PRAISE FOR
THE BANTAM NEW COLLEGE
ITALIAN AND ENGLISH DICTIONARY

". . . thorough, accurate, well-organized, clear, and up to date . . . Relevant to the student's contemporary life . . . It is bound to become a mainstay in the field."
—Albert N. Mancini, Professor of Romance Languages, The Ohio State University

"Both the method and the execution seem to me excellent . . . It would be impossible to find elsewhere as good a dictionary of this size."
—Beatrice Corrigan, Professor Emeritus, Editor, University of Toronto Press

"Apart from its accurate philological approach, its most useful grammatical apparatus, and other singular features, this concise dictionary is the first which is based primarily on *American* English usage . . . It contains numerous up-to-date colloquial and technical terms which cannot be found in any other similar dictionary."
—M. Ricciardelli, Professor of Italian and Comparative Literatures, Editor of *Forum Italicum*

Comprehensive, authoritative, and completely modern, **THE BANTAM NEW COLLEGE ITALIAN AND ENGLISH DICTIONARY** is a landmark in foreign language reference works.

THE BANTAM NEW COLLEGE DICTIONARY SERIES

Robert C. Melzi, Author

ROBERT C. MELZI, D. in L., A.M., Ph.D., was trained in Italy, at the University of Padua, and in the United States, at the University of Pennsylvania. He has done extensive linguistic research, traveling frequently to his native country. Now professor of Romance Languages at Widener College, he has contributed articles and reviews to many learned journals, is the author of *Castelvetro's Annotations to the Inferno,* The Hague and Paris, 1966 (Castelvetro was one of Italy's foremost philologists), and is an associate editor of *The Scribner-Bantam English Dictionary* (Scribner's, 1977; Bantam Books, 1979). Professor Melzi is a Cavaliere in the Order of Solidarity of the Republic of Italy.

Edwin B. Williams, General Editor

EDWIN B. WILLIAMS (1891–1975), A.B., A.M., Ph.D., Doct. d'Univ., LL.D., L.H.D., was chairman of the Department of Romance Languages, dean of the Graduate School, and provost of the University of Pennsylvania. He was a member of the American Philosophical Society and the Hispanic Society of America. Among his many lexicographical works are *The Williams Spanish and English Dictionary* (Scribner's, formerly Holt) and *The Bantam New College Spanish and English Dictionary*. He created and coordinated the Bantam series of original dictionaries—English, French, German, Italian, Latin, and Spanish. The University of Pennsylvania named "Williams Hall" in honor of Edwin B. Williams and his wife, Leonore, and is establishing the "Williams Chair in Lexicography," as the first chair in lexicography in an English-speaking country.

THE BANTAM NEW COLLEGE
ITALIAN & ENGLISH DICTIONARY

ROBERT C. MELZI, Ph.D.
Widener College, Philadelphia

BANTAM BOOKS
TORONTO · NEW YORK · LONDON · SYDNEY · AUCKLAND

THE BANTAM NEW COLLEGE
ITALIAN & ENGLISH DICTIONARY
A Bantam Book / April 1976
10 printings through June 1986

ISBN 0-553-26306-4

Published simultaneously in the United States and Canada

PRINTED IN THE UNITED STATES OF AMERICA

KR   19 18 17 16 15 14 13 12 11

CONTENTS

Preface   vii

Prefazione   vii

Labels and Abbreviations   xii

Sigle ed abbreviazioni   xii

Part One   Italian-English

Italian Spelling and Pronunciation   3

Grammatical Tables   7

Table of Regular Endings of Italian Verbs   15

Model Verbs   17

ITALIAN-ENGLISH   37–364

Part Two   Inglese-Italiano

La pronunzia dell'inglese   3

La pronunzia delle parole composte   5

La pronunzia dei participi passati   5

INGLESE-ITALIANO   7–355

PREFACE

Inasmuch as the basic function of a bilingual dictionary is to provide semantic equivalences, syntactical constructions are shown in both the source and the target languages on both sides of the Dictionary. In performing this function, a bilingual dictionary must fulfill six purposes. That is, an Italian and English dictionary must provide (1) Italian words which an English-speaking person wishes to use in speaking and writing (by means of the English-Italian part), (2) English meanings of Italian words which an English-speaking person encounters in listening and reading (by means of the Italian-English part), (3) the spelling, pronunciation, and inflection of Italian words and the gender of Italian nouns which an English-speaking person needs in order to use Italian words correctly (by means of the Italian-English part), (4) English words which an Italian-speaking person wishes to use in speaking and writing (by means of the Italian-English part), (5) Italian meanings of English words which an Italian-speaking person encounters in listening and reading (by means of the English-Italian part), and (6) the spelling, pronunciation, and inflection of English words which an Italian-speaking person needs in order to use English words correctly (by means of the English-Italian part).

It may seem logical to provide the pronunciation and inflection of English words and the pronunciation and inflection of Italian words and the gender of Italian nouns where these words appear as target words inasmuch as target words, according to (1) and (4) above, are sought for the purpose of speaking and writing. Thus the user would find not only the words he seeks but all the information he needs about them in one and the same place. But this technique is impractical because target words are not alphabetized and could, therefore, be found only by the roundabout and uncertain way of seeking them through their translations in

PREFAZIONE

Dato che la funzione principale di un dizionario bilingue è quella di fornire all'utente equivalenze semantiche, le costruzioni sintattiche sono indicate in entrambe le lingue, quella di partenza e quella di arrivo, in entrambe le parti del Dizionario. Per compiere questa funzione, un dizionario bilingue deve raggiungere sei scopi differenti. Cioè, un dizionario italiano e inglese deve fornire (1) nella parte inglese-italiano, le parole italiane che la persona anglofona vuole adoperare parlando e scrivendo l'italiano; (2) nella parte italiano-inglese, il significato in inglese delle parole italiane che tale persona oda nella lingua parlata o legga in libri o giornali; (3) nella parte italiano-inglese, l'ortografia, la pronunzia, la flessione delle parole italiane e il genere dei nomi italiani che la persona anglofona deve conoscere per servirsi correttamente della lingua italiana; (4) nella parte italiano-inglese, le parole inglesi che la persona italofona vuole adoperare parlando o scrivendo l'inglese; (5) nella parte inglese-italiano, il significato in italiano delle parole inglesi che tale persona oda nella lingua parlata o legga in libri o giornali; (6) nella parte inglese-italiano, l'ortografia, la pronunzia figurata e la flessione delle parole inglesi che la persona italofona deve conoscere per servirsi correttamente della lingua inglese.

A prima vista potrebbe sembrare logico che la pronunzia e la flessione delle parole inglesi e la pronunzia e la flessione delle parole italiane e il genere dei nomi italiani fossero indicati dove queste parole si trovano nella lingua d'arrivo, dato che le parole della lingua d'arrivo, secondo i punti (1) e (4) enunciati più sopra, sono consultate da coloro che vogliono parlare e scrivere in lingua straniera. In questa maniera l'utente troverebbe non solo le parole che cerca, ma tutte le informazioni che gli sono necessarie, nello stesso luogo. Questa tecnica, peraltro, non è pratica poiché le parole della lingua d'arrivo non si trovano in ordine

the other part of the dictionary. And this would be particularly inconvenient for persons using the dictionary for purposes (2) and (5) above. It is much more convenient to provide immediate alphabetized access to pronunciation and inflection where the words appear as source words.

alfabetico e potrebbero quindi essere trovate solo in maniera complicata nella parte opposta del dizionario. E ciò sarebbe specialmente scomodo per coloro che usano il dizionario per gli scopi (2) e (5) menzionati più sopra. È molto più semplice aggiungere la pronunzia e la flessione nella serie alfabetica in cui le parole si trovano nella loro lingua di partenza.

Since Italian is an almost perfectly phonetic language, IPA transcription of Italian words has been omitted. The only elements of pronunciation not shown by standard spelling are the values of tonic e and o (§1; pp. 3, 4) the stress of words stressed on the third syllable from the end (§3,3; p. 5), the value of intervocalic s when unvoiced, and the values of z and zz when voiced (§1; p. 4); these are shown in the entry words themselves.

Dato che l'italiano è una lingua quasi perfettamente fonetica, non si è data la trascrizione delle parole italiane nell'alfabeto dell'Associazione Fonetica Internazionale. Considerando che l'ortografia comune non mostra il vario timbro della e (§1, p. 3) e della o (§1, p. 4) quando esse sono toniche, l'accento delle parole sdrucciole (§3,3, p. 5), la pronunzia della s sorda (§1, p. 4) e la pronunzia delle z e zz sonore (§1, p. 4), si è data tale informazione nell'esponente stesso.

All words are treated in a fixed order according to the parts of speech and the functions of verbs, as follows: adjective, article, substantive, pronoun, adverb, preposition, conjunction, transitive verb, intransitive verb, reflexive verb, auxiliary verb, impersonal verb, interjection.

Ogni singola voce è trattata secondo uno schema fisso che si riferisce alle parti del discorso o alle funzioni del verbo, nel seguente ordine: aggettivo, articolo, sostantivo, pronome, avverbio, preposizione, congiunzione, verbo transitivo, verbo intransitivo, verbo riflessivo, verbo ausiliare, verbo impersonale e interiezione.

Meanings with labels come after more general meanings. Labels (printed in roman and in parentheses) refer to the preceding entry or phrase (printed in boldface).

I significati accompagnati da sigle si trovano dopo quelli di accezione più generale. Tali sigle (che sono sempre stampate in carattere romano e in parentesi) si riferiscono all'esponente precedente, stampato in grassetto, o alla frase precedente, ugualmente stampata in grassetto.

In view of the fact that the users of this Italian and English bilingual dictionary are for the most part English-speaking people, definitions and discriminations are provided in English. They are printed in italics and in parentheses and refer to the English word which they particularize:

Dato che gli utenti di questo dizionario bilingue italiano e inglese sono per lo più anglofoni, definizioni e locuzioni esplicative sono apportate in inglese. Sono stampate in corsivo e in parentesi e si riferiscono sempre alla parola inglese il cui significato cercano di spiegare:

porter [ˈportər] *s* (*doorman*) portiere *m;* (*man who carries luggage*) facchino; . . .
órdine *m* order; . . . series (*e.g., of years*); college (*e.g., of surgeons*); . . .

English adjectives are always translated by the Italian masculine form

Gli aggettivi inglesi sono sempre tradotti in maschile italiano, anche se il

regardless of whether the translation of the exemplary noun modified would be masculine or feminine:

nome che qualificano sia un femminile italiano:

tough [tʌf] *adj* duro; . . . ; (*luck*) cattivo; . . .

In order to facilitate the finding of the meaning and use sought for, changes within a vocabulary entry in part of speech and function of verb, in irregular inflection, in the use of an initial capital, in the gender of Italian nouns, and in the pronunciation of English words are marked with parallels: ‖, instead of the usual semicolons.

Per facilitare l'uso del Dizionario, i raggruppamenti sono stati fatti secondo le parti del discorso, la funzione del verbo, la flessione irregolare, l'uso della maiuscola iniziale, il genere dei nomi italiani e la pronunzia delle parole inglesi e sono separati da sbarrette verticali: ‖, invece del punto e virgola che è stato usato.

Since vocabulary entries are not determined on the basis of etymology, homographs are included in a single entry. When the pronunciation of an English homograph changes, this is shown in the proper place after parallels:

Dato che gli esponenti in questo Dizionario non sono stati selezionati su base etimologica, tutti gli omografi sono inclusi sotto il medesimo esponente. Il cambio di pronunzia di un omografo inglese è indicato al posto adatto dopo sbarrette verticali:

frequent [ˈfrikwənt] *adj* frequente ‖ [frɪˈkwent] or [ˈfrikwənt] *tr* . . .

However, when the pronunciation of an Italian homograph changes, the words are entered separately:

Però, quando la pronunzia di un omografo italiano cambia, si hanno esponenti separati:

retina *f* small net
rètina *f* (anat) retina
tóc·co -ca (-chi -che) *adj* . . . ‖ *m* touch; . . .
tòc·co *m* (-chi) chunk, piece; . . .

Periods are omitted after labels and grammatical abbreviations and at the end of vocabulary entries.

Il punto è stato omesso dopo sigle, abbreviazioni grammaticali, ed alla fine di ogni articolo.

Proper nouns are listed in their alphabetical position in the main body of the Dictionary. Thus **Svezia** and **svedese** do not have to be looked up in two different sections of the book. And all subentries are listed in strictly alphabetical order.

Tutti i nomi propri sono posti nella loro posizione alfabetica nel corpo del Dizionario: quindi **Svezia** e **svedese** non si trovano in sezioni separate di questo libro. Per la medesima ragione di semplicità d'uso, le parole e frasi contenute sotto ogni esponente sono poste in ordine alfabetico.

The gender of Italian nouns is shown on both sides of the Dictionary, except that the gender of masculine nouns ending in -o, feminine nouns ending in -a and -ione, masculine nouns modified by an adjective ending in -o, and feminine nouns modified by an adjective

Il genere dei nomi italiani è indicato in entrambe le parti del Dizionario, eccezion fatta nella parte inglese-italiano, per le parole maschili che terminano in -o, per le parole femminili che terminano in -a e in -ione, per i nomi maschili accompagnati da un

ending in **-a** is not shown on the English-Italian side.

aggettivo che termina in **-o** e per i nomi femminili accompagnati da un aggettivo che termina in **-a**.

The feminine form of an Italian adjective used as a noun (or an Italian feminine noun having identical spelling with the feminine form of an adjective) which falls alphabetically in a separate position from the adjective is treated in that position and is listed again as a cross reference under the adjective:

Quando un nome femminile italiano ha la medesima grafia della forma femminile di un aggettivo o quando tale forma femminile di aggettivo è usata come nome, lo si trova elencato nella sua posizione alfabetica come nome e poi di nuovo come rinvio interno sotto l'aggettivo:

> **nòta** *f* mark, score, . . .
> **nò·to -ta** *adj* . . . || *m* . . . || *f* see **nota**

The centered period is used in vocabulary entries of inflected words to mark off, according to standard orthographic principles in the two languages, the final syllable that has to be detached before the syllable showing the inflection is added:

Qualora l'esponente italiano o inglese sia un vocabolo a flessione, un punto leggermente elevato sopra il rigo è stato usato per separare, secondo le regole ortografiche di ciascuna delle due lingue, la sillaba finale che dev'essere rimossa prima che la nuova desinenza di flessione possa essere attaccata al corpo dell'esponente, per es.:

> **vèc·chio -chia (-chi -chie)** *adj* . . .
> **put·ty** [ˈpʌti] *s* (**-ties**) . . . || *v* (*pret & pp* **-tied**) . . .
> **hap·py** [ˈhæpi] *adj* (**-pier; -piest**) . . .

If the entry word cannot be divided by a centered period the full form is given in parentheses:

Se l'esponente non può essere scisso a mezzo del suddetto punto, la forma completa è indicata in parentesi:

> **mouse** [maʊs] *s* (**mice** [maɪs]) . . .
> **mouth** [maʊθ] *s* (**mouths** [maʊðz]) . . .
> **die** [daɪ] *s* (**dice** [daɪs]) . . . || *s* (**dies**) . . . || *v* (*pret & pp* **died**; *ger* **dying**) *intr* . . .

Many Italian verbs which take an indirect object have, as their equivalent, English verbs which take a direct object. This is shown on both sides of this Dictionary by the insertion of (with *dat*) after the Italian verb, e.g.,

Molti verbi italiani che reggono un oggetto indiretto hanno come equivalenti inglesi verbi che reggono un oggetto diretto. Questa equivalenza è indicata in entrambe le parti del Dizionario con l'aggiunta di (with *dat*) dopo il verbo italiano, per es.:

> **ubbidire** §176 *intr* . . . ; (with *dat*) to obey
> **obey** [oˈbe] *tr* ubbidire (with *dat*)

On the Italian-English side inflection is shown by: a) numbers that refer to the grammatical tables of articles, pronouns, etc., and to the tables of model verbs; they are placed before the abbreviation indicating the part of speech:

Nella parte italiano-inglese la flessione si indica: a) con numeri che si riferiscono alle tavole grammaticali degli articoli, dei pronomi, ecc., e alle tavole dei verbi modello; questi numeri sono posti innanzi all'abbreviazione indicante la parte del discorso:

> **mì·o -a** §6 *adj & pron poss*
> **lui** §5 *pron pers*
> **congiùngere** §183 *tr & ref*

b) the first person singular of the present indicative of verbs in which the stress falls on either an e or an o not stressed in the infinitive or on the third syllable from the end, whatever the vowel may be:

b) con la prima persona singolare del presente dell'indicativo dei verbi non sdruccioli all'infinito in cui l'accento tonico cade o su una e o su una o, o su qualsiasi vocale di una parola sdrucciola:

> ritornare (ritórno) tr ...
> visitare (vìsito) tr ...

c) the feminine endings of all adjectives which end in -o:

c) con la desinenza femminile di tutti gli aggettivi che terminano in -o nel maschile:

> laborió•so -sa [s] adj ...

d) the plural endings of nouns and adjectives which are formed irregularly:

d) con la desinenza plurale dei nomi e aggettivi che si formano in maniera irregolare:

> bràc•cio m (-cia fpl) ... || m (-ci) ...
> cit•tà f (-tà) ...
> dià•rio -ria (-rì -rie) adj ... || m ... || f ...
> fotogram•ma m (-mi) ...
> fràn•gia f (-ge) ...
> laburi•sta (-sti -ste) adj ... || mf ...
> la•go m (-ghi) ...
> òr•co m (-chi) ...
> òtti•co -ca (-ci -che) adj ... || m ... || f ...

e) the full plural forms of all nouns that cannot be divided by a center period or whose plural cannot be shown by such division:

e) con la completa forma plurale di quei nomi che non possono essere scissi col suddetto punto o che hanno mutamenti interni:

> re m (re) ...
> caporeparto m (capireparto) ...

I wish to express my gratitude to many persons who helped me in the production of this book and particularly to Dr. Edwin B. Williams who, ever since graduate school, has been a constant inspiration and who has established the principles upon which this book was compiled, to my wife and children, who patiently aided and abetted me through ten years of research and compilation, to Richard J. Nelson, Sebastiano DiBlasi, Walter D. Glanze, and to Giacomo De Voto, Miro Dogliotti, and Michele Ricciardelli.

xi

Labels and abbreviations

Sigle ed abbreviazioni

abbr abbreviation—abbreviazione
(acronym) word formed from the initial letters or syllables of a series of words—parola costituita dalle lettere o sillabe iniziali di una serie di parole
adj adjective—aggettivo
adv adverb—avverbio
(aer) aeronautics—aeronautica
(agr) agriculture—agricoltura
(alg) algebra—algebra
(anat) anatomy—anatomia
(archaic) arcaico
(archeol) archeology—archeologia
(archit) architecture—architettura
(arith) arithmetic—aritmetica
art article—articolo
(astr) astronomy—astronomia
(astrol) astrology—astrologia
(aut) automobile—automobile
aux auxiliary verb—verbo ausiliare
(bact) bacteriology—batteriologia
(baseball) baseball
(basketball) pallacanestro
(bb) bookbinding—legatoria
(Bib) Biblical—biblico
(billiards) biliardo
(biochem) biochemistry—biochimica
(biol) biology—biologia
(bot) botany—botanica
(bowling) bowling
(boxing) pugilato
(bridge) bridge
(Brit) British—britannico
(cards) carte da gioco
(carp) carpentry—falegnameria
(checkers) gioco della dama
(chem) chemistry—chimica
(chess) scacchi
(coll) colloquial—familiare
(com) commercial—commerciale
comb form elemento di parola composta
comp comparative—comparativo
cond conditional—condizionale
conj conjunction—congiunzione
(cricket) cricket
(culin) cooking—cucina
dat dative—dativo
def definite—determinativo, definito
dem demonstrative—dimostrativo
(dentistry) medicina dentaria
(dial) dialectal—dialettale
(dipl) diplomacy—diplomazia

(disparaging) sprezzante
(eccl) ecclesiastical—ecclesiastico
(econ) economics—economia
(educ) education—istruzione
e.g., or *e.g.*, per esempio
(elec) electricity—elettricità
(electron) electronics—elettronica
(ent) entomology—entomologia
(equit) horseback riding—equitazione
f feminine noun—nome femminile
(fa) fine arts—belle arti
fem feminine—femminile
(fencing) scherma
(fig) figurative—figurato
(fin) financial—finanziario
(football) football americano
fpl feminine noun plural—nome femminile plurale
fut future—futuro
(geog) geography—geografia
(geol) geology—geologia
(geom) geometry—geometria
ger gerund—gerundio
(golf) golf
(gram) grammar—grammatica
(herald) heraldry—araldica
(hist) history—storia
(hort) horticulture—orticoltura
(hunt) hunting—caccia
(ichth) ichthyology—ittiologia
i.e., cioè
imperf imperfect—imperfetto
impers impersonal verb—verbo impersonale
impv imperative—imperativo
ind indicative—indicativo
indef indefinite—indefinito, indeterminativo
inf infinitive—infinito
(ins) insurance—assicurazione
interj interjection—interiezione
interr interrogative—interrogativo
intr intransitive verb—verbo intransitivo
invar invariable—invariabile
(Italian cards) carte italiane
(jewelry) gioielleria
(joc) jocular—faceto
(journ) journalism—giornalismo
(law) diritto, legge
(letterword) word in the form of an abbreviation which is pronounced by sounding the names of its letters in

succession and which functions as a part of speech—parola in forma di abbreviazione che si ottiene pronunziando consecutivamente la denominazione di ciascuna lettera e che funziona come parte del discorso

(lexicography) lessicografia
(ling) linguistics—linguistica
(lit) literary—letterario
(log) logic—logica
m masculine noun—nome maschile
(mach) machinery—macchinario
masc masculine—maschile
(math) mathematics—matematica
(mech) mechanics—meccanica
(med) medicine—medicina
(metallurgy) metallurgia
(meteor) meteorology—meteorologia
mf masculine or feminine noun according to sex—nome maschile o nome femminile secondo il sesso
m & f see below between (mythol) and (naut)
(mil) military—militare
(min) mining—lavorazione delle miniere
(mov) moving pictures—cinematografo
mpl masculine noun plural—nome maschile plurale
(mus) music—musica
(mythol) mythology—mitologia
m & f masculine and feminine noun without regard to sex—nome maschile e femminile senza distinzione di sesso
(naut) nautical—nautico
(nav) naval—navale
neut neuter—neutro
num number—numero
(obs) obsolete—in disuso
(obstet) obstetrics—ostetricia
(opt) optics—ottica
(orn) ornithology—ornitologia
(painting) pittura
(pathol) pathology—patologia
(pej) pejorative—peggiorativo
perf perfect—perfetto, passato
pers personal—personale; person—persona
(pharm) pharmacy—farmacia
(philately) filatelia
(philol) philology—filologia
(philos) philosophy—filosofia
(phonet) phonetics—fonetica
(phot) photography—fotografia
(phys) physics—fisica
(physiol) physiology—fisiologia
pl plural—plurale
(poet) poetical—poetico
(poker) poker
(pol) politics—politica
pp past participle—participio passato
poss possessive—possessivo
pref prefix—prefisso
prep preposition—preposizione

prep phrase prepositional phrase—frase preposizionale
pres present—presente
pret preterit—passato remoto
pron pronoun—pronome
(pros) prosody—prosodia
(psychoanal) psychoanalysis—psicanalisi
(psychol) psychology—psicologia
(psychopath) psychopathology—psicopatologia
qlco or *qlco* qualcosa—something
qlcu or *qlcu* qualcuno—someone
(racing) corse
(rad) radio—radio
ref reflexive verb—verbo riflessivo o pronominale
rel relative—relativo
(rel) religion—religione
(rhet) rhetoric—retorica
(rok) rocketry—studio dei razzi
(rowing) canottaggio
(rr) railroad—ferrovia
(rugby) rugby
s substantive—sostantivo
(scornful) sprezzante
(Scot) Scottish—scozzese
(sculp) sculpture—scultura
(sew) sewing—cucito
sg singular—singolare
(slang) gergo
s.o. or *s.o.* someone—qualcuno
(soccer) calcio
spl substantive plural—sostantivo plurale
(sports) sport
ssg substantive singular—sostantivo singolare
s.th or *s.th* something—qualcosa
subj subjunctive—congiuntivo
suf suffix—suffisso
super superlative—superlativo
(surg) surgery—chirurgia
(surv) surveying—agrimensura, topografia
(taur) bullfighting—tauromachia
(telg) telegraphy—telegrafia
(telp) telephone—telefonia
(telv) television—televisione
(tennis) tennis
(tex) textile—tessile
(theat) theater—teatro
(theol) theology—teologia
tr transitive verb—verbo transitivo
(trademark) marchio di fabbrica
(typ) printing—tipografia
(U.S.A.) S.U.A.
v verb—verbo
var variant—variante
(vet) veterinary medicine—medicina veterinaria
(vulg) vulgar—volgare, ordinario
(wrestling) lotta
(zool) zoology—zoologia

PART ONE

Italian-English

Italian Spelling and Pronunciation

§1. The Italian Alphabet. 1. The twenty-one letters of the Italian alphabet are listed below with their names and their sounds in terms of approximate equivalent English sounds. Their gender is masculine or feminine.

LETTER	NAME	APPROXIMATE SOUND
a	a	Like *a* in English *father*, e.g., **facile, padre.**
b	bi	Like *b* in English *boat*, e.g., **bello, abate.**
c	ci	When followed by **e** or **i**, like *ch* in English *cherry*, e.g., **cento, cinque;** if the **i** is unstressed and followed by another vowel, its sound is not heard, e.g., **ciarla, cieco.** When followed by **a, o, u,** or a consonant, like *c* in English *cook*, e.g., **casa, come, cura, credere.** The digraph **ch,** which is used before **e** and **i,** has likewise the sound of *c* in English *cook*, e.g., **chiesa, perché.**
d	di	Like *d* in English *dance*, e.g., **dare, madre.**
e	e	Has two sounds. One like *a* in English *make*, shown on stressed syllables in this DICTIONARY by the acute accent, e.g., **séra, trénta;** and one like *e* in English *met*, shown on stressed syllables in this DICTIONARY by the grave accent, e.g., **fèrro, fèsta.**
f	effe	Like *f* in English *fool*, e.g., **farina, efelide.**
g	gi	When followed by **e** or **i**, like *g* in English *general*, e.g., **gelato, ginnasta;** if the **i** is unstressed and followed by another vowel, its sound is not heard, e.g., **giallo, giorno.** When followed by **a, o, u,** or a consonant, like *g* in English *go*, e.g., **gamba, goccia, gusto, grado.** The digraph **gh,** which is used before **e** and **i,** has likewise the sound of *g* in English *go*, e.g., **gherone, ghisa.** When the combination **gli** (a) is a form of the definite article or the personal pronoun, (b) is final in a word, or (c) is intervocalic, it has the sound of Castilian *ll*, which is somewhat like *lli* in English *million*, e.g., (a) **gli uomini, gli ho parlato ieri,** (b) **battagli,** (c) **figlio, migliore.** When it is (a) initial (except in the word **gli,** above), (b) preceded by a consonant, or (c) followed by a consonant, it is pronounced like *gli* in English *negligence*, e.g., (a) **glioma,** (b) **ganglio,** (c) **negligenza.** The combination **gl** followed by **a, e, o,** or **u** is pronounced like *gl* in English *globe*, e.g., **glabro, gleba, globo, gluteo, inglese, poliglotto.** The digraph **gn** has the sound of Castilian **ñ,** which is somewhat like *ni* in English *onion*, e.g., **signore, gnocco.**
h	acca	Always silent, e.g., **ah, hanno.** See **ch** under **c** above and **gh** under **g** above.
i	i	Like *i* in English *machine*, e.g., **piccolo, sigla.** When unstressed and followed by another vowel, like *y* in English *yes*, e.g., **piatto, piede, fiore, fiume.** For **i** in **ci,** see **c** above, in **gi,** see **g** above, and in **sci,** see **s** below.

3

LETTER	NAME	APPROXIMATE SOUND
l	elle	Like *l* in English *lamb*, e.g., **labbro, lacrima.**
m	emme	Like *m* in English *money*, e.g., **mano, come.**
n	enne	Like *n* in English *net*, e.g., **nome, cane.**
o	o	Has two sounds. One like *o* in English *note*, shown on stressed syllables in this DICTIONARY by the acute accent, e.g., **dópo, sóle;** and one like *ou* in English *ought*, shown on stressed syllables in this DICTIONARY by the grave accent, e.g., **còsa, dònna.**
p	pi	Like *p* in English *pot*, e.g., **passo, carpa.**
q	cu	This letter is always followed by the letter **u** and the combination has the sound of *qu* in English *quart*, e.g., **quanto, questo.**
r	erre	Like *r* in English *rubber*, with a slight trill, e.g., **roba, carta.**
s	esse	Has two sounds. When initial and followed by a vowel, when preceded by a consonant and followed by a vowel, and when followed by **c** [k] **f, p, q,** or **t,** like *s* in English *see*, e.g., **sale, falso, scappare, spazio, stoffa;** and when standing between two vowels and when followed by **b, d, g** [g], **l, m, n, r** or **v,** like *z* in English *zero*, e.g., **paese, sbaglio, svenire.** However, **s** standing between two vowels in some words and initial **s** followed by **b, d, g** [g], **l, m, n, r,** or **v** in some foreign borrowings are pronounced like *s* in *see*, e.g., **casa*, tesa, smoking, slam** In this DICTIONARY this is indicated by the insertion of [s] immediately after the entry word. However, when initial **s** stands between two vowels in a compound, its pronunciation remains that of initial **s,** e.g., **autoservizio** and this is not indicated. The digraph **sc,** when followed by **e** or **i** has the sound of *sh* in English *shall*, e.g., **scelta, scimmia;** if the **i** is unstressed and followed by another vowel, its sound is not heard, e.g., **sciame, sciopero.** The trigraph **sch** has the sound of *sc* in English *scope*, e.g., **scherzo, schiavo.**
t	ti	Like *t* in English *table*, e.g., **terra, pasto.**
u	u	Like *u* in English *rule*, e.g., **luna, mulo.** When followed by a vowel, like *w* in English *was*, e.g., **quanto, guerra, nuovo.**
v	vu	Like *v* in English *vain*, e.g., **vita, uva.**
z	zeta	Has two sounds. One like *ts* in English *nuts*, e.g., **grazia, zucchero;** and one like *dz* in English *adze*, e.g., **zero, mezzo.** In this DICTIONARY the sound of *dz* in *adze* is indicated by the insertion of [dz] immediately after the entry word. If the sound is long, [ddzz] is inserted

---

* Intervocalic **s** is generally voiced in the north of Italy.

2. The following five letters are found in borrowings from other languages.

LETTER	NAME	EXAMPLES
j	i lunga	**jazz, jingo**
k	cappa	**kiosco, kodak**
w	doppia vu	**water-polo, whisky**
x	ics	**xenofobo, xilofono**
y	ìpsilon	**yacht, yoghurt**

3. Consonants written double are longer than consonants written single, that is, it takes a longer time to pronounce them, e.g., **camino** *chimney* and **cam-**

4

mino *road*, **capello** *hair* and **cappello** *hat*. Special attention is called to the following double consonants: **cc** followed by **e** or **i** has the sound of *ch ch* in English *beach chair*, that is, a lengthened *ch* (not the sound of *ks*), *e.g.*, **accento**; **cch** has the sound of *kk* in English *bookkeeper*, *e.g.*, **becchino**; **cq** has the sound of *kk* in English *bookkeeper*, *e.g.*, **acqua**; **gg** followed by **e** or **i** has the sound of *ge j* in English *carriage joiner*, *e.g.*, **peggio**; **ggh** has the sound of *g g* in English *tag game*, *e.g.*, **agghindare**.

§2. Division of Syllables. In the application of the following rules for the syllabic division of words, the digraphs **ch**, **gh**, **gl**, **gn**, and **sc** count as single consonants.

(a) When a single consonant stands between two vowels it belongs to the following syllable, e.g., **ca·sa**, **fu·mo**, **ami·che**, **la·ghi**, **fi·glio**, **biso·gno**, **la·sciare**.

(b) When a consonant group consisting of two consonants of which the second is **l** or **r** stands between two vowels, the group belongs to the following syllable, e.g., **nu·cleo**, **so·brio**, **qua·dro**.

(c) When a consonant group consisting of two or more consonants of which the first or the second is **s** stands between two vowels, that part of the group beginning with **s** belongs to the following syllable, e.g., **ta·sca**, **bo·schi**, **fine·stra**, **super·sti·zione**, **sub·strato**.

(d) When a consonant group consisting of two or three consonants of which the first is **l**, **m**, **n**, or **r** stands between two vowels, the **l**, **m**, **n**, or **r** belongs to the preceding syllable, the other consonant or consonants to the following syllable, e.g., **al·bero**, **am·pio**, **prin·cipe**, **mor·te**, **in·flazione**, **com·pleto**.

(e) When a double consonant stands between two vowels or between a vowel and **l** or **r**, the first belongs to the preceding syllable, the second to the following syllable, e.g., **bab·bo**, **caval·lo**, **an·no**, **car·ro**, **mez·zo**, **sup·plica**, **lab·bro**, **quat·tro**.

§3. Stress and Accent Marks. 1. Whenever stress is shown as part of regular spelling, it is shown on **a**, **i**, and **u** by the grave accent mark, e.g., **libertà**, **giovedì**, **gioventù**, on close **e** and **o** by the acute accent mark, e.g., **perché**, and on open **e** and **o** by the grave accent mark, e.g., **caffè**, **parlò**. This occurs (a) in words ending in a stressed vowel, as in the above examples, (b) in stressed monosyllables in which the vocalic element is a diphthong of which the first letter is unstressed **i** or **u**, e.g., **già**, **più**, **può**, and (c) on the stressed monosyllable of any pair of monosyllables of which one is stressed and the other unstressed, in order to distinguish one from the other, e.g., **dà** *he gives* and **da** *from*, **è** *is* and **e** *and*, **sé** *himself* and **se** *if*, **sì** *yes* and **si** *himself*.

2. Whenever stress is not shown as part of regular spelling, it is often difficult to determine where it falls.

(a) In words of two syllables, the stress falls on the syllable next to the last, e.g., **ca'sa**, **mu'ro**, **ter'ra**. If the syllable next to the last contains a diphthong, that is, a combination of a strong vowel (**a**, **e**, or **o**) and a weak vowel (**i** or **u**), the strong vowel is stressed, regardless of which vowel comes first, e.g., **da'ino**, **ero'ico**, **ne'utro**, **fia'to**, **dua'le**, **sie'pe**, **fio're**, **buo'no**.

(b) In words of more than two syllables, the stress may fall on the syllable next to the last, e.g., **anda'ta**, **canzo'ne**, **pasto're** or on a preceding syllable, e.g., **fis'sile**, **gon'dola**, **man'dorla**. In these positions also the stressed syllable may contain a diphthong, e.g., **inca'uto**, **idra'ulico**, **fio'cina**.

(c) If a weak vowel in juxtaposition with a strong vowel is stressed, the two vowels constitute two separate syllables, e.g., **abba·i'no**, **ero·i'na**, **pa·u'ra**, **miri'ade**, **vi'a**.

(d) Two strong vowels in juxtaposition constitute two separate syllables, e.g., **pa·e'se**, **aure'ola**, **ide'a**, **oce'ano**.

(e) Two weak vowels in juxtaposition generally constitute a diphthong in which the first vowel is stressed in some words, e.g., **flu'ido** and the second vowel in others, e.g., **piu'ma**.

(f) If a word ends in a diphthong, the diphthong is stressed, e.g., **marina'i**, **parla'i**, **ero'i**.

3. In this DICTIONARY, stress is understood or shown on all words that do not bear an accent mark as part of regular spelling according to the following principles. In the application of these principles, individual vowels and not diphthongs are counted as units. In some words in which it is not necessary to show stress, an accent mark is used to show the quality of the stressed vowels **e** and **o**.

As in regular Italian spelling, stress is shown on **a**, **i**, and **u** by the grave accent mark, on close **e** and **o** by the acute accent mark, and on open **e** and **o** by the grave accent mark.

(a) It is understood that in words of more than one syllable in which no accent mark is shown, the stress falls on the vowel next to the last, e.g., **casa**,

5

fiato, duale, abbaino, paura. In such words as **sièpe, fióre, buòno, paése, fluènte, eròe, nói, pòi,** the accent mark is used to show the quality of the vowel.

(b) An accent mark is placed on the stressed vowel if the word is stressed on the third vowel from the end, e.g., **mùsica, sìmbolo, dàino, incàuto, marinàio, contìnuo, infànzia.** If this vowel is **e** or **o**, the acute or grave accent mark must correspond to the quality of the vowel, e.g., **fiòcina, rómpere, nèutro, eròico, assèdio, filatóio.**

(c) Contrary to the above-mentioned principle of counting vowels, an accent mark is placed on the strong vowel of a final diphthong, e.g., **marinài, assài.**

(d) Contrary to the above-mentioned principle of counting vowels, an accent mark is placed on the **i** of final **ia, ie, ii,** and **io,** e.g., **farmacìa, scìa, farmacìe, mormorìi, gorgoglìo, fìo.**

(e) An accent mark is placed on some borrowings ending in a consonant, e.g., **hàrem, revòlver.**

(f) The loss of the last vowel or last syllable of a word does not alter the position of the stress of the word, e.g., **la maggior parte, in alcun modo, fan bene.**

84. The Definite Article and Combinations with Prepositions.

		MASC BEFORE CONSONANT	MASC BEFORE S IMPURE OR Z[1]	MASC BEFORE VOWEL	FEM BEFORE CONSONANT	FEM BEFORE VOWEL
	SG	il	lo	l'[2]	la	l'[3]
	PL	i	gli	gli[2]	le	le[3]
WITH **a**	SG	al	allo	all'[2]	alla	all'[3]
	PL	ai	agli	agli[2]	alle	alle[3]
WITH **di**	SG	del	dello	dell'[2]	della	dell'[3]
	PL	dei	degli	degli[2]	delle	delle[3]
WITH **con**	SG	col	collo	coll'[2]	colla	coll'[3]
	PL	coi	cogli	cogli[2]	colle	colle[3]
WITH **da**	SG	dal	dallo	dall'[2]	dalla	dall'[3]
	PL	dai	dagli	dagli[2]	dalle	dalle[3]
WITH **in**	SG	nel	nello	nell'[2]	nella	nell'[3]
	PL	nei	negli	negli[2]	nelle	nelle[3]
WITH **su**	SG	sul	sullo	sull'[2]	sulla	sull'[3]
	PL	sui	sugli	sugli[2]	sulle	sulle[3]

[1] Other letters and groups of letters, which occur in a few words, are **gn, pn, ps, sc, x,** and **i** before a vowel, sometimes spelled **j** or **y.**

[2] These forms may drop the **l** before words beginning with **l,** e.g., **gl'Inglesi.**

[3] The **e** of these forms is not elided, e.g., **le erbe.**

7

85. Personal and Reflexive Pronouns.

PERSONS	SUBJECT	PERSONAL DIRECT OBJECT	PERSONAL INDIRECT OBJECT	REFLEX. & RECIPROCAL DIRECT & INDIRECT OBJECT	PERSONAL PREPOSITIONAL OBJECT	REFLEX. & RECIPROCAL PREPOSITIONAL OBJECT
SG						
1	io *I*	mi *me*	mi *to me*	mi *myself; to myself*	me *me*	me *myself*
2	tu *you*	ti *you*	ti *to you*	ti *yourself; to yourself*	te *you*	te *yourself*
3 MASC	egli, lui *he*	lo *him or it*	gli *to him*	si *himself; to himself*	lui *him*	sé *himself*
3 FEM	lei, essa *she*	la *her or it*	le *to her*	si *herself; to herself*	lei, essa *her*	sé *herself*
2 FORMAL	Lei *you*	La *you*	Le *to you*	si *yourself; to yourself*	lei, essa *her* Lei *you*	sé *yourself*
PL						
1	noi *we*	ci *us*	ci *to us*	ci *ourselves; to ourselves; each other; to each other*	noi *us*	noi *ourselves; each other*
2	voi *you*	vi *you*	vi *to you*	vi *yourself; yourselves; to yourself; to yourselves; each other*	voi *you*	voi *yourself; yourselves; each other*
3 MASC	loro, essi *they*	li *them*	loro *to them*	si *themselves; to themselves; each other; to each other*	loro, essi *them*	sé *themselves; each other*
3 FEM	loro, esse *they*	le *them*	loro *to them*	si *themselves; to themselves; each other; to each other*	loro, esse *them*	sé *themselves; each other*
2 FORMAL	Loro *you*	Li Le } *you*	Loro *to you*	si *yourselves; to yourselves; each other; to each other*	Loro *you*	sé *yourselves; each other*

ci and vi both mean also *here, there, to it, in it, to them, in them, about it.*

ne means *of, from,* or *with him, her, it, them; some, any; from here, from there, thence, about it.*

meco *with me,* teco *with you,* and seco *with him, with himself; with her, with herself; with you, with yourself, with yourselves; with them, with themselves; with each other* may be used instead of con me, con te, and con sé respectively.

8

COMBINATION OF DIRECT AND INDIRECT OBJECT

PERSONS		
1 SG & 3 SG	me lo } *him, her, it to me* me la }	
1 SG & 3 PL	me li } *them to me* me le }	
2 SG & 3 SG	te lo } *him, her, it to you* te la }	
2 SG & 3 PL	te li } *them to you* te le }	
3 SG & 3 SG	glielo } *him, her, it to him* gliela } *him, her, it to her*	
3 SG & 3 PL	glieli } *them to him* gliele } *them to her*	
2 SG FORMAL & 3 SG	Glielo } *him, her, it to you* Gliela }	
2 SG FORMAL & 3 PL	Glieli } *them to you* Gliele }	

PERSONS		
1 PL & 3 SG	ce lo } *him, her, it to us* ce la }	
1 PL & 3 PL	ce li } *them to us* ce le }	
2 PL & 3 SG	ve lo } *him, her, it to you* ve la }	
2 PL & 3 PL	ve li } *them to you* ve le }	
3 SG & 3 PL	lo } VERB loro *him, her, it to them* la }	
3 PL & 3 PL	li } VERB loro *them to them* le }	
3 SG & 2 PL FORMAL	lo } VERB Loro *him, her, it to you* la }	
3 PL & 2 PL FORMAL	li } VERB Loro *them to you* le }	

The form si (third singular and plural reflexive and reciprocal indirect object) changes to se before one of the direct objects lo, la, li, and le, and before ne, e.g., se lo mette he puts it on; se n'è andato he went away.

In combinations, ne occupies the same position as lo, la, li, and le, e.g. me ne, and forms one word with gli, namely, gliene.

86 Possessive Adjectives and Pronouns

PERSON, NUMBER & SEX OF POSSESSOR	GENDER & NUMBER OF POSSESSIVE ADJECTIVE OR PRONOUN ACCORDING TO THE GENDER & NUMBER OF THE PERSON OR THING POSSESSED				MEANING OF ADJECTIVE	MEANING OF PRONOUN
SG	MSG	MPL	FSG	FPL		
1	il mio	i miei	la mia	le mie	*my*	*mine*
2	il tuo	i tuoi	la tua	le tue	*your*	*yours*
3 MASC	il suo	i suoi	la sua	le sue	*his*	*his*
3 FEM	il suo	i suoi	la sua	le sue	*her*	*hers*
3 NEUT	il suo	i suoi	la sua	le sue	*its*	*its*
2 FORMAL	il Suo	i Suoi	la Sua	le Sue	*your*	*yours*
PL						
1	il nostro	i nostri	la nostra	le nostre	*our*	*ours*
2	il vostro	i vostri	la vostra	le vostre	*your*	*yours*
3	il loro	i loro	la loro	le loro	*their*	*theirs*
2 FORMAL	il Loro	i Loro	la Loro	le Loro	*your*	*yours*

The definite article, shown here, is not generally used (a) in direct address, e.g., **mio caro amico** *my dear friend*, (b) after the verb **essere**, e.g., **la casa è nostra** *the house is ours*, and (c) when a singular form modifies the name of a relative, e.g., **sua sorella** *his sister*.

With forms of the indefinite article, the possessive adjective, whether standing before or after the noun, is translated by *of*

plus the possessive pronoun, e.g., **un amico mio** *a friend of mine*; **una sua zia** *an aunt of his* (or *of hers*).

The forms of the possessive pronouns also have the force of nouns, e.g., **il mio** *my property, my belongings*; **i suoi** *his people, relatives, followers, troops, retinue*, etc.; **la mia** *my letter*; **la sua** *his opinion*.

§7. The Demonstrative Adjective.

	MASC BEFORE CONSONANT	MASC BEFORE **s** IMPURE OR **z** (see note 1, p. 7)	MASC BEFORE VOWEL	FEM BEFORE CONSONANT	FEM BEFORE VOWEL
SG	quel *that*	quello	quell'	quella	quell'
PL	quei *those*	quegli	quegli	quelle	quelle
SG	questo *this*	questo	questo or quest'	questa	questa or quest'
PL	questi *these*	questi	questi	queste	queste

11

§8. The Demonstrative Pronoun.

	MASC	FEM	MASC
SG	**quello** *that one*	**quella**	**quegli** *that one; the former*
PL	**quelli** *those*	**quelle**	
SG	**questo** *this one*	**questa**	**questi** *this one; the latter*
PL	**questi** *these*	**queste**	

The demonstrative pronoun **quello** is often followed by **che, di,** or **da** and the masculine singular form may be shortened to **quel** before these words.

SG	**colui** *that one*	**colei**
PL	**coloro** *those*	**coloro**
SG	**costui** *this one*	**costei**
PL	**costoro** *these*	**costoro**

code•sto -sta -sti -ste and **cote•sto -sta -sti -ste** are demonstrative adjectives and demonstrative pronouns and mean *that* (*of yours*).

§9. Indefinite Article and Numeral Adjective.

MASC	MASC	MASC	FEM	FEM
BEFORE CONSONANT	BEFORE S IMPURE OR Z (see note 1, p. 7)	BEFORE VOWEL	BEFORE CONSONANT	BEFORE VOWEL
un *a, an; one*	uno	un	una	un'

13

§10. Indefinite Pronoun uno.

MASC	FEM
uno *one*	una

§11. Correlative Indefinite Pronoun.

	MASC	FEM
SG	l'uno . . . l'altro *one . . . the other*	l'una . . . l'altra
PL	gli uni . . . gli altri *some . . . the others*	le une . . . le altre

§12. Reciprocal Indefinite Pronoun.

	MASC	FEM
SG	l'un l'altro *each other, one another*	l'una l'altra
PL	gli uni gli altri	le une le altre

Table of Regular Endings of Italian Verbs

The stem to which the endings of the gerund, past participle, present participle, imperative, present indicative, present subjunctive, imperfect indicative, preterit indicative, and imperfect subjunctive are attached is obtained by dropping the ending of the infinitive, viz., -are, -ere, -ire.

The stem to which the endings of the future indicative and present conditional are attached is obtained by dropping the -e of the ending of the infinitive of all conjugations and changing the a of the ending of the infinitive of the first conjugation to e.

The letters before the names of some of the tenses of this table correspond to the designation of the tenses shown on the following page.

Letters printed in italics have a written accent that is not part of the regular spelling.

TENSE	FIRST CONJUGATION	SECOND CONJUGATION	THIRD CONJUGATION
inf	**-are**	**-ére (or -ere)**	**-ire**
ger	-ando	-èndo	-èndo
pp	-ato	-uto	-ito
pres part	-ante	-ènte	-ènte
(a) *impv*	-a -ate	-i -éte	-i -ite
(b) *pres ind*	-o -i -a -iamo -ate -ano	-o -i -e -iamo -éte -ono	-o -i -e -iamo -ite -ono
(c) *pres subj*	-i -i -i -iamo -iate -ino	-a -a -a -iamo -iate -ano	-a -a -a -iamo -iate -ano
(d) *imperf ind*	-avo -avi -ava -avamo -avate -àvano	-évo -évi -éva -evamo -evate -évano	-ivo -ivi -iva -ivamo -ivate -ìvano
(e) *pret ind*	-ài -asti -ò -ammo -aste -àrono	-éi -ésti -è -émmo -éste -érono	-ìi -isti -ì -immo -iste -ìrono
imperf subj	-assi -assi -asse -àssimo -aste -àssero	-éssi -éssi -ésse -éssimo -éste -éssero	-issi -issi -isse -ìssimo -iste -ìssero
(f) *fut ind*	-er-ò -er-ài -er-à -er-émo -er-éte -er-anno	-ò -ài -à -émo -éte -anno	-ò -ài -à -émo -éte -anno

TENSE	FIRST CONJUGATION	SECOND CONJUGATION	THIRD CONJUGATION
pres cond	-er-èi	-èi	-èi
	-er-ésti	-ésti	-ésti
	-er-èbbe	-èbbe	-èbbe
	-er-émmo	-émmo	-émmo
	-er-éste	-éste	-éste
	-er-èbbero	-èbbero	-èbbero

MODEL VERBS
ORDER OF TENSES

(a) imperative
(b) present indicative
(c) present subjunctive

(d) imperfect indicative
(e) preterit indicative
(f) future indicative

In addition to the infinitive, gerund, and past participle, which are shown in line one of these tables, all simple tenses are shown if they contain at least one irregular form, except (1) the present conditional, which is always formed on the stem of the future indicative, (2) the imperfect subjunctive, which is always formed on the stem of the *2nd sg* of the preterit indicative, and (3) the present participle, which is generally formed by changing the final **-do** of the gerund to **-te** (exceptions being shown in parentheses after the gerund).

Letters printed in italics have a written accent that is not part of the regular spelling.

§100 **ACCÈDERE**—accedèndo—acceduto
    (e) accedètti *or* accedéi *or* accèssi; accedésti; accedètte *or* accedé *or* accèsse; accedémmo; accedéste; accedèttero *or* accedérono *or* accèssero

§101 **ACCÈNDERE**—accendèndo—accéso
    (e) accési, accendésti, accése, accendémmo, accendéste, accésero

§102 **ADDURRE**—adducèndo—addótto
    (b) adduco, adduci, adduce, adduciamo, adducéte, add*ù*cono
    (c) adduca, adduca, adduca, adduciamo, adduciate, add*ù*cano
    (d) adducévo, adducévi, adducéva, adducevamo, adducevate, adducévano
    (e) addussi, adducésti, addusse, adducémmo, adducéste, add*ù*ssero

§103 **AFFÌGGERE**—affiggèndo—affisso
    (e) affissi, affiggésti, affisse, affiggémmo, affiggéste, aff*ì*ssero

17

§104 AFFLÌGGERE—affliggèndo—afflitto
    (e) afflissi, affliggésti, afflisse, affliggémmo, affliggéste, afflìssero

§105 ALLÙDERE—alludèndo—alluso
    (e) allusi, alludésti, alluse, alludémmo, alludéste, allùsero

§106 ANDARE—andando—andato
    (a) va *or* va' *or* vai, andate
    (b) vò *or* vado, vai, va, andiamo, andate, vanno
    (c) vada, vada, vada, andiamo, andiate, vàdano
    (f) andrò, andrài, andrà, andrémo, andréte, andranno

§107 ANNÈTTERE—annettèndo—annèsso *or* **annéttere,** annetténdo, annésso
    (e) annettéi *or* annèssi *or* annéssi; annettésti; annetté *or* annèsse *or* annésse; annettémmo; annettéste; annettérono *or* annèssero *or* annéssero

§108 APPARIRE—apparèndo—apparso
    (a) apparisci *or* appari; apparite
    (b) apparisco *or* appàio; apparisci *or* appari; apparisce *or* appare; appariamo; apparite; apparìscono *or* appàiono
    (c) apparisca *or* appàia; apparisca *or* appàia; apparisca *or* appàia; appariamo; appariate; apparìscano *or* appàiano
    (e) apparvi *or* apparìi *or* apparsi; appariti; apparve *or* apparì *or* apparse; apparimmo; appariste; appàrvero *or* apparìrono *or* appàrsero

§109 APPÈNDERE—appendèndo—appéso
    (e) appési, appendésti, appése, appendémmo, appendéste, appésero

§110 APRIRE—aprèndo—apèrto
    (e) aprìi *or* apèrsi; apristi; aprì *or* apèrse; aprimmo; apriste; aprìrono *or* apèrsero

§111 ÀRDERE—ardèndo—arso
    (e) arsi, ardésti, arse, ardémmo, ardéste, àrsero

§112 ASPÈRGERE—aspergèndo—aspèrso
    (e) aspèrsi, aspergésti, aspèrse, aspergémmo, aspergéste, aspèrsero

§113 ASSÌDERE—assidèndo—assiso
    (e) assisi, assidésti, assise, assidémmo, assidéste, assìsero

§114 ASSÌSTERE—assistèndo—assistito
    (e) assistéi *or* assistètti; assistésti; assisté *or* assistètte; assistémmo; assistéste; assistérono *or* assistèttero

§115 ASSÒLVERE—assolvèndo—assòlto *or* assoluto
    (e) assolvéi *or* assolvètti *or* assòlsi; assolvésti; assolvé *or* assolvètte *or* assòlse; assolvémmo; assolvéste; assolvérono *or* assolvèttero *or* assòlsero

§116 ASSÙMERE—assumèndo—assunto
    (e) assunsi, assumésti, assunse, assumémmo, assuméste, assùnsero

§117 ASSÙRGERE—assurgèndo—assurto
    (e) assursi, assurgésti, assurse, assurgémmo, assurgéste, assùrsero

§118 AVÈRE—avèndo—avuto
    (a) abbi, abbiate
    (b) ho, hai, ha, abbiamo, avete, hanno
    (c) àbbia, àbbia, àbbia, abbiamo, abbiate, àbbiano
    (e) èbbi, avésti, èbbe, avémmo, avéste, èbbero
    (f) avrò, avrài, avrà, avrémo, avréte, avranno

§119 AVVIARE—avviando—avviato
    (b) avvìo, avvìi, avvìa, avviamo, avviate, avvìano
    (c) avvìi, avvìi, avvìi, avviamo, avviate, avvìino

§120 BÉRE—bevèndo—bevuto
    (a) bévi, bevéte
    (b) bévo, bévi, béve, beviamo, bevéte, bévono
    (c) béva, béva, béva, beviamo, beviate, bévano
    (d) bevévo, bevévi, bevéva, bevevamo, bevevate, bevévano
    (e) bévvi *or* bevéi *or* bevètti; bevésti, bévve *or* bevé *or* bevètte; bevémmo; bevéste; bévvero *or* bevérono *or* bevèttero
    (f) berrò, berrài, berrà, berrémo, berréte, berranno

§121 CADÉRE—cadèndo—caduto
    (e) caddi, cadésti, cadde, cadémmo, cadéste, càddero
    (f) cadrò, cadrài, cadrà, cadrémo, cadréte, cadranno

§122 CECARE—cecando—cecato
    (a) cièca *or* cèca; cecate
    (b) cièco *or* cèco; cièchi *or* cèchi; cièca *or* cèca; cechiamo; cecate; ciècano *or* cècano
    (c) cièchi *or* cèchi; cièchi *or* cèchi; cièchi *or* cèchi; cechiamo; cechiate; cièchino *or* cèchino
    (f) cecherò, cecherài, cecherà, cecherémo, cecheréte, cecheranno

§123 CÈDERE—cedèndo—ceduto
    (e) cedéi *or* cedètti; cedésti; cedé *or* cedètte; cedémmo; cedéste; cedérono *or* cedèttero

§124 CHIÈDERE—chiedèndo—chièsto
(e) chièsi, chiedésti, chièse, chiedémmo, chiedéste, chièsero

§125 CHIÙDERE—chiudèndo—chiuso
(e) chiusi, chiudésti, chiuse, chiudémmo, chiudéste, chiùsero

§126 CÌNGERE—cingèndo—cinto
(e) cinsi, cingésti, cinse, cingémmo, cingéste, cìnsero

§127 CÒGLIERE—coglièndo—còlto
(a) còglì, cogliéte
(b) còlgo, còglì, còglie, cogliamo, cogliéte, còlgono
(c) còlga, còlga, còlga, cogliamo, cogliate, còlgano
(e) còlsi, cogliésti, còlse, cogliémmo, cogliéste, còlsero

§128 COMINCIARE—cominciando—cominciato
(b) comìncio, cominci, comìncia, cominciamo, cominciate, comìnciano
(c) cominci, cominci, cominci, cominciamo, cominciate, comìncino
(f) comincerò, comincerài, comincerà, comincerémo, cominceréte, cominceranno

§129 COMPÈTERE—competèndo—*pp* missing

§130 CÒMPIERE—compièndo—compiuto
(a) cómpi, compite
(b) cómpio, cómpi, cómpie, compiamo, compite, cómpiono
(c) cómpia, cómpia, cómpia, compiamo, compiate, cómpiano
(d) compivo, compivi, compiva, compivamo, compivate, compìvano
(e) compiéi *or* compìi; compiésti *or* compisti; compié *or* compì; compiémmo *or* compimmo; compiéste *or* compiste; compiérono *or* compìrono

§131 COMPRÌMERE—comprimèndo—comprèsso
(e) comprèssi, comprimésti, comprèsse, comprimémmo, compriméste, comprèssero

§132 CONCÈDERE—concedèndo—concèsso
(e) concedéi *or* concèssi *or* concedètti; concedésti; concedé *or* concèsse *or* concedètte; concedémmo; concedéste; concedérono *or* concèssero *or* concedèttero

§133 CONCÈRNERE—concernèndo—*pp* missing
(e) concernéi *or* concernètti; concernésti; concerné *or* concernètte; concernémmo; concernéste; concernérono *or* concernèttero

§134 CONÓSCERE—conoscèndo—conosciuto
    (e) conóbbi, conoscésti, conóbbe, conoscémmo, conoscéste, conóbbero

§135 CONQUÌDERE—conquidèndo—conquiso
    (e) conquisi, conquidésti, conquise, conquidémmo, conquidéste, conquìsero

§136 CONSÙMERE—*ger* missing—consunto
    (a) missing
    (b) missing
    (c) missing
    (d) missing
    (e) consunsi, consunse, consùnsero
    (f) missing

§137 CONVÈRGERE—convergèndo—convèrso
    (e) convèrsi *or* convergéi; convergésti; convèrse *or* convergé; convergémmo; convergéste; convèrsero *or* convergérono

§138 CONVERTIRE—convertèndo—convertito
    (e) convertìi *or* convèrsi; convertisti; convertì or convèrse; convertimmo; convertiste; convertìrono *or* convèrsero

§139 CÓRRERE—corrèndo—córso
    (e) córsi, corrésti, córse, corrémmo, corréste, córsero

§140 COSTRUIRE—costruèndo—costruito
    (a) costruisci, costruite
    (b) costruisco, costruisci, costruisce, costruiamo, costruite, costruìscono
    (c) costruisca, costruisca, costruisca, costruiamo, costruiate, costruìscano
    (e) costruìi *or* costrussi; costruisti; costruì *or* costrusse; costruimmo; costruiste; costruìrono *or* costrùssero

§141 CRÉDERE—credèndo—creduto
    (e) credéi *or* credètti; credésti; credé *or* credètte; credémmo; credéste; credérono *or* credèttero

§142 CRÉSCERE—crescèndo—cresciuto
    (e) crébbi, crescésti, crébbe, crescémmo, crescéste, crébbero

§143 CUCIRE—cucèndo—cucito
    (b) cùcio, cuci, cuce, cuciamo, cucite, cùciono
    (c) cùcia, cùcia, cùcia, cuciamo, cuciate, cùciano

§144a CUÒCERE—cuocèndo *or* cocèndo (cocènte)—còtto *or* cociuto

(a) cuòci, cocéte
(b) cuòcio, cuòci, cuòce, cociamo, cocéte, cuòciono
(c) cuòcia, cuòcia, cuòcia, cociamo, cociate, cuòciano
(d) cocévo, cocévi, cocéva, cocevamo, cocevate, cocévano
(e) còssi, cocésti, còsse, cocémmo, cocéste, còssero
(f) cocerò, cocerài, cocerà, cocerémo, coceréte, coceranno

§144b **DARE**—dando—dato
  (a) dà *or* dài *or* da'; date
  (b) dò *or* dò; dài; dà; diamo; date; danno
  (c) dìa, dìa, dìa, diamo, diate, dìano
  (e) dièdi *or* dètti; désti; diède *or* dètte *or* diè; démmo; déste; dièdero *or* dèttero
  (f) darò, dardi, darà, darémo, daréte, daranno

§145 **DECÌDERE**—decidèndo—deciso
  (e) decisi, decidésti, decise, decidémmo, decidéste, decìsero

§146 **DELÌNQUERE**—delinquèndo—*pp* missing
  (a) missing
  (c) missing
  (e) missing

§147 **DEVÒLVERE**—devolvèndo—devoluto
  (e) devolvéi *or* devolvètti; devolvésti; devolvé *or* devolvètte; devolvémmo; devolvéste; devolvérono *or* devolvèttero

§148 **DIFÈNDERE**—difendèndo—diféso
  (e) difési, difendésti, difése, difendémmo, difendéste, difésero

§149 **DILÌGERE**—diligèndo—dilètto
  (a) missing
  (b) missing
  (c) missing
  (d) missing
  (e) dilèssi, diligésti, dilèsse, diligémmo, diligéste, dilèssero
  (f) missing

§150 **DIPÈNDERE**—dipendèndo—dipéso
  (e) dipési, dipendésti, dipése, dipendémmo, dipendéste, dipésero

§151 **DIRE**—dicèndo—détto
  (a) di' *or* dì; dite
  (b) dico, dici, dice, diciamo, dite, dìcono
  (c) dica, dica, dica, diciamo, diciate, dìcano
  (d) dicévo, dicévi, dicéva, dicevamo, dicevate, dicévano
  (e) dissi, dicésti, disse, dicémmo, dicéste, dìssero
  (f) dirò, dirdi, dirà, dirémo, diréte, diranno

§152 DIRÌGERE—dirigèndo—dirètto
(e) dirèssi, dirigésti, dirèsse, dirigémmo, dirigéste, dirèssero

§153 DISCÈRNERE—discernèndo—*pp* missing
(e) discernéi; discernésti; discerné *or* discernètte; discernémmo; discernéste; discernérono *or* discernèttero

§154 DISCÙTERE—discutèndo—discusso
(e) discussi, discutésti, discusse, discutémmo, discutéste, discùssero

§155 DISSÒLVERE—dissolvèndo—dissòlto
(e) dissòlsi *or* dissolvéi *or* dissolvètti; dissolvésti; dissòlse *or* dissolvé *or* dissolvètte; dissolvémmo; dissolvéste; dissòlsero *or* dissolvérono *or* dissolvèttero

§156 DISTÌNGUERE—distinguèndo—distinto
(e) distinsi, distinguésti, distinse, distinguémmo, distinguéste, distìnsero

§157 DIVÈRGERE—divergèndo—*pp* missing
(e) obsolete

§158 DIVÌDERE—dividèndo—diviso
(e) divisi, dividésti, divise, dividémmo, dividéste, divìsero

§159 DOLÉRE—dolèndo—doluto
(a) duòli, doléte
(b) dòlgo, duòli, duòle, doliamo, doléte, dòlgono
(c) dòlga, dòlga, dòlga, doliamo, doliate, dòlgano
(e) dòlsi, dolésti, dòlse, dolémmo, doléste, dòlsero
(f) dorrò, dorràI, dorrà, dorrémo, dorréte, dorranno

§160 DOVÉRE—dovèndo—dovuto
(b) dèbbo *or* dèvo; dèvi; dève; dobbiamo; dovéte; dèbbono *or* dèvono
(c) dèva *or* dèbba; dèva *or* dèbba; dèva *or* dèbba; dobbiamo; dobbiate; dèvano *or* dèbbano
(e) dovéi *or* dovètti; dovésti; dové *or* dovètte; dovémmo; dovéste; dovérono *or* dovèttero

§161 ELÌDERE—elidèndo—eliso
(e) elisi, elidésti, elise, elidémmo, elidéste, elìsero

§162 EMÈRGERE—emergèndo—emèrso
(e) emèrsi, emergésti, emèrse, emergémmo, emergéste, emèrsero

§163 ÉMPIERE & EMPIRE—empièndo—empito *or* empiuto
(a) émpi, empite

- (b) émpio, émpi, émpie, empiamo, empite, émpiono
- (c) émpia, émpia, émpia, empiamo, empiate, émpiano
- (d) empivo, empivi, empiva, empivamo, empivate, empìvano
- (e) empiéi or empìi; empiésti; or empisti; empié or empì; empiémmo or empimmo; empiéste or empiste; empiérono or empìrono
- (f) empirò, empirài, empirà, empirémo, empiréte, empiranno

§164 ÈRGERE—ergèndo—èrto
- (e) èrsi, ergésti, èrse, ergémmo, ergéste, èrsero

§165 ESÌGERE—esigèndo—esatto
- (e) esigéi or esigètti; esigésti; esigé or esigètte; esigémmo; esigéste; esigérono or esigèttero

§166 ESÌMERE—esimèndo—*pp* missing
- (e) esiméi or esimètti; esimésti; esimé or esimètte; esimémmo; esiméste; esimérono or esimèttero

§167 ESPÀNDERE—espandèndo—espanso
- (e) espandéi or espandètti or espansi; espandésti; espandé or espandètte or espanse; espandémmo; espandéste; espandérono or espandèttero or espànsero

§168 ESPÈLLERE—espellèndo—espulso
- (e) espulsi, espellésti, espulse, espellémmo, espelléste, espùlsero

§169 ESPLÒDERE—esplodèndo—esplòso
- (e) esplòsi, esplodésti, esplòse, esplodémmo, esplodéste, esplòsero

§170 ÈSSERE—essèndo—stato
- (a) sii, siate
- (b) sóno, sèi, è, siamo, siète, sóno
- (c) sìa, sìa, sìa, siamo, siate, sìano
- (d) èro, èri, èra, eravamo, eravate, èrano
- (e) fui, fósti, fu, fummo, fóste, fùrono
- (f) sarò, sarài, sarà, sarémo, saréte, saranno

§171 ESTÒLLERE—estollèndo—*pp* missing
- (e) missing

§172 EVÀDERE—evadèndo—evaso
- (e) evasi, evadésti, evase, evadémmo, evadéste, evàsero

§173 FARE—facèndo—fatto
- (a) fa or fài or fa'; fate

(b) fàccio *or* fò; fài; fa; facciamo; fate; fanno
(c) fàccia, fàccia, fàccia, facciamo, facciate; fàcciano
(d) facévo, facévi, facéva, facevamo, facevate, facévano
(e) féci, facésti, féce, facémmo, facéste, fécero
(f) farò, faràì, farà, farémo, faréte, faranno

§174 **FÈNDERE**—fendèndo—fenduto *or* fésso
(e) fendéi *or* fendètti; fendésti; fendé *or* fendètte; fendémmo; fendéste; fendérono *or* fendèttero

§175 **FÈRVERE**—fervèndo—*pp* missing
(e) fervéi *or* fervètti; fervésti; fervé *or* fervètte; fervémmo; fervéste; fervérono *or* fervèttero

§176 **FINIRE**—finèndo—finito
(a) finisci, finite
(b) finisco, finisci, finisce, finiamo, finite, finìscono
(c) finisca, finisca, finisca, finiamo, finiate, finìscano

§177 **FLÈTTERE**—flettèndo—flèsso
(e) flettéi *or* flèssi; flettésti; fletté *or* flèsse; flettémmo; flettéste; flettérono *or* flèssero

§178 **FÓNDERE**—fondèndo—fuso
(e) fusi, fondésti, fuse, fondémmo, fondéste, fùsero

§179 **FRÀNGERE**—frangèndo—franto
(e) fransi, frangésti, franse, frangémmo, frangéste, frànsero

§180 **FRÌGGERE**—friggèndo—fritto
(e) frissi, friggésti, frisse, friggémmo, friggéste, frìssero

§181 **GIACÉRE**—giacèndo—giaciuto
(b) giàccio; giaci; giace; giacciamo *or* giaciamo; giacete; giàcciono
(c) giàccia, giàccia, giàccia, giacciamo, giacciate, giàcciano
(e) giàcqui, giacésti, giàcque, giacémmo, giacéste, giàcquero

§182 **GIOCARE**—giocando—giocato
(a) giuòca *or* giòca; giocate
(b) giuòco *or* giòco; giuòchi *or* giòchi; giuòca *or* giòca; giochiamo; giocate; giuòcano *or* giòcano
(c) giuòchi *or* giòchi; giuòchi *or* giòchi; giuòchi *or* giòchi; giochiamo; giochiate; giuòchino *or* giòchino
(f) giocherò, giocheràì, giocherà, giocherémo, giocheréte, giocheranno

§183 **GIÙNGERE**—giungèndo—giunto
(e) giunsi, giungésti, giunse, giungémmo, giungéste, giùnsero

25

§184 GODÉRE—godèndo—goduto
  (e) godéi *or* godètti; godésti; godé *or* godètte; godémmo; godéste; godérono *or* godèttero
  (f) godrò, godrài, godrà, godrémo, godréte, godranno

§185 IMBÉVERE—imbevèndo—imbevuto
  (e) imbévvi, imbevésti, imbévve, imbevémmo, imbevéste, imbévvero

§186 INCÓMBERE—incombèndo—*pp* missing
  (e) incombéi *or* incombètti; incombésti; incombé *or* incombètte; incombémmo; incombéste; incombérono *or* incombèttero

§187 INDÙLGERE—indulgèndo—indulto
  (e) indulsi, indulgésti, indulse, indulgémmo, indulgéste, indùlsero

§188a INFERIRE—inferèndo—inferito *or* infèrto
  (a) inferisci, inferite
  (b) inferisco, inferisci, inferisce, inferiamo, inferite, inferìscono
  (c) inferisca, inferisca, inferisca, inferiamo, inferiate, inferìscano
  (e) inferìi *or* infèrsi; inferisti; inferì *or* infèrse; inferimmo; inferiste; inferìrono *or* infèrsero

§188b INSTARE—instando—*pp* missing

§189 INTRÌDERE—intridèndo—intriso
  (e) intrisi, intridésti, intrise, intridémmo, intridéste, intrìsero

§190 INTRÙDERE—intrudèndo—intruso
  (e) intrusi, intrudésti, intruse, intrudémmo, intrudéste, intrùsero

§191 IRE—*ger* missing—ito
  (a) *sg* missing, ite
  (b) missing
  (c) missing
  (d) ivo, ivi, iva, ivamo, ivate, ìvano
  (e) *1st sg* missing, isti, *3rd sg* missing, *1st pl* missing, iste, ìrono

§192 LÈDERE—ledèndo—léso *or* lèso
  (e) lési, ledésti, lése, ledémmo, ledéste, lésero

§193 LÈGGERE—leggèndo—lètto
  (e) lèssi, leggésti, lèsse, leggémmo, leggéste, lèssero

26

§194 LIQUEFARE—liquefacèndo—liquefatto
(a) liquefà, liquefate
(b) liquefò or liquefàccio; liquefài; liquefà liquefacciamo; liquefate; liquefanno
(c) liquefàccia, liquefàccia, liquefàccia, liquefacciamo, liquefacciate, liquefàcciano
(d) liquefacévo, liquefacévi, liquefacéva, liquefacevamo, liquefacevate, liquefacévano
(e) liqueféci, liquefacésti, liqueféce, liquefacémmo, liquefacéste, liquefécero
(f) liquefarò, liquefarài, liquefarà, liquefarémo, liquefaréte, liquefaranno

§195 MALEDIRE—maledicèndo—maledétto
(a) maledici, maledite
(b) maledico, maledici, maledice, malediciamo, maledite, maledìcono
(c) maledica, maledica, maledica, malediciamo, malediciate, maledìcano
(d) maledicévo or maledivo; maledicévi or maledivi; maledicéva or malediva; maledicevamo or maledivamo; maledicevate or maledivate; maledicévano or maledìvano
(e) maledìi or maledissi; maledisti or maledicésti; maledì or maledisse; maledimmo or maledicémmo; malediste or maledicéste; maledìrono or maledìssero
(f) maledirò, maledirài, maledirà, maledirémo, malediréte, malediranno

§196 MALVOLÉRE—*ger* missing—malvoluto
(a) missing
(b) missing
(c) missing
(d) missing
(e) missing
(f) missing

§197 MANCARE—mancando—mancato
(b) manco, manchi, manca, manchiamo, mancate, màncano
(c) manchi, manchi, manchi, manchiamo, manchiate, mànchino
(f) mancherò, mancherài, mancherà, mancherémo, mancheréte, mancheranno

§198 MÉTTERE—mettèndo—mésso
(e) misi, mettésti, mise, mettémmo, mettéste, mìsero

§199 MÌNGERE—mingèndo—minto
(e) minsi, mingésti, minse, mingémmo, mingéste, mìnsero

§200 MÒRDERE—mordèndo—mòrso
    (e) mòrsi, mordésti, mòrse, mordémmo, mordéste, mòrsero

§201 MORIRE—morèndo—mòrto
    (a) muòri, morite
    (b) muòio, muòri, muòre, moriamo, morite, muòiono
    (c) muòia. muòia, muòia, moriamo, moriate, muòiano
    (f) morrò or morirò; morrài or morirài; morrà or morirà;
        morrémo or morirémo; morréte or moriréte; mor-
        ranno or moriranno

§202 MUÒVERE—muovèndo or movèndo (movènte)—mòsso
    (a) muòvi, movéte
    (b) muòvo, muòvi, muòve, moviamo, movéte, muòvono
    (c) muòva, muòva, muòva, moviamo, moviate, muòvano
    (d) movévo, movévi, movéva, movevamo, movevate,
        movévano
    (e) mòssi, movésti, mòsse, movémmo, movéste, mòssero
    (f) moverò, moverài, moverà, moverémo, moveréte, move-
        ranno

§203 NÀSCERE—nascèndo—nato
    (e) nàcqui, nascésti, nàcque, nascémmo, nascéste, nàcquero

§204 NASCÓNDERE—nascondèndo—nascósto
    (e) nascósi, nascondésti, nascóse, nascondémmo, nas-
        condéste, nascósero

§205 NEGLÌGERE—negligèndo—neglètto
    (a) missing
    (b) missing
    (c) missing
    (e) neglèssi, negligésti, neglèsse, negligémmo, negligéste,
        neglèssero

§206 NUÒCERE—nuocèndo—nociuto
    (a) nuòci, nocéte
    (b) nuòccio or nòccio; nuòci; nuòce; nociamo; nocéte;
        nuòcciono or nòcciono
    (c) nòccia, nòccia, nòccia, nociamo, nociate, nòcciano
    (d) nocévo, nocévi, nocéva, nocevamo, nocevate, nocévano
    (e) nòcqui, nocésti, nòcque, nocémmo, nocéste, nòcquero
    (f) nocerò, nocerài, nocerà, nocerémo, noceréte, noceranno

§207 OFFRIRE—offrèndo (offerènte)—offèrto
    (e) offrìi or offèrsi; offristi; offrì or offèrse; offrimmo;
        offriste; offrìrono or offèrsero

§208 OTTÙNDERE—ottundèndo—ottuso
    (e) ottusi, ottundésti, ottuse, ottundémmo, ottundéste,
        ottùsero

§209 PAGARE—pagando—pagato
(b) pago, paghi, paga, paghiamo, pagate, pàgano
(c) paghi, paghi, paghi, paghiamo, paghiate, pàghino
(f) pagherò, pagherài, pagherà, pagherémo, pagheréte, pagheranno

§210 PARÉRE—parèndo (parvènte)—parso
(a) missing
(b) pàio; pari; pare; pariamo *or* paiamo; paréte; pàiono
(c) pàia; pàia; pàia; pariamo *or* paiamo; pariate *or* paiate; pàiano
(e) parvi, parésti, parve, parémmo, paréste, pàrvero
(f) parrò, parrài, parrà, parrémo, parréte, parranno

§211 PÀSCERE—pascèndo—pasciuto
(a) pascéi *or* pascètti; pascésti; pascé *or* pascètte; pascémmo; pascéste; pascérono *or* pascèttero

§212 PÈRDERE—perdèndo—pèrso *or* perduto
(e) perdéi *or* pèrsi *or* perdètti; perdésti; perdé, *or* pèrse *or* perdètte; perdémmo; perdéste; perdérono *or* pèrsero *or* perdèttero

§213 PERSUADÉRE—persuadèndo—persuaso
(e) persuasi, persuadésti, persuase, persuadémmo, persuadéste, persuàsero

§214 PIACÉRE—piacèndo—piaciuto
(b) piàccio, piaci, piace, piacciamo, piacéte, piàcciono
(c) piàccia, piàccia, piàccia, piacciamo, piacciate, piàcciano
(e) piàcqui, piacésti, piàcque, piacémmo, piacéste, piàcquero

§215 PIÀNGERE—piangèndo—pianto
(e) piansi, piangésti, pianse, piangémmo, piangéste, piànsero

§216 PIÒVERE—piovèndo—piovuto
(e) piòvvi, piovésti, piòvve, piovémmo, piovéste, piòvvero

§217 PÒRGERE—porgèndo—pòrto
(e) pòrsi, porgésti, pòrse, porgémmo, porgéste, pòrsero

§218 PÓRRE—ponèndo—pósto
(a) póni, ponéte
(b) póngo, póni, póne, poniamo, ponéte, póngono
(c) pónga, pónga, pónga, poniamo, poniate, póngano
(d) ponévo, ponévi, ponéva, ponevamo, ponevate, ponévano
(e) pósi, ponésti, póse, ponémmo, ponéste, pósero

§219 POTÉRE—potèndo (potènte *or* possènte)—potuto
(a) missing
(b) pòsso, puòi, può, possiamo, potéte, pòssono

29

    (c) pòssa, pòssa, pòssa, possiamo, possiate, pòssano

    (e) potéi *or* potètti; potésti, poté *or* potètte; potémmo; potéste; potérono *or* potèttero

    (f) potrò, potrài, potrà, potrémo, potréte, potranno

§220 PRÈNDERE—prendèndo—préso
    (e) prési, prendésti, prése, prendémmo, prendéste, présero

§221 PROVVEDÉRE—provvedèndo—provveduto *or* provvisto
    (e) provvidi, provvedésti, provvide, provvedémmo, provvedéste, provvìdero

§222 PRÙDERE—prudèndo—*pp* missing
    (e) *1st sg* missing; *2nd sg* missing; prudé *or* prudètte; *1st pl* missing; *2nd pl* missing; prudérono *or* prudèttero

§223 RÀDERE—radèndo—raso
    (e) rasi, radésti, rase, radémmo, radéste, ràsero

§224 REDÌGERE—redigèndo—redatto
    (e) redassi, redigésti, redasse, redigémmo, redigéste, redàssero

§225 REDÌMERE—redimèndo—redènto
    (e) redènsi, redimésti, redènse, redimémmo, rediméste, redènsero

§226 RÈGGERE—reggèndo—rètto
    (e) rèssi, reggésti, rèsse, reggémmo, reggéste, rèssero

§227 RÈNDERE—rendèndo—réso
    (e) rési *or* rendéi *or* rendètti; rendésti; rése *or* rendé *or* rendètte; rendémmo; rendéste; résero *or* rendérono *or* rendèttero

§228 RETROCÈDERE—retrocedèndo—retrocèsso *or* retroceduto
    (e) retrocèssi *or* retrocedéi *or* retrocedètti; retrocedésti; retrocèsse *or* retrocedé *or* retrocedètte; retrocedémmo; retrocedéste; retrocèssero *or* retrocedérono *or* retrocedèttero

§229 RIAVÉRE—riavèndo—riavuto
    (a) riabbi, riabbiate
    (b) riò, riài, rià, riabbiamo, riavéte, rianno
    (c) riàbbia, riàbbia, riàbbia, riabbiamo, riabbiate, riàbbiano
    (e) rièbbi, riavésti, rièbbe, riavémmo, riavéste, rièbbero
    (f) riavrò, riavrài, riavrà, riavrémo, riavréte, riavranno

§230 RIDARE—ridando—ridato
    (a) ridài *or* ridà; ridate
    (b) ridò, ridài, ridà, ridiamo, ridate, ridanno
    (c) ridìa, ridìa, ridìa, ridiamo, ridiate, ridìano

(e) ridièdi *or* ridètti; ridésti; ridiède *or* ridètte; ridémmo; ridéste; ridièdero *or* ridèttero

(f) ridarò, ridarài, ridarà, ridarémo, ridaréte, ridaranno

§231 RÌDERE—ridèndo—riso
  (e) risi, ridésti, rise, ridémmo, ridéste, rìsero

§232 RIFLÈTTERE—riflettèndo—riflèsso *or* riflettuto

§233 RIFÙLGERE—rifulgèndo—rifulso
  (e) rifulsi, rifulgésti, rifulse rifulgémmo, rifulgéste, rifùlsero

§234 RILÙCERE—rilucèndo—*pp* missing

§235 RIMANÉRE—rimanèndo—rimasto
  (b) rimango, rimani, rimane, rimaniamo, rimanéte, rimàngono
  (c) rimanga, rimanga, rimanga, rimaniamo, rimaniate, rimàngano
  (e) rimasi, rimanésti, rimase, rimanémmo, rimanéste, rimàsero
  (f) rimarrò, rimarrài, rimarrà, rimarrémo, rimarréte, rimarranno

§236 RINCORARE—rincorando—rincorato
  (a) rincuòra, rincorate
  (b) rincuòro, rincuòri, rincuòra, rincoriamo, rincorate, rincuòrano
  (c) rincuòri, rincuòri, rincuòri, rincoriamo, rincoriate, rincuòrino

§237 RISOLARE—risolando—risolato
  (a) risuòla, risolate
  (b) risuòlo, risuòli, risuòla, risoliamo, risolate, risuòlano
  (c) risuòli, risuòli, risuòli, risoliamo, risoliate, risuòlino

§238 RISPÓNDERE—rispondèndo—rispósto
  (e) rispósi, rispondésti, rispóse, rispondémmo, rispondéste, rispósero

§239 RÓDERE—rodèndo—róso
  (e) rósi, rodésti, róse, rodémmo, rodéste, rósero

§240 RÓMPERE—rompèndo—rótto
  (e) ruppi, rompésti, ruppe, rompémmo, rompéste, rùppero

§241 ROTARE—rotando—rotato
  (a) ruòta, rotate
  (b) ruòto, ruòti, ruòta, rotiamo, rotate, ruòtano
  (c) ruòti, ruòti, ruòti, rotiamo, rotiate, ruòtino

§242 SALIRE—salèndo—salito
  (b) salgo, sali, sale, saliamo, salite, sàlgono
  (c) salga, salga, salga, saliamo, saliate, sàlgano

§243 SAPÉRE—sapèndo (sapiènte)—saputo
  (a) sappi, sappiate
  (b) sò, sai, sa, sappiamo, sapéte, sanno
  (c) sàppia, sàppia, sàppia, sappiamo, sappiate, sàppiano
  (e) sèppi, sapésti, sèppe, sapémmo, sapéste, sèppero
  (f) saprò, saprài, saprà, saprémo, sapréte, sapranno

§244 SCÉGLIERE—sceglièndo—scélto
  (a) scégli, scegliéte
  (b) scélgo, scégli, scéglie, scegliamo, scegliéte, scélgono
  (c) scélga, scélga, scélga, scegliamo, scegliate, scélgano
  (e) scélsi, scegliésti, scélse, scegliémmo, scegliéste, scélsero

§245 SCÉNDERE—scendèndo—scéso
  (e) scési, scendésti, scése, scendémmo, scendéste, scésero

§246 SCÈRNERE—scernèndo—*pp* missing
  (e) scernéi *or* scernètti; scernésti; scerné *or* scernètte; scer-
      némmo; scernéste; scernérono *or* scernèttero

§247 SCÌNDERE—scindèndo—scisso
  (e) scissi, scindésti, scisse, scindémmo, scindéste, scìssero

§248 SCOIARE—scoiando—scoiato
  (a) scuòia, scoiate
  (b) scuòio, scuòi, scuòia, scoiamo, scoiate, scuòiano
  (c) scuòi, scuòi, scuòi, scoiamo, scoiate, scuòino

§249 SCÒRGERE—scorgèndo—scòrto
  (e) scòrsi, scorgésti, scòrse, scorgémmo, scorgéste, scòrsero

§250 SCRÌVERE—scrivèndo—scritto
  (e) scrissi, scrivésti, scrisse, scrivémmo, scrivéste, scrìssero

§251 SCUÒTERE—scotèndo—scòsso
  (a) scuòti, scotéte
  (b) scuòto, scuòti, scuòte, scotiamo, scotéte, scuòtono
  (c) scuòta, scuòta, scuòta, scotiamo, scotiate, scuòtano
  (d) scotévo, scotévi, scotéva, scotevamo, scotevate, scoté-
      vano
  (e) scòssi, scotésti, scòsse, scotémmo, scotéste, scòssero

§252 SEDÉRE—sedéndo—seduto
  (a) sièdi, sedéte
  (b) sièdo *or* sèggo; sièdi; sième; sediamo; sedéte; sièdono
      or sèggono
  (c) sièda *or* sègga; sièda *or* sègga; sièda *or* sègga; sediamo;
      sediate; sièdano *or* sèggano
  (e) sedéi *or* sedètti; sedésti; sedé *or* sedètte; sedémmo;
      sedéste; sedérono *or* sedèttero

§253 SEPPELLIRE—seppellèndo—sepólto *or* seppellito
- (a) seppellisci, seppellite
- (b) seppellisco, seppellisci, seppellisce, seppelliamo, seppellite, seppellìscono
- (c) seppellisca, seppellisca, seppellisca, seppelliamo, seppelliate, seppellìscano

§254 SODDISFARE—soddisfacèndo—soddisfatto
- (a) soddisfa *or* soddisfài *or* soddisfa'
- (b) soddisfàccio *or* soddisfò *or* soddisfo; soddisfài *or* soddisfi; soddisfà *or* soddisfa; soddisfacciamo; soddisfate; soddisfanno *or* soddìsfano
- (c) soddisfàccia *or* soddisfi; soddisfàccia *or* soddisfi; soddisfàccia *or* soddisfi; soddisfacciamo; soddisfacciate; soddisfàcciano *or* soddìsfino
- (d) soddisfacévo, soddisfacévi, soddisfacéva, soddisfacevamo, soddisfacevate, soddisfacévano
- (e) soddisféci, soddisfacésti, soddisféce, soddisfacémmo, soddisfacéste, soddisfécero
- (f) soddisfarò, soddisfarài, soddisfarà, soddisfarémo, soddisfaréte, soddisfaranno

§255 SOLÉRE—solèndo—sòlito
- (a) missing
- (b) sòglio, suòli, suòle, sogliamo, soléte, sògliono
- (c) sòglia, sòglia, sòglia, sogliamo, sogliate, sògliano
- (e) missing
- (f) missing

§256 SÒLVERE—solvèndo—soluto
- (e) solvéi *or* solvètti; solvésti; solvé *or* solvètte; solvémmo; solvéste; solvérono *or* solvèttero

§257 SONARE—sonando—sonato
- (a) suòna, sonate
- (b) suòno, suòni, suòna, soniamo, sonate, suònano
- (c) suòni, suòni, suòni, soniamo, soniate, suònino

§258 SÓRGERE—sorgèndo—sórto
- (e) sórsi, sorgésti, sórse, sorgémmo, sorgéste, sórsero

§259 SOSPÈNDERE—sospendèndo—sospéso
- (e) sospési, sospendésti, sospése, sospendémmo, sospendéste, sospésero

§260 SPÀNDERE—spandèndo—spanto
- (e) spandéi *or* spandètti *or* spansi; spandésti; spandé *or* spandètte *or* spanse; spandémmo; spandéste; spandérono *or* spandèttero *or* spànsero

§261 SPÀRGERE—spargèndo—sparso
- (e) sparsi, spargésti, sparse, spargémmo, spargéste, spàrsero

§262 SPÈGNERE—spegnèndo—spènto
- (b) spéngo *or* spèngo; spégni *or* spègni; spégne *or* spègne; spegniamo; spegnéte; spéngono *or* spèngono
- (c) spénga *or* spènga; spénga *or* spènga; spénga *or* spènga; spegniamo; spegniate; spéngano *or* spèngano
- (e) spènsi, spegnésti, spènse, spegnémmo, spegnéste, spènsero

§263 STARE—stando—stato
- (a) sta *or* stai *or* sta'; state
- (b) stò, stài, sta, stiamo, state, stanno
- (c) stìa, stìa, stìa, stiamo, stiate, stìano
- (e) stètti, stésti, stètte, stémmo, stéste, stèttero
- (f) starò, starài, starà, starémo, staréte, staranno

§264 STRÌDERE—stridèndo—*pp* missing
- (e) stridéi *or* stridètti; stridésti; stridé *or* stridètte; stridémmo; stridéste; stridérono *or* stridèttero

§265 STRÌNGERE—stringèndo—strétto
- (e) strinsi, stringésti, strinse, stringémmo, stringéste, strìnsero

§266 STRÙGGERE—struggèndo—strutto
- (e) strussi, struggésti, strusse, struggémmo, struggéste, strùssero

§267 SVÈLLERE—svellèndo—svèlto
- (b) svèllo *or* svèlgo; svèlli; svèlle; svelliamo; svelléte; svèllono *or* svèlgono
- (c) svèlla *or* svèlga; svèlla *or* svèlga; svèlla *or* svèlga; svelliamo; svelliate; svèllano *or* svèlgano
- (e) svèlsi, svellésti, svèlse, svellémmo, svelléste, svèlsero

§268 TACÉRE—tacèndo—taciuto
- (b) tàccio, taci, tace, taciamo, tacéte, tàcciono
- (c) tàccia, tàccia, tàccia, taciamo, taciate, tàcciano
- (e) tàcqui, tacésti, tàcque, tacémmo, tacéste, tàcquero

§269 TÀNGERE—tangèndo—*pp* missing
- (a) missing
- (b) *1st sg* missing; *2nd sg* missing; tange; *1st pl* missing; *2nd pl* missing; tàngono
- (c) *1st sg* missing; *2nd sg* missing; tanga; *1st pl* missing; *2nd pl* missing; tàngano
- (d) *1st sg* missing; *2nd sg* missing; tangéva; *1st pl* missing; *2nd pl* missing; tangévano
- (e) missing
- (f) *1st sg* missing; *2nd sg* missing; tangerà; *1st pl* missing; *2nd pl* missing; tangeranno

§270 TÈNDERE—tendèndo—téso
(e) tési, tendésti, tése, tendémmo, tendéste, tésero

§271 TENÉRE—tenèndo—tenuto
(a) tièni, tenéte
(b) tèngo, tièni, tiène, teniamo, tenéte, tèngono
(c) tènga, tènga, tènga, teniamo, teniate, tèngano
(e) ténni, tenésti, ténne, tenémmo, tenéste, ténnero
(f) terrò, terrài, terrà, terrémo, terréte, terranno

§272 TÒRCERE—torcèndo—tòrto
(e) tòrsi, torcésti, tòrse, torcémmo, torcéste, tòrsero

§273 TRARRE—traèndo—tratto
(a) trài, traéte
(b) traggo, trài, trae, traiamo, traéte, tràggono
(c) tragga, tragga, tragga, traiamo, traiate, tràggano
(d) traévo, traévi, traéva, traevamo, traevate, traévano
(e) trassi, traésti, trasse, traémmo, traéste, tràssero

§274 UCCÌDERE—uccidèndo—ucciso
(e) uccisi, uccidésti, uccise, uccidémmo, uccidéste, uccìsero

§275 UDIRE—udèndo *or* udièndo—udito
(a) òdi, udite
(b) òdo, òdi, òde, udiamo, udite, òdono
(c) òda, òda, òda, udiamo, udiate, òdano
(f) udirò *or* udrò; udirài *or* udrài; udirà *or* udrà; udirémo *or* udrémo; udiréte *or* udréte; udiranno *or* udranno

§276 ÙRGERE—urgèndo—*pp* missing
(a) missing
(e) missing

§277 USCIRE—uscèndo—uscito
(a) èsci, uscite
(b) èsco, èsci, èsce, usciamo, uscite, èscono
(c) èsca, èsca, èsca, usciamo, usciate, èscano

§278 VALÉRE—valèndo—valso
(b) valgo, vali, vale, valiamo, valéte, vàlgono
(c) valga, valga, valga, valiamo, valiate, vàlgano
(e) valsi, valésti, valse, valémmo, valéste, vàlsero
(f) varrò, varrài, varrà, varrémo, varréte, varranno

§279 VEDÉRE—vedèndo—veduto *or* visto
(e) vidi, vedésti, vide, vedémmo, vedéste, vìdero
(f) vedrò, vedrài, vedrà, vedrémo, vedréte, vedranno

§280 VEGLIARE—vegliando—vegliato
(b) véglio, végli, véglia, vegliamo, vegliate, végliano
(c) végli, végli, végli, vegliamo, vegliate, véglino

§281 VÉNDERE—vendèndo—venduto
    (e) vendéi *or* vendètti; vendésti; vendé *or* vendètte; ven-
    démmo; vendéste; vendérono *or* vendèttero

§282 VENIRE—venèndo (veniènte)—venuto
    (a) vièni, venite
    (b) vèngo, vièni, viène, veniamo, venite, vèngono
    (c) vènga, vènga, vènga, veniamo, veniate, vèngano
    (e) vénni, venisti, vénne, venimmo, veniste, vénnero
    (f) verrò, verrài, verrà, verrémo, verréte, verranno

§283 VÈRTERE—vertèndo—*pp* missing

§284 VÌGERE—vigèndo—*pp* missing
    (a) missing
    (b) *1st sg* missing; *2nd sg* missing; vige; *1st pl* missing;
        2d pl missing; vìgono
    (c) *1st sg* missing; *2d sg* missing; viga; *1st pl* missing;
        2d pl missing; vìgano
    (d) *1st sg* missing; *2d sg* missing; vigéva; *1st pl* missing;
        2d pl missing; vigévano
    (e) missing

§285 VÌNCERE—vincèndo—vinto
    (e) vinsi, vincésti, vinse, vincémmo, vincéste, vìnsero

§286 VÌVERE—vivèndo—vissuto
    (e) vissi, vivésti, visse, vivémmo, vivéste, vìssero
    (f) vivrò, vivrài, vivrà, vivrémo, vivréte, vivranno

§287 VIZIARE—viziando—viziato
    (b) vìzio, vizi, vìzia, viziamo, viziate, vìziano
    (c) vizi, vizi, vizi, viziamo, viziate, vìzino

§288 VOLÉRE—volèndo—voluto
    (a) vògli, vogliate
    (b) vòglio, vuòi, vuòle, vogliamo, voléte, vògliono
    (c) vòglia, vòglia, vòglia, vogliamo, vogliate, vògliano
    (e) vòlli, volésti, vòlle, volémmo, voléste, vòllero
    (f) vorrò, vorrài, vorrà, vorrémo, vorréte, vorranno

§289 VÒLGERE—volgèndo—vòlto
    (e) vòlsi, volgésti, vòlse, volgémmo, volgéste, vòlsero

§290 VOLTEGGIARE—volteggiando—volteggiato
    (b) voltéggio, voltéggi, voltéggia, volteggiamo, volteggiate,
        voltéggiano
    (c) voltéggi, voltéggi, voltéggi, volteggiamo, volteggiate,
        voltéggino
    (f) volteggerò, volteggerài, volteggerà, volteggerémo, vol-
        teggeréte, volteggeranno

A

A, a [α] *m* & *f* first letter of the Italian alphabet

a *prep* (ad in front of a vowel) to, e.g., **diede il libro a Giovanni** he gave the book to John; in, e.g., **a Milano** in Milan; at, e.g., **a casa** at home; within, e.g., **a tre miglia da qui** within three miles from here; on, e.g., **portare una catena al collo** to wear a chain on one's neck; e.g., al **sabato** on Saturdays; for, e.g., **a vita** for life; by, e.g., **fatto a mano** made by hand; with, e.g., **una gonna a pieghe** a skirt with pleats; as, e.g., **eleggere a presidente** to elect as chairman; into, e.g., **fu gettato a mare** he was thrown into the sea; of, e.g., **un quarto alle due** fifteen minutes of two

àba·co *m* (-chi) (archit) abacus

abate *m* abbot

abbacchiare §287 *tr* to knock down (e.g., olives); to sell too cheap || *ref* to lose courage; to be dejected

abbacchia·to -ta *adj* (coll) dejected

abbàc·chio *m* (-chi) baby lamb (slaughtered)

abbacinare (abbàcino) *tr* to dazzle; to deceive

abbadéssa *f* var of **badessa**

abbagliante *adj* dazzling || *m* (aut) bright light, high beam

abbagliare §280 *tr* to dazzle; to deceive; to blind (with the lights of a car)

abbà·glio *m* (-gli) error; **prendere abbaglio** to make a mistake

abbaiaménto *m* bark (of dog)

abbaiare §287 *intr* to bark; to yelp

abbaino *m* dormer window; skylight; attic

abbambinare *tr* to walk (a heavy piece of furniture)

abbandonare (abbandóno) *tr* to abandon; to give up; to let go (e.g., the reins); to let fall; (sports) to withdraw from || *ref* to yield; to lose courage

abbandóno *m* abandon, abandonment; desertion; neglect; relaxation; renunciation (of a right); cession (of property); withdrawal (from a fight)

abbarbicare §197 (abbàrbico) *intr* & *ref* to cling; to hold on

abbassalin·gua *m* (-gua) tongue depressor

abbassaménto *m* lowering; reduction; drop, fall

abbassare *tr* to lower; to dim (lights); to turn (the radio) lower; **abbassare le armi** to surrender; **abbassare la cresta** to yield || *ref* to lower oneself; to drop

abbàs·so *m* (-so) angry shout (of a crowd) || *adv* down, below; downstairs || *interj* down with!

abbastanza *adj invar* enough || *adv* enough; rather, fairly

abbàttere *tr* to demolish; to fell; to shoot down; to refute (an argument); to depress || *ref* to be depressed, be downcast

abbattiménto *m* demolition; felling; shooting down; chill; (fig) depression; **abbattimento alla base** (econ) basic exemption (from taxes)

abbattu·to -ta *adj* dejected, downcast || *f* clearing (of trees)

abbazìa *f* abbey; abbacy

abbecedà·rio *m* (-ri) speller, primer

abbelliménto *m* embellishment, ornamentation

abbellire §176 *tr* to embellish, adorn; to landscape

abbeverare (abbévero) *tr* to water (animals) || *ref* to quench one's thirst

abbevera·tóio *m* (-tói) watering trough

abbic·cì *m* (-cì) alphabet; speller, primer; ABC's, rudiments

abbiènte *adj* well-to-do || *m*—**gli abbienti** the haves; **gli abbienti e nullatenenti** the haves and the have-nots

abbiettézza or **abiettézza** *f* abjectness, baseness

abbièt·to -ta or **abièt·to -ta** *adj* abject, base, low

abbiezióne or **abiezióne** *f* wretchedness, baseness

abbigliaménto *m* attire, wear

abbigliare §280 *tr* & *ref* to dress; to dress up

abbinaménto *m* coupling; merger

abbinare *tr* to couple; to join, merge

abbindolare (abbìndolo) *tr* to dupe, deceive

abbiosciare §128 *ref* to fall down; to lose heart, be downcast

abbisognare (abbisógno) *intr* to be in need

abboccaménto *m* interview, conversation

abboccare §197 (abbócco) *tr* to swallow (the hook); to fit (pipes) || *intr* to bite (said of fish); to fall; to fit (said of pipes) || *ref* to confer

abbocca·to -ta *adj* palatable; slightly sweet (wine)

abbonacciare §128 *ref* to calm down, abate (said of weather)

abbonaménto *m* subscription; **abbonamento postale** mailing permit

abbonare (abbòno) *tr* to take out a subscription for (s.o.) || *ref* to subscribe || §257 *tr* to remit (a debt); to forgive

abbona·to -ta *mf* subscriber; commuter

abbondante *adj* abundant, plentiful; heavy (rain)

abbondanza *f* abundance, plenty

abbondare (abbóndo) *intr* (ESSERE & AVERE) to abound; to exceed; **abbondare di** or **in** to abound in

abbonire §176 *tr* to calm; to placate || *ref* to calm down

abbordàbile *adj* accessible, approachable; negotiable (curve)

abbordàg·gio m (-gi) boarding (of an enemy ship); **andare all'abbordàggio di** to board

abbordare (abbórdo) tr to board (an enemy ship); to negotiate (a curve); to face (a problem); (fig) to button-hole

abborracciare §128 tr to botch, bungle

abborracciatura f botch, bungle

abbottonare (abbottóno) tr to button || ref (coll) to keep to oneself

abbottonatura f buttoning; row of buttons

abbozzare (abbòzzo) tr to sketch; to hew (e.g., a statue); (naut) to tie up || intr (coll) to take it

abbòzzo m sketch, draft

abbracciabò·sco m (-schi) (bot) woodbine

abbracciare m embrace, embracing || §128 tr to embrace, hug; to seize (an opportunity); to become converted to (e.g., Christianity); to enter (a profession); to span, encompass || ref to cling; to embrace one another

abbràc·cio m (-ci) embrace, hug

abbrancare §197 tr to grab; to herd || ref to cling; to join a herd

abbreviaménto m abbreviation, shortening

abbreviare §287 (abbrèvio) tr to abbreviate, shorten, abridge

abbreviatura f shortening, abridgment

abbreviazióne f abbreviation

abbrìvo or **abbrìvio** m headway (of a ship); **prendere l'abbrìvio** to gather momentum

abbronzante [dz] adj suntanning || m suntan lotion

abbronzare [dz] (abbrónzo) tr & ref to bronze; to tan

abbronza·to -ta [dz] adj tanned, suntanned

abbronzatura [dz] f tan, suntan

abbruciacchiare §287 tr to singe

abbrunare tr to brown; to hang crepe on || ref to wear mourning

abbrunire §176 tr to turn brown; to tan; to burnish

abbrustolire §176 tr to toast; to singe || ref to tan; to become sunburned

abbrutiménto m degradation, brutishness

abbrutire §176 tr to degrade; to brutalize || intr & ref to become brutalized

abbuiare §287 tr to darken; to hush up, hide || ref to grow dark; to become gloomy || impers—**abbuia** it's growing dark

abbuòno m allowance, discount; handicap (in racing)

abburattaménto m sifting

abburattare tr to sift, bolt

abdicare §197 (àbdico) tr & intr to abdicate; **abdicare a** to give up, renounce; to abdicate (e.g., the throne)

abdicazióne f abdication

aberrare (abèrro) intr to deviate

aberrazióne f aberration

abéte m fir

abetina f forest of fir trees

abiàti·co m (-ci) (coll) grandson

abièt·to -ta adj abject, base, low

abigeato m (law) cattle rustling

àbile adj able, clever, capable; (mil) fit

abili·tà f (tà) ability, skill

abilitare (abìlito) tr to certify (e.g., a teacher); to qualify, license

abilita·to -ta adj certified (teacher)

abilitazióne f qualification; certification (of teachers)

abissale adj abysmal

Abissìnia, l' f Abyssinia

abissì·no -na adj & mf Abyssinian

abisso m abyss; fountain (of knowledge); slough (of degradation)

abitàbile adj inhabitable

abitàcolo m (aer) cockpit; (aut) cab, interior; (naut) compass bowl; abitacolo eiettàbile (aer) ejection capsule

abitante mf inhabitant; resident

abitare (àbito) tr to inhabit; to occupy || intr to dwell, live, reside

abitati·vo -va adj living, e.g., **condizioni abitative** living conditions

abita·to -ta adj inhabited, populated || m built-up area

abitatóre -**trice** mf dweller

abitazióne f dwelling; housing

àbito m suit (for men); dress (for women); garb, attire; habit; **abiti** clothes; **abito da ballo** evening gown; **abito da cerimonia** formal dress; **abito da inverno** winter suit; winter clothes; **levarsi l'abito** to doff the cassock; **prender l'abito** to enter the Church

abituale adj habitual

abituare (abìtuo) tr to accustom || ref to grow accustomed

abitudinà·rio -**ria** adj (-ri -rie) set in his ways

abitùdine f habit, custom

abituro m (poet) shanty, hut

abiura f abjuration

abiurare tr to abjure

ablati·vo -va adj & m ablative

ablazióne f (med) removal; (geol) erosion

abluzióne f ablution

abnegare §209 (abnégo & abnègo) tr to renounce, abnegate

abnegazióne f abnegation, self-denial

abnòrme adj abnormal

abolire §176 tr to abolish

abolizióne f abolition

abominàbile adj abominable

abominare (abòmino) tr to abominate, detest

abominazióne f abomination

abominévole adj abominable

aborìge·no -na adj aboriginal || m aborigine; aborigeni aborigines

aborrire §176 & (abòrro) tr to abhor, loathe || intr—**aborrire da** to shun, shrink from

abortire §176 intr to abort

abòrto m abortion, miscarriage; **aborto di natura** monstrosity

abrasióne f abrasion; erosion

abrasi·vo -va adj & m abrasive

abrogare §209 (àbrogo) tr to abrogate

abrogazióne f abrogation

abruzzése adj of the Abruzzi || mf person of the Abruzzi || m dialect of the Abruzzi

àbside f (archit) apse

abusare intr—**abusare di** to go to excesses in (e.g., smoking); to take advantage of; to impose on

abusí·vo -va adj illegal, abusive; unwarranted

abuso m abuse, excess

acà·cia f (-cie) acacia

acanto m acanthus

àcaro m (ent) acarus, mite, tick; **acaro della scabbia** itch mite

ac·ca m & f (-ca or -che) h (letter); **non valere un'acca** (coll) to not be worth a fig

accadèmia f academy

accadèmi·co -ca (-ci -che) adj academic || mf academician

accadére §121 intr (ESSERE) to happen, occur

accadu·to -ta adj happened, occurred || m fact, event; what has taken place

accagliare §280 tr, intr (ESSERE) & ref to curdle, coagulate

accalappiaca·ni m (-ni) dogcatcher

accalappiare §287 tr to catch (a dog); to snare; (fig) to fool

accalcare §197 tr to crowd || ref to throng

accaldare ref to get hot; to become flushed

accalda·to -ta adj hot; perspired

accalorare (accalóro) tr to excite || ref to get excited

accalora·to -ta adj excited, animated

accampaménto m encampment, camp; camping

accampare tr to encamp; to advance, lay (a claim) || ref to camp, encamp

accaniménto m animosity, bitterness, obstinacy, stubbornness

accanire §176 tr to persist; to work doggedly; **accanirsi contro** to harass

accani·to -ta adj obstinate, persistent; furious; fierce, ruthless, bitter (fight)

accanto adv near, nearby; **accanto a** near

accantonaménto m tabling (e.g., of a discussion); reserve (of money); (mil) billeting; (sports) camping

accantonare (accantóno) tr to set aside (money); (mil) to billet

accaparraménto m cornering (of market)

accaparrare tr to corner (merchandise); to hoard; to put a down payment on (e.g., a house); (coll) to gain (somebody's affection)

accaparra·tóre -trice mf monopolizer; hoarder

accapigliare §280 tr to pull each other's hair; to scuffle; to come to blows

accapo or **a capo** m paragraph

accappa·tóio m (-tói) bathrobe

accapponare (accappóno) tr to castrate (a rooster) || ref to wrinkle; **mi si accappona la pelle** I get gooseflesh

accarezzare (accarézzo) tr to caress, fondle; to pet; to nurture (e.g., a hope); **accarezzare le spalle di** to strike; to club

accartocciare §128 (**accartòccio**) tr to wrap up in a cone || ref to curl up

accartoccia·to -ta adj curled up

accasare [s] tr & ref to marry

accasciaménto m dejection

accasciare §128 tr to weaken, enfeeble; to depress || ref to weaken; to lose heart

accasermare [s] (**accasèrmo**) tr to quarter, billet

accatastare tr to register (real estate); to pile, heap up

accattabri·ghe mf (-ghe) quarrelsome person, scrapper

accattare tr to beg for; to borrow (e.g., ideas) || intr to beg

accattonàg·gio m (-gi) begging, mendicancy

accattó·ne -na mf mendicant, beggar

accavalcare §197 tr to straddle; to go over

accavalciare §128 tr to bestride

accavallare tr to superimpose; to cross (one's legs) || ref to pour forward, run high (said of waves)

accecaménto m blinding

accecare §122 tr to blind; to countersink || intr (ESSERE) to become blind || ref to blind oneself

acceca·tóio m (-tói) countersink

accèdere §100 intr (ESSERE) to enter, approach; to accede

acceleraménto m acceleration

accelerare (accèlero) tr & intr to accelerate

accelera·to -ta adj accelerated; intensive (course); local (train) || m local train

acceleratóre m accelerator

accelerazióne f acceleration

accèndere §101 tr to kindle; to turn on (e.g., the light); to light (e.g., a match, a cigar) || ref to catch fire; to become lit; **accendersi in viso** to become flushed

accendisigaro m lighter

accendi·tóio m (-tói) candle lighter

accenditóre m lighter

accennare (accénno) tr to nod; to point at; to sketch || intr to refer; to hint

accénno m nod; sign; allusion

accensióne f lighting, kindling; (aut) ignition; (law) contraction (of a debt); **accensione improvvisa** spontaneous combustion

accentare (accénto) tr to accent

accènto m accent; stress; (poet) accent (word); **accento tonico** stress accent

accentraménto m centralization

accentrare (accèntro) tr to concentrate, centralize

accentuare (accèntuo) tr to accentuate || ref to become aggravated

accentuazióne f accentuation

accerchiaménto m encirclement

accerchiare §287 (**accérchio**) tr to encircle, surround

accertàbile adj verifiable

accertaménto m ascertainment, verification; determination (e.g., of taxes)

accertare (accèrto) *tr* to assure; to ascertain, verify; to determine (*the tax due*) ‖ *ref* to make sure

accé·so -sa [s] *adj* lit; turned on; on (*e.g., radio*); excited, aroused; bright (*color*)

accessìbile *adj* accessible; moderate (*price*)

accessióne *f* accession

accèsso *m* access, approach; admittance, entry; fit (*of anger, of coughing*)

accessò·rio -ria (-ri -rie) *adj* accessory ‖ *m* accessory; (mach) accessory, attachment

accètta *f* hatchet, axe, cleaver; **tagliato con l'accetta** rough-hewn

accettàbile *adj* acceptable

accettare (accètto) *tr* to accept

accettazióne *f* acceptance; receiving room; (econ) acceptance

accèt·to -ta *adj* agreeable; welcome; **male accetto** unwelcome

accezióne *f* meaning, acceptation

achiappafarfal·le *m* (-le) butterfly net

achiappamó·sche *m* (-sche) fly catcher

achiappare *tr* to grab, seize; (coll) to catch in the act

acchito *m* (billiards) break; **di primo acchito** at first

acciaccare §197 *tr* to crush; to trample upon; (coll) to lay low (*e.g., by illness*)

acciac·co·m (-chi) illness, infirmity, ailment

acciaiare §287 *tr* to convert into steel; to strengthen with steel

acciaierìa *f* steel mill, steelworks

ac·ciàio *m* (-ciài) steel; **acciaio inossidabile** stainless steel

acciaiòlo *m* whetstone

acciambellare (acciambèllo) *tr* to shape in the form of a doughnut ‖ *ref* to curl up

acciarino *m* flintlock; linchpin; (nav) war nose (*of a torpedo*)

accidèmpoli *interj* (slang) darn it!

accidentale *adj* accidental

accidenta·to -ta *adj* paralyzed; uneven, rough (*road*); broken (*ground*)

accidènte *m* accident; crack-up; (coll) paralytic stroke; (coll) hoot, fig; (coll) pest, menace (*child*); (mus) accidental; **accidènti!** (coll) darn!, damn!; **correre come un accidente** to run like the devil; **mandare un accidente a** to wish ill luck to; **per accidente** perchance

accìdia *f* sloth

accidió·so -sa [s] *adj* slothful

acciglìare §280 *ref* to frown, knit one's brow

accìngere §126 *ref*—**accingersi a** to get ready to

-àccio -àccia *suf adj & mf* (-acci -acce) no good, e.g., **gentaccia** no good people; good-for-nothing, e.g., **ragazzaccio** good-for-nothing boy

acciò or **acciocché** *conj* (poet) so that

acciottolare (acciòttolo) *tr* to pave with cobblestones

acciottola·to -ta *adj* cobblestone ‖ *m* cobblestone pavement

acciottolì·o *m* (-ì) clatter (*e.g., of dishes*)

accipicchia *interj* (coll) darn it!

acciuffare *tr* to seize, grab, pinch (*a thief*)

acciu·ga *f* (-ghe) anchovy

acclamare *tr* to acclaim ‖ *intr* to voice one's approval

acclamazióne *f* acclamation

acclimatare (acclìmato) *tr & ref* to acclimate

acclimatazióne *f* acclimatation

acclìve *adj* (poet) steep

acclivi·tà *f* (-tà) acclivity

acclùdere §105 *tr* to enclose

acclu·so -sa *adj* enclosed

accoccare §197 (**accòcco & accócco**) *tr* (poet) to nock (*the arrow*)

accoccolare (accòccolo) *ref* to squat down

accodare (accódo) *tr* to line up ‖ *ref* to line up, queue

accogliènte *adj* cozy, hospitable, inviting

accogliènza *f* reception, welcome

accògliere §127 *tr* to receive; to welcome; to grant (*a request*) ‖ *ref* (poet) to gather

accoglitrice *f* receptionist

accòlito *m* acolyte, altar boy; follower

accollare (accòllo) *tr* to overload (*a cart*); **accollare qlco a qlcu** to charge s.o. with s.th ‖ *intr* to go up to the neck (*said of a dress*) ‖ *ref* to assume, take upon oneself

accolla·to -ta *adj* high-necked (*dress*); high-cut (*shoes*) ‖ *f* accolade

accollatura *f* neck, neckhole

accòlta *f* (poet) gathering

accoltellare (accoltèllo) *tr* to knife

accomandante *m* limited partner

accomandatà·rio *m* (-ri) (law) general partner

accomàndita *f* (law) limited partnership

accomiatare *tr* to dismiss ‖ *ref* to take leave

accomodaménto *m* arrangement; compromise; settlement

accomodante *adj* accommodating, obliging

accomodare (accòmodo) *tr* to arrange; to fix; to settle ‖ *intr* to be convenient ‖ *ref* to adapt oneself; to agree; to sit down; **si accomodi** have a seat, make yourself comfortable

accomodatura *f* arrangement; repair

accompagnaménto *m* retinue; cortege; (mus) accompaniment; (law) writ of mandamus; (mil) softening-up (*by gunfire*)

accompagnare *tr* to accompany; to escort; to follow; to match ‖ *ref*—**accompagnarsi a** or **con** to join

accompagna·tóre -trice *mf* escort; guide; (mus) accompanist

accomunare *tr* to mingle, mix; to unite, associate; to share

acconciaménto *m* arrangement

acconciare §128 (**accóncio**) *tr* to prepare for use; to arrange; to set (*e.g., the hair*) ‖ *ref* to adorn oneself; to dress one's hair; to adapt oneself

acconcia·tóre -trice *mf* hairdresser

acconciatura f hairdo; headdress

accón·cio -cia adj (**-ci -ce**) proper, fitting

accondiscendènte adj acquiescing, acquiescent

accondiscendènza f acquiescence

accondiscéndere §245 intr to acquiesce, consent; to yield

acconsentire (**acconsènto**) intr to consent, acquiesce

acconsenziènte adj consenting, acquiescing

accontentare (**accontènto**) tr to satisfy, please || ref to be satisfied, be pleased

accónto m installment

accoppare (**accòppo**) tr (coll) to kill; (coll) to beat to death || ref (coll) to get killed

accoppiaménto m pairing; mating; (mach) parallel operation

accoppiare §287 (**accòppio**) tr to couple, pair, cross (e.g., animals) || ref to mate, copulate

accoppiata f daily double (in races)

accoraménto m sadness, sorrow

accorare (**accòro**) tr to stab to death; to sadden || ref to sadden, grieve

accora·to -ta adj saddened, grieving

accorciare §128 (**accórcio**) tr & ref to shorten; to shrink

accorciatura f shortening; shrinking

accordare (**accòrdo**) tr to harmonize (colors); to reconcile (people); to tune up; to grant; (gram) to make agree || ref to agree; to match

accorda·to -ta adj tuned up || m (econ) credit limit

accorda·tóre -trice mf (mus) tuner

accordatura f tuning

accòrdo m agreement, accordance; (law) mutual consent; (mus) harmony; **d'accordo** O.K., agreed; **d'accordo con** in accord with; **di comune accordo** with one accord; **essere d'accordo** to agree; **mettersi d'accordo** to come to an agreement

accòrgere §249 ref to perceive, notice; **accorgersi di** to become aware of, realize; **senza accorgersi** inadvertently

accorgiménto m smartness; device, trick

accórrere §139 intr (ESSERE) to run up, rush up

accortézza f alertness; shrewdness, perspicacity

accòr·to -ta adj alert; shrewd, perspicacious

accosciare §128 (**accòscio**) ref to squat

accostàbile adj approachable

accostaménto m approach; combination (e.g., of colors)

accostare (**accòsto**) tr to approach; to bring near; to leave (a door) ajar || intr to be near; to cling, adhere; (naut) to come alongside; (naut) to maneuver alongside a pier; (naut) to change direction, haul || ref to approach, come near; to cling (e.g., to a faith)

accosta·to -ta adj ajar

accò·sto -sta adj (coll) near || m approach; help || **accosto** adv near; **accosto a** near, close to

accovacciare §128 ref to crouch

accovonare (**accovóno**) tr to sheave

accozzàglia f hodgepodge; motley crowd

accozzare (**accòzzo**) tr to jumble up; to collect, gather (people) together || ref to collect, congregate

accòzzo m jumble, medley

accreditàbile adj chargeable (e.g., account); creditable

accreditaménto m crediting

accreditare (**accrédito**) tr to credit, believe; to accredit (an ambassador); to credit (one's account)

accredita·to -ta adj confirmed (news); accredited

accréscere §142 tr & ref to increase

accresciménto m increase

accucciare §128 ref to curl up (said of dogs)

accudire §176 tr (coll) to attend (a sick person) || intr—**accudire a** to take care of

acculturazióne f acculturation

accumulare (**accùmulo**) tr, intr & ref to accumulate; to gather

accumulatóre m storage battery

accumulazióne f accumulation

accuratézza f care, carefulness

accura·to -ta adj careful, painstaking

accusa f accusation, charge; **pubblica accusa** (law) public prosecutor

accusare tr to accuse, charge; to betray; to acknowledge (receipt); (cards) to declare, bid

accusati·vo -va adj & m accusative

accusa·to -ta adj accused || mf defendant

accusató·re -trice mf accuser; **pubblico accusatore** (law) public prosecutor, district attorney

accusatò·rio -ria adj (**-ri -rie**) accusatory, accusing

acèfa·lo -la adj headless; without the first page (said of a manuscript)

acèr·bo -ba adj unripe, green, sour

àcero m maple tree, sugar maple

acèrri·mo -ma adj bitter, fierce

acetato m acetate

acèti·co -ca adj (**-ci -che**) acetic

acetificare §197 (**acetìfico**) tr to acetify

acetilène m acetylene

acéto m vinegar; **aceto aromatico** aromatic spirits; **sotto aceto** pickled

acetóne m acetone

acetósa [s] f (bot) sorrel

acetosèlla [s] f wood sorrel

acetó·so -sa [s] adj vinegarish || f see **acetosa**

Acherónte m Acheron

Achille m Achilles

acidificare §197 (**acidìfico**) tr to acidify

acidi·tà f (**-tà**) acidity; **acidità di stomaco** heartburn

àci·do -da adj acid, sour || m acid; **sapere d'acido** to taste sour

acidu·lo -la adj acidulous

àcino m berry (of grapes); bead (of rosary)

acme f acme; crisis

acne f acne

acònito m (bot) monkshood

àcqua f water; rain; purity (e.g., of a diamond); **acqua a catinelle** pouring rain; **acqua alta** high water; **acqua corrente** running water; **acqua dolce** fresh water; drinking water; **acqua in bocca!** mum's the word!; **acqua morta** stagnant water; **acqua ossigenata** hydrogen peroxide; **acqua potabile** drinking water; **acqua salata** salt water; **acqua viva** spring; **all'acqua di rose** very mild; **avere l'acqua alla gola** to be in dire straits; **della più bell'acqua** of the first water; **fare acqua** to leak (said of a boat); **fare un buco nell'acqua** to waste one's efforts; **portare acqua al mare** to carry coals to Newcastle; **prendere l'acqua** to get wet; **sott'acqua** (fig) underhand; **tirare l'acqua al proprio mulino** to be grist to one's mill; **versare acqua in un cesto** to waste one's efforts

acquafòrte f (acquefòrti) etching

acquaforti·sta mf (-sti -ste) etcher

ac·quàio -quàia (-quài -quàie) adj watering (trough) || m sink

acquaiò·lo -la (-lai) adj water || m water carrier; (sports) water boy

acquamarina f (acquemarine) aquamarine

acquaplano m aquaplane

acquaràgia f turpentine

acquarèllo m var of acquerello

acquà·rio m (-ri) aquarium || **Acquario** m (astr) Aquarius

acquartierare (acquartièro) tr (mil) to quarter || ref to be quartered

acquasanta f holy water

acquasantièra f (eccl) stoup

acquàti·co -ca adj (-ci -che) aquatic, water

acquattare ref to crouch, squat

acquavite f brandy; liquor, rum

acquazzóne m downpour, heavy shower

acquedótto m aqueduct

àcque·o -a adj aqueous, watery

acquerelli·sta mf (-sti -ste) watercolorist

acquerèllo m watercolor; watered-down wine

acquerùgiola f fine drizzle

acquiescènte adj acquiescent

acquietare (acquièto) tr to pacify, placate || ref to quiet down

acquirènte mf buyer, purchaser; **il miglior acquirente** the highest bidder

acquisire §176 tr to acquire

acquisi·tóre -trice mf salesperson, agent || m salesman || f saleswoman

acquistare tr to purchase, buy; to acquire; to gain (e.g., ground) || intr to improve

acquisto m buy, purchase; acquisition

acquitrino m marsh

acquitrinó·so -sa [s] adj marshy

acquolina f—**far venire l'acquolina in bocca** to make one's mouth water

acquó·so -sa [s] adj watery

acre adj sour; pungent; acrid; bitter (words)

acrèdine f acrimony, sourness

acrimònia f acrimony

acro m acre

acròba·ta mf (-tí -te) acrobat

acrobàti·co -ca (-ci -che) adj acrobatic || f acrobatics

acrobatismo m acrobatics

acrobazìa f acrobatics; stunt, feat

acrocòro m plateau

acrònimo m acronym

acròpo·li f (-li) acropolis

acròsti·co m (-ci) acrostic

acuire §176 tr to sharpen, whet

acuità f acuity

acùle·o m (-i) quill; prickle, thorn; stinger (of an insect)

acume m acumen

acuminare (acùmino) tr to sharpen, whet

acumina·to -ta adj pointed, sharp

acùsti·co -ca (-ci -che) adj acoustic(al) || f acoustics

acutézza f acuteness, sharpness

acutizzare [ddzz] tr & ref to sharpen

acu·to -ta adj acute, sharp || m high note

ad prep var of **a** before words beginning with a vowel

adagiare §290 tr to lay down gently; to lower gently || ref to lie down; to stretch out

adà·gio m (-gi) adage; (mus) adagio || adv slowly; gently; (mus) adagio

Adamo m Adam

adattàbile adj adaptable

adattaménto m adaptation; adaptability

adattare tr to adapt, fit || ref to adapt oneself; to become adapted; **adattarsi a** to go with; to match; to be becoming to

adat·to -ta adj suitable, adequate

addebitaménto m debiting

addebitare (addèbito) tr to debit; **addebitare una spesa a qlcu** to debit s.o. with an expense

addèbito m charge; (com) debit; **elevare l'addebito di qlco a qlcu** (law) to charge s.o. with s.th

addènda mpl addenda

addèndo m (math) addend

addensare (addènso) tr to thicken || ref to thicken; to gather, throng

addentare (addènto) tr to bite || ref (mach) to mesh

addentatura f bite; (carp) tongue (of tongue and groove)

addentellà·to -ta adj toothed, notched || m chance, occasion; (archit) toothing

addentrare (addèntro) tr to penetrate || ref to penetrate; to proceed

addéntro adv inside; **addentro in** into; inside of

addestraménto m training

addestrare (addèstro) tr & ref to train

addestra·tóre -trice mf trainer

addét·to -ta adj assigned; attached; pertaining || m attaché; **addetto stampa** press secretary

addì adv the (+ a certain date), e.g., **addì 27 gennaio** the 27th of January

addiàc·cio m (-ci), sheepfold; bivouac

addiètro m (naut) stern; **per l'addietro** in the past || adv behind; ago; **dare**

addietro to back up; **lasciarsi addietro** to delay; **tempo addietro** some time ago; **tirarsi addietro** to back away

addì·o *m* (-i) farewell; **dare l'addio to** say good-bye; **dare l'estremo addio** to pay one's last respects; **fare gli addii** to say good-bye || *interj* farewell!, good-bye!

addire §151 *tr* (poet) to consecrate || *ref* to be suitable, be becoming; **addirsi a** to be becoming to

addirittura *adv* directly; even, without hesitation; absolutely, positively

addirizzare *tr* to straighten up; **addirizzare le gambe ai cani** to try the impossible

additare *tr* to point out

additi·vo -va *adj & m* additive

addivenire §282 *intr* (ESSERE)—**addivenire a** to come to, reach (*e.g., an agreement*)

addizionale *adj* additional || *f* supplementary tax

addizionare (addizióno) *tr & intr* to add

addizionatrice *f* adding machine

addizione *f* addition

addobbaménto *m* adornment, decoration

addobbare (addòbbo) *tr* to adorn, bedeck, decorate

addobba·tóre -trice *mf* decorator

addòbbo *m* adornment, decoration; hangings (*in a church*)

addolcire §176 *tr* to soften up

addolcire §176 *tr* to sweeten; to calm down || *ref* to mellow, soften

addolorare (addolóro) *tr & ref* to grieve; **addolorarsi per** to grieve over, lament

addolora·to -ta *adj* sorrowful || **l'Addolorata** *f* (eccl) Our Lady of Sorrows

addòme *m* abdomen

addomesticàbile *adj* tamable

addomesticaménto *m* taming

addomesticare §197 **(addomèstico)** *tr* to tame; to accustom || *ref* to become accustomed

addomestica·to -ta *adj* tame, domesticated

addominale *adj* abdominal

addormentare (addorménto) *tr* to put to sleep; to numb || *ref* to fall asleep; to be asleep (*said of a limb*)

addormenta·to -ta *adj* asleep; numbed

addossare (addòsso) *tr* to put on; **addossare qlco a qlco** to lean s.th against s.th; **addossare qlco a qlcu** to put s.th on s.o.; (fig) to entrust s.o. with s.th || *ref* to take upon oneself; to crowd together; **addossarsi a** to lean against; to crowd

addossa·to -ta *adj* leaning

addòsso *adv* on; on oneself, on one's back; about oneself; **addosso a** on, upon; against; **avere la sfortuna addosso** to be always unlucky; **dare addosso a qlcu** to assail s.o.; **levarsi d'addosso** to get rid of; **levarsi i panni d'addosso** to take the shirt off one's back

addót·to -ta *adj* adduced, alleged

addottorare (addottóro) *tr* to confer the doctor's degree on || *ref* to receive the doctor's degree

addurre §102 *tr* to adduce; to allege; (poet) to bring

Ade *m* Hades

adeguare (adéguo) *tr* to equalize; to bring in line || *ref* to conform, adapt oneself

adegua·to -ta *adj* adequate

adeguazione *f* equalization

adémpiere §163 *tr* to fulfill, accomplish || *ref* to come true

adempiménto *m* fulfillment, discharge (*of one's duty*)

adempire §176 *tr* to fulfill, accomplish || *ref* to come true

adenòide *adj* adenoid || **adenoidi** *fpl* adenoids

adèpto *m* follower; initiate

aderènte *adj* adherent || *mf* adherent, supporter

aderènza *f* adherence; (mach) friction; (pathol) adhesion; **aderenze** connections

aderire §176 *intr* to adhere; to stick; **aderire a** to grant (*e.g., a request*); to concur with; to subscribe to

adescare §197 **(adésco)** *tr* to lure, bait, entice; (mach) to prime (*a pump*)

adesióne *f* adhesion; support; (phys) adherence

adesi·vo -va *adj & m* adhesive

adèsso *adv* now, just now; **da adesso in poi** from now on; **per adesso** for the time being

adiacènte *adj* adjacent

adiacènza *f* adjacency; **adiacenze** vicinity

adianto *m* (bot) maidenhair

adibire §176 *tr* to assign; to use

àdipe *m* fat

adipó·so -sa [s] *adj* adipose

adirare *ref* to get angry

adira·to -ta *adj* angry, mad

adire §176 *tr* to apply to (*the court*); to enter into possession of (*an inheritance*)

adocchiare §287 **(adòcchio)** *tr* to eye; to ogle; to spot

adolescènte *adj & mf* adolescent

adolescènza *f* adolescence

adombrare (adómbro) *tr* to shade; to hide, veil || *ref* to shy (*said of a horse*); (fig) to take umbrage

Adóne *m* Adonis

adontare (adónto) *tr* (obs) to offend || *ref* to take offense

adoperare (adòpero & adópero) *tr* to use, employ || *ref* to exert oneself; to do one's best

adoràbile *adj* adorable

adorare (adóro) *tr* to adore; to worship || *intr* (archaic) to pray

adora·tóre -trice *mf* worshiper || *m* (joc) admirer, suitor

adorazióne *f* adoration, worship

adornare (adórno) *tr* to adorn || *ref* to bedeck oneself

adór·no -na *adj* adorned, bedecked; (poet) fine, beautiful

adottante *mf* (law) adopter

adottare (adòtto) *tr* to adopt
adotti·vo -va *adj* adoptive; foster (*child*)
adozióne *f* adoption
Adriàti·co -ca *adj* (*-ci -che*) Adriatic || **Adriàtico** *m* Adriatic
adulare (àdulo) *tr* to flatter; to fawn on
adula·tóre -trice *mf* flatterer
adulatò·rio -ria *adj* (*-ri -rie*) flattering; fawning
adulazióne *f* adulation; fawning
adulterante *adj & m* adulterant
adulteri·no -na *adj* bastard; adulterated
adultè·rio *m* (*-ri*) adultery
adùlte·ro -ra *adj* adulterous || *m* adulterer || *f* adulteress
adul·to -ta *adj & mf* adult
adunanza *f* assembly
adunare *tr & ref* to assemble, gather
adunata *f* reunion, meeting; (mil) muster
adun·co -ca *adj* (*-chi -che*) hooked, crooked
adunghiare §287 *tr* (poet) to claw
adu·sto -sta *adj* skinny; (poet) burnt
aerare (àero) *tr* to air, ventilate
aerazióne *f* aeration; airing
aère·o -a *adj* aerial; air; overhead; high, lofty; airy, fanciful || *m* airplane; (rad & telv) aerial
aerobrigata *f* (mil) wing
aerocistèrna *f* (aer) tanker
aerodinàmi·co -ca (*-ci -che*) *adj* aerodynamic(al); streamlined || *f* aerodynamics
aeròdromo *m* airfield, airdrome
aerofaro *m* airport beacon
aerofotogram·ma *m* (*-mi*) aerial photograph
aerogiro *m* helicopter
aerògrafo *m* spray gun (*for painting*)
aerolìnea *f* airline; **aerolinea principale** trunkline
aeròlito *m* aerolite, meteorite
aeromarìtti·mo -ma *adj* air-sea
aeròmetro *m* aerometer
aeromòbile *m* aircraft; **aeromobile senza pilota** drone, pilotless aircraft
aeromodellismo *m* model-airplane building
aeromodelli·sta *mf* (*-sti -ste*) model-airplane builder
aeromodèllo *m* model airplane
aeromotóre *m* windmill; aircraft motor
aeronàu·ta *m* (*-ti*) aeronaut
aeronàuti·co -ca (*-ci -che*) *adj* aeronautic(al) || *f* aeronautics
aeronave *f* airship, aircraft
aeroplano *m* airplane
aeropòrto *m* airport, airfield
aeroportuale *adj* airport
aerorazzo [ddzz] *m* rocket spaceship
aerorimèssa *f* hangar
aerosbar·co *m* (*-chi*) landing of airborne troops
aeroservì·zio [s] *m* (*-zi*) air service
aerosilurante [s] *f* torpedo plane
aerosiluro [s] *m* aerial torpedo
aerosòl [s] *m* aerosol
aerosostenta·to -ta [s] *adj* airborne
aerospaziale *adj* aerospace
aerospà·zio *m* (*-zi*) aerospace

aerostàti·co -ca (*-ci -che*) *adj* aerostatic(al) || *f* aerostatics
aeròstato *m* aerostat
aerostazióne *f* air terminal
aerotas·sì *m* (*-sì*) taxiplane
aerotrasportare (aerotraspòrto) *tr* to airlift
aerotrasporta·to -ta *adj* airlifted; airborne
aerovìa *f* (aer) beam (*course indicated by a radio beam*); (aer) air lane
afa *f* sultriness; **fare afa a** (coll) to be a pain in the neck to
afèresi *f* apheresis
affàbile *adj* affable, agreeable
affaccendare (affaccèndo) *tr* to busy || *ref* to busy oneself, bustle
affaccenda·to -ta *adj* busy, bustling; occupied with busywork
affacciare §128 *tr* to show or display at the window; to bring forward (*e.g., an objection*); to raise (*a doubt*) || *ref* to show oneself (*at the door or window*); to present itself (*said of a doubt*)
affaccia·to -ta *adj* facing
affagottare (affagòtto) *tr* to bundle || *ref* to bundle up; to dress sloppily
affamare *tr* to starve
affama·to -ta *adj* starved, ravenous || *mf* starveling; hungry person; wretch
affannare *tr* to worry, to afflict || *intr* to pant; to be out of breath || *ref* to worry; to bustle around
affanna·to -ta *adj* panting; out of breath; worried
affanno *m* shortness of breath; grief, sorrow
affannó·so -sa [s] *adj* panting; wearisome
affardellare (affardèllo) *tr* to bundle together; (mil) to pack
affare *m* affair, matter; business; condition, quality; deal; **affari** business; **affari esteri** foreign affairs; **un buon affare** a good deal; a bargain
affarismo *m* sharp business practice
affari·sta *mf* (*-sti -ste*) unscrupulous operator
affarìsti·co -ca *adj* (*-ci -che*) sharp
affascinante *adj* fascinating, charming
affascinare (affàscino) *tr* to fascinate; charm; to seduce; to spellbind || (affàscino) *tr* to bundle, to sheave
affascina·tóre -trice *adj* fascinating, charming || *mf* charmer, spellbinder
affastellare (affastèllo) *tr* to fagot (*twigs*): to sheave, bundle (*e.g., hay*); to pile, heap (*wood, crops, etc*); (fig) to jumble up
affaticare §197 *tr* to fatigue, tire, weary || *ref* to get tired; to weary; to toil
affatica·to -ta *adj* weary, tired
affatto *adv* quite, entirely; **niente affatto** not at all; **non . . . affatto** not at all
affatturare *tr* to bewitch; to adulterate (*e.g., food*)
affermare (affèrmo) *tr* to affirm, assert || *intr* to nod assent || *ref* to take hold (*said, e.g., of a new product*)
affermati·vo -va *adj & f* affirmative
affermazióne *f* affirmation; assertion;

statement; success (*e.g., of a new product*); (sports) victory

afferrare (affèrro) *tr* to grab, grasp; to catch, nab || *ref* to cling

affettare (affètto) *tr* to slice; to cut up || (affètto) *tr* to affect

affetta·to -ta *adj* affected || *m* cold cuts

affettatrice *f* slicing machine

affettazióne *f* affectation

affetti·vo -va *adj* emotional

affèt·to -ta *adj* afflicted, burdened || *m* affection, love; feeling

affettuosi·tà [s] *f* (-tà) love, affection

affettuó·so -sa [s] *adj* affectionate, loving, tender

affezionare (affezióno) *tr* to inspire affection in || *ref*—**affezionarsi a** to become fond of

affeziona·to -ta *adj* affectionate, loving; **Suo affezionatissimo** best regards; **tuo affezionatissimo** love, as ever

affezióne *f* affection

affiancare §197 *tr* to place next; to favor, help; (mil) to flank

affiatamento *m* harmony; teamwork

affiatare *tr* to harmonize

affibbiare §287 *tr* to buckle, fasten; to deliver (*a blow*); to play (*a trick*); to slap (*a fine*)

affidaménto *m* consignment, delivery; trust, confidence; **dare affidamento** to be trustworthy; **fare affidamento su** to rely upon

affidare *tr* to entrust; to commit (*to memory*); **affidare qlco a qlcu** to entrust s.o with s.th || *ref* to trust; **affidarsi a** to trust in

affievolimento *m* weakening

affievolire §176 *tr* to weaken || *ref* to grow weaker

affiggere §103 *tr* to post; to fix (*one's eyes or glance*) || *ref* to gaze, stare

affigliare §280 *tr* & *ref* var of **affiliare**

affilacoltèl·li *m* (-li) steel (*for sharpening knives*)

affilara·sóio *m* (-sói) strop

affilare *tr* to sharpen, hone, whet; to make thin || *ref* to become thin

affila·to -ta *adj* sharp, sharpened; thin || *f* sharpening

affila·tóio *m* (-tói) sharpener

affilatrice *f* grindstone

affiliare §287 *tr* to affiliate || *ref* to become affiliated; **affiliarsi a** to become a member of

affilia·to -ta *adj* affiliated || *mf* affiliate; foster child; member of a secret society

affiliazióne *f* affiliation

affinare *tr* to sharpen; to refine, purify; to improve (*e.g., one's style*) || *ref* to improve

affinché *conj* so that, in order that; **affinché non** lest

affine *adj* akin, related; similar || *mf* in-law || *m* kinsman || *f* kinswoman || *adv*—**affine di** in order to

affini·tà *f* (-tà) affinity

affiochire §176 *tr* to make hoarse; to weaken || *ref* to become hoarse; to grow dim (*said of a candle*)

affioraménto *m* surfacing; (min) outcrop

affiorare (affióro) *intr* to surface, emerge; to appear, to show

affissare *tr* (poet) to fix || *ref* to concentrate; (poet) to gaze

affissióne *f* posting, bill posting

affìs·so -sa *adj* fixed; posted || *m* bill, poster; door or window; (gram) affix

affittacàme·re *m* (-re) landlord || *f* landlady

affittanza *f* rent

affittare *tr* to rent || *ref*—**si affitta** for rent

affitto *m* rent, rental; **dare in affitto** to rent (*to grant by lease*); **prendere in affitto** to rent (*to take by lease*)

affittuà·rio -ria *mf* (-ri -rie) renter; tenant

affliggènte *adj* tormenting, distressing

affliggere §104 *tr* to afflict, distress || *ref* to grieve

afflit·to -ta *adj* afflicted, grieving || *mf* afflicted person, wretch

afflizióne *f* affliction, distress

afflosciare §128 (afflòscio) *tr* to cause to sag; to weaken || *ref* to droop; to sag; to be deflated; to faint

affloscire §176 *tr* & *ref* var of **afflosciare**

affluènte *adj* & *m* confluent

affluènza *f* confluence; abundance; crowd

affluire §176 *intr* (ESSERE) to flow (*said of river*); to flock (*said of people*); to pour in (*said of earnings*)

afflusso *m* flow

affogaménto *m* drowning

affogare §209 (affógo) *tr* to drown; to smother || *intr* (ESSERE) to drown

affoga·to -ta *adj* drowned; poached (*egg*)

affollaménto *m* crowd, throng

affollare (affóllo & affòllo) *tr* to crowd; to overcome || *ref* to crowd

affolla·to -ta *adj* crowded

affondaménto *m* sinking

affondami·ne *m* (-ne) mine layer

affondare (affóndo) *tr* to sink; to stick || *ref* to sink

affondata *f* (aer) nosedive

affóndo *m* (fencing) lunge || *adv* deeply

afforestare (afforèsto) *tr* to reforest

affossare (affòsso) *tr* to ditch; (fig) to table (*e.g., a proposal*); to hollow out || *ref* to become sunken or hollow (*said, e.g., of cheeks*)

affossatóre *m* ditchdigger; gravedigger

affrancare §197 *tr* to set free; to free; to redeem (*a property*); to stamp || *ref* to free oneself; to take heart

affrancatrice *f* postage meter

affrancatura *f* stamp, stamping

affràngere §179 *tr* to weary; (obs) to break down (*the spirit*)

affran·to -ta *adj* weary; broken down, broken-hearted

affratellaménto *m* fraternization

affratellare (affratèllo) *tr* to bind in brotherly love || *ref* to fraternize

affrescare §197 (affrésco) *tr* to fresco; to paint in fresco

affré·sco m (-schi) fresco

affrettare (**affrétto**) tr & ref to hurry, hasten

affretta·to -ta adj hurried

affrontare (**affrónto**) tr to face, confront || ref to meet in combat; to come to blows

affronta·to -ta adj—**affrontati** (herald) combattant

affrónto m affront, offense

affumicare §197 (**affùmico**) tr to smoke; to blacken; to smoke out; to smoke (meat or fish)

affumica·to -ta adj smoked; dark (glasses)

affusolare [s] (**affùsolo**) tr & ref to taper

affusola·to -ta [s] adj tapered; slender

affusto m gun carriage

afga·no -na adj & mf Afghan

àfo·no -na adj voiceless

afori·sma m (-smi) aphorism

afó·so -sa [s] adj sultry

Africa, l' f Africa

africa·no -na adj & mf African

afrodisìa·co -ca adj & m (-ci -che) aphrodisiac

afta m mouth ulcer; **afta epizootica** (vet) foot-and-mouth disease

àgata f agate || **Agata** f Agatha

agènda f notebook; agenda

agènte adj active || m agent; broker; merchant; officer; **agente delle tasse** tax collector; **agente di cambio** stockbroker; money changer; **agente di commercio** broker, commission merchant; **agente di custodia** jailer; **agente di polizia** police officer, policeman; **agente di spionaggio** informer; **agente provocatore** agent provocateur

agenzìa f agency; office, branch; **agenzia immobiliare** real-estate office

agevolare (**agévolo**) tr to facilitate, help

agevolazióne f facility; **agevolazione di pagamento** easy terms

agévole adj easy

agevolézza f facility

aggallare intr to come to the surface

agganciaménto m docking (in space); (rr) coupling

agganciare §128 tr to hook; (rr) to couple; (mil) to engage (the enemy)

aggàn·cio m (-ci) docking (in space); (rr) coupling

aggég·gio m (-gi) gadget

aggettivale adj adjectival

aggettivo m adjective

agghiacciaménto m freezing

agghiacciante adj hair-raising, frightful

agghiacciare §128 tr to freeze || ref to freeze; to be horrified

agghiaccia·to -ta adj frozen, icy

agghindare tr & ref to preen, primp

àg·gio m (-gi) agio; **fare aggio** to be at a premium

aggiogare §209 (**aggiógo**) tr to yoke

aggiornaménto m adjournment (e.g., of a meeting); bringing up to date

aggiornare (**aggiórno**) tr to bring up to date; to adjourn || ref to keep up with the times

aggiraménto m surrounding, outflanking

aggirare tr to surround, outflank; to swindle || ref to roam, wander; **aggirarsi su** to approximate; to be almost

aggiudicare §197 (**aggiùdico**) tr to adjudicate, award || ref to win

aggiudicazióne f adjudication, award

aggiùngere §183 tr to add; to join, connect || ref to be added; to join

aggiunta f addition

aggiuntare tr to attach, join

aggiun·to -ta adj & m associate, assistant, deputy || f see **aggiunta**

aggiustàbile adj repairable

aggiustaménto m settlement; adjustment; (mil) correction (of fire)

aggiustare tr to fix, repair; to adjust; (mil) to correct (cannon fire); **aggiustare per le feste** (coll) to fix; (coll) to give a good beating to || ref (archaic) to come closer; (coll) to manage; (coll) to come to an agreement

aggiusta·tóre -trice mf repairer, fixer || m repairman

aggiustatura f fixing, repairing, repair

agglomerare (**agglòmero**) tr & ref to pile up; to crowd together

agglomerato m built-up area; **agglomerato urbano** urban center

agglutinare (**agglùtino**) tr & ref to agglutinate

agglutinazióne f agglutination

aggobbire §176 tr to bend, bend over || intr (ESSERE) & ref to hunch over

aggomitolare (**aggomìtolo**) tr to coil || ref to curl up

aggradare intr (with dat) (poet) to please; **come Le aggrada** as you please

aggradire §176 tr to appreciate || intr (poet) (with dat) to please

aggraffare tr to hook; to grab; to join (metal sheets) with a double seam; to stitch, staple

aggraffatrice f folding machine; (mach) can sealer

aggranchire §176 tr to benumb; to deaden, stupefy || intr to become numb

aggrappare tr to grab; to clamp || ref to cling

aggravaménto m aggravation

aggravante adj (law) aggravating (circumstances)

aggravare tr to aggravate; to overload (e.g., one's stomach) || ref to get worse

aggrà·vio m (-vi) burden (e.g., of taxes); **fare aggravio a qlcu di qlco** to impute s.th to s.o.

aggraziare §287 tr to embellish; to render graceful || ref to win, gain; to ingratiate oneself

aggrazia·to -ta adj graceful; polite

aggredire §176 tr to assail, attack, assault

aggregare §209 (**aggrègo**) tr & ref to join, unite

aggrega·to -ta adj adjunct || m aggregation

aggressióne f aggression

aggressi·vo -va *adj* aggressive || *m* (mil) poison gas

aggressóre *m* aggressor

aggricciare §128 *tr* to wrinkle; (slang) to knit (*e.g., the brow*) || *ref* (poet) to shiver

aggrinzare *tr & ref* to wrinkle

aggrinzire §176 *tr & ref* var of **aggrinzare**

aggrondare (aggróndo) *tr* to knit (*the brow*)

aggrottare (aggròtto) *tr* to knit (*the brow*)

aggrovigliare §280 *tr* to tangle, entangle || *ref* to become entangled

aggrumare *tr & ref* to clot; to coagulate

aggruppare *tr* to group

agguagliare §280 *tr* to level; to equalize; to compare

agguantare *tr* to grab; to nab; (coll) to hit; **agguantare per il collo** to grab by the neck || *ref*—**agguantarsi a** to get hold of

agguato *m* ambush; **cadere in un agguato** to fall into a trap; **stare in agguato** to wait in ambush

agguerrire §176 *tr* to train for war; to inure to war; to inure

aghétto *m* shoestring; (mil) lanyard

agiatézza *f* comfort, wealth; **vivere nell'agiatezza** to live in comfort

agia·to -ta *adj* well-to-do, comfortable

àgile *adj* agile, nimble; prompt

agili·tà *f* (**-tà**) agility, nimbleness; promptness

à·gio *m* (**-gi**) comfort; opportunity; ease; **agi** conveniences, comforts; **a Suo agio** at your convenience; **aver agio** to have time; **stare a proprio agio** to feel at ease; to be comfortable; **vivere negli agi** to live comfortably

agiografia *f* hagiography

agiògrafo *m* hagiographer

agire §176 *intr* to act; to work; (theat) to act, perform

agitare (àgito) *tr* to agitate, shake; to stir; to stir up; to discuss (*e.g., a problem*) || *ref* to toss; to shake; to stir; to get excited

agita·to -ta *adj* rough, choppy (*sea*); troubled, upset || *mf* violently insane person

agita·tóre -trice *mf* agitator || *m* shaker

agitazióne *f* agitation

agli §4

agliàce·o -a *adj* garlicky

à·glio *m* (**-gli**) garlic

agnellino *m* little lamb, lambkin

agnèllo *m* lamb

agnizióne *f* recognition

agnòsti·co -ca *adj & mf* (**-ci -che**) agnostic

a·go *m* (**-ghi**) needle; pointer (*of scales*); stem (*of valve*)

agognare (agógno) *tr* to covet

agóne *m* contest; arena

agonia *f* agony, death struggle; anguish

agonìsti·co -ca *adj* (**-ci -che**) competitive, aggressive (*spirit*); athletic (*competition*) || *f* athletics

agonizzare [ddzz] *intr* to agonize, be in agony; (fig) to die out

agopuntura *f* acupuncture

ago-ràio *m* (**-rài**) needle case

agosta·no -na *adj* August, e.g., **pomeriggio agostano** August afternoon

agostinia·no -na *adj & m* Augustinian

agósto *m* August

agrà·rio -ria (**-ri -rie**) *adj & m* agrarian || *m* landlord || *f* agriculture

agrèste *adj* country

agrìco·lo -la *adj* agricultural

agricoltóre *m* farmer; agriculturist

agricoltura *f* agriculture

agrifò·glio *m* (**-gli**) holly

agrimensóre *m* surveyor

agrimensura *f* surveying

a·gro -gra *adj* sour, bitter || *m* citrus juice; sourness, bitterness; surrounding country

agrodólce *adj* sweet and sour; (fig) acidulous (*tone*)

agronomia *f* agronomy

agrònomo *m* agronomist

agrume *m* citrus (*tree and fruit*); **agrumi** citrus fruit

agucchiare §287 *intr* to knit or sew idly

agùglia *f* spire; top; (ichth) gar; (poet) eagle; (obs) needle

aguzzare *tr* to sharpen; to whet (*the appetite*)

aguzzino [ddzz] *m* slave driver; jailer

aguz·zo -za *adj* sharp, pointed

ah *interj* ah!, aha!; ha!

ahi *interj* ouch!

ahimè *interj* alas!

àia *f* yard, barnyard; threshing floor; governess || **L'Àia** *f* the Hague

Aiace *m* Ajax

àio *m* (**ài**) tutor

aiòla *f* lawn; flower bed

àire *m* push; short run (*preparing for a jump*); **dare l'aire a** to start off; **prendere l'aire** to take off

airóne *m* heron

aitante *adj* robust, stalwart

aiuòla *f* (poet) var of **aiola**

aiutante *adj* helping || *mf* assistant || *m* (mil) adjutant; **aiutante di campo** aide-de-camp; **aiutante di sanità** orderly

aiutare *tr* to help || *ref* to strive; to help oneself; to help one another

aiutato *m* first assistant (*e.g., of a surgeon*)

aiuto *m* aid, help; assistant; first assistant (*of a surgeon*)

aizzare [aìzzo] *tr* to incite, to incite to riot; to sic (*a dog*)

al §4

a·la *f* (**-li** & **-le**) wing; sail, vane (*of windmill*); blade (*e.g., of fan*); brim (*of hat*); (football) end; **ala a freccia** backswept wing; **ala di popolo** throng; **fare ala a** to line up along

alabarda *f* halberd

alabardière *m* halberdier

alabastri·no -na *adj* alabaster; white as alabaster

alabastro *m* alabaster

àlacre *adj* eager, lively

alacrità *f* alacrity

alàg·gio *m* (-gi) hauling, towing

alamaro *m* braid, gimp

alambic·co *m* (-chi) still

alano *m* Great Dane

alare *adj* wing (*e.g., span*) ‖ *m* andiron ‖ *tr* to haul

Alasca, l' *f* Alaska

ala·to -ta *adj* winged, sublime

alba *f* dawn, daybreak

albagìa *f* haughtiness

albanése [s] *adj & mf* Albanian

Albania, l' *f* Albania

àlbatro *m* (orn) albatross

albeggiaménto *m* dawning

albeggiare §290 (albéggio) *intr* (ESSERE) to dawn; (poet) to sparkle (*said, e.g., of ice*) ‖ *impers* (ESSERE)—albeggia the day dawns

alberare (àlbero) *tr* to plant (*trees*); to reforest; to hoist (*a mast*); to mast (*a ship*)

albera·to -ta *adj* tree-lined; (naut) masted

alberèllo *m* small tree; apothecary's jar

albergare §209 (albèrgo) *tr* to lodge; to put up at a hotel; (fig) to harbor ‖ *intr* to lodge; to put up

alberga·tóre -trice *mf* hotelkeeper

alberghiè·ro -ra *adj* hotel

albèr·go *m* (-ghi) hotel; refuge; hospitality; **albergo diurno** day hostel; **albergo per la gioventù** youth hostel

àlbero *m* tree; poplar; (mach) shaft; (naut) mast; **albero a camme** (aut) camshaft; **albero a gomito** (aut) crankshaft; **albero di distribuzione** (aut) camshaft; **albero di Natale** Christmas tree; **albero di trasmissione** (aut) transmission; **albero genealogico** family tree

albicòc·ca *f* (-che) apricot

albicòc·co *m* (-chi) apricot tree

al·bo -ba *adj* (poet) white ‖ *m* album; bulletin board; (law) roll; comic book; **albo d'onore** honor roll ‖ *f see* alba

albóre *m* (poet) whiteness; (poet) dawn

album *m* (album) album, scrapbook

albume *m* albumen

albumina *f* albumin

àlca·li *m* (-li) alkali

alcali·no -na *adj* alkaline

alce *m* moose; elk

alchimìa *f* alchemy

alchimi·sta *m* (-sti) alchemist

alcióne *m* halcyon

alciò·nio -nia *adj* (-ni -nie) halcyon

àlco·le *m* alcohol

alcolici·tà *f* (-tà) alcoholic content

alcòli·co -ca *adj* (-ci -che) alcoholic ‖ *m* alcoholic beverage

alcolismo *m* alcoholism

alcolizzare [ddzz] *tr* to intoxicate ‖ *ref* to become intoxicated

alcolizza·to -ta [ddzz] *adj* intoxicated ‖ *mf* alcoholic

alcool *m* (alcool) var of alcole

alcoolici·tà *f* (-tà) var of alcolicità

alcòli·co -ca (-ci -che) *adj & m* var of alcolico

alcoolismo *m* var of alcolismo

alcoolizzare [ddzz] *tr* var of alcolizzare

alcoolizza·to -ta [ddzz] *adj & mf* var of alcolizzato

alcòva *f* bedroom; bed; alcove

alcunché *pron* something, anything

alcu·no -na *adj & pron* some; **alcu·ni -ne** some; quite a few, several, a good many

aldilà *m* life beyond, afterlife

àlea *f* chance, hazard; **correre l'alea to** try one's luck

aleggiare §290 (aléggio) *intr* to flutter; to flap the wings; to hover

aleróne *m* var of alettone

alesàg·gio *m* (-gi) (mach) bore

alesare (alèso) *tr* (mach) to bore

alesatóre *m* reamer

alesatrice *s* boring machine

Alessandria d'Egitto *f* Alexandria

alessandri·no -na *adj & mf* Alexandrian ‖ *m* Alexandrine (*verse*)

Alessandro *m* Alexander; **Alessandro Magno** Alexander the Great

alétta *f* small wing; fin (*of fish*); (aer) tab; **aletta di compensazione** trim tab; **aletta parasole** (aut) sun visor

alettóne *m* (aer) aileron, flap

Aleuti·ne -na *adj*—**Isole Aleutine** Aleutian Islands

al·fa *m* (-fa) alpha ‖ *f* esparto

alfabèti·co -ca *adj* (-ci -che) alphabetical

alfabetizzazióne [ddzz] *f* teaching to read; learning to read

alfabèto *m* alphabet; code (*e.g., Morse*)

alfière *m* flagbearer, standardbearer; (chess) bishop

alfine *adv* finally, at last

al·ga *f* (-ghe) alga; **alga marina** seaweed

àlgebra *f* algebra

algèbri·co -ca *adj* (-ci -che) algebraic

Algèri *f* Algiers

Algerìa, l' *f* Algeria

algeri·no -na *adj & mf* Algerian

aliante *m* (aer) glider

alianti·sta *mf* (-sti -ste) glider pilot

àli·bi *m* (-bi) alibi

alice *f* anchovy

alienàbile *adj* alienable

alienare (alièno) *tr* to alienate; to transfer, convey ‖ *ref*—**alienarsi dalla ragione** to go out of one's mind

aliena·to -ta *adj* alienated ‖ *mf* insane person; dispossessed person

alienazióne *f* alienation

alieni·sta *mf* (-sti -ste) alienist

alièno -na *adj* disinclined; (poet) foreign, alien

alimentare *adj* alimentary ‖ **alimentari** *mpl* food, foodstuff ‖ *v* (aliménto) *tr* to feed; to fuel

alimentari·sta *m* (-sti) food merchant; food-industry worker

alimenta·tóre -trice *mf* stoker ‖ *m* (mach) stoker, feeder

alimentazióne *f* nourishment; feeding; (mil) loading; **alimentazione artificiale** intravenous feeding

aliménto *m* food, nourishment; feed; **alimenti** alimony (*maintenance*)

alimònia *f* alimony

alìnea *f* (law) paragraph, section

alìquota f share; parcel, quota

aliscafo m hydrofoil

alìse·o -a adj trade (wind) || m trade wind

alitare (**àlito**) intr to breathe; to blow gently; **non alitare** to not breathe a word

àlito m breath; (fig) breeze

alìvo·lo -la adj (poet) winged; (fig) swift

alla §4

allacciaménto m binding; connection, linking

allacciare §128 tr to bind, tie; to connect; to buckle; (fig) to deceive

allacciatura f lacing; buckling

allagare §209 tr to flood, overflow

allampana·to -ta adj tall and lean, lanky

allargare §209 tr to broaden, widen; **allargare la mano** to be lenient; to be liberal; **allargare il freno** to give free rein || ref to widen, spread out; **mi si allarga il cuore** I feel relieved

allargatura f widening

allarmante adj alarming

allarmare tr to alarm || ref to worry, become alarmed

allarme m alarm; **allarme aereo** air-raid warning; **cessato allarme** all clear; **falso allarme** false alarm; **stare in allarme** to be alarmed

allascare §197 tr (naut) to ease, slacken (a rope)

allato adv (poet) near; **allato a** near; beside; in comparison with

allattaménto m nursing, feeding; **allattamento artificiale** bottle feeding

allattare tr to nurse (at the breast); to feed (with a bottle)

alle §4

alleanza f alliance

alleare (**allèo**) tr to ally || ref to become allied; to be connected

allea·to -ta adj allied || mf ally

allegare §209 (**allégo**) tr to enclose; to adduce; to allege; **allegare i denti** to set the teeth on edge || intr (hort) to ripen

allega·to -ta adj enclosed || m enclosure

alleggeriménto m lightening, easing

alleggerire §176 tr to lighten; to alleviate || ref to put on lighter clothes; **alleggerirsi di** (naut) to jettison

allegoria f allegory

allegòri·co -ca adj (**-ci -che**) allegorical

allegraménte adv cheerfully, merrily; thoughtlessly

allegrézza f joy, cheerfulness

allegrìa f cheer, gaiety; **stare in allegria** to be merry || interj good cheer!

allé·gro -gra adj cheerful, merry, gay || m (mus) allegro

allelùia m hallelujah

allenaménto m training

allenare (**allèno**) tr & ref to train

allena·tóre -trice adj training || mf trainer, coach

allentare (**allènto**) tr to loosen, slacken; to mitigate; (coll) to deliver (a blow); **essere allentato** to have a hernia || ref to slow up; to loosen up; to diminish

allergìa f allergy

allèrgi·co -ca adj (**-ci -che**) allergic

allérta f alert || adv alert, on the alert

allessare (**allésso**) tr to boil

allés·so -sa adj boiled || m boiled meat, boiled beef

allestire §176 tr to prepare, make ready; to rig (e.g., a ship); to produce (e.g., a play)

allettaménto m allure, fascination

allettante adj alluring, enticing

allettare (**allètto**) tr to allure, entice; to confine to bed; to bend (plants) to the ground || ref to be confined to bed

allevaménto m raising, breeding; flock

allevare (**allèvo**) tr to raise, breed; to rear

alleva·tóre -trice mf raiser, breeder

alleviare §287 (**allèvio**) tr to alleviate, lighten

allibire §176 intr (ESSERE) to turn pale; to be astonished, be dismayed

allibraménto m registration, entry; booking (of bets)

allibrare tr to register, enter; to book (a bet) on a horse

allibratóre m bookmaker (at races)

allietare (**allièto**) tr to cheer, enliven

alliè·vo -va mf pupil, student; follower, disciple || m trainee; **allievo ufficiale** cadet

alligatóre m alligator

allignare intr to take root; to do well, prosper

allineaménto m alignment; falling in line

allineare (**allìneo**) tr to align; (typ) to justify || ref to align oneself, be aligned

allinea·to -ta adj aligned; **non allineato** nonaligned, uncommitted

allitterazióne f alliteration

allo §4

allòc·co m (**-chi**) horned owl; (fig) dolt, nincompoop

allocu·tóre -trice mf (poet) speaker

allocuzióne f (poet) speech, address

allòdola f lark, skylark

allogare §209 (**allògo**) tr to place; to let, lease; to find employment for; to invest (money); to marry off (a daughter)

allòge·no -na adj minority || mf member of an ethnic minority

alloggiaménto m (mil) lodging, quarters; (carp, mach) housing

alloggiare §290 (**allòggio**) tr to lodge, put up || intr to lodge, stay

allòg·gio m (**-gi**) lodging, living quarters; accommodations

allontanaménto m removal; estrangement

allontanare tr to remove; to send away; to exonerate; to dismiss; to alienate || ref to go away; to withdraw; to become estranged

allóra adj then || adv then; at that time; in that case; **da allora** ever since; **da allora in poi** from that time on; **fino allora** until then; **per allora** at that time

allorché *conj* when

allòro *m* laurel; **riposare sugli allori** to rest on one's laurels

allorquando *conj* (poet) when

àlluce *m* big toe

allucinante *adj* hallucinating; dazzling; deceptive

allucinare (allùcino) *tr* to hallucinate; to dazzle; to deceive

allucinazióne *f* hallucination

allùdere §105 *intr* to allude

allume *m* alum

alluminare (allùmino) *tr* to illuminate (*a manuscript*); (poet) to light

allumìnio *m* aluminum

allunàg·gio *m* (-gi) lunar landing; **allunaggio morbido** soft lunar landing

allunare *intr* to land on the moon

allunga *f* (mach) adapter

allungàbile *adj* extensible; extension (*table*)

allungaménto *m* lengthening

allungare §209 *tr* to lengthen; to stretch out (*e.g., the hand*); to dilute (*e.g., wine*); (coll) to deliver (*e.g., a slap*); (sports) to pass (*the ball*); **allungare il collo** to crane the neck; **allungare il passo** to walk faster ‖ *ref* to grow longer; to stretch; to grow taller

allun·go *m* (-ghi) (sports) sprint; (sports) forward pass

allusióne *f* allusion

alluvióne *m* flood

almanaccare §197 *tr* to dream of ‖ *intr* to dream, muse

almanac·co *m* (-chi) almanac

alméno *adv* at least; if only

alno *m* (bot) alder

àloe *m & f* aloe

alògeno *m* halogen

alogenuro *m* halide

alóne *m* halo

alòsa *f* (ichth) shad

alpacca *f* German silver

alpe *f* high mountain, alp ‖ **le Alpi** the Alps

alpèstre *adj* mountainous; (fig) uncouth

alpigia·no -na *adj* mountain, mountainous; (fig) uncouth ‖ *mf* mountaineer

alpinismo *m* mountain climbing

alpini·sta *mf* (-sti -ste) mountain climber

alpinìsti·co -ca *adj* (-ci -che) mountain-climbing

alpi·no -na *adj* alpine; Alpine ‖ *m* alpine soldier

alquan·to -ta *adj & pron* some; **alquanti -te** some; quite a few, several, a good many ‖ **alquanto** *adv* somewhat, rather

Alsàzia, l' *f* Alsace

alsazia·no -na *adj & mf* Alsacian

alt *m* (alt) halt, stop ‖ *interj* halt!, stop!

altaléna *f* seesaw; swing; (fig) ups and downs; **altalena a bilico** seesaw; **altalena sospesa** swing

altalenare (altaléno) *intr* to seesaw; to swing

altana *f* roof terrace

altare *m* altar

altarino *m* small altar; **svelare gli alta-**

rini (joc) to expose the skeleton in the closet

altèa *f* marsh mallow

alterare (àltero) *tr* to alter; to falsify; to adulterate; to anger ‖ *ref* to alter; to become adulterated; to get angry

altera·to -ta *adj* altered; adulterated; feverish; angry

alterazióne *f* change, alteration; adulteration; slight fever

altercare §197 (altèrco) *intr* to dispute, quarrel

altèr·co *m* (-chi) altercation; **venire a un alterco** to get into a quarrel

alterìgia *f* haughtiness

alternare (altèrno) *tr & ref* to alternate

alternati·vo -va *adj* alternating ‖ *f* alternative; choice

alterna·to -ta *adj* alternate; alternating (*current*)

alternatóre *m* (elec) alternator

altèr·no -na *adj* alternate

altè·ro -ra *adj* proud, haughty

altézza *f* height; width (*of cloth*); depth (*of water*); pitch (*of sound*); (astr, geom) altitude; (fig) loftiness, nobility; (naut) latitude; (typ) size; **essere all'altezza di** to be up to, be equal to; (naut) to be off ‖ **Altezza** *f* Highness

altezzó·so -sa [s] *adj* haughty

altíc·cio -cia *adj* (-ci -ce) tipsy

altìmetro *m* altimeter

altipiano *m* var of **altopiano**

altisonante [s] *adj* high-sounding

altìssi·mo -ma *adj* very high, highest ‖ **l'Altissimo** *m* the Most High

altitùdine *f* altitude

al·to -ta *adj* high; tall; wide (*cloth*); deep (*water*); upper; full (*day*); late (*e.g., Easter*); deep (*sleep*); early (*Middle Ages*); loud (*voice*); lofty (*peak*) ‖ *m* top; upper part; high quarters; **alti e bassi** ups and downs; **fare alto e basso** to be the undisputed boss; **guardare qlcu dall'alto in basso** to look down one's nose at s.o.; **in alto** up ‖ **alto** *adv* up

altofórno *m* (**altifórni**) blast furnace

altoloca·to -ta *adj* high-placed, high-ranking

altoparlante *m* loudspeaker

altopiano *m* (**altipiani**) plateau

altrettan·to -ta *adj & pron* as much; the same; **altrettan·ti -te** as many ‖ **altrettanto** *adv* as much; the same

altri *indef pron invar* someone; someone else; **non altri che** no one else but

altrièri *m & adv* day before yesterday

altriménti *adv* otherwise

al·tro -tra *adj* other; next (*world*); **altro ieri** day before yesterday; **chi altro?** who else?; **domani l'altro** the day after tomorrow; **fra l'altro** among other things; **ieri l'altro** the day before yesterday; **l'altro anno** last year; **l'altro giorno** the other day; **noi altri** we; **qualcun altro** somebody else; anybody else; **quest'altro (giorno, mese, anno)** next (day, month, year) ‖ *pron* other; anything else; **altro che!** why yes! || **l'altro §11** *correlative indef pron* || **l'altro §12** *reciprocal pron*

altrónde *adv* (poet) somewhere else; **d'altronde** besides; on the other hand

altróve *adv* elsewhere, somewhere else

altrui *adj invar* somebody else's, other people's || *pron invar* somebody else || *m*—**l'altrui** what belongs to someone else

altrui·sta (**-sti -ste**) *adj* altruistic || *mf* altruist

altura *f* height; (naut) high seas

alun·no -na *mf* pupil, student

alveare *m* beehive

àlveo *m* bed (*of a river*)

alvèolo *m* alveolus; socket (*of tooth*); cell (*of honeycomb*)

alzabandiè·ra *m* (**-ra**) raising of the flag

alzacristal·li *m* (**-li**) (aut) crank (*to raise a window*)

alzàia *f* tow line; towpath

alzare *tr* to lift, raise; to cut (*cards*); to shrug (*one's shoulders*); to set (*sail*); **alzare al cielo** to praise to the sky; **alzare i tacchi** to show a clean pair of heels; **alzare la cresta** to get cocky || *ref* to rise; to get up; **alzarsi in piedi** to stand up

alzata *f* raising, lifting; shrugging (*of shoulders*); standing up; riser (*of step*); three-tier candy tray; **alzata di scudi** rebellion; **alzata di testa** whim, caprice

alzavàlvo·le *m* (**-le**) (aut) valve lifter

alzo *m* gunsight

amàbile *adj* amiable; sweetish (*wine*)

amabili·tà *f* (**-tà**) amiability, kindness

ama·ca *f* (**-che**) hammock

amàlga·ma *m* (**-mi**) amalgam

amalgamare (**amàlgamo**) *tr* to amalgamate || *ref* to amalgamate; to blend

amalgamazióne *f* amalgamation

amante *adj* loving, fond || *m* lover || *f* mistress

amanuènse *m* amanuensis, scribe

amare *tr* to love; to like || *ref* to love one another

amareggiare §290 (**amaréggio**) *tr* to make bitter; to sadden || *ref* to become bitter; to sadden

amarèna *f* sour cherry

amarétto *m* macaroon

amarézza *f* bitterness

ama·ro -ra *adj* bitter || *m* bitters; bitterness

amarógno·lo -la *adj* bitterish

amarra *f* (naut) hawser

amarrare *tr* & *intr* var of **ammarrare**

ama·tóre -trice *mf* lover; amateur

amató·rio -ria *adj* (**-ri -rie**) amatory, of love

amàzzone [ddzz] *f* horsewoman; female jockey; (obs) riding habit; **cavalcare all'amazzone** to ride sidesaddle || **Amazzone** *f* (myth) Amazon

ambage *f* winding path; **ambagi** circumlocutions; **senz'ambagi** without beating about the bush

ambascerìa *f* embassy

ambà·scia *f* (**-sce**) shortness of breath; grief, sorrow

ambasciata *f* embassy; ambassadorship; errand, mission

ambasciatóre *m* ambassador

ambasciatrice *f* ambassadress

ambedùe *adj invar*—**ambedue i** or **le** both || *pron invar* both

ambiare §287 *intr* to amble, pace (*said of a horse*)

ambiatura *f* pacing (*said of a horse*)

ambidè·stro -stra *adj* ambidextrous

ambidùe *adj* & *pron invar* var of **ambedue**

ambientare (**ambiènto**) *tr* to accustom; to place (*a story in a certain period*) || *ref* to get accustomed to one's surroundings; to orient oneself

ambienta·tóre -trice *mf* interior decorator; (theat) decorator

ambiènte *adj* room, e.g., **temperatura ambiente** room temperature || *m* environment; habitat; milieu; room; **trovarsi fuori del proprio ambiente** to be out of one's element

ambigui·tà *f* (**-tà**) ambiguity

ambi·guo -gua *adj* ambiguous

àm·bio *m* (**-bi**) amble, pacing

ambire §176 *tr* to be eager for || *intr* to be ambitious; **ambire a** to be ambitious for

àmbito *m* range, circle; (mus) range; **nell'ambito di** within

ambizióne *f* ambition

ambizióso -sa [s] *adj* ambitious || *mf* ambitious person

ambo or **am·bi -be** *adj pl*—**ambo i, ambo le, ambi le, ambe le** both

ambosèssi *adj invar* of both sexes, e.g., **giovani ambosessi** young people of both sexes

ambra *f* amber; **ambra grigia** amber-gris

ambròsia *f* ambrosia; (bot) ragweed

ambulante *adj* itinerant; circulating; ambulant || *m* mail car

ambulanza *f* ambulance

ambulare (**àmbulo**) *intr* (coll) to ambulate

ambulatòrio -ria (**-ri -rie**) *adj* ambulatory || *m* clinic, first-aid department

Amburgo *m* Hamburg

amèba *f* amoeba

a·men *m* (**-men**) amen || *interj* amen!

ameni·tà *f* (**-tà**) *f* amenity; pleasantry

amèno -na *adj* pleasant, agreeable; amusing (*fellow*)

Amèrica, *l'* *f* America; **l'America del Nord** North America; **l'America del Sud** South America

americana *f* bicycle race between pairs

americanismo *m* Americanism

americanizzare [ddzz] *tr* to Americanize || *ref* to become Americanized

america·no -na *adj* & *mf* American || *m* vermouth with bitters || *f* see **americana**

ametista *f* amethyst

amianto *m* asbestos

amicale *adj* (poet) friendly

amichévole *adj* friendly; (sports) non-competitive

amicìzia *f* friendship; **stringere amicizia con** to make friends with

ami·co -ca (-ci -che) *adj* friendly || *mf* friend; beloved || *m* boy friend; lover, paramour; **amico del cuore** bosom friend || *f* girl friend; mistress

amidàce·o -a *adj* starchy

amidatura *f* starching

àmido *m* starch

Amlèto *m* Hamlet

ammaccare §197 *tr* to crush; to pound; to bruise; to dent

ammaccatura *f* bruise; dent

ammaestraménto *m* instruction, teaching; training

ammaestrare (ammaèstro & ammaéstro) *tr* to teach, to educate; to train (*animals*)

ammainare (ammàino) *tr* to lower (*e.g., a flag*)

ammalare *intr* (ESSERE) to fall ill || *ref* to fall ill; **ammalarsi di** to come down with

ammala·to -ta *adj* ill, sick || *mf* patient

ammaliare §287 *tr* to cast a spell on; to charm, enchant, fascinate; to bewitch

ammalia·tóre -trice *adj* charming, enchanting || *mf* charmer || *m* enchanter, sorcerer || *f* enchantress, sorceress

amman·co *m* (-chi) shortage

ammanettare (ammanétto) *tr* to handcuff

ammaniglia·to -ta *adj* shackled; (fig) closely bound, closely tied

ammannare *tr* to sheave (*grain*)

ammannire §176 *tr* to prepare (*a dish*); to dish up (*a meal*)

ammansare *tr & ref* var of **ammansire**

ammansa·tóre -trice *mf* (poet) tamer

ammansire §176 *tr* to tame; to calm || *ref* to become tamed; to calm down

ammantare *tr* to mantle, clothe; to cover; to hide (*the truth*)

ammanto *m* mantle, cloak; (fig) authority

ammaràg·gio *m* (-gi) landing on water; splashdown (*of a space vehicle*)

ammaraménto *m* var of **ammaraggio**

ammarare *intr* (aer) to land on water; (rok) to splash down

ammarrare *tr* (naut) to moor

ammassare *tr* to amass || *ref* to crowd, throng

ammasso *m* heap, pile; cluster (*of stars*); government stockpile

ammattiménto *m* worry, nuisance

ammattire §176 *intr* (ESSERE) to go crazy; **fare ammattire** to drive crazy

ammattonare (ammattóno) *tr* to floor with bricks

ammattona·to -ta *adj* floored with bricks || *m* brick floor; bricklaying

ammazzare *tr* to kill || *ref* to kill oneself; to get killed

ammazzasèt·te *m* (-te) braggart

ammazza·tóio *m* (-tói) slaughterhouse

ammènda *f* fine; satisfaction (*for injury*); **fare ammenda** to make amends

ammendaménto *m* emendation: improvement (*of land*)

ammendare (ammèndo) *tr* to emendate; to improve (*land*)

ammennìcolo *m* excuse; trifle; **ammennicoli** extras

ammés·so -sa *adj* admitted; **ammesso che** supposing that; **ammesso e non concesso** for the sake of argument

amméttere §198 *tr* to admit; to accept, suppose

ammezzare [ddzz] (ammèzzo) *tr* to leave half-finished (*a piece of work*); to fill halfway; to empty halfway

ammezzato [ddzz] *m* mezzanine

ammiccare §197 *intr* to wink; to cock one's eye

amministrare *tr* to administer, manage

amministra·tóre -trice *mf* administrator, manager; **amministratore delegato** chairman of the board

amministrazióne *f* administration, management: **ordinaria amministrazione** run-of-the-mill business

ammiràbile *adj* admirable

ammiràglia *f* (nav) flagship

ammiragliato *m* admiralty

ammirà·glio *m* (-gli) admiral; **ammiraglio d'armata** admiral; **ammiraglio di divisione** rear admiral; **ammiraglio di squadra** vice admiral; **grande ammiraglio** admiral of the fleet

ammirare *tr* to admire || *intr* to wonder

ammirati·vo -va *adj* admiring; exclamation (*mark*)

ammira·tóre -trice *mf* admirer || *m* suitor

ammirazióne *f* admiration

ammirévole *adj* admirable

ammissìbile *adj* admissible; permissible

ammissióne *f* admission; (mach) intake; **ammissione comune** consensus

ammobiliaménto *m* furnishing; furniture

ammobiliare §287 *tr* to furnish

ammodernare (ammodèrno) *tr* to modernize

ammòdo *adj invar* well-mannered, polite || *adv* properly

ammogliare §280 **(ammóglio)** *tr* to marry, give in marriage || *ref* to marry, get married

ammoglia·to *adj* married || *m* married man

ammollare (ammòllo) *tr* to soften; to soak; to slacken (*e.g., a hawser*); to deliver (*a slap*) || *ref* to get soaked

ammollire §176 *tr* to soften; to weaken || *ref* to soften; to mellow

ammonìaca *f* ammonia

ammoniménto *m* warning

ammonire §176 *tr* to admonish, reprimand

ammoni·tóre -trice *adj* warning

ammonizióne *f* admonition, warning

ammontare *m* amount, total || *v* (ammónto) *tr* to pile up || *intr* (ESSERE) to amount

ammonticchiare §287 *tr* to pile up, heap up

ammorbare (ammòrbo) *tr* to infect, contaminate

ammorbidènte *m* softener

ammorbidire §176 *tr* to soften; to mitigate || *ref* to soften

ammortaménto *m* amortization; payment, redemption (*of a loan*)

ammortare (ammòrto) *tr* to amortize

ammortire §176 *tr* to deaden; to weaken, soften

ammortizzamento [ddzz] *m* amortization, amortizement

ammortizzare [ddzz] *tr* to amortize; (aut) to absorb (*shocks*)

ammortizzatóre [ddzz] *m* (aut) shock absorber

ammosciare §128 (ammòscio) *tr, intr & ref* var of **ammosciare**

ammoscia·to -ta *adj* (coll) downcast

ammosciare §176 *tr* to make sag; to make flabby ‖ *intr & ref* to sag; to become flabby; to droop

ammucchiare §287 *tr* to heap up, pile up ‖ *ref* to crowd together

ammuffire §176 *intr* (ESSERE) to become moldy

ammusare *tr & intr* to nuzzle

ammutinaménto *m* mutiny, riot

ammutinare (ammùtino & ammutino) *tr* to incite to riot ‖ *ref* to mutiny

ammutinato *m* mutineer

ammutolire §176 *intr* (ESSERE) to become silent; to be dumbfounded

amnesìa *f* amnesia

amnistìa *f* amnesty

amnistiare §287 or §119 *tr* to amnesty

amo *m* hook; **abboccare all'amo** to bite, to swallow the hook

amorale *adj* immoral; amoral

amorali·tà *f* (-tà) immorality; amorality

amóre *m* love; eagerness; **amor proprio** amour-propre, self-esteem; **con amore** with pleasure; **d'amore e d'accordo** in perfect agreement; **fare all'amore** to make love; **fare l'amore** to flirt; **per amor del cielo** for heaven's sake; **per amore di** for the sake of; **un amore di bambino** a charming child; **un amore di cappello** a darling hat

amoreggiare §290 (amoréggio) *intr* to flirt; to play around

amorévole *adj* loving; kindly

amòr·fo -fa *adj* amorphous; safety (*match*)

amorino *m* cupid; cute child; love seat; (bot) mignonette

amoró·so -sa [s] *adj* loving; kindly; amorous; love (*e.g., life*) ‖ *mf* lover ‖ *m* fiancé ‖ *f* fiancée

amovìbile *adj* removable

amperàg·gio *m* (-gi) amperage

ampère *m* ampere

amperòmetro *m* ammeter

amperóra *f* ampere-hour

ampiézza *f* width, breadth; trajectory (*of a missile*); amplitude; **ampiezza di vedute** open-mindedness

àm·pio -pia *adj* (-pì -pie) ample; wide; roomy

amplèsso *m* (poet) embrace

ampliaménto *m* amplification, extension

ampliare §287 *tr* to enlarge, widen ‖ *ref* to widen

amplificare §197 (amplìfico) *tr* to amplify; to widen; to exaggerate

amplifica·tóre *m* (rad & telv) amplifier

amplificazióne *f* amplification

amplitùdine *f* amplitude

ampólla *f* cruet; (eccl) ampulla

ampollièra *f* cruet stand

ampollosi·tà [s] *f* (-tà) grandiloquence, turgidity

ampolló·so -sa [s] *adj* grandiloquent, turgid

amputare (àmputo) *tr* to amputate

amputazióne *f* amputation

amulèto *m* amulet, charm

anabbagliante *m* (aut) low beam; **anabbaglianti** (aut) dimmers

anacàr·dio *m* (-di) cashew

ànace *m* var of **anice**

anacorè·ta *m* (-ti) anchorite, hermit

anacronismo *m* anachronism

anacronìsti·co -ca *adj* (-ci -che) anachronistic(al)

anàgrafe *m* bureau of vital statistics; registry of births, deaths, and marriages

anagram·ma *m* (-mi) anagram

analcòli·co -ca *adj* (-ci -che) nonalcoholic; soft (*drink*) ‖ *m* soft drink

analfabè·ta *mf* (-ti -te) illiterate

analfabèti·co -ca *adj* (-ci -che) unalphabetized, unalphabetic

analfabetismo *m* illiteracy

analgèsi·co -ca *adj & m* (-ci -che) analgesic

anàli·si *f* (-si) analysis; breakdown; **analisi grammaticale** parsing; **analisi dell'urina** urinalysis

anali·sta *mf* (-sti -ste) analyst; **analista finanziario** financial analyst; **analista tempi e metodi** efficiency expert, efficiency engineer

analìti·co -ca *adj* (-ci -che) analytic(al)

analizzare [ddzz] *tr* to analyze; to assay (*ores*); (telv) to scan

analogìa *f* analogy

anàlo·go -ga *adj* (-ghi -ghe) analogous; similar

anamnè·si *f* (-si) (med) case history

ananasso *m* pineapple

anarchìa *f* anarchy

anàrchi·co -ca *adj* (-ci -che) anarchical ‖ *m* anarchist

anatè·ma or **anàte·ma** *m* (-mi) anathema

anatomìa *f* anatomy

anatòmi·co -ca *adj* (-ci -che) anatomic(al)

ànatra *f* duck; drake

anatròccolo *m* duckling

an·ca *f* (-che) hip; (coll) thigh (*e.g., of a chicken*); **dare d'anche** to run away; **menare anca** to walk

ancèlla *f* maidservant

ancestrale *adj* ancestral

anche *adv* also, too; even; (poet) yet; **anche a + inf** even if + *ind*

anchilosare (anchilòso) *tr* to paralyze ‖ *ref* to become paralyzed

anchilòsto·ma *m* (-mi) hookworm

àn·cia *f* (-ce) (mus) reed

ancillare *adj* servant

ancòra *adv* still, yet; again; more e.g., **ancora cinque minuti** five minutes more

àncora *f* anchor; keeper (*of magnet*); armature (*of buzzer or electric bell*); **ancora di salvezza** last hope; **gettar l'ancora** to cast anchor; **salpare** or **levar l'ancora** to weigh anchor

ancoràg·gio *m* (-gi) anchorage, berth

ancorare (àncoro) *tr* to anchor; to tie (*e.g., a currency to gold*) ‖ *ref* to anchor; to hold fast

ancorché *conj* although

andalu·so -sa *adj & mf* Andalusian

andaménto *m* course, progress

andante *adj* ordinary, common; continuous

andare *m* going; gait; **a lungo andare** in the long run ‖ §106 *intr* (ESSERE) to go; to spread (*said of news*); to be (*e.g., proud*); to work (*said of machinery*); (with *dat*) to fit, e.g., **quel vestito non gli va** that suit does not fit him; (with *dat*) to please, e.g. **quel vestito non le va** that dress does not please her; **andare a cavallo** to go horseback riding; **andare a finire** to wind up; **andare a male** to spoil; **andare a picco** to sink; **andare d'accordo** to agree; **andare in cerca di** to seek; **andare in macchina** to be in press; **andare in onda** (rad & telv) to go on the air; **andare per i vent'anni** to be bordering on twenty years; **andare pazzo per** to be crazy about; **andare soldato** to be drafted; **andare via** to go away; **come va?** how are things?; **mi va il vino dolce** I like sweet wine; **ne va della vita** life is at stake; **va da sé** it goes without saying ‖ *ref*—**andarsene** to go away, leave

anda·to -ta *adj* gone, past; finished; (coll) spoiled (*e.g., meat*) ‖ *f* going; journey, trip; **a lunga andata** in the long run; **andata e ritorno** round trip; **dare l'andata** *f* to give the go-ahead to

andatura *f* gait; pace; **fare l'andatura** to set the pace

andazzo *m* bad practice, bad habit; fad

Ande, le the Andes

andicappare *tr* to handicap

andi·no -na *adj* Andean

andirivìè·ni *m* (-ni) coming and going; maze; ado

àndito *m* corridor, hallway

andróne *m* hall, lobby

aneddòti·co -ca *adj* (-ci -che) anecdotal

anèddoto *m* anecdote

anelante *adj* panting

anelare (anèlo) *tr* to long for ‖ *intr* to yearn; (poet) to pant

anèlito *m* last breath; yearning; (poet) panting; **mandare l'ultimo anelito** to breathe one's last

anellino *m* ringlet

anèllo *m* ring; link (*of a chain*); traffic circle; segment (*of a worm*); (sports) track; **ad anello** ring-shaped; **anello di congiunzione** (fig) link; **anello di fidanzamento** engagement ring ‖ **anella** *fpl* (poet) ringlets; (archaic) rings

anemìa *f* anemia

anèmi·co -ca *adj* (-ci -che) anemic

anestesìa *f* anesthesia

anestesi·sta *mf* (-sti -ste) anesthetist

anestèti·co -ca *adj & m* (-ci -che) anesthetic

anestetizzare [ddzz] *tr* to anesthetize

aneuri·sma *m* (-smi) aneurysm

anfi·bio -bia (-bi -bie) *adj* amphibian; (fig) ambiguous ‖ *m* amphibian

anfiteatro *m* amphitheater

anfitrióne *m* (lit) generous host

anfratto *m* ravine; narrow, winding, rugged spot

anfrattuosi·tà [s] *f* (-tà) rough broken ground; winding, rough spot

anfrattuó·so -sa [s] *adj* winding, rough, craggy

angariare §287 *tr* to pester, oppress

angèli·co -ca *adj* (-ci -che) angelic(al)

àngelo *m* angel; **angelo custode** guardian angel

angherìa *f* vexation; outrage; imposition

angina *f* quinsy; **angina pectoris** angina pectoris

angipòrto *m* blind alley; narrow lane

anglica·no -na *adj & mf* Anglican

anglicismo *m* Anglicism

anglicizzare [ddzz] *tr* to Anglicize ‖ *ref* to become Anglicized

anglòfo·no -na *adj* English-speaking ‖ *m* English-speaking person

anglosàssone *adj & mf* Anglo-Saxon

angolare *adj* angular; corner (*stone*) ‖ *m* angle iron ‖ *v* (àngolo) *tr* to take an angle shot of; (sports) to kick (*the ball*) into the corner of the goal

angolazióne *f* (mov) angle shot

angolièra *f* corner shelving; corner cupboard

àngolo *m* angle; corner

angoló·so -sa [s] *adj* angular

àngora *f* Angora cat; Angora goat

angò·scia *f* (-sce) anxiety, distress, anguish

angosciare §128 (angòscio) *tr* to distress

angoscia·to -ta *adj* tormented, distressed

angosció·so -sa [s] *adj* agonizing

anguilla *f* eel

anguillé·sco -sca *adj* (-schi -sche) as slippery as an eel

angùria *f* watermelon

angùstia *f* narrowness; scarcity; **stare in angustia** to be worried

angustiare §287 *tr* to distress, grieve ‖ *ref* to worry

angu·sto -sta *adj* narrow

ànice *m* anise

anicino *m* anise cookie

anidride *f* anhydride

àni·dro -dra *adj* anhydrous

anilina *f* aniline

ànima *f* soul; life (*e.g., of the party*); core; kernel; bore (*of gun*); mold (*of button*); mind; enthusiasm; pith (*of fruit*); sounding post (*of violin*); web (*of rail*); **anima dannata** evil counselor; **anima mia!** darling!; **anima nera** villain; **anima viva** living soul; **buon'anima** late, e.g., **mio padre, buon'anima** my late father; **dannare l'anima** to lose patience; **la buon'anima di** the late; **rompere l'anima a** to annoy

animale *adj* animal; (poet) of the soul; (poet) animate ‖ *m* animal; (fig) boor, lout

animalé·sco -sca *adj* (**-schi -sche**) animal, bestial

animare (**ànimo**) *tr* to animate, to enliven; to promote ‖ *ref* to become lively or heated

anima·to -ta *adj* animated (*cartoon*); animated, lively; animal

anima·tóre -trice *adj* animating ‖ *m* moving spirit; (*mov*) animator

animazióne *f* animation

animèlla *f* sweetbread

ànimo *m* mind; heart, affection; courage; **aprire l'animo** to open one's heart; **avere in animo di** to have a mind to; **mal animo** ill will; **mettersi l'animo in pace** to resign oneself; **perdersi d'animo** to lose heart; **serbare nell'animo** to keep in mind

animosi·tà [s] *f* (**-tà**) animosity, ill will

animó·so -sa [s] *adj* bold; spirited (*animal*); hostile

anióne *m* anion

anisétta *f* anisette

ànitra *f* var of **anatra**

anitròccolo *m* var of **anatroccolo**

annacquare (**annàcquo**) *tr* to water; to water down

annaffiare §287 *tr* to sprinkle; to water (*wine*)

annaffia·tóio *m* (**-tói**) sprinkling can

annaffia·tóre -trice *adj* watering, sprinkling

annali *mpl* annals *spl*

annaspare *tr* to reel ‖ *intr* to gesticulate; to grope; to flounder

annata *f* year; year's activity; year's rent; year's issues (*of a magazine*)

annebbiare §287 (**annébbio**) *tr* to befog; to dim ‖ *ref* to become foggy; to become dim

annegaménto *m* drowning

annegare §209 (**annégo**) *tr* & *intr* (ESSERE) to drown

anneriménto *m* blackening

annerire §176 *tr* to blacken ‖ *ref* to turn black

annessióne *f* annexation

annès·so -sa *adj* united, attached ‖ *m* annex; **con tutti gli annessi e connessi** everything included

annèttere §107 *tr* to annex; to attach, enclose; to unite; to ascribe (*importance*)

annichilante *adj* annihilating; devastating (*e.g., reply*)

annichilare (**annìchilo**) *tr* to annihilate ‖ *ref* to destroy oneself; (fig) to humble oneself

annichilire §176 *tr* & *ref* var of **annichilare**

annidare *tr* to nest; (fig) to nourish, cherish ‖ *ref* to nest; to hide; (fig) to settle

annientaménto *m* annihilation

annientare (**anniènto**) *tr* to annihilate; to knock down, demolish; (fig) to crush ‖ *ref* to humble oneself

anniversà·rio -ria *adj* & *m* (**-ri -rie**) anniversary

anno *m* year; **anno bisestile** leap year; **anno luce** light-year; **anno nuovo** New Year; **anno scolastico** school year; **avere . . . anni** to be . . . years old; **l'anno che viene** next year; **l'anno corrente** this year; **quest'altr'anno** next year; **un anno dopo l'altro** year in, year out

annobilire §176 *tr* to ennoble

annodare (**annòdo**) *tr* to knot, tie; (fig) to tie up ‖ *ref* to get entangled

annoiare §287 (**annòio**) *tr* to bore ‖ *ref* to become bored

annòna *f* food; food-control agency

annonà·rio -ria *adj* (**-ri -rie**) food; rationing (*card*)

annó·so -sa [s] *adj* old, aged

annotare (**annòto**) *tr* to jot down; to chalk up; to annotate; to comment

annotazióne *f* note; notation, annotation

annottare (**annòtta**) *impers* (ESSERE) & *ref* to grow dark, e.g., **si annotta** it's growing dark; **è annottato** it grew dark

annoverare (**annòvero**) *tr* to count, number

annuale *adj* annual ‖ *m* anniversary

annuà·rio *m* (**-ri**) annual, yearbook

annuire §176 *intr* to nod assent; to consent

annullaménto *m* nullification, annulment

annullare *tr* to annul, nullify, cancel; to call off ‖ *ref* to cancel one another

annunciare §128 *tr* var of **annunziare**

Annunciazióne *f* Annunciation

annunziare §287 (**annùnzio**) *tr* to announce; (fig) to forecast, foreshadow

annunzia·tóre -trice *mf* announcer, newscaster

annùn·zio *m* (**-zi**) announcement, notice; **annunzio economico** classified ad; **annunzio pubblicitario** advertisement; **annunzio pubblicitario radiofonico** (rad) commercial

ànnu·o -a *adj* yearly, annual

annusare [s] *tr* to smell; to snuff (*tobacco*)

annuvolaménto *m* cloudiness

annuvolare (**annùvolo**) *tr* to cloud, becloud ‖ *ref* to become cloudy; to turn somber

anòdi·no -na *adj* pain-relieving; ineffective; weak, colorless (*person*)

ànodo *m* anode

anomalìa *f* anomaly

anòma·lo -la *adj* anomalous

anonimìa *f* anonymity

anòni·mo -ma *adj* anonymous ‖ *m* anonymous author; **serbare l'anonimo** to preserve one's anonymity

anormale *adj* abnormal ‖ *m* queer fellow

anormali·tà *f* (**-tà**) abnormality

ansa *f* handle (*of vase*); pretext; bend (*of a river*)

ansante *adj* panting

ansare *intr* to pant

ànsia *f* anxiety; **essere in ansia** to be worried

ansie·tà *f* (**-tà**) anxiety

ansimare (**ànsimo**) *intr* to pant

ansió·so -sa [s] *adj* anxious

antagonismo *m* antagonism

antagoni·sta (**-sti -ste**) *adj* antagonistic ‖ *mf* antagonist, opponent

antagonìsti·co -ca *adj* (**-ci -che**) antagonistic

antàrti·co -ca *adj* (**-ci -che**) antarctic ‖ **Antàrtico** *m* Antarctic

antecedènte *adj* preceding ‖ *m* antecedent

antecedènza *f* antecedence

antecessóre *m* predecessor

antefatto *m* background, antecedents

anteguèr·ra (**-ra**) *adj* prewar ‖ *m* prewar period

anteluca·no -na *adj* (poet) predawn

antenato *m* ancestor

anténna *f* lance; (naut) yard; (rad & telv) aerial, antenna; (zool) antenna

antepórre §218 *tr* to prefer; to place before

anteprima *f* (mov & theat) preview

anteriore *adj* fore, front; previous; earlier

antesignano [s] *m* forerunner

anti- *pref adj* anti-, e.g., **anticomunìstico** anticommunist; un-, e.g., **antieconòmico** uneconomical ‖ *pref mf* anti-, e.g., **anticomunista** anticommunist

antiabbagliante *adj* antiglare ‖ *m* low beam

antiàci·do -da *adj & m* antacid

antiaère·o -a *adj* antiaircraft ‖ *f* antiaircraft defense

antibattèri·co -ca (**-ci -che**) *adj* antibacterial ‖ *m* bactericide

antibiòti·co -ca *adj & m* (**-ci -che**) antibiotic

anticà·glia *f* (**-glie**) antique, curio; rubbish, junk

anticàmera *f* waiting room, anteroom; **fare anticamera** to cool one's heels

anticarro *adj invar* antitank

antichi·tà *f* (**-tà**) antiquity; **antichità** *fpl* antiques

anticipare (**antìcipo**) *tr* to advance; to speed up; to pay in advance; to leak (*news*); to expect, anticipate ‖ *intr* to be early

anticipa·to -ta *adj* in advance (*e.g., payment*)

anticipazióne *f* advance; collateral loan; expectation, anticipation

antìcipo *m* advance; loan (*on accounts receivable*); **in anticipo** in advance

antì·co -ca *adj* (**-chi -che**) antique, ancient, old; **all'antica** in the old-fashioned manner; **gli antichi** the ancients; the forefathers; **in antico** in olden times

anticoncezionale *adj & f* contraceptive

anticonformì·sta *mf* (**-sti -ste**) nonconformist

anticonformìsti·co -ca *adj* (**-ci -che**) unconventional

anticongelante *adj & m* antifreeze

anticongiunturale *adj* crisis, emergency

anticòrpo *m* antibody

anticristo *m* Antichrist

antidatare *tr* to predate

antiderapante *adj* nonskid

antidetonante *adj* antiknock ‖ *m* antiknock compound

antidiluvia·no -na *adj* antediluvian

antìdoto *m* antidote

antievanescènza *f* (rad) antifading device

antifecondati·vo -va *adj & m* contraceptive

antìfona *f* antiphon; **capire l'antifona** (fig) to get the message

antifurto *adj invar* antitheft ‖ *m* antitheft device

antigàs *adj invar* gas (*e.g., mask*)

antigièni·co -ca *adj* (**-ci -che**) unsanitary

antìlope *f* antelope

antimeridia·no -na *adj* antemeridian, A.M.

antimìssile *adj invar* antimissile

antimònio *m* antimony

antincèndio *adj invar* fire-fighting; fire, e.g., **scala antincendio** fire escape

antinéb·bia *adj invar* fog ‖ *m* (**-bia**) fog light

antinéve *adj invar* snow, e.g., **catena antineve** snow chain

antioràrio -ria *adj* (**-ri -rie**) counterclockwise

antipatìa *f* antipathy, dislike

antipàti·co -ca *adj* (**-ci -che**) antipathetic; disagreeable; uncongenial

antipièga *adj invar* crease-resistant, wrinkle-proof

antìpodi *mpl* antipodes

antipòlio *adj invar* polio (*e.g., vaccine*)

antipòrta *f* stormdoor; corridor

antiquàrio -ria (**-ri -rie**) *adj* antiquarian ‖ *m* antiquary, antiquarian

antiqua·to -ta *adj* obsolete; antiquated

antireligió·so -sa [s] *adj* antireligious, irreligious

antirùggine *adj invar* antirust

antirumóre *adj invar* antinoise

antisala [s] *f* anteroom, waiting room

antisassi [s] *adj invar* protecting against falling stones

antischiavì·sta *adj & mf* (**-sti -ste**) abolitionist

antisemì·ta [s] *adj* (**-ti -te**) anti-Semitic ‖ *mf* anti-Semite

antisemìti·co -ca [s] *adj* (**-ci -che**) anti-Semitic

antisemitìsmo [s] *m* anti-Semitism

antisètti·co -ca [s] *adj & m* (**-ci -che**) antiseptic

antisociale [s] *adj* antisocial

antisóle [s] *adj invar* sun (*glasses*); suntan (*lotion*)

antisommergìbile [s] *adj* antisubmarine

antistatale *adj* antigovernment

antitàrmi·co -ca *adj* (**-ci -che**) mothproof

antitèmpo *adv* early, prematurely

antìte·si *f* (**-si**) antithesis

antitèti·co -ca *adj* (**-ci -che**) antithetic(al)

antitossìna *f* antitoxin

antiuòmo *adj invar* (mil) antipersonnel

antivigìlia *f*—**l'antivigilia di** two days before

antologìa *f* anthology

antònimo *m* antonym

antrace *m* anthrax

antracite *f* anthracite

antro *m* cave; den, hovel

antròpi·co -ca *adj* (**-ci -che**) human

antropofagìa *f* cannibalism

antropòfa·go -ga (**-gi -ghe**) *adj* cannibalistic ‖ *m* cannibal

antropòide *adj* anthropoid

antropologìa *f* anthropology

antropomòrfi·co -ca *adj* (**-ci -che**) anthropomorphic

antropomòr·fo -fa *adj* see **scimmia**

anulare *adj* ring-shaped, annular ‖ *m* ring finger

Anvèrsa *f* Antwerp

anzi *adv* on the contrary, rather; **anzi che no** rather ‖ *prep* (poet) before

anziani·tà *f* (**-tà**) seniority

anzia·no -na *adj* old, elderly; senior ‖ *m* senior

anziché *conj* rather than

anzidét·to -ta *adj* aforesaid

anzitutto *adv* above all, first of all

apatìa *f* apathy

apàti·co -ca *adj* (**-ci -che**) apathetic

ape *f* bee; **ape operaia** worker; **ape regina** queen bee

aperitivo *m* apéritif

apèr·to -ta *adj* open; frank, candid ‖ *m* open space; **all'aperto** in the open

apertura *f* opening; aperture; approach; **ad apertura di libro** at sight; **apertura alare** (*of a bird*) wingspread; (aer) wingspan

apià·rio *m* (**-ri**) apiary

àpice *m* apex, top; climax

apicol·tóre -trice *mf* beekeeper, apiarist

apicoltura *f* beekeeping, apiculture

Apocalisse *f* Apocalypse, Revelation

apocalìtti·co -ca *adj* (**-ci -che**) apocalyptic(al)

apòcri·fo -fa *adj* apocryphal

apofonìa *f* ablaut

apogèo *m* apogee

apòlide *adj* stateless ‖ *m* man without a country

apolìti·co -ca *adj* (**-ci -che**) nonpolitical, nonpartisan

apologè·ta *m* (**-ti**) apologist

apologèti·co -ca *adj* (**-ci -che**) apologetic

apologìa *f* apology

apòlo·go *m* (**-ghi**) apologue

apoplessìa *f* apoplexy

apoplètti·co -ca *adj & m* (**-ci -che**) apoplectic

apostasìa *f* apostasy

apòsta·ta *mf* (**-ti -te**) apostate

apostolato *m* apostolate

apostòli·co -ca *adj* (**-ci -che**) apostolic(al)

apòstolo *m* apostle

apostrofare (**apòstrofo**) *tr* to write with an apostrophe; to apostrophize

apòstrofe *f* apostrophe (*to a person*)

apòstrofo *m* (gram) apostrophe

apoteò·si *f* (**-si**) apotheosis

appagare §209 *tr* to satisfy, gratify ‖ *ref*—**appagarsi di** to be content with

appaiare §287 *tr* to pair, couple; to match ‖ *ref* to match (*said, e.g., of colors*)

appallottolare (**appallòttolo**) *tr* to crumple into a ball ‖ *ref* to become lumpy

appaltare *tr* to contract for

appalta·tóre -trice *mf* contractor

appalto *m* contract; state monopoly; **appalto di sali e tabacchi** tobacco shop

appannàg·gio *m* (**-gi**) appanage; (fig) prerogative

appannare *tr* to tarnish; to befog, becloud ‖ *ref* to become clouded (*said, e.g., of one's eyesight*)

apparato *m* decoration; display; appliance; leadership (*of political party*); (rad, telv) set

apparecchiare §287 (**apparécchio**) *tr* to prepare; to set (*the table*) ‖ *ref* to get ready

apparecchiatura *f* sizing (*of paper; of a wall*); preparation (*of a canvas*); apparatus

apparéc·chio *m* (**-chi**) apparatus; sizing; preparation; gadget; (rad, telv) set; airplane; **apparecchio da caccia** fighter plane; **apparecchio telefonico** telephone

apparentare (**apparènto**) *tr* to tie, unite (*through marriage*) ‖ *ref* to become related; to become intimate; (pol) to form a coalition

apparènte *adj* apparent, seeming

apparènza *f* appearance; **in apparenza** seemingly

apparigliare §280 *tr* to pair, team (*horses*)

apparire §108 *intr* (ESSERE) to appear, seem; to look

appariscènte *adj* showy, flashy, gaudy

apparizióne *f* apparition; appearance

appartaménto *m* apartment

appartare *tr* to set aside ‖ *ref* to withdraw, retire

apparta·to -ta *adj* secluded, solitary

appartenènza *f* belonging, membership; **appartenenze** accessories; annexes

appartenére §271 *intr* (ESSERE & AVERE) to belong; to pertain ‖ *impers* (ESSERE & AVERE)—**appartiene a it** behooves, it is up to

appassionaménto *m* excitement, interest, enthusiasm

appassionare (**appassióno**) *tr* to move; to interest; to excite ‖ *ref* to be deeply interested

appassiona·to -ta *adj* impassioned; deep, ardent ‖ *m* fan, amateur

appassire §176 *intr* (ESSERE) to wilt, wither; to decay; to dry up (*said, e.g., of grapes*)

appellare (**appèllo**) *tr* (law) to appeal; (poet) to call ‖ *ref* to appeal; **appellarsi da** or **contro** (law) to appeal

appèllo *m* call, roll call; **fare appello a** to summon (*e.g., one's strength*); **fare l'appello** to call the roll; **mancare all'appello** to be absent

appèna *adv* hardly, scarcely; only; just ‖ *conj* as soon as; **non appena** as soon as, no sooner

appèndere §109 *tr* to hang

appéndice *f* appendix; feuilleton

appendicectomìa *f* appendectomy

appendicite *f* appendicitis

Appennino, l' *m* the Appennines

appesantire [s] §176 *tr* to make heavy; to burden, overwhelm || *ref* to get heavy; to get fat

appestare (appèsto) *tr* to infect; to stink up

appesta·to -ta *adj* plague-ridden || *m* plague victim

appetire §176 *tr* to crave, long for || *intr* (ESSERE & AVERE) to be appetizing

appetito *m* appetite

appetitó·so -sa [s] *adj* appetizing, tempting

appètto *adv* opposite; **appetto a** opposite; in comparison with

appezzamento *m* plot, parcel (*of land*)

appianare *tr* to smooth, level; to settle (*a dispute*); to get around (*a difficulty*)

appiana·tóio *m* (-tói) road grader

appiattare *tr* & *ref* to hide

appiattimento *m* leveling; equalization

appiattire §176 *tr* & *ref* to flatten, to level

appiccare §197 *tr* to hang; **appiccare il fuoco a** to set on fire; **appiccare una lite** to pick a fight

appicciare §128 *tr* (coll) to string together; (coll) to kindle, light

appicciare §197 (appìccico) *tr* to stick, glue; **appicciare uno schiaffo a** to slap || *ref* to stick, adhere

appiccicatic·cio -cia *adj* (-ci -ce) sticky

appic·co *m* (-chi) grip; steep wall (*of mountain*); (fig) pretext

appiè *adv*—**appiè di** at the foot of; at the bottom of

appiedare (appièdo) *tr* to order (*a cavalryman*) off a horse; to order (*e.g., troops*) off a vehicle; to force out of a car (*said, e.g., of motor trouble*)

appièno *adv* fully

appigionare (appigióno) *tr* to rent || *ref*—**appigionasi** for rent

appigiónasi [s] *m* for-rent sign

appigliare §280 *ref* to cling, adhere; **appigliarsi a un pretesto** to seize a pretext

appi·glio *m* (-gli) grip; (fig) pretext

appiómbo *m* perpendicular || *adv* plumb, perpendicularly

appioppare (appiòppo) *tr* to plant with poplar trees; to tie (*a vine*) to a poplar tree; (coll) to deliver (*a blow*); (coll) to pass off (*e.g., inferior goods*)

appisolare (appìsolo) *ref* to snooze, doze

applaudire §176 & (applàudo) *tr* to applaud` || *intr* to applaud, clap the hands; (with *dat*) to applaud

applàuso *m* applause; **applausi** applause

applicàbile *adj* applicable

applicare §197 (àpplico) *tr* to apply; to attach; to give (*e.g., a slap*); to put into effect (*a law*); to assign || *ref* to apply oneself

applica·to -ta *adj* applied; appliqué || *m* clerk

applicazióne *f* application; appliqué

applique *m* (elec) wall fixture

appoggiaca·po *m* (-po) headrest; tidy (*on back of chair*)

appoggiagómi·ti *m* (-ti) elbowrest

appoggiama·no *m* (-no) mahlstick

appoggiare §290 (appòggio) *tr* to lean; to rest; to prop, support; to raise (*the tone of voice*); to give (*a slap*); to second (*a motion*); (fig) to back, support || *intr* to lean; to rest || *ref*—**appoggiarsi a** or **su** to lean on

appoggia·tóio *m* (-tói) support, rest; banister

appoggiatura *f* (mus) grace note

appòg·gio *m* (-gi) support, prop; backer; backing, support; grip; (mach) bearing

appollaiare §287 *ref* to roost

appórre §218 *tr* to affix, append

apportare (appòrto) *tr* to cause; to presage; (poet) to carry

appòrto *m* carrying; contribution; (law) share

appositaménte *adv* expressely, on purpose

appòsi·to -ta *adj* proper, fitting

apposizióne *f* apposition

appòsta *adj invar* suitable || *adv* on purpose, expressly, intentionally

appostaménto *m* ambush

appostare (appòsto) *tr* to ambush || *ref* to lie in ambush

apprèndere §220 *tr* to learn || *ref* (poet) to take hold

apprendi·sta *mf* (-sti -ste) apprentice

apprendistato *m* apprenticeship

apprensióne *f* apprehension, fear

apprensi·vo -va *adj* apprehensive

appressare (apprèsso) *tr* (poet) to approach || *ref* to come near

appresso *adj invar* next, following || *adv* near; later on; **appresso a** near; after

apprestare (apprèsto) *tr* to prepare; to supply, provide (*e.g., help*) || *ref* to prepare, get ready

apprettare (apprètto) *tr* to dress (*leather*); to size (*cloth*)

apprètto *m* tan (*for leather*); sizing (*for cloth*)

apprezzàbile *adj* appreciable

apprezzaménto *m* appreciation; estimation

apprezzare (apprèzzo) *tr* to appreciate

apprezza·to -ta *adj* esteemed

appròc·cio *m* (-ci) approach; **approcci** advances

approdare (appròdo) *intr* (ESSERE & AVERE) to land; (with *dat*) (poet) to benefit; **approdare a** to come to

appròdo *m* landing

approfittare *intr*—**approfittare di** to capitalize on || *ref*—**approfittarsi di** to take advantage of

approfondire §176 *tr* to make deep; to study thoroughly || *ref*—**approfondirsi in** to go deep into

approntare (apprónto) *tr* to prepare, make ready

appropriare §287 (appròprio) *tr* to adapt; to bestow || *ref*—**appropriarsi a** to befit; **appropriarsi di** to appropriate; to embezzle

appropria·to -ta *adj* appropriate
appropriazióne *f* appropriation; **appropriazione indebita** fraudulent conversion, embezzlement
approssimare (appròssimo) *tr* to bring near || *ref* to approach, come near
approssimati·vo -va *adj* approximate
approssimazióne *f* approximation
approvàbile *adj* laudable
approvare (appròvo) *tr* to approve, countenance; to subscribe to (*an opinion*); to pass (*a student; a law*); to confirm
approvazióne *f* approval; confirmation; passage (*of a law*)
approvvigionaménto *m* supply
approvvigionare (approvvigióno) *tr* to supply || *ref* to be supplied
appuntaménto *m* appointment; date; **appuntamento amoroso** assignation
appuntare *tr* to sharpen; to fasten, pin; to stick (*a pin*) in; to point; to jot down, take note of; to prick up (*one's ears*); (fig) to reproach || *ref* to be turned; to aim
appunta·to -ta *adj* sharpened || *m* corporal (*of Italian police*)
appuntellare (appuntèllo) *tr* to shore up, prop up
appuntellatura *f* shoring up, propping up
appuntino *adv* precisely, meticulously
appuntire §176 *tr* to sharpen
appunti·to -ta *adj* sharp, pointed
appunto *m* note; blame, charge; **muovere un appunto a** to blame; **per l'appunto** just, precisely || *adv* exactly, precisely
appurare *tr* to ascertain
appuzzare *tr* to befoul, pollute
apribottì·glie *m* (-glie) bottle opener
apri·co -ca *adj* (-chi -che) (poet) sunny, bright
aprile *m* April
apripi·sta *m* (-sta) blade (*of bulldozer*); bulldozer
aprire §110 *tr* to open; to turn on; to dig (*e.g., a grave*) || *ref* to open; to clear up (*said of the weather*); **aprirsi con** to open one's heart to; **aprirsi il varco tra** to press through
apriscàto·le *m* (-le) can opener
aquà·rio *m* (-ri) aquarium || **Aquario** *m* (astr) Aquarius
aquàti·co -ca *adj* (-ci -che) aquatic
àquila *f* eagle; genius
aquili·no -na *adj* aquiline
aquilóne *m* north wind; kite
aquilòtto *m* eaglet; cadet (*in Italian Air Force Academy*)
Aquinate, l' *m* Saint Thomas Aquinas
ara *f* (poet) altar; are (*100 square meters*)
arabé·sca *f* (-sche) (mus) arabesque
arabesca·to -ta *adj* arabesque
arabé·sco -sca (-schi -sche) *adj* arabesque || *m* arabesque; doodle || *f* see **arabesca**
Aràbia, l' *f* Arabia
aràbi·co -ca *adj* (-ci -che) Arabic
aràbile *adj* tillable

àra·bo -ba *adj* Arabic, Arabian || *mf* Arab (*person*) || *m* Arabic (*language*)
aràchide *f* peanut (*vine*)
aragonése [s] *adj & mf* Aragonese
aragósta *f* (*Palinurus vulgaris*) lobster
aràldi·co -ca (-ci -che) *adj* heraldic || *f* heraldry
araldo *m* herald
arancéto *m* orange grove
aràn·cia *f* (-ce) orange
aranciata *f* orangeade
aràn·cio *adj invar* orange (*in color*) || *m* (-ci) orange tree
arancióne *adj & m* orange (*color*)
arare *tr* to plow; (naut) to drag (*the anchor*)
aratro *m* plow
arazzo *m* tapestry, arras
arbitràg·gio *m* (-gi) (sports) umpiring; (com) arbitrage
arbitrale *adj* judge's, umpire's
arbitrare (àrbitro) *tr* to umpire, referee || *intr* to arbitrate || *ref*—**arbitrarsi di** to take the liberty to
arbitrà·rio -ria *adj* (-ri -rie) arbitrary; wanton
arbitrato *m* arbitration
arbì·trio *m* (-tri) will; abuse, violation; **libero arbitrio** free will
àrbitro *m* arbiter; judge, referee, umpire
arboscèllo *m* small tree
arbusto *m* shrub, bush
ar·ca *f* (-che) sarcophagus; ark; chest; **arca di Noè** Noah's Ark; **arca di scienza** (fig) fountain of knowledge
àrcade *adj & m* Arcadian
Arcàdia *f* Arcadia, Arcady
arcài·co -ca *adj* (-ci -che) archaic
arcaismo *m* archaism
arcàngelo *m* archangel
arca·no -na *adj* mysterious, arcane || *m* mystery
arcata *f* arch; arcade
archeologia *f* archaeology
archeològi·co -ca *adj* (-ci -che) archaeological
archeòlo·go -ga *mf* (-gi -ghe) archaeologist
archètipo *m* archetype
archétto *m* (archit) small arch; (elec) trolley pole; (mus) bow
archi- *pref adj* archi-, e.g., **architettonico** architectonic || *pref m & f* archi-, e.g., **architettura** architecture
archibù·gio *m* (-gi) harquebus
Archimède *m* Archimedes
architettare (architétto) *tr* to plan (*a building*); (fig) to contrive, plot
architétto *m* architect
architettòni·co -ca *adj* (-ci -che) architectural
architettura *f* architecture
architetturale *adj* architectural
architrave *m* architrave; doorhead, lintel
archiviare §287 *tr* to file; to lay aside, shelve; (law) to throw out
archi·vio *m* (-vi) archives; record office; chancery, public records
archivi·sta *mf* (-sti -ste) archivist, file clerk

arci- *pref adj* archi-, e.g., **arcivescovile** archiepiscopal || *pref m & f* arch-, e.g., **arciprete** archpriest

arcicontèn·to -ta *adj* (coll) very glad

arcidiàcono *m* archdeacon

arcidu·ca *m* (**-chi**) archduke

arciduchéssa *f* archduchess

arcière *m* archer, bowman

arci·gno -gna *adj* gruff, surly

arcióne *m* saddlebow; **montare in arcioni** to mount, to mount a horse

arcipèla·go *m* (**-ghi**) archipelago

arciprète *m* archpriest; dean

arcivescovado *m* archbishopric

arcivéscovo *m* archbishop

ar·co *m* (**-chi**) bow; (archit) arch; (geom, elec) arc; **arco rampante** flying buttress

arcobaléno *m* rainbow

arco·làio *m* (**-lài**) reel; **girare come un arcolaio** to spin like a top

arcuare (**àrcuo**) *tr* to arch; to bend; to camber

arcua·to -ta *adj* bent, curved; bow (*e.g., legs*); **avere le gambe arcuate** to be bowlegged

ardènte *adj* burning; hot; ardent, impassioned

àrdere §111 *tr* to burn || *intr* to burn; to be in full swing (*said, e.g., of a war*)

ardèsia *f* slate

ardiménto *m* boldness, daring

ardire *m* boldness; presumption, impudence || §176 *intr*—**ardire** + *inf* or **ardire di** + *inf* to dare to + *inf*

arditézza *f* daring; temerity

ardi·to -ta *adj* daring; rash || *m* (hist) shock trooper

ardóre *m* intense heat; ardor

àr·duo -dua *adj* arduous

àrea *f* area, surface; group, camp; **area arretrata** backward area

àrem *m* (**àrem**) harem

arèna *f* arena; **scendere nell'arena** to throw one's hat in the ring

aréna *f* sand

arenare (**aréno**) *intr* (ESSERE) & *ref* to run aground

arenària *f* sandstone

arén·go *m* (**-ghi**) (hist) town meeting

arenile *m* sandy beach

arenó·so -sa [*s*] *adj* sandy

areòmetro *m* hydrometer

aeronàuti·co -ca *adj & f* (**-ci -che**) var of **aeronautico**

areoplano *m* var of **aeroplano**

areopòrto *m* var of **aeroporto**

areòstato *m* var of **aerostato**

àrgano *m* winch; (naut) capstan

argentare (**argènto**) *tr* to silver; to silver-plate; to back (*a mirror*) with foil

argenta·to -ta *adj* silver; silvery; silver-plated

argentatura *f* silver plating; silver plate; foil (*of mirror*)

argènte·o -a *adj* silver, silvery

argentería *f* silverware

argentière *m* silversmith; jeweler

argenti·no -na *adj* silver, silvery; Argentine || *mf* Argentine || *f* high-necked sweater || **l'Argentina** *f* Argentina

argènto *m* silver; (archaic) money; **argenti** silverware; **argento vivo** quicksilver

argentóne *m* German silver

argilla *f* clay

argilló·so -sa [*s*] *adj* clayey

arginare (**àrgino**) *tr* to dam, dike; to hold back, check

àrgine *m* embankment, dam; (fig) defense

ar·go *m* (**-ghi**) (chem) argon; (orn) grouse || **Argo** *m* Argus

argomentare (**argoménto**) *tr & intr* to argue

argomentazióne *f* argumentation, discussion

argoménto *m* argument; pretext; subject; **fuori dell'argomento** beside the point

argonàu·ta *m* (**-ti**) Argonaut

arguire §176 *tr* to deduce, infer; (archaic) to denote

argutézza *f* wit; witty remark

argu·to -ta *adj* keen, acute; witty

argùzia *f* keenness; wit

ària *f* air; climate; look; mien; aria, tune; poem; **all'aria aperta** in the open air; **a mezz'aria** in midair; halfway; **andare all'aria** to fail; **aria condizionata** air conditioning; **avere l'aria di** to seem to; to look like; **dare aria a** to air; **in aria** in the air; **tira un'aria pericolosa** a mean wind is blowing

aria·no -na *adj & mf* Aryan

aridi·tà *f* (**-tà**) dryness, aridity; dearth

àri·do -da *adj* arid, dry, barren; (fig) dry

arieggiare §290 (**ariéggio**) *tr* to air; to imitate || *ref*—**arieggiarsi a** to give oneself the airs of

ariète *m* ram; (mil) battering ram || **Ariete** *m* (astr) Aries

ariétta *s* breeze; (mus) short aria

arin·ga *f* (**-ghe**) herring; **aringa affumicata** kippered herring, kipper

arin·go *m* (**-ghi**) assembly; field; joust; **scendere nell'aringo** to throw one's hat in the ring

arió·so -sa [*s*] *adj* airy, breezy; (fig) of wide scope

àrista *f* loin of pork

arista *f* (bot) awn

aristocràti·co -ca (**-ci -che**) *adj* aristocratic || *mf* aristocrat

aristocrazìa *f* aristocracy

Aristòtele *m* Aristotle

aristotèli·co -ca *adj & m* (**-ci -che**) Aristotelian

aritmèti·co -ca (**-ci -che**) *adj* arithmetical || *m* arithmetician || *f* arithmetic

arlecchino *adj invar* harlequin; fiesta (*e.g., dishes*) || **Arlecchino** *m* Harlequin

ar·ma *f* (**-mi**) arm, weapon; (fig) army; (mil) corps, service; **alle prime armi** at the beginning; **arma bianca** steel blade; **arma da taglio** cutting weapon; **arma delle trasmissioni** signal corps

armacòllo *m*—**ad armacollo** slung across the shoulders (*said of a rifle*)

armà·dio *m* (**-di**) cabinet; closet; **armadio a muro** built-in closet; **armadio**

d'angolo corner cupboard; **armadio farmaceutico** medicine cabinet; **armadio guardaroba** armoire

armaiòlo *m* gunsmith

armamentà·rio *m* (**-ri**) outfit, set (*of tools*)

armaménto *m* armament; crew; gun crew; crew (*of rowboat*); outfit, equipment

armare *tr* to arm; to dub (*s.o. a knight*); to outfit, commission (*a ship*); to cock (*a gun*); to brace, shore up (*a building*); (rr) to furnish with track || *ref* to arm oneself; to outfit oneself

arma·to -ta *adj* armed; reinforced (*concrete*) || *m* soldier || *f* army; navy; fleet; (nav) task force

arma·tóre -trice *adj* outfitting || *m* shipowner; (min) carpenter; (rr) trackwalker

armatura *f* armor; scaffold; framework, support; reinforcement (*for concrete*); (elec) plate (*of condenser*)

armeggiare §290 (**arméggio**) *intr* to fumble, fool around; to scheme; (archaic) to handle arms; (archaic) to joust

armeggì·o *m* (**-i**) fooling around; scheming, intriguing

armè·no -na *adj & mf* Armenian

arménto *m* herd

armerìa *f* armory

armière *m* (aer) gunner

armìge·ro -ra *adj* warlike, bellicose || *m* warrior; bodyguard

armistiziale *adj* armistice

armistì·zio *m* (**-zi**) *m* armistice

armonìa *f* harmony; **in armonia con** according to

armòni·co -ca (**-ci -che**) *adj* harmonic; resonant; harmonious || *f* harmonica; **armonica a bocca** mouth organ

armonió·so -sa [s] *adj* harmonious

armonizzare [ddzz] *tr & intr* to harmonize

arnése [s] *m* tool, implement; garb, dress; (coll) gadget; **bene in arnese** well-heeled; **male in arnese** down at the heels

àrnia *f* beehive

arò·ma *m* (**-mi**) aroma, odor; zest

aromàti·co -ca *adj* (**-ci -che**) aromatic

aromatizzare [ddzz] *tr* to flavor; to spice

arpa *f* harp

arpeggiare §290 (**arpéggio**) *intr* to play arpeggios; to play a harp; to strum

arpég·gio *m* (**-gi**) arpeggio

arpìa *f* Harpy; (coll) harpy

arpionare (**arpióno**) *tr* to harpoon

arpióne *m* hinge (*of door*); hook; harpoon; spike (*for mountain climbing*)

arpionismo *m* ratchet

arpi·sta *mf* (**-sti -ste**) harpist

arrabattare *ref* to exert oneself, to strive, to endeavor

arrabbiare §287 *intr* (ESSERE) to go mad (*said of dogs*) || *ref* to become angry (*said of people*)

arrabbia·to -ta *adj* mad (*dog*); angry; obstinate; confirmed

arrabbiatura *f* rage; **prendersi un'arrabbiatura** to burn up (*with rage*)

arraffare *tr* to snatch

arrampicare §197 (**arràmpico**) *ref* to climb, climb up

arrampicata *f* climbing

arrampica·tóre -trice *mf* climber; mountain climber; **arrampicatore sociale** social climber

arrancare §197 *intr* to hobble, limp; to struggle, work hard; to row hard

arrangiaménto *m* agreement; (mus) arrangement

arrangiare §290 *tr* to arrange; to fix; (coll) to steal || *ref* to manage, get along

arrecare §197 (**arrèco**) *tr* to cause; to carry, deliver

arredaménto *m* furnishing; furnishings; equipment

arredare (**arrèdo**) *tr* to furnish; to equip

arreda·tóre -trice *mf* interior decorator; upholsterer; (mov) property man

arrèdo *m* furnishings, furniture; piece of furniture; **arredi sacri** church supplies

arrembàg·gio *m* (**-gi**) boarding (*of a ship*)

arrenare (**arréno**) *tr* to sand

arrèndere §227 *tr* (archaic) to surrender || *ref* to surrender; **arrendersi a discrezione** to surrender unconditionally

arrendévole *adj* yielding, compliant, flexible

arrendevolézza *f* suppleness; compliance

arrestare (**arrèsto**) *tr* to stop; to arrest || *ref* to stop, stay

arrèsto *m* arrest; stop; pause; (mach) stop, catch; **arresti** (mil) house arrest; **in stato d'arresto** under arrest

arretrare (**arrètro**) *tr* to withdraw || *intr* (ESSERE & AVERE) & *ref* to withdraw

arretra·to -ta *adj* withdrawn; backward; back (*issue*); overdue || **arretrati** *mpl* arrears

arricchimento *m* enrichment

arricchire §176 *tr* to enrich || *intr* (ESSERE) & *ref* to get rich

arricchi·to -ta *mf* nouveau riche

arricciacapé·li *m* (**-li**) curler

arricciare §128 *tr* to curl; to wrinkle; to screw up (*one's nose*); **arricciare il pelo** to bristle (*said of a person*); to bristle up (*said of an animal*) || *ref* to curl up

arriccia·to -ta *adj* curled up || *m* first coat (*of cement*)

arricciatura *f* curling (*of hair*); pleating (*of a skirt*); kink (*in a rope*)

arrìdere §231 *tr* (poet) to grant || *intr* to smile

arrin·ga *f* (**-ghe**) harangue; (law) lawyer's plea

arringare §209 *tr* to harangue; (law) to plead

arrischiare §287 *tr* to endanger; to risk || *ref* to dare, venture

arrischia·to -ta *adj* risky; daring

arrivare *tr* to reach || *intr* (ESSERE) to arrive; to happen; to get along, be successful; **arrivare a** to reach; to succeed in

arriva·to -ta *adj* arrived; successful; **ben arrivato** welcome

arrivedér·ci *m* (**-ci**) good-bye || *interj* good-bye!, so long!

arrivedérla *interj* good-bye!

arrivismo *m* social climbing, ruthless ambition

arrivi·sta *mf* (**-sti -ste**) social climber

arrivo *m* arrival; (sports) goal line; (sports) finishing line

arroccare §197 (**arrócco**) *tr* to put (*e.g.*, flax) on the distaff || §197 (**arròcco**) *tr* to shelter; (chess) to castle || *ref* to seek shelter; (chess) to castle

arròc·co *m* (**-chi**) castling

arrochire §176 *tr* to make hoarse || *intr* (ESSERE) to become hoarse

arrogante *adj* arrogant, insolent

arroganza *f* arrogance, insolence

arrogare §209 (**arrògo**) *tr—***arrogare a sé** to arrogate to oneself || *ref* to arrogate to oneself

arrolare §237 *tr* var of **arruolare**

arrossare (**arrósso**) *tr* to redden

arrossire §176 *intr* (ESSERE) to blush; to change color

arrostire §176 *tr* to roast; to toast; **arrostire allo spiedo** to barbecue on the spit || *intr* (ESSERE) & *ref* to roast

arrò·sto *m* (**-sto** & **-sti**) roast

arrotare (**arròto**) *tr* to grind, hone; to smooth; to strike, run over; to grit (*one's teeth*) || *ref* to grind (*to work hard*); to sideswipe

arrotatrice *f* floor sander

arrotatura *f* sharpening

arrotino *m* grinder

arrotolare (**arròtolo**) *tr* to roll

arrotondaménto *m* rounding; rounding out; increase (*in salary*)

arrotondare (**arrotóndo**) *tr* to make round; to round out; to supplement (*a salary*) || *ref* to round out, become plump

arrovellare (**arrovèllo**) *tr* to vex || *ref* to become angry; to strive, endeavor; **arrovellarsi il cervello** to rack one's brains

arroventare (**arrovènto**) *tr* to make red-hot || *ref* to become red-hot

arroventire §176 *tr* & *ref* var of **arroventare**

arruffapòpo·li *m* (**-li**) rabble-rouser

arruffare *tr* to tangle; to muss, rumple; to confuse

arruf·fio *m* (**-fii**) tangle; confusion, mess

arruffó·ne -na *mf* blunderer; swindler

arrugginire §176 *tr*, *intr* (ESSERE) & *ref* to rust

arruolaménto *m* enlistment; draft

arruolare (**arruòlo**) *tr* to recruit; to draft || *ref* to enlist

arruvidire §176 *tr* to make rough, roughen || *intr* (ESSERE) to become rough

arsenale *m* arsenal; navy yard

arsèni·co -ca (**-ci -che**) *adj* arsenic, arsenical || *m* arsenic

ar·so -sa *adj* burnt; dry, parched; **arso di** consumed with

arsura *f* sultriness; dryness

arte *f* art; ability; guile; **ad arte** on purpose; **arti e mestieri** arts and crafts

artefare §173 *tr* to adulterate

artefat·to -ta *adj* adulterated; artificial

artéfice *m* craftsman; creator

artèria *f* artery

arteriosclerosi *m* arteriosclerosis

arterió·so -sa [s] *adj* arterial

artesia·no -na *adj* artesian

àrti·co -ca *adj* (**-ci -che**) arctic || **Artico** *m* Arctic

articolare *adj* articular || *v* (**artícolo**) *tr* & *ref* to articulate

articola·to -ta *adj* articulated; articulate; (gram) combined; jagged (*coastline*)

articolazióne *f* articulation

articoli·sta *mf* (**-sti -ste**) columnist; feature writer

artícolo *m* article; item; paragraph; **articolo di fondo** editorial; **articolo di spalla** comment

artificiale *adj* artificial

artificière *m* pyrotechnist; (mil) demolition expert

artifi·cio *m* (**-ci**) artifice; sophistication, affectation; **artificio d'illuminazione** (mil) flare

artificiosi·tà [s] *f* (**-tà**) artfulness, craftiness; artificiality

artifició·so -sa [s] *adj* artful, crafty; artificial, affected

artigianato *m* craftsmanship

artigia·no -na *adj* of craftsmen || *m* craftsman

artigliare §280 *tr* (poet) to claw

artiglière *m* artilleryman

artiglieria *f* artillery; **artiglieria a cavallo** mounted artillery

artì·glio *m* (**-gli**) claw; **cadere negli artigli di** to fall into the clutches of

arti·sta *mf* (**-sti -ste**) artist; actor

artìsti·co -ca *adj* (**-ci -che**) artistic

ar·to -ta *adj* (poet) narrow || *m* limb

artrite *f* arthritis

artríti·co -ca *adj* & *mf* (**-ci -che**) arthritic

arturia·no -na *adj* Arthurian

arzigogolare [dz] (**arzigògolo**) *intr* to muse; to cavil

arzigògolo [dz] *m* fantasy; cavil

arzil·lo -la [dz] *adj* lively, sprightly; (coll) sparkling (*wine*)

arzin·ga *f* (**-ghe**) tong (*of a blacksmith*)

asbèsto *m* asbestos

ascèlla *f* armpit

ascendènte *adj* ascendant || *m* upper hand, ascendancy; **ascendenti** forefathers

ascendènza *f* ancestry, lineage

ascéndere §245 *tr* to climb || *intr* (ESSERE & AVERE) to ascend, climb

ascensionale *adj* rising; lifting

ascensióne *f* ascent, climb || **Ascensione** *f* Ascension, Ascension Day

ascensóre *m* elevator

ascésa [s] *f* ascent

ascèsso *m* abscess

ascè·ta *mf* (**-ti -te**) ascetic

ascèti·co -ca *adj* (**-ci -che**) ascetic

ascetismo *m* asceticism

à·scia *f* (**-sce**) adze

asciugacapél·li *m* (**-li**) hair drier
asciugamano *m* towel; **asciugamano spugna** Turkish towel
asciugante *adj* drying; blotting; soaking ‖ *m* dryer
asciugare §209 *tr* to dry, dry up; to wipe; to drain (*e.g., a glass of wine*) ‖ *ref* to dry oneself; to dry, dry up
asciuga·tóio *m* (**-tói**) towel; bath towel
asciugatrice *f* dryer
asciut·to **-ta** *adj* dry; skinny; blunt (*in speech*) ‖ *m* dry land; dry climate; **all'asciutto** pennyless
ascoltare (**ascólto**) *tr* to listen to ‖ *intr* to listen
ascolta·tóre **-trice** *mf* listener
ascólto *m* listening; **stare in ascolto** to listen
ascòrbi·co **-ca** *adj* (**-ci -che**) ascorbic
ascrit·to **-ta** *adj* ascribed; belonging ‖ *m* member
ascrìvere §250 *tr* to inscribe, register; to ascribe, attribute
ascultare *tr* to sound (*s.o.'s chest*)
asèpsi [s] *f* asepsis
asètti·co **-ca** [s] *adj* (**-ci -che**) aseptic
asfaltare *tr* to tar, pave
asfalto *m* asphalt
asfissìa *f* asphyxia
asfissiante *adj* asphyxiating; poison (*gas*); boring
asfissiare §287 *tr* to asphyxiate; to bore ‖ *intr* (ESSERE) to be asphyxiated
asfodèlo *m* asphodel
Àsia, l' *f* Asia; **l'Asia Minore** Asia Minor
asiàti·co **-ca** *adj* & *mf* (**-ci -che**) Asian, Asiatic
asilo *m* shelter; asylum; home; **asilo di mendicità** poorhouse; **asilo infantile** kindergarten; **asilo per i vecchi** old-age home, nursing home
asimmetria [s] *f* asymmetry
asimmètri·co **-ca** [s] *adj* (**-ci -che**) asymmetric(al)
asinàggine [s] *f* stupidity, asininity
asi·nàio [s] *m* (**-nài**) donkey driver
asinata [s] *f* stupidity, folly
asineria [s] *f* asininity
asiné·sco **-sca** [s] *adj* (**-schi -sche**) asinine
asini·no **-na** [s] *adj* asinine
àsino [s] *m* ass, donkey; **fare l'asino a** (*slang*) to play up to; **qui casca l'asino** here is the rub
asma *f* asthma
asmàti·co **-ca** *adj* & *mf* (**-ci -che**) asthmatic
àsola *f* buttonhole; buttonhole hem
aspàra·go *m* (**-gi**) asparagus; piece of asparagus; **asparagi** asparagus (*as food*)
aspèrgere §112 *tr* to sprinkle
aspersióne *f* asperging, sprinkling
aspettare (**aspètto**) *tr* to wait for, await; to expect; **aspettare al varco** to be on the lookout for ‖ *intr* to wait; **fare aspettare** to keep waiting ‖ *ref* to expect
aspettativa *f* expectancy, expectation; leave of absence without pay
aspètto *m* waiting; aspect, look; **al primo aspetto** at first sight

àspide *m* asp
aspirante *adj* suction (*pump*) ‖ *m* aspirant; applicant, candidate; suitor; upperclassman (*in naval academy*)
aspirapólve·re *m* (**-re**) vacuum cleaner
aspirare *tr* to inhale, breathe in; to suck (*e.g., air*); (*phonet*) to aspirate ‖ *intr* to aspire
aspiratóre *m* exhaust fan
aspirazióne *f* aspiration; (*aut*) intake
aspirina *f* aspirin
aspo *m* reel
asportàbile *adj* removable
asportare (**aspòrto**) *tr* to remove, take away
asportazióne *f* removal
asprézza *f* sourness; roughness, harshness
a·spro **-spra** *adj* sour; rough, harsh
assaggiare §290 *tr* to taste; to sample, test; **assaggiare il terreno** (*fig*) to see how the land lies
assaggia·tóre **-trice** *mf* taster
assàg·gio *m* (**-gi**) taste, sample; tasting; test, trial
assài *adj invar* a lot of ‖ *m* much ‖ *adv* enough; fairly; very
assale *m* axle
assalire §242 *tr* to attack, assail; (*fig*) to seize
assali·tóre **-trice** *mf* assailant
assaltare *tr* to assault; **assaltare a mano armata** to stick up
assalto *m* assault, attack; (*law*) battery; **cogliere d'assalto** to catch unawares; **prendere d'assalto** to assault
assaporare (**assapóro**) *tr* to taste; to relish, enjoy
assassinare *tr* to assassinate; (*fig*) to murder
assassì·nio *m* (**-ni**) assassination, murder
assassi·no **-na** *adj* murderous ‖ *mf* assassin, murderer
asse *m* axle; shaft, spindle; (*geom, phys*) axis; **asse ereditario** estate; **asse stradale** median strip ‖ *f* plank; **asse da stiro** ironing board
assecondare (**assecóndo**) *tr* to help; to second; to uphold
assediante *adj* besieging ‖ *m* besieger
assediare §287 (**assèdio**) *tr* to lay siege to, besiege
assè·dio *m* (**-di**) siege; **assedio economico** economic sanctions; **cingere d'assedio** to besiege
assegnaménto *m* awarding; allowance; faith, reliance; **fare assegnamento su** to rely upon
assegnare (**asségno**) *tr* to assign; to prescribe; to distribute; to award
assegnatà·rio **-ria** *mf* (**-ri -rie**) assignee
assegnazióne *f* assignment; awarding
asségno *m* allowance; check; **assegni fringe benefits; assegni familiari** family allowance; **assegno a copertura garantita** certified check; **assegno a vuoto** worthless check; **assegno di studio** (*educ*) stipend; **assegno turistico** traveler's check; **assegno vademecum** certified check; **contro assegno** C.O.D.

assemblàg·gio *m* (**-gi**) (mach) assembling, assembly

assemblèa *f* assembly

assembraménto *m* gathering

assembrare (**assémbro**) *tr* & *ref* to gather

assennatézza *f* good judgment, discretion

assenna·to -ta *adj* sensible, prudent

assènso *m* approval, consent

assentare (**assènto**) *ref* to be absent, to absent oneself

assènte *adj* absent || *mf* absentee

assenteìsmo *m* absenteeism

assentire (**assènto**) *tr* (poet) to grant || *intr* to assent, acquiesce; **assentire con un cenno** to nod assent

assènza *f* absence

assenzìente *adj* consenting, approving

assèn·zio *m* (**-zi**) absinthe; (bot) wormwood

asserire §176 *tr* to affirm, assert

asserragliare §280 *tr* to barricade || *ref* to barricade oneself

assèrto *m* (poet) assertion

asser·tóre -trice *mf* advocate, supporter

asserviménto *m* enslavement

asservire §176 *tr* to enslave; to subjugate

asserzióne *f* assertion

assessóre *m* councilman; alderman

assestaménto *m* arrangement; settling (*of a building*)

assestare (**assèsto**) *tr* to arrange; to adapt, regulate; to deliver, deal (*a blow*) || *ref* to become organized; to settle (*said of a building*)

assesta·to -ta *adj* sensible, prudent

assetare (**assèto**) *tr* to make thirsty; (fig) to inflame

asseta·to -ta *adj* thirsty; parched; eager || *mf* thirsty person

assettare (**assètto**) *tr* to tidy, straighten up || *ref* to straighten oneself up

assetta·to -ta *adj* tidy

assètto *m* arrangement; order; (naut) trim; **assetto longitudinale** (aer) pitch, attitude; **in assetto di guerra** ready for war; **male in assetto** in poor shape

asseverare (**assèvero**) *tr* to asseverate, assert

assicèlla *f* roofing board, lath; batten

assicuràbile *adj* insurable

assicurare *tr* to assure; to insure; to protect; to fasten; to deliver (*e.g., a thief*) || *ref* to make sure; to take out insurance

assicura·to -ta *adj* & *mf* insured || *f* insured letter

assicura·tóre -trice *mf* insurer

assicurazióne *f* assurance; insurance; **assicurazione contro gli infortuni sul lavoro** workman's compensation insurance; **assicurazione contro i danni** casualty insurance; **assicurazione incendio** fire insurance; **assicurazione infortuni** accident insurance; **assicurazione per la vecchiaia** old age insurance; **assicurazione sociale** social security; **assicurazione sulla vita** life insurance

assideraménto *m* freezing; frostbite

assiderare (**assìdero**) *ref* to freeze; to become frostbitten

assidere §113 *ref* (poet) to take one's seat (*e.g., on the throne*)

assì·duo -dua *adj* assiduous, diligent

assième *m* ensemble || *adv* together; **assieme a** together with

assiepare (**assièpo**) *tr* & *ref* to crowd

assillante *adj* disturbing, troublesome

assillare *tr* to beset, trouble

assillo *m* gadfly; (fig) stimulus, goad

assimilare (**assìmilo**) *tr* to assimilate; to compare

assimilazióne *f* assimilation

assiòlo *m* horned owl

assiò·ma *m* (**-mi**) axiom

assiomàti·co -ca *adj* (**-ci -che**) axiomatic

assi·ro -ra *adj* & *mf* Assyrian

assisa *f* (poet) uniform, livery; (geol) layer; (archaic) duty, tax; **assise** criminal court; assembly, session; (hist) assises

assistènte *mf* assistant; **assistente sanitario** practical nurse; **assistente sociale** social worker || *m*—**assistente ai lavoro** foreman || *f*—**assistente di volo** (aer) hostess

assistènza *f* assistance, help; intervention; **assistenza pubblica** relief

assistenziale *adj* welfare, charity

assistere §114 *tr* to assist, help || *intr*—**assistere a** to attend, be present at

assito *m* flooring, boarding

assiuòlo *m* var of **assiolo**

asso *m* ace; **asso del volante** speed king; **piantare in asso** to walk out on

associare §128 (**assòcio**) *tr* to associate; **associare alle carceri** to take to prison || *ref* to associate; to become a member; to subscribe; to participate

associa·to -ta *adj* associate || *mf* associate, partner

associazióne *f* association; union; subscription; membership

assodare (**assòdo**) *tr* to solidify; to strengthen; to ascertain || *ref* to solidify; to strengthen

assoggettare (**assoggètto**) *tr* to subject, subdue || *ref* to submit

assola·to -ta *adj* sunny, exposed to the sun

assolcare §197 (**assólco**) *tr* to furrow

assoldare (**assòldo**) *tr* to hire, recruit

assólo *m* (mus) solo

assolutìsmo *m* absolutism

assolutìsti·co -ca *adj* (**-ci -che**) absolutist, despotic

assolu·to -ta *adj* & *m* absolute

assoluzióne *f* absolution

assòlvere §115 *tr* to absolve; to fulfill

assomigliare §280 *tr* to compare; to make similar, make equal || *intr* (ESSERE & AVERE) (with *dat*) to resemble, to look like; to be like || *ref* to resemble each other, look alike; **assomigliarsi a** to resemble

assommare (**assómmo**) *tr* to add; to be the epitome of; (archaic) to complete || *intr* (ESSERE) to amount

assonna·to -ta *adj* sleepy

assopire §176 *tr* to lull to sleep; to

soothe || *ref* to drowse, to nod; to calm down

assorbènte *adj* absorbent || *m* sanitary napkin

assorbiménto *m* absorption

assorbire §176 & (**assòrbo**) *tr* to absorb

assorbi·to -ta *adj* absorbed; **assorbito da** consumed with

assordare (**assòrdo**) *tr* to deafen || *ref* to become deaf; to dim; to lessen

assortiménto *m* assortment; **avere in assortimento** (com) to carry, stock

assortire §176 *tr* to assort, sort out; to stock

assorti·to -ta *adj* assorted; **bene assortito** well matched

assòr·to -ta *adj* engrossed, absorbed

assottigliare §280 *tr* to thin; to sharpen; to reduce || *ref* to grow thinner

assuefare §173 *tr* to accustom || *ref* to become accustomed

assuefazióne *f* habit, custom

assùmere §116 *tr* to assume; to hire; to raise, elevate; (law) to accept in evidence

Assunta *f* Assumption

assunto *m* thesis, argument; (poet) task

assun·tóre -trice *mf* contractor

assunzióne *f* assumption; hiring; (law) examination || **Assunzione** *f* Assumption

assurdi·tà *f* (**-tà**) absurdity

assùr·do -da *adj* absurd || *m* absurdity

assùrgere §117 *intr* (ESSERE) (poet) to rise

asta *f* staff; rod; arm (*e.g., of scale*); lance; leg (*of compass*); stroke (*in handwriting*); shaft (*of arrow*); auction; (naut) boom; (naut) mast; (elec) trolley pole; **a mezz'asta** half-mast; **vendere all'asta** to auction, auction off

astante *mf* bystander || *m* physician on duty (*in a hospital*)

astanterìa *f* receiving ward

astato *m* (chem) astatine

astè·mio -mia *adj* abstemious, temperate || *mf* teetotaler

astenére §271 *ref* to abstain

astensióne *f* abstension

astenuto *m* person who abstains from voting; abstention (*vote withheld*)

astèrgere §164 (*pp* **astèrso**) *tr* to wipe

asteri·sco *m* (**-schi**) asterisk

asticciòla *f* penholder; rib (*of umbrella*); temple (*of eyeglasses*)

àstice *m* (*Hommarus vulgaris*) lobster

asticèlla *f* (sports) bar

astinènte *adj* abstinent

astinènza *f* abstinence

à·stio *m* (**-stii**) grudge, rancor

astió·so -sa [s] *adj* full of malice, spiteful

astóre *m* goshawk

astràgalo *m* astragalus, anklebone

astrakàn *m* Persian lamb

astrarre §273 *tr* to abstract || *intr*—**astrarre da** to leave aside, overlook

astrat·to -ta *adj* abstract || *m* abstract

astrazióne *f* abstraction

astringènte *adj & m* astringent

-astro -astra *suf adj* -ish, *e.g.,* **verdastro**

greenish || *suf mf* -aster, *e.g.,* **poetastro** poetaster

astro *m* star, heavenly body; (bot) aster; (fig) star

astrologìa *f* astrology

astrològi·co -ca *adj* (**-ci -che**) astrological

astròlo·go m (**-gi** or **-ghi**) astrologer

astronàu·ta *mf* (**-ti -te**) astronaut

astronàuti·co -ca (**-ci -che**) *adj* astronautic(al) || *f* astronautics

astronave *f* spaceship, spacecraft

astronomìa *f* astronomy

astrònomo *m* astronomer

astronòmi·co -ca *adj* (**-ci -che**) astronomic(al)

astruserìa *f* abstruseness

astrusi·tà *f* (**-tà**) abstruseness

astru·so -sa *adj* abstruse

astùc·cio *m* (**-ci**) case, box

astu·to -ta *adj* astute, crafty

astùzia *f* astuteness, craftiness

à·ta·vo -va *mf* ancestor

ateìsmo *m* atheism

ateì·sta *mf* (**-sti -ste**) atheist

Atène *f* Athens

atenèo *m* athenaeum; university

ateniése [s] *adj & mf* Athenian

àte·o -a *adj* atheistic || *mf* atheist

atlante *m* atlas || **Atlante** *m* Atlas

atlànti·co -ca *adj* (**-ci -che**) Atlantic || **Atlantico** *m* Atlantic

atlè·ta *mf* (**-ti -te**) athlete

atletéssa *f* female athlete

atlèti·co -ca (**-ci -che**) *adj* athletic || *f* athletics; **atletica leggera** track and field

atmosfèra *f* atmosphere

atmosfèri·co -ca *adj* (**-ci -che**) atmospheric

atòllo *m* atoll

atòmi·co -ca *adj* (**-ci -che**) atomic; (coll) stunning

atomizzare [dzz] *tr* to atomize

atomizzatóre [dzz] *m* atomizer

àtomo *m* atom

atòni·co -ca *adj* (**-ci -che**) (pathol) weak

àto·no -na *adj* (gram) atonic

atout *m* (atouts) trump

à·trio *m* (**-tri**) entrance hall, lobby

atróce *adj* atrocious

atroci·tà *f* (**-tà**) atrocity

atrofìa *f* atrophy

atròfi·co -ca *adj* (**-ci -che**) atrophied

atrofizzare [dzz] *tr & ref* to atrophy

attaccabottó·ni *mf* (**-ni**) bore, pest, buttonholer

attaccabri·ghe *mf* (**-ghe**) (coll) quarrelsome person, scrapper

attaccaménto *m* attachment, affection

attaccapan·ni *m* (**-ni**) coathanger

attaccare §197 *tr* to attach; to bind, unite; to sew on; to stick; to hitch (*a horse*); to hang; to attack; to strike up (*a conversation*); to begin; to communicate (*a disease*); **attaccare un bottone a** (fig) to buttonhole || *intr* to stick; to gain a foothold, take root; to begin || *ref* to stick; to cling; to spread (*said of a disease*); (fig) to become attached

attaccatìc·cio -cia *adj* (**-ci -ce**) sticky

attacchino *m* billposter

attac·co *m* (**-chi**) attachment; onslaught; fastening; beginning; seizure (*e.g., of epilepsy*); spell (*e.g., of coughing*); (elec) plug; (rad) jack; (sports) forward line; **attacco cardiaco** heart attack

attagliare §280 *ref*—**attagliarsi a** to fit, become

attanagliare §280 *tr* to grip; to seize; to hold (*e.g., with tongs*)

attardare *ref* to tarry, delay

attecchire §176 *intr* to take root; to take hold

atteggiamento *m* attitude

atteggiare §290 (**attéggio**) *tr* to compose (*e.g., one's face*); to place ‖ *ref* to pose; to strike an attitude

attempà·to -ta *adj* elderly

attendamento *m* camping; jamboree (*of Boy Scouts*)

attendare (**attèndo**) *ref* to encamp; to pitch one's tent

attendènte *m* (mil) orderly

attèndere §270 *tr* to await; (archaic) to keep; **attendere l'ora propizia** to bide one's time ‖ *intr*—**attendere a** to attend to

attendìbile *adj* reliable

attendismo *m* wait-and-see attitude

attendì·sta (**-sti -ste**) *adj* wait-and-see ‖ *mf* fence-sitter

attenére §271 *tr* to keep (*a promise*) ‖ *intr*—**attenere** (with *dat*) to concern, e.g., **ciò non gli attiene** this does not concern him ‖ *ref*—**attenersi a** to conform to

attentare (**attènto**) *intr*—**attentare a** to attempt (*s.o.'s life*) ‖ *ref* to make an attempt, dare

attentato *m* attempt

attenta·tóre -trice *mf* would-be murderer; attacker

attèn·ti *m* (**-ti**) attention ‖ *interj* (mil) attention!

attèn·to -ta *adj* attentive; careful

attenuare (**attènuo**) *tr* to extenuate, play down; to attenuate; to mitigate

attenzióne *f* attention; **fare attenzione** to take care; **prestare attenzione** to pay attention

atterràg·gio *m* (**-gi**) landing; **atterraggio di fortuna** emergency landing; **atterraggio senza carrello** crash-landing

atterramento *m* landing; pinning, pin (*in wrestling*); (boxing) knocking down; **atterramento frenato** (aer) arrested landing

atterrare (**attèrro**) *tr* to fell; to knock down; to pin (*in wrestling*); (fig) to humiliate ‖ *intr* to land; **atterrare scassando** or **atterrare senza carrello** to crash-land

atterrire §176 *tr* to frighten, terrify ‖ *ref* to become frightened

atté·so -sa [s] *adj* awaited, expected; **atteso che** considering that ‖ *f* waiting; expectation; **in attesa (di)** waiting (for)

attestare (**attèsto**) *tr* to certify, attest; to prove; to join; (mil) to deploy ‖ *ref* (mil) to take a stand

attestato *m* certificate

attestazióne *f* testimony; affidavit; attestation, proof

àtti·co -ca (**-ci -che**) *adj* & *mf* Attic ‖ *m* attic

attì·guo -gua *adj* adjacent, contiguous

attillare *tr* & *ref* to preen

attillà·to -ta *adj* tight, close-fitting; tidy, all dressed up

àttimo *m* moment, split second; **di attimo in attimo** any moment

attinènte *adj* related, pertinent

attinènza *f* relation; **attinenze** appurtenances; annexes

attìngere §126 *tr* to draw (*water*); to get; (poet) to attain (*e.g., glory*)

attingi·tóio *m* (**-tói**) ladle

attirare *tr* to draw, attract

attitùdine *f* aptitude; attitude

attivare *tr* to activate; to expedite

attivazióne *f* activation; reassessment

attivì·tà *f* (**-tà**) activity; **attività** *fpl* assets

attì·vo -va *adj* active; profit-making ‖ *m* assets

attizzare *tr* to stir, poke (*a fire*); (fig) to stir up

attizza·tóio *m* (**-tói**) poker

at·to -ta *adj* apt, fit ‖ *m* act, action; gesture; (law) instrument; **all'atto pratico** in reality; **atti** proceedings (*of a learned society*); **atti notarili** legal proceedings; **atto di nascita** birth certificate; **fare atto di presenza** to put in a brief formal appearance; **atto di vendita** bill of sale; **nell'atto o sull'atto** in the act

attòni·to -ta *adj* astonished

attorcigliare §280 *tr* to twist ‖ *ref* to wind; to coil up

attóre *m* actor; (law) plaintiff; **attore giovane** (theat) juvenile; **primo attore** (theat) lead

attorniare §287 (**attórnio**) *tr* to surround; (fig) to dupe

attórno *adv* around; **andare attorno** to walk around; **attorno a** around, near; **darsi d'attorno** to busy oneself; **levarsi qlcu d'attorno** to get rid of s.o.

attortigliare §280 *tr* to twist ‖ *ref* to wind; to coil up

attraccare §197 *tr* & *intr* to moor, dock

attrac·co *m* (**-chi**) mooring, docking

attraènte *adj* attractive

attrarre §273 *tr* to attract, draw

attrattì·vo -va *adj* attractive; alluring ‖ *f* attraction, charm

attraversaménto *m* crossing; **attraversamento pedonale** pedestrian crossing

attraversare (**attravèrso**) *tr* to cross; to go through; to thwart; **attraversare il passo a** to stand in the way of

attravèrso *adv* across; crosswise; **andare attraverso** to go down the wrong way (*said of food or drink*); (fig) to go wrong; **attraverso a** through, across ‖ *prep* through, across

attrazióne *f* attraction

attrezzare (**attrézzo**) *tr* to outfit, equip

attrezzatura f outfit; gear, equipment; **attrezzatura di una nave** rigging; **attrezzature** facilities

attrezzi·sta (**-sti -ste**) mf gymnast || m toolmaker; (theat) property man

attrézzo m tool, utensil; **attrezzi** gymnastic equipment

attribuire §176 tr to award; to attribute; **attribuire qlco a qlcu** to credit s.o. with s.th || ref to ascribe to oneself, claim for oneself

attributo m attribute

attribuzióne f attribution

attrice f actress; (law) plaintiff; **prima attrice** (theat) lead

attristare tr (poet) to sadden || ref to become sad

attri·to -ta adj worn, worn-out || m attrition; disagreement

attruppare tr to band, group || ref to mill about, throng

attuàbile adj feasible

attuale adj present; present-day, current

attuali·tà f (**-tà**) timeliness; reality; **attualità** fpl current events; **di viva attualità** newsworthy; timely; **in the news**

attualizzare [ddzz] tr to bring up to date || ref to become a reality

attuare (**àttuo**) tr to carry out, make come true || ref to come true

attuà·rio -ria (**-ri -rie**) adj (hist) transport (e.g., ship) || m actuary

attuazióne f realization

attutire §176 tr to mitigate; to deaden (a sound, a blow) || ref to diminish (said of a sound)

audace adj audacious

audàcia f audacity

audiofrequènza f audio frequency

audiovisi·vo -va adj audio-visual

auditi·vo -va adj var of uditivo

auditóre m var of uditore

auditò·rio -rio m (**-ri**) auditorium

audizióne f program; audition; (law) hearing

àuge f acme; **essere in auge** to enjoy a great reputation; to be in vogue; to be on top of the world

augurale adj well-wishing; salutatory

augurare (**àuguro**) tr to wish; to bid (good day) || intr to augur || ref to hope; to expect

àugure m augur

augù·rio m (**-ri**) wish; augury, omen

augustè·o -a adj Augustan

augu·sto -sta adj august, venerable

àula f hall; classroom; (poet) chamber (of a palace)

àuli·co -ca adj (**-ci -che**) courtly; noble, elevated

aumentare (**auménto**) tr to augment, increase || intr (ESSERE) to increase, rise

auménto m increase

àura f (poet) breeze; (poet) breath

àure-o -a adj golden, gold

aurèola f halo

auricolare adj ear; first-hand || m (telp) receiver; (rad) earphone

auròra f dawn; (fig) aurora

ausiliare adj auxiliary || m collaborator, helper

ausilià·rio -ria (**-ri -rie**) adj auxiliary; (mil) supply || m helper; (mil) reserve officer || f female member of the armed forces

ausì·lio m (**-li**) (poet) help

auspicare §197 (**àuspico**) tr to wish, augur

àuspice m sponsor; (hist) augur

auspì·cio m (**-ci**) sponsorship; (hist, poet) augury, omen; **sotto gli auspici di** under the auspices of

austeri·tà f (**-tà**) austerity

austè·ro -ra adj austere

australe adj austral, southern

Austràlia, l' f Australia

australia·no -na adj & mf Australian

Austria, l' f Austria

austria·co -ca adj & mf (**-ci -che**) Austrian

autarchìa f autarky; autonomy (of an administration)

autàrchi·co -ca adj (**-ci -che**) autonomous, independent

autènti·ca f (**-che**) authentication of a signature or a document

autenticare §197 (**autèntico**) tr to authenticate

autentici·tà f (**-tà**) authenticity

autènti·co -ca (**-ci -che**) adj authentic, genuine || f see autentica

autière m (mil) driver

auti·sta mf (**-sti -ste**) (aut) driver

au·to f (**-to**) auto

autoabbronzante [dz] adj tanning || m tanning lotion

autoaffondaménto m scuttling

autoambulanza f ambulance

autobiografìa f autobiography

autobiogràfi·co -ca adj (**-ci -che**) autobiographical

autoblinda·to -ta adj armored

autoblin·do m (**-do**) armored car

autobótte f tank truck

àuto·bus m (**-bus**) bus

autocarro m truck, motor truck

autocèntro m (mil) motor pool

autocistèrna f tank truck

autocivétta f unmarked police car

autocolónna f row of cars

autocombustióne f spontaneous combustion

autocontròllo m self-control

autocorrièra f intercity bus, highway bus

autocrazìa f autocracy

autocrìti·ca f (**-che**) self-criticism

autòcto·no -na adj autochthonous, independent

autodecisióne m free will

autodeterminazióne f self-determination

autodidat·ta mf (**-ti -te**) self-taught person

autodidàtti·co -ca adj (**-ci -che**) self-instructional

autodifésa [s] f self-defense

autodisciplina f self-discipline

autòdromo m automobile race track

autoemotè·ca f (**-che**) bloodmobile

autofilettante adj self-threading

autofurgóne m van; **autofurgone cellu-**

lare police van; **autofurgone funebre** hearse

autogiro *m* autogyro

autogovèrno *m* self-government

autò·gra·fo -fa *adj* autographic(al) || *m* autograph

auto·grù *f* (**-grù**) tow truck

autolesioni·sta *mf* (**-sti -ste**) person who wounds himself to avoid the draft or collect insurance

autoletti·ga *f* (**-ghe**) ambulance

autolibro *m* bookmobile

autolìnea *f* bus line

autò·ma *m* (**-mi**) automaton, robot

automàti·co -ca (**-ci -che**) *adj* automatic || *m* snap

automatizzare [dzz] *tr* to automate

automazióne *f* automation

automèzzo [dzz] *m* motor vehicle

automòbile *f* automobile, car; **automobile da corsa** racing car; **automobile di serie** stock car; **automobile fuori serie** custom-made car

automobilismo *m* motoring

automobili·sta *mf* (**-sti -ste**) motorist

automobilìsti·co -ca *adj* (**-ci -che**) car, automobile

automo·tóre -trice *adj* self-propelled || *f* (**rr**) automotive rail car

autonolég·gio *m* (**-gi**) car rental agency

autonomia *f* autonomy; (aer, naut) cruising radius

autonomi·sta *adj* (**-sti -ste**) autonomous

autòno·mo -ma *adj* autonomous, independent

autoparchég·gio *m* (**-gi**) parking; parking lot

autopar·co *m* (**-chi**) parking; parking lot

autopiano *m* player piano

autopilò·ta *m* (**-ti**) (aer) automatic pilot

autopómpa *f* fire engine

autopsìa *f* autopsy

autorà·dio *f* (**-dio**) car radio

autóre *m* author; perpetrator; creator, maker

autoreattóre *m* ramjet engine

autorespiratóre *m* aqualung

autorévole *adj* authoritative

autoriméssa *f* garage

autori·tà *f* (**-tà**) authority

autorità·rio -ria *adj* (**-ri -rie**) authoritarian

autoritratto *m* self-portrait

autorizzare [dzz] *tr* to authorize

autorizzazióne [dzz] *f* authorization

autoscala *f* hook and ladder; ladder (of hook and ladder)

autoscuòla *f* driving school

autoservì·zio *m* (**-zi**) bus service, bus line; self-service

autosilo *m* parking garage

autostazióne *f* bus station

autostèllo *m* roadside motel

auto·stòp *m* (**-stòp**) hitchhiking; **fare l'autostop** to hitchhike

autostoppi·sta *mf* (**-sti -ste**) hitchhiker

autostrada *f* highway, turnpike

autosufficiènte *adj* self-sufficient

autote·làio *m* (**-lài**) (aut) frame

autotrasportare (**autotraspòrto**) *tr* to truck

autotrasportatóre *m* trucker

autotreni·sta *m* (**-sti**) truck driver, teamster

autotrèno *m* tractor trailer

autoveìcolo *m* motor vehicle

autovettura *f* car, automobile

autrice *f* authoress

autunnale *adj* autumnal, fall

autunno *m* autumn, fall

avallare *tr* to endorse (a promissory note); to guarantee

avallo *m* endorsement (of a promissory note)

avambràc·cio *m* (**-ci**) forearm

avampósto *m* outpost

avancàrica *f*—**ad avancarica** muzzle-loading

avanguàrdia *f* vanguard; avant-garde

avanguardismo *m* avant-garde

avanguardi·sta *m* (**-sti**) avant-gardist; (hist) member of Fascist youth organization

avannòtto *m* small fry (young freshwater fish)

avanti *adj* preceding || *m* forward || *adv* forward, ahead; **andare avanti** to proceed, to go ahead; **andare avanti negli anni** to be up in years; **avanti a** in front of; **avanti che** rather than; **avanti di** before; **essere avanti** to be advanced (in work or study); **in avanti** ahead || *prep*—**avanti Cristo** before Christ; **avanti giorno** before daybreak || *interj* come in!

avantièri *adv* day before yesterday

avantrèno *m* (aut) front-axle assembly; (mil) limber

avanzaménto *m* advancement

avanzare *tr* to advance; to overcome; to be creditor for, e.g., **avanza cento dollari da suo fratello** he is his brother's creditor for one hundred dollars; to save || *intr* (mil) to advance || *intr* (ESSERE) to advance; to stick out; to be abundant; to be left over, e.g., **avanzano due polpette** two meatballs are left over; **avanzare negli anni** to grow older || *ref* to advance, come forward

avanza·to -ta *adj* advanced; progressive || *f* (mil) advance

avanzo *m* remainder; **avanzi** remains

avarìa *f* damage, breakdown; (naut) average

avariare §287 *tr* to damage, spoil || *intr* to spoil

avarìa·to -ta *adj* damaged, spoiled

avarìzia *f* avarice, greed

ava·ro -ra *adj* avaricious, stingy || *mf* miser

avellana *f* filbert

avellano *m* filbert tree

avèllo *m* (poet) tomb

avéna *f* oats

avére *m* belongings, property; assets, credit; amount due || §118 *tr* to have; to hold; to wear; to receive, get; to stand (a chance); to be, e.g., **avere . . . anni** to be . . . years old; **avere caldo** to be hot; to be warm; **avere fame** to be hungry; **avere freddo** to be cold; **avere fretta** to be in a hurry;

avere paura to be afraid; **avere ragione** to be right; **avere sete** to be thirsty; **avere sonno** to be sleepy; **avere torto** to be wrong; **avere vergogna** to be ashamed; **avere voglia di** to be anxious to; **avere qlco da** + *inf* to have s.th to + *inf*, e.g., **ho molto lavoro da fare** I have a lot of work to do; **averla con** to be angry at; **non avere niente a che fare con** to have nothing to do with ‖ *impers*— **v'ha** there is ‖ *aux* to have, e.g., **ha letto il giornale** he has read the newspaper; **avere da** + *inf* to have to + *inf*, e.g., **avevo da lavorare** I had to work; **to be to** + *inf*, e.g., **ha da venire alle cinque** he is to arrive at five o'clock

avià·rio -ria (-**ri -rie**) *adj* bird ‖ *m* aviary

avia·tóre -tóra *mf* aviator ‖ *f* aviatrix

aviazióne *f* aviation

avicoltóre *m* bird raiser; poultry farmer

avidi·tà *f* (-**tà**) avidity, greediness

àvi·do -da *adj* avid, greedy

avière *m* airman

aviogètto *m* jet plane

aviolinea *f* airline

aviopista *f* (aer) airstrip

avioriméssa *f* (aer) hangar

aviotrasporta·to -ta *adj* airborne

avi·to -ta *adj* ancestral

a·vo -va *mf* grandparent; ancestor ‖ *m* grandfather ‖ *f* grandmother

avocare §197 (**àvoco**) *tr* to demand (*jurisdiction*); to expropriate

avò·rio *m* (-**ri**) ivory

avul·so -sa *adj* (poet) torn, uprooted; (poet) separated

avvalére §278 *ref*—**avvalersi di** to avail oneself of

avvallaménto *m* sinking, settling

avvallare *tr* (poet) to lower (*e.g., one's eyes*) ‖ *ref* to sink; (lit) to humiliate oneself

avvalorare (**avvalóro**) *tr* to strengthen, confirm ‖ *ref* to gain strength

avvampare *tr* (poet) to inflame ‖ *intr* (ESSERE) to burn

avvantaggiare §290 *tr* to be profitable to; to benefit ‖ *ref* to profit; **avvantaggiarsi su** to overcome; to beat

avvedére §279 *ref*—**avvedersi di** to notice, become aware of

avvedutézza *f* discernment; shrewdness

avvedu·to -ta *adj* prudent; shrewd; **fare qlcu avveduto di** to inform s.o. of

avvelenaménto *m* poisoning

avvelenare (**avveléno**) *tr* to poison ‖ *ref* to take poison; to be poisoned

avveniménto *m* happening, event

avvenire *adj invar* future, to come ‖ *m* future; **in avvenire** in the future ‖ §282 *intr* (ESSERE) to happen, occur; **avvenga quel che vuole** come what may

avventare (**avvènto**) *tr* to hurl; to deliver (*a blow*); to venture (*an opinion*) ‖ *ref* to throw oneself

avventatézza *f* thoughtlessness, heedlessness

avventa·to -ta *adj* thoughtless, heedless; **all'avventata** heedlessly

avventi·zio -zia *adj* (-**zi -zie**) outside, exterior; temporary, occasional

avvènto *m* advent; elevation, rise

avven·tóre -tóra *mf* customer, consumer

avventura *f* adventure

avventuriè·ro -ra *adj* adventurous ‖ *m* adventurer ‖ *f* adventuress

avventuró·so -sa [s] *adj* adventurous, adventuresome

avverare (**avvéro**) *tr* to make true ‖ *ref* to come true

avvèr·bio *m* (-**bi**) adverb

avversà·rio -ria (-**ri -rie**) *adj* opposing, contrary ‖ *mf* adversary, opponent

avversióne *f* aversion

avversi·tà *f* (-**tà**) adversity

avvèr·so -sa *adj* adverse; (obs) opposite ‖ **avverso** *prep* (law) against

avvertènza *f* prudence, caution; advice; **avvertenze** instructions, directions

avvertiménto *m* caution, warning; advice

avvertire (**avvèrto**) *tr* to caution, warn; to notice

avvezzare (**avvézzo**) *tr* to accustom; to inure; to train; **avvezzar male** to spoil ‖ *ref* to get accustomed

avvéz·zo -za *adj* accustomed

avviaménto *m* starting; introduction; trade school; good shape (*of a business*); (mach) starting; (typ) adjustment (*of printing press*)

avviare §119 *tr* to start, set in motion; to introduce; to initiate; to begin ‖ *ref* to set out

avvia·to -ta *adj* going, thriving (*concern*)

avvicendaménto *m* alteration, rotation (*of crops*)

avvicendare (**avvicèndo**) *tr & ref* to alternate

avvicinaménto *m* approach; rapprochement

avvicinare *tr* to bring near or closer; to approach, go or come near to ‖ *ref* to approach, come near; **avvicinarsi a** to come closer, approach

avviliménto *m* discouragement, dejection

avvilire §176 *tr* to degrade; to deject ‖ *ref* to become dejected, become discouraged

avviluppare *tr* to entangle, snarl; to wrap

avvinazza·to -ta *adj & mf* drunk

avvincènte *adj* fascinating

avvincere §285 *tr* to fascinate, charm; (poet) to twine

avvinghiare §287 *tr* to claw; to clasp, clutch ‖ *ref* to grip one another

avvì·o *m* (-**vi**) beginning

avvisàglia *f* skirmish; **prime avvisaglie** onset; first signs

avvisare *tr* to inform, advise; (archaic) to observe, notice

avvisa·tóre -trice *mf* announcer, messenger ‖ *m* alarm; (theat) callboy; **avvisatore acustico** (aut) horn; **avvisatore d'incendio** fire alarm

avviso *m* advise; notice, poster; opinion; **avviso di chiamata alle armi**

notice of induction; **sull'avviso** on one's guard

avvistare *tr* to sight

avvitaménto *m* (aer) tailspin

avvitare *tr* to screw; to fasten || *ref* (aer) to go into a tailspin

avviticchiare §287 *tr* to entwine || *ref* to cling

avvivare *tr* to revive; to stir up

avvizzire §176 *tr & intr* (ESSERE) to wither

avvocatéssa *f* woman lawyer

avvocato *m* lawyer, attorney

avvocatura *f* law, legal profession

avvòlgere §289 *tr* to wind; to wrap up; to spread over, surround || *ref* to wind around; to wrap oneself up

avvolgiménto *m* winding; wrapping; (elec) coil; (mil) envelopment

avvol·tóio *m* (-tói) vulture

avvoltolare (avvòltolo) *tr* to roll up || *ref* to roll around, wallow

aziènda [dz] *f* business, firm

azionare (azióno) *tr* to start; to drive, propel

aziona·rio -ria *adj* (-ri -rie) (com) stock

azióne *f* action, act; (law) suit; (com) share (*of stock*); **azione legale** prosecution; **azione privilegiata** preferred stock

azioni·sta *mf* (-sti -ste) stockholder, shareholder

azòto [dz] *m* nitrogen

azoturo [dz] *m* nitride

aztè·co -ca *adj & mf* (-chi -che) Aztec

azzannare *tr* to seize with the fangs

azzardare [ddzz] *tr* to risk; to advance || *ref* to dare

azzarda·to -ta [ddzz] *adj* daring

azzardo [ddzz] *m* chance, hazard

azzardó·so -sa [ddzz] [s] *adj* hazardous, risky

azzeccagarbu·gli *m* (-gli) shyster

azzeccare §197 (azzécco) *tr* to hit; to deliver; to pass off (*counterfeit money*); **azzeccarla** (coll) to hit the mark

azzimare [ddzz] (àzzimo) *tr & ref* to spruce up

àzzi·mo -ma [ddzz] *adj* unleavened (*bread*)

azzittare & azzittire §176 *tr* to hush || *ref* to keep quiet

azzoppare (azzòppo) *tr* to cripple || *ref* to become lame or crippled

Azzòrre [ddzz] *fpl* Azores

azzuffare *ref* to come to blows; to scuffle

azzur·ro -ra [ddzz] *adj* blue || *m* blue; Italian athlete (*in international competition*)

azzurrógno·lo -la [ddzz] *adj* bluish

B

B, b [bi] *m & f* second letter of the Italian alphabet

ba·bàu *m* (-bàu) bogey, bugbear

babbè·o -a *adj* foolish || *mf* fool

babbo *m* (coll) daddy, father

babbù·cia *f* (-ce) babouche; bedroom slipper

babbuino *m* baboon

babèle *f* babel || **Babele** *f* Babel

babilònia *f* confusion || **Babilònia** *f* Babylon

babórdo *m* (naut) port

bacare §197 *ref* to become worm-eaten

baca·to -ta *adj* worm-eaten; rotten

bac·ca *f* (-che) berry

bacca·là *m* (-là) dried codfish; (coll) skinny person; (coll) lummox

baccalaureato *m* baccalaureate, bachelor's degree

baccanale *m* bacchanal

baccano *m* noise, hubbub; **fare baccano** to carry on

baccante *f* bacchant

baccellière *m* (hist) bachelor

baccèllo *m* pod

baccellóne *m* simpleton, fool

bacchétta *f* rod, wand, baton; **bacchetta magica** magic wand; **bacchette del tamburo** drumsticks

bacchétto·ne -na *mf* bigot

bàcchi·co -ca *adj* (-ci -che) Bacchic

Bacco *m* Baccus

bachè·ca *f* (-che) showcase

bachelite *f* bakelite

bacheròzzo *m* worm; earthworm; (coll) cockroach

bachicoltura *f* silkworm raising

baciama·no *m* (-ni) kissing of the hand

baciapi·le *mf* (-le) bigot

baciare §128 *tr* to kiss; **baciare la polvere** to bite the dust || *ref* to kiss one another

bacia·to -ta *adj* kissed; rhymed (*couplet*)

bacile *m* basin

bacillo *m* bacillus

bacinèlla *f* small basin; (phot) tray

bacino *m* basin; reservoir; cove; (anat) pelvis; **bacino carbonifero** coal field; **bacino di carenaggio** drydock; **bacino fluviale** river basin

bà·cio *m* (-ci) kiss; **a bacio** with a northern exposure

baciucchiare §287 *tr* to keep on kissing || *ref* to pet

ba·co *m* (-chi) worm; **baco da seta** silkworm

bacuc·co -ca *adj* (-chi -che)—**vecchio bacucco** dotard

bada *f*—**tenere a bada** to stave off; to delay

badare *tr* to tend, take care of || *intr* to attend; to take care; to pay attention; **badare a** to mind; to watch over; to attend to; **badare alla salute** to take care of one's health

badéssa f abbess

badìa f abbey

badilata f shovelful

badile m shovel

baffo m whiskers; whisker; **baffi** mustache; whiskers; **baffo di gatto** (rad) cat's whiskers; **leccarsi i baffi** to lick one's chops; **sotto i baffi** up one's sleeve

baga·gliàio m (**-gliài**) (rr) baggage car; (rr) baggage room; (aut) baggage rack

bagaglièra f baggage room

bagaglière m baggage master

bagà·glio m (**-gli**) baggage, luggage; (of knowledge) fund

bagagli·sta m (**-sti**) porter (in a hotel)

bagarinàg·gio m (**-gi**) profiteering; (theat) scalping

bagarino m profiteer; scalper

bagà·scia f (**-sce**) harlot, prostitute

bagattèlla f trifle, bauble

baggiano m nitwit, simpleton

bà·glio m (**-gli**) (naut) beam

bagliore m shine, gleam

bagnante mf bather, swimmer; vacationer at the seashore

bagnare tr to bathe; to wet; to soak; to water, sprinkle; to moisten; (fig) to celebrate || ref to bathe; to wet one another

bagnaròla f (coll) bathtub

bagnasciu·ga f (**-ghe**) (naut) waterline

bagnino m lifeguard

bagno m bath; bathroom; bathtub; **bagno di luce** diathermy; **bagno di schiuma** bubble bath; **bagno di sole** sun bath; **bagno di vapore** steam bath; **bagno turco** Turkish bath; **essere in un bagno di sudore** to be soaked with perspiration; **fare il bagno** to take a bath

bagnomaria m (**bagnimarìa**) double boiler; bain-marie; **a bagnomaria** in a double boiler

bagórdo m carousal, revelry; **far bagordi** to carouse, revel

bàio bàia (**bài bàie**) adj & m bay || f bay; jest; trifle; **dare la baia a** to make fun of, tease

baionétta f bayonet; **baionetta in canna** with fixed bayonet

bàita f mountain hut

balaustrata f balustrade

balaùstro m baluster

balbettaménto m stammering

balbettare (**balbétto**) tr to stammer; to speak poorly (a foreign language) || intr to stammer; to babble (said of a baby)

balbettì·o m (**-i**) babble (of a baby); stammering

balbùzie f stammering

balbuziènte adj stammering || mf stammerer

Balcani, i the Balkans

balcàni·co -ca adj (**-ci -che**) Balkan

balconata f balcony; (theat) upper gallery

balcóne m balcony

baldacchino m canopy, baldachin

baldanza f boldness; aplomb, assurance

baldanzó·so -sa [s] adj bold; self-assured

bal·do -da adj bold; self-assured

baldòria f carousal, revelry; **fare baldoria** to carouse, revel

baldrac·ca f (**-che**) harlot, prostitute

baléna f whale

balenare (**baléno**) intr to stagger || intr (ESSERE) to flash, e.g., **gli balena un pensiero** a thought flashes through his mind || impers (ESSERE)—**balena, it is lightning**

balenièra f whaler, whaleboat

baléno m flash; flash of lightning; **in un baleno** in a flash

balenòttera f rorqual

balèstra f crossbow; (aut) spring, leaf spring

balestrière m crossbowman

bàlia f wet nurse; **balia asciutta** dry nurse; **prendere a balia** to wet-nurse

balìa f power; **in balìa di** at the mercy of

balisti·co -ca (**-ci -che**) adj ballistic || f ballistics

balla f bale; (vulg) lie

ballàbile adj dance || m dance tune

ballare tr to dance || intr to dance; to shake; to be loose; to wobble (said, e.g., of a chair)

ballata f ballad; (mus) ballade

balla·tóio m (**-tói**) gallery; perch (in birdcage)

balleri·no -na adj dancing || m ballet dancer; dancer; dancing partner || f dancing girl; ballerina; chorus girl; ballet slipper; (orn) wagtail

ballétto m ballet; chorus

ballo m dance; chorus; ball; stake; **ballo di San Vito** Saint Vitus's dance; **ballo in maschera** masked ball; **in ballo** at stake; in question; **tirare in ballo** to drag in

ballonzolare (**ballónzolo**) intr to hop around

ballottàg·gio m (**-gi**) runoff

ballottare (**ballòtto**) tr to ballot (e.g., a candidate)

balneare adj bathing; water, watering

baloccare §197 (**balòcco**) tr to amuse with toys || ref to play; to trifle, to fool around

balòc·co m (**-chi**) toy; hobby

balordàggine f silliness

balór·do -da adj silly, foolish

balsàmi·co -ca adj (**-ci -che**) balmy; antiseptic

balsamina f balsam

bàlsamo m balm, balsam

bàlti·co -ca adj (**-ci -che**) Baltic

baluardo m bastion, bulwark

baluginare (**balùgino**) intr (ESSERE) to flicker; to flash (through one's mind)

balza f crag, cliff; flounce (on dress); fringe (on curtains, bedspreads, etc.)

balza·no -na adj white-footed (horse); odd, funny || f flounce; fringe; white mark (on horse's foot)

balzare tr to throw (a rider; said of a horse) || intr (ESSERE) to jump, leap;

to bounce; **balzare in mente a** to suddenly dawn on

balzellare (balzèllo) *intr* to hop

balzèllo *m* hop; tribute; tax; toll; **stare a balzello** to lie in wait

balzellóni *adv*—**a balzelloni** leaping, skipping

balzo *m* leap; bounce; **pigliare la palla al balzo** to take time by the forelock

bambàgia *f* cotton wool

bambinàggine *f* childishness

bambinàia *f* nursemaid; **bambinaia ad ore** baby sitter

bambiné·sco -sca *adj* (-schi -sche) childish

bambi·no -na *adj* childish ‖ *mf* child

bambòc·cio *m* (-ci) fat baby; doll; rag doll

bàmbola *f* doll; **bambola di pezza** rag-doll

bam·bù *m* (-bù) bamboo

banale *adj* banal, commonplace

banali·tà *f* (-tà) banality, commonplaceness, triviality

banana *f* banana; hair with curls shaped as rolls

bananièra *f* banana boat

banano *m* banana plant

ban·ca *f* (-che) bank; embankment

bancàbile *adj* negotiable

bancarèlla *f* cart, pushcart; stall

banca·rio -ria (-ri -rie) *adj* bank, banking ‖ *m* bank clerk

bancarótta *f* bankruptcy; **fare bancarotta** to go bankrupt

banchettare (banchétto) *intr* to feast, banquet

banchétto *m* banquet

banchière *m* banker

banchina *f* garden bench; bicycle path; sidewalk; shoulder (*of highway*); dock, pier; (rr) platform; (mil) banquette

ban·co *m* (-chi) bench; seat; bank; witness stand; school (*of fish*); **banco di coralli** coral reef; **banco di ghiaccio** ice pack; **banco di nebbia** fog bank; **banco di prova** (mach) bench; **banco di sabbia** sandbar; **banco d'ostriche** oyster bed; **banco lotto** lottery office

bancogiro *m* (com) transfer of funds

bancóne *m* counter; bench

banconòta *f* banknote

banda *f* band; **andare alla banda** (naut) to list; **da ogni banda** from every side; **mettere da banda** to put aside

bandèlla *f* hinge (*of door or window*); hinged leaf (*of table*)

banderuòla *f* banderole; weather vane

bandièra *f* flag; banner; **battere la bandiera** (e.g., **italiana**) to fly the (*e.g Italian*) flag; **mutar bandiera** to change sides

bandierare (bandièro) *tr* (aer) to feather

bandire §176 *tr* to announce (*e.g., a competitive examination*); to banish

bandìsti·co -ca *adj* (-ci -che) (mus) band

bandi·to -ta *adj* announced; open (*house*) ‖ *m* bandit ‖ *f* preserve (*for hunting or fishing*)

bandi·tóre -trice *mf* town crier; auctioneer; barker

bando *m* announcement; banishment; **bandi matrimoniali** (eccl) banns; **mandare in bando** to exile, banish

bandolièra *f* bandoleer; **a bandoliera** slung across the shoulders

bàndolo *m* end of a skein; **perdere il bandolo** to lose the thread (*e.g., of a story*)

bara *f* bier, coffin

barac·ca *f* (-che) hut, cabin; (fig) household; **fare baracca** to carouse around

baracca·to -ta *adj* lodged in a hut or a cabin; slum (*e.g., section*) ‖ *m* dweller in a hut or a cabin; slum dweller

baraccóne *m* big circus tent

baraónda *f* hubbub; mess

barare *intr* to cheat (*e.g., at cards*)

bàratro *m* abyss, chasm

barattare *tr* to barter; **barattare le carte in mano a uno** to distort someone's words; **barattar parole** to chat, talk ‖ *intr* to barter

barattière *m* grafter

baratto *m* barter

baràttolo *m* can, canister, jar

barba *f* beard; whiskers; barb, vane (*of feather*); (naut) line; **barba a punta** imperial, goatee; **fare la barba (a)** to shave; **farla in barba a qlcu** to act in spite of s.o.; to dupe s.o.; **mettere barbe** to take root; **radersi la barba** to shave

barbabiètola *f* beet; sugar beet

barbafòrte *m* horseradish

barbagia·ni *m* (-ni) owl; (fig) jackass

barbà·glio *m* (-gli) glitter, dazzle

barbaré·sco -sca (-schi -sche) *adj* Barbary ‖ *m* inhabitant of the Barbary States

barbàri·co -ca *adj* (-ci -che) barbaric

barbà·rie *f* (-rie) barbarism, barbarity

barbarismo *m* barbarism

bàrba·ro -ra *adj* barbarous, barbaric ‖ *m* barbarian

barbazzale *m* curb (*of bit*)

Barberìa, la Barbary States

barbétta *f* fetlock (*tuft of hair on horse*); goatee; (mil) barbette; (naut) painter

barbière *m* barber

barbierìa *f* barbershop

barbì·glio *m* (-gli) barb (*of arrow*)

barbi·no -na *adj* shoddy; botched; stingy

bàr·bio *m* (-bi) (ichth) barbel

barbiturato *m* barbiturate

barbitùri·co -ca *adj* (-ci -che) barbituric ‖ *m* barbiturate

barbo *m* var of **barbio**

barbò·gio -gia *adj* (-gi -gie) senile

barbóne *m* long beard, thick beard; poodle; (coll) bum, hobo

barbó·so -sa [s] *adj* boring

barbugliare §280 *tr* to stutter (*e.g., a word*) ‖ *intr* to stutter; to bubble, gurgle

barbu·to -ta *adj* bearded

bar·ca *f* (-che) boat; heap; (fig) family

affairs; **barca a motore** motorboat; **barca da pesca** fishing boat; **barca a remi** rowboat

barcàc·cia f (-ce) (theat) stage box

barcaiòlo m boatman

barcamenare (barcaméno) ref to manage, get along

barcarizzo m (naut) gangway

barcaròla f barcarole

barcata f boatful

barchéssa f tool shed

barchétta f small boat; (naut) log chip

barcollare (barcòllo) intr to totter, stagger

barcollóni adv staggering, tottering

barcóne m barge

bardare tr to harness || ref to get dressed

bardatura f harnessing; harness

bardo m bard

bardòsso m —a bardosso (archaic) bareback

barèlla f stretcher

barellare (barèllo) tr to carry on a stretcher || intr to totter, stagger

barenatura f (mach) boring

bargèllo m (hist) chief of police; (hist) police headquarters

bargì·glio m (-gli) wattle

baricèntro m center of gravity; (fig) essence, gist

barile m barrel, cask

barilòtto m keg

bàrio m barium

bari·sta mf (-sti -ste) bartender, barkeeper || m barman || f barmaid

baritonale adj baritone

baríto·no -na adj barytone || m baritone

barlume m glimmer, gleam

baro m cheat, cardsharp

baròc·co -ca adj & m (-chi -che) baroque

baròmetro m barometer

baróne m baron

baronéssa f baroness

barra f bar; link; rod; sandbar; **andare alla barra** to plead a case; **barra del timone** (naut) tiller; **barra di torsione** (aut) torsion bar; **barra spaziatrice** space bar (of typewriter)

barrare tr to cross, draw lines across (a check)

barrétta f bar (e.g., of chocolate)

barricare §197 (bàrrico) tr to barricade || ref to barricade oneself

barricata f barricade

barrièra f barrier; bar; **barriera corallina** barrier reef

barrire §176 intr to trumpet (said of elephant)

barrito m trumpeting, cry of an elephant

barroc·ciàio m (-ciài) cart driver

barròc·cio m (-ci) cart

baruffa f fight, quarrel

barzellétta [dz] f joke

basale adj basal

basalto m basalt

basaménto m foundation (of building); baseboard; base (of column)

basare tr to base || ref—**basarsi su** to be based on; to rest on

ba·sco -sca adj & mf (-schi -sche) Basque

basculla f balance, scale

base f base, foundation; (fig) basis; **a base di** composed of, made of; **base navale** naval base, naval station; **in base a** according to

basétta f sideburns

bàsi·co -ca adj (-ci -che) (chem) basic

basilare adj basic, fundamental

Basilèa f Basel

basìli·ca f (-che) basilica

basìli·co m (-ci) basil

basilissa f (fig) queen bee

bàsolo m large paving stone

bassacórte f barnyard

bassézza f baseness

bas·so -sa adj low; shallow; late (e.g., date); (fig) base, vile; **basso di statura** short || m bottom; hovel (in Naples); (mus) basso || **basso** adv low; down; **a basso, da basso** or **in basso** downstairs

bassofóndo m (bassifóndi) (naut) shallows, shallow water; **bassifondi** underworld, slums

bassopiano m lowland

bassorilièvo m bas-relief

bassòt·to -ta adj stocky || m basset hound

bassotuba m bass horn

bassura f lowland; (fig) baseness

basta f hem; basting (with long stitches) || interj enough!

bastante adj sufficient, adequate; comfortable (income)

bastar·do -da adj bastard; irregular || m bastard

bastare intr to suffice, be enough; **basta!** enough!; **basta che** + subj as long as + ind; **bastare a sé stesso** to be self-sufficient; **non basta che** + subj not only + ind

bastévole adj sufficient

bastiménto m ship; shipload

bastióne m bastion; (fig) defense, rampart

basto m packsaddle; (fig) burden

bastonare (bastóno) tr to club, cudgel; **bastonare di santa ragione** to give a good thrashing to

bastonata f clubbing, cudgeling; **darsi bastonate ad orbi** to thrash one another soundly

bastoncino m small stick; roll; (anat) rod

bastóne m stick, cane; pole; club; baton; staff; French bread; **bastone a leva** crowbar; **bastone animato** sword cane; **bastone da golf** club; **bastone da montagna** alpenstock; **bastone da passeggio** walking stick; **bastone da sci** ski pole; **bastoni** suit in Neapolitan cards corresponding to clubs; **mettere il bastone tra le ruote** to throw a monkey wrench into the machinery

batàc·chio m (-chi) clapper (of bell); cudgel

batata f sweet potato

batisfèra f bathysphere
batista f batiste, cambric
batòsta f blow; (fig) blow
bàtrace or **batrace** m batrachian
battà·glia f (-glie) battle; campaign
battagliare §280 intr to fight
battagliè·ro -ra adj fighting, warlike
battà·glio m (-gli) clapper (of bell); knocker
battaglióne m battalion
battèllo m boat; **battello di salvataggio** lifeboat; **battello pneumatico** rubber raft
battènte m leaf (e.g., of door); knocker; tapper (of alarm clock)
bàttere m—**in un batter d'occhio** in the twinkling of an eye || tr to beat; to hit; to strike; to strike (the hour; said of a clock); to click (teeth, heels); to clap (hands); to stamp (one's foot); to mint (coins); to fly (a flag); to beat (time); to scour (the countryside); to flap (the wings); (sports) to bat; (sports) to kick (a penalty); **battere a macchina** to type; **battere il naso in** to chance upon; **battere la fiacca** to goof off; **battere la grancassa per** to ballyhoo; **battere la strada** to be a streetwalker; **senza batter ciglio** without batting an eye || intr (ESSERE) to beat down (said, e.g., of rain); to beat (said of the heart); to chatter (said of teeth); to knock (at the door); **battere in ritirata** to beat a retreat; **battere in testa** (aut) to knock
batteria f battery; set (of utensils); (sports) heat
batterici·da (-**di -de**) adj bactericidal || m bactericide
battèri·co -ca adj (-ci -che) bacterial
battè·rio m (-ri) bacterium
batteriologìa f bacteriology
batteriòlo·go -ga mf (-gi -ghe) bacteriologist
batteri·sta mf (-sti -ste) jazz drummer
battesimale adj baptismal
battésimo m baptism; **tenere a battesimo** to christen
battezzare (**battézzo**) [ddzz] tr to christen || ref to receive baptism; to assume the name of
battibaléno m—**in un battibaleno** in the twinkling of an eye
battibéc·co m (-chi) squabble
batticuòre m palpitation; (fig) trepidation
battilò·ro m (-ro) goldsmith; silversmith
battimano m applause
battimuro m—**giocare a battimuro** to pitch pennies (against a wall)
battipalo m pile driver
battipan·ni m (-ni) clothes beater
battira·me m (-me) coppersmith
battiscó·pa m (-pa) washboard, baseboard
batti·sta adj & mf (-sti -ste) Baptist
battistèro m baptistry
battistra·da m (-da) outrider; (sports) leader; (aut) tread
battitappéto m carpet sweeper
bàttito m beating; palpitation; ticking;

wink; pitter-patter (of rain)
batti·tóio m (-tói) leaf (e.g., of door); casement; cotton beater
battitóre m (hunt) beater; (baseball) batter
battitrice f threshing machine
battitura f thrashing, whipping; threshing (e.g., of wheat)
battu·to -ta adj beaten; hammered || m pavement || f beat; stroke, keystroke; meter (in poetry); witticism, quip; (hunt) battue; (mus) bar; (tennis) service; (theat) line; (theat) cue; **battuta d'aspetto** (mus) pause; **dare la battuta** to give the cue
batùffolo m wad; (fig) bundle
baule m trunk; **baule armadio** wardrobe trunk; **fare i bauli** to be on one's way; **fare il baule** to pack one's trunk
baulétto m small trunk; handbag; jewel case
bava f slobber; foam, froth; burr (on metal edge); **avere la bava alla bocca** to be frothing at the mouth; **bava di vento** breath of air, soft breeze
bavaglino m bib
bavà·glio m (-gli) gag
bavaré·se [s] adj & mf Bavarian || f Bavarian cream; chocolate cream
bàvero m collar
bavièra f beaver (of helmet) || **la Baviera** Bavaria
bavó·so -sa [s] adj slobbering, slobbery
bazza [ddzz] f protruding chin; windfall
bazzana [ddzz] f sheepskin
bazzècola [ddzz] f trifle, bauble
bazzicare §197 (**bàzzico**) tr to frequent
bazzòt·to -ta [ddzz] adj soft-boiled; uncertain (weather)
beare (**bèo**) tr to delight || ref to be delighted, be enraptured
beatificare §197 (**beatìfico**) tr to beatify
beatitùdine f beatitude, bliss
bea·to -ta adj blissful, happy; blessed || mf blessed
be·bè m (-bè) baby
beccàc·cia f (-ce) woodcock
beccaccino m snipe
beccafi·co m (-chi) figpecker, beccafico
bec·càio m (-cài) butcher
beccamòr·ti m (-ti) gravedigger
beccare §197 (**bécco**) tr to peck; to pick; (coll) to catch || ref to peck one another; to quarrel
beccata f peck
beccheggiare §290 (**becchéggio**) intr (naut) to pitch
becchég·gio m (-gi) (naut) pitching
beccherìa f butcher shop
becchìme m food for poultry
becchino m gravedigger
béc·co m (-chi) beak, bill; tip, point; nozzle (e.g., of teapot); billy goat; (vulg) cuckold; **bagnarsi il becco** (joc) to wet one's whistle; **mettere il becco in** (coll; joc) to stick one's nose into; **non avere il becco di un quattrino** to not have a red cent
beccùc·cio m (-ci) small bill; lip, spout
beccuzzare tr to peck || ref to bill (said of doves)

béce·ro -ra adj (coll) boorish || m (coll) boor

beduì·no -na adj & m Bedouin

befana f (coll) Epiphany; old hag

bèffa f jest, mockery; **farsi beffa di** to make fun of

beffar·do -da adj mocking

beffare (**bèffo**) tr to mock, deride || ref —**beffarsi di** to make fun of

beffeggiare §290 (**beffèggio**) tr to scoff at, deride

bè·ga f (-**ghe**) quarrel; trouble

beghina f Beguine; bigoted woman

begònia f begonia

bèl adj apocopated form of **bello**, used only before masculine singular nouns beginning with a consonant except impure **s, z, gn, ps,** and **x,** e.g., **bel ragazzo**

belare (**bèlo**) tr to croon || intr to bleat, baa; to moan

belato m bleat, baa

bèl·ga adj & mf (-**gi -ghe**) Belgian

Bèlgio, il Belgium

bèll' adj apocopated form of **bello**, used only before singular nouns of both genders beginning with a vowel, e.g., **bell'amico; bell'epoca**

bèlla adj fem of **bello** || f belle; girl-friend; final draft; (sports) final game; (sports) rubber match; **alla bell'e meglio** the best one could; **bella di notte** (bot) four-o'clock

belladònna f belladonna

bellétto m rouge, makeup

bellézza f beauty; **che bellezza!** how lovely!; **la bellezza di** as much as

bellici·sta adj (-**sti -ste**) bellicose

bèlli·co -ca adj (-**ci -che**) war, warlike

bellicó·so -sa [s] adj bellicose

belligerante adj & m belligerent

belligeranza f belligerence

bellimbusto m fop, dandy, beau

bèl·lo -la (declined like **quello** §7) adj beautiful; lovely; handsome; good-looking; pleasing; fine; quite, a, e.g., **una bella cifra** quite a sum; fair; pretty; **bell'e fatto** ready-made; taken care of; **farla bella** to start trouble; (coll) to do it, e.g., **l'hai fatta bella** you've done it; **farsi bello** to dress up; **farsi bello di** to appropriate || m beauty; beautiful; climax; fine weather; beau; **il bello è** the funny thing is; **sul più bello** just then; **sul più bello che** just when || f see **bella** || **bello** adv—**bel bello** slowly

bellospìrito m (**begli spìriti**) wit, bel-esprit

bellui·no -na adj wild, fierce

bellumóre m (**begli umóri**) jolly fellow

bel·tà f (-**tà**) beauty (woman); (lit) beauty

bélva f wild beast

belvedére adj (rr) observation (car) || m belvedere; (naut) topgallant

Belzebù m Beelzebub

bemòlle m (mus) flat

benama·to -ta adj beloved

benarriva·to -ta adj welcome

benché conj although, albeit

bènda f bandage; band; blindfold; **benda gessata** cast, surgical dressing

bendàg·gio m (-**gi**) bandage

bendare (**bèndo**) tr to bandage; **bendare gli occhi a** to blindfold

bendispó·sto -sta adj well-disposed

bène adj well; well-born || m goal, aim; good; love; sake; **bene dell'ànima** profound affection; **beni** (econ) assets, goods; **beni di consumo** consumer goods; **beni immobili** real estate; **beni mobili** personal property, chattels; **beni rifugio** hedge (e.g., against inflation); **è un bene** it is a blessing; **fare del bene a** to do good; **per il Suo bene** for your sake; **voler bene a** to love, like; to care for || adv well; all right; properly; **ben bene** quite carefully; **star bene** to be well; **va bene** O.K., all right

benedetti·no -na adj & m Benedictine

benedét·to -ta adj blessed; holy

benedire §195 tr to bless; to praise; **andare a farsi benedire** (coll) to go to wrack and ruin; **mandare a farsi benedire** (coll) to get rid of, dump

benedizióne f benediction; boon

beneduca·to -ta adj well-behaved

benefattóre m benefactor

benefattrice f benefactress

beneficare §197 (**benèfico**) tr to benefit, help

beneficènza f welfare; charity, beneficence

beneficiale adj beneficial

beneficiare §128 intr to benefit

beneficià·rio -ria adj & mf (-**ri -rie**) beneficiary

beneficiata f benefit performance; streak of good luck; streak of bad luck

benefì·cio m (-**ci**) benefice; profit; favor; benefit

benèfi·co -ca adj (-**ci -che**) beneficial; beneficent

benemerènte adj deserving, well-deserving

benemèri·to -ta adj worthy, deserving || m—**benemerito della patria** national hero || f—**la Benemerita** the Carabinieri

beneplàcito m approval, consent; **a beneplacito di** at the pleasure of

benèssere m well-being, comfort; prosperity

benestante adj well-to-do || mf well-to-do person

benestare m approval; prosperity; **dare il benestare a** to approve

benevolènte adj benevolent

benevolènza f benevolence

benèvo·lo -la adj well-meaning; benevolent

benfat·to -ta adj well-done; well-favored; shapely

benga m (-**li** & -**la**) fireworks

benga·li adj & m (-**li**) Bengalese

beniami·no -na mf favorite child; favorite

benigni·tà f (-**tà**) benignity; graciousness; mildness (of climate)

beni-gno -gna *adj* benign; gracious; mild (*climate*)

benintenziona-to -ta *adj* well-meaning

benintéso [s] *adv* of course, naturally

bènna *f* bucket, scoop (*e.g., of dredge*)

benna-to -ta *adj* (lit) well-born

benpensante *m* sensible person; conformist

benportante *adj* well-preserved

benservito *m* testimonial, recommendation; **dare il benservito a** to dismiss, fire

bensì *adv* indeed || *conj* but

bentorna-to -ta *adj* & *m* welcome || *interj* welcome back!

benvenu-to -ta *adj* & *m* welcome; **dare il benvenuto a** to welcome

benvi-sto -sta *adj* well-thought-of

benvolére *tr*—**farsi benvolere da qlcu** to enter the good graces of s.o.; **prendere a benvolere qlcu** to be well-disposed toward s.o.

benvolu-to -ta *adj* liked, loved

benzina *f* gasoline, gas; benzine; **far benzina** (coll) to get gas

benzi-nàio -nàio *m* (**-nài**) gasoline dealer; gas-station attendant

benzòlo *m* benzene

beóne *m* drunkard, toper

bequadro *m* (mus) natural

berciare §128 (**bèrcio**) *intr* (coll) to yell

bére *m* drink, drinking || §120 *tr* to drink; (fig) to swallow; **bere come una spugna** to drink like a fish; **darla a bere** to make believe

bergamòt-to -ta *adj* bergamot || *m* bergamot orange || *f* bergamot pear

berìllio *m* beryllium

berlina *f* pillory; berlin, coach; (aut) sedan; **mettere alla berlina** to pillory

berlinése [s] *adj* Berlin || *mf* Berliner

Berlino *m* Berlin

bermuda *mpl* Bermuda shorts || **le Bermude** Bermuda

bernòccolo *m* bump, protuberance; (fig) knack

berrétta *f* biretta

berrétto *m* cap; **berretto a sonagli** cap and bells; **berretto da notte** nightcap; **berretto gogliardico** student cap

bersagliare §280 *tr* to harass, pursue; to bomb, bombard

bersà-glio *m* (**-gli**) target; butt (*of a joke*); target (*of criticism*)

bèrta *f* pile driver; **dar la berta a** to ridicule

bertùc-cia *f* (**-ce**) Barbary ape; **fare la bertuccia di** to ape

bestémmia *f* blasphemy

bestemmiare §287 (**bestémmio**) *tr* to blaspheme, curse

bestemmia-tóre -trice *adj* blasphemous || *mf* blasphemer

béstia *f* beast, animal; **andare in bestia** to fly into a rage; **bestia da soma** beast of burden; **bestia nera** pet aversion, bête noire; **bestie grosse** cattle

bestiale *adj* beastly, bestial

bestiali-tà *f* (**-tà**) beastliness; blunder

bestiame *m* livestock; **bestiame da cortile** barnyard animals; **bestiame grosso** cattle

bestino *m* gamy odor; stench of perspiration

bestiòla *f* tiny animal; pet

bestsèl-ler *m* (**-ler**) best seller

Betlèmme *f* Bethlehem

betonièra *f* cement mixer

béttola *f* tavern

bettolière *m* tavern keeper

bettònica *f* betony; **conosciuto più della bettonica** very well-known

betulla *f* birch

bèuta *f* flask

bevanda *f* drink, beverage

beveràg-gio *m* (**-gi**) beverage, potion

bevìbile *adj* drinkable

bevi-tóre -trice *mf* drinker

bevuta *f* drink, drinking

bezzicare §197 (**bézzico**) *tr* to peck; to vex || *ref* to fight one another

biacca *f* white lead

biada *f* feed; blade harvest

bianca-stro -stra *adj* whitish

biancheria *f* laundry; linen; underwear; **biancheria da letto** bed linen; **biancheria da tavola** table linen; **biancheria di bucato** freshly laundered clothes; **biancheria intima** underclothes

bianchézza *f* whiteness

bianchire §176 *tr* to blanch; to bleach; to polish

bian-co -ca (**-chi -che**) *adj* white; clean; **bianco come un cencio lavato** as white as a ghost || *m* white; **dare il bianco a** to whitewash; **in bianco** blank (*paper*); **mangiare in bianco** to eat a bland or non-spicy diet; **ricamare in bianco** to embroider

biancóre *m* whiteness

biancospino *m* hawthorn

biascicare §197 (**biàscico**) *tr* to chew with difficulty; to peck at (*one's food*); to mumble

biasimare (**biàsimo**) *tr* to blame

biasimévole *adj* blamable, censurable

biàsimo *m* blame, censure; **dare una nota di biasimo a** to censure

biauricolare *adj* binaural

Bìbbia *f* Bible

bibe-rón *m* (**-rón**) nursing bottle

bibita *f* soft drink

bìbli-co -ca *adj* (**-ci -che**) Biblical

bìblio-bus *m* (**-bus**) bookmobile

bibliòfi-lo -la *mf* bibliophile

bibliografìa *f* bibliography

bibliotè-ca *f* (**-che**) library; bookshelf, stack; collection (*of books*); **biblioteca ambulante** walking encyclopedia

bibliotecà-rio -ria *mf* (**-ri -rie**) librarian

bibu-lo -la *adj* absorbent (*e.g., paper*)

bi-ca *f* (**-che**) pile of sheaves

bicarbonato *m* bicarbonate; **bicarbonato di soda** bicarbonate of soda, baking soda

bicchierata *f* (coll) glassful; wine party

bicchière *m* glass

bicchierino *m* small glass, liquor glass; **bicchierino da rosolio** whiskey glass, jigger

biciclétta *f* bicycle

bicilìndri-co -ca *adj* (**-ci -che**) two-cylinder

bicìpite *adj* two-headed || *m* biceps
bicòc·ca *f* (**-che**) castle built on a hill; shanty, hut
bicolóre *adj* two-color
bicòrno *m* two-cornered hat
bidèllo *m* school janitor, caretaker
bidènte *m* two-pronged pitchfork
bidimensionale *adj* two-dimensional
bidóne *m* can (*for milk*); drum (*for gasoline or oil*); jalopy; (slang) fraud
bidon·ville *f* (**-ville**) shantytown
biè·co -ca *adj* (**-chi -che**) awry; sullen; cross; fierce; **guardar bieco** to look askance (at)
bièlla *f* connecting rod
biennale *adj* biennial || *f* biennial show
biènne *adj* biennial
bièn·nio *m* (**-ni**) biennium
biètola *f* Swiss chard
biètta *f* wedge, chock; (naut) batten
bifase *adj* diphase
biffa *f* (surv) rod
biffare *tr* to cross out; (surv) to level
bìfi·do -da *adj* bifurcate
bifocale *adj* bifocal
bifól·co m (**-chi**) ox driver; clodhopper, boor
biforcaménto *m* bifurcation
biforcare §197 (**bifórco**) *tr* to bifurcate
biforcazióne *f* bifurcation, branching off; fork (*of a road*)
biforcu·to -ta *adj* forked; cloven (*e.g., hoof*)
bifrónte *adj* two-faced
bi·ga *f* (**-ghe**) chariot
bigamìa *f* bigamy
bìga·mo -ma *adj* bigamous || *mf* bigamist
bighellonare (**bighellóno**) *intr* to idle, dawdle, dally
bighelló·ne -na *mf* idler, dawdler
bigino *m* (slang) pony (*used to cheat*)
bì·gio -gia *adj* (**-gi -gie**) gray, grayish; (fig) undecided
bigiotterìa *f* costume jewelry; costume jewelry store
bigliardo *m* billiards
bigliet·tàio *m* (**-tài**) ticket agent; (rr) conductor
biglietterìa *f* ticket office; (theat) box office
bigliétto *m* note; card; ticket; **biglietto d'abbonamento** commutation ticket; season ticket; **biglietto d'andata e ritorno** round-trip ticket; **biglietto di banca** banknote; **biglietto di lotteria** lottery ticket, chance; **biglietto d'invito** invitation; **biglietto di visita** calling card; business card; **biglietto di Stato** banknote; **mezzo biglietto** half fare
bigné *m* (**bignè**) puff, creampuff
bigodino *m* curler; roller
bigón·cia *f* (**-ce**) vat; bucket; **a bigonce** abundantly
bigón·cio *m* (**-ci**) vat; tub; (theat) ticket box (*for stubs*)
bigottismo *m* bigotry
bigòt·to -ta *adj* bigoted || *mf* bigot
bilàn·cia *f* (**-ce**) balance, scale; **bilancia commerciale** balance of trade; **bilan-**

cia dei pagamenti balance of payments || **Bilancia** *f* (astr) Libra
bilanciare §128 *tr* & *ref* to balance
bilancière *m* balance; balance wheel; rope-walker's balancing rod
bilàn·cio *m* (**-ci**) **bilancio consuntivo** balance sheet; **bilancio preventivo** budget; **fare il bilancio** to balance; to strike a balance
bile *f* bile; **rodersi dalla bile** to burn with anger
bìlia *f* billiard ball; marble; (billiards) pocket
biliardino *m* pocket billiards; pinball machine
biliardo *m* billiards
biliare *adj* bile; gall (*stone*)
bili·co m (**-chi**) balance, equipoise; **in bilico** in balance; **tenere in bilico** to balance
bilingue *adj* bilingual
bilióne *m* billion; trillion (Brit)
bilió·so -sa [**s**] *adj* bilious
bim·bo -ba *mf* child
bimensile *adj* bimonthly
bimèstre *m* period of two months
bimotóre *adj* twin-engine || *m* twin-engine plane
binà·rio -ria (**-ri -rie**) *adj* binary || *m* (rr) track; **binario morto** (rr) siding; **uscire dai binari** (rr) to run off the track; (fig) to go astray
bina·to -ta *adj* binary; twin (*e.g., guns*)
binda *f* (aut) jack
binòcolo *m* binoculars; **binocolo da teatro** opera glasses
binò·mio -mia (**-mi -mie**) *adj* binomial || *m* binomial; couple, pair
biòccolo *m* wad (*of cotton*); flake (*of snow*); flock (*of wool*)
biochìmi·co -ca (**-ci -che**) *adj* biochemical || *m* biochemist || *f* biochemistry
biodegradàbile *adj* biodegradable
biofisica *f* biophysics
biografìa *f* biography
biogràfi·co -ca *adj* (**-ci -che**) biographic(al)
biògra·fo -fa *mf* biographer
biologìa *f* biology
biòlo·go m (**-gi**) biologist
biondeggiare §290 (**biondéggio**) *intr* to be or become blond; to ripen (*said of grain*)
biòn·do -da *adj* blond, fair || *m* blond; blondness || *f* blonde
biopsìa *f* biopsy
biòssido *m* dioxide
bipartìti·co -ca *adj* (**-ci -che**) two-party, bipartisan
biparti·to -ta *adj* bipartite || *m* two-party government
bipede *adj* & *m* biped
bipènne *f* double-bitted ax
biplano *m* biplane
bipòsto *adj invar* having seats for two || *m* two-seater
birba *f* rascal, rogue
birbante *m* scoundrel, rascal; (joc) madcap, wild young fellow
birbanterìa *f* knavery; trick
birbonata *f* trick

birbó·ne -na *adj* wicked || *mf* rascal, rogue, scoundrel
bireattóre *m* twin jet
birichinata *f* prank
birichi·no -na *adj* prankish; spirited || *mf* rogue; urchin
birillo *m* pin; **birilli** ninepins; tenpins
Birmània, la Burma
birra *f* beer; **birra chiara** light beer; **birra scura** dark beer
bir·ràio *m* (**-rài**) brewer; beer distributor
birreria *f* brewery; tavern; beer saloon
bis *adj invar***—treno bis** (rr) second section || *m* (**bis**) encore || *interj* encore!
bisàc·cia *f* (**-ce**) knapsack; saddlebag; bag (*of mendicant friar*)
Bisànzio *m* Bysantium
bisa·vo -va *mf* great-grandparent; ancestor || *m* great-grandfather || *f* great-grandmother
bisbèti·co -ca (**-ci -che**) *adj* shrewish; crotchety; cantankerous || *f* (fig) shrew
bisbigliare §280 *tr* & *intr* to whisper
bisbì·glio *m* (**-gli**) whisper
bisbòccia *f***—fare bisboccia** to revel
bisboccióne *m* reveler
bis·ca *f* (**-che**) gambling house
Biscàglia *f* Biscay, e.g., **Baia di Biscaglia** Bay of Biscay; **la Biscaglia** Biscay
biscaglina *f* (naut) Jacob's ladder
biscazzière *m* gaming-house operator; habitué of a gaming house; marker (*at billiards*)
bischero *m* (mus) peg
bì·scia *f* (**-sce**) snake; **biscia d'acqua** water snake
biscottare (**biscòtto**) *tr* to toast
biscotteria *f* cookie factory; cookie store
biscottièra *f* cookie jar
biscottifi·cio *m* (**-ci**) cookie factory
biscòt·to -ta *adj* twice-baked || *m* cookie
biscròma *f* (mus) demisemiquaver
bisdòsso *m***—a bisdosso** bareback
bisecare [s] §197 (**bìseco**) *tr* to bisect
bisènso *m* double meaning
bisessuale [s] *adj* bisexual
bisestile *adj* leap (*year*)
bisettimanale [s] *adj* biweekly
bisettrice [s] *f* bisector
bisezióne [s] *f* bisection
bisìlla·bo -ba [s] *adj* disyllabic
bislac·co -ca *adj* (**-chi -che**) queer, extravagant
bislun·go -ga *adj* (**-ghi -ghe**) oblong
bismuto *m* bismuth
bisnòn·no -na *mf* great-grandparent; **bisnonni** ancestors || *m* great-grandfather || *f* great-grandmother
bisógna *f* (lit) task, job
bisognare (**bisógna**) *intr* (with *dat*) to need, e.g., **gli bisognavano tre litri di benzina** he needed three liters of gasoline || *impers*—**bisogna** + *inf* it is necessary to, e.g., **bisogna partire** it is necessary to leave; **bisogna che** + *subj* must, to have to, e.g., **bisogna che me ne vada** I must go,

I have to go; **bisognando** if need be; **non bisogna** one should not; **più che non bisogna** more than necessary
bisognévole *adj* needy
bisógno *m* need; want, lack; **aver bisogno di** to need; **c'è bisogno di** there is need of; **se ci fosse bisogno** if need be
bisognó·so -sa *adj* needy || **i bisognosi** the needy
bisolfato [s] *m* bisulfate
bisolfito [s] *m* bisulfite
bisolfuro [s] *m* bisulfide
bisónte *m* bison
bistec·ca *f* (**-che**) beefsteak, steak; **bistecca al sangue** rare steak
bisticciare §128 *intr* & *ref* to quarrel, bicker
bistic·cio *m* (**-ci**) quarrel, bickering; play on words, pun
bistrattare *tr* to mistreat
bìstu·ri *m* (**-ri**) bistouri, surgical knife
bisul·co -ca *adj* (**-chi -che**) cloven
bisun·to -ta *adj* greasy
bitagliènte *adj* double-edged
bitórzolo *m* wart (*on humans, plants, or animals*); pimple (*on human face*)
bitta *f* (naut) bollard
bitume *m* bitumen, asphalt
bituminó·so -sa [s] *adj* bituminous
bivaccare §197 *intr* to bivouac; to spend the night
bivac·co *m* (**-chi**) bivouac
bì·vio *m* (**-vi**) fork (*of road*); **essere al bivio** (fig) to be at the crossroads
bizanti·no -na [dz] *adj* Byzantine
bizza [ddzz] *f* tantrum; **fare le bizze** to go into a tantrum
bizzarria [ddzz] *f* extravagance, oddity
bizzar·ro -ra [ddzz] *adj* bizarre, odd; skittish (*e.g., horse*)
bizzèffe [ddzz] *adv*— **a bizzeffe** plenty, in abundance
bizzó·so -sa [s] *adj* irritable
blandire §176 *tr* to blandish, coax; to soothe, mitigate
blandizie *fpl* blandishment
blan·do -da *adj* bland
blasfemare (**blasfèmo**) *tr* & *intr* to blaspheme
blasfè·mo -ma *adj* blasphemous
blasona·to -ta *adj* emblazoned
blasóne *m* coat of arms, blazon
blaterare (**blàtero**) *intr* to babble
blatta *f* water bug, cockroach
blenoraggia *f* gonorrhea
blè·so -sa *adj* lisping
blindàg·gio *m* (**-gi**) armor
blindare *tr* to armor
bloccare §197 (**blòcco**) *tr* to block; to blockade; to stop; to jam; to close up; to freeze (*e.g., prices*); (sports) to block || *intr*—**bloccare su** to vote as a block for || *ref* to stop
blòc·co *m* (**-chi**) block; blockade; notebook, pad; freezing (*e.g., of wages*); **in blocco** in bulk
bloc-notes *m* (**-notes**) notebook
blu *adj invar* & *m* blue
blua·stro -stra *adj* bluish
bluffare *intr* to bluff
blusa *f* blouse; smock

bò·a *m* (-a) boa ‖ *f* buoy

boà·rio -ria *adj* (-ri -rie) cattle

boa·ro -ra *adj* ox ‖ *m* stable boy

boato *m* roar; **boato sonico** sonic boom

bobina *f* spool (*of thread*); coil (*of wire*); reel (*of movie film; of magnetic tape*); roll (*of film*); cylinder, bobbin; (elec) coil; **bobina d'accensione** spark coil

bóc·ca *f* (-che) mouth; nozzle; muzzle (*of gun*); pit (*of the stomach*); opening; straits; pass; **a bocca aperta** agape; **bocca da fuoco** cannon; **di buona bocca** easily pleased; **in bocca al lupo!** good luck!; **per bocca** orally; **rimanere a bocca asciutta** to be foiled; to be left high and dry; **tieni la bocca chiusa!** shut up!

boccaccé·sco -sca *adj* (-schi -sche) written by or in the style of Boccaccio; bawdy, licentious

boccàc·cia *f* (-ce) ugly mouth; grimace; **fare le boccacce** to make faces

boccà·glio *m* (-gli) nozzle (*of hose or pipe*); mouthpiece (*of megaphone*)

boccale *adj* oral ‖ *m* jug, tankard

boccapòrto *m* hatch; port; mouth (*of oven or furnace*); **chiudere i boccaporti** to batten the hatches

boccascèna *m* (-na) proscenium, front (*of stage*)

boccata *f* mouthful; **andare a prendere una boccata d'aria** to go out for a breath of fresh air

boccétta *f* small bottle, vial; small billiard ball

boccheggiante *adj* gasping; moribund

boccheggiare §290 (bocchéggio) *intr* to gasp

bocchétta *f* nozzle (*of sprinkling can*); mouthpiece (*of wind instrument*); opening (*of drainage or ventilation system*); **bocchetta stradale** manhole

bocchino *m* cigarette holder; mouthpiece (*of cigarette or of musical instrument*)

bòc·cia *f* (-ce) decanter; ball (*for bowling*); **bocce** bowls

bocciare §128 (bòccio) *tr* to score (*at bowling*); to reject (*a proposal*); to flunk (*a student*)

bocciatura *f* failure

boccino *m* jack (*at bowls*)

bocciòlo *m* bud

bóccola *f* buckle; earring; (mach) bushing

bocconcino *m* morsel; (culin) stew

boccóne *m* mouthful; piece; morsel; **buttar giù un boccone amaro** to swallow a bitter pill; **levarsi il boccone di bocca** to take the bread out of one's mouth (to help someone); **mangiare un boccone** to have a bite ‖ **bocconi** *adv* flat on one's face

boè·mo -ma *adj* & *mf* Bohemian

boè·ro -ra *adj* & *m* Boer

bofonchiare §287 (bofónchio) *intr* to snort, grumble

bò·ia *m* (-ia) hangman, executioner

boiata *f* (slang) infamy; (slang) trash

boicottàg·gio *m* (-gi) boycott

boicottare (boicòtto) *tr* to boycott

bòl·gia *f* (-ge) pit (*in hell*)

bólide *m* (astr) bolide, fireball; (aut) racer; (joc) lummox; **andare come un bolide** to go like a flash

bolina *f* (naut) bowline; **di bolina** (naut) close-hauled

bolivia·no -na *adj* & *mf* Bolivian

bólla *f* bubble; blister; ticket; **bolla di consegna** receipt; **bolla di spedizione** delivery ticket; **bolla di sapone** soap bubble; **bolla papale** papal bull

bollare (bóllo) *tr* to stamp; to brand

bollà·to -ta *adj* stamped; sealed

bollatura *f* stamp; brand; postage

bollènte *adj* boiling, scalding hot

bollétta *f* ticket; receipt; bill; **essere in bolletta** (coll) to be broke

bollettà·rio *m* (-ri) receipt book

bollettino *m* bulletin; receipt; **bollettino dei prezzi correnti** price list; **bollettino di versamento** (com) deposit ticket; **bollettino meteorologico** weather forecast

bollire (bóllo) *tr* & *intr* to boil

bolli·to -ta *adj* boiled ‖ *m* boiled beef

bollitura *f* boiling

bóllo *m* mark, cancellation; revenue stamp; postmark; seal; **bollo a freddo** seal (*embossed*); **bollo postale** cancellation, postmark

bollóre *m* boiling; sultriness; (fig) passion, excitement; **alzare il bollore** to begin to boil

bollò·so -sa [s] *adj* blistery

bolscevi·co -ca *adj* & *mf* (-chi -che) Bolshevik

bolscevismo *m* Bolshevism

ból·so -sa *adj* broken-winded (*horse*); asthmatic

bòma *f* (naut) boom

bómba *f* bomb; bubble gum; fireworks; (aer) double loop; (journ) scandal; **bomba a idrogeno** hydrogen bomb; **bomba a mano** hand grenade; **bomba antisommergibile** depth charge; **bomba a orologeria** time bomb; **bomba atomica** atom bomb; **bomba H** (acca) H bomb; **tornare a bomba** (fig) to get back to the point

bombàggio *m* swelling (*of a spoiled can of food*)

bombardaménto *m* bombing, bombardment

bombardare *tr* to bomb, bombard; to besiege (*with questions*)

bombardière *m* (aer) bomber; (mil) artilleryman

bombétta *f* derby (*hat*)

bómbola *f* bottle; cylinder; **bombola d'ossigeno** oxygen tank

bombonièra *f* candy box

bomprèsso *m* (naut) bowsprit

bonàc·cia *f* (-ce) calm; calm sea; (fig) normalcy; (com) stagnation

bonacció·ne -na *adj* good-hearted, good-natured

bonarie·tà *f* (-tà) kindheartedness, good nature

bonà·rio -ria *adj* (-ri -rie) kindhearted, good-natured

boncinèllo *m* hasp

bonì·fica *f* (-che) reclamation; reclaimed land; improvement (e.g., of morals); clearing of mines; (metallurgy) hardening and tempering

bonificare §197 (**bonifico**) tr to reclaim; to discount, make a reduction of; to clear of mines

bonifi·co m (-ci) discount

bonomía f good nature; simple-heartedness

bon·tà f (-tà) goodness; kindness; **avere la bontà di** to be kind enough to; **bontà mia** (**sua**, **etc.**) through my (his, her, etc.) kindness; **per mia** (**sua**, **etc.**) **bontà** through my (his, her, etc.) efforts

bòra f northeast wind

boráce m borax

borbogliare §280 (**borbóglio**) intr to gurgle; to rumble

borbòni·co -ca (-ci -che) adj Bourbon ‖ m Bourbonist

borbottare (**borbòtto**) tr to mutter ‖ intr to mutter; to gurgle; to rumble (said, e.g., of thunder)

borbotti·o m (-i) mutter; gurgle; rumble

bòrchia f upholsterer's nail; boss, stud

bordare (**bórdo**) tr to border, hem

bordata f (naut) tack; (nav) broadside

bordatura f border, hem

bordeggiare §290 (**bordéggio**) intr (naut) to tack

bordèllo m brothel

borde·rò m (-rò) list; note; (theat) box office; receipts

bórdo m side (of ship); border, hem; edge, rim; (naut) tack; (naut) board; **a bordo** on board; **a bordo di** on board; on, in; **bordo d'entrata** (aer) leading edge; **bordo d'uscita** (aer) trailing edge; **d'alto bordo** (naut) big, sea-going; (fig) high-toned; **virare di bordo** (naut) to change course

bordóne m staff; bass stop (of organ); drone (of insect); **tener bordone a** (mus) to accompany; (fig) to hold the bag for

bordura f hem, edge; rim

boreale adj northern, boreal

borgáta f hamlet, village

borghése [s] adj middle-class ‖ mf bourgeois, person of the middle class; civilian; **in borghese** in civilian clothes; in plainclothes

borghesía f bourgeoise, middle class; **alta borghesia** upper middle class

bór·go m (-ghi) borough; small town; suburb

borgógna m Burgundy (wine) ‖ **la Borgogna** Burgundy

borgognóne m iceberg

borgomastro m burgomaster

bòria f haughtiness, vainglory

bòri·co -ca adj (-ci -che) boric

borió·so -sa (-si) adj haughty, puffed-up; blustery

bòro m boron

borotal·co m (-chi) talcum powder

bórra f flock (for pillows); (fig) rubbish, filler

borràc·cia f (-ce) canteen (e.g., for carrying water)

bórro m gully

bórsa f bag; pouch; bourse, exchange; (sports) purse; **borsa da viaggio** traveling bag; **borsa dell'acqua** hot-water bag; **borsa della spesa** shopping bag; **borsa di ghiaccio** ice bag; **borsa di studio** scholarship; **borsa merci** commodity exchange; **borsa nera** black market; **borsa valori** stock exchange; **essere di borsa larga** to be generous; **o la borsa o la vita!** your money or your life!; **pagare di borsa propria** to pay out of one's own pocket

borsaiòlo m pickpocket

borsanéra f black market

borsaneri·sta mf (-sti -ste) black marketeer

borseggiare §290 (**borséggio**) tr to pick the pocket of; to rob

borseggia·tóre -trice mf pickpocket

borség·gio m (-gi) theft

borsellino m purse

borsétta f handbag, pocketbook

borsétto m man's purse

borsi·sta mf (-sti -ste) recipient of a scholarship; stockbroker

borsisti·co -ca adj (-ci -che) stock-exchange

borsite f bursitis

boscàglia f thicket, underbrush

boscaiòlo m woodcutter

boscheréc·cio -cia adj (-ci -ce) wood, woodland; rustic; pastoral

boschétto m coppice, copse

boschi·vo -va adj wooded, wood

bò·sco m (-schi) woods, forest; **bosco ceduo** or **da taglio** tree farm

boscó·so -sa [s] adj wooded, woody

bòsforo m (lit) straits ‖ **Bosforo** m Bosphorus

bòsso m boxwood

bòssolo m box; cartridge case

botàni·co -ca (-ci -che) adj botanic(al) ‖ m botanist ‖ f botany

bòtola f trap door

bòtolo m small snarling dog

bòtta f hit; bump; rumble (e.g., of an explosion); thrust, lunging (in fencing); (fig) disaster; **botta dritta** (fencing) lunge; **botta e risposta** give-and-take; **botte da orbi** severe beating

bot·tàio m (-tài) cooper

bótte f barrel, cask, casket

botté·ga f (-ghe) store, shop; **chiudere bottega** to close up shop

botte·gàio -gàia (-gài -gàie) adj store, shop ‖ mf storekeeper, shopkeeper

botteghino m box office; lottery agency

bottíglia f bottle; **bottiglia Molotov** Molotov cocktail

bottiglierìa f wine store, liquor store

bottino m booty, spoil; capture; cesspool; sewage

bòtto m hit, bump; explosion; noise; toll (of bell); **di botto** all of a sudden

bottoncino m small button; cuff button; **bottoncino di rosa** rosebud

bottóne m button; stud; bud; **attaccare un bottone a** (fig) to buttonhole; **botton d'oro** (bot) buttercup; **bottone automatico** snap; **bottone della**

luce (elec) pushbutton; **bottoni gemelli** cuff links; **bottoni gustativi**
taste buds
bottonièra f row of buttons; buttonhole; (elec) panel (with buttons)
bova·ro -ra adj & m var of **boaro**
bovile m ox stable
bovi·no -na adj cattle, cow; bovine ||
m bovine
box m (box) locker (e.g., in a station);
box stall (for a horse); pit (in auto
racing); garage (on the ground floor
of a split-level); play pen
boxare (bòxo) intr to box
boxe f boxing
bòzza f stud, boss; bump (caused by
blow); rough copy, draft; **bozze** (typ)
galleys, galley proof
bozzèllo m (mach) block and tackle
bozzétto m sketch
bòzzolo m cocoon; lump (of flour)
bra·ca f (-che) safety belt; (naut) sling;
brache (archaic) breeches; (joc)
trousers
braccare §197 tr to stalk; to hunt out
braccétto—a braccetto arm in arm
bracciale m armlet, armband; arm rest
braccialétto m bracelet
bracciante m laborer
bracciata f armful; stroke (in swimming); **bracciata a rana** breaststroke;
bracciata sul dorso backstroke
bràc·cio m (-cia fpl) arm (of body);
unit of length (about 60 centimeters);
a braccia aperte with open arms;
avere le braccia legate to have one's
hands tied; **braccia** laborers; **braccio
destro** right-hand man; **braccio di
ferro** Indian wrestling; **fare a braccio
di ferro** to play at Indian wrestling;
sentirsi cascare le braccia to lose
courage || m (-ci) arm (e.g., of sea,
chair, lamp, etc.); beam (of balance);
braccio diretto cutoff (of river)
bracciòlo m arm; arm rest; banister
brac·co m (-chi) hound, beagle
bracconàg·gio m (-gi) poaching
bracconière m poacher
brace f embers; (coll) charcoal; **farsi
di brace** to blush
brachétta f flap (of trousers); (bb) joint;
brachette shorts
brachière m truss (for hernia)
bracière m brazier
braciòla f chop, cutlet
bra·do -da adj wild, untamed
bra·go m (-ghi) (lit) mud, slime
brama f ardent desire; covetousness;
longing
bramare tr to desire intensely; to covet;
to long for
bramino m Brahmin
bramire §176 intr to roar; to bell (said
of a deer)
bramito m bell (of deer)
bramosìa [s] f covetousness; greed
bramó·so -sa [s] adj (lit) covetous,
greedy
bran·ca f (-che) branch (of tree); flight
(of stairs); **branche** (poet) clutches
brànchia f gill
brancicare §197 (bràncico) tr to finger,
handle || intr to grope

bran·co m (-chi) flock, herd; (pej)
crowd
brancolare (bràncolo) intr to grope
branda f cot
brandèllo m tatter, shred
brandire §176 tr to brandish
brando m (lit) sword
brano m shred, bit; excerpt; **cadere a
brani** to fall apart; **fare a brani** to
tear apart
brasare tr to braze (to solder with
brass); (culin) to braise
brasile m brazil (nut) || **il Brasile**
Brazil
brasilià·no -na adj & mf Brazilian
bravàc·cio m (-ci) braggart, swaggerer
bravare tr to challenge; to threaten ||
intr to brag
bravata f swagger, bluster; boast; stunt
bra·vo -va adj good, able; honest; good-
hearted; brave; **alla brava** rapidly;
bravo ragazzo good boy; **fare il bravo**
to boast, be a braggart || m mer-
cenary soldier; bravo, hired assassin
|| **bravo!** interj well done!, bravo!
bravura f ability; bravery; bravura
brèc·cia f (-ce) breach, gap; crushed
stone
brefotrò·fio m (-fi) foundling hospital
Bretagna, la Britanny
bretèlla f suspenders; strap, shoulder
strap
bretóne adj Breton; Arthurian
brève adj brief, short; **in breve** in a nut-
shell; **per farla breve** in short || m
(eccl) brief || adv (lit) in short
brevettare (brevétto) tr to patent
brevétto m patent; (aer) license; (obs)
commission
brevià·rio m (-ri) compendium; handbook, vade mecum; (eccl) breviary
brevi·tà f (-tà) brevity
brézza [ddzz] f breeze
brezzare (brézzo) [ddzz] tr to winnow
|| intr to blow gently
bricchétta f briquet
bric·co m (-chi) kettle, pot
bricconata f rascality
briccó·ne -na mf rascal
bricconerìa f rascality
briciola f crumb; **ridurre in briciole** to
crumb, crumble
briciolo m bit, fragment; (fig) least bit;
andare in bricioli to crumble; **mandare in bricioli** to crumble
bri·ga f (-ghe) worry, trouble, **attaccar
briga** to pick a fight; **darsi la briga di**
to worry about; **trovarsi in una briga**
to be in trouble
brigadière m noncommissioned officer
(in carabinieri); (hist) brigadier
brigantàg·gio m (-gi) brigandage
brigante m brigand
brigantino m (naut) brig, brigantine;
brigantino goletta (naut) brigantine
brigare §209 tr to plot; to scheme to get
|| intr to plot, scheme
brigata f company; (mil) brigade
brì·glia f (-glie) bridle; harness (for
holding baby); (naut) bobstay; **a
briglia sciolta** at full speed; **tirare le
briglie** to bridle
brillante adj brilliant || m cut diamond

brillare *tr* to husk, hull (*rice*); to explode (*e.g., a mine*) || *intr* to shine, sparkle; **far brillare** to explode, blow up

brillì·o *m* (**-i**) shine, sparkle

bríl·lo -la *adj* tipsy

brína *f* frost

brinare *intr* to frost; to turn (*e.g., hair*) gray || *impers* (ESSERE) **è brinato** there was frost; **brina** there is frost

brinata *f* frost

brindare *intr* to toast; **brindare alla salute di** to toast

bríndisi *m* (**-si**) toast; pledge; **fare un bríndisi a** to toast

brì·o *m* (**-i**) sprightliness, liveliness, verve, spirit

briò·scia *f* (**-sce**) brioche

briò·so -sa [s] *adj* sprightly, lively

brìscola *f* briscola (*game*); trump (*card*)

britànni·co -ca *adj* (**-ci -che**) British, Britannic

britàn·no -na *adj* British || *mf* Briton

brìvido *m* shake, shiver; thrill; **brivido di freddo** chill, shiver

brizzolà·to -ta *adj* grizzled

bròc·ca *f* (**-che**) pitcher; pitcherful; shoot, bud; hobnail

broccatèllo *m* brocatel

broccato *m* brocade

bròc·co *m* (**-chi**) twig; shoot; center pin (*of shield or target*); (coll) nag; **dar nel brocco** to hit the bull's eye

bròccolo *m* (bot) broccoli; **broccoli** broccoli (*as food*)

bròda *f* slop, thin or tasteless soup; mud

brodàglia *f* slop

brodétto *m* fish soup

bròdo *m* broth; **andar in brodo di giuggiole** (fig) to swoon with joy; **brodo in dadi** cube bouillon; **brodo ristretto** consommé

brodó·so -sa [s] *adj* thin, watery (*soup*)

brogliàc·cio *m* (**-ci**) (com) daybook, first draft; (naut) first draft of logbook

bròglio *m* (**-gli**) plot, intrigue; maneuver; **broglio elettorale** political maneuver

bròlo *m* (archaic) garden; (lit) garland

bromìdri·co -ca *adj* (**-ci -che**) hydrobromic

bròmo *m* bromine

bromuro *m* bromide

bronchite *f* bronchitis

brón·cio *m* (**-ci**) pout, pouting; **fare il broncio** to sulk; **tenere il broncio a** to harbor a grudge against

brón·co *m* (**-chi**) bronchial tube; thorny branch; ramification (*of antlers*)

brontolare (**bróntolo**) *tr* to grumble (*to express with a grumble*) || *intr* to grumble at || *intr* to grumble, mutter; to rumble; to gurgle (*said of water*)

brontolì·o *m* (**-i**) grumble, mutter; rumble; gurgle

brontolì·ne -na *mf* grumbler; curmudgeon

bronzare [dz] (**brónzo**) *tr* to bronze

brónze·o -a [dz] *adj* bronze; tanned

bronzina [dz] *f* little bell; (mach) bearing; (mach) bushing

brónzo [dz] *m* bronze

brossura *f* brochure; **in brossura** paperback

brucare §197 *tr* to browse, graze

bruciacchiare §287 *tr* to singe

bruciante *adj* burning

bruciapélo *m*—**a bruciapelo** point-blank

bruciare §128 *tr* to burn; to burn down; to singe; to scorch; to cauterize (*a wound*); (sports) to overcome with a burst of speed; **bruciare le tappe** to go straight ahead; to press on || *intr* (ESSERE) to burn; to smart, sting || *ref* to burn (*e.g., one's fingers*); to get burnt; to blow (*one's brains*) out; to burn out (*said of an electric light or fuse*); **bruciarsi i vascelli alle spalle** to burn one's bridges behind one

bruciatìc·cio *m* (**-ci**) burnt material; **sapere di bruciaticcio** to taste burnt

bracia·to -ta *adj* burnt; burnt out || *m* burnt taste or smell || *f* roast chestnut

bruciatóre *m* burner; heater; **bruciatore a gas** gas burner; **bruciatore a nafta** oil burner

bruciatorì·sta *m* (**-sti**) oil burner mechanic

bruciatura *f* burn

bruciôre *m* burning; burn; inflammation; **bruciore agli occhi** eye inflammation; **bruciore di stomaco** heartburn

bru·co *m* (**-chi**) caterpillar; worm

brùffolo *m* (coll) small boil

brughièra *f* waste land; heath

brulicare §197 (**brùlico**) *intr* to crawl; to swarm (*e.g., with bees*); to teem (*with people*)

brulichì·o *m* (**-i**) crawling; swarming; teeming

brúl·lo -la *adj* barren, bare

bruma *f* shipworm; (lit) fog; (lit) winter

bruna·stro -stra *adj* brownish

brunire §176 *tr* to burnish

brú·no -na *adj* brown; dark (*bread, complexion*) || *m* brown; dark; brunet; **vestire a bruno** to dress in black || *f* brunette

brú·sca *f* (**-sche**) horse brush; **con le brusche** curtly

bruschézza *f* brusqueness

bruschino *m* scrub brush

brú·sco -sca (**-schi -sche**) *adj* sour; curt, gruff; sharp (*weather*); dangerous; sudden || *m* twig || *f see* **brusca**

brùscolo *m* speck, mote; **fare di un bruscolo una trave** to make a mountain out of a molehill

brusì·o *m* (**-i**) buzz, buzzing; (fig) whispering (*gossip*)

brutale *adj* brutal

brutali·tà *f* (**-tà**) brutality

brutalizzare [ddzz] *tr* to brutalize

bru·to -ta *adj & m* brute

brutta *f* rough copy

bruttare *tr* (lit) to soil

bruttézza *f* ugliness; (fig) lowliness

brút·to -ta *adj* ugly, homely; foul (*weather*); bad (*news*); **alle brutte** at the worst; **con le brutte** harshly; **farla brutta a** to play a mean trick on;

guardare **brutto** to look irritated; **vedersela brutta** to foresee trouble || *m* worst; bad weather || *f* see **brutta**

bruttura *f* ugliness

bùbbola *f* lie; trifle

bùbbolo *m* jingle bell (*on horse*)

bubbòni·co -ca *adj* (**-ci -che**) bubonic

bu·ca *f* (**-che**) hole; pit; hollow; **buca cieca** trap (*for hunting*); **buca del biliardo** pocket; **buca delle lettere** mailbox; **buca del suggeritore** prompter's box; **buca sepolcrale** grave

bucané·ve *m* (**-ve**) snowdrop

bucanière *m* buccaneer

bucare §197 *tr* to pierce; to prick; to puncture (*a tire*)

bucato *m* wash; laundry; **di bucato** freshly laundered; **fare il bucato in famiglia** (fig) to not air one's family affairs, to not wash one's dirty linen in public

bucatura *f* piercing; puncturing; puncture; **bucatura di una gomma** flat tire

bùc·cia *f* (**-ce**) rind, peel; skin (*of a person; of fruit and vegetables*); tender bark; **fare le bucce a** (coll) to thwart, frustrate

bucherellare (**bucherèllo**) *tr* to riddle

bu·co *m* (**-chi**) hole; **fare un buco nell'acqua** to fail miserably

bucòli·co -ca *adj* (**-ci -che**) bucolic, pastoral

Budda *m* Buddha

buddismo *m* Buddhism

buddi·sta *mf* (**-sti -ste**) Buddhist

budèl·lo *m* (**-la** *fpl*) bowel; **budella** bowels; guts || *m* (**-li**) casing (*for salami*); pipe; blind alley

budino *m* pudding

bùe *m* (**buòi**) ox (*for draft*); steer (*for meat*); **bue muschiato** musk ox

bùfalo *m* buffalo

bufèra *f* storm; **bufera di neve** snowstorm; **bufera di pioggia** rainstorm; **bufera di vento** windstorm

buffa *f* cowl; gust of wind; (archaic) trick, jest

buffare *tr* to huff (*at checkers*) || *intr* to joke; (archaic) to blow

buffettería *f* (mil) accouterments

buffétto *m* tap, slight blow

buf·fo -fa *adj* funny, comical || *m* gust of wind; comic || *f* see **buffa**

buffonata *f* buffoonery; antics

buffóne *m* buffoon, clown; (hist) jester; **buffone di corte** court jester

buffonería *f* buffoonery

buffoné·sco -sca *adj* (**-schi -sche**) clownish

bugìa *f* lie; candlestick; **bugia ufficiosa** white lie

bugiar·do -da *adj* lying, false || *mf* liar

bugigàttolo *m* cubbyhole

bugna *f* ashlar; (naut) clew

bugnato *m* ashlar; (archit) boss

bù·io -ia (*pl* **-i -ie**) *adj* dark || *m* darkness; **buio pesto** pitch dark

bulbo *m* bulb

bùlga·ro -ra *adj & mf* Bulgarian || *m* Russian leather

bulinare *tr* to engrave

bulino *m* burin

bullétta *f* tack

bullonare (**bullóno**) *tr* to bolt

bullóne *m* bolt

buon *adj* apocopated form of **buono**, used before masculine singular nouns except those beginning with impure s, z, gn, ps, and x

buon' *adj* apocopated form of **buona** used before feminine singular nouns beginning with a vowel, e.g., **buon'ora**

buonagràzia *f* (**buonegràzie**) courtesy, good manners; **con Sua buonagrazia** with your permission

buonamano *f* (**buonemani**) tip, gratuity

buonànima *f* departed; **la buonanima di** the late lamented

buonavò·glia *m* (**-glia**) intern (*in a hospital*); (coll) lazybones || *f* good will

buoncostume *m* morals

buongu·stàio *m* (**-stài**) gourmet; connoisseur

buò·no -na *adj* good; kind; high (*society*); cheap (*price*); **alla buona** plainly; without ceremony; **buono a nulla** good-for-nothing; **con le buone** kindly, gently; **che Dio la mandi buona** a may God be kind with; **essere in buona con** to be on good terms with || *m* good person; bond; ticket; **buono a nulla** ne'er-do-well; **buono del tesoro** government bond; **buono di consegna** delivery order; **buono premio** trading stamp

buonsènso *m* common sense

buontempó·ne -na *adj* jolly || *m* playboy || *f* fun-loving girl; playgirl

buonumóre *m* good humor, good cheer

buonuscita *f* indemnity, bonus; severance pay

burattare *tr* to sift

buratti·nàio *m* (**-nài**) puppeteer; puppet maker

burattinata *f* clowning

burattino *m* puppet

burato *m* sifter, sifting machine

burbanza *f* haughtiness, arrogance

burbanzó·so -sa [s] *adj* haughty, arrogant

bùrbe·ro -ra *adj* gruff, surly

bùr·chio *m* (**-chi**) (naut) lighter

burgun·do -da *adj & mf* Burgundian

burla *f* joke, jest; prank; **mettere in burla** to ridicule; **fuori di burla** joking aside

burlare *tr* to ridicule || *intr* to be joking || *ref*—**burlarsi di** to make fun of

burlé·sco -sca (**-schi -sche**) *adj* funny; mocking; burlesque; jocose || *m* burlesque; mock-heroic

burletta *f* joke, jest; **mettere in burletta** to ridicule

burló·ne -na *mf* joker, jester

burócrate *m* bureaucrat

burocràti·co -ca *adj* (**-ci -che**) bureaucratic; clerical (*error*)

burocrazìa *f* bureaucracy; red tape

burra·sca *f* (**-sche**) storm

burrascó·so -sa [s] *adj* stormy

burrièra *f* butter dish

burrifi·cio *m* (**-ci**) butter factory; dairy

burro *m* butter

burróne *m* canyon, ravine

burró·so -sa [s] *adj* buttery

buscare §197 *tr* to get; to catch || *intr* to be damaged || *ref*—**buscarsi un malanno** to catch a cold

busécchia *f* casing (*for sausage*)

busìllis *m*—**qui sta il busillis** here's the rub, that's the trouble

bussa *f* hit, blow; **venire alle busse** to come to blows

bussare *intr* to knock; **bussare a quat-trini** (fig) to hit somebody for a loan

bussata *f* knock (*at the door*)

bussa-tòio *m* (-tòi) knocker

bùssola *f* sedan chair; door; revolving door; swinging door; ballot box; (mach) bushing; (aer & naut) com-pass; **perdere la bussola** to lose one's bearings

bussolòtto *m* dice box

busta *f* envelope; briefcase; **busta a finestrella** window envelope; **busta primo giorno** first-day cover; **in busta a parte** under separate cover

bustapa-ga *f* (-ga) pay envelope

bustarèlla *f* bribery; kickback

bustina *f* powder, dose; small envelope; (mil) cap, fatigue cap

busto *m* chest, trunk; bust; corset

butirró-so -sa [s] *adj* buttery

buttafuò-ri *m* (-ri) bouncer (*in a night club*); (theat) callboy; (naut) out-rigger

buttare *tr* to throw; to waste (*e.g., time*); to give off (*e.g., smoke*); **buttar giù** to demolish; to swallow; (fig) to discredit; to jot down; **buttar via** to throw away; to cast aside || *intr* to secrete, ooze || *ref* to throw oneself; to let oneself fall; **buttarsi giù** (fig) to become downcast

butterare (bùttero) *tr* to pock, pit

bùttero *m* pockmark; cowboy

buzzo [ddzz] *m* (vulg) belly; **di buzzo buono** with energy; willingly

C

C, c [t/i] *m & f* third letter of the Italian alphabet

càbala *f* cabala; cabal, intrigue

cabina *f* cabin, stateroom; car, cage (*of elevator*); cockpit (*of airplane*); booth (*of telephone*); cab (*of loco-motive*)

cablàg-gio *m* (-gi) (elec) cable (*in auto or radio*)

cablare *tr* to cable

cablografare (cablògrafo) *tr* to cable

cablogram-ma *m* (-mi) cablegram, cable

cabotàg-gio *m* (-gi) coasting trade, coastal traffic

cabrare *intr* to zoom

cabrata *f* zoom

cacào *m* cocoa

cacasènno *m* (slang) wiseacre

cacatò-a *m* (-a) cockatoo

càc-cia *m* (-cia) pursuit plane, fighter; (nav) destroyer || *f* chase, hunt; pur-suit; **caccia alle streghe** witch hunt

cacciagióne *f* small game; venison; kill (*e.g., of game birds*)

cacciapiè-tre *m* (-tre) (rr) cowcatcher

cacciare §128 *tr* to hunt; to chase; to rout; to send out; to stick, thrust; to utter (*e.g., a cry*); **cacciar fuori** to pull out; **cacciar via** to chase away || *ref* to hide; to intrude; to get; to wind up; to thrust oneself; **cacciarsi negli affari di** to butt into the affairs of

cacciasommergìbi-li *m* (-li) subchaser, submarine chaser

cacciata *f* hunting party; expulsion

cacciatóra *f* hunting jacket; **alla caccia-tora** (culin) stewed with herbs

cacciatóre *m* hunter; (aer) fighter pilot; **cacciatore di frodo** poacher; **caccia-tore di teste** headhunter

cacciatorpediniè-re *m* (-re) destroyer

cacciatrice *f* huntress

cacciavì-te *m* (-te) screwdriver

càccola *f* gum (*on edge of eyelid*); (slang) snot

caccoló-so -sa [s] *adj* gummy (*eyelid*); (slang) snotty

ca-chi (-chi) *adj* khaki || *m* Japanese persimmon; khaki

cacìc-co *m* (-chi) Indian chief; boss (*in Latin America*)

cà-cio *m* (-ci) cheese; **come il cacio sui maccheroni** (coll) at the right mo-ment

cacofóni-co -ca *adj* (-ci -che) cacoph-onous

cac-tus *m* (-tus) cactus

cadau-no -na *adj* each || *pron* each one

cadàvere *m* corpse, cadaver

cadavèri-co -ca *adj* (-ci -che) cadaver-ous

cadènte *adj* falling (*star*); rickety (*house*); run-down, decrepit (*person*)

cadènza *f* cadence, rhythm; accent (*peculiar to a region*)

cadére §121 *intr* (ESSERE) to fall; to sink; to slough (*said, e.g., of crust*); to fail; (gram) to end; **cadere a pro-posito** to come in handy; to come at the right moment; **cadere dalle nuvole** to be dumfounded

cadétto *m* cadet

càdmio *m* cadmium

caducità *f* transiency, brevity

cadu-co -ca *adj* (-ci -che) fleeting; de-ciduous

cadu-no -na *adj & pron* var of **cadauno**

cadu-to -ta *adj* fallen; lost, gone astray; **i caduti** the fallen, the dead || *f* fall; crash (*of stock market*); slump (*of prices*)

caf-fè *m* (-fè) coffee; café

caffeina *f* caffeine

caffetteria *f* cafeteria

caffettièra *f* coffeepot

cafó·ne -na adj loud, gaudy ‖ m boor, lout

cagionare (cagióno) tr to cause, produce

cagióne f cause, reason; **a cagione di** because of

cagionévole adj sickly, delicate

cagliare §280 tr, intr (ESSERE) & ref to curdle, curd

cagliata f curd

cà·glio m (-gli) rennet

cagna f bitch

cagnara f barking (of dogs); uproar, confusion

cagné·sco -sca (-schi -sche) adj dog-like, doggish ‖ m—**guardare in cagnesco** to look askance at; **stare in cagnesco con** to be angry with

Caino m Cain

Càiro, il Cairo

cala f cove; (naut) hold

calabrése [s] adj & mf Calabrian

calabróne m hornet

calafatare tr (naut) to caulk

cala·màio m (-mài) inkwell

calamaro m squid

calamita f magnet; (mineral) loadstone; (fig) magnet, attraction

calami·tà f (-tà) calamity, disaster

calamitare tr to magnetize

calamitó·so -sa [s] adj calamitous

càlamo m reed, quill

calandra f calender; (aut) grille

calandrare tr to calender

calante adj waning (moon)

calàp·pio m (-pi) snare; noose

calapran·zi m (-zi) dumbwaiter

calare tr to lower; to strike (sails) ‖ intr (ESSERE) to fall, sag (said, e.g., of prices); to grow shorter (said of days); to come down; to shrink (said, e.g., of meat); to lose weight; to set (said, e.g., of the sun); to wane (said of the moon); (mus) to drop in pitch ‖ ref to let oneself down; to dive

calata f lowering; descent; invasion; fall; wharf; (coll) intonation; **calata del sole** sunset

cal·ca f (-che) crowd, throng

calca·gno m (-gni) heel ‖ m (-gna fpl) (fig) heel; **alle calcagna di** at the heels of

calcare m limestone ‖ §197 tr to trample; to trace (on paper); to tread (the boards); to emphasize; **calcare la mano** to exaggerate; **calcare le orme di** to follow in the footsteps of

calce m—**in calce** at the foot of the page; **in calce a** at the foot of ‖ f lime; **calce viva** quicklime

calcedònio m chalcedony

calcestruzzo m concrete

calciare §128 tr & intr to kick

calciatóre m soccer player; football player

calcificare §197 (calcìfico) tr & ref to calcify

calcificazióne f calcification

calcina f mortar; lime

calcinàc·cio m (-ci) flake of plaster; **calcinacci** ruins, rubble

calci·nàio m (-nài) lime pit

calcinare tr to calcine; to lime (e.g., a field)

càl·cio m (-ci) kick; soccer; calcium; (e.g., of rifle) butt; **calcio d'inizio** (sports) kickoff

calciocianamide m calcium cyanamide

cal·co m (-chi) tracing; cast; imprint

calcografia f copper engraving

calcolare (càlcolo) tr to calculate; to estimate, reckon; to compute; to consider

calcola·tóre -trice adj calculating ‖ m calculator; computer; schemer ‖ f calculating machine, adding machine

càlcolo m calculation; estimate; planning; calculus; (pathol) calculus, stone; **calcolo biliare** gallstone; **calcolo errato** miscalculation; **fare calcolo su** to count upon

calcolò·si f (-si) (pathol) stones

calcomanìa f decalcomania

caldàia f boiler

cal·dàio m (-dài) cauldron, boiler

caldalléssa f boiled chestnut

caldana f flush

caldano m brazier

caldarròsta f roast chestnut

caldeggiare §290 (caldéggio) tr to favor, support; to recommend

calde·ràio m (-rài) coppersmith; boilermaker

calderóne m cauldron

cal·do -da adj warm; hot; rich (voice); caldo, **caldo** quite recent ‖ m heat; warmth; **aver caldo** to be warm (said of people); to be hot (said of people); **fa caldo** it is warm; it is hot; **non mi fa nè caldo nè freddo** it leaves me cold, it does not move me

calefazióne f heating

caleidoscò·pio m (-pi) kaleidoscope

calendà·rio m (-ri) calendar

calènde fpl—**calende greche** Greek calends

calendimàggio m May Day

calèsse m buggy, gig

calére impers—**non mi cale** (lit) I don't care

calettare (calétto) tr to dovetail, mortise ‖ intr to fit

calibrare (càlibro) tr to gauge, calibrate

càlibro m caliber; (mach) calipers; (fig) quality, importance

càlice m wine cup; (bot) calyx; (eccl) chalice

cali·cò m (-cò) calico

califfo m caliph

caligine f fog, mist; (fig) darkness

caliginó·so -sa [s] adj foggy, misty; (fig) dark, gloomy

calla f—**calla dei fioristi** calla lily

calle f lane, alley

callìfu·go m (-ghi) corn remedy

calligrafia f penmanship; handwriting

calli·sta mf (-sti -ste) chiropodist

callo m corn; callus; **fare il callo a** to get used to; **pestare i calli a qlcu** to step on s.o.'s feet

callosi·tà [s] f (-tà) callosity; callus

calló·so -sa [s] adj corny; callous; hard

calma f calm, tranquillity

calmante *adj* sedative, calming, soothing ‖ *m* sedative

calmare *tr* to calm, soothe, appease ‖ *ref* to calm down; to subside, abate

calmierare (calmièro) *tr* to fix the price of

calmière *m* ceiling price; price control

cal·mo -ma *adj* calm, quiet, still ‖ *f see* **calma**

calo *m* decrease; shrinkage

calomelano *m* calomel

calóre *m* heat; warmth; fervor, ardor; (pathol) rash, inflammation; (vet) rut, mating season

caloria *f* calorie

calòri·co -ca *adj* (**-ci -che**) caloric

calorifero *m* heater, radiator

caloró·so -sa [s] *adj* warm; hot; cordial; heated

calò·scia *f* (**-sce**) var of **galoscia**

calòtta *f* skullcap; case (*e.g., of watch*); (aut) hubcap; (mach) cap; **calotta cranica** skull

calpestare (calpésto) *tr* to trample

calpestí·o *m* (**-í**) trampling

calúgine *f* down (*of bird*)

calùnnia *f* calumny, slander

calunniare §287 *tr* to calumniate, slander

calunnia·tóre -trice *mf* slanderer

calunnió·so -sa [s] *adj* slanderous

Calvàrio *m* (Bib) Calvary

calvìzie *f* baldness

cal·vo -va *adj* bald

calza *f* sock; stocking; wick; **calza di donna** stocking; **calze** hose, hosiery; **fare la calza** to knit

calzamàglia *f* tights

calzare *m* footwear ‖ *tr* to wear, put on (*shoes, gloves, or socks*) ‖ *intr* to fit (*said of any garment*); to suit

calzascar·pe *m* (**-pe**) shoehorn

calza·tóio *m* (**-tói**) shoehorn

calzatura *f* footwear; **calzature** footwear

calzaturière *m* shoe manufacturer

calzaturiè·ro -ra *adj* shoe (*e.g., industry*) ‖ *m* shoe worker

calzaturifì·cio *m* (**-ci**) shoe factory

calzeròtto *m* woolen sock

calzet·tàio *m* (**-tài**) hosier

calzettóne *m* knee-high woolen sock (*for mountain boots*)

calzifì·cio *m* (**-ci**) hosiery mill

calzino *m* sock; **calzini corti** socks; half hose; **calzini lunghi** knee-high socks

calzo·làio *m* (**-lài**) shoemaker; cobbler

calzolería *f* shoemaker's shop; shoe store

calzoncini *mpl* shorts

calzóne *m* trouser leg; **calzoni** trousers, pants; slacks; **calzoni a zampe d'elefante** bell-bottom trousers, flares

camaleònte *m* chameleon

camarilla *f* cabal, clique

cambiadí·schi *m* (**-schi**) record changer

cambiale *f* promissory note, IOU

cambiaménto *m* change, modification

cambiare §287 *tr* to change, exchange; to shift (*gears*) ‖ *intr* to change, switch ‖ *ref* to change (*clothing*); **cambiarsi in** to turn into

cambiavalu·te *m* (**-te**) moneychanger

càm·bio *m* (**-bi**) change; switch; rate of exchange; (mil) relief; **cambio a cloche** shift lever, stick; **cambio di velocità** gearshift; **in cambio di** in exchange for, in place of

cambrètta *f* staple (*to hold a wire*)

cam·brì *m* (**-brì**) cambric

cambusa *f* (naut) galley

cambusière *m* steward

càmera *f* room; bedroom; chamber; **camera ardente** funeral parlor; **Camera dei comuni** House of Commons; **Camera dei deputati** House of Representatives; **camera d'aria** inner tube; **camera di sicurezza** detention cell; vault (*of bank*)

camera·ta *m* (**-ti**) friend, comrade ‖ *f* dormitory; barracks; roomful (*of students or soldiers*)

cameratismo *m* comradeship

camerièra *f* waitress; maid, chambermaid

camerière *m* waiter; steward; valet

camerino *m* small room; toilet, lavatory; (nav) noncommissioned officer's quarters; (theat) dressing room

càmice *m* gown (*of physician*); smock (*of painter*); (eccl) alb

camicería *f* shirt store; shirt factory

camicétta *f* blouse

camìcia *f* shirt; casing, jacket (*e.g., of boiler*); lining (*e.g., of furnace*); vest (*of sailor*); folder; **camicia da giorno** chemise; **camicia da notte** nightgown; **camicia di forza** strait jacket; **camicia di maglia** coat of mail; **camicia nera** black shirt (*Fascist*); **camicia rossa** red shirt (*Garibaldine*); **dare la camicia** to give the shirt off one's back; **essere nato con la camicia** to be born with a silver spoon in one's mouth; **perdere la camicia** to lose one's shirt

cami·ciàio -ciàia *mf* (**-ciài -ciàie**) shirtmaker, haberdasher

camiciòla *f* sport shirt; undershirt; T-shirt; (obs) vest

camiciòtto *m* smock (*of mechanic*); jumper; sport shirt

caminétto *m* small fireplace; fireplace

camino *m* fireplace; chimney, smokestack; shaft (*in mountain*); mouth (*of volcano*); (naut) funnel

cà·mion *m* (**-mion**) truck

camionale *f* highway

camioncino *m* small truck; panel truck; pickup truck

camionétta *f* small truck; van (*e.g., of police*)

camioni·sta *m* (**-sti**) truckdriver, teamster

camma *f* (mach) cam; (mach) wiper

cammellière *m* camel driver

cammèllo *m* camel

cammèo *m* cameo

camminaménto *m* (mil) communication trench

camminare *intr* to walk; to go, run

camminata *f* walk; gait; (obs) hall with fireplace

cammina·tóre -trice *mf* walker; runner

cammino *m* road, way, route; path (*e.g., of the moon*); course; journey; **cammin facendo** on the way; **cammino battuto** beaten path; **cammino coperto** (mil) covered way; **mettersi in cammino** to set out, start out

camomilla *f* camomile

camòrra *f* underworld

camò·scio *m* (**-sci**) chamois

campagna *f* country; countryside; country property; season (*for harvesting*); campaign; **andare in campagna** to go on vacation (in the country)

campagnò·lo -la *adj* country, rural || *mf* peasant

campale *adj* field (*artillery*); pitched, decisive (*battle*)

campana *f* bell; bell glass, bell jar; lamp shade; (archit) bell; **a campana** bell-bottomed; **campana a martello** alarm bell, tocsin; **campana di vetro** bell glass; **campana pneumatica** caisson

campanàc·cio *m* (**-ci**) cowbell

campanaro *m* bell ringer; (archaic) bell founder

campanèlla *f* small bell; door knocker; curtain ring; (bot) bluebell

campanèllo *m* bell; small bell; doorbell, chimes; **campanello d'allarme** alarm bell

campanile *m* steeple, belfry; native city or town

campanilismo *m* parochialism

campano *m* cowbell

campare *tr* to keep alive; to save; to bring out the details of || *intr* (ESSERE) to live; to survive; **si campa** one ekes out a living

campa·to -ta *adj*—**campato in aria** without any foundation || *f* span

campeggiare §290 (**campéggio**) *intr* to camp, encamp; to stand out

campeggia·tóre -trice *mf* camper

campég·gio *m* (**-gi**) camping, outing; campground; (bot) logwood

campeggi·sta *mf* (**-sti -ste**) camper

campèstre *adj* field, country; (sports) cross-country

campidò·glio *m* (**-gli**) capitol || **Campidoglio** *m* Capitoline (*hill*); Capitol (*temple*)

campionare (**campióno**) *tr* to sample

campionà·rio -ria (**-ri -rie**) *adj* of samples; trade (*exposition*) || *m* sample book, catalogue, pattern book

campionato *m* championship, title

campióne *m* champion; sample; specimen; standard; **campione senza valore** uninsured parcel, sample post

campionéssa *f* championess

campionissimo *m* world champion, ace

campo *m* field; camp; ground; tennis court; golf course; center (*e.g., for refugees*); **campo addestramento** training camp; **campo d'aviazione** airfield, airport; **campo di battaglia** battlefield; **campo petrolifero** oil field; **lasciare il campo** to retreat; **mettere in campo** to bring up, adduce; **piantare il campo** to pitch camp

camposanto *m* cemetery, churchyard

camuffare *tr* to disguise, mask; to camouflage || *ref* to disguise oneself

camu·so -sa *adj* snub-nosed

Canadà, il Canada

canadése [s] *adj & mf* Canadian

canàglia *f* scoundrel; rabble

canagliata *f* knavery, mean trick

canale *m* canal; irrigation ditch; network (*of communications*); pipe, drain; (anat) duct, tract; (rad, telv) channel; (theat) aisle; **Canale della Manica** English Channel; **Canale di Panama** Panama Canal; **Canale di Suez** Suez Canal

canalizzare [ddzz] *tr* to channel; to install pipes in; (elec) to wire

canalizzazióne [ddzz] *f* channeling; piping; ductwork; (elec) wiring

canalóne *m* ravine

cànapa *f* hemp

cana·pè *m* (**-pè**) sofa, couch; (culin) canapé

cànapo *m* rope, cable

Canàrie, le the Canaries

canarino *m* canary

cancàn *m* noise, racket

cancellare (**cancèllo**) *tr* to cancel, erase; to obliterate; to write off (*a debt*); to scratch (*a horse*) || *ref* to vanish, fade

cancellata *f* railing

cancellatura *f* erasure

cancellazióne *f* cancellation; erasure (*of a tape*)

cancelleria *f* chancellery; stationery

cancellière *m* chancellor; court clerk; registrar, recorder

cancèllo *m* gate, railing, grating

canceró·so -sa [s] *adj* cancerous || *mf* cancer victim

cànchero *m* trouble; troublesome person; (coll) cancer

cancrèna *f* gangrene; **andare in cancrena** to become gangrenous

cancrenó·so -sa [s] *adj* gangrenous

cancro *m* cancer; (bot) canker || **Cancro** *m* (astr) Cancer

candeggiante *adj* bleaching || *m* bleaching agent, bleach

candeggiare §290 (**candéggio**) *tr* to bleach

candeggina *f* bleach

candég·gio *m* (**-gi**) bleaching

candéla *f* candle; candlestick; candlepower; (aut) spark plug; **studiare a lume di candela** to burn the midnight oil; **tenere la candela a** to favor the love affair of

candelabro *m* candelabrum

candelière *m* candlestick

candelòra *f* Candlemas

candelòtto *m* big wax candle; **candelotto lacrimogeno** tear-gas canister

candida·to -ta *mf* candidate

candidatura *f* candidature, candidacy

càndi·do -da *adj* white; candid

candire §176 *tr* to candy

candi·to -ta *adj* candied || *m* candied fruit

candóre *m* whiteness; candor

cane *m* dog; hound; hammer, cock (*of gun*); ham actor; **cane barbone**

poodle; **cane bastardo** mongrel; **cane da ferma** setter; **cane da guardia** watchdog; **cane da presa** retriever; **cane da punta** pointer; **cane grosso** big shot; **cane guida per ciechi** seeing eye dog; **cane sciolto** (pol) lone wolf; **come un cane** all alone; **come un cane in chiesa** as an unwelcome guest; **da cani** poorly; **menare il can per l'aia** to beat around the bush; **non c'è un cane** there is nobody there; **raddrizzare le gambe ai cani** to perform an impossible task

canèstro m basket

cànfora f camphor

cangiante adj changeable (color); changing, iridescent

canguro m kangaroo

canìcola f dog days

canile m doghouse, kennel

canino adj canine ‖ m canine tooth

canìzie f gray hair; head of gray hair; old age

canna f cane, reed; rod (for fishing or measuring); pipe (of organ); barrel (of gun); **canna da zucchero** sugar cane; **canna di caduta** disposal chute; **canna fumaria** chimney; **canna della gola** (coll) windpipe

cannèlla f small tube; tap (of barrel); cinnamon

cannèllo m pipe, tube; stick (e.g., of licorice); (chem) pipette; **cannello ossiacetilenico** acetylene torch; **cannello ossidrico** oxyhydrogen blowpipe

cannellóni mpl cannelloni

cannéto m cane field

cannìbale m cannibal

cannìc·cio m (-ci) wicker frame; shade made out of rushes

cannocchiale m spyglass; **cannocchiale astronomico** telescope

cannonata f cannonade, cannon shot; (slang) hit

cannoncino m small gun; **cannoncino antiaereo** antiaircraft gun

cannóne m gun, cannon; pipe, stovepipe; box pleat; shin (of cattle); **è un cannone** (coll) he's the tops

cannoneggiare §290 (cannonéggio) tr to cannonade, shell

cannonièra f gunboat

cannonière m gunner, artilleryman; kicker (in soccer)

cannùc·cia f (-ce) reed; thin tube; stem (e.g., of pipe); straw (for drinking); (chem) pipette

canòa f canoe; launch

canòcchia f mantis shrimp

cànone m canon; rule; rent; fee, charge (for use of radio)

canonicato m canonry

canòni·co -ca (-ci -che) adj canonical, canon (law) ‖ m canon; priest ‖ f parsonage, rectory

canonizzare [ddzz] tr to canonize

canò·ro -ra adj song (bird); melodious

canottàg·gio m (-gi) boating, rowing

canottièra f undershirt, T-shirt; skimmer, boater

canottière m oarsman

canòtto m skiff, scull, shell

canovàc·cio m (-ci) dishcloth; embroidery cloth; plot (of novel or play)

cantàbile adj singable; songlike; cantabile ‖ m song

cantamban·co m (-chi) jongleur, wandering minstrel; mountebank

cantante adj singing, song ‖ mf singer

cantare m song; chant; laisse, epic strophe ‖ tr to sing; to chant ‖ intr to sing; to chant; (coll) to squeal

cantàride f Spanish fly

càntaro m urn

cantastò·rie mf (-rie) minstrel

canta·tóre -trice adj singing ‖ mf singer

cantau·tóre -trice mf singer composer

canterano m chest of drawers

canterellare (**canterèllo**) tr & intr to sing in a low voice, hum

canteri·no -na adj singing, warbling; decoy (bird) ‖ mf songster, singer

càntero m urinal

canticchiare §287 tr & intr to hum

cànti·co m (-ci) canticle

cantière m shipyard, dockyard; navy yard; undertaking, work in progress; **avere in cantiere** to have in hand, be working at; **cantiere edile** building site; builder's yard

cantilèna f singsong; **la stessa cantilena** the same old tune

cantimban·co m (-chi) var of **cantimbanco**

cantina f cellar; wine cellar; wine shop, canteen

cantinière m cellarman; butler; wineshop keeper; sommelier

canto m song, singing; chant; canto; crow (of rooster); chirping (of grasshopper); corner, edge; (mus) voice part; **canto del cigno** swan song; **dal canto mio** for my part; **d'altro canto** on the other hand; **da un canto** on the one hand

cantonata f corner (of street); **prendere una cantonata** to make a blunder

cantóne m corner (of room or building); canton

cantonièra f corner cupboard; (rr) section worker's house

cantonière m road laborer; (rr) section hand

cantóre m choir singer; cantor; (poet) singer

cantùc·cio m (-ci) nook, niche

canutézza f hoariness

canutìglia f gold thread

canu·to -ta adj gray-haired; whitehaired; (poet) white

canzonare (**canzóno**) tr to mock, ridicule

canzonatò·rio -ria adj (-ri -rie) mocking

canzonatura f mockery, gibe

canzóne f song; canzone

canzonétta f canzonet; popular song

canzonetti·sta mf (-sti -ste) singer (e.g., in a nightclub) ‖ m songster ‖ f songstress

canzonière m songbook; collection of poems; song writer

caolino m kaolin

caos m chaos
caòti·co -ca adj (-ci -che) caotic
capace adj capacious; capable, intelligent; legally qualified; capace di with a capacity of (e.g., fifty people); essere capace di to be able to; fare capace di to convince of
capaci·tà f (-tà) capacity; capability
capacitare (capàcito) tr to persuade || ref to become convinced
capanna f hut, cabin; thatched cottage; bathhouse
capannèllo m group, crowd
capanno m hunting box; cabana, bathhouse
capannóne m large shed; hangar
caparbiàggine f var of caparbietà
caparbie·tà f (-tà) obstinacy, stubborness
capàr·bio -bia adj (-bi -bie) stubborn, hard-headed
caparra f down payment, deposit; performance bond
capatina f short visit
capeggiare §290 (capéggio) tr to lead
capeggia·tóre -trice mf leader
capellini mpl small vermicelli
capéllo m hair; averne fin sopra i capelli to have one's fill; capelli hair; capelli a spazzola crew cut; c'è mancato un capello che + subj he came close to + ger; far rizzare i capelli a qlcu to make s.o.'s hair stand on end
capellóne m hippie, beatnik
capellu·to -ta adj hairy; long-haired
capelvènere m maidenhair
capèstro m halter; gallows
capezzale m bolster; (fig) bedside
capézzolo m nipple, teat; udder
capidò·glio m (-gli) var of capodoglio
capiènza f capacity (e.g., of bus)
capigliatura f head of hair
capillare adj capillary; (fig) far-reaching
capinéra f (orn) blackcap
capintè·sta m (-sti -ste) boss; (sports) head, leader
capire §176 tr to understand; capire a volo to grasp immediately || intr—non capire dalla contentezza to be bursting with joy || ref to understand each other; to agree
capitale adj capital; mortal (sin) || m capital; principal; capitale sociale capital stock || f capital (of country)
capitalismo m capitalism
capitali·sta mf (-sti -ste) capitalist
capitalisti·co -ca adj (-ci -che) capitalistic
capitalizzare [ddzz] tr to capitalize; to compound (interest)
capitana f flagship
capitanare tr to lead, captain
capitanerìa f (hist) captaincy; capitaneria di porto harbor-master's office; coast guard office; port authority's office
capitano m captain; skipper, master (of ship); commander (in air force); capitano di corvetta or capitano di fregata (nav) lieutenant commander;

capitano di gran cabotaggio master; capitano di lungo corso master; capitano di porto harbor master; capitano di vascello (nav) commander
capitare (càpito) intr (ESSERE) to arrive; to happen, occur; to happen to get, e.g., capitò a casa mia alle tre he happened to get to my house at three; capitare bene to be lucky; dove capita at random
capitazióne f poll tax
capitèllo m (archit) capital; (bb) headband
capitolare adj & m capitular || v (capìtolo) intr to capitulate, surrender
capitolato m (com) specifications
capitolazióne f capitulation
capìtolo m chapter; article, paragraph (of contract)
capitombolare (capitómbolo) intr to tumble
capitómbolo m tumble; fare un capitombolo (fig) to collapse
capitóne m big eel
capitozzare (capitòzzo) tr to poll (a tree)
capo m head; chief; boss, leader; top; (geog) cape; (nav) chief petty officer; a capo scoperto bareheaded; capo d'accusa (law) charge; capo del governo prime minister; capo dello stato president, chief of state; capo di vestiario garment; capo scarico scatterbrain; col capo nel sacco (fig) heedlessly; da capo all over (again); fare capo a to flow into; in capo a at the end of (e.g., one month); in capo al mondo at the end of the world; per sommi capi briefly; rompersi il capo to rack one's brain; scoprirsi il capo to take one's hat off; senza capo né coda without rhyme or reason; venire a capo di to come to the end of
capobanda m (capibanda) bandmaster; ringleader
capocamerière m headwaiter
capocannonière m (capicannonièri) petty gunnery officer; (soccer) leader in number of goals
capòcchia f head (e.g., of a match)
capòc·cia m (-ci & -cia) head of household; foreman, boss (e.g., of roadworkers or farmers)
capocòmi·co m (-ci) head of dramatic company
capocòr·da m (capicòrda) (elec) binding post, terminal
capocrònaca m (capicrònaca) leading article
capocronista m (capicronisti) city editor
capocuòco m (capocuòchi & capicuòchi) chef
capodanno m (capodanni & capi d'anno) New Year's Day
capodò·glio m (-gli) sperm whale
capofàbbrica m (capifàbbrica) foreman, superintendent
capofabbricato m (capifabbricato) airraid warden

capofamìglia *m* (capifamìglia) head of the family

capofila *m* (capifila) head of a line || *f* (capofila) head of a line

capofitto *adj invar*—a capofitto headlong

capogiro *m* vertigo, dizziness; da capogiro dizzying, e.g., prezzi da capogiro dizzying prices

capolavó·ro *m* (-ri) masterpiece

capolèttera *m* (capilèttera) letterhead; (typ) first large bold letter of a paragraph

capolìnea *m* (capilìnea) terminal, terminus

capolino *m*—fare capolino to peep

capolista *m* (capilista) first (*of a list*); (sports) leader || *f* (capolista) first (*of a list*)

capoluò·go *m* (-ghi) capital (*of province*); county seat

capomacchini·sta *m* (-sti) chief engineer

capomastro *m* (capomastri & capimastri) foreman; building contractor

capomùsica *m* (capimùsica) bandmaster

capoofficina *m* (capiofficina) superintendent (*of shop*)

capopàgina *m* (capipàgina) heading (*of newspaper*)

capopèzzo *m* (capipèzzo) gunnery sergeant

capopòpolo *m* (capipòpolo) demagogue

caporale *m* corporal

caporeparto *m* (capireparto) department manager, floor walker; shop foreman

caporióne *m* ringleader

caposaldo *m* (capisaldi) (fig) main point, basis; (mil) stronghold; (surv) datum

caposezióne *m* (capisezióne) department head

caposquadra *m* (capisquadra) group leader; (sports) team captain

capostazióne *m* (capistazióne) station master

capostìpite *m* founder (*of family*); prototype, archetype

capotaménto *m var of* cappottamento

capotare (capòto) *intr var of* cappottare

capotàvola *m* (capitàvola) head of the table, honored guest

capòte *f* (aut) top

capotrèno *m* (capitrèno & capotrèni) (rr) conductor

capottaménto *m var of* cappottamento

capottare (capòtto) *intr var of* cappottare

capoufficio *m* (capiufficio) office manager

capovèrso *m* paragraph; (typ) indentation

capovòlgere §289 *tr* to overturn; (fig) to upset || *ref* to overturn; (fig) to be or become reversed

capovolgiménto *m* upset; (fig) reversal

capovòlta *f* overturn; turn (*in swimming*)

cappa *f* cape, cloak; mantle; letter K; shroud (*of clouds*); (naut) trysail;

cappa del cielo vault of heaven; navigare alla cappa (naut) to lay to

cappèlla *f* chapel; cappella mortuaria undertaker's parlor || Cappella Sistina Sistine Chapel

cappel·làio *m* (-lài) hatter, hat maker or dealer

cappellano *m* chaplain

cappellata *f* hatful

cappelleria *f* hat store

cappellièra *f* hatbox

cappèllo *m* hat; bonnet; cap (*of mushroom*); head (*of nail*); cowl (*of chimney*); preamble (*of newspaper article*); cappello a cencio slouch hat; cappello a cilindro top hat; cappello a cono dunce cap; cappello a due punte cocked hat; cappello a tre punte three-cornered hat; cappello del lume lampshade; cappello di feltro felt hat; cappello di paglia straw hat; cappello floscio fedora; fare di cappello to take one's hat off; prendere cappello to take offense

cappellóne *adj invar* Western (*movie*) || *m* big hat; (coll) recruit; (mov) Western character

càppero *m* (bot) caper; capperi! (coll) wow!

càp·pio *m* (-pi) bow; noose; loop

capponàia *f* chicken coop

cappóne *m* capon

cappòtta *f* cape; navy coat; hood (*of car*)

cappottaménto *m* upset, rolling over

cappottare (cappòtto) *intr* to upset, roll over

cappottatura *f* (aer) cowl

cappòtto *m* overcoat; lurch (*at the close of game*); (cards) slam; cappotto da mezza stagione lightweight coat

cappuccino *m* espresso with cream; Capuchin (*friar*)

Cappuccétto *m*—Cappuccetto Rosso Little Red Ridinghood

cappùc·cio *m* (-ci) hood, cowl; cabbage; cap (*of fountain pen*)

capra *f* goat; nanny goat; tripod

ca·pràio -pràia *mf* (-prài -pràie) goatherd

caprét·to -ta *mf* kid

capriata *f* truss (*to support roof*)

capric·cio *m* (-ci) whim, fancy, caprice; tantrum; flirting; (mus) capriccio

capricció·so -sa [s] *adj* whimsical, capricious; naughty; fanciful, bizarre

Capricòrno *m* (astr) Capricorn

caprifò·glio *m* (-gli) honeysuckle

caprimul·go *m* (-gi) (orn) goatsucker

capri·no -na *adj* goatlike, goatish || *m* smell of goat

capriòla *f* female roe deer; caper, somersault; fare capriole to cut capers, to caper

capriòlo *m* roe deer; roebuck

capro *m* he-goat, billy goat; capro espiatorio scapegoat

capróne *m* he-goat, billy goat

càpsula *f* capsule; percussion cap; cap (*of bottle*); (rok) capsule

captare *tr* to captivate; to catch, intercept; to harness (*a waterfall*); (rad, telv) to pick up (*a signal*)

captazióne *f* undue influence (*to secure an inheritance*)

capzió·so -sa [s] *adj* insidious, treacherous

carabàttola *f* (coll) trifle

carabina *f* carbine

carabinière *m* carabineer; Italian military policeman, carabiniere; (*hist*) cavalryman

caracollare (caracòllo) *intr* to caracole, caper; (coll) to trot along

caracòllo *m* caracole, caper

caraffa *f* carafe, decanter

caràmbola *f* carom

carambolare (caràmbolo) *intr* to carom

caramèlla *f* piece of hard candy; taffy; (coll) monocle; **caramelle** hard candy

caramellare (caramèllo) *tr* to caramel; to candy

caramèllo *m* caramel (*burnt sugar*)

caraménte *adv* affectionately

carati·sta *m* (-**sti**) shareholder (*in ship or business*)

carato *m* carat; share (*of ship*)

caràttere *m* character; type; handwriting; characteristic; disposition; **carattere corsivo** (typ) italic; **carattere maiuscolo** capital; **carattere minuscolo** small letter, lower case; **carattere neretto** or **grassetto** (typ) boldface

caratteri·sta *m* (-**sti**) character actor || *f* (-**ste**) character actress

caratteristi·co -ca (-**ci -che**) *adj & f* characteristic

caratterizzare [ddzz] *tr* to characterize

caratura *f* share (*in business or ship*)

cara·vàn *m* (-**vàn**) trailer, mobile home

caravanserrà·glio *m* (-**gli**) caravansary

caravèlla *f* caravel; carpenter's glue

carbo·nàio -nàia (-**nài -nàie**) *adj* coal || *m* coal man, coal dealer || *f* charcoal pit; coalbin, bunker; coal yard

carbonato *m* carbonate

carbón·chio *m* (-**chì**) (agr) smut (*on wheat*); (jewelry) carbuncle

carboncino *m* charcoal (*pencil and drawing*)

carbóne *m* coal; charcoal; carbon (*of arc light or primary battery*); **carbone bianco** hydroelectric power; **carbone dolce** charcoal; **carbone fòssile** coal; **fare carbone** to coal

carbòni·co -ca *adj* (-**ci -che**) carbonic

carbonièra *f* coal yard; (naut) collier; (rr) tender

carbonile *m* (naut) bunker

carbònio *m* (chem) carbon

carbonizzare [ddzz] *tr* to carbonize; to char

carbùncolo *m* boil, carbuncle; (archaic) ruby

carburante *m* fuel

carburatóre *m* carburetor

carburazióne *f* (aut) mixture

carburo *m* carbide

carcassa *f* carcass; framework; (aut) jalopy; (fig) wreck

carcerare (càrcero) *tr* to jail

carcerà·rio -ria *adj* (-**ri -rie**) jail, prison

carcera·to -ta *adj* imprisoned || *mf* prisoner

càrce·re *m* (-**ri** *fpl*) jail, prison

carcerière *m* jailer, prison guard

carciòfo *m* artichoke

cardàni·co -ca *adj* (-**ci -che**) universal (*e.g., joint*)

cardano *m* universal joint

cardatrice *f* carding machine

cardellino *m* goldfinch

cardìa·co -ca (-**ci -che**) *adj* heart, cardiac || *m* heart patient

cardinale *adj* cardinal || *m* (eccl, orn) cardinal

cardinalì·zio -zia *adj* (-**zi -zie**) cardinal, cardinal's

càrdine *m* hinge; (fig) pivot, mainstay (*e.g., of theory*)

càr·dio *m* (-**di**) cockle (*mollusk*)

cardiochirurgia *f* heart surgery

cardiogram·ma *m* (-**mi**) cardiogram

cardiòlo·go *m* (-**gi**) cardiologist

cardiopalmo *m* tachycardia

cardiopatìa *f* heart disease

cardo *m* (bot) thistle; (bot) cardoon

carèna *f* ship's bottom; (aer) outer cover (*of airship*); (bot) rib

carenàg·gio *m* (-**gi**) careening a ship; careen

carenare (carèno) *tr* to careen (*a ship*)

carenatura *f* streamlining; **carenatura di fusoliera** (aer) turtleback

carènza *f* lack, want

carestìa *f* famine; scarcity (*e.g., of manpower*)

carézza *f* caress; **fare una carezza a** to caress

carezzare (carézzo) *tr* to caress

carezzévole *adj* caressing, fondling; sweet, suave; blandishing

cariare §287 *tr* to cause (*a tooth*) to decay; to corrode || *ref* to decay; to rot

cariàtide *f* caryatid

caria·to -ta *adj* decayed

càri·ca *f* (-**che**) office, appointment; charge; (fig) insistence

caricaménto *m* loading

caricare §197 (**càrico**) *tr* to load; to burden; to wind (*a watch*); to fill (*a pipe*); to charge (*a battery*); to deepen (*a color*); **caricare la mano** to exceed; **caricare le dosi** to exaggerate || *ref* to burden oneself

carica·to -ta *adj* exaggerated, affected

carica·tóre -trice *adj* loading || *m* clip, magazine (*for rifle*); loader (*of gun*); cassette (*of tape recorder*); charger (*of battery*); longshoreman; (phot) cartridge, cassette

caricatura *f* caricature, cartoon; **mettere in caricatura** to ridicule

caricaturi·sta *mf* (-**sti -ste**) cartoonist, caricaturist

càrice *m* (bot) sedge

càri·co -ca (-**chi -che**) *adj* loaded; burdened; vivid (*color*); strong (*tea*); charged (*battery*) || *m* loading; load, burden; charge; cargo || *f* see **carica**

càrie *f* caries, decay

cari·no -na *adj* nice, pretty, cute; **questa è carina!** this is funny!

cari·tà *f* (**-tà**) charity; alms; (poet) love; **per carità** please

caritatévole *adj* charitable

caritati·vo -va *adj* (obs) charitable

carlin·ga *f* (**-ghe**) fuselage

Carlo *m* Charles

Carlomagno *m* Charlemagne

carlóna *f*—**alla carlona** carelessly, haphazardly

carlòtta *f* charlotte ‖ **Carlòtta** Charlotte

carme *m* poem, lyric poem

carmi·nio *m* (**-ni**) carmine

carnagióne *f* complexion

car·nàio *m* (**-nài**) carnage; slaughter house; mass of humanity

carnale *adj* carnal, sensual; full (*e.g.*, *brother, cousin*)

carname *m* carrion

carne *f* flesh; meat; **bene in carne** plump; **carne da macello** cannon fodder; **carne suina** pork; **carne viva** open wound; **essere solo carne ed ossa** to be nothing but skin and bones; **in carne ed ossa** in person, in the flesh; **troppa carne al fuoco** too many irons in the fire

carnéfice *m* executioner

carneficina *f* slaughter, carnage

càrne·o -a *adj* fleshy, meaty; flesh-colored

carnet *m* (**carnet**) notebook; checkbook; backlog

carnevale *m* carnival

carnièra *f* hunting jacket; gamebag

carnière *m* gamebag

carnì·voro -ra *adj* carnivorous ‖ *mpl* carnivores; Carnivora

carnò·so -sa [*s*] *adj* fleshy

ca·ro -ra *adj* dear (*beloved; high in price*); **caro** *adv* dear ‖ *m* high price; beloved; **i miei cari** my parents; my relatives; my friends

carógna *f* carcass; cad, rotter; **carogne** carrion

carosèllo *m* tournament; carousel, merry-go-round

caròta *f* carrot; (fig) lie

caròtide *f* carotid artery

carovana *f* caravan; group, crowd; union of longshoremen; apprenticeship; (naut, nav) convoy; **far carovana** to join a tour; **fare la carovana** to be an apprentice

carovaniè·ro -ra *adj* caravan ‖ *f* desert trail

carovi·ta *m* (**-ta**) high cost of living; cost-of-living increase

carovive·ri *m* (**-ri**) high cost of living; cost-of-living increase

carpa *f* (ichth) carp

carpentière *m* carpenter

carpire §176 *tr* to snatch, seize; to extract, worm (*a secret*)

carpóni *adv* on all fours; **avanzare carponi** to crawl

carradóre *m* cart maker, wheelwright

car·ràio -ràia (**-rài -ràie**) *adj* passable for vehicles ‖ *f* cart road

carrarèc·cia *f* (**-ce**) country road; rut

carreggiata *f* paved road; track (*of vehicles*); (fig) right path

carrellare (**carrèllo**) *intr* (mov, telv) to dolly

carrellata *f* (mov) dolly shot, tracking shot

carrèllo *m* car (*for narrow-gauge track*); carriage (*of typewriter*); cart (*for shopping*); (aer) landing gear; (mach, rr) truck; (mov, telv) dolly; **carrello d'atterraggio** (aer) undercarriage, landing gear; **carrello elevatore** fork-lift truck

carrétta *f* cart; tramp steamer

carrettata *f* cartful; **a carrettate** abundantly

carrettière *m* cart driver, drayman; teamster

carrétto *m* small cart; **carretto a mano** pushcart

carriàg·gio *m* (**-gi**) wagon; **carriaggi** (mil) baggage train

carrièra *f* career; **di gran carriera** at top speed

carrieri·sta *mf* (**-sti -ste**) unscrupulous go-getter

carriòla *f* wheelbarrow

carro *m* wagon; cart; wagonload; cartload; carload; (rr) car; (astr) Plough; (poet) chariot; **carri armati** (mil) armor; **carro allegorico** float (*in a pageant*); **carro armato** (mil) tank; **carro attrezzi** (aut) tow truck, wrecker; **carro bestiame** (rr) cattle car; **carro botte** or **carro cisterna** (aut) tank truck; (rr) tank car; **carro di Tespi** traveling show; **carro funebre** hearse; **carro gru** (rr) wrecking crane; **carro marsupio** (rr) double decker (*used to transport automobiles*); **carro merci** (rr) freight car; **Gran Carro** (astr) Big Dipper; **mettere il carro innanzi ai buoi** to put the cart before the horse; **Piccolo Carro** (astr) Little Dipper ‖ *m* (**carra** *fpl*) carload; wagonload; cartload

carròzza *f* wagon carriage; **carrozza letti** (rr) sleeping car; **carrozza ristorante** (rr) dining car; **carrozza salone** (rr) club car; **con la carrozza di S. Francesco** on shank's mare; **signori, in carrozza!** (rr) all aboard!

carrozzàbile *adj* open to vehicular traffic ‖ *f* road open to vehicular traffic

carrozzèlla *f* small wagon; baby carriage; wheelchair; hackney

carrozzino *m* baby carriage; sidecar

carrozzóne *m* wagon; hearse; caravan (*e.g., of gypsies*); (rr) car

carruba *f* carob

carrubo *m* carob tree

carrùcola *f* pulley

carta *f* paper; document (*e.g., of identification*); **alla carta** à la carte; **carta assorbente** blotter; **carta astronomica** astronomical map; **carta bianca** carte blanche; **carta bollata** stamped paper (*for official documents*); **carta carbone** carbon paper; **carta catramata** tar paper; **carta da disegno** drawing paper; **carta da gioco** playing card; **carta da giornale** newsprint; **carta da imballaggio** or **da impacco** wrapping paper; **carta da lettera** or **da scrivere** writing paper; **carta geografica** map, chart; **carta igienica** toilet paper; **carta oleata** wax paper; **carta torna-**

sole litmus paper; **carta velina** India paper; tissue paper; **carta vetrata** sandpaper; **carte** papers, writings; **carte francesi** cards in the four suits spades, hearts, diamonds, and clubs; **carte napoletane** cards in the four suits gold coins, cups, swords, and clubs; **fare le carte** to shuffle the cards; **fare le carte a qlcu** to tell s.o.'s fortune with cards

cartacarbóne f (**cartacarbóne**) carbon paper

cartàc·cia f (**-ce**) waste paper

cartàce·o -a adj (**-i -e**) paper

Cartàgine f Carthage

car·tàio m (**-tài**) papermaker; paper dealer; (cards) dealer

cartamonéta f paper money

cartapècora f parchment

cartapésta f papier-mâché

cartà·rio -ria adj (**-ri -rie**) paper

cartastràccia f (**cartestracce**) wrapping paper; wastepaper

cartég·gio m (**-gi**) correspondence; (aer, naut) reckoning

cartèlla f lottery ticket; card (e.g., of bingo); page of manuscript; Manila folder; schoolbag; briefcase; binding (of book); **cartella clinica** clinical chart; **cartella di rendita** government bond; **cartella esattoriale** tax bill; **cartella fondiaria** bond certificate

cartellino m label; nameplate (on door); file; (sports) contract; **cartellino di presenza** timecard; **cartellino signaletico** criminal record

cartèllo m poster; sign (on store); (com) cartel, trust; **cartello di sfida** challenge; **cartello stradale** traffic sign

cartellóne m show bill, theater poster; bill (for advertising); **tenere il cartellone** to find public favor, make a hit, be the rage

car·ter m (**-ter**) chain guard (of bicycle); (aut) crankcase

cartièra f papermill

cartilàgine f cartilage, gristle

cartina f dose; cigarette paper; small map

cartòc·cio m (**-ci**) paper cone; charge (of gun); cornhusk; (archit) scroll

cartògrafo m cartographer

carto·làio m (**-lài**) stationer

cartoleria f stationery store

cartolina f card, post card; **cartolina precetto** induction notice

cartomante mf fortuneteller

cartoncino m light cardboard, calling card; **cartoncino natalizio** Christmas card

cartóne m cardboard, carton; **cartone animato** (mov) animated cartoon

cartùc·cia f (**-ce**) cartridge; shot, shell; **mezza cartuccia** (fig) half pint

cartuccièra f cartridge belt

casa [s] f house; dwelling; home; household; **andare a casa** to go home; **casa base** (baseball) home base; **casa colonica** farm house; **casa da gioco** gambling house; **casa del diavolo** faraway place; **casa di bambole** playhouse, doll's house; **casa di correzione** reform school; **casa di cura** sanatorium, private clinic; **casa di riposo** convalescent home, nursing home; **casa di spedizione** shipping agency; **casa di tolleranza** bawdyhouse; **casa madre** home office, headquarters; **esser di casa** to be intimate; **fuori casa** (sports) away; **in casa** (sports) home; **metter su casa** to set up housekeeping; **sentirsi a casa** to feel at home; **stare a casa** to stay at home; **star di casa** to dwell, live

casac·ca f (**-che**) coat; **voltar casacca** to be a turncoat

casàccio m—**a casaccio** at random; heedlessly

casalin·go -ga (**-ghi -ghe**) [s] adj home, domestic; stay-at-home; homey; home-made || **casalinghi** mpl household articles || f housewife

casamatta [s] f casemate, bunker

casaménto [s] m apartment house, tenement; tenants

casata [s] f house, lineage

casato [s] m birth, family; (obs) family name

cascame m waste; remnants (e.g., of silk)

cascante adj flabby, loose; (poet) languid, dull

cascare §197 intr (ESSERE) to fall, droop; to fit (said of clothes); **cascare dalla noia** to be bored to death; **cascare dal sonno** to be overwhelmed with sleep; **cascare diritto** to escape unscathed; **non casca il mondo** the world is not coming to an end

cascata f fall, waterfall; necklace (e.g., of pearls); **a cascata** flood of, e.g., telefonate **a cascata** flood of telephone calls || **le Cascate del Niagara** Niagara Falls

cascina f farm house; dairy barn

ca·sco m (**-schi**) helmet, crash helmet; electric hairdrier; cluster (e.g., of bananas)

caseggiato [s] m built-up zone; block, row of houses; apartment house

caseifi·cio m (**-ci**) dairy, creamery, cheese factory

casèlla [s] f pigeonhole; square (of paper); **casella postale** post-office box

casellante [s] mf gatekeeper || m (rr) trackwalker

casellà·rio [s] m (**-ri**) filing cabinet; row of post-office boxes; **casellario giudiziale** criminal file

casèllo [s] m tollgate (on turnpike); (rr) trackwalker's house

casèrma f barracks; fire station

casino [s] m country house; clubhouse; (slang) whorehouse; (slang) noise, racket

casìsti·ca f (**-che**) case study; (eccl) casuistry

caso m case; chance; fate; vicissitude; opportunity; **a caso** inadvertently; **al caso** eventually; **caso fortuito** (law) act of God; **caso mai** assuming that, in the event that; **è il caso** it is the moment; **far caso a qlco** to notice s.th; **in ogni caso** in any event; **mettere il caso che** suppose; **mi fa caso** I am surprised; **non fare caso a** to make nothing of, pay no attention to; **per caso** perchance

casolare [s] *m* hut, hovel; isolated farmhouse

casòtto [s] *m* cabana, bathhouse; sentry box

Càspio *adj* Caspian

càspita *interj* you don't say!

cassa *f* box; chest; case; stock (*of rifle*); cash; cash register; desk (*e.g., in hotel*); check-out (*in a supermarket*); **a pronta cassa** by cash; **cassa acustica** loudspeaker; **cassa di risparmio** savings bank; **cassa malattia** health insurance; **cassa rurale** farmers' credit cooperative; **in cassa** in hand (*said of money*)

cassafórma *f* (**casseforme**) (archit) form (*for cement*)

cassaforte *f* (**casseforti**) safe

cassapanca *f* (**cassapanche** & **cassepanche**) wooden chest

cassare *tr* to erase, cancel; to cross off; (law) to annull

cassata *f* Neapolitan ice cream with soft core; Sicilian cake

cassazióne *f* annulment, abolition; cancellation

casserétto *m* (naut) poop

càssero *m* (naut) quarterdeck; **cassero di poppa** (naut) cockpit

casseruòla *f* saucepan

cassétta *f* small box; coach box; (theat) box office; **cassetta dei ferri** workbox; **cassetta delle lettere** mail box; **cassetta di cottura** dish warmer; **cassetta di sicurezza** safe-deposit box; **cassetta per ugnature** miter box

cassettièra *f* chest of drawers

cassétto *m* drawer; **cassetto di distribuzione** (mach) slide valve

cassettóne *m* chest of drawers; (archit) coffer, caisson

cassiè·re -ra *mf* cashier; teller

cassóne *m* large case, large box; chest; caisson (*for underwater construction*); body (*of truck*); (mil) caisson

cassonétto *m* cornice

cast *m* cast (*of actors*)

casta *f* caste

castagna *f* chestnut; **castagna d'India** horse chestnut

castagnéto *m* chestnut grove

castagno *m* chestnut tree; chestnut (*lumber*); **castagno d'India** horse chestnut tree

casta·no -na *adj* chestnut (*color*)

castellana *f* chatelaine

castellano *m* lord of the castle, squire

castellétto *m* scaffold; (min) gallows, headframe

castèl·lo *m* castle; works (*e.g., of watch*); scaffold; jungle gym; hydraulic boom, bucket lift (*on truck*); (naut) forecastle; **castello di menzogne** pack of lies; **castello in aria** castle in Spain ǁ *m* (**-la** *fpl*) (archaic) castle

castigare §209 *tr* to punish; (poet) to correct, castigate

castigatézza *f* purity (*e.g., of style*)

castiga·to -ta *adj* decent, modest; pure (*language*)

Castiglia, la Castile

castiglia·no -na *adj & mf* Castilian

casti·go *m* (**-ghi**) punishment; (fig) scourge; **mettere in castigo** (coll) to punish

casti·tà *f* (**-tà**) chastity; (fig) purity

ca·sto -sta *adj* chaste; pure, elegant (*language or style*)

castóne *m* setting (*of stone*)

castòro *m* beaver

castrare *tr* to castrate; to spay; (fig) to expurgate

castra·to -ta *adj* castrated; spayed; (fig) effeminate ǁ *m* mutton (*of castrated sheep*); eunuch

castróne *m* wether (*sheep*); gelding (*horse*); (fig) nincompoop

castroneria *f* (vulg) stupidity

casuale *adj* fortuitous, casual; sundry (*e.g., expenses*)

casuali·tà *f* (**-tà**) chance, accident

casùpola [s] *f* hut, hovel

catacli·sma *m* (**-smi**) cataclysm

catacómba *f* catacomb

catafal·co *m* (**-chi**) catafalque

catafàscio *adv*—**a catafascio** topsy-turvy

catalès·si *f* (**-si**) catalepsy

catàli·si *f* (**-si**) catalysis

catalizza·tóre -trice [ddzz] *adj* catalytic ǁ *m* catalyst

catalogare §209 (**catàlogo**) *tr* to catalogue

catàlo·go *m* (**-ghi**) catalogue

catapècchia *f* hovel

catapla·sma *m* (**-smi**) poultice, plaster; (fig) bore

catapulta *f* catapult

catapultare *tr* to catapult

cataratta *f* cataract; sluice (*of canal*)

catarro *m* catarrh

catar·si *f* (**-si**) catharsis

catàrti·co *-ca adj* (**-ci -che**) cathartic

catasta *f* pile, heap

catastale *adj* land (*office*)

catasto *m* real-estate register; land office

catàstrofe *f* catastrophe; wreck

catastròfi·co *-ca adj* (**-ci -che**) catastrophic

catechismo *m* catechism

catechizzare [ddzz] *tr* to catechize

categoria *f* category; weight (*in boxing*); (sports) class

categòri·co *-ca adj* (**-ci -che**) categorical; classified (*telephone directory*)

caténa *f* chain; range (*of mountains*); (archit) tie beam; **catene da neve** tire chains; **mordere la catena** to champ the bit

catenàc·cio *m* (**-ci**) bolt; (fig) jalopy; (journ) giant-size headline

catenèlla *f* chain

cateratta *f* var of **cataratta**

catèrva *f* great quantity, large number

catetère *m* catheter

cateterizzare [ddzz] *tr* to catheterize

catinèlla *f* water basin; **piovere a catinelle** (coll) to rain cats and dogs

catino *m* basin

càtodo *m* cathode

Catóne *m* Cato; **Catone il Maggiore** Cato the Elder

catòr·cio *m* (**-ci**) (coll) piece of junk

catramare *tr* to tar

catramatrice *f* asphalt-paving machine

catrame *m* tar, coal tar

càttedra *f* desk (*of teacher*); chair, professorship

cattedrale *adj* & *f* cathedral

cattedràti·co -ca (**-ci -che**) *adj* pedantic || *m* professor

catte·gù *m* (**-gù**) catgut

cattivare *tr* to captivate

cattivèria *f* wickedness; piece of wickedness

cattivi·tà *f* (**-tà**) captivity

catti·vo -va *adj* bad; wicked; vicious (*animal*); worthless; poor (*reputation; condition*); nasty; naughty; (archaic) cowardly || *mf* wicked person || *m* bad taste; **sapere di cattivo** to taste bad

cattolicità *f* catholicity

cattòli·co -ca (**-ci -che**) *adj* catholic || *adj* & *mf* Catholic

cattura *f* capture, seizure; arrest

catturare *tr* to capture, seize; to arrest

caucàsi·co -ca *adj* & *mf* (**-ci -che**) Caucasian

caucciù *m* (**caucciù**) rubber

càusa *f* cause, motive; fault; lawsuit, action; **a causa di** on account of; **causa civile** civil suit; **causa penale** criminal suit; **fare causa** to take legal action; **intentare causa a** to bring suit against

causale *adj* causal || *f* cause

causare (**càuso**) *tr* to cause

causìdi·co *m* (**-ci**) amicus curiae; (joc) pettifogger

càusti·co -ca *adj* (**-ci -che**) caustic

cautèla *f* caution; precaution; care

cautelare *tr* guaranteeing, protecting || *v* (**cautèlo**) *tr* to guarantee, protect || *ref* to take precautions

cauterizzare [*ddzz*] *tr* to cauterize

càu·to -ta *adj* cautious, prudent; cagey

cauzione *f* security, bail; **dare cauzione** to give bail

cava *f* quarry; cave; (fig) mine

cavadènti *m* (**-ti**) (coll) tooth puller, poor dentist

cavagno *m* (coll) basket

cavalcare §197 *tr* to ride; to cross over (*e.g., a river*) || *intr* to ride; **cavalcare a bisdosso** to ride bareback; **cavalcare all'amazzone** to ride sidesaddle

cavalcata *f* ride; cavalcade

cavalcatura *f* mount

cavalca·vìa *m* (**-via**) bridge (*between two buildings*); overpass

cavalcióni *adj*—**a cavalcióni** (**di**) astride

cavalierato *m* knighthood

cavalière *m* rider (*on horseback*); knight; cavalier; chevalier; **a cavaliere** astride; **cavaliere d'industria** adventurer; **cavaliere errante** knight errant; **essere a cavaliere di** to overlook (*e.g., a valley*); to stretch over (*e.g., two centuries*)

cavalla *f* mare

cavalleggièro *m* cavalryman

cavalleré·sco -sca *adj* (**-schi -sche**) chivalrous, knightly

cavallerìa *f* cavalry; chivalry, knighthood; (fig) chivalry

cavallerizza *f* manège, riding school; horsemanship; horsewoman

cavallerizzo *m* horseman; riding master

cavallétta *f* grasshopper

cavallétto *m* tripod; easel; trestle (*of ski lift*); scaffold (*e.g., of stonemason*); sawhorse, sawbuck

cavalli·no -na *adj* horse, horse-like || *m* foal, colt || *f* foal, filly; **correre la cavallina** to be on the loose; to sow one's wild oats

cavallo *m* horse; knight (*in chess*); crotch (*of pants*); **a cavallo** on horseback; **a cavallo di** someone; **andare col cavallo di San Francesco** to ride shank's mare; **cavallo a dondolo** hobbyhorse; **cavallo di battaglia** battle horse; (fig) specialty, forte; **cavallo da corsa** race horse; **cavallo da tiro** draft horse; **cavallo di Frisia** cheval-de-frise; **cavallo di ritorno** confirmed news; **cavallo vapore** metric horsepower; **essere a cavallo** (fig) to have turned the corner

cavallóne *m* big horse; billow

cavallùc·cio *m* (**-ci**) little horse; **a cavalluccio** on one's shoulders; **cavalluccio marino** (ichth) sea horse

cavare *tr* to dig; to extract (*e.g., a tooth*); to pull out (*e.g., money*); to draw; **cavare il cuore a qlcu** to move s.o. to compassion; **cavare una spina dal cuore a qlcu** to ease s.o.o.'s mind || *ref* to take off (*e.g., one's hat*); **cavarsela** to overcome an obstacle; to get out of trouble; **cavarsi la camicia di dosso** to give the shirt off one's back; **cavarsi la fame** to eat one's fill; **cavarsi la voglia** to satisfy one's wishes

cavastiva·li *m* (**-li**) bootjack

cavatap·pi *m* (**-pi**) corkscrew

cavaturàccio·li *m* (**-li**) corkscrew

cavèrna *f* cave, cavern

cavernó·so -sa [*s*] *adj* cavernous; deep (*voice*)

cavézza *f* halter; (fig) check

càvia *f* guinea pig; **cavia umana** (fig) guinea pig

caviale *m* caviar

cavìc·chio *m* (**-chi**) peg

cavì·glia *f* (**-glie**) ankle; bolt; pin, dowel, peg

caviglièra *f* ankle support

cavillare *intr* to cavil, quibble

cavillo *m* quibble

cavilló·so -sa [*s*] *adj* quibbling, captious

cavi·tà *f* (**-tà**) cavity

ca·vo -va *adj* hollow || *m* hollow; cable; trough (*between two waves*); (naut) hawser; **cavo di rimorchio** towline; **cavo telefonico** telephone cable || *f* see **cava**

cavolfióre *m* cauliflower

càvolo *m* cabbage; **cavolo di Bruxelles** Brussels sprouts (*food*); (bot) Brussels sprout; **non capire un cavolo** (vulg) to not understand a blessed thing

cazzòtto *m* (vulg) punch, sock

cazzuòla *f* trowel

ce §5
cecare §122 *tr* to blind
cèc·ca *f* (-che) magpie; fare cecca to misfire
cecchino *m* sniper
céce *m* chickpea
ceci·tà *f* (-tà) blindness
cè·co -ca *adj & mf* (-chi -che) Czech
Cecoslovàcchia, la Czechoslovakia
cecoslovac·co -ca *adj & mf* (-chi -che) Czechoslovak
cèdere §123 *tr* to cede; to give up; to sell at cost; cedere il passo to let s.o. through; cedere la strada to yield the right of way; non cederla to be second to none ‖ *intr* to give in, yield; to give way, succumb; to sag
cedévole *adj* yielding; soft; pliable
cedìglia *f* cedilla
cediménto *m* cave-in; (fig) yielding
cèdola *f* slip; coupon
cedri·no -na *adj* citron; citron-like; cedar, cedar-like
cédro *m* (*Citrus medica*) citron; (*Cedrus*) cedar; cedro del Libano cedar of Lebanon
CEE *m* (letterword) (Comunità Economica Europea) EEC (*European Economic Community-Common Market*)
cefalèa *f* slight headache; headache
cèfalo *m* (ichth) mullet
cèffo *m* snout; (pej) face; brutto ceffo ugly mug
ceffóne *m* slap in the face
celare (cèlo) *tr* to hide, conceal
cela·to -ta *adj* hidden ‖ *f* sallet
celebèrri·mo -ma *adj* very famous, renowned
celebrare (cèlebro) *tr & intr* to celebrate
celebrazióne *f* celebration
cèlebre *adj* famous, renowned, celebrated
celebri·tà *f* (-tà) celebrity
cèlere *adj* swift, rapid; express (*train*); short, quick; prompt ‖ Celere *f* special police
celeri·tà *f* (-tà) swiftness, rapidity; speed (*e.g., of a machine gun*)
celèste *adj* heavenly, celestial; blue, sky-blue ‖ *m* blue, sky blue; celesti heavenly spirits; (mythol) gods
celestiale *adj* celestial, heavenly
cèlia *f* jest; mettere in celia to deride; per celia in jest
celiare §287 (cèlio) *intr* to jest, joke
celibatà·rio -ria (-ri -rie) *adj* single ‖ *m* old bachelor
celibato *m* celibacy; bachelorhood
cèlibe *adj* single, unmarried ‖ *m* bachelor
cèlla *f* cell; cella frigorifera walk-in refrigerator; cella campanaria belfry
cèllofan or cellofàn *m* cellophane
cèllula *f* cell; cellula fotoelettrica photoelectric cell
cellulare *adj* cellular; ventilated (*fabric*); solitary (*confinement*)
cellulòide *f* celluloid
celluló·so -sa [s] *adj* cell-like, cellular ‖ *f* cellulose
cèl·ta *mf* (-ti -te) Celt

cèlti·co -ca *adj* (-ci -che) Celtic; venereal (*disease*)
cementare (ceménto) *tr* to cement
ceménto *m* cement, concrete; cemento armato reinforced concrete
céna *f* supper; Ultima Cena Last Supper
cenàcolo *m* cenacle
cenare (céno) *intr* to sup, have supper
cenciaiò·lo -la *mf* ragpicker
cén·cio *m* (-ci) rag, duster (*for cleaning*)
cenció·so -sa [s] *adj* tattered, ragged
cénere *adj* ashen ‖ *f* ash; cinder; andare in cenere to go up in smoke; ceneri ashes (*of a person*); ridurre in cenere to burn to ashes ‖ le Ceneri Ash Wednesday
cenerèntola *f* (fig) Cinderella ‖ Cenerèntola *f* (*of the fable*) Cinderella
cén·gia *f* (-ge) ledge (*of a mountain*)
cénno *m* sign; wave (*with hand*); nod; wag; wink; gesture; hint; notice; ai cenni di at the orders of; fare cenno a or di to mention; fare cenno di no to shake one's head; fare cenno di sì to nod assent
cenò·bio *m* (-bi) monastery
cenobi·ta *m* (-ti) monk, cenobite
censiménto *m* census
censire §176 *tr* to take the census of
cènso *m* wealth, income; census (*in ancient Rome*)
censóre *m* censor; faultfinder; (educ) proctor
censuà·rio -ria (-ri -rie) *adj* income; tax (*register*) ‖ *m* taxpayer
censura *f* censure; censorship; fault-finding
censurare *tr* to censure; to criticize, find fault with
centàuro *m* centaur
centellinare *tr* to sip; to take a nip of
centellino *m* sip, nip
centenà·rio -ria (-ri -rie) *adj & mf* centenary, centennial ‖ *m* centenary, centennial (*anniversary*)
centèsi·mo -ma *adj* hundredth ‖ *m* hundredth; centime; cent; penny
centigrado *m* centigrade
centigrammo *m* centigram
centimetro *m* centimeter; tape measure
cèntina *f* (archit) centering; (aer) rib
centi·nàio *m* hundred; un centinaio di about a hundred ‖ *m* (-nàia *fpl*)—a centinaia by the hundreds
cènto *adj, m & pron* a hundred, one hundred; per cento per cent
centomila *adj, m & pron* a hundred thousand, one hundred thousand
centóne *m* cento
centopiè·di *m* (-di) centipede
centrale *adj* central ‖ *f* headquarters, home office; powerhouse, generating station; telephone exchange; centrale di conversione (elec) transformer station; centrale telefonica central
centralini·sta *mf* (-sti -ste) telephone operator
centralino *m* telephone exchange
centralizzare [ddzz] *tr* to centralize
centrare (cèntro) *tr* to center; to hit the center of

centrattac·co *m* (**-chi**) (sports) center forward

centrìfu·go -ga *adj* (**-ghi -ghe**) centrifugal || *f* centrifuge

centrino *m* centerpiece

centrìpe·to -ta *adj* centripetal

centrì·sta *mf* (**-sti -ste**) (pol) centrist

cèntro *m* center; **al centro** downtown: **far centro** to hit the mark

centrocampo *m* (soccer) midfield

centuplicare §197 (**centùplico**) *tr* to multiply a hundredfold

cèntu·plo -pla *adj & m* hundredfold

céppo *m* trunk, stump; log; block (*for beheading*); brake shoe; stock (*of anchor*); **ceppi** stocks, fetters || il **Ceppo** (coll) Christmas

céra *f* wax; face, aspect, air, look; **di cera** waxen; pale; **cera da scarpe** shoe polish; **avere buona cera** to look well; **fare buona cera a** to welcome

ceralac·ca *f* (**-che**) sealing wax

ceràmi·co -ca (**-ci -che**) *adj* ceramic || *f* ceramics

cerare (**céro**) *tr* to wax

Cèrbero *m* Cerberus

cerbiatto *m* fawn

cerbottana *f* blowgun, peashooter

cer·ca *f* (**-che**) search, quest; **in cerca di** in search of

cercare §197 (**cérco**) *tr* to seek, look for; to desire, yearn for; **cercare il pelo nell'uovo** to be a faultfinder, to nitpick || *intr* to try

cerca·tóre -trice *adj* seeking || *mf* seeker; mendicant || *m* prospector

cérchia *f* coterie; compass, limits (*of a wall*); circle (*of friends*)

cerchiare §287 (**cérchio**) *tr* to hoop (*a barrel*); to circle, encircle

cér·chio *m* (**-chi**) circle; hoop; loop; **fare il cerchio della morte** (aer) to loop the loop; **in cerchio** in a circle || *m* (**-chia** *fpl*) (archaic) circle

cerchìone *m* rim; tire (*of metal*)

cereale *adj & m* cereal

cerebrale *adj* cerebral

cère·o -a *adj* waxen; wax-colored, pale

cerfò·glio *m* (**-gli**) chervil

cerimònia *f* ceremony; **fare cerimonie** to stand on ceremony; to make a fuss

cerimoniale *adj & m* ceremonial

cerimonière *m* master of ceremonies (*at court*)

cerimonió·so -sa [*s*] *adj* ceremonious

cerino *m* wax match; taper

cernéc·chio *m* (**-chi**) tuft (*of hair*)

cernièra *f* hinge; clasp (*of handbag*); **a cerniera** hinged; **cerniera lampo** zipper

cèrnita *f* sorting, selection, grading

céro *m* church candle; **offrire un cero** to light a candle

ceróne *m* make-up (*of actor*)

ceròtto *m* adhesive tape; (fig) bore; **cerotto per i calli** corn plaster

certame *m* (poet) combat; competition, contest (*of poets*)

certézza *f* certitude, assurance, conviction, certainty

certificare §197 (**certìfico**) *tr* to certify, certificate

certificato *m* certificate

cèr·to -ta *adj* such, some; convinced; certain; real, positive || *m* certainty; **di certo** or **per certo** for certain || **certi** *pron* some || **certo** *adv* undoubtedly

certósa *f* Carthusian monastery, charterhouse

certosi·no *m* Carthusian monk; chartreuse (*liquor*); **da certosino** with great patience

certu·no -na *adj* (obs) some || **certuni** *pron* some

cerùle·o -a *adj* cerulean

cerume *m* ear wax

cervellétto *m* cerebellum

cervelli·no -na *adj & mf* scatterbrain

cervèllo *m* (**cervèlli & cervèlla** *fpl*) brain; head; mind; **dare al cervello** to go to one's head

cervellòti·co -ca *adj* (**-ci -che**) queer, extravagant

cervice *f* (anat) cervix; (poet) nape of the neck

cerviè·ro -ra *adj* lynx-like; || *m* lynx

cervi·no -na *adj* deer-like || **Cervino** *m* Matterhorn

cèrvo *m* deer; (ent) stag beetle; **cervo volante** kite

Cèsare *m* Caesar

cesàre·o -a *adj* Caesarean; (poet) courtly

cesellare (**cesèllo**) *tr* to chase, chisel; to carve, engrave; to polish (*e.g., a poem*)

cesella·tóre -trice *mf* chaser, engraver, chiseler

cesellatura *f* chasing, engraving; polished writing

cesèllo *m* burin, graver

cesóia *f* shears, metal shears; **cesoie** shears (*for gardening*)

cesoiatrice *f* shearing machine

cèspite *m* source (*of income*); (poet) tuft

céspo *m* tuft

cespù·glio *m* (**-gli**) bush, shrub, thicket

cèssa *f*—**senza cessa** without letup

cessare (**cèsso**) *tr* to stop, interrupt || *intr* to cease, stop; **cessare di** + *inf* to stop + *ger*

cessazióne *f* cessation, discontinuance; **cessazione d'esercizio** going out of business

cessionà·rio *m* (**-ri**) assignee

cèsso *m* (vulg) privy, outhouse

césta *f* basket, hamper

cestinare *tr* to throw into the wastebasket; to reject (*a book, article, etc.*)

césto *m* basket; tuft; head (*e.g., of lettuce*)

cesura *f* caesura

cetàceo *m* cetacean

cèto *m* class; **ceto medio** middle class

cétra *f* lyre; cither; inspiration

cetriolino *m* gherkin

cetriòlo *m* cucumber; (fig) dolt

che *adj* what; which; what a, e.g., **che bella giornata!** what a beautiful day! || *pron interr* what || *pron rel* who; whom; that; which; (coll) in which || *m*—**essere un gran che** to be a big

shot, **to be somebody** || *adv* how,
e.g., **che bello!** how nice!; **non** . . .
che only, e.g., **non venne che Luigi**
only Luigi came; no one but, e.g.,
non restò che mio cugino no one but
my cousin stayed || *conj* that; (*after
comparatives*) than, as

ché *adv* (coll) why || *conj* (coll) because; (coll) so that

checché *pron* (lit) whatever, no matter
what

checchessìa *pron* (lit) anything, everything

chèla *f* claw

che·pì *m* (**-pì**) kepi

cherubino *m* cherub

chetare (**chéto**) *tr* to quiet; to placate ||
ref to quiet down, become quiet

chetichèlla *f*—**alla chetichèlla** surreptitiously, stealthily

ché·to -ta *adj* quiet, still

chi *pron interr* who; whom || *pron rel*
who; whom; **chi . . . chi** some . . .
some

chiàcchiera *f* chatter, idle talk; gossip;
glibness; **fare quattro chiacchiere** to
have a chat

chiacchierare (**chiàcchiero**) *intr* to chat;
to gossip

chiacchierata *f* talk, chat; **fare una
chiacchierata** to visit

chiacchierì·no -na *adj* talkative, loquacious

chiacchierì·o *m* (**-i**) chattering, jabbering (*of a crowd*)

chiacchieró·ne -na *adj* talkative, loquacious || *mf* chatterbox

chiama *f* roll call; **fare la chiama** to call
the roll; **mancare alla chiama** to be
absent at the roll call

chiamare *tr* to call; to hail (*a cab*);
to invoke, call upon; **chiamare al
telefono** to call up; **esser chiamato a**
to have the vocation for || *ref* to be
named; **si chiama Giovanni** his name
is John

chiamata *f* call; (law) designation (*of
an heir*); (telp) ring; (theat) curtain
call; (typ) catchword

chiappa *f* (vulg) buttock; (slang) catch
(*e.g., of fish*)

chiarét·to -ta *adj & m* claret

chiarézza *f* clarity, clearness

chiarificare §197 (**chiarìfico**) *tr* to
clarify

chiarificazióne *f* clarification

chiariménto *m* explanation

chiarire §176 *tr* to clear up, explain;
to unravel || *intr* (ESSERE) to clear,
become clear || *ref* to make oneself
clear; to assure oneself

chia·ro -ra *adj* clear; bright; light
(*color*); honest; clear-cut; plain (*language*); illustrious, famous || *m* light;
bright color; brightness; **chiaro di
luna** moonlight; **con questi chiari di
luna** in these troubled times; **mettere
in chiaro** to clarify, explain || **chiaro**
adv plainly; **chiaro e tondo** bluntly,
frankly

chiaróre *m* light, glimmer

chiaroveggènte *adj & mf* clairvoyant

chiaroveggènza *f* clairvoyance

chiassata *f* uproar, disturbance, racket;
noisy scene

chiasso *m* noise; uproar; alley; **fare
chiasso** to cause a sensation

chiàsso·so -sa [*s*] *adj* noisy; gaudy

chiatta *f* barge; pontoon

chiavarda *f* bolt

chiave *f* key; wrench; (archit) keystone;
(mus) clef; **avere le chiavi di** to own;
chiave a rollino adjustable wrench;
chiave a tubo socket wrench; **chiave
di volta** keystone; **chiave inglese**
monkey wrench; **fuori chiave** off
key; **sotto chiave** under lock and key

chiavétta *f* key; cock; cotter pin

chiàvi·ca *f* (**-che**) sewer

chiavistèllo *m* bolt

chiazza *f* spot, blotch

chiazzare *tr* to spot, blotch; to mottle

chiazza·to -ta *adj* spotted, mottled

chìc·ca *f* (**-che**) sweet, candy

chìcchera *f* cup

chicchessìa *pron indef* anyone, anybody

chicchirichì *m* cock-a-doodle-doo

chìc·co *m* (**-chi**) grain, seed; bead (*of
rosary*); bean (*of coffee*); **chicco di
grandine** hailstone; **chicco d'uva**
grape

chièdere §124 *tr* to ask; to ask for; to
beg (*pardon*); to require; to sue (*for
damages or peace*); **chiedere a qlcu
di** + *inf* to ask s.o. to + *inf*; **chiedere
in prestito** to borrow; **chiedere qlco
a qlcu** to ask s.o. for s.th || *ref* to
wonder

chiéri·ca *f* (**-che**) tonsure; priesthood

chiéri·co *m* (**-ci**) clergyman; altar boy;
(archaic) clerk

chièsa *f* church

chiesuòla *f* small church; clique, set
(*e.g., of artists*); (naut) binnacle

chì·glia *f* (**-glie**) keel; **chiglia mobile**
(naut) centerboard

chilo *m* kilo, kilogram; **fare il chilo** to
take a siesta

chilociclo *m* kilocycle

chilogrammo *m* kilogram

chilohèrtz *m* kilohertz

chilometràg·gio *m* (**-gi**) distance in
kilometers

chilomètri·co -ca *adj* (**-ci -che**) kilometric; interminable (*e.g., speech*)

chilòmetro *m* kilometer

chilo·watt *m* (**-watt**) kilowatt

chimèra *f* chimera; daydream, utopia

chimèri·co -ca *adj* (**-ci -che**) chimerical

chìmi·co -ca (**-ci -che**) *adj* chemical ||
m chemist || *f* chemistry

chimòno *m* kimono

china *f* slope, decline; India ink; cinchona

chinare *tr* to bend; to lower (*one's
eyes*); **chinare il capo** to nod assent;
chinare la fronte to yield, give in ||
ref to bend, stoop

china·to -ta *adj* bent, lowered; bitter;
with quinine, e.g., **vino chinato** wine
with quinine

chincàglie *fpl* notions, knicknacks, sundries

chincaglière *m* notions or knicknack dealer

chincaglieria *f* knicknack; **chincaglierie** knicknacks, notions

chinina *f* quinine (*alkaloid*)

chinino *m* quinine (*salt of the alkaloid*)

chi·no -na *adj* bent, lowered || *f* see **china**

chiòc·cia *f* (**-ce**) brooding hen

chiocciare §128 (**chiòccio**) *intr* to cluck; to sit, brood; to crouch

chiocciata *f* brood

chiòc·cio -cia (**-ci -ce**) *adj* hoarse || *f* see **chioccia**

chiòcciola *f* snail; (anat) cochlea; (mach) nut

chioccolì·o *m* (**-i**) cackle (*of hen*); gurgle (*of water*)

chiodare (**chiòdo**) *tr* to nail

chioda·to -ta *adj* nailed shut; hobnailed

chiòdo *m* nail; spike; obsession; craze; (coll) debt; **chiodi** climbing irons; **chiodo a espansione** expansion bolt; **chiodo da cavallo** horseshoe nail; **chiodo di garofano** clove; **chiodo ribattino** rivet

chiòma *f* hair; mane; foliage; (astr) coma

chioma·to -ta *adj* hairy, long-haired; leafy

chiòsa *f* gloss

chiosare (**chiòso**) *tr* to gloss, comment on

chiò·sco *m* (**-schi**) kiosk, stand, newsstand; pavilion, bandstand

chiòstra *f* circular range (*of mountains*); (poet) enclosure; (poet) set (*of teeth*); (poet) zone, region

chiòstro *m* cloister

chiòt·to -ta *adj* quiet, still; **chiotto chiotto** still as a mouse

chiromante *mf* palmist

chiromanzia *f* palmistry

chiropràtica *f* chiropractice

chirurgia *f* surgery

chirùrgi·co -ca *adj* (**-ci -che**) surgical

chirur·go *m* (**-ghi** & **-gi**) surgeon

chissà *adv* maybe

chitarra *f* guitar; **chitarra hawaiana** ukulele

chitarri·sta *mf* (**-sti -ste**) guitar player

chiùdere §125 *tr* to shut, close; to lock; to turn off; to fasten; to block (*a road*); to fence in; to nail shut (*a box*); to strike (*a balance*); to conclude, wind up; **chiudere a chiave** to lock; **chiudere bottega** to go out of business; **chiudere il becco** (slang) to shut up || *intr* to shut, close; to lock || *ref* to shut, close; to lock; to withdraw; to cloud over

chiùnque *pron indef invar* anybody, anyone || *pron rel invar* whoever, whomever; anyone who, anyone whom

chiurlo *m* (orn) curlew

chiusa *f* fence; lock (*of canal*); end, conclusion (*e.g., of letter*)

chiusino *m* manhole

chiu·so -sa [s] *adj* shut, closed, locked; stuffy (*air*); high-bodiced (*dress*); close (*vowel*) || *m* enclosure, corral; close || *f* see **chiusa**

chiusura [s] *f* closing, end; fastener; lock; **chiusura lampo** zipper, slide fastener

ci §5

ciabatta *f* slipper; old shoe

ciabat·tàio *m* (**-tài**) cobbler

ciabattare *intr* to shuffle along

ciabattino *m* cobbler, shoemaker

ciàc *f* (mov) clappers

cialda *f* wafer; thin waffle

cialdóne *m* cone (*for ice cream*)

cialtró·ne -na *mf* rogue, scoundrel; slovenly person

ciambèlla *f* doughnut; **ciambella di salvataggio** life saver

ciambellano *m* chamberlain

ciampicare §197 (**ciàmpico**) *intr* to stumble along

ciana *f* (slang) fishwife

cianamide *f* cyanamide

ciàn·cia *f* (**-ce**) chatter, prattle, idle gossip

cianciare §128 (**ciàncio**) *intr* to chatter, prattle

cianciafrùscola *f* trifle, bagatelle

cianfrusà·glia *f* (**-glie**) trifle, trinket; rubbish, trash, junk

cianìdri·co -ca *adj* (**-ci -che**) hydrocyanic

cianògeno *m* cyanogen

cianuro *m* cyanide

ciao *interj* (coll) hi!, hello!; (coll) goodbye!, so long!

ciarla *f* chatter, prattle, idle talk; gossip

ciarlare *intr* to chatter, prattle

ciarlatanata *f* charlatanism, quackery

ciarlataneria *f* charlatanism

ciarlatané·sco -sca *adj* (**-schi -sche**) charlatan

ciarlatano *m* charlatan, quack

ciarliè·ro -ra *adj* talkative, garrulous

ciarpame *m* rubbish, junk

ciaschedu·no -na *adj indef* each || *pron indef* each one, everyone

ciascu·no -na *adj indef* each || *pron indef* each one, everyone

cibare *tr* & *ref* to feed

cibà·rio -ria (**-ri -rie**) *adj* alimentary || **cibarie** *fpl* foodstuffs, victuals

cibo *m* food; meal; (fig) dish

cicala *f* cicada; grasshopper; locust; (fig) chatterbox; (naut) anchor ring

cicalare *intr* to prattle, babble; to chatter

cicalé·cio *m* (**-ci**) prattle, babble; chatter

cicatrice *f* scar

cicatrizzare [ddzz] *tr* to heal (*a wound*) || *intr* (ESSERE) & *ref* to heal, scar

cicatrizzazióne [ddzz] *f* closing, healing (*of a wound*)

cic·ca *f* (**-che**) butt (*of cigar or cigarette*); (slang) chewing gum

ciccare §197 *intr* to chew tobacco; (coll) to boil with anger

cicchettare (**cicchétto**) *tr* (slang) to prime (*a carburetor*); (slang) to dress down, reprimand || *intr* to tipple

cicchétto *m* nip (*of liquor*); (slang) dressing down

cìc·cia *f* (-ce) (joc) flesh; (joc) fat

cicció·ne -na *mf* fatty

ceceróne *m* guide || **Cicerone** *m* Cicero

ciclàbile *adj* open to bicycles; bicycle, e.g., **pista ciclabile** bicycle trail

cìcli·co -ca *adj* (-ci -che) cyclic(al)

cicli·sta *mf* (-sti -ste) cyclist, bicyclist

cìclo *m* cycle; (coll) bicycle; **ciclo operativo** (econ) turnover

ciclomotóre *m* motorbike

ciclomotori·sta *mf* (-sti -ste) driver of motorbike

cicióne *m* cyclone

ciclòpe *m* cyclops

ciclòpi·co -ca *adj* (-ci -che) cyclopean, gigantic

ciclopista *f* bicycle trail

ciclostilare *tr* to mimeograph

ciclostile or **ciclostìlo** *m* mimeograph

ciclotróne *m* cyclotron

cicógna *f* stork

cicòria *f* chicory; endive

cicuta *f* hemlock

ciè·co -ca (-chi -che) *adj* blind; **alla cieca** blindly || *mf* blind person || *m* blind man; **i ciechi** the blind

cièlo *m* sky; heaven; weather, climate; roof (*e.g., of wagon*); **a ciel sereno** in the open air; **cielo a pecorelle** mackerel or fleecy sky; **dal cielo** from above; **non stare né in cielo né in terra** to be utterly absurd; **per amor del cielo** for heaven's sake; **portare al cielo** to praise to the skies; **santo cielo!** good heavens!; **volesse il cielo che . . . !** would that . . . !

cifra *f* number, figure; Arabic numeral; sum, total; digit; initial, monogram; cipher, code; **cifra d'affari** amount of business, turnover; **cifra tonda** round number

cifrare *tr* to cipher, code; to embroider (*a monogram*)

cifrà·rio *m* (-ri) code, cipher

cì·glio *m* (-glia *fpl*) eyelash; eyebrow; **a ciglio asciutto** with dry eyes; **ciglia** (zool) cilia; **senza batter ciglio** without batting an eye || *m* (-gli) (fig) edge, brow

ciglióne *m* bank, embankment

cigno *m* swan; cob

cigolante *adj* creaky, squeaky

cigolare (**cìgolo**) *intr* to squeak, creak

cigolì·o *m* (-ìi) squeak, creak

Cile, il Chile

cilécca *f*—**fare cilecca** to misfire

cileccare §197 (**cilécco**) *intr* to goof, blunder; to fail

cilè·no -na *adj & mf* Chilean

cilè·stro -stra *adj* (poet) azure, blue

cilì·cio *m* (-ci) sackcloth

ciliè·gia *f* (-gie & -ge) cherry

ciliè·gio *m* (-gi) cherry tree

cilindrare *tr* to calender (*e.g., paper*); to roll (*a road*)

cilindrata *f* (aut) cylinder capacity, piston displacement

cilìndri·co -ca *adj* (-ci -che) cylindric(al)

cilìndro *m* cylinder; top hat; roll, roller

cìma *f* top, summit; tip (*e.g., of a pole*); peak (*of mountain*); edge, end; rope, cable; head (*e.g., of lettuce*); (coll) genius; **da cima a fondo** from top to bottom

cimare *tr* to cut the tip off; to shear; (agr) to prune

cimasa *f* (archit) coping

cìmbalo *m* gong; (obs) cymbal; **in cimbali** tipsy; in a tizzy

cimè·lio *m* (-li) relic, souvenir, memento

cimentare (**ciménto**) *tr* to risk (*e.g., one's life*); to provoke; (archaic) to assay || *ref* to expose oneself; to venture

ciménto *m* risk, danger; (archaic) assay

cìmice *f* bug; bedbug; (coll) thumbtack

cimièro *m* crest; (poet) helmet

ciminièra *f* chimney (*of factory*); smokestack (*of locomotive*); funnel (*of steamship*)

cimitèro *m* cemetery, graveyard; (fig) ghosttown

cimòsa [s] or **cimòssa** *f* selvage; blackboard eraser

cimurro *m* distemper; (joc) cold

Cina, la China

cinabro *m* cinnabar; crimson; red ink

cìn·cia *f* (-ce) titmouse

cinciallègra *f* great titmouse

cincilla *f* chinchilla

cincischiare §287 *tr* to shred; to wrinkle, crease; to waste (*time*); to mumble (*words*) || *intr* to wrinkle, crease

cine *m* (coll) cinema

cineamatóre *m* amateur movie maker

cine·asta *m* (-sti) motion-picture producer; movie fan; movie actor || *f* movie actress

cinecàmera *f* movie camera

cinedilettante *mf* amateur movie maker

cinegiornale *m* newsreel

cinelàndia *f* movieland

cìne·ma *m* (-ma) movies; movie house

cinematografare (**cinematògrafo**) *tr* to film, shoot

cinematografìa *f* cinema, motion pictures, movie industry

cinematogràfi·co -ca *adj* (-ci -che) movie, motion-picture; movie-like

cinematògrafo *m* motion picture; movie theater; (fig) hubbub; (fig) funny sight

cineparchég·gio *m* (-gi) drive-in movie

cinepar·co *m* (-chi) drive-in movie

cineprésa [s] *f* movie camera

cinère·o -a *adj* ashen

cinescò·pio *m* (-pi) kinescope, TV tube

cinése [s] *adj & mf* Chinese

cineteatro *m* movie house; **cineteatro all'aperto** outdoor movie

cinetè·ca *f* (-che) film library

cinèti·co -ca *adj* (-ci -che) kinetic || *f* kinetics

cingallègra *f* var of **cinciallegra**

cìngere §126 *tr* to surround; to gird (*e.g., the head*); to gird on (*e.g., the sword*); **cìngere cavalière** to dub a knight; **cìngere d'assedio** to besiege

cinghia *f* belt, strap; **tirare la cinghia** to tighten one's belt

cinghiale *m* wild boar

cinghiata *f* lash

cìngola·to -ta *adj* track-driven, caterpillar

cìngolo *m* endless metal belt, track; girdle, belt (*of a priest*)

cinguettare (**cinguétto**) *intr* to chirp, twitter; to babble

cinguettì·o *m* (**-i**) chirp, twitter; (fig) babble

cìni·co -ca (**-ci -che**) *adj* cynical ‖ *m* cynic

ciniglia *f* chenille

cinismo *m* cynicism

cinòfilo *m* dog lover

cinquanta *adj, m & pron* fifty

cinquantenà·rio -ria (**-ri -rie**) *adj* fifty-year-old; occurring every fifty years ‖ *m* fiftieth anniversary

cinquantènne *adj* fifty-year-old ‖ *mf* fifty-year-old person

cinquantèn·nio *m* (**-ni**) period of fifty years, half century

cinquantèsi·mo -ma *adj, m & pron* fiftieth

cinquantina *f* about fifty; **sulla cinquantina** about fifty years old

cìnque *adj & pron* five; **le cinque** five o'clock ‖ *m* five; fifth (*in dates*)

cinquecenté·sco -sca *adj* (**-schi -sche**) sixteenth-century

cinquecènto *adj, m & pron* five hundred ‖ *f* small car ‖ **il Cinquecento** the sixteenth century

cinquina *f* set of five; five numbers (*drawn at Italian lotto*); (mil) pay

cinta *f* fence, wall; circuit, enclosure; circumference (*of a city*)

cintare *tr* to surround; to fence in; to hold (*in wrestling*)

cìn·to -ta *adj* surrounded, girded ‖ *m* belt; girdle; **cinto erniario** truss ‖ *f* see **cinta**

cìntola *f* waist; belt; **con le mani alla cintola** idling, loafing

cintura *f* belt; waist; waistband; lock (*in wrestling*); **cintura di salvataggio** life preserver; **cintura di sicurezza** safety belt

cinturare *tr* to surround

cinturino *m* strap (*of watch or shoes*); hem (*e.g., of cuffs*)

cinturóne *m* belt; Sam Browne belt

ciò *pron* this; that; **a ciò** for that purpose; **a ciò che** so that; **ciò nondimeno** or **ciò nonostante** though, nevertheless; **con tutto ciò** in spite of everything; **per ciò** therefore

ciòc·ca *f* (**-che**) lock (*of hair*); cluster (*e.g., of cherries*)

ciòc·co *m* (**-chi**) log; **dormire come un ciocco** to sleep like a log

cioccolata *adj invar* chocolate ‖ *f* chocolate (*beverage*)

cioccolatino *m* chocolate candy

cioccolato *m* chocolate; **cioccolato al latte** milk chocolate

cioè *adv* that is to say, namely; to wit; rather

ciondolare (**cióndolo**) *tr* to dangle ‖ *intr* to dawdle; to stroll, saunter

cióndolo *m* pendant, charm

ciondolóne *m* idler ‖ *adv* dangling

ciòtola *f* bowl

ciòttolo *m* pebble, small stone; cobblestone

ciottoló·so -sa [s] *adj* pebbly

cip *m* (**cip**) chip (*in gambling*)

cìpì·glio *m* (**-glì**) frown

cipólla *f* onion; bulb (*e.g., of a lamp*); nozzle (*of sprinkling can*)

cippo *m* column; bench mark

ciprèsso *m* cypress

cipria *f* face powder; **cipria compatta** compact

ciprió·ta *adj & mf* (**-ti -te**) Cypriot

Cipro *m* Cyprus

circa *adv* about, nearly ‖ *prep* concerning, regarding, as to

cir·co *m* (**-chi**) circus; **circo equestre** circus; **circo glaciale** cirque; **circo lunare** walled plain

circolante *adj* circulating; lending (*library*) ‖ *m* available cash (*of a corporation*)

circolare *adj* circular; cashier's (*check*) ‖ *f* circular (*letter*); (rr) beltline ‖ *v* (**cìrcolo**) *intr* to circulate

circolazióne *f* circulation; traffic; currency; **circolazione sanguigna** bloodstream; circulation of blood

cìrcolo *m* circle; circulation (*of blood*); reception (*e.g., at court*); club, set, group

circoncidere §145 *tr* to circumcise

circoncisióne *f* circumcision

circonci·so -sa *adj* circumcised

circondare (**circóndo**) *tr* to surround, encircle; to overwhelm (*e.g., with kindness*) ‖ *ref* to surround oneself; to be surrounded

circondà·rio *m* (**-ri**) district; surrounding territory

circonduzióne *f* rotation (*e.g., of the body in calisthenics*)

circonferènza *f* circumference

circonflès·so -sa *adj* circumflex

circonlocuzióne *f* circumlocution

circonvallazióne *f* city-line road; (rr) beltline

circonvenire §282 *tr* to circumvent; to outwit

circonvenzióne *f* circumvention

circonvici·no -na *adj* neighboring, nearby

circoscrit·to -ta *adj* circumscribed

circoscrìvere §250 *tr* to circumscribe

circoscrizióne *f* district; circuit

circospèt·to -ta *adj* circumspect, cautious

circospezióne *f* circumspection

circostante *adj* neighboring, surrounding, nearby ‖ **circostanti** *mpl* neighbors; bystanders, onlookers

circostanza *f* circumstance

circostanziale *adj* circumstantial

circostanziare §287 *tr* to describe in detail; to circumstanciate

circostanzia·to -ta *adj* detailed, circumstantial

circuire §176 *tr* to circumvent

circùito *m* circuit; race (*of automobiles or bicycles*); **circuito stampato** (rad, telv) printed circuit

circumnavigare §209 (**circumnàvigo**) *tr* to circumnavigate

circumnavigazióne *f* circumnavigation

cirìlli·co -ca *adj* (**-ci -che**) Cyrillic

Ciro m Cyrus
cirro m cirrus
cirrò·si f (**-si**) cirrhosis
cispa f gum (*on edge of eyelids*)
cisposità [s] f gum; gumminess
cispó·so -sa [s] *adj* gummy
ciste f cyst
cistèrna f cistern; tank
cisti f cyst
cistifèllea f gall bladder
citante mf (law) plaintiff
citare tr to cite, quote; to mention;
(law) to summon, subpoena
citazióne f citation, quotation; mention; (law) summons, subpoena;
(mil) commendation
citillo m (zool) gopher
citòfono m intercom
citostàti·co -ca *adj* (**-ci -che**) (biochem)
cancer-inhibiting
citrato m citrate
citri·co -ca *adj* (**-ci -che**) citric
citrul·lo -la *adj* simple, foolish || m
simpleton, fool
cit·tà f (**-tà**) city, town || **Città del Capo**
Cape Town; **Città del Messico** Mex-
ico City; **Città del Vaticano** Vatican
City; **città fungo** boom town
cittadèlla f citadel
cittadinanza f citizenship
cittadi·no -na *adj* city, town, civic ||
mf citizen; city dweller, urbanite ||
m townsman
ciù·co m (**-chi**) (coll) donkey, ass
ciuffo m lock, forelock; tuft; (bot)
tassel
ciuffolòtto m (orn) bullfinch
ciurlare *intr*—**ciurlare nel manico** to
play fast and loose
ciurma f crew, gang, mob
ciurmare tr (archaic) to charm; (archaic) to trick, inveigle
ciurmatóre m swindler, charlatan
civétta f barn owl, little owl; unmarked
police car; ship used as decoy; (fig)
coquette, flirt
civettare (**civétto**) *intr* to flirt
civetteria f coquettishness, coquetry
civettuò·lo la *adj* coquettish; attractive
civi·co -ca *adj* (**-ci -che**) civic; town,
city
civile *adj* civil; civilian || mf civilian
civili·sta mf (**-sti -ste**) attorney, solicitor
civilizzare [ddzz] tr to civilize || ref to
become civilized
civilizzazióne [ddzz] f civilizing (e.g.,
of barbarians); civilization
civil·tà f (**-tà**) civilization; civility
civismo m good citizenship
clac·son m (**-son**) horn (of a car)
claire f (**claire**) grating (in front of a
store window)
clamóre m clamor, uproar
clamoró·so -sa [s] *adj* noisy; clamorous
clan m (clan) clan; clique
clandesti·no -na *adj* clandestine
clangóre m clangor, clang
clarinetti·sta mf (**-sti -ste**) clarinet
player
clarinétto m clarinet
clarino m clarion
classe f class

classicheggiante *adj* classicistic
classicismo m classicism
classici·sta mf (**-sti -ste**) classicist
classici·tà f (**-tà**) classical spirit; classical antiquity
clàssi·co -ca *adj* (**-ci -che**) classic(al) ||
m classic
classìfi·ca f (**-che**) rank, rating (in
competitive testing); classification;
(sports) rating
classificare §197 (**classìfico**) tr to
classify; to rate, rank || ref to score
classificazióne f classification
claudicante *adj* lame, limping
claudicare §197 (**clàudico**) *intr* to limp
clauné·sco -sca *adj* (**-schi -sche**) clownish
clàusola f provision, proviso; clause;
close, conclusion (e.g., of a speech);
clausola rossa instructions for payment (in bank-credit documents);
clausola verde shipping instructions
(in bank-credit documents)
clausura f (eccl) seclusion; (fig) secluded place
clava f club, bludgeon
clavicémbalo m harpsichord
clavìcola f clavicle, collarbone
clemàtide f clematis
clemènte *adj* clement, indulgent; mild
(climate)
clemènza f clemency; mildness
cleptòmane *adj & mf* kleptomaniac
clericale *adj* clerical || m clericalist
clericalismo m clericalism
clèro m clergy
clessidra f water clock; sandglass
clicchetti·o m (**-i**) clicking, click-clack
(e.g., of a typewriter)
cli·ché m (**-ché**) cliché; stereotype
(plate)
cliènte m client, customer, patron
clientèla f clientele, customers; practice (of a professional man)
cli·ma m (**-mi**) climate
climatèri·co -ca *adj* (**-ci -che**) climacteric; crucial
climatè·rio m (**-ri**) climacteric; crucial
period
climàti·co -ca *adj* (**-ci -che**) climatic
climatizzazióne [ddzz] f air conditioning
clìni·co -ca (**-ci -che**) *adj* clinic || m
clinician; highly skilled physician ||
f clinic; private hospital
cli·sma m (**-smi**) enema
clistère m enema; **clistere a pera** fountain syringe
cloa·ca f (**-che**) sewer
cioche f (**cioche**) woman's wide-
brimmed hat; (aer) stick; (aut) floor
gearshift
clorare (**clòro**) tr to chlorinate
clorato m chlorate
cloridri·co -ca *adj* (**-ci -che**) hydrochloric
clòro m chlorine
clorofilla f chlorophyll
clorofòr·mio m (**-mi**) chloroform
cloroformizzare [ddzz] tr to chloroform
cloruro m chloride

coabitare (coàbito) *intr* to live together; to cohabit

coabitazióne *f* sharing (*of an apartment*)

coaccusa·to -ta *adj* jointly accused || *m* codefendant

coacèrvo *m* accumulation (*e.g., of interest*)

coadiutóre *m* coadjutor

coadiuvante *adj* helping || *m* helper

coadiuvare (coàdiuvo) *tr* to assist, advise

coagulare (coàgulo) *tr & ref* to coagulate, clot

coagulazióne *f* coagulation, clotting

coàgulo *m* clot

coalescènza *f* coalescence

coalizióne *f* coalition

coalizzare [ddzz] *tr & ref* to unite, rally

coartare *tr* to coerce, force

coartazióne *f* coercion, forcing

coatti·vo -va *adj* forceful, compelling

coat·to -ta *adj* coercive

coautóre *m* coauthor

coazióne *f* coercion

cobalto *m* cobalt

cocaina *f* cocaine

cocainòmane *mf* cocaine addict

coc·ca *f* (-che) notch (*of arrow*); corner, edge (*e.g., of a handkerchief*); three-mast galley

coccarda *f* cockade

cocchière *m* coachman, cab driver

còc·chio *m* (-chi) coach; chariot

cocchiume *m* bung

còc·cia *f* (-ce) sword guard; (coll) head, noggin

còccige *m* coccyx

coccinèlla *f* ladybug

cocciniglia *f* cochineal

còc·cio *m* (-ci) earthenware; broken piece of pottery

cocciutàggine *m* stubborness

cocciu·to -ta *adj* stubborn

còc·co·m *m* (-chi) coconut (*tree and nut*); (bact) coccus; (coll) egg; (coll) darling, favorite

cocco·dè *m* (-dè) cackle

coccodrillo *m* crocodile

còccola *f* berry (*of cypress*); darling girl

coccolare (còccolo) *tr* to fondle, cuddle || *ref* to nestle, cuddle up; to bask

còcco·lo ·la (coll) nice, darling || *m* darling boy || *f* see **coccola**

coccolóne *or* coccolóni *adv* squatting

cocènte *adj* burning

cocktail *m* (cocktail) cocktail; cocktail party

còclea *f* dredge; (anat) cochlea

cocómero *m* watermelon; (coll) simpleton

cocorita *f* parakeet

cocuzza *f* (coll) pumpkin; (coll) head, noggin

cocùzzolo *m* crown (*of hat*); peak (*of mountain*)

códa *f* tail; train (*of skirt*); pigtail (*of hair*); coda di paglia (coll) uneasy conscience; con la coda dell'occhio out of the corner of the eye; con la coda tra le gambe with its tail between its legs; (fig) crestfallen; di

coda last; fare la coda to stand in line; in coda in a row; at the tail end

codardia *f* (lit) cowardice

codar·do -da *adj* cowardly || *mf* coward

codazzo *m* (pej) trail (*of people*)

codeina *f* codein

codé·sto -sta §7 *adj* || §8 *pron*

còdice *m* code; codex; codice della strada traffic laws; codice di avviamento postale zip code

codicillo *m* codicil

codificare §197 (codìfico) *tr* to codify

codi·no -na *adj* reactionary; conformist || *m* pigtail (*of a man*); (fig) reactionary; conformist || *f* small tail

códolo *m* tang, shank (*e.g., of knife*); handle (*of spoon or knife*); head (*of violin*)

coeducazióne *f* coeducation

coefficiènte *m* coefficient

coerciti·vo -va *adj* coercive

coercizióne *f* coercion

coerède *mf* coheir

coerènte *adj* coherent; consistent

coerènza *f* coherence; consistency

coesióne *f* cohesion

coesistènza *f* coexistence

coesìstere §114 *intr* to coexist

coesi·vo -va *adj* cohesive

coetàne·o -a *adj & m* contemporary

coè·vo -va *adj* contemporaneous, coeval

cofanétto *m* small chest, small coffer

còfano *m* chest, coffer; box, case (*for ammunition*); (aut) hood

còffa *f* masthead, crow's-nest

cofirmatà·rio -ria *adj & mf* (-ri -rie) cosigner

cogitabón·do -da *adj* (poet & joc) thoughtful, meditative

cogitare (còngito) *tr & intr* (poet & joc) to cogitate

cógli §4

cògliere §127 *tr* to gather; to hit (*the target*); to pluck (*flowers*); to grab, seize; (fig) to guess; cogliere in flagrante to catch in the act; cogliere la palla al balzo to seize time by the forelock; cogliere nel giusto to hit the nail on the head; cogliere qlcu alla sprovvista to catch s.o. napping; cogliere sul fatto to catch in the act

coglióne *m* (vulg) testicle; (vulg) simpleton, fool

coglioneria *f* (vulg) great stupidity

cognata *f* sister-in-law

cognato *m* brother-in-law

cògni·to -ta *adj* (poet & law) wellknown

cognizióne *f* cognition, knowledge

cognóme *m* surname, family name

coguaro *m* cougar

cói §4

coibènte *adj* nonconducting || *m* nonconductor

coincidènza *f* coincidence; harmony, identity; transfer (*from one streetcar or bus to another*); (rr) connection

coincìdere §145 *intr* to coincide

coinquilino *m* fellow tenant

cointeressare (cointerèsso) *tr* to give a share (*of profit*) to

cointeressa·to -ta *adj* jointly interested || *mf* party having a joint interest
cointeressènza *f* interest, share
coinvòlgere §289 *tr* to involve
còito *m* coitus, intercourse
cól §4
colà *adv* over there
colabròdo *m* colander, strainer
colàg·gio *m* (-gi) loss, leak
colapa·sta *m* (-sta) colander
colare (**cólo**) *tr* to filter, strain; to sift (*wheat*); to cast (*metals*); **colare a picco** to sink || *intr* to leak, drip; to flow (*said of blood*); **colare a picco** to sink
colata *f* casting (*of metal*); stream of lava; slide (*of snow or rocks*)
colatíc·cio *m* (-ci) drip, dripping
cola·tóio *m* (-tói) colander, strainer
colazione *f* breakfast; lunch; **colazione al sacco** picnic; **prima colazione** breakfast; **seconda colazione** lunch
colbac·co *m* (-chi) busby
colèi §8 *pron dem*
colèn·do -da *adj* (archaic) honorable
colè·ra *m* (-ra) cholera
colesterina *f* cholesterol
coli·brì *m* (-brì) hummingbird
còli·co -ca *adj* & *f* (-ci -che) colic
colino *m* strainer
cólla §4
còlla *f* glue; paste; **colla di pesce** isinglass
collaborare (**collàboro**) *intr* to collaborate; to contribute (*to newspaper or magazine*)
collaboratóre *m* collaborator; contributor (*to newspaper or magazine*)
collaborazióne *f* collaboration
collaborazioni·sta *mf* (-sti -ste) collaborationist
collana *f* necklace; series, collection (*of literary works*)
collante *adj* & *m* adhesive
collare *m* collar || *v* (**còllo**) *tr* to lift or lower (*with a rope*)
collasso *m* collapse
collaterale *adj* & *m* collateral
collaudare (**collàudo**) *tr* to test; to approve; to pass
collauda·tóre -trice *mf* tester
collàudo *m* test
collazionare (**collazióno**) *tr* to collate
cólle §4
còlle *m* hill; low peak; mountain pass
collè·ga *mf* (-ghi -ghe) colleague, associate
collegaménto *m* connection, telephone connection; contact; (mil) liaison
collegare §209 (**collégo**) *tr* to join, connect || *intr* to agree, be in harmony || *ref* to become allied; to make contact, make connection (*e.g., by phone*)
collegiale *adj* collegiate || *mf* boarding-school student
collegiata *f* collegiate church
collè·gio *m* (-gi) college (*e.g., of surgeons*); boarding school, academy
còllera *f* anger, wrath; **montare in collera** to become angry
collèri·co -ca *adj* (-ci -che) hot-tempered, choleric

collètta *f* collection; collect (*in church*)
collettivismo *m* collectivism
collettivi·tà *f* (-tà) collectivity, community
colletti·vo -va *adj* collective || *m* party worker (*of leftist party*)
collétto *m* collar; flank (*of a tooth*)
collet·tóre -trice *adj* connecting; collecting (*pipe*) || *m* collector; tax collector; manifold; (elec) commutator (*of D.C. device*); (elec) collector (*of A.C. device*); **collettore d'ammissione** intake manifold; **collettore di scarico** exhaust manifold
collettoria *f* tax office; small post office
collezionare (**collezióno**) *tr* to collect (*e.g., stamps*)
collezióne *f* collection; collection, series (*of literary works*)
collezioni·sta *mf* (-sti -ste) collector
collìdere §135 *intr* to collide
collimare *tr* to point (*a telescope*) || *intr* to coincide; match; to dovetail
collina *f* hill; **in collina** in the hill country
collinó·so -sa [*s*] *adj* hilly
colli·rio *m* (-ri) eyewash
collisióne *f* collision; (fig) conflict; **entrare in collisione** to collide
còllo §4
còllo *m* neck; piece (*of baggage*); package, parcel; **al collo** in a sling; (fig) downhill; **collo del piede** instep; **collo d'oca** crankshaft; **in collo** in one's arms (*said of a baby*)
collocaménto *m* placement, employment; **collocamento a riposo** retirement; **collocamento in aspettativa** leave of absence without pay; **collocamento in malattia** sick leave
collocare §197 (**còlloco**) *tr* to place; to find employment for; to sell; **collocare a riposo** to retire; **collocare in aspettativa** to give a leave of absence without pay; **collocare in malattia** to grant sick leave to
collocazióne *f* location (*of a book in a library*); catalogue card
colloidale *adj* colloidal
collòide *m* colloid
colloquiale *adj* colloquial
collò·quio *m* (-qui) talk, conference; colloquy; colloquium, symposium
colló·so -sa [*s*] *adj* gluey, sticky
collotòrto *m* (**collitòrti**) bigot, hypocrite
collòttola *f* nape or scruff of the neck
collùdere §105 *intr* to be in collusion
collusióne *f* collusion
collutó·rio *m* (-ri) mouthwash
colluttare *intr* to scuffle, fight
colluttazióne *f* scuffle, fight
cólma *f* high-water level (*during high tide*)
colmare (**cólmo**) *tr* to fill, fill up; fill in (*with dirt*); to overwhelm; **colmare una lacuna** to bridge a gap
colmata *f* silting; reclaimed land; sand bank
cól·mo -ma *adj* full, filled up || *m* top, peak, summit; (archit) ridgepole; (fig) acme; **al colmo di** at the height

of; **è il colmo** that's the limit || *f* see **colma**

colofóne *m* colophon

colofònia *f* rosin

colombàia *f* dovecot

colombèlla *f* ingenue; **a colombella** vertically

colóm·bo -ba *mf* pigeon, dove || **Colombo** *m* Columbus

colònia *f* colony; cologne; settlement; summer camp; **colonia penale** penal colony; penitentiary || **Colonia** *f* Cologne

coloniale *adj* colonial || *m* colonial; colonist; **coloniali** imported foods

colòni·co -ca *adj* (**-ci -che**) farm (*e.g., house*)

colonizzare [ddzz] *tr* to colonize; to settle

colonizzazióne [ddzz] *f* colonization

colonna *f* column; row; **colonna sonora** sound track; **Colonne d'Ercole** Pillars of Hercules

colonnato *m* colonnade

colonnèllo *m* colonel

colonnétta *f* small column; gasoline pump

colò·no -na *mf* sharecropper; colonist; settler; (*poet*) farmer

colorante *adj* coloring || *m* dye; stain

colorare (**colóro**) *tr & ref* to color; to stain

colora·to -ta *adj* colored; stained (*glass*)

colorazióne *f* coloring

colóre *m* color; paint; suit (*of cards*); flush (*at poker*); shade; character (*of a deal*); **di colore** colored (*man*); **farne di tutti i colori** to be up to all kinds of deviltry; **farsi di tutti i colori** to change countenance

colorifí·cio *m* (**-ci**) paint factory; dye factory

colorire §176 *tr* to color

colori·to -ta *adj* colored, flushed; expressive || *m* color, complexion; (*fig*) expression

coloritura *f* coloring; characteristic; political complexion

colóro §8

colossale *adj* colossal

Colossèo *m* Coliseum

colòsso *m* colossus

cólpa *f* fault; sin; guilt; (*law*) injury; **avere la colpa** to be guilty; to be wrong; **essere in colpa** to be guilty

colpévole *adj* guilty || *mf* guilty person, culprit

colpevolí·sta *mf* (**-sti -ste**) person who prejudges s.o. guilty

colpire §176 *tr* to hit, strike; to harm; to impress; **colpire nel segno** to hit the mark

cólpo *m* hit, blow; strike; tip, rap; knock; shot; round (*of gun*); cut, slash (*of knife*); thrust (*e.g., of spear*); lash (*of animal's tail*); toot (*of car's horn*); **andare a colpo sicuro** to know where to hit; **colpo apoplettico** stroke; **colpo da maestro** master stroke; **colpo d'aria** draft; **colpo d'ariete** water hammer; **colpo di fortuna** stroke of luck; **colpo di fulmine** love at first sight; **colpo di**

grazia coup de grâce; **colpo di mano** surprise attack; **colpo di scena** dramatic turn of events; **colpo di sole** sunstroke; **colpo di spugna** wiping the slate clean; **colpo di stato** coup d'état; **colpo di telefono** telephone call; **colpo di testa** sudden decision, inconsiderate action; **colpo di vento** gust of wind; **colpo d'occhio** view; glance, look; **di colpo** at once; **fallire il colpo** to miss the mark; **fare colpo** to make a hit; **sul colpo** then and there; **tutto in un colpo** all at once

colpó·so -sa [s] *adj* unpremeditated; involuntary (*e.g., manslaughter*)

coltèlla *f* butcher knife; (elec) knife switch

coltellàc·cio *m* (**-ci**) hunting knife; butcher knife; (naut) studding sail

coltellata *f* stab, gash, slash; **fare a coltellate** to fight with knives

coltellerìa *f* cutlery

coltelli·nàio *m* (**-nài**) cutler

coltèllo *m* knife; **a coltello** edgewise (*said of bricks*); **avere il coltello per il manico** to have the upper hand; **coltello a serramanico** switchblade knife; pocketknife

coltivare *tr* to cultivate

coltiva·to -ta *adj* cultivated

coltivatóre *m* farmer

coltivazióne *f* cultivation

cól·to -ta *adj* cultivated; learned (*word*) || *m* garden; (archaic) worship

cóltre *f* blanket; comforter; (fig) pall; **coltri** bedclothes

coltróne *m* quilt

coltura *f* cultivation; crop; culture (*e.g., of silkworms, bacteria*)

colubrina *f* culverin

colùi §8 *pron dem*

comandaménto *m* commandment

comandante *m* commanding officer; commandant; (nav) captain; **comandante del porto** harbor master; **comandante in seconda** (naut) first mate

comandare *tr* to command, order; to direct (*employees*); to register (*a letter*); (mach) to regulate; (mach) to control; (poet) to overlook, command the view of (*e.g., a valley*); **comandare a bacchetta** to command in a dictatorial manner || *intr* to command; **comandi!** (mil) at your orders!

comando *m* command, order

comare *f* godmother; (coll) friend, neighbor; (coll) gossip

combaciare §128 *tr* (archaic) to gather || *intr* to fit closely together; to tally, dovetail; to coincide

combattènte *adj* fighting || *m* combatant

combàttere *tr & intr* to combat || *ref* to fight one another

combattiménto *m* combat; fight; battle; **fuori combattimento** knockout, K.O.; **fuori combattimento tecnico** technical knockout, T.K.O.; **mettere fuori combattimento** to knock out; (fig) to weaken

combatti·vo -va *adj* pugnacious, combative

combattu·to -ta *adj* heated (*discussion*); overcome (*by doubt*); torn (*between two opposing feelings*)

combinare *tr* to combine; to match (*e.g., colors*); to organize || *intr* to agree; **combinare a** to succeed in || *ref* to agree; to chance, happen; to combine

combinazióne *f* combination; chance; coverall (*for mechanics or flyers*)

combrìccola *f* gang

combustìbile *adj* combustible || *m* fuel, combustible

combustióne *f* combustion; (poet) upheaval

combutta *f* gang, band; **essere in combutta** to be in cahoots

cóme *m* manner, way; **il come e il perchè** the why and the wherefore || *adv* as; like; as for; how; **come mai?** why?; **e come!** and how!; **ma come?** what?, how is it? || *conj* as; as soon as; while; how; because; since; **come se** as if

comecché *conj* (lit) although; (poet) wherever

comedóne *m* blackhead

cométa *f* comet

comici·tà *f* (-tà) comicalness

còmi·co -ca (-ci -che) *adj* comic(al) || *m* comic; author of comedies; comic actor

comignolo *m* chimney pot; ridge (*of roof*)

cominciare §128 *tr & intr* to begin, start, commence

comitato *m* committee

comitiva *f* group, party; (poet) retinue

comi·zio -zi (-zi) (pol) meeting, rally; (hist) comitia

còm·ma -mi (-mi) paragraph, article (*of law or decree*)

commèdia *f* comedy; play, drama; (fig) farce; **commedia di carattere** comedy of character; **commedia d'intreccio** comedy of intrigue; **far la commedia** to pretend, feign; **finire in commedia** to end ludicrously; **finire la commedia** to stop faking

commediante *mf* actor; comedian (*amusing person*); (fig) hypocrite

commediògra·fo -fa *mf* playwright, comedian

commemorare (**commèmoro**) *tr* to commemorate

commemorati·vo -va *adj* commemorative, memorial

commemorazióne *f* commemoration

commènda *f* commandership (*of an order*); (eccl) commendam

commendàbile *adj* commendable

commendare (**commèndo**) *tr* (lit) to commend, praise; (obs) to entrust

commendati·zio -zia (-zi -zie) *adj* introductory || *f* letter of introduction; recommendation

commendatóre *m* commander (*of an order*)

commendévole *adj* commendable

commensale *mf* guest; table companion

commensurare (**commènsuro** & **commensuro**) *tr* to compare; to proportion, prorate

commentare (**commènto**) *tr* to comment, comment on

commentà·rio *m* (-ri) commentary; diary, journal

commenta·tóre -trice *mf* commentator

commènto *m* comment; **fare commenti** to criticize; **non far commenti!** don't waste your time talking!

commerciàbile *adj* marketable

commerciale *adj* commercial; common, ordinary

commerciali·sta *mf* (-sti -ste) business-administration major; attorney specializing in commercial law

commerciante *mf* merchant, dealer

commerciare §128 (**commèrcio**) *tr* to deal in; to buy and sell || *intr* to deal

commèr·cio *m* (-ci) commerce, trade; illegal traffic; (poet) intercourse; **commercio all'ingrosso** wholesale (trade); **commercio al minuto** retail (trade); **fuori commercio** not for sale; **in commercio** for sale

commès·so -sa *adj* committed || *mf* clerk (*in a store*) || *m* salesman; clerk (*in a court*); janitor (*in a school*); **commesso viaggiatore** traveling salesman || *f* saleslady; order (*of merchandise*)

commestìbile *adj* edible || **commestìbili** *mpl* staples, groceries; foodstuffs

commèttere §198 *tr* to join, connect; to commit; to charge, commission; to peg; (poet) to entrust || *intr* to join, fit

commettitura *f* joint, seam

commiato *m* leave; **dare commiato a** to dismiss; **prender commiato** to take one's leave

commilitóne *m* comrade, comrade in arms

comminare *tr* (law) to determine, fix (*a penalty*)

comminatò·rio -ria *adj* threatening

commiserare (**commisero**) *tr* to pity, feel sorry for

commiserazióne *f* commiseration

commissariale *adj* commissioner's, e.g., **funzioni commissariali** commissioner's functions; commissar's functions

commissariato *m* commissary; inspector's office

commissà·rio *m* (-ri) commissary; inspector; commissioner; **commissario del popolo** commissar; **commissario di bordo** purser; **commissario di pubblica sicurezza** police inspector; **commissario tecnico** (sports) soccer commissioner

commissionare (**commissióno**) *tr* to commission, order

commissionà·rio -ria (-ri -rie) *adj* commission || *m* commission merchant

commissióne *f* commission, agency; order (*of merchandise*); committee; errand; commitment (*of an act*)

commisurare *tr* to proportion (*e.g., crime to punishment*)

committènte *mf* buyer, customer

commodòro _m_ commodore

commòs·so -sa _adj_ moved; moving

commovènte _adj_ moving, touching

commozióne _f_ commotion; emotion; **commozione cerebrale** (pathol) concussion

commuòvere §202 _tr_ to move; to touch; to stir || _ref_ to be moved; to be touched

commutare _tr_ to commute; to switch || _ref_ to turn

commuta·tóre -trice _adj_ commutative || _m_ (elec) change-over switch; (elec) commutator (_switch_); (telp) plugboard || _f_ converter

commutatori·sta _mf_ (-sti -ste) (telp) operator

commutazióne _f_ commutation; (telp) selection; (elec) switchover

co·mò _m_ (-mò) chest; chest of drawers

còmoda _f_ commode

comodare (**còmodo**) _tr_ to lend || _intr_ (with _dat_) to please, e.g., **non le comoda** it doesn't please her

comodino _m_ night table; (theat) bit player; **fare il comodino a** (coll) to follow sheepishly

comodi·tà _f_ (-tà) comfort; convenience; opportunity

còmo·do -da _adj_ comfortable; convenient; easy; loose-fitting; calm || _m_ convenience; ease; advantage; comfort; opportunity; **a Suo comodo at your convenience; comodo di cassa credit** (_at the bank_); **con comodo** without hurrying; **fare comodo** to come in handy; (with _dat_) to please, e.g., **non gli fa comodo** it doesn't please him; **fare il proprio comodo** to think only of oneself; **stia comodo!** make yourself at home! || _f_ see **comoda**

compaesa·no -na _mf_ fellow citizen || _m_ fellow countryman || _f_ fellow countrywoman

compàgine _f_ strict union; connection; assemblage; (fig) cohesion

compagna _f_ companion, mate; (archaic) company

compagnìa _f_ company; **Compagnia di Gesù** Society of Jesus; **compagnia stabile** (theat) stock company

compa·gno -gna _adj_ like, similar || _m_ fellow; companion, comrade; mate; partner; **compagno d'armi** comrade in arms; **compagno di viaggio** fellow traveler || _f_ see **compagna**

companàti·co _m_ (-ci) food to eat with bread

comparàbile _adj_ comparable

comparati·vo -va _adj & m_ comparative

compara·to -ta _adj_ comparative

comparazióne _f_ comparison

compare _m_ godfather; best man (_at wedding_); fellow; confederate

comparire §108 _intr_ to appear; to be known; to cut a figure

comparizióne _f_ appearance (_in court_)

comparsa _f_ appearance; (theat) extra, supernumerary; (law) petition, brief; **far comparsa** to cut a figure

compartecipare (**compartécipo**) _intr_ to share

compartecipazióne _f_ sharing; **compartecipazione agli utili** profit sharing

compartécipe _adj_ sharing

compartiménto _m_ circle, clique; district; (naut, rr) compartment

compartire §176 & (**comparto**) _tr_ to divide up, distribute

compassa·to -ta _adj_ measured; stiff, formal; reserved; self-controlled

compassionare (**compassióno**) _tr_ to pity

compassióne _f_ compassion, pity

compassionévole _adj_ compassionate; pitiful

compasso _m_ compass; **compasso a grossezza** calipers

compatìbile _adj_ excusable; compatible

compatiménto _m_ compassion; condescension

compatire §176 _tr_ to pity; to forgive, overlook; to bear with; **farsi compatire** to become an object of ridicule || _intr_ to pity

compatriò·ta _mf_ (-ti -te) compatriot

compattézza _f_ compactness

compat·to -ta _adj_ compact, tight

compendiare §287 (**compèndio**) _tr_ to epitomize, summarize

compèn·dio _m_ (-di) compendium, summary; **fare un compendio di** to abstract

compendió·so -sa [s] _adj_ compendious, brief, succinct

compenetràbile _adj_ penetrable

compenetrabilità _f_ penetrability

compenetrare (**compènetro**) _tr_ to penetrate; to permeate; to pervade || _ref_ to be overcome; **compenetrarsi di** to be conscious of

compensare (**compènso**) _tr_ to compensate, pay; to balance, offset; to clear (_checks_)

compensa·to -ta _adj_ compensated; laminated || _m_ laminate; plywood

compensazióne _f_ compensation; offset; (com) clearing (_of checks_)

compènso _m_ reward; retribution, pay; **in compenso** on the other hand

cómpera _f_ var of **compra**

comperare (**cómpero**) _tr & intr_ var of **comprare**

competènte _adj_ competent

competènza _f_ competence; jurisdiction; **competenze honoraria**

compètere §129 _intr_ to compete; to concern; to have jurisdiction

competiti·vo -va _adj_ competitive

competi·tóre -trice _mf_ competitor, contender

competizióne _f_ competition, contest

compiacènte _adj_ complaisant, obliging

compiacènza _f_ complaisance, kindness; pleasure

compiacére §214 _tr_ to gratify || _intr_ (with _dat_) to please, e.g., **non posso compiacere a tutti** I cannot please everybody || _ref_ to be pleased; **compiacersi con** to congratulate; **compiacersi di** to be kind enough to

compiacimÃ©nto _m_ pleasure; congratulation; approval

compiaciu·to -ta *adj* pleased, satisfied
compiàngere §215 *tr* to pity || *ref* to feel sorry
compian·to -ta *adj* lamented (*departed person*) || *m* sympathy; (poet) sorrow; (poet) lament
compiegare §209 (**compiègo**) *tr* to enclose (*in a letter*)
cómpiere §130 *tr* to complete, finish; to fulfill, accomplish; **compiere . . . anni** to be . . . years old; **compiere gli anni** to have a birthday || *ref* to happen; to come true
compilare *tr* to compile
compila·tóre -trice *mf* compiler
compilazióne *f* compilation
compiménto *m* fulfillment, accomplishment
compire §176 *tr* to complete, finish; to fulfill, accomplish; **per compir l'opera** as if it weren't enough || *ref* to happen; to come true
compitare (**cómpito**) *tr* to syllabify; to read poorly; to spell, spell letter by letter
compitazióne *f* spelling letter by letter
compitézza *f* courtesy, politeness
cómpito *m* task; exercise; homework
compi·to -ta *adj* courteous, polite; (poet) adequate
compiu·to -ta *adj* accomplished
compleanno *m* birthday; **buon compleanno** happy birthday
complementare *adj* complementary; additional (*tax*) || *f* graduated income tax
compleménto *m* complement; (mil, nav) reserve
complessióne *f* build, physique
complessi·tà *f* (-tà) complexity
complessi·vo -va *adj* total, aggregate
complès·so -sa *adj* complex, complicated; compound (*fracture*) || *m* whole; complex; **in complesso** in general
completare (**complèto**) *tr* to complete, carry through; to supplement, round off
complè·to -ta *adj* complete, full; overall, thoroughgoing; **al completo** full (*e.g., bus*) || *m* set (*of matching items*); suit of clothes; **completo femminile** lady's tailor-made suit; **completo maschile** suit
complicare §197 (**còmplico**) *tr* to complicate || *ref* to become complicated
complica·to -ta *adj* complicated, complex
complicazióne *f* complication
còmplice *mf* accomplice, accessory
complici·tà *f* (-tà) complicity
complimentare (**compliménto**) *tr* to compliment || *ref*—**complimentarsi con** to congratulate
compliménto *m* compliment; congratulation; favor; **complimenti** regards; **complimenti!** congratulations!; **fare complimenti** to stand on ceremony; **senza complimenti** without ceremony; without any further ado
complimentó·so -sa [s] *adj* ceremonious; complimentary

complottare (**complòtto**) *intr* to plot
complòtto *m* plot, machination
compliù·vio *m* (-vi) valley (*of roof*)
componènte *adj* component || *mf* member || *m* component (*component part*) || *f* component (*force*)
componìbile *adj* sectional (*e.g., bookcase*)
componiménto *m* composition, settlement (*of a dispute*)
compórre §218 *tr* to compose; to arrange; to settle (*a quarrel*); to lay out (*a corpse*); (typ) to set
comportaménto *m* behavior
comportare (**compòrto**) *tr* to allow, tolerate; to entail || *ref* to behave; to handle (*said, e.g., of a motor*); **comportarsi male** to misbehave
compòrto *m* (com) delay
compòsi·to -ta *adj* composite || **composite** *fpl* (bot) Compositae
composi·tóio *m* (-tói) (typ) composing stick
composi·tóre -trice *mf* compositor, typesetter; composer || *f* typesetting machine
composizióne *f* composition; settlement
compósta *f* compote; **composta di frutta** stewed fruit
compostézza *f* neatness, tidiness; good behavior; orderliness
compostièra *f* compote, compotier
compó·sto -sta *adj* compound; neat, tidy; well-behaved || *m* compound || *f* see **composta**
cómpra *f* purchase; shopping; **compre** shopping
comprare (**cómpro**) *tr* to buy, purchase; to buy off || *intr* to buy, shop; to trade
compra·tóre -trice *mf* buyer, purchaser
compravéndere §281 *tr* to make a deal in, to transfer (*e.g., a house*)
compravéndita *f* transaction; transfer (*e.g., of real estate*)
comprèndere §220 *tr* to comprehend, include, comprise; to overwhelm; to understand; to forgive
comprendò·nio *m* (-ni) (joc) understanding
comprensìbile *adj* understandable, comprehensible
comprensióne *f* comprehension, understanding
comprensi·vo -va *adj* comprehensive; understanding
compensò·rio *m* (-ri) land to be reclaimed; area, zone, e.g., **comprensorio turistico** tourist area
comprè·so -sa [s] *adj* comprised, included; understood; deeply touched; immersed
comprèssa *f* compress
compressióne *f* compression
comprès·so -sa *adj* compressed; (fig) repressed; (aut) supercharged || *f* see **compressa**
compressóre *m* compressor; **compressore stradale** road roller
comprimà·rio *m* (-ri) (med) associate chief of staff; (theat) second lead

comprìmere §131 *tr* to compress; to repress, restrain; to tamp

compromés·so -sa *adj* jeopardized, in danger || *m* compromise; referral (*to arbitration*)

compromettènte *adj* compromising

comprométtere §198 *tr* to compromise; to endanger; to involve, commit; (law) to refer (*to arbitration*)

comproprie·tà *f* (-tà) joint ownership

comproprietà·rio -ria *mf* (-ri -rie) joint owner

compròva *f* confirmation

comprovare (compròvo) *tr* to confirm; to circumstantiate

compulsare *tr* to consult, peruse; to summon (*to appear in court*)

compulsi·vo -va *adj* compulsive

compun·to -ta *adj* contrite, repentant

compunzióne *f* compunction

computàbile *adj* computable

computare (còmputo) *tr* to compute

computi·sta *mf* (-sti -ste) bookkeeper

computistería *f* bookkeeping

còmputo *m* computation, reckoning

comunale *adj* municipal, town (*e.g., hall*); community-owned; (poet) common

comunanza *f* community; **in comunanza** in common

comune *adj* common || *m* normalcy; commune, municipality, town; town hall; (hist) guild; (nav) common seaman; **in comune** in common || *f* commune (*in communist countries*); (theat) main stage entrance; **andare per la comune** to follow the crowd; **per la comune** commonly

comunèlla *f* cabal, clique; passkey (*in a hotel*); (law) mutual insurance (*of cattlemen*); **fare comunella con** to consort with

comunicàbile *adj* communicable

comunicante *adj* communicant; communicating || *m* priest who gives communion

comunicare §197 (comùnico) *tr* to communicate; to administer communion to || *intr* to communicate || *ref* to spread; to receive communion, to commune

comunicati·vo -va *adj* communicable, spreading; communicative

comunicato *m* communiqué; **comunicato commerciale** advertisement, ad; **comunicato stampa** press release

comunicazióne *f* communication; statement; (telp) connection; **comunicazioni** communications

comunióne *f* community; (law) community property || **Comunione** *f* Communion

comunismo *m* communism

comuni·sta (-sti -ste) *adj* communist || *mf* communist; (law) joint tenant

comunìsti·co -ca *adj* (-ci -che) communistic

comuni·tà *f* (-tà) community

comunità·rio -ria *adj* (-ri -rie) community, e.g., **interessi comunitari** community interests

comùnque *adv* however, nevertheless || *conj* however, no matter how

cón §4 *prep* with; by (*e.g., boat*); **con + art + inf** by + ger, e.g., **col leggere** by reading

conato *m* effort, attempt

cón·ca *f* (-che) washbowl, washbasin; copper water jug; valley, hollow; (poet) shell; **conca idraulica** drydock

concatenaménto *m* (poet) concatenation

concatenare (concaténo) *tr* to link || *ref* to unfold, ensue

concatenazióne *f* concatenation

concàusa *f* joint cause; (law) aggravation

cònca·vo -va *adj* concave; hollow || *m* hollow

concèdere §132 *tr* to grant, concede; to stretch (*a point*) || *ref* to let oneself go, give oneself over

concènto *m* harmony; (fig) agreement

concentraménto *m* concentration

concentrare (concèntro) *tr* to concentrate; to center || *ref* to concentrate, focus; to center

concentra·to -ta *adj* concentrated; condensed (*e.g., milk*) || *m* purée (*e.g., of tomatoes*)

concentrazióne *f* concentration; (chem) condensation

concèntri·co -ca *adj* (-ci -che) concentric

concepìbile *adj* conceivable

concepiménto *m* conception; (fig) formulation

concepire §176 *tr* to conceive; (fig) to nurture

concería *f* tannery

concèrnere §133 *tr* to concern

concertare (concèrto) *tr* to scheme, concert; (mus) to orchestrate, arrange || *ref* to agree

concerta·to -ta *adj* agreed upon; (mus) with accompaniment || *m* ensemble (*of orchestra, soloists, and chorus*)

concerta·tóre -trice *mf* arranger || *m* plotter, schemer

concertazióne *f* (mus) arrangement

concerti·sta *mf* (-sti -ste) concert performer, soloist

concèrto *m* concert; concerto; (fig) choir

concessionà·rio -ria *m* (-ri) sole agent, concessionaire; dealer; lessee (*of business establishment*)

concessióne *f* concession; dealership; admission

concessi·vo -va *adj* concessive

concès·so -sa *adj* granted, admitting

concètto *m* concept; opinion

concettó·so -sa [*s*] *adj* concise; full of ideas; full of conceits

concettuale *adj* conceptual

concezióne *f* conception; formulation

conchìglia *f* shell, conch; (sports) jock guard, protective cup

conchiùdere §125 *tr, intr & ref* var of concludere

cón·cia *f* (-ce) tanning

conciapèl·li *m* (-li) tanner

conciare §128 (cóncio) *tr* to tan; to cure (*e.g., tobacco*); to arrange; to straighten up; to reduce; to cut (*a precious stone*); **conciare per le feste** (coll) to give a good beating to ‖ *ref* to get messed up, get dirty

conciatét·ti *m* (**-ti**) roofer

conciató·re -trice *mf* tanner

conciliàbile *adj* reconcilable

conciliàbolo *m* conventicle, secret meeting

conciliante *adj* conciliatory

conciliare *adj* council ‖ *m* member of an ecclesiastical council ‖ §287 *tr* to conciliate, reconcile; to settle (*a fine*); to promote (*e.g., sleep*); to obtain (*a favor*) ‖ *ref* to become reconciled

concilia·tóre -trice *adj* conciliatory ‖ *mf* conciliator, peacemaker ‖ *m* justice of the peace

conciliazióne *f* conciliation ‖ **la Conciliazione** the Concordat (*of 1929 between Italy and the Vatican*)

concì·lio *m* (**-li**) council; church council

concimàia *f* manure pit

concimare *tr* to manure

concimazióne *f* spreading of manure; chemical fertilization

concime *m* manure; fertilizer

cón·cio -cia (**-ci -ce**) *adj* tanned ‖ *m* ashlar; dung, manure; (*archaic*) agreement; **concio di scoria** cinder block ‖ *f* see **concia**

conciofossecosaché *conj* (archaic) since

concionare (concióno) *intr* (archaic) to harangue

concióne *f* (archaic) harangue; (archaic) assembly

conciossiacosaché *conj* (archaic) since

concisióne *f* concision, brevity

conci·so -sa *adj* concise, brief

concistòro *m* consistory; (fig) assembly

concitare (còncito) *tr* to excite, stir up

concita·to -ta *adj* excited; (poet) decisive

concitazióne *f* impetus; excitement

concittadi·no -na *mf* fellow citizen

conclave *m* conclave

conclùdere §105 *tr* to conclude ‖ *intr* to conclude; to be convincing ‖ *ref* to conclude, end; **concludersi con** to end with; to result in

conclusionale *adj* (law) summary

conclusióne *f* conclusion; **conclusioni** (law) summation

conclusi·vo -va *adj* conclusive

conclu·so -sa *adj* concluded; terminated; (poet) closed

concomitante *adj* concomitant

concordanza *f* concordance, agreement; (gram) concord; **concordanze** concordance (*e.g., to the Bible*)

concordare (concòrdo) *tr* to agree on; to make agree ‖ *intr* & *ref* to come to an agreement

concordato *m* agreement; concordat; settlement (*with creditors*)

concòrde *adj* in agreement

concòrdia *f* concord, harmony

concorrènte *adj* competitive ‖ *m* (com) competitor; (sports) contestant

concorrènza *f* competition

concorrenziale *adj* competitive (*e.g., price*)

concórrere §139 *intr* to converge; to concur; to compete

concórso *m* attendance; concurrence; combination (*of circumstances*); competition; competitive examination; contest; **concorso di bellezza** beauty contest; **concorso di pubblico** turnout; **fuori concorso** not entering the competition; in a class by itself

concretare (concrèto) *tr* to realize (*e.g., a dream*); to conclude, accomplish ‖ *ref* to come true

concretézza *f* concreteness, consistency

concrè·to -ta *adj* concrete, real; practical ‖ *m* practical matter; **in concreto** really, in reality

concubina *f* concubine

concubinàg·gio *m* (**-gi**) concubinage

concubinato *m* var of **concubinaggio**

conculcare §197 *tr* (lit) to trample under foot; (lit) to violate

concupire §176 *tr* (poet) to lust for

concupiscènza *f* concupiscence, lust

concussióne *f* extortion, shakedown; **concussione cerebrale** (pathol) concussion

condanna *f* conviction; sentence; (fig) blame, condemnation

condannare *tr* to condemn; to find guilty, convict; to sentence; to damn (*to eternal punishment*); to declare incurable; to wall up

condanna·to -ta *adj* condemned ‖ *m* convict

condensare (condènso) *tr* & *ref* to condense

condensa·to -ta *adj* condensed (*e.g., milk*)

condensatóre *m* condenser

condensazióne *f* condensation

condiménto *m* condiment, seasoning

condire §176 *tr* to season

condiret·tóre -trice *mf* associate manager

condiscendènte *adj* condescending

condiscendènza *f* condescension

condiscéndere §245 *intr* to condescend

condiscépo·lo -la *mf* schoolmate, school companion

condividere §158 *tr* to share

condizionale *adj* & *m* conditional ‖ *f* (law) suspended sentence

condizionare (condizióno) *tr* to condition; to treat (*to prevent spoilage*)

condizionatóre *m* air conditioner

condizióne *f* condition; term (*of sale*); **a condizione che** provided that; **condizioni** condition, shape (*e.g., of a shipment*); **essere in condizione di** to be in a position to

condoglianza *f* condolence; **fare le condoglianze a** to extend one's sympathy to

condolére §159 *ref* to condole

condomì·nio *m* (**-ni**) condominium

condòmi·no -na *mf* joint owner (*of real estate*)

condonare (condóno) *tr* to condone; to remit

condóno *m* pardon, parole

condót·to -ta *adj* country (*doctor*) ‖ *m* duct, canal; conduit ‖ *f* behavior, conduct; district (*of country doctor*); transportation; pipeline; (theat) baggage; **condotta forzata** flume

conducènte *m* driver; bus driver; motorman

condù·plex *mf* (**-plex**) (telp) party-line user

condurre §102 *tr* to lead; to drive (*a car*); to round up (*cattle*); to pipe (*e.g., gas*); to conduct; to trace (*a line*); to take; to bring; to manage; **condurre a termine** to bring to fruition, realize || *intr* to lead || *ref* to behave; to betake oneself, go; **condursi** (a poet) to be reduced to (*e.g., poverty*)

conduttivi·tà *f* (**-tà**) conductivity

condutti·vo -va *adj* conductive

condut·tóre -trice *adj* guiding, leading || *m* operator (*of a bus*); driver (*of a car*); (rr) engineer; (rr) ticket collector; (phys) conductor

conduttura *f* conduit, pipeline

conduzióne *f* conduction; leasing

conestàbile *m* constable (*keeper of a castle*)

confabulare (**confàbulo**) *intr* to confabulate, commune; to connive, scheme

confacènte *adj* suitable, appropriate; helpful

confare §173 *ref*—**confarsi a** to agree with, e.g., **le uova non gli si confanno** eggs do not agree with him

confederare (**confèdero**) *tr* & *ref* to confederate

confedera·to -ta *adj* & *m* confederate

confederazióne *f* confederation

conferènza *f* conference; lecture; **conferenza illustrata** chalk talk; **conferenza stampa** press conference

conferenziè·re -ra *mf* speaker, lecturer

conferiménto *m* conferring, bestowal

conferire §176 *tr* to confer, bestow; to add; to contribute || *intr* to confer; to contribute; **conferire alla salute** to be healthful

conférma *f* confirmation; **a conferma di** (com) in reply to, confirming

confermare (**conférmo**) *tr* to confirm; to verify; to retain (*in office*) || *ref* to become more sure of oneself; to prove to be; to remain (*in the conclusion of a letter*)

confessare (**confèsso**) *tr* & *ref* to confess

confessionale *adj* confessional; church; church-related, parochial (*e.g., school*) || *m* confessional

confessióne *f* confession

confès·so -sa *adj* acknowledged, self-admitted; **confesso e comunicato** having made one's confession and taken communion

confessóre *m* confessor

confetterìa *f* candy store, confectioner's shop

confettièra *f* candy box

confettière *m* candy maker; candy dealer, confectioner

confètto *m* sugar-covered nut, sweetmeat; losenge, drop

confettura *f* candy; preserves, jam; **confetture** confectionery

confezionare (**confezióno**) *tr* to make; to tailor (*a suit*)

confezióne *f* preparation, manufacturing; packaging; **confezioni** ready-made clothes

confezioni·sta *mf* (**-sti -ste**) ready-made clothier

conficcare §197 *tr* to drive (*a nail*); to thrust (*a knife*) || *ref* to become embedded

confidare *tr* to trust (*a secret*) || *intr* to trust || *ref* to confide

confidènte *adj* confident || *mf* confident; informer

confidènza *f* confidence; secret; familiarity

confidenziale *adj* confidential; friendly

configgere §104 *tr* to plunge, thrust

configurazióne *f* configuration

confinante *adj* bordering || *mf* neighbor

confinare *tr* to exile; to confine || *intr* to border

confinà·rio -ria *adj* (**-ri -rie**) border (*e.g., zone*)

Confindùstria *f* (acronym) **Confederazione Nazionale degli Industriali** National Confederation of Industrialists

confine *m* border, boundary line; boundary mark, landmark

confino *m* exile (*in a different town*)

confi·sca *f* (**-sche**) confiscation

confiscare §197 *tr* to confiscate

confit·to -ta *adj* nailed; bound; tied; **confitto in croce** nailed to the cross

conflagrazióne *f* conflagration

conflitto *m* conflict

conflittualità *f* confrontation; belligerent attitude

confluènte *m* confluent

confluènza *f* confluence

confluire §176 *intr* to flow together, join; to converge

confóndere §178 *tr* to confuse; to overwhelm (*with kindness*); to humiliate; **confondere con** to mistake for || *ref* to mix; to become confused

conformare (**confórmo**) *tr* to shape; to conform || *ref* to conform

conformazióne *f* conformation

confórme *adj* faithful, exact; in agreement; true (*copy*)

conformeménte *adv* in conformity

conformi·sta *mf* (**-sti -ste**) conformist

conformi·tà *f* (**-tà**) conformity; **in conformità di** in conformity with, in accord with

confortante *adj* comforting

confortare (**confòrto**) *tr* to comfort

confortévole *adj* comforting, consoling; comfortable

confòrto *m* comfort, solace; convenience; corroboration; **conforti religiosi** last rites

confratèllo *m* brother, confrere

confratèrnita *f* brotherhood

confricare §197 *tr* to rub

confrontare (**confrónto**) *tr* to compare, confront; to consult || *intr* to correspond

confrónto *m* comparison; (law) cross examination; **a confronto di** or **in confronto a** in comparison with; with regard to

confusaménte *adv* vaguely, hazily

confusionale *adj* confusing; confused

confusionà·rio -ria (-ri -rie) *adj* blundering; scatterbrain || *mf* blunderer; scatterbrain

confusióne *f* confusion, disorder; noise; error; embarrassment; shambles

confu·so -sa *adj* confused, mixed; vague, hazy; **in confuso** indistinctly

confutare (cònfuto) *tr* to confute

confutazióne *f* confutation

congedare (congèdo) *tr* to dismiss; to let (*a tenant*) go; (mil) to discharge || *ref* to take leave

congedà·to -ta *adj* discharged || *m* discharged soldier

congèdo *m* dismissal; leave; permission to leave; (mil) discharge; envoy, envoi; **congedo per motivi di salute** sick leave; **dare il congedo a** to discharge; **prender congedo** to take leave

congegnare (congégno) *tr* to assemble (*machinery*); to contrive, cook up

congégno *m* contrivance, gadget; mechanism; design (*of a play*)

congelaménto *m* freezing; frostbite

congelare (congèlo) *tr & ref* to freeze, congeal

congela·tóre -trice *adj* freezing || *m* freezer; freezer unit; freezing compartment (*of a refrigerator*)

congènere *adj* similar, alike

congeniale *adj* congenial

congèni·to -ta *adj* congenital

congèrie *f* congeries

congestionare (congestióno) *tr* to congest

congestióne *f* congestion

conguttura *f* conjecture

congetturare *tr* to conjecture

congiùngere §183 *tr & ref* to unite, join

congiuntíva *f* (anat) conjunctiva

congiuntivite *f* (pathol) conjunctivitis

congiunti·vo -va *adj* conjunctive; subjunctive || *m* subjunctive || *f* see **congiuntiva**

congiun·to -ta *adj* joined; joint || *m* relative

congiuntura *f* juncture; joint; circumstance, situation; **bassa congiuntura** (econ) unfavorable circumstance; (econ) crisis

congiunzióne *f* conjunction

congiura *f* conspiracy, plot

congiurare *intr* to conspire, plot

congiura·to -ta *adj & m* conspirator

conglobare (conglòbo) *tr* to lump together

conglomerare (conglòmero) *tr & ref* to pile up, conglomerate

conglomera·to -ta *adj & m* conglomerate

congratulare (congràtulo) *intr* to rejoice || *ref*—**congratularsi con** to congratulate

congratulazióne *f* congratulation

congrèga *f* gang; cabal; religious brotherhood

congregare §209 (**congrègo**) *tr & ref* to congregate

congregazióne *f* congregation

congressi·sta *mf* (**-sti -ste**) delegate || *m* congressman || *f* congresswoman

congrèsso *m* congress, assembly; conference; convention

congruènte *adj* congruous

congruènza *f* congruence

còn·gruo -grua *adj* congruous; congruent

conguagliare §280 *tr* to adjust; to make up (*what is owed*)

conguà·glio *m* (**-gli**) balance; adjustment (*of wages*)

coniare §287 (**cònio**) *tr* to mint, coin

coniatura *f* mintage, coinage

còni·co -ca (**-ci -che**) *adj* conic(al) || *f* conic section

conìfera *f* conifer

coniglièra *f* warren, rabbit hutch

coni·glio·m (**-gli**) rabbit

cò·nio *m* (**-ni**) die (*to mint coins*); mintage; wedge; **dello stesso conio** (fig) of the same feather; **di nuovo conio** newly-minted; new-fangled

coniugale *adj* conjugal

coniugare §209 (**còniugo**) *tr* to conjugate || *ref* to marry, get married

coniuga·to -ta *adj* coupled, paired || *mf* spouse, consort

coniugazióne *f* conjugation

còniuge *mf* spouse; **coniugi** *mpl* husband and wife

connaturale *adj* inborn, innate

connatura·to -ta *adj* deep-seated, deep-rooted; congenital

connazionale *mf* fellow countryman

connessióne *f* connection

connés·so -sa & connès·so -sa *adj* connected, tied

connéttere & connèttere §107 *tr* to connect, link || *ref* to refer

connetti·vo -va *adj* connective

connivènte *adj* conniving

connivènza *f* connivance

connotare (connòto) *tr* to connote

connotato *m* personal characteristic

connù·bio *m* (**-bi**) wedding, union

còno *m* cone

conòcchia *f* distaff

conoscènte *mf* acquaintance

conoscènza *f* knowledge; acquaintance; understanding; consciousness; **conoscenza di causa** full knowledge; **essere a conoscenza di** to be acquainted with; **prendere conoscenza di** to take cognizance of

conóscere §134 *tr* to know; to recognize; **conoscere i propri polli** to know one's onions; **conoscere per filo e per segno** to know thoroughly; **conoscere ragioni** to listen to reason; **darsi a conoscere** to make oneself known; to reveal oneself || *intr* to reason || *ref* to acknowledge oneself to be; to know one another

conoscìbile *adj* knowable

conosci·tóre -trice *mf* connoisseur, expert

conosciù·to -ta *adj* known, well-known; proven

conquìdere §135 *tr* (poet) to conquer

conquista _f_ conquest
conquistare _tr_ to conquer, win
conquista·tóre -trice _adj_ conquering ||
_m_ conqueror; lady killer
consacrare _tr_ to consecrate || _ref_ to
dedicate oneself
consacrazióne _f_ consecration
consanguineità _f_ consanguinity
consanguìne·o -a _adj_ consanguineous;
fratello consanguineo half brother on
the father's side || _m_ kin
conspapévole _adj_ aware, conscious
conspapevolézza _f_ awareness, consciousness
còn·scio -scia _adj_ (**-sci -sce**) conscious
consecutì·vo -va _adj_ consecutive
conségna _f_ delivery; (mil) order; (mil)
confinement (_to barracks_); **in consegna** (com) on consignment
consegnare (**conségno**) _tr_ to deliver; to
entrust; (mil) to confine (_to barracks_)
consegnatà·rio _m_ (**-ri**) consignee
conseguènte _adj_ consequent; consistent;
conseguente a resulting from; consistent with
conseguènza _f_ consequence; consistency; **in conseguenza di** as a result
of
conseguìbile _adj_ attainable
conseguiménto _m_ attainment
conseguire (**conséguo**) _tr_ to attain; to
obtain || _intr_ to ensue, result
consènso _m_ consent, approval; consensus
consensuale _adj_ mutual-consent (_e.g._,
agreement)
consentiménto _m_ consent
consentire (**consènto**) _tr_ to allow, per-
mit || _intr_ to agree, consent; to yield;
to admit
consenziènte _adj_ consenting
consèr·to -ta _adj_ intertwined; folded
(_arms_); **di conserto** in agreement
consèrva _f_ preserve; purée (_e.g._, _of
tomatoes_); tank (_for water_); sauce
(_e.g._, _of cranberries_); **conserve alimentari** canned goods; **di conserva**
together, in a group; **far conserva di**
to preserve
conservare (**consèrvo**) _tr_ to preserve;
to keep; to cure (_e.g._, _meat_); to
cherish (_a memory_) || _ref_ to keep; to
remain; to keep in good health
conservatì·vo -va _adj_ preserving; con-
servative || _m_ conservative
conserva·tóre -trice _adj_ preserving; con-
servative || _mf_ keeper, curator; con-
servative
conservatorìa _f_ registrar's office (_in a
court house_)
conservatò·rio _m_ (**-ri**) conservatory;
girl's boarding school (_run by nuns_)
conservatorismo _m_ conservatism
conservazióne _f_ conservation; preservation; self-preservation; canning
consèsso _m_ assembly
consideràbile _adj_ considerable; large,
important
considerare (**consìdero**) _tr_ to consider;
to rate; (law) to provide for
considera·to -ta _adj_ considered; **considerato che** considering that, since;

tutto considerato all in all, considering
considerazióne _f_ consideration
considerévole _adj_ considerable
consigliare _adj_ council, councilmanic ||
§280 _tr_ to advise, counsel || _ref_ to
consult
consigliè·re -ra _mf_ counselor, advisor ||
_m_ chancellor (_of embassy_); councilman; **consigliere delegato** chairman
of the board
consì·glio _m_ (**-gli**) advice, counsel; will
(_of God_); decision, idea; council;
consiglio d'amministrazione (com)
board of directors; **consiglio dei mini-
stri** cabinet; **consiglio municipale** city
council; **l'eterno consiglio** the will of
God; **venire a più miti consigli** to
become more reasonable
consìmile _adj_ similar
consistènte _adj_ consistent, solid; trustworthy
consistènza _f_ consistency, resistance;
foundation, grounds
consistere §114 _intr_ to consist; **consistere in** to consist of
consociare §128 (**consòcio**) _tr_ to syndicate, unite
consocia·to -ta _adj_ syndicated, united
consociazióne _f_ syndicate, association,
group
consò·cio -cia _mf_ (**-ci -cie**) fellow shareholder; associate, partner
consolare _adj_ consular || _v_ (**consòlo**) _tr_
to console, cheer, comfort || _ref_ to
rejoice; to take comfort
consolato _m_ consulate
consola·tóre -trice _adj_ comforting || _mf_
comforter
consolazióne _f_ consolation
cònsole _m_ consul
consò·le _f_ (**-le**) console
consòlida _f_—**consolida maggiore** com-
frey; **consolida reale** field larkspur
consolidaménto _m_ consolidation
consolidare (**consòlido**) _tr_ to consoli-
date || _ref_ to consolidate; to harden
consolida·to -ta _adj_ consolidated; joint
(_e.g._, _balance sheet_); hardened || _m_
funded public debt; government
bonds
consonante _adj_ & _f_ consonant
consonànti·co -ca _adj_ (**-ci -che**) consonant
consonanza _f_ consonance; agreement;
(mus) harmony
cònso·no -na _adj_ consonant
consorèlla _adj_ sister (_e.g._, _company_) ||
_f_ sister of charity; sister branch;
sister firm
consòrte _adj_ (poet) equally fortunate;
(poet) united || _mf_ consort, mate,
spouse
consorterìa _f_ political clique
consò·rzio _m_ (**-zi**) syndicate, consor-
tium; (poet) society
constare (**cònsto**) _intr_ to consist ||
impers to be known; to be proved;
to understand, _e.g._, **gli consta che
Lei ha torto** he understands that you
are wrong
constatare (**constato** & **cònstato**) _tr_ to
verify, ascertain, establish

constatazióne f ascertainment, verification

consuè·to -ta adj usual, customary; consueto a accustomed to, used to || m manner, custom; di consueto generally

consuetudinà·rio -ria adj (-ri -rie) customary; common (law)

consuetùdine f custom; common law; (poet) familiarity

consulènte adj advising, consulting || mf adviser, expert

consulènza f expert advice

consulta f council

consultare tr to consult || ref to take counsel; to counsel with one another; consultarsi con to take counsel with

consultazióne f consultation; reference; consultazione popolare referendum

consulti·vo -va adj advisory

consulto m consultation (of physicians); legal conference

consul·tóre -trice mf adviser, expert || m councilman

consultò·rio m (-ri) clinic, dispensary

consumare tr to consume; to perform, to consummate || ref to be consumed, to waste away

consuma·to -ta adj consummate, accomplished; consummated (marriage); consumed, worn out

consuma·tóre -trice adj consuming || mf consumer; customer (of a restaurant)

consumazióne f consummation (e.g., of a crime); consumption (of food); food or drink

consumismo m consumerism

consumo m consumption; wear

consunti·vo -va adj end-of-year (e.g., report); (econ) consumption || m balance sheet

consun·to -ta adj worn-out

consunzióne f consumption

contàbile adj bookkeeping || mf accountant; bookkeeper, clerk; esperto contabile certified public accountant

contabili·tà f (-tà) accounting, bookkeeping; accounts

contachìlome·tri m (-tri) odometer; (coll) speedometer

contadine·sco -sca adj (-schi -sche) farm, farmer; rustic

contadi·no -na adj rustic || mf peasant, farmer

contado m country, countryside

contagiare §290 tr to infect

contà·gio m (-gi) contagion

contagió·so -sa [s] adj contagious

contagi·ri m (-ri) tachometer

contagóc·ce m (-ce) dropper, eye-dropper

contaminare (contàmino) tr to contaminate; to pollute

contaminazióne f contamination; pollution

contante adj & m cash; in contanti cash

contare (cónto) tr to count; to limit; to regard, value; to propose; contarle grosse (coll) to tell tall tales || intr to count; contare su to count on

contasecón·di m (-di) watch with second hand

conta·to -ta adj limited; numbered (e.g., days)

conta·tóre -trice adj counting || mf counter || m meter; contatore dell'acqua water meter; contatore della luce electric meter

contattare tr to contact

contatto m contact

cónte m count

contèa f county

conteggiare §290 (contéggio) tr to charge (e.g., a bill) || intr to count

contég·gio m (-gi) reckoning, calculation; (sports) count; conteggio alla rovescia countdown

contégno m behavior; reserve, reserved attitude; air

contegnó·so -sa [s] adj reserved, dignified

contemperare (contèmpero) tr to adapt; to mitigate, moderate

contemplare (contèmplo) tr to contemplate

contemplati·vo -va adj contemplative

contemplazióne f contemplation

contèmpo m—nel contempo meanwhile

contemporaneaménte adv at the same time

contemporàne·o -a adj contemporaneous || mf contemporary

contendènte adj fighting || m contender, fighter; (law) contestant

contèndere §271 tr to contest, oppose || intr to contend, fight || ref to fight

contenére §271 tr to contain || ref to restrain oneself; to behave

conteniménto m containment

contenitóre m container

contentare (contènto) tr to satisfy, content || ref to be satisfied

contentézza f gladness, contentedness, contentment

contentino m gratuity, makeweight, gift to a customer

contèn·to -ta adj contented, glad, happy; satisfied || m (poet) happiness, contentedness

contenuto m content; contents

contenzióne f contention

contenzióso [s] m legal matter; legal department (of a corporation)

conterìe fpl beads, sequins

conterrà·neo -nea adj from the same country || m fellow countryman || f fellow countrywoman

conté·so -sa [s] adj coveted || f contest; dispute; venire a contesa to dispute

contéssa f countess

contestare (contèsto) tr to serve (e.g., a summons); to deny; to challenge, contest; contestare qlco a qlcu to charge s.o. with s.th

contestazióne f notification, summons; dispute, confrontation; challenge

contè·sto -sta adj (poet) intertwined || m context

contì·guo -gua adj contiguous

continentale adj continental

continènte adj & m continent

continènza f continence

contingentaménto m import quota

contingentare (contingènto) tr to assign a quota to (imports)

contingènte *adj* possible, contingent; (obs) due ‖ *m* contingent; import quota; **contingente di leva** draft quota

contingènza *f* contingency

continuare (contìnuo) *tr* to continue ‖ *intr* to last, continue; **continuare a** + *inf* to keep on + *ger*

continuazióne *f* continuation

continui·tà *f* (-tà) continuity

contì·nuo -nua *adj* continuous; direct *(current)*; **di continuo** continuously

cón·to -ta *adj* (archaic) well-known; (poet) gentle; (poet) narrated ‖ *m* figuring; account; bill, invoice; check *(in a restaurant)*; opinion; worth, value; **a conti fatti** everything considered; **chiedere conto di** to call to account; **conto all'indietro** countdown; **di conto** valuable; **estratto conto** (com) statement; **fare conto di** + *inf* to intend to + *inf*; **fare conto su** to count on; **fare di conto** to count; **fare i conti senza l'oste** to reckon without one's host; **il conto non torna** the sums do not jibe; **in conto** on account; **in conto di** in one's position as; **per conto di** in the name of; **per conto mio** as far as I am concerned; **render conto di** to give an account of; **rendersi conto di** to realize, be aware of; **tener conto di** to reckon with; **tener di conto** to treat with care; **torna conto** it is worthwhile

contòrcere §272 *tr* to twist ‖ *ref* to writhe

contorciménto *m* contortion, writhing

contornare (contórno) *tr* to surround

contórno *m* outline; contour; circle *(of people)*; side dish *(of vegetables)*

contorsióne *f* contorsion; gyration *(e.g., of a dancer)*; squirm

contòr·to -ta *adj* twisted *(e.g., face)*

contrabbandare *tr* to smuggle

contrabbandiè·re -ra *adj* smuggling ‖ *mf* smuggler; bootlegger

contrabbando *m* contraband; smuggling; **di contrabbando** by smuggling; (fig) without paying

contrabbasso *m* contrabass, bass viol

contraccambiare §287 *tr* to reciprocate, return ‖ *intr* to reciprocate

contraccàm·bio *m* (-bi) exchange; **in contraccambio di** in exchange for, in return for

contraccólpo *m* shock, rebound; recoil *(of a rifle)*; backlash *(of a machine)*

contrada *f* road; (poet) region

contraddire §151 *(impv sg* **contraddici)** *tr* to contradict ‖ *ref* to contradict oneself; to contradict one another

contraddistìnguere §156 *tr* to earmark ‖ *ref* to stand out

contraddittò·rio -ria *(-ri -rie) adj* contradictory; incoherent ‖ *m* open discussion, debate

contraddizióne *f* contradiction

contraènte *adj* contracting; acting ‖ *mf* contractor *(person who makes a contract)*; (law) party

contrère·o -a *adj* antiaircraft

contraffare §173 *tr* to counterfeit; to fake, sham ‖ *intr* (archaic) to disobey ‖ *ref* to camouflage oneself, disguise oneself

contraffat·to -ta *adj* counterfeit; adulterated; apocryphal

contraffat·tóre -trice *mf* counterfeiter; falsifier

contraffazióne *f* forgery; fake; imitation; piracy *(of book)*; mockery *(of justice)*

contraffòrte *m* spur *(of mountain)*; crossbar *(to secure door)*; (archit) buttress

contraggènio *m*—**a contraggenio** against one's will

contral·to -(to) adj alto ‖ *m* contralto *(voice)* ‖ *f* contralto *(singer)*

contrammirà·glio *m* (-gli) rear admiral

contrappasso *m* retributive justice

contrappesare [s] **(contrappéso)** *tr* to counterweight, counterbalance

contrappéso [s] *m* counterweight, counterpoise

contrappórre §218 *tr* to oppose; to compare ‖ *ref*—**contrapporsi a** to oppose

contrappó·sto -sta *adj* opposing ‖ *m* opposite, antithesis

contrappunto *m* counterpoint

contrare (cóntro) *tr* (boxing) to counter; (bridge) to double

contrariare §287 *tr* to oppose, counter; to thwart; to contradict; to bother, vex

contrarie·tà *f* (-tà) contrariety, vexation; setback

contrà·rio -ria *(-ri -rie) adj* contrary, opposite ‖ *m* opposite; **al contrario** on the contrary; **al contrario di** unlike; **avere qlco in contrario** to have some objection, object

contrarre §273 *tr & ref* to contract

contrassegnare (contrasségno) *tr* to earmark, mark

contrasségno *m* earmark; proof

contrastare *tr* to oppose; to obstruct; to prevent ‖ *intr* to contrast; to disagree; (poet) to quarrel ‖ *ref* to contend

contrasto *m* contrast; fight, dispute; (telv) contrast knob

contrattàbile *adj* negotiable

contrattaccare §197 *tr* to counterattack

contrattac·co *m* (-chi) counterattack

contrattare *tr* to contract for, negotiate a deal for ‖ *intr* to bargain

contrattèmpo *m* mishap

contrat·to -ta *adj* contracted ‖ *m* contract

contrattuale *adj* contractual

contravveléno *m* antidote

contravvenire §282 *intr* (with *dat*) to contravene; **contravvenire a** to infringe upon

contravvenzióne *f* violation; ticket, fine; **in contravvenzione** in the wrong; **intimare una contravvenzione a** to give a ticket to

contrazióne *f* contraction

contribuènte *mf* taxpayer

contribuire §176 *intr* to contribute

contributo *m* contribution

contribu·tóre -trice *mf* contributor

contribuzióne *f* contribution
contristare *tr & ref* to sadden
contri·to -ta *adj* contrite
contrizióne *f* contrition
cóntro *m* con, contrary opinion || *adv*
—contro di against, versus; dar contro a to oppose; di contro opposite,
facing; per contro on the other hand
|| *prep* against, versus; at; contro
pagamento upon payment; contro
vento into the wind; contro voglia
unwillingly
controbàttere *tr* (mil) to counterattack;
(fig) to contest
controbilanciare §128 *tr* to counterpoise, counterbalance
controcanto *m* (mus) counterpoint
controcarro *adj invar* antitank
controchiglia *f* keelson
controcorrènte *f* countercurrent; under-
tow; (fig) undercurrent || *adv* up-
stream
controdado *m* lock nut
controffensiva *f* counteroffensive
controfigura *f* (mov) stand-in; (mov)
stuntman
controfilo *m*—a controfilo against the
grain
controfinèstra *f* storm window
controfirma *f* countersign
controfirmare *tr* to countersign
controfòdera *f* inner facing (*of a suit,
between lining and cloth*)
controfuò·co *m* (-chi) backfire (*to check
the advance of a forest fire*)
controindicare §197 (controìndico) *tr*
to contraindicate
controllare (contròllo) *tr* to control,
check || *ref* to control oneself
contròllo *m* control, check; restraint;
(rad, telv) knob
controllóre *m* (com) comptroller; (rr)
ticket collector, conductor
controluce *f* picture taken against the
light || *adv* against the light
contromano *adv* against traffic
contromar·ca *f* (-che) check, stub (*e.g.,
of ticket*)
contromàr·cia *f* (-ce) countermarch;
(aut) reverse, reverse gear
contromezzana [ddzz] *f* (naut) topsail
contronòta *f* countermanding note
contropalo *m* strut
controparte *f* (law) opponent
contropedale *m* foot brake (*of a bicycle*)
contropélo *m* close shave (*in the oppo-
site direction of hair's growth*) || *adv*
against the grain; the wrong way
(*said of the hair*); against the nap;
accarezzare contropelo to stroke the
wrong way
contropiède *m* counterattack; cogliere
in contropiede to catch off balance
contropòrta *f* storm door
controproducènte *adj* counterproduc-
tive, self-defeating
contropropósta *f* counterproposition
contropròva *f* proof; second balloting
contrórdine *m* countermand
controrèplica *f* retort; (law) rejoinder
controrifórma *f* Counter Reformation

controrivoluzióne *f* counterrevolution
controsènso *m* nonsense; mistranslation
controspallina *f* (mil) epaulet
controspionàg·gio *m* (-gi) counter-
espionage
controvalóre *m* equivalent
controvènto *m* (archit) strut; (archit)
crossbrace || *adv* windward
controvèrsia *f* controversy
controvèr·so -sa *adj* controversial, moot
controvòglia *adv* unwillingly
contumace *adj* (archaic) contumacious;
(law) absent from court; (law) guilty
of nonappearance
contumàcia *f* quarantine; (archaic) con-
tumacy; (law) nonappearance; in
contumacia (law) in absentia
contumèlia *f* contumely
contundènte *adj* blunt
conturbante *adj* disturbing, upsetting
conturbare *tr* to disturb, upset || *ref*
to become perturbed
contusióne *f* bruise, contusion
contu·so -sa *adj* bruised
contuttoché *conj* although
contuttociò *conj* although
convalescènte *adj* convalescent
convalescènza *f* convalescence
convalescenzià·rio *m* (-ri) convalescent home
convàlida *f* validation; confirmation
convalidare (convàlido) *tr* to validate;
to confirm; to strengthen (*e.g., a
suspicion*)
convègno *m* meeting, convention
conveniènte *adj* convenient; adequate;
useful; profitable (*business*); cheap,
reasonable
conveniènza *f* convenience; suitability,
fitness; propriety; profit; convenienze
conventions
convenire §282 *tr* to fix (*e.g., a price*);
(law) to summon || *intr* (ESSERE) to
convene; to agree; to fit, be appro-
priate; (poet) to flow together || *ref*
to be proper; (with *dat*) to behoove,
befit, e.g., gli si conviene it behooves
him || *impers*—conviene it is neces-
sary
convènto *m* convent; monastery
convenu·to -ta *adj* agreed upon || *m*
agreement; (law) defendant; conve-
nuti conventioners, delegates
convenzionale *adj* conventional
convenzióne *f* convention
convergènte *adj* converging, convergent
convergènza *f* convergence
convèrgere §137 *intr* to converge
convèrsa *f* lay sister; flashing (*on a
roof*)
conversare (convèrso) *intr* to converse
conversazióne *f* conversation
conversióne *f* conversion; change of
heart; (mil) wheeling
convèrso *m* lay brother
convertibile *adj* convertible || *m* (aer)
fighter-bomber || *f* (aut) convertible
convertibili·tà *f* (-tà) convertibility
convertire §138 *tr* to convert, change;
to translate || *ref* to convert, change;
(poet) to address oneself

converti·to -ta *adj* converted ‖ *mf* convert
convertitóre *m* converter
convès·so -sa *adj* convex
convincènte *adj* convincing
convìncere §285 *tr* to convince; to convict ‖ *ref* to become convinced
convincimènto *m* conviction
convin·to -ta *adj* convinced, confirmed; convicted
convinzióne *f* conviction
convita·to -ta *adj* invited ‖ *mf* guest (*at a banquet*)
convito *m* banquet
convitto *m* boarding school
convit·tóre -trice *mf* boarding-school student
convivènte *adj* living together
convivènza *f* living together; **convivenza illecita** cohabitation; **convivenza umana** human society
convìvere §286 *intr* to live together; to cohabit
conviviale *adj* convivial
convì·vio *m* (-vi) banquet
convocare §197 (cònvoco) *tr* to summon, convoke; to convene
convocazióne *f* convocation
convogliare §280 (convòglio) *tr* to convoy, escort; to convey, carry
convò·glio *m* (-gli) convoy; cortege; (rr) train
convolare (convòlo) *intr*—**convolare a nozze** to get married
convòlvolo *m* (bot) morning-glory
convulsióne *f* convulsion
convul·so -sa *adj* convulsive; convulsed; choppy (*style*)
coonestare (coonèsto) *tr* to justify, palliate
cooperare (coòpero) *intr* to cooperate
cooperati·vo -va *adj & f* cooperative
coopera·tóre -trice *adj* coadjutant, cooperating ‖ *m* coadjutor
cooperazióne *f* cooperation
coordinaménto *m* coordination
coordinare (coórdino) *tr* to coordinate; to collect (*ideas*)
coordinati·vo -va *adj* (gram) coordinate
coordina·to -ta *adj & f* coordinate
coordinazióne *f* coordination
coòrte *f* cohort
copèr·chio *m* (-chi) lid, cover; top (*of box*)
copertina *f* small blanket, child's blanket; cover (*of book*)
copèr·to -ta *adj* covered; protected; cloudy; obscure ‖ *m* cover; shelter; **al coperto** under cover; indoors; secure ‖ *f* blanket, cover; seat cover; case, sheath; (naut) deck; **coperta da viaggio** steamer rug, lap robe; **far coperta a** to cover up for
copertóne *m* canvas; casing, shoe (*of tire*); **copertone cinturato** belted tire
copertura *f* covering; cover; coverage; whitewash; (boxing) defensive stance; (archit) roof
còpia *f* copy; (poet) abundance; (archaic) opportunity; **brutta copia** first draft; **copia a carbone** carbon copy; **copia dattiloscritta** typescript; **per**

copia conforme certified copy (*formula appearing on a document*)
copialètte·re *m* (-re) letter file; copying press
copiare §287 (còpio) *tr* to copy
copiati·vo -va *adj* indelible; copying
copiatura *f* copying; copy; plagiarism
copiglia *f* cotterpin
copilò·ta *m* (-ti -te) copilot
copióne *m* (theat) script
copiosi·tà [s] *f* (-tà) copiousness
copió·so -sa [s] *adj* copious
copi·sta *m* (-sti -ste) scribe; copyist
copisteria *f* copying office; public typing office
còppa *f* cup, goblet; bowl; pan (*of balance*); trophy; (aut) crankcase; (aut) housing; **coppe** suit of Neapolitan cards corresponding to hearts
coppàia *f* chuck (*of lathe*)
còppia *f* couple; pair; **a coppie** two by two; **far coppia fissa** to go steady
coppière *m* cupbearer
coppiglia *f* var of **copiglia**
còppo *m* earthenware jar (*for oil*); roof tile
copribu·sto *m* (-sto) bodice
copricapo *m* headgear
copricaté·na *m* (-na) chain guard (*on bicycle or motorcycle*)
coprifuò·co *m* (-chi) curfew
coprinu·ca *m* (-ca) havelock
coprire §110 *tr* to cover; to occupy (*a position*); to coat (*e.g., a wall*); to drown (*a noise*) ‖ *ref* to cover oneself; (econ) to hedge
copriteiè·ra *m* (-ra) cozy
coprivivan·de *m* (-de) dish cover
cò·pto -pta *adj* Coptic ‖ *mf* Copt
còpula *f* copulation; (gram) copula
coque *f* see **uovo**
coràg·gio *m* (-gi) courage; effrontery; (obs) heart; **fare coraggio a** to hearten, encourage; **prendere il coraggio a quattro mani** to screw up one's courage
coraggió·so -sa [s] *adj* courageous
corale *adj* choral; (archaic) cordial; (fig) unanimous ‖ *m* chorale
coralli·no -na *adj* coral
corallo *m* coral
corame *m* engraved leather
coramèlla *f* razor strop
Corano *m* Koran
corata *f* haslet
coratèlla *f* giblets
corazza *f* breastplate, cuirass; shoulder pad (*in football*); armor plate; carapace, shell
corazzare *tr* to armor ‖ *ref* to armor, protect oneself
corazza·to -ta *adj* armor-plated, armored; plated; protected ‖ *f* battleship, dreadnought
corazzière *m* cuirassier; mounted carabineer
còrba *f* basket
corbelleria *f* (coll) blunder
corbèllo *m* basket; basketful
corbézzolo *m* (bot) arbutus; **corbezzoli!** gosh!
còrda *f* rope; tightrope; string (*of an*

instrument); chord; woof; cord; plumbline; **dare la corda a** to wind (*a clock*); **essere con la corda al collo** to have a rope around one's neck; **mostrare la corda** to be threadbare; **tagliare la corda** to take off, leave; **tenere sulla corda** to keep in suspense

cordame *m* cordage

cordata *f* group of climbers tied together

cordellina *f* (mil) braided cord, braid; (mil) lanyard

cordiale *adj* & *m* cordial

cordiali·tà *f* (-tà) cordiality

cordièra *f* (mus) tailpiece

cordò·glio *m* (-gli) sorrow, grief

cordonata *f* gradient

cordóne *m* cordon; (anat, elec) cord; curbstone; **cordone litorale** sandbar; **cordone sanitario** sanitary cordon

corèa *f* St. Vitus's dance || **Corea** *f* Korea

corea·no -na *adj* & *mf* Korean

coréggia *f* leather strap

coreografia *f* choreography

coreògrafo *m* choreographer

coriàce·o -a *adj* tough, leathery

coriàndolo *m* (bot) coriander; **coriandoli** confetti

coricare §197 (còrico) *tr* to put to bed || *ref* to lie down, go to bed

corindóne *m* corundum

corìn·zio -zia *adj* & *mf* (-zi -zie) Corinthian

cori·sta *mf* (-sti -ste) choir singer, choirmaster || *m* chorus man; (mus) tuning fork; (mus) pitch pipe

coriza [dz] or **corizza** [ddzz] *f* coryza

cormorano *m* cormorant

cornàcchia *f* rook, crow

cornamusa *f* bagpipe

cornata *f* butt; hook, goring (*by bull*)

còrne·o -a *adj* horn, horn-like || *f* cornea

cornétta *f* (mus) cornet; (mus) cornet player; (telp) receiver; (hist) pennon (*of cavalry*)

cornétto *m* little horn; amulet (*in shape of horn*); crescent (*bread*); ear trumpet

cornice *f* cornice; frame; (typ) box; (archit) pediment

cornicióne *m* (archit) ledge; (archit) cornice

cornificare §197 (cornìfico) *tr* (joc) to cuckold

corniòla *f* carnelian

còrniola *f* (bot) dogberry

còrniolo *m* (bot) dogwood

còrno *m* horn; wing (*of army*); edge, end; (mus) horn; **corno da caccia** hunting horn; **corno da scarpe** shoe horn; **corno dell'abbondanza** horn of plenty; **corno dogale** (hist) Doge's hat; **corno inglese** (mus) English horn; **non capire un corno** to not understand a blessed thing; **non valere un corno** to not be worth a fig; **un corno!** (slang) heck no! || *m* (**còrna** *fpl*) horn (*of animal*); **alzare le corna** to raise one's head; to be-

come rambunctious; **dire corna di** to speak evil of; **fare le corna** to make horns, to touch wood (*to ward off the evil eye*); **mettere le corna a** to cuckold (*one's husband*); to be unfaithful to (*one's wife*); **portare le corna** to be cuckolded; **rompersi le corna** to get the worst of it

cornu·to -ta *adj* horny; horn-shaped; (vulg) cuckolded

còro *m* choir; chorus; chancel

corollà·rio *m* (-ri) corollary

coróna *f* crown; coronet; wreath, garland; range (*of mountains*); collection (*e.g., of sonnets*); stem (*of watch*); felloe (*of wheel*); (astr) corona; (rel) string (*of beads*); (mus) pause; **fare corona a** to surround

coronaménto *m* crowning; (archit) capstone; (naut) taffrail

coronare (coróno) *tr* to crown; to top, surmount

coronà·rio -ria *adj* (-ri -rie) coronary; (hist) rewarded with a garland

corpétto *m* baby's shirt; waistcoat, vest

corpino *m* bodice; vest

còrpo *m* body; substance; staff (*of teachers*); (mil) corps; (typ) em quad; **a corpo a corpo** hand-to-hand (*fight*); (sports) in a clinch; **a corpo morto** heavily; doggedly; **andare di corpo** to have a bowel movement; **avere in corpo** (fig) to have inside; **corpo del reato** corpus delicti; **corpo di Bacco!** good Heavens!; **corpo di ballo** ballet; **corpo di commissariato** (mil) supply corps; **corpo di guardia** guard, guardhouse; **corpo semplice** (chem) simple substance; **prendere corpo** to materialize

corporale *adj* bodily, body || *m* (eccl) corporal, Communion cloth

corporativismo *m* corporatism (*e.g., of Fascist Italy*)

corporati·vo -va *adj* corporative, corporate

corpora·to -ta *adj* corporate

corporatura *f* size, build

corporazióne *f* corporation

corpòre·o -a *adj* corporeal

corpó·so -sa [s] *adj* heavy-bodied

corpulèn·to -ta *adj* corpulent

corpùscolo *m* particle; (phys) corpuscle

Corpus Dòmini *m* (eccl) Corpus Christi

corredare (corrèdo) *tr* to provide, furnish; to annotate, accompany

corredino *m* layette

corrèdo *m* trousseau; outfit, garb; actor's kit; furniture; equipment; apparatus (*e.g., footnotes*)

corrèggere §226 *tr* to correct; to straighten (*e.g., a road*); to rewrite, revise (*news*); to touch up the flavor of || *ref* to reform

corrég·gia *f* (-ge) leather strap

corregionale *adj* fellow || *mf* person of the same section of the country

correità *f* complicity

correlare (corrèlo) *tr* to correlate

correlati·vo -va *adj* correlative

correla·tóre -trice *mf* second reader (*of a doctoral dissertation*)

correlazióne *f* correlation; (gram) sequence

corrènte *adj* current; running; fluent; recurring; run-of-the-mill || *m*—**essere al corrente di** to be acquainted with; to be abreast of; **mettere al corrente di** to acquaint with || *f* current; draft (*of air*); stream (*of water*); mass (*of lava*); (elec) current; (fig) tide; **contro corrente** upstream; **corrente alternata** (elec) alternating current; **corrente continua** (elec) direct current; **corrente di rete** (elec) house current

córrere §139 *tr* to travel; to run (*a risk; a race*); **correre la cavallina** to sow one's wild oats || *intr* (ESSERE & AVERE) to run; to speed; to race; to flow; to fly (*said of time*); to elapse; to be (*e.g., the year 1820*); to be current (*said of coins*); to spread (*said of gossip*); to mature (*said of interest*); to intervene (*said of distance*); to have dealings; **ci corre!** there is quite a difference!; **ci corre poco che cadesse** he narrowly escaped falling; **correre a gambe levate** to run at breakneck speed; **corre l'uso** it is the fashion; **corrono parole grosse** they are having words; **non corre buon sangue fra loro** there is bad blood between them

corresponsàbile *adj* jointly responsible

corresponsióne *f* payment; (fig) gratitude

correttézza *f* correctness

corretti·vo -va *adj* corrective || *m* flavoring

corrèt·to -ta *adj* correct; flavored; spiked

correttóre -trice *mf* corrector; **correttore di bozze** proofreader

correzionale *adj* correctional

correzióne *f* correction

còrri còrri *m* rush

corri·dóio *m* (**-dói**) corridor; hallway; (tennis) alley; (theat) aisle

corridóre *adj* running || *m* racer; runner (*in baseball*)

corrièra *f* mail coach; bus

corrière *m* courier; mail; carrier (*of merchandise*)

corrispetti·vo -va *adj* equivalent, proportionate || *m* requital, compensation

corrispondènte *adj* corresponding, equivalent || *mf* correspondent

corrispondènza *f* correspondence

corrispóndere §238 *tr* to pay, compensate || *intr* to correspond

corri·vo -va *adj* rash; indulgent

corroborante *adj* corroborating || *m* tonic

corroborare (**corròboro**) *tr* to corroborate; to invigorate

corroborazióne *f* corroboration

corródere §239 *tr* to corrode; to erode

corrómpere §240 *tr* to spoil; to corrupt; to suborn || *ref* to putrefy, rot

corrosióne *f* corrosion

corrosi·vo -va *adj & m* corrosive

corró·so -sa *adj* corroded; eroded

corrót·to -ta *adj* corrupted, corrupt; putrefied, rotten || *m* (archaic) lament

corrucciare §128 *tr* to anger, vex || *ref* to get angry

corrùc·cio *m* (**-ci**) anger, vexation

corrugaménto *m* wrinkling; (geol) fold

corrugare §209 *tr* to wrinkle, knit (*one's brow*) || *ref* to frown

corruscare §197 *intr* (poet) to shine

corruttèla *f* corruption

corruttìbile *adj* corruptible

corrut·tóre -trice *adj* corrupting, depraving || *m* seducer; briber

corruzióne *f* corruption; putrefaction, decomposition

córsa *f* race; run; trip; fare; (mach) stroke; (hist) privateering; **a tutta corsa** at full speed; **corsa al galoppo** flat race; **corsa al trotto** harness racing; **corsa semplice** one-way ticket; **corse** horse racing; **da corsa** race, for racing, e.g., **cavallo da corsa** race horse; **di corsa** running, in a hurry; **fare una corsa** to run an errand; **prendere la corsa** to begin to run

corsalétto *m* corselet

corsa·ro -ra *adj* privateering || *m* privateer, corsair, pirate

corsétto *m* corset

corsìa *f* aisle; ward (*in hospital*); runner (*of carpet*); lane (*of highway*); **corsia d'accesso** entrance lane; **corsia d'uscita** exit lane

Còrsica, la Corsica

corsivi·sta *mf* (**-sti -ste**) (journ) political writer

corsi·vo -va *adj* cursive; (poet) running; (poet) current || *m* cursive handwriting; (typ) italics

córso *m* course; navigation (*by sea*); path (*of stars*); parade; large street; boulevard; tender (*of currency*); current rate, current price (*of stock at the exchange*); **corso d'acqua** watercourse; **fuori corso** (coin) no longer in circulation; **in corso** in circulation; in progress; **in corso di** in the course of; **in corso di stampa** in press

còr·so -sa *adj & mf* Corsican

cor·sóio -sóia (**-sói -sóie**) *adj* running (*knot*); (mach) on rollers || *m* slide (*of slide rule*); (mach) slide

córte *f* court; **corte bandita** open house; **Corte d'appello** appellate court; **Corte di cassazione** Supreme Court; **fare la corte a** to pay court to, woo

cortéc·cia *f* (**-ce**) bark; crust (*of bread*); (fig) appearance; (anat) cortex

corteggiaménto *m* courtship

corteggiatóre *m* wooer, suitor

cortég·gio *m* (**-gi**) retinue; cortege

cortèo *m* procession; parade; funeral train; wedding party

cortése *adj* courteous, polite; (lit) liberal; (poet & hist) courtly

cortesìa *f* courtesy, politeness; (lit) liberality; (poet & hist) courtliness; **per cortesia** please

còrtice *f* cortex

cortigia·no -na *adj* flattering; courtly || *mf* courtier; flatterer || *f* courtesan

cortile *m* courtyard; barnyard

cortina f curtain; **cortina di ferro** iron curtain; **cortina di fumo** smoke screen; **oltre cortina** behind the iron curtain

cortisóne m cortisone

cór·to -ta adj short; close (haircut); **alle corte** in short; **essere a corto di** to be short of; **per farla corta, in short**

cortocircùito m short circuit

cortometràg·gio m (-gi) (mov) short

cor·vè f (-vè) tiresome task, drudgery; **corvè di cucina** kitchen police

corvétta f corvette

corvi·no -na adj raven-black

còrvo m raven; crow

còsa [s] f thing; **belle cose!** or **buone cose!** regards!; **che cosa** what; **cosa da nulla** a mere trifle, nothing at all; **cos'ha?** what's the matter with you (him, her)?; **cosa pubblica** commonweal; **cosa strana** no wonder; **cose belongings; per la qual cosa** wherefore; **per prima cosa** first of all; **sopra ogni cosa** above all; **tante belle cose!** best regards!; **una cosa** something; **una cosa nuova** a piece of news

cosac·co -ca (-chi -che) adj Cossack's || mf Cossack

cò·scia f (-sce) thigh; haunch; leg (of gun); (archit) abutment; **coscia di montone** leg of lamb

cosciènte adj conscious; sensible; aware

cosciènza f conscience; consciousness; conscientiousness; awareness

coscienzió·so -sa [s] adj conscientious

cosciòtto m leg; leg of lamb

coscrit·to -ta adj conscript || m conscript, recruit, draftee

coscrìvere §250 tr to conscript

coscrizióne f conscription, draft

così [s] adj invar—**un così**... or **un**... **così** such a || adv thus; like this; so; **così**... **come** as ... as; **così così** so so; **e così via** and so on, and so forth; **per così dire** so to speak

cosicché [s] conj so that

cosiddét·to -ta [s] adj so-called

cosiffat·to -ta [s] adj such, similar

cosino [s] m (coll) little fellow

cosmèti·co -ca adj & m (-ci -che) cosmetic

còsmi·co -ca adj (-ci -che) cosmic; outer (space)

còsmo m cosmos; outer space

cosmòdromo m space center

cosmologìa f cosmology

cosmonàu·ta mf (-ti -te) cosmonaut, astronaut

cosmopòli·ta adj & mf (-ti -te) cosmopolitan

còso [s] m (coll) thing, what-d'you-call-it

cospàrgere §261 tr to spread; to sprinkle

cospèrgere §112 tr (poet) to wet, sprinkle

cospètto m presence; **al cospetto di** in the presence of

cospì·cuo -cua adj distinguished, outstanding, huge, immense; (poet) conspicuous

cospirare intr to conspire, plot

cospira·tóre -trice mf conspirator

cospirazióne f conspiracy, plot

còsta f side; rib; coast, seashore; slope; welt (along seam); wale (in fabric); (naut) frame

costà adv there; over there

costaggiù adv down there

costante adj & f constant

Costantinòpoli f Constantinople

costanza f constancy || **Costanza** f Constance

costare (còsto) intr (ESSERE) to cost; to be expensive; **costare caro** to cost dear; **costare un occhio della testa** to cost a fortune

costarica·no -na or **costaricènse** adj & mf Costa Rican

costassù adv up there

costata f rib roast; side

costeggiare §290 (costéggio) tr to sail along; to run along; to border on || intr to coast

costèi §8 pron dem

costellare (costèllo) tr to stud, star

costellazióne f constellation

costernare (costèrno) tr to dismay, cause consternation to

costernazióne f consternation

costì adv there

costiè·ro -ra adj coast, coastal; offshore || f coastline; gentle slope

costipare tr to constipate; to heap, pile || ref to become constipated

costipazióne f constipation

costituènte adj constituent; constituting || m member of constituent assembly; (chem) constituent

costituire §176 tr to constitute; to form || ref to form; to become; to appoint oneself; to give oneself up (to justice); **costituirsi in giudizio** (law) to sue (in civil court); **costituirsi parte civile** (law) to appear as a plaintiff (in civil court)

costituto m (law) pact, agreement; (naut) master's declaration (to health authorities)

costituzionale adj constitutional

costituzióne f constitution; charter; composition; (law) appearance; surrender (to justice)

còsto m cost; **a costo di** at the price of; **ad ogni costo** at any cost; **a nessun costo** by no means; **a tutti i costi** at any cost, in any event; **costo della vita** cost of living; **sotto costo** below cost

còstola f rib; spine (of book); back (of knife); **avere qlcu alle costole** to have s.o. at one's heels; **rompere le costole a** (fig) to break the bones of; **stare alle costole di** to be at the back of

costolétta f chop, cutlet

costolóne m (archit) groin

costóro §8 pron dem

costó·so -sa [s] adj costly

costrìngere §265 tr to force, constrain; (poet) to compress

costritti·vo -va adj constrictive

costrizióne f constriction

costruire §140 tr to construct, build

costrut·to -ta adj constructed || m profit; sense; (gram) construction; **dov'è il costrutto?** what's the point?

costruttóre m builder

costruzióne f construction; building

costùi §8 pron dem

costumanza f custom

costumare intr (+ inf) to be in the habit of (+ ger) || intr (ESSERE) to be the custom; to be in use

costumatézza f good manners

costuma·to -ta adj polite, well-bred

costume m custom, manner; costume, dress; bathing suit

costumi·sta mf (-sti -ste) (theat) costumer

costura f seam

cotale adj & pron such || adv (archaic) thus

cotan·to -ta adj & pron (poet) so much || **cotanto** adv (poet) such a long time

côte f flint

coténna f pigskin; rind; (coll) hide, skin

coté·sto -sta §7 adj dem || §8 pron dem

cóti·ca f (-che) (coll) hide, skin (of porker)

cotógna f quince (fruit)

cotognata f quince jam

cotógno m quince (tree)

cotolétta f chop, cutlet

cotóne m cotton; thread; **cotone fulminante** guncotton; **cotone idrofilo** absorbent cotton; **cotone silicato** mineral wool

cotonière m cotton manufacturer

cotoniè·ro -ra adj cotton || mf cotton worker

cotonifi·cio m adj (-ci) cotton mill

cotonó·so -sa [s] adj cotton; cottony

còtta f cooking; baking; drying (of bricks); (sports) exhaustion; (coll) drunkenness; (joc) infatuation, love; (eccl) surplice; **cotta d'armi** coat of mail

cottimi·sta mf (-sti -ste) pieceworker

còttimo m piecework

còt·to -ta adj cooked; baked; burnt; suntanned; (joc) half-baked; (joc) in love; (sports) exhausted || m brick || f see **cotta**

cottura f cooking; **a punto di cottura** (culin) done just right

coutènte mf (law) joint user; (telp) party-line user

cóva f brooding; nest

covare (cóvo) tr to brood, to hatch; to harbor or nurse (an enmity); to nurture (a disease); **covare con gli occhi** to look fondly at; **covare le lenzuola** to loll around || intr to smolder (said of fire or passion)

covata f brood, covey

covile m doghouse; den

cóvo m shelter; den, lair; **farsi il covo** (fig) to gather a nestegg; **uscire dal covo** to stick one's nose out of the house

covóne m sheaf; cock (of hay)

còzza f cockle

cozzare (còzzo) tr to hit; to butt (one's head) || intr to butt; (fig) to clash;

cozzare contro to bump into || ref to hit one another; to fight

còzzo m butt; clash, conflict

crac m crash

crampo m cramp

cràni·co -ca adj (-ci -che) cranial

crà·nio m (-ni) cranium, skull

cràpula f excess (in eating and drinking)

cras·so -sa adj crass, gross; large (intestine)

cratère m crater; bomb crater

cràuti mpl sauerkraut

cravatta f tie, necktie; **cravatta a farfalla** bow tie; **fare cravatte** to be a usurer

creanza f politeness; **buona creanza** good manners

creare (crèo) tr to create; to name, elect

creati·vo -va adj creative

crea·to -ta adj created || m creation, universe

crea·tóre -trice adj creative || mf creator

creatura f creature; baby; **povera creatura!** poor thing!

creazióne f creation; (poet) election

credènte adj believing || mf believer

credènza f credence, faith, belief; sideboard, buffet; (coll) credit

credenziale f letter of credit; **credenziali** credentials

credenzière m butler

crédere §141 tr to believe; to think; **lo credo bene!** I should say so! || intr to believe; to trust; **credere a** to believe in; **credere in Dio** to believe in God || ref to believe oneself to be

credìbile adj credible

credibilità f credibility

crédito m credit

credi·tóre -trice mf creditor

crèdo m credo, creed

credulità f credulity

crèdu·lo -la adj credulous

crèma f cream; custard; **crema da scarpe** shoe polish; **crema di bellezza** beauty cream; **crema di pomodoro** cream of tomato soup; **crema evanescente** vanishing cream; **crema per barba** shaving cream

cremaglièra f rack; cogway, cograil

cremare (crèmo) tr to cremate

crema·tóio m (-tói) crematory

crema·tó·rio m (-ri) crematory

cremazióne f cremation

cremerìa f creamery

crèmisi adj & m crimson

Cremlino m Kremlin

cremlinologia f Kremlinology

cremortàrtaro m cream of tartar

cremó·so -sa [s] adj creamy

crèn m horseradish

creolina f creolin

crèo·lo -la adj & mf Creole

creosòto m creosote

crèpa f crack, crevice; rift

crepàc·cio m (-ci) crevasse; fissure

crepacuòre m heartbreak

crepapància m—**mangiare a crepapancia** to burst from eating too much

crepapèlle m—**ridere a crepapelle** to split one's sides laughing

crepare (**crèpo**) *intr* to burst; to crack; to chip; (slang) to croak; **crepare dalla sete** to die of thirst; **crepare dalle risa** to die laughing; **crepare d'invidia** to be green with envy

crepitare (**crèpito**) *intr* to crackle (*said of fire or weapons*); to rustle (*said of leaves*)

crepiti·o *m* (-**i**) crackle; rustle; pitter-patter (*of rain*)

crepuscolare *adj* twilight; (fig) dim

crepùscolo *m* twilight

crescènte *adj* rising, growing; crescent (*moon*) ‖ *m* (astr & heral) crescent

crescènza *f* growth

créscere §142 *tr* to grow, raise; to increase ‖ *intr* (ESSERE) to grow; to increase; to rise (*said, e.g., of prices*); to wax (*said of the moon*); **farsi crescere** to grow (*a beard*)

crescióne *m* watercress

créscita *f* growth; outgrowth; rise (*of water*)

crèsima *f* confirmation

cresimare (**crèsimo**) *tr* to confirm

Crèso *m* (mythol) Croesus

cré·spo -spa *adj* crispy, kinky; (archai) wrinkled ‖ *m* crepe ‖ *f* wrinkle; ruffle

crèsta *f* comb (*of chicken*); crest; abbassare la cresta to come down a peg or two; **alzare la cresta** to become insolent

crestàia *f* (coll) milliner

créta *f* clay

cretése [s] *adj* & *mf* Cretan

cretinerìa *f* idiocy

creti·no -na *adj* & *mf* idiot, cretin

cribro *m* (poet) sieve

cric·ca *f* (-**che**) clique, gang; group; crevice

cric·co *m* (-**chi**) (aut) jack

cricéto *m* hamster

cri cri *m* chirping (*of crickets*)

criminale *adj* criminal; (law) penal ‖ *mf* criminal

criminali·sta *mf* (-**sti -ste**) penal lawyer, criminal lawyer

criminalità *f* criminality

crìmine *m* crime

criminologìa *f* criminology

criminòlo·go m (-**gi**) criminologist

criminó·so -sa [s] *adj* criminal

crinale *adj* (poet) hair ‖ *m* ridge (*of mountains*)

crine *m* horsehair; (poet) hair; (poet) sunbeam

crinièra *f* mane

crinolìna *f* crinoline

cripta *f* crypt

criptocomuni·sta *mf* (-**sti -ste**) fellow traveler

crisàlide *f* chrysalis

crisantèmo *m* chrysanthemum

cri·si *f* (-**si**) crisis; shortage (*of houses*); attack (*e.g., of fever*); outburst (*of tears*); (econ) slump; **crisi ancillare** or **domestica** servant problem; **in crisi** in difficulties

cristallerìa *f* glassware; crystal service; glassware shop; glassworks

cristallièra *f* china closet

cristalli·no -na *adj* crystalline ‖ *m* crystalline lens

cristallizzare [ddzz] *tr* & *ref* to crystallize

cristallo *m* crystal; glass; pane (*of glass*); windshield; **cristallo di rocca** rock crystal; **cristallo di sicurezza** (aut) safety glass

cristianaménte *adv* in a Christian manner, like a Christian; (coll) decently; **morire cristianamente** to die in the faith

cristianésimo *m* Christianity

cristianità *f* Christendom

cristia·no -na *adj* & *mf* Christian

Cristo *m* Christ; **avanti Cristo** before Christ (B.C.); **dopo Cristo** after Christ (A.D.); **un povero cristo** (slang) a poor guy

critè·rio *m* (-**ri**) criterion; judgment

crìti·ca *f* (-**che**) criticism; critique; slur

criticare §197 (**crìtico**) *tr* to criticize, censure; to find fault with

crìti·co -ca (-**ci -che**) *adj* critical ‖ *mf* critic; (coll) faultfinder ‖ *f* see **critica**

crittografìa *f* cryptography

crittogram·ma *m* (-**mi**) cryptogram

crivellare (**crivèllo**) *tr* to riddle

crivèllo *m* sieve, riddle

croa·to -ta *adj* & *mf* Croatian

Croàzia, la Croatia

croccante *adj* crisp, crunchy ‖ *m* almond brittle, peanut brittle

crocchétta *f* croquette

cròcchia *f* chignon, topknot

crocchiare §287 (**cròcchio**) *intr* to crackle; to sound cracked or broken; to cluck (*said of a hen*); to crack (*said of joints*)

cròc·chio *m* (-**chi**) group (*of people*); **far crocchio** to gather around

cróce *f* cross; x (*mark made by illiterate person*); tail (*of coin*); (fig) trial; **Croce del Sud** Southern Cross; **croce di Malta** Maltese cross; **Croce Rossa** Red Cross; **croce uncinata** swastika; **fare una croce sopra** to forget about; **gettare la croce addosso** (fig) to put the blame on; **mettere in croce** to crucify

crocefisso *m* crucifix

crocerossina *f* Red Cross worker

croceségno *m* cross, x (*mark made instead of signature*)

crocétta *f* (naut) crosstree

croce·vìa *m* (-**vìa**) crossroads, intersection

crocia·to -ta *adj* crossed; crusading; see **parola** ‖ *m* crusader ‖ *f* crusade

crocièra *f* cruise; (archit) cross (*vault*); (mach) cross (*of universal joint*)

crocière *m* (orn) crossbill

crocifìggere §104 *tr* to crucify

crocifissióne *f* crucifixion

crocifis·so -sa *adj* crucified ‖ *m* crucifix

crò·co *m* (-**chi**) crocus

crogiolare (**c/*crògiolo**) *tr* to cook on a low fire; to simmer; to temper (*glass*) ‖ *ref* to bask; to snuggle (*e.g., in bed*)

crògiolo *m* cooking on a low fire; simmering; tempering (*of glass*)

crogiòlo *m* crucible; (fig) melting pot

crollare (**cròllo**) *tr* to shake (*e.g., one's head*) ‖ *intr* (ESSERE) to fall down, collapse ‖ *ref* to shake

cròllo *m* shake; fall, collapse

cròma *f* (mus) quaver

cromare (cròmo) *tr* to plate with chromium

croma·to -ta *adj* chromium-plated; chrome || *m* chrome yellow

cromatura *f* chromium plating

cròmo *m* chrome, chromium

cromosfèra *f* chromosphere

cromosò·ma [s] *m* (-**mi**) chromosome

cròna·ca -ca (-**che**) chronicle; report, news; **cronaca bianca** news of the day; **cronaca giudiziaria** court news; **cronaca mondana** social column; **cronaca nera** police and accident report; **cronaca rosa** wedding column; stork news

cròni·co -ca (-**ci -che**) *adj* chronic || *mf* incurable

croni·sta *mf* (-**sti -ste**) reporter; chronicler

cronistòria *f* chronicle

cronologìa *f* chronology

cronològi·co -ca *adj* (-**ci -che**) chronologic(al)

cronometrare (cronòmetro) *tr* to time

cronomètri·co -ca *adj* (-**ci -che**) chronometric(al); split-second

cronometri·sta *m* (-**sti**) (sports) timekeeper

cronòmetro *m* stopwatch; chronometer

crosciare §128 (cròscio) *tr* (archaic) to heave, throw || *intr* to rustle (*said of dry leaves*); to pitter-patter (*said of rain*)

cròsta *f* crust; bark (*of tree*); scab; slough; shell (*of crustacean*); poor painting

crostàceo *m* crustacean

crostata *f* pie

crostino *m* toast

crostó·so -sa [s] *adj* crusty

croupier *m* (croupier) croupier

crucciare §128 *tr* to worry, vex; to chagrin || *ref* to worry; to become angry

cruccia·to -ta *adj* afflicted; worried; angry; chagrined

crùc·cio *m* (-**ci**) sorrow; (obs) anger; **darsi cruccio** to fret

cruciale *adj* crucial

crucivèr·ba *m* (-**ba**) crossword puzzle

crudèle *adj* cruel

crudel·tà *f* (-**tà**) cruelty

crudézza *f* crudity; harshness

cru·do -da *adj* raw; rare (*meat*); (poet) cruel

cruèn·to -ta *adj* (lit) bloody

crumiro *m* scab (*in strikes*)

cruna *f* eye (*of a needle*)

cru·sca *f* (-**sche**) bran; (coll) freckles

cruscante *adj* Della-Cruscan; affected || *m* member of the Accademia della Crusca

cruschèllo *m* middlings

cruscòtto *m* (aut) dashboard; (aer) instrument panel

cuba·no -na *adj* & *mf* Cuban

cubatura *f* volume

cùbi·co -ca *adj* (-**ci -che**) cubic; cube (*root*)

cubitale *adj* very large (*handwriting or type*)

cùbito *m* cubit; (poet) elbow

cubo *m* cube

cuccagna *f* plenty; windfall; Cockaigne

cuccétta *f* berth

cucchiàia *f* large spoon; ladle; trowel; bucket (*of power shovel*); **cucchiaia bucata** skimmer

cucchiaiàta *f* spoonful; tablespoonful

cucchiaino *m* teaspoon; teaspoonful; spoon (*lure*)

cuc·chiàio *m* (-**chiài**) spoon; spoonful; tablespoon; **cucchiaio da minestra** soupspoon

cucchiaióne *m* ladle

cùc·cia *f* (-**ce**) dog's bed; **a cuccia!** lie down!

cucciare §128 *intr* (ESSERE) & *ref* to lie down (*said of a dog*)

cucciolata *f* litter (*e.g., of puppies*)

cùcciolo *m* puppy; cub; (fig) greenhorn

cuc·co *m* (-**chi**) cuckoo; simpleton; darling (*child*)

cuccuru·cù *m* (-**cù**) cock-a-doodle-doo

cucina *f* kitchen; cuisine; kitchen range; **cucina componibile** kitchen with sectional cabinets; **cucina economica** kitchen range; **fare da cucina** to prepare a meal

cucinare *tr* to cook; (fig) to fix

cucinétta *f* kitchenette

cuciniè·re -ra *mf* cook

cucire §143 *tr* to sew; to stitch || *ref*—**cucirsi la bocca** to keep one's mouth shut

cucirino *m* sewing thread

cuci·tóre -trice *adj* sewing || *mf* sewing machine operator || *f* seamstress; sewing machine (*for bookbinding*); **cucitrice a grappe** stapler

cuci·to -ta *adj* sewn || *m* sewing; needle work

cucitura *f* seam; sewing; stitches

cu·cù *m* (-**cù**) cuckoo

cuculo or **cùculo** *m* cuckoo

cùffia *f* bonnet (*for baby*); coif; (rad) headset; (telp) headpiece; (theat) prompter's box

cugi·no -na *mf* cousin

cui *pron invar* whose; to which; whom; which; of whom; of which; **per cui** (coll) therefore

culatta *f* breech (*of a gun*)

culinà·rio -ria (-**ri -rie**) *adj* culinary || *f* gastronomy

culla *f* cradle

cullare *tr* to rock (*a baby*); (fig) to delude || *ref* to have delusions

culminante *adj* highest; culminating

culminare (cùlmino) *intr* to culminate

cùlmine *m* top, summit

culo *m* (vulg) behind; (slang) bottom (*of glass or bottle*); **culi di bicchiere** (coll) fake diamonds

cul·to -ta *adj* cultivated; learned (*e.g., word*) || *m* cult, worship

cul·tóre -trice *mf* devotee

cultura *f* culture; **cultura fisica** physical culture

culturale *adj* cultural

cumino *m* (bot) caraway seed; (bot) cumin

cumulati·vo -va *adj* cumulative

cùmulo *m* heap, pile; concurrence (*of penal sentences*); cumulus
cuna *f* cradle
cùneo *m* wedge; chock; (archit) voussoir
cunétta *f* ditch; gutter
cunìcolo *m* small tunnel; burrow
cuòcere §144a *tr* to cook; to bake (*bricks*); to burn, dry up; (fig) to stew ‖ *intr* to cook; to burn; to dry up; (*with dat*) to grieve, to pain
cuò·co -ca *mf* (**-chi -che**) cook
cuòio *m* (**cuòi**) leather; **avere il cuoio duro** to have a tough hide; **cuoio capelluto** scalp ‖ *m* (**cuoia** *fpl*) (archaic) leather; **tirare le cuoia** (slang) to croak, to kick the bucket
cuòre *m* heart; **avere il cuore da coniglio** to be chicken-hearted; **avere il cuore da leone** to be lion-hearted; **cuori** (cards) hearts; **di cuore** gladly; heartily; **fare cuore a** to encourage; **stare a cuore** to be important
cupidigia *f* cupidity, greed, covetousness
Cupido *m* Cupid
cùpi·do -da *adj* greedy, covetous
cu·po -pa *adj* dark; deep (*color, voice*); sad, gloomy
cùpola *f* dome, cupola; crown (*of hat*)
cura *f* care; interest; cure; ministry; (poet) anxiety; **a cura di** edited by (*e.g., text*)
curare *tr* to take care of; to heed ‖ *intr* to see to it ‖ *ref* to take care of oneself; to care; to deign; **curarsi di** to care for
curatèla *f* (law) guardianship
curati·vo -va *adj* curative
cura·to -ta *adj* cured; healed ‖ *m* curate
cura·tóre -trice *mf* curator; trustee; editor (*of critical edition*); receiver (*in bankruptcy*)
curculióne *m* (ent) weevil
cur·do -da *adj & mf* Kurd
cùria *f* curia; bar
curiale *adj* curia; legal

curialé·sco -sca *adj* (**-schi -sche**) hairsplitting, legalistic
curiosare [s] (**curióso**) *intr* to pry around, snoop; to browse around
curiosi·tà [s] *f* (**-tà**) curiosity; whim; curio
curió·so -sa [s] *adj* curious; bizarre, quaint
curro *m* roller
cursóre *m* process server; court messenger; slide (*of slide ruler*)
curva *f* curve, bend; sweep; **curva di livello** contour line
curvare *tr* to curve, bend; **curvare la fronte** to bow down, yield ‖ *intr* to curve (*said of a road*); to take a curve, negotiate a curve ‖ *ref* to curve, bend; to bow; to become bent; to warp
curvatura *f* curving, bending; warp; stoop, curvature; camber
cur·vo -va *adj* bent, curved ‖ *f* see **curva**
cuscinétto *m* small pillow; pad (*for ink*); buffer (*zone*); (mach) bearing; **cuscinetto a rulli** roller bearing; **cuscinetto a sfere** ball bearing
cuscino *m* pillow; cushion
cùspide *f* point (*e.g., of arrow*); (archit) steeple
custòde *adj* guardian (*angel*) ‖ *m* custodian; janitor; warden; guard; (coll) policeman, cop
custòdia *f* safekeeping, custody; case (*e.g., of violin*); trust; (mach) housing
custodire §176 *tr* to keep; to protect, guard; to be in charge of (*prisoners*); to take care of; to cherish (*a memory*)
cutàne·o -a *adj* cutaneous
cute *f* (anat) skin
cuticagna *f* (joc) nape of the neck
cuticola *f* epidermis; cuticle; dentine
cutireazióne *f* skin test (*for allergic reactions*)
cutréttola *f* (orn) wagtail

D

D, d [di] *m & f* fourth letter of the Italian alphabet
da *prep* from; to; at; on; through; between; since; with; by, e.g., **è stato arrestato dalla polizia** he was arrested by the police; worth, e.g., **un libro da mille lire** a book worth a thousand lire; worthy of, e.g., **azione da gentiluomo** action worthy of a gentleman; at the house, office, shop, etc., of, e.g., **dal pittore** at the house of the painter; **da Giovanni** at John's; **dall'avvocato** at the lawyer's office; **d'altro lato** on the other hand; **d'ora in poi** from now on
dabbasso *adv* downstairs; down below
dabbenàggine *f* simplicity, foolishness
dabbène *adj invar* honest, upright, e.g., **un uomo dabbene** an honest man;

simple, foolish, e.g., **un dabben uomo** a Simple Simon
daccanto *adv* near, nearby
daccapo *adv* again, all over again; **andar daccapo** to begin a new paragraph; **daccapo a piedi** from top to bottom
dacché *conj* since
dado *m* cube; pedestal (*of column*); (mach) nut; (mach) die (*to cut threads*); **dadi** dice; **giocare ai dadi** to shoot craps; **il dado è tratto** the die is cast
daffare *m* things to do; bustle; **darsi daffare** to bustle, bustle about
da·ga *f* (**-ghe**) dagger
dagli §4 ‖ *interj*—**dagli al ladro!** stop thief!; **e dagli!** cut it out!
dài §4

dài·no -na *mf* fallow deer || *m* fallow deer; buckskin
dal §4
dàlia *f* dahlia
dalla §4
dallato *adv* aside; sideways
dalle §4
dalli *interj*—**dalli al ladro!** stop thief!; e dalli! cut it out!
dallo §4
dàlma·ta *adj & mf* (**-ti -te**) Dalmatian
Dalmàzia, la Dalmatia
daltòni·co -ca *adj* (**-ci -che**) color-blind
daltonismo *m* color blindness
dama *f* lady; dancing partner; checkers; andare a dama (checkers) to be crowned; **dama di compagnia** companion; **dama di corte** lady-in-waiting
damare *tr* (checkers) to crown
damascare §197 *tr* to damask
damaschinare *tr* to damascene
dama·sco -m (**-schi**) damask || **Damasco** *f* Damascus
damerino *m* fop, dandy
damigèlla *f* (lit) damsel; (orn) demoiselle; **damigella d'onore** bridesmaid
damigiana *f* demijohn
danaro *m* var of denaro
danaró·so -sa [s] *adj* wealthy, rich
dande *fpl* leading strings
danése [s] *adj* Danish || Danish || *mf* Dane || *m* Danish (*language*); Great Dane
Danimarca, la Denmark
dannare *tr* to damn; to bedevil || *ref* to be damned; to fret
danna·to -ta *adj* damned; wicked; terrible (*e.g., fear*) || *m* damned soul
dannazióne *f* damnation
danneggiare §290 (**dannéggio**) *tr* to damage; to injure, impair
danneggia·to -ta *adj* damaged; injured, impaired || *mf* victim
danno *m* damage; injury; (ins) loss; chiedere i danni to ask for indemnification; far danni a to damage; rifare i danni a to indemnify; tuo danno so much the worse for you
dannó·so -sa [s] *adj* damaging, harmful
dante *m*—**pelle di dante** buckskin
danté·sco -sca *adj* (**-schi -sche**) Dantean, Dantesque
danti·sta *mf* (**-sti -ste**) Dante scholar
Danùbio *m* Danube
danza *f* dance; dancing
danzare *tr & intr* to dance
danza·tóre -trice *mf* dancer
dappertutto *adv* everywhere
dappiè *adv*—**dappiè di** at the foot of
dappiù *adv*—**dappiù di** more than
dappòco *adj invar* worthless
dappòi *adv* (obs) afterwards, after
dapprèsso *adv* near, nearby, close
dapprima *adv* first, in the first place
dapprincipio *adv* first, in the beginning; over again
dardeggiare §290 (**dardéggio**) *tr* to hurl darts at; to beat down on; to look daggers at || *intr* to hurl darts; to beat down
dardo *m* dart, arrow; tip (*of blowtorch*)
da·re *m* (**-re**) (com) debit; **dare e avere**

debit and credit || §144b *tr* to give; to set (*fire*); to hand over; to lay down (*one's life*); to render (*e.g., unto Caesar*); to give away (*a bride*); to take (*an examination*); to tender (*one's resignation*); to say (*good night*); to shed (*tears*); **dare acqua a** to water; **dare alla luce** to give birth to; to bring out (*e.g., a book*); **dare aria a** to air; **dare . . . anni a qlcu** to think that s.o. is . . . years old; **dare a ridire** to give rise to complaint; **dare da intendere** to lead to believe; **dare fastidio a** to bother, annoy; **dare fondo a** to use up; **dare gli otto giorni a** to dismiss, fire; **dare il benvenuto a** to welcome; **dare il via a** to start (*e.g., a race*); **dare la colpa a** to declare guilty; to put the blame on; **dare la mano a** to shake hands with; **dare l'assalto a** to assault; **dare luogo a** to give rise to; **dare noia a** to bother; **dare per certo a** to assure; **dare ragione a** to agree with; **dare torto a** to disagree with; **dare via** to give away || *intr* to burst; to begin; to beat down (*said of the sun*); **dare a** to verge on; to face, overlook; **dare addosso a** to attack, persecute; **dare ai** or **sui nervi di** to irritate, irk; **dare alla testa a** to go to one's head, e.g., **il vino gli dà alla testa** wine goes to his head; **dare contro a** to disagree with; **dare del porco a** to call (s.o.) a thief; **dare del Lei a** to address formally; **dare del tu a** to address familiarly; **dare di volta il cervello a** to go raving mad, e.g., **gli ha dato di volta il cervello** he went raving mad; **dare giù** to abate; **dare in** to hit; **dare in affitto** to rent, lease; **dare nell'occhio** to attract attention; to hit the eye; **dare nel segno** to hit the target || *ref* to put on, e.g., **darsi la cipria** to put powder on; **darsela a gambe** to take to one's heels; **darsela per intesa** to become convinced; to take for granted; **darsele** to strike one another; **darsi a** to give oneself over to; **darsi delle arie** to put on airs; **darsi il vanto di** to boast of; **darsi un bacio** to kiss one another; **darsi la mano** to shake hands; **darsi la morte** to commit suicide; **darsi pace** to resign oneself; **darsi pensiero** to worry; **darsi per malato** to declare oneself ill; to fall ill; **darsi per vinto** to give in, submit; **può darsi** it's possible, maybe; **si dà il caso** it happens
dàrsena *f* dock; basin
data *f* date; deal (*of cards*); **a . . . data** (com) . . . days hence, on or before . . . days; **di fresca data** new (*e.g., friend*); **di vecchia data** old (*e.g., friend*)
datare *tr* to date || *intr*—**a datare da** beginning with
datà·rio *m* (**-ri**) date stamp
dati·vo -va *adj & m* dative
da·to -ta *adj* inclined, bent; addicted; given; appointed (*date*); **dato e non concesso** assumed for the sake of

argument; **dato che** since ‖ *m* datum ‖ *f* see **data**

da·tóre -trice *mf* giver, donor; **datore di lavoro** employer; **datore di sangue** blood donor; **datori di lavoro** management

dàttero *m* date; (zool) date shell

dattilografare (dattilògrafo) *tr* to typewrite, type

dattilografìa *f* typewriting

dattilògra·fo -fa *mf* typist

dattiloscopìa *f* examination of fingerprints

dattiloscrìt·to -ta *adj* typewritten ‖ *m* typescript

dattórno *adv* near, nearby; **darsi dattorno** to strive; **stare dattorno a** to cling to; **togliersi dattorno qlcu** to get rid of s.o.

davanti *adj invar* fore, front ‖ **davan·ti** *m* (-ti) front, face ‖ *adv* ahead, in front; **davanti a** in front of; **levarsi davanti a qlcu** to get out of someone's way; **passare davanti a** to pass, outstrip

davanzale *m* window sill

davanzo *adv* more than enough

davvéro *adv* indeed; **dire davvero** to speak in earnest

daziare §287 *tr* to levy a duty on

dà·zio *m* (-zi) duty, custom; **custom office**

dèa *f* goddess

debellare (debèllo) *tr* (lit) to crush

debilitare (debìlito) *tr* to debilitate

debilitazióne *f* debilitation

débi·to -ta *adj* due ‖ *m* debit; debt; **debito pubblico** national debt

debi·tóre -trice *mf* debtor

débole *adj* weak; faint; gentle (*sex*); **debole di mente** feeble-minded ‖ *m* weakness, weak point; weakness, foible; weakling

debolézza *f* weakness, debility

debordare (debórdo) *intr* (ESSERE & AVERE) to overflow

debòscia *f* debauchery

deboscia·to -ta *adj* debauched ‖ *mf* debauchee

debuttante *adj* beginning ‖ *mf* beginner ‖ *f* debutante

debuttare *intr* to come out, make one's debut; (theat) to perform for the first time; (theat) to open

debutto *m* debut; (theat) opening night, opening

dècade *f* ten; period of ten days; (mil) ten days' pay

decadènte *adj* & *m* decadent

decadènza *f* decadence; lapse (*of insurance policy*); (law) forfeiture

decadére §121 *intr* (ESSERE) to decline; to lose one's standing; (ins) to lapse; **decadere da** (law) to forfeit

decadiménto *m* decadence; (law) forfeiture

decadu·to -ta *adj* fallen upon hard times

decaffeinizzare [ddzz] *tr* to decaffeinate

decalcificatóre *m* water softener

decalcomanìa *f* decalcomania

decàlo·go *m* (-ghi) decalogue

decampare *intr* to decamp; **decampare da** to abandon (*a plan*)

decano *m* dean

decantare *tr* to praise, extol; to decant; (lit) to purify ‖ *intr* to undergo decantation

decapàggio *m* (metallurgy) pickling

decapitare (decàpito) *tr* to behead, decapitate

decapitazióne *f* beheading

decappottàbile *adj* & *f* (aut) convertible

decèdere §123 *intr* (ESSERE) to die; to decease

decelerare (decèlero) *tr* & *intr* to decelerate

decennale *adj* & *m* decennial

decènne *adj* & *mf* ten-year-old

decèn·nio *m* (-ni) decade

decènte *adj* decent; proper

decentralizzare [ddzz] *tr* to decentralize

decentrare (decèntro) *tr* to decentralize

decènza *f* decency; propriety

decèsso *m* decease, demise

decìdere §145 *tr* to decide; to persuade ‖ *intr* & *ref* to decide; **diciditi!** make up your mind!

decifràbile *adj* decipherable

decifrare *tr* to decipher, decode; (fig) to puzzle out (*e.g., somebody's intentions*); (mus) to sight-read

dècima *f* tithe

decimale *adj* & *m* decimal

decimare (decìmo) *tr* to decimate

decìmetro *m* decimeter; **doppio decimetro** ruler

dèci·mo -ma *adj, m* & *pron* tenth ‖ *f* see **decima**

decisionale *adj* decision-making

decisióne *f* decision

decisì·vo -va *adj* decisive, conclusive

decì·so -sa *adj* determined, resolute; appointed (*time*)

declamare *tr* to declaim ‖ *intr* to declaim; to inveigh

declamazióne *f* declamation

declaratò·rio -ria *adj* (-ri -rie) declarative

declinare *tr* to decline; to declare, show; (gram) to decline; (lit) to bend ‖ *intr* to set (*said, e.g., of a star*); to slope; to diminish

declinazióne *f* declination; (gram) declension

declino *m* decline

declì·vio *m* (-vi) declivity, slope

decollàg·gio *m* (-gi) take-off; lift-off

decollare (decòllo) *tr* to decapitate ‖ *intr* (aer) to take off; (rok) to lift off

decòllo *m* take-off; lift-off

decolorante *adj* bleaching ‖ *m* bleach

decompórre §218 *tr, intr* & *ref* to decompose

decomposizióne *f* decomposition

decompressióne *f* decompression

decongelare (decongèlo) *tr* to thaw; (com) to unfreeze

decontaminare (decontàmino) *tr* to decontaminate

decorare (decòro) *tr* to decorate

decoratì·vo -va *adj* decorative

decora·tóre -trice *mf* decorator

decorazióne *f* decoration

decòro *m* decorum, propriety; decor; dignity; decoration

decoró·so -sa [s] *adj* fitting, decorous, proper; dignified

decorrènza *f* beginning, effective date; lapse

decórrere §139 *intr* (ESSERE) to elapse; to begin; (lit) to run; a decorrere da effective, beginning with

decór·so -sa *adj* past || *m* period, span; course; development; nel decorso di in the course of

decòt·to -ta *adj* (com) insolvent || *m* decoction

decozióne *f* (com) insolvency

decrèpi·to -ta *adj* decrepit

decréscere §142 *intr* (ESSERE) to decrease

decretare (decréto) *tr* to decree

decréto *m* decree; decreto legge decree law

decùbito *m* recumbency

decuplicare §197 (decùplico) *tr* to multiply tenfold

dècu·plo -pla *adj* tenfold || *m* tenfold part

decurtare *tr* to diminish, decrease

decurtazióne *f* decrease

dèda·lo -la *adj* (lit) ingenious || *m* maze, labyrinth

dèdi·ca *f* (-che) dedication; inscription (in a book)

dedicare §197 (dèdico) *tr* to dedicate; to inscribe (a book) || *ref* to devote oneself

dèdi·to -ta *adj* devoted; addicted

dedizióne *f* devotion; (obs) surrender

dedurre §102 *tr* to deduce; to deduct; to derive; (hist) to found (a colony)

deduzióne *f* deduction

defalcàbile *adj* deductible

defalcare §197 *tr* to deduct, withhold

defal·co *m* (-chi) deduction, withholding

defecare §197 (defèco) *tr* (chem) to purify || *intr* to defecate

defenestrare (defenèstro) *tr* to throw out of the window; (fig) to fire; (pol) to unseat

defenestrazióne *f* defenestration; (fig) firing, dismissal

deferènte *adj* deferential; (anat) deferent

deferènza *f* deference

deferire §176 *tr* to submit; (law) to commit; deferire il giuramento a qlcu to put s.o. under oath || *intr* to defer

defezionare (defezióno) *intr* to desert, defect

defezióne *f* defection

deficiènte *adj* deficient, lacking || *mf* idiot

deficiènza *f* deficiency; idiocy

dèfi·cit *m* (-cit) deficit

deficità·rio -ria *adj* (-ri -rie) lacking; deficit (e.g., budget)

defilare *tr* to defilade || *ref* to protect oneself

denfinìbile *adj* definable

definire §176 *tr* to define; to settle (an argument)

definiti·vo -va *adj* definitive; in definitiva after all

defini·to -ta *adj* definite

definizióne *f* definition; settlement (of an argument)

deflagrare *intr* to burst into flame; (fig) to burst out

deflazionare (deflazióno) *tr* (com) to deflate

deflazióne *f* deflation

deflèttere §177 *intr* to deflect

deflettóre *m* (aut) vent window; (mach) baffle

deflorare (deflòro) *tr* to deflower

defluire §176 *intr* (ESSERE) to flow down; (fig) to pour out

deflusso *m* flow; outflow, outpour; ebbtide

deformare (defórmo) *tr* to deform; to cripple; to alter (a word)

defórme *adj* deformed, crippled

deformi·tà *f* (-tà) deformity

defraudare (defràudo) *tr* to defraud, bilk

defun·to -ta *adj* dead; deceased; defunct; late || *mf* dead person, deceased || *m* deceased; i defunti the deceased

degenerare (degènero) *intr* (ESSERE & AVERE) to degenerate; to worsen

degenera·to -ta *adj* degenerate, perverted || *mf* degenerate, pervert

degenerazióne *f* degeneracy, degeneration

degènere *adj* degenerate

degènte *adj* bedridden; hospitalized || *mf* patient; inpatient

degènza *f* confinement; hospitalization

dégli §4

deglutire §176 *tr* to swallow

degnare (dégno) *tr* to honor || *ref* to deign, condescend

degnazióne *f* condescension

dé·gno -gna *adj* worthy; degno di nota noteworthy

degradante *adj* degrading

degradare *tr* to degrade; to downgrade; (mil) to break || *ref* to become degraded

degradazióne *f* degradation

degustare *tr* to taste

degustazióne *f* tasting

dèh *interj* oh!

déi §4

deiezióne *f* excrement; (geol) detritus

deificare §197 (deìfico) *tr* to deify

dei·tà *f* (-tà) deity

dél §4

dela·tóre -trice *mf* informer

delazióne *f* informing; (law) administration of an oath

dèle·ga *f* (-ghe) proxy, power of attorney

delegare §209 (dèlego) *tr* to delegate

delega·to -ta *adj* delegated || *m* delegate; (eccl) legate

delegazióne *f* delegation

deletè·rio -ria *adj* (-ri -rie) deleterious

delfino *m* dolphin; (hist) dauphin

delibare *tr* to relish; to touch on; to ratify (a foreign decree)

delibazióne *f* ratification (*of a foreign decree*)

deliberare (**delìbero**) *tr* to deliberate; to decide; to award (*at auction*) || *intr* to deliberate

delibera·to -ta *adj* deliberate; resolved

deliberazióne *f* deliberation; decision

delicatézza *f* delicacy; gentleness; tactfulness; luxury

delica·to -ta *adj* delicate; gentle; tactful

delimitare (**delìmito**) *tr* to delimit

delineare (**delìneo**) *tr* to outline, sketch || *ref* to take shape; to appear

delinquènte *m* criminal

delinquènza *f* delinquency; **delinquenza minorile** juvenile delinquency

delinquere §146 *intr* to commit a crime

delì·quio *m* (**-qui**) fainting spell, swoon; **cadere in deliquio** to faint

delirare *intr* to be delirious; to rave; (lit) to stray

delì·rio *m* (**-ri**) delirium; frenzy; **andare in delirio** to go wild; **cadere in delirio** to become delirious

delitto *m* crime

delittuó·so -sa [s] *adj* criminal

delìzia *f* delight; (hort) Delicious (*variety of apple*)

deliziare §287 *tr* & *ref* to delight

delizió·so -sa [s] *adj* delicious; delightful

délla §4

délle §4

déllo §4

dèl·ta *m* (**-ta**) delta

delucidare (**delùcido**) *tr* to elucidate; to remove the sheen from

delucidazióne *f* elucidation; removal of sheen

delùdere §105 *tr* to disappoint; to deceive; to foil

delusióne *f* disappointment; deception

delu·so -sa *adj* disappointed; deceived

demagnetizzare [ddzz] *tr* to demagnetize

demagogìa *f* demagogy

demagò·go -ga (**-ghi**) demagogue

demandare *tr* (law) to commit

demà·nio *m* (**-ni**) state land, state property

demarcare §197 *tr* to demarcate

demarcazióne *f* demarcation

demènte *adj* demented, crazy; idiotic || *mf* insane person; idiot

demènza *f* insanity, madness; idiocy

demèrito *m* demerit

demilitarizzare [ddzz] *tr* to demilitarize

democrà·tico -ca (**-ci -che**) *adj* democratic || *mf* democrat

democrazìa *f* democracy || **Democrazia Cristiana** Christian Democratic Party

democristia·no -na *adj* Christian Democratic || *mf* Christian Democrat

demogrà·fico -ca *adj* (**-ci -che**) demographic

demolire §176 *tr* to demolish

demoli·tóre -trice *adj* wrecking; destructive || *mf* wrecker

demolizióne *f* demolition

dèmone *m* demon

demonìa·co -ca *adj* (**-ci -che**) fiendish; demoniacal

demò·nio *m* (**-ni**) demon; **avere il demonio addosso** to be full of the devil

demoralizzare [ddzz] *tr* to demoralize || *ref* to become demoralized

demoralizza·to -ta [ddzz] *adj* demoralized, dejected

denaro *m* money; denier (*of nylon thread*); **avere il denaro contato** to be short of money; **denari** suit of Neapolitan cards corresponding to diamonds

denatura·to -ta *adj* denatured

denegare §209 (**dènego** or **denégo**) *tr* to deny

denigrare *tr* to denigrate; to backbite

denominare (**denòmino**) *tr* to call, designate

denomina·tóre -trice *adj* designating || *m* denominator

denominazióne *f* denomination; designation

denotare (**denòto**) *tr* to denote

densi·tà *f* (**-tà**) density

dèn·so -sa *adj* dense, thick

dentale *adj* & *f* dental

dentare (**dènto**) *tr* to notch, scallop || *intr* to teethe

dentaruòlo *m* teething ring

denta·to -ta *adj* toothed

dentatura *f* set of teeth; teeth (*of gear*)

dènte *m* tooth; peak (*of mountain*); pang (*of jealousy*); fluke (*of anchor*); prong (*of fork*); **battere i denti** to shiver; **dente canino** canine tooth; **dente del giudizio** wisdom tooth; **dente di latte** baby tooth; **dente di leone** (bot) dandelion; **mettere i denti** to teethe

dentellare (**dentèllo**) *tr* to notch, scallop; to perforate (*stamps*)

dentellatura *f* notch; perforation (*of postage stamps*); (archit) denticulation

dentèllo *m* notch, scallop; lace; (archit) dentil

dentièra *f* denture, plate; cog

dentifrì·cio -cia (**-ci -cie**) *adj* tooth || *m* dentifrice

denti·sta *mf* (**-sti -ste**) dentist

dentizióne *f* teething

déntro *adv* inside, in; **dentro di** inside of; within; **essere dentro** (coll) to be behind bars; **in dentro** inward || *prep* inside of

denuclearizzare [ddzz] *tr* to denuclearize

denudare *tr* to denude; to strip; (lit) to unveil

denunciare §128 *tr* var of **denunziare**

denùnzia *f* denunciation; announcement; report

denunziare §287 *tr* to denounce; to accuse; to announce; to report

denutrì·to -ta *adj* undernourished

denutrizióne *f* undernourishment

deodorante *adj* & *m* deodorant

deodorare (**deodóro**) *tr* to deodorize

depauperare (**depàupero**) *tr* to impoverish

depennare (**depènno**) *tr* to strike out, expunge

deperìbile *adj* perishable

deperiménto *m* deterioration; decline

deperire §176 *intr* (ESSERE) to deteriorate; to perish; to decay

depilató·rio -ria *adj & m* (**-ri -rie**) depilatory

deplorare (**deplòro**) *tr* to deplore; to reproach

deplorévole *adj* deplorable; reproachable

depolarizzare [ddzz] *tr* to depolarize

depórre §218 *tr* to lay; to lay down (*crown, arms*); to depose (*e.g., a king*); to take off (*clothes*); to give up (*hope*); to renounce; **deporre l'abito talare** to doff the cassock

deportare (**depòrto**) *tr* to deport

deporta·to -ta *adj* deported ‖ *mf* deportee

deportazióne *f* deportation

depositare (**depòsito**) *tr* to deposit; to register, check ‖ *intr* to settle (*said, e.g., of sand*)

depositá·rio -ria (**-ri -rie**) *adj* deposit ‖ *mf* depositary

depòsito *m* deposit; checking (*e.g., of a suitcase*); registration; heap (*e.g., of refuse*); warehouse; morgue; receiving ward; (mil) depot; **deposito bagagli** baggage room

deposizióne *f* deposition; Descent from the Cross

deprava·to -ta *adj* depraved

depravazióne *f* depravation

deprecare §197 (**dèpreco**) *tr* to deprecate

depredare (**deprèdo**) *tr* to plunder

depredazióne *f* depredation

depressióne *f* depression

deprès·so -sa *adj* depressed

deprezzaménto *m* depreciation

deprezzare (**deprèzzo**) *tr* to depreciate; to underestimate ‖ *intr* (ESSERE) to depreciate

depriménte *adj* depressing

deprimere §131 *tr* to humble, discourage; to depress

depurare *tr* to purify

deputare (**dèputo**) *tr* to deputize, delegate

deputa·to -ta *mf* deputy, delegate; representative

deputazióne *f* deputation, delegation

deragliaménto *m* derailment

deragliare §280 *intr* to be derailed, to run off the track

derapàg·gio *m* (**-gi**) skidding

derapare *intr* to skid

derelìt·to -ta *adj & mf* derelict

derelizióne *f* dereliction

dereta·no -na *adj & m* posterior

deridere §231 *tr* to deride, mock

derisióne *f* derision, ridicule

derisò·rio -ria *adj* (**-ri -rie**) derisory, derisive

deriva *f* (aer) vertical stabilizer; (aer, naut) leeway; (naut) drift; **alla deriva** adrift

derivare *tr* to derive; to branch off (*e.g., a canal*) ‖ *intr* (ESSERE) to be derived, arise; to drift

deriva·to -ta *adj* derivative ‖ *m* derivative (*word*) ‖ *f* (math) derivative

derivazióne *f* derivation; (elec) shunt; (telp) extension

dermatòlo·go *m* (**-gi**) dermatologist

dermòide *f* imitation leather

dèro·ga *f* (**-ghe**) exception; **in deroga a** deviating from

derogare §209 (**dèrogo**) *intr* to transgress; **derogare a** to deviate from

derrata *f* foodstuff; **derrate** foodstuff, produce

derubare *tr* to rob

dèr·vis *m* (**-vis**) or **dervì·scio** *m* (**-sci**) dervish

desalazióne [s] *f* desalinization

desalificare §197 (**desalìfico**) *tr* to desalt

dé·sco *m* (**-schi**) dinner table; meal

descrìtti·vo -va *adj* descriptive

descrìvere §250 *tr* to describe

descrizióne *f* description

desegregazióne [s] *f* desegregation

desensibilizzare [s] [ddzz] *tr* to desensitize

desèrti·co -ca *adj* (**-ci -che**) desert, wild

desèr·to -ta *adj* deserted; **andare deserto** to be unattended ‖ *m* desert

desideràbile [s] *adj* desirable

desiderare (**desìdero**) [s] *tr* to desire; **farsi desiderare** to make oneself scarce; to be dilatory

desidè·rio [s] *m* (**-ri**) desire; craving; lust; **lasciar desiderio di sé** to be greatly missed

desideró·so -sa [s] *adj* desirous

designare [s] *tr* to designate

designazióne [s] *f* designation

desinare *m* dinner ‖ *intr* to dine

desinènza *f* (gram) ending

desì·o *m* (**-ì**) (lit) desire

desìstere §114 *intr* to desist

desolante [s] *adj* distressing

desolare (**dèsolo**) *tr* to distress; (lit) to devastate

desola·to -ta *adj* desolate; distressed

desolazióne *f* desolation; distress

dèspo·ta *m* (**-ti**) despot

despòti·co -ca *adj* (**-ci -che**) var of dispotico

despotismo *m* var of dispotismo

des·sèrt *m* (**-sèrt**) dessert

destare (**dèsto**) *tr* to awaken; to stir up ‖ *ref* to wake up

destinare *tr* to destine; to assign; to address

destinatà·rio -ria *mf* (**-ri -rie**) consignee; addressee

destinazióne *f* destination; assignment

destino *m* destiny; (com) destination

destituire §176 *tr* to demote; to dismiss; to deprive

destituzióne *f* demotion; dismissal

dé·sto -sta *adj* awake; (fig) wide-awake

dèstra *f* right, right hand

destreggiare §290 (**destréggio**) *intr* to maneuver ‖ *ref* to manage shrewdly

destrézza *f* skill, dexterity

destrière or **destriéro** *m* (lit) steed

dè·stro -stra *adj* right; skillful ‖ *f* see destra

destròr·so -sa *adj* clockwise; right-hand; (bot) dextrorse

destròsio *m* dextrose

desùmere [s] §116 *tr* to obtain; to infer

detecti·ve *m* (-ve) detective

detèc·tor *m* (-tor) (rad) detector

detenére §271 *tr* to hold; to detain

deten·tóre -trice *mf* holder; receiver (*of stolen goods*)

detenu·to -ta *m* prisoner

detenzióne *f* illegal possession; detention

detergènte *adj & m* detergent

detèrgere §164 (*pp* **detèrso**) *tr* to cleanse; to wipe

deterioràbile *adj* perishable

deteriorare (**deterióro**) *tr* to spoil || *intr* (ESSERE) & *ref* to deteriorate, spoil

determinare (**detèrmino**) *tr* to determine; to fix; to decide; to cause || *ref* to decide; to happen

determinatézza *f* determination; precision

determinati·vo -va *adj* (gram) definite

determina·to -ta *adj* given; resolved, determined

determinazióne *f* determination

deterrènte *adj & m* deterrent

detersi·vo -va *adj* cleansing || *m* cleanser; detergent

detestàbile *adj* detestable

detestare (**detèsto**) *tr* to detest

detettóre *m* detector; **detettore di bugie** lie detector

detonare (**detòno**) *intr* to explode, detonate

detonatóre *m* blasting cap, detonator

detonazióne *f* detonation; report

detrarre §273 *tr* to take away; (lit) to detract

detrat·tóre -trice *mf* detractor

detrazióne *f* detraction; deduction

detriménto *m* detriment

detrito *m* debris; detritus; (fig) outcast, outlaw

detronizzare [ddzz] *tr* to dethrone

détta *f*—**a detta di** according to

dettagliante *m* retailer

dettagliare §280 *tr* to tell in detail; to itemize; to retail || *intr*—**pregasi dettagliare** please send detailed information

dettà·glio *m* (-gli) detail; retail

dettame *m* (lit) law, norm

dettare (**détto**) *tr* to dictate; (lit) to compose, write; **dettar legge** to impose one's will

dettato *m* dictation; (lit) style

dettatura *f* dictation

dét·to -ta *adj* called, named; **detto (e) fatto** no sooner said than done || *m* saying || *f* see **detta**

deturpare *tr* to disfigure, mar

deturpazióne *f* disfigurement, disfiguration

devalutazióne *f* devaluation

devastare *tr* to devastate, lay waste; (fig) to disfigure

devasta·tóre -trice *adj* devastating || *m* devastator

devastazióne *f* devastation

deviaménto *m* switching; derailment; (fig) straying

deviare §119 *tr* to turn aside; to lead astray; (rr) to switch; (rr) to derail

|| *intr* to deviate; to wander; to go astray; (rr) to run off the track

deviatóre *m* (rr) switchman; (elec) two-way switch

deviazióne *f* deviation; detour; curvature (*of the spine*); (phys) declination; (phys) deflection; (rr) switching

deviazionismo *m* deviationism

deviazioni·sta *mf* (-sti -ste) deviationist

devoluzióne *f* transfer

devòlvere §147 *tr* to transfer || *intr & ref* (lit) to roll down

devò·to -ta *adj* devoted; devout, pious || *m* devout person; worshiper

devozióne *f* devotion

di §4 *prep* of; in, e.g., **la più bella della famiglia** the prettiest one in the family; (*with definite article*) some, e.g., **mi occorrono dei fiammiferi** I need some matches; than, e.g., **più veloce del baleno** faster than lightning; from, e.g., **è di Milano** he is from Milan; off, e.g., **smontare di sella** to get off the saddle; about, e.g., **discutere di politica** to talk about politics; with, e.g., **ornare di fiori** to adorn with flowers; made of, e.g., **una casa di mattoni** a house made of bricks; by, e.g., **di notte** by night; for, e.g., **amor di patria** love for one's country; worth, e.g., **casa di dieci milioni** house worth ten million; in the amount of, e.g., **multa di mille lire** fine in the amount of one thousand lire; son of, e.g., **Carlo Giovannini di Filippo** Carlo Giovannini son of Philip; daughter of, e.g., **Anna Ponti di Antonio** Anna Ponti daughter of Anthony; **di corsa** running; **di gran lunga** greatly; by far; **di . . . in** from . . . to; **di là da** beyond; **di nascosto** stealthily; **di qua da** on this side of; **di quando in quando** from time to time; **di tre metri** three meters long or wide or high

dì *m* (**dì**) day; **a dì** (e.g., **ventisei**) this (e.g., twenty-sixth) day; **conciare per il dì delle feste** (coll) to beat up

diabète *m* diabetes

diabèti·co -ca *adj & mf* (-ci -che) diabetic

diabòli·co -ca *adj* (-ci -che) diabolic(al)

diàcono *m* deacon

diadè·ma *m* (-mi) diadem (*of king*); tiara (*of lady*)

diàfa·no -na *adj* diaphanous

diafonia *f* (telp) cross talk

diafram·ma *m* (-mi) diaphragm; (fig) partition

diàgno·si *f* (-si) diagnosis

diagnosticare §197 (**diagnòstico**) *tr* to diagnose

diagonale *adj & f* diagonal

diagram·ma *m* (-mi) diagram; chart

diagrammare *tr* to diagram

dialettale *adj* dialectal

dialètti·co -ca (-ci -che) *adj* dialectic(al) || *m* dialectician || *f* dialectic; (philos) dialectics

dialètto *m* dialect

dialettòfo·no -na *adj* dialect-speaking || *m* dialect-speaking person

dialogare §209 (dià̀logo) *intr* to carry on a dialogue

dialoga·to -ta *adj* written in the form of a dialogue ‖ *m* dialogue

diàlo·go *m* (-ghi) dialogue

diamante *m* diamond; **diamante tagliavetro** glass cutter

diametrale *adj* diametric(al)

diàmetro *m* diameter

diàmine *interj* good heavens!; the devil!; sure!

diana *f* (mil) reveille ‖ **Diana** *f* Diana

dianzi *adv* (lit) a short while ago

diàpa·son *m* (-son) (mus) pitch; (mus) tuning fork

diapositiva *f* (phot) slide, transparency

dià·rio -ria (-ri -rie) *adj* daily ‖ *m* diary; journal; **diario scolastico** homework book ‖ *f* per diem

diarrèa *f* diarrhea

diascò·pio *m* (-pi) slide projector

diaspro *m* jasper

diàstole *f* diastole

diatermìa *f* diathermy

diatriba *f* diatribe

diavolàc·cio *m* (-ci) devil; **buon diavolaccio** good fellow

diavolerìa *f* deviltry; devilment; evil plot

diavolè·rio *m* (-ri) hubbub, uproar

diavoléto *m* hubbub, uproar

diavolétto *m* little devil, imp

diàvolo *m* devil; **avere il diavolo in corpo** to be nervous; **avere un diavolo per capello** to be in a horrible mood; **buon diavolo** good fellow; **essere come il diavolo e l'acqua santa** to be at opposite poles; **fare il diavolo a quattro** to make a racket; to try very hard

dibàttere *tr* to debate ‖ *ref* to struggle; to writhe

dibattiménto *m* debate; (law) pleading, trial

dibàttito *m* debate

dicastèro *m* department, ministry

dicèmbre *m* December

dicerìa *f* rumor, gossip

dichiarare *tr* to declare, state; to find (guilty); to proclaim; to nominate, name ‖ *ref* to declare oneself to be; to declare one's love; to plead (e.g., guilty)

dichiarazióne *f* declaration; avowal (of love); return (of income tax); **dichiarazioni** representations

diciannòve *adj & pron* nineteen; **le diciannove** seven P.M. ‖ *m* nineteen; nineteenth (in dates)

diciannovèsi·mo -ma *adj, m & pron* nineteenth

diciassètte *adj & pron* seventeen; **le diciassette** five P.M. ‖ *m* seventeen; seventeenth (in dates)

diciassettèsi·mo -ma *adj, m & pron* seventeenth

diciottèsi·mo -ma *adj, m & pron* eighteenth

diciòtto *adj & pron* eighteen; **le diciotto** six P.M. ‖ *m* eighteen; eighteenth (in dates)

dici·tóre -trice *mf* reciter

dicitura *f* caption, legend; (lit) wording, language

dicotomìa *f* dichotomy

didascalìa *f* note, notice; caption; legend (e.g., on coin); (mov) subtitle

didascàli·co -ca *adj* (-ci -che) didactic

didàtti·co -ca (-ci -che) *adj* didactic; elementary school (director, principal) ‖ *f* didactics

didéntro *m* (coll) inside

didiètro *m* behind; back (of house) ‖ *adv* behind

dièci *adj & pron* ten; **le dieci** ten o'clock ‖ *m* ten; tenth (in dates)

diecimila *adj, m & pron* ten thousand

diecina *f* about ten

dière·si *f* (-si) dieresis

diè·sis *m* (-sis) (mus) sharp

dièta *f* diet; **dieta idrica** fluid diet

dietèti·co -ca (-ci -che) *adj* dietetic ‖ *f* dietetics

dieti·sta *mf* (-sti -ste) dietitian

diètro *adj invar* back, rear ‖ *m* back, rear ‖ *adv* back, behind; **dal di dietro** from behind; **di dietro** hind (legs); back (side); behind, back (e.g., of cupboard) ‖ *prep* behind; beyond; after; upon; **dietro a** behind; beyond; after; according to; **dietro consegna** on delivery; **dietro domanda** upon application; **dietro versamento** upon payment; **essere dietro a** to be in the process of

dietrofrónt *m* (mil) about face

difatti *adv* indeed

difèndere §148 *tr* to defend, protect ‖ *ref* to protect oneself; (coll) to get along

difensì·vo -va *adj & f* defensive

difen·sóre -sóra or **difenditrice** *adj* defense ‖ *mf* defender

difésa [s] *f* defense; bulwark; protection; **legittima difesa** self-defense; **pigliare le difese di** to defend, back up; **venire in difesa di** to go to the defense of

difettare (difètto) *intr* to be lacking; to be defective; **difettare di** to lack

difetti·vo -va *adj* defective

difètto *m* lack; blemish; fault; defect; **essere in difetto** to be at fault; **far difetto a** to lack, e.g., **gli fa difetto il denaro** he lacks money

difettó·so -sa [s] *adj* defective

diffamare *tr* to defame, slander

diffama·tóre -trice *mf* defamer, slanderer

diffamazióne *f* defamation, slander

differènte *adj* different

differènza *f* difference; spread; variance; **a differenza di** unlike; **c'è una bella differenza** it's a horse of another color

differenziale *adj & m* differential

differenziare §287 (differènzio) *tr* to differentiate

differiménto *m* deferment

differire §176 *tr* to postpone, defer ‖ *intr* to be different; to differ

difficile *adj* hard, difficult; awkward (situation); hard-to-please; unlikely

‖ *mf* hard-to-please person ‖ *m*— **fare il difficile** to be hard to please; **qui sta il difficile!** here's the trouble!

difficol·tà *f* (**-tà**) difficulty; defect; obstacle; objection

difficoltó·so -sa [s] *adj* difficult, troublesome; fastidious

diffida *f* notice; warning

diffidare *tr* to give notice to; to warn ‖ *intr* to mistrust

diffidènte *adj* distrustful

diffidènza *f* mistrust

diffóndere §178 *tr* to spread; to circulate; to broadcast ‖ *ref* to spread; to dwell at length

diffórme *adj* unlike; (obs) deformed

diffrazióne *f* diffraction

diffusióne *f* spreading; circulation (*of a newspaper*); diffusion; (rad) broadcast

diffu·so -sa *adj* diffuse; widespread

diffusóre *m* diffuser (*to soften light*); baffle (*of loudspeaker*); (mach) choke

difilato *adv* forthwith, right away

difrónte *adj invar* in front

difterite *f* diphtheria

di·ga *f* (**-ghe**) dike; dam

digerènte *adj* alimentary (*canal*), digestive (*tube*)

digeríbile *adj* digestible

digerire §176 *tr* to digest; to tolerate, stand

digestióne *f* digestion

digesti·vo -va *adj* digestive

digèsto *m* digest

digitale *adj* digital ‖ *f* (bot) digitalis

digitalina *f* (pharm) digitalin

digiunare *intr* to fast

digiu·no -na *adj* without food; deprived; **digiuno di cognizioni** ignorant; **tenere digiuno** to keep in ignorance ‖ *m* fast; **a digiuno** on an empty stomach; **fare digiuno** to fast

digni·tà *f* (**-tà**) dignity; **dignità** *fpl* dignitaries

dignità·rio *m* (**-ri**) dignitary

dignitó·so -sa [s] *adj* dignified

digradare *tr* to shade (*colors*) ‖ *intr* to slope; to fade

digredire §176 *intr* to digress

digressióne *f* digression

digrignare *tr* to show (*one's or its teeth*); to grit (*one's teeth*)

digrossare (**digròsso**) *tr* to rough-hew; to whittle down; (fig) to refine ‖ *ref* to become refined

diguazzare *tr* to beat (*a liquid*) ‖ *intr* to wallow; to splash

dilagare §209 *intr* to flood, to overflow; to spread abroad

dilaniare §287 *tr* to tear to pieces ‖ *ref* to slander one another

dilapidare (**dilàpido**) *tr* to squander

dilatare *tr* to expand; to dilate ‖ *ref* to expand; to spread

dilatazióne *f* expansion; dilation

dilatò·rio -ria *adj* (**-ri -rie**) delaying; dilatory

dilavare *tr* to wash away, erode

dilava·to -ta *adj* dull, flat; wan

dilazionare (**dilazióno**) *tr* to delay, put off; (com) to extend

dilazióne *f* delay; (com) extension

dileggiare §290 (**diléggio**) *tr* to mock

dilég·gio *m* (**-gi**) mockery, scoffing; **mettere in dileggio** to scoff at

dileguare (**diléguo**) *tr* to scatter ‖ *intr* (ESSERE) to disappear, vanish; to melt

dilèm·ma *m* (**-mi**) dilemma

dilettante *mf* amateur; dilettante

dilettané·sco -sca *adj* (**-schi -sche**) amateurish

dilettare (**dilètto**) *tr* to delight ‖ *ref* to delight; **dilettarsi a** + *inf* to delight in + *ger*; **dilettarsi di** to pursue as a hobby, e.g., **si diletta di pittura** he pursues painting as a hobby

dilettévole *adj* delectable, delightful

dilèt·to -ta *adj* beloved ‖ *m* loved one; pleasure; hobby

diligènte *adj* diligent

diligènza *f* diligence; stagecoach

dilucidare (**dilùcido**) *tr* to elucidate

diluire §176 *tr* to dilute

dilungare §209 *tr* (archaic) to stretch ‖ *ref* to expatiate; to be ahead by several lengths (*said of a race horse*)

dilungo *m*—**a un dilungo** more or less

diluviare §287 *tr* to devour ‖ *intr* (ESSERE & AVERE) to rain (*said, e.g., of bullets*) ‖ *impers* (ESSERE)—**diluvia** it is pouring

dilù·vio *m* (**-vi**) deluge, flood; **diluvio universale** Flood

dimagrante *adj* reducing

dimagrare *tr* to thin down ‖ *intr* (ESSERE) to become thin; to lose weight; to become exhausted (*said of land*); (fig) to become meager

dimagrire §176 *intr* (ESSERE) to become thin; to lose weight, reduce

dimanda *f var of* **domanda**

dimane *adv* (coll) tomorrow

dimani *m & adv var of* **domani**

dimenare (**diméno**) *tr* to wag (*the tail*); to beat (*eggs*); to wave (*one's arms*); to stir up (*a question*) ‖ *ref* to toss; to busy oneself

dimensióne *f* dimension; (fig) nature

dimenticanza *f* oversight, neglect; **andare in dimenticanza** to be forgotten

dimenticare §197 (**diméntico**) *tr* to forget; to forgive ‖ *ref* to forget; **dimenticarsi di** to forget; to neglect

dimenticatóio *m*—**mettere nel dimenticatoio** (coll) to forget

diménti·co -ca *adj* (**-chi -che**) forgetful; neglectful

dimés·so -sa *adj* humble, modest (*demeanor*); low (*voice*); shabby (*clothes*)

dimestichézza *f* familiarity

diméttere §198 *tr* to dismiss; to release ‖ *ref* to resign

dimezzare [ddzz] (**dimèzzo**) *tr* to halve

diminuire §176 *tr* to lessen, reduce; to lower (*prices*) ‖ *intr* (ESSERE) to diminish

diminuti·vo -va *adj & m* diminutive

diminuzióne *f* diminution

dimissionare (**dimissióno**) *tr* to dismiss, discharge ‖ *ref* to resign

dimissionà·rio -ria *adj* (**-ri -rie**) resigning, outgoing

dimissióne f resignation; **dare le dimissióni** to resign

dimól·to -ta adj & m (coll) much || **dimolto** adv (coll) much

dimòra f stay; residence; (lit) delay; **mettere a dimora** to install; to plant (trees); **senza dimora** (lit) without delay; **senza fissa dimora** vagrant

dimorare (dimòro) intr to stay; to reside; (lit) to delay

dimostràbile adj demonstrable

dimostrante m demonstrator

dimostrare (dimóstro) tr to demonstrate; to register (e.g., anger); **dimostrare trent'anni** to look thirty || intr to demonstrate || ref to prove oneself to be

dimostrati·vo -va adj demonstrative; (mil) diverting

dimostra·tóre -trice mf demonstrator

dimostrazióne f demonstration

dinàmi·co -ca (-ci -che) adj dynamic || f dynamics

dinamismo m dynamism

dinamite f dynamite

dìna·mo f (-mo) generator, dynamo

dinanzi adj invar front, e.g., **la porta dinanzi** the front door; preceding, e.g., **il mese dinanzi** the preceding month || adv ahead; beforehand; (lit) before; **dinanzi a** before, in front of

dina·sta m (-sti) dynast

dinastia f dynasty

dinàsti·co -ca adj (-ci -che) dynastic

dindo m (coll) turkey

dindòn m ding-dong || interj ding-dong!

diniè·go m (-ghi) denial

dinoccola·to -ta adj gangling; clumsy (gait)

dinosàuro [s] m dinosaur

dintórno m—**dintorni** surroundings, neighborhood || adv around; **dintorno a** around

dì·o -a adj (-i -e) (poet) godly || m (dèi) god; **gli dei** the gods || **Dio** m God; **che Dio ce la manda** cats and dogs (said of rain); **come Dio volle** at long last; **come Dio vuole** botched (piece of work); **Dio ci scampi!** God forbid!; **Dio santo!** good heavens!; **grazie a Dio** God willing; thank God!; **voglia Dio** God grant

diòce·si f (-si) diocese

diodo m (electron) diode

diomedèa f (orn) albatross

diottrìa f (opt) diopter

dipanare tr to unravel, unwind

dipartiménto m department

dipartire §176 tr (archaic) to divide || intr (**diparto**) (ESSERE) & ref (lit) to depart

dipartita f (lit) departure; (lit) demise

dipendènte adj dependent || mf employee

dipendènza f dependence; employment; annex; (com) branch; **in dipendenza di** as a consequence of

dipèndere §150 intr (ESSERE) to depend; **dipendere da** to depend on

dipingere §126 tr to paint; **dipingere a olio** to paint in oils; **dipingere a tempera** to distemper || ref to paint one-self; to put make-up on; to appear, e.g., **gli si dipinse in volto la paura** fear appeared on his face

dipin·to -ta adj painted || m painting, picture

diplò·ma m (-mi) diploma, certificate

diplomare (diplòmo) tr to grant a degree to; to graduate || ref to receive a degree; to graduate

diplomàti·co -ca (-ci -che) adj diplomatic; true, faithful (copy) || m diplomat || f diplomatics

diploma·to -ta adj graduated || mf graduate || m alumnus || f alumna

diplomazìa f diplomacy

dipòi adv after, thereafter

diportare (dipòrto) ref (lit) to behave; (obs) to have a good time

dipòrto m recreation; (obs) sport; **andare a diporto** to go on an outing; to go for a walk

diprèsso adv—**a un dipresso** about, approximately

diradare tr to thin out (vegetation); to disperse; to space out (one's visits) || intr (ESSERE) & ref to diminish; to disperse

diramare tr to prune; to circulate (notices); to issue (a communiqué) || ref to branch out; to spread

diramazióne f branch; ramification; issuance

dire m talk; **per sentito dire** by hearsay; **stando al dire** according to his words || §151 tr & intr to say; to tell; to call (e.g., s.o. a genius); to talk; **detto (e) fatto** no sooner said than done; **dica pure!** go ahead!; speak up!; **dire bene di** to speak well of; **dire di no** to say no; **dire di sì** to say yes; **direi quasi** I dare say; **dire la sua** to have one's say; **dire male di** to speak ill of; **dirla grossa** to make a blunder; to tell a tall tale; **dirlo chiaro e tondo** to speak bluntly; **dirne un sacco e una sporta a** to pour insults upon; **è tutto dire** that's all; **non c'è che dire** it's a fact; **non fo per dire** I do not want to boast; **per così dire** so to speak; **per meglio dire** rather; **trovarci a dire** to find fault with; **trovare da dire con** to have words with; **voler ben dire** to be sure; **voler dire** to mean || ref—**dirsela con** to connive with; **si dice** it is said

dirètro m & adv (archaic) behind, back

direttìssima f (rr) high-speed line; **per direttissima** straight up (in mountain climbing)

direttissimo m express train

diretti·vo -va adj managerial || m board of directors || f directive; direction; guideline

dirèt·to -ta adj direct; **diretto a** addressed to; directed at; bound for || m through train

diret·tóre -trice mf manager; principal || m director; **direttore di macchina** (naut, nav) chief engineer; **direttore di tiro** (nav) gunnery officer; **direttore di un giornale** editor; **direttore d'or-**

chestra orchestra leader; **direttore responsabile** publisher; **direttore tecnico** (sports) manager ‖ *f* see **direttrice**

direttò·rio -ria (-ri -rie) *adj* directorial ‖ *m* directory

direttrice *adj fem* directing; guiding; front (*wheels*) ‖ *f* directress; line of action

direzionale *adj* directional; managerial

direzióne *f* direction; management; run (*of events*)

dirigènte *adj* leading; managerial ‖ *m* employer; boss; leader; executive

dirigere §152 *tr* to direct; to turn; to lead ‖ *ref* to address oneself; **dirigersi verso** to head for

dirigìbile *adj & m* dirigible

dirimpètto *adj invar & adv* opposite; **dirimpetto a** opposite to; in comparison with

dirìt·to -ta *adj* straight; right; unswerving; (coll) smart ‖ *m* law; obverse, face (*of coin*); fee, dues; (fin) right; **a buon diritto** rightly so; **di diritto** by law; **diritti d'autore** copyright; **diritti di segreteria** registration fee; **diritti doganali** customs duty; **diritti speciali di prelievo** (econ) special drawing rights; **diritto canonico** canon law; **diritto consuetudinario** common law; **diritto internazionale** international law; **in diritto** according to law ‖ *f* right, right hand ‖ **diritto** *adv* straight; **tirare diritto** to go straight ahead

dirittura *f* direction; uprightness; (sports) straightaway, home stretch

dirizzóne *m* blunder

diroccare §197 (**diròcco**) *tr* to knock down ‖ *intr* (ESSERE) (archaic) to fall down

dirocca·to -ta *adj* dilapidated, rickety

dirompènte *adj* fragmentation (*bomb*)

dirottaménto *m* hijacking; skyjacking (*of an airplane*)

dirottare (**diròtto**) *tr* to detour (*traffic*); to hijack (*e.g., a ship*); to skyjack (*an airplane*) ‖ *intr* to change course

dirottatóre *m* hijacker; skyjacker (*of a plane*)

dirót·to -ta *adj* copious, heavy (*rain, tears*); (lit) craggy; **a dirotto** cats and dogs (*said of rain*)

dirozzare [ddzz] (**diròzzo**) *tr* to roughhew; to refine ‖ *ref* to become polished

diruggìnire §176 *tr* to take the rust off; to limber up; to gnash (*one's teeth*); to clear (*one's mind*)

dirupa·to -ta *adj* rocky, craggy

dirupo *m* rock; crag, cliff

disabbigliare §280 *tr & ref* to undress, disrobe

disabita·to -ta *adj* uninhabited

disabituare (**disàbituo**) *tr* to disaccustom ‖ *ref* to become unaccustomed

disaccenta·to -ta *adj* unaccented

disaccòrdo *m* disagreement

disadat·to -ta *adj* unfit

disadór·no -na *adj* unadorned, bare

disaffezionare (**disaffezióno**) *tr* to alienate the affection of; to estrange ‖ *ref* to become estranged

disaffezióne *f* dislike

disagévole *adj* troublesome, uncomfortable

disagiare §290 *tr* to trouble, inconvenience

disagia·to -ta *adj* uncomfortable; needy

disà·gio *m* (**-gi**) discomfort; need

disalberare (**disàlbero**) *tr* to dismast

disambienta·to -ta *adj* bewildered, strange

disàmina *f* examination, scrutiny

disaminare (**disàmino**) *tr* to scrutinize; to weigh

disamorare (**disamóro**) *tr* to alienate the affection of; to estrange ‖ *ref* to become estranged

disancorare (**disàncoro**) *intr* to weigh anchor; to leave port ‖ *ref* to weigh anchor; (fig) to free oneself

disanimare (**disànimo**) *tr* to dishearten

disappetènza *f* loss of appetite

disapprovare (**disappròvo**) *tr* to disapprove

disapprovazióne *f* disapproval

disappunto *m* disappointment

disarcionare (**disarcióno**) *tr* to unsaddle, unhorse; to kick out

disarmare *tr* to disarm; to dismantle (*a scaffold*); to ship (*oars*); (naut) to unrig ‖ *intr* to disarm; (fig) to give up

disarma·to -ta *adj* unarmed, defenseless

disarmo *m* disarmament; dismantling; unrigging

disarmonìa *f* discord; contrast

disarmòni·co -ca *adj* (**-ci -che**) discordant

disarticolare (**disartìcolo**) *tr* to limber up; to disjoint ‖ *ref* to become dislocated

disassociare §128 (**disassòcio**) *tr* to disassociate

disastra·to -ta *adj* damaged ‖ *mf* victim

disastro *m* disaster, calamity; wreck

disastró·so -sa [s] *adj* disastrous

disattèn·to -ta *adj* inattentive; careless

disattenzióne *f* inattention; carelessness

disattivare *tr* to deactivate (*e.g., a mine*)

disavanzo *m* (com) deficit

disavvedu·to -ta *adj* heedless

disavventura *f* misfortune

disavvertènza *f* inadvertence

disavvezzare (**disavvèzzo**) *tr* to break (*s.o.*) of a habit ‖ *ref*—**disavvezzarsi da** to give up or lose the habit of

disavvéz·zo -za *adj* unaccustomed

disbórso *m* disbursement, outlay

disboscare §197 (**disbòsco**) *tr* to deforest

disbrigare §209 *tr* to dispatch ‖ *ref* to extricate oneself

disbri·go *m* (**-ghi**) prompt execution, dispatch

discacciare §128 *tr* (lit) to chase away

discanto *m* (mus) harmonizing

discàpito *m* damage; **tornare a discapito di** to be detrimental to

discàri·ca *f* (**-che**) discharge (*e.g., of pollutants*); dumping (*of refuse*); unloading (*of a ship*)

discàri·co *m* (**-chi**) exculpation; **a discarico di** in defense of

discatóre *m* hockey player; discus thrower

discendènte *adj* descending; sloping; down (*train*) ‖ *mf* descendant

discendènza *f* descent; pedigree

discéndere §245 *tr* to go down ‖ *intr* (ESSERE & AVERE) to descend, go down; to slope; to fall (*said, e.g., of thermometer*); to get off; **discendere in picchiata** (aer) to nose-dive

discènte *mf* student, pupil

discépo·lo -la *mf* disciple

discèrnere §153 *tr* to discern

discerníbile *adj* discernible

discerniménto *m* discernment

discésa [s] *f* descent; slope; drop

discettare (**discètto**) *tr* (lit) to discuss

dischiodare (**dischiòdo**) *tr* to take the nails out of

dischiùdere §125 *tr* to open; to reveal

discin·to -ta *adj* scantily dressed; untidy; in disarray

disciògliere §127 *tr* to dissolve, melt; (lit) to untie ‖ *ref* to dissolve, melt

disciplína *f* discipline; whip, scourge

disciplinare *adj* disciplinary ‖ *m* regulation ‖ *tr* to discipline

disciplina·to -ta *adj* obedient

di·sco *m* (**-schi**) disk; (phonograph) record; bob (*of pendulum*); (ice hockey) puck; (sports) discus; (rr) signal; (pharm) tablet; **disco combinatore** (telp) dial; **disco microsolco** microgroove record; **disco volante** flying saucer

discòfilo *m* record lover

discòide *m* (pharm) tablet, pill

dìsco·lo -la *adj* undisciplined, wild ‖ *m* rogue, rascal

discolorare (**discolóro**) *tr* to discolor ‖ *ref* to pale

discolorazióne *f* discoloration; paleness

discólpa *f* defense

discolpare (**discólpo**) *tr* to defend

disconnèttere §107 *tr* to disconnect

disconóscere §134 *tr* to ignore, to disregard; to be ungrateful for

discontinuare (**discontìnuo**) *tr* to perform sporadically ‖ *intr* to lose continuity

discontì·nuo -nua *adj* uneven

disconvenire §282 *intr* (ESSERE) (lit) to disagree ‖ *impers* (ESSERE) (lit) to be improper

discoprire §110 (**discòpro**) *tr* to discover

discordante *adj* discordant

discordare (**discòrdo**) *intr* (ESSERE) to disagree, differ

discòrde *adj* discordant; opposing

discòrdia *f* discord, dissension

discórrere §139 *intr* to talk, chat; (coll) to keep company; **discorrere del più e del meno** to make small talk; **e via discorrendo** and so forth

discórso *m* discourse; conversation; speech; **pochi discorsi!** (coll) cut it out!

discostare (**discòsto**) *tr* to remove ‖ *ref* to withdraw; to differ

discò·sto -sta *adj* distant ‖ **discosto** *adv* far

discotè·ca *f* (**-che**) record library; discotheque

discreditare (**discrédito**) *tr* to discredit

discrédito *m* discredit

discrepanza *f* discrepancy

discretaménte *adv* rather; fairly well

discré·to -ta *adj* discreet; fairly large; fair

discrezióne *f* discretion

discriminante *adj* discriminatory; extenuating ‖ *m* (math) discriminant

discriminare (**discrìmino**) *tr* to discriminate; to extenuate

discriminazióne *f* discrimination

discussióne *f* discussion; argument

discus·so -sa *adj* controversial

discùtere §154 *tr* to discuss ‖ *intr* to discuss; to argue

discutìbile *adj* moot, debatable

disdegnare (**disdégno**) *tr* to disdain, scorn ‖ *ref* (obs) to be angry

disdégno *m* disdain, scorn

disdegnó·so -sa [s] *adj* disdainful

disdétta *f* ill luck; (law) notice

disdicévole *adj* unbecoming, unseemly

disdire §151 *tr* to retract; to belie; to cancel; to countermand; to terminate the contract of ‖ *ref* to retract; **disdire a** to be unbecoming to

disdòro *m* shame; **tornare a disdoro di** to bring shame on

disegnare [s] (**diségno**) *tr* to draw; to sketch; to design; (obs) to elect

disegna·tóre -trice [s] *mf* cartoonist; designer ‖ *m* draftsman

diségno [s] *m* drawing; sketch; outline; plan; design; **disegno animato** (mov) cartoon; **disegno di legge** (law) bill

disellare [s] (**disèllo**) *tr* var of **dissellare**

diserbante *adj* weed-killing ‖ *m* weed-killer

diseredare (**diserèdo**) *tr* to disinherit

disereda·to -ta *adj* disinherited ‖ **i diseredati** the underprivileged

disertare (**disèrto**) *tr* to desert; (lit) to lay waste ‖ *intr* to desert

disertóre *m* deserter

diserzióne *f* desertion

disfaciménto *m* disintegration

disfare §173 *tr* to undo; to defeat; to melt; to unknit; to break up (*housekeeping*); **disfare il letto** to remove the bedclothes ‖ *ref* to spoil (*said, e.g., of meat*); **disfarsi di** to get rid of

disfatta *f* defeat

disfattismo *m* defeatism

disfattì·sta *mf* (**-sti -ste**) defeatist

disfat·to -ta *adj* undone; defeated; melted; broken up; ravaged ‖ *f* see **disfatta**

disfida *f* (lit) challenge

disfunzióne *f* malfunction

disgelare (**disgèlo**) *tr* & *intr* to thaw

disgèlo *m* thaw

disgiùngere §183 *tr* & *ref* to separate

disgiuntì·vo -va *adj* disjunctive

disgràzia *f* disfavor; bad luck, misfortune; accident; **per disgrazia** unfortunately

disgrazia·to -ta adj unlucky; wretched
disgregaménto m disintegration
disgregare §209 (**disgrègo**) tr & ref to disintegrate
disgregazióne f disintegration
disguido m miscarriage, missending (of a letter)
disgustare tr to disgust, sicken ‖ ref to become disgusted, sicken; to have a falling-out, to part company
disgusto m disgust, repugnance
disgustó·so -sa [s] adj disgusting
disidratare tr to dehydrate
disilla·bo -ba adj disyllabic ‖ m disyllable
disillúdere §105 tr to delude, deceive ‖ ref to become disillusioned
disillusióne f disillusion
disimboscare §197 (**disimbòsco**) tr to put back in circulation
disimparare tr to unlearn, forget
disimpegnare (**disimpégno**) tr to release; to free, to open; to loosen; to redeem (a pledge); to clear; to perform ‖ ref to succeed
disimpégno m release; redemption; performance; disengagement; **di disimpegno** for every day (e.g., a suit); main (e.g., hallway)
disimpiè·go m (-ghi) unemployment; (mil) withdrawal
disincagliare §280 tr to set afloat; (fig) to disentangle
disincantare tr disenchant
disinfestare (**disinfèsto**) tr to exterminate
disinfestazióne f extermination
disinfettante adj & m disinfectant
disinfettare (**disinfètto**) tr to disinfect
disingannare tr to disillusion ‖ ref to become disillusioned
disinganno m disillusion
disinnescare §197 (**disinnésco**) tr to defuse
disinnestare (**disinnèsto**) tr to disconnect; to throw out, disengage
disinserire §176 tr (elec) to disconnect; (aut) to disengage
disintasare [s] tr to unclog
disintegrare (**disintègro**) tr & ref to disintegrate
disintegrazióne f disintegration
disinteressare (**disinterèsso**) tr to make (s.o.) lose interest ‖ ref to lose interest; to take no interest
disinteressa·to -ta adj selfless, unselfish
disinterèsse m disinterest; unselfishness
disintossicare §197 (**disintòssico**) tr to free of poison; (fig) to clean the air in ‖ ref to shake the drug habit
disinvòl·to -ta adj free and easy; fresh, forward
disinvoltura f naturalness, ease of manners, offhandedness; freshness; impudence
disì·o m (-ì) (poet) desire
disistima f scorn, low regard, disesteem
disistimare tr to scorn, hold in low regard
dislivèllo m difference of level; disparity
dislocaménto m transfer of troops; (naut) displacement

dislocare §197 (**dislòco**) tr to transfer (troops); to post (sentries); (naut) to displace
dislocazióne f (mil) transfer; (geog, naut, psychol) displacement
dismisura f excess; **a dismisura** excessively
disobbedire §176 intr var of **disubbidire**
disobbligare §209 (**disòbbligo**) tr to free from an obligation ‖ ref to repay a favor
disoccupa·to -ta adj unemployed, jobless; idle; unoccupied ‖ m unemployed person; **i disoccupati** the jobless
disoccupazióne f unemployment
disone·stà f (-stà) dishonesty; shamelessness
disonè·sto -sta adj dishonest; shameless; immoral
disonorante adj disgraceful
disonorare (**disonóro**) tr to dishonor, disgrace; to seduce
disonóre m dishonor, shame
disonorévole adj dishonorable; shameful
disoppilare (**disòppilo**) tr to clear of obstructions
disópra adj invar upper ‖ m (**disópra**) upper part, top; **prendere il disopra** to have the upper hand ‖ adv above; **al disopra di** above
disordinare (**disórdino**) tr to cancel, countermand; to confuse; to mess up ‖ intr to indulge ‖ ref to become disorganized
disordina·to -ta adj confused; messy; untidy; intemperate
disórdine m confusion; mess; disarray; disorder; intemperance
disorganizzare [ddzz] tr to disorganize; to disrupt
disorganizzazióne [ddzz] f disorganization, disorder; disruption
disorientaménto m disorientation; confusion, bewilderment
disorientare (**disoriènto**) tr to cause (s.o.) to lose his way; to confuse; to disorient ‖ ref to be bewildered; to lose one's bearings
disorienta·to -ta adj disoriented; confused, bewildered; lost, astray
disormeggiare §290 (**disorméggio**) tr to unmoor
disossare (**disòsso**) tr to bone ‖ ref (lit) to lose weight
disótto [s] adj invar below ‖ m (**disótto**) lower part, bottom ‖ adv below; **al disotto di** below, underneath
disotturare tr to unclog
dispàc·cio m (-ci) dispatch; urgent letter; **dispaccio telegrafico** telegram
dispara·to -ta adj disparate
disparére m disagreement
dìspari adj invar odd, uneven
dispari·tà f (-tà) disparity
dispàrte adv—**in disparte** apart, aside; **starsene in disparte** to keep aloof
dispèn·dio m (-di) expenditure; waste
dispendió·so -sa [s] adj expensive; wasteful

dispènsa *f* cupboard; pantry; distribution; number (*of magazine*); installment (*of book*); dispensation; (naut) storeroom; (coll) store

dispensare (**dispènso**) *tr* to exempt, free; to distribute ‖ *ref*—**dispensarsi da** to get out of

dispensà·rio *m* (**-ri**) dispensary

dispensa·tóre -trice *mf* dispenser

dispensiè·re -ra *mf* dispenser ‖ *m* steward

dispepsìa *f* dyspepsia

dispèpti·co -ca *adj & mf* (**-ci -che**) dyspeptic

disperare (**dispèro**) *intr* to despair; **fare disperare** to drive crazy ‖ *ref* to despair

dispera·to -ta *adj* hopeless ‖ *m* poor wretch; **come un disperato** desperately ‖ *f*—**alla disperata** with all one's might

disperazióne *f* desperation, despair

dispèrdere §212 *tr* to scatter; to waste ‖ *ref* to disperse; (fig) to waste one's energies

dispersióne *f* dispersion; loss; (elec) leakage

dispersività *f* tendency toward disorganization

dispersì·vo -va *adj* dispersive; disorganized

dispèr·so -sa *adj* scattered; lost; dispersed; missing in action

dispersóre *m* (elec) leakage conductor

dispètto *m* spite; (lit) haughtiness; **a dispetto di** in spite of; **far dispetto a** to provoke

dispettó·so -sa [s] *adj* pestiferous; spiteful, resentful

dispiacènte *adj* sorry; distressing

dispiacére *m* sorrow, displeasure ‖ §214 *intr* (ESSERE) to be displeasing; to be sorry, e.g., **mi dispiace** I am sorry; (with *dat*) to displease; (with *dat*) to dislike, e.g., **le mie parole gli dispiacciono** he dislikes my words; **Le dispiace?** would you please?; **se non Le dispiace** if you don't mind

dispiegare §209 (**dispiègo**) *tr* to manifest; (lit) to unfurl ‖ *ref* to spread out; to flow out

displù·vio *m* (**-vi**) divide, watershed; ridge (*of roof*)

disponìbile *adj* available; open-minded

disponibili·tà *f* (**-tà**) availability; inactive status; **disponibilità** *fpl* available funds

dispórre §218 *tr* to dispose; to prepare ‖ *intr* to provide; to dispose; **disporre di** to have (*available*) ‖ *ref* to get ready

dispositivo *m* gadget; device; (mil) deployment

disposizióne *f* arrangement; inclination; disposition; disposal; instruction; (law) provision

dispó·sto -sta *adj* arranged; disposed; provided; willing; **ben disposto** disposed ‖ *m* (law) proviso

dispòti·co -ca *adj* (**-ci -che**) despotic

dispotismo *m* despotism

dispregiati·vo -va *adj* disparaging; (gram) pejorative

disprè·gio *m* (**-gi**) contempt; disrepute

disprezzàbile *adj* contemptible; negligible

disprezzare (**disprèzzo**) *tr* to despise

disprèzzo *m* contempt, scorn

dìsputa *f* dispute; debate

disputàbile *adj* debatable

disputare (**dìsputo**) *tr* to contest; to discuss; to vie for (*victory*) ‖ *intr* to dispute, debate; to vie ‖ *ref* to vie for

disqualificare §197 (**disqualìfico**) *tr* to disqualify

disquisizióne *f* disquisition

dissacrare *tr* to desecrate

dissacrazióne *f* desecration

dissaldare *tr* to unsolder

dissanguare (**dissànguo**) *tr* to bleed ‖ *ref* to bleed; to ruin oneself

dissangua·to -ta *adj* bled white; **morire dissanguato** to bleed to death

dissapóre *m* disagreement

disseccare §197 (**dissécco**) *tr* to dry ‖ *ref* to dry; to dry up

disselciare §128 (**dissélcio**) *tr* to remove the cobblestones from

dissellare (**dissèllo**) *tr* to unsaddle

disseminare (**dissémino**) *tr* to disseminate; to scatter

dissenna·to -ta *adj* foolish, unwise; crazy, mad

dissensióne *f* dissension

dissènso *m* dissent; disagreement

dissenterìa *f* dysentery

dissentire (**dissènto**) *intr* to dissent

dissenziènte *adj* dissenting ‖ *mf* dissenter

disseppellire §176 *tr* to exhume

dissertare (**dissèrto**) *intr* to discourse

dissertazióne *f* dissertation

disservì·zio *m* (**-zi**) poor service

dissestare (**dissèsto**) *tr* to unsettle; to disarrange

dissesta·to -ta *adj* financially embarrassed; mentally deranged

dissèsto *m* financial embarrassment; mental derangement

dissetante *adj* thirst-quenching

dissetare (**dissèto**) *tr* to quench the thirst of ‖ *ref* to quench one's thirst

dissezióne *f* dissection

dissidènte *adj & m* dissident

dissidènza *f* dissent

dissì·dio *m* (**-di**) dissent; disagreement

dissigillare *tr* to unseal ‖ *ref* (lit) to melt

dissìmile *adj* unlike

dissimulare (**dissìmulo**) *tr* to dissimulate, disguise ‖ *intr* to dissimulate

dissimulazióne *f* dissimulation

dissipare (**dìssipo**) *tr* to dissipate; to squander; to clear up (*a doubt*) ‖ *ref* to dissipate

dissipa·to -ta *adj & mf* profligate

dissipa·tóre -trice *mf* squanderer

dissipazióne *f* dissipation

dissociare §128 (**dissòcio**) *tr* to dissociate, disassociate ‖ *ref* to dissociate or disassociate oneself

dissociazióne *f* dissociation

dissodare (dissòdo) *tr* to cultivate
dissolutézza *f* profligacy
dissolu·to *-ta adj & mf* profligate
dissoluzióne *f* dissolution
dissolvènza *f* (mov) fade-out; **dissolvenza incrociata** (mov) lap dissolve
dissólvere §155 *tr* to dissolve; to clear up (*a doubt*); (obs) to untie ‖ *ref* to dissolve
dissomiglianza *f* dissimilarity
dissonanza *f* dissonance
dissotterrare (dissottèrro) *tr* to exhume; to unearth
dissuadére §213 *tr* to dissuade
dissuè·to *-ta adj* (lit) unaccustomed
dissuggellare (dissuggèllo) *tr* to unseal
distaccaménto *m* (mil) detachment
distaccare §197 *tr* to detach; to remove; to transfer; to outdistance ‖ *ref* to stand out; to withdraw, become separated
distacca·to *-ta adj* detached; branch (*office*)
distac·co *m* (**-chi**) detachment; separation; (sports) spread (*in points*)
distante *adj* distant; aloof; different ‖ *adv* far away
distanza *f* distance; **mantenere le distanze** to keep one's distance; **tenere a distanza** to keep at arm's length
distanziare §287 *tr* to outdistance
distare *intr* to be distant
distèndere §270 *tr* to stretch; to spread; to unfurl; to relax; to knock down; to write ‖ *ref* to stretch; to spread out; to relax
distensióne *f* relaxation; relaxation of tension
disté·so *-sa* [s] *adj* stretched out; full (*voice*); lank (*hair*) ‖ *m*—**per disteso** in full ‖ *f* expanse; row; **a distesa** with full voice; at full peal
distillare *tr* to distill; to exude; to pour; to trickle ‖ *intr* (ESSERE) to trickle ‖ *ref*—**distillarsi il cervello** to rack one's brain
distilla·to *-ta adj* distilled ‖ *m* distillate
distilla·tóre *-trice mf* distiller ‖ *m* still
distilleria *f* distillery
distinguibile *adj* distinguishable
distinguere §156 *tr* to distinguish; to make out; to tell (*one thing from another*); to divide
distinta *f* note, list; **distinta di versamento** deposit slip
distintaménte *adj* distinctly; sincerely yours
distinti·vo *-va adj* distinctive ‖ *m* emblem, insignia, badge
distin·to *-ta adj* distinct; distinguished; sincere (*greetings*); reserved (*seat*); **Distinto Signor . . .** (*on an envelope*) Mr. . . . ‖ *f see* **distinta**
distinzióne *f* distinction
distògliere §127 *tr* to dissuade; to deter; to distract; to turn (*one's eyes*) away
distòrcere §272 *tr* to distort; to twist ‖ *ref* to become distorted; to sprain (*e.g., one's ankle*)
distorsióne *f* distortion; sprain; **distorsione acustica** wow
distrarre §273 *tr* to distract; to divert;

to amuse; to pull (*a muscle*) ‖ *ref* to become distracted; to relax
distrat·to *-ta adj* absent-minded
distrazióne *f* absent-mindedness; distraction; diversion (*of money*); pull (*of muscle*)
distrét·to *-ta adj* (obs) close; (obs) hard-pressed ‖ *m* district; precinct (*e.g., of police*); circuit (*of court*); ward (*in city*); **distretto militare** draft board; **distretto postale** postal zone ‖ *f* stricture; necessity
distrettuale *adj* district
distribuire §176 *tr* to distribute; to pass out; to allot; to deploy (*troops*); (theat) to cast (*roles*); (mov) to release; (mil) to issue (*e.g., clothing*)
distribu·tóre *-trice adj* distributing, dispensing ‖ *mf* distributor, dispenser ‖ *m* distributor; **distributore automatico** vending machine; **distributore di benzina** gasoline pump
distribuzióne *f* distribution; issue; delivery; (aut) timing gears; (mov) release; (fig) dispensation
districare §197 *tr* to unravel ‖ *ref* to extricate oneself
distrofia *f* dystrophy
distrúggere §266 *tr* to destroy; to ruin
distrutti·vo *-va adj* destructive
distruzióne *f* destruction
disturbare *tr* to disturb, bother; **disturbo?** may I come in? ‖ *ref* to bother; to go out of one's way
disturba·tóre *-trice mf* disturber; **disturbatore della quiete pubblica** disturber of the peace
disturbo *m* trouble, bother; disturbance; (rad) interference; **disturbi atmosferici** static, atmospherics; **togliere il disturbo a** to take leave of
disubbidiènte *adj* disobedient
disubbidiènza *f* disobedience
disubbidire §176 *intr* to disobey; (with *dat*) to disobey
disuguaglianza *f* inequality; disparity
disuguale *adj* uneven; unequal
disuma·no *-na adj* inhumane; unbearable
disunióne *f* disunion
disunire §176 *tr* to disunite
disusa·to *-ta adj* obsolete, out of use
disuso *m* disuse; **in disuso** obsolete
disùtile *adj* useless; burdensome ‖ *m* worthless fellow; (com) loss
disvìo *m* (**-i**) miscarriage, missending (*of a letter*)
ditale *m* thimble; fingerstall
ditata *f* poke with a finger; finger mark; dab (*with a finger*)
dito *m* (**dita** *fpl*) finger; toe; **avere le dita d'oro** to have a magic touch; **dita della mano** fingers; **dita del piede** toes; **legarsela al dito** to never forget ‖ *m* (**diti**) finger, e.g., **dito indice** index finger; **dito anulare** ring finger; **dito medio** middle finger; **dito mignolo** little finger; **dito pollice** thumb
ditta *f* firm, house; office
dittàfono *m* intercom; dictaphone
dittatóre *m* dictator

dittatura *f* dictatorship

dittongare §209 (dittòngo) *tr* to diphthongize

dittòn·go *m* (-ghi) diphthong

diurèti·co -ca *adj* & *m* (-ci -che) diuretic

diur·no -na *adj* daily; daytime || *f* (theat) matinée

diutur·no -na *adj* long-lasting

diva *f* diva; (mov) star; (lit) goddess

divagare §209 *tr* to amuse; to distract || *intr* to digress || *ref* to relax

divagazióne *f* distraction; digression; relaxation

divampare *intr* (ESSERE & AVERE) to blaze, flare

diváno *m* divan; couch, sofa

divaricare §197 (divàrico) *tr* to spread (one's legs); to open up (an incision)

divà·rio *m* (-ri) difference

divèllere §267 *tr* to eradicate, uproot

diveni·re *m* (-re) (philos) becoming || §282 *intr* (ESSERE) (lit) to become; (archaic) to come

diventare (divènto) *intr* (ESSERE) to become; **diventare di tutti i colori** to blush; to be embarrassed; **diventare grande** to grow up; **diventare matto** to go mad; **diventare pallido** to turn pale; **diventare piccolo** to grow smaller; **diventare rosso** to blush

divèr·bio *m* (-bi) argument; **venire a diverbio** to have an altercation

divergènza *f* divergency

divèrgere §157 *intr* to diverge

diversificare §197 (diversìfico) *tr* to diversify || *ref* to be diversified; to differ

diversióne *f* diversion

diversi·tà *f* (-tà) diversity

diversi·vo -va *adj* diverting || *m* diversion

diver·so -sa *adj* different; **diver·si -se** several, e.g., **diverse ragazze** several girls || **diver·si -se** *pron* several

divertènte *adj* diverting, amusing

divertiménto *m* amusement, pastime; fun; (mus) divertimento

divertire (divèrto) *tr* to amuse, entertain; (lit) to turn aside || *ref* to have fun, enjoy oneself; (lit) to go away

diverti·to -ta *adj* amused; amusing

divètta *f* starlet

divezzare (divèzzo) *tr* to wean || *ref*— **divezzarsi da** to get out of the habit of

dividèndo *m* dividend

dividere §158 *tr* to divide; to partition; to split; to share in (e.g., s.o.'s grief) || *ref* to be divided; to become separated; **dividersi fra** to divide one's time between

divièto *m* prohibition; **divieto di affissione** post no bills; **divieto di parcheggio** no parking; **divieto di sosta** no stopping; **divieto di svolta** no turns; **divieto di transito** no thoroughfare

divinare *tr* (lit) to divine

divina·tóre -trice *adj* divining || *m* diviner

divinazióne *f* divination

divincolare (divìncolo) *tr* & *ref* to wriggle

divini·tà *f* (-tà) divinity

divinizzare [ddzz] *tr* to deify

divi·no -na *adj* divine

divisa *f* uniform; motto; part (in hair); **divise** foreign exchange

divisare *tr* (lit) to intend

divisibile *adj* divisible

divisióne *f* division; partition; (sports) league

divisionismo *m* (painting) divisionism; (pol) separatism

divismo *m* (mov) star system; (mov) adulation of stars

divisóre *m* (math) divisor

divisò·rio -ria (-ri -rie) *adj* dividing || *m* partition; (math) divisor

di·vo -va *adj* (lit) divine || *m* (theat, mov) star; (lit) god || *f* see **diva**

divolgare §209 *tr* & *ref* var of **divulgare**

divorare (divóro) *tr* to devour; to gulp down; to consume; **divorare la via** to burn up the road

divora·tóre -trice *adj* consuming || *mf* consumer (e.g., of food, books)

divorziare §287 (divòrzio) *intr* to become divorced; **divorziare da** to divorce

divorzia·to -ta *adj* divorced || *m* divorcé || *f* divorcée

divòr·zio *m* (-zi) divorce

divulgare §209 *tr* to divulge; to publicize; to popularize || *ref* to spread; to become popular

divulga·tóre -trice *adj* popularizing || *mf* popularizer; **divulgatore di calunnie** scandalmonger; **divulgatore di notizie** telltale

divulgazióne *f* publicizing; popularization

divulsióne *f* (surg) dilation

dizionà·rio *m* (-ri) dictionary; **dizionario geografico** gazetteer

dizióne *f* diction; reading (of poetry)

do [do] *m* (do) (mus) do; (mus) C

dóc·cia *f* (-ce) shower; gutter (on roof); spout; (fig) dash of cold water; **fare la doccia** to take a shower

docciare §128 (dóccio) *tr*, *intr* (ESSERE) & *ref* to shower

doccióne *m* trough, gutter; gargoyle

docènte *adj* teaching || *m* teacher; **libero docente** certified university teacher

docènza *f* teaching post; **libera docenza** lectureship

dòcile *adj* docile; tame; amenable (person); workable (material)

documentare (documénto) *tr* to document || *ref* to gather information

documentà·rio -ria *adj* & *m* (-ri -rie) documentary

documénto *m* document; paper; **documenti di bordo** ship's papers

dodecafonìa *f* twelve-tone system

dodecasìlla·bo -ba *adj* twelve-syllable, dodecasyllable

dodicèsi·mo -ma *adj*, *m* & *pron* twelfth

dódici *adj* & *pron* twelve; **le dódici**

twelve o'clock || *m* twelve; twelfth (*in dates*)

dó·ga *f* (-ghe) stave

dogale *adj* (hist) of the doge

dogana *f* duty; customs; custom house

doganière *m* customs officer

dòge *m* (hist) doge

dò·glia *f* (-glie) (lit) pain, pang; **doglie** labor pains

dò·glio *m* (-gli) barrel; (lit) large jar

doglió·so -sa [s] *adj* (lit) sorrowful

dòg·ma *m* (-mi) dogma

dogmàti·co -ca (-ci -che) *adj* dogmatic || *mf* dogmatist

dogmatismo *m* dogmatism

dólce *adj* sweet; soft; gentle; fresh (*water*); mild (*climate*); delicate (*feet*); **dolce far niente** sweet idleness || *m* sweet; sweet dish; **dolci** candy

dolceama·ro -ra *adj* bittersweet

dolcézza *f* sweetness; mildness; gentleness

dolcia·stro -stra *adj* sweetish

dolcière *m* candy maker; pastry baker

dolcificare §197 (**dolcifico**) *tr* to sweeten

dolciume *m* sweet; **dolciumi** candy

dolènte *adj* aching; sorrowful; sorry

dolére §159 *intr* (ESSERE & AVERE) to ache, e.g., **gli dolgono i denti** his teeth ache || *ref* to grieve || *impers* (ESSERE) to be sorry, e.g., **mi duole che Lei non possa venire** I am sorry that you won't be able to come

dolicònice *m* bobolink

dòllaro *m* dollar

dòlo *m* fraud, malice, guile

dolomite *f* dolomite || **Dolomiti** *fpl* Dolomites

dolorante *adj* aching

dolorare (**doloro**) *intr* (lit) to ache

dolóre *m* ache; sorrow; contrition

doloró·so -sa [s] *adj* painful; sorrowful

doló·so -sa [s] *adj* intentional, fraudulent; (law) felonious

domàbile *adj* tamable

domanda *f* question; application; appeal; (econ) demand; **domanda suggestiva** (com) leading question; **fare una domanda** to ask a question

domandare *tr* to ask; to ask for; **domandare la parola** to ask for the floor || *intr* to inquire || *ref* to wonder; (lit) to be called

doma·ni *m* (-ni) tomorrow || *adv* tomorrow; **a domani** until tomorrow; **domani a otto** a week from tomorrow; **domani l'altro** the day after tomorrow

domare (**domo**) *tr* to tame; to extinguish; to quell

doma·tóre -trice *mf* tamer

domattina *adv* tomorrow morning

doméni·ca *f* (-che) Sunday

domenicale *adj* Sunday (*e.g., rest*)

domenica·no -na *adj* & *m* Dominican (*e.g., order*)

domesticare §197 (**domèstico**) *tr* to domesticate

domèsti·co -ca (-ci -che) *adj* family; household; familiar; domestic || *mf* domestic, servant || *f* maid; **alla**

domestica family style; **domestica a mezzo servizio** part-time domestic

domiciliare *adj* house || §287 *tr* (com) to draw || *ref* to dwell; to settle

domicília·to -ta *adj* residing

domici·lio *m* (-li) domicile, residence; principal office; **domicilio coatto** imprisonment; **franco domicilio** free delivery

dominare (**dòmino**) *tr* to dominate, rule; to master; to overlook || *intr* to prevail; to reign || *ref* to control oneself

domina·tóre -trice *mf* ruler

dominazióne *f* domination; rule

domineddìo *m invar* (coll) the Lord God

dominica·no -na *adj* & *mf* Dominican (*e.g., Republic*)

domi·nio *m* (-ni) dominion; domain

dòmi·no *m* (-no) domino (*cloak*); dominoes (*game*)

dòn *m* (used only before singular Christian name) don (*Spanish title*); Don (*priest*); uncle (*familiar title of elderly man*)

donare (**dóno**) *tr* to donate; to give as a present || *intr*—**donare a** to be becoming to

dona·tóre -trice *mf* donor; **donatore di sangue** blood donor

donazióne *f* gift, donation

donchisciottè·sco -sca *adj* (-schi -sche) quixotic

dónde *adv* wherefrom, whence

dondolare (**dóndolo**) *tr* to swing, rock || *ref* to swing, rock; to loaf around

dondolì·o *m* (-i) swinging, rocking

dóndolo *m*—**a dondolo** rocking (*chair, horse*); **andare a dondolo** to loaf around

dondoló·ne -na *mf* idler, loafer

dongiovan·ni *m* (-ni) Don Juan

dònna *f* woman; ladyship; (lit) lady; (coll) Mrs.; (coll) maid; (cards) 'queen; **da donna** woman's, e.g., **scarpe da donna** woman's shoes; **donna cannone** fat lady (*of circus*); **donna di casa** housewife; **Nostra Donna** Our Lady

donnaiòlo *m* ladies' man, philanderer

donnè·sco -sca *adj* (-schi -sche) womanly, feminine

dònnola *f* weasel

dóno *m* gift; **in dono** as a gift

donzèlla [dz] *f* (lit) damsel

donzèllo [dz] *m* (coll) doorman; (lit) page

dópo *adv* afterwards, later; **dopo che** after; **dopo di** after || *prep* after; **dopo** + *pp* after having + *pp*

dopobar·ba *adj invar* after-shaving || *m* (-ba) after-shaving lotion

dopodomani *m* & *adv* the day after tomorrow

dopoguèr·ra *m* (-ra) postwar era

dopolavóro *m* government office designed to organize workers' leisure time

dopopranzo *m* afternoon || *adv* in the afternoon

doppiàg·gio *m* (-gi) (mov) dubbing

doppiare §287 (**dóppio**) *tr* to double; (mov) to dub

doppière *m* candelabrum

doppiétta *f* double-barreled shotgun; (aut) double shift

doppiézza *f* duplicity

dóp·pio -pia (-pi -pie) *adj* double; coupled; double-dealing ‖ *adv* twice, twofold ‖ *m* double; twice as much; (tennis) doubles; (theat) understudy

doppióne *m* duplicate; (philol) doublet

doppiopèt·to *adj invar* double-breasted ‖ *m* (**-to**) double-breasted suit

dorare (**dòro**) *tr* to gild; (culin) to brown; **dorare la pillola** to sugar-coat the pill

dora·to -ta *adj* gilt, golden

doratura *f* gilding

dormicchiare §287 *intr* to doze

dormiènte *adj* sleeping ‖ *mf* sleeper

dormiglió·ne -na *mf* sleepyhead

dormire (**dòrmo**) *tr & intr* to sleep; **dormire a occhi aperti** to be overcome with sleep; **dormire della grossa** to sleep profoundly; **dormire tra due guanciali** to be safe and secure

dormita *f* long sleep; **fare una bella dormita** to have a long sleep

dormitò·rio *m* (**-ri**) dormitory

dormivé·glia *m* (**-glia**) drowsiness

dorsale *adj* dorsal; back (*bone*) ‖ *m* head (*of bed*); back (*of chair*) ‖ *f* (geog) ridge

dòrso *m* back; (sports) backstroke

dosàg·gio *m* (**-gi**) dosage

dosare (**dòso**) *tr* to dose

dosatura *f* dosage

dòse *f* dose

dòsso *m* back; (lit) summit; **levarsi di dosso** to take off; **mettersi in dosso** to put on

dotare (**dòto**) *tr* to provide with a dowry; to endow; to bless

dotazióne *f* dowry; endowment; supply

dòte *f* dowry; gift; endowment

dòt·to -ta *adj* learned, erudite ‖ *m* scholar; (anat) duct

dottorale *adj* doctoral

dottó·re -réssa *mf* doctor

dottrina *f* doctrine; Christian doctrine

dóve *m* where; **per ogni dove** everywhere ‖ *adv* where; **da dove** or **di dove** from where; which way; **fin dove** up to what point; **per dove** which way ‖ *conj* where; whereas

dovére *m* duty, obligation; homework; **a dovere** properly; **doveri** regards; **farsi un dovere di** to feel duty-bound to; **mettere qlcu a dovere** to put s.o. in his place; **più del dovere** more than one should; **sentirsi in dovere di** to feel duty-bound to ‖ §160 *tr & intr* to owe ‖ *aux* (ESSERE & AVERE) must, e.g., **deve farlo** you must do it; to have to, e.g., **dovei partire** I had to leave; ought to, e.g., **dovrebbe lucidare la macchina** he ought to polish the car; should, e.g., **dovresti immaginarti** you should imagine; to be to, e.g., **il treno doveva arrivare alle sei** the train was to arrive at six; to be supposed to, e.g., **deve aver fatto un lungo viaggio** he is supposed to have taken a long journey

doveró·so -sa [s] *adj* proper, right

dovizia *f* (lit) abundance, wealth

dovunque *adv* wherever, anywhere; everywhere

dovu·to -ta *adj & m* due

dozzina [dzz] *f* dozen; room and board; **da** or **di dozzina** common, ordinary; **tenere a dozzina** to board

dozzinale [dzz] *adj* common, ordinary

dozzinante [dzz] *mf* boarder

dra·ga *f* (**-ghe**) dredge

dragàg·gio *m* (**-gi**) dredging

dragami·ne *m* (**-ne**) minesweeper

dragare §209 *tr* to dredge

dràglia *f* (naut) stay

dra·go *m* (**-ghi**) dragon; **drago volante** kite

dragóna *f* sword strap

dragoncèllo *m* (bot) tarragon

dragóne *m* dragon; dragoon

dram·ma *m* (**-mi**) drama, play; **dramma musicale** (hist) melodrama ‖ *f* drachma; dram

drammàti·co -ca (-ci -che) *adj* dramatic ‖ *f* drama, dramatic art

drammatizzare [dzz] *tr* to dramatize

drammatur·go *m* (**-ghi**) playwright, dramatist

drappég·gio *m* (**-gi**) drape; pleats

drappeggiare §290 (**drappéggio**) *tr* to drape ‖ *ref* to be draped

drappèlla *f* pennon (*on bugler's trumpet*)

drappèllo *m* squad, platoon

drapperia *f* dry goods; dry-goods store

drappo *m* cloth, silk cloth; (billiards) green cloth, baize

dràsti·co -ca *adj* (**-ci -che**) drastic

drenàg·gio *m* (**-gi**) drainage

drenare (**drèno**) *tr* to drain

dressàg·gio *m* (**-gi**) *m* training (*of animals*)

dribblare *tr & intr* (sports) to dribble

drit·to -ta *adj* straight; (lit) correct; **dritto come un fuso** straight as a ramrod ‖ *m* (fig) old fox ‖ *f* right; (naut) starboard

drizza *f* (naut) halyard

drizzare *tr* to straighten; to address; to erect; to cock (*the head*); to direct (*a blow*); **drizzare le gambe ai cani** to do the impossible; **drizzare le orecchie** to prick up one's ears ‖ *intr* (naut) to hoist the halyard ‖ *ref* to stand erect

drò·ga *f* (**-ghe**) drug; spice; seasoning

drogare §209 (**drògo**) *tr* to drug; to spice, season

drogheria *f* grocery (store)

droghière *m* grocer

dromedà·rio *m* (**-ri**) dromedary

dru·do -da *adj* (archaic) faithful; (lit) strong ‖ *m* (obs) vassal; (lit) lover

drùi·da *m* (**-di**) druid

drupa *f* (bot) drupe, stone fruit

duale *adj & m* dual

dualismo *m* dualism

duali·tà *f* duality

dùb·bio -bia (-bi -bie) *adj* doubtful ‖ *m* doubt; misgiving; **mettere in dub-**

bio to question; to risk; **senza dubbio** no doubt

dubbió·so -sa [s] *adj* dubious; doubtful; (*lit*) dangerous

dubitare (**dùbito**) *intr* to doubt; to suspect; **dubitare di** to mistrust; to doubt; **non dubitare!** don't worry!

du·ca *m* (**-chi**) duke; (*lit*) leader

ducato *m* duchy; ducat

duce *m* leader; duce

duchéssa *f* duchess

duchessina *f* young duchess

duchino *m* young duke

due *adj & pron* two; **le due** two o'clock ‖ *m* two; second (*in dates*) ‖ *f*—**fra le due** between two alternatives

ducenté·sco -sca *adj* (**-schi -sche**) thirteenth-century

duecentèsi·mo -ma *adj, m & pron* two hundredth

duecènto *adj, m & pron* two hundred ‖ **il Duecento** the thirteenth century

duellante *adj* dueling ‖ *m* duelist

duellare (**duèllo**) *intr* to duel

duèllo *m* duel; contest; debate; **sfidare a duello** to challenge to a duel

duemila *adj, m & pron* two thousand ‖ **Duemila** *m* twenty-first century

duepèz·zi *m* (**-zi**) two-piece bathing suit

duétto *m* (mus) duet

dulcamara *f* (bot) bittersweet

dulcina *f* artificial sweetening

duna *f* dune

dunque *m*—**venire al dunque** to come

to the point ‖ *adv* then ‖ *conj* therefore, hence ‖ *interj* well!

duodèno *m* (anat) duodenum

duòlo *m* (lit) grief

duòmo *m* cathedral; dome (*e.g., of a boiler*)

du·plex *m* (**-plex**) (telp) party line

duplicare §197 (**dùplico**) *tr* to duplicate

duplica·to -ta *adj & m* duplicate

duplicatóre *m* duplicator

dùplice *adj* twofold, double ‖ *f* (racing) daily double

duplici·tà *f* (**-tà**) duplicity

duràbile *adj* durable, lasting

duràci·no -na *adj* clingstone ‖ *f* clingstone peach

duralumìnio *m* duralumin

durare *tr* to endure, bear ‖ *intr* to last; **durare a** + *inf* to keep on + *ger*; **durare in carica** to remain in office

durata *f* duration; lasting quality; **di lunga durata** long-lasting

durante *prep* during; throughout

duratu·ro -ra *adj* enduring, lasting

durévole *adj* lasting, durable

durézza *f* hardness; toughness; rigidity

du·ro -ra *adj* hard; hard-boiled (*egg*); durum (*wheat*); tough (*skin*); harsh; (phonet) voiceless ‖ *m* hard part; hard floor; hard soil; **il duro sta che . . . .** the trouble is that . . . ; **tener duro** to hold out

duróne *m* callousness, callosity

dùttile *adj* ductile; tractable

E

E, e [e] *m & f* fifth letter of the Italian alphabet

e *conj* and

ebani·sta *m* (**-sti**) cabinetmaker

ebanisterìa *f* cabinetmaking; cabinetmaker's shop

ebanite *f* ebonite, vulcanite

èbano *m* ebony

ebbène *interj* well!

ebbrézza *f* intoxication, drunkenness

èb·bro -bra *adj* intoxicated ‖ *mf* drunk

ebdomadà·rio -ria *adj & m* (**-ri -rie**) weekly

èbete *adj* stupid, dull, dumb

ebollizióne *f* boil, boiling

ebrài·co -ca (**-ci -che**) *adj* Hebrew, Hebraic ‖ *m* Hebrew (*language*)

ebrè·o -a *adj & mf* Hebrew ‖ *m* Hebrew (*language*); Jew; **ebreo errante** Wandering Jew

è·bro -bra *adj & mf* var of ebbro

ebùrne·o -a *adj* (lit) ivory

ecatòmbe *f* hecatomb, slaughter

eccedènte *adj* exceeding ‖ *m* excess

eccedènza *f* excess, surplus

eccèdere §123 *tr* to exceed ‖ *intr* to go too far

eccellènte *adj* excellent

eccellènza *f* excellence ‖ **Eccellenza** *f* Excellency

eccèllere §162 *intr* (ESSERE) to excel

eccèl·so -sa *adj* unexcelled; very high ‖ **—l'Eccelso** *m* the Most High

eccentrici·tà *f* (**-tà**) eccentricity

eccèntri·co -ca (**-ci -che**) *adj* eccentric; suburban ‖ *mf* vaudeville performer ‖ *m* (mach) eccentric

eccepìbile *adj* objectionable

eccepire §176 *tr* (law) to take exception to ‖ *intr* (law) to object

eccessi·vo -va *adj* excessive; overweening (*opinion*)

eccèsso *m* excess; **all'eccesso** excessively; **andare agli eccessi** to go to extremes; **dare in eccessi** to fly into a rage; **eccesso di peso** excess weight

eccètera *adv* and so forth, et cetera

eccètto *prep* except, but; **eccetto che** except that; unless

eccettuare (**eccèttuo**) *tr* to except

eccettua·to -ta *adj* excepted ‖ **eccettuato** *prep* except

eccezionale *adj* exceptional

eccezióne *f* exception; objection; **ad eccezione di** with the exception of; **d'eccezione** extraordinary; **sollevare un'eccezione** (law) to take exception

ecchimò·si *f* (**-si**) bruise

eccì·dio *m* (**-di**) massacre

eccitàbile *adj* excitable

eccitaménto *m* instigation; excitement

eccitante *adj* stimulating ‖ *m* stimulant

eccitare (èccito) *tr* to excite ‖ *ref* to become excited or aroused; (sports) to warm up

eccitazióne *f* excitement; (elec) excitation

ecclesiàsti·co -ca (-ci -che) *adj* ecclesiastical ‖ *m* clergyman

ècco *tr invar* here is (are), there is (are); ecco che here, e.g., ecco che viene here he comes; eccoci here we are; ecco fatto that's it; eccola here she is; here it is; eccomi here I am; eccone here are some ‖ *intr invar* here I am; here it is; quand'ecco suddenly ‖ *interj* look!

eccóme *interj* and how!, indeed!

echeggiare §290 (echéggio) *intr* (ESSERE & AVERE) to echo

eclètti·co -ca *adj & mf* (-ci -che) eclectic

eclissare *tr* to eclipse ‖ *ref* to be eclipsed; (coll) to vanish, sneak away

eclìs·si *f* (-si) eclipse

eclìtti·ca *f* (-he) ecliptic

èclo·ga *f* (-ghe) var of egloga

è·co *m & f* (-chi *mpl*) echo; far eco a to echo

ecogonìòmetro *m* sonar

ecologìa *f* ecology

economato *m* comptroller's or administrator's office

economìa *f* administration; management; economy; economics; economìa aziendale business management; economìa di mercato free enterprise; economìa doméstica home economics; economìa polìtica political economy; economics; economìe savings; fare economìa to save

econòmi·co -ca *adj* (-ci -che) economic(al); cheap

economi·sta *mf* (-sti -ste) economist

economizzare [ddzz] *tr & intr* to economize, save

ecòno·mo -ma *adj* thrifty ‖ *m* comptroller; administrator

ecosistè·ma [s] *m* (-mi) ecosystem

ecumèni·co -ca *adj* (-ci -che) ecumenical

eczè·ma [dz] *m* (-mi) eczema

édera *f* ivy

edìcola *f* shrine; newsstand

edificante *adj* edifying

edificare §197 (edìfico) *tr* to build; to edify ‖ *intr* to build

edifica·tóre -trice *adj* building ‖ *mf* builder

edificazióne *f* building; edification

edifì·cio *m* (-ci) building, edifice; pack (*e.g., of lies*); structure

edìle *adj* building, construction ‖ *m* builder, construction worker

edilì·zio -zia (-zi -zie) *adj* building, construction ‖ *f* building trade

edìpi·co -ca *adj* (-ci -che) Oedipus (*e.g., complex*)

Edipo *m* Oedipus

èdi·to -ta *adj* published

edi·tóre -trice *adj* publishing ‖ *mf* publisher; editor (*e.g., of a text*)

editorìa *f* publishing; publishers

editoriale *adj* editorial; publishing ‖ *m* editorial

editoriali·sta *mf* (-sti -ste) editorial writer

editto *m* edict

edizióne *f* edition; performance; (fig) vintage

edonismo *m* hedonism

edoni·sta *mf* (-sti -ste) hedonist

edòt·to -ta *adj* (lit) informed, acquainted; rendere qlcu edotto su qlco (lit) to inform s.o. of s.th

edredóne *m* eider, eider duck

educanda *f* boarding-school girl; convent-school girl

educandato *m* (convent) boarding school for girls

educare §197 (èduco) *tr* to educate; to rear, bring up; to train; to accustom, inure; (lit) to grow

educati·vo -va *adj* educational

educa·to -ta *adj* educated; polite, well-bred

educa·tóre -trice *mf* educator

educazióne *f* education; breeding, manners; educazione cìvica civics

edule *adj* edible

efèbo *m* (coll) sissy

efèlide *f* freckle

effeminatézza *f* effeminacy

effemina·to -ta *adj* effeminate; frivolous

efferatézza *f* savagery

effervescènte *adj* effervescent

effervescènza *f* effervescence

effettivamènte *adv* really

effetti·vo -va *adj* real, true; effective; full (*e.g., member*); regular (*e.g., army officer*) ‖ *m* effective; total amount; (mil) manpower

effètto *m* effect, result; (com) promissory note; (billiards) English; (sports) spin; a questo effetto for this purpose; effetti effects, belongings; effetto di luce play of light; effetto òttico optical illusion; fare effetto to make a sensation; fare l'effetto di to give the impression of; in effetto in fact; mandare a effetto to carry out; porre in effetto to put into effect

effettuàbile *adj* feasible

effettuare (effèttuo) *tr* to bring about; to contrive; to actuate; effettuare (una corsa, un servizio) to run, e.g., l'autobus effettua una corsa ogni mezz'ora the bus runs every half hour

efficace *adj* effective; forceful (*writer*)

effìca·cia *f* (-cie) effectiveness, efficacy; (law) validity

efficiènte *adj* efficient

efficiènza *f* efficiency; in piena efficienza in full working order; in top condition

effigiare §290 *tr* to portray, represent

effì·gie *f* (-gie or -gi) effigy; image

effìme·ro -ra *adj* ephemeral

efflusso *m* flow, outflow

efflù·vio *m* (-vi) effluvium; emanation (*e.g., of light*)

effrazióne *f* (law) burglary

effusióne *f* effusion; outflow; shedding (*of blood*); effusiveness

egemonìa *f* hegemony

egè·o -a *adj* Aegean

ègida *f* aegis

Egitto, l' *m* Egypt

egizia·no -na *adj* & *mf* Egyptian

eglantina *f* sweetbrier

eglefino *m* haddock

èglo·ga *f* (-ghe) eclogue

egocèntri·co -ca *adj* & *mf* (-ci -che) egocentric

egoismo *m* egoism, selfishness

egoi·sta (-sti -ste) *adj* selfish || *mf* egoist

egoìsti·co -ca *adj* (-ci -che) egoistic(al)

egotismo *m* egotism

egoti·sta (-sti -ste) *adj* egotistic || *mf* egotist

egrè·gio -gia *adj* (-gi -gie) (lit) outstanding; Egregio Signore Mr. (*before a man's name in an address on a letter*); Dear Sir

eguaglianza *f* equality

eguale *adj* var of uguale

egualità·rio -ria *adj* & *m* (-ri -rie) equalitarian

éhi *interj* hey!

éi *pron* (lit) he; (archaic) they

eiaculazióne *f* ejaculation

eiettàbile *adj* ejection (*seat*)

eiezióne *f* ejection

él *pron* (archaic) he

elaborare (elàboro) *tr* to elaborate; to digest; to secrete

elabora·to -ta *adj* elaborate || *m* written exercise

elaboratóre *m* computer

elaborazióne *f* elaboration; data processing

elargire §176 *tr* to donate

elargizióne *f* donation

elastici·tà *f* (-tà) elasticity; agility; (com) oscillation; (com) upswing

elàsti·co -ca (-ci -che) *adj* elastic || *m* rubber band; bedspring

élce *m* & *f* holm oak

elefante *m* elephant; elefante marino sea elephant

elefantéssa *f* female elephant

elegante *adj* elegant, fashionable

elegantó·ne -na *mf* fashion plate || *m* dandy, dude

eleganza *f* elegance, stylishness

elèggere §193 *tr* to elect

eleggìbile *adj* eligible

elegia *f* elegy

elegìa·co -ca *adj* elegiac

elementare *adj* elementary || elementari *fpl* elementary schools

eleménto *m* element; rudiment; member; cell (*of battery*); elementi personnel, e.g., elementi femminili female personnel

elemòsina *f* alms; (eccl) collection; chiedere l'elemosina to beg; vivere d'elemosina to live on charity

elemosinare (elemòsino) *intr* to beg

Èlena *f* Helen

elencare §197 (elènco) *tr* to list; to enumerate

elèn·co *m* (-chi) list; elenco telefonico telephone directory

eletti·vo -va *adj* elective

elèt·to -ta *adj* elect; distinguished (*audience*); precious (*metal*); chosen (*people*) || *mf* elect

elettorato *m* electorate, constituency

elet·tóre -trice *mf* voter; elector

elettràuto *m* automobile electrician; automotive electric shop

elettrici·sta *mf* (-sti -ste) electrician

elettrici·tà *f* (-tà) electricity

elèttri·co -ca (-ci -che) *adj* electrical || *m* electrical worker

elettrificare §197 (elettrìfico) *tr* to electrify

elettrizzare [ddzz] *tr* to electrify (*e.g., a person*) || *ref* to become electrified

elèttro *m* amber

elettrocalamita *f* electromagnet

elettrocardiògrafo *m* electrocardiograph

elettrocardiogram·ma *m* (-mi) electrocardiogram

elettrodinàmi·co -ca (-ci -che) *adj* electrodynamic || *f* electrodynamics

elèttrodo *m* electrode

elettrodomèsti·co -ca (-ci -che) *adj* electric household || *m* electric household appliance

elettroesecuzióne *f* electrocution

elettròge·no -na *adj* generating (*unit*)

elettròli·si *f* (-si) electrolysis

elettrolìti·co -ca *adj* (-ci -che) electrolytic

elettròlito *m* electrolyte

elettromagnèti·co -ca *adj* (-ci -che) electromagnetic

elettromo·tóre -trice *adj* electromotive || *m* electric motor || *f* electric train; electric railcar

elettróne *m* electron

elettròni·co -ca (-ci -che) *adj* electronic || *f* electronics

elettropómpa *f* electric pump

elettrosquasso *m* electroshock

elettrostàti·co -ca (-ci -che) *adj* electrostatic || *f* electrostatics

elettrotècni·co -ca (-ci -che) *adj* electrotechnical || *m* electrician; electrical engineer || *f* electrical engineering

elettrotrèno *m* electric train

elevaménto *m* elevation

elevare (èlevo & elèvo) *tr* to lift, elevate; (math) to raise || *ref* to rise

elevatézza *f* loftiness, dignity

eleva·to -ta *adj* high, lofty

eleva·tóre -trice *adj* elevating || *m* elevator

elevazióne *f* elevation; (sports) jump; (math) raising

elezióne *f* election; choice

èlfo *m* elf

èli·ca *f* (-che) propeller; (geom) helix

elicoidale *adj* helicoidal

elicòttero *m* helicopter

elìdere §161 *tr* to annul; to elide || *ref* to neutralize one another

eliminare (elìmino) *tr* to eliminate

eliminatò·rio -ria (-ri -rie) *adj* eliminating || *f* (sports) heat

eliminazióne *f* elimination; extermination

èlio- *comb form adj* helio-, e.g., eliocentrico heliocentric || *comb form*

m & *f* helio-, e.g., **elioterapìa** helio-
therapy
èlio *m* helium
eliocèntri·co -ca *adj* (**-ci -che**) helio-
centric
eliògrafo *m* heliograph
elioteràpi·co -ca *adj* (**-ci -che**) sunshine
(*treatment*); sunbathing (*establishment*)
eliotrò·pio *m* (**-pi**) heliotrope; blood-
stone
elipòrto *m* heliport
elisabettia·no -na *adj* Elizabethan
elì·sio -ia *adj* (**-si -sie**) Elysian
elisióne *f* elision
elì·sir *m* (**-sir**) elixir
èlitra *f* elytron, shard
Ella *pron* (lit) she ‖ **Ella** *pron* (lit) you
ellèboro *m* hellebore
ellèni·co -ca *adj* (**-ci -che**) Hellenic
ellisse *f* ellipse
ellìs·si *f* (**-si**) (gram) ellipsis
ellìtti·co -ca *adj* (**-ci -che**) elliptical
-èllo -èlla *suf adj* little, e.g., **poverello**
poor little
elmétto *m* helmet; tin hat
élmo *m* helmet
elogiare §290 (**elògio**) *tr* to praise
elò·gio *m* (**-gi**) praise, encomium;
write-up; **elogio funebre** eulogy
eloquènte *adj* eloquent
eloquènza *f* eloquence
elò·quio *m* (**-qui**) (lit) speech, diction
élsa *f* hilt
elucidare (**elùcido**) *tr* to elucidate
elùdere §105 *tr* to elude, evade
elusì·vo -va *adj* elusive
elvèti·co -ca *adj* & *mf* (**-ci -che**)
Helvetian
elzevì·ro -ra [dz] *adj* Elzevir ‖ *m*
Elzevir book; (journ) literary article
emacia·to -ta *adj* emaciated, lean
emanare *tr* to send forth; to issue ‖
intr (ESSERE) to emanate; to come
forth
emanazióne *f* emanation; issuance
emancipare (**emàncipo**) *tr* to emancipate ‖ *ref* to become emancipated
emancipazióne *f* emancipation
emarginare (**emàrgino**) *tr* to note in
the margin; (fig) to put aside, neglect
emarginato *m* marginal note
emàti·co -ca *adj* (**-ci -che**) blood,
hematic
ematite *f* hematite
embar·go *m* (**-ghi**) embargo
emblè·ma *m* (**-mi**) emblem
emblemàti·co -ca *adj* (**-ci -che**) em-
blematic
embolìa *f* embolism
èmbrice *m* flat roof tile; shingle
embriologìa *f* embryology
embrionale *adj* embryonic
embrióne *m* embryo
emendaménto *m* emendation (*of a
text*); amendment (*to a law*)
emendare (**emèndo**) *tr* to correct; to
emend; to amend (*a law*) ‖ *ref* to
reform
emergènza *f* emergence; emergency
emèrgere §162 *intr* (ESSERE) to emerge;

to surface (*said of a submarine*); to
loom; to stand out
emèri·to -ta *adj* emeritus (*professor*);
famous
emerotè·ca *f* (**-che**) periodical library
emersióne *f* emersion; surfacing
emèr·so -sa *adj* emergent
emèti·co -ca *adj* & *m* (**-ci -che**) emetic
eméttere §198 *tr* to emit, send forth;
to utter (*a statement*); (com) to issue
emicìclo *m* hemicycle; floor (*of legislative body*)
emicrània *f* migraine, headache
emigrante *adj* & *mf* emigrant
emigrare *intr* (ESSERE & AVERE) to emigrate
emigra·to -ta *adj* & *mf* emigrant
emigrazióne *f* emigration; migration
(e.g., of birds)
eminènte *adj* eminent
eminènza *f* eminence; (eccl) Eminence
emisfèro *m* hemisphere
emissà·rio *m* (**-ri**) emissary; outlet
(*river or lake*); drain
emissióne *f* emission; issuance; (rad)
broadcast
emistì·chio *m* (**-chi**) hemistich
emittènte *adj* emitting; issuing; (rad)
broadcasting ‖ *f* (rad) transmitting
set; broadcasting station
emofilìa *f* hemophilia
emoglobìna *f* hemoglobin
emolliènte *adj* & *m* emollient
emoluménto *m* fee, emolument
emorragìa *f* hemorrhage
emorròidi *fpl* hemorrhoids, piles
emostàti·co -ca (**-ci -che**) *adj* hemo-
static ‖ *m* hemostat
emotè·ca *f* (**-che**) blood bank
emotivi·tà *f* (**-tà**) emotionalism
emotì·vo -va *adj* emotional ‖ *mf* emotional person
emottìsi *f* (pathol) hemoptysis
emozionale *adj* emotional, moving
emozionare (**emozióno**) *tr* to move,
stir; to thrill
emozióne *f* emotion
empiastro *m* var of **impiastro**
empiere §163 *tr* & *ref* var of **empire**
empie·tà *f* (**-tà**) impiety; cruelty
ém·pio -pia *adj* (**-pi -pie**) impious;
pitiless, wicked
empire §163 *tr* to fill; (lit) to fulfill;
empire qlcu di insulti to heap insults
on s.o. ‖ *ref* to get full
empìre·o -a *adj* heavenly, sublime ‖
m empyrean
empìri·co -ca (**-ci -che**) *adj* empirical ‖
mf empiricist
empirìsmo *m* empiricism
empirì·sta *mf* (**-sti -ste**) empiricist
émpito *m* (lit) rush; fury
empò·rio *m* (**-ri**) emporium, mart
emulare (**èmulo**) *tr* to emulate
emulazióne *f* emulation, rivalry; (law)
evil intent
èmu·lo -la *adj* emulous ‖ *mf* emulator
emulsionare (**emulsióno**) *tr* to emulsify
emulsióne *f* emulsion
encefalite *f* encephalitis
encìcli·ca *f* (**-che**) encyclical
enciclopedìa *f* encyclopedia

enciclopèdi·co -ca *adj* (-ci -che) encyclopedic

enclave *f* enclave

enclìti·co -ca *adj* & *f* (-ci -che) enclitic

encomiàbile *adj* praiseworthy

encomiare §287 (encòmio) *tr* to praise

encò·mio *m* (-mi) encomium, praise

endecasìlla·bo -ba *adj* hendecasyllabic || *m* hendecasyllable

endemìa *f* endemic

endèmi·co -ca *adj* (-ci -che) endemic

èndice *m* nest egg; (obs) souvenir

endocàr·dio *m* (-di) (anat) endocardium

endocarpo *m* (bot) endocarp

endòcri·no -na *adj* endocrine

endourba·no -na *adj* inner-city

endovenó·so -sa [s] *adj* intravenous

energèti·co -ca *adj* (-ci -che) energy (*e.g., crisis*); (med) tonic || *m* (med) tonic

energìa *f* energy, power

enèrgi·co -ca *adj* (-ci -che) energetic

energùme·no -na *mf* wild or mad person

ènfa·si *f* (-si) emphasis; forcefulness

enfàti·co -ca *adj* (-ci -che) emphatic

enfiare §287 (énfio) *tr* & *ref* to swell

enfisè·ma *m* (-mi) emphysema

enfitèu·si *f* (-si) lease (*of land*)

enig·ma *m* (-mi) enigma, riddle, puzzle

enigmàti·co -ca *adj* (-ci -che) enigmatic, puzzling

-ènne *suf adj* -year-old, e.g., **ragazzo diciassettenne** seventeen-year-old boy || *suf mf* -year-old person, e.g., **diciassettenne** seventeen-year-old person

ennèsi·mo -ma *adj* nth

-èn·nio *suf m* (-ni) period of ... years, e.g., **ventennio** period of twenty years

enòlo·go -ga *mf* (-gi -ghe) oenologist

enórme *adj* enormous

enormeménte *adv* enormously

enormi·tà *f* (-tà) enormity; outrage; absurdity

Enrico *m* Henry

ènte *m* being; entity; corporation; agency, body

enteroclì·sma *m* (-smi) enema

enti·tà *f* (-tà) entity; value, importance

entomologìa *f* entomology

entram·bi -be *adj*—**entrambi i** both || *pron* both

entrante *adj* next (*e.g., week*)

entrare (éntro) *intr* (ESSERE) to enter; to go (*said of numbers*); to get (*into one's head*); **entrarci** to make it, e.g., **con questi soldi non c'entro I can't make it with this money; entrarci come i cavoli a merenda** to be completely out of line; **entrare a** to begin to; **entrare in** to enter (*e.g., a room*); to fit in; to go in (*said of a number*); to get into (*one's head*); **entrare in amore** to be in heat (*said of animals*); **entrare in ballo** to come into play; **entrare in carica** to take up one's duties; **entrare in collera** to get angry; **entrare in collisione** to collide; **entrare in contatto** to establish contact; **entrare in gioco** to come into play; **entrare in guerra** to go to war; **entrare in società** to make one's debut; **entrare nella parte di** (theat)

to play the role of; **entrare in vigore** to become effective; **Lei non c'entra** this is none of your business; **questo non c'entra** this is beside the point

entrata *f* entry; entrance; **entrata di favore** (theat) complimentary ticket; **entrate income**

entratura *f* entry; entrance; assumption (*of a position*); familiarity

éntro *adv* inside || *prep* within; **entro di** within, inside of

enrobórdo *m* inboard motorboat

entrotèrra *f* inland, hinterland

entusiasmare *tr* to carry away, enthuse || *ref* to be carried away, to become enthused

entusiasmo *m* enthusiasm

entusia·sta -sti -ste) *adj* enthusiastic || *mf* enthusiast, devotee

entusiàsti·co -ca *adj* (-ci -che) enthusiastic

enucleare (enùcleo) *tr* to elucidate; (surg) to remove

enumerare (enùmero) *tr* to enumerate

enumerazióne *f* enumeration

enunciare §128 *tr* to enunciate, state

enunciatì·vo -va *adj* (gram) declarative

enunciazióne *f* enunciation, statement

enzi·ma [dz] *m* (-mi) enzyme

èpa *f* (lit) belly, paunch

epàti·co -ca *adj* (-ci -che) hepatic, liver

epatite *f* (pathol) hepatitis

epènte·si *f* (-si) epenthesis

eperlano *m* (ichth) smelt

èpi·co -ca *adj* & *f* (-ci -che) epic

epicurè·o -a *adj* & *m* epicurean

epidemìa *f* epidemic

epidèmi·co -ca *adj* (-ci -che) epidemic (al)

epidèrmi·co -ca *adj* (-ci -che) epidermal; (fig) superficial, skin-deep

epidèrmide *f* epidermis

Epifanìa *f* Epiphany

epiglòttide *f* (anat) epiglottis

epìgono *m* follower; descendant

epìgrafe *f* epigraph

epigram·ma *m* (-mi) epigram

epigrammàti·co -ca *adj* (-ci -che) epigrammatic

epilessìa *f* (pathol) epilepsy

epilètti·co -ca *adj* & *m* (-ci -che) epileptic

epìlo·go -ga (-ghi) epilogue; conclusion

episcopale *adj* episcopal

episcopalia·no -na *adj* & *mf* Episcopalian

episcopato *m* episcopate, bishopric

episòdi·co -ca *adj* (-ci -che) episodic

episò·dio *m* (-di) episode

epìstola *f* epistle

epistolà·rio *m* (-ri) letters, correspondence

epitàf·fio *m* (-fi) epitaph

epitè·lio *m* (-li) epithelium

epìteto *m* epithet; insult

epitomare (epìtomo) *tr* to epitomize

epìtome *f* epitome

èpo·ca *f* (-che) epoch; period; moment; **fare epoca** to be epoch-making

epopèa *f* epic

eppure *conj* yet, and yet

epsomite *f* Epsom salt

epurare *tr* to cleanse; to purge
epurazióne *f* purification; purge
equànime *adj* calm, composed; impartial
equanimità *f* equanimity; impartiality
equatóre *m* equator
equatoriale *adj & m* equatorial
equazióne *f* equation
equèstre *adj* equestrian
equilàte·ro -ra *adj* equilateral
equilibrare *tr* to balance; (aer) to trim || *ref* to balance one another
equilibra·to -ta *adj* level-headed
equilibra·tóre -trice *adj* stabilizing || *m* (aer) horizontal stabilizer
equili·brio *m* (-bri) equilibrium, balance; (fig) proportion; **equilibrio politico** balance of power
equilibri·sta *mf* (-sti -ste) acrobat, equilibrist
equi·no -na *adj & m* equine
equinoziale *adj* equinoctial
equinò·zio *m* (-zi) equinox
equipaggiamento *m* equipment, outfit
equipaggiare §290 *tr* to equip, outfit; (naut) to fit out; (naut) to man
equipàg·gio *m* (-gi) equipage; (naut) crew, complement; (sports) team; (rowing) crew
equiparare *tr* to equalize (*e.g.*, *salaries*)
équipe *f* team
equipollènte *adj* equivalent
equi·tà *f* (-tà) equity, fair-mindedness
equitazióne *f* horsemanship
equivalènte *adj & m* equivalent
equivalére §278 *intr* (ESSERE & AVERE) —**equivalere a** to be equivalent to || *ref* to be equal
equivocare §197 (equìvoco) *intr*—**equivocare su** to mistake, misunderstand
equivo·co -ca (-ci -che) *adj* equivocal; ambiguous || *m* misunderstanding
è·quo -qua *adj* equitable, fair
èra *f* era, age; era spaziale space age
erà·rio *m* (-ri) treasury
èrba *f* grass; **erba limoncina** lemon verbena; **erba medica** alfalfa; **erbe** vegetables; **erbe aromatiche** herbs; **far l'erba** to cut the grass; **in erba** (fig) budding; **metter a erba** to put to pasture
erbàc·cia *f* (-ce) weed
erbaggi *mpl* vegetables
erbaiò·lo -la *mf* fresh vegetable retailer
erbici·da *m* (-di) weed-killer
erbivéndo·lo -la *mf* fresh fruit and vegetable retailer
erbìvo·ro -ra *adj* herbivorous
erbori·sta *mf* (-sti -ste) herbalist
erbó·so -sa [s] *adj* grassy
Èrcole *m* Hercules
ercùle·o -a *adj* Herculean
erède *m* heir || *f* heiress
eredi·tà *f* (-tà) inheritance; heredity
ereditare (erèdito) *tr* to inherit
eredità·rio -ria *adj* (-ri -rie) hereditary; crown (*prince*)
ereditièra *f* heiress
eremi·ta *m* (-ti) hermit
eremitàg·gio *m* (-gi) hermitage
èremo *m* hermitage
eresìa *f* heresy

eresiar·ca *m* (-chi) heretic
erèti·co -ca (-ci -che) *adj* heretical || *mf* heretic
erèt·to -ta *adj* erect, straight
erezióne *f* erection
ergastola·no -na *mf* lifer
ergàstolo *m* life imprisonment; prison for persons sentenced to life imprisonment
èrgere §164 *tr* (lit) to erect; (lit) to lift || *ref* to rise (*said, e.g., of a mountain*)
èrgo *m* *invar*—**venire all'ergo** to come to a conclusion || *adv* thus, hence
èri·ca *f* (-che) heather
erìgere §152 *tr* to erect, build || *ref* to rise; **erigersi a** to set oneself up as
eritrè·o -a *adj & mf* Eritrean
ermafrodi·to -ta *adj & m* hermafrodite
ermellino *m* ermine
ermèti·co -ca (-ci -che) *adj* airtight; watertight; hermetic
èrnia *f* hernia; **ernia del disco** (pathol) herniated disk
eródere §239 *tr* to erode
eròe *m* hero
erogare §209 (èrogo) *tr* to distribute; to bestow
erogazióne *f* distribution; bestowal
eròi·co -ca *adj* (-ci -che) heroic
eroicòmi·co -ca *adj* (-ci -che) mock-heroic
eroìna *f* heroine; (pharm) heroin
eroìsmo *m* heroism
erómpere §240 *intr* to erupt, burst out
erosióne *f* erosion
eròti·co -ca *adj* (-ci -che) erotic
erotìsmo *m* eroticism
èrpete *m* (pathol) herpes, shingles
erpicare §197 (èrpico) *tr* to harrow
érpice *m* harrow
errabón·do -da *adj* (lit) wandering
errante *adj* errant; wandering
errare (èrro) *intr* to wander; to err; (lit) to stray
erra·to -ta *adj* mistaken, wrong
errò·ne·o -a *adj* erroneous
erróre *m* error, mistake; fault; (lit) wandering; **errore di lingua** slip of the tongue; **errore di scrittura** slip of the pen; **errore di stampa** misprint; **errore giudiziario** miscarriage of justice; **salvo errore od omissione** barring error or omission
érto -ta *adj* arduous, steep; erect || *f* arduous ascent; **all'erta** on the alert
erudire §176 *tr* to educate, instruct
erudi·to -ta *adj* erudite, learned || *m* scholar, savant
erudizióne *f* erudition, learning
eruttare *tr* to belch forth (*e.g., lava*); to utter (*obscenities*) || *intr* to belch
erutti·vo -va *adj* eruptive
eruzióne *f* eruption
esacerbare (esacèrbo) *tr* to embitter; to exacerbate || *ref* to become embittered
esagerare (esàgero) *tr & intr* to exaggerate
esagera·to -ta *adj* exaggerated, excessive || *mf* exaggerator
esagerazióne *f* exaggeration

esagitare (esàgito) *tr* to perturb

esàgono *m* hexagon

esalare *tr* to exhale; **esalare l'ultimo respiro** to breathe one's last ‖ *intr* to spread (*said of odors*)

esalazióne *f* exhalation; fume, vapor

esaltare *tr* to exalt; to excite ‖ *ref* to glorify oneself; to become excited

esalta·to -ta *adj* frenzied, excited ‖ *mf* hothead

esame *m* examination; checkup, test; **dare gli esami** to take an examination; **esame attitudinale** aptitude test; **esame del sangue** blood test; **esame di riparazione** make-up test; **fare gli esami** to prepare a test (*for a student*); **prendere in esame** to take in consideration

esàmetro *m* hexameter

esaminan·do -da *mf* candidate; examinee

esaminare (esàmino) *tr* to examine; to test

esamina·tóre -trice *mf* examiner

esàngue *adj* bloodless; (fig) pale

esànime *adj* lifeless

esasperante *adj* exasperating

esasperare (esàspero) *tr* to exasperate ‖ *ref* to become exasperated

esasperazióne *f* exasperation

esattézza *f* exactness; punctuality

esat·to -ta *adj* exact; punctual

esattore *m* tax collector; bill collector

esattorìa *f* tax collector's office; bill collector's office

esaudire §176 *tr* to grant

esauriènte *adj* exhaustive; convincing

esaurimento *m* depletion (*e.g., of merchandise*); (pathol) exhaustion; (naut) drainage

esaurire §176 *tr* to exhaust; to play out (*e.g., a hooked fish*); to use up ‖ *ref* to be exhausted; to be depleted; to be sold out

esauri·to -ta *adj* exhausted; depleted; sold out; out of print

esau·sto -sta *adj* exhausted; empty

esautorare (esàutoro) *tr* to deprive of authority; to discredit (*a theory*)

esazióne *f* exaction; collection

é·sca /f (-sche) bait; punk (*for lighting fireworks*); tinder (*for lighting powder*): **dare esca a** to foment

escandescènza /—**dare in escandescenze** to fly off the handle

escava·tóre -trice *mf* excavator, digger ‖ *m* excavator; **escavatore a vapore** steam shovel ‖ *f* (mach) excavator

escavazióne *f* excavation

eschimése [s] *adj & mf* Eskimo

esclamare *tr & intr* to exclaim

esclamati·vo -va *adj* exclamatory; exclamation (*mark*)

esclùdere §105 *tr* to exclude; to keep or shut out

esclusióne *f* exclusion; **a esclusione di** with the exception of

esclusiva *f* sole right, monopoly; (journ) scoop

esclusivi·sta (-sti -ste) *adj* clannish; bigoted ‖ *mf* bigot; (com) sole agent

esclusi·vo -va *adj* exclusive; intolerant, bigoted ‖ *f* see **esclusiva**

esclu·so -sa *adj* excluded, excepted

escogitare (escògito) *tr* to think up, invent; to think out

escoriare §287 (**escòrio**) *tr & ref* to skin

escoriazióne *f* abrasion

escremento *m* excrement

escrescènza *f* excrescence

escrè·to -ta *adj* excreted ‖ *m* excreta

escursióne *f* excursion; (mach) sweep; (mil) transfer; **escursione termica** (meteor) temperature range

escursioni·sta *mf* (-sti -ste) excursionist, sightseer

escussióne *f* (law) examination, cross-examination

esecrare (esècro) *tr* to execrate

esecrazióne *f* execration

esecuti·vo -va *adj & m* executive

esecu·tóre -trice *mf* (mus) performer ‖ *m* executor; **esecutore di giustizia** executioner ‖ *f* executrix

esecuzióne *f* accomplishment, completion; performance; execution; **esecuzione capitale** capital punishment

esegè·si *f* (-si) exegesis

eseguire (eséguo) & §176 *tr* to execute, carry out; to perform

esèm·pio *m* (-pi) example; **a mo' d'esempio** as an illustration; **dare il buon esempio** to set a good example; **per esempio** for instance

esemplare *adj* exemplary ‖ *m* copy; specimen ‖ *v* (esèmplo) *tr* (lit) to copy

esemplificare §197 (**esemplìfico**) *tr* to exemplify

esentare (esènto) *tr* to exempt

esènte *adj* exempt, free

esenzióne *f* exemption

esèquie *fpl* obsequies, funeral rites

esercènte *adj* practicing ‖ *mf* dealer, merchant

esercire §176 *tr* to practice; to run (*a store*)

esercitare (esèrcito) *tr* to exercise; to tax (*e.g., s.o.'s patience*); to practice, ply (*a trade*); to wield (*e.g., power*) ‖ *ref* to practice

esercitazióne *f* exercise, training; **esercitazioni militari** drilling

esèrcito *m* army; (fig) flock; **Esercito della Salvezza** Salvation Army

eserci·zio *m* (-zi) exercise; practice; training; homework; occupation; drill; **d'esercizio** (com) administrative (*expenses*); **esercizio finanziario** fiscal year; **esercizio provvisorio** (law) emergency appropriation; **esercizio pubblico** establishment open to the public; **esercizio spirituale** (eccl) retreat

esibire §176 *tr* to exhibit ‖ *ref* to show oneself, appear; **esibirsi di** to offer to

esibizióne *f* exhibition

esigènte *adj* demanding, exigent

esigènza *f* demand, requirement, exigency

esìgere §165 *tr* to demand; to require; to exact; to collect

esigìbile *adj* due; collectable

esigui·tà *f* (-tà) meagerness, scantiness

esì·guo -gua *adj* meager, scanty

esilarante *adj* exhilarating; laughing (gas)

esilarare (esìlaro) *tr* to amuse || *ref* to be amused

èsile *adj* slender, thin; weak

esiliare §287 *tr* to exile || *ref* to go into exile; to withdraw

esìlia·to -ta *adj* exiled || *m* exile (person)

esì·lio *m* (-li) exile, banishment

esìmere §166 *tr* to exempt || *ref—esimersi da* to avoid (an obligation)

esì·mio -mia *adj* (-mi -mie) distinguished, eminent

-èsi·mo -ma *suf adj & pron* -eth, e.g., **ventesimo** twentieth; -th, e.g., **diciannovesimo** nineteenth

esistènte *adj* existent; extant

esistènza *f* existence

esistenzialismo *m* existentialism

esìstere §114 *intr* (ESSERE) to exist

esitante *adj* hesitant

esitare (èsito) *tr* to retail || *intr* to hesitate; (med) to resolve itself

esitazióne *f* hesitation; haw (in speech)

èsito *m* result, outcome; sale; outlet; (philol) late form; **dare esito a** (com) to reply

esiziale *adj* ruinous, fatal

èsodo *m* exodus, flight

esòfa·go *m* (-gi) esophagus

esonerare (esònero) *tr* to exempt, release

esònero *m* exemption, release

Esòpo *m* Aesop

esorbitante *adj* exorbitant

esorbitare (esòrbito) *intr—esorbitare da* to go beyond

esorcismo *m* exorcism

esorcizzare [ddzz] *tr* to exorcise

esordiènte *adj* beginning, budding || *mf* beginner || *f* debutante

esòr·dio *m* (-di) beginning

esordire §176 *intr* to make a start; (theat) to debut; (theat) to open

esortare (esòrto) *tr* to exhort

esortazióne *f* exhortation

esò·so -sa *adj* greedy, avaricious; hateful; exorbitant (price)

esòti·co -ca *adj* (-ci -che) exotic

esotismo *m* exoticism; borrowing (from a foreign language)

espàndere §167 *tr* to expand || *ref* to spread out; to confide

espansióne *f* expansion; effusiveness

espansionismo *m* expansionism

espansivi·tà *f* (-tà) effusiveness

espansi·vo -va *adj* expansive; effusive

espan·so -sa *adj* flared; expanded, dilated

espatriare §287 *intr* to emigrate

espà·trio *m* (-tri) emigration

espediènte *m* expedient, makeshift; ruse; **vivere di espedienti** to live by one's wits

espedire §176 *tr* to expedite || *ref—espedirsi di* to get rid of

espèllere §168 *tr* to expel, eject

esperiènza *f* experience; experiment

esperiménto *m* experiment; test

espèr·to -ta *adj & m* expert

espettorare (espèttoro) *tr & intr* to expectorate

espiare §119 *tr* to expiate; to placate (the gods); **espiare una pena** to serve a sentence

espiató·rio -ria *adj* (-ri -rie) expiatory

espiazióne *f* expiation

espirare *tr & intr* to breath out, to exhale

espirazióne *f* exhaling

espletare (esplèto) *tr* to dispatch, complete

esplicare §197 (èsplico) *tr* to carry out; (lit) to explain

esplicati·vo -va *adj* explanatory

esplìci·to -ta *adj* explicit

esplòdere §169 *tr* to shoot; to fire (a shot) || *intr* (ESSERE & AVERE) to explode; to burst forth

esploditóre *m* blasting machine

esplorare (esplòro) *tr* to explore; to search, probe; (telv) to scan

esplora·tóre -trice *mf* explorer || *m* (nav) gunboat; **giovane esploratore** boy scout

esplorazióne *f* exploration; (telv) scanning

esplosióne *f* explosion, blast; (fig) outburst

esplosi·vo -va *adj & m* explosive

esponènte *adj* (typ) superior || *m* spokesman; dictionary entry; catchword (of dictionary); (math) exponent; (naut) net weight

espórre §218 *tr* to expose, show; to expound; to abandon (a baby); to lay out (a corpse); to lay open (to danger) || *intr* to show, exhibit || *ref* to expose oneself

esportare (espòrto) *tr* to export

esporta·tóre -trice *mf* exporter

esportazióne *f* export, exportation

esposìmetro *m* exposure meter

esposi·tóre -trice *mf* commentator; exhibitor

esposizióne *f* exposition; abandonment (of a baby); exhibit, fair; line (of credit); exposure (of a house); (phot) exposure

espó·sto -sta *adj* exposed; aforementioned || *m* petition, brief; foundling

espressióne *f* expression; feeling

espressi·vo -va *adj* expressive

esprès·so -sa *adj* manifest; express; prepared on the spot || *m* espresso; messenger; special-delivery letter; special-delivery stamp

esprìmere §131 *tr* to express; to convey (an opinion); (lit) to squeeze || *ref* to express oneself

espropriare §287 (espròprio) *tr* to expropriate || *ref* to deprive onself; **espropriarsi di** to divest oneself of

espró·prio *m* (-pri) expropriation

espugnare *tr* to take by storm

espulsióne *f* expulsion; (mach) ejection

espulsóre *m* ejector

espurgare §209 *tr* to expurgate

éssa §5 *pron pers* she; it

ésse §5 *pron pers* they

essènza *f* essence

essenziale *adj* essential || *m* main point

èssere *m* being; existence; condition; (coll) character; **in essere** in good shape || §170 *intr* (ESSERE) to be;

c'è there is; ci sono there are; ci sono! I get it!; come sarebbe a dire? what do you mean?; come se nulla fosse as if nothing had happened; esserci to have arrived, to be there; essere di to belong to; essere per to be about to; può essere maybe; sarà maybe; sia . . . sia both . . . and; whether . . . or || *aux* (ESSERE) (to form passive) to be, e.g., fu investito da un tassametro he was run over by a taxi; (to form the compound tenses of certain intransitive verbs and all reflexive verbs) to have, e.g., sono arrivati they have arrived; mi sono appena alzato I have just got up || *impers* (ESSERE) to be, e.g., è giusto it is fair

éssi §5 *pron pers* they
essiccare §197 *tr* to dry || *ref* to dry up
essicca-tóio *m* (-tói) drier
essiccazióne *f* drying
èsso §5 *pron pers* he; it; chi per esso his representative
essudare *intr* to exude
èst *m* east
èsta-si *f* (-si) ecstasy; andare in estasi to become enraptured
estasiare §287 *tr* to enrapture, delight || *ref* to become enraptured
estate *f* summer
estàti-co -ca *adj* (-ci -che) ecstatic, enraptured
estemporàne-o -a *adj* extemporaneous
estèndere §270 *tr* to extend; to broaden (e.g., one's knowledge); to draw up (a document) || *ref* to extend
estensìbile *adj* applicable; inviare saluti estensibili a to send greetings to be extended to (e.g., another person)
estensióne *f* extension; extent; expanse (e.g., of water); (mus) compass, range
estensi-vo -va *adj* extensive
estèn-so -sa *adj*—per esteso fully
estensóre *adj* extensible || *m* compiler (e.g., of a dictionary); (sports) exerciser, chest expander
estenuante *adj* exhausting
estenuare (estènuo) *tr* to exhaust || *ref* to become exhausted
esterióre *adj* exterior || *m* outside appearance
esteriori-tà *f* (-tà) appearance
esternare (estèrno) *tr* to reveal, manifest || *ref* to confide
estèr-no -na *adj* external; outside; day (student) || *m* exterior, outside; (baseball) outfielder; all'esterno outside; in esterno (mov) on location
èste-ro -ra *adj* foreign || *m* foreign countries; all'estero abroad
esterrefat-to -ta *adj* terrified
esté-so -sa [s] *adj* extended, wide; per esteso in full
estè-ta *mf* (-ti -te) aesthete
estèti-co -ca *adj* (-ci -che) aesthetic || *f* aesthetics
esteti-sta *mf* (-sti -ste) beautician
estima-tóre -trice *mf* appraiser; admirer
èstimo *m* appraisal; assessment
estìnguere §156 *tr* to extinguish; to quench (thirst); to pay off (a debt) || *ref* to die out

estinguìbile *adj* extinguishable; payable
estìn-to -ta *adj* extinguished; extinct || *m* deceased, dead person
estintóre *m* fire extinguisher
estirpare *tr* to uproot; to eradicate; to pull (a tooth)
estirpa-tóre -trice *mf* eradicator || *m* (agr) weeder
estivare *tr & intr* to summer
esti-vo -va *adj* summer; summery
estòllere §171 *tr* to extol
èstone *adj & mf* Estonian
estòrcere §272 *tr* to extort; estorcere qlco a qlcu to extort s.th from s.o.
estorsióne *f* extortion
estradare *tr* (law) to extradite
estradizióne *f* extradition
estràne-o -a *adj* extraneous, foreign; aloof || *mf* outsider
estrapolare (estràpolo) *tr* to extrapolate
estrarre §273 *tr* to extract, draw; to pull (a tooth)
estrat-to -ta *adj* extracted || *m* extract; abstract; certified copy; (typ) offprint; estratto conto bank statement; estratto dell'atto di nascita copy of one's birth certificate
estrazióne *f* extraction; drawing (of lottery)
estrèma *f* (sports) wing, end
estremi-sta *adj & mf* (-sti -ste) extremist
estremi-tà *f* (-tà) end; tip, top; extremity; le estremità the extremities
estrè-mo -ma *adj* extreme; esalare l'estremo respiro to breath one's last || *m* extremity; end, extreme; essere agli estremi to be near the end; estremi essentials || *f* see estrema
estrìnse-co -ca *adj* (-ci -che) extrinsic
èstro *m* horsefly; whim, fancy; inspiration; estro venereo heat (of female animal)
estromèttere §198 *tr* to oust, expel
estró-so -sa [s] *adj* fanciful, whimsical; inspired
estrovèr-so -sa or estroverti-to -ta *adj & mf* extrovert
estrùdere §190 *tr* to extrude
estuà-rio *m* (-ri) estuary
esuberante *adj* exuberant; buoyant
esuberanza *f* exuberance; buoyancy; a esuberanza abundantly
esulare (èsulo) *intr* (ESSERE & AVERE) to go into exile; esulare da to be alien to
esulcerare (esùlcero) *tr* to ulcerate on the surface; (fig) to exacerbate
esulcerazióne *f* superficial ulceration; (fig) exasperation, exacerbation
èsule *mf* exile (person)
esultante *adj* exultant, jubilant
esultare *intr* to exult
esumare *tr* to exhume; to revive (e.g., a custom)
esumazióne *f* exhumation; revival
e-tà *f* (-tà) age; che età ha? how old is he (or she)?; ha la sua età he (or she) is no longer a youngster; l'età di mezzo Middle Ages; maggiore età majority; mezza età middle age; minore età minority
etamine *f* cheesecloth
ètere *m* ether

etère·o -a *adj* ethereal
eternare (etèrno) *tr* to immortalize || *ref* to become immortal
eterni·tà *f* (-tà) eternity
etèr·no -na *adj* eternal, everlasting || *m* eternity; in eterno forever
eterodòs·so -sa *adj* heterodox
eterogène·o -a *adj* heterogeneous
èti·ca *f* (-che) ethics
etichétta *f* label; card (*e.g., of a library*); etiquette; etichetta gommata sticker
etichettare (etichétto) *tr* to label
èti·co -ca (-ci -che) *adj* ethical; consumptive || *m'* consumptive || *f* see etica
etile *m* ethyl
etilène *m* ethylene
etìli·co -ca *adj* (-ci -che) ethyl
ètimo *m* etymon
etimologìa *f* etymology
etìope *adj* & *mf* Ethiopian
Etiòpia, l' *f* Ethiopia
etiòpi·co -ca *adj* (-ci -che) Ethiopian
etisìa *f* tuberculosis
ètni·co -ca *adj* (-ci -che) ethnic(al)
etnografìa *f* ethnography
etnologìa *f* ethnology
etru·sco -sca *adj* & *mf* (-schi -sche) Etruscan
ettàgono *m* heptagon
èttaro *m* hectare
ètte *m* (coll) particle, jot, whit, tittle
ètto or ettogrammo *m* hectogram
-étto -étta *suf adj* rather, e.g., piccoletto rather small; -ish, e.g., rotondetto roundish
ettòlitro *m* hectoliter
eucalipto *m* eucalyptus
eucaristìa *f* Eucharist
eufemismo *m* euphemism
eufonìa *f* euphony
eufòni·co -ca *adj* (-ci -che) euphonic
euforìa *f* euphoria
eufòri·co -ca *adj* (-ci -che) euphoric
eufuismo *m* euphuism
eugèni·co -ca -ca (-ci -che) *adj* eugenic || *f* eugenics
eunu·co *m* (-chi) eunuch
europè·o -a *adj* & *mf* European
Europa, l' *f* Europe
eurovisióne *f* European television chain
eutanasìa *f* euthanasia
Èva *f* Eve
evacuaménto *m* evacuation
evacuare (evàcuo) *tr* to evacuate || *intr* to evacuate; to have a bowel movement
evacuazióne *f* evacuation; bowel movement

evàdere §172 *tr* to evade; to complete (*a deal*); to answer (*a letter*); to execute (*orders*) || *intr* (ESSERE) to flee, escape
evanescènza *f* evanescence; (rad) fading
evanescènte *adj* evanescent; vanishing
evangèli·co -ca *adj* (-ci -che) evangelic(al)
evangeli·sta *m* (-sti) evangelist
evangelizzare [ddzz] *tr* to evangelize; to campaign for; to subject to political propaganda
evaporare (evapóro) *tr* & *intr* to evaporate
evaporatóre *m* evaporator; humidifier
evaporazióne *f* evaporation
evasióne *f* evasion, escape; (com) reply; dare evasione a to complete (*an administrative matter*)
evasi·vo -va *adj* evasive
eva·so -sa *adj* escaped || *m* escapee
evasóre *m* tax dodger
eveniènza *f* eventuality, contingency; nell'evenienza che in the event (that); per ogni evenienza just in case
evènto *m* event; eventi correnti current events; fausto or lieto evento happy event
eventuale *adj* contingent
eventuali·tà *f* (-tà) eventuality
eversi·vo -va *adj* upsetting; destructive
evidènte *adj* evident; clear
evidènza *f* evidence; clearness; mettersi in evidenza to make oneself conspicuous; tenere in evidenza (com) to keep active
evirare *tr* to emasculate
evitare (èvito) *tr* to avoid, shun; evitare qlco a qlcu to spare s.o. s.th, to save s.o. from s.th
èvo *m* age, era; evo antico ancient times; evo moderno modern times; medio evo Middle Ages
evocare §197 (èvoco) *tr* to evoke
evoluìre §176 *intr* (aer, nav) to maneuver
evolu·to -ta *adj* developed; progressive; modern
evoluzióne *f* evolution
evòlvere §115 *tr* to develop || *ref* to evolve
evvi·va *m* (-va) cheer || *interj* long live!, hurrah for!
èx *adj invar* ex-, e.g., la sua ex moglie his ex-wife; ex, e.g., ex dividendo ex dividend
ex li·bris *m* (-bris) bookplate
extraconiugale *adj* extramarital
extraeuropè·o -a *adj* non-European
ex vó·to *m* (-to) votive offering
eziologìa *f* etiology

F

F, f ['effe] *m* & *f* sixth letter of the Italian alphabet
fa *m* (fa) (mus) F, fa
fabbisógno *m invar* need; requirement
fàbbri·ca *f* (-che) building, construction; factory, plant

fabbricante *mf* builder, manufacturer
fabbricare §197 (fàbbrico) *tr* to manufacture; to fabricate
fabbrica·to -ta *adj* built || *m* building
fabbricazióne *f* building; erection; manufacturing; fabrication (*invention*)

fabbro *m* blacksmith; locksmith; (fig) master; **fabbro ferraio** blacksmith

faccènda *f* business, matter; **faccende domestiche** household chores

faccendiè·re -ra *mf* operator, schemer

faccétta *f* small face; face, facet

facchinàg·gio *m* (-gi) porterage; (fig) drudgery

facchino *m* porter; **lavorare come un facchino** to work like a slave

fàc·cia *f* (-ce) face; countenance; **avere la faccia di** to have the gall to; **di faccia a** opposite; **faccia da galeotto** (coll) gallows bird; **faccia tosta** cheek, gall; **in faccia a** in front of

facciale *adj* facial

facciata *f* façade; page; (fig) surface appearance

face *f* (lit) torch

facè·to -ta *adj* facetious

facèzia *f* pleasantry, banter; **scambiar facezie** to banter with each other

fachiro *m* fakir

fàcile *adj* easy; inclined; loose (*morals*); glib (*tongue*); **è facile** it is probable || *m* something easy

facili·tà *f* (-tà) facility, ease; inclination; **facilità di pagamento** easy payments, easy terms; **facilità di parola** glibness

facilitare (**facìlito**) *tr* to facilitate; to grant (*credit*); to give (*easy terms*)

facilitazióne *f* facilitation; easy terms; cut rate

facinoró·so -sa [s] *adj* criminal || *m* hoodlum, thug

facoltà *f* (-tà) faculty; power; school (*of a university*); **facoltà** *fpl* means, wealth

facoltati·vo -va *adj* optional

facoltó·so -sa [s] *adj* wealthy, affluent

facóndia *f* loquacity, gift of gab

facón·do -da *adj* loquacious

facsìmi·le *m* (-le) facsimile

faènza *f* faïence || **Faenza** *f* Faenza

fàg·gio *m* (-gi) (bot) beech

fagia·no -na *mf* pheasant

fagiolino *m* string bean

fagiòlo *m* bean; (coll) sophomore; **andare a fagiolo** (coll) to fit perfectly; **fagiolo bianco** lima bean

fà·glia *f* (-glie) (geol) fault

fagòtto *m* bundle; (mus) bassoon; **far fagotto** (coll) to pack up

fàida *f* vengeance, vendetta

faìna *f* stone marten

falange *f* phalanx

fal·bo -ba *adj* tawny

falcata *f* step, stride; bucking

falce *f* scythe; crescent (*of moon*); **falce messoria** sickle

falcétto *m* sickle

falciare §128 *tr* to mow

falcia·tóre -trice *mf* mower || *f* mowing machine

falcidiare §287 *tr* to reduce; to cut down

fal·co *m* (-chi) hawk; **falco pescatore** osprey

falcóne *m* falcon

falconeria *f* falconry

falconière *m* falconer

falda *f* band, strip; flake (*of snow*); gable (*of roof*); brim (*of hat*); foot (*of mountain*); slab (*of stone*); waist plate (*of armor*); hem (*of suit*); flounce (*of dress*); layer (*of rock*); flap, coattail; **falda della camicia** shirttail; **falda straps** (*to hold a baby*); **mettersi in falde** to wear tails

falegname *m* carpenter; cabinetmaker

falegnameria *f* carpentry; cabinetmaking; carpenter shop; woodworker shop

falèna *f* moth

falla *f* hole, leak; (archaic) fault

fallace *adj* fallacious, deceptive

fallà·cia *f* (-cie) fallacy

fallare *intr* & *ref* (lit) to be mistaken

fallìbile *adj* fallible

fallimentare *adj* bankrupt; ruinous

fallimènto *m* bankruptcy; (fig) collapse, failure

fallire §176 *tr* to miss (*the target*) || *intr* (ESSERE) to go bankrupt; to fail || *intr* (AVERE) (lit) to be mistaken

falli·to -ta *adj* & *mf* bankrupt

fallo *m* error, fault; sin; flaw; phallus; (sports) penalty; (sports) foul; **cadere in fallo** to make the wrong move; to be mistaken; **cogliere in fallo** to catch in the act; **far fallo a** to fail, e.g., **gli faccio fallo** I fail him; **senza fallo** without fail

fa·lò *m* (-lò) bonfire

falpa·là *f* (-là) flounce, furbelow

falsare *tr* to falsify, alter; (lit) to forge

falsari·ga *f* (-ghe) guideline (*for writing*); model, pattern; **seguire la falsariga di** to follow in the footsteps of

falsà·rio -ria (-ri) forger; counterfeiter

falsétto *m* falsetto

falsificare §197 (**falsìfico**) to falsify; to forge, fake

falsificazióne *f* falsification; forgery; misrepresentation

falsi·tà *f* (-tà) falsehood; falsity

fal·so -sa *adj* false; wrong (*step*); assumed (*name*); bogus, counterfeit, fake (*money*); phony || *m* falsehood; perjury; forgery; **commettere un falso** to perjure oneself; to commit forgery; **giurare il falso** to bear false witness; to perjure oneself

fama *f* fame; reputation; **cattiva fama** notoriety

fame *f* hunger; dearth; **aver fame** to be hungry; **avere una fame da lupo** to be as hungry as a wolf, to be as hungry as a bear; **morire di fame** to starve to death; to be ravenous

famèli·co -ca *adj* (-ci -che) starving, famished

famigera·to -ta *adj* notorious

famìglia *f* family; community; **di famiglia** intimate; **in famiglia** at home

famì·glio *m* (-gli) beadle, usher; hired man

familiare *adj* family; familiar, intimate; homelike || *m* member of the family

familiari·tà *f* (-tà) familiarity; **avere familiarità con** to be familiar with

familiarizzare [ddzz] *tr* to familiarize

famó·so -sa [s] *adj* famous, illustrious

fanale *m* lamp, lantern; (rr) headlight; **fanale di coda** taillight

fanalino *m* small light; (aut) parking light; (aut) tail light

fanàti·co -ca (-ci -che) *adj* fanatic, fanatical || *mf* fanatic

fanatismo *m* fanaticism

fanatizzare [ddzz] *tr* to make a fanatic of

fanciulla *f* girl; spinster; bride

fanciullè·sco -sca *adj* (**-schi -sche**) childish; children's

fanciullézza *f* childhood; (fig) infancy

fanciulo·lo -la *adj* childish; childlike || *mf* child || *m* boy || *f* see **fanciulla**

fandònia *f* fib, tale, yarn

fanèllo *m* (orn) linnet; (orn) finch

fanfara *f* military band; fanfare

fanfaróne *m* braggart

fangatura *f* mud bath

fanghìglia *f* mud, slush

fan·go *m* (**-ghi**) mud; **fare i fanghi** to take mud baths

fangó·so -sa [s] *adj* muddy

fannullo·ne -na *mf* idler, loafer

fanóne *m* whalebone

fantaccino *m* infantryman, foot soldier

fantascientífi·co -ca *adj* (**-ci -che**) science-fiction

fantasciènza *f* science fiction

fantasìa *f* fantasy, fancy, whim; (mus) fantasia; **di fantasia** fancy

fantasió·so -sa [s] *adj* fanciful; imaginative

fanta·sma *m* (**-smi**) ghost, spirit; phantom; **fantasma poetico** poetic fancy

fantasticare §197 (**fantàstico**) *tr* to imagine, dream up || *intr* to daydream

fantastichería *f* imagination, daydreaming

fantàsti·co -ca *adj* (**-ci -che**) fantastic || **fantàstico** *interj* unbelievable!

fante *m* infantryman, foot soldier; (cards) jack; (obs) youth

fanterìa *f* infantry

fanté·sca *f* (**-sche**) (joc, lit) housemaid

fantino *m* jockey

fantòc·cio *m* (**-ci**) puppet

fantomàti·co -ca *adj* (**-ci -che**) ghostly; mysterious

farabutto *m* scoundrel, heel

faraóna *f* guinea fowl

faraóne *m* Pharaoh; (cards) faro

farcire §176 *tr* to stuff

fardèllo *m* bundle; burden; **far fardello** to pack one's bags

fare *m* doing; break (*of day*); way (*of acting*); **sul far della sera** at nightfall || §173 *tr* to do; to make; to work; to take (*e.g., a walk, a step*); to give (*a sigh*); to deal (*cards*); to suffer (*hunger*); to lead (*a good or bad life*); to render (*service*); to log (*e.g., 15 m.p.h.*); to be, e.g., **tre volte tre fa nove** three times three is nine; to build (*e.g., a house*); to put together (*a collection*); to prepare (*dinner*); to say, utter (*a word*); to have (*a dream*); to give (*fruit*); to pay (*atten-*

tion); to play (*a role*); to stir up (*pity*); to mention (*a name*); **fare il** (or **la**) to be a (*e.g., carpenter*); **fare + inf** to have + inf, e.g., **gli ho fatto ...** I had him ...; to make + inf, e.g., **il medico mi fece ...** the doctor made me ...; to have + pp, e.g., **farò fare ...** I shall have ... done; **fare acqua** to leak, to take in water; to get a supply of water; (coll) to urinate; **fare a metà** to divide in half; **fare a pugni** to come to blows; **fare a tempo** to be on time; **fare benzina** to buy gasoline; **fare caldo a** to keep warm, e.g., **questa coperta gli fa caldo** this blanket keeps him warm; **fare carbone** to coal; **fare ... che** to have been ... since, e.g., **fanno tre mesi che siamo in questa città** it has been three months since we have been in this city; **fare che + subj** to see to it that + ind, e.g., **faccia che comincino a lavorare subito** see to it that they begin to work at once; **fare colpo** to make an impression; **fare corona a** to crown; **fare cuore a** to encourage; **fare del male a** to harm; **fare di + inf** to see to it that + ind; **fare di tutto** to do one's best; **fare festa** to cheer; **fare fiasco** to fail; **fare finta di** to pretend to; **fare fronte a** to face, meet; **fare fuoco su** to fire upon; **fare il gioco di** to play into the hands of; **fare il pappagallo** to parrot, ape; **fare il pieno** to fill up (*with gasoline*); **fare la bocca a** to get used to; **fare la calza** to knit; **fare la coda** to queue up, line up; **fare la festa a** to kill; **fare la guardia** to stand guard; **fare la mano a** to get used to; **fare le cose in famiglia** to wash one's dirty linen at home; **fare le cose in grande stile** to splurge; **fare legna** to gather firewood; **fare l'occhio** to become accustomed; **fare mente** to pay attention; **fare onore a** to do honor to; **fare paura a** to frighten; **fare sangue** to bleed; **fare sapere a qlcu** to let s.o. know; **fare scalo** (aer, naut) to make a call; **fare sì che** to act in such a way that; to see to it that; **fare silenzio** to keep silent; **fare specie a** to amaze, e.g., **il tuo comportamento gli fa specie** your behavior amazes him; **fare tesoro di** to prize; **fare una bella figura** to look good; to make a fine appearance; **fare una mala figura** to look bad; to make a bad showing; **fare una malattia** (coll) to get sick; **fare vela** to set sail; **fare venire** to send for; **fare vigilia** to fast; **farla corta** to cut it short; **farla franca** to get off scot-free; **farla grossa** to commit a blunder; **farla in barba a** to outwit; **farne di cotte e di crude, farne di tutti i colori,** or **farne più di Carlo in Francia** to engage in all sorts of mischief; to paint the town red; **non fare che + ind** to do nothing but + inf || *intr*—**averla a che fare con** to have words with; to have to deal with; **fare a coltellate** to have a fight with knives; **fare a girotondo** to play ring-around-the-rosy; **fare al caso di** to fit; to suit; **fare a meno di** to do without; **fare da** to serve as, e.g., **fare da cuscino** to serve as a pillow; **fare da cena** to fix dinner; **fare di cappello** to take one's hat off; **fare presto** to hurry; **fare per** to be just the thing for; **fare tardi** to be late || *ref* to become; to cut (*e.g., one's hair*); to move, e.g., **farsi in là** to move farther; **farsi avanti** to come forward; **farsi beffe di** to make fun of; **farsi bello** to bedeck oneself; to dress up; **farsi bello di** to boast about; to appropriate; **farsi gioco di** to make fun of; **farsi le labbra** to put lipstick on; **farsi strada** to make one's way; **farsi una ragione di** to rationalize, explain to oneself; **farsi un baffo** to not give a hoot; **si fa giorno** it is getting light; **si fa tardi** it is getting late || *impers*—**che tempo fa?** what's the weather like?; **fa** ago, e.g., **alcune settimane fa** a few weeks ago; **fa estate** it is like summer; **fa fino** it is smart; **fa freddo** it is cold; **fa luna** there is moonlight, the moon is out; **fa nebbia**.it is foggy; **fa notte** it is nighttime; it is dark; it is getting dark; **fa sole** it is sunny, the sun is out; **fa tipo** or **fa tono!** that's classy!; **non fa nulla** it doesn't matter, never mind

farètra *f* quiver
farfalla *f* butterfly; bow tie; (mach) butterfly valve; (coll) promissory note
farfallóne *m* large butterfly; blunder; Don Juan
farfugliare §280 *intr* to mumble, mutter
farina *f* flour; **farina d'avena** oatmeal; **farina di legno** sawdust; **farina di ossa** bone meal; **farina gialla** yellow corn meal
farinàce·o -a *adj* farinaceous || **farinacei** *mpl* flour-yielding cereals
farinata *f* porridge
faringe *f* pharynx
faringite *f* pharingitis
farinó·so -sa [s] *adj* floury; powdery (*snow*); crumbly, friable
farisèo *m* Pharisee; (fig) pharisee
farmacèuti·co -ca *adj* (**-ci -che**) pharmaceutical, drug
farmacìa *f* pharmacy; drugstore; medicine cabinet; **farmacia di guardia** or **di turno** drugstore open all night and Sunday
farmaci·sta *mf* (**-sti -ste**) pharmacist, druggist
fàrma·co *m* (**-ci** or **-chi**) remedy, medicine
farneticare §197 (**farnètico**) *intr* to rave
farnèti·co -ca (**-chi -che**) *adj* raving || *m* delirium; craze
faro *m* lighthouse, beacon; (aut) headlight; **faro retromarcia** (aut) back-up light
farràgine *f* hodgepodge
farraginó·so -sa [s] *adj* confused, mixed

farsa *f* farce; burlesque
farsè·sco -sca *adj* (**-schi -sche**) farcical, ludicrous
farsétto *m* sweater; (hist) doublet
fascétta *f* girdle; band; wrapper; clamp; **fascetta editoriale** advertising band (*of book*)
fà·scia *f* (**-sce**) band; belt; bandage; newspaper wrapper; **fascia del cappello** hatband; **fascia di garza** gauze bandage; **fascia elastica** abdominal supporter; (aut) piston ring; **fasce del neonato** swaddling clothes; **in fasce** newborn; **sotto fascia** in a wrapper
fasciame *m* (naut) planking; (naut) plating
fasciare §128 to bind; to bandage; to wrap; to surround
fasciatura *f* bandaging, dressing
fascìcolo *m* number, issue; pamphlet; file, dossier; (bb) fasciculus
fascina *f* fagot
fascina·tóre -trice *mf* charmer
fàscino *m* fascination, charm
fà·scio *m* (**-sci**) bundle; sheaf; bunch (*of flowers*); pencil or beam (*of rays*); fascist party
fascismo *m* fascism
fasci·sta *adj & mf* (**-sti -ste**) fascist
fase *f* phase, stage; (aut) cycle; (astr, elec, mach) phase
fastèllo *m* bundle, fagot
fasti *mpl* records, annals; notable events; (hist) Roman calendar
fastì·dio *m* (**-di**) annoyance; (coll) loathing, nausea; **avere in fastidio** to loathe; **dar fastidio a** to annoy; **fastidi** troubles, worries
fastidió·so -sa [s] *adj* annoying, irksome; irritable; (obs) disgusting
fastì·gio *m* (**-gi**) top, summit
fa·sto -sta *adj* (lit) propitious || *m invar* pomp, display || *mpl* see **fasti**
fastó·so -sa [s] *adj* pompous, ostentatious
fata *f* fairy; **buona fata** fairy godmother; **Fata Morgana** Fata Morgana (*mirage; Morgan le Fay*)
fatale *adj* fatal; inevitable; irresistible (*woman*)
fatalismo *m* fatalism
fatali·sta *mf* (**-sti -ste**) fatalist
fatali·tà *f* (**-tà**) fatality, fate
fatalóna *f* vamp
fata·to -ta *adj* fairy, enchanted; (lit) predestined
fatì·ca *f* (**-che**) fatigue, weariness; labor; **a fatica** with difficulty; **da fatica** draft (*e.g., horse*); of burden (*beast*); **durar fatica a** + *inf* to have trouble in + *ger*
faticare §197 *intr* to toil; **faticare a** to be hardly able to
faticó·so -sa [s] *adj* burdensome, heavy; (lit) weary
fatìdi·co -ca *adj* (**-ci -che**) fatal
fato *m* fate, destiny
fatta *f* kind, sort; **essere sulla fatta di** to be on the trail of
fattàc·cio *m* (**-ci**) (coll) crime
fattézze *fpl* features

fattìbile *adj* feasible, possible

fattispècie *f*—**nella fattispecie** in this particular case

fat·to -ta *adj* made, e.g., **fatto a mano** handmade; broad (*daylight*); deep (*night*); ready-made (*e.g., suit*); **ben fatto** well-done; shapely; **esser fatto per** to be cut out for; **fatto di** made of; **venir fatto a** to happen, chance, e.g., **gli venne fatto d'incontrarmi** he happened to meet me ‖ *m* fact; act, deed; feat; action; business, affair; **badare ai fatti propri** to mind one's own business; **cogliere sul fatto** to catch in the act; **dire a qlcu il fatto suo** to give s.o. a piece of one's mind; **fatto compiuto** fait accompli; **fatto d'arme** feat of arms; **fatto si è** the fact remains that; **in fatto di** concerning; as of; **sapere il fatto proprio** to know one's business; **venire al fatto** to come to the point ‖ *f* see **fatta**

fat·tóre -tóra or **-toréssa** *mf* farm manager ‖ *m* maker; factor; steward ‖ *f* stewardess; manager's wife

fattoria *f* farm; stewardship

fattorino *m* delivery boy, messenger boy; conductor (*of streetcar*)

fattrice *f* (zool) dam

fattucchiè·re -ra *mf* magician ‖ *m* sorcerer ‖ *f* sorceress, witch

fattura *f* preparation; workmanship; bill, invoice; (coll) witchcraft; (lit) creature

fatturare *tr* to adulterate; to invoice, bill

fattura·to -ta *adj* adulterated ‖ *m* (com) turnover

fatturi·sta *mf* (**-sti -ste**) billing clerk

fà·tuo -tua *adj* fatuous

fàuci *fpl* jaws; (fig) mouth

fàuna *f* fauna

fàuno *m* faun

fàu·sto -sta *adj* propitious, lucky

fau·tóre -trice *mf* supporter, promoter

fava *f* broad bean; **pigliare due piccioni con una fava** to catch two birds with one stone

favèlla *f* speech; (lit) tongue

favilla *f* spark; **far** or **mandare faville** to sparkle

favo *m* honeycomb

fàvola *f* fable; tale; **favola del paese** talk of the town

favoló·so -sa [s] *adj* fabulous; mythical

favóre *m* favor; help; cover (*e.g., of night*); **a favore di** for the benefit of; **di favore** special (*price*); complimentary (*ticket*); **favore politico** patronage; **per favore** please; **per favore di** courtesy of

favoreggiaménto *m* abetting, support

favoreggiare §290 (**favoréggio**) *tr* to abet, support

favoreggia·tóre -trice *mf* abettor, supporter, backer

favorévole *adj* favorable; propitious

favorire §176 *tr* to favor; to accept; to oblige, accommodate; **favorire qlcu di qlco** to oblige s.o. with s.th; **favorisca** + *inf* please + *inf*, be kind

enough to + *inf*; **favorisca alla cassa** please pay the cashier; **favorisca uscire!** please leave!; **tanto per favorire** just to keep you company; **vuol favorire?** won't you please join us (*at a meal*)?; please help yourself!

favorita *f* royal mistress

favoritismo *m* favoritism

favori·to -ta *adj & mf* favorite ‖ *m* protegé; **favoriti** sideburns ‖ *f* see **favorita**

fazióne *f* faction; **essere di fazione** to be on guard duty

fazió·so -sa [s] *adj* factious ‖ *m* partisan

fazzolétto *m* handkerchief; **fazzoletto da collo** neckerchief

fé *f* var of **fede**

feb·bràio *m* (**-brài**) February

fèbbre *f* fever; fever blister; **febbre da cavallo** (coll) very high fever; **febbre da fieno** hay fever; **febbre dell'oro** gold fever

febbricitante *adj* feverish

febbrile *adj* feverish

Fèbo *m* Phoebus

féc·cia *f* (**-ce**) dregs; (fig) dregs (*of society*); **fino alla feccia** to the bitter end

fèci *fpl* feces

fècola *f* starch

fecondare (**fecóndo**) *tr* to fecundate

fecondazióne *f* fecundation; **fecondazione artificiale** artificial insemination

fecondi·tà *f* (**-tà**) fecundity

fecón·do -da *adj* fecund, prolific

féde *f* faith; certificate; wedding ring; faithfulness; **far fede** to bear witness; **in fede di che** in testimony whereof; **in fede mia!** upon my word! **prestar fede a** to put one's faith in; **tener fede alla parola data** to keep one's word

fedecommésso *m* fideicommissum; trusteeship

fedéle *adj* faithful, devoted ‖ *mf* faithful person; **i fedeli** the faithful

fedel·tà *f* (**-tà**) faithfulness, allegiance; fidelity; **ad alta fedeltà** hi-fi

fèdera *f* pillowcase

federale *adj* federal

federali·sta *mf* (**-sti -ste**) federalist

federati·vo -va *adj* federative

federa·to -ta *adj* federate, federated

federazióne *f* federation; (sports) league

Federico *m* Frederick

fedìfra·go -ga *adj* (**-ghi -ghe**) unfaithful, treacherous

fedina *f* police record; **avere la fedina sporca** to have a bad record; **fedine** sideburns

fégato *m* liver; courage; **fegato d'oca** pâté de foie gras; **rodersi il fegato** to be consumed with rage

féice *f* fern

feldspato *m* feldspar

felice *adj* happy; blissful; glad; felicitous

felici·tà *f* (**-tà**) happiness; bliss

felicitare (**felicìto**) *tr* to make happy; **che Dio vi feliciti!** God bless you! ‖

ref to rejoice; **felicitarsi con qlcu per qlco** to congratulate s.o. for or on s.th

felicitazióne *f* congratulation

felì·no -na *adj & m* feline

fellóne *m* (lit) traitor

félpa *f* plush

felpa·to -ta *adj* covered with plush; soft (*e.g., step*)

féltro *m* felt; felt hat

felu·ca *f* (-che) two-cornered hat; (naut) felucca

fémmina *adj & f* female

femminile *adj* feminine, female || *m* feminine gender

femminili·tà *f* (-tà) femininity, womanliness

femminismo *m* feminism

fèmore *m* femur; thighbone

fendènte *m* slash with a sword

fèndere §174 *tr* to split, cleave; to plow (*water*); to rend (*air*); to make one's way through (*a crowd*) || *ref* to split; to come apart

fenditura *f* split, breach, fissure

fenice *f* phoenix

fenì·cio -cia (-ci -cie) *adj & mf* Phoenician || **la Fenicia** Phoenicia

fèni·co -ca *adj* (-ci -che) carbolic

fenicòttero *m* flamingo

fenòlo *m* phenol

fenomenale *adj* phenomenal

fenòmeno *m* phenomenon; freak, monster; **essere un fenomeno** to be unbelievable

ferace *adj* (lit) fertile

ferale *adj* (lit) mortal, deadly

fèretro *m* bier, coffin

feriale *adj* working (*day*); weekday

fèrie *fpl* vacation; **ferie retribuite** vacation with pay

ferire §176 *tr* to wound; to strike; **senza colpo ferire** without striking a blow || *ref* to wound oneself

ferì·to -ta *adj* wounded, injured || *m* wounded person; injured person; **i feriti** the wounded; the injured || *f* wound, injury

feritóia *f* loophole; embrasure

feri·tóre -trice *mf* assailant

fèrma *f* setting (*of setter or pointer*); (mil) service; (mil) enlistment

fermacarro *m* (rr) buffer

fermacar·te *m* (-te) paperweight; large paper clip

fermacravat·ta *m* (-ta) tiepin

fermà·glio *m* (-gli) clasp; buckle; clip; brooch

fermare (**férmo**) *tr* to stop; to pay (*attention*); to fasten; to close, shut; to detain (*in police station*); to set (*game*); to reserve (*seats*) || *ref* to stop; to stay

fermata *f* stop; **fermata a richiesta** or **facoltativa** stop on signal

fermentare (**ferménto**) *tr & intr* to ferment

fermentazióne *f* fermentation

ferménto *m* ferment

fermézza *f* firmness; steadfastness

fér·mo -ma *adj* firm; stopped; quiet (*water*); (fig) steadfast; **fermo in**

posta general delivery; **fermo restando che** seeing that; **stare fermo** to be quiet || *m* stop; detention; **mettere il fermo a** to stop (*a check*)

fermopòsta *m* general delivery || *adv* care of general delivery

feróce *adj* fierce; wild

feró·cia *f* (-cie) ferocity, ferociousness, fierceness

feròdo *m* (aut) brake lining

ferragósto *m* Assumption; mid-August holiday

ferrame *m* ironware

ferramén·to *m* (-ti) iron or metal bracket; iron or metal trimming || *m* (-ta *fpl*)—**ferramenta** hardware

ferrare (**fèrro**) *tr* to shoe (*a horse*); to hoop (*a barrel*)

ferra·to -ta *adj* iron; ironclad; shod (*horse*); spiked (*shoe*); well-versed || *f* pressing, ironing; mark or burn (*caused by ironing*); (coll) iron grate

ferravèc·chio *m* (-chi) scrap-iron dealer, junkman

fèrre·o -a *adj* iron; ironclad

ferrièra *f* ironworks; (obs) iron mine

fèrro *m* iron; tool; anchor; sword; **al ferri** on the grill, broiled (*e.g., steak*); **essere sotto i ferri del chirurgo** to go under the knife; **ferri** shackles; **ferri del mestiere** tools of the trade; **ferro battuto** wrought iron; **ferro da arricciare** curling iron; **ferro da calza** knitting needle; **ferro da cavallo** horseshoe; **ferro da stiro** iron, flatiron; **ferro fuso** cast iron; **ferro grezzo** pig iron; **mettere a ferro e fuoco** to put to fire and sword; **venire ai ferri corti** to get into close quarters

ferromodellismo *m* hobby of model railroads

ferrotranvièri *mpl* transport workers

ferrovìa *f* railroad; **ferrovia a dentiera** rack railway; **ferrovia sopraelevata** elevated railroad

ferrovià·rio -ria *adj* (-ri -rie) railroad

ferrovière *m* railroader

fèrtile *adj* fertile

fertilizzante [ddzz] *adj* fertilizing || *m* fertilizer

fertilizzare [ddzz] *tr* to fertilize

fervènte *adj* fervent

fervere §175 *intr* to be fervent; to rage (*said, e.g., of a battle*); to go full blast

fèrvi·do -da *adj* fervent

fervóre *m* fervor; (fig) heat

fervorino *m* lecture, sermon

fesserìa *f* (slang) stupidity, nonsense; (slang) trifle

fés·so -sa *adj* cracked; cleft; (slang) dumb || *m* (lit) cranny; **fare fesso qlcu** (slang) to play s.o. for a sucker

fessura *f* crack; cranny

fèsta *f* feast; holiday; birthday; saint's day; **a festa** festively; **buone feste!** happy holiday!; **conciare per le feste** to drub the daylights out of; **fare festa a** to welcome; **fare le feste** to spend the holidays; **far festa** to celebrate; to take the day off; **far la festa**

a to do in, kill; **festa del ceppo** Christmas; **festa da ballo** or **danzante** dancing party; **festa della mamma** Mother's Day; **festa del papà** Father's Day; **festa di precetto** (eccl) day of obligation; **festa nazionale** national holiday; **mezza festa** half holiday

festante *adj* cheerful

festeggiaménto *m* celebration

festeggiare §290 (festéggio) *tr* to celebrate, fete; to cheer

festi·no -na *adj* (lit) rapid || *m* party

festivi·tà *f* (-tà) festivity

festi·vo -va *adj* festive, holiday

festóne *m* festoon

festó·so -sa [s] *adj* cheerful, merry

festu·ca *f* (-che) straw; (fig) mote

fetènte *adj* stinking; stink (*bomb*) || *mf* (fig) stinker, louse

fetìc·cio *m* (-ci) fetish

feticismo *m* fetishism

fèti·do -da *adj* stinking, fetid

fèto *m* fetus

fetóre *m* stench

fétta *f* slice; **tagliare a fette** to slice

fettìna *f* thin slice; twist (*of lemon*); **fettina di vitello** veal cutlet

fettùc·cia *f* (-ce) tape, ribbon

fettuccìne *fpl* noodles

feudale *adj* feudal

feudalismo *m* feudalism

feudatà·rio -ria (-ri -rie) *adj* feudatory || *m* feudal vassal

fèudo *m* fief

fiaba *f* fairy tale; tale, yarn

fiacca *f* tiredness; sluggishness; **batter la fiacca** to loaf, to goof off

fiaccare §197 *tr* to weaken; to weary; to break || *ref* to weaken; to break (*e.g., one's neck*)

fiacche·ràio *m* (-rài) (coll) hackman, cabman

fiacchézza *f* weakness; sluggishness

fiàc·co -ca *adj* (-chi -che) weak; sluggish; slack || *f* see **fiacca**

fiàccola *f* torch; **fiaccola della discordia** firebrand

fiaccolata *f* torchlight procession

fiala *f* vial, phial

fiamma *f* flame; blaze; (mil) insignia; (nav) pennant; **alla fiamma** (culin) flaming; **dare alle fiamme** to set on fire; **diventare di fiamma** to blush; **in fiamme** afire

fiammante *adj* blazing; **nuovo fiammante** brand-new

fiammata *f* blaze; flare-up

fiammeggiante *adj* flaming, blazing; (archit) flamboyant

fiammeggiare §290 (fiamméggio) *tr* to singe || *intr* to flame, blaze

fiammìfero *m* match

fiammìn·go -ga (-ghi -ghe) *adj* Flemish; Dutch (*e.g., master*) || *mf* Fleming || *m* Flemish (*language*); (orn) flamingo

fiancata *f* blow with one's hip; dig, sarcastic remark; side, flank; (nav) broadside

fiancheggiare §290 (fianchéggio) *tr* to flank; to border (*a road*); to support

fiancheggia·tóre -trice *mf* supporter, backer

fiàn·co *m* (-chi) flank, side; hip; **di fianco** sideways; **fianco a fianco** side by side; **fianco destr'l** (mil) right face!; **fianco destro** (naut) starboard; **fianco sinistr'l** (mil) left face!; **fianco sinistro** (naut) port; **prestare il fianco a** to leave oneself wide open to; **tenersi i fianchi dal ridere** to split one's sides laughing

Fiandre, le *fpl* Flanders

fia·sca *f* (-sche) flask

fiaschetterìa *f* tavern, wine shop

fia·sco *m* (-schi) straw-covered wine bottle; flask; fiasco

fiata *f* (archaic) time

fiatare *intr* to breathe; **senza fiatare** without breathing a word

fiato *m* breath; (archaic) stench; **avere il fiato grosso** to be out of breath; **bere d'un fiato** to gulp down; **col fiato sospeso** holding one's breath; **dare fiato a** to blow, sound (*a trumpet*); **d'un fiato** or **in un fiato** without interruption; in one gulp; **fiati** (mus) winds; **senza fiato** out of breath

fiatóne *m*—**avere il fiatone** to be out of breath

fìbbia *f* clasp, buckle

fibra *f* fiber

fibró·so -sa [s] *adj* fibrous

ficcana·so [s] *mf* (-si *mpl* -so *fpl*) (coll) busybody, meddler; nosy person

ficcare §197 *tr* to stick; to drive (*e.g., a nail*); to push; **ficcare gli occhi addosso a** to gaze at, stare at; **ficcare il naso negli affari degli altri** to poke one's nose in other people's business || *ref* to hide; to butt in; to get involved

fì·co *m* (-chi) fig; fig tree

ficodindia *m* (*pl* fichidindia) prickly pear

fidanzaménto *m* engagement, betrothal

fidanzare *tr* to betroth || *ref* to become engaged

fidanza·to -ta *adj* engaged || *m* fiancé || *f* fiancée

fidare *tr* to entrust || *intr* to trust || *ref* to have confidence; **fidarsi a** (coll) to dare to; **fidarsi di** to trust, rely on

fida·to -ta *adj* trustworthy, reliable

fì·do -da *adj* (lit) faithful, trusted || *m* loyal follower; credit; **far fido** to extend credit

fidùcia *f* faith, confidence; (com) credit; **di fiducia** trustworthy

fiducià·rio -ria (-ri -rie) *adj* fiduciary || *mf* fiduciary, trustee

fidució·so -sa [s] *adj* confident, hopeful

fièle *m* *invar* gall, bile; acrimony

fienìle *m* hayloft

fièno *m* hay

fierìsti·co -ca *adj* (-ci -che) of a fair, e.g., **attività fieristica** activity of a fair

fiè·ro -ra *adj* fierce; dignified; proud || *f* fair; exhibit; wild beast

fièvole adj feeble, weak

fifa f (coll) scare; **avere la fifa** (coll) to be chicken; **avere una fifa blu** (coll) to be scared stiff

fifó·ne -na mf (coll) scaredy-cat

figgere §104 tr (lit) to drive, thrust || ref—**figgersi in capo** to get into one's head

figlia f daughter; (com) stub; **figlia consanguinea** stepdaughter on the father's side

figliare §280 tr & intr to whelp (said of animals)

figlia·stro -stra mf stepchild || m stepson || f stepdaughter

figliata f litter (e.g., of pigs)

fi·glio -glia mf child, offspring || m son; **figli** children; **figlio consanguineo** stepson on the father's side || f see **figlia**

figliòc·cio -cia (-ci -ce) mf godchild || m godson || f goddaughter

figliolanza f children, offspring

figliò·lo -la mf child || m son, boy || f daughter, girl

figura f figure; illustration; figurehead; face card; **far bella figura** to make a good showing; **far cattiva figura** to make a poor showing; **far figura** to look good; **figura retorica** figure of speech

figurante mf (theat) extra, super

figurare tr to feign; to represent || intr to figure; to appear; to make a good showing || ref to imagine; **si figuri!** imagine!

figurati·vo -va adj (fa) figurative

figura·to -ta adj figurative (speech); transcribed (pronunciation); illustrated (book)

figurina f figurine; card, picture (of a series of athletes or entertainment celebrities)

figurini·sta mf (-sti -ste) dress designer; costume designer

figurino m fashion plate; fashion magazine

figuro m scoundrel; gangster

figuróne m—**fare un figurone** to make a very good showing

fila f row; file, line; series; **di fila in a row**; **fare la fila** to wait in line; **file ranks**

filàc·cia f (-ce) lint

filacció·so -sa [s] or **filaccio·so -sa** [s] adj thready, stringy

filamento m filament

filamentó·so -sa [s] adj thready, stringy; thread-like

filanda f spinning mill; silk spinning mill

filante adj spinning; shooting (star); thready; flowing (e.g., line)

filantropia f philanthropy

filantròpi·co -ca adj (-ci -che) philanthropic

filàntro·po -pa mf philanthropist

filare m row, line || tr to spin; to drip, ooze; to rest on (one's oars); to make (e.g., ten knots); (naut) to pay out; (mus) to hold (a note); **filare l'amore** to be in love || intr to spin (said of a spider); to rope, thread (said of wine

or syrup); to make sense; to drip; **fare filare dritto qlcu** to keep s.o. in line; **filare a to do** (e.g., twenty miles an hour); **filare all'inglese** to take French leave; **fila via!** (coll) get out!

filarmòni·co -ca (-ci -che) adj philharmonic || f philharmonic society

filastròc·ca f (-che) rigmarole; nursery rhyme

filatelìa f philately

filatèli·co -ca (-ci -che) adj philatelic(al) || mf philatelist

fila·to -ta adj spun; well-constructed (speech) || m yarn

fila·tóio m (-tói) spinning wheel

filatura f spinning; spinning mill

filettare (filétto) tr to fillet; (mach) to thread

filettatura f stripe (on a cap); (mach) thread

filétto m fillet; stripe; snaffle (on a horse's bit); fine stroke (in handwriting); (mach) thread; (typ) ornamental line, headband; (typ) rule

filiale adj filial || f branch office

filiazióne f filiation

filibustière m filibuster, buccaneer; adventurer

filièra f (mach) drawplate; (mach) die (to cut threads)

filigrana f filigree; watermark (in paper)

filippi·no -na adj Philippine || m Filipino || **le Filippine** the Philippines

Filippo m Philip

filistè·o -a adj & m philistine; Philistine

Fìllide f Phyllis

film m (film) film; movie, motion picture; **film parlato** or **sonoro** talking picture

filmare tr to film

filmina f filmstrip

filmìsti·co -ca adj (-ci -che) movie, motion-picture

filmotè·ca f (-che) film library

fi·lo m (-li) thread; wire; yarn; blade (of grass); breath (of air); string (of pearls); edge (of razor); **dare del filo da torcere** to cause trouble; **essere ridotto a un filo** to be only skin and bones; **fil di voce** thin voice; **filo a piombo** plumb line; **filo d'acqua** thin stream; **filo della schiena** or **delle reni** spine; **filo spinato** barbed wire; **passare a fil di spada** to put to the sword; **per filo e per segno** in detail; from beginning to end; **senza fili** wireless; **stare a filo** to stand upright; **tenere i fili** (fig) to pull wires; **tenere in filo** to keep in line; **un filo di** a bit of || m (-la fpl) string (e.g., of cooked cheese); (archaic) file, row

filo·bus m (-bus) trolley bus

filodiffusióne f wired wireless; cable TV

filodrammàti·co -ca adj & mf (-ci -che) (theat) amateur

filogovernati·vo -va adj on the government side

filologìa f philology

filòlo·go -ga (-gi -ghe) adj philologic(al) || m philologist

filóne m vein (of ore); ripple (of a cur-

rent); stream; loaf (*of bread*); (lit) mainstream; **filone d'oro** gold lode
filó·so -sa [s] *adj* stringy
filosofìa *f* philosophy
filosòfi·co -ca *adj* (**-ci -che**) philosophic(al)
filòso·fo -fa *mf* philosopher
filovìa *f* trolley bus line
filtrare *tr* to filter; to percolate (*coffee*) || *intr* to filter, permeate
filtrazióne *f* filtering, filtration
filtro *m* filter; philter
filugèllo *m* silkworm
filza *f* string (*of pearls*); series (*of errors*); row; dossier, file; basting (*of dress*)
finale *adj* final, last; consumer (*goods*) || *m* end, ending; (mus) finale; (sports) finish || *f* end, ending; (sports) finals
finali·sta *mf* (**-sti -ste**) finalist
finali·tà *f* (**-tà**) end, purpose
finanche *adv* even
finanza *f* finance
finanziaménto *m* financing
finanziare §287 *tr* to finance
finanzià·rio -ria (**-ri -rie**) *adj* finance, financial || *f* (com) holding company
finanzia·tóre -trice *mf* financial backer
finanzièra *f* frock coat; **alla finanziera** with giblet gravy
finanzière *m* financier; (coll) customs officer
fin·ca *f* (**-che**) column, row (*of ledger*)
finché *conj* until, as long as; **finché non** until
fine *adj* fine, thin; choice, nice || *m* end, purpose; conclusion; (lit) limit, border; **a fin di bene** to good purpose, for the best; **secondo fine** ulterior motive || *f* end, conclusion; **condurre a fine** to bring to fruition; **fine di settimana** weekend; **in fin dei conti** after all; **senza fine** endless
fine-settimà·na *m* or *f* (**-na**) weekend
finèstra *f* window; (lit) gash, wound; **finestra a ganghero** casement window; **finestra a ghigliottina** sash window; **finestra panoramica** picture window; **finestre** (lit) eyes
finestrino *m* (aut, rr) window
finézza *f* thinness; delicacy; finesse; kindness
fìngere §126 *tr* to feign, pretend; (lit) to invent || *intr* to feign, pretend || *ref* to pretend to be
finiménto *m* finishing touch; **finimenti** harness
finimóndo *m* fracas, uproar
finìre §176 *tr* to end; to put an end to; **finìscila!** cut it out! || *intr* (ESSERE) to end, to be over; to abut; to wind up; **finire con** + *inf* to wind up + *ger*; **finire di** + *inf* to finish + *ger*, e.g., **ho finito di farmi la barba** I have finished shaving
finì·to -ta *adj* finished; accomplished; finite; exhausted; **aver finito** to be through; **falla finita!** cut it out!; **farla finita con** to be through with; **farla finita con la vita** to end one's life
finitura *f* finish, finishing touch

finlandése [s] *adj* Finnish || *mf* Finlander, Finn || *m* Finnish (*language*)
Finlàndia, la Finland
fìnni·co -ca *adj* & *mf* (**-ci -che**) Finnic
fì·no -na *adj* fine, thin; refined; pure; sheer; **fare fino** (coll) to be refined || *adv* even; **fin a quando?** till when?; **fin da domani** beginning tomorrow; **fin da ora** beginning right now; **fin dove?** how far?; **fin in cima** up to the top; **fino a** until; down to; up to; as far as; **fin qui** up to now; up to this point
finòc·chio *m* (**-chi**) fennel; (vulg) fairy, queer
finóra *adv* up to now, heretofore
finta *f* pretense; fly (*of trousers*); (sports) feint; **far finta di** + *inf* to pretend to + *inf*, to feign + *ger*
fintantoché *conj* until
fìn·to -ta *adj* false (*teeth*); fake; fictitious; sham (*battle*) || *mf* hypocrite || *f* see **finta**
finzióne *f* pretense; fiction; figment
fìo *m*—**pagare il fio** to pay the piper; **pagare il fio di** to pay the penalty for
fioccare §197 (**fiòcco**) *intr* (ESSERE) to fall (*said of snow*); to flow (*said, e.g., of complaints*) || *impers* (ESSERE) —**fiocca** it is snowing
fiòc·co *m* (**-chi**) bow, knot; flake (*of snow*); flock, tuft (*of wool*); (naut) jib; **coi fiocchi** excellent; made to perfection; **fiocco pallone** (naut) spinnaker
fioccó·so -sa [s] *adj* flaky
fiòcina *f* harpoon
fiò·co -ca *adj* (**-chi -che**) feeble, faint
fiónda *f* sling; slingshot
fio·ràio -ràia (**-rài -ràie**) *mf* florist || *f* flower girl
fiorami *mpl*—**a fiorami** with flower design
fiordalìso *m* fleur-de-lis; (bot) iris; (lit) lily
fiòrdo *m* fjord
fióre *m* flower; prime (*of life*); best, pick; bloom; **a fior d'acqua** on the surface; skimming the water; **a fior di labbra** in a low tone, sottovoce; **a fior di pelle** skin-deep, superficial; **fior di** (coll) a lot of; **fiore di latte** cream; **fiori** (cards) clubs; **primo fiore** down (*soft hairy growth*)
fiorènte *adj* flourishing, thriving
fiorentì·no -na *adj* & *mf* Florentine
fiorettare (**fiorétto**) *tr* (fig) to overembellish
fiorétto *m* little flower; choice, pick; overembellishment; choice passage (*from life of saint*); foil; button of foil
fioricoltóre *m* var of **floricoltore**
fioricoltura *f* var of **floricoltura**
fiorino *m* florin
fiorìre §176 *tr* to cause to flower; to adorn with flowers || *intr* (ESSERE) to flower, bloom; to flourish; to break out (*said of skin eruption*); to get moldy
fiorì·sta *mf* (**-sti -ste**) florist
fiorì·to -ta *adj* flowering; flowery;

mottled; moldy; studded (e.g., with errors)

fioritura f flowering; flourish; mold; (pathol) eruption

fiorrancino m (orn) kinglet, firecrest

fiorràn·cio m (-ci) marigold

fiòtto m gush, surge; (obs) wave

Firènze f Florence

firma f signature; power of attorney; good reputation; (mil) enlisted man; **buona firma** famous writer; **farci la firma** (coll) to accept quite willingly; **firma di favore** guarantor's signature

firmaiòlo m (mil) enlisted man

firmaménto m firmament

firmare tr to sign

firmatà·rio -ria (-ri -rie) adj signatory || mf signer, signatory

fisarmòni·ca f (-che) accordion

fiscale adj fiscal, tax

fischiare §287 tr to whistle; to boo || intr to whistle; to ring (said of ears); to blow (said, e.g., of a factory whistle)

fischiettare (fischiétto) tr & intr to whistle

fischiétto m whistle (instrument)

fi·schio m (-schi) whistle; hiss, boo; blow (of whistle); ringing (in the ears)

fi·sciù m (-sciù) kerchief, fichu

fisco m invar treasury; internal revenue service

fìsi·co -ca (-ci -che) adj physical; bodily || m physicist; physique; (obs) physician || f physics

fìsima f whim, fancy, caprice

fisiologìa f physiology

fisiològi·co -ca adj (-ci -che) physiological

fisionomìa or **fisonomìa** f physiognomy; countenance, face; appearance

fisionomi·sta mf (-sti -ste) person good at faces; physiognomist

fì·so -sa adj (lit) fixed

fissàg·gio m (-gi) (phot) fixing

fissare tr to fix; to fasten; to gaze at; to reserve; to hire; **fissare lo sguardo** to gaze || ref to gaze, stare; to become obsessed; to settle down

fissatì·vo -va adj fixing

fissa·to -ta adj fixed; (coll) cracked || mf (coll) crackpot

fissa·tóre -trice adj (phot) fixing || m fixer; **fissatore per capelli** hair spray; hair dressing

fissazióne f fixation; fixed idea

fissile adj fissionable

fissionàbile adj fissionable

fissióne f fission

fis·so -sa adj fixed; regular || m pay

fìstola f (pathol) fistula; (lit) pipe

fitta f pang, stitch; crowd; great amount; (coll) blow; (obs) quagmire

fittàvolo m tenant farmer

fitti·zio -zia adj (-zi -zie) fictitious

fit·to -ta adj fixed, dug in; thick, dense; pitch (dark) || m thick; rent; tenancy || f see **fitta**

fittóne m (bot) taproot

fiuma·no -na adj river; from Fiume || m person from Fiume || f flood, stream

fiumara f torrent

fiume m river; **a fiumi** like a river

fiutare tr to snuff, sniff; to smell

fiutata f snuff, sniff

fiuto m sense of smell; snuff; flair

flàcci·do -da adj flabby

flacóne m flacon

flagellare (flagèllo) tr to scourge, lash, flagellate

flagèllo m whip, scourge; pest, plague; (coll) mess

flagrante adj flagrant; **in flagrante (delitto)** in the act

flan m (flan) pudding; (typ) mat

flanèlla f flannel

flàn·gia f (-ge) flange

flato m gas, flatus

flatulènza f flatulence

flautino m flageolet

flauti·sta mf (-sti -ste) flutist

flàuto m flute; **flauto diritto** or **dolce** (mus) recorder

fla·vo -va adj (lit) blond, golden

flèbile adj mournful

flebite f phlebitis

flèmma f apathy; coolness; phlegm

flemmàti·co -ca adj (-ci -che) phlegmatic(al)

flessìbile adj flexible, pliable

flessióne f bending; (com) fall, drop; (gram) inflection

flessuó·so -sa [s] adj lithe, willowy; winding; flowing (style)

flèttere §177 tr to flex; (gram) to inflect

flirtare intr to flirt

flòra f flora

floreale adj floral

floricoltóre m floriculturist

floricoltura f floriculture

flòri·do -da adj florid; flourishing

flò·scio -scia adj (-sci -sce) flabby; soft (hat)

flòtta f fleet

flottante adj floating || m (com) floating stock

flottare (flòtto) tr & intr to float

flottìglia f flottilla

fluènte adj flowing

fluidità f fluidity

flùi·do -da adj & m fluid; fluent (style)

fluire §176 intr (ESSERE) to flow; to pour

fluitazióne f log driving

fluorescènte adj fluorescent

fluorescènza f fluorescence

fluorìdri·co -ca adj (-ci -che) hydrofluoric

fluorite f fluor, fluorite

fluorizzazióne [ddzz] f fluoridation

fluòro m fluorine

fluoruro m fluoride

flusso m flow; flood (of tide); high tide; (pathol) flow (e.g., of blood); (phys) flux

flutto m (lit) wave

fluttuare (flùttuo) intr to fluctuate; to bob, toss; to waver; to surge, stream

fluviale adj fluvial, river

fobìa f phobia

fò·ca f (-che) seal; sealskin

focàc·cia f (-ce) flat, rounded loaf; cake

focaccina f bun

fo·càia adj fem (-càie) flint

focale adj focal

fóce f mouth (of river)

focèna f porpoise

fochi·sta m (-sti) fireman, stoker; fireworks manufacturer

foco·làio m (-lài) (pathol) focus; (fig) hotbed

focolare m hearth; firebox; fireside, home

focó·so -sa [s] adj fiery, high-spirited

fòdera f lining (of suit); cover, case

foderare (fòdero) tr to line; to cover

fòdero m sheath, scabbard; raft

fó·ga f (-ghe) ardor, impetus

fòg·gia f (-ge) fashion, shape; a foggia di shaped like

foggiare §290 (fòggio) tr to shape, fashion

fòglia f leaf; petal; foil (of gold); mangiare la foglia (fig) to get wise, catch on

fogliame m foliage

fò·glio m (-gli) sheet; bill, banknote; folio; newspaper; permit; foglio d'avviso notice; foglio di congedo (mil) discharge; foglio d'iscrizione application; foglio di via (mil) travel orders; foglio modello blank form; foglio rosa (aut) permit; foglio volante flier, handbill

fógna f sewer, drain

fognatura f sewerage

fòla f tale, fable

fola·ga f (-ghe) (zool) coot

folata f gust; (lit) flight (of birds)

folclóre m folklore

folgorante adj striking; flashing; meteoric (career)

folgorare (fólgoro) tr to strike (with lightning) || intr to flash by || impers —folgora it is thundering

fólgore m (lit) thunderbolt || f flash of lightning; thunderbolt

fólla f crowd; (fig) flock

follare (fòllo) tr to full

fòlle adj mad, crazy; (aut) neutral; (mach) loose (pulley)

folleggiare §290 (follèggio) intr to act foolishly; to frolic

follemente adv desperately, madly

follétto m elf; little imp

follìa f madness, lunacy; folly; alla follia madly; far follie per to be crazy about

follìcolo m follicle

fól·to -ta adj thick; beetle (brow); deep (night) || m depth (e.g., of the night); thick (e.g., of the battle)

fomentare (foménto) tr to foment

fòmite m (lit) instigation; impetus

fónda f anchorage; lowland; saddlebag; alla fonda at anchor

fónda·co m (-chi) (hist) warehouse

fondale m depth (of river, sea); (theat) backdrop

fondamentale adj fundamental, basic

fondamén·to m (-ti) ground, foundation; basis; fare fondamento su to count on; fondamenti elements; senza fondamento baseless; without getting anywhere || m (-ta fpl)—fondamenta foundations (of a building)

fondare (fóndo) tr to found; to build; to charter || ref—fondarsi su to rely on; to be based upon

fondatézza f basis, ground, foundation

fonda·to -ta adj well-founded

fonda·tóre -trice mf founder

fondazióne f foundation

fondèllo m bottom, base

fondènte m flux

fóndere §178 tr to smelt; to melt; to blow (a fuse); to cast (a statue); to blend (colors) || intr to melt; to blend || ref to melt; to blend; to burn out

fondería f foundry

fondià·rio -ria (-ri -rie) adj real-estate, land || f real-estate tax

fondina f holster; (coll) soup dish

fondi·sta mf (-sti -ste) editorialist; (sports) long-distance runner

fóndita f (typ) font

fonditóre m smelter, founder

fón·do -da adj deep || m bottom; fund; innermost nature; seat; end; background; land, property; a doppio fondo with a false bottom; a fondo thoroughly; a fondo perduto as an outright grant; dar fondo (naut) to cast anchor; dar fondo a to exhaust; di fondo (journ) editorial; (sports) long-distance; fondi funds; lees; fondi di bottega remnants; fondi di caffè coffee grounds; fondo comune d'investimento mutual fund; fondo d'ammortamento sinking fund; fondo di beneficenza community chest; fondo tinta foundation (in make-up); in fondo in the end; at the bottom; after all

fonè·ma m (-mi) phoneme

fonèti·co -ca (-ci -che) adj phonetic || f phonetics

fonògeno m pickup (of record player)

fonògrafo m phonograph, Gramophone

fonogram·ma m (-mi) telegram delivered by telephone

fonologia f phonology

fonorivelatóre m pickup (of record player)

fonovaligia f portable phonograph

fontana f fountain; spring; source

fónte m (lit) spring, source; fonte battesimale font || f spring; fountain; source; da fonte autorevole on good authority

foraggiare §290 tr to subsidize || intr to forage

foràg·gio m (-gi) forage, provender, fodder

foràne·o -a adj rural; outer; (naut) outer (dock)

forare (fóro) tr to pierce; to bore; to puncture || intr to have a flat tire || ref to be punctured

foratura f puncture

fòrbice f—a forbice (sports) scissors (e.g., kick); forbici scissors; clippers; forbici per le unghie nail clippers

forbire §176 tr to wipe; to polish; to shine

fór·ca f (-che) fork; pitchfork; gallows; mountain pass; fare la forca a qlcu (slang) to betray s.o.; (slang) to do s.o. dirt; fatto a forca V-shaped

forcèlla *f* fork (*of bicycle or motor-cycle*); mountain pass; fork-shaped pole; hairpin; cradle (*of handset*); (coll) wishbone (*of chicken*)

forchétta *f* fork; (coll) wishbone (*of chicken*); **alla forchetta** (culin) cold (*e.g., lunch*)

forchettata *f* forkful; blow with a fork

forchettóne *m* carving fork

forcina *f* hairpin

fòrcipe *m* forceps

forcóne *m* pitchfork

forellino *m* pinhole

forèsta *f* forest

forestale *adj* forest, park

foresterìa *f* guest quarters (*in college or monastery*)

forestierismo *m* borrowing (*from another language*)

forestiè·ro ·ra *adj* foreign ‖ *mf* foreigner; stranger; outsider

forfettà·rio ·ria *adj* (·ri ·rie) job, e.g., **contratto forfettario** job contract; all-inclusive, e.g., **combinazione forfettaria** all-inclusive price agreement

fórfora *f* dandruff

fòr·gia *f* (·ge) forge; smithy

forgiare §290 (fòrgio) *tr* to forge

foriè·ro ·ra *adj* forerunning ‖ *mf* forerunner, harbinger

fórma *f* shape; form; mold (*e.g., for cakes*); wheel (*of cheese*); (typ) form; **forma da cappelli** hat block; **forma da scarpe** shoe tree; shoe last (*used by shoemaker*); **forme shape, body; good manners; **salvare le forme** to save face

formaggièra *f* dish for grated cheese

formàg·gio *m* (·gi) cheese

formaldèide *f* formaldehyde

formale *adj* formal; prim

formalismo *m* formalism

formali·tà *f* (·tà) formality

formalizzare [ddzz] *tr* to scandalize ‖ *ref* to be shocked

formare (fórmo) *tr* & *ref* to form

forma·to ·ta *adj* formed ‖ *m* format

formazióne *f* formation

fòrmica *f* (trademark) Formica

formi·ca *f* (·che) ant

formi·càio *m* (·cài) anthill; (fig) swarm

formichière *m* anteater

formicolare (formìcolo) *intr* to swarm; to crawl ‖ *intr* (ESSERE) to creep (*said, e.g., of a leg*)

formicolì·o *m* (·i) swarm; creeping sensation, numbness

formidàbile *adj* formidable

formó·so ·sa [s] *adj* shapely, buxom

fòrmula *f* formula; (aut) category, class; **formula dubitativa** (law) lack of evidence; **formula piena** (law) acquittal

formulare (fòrmulo) *tr* to formulate

formulà·rio *m* (·ri) formulary; form

fornace *f* furnace, kiln

for·nàio ·nàia *mf* (·nài ·nàie) baker

fornèllo *m* stove, range; (*of boiler*) firebox; bowl (*of pipe*); (min) shaft; **fornello a gas** gas range; **fornello a spirito** kerosene stove; chafing dish

fornire §176 *tr* to furnish, supply

forni·tóre ·trice *mf* supplier, purveyor

fornitura *f* supply; order; delivery

fórno *m* oven; furnace; kiln; bakery; (theat) empty house; **al forno** or **in forno** baked; **alto forno** blast furnace; **forno crematorio** crematorium; **far forno** (theat) to play before an empty house

fóro *m* hole

fòro *m* forum; (law) bar

forosétta [s] *f* (lit) peasant girl

fórse *m* doubt; **mettere in forse** to endanger; to put in doubt ‖ *adv* perhaps, maybe

forsenna·to ·ta *adj* mad, insane ‖ *mf* lunatic

fòrte *adj* strong; firm; bad (*cold*); fat, hefty; fast (*color*); offensive (*joke*); hard (*smoker*); main (*dish*); (lit) thick ‖ *m* strong person; fortress; bulk, main body; forte; (lit) thick; **sapere di forte** to have a strong flavor; **farsi forte** to bear up; **farsi forte di** to appropriate, use; to be cocksure of ‖ *adv* hard; strong; much; loud; openly; a lot; fast; swiftly

fortézza *f* fortress; strength; fortitude

fortificare §197 (fortìfico) *tr* to fortify ‖ *ref* to be strengthened; to dig in

fortificazióne *f* fortification

fortino *m* blockhouse, redoubt

fortùi·to ·ta *adj* fortuitous

fortuna *f* fortune; luck; good luck; fate, destiny; (lit) storm; **avere fortuna** to be lucky; to be a hit; **buona fortuna!** good luck!; **di fortuna** makeshift, emergency; **non aver la fortuna di** to not be fortunate enough to; **per fortuna** luckily

fortunale *m* storm, tempest

fortuna·to ·ta *adj* fortunate, lucky

fortunó·so ·sa [s] *adj* eventful

forùncolo *m* boil; pimple

forviare §119 *tr* to mislead, lead astray ‖ *intr* to go astray

fòrza *f* strength; force; power; police; (phys) force; **a forza di** by dint of; **a tutta forza** at full speed; **bassa forza** (mil) enlisted personnel; **di forza** by force; **di prima forza** first-rate; **far forza a** to encourage; to force; **fare forza a sé stesso** to restrain oneself; **forza!** courage!; **forza di corpo** (typ) height-to-paper; **forza maggiore** force majeure, act of God; **forza muscolare** brawn; **forza pubblica** police; **forza viva** kinetic energy; **per forza** of course; under duress

forzare (fòrzo) *tr* to force; to strain; to rape; to tamper with (*a lock*); **forzare il passo** to hasten one's step; **forzare la consegna** (mil) to violate orders

forza·to ·ta *adj* forced; force (*e.g., feed*) ‖ *m* convict

forzière *m* chest, coffer

forzó·so ·sa [s] *adj* compulsory; imposed by law

forzu·to ·ta *adj* husky, robust

foschìa *f* smog; mist; haze

fó·sco -sca *adj* (**-schi -sche**) dark; gloomy; misty
fosfato *m* phosphate
fosforeggiare §290 (**fosforéggio**) *intr* to phosphoresce; to glow
fosforescènte *adj* phosphorescent
fòsforo *m* phosphorus
fòssa *f* grave; hollow; hole, ditch; moat; pit; den (*of lions*); **fossa biologica** sewage-treatment plant; **fossa di riparazione** (aut) pit; **fossa settica** septic tank
fossato *m* ditch; moat
fossétta *f* dimple
fòssile *adj & m* fossil
fossilizzare [*ddzz*] *tr* to fossilize ǁ *ref* to become fossilized
fòsso *m* ditch; moat
fò·to *f* (**-to**) photo
fotocopia *f* photocopy
fotocopiare §287 (**fotocòpio**) *tr* to photocopy
fotoelèttri·co -ca (**-ci -che**) *adj* photoelectric ǁ *f* (mil) searchlight
fotogèni·co -ca *adj* (**-ci -che**) photogenic
fotogiornale *m* pictorial magazine
fotografare (**fotògrafo**) *tr* to photograph
fotografia *f* photography; photograph
fotogràfi·co -ca *adj* (**-ci -che**) photographic
fotògrafo *m* photographer
fotogram·ma *m* (**-mi**) (phot) frame
fotoincisióne *f* photoengraving
fotolampo *m* flashlight
fotòmetro *m* exposure meter
fotomontàg·gio *m* (**-gi**) photomontage
fototubo *m* phototube
fra *m invar* brother, e.g., **fra Cristoforo** Brother Christopher ǁ *prep* among; between; in, within
frac *m* (**frac**) swallow-tailed coat
fracassare *tr* to crash, smash ǁ *ref* to crash
fracasso *m* crash; uproar; (coll) slew
frà·dicio -cia (**-ci -cie**) *adj* rotten; soaked ǁ *m* rotten part; decay; wet ground
fràgile *adj* fragile; brittle; frail
fragilità *f* fragility, frailty
fràgola *f* strawberry
fragóre *m* din; peal; roar
fragoró·so -sa [*s*] *adj* noisy
fragrante *adj* fragrant
fraintèndere §270 *tr* to misunderstand
frammassóne *m* Freemason
frammassoneria *f* Freemasonry
frammentare (**framménto**) *tr* to fragment
frammentà·rio -ria *adj* (**-ri -rie**) fragmentary
framménto *m* fragment
framméttere §198 *tr* to interpose ǁ *ref* to meddle; **frammettersi in** to intrude in, to butt into
frammèzzo [*ddzz*] *adv* in the middle ǁ *prep* in the midst of
frammischiare §287 *tr* to mix ǁ *ref* to concern oneself
frana *f* landslide; (fig) collapse
franare *intr* to slide; to collapse

francesca·no -na *adj & mf* Franciscan
francé·sco -sca (**-schi -sche**) *adj* (archaic) French ǁ **Francesco** *m* Francis ǁ **Francesca** *f* Frances
francése *adj* French ǁ *m* French (*language*); Frenchman (*person*); **i francesi** the French ǁ *f* Frenchwoman
francesismo *m* gallicism
francesizzare [*ddzz*] *tr* to Frenchify
franchézza *f* frankness
franchi·gia *f* (**-gie**) franchise; exemption; deductible insurance; (naut) shore leave; **franchigia postale** franking privilege
Frància, la France
fran·co -ca (**-chi -che**) *adj* free; frank; Frankish; **farla franca** to get off scot free; **franco di porto** prepaid, postpaid; **franco domicilio** home delivery, free delivery ǁ *m* franc ǁ **Franco** *m* Frank
francobóllo *m* postage stamp, stamp
frangènte *m* breaker, surf; **essere nei frangenti** to be in bad straits
fràngere §179 *tr* to crush; (lit) to break ǁ *ref* to break, comb (*said of waves*)
frangétta *f* bangs
fràn·gia *f* (**-ge**) fringe; embellishment; shoreline; bangs; **frangia di corallo** coral reef
frangibile *adj* breakable
frangiflut·ti *m* (**-ti**) breakwater
frangi-vènto *m* (**-vènto**) windbreak
frangizòl·le *m* (**-le**) disc harrow
Frankfur·ter *m* (**-ter**) hot dog
fran·tóio *m* (**-tói**) crusher; **frantoio a mascelle** jawbreaker
frantumare *tr* to crush; to break to pieces ǁ *ref* to be crushed; to go to pieces
frantume *m* fragment; **andare in frantumi** to go to pieces
frappé *m* (**frappé**) shake; frappé; **frappé alla menta** mint julep; **frappé di latte** milk shake
frappórre §218 *tr* to interpose ǁ *ref* to interfere; to intervene
frasà·rio *m* (**-ri**) language, speech
fra·sca *f* (**-sche**) branch; bush; ornament; whim; frivolous woman, flirt
frase *f* sentence; (mus) phrase; **frase fatta** cliché; **frase idiomàtica** idiom; **frasi** words; **frasi di commiserazione** condolences
fraseggiare §290 (**fraséggio**) *intr* to use phrasing; to use big words; (mus) to phrase
fraseologia *f* phraseology
fràssino *m* ash tree
frastagliare §280 *tr* to cut out (*e.g., paper*)
frastaglia·to -ta *adj* indented, jagged; ornamented
frastornare (**frastórno**) *tr* to disturb; (lit) to prevent
frastuòno *m* din, roar
frate *m* friar, monk, brother
fratellanza *f* brotherhood
fratellastro *m* stepbrother; half brother
fratèllo *m* brother; **fratelli** brothers and sisters; **fratello consanguineo** half brother on the father's side; **fratello**

di latte foster brother; **fratello ge-mello** twin
fraterni·tà f (-**tà**) fraternity
fraternizzare [ddzz] intr to fraternize
fratèr·no -na adj fraternal, brotherly
fratrici·da (-**di -de**) adj fratricidal ‖ mf fratricide
fratrici·dio m (-**di**) fratricide
fratta f brushwood; (coll) hedge
frattàglie fpl giblets, chitterlings, offal
frattanto adv meantime, meanwhile
frattèmpo m—**nel frattempo** meanwhile
frattura f fracture; break; breach
fratturare tr & ref to fracture, break
fraudolènte adj fraudulent
frazionà·rio (-**frazióno**) tr to fractionate; to break up
frazionà·rio adj (-**ri -rie**) fractional
frazióne f fraction; hamlet; (eccl) breaking of the host
fréc·cia f (-**ce**) arrow, bolt; steeple, spire; clock (on hosiery); (archit) rise; (fig) aspersion; **freccia consen-siva** arrow (on traffic light); **freccia direzionale** (aut) turn signal
frecciata f arrow shot; taunt, gibe; **dare una frecciata** a to hit for a loan
freddare (**fréddo**) tr to chill; to kill
freddézza f chill; cold, coldness; cool-ness, cold shoulder; sang-froid
fréd·do -da adj cool; cool, chilly; frigid ‖ m cold, cold weather; chill; **a freddo** cold; cooly; **avere freddo** to be cold (said of people); **fare freddo** to be cold (said of weather); **freddo cane** biting cold; **sentire freddo** to feel cold; **sudare freddo** to be in a cold sweat
freddoló·so -sa [s] adj chilly (person)
freddura f joke, pun; cold weather
fredduri·sta mf (-**sti -ste**) punster
fregagióne f rubbing, rubdown, mas-sage
fregare §209 (**frégo**) tr to rub; to strike (a match); (slang) to steal; (slang) to cheat, dupe; (vulg) to make love with ‖ ref to rub (e.g., one's hands); **fregarsene di** (vulg) to not give a hoot about
fregata f rubbing; (nav) frigate; (orn) frigate bird; (slang) cheating
fregatura f (slang) cheating; (slang) hitch, halt
fregiare §290 (**frégio**) tr to decorate; to fret
fré·gio m (-**gi**) decoration; insignia (on cap of officer); (archit) frieze
fré·go m (-**ghi**) line, stroke
frégola f rut, heat; (slang) mania, craze
fremènte adj throbbing; thrilling
frèmere §123 tr (lit) to beg insistently ‖ intr to throb; to be thrilled; to shake, tremble, rustle; to shudder (with horror); (fig) to boil; (fig) to fret
frèmito m throb; thrill; shudder; roar; quiver
frenare (**fréno**) tr to brake, stop; to bridle (a horse); to curb (passions); to restrain (e.g., laughter); **frenare la corsa** to slow down ‖ intr to put the brakes on ‖ ref to control oneself

frenatóre m (**rr**) brakeman
frenesìa f frenzy; (fig) craze, fever; (lit) thought
frenèti·co -ca adj (-**ci -che**) frenzied; frantic, crazy, enthusiastic
fréno m bit, bridle; brake; (fig) check; (mach) lock; **freno ad aria compressa** air brake; **mordere il freno** to champ the bit; **senza freno** wild, unbridled; **tenere a freno** to keep in check
frenologìa f phrenology
frequentare (**frequènto**) tr to frequent; to attend ‖ intr to associate
frequenta·tóre -trice mf patron, cus-tomer; frequenter, habitué
frequènte adj frequent; rapid (pulse); (lit) crowded
frequènza f frequency; attendance; **fre-quenza ultraelevata** ultrahigh fre-quency
frèsa f milling cutter; burr (of dentist's drill)
fresatrice f milling machine
fresatura f (mach) milling
freschézza f freshness; coolness
fré·sco -sca (-**schi -sche**) adj fresh; cool; **fresco di malattia** just recov-ered; **fresco di stampa** fresh off the press; **fresco di studi** fresh out of school; **star fresco** to be in a fix; to be all wrong ‖ m cool weather; tropi-cal fabric; **di fresco** recently; **fare fresco** to be cool (said of weather); **mettere al fresco** (coll) to put in the clink; **per il fresco** in cool weather
frescó·ne -na mf (slang) dumbell
frescura f coolness, freshness
frétta f hurry, haste; **avere fretta** to be in a hurry; **in fretta** in a hurry; **in fretta e furia** in a rush
frettazzo m plasterer's wooden trowel; steel brush
frettoló·so -sa [s] adj hurried, hasty
freudismo m Freudianism
friàbile adj friable, crumbly
friabilità f friableness
fricassèa f fricassee
frìggere §180 tr to fry; **mandare qlcu a farsi friggere** to tell s.o. to go to the devil ‖ intr to fry; to sizzle; to fret
friggitorìa f fried-food shop
frigidézza f frigidity
frigidi·tà f (-**tà**) coldness; frigidity
frìgi·do -da adj cold; frigid
frì·gio -gia adj (-**gi -gie**) Phrygian
frignare intr to whimper
frigorìfe·ro -ra adj refrigerating ‖ m refrigerator; (journ) morgue
fringuèl·lo -la mf chaffinch, finch
frinire §176 intr to chirp
frisata f gunnel
frittata f omelet; **fare la frittata** (coll) to make a mess of it
frittèlla f fritter; pancake; (coll) grease spot
frit·to -ta adj fried; cooked, ruined ‖ m fry, fried platter
frittura f frying; fry, fried platter
frivolézza f frivolity
frìvo·lo -la adj frivolous; flighty
frizionare (**frizióno**) tr to massage

frizióne *f* friction; massage; (aut) clutch

frizzante [ddzz] *adj* crisp, brisk (*weather*); sparkling (*wine*)

frizzare [ddzz] *intr* to tingle; to sparkle, fizz (*said of wine*); (fig) to sting

frizzo [ddzz] *m* jest, witticism; gibe, dig

frodare (**fròdo**) *tr* to cheat, swindle

fròde *f* fraud; **frode fiscale** tax evasion or fraud

fròdo *m invar* customs evasion; **di frodo** smuggled

frò·gia *f* (-ge *or* -gie) nostril (*of horse*)

fròl·lo -la *adj* high (*meat*); soft, tender; (fig) weak

frónda *f* branch, bough; political opposition; **fronde** foliage; ornaments

frondó·so -sa [s] *adj* leafy

frontale *adj* front; frontal

frónte *m* (mil, pol) front; **far fronte a** to face; to face up to; to meet (*expenses*); **tenere fronte a** to face, resist || *f* forehead, brow; countenance; title page; headline; (fig) face; **a fronte** opposite, facing; **a fronte di** (com) in reference to; **dietro fronte!** (mil) about face!; **di fronte a** in the face of; facing; **di fronte a tutti** in plain view; **fronte destr'!** (mil) right face!; **mettere a fronte** to compare; **tenere a fronte** to have in front of one's eyes

fronteggiare §290 (**frontéggio**) *tr* to face, front || *ref* to face one another

frontespì·zio *m* (-zi) title page

frontièra *f* border, frontier

frontóne *m* (archit) pediment; (archit) gable

frónzolo *m* bauble, gewgaw; **fronzoli** finery, frippery

fròtta *f* crowd; swarm; flock

fròttola *f* fib; popular poem; **frottole** humbug

frugale *adj* frugal (*meal; life*); temperate (*in eating or drinking*)

frugare §209 *tr* to rummage through; to search (*a person*) || *intr* to rummage, poke around

frùgo·lo -la *mf* restless child, imp

fruire §176 *tr* to enjoy || *intr*—**fruire di** to enjoy

fruitóre *m* user

frullare *tr* to beat, whip || *intr* to flutter; to spin; **frullare per il capo a** to get into the head of, e.g., **cosa gli è frullato per il capo?** what got into his head?

frulla·to -ta *adj* whipped || *m* shake (*drink*)

frullatóre *m* electric beater

frullino *m* egg beater

fruménto *m* wheat

frumentóne *m* corn

frusciare §128 *intr* to rustle

frusci·o *m* (-i) rustle, rustling

frusta *f* whip; egg beater

frustare *tr* to whip, lash; (fig) to censure; (coll) to wear out (*clothes*)

frustata *f* lash; (fig) censure

frustino *m* whip, crop

frù·sto -sta *adj* worn out, threadbare || *f see* **frusta**

frustrare *tr* to frustrate, baffle; to discomfit

frut·ta *f* (-ta & -te) fruit; **essere alle frutta** to be at the end of the meal, to be having one's dessert

fruttare *tr & intr* to yield

frutféto *m* orchard

frutticoltóre *m* fruit grower

fruttièra *f* fruit dish

fruttífe·ro -ra *adj* fruit-bearing; fruitful, profitable; (lit) fecund

fruttificare §197 (**fruttífico**) *intr* to fructify; to yield

fruttivéndo·lo -la *mf* fruit dealer

frutto *m* fruit; **frutti di mare** shellfish; **mettere a frutto** to make yield

fruttuó·so -sa [s] *adj* fruitful, profitable

fu *adj invar* late (*deceased*); son of the late . . . ; daughter of the late . . .

fucilare *tr* to shoot

fucilata *f* rifle shot

fucilazióne *f* execution by a firing squad

fucile *m* rifle, gun; **fucile ad aria compressa** air gun; **fucile da caccia** shotgun; **un buon fucile** a good shot

fucilería *f* fusillade

fucilière *m* rifleman

fucina *f* forge, smithy

fu·co *m* (-chi) (bot) rockweed; (zool) drone

fùcsia *f* fuchsia

fu·ga *f* (-ghe) flight; leak; row (*e.g., of rooms*); spurt (*in bicycle race*); (mus) fugue; **di fuga** hastily; **prendere la fuga** to take flight; **volgere in fuga** to put to flight; to take flight

fugace *adj* passing, fleeting

fugare §209 *tr* (lit) to avoid; (lit) to put to flight; (lit) to dispel

fuggènte *adj* passing, fleeting

fuggévole *adj* fleeting

fuggia·sco -sca (-schi -sche) *adj* fleeing, fugitive || *mf* fugitive; refugee

fuggi fug·gi *m* (-gi) stampede

fuggire *tr* to flee; to avoid || *intr* (ESSERE) to flee, run away; (sports) to take the lead; **fuggire a** to flee from

fuggití·vo -va *adj & mf* fugitive

fulcro *m* fulcrum; (fig) pivot

fulgènte *adj* (lit) resplendent

fùlgi·do -da *adj* resplendent

fulgóre *m* resplendency, radiance

fuliggine *f* soot

fuligginó·so -sa [s] *adj* sooty

fulmicotóne *m* guncotton

fulminante *adj* crushing (*illness*); withering (*look*); explosive || *m* exploding cap; (coll) match

fulminare (**fùlmino**) *tr* to strike by lightning; to strike down; to confound, astound || *ref* (elec) to burn out, to blow out || *impers* (ESSERE)— **fulmina** it is lightning

fùlmine *m* lightning, thunderbolt; **fulmine a ciel sereno** bolt out of the blue

fulmìne·o -a *adj* swift, instant

ful·vo -va *adj* tawny

fumaiòlo *m* chimney; smokestack; (naut) funnel

fumante *adj* smoking; steaming; dusty
fumare *tr* to smoke; (lit) to exhale ‖ *intr* to smoke; to steam; to fume; **fumare come un turco** to smoke like a chimney
fumata *f* smoking; smoke signal; **fare una fumata** to have a smoke
fuma·tóre -trice *mf* smoker
fumettí·sta *mf* (-sti -ste) cartoonist
fumétto *m* cartoon; **fumetti** comics
fumigare §209 (fùmigo) *tr* (obs) to fumigate ‖ *intr* to steam, smoke
fumigazióne *f* fumigation
fumi·sta *m* (-sti) heater man; joker, hoaxer
fumisteria *f* fondness for practical jokes; bamboozling
fumo *m* smoke; vapor, steam; smoking; (coll) hot air; **andare in fumo** to go up in smoke; **fumi** vapors, fumes; **mandare in fumo** to squander; to thwart; **sapere di fumo** to taste smoky; **vedere qlcu come il fumo negli occhi** to not be able to stand s.o.; **vender fumo** to peddle influence
fumòge·no -na *adj* smoke, e.g., **cortina fumogena** smoke curtain
fumó·so -sa [s] *adj* smoky; obscure
funambolismo *m* tightrope walking; (fig) acrobatics
funàmbo·lo -la *mf* tightrope walker; (fig) acrobat
fune *f* rope, cable; **fune portante** suspension cable
fùnebre *adj* funeral; funereal, gloomy
funerale *adj* & *m* funeral
funerà·rio -ria *adj* (-ri -rie) funeral
funère·o -a *adj* funereal; funeral
funestare (funèsto) *tr* to afflict
funè·sto -sta *adj* baleful; mournful
fungàia *f* mushroom farm; mushroom bed; flock, swarm
fùngere §183 *intr*—**fungere da** to act as
fun·go *m* (-ghi) mushroom; fungus; **fungo atomico** mushroom cloud; **venir su come i funghi** to mushroom
fungó·so -sa [s] *adj* fungous
funicolare *adj* cable, cable-driven ‖ *f* funicular railway
funivìa *f* cableway
funzionale *adj* functional
funzionalità *f* functionalism
funzionaménto *m* working order; functioning
funzionare (funzióno) *intr* to work; to function; **funzionare da** to act as
funzionà·rio -ria *mf* (-ri -rie) functionary, official; public official
funzióne *f* function; office; duty; (eccl) service; **facente funzione** acting; **mettere in funzione** to make (*s.th*) work
fuò·co *m* (-chi) fire; burner (*of gas range*); focus; (fig) home; (lit) thunderbolt; **al fuoco!** fire! (*warning*); **andare per il fuoco** (culin) to boil over; **cuocere a fuoco lento** (culin) to simmer; **dar fuoco a** to set fire to; **di fuoco** fiery; blushing; **far fuoco** to fire; **fuochi artificiali** fireworks; **fuoco di fila** enfilade; **fuoco!** (mil) fire!; **fuoco di paglia** (fig) flash in the pan; **fuoco di segnalazione** flare; **fuoco fatuo** will-o'-the-wisp; **fuoco**

incrociato cross fire; **fuoco nutrito** drumfire; **mettere a fuoco** to focus; **mettere una mano sul fuoco** to be absolutely sure, to swear by it
fuorché *prep* except; **fuorché di** except to
fuòri *adv* outside, out; aside; e.g., **lasciar fuori** to leave aside; **andar di fuori** (culin) to boil over; **dar fuori** to do away with; to squander; **di fuori** outside; **far fuori** to publish; **fuori di** out of; outside of; beyond (*a doubt*); off (*the road*); beside (*oneself*); **fuori d'uso** out of style; obsolete; **il di fuori** the outside; **in fuori** protruding; forward; **mettere fuori** to throw out; to spread; to exhibit ‖ *prep* beyond; out of; outside; **fuori commercio** not for sale; **fuori concorso** in a class by itself (himself, etc.); **fuori luogo** untimely, out of place; **fuori (di) mano** far away; solitary; **fuori testo** inserted, tipped in
fuoribór·do *m* (-do) outboard; outboard motor
fuoricombattimén·to (-to) *adj* knocked out ‖ *m* knockout
fuorigiò·co *m* (-co) (sports) offside
fuorilég·ge *mf* (-ge) outlaw
fuorisè·rie (-rie) *adj* custom-built ‖ *m* & *f* custom model ‖ *f* custom-built car
fuoristra·da *m* (-da) land rover
fuoriusci·to -ta *adj* exiled ‖ *mf* political exile ‖ *f* leak; flow; protrusion
fuorvia·to -ta *adj* mislead, misguided
furbacchió·ne -na *mf* slippery person
furberia *f* slyness, cunning
fur·bo -ba *adj* sly, cunning ‖ *mf* knave; **furbo di tre cotte** slicker
furènte *adj* furious
fureria *f* (mil) company headquarters
furétto *m* ferret
furfante *m* sharper, scoundrel
furfanteria *f* rascality
furgoncino *m* small delivery van
furgóne *m* truck; patrol wagon; hearse; **furgone cellulare** prison van
furgoni·sta *mf* (-sti -ste) truck driver, teamster
fùria *f* fury; strength; violence; hurry; **a furia di** by dint of; **con furia** in a hurry; **far furia a** to urge; **montare in furia** to go berserk; to fly off the handle
furibón·do -da *adj* furious, wild
furière *m* soldier attached to company headquarters
furió·so -sa [s] *adj* furious; fierce; mad
furóre *m* furor, frenzy; violence; longing; **far furore** to be a hit, to be all the rage
foroeggiare §290 (furoréggio) *intr* to be a hit, be all the rage
furti·vo -va *adj* stealthy; furtive; stolen (*e.g., goods*)
furto *m* theft; stolen goods; **di furto** stealthily; **furto con scasso** burglary
fusa [s] *fpl*—**fare le fusa** to purr
fuscèllo *m* twig
fusciac·ca *f* (-che) sash (*around the waist*)

fusèllo [s] *m* spindle; axle, shaft
fusìbile *adj* fusible || *m* (elec) fuse
fusióne *f* fusion; melting; merger; blending (*of colors*)
fu·so -sa *adj* melted; molten
fuso [s] *m* spindle; shank (*of anchor*); shaft (*of column*); (aut) axle; **fuso orario** time zone
fusolièra *f* (aer) fuselage
fustagno *m* fustian
fustàia *f* adult forest, full-grown forest
fustèlla *f* (perforating) punch; (pharm) price stub

fustigare §209 (**fùstigo**) *tr* to whip
fusto *m* trunk (*of tree*); stalk; stem (*of key*); beam (*of balance*); butt (*of gun*); trunk, body; frame (*of armchair*); tank (*for holding liquids*); drum (*metal receptacle*); holding stick (*of umbrella*); shaft (*of column*); **d'alto fusto** full-grown (*tree*)
fùtile *adj* futile, trifling
futilità *f* futility
futurismo *m* futurism
futuri·sta *mf* (**-sti -ste**) futurist
futu·ro -ra *adj* & *m* future

G

G, g [dʒi] *m* & *f* seventh letter of the Italian alphabet
gabardi·ne *f* (**-ne**) gabardine; gabardine raincoat or topcoat
gabbamón·do *m* (**-do**) cheat, sharper
gabbanèlla *f* gown (*of physician or patient*); robe
gabbano *m* cloak; frock; **mutare gabbano** to be a turncoat
gabbare *tr* to dupe, cheat || *ref*—**gabbarsi di** to make fun of
gàbbia *f* cage; ox muzzle; dock (*in courtroom*); (mach) housing; (naut) top; (naut) topsail; **gabbia d'imballaggio** crate; **gabbia toracica** rib cage
gabbiano *m* sea gull
gabbo *m*—**farsi gabbo di** to make fun of; **prendere a gabbo** to make light of
gabèlla *f* (obs) customs, duty
gabellare (**gabèllo**) *tr* to palm off; to swallow (*e.g., a tall story*); (obs) to tax
gabinétto *m* office (*of doctor, dentist, lawyer*); cabinet; chamber (*of judge*); toilet; closet; laboratory; **gabinetto da bagno** bathroom; **gabinetto di decenza** toilet, bathroom
ga·gà *m* (**gà**) fop, dandy; lounge lizard
gaggìa *f* acacia
gagliardétto *m* pennon; pennant
gagliardìa *f* (lit) vigor; (lit) prowess
gagliar·do -da *adj* vigorous; stalwart; hearty (*e.g., voice*)
gagliòf·fo -fa *adj* loutish; rascal || *mf* lout; rascal
gaiézza *f* gaiety, vivacity
gàio gàia *adj* (**gài gàie**) gay, vivacious
gala *m* & *f* gala; gala affair; **di gala** formal; **mettersi in gala** to dress up || *f* frill; bow tie (*for formal attire*); (naut) bunting
galalite *f* casein plastic, galalith
galante *adj* gallant, courtly; amorous; pretty, graceful
galanterìa *f* gallantry, courtliness
galantuò·mo *m* (**-mini**) honest man; (coll) my good fellow
galàssia *f* galaxy
galatèo *m* good manners
galèna *f* (min) galena
galeóne *m* galleon
galeòt·to -ta *adj* (archaic) intermediary

(*in love affairs*) || *m* galley slave; convict; (archaic) procurer
galèra *f* galley; forced labor
gali·lèo -lèa (**-lèi -lèe**) *adj* & *m* Galilean
galla *f* (bot) gall; (pathol) blister; **a galla** afloat; **tenersi a galla** (fig) to keep alive; to manage; **venire a galla** to come to the surface
galleggiante *adj* floating || *m* float
galleggiare §290 (**galléggio**) *intr* to float
galleria *f* tunnel; gallery; balcony; mall, arcade; wind tunnel
Galles, il Wales
gallése [s] *adj* Welsh || *m* Welshman; Welsh (*language*) || *f* Welsh woman
gallétta *f* cracker; hardtack; (naut) ball on top of flagpole
gallétto *m* cockerel; (fig) gallant; (fig) whippersnapper; (mach) wing nut; **fare il galletto** to swagger
gàlli·co -ca *adj* & *m* (**-ci -che**) Gallic
gallina *f* hen; **gallina faraona** guinea fowl
gal·lo -la *adj* Gallic; (sports) Bantam (*weight*) || *m* rooster, cock; weathercock; Gaul; Gallic (*language*); **fare il gallo** to strut; **gallo cedrone** wood grouse; **gallo d'India** turkey
gallòc·cia *f* (**-ce**) (naut) cleat
gallóne *m* braid; stripe; chevron; gallon
galoppare (**galòppo**) *intr* to gallop; (fig) to rush around
galoppata *f* gallop
galoppa·tóio *m* (**-tói**) bridle path
galoppino *m* errand boy; **galoppino elettorale** ward heeler
galòppo *m* gallop; **andare al piccolo galoppo** to canter; **di gran galoppo** at full speed; **piccolo galoppo** canter
galò·scia *f* (**-sce**) overshoe, rubber
galvanizzare [ddzz] *tr* to electroplate; (fig) to galvanize
galvanoplàsti·ca *f* (**-che**) electroplating
gamba *f* leg; stem; (aer) shock strut; **a gambe all'aria** upside down; **a gambe levate** at top speed; upside down; **darsela a gambe** to take to one's heels; **essere in gamba** to be in good shape; to be on the ball; **essere male in gamba** to be in bad shape; **gamba di legno** peg leg; **gambe a ciambella** bowlegs; **le gambe mi fanno giacomo** my knees shake;

prendere qlcu sotto gamba to make light of s.o.; **raddrizzare le gambe ai cani** to try the impossible
gambale *m* legging, gaiter; boot last; leg (*of boot*)
gamberétto *m* shrimp
gàmbero *m* (*Astacus, Cambarus*) crawfish
gambétto *m* stumble; trip; (chess) gambit
gambo *m* stem
gamèlla *f* (mil) mess kit, mess tin
gamma *f* gamut; range; **gamma d'onda** (rad) wave band
ganà·scia *f* (-sce) jaw; (aut) brake shoe; **mangiare a quattro ganasce** to eat like a horse
gàn·cio *m* (-ci) hook; clasp; hanger
gan·ga *f* (-ghe) gang; (min) gangue
gànghero *m* hinge; clasp; **uscire dai gangheri** to fly off the handle
gàn·glio *m* (-gli) ganglion
ganzo [dz] *m* (slang) lover; (coll) slicker
gara *f* competition, match; **fare a gara** to compete; **gara d'appalto** competitive bidding
garagi·sta *m* (-sti) garage man
garante *adj* responsible ‖ *m* guarantor; **farsi garante per** to vouch for
garantire §176 *tr* to guarantee; to secure (*a mortgage*)
garanti·to -ta *adj* guaranteed, warranted; downright, absolute (*liar*)
garanzia *f* guarantee, warranty; insurance, assurance
garbare *tr* (naut) to shape (*a hull*) ‖ *intr* (ESSERE) (with *dat*) to like, e.g., **non gli garbano le Sue parole** he does not like your words
garbatézza *f* politeness, courtesy
garba·to -ta *adj* polite, courteous
garbo *m* politeness, good manners; gesture; act; shape (*of a hull*); good cut (*of clothes*); elegance (*in painting or writing*); a **garbo** correctly
garbù·glio *m* (-gli) tangle, confusion; mess
gardènia *f* gardenia
gareggiare §290 (garéggio) *intr* to compete, vie
garétta *f* var of **garitta**
garétto *m* var of **garretto**
garganèlla *f*—**bere a garganella** to gulp down
gargarismo *m* gargling; gargle
gargarizzare [ddzz] *intr* & *ref* to gargle
gargaròzzo *m* throat, gullet
garitta *f* railroad-crossing box; (mil) sentry box; (rr) brakeman's box
garòfano *m* carnation, pink
garrése [s] *m* withers
garrétto *m* ankle (*of man*); hock (*of horse*)
garrire §176 *intr* to chirp, twitter; to flap; (archaic) to quarrel
garrito *m* chirp, twitter
garròtta *f* garrote
gàrru·lo -la *adj* garrulous
garza [dz] *f* gauze
garzonato [dz] *m* apprenticeship
garzó·ne -na [dz] *mf* helper ‖ *m*

helper, boy; apprentice; (archaic) bachelor; **garzone di stalla** stableboy
gas *m* (gas) gas; gasoline; **gas asfissiante** poison gas; **gas delle miniere** firedamp; **gas esilarante** laughing gas; **gas illuminante** illuminating gas; **gas lacrimogeno** tear gas
gasdótto *m* gas pipeline
gasificare §197 (gasìfico) *tr* var of **gassificare**
gasòlio *m* Diesel oil
gasòmetro *m* var of **gassometro**
gassificare §197 (gassìfico) *tr* to gasify
gassi·sta *m* (-sti) gasworker; gas fitter; gas-meter reader
gassòmetro *m* gasholder, gas tank
gassó·so -sa [s] *adj* gaseous, gassy ‖ *f* soda, pop
gastronomìa *f* gastronomy
gatta *f* she-cat, tabby; **comprare la gatta nel sacco** to buy a pig in a poke; **gatta ci cova** something is rotten in Denmark; **pigliare una gatta da pelare** to take on a heavy burden, to get a tiger by the tail
gattabùia *f* (coll) clink, lockup
gattamòrta *f* (**gattemòrte**) hypocrite
gattino *m* kitten; (bot) catkin
gat·to -ta *mf* cat ‖ *m* tomcat; tamper, pile driver; **gatto a nove code** cat-o'-nine-tails; **gatto soriano** tortoiseshell cat; **quattro gatti** a handful of people ‖ *f* see **gatta**
gattóni *adv* on all fours
gattopardo *m* (zool) serval; **gattopardo americano** ocelot
gattùc·cio *m* (-ci) compass saw; (ichth) small dotted dogfish
gaudènte *adj* jovial ‖ *m* bon vivant
gàu·dio *m* (-di) joy, happiness
gavazzare *intr* (lit) to revel
gavétta *f* mess kit, mess gear; **venire dalla gavetta** to come up through the ranks
gavitèllo *m* buoy
gazza [ddzz] *f* magpie
gazzarra [ddzz] *f* racket, uproar
gazzèlla [ddzz] *f* gazelle
gazzétta [ddzz] *f* newspaper; gazette; newsmonger, gossip; **Gazzetta Ufficiale** Official Gazette (*in Italy*); Congressional Record (*U.S.A.*)
gazzettino [ddzz] *m* small newspaper; column, e.g., **gazzettino rosa** social column; newsmonger, gossip
gazzósa [ddzz] *f* var of **gassosa**
gèl *m* gel
gelare (**gèlo**) *tr* to freeze; to nip ‖ *intr* (ESSERE) & *ref* to freeze ‖ *impers* (ESSERE & AVERE)—**gela** it is freezing
gelata *f* frost
gela·tàio -tàia *mf* (-tài -tàie) ice-cream dealer
gelaterìa *f* ice-cream parlor
gelatièra *f* ice-cream freezer
gelatière *m* ice-cream dealer
gelatina *f* gelatin; jelly; **gelatina di frutta** fruit jelly; gum drop
gelatinizzare [ddzz] *tr* & *ref* to gelatinize; to jell
gela·to -ta *adj* frozen ‖ *m* ice cream;

gelato da passeggio ice cream on a stick, popsicle

gèli·do -da *adj* icy, ice-cold

gèlo *m* frost; ice; cold; **diventare di gelo** to remain dumfounded; **farsi di gelo** to be cold or aloof; **sentirsi il gelo addosso** to get a chill

gelóne *m* chilblain

gelosìa [s] *f* jealousy; great care; shutter

gelò·so -sa [s] *adj* jealous; solicitous

gèlso *m* mulberry

gelsomino *m* jasmine

gemebón·do -da *adj* (lit) moaning

gemèllàggio *m* sisterhood (*of two cities*)

gemèl·lo -la *adj* twin; sister (*ship*) || *mf* twin || **gemelli** *mpl* cufflinks | **Gemelli** *mpl* (astr) Gemini

gèmere §123 *tr* (lit) to lament || *intr* (ESSERE & AVERE) to moan, groan; to suffer; to squeak (*said of a wheel*); to ooze; to coo (*said of a dove*)

gèmito *m* moan; howl (*of wind*)

gèmma *f* gem; (bot) bud

gemma·to -ta *adj* gemmate; jeweled

gendarme *m* gendarme, policeman

genealogìa *f* genealogy

generalato *m* generalship

generale *adj* general || *m* general; **generale d'armata** (mil) general; **generale di brigata** brigadier general; **generale di corpo d'armata** lieutenant general; **generale di divisione** major general || *f* (mil) assembly; **stare sulle generali** to speak in vague generalities

generali·tà *f* (-tà) generality; majority; **generalità** *fpl* personal data

generalizzare [ddzz] *tr* to generalize; to bring into general use || *intr* to generalize, deal in generalities

generare (gènero) *tr* to beget; to generate || *ref* to occur

genera·tóre -trice *adj* generating || *m* generator || *f* generatrix

generazióne *f* generation

gènere *m* genus; kind, type; genre; (gram) gender; **del genere** similar, alike; **farne di ogni genere** to commit all sorts of mischief; **genere umano** mankind; **generi alimentari** foodstuffs; **generi diversi** sundries, assorted articles; **in genere** generally

genèri·co -ca (-ci -che) *adj* generic; vague; all-round; general (*e.g., practitioner*) || *mf* (theat) actor playing bit parts || *m* vagueness, imprecision

gènero *m* son-in-law

generosi·tà [s] *f* (-tà) generosity

generó·so -sa [s] *adj* generous; rich (*wine*)

gène·si *f* (-si) genesis || **il Genesi** Genesis

genèti·co -ca (-ci -che) *adj* genetic(al) || *f* genetics

genetlìa·co -ca (-ci -che) *adj* birth || *m* birthday

gengiva *f* (anat) gum

genìa *f* set, gang; (lit) breed

geniale *adj* clever; genial; inspired, genius-like

geniali·tà *f* (-tà) cleverness, ingeniousness; genius; (lit) geniality

genière *m* (mil) engineer

gè·nio *m* (-ni) genius; (mil) corps of engineers; **andare a genio** (with *dat*) to like, e.g., **la musica moderna non gli va a genio** he does not like modern music; **fare qlco di genio** to do s.th willingly

genitale *adj* genital || **genitali** *mpl* genitals

geniti·vo -va *adj & m* genitive

geni·tóre -trice *mf* parent

gen·nàio *m* (-nài) January

genocìdio *m* genocide

Gènova *f* Genoa

genovése [s] *adj & mf* Genoese

gentàglia *f* riffraff, rabble, scum

gènte *adj* (archaic) gentle || *f* people; nation; family; (nav) crew; **gente d'arme** soldiers; **gente di mal affare** riffraff; **gente di mare** sailors

gentildònna *f* gentlewoman

gentile *adj* gentle; nice; genteel || **Gentili** *mpl* heathen

gentilézza *f* gentleness; kindness; **per gentilezza** kindly, please

gentili·zio -zia *adj* (-zi -zie) of noble family; (lit) ancestral

gentiluò·mo *m* (-mini) gentleman, nobleman

genuflèttere §177 *ref* to kneel down

genui·no -na *adj* genuine

genziana *f* gentian

geofìsi·co -ca (-ci -che) *adj* geophysical || *f* geophysics

geografìa *f* geography

geogràfi·co -ca (-ci -che) *adj* geographic(al)

geògra·fo -fa *mf* geographer

geologìa *f* geology

geòlo·go -ga *mf* (-gi -ghe) geologist

geòme·tra *m* (-tri) geometrician; land surveyor

geometrìa *f* geometry

gerà·nio *m* (-ni) geranium

gerar·ca *m* (-chi) leader

gerarchìa *f* hierarchy

geràrchi·co -ca *adj* (-ci -che) hierarchical; **per via gerarchica** through proper channels

Geremìa *f* Jeremiah

geremìade *f* jeremiad

gerènte *m* manager, director; **gerente responsabile** (journ) managing editor

gèr·go *m* (-ghi) jargon

geriatrìa *f* geriatrics

Gèrico *f* Jericho

gèrla *f* pannier (*carried on the back*)

Germània, la Germany

germàni·co -ca *adj* (-ci -che) Germanic

germànio *m* germanium

germanizzare [ddzz] *tr* to Germanize

germa·no -na *adj* german, e.g., **fratello germano** brother-german; Germanic || *m* (lit) brother-german; **germano nero** (orn) coot; **germano reale** (orn) mallard

gèrme *m* germ; (lit) offspring

germici·da (-di) *adj* germicidal || *m* germicide

germinare (gèrmino) *intr* (ESSERE & AVERE) to germinate

germogliare §280 (germóglio) *tr* to put forth ‖ *intr* (ESSERE & AVERE) to bud, sprout

germó·glio *m* (-gli) bud, sprout

geroglìfi·co -ca *adj* & *m* (-ci -che) hieroglyphic

Geròlamo *m* Jerome

gerontocò·mio *m* (-mi) or **gerotrò·fio** *m* (-fi) old people's home, nursing home

gerùn·dio *m* (-di) gerund

Gerusalèmme *f* Jerusalem

gessare (gèsso) *tr* to plaster; to lime (*a field*)

gèsso *m* gypsum; plaster; chalk; (sculp) plaster cast

gessó·so -sa [s] *adj* plastery, chalky; chalklike

gèsta *f* (archaic) army; **gesta** *fpl* deeds, exploits

gestante *f* pregnant woman

gestazióne *f* gestation

gesticolare (gesticolo) *intr* to gesticulate

gestióne *f* management, operation; data processing

gestire §176 *tr* to manage, operate ‖ *intr* to gesticulate; (theat) to make gestures

gèsto *m* gesture; attitude; act, deed

ge·stóre -strìce *mf* manager, operator; **gestore di stazione** (rr) station agent

gestualità *f* bodily movements (*e.g., of an actor*)

Gesù *m* Jesus; **Gesù Cristo** Jesus Christ

gesuì·ta *m* (-ti) Jesuit

gesuìti·co -ca *adj* (-ci -che) Jesuitic(al)

gettare (gètto) *tr* to throw; to cast; to pour; to lay (*e.g., a floor*); to send forth; to yield; to broadcast (*seed*); to risk (*one's life*); **gettare la colpa addosso a qlcu** to lay the blame on s.o.; **gettare le armi** to lay down one's arms; **gettar giù** to fell, knock down; **gettar sangue** to bleed ‖ *ref* to throw oneself; to plunge; to flow, empty (*said of a river*)

gettata *f* pour, pouring; jetty; shoot, sprout; cast; range (*of a gun*); **gettata cardiaca** (med) rate of flow of blood

gèttito *m* yield; waste; **far gettito di** to waste

gètto *m* throw; gush; shoot, sprout; cast; precast concrete slab; (aer) jet; **a getto** (aer) jet; **a getto continuo** continuously; **di getto** spontaneously; **far getto di** to waste; **primo getto** first draft

gettonare (gettóno) *tr* (coll) to call up from a pay station; (coll) to make the selection of (*a record in a juke-box*)

gettóne *m* counter, token; attendance fee; (cards) chip

gettopropulsióne *f* jet propulsion

ghepardo *m* cheetah

ghép·pio *m* (-pi) kestrel

gherì·glio *m* (-gli) kernel, meat (*of nut*)

gherlino *m* (naut) warp, line

gherminèlla *f* trick, sleight of hand; trickery

ghermire §176 *tr* to claw; to seize

gheróne *m* gusset

ghétta *f* gaiter; **ghette** spats

ghétto *m* ghetto

ghiac·ciàia *f* icebox, cooler

ghiac·ciàio *m* (-ciài) glacier; **ghiacciaio continentale** polar cap

ghiacciare §128 *tr* to freeze ‖ *intr* (ESSERE) to freeze ‖ *impers* (ESSERE) —**ghiaccia** it is freezing

ghiaccia·to -ta *adj* iced; ice-cold; frozen ‖ *f* flavored crushed ice

ghiàc·cio -cia (-ci -ce) *adj* icy, ice-cold ‖ *m* ice; **ghiaccio secco** dry ice

ghiacciò·lo -la *adj* crumbly, breakable ‖ *m* icicle; popsicle

ghiàia *f* gravel, crushed stone

ghianda *f* (fringe or a curtain); (bot) acorn; **ghiande** mast (*for swine*)

ghiandàia *f* (orn) jay

ghiàndola *f* gland

ghibelli·no -na *adj* & *m* Ghibelline

ghièra *f* ferrule; ring

ghigliottina *f* guillotine; **a ghigliottina** sash (*window*)

ghigliottinare *tr* to guillotine

ghigna *f* (coll) grimace

ghignare *intr* to grimace; to sneer

ghigno *m* sneer, smirk; grin

ghinèa *f* guinea

ghìngheri *m invar*—**in ghìngheri** dressed up

ghiót·to -ta *adj* fond; gluttonous; eager; dainty (*food*) ‖ *f* (culin) dripping pan

ghiottó·ne -na *mf* glutton; (zool) glutton, wolverine

ghiottonerìa *f* gluttony; tidbit; (fig) rarity

ghiòzzo [ddzz] *m* dolt; (ichth) gudgeon

ghirba *f* jar; (coll) skin, life

ghiribìzzo [ddzz] *m* (coll) whim, caprice

ghirigòro *m* doodle, curlicue

ghirlanda *f* garland, wreath

ghiro *m* dormouse; **dormire come un ghiro** to sleep like a log

ghisa *f* cast iron

già *adv* already; once upon a time; formerly ‖ *interj* indeed!

giac·ca *f* (-che) jacket, coat; **giacca a due petti** double-breasted coat; **giacca a vento** windbreaker

giacché *conj* since

giacènte *adj* lying, idle (*capital*); unclaimed (*letter*); in abeyance

giacènza *f* lying; stay, abeyance; **giacenze di capitali** idle capital; **giacenze di magazzino** unsold stock of merchandise

giacére §181 *intr* (ESSERE) to lie; to be in abeyance; (lit) to be prostrate

giacì·glio *m* (-gli) pallet, cot

giacimento *m* field, bed; **giacimento petrolifero** oil field

giacinto *m* hyacinth

Giàcomo *m* James

giaculatòria *f* ejaculation (*prayer*); litany (*monotonous account*); curse

giada *f* jade

giaggiòlo *m* (bot) iris

giaguaro *m* jaguar

giaiétto *m* jet (*black coal*)

gialappa *f* (pharm) jalap

gialla-stro -stra *adj* yellowish

gial·lo -la *adj* yellow; detective (*book or picture*); white (*with fear*) || *m* yellow; detective story, whodunit; suspense movie; giallo dell'uovo egg yolk

giamaica·no -na *adj & mf* Jamaican

giàmbi·co -ca *adj* (-ci -che) iambic

giambo *m* iamb

giammài *adv* never

giansenismo *m* Jansenism

Giappóne, il Japan

giapponése [*s*] *adj & mf* Japanese

giara *f* crock, jar

giardinàg·gio *m* (-gi) gardening

giardiniétta *f* station wagon

giardinié·re -ra *mf* gardener || *f* jardiniere; mixed pickles; mixed salad; wagonette; station wagon

giardino *m* garden; giardino d'infanzia kindergarten; giardino pensile roof garden; giardino zoologico zoological garden

giarrettièra *f* garter

Giasóne *m* Jason

giavanése [*s*] *adj & mf* Javanese

giavellòtto *m* javelin

gibbó·so -sa [*s*] *adj* gibbous, humped; humpbacked; rough (*ground*)

gibèrna *f* cartridge box; cartridge belt

gi·bus *m* (-bus) opera hat

gi·ga *f* (-ghe) gigue, jig

gigante *adj & m* giant

giganté·sco -sca *adj* (-schi -sche) gigantic

gigantéssa *f* giantess

gigióne *m* ham actor

gi·glio *m* (-gli) Madonna lily; fleur-de-lys

gilda *f* guild

gi·lè *f* (-lè) vest, waistcoat

gimnòto *m* electric eel

ginecologìa *f* gynecology

ginecòlo·go -ga *mf* (-gi -ghe) gynecologist

gine-pràio *m* (-prài) juniper thicket; (fig) mess

ginépro *m* juniper

ginèstra *f* (bot) Spanish broom

Ginèvra *f* Geneva

ginevri·no -na *adj & mf* Genevan

gingillare *ref* to trifle; to idle

gingillo *m* trifle, bauble

ginnà·sio *m* (-si) secondary school; gymnasium

ginna·sta *mf* (-sti -ste) gymnast

ginnàsti·co -ca *adj* (-ci -che) gymnastic || *f* gymnastics; ginnastica a corpo libero or ginnastica da camera calisthenics

ginni·co -ca *adj* (-ci -che) gymnastic

ginocchiata *f* blow with the knee; blow on the knee

ginocchièra *f* kneepad; elastic bandage (*for knee*); kneepiece (*of armor*)

ginòc·chio *m* (-chi) knee; avere il ginocchio valgo to be bowlegged; avere il ginocchio varo to be knock-kneed; in ginocchio on one's knees

|| *m* (-chia *fpl*) knee; fino alle ginocchia knee-deep; gettarsi alle ginocchia di to go down on one's knees to; mettere qlcu in ginocchio to bring s.o. to his knees

ginocchióni *adv* on one's knees

giocare §182 *tr* to play; to stake, bet, risk, gamble; to make a fool of || *intr* to play; to gamble; to circulate (*said of air*); (fig) to play a role; giocare a to play; to wager; giocare a mosca cieca to play blindman's buff; giocare con to resist; giocare d'armi to fence; giocare d'azzardo to gamble; giocare di to use (*e.g., one's wits*); giocare di gomiti to elbow one's way; giocare di mano to steal; giocare sulle parole to play on words; to pun || *ref* to risk (*e.g., one's life*); to gamble away

giocata *f* wager, stake; game, play

gioca-tóre -trice *mf* player; gambler; speculator

giocàttolo *m* toy, plaything

giocherellare (giocherèllo) *intr* to play, trifle

giochétto *m* children's game; child's play; dirty trick

giò·co *m* (-chi) game; gambling; play; wager, stake; set; joke; (cards) hand; entrare in gioco to come into play; fare gioco a to come in handy to; fare il doppio gioco to be guilty of duplicity; fare il gioco di to play into the hands of; giochi di equilibrio balancing act; gioco da ragazzi child's play; gioco d'azzardo gambling; game of chance; gioco dei bussolotti (fig) jugglery; gioco di destrezza game of skill; gioco di parole play on words, pun; gioco di prestigio sleight of hand; gioco di società parlor game; metter in gioco to risk; to stake; per gioco for fun; prendersi gioco di to make fun of

giocoforza *m*—è giocoforza + *inf* it is necessary + *inf*

giocolière *m* juggler

giocón·do -da *adj* merry, joyful

giocó·so -sa [*s*] *adj* jocose, jolly

giogàia *f* dewlap; chain of mountains

giò·go *m* (-ghi) yoke; beam (*of balance*); rounded peak; pass

giòia *f* joy, happiness; darling; jewel; darsi alla pazza gioia to have a wild time

gioiellerìa *f* jewelry; jewelry store

gioiellière *m* jeweler

gioièllo *m* jewel

gioió·so -sa [*s*] *adj* joyful

gioire §176 (*pres part* missing) *intr* to rejoice

Giòna *m* Jonas

Giordània, la Jordan (*country*)

giorda·no -na *adj & mf* Jordanian || Giordano *m* Jordan (*river*)

Giórgio *m* George

giorna-làio -làia *mf* (-lài -làie) newsdealer

giornale *m* newspaper; magazine; (com) journal; giornale di bordo log, logbook; giornale murale poster; giornale radio newscast

giornaliè·ro -ra *adj* daily || *mf* day laborer

giornalismo *m* journalism

giornali·sta *mf* (**-sti -ste**) journalist; **giornalista pubblicista** free-lance writer || *m* newspaperman || *f* newspaperwoman

giornalménte *adv* daily

giornata *f* day; day's work; birthday; pay, salary; battle; day's march; **giornata campale** pitched battle; **giornata della mamma** Mother's Day; **giornata lavorativa** workday; **vivere alla giornata** to live from hand to mouth

giórno *m* day; **a giorni** within the next few days; **a giorni . . . a giorni** some days . . . others; **a giorno** open, openwork (*needlework*); full (*light*); **ai giorni nostri** nowadays; **al giorno d'oggi** nowadays; **buon giorno** good day; good morning; good-bye; **dare gli otto giorni a** to dismiss, fire; **di ogni giorno** everyday (*e.g., clothes*); **essere a giorno** to be up to date; **giorno dei morti** All Souls' Day; **giorno di lavoro** workday; **giorno di paga** payday; **giorno fatto** broad daylight; **giorno feriale** weekday; **giorno festivo** holiday; **mettere a giorno** to bring up to date; **otto giorni oggi** one week from today; **passare un brutto giorno** to have a bad time; **un giorno o l'altro** one of these days

giòstra *f* joust; merry-go-round

giostrare (**giòstro**) *intr* to joust; to get along, manage; to idle, loiter

Giosuè *m* Joshua

Giotté·sco -sca *adj* (**-schi -sche**) of the school of Giotto

giovaménto *m* benefit, advantage

gióvane *adj* young; youthful; fresh (*e.g., cheese*); Younger, e.g., **Plinio il Giovane** Pliny the Younger || *m* young man; boy, apprentice; **i giovani** the young || *f* young woman

giovanile *adj* youthful

Giovanni *m* John; **Giovanni Battista** John the Baptist

giovanòtta *f* young woman

giovanòtto *m* young man; (*coll*) bachelor

giovare (**gióvo**) *tr* (*lit*) to help || *intr* (**with dat**) to help, to be of use to || *ref* to avail oneself || *impers* (ESSERE) **—non giova** it's no use

Giòve *m* Jupiter

giove·dì *m* (**-dì**) Thursday; **giovedì santo** Maundy Thursday

giovèn·ca *f* (**-che**) heifer

gioventù *f* youth

giovévole *adj* helpful, beneficial

gioviale *adj* jovial

giovinézza *f* youth

gip *f* (**gip**) jeep

gippóne *m* large jeep, panel truck

giràbile *adj* endorsable

giradi·schi *m* (**-schi**) record player

giradito *m* (pathol) felon

giraffa *f* giraffe; (mov, telv) boom, crane

girafilièra *f* diestock

giramà·schio *m* (**-schi**) tap wrench

giraménto *m* **—giramento di testa** vertigo, dizziness

giramón·do *m* (**-do**) globetrotter

giràndola *f* girandole; pinwheel; (fig) weathercock

girandolare (**giràndolo**) *intr* to stroll, saunter

girante *mf* endorser || *f* blade (*e.g., of fan*)

girare *tr* to turn; to tour; to go around, travel over; to switch (*the conversation*); to film, shoot; to transfer (*a phone call*); to endorse; (mil) to surround || *intr* to turn; to circulate; to spin (*said of one's head*) || *ref* to turn; to toss and turn

girarrósto *m* turnspit; **girarrosto a motore** rotisserie

girasóle *m* sunflower

girata *f* turn; walk, ramble; (com) endorsement; (cards) deal; (coll) tongue-lashing

giratà·rio -ria *mf* (**-ri -rie**) endorsee

giravòlta *f* turn, pirouette; bend; sudden change of mind

girellare (**girèllo**) *intr* to stroll, wander around

girèllo *m* rump; go-cart, walker

girévole *adj* revolving

girino *m* tadpole; bicycle rider competing on the Tour of Italy

giro *m* periphery; turn, revolution; ride; size (*of hat*); edge (*of glass*); round (*of a doctor*); (sports) tour; (sports) lap; (com) transfer; (cards) hand; (theat) tour; **a giro di posta** by return mail; **andare in giro** to poke along; **giro collo** neckline; **giro d'affari** volume of business, turnover; **giro di parole** circumlocution; **fare il giro di** to tour; **mettere in giro** to spread (*news, gossip*); **nel giro di** within (*a period*); **prendere in giro** to poke fun at

girobùssola *f* gyrocompass

girondolare (**giróndolo**) *intr* var of girandolare

giróne *m* (sports) conference; (sports) division; (sports) league; (archaic) circle

gironzolare [dz] (**girónzolo**) *intr* to stroll, saunter

giropilò·ta *m* (**-ti**) gyropilot

giroscò·pio *m* (**-pi**) gyroscope

girotóndo *m* ring-around-a-rosy

giròtta *f* weather vane

girovagare §209 (**giròvago**) *intr* to roam, wander

giròva·go -ga (**-ghi -ghe**) *adj* wandering; strolling (*player*) || *m* vagrant, hobo

gita *f* trip, excursion, outing

gita·no -na *adj* & *mf* Gypsy

gitante *mf* excursionist, vacationist

gittata *f* range (*of gun*)

giù *adv* down; **andar giù** to go down; to deteriorate; to get worse; **buttar giù** to throw down; (culin) to start to cook, e.g., **buttar giù gli spaghetti** to start to cook the spaghetti; (fig) to jot down; **da . . . in giù** for the past . . . ; **dar giù** to look worse (*said* *of a sick person*); **esser giù** to be downcast; **giù di lì** thereabouts; **in giù** down; downstream; **mandar giù** to swallow; **non andar giù** to not be able to stomach or swallow, e.g., **non gli vanno giù i bugiardi** he cannot stomach liars; **venire giù** to come down; to crumble; to collapse

giubba *f* coat, jacket; mane

giubbétto *m* small coat; bodice; jerkin

giubbòtto *m* jacket (*e.g., of a motorcyclist*); **giubbotto salvagente** (aer, naut) life jacket

giubilare (**giùbilo**) *tr* to retire, to pension || *intr* to rejoice

giubilèo *m* jubilee

giùbilo *m* jubilation, exultation

giuda || **Giuda** *m* Judas

giudài·co -ca *adj* (**-ci -che**) Judaic

giudaismo *m* Judaism

giudè·o -a *adj* Judean; Jewish || *mf* Judean; Jew

giudicare §197 (**giùdico**) *tr* to judge; to find (*e.g., s.o. innocent*); to try (*a case*) || *intr* to judge, deem

giudicato *m* (hist) Sardinian region; **passare in giudicato** (law) to become final

giùdice *m* judge; magistrate, justice; **giudice conciliatore** justice of the peace; **giudice popolare** member of the jury

giudizià·rio -ria *adj* (**-ri -rie**) judicial, judiciary

giudì·zio *m* (**-zi**) judgment; wisdom; trial; sentence; **giudizio di Dio** (hist) ordeal; **giudizio finale** Last Judgment; **metter giudizio** to mend one's ways

giudizió·so -sa [s] *adj* judicious, wise

giùggiola *f* jujube; (joc) trifle; **andare in brodo di giuggiole** to swoon, become ecstatic

giugno *m* June

giugulare *adj* jugular || *v* (**giùgolo**) *tr* to cut the throat of

giulèbbe *m* julep

giuliana *f* (culin) julienne || **Giuliana** Juliana

giuli·vo -va *adj* gay

giullare *m* jongleur; (pej) mountebank

giumén·to -ta *mf* beast of burden || *f* female saddle horse

giun·ca *f* (**-che**) (naut) junk

giunchìglia *f* (bot) jonquil

giun·co *m* (**-chi**) (bot) rush

giùngere §183 *tr* to join (*e.g., one's hands*) || *intr* (ESSERE) to arrive; **giungere a** or **in** to arrive at, reach; **giungere a** + *inf* to succeed in + *ger*; **mi giunge nuovo** it's news to me

giungla *f* jungle

Giunóne *f* Juno

giunòni·co -ca *adj* (**-ci -che**) Junoesque

giunta *f* addition; makeweight; strip (*of cloth*); junta; committee; **di prima giunta** at the very beginning; **per giunta** in addition

giuntare *tr* to join

giuntatrice *f* (mov) splicer

giunto *m* (**-chi**) (mach) joint, coupling;

giunto a sfere ball-and-socket joint; **giunto cardanico** universal joint

giuntura or **giunzióne** *f* joint; juncture, seam

giuò·co *m* (**-chi**) var of **gioco**

giuraménto *m* oath; **deferire il giuramento a** to put under oath

giurare *tr* to swear, pledge || *intr* to swear

giura·to -ta *adj* sworn || *m* juror

giurìa *f* committee; jury

giurìdi·co -ca *adj* (**-ci -che**) juridical

giurisdizióne *f* jurisdiction

giurisprudénza *f* jurisprudence

giuri·sta *mf* (**-sti -ste**) jurist

Giusèppe *m* Joseph

Giuseppina *f* Josephine

giusta *prep* according to; in accordance with

giustappórre §218 *tr* to juxtapose

giustézza *f* correctness, justness; (typ) measure

giustificàbile *adj* justifiable

giustificare §197 (**giustìfico**) *tr* to justify || *ref* to excuse oneself

giustificazióne *f* justification

giustìzia *f* justice; **far giustizia a** to execute; **farsi giustizia da sé** to take the law into one's own hands; **render giustizia a** to do justice to

giustiziare §287 *tr* to execute

giustizière *m* executioner; (obs) judge

giu·sto -sta *adj* just; opportune || *m* just man; just price; rights, due || **giusto** *adv* just, justly

gla·bro -bra *adj* smooth (*face*)

glaciale *adj* glacial; (fig) icy

gladiatóre *m* gladiator

gladiòlo *m* gladiolus

glàndola *f* var of **ghiandola**

glassa *f* glaze, icing

glassare *tr* to glaze, ice

glèba *f* clod, lump of earth

gli §4 *art* || §5 *pers pron*

glicerina *f* glycerin

glìcine *m* wistaria

gliéla; gliéle; gliéli; gliélo; gliéne §5

globale *adj* total, aggregate

glòbo *m* globe; **globo oculare** eyeball

globulare *adj* globular, global

glòbulo *m* globule; (physiol) corpuscle

gloglottare (**gloglòtto**) *intr* to gobble; to gurgle

gloglottì·o *m* (**-i**) gobble, gobbling; gurgle

glòria *f* glory

gloriare §287 (**glòrio**) *tr* (lit) to exalt || *ref* to boast; to glory

glorificare §197 (**glorìfico**) *tr* to glorify

glorió·so -sa [s] *adj* glorious; proud

glòssa *f* gloss

glossà·rio *m* (**-ri**) glossary

glòttide *f* glottis

glottòlo·go -ga *mf* (**-gi -ghe**) linguist

glucòsio *m* glucose

glùtine *m* gluten

gnòc·co *m* (**-chi**) potato dumpling

gnòmo *m* gnome

gnòrri *m invar*—**fare lo gnorri** to feign ignorance

gòb·bo -ba *adj* hunchbacked || *mf*

hunchback || *f* hump; hunch; hump (*of gibbous moon*); hook (*of nose*)

góc·cia *f* (**-ce**) drop; bead; **avere la goccia al naso** to have a runny nose; **goccia d'acqua** raindrop

góc·cio *m* (**-ci**) drop, swallow

gócciola *f* drop; bead

gocciolare §290 (**gócciolo**) *tr & intr* to drip

gocciola·tóio *m* (**-tói**) dripstone

gocciolì·o *m* (**-ì**) drip, trickle

godére §184 *tr* to enjoy || *intr* to take pleasure; to revel; to profit || *ref* to enjoy; **godersela** to have a good time

godìbile *adj* enjoyable

godiménto *m* enjoyment, pleasure

goffàggine *f* clumsiness

gòf·fo -fa *adj* awkward; ill-fitting

gógna *f* pillory; **mettere alla gogna** to pillory

góla *f* throat; neck; gluttony; gorge (*of mountain*); mouth (*of cannon*); flue (*of chimney*); (archit) ogee; **far gola a** to tempt; **mentire per la gola** to lie shamelessly; **tornare a gola** to repeat (*said of food*)

golétta *f* neck (*of shirt*); (naut) schooner

gòlf *m* (**gòlf**) sweater, cardigan; (sports) golf

gólfo *m* gulf; **golfo mistico** orchestra pit || **Golfo Persico** Persian Gulf

Gòlgota, il Golgotha

goliardo *m* goliard; university student

golosi·tà [s] *f* (**-tà**) gluttony; tidbit

golό·so -sa [s] *adj* gluttonous; appetizing

gómena *f* hawser

gomitata *f* blow with the elbow; nudge

gómito *m* elbow; bend; **alzare il gomito** to crook the elbow; **dare di gomito a** to nudge

gomìtolo *m* skein, clew

gómma *f* gum; rubber; eraser; tire; **bucare una gomma** to have a flat tire; **gomma arabica** gum arabic; **gomma a terra** flat tire; **gomma da masticare** chewing gum; **gomma lacca** shellac

gommapiuma *f* foam rubber

gomma·to -ta *adj* gummed; with tires

gommatura *f* gumming; (aut) tires

gommi·sta *m* (**-sti**) tire dealer; tire repairman

gommό·so -sa [s] *adj* gummy

góndola *f* gondola; (aer) pod

gonfalóne *m* gonfalon

gonfiare §287 (**gónfio**) *tr* to inflate, blow up; to bloat; to swell; to exaggerate; to puff up || *intr* (ESSERE) to swell || *ref* to swell; to puff up; to bulge, balloon

gonfiatura *f* inflation; exaggeration

gonfiézza *f* swelling; grandiloquence

gón·fio -fia (**-fi -fie**) *adj* inflated, swollen; conceited || *m* swelling, bulge

gonfióre *m* swelling

gongolare (**góngolo**) *intr* to rejoice; to be elated

goniòmetro *m* goniometer; protractor

gònna *f* skirt; **gonna pantaloni** culottes

gonnèlla *f* skirt; (fig) petticoat

gonnellino *m* kilt; ballerina skirt

gón·zo -za [dz] *mf* simpleton, fool

gòra *f* millpond; marsh; (coll) spot

górbia *f* tip (*of umbrella*)

gorgheggiare §290 (**gorghéggio**) *tr & intr* to warble; to trill

gorghég·gio *m* (**-gi**) warbling; trill

gór·go *m* (**-ghi**) whirlpool; (lit) river

gorgogliare §280 (**gorgóglio**) *intr* to gurgle

gorgό·glio *m* (**-gli**) gurgle

gorgogli·o *m* (**-i**) gurgling

goril·la *m* (**-la**) gorilla

gòta *f* cheek; (lit) side

gòti·co -ca *adj & m* (**-ci -che**) Gothic

Gòto *m* Goth

gótta *f* (pathol) gout

gottazza *f* (naut) scoop

gottό·so -sa [s] *adj* gouty

governale *m* fin (*of bomb*); (obs) rudder

governante *adj* governing || *m* ruler || *f* governess; housekeeper

governare (**govèrno**) *tr* to rule, govern; to steer (*a ship*); to tend (*animals*); to wash and dry (*dishes*); to run (*e.g., a bank*) || *intr* to steer

governati·vo -va *adj* government

govèrno *m* government; tending (*e.g., of animals*); running (*of household*); cleaning (*of house*); blending (*of wine*); (archaic) steering

gόzzo *m* crop, craw (*of bird*); (pathol) goiter

gozzovigliare §280 *intr* to go on a spree

gracchiare §287 *intr* to caw

gràc·chio *m* (**-chi**) caw; (orn) chough

gracidare (**gràcido**) *intr* to croak; to honk (*said, e.g., of a goose*)

gràcile *adj* weak, frail; thin, delicate

gradasso *m* swaggerer, braggadocio

grada·to -ta *adj* graded; gradual

gradazióne *f* gradation; alcoholic proof; **gradazione vocalica** (phonet) ablaut

gradévole *adj* pleasant

gradiménto *m* pleasure; acceptance (*of a product*); liking

gradinata *f* steps; tier (*of seats*)

gradino *m* step; (fig) stepping stone

gradire §176 *tr* to like; to welcome

gradi·to -ta *adj* agreeable; welcome (*guest*); kind (*letter*)

grado *m* degree; rank; (nav) rating; (archaic) step; **a buon grado o a mal grado** willy-nilly; **a grado a grado** little by little; **a Suo grado** according to your wishes; **di buon grado** willingly; **di secondo grado** secondary (*school*); **essere in grado di** to be in a position to; **saper grado a** (lit) to be grateful to

graduale *adj & m* gradual

graduare (**gràduo**) *tr* to graduate

gradua·to -ta *adj* graduated || *m* noncommissioned officer

graduatória *f* ranking; rank

graffa *f* clamp; brace, bracket

graffiare §287 *tr* to scratch; (coll) to swipe

graffiétto *m* tiny scratch; marking gage

gràf·fio *m* (**-fi**) scratch

grafia *f* writing, spelling; (gram) graph

gràfi·co -ca (-ci -che) *adj* graphic ‖ *m* graph, diagram; designer (*for printing industry*); member of printers' union ‖ *f* graphic arts

grafite *f* graphite

grafologia *f* graphology

gragnòla *f* hail

gramàglia *f* crepe; widow's weeds; **in gramaglie** in mourning

gramigna *f* couch grass; weed

grammàti·co -ca (-ci -che) *adj* grammatical ‖ *m* grammarian ‖ *f* grammar

grammo *m* gram

grammofòni·co -ca *adj* **(-ci -che)** phonograph, recording

grammòfono *m* phonograph, record player

gra·mo -ma *adj* poor, sad; wretched, miserable; frail, sickly

gran *adj* apocopated form of **grande**, used before singular and plural nouns beginning with a consonant sound other than *gn, pn, ps,* impure *s, x,* and *z*

gra·na *m* **(-na)** Parmesan cheese ‖ *f* **(-ne)** cochineal; grain (*of wood, metal, etc*); (slang) dough; (coll) trouble

granàglie *fpl* grain, cereals

gra·nàio *m* **(-nài)** granary, barn

granata *adj invar & m* garnet (*color*) ‖ *f* pomegranate (*fruit*); garnet; broom; grenade

granatière *m* grenadier

granatina *f* grenadine

Gran Bretagna, la Great Britain

grancassa *f* bass drum

grancèvola *f* spider crab

gràn·chio *m* **(-chi)** crab; claw (*of hammer*); (coll) cramp; **prendere un granchio** to make a blunder

grandangolare *adj* wide-angle

grande *adj* big, large; great; tall; high (*mass; voice*); long (*time*); capital (*letter*); full (*speed*); grown-up ‖ *m* grownup; grandeur; grandee; **fare il grande** to show off; **i grandi** the great; **in grande** on a large scale; lavishly

grandézza *f* size; enormity; greatness; quantity; **in grandezza naturale** lifesize; **grandezze** ostentatiousness

grandezzó·so -sa [s] *adj* ostentatious

grandiloquènza *f* grandiloquence

grandinare (gràndino) *tr* (obs) to hail ‖ *intr* to hail ‖ *impers* (ESSERE & AVERE)—**grandina** it is hailing

grandinata *f* hailstorm

gràndine *f* hail

grandiosi·tà [s] *f* **(-tà)** grandeur, magnificence

grandió·so -sa [s] *adj* grandiose, grand

grandu·ca *m* **(-chi)** grand duke

granduchéssa *f* grand duchess

granèllo *m* grain, seed; speck

grànfia *f* clutch

granìco·lo -la *adj* grain, wheat

granire §176 *tr* to grain; to stipple; (mus) to make (*the notes*) clear-cut ‖ *intr* to teethe

granita *f* sherbet, water ice

granito *m* granite

granitura *f* knurl, milled edge

grano *m* wheat; grain of wheat; grain; speck; **grano duro** durum wheat; **grano saraceno** buckwheat; **grano turco** corn

granturco *m* corn

granulare *adj* granular ‖ *v* **(grànulo)** *tr* to granulate

granulatóre *m* crusher

grànulo *m* granule, pellet, bud

granuló·so -sa [s] *adj* granular; lumpy; gritty; friable, crumbly

grappa *f* eau de vie; clamp, brace

grappétta *f* staple; crampon

grappino *m* (naut) grapnel

gràppolo *m* bunch, cluster

grassàg·gio *m* **(-gi)** (aut) lubrication

grassatóre *m* highwayman

grassazióne *f* holdup

grassétto *m* boldface

grassézza *f* fatness; richness

gras·so -sa *adj* fat; rich; greasy; risqué ‖ *m* fat, suet; grease; shortening

grassòc·cio -cia *adj* **(-ci -ce)** pudgy, plump

grata *f* grate, grating

gratèlla *f* strainer; sieve; broiler

gratic·cia *f* **(-ce)** (theat) gridiron

gratic·cio *m* **(-ci)** lattice, trellis

graticola *f* gridiron; grating; graticule

gratìfi·ca *f* **(-che)** bonus

gratificare §197 **(gratìfico)** *tr* to give a bonus to; (fig) to pelt (*with insults*)

gratificazióne *f* bonus

gratis *adv* gratis, free, for nothing

gratitùdine *f* gratitude

gra·to -ta *adj* grateful, appreciative ‖ *f* see **grata**

grattacapo *m* trouble, worry

grattacièlo *m* skyscraper

grattare *tr* to scratch; to scrape; to grate; (slang) to snitch ‖ *intr* to scratch; to grate

grattùgia *f* grater

grattugiare §290 *tr* to grate

gratùi·to -ta *adj* gratuitous, free

gravame *m* burden; tax; (law) appeal; **fare gravame a qlcu di qlco** to impute s.th to s.o.

gravare *tr* to burden, oppress; (obs) to seize ‖ *intr* (ESSERE & AVERE) to weigh; to lie; to be sorry, e.g., **gli grava d'avermi disturbato** he is sorry to have bothered me ‖ *ref*—**gravarsi di** to take upon oneself

grave *adj* heavy; burdensome; grave, serious ‖ *m* (phys) body; **stare sul grave** to put on airs

graveolènte *adj* stinking

gravézza *f* heaviness; burden; oppression; (obs) taxation

gravidanza *f* pregnancy

gràvi·do -da *adj* pregnant; fraught

gravi·tà *f* **(-tà)** gravity

gravitare (gràvito) *intr* to gravitate; to weigh, lie

gravitazióne *f* gravitation

gravó·so -sa [s] *adj* heavy; hard, burdensome; oppressive

gràzia *f* grace; pardon, mercy; delicacy; kindness; **di grazia!** please!;

essere nelle grazie di qlcu to be in s.o.'s good graces; **fare grazia di qlco a qlcu** to spare s.o. s.th; **grazia di Dio** abundance, bounty; **grazie!** thank you!; **grazie tante!** thanks a lot!; **in grazia di** thanks to; **male grazie** bad manners; **per grazie** as a favor; **render grazia a** to thank; **saper grazia a** to be thankful to

graziare §287 *tr* to pardon; **graziare qlcu di qlco** to grant s.th to s.o.

grazió·so -sa [s] *adj* graceful, pretty; gracious; (lit) free, gratuitous

Grècia, la Greece

grè·co -ca (-ci -che) *adj & mf* Greek ‖ *f* fret, fretwork; bullion (*on Italian general's hat*); tunic

gregà·rio -ria (-ri -rie) *adj* gregarious ‖ *m* private; follower

grég·ge m (-gi or -ge fpl) flock, herd

grég·gio -gia (-gi -ge) *adj* coarse; raw, unrefined ‖ *m* crude oil

gregoria·no -na *adj* Gregorian

grembiale *m* var of grembiule

grembiule *m* apron; frock; smock

grembiulino *m* pinafore

grèmbo *m* lap; womb; bosom

gremire §176 *tr* to crowd ‖ *ref* to become crowded

gremi·to -ta *adj* overcrowded

gréppia *f* manger, crib

gréto *m* dry gravel bed of a river

grettézza *f* stinginess; narrow-mindedness

grét·to -ta *adj* stingy; narrow-minded

grève *adj* heavy; uncouth; (lit) grievous

gréz·zo -za [ddzz] *adj* raw, crude; coarse

gridare *tr* to cry out; to cry for (*help*); (coll) to scold ‖ *intr* to cry out, shout

grido *m* cry (*of animal*) ‖ *m* (**grida** fpl) cry; scream; shout; yell; fame; **di grido** famous; **grido di guerra** war cry; **ultimo grido** latest fashion

grifa·gno -gna *adj* rapacious, fierce

griffa *f* hobnail; (mov, phot) sprocket

grifo *m* snout (*of pig*); (pej) snoot; (lit) griffin

grifóne *m* vulture; (mythol) griffin

grigia·stro -stra *adj* grayish

grì·gio -gia (-gi -ge) *adj & m* (**-gi -gie**) grey

grigiovérde *adj invar* olive-drab ‖ *m* olive-drab uniform

griglia *f* gridiron, broiler; grate, grille; (elec) grid (*of vacuum tube*)

grillare *tr* to grill, broil ‖ *intr* to sizzle; to bubble (*said of fermenting wine*); to have a sudden whim

grillétto *m* trigger

grillo *m* cricket; whim, fancy

grimaldèllo *m* picklock

grìnfia *f* claw, clutch; **grinfie** clutches

grinta *f* grim or foreboding face

grinza *f* wrinkle; crease; **non fare una grinza** to be perfect

grinzó·so -sa [s] *adj* wrinkled; creased

grippare *intr & ref* to bind, jam

grisèlla *f* (naut) ratline

gri·sou *m* (-sou) firedamp

grissino *m* breadstick

Groenlàndia, la Greenland

grómma *f* incrustation, deposit

grónda *f* eaves; slope (*of ground*)

grondàia *f* gutter (*of roof*)

grondare (**gróndo**) *tr* to drip ‖ *intr* (ESSERE) to ooze (*said, e.g., of perspiration*); to drip; **grondare di sangue** to stream with blood

gròppa *f* back (*of animal*); top (*of mountain*); **restare sulla groppa a** to be stuck with, e.g., **gli sono restati sulla groppa cento esemplari** he is stuck with one hundred copies

groppata *f* bucking (*of horse*)

gróppo *m* knot, tangle; lump (*in throat*); squall

groppóne *m* back, rump

gròssa *f* gross; **dormire della grossa** to sleep like a log

grossézza *f* bigness; thickness; density; swelling (*of river*); (fig) coarseness; **grossezza d'udito** hardness of hearing

grossi·sta *mf* (**-sti -ste**) wholesaler

gròs·so -sa *adj* big, large; thick; heavy (*seas*); swollen (*river*); hard (*breathing*); offensive (*words*); coarse (*e.g., salt*); pregnant; deep (*voice*); (coll) important; **alla grossa** approximately; **di grosso** a lot, very much; **dirla grossa** to talk nonsense; **farla grossa** to make a blunder; **grosso d'udito** hard of hearing; **in grosso** wholesale; **spararle grosse** to tell tall tales ‖ *m* bulk; main body (*e.g., of an army*) ‖ *f see* grossa

grossola·no -na *adj* coarse; boorish, uncouth; big (*blunder*)

gròtta *f* grotto; (coll) inn

grotté·sco -sca (-schi -sche) *adj & m* grotesque ‖ *f* (hist) grotesque painting

grovièra *f* Gruyère cheese

grovì·glio m (-gli) tangle, snarl

gru *f* (**gru**) (orn, mach) crane

grùc·cia *f* (**-ce**) crutch; clothes hanger; (obs) wooden leg

grufolare (**grùfolo**) *intr* to nuzzle ‖ *ref* to wallow (*in mud*)

grugnire §176 *tr & intr* to grunt

grugnito *m* grunt

grugno *m* snout; (pej) snoot; **fare il grugno** to sulk

grui·sta *m* (**-sti**) crane operator

grulleria *f* foolishness

grul·lo -la *adj* silly, simple

gruma *f* deposit, incrustation

grumo *m* lump; clot

grùmolo *m* heart (*e.g., of lettuce*); small lump

grumó·so -sa [s] *adj* lumpy; incrusted, scaly

gruppo *m* group; main body (*e.g., of runners*); club; **gruppo elettrogeno** generating unit; **gruppo motore** (aut) power plant

grùzzolo *m* hoard, pile; **farsi il gruzzolo** to feather one's nest

guadagnare *tr* to earn; to win; to gain; to pick up (*speed*); to reach (*port*) ‖ *intr* to win; to look better ‖ *ref* to win; to win over; **guadagnarsi il pane** or **la vita** to earn one's living

guadagno *m* earnings; profit; **a basso**

guadagno (rad, telv) low-gain; **ad alto guadagno** (rad, telv) high-gain
guadare tr to wade, ford
guado m ford; (bot) woad; **passare a guado** to ford
guài interj woe!
guaina f case; scabbard, sheath; corset; (aut) seat cover
guàio m (**guài**) trouble ‖ interj see **guài**
guaire §176 intr to yelp; to whine
guaito m yelp, whine
gualcire §176 tr to crumple
gualdrappa f saddlecloth
Gualtièro m Walter
guàn·cia f (-ce) cheek; moldboard; cheek side (of gunstock)
guanciale m pillow; **dormire tra due guanciali** to sleep safe and sound
guan·tàio -tàia mf (-tài -tàie) glove maker; glove merchant
guanterìa f glove factory
guantièra f glove case; tray
guanto m glove; **gettare il guanto** to fling down the gauntlet; **raccogliere il guanto** to take up the gauntlet; **trattare con i guanti gialli** to handle with kid gloves
guantóne m big glove; **guantoni da pugilato** boxing gloves
guardabarriè·re m (-re) (rr) gatekeeper, crossing watchman
guardabò·schi m (-schi) forester
guardacà·cia m (-cia) gamekeeper
guardacò·ste m (-ste) coast guard; coast-guard cutter
guardafi·li m (-li) (elec) lineman
guardal·nee m (-nee) (rr) trackwalker; (sports) linesman
guardama·no m (-no) guard (of sabre or rifle); work glove; (naut) handrail
guardaportó·ne m (-ne) doorman
guardare tr to look at; to protect, watch; to pay attention to; to face, overlook; (obs) to keep to (one's bed); (obs) to keep (a holiday); **guardare a vista** to keep under close watch; **guardare dall'alto in basso** to look down one's nose at; **guardare di sotto in su** to leer at ‖ intr to look; to pay attention; **Dio guardi!** God forbid!; **guardare a** to face (said, e.g., of a room); **guardare di non** + inf to be careful not to + inf; **guardare in faccia** to face (e.g., danger); **stare a guardare** to keep on the sidelines ‖ ref to look at one another; to look at oneself; **guardarsi da** to keep from; to guard against
guardaro·ba m (-ba) wardrobe; linen closet; checkroom, cloakroom
guardarobiè·re -ra mf checkroom attendant ‖ f hatcheck girl
guardasigil·li m (-li) minister of justice (in Italy); (Brit) Lord Privy Seal; (U.S.A.) attorney general; (hist) keeper of the seals
guardaspal·le m (-le) bodyguard
guardata f quick look, glance
guarda·vìa m (-vìa) guardrail; median strip
guàrdia f watch; guard; top water level; flyleaf; **di guardia** on duty;

fare la guardia a to watch; **guardia campestre** forester; **guardia carceraria** prison guard; **guardia del corpo** guard, body guard; **guardia di finanza** customs officer; **guardia d'onore** honor guard; **guardia forestale** forester; park guard; **guardia giurata** private policeman; **guardia medica** emergency clinic; **guardia municipale** police officer; **guardia notturna** night watch; **mettere qlcu in guardia** to warn s.o.; **montare la guardia** to be on guard duty, keep guard; **stare in guardia** to be on one's guard
guardiamari·na m (-na) (nav) ensign
guardiano m keeper; warden; watchdog; (eccl) superior; **guardiano notturno** night watchman
guardina f lockup; **in guardina** in jail
guardinfante m bustle (worn under the back of a woman's skirt)
guardin·go -ga adj (-ghi -ghe) wary
guàrdolo m welt (in shoe)
guardóne m peeping tom
guarenti·gìa f (-gìe) guarantee
guaribile adj curable
guarigióne f cure, recovery
guarire §176 tr to cure; to heal ‖ intr (ESSERE) to recover; to heal
guaritóre m healer; quack
guarnigióne f (mil) garrison
guarnìre §176 tr to equip; to rig; to trim; (naut) to rig; (culin) to garnish ‖ intr to add beauty
guarnizióne f decoration; trimming; lining; (culin) garniture; (mach) gasket; (mach) washer
Guascógna, la Gascony
guascó·ne -na adj & mf Gascon
guastafè·ste mf (-ste) kill-joy
guastare tr to ruin, spoil; to undo; to wreck; (obs) to lay waste; **guastare le uova nel paniere a** to spoil the plans of ‖ ref to spoil; to worsen (said, e.g., of the weather); (mach) to break down; **guastarsi con qlcu** to quarrel with s.o.; **guastarsi il sangue** to blow one's top
guastatóre m commando
gua·sto -sta adj ruined, spoiled; wrecked ‖ m breakdown; corruption; discord
guatare tr (lit) to look askance or with fear at
Guayana, la Guyana
guazza f dew
guazzabù·glio m (-gli) muddle, mess
guazzare tr to make (an animal) wade in a river ‖ intr to wallow
guazzétto m stew, ragout
guazzo m puddle, pool; gouache
guèl·fo -fa adj & mf Guelph
guèr·cio -cia (-ci -ce) adj cross-eyed; one-eyed; almost blind ‖ mf cross-eyed person; one-eyed person
guèrra f war; warfare; **guerra a coltello** internecine feud; **guerra di Troia** Trojan war; **guerra fredda** cold war; **guerra lampo** blitzkrieg; **guerra mondiale** world war

guerrafon·dàio -dàia (-dài -dàie) *adj* warmongering ‖ *mf* warmonger

guerreggiare §290 **(guerréggio)** *tr* to fight, war against ‖ *intr* to fight ‖ *ref* to make war on one another

guerré·sco -sca *adj* **(-schi -sche)** warlike

guerriè·ro -ra *adj* war, warlike ‖ *mf* fighter ‖ *m* warrior

guerrìglia *f* guerrilla

guerriglièro *m* guerrilla (*soldier*)

gufo *m* misanthrope; (orn) horned owl

gùglia *f* spire; peak

gugliata *f* needleful

Guglièlmo *m* William

guida *f* guide; guidance; driving; runner (*rug*); guidebook; manual (*of instruction*); (aut) steering; **guida a destra** right-hand drive; **guide reins** (*of horse*); (mach) slide

guidaiòlo *m* leader (*among animals*)

guidare *tr* to guide, lead; to steer; to drive ‖ *intr* to drive ‖ *ref* to restrain oneself

guida·tóre -trice *mf* driver

guiderdóne *m* (lit) premium, prize

guidóne *m* pennant, pennon

guidoslitta *f* bobsled

guidovìa *f* ski lift

Guinèa, la Guinea

guinzà·glio *m* **(-gli)** leash; (fig) fetter, shackle

guisa *f* way, manner; **in guisa che** so that; **in guisa di** under the guise of

guit·to -ta *adj* miserly, niggardly ‖ *m* strolling player

guizzare *intr* to dart; to wriggle; to flash (*said of lightning*); (naut) to yaw ‖ *intr* (ESSERE) to slip away

guizzo *m* dart; wriggle; flash

gù·scio *m* **(-sci)** shell; pod (*of pea*); tick (*of mattress*); **guscio di noce** nutshell; **guscio d'uovo** eggshell

gustare *tr* to taste; to relish ‖ *intr* (ESSERE & AVERE) to please; to like, e.g., **gli gustano le gite in barca** he likes boat rides

gusto *m* taste; pleasure, fun; whim; style; **di cattivo gusto** tasteless; **di gusto** gladly, with gusto; **prendere gusto per** to take a liking for; **prendersi il gusto di** to relish; **provar gusto** to have fun

gustó·so -sa [s] *adj* tasty

guttapèrca *f* gutta-percha

gutturale *adj* & *f* guttural

H

H, h ['akka] *m* & *f* eighth letter of the Italian alphabet

handicappare *tr* var of **andicappare**

hangar *m* **(hangar)** hangar

havaia·no -na *adj* & *mf* Hawaiian

henné *m* henna

hertz *m* hertz

hertzia·no -na *adj* Hertzian

hi-fi *f* (coll) hi-fi

hockei·sta *m* **(-sti)** hockey player

hollywoodia·no -na *adj* Hollywood, Hollywood-like

hurrà *interj* hurrah!

I

I, i, [i] *m* & *f* ninth letter of the Italian alphabet

i §4 *def art* the

iarda *f* yard

iato *m* hiatus

iattanza *f* boasting, bragging

iattura *f* misfortune, calamity

ibèri·co -ca *adj* **(-ci -che)** Iberian

ibernare (ibèrno) *intr* to hibernate

ibi·sco *m* **(-schi)** hibiscus

ibridare (ìbrido) *tr* & *intr* to hybridize

ìbri·do -da *adj* & *m* hybrid

icàsti·co -ca *adj* **(-ci -che)** figurative; realistic

-ìccio -ìccia *suf adj* -ish, e.g., **gialliccio** yellowish

iconocla·sta *mf* **(-sti -ste)** iconoclast

iconografìa *f* iconography

iconoscò·pio *m* **(-pi)** iconoscope

iddì·o *m* **(-i)** god ‖ **Iddìo** *m* God

idèa *f* idea; goal, purpose; bit; touch; **avere idea di** to have a mind to; **dare l'idea di** to seem; **farsi un'idea di** to grasp the notion of; **idea fissa** fixed idea; **neanche per idea** not in the least

ideale *adj* & *m* ideal

idealismo *m* idealism

ideali·sta *mf* **(-sti -ste)** idealist

idealìsti·co -ca *adj* **(-ci -che)** idealistic

idealizzare [ddzz] *tr* to idealize

ideare (idèo) *tr* to conceive

idea·tóre -trice *mf* inventor

idem *adv* ditto

idènti·co -ca *adj* **(-ci -che)** identical

identificare §197 **(identìfico)** *tr* to identify ‖ *ref* to resemble each other; **identificarsi con** to identify with

identificazióne *f* identification

identi·tà *f* **(-tà)** identity

ideologìa *f* ideology

idi *mpl* & *fpl* ides

idillìa·co -ca *adj* **(-ci -che)** idyllic

idìl·lio *m* **(-li)** idyll; romance

idiò·ma *m* **(-mi)** language, idiom

idiomàti·co -ca *adj* **(-ci -che)** idiomatic

idiosincrasìa _f_ aversion; (med) idiosyncrasy
idiò·ta (**-ti -te**) _adj_ idiotic || _mf_ idiot
idiotismo _m_ idiom; idiocy
idiozìa _f_ idiocy
idolatrare _tr & intr_ to idolize
idolatrìa _f_ idolatry
ìdolo _m_ idol
idonei·tà _f_ (**-tà**) fitness, aptitude; qualification
idòne·o -a _adj_ fit; qualified; opportune
idra _f_ hydra
idrante _m_ hydrant, fireplug
idratante _adj_ moisturizing
idratare _tr & ref_ to hydrate
idrato _m_ hydrate
idràuli·co -ca (**-ci -che**) _adj_ hydraulic || _m_ plumber || _f_ hydraulics
idri·co -ca _adj_ (**-ci -che**) water, e.g., **forza idrica** water power
idrocarburo _m_ hydrocarbon
idroelèttri·co -ca _adj_ (**-ci -che**) hydroelectric
idròfi·lo -la _adj_ absorbent
idrofobìa _f_ hydrophobia, rabies
idròfo·bo -ba _adj_ hydrophobic, rabid
idròfu·go -ga _adj_ (**-ghi -ghe**) waterproof
idrogenare (**idrògeno**) _tr_ to hydrogenate
idrògeno _m_ hydrogen
idròpi·co -ca (**-ci -che**) _adj_ dropsical || _mf_ patient suffering from dropsy
idropisìa _f_ dropsy
idroplano _m_ hydroplane (_boat_)
idropòrto _m_ seaplane airport
idrorepellènte _adj_ water-repellent
idroscalo _m_ seaplane airport
idro·scì _m_ (**-scì**) water ski
idroscivolante _m_ (naut) hydroplane
idrosilurante _m_ torpedo plane
idròssido _m_ hydroxide
idroterapìa _f_ hydrotherapy
idrovìa _f_ inland waterway
idrovolante _m_ seaplane, hydroplane
idròvo·ro -ra _adj_ suction (_pump_) || _f_ suction pump
ièna _f_ hyena
ièri _m & adv_ yesterday; **ieri l'altro** the day before yesterday; **ieri notte** last night; **ieri sera** last evening, last night, yesterday evening
iettatóre -trice _mf_ hoodoo
iettatura _f_ evil eye; bad luck, jinx
igiène _f_ hygiene; sanitation
igièni·co -ca _adj_ (**-ci -che**) hygienic, sanitary
igname _m_ yam
igna·ro -ra _adj_ unaware; inexperienced
igna·vo -va _adj_ (lit) slothful
ignizióne _f_ ignition
ignòbile _adj_ (lit) ignoble
ignominìa _f_ ignominy; outrage
ignominió·so -sa [_s_] _adj_ ignominious
ignorante _adj_ ignorant; illiterate || _mf_ ignoramus
ignoranza _f_ ignorance
ignorare (**ignòro**) _tr_ to not know; to ignore
ignò·to -ta _adj & m_ unknown
ignu·do -da _adj_ (lit) naked || _m_ (lit) naked person
il §4 _def art_ the
ìlare _adj_ cheerful

ilari·tà _f_ (**-tà**) cheerfulness; laughter
ilice _f_ (lit) ilex, holm oak
ìlio _m_ (anat) ilium
illanguidire §176 _tr_ to weaken || _intr_ (ESSERE) to get weak
illazióne _f_ inference
illéci·to -ta _adj_ illicit, unlawful || _m_ unlawful act
illegale _adj_ illegal
illeggiadrire §176 _tr_ to embellish
illeggìbile _adj_ illegible
illegìtti·mo -ma _adj_ illegitimate
illé·so -sa _adj_ unhurt, unharmed
illettera·to -ta _adj & mf_ illiterate
illiba·to -ta _adj_ spotless, pure
illimita·to -ta _adj_ unlimited
illìri·co -ca _adj_ (**-ci -che**) Illyrian
illògi·co -ca _adj_ (**-ci -che**) illogical
illùdere §105 _tr_ to delude
illuminare (**illùmino**) _tr_ to illuminate; to brighten; to enlighten || _ref_ to grow bright
illumina·to -ta _adj_ illuminated; enlightened; educated
illuminazióne _f_ illumination; enlightenment
illuminismo _m_ Age of Enlightenment
illusióne _f_ illusion; delusion; **farsi illusioni** to indulge in wishful thinking
illusionismo _m_ sleight of hand; magic
illusioni·sta _mf_ (**-sti -ste**) magician
illu·so -sa _adj_ deluded || _mf_ deluded person
illusò·rio -ria _adj_ (**-ri -rie**) illusory, illusive
illustrare _tr_ to illustrate; to explain, elucidate || _ref_ to become famous
illustra·to -ta _adj_ illustrated, pictorial
illustra·tóre -trice _mf_ illustrator
illustrazióne _f_ illustration; illustrious person
illustre _adj_ illustrious, famous
illustrìssi·mo -ma _adj_ distinguished; honorable; **Illustrissimo Signore** Dear Sir; Mr. (_addressing a letter_)
imbacuccare §197 _tr & ref_ to muffle up; to wrap up
imbaldanzire §176 _tr_ to embolden || _intr_ (ESSERE) & _ref_ to grow bold
imballàg·gio _m_ (**-gi**) wrapping, packaging
imballare _tr_ to wrap up, package; to bale; to race (_the motor_); **imballare in una gabbia** to crate || _ref_ to race (_said of a motor_)
imballa·tóre -trice _mf_ packer
imballo _m_ packing; packaging, wrapping; racing (_of motor_)
imbalsamare (**imbàlsamo**) _tr_ to embalm; to stuff (_animals_)
imbambola·to -ta _adj_ gazing, staring; stunned, dumfounded; sleepy-eyed; sluggish
imbandierare (**imbandièro**) _tr_ to bedeck with flags
imbandire §176 _tr_ to prepare (_food, a meal, a table_) lavishly
imbarazzante _adj_ embarrassing, awkward
imbarazzare _tr_ to embarrass; to encumber, hamper; to upset (_the stomach_)

imbarazza·to -ta *adj* embarrassed, perplexed; upset (*stomach*); ill-at-ease

imbarazzo *m* embarrassment; annoyance; **imbarazzo di stomaco** upset stomach

imbarbarire §176 *tr & ref* to make barbarous; to corrupt (*a language*)

imbarcadèro *m* landing pier

imbarcare §197 *tr* to ship; to load, embark; to ship (*water*) ‖ *ref* to sail; to embark; to curve (*said of furniture*)

imbarca·tóio *m* (**-tói**) landing pier

imbarcazióne *f* boat; **imbarcazione di salvataggio** lifeboat

imbar·co *m* (**-chi**) embarkation; port of embarkation

imbardare *intr & ref* (aer) to yaw; (aut) to swerve, lurch

imbardata *f* (aer) yaw; (aut) swerve, lurch

imbarilare *tr* to barrel

imbastardire §176 *tr* to corrupt ‖ *ref* to become corrupt

imbastire §176 *tr* (sew) to baste; (fig) to sketch out

imbastitura *f* (sew) basting

imbàttere *ref*—**imbattersi bene** to be lucky; **imbattersi in** to come across; **imbattersi male** to have bad luck

imbattìbile *adj* unbeatable

imbavagliare §280 *tr* to gag

imbeccare §197 (**imbécco**) *tr* to feed (*a fledgling*); (fig) to prompt

imbeccata *f* beakful; (fig) prompting

imbecillàggine *f* imbecility

imbecille *adj & mf* imbecile

imbecilli·tà *f* (**-tà**) imbecility

imbèlle *adj* unwarlike; cowardly

imbellettare (**imbellétto**) *tr* to apply rouge to, apply make-up on ‖ *ref* to put on make-up

imbellire §176 *tr* to embellish

imbèrbe *adj* beardless; callow

imbestialire §176 *tr* to enrage ‖ *intr* (ESSERE) & *ref* to become enraged

imbévere §185 *tr* to soak; to soak up; to imbue ‖ *ref* to become soaked; to become imbued

imbiancare §197 *tr* to whiten; to bleach; to whitewash ‖ *intr* (ESSERE) & *ref* to turn white (*said, e.g., of hair*); to clear up (*said of weather*)

imbiancatura *f* bleaching (*of laundry*); whitening; whitewashing

imbianchimento *m* bleaching

imbianchino *m* whitewasher; house painter; (pej) dauber

imbianchire §176 *tr* to whiten; to bleach ‖ *ref* to turn white

imbiondire §176 *tr* to bleach (*hair*) ‖ *intr* to become blond; to ripen (*said of wheat*)

imbizzarrire [ddzz] *intr* (ESSERE) & *ref* to become skittish (*said of a horse*); to become infuriated

imbizzire [ddzz] §176 *intr* (ESSERE) to get angry

imboccare §197 (**imbócco**) *tr* to feed by mouth; to put (*an instrument*) in one's mouth; to take, enter (*a road*); to prompt ‖ *intr* (ESSERE) to

flow; to open (*said of a road*); (mach) to fit

imboccatura *f* entrance (*of street*); inlet; opening, top (*e.g., of bottle*); bit (*of bridle*); (mus) mouthpiece; **avere l'imboccatura a** to be experienced in

imbóc·co *m* (**-chi**) entrance; inlet; opening

imbonimento *m* claptrap

imbonire §176 *tr* to lure, entice (*s.o. to buy or enter*)

imbonitóre *m* barker

imborghesire §176 *tr* to render middle-class ‖ *intr* (ESSERE) to become middle-class

imboscare §197 (**imbòsco**) *tr* to hide; to hide (*s.o.*) underground ‖ *ref* to shirk; to be a slacker

imbosca·to -ta *adj* (mil) shirking, draft-dodging ‖ *m* (mil) slacker; (mil) goldbrick ‖ *f* ambush; **tendere un'imboscata** to set an ambush

imboscatóre *m* accomplice of a draft dodger; hoarder (*of scarce items*)

imboschire §176 *tr* to forest

imbottare (**imbótto**) *tr* to barrel

imbottigliare §280 *tr* to bottle; to bottle up ‖ *ref* to get bottled up (*said of traffic*)

imbottire §176 *tr* to pad, fill; to stuff; to pad (*a speech*)

imbottita *f* bedspread, quilt

imbottitura *f* padding

imbra·ca *f* (**-che**) breeching strap (*of harness*); safety belt; (naut) sling

imbracare §197 *tr* to sling

imbracciare §128 *tr* to fasten (*shield*); to level (*gun*)

imbrancare §197 *tr & ref* to herd

imbrattacar·te *mf* (**-te**) scribbler

imbrattamu·ri *mf* (**-ri**) dauber

imbrattare *tr* to soil, dirty; to smudge, smear

imbrattate·le *mf* (**-le**) dauber

imbratto *m* dirt; smudge, smear; daub; scribble; swill

imbrigliare §280 *tr* to bridle

imbroccare §197 (**imbròcco**) *tr* to hit (*the target*); to guess right

imbrodare (**imbròdo**) *tr* to soil

imbrogliare §280 (**imbròglio**) *tr* to cheat; to mix up; to tangle; to confuse; **imbrogliare le vele** (naut) to take in the reef ‖ *ref* to get tangled up; to get confused; to turn bad (*said of weather*)

imbrò·glio *m* (**-gli**) cheat; tangle; (naut) reef; **cacciarsi in un imbroglio** to get involved in a mess

imbroglió·ne -na *mf* swindler

imbronciare §128 (**imbróncio**) *intr* (ESSERE) & *ref* to pout, sulk ‖ *ref* to lower (*said of the weather*)

imbroncia·to -ta *adj* sulky, surly; cloudy, overcast

imbrunire *m*—**sull'imbrunire** at nightfall ‖ §176 *intr* (ESSERE) to turn brown ‖ *impers* (ESSERE)—**imbrunisce** it is growing dark

imbruttire §176 *tr* to mar; to make ugly ‖ *intr* (ESSERE) & *ref* to grow ugly

imbucare §197 *tr* to mail; to put in a hole ‖ *ref* to hide

imburrare *tr* to butter
imbuto *m* funnel
imène *m* (anat) hymen, maidenhead
imitare (**ìmito**) *tr* to imitate
imita·tóre -trice *mf* imitator; (theat) mimic
imitazióne *f* imitation
immacola·to -ta *adj* immaculate
immagazzinare [ddzz] *tr* to store, store up
immaginare (**immàgino**) *tr* to imagine; to guess; to invent || *ref*—**si immagini!** of course!; not at all!
immaginà·rio -ria *adj* (**-ri -rie**) imaginary
immaginativa *f* imagination
immaginazióne *f* imagination
immàgine *f* image; picture
immaginó·so -sa [s] *adj* imaginative
immalinconire §176 *tr* to sadden || *intr* (ESSERE) & *ref* to become melancholy
immancàbile *adj* unfailing; certain
immane *adj* monstrous; gigantic
immangiàbile *adj* uneatable, inedible
immantinènte *adv* (lit) immediately
immarcescìbile *adj* incorruptible
immateriale *adj* immaterial
immatricolare (**immatrìcolo**) *tr* to matriculate
immatricolazióne *f* matriculation
immatu·ro -ra *adj* immature; premature
immedesimare (**immedésimo**) *tr* to identify; to blend || *ref* to identify oneself
immediataménte *adv* immediately
immediatézza *f* immediacy
immedia·to -ta *adj* immediate
immemoràbile *adj* immemorial
immèmore *adj* forgetful
immèn·so -sa *adj* immense, huge
immèrgere §162 *tr* to immerse; to plunge || *ref* to plunge; to become absorbed
immerita·to -ta *adj* undeserved
immeritévole *adj* undeserving
immersióne *f* immersion; submersion (*of a submarine*); (naut) draft
immèttere §198 *tr* to let in; **inmettere qlcu nel possesso di** (law) to grant s.o. possession of
immigrante *adj* & *mf* immigrant
immigrare *intr* (ESSERE) to immigrate
immigrazióne *f* immigration; (biol) migration
imminènte *adj* imminent
imminènza *f* imminence
immischiare §287 *tr* to involve || *ref* to meddle
immiserire §176 *tr* to impoverish || *intr* (ESSERE) & *ref* to become impoverished; to become debased
immissà·rio *m* (**-ri**) tributary
immissióne *f* letting in, introduction; intake; insertion (*in lunar orbit*)
immòbile *adj* motionless, immobile; real (*property*) || **immobili** *mpl* real estate
immobiliare *adj* real, e.g., **proprietà immobiliare** real estate; real-estate, e.g., **imposta immobiliare** real-estate tax
immobilizzare [ddzz] *tr* to immobilize; to pin down; to tie up (*capital*)

immodè·sto -sta *adj* indecent; immodest
immolare (**immòlo**) *tr* to immolate
immondézza *f* filth; impurity
immondez·zàio *m* (**-zài**) rubbish heap, dump; garbage can
immondìzia *f* trash; garbage; filth
immón·do -da *adj* filthy, dirty; unclean
immorale *adj* immoral
immorali·tà *f* (**-tà**) immorality
immortalare *tr* to immortalize
immortale *adj* immortal
immortali·tà *f* immortality
immò·to -ta *adj* (lit) motionless
immune *adj* immune
immunizzare [ddzz] *tr* to immunize
immutàbile *adj* immutable
immuta·to -ta *adj* unchanged
i·mo -ma *adj* (lit) bottom, lowest || *m* (lit) bottom; (lit) depth
impaccare §197 *tr* to pack, wrap up
impacchettare (**impacchétto**) *tr* to pack, bundle
impacciare §128 *tr* to hamper; to embarrass || *ref* to meddle
impaccia·to -ta *adj* hampered; clumsy
impàc·cio *m* (**-ci**) embarrassment; hindrance; trouble; **essere d'impaccio** to be in the way
impac·co *m* (**-chi**) wrapping; (med) compress
impadronire §176 *ref*—**impadronirsi di** to seize; to take possession of; to master (*a language*)
impagàbile *adj* invaluable, priceless
impaginare (**impàgino**) *tr* (typ) to make up (*in pages*), paginate
impaginato *m* (typ) page proof
impagliare §280 *tr* to cane (*a chair*), to stuff (*an animal; a doll*); to pack in straw
impalare *tr* to impale; to tie to a pole or stake || *ref* to stiffen up
impala·to -ta *adj* stiff, rigid
impalcatura *f* scaffold; frame, framework
impallidire §176 *intr* to turn pale; to blanch; to grow dim (*said of a star*); (fig) to wane
impalmare *tr* (lit) to wed
impalpàbile *adj* impalpable
impaludare *tr* to make swampy or marshy || *intr* to become marshy
impanare *tr* to bread; to thread (*a screw*) || *intr* to screw in
impaniare §287 *tr* to trap, ensnare || *ref* to fall into the trap
impantanare *tr* to turn into a swamp || *ref* to get stuck, to sink (*in vice*)
impaperare (**impàpero**) *ref* to fluff, make a slip
impappinare *tr* to confuse || *ref* to blunder; to stammer
imparare *tr* to learn; **imparare a memoria** to learn by heart || *intr* **imparare a** to learn to, to learn how to
impareggiàbile *adj* peerless, unmatched
imparentare (**imparènto**) *tr* to bring into the family || *ref*—**imparentarsi con** to marry into
impari *adj* odd, uneven
imparrucca·to -ta *adj* bewigged
impartire §176 *tr* to impart
imparziale *adj* impartial

impasse *f* blind alley; deadlock; (cards) finesse

impassìbile *adj* impassible, impassive

impastare *tr* to knead; to mix; to smear with paste

impasta·to -ta *adj* kneaded; smeared; impastato di tainted with; overwhelmed with (*sleep*)

impasto *m* paste; pastiche

impastoiare §287 (impastóio) *tr* to fetter, hamstring

impataccare §197 *tr* to besmear, soil

impattare *tr* to even up; to tie (*a game*); impattarla con to tie (*a person*)

impatto *m* impact

impaurire §176 *tr* to scare || *ref* to get scared

impàvi·do -da *adj* fearless

impaziente *adj* impatient

impazientire §176 *intr* (ESSERE) & *ref* to get impatient

impaziènza *f* impatience

impazzare *intr* (ESSERE) to be wild with excitement; to go mad; (culin) to curdle

impazzata *f*—all'impazzata at top speed; berserk

impazzire §176 *intr* (ESSERE) to go crazy; fare impazzire to drive crazy

impeccàbile *adj* impeccable

impeciare §128 (impécio) *tr* to tar

impedènza *f* impedance

impedimén̄to *m* hindrance, obstacle, impediment

impedire §176 *tr* to impede, hinder; to obstruct || *intr* to prevent; impedire (with *dat*) di + *inf* or che + *subj* to prevent from + *ger*

impegnare (impégno) *tr* to pawn; to reserve (*a room*); to engage (*the enemy*); to keep occupied; to pledge || *ref* to obligate oneself; to go all out; to become engaged

impegnati·vo -va *adj* demanding (*activity*); binding (*promise*)

impegna·to -ta *adj* pawned; pledged; occupied; committed

impégno *m* commitment; obligation; task; zeal; senza impegno without promising

impegolare (impégolo) *tr* to tar || *ref* to become entangled

impelagare §209 (impèlago) *ref* to bog down; to become entangled

impellicciare §128 *tr* to fur; to veneer

impenetràbile *adj* impenetrable

impenitènte *adj* impenitent; confirmed

impennàg·gio *m* (-gi) (aer) empennage

impennare (impénno) *tr* to feather; (fig) to give wings to || *ref* to rear (*said of a horse*); to take umbrage; (aer) to zoom

impennata *f* rearing (*of horse*); (aer) zoom

impensàbile *adj* unthinkable

impensa·to -ta *adj* unexpected

impensierire §176 *tr* & *ref* to worry

imperante *adj* prevailing

imperare (impèro) *intr* to rule, reign; to prevail; imperare su to rule over

imperati·vo -va *adj* & *m* imperative

imperatóre *m* emperor

imperatrice *f* empress

impercettìbile *adj* imperceptible

imperdonàbile *adj* unforgivable

imperfèt·to -ta *adj* & *m* imperfect

imperfezióne *f* imperfection

imperiale *adj* imperial || *m* upper deck (*of bus or coach*); imperiali imperial troops

imperiali·sta *adj* & *mf* (-sti -ste) imperialist

impè·rio *m* (-ri) empire; rule

imperió·so -sa [s] *adj* imperious; imperative

imperi·to -ta *adj* (lit) inexperienced

imperitu·ro -ra *adj* immortal; everlasting, imperishable

imperìzia *f* inexperience

imperlare (impèrlo) *tr* to bead; to cover with beads (*of perspiration*)

impermalire §176 *tr* to provoke || *ref* to become provoked

impermeàbile *adj* waterproof || *m* raincoat

imperniare §287 (impèrnio) *tr* to pivot; (fig) to base

impèro *adj invar* Empire || *m* empire; control, sway

imperscrutàbile *adj* inscrutable

impersonale *adj* impersonal

impersonare (impersóno) *tr* to impersonate || *ref*—impersonarsi in to be the embodiment of; (theat) to impersonate

impertèrri·to -ta *adj* undaunted

impertinènte *adj* impertinent, pert

impertinènza *f* impertinence

imperturbàbile *adj* imperturbable

imperturba·to -ta *adj* unperturbed

imperversare (impervèrso) *intr* to storm, rage; to be the rage

impèr·vio -via *adj* (-vi -vie) impassable

ìmpeto *m* impetus; onslaught; violence; outburst; d'impeto rashly

impetrare (impètro) *tr* to beg for; to obtain by entreaty || *intr* (ESSERE) (lit) to turn to stone

impetti·to -ta *adj* puffed up with pride

impetuó·so -sa [s] *adj* impetuous

impiallacciare §128 *tr* to veneer

impiallacciatura *f* veneer, veneering

impiantare *tr* to install (*a machine*); to set up (*a business*); to open (*an account*)

impiantito *m* floor, flooring

impianto *m* installation; plant; system

impiastrare *tr* to plaster; to dirty

impiastricciare §128 *tr* to plaster; to daub; to soil

impiastro *m* (med) plaster; (fig) bore

impiccagióne *f* hanging

impiccare §197 *tr* to hang

impicciare §128 *tr* to hinder; to bother || *ref* to meddle, butt in; impicciarsi degli affari propri to mind one's own business

impìc·cio *m* (-ci) hindrance; trouble; essere d'impiccio to be in the way

impicció·ne -na *mf* meddler

impiccolire §176 *tr* to reduce in size || *ref* to shrink in size

impiegare §209 (impiègo) *tr* to employ;

to use; to devote (*one's energies*); to spend (*time*); to invest (*capital*); to take (*time*) || *ref* to have a job

impiegati·zio -zia *adj* (*-zi -zie*) employee, white-collar

impiega·to -ta *mf* employee; clerk

impiè·go *m* (*-ghi*) employment; use; job; place of business; investment

impietosire [*s*] §176 *tr* to move to pity || *ref* to be moved to pity

impietrire §176 *tr, intr* (ESSERE) & *ref* to turn to stone

impigliare §280 *tr* to entangle || *ref* to become entangled

impigrire §176 *tr* to make lazy || *intr* (ESSERE) & *ref* to get lazy

impinguare (**impìnguo**) *tr* & *ref* to fatten

impinzare *tr* to stuff || *ref* to stuff oneself; **impinzarsi il cervello** to stuff one's brain (*with knowledge*)

impiombare (**impiómbo**) *tr* to lead; to plumb, seal with lead; to fill (*a tooth*); (naut) to splice (*a cable*)

impiombatura *f* seal; filling (*of tooth*); (naut) splicing

impipare *ref*—**impiparsi di** (slang) to not give a hoot about

implacabile *adj* implacable

implicare §197 (**ìmplico**) *tr* to implicate; to imply

implìci·to -ta *adj* implicit, implied

implorare (**implòro**) *tr* to implore

implume *adj* unfledged, featherless

impolìti·co -ca *adj* (*-ci -che*) unpolitical; impolitic, injudicious

impollinare (**impòllino**) *tr* to pollinate

impoltronire §176 *tr* to make lazy || *ref* to get lazy

impolverare (**impólvero**) *tr* to cover with dust || *ref* to get covered with dust

impomatare *tr* to pomade; to smear with pomade

imponderàbile *adj* imponderable; weightless

imponderabilità *f* imponderability; weightlessness

imponènte *adj* imposing; stately

imponìbile *adj* taxable || *m* taxable income

impopolare *adj* unpopular

impopolarità *f* unpopularity

impórre §218 *tr* to place, put; to impose; to order; to compel; to give (*a name*) || *intr* (ESSERE) to be imposing; (*with dat*) to order, command || *ref* to command respect; to win favor; to be necessary

importante *adj* important; sizable || *m* important thing

importanza *f* importance; size; **darsi importanza** to assume an air of importance

importare (**impòrto**) *tr* to import; to imply; to involve || *intr* (ESSERE) to be of consequence || *impers* (ESSERE) —**importa** it matters; **non importa** never mind

importa·tóre -trice *mf* importer

importazióne *f* importation; import

impòrto *m* amount

importunare *tr* to bother, importune

importu·no -na *adj* importunate, bothersome || *mf* bore

imposizióne *f* imposition; giving (*of a name*); order, command; taxation

impossessare (**impossèsso**) *ref*—**impossessarsi di** to seize; to master (*a language*)

impossibile *adj* & *m* impossible

impossibili·tà *f* (*-tà*) impossibility

impossibilitare (**impossibilìto**) *tr* to make impossible; to make unable or incapable

impossibilita·to -ta *adj* unable

impòsta *f* tax; shutter; (archit) impost; **imposta complementare** surtax; **imposta sul valore aggiunto** value-added tax

impostare (**impòsto**) *tr* to start, begin; to state (*a problem*); to mail; to lay (*a stone*); to open (*an account*); to attune (*one's voice*); to lay the keel of (*a ship*) || *ref* to take one's position, get ready

impostazióne *f* beginning, starting; laying; mail, mailing; (com) posting

impo·stóre -stóra *mf* impostor

impostura *f* imposture

impotènte *adj* weak; impotent

impotènza *f* impotence

impoverimén·to *m* impoverishment

impoverire §176 *tr* to impoverish || *intr* (ESSERE) & *ref* to become impoverished

impraticàbile *adj* impracticable; impassable

impratichire §176 *tr* to train, familiarize || *ref* to become familiar (*e.g., with a task*)

imprecare §197 (**imprèco**) *tr* to wish (*e.g., s.o.'s death*) || *intr* to curse

imprecazióne *f* imprecation, curse

imprecisàbile *adj* undefinable

imprecisióne *f* inexactness, inaccuracy

imprecì·so -sa *adj* vague, inexact

impregnare (**imprégno**) *tr* to impregnate

impremedita·to -ta *adj* unpremeditated

imprendìbile *adj* impregnable

imprendi·tóre -trice *mf* contractor || *m*—**imprenditore di pompe funebri** undertaker

imprenditoriale *adj* managerial

imprepara·to -ta *adj* unprepared

impreparazióne *f* unpreparedness

imprésa [*s*] *f* enterprise; undertaking; achievement; firm, concern; (theat) management; **impresa (di) pompe funebri** undertaking establishment

impresà·rio [*s*] *m* (*-ri*) manager; (theat) impresario

imprescindìbile *adj* essential, indispensable; unavoidable

impresentàbile *adj* unpresentable

impressionàbile *adj* impressionable

impressionante *adj* striking, impressive; frightening

impressionare (**impressióno**) *tr* to impress; (phot) to expose || *ref* to become frightened; (phot) to be exposed

impressióne *f* impression

imprestare (**imprèsto**) *tr* (coll) to lend

imprèstito *m* (philol) borrowing
imprevedìbile *adj* unforeseeable
imprevedù·to -ta *adj* unforeseen
imprevidènte *adj* improvident
imprevì·sto -sta *adj* unforeseen, unexpected || **imprevisti** *mpl* unforeseen events
imprigionare (**imprigióno**) *tr* to imprison
imprìmere §131 *tr* to impress; to imprint; to impart (*e.g., motion*)
improbàbile *adj* improbable, unlikely
impro·bo -ba *adj* dishonest; laborious
improdutti·vo -va *adj* unproductive
imprónta *f* print, imprint; mark; **impronta digitale** fingerprint
improntare (**imprónto**) *tr* to impress, imprint; to mark
improntitùdine *f* audacity, impudence
impronunziàbile *adj* unpronounceable
impropè·rio *m* (-ri) insult
improprie·tà *f* (-tà) impropriety; error
imprò·prio -pria *adj* (-pri -prie) improper, inappropriate; (math) improper
improrogàbile *adj* unextendible
improvvi·do -da *adj* improvident
improvvisare *tr* to improvise || *ref* to suddenly decide to become
improvvisa·to -ta *adj* improvised; impromptu || *f* surprise; surprise party
improvvisazióne *f* improvisation
improvvì·so -sa *adj* sudden || *m* (mus) impromptu; **all'improvviso** or **d'improvviso** suddenly
imprudènte *adj* imprudent; rash
imprudènza *f* imprudence; rashness
impudènte *adj* shameless; brazen; impudent
impudènza *f* shamelessness; impudence
impudicìzia *f* immodesty
impudì·co -ca *adj* (-chi -che) immodest, indecent
impugnare *tr* to grip, seize; to take up (*arms*); to impugn, contest
impugnatura *f* handle; grip, hold; hilt, haft
impulsì·vo -va *adj* impulsive
impulso *m* impulse; **dare impulso a** to promote, foment
impunemènte *adv* with impunity
impunità *f* impunity
impunì·to -ta *adj* unpunished
impuntare *intr* to stumble, trip; to stutter || *ref* to stutter; to balk; to be stubborn; **impuntarsi a** or **di** + *inf* to stubbornly insist on + *ger*
impuntigliare §280 *ref* to persist, insist
impuntire §176 *tr* to tuft (*e.g., a pillow*)
impuntura *f* backstitch
impuri·tà *f* (-tà) impurity; unchastity
impu·ro -ra *adj* impure; unchaste
imputàbile *adj* attributable
imputare (**ìmputo**) *tr* to impute; to charge, accuse; (com) to post
imputà·to -ta *mf* accused, defendant
imputazióne *f* imputation; charge, accusation; (com) posting
imputridire §176 *ir & intr* (ESSERE) to rot
in *prep* in; at; into; to; on; upon; through; during; married to, e.g.,

Maria Roberti in Bianchi Marie Roberti married to Bianchi; as, e.g., **in premio** as a prize; by, e.g., **in automobile** by car; of, e.g., **studente in legge** student of law; **essere in quattro** to be four; in **alto up**; in **breve** soon; in a word; in **giù** down; in **là** there; in **qua** here; in **realtà** really; in **seguito a** because of
-ina *suf fem* about, e.g., **cinquantina** about fifty
inabbordàbile *adj* unapproachable
inàbile *adj* unfit; ineligible; awkward
inabili·tà *f* (-tà) unfitness; awkwardness; inability
inabilitare (**inabìlito**) *tr* to incapacitate; to render unfit; to disqualify
inabilitazióne *f* disqualification
inabissare *tr* to plunge || *ref* to sink
inabitàbile *adj* uninhabitable
inabita·to -ta *adj* uninhabited
inaccessìbile *adj* inaccessible; unfathomable
inaccettàbile *adj* unacceptable
inacerbire §176 *tr* to exacerbate || *ref* to grow bitter
inacidire §176 *tr & ref* to sour
inadattàbile *adj* unadaptable; maladjusted
inadat·to -ta *adj* inadequate
inadegua·to -ta *adj* inadequate
inadempiènte *adj* not fulfilling; **inadempiente agli obblighi di leva** draft-dodging
inafferràbile *adj* that cannot be caught or captured; incomprehensible; elusive
inalare *tr* to inhale
inalatóre *m* inhaler
inalberare (**inàlbero**) *tr* to hoist || *ref* to rear; to fly into a rage
inalteràbile *adj* unalterable
inamidare (**inàmido**) *tr* to starch
inamida·to -ta *adj* starched; pompous, starchy
inammissìbile *adj* inadmissible
inamovìbile *adj* irremovable
inamovibili·tà *f* (-tà) irremovability; tenure
inane *adj* inane; futile
inanella·to -ta *adj* curly; beringed
inanima·to -ta *adj* inanimate; lifeless
inanizióne *f* starvation
inappagàbile *adj* unquenchable
inappaga·to -ta *adj* unsatisfied
inappellàbile *adj* definitive, final
inappetènza *f* lack of appetite
inapprezzàbile *adj* inappreciable, imperceptible; inestimable
inappuntàbile *adj* faultless, impeccable
inarcare §197 *tr* to arch; to raise (*one's eyebrows*)
inargentare (**inargènto**) *tr* to silver
inaridire §176 *tr* to dry; to parch || *ref* to dry up
inarrestàbile *adj* irresistible
inarrivàbile *adj* unattainable; inimitable
inarticola·to -ta *adj* indistinct, inarticulate
inascolta·to -ta *adj* unheeded
inaspetta·to -ta *adj* unexpected
inasprimènto *m* exacerbation

inasprire §176 *tr* to aggravate || *ref* to sour; to become embittered; to become sharper; to become fierce or furious

inastare *tr* to hoist (*flag*); to fix (*bayonets*)

inattaccàbile *adj* unattackable; unassailable; **inattacàbile da** resistant to

inattendìbile *adj* unreliable

inattè·so -sa [s] *adj* unexpected

inatti·vo -ta *adj* inactive

inaudi·to -ta *adj* unheard-of

inaugurale *adj* inaugural; maiden (*voyage*)

inaugurare (**inàuguro**) *tr* to inaugurate; to usher in (*the New Year*); to open (*e.g., an exhibit*); to unveil (*a statue*); to sport for the first time

inaugurazióne *f* inauguration

inauspica·to -ta *adj* (lit) inauspicious

inavvedu·to -ta *adj* careless, rash

inavvertènza *f* inadvertence, oversight

inavverti·to -ta *adj* unnoticed; inadvertent, thoughtless

inazióne *f* inaction

incagliare §280 *tr* to hamper; to run aground || *intr* (ESSERE) & *ref* to run aground; (fig) to get stuck

incà·glio *m* (**-gli**) running aground; hindrance, obstacle

incalcinare *tr* to whitewash; to lime (*a field*)

incalcolàbile *adj* incalculable

incallire §176 *tr* to make callous || *intr* (ESSERE) to become callous; to become inured

incalli·to -ta *adj* callous; inveterate

incalzante *adj* pressing

incalzare *tr* to press, pursue || *intr* to be imminent; to be pressing || *ref* to follow one another in rapid succession

incamerare (**incàmero**) *tr* to confiscate

incamminare *tr* to launch; to guide, direct || *ref* to set out; to be on one's way

incanagli·to -ta *adj* vile, despicable

incanalare *tr* to channel || *ref* to flow

incancrenire §176 *tr* to affect with gangrene || *ref* to become gangrenous; (fig) to become callous

incandescènte *adj* incandescent; (fig) red-hot

incandescènza *f* incandescence

incannare *tr* to reel, wind

incantare *tr* to bewitch; to auction off || *ref* to become enraptured; to be spellbound; to jam, get stuck (*said of machinery*)

incanta·tóre -trice *adj* enchanting || *m* enchanter || *f* enchantress

incantésimo *m* enchantment, spell

incantévole *adj* enchanting, charming

incanto *m* enchantment; bewitchery; auction; **d'incanto** marvelously well

incanutire §176 *tr*, *intr* (ESSERE) & *ref* to turn gray-headed; to turn gray (*said of a person*)

incanuti·to -ta *adj* hoary

incapace *adj* incapable; (law) incompetent || *mf* oaf; (law) incompetent

incapaci·tà *f* (**-tà**) incapacity; (law) incompetence

incaparbire §176 *intr* (ESSERE) & *ref* to be obstinate; to be determined

incaponire §176 *ref* to get stubborn; to be determined

incappare *intr* (ESSERE) to stumble

incappottare (**incappòtto**) *tr* to cover with a coat || *ref* to wrap oneself in a coat

incappucciare §128 *tr* to cover with a hood

incapricciare §128 *ref*—**incapricciarsi di** to take a fancy to; to become infatuated with

incapsulare (**incàpsulo**) *tr* to encapsulate; to cap

incarcerare (**incàrcero**) *tr* to jail, incarcerate; (fig) to confine

incaricare §197 (**incàrico**) *tr* to charge || *ref*—**incaricarsi di** to take charge of; to take care of

incarica·to -ta *adj* in charge; visiting (*professor*) || *mf* deputy; **incaricato d'affari** chargé d'affaires

incàri·co *m* (**-chi**) task; appointment, position; **per incarico di** on behalf of

incarnare *tr* to incarnate, embody

incarna·to -ta *adj* incarnate || *m* pink complexion

incarnazióne *f* incarnation

incarnire §176 *intr* (ESSERE) & *ref* to grow in (*said of a toenail*)

incarni·to -ta *adj* ingrown (*toenail*)

incartaménto *m* file, dossier

incartapecori·to -ta *adj* shriveled up

incartare *tr* to wrap up (*in paper*)

incasellare [s] (**incasèllo**) *tr* to file; to sort out

incasellatóre [s] *m* post-office file clerk

incassare *tr* to box up; to put (*a watch*) in a case; to mortise (*a lock*); to channel (*a river*); to cash (*a check*); (fig) to take (*e.g., blows*) || *intr* to fit; to take it

incasso *m* receipts

incastellatura *f* scaffolding

incastonare (**incastóno**) *tr* to set, mount (*a gem*); **incastonare citazioni in un discorso** to stud a speech with quotations

incastrare *tr* to insert; to mortise; (fig) to corner || *intr* to fit || *ref* to fit; to become imbedded; to telescope (*said, e.g., of a train in a collision*)

incastro *m* joint; insertion; (carp) tenon; (carp) mortise

incatenare (**incaténo**) *tr* to chain, put in chains; to tie down, restrain

incatramare *tr* to tar

incàu·to -ta *adj* unwary, careless

incavallatura *f* truss (*to support roof*)

incavare *tr* to hollow out; to groove

incava·to -ta *adj* hollow

incavatura *f* hollow

incavicchiare §287 *tr* to peg

incavigliare §280 *tr* to peg

incavo *m* hollow; cavity; **incavo dell'ascella** armpit

incazzottare (**incazzòtto**) *tr* (naut) to furl

incèdere m stately walk || §123 intr to walk stately

incendiare §287 (incèndio) tr to set on fire; (fig) to inflame || ref to catch fire

incendià·rio -ria adj & mf (-ri -rie) incendiary

incèn·dio m (-di) fire; incendio doloso arson

incenerire §176 tr to reduce to ashes; to wither (e.g., with a look) || ref to turn to ashes

inceneritóre m incinerator

incensare (incènso) tr (eccl) to incense; (fig) to flatter

incensa·tóre -trice mf incense burner; (fig) flatterer

incensière m incense burner

incènso m incense

incensura·to -ta adj uncensored; (law) having no previous record

incentivo m incentive

inceppare (incéppo) tr to hinder; to shackle || ref to jam (said of firearm)

incerare (incéro) tr to wax

incerata f oilcloth; (naut) raincoat

incernierare (incernièro) tr to hinge

incertézza f uncertainty, incertitude

incèr·to -ta adj uncertain; irresolute || m uncertainty; incerti extras; incerti del mestiere cares of office, occupational annoyances, occupational hazards

incespicare §197 (incéspico) intr to stumble

incessàbile adj (lit) ceaseless

incessante adj unceasing, incessant

incèsto m incest

incestuó·so -sa [s] adj incestuous

incètta f cornering (of market)

incettare (incètto) tr to corner (market)

incetta·tóre -trice mf monopolizer

inchiavardare tr to key, bolt

inchièsta f probe, inquest; (journ) inquiry

inchinare tr to bend; to bow (the head) || intr (lit) to go down (said of stars) || ref to bow; to yield

inchi·no -na adj bent; bowing || m bow; curtsy

inchiodare (inchiòdo) tr to nail; to spike; to rivet; to tie, bind; to stop (a car) suddenly; to transfix || ref to freeze (said, e.g., of brakes); (fig) to be tied down; (fig) to go into debt

inchiostrare (inchiòstro) tr (typ) to ink

inchiòstro m ink; inchiostro di china India ink, Chinese ink

inciampare intr to trip, stumble

inciampo m stumbling block, obstacle; essere d'inciampo a to be in the way of

incidentale adj incidental

incidènte adj incidental || m incident; accident; argument, question

incidènza f incidence

incìdere §145 tr to engrave; to cut; to record (a record, a tape; a song); incidere all'acqua forte to etch || intr—incidere su to weigh heavily on (expenses, a budget); to leave a mark on

incinerazióne f incineration; cremation

incinta adj fem pregnant

incipiènte adj incipient

incipriare §287 tr to powder || ref to powder oneself

incirca adv about; all'incirca more or less

incisióne f engraving; cutting (of a record); recording (of a tape; of a song); incision; incisione all'acquaforte etching

incisi·vo -va adj incisive; sharp (photograph) || m incisor

inciso m (gram) parenthetical clause; (mus) theme; per inciso incidentally

incisóre m engraver, etcher

incitare tr to incite, provoke

incivile adj uncivilized; uncouth

incivilire §176 tr to civilize || ref to become civilized

inclemènte adj inclement, harsh

inclemènza f inclemency, harshness

inclinare tr to tilt; to bow, bend; to incline || intr (fig) to lean || ref to bend

inclinazióne f inclination; slope; inclinazione laterale (aer) bank; inclinazione magnetica magnetic dip

incline adj inclined

ìncli·to -ta adj famous; noble

inclùdere §105 tr to enclose, include

inclusi·vo -va adj including; inclusivo di including

inclu·so -sa adj enclosed; included; inclusive || f enclosed letter

incoerènte adj incoherent

incògliere §127 tr (lit) to catch in the act || intr—incogliere a to happen to

incògni·to -ta adj unknown || m incognito; unknown; in incognito incognito || f (math) unknown quantity; (fig) puzzle

incollare (incòllo) tr to glue, paste; to size (paper) || intr to stick || ref to stick; to take on one's shoulders

incollatura f neck (of horse); glueing, sticking

incollerire §176 intr & ref to get angry

incolloca·to -ta adj unemployed

incolonnare (incolónno) tr to set up in columns

incolonnatóre m tabulator

incolóre adj colorless

incolpàbile adj blamable; (lit) guiltless

incolpare (incólpo) tr—incolpare di to charge with

incól·to -ta adj uncultivated; unkempt

incòlume adj unharmed, unhurt

incolumità f safety, security

incombènte adj (danger) impending; (duty) incumbent

incombènza f task, charge, incumbency

incómbere §186 intr (ESSERE) to be impending; to be incumbent

incombustibile adj incombustible

incominciare §128 tr & intr (ESSERE) to begin

incommensuràbile adj immeasurable; (math) incommensurable

incomodare (incòmodo) tr to bother, disturb || ref to bother; non s'incomodi! don't bother!

incòmo·do -da adj bothersome, inconvenient || m inconvenience; ailment;

levare l'incomodo a to get out of the way of
incomparàbile *adj* incomparable
incompatìbile *adj* incompatible; unforgivable
incompetènte *adj & mf* incompetent
incompiu·to -ta *adj* unfinished
incomplè·to -ta *adj* incomplete
incompó·sto -sta *adj* untidy; unkempt; unbecoming (*behavior*)
incomprensìbile *adj* incomprehensible
incomprensióne *f* lack of understanding
incompré·so -sa [s] *adj* misunderstood
incomprimìbile *adj* irrepressible; incompressible
inconcepìbile *adj* inconceivable
inconciliàbile *adj* irreconcilable
inconcludènte *adj* inconclusive; insignificant
inconcus·so -sa *adj* (lit) unshaken
incondiziona·to -ta *adj* unconditional
inconfessàbile *adj* unspeakable, vile
inconfessa·to -ta *adj* unavowed
inconfondìbile *adj* unmistakable
inconfutàbile *adj* irrefutable
incongruènte *adj* inconsistent
incòn·gruo -grua *adj* incongruous
inconoscìbile *adj* unknowable
inconsapévole *adj* unaware, unconscious
incòn·scio -scia *adj & m* (-sci -sce) unconscious
inconseguènte *adj* inconsistent, inconsequential
inconsidera·to -ta *adj* inconsiderate
inconsistènte *adj* flimsy; inconsistent
inconsistènza *f* flimsiness; inconsistency
inconsolàbile *adj* inconsolable
inconsuè·to -ta *adj* unusual
inconsul·to -ta *adj* ill-advised, rash
incontaminà·to -ta *adj* uncontaminated
incontenìbile *adj* irrepressible
incontentàbile *adj* insatiable; hard to please; exacting
incontinènza *f* incontinence
incontrare (incóntro) *tr* to meet; to encounter, meet with || *intr* (ESSERE) to catch on (*said, e.g., of fashions*) || *ref* to meet; to agree || *impers* (ESSERE) to happen
incontrastàbile *adj* indisputable
incontrasta·to -ta *adj* undisputed
incóntro *m* meeting; encounter; success; meet; game, fight, match; occasion, opportunity; **all'incontro** on the other hand; opposite; **andare incontro a** to go towards; to go to meet; to face; to meet (*expenses*); to accommodate; **farsi incontro a** to advance toward
incontrollàbile *adj* uncontrollable
incontrolla·to -ta *adj* unchecked
incontrovertìbile *adj* incontrovertible
inconveniènte *adj* inconvenient || *m* inconvenience, disadvantage
incoraggiante *adj* encouraging
incoraggiare §290 *tr* to encourage
incorare §257 (incuòro) *tr* to hearten
incordare (incòrdo) *tr* to string (*e.g., a racket*); to tie up (*with a cord*) || *ref* to stiffen (*said of a muscle*)
incornare (incòrno) *tr* (taur) to gore

incorniciare §128 *tr* to frame; (journ) to border; (slang) to cuckold
incoronare (incoróno) *tr* to crown
incoronazióne *f* coronation
incorporàbile *adj* absorbable; adaptable
incorporare (incòrporo) *tr* to incorporate; to absorb || *ref* to incorporate
incorpòre·o -a *adj* incorporeal
incorreggìbile *adj* incorrigible
incórrere §139 *intr* (ESSERE)—**incorrere in** to incur
incorrót·to -ta *adj* uncorrupt
incosciènte *adj* unconscious; unaware; irresponsible || *mf* irresponsible person
incosciènza *f* unconsciousness; irresponsibility; madness
incostante *adj* inconstant, fickle
incredìbile *adj* incredible, unbelievable
incrèdu·lo -la *adj* incredulous || *mf* disbeliever; doubter
incrementare (increménto) *tr* to increase, boost
increménto *m* increase, increment, boost
incresció·so -sa [s] *adj* disagreeable, unpleasant
increspare (incréspo) *tr* to ripple; to wrinkle; to knit (*the brow*); to pleat || *ref* to ripple
incretinire §176 *tr* to make stupid; (fig) to deafen || *intr* (ESSERE) to become stupid; to lose one's mind
incriminare (incrìmino) *tr* to incriminate
incrinare *tr* to flaw; to ruin
incrinatura *f* crack, flaw
incrociare §128 (incrócio) *tr* to cross || *intr* (naut) to cruise || *ref* to cross one another; to interbreed
incrociatóre *m* (nav) cruiser
incró·cio -cio *m* (-ci) crossing; cross; crossroads; crossbreed
incrollàbile *adj* unshakable
incrostare (incròsto) *tr* to incrust; to inlay (*e.g., with mosaic*) || *ref* to become incrusted
incrostazióne *f* incrustation
incrudelire §176 *tr* to enrage || *intr* to commit cruelties || *intr* (ESSERE) to become cruel; **incrudelire su** to commit cruelties upon
incruèn·to -ta *adj* bloodless
incubare (ìncubo & incùbo) *tr* to incubate
incubatrice *f* incubator; brooder
incubazióne *f* incubation; **in incubazione** brewing (*said of an infectious disease*)
ìncubo *m* nightmare
incùdine *f* anvil; **essere tra l'incudine e il martello** to be between the devil and the deep blue sea
inculcare §197 *tr* to inculcate
incunàbolo *m* incunabulum
incuneare (incùneo) *tr & ref* to wedge
incuràbile *adj & mf* incurable
incurante *adj* careless, indifferent
incùria *f* malpractice; neglect
incuriosire [s] **§176** *tr* to intrigue || *ref* to be intrigued
incursióne *f* incursion; **incursione aerea** air raid

incurvare *tr* to bend; (lit) to lower || *intr* (ESSERE) & *ref* to bend; to warp

incurvatura *f* bend, curve

incustodi·to -ta *adj* unguarded, unwatched

incùtere §154 *tr* to inspire; **incutere terrore a** to strike with terror

ìndaco *adj* & *m* indigo

indaffara·to -ta *adj* busy

indagare §209 *tr* & *intr* to investigate; **indagare su** to investigate

indaga·tóre -trice *adj* probing, searching || *mf* investigator

indàgine *f* investigation, inquiry

indarno *adv* (lit) in vain

indebitare (**indébito**) *tr* to burden with debts || *ref* to run into debt

indebita·to -ta *adj* indebted

indébi·to -ta *adj* undue; unjust; fraudulent (*conversion*) || *m* what one does not owe; excess payment

indebolimènto *m* weakening

indebolire §176 *tr*, *intr* (ESSERE) & *ref* to weaken

indecènte *adj* indecent

indecènza *f* indecency; outrage

indecifràbile *adj* indecipherable

indecisióne *f* indecision

indeci·so -sa *adj* uncertain; undecided; indecisive

indecoró·so -sa [s] *adj* indecorous, unseemly

indefès·so -sa *adj* indefatigable

indefinìbile *adj* indefinable

indefini·to -ta *adj* indefinite; undefined

indégno -gna *adj* unworthy; disgraceful

indelèbile *adj* indelible

indelica·to -ta *adj* indelicate

indemagliàbile *adj* runproof

indemonia·to -ta *adj* possessed by the devil; restless

indènne *adj* undamaged, unscathed; **tener indenne** to guarantee against harm or damage

indenni·tà *f* (-**tà**) indemnity; indemnification; **indennità di carica** special emolument; bonus; **indennità di carovita** cost-of-living allowance; **indennità di preavviso** severance pay; **indennità di trasferta** per diem

indennizzare [ddzz] *tr* to indemnify

indennizzo [ddzz] *m* indemnification; indemnity

inderogàbile *adj* inescapable

indescrivìbile *adj* indescribable

indesideràbile *adj* undesirable

indesidera·to -ta *adj* unwished-for; undesirable

indeterminati·vo -va *adj* indefinite

indetermina·to -ta *adj* indeterminate; (gram) indefinite

indi *adv* (lit) then; (lit) thence; **da indi innanzi** (lit) from that moment on

India, l' *f* India; **le Indie Occidentali** the West Indies; **le Indie Orientali** the East Indies

india·no -na *adj* & *m* Indian; **fare l'indiano** to feign ignorance || *f* printed calico

indiavola·to -ta *adj* devilish, fierce; impish (*child*)

indicare §197 (**indico**) *tr* to indicate; to show

indicati·vo -va *adj* & *m* indicative

indica·to -ta *adj* appropriate, fitting; recommended, advisable

indica·tóre -trice *adj* indicating, pointing || *m* indicator; **indicatore di direzione** (aut) turn signal; **indicatore di livello** gauge; **indicatore di pressione** pressure gauge; **indicatore di velocità** (aut) speedometer; **indicatore stradale** road sign; **indicatore telefonico** telephone directory

indicazióne *f* indication; direction; **indicazioni per l'uso** instructions

ìndice *m* index finger; pointer, gauge; indicator; sign, indication; index; (typ) fist; **indice delle materie** table of contents || **Indice** *m* Index; **mettere all'Indice** to put on the Index; to ban, index

indicìbile *adj* inexpressible, unspeakable

indietreggiare §290 (**indietréggio**) *intr* (ESSERE & AVERE) to withdraw

indiètro *adv* back; behind; **all'indietro** backwards; **dare indietro** to return, give back; **domandare indietro** to ask back; **essere indietro** to be slow (*said of a watch*); to be behind; to be backward, be slow; **tirarsi indietro** to withdraw; to step back

indifendìbile *adj* indefensible

indifé·so -sa [s] *adj* defenseless

indifferènte *adj* indifferent; **essere indifferente a** to be the same to; **lasciare indifferente** to leave cold

indifferènza *f* indifference

indìge·no -na *adj* indigenous || *m* native

indigènte *adj* indigent, poor

indigestìbile *adj* indigestible

indigestióne *f* indigestion

indigè·sto -sta *adj* indigestible; (fig) dull, boring

indignare *tr* to anger, shock || *ref* to be aroused, be indignant

indigna·to -ta *adj* indignant, outraged

indignazióne *f* indignation

indigni·tà *f* (-**tà**) indignity

indimenticàbile *adj* unforgettable

indipendènte *adj* & *m* independent

indipendènza *f* independence

indire §151 *tr* to announce publicly; (lit) to declare (*war*)

indirèt·to -ta *adj* indirect

indirizzare *tr* to direct; to address

indirizzà·rio *m* (-**ri**) mailing list

indirizzo *m* address; direction

indiscernìbile *adj* indiscernible

indisciplina *f* lack of discipline

indisciplina·to -ta *adj* undisciplined

indiscré·to -ta *adj* indiscreet; tactless

indiscrezióne *f* indiscretion; gossip; news leak

indiscus·so -sa *adj* unquestioned

indiscutìbile *adj* indisputable

indispensàbile *adj* indispensable || *m* essential

indispettire §176 *tr* to annoy || *ref* to get annoyed

indisponènte *adj* vexing, irritating

indispórre §218 *tr* to indispose; to disgust
indisposizióne *f* indisposition
indispó·sto -sta *adj* indisposed
indissolùbile *adj* indissoluble
indistìn·to -ta *adj* indistinct
indistruttìbile *adj* indestructible
indisturba·to -ta *adj* undisturbed
indìvia *f* endive
individuàbile *adj* distinguishable
individuale *adj* individual
individuali·tà *f* (-**tà**) individuality
individuare (**indivìduo**) *tr* to individuate; to outline; to single out
indivìduo *m* individual; fellow
indivisìbile *adj* indivisible
indivi·so -sa *adj* undivided
indiziare §287 *tr* to cast suspicion on
indizià·rio -ria *adj* (**-ri -rie**) circumstancial
indì·zio *m* (**-zi**) clue; token; symptom
indòcile *adj* indocile, unteachable
Indocìna, l' *f* Indochina
indocinése [s] *adj* & *mf* Indochinese
indoeuropè·o -a *adj* & *m* Indo-European
indolcíre §176 *tr* to sweeten ‖ *ref* to become sweet
ìndole *f* temper, disposition; nature
indolènte *adj* indolent
indolenziménto *m* soreness, stiffness; numbness
indolenzíre §176 *tr* to make sore or stiff; to benumb ‖ *ref* to become sore or stiff
indolenzì·to -ta *adj* sore, stiff; numb
indolóre *adj* painless
indomàbile *adj* indomitable
indoma·ni *m* (**-ni**) morrow, next day; l'indomani di . . . the day after . . .
indoma·to -ta *adj* (lit) indomitable, untamed
indòmi·to -ta *adj* (lit) indomitable, untamed
Indonèsia l' *f* Indonesia
indonesia·no -na *adj* & *mf* Indonesian
indorare (**indòro**) *tr* to gild; (culin) to brown; (fig) to sugar-coat
indoratura *f* gilding
indossare (**indòsso**) *tr* to wear; to put on
indossatrice *f* mannequin, model
indòsso *adv* on, on one's back; **avere indosso** to have on, wear
Indostàn, l' *m* Hindustan
indosta·no -na *adj* & *mf* Hindustani
indòtto *m* (elec) armature (*of motor*)
indottrinare *tr* to indoctrinate
indovinare *tr* to guess; **indovinarla** to guess right; **non indovinarne una** to never hit the mark
indovina·to -ta *adj* felicitous
indovinèllo *m* puzzle, riddle
indovi·no -na *mf* soothsayer, fortuneteller
indù *adj invar* & *mf* Hindu
indùb·bio -bia *adj* (**-bi -bie**) undoubted, undisputed
indubita·to -ta *adj* undeniable
indugiare §290 *tr* to delay ‖ *intr* to linger; to hesitate ‖ *ref* to linger
indù·gio *m* (**-gi**) delay; **rompere gli**

indugi to come to a decision; **senza ulteriore indugio** without further delay
indulgènte *adj* indulgent
indulgènza *f* indulgence
indùlgere §187 *tr* to grant; to forgive ‖ *intr* to be indulgent; **indulgere a** to indulge; to yield to
indulto *m* (law) pardon
indumento *m* garment; **indumenti intimi** undergarments, unmentionables
induríre §176 *tr* to harden ‖ *intr* (ESSERE) to harden; to get stiff
indurre §102 *tr* to induce
indùstria *f* industry; **grande industria** heavy industry
industriale *adj* industrial ‖ *m* industrialist
industrializzare [ddzz] *tr* to industrialize
industriare §287 *ref* to try, try hard; **industriarsi a** or **per** + *inf* to try to + *inf*, to do one's best to + *inf*
industrió·so -sa [s] *adj* industrious
indut·tóre -trice *adj* inducing, provoking ‖ *m* (elec) field (*of motor*)
induzióne *f* induction
inebetíre §176 *tr* to dull; to stun ‖ *intr* (ESSERE) & *ref* to become dull; to be stunned
inebriare §287 (**inèbrio**) *tr* to intoxicate ‖ *ref* to get drunk
inebriante *adj* intoxicating
ineccepìbile *adj* unexceptionable
inèdia *f* starvation, inanition; boredom
inèdi·to -ta *adj* unpublished; new, novel
ineduca·to -ta *adj* uneducated; ill-mannered
ineffàbile *adj* ineffable
inefficace *adj* ineffectual, ineffective
inefficàcia *f* inefficacy
inefficiènte *adj* inefficient
ineguale *adj* unequal; uneven
inelegante *adj* inelegant; shabby
ineleggìbile *adj* ineligible
ineluttàbile *adj* inevitable, inescapable
inenarràbile *adj* unspeakable
inerènte *adj* inherent
inèrme *adj* unarmed, defenseless
inerpicare §197 (**inérpico**) *ref* to clamber
inèrte *adj* inert
inèrzia *f* inertia; inactivity
inesattézza *f* inaccuracy
inesat·to -ta *adj* inaccurate, inexact; uncollected
inesaudì·to -ta *adj* unanswered
inesauríbile *adj* inexhaustible
inescusàbile *adj* inexcusable
inesigìbile *adj* uncollectable
inesistènte *adj* inexistent
inesoràbile *adj* inexorable
inesperiènza *f* inexperience
inespèr·to -ta *adj* inexperienced; unskilled
inesplicàbile *adj* inexplicable
inesplica·to -ta *adj* unexplained
inesplora·to -ta *adj* unexplored
inesplò·so -sa *adj* unexploded
inespressi·vo -va *adj* inexpressive
inesprimìbile *adj* inexpressible

inespugnàbile *adj* impregnable; incorruptible
inespugna·to -ta *adj* unconquered
inestimàbile *adj* priceless, invaluable
inestinguìbile *adj* inextinguishable
inestirpàbile *adj* ineradicable
inestricàbile *adj* inextricable
inèt·to -ta *adj* inept
ineva·so -sa *adj* unfinished (*business*); unanswered (*mail*)
inevitàbile *adj* unavoidable, inevitable
inèzia *f* trifle, bagatelle
infagottare (**infagòtto**) *tr* & *ref* to bundle up
infallìbile *adj* infallible
infamante *adj* shameful, disgraceful
infamare *tr* to disgrace; to slander
infame *adj* infamous; villainous; (coll) horrible || *mf* villain
infàmia *f* infamy; (coll) botch, bungle
infangare §209 *tr* to splash with mud; (fig) to stain, spot
infante *adj* & *mf* infant, baby || *m* infante || *f* infanta
infantile *adj* infantile, childish
infànzia *f* infancy, childhood
infarcire §176 *tr* to cram; (culin) to stuff
infarinare *tr* to sprinkle with flour; to powder; (fig) to cram || *ref* to be covered with flour
infarinatura *f* sprinkling with flour; (fig) smattering
infastidire §176 *tr* to annoy || *ref* to be annoyed, lose one's patience
infaticàbile *adj* indefatigable, tireless
infatti *adv* indeed; really
infatuare (**infàtuo**) *tr* to infatuate || *ref* to become infatuated
infatua·to -ta *adj* infatuated
infàu·sto -sta *adj* unlucky, fatal
infecón·do -da *adj* barren
infedéle *adj* unfaithful; inaccurate || *mf* infidel
infedel·tà *f* (**-tà**) unfaithfulness; inaccuracy; infidelity
infelice *adj* unhappy, unfortunate; unfavorable || *mf* wretch
infelici·tà *f* (**-tà**) unhappiness
inferiore *adj* inferior; lower; **inferiore a** a lower than; less than; smaller than
inferiorità *f* inferiority
inferire §188a *tr* to inflict; to infer; (naut) to bend (*a sail*)
infermare (**infèrmo**) *tr* (lit) to weaken || *intr* (ESSERE) to get sick
infermerìa *f* infirmary
infermiè·re -ra *adj* nursing || *m* male nurse || *f* nurse; **infermiera diplomata** trained nurse
infermierìsti·co -ca *adj* (**-ci -che**) nursing
infermi·tà *f* (**-tà**) infirmity
infér·mo -ma *adj* infirm; sick || *m* patient
infernale *adj* infernal
infèr·no -na *adj* (lit) lower (*region*) || *m* hell; inferno
inferocire §176 *tr* to infuriate || *intr*—**inferocire su** to be pitiless to || *intr* (ESSERE) to become infuriated
inferriata *f* grating, grill

infervorare (**infèrvoro** & **infervóro**) *tr* to excite, stir up || *ref* to get excited; to become absorbed
infestare (**infèsto**) *tr* to infest
infettare (**infètto**) *tr* to infect
infetti·vo -va *adj* infectious
infèt·to -ta *adj* infected; corrupted
infezióne *f* infection
infiacchire §176 *tr* to weaken || *intr* (ESSERE) & *ref* to grow weak
infiammàbile *adj* inflammable
infiammare *tr* to inflame; to ignite || *ref* to catch fire, ignite
infiamma·to -ta *adj* burning; aflame; inflamed, excited
infiammazióne *f* inflammation
infi·do -da *adj* untrustworthy
infierire §176 *intr* to become cruel; to be merciless to; to rage (*said, e.g., of a disease*)
infievolire §176 *tr* to weaken
infìggere §103 *tr* to thrust, stick, sink || *ref*—**infìggersi in** to creep in; to work in
infilare *tr* to thread (*a needle*); to insert (*a key*); to transfix (*with a sword*); to put on (*e.g., a coat*); to pull on (*one's pants*); to slip on (*a dress*); to slip (*e.g., one's arm into a sleeve*); to string (*beads*); to hit (*the target*); to take (*a road*); to enter through (*a door*); **infilare l'uscio** to slip away; **infilarle tutte** to succeed all the time; **non infilarne mai una** to never succeed || *ref* to slip; to sink; to slide (*e.g., through a crowd*)
infilata *f* row; string (*e.g., of insults*); (mil) enfilade; **d'infilata** lengthwise
infiltrare *ref* to infiltrate; to seep; (fig) to creep
infilzare *tr* to pierce; to string; (sew) to baste
infilzata *f* string (*of pearls, of lies, etc.*)
infi·mo -ma *adj* lowest, bottom
infine *adv* finally
infingar·do -da *adj* lazy, slothful
infini·tà *f* (**-tà**) infinity
infinitèsi·mo -ma *adj* & *m* infinitesimal
infiniti·vo -va *adj* (gram) infinitive
infini·to -ta *adj* infinite || *m* infinite; infinity; (gram) infinitive; (math) infinity; **all'infinito** ad infinitum
infino *adv* (lit)—**infino a** until; as far as; **infino a che** as long as
infinocchiare §287 (**infinòcchio**) *tr* (coll) to fool, bamboozle
infioccare §197 (**infiòcco**) *tr* to adorn with tassels
infiorare (**infióro**) *tr* to adorn with flowers; (fig) to sprinkle; (fig) to embellish || *ref* to be covered with flowers
infiorescènza *f* inflorescence
infirmare *tr* to weaken; to invalidate
infischiare §287 *ref*—**infischiarsi di** to not care a hoot about
infisso *m* frame (*e.g., of door*); fixture
infittire §176 *tr, intr* (ESSERE) & *ref* to thicken
inflazionare (**inflazióno**) *tr* to inflate
inflazióne *f* inflation
inflessìbile *adj* inflexible

inflessióne f inflection
inflèttere §177 tr (lit) to inflect
inflìggere §104 tr to inflict
influènte adj influential
influènza f influence; (pathol) influenza
influenzare (influènzo) tr to influence, sway
influíre §176 intr to have an influence; **influíre su** to influence || intr (ESSERE) —**influíre in** to flow into
influsso m influence; (lit) plague
infocare §182 tr to make glow with heat || ref to catch fire; to get excited
infocà·to -ta adj red-hot; sultry
infognare (infógno) ref (coll) to sink (e.g., in vice); (coll) to get stuck (e.g., in debt)
infoltíre §176 tr & intr (ESSERE) to thicken
infondà·to -ta adj unfounded, groundless
infóndere §178 tr to infuse, instill
inforcare §197 (infórco) tr to pitch (hay); to bestride; to mount (a horse or bicycle); to put on (one's eyeglasses)
inforcatura f pitching with a fork; crotch
informare (infórmo) tr to inform; (fig) to mold || ref to conform; to inquire; **informarsi da** to seek or get information from; **informarsi di** or **su** to inquire about; to find out about
informatí·vo -va adj informative, informational
informa·tóre -trice adj underlying || mf informer; (journ) reporter || m informant (of a foreign language)
informazióne f piece of information; **chiedere informazioni sul conto di** to inquire about; **informazioni** information
infórme adj shapeless
informicolíre §176 ref to tingle; **informicolirsi a** to go to sleep, e.g., **gli si è informicolita la gamba** his leg went to sleep
infornare (infórno) tr to put in the oven; to bake
infornata f batch (of bread); (coll) flock
infortunare ref to get hurt
infortunà·to -ta adj injured || mf casualty, victim
infortú·nio m (-ni) accident, mishap; **infortunio sul lavoro** job-connected injury
infossare (infòsso) tr to bury || ref to cave in, settle; to become sunken (said of eyes or cheeks)
infracidare (infràcido) tr var of **infradiciare**
infracidíre §176 intr to rot
infradiciare §128 (infràdicio) tr to drench || ref to get drenched; to rot (said of fruit)
inframmettènza f interference, meddling
inframméttere §198 tr to interpose || ref to meddle, interfere
inframmezzare [ddzz] (inframmèzzo) tr to intersperse

infràngere §179 tr & ref to break
infrangìbile adj unbreakable
infran·to -ta adj broken, shattered
infrarós·so -sa adj & m infrared
infrascrit·to -ta adj mentioned below
infrastruttura f underpinning; infrastructure; (rr) roadbed
infrazióne f infraction, breach
infreddatura f mild cold
infreddolíre §176 ref to feel cold, to be chilled
infrenàbile adj irrepressible
infrequènte adj infrequent
infrollíre §176 tr to make (meat) high || intr (ESSERE) & ref to get high (said of meat); (fig) to soften
infruttuó·so -sa [s] adj unprofitable
infuòri adv out; **all'infuori** outward; **all'infuori di** except
infuriare §287 tr to infuriate, enrage || intr to get blustery; to rage || intr (ESSERE) to lose one's temper
infusióne f infusion; sprinkling (of holy water)
infuso m infusion
ingabbiare §287 tr to cage; to jail; to corner; to build the framework of
ingabbiatura f frame, framework
ingaggiare §290 tr to hire; to engage || ref to sign up; to get tangled up
ingàg·gio m (-gi) engagement; (sports) bonus (for signing up)
ingagliardíre §176 tr to strengthen || ref to become strong
ingannare tr to deceive; to cheat; to elude; to beguile || ref to be mistaken
ingannatóre -trice adj deceptive || mf impostor
ingannévole adj deceitful; deceptive
inganno m deception; illusion
ingarbugliare §280 tr to entangle; to jumble || ref to get mixed up; to become embroiled
ingegnare (ingégno) ref to manage; to scheme
ingegnère m engineer
ingegnería f engineering; **ingegneria civile** civil engineering; **ingegneria meccanica** mechanical engineering
ingégno m brain, intelligence; talent; genius; expediency; (lit) machinery
ingegnosità [s] f ingeniousness
ingegnó·so -sa [s] adj ingenious; euphuistic
ingelosire [s] §176 tr to make jealous || intr (ESSERE) & ref to become jealous
ingemmare (ingèmmo) tr to adorn or stud with gems
ingenerare (ingènero) tr to engender
ingèni·to -ta adj inborn
ingènte adj huge, vast
ingentilíre §176 tr to refine
ingenui·tà f (-tà) ingenuousness; ingenuous act
ingè·nuo -nua adj ingenuous, artless || m (theat) artless character || f (theat) ingénue
ingerènza f interference
ingerire §176 tr to ingest, swallow || ref to meddle

ingessare (ingèsso) *tr* to put in a plaster cast; to plaster up

ingessatura *f* (surg) plaster cast

inghiaiare §287 *tr* to gravel, cover with gravel

Inghilterra, l' *f* England; **la Nuova Inghilterra** New England

inghiottire (inghiótto) & §176 *tr* to swallow; to swallow up; to pocket (*one's pride*)

inghirlandare *tr* to bedeck with garlands; (lit) to encircle

ingiallire §176 *tr* & *intr* (ESSERE) to turn yellow

ingigantire §176 *tr* to exaggerate || *intr* (ESSERE) to grow larger, increase

inginocchiare §287 (inginòcchio) *ref* to kneel down

inginocchia-tóio *m* (-tói) prie-dieu

ingioiellare (ingioièllo) *tr* to bejewel; (fig) to stud

ingiù *adv* down; **all'ingiù** downwards

ingiùngere §183 *tr* to order, command || *intr* (with *dat*) to order, command, e.g., **il giudice ingiunse all'imputato di rispondere** the judge ordered the accused to answer

ingiunzióne *f* order; (law) injunction

ingiuria *f* insult, abuse; damage, wear

ingiuriare §287 *tr* to insult

ingiurió·so -sa [s] *adj* insulting

ingiustificàbile *adj* unjustifiable

ingiustifica·to -ta *adj* unjustified

ingiustizia *f* injustice

ingiu·sto -sta *adj* unjust, unfair || *m* unjust person

inglése [s] *adj* English; **all'inglese** in the English fashion; **andarsene all'inglese** to take French leave || *m* Englishman; English (*language*) || *f* Englishwoman

ingoiare §287 (ingóio) *tr* to swallow; to gulp down; **ingoiare un rospo** (fig) to swallow one's pride

ingolfare (ingólfo) *tr* (aut) to flood || *ref* to form a gulf; to get involved; (aut) to flood

ingollare (ingóllo) *tr* to swallow, gulp down

ingolosire [s] §176 *tr* to make the mouth of (*s.o.*) water || *intr* (ESSERE) & *ref* to have a craving

ingombrante *adj* cumbersome

ingombrare (ingómbro) *tr* to clutter

ingóm·bro -bra *adj* encumbered, cluttered || *m* encumbrance; **essere d'ingombro** to be in the way

ingommare (ingómmo) *tr* to glue

ingordìgia *f* greed

ingór·do -da *adj* greedy, covetous

ingorgare §209 (ingórgo) *ref* to get clogged up

ingór·go *m* (-ghi) blocking, congestion; **ingorgo stradale** traffic jam

ingovernàbile *adj* uncontrollable

ingozzare (ingózzo) *tr* to gobble, gulp down; to swallow; to cram (*e.g., a goose for fattening*)

ingranàg·gio *m* (-gi) gear, gearwheel; (fig) meshes; **ingranaggio di distribuzione** (aut) timing gear; **ingranaggio elicoidale** worm gear

ingranare *tr* to engage (*a gear*); **ingranare la marcia** to throw into gear || *intr* to be in gear; to succeed

ingrandimẻnto *m* enlargement; increase

ingrandire §176 *tr* to enlarge; to increase; || *intr* (ESSERE) & *ref* to increase, get larger

ingrassare *tr* to fatten; to lubricate || *intr* (ESSERE) & *ref* to get fat; to get rich

ingrassa·tóre -trice *mf* greaser, lubricator || *f* grease gun; lubricating machine

ingratitùdine *f* ingratitude

ingra·to -ta *adj* ungrateful; thankless || *mf* ingrate

ingraziare §287 *ref* to ingratiate oneself with

ingrediénte *m* ingredient

ingrèsso *m* entrance; admittance, entry; **ingressi** hallway furniture; **primo ingresso** debut

ingrossaménto *m* enlargement; swelling

ingrossare (ingròsso) *tr* to enlarge; to swell; to make bigger; to dull (*the mind*); to raise (*one's voice*) || *intr* (ESSERE) & *ref* to swell; to thicken; to become fat; to become pregnant; to become important

ingròsso *m*—**all'ingrosso** wholesale; approximately, more or less

ingrullire §176 *tr* to drive crazy || *intr* (ESSERE) & *ref* to become silly; **fare ingrullire** to drive crazy

inguadàbile *adj* not fordable

inguainare (inguaìno) *tr* to sheathe

ingualcìbile *adj* wrinkle-free, wrinkleproof

inguanta·to -ta *adj* with gloves on; **con le mani inguantate** with gloves on

inguaribile *adj* incurable

inguine *f* (anat) groin

ingurgitare (ingùrgito) *tr* to swallow, gulp down

inibire §176 *tr* to inhibit

inibi·tóre -trice *adj* inhibiting || *m* inhibitor

inidòne·o -a *adj* unfit, unqualified

iniettare (iniètto) *tr* to inject || *ref* to become bloodshot; **iniettarsi di sangue** to become bloodshot

iniezióne *f* injection

inimicare §197 *tr* to make an enemy of; to alienate || *ref*—**inimicarsi con** to fall out with

inimicizia *f* enmity

inimitàbile *adj* inimitable, matchless

ininterrót·to -ta *adj* uninterrupted

iniqui·tà *f* (-tà) injustice; iniquity

inì·quo -qua *adj* unjust; wicked

iniziale *adj* & *f* initial

iniziare §287 *tr* to initiate || *ref* to begin

iniziativa *f* initiative; sponsorship; **iniziativa privata** private enterprise

inizia·tóre -trice *adj* initiating || *mf* initiator, promoter

iniziazióne *f* initiation

inì·zio *m* (-zi) beginning, start

inaffiare §287 *tr* var of **annaffiare**

innaffia·tóio *m* (-tói) var of **annaffiatoio**

innalzaménto *m* elevation

innalzare *tr* to raise; to elevate; **innalzare al cielo** to praise to the sky. || *ref* to rise; to tower

innamorare (innamóro) *tr* to charm, fascinate; to inspire with love || *ref* to fall in love

innamorà·to -ta *adj* in love, enamored; fond || *mf* sweetheart || *m* boyfriend || *f* girl friend

innanzi *adj invar* previous, prior (e.g., day) || *adv* ahead, before; **innanzi a** in front of; **innanzi di** + *inf* before + *ger*; **mettere innanzi** to prefer; to place before; to advance (an excuse); **per l'innanzi** before, in the past; **tirare innanzi** to get along || *prep* before; above; **innanzi tempo** ahead of time; **innanzi tutto** above all

innà·rio *m* (-ri) hymnal

inna·to -ta *adj* inborn, innate

innegàbile *adj* undeniable

inneggiare §290 (**innéggio**) *intr*—**inneggiare a** to sing the praises of

innervosire [s] §176 *tr* to make nervous

innescare §197 (**innésco**) *tr* to bait (a hook); to prime (a bomb)

inné·sco *m* (-schi) primer; detonator

innestare (innèsto) *tr* (hort & surg) to graft; (surg) to implant; (med) to inoculate (a vaccine); (mach) to engage; (elec) to plug in (e.g., a plug); **innestare la marcia** (aut) to throw into gear || *ref* to be grafted; **innestarsi in** to merge with; **innestarsi su** to connect with

innèsto *m* (hort & surg) graft; (surg) implant; (med) inoculation; (mach) engagement; (mach) coupling; (elec) plug

inno *m* hymn; **inno nazionale** national anthem

innocènte *adj* innocent || *m* innocent; **innocenti** foundlings

innocènza *f* innocence

innò·cuo -cua *adj* innocuous, harmless

innominàbile *adj* unmentionable

innomina·to -ta *adj* unnamed

innovare (innòvo) *tr* to innovate

innovazióne *f* innovation

innumerévole *adj* countless, innumerable

-ino -ina *suf adj* little, e.g., **poverino** poor little; hailing from, e.g., **fiorentino** hailing from Florence, Florentine || *suf f see* **-ina**

inoccupa·to -ta *adj* unoccupied || *m* person looking for his first job

inoculare (inòculo) *tr* to inoculate

inoculazióne *f* inoculation

inodó·ro -ra *adj* odorless

inoffensi·vo -va *adj* inoffensive

inoltrare (inóltro) *tr* (com) to forward (e.g., a request) || *ref* to advance

inóltre *adv* besides, in addition

inóltro *m* (com) forwarding

inondare (inóndo) *tr* to inundate, flood; to swamp

inondazióne *f* flood, inundation

inoperosità [s] *f* idleness

inoperó·so -sa [s] *adj* idle

inopina·to -ta *adj* (lit) unexpected

inopportu·no -na *adj* inopportune, untimely

inoppugnàbile *adj* incontestable; indisputable

inorgàni·co -ca *adj* (-ci -che) inorganic

inorgoglire §176 *tr* to make proud || *intr* (ESSERE) & *ref* to grow proud

inorridire §176 *tr* to horrify || *intr* (ESSERE) to be horrified

inospitale *adj* inhospitable

inosservante *adj* unobservant

inosserva·to -ta *adj* unnoticed; unperceived

inossidàbile *adj* stainless

inquadrare *tr* to frame; to arrange

inquadratura *f* framing; (mov, phot) frame

inqualificàbile *adj* unspeakable

inquietante *adj* disquieting

inquietare (inquièto) *tr* to worry || *ref* to worry; to get angry

inquiè·to -ta *adj* worried; restless; angry; (lit) stormy

inquietùdine *f* worry; restlessness; preoccupation

inquili·no -na *mf* tenant

inquinaménto *m* pollution

inquinare *tr* to pollute

inquirènte *adj* investigating

inquisi·tóre -trice *adj* inquiring || *m* inquisitor

inquisizióne *f* inquisition

insabbiare §287 *tr* to cover with sand; to pigeonhole; to shelve || *ref* to get covered with sand; to bury oneself in sand; to get stuck

insaccare §197 *tr* to bag; to stuff (e.g., salami); (mil) to hem in; (fig) to bundle up; (coll) to gulp down || *ref* to be packed in; to crumple up; to disappear behind a thick bank of clouds (said, e.g., of the sun)

insaccato *m* participant in a sack race; **insaccati** cold cuts, lunch meat

insalata *f* salad; (fig) mess

insalatièra *f* salad bowl

insalubre *adj* unhealthy

insaluta·to -ta *adj* unsaluted; **andarsene insalutato ospite** to take French leave

insanàbile *adj* incurable; implacable

insanguinare (insànguino) *tr* to bloody; to cover with blood; to bathe in blood

insa·no -na *adj* insane

insaponare (insapóno) *tr* to soap; to lather; (fig) to soft-soap

insaporire §176 *tr* to flavor || *intr* (ESSERE) to become tasty

insaputa *f*—**all'insaputa di** without the knowledge of, unbeknown to

insaziàbile *adj* insatiable

insazia·to -ta *adj* insatiate, unsatisfied

inscatolare (inscàtolo) *tr* to can

inscenare (inscèno) *tr* to stage

inscindìbile *adj* inseparable

inscrìvere §250 *tr* (geom) to inscribe

inscrutàbile *adj* inscrutable

inscurire §176 *tr*, *intr* (ESSERE) & *ref* to darken

insecchire §176 *tr* to dry || *intr* (ESSERE) & *ref* to dry up

insediaménto *m* installation (*into an office*); assumption (*of an office*)

insediare §287 (**insèdio**) *tr* to install || *ref* to be installed; to take one's seat; to settle

inségna *f* badge, insignia, emblem; ensign, flag; coat of arms; motto; sign (*e.g., on a restaurant*); traffic sign

insegnaménto *m* education, instruction

insegnante *adj* teaching || *mf* teacher

insegnare (**inségno**) *tr* to teach; to show || *intr* to teach

inseguiménto *m* pursuit

inseguire (**inséguo**) *tr* to pursue, chase; to chase after

insellare (**insèllo**) *tr* to saddle; to put on (*e.g., one's glasses*); to bend

insellatura *f* saddling; bending

insenatura *f* inlet, cove

insensatézza *f* nonsense, folly

insensa·to -ta *adj* nonsensical, foolish || *mf* scatterbrain

insensìbile *adj* insensible; unresponsive; insensitive

inseparàbile *adj* inseparable || *m* (orn) lovebird

insepól·to -ta *adj* unburied

inserire §176 *tr* to insert; to plug in || *ref* to slip in; to butt in

inseri·tóre -trice *adj* (elec) connecting || *m* (elec) connector, plug || *f* sorter (*of punch cards*)

insèrto *m* file, folder; insert; spliced film

inservìbile *adj* useless, worthless

inserviènte *m* attendant, porter; (eccl) server

inserzionare (**inserzióno**) *intr* to advertise

inserzióne *f* insertion; advertisement

inserzioni·sta (**-sti -ste**) *adj* advertising || *mf* advertiser

insettici·da *adj* & *m* (**-di -de**) insecticide

insettìfu·go *m* (**-ghi**) insect repellent

insètto *m* insect; **insetti** vermin

insìdia *f* trap, ambush; **insidie** lure

insidiare §287 *tr* to ensnare; to try to trap; to try to seduce; to attempt (*someone's life*)

insidió·so -sa [s] *adj* insidious

insième *m* whole, entirety; harmony; ensemble; set; **d'insieme** general, comprehensive; **nell'insieme** as a whole || *adv* together

insigne *adj* famous; notable; arrant (*knave*)

insignificante *adj* insignificant; petty

insignire §176 *tr* to decorate; **insignire qlcu di un titolo** to bestow a title upon s.o.

insignorire §176 *tr* (lit) to invest with a fief || *intr* (ESSERE) to enrich oneself || *ref* to enrich oneself; **insignorirsi di** to seize; to take possession of

insilare *tr* to silo, ensile

insilato *m* ensilage

insincè·ro -ra *adj* insincere

insindacàbile *adj* final, indisputable

insino *adv* (lit)—**insino a** until; as far as; **insino a che** as long as

insinuante *adj* insinuating

insinuare (**insìnuo**) *tr* to stick, thrust; to insinuate; (law) to register || *ref* to creep, filter; to ingratiate oneself; **insinuarsi in** to worm one's way into

insinuazióne *f* insinuation, hint

insìpi·do -da *adj* insipid, vapid

insistènte *adj* insistent

insistere §114 *intr* to insist

insì·to -ta *adj* inborn, inherent

insociévole *adj* unsociable

insoddisfat·to -ta *adj* dissatisfied

insofferènte *adj* intolerant

insoffrìbile *adj* unbearable, insufferable

insolazióne *f* sunning; sun bath; sunstroke; sunny exposure

insolènte *adj* insolent

insolentire §176 *tr* to insult, abuse || *intr* to be insolent

insolènza *f* insolence; insult

insòli·to -ta *adj* unusual

insolùbile *adj* insoluble

insolu·to -ta *adj* unsolved; not dissolved; unpaid

insolvènza *f* insolvency

insolvìbile *adj* insolvent; bad (*debt*)

insómma *adv* in conclusion || *interj* well!

insommergìbile *adj* unsinkable

insondàbile *adj* unfathomable

insònne *adj* sleepless

insònnia *f* insomnia

insonnoli·to -ta *adj* sleepy, drowsy

insonorizzazióne [ddzz] *f* soundproofing

insopportàbile *adj* unbearable

insorgènte *adj* appearing || *mf* insurgent

insorgènza *f* appearance (*of illness*)

insórgere §258 *intr* (ESSERE) to rise up, revolt; to appear

insormontàbile *adj* unsurmountable, insurmountable

insór·to -ta *adj* & *m* insurgent

insospettàbile *adj* above suspicion; unexpected

insospetta·to -ta *adj* not suspect; unexpected

insospettire §176 *tr* to make suspicious || *intr* (ESSERE) & *ref* to become suspicious

insostenìbile *adj* indefensible; unbearable

insostituìbile *adj* irreplaceable

insozzare (**insózzo**) *tr* to soil, sully

inspera·to -ta *adj* unexpected; unhoped-for

inspiegàbile *adj* unexplainable

inspirare *tr* to inhale, breathe in

inspirazióne *f* inhalation

instàbile *adj* unstable

installare *tr* to install; to set up, settle; to induct (*in an office*) || *ref* to settle

installatóre *m* plumber; erector

installazióne *f* installation; plumbing

instancàbile *adj* untiring

instante *adj* insistent; impending || *m* petitioner

instare (*pp* missing) *intr* to insist; to threaten, be imminent

instaurare (**instàuro**) *tr* to establish

instaurazióne *f* establishment

instigare §209 *tr* var of **istigare**

instillare *tr* var of **istillare**

instituire §176 *tr* var of **istituire**

instruire §176 *tr* var of istruire
instrumento *m* var of istrumento
instupidire §176 *tr* var of istupidire
insù *adv* up; **all'insù** up
insubordina·to -ta *adj* insubordinate
insuccèsso *m* failure
insudiciare §128 (**insùdicio**) *tr* to soil, dirty; to sully ‖ *ref* to get dirty
insufficiènte *adj* insufficient; failing (*in school*)
insufficiènza *f* insufficiency; failure (*in school*)
insulare *adj* insular
insulina *f* insulin
insulsàggine *f* silliness, nonsense
insul·so -sa *adj* insipid; simple, silly
insultante *adj* insulting
insultare *tr* to insult ‖ *intr* (with *dat*) to insult
insulto *m* insult; (pathol) attack
insuperàbile *adj* insuperable; unparalleled
insupera·to -ta *adj* unsurpassed
insuperbire §176 *tr*, *intr* (ESSERE) & *ref* to swell with pride
insurrezióne *f* insurrection
insussistènte *adj* nonexistent, unfounded
intabarrare *tr* to wrap up
intaccare §197 *tr* to notch; to corrode; to scratch; to attack (*said of a disease*); to damage (*e.g., a reputation*); to cut into (*capital*) ‖ *intr* to stutter
intaccatura *f* notch; (carp) mortise
intagliare §280 *tr* to carve; to engrave
intà·glio *m* (**-gli**) carving; intaglio
intanare *ref* to hide
intangìbile *adj* intangible; inviolable
intanto *adv* meanwhile; (coll) yet; (coll) finally; **intanto che** while; **per intanto** at present; in the meantime
intarsiare §287 *tr* to inlay; (fig) to stud
intarsia·to -ta *adj* inlaid
intàr·sio *m* (**-si**) inlay; inlaid work
intasare [s] *tr* to clog; to tie up (*traffic*); to stop up ‖ *ref* to be clogged up; to be tied up; to be stopped up (*said of nose*)
intascare §197 *tr* to pocket
intat·to -ta *adj* intact, untouched
intavolare (**intàvolo**) *tr* to start (*a conversation*); to broach (*a subject*); to launch (*negotiations*)
intavolato *m* boarding, planking
integèrri·mo -ma *adj* of the utmost honesty
integrale *adj* integral; whole; wholewheat (*bread*); built-in ‖ *m* integral
integralismo *m* policy of the complete absorption of the body politic by an ideology
integrante *adj* constituent, integral
integrare (**ìntegro**) *tr* to integrate ‖ *ref* to complement each other
integrazióne *f* integration
integrità *f* integrity
ìnte·gro -gra *adj* whole, complete; honest, upright; intact
intelaiatura *f* frame; framework
intellètto *m* intellect, mind; understanding
intellettuale *adj* & *mf* intellectual

intellettuali·tà *f* (**-tà**) intellectuality; intelligentsia
intellettualòide *mf* highbrow
intelligènte *adj* intelligent; clever
intelligènza *f* intelligence; understanding; **essere d'intelligenza con** to be in collusion with
intellighènzia *f* intelligentsia
intelligìbile *adj* intelligible
intemera·to -ta *adj* pure, spotless ‖ *f* reprimand, scolding; long, boring speech
intemperante *adj* intemperate
intemperanza *f* intemperance
intempèrie *fpl* inclement weather
intempesti·vo -va *adj* untimely
intendènte *m* district director; **intendente di finanza** director of customs office; **intendente militare** commissary, quartermaster
intendènza *f* office of the district director; intendance; **intendenza militare** quartermaster corps
intèndere §270 *tr* to understand; to hear; to intend; to turn (*e.g., one's eyes*); to mean; **dare ad intendere a** to lead (*s.o.*) to believe (*s.th*); **far intendere** to give to understand; **farsi intendere** to force obedience; to make oneself understood; **intender dire che** to hear that; **intendere a rovescio** to misunderstand; **intendere a volo** to catch on quickly (to); **intendere ragione** to listen to reason; **lasciare intendere** to give to understand ‖ *intr* to aim (*toward a goal*) ‖ *ref* to come to an agreement; **intendersela con** to be in collusion with; to have an affair with; **intendersi di** to be a good judge of; to be an expert in
intendiménto *m* understanding, comprehension; aim, goal
intendi·tóre -trice *mf* connoisseur, expert; **a buon intenditore poche parole** a word to the wise is sufficient
intenerire §176 *tr* to soften; (fig) to move ‖ *ref* to soften; (fig) to be moved
intensificare §197 (**intensìfico**) *tr* & *ref* to intensify
intensi·tà *f* (**-tà**) intensity
intensi·vo -va *adj* intensive
intèn·so -sa *adj* intense
intentare (**intènto**) *tr* (law) to bring (*action*)
intenta·to -ta *adj* unattempted
intèn·to -ta *adj* intent ‖ *m* intent, goal; **coll'intento di** with the purpose of
intenzionale *adj* intentional
intenziona·to -ta *adj*—**bene intenzionato** well-meaning; **essere intenzionato di** to intend to
intenzióne *f* intention; purpose; **con intenzione** on purpose
intepidire §176 *tr* & *ref* var of intiepidire
interbase *f* (baseball) shortstop
intercalare *m* refrain; pet word or phrase ‖ *tr* to intercalate; to inset
intercalazióne *f* intercalation; inset
intercapèdine *f* air space
intercèdere §123 *tr* to seek, get (*a par-*

don for s.o.) || *intr* to intercede || *intr* (ESSERE)—**intercedere tra** to intervene or elapse between; to extend between; to exist between

intercettare (intercètto) *tr* to intercept; to tap (*a phone*)

intercetta·tóre -trice *mf* interceptor

intercettóre *m* (aer) interceptor

intercomunale *adj* long-distance (*call*)

intercórrere §139 *intr* (ESSERE) to elapse; to happen; to be, to stand

interdét·to -ta *adj* dumfounded; forbidden || *m* interdict; (coll) dumbell

interdire §151 *tr* to prohibit; (eccl) to interdict; (law) to disqualify

interessaménto *m* interest, concern

interessante *adj* interesting; **in stato interessante** in the family way

interessare (interèsso) *tr* to interest; to concern || *intr* to be of interest || *ref*—**interessarsi a** to take an interest in; **interessarsi di** to concern oneself with

interessa·to -ta *adj* interested; selfish || *m* interested party

interèsse *m* interest; self-interest

interessènza *f* (com) share, interest

interferènza *f* interference

interferire §176 *intr* to interfere

interfogliare §280 **(interfòglio)** *tr* to interleave

interiezióne *f* interjection

interinato *m* temporary office or tenure

interì·no -na *adj* acting || *m* temporary appointee

interióra *fpl* entrails

interióre *adj* interior || **interiori** *mpl* entrails

interlinea *f* interlining; (typ) leading

interlineare *adj* interlinear || *v* **(interlìneo)** *tr* (typ) to lead

interlocu·tóre -trice *mf* participant (*in a discussion*); person speaking

interloquire §176 *intr* to take part in a discussion; to chime in

interlù·dio *m* **(-di)** interlude

intermedià·rio -ria (-ri -rie) *adj & mf* intermediary || *m* middleman

intermè·dio -dia (-di -die) *adj* intermediate || *mf* supervisor

intermèzzo [ddzz] *m* intermezzo; entr'acte; interval

interminàbile *adj* interminable, endless

intermissióne *f* intermission

intermittènte *adj* intermittent

internaménto *m* internment

internare (intèrno) *tr* to intern; to confine; to commit (*an insane person*) || *ref* to go deep (*into a problem*)

interna·to -ta *adj* interned || *m* internee; inmate; boarder; boarding school

internazionale *adj* international

internazionalizzare [ddzz] *tr* to internationalize

internì·sta *mf* **(-sti -ste)** internist

intèr·no -na *adj* inside, internal; inland; interior; boarding (*student*) || *m* inside; interior; (med) intern; lining (*of coat*); **all'interno** inside; **interni** (mov) indoor shots || **gli Interni** the Italian Ministry of Internal Affairs

inté·ro -ra *adj* entire, whole; full (*price*); (lit) upright, honest || *m* whole; **per intero** completely

interpellare (interpèllo) *tr* to interpellate; to question; to consult

interpetrare (intèrpetro) *tr* var of **interpretare**

interplanetà·rio -ria *adj* **(-ri -rie)** interplanetary

interpolare (intèrpolo) *tr* to interpolate

interpolazióne *f* interpolation

interpónte *m* (naut) between-deck

interpórre §218 *tr* to interpose || *ref* to intervene

interpretare (intèrpreto) *tr* to interpret

interpretazióne *f* interpretation

intèrprete *mf* interpreter

interpunzióne *f* punctuation

interrare (intèrro) *tr* to bury, inter; to fill in (*e.g., a marsh*) || *ref* to become silted

interra·to -ta *adj* underground; **piano interrato** basement

interrogare §209 **(intèrrogo)** *tr* to question; to interrogate

interrogatì·vo -va *adj* interrogative || *m* why; question

interrogatò·rio -ria (-ri -rie) *adj* questioning || *m* (law) interrogatory; **interrogatorio di terzo grado** third degree

interrogazióne *f* interrogation; quiz, examination; **interrogazione retorica** rhetorical question

interrómpere §240 *tr* to interrupt

interruttóre *m* (elec) switch; **interruttore di linea** (elec) controller

interruzióne *f* interruption

interscàm·bio *m* **(-bi)** interchange

interscolàsti·co -ca *adj* **(-ci -che)** interscholastic; intercollegiate

intersecare §197 **(intèrseco)** *tr & ref* to intersect

intersezióne *f* intersection

interstellare *adj* interstellar

interstì·zio *m* **(-zi)** interstice

interurbà·no -na *adj* interurban, intercity; (telp) long-distance || *f* (telp) long-distance call

intervallo *m* interval; pause; (educ) recess; (theat) intermission

intervenire §282 *intr* (ESSERE) to intervene; (surg) to operate; **intervenire a** to take part in

interventì·sta *mf* **(-sti -ste)** interventionist

intervènto *m* intervention; attendance; (surg) operation

intervenzióne *f* intervention

intervista *f* interview; **fare un'intervista a** to interview

intervistare *tr* to interview

inté·so -sa [s] *adj* understood; intended, designed; **bene inteso** of course; **non darsene per inteso** to not pay attention; **rimanere inteso** to agree || *f* understanding, agreement; entente

intèssere (intèsso) *tr* to interweave; to wreathe (*a garland*)

intestardire §176 *ref* to get obstinate; to be determined

intestare (intèsto) *tr* to caption; to label; (typ) to head (*a page*); **intestare qlco a qlcu** to register s.th in the name of s.o.; **intestare una fattura a** to issue a bill in the name of || *ref* to become obstinate; to take it into one's head

intesta·to -ta *adj* headed; registered (*stock*); obstinate; (law) intestate

intestazióne *f* heading; registration (*of stock*)

intestinale *adj* intestinal

intesti·no -na *adj & m* intestine; **intestino crasso** large intestine; **intestino tenue** small intestine

intiepidire §176 *tr & ref* to warm up; to cool off

intiè·ro -ra *adj & m* var of **intero**

intimare (intìmo & intimo) *tr* to intimate; to order, command; to declare (*war*); to impose (*a fine*); (law) to enjoin

intimazióne *f* intimation; order; (law) injunction

intimidazióne *f* intimidation

intimidire §176 *tr* to intimidate; to threaten || *ref* to become bashful

intimi·tà *f* (-tà) intimacy; privacy

inti·mo -ma *adj* intimate; inmost; **biancheria intima** underwear, lingerie || *m* intimate friend; depth (*of one's heart*)

intimorire §176 *tr* to frighten

intingere §126 *tr* to dip || *intr*—**intingere in** to dip in || *ref*—**intingersi in un affare** to have a finger in the pie

intingolo *m* sauce, gravy; fancy dish

intirizzire [ddzz] §176 *tr* to benumb || *intr* (ESSERE) & *ref* to become numb or stiff; to become stiff and frostbitten

intirizzi·to -ta [ddzz] *adj* numb

intisichire §176 *tr* to make tubercular; (fig) to weaken || *intr* (ESSERE) to become tubercular; to wither

intitolare (intìtolo) *tr* to title; to dedicate || *ref* to be named; to assume the title of

intoccàbile *adj & m* untouchable

intolleràbile *adj* intolerable

intollerante *adj* intolerant

intonacare §197 (intònaco) *tr* to plaster; to whitewash; to cover (*e.g., with tar*) || *ref*—**intonacarsi la faccia** (joc) to put on one's warpaint

intòna·co *m* (-chi) plaster; roughcast

intonare (intòno) *tr* to intone; to harmonize; (mus) to tune || *ref* to harmonize, go

intonazióne *f* intonation; harmony

intòn·so -sa *adj* uncut; (lit) unsheared

intontire §176 *tr* to stun || *intr* (ESSERE) & *ref* to become stunned

intoppare (intòppo) *tr* to stumble upon || *intr* (ESSERE) & *ref* to stumble

intòppo *m* obstacle, hindrance

intorbidare (intórbido) *tr* to cloud; to muddy; to obfuscate; to upset (*friendship*); to stir up (*passions*) || *ref* to become cloudy or muddy; to become obfuscated

intorbidire §176 *tr & ref* to cloud; to muddy

intormentire §176 *tr* to benumb || *intr* (ESSERE) to become numb

intórno *adv* around, about; **all'intorno** all around; **intorno a** around; about; **levarsi qlcu d'intorno** to get rid of s.o.

intorpidire §176 *tr* to benumb || *ref* to become numb

intossicare §197 (intòssico) *tr* to poison, intoxicate

intossicazióne *f* poisoning, intoxication

intraducibile *adj* untranslatable; inexpressible

intrafèrro *m* spark gap; air gap

intralciare §128 *tr* to hamper; to intertwine || *ref* to become hampered

intràl·cio *m* (-ci) hindrance; **essere d'intralcio** to be in the way; **intralcio del traffico** traffic congestion

intralicciatura *f* lattice truss (*of high-tension tower*)

intrallazzare *intr* to deal in the black market

intrallazza·tóre -trice *mf* black marketeer

intrallazzo *m* black-market dealing; kickback

intramezzare [ddzz] (intramèzzo) *tr* to alternate

intramontàbile *adj* undying, immortal

intransigènte *adj & mf* intransigent, die-hard

intransitàbile *adj* impassable

intransiti·vo -va *adj* intransitive

intrappolare (intràppolo) *tr* to entrap

intraprendènte *adj* enterprising

intraprendènza *f* enterprise, initiative

intraprèndere §220 *tr* to undertake

intrattàbile *adj* unmanageable, intractable

intrattenére §271 *tr* to entertain || *ref* to linger; **intrattenersi su** to dwell upon

intrattenimento *m* entertainment

intravedére §279 *tr* to glimpse, catch a glimpse of; to foresee

intraveno·so -sa [s] *adj* intravenous

intrecciare §128 (intréccio) *tr* to braid; to twine; to cross (*one's fingers*); (fig) to weave; to begin (*a dance*) || *ref* to become embroiled; to become intertwined; to crisscross

intréc·cio *m* (-ci) knitting; intertwining; plot (*of novel*); (theat) intrigue

intrepidézza *f* intrepidness, intrepidity

intrèpi·do -da *adj* intrepid

intricare §197 *tr* (lit) to entangle

intrica·to -ta *adj* tangled; intricate

intri·co *m* (-chi) tangle, jumble

intrìdere §189 *tr* to soak; to knead

intrigante *adj* intriguing || *mf* schemer

intrigare §209 *tr* to tangle || *intr* to intrigue || *ref* (coll) to meddle

intri·go *m* (-ghi) intrigue; trouble

intrìnse·co -ca (-ci -che) *adj* intrinsic; intimate || *m* intimate nature, core

intri·so -sa *adj* soaked || *m* mash

intristire §176 *intr* (ESSERE) to wither; to waste away

introdót·to -ta *adj* introduced; well-known; knowledgeable, expert

introdurre §102 *tr* to introduce; to insert; to open (*a speech*); to show in || *ref* to slip in

introdutti·vo -va *adj* introductory

introduzióne *f* introduction

introitare (intròito) *tr* to collect, take in

intròito *m* receipts, collection; (eccl) introit

introméttere §198 *tr* to insert; to introduce; to involve || *ref* to meddle; to pry

intromissióne *f* meddling; intrusion; intervention

intronare (intròno) *tr* to deafen; to stun

intronizzare [ddzz] *tr* to enthrone

introspetti·vo -va *adj* introspective

introspezióne *f* introspection

introvàbile *adj* unobtainable; inaccessible

introvèr·so -sa *adj & mf* introvert

intrùdere §190 *tr* (lit) to slip in || *ref* to intrude; to trespass

intrufolare (intrùfolo) *tr* (coll) to slip (*e.g.*, *one's hand into somebody's pocket*) || *ref* to slip in, intrude

intrù·glio *m* (**-gli**) concoction, brew; hodgepodge; imbroglio; mess

intrusióne *f* intrusion

intru·so -sa *adj* intrusive || *mf* intruder

intuire §176 *tr* to know by intuition; to guess; to sense

intuiti·vo -va *adj* intuitive; obvious

intùito *m* intuition; insight

intuizióne *f* intuition

inturgidire §176 *intr* (ESSERE) & *ref* to swell

inuma·no -na *adj* inhuman; inhumane

inumare *tr* to bury, inhume

inumazióne *f* burial, inhumation

inumidire §176 *tr* to moisten || *ref* to get wet

inurbaménto *m* migration to the city

inurba·no -na *adj* uncouth, unmannerly

inurbare *ref* to move into the city; to become citified

inusa·to -ta *adj* unused; unusual

inusita·to -ta *adj* unusual; out-of-the-way

inùtile *adj* useless; worthless

inutilizzàbile [ddzz] *adj* unusable

inutilizzare [ddzz] *tr* to waste (*e.g.*, *time*)

inutilizza·to -ta [ddzz] *adj* unused

inutilménte *adv* needlessly, to no purpose || *interj* no use!

invadènte *adj* meddlesome, intrusive

invàdere §172 *tr* to invade; to encroach on; to spread over; to overcome

invaghire §176 *tr* to charm || *ref* to fall in love

invalére §278 *intr* (ESSERE) to become established; to prevail

invalicàbile *adj* impassable, unsurmountable

invalidàbile *adj* voidable

invalidaménto *m* invalidity; invalidation

invalidare (invàlido) *tr* to void, invalidate; to negate (*e.g.*, *evidence*)

invalidi·tà *f* (**-tà**) invalidity; invalidation; sickness, disability

invàli·do -da *adj* void, invalid; sick, disabled || *m* disabled person; invalid

inval·so -sa *adj* prevailing

invano *adv* in vain, vainly

invariàbile *adj* invariable

invaria·to -ta *adj* unchanging; unchanged

invasare *tr* to pot (*a plant*); to fill up (*a reservoir*); to possess, obsess

invasa·to -ta *adj* possessed, obsessed

invasióne *f* invasion

inva·so -sa *adj* invaded || *m* potting (*of plant*); capacity (*of reservoir*)

inva·sóre -ditrice *adj* invading || *m* invader

invecchiaménto *m* aging

invecchiare §287 **(invècchio)** *tr & intr* (ESSERE) to age

invéce *adv* on the contrary, instead; **invece di** instead of

inveire §176 *intr* to inveigh, rail

invelenire §176 *tr* to envenom; to embitter || *intr* (ESSERE) & *ref* to grow bitter

invendìbile *adj* unsalable

invendica·to -ta *adj* unavenged

invendu·to -ta *adj* unsold

inventare (invènto) *tr* to invent

inventariare §287 *tr* to inventory

inventà·rio *m* (**-ri**) inventory

inventi·vo -va *adj* inventive || *f* inventiveness

inven·tóre -trice *adj* inventive || *mf* inventor

invenzióne *f* invention; (lit) find

inverdire §176 *intr* (ESSERE) to turn green

inverecóndia *f* immodesty

inverecón·do -da *adj* immodest

invernale *adj* winter; wintry

inverniciare §128 *tr* to paint; to varnish

invèrno *m* winter

invéro *adv* (lit) truly, indeed

inverosimiglianza [s] *f* unlikelihood

inverosìmile [s] *adj* unlikely

inversióne *f* inversion

invèr·so -sa *adj* inverse, opposite; (coll) cross || *m* inverse

inversóre *m* inverter; **inversore di spinta** (aer) thrust reverser

invertebra·to -ta *adj & m* invertebrate

invertire §176 & **(invèrto)** *tr* to invert; to reverse

inverti·to -ta *adj* inverted || *m* invert

investigare §209 **(invèstigo)** *tr* to investigate

investiga·tóre -trice *adj* investigating || *mf* investigator; detective

investigazióne *f* investigation

investiménto *m* investment; collision

investire (invèsto) *tr* to invest; to collide with; **investire di insulti** to cover with insults || *ref*—**investirsi di** to become conscious of (*e.g.*, *one's authority*); (theat) to become identified with (*a character*)

investi·tóre -trice *mf* investor

investitura *f* investiture

invetera·to -ta *adj* inveterate, confirmed

invetria·to -ta *adj* glazed || *f* window; window pane

invettiva *f* invective

inviare §119 *tr* to send

invia·to -ta *mf* envoy; correspondent

invidia *f* envy

invidiàbile *adj* enviable

invidiare §287 *tr* to envy; to begrudge; **non aver niente da invidiare a** to be just as good as

invidió·so -sa [s] *adj* envious

invigorire §176 *tr* to strengthen, invigorate || *intr* (ESSERE) & *ref* to grow stronger

invilire §176 *tr* to dishearten; to vilify; to lower (*prices*) || *intr* (ESSERE) & *ref* to lose heart; to lose one's reputation

inviluppare *tr* to envelop; to wrap up

invincibile *adj* invincible

invì·o *m* (-i) dispatch; shipment; remittance; envoy (*of a poem*)

inviolàbile *adj* inviolable

inviperire §176 *ref* to become enraged

invischiare §287 *tr* to smear with birdlime; to ensnare || *ref* to become ensnared

invisibile *adj* invisible

invi·so -sa *adj* disliked, hated

invitante *adj* attractive, inviting

invitare *tr* to invite; to summon; (*cards*) to bid; (*cards*) to open; (*mach*) to screw (*e.g., a light bulb*) in; to screw (*e.g., a lid*) on

invita·to -ta *adj* invited || *m* guest

invito *m* invitation; inducement; bottom of stairway; (*cards*) opening

invit·to -ta *adj* unvanquished

invocare §197 (invòco) *tr* to invoke

invocazióne *f* invocation

invogliare §280 (invòglio) *tr* to induce, entice || *ref* to yearn, long

involare (invólo) *tr* to steal; to abduct || *intr* (ESSERE) (aer) to take off || *ref* to disappear; to fly away

invòlgere §289 *tr* to wrap, envelop; to involve || *ref* to become entangled

invòlo *m* (aer) take-off

involontà·rio -ria *adj* (-ri -rie) involuntary

invòlto *m* bundle; wrapper

invòlucro *m* wrapping; shell (*of boiler*); (aer) envelope

involu·to -ta *adj* (fig) involved; (lit) enveloped

invòlvere §147 (*pret* missing; *pp* also **invòlto**) *tr* (lit) to envelop

invulneràbile *adj* invulnerable

inzaccherare (inzàcchero) *tr* to bespatter

inzeppare (inzéppo) *tr* to cram, stuff

inzuccherare (inzùcchero) *tr* to sweeten

inzuppare *tr* to soak || *ref* to get drenched

io *m* ego; self || §5 *pron pers*

iòdio *m* iodine

iodìdri·co -ca *adj* (-ci -che) hydriodic

ioduro *m* iodide

iògurt *m* yogurt

iò·le *f* (-le) (naut) yawl; (sports) shell

ióne *m* ion

iòni·co -ca *adj* & *m* (-ci -che) Ionic

ionizzare [ddzz] *tr* to ionize

iòsa [s] *f*—**a iosa** in abundance

iperacidità *f* hyperacidity

ipèrbole *f* (geom) hyperbola; (rhet) hyperbole

iperbòli·co -ca *adj* (-ci -che) hyperbolic(al)

ipereccita·to -ta *adj* overexcited

ipermercato *m* shopping center

ipersensibile *adj* hypersensitive; supersensitive

ipersostentatóre *m* landing flap

ipertensióne *f* hypertension

ipnò·si *f* (-si) hypnosis

ipnòti·co -ca *adj* & *m* (-ci -che) hypnotic

ipnotismo *m* hypnotism

ipnotizzare [ddzz] *tr* to hypnotize

ipnotizza·tóre -trice [ddzz] *adj* hypnotizing || *m* hypnotizer

ipocondria·co -ca *adj* & *mf* (-ci -che) hypochondriac

ipocrisìa *f* hypocrisy

ipòcri·ta (-ti -te) *adj* hypocritical || *mf* hypocrite

ipodèrmi·co -ca *adj* (-ci -che) hypodermic

iposolfito [s] *m* hyposulfite

ipotè·ca *f* (-che) mortgage

ipotecare §197 (ipotèco) *tr* to mortgage

ipotecà·rio -rio *adj* (-ri -rie) mortgage

ipotenusa *f* hypotenuse

ipòte·si *f* (-si) hypothesis; **nella miglior delle ipotesi** at best; **nell'ipotesi che** in the event; **per ipotesi** by supposition

ipotèti·co -ca *adj* (-ci -che) hypothetic(al)

ipotizzare [ddzz] *tr* to hypothesize

ìppi·co -ca (-ci -che) *adj* horse, horseracing || *f* horse racing

ippocampo *m* sea horse

ippocastano *m* horse chestnut tree

ippòdromo *m* race track

ippoglòsso *m* (ichth) halibut

ippopòtamo *m* hippopotamus

iprite *f* mustard gas

ira *f* wrath, anger, ire

irachè·no -na *adj* & *mf* Iraqi

iracóndia *f* wrath, anger

iracón·do -da *adj* wrathful

irania·no -na *adj* & *mf* Iranian

irascibile *adj* irascible

ira·to -ta *adj* irate, angry

ire §191 *intr* (ESSERE) (lit) to go

irida·to -ta *adj* rainbow-hued || *m* world bicycle champion

iride *f* rainbow; (anat, bot) iris

Irlanda, l' *f* Ireland

irlandése [s] *adj* Irish || *m* Irishman; Irish (*language*) || *f* Irishwoman

ironìa *f* irony

iròni·co -ca *adj* (-ci -che) ironic(al)

iró·so -sa [s] *adj* angry, wrathful

irradiare §287 *tr* to illuminate; to irradiate, radiate; to brighten; (rad) to broadcast || *intr* to radiate || *ref* to radiate; to spread

irraggiare §290 *tr* to illuminate; to irradiate, radiate, beam; to brighten; (rad) to broadcast || *intr* to radiate || *ref* to radiate; to spread

irraggiungìbile *adj* unattainable
irragionévole *adj* unreasonable
irrancidire §176 *intr* (ESSERE) & *ref* to get rancid
irrazionale *adj* irrational
irreale *adj* unreal
irreconciliàbile *adj* irreconcilable
irrecuperàbile *adj* irretrievable, irrecoverable
irredentismo *m* irredentism
irredenti·sta *mf* (-sti -ste) irredentist
irredèn·to -ta *adj* not yet redeemed
irredimìbile *adj* irredeemable
irrefrenàbile *adj* unrestrainable
irrefutàbile *adj* irrefutable
irregimentare (irregiménto) *tr* to regiment
irregolare *adj* irregular
irregolari·tà *f* (-tà) irregularity
irreligió·so -sa [s] *adj* irreligious
irremovìbile *adj* irremovable; obstinate
irreparàbile *adj* irreparable; unavoidable
irreperìbile *adj* not to be found; unaccounted for (*e.g., soldier*)
irreprensìbile *adj* irreproachable
irreprimìbile *adj* irrepressible
irrequiè·to -ta *adj* restless, restive
irresistìbile [s] *adj* irresistible
irresolùbile [s] *adj* unbreakable (*bond; contract*); insoluble; unsolvable
irresolu·to -ta [s] *adj* irresolute
irrespiràbile *adj* unbreathable
irresponsàbile *adj* irresponsible
irrestringìbile *adj* unshrinkable
irretire §176 *tr* to ensnare, entrap
irrevocàbile *adj* irrevocable
irriconoscìbile *adj* unrecognizable
irriducìbile *adj* irreducible; stubborn
irriflessì·vo -va *adj* thoughtless, rash
irrigare §209 *tr* to irrigate
irrigazióne *f* irrigation
irrigidire §176 *tr* to chill || *intr* & *ref* to stiffen, harden; to get cool
irrì·guo -gua *adj* well-watered; irrigating
irrilevante *adj* irrelevant
irrilevanza *f* irrelevance
irrimediàbile *adj* irremediable
irripetìbile *adj* unrepeatable
irrisióne *f* (lit) derision, mockery
irrisò·rio -ria *adj* (-ri -rie) mocking; paltry
irritàbile *adj* peevish; irritable
irritante *adj* irritating || *m* irritant
irritare (irrito) *tr* to irritate; to anger; to chafe || *ref* to become irritated
irritazióne *f* irritation
irriverènte *adj* irreverent
irrobustire §176 *tr* & *ref* to strengthen
irrómpere §240 (*pp* missing) *intr* to burst
irrorare (irròro) *tr* to sprinkle; to bathe, wet; to spray
irroratrice *f* sprayer; irroratrice a zaino portable sprayer
irruènte *adj* impetuous, rash
irruzióne *f* foray, raid; irruption
irsu·to -ta *adj* hairy, bristling
ir·to -ta *adj* prickly; shaggy (*hair*); irto di bristling with
iscrìvere §250 *tr* to inscribe; to register || *ref* to register; to sign up

iscrizióne *f* inscription; registration
Islam, l' *m* Islam
Islanda, l' *f* Iceland
islandése [s] *adj* Icelandic || *mf* Icelander || *m* Icelandic (*language*)
ìsola *f* island; block; isola spartitraffico traffic island
isolaménto *m* isolation; (elec) insulation
ìsola·no -na *adj* island || *mf* islander
isolante *adj* insulating || *m* (elec) insulation
isolare (ìsolo) *tr* to isolate; (elec) to insulate || *ref* to keep apart
ìsola·to -ta *adj* isolated; (elec) insulated || *m* city block; (sports) independent
isolatóre *m* (elec) insulator
isolazionismo *m* isolationism
isolazioni·sta *mf* (-sti -ste) isolationist
isolétta *f* isle
isòscele *adj* isosceles
isòto·po -pa *adj* isotopic || *m* isotope
ispani·sta *mf* (-sti -ste) Hispanist
ispa·no -na *adj* Hispanic
ispanoamerica·no -na *adj* & *mf* Spanish-American
ispessire §176 *tr* & *ref* to thicken
ispettorato *m* inspectorship
ispet·tóre -trice *mf* inspector; ispettore di produzione (mov) production manager
ispezionare (ispezióno) *tr* to inspect
ispezióne *f* inspection
ìspi·do -da *adj* bristly
ispirare *tr* to inspire || *ref* to be inspired
ispirazióne *f* inspiration
Israèle *m* Israel
israelia·no -na *adj* & *mf* Israeli
israeli·ta *adj* & *mf* (-ti -te) Israelite
issare *tr* to hoist
issòpo *m* hyssop
istallare *tr* & *ref* var of installare
istantàne·o -a *adj* instantaneous || *f* snapshot
istante *m* instant, moment; petitioner
istanza *f* petition; request, application; (law) instance; in ultima istanza as a final decision
istèri·co -ca (-ci -che) *adj* hysteric(al) || *mf* hysteric
isterilire §176 *tr* to make barren || *ref* to become barren
isterismo *m* hysteria, hysterics
istigare §209 *tr* to instigate, prompt
istiga·tóre -trice *mf* instigator
istillare *tr* to instill, implant; istillare il collirio negli occhi to put drops in the eyes
istintì·vo -va *adj* instinctive
istinto *m* instinct
istituire §176 *tr* to institute, found; (lit) to decide
istituto *m* institute; institution; bank; istituto di bellezza beauty parlor
istitu·tóre -trice *mf* founder; teacher, instructor || *m* tutor || *f* governess; nurse
istituzionalizzare [ddzz] *tr* to institutionalize
istituzióne *f* institution
istmo *m* isthmus
istologìa *f* histology

istoriare §287 (istòrio) *tr* to adorn with historical figures

istradare *tr* to direct || *ref* to wend one's way

istrice *m & f* (European) porcupine

istrióne *m* ham actor; buffoon

istrióni·co -ca *adj* (-ci -che) histrionic

istrionismo *m* histrionics

istruire §176 *tr* to instruct; to train; (law) to draw up, prepare (*a case*) || *ref* to learn

istruì·to -ta *adj* learned, educated

istruménto *m* (law) instrument

istrutti·vo -va *adj* instructive

istrut·tóre -trice *mf* instructor; (sports) coach

istruttò·rio -ria (-ri -rie) *adj* investigating, preliminary || *f* (law) preliminary investigation

istruzióne *f* instruction; (law) prelimi-nary investigation; **istruzioni** instruc-tions; directions

istupidire §176 *tr* to make dull; to stupefy

**Italia, l' *f* Italy

italia·no -na *adj & mf* Italian

itàli·co -ca *adj* (-ci -che) italic; Italic; (lit) Italian || *m* italics

italòfo·no -na *adj* Italian-speaking || *m* Italian-speaking person

itinerante *adj* itinerant

itinerà·rio *m* (-ri) itinerary

ittèri·co -ca *adj* (-ci -che) jaundiced

itterizia *f* jaundice

ittiologìa *f* ichthiology

Iugoslàvia, la Yugoslavia

iugosla·vo -va *adj & mf* Yugoslav

iugulare *adj & tr* var of giugulare

iuta *f* jute

ivi *adv* (lit) there

J
K
L

L, l ['elle] *m & f* tenth letter of the Italian alphabet

la §4 *def art* the || *m* (mus) la, A; **dare il la** to set the tone || §5 *pers pron*

là *adv* there; **al di là da venire** to come, future; **al di là (di)** beyond; **andare di là** to go in the next room; **andare troppo in là là (di) beyond; farsi in là** to move aside; **in là con gli anni** advanced in years; **l'al di là** the life beyond; **più in là** further; **più in là di beyond; va' là!** come on!

lab·bro *m* (-bri) edge (*of wound*); (lit) lip || *m* (-bra *fpl*) lip; **labbro lepo-rino** harelip

labiale *adj & f* labial

làbile *adj* (coll) weak; (lit) fleeting

labiolettura *f* lip reading

labirinto *m* labyrinth, maze

laboratò·rio *m* (-ri) laboratory; work-shop; **laboratorio linguistico** lan-guage laboratory

laborió·so -sa [s] *adj* hard-working, laborious; labored (*e.g., digestion*)

laburi·sta (-sti -ste) *adj* Labour || *mf* Labourite

lac·ca *f* (-che) lacquer

laccare §197 *tr* to lacquer; to japan; to polish (*nails*)

lac·chè *m* (-chè) lackey

lac·cio *m* (-ci) lasso; snare; noose; string; (fig) bond; **laccio delle scarpe** shoelace; **laccio emostatico** tourni-quet

lacciòlo *m* snare

lacerare (làcero) *tr* to lacerate; to tear || *ref* to tear

làce·ro -ra *adj* torn; tattered

lacèrto *m* (lit) shred of flesh; (lit) biceps

lacòni·co -ca *adj* (-ci -che) laconic

làcrima *f* tear; drop

lacrimare (làcrimo) *tr* (lit) to weep over || *intr* to water (*said of the eyes*); (lit) to weep

lacrima·to -ta *adj* (lit) lamented

lacrimévole *adj* pitiful

lacrimò·ge·no -na *adj* tear (*e.g., gas*)

lacrimó·so -sa [s] *adj* teary, watery (*eyes*); tearful; lachrymose

lacuna *f* gap, lacuna; blank (*in one's mind*); **colmare una lacuna** to bridge a gap

lacustre *adj* lake

laddóve *conj* while, whereas

ladré·sco -sca *adj* (-schi -sche) thievish

la·dro -dra *adj* thieving; foul (*weather*); bewitching (*eyes*) || *mf* thief; **ladro di strada** highwayman || *f* inside pocket (*of suit*)

ladróne *m* thief; highwayman; **ladrone di mare** pirate

ladrùncolo *m* petty thief, pilferer

laggiù *adv* down there

lagnanza *f* complaint

lagnare *ref* to complain; to moan

lagno *m* complaint, lament

la·go *m* (-ghi) lake; pool (*of blood*)

làgrima *f* var of lacrima

laguna *f* lagoon

lai *m* (lai) lay; **lai** *mpl* (lit) lamen-tations

laicato *m* laity

lài·co -ca *adj* (-ci -che) lay || *m* layman

lài·do -da *adj* foul; obscene

la·ma *m* (-ma) llama; **lama** || *f* (-me) blade (*of knife*); marsh; (lit) lowland

lambiccare §197 *tr* to distill || *ref* to strive; **lambiccarsi il cervello** to rack one's brains

lambìc·co *m* (-chi) still

lambire §176 *tr* to lap; to graze, to touch lightly

lamèlla *f* thin sheet

lamentare (laménto) *tr* to bemoan, lament || *ref* to moan; to complain

lamentazióne *f* lamentation

lamentévole *adj* plaintive; lamentable
laménto *m* complaint, lament; moan
lamentó·so -sa [s] *adj* plaintive, doleful
lamétta *f* razor blade
lamièra *f* plate; armor plate
lamierino *m* sheet metal, lamina
làmina *f* sheet, lamina
laminare (**làmino**) *tr* to laminate; to roll (*steel*)
lamina·tóio *m* (**-tói**) rolling mill
làmpada *f* lamp, light; **lampada al neon** neon lamp; **lampada a petrolio** oil lamp; **lampada a stelo** pole lamp; **lampada di sicurezza** (min) safety lamp; **lampada fluorescente** fluorescent lamp; **lampada lampo** (phot) flash bulb
lampadà·rio *m* (**-ri**) chandelier
lampadina *f* bulb; **lampadina tascabile** flashlight
lampante *adj* shiny; clear; lamp (*oil*)
lampeggiare §290 (**lampéggio**) *tr* (lit) to flash (*a smile*) || *intr* to flash; (aut) to blink; (coll) to flash the turn signals || *impers* (ESSERE & AVERE)—**lampeggia** it lightens, it is lightning
lampeggiatóre *m* (aut) turn signal; (phot) flashlight
lampio·nàio *m* (**-nài**) lamplighter
lampióne *m* street lamp
lampìride *f* glowworm
lampo *m* lightning; flash of lightning; (fig) flash
lampóne *m* raspberry
lana *f* wool; **buona lana** (coll) rogue, rascal; **lana d'acciaio** steel wool; **lana di vetro** fiberglass, glass wool
lancétta *f* lancet; hand (*of watch*); pointer (*of instrument*)
làn·cia *f* (**-ce**) lance, spear; nozzle (*of fire hose*); launch; **lancia di salvataggio** lifeboat
lanciabóm·be *m* (**-be**) trench mortar
lanciafiam·me *m* (**-me**) flamethrower
lanciamìssi·li (**-li**) *adj* missile-launching || *m* missile launcher
lanciaraz·zi [ddzz] *m* (**-zi**) rocket launcher
lanciare §128 *tr* to throw, hurl; to drop (*from an airplane*); to launch (*e.g., an advertising campaign*) || *ref* to hurl oneself; (rok) to blast off; **lanciarsi col paracadute** to parachute, bail out
lanciasilu·ri *m* (**-ri**) torpedo tube
lancia·to -ta *adj* hurled, flung; flying, e.g., **partenza lanciata** flying start
lancia·tóre -trice *mf* hurler, thrower; (baseball) pitcher
lancière *m* lancer
lancinante *adj* piercing
làn·cio *m* (**-ci**) throw; publicity campaign; (aer) drop; (aer) release (*of bombs*); (baseball) pitch; (rok) launch; **lancio del peso** shot put
landa *f* moor; wasteland
lanerie *fpl* woolens
languidézza *f* languidness, languor
làngui·do -da *adj* languid; sad (*eyes*)
languire (**lànguo**) & §176 *intr* to languish
languóre *m* languor; languishing; weakness; tenderness

laniè·ro -ra *adj* wool (*industry*)
lanifì·cio *m* (**-ci**) woolen mill
lanó·so -sa [s] *adj* woolly; kinky (*hair*); bushy (*face*)
lantèrna *f* lantern
lanùgine *f* down
lanzichenéc·co *m* (**-chi**) landsknecht
laónde *conj* (lit) wherefore
laotia·no -na *adj* & *mf* Laotian
lapalissia·no -na *adj* self-evident
lapidare (**làpido**) *tr* to stone (to death); (fig) to pick to pieces
làpide *f* stone tablet; tombstone
lapillo *m* lapillus
là·pis *m* (**-pis**) pencil
lappare *intr* to lap
làppola *f* (bot) burdock; (bot) bur
lappóne *adj* Lappish || *mf* Lapp || *m* Lapp (*language*)
Lappónia, la Lapland
lardellare (**lardèllo**) *tr* to lard; to stuff with bacon
lardo *m* lard; **nuotare nel lardo** to live on easy street
largheggiare §290 (**larghéggio**) *intr* to be liberal; to be lavish
larghézza *f* width; liberality; abundance; **larghezza di vedute** broad-mindedness
largire §176 *tr* (lit) to bestow liberally
largizióne *f* bestowal; donation
lar·go -ga (**-ghi -ghe**) *adj* broad, wide; ample; liberal; abundant; (phonet) open; **prenderla larga** to keep away || *m* width; open sea; square; (mus) largo; **al largo di** (naut) off; **fare largo a** to open the way to; **farsi largo** to elbow one's way; **prendere il largo** to run away; (naut) to put to sea; **tenersi al largo** to keep at a distance || *f*—**alla larga!** keep away! || **largo** *adv*—**girare largo** to keep away
làrice *m* larch
laringe *f* larynx
laringite *f* laryngitis
laringoia·tra *mf* (**-tri -tre**) laryngologist
laringoscò·pio *m* (**-pi**) laryngoscope
larva *f* (ent) larva; (lit) ghost; (lit) skeleton; (lit) sham
lasagne *fpl* lasagne
lasciapassa·re *m* (**-re**) safe-conduct; permit
lasciare §128 *tr* to leave; to let; to let go of; **lasciar cadere** to drop; **lasciarci le penne** (coll) to die; (coll) to be skinned alive; **lasciar correre** to let go; **lasciar detto** to leave word; **lasciar fare** to leave alone; **lasciare in pace** to leave alone; **lasciar libero** to let go; **lasciare scritto** to leave in writing || *ref* to abandon oneself; to abandon one another
làscito *m* (law) bequest
lascìvia *f* lasciviousness
lascì·vo -va *adj* lascivious
lassati·vo -va *adj* mildly laxative || *m* mild laxative
lassismo *m* laxity
las·so -sa *adj* lax || *m* lasso; **lasso di tempo** period of time
lassù *adv* up there, up above
lastra *f* slab; paving stone; (phot)

plate; exposed X-ray film; **farsi le lastre** (coll) to be X-rayed

lastricare §197 (làstrico) *tr* to pave

lastricato *m* paving, pavement

làstri·co *m* (-ci or -chi) pavement; roadway; **ridursi sul lastrico** to fall into abject poverty

lastróne *m* slab; plate glass

latènte *adj* latent

laterale *adj* lateral ‖ *m* (soccer) halfback

laterì·zio -zia (-zi -zie) *adj* brick ‖ **laterizi** *mpl* bricks, tiles

làtice *m* latex

latifondi·sta *mf* (-sti -ste) rich landowner

latifóndo *m* large landed estate

lati·no -na *adj* Latin; lateen (*sail*) ‖ *m* Latin

latitante *adj* hiding ‖ *mf* fugitive

latitanza *f* flight from justice

latitùdine *f* latitude

la·to -ta *adj* wide; broad (*meaning*) ‖ *m* side; **d'altro lato** on the other hand

la·tóre -trice *mf* bearer

latrare *intr* to bark

latrato *m* bark

latrina *f* toilet, lavatory, washroom

latta *f* tin; can

lattàia *f* milkmaid

lat·tàio *m* (-tài) milkman, dairyman

lattante *adj & m* suckling

latte *m* milk; **latte detergente** cleansing cream; **latte di gallina** flip; (bot) star-of-Bethlehem; **latte in polvere** powdered milk; **latte magro** or **scremato** skim milk

lattemièle *m* whipped cream

làtte·o -a *adj* milky

lattería *f* dairy; creamery

làttice *m* var of latice

latticèllo *m* buttermilk

lattici·nio *m* (-ni) dairy product

lattiginó·so -sa [s] *adj* milky

lattonière *m* tinsmith

lattu·ga *f* (-ghe) lettuce; head of lettuce; frill

làudano *m* paregoric, laudanum

laudati·vo -va *adj* laudatory

làurea *f* wreath; doctorate; doctoral examination

laurean·do -da *mf* candidate for the doctorate

laureare (làureo) *tr* to confer the doctorate on; to award (*s.o.*) the title of; (lit) to wreathe ‖ *ref* to receive the doctorate; (sports) to get the tile of

laurea·to -ta *adj* laureate ‖ *m* alumnus, graduate

làuro *m* laurel

làu·to -ta *adj* sumptuous, rich

lava *f* lava

lavabianche·rìa *f* (-rìa) washing machine

lavàbile *adj* washable

lavabo *m* washstand; lavatory

lavacristallo *m* windshield washer

lavacro *m* washing; font; purification; **santo lavacro** baptism

lavàg·gio *m* (-gi) washing; **lavaggio a secco** dry cleaning; **lavaggio del cervello** brainwashing

lavagna *f* slate; blackboard; **lavagna di panno** felt board; **lavagna luminosa** overhead projector

lavama·no *m* (-no) washstand

lavanda *f* washing; pumping (*of stomach*); lavender

lavandàia *f* laundrywoman; **lavandaia stiratrice** laundress (*woman who washes and irons*)

lavan·dàio *m* (-dài) laundryman; **lavandaio stiratore** launderer

lavandería *f* laundry; **lavanderia a gettone** laundromat; **lavanderia a secco** dry-cleaning establishment

lavandino *m* sink

lavapiat·ti *mf* (-ti) dishwasher (*person*)

lavare *tr* to wash; to cleanse; **lavare a secco** to dry-clean; **lavare il capo a** to scold ‖ *ref* to wash oneself; **lavarsi le mani** to wash one's hands

lavastovì·glie *mf* (-glie) dishwasher ‖ *m & f* dishwasher (*machine*)

lavata *f* washing; **lavata di capo** scolding

lavativo *m* (coll) enema; (coll) bore; (coll) goldbricker

lava·tóio *m* (-tói) laundry room; washtub

lava·tóre -trice *mf* washer ‖ *m* washerman; (mach) purifier ‖ *f* washerwoman; washing machine

lavatura *f* washing; **lavatura a secco** dry cleaning; **lavatura di piatti** dishwater; washing of dishes; (fig) watery soup

lavèllo *m* wash basin; sink

lavoràbile *adj* workable

lavorante *mf* helper, apprentice

lavorare (lavóro) *tr* to work; to till ‖ *intr* to work; to perform; to be busy; to trade; **lavorare ai ferri** to knit; **lavorare di fantasia** to daydream; **lavorare di ganasce** to eat voraciously; **lavorare di gomiti** to elbow one's way; **lavorare di mano** to pilfer; **lavorare di traforo** to work with a jig saw

lavorati·vo -va *adj* working; workable

lavora·to -ta *adj* wrought; tilled

lavora·tóre -trice *mf* worker ‖ *m* workman; workingman ‖ *f* workingwoman

lavorazióne *f* working; manufacturing; tilling

lavorì·o *m* (-ì) bustle; steady work; scheming

lavóro *m* work; labor; steady work; homework; piece of work; (coll) trouble; **a lavori ultimati** when the work is finished; **lavori forzati** hard labor; **lavori in economia** time and material contract work; **lavori teatrali** theatrical productions; **lavoro a cottimo** piecework; **lavoro a maglia** knitting; **lavoro di cucito** needlework; **mettere al lavoro** to press into service

lazzarétto [ddzz] *m* lazaretto

lazzaróne [ddzz] *m* cad; (coll) goldbricker

le §4 *def art* the ‖ §5 *pers pron*

leale *adj* loyal; sincere

leali·sta *mf* (-sti -ste) loyalist

leal·tà *f* (-tà) loyalty; sincerity

lébbra f leprosy

lebbró·so -sa [s] adj leprous || mf leper

lécca-léc·ca m (-ca) (coll) lollypop

leccapiat·ti m (-ti) glutton; sponger

leccapiè·di mf (-di) bootlicker

leccarda f dripping pan

leccare §197 (**lécco**) tr to lick; to fawn on; (fig) to polish || ref to make oneself up

lecca·to -ta adj affected; polished || f licking

léc·cio m (-ci) holm oak

leccornìa f dainty morsel, delicacy

léci·to -ta adj licit, permissible; **mi sia lecito** may I || m right

lèdere §192 tr to damage, injure

lé·ga f (-ghe) league; alloy; **di bassa lega** poor, in poor taste; **fare lega** to unite

legale adj legal; lawyer's; official || m lawyer

legali·tà f (-tà) legality, lawfulness

legalità·rio -ria adj (-ri -rie) (pol) observing the rule of law

legalizzare [ddzz] tr to legalize; to authenticate

legame m bond; connection; relationship

legaménto m tie, bond; ligament; (phonet) liaison

legare §209 (**légo**) tr to tie; to bind; to unite; to set (a stone); to bequeath; to alloy; (bb) to bind || intr to bond; to mix (said of metals); to go together || ref to unite; **legarsela al dito** to never forget

legatà·rio -ria mf (-ri -rie) legatee

lega·to -ta adj muscle-bound || m legate; bequest; (mus) legato

lega·tóre -trice mf bookbinder

legatorìa f bookbindery

legatura f typing; binding; ligature; bookbinding; (mus) tie

legazióne f legation

légge f law; act; **dettar legge** to lay down the law; **è fuori della legge** he is an outlaw; **legge stralcio** emergency law

leggènda f legend; story, tall tale; (journ) caption

leggendà·rio -ria adj (-ri -rie) legendary

lèggere §193 tr, intr & ref to read

leggerézza f lightness; nimbleness; thoughtlessness; fickleness

leggè·ro -ra adj light; nimble; thoughtless; slight; fickle; **alla leggera** lightly || **leggero** adv lightly

leggia·dro -dra adj graceful, lovely

leggìbile adj legible, readable

leggì·o m (-i) lectern; music stand

legiferare (**legìfero**) intr to legislate

legionà·rio -ria adj & m (-ri -rie) legionary

legióne f legion

legislati·vo -va adj legislative

legisla·tóre -trice mf legislator

legislatura f legislature

legittimare (**legìttimo**) tr to legitimize

legittimi·tà f (-tà) legitimacy

legìtti·mo -ma adj legitimate; pure; just, right || f (law) legitim

lé·gna f (-gna & -gne) firewood; (fig) fuel

legnàia f woodpile; woodshed

legname m timber, lumber

legnata f clubbing, thrashing

légno m wood; stick; ship; coach; timber; **legno compensato** plywood; **legno dolce** softwood; **legno forte** hardwood

legnòlo m ply (e.g., of a cable)

legnó·so -sa [s] adj wooden; tough (meat); dry (style)

legu-lèio m (-lèi) pettifogger

legume m legume; **legumi** vegetables; legumes

leguminósa [s] f leguminous plant; leguminose legumes

lèi §5 pron pers; **dare del Lei a** to address formally

lémbo m edge, border; patch (of land)

lèm·ma m (-mi) entry (in a dictionary)

lèmme lèmme adv (coll) slowly

léna f energy; enthusiasm; (lit) breath

lèndine m nit

lène adj (lit) light, soft, gentle; (phonet) voiced

lenire §176 tr to soothe, assuage

lenóne m panderer, procurer

lenóna f procuress

lènte f lens; bob, pendulum bob; **lente d'ingrandimento** magnifying glass; **lenti** glasses

lentézza f slowness

lenticchia f lentil

lentìggine f freckle

lentiginó·so -sa [s] adj freckly

lèn·to -ta adj slow; slack; (lit) loose (hair); (lit) loose-fitting (garment) || **lento** adv slowly

lènza f fishline

lenzuò·lo m (-li) sheet; (fig) blanket; **lenzuolo a due piazze** double sheet; **lenzuolo funebre** winding sheet, shroud || m (-la fpl) sheet; **lenzuola** pair of sheets (in a bed)

leoncino m lion cub

leóne m lion; **leone d'America** cougar; **leone marino** sea lion || **Leone** m (astr) Leo

leonéssa f lioness

leopardo m leopard

lepidézza f wit; witticism

lèpi·do -da adj witty, facetious

lepisma f (ent) silverfish

lèpre adj invar rendezvous, e.g., **razzo lepre** rendezvous rocket || f hare

lepròtto m leveret, young hare

lèr·cio -cia adj (-ci -ce) filthy

lerciume m filth, dirt

lèsbi·co -ca (-ci -che) adj & mf Lesbian || f Lesbian (female homosexual)

lésina f awl; stinginess; miser

lesinare (**lésino** & **lèsino**) tr to begrudge || intr to be miserly

lesionare (**lesióno**) tr to damage; to crack open

lesióne f damage; injury; lesion

lé·so -sa adj damaged; injured

lessare (**lésso**) tr to boil

lessicale adj lexical

lèssi·co -ca (-ci) lexicon

lessicografìa f lexicography

lessicogràfi·co -ca adj (-ci -che) lexicographic(al)

lessicògrafo m lexicographer

lessicologìa f lexicology
lés·so -sa adj boiled || m boiled meat; soup meat
lè·sto -sta adj swift; nimble; quick; **alla lesta** hastily; **lesto di lingua** ready-tongued; **lesto di mano** light-fingered
lestofante m swindler
letale adj lethal, deadly
leta·màio m (**-mài**) dunghill
letame m manure, dung
letàrgi·co -ca adj (**-ci -che**) lethargic
letar·go m (**-ghi**) lethargy; hibernation
letìzia f happiness, joy
lèttera f letter; **alla lettera** literally; **lettera morta** unheeded, e.g., **le sue parole rimasero lettera morta** his words remained unheeded; **lettere** literature; **lettere credenziali** credentials; **scrivere in tutte lettere** to spell out
letterale adj literal
letterà·rio -ria adj (**-ri -rie**) literary; learned (word)
letterà·to -ta adj literary; literate || m man of letters; (coll) literate, learned person
letteratura f literature
lettièra f litter, bedding
letti·ga f (**-ghe**) sedan chair; stretcher
lètto m bed; bedding; **di primo letto** born of the first marriage; **letti gemelli** twin beds; **letto a castello** bunk bed; **letto a due piazze** double bed; **letto a scomparsa** Murphy bed; **letto a una piazza** single bed; **letto bastardo** oversize bed; **letto caldo** hot-bed; **letto di morte** deathbed; **letto operatorio** operating table
lèttone or **lettóne** adj Lettish || mf Lett || m Lett, Lettish (language)
Lettònia, La Latvia
let·tóre -trice mf reader; lecturer; meter reader || m reader (e.g., for microfilm); **lettore perforatore** reader (of punch cards)
lettura f reading; lecture; **lettura del pensiero** mind reading
letturi·sta m (**-sti**) meter reader
leucemìa f leukemia
leucorrèa f leucorrhea
lèva f lever; (mil) draft; (mil) class; **essere di leva** to be of draft age; **fare leva su** to use (s.o.'s emotions)
levachio·di m (**-di**) claw hammer
levante adj rising || m east; Levant
levanti·no -na adj & mf Levantine
levare (**lèvo**) tr to lift, raise; to weigh (anchor); to pull (a tooth); to break (camp); to collect (mail); to remove, take away; to subtract; **levare alle stelle** to praise to the sky; **levare il disturbo** a to take leave of || ref to arise; to get up; to take off; to satisfy (e.g., one's hunger); to rise (said of wind); **levarsi dai piedi** to get out of the way; **levarsi dai piedi** or **di mezzo qicu** to get rid of s.o.
levata f rise; reveille; collection (of mail); withdrawal (of merchandise from warehouse); **levata di scudi** uprising
levatàc·cia f (**-ce**) getting up at an im-

possible hour; **ho dovuto fare una levataccia** I had to get up way too early
leva·tóio -tóia adj (**-tói -tóie**)—**ponte levatoio** drawbridge
levatrice f midwife
levatura f intellectual breadth
leviatano m leviathan
levigare §209 (**lèvigo**) tr to polish
levigatrice f sander; buffer
levi·tà f (**-tà**) (lit) levity
levitazióne f levitation
levrière m greyhound
lezióne f lesson; lecture; reading
lezió·so -sa [s] adj affected, mincing
lézzo [ddzz] m stench; filth
lì def art masc plur (obs) the; **li tre novembre** the third of November (in official documents) || §5 pers pron
lì adv there; **di lì** that way; **di lì a un anno** a year hence; **essere lì lì per** to be about to; **fin lì** up to that point; **giù di lì** more or less; **lì per lì** on the spot
libanése [s] adj & mf Lebanese
Lìbano, il Lebanon
libare tr to toast; to taste || intr to toast
libazióne f libation
lìbbra f pound
libéc·cio m (**-ci**) southwest wind
libèllo m libel; (law) brief
libèllula f dragonfly
liberale adj & m liberal
liberali·tà f (**-tà**) liberality
liberare (**lìbero**) tr to free; to pay in full for; to open into (said, e.g., of a hall opening into a room); to clear, empty (a room) || ref—**liberarsi da** or **di** to get rid of
libera·tóre -trice adj liberating || mf liberator
liberismo m free trade
lìbe·ro -ra adj free; vacant; without a revenue stamp (document); open (syllable; heart); outspoken
liber·tà f (**-tà**) freedom; release (e.g., from mortgage); **libertà provvisoria** bail, parole; **libertà vigilata** probation; **mettersi in libertà** to put comfortable house clothes on; **rimettere in libertà** to set free
liberti·no -na adj & mf libertine
Lìbia, la Libya
lìbi·co -ca adj & mf (**-ci -che**) Libyan
libìdine f lust; greed
libidinó·so -sa [s] adj lustful
lìbido f libido
li·bràio m (**-brài**) bookseller
librare ref to balance; to soar; (aer) to glide
libratóre m glider
librerìa f bookstore; library (room); bookshelf; book collection
libré·sco -sca adj (**-schi -sche**) bookish
librétto m booklet; card; (mus) libretto; **libretto di banca** passbook; **libretto degli assegni** checkbook; **libretto di circolazione** car registration; **libretto ferroviario** railroad pass; **libretto di risparmio** passbook (of savings bank)
libro m book; ledger; register (e.g., of births); **a libro** folding; **libro di**

bordo log; **libro in brossura** paperback; **libro mastro** ledger; **libro paga (com)** payroll

liceale *adj* high-school ‖ *mf* high-school student

licènza *f* permit; license; diploma; (mil) leave; **con licenza parlando!** excuse my language!; **dar licenza a** to dismiss; **prender licenza da** to take leave of

licenziaménto *m* dismissal; **licenziamento in tronco** firing on the spot

licenziare §287 (**licènzio**) *tr* to dismiss; to O.K. (*a book to be published*); to graduate ‖ *ref* to take leave; to give notice, resign; to graduate

licenzió·so -sa [*s*] *adj* licentious

licèo *m* high school; lycée

lichène *m* lichen

licitazióne *f* auction; (bridge) bidding

lido *m* shore; sand bar

liè·to -ta *adj* glad; blessed (*event*)

lième *adj* light; slight

lievitare (**lièvito**) *tr* to leaven ‖ *intr* (ESSERE & AVERE) to rise; to ferment

lièvito *m* yeast; leaven; **lievito in polvere** baking powder

li·gio -gia *adj* (-**gi -gie**) devoted

lignàg·gio *m* (-**gi**) ancestry, lineage

ligustro *m* privet

lil·la (-**la**) *adj invar & m* lilac

lilliputia·no -na *adj & mf* Lilliputian

lima *f* file; **lima per le unghie** nail file

limacció·so -sa [*s*] *adj* miry, muddy

limare *tr* to file; to polish (*e.g., a speech*); to gnaw, plague

limatura *f* filing; filings

limbo *m* (lit) edge; (fig) limbo ‖ **Limbo** *m* (theol) Limbo

limétta *f* nail file; (bot) lime

limitare *m* threshold ‖ *v* (**limito**) *tr* to limit; to bound

limitazióne *f* limitation

limite *m* limit; boundary; check; (soccer) penalty line; **limite di carico** maximum weight; **limite di età** retirement age; **limite di velocità** speed limit; **senza limiti** limitless

limìtro·fo -fa *adj* neighboring (*country*)

limo *m* mud, mire

limonare (**limóno**) *intr* (coll) to spoon

limonata *f* lemonade; (med) citrate of magnesia

limóne *m* lemon tree; lemon

limó·so -sa [*s*] *adj* slimy

limpi·do -da *adj* limpid, clear

lince *f* lynx, wildcat

linciàg·gio *m* (-**gi**) lynching

linciare §128 *tr* to lynch

lin·do -da *adj* neat; clean

linea *f* line; degree (*of temperature*); **conservare la linea** to keep one's figure; **in linea abreast**; (telp) connected; **in linea d'aria** as the crow flies; **linea del fuoco** firing line; **linea del cambiamento di data** international date line; **linea di circonvallazione** (rr) beltline; **linea di condotta** policy; **linea di partenza** starting line; **linea laterale** (sports) side line

lineaménti *mpl* lineaments; elements

lineare *adj* linear ‖ *v* (**lìneo**) *tr* to delineate

lineétta *f* dash; hyphen

linfa *f* (anat) lymph; (bot) sap; **dar linfa** (bot) to bleed

lingòtto *m* (metallurgy) pig, ingot; **lingotto d'oro** bullion

lingua *f* tongue; language; strip (*of land*); **essere di due lingue** to speak with a forked tongue; **in lingua** in the correct language; **lingua di gatto** ladyfinger; **lingua lunga** backbiter; **lingua sciolta** glib tongue; **mala lingua** wicked tongue

linguacciu·to -ta *adj* talkative; sharp-tongued

linguàg·gio *m* (-**gi**) language

linguèlla *f* (philately) gummed strip

linguétta *f* tongue (*of shoe*); (mach) pin; (mus) reed

linguìsti·co -ca (-**ci -che**) *adj* linguistic ‖ *f* linguistics

linifi·cio *m* (-**ci**) flax-spinning mill

liniménto *m* liniment

lino *m* flax; linen

linósa [*s*] *f* flaxseed, linseed

linotipì·sta *mf* (-**sti -ste**) linotypist

liocòrno *m* unicorn

liofilizzare | ddzz] *tr* to freeze-dry

liquefare §194 *tr & ref* to liquefy

liquefazióne *f* liquefaction

liquidare (**liquido**) *tr* to liquidate; to close out; to dismiss; to settle

liquidazióne *f* liquidation; clearance; **liquidazione del danno** (ins) adjustment

liquidità *f* liquidity

liqui·do -da *adj* liquid; (com) due ‖ *m* liquid; cash ‖ *f* liquid

liqui·gàs *m* (-**gàs**) liquid gas

liquirìzia *f* licorice

liquóre *m* liqueur; (pharm) liquor

liquorì·sta *mf* (-**sti -ste**) liqueur manufacturer or dealer

lira *f* lira; pound; (mus) lyre ‖ **Lira** *f* (astr) Lyra

lìri·co -ca (-**ci -che**) *adj* lyric; (mus) operatic ‖ *m* lyric poet ‖ *f* lyric; lyric poetry; opera

lìrismo *m* lyricism

Lisbóna *f* Lisbon

li·sca *f* (-**sche**) fishbone; lisp

lisciare §128 *tr* to smooth; **lisciare il pelo a** to butter up, flatter; to beat up ‖ *ref* to preen

lì·scio -scia *adj* (-**sci -sce**) smooth; straight (*drink*); black (*coffee*); **passarla liscia** to get away scot-free

lisciva *f* lye; bleach

lisciviatrice *f* washing machine

li·so -sa *adj* worn-out, threadbare

lista *f* list; strip, band; stripe; **lista delle spese** shopping list; **lista delle vivande** bill of fare; **lista elettorale** slate (*of candidates*)

listare *tr* to border; to stripe

listèllo *m* lath; (archit) listel

listino *m* price list; market quotation

litanìa *f* litany

lite *f* quarrel; lawsuit

litigante *adj* quarreling ‖ *mf* quarreler; (law) litigant

litigare §209 (lìtigo) *tr*—litigare qlco a qlcu to fight with s.o. for s.th || *intr* to quarrel; to litigate || *ref*—litigarsi qlco to strive for s.th
lìti·gio *m* (-gi) quarrel, litigation
litigió·so -sa [s] *adj* quarrelsome
lìtio *m* lithium
litografìa *f* lithography
litògrafo *m* lithographer
litorale *adj* littoral || *m* seashore, coast-line
litro *m* liter
Lituània, la Lithuania
litua·no -na *adj & mf* Lithuanian || *m* Lithuanian (*language*)
liturgìa *f* liturgy
litùrgi·co -ca *adj* (-ci -che) liturgical
liu·tàio *m* (-tài) lute maker
liuto *m* lute
livèlla *f* level; **livella a bolla d'aria** spirit level
livellaménto *m* leveling; equalization
livellare (livèllo) *tr* to level; to equalize; to survey || *intr* (ESSERE) & *ref* to become level
livella·tóre -trice *adj* leveling || *mf* surveyor || *f* bulldozer
livellazióne *f* leveling
livèllo *m* level; **livello delle acque sea** level
lìvi·do -da *adj* livid, black-and-blue || *m* bruise
lividóre *m* bruise
livóre *m* grudge; hatred
Livórno *f* Leghorn
livrèa *f* livery
lizza *f* tilting ground; **entrare in lizza** to enter the lists
lo §4 *def art* the || §5 *pers pron*
lòb·bia *m & f* (-bia *mpl & fpl*) homburg
lòbo *m* lobe
locale *adj* local || *m* room; place (of *business*); (naut) compartment; **locale notturno** night spot
locali·tà *f* (-tà) locality, spot
localizzare [ddzz] *tr* to localize; to locate || *ref* to become localized
localizzazióne [ddzz] *f* localization; **localizzazióne dei guasti** troubleshooting
locanda *f* inn
locandiè·re -ra *mf* innkeeper
locandìna *f* playbill; flyer; small poster
locare §197 (lòco) *tr* to rent, lease
locatà·rio -ria *mf* (-ri -rie) lessee, renter
loca·tóre -trice *mf* lessor
locazióne *f* rent; lease; **dare in locazióne** to rent
locomotiva *f* locomotive, engine
locomo·tóre -trice *adj* locomotive || *m & f* (rr) electric locomotive
locomotorì·sta *m* (-stì) (rr) engineer
locomozióne *f* locomotion; transportation
lòculo *m* burial niche
locusta *f* locust
locuzióne *f* locution, expression; phrase; idiom
lodàbile *adj* praiseworthy
lodare (lòdo) *tr* to praise || *ref* to praise oneself, brag; **lodarsi di** (poet) to be pleased with

lodati·vo -va *adj* laudatory
lòde *f* praise; **con la lode cum laude; con lode** plus (*on a report card*)
lodévole *adj* praiseworthy, commendable
lòdo *m* arbitration
logaritmo *m* logarithm
lòg·gia *f* (-ge) lodge; (archit) loggia
loggióne *m* (theat) upper gallery
lògi·co -ca (-ci -che) *adj* logical; **esser logico** to think logically || *m* logician || *f* logic
logìsti·co -ca (-ci -che) *adj* logistic || *f* logistics
lò·glio *m* (-gli) cockle
logoraménto *m* wear; attrition
logorare (lógoro) *tr* to wear out; to fray || *ref* to wear away; to become threadbare
logorì·o *m* (-ì) wear and tear
lógo·ro -ra *adj* worn out; threadbare
lòlla *f* chaff
lombàggine *f* lumbago
lombar·do -da *adj & mf* Lombard
lombata *f* loin, sirloin
lómbo *m* loin; hip; (lit) ancestry
lombrì·co *m* (-chi) earthworm
londinése [s] *adj* London || *mf* Londoner
Londra *f* London
longànime *adj* patient, forbearing
longanimi·tà *f* (-tà) patience, forbearance
longevità *f* longevity
longè·vo -va *adj* long-lived
longherìna *f* beam, girder
longheróne *m* (aer) longeron; (aer) spar; (aut) main frame member
longitùdine *f* longitude
longobar·do -da *adj & mf* Lombard
lontananza *f* distance
lonta·no -na *adj* distant, remote; vague; indirect || *m* (lit) far-away place || *f*—alla lontana from a distance; vaguely; distant (*e.g., relative*) || **lontano** *adv* far; **da lontano** from afar; **lontano da** away from; far from; **rifarsi da lontano** to start from the very beginning
lóntra *f* otter
lónza *f* pork loin; (poet) leopard
lòppa *f* chaff; skin (*of plant*); slag, dross
loquace *adj* loquacious; (fig) eloquent
loquèla *f* (lit) tongue; (lit) style
lordare (lórdo) *tr* to soil, dirty
lór·do -da *adj* soiled, dirty; gross (*weight*)
lordume *m* dirt, filth
lordura *f* dirt, filth; soil
lóro §5 *pron pers* || §6 *adj poss & pron*
losan·ga *f* (-ghe) rhombus; (herald) lozenge
ló·sco -sca *adj* (-schi -sche) squint-eyed; cross-eyed; (fig) shady
lóto *m* mud
lòto *m* lotus
lòtta *f* fight; struggle; wrestling; **essere in lotta** to be at war; **lotta libera** catch-as-catch-can
lottare (lòtto) *intr* to fight; to quarrel; to struggle; to wrestle

lotta·tóre -trice *mf* fighter; wrestler
lotteria *f* lottery
lottizzare [ddzz] *tr* to divide into lots
lòtto *m* lotto; parcel, lot
lozióne *f* lotion
lùbri·co -ca *adj* (**-ci -che**) lewd; (lit) slippery
lubrificante *adj & m* lubricant
lubrificare §197 (**lubrìfico**) *tr* to lubricate
lucchétto *m* padlock
luccicare §197 (**lùccico**) *intr* to sparkle; to shine
luccichì·o *m* (**-i**) glittering; shining; sparkle
luccicóne *m* big tear
lùc·cio *m* (**-ci**) pike
lùcciola *f* firefly; usherette (*in movie*); **prendere lucciole per lanterne** to make a blunder; to be seeing things
luce *f* light; sunlight; opening; glass (*of mirror*); leaf (*e.g., of door*); (archit) span; (coll) electricity; **alla luce del sole** in plain view; **fare luce** to shed light; **luce degli occhi** eyesight; **luce del giorno** daylight; **luce della luna** moonlight; **luce di arresto** (aut) stoplight; **luce di incrocio** (aut) dimmer, low beam; **luce di posizione** (aut) parking light; **luce di profondità** (aut) high beam; **luci** (poet) eyes; **luci della ribalta** (fig) stage, boards; **mettere alla luce** to give birth to; **mettere in luce** to reveal; to publish; **venire alla luce** to be born; to come to light
lucènte *adj* shiny, shining
lucentézza *f* brightness; sheen
lucèrna *f* lamp; light; **lucerne** (lit) eyes || **Lucerna** *f* Lucerne
lucernà·rio *m* (**-ri**) skylight
lucèrtola *f* lizard
lucherino *m* (orn) siskin
Lucìa *f* Lucy
lucidare (**lùcido**) *tr* to shine, polish; to trace (*a figure*)
lucida·tóre -trice *mf* polisher (*person*) || *f* (mach) floor polisher
lucidatura *f* polish; tracing (*on paper*)
lucidi·tà *f* (**-tà**) polish; lucidity
lùci·do -da *adj* bright; lucid || *m* shine; tracing; **lucido per le scarpe** shoe polish
lucìfe·ro -ra *adj* (poet) light-bringing || **Lucifero** *m* Lucifer, morning star
lucignolo *m* wick
lucrare *tr* to win, acquire
lucratì·vo -va *adj* lucrative
lucro *m* gain, earnings, lucre; **lucro cessante** (law) loss of earnings
lucró·so -sa [s] *adj* lucrative
ludì·brio *m* (**-bri**) mockery; laughing-stock
lù·glio *m* (**-gli**) July
lùgubre *adj* gloomy, dismal
lui §5 *pron pers*
luigi *m* louis || **Luigi** *m* Louis
luma·ca *f* (**-che**) snail
lume *m* light; lamp; **lume degli occhi** eyesight; **lume delle stelle** starlight; **lumi** eyesight; **lumi di luna** hard times; **perdere il lume degli occhi**

to lose one's self-control; **reggere il lume a** to close one's eyes to; **studiare al lume di candela** to burn the midnight oil
lumeggiare §290 (**luméggio**) *tr* to illuminate, to shed light on
lumicino *m* faint light; **essere al lumicino** to be on one's last legs
luminare *m* star; luminary
luminària *f* illumination
lumino *m* night light; votive light; rush light
luminó·so -sa [s] *adj* luminous; bright (*idea*)
luna *f* moon; **andare a lune** to be fickle; **avere la luna di traverso** to be in a bad mood; **luna calante** waning moon; **luna crescente** crescent moon; **luna di miele** honeymoon
lunare *adj* lunar, moon
lunària *f* (min) moonstone; (bot) honesty
lunà·rio *m* (**-ri**) almanac; **sbarcare il lunario** to live from hand to mouth
lunàti·co -ca *adj* (**-ci -che**) moody; whimsical
lune·dì *m* (**-dì**) Monday
lunétta *f* lunette; fanlight
lunga *f*—**alla lunga** in the long run; **alla più lunga** at the latest; **andare per le lunghe** to last a long time, drag on; **di gran lunga** by far; **farla lunga** to dillydally
lungàggine *f* delay, procrastination
lunghézza *f* length; **lunghezza d'onda** wave length; **prendere la lunghezza di** to measure
lungi *adv* (lit) far
lungimirante *adj* (fig) far-sighted
lun·go -ga (**-ghi -ghe**) *adj* long; sharp (*tongue*); nimble (*fingers*); tall; thin (*soup*); (coll) slow; **a lungo** for a long time; at length; **a lungo andare** in the long run; **lungo disteso** sprawling || *m* length; **in lungo e in largo** far and wide; **per il lungo** lengthwise || *f* see **lunga** || **lungo** *prep* along; during
lungofiume *m* river road
lungola·go·m (**-ghi**) lakeshore road
lungomare *m* seashore road
lungometràg·gio *m* (**-gi**) full-length movie, feature film
lunòtto *m* (aut) rear window
luò·go·m (**-ghi**) place; passage; site; (geom) locus; **aver luogo** to take place; **aver luogo in** to be laid in (*e.g., a certain place*); **dar luogo a** to give rise to; **del luogo** local; **far luogo** to make room; **fuori luogo** inopportune(ly); **in alto luogo** high-placed; **in luogo di** instead of; **luogo comune** commonplace; **luogo di decenza** toilet; **luogo di nascita** birthplace; **luogo di pena** penitentiary; **non luogo a procedere** (law) no ground for prosecution; (law) **nolle prosequi**; **sul luogo** on the spot; **on the premises**
luogotenènte *m* lieutenant
lupa *f* she-wolf
lupanare *m* (lit) brothel

lupé·sco -sca *adj* (**-schi -sche**) wolfish
lupétto *m* young wolf; cub (*in Boy Scouts*)
lupinèlla *f* sainfoin
lupi·no -na *adj* wolfish
lu·po -pa *mf* wolf; **lupo cerviero** lynx; **lupo di mare** seadog; **lupo mannaro** werewolf ‖ *f* see **lupa**
lùppolo *m* hops
lùri·do -da *adj* filthy, dirty
lusco *m*—**tra il lusco e il brusco** at twilight
lusin·ga *f* (**-ghe**) flattery; illusion
lusingare §209 *tr* to flatter ‖ *ref* to be flattered; to hope
lusinghiè·ro -ra *adj* flattering; promising
lussare *tr* to dislocate
lussazióne *f* dislocation

lusso *m* luxury; **di lusso** de luxe; **lusso di** abundance of
lussuó·so -sa [s] *adj* luxurious, sumptuous
lussureggiante *adj* luxuriant
lussùria *f* lust
lussurió·so -sa [s] *adj* lustful, lecherous
lustrare *tr* to polish, shine; to lick (*s.o.'s boots*) ‖ *intr* to shine, be shiny
lustrascar·pe *m* (**-pe**) bootblack
lustrino *m* sequin; tinsel
lu·stro -stra *adj* shiny, polished ‖ *m* shine, polish; period of five years; **dare il lustro a** to shine, polish
lutto *m* mourning; bereavement; **a lutto** black-edged (*e.g., stationery*); **lutto stretto** deep mourning
luttuó·so -sa [s] *adj* mournful

M

M, m ['emme] *m & f* eleventh letter of the Italian alphabet
ma *m* but; **ma e se** ifs and buts ‖ *conj* but; yet ‖ *interj* who knows?; too bad!
màca·bro -bra *adj* macabre
maca·co *m* (**-chi**) macaque; (fig) dumbell
macadàm *m* macadam
macadamizzare [ddzz] *tr* to macadamize
mac·ca *f* (**-che**) abundance; **a macca** (coll) abundantly; (coll) without paying
maccarèllo *m* mackerel
maccheróni *mpl* macaroni
màcchia *f* spot, stain; brushwood; thicket; (fig) blot; **alla macchia** clandestinely; (painting) done in pointillism; **darsi alla macchia** to join the underground; to escape the law; **macchia solare** sunspot; **senza macchia** spotless
macchiare §287 *tr* to stain, soil ‖ *ref* to become stained; **macchiarsi d'infamia** to soil one's reputation
macchiétta *f* caricature; comedian; **fare la macchietta di** to impersonate, to parody
macchiettare (**macchiétto**) *tr* to speckle
macchietti·sta *mf* (**-sti -ste**) cartoonist; comedian; impersonator
màcchina *f* machine; engine; car, automobile; machination; **andare in macchina** to go to press; **fatto a macchina** machine-made; **macchina da presa** (mov) camera; **macchina da proiezione** projector; **macchina fotografica** camera; **macchina per o da cucire** sewing machine; **macchina per or da scrivere** typewriter; **scrivere a macchina** to typewrite
macchinale *adj* mechanical
macchinare (**màcchino**) *tr* to plot
macchinà·rio *m* (**-ri**) machinery
macchinazióne *f* machination

macchinétta *f* gadget; **macchinetta del caffé** coffee maker
macchini·sta *m* (**-sti**) engineer; (theat) stagehand
macchinó·so -sa [s] *adj* heavy, ponderous; complicated
macedònia *f* fruit salad, fruit cup
macel·làio *m* (**-lài**) butcher
macellare (**macèllo**) *tr* to butcher
macelleria *f* butcher shop
macèllo *m* slaughterhouse; butchering; carnage; disaster
macerare (**màcero**) *tr* to soak; to mortify (*the flesh*) ‖ *ref* to waste away
macèria *f* low wall; **macerie** ruins
màce·ro -ra *adj* emaciated; skinny ‖ *m* soaking vat (*for papermaking*)
machiavèlli·co -ca *adj* (**-ci -che**) Machiavellian
macigno *m* boulder
macilèn·to -ta *adj* emaciated, pale, wan
màcina *f* millstone; (coll) grind
macinacaf·fè *m* (**-fè**) coffee grinder
macinapé·pe *m* (**-pe**) pepper mill
macinare (**màcino**) *tr* to grind, mill; to burn up (*e.g., the road*)
macina·to -ta *adj* ground ‖ *m* grindings; ground meat ‖ *f* grinding
macinino *m* grinder; (coll) jalopy
mà·cis *m & f* (**-cis**) mace (*spice*)
maciste *m* strong man (*in circus*)
maciullare *tr* to brake (*flax or hemp*); to crush
macrocòsmo *m* macrocosm
màdia *f* bread bin; kneading trough
màdi·do -da *adj* wet, perspiring
madònna *f* lady ‖ **Madonna** *f* Madonna
madornale *adj* huge; gross (*error*)
madre *f* mother; stub; mold; **madre nubile** unwed mother
madreggiare §290 (**madréggio**) *intr* to take after one's mother
madrelingua *f* mother tongue
madrepàtria *f* mother country
madrepèria *f* mother-of-pearl
madresélva *f* (coll) honeysuckle

madrevite f (mach) nut; die; **madrevite ad alette** wing nut

madrigna f stepmother

madrina f godmother; **madrina di guerra** war mother

mae·stà f (-stà) majesty; **lesa maestà** lese majesty

maestó·so -sa [s] adj majestic, stately

maèstra f teacher; (fig) master; **maestra giardiniera** kindergarten teacher

maestrale m northwest wind (in Mediterranean)

maestranze fpl workmen

maestrìa f skill, mastery

mae·stro -stra adj masterly; main || m teacher; master; instructor; northwester (in Mediterranean); **maestro di cappella** choirmaster || f see **maestra**

mafió·so -sa [s] adj Mafia || mf member of the Mafia; gaudy dresser

ma·ga f (-ghe) sorceress

magagna f fault, weak spot

magagna·to -ta adj spoiled (fruit)

magari adv even, maybe || conj even if || interj would that . . . !

magazzinàg·gio [ddzz] m (-gi) storage

magazziniè·re -ra [ddzz] mf stockroom attendant || m warehouseman

magazzino [ddzz] m warehouse; store; inventory; (phot, journ) magazine; **grandi magazzini** department store

maggése [s] adj May || m (agr) fallow

màg·gio m (-gi) May; May Day

maggiolino m cockchafer

maggiorana f sweet marjoram

maggioranza f majority

maggiorare (**maggióro**) tr to increase

maggiorazióne f increase, appreciation

maggiordòmo m butler; majordomo

maggióre adj bigger, greater; major; main; higher (bidder); older, elder; (mil) master (e.g., sergeant); biggest, greatest; highest; oldest, eldest; **andare per la maggiore** to be all the rage; **maggiore età** majority || m (mil) major; oldest one; **maggiori** ancestors

maggiorènne adj of age || mf grown-up, adult

maggiorènte mf notable

maggiori·tà f (-tà) (mil) C.O.'s office

maggioritá·rio -ria adj (-ri -rie) majority

magìa f magic

màgi·co -ca adj (-ci -che) magic

Magi mpl Magi, Wise Men

magióne f (lit) home, dwelling

magistèro m education, teaching; mastery; (chem) precipitation

magistrale adj teacher's; masterly || f teacher's college

magistrato m magistrate

magistratura f judiciary

màglia f knitting; stitch; link; undershirt; sports shirt; (hist) mail; (fig) web; **lavorare a maglia** to knit

maglierìa f knitting mill; yarn shop; knitwear store

magliétta f polo shirt, T-shirt; buckle (to secure rifle strap); picture hook; buttonhole

maglifi·cio m (-ci) knitwear factory

mà·glio m (-gli) sledge hammer; mallet; drop hammer

magli óne m heavy sweater, jersey

magnàni·mo -ma adj magnanimous

magnano m (coll) locksmith

magnate m (lit) magnate, tycoon

magnèsio m magnesium

magnète m magnet; magneto

magnèti·co -ca adj (-ci -che) magnetic

magnetismo m magnetism

magnetite f loadstone

magnetizzare [ddzz] tr to magnetize

magnetòfono m tape recorder

magnificare §197 (**magnìfico**) tr to extol, praise; to magnify (to exaggerate)

magnificènza f magnificence

magnìfi·co -ca adj (-ci -che) magnificent; munificent; wonderful, splendid

ma·gno -gna adj (lit) great; the Great, e.g., **Alessandro Magno** Alexander the Great

magnòlia f magnolia

ma·go m (-ghi) magician; wizard

magóne m (coll) gizzard; (coll) grief; **avere il magone** (coll) to be in the dumps

magra f low water; (fig) dearth, want

magrézza f leanness; scarcity

ma·gro -gra adj lean, thin; meager || m lean meat; meatless day || f see **magra**

mài adv never; ever; **non . . . mai** never, not ever; **come mai?** how come?

maiá·le -la mf pig; hog || m pork || f sow

maialé·sco -sca adj (-schi -sche) piggish

maiòli·ca f (-che) majolica

maionése [s] f mayonnaise

mà·is m (-is) corn, maize

maiuscolétto m (typ) small capital

maiùsco·lo -la adj capital || m—**scrivere in maiuscolo** to capitalize || f capital letter

Malacca, la Malay Peninsula

malaccèt·to -ta adj unwelcome

malaccòr·to -ta adj imprudent; awkward

malacreanza f (**malecreanze**) instance of bad manners; **malecreanze** bad manners

malafatta f (**malefatte**) defect; **malefatte** evildoings

malaféde f (**malefédi**) bad faith

malaffare m—**donna di malaffare** prostitute; **gente di malaffare** underworld

malagévole adj rough (road); hard (work)

malagràzia f (**malegràzie**) rudeness, uncouthness

malalingua f (**malelingue**) slanderer, backbiter

malanda·to -ta adj run-down; shabby

malandri·no -na adj dishonest; bewitching (eyes) || m highwayman

malànimo m ill will; **di malanimo** reluctantly

malanno m misfortune; illness; (joc) menace

malaparata f (coll) danger, dangerous situation

malapéna f—**a malapena** hardly

malària *f* malaria

malatìc·cio -cia *adj* (**-ci -ce**) sickly

mala·to -ta *adj* sick, ill; **essere malato agli occhi** to have sore eyes; **fare il malato** to play sick || *mf* patient; **i malati** the sick

malattìa *f* sickness; illness; disease; **malattie del lavoro** occupational diseases

malaugura·to -ta *adj* unfortunate; ill-omened

malaugù·rio *m* (**-ri**) ill omen

malavita *f* underworld

malavòglia *f* (**malevòglie**) unwillingness; **di malavoglia** reluctantly

malcapita·to -ta *adj* unlucky || *m* unlucky person

malcàu·to -ta *adj* rash, heedless

malcòn·cio -cia *adj* (**-ci -ce**) battered

malcontèn·to -ta *adj* dissatisfied, malcontent || *mf* malcontent || *m* dissatisfaction

malcostume *m* immorality; bad practice

malcrea·to -ta *adj* ill-bred

maldè·stro -stra *adj* clumsy, awkward

maldicènte *adj* gossipy, slanderous || *mf* gossip, slanderer, backbiter

maldicènza *f* gossip, slander

male *m* evil; ill; trouble; **andare a male** to go to pot; **aversela a male** to take offense; **di male in peggio** from bad to worse, worse and worse; **fare del male** to do ill; **fare male** to be in error; **fare male a** to hurt; **farsi male** to get hurt; to hurt oneself; **far venire il mal di mare a** to make seasick; (fig) to nauseate; **Lei fa male** you should not; **mal d'aereo** airsickness; **mal di capo** headache; **mal di cuore** heart disease; **mal di denti** toothache; **mal di gola** sore throat; **mal di mare** sea-sickness; **mal di montagna** mountain sickness; **mal di pancia** bellyache; **mal di schiena** backache; **mandare a male** to spoil; **mettere male** to sow discord; **prendere a male** to take amiss; **voler male a** to bear a grudge against || *adv* badly, poorly; **male educato** ill-bred; **meno male!** fortunately!; **restar male** to be disappointed; **sentirsi male** to feel sick; **stare male** to be ill; **star male a** to not fit, e.g., **questo vestito gli sta male** this suit does not fit him; **veder male** qlco to disapprove of s.th; **veder male qlcu** to dislike s.o.

maledettaménte *adv* (coll) damned

maledét·to -ta *adj* cursed, damned

maledire §195 *tr* to curse

maledizióne *f* malediction, curse || *interj* damn it!, confound it!

maleduca·to -ta *adj* ill-bred || *mf* boor

malefatta *f* var of **malafatta**

malefì·cio *m* (**-ci**) curse, spell; witchcraft; wickedness

malèfi·co -ca *adj* (**-ci -che**) maleficent

maleolènte *adj* (lit) malodorous

malèrba *f* weed, weeds

malése *adj* & *mf* Malay

Malésia, la Malaysia

malèssere *m* malaise; uneasiness; worry

malevolènza *f* malevolence; malice

malèvo·lo -la *adj* malevolent; malicious

malfama·to -ta *adj* ill-famed; notorious

malfat·to -ta *adj* botched; misshapen || *m* misdeed

malfat·tóre -trice *mf* malefactor

malfér·mo -ma *adj* wobbly, unsteady

malfì·do -da *adj* untrustworthy

malgarbo *m* bad manners, rudeness

malgovèrno *m* misrule; mismanagement; neglect

malgrado *prep* in spite of; **mio malgrado** in spite of me || *conj* although

malìa *f* spell, charm

maliar·do -da *adj* enchanting, charming || *mf* magician || *f* enchantress, witch

malignare *intr* to gossip

malignì·tà *f* (**-tà**) maliciousness; malevolence; malignancy

malì·gno -gna *adj* malicious, evil; unhealthy; malignant || **il Maligno** the Evil One

malinconìa *f* melancholy; melancholia

malincòni·co -ca *adj* (**-ci -che**) melancholy, wistful

malincuòre *m*—**a malincuore** unwillingly, against one's will

malintenziona·to -ta *adj* evil-minded || *mf* evildoer

malinté·so -sa [s] *adj* misunderstood; misapplied || *m* misunderstanding

maliò·so -sa [s] *adj* malicious; cunning; mischievous; bewitching

malìzia *f* malice; trick; mischief

maliziò·so -sa [s] *adj* malicious; clever, artful; mischievous

malleàbile *adj* malleable; manageable

malleva·dóre -drice *mf* guarantor

malleverìa *f* surety

mallo *m* hull, husk

mallòppo *m* bundle; (aer) trail cable; (coll) lump (*in one's throat*); (slang) swag, booty

malmenare (**malméno**) *tr* to manhandle

malmés·so -sa *adj* shabby, seedy; tasteless

malna·to -ta *adj* uncouth; unfortunate; harmful

malnutri·to -ta *adj* undernourished

malnutrizióne *f* malnutrition

ma·lo -la *adj* (lit) bad

malòc·chio *m* (**-chi**) evil eye

malóra *f* ruin; **mandare in malora** to ruin; **va in malora!** go to the devil!

malóre *m* malaise; fainting spell

malpràti·co -ca *adj* (**-ci -che**) inexperienced

malsa·no -na *adj* unhealthy; unsound

malsicù·ro -ra *adj* unsafe; insecure

malta *f* (mortar; plaster; (obs) mud

maltèmpo *m* bad weather

malto *m* malt

maltòlto *m* ill-gotten gains

maltrattaménto *m* mistreatment

maltrattare *tr* to mistreat, maltreat

malumóre *m* bad humor; **di malumore** in a bad mood

malva *f* mallow

malvà·gio -gia (**-gi -gie**) *adj* wicked || *mf* wicked person || **il Malvagio** the Evil One

malversare (malvèrso) *tr* to embezzle; to misappropriate

malversazióne *f* embezzlement; misappropriation

malvésti·to -ta *adj* shabby, seedy

malvi·sto -sta *adj* disliked; unpopular

malvivènte *mf* criminal; (lit) profligate

malvolentièri *adv* unwillingly

malvolére *m* malevolence; indolence ‖ §196 *tr* to dislike

mamma *f* mother, mom; (lit) breast; **mamma mia** dear me!

mammaluc·co m (-chi) simpleton

mammèlla *f* breast; udder

mammíf·ero -ra *adj* mammalian ‖ *m* mammal

màmmola *f* violet; (fig) shrinking violet

mam·mùt *m* (**-mut**) mammoth

manata *f* slap; handful; **dare una manata a** to slap

man·ca *f* (**-che**) left hand, left

mancante *adj* missing, lacking; unaccounted for

mancanza *f* lack; absence; defect; mistake; **in mancanza di** for lack of

mancare §197 *tr* to miss ‖ *intr* (AVERE) to be at fault; **mancare a** to break (*e.g., one's word*); **mancare di** to be wanting; to lack; **mancare di parola** to break one's word ‖ *intr* (ESSERE) to fail (*said, e.g., of electric power*); to be lacking, e.g., **manca il sale nell'arrosto** salt is lacking in the roast; to be missing; to be absent, e.g., **mancano tre soci** three members are absent; to be, e.g., **mancano dieci minuti alle quattro** it is ten minutes to four; (with *dat*) to lack, e.g., **gli mancano le forze** he lacks the strength; to miss, e.g., **mi manca la sua compagnia** I miss his company; **mancare a** to be absent from (*e.g., the roll call*); to be . . . from, e.g., **mancano dieci chilometri all'arrivo** we are ten kilometers from the journey's end; **mancare ai vivi** (lit) to pass away; **sentirsi mancare** to feel faint ‖ *impers*—**mancare poco che** + *subj* to narrowly miss + *ger*, e.g., **ci mancò poco che fosse investito da un'automobile** he narrowly missed being hit by a car; **non ci mancherebbe altro!** that would be the last straw!, I should say not!

manca·to -ta *adj* unsuccessful; missed (*opportunity*); abortive (*attempt*), e.g., **omicidio mancato** abortive attempt to murder; manqué, e.g., **un poeta mancato** a poet manqué

manchévole *adj* faulty

manchevolézza *f* fault, shortcoming

màn·cia *f* (**-ce**) tip, gratuity; **mancia competente** reward

manciata *f* handful

manci·no -na *adj* left-handed; underhanded ‖ *mf* left-handed person ‖ *f* left hand, left; (mach) floating crane

man·co -ca *adj* (**-chi -che**) *adj* left; (lit) sinister, ill-omened; (lit) lacking ‖ *m* (lit) lack; **senza manco** (coll) without fail ‖ **manco** *adv*—**manco male!**

(coll) at least!; **manco per idea!** (coll) not at all! ‖ *f* see **manca**

mandaménto *m* jurisdiction

mandante *m* (law) principal

mandare *tr* to send; to condemn (*to death*); to commit (*to memory*); to send forth (*e.g., smoke, buds*); to operate (*a machine*); **che Dio ce la mandi buona!** may God help us!; **mandare ad effetto** to carry out; **mandare all'altro mondo** to dispatch, kill; **mandare a effetto** to carry out; **mandare a monte** to ruin; **mandare a picco** to sink; **mandare a quel paese** to send to the devil; **mandare a spasso** to fire, dismiss; to get rid of; **mandar giù** to swallow; **mandare in malora** to ruin; **mandare in pezzi** to break to pieces; **mandare per le lunghe** to delay ‖ *intr*—**mandare a chiamare** to send for; **mandare a dire** to send word

mandarino *m* mandarin; (*Citrus nobilis*) tangerine; (*Citrus reticulata*) mandarin orange

mandata *f* sending; delivery (*of merchandise*); group; gang (*e.g., of thieves*); turn (*of key*); **chiudere a doppia mandata** to double-lock

mandatà·rio m (-ri) mandatary, trustee

mandato *m* mandate; order; **mandato di cattura** arrest warrant; **mandato di comparizione** subpoena; **mandato di perquisizione** search warrant

mandíbola *f* jaw

mandolino *m* mandolin

màndorla *f* almond; kernel (*of fruit*)

mandorla·to -ta *adj* almond ‖ *m* nougat

màndorlo *m* almond tree

mandràgola *f* mandrake

màndria *f* herd

mandriano *m* herdsman

mandrillo *m* mandrill

mandrino *m* (mach) mandrel; (mach) driftpin

mandritta *f*—**a mandritta** to the right

mane *f*—**da mane a sera** from morning till night

maneggévole *adj* usable; manageable; accessible to small craft (*sea*)

maneggiare §290 (**manéggio**) *tr* to work (*e.g., clay*); to handle; to wield (*a sword*); to knead (*dough*); to manage; (equit) to train

manég·gio m (-gi) handling; intrigue; horsemanship; management; riding school; manège

mané·sco -sca *adj* (**-schi -sche**) ready-fisted; hand (*e.g., weapons*)

manétta *f* throttle (*on a motorcycle*); **manette** handcuffs, manacles

manfòrte *f*—**dar manforte a** to help

manganèllo *m* bludgeon, cudgel

manganése [s] *m* manganese

màngano *m* calender; mangle

mangeréc·cio -cia *adj* (**-ci -ce**) edible

mangería *f* graft, peculation

mangiàbile *adj* edible

mangiana·stri *m* (**-stri**) tape recorder

mangia-pane *m* (**-pane**) idler

mangia·prèti *m* (**-prèti**) priest hater

mangiare *m* eating; food ‖ *v* §290 *tr*

to eat; to bite, gnaw; to erode; to embezzle, graft; (cards, chess) to take; **mangiar la foglia** to get wise || *intr* to eat; **mangiare alle spalle di qlcu** to eat at the expense of s.o. || *ref* to eat up; **mangiarsi il fegato** to be green with envy; **mangiarsi la parola** to break one's promise; **mangiarsi le unghie** to bite one's nails; **mangiarsi una promessa** to break one's promise

mangiasòldi *adj invar* money-eating, e.g., **macchina mangiasoldi** money-eating contraption

mangiata *f* (coll) fill, hearty meal, bellyful

mangiatóia *f* manger, crib

mangia·tóre -trice *mf* eater

mangime *m* fodder; feed; poultry feed

mangimìsti·co -ca *adj* (-ci -che) feed, e.g., **attrezzature mangimistiche** feed machinery

mangió·ne -na *mf* great eater, glutton

mangiucchiare §287 (**mangiùcchio**) *tr* to nibble

mangusta *f* mongoose

manìa *f* mania, craze; complex; whim; **mania di grandezza** delusions of grandeur

manìa·co -ca (-ci -che) *adj* maniacal; enthusiastic || *m* maniac; fan, enthusiast

màni·ca *f* (-che) sleeve; hose; (coll) crowd, bunch; **essere di manica larga** to be broad-minded; **essere nelle maniche di qlcu** to be in the favor of s.o.; **è un altro paio di maniche** this is a horse of another color; **in maniche di camicia** in shirt sleeves; **manica a vento** air sleeve, windsock; **manica per l'acqua** hose || **la Manica** the English Channel

manicarétto *m* dainty, delicacy

manichino *m* mannequin; cuff; (obs) handcuff; **fare il manichino** to model

màni·co *m* (-chi & -ci) handle; stock (*of rifle*); shaft (*of golf club*); stem (*of spoon*); (mus) neck; **manico di scopa** broomstick

manicò·mio *m* (-mi) insane asylum, madhouse

manicòtto *m* muff; (mach) collar; (mach) nipple; (mach) sleeve

manicu·re *mf* (-re) manicure, manicurist (*person*) || *f* (-re) manicure (*treatment*)

manicuri·sta *mf* (-sti -ste) manicurist

manièra *f* manner, fashion, way; **belle maniere** good manners; **di maniera** (lit, painting) Manneristic; **di maniera che** so that; **in nessuna maniera** by no means; **maniere** bad manners

manierà·to -ta *adj* mannered, affected; genteel

maniè·ro -ra *adj* tame, gentle || *m* manor house, mansion || *f* see **maniera**

manieró·so -sa [s] *adj* genteel; mannered

manifattura *f* manufacture; factory; product; ready-made wear

manifestare (**manifèsto**) *tr* to manifest

|| *intr* to demonstrate || *ref* to turn out to be

manifestazióne *f* manifestation; demonstration

manifestino *m* leaflet, handbill

manifè·sto -sta *adj* manifest, clear || *m* poster, placard; manifest; (pol) manifesto; **manifesto di carico** (naut) manifest

manìglia *f* handle; knob; (naut) link (*of chain*)

manigóldo *m* criminal; scoundrel

manipolare (**manìpolo**) *tr* to concoct; to adulterate; (telg) to transmit

manipola·tóre -trice *mf* schemer || *m* telegraph key

manìpolo *m* sheaf; (eccl; hist) maniple; (fig) handful

maniscàl·co *m* (-chi) blacksmith

manna *f* manna; godsend

mannàia *f* axe; knife (*of guillotine*)

mano *f* hand; way (*in traffic*); coat (*of paint*); (lit) handful; (fig) finger; fingertip; **alla mano** plain, affable; **a mani nude** barehanded; **a mano** by hand; **a mano a mano** little by little; **a mano armata** armed (*e.g., robbery*); **at gunpoint**; **andare contro mano** to buck traffic; **a quattro mani** four-handed; **avere le mani bucate** to be a spendthrift; **avere le mani in pasta** to have one's fingers in the pie; **avere le mani lunghe** to be light-fingered; **battere le mani** to clap; **con le mani in mano** idle; **dare la mano a** to shake hands with; **dare man forte a** to help; **dare una mano** to pitch in; **dare una mano a** to lend a hand to; **di lunga mano** beforehand; **essere colto con le mani nel sacco** to be caught red-handed; **essere svelto di mano** to be light-fingered; **far man bassa (su)** to plunder; **fuori mano** out of the way; **mani di burro** butterfingers; **mani in alto!** hands up!; **man mano (che)** as; **mettere mano a** to begin; **mettere le mani sul fuoco** to guarantee; to swear; **per mano di** at the hands of; **prendere la mano** to balk; to get out of hand; **tenere la mano a** to abet; **venire alle mani** to come to blows

manodòpera *f* labor, manpower; **manodopera qualificata** skilled labor

manòmetro *m* manometer

manomèttere §198 *tr* to tamper with

manomissióne *f* tampering

manomòrta *f* (law) mortmain

manòpola *f* mitten; handgrip; strap (*to hold on to*); (rad, telv) knob; (hist) gauntlet

manoscrìt·to -to *adj & m* manuscript

manoscrìvere §250 *intr* to write in one's own handwriting

manovale *m* laborer, helper; hod carrier

manovèlla *f* handle, crank; lever

manòvra *f* maneuver; (rr) shifting; **fare manovra** to maneuver; (rr) to shift

manovrare (**manòvro**) *tr* to maneuver; to handle, drive; (rr) to shift || *intr* to maneuver; (rr) to shunt, shift; (fig) to plot

manovratóre *m* motorman; driver; (rr) brakeman; (rr) flagman

manrovè·scio *m* (-sci) backhanded slap

mansalva *f*—**rubare a mansalva** to help oneself freely (*e.g., to the till*)

mansarda *f* mansard

mansióne *f* duty, function

mansuè·to -ta *adj* tame; meek

mansuetùdine *f* tameness; meekness

mantèlla *f* coat; (mil) cape

mantellina *f* (mil) cape

mantèllo *m* woman's coat; coat (*of animal*); (fig) cloak; (mil) cape; (mach) casing

mantenére §271 *tr* to keep; to maintain; to hold (*e.g., a position*) || *ref* to stay alive; to last; to remain, stay, continue

manteniménto *m* keeping; maintenance

mantenu·to -ta *adj* kept || *m* gigolo || *f* kept woman

màntice *m* bellows; folding top (*of carriage*); (aut) convertible top

manto *m* mantle; coat; cloak

Màntova *f* Mantua

mantovana *f* valance

manuale *adj & m* manual

manualizzare [ddzz] *tr* to make (*e.g., a machine*) hand-operated; to include in a manual; to prepare a manual of

manù·brio *m* (-bri) handlebar; handle; dumbbell

manufat·to -ta *adj* manufactured || *m* manufactured product; manufacture

manutèngolo *m* accomplice

manutenzióne *f* maintenance, upkeep

manza [dz] *f* heifer

manzo [dz] *m* steer; beef

maomettà·no -na *adj & mf* Mahometan, Mohammedan

maomettismo *m* Mahometanism, Mohammedanism

Maométto *m* Mahomet

maóna *f* barge

mappa *f* map; bit (*of key*)

mappamóndo *m* globe; map of the world

marachèlla *f* mischief

maramèo *m*—**fare marameo** to thumb one's nose

mara·sma *m* (-smi) utter confusion; (pathol) decrepitude, feebleness

maratóna *f* marathon

maratonè·ta *m* (-ti) Marathon runner

mar·ca *f* (-che) mark, label; make, brand; token; ticket; (hist, geog) march; **di marca** of quality; **marca da bollo** revenue stamp; **marca di fabbrica** trademark

marcare §197 *tr* to mark; to label; to brand; to keep the score of; to score (*e.g., a goal*); to accentuate

marcatèm·po *m* (-po) timekeeper

marca·to -ta *adj* marked, pronounced

marchésa *f* marchioness, marquise

marchése *m* marquess, marquis

marchia·no -na *adj* gross (*error*)

marchiare §287 *tr* to brand

màr·chio *m* (-chi) brand; initials; characteristic; trademark

màr·cia *f* (-ce) march; operation; pus; (aut) gear, speed; (mil) hike; (sports) walk; **far marcia indietro** to back up; (naut) to back water; **marcia indietro** (aut) reverse; **marcia nuziale** wedding march

marciapiède *m* sidewalk; (rr) platform

marciare §128 *intr* to march; (mil) to advance; (sports) to walk; (coll) to function; **far marciare qlcu** to keep s.o. in line

màr·cio -cia (-ci -ce) *adj* rotten; infected; corrupt || *m* rotten part; decayed part; corruption || *f see* **marcia**

marcire §176 *intr* (ESSERE) to rot

marciume *m* rot; pus; decay

marconigram·ma *m* (-mi) radiogram

marconi·sta *mf* (-sti -ste) radio operator

mare *m* sea; bunch, heap; **al mare** at the seashore; **alto mare** high sea; **fa mare** the sea is rough; **gettare a mare** to throw overboard; **mare grosso** rough sea; **mare territoriale** territorial waters; **promettere mari e monti** to promise the moon; **tenere il mare** to be seaworthy

marèa *f* tide; sea (*e.g., of mud*); **alta marea** high tide; **bassa marea** low tide; **marea di quadratura** neap tide; **marea di sizigia** spring tide

mareggiata *f* coastal storm

maremòto *m* seaquake

mareògrafo *m* tide-level gauge

maresciallo *m* marshall; warrant officer

marétta *f* choppy sea; instability

margarina *f* margarine

margherita *f* daisy; **margherite** beads

marginale *adj* marginal

marginatóre *m* margin stop (*of typewriter*); (typ) try square

màrgine *m* margin; edge; **margine a scaletta** thumb index

marijuana *f* marijuana, marihuana

marina *f* seashore; seascape; navy; **marina mercantile** merchant marine

mari·nàio *m* (-nài) seaman, sailor

marinara *f* middy blouse

marinare *tr* to marinate; **marinare la scuola** to cut school, play truant

marinaré·sco -sca *adj* (-schi -sche) sailor, seamanlike

marina·ro -ra *adj* sea, sailor; seamanlike; nautical || *m* (coll) sailor || *f see* **marinara**

mari·no -na *adj* marine, nautical || *f see* **marina**

mariòlo *m* rascal

marionétta *f* puppet, marionette

maritale *adj* marital

maritare *tr* to marry || *ref* to get married

marito *m* husband

marìtti·mo -ma *adj* maritime, sea || *m* merchant seaman

marmàglia *f* riffraff, rabble

marmellata *f* jam, preserves; **marmellata di arancia** orange marmalade

marmi·sta *m* (-sti) marble worker; marble cutter

marmitta *f* pot, kettle; (aut) muffler

marmittóne *m* (coll) sad sack

marmo *m* marble

marmòc·chio *m* (-chi) brat

marmòre·o -a *adj* marble
marmorizzare [ddzz] *tr* to marble
marmòtta *f* marmot; woodchuck; (fig) sluggard; (rr) switch signal
marmottina *f* salesman's sample case
marna *f* marl
marnare *tr* to marl
marocchi·no -na *adj & mf* Moroccan ‖ *m* morocco leather
Maròcco, il Morocco
maróso [s] *m* billow, surge
marra *f* hoe; fluke (*of anchor*)
marrano *m* Marrano; (fig) scoundrel; (lit) traitor
marronata *f* (coll) blunder, boner
marróne *adj invar* maroon, tan ‖ *m* chestnut; (coll) blunder
Marsiglia *f* Marseille
marsigliése [s] *adj* Marseilles ‖ *m* native or inhabitant of Marseilles ‖ *f* Marseillaise
marsina *f* swallow-tailed coat
Marte *m* Mars
marte·dì -m (-dì) Tuesday; **martedì grasso** Shrove Tuesday
martellare (martèllo) *tr* to hammer; to pester (*with questions*) ‖ *intr* to throb; (fig) to insist
martellata *f* hammer blow
martellétto *m* hammer (*of piano or bell*); lever (*of typewriter*)
martèllo *m* hammer; **martello dell'uscio** knocker; **martello perforatore** jack-hammer
martinétto *m* jack; **martinetto a vite** screw jack
martingala *f* half belt (*sewn in back of sports jacket*); martingale (*of harness*)
martinic·ca *f* (-che) wagon brake
martin pescatóre *m* kingfisher
màrtire *m* martyr
marti·rio *m* (-ri) martyrdom
martirizzare [ddzz] *tr* to martyrize
màrtora *f* marten
martoriare §287 (martòrio) *tr* to torment
marxi·sta *adj & mf* (-sti -ste) Marxist
marzapane *m* marzipan
marziale *adj* martial
marzia·no -na *adj & mf* Martian
marzo *m* March
mas *m* (**mas**) torpedo boat
mascalzóne *m* cad, rascal
mascèlla *f* jaw; jawbone
màschera *mf* usher ‖ *f* mask; masque; **maschera antigas** gas mask; **maschera di bellezza** beauty pack; **maschera respiratoria** oxygen mask; **maschera subacquea** diving helmet
mascheraménto *m* camouflage
mascherare (màschero) *tr, intr & ref* to mask; to camouflage
mascherata *f* masquerade
mascherina *f* little mask, loup; tip (*of shoe*); (aut) grille; (phot) mask
maschiare §287 *tr* (mach) to tap
maschiétta *f* tomboy; **alla maschietta** bobbed (*hair*); **tagliare i capelli alla maschietta** to bob the hair
maschiétto *m* baby boy; pintle
maschile *adj* masculine; manly; men's;

male (*sex*); boys' (*school*) ‖ *m* masculine
mà·schio -schia *adj* manly, virile; male ‖ *m* male; keep, donjon; tenon; (mach) tap; (carp) tongue
mascolinizzare [ddzz] *tr* to make masculine or mannish ‖ *ref* to act like a man
mascoli·no -na *adj* masculine; mannish (*woman*)
masnada *f* mob, gang; (obs) group
masnadière *m* highwayman
massa *f* mass; body (*of water*); (elec) ground; **mettere a massa** (elec) to ground; **in massa** in a body; **massa ereditaria** (law) estate
massacrante *adj* killing, fatiguing
massacrare *tr* to massacre; to ruin; to wear out, fatigue
massacro *m* massacre
massaggiare §290 *tr* to massage
massaggiatóre *m* masseur
massaggiatrice *f* masseuse
massàg·gio *m* (-gi) massage
massàia *f* housewife
massèllo *m* block (*of stone*); (metallurgy) pig, ingot
masseria *f* farm
masserizie *fpl* household goods
massicciata *f* roadbed; (rr) ballast
massic·cio -cia (-ci -ce) *adj* massive; bulky; heavy; (fig) gross ‖ *m* massif
màssi·mo -ma *adj* maximum; top ‖ *m* maximum; limit; **al massimo** at the most ‖ *f* maxim; maximum temperature
massi·vo -va *adj* massive
masso *m* rock, boulder
Massóne *m* Mason
Massoneria *f* Masonry
mastèllo *m* washtub
masticare §197 (màstico) *tr* to chew, masticate; to mumble (*words*); to speak (*a language*) poorly; **masticare amaro** to grumble
masticazióne *f* mastication
màstice *m* mastic; glue; putty
mastino *m* mastiff
mastodònti·co -ca *adj* (-ci -che) mammoth
ma·stro -stra (*adj*) master ‖ *m* ledger; master, e.g., **mastro meccanico** master mechanic
masturbare *tr & ref* to masturbate
matassa *f* skein; trouble
matemàti·co -ca (-ci -che) *adj* mathematical ‖ *m* mathematician ‖ *f* mathematics
materassino *m* (sports) mat; **materassino pneumatico** air mattress
materasso *m* mattress; (boxing) sparring partner
matèria *f* matter; substance; subject; (coll) pus; **dare materia a** to give ground for; **materia grigia** gray matter; **materie coloranti** dyestuffs; **materie prime** raw materials
materiale *adj* material; rough, bulky ‖ *m* material; equipment, supplies; (fig) makings, stuff; **materiale ferroviario** (rr) rolling stock; **materiale stabile** (rr) permanent way

materni·tà f (-tà) maternity; maternity hospital; maternity ward

matèr·no -na adj maternal; mother (tongue, country)

matita f pencil; **matita per gli occhi** eye-shadow pencil; **matita per le labbra** lipstick; cosmetic pencil

matrice f matrix; stub

matrici·da mf (-di -de) matricide

matrici·dio m (-di) matricide

matrìcola f register, roll; registration (number); registry; beginner, novice; freshman (in university); **far la matricola** a to haze

matrigna f stepmother

matrimoniale adj matrimonial; double (bed); married (life)

matrimonialménte adv as husband and wife

matrimò·nio m (-ni) matrimony, marriage; wedding

matròna f matron

matronale adj matronly

matta f joker, wild card

mattacchió·ne -na mf jester, prankster

mattana f tantrum; fit of laughter

matta·tóio m (-tói) slaughterhouse

matterèllo m rolling pin

mattina f morning; **di prima mattina** early in the morning; **la mattina in** the morning

mattinale adj morning ‖ m morning report

mattinata f morning; (theat) matinée

mattiniè·ro -ra adj early-rising

mattino m morning; **di buon mattino** early in the morning

mat·to -ta adj crazy; whimsical; dull; false (jewelry); wild (desire); **andare matto per** to be crazy about; **da matti** unbelievable; **fare il matto** to cut a caper; **matto da legare** raving mad ‖ f see **matta**

mattòide adj & mf madcap

mattonare (**mattóno**) tr to pave with bricks

mattonato m brick floor; **restare sul mattonato** to be utterly destitute

mattóne m brick; (fig) bore

mattonèlla f tile; cushion (of billiard table)

mattuti·no -na adj morning ‖ m matins

maturan·do -da mf lycée student who has to take the baccalaureate examination

maturare tr to ripen; to ponder; to pass (a lycée pupil) ‖ intr (ESSERE) to ripen, mature; to fall due

maturazióne f ripening

maturi·tà f (-tà) maturity; ripening; lycée final

matu·ro -ra adj ripe; mature; due

Matusalèmme m Methuselah

mausolèo m mausoleum

mazza f club; mallet; sledge hammer; cane; mace; golf club; (baseball) bat

mazzacavallo m well sweep

mazzapìc·chio m (-chi) mallet; sledge

mazzata f heavy blow, wallop (with club)

mazzeran·ga f (-ghe) (mach) tamper

mazzière m macer; (cards) dealer

mazzo m bunch; bouquet; deck (of cards); **fare il mazzo** to shuffle the cards

mazzuòla f sledge hammer

mazzuòlo m sledge; mallet; wedge (of golf club); drumstick (for bass drum)

me §5 pron pers

meandro m meander; labyrinth

MEC m (letterword) (**Mercato Europeo Comune**) European Economic Community, Common Market

Mècca, la Mecca; (fig) the Mecca

meccàni·co -ca (-ci -che) adj mechanical ‖ m mechanic ‖ f mechanics; process (e.g., of digestion); machinery

meccanismo m machinery; mechanism; movement (of watch)

meccanizzare [ddzz] tr to mechanize ‖ ref to become mechanized

mecenate m patron (of the arts)

méco §5 prep phrase (lit) with me

medàglia f medal

medaglióne m medallion; locket; biographical sketch

medési·mo -ma adj & pron same; -self, e.g., **egli medesimo** he himself; very e.g., **la verità medesima** the very truth

mèdia f average; secondary school, middle school; (math) mean; **media oraria** average speed ‖ **mèdia** mpl media (of communication)

mediana f median; (soccer) middle line

mediàni·co -ca adj (-ci -che) medium

media·no -na adj median ‖ m (sports) halfback ‖ f see **mediana**

mediante prep by means of

mediare §287 (**mèdio**) tr & intr (ESSERE) to mediate

media·to -ta adj indirect

media·tóre -trice adj mediating ‖ mf mediator; broker; commission merchant

mediazióne f mediation; brokerage; broker's fee, commission

medicaménto m medicine

medicaménto·so -sa [s] adj medicinal

medicare §197 (**mèdico**) tr to medicate; to treat

medicastro m quack

medicazióne f medication; dressing

medichéssa f (pej) lady doctor

medicina f medicine

medicinale adj medicinal ‖ m medicine

mèdi·co -ca (-ci -che) adj medical ‖ m doctor, physician; healer; **fare il medico** to practice medicine; **medico chirurgo** surgeon; **medico condotto** board-of-health doctor; country doctor; **medico curante** family physician

medievale adj medieval

medievali·sta mf (-sti -ste) medievalist

mè·dio -dia (-di -die) adj average; median; middle; secondary (school); medium ‖ m middle finger ‖ f see **media**

mediòcre adj mediocre

mediocri·tà f (-tà) mediocrity

medioèvo m Middle Ages

medioleggèro m welterweight

mediomàssimo *m* light heavyweight

meditabón·do -da *adj* meditative

meditare (mèdito) *tr & intr* to meditate

medita·to -ta *adj* considered

meditazióne *f* meditation

mediterrà·neo -nea *adj* inland (*sea*) ‖ **Mediterraneo** *adj & m* Mediterranean

mè·dium *mf* (**-dium**) medium

medusa *f* jellyfish

mefistofèli·co -ca *adj* (**-ci -che**) Mephistophelian

mefiti·co -ca *adj* (**-ci -che**) mephitic

megaciclo *m* megacycle

megàfono *m* megaphone

megalomanìa *f* megalomania

megalòpo·li *f* (**-li**) megalopolis

mega·òhm *m* (**-òhm**) megohm

megèra *f* hag, termagant, vixen

mèglio *adj invar* better; (coll) best ‖ *m*—**il meglio** the best; **nel meglio di** (coll) in the middle of ‖ *f*—**avere la meglio** to get the upper hand; **avere la meglio di** to get the better of ‖ *adv* better; best; rather; **stare meglio** to feel better; to be becoming; to fit better; **stare meglio a** to be becoming to; to fit; **tanto meglio!** so much the better!

méla *f* apple; nozzle (*of sprinkling can*); **mela cotogna** quince (*fruit*); **mela renetta** pippin

melagrana *f* pomegranate

melanzana [dz] *f* eggplant

melassa *f* molasses, treacle

mela·to -ta *adj* honey, honeyed

melèn·so -sa *adj* dull, silly

melissa *f* (bot) balm

mellìflu·o -a *adj* mellifluous

mélma *f* mud, slime

melmó·so -sa [s] *adj* muddy, slimy

mélo *m* apple tree

melodìa *f* melody

melòdi·co -ca *adj* (**-ci -che**) melodic

melodió·so -sa [s] *adj* melodious

melodram·ma *m* (**-mi**) melodrama; lyric opera; (fig) melodrama

melodrammàti·co -ca *adj* (**-ci -che**) melodramatic

melograno *m* pomegranate tree

melóne *m* melon; cantaloupe; **melone d'acqua** watermelon

membrana *f* membrane; parchment; diaphragm (*of telephone*); (zool) web

membratura *f* frame

mèm·bro *m* (**-bri**, *considered individually*) limb; member; penis ‖ *m* (**-bra** *fpl*, *considered collectively*) limb (*of human body*)

membru·to -ta *adj* burly, husky

memoràbile *adj* memorable

memoràn·dum *m* (**-dum**) memorandum; agenda, calendar; note; note paper

mèmore *adj* (lit) mindful, grateful

memòria *f* memory; souvenir; memoir; dissertation; (law) brief

memoriale *m* memoir; memorial

memorizzare [ddzz] *tr* to memorize

ména *f* intrigue

mena·bò *m* (**-bò**) (typ) layout, dummy

menadito *m*—**a menadito** at one's fingertips; perfectly

menare (méno) *tr* to lead; to bring

(*luck*); to wag (*the tail*); to deliver (*a blow*); (coll) to hit; **menare a effetto** to carry out; **menare buono di** to approve of; **menare il can per l'aia** to beat around the bush; **menare per le lunghe** to delay; **menare vanto** to boast

mènda *f* (lit) fault, flaw

mendace *adj* lying, false, mendacious

mendà·cio *m* (**-ci**) (law) falsehood

mendicante *adj & m* mendicant

mendicare §197 **(méndico)** *tr & intr* to beg

mendici·tà *f* (**-tà**) indigence, poverty

mendi·co -ca *adj & mf* (**-chi -che**) mendicant

menefreghismo *m* I-don't-care attitude

menestrèllo *m* minstrel

méno *adj invar* less ‖ *m* less; least; minus (*sign*); **i meno** the few; **per lo meno** at least ‖ *adv* less; least; minus; **a meno che** unless; **da meno** inferior; **fare a meno di** to do without; to spare; **meno . . . di** less . . . than; **meno male** fortunately; **meno . . . meno** the less . . . the less; **non poter fare a meno di** + *inf* to not be able to help + *ger*, e.g., **la conferenza non poteva fare a meno di essere un successo** the conference could not help being a success; **quanto meno** at least; **senza meno** without fail; **venir meno** to swoon, pass out; to fail; to lose, e.g., **gli venne meno il cuore** he lost his courage; **venir meno di** to break (*one's word*) ‖ *prep* except; less, minus; of, e.g., **le sette meno dieci** ten minutes of seven

menomare (mènomo) *tr* to lessen, diminish; (fig) to hurt, damage

mèno·mo -ma *adj* least

menopàusa *f* menopause

mènsa *f* (prepared) table; mess, mess hall; (eccl) altar; communion table; (poet) mass; (poet) altar; **mensa aziendale** company cafeteria

mensile *adj* monthly ‖ *m* monthly salary or allowance

mensili·tà *f* (**-tà**) monthly installment

mènsola *f* bracket; corner shelf; neck (*of harp*); mantel (*of chimney*); console

ménta *f* mint

mentale *adj* mental; (anat) chin

mentali·tà *f* (**-tà**) mentality, mind

ménte *f* mind; **a mente di** according to; **avere in mente** to mean; to intend; **di mente** mental; **mente direttiva** mastermind; **scappare di mente a qlcu** to escape s.o.'s mind, e.g., **gli è scappato di mente** it escaped his mind; **uscire di mente** to go out of one's mind; **venire in mente a qlcu** to remember, e.g., **non gli è venuto in mente di spedire la lettera** he did not remember to mail the letter

mentecat·to -ta *adj & mf* lunatic

mentìna *f* mint; **mentina digestiva** after-dinner mint

mentire §176 & **(mènto)** *intr* to lie;

mentire per la gola to lie through one's teeth

menti·to -ta *adj* false; disguised

menti·tóre -trice *adj* lying || *mf* liar

ménto *m* chin

mentòlo *m* menthol

méntre *m*—in quel mentre at that very moment; nel mentre che at the time when || *conj* while; whereas

me·nù *m* (-nù) menu

menzionare (menzióno) *tr* to mention

menzióne *f* mention

menzógna *f* lie

menzognè·ro -ra *adj* false, deceptive; lying, untruthful

meraviglia *f* marvel, wonder; a meraviglia wonderfully; destare le meraviglie di to amaze; dire meraviglie di to praise to the skies; fare meraviglia (with *dat*) to amaze; far meraviglie to work wonders

meravigliare §280 (meravìglio) *tr* to amaze; to astonish || *ref* to be astonished

meravìglió·so -sa [*s*] *adj* marvelous, wonderful || *m* (lit) supernatural

mercan·te -téssa *mf* merchant, dealer

mercanteggiare §290 (mercantéggio) *tr* to sell || *intr* to deal; to haggle

mercantile *adj* mercantile; merchant (*marine*) || *m* cargo boat, freighter

mercanzìa *f* merchandise; (coll) junk

mercato *m* market; trafficking; a buon mercato cheap; far mercato di to traffic in; sopra mercato besides; into the bargain

mèrce *f* merchandise, goods; commodity

mercé *f* favor, grace; mercy; alla mercé di at the mercy of; mercé a thanks to; mercé sua thanks to him (her, etc.)

mercéde *f* pay; (lit) reward

mercenà·rio -ria *adj & m* (-ri -rie) mercenary

mercerìa *f* notions store; mercerie notions

mercerizzare [ddzz] *tr* to mercerize

mèr·ci *adj invar* freight (*train, car, etc.*) || *m* (-ci) freight train

mer·ciàio -ciàia *mf* (-ciài -ciàie) notions store owner

merciaiòlo *m* small businessman; merciaiolo ambulante peddler

mercole·dì *m* (-dì) Wednesday

mercuriale *f* market report; price ceiling

mercùrio *m* mercury || Mercùrio *m* Mercury

merènda *f* afternoon snack, bite

meretrice *f* harlot

meridia·no -na *adj & m* meridian || *f* sundial

meridionale *adj* meridional, southern || *mf* southerner

meridióne *m* south; South

merig·gio *m* (-gi) noon

merìn·ga *f* (-ghe) meringue

meritare (mèrito) *tr* to deserve; to win || *intr* (eccl) to merit; bene meritare di to deserve the gratitude of || *impers*—merita it is worth while to

meritévole *adj* deserving, worthy

mèrito *m* merit; in merito a concerning; per merito di thanks to; render merito a to reward

meritò·rio -ria *adj* (-ri -rie) meritorious

merlan·go *m* (-ghi) whiting

merlatura *f* battlement

merlétto *m* lace, needlepoint

mèrlo *m* blackbird; merlon; (fig) simpleton

merluzzo *m* cod

mè·ro -ra *adj* bare, mere; (poet) pure

merovìngi·co -ca (-ci -che) *adj* Merovingian || *f* Merovingian script

mesata [*s*] *f* month's wages

méscere (*pp* mesciuto) *tr* to pour (*e.g., wine*); (poet) to mix

meschini·tà *f* (-tà) pettiness; narrowmindedness; meanness, stinginess

meschi·no -na *adj* petty; narrowminded; wretched; puny || *m* wretch

méscita *f* pouring; counter; bar

mescolanza *f* mixture, blend

mescolare (méscolo) *tr* to mix, blend; to shuffle (*cards*); to stir (*e.g., coffee*) || *ref* to mix, blend; to mingle; to consort; mescolarsi in to mind (*somebody else's business*)

mescolatrice *f* mixer, blender

mése [*s*] *m* month; month's pay

mesétto [*s*] *m* short month

mesóne *m* (phys) meson

méssa *f* (eccl & mus) Mass; messa a fuoco (phot) focusing; messa a punto adjustment; clear statement, outline of a problem; (aut) tune-up; messa a terra (elec) grounding; messa cantata high mass; messa in marcia or in moto (mach) starting; messa in orbita (rok) orbiting; messa in piega waving (*of hair*); messa in scena staging; messa in vendita putting up for sale

messaggerìe *fpl* delivery service

messaggè·ro -ra *mf* messenger; postal clerk

messàg·gio *m* (-gi) message

messale *m* missal

mèsse *f* harvest; crop

Messìa *m* Messiah

messiàni·co -ca *adj* (-ci -che) Messianic

messica·no -na *adj & mf* Mexican

Mèssico, il Mexico

messinscèna *f* staging; faking

mésso *m* clerk; (poet) messenger

mestare (mésto) *tr* to stir || *intr* to intrigue

mesta·tóre -trice *mf* ringleader; schemer

mèstica *f* (painting) filler

mesticare §197 (mèstico) *tr* to prime (*a canvas*); to mix (*colors*)

mestierante *mf* potboiler (*person*); tradesman, craftsman

mestière *m* trade, craft; (archaic) task; di mestiere by trade; habitual; essere del mestiere to be up in one's line

mestièri *m*—essere di or far mestièri to be necessary

mestizia *f* sadness

mè·sto -sta *adj* sad

méstola *f* làdle; trowel

méstolo *m* kitchen spoon; avere il mestolo in mano to be the boss

mèstruo *m* menses, menstruation

mèta *f* goal, aim; (rugby) goal line

méta *f* heap, stack (*e.g., of hay*)

me·tà *f* (-tà) half; middle; halfway; better half; **a metà** halfway, in the middle; **aver qlco a metà con qlcu** to go half and half with s.o.

metabolismo *m* metabolism

metafisi·co -ca (-ci -che) *adj* metaphysical ‖ *m* metaphysician ‖ *f* metaphysics

metafonèsi *f* umlaut, metaphony

metafonìa *f* umlaut, metaphony

metàfora *f* metaphor

metafòri·co -ca *adj* (-ci -che) metaphoric(al)

metàlli·co -ca *adj* (-ci -che) metallic

metallizzare [ddzz] *tr* to cover with metal

metallo *m* metal; timbre (*of voice*); (poet) metal object; **il vile metallo** filthy lucre

metallòide *m* nonmetal

metallurgia *f* metallurgy

metallùrgi·co -ca (-ci -che) *adj* metallurgic(al) ‖ *m* metalworker

metalmeccàni·co -ca (-ci -che) *adj* metallurgic(al) and mechanical ‖ *m* metalworker

metamòrfo·si *f* (-si) metamorphosis

metanizzare [ddzz] *tr* to provide with methane

metano *m* methane

metanodótto *m* natural gas pipeline

metàte·si *f* (-si) metathesis

metèora *f* meteor; atmospheric phenomenon

meteorite *m & f* meteorite

meteorologia *f* meteorology

meteorològi·co -ca *adj* (-ci -che) meteorologic(al); weather (*forecast*)

meteoròlo·go -ga *mf* (-gi -ghe) meteorologist

metic·cio -cia *adj & mf* (-ci -ce) half-breed

meticoló·so -sa [s] *adj* meticulous

metìli·co -ca *adj* (-ci -che) methyl

metòdi·co -ca (-ci -che) *adj* methodical; subject (*e.g., index*) ‖ *mf* methodical person ‖ *f* methodology

metodi·sta *adj & mf* (-sti -ste) Methodist

mètodo *m* method

metràg·gio *m* (-gi) length in meters; **corto metraggio** short; **lungo metraggio** full-length movie, feature film

metratura *f* length in meters

mètri·co -ca *adj* (-ci -che) metric(al) ‖ *f* metrics, prosody

mètro *m* meter; (fig) yardstick; (lit) words

métro *m* (coll) subway

metrònomo *m* (mus) metronome

metronòt·te *m* (-te) night watchman

metròpo·li *f* (-li) metropolis

metropolita·no -na *adj* metropolitan ‖ *m* policeman, traffic cop ‖ *f* subway

metrovìa *f* subway

méttere §198 *tr* to put, place; to set (*e.g., foot*); to run (*e.g., a nail into a board*); to cause (*fear; fever*); to employ; to admit; to put forth; to give out; (coll) to charge; (coll) to install; (aut) to engage (*a gear*); **metterci** to take (*e.g., an hour*); **mettere a confronto** to compare; **mettere a freno** to check; **mettere a fuoco** (phot) to focus; **mettere al bando** to banish; **mettere all'asta** to auction off; **mettere al mondo** to give birth to; **mettere a nudo** to lay bare; **mettere fuori** to pull out; to give out (*news*); to throw (*s.o.*) out; **mettere giù** to lower; **mettere in onda** to broadcast; **mettere in pericolo** to endanger; **mettere la pulce nell'orecchio a** to put a bug in the ear of; **mettere qlcu alla porta** to show s.o. the door; **mettere su** to set up; (coll) to put (*e.g., a coat*) on; **mettere su qlcu contro qlcu** to excite s.o. against s.o. ‖ *intr* to sprout; to lead (*said, e.g., of a road*) ‖ *ref* to lead on, to don; to place oneself, put oneself; to take shape; **mettersi a** to begin to; **mettersi al bello** to clear up (*said of weather*); **mettersi a letto** to go to bed; **mettersi a sedere** to sit down; **mettersi con** to start to work with; **mettersi in ferie** to take one's vacation; **mettersi in malattia** to fall ill; **mettersi in mare** to put to sea; **mettersi in maschera** to wear a masked costume; **mettersi in salvo** to get out of danger; to save oneself; **mettersi in viaggio** to set out on a journey; **mettersi in vista** to make oneself conspicuous ‖ *impers*—**mette conto** it is worth while

mettima·le *mf* (-le) troublemaker

mezzadrìa [ddzz] *f* sharecropping

mezza·dro -dra [ddzz] *mf* sharecropper

mezzaluna [ddzz] *f* (**mezzelune**) half-moon; crescent (*symbol of Turkey and Islam*); curved chopping knife; lunette (*of fortification*)

mezzana [ddzz] *f* procuress; (naut) mizzen

mezzanave [ddzz] *f—***a mezzanave** amidships

mezzanino [ddzz] *m* mezzanine

mezza·no -na [ddzz] *adj* median; medium; middle ‖ *m* procurer ‖ *f* see **mezzana**

mezzanòtte [ddzz] *f* (**mezzenòtti**) midnight

mezzatinta [ddzz] *f* (**mezzetinte**) halftone

méz·zo -za *adj* overripe, rotten

mèz·zo -za [ddzz] *adj* half; middle ‖ *m* half; middle; medium; means; vehicle; **a mezzo (di)** by (*e.g., messenger*); **andar di mezzo** to suffer the consequences; to be the loser; **entrare di mezzo** to interpose oneself; **esserci di mezzo** to be present; to be at stake; **giusto mezzo** happy medium; **in mezzo a** among; in the lap of, e.g., **in mezzo alle delicatezze** in the lap of luxury; **in quel mezzo** meanwhile; **levar di mezzo** to get rid of; **mezzi** means; facilities; **mezzi di comunicazione di massa** mass media; **per mezzo di** by means of

mezzobusto [ddzz] *m* (**mezzibusti**) (sculp) bust; **a mezzobusto** half-length (*e.g., portrait*)

mezzo·dì [ddzz] *m* (**-dì**) noon; south; South

mezzogiórno [ddzz] *m* noon; south; South

mezzùc·cio [ddzz] *m* (**-ci**) expedient

mi §5 *pron*

miagolare (miàgolo) *intr* to meow

miagoli·o *m* (**-i**) meow, mew

mi·ca *f* (**-che**) mica; (obs) crumb ‖ *adv*—**mica male** (coll) not too bad!; **non . . . mica** not . . . ever; not at all

mìc·cia *f* (**-ce**) fuse

michelàc·cio *m* (**-ci**) (coll) lazy bum

micidiale *adj* deadly; (fig) unbearable

mì·cio -cia *mf* (**-ci -cie**) (coll) pussy cat

micrò·bio *m* (**-bi**) microbe

microbiologìa *f* microbiology

micròbo *m* microbe

microfà·rad *m* (**-rad**) microfarad

microferrovìa *f* model railroad

micro·film *m* (**-film**) microfilm

microfilmare *tr* to microfilm

micròfono *m* microphone

microlettóre *m* microfilm reader

micromotóre *m* small motor; motorcycle

microónda *f* microwave

microschèda *f* microcard

microscòpi·co -ca *adj* (**-ci -che**) microscopic(al)

microscò·pio *m* (**-pi**) microscope

microsól·co *adj invar* microgroove ‖ *m* (**-chi**) microgroove; microgroove, long-playing record

microtelèfono *m* French telephone, handset

midólla *f* crumb; (coll) marrow

midól·lo *m* (**-la** *fpl*) marrow; (bot & fig) pith; **midollo spinale** (anat) spinal cord

mièle *m* honey

mièter (mièto) *tr* to reap; (lit) to kill

mietitrebbiatrice *f* combine

mieti·tóre -trice *mf* reaper, harvester

mietitura *f* harvesting

mi·gliàlo *m* (**-gliàia** *fpl*) thousand

mì·glio *m* (**-glia** *fpl*) mile; milestone; **miglio marino** nautical mile; **miglio terrestre** mile ‖ *m* (**-gli**) millet

miglioraménto *m* improvement

migliorare (miglióro) *tr, intr* (ESSERE & AVERE) & *ref* to improve

migliore *adj* better; best

migliorìa *f* improvement (*e.g., of real estate*)

mignatta *f* leech

mìgnolo *adj masc* little (*finger or toe*) ‖ *m* little finger; little toe

migrare *intr* to migrate

migra·tóre -trice *adj* & *m* migrant

migrazióne *f* migration

Milano *f* Milan

miliardà·rio -ria *adj* & *mf* (**-ri -rie**) billionaire

miliardo *m* billion

milionà·rio -ria *adj* & *mf* (**-ri -rie**) millionaire

milióne *m* million

milionèsi·mo -ma *adj* & *m* millionth

militante *adj* & *m* militant

militare *adj* military ‖ *m* soldier ‖ *v* (**milito**) *intr* to be a member; to mili-

tate; to be in the armed forces; **militare in** to be a member of (*e.g., a party*)

militaré·sco -sca *adj* (**-schi -sche**) military, soldierly

militarismo *m* militarism

militari·sta -sti -ste) *adj* militaristic ‖ *mf* militarist

militarizzare [ddzz] *tr* to militarize; to fortify

milite *m* militiaman; soldier; **milite del fuoco** fireman; **Milite Ignoto** Unknown Soldier

militesènte *adj* exempt from military service ‖ *m* man exempt from military service

milìzia *f* militia; (mil) service; struggle; **milizie celesti** heavenly host

miliziano *m* militiaman

millantare *tr* to boast of ‖ *ref* to brag, boast

millanta·tóre -trice *mf* braggart

millanterìa *f* bragging

mille *adj, m* & *pron* (**mila**) thousand, a thousand, one thousand ‖ **il Mille** the eleventh century; the year one thousand

millecènto *m* eleven hundred ‖ *f* car with a 1100 cc. motor

millefò·glie *m* (**-glie**) puff-paste cake

millenà·rio -ria (**-ri -rie**) *adj* millennial ‖ *m* millennium

millèn·nio *m* (**-ni**) millennium

millepiè·di *m* (**-di**) millipede

millèsi·mo -ma *adj* & *m* thousandth

milliam·père *m* (**-père**) milliampere

milligrammo *m* milligram

millimetra·to -ta *adj* divided into squares of one millimeter square

millìmetro *m* millimeter

milli·vòlt *m* (**-vòlt**) millivolt

milza *f* spleen

mimare *tr* & *intr* to mime

mimetizzare [ddzz] *tr* (mil) to camouflage

mimetizzazióne [ddzz] *f* (mil) camouflage

mìmi·co -ca (**-ci -che**) *adj* mimic; sign (*language*) ‖ *f* mimicry; (theat) gestures; (theat) miming

mì·mo -ma *mf* mime ‖ *m* (orn) mockingbird

mina *f* lead (*of pencil*); (mil) mine; **mina anticarro** antitank mine; **mina antiuomo** antipersonnel mine

minaccévole *adj* (lit) threatening

minàc·cia *f* (**-ce**) threat, menace

minacciare §128 *tr* to threaten, menace

minacció·so -sa [s] *adj* threatening

minare *tr* to mine; to undermine

minaréto *m* minaret

minatóre *m* miner

minatò·rio -ria *adj* (**-ri -rie**) threatening

minchionare (minchióno) *tr* (slang) to make a sucker of

minchióne *m* (slang) sucker

minerale *adj* mineral ‖ *m* mineral; ore

mineralogìa *f* mineralogy

minerà·rio -ria *adj* (**-ri -rie**) mining

minèr·va *m* (**-va**) safety match

minèstra *f* vegetable soup

minestróne *m* minestrone; hodgepodge

mìngere §199 *intr* to urinate

mingherli·no -na *adj* frail, thin

miniare §287 *tr* to paint in miniature; to illuminate

miniatura *f* miniature

miniaturizzare [ddzz] *tr* to miniaturize

miniaturizzazióne [ddzz] *f* miniaturization

minièra *f* mine

mini-gòlf *m* (**-gòlf**) miniature golf

minigònna *f* miniskirt

mìnima *f* lowest temperature; (mus) minim

minimizzare [ddzz] *tr* to minimize

mìni·mo -ma *adj* smallest, least; minimum || *m* minimum; **al minimo** at the least; **girare al minimo** or **tenere il minimo** (aut) to idle || *f* see **minima**

mìnio *m* red lead; rouge

ministeriale *adj* ministerial

ministèro *m* ministry; cabinet; department; **pubblico ministero** public prosecutor

ministra *f* (joc) wife of minister; (joc) female minister; (poet) minister

ministro *m* minister; secretary; administrator; **ministro degli Esteri** foreign minister; (U.S.A.) Secretary of State

minoranza *f* minority

minorare (**minóro**) *tr* to lessen; to disable

minora·to -ta *adj* disabled || *mf* disabled person

minorazióne *f* reduction; disability

minóre *adj* smaller, lesser; minor; smallest, least; younger; youngest || *m* minor

minorènne *adj* underage || *mf* minor

minorile *adj* juvenile (*e.g.*, *court*)

minori·tà *f* (**-tà**) minority

minuétto *m* minuet

minù·gia *f* (**-gia** & **-gie**) (mus) catgut

minùsco·lo -la *adj* small (*letter*); diminutive || *m* & *f* small letter

minuta *f* first draft, rough copy

minutàglia *f* trifles; small fry

minutante *m* secretary; retailer

minuterìa *f* trinkets, notions

minu·to -ta *adj* minute; small (*change*); common (*people*) || *m* minute; **al minuto** retail; **di minuto in minuto** at any moment; **minuto secondo** second; **nel minuto** in detail; **per minuto** minutely || *f* see **minuta**

minùzia *f* trifle; **minuzie** minutiae

minuzió·so -sa [s] *adj* meticulous

minùzzolo *m* scrap, crumb; small boy

mìo mìa §6 *adj* & *pron poss* (**mièi mìe**)

mìope *adj* nearsighted || *mf* nearsighted person

miopìa *f* nearsightedness

mira *f* aim; sight; target, goal; **prendere di mira** to aim at; to torment

miràbile *adj* admirable || *m* wonder

mirabìlia *fpl* wonders; **far mirabilia** to perform wonders; **dir mirabilia di** to speak highly of

mirabolante *adj* amazing, astonishing

miracola·to -ta *adj* miraculously cured || *mf* miraculously cured person

miràcolo *m* miracle; wonder; **dir mira-**

coli di to praise to the skies; **per miracolo** by mere chance

miracoló·so -sa [s] *adj* miraculous; wonderful

miràg·gio *m* (**-gi**) mirage

mirare *tr* (lit) to look at; (lit) to aim at || *intr* to aim; **mirare a** to aim at; **mirare a** + *inf* to aim to + *inf*; **to intend to** + *inf*

mirìade *f* myriad

mirino *m* sight (*of gun*); (phot) finder

mirra *f* myrrh

mirtillo *m* blueberry; whortleberry, huckleberry

mirto *m* myrtle

misantropìa *f* misanthropy

misàntro·po -pa *adj* misanthropic || *mf* misanthrope

miscèla *f* mixture, blend

miscelare (**miscèlo**) *tr* to mix, blend

miscellàne·o -a *adj* miscellaneous || *f* miscellany

mischia *f* fight; (sports) scrimmage

mischiare §287 *tr* to mix, blend; to shuffle (*cards*) || *ref* to mix

misconóscere §134 *tr* to not appreciate, undervalue

miscredènte *adj* misbelieving || *mf* misbeliever

miscù·glio *m* (**-gli**) mixture, blend

miseràbile *adj* pitiful, miserable; poor, wretched

miseran·do -da *adj* pitiable

miserère *m* Miserere; **essere al miserere** to be in one's last hours

miserévole *adj* pitiful; pitiable

misèria *f* destitution, misery; wretchedness; lack, want; trifle; **piangere miseria** to cry poverty

misericòrdia *f* mercy

misericordió·so -sa [s] *adj* merciful

mìse·ro -ra *adj* unhappy, wretched; poor; meager; mean; too small, too short

misfatto *m* misdeed, misdoing

misirìz·zi [s] *m* (**-zi**) tumbler (*toy*); (fig) chameleon

misògi·no -na *adj* misogynous || *m* misogynist

mìssile *adj* & *m* missile; **missile antimissile** antimissile missile; **missile intercontinentale** I.C.B.M.; **missile teleguidato** guided missile

missilìsti·co -ca *adj* (**-ci -che**) missile

missionà·rio -ria *adj* & *m* (**-ri -rie**) missionary

missióne *f* mission

missiva *f* missive

misterió·so -sa [s] *adj* mysterious

mistèro *m* mystery

mìstica *f* mysticism; mystical literature

misticismo *m* mysticism

mìsti·co -ca *adj* (**-ci -che**) *adj* & *mf* mystic || *f* see **mistica**

mistificare §197 (**mistìfico**) *tr* to hoax

mistificazióne *f* hoax

mì·sto -sta *adj* mixed || *m* mixture; mixed train

mistura *f* mixture

misura *f* measure; size; bounds; fitting; **a misura che** in proportion as; **di**

misura (sports) with a narrow margin; **su misura** made-to-order
misuràbile adj measurable
misurare tr to measure; to deliver (e.g., a slap); to budget (expenses); to try on (clothes); to weigh (the outcome) || intr to measure || ref to compete; to limit oneself; **misurarsi con** to try conclusions with
misura·to -ta adj moderate; scanty
misurino m measuring spoon or cup
mite adj mild; tame; low (price)
mìti·co -ca adj (-ci -che) mythical
mitigare §209 (mìtigo) tr to mitigate; to assuage, allay || ref to abate
mìtilo m mussel
mito m myth
mitologìa f mythology
mitològi·co -ca adj (-ci -che) mythologic(al)
mitòmane mf compulsive liar
mi·tra m (-tra) submachine gun || f miter
mitràglia f grapeshot; scrap iron; (coll) machine gun
mitragliare §280 (mitràglio) tr to machine-gun
mitragliatrice f machine gun
mitraglièra f heavy machine gun
mitraglière m machine gunner
mittènte mf sender; shipper
mo' m—apocopated form of **modo** by way of; **a mo' d'esempio** as an illustration
mòbile adj movable; personal (property); (fig) fickle; (rr) rolling (stock) || m piece of furniture; cabinet; (phys) body; **mobili** furniture
mobìlia f furniture
mobiliare adj (fin) security; (law) movable || §287 (mobìlio) tr to furnish
mobilière m furniture maker; furniture dealer
mobilità f mobility
mobilitare (mobìlito) tr & intr to mobilize
mobilitazióne f mobilization
mò·ca m (-ca) mocha; **caffè moca** Mocha coffee
mocassino m mocassin
moccicare §197 (móccico) intr (slang) to snivel; (slang) to run (said of the nose); (slang) to whimper
moccicó·so -sa [s] adj (slang) snotty
móc·cio m (-ci) snot, snivel
mocció·so -sa [s] adj snotty || m brat
mòccolo m end of candle, snuff; (joc) snot; (slang) curse word; **reggere il moccolo a qlcu** to be a third party to a couple's necking
mòda f fashion, vogue; **andar di moda** to be fashionable; to be all the rage; **fuori moda** outdated
modali·tà f (-tà) modality; method
modanatura f molding
mòdano m mold
modèlla f model
modellare (modèllo) tr to model; to mold || ref to pattern oneself
modella·tóre -trice mf pattern maker; molder

modellino m (archit) model, maquette
modèllo adj invar model || m model; fashion; style; pattern
moderare (mòdero) tr to moderate, control
moderatézza f moderation
modera·to -ta adj moderate; (mus) moderato || m middle-of-the-roader
modera·tóre -trice adj moderating || m moderator
modernizzare [ddzz] tr & ref to modernize
modèr·no -na adj & m modern
modèstia f modesty; scantiness, meagerness
modè·sto -sta adj modest; humble
mòdi·co -ca adj (-ci -che) reasonable
modìfi·ca f (-che) modification; alteration
modificare §197 (modìfico) tr to modify; to change; to alter
modiglióne m (archit) modillion
modista f milliner
modisterìa f millinery; millinery shop
mòdo m manner, mode, way; custom; idiom; (gram) mood; (mus) mode; **ad ogni modo** anyhow; nevertheless; **ad un modo** equally; **a modo** proper; properly; **a suo modo** in his own way; **bei modi** good manners; **di modo che** so that; **in malo modo** poorly; **in modo da** so as to; **in nessun modo** by no means; **in ogni modo** anyhow; **in qualche modo** somehow; **modo di dire** idiom; turn of phrase; **modo di fare** behavior; **modo di vedere** opinion; **per modo di dire** so to speak
modulare (mòdulo) tr to modulate
modulazióne f modulation; **modulazione d'ampiezza** amplitude modulation; **modulazione di frequenza** frequency modulation
mòdulo m module; blank, form
moffétta f skunk
mògano m mahogany
mòg·gio m (-gi) bushel
mò·gio -gia adj (-gi -gie) downcast, crestfallen
mó·glie f (-gli) wife
moìne fpl blandishments
mòla f grindstone; (coll) millstone
molare adj grinding; molar || m molar || v (mòlo) tr to grind
molassa f molasse, sandstone
molatóre m grinder (person); sander (person)
molatrice f grinder (machine); sander (machine); **molatrice di pavimenti** floor sander
mòle f size; pile; bulk, mass; huge structure
molècola f molecule
molestare (molèsto) tr to bother, annoy
molèstia f bother, trouble, annoyance
molè·sto -sta adj bothersome, troublesome
molibdèno m molybdenum
molinétto m (naut) winch
mòlla f spring; (fig) mainspring; **molla a balestra** leaf spring; **molle** tongs; **molle del letto** bedspring; **prendere**

qlco con le molle to keep at a reasonable distance from s.th

mollare (mòllo) *tr* to let go; to slacken; to drop (*anchor*); (coll) to soak || *intr* to give up; (coll) to soak; **molla!** (coll) cut it out!

mòlle *adj* wet, soaked; soft; mild; easy (*life*); weak (*character*); flexible || *m* softness; soft ground; **tenere a molle** to soak

mollécca *f* soft-shell crab

molleggiaménto *m* suspension; springiness

molleggiare §290 (mollèggio) *tr* to provide with springs, to make elastic; (aut) to provide with suspension || *intr* to be springy, to have bounce || *ref* to bounce along

mollég·gio *m* (-gi) springs; (aut) suspension; springiness

mollétta *f* hairpin; clothespin; **mollette sugar tongs**

mollettièra *f* puttee

mollettóne *m* swansdown

mollézza *f* softness

molli·ca *f* (-che) crumb (*soft inner portion of bread*); **molliche crumbs**

mollificare §197 (mollìfico) *tr* & *ref* to mollify; to soften

mòl·lo -la *adj* soft || *m*—**mettere a mollo** to soak || *f* see **molla**

mollu·sco *m* (-schi) mollusk

mòlo *m* pier, wharf

moltéplice *adj* multiple, manifold

moltilaterale *adj* multilateral, many-sided

moltìpli·ca *f* (-che) front sprocket (*of bicycle*)

moltiplicare §197 (moltìplico) *tr* & *ref* to multiply

moltitùdine *f* multitude, crowd

mól·to -ta *adj* much, a lot of; very, e.g., **ho molta sete** I am very thirsty || *pron* much; a lot; **a dir molto** mostly; **ci corre molto** there is a great difference || **mol·ti -te** *adj* & *pron* many || **molto** *adv* very; quite; much; a lot; widely; long; **fra non molto** before long; **non . . . molto** (coll) not . . . at all

momentàne·o -a *adj* momentary

moménto *m* moment; opportune time; (slang) trifle; (phys) momentum; **dal momento che** since; **per il momento** for the time being; **sul momento** this very moment

mòna·ca *f* (-che) nun

monacale *adj* monachal, conventual

monacato *m* monkhood

monachésimo *m* monachism, monasticism

monachina *f* little nun; **monachine sparks**

mòna·co *m* (-ci) monk; (archit) king post || **Monaco** *m* Monaco || *f* Munich

monar·ca *m* (-chi) monarch

monarchìa *f* monarchy

monàrchi·co -ca *adj* (-ci -che) monarchical; monarchist(ic) (*advocating a monarch*) || *mf* monarchist

monastèro *m* monastery

monàsti·co -ca *adj* (-ci -che) monastic(al)

moncherino *m* stump (*without hand*)

món·co -ca *adj* (-chi -che) one-handed; one-armed; incomplete || *mf* cripple

moncóne *m* stump

mondana *f* prostitute

mondani·tà *f* (-tà) worldliness

monda·no -na *adj* mundane; worldly; society; fashionable || *m* playboy || *f* see **mondana**

mondare (móndo) *tr* to peel, pare; to thresh; to weed; to prune; (fig) to cleanse

mondari·so *mf* (-so) rice weeder

mondez·zàio *m* (-zài) dump

mondiale *adj* world, world-wide; (coll) stupendous

mondìglia *f* chaff; trash; refuse

mondina *f* rice weeder

món·do da *adj* clean-peeled; (lit) pure || *m* world; hopscotch; (coll) heap, bunch; **bel mondo** smart set; **cascasse il mondo!** (coll) come what may!; **da che mondo è mondo** since the world began; **essere nel mondo della luna** to be absent-minded; **mandare all'altro mondo** (coll) to send packing; **mettere al mondo** to give birth to; **mondo della luna** world of fancy; **un mondo a lot; venire al mondo** to be born || **Mondo** *m*—**Terzo Mondo** Third World

monega·sco -sca *adj* & *mf* (-schi -sche) Monacan

monellerìa *f* prank

monèl·lo -la *mf* urchin, brat || *f* romp

monéta *f* money; coin; piece of money; purse (*in horse races*); change; **batter moneta** to mint money; **moneta sonante** cash

monetà·rio -ria (-ri -rie) *adj* monetary || *m*—**falso monetario** counterfeiter

monetizzare [ddzz] *tr* to express in money; to transform into cash

mòngo·lo -la *adj* & *mf* Mongolian

monile *m* necklace; jewel

mònito *m* admonition, warning

monitóre *m* monitor

mònna *f* (obs) lady; (coll) monkey

monoàlbero *adj invar* (aut) single-camshaft, valve-in-head (*distribution*)

monoaurale *adj* monaural

monoblòc·co *adj* (-co) single-block || *m* (aut) cylinder block

monocilìndri·co -ca *adj* (-ci -che) (mach) single-cylinder

monòco·lo -la *adj* one-eyed || *m* monocle

monocolóre *adj invar* one-color; one-party

monofa·se *adj* (-si & -se) single-phase

monogamìa *f* monogamy

monòga·mo -ma *adj* monogamous || *m* monogamist

monografìa *f* monograph

monogram·ma *m* (-mi) monogram

monolìti·co -ca *adj* (-ci -che) monolithic

monolito *m* monolith

monòlo·go *m* (-ghi) monologue

monomanìa *f* monomania

monò·mio *m* (**-mi**) monomial
monopàttino *m* scooter
monopèt·to (**-to**) *adj* single-breasted ‖ *m* single-breasted suit
monoplano *m* (aer) monoplane
monopò·lio *m* (**-li**) monopoly
monopolizzare [ddzz] *tr* to monopolize
monopósto *adj invar* one-man ‖ *m* single-seater
monorotàia *adj invar* single-track ‖ *f* monorail
monoscò·pio *m* (**-pi**) (telv) test pattern
monosìlla·bo -ba *adj* monosyllabic ‖ *m* monosyllable
monòssido *m* monoxide
monoteìsti·co -ca *adj* (**-ci -che**) monotheistic
monotìpìa *f* monotype
monotipo *m* monotype
monotonìa *f* monotony
monòto·no -na *adj* monotonous
monsignóre *m* monsignor
monsóne *m* monsoon
mónta *f* horseback riding; stud; jockey
montacàri·chi *m* (**-chi**) freight elevator
montàg·gio *m* (**-gi**) (mach) assembly; (mov) editing; (mov) montage
montagna *f* mountain; **montagna di ghiaccio** iceberg; **montagne russe** roller coaster
montagnó·so -sa [s] *adj* mountainous
montana·ro -ra *adj* mountain ‖ *mf* mountaineer
monta·no -na *adj* mountain
montante *adj* rising ‖ *m* riser, upright; (football) goal post; (aer) strut; (boxing) uppercut; (com) aggregate amount
montare (**mónto**) *tr* to mount; to go up (*the stairs*); to set (*jewels*); to frame (*a painting*); to whip (*e.g., eggs*); to excite; to exaggerate (*news*); to decorate (*a house*); to cover (*said of a male animal*); (mach) to assemble; (mov) to edit; **montare la testa a** to excite; to give a swell head to ‖ *intr* (ESSERE) to jump; to climb; to go up; to rise; to swell; **montare alla testa a** to go to the head of; **montare in collera** to get angry ‖ *impers*—**non monta** it doesn't matter, never mind
monta·tóre -trice *mf* (mach) assembler; (mov) editor
montatura *f* assembly; frame (*of glasses*); appliqué; setting (*of gem*); (journ) ballyhoo; (mov) editing; **montatura pubblicitaria** publicity stunt
montavivan·de *m* (**-de**) dumbwaiter
mónte *m* mountain; bank; mount (*in palmistry*); (cards) discard; **a monte** uphill; upstream; **andare a monte** to fail; **mandare a monte** to cause to fail; **monte di pietà** pawnbroker's; **monte di premi** pot (*in a lottery*)
montenegri·no -na *adj & mf* Montenegrin
montessoria·no -na *adj* Montessori
montóne *m* ram; mutton; rounded stone
montuó·so -sa [s] *adj* mountainous
montura *f* uniform

monumentale *adj* monumental
monuménto *m* monument
moquètte *f* (**moquètte**) wall-to-wall carpeting
mòra *f* mulberry; blackberry; brunette; Moorish woman; arrears; penalty (*for arrears*); (archaic) heap of stones
morale *adj* moral ‖ *m* morale; **giù di morale** downcast; **su di morale in high spirits** ‖ *f* morals, ethics; moral (*of a fable*)
moraleggiare §290 (**moraléggio**) *intr* to moralize
moralismo *m* moralism
morali·tà *f* (**-tà**) morality; morals
moralizzare [ddzz] *tr & intr* to moralize
moratòria *f* moratorium
morbidézza *f* softness
mòrbi·do -da *adj* soft; sleek; pliable ‖ *m* soft ground
morbillo *m* measles
mòrbo *m* disease; plague
morbó·so -sa [s] *adj* morbid
mòrchia *f* sediment; dregs of oil
mordace *adj* biting, mordacious
mordènte *adj* biting; (chem) mordant; (mach) interlocking ‖ *s* strength; (chem) mordant
mòrdere §200 *tr* to bite; to grab; to corrode; **mordere il freno** to champ the bit
mordicchiare §287 (**mordìcchio**) *tr* to nibble
morèl·lo -la *adj* blackish; black (*horse*) ‖ *m* black horse
morènte *adj* dying ‖ *mf* dying person
moré·sco -sca (**-schi -sche**) *adj* Moresque, Moorish ‖ *f* Moorish dance
morét·to -ta *adj* brunet ‖ *m* Negro boy; dark-skinned boy; chocolate-covered ice-cream bar ‖ *f* Negro girl; dark-skinned girl; mask; (orn) scaup duck
morfè·ma *m* (**-mi**) morpheme
morfina *f* morphine
morfinòmane *mf* morphine addict
morfologìa *f* morphology
morìa *f* pestilence; high mortality
moribón·do -da *adj* moribund
morigera·to -ta *adj* temperate, moderate
morire §201 *intr* (ESSERE) to die; to die out; to end (*said of a street*); **morire di noia** to be bored to death
moritu·ro -ra *adj* about to die, doomed
mormóne *mf* Mormon
mormorare (**mórmoro**) *tr* to murmur; to whisper ‖ *intr* to murmur; to whisper; to babble (*said of a brook*); to rustle; to gossip
mormorì·o *m* (**-i**) whisper; murmur
mò·ro -ra *adj* Moorish; dark-skinned; dark-brown ‖ *mf* Moor ‖ *m* mulberry tree ‖ *f* see **mora**
morosi·tà [s] *f* (**-tà**) delinquency (*in paying one's bills*)
moró·so -sa [s] *adj* delinquent (*in paying one's bills*) ‖ *m* (coll) boyfriend; **i morosi** (coll) the lovers ‖ *f* (coll) girl friend
mòrsa *f* vise; (archit) toothing
morsétto *m* clamp; (elec) binding post

morsicare §197 (**mòrsico**) *tr* to bite
morsicatura *f* bite
morsicchiare §287 (**morsìcchio**) *tr* to nibble
mòrso *m* bite; bit
mor·tàio *m* (**-tài**) mortar
mortale *adj* mortal; deadly || *m* mortal
mortali·tà *f* (**-tà**) mortality
mortarétto *m* firecracker
mòrte *f* death; end; **averla a morte** con to harbor hatred for; **morte civile** (law) attainder, loss of civil rights
mortèlla *f* myrtle
mortificare §197 (**mortìfico**) *tr* to mortify || *ref* to feel ashamed
mòr·to -ta *adj* dead; still (*life*); **morto di fame** dying of hunger; **morto di paura** scared to death || *mf* dead person, deceased || *m* hidden treasure; (cards) dummy, widow; **fare il morto** to float on one's back; to play possum; **morto di fame** ne'er-do-well, good-for-nothing; **suonare a morto** to toll
mortò·rio *m* (**-ri**) funeral
mortuà·rio -ria *adj* (**-ri -rie**) mortuary
mosài·co -ca (**-ci -che**) *adj* Mosaic || *m* mosaic
mó·sca *f* (**-sche**) fly; imperial (*beard*); **mosca bianca** one in a million; **mosca cieca** blindman's buff; **fare venire la mosca al naso** a to make angry || **Mosca** *f* Moscow
moscaiòla *f* fly netting; flytrap
moscardino *m* dandy; (zool) dormouse
moscatèl·lo -la *adj* muscat || *m* muscatel
moscato *m* muscat grape; muscat wine
moscerino *m* gnat
moschèa *f* mosque
moschettière *m* musketeer; Italian National soccer player
moschétto *m* musket
moschettóne *m* snap hook
moschici·da *adj* (**-di -de**) fly-killing
mó·scio -scia *adj* (**-sci -sce**) flabby, soft
moscóne *m* big fly; pesky suitor
moscovi·ta *adj* & *mf* (**-ti -te**) Muscovite
Mosè *m* Moses
mòssa *f* gesture; movement; move; fake; post; **fare la mossa** to sprout (*said of plants*); **mossa di corpo** bowel movement; **prendere le mosse** to begin; **stare sulle mosse** to be about to begin; to be eager to take off (*said of a horse*)
mossière *m* starter (*in a race*)
mòs·so -sa *adj* moved; in motion; plowed; rough (*sea*); blurred (*picture*); wavy (*hair; ground*) || *f* see **mossa**
mostarda *f* mustard; candied fruit
mósto *m* must
móstra *f* show; pretense; simulation; exhibit; display window; lapel; face (*of watch*); sample; (mil) insignia; (obs) military parade; **far mostra di sé** to show off; **mettersi in mostra** to show off
mostrare (**móstro**) *tr* to show; to put on; **mostrare a dito** to point to;

mostrare la corda to be threadbare || *ref* to show up; to show oneself
mostreggiatura *f* lapel; cuff
mostrina *f* (mil) insignia
móstro *m* monster
mostruó·so -sa [*s*] *adj* monstrous
mòta *f* mud, mire
mo·tèl *m* (**-tèl**) motel
motivare *tr* to cause; to justify
motivazióne *f* justification, reason
motivo *m* motive, reason; motif; theme; (coll) tune; **a motivo di** because of; **motivo per cui** wherefore
mò·to *m* (**-ti**) motion; movement; emotion; riot; **mettere in moto** to start || *f* (**-to**) (coll) motorcycle
motobar·ca *f* (**-che**) motorboat
motocannonièra *f* gunboat
motocarro *m* three-wheeler (*truck*)
motocarrozzétta *f* three-wheeler (*vehicle with sidecar*)
motociclétta *f* motorcycle
motocicli·sta *mf* (**-sti -ste**) motorcyclist
motocorazza·to -ta *adj* armored, panzer
motofalciatrice *f* power mower
motofurgóne *m* delivery truck
motolàn·cia *f* (**-ce**) motorboat, speedboat
motonàuti·co -ca (**-ci -che**) *adj* motorboat || *f* motorboating
motonave *f* motor ship
motopescheréc·cio *m* (**-ci**) motor fishing boat
mo·tóre -trice *adj* motive (*power*); (mach) drive || *m* motor; engine; car; **a motore** motorized; motor; **motore rotativo** (aut) rotary engine; **primo motore** prime mover || *f* see **motrice**
motorétta *f* motor scooter
motorino *m* small motor; motor bicycle; **motorino d'avviamento** (aut) starter
motori·sta *m* (**-sti**) mechanic
motoristi·co -ca *adj* (**-ci -che**) motor
motorizzare [*ddzz*] *tr* to motorize
motoscafo *m* motorboat; **motoscafo da corsa** speedboat
motosé·ga *f* (**-ghe**) chain saw
motosilurante *f* torpedo boat
motoveicolo *m* motor vehicle
motovelièro *m* motor sailer
motrice *f* (rr) engine, motor; (aut) tractor; **motrice a vapore** steam engine
motteggiare §290 (**mottéggio**) *tr* to mock, jeer at || *intr* to jest
mottég·gio *m* (**-gi**) mockery, jest
mòtto *m* witticism; motto; (lit) word
movènte *m* stimulus, motive
movènza *f* bearing, carriage; flow (*of a sentence*); cadence
movìbile *adj* movable
movimenta·to -ta *adj* lively; eventful
moviménto *m* motion, movement; traffic; **movimento di cassa** cash turnover
moviòla *f* (mov) viewer and splicer
mozióne *f* motion; (lit) movement
mozzare (**mózzo**) *tr* to lop off; to sever; **mozzare la testa** a to cut off the head of

mozzicóne *m* stump; butt (*e.g., of cigar*)

móz·zo -za *adj* cut off; truncated; cropped (*ears*); docked (*tail*); hard (*breathing*) ‖ *m* cabin boy; **mozzo di stalla** stable boy

mòzzo [ddzz] *m* hub

muc·ca *f* (*-che*) milch cow

mùc·chio *m* (*-chi*) pile, heap; bunch

mucillàgine *f* mucilage

mu·co *m* (*-chi*) mucus, phlegm

mucó·so -sa [s] *adj* mucous ‖ *f* mucous membrane

muda *f* molt

muffa *f* mold; mildew; **fare la muffa** to be musty

muffire §176 *intr* (ESSERE) to be musty

mùffola *f* mitten; muffle (*of furnace*)

muflóne *m* mouflon

mugghiare §287 (**mùgghio**) *intr* to bellow; to roar

mùggine *m* (ichth) mullet

muggire §176 & (**muggo**) *intr* to moo, low; to roar; to howl

muggito *m* bellow; moo, low; roar

mughétto *m* lily of the valley

mu·gnàio -gnàia *mf* (*-gnài -gnàie*) miller

mugolare (**mùgolo**) *intr* to yelp; to moan

mugolì·o *m* (*-i*) yelp; moan

mugò·lio *m* (*-li*) pine tar

mugugnare *intr* (coll) to mumble; (coll) to grumble

mugugno *m* (coll) grumble

mulattière *m* mule driver, muleteer

mulattì·ero -ra *adj* mule ‖ *f* mule track

mulat·to -ta *adj* & *mf* mulatto

muliebre *adj* womanly, feminine

mulinare *tr* to twirl; to scheme ‖ *intr* to whirl; to muse; to buzz (*in the mind*)

mulinèllo *m* twirl; whirlpool; whirlwind; fishing reel; whirligig; **fare mulinello con** to twirl

mulino *m* mill; **mulino ad acqua** water mill; **mulino a vento** windmill

mu·lo -la *mf* mule; (slang) bastard

multa *f* penalty, fine

multare *tr* to fine

multilaterale *adj* multilateral, many-sided

mùlti·plo -pla *adj* & *m* multiple

mùmmia *f* mummy

mummificare §197 (**mummìfico**) *tr* to mummify

mùngere §183 *tr* to milk

mungi·tóre -trice *mf* milker ‖ *f* milking machine; milk maid

mungitura *f* milking

municipale *adj* municipal, city

municipalizzazióne [ddzz] *f* municipalization; city management

munici·pio *m* (*-pi*) municipality; city council; city hall

munificènza *f* munificence

munìfi·co -ca *adj* (*-ci -che*) munificent

munire §176 *tr* to fortify; to provide; **munire di** to equip with ‖ *ref* to provide oneself

munizióne *f* (obs) fortification; **munizioni** ammunition; building supplies

muòvere §202 *tr* to move; to wag; to propel, run; to lift (*one's finger*); to take (*a step*); to pose (*a question*); to stir up (*laughter*); to institute (*a lawsuit*); **muovere accusa a** to reproach ‖ *intr* (ESSERE) to begin; to move, start ‖ *ref* to move; to travel; to stir; to set out; to be moved; **muoviti!** hurry up!

mura *fpl* see **muro**

muràglia *f* wall; (fig) obstacle; **muraglia cinese** Chinese Wall

muraglióne *m* high wall, rampart

murale *adj* & *m* mural

murare *tr* to wall; to wall in ‖ *intr* to build a wall; **murare a secco** to build a dry wall ‖ *ref* to close oneself in

murata *f* (naut) bulwark

muratóre *m* bricklayer, mason

muratura *f* bricklaying, stonework

muriàti·co -ca *adj* (*-ci -che*) muriatic

mu·ro *m* (*-ri*) wall; **muro del pianto** Wailing Wall; **muro del suono** sound barrier ‖ *m* (*-ra fpl*)—**mura** walls (*of a city*)

musa *f* muse

muschia·to -ta *adj* musk (*e.g., ox*)

mù·schio *m* (*-schi*) musk; (coll) moss

mu·sco *m* (*-schi*) moss

mùscolo *m* muscle; (fig) sinew; (coll) mussel

muscoló·so -sa [s] *adj* muscular

muscó·so -sa [s] *adj* (lit) mossy

musèo *m* museum

museruòla *f* muzzle

musétta *f* nose bag

mùsi·ca *f* (*-che*) music; band; **cambiare musica** to change one's tune

musicale *adj* musical

musicante *adj* music-playing (*angels*) ‖ *mf* band player; second-rate musician

musicare §197 (**mùsico**) *tr* to set to music

musicassétta *f* cassette, tape cartridge

music-hall *m* (*-hall*) *m* vaudeville, burlesque

musici·sta *mf* (*-sti -ste*) musician

musicologìa *f* musicology

musicòlo·go *m* (*-gi*) musicologist

muso *m* muzzle, snout; (coll) mug; (fig) nose; **avere il muso lungo** to make a long face; **mettere il muso** to pout

musó·ne -na *mf* pouter, sulker

mussare *tr* to publish with great fanfare (*a piece of news*) ‖ *intr* to foam (*said of wine*)

mùssola or **mussolina** *f* muslin

mussolinia·no -na *adj* & *m* of Mussolini

mùssolo *m* mussel

mustàc·chio *m* (*-chi*) shroud (*of bowsprit*); **mustacchi** moustache

musulma·no -na [s] *adj* & *m* Moslem

muta *f* change; shift; molt; set (*of sails*); pack (*of hounds*); (mil) watch

mutàbile *adj* changeable

mutande *fpl* shorts, briefs, drawers

mutandine *fpl* panties; **mutandine da bagno** trunks

mutare *tr*, *intr* (ESSERE) & *ref* to change

mutazióne *f* mutation; (biol) mutation, sport

mutévole *adj* changeable; fickle

mutilare (mùtilo) *tr* to mutilate, maim
mutila·to -ta *adj* mutilated ‖ *mf* cripple; amputee; **mutilato di guerra** disabled veteran
mutismo *m* silence, willful silence; (pathol) dumbness
mu·to -ta *adj* mute; dumb; silent (*movie*); unexpressed ‖ *mf* mute ‖ *f* see **muta**
mùtria *f* sulking attitude; proud demeanor

mùtua *f* mutual benefit society; medical insurance; **mettersi in mutua** to go on sick leave
mutuali·tà *f* (**-tà**) mutuality; mutual benefit institutions
mutuare (mùtuo) *tr* to borrow; to lend
mutua·to -ta *mf* person insured by mutual benefit society; person insured by medical insurance
mù·tuo -tua *adj* mutual; borrowing ‖ *m* loan ‖ *f* see **mutua**

N

N, n ['enne] *m & f* twelfth letter of the Italian alphabet
nababbo *m* nabob
Nabucodònosor *m* Nebuchadnezzar
nàcchera *f* castanet
nafta *f* crude oil; naphta; Diesel oil
naftalina *f* naphthalene
nàia *f* cobra; (slang) army discipline; (slang) military service
nàiade *f* naiad
nàilon *m* nylon
nanna *f* sleep (*of child*); **fare la nanna** to sleep (*said of child*)
na·no -na *adj & mf* dwarf
nàpalm *m* napalm
napoleòne *m* napoleon (*gold coin*) ‖ **Napoleone** *m* Napoleon
napoleòni·co -ca *adj* (**-ci -che**) Napoleonic
napoleta·no -na *adj & mf* Neapolitan ‖ *f* espresso coffee machine
Nàpoli *f* Naples
nappa *f* tassel; tuft; kid (*leather*)
narciso *m* narcissus
narcòti·co -ca *adj & m* (**-ci -che**) narcotic
narcotizzare [ddzz] *tr* to drug, dope; to anesthetize
narghi·lè *m* (**-lè**) hookah
narice *f* nostril
narrare *tr* to narrate, tell, recount
narrati·vo -va *adj* narrative; fictional ‖ *f* narrative; fiction
narra·tóre -trice *mf* narrator, storyteller
narrazióne *f* narration; tale, story; narrative
nasale [s] *adj & f* nasal
nascènte *adj* nascent; budding; rising (*sun*); dawning (*day*)
nàscere *m* beginning, origin ‖ §203 *intr* (ESSERE) to be born; to bud; to shoot; to dawn; to rise; to spring up; **nascere con la camicia** to be born with a silver spoon in one's mouth
nàscita *f* birth; birthday; origin
nascitu·ro -ra *adj* unborn, future ‖ *mf* unborn child
nascóndere §204 *tr* to hide; **nascondere a** to hide from ‖ *ref* to hide; to lurk
nascondi·glio *m* (**-gli**) hiding place; hideout; cache
nascondino *m* hide-and-seek; **giocare a nascondino** to play hide-and-seek
nascó·sto -sta *adj* hidden, concealed; secret; **di nascosto** secretly

nasèllo [s] *m* catch (*of latch*); (ichth) hake
nasièra [s] *f* nose ring
naso [s] *m* nose; (fig) face; **aver buon naso** to have a keen sense of smell; **ficcare il naso negli affari degli altri** to pry into the affairs of others; **menare per il naso** to lead by the nose; **naso adunco** hooknose; **restare con un palmo di naso** to be duped
nassa *f* pot (*for fishing*); **nassa per aragoste** lobster pot
nastrino *m* ribbon; badge
nastro *m* ribbon; band; tape; streamer; tape measure; **nastro del cappello** hatband; **nastro isolante** friction tape; **nastro per capelli** hair ribbon
nastùr·zio *m* (**-zi**) nasturtium
natale *adj* native, natal ‖ **natali** *mpl* birth; birthday; **dare i natali a** to be the birthplace of ‖ **Natale** *m* Christmas
natali·tà *f* (**-tà**) birth rate
natalì·zio -zia (**-zi -zie**) *adj* natal; Christmas ‖ *m* birthday
natante *adj* swimming; floating ‖ *m* craft
natatóia *f* fin
natató·rio -ria *adj* (**-ri -rie**) swimming
nàti·ca *f* (**-che**) buttock
natì·o -a *adj* (**-i -e**) (poet) native
nativi·tà *f* (**-tà**) birth, nativity ‖ **Nativi-tà** *f* Nativity
nati·vo -va *adj* native; natural, inborn ‖ *mf* native
N.A.T.O. *f* (acronym) (**North Atlantic Treaty Organization**)—**la N.A.T.O.** NATO
na·to -ta *adj* born; **nata née**; **nato e sputato** the spit and image of; **nato morto** stillborn ‖ *mf* child
natura *f* nature; **natura morta** still life; **in natura** in kind
naturale *adj* natural ‖ *m* nature, disposition; **al naturale** life-size
naturalézza *f* naturalness; spontaneity
naturalismo *m* naturalism
naturali·sta *mf* (**-sti -ste**) naturalist
naturali·tà *f* (**-tà**) naturalization
naturalizzare |ddzz| *tr* to naturalize ‖ *ref* to become naturalized
naturalizzazióne [ddzz] *f* naturalization
naturalménte *adv* naturally; of course
naufragare §209 (nàufrago) *intr* (ESSERE

& AVERE) to be shipwrecked; to sink, to fail

naufrà·gio m (-gi) shipwreck; failure

nàufra·go -ga (-ghi -ghe) adj shipwrecked ‖ mf shipwrecked person; (fig) outcast

nàusea f nausea; disgust; **avere la nausea** to be sick at one's stomach

nauseabón·do -da adj sickening, nauseating; (fig) unsavory

nauseante adj sickening, nauseous

nauseare (nàuseo) tr to nauseate, sicken

nausea·to -ta adj sickened, disgusted

nàuti·co -ca (-ci -che) adj nautical ‖ f sailing, navigation

navale adj naval, navy, sea

navata f nave; **navata centrale** nave; **navata laterale** aisle

nave f ship, vessel, boat; craft; **nave ammiraglia** flagship; **nave a motore** motorboat; **nave appoggio** tender; **nave a vela** sailboat; **nave da carico** freighter; **nave da guerra** warship; **nave petroliera** tanker; **nave portaerei** aircraft carrier; **nave rompighiaccio** icebreaker; **nave traghetto** ferryboat

navétta f shuttle; **fare la navetta** to shuttle

navicèlla f nacelle, cabin (of airship); car (of balloon)

navigàbile adj navigable

navigabili·tà f (-tà) navigability; seaworthiness

navigante adj sailing ‖ m sailor

navigare §209 (nàvigo) tr & intr to navigate, to sail

naviga·to -ta adj seawise; wordly-wise

naviga·tóre -trice mf navigator

navigazióne f navigation

navi·glio m (-gli) ship, craft, boat; fleet; navy; canal; **naviglio mercantile** merchant marine

nazionale adj national ‖ f national team

nazionalismo m nationalism

nazionali·sta mf (-sti -ste) nationalist

nazionalisti·co -ca adj (-ci -che) nationalistic

nazionali·tà f (-tà) nationality

nazionalizzare [ddzz] tr to nationalize

nazionalizzazióne [ddzz] f nationalization

nazióne f nation

nazi·sta adj & mf (-sti -ste) Nazi

nazzarè·no -na [ddzz] adj & mf Nazarene ‖ **il Nazzareno** the Nazarene

ne §5 pron & adv

né conj neither, nor; **né . . . né** neither . . . nor

neanche adv not even; nor; not . . . either

nébbia f fog, haze, mist; **fa nebbia** it is foggy; **nebbia artificiale** smoke screen

nebbióne m thick fog, pea soup

nebbió·so -sa [s] adj foggy, hazy, misty

nebulare adj nebular

nebulizzare [ddzz] tr to atomize

nebulizzatóre [ddzz] m atomizer

nebulósa [s] f nebula

nebulosi·tà [s] f (-tà) fogginess, haziness, mistiness

nebuló·so -sa [s] adj foggy, hazy, misty ‖ f see **nebulosa**

néces·saire m (-saire) vanity case; sewing kit

necessariaménte adv necessarily

necessà·rio -ria (-ri -rie) adj necessary, needed; essential ‖ m necessity; necessities (of life)

necessi·tà f (-tà) necessity; need, want; **di necessità** necessarily

necessitare (necèssito) tr to require; to force ‖ intr to be in want; to be necessary; **necessitare di** to need

necrologìa f necrology, obituary

necrològi·co -ca adj (-ci -che) obituary

necromanzìa f necromancy

necròsi f necrosis, gangrene

nefan·do -da adj heinous, nefarious

nefa·sto -sta adj ill-fated; ominous

nefrite f nephritis

negare §209 (négo & nègo) tr to deny, negate; to refuse

negati·vo -va adj & f negative

nega·to -ta adj unfit, unsuited

negazióne f negation, denial; (gram) negative

neghittó·so -sa [s] adj lazy, slothful

neglèt·to -ta adj neglected; untidy

négli §4

negligènte adj negligent, careless

negligènza f negligence, carelessness; dereliction (of duty)

negligere §205 tr to neglect

negoziàbile adj negotiable

negoziante mf merchant, shopkeeper; dealer; **negoziante all'ingrosso** wholesaler; **negoziante al minuto** retailer; shopkeeper, storekeeper

negoziare §287 (negòzio) tr to negotiate, transact ‖ intr to negotiate, deal

negoziati mpl negotiations

negozia·tóre -trice mf negotiator

negò·zio m (-zi) business; transaction; store, shop; **negozio di cancellerìa** stationery store

negrière m slave trader; slave driver

negriè·ro -ra adj slave ‖ m slave trader; slave driver

né·gro -gra adj & mf Negro

negromante m sorcerer

néi §4

nél §4

nélla §4

nélle §4

néllo §4

némbo m rain cloud; cloud (e.g., of dust)

Nembròd m Nimrod

nèmesi f invar nemesis ‖ **Nemesi** f Nemesis

nemi·co -ca (-ci -che) adj inimical, hostile, unfriendly; enemy; (fig) adverse ‖ mf enemy, foe; **Il Nemico** the Evil One

nemméno adv not even; nor; not . . . either

nènia f funeral dirge; lamentation

nenùfaro m water lily

nèo m mole (on the skin); flaw, blemish; neon; beauty spot

neoclassicheggiante adj in the direction of the neoclassical

neòfi·ta *mf* (**-ti -te**) neophite
neolati·no -na *adj* Neo-Latin, Romance
neologismo *m* neologism
neomicina *f* neomycin
nèon *m* neon
neona·to -ta *adj* newborn || *mf* infant, baby; newborn child
neozelandése [dz] [s] *adj* New Zealand || *mf* New Zealander
nepènte *f* nepenthe
Nepóte *m* Nepos
neppure *adv* not even; nor; not . . . either
nequìzia *f* iniquity, wickedness
nera·stro -stra *adj* blackish
nerbata *f* heavy blow
nèrbo *m* whip; sinew; bulk; strength (*of an opposing force*)
nerboru·to -ta *adj* muscular, sinewy
nereggiare §290 (**neréggio**) *intr* to look black; to be blackish
nerétto *m* (*typ*) boldface
né·ro -ra *adj* black; dark; gloomy; dark-red (*wine*) || *mf* black; Negro || *m* black
nerofumo *m* lampblack
Neróne *m* Nero
nervatura *f* ribbing
nervi·no -na *adj* nerve (*gas*); nervine (*medicine*)
nèrvo *m* nerve; sinew; **avere i nervi** to be in a bad mood
nervosismo [s] *m* nervousness, irritability
nervó·so -sa [s] *adj* nervous, irritable; sinewy, vigorous (*style*) || *m* bad mood; **avere il nervoso** to be in a bad mood
nèsci *m*—**fare il nesci** to feign ignorance
nèspola *f* medlar; **nespole** (coll) blows
nèspolo *m* medlar tree
nèsso *m* connection, link; **avere nesso** to cohere
nessu·no -na *adj* no, not any || **nessuno** *pron* nobody, no one; none; not anybody; not anyone; **nessuno dei due** neither one
nettapén·ne *m* (**-ne**) penwiper
nettare (**nétto**) *tr* to clean, to cleanse
nèttare *m* nectar
nettézza *f* cleanness, cleanliness; neatness; **nettezza urbana** department of sanitation; garbage collection
nét·to -ta *adj* clean; clear; sharp; net || **netto** *adv* clearly, distinctly
nettùnio *m* neptunium
Nettuno *m* Neptune
netturbino *m* street cleaner
neurologìa *f* neurology
neuró·si *f* (**-si**) neurosis
neuròti·co -ca *adj* (**-ci -che**) neurotic
neutrale *adj* & *mf* neutral
neutrali·sta *adj* & *mf* (**-sti -ste**) neutralist
neutrali·tà *f* (**-tà**) neutrality
neutralizzare [ddzz] *tr* to neutralize
nèu·tro -tra *adj* neuter; neutral
neutróne *m* neutron
ne·vàio *m* (**-vài**) snowfield; snowdrift
néve *f* snow; **neve carbonica** dry ice
nevicare §197 (**névica**) *impers* (ESSERE) —**nevica** it is snowing

nevicata *f* snowfall
nevìschio *m* sleet
nevó·so -sa [s] *adj* snowy
nevralgìa *f* neuralgia
nevrastèni·co -ca *adj* & *mf* (**-ci -che**) neurasthenic
nevvéro (i.e., **n'è vero** for **non è vero**) see **non**
niacina *f* niacin
nìb·bio *m* (**-bi**) (orn) kite
nicchia *f* niche; nook, recess
nicchiare §287 (**nicchio**) *intr* to waver
nìc·chio *m* (**-chi**) shell; nook
nichel *m* nickel
nichelare (**nichelo**) *tr* to nickel, to nickel-plate
nichelatura *f* nickel-plating
nichelino *m* nickel (*coin*)
nichèlio *m* var of **nichel**
Nicòla *m* Nicholas
nicotina *f* nicotine
nidiata *f* nestful; brood
nidificare §197 (**nidifico**) *intr* to build a nest, to nest
nido *m* nest; home; nursery; den (*of thieves*)
niènte *m* nothing; nothingness; **dal niente** from scratch; **di niente** you're welcome || *pron* nothing; not . . . anything; **quasi niente** next to nothing
nientediméno *adv* no less, nothing less
Nilo *m* Nile
ninfa *f* nymph
ninfèa *f* white water lily
ninnananna *f* lullaby, cradlesong
nìnnolo *m* toy; trinket
nipóte *mf* grandchild || *m* grandson; nephew; **nipoti** descendants || *f* granddaughter; niece
nippòni·co -ca *adj* (**-ci -che**) Nipponese
nirvana, il nirvana
nìti·do -da *adj* clear, distinct
nitóre *m* brightness; elegance
nitrato *m* nitrate
nitrire §176 *intr* to neigh
nitrito *m* neigh; (chem) nitrite
nitro *m* niter; **nitro del Cile** Chile saltpeter
nitroglicerina *f* nitroglycerin
nitruro *m* nitride
niu·no -na *adj* (poet) var of **nessuno**
nìve·o -a *adj* snow-white
Nizza *f* Nice
no *adv* no; not; **come no?** why not; certainly; **dire di no** to say no; **no?** is it not so?; **non dir di no** to consent; **proprio no** certainly not
nòbile *adj* noble; second (*floor*) || *m* nobleman || *f* noblewoman
nobiliare *adj* noble, of nobility
nobilitare (**nobìlito**) *tr* to ennoble
nobil·tà *f* (**-tà**) nobility
nòc·ca *f* (**-che**) knuckle
nocchière *m* or **nocchiero** *m* petty officer; (poet) pilot, helmsman
nocchieru·to -ta *adj* knotty
nòc·chio *m* (**-chi**) knot (*in wood*)
nocciòla *adj invar* hazel (*in color*) || *f* hazelnut; filbert
nocciolina *f* little nut; **nocciolina americana** peanut; roasted peanut
nòcciolo *m* stone, pit, kernel; **il noc-**

ciolo della questione the crux of the matter

nocciòlo *m* hazel (*tree*); filbert (*tree*)

nóce *m* walnut tree || *f* walnut (*fruit*); **noce del collo** Adam's apple; **noce di cocco** coconut; **noce di vitello** filet of veal; **noce moscata** nutmeg

nocévole *adj* harmful

noci·vo -va *adj* harmful, detrimental

nòdo *m* knot; crux, gist (*of a question*); junction; lump (*in one's throat*); (naut) knot; (phys) node; **fì è il nodo** there's the rub; **nodo d'amore** true-love knot; **nodo ferroviario** rail center, junction; **nodo scorsoio** noose; **nodo stradale** highway center, cross-roads

nodó·so -sa [s] *adj* knotty

Noè *m* Noah

noi §5 *pron pers* we; us; **noi altri** we, e.g., **noi altri italiani** we Italians

nòia *f* boredom; bother, trouble; bug (*in a motor*); **venire a noia** (with *dat*) to weary; **dar noia** (with *dat*) to bother

noial·tri -tre *pron* we; us; **noialtri italiani** we Italians

noió·so -sa [s] *adj* boring, annoying

noleggiare §290 (**noléggio**) *tr* to rent; to hire, to charter || *ref*—**si noleggia, si noleggiano** for rent

noleggiatóre *m* hirer; lessor (*e.g., of a car*)

nolég·gio *m* (**-gi**) rent, lease; car rental; chartering; freightage

nolènte *adj* unwilling

nòlo *m* rent, hire; **a nolo** for hire

nòmade *adj* nomad, nomadic || *mf* nomad

nóme *m* name; fame; reputation; (gram) noun; **a nome di** on behalf of; **in nome di** in the name of; **nome commerciale** firm name; **nome depositato** registered name; **nome di battesimo** Christian name; **nome e cognome** full name

nomèa *f* name, reputation; notoriety

nomìgnolo *m* nickname; **affibbiare un nomignolo a** to nickname

nòmina *f* appointment; **di prima nomina** newly appointed

nominale *adj* nominal; noun

nominare (**nòmino**) *tr* to name, call; to mention; to elect; to appoint

nominati·vo -va *adj* nominative; with names in alphabetical order; (fin) registered || *m* nominative; name; model number

non *adv* no, not; none, e.g., **non troppo presto** none too soon; **non appena** as soon as; **non c'è di che** you are welcome; **non . . . che** but, only; **non è vero?** is it not so?, isn't it so? La traduzione in inglese di questa domanda dipende generalmente dalla proposizione che la precede. Se la proposizione è affermativa, l'interrogazione sarà negativa, p.es. **Lei mi scriverà, non è vero?** You will write me. Won't you? Se la proposizione è negativa, l'interrogazione sarà positiva, p.es. **Lei non beve birra, non è**

vero? You do not drink beer. Do you? Se il soggetto della proposizione è un nome sostantivo, sarà rappresentato nell'interrogazione da un pronome personale, p.es. **Giovanni ha finito, non è vero?** John has finished. Hasn't he?

nonagenà·rio -ria *adj* & *mf* (**-ri -rie**) nonagenarian

nonagèsi·mo -ma *adj, pron* & *m* ninetieth

nonconformi·sta *mf* (**-sti -ste**) nonconformist

noncurante *adj* careless, indifferent

noncuranza *f* carelessness, indifference

nondiméno *conj* yet, nevertheless

nòn·no -na *mf* grandparent || *m* grandfather || *f* grandmother

nonnulla *m invar* nothing, trifle

nò·no -na *adj, m* & *pron* ninth

nonostante *prep* in spite of, notwithstanding; **nonostante che** although, even though

nonpertanto *adv* nevertheless, still, yet

non plus ultra *m* ne plus ultra, acme

nonsènso *m* nonsense

non so ché *adj invar* indefinable || *m invar* something indefinable

nontiscordardi·mé *m* (**-mé**) forget-me-not

nòrd *m* north

nòrdi·co -ca (**-ci -che**) *adj* Nordic; northern, north || *mf* northerner

nòrma *f* rule, regulation; **a norma di legge** according to law; **per Sua norma** for your guidance

normale *adj* normal; normative; perpendicular || *f* perpendicular line

normali·tà *f* (**-tà**) normality, normalcy

normalizzare [ddzz] *tr* to normalize, to standardize

Normandìa, la Normandy

norman·no -na *adj* & *mf* Norman || *m* Norseman

normati·vo -va *adj* normative || *f* normativeness

normògrafo *m* stencil

norvegése [s] *adj* & *mf* Norwegian

Norvègia, la Norway

nosocò·mio *m* (**-mi**) hospital

nossignóra (*i.e.,* **no signora**) *adv* no, Madam

nossignóre (*i.e.,* **no signore**) *adv* no, Sir

nostalgìa *f* nostalgia, longing; homesickness

nostàlgi·co -ca (**-ci -che**) *adj* nostalgic; homesick || *m* worshiper of the good old days (*esp. of Fascism*)

nostra·no -na *adj* domestic, national; home-grown; regional

nò·stro -stra §6 *adj* & *pron poss*

nostròmo *m* boatswain

nòta *f* mark; score; memorandum; list; bill, invoice; report (*on a subordinate*); (mus) note; **note caratteristiche** personal folder, efficiency report (*of an employee*); **prender nota di** to take down

notàbile *adj* notable, noteworthy || *m* notable

no·tàio *m* (**-tài**) notary (public); lawyer

notare (**nòto**) *tr* to mark, check; to note, to jot down; to observe; to bring out; **farsi notare** to attract attention, make oneself conspicuous; **nota bene** note well, take notice

notariale or **notarile** *adj* notarial

notazióne *f* notation; annotation; observation

nò·tes *m* (**-tes**) notebook

notévole *adj* noteworthy, remarkable

notìfi·ca *f* (**-che**) notification, notice; service (*e.g., of a summons*)

notificare §197 (**notìfico**) *tr* to report; to serve (*a summons*); to declare ..(*e.g., one's income*)

notificazióne *f* notification, notice; service (*e.g., of a summons*)

notìzia *f* knowledge; report; piece of news; **aver notizie di** to hear from; **notizie** news; **una notizia** a news item

notizià·rio *m* (**-ri**) news; news report, news bulletin; (rad) newscast; **notiziario sportivo** sports page; (rad, telv) sports news

nò·to -ta *adj* known, well-known ‖ *m* south wind; (coll) swimming ‖ *f* see **nota**

notorie·tà *f* (**-tà**) general knowledge; affidavit; notoriety

notò·rio -ria *adj* (**-ri -rie**) well-known

nottàmbu·lo -la *adj* nighttime; night-wandering ‖ *mf* nightwalker; night owl

nottata *f* night; **far nottata bianca** to spend a sleepless night

nòtte *f* night; **buona notte** good night; **di notte** at night, by night, in the nighttime; **la notte di lunedì** Sunday night; Monday night; **lunedì notte** Monday night; **notte bianca** sleepless night; **notte di San Silvestro** New Year's Eve; watch night

nottetèmpo *adv*—**di nottetempo** at night, in the nighttime

nòttola *f* wooden latch; (zool) bat

nottolino *m* small wooden latch; ratchet, catch

nottur·no -na *adj* nocturnal, night ‖ *m* nocturne

novanta *adj, m & pron* ninety

novantènne *adj* ninety-year-old ‖ *mf* ninety-year-old person

novantèsi·mo -ma *adj, m & pron* ninetieth

novantina *f* about ninety; **sulla novantina** about ninety years old

nòve *adj & pron* nine; **le nove** nine o'clock ‖ *m* nine; ninth (*in dates*)

novecentèsmo *m* twentieth-century arts and letters

novecenti·sta (**-sti -ste**) *adj* twentieth-century ‖ *mf* artist of the twentieth century

novecènto *adj, m & pron* nine hundred ‖ **il Novecento** the twentieth century

novèlla *f* short story; (poet) news

novelliè·re -ra *mf* storyteller; short-story writer

novelli·no -na *adj* early, tender; inexperienced, green

novellìstica *f* storytelling; fiction

novèl·lo -la *adj* fresh, young, tender; new ‖ *f* see **novella**

novèmbre *m* November

novenà·rio -ria *adj* (**-ri -rie**) nine-syllable

noverare (**nòvero**) *tr* to count; to enumerate; (poet) to remember

nòvero *m* number; class

novilù·nio *m* (**-ni**) new moon

novìssi·mo -ma *adj* (lit) last, newest

novi·tà *f* (**-tà**) newness, originality; novelty, innovation; latest idea; late news

noviziato *m* novitiate; apprenticeship

novi·zio -zia (**-zi -zie**) *mf* novice; apprentice ‖ *f* novice (*in a convent*)

novocaina *f* novocaine

nozióne *f* notion, conception

nòzze *fpl* wedding, marriage; **nozze d'argento** silver wedding; **nozze d'oro** golden wedding

nube *f* cloud

nubifrà·gio *m* (**-gi**) cloudburst

nùbile *adj* unmarried, single (*woman*); marriageable ‖ *f* unmarried girl

nu·ca *f* (**-che**) nape of the neck, scruff

nucleare *adj* nuclear

nùcleo *m* nucleus; group; (elec) core

nudismo *m* nudism

nudi·sta *adj & mf* (**-sti -ste**) nudist

nudi·tà *f* (**-tà**) nudity, nakedness

nu·do -da *adj* naked, bare; barren; simple; **mettere a nudo** to lay bare; **nudo e crudo** stark-naked; destitute ‖ *m* nude

nùgolo *m* cloud; throng, swarm

nulla *pron* nothing ‖ *m invar* nothing; nothingness

nulla òsta *m* permission; visa

nullatenènte *adj* poor ‖ *mf* have-not

nullificare §197 (**nullìfico**) *tr* to nullify

nulli·tà *f* (**-tà**) nothingness; nonentity; invalidity (*of a document*)

nul·lo -la *adj* void, worthless ‖ **nullo** *pron* (poet) none, no one ‖ **nulla** *m & pron* see **nulla**

nume *m* divinity, deity

numerare (**nùmero**) *tr* to number

numeratóre *m* numerator; numbering machine

numèri·co -ca *adj* (**-ci -che**) numerical

nùmero *m* number; lottery ticket; size (*of shoes*); **numero dispari** odd number; **numero legale** quorum; **numero pari** even number

numeró·so -sa [s] *adj* numerous, large; harmonious

nùn·zio *m* (**-zi**) nuncio; (poet) news

nuòcere §206 *intr* to be harmful; (with *dat*) to harm

nuòra *f* daughter-in-law

nuotare (**nuòto**) *intr* to swim; to float; to wallow (*in wealth*)

nuotata *f* swim, dip, plunge

nuota·tóre -trice *mf* swimmer

nuòto *m* swimming; **gettarsi a nuoto** to jump into the water; **traversare a nuoto** to swim across

nuòva *f* news; late news

Nuòva York *f* New York
Nuova Zelanda, la [dz] New Zealand
nuòvo -va *adj* new; **di nuovo** again; **nuovo di zecca** brand-new; **nuovo fiammante** brand-new; **nuovo venuto** new arrival ‖ *m*—**il nuovo** the new ‖ *f* see **nuova**
nùtria *f* coypu
nutrice *f* wet nurse; (lit) provider
nutriènte *adj* nourishing
nutriménto *m* nourishment
nutrire §176 & (**nutro**) *tr* to nourish;

to nurture; to harbor · (*e.g., hatred*) ‖ *ref*—**nutrirsi di** to feed on or upon
nutriti·vo -va *adj* nutritious, nutritive
nutri·to -ta *adj* well-fed; strong; rich (*food*); brisk, heavy (*gunfire*)
nutrizióne *f* nutrition; food
nùvo·lo -la *adj* cloudy ‖ *m* cloudy weather; (lit) cloud; (fig) swarm ‖ *f* cloud
nuvoló·so -sa [s] *adj* cloudy
nuziale *adj* wedding, nuptial
nuzialità *f* marriage rate

O

O, o [o] *m* & *f* thirteenth letter of the Italian alphabet
o *conj* or; now; **o . . . o** either . . . or; whether . . . or ‖ *interj* oh!
òa·si *f* (**-si**) oasis
obbediènte *adj* var of **ubbidiente**
obbediènza *f* obedience
obbedire §176 *tr* & *intr* var of **ubbidire**
obbiettare (**obbiètto**) *tr* & *intr* var of **obiettare**
obbligare §209 (**òbbligo**) *tr* to oblige; to compel, to force ‖ *ref* to obligate oneself
obbligatissi·mo -ma *adj* much obliged
obbligatò·rio -ria *adj* (**-ri -rie**) compulsory, obligatory
obbligazióne *f* obligation; burden; (com) debenture, bond
obbligazioni·sta *mf* (**-sti -ste**) bondholder
òbbli·go *m* (**-ghi**) obligation; duty; **d'obbligo** obligatory, mandatory; **fare d'obbligo a qlcu** + *inf* to be necessary for s.o. to + *inf, e.g.,* **gli fa d'obbligo lavorare** it is necessary for him to work
obbrò·brio *m* (**-bri**) opprobrium, disgrace; **obbrobri** insults
obbrobrió·so -sa [s] *adj* opprobrious, disgraceful
obeli·sco *m* (**-schi**) obelisk
obera·to -ta *adj* overburdened
obesità *f* obesity
obè·so -sa *adj* obese, stout
òbice *m* howitzer
obiettare (**obiètto**) *tr* & *intr* to argue; to object
obietti·vo -va *adj* & *m* objective
obiettóre *m* objector; **obiettore di coscienza** conscientious objector
obiezióne *f* objection
obitò·rio *m* (**-ri**) morgue
oblare (**òblo**) *tr* to willingly pay (*a fine*)
obla·tóre -trice *mf* donor
oblazióne *f* donation; (eccl) oblation; (law) payment of a fine
obliare §119 *tr* (lit) to forget
oblì·o *m* (**-i**) (lit) oblivion
oblì·quo -qua *adj* oblique
obliterare (**oblìtero**) *tr* to obliterate, cancel
o·blò *m* (**-blò**) (naut) porthole; **oblò di accesso** door (*of space capsule*)

oblun·go -ga *adj* (**-ghi -ghe**) oblong
òbo·e *m* (**-e**) oboe
oboi·sta *mf* (**-sti -ste**) oboist
òbolo *m* mite
ò·ca *f* (**-che**) goose; gander
ocarina *f* ocarina, sweet potato
occasionale *adj* chance; immediate (*cause*)
occasionare (**occasióno**) *tr* to occasion
occasióne *f* occasion; opportunity; ground, pretext; bargain; **all'occasione** on occasion; **d'occasione** second-hand; occasional (*verses*)
occhiàia *f* eye socket; **occhiaie** rings under the eyes
occhia·làio *m* (**-lài**) optician
occhiale *adj* eye, ocular ‖ **occhiali** *mpl* glasses; goggles; **occhiali antisole** sunglasses; **occhiali a stringinaso** nose glasses
occhialétto *m* lorgnon; monocle
occhiata *f* glance
occhieggiare §290 (**occhiéggio**) *tr* to eye ‖ *intr* to peep
occhièllo *m* buttonhole; boutonniere; eyelet; half title; subhead
occhièra *f* eyecup
òc·chio *m* (**-chi**) eye; speck of grease (*in soup*); handle (*of scissors*); ring (*of stirrup*); (typ) face; (fig) bit; **a occhio e croce** at a rough guess; **a quattr'occhi** in private; **battere gli occhi** to blink; **cavarsi gli occhi** to strain one's eyes; **dar nell'occhio** to attract attention; **di buon occhio** favorably; **fare l'occhio a** to get used to; **fare tanto d'occhi** to be amazed, to open one's eyes wide; **lasciare gli occhi su** to covet; **non chiudere un occhio** not to sleep a wink; **occhio!** watch out!; **occhio della testa** outrageous price; **occhio di bue** (naut) porthole; **occhio di cubia** (naut) hawsehole; **occhio di pavone** (zool) peacock butterfly; **occhio di triglia** sheep's eyes; **occhio pesto** black eye; **occhio pollino** corn (*on toes*); **tenere d'occhio** to keep an eye on
occhiolino *m* small eye; **far l'occhiolino** to wink
occidentale *adj* western, occidental
occidènte *adj* (poet) setting (*sun*) ‖ *m* west, occident

occìpite *m* occipital bone

occlusióne *f* occlusion

occlusì·vo -va *adj & f* occlusive

occlu·so -sa *adj* occluded

occorrènte *adj* necessary ǁ *m* necessary; (lit) occurrence

occorrènza *f* necessity; **all'occorrenza** if need be

occórrere §139 *intr* (ESSERE) to happen; (with *dat*) to need, e.g., **gli occorre dell'olio** he needs oil ǁ *impers* (ESSERE)—**occorre** it is necessary

occultaménto *m* concealment

occultare *tr & ref* to hide

occul·to -ta *adj* occult; (lit) hidden

occupante *adj* occupying ǁ *m* occupant

occupare (òccupo) *tr* to occupy; to employ ǁ *ref* to take employment; **occuparsi di** to busy oneself with, to mind; to attend to

occupa·to -ta *adj* occupied; busy

occupazionale *adj* occupational

occupazióne *f* occupation

oceàni·co -ca *adj* (-ci -che) oceanic

ocèano *m* ocean

òcra *f* ocher

oculare *adj* ocular; see **testimone** ǁ *m* eyepiece

oculatézza *f* circumspection, prudence

ocula·to -ta *adj* circumspect, prudent

oculi·sta *mf* (-sti -ste) oculist

od *conj* or

odali·sca *f* (-sche) odalisque

òde *f* ode

odepòri·co -ca (-ci -che) *adj* (lit) travel ǁ *m* (lit) travelogue

odiare §287 (òdio) *tr* to hate

odièr·no -na *adj* today's, current

ò·dio -a (-dì) hatred; **avere in odio** to hate; **essere in odio a** to be hated by

odió·so -sa [s] *adj* hateful, odious

odissèa *f* odyssey ǁ **Odissea** *f* Odyssey

Odissèo *m* Odysseus

odontoia·tra *mf* (-tri -tre) doctor of dental surgery, dentist

odontoiatrìa *f* odontology, dentistry

odorare (odóro) *tr & intr* to smell

odora·to -ta *adj* (poet) fragrant ǁ *m* smell

odóre *m* smell, odor, scent; **cattivo odore** bad odor; **odori** herbs, spice

odoró·so -sa [s] *adj* odorous, fragrant

offèndere §148 *tr & intr* to offend ǁ *ref* to take offense

offensì·vo -va *adj & f* offensive

offensóre *m* offender

offerènte *mf* bidder; **miglior offerente** highest bidder

offèrta *f* offer; offering, donation; (at an auction) bid; (com) supply

offésa [s] *f* offense; wrongdoing; ravage (of time); **da offesa** (mil) offensive; **recarsi a offesa** qlco to regard s.th as offensive

officìna *f* shop, workshop; **officina meccanica** machine shop

offició·so -sa [s] *adj* helpful, obliging

offrire §207 *tr* to offer; to sponsor (a radio or TV program); to dedicate (a book); to bid (at an auction); (com) to tender ǁ *ref* to offer oneself, to volunteer

offuscare §197 *tr* to darken, obscure; to obfuscate; to dim (mind; eyes) ǁ *ref* to grow dark; to grow dim

oftàlmi·co -ca *adj* (-ci -che) opthalmic

oftalmòlo·go -ga *mf* (-gi -ghe) ophthalmologist

oggettività *f* objectivity

oggettì·vo -va *adj & m* objective

oggètto *m* object; subject, argument; article; **oggetti preziosi** valuables

òggi *m* today; **dall'oggi al domani** suddenly; overnight ǁ *adv* today; **d'oggi in poi** henceforth; **oggi a otto** a week hence; **oggi come oggi** at present; **oggi è un anno** one year ago

oggidì *m invar & adv* nowadays

oggigiórno *m invar & adv* nowadays

ogìva *f* ogive, pointed arch; nose cone

ógni *adj indef invar* each; every, e.g., **ogni due giorni** every two days; **ogni cosa** everything; **ogni tanto** every now and then; **per ogni dove** (lit) everywhere

ogniqualvòlta *conj* whenever

Ognissan·ti *m* (-ti) All Saints' Day

ognitèmpo *adj invar* all-weather

-ógno·lo -la *suf adj* -ish, e.g., **giallognolo** yellowish

ognóra *adv* (lit) always

ognu·no -na *adj* (obs) each ǁ *pron* each one, everyone

oh *interj* oh!

òhi *interj* ouch!

ohibò *interj* fie!

ohimè *interj* alas!

ohm *m* (ohm) ohm

olanda *f* Dutch linen ǁ **l'Olanda** *f* Holland

olandése [s] *adj* Dutch ǁ *m* Dutch (language); Dutchman; Dutch cheese ǁ *f* Dutch woman

oleandro *m* oleander

oleà·rio -ria *adj* (-ri -rie) oil

olea·to -ta *adj* oiled

oleifì·cio *m* (-ci) oil mill

oleodótto *m* pipeline

oleó·so -sa [s] *adj* oily

olezzare [ddzz] (olézzo) *intr* (lit) to smell sweet

olézzo [ddzz] *m* perfume, fragrance

olfatto *m* smell

oliare §287 (òlio) *tr* to oil

oliatóre *m* oiler, oil can

olìbano *m* frankincense

olièra *f* cruet

oligarchìa *f* oligarchy

olimpìade *f* Olympiad

olìmpi·co -ca *adj* (-ci -che) Olympic; Olympian

olimpiòni·co -ca *adj* (-ci -che) Olympic ǁ *mf* Olympic athlete

ò·lio -a (-li) oil; **ad olio** oil, e.g., **quadro ad olio** oil painting; **olio di fegato di merluzzo** cod-liver oil; **olio di lino** linseed oil; **olio di ricino** castor oil; **olio solare** sun-tan lotion

olìva *f* olive

oliva·stro -stra *adj* livid; swarthy ǁ *m* wild olive (tree)

olivéto *m* olive grove

Olivièro *m* Oliver

olivo *m* olive tree

ólmo *m* elm tree

olocàu·sto -sta *adj* (lit) burnt; (lit) sacrificed ‖ *m* holocaust; sacrifice

ològra·fo -fa *adj* holographic

olóna *f* sailcloth, canvas

oltracciò *adv* besides

oltraggiare §290 *tr* to outrage; to insult

oltràg·gio *m* (-gi) outrage; offense; ravages (*of time*); **oltraggio al pudore** offense to public morals; **oltraggio al tribunale** contempt of court

oltraggió·so -sa [s] *adj* outrageous

oltranza *f*—**a oltranza** to the bitter end

oltranzi·sta *mf* (-sti -ste) (pol) extremist

óltre *adv* beyond; ahead; further; **oltre a** apart from; in addition to; **troppo oltre** too far ‖ *prep* beyond; past; more than

oltrecortina *adj invar* beyond-the-iron-curtain ‖ *m* country beyond the iron curtain

oltremare *m invar* country overseas ‖ *adv* overseas

oltremisura *adv* (lit) beyond measure

oltremòdo *adv* (lit) exceedingly

oltrepassare *tr* to overstep; to cross (*a river*); to be beyond (. . . *years old*); (sports) to overtake

oltretómba *m*—**l'oltretomba** the life beyond

omàg·gio *m* (-gi) homage; compliment; **in omaggio** complimentary; **rendere omaggio a** to pay tribute to

òmaro *m* Norway lobster

ombeli·co *m* (-chi) navel

ómbra *f* shade; shadow; umbrage; form, mass; **nemmeno per ombra** not in the least

ombreggiare §290 (**ombréggio**) *tr* to shade

ombrèlla *f* shade (*of trees*); (bot) umbel; (coll) umbrella

ombrel·làio *m* (-lài) umbrella maker

ombrellino *m* parasol

ombrèllo *m* umbrella

ombrellóne *m* beach umbrella

ombró·so -sa [s] *adj* shady; touchy; skittish (*horse*)

omelette *f* (**omelette**) omelet

omelìa *f* homily

omeopàti·co -ca (-ci -che) *adj* homeopathic ‖ *m* homeopathist

omèri·co -ca *adj* (-ci -che) Homeric

òmero *m* (anat) humerus; (lit) shoulder

omertà *f* code of silence of underworld

ométtere §198 *tr* to omit

ométto *m* little man; (coll) clothes hanger; (billiards) pin; (archit) king post

omici·da (-di -de) *adj* homicidal, murderous ‖ *mf* homicide, murderer

omici·dio *m* (-di) homicide, murder; **omicidio colposo** (law) manslaughter; **omicidio doloso** (law) first-degree murder

ominó·so -sa [s] *adj* (lit) ominous

omissióne *f* omission

òmni·bus *m* (-bus) omnibus; way train

omnisciènte *adj* all-knowing, omniscient

omogène·o -a *adj* homogeneous

omologare §209 (**omòlogo**) *tr* to con-firm, ratify; to probate (*a will*); (sports) to validate

omòni·mo -ma *adj* of the same name ‖ *m* namesake; homonym

omosessuale [s] *adj & mf* homosexual

ón·cia *f* (-ce) ounce; **oncia a oncia** little by little

ónda *f* wave; **a onde** wavy; wavily; **essere in onda** (rad, telv) to be on the air; **farsi le onde** to have one's hair waved; **mettere in onda** (rad, telv) to put on the air; **onda crespa** whitecap; **onda portante** (rad, telv) carrier wave

ondata *f* wave, billow; gust (*e.g., of smoke*); rush (*of blood*); wave (*of cold weather*)

ondatra *f* muskrat

ónde *pron* from which; of which ‖ *adv* whereof; hence; (poet) wherefrom ‖ *prep* **onde** + *inf* in order to ‖ *conj* **onde** + *subj* so that

ondeggiante *adj* waving, swaying

ondeggiare §290 (**ondéggio**) *intr* to wave, sway; to waver

ondina *f* mermaid; (mythol) undine; (mythol) mermaid

ondó·so -sa [s] *adj* wavy

ondulare (**óndulo & òndulo**) *tr* to wave; to corrugate (*e.g., metal*) ‖ *intr* to sway

ondula·to -ta *adj* wavy (*hair*); corrugated (*e.g., metal*); bumpy (*road*)

ondulazióne *f* undulation; **ondulazione permanente** permanent wave

-óne -óna *suf m* big, e.g., **librone** big book; **dormigliona** big sleeper ‖ **-óne** *suf m* (applies to both sexes) big, e.g., **donnone** *m* big woman

ònere *m* (lit) onus, burden

oneró·so -sa [s] *adj* onerous, burdensome

onestà *f* honesty; (poet) modesty

onè·sto -sta *adj* honest; fair; (poet) modest ‖ *m* moderate amount; honest gain; honest person

ònice *m* onyx

onnipossènte & onnipotènte *adj* almighty, omnipotent

onnisciènte *adj* omniscient

onniveggènte *adj* all-seeing

onnìvo·ro -ra *adj* omnivorous

onomàsti·co -ca *adj* (-ci -che) *adj* onomastic ‖ *m* name day ‖ *f* study of proper names

onomatopèi·co -ca *adj* (-ci -che) onomatopeic

onoràbile *adj* honorable

onoranza *f* honor; **onoranze** homage; **onoranze funebri** obsequies

onorare (**onóro**) *tr* to honor ‖ *ref* to deem it an honor

onorà·rio -ria (-ri -rie) *adj* honorary ‖ *m* fee, honorarium

onora·to -ta *adj* honored; honest; honorable

onóre *m* honor; **d'onore** honest, e.g., **uomo d'onore** honest man; **estremi onori** last rites; **fare gli onori di casa** to receive guests; **fare onore a** to honor; **onore al merito** credit where credit is due; **onor del mento** (lit) beard

onoré·vole *adj* honorable || *m* honorable member (*of parliament*)

onorificènza *f* dignity; decoration

onorífi·co -ca *adj* (-ci -che) honorific; honorary (*e.g., title*)

ónta *f* dishonor, shame; **a onta di** in spite of; **avere onta** to be ashamed; **fare onta a** to bring shame upon; **in onta a** against

ontano *m* alder

O.N.U. (acronym) *f* (**Organizzazione delle Nazioni Unite**) United Nations, U.N.

onu·sto -sta *adj* (poet) laden

opa·co -ca *adj* (-chi -che) opaque

opale *m* opal

opalí·no -na *adj* opaline || *f* shiny cardboard; luster (*fabric*)

òpera *f* work; organization, foundation; day's work; (mus) opera; **mettere in opera** to install; to start work on; to make ready; to begin using; **opera di consultazione** reference work; **opera morta** (naut) upper works; **opera viva** (naut) quickwork; **per opera di** thanks to

ope·ràio -ràia (-rài -ràie) *adj* workman's, worker's; working || *m* workman, worker; **operaio a cottimo** pieceworker; **operaio a giornata** day laborer; **operaio specializzato** craftsman, skilled workman || *f* workwoman

operante *adj* actively engaged; operative

operare (**òpero**) *tr* to operate; to work (*a miracle*); (surg) to operate on || *intr* to operate; to be actively engaged || *ref* to be operated on; to occur, take place

operati·vo -va *adj* operative; operations, e.g., **ricerca operativa** operations research

opera·to -ta *adj* operated; embossed || *m* behavior; patient operated on

opera·tóre -trice *mf* operator || *m* (mov) cameraman

operatò·rio -ria *adj* (-ri -rie) surgical (*operation*); operating (*room*); (math) operational

operazióne *f* operation; transaction

operétta *f* short work; (mus) operetta

operìsti·co -ca *adj* (-ci -che) operatic

operosi·tà [s] *f* (-tà) industry

operó·so -sa [s] *adj* industrious; active

opi·mo -ma *adj* (lit) fat; rich, fertile

opinare *intr* to opine, deem

opinióne *f* opinion

opòs·sum *m* (-sum) opossum

oppia·to -ta *adj* opiate (*mixed with opium*); dulled by drugs || *m* opiate (*medicine containing opium*)

òppio *m* opium

oppiòmane *adj* opium-eating; opium-smoking || *mf* opium addict

oppórre §218 *tr* to oppose; to offer, put up (*resistance*) || *ref* to be opposite; **opporsi a** to oppose, to be against

opportuni·sta *mf* (-sti -ste) opportunist

opportuni·tà *f* (-tà) opportunity; opportuneness

opportu·no -na *adj* opportune

opposi·tóre -trice *mf* opponent

opposizióne *f* opposition; (law) appeal; **fare opposizione a** to object to

oppó·sto -sta *adj* opposite; contrary || *m* opposite; **all'opposto** on the contrary

oppressióne *f* oppression

oppressi·vo -va *adj* oppressive

opprès·so -sa *adj* oppressed; overcome, overwhelmed || **oppressi** *mpl* oppressed people

oppressóre *m* oppressor

opprimènte *adj* oppressive

opprimere §131 *tr* to oppress; to overcome, overwhelm; to weigh down

oppugnare *tr* to refute, contradict

oppure *adv* otherwise || *conj* or else; or rather

optare (**òpto**) *intr* to choose; (com) to exercise an option

optometri·sta *mf* (-sti -ste) optometrist

opulèn·to -ta *adj* opulent

opùscolo *m* booklet, brochure, pamphlet; **opuscolo d'informazioni** instruction manual

opzióne *f* option

ór *adv* now; **or ora** right now; **or sono** ago

óra *f* hour; time; period (*in school*); **alla buon'ora!** finally!; **a ore by the** hour; **a tarda ora** late; **che ora è?** or **che ore sono?** what time is it?; **da un'ora all'altra** from one moment to the next; **dell'ultima ora** up-to-date (*news*); **di buon'ora** early; early in the morning; **di ora in ora** at any moment; **d'ora in avanti** from this moment on; **d'ora in poi** from now on; **far l'ora** to kill time; **fin ora** until now; **non vedere l'ora di** + *inf* to be hardly able to wait until + *ind*; **ora di cena** suppertime; **ora di punta** rush hour, peak hour; **ora legale** daylight-saving time; **ore piccole** late hours; **un'ora di orologio** one full hour || *adv* now

oràcolo *m* oracle

òra·fo -fa *adj* goldsmith's || *m* goldsmith

orale *adj* & *m* oral

oralménte *adv* orally; by word of mouth

oramài *adv* now; already

oran·go *m* (-ghi) orangutan

orà·rio -ria (-ri -rie) *adj* hourly; per hour; clockwise || *m* timetable; schedule; roster; **essere in orario** to be on time; **orario di lavoro** working hours; **orario d'ufficio** office hours

ora·tóre -trice *mf* orator

oratò·rio -ria (-ri -rie) *adj* oratorical || *m* (eccl) oratory; (mus) oratorio || *f* oratory, public speaking

orazióne *f* oration; prayer; **orazione domenicale** Lord's Prayer

orbare (**òrbo**) *tr* (lit) to bereave; (lit) to deprive

òrbe *f* (lit) orb; (lit) world

orbène *adv* well

òrbita f orbit; (fig) sphere
orbitare (**òrbito**) intr to orbit
orbitazióne f orbiting
òr·bo -ba adj bereaved; deprived; blind ‖ m blind man
òrca f killer whale
Òrcadi fpl Orkney Islands
orchèstra f orchestra; band; orchestra pit
orchestrale adj orchestral ‖ mf orchestra player, orchestra performer
orchestrare (**orchèstro**) tr to orchestrate; (fig) to organize
orchestrina f dance band; dance-band music
orchidèa f orchid
ór·cio m (-ci) jar, jug, crock
orciòlo m—a oriciolo puckered up (lips)
òr·co m (-chi) ogre
òrda f horde
ordàlia f (hist) ordeal
ordigno m gadget, contrivance; tool; ordigno esplosivo infernal machine
ordinale adj & m ordinal
ordinaménto m disposition; regulation
ordinanza f ordinance; (mil) orderly; d'ordinanza regulation (e.g., uniform); in ordinanza (mil) in formation
ordinare (**órdino**) tr to order; to straighten up; to range; to regulate; to ordain; to trim
ordinà·rio -ria (-ri -rie) adj ordinary; plain; inferior; workday (suit) ‖ m ordinary; full professor; d'ordinario ordinarily, usually
ordina·to -ta adj orderly, tidy; ordained ‖ f ordinate; straightening up; (aer) frame; (naut) bulkhead
ordinazióne f order; ordination
órdine m order; row; tier; series (e.g., of years); college (e.g., of surgeons); nature (of things); (law) warrant, writ; in ordine a concerning; ordine del giorno order of the day; ordine d'idee train of thought
ordire §176 tr to warp (cloth); to hatch (a plot)
ordi·to -ta adj plotted ‖ m warp (of fabric)
orécchia f ear; dog-ear; con le orecchie tese all ears
orecchiale m earphone (of sonar equipment)
orecchiétta f (anat) auricle
orecchino m earring
oréc·chio m (-chi) ear; hearing; dog-ear; moldboard; fare orecchio da mercante to turn a deaf ear ‖ m (orécchia fpl) (archaic) ear
orecchióne m long-eared bat; (mil) trunnion; orecchioni (pathol) mumps
oréfice m goldsmith; jeweler
oreficeria f goldsmith shop; jewelry shop
orfanézza f orphanage (condition)
òrfa·no -na adj orphaned ‖ mf orphan
orfanotrò·fio m (-fi) orphanage (institution)
Orfèo m Orpheus
organdi m organdy
organétto m hand organ; mouth organ; organetto di Barberia hand organ

orgàni·co -ca (-ci -che) adj organic ‖ m personnel, staff ‖ f (mil) organization
organigram·ma m (-mi) organization chart
organino m hand organ, barrel organ
organismo m organism
organi·sta mf (-sti -ste) organist
organizzare | ddzz| tr to organize
organizza·tóre -trice [ddzz] mf organizer
organizzazióne [ddzz] f organization; Organizzazione delle Nazioni Unite United Nations
òrgano m organ; part (of a machine); organo di stampa mouthpiece
orgasmo m orgasm; agitation, excitement
òr·gia f (-ge) orgy
orgó·glio m (-gli) pride
orgoglio·so -sa [s] adj proud
orientale adj & mf oriental; Oriental
orientaménto m orientation; bearing; trend; trim (of sail); orientamento scolastico e professionale aptitude test; vocational guidance
orientare (**oriènto**) tr to orient; to guide; to trim (a sail) ‖ ref to find one's bearings
oriènte m orient; grand'oriente grand lodge ‖ Oriente m Orient, East; Estremo Oriente Far East; Medio Oriente Middle East; Vicino Oriente Near East
orifi·zio m (-zi) orifice, opening
origano m wild marjoram
originale adj original; odd ‖ mf queer character, odd person ‖ m original; copy (for printer)
originare (**orìgino**) tr to originate ‖ intr (ESSERE) & ref to originate
originà·rio -ria adj (-ri -rie) originating; native; original
origine f origin; source; extraction
origliare §280 intr to eavesdrop
origlière m (lit) pillow
orina f var of urina
orinale m chamber pot, urinal
orinare tr & intr to urinate
orina·tóio m (-tói) urinal, comfort station
oriòlo m (orn) oriole
oriun·do -da adj native ‖ m (sports) native son
orizzontale [ddzz] adj horizontal ‖ orizzontali fpl horizontal words (in crossword puzzle)
orizzontare [ddzz] (**orizzónto**) tr to orient ‖ ref to get one's bearings
orizzónte | ddzz| m horizon
Orlando m Roland
orlare (**órlo**) tr to hem, border; orlare a zigzag to pink
órlo m edge; brim; hem, border; (fig) brink; orlo a giorno hemstitch
órma f footprint; orme remains, vestiges; calcare le orme di to follow the footsteps of
ormeggiare §290 (**orméggio**) tr & ref (naut) to moor
ormég·gio m (-gi) mooring; mollare gli ormeggi (naut) to cast off
ormóne m hormone

ornamentale *adj* ornamental
ornaménto *m* ornament
ornare (órno) *tr* to adorn
orna·to -ta *adj* adorned; ornate ‖ *m* ornament; ornamental design
ornitòlo·go -ga *mf* (-gi -ghe) ornithologist
òro *m* gold; (fig) money; **d'oro** gold, golden; **ori** gold objects; jewels; suit of Neapolitan cards corresponding to diamonds; **oro zecchino** pure gold; **per tutto l'oro del mondo** for all the world
orologerìa *f* watchmaking; clockmaking; watchmaker's shop
orolo·giàio -ia *m* (-giài) watchmaker; clockmaker
orolò·gio *m* (-gi) watch; clock; **orologio a pendolo** clock; **orologio a polvere** sandglass; **orologio a scatto** digital clock; **orologio da polso** wristwatch; **orologio della morte** deathwatch; **orologio solare** sundial
oròscopo *m* horoscope
orpèllo *m* Dutch gold; (fig) tinsel
orrèndo *m* horrible
orrìbile *adj* horrible
òrri·do -da *adj* horrid ‖ *m* horridness; gorge, ravine
orripilante *adj* bloodcurdling, hair-raising
orróre *m* horror; awe; **aver in** or **per orrore** to loath; **fare orrore a** to horrify
órsa *f* she-bear ‖ **Orsa** *f*—**Orsa maggiore** Great Bear; **Orsa minore** Little Bear
orsacchiòtto *m* bear cub; Teddy bear
ór·so -sa *mf* bear; **orso bianco** polar bear; **orso grigio** grizzly bear ‖ *f* see **orsa**
orsù *interj* come on!
ortàg·gio *m* (-gi) vegetable
ortàglia *f* vegetable garden; vegetable
ortènsia *f* hydrangea
orti·ca *f* (-che) nettle; hives
orticària *f* hives, nettle rash
orticoltóre *m* truck gardener; horticulturist
òrto *m* garden, vegetable garden; (lit) sunrise; **orto botanico** botanical garden; **orto di guerra** Victory garden
ortodòs·so -sa *adj* orthodox ‖ *m* Greek Catholic
ortografìa *f* orthography; spelling
ortola·no -na *adj* garden ‖ *m* truck farmer, gardener
ortopèdi·co -ca (-ci -che) *adj* orthopedic ‖ *m* orthopedist
òrza *f* bowline; windward; **andare all'orza** to sail close to the wind
orzaiòlo [dz] *m* (pathol) sty
orzare (òrzo) *intr* to sail close to the wind; to luff
orzata [dz] *f* orgeat
orzata *f* (naut) luff
òrzo [dz] *m* barley
osannare *intr* to cry or sing hosanna; **osannare a** to acclaim, applaud
osare (òso) *intr* to dare
osceni·tà *f* (-tà) obscenity
oscè·no -na *adj* obscene; (coll) horrible
oscillante *adj* oscillating

oscillare *intr* to oscillate; to swing; to wobble; to waver, hesitate
oscillazióne *f* oscillation; fluctuation
oscuraménto *m* darkening, dimming; blackout
oscurare *tr* to darken; to blot out; to dim ‖ *ref* to get dark; **oscurarsi in volto** to frown
oscuri·tà *f* (-tà) obscurity; darkness; ignorance
oscu·ro -ra *adj* obscure, dark; opaque (*style*) ‖ *m* obscurity, darkness; **essere all'oscuro di** to be in the dark about
osmòsi *f* osmosis
ospedale *m* hospital
ospedalière *m* hospital worker
ospedaliè·ro -ra *adj* hospital ‖ *m* hospitaler
ospedalizzare [ddzz] *tr* to hospitalize
ospitale *adj* hospitable ‖ *m* hospital
ospitali·tà *f* (-tà) hospitality
ospitare (òspito) *tr* to lodge, shelter, accommodate; to entertain; (sports) to play (*an opposing team*) at home
òspite *mf* host; guest; **andarsene insalutato ospite** to take French leave; **ospiti** company (*guests at home*)
ospi·zio *m* (-zi) hospice; hostel; (lit) hospitality; **ospizio dei vecchi** nursing home; **ospizio di mendicità** poorhouse
ossatura *f* frame, framework; skeleton
òsse·o -a *adj* bony
ossequènte *adj* (lit) respectful; (lit) reverent
ossequiare §287 (ossèquio) *tr* to pay one's respects to; to honor
ossè·quio *m* (-qui) respect; reverence; **i miei ossequi** my best regards; **in ossequio a** in conformity with; **porgere i propri ossequi a** to pay one's respects to
ossequió·so -sa [s] *adj* obsequious; respectful
osservante *adj & m* observant
osservanza *f* observance; deference
osservare (ossèrvo) *tr* to observe
osserva·tóre -trice *adj* observing, observant ‖ *m* observer
osservatò·rio *m* (-ri) observatory
osservazióne *f* observation; rebuke
ossessionare (ossessióno) *tr* to obsess; to harass, bedevil
ossessióne *f* obsession
ossès·so -sa *adj* possessed ‖ *mf* person possessed
ossìa *conj* or; to wit
ossidante *adj* oxidizing ‖ *m* oxidizer
ossidare (òssido) *tr & ref* to oxidize
òssido *m* oxide; **ossido di carbone** carbon monoxide
ossìdulo *m* protoxide; **ossidulo di azoto** nitrous oxide
ossificare §197 (ossìfico) *tr & ref* to ossify
ossigenare (ossìgeno) *tr* to oxygenate; to bleach (*the hair*); to infuse strength into ‖ *ref* to bleach (*the hair*)
ossìgeno *m* oxygen; (fig) transfusion, shot in the arm
ossìto·no -na *adj & m* oxytone

òs·so *m* (-si) bone (*of animal*); stone (*of fruit*); **osso di balena** whalebone; **osso di seppia** cuttlebone; **osso duro da rodere** hard nut to crack; **osso sacro** sacrum; **rimetterci l'osso del collo** to be thoroughly ruined; **rompersi l'osso del collo** to break one's neck ‖ *m* (-sa *fpl*) bone (*of a person*); **avere le ossa rotte** to be dead-tired

ossu·to -ta *adj* bony; scrawny

ostacolare (ostàcolo) *tr* to hinder; to obstruct; **ostacolare l'azione** (sports) to interfere

ostàcolo *m* obstacle; obstruction; (golf) hazard; (sports) hurdle

ostàg·gio *m* (-gi) hostage

ostare (òsto) *intr* (lit) to be in the way; (with *dat*) to hinder; **nulla osta** no objection, permission granted

òste ostéssa *mf* innkeeper ‖ **oste** *m* & *f* (lit) army in the field ‖ *m* (poet) enemy

ostèllo *m* hostel; (poet) abode

ostentare (ostènto) *tr* to show, display; to affect, feign

ostenta·to -ta *adj* affected, ostentatious

ostentazióne *f* show, ostentation

osteopatìa *f* osteopathy

osterìa *f* tavern, inn, taproom

ostéssa *f* see **oste**

ostètri·ca *f* (-che) midwife

ostetrìcia *f* obstetrics

ostètri·co -ca (-ci -che) *adj* obstetrical ‖ *m* obstetrician ‖ *f* see **ostetrica**

òstia *f* wafer; Host; sacrificial victim

òsti·co -ca *adj* (-ci -che) hard; (lit) repugnant, distasteful

ostile *adj* hostile

ostili·tà *f* (-tà) hostility

ostinare *ref* to be stubborn; to persist

ostina·to -ta *adj* obstinate; persistent

ostinazióne *f* obstinacy

ostracismo *m* ostracism; **dare l'ostracismo a** to ostracize

ostracizzare [ddzz] *tr* (poet) to ostracize

òstri·ca *f* (-che) oyster; **ostrica perlifera** pearl oyster

ostri·càio *m* (-cài) oyster bed; oyster-man

ostruire §176 *tr* to obstruct; to stop up

ostruzióne *f* obstruction

Otèllo *m* Othello

otorinolaringoia·tra *mf* (-tri -tre) ear, nose, and throat specialist, otorhino-laryngologist

ótre *f* wineskin; **otre di vento** windbag (*person*)

ottàni·co -ca *adj* (-ci -che) octane

ottano *m* octane

ottanta *adj, m* & *pron* eighty

ottantènne *adj* eighty-year-old ‖ *mf* eighty-year-old person

ottantèsi·mo -ma *adj, m* & *pron* eightieth

ottantina *f* about eighty; **essere sull'ottantina** to be about eighty years old

ottava *f* octave

Ottaviano *m* Octavian

ottavino *m* (mus) piccolo; (com) commission of ⅛ of 1%

otta·vo -va *adj* & *pron* eighth ‖ *m* eighth; octavo ‖ *f* see **ottava**

ottemperare (ottèmpero) *intr* (with *dat*) to obey; **ottemperare a** to comply with

ottenebrare (ottènebro) *tr* to becloud

ottenére §271 *tr* to obtain, get

ottétto *m* octet

òtti·co -ca (-ci -che) *adj* optic(al) ‖ *m* optician ‖ *f* optics

ottimismo *m* optimism

ottimi·sta *mf* (-sti -ste) optimist

ottimìsti·co -ca *adj* (-ci -che) optimistic

òtti·mo -ma *adj* very good, excellent ‖ *m* best; highest rating

òtto *adj* & *pron* eight; **le otto** eight o'clock ‖ *m* eight; eighth (*in dates*); (sports) racing shell with eight oarsmen; **otto giorni** a week; **otto volante** roller coaster

ottóbre *m* October

ottocené·sco -sca *adj* (-schi -sche) nineteenth-century

ottocènto *adj, m* & *pron* eight hundred ‖ **l'Ottocento** the nineteenth century

ottoma·no -na *adj* & *m* Ottoman ‖ *m* ottoman (*fabric*) ‖ *f* ottoman (*sofa*)

ottomila *adj, m* & *pron* eight thousand

ottoname *m* brassware

ottonare (ottóno) *tr* to coat with brass

ottóne *m* brass; **ottoni** (mus) brasses ‖ **Ottone** *m* Otto

ottuagenà·rio -ria *adj* & *mf* (-ri -rie) octogenerian

ottùndere §208 *tr* (fig) to deaden; (lit) to blunt

otturare *tr* to fill; to plug; to stop; to obstruct, stop up (*e.g., a channel*) ‖ *ref* to clog up

otturatóre *m* breechblock; (phot, mov) shutter; (mach) cutoff (*of cylinder*)

otturazióne *f* filling (*of tooth*)

ottu·so -sa *adj* obtuse; blunt

ovàia *f* ovary

ovale *adj* oval ‖ *m* oval; oval face

ovatta *f* wadding; absorbent cotton

ovattare *tr* to pad, wad; to muffle

ovazióne *f* ovation

óve *adv* (lit) where ‖ *conj* (lit) if; (poet) while

òvest *m* west

Ovìdio *m* Ovid

ovile *m* sheepcote, fold

ovi·no -na *adj* ovine ‖ **ovini** *mpl* sheep

òvo *m* var of **uovo**

ovoidale *adj* egg-shaped

òvulo *m* pill shaped like an egg; (biol) ovum; (bot) ovule

ovùnque *adv* (lit) wherever; (lit) every-where

ovvéro *conj* or; to wit

ovvìa *interj* come on!

ovviare §119 *intr*—(with *dat*) to obviate

òv·vio -via *adj* (-vi -vie) obvious

oziare §287 **(òzio)** *intr* to idle, loiter

ò·zio *m* (-zi) idleness; leisure

oziosi·tà [s] *f* (-tà) idleness

oziò·so -sa [s] *adj* idle; useless, vain

ozòno [dz] *m* ozone

P, p [pi] *m & f* fourteenth letter of the Italian alphabet

pacare §197 *tr* (poet) to placate

pacatézza *f* tranquillity, serenity

paca·to -ta *adj* serene, tranquil

pac·ca *f* (-che) slap

pacchétto *m* parcel, package; book (*of matches*); pack (*of cigarettes*)

pàcchia *f* (coll) hearty meal; (coll) godsend, windfall

pacchia·no -na *adj* boorish, uncouth ‖ *mf* boor

pacciamantura *f* mulching

pacciame *m* mulch

pac·co *m* (-chi) package; **pacchi postali** parcel post (*service*); **pacco dono** gift package; **pacco postale** parcel by mail

paccottiglia *f* shoddy goods, junk; trinkets

pace *f* peace; **lasciare in pace** to leave alone; **mettersi il cuore in pace** to resign oneself

pachidèr·ma *m* (-mi) pachyderm

pachista·no -na *adj & mf* Pakistani

paciè·re -ra *mf* peacemaker

pacificare §197 (**pacifico**) *tr* to pacify; to appease; to mediate ‖ *ref* to make one's peace

pacifica·tóre -trice *adj* pacifying ‖ *mf* peacemaker

pacificazióne *f* pacification; appeasement

pacifi·co -ca (-ci -che) *adj* peaceful, pacific; **è pacifico che** it goes without saying that ‖ *m* peaceable person ‖ **Pacifico** *adj & m* Pacific

pacifismo *m* pacifism

pacifi·sta *mf* (-sti -ste) pacifist

paciccó·ne -na *adj* chubby, easygoing person

padèlla *f* frying pan; bedpan; **cadere dalla padella nella brace** to jump from the frying pan into the fire

padiglióne *m* pavilion; hunting lodge; roof (*of car*); ward (*of a hospital*); (naut) rigging, tackle; **padiglione auricolare** (anat) auricle of the ear

Pàdova *f* Padua

padre *m* father; sire; **padre di famiglia** provider; (law) head of household; **Padre Eterno** Heavenly Father

padreggiare §290 (**padréggio**) *intr* to resemble one's father

padrino *m* godfather; second (*in duel*)

padrona *f* owner, boss, mistress; **padrona di casa** lady of the house

padronale *adj* proprietary; private (*e.g., car*)

padronanza *f* command; **padronanza di sé stesso** self-control

padróne *m* owner, boss, master; **essere padrone di** + *inf* to have the right to + *inf*; **padrone di casa** landlord; **padrone di sé** cool and collected

padroneggiare §290 (**padronéggio**) *tr* to master, control

paesàg·gio *m* (-gi) landscape

paesaggi·sta *mf* (-sti -ste) landscapist

paesa·no -na *adj* country ‖ *mf* villager ‖ *m* countryman ‖ *f* countrywoman; **alla paesana** according to local tradition

paése *m* country; village; **i Paesi Bassi** the Netherlands; (hist) the Low Countries; **mandare a quel paese** to send to blazes

paesi·sta *mf* (-sti -ste) landscapist

paffu·to -ta *adj* chubby, plump

pa·ga *f* (-ghe) salary; wages; repayment; **mala paga** poor pay (*person*)

pagàbile *adj* payable

pagàia *f* paddle

pagaménto *m* payment; **pagamento alla consegna** c.o.d.

paganésimo *m* paganism

paga·no -na *adj & mf* pagan, heathen

pagare §209 *tr* to pay; to pay for; **far pagare** to charge; **pagare di egual moneta** to repay in kind; **pagare il fio** per to pay (the penalty) for; **pagare in natura** to pay in kind; **pagare salato** to pay dearly; **pagare un occhio della testa** to pay through the nose ‖ *intr* to pay

paga·tóre -trice *mf* payer

pagèlla *f* report card

pàg·gio *m* (-gi) page (*boy attendant*)

paghe·rò *m* (-rò) promissory note, I.O.U.

pàgina *f* page (*e.g., of book*)

paginatura *f* pagination

pàglia *f* straw; thatch (*for roof*); **paglia di ferro** steel wool; **paglia di legno** excelsior

pagliac·cé·sco -sca *adj* (-schi -sche) clownish

pagliaccétto *m* rompers

pagliacciata *f* buffoonery, antics

pagliàc·cio *m* (-ci) clown, buffoon; **fare il pagliaccio** to clown

pa·gliàio *m* (-gliài) heap of straw; haystack

paglieric·cio *m* (-ci) straw mattress

paglieri·no -na *adj* straw-colored

pagliétta *f* skimmer, boater; steel wool; (coll) pettifogger

pagnòtta *f* loaf of bread; (coll) bread

pa·go -ga *adj* (-ghi -ghe) satisfied ‖ *f* see **paga**

paguro *m* (zool) hermit crab

pà·io *m* (*fpl* **pàia**) pair, couple; **è un altro paio di maniche** this is a horse of another color; **fare il paio** to match perfectly

paiòlo *m* caldron, kettle; (mil) platform

Pakistan, il Pakistan

pala *f* shovel; blade (*e.g., of turbine*); paddle (*of waterwheel*); peel (*of baker*); **pala d'altare** altarpiece

paladi·no -na *mf* champion ‖ *m* paladin; **farsi paladino di** to champion

palafitta *f* pile dwelling; piles (*to support a structure*)

palafrenière *m* groom

palafréno *m* palfrey

palan·ca *f* (-che) beam, board; (naut)

gangplank; copper coin; **palanche** (coll) money

palanchino *m* palanquin; (naut) pulley

palandrana *f* (joc) long, full coat

palata *f* shovelful; stroke (*of oar*); **a palate** by the bucketful

palatale *adj* & *f* palatal

palati·no **-na** *adj* palatine; (anat) palatal

palato *m* palate

palazzina *f* villa

palazzo *m* palace; large office or government building; mansion; **palazzo dello sport** sports arena; **palazzo di città** city hall; **palazzo di giustizia** courthouse

palchetti·sta (**-sti** **-ste**) *mf* (theat) box-holder || *m* person who lays floors

palchétto *m* shelf; (theat) small box; (journ) box

pal·co *m* (**-chi**) flooring; scaffold; stand, platform; (theat) box; (theat) stage

palcoscèni·co *m* (**-ci**) (theat) stage

palesare (**paléso**) *tr* to reveal, manifest || *ref* to show oneself

palése *adj* plain, manifest; **fare palese** to manifest, reveal

palèstra *f* gymnasium; palestra

palétta *f* small shovel, scoop; blade (*of turbine*)

palettata *f* shovelful

palétto *m* stake; bolt (*of door*)

palificazione *f* pile work (*in the ground for foundation*); line of telephone poles

pà·lio *m* (**-lii**) embroidered cloth (*given as prize*); **metter in palio** to offer as a prize; **palio di Siena** colorful horse-race at Siena

palissandro *m* Brazilian rosewood

palizzata *f* palisade; picket fence

palla *f* ball; bullet; sphere; **dar palla nera a** to blackball; **palla da cannone** cannon ball; **palla di neve** snowball; **prendere la palla al balzo** to seize the opportunity

pallabase *f* baseball

pallacanè·stro *f* (**-stro**) basketball

pallamuro *m* handball

pallanuòto *f* water polo

pallavó·lo *m* (**-lo**) volleyball

palleggiare §290 (**palléggio**) *tr* to toss (*e.g., a javelin*); from one hand to another || *intr* (tennis) to knock a few balls; (soccer) to dribble || *ref*—**palleggiarsi la responsabilità** to shift the responsibility

pallég·gio *m* (**-gi**) (tennis) knocking back and forth; (soccer) dribbling

palliati·vo **-va** *adj* & *m* palliative

pallidézza *f* paleness

pàlli·do **-da** *adj* pale; faint

pallina *f* marble; small ball; **pallina antitarmica** mothball

pallino *m* little ball; (bowling) jack; bullet; **a pallini** polka-dot; **avere il pallino di** to be crazy about; **pallini** buckshot; polka dots

palloncino *m* child's balloon; Chinese lantern

pallóne *m* (soccer) ball; (aer) balloon;

pallone di sbarramento barrage balloon; **pallone gonfiato** (fig) stuffed shirt; **pallone sonda** trial balloon

pallonétto *m* (tennis) lob

pallóre *m* pallor, paleness

pallòttola *f* pellet; ball; bullet

pallottolière *m* abacus

pallovale *f* rugby

palma *f* palm; **tenere in palma di mano** to hold in the highest esteem

palmare *adj* evident, plain

palménto *m* millstone; **mangiare a quattro palmenti** (coll) to stuff oneself eating

palméto *m* palm grove

palmipede *adj* palmate, web-footed

palmi·zio *m* (**-zi**) palm

palmo *m* span; palm (*of hand*); foot (*measure*); **a palmo a palmo** little by little; **restare con un palmo di naso** to be disappointed

palo *m* pole (*of wood or metal*); beam; pile; (soccer, football) goal post; **fare il palo** to be on the lookout (*said of thieves*); **palo indicatore** signpost; **saltare di palo in frasca** to digress

palombaro *m* diver

palómbo *m* dogfish

palpàbile *adj* palpable

palpare *tr* to touch; to palpate

pàlpebra *f* eyelid; **battere le palpebre** to blink

palpeggiare §290 (**palpéggio**) *tr* to finger, touch repeatedly

palpitante *adj* throbbing; burning (*question*); fluttering (*e.g., with love*)

palpitare (**pàlpito**) *intr* to palpitate, pulsate; (fig) to pine

palpitazióne *f* palpitation

pàlpito *m* heartbeat; (fig) throb

pal·tò *m* (**-tò**) overcoat

paltoncino *m* child's winter coat; lady's topcoat

paludaménto *m* (joc) array, attire

palude *f* marsh, bog

paludó·so **-sa** [s] *adj* marshy

palustre *adj* marshy

pàmpino *m* grape leaf

panacèa *f* panacea, cure-all

pàna·ma *m* (**-ma**) Panama hat

panamé·gno·gna *adj* & *mf* Panamenian

panamènse *adj* & *mf* Panamenian

panare *tr* (culin) to bread

pan·ca *f* (**-che**) bench; **scaldare le panche** (coll) to loaf around; (coll) to waste one's time at school

pancétta *f* potbelly; bacon

panchétto *m* footstool

panchina *f* bench

pàn·cia *f* (**-ce**) belly; **a pancia all'aria** on one's back; **mangiare a crepa pancia** to stuff oneself like a pig; **mettere su pancia** to grow a potbelly; **salvar la pancia per i fichi** to not take any chances; **tenersi la pancia dalle risate** to split one's side laughing

panciata *f* belly flop

pancièra *f* bellypiece; body girth

panciòlle *m*—**in panciolle** frittering one's time away

panciòtto *m* waistcoat; vest; **panciotto a maglia** cardigan
panciu·to -ta *adj* potbellied
pàncre·as *m* (-as) pancreas
pandemò·nio *m* (-ni) pandemonium
pane *m* bread; thread (*of screw*); cake (*e.g., of butter*); loaf (*of sugar*); (metallurgy) pig; **a pane di zucchero** conic(al); **dire pane al pane e vino al vino** to call a spade a spade; **essere come pane e cacio** to be hand and glove; **essere pane per i propri denti** to be a match for s.o.; **guadagnarsi il pane** to earn one's living; **pane a cassetta** sandwich bread; **pane azzimo** unleavened bread, matzoth; **pan di Spagna** angel food cake, sponge cake; **pane integrale** graham bread; **render pan per focaccia** to give tit for tat
panegìri·co *m* (-ci) panegyric
panetterìa *f* bakery
panettière *m* baker
panétto *m* pat (*e.g., of butter*)
pànfilo *m* yacht
panfrutto *m* plum cake
pangrattato *m* bread crumbs
pània *f* birdlime; **cadere nella pania** to fall into the trap
pàni·co -ca (-ci -che) *adj* panicky ‖ *m* panic
pani·co *m* (-chi) (bot) Italian millet
panièra *f* basket; basketful
panière *m* basket; basketful
panificazióne *f* breadmaking
panifì·cio *m* (-ci) bakery
panino *m* roll, bun; **panino imbottito** sandwich
panna *f* cream, heavy cream; **essere in panna** (naut) to lie to; (aut) to have a breakdown; **mettere in panna** (naut) to heave to; **panna montata** whipped cream
panne *f* (aut) breakdown; **essere in panne** (aut) to have a breakdown
pannèllo *m* linen cloth; pane; panel (*of machine*); (archit; elec) panel
pannicolo *m* (anat) membrane, tissue
panno *m* cloth; woolen cloth; film, membrane; **bianco come un panno** as white as a ghost; **mettersi nei panni di** to put oneself in the boots of; **non stare più nei propri panni** to be beside oneself with joy; **panni** clothes; **panno verde** baize
pannòcchia *f* ear (*of corn*)
pannolino *m* linen cloth; diaper; sanitary napkin
panòplia *f* panoply
panora·ma *m* (-mi) panorama
panoràmi·co -ca *adj* (-ci -che) panoramic ‖ *f* panoramic view; (mov) panoramic scene
pantaloncini *mpl* trunks
pantalóni *mpl* trousers; **pantaloni da donna** slacks
pantano *m* bog, quagmire
panteismo *m* pantheism
pànteon *m* pantheon
pantèra *f* panther; (slang) police car
pantòfola *f* slipper
pantomima *f* pantomine, mimicry

panzana *f* (lit) fib, lie
Pàolo *m* Paul
paonaz·zo -za *adj & m* purple
pa·pa *m* (-pi) pope; **ad ogni morte di papa** once in a blue moon; **morto un papa se ne fa un altro** nobody is indispensable
pa·pà *m* (-pà) daddy, papa
papàbile *adj* likely to be elected ‖ *mf* front runner ‖ *m* cardinal likely to be elected to the papacy
papale *adj* papal (*e.g., benediction*); Papal (*States*)
papali·no -na *adj* papal ‖ *m* advocate of papal temporal power ‖ *f* skullcap
paparazzo *m* freelance photographer
papato *m* papacy
papàvero *m* poppy; **alto papavero** (fig) big shot
pàpera *f* young goose; slip of the tongue; spoonerism; **fare una papera** to make a boner
pàpero *m* gander
papiro *m* papyrus
pappa *f* bread soup, farina, pap; **pappa molla** (fig) jellyfish
pappafì·co *m* (-chi) (naut) topgallant; (slang) goatee
pappagallo *m* parrot; bedpan; (slang) masher
pappagòr·gia *f* (-ge) double chin, jowl
pappare *tr* (coll) to gulp; (fig) to gobble up fraudulently
pappata·ci *m* (-ci) gnat
pappina *f* light pap; poultice
pàpri·ca *f* (-che) paprika
para *f* crepe rubber
paràbola *f* parable; (geom) parabola
parabórdo *m* (naut) fender
parabréz·za [ddzz] *m* (-za) windshield
paracadutare *tr* to parachute, airdrop ‖ *ref* to parachute
paracadu·te *m* (-te) parachute
paracadutismo *m* parachute jumping; (sports) sky diving
paracadutì·sta *mf* (-sti -ste) parachutist; skydiver ‖ *m* paratrooper
paracarro *m* spur stone
paracól·pi *m* (-pi) doorstop
paràcqua *m* (paràcqua) umbrella
paradèn·ti *m* (-ti) (sports) mouthpiece
paradisìa·co -ca *adj* (-ci -che) heavenly
paradiso *m* paradise
paradossale *adj* paradoxical
paradòsso *m* paradox
parafa *f* initials
parafan·go *m* (-ghi) fender, mudguard
parafare *tr* to initial
paraffina *f* paraffin
parafiam·ma *m* (-ma) fire-proof partition
parafrasare (paràfraso) *tr* to paraphrase
paràfra·si *f* (-si) paraphrase
parafùlmine *m* lightning rod
parafuò·co *m* (-co) screen, fender (*in front of fireplace*)
paràg·gio *m* (-gi) lineage; **paraggi** neighborhood, vicinity
paragonàbile *adj* comparable
paragonare (paragóno) *tr* to compare
paragóne *m* comparison; **a paragone di**

in comparison with; **mettere a paragone** to compare; **senza paragone** beyond compare

paragrafare (paràgrafo) *tr* to paragraph

paràgrafo *m* paragraph

paraguaia·no -na *adj & mf* Paraguayan

paràli·si *f* (-si) paralysis

paraliti·co -ca *adj & mf* (-ci -che) paralytic

paralizzare [ddzz] *tr* to paralyze

parallè·lo -la *adj & m* parallel ‖ *f* (geom) parallel line; **parallele** (sports) parallel bars

paralume *m* lamp shade

paramano *m* cuff, wristband; (archit) facing brick

paraménto *s* facing (*of a wall*); (eccl) vestment

parami·ne *m* (-ne) (nav) paravane

paramó·sche *m* (-sche) fly net

paran·co *m* (-chi) tackle

paranin·fo -fa *mf* matchmaker

paranòi·co -ca *adj & mf* (-ci -che) paranoiac

paraòc·chi *m* (-chi) blinker (*on horse*)

parapètto *m* parapet

parapì·glia *m* (-glia) hubbub

parapiòg·gia *m* (-gia) umbrella

parare *tr* to adorn; to hang; to protect; to parry (*a thrust*); to offer; to drive (*e.g., cattle*) ‖ *intr*—**dove va a parare?** what are you driving at? ‖ *ref* to protect oneself; (eccl) to don the vestments; **pararsi dinanzi a** to loom up in front of

parasóle *m* parasol; (aut) sun visor

paraspal·le *m* (-le) (sports) shoulder pad

parassi·ta (-ti -te) *adj* parasitic ‖ *m* parasite

parassità·rio -ria *adj* (-ri -rie) parasitic(al)

parassiti·co -ca *adj* (-ci -che) parasitic(al)

parastatale *adj* government-controlled ‖ *mf* employee of government-controlled agency

parastin·chi *m* (-chi) (sports) shin guard

parata *f* fence, bar; (fencing) parry; (soccer) catch; (mil) parade; **mala parata** dangerous situation

paratìa *f* bulkhead

parato *m* hangings; **parati** hangings; (naut) bilgeways

paratóia *f* sluice gate

paraur·ti *m* (-ti) (aut) bumper; (rr) buffer

paravènto *m* screen

Par·ca *f* (-che) Fate

parcare §197 *tr & intr* to park

parcèlla *f* bill, fee, honorarium; parcel, lot (*of land*)

parcheggiare §290 (parchéggio) *tr & intr* to park

parchég·gio *m* (-gi) parking; parking lot

parchìmetro *m* parking meter

par·co -ca (-chi -che) *adj* frugal; parsimonious ‖ *m* park; parking; parking lot; **parco dei divertimenti** amusement park

paréc·chio -chia (-chi -chie) *adj indef*

a good deal of, a lot of; **parecchi** several ‖ *pron* a good deal, a lot; **parecchi** several ‖ **parecchio** *adv* a lot; rather

pareggiare §290 (paréggio) *tr* to level; to equal; to match; to balance; to recognize ‖ *intr* (sports) to tie

pareggia·to -ta *adj* accredited (*school*)

parég·gio *m* (-gi) leveling; matching; (sports) tie; **pareggio del bilancio** balancing of the budget

parentado *m* kinsfolk, kindred; relationship; **concludere il parentado di** to arrange for the wedding of

parènte *mf* relative; (lit) parent; **parenti kin**

parentèla *f* relationship; relations

parènte·si *f* (-si) parenthesis; break, interval; **fra parentesi** parenthetically; in parentheses; **parentesi quadra** bracket

parére *m* opinion, mind; advice; **a mio parere** in my opinion ‖ §210 *intr* (ESSERE) to seem; **che Le pare?** what is your opinion?; **ma Le pare!** not at all!; **mi pare che** + *subj* it seems to me that + *ind*; I guess that + *ind*; **non Le pare?** don't you think so?; **non mi pare vero** I can't believe it

paréte *f* wall; **tra le pareti domestiche** within the four walls of the home

pargolét·to -ta *adj* (poet) infantile ‖ *mf* (poet) child

pàrgo·lo -la *adj* (poet) infantile ‖ *mf* (poet) child

pari *adj invar* equal, even; **camminare di pari passo** to walk at the same rate; **essere pari** to be quits; **essere pari al proprio compito** to be equal to the task; **fare un salto a piè pari** to jump with feet together; **pari pari** verbatim; **rimanere pari con** (sports) to be tied with; **saltare a piè pari** to skip (*e.g., a page*); to dodge (*a difficulty*); **trattare da pari a pari** to treat as an equal ‖ *m* peer; **al pari di** as, like; **del pari** also; **in pari** even, leveled; **senza pari** matchless, peerless ‖ *f*—**stare alla pari con** to be an even match for

parìa *f* peerage

pà·ria *m* (-ria) pariah

parificare §197 (parìfico) *tr* to level; to match; to accredit (*a school*); to balance

Parigi *f* Paris

parigi·no -na *adj & mf* Parisian ‖ *f* slow-burning stove; Parisian woman; (rr) switching spur

parìglia *f* pair, couple; team (*of horses*); (cards) two of a kind; **rendere la pariglia** to give tit for tat

parimémti *adv* likewise

pari·tà *f* (-tà) parity

paritèti·co -ca *adj* (-ci -che) joint (*e.g., committee*)

parlamentare *adj* parliamentary ‖ *mf* member of parliament ‖ *m* (mil) envoy ‖ *v* (parlaménto) *intr* to parley

parlaménto *m* parliament

parlante *adj* talking; life-like ‖ *mf* speaker

parlantìna *f* glibness

parla·to *m* talk, speech; dialect ‖ *tr* to speak (*a language*) ‖ *intr* to speak, talk; to discuss; **chi parla?** (telp) hello!; **far parlare di sé** to be talked about; **parlare chiaro** to speak bluntly; **parlare del più e del meno** to make small talk; **parlare tra sé e sé** to talk to oneself ‖ *ref* to talk to one another

parla·to -ta *adj* spoken; current (*speech*); talking (*movie*) ‖ *m* talkie; (mov) sound track; (theat) dialogue ‖ *f* speech, talk; dialect

parla·tóre -trice *mf* speaker

parlató·rio *m* (**-ri**) visting room (*e.g., in jail*)

parlottare (**parlòtto**) *intr* to whisper in secret

parmigia·no -na *adj & mf* Parmesan ‖ *m* Parmesan cheese

parnaso *m* Parnassus (*poetry, poets*) ‖ **il Parnaso** Mount Parnassus

paro *m*—in un **par d'ore** in a couple of hours ‖ *adv*—**andare a paro** to keep abreast; **mettere a paro** to compare

parodìa *f* parody; **fare la parodia di** to parody

parodiare §287 (**paròdio**) *tr* to parody

paròla *f* word; speech; **avere parole con** to have words with; **buttare la mezza parola** to make an allusion; **dare la parola a** to give the floor to; **di poche parole** of few words; **domandare la parola a** to ask for the floor; **essere di parola** to keep one's word; **essere in parola con** to have dealings with; **mangiarsi la parola** to break one's word; **mangiarsi le parole** to slur one's words; **non far parola** to not breathe a word; **parola crociata** crossword puzzle; **parola d'ordine** password; **parola macedonia** acronym **parola sdrucciola** proparoxytone; **parole lyrics; parole di circostanza** occasional words; **prendere la parola** to take the floor; **rivolgere la parola a** to address; **venire a parole** to begin to quarrel

parolàc·cia *f* (**-ce**) dirty word; swear-word

paro·làio -làia (**-lài -làie**) *adj* wordy, verbose ‖ *mf* windbag

parolière *m* lyricist

parossismo *m* paroxysm; climax

parossìto·no -na *adj* paroxytone

parotite *f* (pathol) parotitis; **parotite epidemica** (pathol) mumps

parrici·da *mf* (**-di -de**) patricide

parrocchétto *m* parakeet; (naut) fore-topsail; (naut) fore-topmast

parròcchia *f* parish

parrocchia·no -na *mf* parishioner

pàrro·co *m* (**-ci**) rector, parson

parruc·ca *f* (**-che**) wig; (fig) old fogey

parsimònia *f* parsimony

parsimonió·so -sa [s] *adj* parsimonious

partàc·cia *f*—**fare una partaccia** to break one's word; **fare una partaccia a** to make a scene in front of; to rebuke loudly

parte *f* part; share; section; side; party; partiality; (theat) role; **a parte** sepa-

rately; (theat) aside; **d'altra parte** on the other hand; **da parte** aside; **da parte mia** as for me; **fare le parti** to divide in shares; **gran parte di** a great deal of; **in parte** partially; **la maggior parte di** most of; **parte civile** (law) plaintiff; **parte . . . parte** some . . . some; **part . . . part; prendere in mala parte** to take amiss

partecipante *adj* participating ‖ *mf* participant; (sports) contestant

partecipare (**partécipo**) *tr* to announce; (lit) to share in ‖ *intr*—**partecipare a** to share in; to participate in; **partecipare di** to partake of (*e.g., the nature of an animal*)

partecipazióne *f* announcement; card; announcement (*of a wedding*); share in a business); participation (*in some action*)

partécipe *adj* sharing, partaking

parteggiare §290 (**partéggio**) *intr* to side; **parteggiare per** to side with

Partenóne *m* Parthenon

partènte *adj* departing ‖ *mf* person departing, traveler; (sports) starter

partènza *f* departure; sailing; (sports) start; **di partenza** in or **in partenza** about to leave; **partenza lanciata** (sports) running start

particèlla *f* particle

partici·pio *m* (**-pi**) participle

particolare *adj* particular; private; **in particolare** especially ‖ *m* detail

particolareggiare §290 (**particolaréggio**) *tr* to detail

particolarismo *m* regionalism, particularism

particolarìsti·co -ca *adj* (**-ci -che**) particularistic; individualistic

particolari·tà *f* (**-tà**) peculiarity; detail

partigianerìa *f* partisanship, factionalism

partigia·no -na *adj & mf* partisan

partire §176 *tr* (lit) to divide ‖ *v* (parto) *intr* to depart; (fig) to arise; **a partire da** beginning with; **far partire** to start (*e.g., a car*) ‖ *ref* to depart, leave

parti·to -ta *adj* parted ‖ *m* match (*in marriage*); (pol) party; **ridotto a mal partito** in bad shape; **mettere la testa a partito** to reform; **partito preso** parti pris; **prendere partito** to take sides; to make up one's mind; **trarre il miglior partito da** to make the best of ‖ *f* panel (*e.g., of door*); lot (*of goods*); game; match; party; round (*of golf*); (com) entry; **partita di caccia** hunting party; **partita doppia** (com) double entry; **partita semplice** (com) single entry

partitura *f* (mus) score

partizióne *f* partition, division

parto *m* birth, childbirth

partorìre §176 *tr* to bear, bring forth

parvènza *f* (lit) appearance

parziale *adj* partial, one-sided

parziali·tà *f* (**-tà**) partiality

pàscere §211 *tr, intr & ref* to pasture, graze

pa·scià *m* (**-scià**) pasha

pasciu·to -ta *adj* well-fed

pascolare (pàscolo) *tr & intr* to pasture
pàscolo *m* pasture
Pàsqua *f* Easter; **contento come una Pasqua** as happy as a lark; **Pasqua fiorita** Palm Sunday
pasquale *adj* paschal (*e.g., lamb*)
passàbile *adj* passable, tolerable
passàg·gio *m* (**-gi**) passage; transfer; crossing; traffic; passageway; ride; promotion; (sports) pass; **aprirsi il passaggio** to make one's way; **di passaggio** in passing; transient (*visitor*); **essere di passaggio** to be passing by; **passaggio a livello** railroad crossing; **passaggio zebrato** zebra crossing; **vietato il passaggio** no thoroughfare
passamano *m* passing from hand to hand; ribbon; (coll) railing, handrail
passante *adj* passing (*shot*) || *mf* passer-by || *m* strap
passapòrto *m* passport
passare *tr* to cross; to pass; to undergo (*a medical examination*); to move; to hand; to pay; to send (*word*); to pierce; to spend (*time*); to strain; to go over; to let have (*e.g., a slap*); to overstep (*the bounds*); **passare in rassegna** to pass in review; **passare per le armi** to execute; **passare un brutto quarto d'ora** to have a bad ten minutes; **passare un guaio** to have a hard time; **passarla a qlcu** (coll) to forgive s.o.; **passarla liscia** (coll) to get off unscathed; **passarsela bene** (coll) to have a good time || *intr* (ESSERE) to pass; to go; to filter (*said of air, light*); to move; to spoil (*said of food*); to be overcooked; to be promoted; to become; to enter; (lit) to be over; **fare passare qlcu** to let s.o. come in; **passare a nozze** to get married; **passare a seconde nozze** to remarry; **passare avanti a** to overcome; **passare di mente a** to forget, *e.g.*, **gli è passata di mente la riunione** he forgot the meeting; **passare di moda** to go out of style; **passare in giudicato** (law) to be no longer appealable; **passare per** to pass by; **passare per il rotto della cuffia** to barely make it; **passare sopra qlco** to overlook s.th.; **passi!** come in!; **passo!** (rad) over!; **passo** (cards) pass
passata *f* purée; **dare una passata a** to glance at; **dare una passata di straccio a** to rub lightly with a rag; to give a lick and a promise to; **di passata** hurriedly
passatèmpo *m* pastime; hobby
passati·sta *mf* (**-sti** **-ste**) traditionalist
passa·to -ta *adj* past; last; overcooked; **essere passato** (coll) to be no longer in one's prime; **passato di moda** out of fashion || *m* past; purée; **passato prossimo** present perfect; **passato remoto** preterit || *f* see **passata**
passatóia *f* runner (*rug*)
passa·tóio -tói *m* (**-tói**) stepping stone
passeggè·ro -ra *adj* passing || *mf* passenger; **passeggero clandestino** stowaway

passeggiare §290 (passéggio) *tr* to walk (*e.g., a horse*) || *intr* to walk, promenade
passeggiata *f* promenade; walk; drive, ride; drive, road; **fare una passeggiata** to take a walk; to take a ride
passeggiatrice *f* streetwalker
passég·gio *m* (**-gi**) walk; promenade; **andare a passeggio** to take a walk
passerèlla *f* gangway; catwalk; footbridge
pàsse·ro -ra *mf* sparrow || *f*—**passera di mare** (ichth) flounder
passibile *adj*—**passibile di** subject to, liable to
passiflòra *f* passionflower
passino *m* colander, strainer
passióne *f* passion
passivi·tà *f* (**-tà**) passivity; (com) deficit
passi·vo -va *adj* passive || *m* (com) liabilities; (com) debit side; (gram) passive
pas·so -sa *adj*—see **uva** || *m* step; passage; pass (*in mountain*); pace; footstep; pitch (*of screw, helix, etc.*); (aut) wheelbase; (phot) tread; (phot) size (*of roll*); **a grandi passi** with great strides; **andare al passo** to march in step; to walk (*said of a horse*); **a passi di gigante** by leaps and bounds; **a passo di corsa** running; **a passo d'uomo** walking, at a walk; **aprire il passo** to open the way; **di buon passo** at a good clip; **di pari passo** at the same rate; **fare quattro passi** to take a stroll; **passo doppio** paso doble; **passo d'uomo** manhole; step; **passo falso** misstep; (fig) stumble; **sbarrare il passo** to block the way; **seguire i passi di** to walk in the footsteps of || *interj* (cards) pass!; over!
pasta *f* paste; dough; (fig) disposition; **pasta grossa** uncouth, coarse; **pasta alimentare** pasta, macaroni products; **pasta all'uovo** egg noodles; **pasta asciutta** pasta with sauce and cheese; **pasta dentifricia** toothpaste; **una pasta d'uomo** a good-natured man
pastasciutta *f* pasta with sauce and cheese
pasteggiare §290 (pastéggio) *intr* to dine
pastèllo *adj invar & m* pastel || *m* crayon
pastétta *f* batter; (coll) trickery
pastic·ca *f* (**-che**) lozenge, tablet; **pasticche per la tosse** cough drops
pasticceria *f* pastrymaking; pastry; pastry shop
pasticciare §128 (pasticcio) *tr & intr* to bungle; to scribble
pasticciè·re -ra *mf* pastry cook; confectioner
pasticcino *m* cookie; patty
pastíc·cio *m* (**-ci**) pie (*of meat, macaroni, etc*); bungle; mess; **cacciarsi nei pasticci** to wind up in the soup
pasticció·ne -na *mf* bungler
pastifí·cio *m* (**-ci**) spaghetti and macaroni factory
pastìglia *f* lozenge, tablet; **pastiglia per la tosse** cough drop

pastina·ca f (-che) parsnip
pa·sto -sta adj (archaic) fed ‖ m meal; **pasto a prezzo fisso** table d'hôte ‖ f see **pasta**
pastóia f hobble; (fig) shackle
pastóne m mash
pastóra f shepherdess
pastorale adj pastoral
pastóre m shepherd; pastor
pastorì·zio -zia (-zi -zie) adj shepherd ‖ f sheep raising
pastorizzare [ddzz] tr to pasteurize
pastó·so -sa [s] adj pasty; mellow
pastrano m overcoat
pastura f pasture; hay; fodder
patac·ca f (-che) large, worthless coin; fake; (coll) medal; (coll) spot
patata f potato
patatràc m (patatràc) crash
patèlla f kneecap; (zool) limpet
patè·ma m (-mi) affliction; **patema d'animo** anxiety
patenta·to -ta adj licensed; (coll) well-known
patènte adj patent ‖ f license; driver's license; **patente sanitaria** (naut) bill of health
patentino m (aut) permit
pateréc·cio m (-ci) whitlow
paternale adj (obs) paternal ‖ f reprimand
paterni·tà f (-tà) paternity; authorship
patèr·no -na adj paternal; fatherly
paternòstro m Lord's Prayer; **è vero come il paternostro** it is the gospel truth
patèti·co -ca (-ci -che) adj pathetic; mawkish ‖ m pathos; mawkishness
pathos m pathos
patibile adj endurable
patibolare adj gallows
patibolo m executioner's instrument; scaffold
patimento m suffering
pàtina f patina; coating (on paper); varnish; fur (on tongue)
patinare (pàtino) tr to gloss, glaze (e.g., paper)
patire §176 tr to suffer; (gram) to be the recipient of (an action) ‖ intr to suffer
pati·to -ta adj suffering, sickly ‖ mf fan ‖ m boyfriend ‖ f girlfriend
patòge·no -na adj pathogenic
patologìa f pathology
patològi·co -ca adj (-ci -che) patho-logic(al)
patos m var of **pathos**
patrasso m—**andare a patrasso** to die; to go to ruin; **mandare a patrasso** to kill; to ruin
pàtria f fatherland, native land
patriar·ca m (-chi) patriarch
patriarcale adj patriarchal
patrigno m stepfather
patrimoniale adj patrimonial; property (tax); capital (e.g., transaction)
patrimò·nio m (-ni) patrimony; estate; fortune; (fig) heritage
pà·trio -tria (-tri -trie) adj paternal; of one's country (e.g., love) ‖ f see **patria**

patriò·ta mf (-ti -te) patriot; (coll) fellow citizen
patriòtti·co -ca adj (-ci -che) patriotic
patriottismo m patriotism
patrì·zio -zia (-zi -zie) adj & m patrician ‖ **Patrizio** m Patrick
patrocinante adj pleading (lawyer)
patrocinare tr to favor, sponsor; to plead
patrocina·tóre -trice mf defender; pleader
patroci·nio m (-ni) support; sponsorship; (law) defense; **patrocinio gratuito** public defense
patronato m patronage; charitable institution, foundation; **patronato scolastico** state aid fund
patronéssa f sponsor; trustee (of charitable institution)
patròno m patron saint; patron; sponsor; trustee (of charitable institution); (law) counsel
patta f flap (of garment); bill (of anchor); (coll) potholder; **essere or far patta** to be even, tie
patteggiamento m negotiation
patteggiare §290 (pattéggio) tr & intr to negotiate
pattinàggio m skating
pattinare (pàttino) intr to skate; to skid (said of a car)
pattina·tóio m (-tói) skating rink
pattina·tóre -trice mf skater
pàttino m skate; guide block (of an elevator); (aer) skid, runner; **pattino a rotelle** roller skate
pattino m racing shell with outrigger floats
patto m pact; **a nessun patto** by no means; **a patto che** provided (that); **patto sociale** social contract; **venire a patti** to come to terms
pattùglia f patrol
pattugliare §280 tr & intr to patrol
pattuire §176 tr & intr to negotiate
pattuì·to -ta adj agreed ‖ m agreement
pattume m litter, garbage
pattumièra f dustpan; trash bin
patùrnie fpl—**avere le paturnie** (coll) to be in the dumps
paura f fear; **aver paura di** to be afraid of; **da far paura** frightful; **dar or metter paura a** to frighten; **per paura che** for fear that, lest
pauró·so -sa [s] adj fearful
pàusa f pause
pausare (pàuso) tr (lit) to interrupt ‖ intr (lit) to pause
paventare (pavènto) tr & intr to fear
pavesare (pavéso) tr to deck with flags; to dress (a ship)
pavése [s] adj—see **zuppa** ‖ m pavis (shield); (naut) bunting
pàvi·do -da adj cowardly, timid
pavimentare (paviménto) tr to pave
pavimentazióne f paving, pavement
paviménto m floor; bottom (of sea); paving (of street)
pavoncèlla f lapwing
pavó·ne -na or **-néssa** mf peacock
pavoneggiare §290 (pavonéggio) ref to swagger, strut
pazientare (paziènto) intr to be patient

paziènte *adj* & *mf* patient

paziènza *f* patience; **fare scappare la pazienza a** to drive mad; **pazienza!** too bad!

pazzé·sco -sca *adj* (-schi -sche) crazy, wild

pazzia *f* madness, insanity; folly; **fare pazzie** to act like a fool

paz·zo -za *adj* crazy, insane; **andar pazzo per** to be crazy about ‖ *mf* crazy person

pèc·ca *f* (-che) imperfection

peccamino·so -sa [s] *adj* sinful

peccare §197 (pècco) *intr* to sin; to be lacking; to be at fault

peccato *m* sin; **che peccato!** what a pity!; **è un peccato** it's a shame

pecca·tóre -trice *mf* sinner

pécchia *f* bee

pecchióne *m* drone

péce *f* pitch; **pece greca** rosin

pechinése [s] *adj* & *mf* Pekingese

Pechino *f* Peking

pècora *f* sheep

peco·ràio *m* (-rài) shepherd

pecorèlla *f* small sheep, lamb

pecorì·no -na *adj* sheep; sheepish ‖ *m* sheep-milk cheese ‖ *f* sheep manure

peculato *m* embezzlement, peculation

peculiare *adj* peculiar

peculiari·tà *f* (-tà) peculiarity

pecù·lio *m* (-li) nest egg, savings; (obs) cattle

pecùnia *m* (lit) money

pecunià·rio -ria *adj* (-ri -rie) pecuniary

pedàg·gio *m* (-gi) toll

pedagogìa *f* pedagogy, pedagogics

pedagògi·co -ca *adj* (-ci -che) pedagogic(al)

pedagò·go -ga *mf* (-ghi -ghe) pedagogue

pedalare *intr* to pedal

pedale *m* trunk (*of tree*); pedal; treadle (*e.g., of sewing machine*)

pedalièra *f* pedals, pedal keyboard; (aer) rudder bar

pedalino *m* (coll) sock, short stocking

pedana *f* footrest; platform; bedside rug; hem (*of skirt*); (aut) running board; (sports) springboard

pedante *adj* pedantic ‖ *m* pedant

pedantería *f* pedantry

pedanté·sco -sca *adj* (-schi -sche) pedantic

pedata *f* kick; footprint; tread (*of step*)

pedèstre *adj* pedestrian

pedia·tra *mf* (-tri -tre) pediatrician

pediatrìa *f* pediatrics

pedicu·re *mf* (-re) pedicure

pedicu·ro -ra *mf* var of **pedicure**

pedilù·vio *m* (-vi) foot bath

pedina *f* (checkers) checker, man; (chess) pawn

pedinare *tr* to shadow, follow about

pedìsse·quo -qua *adj* servile

pedivèlla *f* pedal crank

pedóne *m* pedestrian; (chess) pawn

pedule *m* stocking foot ‖ *fpl* climbing shoes, sneakers

pedùncolo *m* (anat, bot, zool) peduncle

pegamòide *f* imitation leather

pèggio *adj invar* worse; **il peggio** the worst, e.g., **il peggio ragazzo** the worst boy; ‖ *m* worst; **andare per il peggio** to be getting worse ‖ *f* worst; **alla peggio** if worst comes to worst; **averne la peggio** to get the worst of it ‖ *adv* worse; worst; at worst; **peggio + pp** less + pp; least + pp; **tanto peggio** so much the worse

peggioraménto *m* deterioration, worsening

peggiorare (peggióro) *tr* & *intr* to worsen

peggió·re (-ri) *adj* worse; worst ‖ *m* worst

pégli §4

pégno *m* pledge, pawn

pégola *f* pitch; (coll) bad luck

péi §4

pél §4

pèla·go *m* (-ghi) (poet) open sea; (coll) mess; **pelago di guai** sea of trouble

pelame *m* hair, coat

pelandróne *m* (coll) shirker, do-nothing

pelapata·te *m* (-te) potato peeler

pelare (pélo) *tr* to fleece; to pluck; to pare, peel; to clear (*land*); (fig) to strip; to scald, burn ‖ *ref* (coll) to shed; to become bald

pela·to -ta *adj* peeled; hairless, bald; barren ‖ *m* (coll) baldy; **pelati** peeled tomatoes ‖ *f* fleecing, plucking; (joc) baldness, bald spot

pélla §4

pellàc·cia *f* (-ce) tough hide

pellame *m* skins, hides

pèlle *f* skin, hide; **a fior di pelle** slightly, superficially; **essere nella pelle di** to be in the boots of; **fare la pelle a** to bump off; **non stare più nella pelle** to be beside oneself with joy; **pelle di dante** buckskin; **pelle d'oca** goose skin, goose flesh; **pelle d'uovo** mull; **pelle pelle** skin-deep, superficial

pélle §4

pellegrinàg·gio *m* (-gi) pilgrimage

pellegrinare *intr* (lit) to go on a pilgrimage

pellegrì·no -na *adj* wandering; (lit) foreign; (lit) strange, quixotic ‖ *mf* pilgrim, traveler

pelleróssa *mf* (pellirosse) redskin

pellettería *f* leather goods; leather goods store

pellicano *m* pelican

pellicceria *f* furrier's store; furrier's trade, fur industry

pellìc·cia *f* (-ce) fur

pellic·ciàio -ciàia *mf* (-ciài -ciàie) furrier

pelliccióne *m* fur jacket

pellìcola *f* film; **pellicola in rotolo** roll film; **pellicola piana** film pack; **pellicola sonora** sound film; **pellicola vergine** unexposed film

pellirós·sa *mf* (-se) var of **pellerossa**

pélo *m* hair (*of beard*); pile (*of carpet*); fur; **avere pelo sul cuore** not to be easily moved; **cercare il pelo nell'uovo** to split hairs; **di primo pelo** green, inexperienced; **non avere peli sulla lingua** to not mince one's words; **pelo dell'acqua** water surface; **per un pelo** by a hair's breadth

peloponnesìa·co -ca *adj* (**-ci -che**) Peloponnesian

peló·so -sa [s] *adj* hairy; self-serving (*e.g.*, *charity*)

péltro *m* pewter

pelùria *f* down, soft hair

péna *f* penalty; concern; compassion; pain, suffering; grief; **a mala pena** barely; **essere in pena per** to worry about; **fare pena** to arouse compassion; **pena infamante** degrading punishment; loss of civil rights; **sotto pena di** under penalty of; **valere la pena** to be worthwhile

penale *adj* penal || *f* penalty

penali·sta *mf* (**-sti -ste**) criminal lawyer

penali·tà *f* (**-tà**) penalty

penalizzare [ddzz] *tr* (sports) to penalize

penare (**péno**) *intr* to suffer; to find it difficult

pencolare (**pèncolo**) *intr* to totter; to waver

pendà·glio *m* (**-gli**) pendant; **pendaglio da forca** gallows bird

pendènte *adj* leaning; hanging; pending || *m* pendant

pendènza *f* inclination, pitch; controversy; balance; **in pendenza** pending

pèndere §123 *intr* to hang; to lean; to slope; to pitch

pendìce *f* slope, declivity

pen·dìo *m* (**-dìi**) slant; slope

pèndola *f* clock

pendolare *adj* pendulum-like; commuting; transient (*tourist*) || *mf* commuter || *v* (**pèndolo**) *intr* to sway back and forth; to waver; (nav) to cruise back and forth

pèndolo *m* pendulum; clock

pèndu·lo -la *adj* (lit) hanging

penetrante *adj* penetrating, piercing

penetrare (**pènetro**) *tr* to penetrate, pierce || *intr* to penetrate || *ref*—**penetrarsi di** to be convinced of; to become aware of

penicillìna *f* penicillin

peninsulare *adj* peninsular

penìsola *f* peninsula

penitènte *adj* & *mf* penitent

penitènza *f* penitence; punishment

penitenzià·rio -ria *adj* & *mf* (**-ri -rie**) penitentiary

pénna *f* feather; pen; peen (*of hammer*); (mus) plectrum; **penna a sfera** ball-point pen; **penna d'oca** quill; **penna stilografica** fountain pen

pennàc·chio *m* (**-chi**) panache; plume, tuft; cloud (*of smoke*)

pennaiòlo *m* hack writer

pennarèllo *m* felt-tip pen

pennellare (**pennèllo**) *intr* to brush; (med) to pencil

pennellata *f* brush stroke

pennèllo *m* brush; (naut) signal flag; (naut) kedge; **pennello per la barba** shaving brush; **stare a pennello** to fit to a T

pennìno *m* pen; penpoint, nib

pennóne *m* flagpole; (naut) yard; (mil) pennant

pennu·to -ta *adj* feathered || **pennuti** *mpl* birds

penómbra *f* penumbra; semidarkness; faint light; **vivere in penombra** to live in obscurity

penó·so -sa [s] *adj* painful

pensàbile *adj* thinkable

pensante *adj* thinking

pensare (**pènso**) *tr* to think; to think of || *intr* to think; to worry; **dar da pensare a** to cause worry to, *e.g.*, **suo figlio gli dà da pensare** his son causes him worry; **pensa ai fatti tuoi** (coll) mind your own business; **pensa alla salute** (coll) don't worry!; **pensare a** to think of; **pensare di** to plan, intend to

pensata *f* bright idea, brainstorm

pensa·tóre -trice *mf* thinker

pensièro *m* thought; **dare pensiero a** to cause worry to; **darsi pensiero per** to worry about; **essere sopra pensiero** to be absorbed in thought

pensieró·so -sa [s] *adj* thoughtful, pensive

pènsile *adj* hanging, overhead

pensilina *f* marquee

pensionaménto *m* retirement

pensionante *mf* boarder, paying guest

pensionare (**pensióno**) *tr* to pension

pensiona·to -ta *adj* pensioned || *mf* pensioner || *m* boarding school

pensióne *f* pension; boarding house; **in pensione** retired; **tenere a pensione** to board (*a lodger*); **vivere a pensione** to board (*said of a lodger*)

pensó·so -sa [s] *adj* thoughtful, pensive

pentàgono *m* pentagon

pentagram·ma *m* (**-mi**) (mus) staff, stave

pentàmetro *m* pentameter

Pentecòste, la Pentecost, Whitsunday

pentiménto *m* repentance; correction (*e.g.*, *in a manuscript*); change of heart

pentire (**pènto**) *ref* to repent; to change one's mind; **pentirsi di** to repent

penti·to -ta *adj* repentant, repenting; **pentito e contrito** in sackcloth and ashes

péntola *f* pot, kettle; potful; **pentola a pressione** pressure cooker

penùlti·mo -ma *adj* next to the last || *f* penult

penùria *f* shortage, scarcity

penzolare (**pènzolo**) [dz] *intr* to dangle, hang down

penzolóni [dz] *adv* dangling

peònia *f* peony

pepaiòla *f* pepper shaker; pepper mill

pepare (**pépo**) *tr* to pepper

pepa·to -ta *adj* peppered; peppery

pépe *m* pepper; **pepe della Giamaica** allspice; **pepe di Caienna** red pepper, cayenne pepper

peperóne *m* (bot) pepper

pepita *f* nugget

per *prep* by; through; throughout; for; because of; to, in order to; in favor of; considering; **essere per** to be about to; **per + adj or adv + che + subj** however **+ adj or adv + ind**, e.g., **per intelligente che sia** however intelligent he is; **per caso** perchance; **per che cosa?** what for?; **per l'appunto** exactly, just; **per lungo** lengthwise; **per me as** for me; **per ora** now; **per parte mia** as for me; **per poco** hardly, scarcely, **per quanto** + *adj* or *adv* + *subj* however + *adj* or *adv* + *pres ind*, e.g., **per quanto disperatamente provi** however desperately he attempts; **per tempo** early; **per traverso** diagonally; **per via che** (coll) because; **stare per** to be about to

péra *f* pear (*fruit*); bulb, light bulb; (joc) head

peraltro *adv* besides, moreover

peranco *adv* yet

perbacco *interj* by Jove!

perbène *adj invar* nice, well brought up

percalle *m* percale

percènto *m* percent; percentage

percentuale *adj* percentage || *f* percent; commission, bonus

percepibile *adj* collectable

percepire §176 *tr* to perceive; to receive (*a salary*)

percettibile *adj* perceptible

percetti•vo -va *adj* perceptive

percezióne *f* perception

perché *m* why, reason; **il perché e il percome** the why and the wherefore || *pron rel* for which || *adv* why || *conj* because; so that

perciò *conj* therefore, accordingly

percóme *m* & *conj* wherefore

percorrènza *f* stretch, distance

percórrere §139 *tr* to cross; to cover, go through

percórso *m* crossing, distance

percòssa *f* hit, blow; contusion

percuòtere §251 *tr* to hit, beat; (fig) to shake || *intr* to strike

percussióne *f* percussion

percussóre *m* firing pin

perdènte *adj* losing || *mf* loser

pèrdere §212 *tr* to lose; to waste; to miss (*e.g., a train*); to ruin; to leak || *intr* to lose; to leak; to be inferior || *ref* to get lost; to waste one's time; **perdersi d'animo** to lose heart; **perdersi in un bicchier d'acqua** to become discouraged for nothing

perdifiato *m*—**a perdifiato** at the top of one's lungs

perdigiór•no *mf* (*-no*) idler

perdinci *interj* good Heavens!

pèrdita *f* loss; leak; **a perdita d'occhio** as far as the eye can see; **perdite** (mil) casualties

perditèm•po *mf* (*-po*) idler || *m* waste of time

perdizióne *f* perdition

perdonàbile *adj* pardonable

perdonare (**perdóno**) *tr* to forgive; to spare; **perdonare a qlcu qlco** or **perdonare qlcu di qlco** to forgive s.o. for s.th || *intr* (with *dat*) to pardon

perdóno *m* forgiveness, pardon

perdurare *intr* (ESSERE & AVERE) to last; to persevere

perdu•to -ta *adj* lost; **andar perduto** to be desperately in love; to get lost

peregrinare *intr* to wander

peregrinazióne *f* wandering

peregri•no -na *adj* far-fetched, outlandish

perènne *adj* everlasting; perennial

perentò•rio -ria *adj* (**-ri -rie**) peremptory

perequare (**perèquo**) *tr* to equalize

perequazióne *f* equalization

perfèt•to -ta *adj* & *m* perfect

perfezionaménto *m* improvement; (educ) specialization

perfezionare (**perfezióno**) *tr* to improve, polish up; to perfect || *ref* to improve; (educ) to specialize

perfezióne *f* perfection; **a** or **alla perfezione** to perfection

perfidia *f* perfidy

pèrfi•do -da *adj* perfidious, treacherous; (coll) foul, nasty

perfini•re *m* (*-re*) punch line

perfino *adv* even

perforante *adj* piercing, perforating

perforare (**perfóro**) *tr* to pierce; to perforate; to punch; to bore

perfora•tóre -trice *mf* key-punch operator || *m* drill || *f* punch; drill; pneumatic drill, rock drill

perforazióne *f* perforation

pergamèna *f* parchment, vellum

pèrgamo *m* (lit) pulpit

pèrgola *f* bower, pergola

pergolato *m* arbor, pergola; grape arbor

pericolante *adj* tottering, unsafe

perìcolo *m* danger; **non c'è pericolo** don't worry

pericoló•so -sa [s] *adj* dangerous

periferìa *f* periphery; suburbs

perifèri•co -ca *adj* (**-ci -che**) peripheral

perìfra•si *f* (*-si*) periphrasis

perìmetro *m* perimeter

periodare *m* writing style || *v* (**perìodo**) *intr* to turn a phrase

periòdi•co -ca *adj* (**-ci -che**) periodic(al) || *m* periodical

perìodo *m* period; age; (gram) sentence; (phys) cycle; **il periodo delle feste** holiday time

peripezìa *f* vicissitude

perìplo *m* circumnavigation

perire §176 *intr* (ESSERE) to perish

periscò•pio *m* (*-pi*) periscope

peritale *adj* expert

peritare (**pèrito**) *ref* (lit) to hesitate

perì•to -ta *adj* expert, skilled || *mf* expert; person skilled; **perito agrario** land surveyor; **perito calligrafo** handwriting expert; **perito chimico** chemist; **perito industriale** industrial engineer

peritonèo *m* peritoneum

perìzia *f* skill; survey; appraisal

periziare §287 (**perìzio**) *tr* to estimate, appraise

pèrla *f* pearl; (med) capsule

perlàce•o -a *adj* pearly

perla•to -ta *adj* pearly, smooth

perlìfe•ro -ra *adj* pearl-producing

perlina *f* bead

perloméno *adv* at least

perlopiù *adv* mostly, generally

perlustrare *tr* to patrol

perlustrazióne *f* patrol, patrolling

permaló·so -sa [s] *adj* touchy, grouchy
permanènte *adj* permanente || *f* permanent wave
permanènza *f* permanence; stay; continuance (*in office*); duration (*of a disease*); **in permanenza** permanent (*employee*); **buona permanenza!** may your stay be happy!
permanére §235 (*pp* **permaso**) *intr* (ESSERE) to remain, stay
permeàbile *adj* permeable
permeare (**pèrmeo**) *tr* to permeate
permés·so -sa *adj* permitted, allowed; **è permesso?** may I come in? || *m* permit; (mil) pass, leave
permèttere §198 *tr* to permit, allow, let; **permette?** do you mind? || *ref* to take the liberty; to afford
permissíbile *adj* permissible
pèrmuta *f* barter; exchange
permutàbile *adj* tradable, exchangeable
permutare (**pèrmuto**) *tr* to barter; (math) to permute
pernàcchia *f* (vulg) raspberry
pernice *f* partridge
pernició·so -sa [s] *adj* pernicious || *m* pernicious malaria
pèr·nio *m* (-ni) var of **perno**
pèrno *m* pivot; pin; kingbolt; swivel; heart (*of the matter*); kernel (*of the story*); support (*of the family*); (mach) journal; **fare perno** to pivot
pernottare (**pernòtto**) *intr* to spend the night, stay overnight
péro *m* pear tree
però *conj* but, yet; however, nevertheless; **e però** (lit) therefore
peróne *m* fibula
peronòspora *f* downy mildew
perorare (**pèroro**) *tr & intr* to perorate; (law) to plead
perorazióne *f* peroration; (law) pleading
peròssido *m* peroxide; **perossido d'idrogeno** hydrogen peroxide
perpendicolare *adj & f* perpendicular
perpendícolo *m* plumb line; **a perpendicolo** perpendicularly
perpetrare (**pèrpetro & perpètro**) *tr* (lit) to perpetrate
perpètua *f* priest's housekeeper
perpetuare (**perpètuo**) *tr* to perpetuate
perpè·tuo -tua *adj* perpetual, life || *f* see **perpetua**
perplessi·tà *f* (-tà) perplexity
perplès·so -sa *adj* perplexed; (lit) ambiguous
perquisíre §176 *tr* to search
perquisizióne *f* search
persecu·tóre -trice *mf* persecutor, oppressor
persecuzióne *f* persecution
perseguíre (**perséguo**) *tr* to pursue; to persecute; to pester
perseguitare (**perséguito**) *tr* to persecute; to pursue; to pester
perseveranza *f* perseverance
perseverare (**persèvero**) *intr* to persevere
persia·no -na *adj* Persian || *m* Persian; Persian lamb || *f* slatted shutter; **persiana avvolgibile** Venetian blind

pèrsi·co -ca (**-ci -che**) *adj* Persian || *m* (ichth) perch; (obs) peach || *f* (coll) peach
persino *adv* var of **perfino**
persistènte *adj* persistent
persistènza *f* persistence
persistere §114 *intr* to persist
pèr·so -sa *adj* lost, wasted; (archaic) reddish-brown; **a tempo perso** in one's spare time
persóna *f* person; **per persona** apiece; **per capita**; **persona di servizio** servant; **persone** people
personàg·gio *m* (-gi) personage; character
personale *adj* personal || *m* figure, body; personnel, staff; crew || *f* oneman show
personali·tà *f* (-tà) personality; personage
personificare §197 (**personífico**) *tr* to personify
perspicace *adj* perspicacious; farsighted
perspicàcia *f* perspicacity
perspí·cuo -cua *adj* perspicuous
persuadére §213 *tr* to persuade || *ref* to become convinced
persuasióne *f* persuasion
persuasí·vo -va *adj* persuasive; pleasing || *f* persuasiveness
persua·so -sa *adj* convinced; resigned
pertanto *conj* therefore; **non pertanto** nevertheless
pèrti·ca *f* (-che) perch; pole
pertinace *adj* pertinacious, persistent
pertinà·cia *f* (-cie) pertinacity, obstinacy
pertinènte *adj* pertinent, relevant
pertinènza *f* pertinence; competence
pertósse *f* whooping cough
pertù·gio *m* (-gi) hole
perturbare *tr* to perturb || *ref* to be perturbed
perturbazióne *f* perturbation; disturbance
Perù, il Peru; **valere un Perù** to be worth a king's ransom
peruvia·no -na *adj & mf* Peruvian
pervàdere §172 *tr* (lit) to pervade
perveníre §282 *intr* (ESSERE) to arrive; to come; **pervenire a** to reach
perversióne *f* perversion
perversi·tà *f* (-tà) perversity
pervèr·so -sa *adj* perverse; wicked
pervertiménto *m* perversion
pervertíre (**pervèrto**) *tr* to pervert || *ref* to become perverted
perverti·to -ta *adj* perverted || *mf* pervert
pervicace *adj* (lit) obstinate
pervín·ca *f* (-che) periwinkle
pésa [s] *f* weighing; scale
pesage *m* (pesage) weigh-in; place for weighing in jockeys
pesalètte·re [s] *m* (-re) postal scale
pesante [s] *adj* heavy
pesantézza [s] *f* heaviness; weight
pesare (**péso**) [s] *tr* to weigh || *intr* to weigh; **pesare a qlcu** to weigh upon s.o.
pesa·tóre -trice [s] *mf* scale or weigh-

bridge operator; **pesatore pubblico** inspector for the department of weights and measures

pesatura [s] *f* weighing

pé·sca *f* (-sche) fishing; catch (*of fish*) **pesca alla traina** trawling; **pesca d'altura** deep-sea fishing; **pesca di beneficenza** benefit lottery

pè·sca *f* (-sche) peach

pescàg·gio *m* (-gi) (naut) draft

pescàia *f* dam, weir

pescare §197 (**pésco**) *tr* to fish; to draw (*a card*); to dig up (*a piece of news*); to dive for (*pearls*); **pescare con la lenza** to angle for (*fish*) || *intr* to fish; (naut) to displace; **pescare con la lenza** to angle; **pescare di frodo** to poach; **pescare nel torbido** to fish in troubled waters

pesca·tóre -trice *mf* fisher; **pescatore di canna** angler; **pescatore di frodo** poacher

pésce *m* fish; (typ) omission; (coll) biceps; **a pesce** headlong; **non sapere che pesci pigliare** to not know which way to turn; **pesce d'aprile** April fool; **pesce gatto** catfish; **pesce martello** hammerhead || **Pesci** *mpl* (astr) Pisces

pescecane *m* (**pescecani** & **pescicani**) shark; (fig) war profiteer

pescheréc·cio -cia (-ci -ce) *adj* fishing || *m* fishing boat

pescherìa *f* fish market

peschièra *f* fishpond; fishpound (*net*)

pescivéndo·lo -la *mf* fishmonger, fish dealer || *f* fishwife, fishwoman

pè·sco *m* (-schi) peach tree

pesi·sta [s] *m* (-sti) (sports) weight lifter

péso -sa [s] *adj* (coll) heavy || *m* weight; burden; bob (*of clock*); (racing) weigh-in; (sports) shot; **di peso** bodily; **peso lordo** gross weight; **peso massimo** (sports) heavyweight; **peso specifico** specific gravity; **rubare sul peso** to give short weight; **usare due pesi e due misure** to have a double standard || *f* see pesa

pessimismo *m* pessimism

pessimi·sta *mf* (-sti -ste) pessimist

pessimìsti·co -ca *adj* (-ci -che) pessimistic

pèssi·mo -ma *adj* very bad, very poor

pésta *f* track, footprint; **lasciar nelle peste** to leave in the lurch; **seguir le peste di** to follow in the footsteps of

pestàggio *m* beating, clubbing

pestare (**pésto**) *tr* to pound; to trample; to step on; **pestare le orme di** to follow in the footsteps of; **pestare i piedi** to stamp the feet; **pestare sodo** to beat up

pèste *f* plague, pest

pestèllo *m* pestle

pestìfe·ro -ra *adj* pestiferous

pestilènza *f* pestilence; stench

pestilenziale *adj* pestilential; pernicious

pé·sto -sta *adj* crushed; thick (*darkness*) || *m* Genoese sauce || *f* see pesta

pètalo *m* petal

petardo *m* petard, firecracker

petènte *mf* petitioner

petizióne *f* petition; **petizione di principio** begging the question

péto *m* wind, gas

Petrarca *m* Petrarch

petrarché·sco -sca *adj* (-schi -sche) Petrarchan

petrolièra *f* (naut) tanker

petrolière *adj* incendiary || *m* petroleum-industry worker; incendiary; oilman (*producer*)

petrolìfe·ro -ra *adj* oil-yielding

petrò·lio *m* (-li) petroleum; coal oil, kerosene

petró·so -sa [s] *adj* (lit) stony

pettegolare (**pettégolo**) *intr* to gossip

pettegolézzo [ddzz] *m* gossip, rumor

pettégo·lo -la *adj* gossipy || *mf* gossip

pettinare (**pèttino**) *tr* to comb; to card; (coll) to scold

pettinatóre *m* carder

pettinatrice *f* hairdresser; carding machine

pettinatura *f* coiffure, hairstyling

pèttine *m* comb; (zool) scallop; **a pettine** perpendicular (*parking*)

pettìno *m* dickey; bib (*of an apron*); plastron

pettirósso *m* robin redbreast

pètto *m* breast, chest; bust; bosom; **a un petto** single-breasted; **avere al petto** to feed at the breast; **a due petti** or **a doppio petto** double-breasted; **stare a petto** to be equal

pettorale *adj* pectoral || *m* pectoral; breast collar (*of horse*)

pettorina *f* var of pettino

pettorù·to -ta *adj* strutting, haughty

petulante *adj* importunate; impertinent

petulanza *f* importunity; impertinence

petùnia *f* petunia

pèzza *f* piece (*of cloth*); diaper; patch (*in suit or tire*); bolt (*of paper or cloth*); **pezza d'appoggio** supporting document, voucher; **trattare come una pezza da piedi** to wipe one's boots on

pezza·to -ta *adj* spotted, dappled

pezzatura *f* dapple (*on a horse*); size (*e.g., of a loaf of bread*)

pezzènte *mf* beggar

pezzétto *m* little bit; scrap, snip

pèzzo *m* piece; cut (*of meat*); coin; (journ) article; **andare** or **cadere a pezzi** to fall apart; **a pezzi e bocconi** by fits and starts; **fare a pezzi** to break to pieces; to blow to bits; **pezzo di ricambio** spare part; **pezzo d'uomo** hunk of a man; **pezzo duro** brick ice cream; **pezzo forte** forte; **pezzo fuso** cast, casting; **un bel pezzo** a good while; **un pezzo grosso** a big shot

pezzuòla *f* small piece of cloth; (coll) handkerchief

phy·lum *m* (-la) phylum

piacènte *adj* attractive, pleasant

piacére *m* pleasure; **a piacere** at will; **a Suo piacere** as you please; **fare piacere a** to do a favor for; to please; **per piacere** please; **piacere!**

pleased to meet you! || §214 *intr*
(ESSERE) to please; to be pleasing;
(with *dat*) to please, e.g., **come piace
a Dio** as it pleases God; to like, e.g.,
gli piace il ballo he likes dancing

piacévole *adj* pleasant, pleasing

piacevolézza *f* pleasantness; off-color
joke

pia·ga *f* (-**ghe**) sore; ulcer; wound;
plague; (joc) bore; **piaga di decubito**
bedsore

piagare §209 *tr* to make sore, injure

piàg·gia *f* (-**ge**) (archaic) declivity; (lit)
clime, country

piaggiare §290 *tr* (lit) to flatter, blan-
dish || *intr* (archaic) to coast

piagnistèo *m* whining

piagnó·ne -na *mf* (coll) weeper, crybaby

piagnucolare (**piagnùcolo**) *intr* to
whimper, whine

piagnucoló·ne -na *mf* whimperer, crybaby

piagnucoló·so -sa [s] *adj* whimpering,
whining

pialla *f* (carp) plane

piallàc·cio *m* (-**ci**) veneer

piallare *tr* (carp) to plane

piallatrice *f* (carp) planer

piallatura *f* (carp) planing

piana *f* plain; wide table

pianale *m* plain; platform; (rr) flatcar,
platform car

pianeggiante *adj* plane, level

pianèlla *f* mule (*slipper*); tile

pianeròttolo *m* landing (*of stairs*);
ledge

piané·ta *m* (-**ti**) planet; horoscope
|| *f* (eccl) chasuble

piàngere §215 *tr* to shed (*tears*); to
mourn, lament; **piangere miseria** to
cry poverty || *intr* to cry, weep

piangimisè·ria *mf* (-**ria**) poverty-crying
penny pincher

piangiucchiare §287 *intr* to whimper

pianificare §197 (**pianifico**) *tr* to level;
(econ) to plan

pianifica·tóre -trice *mf* planner

pianino *m* (coll) barrel organ

piani·sta *mf* (-**sti -ste**) pianist

pia·no -na *adj* plane; plain, flat || *m*
plain; plane; floor; plateau; plan;
map; (mus) piano; **di primo piano**
first-class; **in piano** horizontal; **piano
di coda** (aer) tail assembly; **piano di
studio** curriculum; **piano regolatore**
building plan; **piano terra** ground
floor; **primo piano** (phot) close-up;
(theat) foreground || *f* see **piana** ||
piano *adv* slowly; softly

pianofòrte *m* piano; **pianoforte a coda**
grand piano

pianòla *f* player piano

pianòro *m* plateau

pianotèr·ra *m* (-**ra**) ground floor

pianta *f* plant; sole (*of foot*); plan,
map; floor plan; **di sana pianta**
wholly; **in pianta stabile** permanent
(*employee*); **pianta rampicante** (bot)
climber

piantagióne *f* plantation

piantana *f* scaffolding

piantare *tr* to plant; to set up (*e.g., a
gun emplacement*); to pitch (*a tent*);
piantala! (slang) cut it out!; **piantare
baracca e burattini** (coll) to clear
out; **piantar chiodi** (coll) to go into
debt; **piantare gli occhi addosso a**
to stare at; **piantare in asso** to leave
in the lurch || *ref* to place oneself;
to abandon one another

pianta·to -ta *adj* planted; stuck; driven;
bien piantato well-built (*person*)

pianta·tóre -trice *mf* planter

pianterréno *m* ground floor

piantito *m* (coll) floor

pianto *m* weeping, tears; sadness; (bot)
sap; (coll) sight, mess

piantonare (**piantóno**) *tr* to watch,
guard

piantóne *m* watchman; (mil) orderly;
(mil) sentry; (bot) cutting, shoot;
piantone di guida (aut) steering
wheel column

pianura *f* plain

piastra *f* plate; piaster (*coin*)

piastrèlla *f* tile; small flat stone; bounce
(*of an airplane on landing*)

piastrellaménto *m* bump, bounce (*of
motorboat or airplane*)

piastrelli·sta *m* (-**sti**) tiler, tile layer

piastrina *f* or **piastrino** *m* small plate;
(mil) dog tag; (biol) platelet

piatire §176 *intr* (lit) to argue; (coll) to
beg insistently

piattafórma *f* platform; roadbed (*of
highway*); (rr) turntable; (pol) plank;
piattaforma di lancio launching pad

piattèllo *m* small dish; bobêche; clay
pigeon

piattina *f* electric cord; metal band;
(min) wagon

piattino *m* saucer

piat·to -ta *adj* flat || *m* dish, plate; pan
(*of scale*); pot (*in gambling*); course
(*of meal*); cover (*of book*); flat (*e.g.,
of blade*); **piatti** (mus) cymbals;
piatto del grammofono turntable;
piatto del giorno plat du jour; **piatto
di lenticchie** (Bib & fig) mess of pot-
tage; **piatto fondo** soup dish; **piatto
forte** pièce de résistance

piàttola *f* (zool) crab louse; (coll) cockroach; (vulg) bore

piazza *f* square; plaza; crowd; market;
fortress; **andare in piazza** (coll) to
become bald; **da piazza** common,
ordinary; **di piazza** for hire (*e.g.,
cab*); **fare la piazza** (com) to canvass
for customers; **far piazza pulita di**
to get rid of; to clean out; **mettere in
piazza** to noise abroad; **piazza d'armi**
parade ground; **scendere in piazza**
to take to the streets

piazzafòrte *f* (**piazzefòrti**) stronghold,
fortress

piazzale *m* large square, esplanade,
plaza

piazzaménto *m* placement; (sports) position (*of a team*)

piazzare *tr* to place; to sell || *ref* to
place; to show (*said of a racing
horse*)

piazza·to -ta *adj* placed; arrived (*at a high position*) || *f* row, brawl

piazzi·sta *m* (**-sti**) salesman; traveling salesman

piazzòla *f* court, place; rest area (*off a highway*); (mil) emplacement; **piazzola di partenza** (golf) tee

pi·ca *f* (**-che**) (orn) magpie

picaré·sco -sca *adj* (**-schi -sche**) picaresque

pic·ca *f* (**-che**) pike; pique; **per picca** out of spite; **picche** (cards) spades; **rispondere picche** (fig) to answer no

piccante *adj* piquant, racy

piccare §197 *tr* (obs) to prick || *ref* to become angry; **piccarsi di** to pride oneself on

pic·chè *f* (**-chè**) piqué

picchettaménto *m* picketing

picchettare (**picchétto**) *tr* to stake out; to picket

picchétto *m* stake; picket; (mil) detail

picchiare §287 *tr* to hit, strike || *intr* to knock; to strike; to tap (*said, e.g., of rain*); (aer) to nose-dive; **picchiare in testa** (aut) to knock || *ref* to hit one another

picchiata *f* hit, blow; (aer) nose dive

picchia·tóre -trice *mf* hitter || *m* (boxing) puncher

picchierellare (**picchierèllo**) *tr* & *intr* to tap

picchiettare (**picchiétto**) *tr* to tap; to scrape; to speckle || *intr* to tap

picchiet·tìo *m* (**-tìi**) patter (*e.g., of rain*)

pic·chio *m* (**-chi**) knock; (orn) woodpecker; **di picchio** all of a sudden

picchiòtto *m* knocker (*on door*)

piccinerìa *f* pettiness

picci·no -na *adj* little, tiny; petty || *mf* child; baby

picciòlo *m* stem (*e.g., of cherry*); leafstalk, petiole

piccionàia *f* dovecote; loft; attic; (theat) upper gallery

piccióne -na *mf* pigeon; **pigliare due piccioni con una fava** to hit two birds with one stone

pic·co *m* (**-chi**) peak; (naut) gaff; **andare a picco** to sink; to go to ruin; **a picco** vertically; **picco di carico** (naut) derrick

piccolézza *f* smallness; trifle

pìcco·lo -la *adj* small; low (*speed*); short (*distance*); young; petty; **da piccolo** when young; **in piccolo** on a small scale; **nel mio piccolo** with my modest abilities || *mf* child

piccóne *m* pick

piccòzza *f* mattock (*for mountain climbing*)

pidocchierìa *f* stinginess; meanness

pidòc·chio *m* (**-chi**) louse; **pidocchio rifatto** (slang) parvenu

pidocchió·so -sa *adj* lousy; stingy

piè *m* (**piè**) (lit) foot; **ad ogni piè sospinto** on every occasion; **saltare a piè pari** to skip with the feet together; (fig) to skip over

piède *m* foot; leg (*of table*); stalk (*of salad*); bottom (*of column*); trunk (*of tree*); footing; **alzarsi in piedi** to stand up; **a piede libero** free; **a piedi**

on foot; **a piedi nudi** barefooted; **con i piedi di piombo** cautiously; **essere in piedi** to be up and around; **fare con i piedi** to botch; **mettere un piede in fallo** to stumble; **piede di porco** crowbar; **prendere piede** to take hold; **puntare i piedi** to balk; **su due piedi** offhand; **tenere il piede in due staffe** to carry water on both shoulders

piedestallo or **piedistallo** *m* pedestal

piedritto *m* buttress

piè·ga *f* (**-ghe**) bend; crease; pleat; crimp; wrinkle; (fig) turn; **prendere una cattiva piega** to take a turn for the worse

piegare §209 (**piègo**) *tr* to bend; to wave (*hair*); to fold; to pleat; to bow (*head*) || *intr* to turn || *ref* to bow; to bend; to buckle; to yield

piega·tóre -trice *mf* folder || *f* folding machine

piegatura *f* fold, crease

pieghettare (**pieghétto**) *tr* to pleat

pieghévole *adj* folding; pliant; (fig) versatile || *m* folder

pieghevolézza *f* flexibility

piè·go *m* (**-ghi**) folder; bundle of papers

pièna *f* flood; rise (*of river*); crowd; (fig) overflow; **in piena** overflowing

pienézza *f* plenitude, fullness

piè·no -na *adj* full; solid; broad (*daylight*); full (*honors*); **a pieno** or **in pieno** to the full; **colpire nel pieno** to hit the bull's eye; **pieno di alive with; **pieno di sé** conceited; **pieno zeppo** replete, chock-full || *m* fullness; height (*e.g., of winter*); **fare il pieno** (aut) to fill up || *f* see **piena**

pie·tà *f* (**-tà**) mercy; pity; (lit) piety

pietanza *f* main course

pietó·so -sa [s] *adj* pitiful, piteous; merciful

pièra *f* stone; rock; **pietra angolare** cornerstone; **pietra da affilare** whetstone; **pietra da sarto** French chalk; **pietra dello scandalo** source of scandal; **pietra di paragone** touchstone; **pietra focaia** flint; **pietra miliare** milestone; **pietra tombale** tombstone; **posare la prima pietra** to lay the cornerstone

pietrificare §197 (**pietrìfico**) *tr* & *ref* to petrify

pietrina *f* flint (*for lighter*)

pietri·sco *m* (**-schi**) rubble; (rr) ballast

Piètro *m* Peter

pietró·so -sa [s] *adj* (lit) stony

pievano *m* parish priest

piffero *m* pipe, fife

pigia *m*—**pigia pigia** crowd, throng

pigia·ma *m* (**-ma** & **-mi**) pajamas

pigiare §290 *tr* to squeeze, press || *intr* to insist || *ref* to squeeze

pigia·tóre -trice *mf* presser (*of grapes*) || *f* wine press

pigiatura *f* pressing, squeezing

pigionante *mf* tenant

pigióne *f* rent, rental; **dare a pigione** to rent; to grant the possession of; **prendere a pigione** to rent; to hold for payment

pigliamó·sche *m* (**-sche**) flypaper; fly-trap; (orn) flycatcher

pigliare §280 *tr* to take, catch; to mistake; **che Le piglia?** what's the matter with you? || *ref*—**pigliarsela** (**con**) to get angry (at)

pì·glio *m* (**-gli**) hold; countenance; **dar di piglio a** to grab

pigménto *m* pigment

pigmè·o -a *adj* & *mf* pygmy; Pygmy

pigna *f* strainer (*at the end of a suction pipe*); bunch (*of grapes*); (bot) pine cone

pignatta *f* pot

pignò·lo -la *adj* finicky, fussy || *m* pine nut

pignóne *m* pinion; embankment

pignoraménto *m* (law) seizure

pignorare (**pìgnoro**) *tr* (law) to seize

pigolare (**pìgolo**) *intr* to peep (*said, e.g., of young birds*)

pigolì·o *m* (**-i**) peep (*e.g., of a young bird*)

pigrìzia *f* laziness

pi·gro -gra *adj* lazy; (lit) sluggish

pila *f* pier; buttress (*of bridge*); heap, sink; font; (elec) cell; (elec) battery; **pila atomica** atomic pile

pilastro *m* pier, pillar

pillàcchera *f* mud splash; (fig) fault

pìllola *f* pill; (slang) bullet; **addolcire la pillola** to sugar-coat the pill

pilóne *m* pier; pylon

pilò·ta (**-ti -te**) *adj* pilot || *mf* pilot; (aut) driver

pilotàg·gio *m* (**-gi**) piloting; steering

pilotare (**pilòto**) *tr* to pilot; to drive

pilotina *f* (naut) pilot boat

piluccare §197 *tr* to pluck (*e.g., grapes one by one*); to nibble, pick at; to scrounge; (lit) to consume

piménto *m* allspice

pinacotè·ca *f* (**-che**) picture gallery

pinéta *f* pine grove

pìngue *adj* fat; rich

pinguèdine *f* fatness, corpulence

pinguino *m* penguin

pinna *f* fin (*of fish*); flipper; (zool) pen shell (*mussel*)

pinnàcolo *m* pinnacle

pino *m* pine tree; **pino marittimo** pinaster; **pino silvestre** Scotch fir

pinòlo *m* pine nut

pinta *f* pint

pinza *f* claw (*of lobster*); **pinza emostatica** hemostat; **pinza tagliafili** wire cutter; **pinze** clippers; pliers; pincers

pinzatrice *f* stapler

pinzétte *fpl* tweezers, pliers

pinzòche·ro -ra *mf* bigot

pì·o -a *adj* (**-i -e**) pious; charitable || **Pio** *m* Pius

piòg·gia *f* (**-ge**) rain

piòlo *m* peg; rung (*of ladder*); picket, stake

piombàggine *f* graphite

piombare (**piómbo**) *tr* to lead; to seal; to knock down; to fill (*a tooth*) || *intr* to fall; to swoop down

piombatura *f* leading; filling (*of tooth*)

piombino *m* weight; seal; plumb; plumb bob

piómbo *m* lead; **a piombo** perpendicularly; **di piombo** suddenly

pionerìsti·co -ca *adj* (**-ci -che**) pioneering

pionière *m* pioneer

pióppo *m* poplar; **pioppo tremolo** aspen

piorrèa *f* pyorrhea

piotare (**piòto**) *tr* to sod

piova·no -na *adj* rain (*water*)

piova·sco -na (**-schi**) rain squall

piovènte *m* pitch, slope

piòvere §216 *intr* (ESSERE) to rain; to pour; to flock (*said of people*); **piovere addosso a** to rain down on; **piovere su** to flow down over || *impers* (ESSERE & AVERE)—**piove** it is raining; it is leaking (*from rain*); **piove a catinelle** or **a dirotto** it is raining cats and dogs

piovigginare (**piovìggina**) *impers* (ESSERE & AVERE)—**pioviggina** it is drizzling

piovigginó·so -sa [*s*] *adj* drizzling, drizzly

piovór·no -na *adj* (lit) var of **piovoso**

piovosi·tà [*s*] *f* (**-tà**) raininess; rainfall

piovó·so -sa [*s*] *adj* rainy

piòvra *f* octopus; (fig) leech

pipa *f* pipe; **non valere una pipa di tabacco** to not be worth a tinker's dam

pipare *intr* to smoke a pipe

pipata *f* pipe, pipeful

pipistrèllo *m* (zool) bat

pipita *f* hangnail; (vet) pip

pira *f* (lit) pyre

piràmide *f* pyramid

pira·ta *adj invar* pirate || *m* (**-ti**) pirate; **pirata dell'aria** skyjacker; **pirata della strada** hit-and-run driver

pirateggiare §290 (**piratéggio**) *intr* to pirate

piraterìa *f* piracy; **pirateria letteraria** piracy of literary works

Pirenèi *mpl* Pyrenees

pìri·co -ca *adj* (**-ci -che**) fireworks; **polvere pirica** gunpowder

pirite *f* pyrite

piroétta *f* pirouette

pirò·ga *f* (**-ghe**) pirogue

pirolisi *f* (chem) cracking

piróne *m* (mus) tuning pin

piròscafo *m* steamship; **piroscafo da carico** (naut) freighter; **piroscafo da passeggeri** passenger ship

piroscissióne *f* (chem) cracking

pirotècni·co -ca (**-ci -che**) *adj* pyrotecnic || *m* pyrotecnist || *f* fireworks, pyrotechnics

pisciare §128 *intr* (vulg) to urinate

piscia·tóio *m* (**-tói**) (vulg) street urinal

piscina *f* swimming pool

pisèllo [*s*] *m* pea; **pisello odoroso** sweet pea

pisolare (**pìsolo**) *intr* (coll) to doze

pìsolo *m* (coll) nap; **schiacciare un pisolo** (coll) to take a nap

pìsside *f* (eccl) pyx; (bot) pyxidium

pista *f* track; ring (*of circus*); race track, speedway (*for car races*); ski run; (aer) runway; **pista ciclabile** bicycle trail; **pista da ballo** dance floor; **seguire una pista** to follow a clue

pistàc·chio *m* (**-chi**) pistachio

pistillo *m* (bot) pistil

pistòla *f* pistol

pistolettàta *f* pistol shot

pistolòtto *m* lecture, talking-to; theatrical peroration

pistóne *m* piston; plunger

pitagòri·co -ca *adj* & *m* (**-ci -che**) Pythagorean

pitale *m* (coll) chamber pot

pitoccàre §197 (**pitòcco**) *intr* to beg

pitòc·co *m* (**-chi**) beggar; miser

pitóne *m* python

pìttima *f* plaster; (fig) bore

pit·tóre -trice *mf* painter

pittóre·sco -sca *adj* (**-schi -sche**) picturesque

pittòri·co -ca *adj* (**-ci -che**) pictorial

pittùra *f* painting; picture; (coll) paint

pitturàre *tr* to paint; to varnish || *ref* to put on make-up

più *adj invar* more; several || *m* (**più**) plus; most; **credersi da più** to believe oneself superior; **dal più al meno** about, more or less; **i più** most, the majority; **parlare del più e del meno** (coll) to make small talk || *adv* more; again; **a più non posso** to the very utmost; **in più** besides; **mai più** never again; **non poterne più** to be exhausted; **per di più** besides; **per lo più** for the most part; **più o meno** more or less; **tanto più** moreover; **tutt'al più** mostly

piuma *f* feather, plume; **piume** (fig) bed

piumàc·cio *m* (**-ci**) feather pillow

piumàg·gio *m* (**-gi**) plumage

piumino *m* down; comforter; puff, powder puff; feather duster

piuttòsto *adv* rather; somewhat

piva *f* bagpipe; **tornare con le pive nel sacco** to return bitterly disappointed

pivèllo *m* greenhorn; whippersnapper

pivière *m* (orn) plover

pizza *f* pizza; (mov) canister; (coll) bore

pizzaiò·lo -la *mf* owner of pizzeria || *m* pizza baker || *f—alla pizzaiola* prepared with tomato and garlic sauce

pizzardóne *m* (coll) cop, officer

pizzicàgno·lo -la *mf* grocer; sausage dealer

pizzicàre §197 (**pìzzico**) *tr* to pinch; to pluck; to bite, burn; (mus) to pick, twang

pizzicherìa *f* delicatessen, grocery

pìzzi·co *m* (**-chi**) pinch

pizzicóre *m* itch

pizzicòtto *m* pinch; **dar pizzicotti a** to pinch

pizzo *m* peak (*of mountain*); goatee; lace

placàre §197 *tr* to placate || *ref* to calm down

plac·ca *f* (**-che**) plate; plaque; tag, badge; (elec, rad) plate; (pathol) blotch, spot

placcàre §197 *tr* to plate; (sports) to tackle

plàci·do -da *adj* placid

plafond *m* (plafond) ceiling; (aer) ceiling; (com) top credit

pla·ga *f* (**-ghe**) (lit) clime, region

plagiàre §290 *tr* to plagiarize

plagià·rio -ria (**-ri -rie**) *adj* plagiaristic || *mf* plagiarist

plà·gio *m* (**-gi**) plagiarism

planàre *intr* (aer) to glide

planàta *f* (aer) gliding

plàn·cia *f* (**-ce**) (naut) gangplank; (naut) bridge

planetà·rio -ria (**-ri -rie**) *adj* planetary || *m* planetarium; (aut) planetary gear

plantàre *m* arch support

pla·sma *m* (**-smi**) plasma

plasmàre *tr* to mold, shape

plàsti·ca *f* (**-che**) plastic art; plastics; plastic surgery; plastic

plasticàre §197 (**plàstico**) *tr* to mold, shape; to cover with plastic

plàsti·co -ca (**-ci -che**) *adj* plastic || *m* relief map; maquette; plastic bomb || *f* see **plastica**

plastilina *f* modeling clay

plastron *m* (plastron) ascot

plàtano *m* plane tree; **platano americano** buttonwood tree

platèa *f* audience; (theat) orchestra; (archit) foundation

plateàle *adj* obvious; plebeian

plàtina *f* (typ) platen

platinàre (**plàtino**) *tr* to platinize; to bleach (*hair*)

plàtino *m* platinum

Platóne *m* Plato

plaudènte *adj* enthusiastic

plàudere (**plàudo**) & **plaudìre** (**plàudo**) *intr* to applaud; (with *dat*) to applaud, e.g., **plaudere alla generosità** to applaud the generosity

plausìbile *adj* plausible

plàuso *m* (lit) applause, praise

plebàglia *f* rabble

plèbe *f* populace; (lit) crowd

plebè·o -a *adj* & *mf* plebeian

plebiscìto *m* plebiscite

plenà·rio -ria *adj* (**-ri -rie**) plenary

plenilù·nio *m* (**-ni**) full moon

plenipotenzià·rio -ria *adj* & *m* (**-ri -rie**) plenipotentiary

plètora *f* plethora

plèttro *m* (mus) pick, plectrum

pleurìte *f* (pathol) pleurisy

pli·co *m* (**-chi**) sealed document; bundle of papers; **in plico a parte** or **in plico separato** under separate cover

plotóne *m* platoon; **plotone d'esecuzione** firing squad

plùmbe·o -a *adj* lead, leaden

plurale *adj* & *m* plural; **al plurale** in the plural

plurilìngue *adj* multilingual

plurimotóre *adj* multimotored || *m* multimotor

pluristàdio *adj invar* (rok) multistage

plusvalènza *f* unearned increment

plusvalóre *m*; surplus value (*in Marxist economics*)

Plutàrco *m* Plutarch

plutocrazìa *f* plutocracy

Plutóne *m* Pluto

plutònio *m* plutonium
pluviale *adj* rain || *m* waterspout
pneumàti·co -ca (**-ci -che**) *adj* pneumatic, air || *m* tire; **pneumatico da neve** snow tire
po' *m* see **poco**
pochézza *f* lack, scarcity
pò·co -ca (**-chi -che**) *adj* little; short (*distance*); poor (*health; memory*); (*with collective nouns*) few, e.g., **poca gente** few people; (*with plural nouns*) a few, e.g., **fra pochi mesi** in a few months; (*with plural nouns having singular meaning in English*) little, e.g., **pochi quattrini** little money || *m invar* little; short distance; short time; **a ogni poco** often; **da poco** a little while ago; of no account; **da un bel po'** quite a while; quite a while ago; **fra poco in a little while**; **manca poco a** it won't be long till; **manca poco che** (*e.g., il ragazzo*) **non** + *subj* (e.g., the boy) almost + *subj;* **per poco non** almost; **poco di buono** good-for-nothing; **poco fa** a little while ago; **saper di poco** to taste flat; **un poco di** or **un po' di** a little || *f—***poca di poco** hussy || **poco** *adv* little; **poco bene** poorly; **poco dopo** shortly after; **poco male** not too poorly
podagra *f* gout
podére *m* farm, country property
poderó·so -sa [s] *adj* powerful
pode·stà *m* (**-stà**) (hist) mayor; (hist) podesta
podia·tra *mf* (**-tri -tre**) chiropodist
pò·dio *m* (**-di**) podium; platform; (archit) base
podismo *m* foot racing
podi·sta *mf* (**-sti -ste**) foot racer
poè·ma *m* (**-mi**) long poem
poesìa *f* poetry; poem
poè·ta *m* (**-ti**) poet
poetéssa *f* poetess
poèti·co -ca (**-ci -che**) *adj* poetic(al) || *f* poetics
pòg·gia *f* (**-ge**) leeward
poggiare §290 (**pòggio**) *tr* to lean || *intr* to be based; (mil) to move; (naut) to sail before the wind; (archaic) to rise
poggiatè·sta *m* (**-sta**) headrest; (aut) head restrainer
pòg·gio *m* (**-gi**) hillock, knoll
poggiòlo *m* balcony
pòi *m* future || *adv* then; later; **a poi** until later; **poi dopo** later on
poiana *f* buzzard
poiché *conj* since, as; (lit) after
pòker *m* poker (*game*); four of a kind; **poker di re** four kings
polac·co -ca (**-chi -che**) *adj* Polish || *mf* Pole || *f* (mus) polonaise
polare *adj* pole, polar
polarizzare [ddzz] *tr* to polarize
pòl·ca *f* (**-che**) polka
polèmi·co -ca (**-ci -che**) *adj* polemical || *f* polemics
polemizzare [ddzz] *intr* to engage in polemics
polèna *f* (naut) figurehead
polènta *f* corn mush

polentina *f* poultice
poliambulanza *f* clinic, emergency ward
policlìni·co·m (**-ci**) polyclinic
polifonìa *f* polyphony
polìga·mo -ma *adj* polygamous || *m* polygamist
poliglòt·ta *adj & mf* (**-ti -te**) polyglot
poliglòt·to *adj & mf* polyglot
polìgono *m* polygon; **poligono di tiro** shooting range
polìgrafo *m* author skilled in many subjects; multigraph
polinesia·no -na *adj & mf* Polynesian
polinò·mio *m* (**-mi**) polynomial
pòlio *f* (coll) polio
poliomielite *f* poliomielitis, infantile paralysis
pòlipo *m* (pathol, zool) polyp
polisìlla·bo -ba *adj* polysyllabic || *m* polysyllable
poli·sta·m (**-sti**) polo player
politea·ma *m* (**-mi**) theater
politècni·co -ca (**-ci -che**) *adj* polytechnic || *m* polytechnic institute
politeì·sta (**-sti -ste**) *adj* polytheistic || *mf* polytheist
politeìsti·co -ca *adj* (**-ci -che**) polytheistic
polìti·ca *f* (**-che**) politics; policy
politicante *mf* petty politician
polìti·co -ca (**-ci -che**) *adj* political || *m* politician || *f* see **politica**
polìtti·co·m (**-ci**) polyptych
polizìa *f* police; **polizia sanitaria** health department; **polizia stradale** highway patrol; **polizia tributaria** income-tax investigation department
polizié·sco -sca *adj* (**-schi -sche**) police (*car*); detective (*story*)
poliziòtto *adj masc* police (*dog*) || *m* policeman; detective; **poliziotto in borghese** plain-clothes man
pòlizza *f* policy; ticket (*e.g., of pawnbroker*); **polizza di carico** bill of lading
pólla *f* spring (*of water*)
pol·làio·m (**-lài**) chicken coop
pollaiò·lo -la *mf* chicken dealer
pollame *m* poultry
pollastra *f* pullet; (coll) chick
pollerìa *f* poultry shop
pòllice *m* thumb; big toe; inch
pollicoltura *f* poultry raising
pólline *m* pollen
pollivéndo·lo -la *mf* poultry dealer
póllo *m* chicken; (fig) sucker; **conoscere i propri polli** (fig) to know one's onions; **pollo d'India** turkey
pollóne *m* (bot) shoot; (fig) offspring
polmóne *m* lung; **a pieni polmoni** at the top of one's lungs; **polmone d'acciaio** iron lung
polmonite *f* pneumonia
pòlo *m* pole; polo shirt; (sports) polo
Polònia, la Poland
pólpa *f* meat; pulp; flesh (*of fruit*); (fig) gist; **in polpe** (hist) in knee breeches
polpàc·cio *m* (**-ci**) calf (*of leg*); cut of meat; ball of thumb

polpastrèllo *m* finger tip
polpétta *f* meat ball; meat patty, cutlet
polpettóne *m* meat loaf; (fig) hash
pólpo *m* (zool) octopus
polpó·so -sa [s] *adj* pulpy, fleshy
polpu·to -ta *adj* meaty
polsino *m* cuff
pólso *m* pulse; wrist; cuff, wristband; strong hand, energy; **di polso** energetic
poltiglia *f* mash; slush
poltrire §176 *intr* to idle; to loll in bed
poltróna *f* armchair; (theat) orchestra seat; **poltrona a orecchioni** wing chair; **poltrona a sdraio** chaise longue; **poltrona letto** day bed
poltroncina *f* parquet-circle seat
poltró·ne -na *mf* lazybones, sluggard ‖ *f* see **poltrona**
poltroneria *f* laziness
poltronìssima *f* (theat) first-row seat
pólvere *f* dust; powder; **in polvere** powdered; **polvere da sparo** gunpowder; **polvere di stelle** stardust; **polvere nera** or **pirica** gunpowder; **polveri** gunpowder
polverièra *f* powder magazine; (fig) tinderbox, trouble spot
polverifi·cio *m* (-ci) powder works
polverina *f* (pharm) powder
polverino *m* pounce, sand
polverizzare [ddzz] *tr* to crush, powder; to atomize; to pulverize
polverizza·to -ta [ddzz] *adj* powdered (*sugar*)
polverizzatóre [ddzz] *m* atomizer
polveróne *m* dust cloud
polveró·so -sa [s] *adj* dusty; powdery (*snow*)
pomata *f* ointment; pomade
pomella·to -ta *adj* dapple-grey
pomèllo *m* cheek; cheekbone; pommel, knob
pomeridia·no -na *adj* afternoon, P.M.
pomerig·gio *m* (-gi) afternoon
pomiciare §128 (pómicio) *tr* to pumice ‖ *intr* (slang) to spoon
pomicione *m* (slang) spooner
pomidòro *m* var of **pomodoro**
pómo *m* apple; knob; pommel (*of saddle*); **pomo della discordia** apple of discord; **pomo di Adamo** Adam's apple; **pomo di terra** potato
pomodòro *m* tomato; **pomodoro di mare** (zool) sea anemone
pómolo *m* (coll) knob, handle
pómpa *f* pump; pomp; state; **in pompa magna** all dressed up; **pompa aspirante** suction pump; **pompa premente** force pump; see **imprenditore** and **impresa**
pompare (pómpo) *tr* to pump; to pump up
pompèlmo *m* grapefruit
pompière *m* fireman
pompó·so -sa [s] *adj* pompous
pòn·ce *m* (-ci) punch
ponderare (pòndero) *tr* to weigh, ponder; to weight ‖ *intr* to think it over
pondera·to -ta *adj* considerate, careful
ponderó·so -sa [s] *adj* ponderous

ponènte *m* west; west wind; West; West Wind
pónte *m* bridge; metal scaffolding; (aut) axle; (naut) deck; **fare il ponte** to take the day off between two holidays; **fare ponti d'oro** a to offer a good way out to; **ponte aereo** airlift; **ponte delle segnalazioni** (rr) gantry; **ponte di chiatte** pontoon bridge; **ponte di comando** (naut) bridge; **ponte di volo** flight deck; **ponte levatoio** drawbridge; **ponte radio** radio communication; **ponte sospeso** suspension bridge
pontéfice *m* pontiff; (hist) pontifex
pontéggio *m* scaffolding
ponticèllo *m* small bridge; nosepiece (*of eyeglasses*); (mus) bridge
pontière *m* (mil) engineer
pontificale *adj* pontifical ‖ *m* pontifical mass
pontifi·cio -cia *adj* (-ci -cie) papal
pontile *m* pier
pontóne *m* pontoon, barge
ponzare (pónzo) *tr* (coll) to strain to accomplish ‖ *intr* (coll) to rack one's brains
popeli·ne *f* (-ne) broadcloth
popola·no -na *adj* popular ‖ *mf* commoner
popolare *adj* popular ‖ *v* (pòpolo) *tr* to people, populate ‖ *ref* to be inhabited
popolarità *f* popularity
popola·to -ta *adj* peopled; crowded
popolazióne *f* population
pòpolo *m* people; crowd; **popolo grasso** (hist) rich bourgeoisie; **popolo minuto** (hist) artisans, common people
popoló·so -sa [s] *adj* populous
popóne *m* (coll) melon
póppa *f* breast; (naut) stern; (lit) ship; **a poppa** astern, aft
poppante *adj* & *mf* suckling
poppare (póppo) *tr* to suckle
poppa·tóio *m* (-tói) nursing bottle
poppavìa *f*—**a poppavia** astern, aft
pòr·ca *f* (-che) ridge (*between furrows*); sow
porcacció·ne -na *m* cad, rake ‖ *f* slut
por·càio *m* (-cài) swineherd; pigsty
porcellana *f* porcelain, china; (bot) purslane
porcellino *m* piggy; **porcellino d'India** guinea pig
porcheria *f* dirt; (coll) dirty trick; (coll) botch
porchétta *f* roast suckling pig
porcile *m* pigsty
porci·no -na *adj* pig ‖ *m* (bot) boletus
pòr·co -ca *m* (-ci -che) pig, hog, swine; pork; **porco mondo!** (slang) heck! ‖ *f* see **porca**
porcospino *m* porcupine
pòrfido *m* porphyry
pòrgere §217 *tr* to hand, offer; to relate; **porgere l'orecchio** to lend an ear ‖ *intr* to declaim ‖ *ref* to appear, show up
pornografia *f* pornography
pòro *m* pore
poró·so -sa [s] *adj* porous
pórpora *f* purple

porpora·to -ta *adj* purple || *m* purple; cardinal

porpori·no -na *adj* purple

pórre §218 *tr* to put; to repose (*trust*); to set (*a limit; one's foot*); to lay (*a stone*); to pose (*a question*); to pay (*attention*); to suppose; to advance (*the candidacy*); **porre gli occhi addosso a** to lay one's eyes on; **porre in dubbio** to cast doubt on; **porre mano a** to set to work at; **porre termine a** to put an end to; **posto che** since, provided || *ref* to place oneself; **porsi in cammino** to set out or forth; **porsi in salvo** to reach safety

pòrro *m* wart; (bot) leek

pòrta *f* door; gate; (cricket) wicket; (sports) goal; **di porta in porta** door-to-door; **fuori porta** outside the city limits; **mettere alla porta** to dismiss, fire; **porta di servizio** delivery entrance; **porta scorrevole** sliding door; **porta stagna** (naut) (theat) safety door

portabagà·gli *m* (-gli) porter; baggage rack

portabandiè·ra *m* (-ra) standard-bearer

portàbile *adj* portable

portàbi·ti *m* (-ti) coat hanger

portabottì·glie *m* (-glie) bottle rack

portacar·te *adj invar* & *m* (-te) folder

portacati·no *adj invar* washstand-supporting || *m* (-no) washstand

portacéne·re *m* (-re) ashtray

portachia·vi *m* (-vi) key ring

portaci·pria *m* (-pria) compact

portadi·schi *m* (-schi) record cabinet, record rack; turntable

portadól·ci *m* (-ci) candy dish

portaère·i *f* (-i) aircraft carrier

portaferi·ti *m* (-ti) (mil) stretcher bearer

portafinèstra *f* (**portefinèstre**) French window

portafió·ri *m* (-ri) flower vase

portafò·gli *m* (-gli) or **portafò·glio** *m* (-gli) billfold, wallet; pocketbook; portfolio

portafortu·na *m* (-na) charm, amulet

portafrut·ta *m* (-ta) fruit dish

portafusìbi·li *m* (-li) fuse box

portagiò·ie *m* (-ie) jewel box

portaimmondì·zie *m* (-zie) trash can, garbage can

portainsé·gna *m* (-gna) standard-bearer

portalàmpa·da *m* (-da) (elec) socket

portale *m* portal

portalètte·re (-re) *mf* letter carrier || *m* postman, mailman

portamaz·ze *m* (-ze) caddie

portaménto *m* posture; gait; (fig) behavior

portami·na *m* (-na) mechanical pencil

portamissì·li (-li) *adj invar* missile-carrying || *m* missile carrier

portamonè·te *m* (-te) purse

portamùsi·ca *m* (-ca) music stand

portante *adj* carrying; (archit) weight-bearing; (aer) lifting; (rad) carrier || *m* amble

portantina *f* sedan chair; stretcher

portantino *m* bearer (*of sedan chair*); stretcher bearer

portanza *f* (archit) capacity; (aer) lift

portaombrèl·li *m* (-li) umbrella stand

portaórdi·ni *m* (-ni) (mil) messenger

portapac·chi *m* (-chi) parcel delivery man; basket (*on bicycle*)

portapén·ne *m* (-ne) penholder

portapiat·ti *m* (-ti) dish rack

portaposa·te [s] *m* (-te) silverware chest

portapran·zi [dz] *m* (-zi) dinner pail

portaraz·zi (-zi) [ddzz] *adj invar* missile-carrying || *m* missile carrier

portare (pòrto) *tr* to carry; to bring; to take; to carry along; to lead; to herald; to praise; to wear; to drive (*car*); to run (*a candidate*); to adduce; to nurture (*hatred*); (aut) to hold (*e.g., five people*); **portare a conoscenza di** to let know; **portare avanti** to carry forward; **portare in alto** to lift; **portare via** to steal; to take away || *intr* to carry (*said of a gun*) || *ref* to move; to behave; to be (*a candidate*)

portaritrat·ti *m* (-ti) picture frame

portasapó·ne *m* (-ne) soap dish

portasigaré·te *m* (-te) cigarette case

portasiga·ri *m* (-ri) cigar case; humidor

portaspìl·li *m* (-li) pincushion

portata *f* course (*of a meal*); capacity; flow (*of river*); compass (*of voice*); range (*of voice or gun*); importance; (naut) burden; (naut) tonnage; **a portata di mano** within reach; **a portata di voce** within call, within earshot

portatèsse·re *m* (-re) card case

portàtile *adj* portable

porta·to -ta *adj* worn; **portato a** leaning toward || *m* result, effect || *f* see **portata**

porta·tóre -trice *mf* bearer

portatovagliòlo *m* napkin ring

portauò·vo *m* (-vo) eggcup

portavó·ce *m* (-ce) megaphone; (fig) mouthpiece

porte-enfant *m* (**porte-enfant**) baby bunting

portèllo *m* wicket; leaf (*of cabinet door*); (naut) porthole

portènto *m* portent

portica·to -ta *adj* arcaded || *m* arcade

pòrti·co *m* (-ci) portico, arcade, colonnade; shed

portiè·re -ra *mf* concierge || *m* janitor, doorman; (sports) goalkeeper || *f* portiere (*in church door*); (aut) door

porti·nàio -nàia (-nài -nàie) *adj* door, door-keeping || *mf* doorkeeper, concierge

portineria *f* janitor's quarters

pòrto *m* port, harbor; transportation charge; port wine; goal; **condurre a buon porto** to carry to fruition; **franco di porto** prepaid, postpaid; **porto a carico del mittente** postage prepaid; **porto assegnato** charges to be paid by addressee; **porto d'armi** permit to carry arms; **porto franco** free port

Portogallo, il Portugal

portoghése [s] *adj* & *mf* Portuguese;

fare il portoghese (theat) to crash the gate
portóne *m* portal
portorica·no -na *adj & mf* Puerto Rican
Portorico *m* Puerto Rico
portuale *adj* port, harbor || *m* dock worker, longshoreman
porzióne *f* portion
pòsa [s] *f* laying (*e.g., of cornerstone*); posing (*for portrait*); posture, affectation, pose; dregs; (phot) exposure; (lit) rest; **senza posa** relentlessly, relentlessly
posami·ne (-ne) [s] *adj invar* minelaying || *f* minelayer
posare [s] (**pòso**) *tr* to lay, put down || *intr* to lie; to settle; to pose; **posare a to pose as** || *ref* to settle; to alight; (lit) to rest
posata [s] *f* cover, place (*at table*); table utensil (*knife, fork or spoon*); **posate** knife, fork and spoon
posatería [s] *f* service (*of knives, forks, and spoons*)
posa·to -ta [s] *adj* sedate, quiet; placed || *f* see **posata**
posa·tóre -trice [s] *mf* poseur || *m* layer, installer (*of cables or pipes*)
pòscia *adv* then, afterwards; **poscia che** after
poscritto *m* postscript
posdatare *tr* var of **postdatare**
posdomani *adv* (lit) day after tomorrow
positivaménte *adv* for sure
positi·vo -va *adj* positive || *f* (phot) positive, print
posizióne *f* position; status; (fig) stand
posporre §218 *tr* to put off, postpone; to put last; **posporre qlco a qlco** to put or place s.th after s.th
pòssa *f* (lit) strength, vigor
possanza *f* (lit) power
possedére §252 *tr* to possess; to own; to master (*a language*); **essere posseduto da** to be enthralled with; to be possessed by
possediménto *m* possession, property
posseditrice *f* owner, possessor
possènte *adj* (lit) powerful
possessióne *f* possession
possessi·vo -va *adj* possessive
possèsso *m* possession
possessóre *m* owner, possessor
possìbile *adj* possible || *m*—**fare il possibile** to do one's best
possibili·sta (-sti -ste) *adj* pragmatically flexible || *mf* pragmatically flexible person, possibilist
possibili·tà *f* (-**tà**) possibility; opportunity; **possibilità** *fpl* means
possidènte *mf* proprietor, owner; **possidente terriero** landowner
pòsta *f* post; mail; post office; box (*in stable*); ambush; bet; **a giro di posta** by return mail; **a posta** on purpose; **darsi la posta** to set up an appointment; **fare la posta a** to have under surveillance; **fermo in posta** general delivery; **levare la posta** to pick up the mail; **posta aerea** air mail; **posta dei lettori** (journ) letters to the editor; **poste** postal department

pòsta *f* (archaic) planting; (archaic) footprint
postagi·ro *m* (**-ro & -ri**) postal transfer of funds
postale *adj* postal, mail || *m* mail; mail train (boat, bus, or plane)
postare (**pòsto**) *tr* (mil) to post || *ref* (mil) to take a position
postazióne *f* (mil) emplacement
postbèlli·co -ca *adj* (**-ci -che**) postwar
postbruciatóre *m* (aer) afterburner
postdatare *tr* to postdate
posteggiare §290 (**postéggio**) *tr & intr* to park
posteggia·tóre -trice *mf* parking-lot attendant; customer (*in a parking lot*); (coll) outdoor merchant; **posteggiatore abusivo** parking violator
postég·gio *m* (**-gi**) parking lot; stand (*in outdoor market*); **posteggio di tassi** cabstand
posterióre *adj* back; subsequent, later
posteri·tà *f* (-**tà**) posterity
pòste·ro -ra *adj* later, subsequent || **posteri** *mpl* posterity, descendants
postìc·cio -cia (**-ci -ce**) *adj* artificial; false (*e.g., tooth*); temporary || *m* wiglet, ponytail || *f* row of trees
posticipare (**posticipo**) *tr* to postpone
posticipa·to -ta *adj* deferred
postièrla *f* postern
postiglióne *m* postilion
postilla *f* marginal note
postillare *tr* to annotate
posti·no -na *mf* letter carrier || *m* mailman, postman
pósto *m* place; room; seat; job, position; spot; (mil) post; **a posto in** order; orderly; **al posto di** instead of; **essere a posto** to have a good job; **mettere a posto** to find a good job for; (coll) to keep quiet; **quel posto** (coll) seat of the pants; (coll) toilet; **posto a sedere** seat; **posto di blocco** road block; (rr) signal tower; **posto di guardia** (mil) guardhouse; **posto di medicazione** or **di pronto soccorso** first-aid station; **posto in piedi** standing room; **posto letto** bed (*e.g., in hospital*); **posto telefonico pubblico** public telephone, pay station; **rimettere a posto** to fix, repair; **saper stare al proprio posto** to know one's place; **sul posto** on the spot
postrè·mo -ma *adj* (lit) last
postrìbolo *m* (lit) brothel
postulante *adj* petitioning || *mf* petitioner, applicant; (eccl) postulant
postulare (**pòstulo**) *tr* to postulate
pòstu·mo -ma *adj* posthumous || **postumi** *mpl* sequel; (pathol) sequelae
potàbile *adj* drinkable
potare (**póto**) *tr* to trim, prune
potassa *f* potash
potàssio *m* potassium
potatura *f* pruning, polling
potentato *m* (lit) potentate
potènte *adj* powerful; influential || **i potenti** the powers that be
potènza *f* power, might; (math) power; **all'ennesima potenza** (math) to the nth power; (fig) to the nth degree; **in potenza** potential; potentially

potenziale *adj* & *m* potential
potére *m* ability; authority, power; **in potere di** in the hands of; **potere d'acquisto** purchasing power; **potere esecutivo** executive; **potere giudiziario** judiciary; **quarto potere** fourth estate || §219 *intr* to be powerful; **non ne posso più** I am at the end of my rope; **si può?** may I come in? || *aux* (ESSERE & AVERE) to be able; **non posso fare a meno di** + *inf* I can't help + *ger*; **non potere fare a meno di** to not be able to do without; **posso**, etc. I can; I may, etc.; **potrei**, etc. I could; I might, etc.
pote·stà *f* (**-stà**) power, authority
poverà·cclo -cia *mf* (**-ci -ce**) poor guy, poor soul
pò·ve·ro -ra *adj* poor; needy, wretched; lean (*gasoline mixture*); **povero in canna** as poor as a church mouse || *mf* pauper; beggar; poor devil || **i poveri** the poor
pover·tà *f* (**-tà**) poverty; paucity, scantiness
poveruòmo *m* (used only in *sg*) poor devil
pozióne *f* potion, brew
pózza *f* pool, puddle
pozzànghera *f* puddle
pozzétto *m* small well; manhole; forecastle (*in small boat*)
pózzo *m* well; shaft; **pozzo artesiano** artesian well; **pozzo delle catene** (naut) chain locker; **pozzo di scienza** fountain of knowledge; **pozzo di ventilazione** (min) air shaft; **pozzo nero** cesspool; **pozzo petrolifero** oil well; **pozzo trivellato** deep well; **un pozzo di** (fig) a barrel of
Praga *f* Prague
prammàti·co -ca (**-ci -che**) *adj* pragmatic || *f* social custom; **di prammatica** obligatory, de rigueur
pranzare [dz] *intr* to dine
pranzo [dz] *m* dinner; **dopo pranzo** afternoon
pras·si *f* (**-si**) practice, praxis
pratería *f* prairie
pràti·ca *f* (**-che**) practice; knowledge; matter; file, dossier; business; experience; (naut) pratique; **aver pratica con** to be familiar with (*people*); **aver pratica di** to be familiar with (*things*); **far pratica** to be an apprentice; **fare le pratiche** to make an application; **in pratica** practically; **insabbiare una pratica** to pigeonhole a matter
praticàbile *adj* practicable; passable || *m* (theat) raised platform
praticante *adj* practicing || *mf* apprentice; novice; churchgoer
praticare §197 (**pràtico**) *tr* to practice; to frequent; to be familiar with; to make (*e.g., a hole*); to grant (*a discount*) || *intr* to practice; **praticare in** to frequent
pratici·tà *f* (**-tà**) utility; practicality
pràti·co -ca (**-ci -che**) *adj* practical; experienced || *f* see pratica
praticó·ne -na *mf* (pej) old hand
prato *m* meadow

pratolina *f* daisy
pra·vo -va *adj* (lit) wicked
preaccennare (**preaccénno**) *tr* to mention in advance
preaccenna·to -ta *adj* aforementioned
preallarme *m* early warning
Prealpi *fpl* foothills of the Alps
preàmbolo *m* preamble
preannunziare §287 (**preannùnzio**) *tr* to foretell, forebode
preannùn·zio *m* (**-zi**) advance information; foreboding
preautunnale *adj* pre-fall
preavvertire (**preavvèrto**) *tr* to forewarn
preavvisare *tr* to give advance notice to; to forewarn
preavviso *m* forewarning; notification of dismissal
prebèlli·co -ca *adj* (**-ci -che**) prewar
prebènda *f* prebend; (fig) easy money, sinecure
precà·rio -ria *adj* (**-ri -rie**) precarious
precauzióne *f* precaution
precedènte *adj* preceding || *m* precedent; **precedenti** background; **precedenti penali** previous offenses, record
precedènza *f* precedence; (aut) right of way; (fig) priority
precèdere §123 *tr* & *intr* to precede
precettare (**precètto**) *tr* (mil) to call back from furlough
precètto *m* precept; (eccl) obligation
precettóre *m* tutor
precipitare (**precìpito**) *tr* to precipitate; to hasten; (chem) to precipitate || *intr* (ESSERE) to fall; to fail; to rush (*said of events*); (chem) to precipitate || *ref* to rush
precipitó·so -sa [s] *adj* hasty, headlong
precipì·zio *m* (**-zi**) precipice, cliff; ruin; **a precipizio** headlong
precì·puo -pua *adj* chief, principal, primary
precisare *tr* to say exactly, specify, clarify; to fix (*a date*)
precisazióne *f* clarification
precisióne *f* precision
preci·so -sa *adj* precise, exact; punctilious; identical, same; sharp, (*e.g.*), **alle sette precise** at seven o'clock sharp
precla·ro -ra *adj* (lit) illustrious
preclùdere §105 *tr* to preclude
precòce *adj* precocious, premature
preconcèt·to -ta *adj* preconceived || *m* preconception; prejudice, bias
preconizzare [ddzz] *tr* to foretell, forecast; (eccl) to preconize
precórrere §139 *tr* (lit) to precede || *intr* (lit) to occur before
precursóre *m* precursor
prèda *f* booty, prize; prey
predace *adj* (lit) preying, predatory
predare (**prèdo**) *tr* to pillage; to prey upon
preda·tóre -trice *adj* predacious, rapacious || *mf* plunderer
predecessóre *m* predecessor
predèlla *f* dais; altar step; platform
predellino *m* footboard
predestinare (**predestino** & **predèstino**) *tr* to predestine

predét·to -ta *adj* aforementioned
prediale *adj* field, rural || *f* land tax
prèdi·ca *f* (-che) sermon
predicare §197 (**prèdico**) *tr* & *intr* to preach
predicato *m* predicate; **essere in predicato di** + *inf* to be rumored to + *inf*; **essere predicato per** to be considered for
predica·tóre -trice *mf* preacher
predicazióne *f* preaching; sermon
predicòzzo *m* (coll) lecture, scolding
predilèt·to -ta *adj* & *m* favorite
predilezióne *f* predilection
prediligere §149 (*pres part* missing) *tr* to prefer; to like best
predire §151 *tr* to foretell
predispórre §218 *tr* to predispose, prearrange || *ref* to prepare oneself
predisposizióne *f* predisposition
predizióne *f* prediction
predominare (**predòmino**) *tr* to overcome || *intr* to predominate; to prevail
predomì·nio *m* (-ni) predominance
predóne *m* marauder; **predone del mare** pirate
preesistere §114 *intr* (ESSERE) to preexist
prefabbricare §197 (**prefàbbrico**) *tr* to prefabricate
prefazióne *f* preface
preferènza *f* preference; **a preferenza** rather; **usar preferenza a** to favor
preferìbile *adj* preferable
preferire §176 *tr* to prefer
preferì·to -ta *adj* preferred, favored || *mf* favorite; pet
prefètto *m* prefect
prefettura *f* prefecture
prèfi·ca *f* (-che) professional mourner, paid mourner; (coll) crybaby
prefiggere §103 *tr* to set, fix; (gram) to prefix || *ref* to plan
prefis·so -sa *adj* appointed; prefixed || *m* (gram) prefix; (telp) area code
prefissòide *m* prefixed combining form
pregare §209 (**prègo**) *tr* to beg, pray; to ask, request; **farsi pregare** to take a lot of asking; **La prego** please; **prego!** please!; beg your pardon!; you are welcome!
pregévole *adj* valuable
preghièra *f* entreaty; prayer
pregiare §290 (**prègio**) *tr* (lit) to praise, esteem || *ref* to be honored, to have the pleasure
pregia·to -ta *adj* precious; esteemed; **la Sua pregiata (lettera)** your favor, your kind letter; **pregiatissimo Signore** (com) dear Sir; **pregiato Signore** (com) dear Sir
prè·gio *m* (-gi) value, worth; esteem; **avere in pregio** to value
pregiudicare §197 (**pregiùdico**) *tr* to damage, harm, jeopardize
pregiudica·to -ta *adj* prejudged; prejudiced; compromised; bound to fail || *m* previous offender
pregiudiziale *adj* (law) pretrial; (pol) essential || *f* (law) pretrial
pregiudiziévole *adj* prejudicial, detrimental

pregiudì·zio *m* (-zi) prejudice, bias; harm, damage
pregnante *adj* pregnant
pré·gno -gna *adj* pregnant; saturated
prè·go *m* (-ghi) (lit) prayer || *interj* please!; beg your pardon!; you are welcome!
pregustare *tr* to foretaste, anticipate with pleasure
preistòri·co -ca *adj* (-ci -che) prehistoric(al)
prelato *m* prelate
prelazióne *f* (law) preemption; (obs) privilege
prelevaménto *m* (com) withdrawal
prelevare (**prelèvo**) *tr* to withdraw (*money*); to capture
preliba·to -ta *adj* excellent, delicious
prelièvo *m* withdrawal; (med) specimen
preliminare *adj* preliminary || **preliminari** *mpl* preliminary negotiations
prelùdere §105 *intr* to make an introductory statement; (with *dat*) to precede, usher in
prelù·dio *m* (-di) prelude; (*of an opera*) overture
prematu·ro -ra *adj* premature
premeditare (**premèdito**) *tr* to premeditate
premeditazióne *f* premeditation; **con premeditazione** (law) with malice prepense
prèmere §123 *tr* to press; to push; to squeeze || *intr* (ESSERE & AVERE) to press; to be urgent; **premere a** to matter to, e.g., **gli preme** it matters to him; **premere su** to press, put pressure on
preméssa *f* premise; introduction (*to a book*)
preméttere §198 *tr* to state at the onset; to place at the beginning
premiare §287 (**prèmio**) *tr* to award a prize to, reward
premiazióne *f* awarding of prizes
preminènte *adj* prominent, preeminent
prè·mio *m* (-mi) prize; premium; bonus; award
prèmito *m* straining (*to defecate*)
premolare *adj* & *m* premolar
premonire §176 *tr* (lit) to foretell
premonizióne *f* premonition
premorire §201 *intr* (ESSERE) (with *dat*) to predecease
premunire §176 *tr* to fortify || *ref*—**premunirsi contro** to provide against; **premunirsi di** to provide oneself with
premura *f* haste; attention, care; **aver premura (di)** to be in a hurry (to); **di premura** hastily; **far premura** (with *dat*) to urge
premuró·so -sa [s] *adj* attentive, careful
prèndere §220 *tr* to take; to catch; to lift; to pick up; to fetch; to get; to receive; **prendere a calci** to kick; **prendere a pugni** to punch; **prendere a servizio** to employ, hire; **prendere commiato** to take leave; **prendere con le buone** to treat with kid gloves; **prendere in castagna** to catch in the act; **prendere il sole** to sun oneself; **prendere la fuga** to take flight;

prendere la mano to run away (said of a horse); **prendere le mosse** to begin (said, e.g., of a story); **prendere lucciole per lanterne** to commit a gross error; **prender paura** to get scared; **prendere per** to take for; **prendere per il naso** to lead by the nose; **prendere quota** (aer) to gain altitude; **prendere sonno** to fall asleep; **prendere un granchio** to make a blunder || intr to take root; to set (said of cement); to catch (said of fire); to turn (left or right); **prendere a + inf** to begin to + inf || ref to grab one another; to get along together; **prendersela con** to become angry with; to lay the blame on; **prendersi a** to take hold of

prendi·tóre -trice mf receiver; payee (of a note); margin buyer || m (baseball) catcher

prenóme m first name, given name

prenotare (prenòto) tr to reserve, book || ref to register

prenotazióne f reservation, booking

preoccupante adj worrisome

preoccupare (preòccupo) tr to preoccupy; **preoccupare la mente di** to win the favor of || ref to worry

preoccupazióne f preoccupation, worry

preordinare (preórdino) tr to foreordain; to prearrange

preparare tr to prepare; to prime; to steep, brew || ref to be prepared; to brew (said, e.g., of a storm)

peparati·vo -va adj preparatory || **preparativi** mpl preparations

prepara·to -ta adj prepared; well-equipped || m patent medicine; (med) preparation; **preparato anatomico** dissection, anatomical specimen

preparatò·rio -ria adj (-ri -rie) preparatory

preparazióne f preparation

preponderante adj preponderant, prevailing

preponderanza f preponderance

prepórre §218 tr to prefix; to place before; to prefer; **preporre (qlcu) a** to place (s.o.) at the head of

preposizióne f preposition

prepósto m chief; (eccl) provost

prepotènte adj arrogant, overbearing; urgent (desire) || m bully

prepotènza f arrogance; outrage; **di prepotenza** by force

prerogativa f prerogative

présa [s] f hold, grip; handle; potholder; capture; pinch (e.g., of salt); setting (of cement); intake; (cards) trick; (elec) jack; (mov) take; **a pronta presa** quick-setting (cement); **dar presa a** to give rise to; **essere alle prese** to come to grips; **far presa** to stick (said of glue); to set (said of cement); to take root; **far presa su** to impress; **mettere alle prese** to pit (e.g., animals); **presa d'acqua** spigot, faucet; **presa d'aria** outlet (of air hose); air shaft; **presa di corrente** (elec) wall socket, outlet, receptacle; **presa di terra** (elec) ground; presa

in giro kidding, joke; **venire alle prese** to come to grips

presà·gio m (-gi) forecast; portent

presagire §176 tr to forecast; to portend

presalà·rio [s] m (-ri) (educ) stipend

prèsbite adj far-sighted || mf far-sighted person

presbiteria·no -na adj & mf Presbyterian

prescégliere §244 tr to choose, select

prescìndere §247 (pret prescindéi & prescissi) intr—a prescindere da except for; **prescindere da** to leave out

prescolàsti·co -ca adj (-ci -che) pre-school

prescrit·to -ta adj prescribed

prescrìvere §250 tr to prescribe || intr (ESSERE) (law) to prescribe, to lapse

prescrizióne f prescription; (law) extinctive prescription

presegnale [s] m warning sign

presentàbile adj presentable

presentare (presènto) tr to present; to introduce; **presentare la candidatura di** to nominate; **presentat'arm!** present arms! || ref to show up, appear; to come, arise (said, e.g., of an opportunity)

presenta·tóre -trice mf presenter; (rad, telv) announcer || m master of ceremonies

presentazióne f presentation; introduction

presènte adj present; **avere presente** to have in mind; **fare presente qlco a qlcu** to bring s.th to s.o.'s attention; **tenere presente** to keep in mind || m present; bystander, onlooker; **al presente** at present; **di presente** immediately || interj here!

presentimento [s] m presentiment, foreboding

presentire [s] (presènto) tr to have a presentiment of

presènza f presence; attendance; **di presenza** in person; **presenza di spirito** presence of mind

presenziare §287 (presènzio) tr to attend; to witness || intr—presenziare a to be present at; to witness

prese·pio m (-pi) Nativity, crèche

preservare [s] (presèrvo) tr to preserve, protect

preservati·vo -va [s] adj & m prophylactic

prèside [s] m principal (of secondary school); **preside di facoltà** dean

presidènte [s] m president; chairman; **presidente del Consiglio** premier

presidentéssa [s] f president; chairwoman

presidènza [s] f presidency; chairmanship

presi·dio [s] m (-di) garrison; (fig) defense, help; **presidi medical aids**

presièdere [s] §141 (presièdo) tr to preside over || intr to preside; **presiedere a** to preside over

prèssa f crowd; haste; (mach) press; **far pressa** (poet) to urge

pressacar·te m (-te) paperweight

pressaforàg·gio m (-gio) baler, hay baler

pressante *adj* pressing, urgent

pressappòco *adv* more or less

pressare (**prèsso**) *tr* to press; to urge

pressióne *f* pressure; **far pressione su** to put pressure on; **pressione sanguigna** blood pressure; **sotto pressione** under steam

prèsso *m*—**nei pressi di** in the neighborhood of || *adv* near, nearby; **a un di presso** approximately; **da presso** close; **press'a poco** more or less || *prep* near; about; at; according to; at the house of; at the office of; care of; with, e.g., **godere fama presso di** enjoy popularity with

pressoché *adv* almost, about, nearly

pressurizzare [ddzz] *tr* to pressurize

prestabilire §176 *tr* to preestablish

prestabili·to -ta *adj* appointed

prestanó·me *m* (**-me**) straw man, figurehead

prestante *adj* strong, vigorous; comely

prestanza *f* vigor; (lit) comeliness

prestare (**prèsto**) *tr* to lend; to loan; to give (*ear; help*); to pay (*attention*); to render (*obedience*); to take (*oath*); to keep (*faith*); **prestar man forte** to give aid; **prestar servizio** to work || *ref* to lend oneself; to be suitable; to be willing; to volunteer

presta·tóre -trice *mf* lender; **prestatore d'opera** worker; **prestatori d'opera** labor

prestazióne *f* service; performance

prestigia·tóre -trice *mf* magician, juggler

presti·gio *m* (**-gi**) prestige; spell, influence; ledgerdemain

prestigió·so -sa [s] *adj* captivating, spellbinding; illusory

prèstito *m* loan; (philol) borrowing; **dare a prestito** to lend; **prendere a prestito** to borrow

prè·sto -sta *adj* (archaic) quick || *m* (mus) presto || **presto** *adv* soon; fast; quick, quickly; early; **al più presto** at the earliest possible time; **ben presto** soon; **far presto** to hurry; **più presto che può** as soon as you can; **presto detto** easy to say

presùmere §116 *tr & intr* to presume

presunti·vo -va *adj* presumptive; budgeted, estimated (*expenditure*)

presun·to -ta *adj* alleged, supposed; estimated (*expenditure*)

presuntuó·so -sa [s] *adj* presumptuous; bumptious

presunzióne *f* presumption; conceit

presuppórre [s] §218 *tr* to presuppose

presuppósto [s] *m* assumption

prète *m* priest; minister; wooden frame (*to hold bed warmer*)

pretendènte *m* suitor; pretender

pretèndere §270 *tr* to demand, claim; **pretenderla a** to pretend to be || *intr*—**pretendere a** to be a suitor for; to claim (*e.g., a throne*)

pretensióne *f* demand; pretention; pretense

pretensió·so -sa [s] *or* **pretenzió·so -sa** [s] *adj* pretentious

preterintenzionale *adj* (law) unintentional; (law) justifiable

prethèri·to -ta *adj & m* preterit

preté·so -sa [s] *adj* alleged, ostensible; assumed (*name*) || *f* pretense; pretension

pretèsto *m* pretext, excuse; **sotto il pretesto di** under pretext of

pretòni·co -ca *adj* (**-ci -che**) pretonic

pretóre *m* judge, magistrate (*of lower court*)

prèt·to -ta *adj* pure, genuine

pretura *f* lower court

prevalènte *adj* prevalent, prevailing

prevalènza *f* prevalence; **essere in prevalenza** to be in the majority; **in prevalenza** for the most part

prevalére §278 *tr* (ESSERE & AVERE) to prevail || *ref* to take advantage

prevaricare §197 (**prevàrico**) *intr* to transgress; to graft

prevarica·tóre -trice *mf* grafter

prevedére §279 *tr* to foresee; to provide for (*said of a statute*)

prevedibile *adj* foreseeable

prevenire §282 *tr* to precede; to anticipate; to forewarn; to prejudice

preventivi·sta *mf* (**-sti -ste**) estimator

preventi·vo -va *adj* preventive; prior; estimated (*budget*) || *m* estimate

prevenu·to -ta *adj* forewarned; biased, prejudiced || *m* defendant

prevenzióne *f* prevention; prejudice, bias

previdènte *adj* provident, prudent

previdènza *f* providence; foresight; **previdenza sociale** social security

previdenziale *adj* social (*e.g., responsibility*); social-security (*e.g., contribution*)

prè·vio -via *adj* (**-vi -vie**) with previous, e.g., **previo accordo** with previous agreement

previsióne *f* foresightedness; **in previsione di** anticipating; **previsioni del tempo** weather forecast

previ·sto -sta *adj* foreseen, expected || *m* expected time; estimated amount

prezió·so -sa [s] *adj* precious, valuable; affected; **fare il prezioso** (coll) to play hard to get || **preziosi** *mpl* valuables, jewels

prezzare (**prèzzo**) *tr* to care about; to price

prezzémolo *m* parsley

prèzzo *m* price; cost; **mettere a prezzo** (fig) to sell; **prezzo di favore** special price; **prezzo d'ingresso** admission; **tenere in gran prezzo** to value highly, to esteem highly; **ultimo prezzo** rock-bottom price

prezzolare (**prèzzolo**) *tr* to hire (*e.g., a gunman*); to bribe

prigióne *f* prison, jail; (naut) brig

prigionia *f* imprisonment; bondage

prigioniè·ro -ra *adj* imprisoned || *mf* prisoner || *m* stud bolt

prillare *intr* to spin, whirl

prima *f* first grade (*in school*); (rr) first class; (theat) first night; (aut) first (gear); **alla prima** *or* **sulle prime** at the outset || *adv* before; first; prior; ahead; **di prima** previous; **prima che** before; **prima di** ahead of; before;

prima o poi sooner or later; **quanto prima** as soon as possible

primàrio ·ria (-ri -rie) *adj* primary ‖ *m* (elec) primary; (med) chief of staff

primati·sta *mf* (**-sti -ste**) (sports) record holder

primato *m* primacy; (sports) record

primavèra *f* spring; springtime; (bot) primrose

primaverile *adj* spring; spring-like

primeggiare §290 (**priméggio**) *intr* to excel

primiè·ro -ra *adj* (lit) prior; (lit) pristine ‖ *f* (cards) meld

primiti·vo -va *adj & m* primitive

primìzia *f* first fruits; scoop, beat

pri·mo -ma *adj* first; early (*dawn*); prime (*cost*); raw (*material*); **sulle prime** at first ‖ *m* first; minute; **primo arrivato** first comer ‖ *f* see **prima**

primogèni·to -ta *adj* first-born; (fig) beloved ‖ *mf* first-born child

primòrdi *mpl* beginning, origin

primordiale *adj* primordial, primeval

primula *f* primrose ‖ **Primula** *f—***la Primula Rossa** the Scarlet Pimpernel

principale *adj* principal, main ‖ *m* (coll) boss, chief

principalménte *adv* chiefly, mainly

principato *m* principality

principe *adj* princeps ‖ *m* prince; **il principe di Galles** the Prince of Wales; **principe ereditario** crown prince

principé·sco -sca *adj* (**-schi -sche**) princely

principéssa *f* princess

principiante *adj* beginning ‖ *mf* beginner

principiare §287 *tr & intr* (ESSERE & AVERE) to begin; **a principiare da** beginning with

princi·pio *m* (**-pi**) beginning; principle; **in principio** at the beginning, at first

princisbécco *m* pinchbeck; **restare o rimanere di princisbecco** to be dumfounded

prióre *m* prior

priori·tà *f* (**-tà**) priority

priorità·rio -ria *adj* (**-ri -rie**) priority, e.g., **progetto prioritario** priority project

pri·sma *m* (**-smi**) prism

privare *tr* to deprive; to remove

privativa *f* government monopoly; salt and tobacco store; patent

priva·to -ta *adj* private ‖ *m* private individual

privazióne *f* privation, loss

privilegiare §290 (**privilègio**) *tr* to privilege; (fig) to endow

privilegia·to -ta *adj* privileged; preferred (*stock*) ‖ *m* privileged person

privilè·gio *m* (**-gi**) privilege

pri·vo -va *adj* deprived; **privo di** lacking

prò *m* (**pro**) profit, advantage; **a che pro?** what's the use?; **buon pro!** good appetite!; **far pro** to be good for the health; **il pro e il contro** the pros and the cons ‖ *prep* pro, in favor of

probàbile *adj* probable

probabili·tà *f* (**-tà**) probability; chance; odds

probante *adj* proving; evidential

probatò·rio -ria *adj* (**-ri -rie**) probative, evidential

problè·ma *m* (**-mi**) problem

prò·bo -ba *adj* (lit) honest

procàc·cia *mf* (**-cia**) messenger; mail carrier

procacciare §128 *tr* to get, procure ‖ *ref* to eke out (*a living*); to get into (*trouble*)

procace *adj* buxom, sexy; saucy, petulant

procèdere §123 (**procèdo**) *intr* to proceed, take action ‖ *intr* (ESSERE) to proceed, go ahead

procediménto *m* procedure; behavior

procedura *f* procedure

procèlla *f* (lit) storm, tempest

procellària *f* (orn) petrel

processare (**procèsso**) *tr* to try, prosecute

processióne *f* procession

procèsso *m* process; trial; **processo verbale** minutes

processuale *adj* trial

procinto *m*—**in procinto di** on the point of

procióne *m* raccoon

procla·ma *m* (**-mi**) proclamation

proclamare *tr* to proclaim

proclamazióne *f* proclamation

proclìti·co -ca *adj & f* (**-ci -che**) proclitic

proclive *adj* inclined, disposed

proclivi·tà *f* (**-tà**) proclivity

procrastinare (**procràstino**) *tr* to procrastinate, put off ‖ *intr* to procrastinate

procreare (**procrèo**) *tr* to procreate

procura *f* agency; power of attorney; **Procura della Repubblica** attorney general's office; district attorney's office

procurare *tr* to procure, to get; to cause; **procurare che** to see to it that; **procurare di** to try to ‖ *ref* to get, acquire

procura·tóre -trice *mf* proxy; agent; attorney-at-law; (sports) manager; **Procuratore della Repubblica** district attorney

pròda *f* shore, bank; (archaic) prow

pròde *adj* brave ‖ *m* brave person, hero

prodézza *f* prowess; accomplishment

prodiè·ro -ra *adj* prow, e.g., **cannone prodiero** prow gun; preceding (*in a row of ships*)

prodigare §209 (**pròdigo**) *tr* to squander, lavish ‖ *ref* to do one's best

prodi·gio *m* (**-gi**) prodigy; wonder

prodigió·so -sa [s] *adj* prodigious; wonderful

pròdi·go -ga *adj* (**-ghi -ghe**) lavish, prodigal; **prodigo di** profuse in

prodótto *m* product; result; **prodotti in scatola** canned goods; **prodotti (orto-frutticoli)** produce

produrre §102 *tr* to produce; to turn out; to yield; to breed; to cause; (lit) to prolong; (law) to exhibit || *ref* (theat) to perform, appear

produtti·vo -va *adj* productive

produttivísti·co -ca *adj* (**-ci -che**) productivity, e.g., **fine produttivístico** productivity policy

produt·tóre -trice *adj* producing || *mf* producer; agent; manufacturer's representative || *m* salesman || *f* saleswoman

produzióne *f* production; output; **produzione in massa** or **in serie** mass production

proè·mio *m* (**-mi**) preamble, proem

profanare *tr* to profane, desecrate

profanazióne *f* profanation, desecration

profa·no -na *adj* profane; lay, uninformed || *m* layman; **il profano** the profane

proferire §176 *tr* (lit) to utter; (lit) to proffer

professare (**professo**) *tr* to profess; to practice (*e.g., law*) || *intr* to practice || *ref* to profess oneself to be

professionale *adj* professional; occupational (*disease*); trade (*school*)

professióne *f* profession; **fare il ladro di professione** to be a confirmed thief; **fare qlco di professione** to pursue the trade of s.th, e.g., **fa il falegname di professione** he pursues the trade of carpenter

professioní·sta *mf* (**-sti -ste**) professional

professorale *adj* professorial; pedantic

profes·sóre -soréssa *mf* professor; teacher; **professore d'orchestra** orchestra member

profè·ta *m* (**-ti**) prophet

profetéssa *f* prophetess

profèti·co -ca *adj* (**-ci -che**) prophetic

profetizzare [*ddzz*] *tr* to prophesy

profezia *f* prophecy

profferire §176 (*pp* **profferto**; *pret* **profferíi** & **profférsi**) *tr* to offer; (lit) to utter

profí·cuo -cua *adj* profitable

profilare *tr* to outline; to sketch; to hem; (mach) to shape || *ref* to be outlined; to loom

profilas·si *f* (**-si**) prophylaxis

profila·to -ta *adj* outlined; hemmed; (mach) shaped || *m* structural piece

profilàtti·co -ca *adj* (**-ci -che**) prophylactic

profilatura *f* hemming; (mach) shaping

profilo *m* profile; sketch; outline

profittare *intr* to profit, benefit

profitta·tóre -trice *mf* profiteer

profittévole *adj* (lit) profitable

profitto *m* profit; progress; **profitti e perdite** profit and loss

proflù·vio *m* (**-vi**) overflow; (pathol) discharge

profondare (**profóndo**) *tr* & *intr* to sink

profóndere §178 *tr* to squander, lavish || *ref* to be profuse

profondi·tà *f* (**-tà**) depth

profón·do -da *adj* deep; profound; searching (*e.g., investigation*) || *m* bottom; depth; subconscious

pro fórma *adj invar* pro forma; perfunctory || *m* (coll) formality

pròfu·go -ga (**-ghi -ghe**) *adj* fugitive || *mf* refugee

profumare *tr* to perfume || *intr* to smell

profumataménte *adv* lavishly

profuma·to -ta *adj* perfumed, fragrant

profumería *f* perfumery; perfume shop

profumo *m* perfume; bouquet (*of wine*)

profusióne *f* profusion; **a profusione** in profusion

profu·so -sa *adj* profuse

progè·nie *f* (**-nie**) progeny, offspring; (pej) breed

progeni·tóre -trice *mf* ancestor

progettare (**progètto**) *tr* to plan; to design

progetti·sta *mf* (**-sti -ste**) planner; designer; wild dreamer

progètto *m* project; plan; draft (*of law*); **far progetti** to plan; **progetto di scala reale** (cards) possible straight flush

prògno·si *f* (**-si**) prognosis

program·ma *m* (**-mi**) program; plan; curriculum; cycle (*of washing machine*); (mov) feature; (theat) playbill; **programma politico** platform

programmare *tr* to program; to plan

programma·tóre -trice *mf* programmer

programmazióne *f* programming

progredire §176 *intr* (ESSERE & AVERE) to progress, advance

progredí·to -ta *adj* advanced

progressióne *f* progression

progressí·sta *adj* & *mf* (**-sti -ste**) progressive

progressí·vo -va *adj* progressive

progrèsso *m* progress; progression, advance; **fare progressi** to progress

proibire §176 *tr* to prohibit; to prevent

proibí·to -ta *adj* forbidden; **è proibito entrare** no admission; **è proibito fumare** no smoking

proibizióne *f* prohibition

proibizionismo *m* prohibition

proiettare (**proiètto**) *tr* to project; to cast (*a shadow*) || *intr* to project || *ref* to be projected, project

proièttile *m* projectile, missile

proiet·tóre *m* projector, projection machine; searchlight; (aut) headlight; **proiettore acustico** sonar projector

proiezióne *f* projection; **proiezione rallentata** slow motion

pròle *f invar* offspring, progeny

proletariato *m* proletariat

proletà·rio -ria *adj* & *mf* (**-ri -rie**) proletarian

proliferare (**prolífero**) *intr* to proliferate

prolificare §197 (**prolífico**) *intr* to proliferate

prolífi·co -ca *adj* (**-ci -che**) prolific

prolís·so -sa *adj* prolix, long-winded; long (*e.g., beard*)

pròlo·go *m* (**-ghi**) prologue; preface

prolun·ga *f* (**-ghe**) extension

prolungaménto *m* prolongation, extension

prolungare §209 *tr* to prolong, extend || *ref* to extend; to speak at great length

prolunga·to -ta *adj* extended, protracted

prolusióne *f* inaugural lecture

promemò·ria or **pro memò·ria** m (**-ria**) reminder

promés·so -sa adj promised ‖ mf betrothed ‖ f promise; promising individual

promettènte adj promising

promèttere §198 tr to promise; to threaten (e.g., a storm) ‖ intr to promise; **promettere bene** to be very promising ‖ ref—**promettersi a Dio** to make a vow to God; **promettersi in matrimonio** to become engaged

prominènte adj prominent

promì·scuo -scua adj promiscuous; co-educational; mixed (marriage; races); (gram) epicene

promontò·rio m (**-ri**) promontory, cliff

promo·tóre -trice adj promoting ‖ mf promoter

promozióne f promotion

promulgare §209 tr to promulgate

promuòvere §202 tr to promote; to pass (a student); to initiate (legal suit); to induce (e.g., perspiration)

pronipóte mf great-grandchild ‖ m great-grandson; grandnephew; **pronipoti** descendants ‖ f great-grand-daughter; grandniece

prò·no -na adj (lit) prone

pronóme m pronoun

pronominale adj (gram) pronominal; (gram) reflexive (verb)

pronosticare §197 (**pronòstico**) tr to prognosticate, forecast

pronòsti·co m (**-ci**) prognostication, forecast; sign, omen

prontézza f readiness; quickness, promptness

prón·to -ta adj ready; first (aid); quick; prompt; ready (cash) ‖ **pronto** interj (telp) hello!

prontuà·rio m (**-ri**) handbook

pronùn·cia f (**-cie**) or **pronùnzia** f pronunciaton; (law) judgment

pronunziare §287 tr to pronounce; to utter; to pass (sentence); to make (a speech) ‖ ref to pass judgment

pronunzià·to -ta adj pronounced, marked; prominent (nose, chin, beard) ‖ m (law) sentence

propaganda f propaganda; advertisement; advertising

propagandí·sta mf (**-sti -ste**) propagandist; advertiser; agent; detail-man

propagandìsti·co -ca adj (**-ci -che**) advertising

propagare §209 tr to propagate; to spread ‖ ref to spread

propàggine f offspring; (geog) spur, counterfort; (hort) layer

propalare tr (lit) to spread, divulge

propellènte adj & m propellent

propèllere §168 tr to propel

propèndere §123 (pp **propènso**) intr to incline, tend

propensióne f propensity, inclination

propèn·so -sa adj inclined, bent

propinare tr to administer (e.g., poison); **propinare qlco a qlcu** to put s.th over on s.o.

propìn·quo -qua adj (lit) near; (lit) related

propiziare §287 tr to propitiate, appease

propì·zio -zia adj (**-zi -zie**) propitious, favorable

proponiménto m intention, plan

propórre §218 tr to propose, present; to propound; **proporre come candidato** to nominate ‖ ref—**proporsi di** to propose to, resolve to

proporzionare (**proporzióno**) tr to proportion, prorate

proporzióne f proportion

propòsito m purpose; **a proposito** opportune; opportunely; proper; by the way; **a proposito di** on the subject of; **di proposito** deliberately; **fuor di proposito** out of place; **parlare a proposito** to speak to the point

proposizióne f proposition; (gram) clause; **proposizione subordinata** dependent clause

propósta f proposal; **proposta di legge** bill

propriaménte adv exactly; properly

proprie·tà f (**-tà**) propriety; ownership; property; **la proprietà** property owners; **proprietà immobiliare** real estate; **proprietà letteraria** copyright; **sulla proprietà** on the premises

proprietà·rio -ria mf (**-ri -rie**) owner, proprietor

prò·prio -pria (**-pri -prie**) adj peculiar, characteristic; proper (e.g., name); own, e.g., **il mio proprio libro** my own book ‖ m one's own; **i propri** one's folks; **lavorare in proprio** to work for oneself ‖ **proprio** adv just, really, exactly; **non . . . proprio** not . . . at all; **proprio adesso** just, just now

propugnare tr to advocate; (lit) to fight for

propugna·tóre -trice mf (lit) advocate

propulsare tr to propel; (lit) to repulse

propulsióne f propulsion

propulsóre m propeller, motor

pròra f prow, bow

proravìa f—**a proravia** (naut) fore

pròro·ga f (**-ghe**) delay, extension

prorogare §209 (**pròrogo**) tr to extend; to put off, delay

prorómpere §240 intr to overflow; to burst (into tears)

prosa f prose

prosài·co -ca adj (**-ci -che**) prose; prosaic

prosàpia f (lit) ancestry

prosa·tóre -trice mf prose writer

proscè·nio m (**-ni**) forestage

prosciògliere §127 tr to free; to exonerate

prosciugare §209 tr to drain, reclaim ‖ ref to dry up

prosciutto m ham; **prosciutto cotto** boiled ham; **prosciutto crudo** prosciutto

proscrìvere §250 tr to proscribe, outlaw

prosecuzióne [s] f prosecution, pursuit

proseguiménto [s] m prosecution, pursuit

proseguire [s] (**proséguo**) tr to follow, pursue ‖ intr (ESSERE & AVERE) to continue

prosèlito m proselyte

prosodìa f prosody

prosopopèa f conceit

prosperare (pròspero) intr to prosper, thrive

prosperi·tà f (-tà) prosperity ǁ interj gesundheit!

pròspe·ro -ra adj prosperous, thriving; flourishing; successful ǁ m (coll) match

prosperó·so -sa [s] adj flourishing; healthy; buxom

prospettare (prospètto) tr to face, overlook; to outline ǁ intr—**prospettare su** to face ǁ ref to look; to appear; to loom up

prospetti·vo -va adj prospective ǁ f perspective; prospect; view

prospètto m prospect, view; front (of building); diagram; outline; prospectus

prospettóre m prospector

prospiciènte adj facing

prossimamènte adv shortly

prossimi·tà f proximity, nearness; **in prossimità di** near

pròssi·mo -ma adj near, close; next; immediate (cause) ǁ m neighbor, fellow man

pròstata f prostate

prosternare (prostèrno) ref to prostrate oneself

prostituire §176 tr to prostitute

prostitùta f prostitute

prostituzióne f prostitution

prostrare (pròstro) ref to prostrate oneself

prostrazióne f prostration

protagoni·sta m (-sti -ste) protagonist

protèggere §193 tr to protect; to help, defend; to favor, promote

proteina f protein

protèndere §270 tr & ref to stretch

pròte·si f (-si) (philol) prothesis; (surg) prosthesis

protèsta f protest, protestation

protestante adj & mf protestant; Protestant

protestare (protèsto) tr to protest; to reject (faulty merchandise) ǁ intr & ref to protest

protestatà·rio -ria (-ri -rie) adj protesting ǁ m protester

protèsto m (com) protest

protèt·to -ta adj protected ǁ m protegé ǁ f protegée

protettorato m protectorate

protet·tóre -trice adj patron ǁ mf protector, guardian ǁ m patron ǁ f patroness

protezióne f protection; patronage

pròto m (typ) foreman

protocòllo adj invar commercial (size) ǁ m protocol; **mettere a protocollo** to register, record

protopla·sma m (-smi) protoplasm

protòtipo m prototype; (fig) epitome

protozòi [dz] mpl protozoa

protrarre §273 tr to protract, extend ǁ ref to continue

protrùdere §190 intr to protrude (said, e.g., of a broken bone)

protuberante adj protruding, bulging

pròva f test, examination; proof; try, attempt; probationary period (of employment); trial; token (e.g., of friendship); (sports) competition, event; (theat) rehearsal; **a prova di bomba** bombproof; foolproof; **a tutta prova** thoroughly tested; **in prova** on approval; **mettere a dura prova** to test (e.g., one's patience); **mettere alla prova** to test (e.g., one's ability); **mettere in prova** to fit (a suit); **prova del fuoco** trial by fire; **prova dell'acido** acid test; **prova generale** dress rehearsal; **prova indiziaria** circumstantial evidence

provare (pròvo) tr to test; to try; to try on; to try out; to taste; to prove; to feel (e.g., anger); (theat) to rehearse ǁ intr to try ǁ ref to compete

proveniènza f origin

provenire §282 intr (ESSERE) to stem, originate

provènto m income, proceeds

provenzale adj & mf Provençal

provèr·bio -bia (-bi) proverb; byword

provètta f test tube

provèt·to -ta adj (lit) masterful

provìn·cia f (-ce) province; **in provincia** outside of the big cities

provinciale adj provincial ǁ mf smalltown person ǁ f provincial highway, state highway

provino m gauge; (mov) screen test

provocare §197 (pròvoco) tr to provoke; to bring about, cause; to arouse; to entice

provoca·tóre -trice adj provoking ǁ mf provoker

provocatò·rio -ria adj (-ri -rie) provoking, provocative

provocazióne f provocation; challenge

provvedére §221 tr to prepare; to supply; **provvedere che** to see to it that ǁ intr to take the necessary steps; **provvedere a** to provide for; **provvedere a** + inf to provide for + ger; **provvedere nei confronti di** to take steps against

provvediménto m measure, step

provvedi·tóre -trice mf provider ǁ m superintendent; **provveditore agli studi** superintendent of schools

provvedu·to -ta adj supplied; careful

provvidènza f providence; windfall; **provvidenze** provisions, help

provvidenziale adj providential

pròvvi·do -da adj (lit) provident

provvigióne f (com) commission

provvisò·rio -ria adj (-ri -rie) provisional, temporary

provvi·sto -sta adj supplied ǁ f supply, provision; **fare le provviste** to shop

prozìa f grandaunt

prozì·o m (-i) granduncle

prua f bow, prow

prudènte adj prudent, cautious

prudènza f prudence, discretion

prùdere §222 intr to itch; **sentirsi prudere le mani** to feel like giving s.o. a beating

prugna f plum; **prugna secca** prune

prugno *m* plum tree
prùgnola *f* sloe
prùgnolo *m* sloe, blackthorn
pruno *m* thorn
prurito *m* itch
pseudònimo *m* pseudonym; alias; pen name
psicanàlisi *f* psychoanalysis
psicanali·sta *mf* (**-sti -ste**) psychoanalyst
psicanalizzare [ddzz] *tr* to psychoanalyze
psiche *f* psyche; cheval glass
psichia·tra *mf* (**-tri -tre**) psychiatrist
psichiatrìa *f* psychiatry
psìchi·co -ca *adj* (**-ci -che**) psychic
psicologìa *f* psychology
psicològi·co -ca *adj* (**-ci -che**) psychological
psicòlo·go -ga *mf* (**-gi -ghe**) psychologist
psicopàti·co -ca (**-ci -che**) *adj* psychopathic || *mf* psychopath
psicò·si *f* (**-si**) psychosis
psicosomàti·co -ca *adj* (**-ci -che**) psychosomatic
psicotècni·co -ca (**-ci -che**) *adj* psychotechnical || *m* industrial psychologist || *f* industrial psychology
psicòti·co -ca *adj* (**-ci -che**) psychotic
pubblicare §197 (**pùbblico**) *tr* to publish
pubblicazióne *f* publication; **pubblicazioni di matrimonio** marriage banns
pubblicismo *m* communications; advertising
pubblici·sta *mf* (**-sti -ste**) free-lance newspaper writer; publicist
pubblicìsti·co -ca *adj* (**-ci -che**) advertising; political-science || *f* newspaper business
pubblicità *f* publicity; advertising
pubblicità·rio -ria (**-ri -rie**) *adj* advertising || *mf* advertising agent
publicizzare [ddzz] *tr* to publicize
publicizzazióne [ddzz] *f* publicizing
pùbbli·co -ca *adj* & *m* (**-ci -che**) public; **mettere in pubblico** to publish
pubertà *f* puberty
pudibón·do -da *adj* (lit) modest, bashful; (lit) prudish
pudicìzia *f* modesty; prudery
pudi·co -ca *adj* (**-chi -che**) modest, chaste; bashful; (lit) reserved
pudóre *m* modesty; decency; shame
puericoltóre *m* pediatrician
puerile *adj* puerile, childish
puerili·tà *f* (**-tà**) puerility, childishness
puèrpera *f* lying-in patient
pugilato *m* boxing
pugilatóre *m* boxer, prize fighter
pùgile *m* boxer, prize fighter
pugili·sta *m* (**-sti**) boxer, prize fighter
pù·glia *f* (**-glie**) stake (*in gambling*)
pugnace *adj* (lit) pugnacious
pugnalare *tr* to stab
pugnalata *f* stab
pugnale *m* dagger
pugno *m* fist; fistful; punch; **avere in pugno** to have in one's grasp; **di proprio pugno** in one's own hand; **fare a pugni** to fight; to clash

pula *f* chaff
pulce *f* flea; **mettere una pulce nell'orecchio di** to put a bug in the ear of; **pulce tropicale** jigger, chigger
pulcinèlla *f*—**pulcinella di mare** (orn) Atlantic puffin || **Pulcinel·la** *m* (**-la**) buffoon; Punch, Punchinello
pulcino *m* chick
pulédra *f* filly
pulédro *m* colt, foal
pulég·gia *f* (**-ge**) pulley
pulire §176 *tr* to clean; to shine (*shoes*); to wipe; to polish
puliscipiè·di *m* (**-di**) doormat
puli·to -ta *adj* clean; polished; clear (*conscience*) || *f*—**dare una pulita a** to give a lick and a promise to
pulitura *f* cleaning; **pulitura a secco** dry cleaning
pulizìa *f* cleaning; cleanliness; **fare le pulizie** to clean house
pullulare (**pùllulo**) *intr* to swarm
pùlpito *m* pulpit
pulsante *m* knob; push button
pulsare *intr* to throb; to pulsate
pulvìscolo *m* fine dust; haze
pulzèlla *f* var of **pulcella**
pu·ma *m* (**-ma**) cougar
pungente *adj* pungent; bitter (*cold*)
pùngere §183 *tr* to sting; (fig) to goad
pungiglióne *m* stinger (*of bee*); (fig) sting; (obs) goad
pungitòpo *m* (bot) butcher's broom
pungolare (**pùngolo**) *tr* to goad, prod
punire §176 *tr* to punish
punizióne *f* punishment; penalty
punta *f* point, tip; prong; brad; bit, trifle; needle (*of phonograph*); avantgarde; point (*of dog*); (lit) wound; (fig) peak; (mach) broach; **averne fino alla punta dei capelli** to be sick and tired; **fare la punta a** to sharpen; **in punta di penna** elegantly; **prendere di punta** to treat roughly; to face up to; **punta delle dita** fingertip; **punta di piedi** tiptoe
puntale *m* tip, ferrule
puntaménto *m* aiming
puntare *tr* to aim; to aim at; to point; to thrust; to dot; to bet; to stare at; to fix (*one's eyes*); **puntare i piedi** to stiffen up; (fig) to balk || *intr* to aim; to point; to pin; to bet; **puntare su** to count on; **puntare verso** to march on; to sail toward
puntaspil·li *m* (**-li**) pincushion
puntata *f* jab (*with weapon*); excursion; bet; issue, number (*of magazine*); installment (*of story*); (mil) incursion
punteggiare §290 (**puntéggio**) *tr* to dot; (gram) to punctuate
punteggiatura *f* dotting; punctuation
puntég·gio *m* (**-gi**) score
puntellare (**puntèllo**) *tr* to prop, brace; to support
puntèllo *m* prop, brace; support
punterìa *f* aiming; aiming gear; (aut) tappet
punteruòlo *m* punch; awl
puntì·glio *m* (**-gli**) obstinacy, stubbornness; punctilio

puntiglió·so -sa [s] *adj* punctilious, scrupulous; obstinate, stubborn

puntina *f* brad; needle; thumbtack

puntino *m* small dot; G-string; **a puntino** to a T

punto *m* point; period; dot; place, spot; extent; stitch; **dare dei punti a** to be superior to; **di punto in bianco** all of a sudden; **di tutto punto** thoroughly; **due punti** colon; **essere a buon punto** to be well advanced; **essere sul punto di + inf** to be about to + inf; **fare il punto** (fig; naut) to take one's bearings; **in punto** on the dot; **in punto franco** in bond; **in un punto** together; **mettere a punto** to get in working order; (aut) to tune up; **mettere i punti sulle i** to dot one's i's; **punto assistenza** service agency; **punto di partenza** starting point; **punto di vista** viewpoint; **punto esclamativo** exclamation point; **punto e virgola** semicolon; **punto fermo** full stop; **punto interrogativo** question mark; **punto morto** (mach) dead center; **punto stimato** (naut) dead reckoning; **qui sta il punto!** here's the rub!; **vincere ai punti** (boxing) to win by points, win by decision || *adv*—**né punto né poco** not at all; **non . . . punto** not at all

puntóne *m* rafter

puntuale *adj* punctual, prompt

puntuali·tà *f* (**-tà**) punctuality, promptness

puntura *f* sting; stitch (*sharp pain*); (coll) injection; **puntura lombare** spinal anesthesia

punzecchiare §287 (**punzécchio**) *tr* to keep on stinging; to tease, torment

punzecchiatura *f* sting, bite

punzonare (**punzóno**) *tr* to mark or stamp with a punch

punzonatrice *f* punch press

punzóne *m* punch; nailset

pupa *f* doll; (zool) pupa

pupazzetti·sta *mf* (**-sti -ste**) cartoonist

pupazzétto *m* caricature; cartoon; **pupazzetto di carta** paper doll

pupazzo *m* puppet; **pupazzo di stoffa** rag doll

pupíl·lo -la *mf* pupil; ward, protégé || *f* pupil (*of eye*); protégée

pupo *m* (coll) baby

purché *conj* provided, providing

pure *adv* too, also; indeed; (lit) only; **pur di** only in order to; **quando pure** even if; **se pure** even if || *conj* though, although; but, yet

pu·rè *m* (**-rè**) purée; **purè di patate** mashed potatoes

purézza *f* purity

pur·ga *f* (**-ghe**) laxative; purification; purge

purgante *adj* purging || *m* laxative

purgare §209 *tr* to purge; to purify; to expurgate || *ref* to take a laxative

purgati·vo -va *adj* laxative

purgatò·rio *m* (**-ri**) purgatory

purificare §197 (**purífico**) *tr* to purify

purismo *m* purism

purità *f* purity

purita·no -na *adj & m* puritan; Puritan

pu·ro -ra *adj* pure; clear; simple, mere

purosàn·gue *adj invar & m* (**-gue**) thoroughbred

purpùre·o -a *adj* (lit) purple

purtròppo *adv* unfortunately

purulèn·to -ta *adj* purulent

pus *m* pus

pusillànime *adj* pusillanimous

pàstola *f* pustule; pimple

puta caso *adv* possibly, maybe

putifè·rio *m* (**-ri**) hubbub

putrefare §173 *intr* (ESSERE) & *ref* to putrefy, rot

putrefazióne *f* putrefaction

putrèlla *f* I beam

pùtri·do -da *adj* putrid || *m* corruption

putta *f* (coll) girl; (lit) prostitute

puttana *f* (vulg) whore

put·to -ta *adj* (archaic) meretricious || *m* figure of a child || *f* see **putta**

puzza *f* var of **puzzo**

puzzare *intr* to stink, smell

puzzo *m* stench, smell, bad odor

pùzzola *f* polecat, skunk

puzzolènte *adj* stinking, smelly

puzzonata *f* (coll) contemptible action; (coll) botch, bungle

puzzóne *m* (coll) skunk (*person*)

Q

Q, q [ku] *m & f* fifteenth letter of the Italian alphabet

qua *adv* here; **da un (giorno, mese, anno) in qua** for the past (day, month, year); **di qua da** on this side of; **in qua** on this side; here

quàcche·ro -ra or **quàcque·ro -ra** *adj & mf* Quaker; **alla quacquera** in a plain fashion

quadèrno *m* copybook; **quaderno di cassa** cash book

quadràngo·lo -la *adj* quadrangular || *m* quadrangle

quadrante *m* quadrant; dial; face (*of watch*); **quadrante solare** sundial

quadrare *tr* to square || *intr* (ESSERE & AVERE) to square; **quadrare a** to be satisfactory to; **quadrare con** to fit

quadra·to -ta *adj* square; sound (*mind*) || *m* square; diaper; (boxing) ring; (nav) wardroom

quadratura *f* squaring; concreteness; (astr) quadrature

quadrèl·lo *m* (**-li**) square ruler; square tile || *m* (**-la** *fpl*) (lit) bolt, arrow

quadrerìa *f* picture gallery; collection

quadretta·to -ta *adj* checkered

quadrétto *m* small painting; checker, small square; (fig) picture

quadriennale adj four-year || f quadrennial

quadrifò·glio m (-gli) four-leaf clover; **a quadrifoglio** cloverleaf

quadrì·glio m (-gli) (cards) quadrille

quadrimensionale adj four-dimensional

quadrimestrale adj four-month

quadrimèstre m four-month period; four-month payment

quadrimotóre adj four-motor || m four-motor plane

quadrireattóre m four-motor jet

qua·dro -dra adj square; (fig) solid || m picture; painting; sight; square; table, summary; panel, switchboard; (theat) scene; **quadri** bulletin board; (mil) cadres; (cards) diamonds

quadrùmane adj quadrumanous || m monkey; ape

quadruplicare §197 (quadrùplico) tr & ref to quadruple

quadrùplice adj quadruple; **in quadruplice copia** in four copies

quàdru·plo -pla adj & m quadruple

quaggiù adv down here

quàglia f quail

quagliare §280 tr, intr (ESSERE) & ref var of **cagliare**

qualche adj invar some, e.g., **qualche giorno** some day; some, e.g., **qualche elefante è bianco** some elephants are white; any, e.g., **ha qualche libro da vendere?** do you have any books to sell?; a few, e.g., **qualche giorno** a few days

qualchedu·no -na pron indef var of **qualcuno**

qualcòsa [s] m (fig) something; (fig) somebody || pron indef something; anything; **qualcosa di buono** something good

qualcu·no -na pron indef some; any; somebody; anybody || m somebody

quale adj which, what; what a, e.g., **quale onore!** what an honor!; as, e.g., **il pane, quale vedi, è fresco** the bread, as you can see, is fresh; **quale che sia** regardless of || pron which; what; (archaic) who; **il quale** who, whom; **per la quale** o.k.; well-bred; commendable; terrific; **quale ... quale** some ... some || prep as, e.g., **quale ministro** as a minister

qualifi·ca f (-che) rating; position; quality, qualification

qualificare §197 (qualìfico) tr to qualify; to classify; to rate, give a rating to || ref to introduce oneself; to qualify

qualifica·to -ta adj aggravated (assault); qualified (personnel); specialized (worker)

quali·tà f (-tà) quality; capacity

qualóra conj if; (lit) whenever

qualsìasi [s] adj invar any; whatever; ordinary

qualunque adj invar any; whatever; common, ordinary; **in qualunque modo** anyway, anyhow; **qualunque altro** anybody else; **qualunque cosa** anything; no matter what

qualvòlta conj (lit) whenever

quando m when || adv when; **di quando**

in quando from time to time; **quando ... quando** sometimes ... sometimes || conj when; whenever; while; **da quando** since

quantisti·co -ca adj (-ci -che) quantum

quanti·tà f (-tà) quantity; number

quantitativo m quantity

quan·to -ta adj how much; as much; how great; how great a; what a; **quan·ti -te** how many; as many || m quantum || pron how much; as much; how great; how long; that which; what; whatever; **a quanto si dice** according to what is rumored; **da quanto** from what; for how long; **fra quanto** how soon; **per quanto io ne sappia** as far as I know; **quanto più** (or **meno**) ... **tanto più** (or **meno**) the more (or the less) ... the more (or the less); **quan·ti -te** how many; all those; as many as; **quanti ne abbiamo?** what's the date? || **quanto** adv how much; as much as; **in quanto** as; **in quanto che** inasmuch as; **per quanto** although; no matter; nevertheless; **quanto a** as to, as for; **quanto mai** as never before; **quanto meno** at least; **quanto prima** as soon as possible

quantunque conj although, though

quaranta adj, m & pron forty; **gli anni quaranta** the forties; **i quaranta** the forties (in age)

quarantèna f quarantine

quarantènne adj forty-year-old || mf forty-year-old person

quarantèsi·mo -ma adj, m & pron fortieth

quarantina f about forty; **essere sulla quarantina** to be about forty years old

quarantòtto adj forty-eight || m forty-eight; (coll) hubbub, uproar

quarésima f Lent

quartabuòno m triangle (in drafting); **tagliare a quartabuono** to miter

quartétto m quartet; **quartetto d'archi** string quartet

quartière m quarter, district; (mil) quarters; (coll) apartment; **quartier generale** headquarters; **senza quartiere** (fight) without quarter

quar·to -ta adj & pron fourth || m fourth; quarter; quarter of a kilo; quarter of a liter; (naut) watch; **l'una e un quarto** a quarter after one; **l'una meno un quarto** a quarter to one

quarzo m quartz

quasi adv almost, nearly; **quasi che** as if; **quasi mai** hardly ever; **senza quasi** without any ifs and buts

quassù adv up here

quat·to -ta adj crouching; squatting; **quatto quatto** stealthy, silent; **starsene quatto quatto** to not make a sound

quattordicènne adj fourteen-year-old || mf fourteen-year-old person

quattordicèsi·mo -ma adj, m & pron fourteenth

quattórdici adj & pron fourteen; **le**

quattòrdici two P.M. ‖ *m* fourteen; fourteenth (*in dates*)

quattrino *m* penny; (fig) bit; **quattrini** money

quattro *adj* four; a few, e.g., **quattro gatti** a few people; **a quattro mani** (mus) for four hands ‖ *pron* four; **dirne quattro** a to upbraid; **farsi in quattro** to go all out; **in quattro e quattr'otto** in a few minutes; **le quattro** four o'clock ‖ *m* four; fourth (*in dates*); racing shell with four oarsmen

quattrocènto *adj, m & pron* four hundred ‖ **il Quattrocento** the fifteenth century

quattromila *adj, m & pron* four thousand

quégli §7 *adj* ‖ §8 *pron*

quéi §7 *adj*

quél §7 *adj* ‖ §8 *pron*

quéll' §7 *adj*

quél·lo -la §7 *adj* ‖ §8 *pron*—**per quello che so io** as far as I know

quèr·cia *f* (-ce) oak tree

querci·no -na *adj* oaken

querèla *f* complaint

querelante *adj* complaining ‖ *mf* plaintiff

querelare (querèlo) *tr* to sue ‖ *ref* (law) to sue; (lit) to complain

querela·to -ta *adj* accused ‖ *mf* defendant

quèru·lo -la *adj* (lit) plaintive

quesito *m* question; problem; (lit) request

quésti §7 *pron*

questionare (questióno) *intr* to quarrel

questionà·rio *m* (-ri) questionnaire

questióne *f* question; (coll) quarrel; **questione di gabinetto** call for a vote of confidence; **venire a questione** to quarrel

qué·sto -sta §7 *adj* ‖ §8 *pron*—**e con questo?** so what?; **per questo** therefore; **questa** this matter; **questo . . . quello** the former . . . the latter

questóre *m* police commissioner; sergeant at arms (*of congress*)

quèstua *f* begging; collection of alms; **andare alla questua** to go begging; **vietata la questua** no begging

questura *f* police department; police headquarters

questurino *m* (coll) policeman

què·to -ta *adj* var of quieto

qui *adv* here; **di qui hence**, from here; this way; **di qui a un anno** one year hence; **di qui in avanti** from now on; **qui vicino** nearby

quiescènza *f* quiescence; retirement

quietanza *f* receipt

quietanzare *tr* to receipt

quietare (quièto) *tr* to quiet, calm; to satisfy (*e.g., thirst*) ‖ *ref* to quiet down

quiète *f* quiet, calmness

quiè·to -ta *adj* quiet, calm; still; **stia quieto!** don't worry! ‖ *m* quiet life

quindi *adv* then; therefore; (archaic) thence, from there

quindicènne *adj* fifteen-year-old ‖ *mf* fifteen-year-old person

quindicèsi·mo -ma *adj, m & pron* fifteenth

quìndici *adj & pron* fifteen; **le quindici** three P.M. ‖ *m* fifteen; fifteenth (*in dates*)

quindicina *f* about fifteen; two weeks, fortnight; semimonthly pay

quindicinale *adj* fortnightly

quinquennale *adj* five-year

quinta *f* (theat) wing; (mus) fifth; **dietro le quinte** behind the scenes

quintale *m* quintal (*100 kilos*)

quintèrno *m* signature of five sheets; (bb) quire

quintessènza *f* quintessence

quintétto *m* quintet

quin·to -ta *adj, m & pron* fifth ‖ *f* see quinta

quisquìlia *f* trifle

quivi *adv* (lit) over there; (lit) then

quòrum *m* quorum

quòta *f* quota; share; altitude; elevation; level (*of stock market*); market average; odds (*in betting*); subscription (*to club*); **quota zero** (fig) point of departure

quotare (quòto) *tr* to quote (*a price*); to value, esteem ‖ *ref* to sign up for, e.g., **si quotò duemila lire** he signed up for two thousand lire

quotazióne *f* quotation

quotidia·no -na *adj & m* daily

quoziènte *m* quotient; (sports) percentage; **quoziente d'intelligenza** I.Q.

R

R, r ['erre] *m & f* sixteenth letter of the Italian alphabet

rabàrbaro *m* rhubarb

rabberciare §128 **(rabbèrcio)** *tr* (coll) to patch up

ràbbia *f* (-ce) rage, anger; rabies

rabbino *m* rabbi

rabbió·so -sa [s] *adj* furious; rabid

rabbonire §176 *tr* to pacify ‖ *ref* to calm down

rabbrividire §176 *intr* (ESSERE) to shiver, shudder

rabbuffare *tr* to rebuke; to dishevel

rabbuffo *m* rebuke; **fare un rabbuffo a** to rebuke

rabbuiare §287 *ref* to darken, turn dark

rabdomante *m* dowser, diviner

rabé·sco *m* (-schi) arabesque; scrawl, scribble

ràbi·do -da *adj* rabid

raccapezzare (raccapézzo) *tr* to put together; to gather (*news*); to find (*one's way*); to make out (*what is* *meant*) ‖ *ref*—non raccapezzarsi to not be able to get one's bearings

raccapricciante *adj* bloodcurdling

raccapric·cio *m* (-ci) horror

raccartocciare §128 (raccartòccio) *tr & ref* to shrivel

raccattare *tr* to pick up; to gather

racchétta *f* racket; racchetta da neve snowshoe; racchetta da sci ski pole

ràc·chio -chia *adj* (-chi -chie) (coll) ugly, homely

racchiùdere §125 *tr* to contain, hold

raccògliere §127 *tr* to pick up; to gather; to collect (*e.g.*, *stamps*); to take up (*the gauntlet*); to receive; to reap; to furl (*sail*); to draw in (*a net*); to fold (*the wings*); to shelter (*e.g.*, *foundlings*); raccogliere i passi to stop walking ‖ *ref* to gather; to concentrate

raccoglimento *m* concentration; meditation

raccogli·tóre -trice *mf* collector, compiler ‖ *m* folder

raccòl·to -ta *adj* crouched; collected; engrossed; snug, intimate ‖ *m* harvest ‖ *f* harvest; collection; chiamare a raccolta to rally

raccomandàbile *adj* recommendable; poco raccomandabile unreliable

raccomandare *tr* to recommend; to secure (*e.g.*, *a boat*); to register (*mail*); to exhort ‖ *ref* to recommend oneself; to entreat; mi raccomando please; raccomandarsi a to beg, implore; raccomandarsi alle gambe to take to one's heels

raccomanda·to -ta *adj* recommended; registered ‖ *m* protégé ‖ *f* protégée; registered letter

raccomandazióne *f* recommendation; registration (*of mail*); exhortation

raccomodare (raccòmodo) *tr* to fix; to mend

racconciare §128 (raccóncio) *tr* to fix; to mend ‖ *ref* to clear up (*said of the weather*); to tidy oneself up

raccontare (raccónto) *tr* to tell; raccontarla bene to be good at telling lies

raccónto *m* tale; story; narrative

raccorciaménto *m* shortening

raccorciare §128 (raccòrcio) *tr* to shorten

raccordare (raccòrdo) *tr* to link, connect

raccòrdo *m* link, connection; raccordo a circolazione rotatoria traffic circle; raccordo anulare (rr) belt line; raccordo ferroviario junction; spur; siding; raccordo stradale connecting road

raccostare (raccòsto) *tr & ref* to draw near

raccozzare (raccòzzo) *tr* to scrape together

ràchide *m & f* backbone; midrib (*of leaf*); shaft (*of feather*)

rachì·tico -ca *adj* (-ci -che) stunted; weak; (pathol) rickety

rachitismo *m* rickets

racimolare (racìmolo) *tr* to glean; to scrape together

rada *f* roadstead; cove

ràdar *m* radar

addobbare (raddòbbo) *tr* (naut) to refit

raddolcire §176 *tr & ref* to sweeten; to mellow

raddoppiare §287 (raddóppio) *tr*, *intr* (ESSERE) *& ref* to double, redouble

raddrizzare *tr* to straighten; (elec) to rectify ‖ *ref* to straighten up

raddrizzatóre *m* (elec) rectifier

ràdere §223 *tr* to shave; to raze; to graze, skim ‖ *ref* to shave

radézza *f* rarity, rareness; thinness; sparsity (*of vegetation*); space, distance (*e.g.*, *between trees*)

radiante *adj* radiating

radiare §287 *tr* to strike off; to expel; to condemn (*a ship*); radiare dall'albo degli avvocati to disbar

radiatóre *m* radiator

radiazióne *f* radiation; expulsion

ràdi·ca *f* (-che) brier; (coll) root

radicale *adj & mf* radical ‖ *m & f* (philol) radical, root ‖ *m* (chem, math) radical

radicare §197 (ràdico) *tr & intr* to root

radice *f* root; base or foot (*e.g.*, *of a mountain or tower*); mettere radice to take root; svellere dalle radici to pull up by the roots; to eradicate

rà·dio *adj invar* radio ‖ *m* (-di) (anat) radius; (chem) radium ‖ *f* (-dio) radio; radio fante (mil) grapevine

radioabbonato *m* (rad) subscriber (*to radio broadcasting*)

radioama·tóre -trice *mf* radio fan; radio ham

radioannunciatóre *m* radio announcer

radioascolta·tóre -trice *mf* radio listener

radioatti·vo -va *adj* radioactive

radiobùssola *f* radio compass

radiocanale *m* radio channel

radiocomanda·to -ta *adj* radio-controlled

radiocròna·ca *f* (-che) newscast

radiocroni·sta *mf* (-sti -ste) newscaster

radiodiffóndere §178 *tr* to broadcast

radiodiffusióne *f* broadcasting

radiofaro *m* radio beacon

radiofòni·co -ca *adj* (-ci -che) radio

radiofonògrafo *m* radiophonograph

radiofò·to *f* (-to) radiophoto

radiofrequènza *f* radiofrequency

radiologìa *f* radiology

radiomontatóre *m* radio assembler

radiónda *f* radio wave; radioonde airwaves

radioricevènte *adj* radio ‖ *f* radio set; radio station

radioriparatóre *m* radio repairman

radiosegnale *m* radio signal

radiosentièro *m* range of a radio beacon

radió·so -sa [s] *adj* radiant

radiosorgènte *f* quasar

radiostazióne *f* radio station

radiostélla *f* quasar

radiotas·sì *m* (-sì) radio-dispatched taxi

radiotelescò·pio *m* (-pi) radiotelescope

radiotrasméttere §198 *tr & intr* to broadcast, radio

radiotrasmissióne *f* broadcast

radiotrasmittènte *adj* broadcasting || *f* broadcasting station

ra·do -da *adj* rare; thin; sheer; sparse, scattered; **di rado** seldom, rarely

radunare *tr & ref* to assemble, gather

radunata *f* gathering; (mil) assembly; **radunata sediziosa** unlawful assembly

raduno *m* assembly, gathering

radura *f* clearing, glade

ràfano *m* (bot) radish

raffazzonare (raffazzóno) *tr* to mend, patch up

raffazzonatura *f* patchwork, hodge-podge

rafférma *f* confirmation; stay (*in office*); return to office; (mil) reenlistment

raffermare (raffèrmo) *tr* to reaffirm; to secure; (coll) to reconfirm; to reappoint, reelect; to return (*e.g., a mayor*) to office || *intr* (ESSERE) & *ref* to reenlist; (coll) to harden

raffér·mo -ma *adj* stale (*bread*) || *f* see **rafferma**

ràffi·ca *f* (-che) gust; blast; burst (*e.g., of machine gun*); **a raffiche** gusty

raffigurare *tr* to represent; to symbolize

raffinare *tr* to refine; to polish || *intr* (ESSERE) to become refined

raffinatézza *f* refinement, polish

raffinatura *f* refinement (*of oil*)

raffinazióne *f* refining

raffinerìa *f* refinery

ràf·fio *m* (-fi) hook; grappling iron

rafforzare (raffòrzo) *tr* to strengthen

raffreddaménto *m* cooling

raffreddare (raffréddo) *tr* to make cold; to cool; **raffreddare gli spiriti di qlcu** to dampen s.o.'s enthusiasm || *intr* (ESSERE) & *ref* to get cold; to cool

raffreddóre *m* cold

raffrontare (raffrónto) *tr* to compare; (law) to bring face to face

raffrónto *m* comparison; confrontation

ràfia *f* raffia

raganèlla *f* rattle; (zool) tree frog

ragazza *f* girl; spinster; (coll) girl friend; **ragazza copertina** cover girl; **ragazza squillo** call girl

ragazzata *f* boyish prank

ragaz·zo -za *mf* youth, young person || *m* boy; (coll) boyfriend || *f* see **ragazza**

raggelare (raggèlo) *intr* (ESSERE) to freeze

raggiante *adj* radiant; beaming

raggiare §290 *tr & intr* to radiate

raggièra *f* rayed halo; **a raggiera** radially

ràg·gio *m* (-gi) ray; beam; spoke; (geom) radius; **raggio d'azione** radius, range of action; **raggio di sole** sunbeam

raggiornare (raggiórno) *tr* (coll) to bring up to date || *intr* (ESSERE) to dawn || *impers* (ESSERE)—**raggiorna** it is dawning

raggirare *tr* to trick, swindle || *ref* to roam, wander; **raggirarsi su** to turn on (*e.g., a certain subject*)

raggiro *m* trickery, swindle

raggiungere §183 *tr* to reach; to catch up with, rejoin

raggiungìbile *adj* attainable

raggomitolare (raggomìtolo) *tr* to roll up || *ref* to curl up; to cuddle

raggranellare (raggranèllo) *tr* to gather; to scrape together

raggrinzire §176 *tr & ref* to crease, wrinkle

raggrumare *tr & ref* to clot, coagulate

raggruppaménto *m* grouping; group

raggruppare *tr & ref* to group, assemble

ragguagliare §280 *tr* to compare; to balance; to inform in detail; to level

ragguà·glio *m* (-gli) comparison; detailed report

ragguardévole *adj* considerable, notable

ragionaménto *m* reasoning; discussion

ragionare (ragióno) *intr* to reason; to discuss || *impers ref*—**si ragiona** it is rumored

ragióne *f* reason; account; rate; justice; (math) ratio; **a maggior ragione** with all the more reason; **a ragione** within reason; **aver ragione** to be right; **aver ragione di** to get the best of; **dar ragione a qlcu** to admit that s.o. is right; **di santa ragione** hard, a great deal; **farsi ragione** to be resigned; **in ragione di** at the rate of; **ragion per cui** and therefore; **ragione sociale** (com) trade name; **rendere di pubblica ragione** to publicize

ragionerìa *f* accounting; bookkeeping

ragionévole *adj* reasonable

ragioniè·re -ra *mf* accountant; bookkeeper

ragliare §280 *intr* to bray

rà·glio *m* (-gli) bray

ragnatéla *f* spider web

ragno *m* spider

ra·gù *m* (-gù) meat gravy; stew

ràion *m* rayon

rallegraménto *m* congratulation, act of congratulating; **rallegramenti** congratulations

rallegrare (rallégro) *tr* to cheer up; to rejoice, gladden || *ref* to cheer up; to rejoice; **rallegrarsi con** to congratulate

rallentare (rallènto) *tr, intr & ref* to slow down; to lessen

rallentatóre *m* slow-motion projector; **al rallentatore** slow-motion

ra·màio *m* (-mài) tinker, coppersmith

ramaiòlo *m* ladle

ramanzina [dz] *f* reprimand

ramare *tr* to copperplate; (agr) to spray with copper sulfate

ramarro *m* green lizard

ramazza *f* broom; (mil) cleaning detail; (mil) soldier on cleaning detail

rame *m* copper; etching

ramerino *m* (coll) rosemary

ramificare §197 (**ramìfico**) *intr & ref* to branch; to branch off; to branch out, ramify

ramin·go -ga *adj* (-ghi -ghe) wandering

ramino *m* copper pot; rummy (*card game*)

rammagliare §280 *tr* to reknit; to mend a run in (*a stocking*)

rammaricare §197 (**rammàrico**) *tr* to afflict || *ref* to be sorry, regret; **rammaricarsi di** to be sorry for

rammàri·co m (-chi) regret

rammendare (rammèndo) tr to darn

rammèndo m darn

rammentare (rammènto) tr to remember; to remind || ref—**rammentarsi di** to remember

rammenta·tóre -trice mf prompter

rammollire §176 tr & ref to soften

rammolli·to -ta adj soft; soft-headed || m dodo, jellyfish

ramo m branch; bough; point (of antler); **ramo di pazzia** streak of madness

ramoscèllo m twig; **ramoscello d'olivo** olive branch

rampa f ramp; flight (of stairs); launching platform

rampicante adj climbing || m (ichth) perch; (orn) climber

rampino m hook; tine, prong; pretext

rampógna f (lit) reprimand

rampóllo m spring (of water); scion; shoot (of a plant); (joc) offspring

rampóne m harpoon; crampon

rana f frog

rànci·do -da adj rancid

ràn·cio -cia (-ci -ce) adj (poet) orange || m (mil) mess

rancóre m rancor; grudge; **serbar rancore** to bear malice

randa f (naut) spanker; (obs) edge

randà·gio -gia adj (-gi -gie) wandering; stray

randellare (randèllo) tr to cudgel; to bludgeon; to blackjack

randèllo m cudgel; bludgeon

ran·go m (-ghi) rank; station

rannicchiare §287 tr to cause to curl up || ref to crouch; to cower; to cuddle up

ranno m lye; **buttar via il ranno e il sapone** to waste one's time and effort

rannuvolare (rannùvolo) tr & ref to cloud; to darken

ranòcchia f frog

ranòc·chio m (-chi) frog

rantolare (ràntolo) intr to wheeze

ràntolo m wheezing; death rattle

ranùncolo m buttercup

rapa f turnip; **valere una rapa** to be not worth a fig

rapace adj rapacious || **rapaci** mpl birds of prey

rapare tr to shave (s.o.'s head) || ref to shave one's head; to have one's head shaved

rapidi·tà f (-tà) rapidity, swiftness

ràpi·do -da adj rapid, swift || m (rr) express || **rapide** fpl rapids

rapiménto m rape, abduction; rapture

rapina f pillage, plunder; misappropriation; prey; (lit) fury; **rapina a mano armata** armed robbery

rapinare tr to rob, plunder; to hold up; **rapinare qlco a qlcu** to rob s.o. of s.th

rapina·tóre -trice mf robber, plunderer

rapire §176 tr to rape, abduct; to kidnap; to enrapture

rapi·tóre -trice mf kidnaper

rappacificare §197 **(rappacìfico)** tr to reconcile || ref to become reconciled

rappezzare (rappèzzo) tr to patch; to

piece; **rappezzarla** to get out of trouble

rappèzzo m patch; patchwork

rapportare (rappòrto) tr to report; to transfer (a design) || ref to refer

rapporta·tóre -trice mf reporter || m protractor

rappòrto m report; relation; relationship; (math) ratio; **chiamare a rapporto** to summon; **chiedere di mettersi a rapporto** to ask for a hearing; **fare rapporto** to report; **in rapporto a** concerning; **mettersi a rapporto** to report; **sotto ogni rapporto** in every respect

rapprèndere §220 tr & ref to coagulate

rappresàglia [s] f reprisal; retaliation

rappresentante adj representing; representative || mf representative; agent; **rappresentante di commercio** agent

rappresentanza f delegation; proxy; agency; representation

rappresentare (rappresènto) tr to represent; to play; to portray

rappresentati·vo -va adj representative

rappresentazióne f representation; description; (theat) performance; **rappresentazione teatrale diurna** matinée; **sacra rappresentazione** (theat) mystery, miracle play

rapsodìa f rhapsody

raraménte adv seldom, rarely

rarefare §173 tr to rarefy || ref to become rarefied

rari·tà f (-tà) rarity

ra·ro -ra adj rare; **di raro** seldom

rasare [s] tr to shave; to mow; to trim; to smooth || ref to shave

raschiare §287 **(ràschio)** tr to scrape; to scratch || intr to clear one's throat

raschiétto m scraper; erasing knife; footscraper

rà·schio m (-schi) clearing one's throat; hoarseness; frog in the throat

rasentare (rasènto) tr to graze; to scrape; to border on; to come close to

rasènte adv close; **rasente a** close to || prep close to

ra·so -sa [s] adj shaved; trimmed; brimful; disreputable (clothes); flush || m satin || adv—**raso terra** downto-earth; **volare raso terra** to skim the ground; to hedgehop

ra·sóio [s] m (-sói) razor; **rasoio a mano libera** straight razor; **rasoio di sicurezza** safety razor

raspa f rasp

raspare tr to rasp; to irritate; to stamp, paw; (coll) to steal || intr to rasp; to scratch (said of a chicken); to scrawl

raspo m grape stalk; scraper; (vet) mange

rasségna f review; exposition

rassegnare (rasségno) tr to resign; **rassegnare le dimissioni** to resign || ref to resign oneself; to submit

rassegnazióne f resignation

rasserenare (rasseréno) tr & ref to brighten; to cheer up

rassettare (rassètto) tr & ref to tidy up

rassicurare *tr* to reassure || *ref* to be reassured

rassodare (rassòdo) *tr* to harden; to strengthen || *intr* (ESSERE) & *ref* to harden

rassomigliare §280 (rassomiglio) *tr* to compare || *intr* (ESSERE) (with *dat*) to resemble || *ref* to resemble each other

rastrellaménto *m* roundup; mop-up operation

rastrellare (rastrèllo) *tr* to rake; to round up; to mop up; to drag (*e.g.*, *the bottom*)

rastrellièra *f* rack; crib

rastrèllo *m* rake

rastremare (rastrèmo) *tr* to taper

rata *f* installment; quota; **a rate on time;** by installments

rateale *adj* installment

rateizzare [ddzz] *tr* to prorate; to divide (*a payment*) into installments

ratifi•ca *f* (**-che**) ratification

ratificare §197 (ratifico) *tr* to ratify

rat•to -ta *adj* (lit) swift || *m* rat; (lit) rape || **ratto** *adv* (lit) swiftly

rattoppare (rattòppo) *tr* to patch, patch up

rattrappire §176 *tr* to cramp; to make numb, benumb || *ref* to become cramped; to become numb

rattristare *tr* & *ref* to sadden

raucèdine *f* hoarseness

ràu•co -ca *adj* (**-chi -che**) hoarse, raucous

ravanèllo *m* radish

ravizzóne *m* (bot) rape

ravvedére §279 (*fut* ravvedrò & ravvedrò); *pp* ravveduto) *ref* to repent; to mend one's ways

ravvedu•to -ta *adj* repentant; reformed

ravviare §119 *tr* to arrange, adjust; to poke (*fire*) || *ref* to tidy up; (lit) to reform

ravvicinaménto *m* approach; reconciliation; rapprochement

ravvicinare *tr* to bring up; to reconcile || *ref* to approach; to become reconciled; **ravvicinarsi a** to approach

ravviluppare *tr* to wrap up; to wind up; to bamboozle || *ref* to become tangled

ravvisare *tr* to recognize

ravvivare *tr* to revive; to enliven; to brighten; to stir (*fire*) || *ref* to revive

ravvòlgere §289 *tr* to wrap up

razioci•nio *m* (**-ni**) reasoning; reason; common sense

razionale *adj* rational

razionalizzare [ddzz] *tr* (com, math) to rationalize

razionaménto *m* rationing

razionare (razióno) *tr* to ration

razióne *f* ration; portion

razza *f* race; breed; kind; **di razza** purebred; **far razza** to reproduce; **passare a razza** to go to stud

razza [ddzz] *f* (ichth) ray; **razza cornuta** manta ray

razzìa *f* raid; foray; insect powder

razziale *adj* racial

razziare §119 *tr* & *intr* to foray

razzismo *m* racism

razzi•sta *mf* (**-sti -ste**) racist

razzo [ddzz] *m* rocket; (coll) spoke; (mil) flare

razzolare (ràzzolo) *intr* to scratch (*said of chickens*); (coll) to rummage

re [e] *m* (re) king

re [e] *m* (re) (mus) re

reagènte *m* reagent

reagire §176 *intr* to react

reale *adj* real, actual; royal, regal

realismo *m* realism; royalism

reali•sta *mf* (**-sti -ste**) realist; royalist

realisti•co -ca *adj* (**-ci -che**) realistic

realizzare [ddzz] *tr* to carry out; to realize; to build || *ref* to come true

realizzazióne [ddzz] *f* realization; **realizzazione scenica** production

realizzo [ddzz] *m* conversion into cash; profit taking; forced sale

realménte *adv* really, indeed

real•tà *f* (**-tà**) reality; actuality; **realtà romanzesca** truth stranger than fiction

reato *m* crime

reatti•vo -va *adj* reactive

reattóre *m* reactor; jet plane; jet engine

reazionà•rio -ria (**-ri -rie**) *adj* & *mf* reactionary

reazióne *f* reaction; (mach) backlash; **a reazione** jet-propelled

réb•bio *m* (**-bi**) prong

recalcitrante *adj* balky, restive; **essere recalcitrante a** to be opposed to, to resist

recalcitrare (recàlcitro) *intr* to be balky; to kick; (with *dat*) to buck, resist

recapitare (recàpito) *tr* to deliver

recàpito *m* address; delivery; **far recapito in** to be domiciled in; **recapiti** (com) notes

recare §197 (rèco) *tr* to bring; to cause; **recare ad effetto** to carry out; **recare qlco alla memoria di qlcu** to remind s.o. of s.th; **recare qlco a lode di qlcu** to praise s.o. for s.th || *ref* to go, betake oneself

recèdere §123 *intr* (ESSERE & AVERE) to recede

recensióne *f* book review; collation

recensire §176 *tr* to review; to collate

recensóre *m* reviewer

recènte *adj* recent; **di recente** recently

recessióne *f* recession

recèsso *m* recess; subsiding (*of fever*); ebb tide

recìdere §145 *tr* to cut off; to chop off

recidiva *f* relapse; second offense

recingere §126 *tr* to enclose, pen in

recinto *m* enclosure; pen, yard; compound; playpen; paddock; **recinto delle grida** floor of the exchange

recipiènte *m* container

reciprocità *f* reciprocity

recipro•co -ca *adj* (**-ci -che**) reciprocal

reci•so -sa *adj* cut off; abrupt

rècita *f* show, performance

recitare (rècito) *tr* to recite; to portray, play; to recite; **recitare la commedia** to put on an act || *intr* to perform, play; **recitare a soggetto** (theat) to improvise

recitazióne *f* recitation; diction; acting

reclamare *tr* to claim, demand || *intr* to complain

récla·me *f* (-me) advertising; advertisement; **fare réclame a** to advertise; to boost

reclami·sta *mf* (-sti -ste) advertising agent; show-off || *m* advertising man

reclamìsti·co -ca *adj* (-ci -che) advertising

reclamo *m* complaint; **fare reclamo a** to complain

reclinare *tr* to bow || *intr* to recline

reclusióne *f* seclusion; imprisonment

reclu·so -sa *adj* recluse || *mf* recluse; prisoner

reclusò·rio *m* (-ri) penitentiary

rècluta *f* recruit; rookie

reclutaménto *m* recruitment

reclutare (**rècluto**) *tr* to recruit

recòndi·to -ta *adj* concealed; inmost; recondite

recriminare (**recrìmino**) *intr* to recriminate

recuperare (**recùpero**) *tr* see **ricuperare**

redarguire §176 *tr* to berate

redat·tóre -trice *mf* compiler; newspaper editor; **redattore capo** managing editor; **redattore pubblicitario** copywriter; **redattore responsabile** publisher; **redattore viaggiante** correspondent

redazionale *adj* editorial, editor's (*e.g., policy*)

redazióne *f* writing; draft; version; (journ) city room

redazza *f* mop; (naut) swab

redditi·zio -zia *adj* (-zi -zie) lucrative

rèddito *m* income, revenue; yield; **reddito nazionale** gross national product

redèn·to -ta *adj* redeemed, set free

reden·tóre -trice *mf* redeemer || **Redentore** *m*—**il Redentore** the Redeemer

redenzióne *f* redemption

redìgere §224 *tr* to compile; to write up, compose

redìmere §225 *tr* to redeem; to ransom; to save

rèdine *f* rein

redivì·vo -va *adj* come back to life

rèduce *adj* back (*from war*) || *mf* veteran

réfe *m* thread

referèn·dum *m* (-dum) referendum; **referendum postale** mail questionnaire

referènza *f* reference

referenziare (**referènzio**) *tr* to give references to; to write references for || *intr* to have good references

referenzia·to -ta *adj* with good references, e.g., **impiegato referenziato** employee with good references

referto *m* report (*of a physician*)

refettò·rio *m* (-ri) refectory

refezióne *f* lunch, light meal; **refezione scolastica** school lunch

refrattà·rio -ria *adj* (-ri -rie) refractory

refrigerante *adj* cooling || *m* refrigerator; (chem) condenser

refrigerare (**refrìgero**) *tr* to refrigerate; to cool || *ref* to cool off

refrigè·rio *m* (-ri) relief, comfort

refurtiva *f* stolen goods

refuso *m* misprint

regalare *tr* to present; to deliver (*a slap*); to throw away (*money*); **è regalato** it's a steal

regale *adj* regal; royal; imposing

regalìa *f* gratuity; bonus

regalità *f* regality, royalty

regalo *m* present, gift

regata *f* regatta

reggènte *adj* & *m* regent

reggènza *f* regency

règgere §226 *tr* to hold, hold up; to stand, withstand; to guide; (gram) to govern; **reggere il sacco a** to connive with; **reggere l'animo di** + *inf* to bear or stand + *ger*, e.g., **non gli regge l'animo di vederla piangere** he cannot stand seeing her cry || *intr* to hold; to be valid; to last, hold out (*said of weather*); **reggere** (with *dat*) to withstand (*e.g., the cold*); **reggere al paragone** to bear comparison || *ref* to stand up; to hold; to be ruled; **reggersi a** to hold on to; to be governed as (*e.g., a republic*); **reggersi a galla** to float

règ·gia *f* (-ge) royal palace

reggical·ze *m* (-ze) girdle

reggilibro *m* book end

reggimentale *adj* regimental

reggiménto *m* regiment

reggipètto *m* brassiere

reggisè·no *m* (-ni & -no) brassiere

regìa *f* monopoly; (mov) direction; (theat) production

regici·da *mf* (-di -de) regicide

regicì·dio *m* (-di) regicide

regime *m* regime; diet; flow (*e.g., of river*); government; authoritarian government; (mach) rate; **regime secco** total abstinence

regina *f* queen; **regina claudia** greengage; **regina madre** queen mother

reginétta *f* young queen; queen (*of a beauty contest*)

rè·gio -gia *adj* (-gi -gie) royal || **i regi** the king's soldiers

regióne *f* region

regi·sta *mf* (-sti -ste) coordinator; (theat) producer; (mov) director

registrare *tr* to register, record; to enter; to tally, log; to adjust; to tune up (*a musical instrument*) || *ref* to register

registra·tóre -trice *mf* registrar || *m* recorder; **registratore di cassa** cash register

registrazióne *f* registration; record, entry; adjustment; (aut) tune-up; (telv) videotaping; (telv) video-taping studio; (telv) video-taped program

registro *m* register; registration; classbook; regulator (*of watch*); stop (*of organ*); **cambiar registro** to change one's tune; **dar registro a** to regulate (*a watch*)

regnante *adj* reigning; prevailing || **i regnanti** the rulers

regnare (**régno**) *intr* to reign, rule; to prevail; to take hold (*said of a root*)

régno *m* kingdom; reign

règola *f* rule; regulation; moderation; **a regola d'arte** to a T; **di regola** as a rule; **in regola** in good order; **mettere in regola** to put in order; **regole menstruation**; **secondo le regole** by the book

regolamentare *adj* regulation ‖ *v* (**regolamènto**) *tr* to regulate

regolamènto *m* regulation; settlement; **regolamento edilizio** building code

regolare *adj* regular; steady (*employment*); stock (*material*) ‖ *v* (**règolo**) *tr* to regulate; to adjust; to set (*a watch*); to focus (*a lens*); to settle (*an account*) ‖ *ref* to behave; to control oneself

regolari·tà *f* (**-tà**) regularity

regolarizzare [ddzz] *tr* to regularize

regolatézza *f* regularity; moderation

regola·to -ta *adj* regular, orderly

regola·tóre -trice *adj* regulating; see **piano** ‖ *m* ruler; regulator (*of watch*); (mach) governor; **regolatore dell'aria** register; **regolatore di volume** (rad, telv) volume control

regolazióne *f* regulation

regolìzia *f* (coll) licorice

règolo *m* ruler; slat; (orn, hist) kinglet; **regolo calcolatore** slide rule

regredire §176 (*pres participle* **regrediènte**; *pp* **regredito** & **regrèsso**) *intr* (ESSERE & AVERE) to retrogress

regrèsso *m* regression; abatement (*of fever*); (com) recourse

reièt·to -ta *adj* rejected ‖ *mf* outcast

reimbarcare §197 *tr* & *ref* to reship; to tranship

reimbar·co *m* (**-chi**) reshipment; transshipment

reincarnare *tr* to reincarnate ‖ *ref* to become reincarnated

reincarnazióne *f* reincarnation

reinserimènto *m* integration

reintegrare (**reìntegro**) *tr* to restore; to reinstate; to indemnify

reità *f* guilt

reiterare (**reìtero**) *tr* to reiterate

relativi·tà *f* (**-tà**) relativity

relati·vo -va *adj* relative

rela·tóre -trice *adj* reporting ‖ *mf* relator (*of proceedings*); presenter (*of a bill*); dissertation supervisor

relazióne *f* relation; relationship; report; **relazione amorosa** affair; **relazioni relations**; connections

re·lè *m* (**-lè**) (elec) relay

relegare §209 (**rèlego**) *tr* to banish; to store away

religióne *f* religion

religió·so -sa [s] *adj* religious ‖ *m* clergyman ‖ *f* nun

relìquia *f* relic

relìt·to -ta *adj* residual ‖ *m* shipwreck; air crash; derelict; shoal, bar

remare (**rèmo** & **rémo**) *intr* to row

rema·tóre -trice *mf* rower ‖ *m* oarsman

reminiscènza *f* reminiscence

remissióne *f* submissiveness; remission

remissi·vo -va *adj* submissive

rèmo *m* oar; **remo alla battana** paddle

rèmora *f* hindrance; (lit) delay

remò·to -ta *adj* remote; **passato remoto** (gram) preterit

réna *f* sand

Renània, la the Rhineland

Renata *f* Renée

rèndere §227 *tr* to return, give back; to give (*thanks*); to render (*justice*); to yield; to translate; to make (*known*); **render conto di** to give an account of; **rendere di pubblica ragione** to publicize; **rendere l'anima a Dio** to give up the ghost; **rendere pan per focaccia** to give tit for tat ‖ *intr* to pay, yield ‖ *ref* to make oneself; to betake oneself; to become; (lit) to surrender; **rendersi conto di** to realize

rendicónto *m* account; report; **rendiconti** proceedings

rendimènto *m* rendering; yield; output; (mech) efficiency

rèndita *f* private income; yield; Italian Government bond

rène *m* kidney

renèlla *f* (pathol) gravel

renétta *f* pippin

réni *fpl* loins; **spezzare le reni a** to break the back of

renitènte *adj* opposed ‖ *m*—**renitente alla leva** draft dodger

rènna *f* reindeer; reindeer skin

Rèno *m* Rhine

rè·o -a *adj* guilty; (lit) wicked ‖ *m* guilty person; accused

reòstato *m* (elec) rheostat

reparto *m* department; (mil) unit; **reparto d'assalto** shock troops

repèllere §168 *tr* to repel

repentàglio *m* jeopardy; **mettere a repentàglio** to jeopardize

repènte *adj*—**di repente** suddenly

repentì·no -na *adj* sudden

reperìbile *adj* available

reperimènto *m* finding

reperire §176 *tr* to find

repèrto *m* (archeol) find; (law) evidence; (law) exhibit; (med) report

repertò·rio *m* (**-ri**) repertory; catalogue

rèpli·ca *f* (**-che**) repetition; replica; (law) rebuttal; (theat) repeat performance; **in replica** in reply

replicare §197 (**rèplico**) *tr* to repeat; to reply, answer; (theat) to repeat (*a performance*)

reportàg·gio *m* (**-gi**) news coverage; reporting

repòr·ter *m* (**-ter**) reporter

repressióne *f* repression; constraint

repressi·vo -va *adj* repressive; controlling, checking (*e.g., a disease*)

reprìmere §131 *tr* to repress; to hold back (*tears*) ‖ *ref* to restrain oneself

rèpro·bo -ba *adj* & *m* reprobate

repùbbli·ca *f* (**-che**) republic

repubblica·no -na *adj* & *mf* republican

repulisti *m*—**fare repulisti** (coll) to make a clean sweep

repulsióne *f* repulsion

repulsi·vo -va *adj* var of **ripulsivo**

reputare (**rèputo**) *tr* to think, esteem, repute

reputazióne *f* reputation

rèquie *m* & *f* (eccl) requiem ‖ *f* rest, respite

Rèquiem *m* & *f* Requiem

requisire §176 *tr* to requisition, commandeer

requisito *m* requisite, requirement

requisitòria *f* scolding, reproach; (law) summation

requisizióne *f* requisition

résa [s] *f* surrender; rendering (*of an account*); delivery (*of merchandise*); return (*e.g., of newspapers*); yield; **resa a discrezione** unconditional surrender

rescindere §247 *tr* to rescind

resezióne [s] *f* (surg) resection

residènte [s] *adj & mf* resident

residènza [s] *f* residence

residenziale [s] *adj* residential

residua·to -ta [s] *adj* residual

resì·duo -dua [s] *adj* residual ‖ *m* residue; remainder; balance

rèsina *f* resin

resipiscènza [s] *f* (lit) repentance

resistènte [s] *adj* resistant; strong; fast (*color*) ‖ *mf* member of the Resistance

resistènza [s] *f* resistance ‖ **Resistènza** *f* Resistance

resìstere [s] §114 *intr* to resist; (with *dat*) to withstand; (with *dat*) to endure; (with *dat*) to resist

rèso [s] *m* rhesus

resocónto [s] *m* report, relation

respingènte *m* (rr) bumper, buffer

respìngere §126 *tr* to drive back, beat off; to reject; to fail (*a student*); to vote down

respìn·to -ta *adj* rejected ‖ *mf* failure (*pupil*)

respirare *tr & intr* to breathe, respire

respiratò·rio -ria *adj* (-ri -rie) respiratory

respirazióne *f* breathing

respiro *m* breath; breathing; respite

responsàbile *adj* responsible; **responsabile di** responsible for

responsabili·tà *f* (-tà) responsibility

respónso *m* decision (*of an oracle*); report (*of a physician*); return (*of an election*); (lit) response

rèssa *f* crowd; **far ressa** to crowd

rèsta *f* string (*of garlic or onions*); awn (*e.g., of wheat*); (coll) fishbone; (*for a lance*) (hist) rest

restante *adj* remaining ‖ *m* remainder

restare (**rèsto**) *intr* (ESSERE) to remain; to stay; to be located; (lit) to stop; **non restare a...che** to have no alternative but to, e.g., **non gli resta che andarsene** he has no alternative but to go; **non restare a qlcu qlco da + inf** to not have s.th + to + inf, e.g., **non gli resta molto da finire** he does not have much to finish; **resta a vedere** it remains to be seen; **restare qlco a qlcu** to have s.th left, e.g., **gli restano tre dollari** he has three dollars left; **restare sul colpo** to die on the spot; **resti comodo** please don't get up!

restaurare (**restàuro**) *tr* to restore, renovate

restaurazióne *f* restoration

restàuro *m* restoration (*of a building*)

restì·o -a (**-i -e**) *adj* balky, restive ‖ *m* balkiness

restituire §176 *tr* to give back, return; (lit) to restore ‖ *ref* (lit) to return

restituzióne *f* restitution, return

rèsto *m* remainder; change; balance; **del resto** besides, after all; **resti** remains

restrìngere §265 (*pp* **ristrétto**) *tr* to narrow down; to shrink; to take in (*a suit*); to limit (*expenses*); to tighten (*a knot*); to bind (*the bowels*); to restrict ‖ *ref* to contract; to narrow

restrizióne *f* restriction

retàg·gio *m* (-gi) (fig) heritage

retata *f* haul; (fig) roundup

réte *f* net; network; (soccer) goal; **rete a strascico** trawl; **rete da pesca** fishing net; **rete del letto** bedspring; **rete metallica** wire mesh; window screen; **rete per i capelli** hair net; **rete viaria** highway network

reticèlla *f* small net; hair net; mantle (*of gas jet*)

reticènte *adj* secretive, dissembling; evasive, noncommittal

reticènza *f* secretiveness; evasiveness

reticolato *m* grid (*on map*); wire entanglement

retìcolo *m* grid

retìna *f* small net

rètina *f* (anat) retina

retino *m* small net; (typ) screen

retòri·co -ca (**-ci -che**) *adj* rhetorical ‖ *m* rhetorician ‖ *f* rhetoric

retràttile *adj* retractile

retribuire §176 *tr* to remunerate

retributi·vo -va *adj* retributive; salary (*e.g., conditions*)

retri·vo -va *adj* backward

rètro *m* back; verso; back of store ‖ *adv* (lit) behind; **retro a** (lit) behind

retroatti·vo -va *adj* retroactive

retrobottè·ga *m & f* (-ga *mpl* -ghe *fpl*) back of store

retrocàmera *f* back room

retrocàrica *f*—**a retrocarica** breechloading

retrocèdere §228 *tr* to demote; (com) to return; (com) to give a discount to ‖ *intr* (ESSERE & AVERE) to retreat

retrocessióne *f* demotion; (sports) assignment to a lower division

retrodatare *tr* to antedate, predate

retrògra·do -da *adj* backward; retrograde

retroguàrdia *f* rearguard

retromàr·cia *f* (-ce) (aut) reverse

retrorazzo [ddzz] *m* retrorocket

retrosapóre *m* aftertaste

retroscè·na *m* (-na) intrigue, maneuver ‖ *f* backstage

retrospetti·vo -va *adj* retrospective

retrotèr·ra *m* (-ra) hinterland; (fig) background

retrotrèno *m* rear end (*of vehicle*); (aut) rear assembly

retroversióne *f* retroversion; retranslation

retrovìe *fpl* zone behind the front

retrovisi·vo -va *adj* rear-view, e.g., **specchietto retrovisivo** rear-view mirror

retrovisóre *m* rear-view mirror

rètta *f* board and lodging; straight line; **dar retta a** to pay attention to

rettangolare *adj* rectangular

rettàngolo *m* rectangle

rettifi·ca *f* (**-che**) straightening; rectification; (mach) grinding; (mach) reboring

rettificare §197 (**rettifico**) *tr* to straighten; to rectify; (mach) to grind; (mach) to rebore

rettifica·tóre -trice *adj* rectifying ‖ *mf* rectifier (*person*) ‖ *m* rectifier (*apparatus*)

rettifilo *m* straightaway

rèttile *m* reptile

rettili·neo -nea *adj* rectilinear ‖ *m* straightaway ‖ *f* straight line

rettitùdine *f* straightness; uprightness, rectitude

rèt·to -ta *adj* straight; correct; upright; (geom) right ‖ *m* right; recto; (anat) rectum ‖ *f* see **retta**

rettóre *m* rector; president (*of university*)

reumàti·co -ca *adj* (**-ci -che**) rheumatic

reumatismo *m* rheumatism

reverèn·do -da *adj* & *m* reverend

reverènte *adj* var of **riverente**

reverènza *f* var of **riverenza**

revisióne *f* revision; (mach) overhaul

revisionismo *m* revisionism

revisóre *m* inspector; **revisore dei conti** auditor; **revisore di bozze** proofreader

reviviscènza *f* rebirth

rèvo·ca *f* (**-che**) revocation; recall; repeal

revocare §197 (**rèvoco**) *tr* to revoke; to recall; to repeal

revòl·ver *m* (**-ver**) revolver

revolverata *f* gun shot

revulsióne *f* (med) revulsion

ri- *pref* re-, e.g., **rivìvere** to relive; again, e.g., **rifare** to do again; back, e.g., **riandare** to go back

riabbonare (**riabbòno**) *tr* to renew the subscription of ‖ *ref* to renew one's subscription

riabbracciare §128 (**riabbràccio**) *tr* to embrace again; to greet again

riabilitare (**riabìlito**) *tr* to rehabilitate ‖ *ref* to reestablish one's good name

riaccèndere §101 *tr* to rekindle ‖ *ref* to become rekindled

riaccompagnare *tr* to take home

riaccostare (**riaccòsto**) *tr* to bring near; to bring together ‖ *ref* to draw near

riacquistare *tr* to buy back; to recover

riaddormentare (**riaddorménto**) *tr* to put back to sleep ‖ *ref* to go back to sleep

riaffacciare §128 (**riaffàccio**) *tr* to present again ‖ *ref* to reappear

riaffermare (**riaffèrmo**) *tr* to reaffirm

riaggravare *tr* to make worse ‖ *ref* to get worse again

rialesare (**rialèso**) *tr* to rebore

riallacciare §128 (**riallàccio**) *tr* to tie again ‖ *ref* to be tied or connected

rialto *m* knoll, height; **fare rialto** (coll) to eat better than usual

rialzare *tr* to lift, raise; to increase ‖ *ref* to rise

rialzi·sta *mf* (**-sti -ste**) bull (*in stock market*)

rialzo *m* rise; raise; knoll, height; **giocare al rialzo** to bull the market

riammobiliare §287 *tr* to refurnish

rianimare (**riànimo**) *tr* to revive; to encourage ‖ *ref* to revive; to recover one's spirits, to rally

riapertura *f* reopening

riapparire §108 *intr* (ESSERE) to reappear

riapparizióne *f* reappearance

riaprire §110 *tr* & *ref* to reopen

riarmare *tr* to rearm; to reinforce; to refit ‖ *intr* & *ref* to rearm

riarmo *m* rearmament

riar·so -sa *adj* dry, parched

riassaporare (**riassapóro**) *tr* to relish again

riassettare (**riassètto**) *tr* to tidy up

riassicurare *tr* to reinsure; to fasten again; to reassure

riassorbire §176 & (**riassòrbo**) *tr* to reabsorb

riassùmere §116 *tr* to hire again; to summarize, sum up

riassunto *m* précis, abstract; résumé

riassunzióne *f* rehiring; resumption

riattaccare §197 *tr* to attach again; (coll) to begin again; (telp) to hang up

riattare *tr* to repair, fix

riattivare *tr* to reactivate

riavére §229 *tr* to get again; to recover; to get back ‖ *ref* to recover

riavvicinaménto *m* var of **ravvicinamento**

riavvicinare *tr* & *ref* var of **ravvicinare**

ribadire §176 *tr* to clinch (*a nail*); to rivet; to drive home (*an idea*); to back up (*a statement*)

ribaldo *m* scoundrel, rogue

ribalta *f* lid with hinge; trap door; (theat) footlights; (theat) forestage; (fig) limelight; **a ribalta** hinged

ribaltàbile *adj* collapsable (*e.g., seat*) ‖ *m* dump-truck lift; dump truck

ribaltare *tr* & *ref* to upset, turn over

ribassare *tr* & *intr* (ESSERE) to lower

ribassi·sta *mf* (**-sti -ste**) bear (*in stock market*)

ribasso *m* fall, decline; discount, rebate; **giocare al ribasso** to be a bear

ribàttere *tr* to clinch (*a nail*); to return (*a ball*); to iron smooth; to belabor (*a point*) ‖ *intr* to answer back

ribattezzare [ddzz] (**ribattézzo**) *tr* to rebaptize

ribattino *m* rivet

ribellare (**ribèllo**) *tr* to rouse to rebellion ‖ *ref* to rebel; **ribellarsi a** to rebel against

ribèlle *adj* rebellious ‖ *mf* rebel

ribellióne *f* rebellion

ri·bes *m* (**-bes**) currant; gooseberry

ribobinazióne *f* rewind (*of a tape*)

riboccare §197 (**ribócco**) *intr* (ESSERE) & AVERE) to overflow

ribollire (**ribóllo**) *tr* to boil again ‖

intr to boil over; to simmer; to ferment

ribrézzo [ddzz] *m* repugnance, disgust

ributtare *tr* to return (*a ball*); to throw up; to reject; to push back ‖ *intr* to sprout; (with *dat*) to disgust, nauseate

ricacciare §128 *tr* to drive back ‖ *intr* to sprout ‖ *ref* to sneak away, disappear

ricadére §121 *intr* (ESSERE) to fall back; to fall down; to relapse; **ricadere su** to devolve upon

ricaduta *f* relapse

ricalcare §197 *tr* to transfer (*a design*); to imitate; **ricalcare le orme di** follow in the footsteps of

rical·co *m* (-chi) copy, copying; a **ricalco** multiple-copy

ricamare *tr* to embroider

ricambiare §287 *tr* to return; to repay ‖ *ref* to change clothes

ricàm·bio *m* (-bi) exchange; spare part; refill; metabolism; **di ricambio** spare (*part*)

ricamo *m* embroidery; needlework; **ricami** (*fig*) embellishments

ricapitolare (**ricapìtolo**) *tr* to recapitulate

ricaricare §197 (**ricàrico**) *tr* to reload; to wind (*a watch*); to charge (*a battery*)

ricattare *tr* to blackmail

ricatta·tóre -trice *mf* blackmailer

ricatto *m* blackmail

ricavare *tr* to draw, extract; to obtain, derive

ricavato *m* proceeds; (fig) fruit, yield

ricavo *m* proceeds

ricchézza *f* wealth; **ricchezza mobile** income from personal property; **ricchezze** riches

ric·cio -cia (-ci -ce) *adj* curly ‖ *m* curl; shaving; burr; scroll (*of violin*); crook (*of crozier*); (zool) hedgehog; **riccio di mare** (zool) sea urchin

ricciolo *m* curl

ricciolu·to -ta *adj* curly

ricciu·to -ta *adj* curly

ric·co -ca *adj* (-chi -che) rich ‖ **i ricchi** the rich

ricér·ca *f* (-che) search; research; **ricerca operativa** operations research

ricercare §197 (**ricérco**) *tr* to search for again; to seek; to investigate; (poet) to pluck (*a musical instrument*)

ricercatézza *f* affectation; sophistication

ricerca·to -ta *adj* sought after, wanted; affected; sophisticated

ricetrasmettitóre *m* two-way radio

ricètta *f* prescription; recipe

ricettàcolo *m* receptacle; depository

ricettare (**ricètto**) *tr* to receive (*stolen goods*); to prescribe

ricettà·rio *m* (-ri) recipe book; prescription pad

ricetta·tóre -trice *mf* fence, receiver of stolen goods

ricetti·vo -va *adj* receptive

ricètto *m* (poet) refuge

ricévere §141 *tr* to receive; to get; to contain; to withstand

riceviménto *m* reception; receipt

ricevi·tóre -trice *mf* addressee ‖ *m* receiver; collector; registrar of deeds; **ricevitore postale** postmaster

ricevitoria *f* collection office; **ricevitoria postale** post office

ricevuta *f* receipt; **accusare ricevuta di** to acknowledge receipt of

ricezióne *f* (rad, telv) reception; **accusare ricezione** to acknowledge receipt

richiamare *tr* to call back; to recall; to call (*e.g., attention*); to quote; to chide ‖ *ref* to refer

richiamato *m* soldier recalled to active duty

richiamo *m* call; recall; admonition; cross reference; advertisement

richièdere §124 *tr* to ask again; to demand; to require; to apply for ‖ *ref* to be required

richiè·sto -sta *adj*—**essere richiesto** to be in demand ‖ *f* request; demand; petition, application

richiùdere §125 *tr & ref* to shut again

riciclare *tr* to recycle (*e.g., in the chemical industry*)

ricino *m* castor-oil plant

ricognitóre *m* scout; reconnaissance plane; (law) recognition

ricognizióne *f* recognition; (mil) reconnaissance

ricollegare §209 (**ricollégo**) *tr* to connect ‖ *ref* to be connected; to refer

ricolmare (**ricólmo**) *tr* to fill to the brim; to overwhelm

ricominciare §128 *tr & intr* (ESSERE) to begin again, resume

ricomparire §108 *intr* (ESSERE) to reappear

ricomparsa *f* reappearance

ricompènsa *f* compensation, recompense; reward; (mil) award

ricompensare (**ricompènso**) *tr* to compensate, recompense; to reward

ricomperare (**ricómpero**) *tr* var of **ricomprare**

ricompórre §218 *tr* to recompose; to plan again ‖ *ref* to regain one's composure

ricomprare (**ricómpro**) *tr* to buy again; to buy back

riconcentrare (**riconcèntro**) *tr* to concentrate again; to gather (*one's thoughts*) ‖ *ref* to be withdrawn

riconciliare §287 (**riconcìlio**) *tr* to reconcile ‖ *ref* to become reconciled

ricondurre §102 *tr* to bring back; to take back ‖ *ref* to go back

riconfermare (**riconfèrmo**) *tr* to reconfirm

riconfortare (**riconfòrto**) *tr* to comfort

ricongiùngere §183 *tr & ref* to reunite

riconoscènte *adj* grateful

riconoscènza *f* gratitude

riconóscere §134 *tr* to recognize; (mil) to reconnoiter

riconosciménto *m* recognition; **in riconoscimento di** in recognition of

riconquistare *tr* to reconquer

riconsegnare (**riconségno**) *tr* to give back, to return

riconsiderare (riconsìdero) tr to reconsider

ricontare (ricónto) tr to recount, count again

riconversióne f reconversion

riconvertire §138 tr to reconvert; to recycle

ricopèr·to -ta adj covered; coated

ricopertura f covering; seat cover

ricopiare §287 **(ricòpio)** tr to make a fair copy of; to recopy; to copy

ricoprire §110 tr to cover; to coat; to hide || ref to become covered

ricordanza f (poet) memory

ricordare (ricòrdo) tr to remember; to remind; to mention || ref to remember; **ricordarsi di** to remember

ricòrdo m memory; souvenir; **ricordo marmoreo** marble statue

ricorrènte adj recurrent, recurring

ricorrènza f recurrence; anniversary

ricórrere §139 intr (ESSERE & AVERE) to run again; to run back; to resort; to recur; (law) to appeal; **ricorrere a** to have recourse to

ricórso m recurrence; recourse; appeal

ricostituènte adj invigorating || m tonic

ricostituire §176 tr to reconstitute, to reform; to reinvigorate

ricostruire §140 tr to rebuild; to reconstruct

ricostruzióne f rebuilding; reconstruction

ricòtta f Italian cottage cheese; **di ricotta** weak

ricoverare (ricóvero) tr to shelter || ref to take shelter

ricóvero m shelter; nursing home; (med) admission; **ricovero antiaereo** air-raid shelter

ricreare (ricrèo) tr to recreate; to refresh || ref to relax

ricreati·vo -va adj refreshing; recreational

ricreatò·rio -ria (-ri -rie) adj recreation, recreational || m recreation room; playground

ricreazióne f recreation; recess

ricrédere §141 intr—**far ricredere qlcu** to make s.o. change his mind || ref to change one's mind

ricréscere §142 intr (ESSERE) to grow again; to swell

ricucire §143 tr to sew up

ricuòcere §144a tr to cook again; to anneal

ricuperare (ricùpero) tr to recover; (naut) to salvage; (sports) to make up for (rained-out game)

ricùpero m recovery; salvage; rally; making up (for lost time or postponed game)

ricur·vo -va adj bent; bent over

ricusare tr to refuse

ridacchiare §287 intr to titter, giggle

ridancia·no -na adj prone to laughter; amusing

ridare §230 (1st sg pres ind ridò) tr to give back; to give again; **ridare fuori** to vomit || intr (coll) to reappear, e.g., **gli ha ridato il foruncolo** his boil has reappeared || intr

(ESSERE)—**ridare giù** to have a relapse

ridda f round; confusion; throng

ridènte adj laughing; bright, pleasant

ridere §231 tr (poet) to laugh at || intr to laugh; (poet) to shine; **far ridere i polli** to be utterly ridiculous; **ridere sotto i baffi** to laugh up one's sleeve || ref—**ridersi di** to laugh at

ridestare (ridèsto) tr & ref to reawaken

ridicolizzare [ddzz] tr to ridicule; to twit

ridìco·lo -la adj ridiculous || m ridicule; ridiculousness

ridipìngere §126 tr to paint again

ridire §151 tr to tell again; to repeat; to tell (to express); **avere** or **trovare a** or **da ridire (su)** to find fault (with)

ridistribuzióne f redistribution

ridivenire §282 or **ridiventare (ridivènto)** intr (ESSERE) to become again

ridonare (ridóno) tr to give back

ridondante adj redundant

ridondare (ridóndo) intr (ESSERE & AVERE) (fig) to overflow; **ridondare a** or **in** to redound to

ridòsso m back; shelter; **a ridosso** sheltered; as a shelter; behind, close behind

ridót·to -ta adj reduced; **mal ridotto** down at the heel || m lounge; (theat) foyer || f (mil) redoubt

ridurre §102 tr to reduce; to adapt; to translate; to lead; to curtail; (mus) to arrange || ref to be reduced; to retire

riduttóre m (mach) reduction gear

riduzióne f reduction; (mus) arrangement

riecheggiare §290 **(riechéggio)** tr & intr to echo

riedificare §197 **(riedìfico)** tr to rebuild

rieducare §197 **(rièduco)** tr to reducate

rielèggere §193 tr to reelect

rielezióne f reelection

riemèrgere §162 intr to resurface

riempiménto m fill

riempire §163 tr to fill; to stuff

riempiti·vo -va adj expletive || m expletive; fill-in

rientrante adj hollow (cheeks); (mil) reentrant

rientranza f recess

rientrare (riéntro) intr (ESSERE) to reenter; to come back; to recede; (coll) to shrink; **rientrare in** to recover (one's expenses); **rientrare in sé** to come to one's senses

riéntro m reentry

riepilogare §209 **(riepìlogo)** tr to sum up, recapitulate

riepìlo·go m (-ghi) recapitulation

riesame m reexamination

riesaminare (riesàmino) tr to reexamine

riesumare tr to exhume; (fig) to dig up; (fig) to bring back

rievocare §197 **(rièvoco)** tr to recall

rifaciménto m adaptation; recasting

rifare §173 (3d sg rifà) tr to do again, redo; to remake; to imitate; to indemnify; to prepare again; to repeat;

to make (*a bed*) || *ref* to recover; to become again; to recoup one's losses; to begin; **rifarsi con** to get even with; **rifarsi da** to begin with

rifasciare §128 *tr* to rebind

riferimento *m* reference

riferire §176 *tr* to wound again; to refer; to relate || *ref*—**riferirsi a** to refer to; to concern

riffa *f* raffle; lottery; (coll) violence; **di riffa o di raffa** by hook or crook

rifilare *tr* to trim; (coll) to reel off (*a list of names*); (coll) to deal (*a blow*); (coll) to palm off

rifinire §176 *tr* to give the finishing touch to; to wear out || *intr* to stop || *ref* to wear oneself out

rifiorire §176 (lit) to revive || *intr* to bloom again || *intr* (ESSERE) to flourish; to grow better; to reappear

rifischiare §287 *tr* to whistle again; (coll) to report || *intr* to talk, gossip

rifiutare *tr* to refuse; (lit) to reject || *intr* (cards) to renege, renounce || *ref* to refuse, deny

rifiuto *m* refusal; refuse, rubbish; rejection; rebuff, spurn; (fig) wreck; (cards) renege; **di rifiuto** waste, e.g., **materiale di rifiuto** waste material

riflessione *f* reflexion

riflessi·vo -va *adj* thoughtful; (gram) reflexive

riflès·so -sa *adj* reflex, e.g., **azione riflessa** reflex action || *m* reflection; (physiol) reflex; **di riflesso** vicarious

riflèttere §177 (*pp* **riflettuto & riflèsso**) *tr & intr* to reflect || *ref* to be reflected

riflettóre *m* searchlight; reflector

rifluire §176 *intr* (ESSERE & AVERE) to flow; to flow back

riflusso *m* flow; ebb, ebb tide

rifocillare *tr* to refresh (*with food*) || *ref* to take refreshment

rifóndere §178 *tr* to melt again; to recast; to refund; to reedit

rifórma *f* reform; (mil) rejection || **Riforma** *f*—**la Riforma** the Reformation

riformare (**rifórmo**) *tr* to reform; to amend; (mil) to reject

riformati·vo -va *adj* reformatory

riforma·tóre -trice *adj* reforming || *mf* reformer

riformatò·rio *m* (**-ri**) reform school, reformatory

rifornimento *m* supply; refueling; **fare rifornimento di** to fill up with; **rifornimenti** supplies

rifornire §176 *tr* to supply; to restock; **rifornire di benzina** to refuel

rifràngere §179 *tr* to crush || *ref* to break (*said of waves*) || §179 (*pp* **rifratto**) *tr* to refract || *ref* to be refracted

rifrat·tóre -trice *adj* refracting || *m* refractor

rifrazione *f* refraction

rifriggere §180 *tr* to fry again; to rehash || *intr* to fry too long or in too much oil

rifrit·to -ta *adj* fried again; (fig) hack-

neyed || *m* taste of stale fat; (fig) rehash

rifuggire *tr* to avoid || *intr*—**rifuggire da** to abhor || *intr* (ESSERE) to take refuge

rifugiare §290 *ref* to take refuge, take shelter

rifugiato *m* refugee

rifù·gio *m* (**-gi**) refuge; **rifugio alpino** mountain hut; **rifugio antiaereo** air-raid shelter; **rifugio antiatomico** fallout shelter

rifùlgere §233 *intr* (ESSERE & AVERE) to shine

rifusióne *f* recast; refund, reimbursement

rìga *f* (**-ghe**) line; row; rank; ruler; part (*in hair*); stripe; (fig) quality

rigàglie *fpl* giblets

rigàgnolo *m* rivulet; gutter (*at the side of a road*)

rigare §209 *tr* to rule, line; to stripe; to mark; to rifle (*gun*) || *intr*—**rigare diritto** to toe the line

rigatino *m* gingham

rigattière *m* second-hand dealer

rigatura *f* ruling; rifling (*of gun*)

rigenerare (**rigènero**) *tr* to regenerate; to reclaim; to recycle || *ref* to become regenerate

rigenera·tóre *m*—**rigeneratore per i capelli** hair restorer

rigettare (**rigètto**) *tr* to throw back; to reject; to recast; (slang) to throw up || *intr* to sprout

rigètto *m* rejection

righèllo *m* ruler

rigidi·tà *f* (**-tà**) rigidity; rigor; stiffness; **rigidità cadaverica** rigor mortis

rìgi·do -da *adj* rigid, stiff; severe

rigirare *tr* to keep turning; to dupe; to invest; to encircle || *intr* to ramble || *ref* to turn around; to tumble

rì·go *m* (**-ghi**) line; **rigo musicale** (mus) staff

rigò·glio *m* (**-gli**) luxuriance; bloom; gurgling

rigonfiare §287 (**rigónfio**) *tr* to inflate || *intr* (ESSERE) & *ref* to swell up

rigóre *m* rigor; severity; precision; **a rigor di termini** strictly speaking; **di rigore** de rigueur; (sports) penalty (*e.g., kick*)

rigorismo *m* rigorism, strictness, severity

rigori·sta *mf* (**-sti -ste**) rigorist || *m* (soccer) kicker of penalty goal

rigoró·so -sa [*s*] *adj* rigorous, strict

rigovernare (**rigovèrno**) *tr* to clean, wash (*dishes*); to groom, tend (*animals*)

riguadagnare *tr* to regain

riguardare *tr* to look again; to look back; to examine; to consider; to take care of; to concern || *intr*—**riguardare** a to look out for; to face (*said of a window*) || *ref* to take care of oneself; **riguardarsi da** to keep away from

riguardo *m* care; esteem; regard; **a questo riguardo** in this regard; **ri-**

guardo a as far as . . . is concerned;
senza riguardo a irrespective of
riguardó·so -sa [s] *adj* considerate
rigurgitare (**rigùrgito**) *tr & intr* to
regurgitate
rilanciare §128 *tr* to toss back; to reestablish (*e.g., fashions*); (poker) to
raise
rilasciare §128 *tr* to free, let go; to
relax; to grant || *ref* to relax
rilà·scio *m* (**-sci**) release; delivery;
granting, issue (*of a document*)
rilassante *adj* relaxing
rilassare *tr & ref* to relax
rilassatézza *f* laxity
rilegare §209 (**rilégo**) *tr* to tie again;
to bind, rebind (*a book*); to set (*a
stone*)
rilega·tó·re -trice *mf* binder
rilegatura *f* binding
rilèggere §193 *tr* to reread
rilènto *m*—a rilento slowly
rilevaménto *m* survey; (naut) bearing
rilevare (**rilèvo**) *tr* to lift again; to observe; to draw; to bring out; to sur-
vey; to take over; to pick up; (mil)
to relieve || *intr* to be delineated;
to be of import || *ref* to rise again;
to recover
rilevatà·rio *m* (**-ri**) successor; (law)
assignee
rilièvo *m* relief; survey; remark; assumption (*of debts*); taking over (*of
business*); mettere in rilievo to bring
out; to set off
rilò·ga *f* (**-ghe**) traverse rod
rilucènte *adj* shiny, shining
rilùcere §234 *intr* to shine
riluttante *adj* reluctant
riluttanza *f* reluctance
rima *f* rhyme; slit; crevice; **rispondere
per le rime** to answer in kind, to
retort
rimandare *tr* to send back; to refer; to
dismiss; to put off, postpone; to refer; **rimandare a ottobre** to condition
(*a student*)
rimando *m* delay; reference; footnote;
repartee; postponement; (sports) return
rimaneggiare §290 (**rimanéggio**) *tr* to
rearrange; to reshuffle; to shake up
(*personnel*); to rewrite (*news*)
rimanènte *adj* remaining || *m* remain-
der; remnant; **i rimanenti** the rest
rimanènza *f* remainder
rimanére §235 *intr* (ESSERE) to remain,
stay; to be left; to be in agreement;
to have left, e.g., **mi sono rimasti solo tre dollari**
I only have three dollars left; to be
located; (poet) to stop; **rimanerci**
(coll) to be killed; (coll) to be duped;
rimanere da to depend on, e.g.,
questo rimane da Lei this depends on
you
rimangiare §290 *tr* to eat again || *ref*—
rimangiarsi la parola to go back on
one's word
rimarcare §197 *tr* to mark again; to
point out
rimar·co *m* (**-chi**) remark, notice
rimare *tr & intr* to rhyme

rimarginare (**rimàrgino**) *tr, intr & ref*
to heal
rimaritare *tr & ref* to marry again
rimasù·glio *m* (**-gli**) leftover
rima·tóre -trice *mf* poet; rhymster
rimbalzare *intr* (ESSERE & AVERE) to
bounce back, rebound
rimbalzo *m* rebound
rimbambire §176 *intr* (ESSERE) & *ref*
to become feeble-minded (*from old
age*)
rimbambi·to -ta *adj* feeble-minded || *mf*
dotard
rimbeccare §197 (**rimbécco**) *tr* to peck;
to retort
rimbecilli·to -ta *adj* feeble-minded
rimboccare §197 (**rimbócco**) *tr* to tuck
up; to tuck in; to fill to the brim
rimbombare (**rimbómbo**) *intr* (ESSERE &
AVERE) to thunder, boom
rimbómbo *m* thunder, boom
rimborsare (**rimbórso**) *tr* to reimburse,
pay back
rimbórso *m* repayment
rimboscare §197 (**rimbósco**) *tr* to re-
forest || *ref* to take to the woods
rimboschiménto *m* reforestation
rimboschire §176 *tr* to reforest || *intr*
(ESSERE) to become wooded
rimbrottare (**rimbròtto**) *tr* to scold
rimbròtto *m* scolding
rimediare §287 (**rimèdio**) *tr* (coll) to
scrape together; (coll) to patch up ||
intr (with *dat*) to remedy; to make
up (*lost time*)
rimè·dio *m* (**-di**) remedy
rimembranza *f* remembrance
rimeritare (**rimèrito**) *tr* to reward
rimescolare (**riméscolo**) *tr* to stir; to
shuffle (*cards*)
rimèssa *f* remittance; shipment; harvest; store; loss; sprout; carriage
house; garage; (sports) return;
(sports) putting in play; **rimessa del
tram** carbarn
rimestare (**rimésto**) *tr* to stir
riméttere §198 *tr* to remit; to put back;
to set back; to sprout; to postpone,
defer; to ship; to vomit; to recover;
to deliver; to straighten up; (sports)
to return; **rimetterci** to lose; **rimettere a nuovo** to renovate; **rimettere
in ordine** to tidy up; **rimettere in
piedi** to rebuild, restore || *intr* (coll)
to sprout; (coll) to grow; (lit) to
abate || *ref* to recover; to quiet down;
to defer; to be clearing (*said of
weather*); **rimettersi a** to go back to
(*e.g., bed*); **rimettersi a** + *inf* to start
+ *ger* + again; **rimettersi in cammino** to start off again
rimirare *tr* to stare at
rìmmel *m* mascara
rimodellare (**rimodèllo**) *tr* to remodel
rimodernare (**rimodèrno**) *tr* to modernize; to remodel; to bring up to date
|| *ref* to become modern
rimónta *f* reassembly; return (*of migratory birds*); revamping (*of shoes*);
(mil) remount
rimontare (**rimónto**) *tr* to rewind; to go
up (*a stream*); to vamp (*shoes*); to

renovate; to regain; to reassemble (*a machine*); (mil) to remount ‖ *intr* (ESSERE & AVERE) to climb again; to go back (*in time*)

rimorchiare §287 (**rimòrchio**) *tr* to tow; to drag along

rimorchiatóre *m* tugboat; tow car

rimòr·chio *m* (**-chi**) tow; trailer; **prendere a rimorchio** to take in tow

rimòrdere §200 *tr* to bite again; to prick (*said, e.g., of conscience*)

rimòrso *m* remorse

rimostranza *f* remonstrance

rimostrare (**rimóstro**) *tr* to show again ‖ *intr* to remonstrate; **rimostrare a** to remonstrate with

rimozióne *f* removal; demotion

rimpannucciare §128 *tr* to outfit better ‖ *ref* to be better dressed; to be better off

rimpastare *tr* to knead again; to re-shuffle, remake

rimpasto *m* reshuffling, rearrangement

rimpatriare §287 *tr* to repatriate ‖ *intr* to be repatriated

rimpà·trio *m* (**-tri**) repatriation

rimpètto *adv* opposite; **di rimpetto a** opposite to; in comparison with

rimpiàngere §215 *tr* to regret; to mourn

rimpianto *m* regret

rimpiattare *tr & ref* to hide; **giocare a rimpiattarsi** to play hide-and-seek

rimpiattino *m* hide-and-seek

rimpiazzare *tr* to replace

rimpiazzo *m* replacement, substitute

rimpiccolire §176 *tr* to make smaller ‖ *intr* (ESSERE) to get smaller

rimpinzare *tr* to stuff, cram

rimproverare (**rimpròvero**) *tr* to chide, reproach; **rimproverare qlcu di qlco** or **rimproverare qlco a qlcu** to reproach s.o. for s.th

rimpròvero *m* reproach, rebuke

rimuginare (**rimùgino**) *tr & intr* to rummage; to stir; to ruminate

rimunerare (**rimùnero**) *tr* to reward ‖ *intr* to pay

rimunerati··vo -va *adj* remunerative; rewarding

rimunerazióne *f* remuneration

rimuòvere §202 *tr* to remove; to demote; to move

rinàscere §203 *intr* (ESSERE) to be born again; to grow again; to revive; **far rinascere** to revive

rinasciménto *m* rebirth ‖ **Rinascimento** *m* Renaissance

rinàscita *f* rebirth

rincagna·to -ta *adj* snub (*nose*)

rincalzare *tr* to hill (*plants*); to underpin; to tuck in

rincalzo *m* reinforcement; support

rincantucciare §128 *tr & ref* to hide in a corner

rincarare *tr* to raise the price of; to raise; **rincarare la dose** to add insult to injury ‖ *intr* (ESSERE) to rise, go up (*said of prices*)

rincasare [s] *intr* (ESSERE) to return home

rinchiùdere §125 *tr* to enclose, shut in

rinchiu·so -sa [s] *adj* shut in; musty ‖ *m*—**saper di rinchiuso** to smell musty

rincitrullire §176 *intr* (ESSERE) to grow stupid

rincóntro *m*—**a rincontro** opposite

rincorare §236 *tr* to encourage ‖ *ref* to take heart

rincórrere §139 *tr* to pursue, chase

rincórsa *f*—**prendere la rincorsa** to take off (*for a jump*); to get a running start

rincréscere §142 *intr* (ESSERE) (with *dat*) to displease; to be sorry, e.g., **gli rincresce** he is sorry; to mind, **Le rincresce?** do you mind?

rincresciménto *m* regret

rincrudire §176 *tr* to sharpen; to embitter ‖ *intr* (ESSERE) to become bitter; to get worse

rinculare *intr* (ESSERE & AVERE) to back up; to recoil

rinculo *m* recoil

rinfacciare §128 *tr* to throw in one's face

rinfarcire §176 *tr* to stuff

rinfiancare §197 *tr* to support

rinfocolare (**rinfòcolo**) *tr* to rekindle; to revive

rinfoderare (**rinfòdero**) *tr* sheathe

rinforzare (**rinfòrzo**) *tr* to reinforce; strengthen ‖ *intr* (ESSERE) & *ref* to become stronger

rinfòrzo *m* reinforcement

rinfrancare §197 *tr* to reassure ‖ *ref* to buck up

rinfrescante *adj* refreshing ‖ *m* mild laxative

rinfrescare §197 (**rinfrésco**) *tr* to refresh; to restore; to renew ‖ *intr* (ESSERE & AVERE) to cool off (*said of the weather*) ‖ *ref* to have some refreshments; to cool off

rinfré·sco *m* (**-schi**) refreshment

rinfusa *f*—**alla rinfusa** at random; pell-mell; in bulk

ringalluzzire §176 *tr & ref* to perk up

ringhiare §287 *intr* to growl, to snarl

ringhièra *f* railing

rin·ghio *m* (**-ghi**) growl, snarl

ringiovanimento *m* rejuvenation

ringiovanire §176 *tr* to rejuvenate ‖ *intr* (ESSERE) to grow or look younger

ringraziaménto *m* thanks

ringraziare §287 *tr* to thank; to dismiss

ringuainare (**ringuaíno**) *tr* to sheathe

rinnegare §209 (**rinnègo & rinnégo**) *tr* to forswear; to repudiate

rinnega·to -ta *adj & m* renegade

rinnovaménto *m* renewal; reawakening

rinnovare (**rinnòvo**) *tr* to renew; to renovate; to restore; to replace ‖ *ref* to occur again; to renew

rinnovellare (**rinnovèllo**) *tr* to repeat; (poet) to renew ‖ *intr* (ESSERE) & *ref* to change; to renew

rinnòvo *m* renewal

rinocerónte *m* rhinoceros

rinomanza *f* renown

rinoma·to -ta *adj* renowned, famous

rinsaldare *tr* to starch; (fig) to strengthen ‖ *ref* to become confirmed (*in one's opinion*)

rinsanguare (rinsànguo) *tr* to give new strength to ‖ *ref* to regain strength; to recover

rinsavire §176 *intr* (ESSERE) to return to reason

rintanare *ref* to burrow; to hide

rintóc·co *m* (-chi) toll (*of bell*)

rintontìre §176 *tr* to stun, to daze

rintracciare §128 *tr* to track down

rintronare (rintròno) *tr* to deafen; to make rumble ‖ *intr* (ESSERE & AVERE) to thunder; to rumble

rintuzzare *tr* to dull, blunt; to repel; to repress

rinùn·cia *f* (-ce) or **rinùnzia** *f* renunciation

rinunziare §287 *tr* to renounce ‖ *intr* (with *dat*) to give up, renounce, e.g., **rinunziò al trono** he renounced the throne

rinvangare §209 *tr* & *intr* var of **rivangare**

rinvenìre §282 *tr* to find ‖ *intr* (ESSERE) to come to; to revive ‖ *far rinvenìre* to bring to, revive

rinviare §119 *tr* to send back; to postpone; to refer; to adjourn; to remit (*to a lower court*)

rinvigorìre §176 *tr* to strengthen ‖ *intr* (ESSERE) & *ref* to regain strength

rinvì·o *m* (-i) return; postponement; adjournment; reference; (law) continuance

rì·o *m* (-i) (lit) sin; (lit) brook; (coll) canal

rioccupare (riòccupo) *tr* to reoccupy

rioccupazióne *f* reoccupation

rionale *adj* neighborhood

rióne *m* district; neighborhood

riordinare (riórdino) *tr* to rearrange; to reorganize; to order again

riorganizzare |ddzz| *tr* to reorganize

riottó·so -sa [s] *adj* (lit) quarrelsome; (lit) unruly, rebellious

ripa *f* (lit) bank (*of river*); (lit) escarpment

ripagare §209 *tr* to repay; to pay again

riparare *tr* to protect; to mend, fix, repair; to make up (*an exam*) ‖ *intr* —**riparare a** to make up for ‖ *intr* (ESSERE) & *ref* to take refuge; to betake oneself

riparazióne *f* repair; reparation; redress; (educ) make-up

riparlare *intr* to speak again; **ne riparleremo!** you will see!

riparo *m* repair; shelter

ripartire §176 *tr* to divide; to distribute; to share ‖ (**riparto**) *intr* (ESSERE) to leave again; to start again ‖ §176 *ref* to split up

ripartizióne *f* division; distribution

riparto *m* division; distribution; allotment

ripassare *tr* to cross again; to brush up, review; to repass; to sift again; to check; to read over; (mach) to overhaul ‖ *intr* (ESSERE) to go by; to come by

ripassata *f* checkup; review; (coll) rebuke

ripassa·tóre -trice *mf* checker

ripasso *m* return (*of birds*); (coll) review

ripensare (ripènso) *intr* to keep thinking; **ripensare a** to think of again; to think over again

ripentìre (ripènto) *ref* to repent; **ripentìrsi di** to repent

ripercórrere §139 *tr* to retrace

ripercuòtere §251 *tr* to reflect; to strike again ‖ *ref* to reverberate

ripescare §197 (ripésco) *tr* to fish again; (fig) to dig up

ripètere *tr* & *intr* to repeat ‖ *ref* to be repeated

ripeti·tóre -trice *mf* repeater; coach; tutor ‖ *m* (rad, telv) rebroadcasting station; (rad) relay

ripetizióne *f* repetition; review; tutoring; **a ripetizione** repeating (*firearm*)

ripiano *m* terrace; ledge; shelf; landing; (com) balancing

ripìc·co *m* (-chi) pique; spite

ripì·do -da *adj* steep

ripiegamènto *m* bend; (mil) withdrawal, retreat

ripiegare §209 (ripiègo) *tr* to fold, fold over ‖ *intr* to do better; (mil) to fall back ‖ *ref* to bend over; to withdraw into oneself

ripiè·go·no (-ghi) *adj* expedient

ripiè·no -na *adj* full; stuffed ‖ *m* stuffing; (culin) filling

ripigliare §280 *tr* to reacquire; to catch again; to begin again ‖ *intr* to recover ‖ *ref* to renew a quarrel

ripiombare (ripiómbo) *tr* to make plumb; (fig) to plunge back ‖ *intr* (ESSERE) (fig) to plunge back

ripopolare (ripòpolo) *tr* to repopulate; to restock (*e.g., a pond*)

ripòrre §218 *tr* to put back; to place (*one's hope*); to repose (*one's trust*) ‖ *ref* to back down; **riporsi a** + *inf* to start + *ger* again

riportare (ripòrto) *tr* to bring back; to report; to get; to transfer (*a design*); (com) to carry forward; (hunt) to retrieve; (math) to carry ‖ *ref* to go back

ripòrto *m* filler; retrieving; (com) balance carried forward; (math) number carried

riposante [s] *adj* restful

riposare [s] (ripòso) *tr, intr* & *ref* to rest

ripòso [s] *m* rest; repose; Requiem; retirement; **buon riposo!** sleep well!; **mettere a riposo** to retire; **riposo!** (mil) at ease

riposti·glio *m* (-gli) closet

ripó·sto -sta *adj* innermost ‖ *m* (coll) pantry

riprèndere §220 *tr* to take back; to take up again; to get back; to take in (*a garment*); to catch (*s.th thrown in the air*); to take up (*arms*); to get; to reconquer; to start again, resume; to reprehend; to recover; (mov, telv) to shoot; **riprendere moglie** to remarry ‖ *intr* to start again; to recover, improve; to pick up (*said of a* *motor*) ‖ *ref* to recover; to catch oneself up

riprésa [s] *f* resumption; (aut) pickup; (theat) revival; (mov) shooting, take; (boxing) round; (soccer) second half; (mus, pros) refrain; **a più riprese** several times

ripresentare (ripresènto) *tr* to present again

ripristinare (ripristino) *tr* to restore; to reestablish

ripristino *m* revival, restoration

riprodurre §102 *tr* to reproduce; to express ‖ *ref* to reproduce; to occur

riprodut·tóre -trice *adj* reproducing ‖ *mf* reproducer ‖ *m* reproducer (*e.g., of sound*)

riproduzióne *f* reproduction; playback (*e.g., of tape*)

rip, rométtere §198 *tr* to promise again ‖ *ref* to hope; to propose; to hope for

ripròva *f* new proof; confirmation

riprovare (ripròvo) *tr* to try again; to try on again; to feel, experience again; to flunk; to censure ‖ *ref* to try again

riprovazióne *f* disapproval

ripudiare §287 *tr* to repudiate

ripugnante *adj* repugnant, repulsive

ripugnanza *f* repugnance; aversion

ripugnare *intr* (with *dat*) to disgust, revolt, be repugnant to

ripulire §176 *tr* to clean again; to tidy up; to clean up; to polish ‖ *ref* to be dressed up; to become polished

ripulita *f*—**dare una ripulita a** to give a lick and a promise to; **fare una ripulita** (fig) to clean house

ripulsi·vo -va *adj* repulsive

riquadrare *tr* to square; to decorate (*a room*) ‖ *intr* to measure; to square

riquadro *m* square

risac·ca [s] *f* (-che) undertow; back-wash

risàia [s] *f* rice field

risalire [s] §242 *tr* to go up again; to stem (*the tide*); **risalire la corrente** to go upstream ‖ *intr* (ESSERE) to climb again; to reascend; (com) to appreciate; to date back

risaltare [s] *tr* to jump again ‖ *intr* (ESSERE & AVERE) to rebound ‖ *intr* to stand out; **far risaltare** to emphasize

risalto [s] *m* emphasis; prominence; relief; foil

risanare [s] *tr* to heal; to reclaim (*land*); to redevelop (*urban areas*); to reorganize ‖ *intr* (ESSERE) to heal; to improve

risapére [s] §243 *tr* to find out

risapu·to -ta [s] *adj* well-known

risarcimento [s] *m* indemnification, redress

risarcire [s] §176 *tr* to indemnify; to compensate

risata [s] *f* outburst of laughter

risatina [s] *f* chuckle

riscaldamento *m* heating; inflammation

riscaldare *tr* to heat; to warm up; to inflame ‖ *ref* to warm up; to go in heat; to perspire; to get excited

riscaldo *m* inflammation; prickly heat; padding (*for clothes*)

riscattare *tr* to ransom; to redeem ‖ *intr* (ESSERE) to click again (*said, e.g., of a ratchet*)

riscatto *m* ransom; redemption

rischiarare, *tr, intr* (ESSERE) & *ref* to clear, clear up

rischiare §287 *tr* to risk ‖ *intr* to run a risk

ri·schio *m* (-schi) risk

rischió·so -sa [s] *adj* risky

risciacquare (risciàcquo) *tr* to rinse

risciacquatura *f* rinse; swill

risciàcquo *m* rinsing (*of mouth*); mouthwash

riscónto *m* (com) discount

riscontrare (riscóntro) *tr* to compare, collate; to check; to reply to ‖ *intr* to reply; to tally ‖ *ref* to tally

riscóntro *m* comparison; check, control; draft; correspondence; reply; **far riscontro** to correspond; **far riscontro con** to correspond to; **far riscontro di** to check; **mettere a riscontro** to compare; **riscontri** drafts (*of air*); parts (*that fit together*)

riscoprire §110 *tr* to rediscover

riscòssa *f* insurrection; recovery, reconquest; (mil) counterattack

riscossióne *f* collection

riscrìvere §250 *tr* to rewrite; to write back

riscuòtere §251 *tr* to shake; to wake up; to collect; to get; to redeem ‖ *ref* to wake up; to come to one's senses

riseccare [s] §197 (riséceo) *tr, intr* (ESSERE) & *ref* to dry up

risecchire [s] §176 *intr* (ESSERE) & *ref* to dry up

risentiménto [s] *m* resentment, pique

risentire [s] (risènto) *tr* to hear again; to feel ‖ *intr*—**risentire di** to feel the effects of ‖ *ref* to take offense; to wake up; to come to one's senses; (telp) to talk again; **a risentirci!** (telp) until we talk again!; **risentirsi con** to resent (*a person*); **risentirsi di** to feel the effects of; **risentirsi per** to resent (*an act*)

risenti·to -ta [s] *adj* heard again; resentful; strong; swift; incisive

riserbare [s] (risèrbo) *tr* var of **riservare**

risèrbo [s] *m* var of **risèrvo**

risèrva [s] *f* preservation; exclusive rights; preserve; reserve; supply; backlog; reservation; circumspection; vintage

riservare [s] (risèrvo) *tr* to reserve

riservatézza [s] *f* reservedness

riserva·to -ta [s] *adj* reserved; private; classified

riservista [s] *m* (-sti) reservist

risèrvo [s] *m* discretion

risguardo *m* end paper

risièdere [s] *intr* to reside

risma [s] *f* ream; (fig) type

riso [s] *m* rice ‖ *m* (risa *fpl*) laugh; laughter; jest; cheer; (lit) smile

risolare [s] §257 *tr* to resole

risolino [s] *m* smile; giggle

risollevare [s] (**risollèvo**) *tr* to raise again; to lift || *ref* to rise

risolutézza [s] *f* resoluteness

risolu·to -ta [s] *adj* resolved, determined

risoluzióne [s] *f* resolution; resolve; dissolution

risòlvere [s] §256 (*pret ind* **risolvéi** or **risolvètti** or **risòlsi**; *pp* **risòlto**) *tr* to resolve; to solve; to dissolve; to persuade || *ref* to dissolve; to resolve

risolvìbile [s] *adj* solvable

risonante [s] *adj* resounding

risonanza [s] *f* resonance; (fig) sensation

risonare [s] §257 *tr* to ring again; (lit) to repeat || *intr* (ESSERE & AVERE) to resonate; to resound; to ring again; to echo

risórgere [s] §258 *intr* (ESSERE) to rise again; to revive, to come back to life; to recover

risorgiménto [s] *m* renaissance; resurgence || **Risorgimento** *m* Risorgimento

risórsa [s] *f* resource

risór·to -ta [s] *adj* arisen; reborn

risòtto [s] *m* risotto, rice cooked with broth

risparmiare §287 *tr* to save; to spare

rispàr·mio -mi (-mi) saving; sparing; savings; **risparmi** savings; **senza risparmio** lavishly

rispecchiare §287 (**rispècchio**) *tr* to reflect

rispedire §176 *tr* to send back; to forward; to reship

rispedizióne *f* reshipment

rispettàbile *adj* respectable

rispettare (**rispètto**) *tr* to respect; **farsi rispettare** to command respect; **rispettare sé stesso** to have self-respect

rispetti·vo -va *adj* respective

rispètto *m* respect; observance; restriction (*e.g., in building*); comparison; regard; **con rispetto parlando** excuse the word; **di rispetto** (naut) spare (*e.g., parts*); **rispetti** regards; **rispetto di sé medesimo** self-respect; **rispetto umano** fear of what people will say

rispettó·so -sa [s] *adj* respectful; respectable (*distance*)

risplendènte *adj* resplendent

risplèndere §281 *intr* (ESSERE & AVERE) to shine

rispóndere §238 *tr* to answer; **risponder picche** (coll) to say no || *intr* to answer; **rispondere a** to answer (*e.g., a letter*); **rispondere con un cenno del capo** to nod assent; **rispondere di** to be responsible for; **rispondere in** faccia, overlook

risposare (**rispòso**) *tr* & *ref* to marry again, remarry

rispósta *f* answer, reply, response

rissa *f* scuffle, brawl

rissó·so -sa [s] *adj* quarrelsome

ristabilire §176 *tr* to reestablish || *ref* to recover

ristagnare *tr* to tin; to solder || *intr* to stagnate

ristampa *f* reprint

ristampare *tr* to reprint

ristorante *m* restaurant

ristorare (**ristòro**) *tr* & *ref* to refresh

ristora·tóre -trice *adj* refreshing || *m* restaurant

ristòro *m* refreshment; compensation

ristrettézza *f* narrowness; scarcity; **ristrettezza d'idee** narrow-mindedness

ristrét·to -ta *adj* narrow; limited; in straitened circumstances; concentrated, condensed (*e.g., broth*)

ristrutturazióne *f* restructuring

risùc·chio [s] *m* (-chi) whirlpool

risultante [s] *adj* resulting || *m* & *f* resultant; (phys) resultant

risultare [s] *intr* (ESSERE) to result; to prove to be, turn out to be; to appear

risultato [s] *m* result

risurrezióne [s] *f* resurrection

risuscitare [s] (**risùscito**) *tr* to resurrect; to revive || *intr* to be resurrected; to be revived

risvegliare §280 (**risvéglio**) *tr* & *ref* to awaken; to reawaken

risvé·glio *m* (-gli) awakening, reawakening

risvòlto *m* cuff; lapel; inside flap (*of book*); minor aspect (*of a question*)

ritagliare §280 *tr* to cut again; to clip; to trim

rità·glio *m* (-gli) clipping (*of paper*); scrap (*of meat*); cutting (*of fabric*); bit (*of time*); **al ritaglio** retail

ritappezzare (**ritappézzo**) *tr* to repaper

ritardare *tr* to delay; to slow down, retard; || *intr* to tarry; to be late; to be slow (*said of a watch*)

ritardatà·rio -ria *mf* (-ri -rie) latecomer; (com) delinquent

ritardo *m* delay; retard; lateness; **essere in ritardo** to be late

ritégno *m* reservation; discretion; **senza ritegno** shamelessly

ritemprare (**ritèmpro**) *tr* to temper again; to invigorate || *ref* to harden

ritenére §271 *tr* to retain; to hold; to withhold; to believe, think || *ref* to restrain oneself; to consider oneself; to be considered

ritentare (**ritènto**) *tr* to try again; (law) to retry

ritirare *tr* to withdraw; to pay (*a note*); to throw back; to shoot again; to accept delivery of; to take back (*a promise*) || *intr* to shrink || *ref* to shrink; to withdraw; to fall back, retreat; to retire

ritirata *f* toilet; (mil) retreat

ritiro *m* withdrawal; retreat; retirement; shrinkage; (metallurgy) shrinking

ritma·to -ta *adj* measured (*step*)

rìtmi·co -ca *adj* (-ci -che) rhythmic(al)

ritmo *m* rhythm; **a ritmo serrato** at a quick pace

rito *m* rite; (fig) ritual, ceremony; **di rito** customary

ritoccare §197 (**ritócco**) *tr* to retouch; to brush up

ritóc·co *m* (-chi) retouch; improvement; change

ritòrcere §272 *tr* to twist, twine; to wring; to retort

ritornare (**ritórno**) *tr* to return, give back || *intr* (ESSERE) to return, go back, come back; **ritornare in sé** to come back to one's senses

ritornèllo *m* refrain; chorus (*of song*)

ritórno *m* return; reoccurrence; **di ritorno** reoccurring; **essere di ritorno** to be back; **far ritorno** to return; **ritorno di fiamma** backfire

ritòr·to -ta *adj* twisted || *m* twist

ritrarre §273 *tr* to retract; to draw; to portray || *intr*—**ritrarre da** to look like || *ref* to retreat; to portray oneself

ritrasméttere §198 *tr* (rad, telv) to retransmit, rebroadcast

ritrattare *tr* to treat again; to retract; (coll) to portray || *ref* to recant

ritrattazióne *f* retraction

ritratti·sta *mf* (-sti -ste) portrait painter

ritratto *m* portrait, picture; photograph; **ritratto parlante** spit and image

ritri·to -ta *adj* (fig) stale, trite

ritrósa [s] *f* (coll) cowlick

ritrosìa [s] *f* coyness, shyness

ritró·so -sa [s] *adj* coy, shy; **a ritroso** backwards || *f* see ritrosa

ritrovare (**ritróvo**) *tr* to discover; to find; to regain; to meet again || *ref* to meet again; to find oneself; to find one's bearings; **non ritrovarcisi** to be out of sorts

ritrovato *m* discovery, find

ritròvo *m* meeting; nightspot; **ritrovo estivo** summer resort; **ritrovo notturno** night club

rit·to -ta *adj* upright; straight; right || *m* face (*of medal*); prop; (sports) post || *f* (lit) right hand

rituale *adj* & *m* ritual

riunióne *f* reunion; meeting; assembly; **riunione alla sommità** summit conference

riunire §176 *tr* to assemble; to reunite; to reconcile || *ref* to gather together; to meet; to be reunited; to rally

riuscire §277 *intr* (ESSERE) to go out again; to turn out, turn out to be; to lead (*said, e.g., of a door*); to succeed; **riuscire a** + *inf* to succeed in + *ger* || *impers*—**riesce** (with *dat*) **di** + *inf* to succeed in + *ger*, e.g., **non gli è riuscito di farsi ricevere** he did not succeed in being received

riuscita *f* success; result; outlet

riva *f* shore; bank; (naut) board

rivale *adj* & *mf* rival

rivaleggiare §290 (**rivaléggio**) *intr* to compete; **rivaleggiare con** to rival

rivalére §278 *ref*—**rivalersi di** to use; **rivalersi su qlcu** to resort to s.o. for compensation; to fall back on s.o., to have recourse to s.o.

rivali·tà *f* (-tà) rivalry

rivalsa *f* compensation; revenge; (com) recourse

rivalutare (**rivàluto** & **rivaluto**) *tr* to revalue

rivalutazióne *f* reassessment

rivangare §209 *tr* to rake up; to mull over || *intr* to reminisce

rivedére §279 *tr* to see again; to review; to check; to reread; to revise; to read (*proof*) || *ref* to see one another; **a rivederci!** good-bye!, au revoir!

rivedìbile *adj* deferred (*for draft*)

rivelare (**rivélo**) *tr* to reveal; to detect; (phot) to develop

rivela·tóre -trice *adj* revealing || *m* (phot) developer; (rad) detector; **rivelatore di mine** mine detector

rivelazióne *f* revelation

rivéndere §281 *tr* to resell; (fig) to surpass

rivendicare §197 (**rivéndico**) *tr* to demand; to claim

rivendicazióne *f* demand; claim

rivéndita *f* resale; shop; **rivendita sali e tabacchi** cigar store

rivendi·tóre -trice *mf* seller, dealer, retailer

rivendùgliolo *m* peddler; huckster

rivèrbero *m* reverberation; reflection; glare; echo

riverènte *adj* reverent

riverènza *f* reverence; curtsy, bow

riverire §176 *tr* to revere; to pay one's respects to

riversare (**rivèrso**) *tr* to pour again; to transfer || *ref* to overflow

rivèr·so -sa *adj* on one's back

rivestiménto *m* coating; covering; lining

rivestire (**rivèsto**) *tr* to dress again; to coat; to line; to cover; to wear; to have (*importance*); to hold (*a rank*) || *ref* to get dressed again; to wear; to be covered

rivièra *f* coast || **Riviera** *f* Riviera

riviera·sco -sca *adj* (-schi -sche) coastal; riverside

rivíncere §285 *tr* to win back

rivincita *f* revenge; return match; **prendersi la rivincita** to get even

rivista *f* review; parade; magazine, journal; revue; proofreading

rivivere §286 *tr* to relive || *intr* (ESSERE) to live again; to revive

rivo *m* (lit) rivulet, brook

rivolare (**rivólo**) *intr* (ESSERE & AVERE) to fly again

rivolére §288 *tr* to want back

rivòlgere §289 *tr* to turn again; to revolve; to overturn; to train (*a weapon*); to address; to deter || *ref* to turn; to turn around; **rivolgersi a** to apply to

rivolgiménto *m* turn; revolution; upheaval

rivòlta *f* revolt; cuff

rivoltante *adj* revolting

rivoltare (**rivòlto**) *tr* to overturn; to turn inside out; to toss (*salad*); to upset || *ref* to turn around; to revolt; to toss

rivoltèlla *f* revolver; spray gun

rivoltellata *f* revolver shot

rivoltó·so -sa [s] *adj* rebellious || *m* rioter; rebel

rivoluzionare (**rivoluzióno**) *tr* to revolutionize

rivoluzionà·rio -ria *adj* & *mf* (**-ri -rie**) revolutionary

rivoluzióne *f* revolution

rizza *f* (naut) rigging

rizzare *tr* to raise; to hoist; to pay (*attention*); to build; (naut) to lash || *ref* to rise; to bristle (*said of hair*); to rear up (*said of a horse*)

ròba *f* things, stuff; property

robìnia *f* locust tree

robivèc·chi *m* (**-chi**) junk dealer

robu·sto -sta *adj* robust; burly

róc·ca *f* (**-che**) distaff

ròc·ca *f* (**-che**) fortress

roccafòrte *f* (**roccheffòrti**) stronghold

rocchétto *m* spool; reel; coil; roll (*of film*); pinion, rear sprocket wheel; (eccl) rochet; **rocchetto d'accensione** ignition coil; **rocchetto d'induzione** induction coil

ròc·cia *f* (**-ce**) rock; crag; cliff

rocció·so -sa [*s*] *adj* rocky

rò·co -ca *adj* (**-chi -che**) hoarse; (poet) faint

rodàg·gio *m* (**-gi**) breaking in, running in; adjustment period (*to a new situation*); **in rodaggio** (aut) being run in

Ròdano *m* Rhone

rodare (**ròdo**) *tr* to break in; (aut) to run in

ródere §239 *tr* to gnaw; to bite; to corrode || *ref* to worry, to fret

Ròdi *f* Rhodes

rodì·o *m* (**-i**) gnawing

rodi·tóre -trice *adj* gnawing || *mf* rodent

rodomónte *m* braggart

rogare §209 (**rògo**) *tr* to draw up (*a contract*); (law) to request

rògito *m* (law) instrument, deed

rógna *f* mange; itch

rognóne *m* (culin) kidney

rognó·so -sa [*s*] *adj* scabby, mangy

rò·go *m* (**-ghi**) pyre; stake

rollì·o *m* (**-i**) roll (*of ship*)

Róma *f* Rome

romané·sco -sca *adj* (**-schi -sche**) Roman (*dialect*)

Romania, la Rumania

romàni·co -ca *adj* & *m* (**-ci -che**) Romanesque

roma·no -na *adj* & *mf* Roman; **pagare alla romana** to go Dutch

romanticismo *m* romanticism

romànti·co -ca (**-ci -che**) *adj* romantic || *mf* romanticist

romanza *f* romance; ballad

romanzare *tr* to fictionalize

romanzé·sco -sca *adj* (**-schi -sche**) romantic; of chivalry; novelistic

romanzière *m* novelist

roman·zo -za *adj* Romance (*language*) || *m* novel; story; romance; fiction; **romanzi** fiction; **romanzo a fumetti** comic strip; comic book; **romanzo d'appendice** serial story, feuilleton; **romanzo giallo** whodunit; **romanzo rosa** love story

rombare (**rómbo**) *intr* to thunder

rómbo *m* thunder, roar

romè·no -na *adj* & *mf* Rumanian

romì·to -ta *adj* (lit) lonely || *m* (coll) hermit

rómpere §240 *tr* to break; to bust; **rompere la testa a** to annoy, pester || *intr* to overflow; to be wrecked; to break; **rompere in pianto** to burst out crying || *ref* to fly to pieces; **rompersi la testa** to rack one's brains

rompicapo *m* annoyance; puzzle; jig-saw puzzle

rompicòllo *m* madcap || **a rompicollo** headlong, rashly; at breakneck speed

rompighiàc·cio *m* (**-cio**) icebreaker; ice pick

rompiscàto·le *m* (**-le**) bore, pest

ronci·glio *m* (**-gli**) (poet) hook

róncola *f* pruning hook

rónda *f* patrol; beat (*of policeman*)

rondèlla *f* (mach) washer

róndine *f* swallow

rondóne *m* European swift

ronfare (**rónfo**) *intr* (coll) to snore; (coll) to purr

ronzare [*dz*] (**rónzo**) *intr* to buzz; to hum

ronzino [*dz*] *m* jade, nag

ronzì·o [*dz*] *m* (**-i**) buzzing; humming

ròsa *adj* *invar* & *m* pink || *f* rose; group; rosette; **rosa dei venti** compass card; **rosa del Giappone** (bot) camelia; **rosa delle Alpi** (bot) rhododendron; **rosa di tiro** (mil) dispersion

ro·sàio *m* (**-sài**) rosebush

rosà·rio *m* (**-ri**) rosary; **recitare il rosario** to count one's beads

rosa·to -ta *adj* rosy

ròse·o -a *adj* rosy

roséto *m* rose garden

rosétta *f* rosette; hard roll; (mach) washer

rosicanti [*s*] *mpl* rodents

rosicchiare [*s*] §287 *tr* to gnaw; to pick (*a bone*); to bite (*one's fingernails*)

rosmarino *m* (bot) rosemary

rosolare (**ròsolo**) *tr* (culin) to brown

rosolìa *f* German measles

rosóne *m* (archit) rosette; (archit) rose window

ròspo *m* toad; ugly person; unsociable person; **ingoiare un rospo** to swallow a bitter pill

rossa·stro -stra *adj* reddish

rossétto *m* rouge; **rossetto per le labbra** lipstick

rós·so -sa *adj* red; red-headed; Red; **diventare rosso** to blush || *mf* red-head; Red (*Communist*) || *m* red

rossóre *m* redness; blush

rosticcerìa *f* grill; rotisserie

rotàbile *adj* open to vehicular traffic (*road*); (rr) rolling (*stock*) || *f* road open to vehicular traffic

rotàia *f* rail; rut; **uscire dalle rotaie** to jump the track; (fig) to go astray

rotare §257 *tr* & *intr* to rotate; to circle

rotativa *f* (typ) rotary press

rotazióne *f* rotation

roteare (**ròteo**) *tr* to roll (*the eyes*); to flourish (*a sword*) || *intr* to circle

rotèlla *f* small wheel; caster; roller; kneecap; disk (*of ski pole*); **gli**

manca una rotella he has a screw loose

rotocàl·co m (-chi) rotogravure

rotolare (ròtolo) tr & intr (ESSERE) to roll || ref to turn over; to wallow

ròtolo m roll; bolt; coil; **a rotoli** to rack and ruin

rotolóne m tumble; **a rotoloni** falling down; to rack and ruin

rotón·do -da adj round; rotund || f rotunda; terrace

ròtta f break; rout; (aer, naut) course; **a rotta di collo** at breakneck speed; **mettere in rotta** to rout

rottame m fragment; wreck; **rottami** scraps, debris; wreckage; **rottami di ferro** scrap iron

ròt·to -ta adj broken; shattered; inured || m break, tear; **e rotti** odd, e.g., **duecento e rotti** two hundred odd; **per il rotto della cuffia** hardly; just about || f see **rotta**

rottura f break; breakage; rupture; breakdown (of relations); crack

ròtula f kneecap

rovèllo m (lit) anger

rovènte adj red-hot

róvere m & f oak tree || m oak (lumber)

rovè·scia f (-sce) cuff; **alla rovescia** inside out; upside down; the wrong way

rovesciamento m upset; overturn

rovesciare §128 (rovèscio) tr to overturn; to upset; to throw back (one's head); to spill (liquid); to pour; to hurl (insults); to turn inside out || intr to throw up || ref to spill; to pour; to upset

rovè·scio -scia (-sci -sce) adj reverse; inverse; inside out; upside down; backwards || m reverse; wrong side; downpour; upset; (com) crash; (tennis) backhand; **a rovescio** upside down; backwards || f see **rovescia**

rovéto m bramble; brier patch

rovina f ruin; blight; **andare in rovina** to go to ruin; **mandare in rovina** to ruin; **rovine** ruins

rovinare tr to ruin || intr (ESSERE) to collapse || ref to go to ruin

rovinì·o m (-ì) clatter; crash

rovinó·so -sa [s] adj ruinous

rovistare tr to rummage through

róvo m bramble

ròzza [ddzz] f nag

róz·zo -za [ddzz] adj rough; coarse

ruba—**andare a ruba** to sell like hot-cakes; **mettere a ruba** to plunder

rubacchiare §287 tr to pilfer

rubacuó·ri (-ri) adj ravishing || m lady-killer || f vamp

rubare tr to steal; **rubare a man salva** to pillage, loot || intr to steal; **rubare sul peso** to give short measure

ruberìa f thieving, stealing

rubicón·do -da adj rubicund

rubinétto m faucet; cock

rubino m ruby; jewel (of watch)

rubiz·zo -za adj well-preserved (person)

rùbri·ca f (-che) title, heading; directory; (journ) section

rude adj (lit) rough; (lit) rude

rùdere m ruin

rudimentale adj rudimentary

rudiménto m rudiment

ruffia·no -na mf go-between || m pimp, panderer || f bawd, procuress

ru·ga f (-ghe) wrinkle; (bot) rocket

ràggine f rust; ill-will; (bot) blight

rugginó·so -sa [s] adj rusty

ruggire §176 tr & intr to roar

ruggito m roar

rugiada f dew

rugó·so -sa adj wrinkled, wrinkly

rullàg·gio m (-gi) (aer) taxiing

rullare tr to roll || intr to roll; to taxi

rullì·o m (-ì) roll; rub-a-dub

rullo m roll; platen (of typewriter); pin (in tenpins); **rullo compressore** road roller

rumè·no -na adj & mf var of **romeno**

ruminare (rùmino) tr & intr to ruminate

rumóre m noise; rumor; ado; **far molto rumore** to create a stir

rumoreggiare §290 (rumoréggio) intr to rumble

rumoró·so -sa [s] adj noisy; rumbling; controversial

ruolino m roster

ruòlo m roll; role; list; **di ruolo** regular, full-time; **fuori ruolo** temporary, part-time

ruòta f wheel; paddle wheel; revolving server (in convent); **a quattro ruote** four-wheel; **dar la ruota a** to sharpen; **esser l'ultima ruota del carro** to be the fifth wheel to a wagon; **fare la ruota** to spread its tail, strut (said, e.g., of a peacock); to turn cart-wheels (said, e.g., of an acrobat); **ruota dentata** cog, cogwheel; **ruota idraulica** water wheel; **seguire a ruota** to follow closely

rupe f cliff

rurale adj rural, farm, farmer

ruscèllo m brook

ruspa f road grader

ruspante m barnyard chicken

russare intr to snore

Rùssia, la Russia

rus·so -sa adj & mf Russian

rustica·no -na adj rustic, boorish

rùsti·co -ca (-ci -che) adj rustic; coarse || m tool shed; cottage; (lit) peasant

rutilante adj (lit) shiny

ruttare tr (lit) to belch || intr (vulg) to belch

rutto m (vulg) belch

ruttóre m (elec) contact breaker

ruvidézza f or **ruvidi·tà** f (-tà) coarse-ness; roughness

rùvi·do -da adj coarse; rough

ruzzare [ddzz] intr to romp

ruzzolare (rùzzolo) tr to roll || intr (ESSERE) to tumble down; to roll

ruzzolóne m tumble; **a ruzzoloni** tum-bling down

S

S, s ['esse] *m & f* seventeenth letter of the Italian alphabet

s- *pref* dis-, e.g., **sleale** disloyal; e.g., **sconto** discount; un-, e.g., **scatenare** to unchain, unleash

sàbato *m* Saturday; (*of Jews*) Sabbath; **sabato inglese** Saturday afternoon off

sabbàti·co -ca *adj* (-**ci -che**) sabbatical

sàbbia *f* sand; **sabbia mobile** quicksand

sabbiatura *f* sand bath; sandblast

sabbièra *f* (rr) sandbox

sabbió·so -sa [s] *adj* sandy

sabotàg·gio *m* (-**gi**) sabotage

sabotare (sabòto) *tr* to sabotage

sac·ca *f* (-**che**) bag; satchel; (mil) pocket; **sacca d'aria** (aer) air pocket; **sacca da viaggio** traveling bag; duffel bag

saccarina *f* saccharine

saccènte *mf* wiseacre, know-it-all

saccheggiare §290 (**sacchéggio**) *tr* to pillage, plunder

sacchég·gio *m* (-**gi**) pillage, plunder

sacchétto *m* little bag, pouch

sac·co *m* (-**chi**) bag; sack; sackcloth; pouch; (boxing) punching bag; (fig) heap, lot; **fare sacco to sag**; **mettere a sacco** to sack; **mettere nel sacco** to outwit; **sacco alpino** knapsack; **sacco a pelo** or **a piuma** sleeping bag; **sacco postale** mailbag

saccòc·cia *f* (-**ce**) (coll) pocket

sacerdòte *m* priest; (fig) devotee

sacerdotéssa *f* priestess

sacerdòzio *m* priesthood; ministry

sacramentale *adj* sacramental; (joc) habitual, ritual

sacraménto *m* sacrament

sacrà·rio *m* (-**ri**) memorial; sanctuary, shrine

sacrestia *f* var of sagrestia

sacrificare §197 (**sacrifico**) *tr* to sacrifice; to waste; to force ‖ *ref* to sacrifice oneself

sacrifi·cio *m* (-**ci**) sacrifice

sacrilè·gio *m* (-**gi**) sacrilege

sacrile·go -ga *adj* (-**ghi -ghe**) sacrilegious

sacri·sta *m* (-**sti**) sexton

sacristia *f* var of sagrestia

sa·cro -cra *adj* sacred

sacrosan·to -ta *adj* sacrosanct; sacred (*truth*)

sàdi·co -ca *adj* (-**ci -che**) *adj* sadistic ‖ *mf* sadist

sadismo *m* sadism

saétta *f* stroke of lightning; hand (*of watch*); (mach) bit; (lit) arrow

saettare (saétto) *tr* to dart; **saettare sguardi a** to look daggers at

saettóne *m* (archit) strut

sagace *adj* sagacious, shrewd

sagà·cia *f* (-**cie**) sagacity

saggézza *f* wisdom

saggiare §290 *tr* to assay; to test; (dial) to taste

saggia·tóre -trice *mf* assayer ‖ *m* assay balance

saggina *f* sorghum

sàg·gio -gia (-**gi -ge**) *adj* wise ‖ *m* sage; assay; sample; proof; theme; test; rate (*of interest*); display; **di saggio** examination (*copy*)

saggi·sta *mf* (-**sti -ste**) essayist

sagittària *f* (bot) arrowhead

sagittà·rio *m* (-**ri**) (obs) archer ‖ **Sagittario** *m* Sagittarius

sàgola *f* (naut) halyard

sàgoma *f* outline; target; model, pattern; (joc) character

sagomare (sàgomo) *tr* to outline; to mold; to shape

sagomato *m* billboard

sagra *f* anniversary consecration (*of church*); festival

sagrato *m* elevated square in front of a church; churchyard; (coll) curse

sagrestano *m* sexton, sacristan

sagrestìa *f* sacristy, vestry

shìa *f* serge

sàio *m* (sài) habit (*of monk or nun*); doublet; frock coat

sala *f* axletree; hall, room; (bot) cattail, reed mace; **sala da ballo** dance hall; **sala da pranzo** dining room; **sala d'aspetto** waiting room; anteroom; **sala operatoria** operating room

salac·ca *f* (-**che**) (coll) sardine; (coll) shad

salace *adj* salacious; pungent

salamandra *f* salamander

salame *m* salami

salamelèc·co *m* (-**chi**) salaam

salamòia *f* brine

salare *tr* to salt; (coll) to cut (*school*)

salaria·to -ta *adj* wage-earning ‖ *m* wage earner

salà·rio *m* (-**ri**) pay, wages

salassare *tr* to bleed

salasso *m* bloodletting

sala·to -ta *adj* salted; salty; dear, expensive; (fig) sharp ‖ *m* salt pork; cold cuts ‖ *f* salting

salda *f* starch solution (*used in laundering*)

saldacón·ti *m* (-**ti**) bookkeeping department; credit department; ledger; bookkeeping machine

saldare *tr* to solder; to set (*a bone*); to weld; to pay, settle ‖ *ref* to knit (*said of a bone*); (lit) to heal

saldatóre *m* solderer; welder; soldering iron

saldatura *f* soldering; setting (*of bones*); joint; continuity; **saldatura autogena** welding

saldézza *f* firmness

sal·do -da *adj* firm; valid (*reason*); flawless ‖ *m* balance; clearance sale; job lot; payment; **saldi** remnants ‖ *f* see **salda**

saldobrasatura *f* soldering

sale *m* salt; wit; (lit) sea; **restare di sale** to be dumbfounded; **sale inglese** Epsom salts; **sali aromatici** smelling salts; **sali da bagno** bath salts

salgèmma *f* rock salt

sàlice *m* willow tree; **salice piangente** weeping willow

salicilato *m* salicylate

saliènte *adj* projecting; (fig) salient ‖ *m* projection

salièra *f* saltcellar, salt shaker

salini·tà *f* (-tà) salinity

sali·no -na *adj* saline; salty ‖ *f* salt bed

salire §242 *tr* to climb ‖ *intr* (ESSERE) to climb; to go up; to rise; **salire in** or **su** to get on (*e.g., a train*)

saliscén·di *m* (-di) latch; **saliscendi** *mpl* ups and downs

salita *f* climbing; ascent, rise; slope; **in salita** uphill

saliva *f* saliva

salma *f* corpse, body

salma·stro -stra *adj* briny; saltish ‖ *m*— **sapere di salmastro** to smell or taste salty

salmerìe *fpl* wagon train; (mil) supplies

salmì *m*—**in salmì** (culin) in a stew

salmo *m* psalm

salmodiare §287 **(salmòdio)** *intr* to chant, sing hymns, intone

salmóne *m* salmon

salnitro *m* saltpeter

Salomóne *m* Solomon

salóne *m* hall; salon, drawing room; (naut) saloon; **salone da barbiere** barber shop; **salone dell'automobile** auto show

salòtto *m* drawing room; living room, parlor; reception room

salpare *tr* to weigh (*anchor*) ‖ *intr* (ESSERE) to weigh anchor

salsa *f* sauce

salsaparìglia *f* sarsaparilla

salsèdine *f* saltiness

salsìc·cia *f* (-ce) sausage

salsièra *f* gravy boat

sal·so -sa *adj* salty; saline ‖ *m* saltiness ‖ *f* see salsa

saltabeccare §197 **(saltabécco)** *intr* to hop

saltaleóne *m* coil spring

saltare *tr* to jump; to skip; to sauté; (sports) to vault, hurdle; **far saltare** to kick out; to blow up (*e.g., a mine*); **saltare la sbarra** (coll) to go A.W.O.L. ‖ *intr* (ESSERE & AVERE) to jump; to pop off, e.g., **mi è saltato un bottone** one of my buttons has popped off; to blow out (*said of a fuse*); **saltare agli occhi** to be self-evident; **saltare a piè pari** to skip with both feet; **saltar fuori** to pop out (*said of the eyes*); to appear suddenly; **saltare in mente** a to come to the mind of; **saltare il ticchio** a (qlcu) **di** to feel like + *ger*, e.g., **gli è saltato il ticchio di cantare** he felt like singing; **saltare la mosca al naso** a (qlcu) to blow one's top, e.g., **le è saltata la mosca al naso** she blew her top; **saltare per aria** to blow up; **saltare su** to start (*to make a sudden jerk*); **saltare su** a + *inf* to begin suddenly to + *inf*

salta·tóre -trice *mf* jumper, hurdler

saltellare (saltèllo) *intr* to skip, hop

saltellóni *adv*—**a saltelloni** skipping, hopping

saltimban·co *m* (-chi) acrobat, tumbler; mountebank

salto *m* jump; leap; fall; skip; (*of animals*) mating; (fig) step; **a salti** skipping, jumping; **al salto sauté** to dance; **fare quattro salti** to dance; **fare un salto** to hop, hurry; **salto a pesce** jackknife (*dive*); **salto coll'asta** pole vaulting; **salto in altezza** high jump; **salto in lunghezza** broad jump; **salto mortale** somersault; **salto nel vuoto** leap in the dark

saltuà·rio -ria *adj* (-ri -rie) desultory, occasional

salubre *adj* salubrious, healthy, healthful

salume *m* pork product

salumerìa *f* pork butcher shop

salumiè·re -ra *mf* pork butcher

salutare *adj* healthful ‖ *tr* to greet; to salute; (lit) to proclaim

salute *f* health; salvation; safety ‖ *interj* good luck; to your health!; gesundheit!

saluto *m* salute; greeting; salutation; **distinti saluti** sincerely yours

salva *f* salvo; outburst; **a salve** with blank cartridges, with blanks

salvacondótto *m* safe-conduct

salvada·nàio *m* (-nài) piggy bank

salvagèn·te *m* (-te & -ti) life preserver; fender (*of trolley car*) ‖ *m* (-te) safety island

salvaguardare *tr* to safeguard

salvaguàrdia *f* safeguard

salvaménto *m* safety

salvamotóre *m* circuit breaker; fuse box

salvapun·te *m* (-te) pencil cap; tap (*on sole of shoe*)

salvare *tr* to save; to spare (*a life*); to rescue ‖ *ref* to save oneself; to be rescued; **si salvi chi può!** every man for himself!

salvatàg·gio *m* (-gi) rescue

salvatóre *m* savior, rescuer ‖ **il Salvatore** the Saviour

salvazióne *f* salvation

salve *interj* hello!, hail!

salvézza *f* salvation; safety

sàlvia *f* (bot) sage

salviétta *f* napkin; paper napkin; paper towel

sal·vo -va *adj* safe; saved; secure ‖ *m* —**mettere in salvo** to put in a safe place; **mettersi in salvo** to reach safety ‖ *f* see salva ‖ **salvo** *prep* except; **salvo che** unless; **salvo il vero** unless I am mistaken

samarita·no -na *adj & mf* Samaritan

sambu·co *m* (-chi) elder tree

san *adj* apocopated and unstressed form of **santo**

sanàbile *adj* curable

sanare *tr* to heal; to remedy; to reclaim (*land*); to normalize

sanatò·rio *m* (-ri) sanatorium

sancire §176 *tr* to ratify, sanction; to establish

sàndalo *m* sandal; sandalwood; flat-bottom boat

sandolino *m* canoe, skiff, kayak

sangue *m* blood; **agitarsi il sangue** to fret; **all'ultimo sangue** (*duel*) to the death; **al sangue rare** (*meat*); **a sangue freddo** in cold blood; cold-blooded; **cavar sangue da una rapa** to draw blood from a stone; **farsi cattivo sangue** to get angry; **il sangue non è acqua** blood is thicker than water; **puro sangue** thoroughbred; **sangue dal naso** nosebleed; **sangue freddo** calmness, composure

sangui·gno -gna *adj* blood (*circulation*); bloody; sanguine, ruddy ‖ *m* (*lit*) color of blood

sanguinante *adj* bloody, bleeding

sanguinare (**sànguino**) *intr* to bleed; to be rare (*said of meat*)

sanguinà·rio -ria *adj* (**-ri -rie**) sanguinary

sanguinó·so -sa [*s*] *adj* bloody; bleeding; (fig) stinging

sanguisu·ga [*s*] *f* (**-ghe**) leech

sani·tà *f* (**-tà**) health; healthfulness; soundness (*of body*); sanity; health department

sanità·rio -ria (**-ri -rie**) *adj* health; sanitary ‖ *m* physician

sa·no -na *adj* healthy; sound; **sano e salvo** safe and sound

sant' *adj* apocopated form of **santo** and **santa**

santa *f* saint

santabàrbara *f* (**santebàrbare**) (nav) powder magazine

santarellina *f* goody-goody girl

santificare §197 (**santifico**) *tr* to sanctify

santissi·mo -ma *adj* most holy ‖ *m* Eucharist

santi·tà *f* (**-tà**) sanctity, holiness; sainthood, saintliness

san·to -ta *adj* saintly, holy; sacred; blessed, livelong, e.g., **tutto il santo giorno** all the livelong day ‖ *m* saint; name day; (fig) someone ‖ *f* see **santa**

santorég·gia *f* (**-ge**) (bot) savory

santuà·rio *m* (**-ri**) sanctuary

sanzionare (**sanzióno**) *tr* to sanction; to ratify

sanzióne *f* sanction

sapére *m* knowledge; **sapere fare** savoir-faire ‖ §243 *tr* to know; to find out; to know how to; **far sapere** to let know; **saperla lunga** to know a thing or two; **un certo non so che** a certain something, something vague ‖ *intr*— **sapere di** to know; to taste; to smell; to smack of; **mi sa che** I think that; **non voler più saperne di** to not want to have anything to do with; **sapere male** (with *dat*) to feel sorry, e.g., **gli sa male** he feels sorry ‖ *ref*—**che io mi sappia** as far as I know

sàpido -da *adj* savory; witty

sapiènte *adj* wise; talented; trained (*dog*) ‖ *m* wise man

sapientó·ne *mf* wiseacre, know-it-all

sapiènza *f* wisdom; knowledge

saponària *f* (bot) soapwort

saponata *f* soapsuds; lather; (fig) soft soap

sapóne *m* soap; **sapone da toletta** toilet soap; **sapone per la barba** shaving soap

saponétta *f* cake of soap

saponière *m* soap maker

saponifi·cio *m* (**-ci**) soap factory

saponó·so -sa [*s*] *adj* soapy

sapóre *m* taste; savor; flavor

saporire §176 *tr* to savor

saporitaménte *adv* heartily; soundly

sapori·to -ta *adj* tasty; flavorful; salty; expensive

saporó·so -sa [*s*] *adj* savory; witty

saputèl·lo -la *adj* cocksure ‖ *m* smart aleck

saracco *m* (**-chi**) hand saw

saracè·no -na *adj* Saracen, Saracenic ‖ *m* Saracen; quintain

saraciné·sca *f* (**-sche**) metal shutter (*of store*); sluice gate; (hist) portcullis

sarcasmo *m* sarcasm

sarcàsti·co -ca *adj* (**-ci -che**) sarcastic

sarchiare §287 *tr* to weed

sarchia·tóre -trice *mf* weeder ‖ *f* (agr) cultivator

sarchièllo *m* weeding hoe

sàr·chio *m* (**-chi**) hoe

sarcòfa·go *m* (**-gi** & **-ghi**) sarcophagus

sarcràuti *mpl* sauerkraut

Sardégna, la Sardinia

sardèlla *f* pilchard; sardine

sardina *f* pilchard; sardine

sar·do -da *adj* & *mf* Sardinian

sardòni·co -ca *adj* (**-ci -che**) sardonic

sarménto *m* vine shoot, running stem

sarta *f* dressmaker

sàrtie *fpl* (naut) shrouds

sarto *m* tailor

sartoria *f* dressmaker's shop; tailor shop; dressmaking; tailoring

sassaiòla *f* shower of stones

sassata *f* blow with a stone

sasso *m* stone, rock; pebble; (poet) tombstone; **di sasso** stony; **restare di sasso** to be taken aback; **tirare sassi in colombaia** to cut one's nose to spite one's face

sassòfono *m* saxophone

sàssone *adj* & *mf* Saxon

sassó·so -sa [*s*] *adj* stony

Sàtana *m* Satan

satanasso *m* Satan; devil

satèllite *m* satellite

sa·tin *m* (**-tin**) sateen

satinare *tr* to gloss

sàtira *f* satire

satireggiare §290 (**satiréggio**) *tr* to satirize, lampoon ‖ *intr* to compose satires

satìri·co -ca *adj* (**-ci -che**) satiric(al) ‖ *m* satirist

sàtiro *m* satyr

satól·lo -la *adj* sated, full

saturare *tr* (**sàturo**) *tr* to saturate; to steep; (fig) to fill; (com) to glut (*a market*)

saturni·no -na *adj* Saturnian; saturnine

Saturno *m* (astr) Saturn

sàtu·ro -ra *adj* saturated; (fig) full; (lit) sated

sàu·ro -ra adj & m sorrel (horse)

Savèrio m Xavier

sà·vio -via (-vi -vie) adj wise ‖ m wise man, sage

savoiar·do -da adj & mf Savoyard ‖ m ladyfinger

saxòfono m saxophone

saziare §287 tr to satisfy; to cloy, satiate

sazietà f satiety, surfeit; **mangiare a sazietà** to eat one's fill

sà·zio -zia adj (-zi -zie) sated; full; satisfied

sbaciucchiare §287 (**sbaciùcchio**) tr to kiss again and again ‖ ref to neck

sbadàggine f carelessness; oversight

sbada·to -ta adj careless; heedless

sbadigliare §280 intr to yawn

sbadì·glio m (-gli) yawn

sbafa·tóre -trice mf sponger

sbafo m—**a sbafo** sponging; **mangiare a sbafo** to sponge

sbagliare §280 tr to miss; to mistake; **sbagliarla** to be sadly mistaken ‖ intr & ref to be mistaken; to make a mistake

sbaglia·to -ta adj wrong; mistaken

sbà·glio m (-gli) error, mistake

sbalestrare (**sbalèstro**) tr to fling with the crossbow; to send (an employee) far away ‖ intr to speak amiss; to ramble; to blunder

sbalestra·to -ta adj unbalanced; ill-at-ease

sballare tr to unpack; **sballarle grosse** to tell tall tales ‖ intr to overbid

sballa·to -ta adj unpacked; absurd, wild

sballottare (**sballòtto**) tr to toss

sbalordire §176 tr to stun; to amaze; to bewilder ‖ intr to lose consciousness; to be dumfounded

sbalorditi·vo -va adj amazing

sbalzare tr to upset; to send far away; to overthrow; to emboss ‖ intr (ESSERE) to bounce

sbalzo m leap, jump; climb; emboss-ment, relief; **a sbalzi** by leaps and bounds; **di sbalzo** all of a sudden

sbancare §197 tr to clear (ground) of rocks; to ruin; (cards) to break (the bank)

sbandaménto m skid; swerve; disband-ment; breaking up; (naut) list

sbandare tr to disband; (naut) to cause to list ‖ intr to list; to skid; to swerve; to deviate ‖ ref to disband; to break up

sbanda·to -ta adj disbanded; stray; alienated ‖ mf alienated person ‖ m straggler ‖ f listing (of ship); skid-ding (of vehicle); **prendere una sbandata per** to get a crush on

sbandierare (**sbandièro**) tr to wave (a flag); to display

sbaragliare §280 tr to rout; to crush

sbaràglio m—**mettere allo sbaraglio** to endanger

sbarazzare tr to clear out; to free ‖ ref —**sbarazzarsi di** to get rid of

sbarazzi·no -na adj mischievous ‖ mf scamp; **alla sbarazzina** cocked, at an angle (said of a hat)

sbarbare tr to shave; to uproot ‖ ref to shave

sbarbatèllo m greenhorn, fledgling

sbarcare §197 tr to unload; to dis-charge; to disembark; to pass; to strew (fodder); **sbarcare il lunario** to make ends meet ‖ intr (ESSERE) to come ashore, land

sbarca·tóio m (-tói) landing pier

sbar·co m (-chi) unloading; landing

sbarra f bar; (typ) dash

sbarraménto m barrage; obstacle

sbarrare tr to bar; to block (the way); to open (one's eyes) wide, e.g., **sbarrò gli occhi** he opened his eyes wide

sbarrétta f bar; **sbarrette verticali** (typ) parallels

sbatacchiare §287 tr to slam; to flap ‖ intr to slam

sbatàc·chio m (-chi) shore, prop

sbàttere tr to flap; to fling; to slam; to beat; to toss; to send away; to make pale; **sbatter fuori** to throw out ‖ intr to flap; to slam

sbattighiàc·cio m (-cio) cocktail shaker

sbattitóre m electric mixer

sbattiuò·va m (-va) egg beater

sbattu·to -ta adj haggard, downcast

sbavare tr to slobber over; (mach) to trim ‖ intr to drivel, slobber; to run (said of colors)

sbavatura f drivel; run (of colors); burr (of metal); deckle edge; verbosity

sbeccare §197 (**sbécco**) tr & ref to chip

sbeffeggiare §290 (**sbefféggio**) tr to make fun of

sbellicare §197 ref—**sbellicarsi dalle risa** to burst with laughter

sbèrla f (coll) slap

sberléffo m scar; grimace; **fare gli sberleffi a** to make faces at

sbevazzare intr to guzzle

sbevucchiare §287 intr to tipple

sbiadire §176 tr & intr (ESSERE) to fade

sbiadi·to -ta adj faded; dull

sbiancare §197 tr to whiten ‖ ref to become white; to pale

sbianchire §176 tr (culin) to blanch

sbiè·co -ca (-chi -che) adj oblique; **di sbieco** on the bias; **guardare di sbieco** to look askance at ‖ m cloth cut diagonally

sbigottire §176 tr to terrify, dismay ‖ intr (ESSERE) & ref to be dismayed

sbilanciare §128 tr to unbalance; to up-set ‖ intr to lose one's balance ‖ ref to commit oneself

sbilàn·cio m (-ci) disequilibrium; (com) deficit

sbilèn·co -ca adj (-chi -che) twisted, crooked

sbirciare §128 tr to leer at, ogle; to eye closely

sbir·ro -ra adj (coll) smart ‖ m (pej) cop

sbizzarrire [ddzz] §176 tr to cure the whims of ‖ ref to indulge one's whims

sbloccare §197 (**sblòcco**) tr to unblock; to raise the blockade of; to free

sbòbba f slop, dishwater

sboccare §197 (**sbócco**) tr to break the

mouth of (a bottle); to remove a few drops from (a bottle) || intr (ESSERE) to flow; to open (said of a street); **sboccare in** to turn out to be

sbocca·to -ta adj foulmouthed; foul (language); chipped at the mouth (said of a bottle)

sbocciare §128 (sbòccio) intr (ESSERE) to bud, burgeon, bloom

sbóc·co m (-chi) outlet; **avere uno sbocco di sangue** to spit blood

sbocconcellare (sbocconcèllo) tr to nibble at; to chip, nick

sbollentare (sbollènto) tr to blanch

sbollire §176 intr to stop boiling; to calm down

sbolognare (sbológno) tr (coll) to palm off; (coll) to get rid of

sbòrnia f (coll) drunk, jag; **smaltire la sbornia** to sober up

sborsare (sbórso) tr to pay out, disburse

sbórso m disbursement, outlay

sbottare (sbòtto) intr—**sbottare a** + inf to burst out + ger

sbottonare (sbottóno) tr to unbutton || ref (fig) to unbosom oneself

sbozzare (sbòzzo) tr to rough-hew; to sketch, outline

sbraca·to -ta adj without pants; slovenly; vulgar

sbracciare §128 intr to gesticulate || ref to roll up one's sleeves; to wear sleeveless clothes; to gesticulate; to do one's best

sbraccia·to -ta adj bare-armed

sbraitare (sbràito) intr to scream

sbraitó·ne -na mf bigmouth

sbranare tr to tear to pieces

sbrano m tear, rent

sbrattare tr to clean; to clear

sbreccare §197 (sbrécco) tr to chip, nick

sbrecciare §128 (sbréccio) tr to open a gap in

sbréndolo m tatter, rag

sbriciolare (sbrìciolo) tr to crumb || ref to crumble

sbrigare §209 tr to transact; to take care of || ref to hasten, hurry; **sbrigarsela** to get out of trouble; **sbrigarsi di** to get rid of; **sbrigati!** make it snappy!, hurry up!

sbrigativ·o -va adj quick, brisk; businesslike

sbrigliare §280 tr to unbridle; to reduce (a hernia); to lance (an infected wound) || ref to cut loose

sbrinare tr to defrost

sbrindella·to -ta adj tattered

sbrodolare (sbròdolo) tr to soil; (fig) to drag out || ref to slobber

sbrogliare §280 (sbròglio) tr to untangle; to clean up || ref to extricate oneself; **sbrogliarsela** to get out of a tight spot

sbronzare (sbrónzo) ref (coll) to get drunk

sbruffare tr to squirt out of the mouth; to spatter; to bribe || intr to tell tall tales

sbruffo m sprinkle, squirt; bribe

sbruffó·ne -na mf braggart

sbucare §197 intr (ESSERE) to pop out, come out

sbucciare §128 tr to peel; to skin || ref to slough (said of snakes); **sbucciarsela** (coll) to goldbrick

sbucciatura f slight abrasion

sbudellare (sbudèllo) tr to disembowel || ref—**sbudellarsi dalle risa** to burst with laughter, split one's sides laughing

sbuffare tr & intr to puff

sbuffo m puff; gust (of wind); **a sbuffo** puffed (sleeve)

sbullonare (sbullóno) tr to unbolt

sc- pref dis-, e.g., **sconto** discount; es-, e.g., **scalare** to escalate; ex-, e.g., **scusare** to excuse

scàbbia f scabies

sca·bro -bra adj rough; stony; tight (style)

scabró·so -sa [s] adj scabrous

scacchièra f checkerboard; chessboard

scacchière m (mil) sector; (obs) checkerboard; exchequer

scacciaca·ni m & f (-ni) toy gun; gun shooting only blanks

scacciamó·sche m (-sche) fly swatter

scacciapensiè·ri m (-ri) jew's-harp

scacciare §128 tr to chase away, drive away; to expel

scaccino m sexton, sacristan

scac·co m (-chi) chessman; checker; check; square; **a scacchi** checkered; **dare scacco matto a** to checkmate; **in scacco** or **sotto scacco** in check; **scacchi** chess; **scacco matto** checkmate

scàccoli mpl cement piles

scaccomatto m checkmate

scadènte adj inferior, poor, shoddy

scadènza f term, maturity; obligation; **a breve scadenza** short-term; **a lunga scadenza** long-term

scadére §121 intr (ESSERE) to decay, to decline; to fall due; to expire; (naut) to drift

scafandro m diving suit; **scafandro astronautico** space suit

scaffale m bookcase; shelf

scafo m hull

scagionare (scagióno) tr to exonerate, exculpate

scàglia f scale (of fish); chip; plate (of medieval armor); flake (of soap); tile (of slate roof)

scagliare §280 tr to hurl, fling, throw; to scale (fish) || ref to dash, to rush; to flake

scaglionare (scaglióno) tr to echelon; to stagger (e.g., payments)

scaglióne m terrace (of mountain); echelon; scale; **a scaglioni** graded (e.g., income tax)

scala f. stairs; ladder; scale; (cards) straight; (rad) dial; **a scala** scaled, graded; **fare le scale** to climb the stairs; **scala a chiocciola** spiral stairway; **scala a gradini** or **a libretto** stepladder; **scala mobile** escalator; (econ) sliding scale; **scala porta** aerial ladder; **scala reale** (poker) straight flush; **su larga scala** large-scale; **su scala nazionale** on a national scale

scalandróne *m* (naut) gangway

scalare *adj* graded, scaled; gradual ‖ *m* (com) running balance ‖ *tr* to climb, ascend; to scale, grade; to reduce

scalata *f* climb, ascent; **dar la scalata a** to climb; to climb up to

scalcagna·to -ta *adj* down-at-the-heel

scalcare §197 *tr* to slice, carve

scalciare §128 *intr* to kick

scalcina·to -ta *adj* (*wall or plaster*) that is peeling off; worn-out; down-at-the-heels

scalda-acqua *m* (**-acqua**) hot-water heater

scaldaba·gno *m* (**-gno**) hot-water heater; **scaldabagno a gas** gas heater

scaldalèt·to *m* (**-ti &** **-to**) bedwarmer

scaldare *tr* to warm, warm up; to heat, heat up ‖ *intr* (mach) to become hot ‖ *ref* to warm up; to heat up; **scaldarsi la testa** to get excited

scaldavivan·de *m* (**-de**) hot plate

scaldino *m* hand warmer

scalèa *f* flight of stairs, stairway

scalèo *m* stepladder

scalétta *f* small ladder; small stairs; (mov) rough draft

scalfire §176 *tr* to graze, scratch; to cut (*e.g.*, *glass*)

scalfittura *f* graze, scratch

scalinata *f* stairway, perron

scalino *m* step (*of a stair*); (fig) ladder

scalmana *f* chill; flush; **prendere una scalmana per** to take a fancy to

scalmanare *tr* to hustle, bustle; to fuss

scalmana·to -ta *adj* panting; hotheaded

scalmo *m* (naut) oarlock

scalo *m* pier, dock; (naut) ways; (naut) port of call; **fare scalo** (naut) to call, stop; (aer) to land; **scalo di alaggio** (naut) slip; **scalo merci** (rr) freight yard; **senza scalo** (aer, naut) nonstop

scalógna *f* (coll) bad luck

scalógno *m* (bot) scallion

scalòppa *f* veal chop

scaloppina *f* veal cutlet, scallop

scalpellare (**scalpèllo**) *tr* to chisel

scalpellino *m* stone cutter

scalpèllo *m* chisel; (surg) scalpel; **scalpello a taglio obliquo** skew chisel

scalpicciare §128 *tr* & *intr* to shuffle

scalpitare (**scàlpito**) *intr* to paw the ground

scalpóre *m* scene; **fare scalpore** to raise a fuss

scaltrézza *f* shrewdness, cunning

scaltrire §176 *tr* to polish, refine; to sharpen the wits of ‖ *ref* to catch on; to improve

scal·tro -tra *adj* shrewd, smart

scalzare *tr* to take the shoes or stockings off of; to undermine ‖ *ref* to take off one's shoes or stockings

scal·zo -za *adj* barefoot

scambiare §287 *tr* to exchange; to mistake ‖ *ref* to exchange (*presents*)

scambiévole *adj* mutual

scàm·bio *m* (**-bi**) exchange; (rr) switch;

libero scambio free trade; **scambio di persona** mistaken identity

scamicia·to -ta *adj* in shirt sleeves; extremist ‖ *m* extremist; tunic, waist

scamoscia·to -ta *adj* chamois, suede

scampagnata *f* excursion, outing

scampanare *intr* to peal, chime; to flare (*said of a garment*)

scampanellare (**scampanèllo**) *intr* to ring loud and clear

scampanì·o *m* (**-ì**) toll, peal

scampare *tr* to save, rescue; **scamparla bella** to have a narrow escape ‖ *intr* (ESSERE)—**scampare a** to escape from; to take refuge in

scampo *m* escape; safety; (zool) Norway lobster; **non c'è scampo** there is no way out

scàmpolo *m* remnant; **scampoli di tempo** free moments

scanalare *tr* to channel, groove, rabbet ‖ *intr* to overflow

scanalatura *f* channel, groove, rabbet

scandagliare §280 *tr* to sound

scandà·glio *m* (**-gli**) sounding lead; **fare uno scandaglio** to make a sounding or survey

scandalismo *m* scandalmongering, yellow journalism

scandalizzare [ddzz] *tr* to scandalize, shock ‖ *ref* to be scandalized

scàndalo *m* scandal

scandaló·so -sa [s] *adj* scandalous

scandina·vo -va *adj* & *mf* Scandinavian

scandire §176 *tr* to scan; to syllabize; (telv) to scan

scàndola *f* wood shingle

scannare *tr* to slaughter, butcher

scanna-tóio *m* (**-tói**) slaughterhouse; gyp joint

scanno *m* bench; seat; sand bar

scansafati·che *mf* (**-che**) loafer

scansare *tr* to move; to avoid ‖ *ref* to get out of the way

scansìa *f* shelf; bookcase

scansióne *f* scansion; (telv) scanning

scanso *m*—**a scanso di** in order to avoid

scantinare *intr* to make a blunder; (mus) to be out of tune

scantinato *m* basement

scantonare (**scantóno**) *tr* to round (*a corner*) ‖ *intr* to duck around the corner

scanzona·to -ta *adj* flippant; unconventional

scapaccióne *m* clout; **dare uno scapaccione a** to clout, slap

scapa·to -ta *adj* scatterbrained ‖ *m* scatterbrain

scapestra·to -ta *adj* & *m* libertine

scapigliare §280 *tr* to dishevel ‖ *ref* to be disheveled

scapiglia·to -ta *adj* disheveled; libertine; unconventional; free and easy

scapitare (**scàpito**) *intr* to lose

scàpito *m* damage; loss; **a scapito di** to the detriment of

scàpola *f* shoulder blade

scapolare *m* scapular ‖ *v* (**scàpolo**) *tr* (coll) to escape, avoid ‖ *intr*—**scapolare da** to get out of (*danger*) scàpo·lo -la *adj* unmarried ‖ *m* bachelor ‖ *f* see scapola

scappaménto *m* escapement (*of watch, of piano*); (aut) exhaust

scappare *tr*—scapparla bella to have a narrow escape ‖ *intr* (ESSERE) to flee; to abscond; to run; to get away; to escape; to stick out; to burst out (*said, e.g., of sun*); far scappare la pazienza a qlcu to make s.o. lose his patience, to tax s.o.'s patience; scappare a gambe levate to run away, beat it; scappare da to burst out, e.g., gli è scappato da ridere he burst out laughing; scappar detto di to blurt out that, e.g., gli scappò detto di non poterne più he blurted out that he could not hold out; scappare di mente to escape one's mind; scappar fuori con to come out with

scappata *f* excursion; sally; escapade; bolt (*of horse*); fare una scappata to take a run; scappata spiritosa witticism

scappatóia *f* subterfuge; loophole

scappellare (scappèllo) *ref* to tip one's hat

scappellòtto *m* smack, slap (on the head); entrare a scappellotto (coll) to squeeze in; passare a scappellotto (coll) to squeeze through with influence

scapricciare §128 *tr* to satisfy the whims of

scarabèo *m* beetle; scarab (*stone*); scarabeo sacro scarab; scarabeo stercorario dung beetle

scarabocchiare §287 (scarabòcchio) *tr* to scribble; to blot (*with ink*)

scarabòc·chio *m* (-chi) ink blot; scribble; scrawl

scarafàg·gio *m* (-gi) cockroach

scaramanzìa *f* exorcism; per scaramanzia to ward off the evil eye, for good luck

scaramazza *adj fem* irregular (*pearl*)

scaramùc·cia *f* (-ce) skirmish

scaravèntare (scaravènto) *tr* to hurl, chuck; to transfer suddenly

scarcerare (scàrcero) *tr* to release from jail

scardinare (scàrdino) *tr* to unhinge

scàri·ca *f* (-che) discharge; volley; evacuation; (elec) discharge; (fig) shower

scaricabarili *m*—giocare a scaricabarili (fig) to pass the buck

scaricare §197 (scàrico) *tr* to unload; to discharge; to hurl (*insults*); to wreak (*anger*); to free (*from responsibility*) ‖ *ref* to unburden oneself; to flow (*said of a river*); to discharge; to run down (*said of a battery or a watch*)

scaricatóre *m* longshoreman; (elec) lightning arrester

scàri·co -ca (-chi -che) *adj* empty, unloaded; discharged; clear (*sky*); free; run-down (*e.g., clock*) ‖ *m* unloading; discharge; exhaust; waste, refuse; a mio (tuo, etc.) scarico in my (your, etc.) defense ‖ *f* see scarica

scarlattina *f* scarlet fever

scarlat·to -ta *adj & m* scarlet

scarmigliare §280 *tr* to dishevel

scarnificare §197 (scarnifico) or scarnire §176 *tr* to bone, take the flesh off; to make thin; to wear down to the bone

scarni·to -ta or scar·no -na *adj* boned; meager; skinny

scaròla *f* escarole, endive

scarpa *f* shoe; wedge, skid; scarp; fare le scarpe a to undercut; scarpe al sole violent death; scarpe da sci ski boots

scarpata *f* escarp, escarpment; slope (*of embankment*); blow with a shoe; scarpata continentale continental slope

scarpétta *f* small shoe; low shoe; scarpette chiodate spikes; scarpette da ginnastica gym shoes

scarpinare *intr* to trudge

scarpóne *m* heavy boot; clodhopper

scarròc·cio *m* (-ci) (aer, naut) leeway

scarrozzare (scarròzzo) *tr* to take for a ride ‖ *intr* to go for a ride; to go for a walk

scarrozzata *f* ride, drive

scarseggiare §290 (scarséggio) *intr* (ESSERE) to be scarce, be in short supply; scarseggiare di to be short of supply

scarsèlla *f* pocket; (obs) purse

scarsézza *f* or scarsi·tà *f* (-tà) scarcity, dearth, lack

scar·so -sa *adj* short; scarce; scanty, scant; weak (*wind*); scarso a short of

scartabellare (scartabèllo) *tr* to leaf through (*a book*)

scartafàc·cio *m* (-ci) note pad, notebook; poorly-bound copybook

scartaménto *m* (rr) gauge; a scartamento ridotto narrow-gauge; small-size; small-scale

scartare *tr* to unpack, unwrap; to discard (*cards*); to remove; to scrap (*e.g., a machine*); (mil) to reject ‖ *intr* to swerve; to side-step

scartata *f* unwrapping; side step; swerving; (fig) scolding

scartina *f* discard

scarto *m* discard; reject; swerve; (mil) rejected soldier; (sports) difference; di scarto inferior

scartocciare §128 (scartòccio) *tr* to unwrap; to unfold; to husk (*corn*)

scartòffie *fpl* old papers, trash

scassare *tr* to uncrate; to plow up; (coll) to ruin, bust ‖ *ref* (coll) to break down

scassinare *tr* to pick (*a lock*); to burglarize; to break open

scassina·tóre -trice *mf* burglar; scassinatore di casseforti safe-cracker

scasso *m* plowing, tilling; burglary

scatenare (scatèno) *tr* to unchain; to trigger; to excite, stir up ‖ *ref* to break loose

scàtola *f* box; can; a scatola chiusa sight unseen; in scatola canned; rompere le scatole a (vulg) to bug, pester; scatola armonica music box; scatola a sorpresa jack-in-the-box;

scatola cranica cranium, skull; **scatola del cambio** (aut) transmission, gear box

scatolame *m* boxes; canned food

scatolifi·cio *m* (-ci) box factory

scattare *tr* to take (*a picture*)` || *intr* (ESSERE & AVERE) to jump, spring; to go off (*said of a trap*); to go up (*said of the cost of living*); to go into action, begin

scatto *m* click (*of camera, gun*); outburst; sprint; automatic increase (*in salary*); shutter release; **a scatti** in jerks; **di scatto** suddenly

scaturire §176 *intr* (ESSERE) to spring; to pour, gush; to stem

scavalcare §197 *tr* to jump over; to pass over; to unsaddle; to skip (*a stitch*) || *intr* (ESSERE) to dismount || *ref* (coll) to rush

scavallare *intr* to caper, cavort

scavare *tr* to dig; to dig up, unearth

scava·tóre -trice *adj* excavating || *m* digger || *f* digger, excavator

scavezzacòllo *m* scamp; daredevil; **a scavezzacollo** headlong, at breakneck speed

scavezzare (scavézzo) *tr* to lop; to burst; to break; to take the halter off (*a horse*)

scavo *m* digging, excavation

scazzottare (scazzòtto) *tr* to beat up

scégliere §244 *tr* to choose; to pick out

sceic·co *m* (-chi) sheik

scelleratàggine *f* or **scelleratézza** *f* wickedness, villainy

scellera·to -ta *adj* wicked || *m* villain

scellino *m* shilling

scél·to -ta *adj* choice; selected; (mil) first-class || *f* choice; pick; selection; **di prima scelta** choice

scemare (scémo) *tr* to diminish, reduce; to lower the level of || *intr* (ESSERE) & *ref* to lessen, diminish

scemènza *f* foolishness, stupidity

scé·mo -ma *adj* silly, foolish || *mf* simpleton, fool

scempiàggine *f* silliness, foolishness

scém·pio -pia (-pi -pie) *adj* simple; single; (lit) wicked || *m* ruination; (lit) slaughter; **fare scempio di** to ruin; (lit) to slaughter

scèna *f* scene; stage; acting; scenery; **esser di scena** (theat) to be on; **mettere in scena** (theat) to stage; **scene di prossima programmazione** (mov) coming attractions

scenà·rio *m* (-ri) scenery; scenario, setting

scenari·sta *mf* (-sti -ste) scenarist; script writer

scenata *f* scene (*outbreak of anger*)

scéndere §245 *tr* to descend, go down; to bring down || *intr* (ESSERE) to descend, go down; to get off; to come (*to an agreement*); to step (*into the ring*); to put up (*at a hotel*); to check in (*at a hotel*)

scendilèt·to *m* (-to) scatter rug; bathrobe

sceneggiare §290 (scenéggio) *tr* to write a scenario for; to adapt for the stage

sceneggia·tóre -trice *mf* scenarist

sceneggiatura *f* (mov) screenplay; (rad, telv) continuity

scenètta *f* (theat) sketch

scenògrafo *m* scene designer

scenotècni·ca *f* (-che) stagecraft

sceriffo *m* sheriff

scèrnere §246 *tr* to discern; to distinguish; to select

scervellare (scervèllo) *ref* to rack one's brains

scervella·to -ta *adj* scatterbrained

scésa [s] *f* discent; slope

scespiria·no -na *adj* Shakesperean

scetticismo *m* skepticism

scètti·co -ca (-ci -che) *adj* skeptic(al) || *m* skeptic

scèttro *m* scepter

sceverare (scévero) *tr* (lit) to distinguish

sce·vro -vra *adj* (lit) free, exempt

schèda *f* card; slip, form; **scheda elettorale** ballot; **scheda perforata** punch card

schedare (schèdo) *tr* to file

schedà·rio *m* (-ri) card index, card catalogue; file cabinet

schég·gia *f* (-ge) splinter; chip

scheggiare §290 (schéggio) *tr & ref* to splinter

schèletri·co -ca *adj* (-ci -che) skeleton, skeletal; succint

schèletro *m* skeleton

schè·ma *m* (-mi) diagram; draft; model; scheme; **schema di montaggio** (electron) hookup

schérma *f* fencing

schermàglia *f* argument

schermare (schérmo) *tr* to screen; (elec) to shield

schermire §176 *tr* to protect; (obs) to fence with || *ref—schermirsi da* to ward off, parry; to protect oneself from

schermi·tóre -trice *mf* fencer

schérmo *m* screen; protection; (elec) shield; **farsi schermo di** to use as protection; **farsi schermo delle mani** to ward off a blow with one's hands

schernire §176 *tr* to deride

schérno *m* derision, ridicule, mockery

scherzare (schérzo) *tr* (coll) to mock || *intr* to play; to joke, trifle

schérzo *m* play; joke, jest; freak (*of nature*); child's play; trick; **neppure per scherzo** under no circumstances; **per scherzo** in jest; **stare allo scherzo** to take a joke

scherzó·so -sa [s] *adj* joking; playful

schiacciaménto *m* crushing; flattening

schiacció·ci *m* (-ci) nutcracker

schiacciante *adj* crushing

schiacciapata·te *m* (-te) ricer

schiacciare §128 *tr* to crush; to take (*a nap*); to squelch (*a rumor*); to subdue (*the details of a painting*); to mash (*potatoes*); to tread on, step on (*s.o.'s foot*); to flatten; to run (*s.o.*) over; to make (*s.o.'s figure*) look squatty; to crack (*nuts*); to flunk; (tennis) to smash

schiacciata *f* hot cake; (tennis) smash

schiaffare *tr* (coll) to fling, clap
schiaffeggiare §290 (schiaffeggio) *tr* to slap; to buffet
schiaffo *m* slap, box
schiamazzare *intr* to squawk, cackle; to honk; to make a racket
schiamazzo *m* squawking, cackle; honk; hubbub
schiantare *tr* to crush, burst || *intr* (ESSERE) (coll) to burst; (coll) to croak || *ref* to break, crack, split
schianto *m* break, crack; crash; bang; knockout (*extraordinary, attractive person or thing*); di schianto all of a sudden; schianto al cuore heartache
schiappa *f* splinter; (coll) good-for-nothing
schiarimento *m* elucidation
schiarire §176 *tr* to make clearer; to make (*the hair*) light; to clear; to explain; to elucidate || *intr* (ESSERE) to become light || *ref* to clear up (*said of the weather*); to clear (*one's throat*); to fade || *impers* (ESSERE) —schiarisce it is getting light
schiarita *f* clearing (*of weather*), improvement (*in relations*)
schiatta *f* race, stock
schiattare *intr* (ESSERE) to burst
schiavi·sta (-sti -ste) *adj* slave (*e.g., state*) || *mf* antiabolitionist
schiavi·tù *f* (-tù) slavery; bondage
schia·vo -va *adj* enslaved || *mf* slave
schiccherare (schicchero) *tr* to scribble; to soil; to sketch; to dash off; to blurt out; (coll) to clean out
schidionare (schidióno) *tr* to put on the spit
schidióne *m* spit
schièna *f* back; divide; crown (*of road*); giocare di schiena to buck
schienale *m* back (*of chair; cut of meat*)
schièra *f* crowd; flock; herd; (mil) rank
schieramento *m* alignment
schierare (schièro) *tr* to line up || *ref* to line up; schierarsi dalla parte di to side with
schiètto -ta *adj* pure; frank, honest
schifare *tr* to loathe; to disgust || *ref*—schifarsi di to feel disgusted with
schifa·to -ta *adj* disgusted
schifiltó·so -sa [s] *adj* fastidious; squeamish
schifo *m* disgust, loathing; skiff; shell; fare schifo a to disgust; to make sick
schifó·so -sa [s] *adj* disgusting; sickening; (slang) tremendous
schioccare §197 (schiocco) *tr* to snap (*the fingers*); to click (*the tongue*); to smack (*the lips*); to crack (*a whip*) || *intr* to crack
schiòc·co *m* (-chi) crack, snap; click; smack
schiodare (schiòdo) *tr* to take the nails out of
schioppettata *f* gunshot; earshot
schiòppo *m* gun, shotgun; a un tiro di schioppo within earshot
schiùdere §125 *tr & ref* to open
schiuma *f* foam, froth; lather; head (*of beer*); dregs, scum; meerschaum

avere la schiuma alla bocca to froth at the mouth
schiumaiòla *f* skimmer
schiumare *tr* to scum; to skim || *intr* to foam, froth; to lather
schiumó·so -sa [s] *adj* foamy
schivare *tr* to avoid; to avert || *ref* to shy
schi·vo -va *adj* averse; bashful, shy
schizzare *tr* to spray; to sprinkle; to ooze (*venom*); to sketch; schizzare fuoco dagli occhi to have fire in one's eyes || *intr* (ESSERE) to gush; to squirt; to dart; gli occhi gli schizzano dall'orbita his eyes are popping out of his head
schizzétto *m* sprayer; syringe; water pistol
schizzinó·so -sa [s] *adj* finicky, fastidious
schizzo *m* spray; splash; sketch; survey (*e.g., of literature*)
sci *m* (sci) ski
scia *f* wake; track; trail; scia di condensazione contrail
sciàbola *f* saber
sciabordare (sciabórdo) *tr* to shake, agitate || *intr* to break (*said of waves*)
sciacallo *m* jackal
sciacquadi·ta *m* (-ta) finger bowl
sciacquare (sciàcquo) *tr* to rinse
sciacquatura *f* rinse
sciacquì·o *m* (-ì) splash, dash
sciàcquo *m* rinsing (*of the mouth*); mouthwash
sciagura *f* calamity, misfortune
sciagura·to -ta *adj* unfortunate; wretched
scialacquare (scialàcquo) *tr* to squander
scialare *tr* to squander || *intr* to be well off; to live it up
scial·bo -ba *adj* pale, faded; wan
scialle *m* shawl; scialle da viaggio traveling blanket
scialo *m* squandering; opulence; a scialo lavishly
scialuppa *f* launch; lifeboat
sciamanna·to -ta *adj* slovenly
sciamannó·ne -na *mf* slovenly person || *f* slattern
sciamare *intr* (ESSERE & AVERE) to swarm
sciame *m* swarm; flock
sciampagna *f* champagne
scianca·to -ta *adj* cripple, lame; wobbly (*table*)
sciangài *m* pick-up-sticks || Sciangài *f* Shanghai
sciarada *f* charade
sciare §119 *intr* to ski; to back water
sciarpa *f* scarf; sash (*e.g., of an officer or of a mayor*)
scias·sì *m* (-sì) chassis
sciàtica *f* (pathol) sciatica
scia·tóre -trice *mf* skier
sciatterìa *f* or sciattézza *f* slovenliness
sciat·to -ta *adj* slovenly, sloppy
scibile *m* knowledge
sciènte *adj* conscious; knowing
scientìfi·co -ca *adj* (-ci -che) scientific
sciènza *f* science; knowledge

scienzia·to -ta *mf* scientist

scilinguágnolo *m* frenum (*of tongue*); avere lo scilinguagnolo sciolto to have a loose tongue

Scilla *f* Scylla; fra Scilla e Cariddi between Scylla and Charibdis

scimitarra *f* scimitar

scimmia *f* monkey; (coll) drunk; fare la scimmia a to ape; scimmia antropomorfa anthropoid ape

scimmié·sco -sca *adj* (-schi -sche) monkeyish; apish

scimmiottare (scimmiòtto) *tr* to ape

scimpan·zé *m* (-zé) chimpanzee

scimuni·to -ta *adj* idiotic || *mf* idiot

scìndere §247 *tr* (lit) to split; to separate

scintilla *f* spark; sparkle; (fig) scintilla; scintilla elettrica jump spark

scintillare *intr* to spark; to sparkle

scintillì·o *m* (-ì) sparkle, brilliance

scioccare §197 *tr* to shock

sciocchézza *f* silliness; trifle

sciòc·co -ca (-chi -che) *adj* silly, foolish || *mf* fool, blockhead

sciògliere §127 *tr* to loosen; to release; to unfasten, untie; to solve; to disperse; to dissolve; to limber; to fulfill (*a promise*); to unfurl (*sails*) || *ref* to loosen up; to get loose; to dissolve; to melt (*into tears*)

scioglilìn·gua *m*(-gue) tongue twister

scioglimento *m* melting; dissolution; fulfillment; denouement

sciolina *f* ski wax

scioltézza *f* nimbleness, agility; freedom (*of movement*); ease

sciòl·to -ta *adj* loose; glib; free; blank (*verse*)

scioperante *adj* striking || *mf* striker

scioperare (sciòpero) *intr* to strike

sciopera·to -ta *adj* loafing; lazy || *m* loafer

sciòpero *m* strike; walkout; sciopero a singhiozzo slowdown strike; sciopero bianco sit-down strike; sciopero della fame hunger strike; sciopero di solidarietà sympathy strike; sciopero pignolo slowdown

sciorinare *tr* to display; to tell (*lies*); to air (*laundry*)

sciovìa *f* ski lift

sciovinismo *m* chauvinism, jingoism

scipì·to -ta *adj* insipid

scippo *m* snatching (*e.g., of a bag*)

sciròc·co *m* (-chi) sirocco; southeast

sciròppo *m* syrup

sci·sma *m* (-smi) schism

scismàti·co -ca *adj* (-ci -che) schismatic

scissióne *f* split; (biol, phys) fission

scis·so -sa *adj* split, rent

scisto *m* schist

sciupare *tr* to spoil; to wear out; to waste; to rumple || *ref* to wear; to run down (*said of health*); to get rumpled

sciupa·to -ta *adj* ruined; worn out; wasted; run down

sciupì·o *m* (-ì) waste

sciupó·ne -na *mf* waster, squanderer

sciu·scià *m* (-scià) bootblack; urchin

scìvola *f* chute

scivolare (scìvolo) *intr* (ESSERE & AVERE) to slide, glide; to steal; scivolare d'ala (aer) to sideslip

scivolata *f* slide, glide; scivolata d'ala (aer) sideslip

scìvolo *m* chute; (aer) slip (*for seaplanes*)

scivolóne *m* slip, slide

scivoló·so -sa [s] *adj* slippery

scoccare §197 (scòcco) *tr* to shoot (*an arrow*); to give (*a buss*); to strike (*the hour*) || *intr* (ESSERE) to dart; to spring; to strike (*said of a clock*); to shoot

scocciare §128 (scòccio) *tr* (coll) to break; (coll) to bother; (naut) to unhook || *ref* to be bored

scoccia·tóre -trice *mf* (coll) nuisance

scocciatura *f* (coll) bother, annoyance

scòc·co *m* (-chi) darting; stroke (*e.g., of three*); (naut) hook; scocco di baci bussing, kissing

scodèlla *f* bowl; soup plate

scodellare (scodèllo) *tr* to dish out

scodellino *m* small bowl; (mil) pan (*of musket lock*)

scodinzolare (scodìnzolo) *intr* to wag its tail; to waddle (*said of a woman*)

scoglièra *f* reef (*of rocks*); scogliera corallina coral reef

scò·glio *m* (-gli) rock; reef; cliff; stumbling block

scoiare §248 *tr* to skin

scoiàttolo *m* squirrel

scolabrò·do *m* (-do) colander, strainer

scolafrit·to *m* (-to) strainer

scolapa·sta *m* (-sta) (coll) colander

scolare (scólo) *tr* to drain; (fig) to polish off || *intr* (ESSERE) to drip || *ref* to melt

scolaré·sco -sca (-schi -sche) *adj* school || *f* schoolchildren; student body

scola·ro -ra *mf* pupil; student

scolàsti·co -ca (-ci -che) *adj* school; scholastic; || *m* scholastic, schoolman || *f* scholasticism

scola·tóio *m* (-tói) drain; strainer

scolatura *f* drip, drippings; dregs

scollaccia·to -ta *adj* low-necked; wearing a low-cut dress; dirty, obscene

scollare (scòllo) *tr* to cut off at the neck; to unglue || *ref* to wear a low-necked dress; to come unglued

scollatura *f* neckline; ungluing; scollatura a barchetta low neck; scollatura a punta V neck

scòllo *m* neck, neckline

scólo *m* drain; drainage; (slang) clap

scolopèndra *f* centipede

scolorare (scolóro) *tr, intr* (ESSERE), & *ref* to fade, discolor; to pale

scolorire §176 *tr, intr* (ESSERE), & *ref* to fade, discolor

scolpare (scólpo) *tr* to excuse

scolpire §176 *tr* to sculpture; to engrave; to emphasize

scólta *f* (lit) sentry; fare la scolta to stand guard

scombaciare §128 *tr* to pull apart, separate

scombinare *tr* to disarrange; to upset

scómbro *m* mackerel

scombù·glio m (-gli) (coll) disorder
scombussolare (scombùssolo) tr to upset
scomméssa f bet, wager
scomméttere §198 tr to bet; to separate
scommetti·tóre -trice mf bettor
scomodare (scòmodo) tr to trouble, disturb || ref to take the trouble
scomodi·tà f (-tà) trouble, inconvenience
scòmo·do -da adj awkward, unwieldy; uncomfortable || m inconvenience
scompaginare (scompàgino) tr to upset; (typ) to pi
scompagna·to -ta adj odd
scomparire §108 intr (ESSERE) to disappear; to make a bad showing
scompar·so -sa adj disappeared; extinct || mf deceased || f disappearance; death
scompartimento m compartment; partition
scompènso m lack of compensation; imbalance
scompigliare §280 tr to disarray; to trouble, upset
scompi·glio m (-gli) disarray; upset
scompisciare §128 tr (vulg) to piss on || ref (vulg) to wet oneself; **scompisciarsi dalle risa** (coll) to split one's sides laughing
scomplè·to -ta adj incomplete
scompórre §218 tr to decompose, disintegrate; to rumple; to dishevel; to upset; to dismantle, take apart; (typ) to pi || ref to lose one's composure
scompo·sto -sta adj unseemly
scomùni·ca f (-che) excommunication
scomunicare §197 (scomùnico) tr to excommunicate; (joc) to ostracize
sconcertare (sconcèrto) tr to upset; to disconcert || ref to become disconcerted
sconcèzza f obscenity, indecency
scón·cio -cia (-ci -ce) adj dirty, filthy, obscene || m obscenity; shame
sconclusiona·to -ta adj inconsequential; incoherent; rambling
sconcordanza f disagreement; (gram) lack of agreement
scondi·to -ta adj unseasoned
sconfessare (sconfèsso) tr to disavow; to retract
sconfessióne f disavowal
sconfiggere §104 tr to defeat, rout; to pull (a nail); to unfasten
sconfinare intr to cross the border; **sconfinare da** to stray from
sconfina·to -ta adj boundless, unlimited
sconfitta f defeat, rout
sconfortante adj discouraging
sconfortare (sconfòrto) tr to discourage; to distress || ref to become discouraged
sconfòrto m depression; distress
scongelare (scongèlo) tr to thaw
scongiurare tr to conjure; to implore
scongiuro m conjuration; entreaty
sconnès·so -sa adj disconnected; incoherent
sconnèttere §107 tr to disconnect; to take apart || intr to be incoherent

sconoscènte adj unappreciative
sconosciu·to -ta adj unknown || mf stranger
sconquassare tr to smash, shatter
sconquassa·to -ta adj broken-down; upset
sconquasso m destruction; confusion; smash-up
sconsacrare tr to desecrate
sconsideratézza f thoughtlessness
sconsidera·to -ta adj inconsiderate
sconsigliare §280 tr to dissuade, discourage
sconsiglia·to -ta adj thoughtless
sconsola·to -ta adj disconsolate
scontare (scónto) tr to expiate; to discount; to serve (time in jail)
scontentare (scontènto) tr to dissatisfy
scontèn·to -ta adj & m discontent
scónto m discount; part payment; (fig) partial remission
scontrare (scóntro) tr to meet; (naut) to turn (the wheel) sharply || ref to clash; to collide; to come to blows
scontrino m check, ticket
scóntro m collision; battle, encounter; clash; ward (of key)
scontró·so -sa [s] adj peevish, cross
sconveniènte adj unfavorable; unseemly, unbecoming; indecent
sconvenire §282 intr (ESSERE) to be unseemly or unbecoming
sconvòlgere §289 tr to upset; to disconcert
sconvolgimento m upsetting; **sconvolgimento di stomaco** stomach upset; **sconvolgimento tellurico** upheaval
sconvòl·to -ta adj upset; disconcerted; distracted
scópa f broom; **scopa per lavaggio** mop
scopare (scópo) tr to sweep
scopata f sweep
scoperchiare §287 (scopèrchio) tr to uncover; to take the lid off
scopèr·to -ta adj uncovered; open; bare; exposed; unpaid || m open ground; open air; overdraft; (econ) short sale; (com) balance; **allo scoperto** in the open; overdrawn (check); short (sale) || f discovery; **alla scoperta** openly
scòpo m purpose, goal, aim
scoppiare §287 (scòppio) tr to uncouple || intr (ESSERE) to burst; to blow; to explode; to break (said, e.g., of news); (fig) to die (e.g., of overeating); **scoppiare a** to burst out (laughing or crying)
scoppiettare (scoppiétto) intr to crackle
scoppiettì·o m (-i) crackle
scòp·pio m (-pi) burst; explosion; outbreak; outburst; blowout (of tire); **a scoppio** internal-combustion (engine); **scoppio di tuono** clap of thunder
scòppola f drop (of plane in air pocket); (coll) rabbit punch
scoprimento m uncovering; unveiling
scoprire §110 tr to uncover; to unveil; to discover; to expose || ref to take off one's clothes; to take one's hat off; to reveal oneself

scopri·tóre -trice *mf* discoverer

scoraggiaménto *m* discouragement

scoraggiante *adj* discouraging

scoraggiare §290 *tr* to discourage, dishearten ‖ *ref* to be or become discouraged

scoraménto *m* (lit) discouragement

scorbuto *m* scurvy

scorciare §128 (**scórcio**) *tr* to shorten; to foreshorten ‖ *intr* (ESSERE) to shorten, grow shorter; to look foreshortened ‖ *ref* to shorten, grow shorter

scorciatóia *f* shortcut, cutoff

scór·cio *m* (**-ci**) foreshortening; end, close (*of a period*); **di scorcio** foreshortened

scordare (**scòrdo**) *tr* to forget; to put out of tune ‖ *ref* to forget; to get out of tune

scoróg·gia *f* (**-ge**) (vulg) fart

scoreggiare §290 (**scoréggio**) *intr* (vulg) to fart

scòrgere §249 *tr* to perceive, to discern

scòria *f* slag, dross; (fig) scum, dregs; **scorie atomiche** atomic waste

scorna·to -ta *adj* humiliated, ridiculed; hornless

scòrno *m* humiliation, ridicule

scorpacciata *f* bellyful; **fare una scorpacciata di** to stuff oneself with

scorpióne *m* scorpion ‖ **Scorpione** *m* (astrol) Scorpio

scorrazzare *tr* to wander over ‖ *intr* to run around; to move about; (fig) to ramble; (mil) to raid

scórrere §139 *tr* to raid; to glance over ‖ *intr* (ESSERE) to flow; to run; to glide

scorrerìa *f* raid, foray, incursion

scorrettézza *f* imprecision; impropriety

scorrèt·to -ta *adj* incorrect; improper

scorrévole *adj* sliding; flowing, fluent ‖ *m* slide (*of slide rule*)

scorribanda *f* raid, foray, incursion

scór·so -sa *adj* past, last ‖ *m* error, slip ‖ *f* glance; short stay

scor·sóio -sóia *adj* (**-sói -sóie**) slip (*knot*)

scòrta *f* escort; provision, stock; **di scorta** spare (*tire*); **fare di scorta a** to escort; **scorta d'onore** (mil) honor guard; **scorte** (com) stockpile; (com) supplies; **scorte morte** agricultural supplies; **scorte vive** livestock

scortare (**scòrto**) *tr* to escort; to foreshorten

scortecciare §128 (**scortéccio**) *tr* to strip the bark from; to peel off; to scrape ‖ *ref* to peel off

scortése *adj* discourteous, impolite

scortesìa *f* discourtesy, impoliteness

scorticare §197 (**scórtico**) *tr* to skin; to be overdemanding with (*students*); to fleece ‖ *ref* to skin (*e.g., one's arm*)

scòrza *f* bark; skin, hide; (fig) appearance; **scorza di limone** lemon peel

scoscendiménto *m* landslide; cliff

scoscé·so -sa [s] *adj* sloping, steep

scòssa *f* shake; jerk; **scossa di pioggia**

downpour; **scossa di terremoto** earth tremor; **scossa elettrica** electric shock; **scossa tellurica** earthquake

scossóne *m* jolt, jerk

scostaménto *m* removal; separation

scostare (**scòsto**) *tr* to move away; to try to avoid ‖ *intr* (ESSERE) to stand away ‖ *ref* to step aside; to stray

scostuma·to -ta *adj* dissolute, debauched

scotennare (**scoténno**) *tr* to scalp; to skin (*an animal*)

sedòtta *f* whey; (naut) sheet

scottante *adj* burning (*question*); outrageous (*offense*)

scottare (**scòtto**) *tr* to burn; to scald; to sear; to boil (*eggs*); (fig) to sting ‖ *intr* to burn; to be hot (*said of stolen goods*) ‖ *ref* to get burnt

scottatura *f* burn; (fig) blow, jolt

scòt·to -ta *adj* overcooked, overdone ‖ *m*—**pagare lo scotto** to foot the bill; **pagare lo scotto di** to expiate ‖ *f* see **scotta**

scoutismo *m* scouting

scovare (**scóvo**) *tr* to rouse (*game*); to find, discover

scovolino *m* pipe cleaner; (mil) small swab

scóvolo *m* (mil) swab

scòzia *f* (archit) scotia ‖ **la Scozia** Scotland

scozzése [s] *adj* Scotch, Scottish ‖ *m* Scotch, Scottish (*language*); Scotchman ‖ *f* Scotchwoman

scozzonare (**scozzóno**) *tr* to break in (*a horse*); to train

scranna *f* (hist) seat

screanza·to -ta *adj* ill-mannered, rude

screditare (**scrédito**) *tr* to discredit

scremare (**scrèmo**) *tr* to cream

scrematrice *f* cream separator

screpolare (**scrèpolo**) *tr*, *intr* (ESSERE), & *ref* to crack; to chap

screpolatura *f* crack; chap (*of skin*)

screziare §287 (**scrèzio**) *tr* to mottle, variegate

scrè·zio *m* (**-zi**) tiff

scri·ba *m* (**-bi**) scribe (*Jewish scholar*)

scribacchiare §287 *tr* to scribble, scrawl

scribacchino *m* scribbler; hack

scricchiolare (**scrìcchiolo**) *intr* to crack, creak

scricchiolì·o *m* (**-i**) crack, creak

scrìcciolo *m* wren

scrigno *m* jewel box

scriminatura *f* part (*in hair*)

scrit·to -ta *adj* written ‖ *m* writing ‖ *f* sign; inscription; contract; **scritta luminosa** electric sign

scrit·tóio *m* (**-tói**) writing desk

scrit·tóre -trice *mf* writer

scrittura *f* handwriting; penmanship; writing; contract; entry; (theat) booking; **Sacra Scrittura** Holy Scripture; **scrittura privata** contract; **scrittura pubblica** deed, indenture; **scrittura a macchina** typing

scritturale *adj* scriptural ‖ *m* clerk; copyist; fundamentalist

scritturare *tr* (theat) to book, engage

scrivanìa *f* desk

scrivano *m* clerk, copyist, typist

scrivere §250 *tr* & *intr* to write; **scrivere a macchina** to type

scroccare §197 (**scròcco**) *tr* to sponge (*a meal*); to manage to get (*a prize*) || *intr* to sponge

scrocca·tóre -trice *mf* sponger

scròc·co *m* (**-chi**) sponging; creaking; **a scrocco** sponging; spring (*lock*); switchblade (*knife*)

scroccó·ne -na *mf* sponger

scròfa *f* sow; slut

scrollare (**scròllo**) *tr* to shake; to shrug (*one's shoulders*) || *ref* to get into action; to pull oneself together

scrollata *f* shake; **scrollata di spalle** shrug

scrosciare §128 (**scròscio**) *intr* (ESSERE & AVERE) to pelt down; (fig) to thunder

scrò·scio *m* (**-sci**) thunder, roar; **scroscio di pioggia** downpour; **scroscio di tuono** thunderclap

scrostare (**scròsto**) *tr* to pick (*a scab*); to scrape; to peel off || *ref* to peel off

scrosta·to -ta *adj* peeling; scaly

scròto *m* scrotum

scrùpolo *m* scruple; scrupulousness

scrupoló·so -sa [s] *adj* scrupulous

scrutare *tr* to scan, scrutinize

scruta·tóre -trice *adj* inquisitive || *mf* teller (*of votes*)

scrutina·tóre -trice *mf* teller (*of votes*)

scruti·nio *m* (**-ni**) poll, vote; evaluation (*of an examination*); count (*of votes*); **scrutinio segreto** secret ballot

scucire §143 *tr* to unstitch; (coll) to cough up || *ref* to come unstitched

scucitura *f* unstitching; rip

scuderìa *f* stable

scudétto *m* badge; escutcheon; (sports) badge of victory

scudièro *m* esquire

scudisciare §128 *tr* to whip

scudì·scio *m* (**-sci**) whip

scudo *m* shield; escutcheon; **far scudo a** to shield

scuffia *f* (coll) load (*intoxication*); **fare scuffia** to capsize; **prendersi una scuffia per** to fall for, to fall in love with

scugnizzo *m* Neapolitan urchin

sculacciare §128 *tr* to spank

sculacciata *f* spank, spanking

sculacción̄e *m* spank, spanking

sculettare (**sculétto**) *intr* to waddle

scul·tóre -trice *mf* sculptor || *f* sculptress

scultura *f* sculpture

scuòla *f* school; **scuola allievi ufficiali** military academy; officers' candidate school; **scuola dell'obbligo** mandatory education; **scuola di danza** dancing school; **scuola di dressaggio** obedience school (*for dogs*); **scuola di guerra** war college; **scuola di guida** driving school; **scuola di perfezionamento per laureati** postgraduate school; **scuola di taglio** sewing school; **scuola materna** kindergarten; **scuola mista** coeducational school

scuòla·bus *m* (**-bus**) school bus

scuòtere §251 *tr* to shake; to shake up; **scuotere di dosso** to shake off

scure *f* ax; cleaver

scurire §176 *tr*, *intr* (ESSERE), & *ref* to darken

scu·ro -ra *adj* dark || *m* darkness; dark; shutter; **essere allo scuro** to be in the dark

scurrile *adj* scurrilous

scusa *f* excuse; apology; pretext; **chiedere scusa** to apologize

scusare *tr* to excuse; to pardon; to apologize for; **scusi!** pardon me! || *ref* to apologize; to beg off

sdaziare §287 *tr* to clear through customs

sdebitare (**sdébito**) *tr* to free from debt || *ref* to become free of debt; **sdebitarsi con** to repay a favor to

sdegnare (**sdégno**) *tr* to scorn; to arouse, enrage || *ref* to get mad

sdégno *m* indignation, anger; (lit) scorn

sdegnó·so -sa [s] *adj* indignant; haughty

sdenta·to -ta *adj* toothless

sdilinquire §176 *tr* to weaken || *intr* (ESSERE) & *ref* to swoon; to become mawkish

sdoganare *tr* to clear through customs

sdolcina·to -ta *adj* mawkish

sdolcinatura *f* mush, slobber

sdoppiare §287 (**sdóppio**) *tr* & *ref* to split

sdoppiaménto *m* splitting

sdottoreggiare §290 (**sdottoréggio**) *intr* to pontificate

sdràia *f* chaise longue; deck chair

sdraiare §287 *tr* to lay down || *ref* to stretch out (*e.g., on the ground*)

sdràio *m* (**sdrài**) stretching out; **mettersi a sdraio** to lie down

sdrucciolare (**sdrùcciolo**) *intr* (ESSERE & AVERE) to slip, slide

sdrucciolévole *adj* slippery

sdrùccio·lo -la *adj* proparoxytone || *m* slip; slope; proparoxytone

sdruccioló̄ni *adv* slipping, sliding

sdrucire (**sdrùcio**) & §176 *tr* to tear, rend, rip

sdrucitura *f* tear, rend, rip

se *m* (**se**) if || §5 *pron* || *conj* if; whether; **se mai** in the event; **se no** otherwise; **se non tu** (lui, lei, etc.) nobody else but you (him, her, etc.), e.g., **non puoi essere stato se non tu** it could not have been anyone else but you; **se non altro** at least; **se non che** but; **se pure** even if

sé §5 *pron* himself; herself; itself; yourself; themselves; yourselves; oneself; **di per sé stesso** by itself; **fuori di sé** beside oneself; **rientrare in sé** to come back to one's senses; **uscire di sé** to be beside oneself

sebbène *conj* although, though

sèbo *m* sebum, tallow

séc·ca *f* (**-che**) sand bank, shoal; drought; **dare in secca** to run aground; **in secca** hard up

seccante *adj* drying; annoying

seccare §197 (**sécco**) *tr* to dry; to bore;

to bother, annoy || *intr* (ESSERE) to dry up || *ref* to dry up; to be annoyed

secca·tóio *m* (**-tói**) drying room; squeegee (*to remove water from wet decks*)

secca·tóre -trice *mf* bore, pest

seccatúra *f* drying; trouble, nuisance

sécchia *f* bucket, pail; **piovere a secchie** to rain cats and dogs

secchièllo *m* little bucket

séc·chio *m* (**-chi**) bucket, pail; bucketful; **secchio dell'immondezza** trash can

séc·co -ca (**-chi -che**) *adj* dry; lanky; sharp || *m* dryness; dry land; drought; **a secco** dry (*cleaning*); **dare in secco** to run aground; **in secco** hard up; **lavare a secco** to dry-clean || *f* see **secca**

secenté·sco -sca *adj* (**-schi -sche**) seventeenth-century

secentèsi·mo -ma *adj, m & pron* six hundredth

secèrnere §153 (*pp* **secrèto**) *tr* to secrete

secessióne *f* secession

séco §5 *prep phrase* (lit) with oneself; along, e.g., **portare seco** to bring along

secolare *adj* secular; century-old; worldly || *m* layman

sècolo *m* century; age; world

secónda *f* second; second-year class; **a seconda** with the wind; **a seconda di** according to; **in seconda** (aut) in second; (mil) second in command

secondare (**secóndo**) *tr* to second

secondà·rio -ria *adj* (**-ri -rie**) secondary

secondíno *m* prison guard, turnkey

secón·do -da *adj* second; (lit) favorable || *m* second; second course; (nav) executive officer || *f* see **seconda** || *pron* second || **secondo** *prep* according to; **secondo me** (**te**, etc.) in my (your, etc.) opinion

secondogèni·to -ta *adj* second-born

secrezióne *f* secretion

sèdano *m* celery

sedare (**sèdo**) *tr* to calm, placate

sedatí·vo -va *adj & m* sedative

sède *f* seat; branch; residence; period; (gram) syllable; (rr) right of way; **in separata sede** in private; (law) **with change of venue**; **Santa Sede** Holy See; **sede centrale** main office, home office

sedentà·rio -ria (**-ri -rie**) *adj* sedentary || *m* sedentary person

sedére §252 *intr* (ESSERE) to sit, to be seated; to be in session; to be located || *ref* to sit down

sèdia *f* chair; seat; see; **sedia a braccioli** armchair; **sedia a dondolo** rocking chair; **sedia a pozzetto** bucket seat; **sedia a sdraio** deck chair; **sedia da posta** (hist) mail coach; **sedia di vimini** wicker chair; **sedia elettrica** electric chair; **sedia girevole** swivel chair

sedicènne *adj* sixteen-year-old || *mf* sixteen-year-old person

sedicènte *adj* so-called, self-styled

sedicèsi·mo -ma *adj, m & pron* sixteenth

sédici *adj & pron* sixteen; **le sedici** four P.M. || *m* sixteen; sixteenth (*in dates*)

sedíle *m* seat; bench; bottom (*of chair*); (aut) bucket seat

sediménto *m* sediment

sedìolo *m* sulky

sedizióne *f* sedition

sedizió·so -sa [s] *adj* seditious

seducènte *adj* seductive; alluring

sedurre §102 *tr* to seduce; to allure; to lead astray; to charm, captivate

seduta *f* sitting; session, meeting; **seduta fiume** (pol) uninterrupted session; **seduta stante** on the spot

sedut·tóre -trice *adj* seductive; alluring; charming || *mf* seducer

seduzióne *f* seduction; allurement; charm

sefardì·ta (**-ti -te**) *adj* Sephardic || *mf* Sephardi

sé·ga *f* (**-ghe**) saw; **a sega** serrated; **sega a nastro** band saw; **sega circolare** buzz saw; **sega da carpentiere** lumberman's saw; **sega intelaiata a lama** bucksaw; **sega meccanica** power saw

ségala *f* rye

segali·gno -gna *adj* rye; lean, wiry

segare §209 (**ségo**) *tr* to saw; to cut

segatrice *f* power saw; **segatrice a disco** circular saw; **segatrice a nastro** band saw

segatura *f* cutting; sawdust

seggétta *f* commode

sèg·gio *m* (**-gi**) seat (*e.g., in congress*); **seggio elettorale** voting commission

sèggiola *f* chair; **seggiola a sdraio** deck chair

seggiolíno *m* child's chair; stool; bucket seat; **seggiolino eiettabile** (aer) ejection seat

seggiolóne *m* highchair; easy chair

seggiovìa *f* chair lift

segherìa *f* sawmill

seghétta·to -ta *adj* serrated

seghétto *m* hacksaw; **seghetto da traforo** coping saw

segménto *m* segment; **segmento elastico** (aut) piston ring

segnaccènto *m* accent mark

segnàcolo *m* (lit) symbol, sign

segnalare *tr* to signal; to point out || *ref* to distinguish oneself

segnalazióne *f* signaling; sign, signal; nomination; recommendation; **dare la segnalazione a** to notify; **fare segnalazioni** to signal; **segnalazioni stradali** road signs

segnale *m* sign; signal; bookmark; **segnale di allarme** (mil) alarm; **segnale di occupato** (telp) busy signal; **segnale di via libera** (telp) dial tone; **segnale orario** (rad, telv) time signal; **segnali stradali** road signs

segnalèti·co -ca *adj* (**-ci -che**) identification (*mark*) || *f* road signs

segnalíbro *m* bookmark

segnalíne·e *m* (**-e**) lineman

segnapósto *m* place card

segnapun·ti *m* (**-ti**) scorekeeper

segnare (ségno) *tr* to mark; to under-score, underline; to jot down; to say (*e.g.*, *five o'clock, said of a watch*); to brand; (sports) to score; **segnare a dito** to point to || *ref* to cross one-self

segnatas·se *m* (-se) postage-due stamp

segnatura *f* signing; signature; library number; (eccl) chancery; (sports) final score; (typ) signature

segnavèn·to m (-to) weather vane

ségno *m* mark; bookmark; symbol; sign; signal; boundary; (mus) signa-ture; **a segno che** so that; **a tal segno** to such a point; **essere fatto segno di** to be the target of; **in segno di** as a token of; **mettere a segno** to check, control; **segno della Croce** sign of the Cross; **segno di croce** cross (*mark*); **segno d'interpunzione,** or **di punteg-giatura,** or **grafico** punctuation mark; **segno di riconoscimento** identifica-tion mark

ségo *m* tallow, suet

segregare §209 (sègrego) *tr* to segre-gate; to secrete || *ref* to withdraw

segregazióne *f* segregation; **segrega-zione cellulare** solitary confinement

segregazioni·sta *mf* (-sti -ste) segrega-tionist

segretariato *m* secretariat

segretà·rio -ria *mf* secretary; clerk

segreterìa *f* secretary's office; secretary-ship

segretézza *f* secrecy

segré·to -ta *adj* secret; secretive || *m* secret; secrecy; **segreto d'alcova** boudoir secret; **segreto di Pulcinella** open secret

seguace *mf* follower

seguènte *adj* following, next

segù·gio m (-gi) bloodhound; (fig) pri-vate eye

seguire (séguo) *tr* to follow; to attend || *intr* (ESSERE) to continue; to follow, ensue; (with *dat*) to follow

seguitare (séguito) *intr*—**seguitare a** + *inf* to keep on + *ger*, e.g., **seguitare a parlare** to keep on talking; **seguiti!** go ahead!

séguito *m* following; retinue; follow-ers; sequence; sequel; pursuit; **di seguito** in succession; **far seguito a** to refer to; **in seguito** thereafter; **in seguito a** as a consequence of

sèi *adj & pron* six; **le sei** six o'clock || *m* six; sixth (*in dates*)

seicènto *adj, m & pron* six hundred || *f* car with a motor displacing 600 cubic centimeters || **il Seicento** the seventeenth century

seimila *adj, m, & pron* six thousand

sélce *f* silica; flint; (lit) stone; **selci** paving blocks

selciare §128 (sélcio) *tr* to pave

selcia·to -ta *adj* paved || *m* paving

seletti·vo -va *adj* selective

selezionare (selezióno) *tr* to select, sort out

selezióne *f* selection; choice

sèlla *f* saddle

sel·làio m (-lài) saddler

sellare (sèllo) *tr* to saddle

sellerìa *f* saddler's shop; saddlery; (aut) upholstery

sélva *f* woods, forest

selvaggina *f* game

selvàg·gio -gia (-gi -ge) *adj* savage; vicious (*horse*) || *m* savage; unsocia-ble person

selvàti·co -ca *adj* (-ci -che) wild

selvicoltura *f* forestry

sèlz m (sèlz) seltzer, club soda

semàforo *m* traffic light; semaphore

semànti·co -ca (-ci -che) *adj* semantic || *f* semantics

sembiante *m* (lit) look; **fare sembianti di** to pretend

sembianza *f* look; (lit) similarity

sembrare (sémbro) *intr* (ESSERE) to seem, look, appear || *impers*—**sembra** it seems

séme *m* seed; stone (*of fruit*); (cards) suit

seménta *f* sowing season; (lit) seed

seménte *f* seed

semènza *f* seed; brads (*used in uphol-stery*)

semenzà·io m (-zài) hotbed, seedbed

semestrale *adj* semiannual, semiyearly

semèstre *m* semester; half year

sèmi- *pref* semi-, e.g., **semicircolare** semicircular; half-, e.g., **semichiuso** half-closed || *pref mf* semi-, e.g., **semicerchio** semicircle; half, e.g., **semitono** half tone; demi-, e.g., **semi-dìo** demigod

semiapèr·to -ta *adj* half-open; ajar

semiasse *m* (mach) axle (*on each side of differential*)

semicér·chio m (-chi) semicircle

semichiu·so -sa [s] *adj* half-closed

semicingola·to -ta *adj & m* half-track

semicircolo m semicircle

semiconduttóre *m* semiconductor

semiconvit·tóre -trice *mf* day student

semicù·pio m (-pi) sitz bath

semi-dìo m (-dèi) demigod

semidòt·to -ta *adj* semilearned

semifinale *f* semifinal

sémina *f* sowing; sowing season

seminare (sémino) *tr* to sow, seed; to plant; (coll) to leave behind

seminà·rio m (-ri) seminary; seminar

seminari·sta *m* (-sti) seminarian

semina·to -ta *adj* sown, seeded || *m* sown land; **uscire dal seminato** to digress

semina·tóre -trice *mf* sower || *f* (mach) seeder, seeding machine

seminterrato *m* basement

seminu·do -da *adj* half-naked

semioscurità *f* partial darkness

semirìgi·do -da *adj* semirigid; inelastic

semirimòr·chio m (-chi) semitrailer

semisè·rio -ria [s] *adj* (-ri -rie) serio-comic

semisfèra *f* (geom) hemisphere

semi·ta (-ti -te) *adj* Semitic || *mf* Semite

semitòno *m* (mus) semitone, half tone

semmài *conj* if ever; in the event that

sémola *f* bran; (coll) freckles

semolino *m* semolina

semovènte *adj* self-propelled

sempitèr·no -na *adj* (lit) everlasting
sémplice *adj* simple; single; plain; mere; (mil) private; (nav) ordinary || *m* medicinal herb; **semplici** simple folk
sempliciò·ne -na *adj* simple || *mf* simpleton
semplici·tà *f* (**-tà**) simplicity
semplificare §197 (**semplìfico**) *tr* to simplify || *ref* to become easier or simpler
sèmpre *adv* always; ever; yet; **da sempre** from time immemorial; **di sempre** same, same old; **e poi sempre** ever and ever; **ma sempre** but only; **per sempre** forever; **sempre che** provided; **sempre meglio** better and better; **sempre meno** less and less; **sempre però** but only; **sempre vostro** very truly yours
semprevérde *adj, m & f* evergreen
sènape *f* mustard
senapismo *m* mustard plaster
senato *m* senate
sena·tóre -trice *mf* senator
senése [s] *adj & mf* Sienese
senile *adj* old; of old age
senilismo *m* (pathol) senility
senilità *f* old age
seniòre *adj & m* elder, senior
Sènna *f* Seine
sénno *m* wisdom; **far senno** to come back to one's senses; **senno di poi** hindsight; **uscir di senno** to go out of one's mind
séno *m* chest; breast; bosom; cove; (anat) sinus; (math) sine; (fig) heart; **in seno a** within
senonché or **se non che** *conj* but
sensale *m* broker; commission merchant
sensa·to -ta *adj* sensible, reasonable; sane
sensazionale *adj* sensational
sensazióne *f* sensation
sensìbile *adj* sensible; perceptible; appreciable; sensitive; responsive (*e.g., to affection*) || *m* world of the senses
sensibili·tà *f* (**-tà**) sensitivity; sensibility
sensibilizzare [ddzz] *tr* to sensitize
sensi·vo -va *adj* sensitive || *m* medium
sènso *m* sense; feeling; meaning; aspect; tone, fashion; direction; **ai sensi di legge** according to law; **senso free** (*translation*); **doppio senso** double entendre; **in senso contrario** in the opposite direction; **perdere i sensi** to lose consciousness; **riprendere i sensi** to come to; **sensi carnal** appetite, flesh; **senso unico** one-way; **senso vietato** no entry, one-way
sensò·rio -ria *adj* (**-ri -rie**) sensory
sensuale *adj* sensual, carnal; sensuous
sensualità *f* sensuality
sentènza *f* sentence; maxim
sentenziare §287 (**sentènzio**) *tr* to pass sentence upon, sentence || *intr* to pontificate
sentenziò·so -sa [s] *adj* sententious
sentièro *m* path, pathway
sentimentale *adj* sentimental; mawkish
sentimentalismo *m* sentimentalism
sentiménto *m* feeling; sentiment; sense;

uscire di sentimento (coll) to go out of one's mind
sentina *f* bilge; sink (*of vice*)
sentinèlla *f* sentry, sentinel
sentire *m* feeling || *v* (**sènto**) *tr* to feel; to hear; to listen to; to consult (*a doctor*); to smell; to taste; **farsi sentire** to make oneself heard || *intr* to feel; to listen; to smell; to taste; **non sentirci di quell'orecchio** to turn a deaf ear; **sentirci bene** to have keen hearing || *ref* to feel; **non sentirsela di** to not have the courage to; **sentirsela** to feel up to it
senti·to -ta *adj* heartfelt
sentóre *m* inkling, feeling; sign; (lit) smell
sènza *prep* without; beyond (*e.g., comparison*); **senza + inf** without + *ger*; **senza che + subj** without + *ger*; **senza di + pron** without + *pron*, e.g., **senza di lui** without him; **senz'altro** without any doubt, of course
senza·dìo *m* (**-dìo**) —**i senzadio** the godless
senzapà·tria *m* (**-tria**) man without a country; renegade
senzatét·to *m* (**-to**) homeless person; **i senzatetto** the homeless
separare *tr & ref* to separate
separazióne *f* separation
sepolcrale *adj* sepulchral
sepolcréto *m* cemetery
sepólcro *m* sepulcher, grave
sepoltura *f* burial; grave
seppellire §253 *tr* to bury
séppia *adj invar* sepia || *f* cuttlefish
seppure *conj* even if
sè·psi *f* (**-psi**) sepsis
sequèla *f* series
sequènza *f* sequence
sequestrare (**sequèstro**) *tr* to seize, confiscate; to kidnap; to confine; to quarantine; (law) to attach, sequester
sequèstro *m* seizure; attachment; **sequestro di persona** unlawful detention
séra *f* evening; night; **da mezza sera** cocktail (*dress*); dark (*suit*); **da sera** evening (*gown*); formal (*attire*)
serac·co *m* (**-chi**) serac
serafino *m* seraph
serale *adj* evening; night
seralménte *adv* in the evening; every evening
serata *f* evening; soiree, evening party; **serata d'addio** (theat) farewell performance; **di beneficenza** benefit performance
serbare (**sèrbo**) *tr* to keep; to save (*e.g., a place*); to bear (*a grudge*) || *ref* to keep oneself; to stay
serba·tóio *m* (**-tói**) tank; reservoir; cartridge clip
sèr·bo -ba *adj & mf* Serbian || *m*—**in serbo** in store
serbocroa·to -ta *adj & mf* Serbo-Croatian
serenata *f* serenade
serenìssi·mo -ma *adj* Serene (*Highness*)
sereni·tà *f* (**-tà**) serenity

seré·no -na *adj* serene; clear, fair (*weather*)

sergènte *m* sergeant; carpenter's clamp; **sergente maggiore** first sergeant

sèri·co -ca *adj* (**-ci -che**) silk

sè·rie *f* (**-rie**) series; (sports) division; **fuori serie** (aut) custom-built; **in serie** (aut) standard; (elec) in series

serietà *f* seriousness; gravity

serigrafia *f* silkscreen process

sè·rio -ria (**-ri -rie**) *adj* serious; stern; **poco serio** unreliable (*man*); loose (*woman*) || *m* seriousness; **sul serio** in earnest; really, e.g., **bello sul serio** really beautiful

sermonare (sermóno) *tr & intr* (lit) to sermonize

sermóne *m* sermon

sermoneggiare §290 (**sermonéggio**) *intr* to preach; to lecture

seròti·no -na *adj* late; (lit) evening

sèrpa *f* coach box

sèrpe *f* snake, serpent; **a serpe** coiled, in a coil; **nutrirsi or scaldarsi la serpe in seno** to nourish a viper in one's bosom

serpeggiare §290 (**serpéggio**) *intr* to zigzag; to wind; to creep, spread

serpènte *m* snake, serpent; **serpente a sonagli** rattlesnake

serpenti·no -na *adj* serpentine || *m* serpentine; coil (*of pipe*) || *f* zigzag, turn (*of winding road*); coil (*of pipe*)

sèrqua *f* dozen; lot, large number

sèrra *f* dike, levee; hothouse; sierra; **un serra serra** a milling crowd

serrafi·la m (**-le**) rear-guard soldier || *f* rear ship (*of convoy*)

serrafilo *m* electrician's pliers; (elec) binding post

serrà·glio *m* (**-gli**) menagerie; seraglio

serramànico m—a serramanico clasp (*knife*); switchblade (*knife*)

serrame *m* lock

serraménto *m* closing, bolting || **serraménti e -ta** *fpl* closing devices, doors, windows, and shutters

serranda *f* shutter (*of store*)

serrare (sèrro) *tr* to shut, close; to pursue (*the enemy*); to increase (*tempo*); to furl (*sails*); to lock; to clench (*one's teeth, one's fists*); to shake (*hands*) || *intr* to shut; to be tight || *ref* to be wrenched, e.g., **gli si serrò il cuore** his heart was wrenched; **serrarsi addosso a** to press (*the enemy*)

serrata *f* lockout

serrate m—serrate finale (sports) finish

serra·to -ta *adj* shut (*e.g., door*); concise (*style*); tight (*game*); rapid (*gallop*); closed (*ranks*); thick (*crowd*) || *f* see **serrata**

serratura *f* lock

sèrto *m* (poet) crown, wreath

sèrva *f* (pej) maidservant, maid

servènte *adj* (*gentleman*) in waiting || *m* gunner; (obs) servant

servibile *adj* usable

serviènte *m* (eccl) server

servì·gio *m* (**-gi**) service; favor

servile *adj* servile; menial; modal (*auxiliary*)

servire (sèrvo) *tr* to serve; to wait on; **in che posso servirLa?** what can I do for you?; may I help you?; **per servirLa** at your service || *intr* to serve || *intr* (ESSERE & AVERE) to serve; to answer the purpose; to last; (with *dat*) (coll) to need, e.g., **gli serve il martello** he needs the hammer; **non servire a nulla** to be of no use; **servire da** to act as || *ref* to help oneself; **servirsi da** to patronize, deal with; **servirsi di** to avail oneself of, use

servitóre *m* servant; tea wagon; **servitor suo umilissimo** your humble servant

servi·tù *f* (**-tù**) servitude; captivity; servants, help; **servitù di passaggio** (law) easement

servizièvole *adj* obliging, accommodating

servì·zio *m* (**-zi**) service; favor; turn; **a mezzo servizio** part-time (*domestic help*); **di servizio** delivery (*entrance*); for hire (*car*); domestic (*help*); **fuori servizio** out of commission; **in servizio in commission**; **servizi** kitchen and bath; facilities; **servizi pubblici** public services; public works; **servizio attivo** active duty; **servizio permanente effettivo** service in the regular army

sèr·vo -va *adj* (lit) enslaved || *m* slave; servant; **servo della gleba** serf || *f* see **serva**

servoassisti·to -ta *adj* servocontrolled

servofréno *m* (aut) power brake

servomotóre *m* servomotor

servostèrzo *m* (aut) power steering

sèsamo *m* sesame; **apriti sesamo!** open sesame!

sessanta *adj, m & pron* sixty

sessantènne *adj* sixty-year-old || *mf* sixty-year-old person

sessantèsi·mo -ma *adj, m & pron* sixtieth

sessantina *f* about sixty

sessióne *f* session

sèsso *m* sex; **il sesso debole** the fair sex

sessuale *adj* sexual

sestante *m* sextant

sestétto *m* sextet

sestière *m* district, section

sè·sto -ta *adj & pron* sixth || *m* sixth; curve (*of an arch*); **fuori sesto** out of sorts; **mettere in sesto** to arrange; to set in order; **sesto acuto** (archit) ogive

sèt *m* (sèt) set; set **all'aperto** (mov) location

séta *f* silk; **seta artificiale** rayon

setacciare §128 *tr* to sift, sieve

setàc·cio *m* (**-ci**) sieve

setàce·o -a *adj* silky

séte *f* thirst; **aver sete** to be thirsty; to lust after; **sete di** thirst for

seterìa *f* silk mill; **seterie** silk goods

setifì·cio *m* (**-ci**) silk mill

sétola *f* bristle; (joc) stubble

sètta *f* sect

settanta *adj, m & pron* seventy

settantènne *adj* seventy-year-old || *mf* seventy-year-old person

settantèsi·mo -ma *adj, m & pron* seventieth

settantina *f* about seventy

settà·rio -ria *adj & mf* (**-ri -rie**) sectarian

sètte *adj & pron* seven; **le sette** seven o'clock || *m* seven; seventh (*in dates*); V-shaped tear (*in clothing*)

settecentèsi·mo -ma *adj, m & pron* seven hundredth

settecènto *adj, m & pron* seven hundred || **il Settecento** the eighteenth century

settèmbre *m* September

settennale *adj* seven-year (*e.g., plan*)

settènne *adj* seven-year-old || *mf* seven-year-old child

settentrionale *adj* northern || *mf* northerner

settentrióne *m* north; (astr) Little Bear

setticemia *f* septicemia

sètti·co -ca *adj* (**-ci -che**) septic

settimana *f* week; week's wages; **settimana corta** five-day week

settimanale *adj & m* weekly

settìmi·no -na *adj* premature (*baby*) || *m* (mus) septet

sètti·mo -ma *adj, m & pron* seventh

sètto *m* septum

settóre *m* sector; section, branch; dissector, anatomist; coroner's pathologist

sevè·ro -ra *adj* severe, stern

seviziare §287 *tr* to torture

sevìzie *fpl* cruelty

sezionale *adj* sectional

sezionare (**sezióno**) *tr* to cut up; to divide up; to dissect

sezióne *f* section; dissection; chapter (*of club*); department (*of agency*); (geom) cross section

sfaccènda·to -ta *adj* loafing || *mf* loafer

sfaccettare (**sfaccétto**) *tr* to facet

sfacchinare *intr* (coll) to toil, drudge

sfacchinata *f* (coll) drudgery, grind

sfacciatàggine *f* brazenness, impudence

sfaccià·to -ta *adj* brazen, impudent; loud, gaudy; **fare lo sfacciato** to be fresh

sfacèlo *m* breakdown, collapse

sfà·glio *m* (**-gli**) swerve (*e.g., of horse*); (cards) discard

sfaldare *tr* to exfoliate; to cut into slices || *ref* to flake, scale; (fig) to collapse, crumble

sfamare *tr* to feed (*the hungry; the family*) || *ref* to get enough to eat

sfare §173 *tr* to undo || *ref* to spoil (*said, e.g., of meat*)

sfarzo *m* pomp, display; luxury

sfarzó·so -sa [s] *adj* sumptuous, luxurious

sfasare *tr* to throw out of phase; (coll) to depress || *intr* (ESSERE) (aut) to misfire; (elec) to be out of phase

sfasciare §128 *tr* to remove the bandage from; to unswathe; to smash, shatter || *ref* to go to pieces; to lose one's figure

sfatare *tr* to discredit; to unmask

sfatìca·to -ta *adj* lazy || *mf* loafer

sfat·to -ta *adj* overdone; overripe; undone (*bed*); ravaged (*by age*)

sfavillare *intr* to spark, sparkle

sfavóre *m* disfavor

sfavorévole *adj* unfavorable

sfebbra·to -ta *adj* free of fever

sfegata·to -ta *adj* (coll) rabid, fanatical

sfèra *f* sphere; (coll) hand (*of clock*); **a sfera** ball-point (*pen*); **a sfere** ball (*bearing*); **sfera di cuoio** (sports) pigskin

sfèri·co -ca *adj* (**-ci -che**) spherical

sferrare (**sfèrro**) *tr* to unshoe (*a horse*); to unchain; to draw (*a weapon from a wound*); to deliver (*a blow*) || *ref* to hurl oneself

sfèrza *f* whip, scourge

sferzare (**sfèrzo**) *tr* to whip, scourge

sfiancare §197 *tr* to break open; to tire out; to fit (*clothes*) too tight || *ref* to burst open; to get worn out

sfiatare *intr* to leak (*said, e.g., of a tire*) || *intr* (ESSERE) to leak (*said of air or gas*) || *ref* to waste one's breath

sfiata·tóio *m* (**-tói**) vent

sfibbiare §287 *tr* to unbuckle, unfasten; to untie (*a knot*)

sfibrante *adj* exhausting

sfibrare *tr* to grind (*wood*) into fibers; to shred (*rags*) into fibers; to weaken, wear out

sfida *f* challenge

sfidare *tr* to challenge, dare; to brave, defy; to endure (*the challenge of time*); **sfidare che** to bet that

sfidù·cia *f* (**-cie**) mistrust; (pol) no confidence

sfiducia·to -ta *adj* downcast, depressed

sfigurare *tr* to disfigure || *intr* to make a bad impression; to lose face

sfilacciare §128 *tr & ref* to ravel, fray

sfilare *tr* to unstring; to take off (*one's shoes*); to count (*beads*); to unthread; to dull (*a blade*); to ravel || *intr* (ESSERE) to march, parade; to follow one another || *ref* to become unthreaded; to become frayed; to run (*said of knitted work*); to break one's back

sfilata *f* parade; row; **sfilata di moda** fashion show

sfilza *f* row, sequence

sfinge *f* sphinx

sfinimento *m* exhaustion

sfinire §176 *tr* to exhaust, wear out || *ref* to be worn out

sfintère *m* sphincter

sfiorare (**sfióro**) *tr* to graze; to barely touch (*a subject*); to skim; (lit) to barely reach

sfioratóre *m* spillway

sfiorire §176 *intr* (ESSERE) to wither, fade

sfit·to -ta *adj* not rented

sfocare §197 (**sfòco**) *tr* to put out of focus; to blur

sfociare §128 (**sfócio**) *tr* to dredge (*the mouth of a river*) || *intr* (ESSERE) to flow; **sfociare in** (fig) to lead to

sfoderare (**sfòdero**) *tr* to unsheathe; to show off, sport, display; to take the cover or lining off || *intr* to be drawn out

sfogare §209 (**sfógo**) *tr* to vent, give vent to || *intr* (ESSERE) to flow; to pour out; **sfogare in** to turn into || *ref*—**sfogarsi a** + *inf* to have one's fill of + *ger;* **sfogarsi con** to unburden oneself to; **sfogarsi su qlcu** to take it out on s.o.

sfoga·tóio *m* (-tói) vent

sfoggiare §290 (sfòggio) *tr* to display, sport; to show off

sfòg·gio *m* (-gi) display, ostentation

sfòglia *f* foil; skin (*of onion*); layer of puff paste; (ichth) sole

sfogliare §280 (sfòglio) *tr* to pluck (*a flower*); to defoliate (*a tree*); to leaf through (*a book*); to deal (*cards*); to husk (*corn*); to press (*dough*) into layers ‖ *ref* to shed its leaves; to flake

sfogliata *f* defoliation; puff paste; **dare una sfogliata a** to glance through

sfó·go *m* (-ghi) exhaust; outlet; vent; (coll) eruption (*of skin*)

sfolgorare (sfólgoro) *intr* (ESSERE & AVERE) to shine, blaze

sfolgorì·o *m* (-i) glittering, blazing

sfollagèn·te *m* (-te) billy

sfollaménto *m* evacuation; layoff

sfollare (sfòllo) *tr* to clear; to cut the staff of ‖ *intr* (ESSERE & AVERE) to disperse, evacuate; to cut down the staff

sfolla·to -ta *adj* driven from home ‖ *mf* evacuee

sfoltire §176 *tr* to thin out

sfondare (sfóndo) *tr* to stave in; to break through; to be heavy on (*the stomach*) ‖ *intr* to give ‖ *ref* to break open

sfóndo *m* background

sfondóne *m* (coll) blunder, error

sforbiciare §128 (sfòrbicio) *tr* to clip, shear

sforbiciata *f* clipping; (sports) scissors; (sports) scissors kick

sformare (sfórmo) *tr* to pull out of shape; to take out of the mold ‖ *intr* to get mad

sforma·to -ta *adj* out of shape ‖ *m* pudding

sfornare (sfórno) *tr* to take out of the oven

sfornire §176 *tr* to deprive; to strip

sfortuna *f* bad luck, misfortune

sfortuna·to -ta *adj* unsuccessful; unlucky, unfortunate

sforzare (sfòrzo) *tr* to strain; to force ‖ *ref* to strive, endeavor

sforza·to -ta *adj* forced, unnatural

sfòrzo *m* effort; strain; stretch (*of imagination*); **senza sforzo** effortlessly

sfóttere *tr* (vulg) to make fun of

sfracassare *tr* to smash, crash

sfracellare (sfracèllo) *tr* & *ref* to shatter, smash

sfrangiare §290 *tr* to ravel

sfrattare *tr* to evict; to deport ‖ *intr* to be evicted

sfratto *m* eviction; notice of eviction

sfrecciare §128 (sfréccio) *intr* (ESSERE & AVERE) to speed by

sfregaménto *m* rubbing

sfregare §209 (sfrégo) *tr* to rub; to scrape; to strike (*a match*)

sfregiare §290 (sfrégio & sfrègio) *tr* to disfigure, slash

sfregia·to -ta *adj* disfigured, slashed ‖ *m* scarface

sfré·gio or **sfrè·gio** *m* (-gi) slash, scar, gash; insult

sfrenare (sfréno & sfrèno) *tr* to take the brake off; to give free rein to ‖ *ref* to kick over the traces

sfriggere §180 *intr* to sizzle

sfrigolì·o *m* (-i) sizzle

sfrondare (sfróndo) *tr* to defoliate; to lop off; to trim down ‖ *ref* to lose leaves

sfrontatézza *f* effrontery, impudence

sfronta·to -ta *adj* brazen, impudent

sfrusciare §128 *intr* to rustle

sfruttare *tr* to exploit; to exhaust (*e.g., a mine*); to take advantage of

sfrutta·tóre -trice *mf* exploiter, developer (*e.g., of an invention*)

sfuggènte *adj* fleeting; receding (*forehead*); shifty (*glance*)

sfuggire *tr* to avoid, flee ‖ *intr* (ESSERE) to flee, escape, get away; (with *dat*) to escape, e.g., **nulla gli sfugge** nothing escapes him; to break, e.g., **sfuggì a una promessa** he broke a promise; **lasciarsi sfuggire** to let slip

sfuggita *f*—**di sfuggita** hastily; incidentally; **dare una sfuggita** to run down (*e.g., to the post office*)

sfumare *tr* to shade down; to tone down; to trim (*hair*) ‖ *intr* (ESSERE) to vanish; to shade

sfumatura *f* nuance, shade; razor clipping

sfumino *m* stump (*in drawing*)

sfuriare §287 *tr* to vent (*one's anger*) ‖ *intr* to rave

sfuriata *f* outburst of anger; gust (*of wind*); **fare una sfuriata a** to give a scolding to

sgabèllo *m* stool, footstool

sgabuzzino *m* cubbyhole

sgambettare (sgambétto) *tr* to trip ‖ *intr* to toddle; to kick (*said of a baby*); to scamper

sgambétto *m* trip, stumble; **dare lo sgambetto a** to trip

sganasciare §128 *tr* to dislocate the jaw of; to break the jaw of; to tear apart ‖ *intr* to steal right and left ‖ *ref* to break one's jaw; **sganasciarsi dalle risa** to split one's sides laughing

sganciare §128 *tr* to unhook; to lay out (*money*); to drop (*bombs*) ‖ *intr* to drop bombs; (coll) to go away ‖ *ref* to get unhooked; (mil) to disengage oneself; **sganciarsi da** to get rid of

sgangherare (sgànghero) *tr* to unhinge; to burst ‖ *ref*—**sgangherarsi dalle risa** to split one's sides laughing

sganghera·to -ta *adj* unhinged; broken down; rickety; coarse (*laughter*)

sgarbatéz·za *f* rudeness, incivility; clumsiness

sgarba·to -ta *adj* rude; clumsy

sgarberìa *f* var of **sgarbatezza**

sgarbo *m*—**fare uno sgarbo a** to be rude to

sgargiante *adj* loud, flashy, showy

sgarrare *intr* to go wrong

sgattaiolare (sgattàiolo) *intr* (ESSERE) to slip away; to wriggle out

sgelare (sgèlo) *tr* & *intr* to thaw, melt

sgèlo *m* thaw

sghém·bo -ba *adj* crooked; **a sghembo** askew || **sghembo** *adv* askew; sideways

sghèrro *m* hired assassin; gendarme

sghiacciare §128 *tr* to thaw

sghignazzare *intr* to guffaw

sghignazzata *f* guffaw

sghimbè·scio -scia *adj*—**a** or **di sghimbescio** askew, crooked

sghiribizzo [ddzz] *m* whim, fancy

sgobbare (sgòbbo) *intr* to drudge, plod, plug

sgobbó·ne -na *mf* plugger, plodder, drudge

sgocciolare (sgócciolo) *tr* to let drip || *intr* to drip (*said of container*) || *intr* (ESSERE) to drip (*said of liquid*)

sgocciola·tóio *m* (-tói) dish rack; drip pan

sgocciolatura *f* dripping; drippings

sgócciolo *m* last drop; **essere agli sgoccioli** to be coming to an end

sgolare (sgólo) *ref* to shout oneself hoarse

sgomberare (sgómbero) *tr* & *intr* var of sgombrare

sgómbero *m* moving

sgombrané·ve *m* (-ve) snowplow (*truck*)

sgombrare (sgómbro) *tr* to clear; to vacate || *intr* to move, vacate

sgóm·bro -bra *adj* clear || *m* moving; (ichth) mackerel

sgomentare (sgoménto) *tr* to frighten; to dismay

sgomén·to -ta *adj* dismayed || *m* dismay; **rimanere di sgomento** to be dismayed

sgominare (sgòmino) *tr* to rout

sgomma·to -ta *adj* unglued; without tires; with poor tires

sgonfiare §287 (sgónfio) *tr* to deflate; to damn with faint praise (*e.g., a play*); (roll) to bore || *intr* (ESSERE) to boast; to balloon || *ref* to go down (*said of swelling*); to go flat (*said of a tire*); (fig) to collapse

sgón·fio -fia *adj* deflated, flat

sgonfiòtto *m* jelly doughnut; puff (*in clothing*)

sgórbia *f* (carp) gouge

sgorbiare §287 (sgòrbio) *tr* to scribble; (carp) to gouge

sgòr·bio *m* (-bi) ink spot; scribble, scrawl

sgorgare §209 (sgórgo) *tr* to unclog || *tur* (ESSERE) to gush

sgottare (sgótto) *tr* to bail out (*a boat*)

sgozzare (sgózzo) *tr* to slaughter; to slit the throat of; (fig) to bleed, fleece

sgradévole *adj* disagreeable, unpleasant

sgradire §176 *tr* to refuse || *intr* to be displeasing

sgradì·to -ta *adj* unpleasant; unwelcome

sgraffignare *tr* to snitch, snatch

sgrammatica·to -ta *adj* ungrammatical

sgranare *tr* to shell (*e.g., peas*); to count (*one's beads*); to seed (*grapes*); to open (*one's eyes*) wide; (mach) to disengage || *ref* to crumble; to scratch oneself

sgranchire §176 *tr* to stretch (*e.g., one's legs*)

sgranocchiare §287 (sgranòcchio) *tr* to crunch, munch

sgrassare *tr* to remove the grease from; to skim (*broth*); to scour (*wool*)

sgravare *tr* to relieve, lighten || *ref* to be relieved; to give birth

sgrà·vio *m* (-vi) lightening, lessening; a **sgravio di coscienza** to ease one's conscience

sgrazia·to -ta *adj* gawky, clumsy

sgretolare (sgrétolo) *tr* & *ref* to crumble

sgretola·to -ta *adj* crumbling, falling down

sgridare *tr* to scold, chide

sgridata *f* scolding; reprimand

sgrondare (sgróndo) *tr* to cause to drip || *intr* to drip, trickle

sgroppare (sgròppo) *tr* to wear (*a horse*) out || *intr* to buck (*said of a horse*)

sgroppare (sgróppo) *tr* to untie

sgrossare (sgròsso) *tr* to rough-hew; (fig) to refine

sgrovigliare §280 *tr* to untangle

sguaiatàggine *f* uncouthness

sguaia·to -ta *adj* crude, vulgar; uncouth || *mf* vulgar person; uncouth person

sguainare *tr* to unsheathe; to show (*one's nails*)

sgualcire §176 *tr* to crumple || *ref* to become crumpled

sgualdrina *f* trollop, strumpet

sguardo *m* glance, look; eyes

sguarnire §176 *tr* to untrim; (mil) to strip, dismantle

sguàtte·ro -ra *mf* dishwasher, scullion || *f* kitchenmaid, scullery maid

sguazzare *tr* to waste, squander || *intr* to splash; to wallow; to be lost (*in shoes too big or clothes too loose*)

sguinzagliare §280 *tr* to unleash, let loose

sgusciare §128 *tr* to shell, hull || *intr* (ESSERE) to slip; **sgusciare di soppiatto** to slip away

shòp·ping *m* (-ping) shopping; shopping bag; **fare lo shopping** to go shopping

shràpnel *m* (shràpnel) shrapnel

si *m* (-si) (mus) si || §5 *pron*

sì *m* (sì) yes; yea; **stare tra il sì e il no** to not be able to make up one's mind; **un . . . sì e l'altro no** every other (*e.g., day*)

sìa *conj* see essere

siamése [s] *adj* & *mf* Siamese

siberia·no -na *adj* & *mf* Siberian

sibilante *adj* & *f* sibilant

sibilare (sìbilo) *intr* to hiss

sibilla *f* sibyl

sibilo *m* hiss, hissing

sicà·rio -ria (-ri) hired assassin

sicché *conj* so that

siccità *f* drought

siccóme *adv* as || *conj* since; as; how

Sicìlia, la Sicily

sicilia·no -na *adj* & *mf* Sicilian

sicomòro *m* sycamore

sicumèra *f* cocksureness, overconfidence

sicura *f* safety lock (*on gun*)

sicurézza f security; assurance; safety; certainty; reliability; **di sicurezza** safety; **sicurezza sociale** social security

sicu·ro -ra adj sure; safe; steady; **di sicuro** certainly ‖ m safety; **camminare sul sicuro** to take no chances ‖ **sicuro** adv certainly ‖ f see **sicura**

sicur·tà f (-tà) insurance

siderale adj sidereal

sidère·o -a adj sidereal

siderùrgi·co -ca (-ci -che) adj iron-and-steel ‖ m iron-and-steel worker

sidro m cider, hard cider

sièpe f hedge; (fig) wall

sièro m serum

sièsta f siesta; **fare la siesta** to take a nap, take a siesta

siffat·to -ta adj such

sifìlide f syphilis

sifóne m siphon; siphon bottle; trap

siga·ràio -ràia (-rài -ràie) mf cigar maker ‖ m (ent) grape hopper; ‖ f cigarette girl

sigarétta f cigarette

sìgaro m cigar

sigillare tr to seal

sigillo m seal; **avere il sigillo alle labbra** to have one's lips sealed; **sigillo sacramentale** seal of confession

sigla f acronym; initials; abbreviation; letterword; **sigla musicale** theme song

siglare tr to initial

significare §197 (**significo**) tr to mean; to signify; **significare qlco a qlcu** to inform s.o. of s.th

significati·vo -va adj significant; meaningful

significato m meaning; **senza significato** meaningless

signóra f Madam, Mrs.; lady; mistress, owner; wife ‖ **Nostra Signora** Our Lady

signóre m sir, Mr.; gentleman; rich man; lord, master, owner; man; **il signore desidera?** what is your pleasure?; **per signori** stag ‖ **Signore** m Lord

signoreggiare §290 (**signoréggio**) tr to rule over; to master; to tower over; to overshadow ‖ intr to be the master

signorìa f seigniory; rule; **La Signoria Vostra** your Honor; **Sua Signoria** his Lordship; your Lordship

signorìle adj seigniorial; gentlemanly; ladylike; elegant, refined

signorìna f miss; Miss; young lady; spinster

signorìno m master, young gentleman

signornò adv no, Sir

signoró·ne -na mf (coll) rich person

signoròtto m lordling

signorsì adv yes, Sir

silenziatóre m silencer (of firearm); (aut) muffler

silèn·zio m (-zi) silence; (mil) taps; **fare silenzio** to be silent; **ridurre al silenzio** (mil) to silence

silenzió·so -sa [s] adj silent; noiseless

sìlfide f sylphid

sìlfo m sylph

silhouèt·te f (-te) silhouette

sìlice f silica

silìcio m silicon

silicóne m silicone

siliquastro m redbud

sìllaba f syllable

sillabare (**sìllabo**) tr to syllabify; **to spell**

sillabà·rio m (-ri) reader, primer

sìllabo m syllabus

silo m silo

silòfono m xylophone

siluétta f silhouette

silurante adj torpedoing, torpedo ‖ f destroyer; torpedo boat

silurare tr to torpedo; (fig) to fire, dismiss; (fig) to undermine

siluro m torpedo

silva·no -na adj sylvan

silvèstre adj (lit) sylvan; (lit) wild; (lit) hard, arduous

simboleggiare §290 (**simboléggio**) tr to symbolize

simbòli·co -ca adj (-ci -che) symbolic

simbolismo m symbolism

sìmbolo m symbol

similari·tà f (-tà) similarity

sìmile adj similar; such ‖ m like; **i propri simili** fellow men

similòro m tombac

simmetrìa f symmetry

simmètri·co -ca adj (-ci -che) symmetrical

simonìa f simony

simpamina f benzedrine

simpatèti·co -ca adj (-ci -che) sympathetic

simpatìa f like, liking; **cattivarsi la simpatia di** to make oneself well liked by

simpàti·co -ca (-ci -che) adj nice, pleasant, congenial ‖ m (anat) sympathetic system

simpatizzante [ddzz] adj sympathizing ‖ mf sympathizer

simpatizzare [ddzz] intr to sympathize; to become friends

simpò·sio m (-si) symposium

simulare (**simulo**) tr to simulate

simula·tóre -trice mf faker, impostor ‖ m simulator

simultàne·o -a adj simultaneous

sin- pref adj syn-, e.g., **sinonimo** synonymous ‖ pref m & f syn-, e.g., **sinonimo** synonym

sin adv—**sin da** ever since

sinagò·ga f (-ghe) synagogue

sincerare (**sincèro**) tr (lit) to convince ‖ ref—**sincerarsi di** to ascertain

sincè·ro -ra adj sincere; pure

sinché conj until

sìncope f fainting spell; (phonet) syncope; (mus) syncopation

sincronismo m syncronism; **sincronismo orrizzontale** (telv) horizontal hold; **sincronismo verticale** (telv) vertical hold

sincronizzare [ddzz] tr to syncronize

sìncro·no -na adj syncronous

sindacale adj mayoral; union

sindacalismo m trade unionism

sindacali·sta mf (-sti -ste) union member; union leader

sindacare §197 (sìndaco) *tr* to criticize; to scrutinize

sindaca·to -ta *adj* controlled, scrutinized || *m* control; labor union; syndicate; **sindacato giallo** company union

sìnda·co *m* (-ci) mayor; controller; auditor

sinecura *f* sinecure

sinfonìa *f* symphony; (*of an opera*) overture; (*coll*) racket (*noise*)

sinfòni·co -ca *adj* (-ci -che) symphonic

singhiozzare (singhiózzo) *intr* to sob; to hiccup; to jerk

singhiòzzo *m* sob; hiccups; **a singhiozzo** in jerks; by fits and spurts

singolare *adj* singular || *m* singular; (*tennis*) singles

sìngo·lo -la *adj* single || *m* individual; shell for one oarsman; (*rr*) roomette; (*telp*) private line; (*tennis*) singles

singulto *m* hiccups; sob

sinistra *f* left hand; left

sinistrare *tr* to ruin; to damage

sinistra·to -ta *adj* injured, damaged, ruined || *mf* victim (*of bombing or flood*)

sinistrismo *m* leftism

sinistri·sta *adj* (-sti -ste) leftish, leftist

sini·stro -stra *adj* left; sinister || *m* accident; (boxing) left || *f* see **sinistra**

sinistròide *adj* & *mf* leftist

sino *adv* var of **fino**

sinologìa *f* Sinology

sinòni·mo -ma *adj* synonymous || *m* synonym

sinò·psi *f* (-psi) (*mov*) synopsis

sinóra *adv* var of **finora**

sinòs·si *f* (-si) synopsis

sinòtti·co -ca *adj* (-ci -che) synoptic(al)

sintas·si *f* (-si) syntax

sìnte·si *f* (-si) synthesis

sintèti·co -ca *adj* (-ci -che) synthetic(al); concise

sintetizzare [ddzz] *tr* to synthesize

sintogram·ma *m* (-mi) (*rad*) dial

sìntomo *m* symptom

sintonìa *f* harmony; (*rad*) tuning

sintonizzare [ddzz] *tr* (*rad*) to tune

sintonizzatóre [ddzz] *m* (*rad*) tuner

sinuó·so -sa [*s*] *adj* sinuous, winding

sionismo *m* Zionism

sipà·rio *m* (-ri) curtain; **sipario di ferro** iron curtain

sirèna *f* siren; mermaid; **sirena da nebbia** foghorn

Sìria, la Syria

siria·no -na *adj* & *mf* Syrian

sirin·ga *f* (-ghe) panpipe; syringe; catheter; grease gun; (*orn*) syrinx

siringare §209 *tr* to catheterize

siròcchia *f* (obs) sister

si·sma *m* (-smi) earthquake

sismògrafo *m* seismograph

sismologìa *f* seismology

sissignóre *adv* yes, Sir!

sistè·ma *m* (-mi) system

sistemare (sistèmo) *tr* to arrange; to put in order; to systematize; to settle; to find a job for; to find a husband for; (coll) to fix || *ref* to settle; to get married

sistemazióne *f* arrangement; settlement; job, position

sìstole *f* systole

sitibón·do -da *adj* (lit) thirsty

si·to -ta *adj* (lit) located || *m* (lit) site, spot, location; (mil) sight; (coll) musty odor

situare (sìtuo) *tr* to locate, place, situate

situazióne *f* situation; condition

slabbrare *tr* to chip; to open (*a wound*) || *intr* to overflow || *ref* to become chipped; to reopen (*said of a cut*)

slacciare §128 *tr* to untie; to unfasten; to unbutton || *ref* to get undone; to get unbuttoned

sladinare *tr* (sports) to train; (mach) to run in, break in

slanciare §128 *tr* to hurl, throw || *ref* to hurl oneself; to rise (*said, e.g., of a tower*)

slancia·to -ta *adj* slender; soaring

slàn·cio *m* (-ci) leap; outburst (*of feeling*); momentum; **di slancio** with a rush; **prendere lo slancio** to get a running start

slargare §209 *tr* to widen; to warm (*the heart*) || *ref* to widen, spread out

slattare *tr* to wean

slava·to -ta *adj* pale, washed out

sla·vo -va *adj* Slav, Slavic || *mf* Slav || *m* Slavic (*language*)

sleale *adj* disloyal; unfair (*competition*)

sleal·tà *f* (-tà) disloyalty

slegare §209 (slégo) *tr* to untie

slega·to -ta *adj* untied; disconnected

slip *m* (slip) briefs; tank suit, bathing suit (*for men*)

slitta *f* sled, sleigh; (mach) carriage

slittaménto *m* skid; slide

slittare *intr* to sled; to skid; to slide

slogare §209 (slògo) *tr* to dislocate || *ref* to become dislocated; to dislocate (*e.g., an arm*)

slogatura *f* dislocation

sloggiare §290 (slòggio) *tr* to dislodge; to evict || *intr* to vacate

slòg·gio *m* (-gi) moving; eviction

slovac·co -ca *adj* & *mf* (-chi -che) Slovak

smacchiare §287 *tr* to clean; to deforest

smacchia·tóre -trice *mf* cleaner || *m* cleaning fluid; spot remover

smac·co *m* (-chi) letdown; slap in the face

smagliante *adj* dazzling, shining

smagliare §280 *tr* to break the links of; to undo the meshes of; to remove (*a fish*) from the net || *intr* to shine, dazzle || *ref* to run (*said, e.g., of knitted fabric*); to free itself from the net

smagliatura *f* run (*in stockings*); (fig) break

smagrire §176 *tr* to impoverish || *intr* (ESSERE) & *ref* to become thin or lean

smaliziare §287 *tr* to make wiser || *ref* to get wiser

smaltare *tr* to enamel; to glaze

smaltire §176 *tr* to digest; to sleep off (*a drunk*); to swallow (*an offense*);

to sell off; to get rid of; to drain off (*water*)

smalti-tóio *m* (**-tói**) drain, sewer

smalto *m* enamel; **smalto per le unghie** nail polish

smancerìe *fpl* affectation; mawkishness

smanceró·so -sa [s] *adj* prissy

smangiare §290 *tr* to erode, eat away || *ref* to be consumed (*e.g., by hatred*)

smània *f* frenzy; craze, yearning; **dare in smanie** to be in a frenzy

smaniare §287 *intr* to be delirious; to yearn, crave

smanió·so -sa [s] *adj* eager; disturbing

smantellare (**smantèllo**) *tr* to dismantle; to demolish; to disable (*a ship*)

smargias·so -sa *mf* braggart, boaster

smarriménto *m* loss; bewilderment; discouragement

smarrire §176 *tr* to lose || *ref* to get lost; to get discouraged

smascellare (**smascèllo**) *ref*—**smascellarsi dalle risa** to split one's sides laughing

smascherare (**smàschero**) *tr* & *ref* to unmask

smazzata *f* (cards) deal; (cards) hand

smembraménto *m* dismemberment

smembrare (**smèmbro**) *tr* to dismember

smemoratàggine *f* forgetfulness

smemora-to -ta *adj* absent-minded; forgetful || *mf* absent-minded or forgetful person

smentire §176 *tr* to belie; to refute; to retract; to be untrue to || *ref* to not be consistent, to contradict oneself

smentita *f* denial; retraction

smeraldo *m* emerald

smerciare §128 (**smèrcio**) *tr* to sell, sell out

smèr·cio *m* (**-ci**) sale

smèr·go *m* (**-ghi**) (zool) merganser

smerigliare §280 *tr* to grind, polish; to sand

smeriglia·to -ta *adj* polished; sand (*paper*); emery (*cloth*); frosted (*glass*)

smerì·glio *m* (**-gli**) emery; (orn) merlin; (ichth) porbeagle

smerlare (**smèrlo**) *tr* to scallop

smèrlo *m* scallop (*along the edge of a garment*)

smés·so -sa *adj* hand-me-down, castoff

sméttere §198 *tr* to stop; to stop wearing; to break up (*housekeeping*); **smetterla** to cut it out || *intr*—**smettere di** + *inf* to stop + *ger*

smezzare [ddzz] (**smèzzo**) *tr* to halve

smidollare (**smidòllo**) *tr* to remove the marrow from; (fig) to emasculate

smilitarizzare [ddzz] *tr* to demilitarize

smil·zo -za *adj* slender; poor, worthless

sminare *tr* to remove mines from

sminuire §176 *tr* to belittle

sminuzzare *tr* to crumble; to mince; to expatiate on || *ref* to crumble

smistaménto *m* sorting (*of mail*); (rr) shunting, shifting

smistare *tr* to sort; (rr) to shift; (soccer) to pass; (rad) to unscramble

smisura-to -ta *adj* immense, huge

smitizzante [ddzz] *adj* debunking, demythologizing

smitizzare [ddzz] *tr* to debunk; to demythologize

smobiliare §287 *tr* to remove the furniture from

smobilizzare (**smobìlito**) *tr* to demobilize

smobilitazióne *f* demobilization

smoccolare (**smòccolo** & **smóccolo**) *tr* to snuff (*a candle*) || *intr* (slang) to swear, curse

smoda-to -ta *adj* excessive, immoderate

smòg *m* smog

smóking *m* (**smóking**) dinner jacket, tuxedo

smontàbile *adj* dismountable

smontàg-gio *m* (**-gi**) disassembling, dismantling

smontare (**smónto**) *tr* to take apart; to dismantle; to cause (*e.g., whipped cream*) to fall; to take (*a precious stone*) out of its setting; to dishearten; to dissuade; to drop (*s.o.*) off; **smontare la guardia** to come off guard duty || *intr* (ESSERE) to dismount; to get off or out (*of a conveyance*); to fade; to drop (*said, e.g., of beaten eggs*) || *ref* to become downcast

smòrfia *f* grimace; mawkishness; **fare le smorfie a** to make faces at

smorfió·so -sa [s] *adj* mawkish, prissy

smòr·to -ta *adj* pale, wan; faded

smorzare (**smòrzo**) *tr* to attenuate; to lessen; to tone down; to turn off (*light*); (phys) to dampen

smorzatóre *m* (mus) damper

smòs·so -sa *adj* moved; loose

smottaménto *m* mud slide

smozzicare §197 (**smózzico**) *tr* to crumble; to mince; to clip, mince (*one's words*)

smun·to -ta *adj* emaciated, pale, wan

smuòvere §202 *tr* to budge; to till; (fig) to move || *ref* to budge; to move away; **smuoviti!** get going!

smussare *tr* to blunt; to bevel; (fig) to soften

snaturalizzare [ddzz] *tr* to denaturalize; to denationalize

snaturare *tr* to change the nature of; to distort, misrepresent

snatura-to -ta *adj* distorted; monstrous, unnatural

snebbiare §287 (**snébbio**) *tr* to drive the fog from; to clear (*e.g., one's mind*)

snellézza *f* slenderness; nimbleness

snellire §176 *tr* & *ref* to slenderize

snèl·lo -la *adj* slender; nimble; lively

snervante (**snèrvo**) *adj* enervating

snervare (**snèrvo**) *tr* to enervate, prostrate || *ref* to become enervated

snidare *tr* to drive out, flush

snòb *adj invar* snobbish || *mf* (**snòb**) snob

snobbare (**snòbbo**) *tr* to snub, slight

snobismo *m* snobbishness, snobbery

snobìsti·co -ca *adj* (**-ci -che**) snobbish

snocciolare (**snòcciolo**) *tr* to spill (*a secret*); to peel off (*sums of money*); to pit, stone (*fruit*)

snodare (**snòdo**) *tr* to untie; to limber up; to exercise; to loosen up (*e.g.,* *s.o.'s tongue*) || *ref* to become loose; to wind (*said, e.g., of a road*)

snòdo *m* (mach) joint; **a snodo** flexible

soave *adj* sweet, gentle

sobbalzare *intr* to jerk, jolt

sobbalzo *m* jerk, jolt; **di sobbalzo** with a jolt

sobbarcare §197 *tr* to overburden || *ref* —**sobbarcarsi a** to take it upon oneself to

sobbór·go *m* (-ghi) suburb

sobillare *tr* to instigate, stir up

sobilla·tóre -trice *mf* instigator

sobrietà *f* sobriety, temperance

sò·brio -bria *adj* sober, temperate; plain

socchiùdere §125 *tr* to half-shut; to leave ajar

socchiu·so -sa [s] *adj* ajar

soccómbere §186 *intr* to succumb

soccórrere §139 *tr* to help || *intr* (lit) to occur

soccórso *m* help, succor; **mancato soccorso** failure to render assistance; hit-and-run driving

sociale *adj* social; company (*e.g., outing*)

socialismo *m* socialism

sociali·sta (-sti -ste) *adj* socialistic || *mf* socialist

sociali·tà *f* (-tà) gregariousness; social responsibility

socie·tà *f* (-tà) society; company; **in società** in partnership; **società anonima** corporation; **società a responsabilità limitata** limited company; **Società delle Nazioni** League of Nations; **società finanziaria** holding company; **società in accomandita** limited partnership; **società per azioni** corporation

sociévole *adj* sociable; gregarious

sò·cio *m* (-ci) member; cardholder; partner; shareholder; **socio fondatore** charter member; **socio sostenitore** patron, sustaining member

sociologìa *f* sociology

sociòlo·go -ga *mf* (-gi -ghe) sociologist

sòda *f* soda

sodalì·zio *m* (-zi) society; brotherhood, fraternity; friendship

soddisfacènte *adj* satisfying, satisfactory

soddisfare §173 (*2d sg pres ind* **soddisfài** *or* **soddisfi**; *3d pl pres* **soddisfanno** *or* **soddisfano**; *1st, 2d & 3d sg pres subj* **soddisfaccia** *or* **soddisfi**; *3d pl pres subj* **soddisfàcciano** *or* **soddisfino**) *tr* to satisfy || *intr* (with *dat*) to satisfy || *ref* to be satisfied

soddisfat·to -ta *adj* satisfied

soddisfazióne *f* satisfaction

sòdi·co -ca *adj* (-ci -che) sodium

sòdio *m* sodium

sò·do -da *adj* hard; hard-boiled; stubborn; solid; **prenderle sode** to get a good thrashing || *m* hard ground; untilled soil; solid foundation; **venire al sodo** to come to the point; **mettere in sodo** to ascertain || *f* see **soda** || *sodo adv* hard

sodomìa *f* sodomy

so·fà *m* (-fà) couch, sofa; **sofà a letto** sofa bed

sofferènte *adj* sickly, ailing; (lit) long-suffering

sofferènza *f* suffering, pain; bad debt; **in sofferenza** overdue

soffermare (**sofférmo**) *tr*—**soffermare il passo** to come to a stop || *ref* to linger, pause

soffiare §287 (**sóffio**) *tr* to blow; to whisper; (checkers) to huff; (coll) to steal || *intr* to blow; to bellow; (slang) to squeal (*about somebody's offense*); **soffiare sul fuoco** to stir up trouble || *ref* to blow (*one's nose*)

soffia·to -ta *adj* blown || *m* soufflé || *f* (slang) squealing, **darsi una soffiata di naso** to blow one's nose

soffiatóre *m* glass blower

sòffice *adj* soft

soffierìa *f* glass factory; blower

soffiétto *m* bellows; hood (*of carriage*); (journ) puff, ballyhoo

sóf·fio *m* (-fi) blow; breath; **in un soffio** in a jiffy; **soffio al cuore** heart murmur

soffióne *m* blowpipe; fumarole; (bot) dandelion; (coll) spy

soffitta *f* attic, garret

soffitto *m* ceiling

soffocaménto *m* choking

soffocante *adj* stifling; oppressive

soffocare §197 (**sòffoco**) *tr* to choke; to stifle; to suffocate; to smother; to repress

sòffo·co *m* (-chi) sultriness

soffóndere §178 *tr* (lit) to suffuse

soffregare §209 (**soffrégo**) *tr* to rub lightly

soffriggere §180 *tr* to fry lightly || *intr* to mutter

soffrire §207 *tr* to suffer; to endure; **non poter soffrire** to not be able to stand || *intr* to suffer; to ail; **soffrire di** to be troubled with

soffritto *m* fried onions and bacon

sofistica·to -ta *adj* adulterated; sophisticated, stunded

sofisti·co -ca *adj* (-ci -che) sophistic; faultfinding || *f* sophistry

soggetti·sta *mf* (-sti -ste) scriptwriter

soggetti·vo -va *adj* subjective

soggèt·to -ta *adj* subject || *m* subject; (coll) character; (law) person; **cattivo soggetto** hoodlum; **recitare a soggetto** to improvise

soggezióne *f* subjection; awe, embarrassment; **mettere a soggezione** to awe

sogghignare *intr* to sneer

soggiacére §181 *intr* (ESSERE & AVERE) to be subject; to succumb

soggiogare §209 (**soggiógo**) *tr* to subjugate, subdue

soggiornare (**soggiórno**) *intr* to sojourn, stay

soggiórno *m* sojourn, stay; living room; sitting room (*in hotel*)

soggiùngere §183 *tr* to add

soggólo *m* wimple (*of nun*); throat-latch (*on horse*); (mil) chin strap

sòglia *f* doorsill; threshhold

sògliola *f* sole

sognare (**sógno**) *tr* to dream of || *intr*

to dream; **sognare ad occhi aperti** to daydream

sogna·tóre -trice *adj* dreaming || *mf* dreamer

sógno *m* dream; **nemmeno per sogno** (coll) by no means

sòia *f* (bot) soy

sòl *m* (sòl) (mus) sol

so·làio m (**-lài**) attic, loft; (agr) crib

solare *adj* solar; bright; clear || *v* §257 *tr* to sole

solàr·rio m (**-ri**) solarium

solati·o -a (**-i -e**) *adj* sunny || *m*—**a solatio** with a southern exposure

solcare §197 (**sólco**) *tr* to furrow; to plow (*the waves*)

sól·co m (**-chi**) furrow; rut; groove (*of phonograph record*); (fig) path; (naut) wake

solcòmetro *m* (naut) log

soldaté·sco -sca (**-schi -sche**) *adj* soldier || *f* soldiery; soldiers; undisciplined troops

soldatino *m* toy soldier

soldato *m* soldier; **andare soldato** to enlist; **soldato di ventura** soldier of fortune; **soldato scelto** private first class; **soldato semplice** private

sòldo *m* soldo (*Italian coin*); coin; money; (mil) pay; (fig) penny; **a soldo a soldo** a penny at a time; **al soldo di** in the pay of; **tirare al soldo** to be a tightwad

sóle *m* sun; sunshine; (fig) day, daytime; **sole artificiale** sun lamp; **sole a scacchi** (joc) hoosegow, calaboose

soleggia·to -ta *adj* sunny

solènne *adj* solemn; (joc) first-class

solenni·tà *f* (**-tà**) solemnity

solennizzare [ddzz] *tr* to solemnize

solére §255 *intr* (ESSERE) + *inf* to be accustomed to + *inf*, *e.g.*, **suole arrivare alle sette** he is accustomed to arrive at seven || *impers* (ESSERE) —**suole** + *inf* it generally + *3d sg ind*, *e.g.*, **suole nevicare** it generally snows

solèrte *adj* (lit) diligent, industrious

solèrzia *f* (lit) diligence

solét·to -ta *adj* (lit) alone, lonely || *f* sole; inner sole; (archit) slab, cement slab

sòlfa *f* (mus) solfeggio; **la solita solfa** the same old story

solfanèllo *m* var of **zofanello**

solfara *f* sulfur mine

solfato *m* sulfate

solfeggiare §290 (**solféggio**) *tr* to sol-fa

solfiè·ro -ra *adj* sulfur

solfito *m* sulfite

sólfo *m* var of **zolfo**

solfòri·co -ca *adj* (**-ci -che**) sulfuric

solforó·so -sa [s] *adj* sulfurous

solfuro *m* sulfide

solidale *adj* solidary; (law) joint; (law) jointly responsible; (mach) built-in; **solidale con** integral with

solidarie·tà *f* (**-tà**) solidarity; (law) joint liability

solidarizzare [ddzz] *intr* to make common cause, become united

solidificare §197 (**solidìfico**) *tr* to solidify; to settle

solidi·tà *f* (**-tà**) solidity; (fig) soundness

sòli·do -da *adj* solid; (law) joint || *m* solid; **in solido** jointly

solilò·quio m (**-qui**) soliloquy

solin·go -ga *adj* (**-ghi -ghe**) (lit) lonely; (lit) solitary (*enjoying solitude*)

solino *m* detachable collar; **solino duro** stiff collar

soli·sta *mf* (**-sti -ste**) soloist

solità·rio -ria (**-ri -rie**) *adj* solitary, lonely || *m* solitaire; solitary

sòli·to -ta *adj* usual, customary; **esser solito** to be accustomed to || *m* habit, custom; **come il solito** as usual; **di solito** usually

solitùdine *f* solitude, loneliness

sollazzare *tr* to amuse || *ref* to have a good time, amuse oneself

sollazzo *m* (lit) amusement; **essere il sollazzo di** to be the laughingstock of

sollecitare (**sollécito**) *tr* to solicit; to urge; to induce; (mach) to stress || *intr & ref* to hasten

sollecitazióne *f* solicitation; urging; (mach) stress

solléci·to -ta *adj* quick, prompt; diligent; solicitous, anxious || *m* (com) solicitation, urging

sollecitùdine *f* solicitude; promptness; diligence; **cortese sollecitudine** (com) prompt attention

solleóne *m* dog days

solleticare §197 (**sollético**) *tr* to tickle; (fig) to flatter

solléti·co m (**-chi**) tickling; stimulation; **fare il solletico a** to tickle

sollevaménto *m* lifting; **sollevamento di pesi** weight lifting

sollevare (**sollèvo**) *tr* to lift; to relieve; to pick up; to raise (*e.g., a question*); to excite; to elevate || *ref* to rise; to lift oneself; to pick up (*said of courage or health*)

sollevazióne *f* uprising

sollièvo *m* relief

sollùchero *m*—**andare in solluchero** to become ecstatic; **mandare in solluchero** to thrill

só·lo -la *adj* lone, lonely, alone; only; single; **fare da solo** to operate all by oneself; **solo soletto** all by myself (yourself, himself, etc.); within oneself; **un solo** only one || *m* (mus) solo || **solo** *adv* only || **solo** *conj* only; **solo che** provided that

solstì·zio m (**-zi**) solstice

soltanto *adv* only

solùbile *adj* soluble

soluzióne *f* solution; installment; **soluzione di comodo** compromise; **soluzione provvisoria** stopgap

solvènte *adj & m* solvent

solvènza *f* solvency

solvìbile *adj* collectable; solvent

sòma *f* burden, load

Somàlia, la Somaliland

sòma·lo -la *adj & mf* Somali

soma·ro -ra *mf* donkey, ass

someggia·to -ta *adj* carried by pack animal; carried on mule back

somigliante *adj* similar; **essere somigliante a** to look like || *m* same thing

somiglianza *f* similarity, resemblance

somigliare §280 *tr* to resemble; (lit) to compare ‖ *intr* (ESSERE & AVERE) (with *dat*) to resemble; to seem to be ‖ *ref* to resemble each other

sómma *f* addition; sum; summary

sommare (sómmo) *tr* to add; to consider; **tutto sommato** all in all ‖ *intr* to amount

sommà·rio -ria (-ri -rie) *adj* summary ‖ *m* summary; abstract; (journ) subheading

sommèrgere §162 *tr* to submerge; (fig) to plunge; (fig) to flood (*with insults*) ‖ *ref* to submerge

sommergìbile *adj & m* submarine

sommés·so -sa *adj* submissive; subdued (*voice*)

somministrare *tr* to administer; to provide; to deliver (*a blow*); to adduce (*proof*)

somministrazióne *f* administration; provision

sommi·tà *f* (-tà) summit

sóm·mo -ma *adj* highest; supreme ‖ *m* top; peak, summit ‖ *f* see **somma**

sommòssa *f* insurrection, riot

sommoviménto *m* tremor (*of earth*); arousal (*of passions*); riot

sommozzatóre *m* skin diver; (nav) frogman

sommuòvere §202 *tr* (lit) to agitate; (lit) to stir up, excite

sonaglièra *f* collar with bells

sonà·glio *m* (-gli) bell; rattle; raindrop; pitter-patter (*of the rain*)

sonante *adj* ringing, sounding; ready (*cash*)

sonare §257 *tr* to sound; to play; to strike (*the hour*); to ring (*a bell*); (coll) to dupe, cheat; (coll) to give a sound thrashing to; **sonare le campane a distesa** to ring a full peal ‖ *intr* (ESSERE & AVERE) to play; to ring (*said of a bell*); to sound; (lit) to spread (*said of reputation*)

sona·to -ta *adj* played; past, e.g., **le tre sonate** past three o'clock; **cinquant'anni sonati** past fifty years of age ‖ *f* ring (*of bell*); (mus) sonata; (coll) thrashing; (coll) cheating

sona·tóre -trice *mf* (mus) player

sónda *f* sound; probe; drill

sondàg·gio *m* (-gi) sounding; probe; drilling; **sondaggio d'opinioni** opinion survey, public opinion poll

sondare (sóndo) *tr* to sound; to probe; to drill; to survey (*public opinion*)

soneria *f* alarm (*of clock*)

sonétto *m* sonnet

sonnacchió·so -sa [s] *adj* sleepy, drowsy

sonnàmbu·lo -la *mf* sleepwalker

sonnecchiare §287 (sonnécchio) *intr* to drowse, take a nap; to nap, nod

sonnellino *m* nap

sonnìfe·ro -ra *adj* soporific; narcotic ‖ *m* sleeping medicine; narcotic

sónno *m* sleep; (lit) dream; **aver sonno** to be sleepy; **far venir sonno a** to bore; **prender sonno** to fall asleep

sonnolèn·to -ta *adj* sleepy; lazy

sonnolènza *f* drowsiness; laziness

sonori·tà *f* (-tà) sonority; acoustics

sonorizzare [ddzz] *tr* to voice; (mov) to dub ‖ *ref* to voice

sonò·ro -ra *adj* sound (*wave*); sonorous; (phonet) sonant, voiced

sontuó·so -sa [s] *adj* sumptuous

sopèr·chio -chia *adj & m* (-chi -chie) var of **soverchio**

sopire §176 *tr* to appease, calm

sopóre *m* drowsiness

soporìfe·ro -ra *adj* soporific

soppanno *m* interlining; lining (*of shoes*)

sopperire §176 *intr*—**sopperire a** to provide for; to make up for

soppesare [s] (soppéso) *tr* to heft; (fig) to weigh

soppiantare *tr* to supplant by scheming; to kick out; to replace; to trick

soppiatto *m*—**di soppiatto** stealthily

sopportàbile *adj* bearable, tolerable

sopportare (soppòrto) *tr* to bear, support; to suffer, endure

sopportazióne *f* forbearance, endurance

soppressióne *f* suppression, abolition

sopprìmere §131 *tr* to suppress, do away with

sópra *adj invar* upper; above, preceding ‖ *m* upper, upper part; **al di sopra** above; **al di sopra di** above, over; beyond; **di sopra** upper ‖ *adv* above; up; on top ‖ *prep* on; upon; on top of; over; beyond; above; versus; **sopra pensiero** absorbed in thought

sopràbito *m* overcoat, topcoat

sopraccàri·co -ca (-chi -che) *adj* overburdened ‖ *m* overload; overweight; (naut) supercargo

sopraccenna·to -ta *adj* above-mentioned

sopracci·glio *m* (-gli & -glia *fpl*) brow, eyebrow; window frame

sopraccita·to -ta *adj* above-mentioned

sopraccopèrta *f* bedspread; book jacket, dust jacket ‖ *adv* (naut) on deck

sopraddét·to -ta *adj* above-mentioned

sopraffare §173 *tr* to overcome, overpower

sopraffazióne *f* overpowering; abuse

sopraffinèstra *f* transom window

sopraffì·no -na *adj* first-class; superfine

sopraggitto *m* (sew) overcasting

sopraggiùngere §183 *intr* (ESSERE) to arrive; to happen

sopraintèndere §270 *tr* var of **soprintendere**

sopralluò·go *m* (-ghi) inspection, investigation on the spot

sopralzo *m* var of **soprelevazione**

soprammercato *m*—**per soprammercato** in addition, to boot

soprammòbile *m* knicknack

soprannaturale *adj & m* supernatural

soprannóme *m* nickname

soprannominare (soprannòmino) *tr* to nickname

soprannùmero *adj invar* in excess; overtime ‖ *m*—**in soprannumero** extra; in excess

sopra·no -na *adj* upper; (lit) supreme

|| **sopra·no** *mf* (**-ni -ne**) soprano (*person*) || *m* soprano (*voice*)

soprappensièro *adj invar & adv* immersed in thought

soprappéso [s] *m*—**per soprappeso** besides, into the bargain

soprap·più *m* (**-più**) plus, extra; **in soprappiù** besides, into the bargain

soprapprèzzo *m* extra charge, surcharge

soprascarpa *f* overshoe

soprascrit·to -ta *adj* written above || *f* address

soprassalto *m* start, jump; **di soprassalto** with a start

soprassedére §252 *intr* to wait; (with *dat*) to postpone

soprassòldo *m* extra pay; (mil) war-zone indemnity

soprastare §263 *intr* (ESSERE) to be the boss

soprattac·co *m* (**-chi**) rubber heel

soprattassa *f* surtax; surcharge

soprattutto *adv* above all, especially

sopravanzare *tr* to overcome || *intr* (ESSERE) to be left over

sopravanzo *m* surplus

sopravvalutare *tr* to overrate

sopravvenire §282 *tr* (lit) to overrun || *intr* (ESSERE) to arrive; to happen, occur; (with *dat*) to befall

sopravvènto *m* windward; **avere il sopravvento** to have the upper hand || *adv* windward

sopravvissu·to -ta *adj* surviving || *mf* survivor

sopravvivènza *f* survival

sopravvivere §286 *intr* (ESSERE) to survive; (with *dat*) to survive, to outlive

soprelevare (**soprelèvo**) *tr* to elevate (*e.g., a railroad*); to increase the height of (*building*)

soprelevazióne *f* elevation; addition of one or more floors

soprintendènte *m* superintendent

soprintendènza *f* superintendency

soprintèndere §270 *tr* to oversee

sopròsso *m* (coll) bony outgrowth

sopruso *m* abuse of power

soqquadro *m*—**a soqquadro** upside down, topsy-turvy

sòrba *f* sorb apple; (coll) hit, blow

sorbettièra *f* ice-cream freezer

sorbétto *m* ice cream; sherbet

sorbire §176 *tr* to sip; (fig) to swallow, endure

sòrbo *m* sorb; service tree

sór·cio *m* (**-ci**) mouse

sòrdi·do -da *adj* sordid; dirty

sordina *f* (mus) sordino, mute; (mus) soft pedal; **in sordina** quietly; stealthily; **mettere in sordina** (mus) to muffle

sór·do -da *adj* deaf; dull (*pain*); deep-seated (*hatred*); hollow (*sound*); (phonet) surd, voiceless; **sordo come una campana** stone-deaf || *mf* deaf person

sordomu·to -ta *adj* deaf and dumb || *mf* deafmute

sorèlla *f* sister

sorellastra *f* stepsister

sorgènte *adj* rising || *f* spring; well (*of oil*); (fig) source; **sorgente del fiume** riverhead

sórgere §258 *intr* (ESSERE) to rise; to arise; to spring forth; **sorgere su un'ancora** (naut) to lie at anchor

sorgi·vo -va *adj* spring (*water*)

sór·go *m* (**-ghi**) sorghum

sormontare (**sormónto**) *tr* to surmount; to overcome || *intr* to fit

sornió·ne -na *adj* cunning, sly || *m* sneak

sorpassare *tr* to get ahead of; to surpass; to overstep; to go above

sorpasso *m* (aut) passing

sorprendènte *adj* surprising, astonishing

sorprèndere §220 *tr* to surprise; to catch; **sorprendere la buona fede di** to take advantage of || *ref* to be surprised

sorprésa [s] *f* surprise; surprise investigation; **di sorpresa** suddenly; unprepared; by surprise

sorrèggere §226 *tr* to sustain, support; to bolster

sorrìdere §231 *tr* (lit) to say with a smile || *intr* to smile; **sorridere a** to appeal to, e.g., **le sorride l'idea di questa gita** the idea of this trip appeals to her; to smile upon, e.g., **gli sorrideva la vita** life was smiling upon him

sorriso [s] *m* smile

sorsata *f* gulp, draught

sorseggiare §290 (**sorséggio**) *tr* to sip

sórso *m* sip; **a sorso a sorso** sipping

sòrta *f* kind, sort

sòrte *f* luck, lot, fate; chance; kind; (com) principal; **per sorte** of each kind; by chance; **tirare a sorte** to cast lots

sorteggiare §290 (**sortéggio**) *tr* to choose by lot; to raffle; **sorteggiare un premio** to draw a prize

sortég·gio *m* (**-gi**) drawing

sortilè·gio *m* (**-gi**) sortilege; sorcery, magic

sortire §176 *tr* (lit) to get by lot; (lit) to have (*results*); (lit) to allot || (**sòrto**) *intr* (ESSERE) to come out (*said, e.g., of a newspaper*); (coll) to be drawn (*by lot*); (coll) to go out; (mil) to make a sally

sortita *f* witticism; (mil) sally, sortie; (theat) appearance

sorvegliante *adj* watchful || *mf* overseer, caretaker; guardian || *m* watchman; foreman

sorveglianza *f* surveillance; supervision

sorvegliare §280 (**sorvéglio**) *tr* to oversee, watch over; to check, control

sorvolare (**sorvólo**) *tr* to fly over; **to** overfly; (fig) to avoid, skip

sorvólo *m* overflight

sò·sia *m* (**-sia**) double, counterpart

sospèndere §259 *tr* to hang; to suspend; (chem) to prepare a suspension of; (law) to stay

sospensióne *f* suspension; suspense; (law) stay; **sospensione cardanica** gimbals

sospensò·rio *m* (**-ri**) jockstrap, supporter

sospé·so -sa [s] *adj* suspended; suspension (*bridge*); **in sospeso** in suspense; in abeyance ‖ *m* employee who has been disciplined by suspension; (com) pending item

sospettare (sospètto) *tr* to suspect ‖ *intr*—**sospettare di** to suspect; to fear

sospèt·to -ta *adj* suspected; suspicious ‖ *m* dash; suspicion

sospettó·so -sa [s] *adj* suspicious

sospìngere §126 *tr* (fig) to drive; (lit) to push

sospirare *tr* to long for, crave; **fare sospirare** to keep waiting ‖ *intr* to sigh

sospiro *m* sigh; longing; (lit) breath; **a sospiri** little by little

sossópra *adv* upside down

sòsta *f* stop; reprieve; (rr) demurrage

sostantì·vo -va *adj & m* substantive

sostanza *f* substance; **sostanza grigia** gray matter

sostanziale *adj* substantial

sostanzió·so -sa [s] *adj* substantial

sostare (sòsto) *intr* to stop, pause

sostégno *m* prop; (fig) support

sostenére §271 *tr* to support; to sustain; to take (*an examination*); to defend (*a thesis*); to prop up; to stand (*alcohol*); to play (*a role*) ‖ *ref* to support oneself; to hold up (*said, e.g., of a theory*); to take nourishment

sosteni·tóre -trice *mf* backer, supporter

sostentaménto *m* sustenance, support

sostentare (sostènto) *tr* to support, keep ‖ *ref* to feed, eat

sostenu·to -ta *adj* reserved, austere; rising (*prices*); bullish (*market*); starchy (*manner*)

sostituìbile *adj* replaceable

sostituìre §176 *tr* to replace, substitute for, take the place of; **sostituire** (*qlco* or *qlcu*) *a* to substitute (*s.th* or *s.o.*) for

sostitu·to -ta *adj* acting; associate, assistant ‖ *m* replacement, substitute

sostituzióne *f* replacement, substitution

sostrato *m* substratum

sottàbito *m* slip

sottacére §268 *tr* (lit) to withhold

sottacéto *adj invar* pickled ‖ **sottaceti** *mpl* pickles

sott'àcqua *adv* underwater

sotta·no -na *adj* lower (*town*) ‖ *f* skirt; petticoat; (eccl) cassock; **gettare la sottana alle ortiche** to doff the cassock

sottécchi *adv*—**di sottécchi** stealthily, secretly; **guardare di sottécchi** to peep, look furtively (at)

sotterrare (sottèntro) *intr* (ESSERE) (with *dat*) to replace

sotterfù·gio *m* (**-gi**) subterfuge

sottèrra *adv* underground

sotterràne·o -a *adj* subterranean, underground; secret, clandestine ‖ *m* cave, vault; dungeon; underground passage ‖ *f* (rr) subway, underground

sotterrare (sottèrro) *tr* to bury

sottigliézza *f* thinness; subtlety

sottile *adj* thin; subtle; (naut) lightweight ‖ *m*—**guardare troppo per il sottile** to split hairs

sottilizzare [ddzz] *intr* to quibble

sottintèndere §270 *tr* to understand ‖ *ref* to be understood, be implied

sottinté·so -sa [s] *adj* understood, implied ‖ *m* innuendo

sótto *adj invar* lower ‖ *m* lower part ‖ *adv* under; underneath; **al di sotto** below; **al di sotto di** under, below; **di sotto** lower; underneath; downstairs; **di sotto a** under, below; **farsi sotto** to sneak up; **metter sotto** to run over (*with a vehicle*); **sotto a** under; **sotto di** under; below; just before; **prendere sotto gamba** to underestimate; **sotto braccio** arm in arm; **sotto carico** (naut) being loaded; **sotto i baffi** up one's sleeve; **sotto le armi** in the service; **sotto mano** within reach; **sotto voce** under one's breath, sottovoce

sottoascèl·la *m* (**-la**) underarm pad

sottobanco *adv* under the counter

sottobicchière *m* coaster

sottobò·sco *m* (**-schi**) underbrush, thicket

sottobràccio *adv* arm in arm

sottòcchio *adv* under one's eyes

sottoccupà·to -ta *adj* underemployed

sottochiave *adv* under lock and key

sottocó·da *m* (**-da**) crupper

sottocommissióne *f* subcommittee

sottocopèrta *adv* (naut) below decks

sottocòp·pa *m* (**-pa**) mat; coaster; (aut) oil pan

sottocòsto *adj invar & adv* below cost

sottocutàne·o -a *adj* subcutaneous

sottofà·scia *m* (**-scia**) wrapper; **spedire sottofascia** to mail (*a newspaper*) in a wrapper ‖ *f* (**-sce**) wrapper (*for cigars*)

sottogamba *adv* lightly; **prendere sottogamba** to underestimate

sottogó·la *m & f* (**-la**) chin strap; throatlatch (*of harness*)

sottolineare (sottolìneo) *tr* to underline, underscore; to emphasize

sott'òlio *adv* in oil

sottomano *m* writing pad ‖ *adv* underhand; within reach

sottomarì·no -na *adj & m* submarine

sottomés·so -sa *adj* conquered; subdued; submissive

sottométtere §198 *tr* to subdue, crush; to defer, postpone; to present (*a bill*); to subject ‖ *ref* to submit, yield

sottomissióne *f* submission

sottopan·cia *m* (**-cia**) bellyband, girth

sottopassàg·gio *m* (**-gi**) underpass; lower level (*of highway*)

sottopiatto *m* saucer

sottopórre §218 *tr* to subject; to submit ‖ *ref* to submit; **sottoporsi a** to submit to; to undergo (*e.g., an operation*)

sottopó·sto -sta *adj* subject; exposed ‖ *m* subordinate

sottoprèzzo *adj invar* cut-rate ‖ *adv* at a cut rate

sottoprodótto *m* by-product

sottórdine *m* suborder; **in sottordine** secondary

sottosca·la *m* (-la) space under the stairs; closet under the stairs

sottoscrit·to -ta *adj & mf* undersigned

sottoscrit·tóre -trice *mf* subscriber

sottoscrìvere §250 *tr* to subscribe; to sign, undersign; to underwrite ‖ *intr* to subscribe

sottoscrizióne *f* subscription

sottosegretà·rio *m* (-ri) undersecretary

sottosópra *adj invar* upset; **mettere sottosopra** to upset; to turn upside down ‖ *m* confusion, disorder ‖ *adv* upside down

sottostante *adj* lower; subordinate ‖ *m* subordinate

sottostare §263 *intr* (ESSERE) to be located below; to be subject; to yield, submit; (with *dat*) to undergo (*e.g., an examination*)

sottosuòlo *m* subsoil; cellar

sottosviluppà·to -ta *adj* underdeveloped

sottotenènte *m* second lieutenant; **sottotenente di vascello** (nav) lieutenant j.g.

sottotèr·ra *m* (-ra) basement ‖ *adv* underground

sottotétto *m* attic, garret

sottotìtolo *m* subtitle; (mov) caption

sottovalutare *tr* to underrate

sottovènto *m & adv* leeward

sottovèste *f* slip (*undergarment*)

sottovóce *adv* sotto voce, under one's breath

sottrarre §273 *tr* to subtract; **sottrarre a** to take away from, steal from ‖ *ref*—**sottrarsi a** to avoid; to escape from

sottrazióne *f* subtraction

sottufficiale *m* noncommissioned officer

sovènte *adv* often

soverchiante *adj* overwhelming

soverchiare §287 (sovèrchio) *tr* to overwhelm; to excel; to bully; (lit) to overflow ‖ *intr* to be in excess

soverchia·tóre -trice *adj* overbearing ‖ *mf* overbearing person, oppressor

sovèr·chio -chia (-chi -chie) *adj* excessive; overbearing ‖ *m* overbearing action

sovè·scio *m* (-sci) plowing under (*of green manure*)

sovièti·co -ca (-ci -che) *adj* Soviet ‖ *mf* Soviet citizen

sovrabbondante *adj* superabundant

sovrabbondare (sovrabbóndo) *intr* (ESSERE & AVERE) to be superabundant; to go to excesses

sovraccaricare §197 (sovraccàrico) *tr* to overload

sovraccàri·co -ca (-chi -che) *adj* overburdened ‖ *m* overload; overweight

sovraespó·sto -sta *adj* overexposed

sovraggiùngere §183 *intr* (ESSERE) var of **sopraggiungere**

sovralimentazióne *f* (aut) supercharging

sovrani·tà *f* (-tà) sovereignty

sovra·no -na *adj & mf* sovereign

sovrappopolare (sovrappòpolo) *tr* to overpopulate

sovrappórre §218 *tr* to overlay; to superimpose; **sovrapporre qlco a** to lay s.th on ‖ *ref* to be superimposed; to be added; **sovrapporsi a** to put oneself above

sovrapproduzióne *f* overproduction

sovrastampa *f* overprint

sovrastante *adj* overlooking, overhanging; impending

sovrastare *tr* to tower over; to hang over; to surpass; to excel ‖ *intr* (ESSERE & AVERE)—**sovrastare a** to tower over; to overlook; to hang over; to surpass; to excel

sovratensióne *f* (elec) surge

sovreccitare (sovrèccito) *tr* to overexcite

sovrespórre §218 *tr* to overexpose

sovrimpòsta *f* surtax

sovrimpressióne *f* double exposure

sovruma·no -na *adj* superhuman

sovvenire §282 *tr* (lit) to help ‖ *intr* (with *dat*) (lit) to help ‖ *impers* (ESSERE)—**sovviene** (with *dat*) **di** remember, e.g., **gli sovviene spesso dei suoi cari** he often remembers his dear ones ‖ *ref*—**sovvenirsi di** to remember

sovvenzionare (sovvenzióno) *tr* to subsidize, grant a subvention to

sovvenzióne *f* subsidy, subvention

sovversi·vo -va *adj & m* subversive

sovvertire (sovvèrto) *tr* to subvert

sóz·zo -za *adj* dirty, filthy, foul

sozzura *f* dirt, filth

spaccalé·gna *m* (-gna) woodcutter

spaccamón·ti *m* (-ti) braggart

spaccaòs·sa *m* (-sa) butcher's cleaver

spaccare §197 *tr* to break, burst; to crack; to unpack; to chop; to split ‖ *ref* to crack; to break; to split

spacca·to -ta *adj* broken; split; (coll) identical; (coll) true ‖ *f* (sports, theat) splits

spaccatura *f* break; crack; cleavage; split

spacchétto *m* vent (*in jacket*)

spacciare §128 *tr* to sell out; to palm off; to spread (*reports*); to expedite; to abandon (*as hopeless*); (slang) to push (*e.g., dope*) ‖ *ref*—**spacciarsi per** to pretend to be, pass oneself off as

spaccia·to -ta *adj* (coll) cooked, done for; (coll) hopeless

spaccia·tóre -trice *mf* passer (*of bad currency or stolen goods*); **spacciatore di notizie false** gossipmonger

spàc·cio *m* (-ci) sale; passing (*of counterfeit money*); spreading (*of false news*); post exchange; tobacco shop

spac·co *m* (-chi) break; split; tear; crack; vent (*in jacket*)

spacconata *f* brag, braggadocio

spaccó·ne -na *mf* braggart, braggadocio

spada *f* sword; **a spada tratta** doggedly; **spade** suit of Neapolitan cards corresponding to spades

spadaccino *m* swordsman; swash-buckler

spadóne *m* two-handed sword

spadroneggiare §290 (spadronéggio) *intr* to be domineering or bossy

spaesa·to -ta *adj* out-of-place

spaghétto *m* (coll) fear, jitters; **avere lo spaghetto** (coll) to be scared stiff; **spaghetti** spaghetti

Spagna, la Spain

spagnòla *f* Spanish woman; Spanish influenza

spagnolétta *f* espagnolette; spool; (coll) cigarette; (coll) peanut

spagnò·lo -la *adj* Spanish || *m* Spaniard (*individual*); Spanish (*language*); **gli spagnoli** the Spanish || *f* see **spagnola**

spa·go *m* (-ghi) string, twine; (coll) fear, jitters

spaiare §287 *tr* to break a pair of

spaia·to -ta *adj* unmatched

spalancare §197 *tr* to open wide || *ref* to open up; to gape

spalare *tr* to shovel; to feather (*oar*)

spalla *f* shoulder; back; abutment (*of bridge*); (theat) stooge, straight man; **alle spalle di qlcu** behind s.o.'s back; **a spalla** on one's back; **fare spalla a** to help; **lavorare di spalle** to elbow one's way; (fig) to worm one's way up; **vivere alle spalle di** to sponge on

spallàrm *interj* (mil) shoulder arms!

spallata *f* push with the shoulder; shrug of the shoulders

spalleggiare §290 (spalléggio) *tr* to back, support; (mil) to carry on one's back

spallétta *f* parapet, retaining wall; jamb

spallièra *f* back (*of chair*); head (*of bed*); foot (*of bed*); espalier

spallina *f* epaulet; shoulder strap

spallùccia *f*—**fare spallucce** to shrug one's shoulders

spalmare *tr* to spread; to smear

spalto *m* glacis; **spalti** seats (*of a stadium*)

spanare *tr* to strip the thread of || *ref* to be stripped (*said, e.g., of the thread of a nut*)

spanciare §128 *tr* to disembowel, gut || *intr* to belly-flop; to bulge (*said of a wall*) || *ref*—**spanciarsi dalle risa** to split one's sides laughing

spanciata *f* belly flop; bellyful; **fare una spanciata** to stuff oneself

spàndere §260 *tr* to spread; to spill; to shed (*tears*); to squander || *ref* to spread

spanna *f* span

spannare *tr* to skim (*milk*)

spannocchiare §287 (spannòcchio) *tr* to husk (*corn*)

spappolare (spàppolo) *tr* to crush, squash || *ref* to become mushy

sparadrappo *m* adhesive tape; (obs) plaster, poultice

sparagnare *tr* (coll) to save

sparare *tr* to gut, disembowel; to shoot; to let go with (*a kick*); to remove

the hangings from; **spararne delle grosse** to tell tall tales

sparato *m* shirt front, dickey

sparatòria *f* shooting

sparecchiare §287 (sparécchio) *tr* to clear (*the table*); to clear away (*one's tools*); to eat up

sparég·gio *m* (-gi) disparity; deficit; (sports) play-off

spàrgere §261 *tr* to spread; to shed; to spill || *ref* to spread

spargimento *m* spreading; **spargimento di sangue** bloodshed

spargisa·le [s] *m* (-le) salt shaker

sparigliare §280 *tr* to break a pair of; to break (*a set*)

spariglia·to -ta *adj* unmatched

sparire §176 *intr* (ESSERE) to disappear

sparlare *intr* to backbite; **sparlare di** to backbite, slander

sparo *m* shot

sparpagliare §280 *tr & intr* to scatter

spar·so -sa *adj* scattered; dotted; speckled; hanging loosely (*e.g., hair*)

sparta·no -na *adj & mf* Spartan

spartiàc·que *m* (-que) watershed

spartiné·ve *m* (-ve) snowplow

spartire §176 *tr* to divide, share; to separate; **non aver nulla da spartire con** to have nothing to do with

spartito *m* (mus) score; (mus) arrange-ment

spartitràffi·co *m* (-co) median strip

spar·to -ta *adj* (lit) spread || *m* esparto grass

sparu·to -ta *adj* lean, wan; meager

sparvière *m* sparrow hawk; mortar-board

spasimante *m* (joc) lover, wooer

spasimare (spàsimo) *intr* to writhe; **spasimare per** to long for; to be madly in love with

spàsimo *m* pang; severe pain; longing

spasmo *m* spasm

spasmòdi·co -ca *adj* (-ci -che) spas-modic

spassare *tr* to amuse || *ref*—**spassarsela** to have a good time

spassiona·to -ta *adj* dispassionate, un-biased

spasso *m* fun, amusement; walk; (coll) funny guy; **andare a spasso** to go out for a walk; **essere a spasso** to be out of a job; **mandare a spasso** to fire, dismiss; to get rid of; **per spasso** for fun; **portare a spasso** to lead by the nose; **prendersi spasso di** to make fun of

spassó·so -sa [s] *adj* amusing, droll

spàsti·co -ca *adj & mf* spastic

spato *m* spar

spatofluòre *m* fluorspar

spàtola *f* spatula; putty knife; slapstick (*of harlequin*)

spauràc·chio *m* (chi) scarecrow; buga-boo, bugbear

spaurare *tr & ref* (lit) var of **spaurire**

spaurire §176 *tr* to frighten || *ref* to be scared

spaval·do -da *adj* bold, swaggering

spaventapàs·seri *m* (-ri) scarecrow

spaventare (spavènto) *tr* to scare, frighten || *ref* to be scared

spaventévole *adj* frightening, dreadful

spavènto *m* fright, fear

spaventó·so -sa [s] *adj* frightful, fearful

spaziale *adj* space

spaziare §287 *tr* (typ) to space || *intr* to soar; to range, rove (*said, e.g., of eye*)

spazia·tóre -trice *adj* spacing || *f* space bar (*of typewriter*)

spaziatura *f* spacing

spazientire §176 *tr* to make (*s.o.*) lose his patience || *intr* (ESSERE) & *ref* to lose patience

spà·zio *m* (-zi) space; (fig) room; **spazio aereo** air space; **spazio cosmico** outer space

spazió·so -sa [s] *adj* spacious, roomy; wide

spazzacamino *m* chimney sweep

spazzami·ne *m* (-ne) mine sweeper

spazzané·ve *m* (-ve) snowplow

spazzare *tr* to sweep; to plow (*snow*); to clean up

spazzata *f*—**dare una spazzata a** to give a lick and a promise to

spazzatrice *f* street sweeper

spazzatura *f* sweeping; sweepings; rubbish, trash

spazzatu·ràio *m* (-rài) or **spazzino** *m* street cleaner; trashman, garbage collector, trash collector

spàzzola *f* brush; **capelli a spazzola** crew cut

spazzolare (spàzzolo) *tr* to brush

spazzolino *m* little brush; (elec) brush; **spazzolino da denti** toothbrush; **spazzolino per le unghie** nailbrush

spazzolone *m* push broom

specchiare §287 **(spècchio)** *tr* (lit) to reflect || *ref* to look at oneself (*in a mirror*); to be reflected; **specchiarsi in qlcu** to model oneself on s.o.

specchièra *f* mirror; dressing table; full-length mirror

specchiétto *m* mirror; synopsis; **specchietto retrovisivo** (aut) rear-view mirror

spèc·chio *m* (-chi) mirror; synopsis; shore (*of lake or river*); panel (*of door or window*); sheet (*of water*); (sports) goal line; (sports) board; **specchio di poppa** (naut) transom; **specchio ustorio** burning glass

speciale *adj* special

speciali·sta *mf* (-sti -ste) specialist

speciali·tà *f* (-tà) specialty; (mil) special services; **specialità farmaceutica** patent or proprietary medicine

specializzare [ddzz] *tr* & *ref* to specialize

spè·cie *f* (-cie) species; kind, sort; appearance, semblance; **fare specie** (with *dat*) (coll) to be surprised, e.g., **gli fa specie** he is surprised; **in specie** especially; **sotto specie di** under pretext of

specifi·ca *f* (-che) itemized list; specification

specificare §197 **(specìfico)** *tr* to specify; to itemize

specìfi·co -ca (-ci -che) *adj* & *m* specific || *f* see **specifica**

specillo *m* (med) probe

speció·so -sa [s] *adj* specious

spè·co *m* (-chi) (lit) cave

spècola *f* observatory

spècolo *m* (med, surg) speculum

speculare (spèculo) *tr* to observe; to meditate on || *intr* to speculate

specula·tóre -trice *adj* speculating || *mf* speculator; **speculatore al rialzo** bull; **speculatore al ribasso** bear

speda·to -ta *adj* footwork

spedire §176 *tr* to expedite; to prepare; to ship, send, forward; (law) to deliver

spedi·to -ta *adj* rapid; free, easy

spedi·tóre -trice *mf* shipper, sender; shipping clerk

spedizióne *f* shipment, shipping; sending, forwarding; expedition; (naut) papers; **di spedizione** expeditionary

spedizionière *m* shipper, forwarder, forwarding agent

spègnere §262 *tr* to extinguish, put out; to turn off; to slake (*lime*); to kill; to mix (*flour*) with water or milk; to quench; to obliterate (*a memory*) || *ref* to burn out; to go out (*said of a light*); to fade, die away; to die

spegni·tóio *m* (-tói) snuffer

spegnitura *f* (theat) blackout

spelacchiare §287 *tr* to strip of hair || *ref* to shed hair or fur

spelacchia·to -ta *adj* mangy; (pej) baldy

spelare (spélo) *tr* to strip of hair; to pluck (*e.g., a chicken*); (fig) to fleece || *ref* to shed hair or fur; to get bald

spellare (spèllo) *tr* to skin; (fig) to skin, fleece

spelón·ca *f* (-che) cave; hovel, den

spème *f* (poet) hope

spendacció·ne -na *mf* spendthrift

spèndere §220 *tr* to spend

spenderéc·cio -cia *adj* (-ci -ce) spendthrift, prodigal

spennacchiare §287 *tr* to pluck; (fig) to fleece || *ref* to lose its feathers

spennare (spénno) *tr* & *ref* var of **spennacchiare**

spennellare (spennèllo) *tr* to dab

spensieratézza *f* thoughtlessness

spensiera·to -ta *adj* thoughtless, careless; carefree, happy-go-lucky

spèn·to -ta *adj* extinguished; turned off; slaked (*lime*); dull (*color*); low (*tone*)

spenzolare [dz] (spènzolo) *tr* & *intr* to hang || *ref*—**spenzolarsi da** to hang out of

speranza *f* hope; prospect, expectation

speranzó·so -sa [s] *adj* hopeful

sperare (spèro) *tr* to candle (*eggs*); to hope for; to expect || *intr* to hope; to trust

spèrdere §212 *tr* (lit) to scatter; (lit) to lose (*one's way*) || *ref* to lose one's way, get lost

sperdu·to -ta *adj* lost, astray; godforsaken (*place*)

sperequazióne *f* disproportion; inequality; unjust distribution

spergiurare *tr* & *intr* to swear falsely; **giurare e spergiurare** to swear over and over again

spergiu·ro -ra *adj* perjured || *mf* perjurer || *m* perjury

spericola·to -ta *adj* reckless, daring

sperimentale *adj* experimental

sperimentare (sperimento) *tr* to test, try out; to experience

sperimenta·to -ta *adj* experienced

spèr·ma *m* (**-mi**) sperm

speronare (speróno) *tr* (naut) to ram

speróne *m* spur; abutment; (nav) ram

sperperare (spèrpero) *tr* to squander

spèrpero *m* squandering

spèr·so -sa *adj* lost, stray

spertica·to -ta *adj* too long; too tall; exaggerated, excessive

spésa [s] *f* expense; shopping; buy, purchase; **fare la spesa** to shop; **fare le spese di** to be the butt of; **lavorare per le spese** to work for one's keep; **pagare le spese** to bear the charges; **spese expenses**; room and board; **spese di manutenzione** upkeep; **spese minute** petty expenses; **spese processuali** (law) costs

spesare [s] (**spéso**) *tr* to support

spesa·to -ta [s] *adj* with all expenses paid

spès·so -sa *adj* thick; many (*times*) || **spesso** *adv* often; **spesso spesso** again and again

spessóre *m* thickness

spettàbile *adj* esteemed; **Spettàbile Ditta** (com) Gentlemen

spettàcolo *m* spectacle, show; sight; **dar spettàcolo di sé** to make a show of oneself; **spettacolo all'aperto** outdoor performance

spettacoló·so -sa [s] *adj* spectacular; (coll) exceptional; (coll) sensational

spettanza *f* concern; pay

spettare (spètto) *intr* (ESSERE)—**spettare a** to belong to || *impers* (ESSERE)—**spetta a** it behooves, it is up to

spetta·tóre -trice *mf* spectator, bystander; **spettatori** public, audience

spettegolare (spettègolo) *intr* to gossip

spettinare (spèttino) *tr* to muss the hair of

spettrale *adj* ghost-like; spectral

spèttro *m* specter, ghost; spectrum

speziale *m* dealer in spices; (coll) pharmacist

spèzie *fpl* spices

spezieria *f* grocery; (coll) drug store, pharmacy; **spezierie** spices

spezzare (spèzzo) *tr* to break; to smash; to interrupt || *ref* to break

spezzatino *m* stew; **spezzatini** change

spezza·to -ta *adj* broken; fragmentary; interrupted || *m* stew; (theat) set piece; **spezzati** change

spezzettare (spezzétto) *tr* to mince

spezzóne *m* small aerial bomb; fragmentation bomb; fragment

spìa *f* spy; indication; peephole; (aut) gauge; (aut) pilot light; **fare la spia** to be an informer

spiacciare §197 (**spiàccio**) *tr* to squash, crush || *ref* to be squashed

spiacènte *adj* sorry; (lit) disliked

spiacére §214 *intr* (ESSERE) (with *dat*) to dislike, e.g., **queste parole gli spiacciono** he dislikes these words; to mind, e.g., **se non Le spiace** if you don't mind || *ref*—**spiacersi di** to be sorry for || *impers* (ESSERE) (with *dat*)—**gli spiace** he is sorry

spiacévole *adj* unpleasant

spiàg·gia *f* (**-ge**) beach, shore

spianare *tr* to grade (*land*); to roll (*dough*); to pave (*the way*); to iron (*pleats*); to raze, demolish; **spianare la fronte** to smooth one's brow || *intr* (ESSERE) to be level

spianata *f* esplanade; **dare una spianata a** to level

spianatóia *f* board (*for rolling dough*)

spiana·tóio *m* (**-tói**) rolling pin

spianatrice *f* grader

spiano *m* leveling; esplanade; **a tutto spiano** at full blast; continuously

spiantare *tr* to uproot; to raze, level; to ruin (*financially*) || *ref* to ruin oneself

spianta·to -ta *adj* ruined || *m* pauper

spiare §119 *tr* to spy on; to keep an eye on

spiattellare (spiattèllo) *tr* to blurt out

spiazzo *m* square; plain; clearing

spiccare §197 *tr* to detach; to pick; to enunciate; to begin; to draw up (*a commercial paper*); to issue (*a warrant*); **spiccare il volo** (aer) to take off || *intr* to stand out || *ref* to separate (*said, e.g., of the stone of a peach*)

spicca·to -ta *adj* clear, distinct; typical; outstanding

spìc·chio *m* (**-chi**) section (*of fruit*); clove (*of garlic*); slice (*e.g., of apple*); arm (*of cross*)

spicciare §128 *tr* to clear up; to wait on; to dispatch (*business*) || *intr* (ESSERE) to flow forth, gush out || *ref* to hurry up, make haste

spicciati·vo -va *adj* expeditious, quick; straightforward; gruff

spiccicare §197 (**spìccico**) *tr* to unglue; to enunciate; to utter || *ref* to come unglued; **spiccicarsi di** to get rid of

spìc·cio -cia (**-ci -ce**) *adj* expeditious, quick; unhampered; small (*change*) || **spìcci** *mpl* change

spicciolata *adj* fem—**alla spicciolata** little by little; a few at a time

spìcciolo·lo -la *adj* small (*change*); (coll) plain || **spiccioli** *mpl* small change

spìc·co -ca (**-chi -che**) *adj* freestone (*e.g., peach*) || *m*—**fare spicco** to stand out

spidocchiare §287 (**spidòcchio**) *tr* to delouse

spièdo *m* spit; **allo spiedo** barbecued

spiegàbile *adj* explainable

spiegaménto *m* (mil) array; (mil) deployment

spiegare §209 (**spiègo**) *tr* to unfold; to let go (*with one's voice*); to unfurl; to spread (*wings*); to deploy (*troops*); to explain; to show, demonstrate; **spiegare il volo** (aer) to take off || *ref* to become unfurled or unfolded;

to make oneself understood; to come to an understanding; to realize

spiega·to -ta *adj* open; full (*voice*)

spiegazióne *f* explanation

spiegazzare *tr* to crumple, rumple

spieta·to -ta *adj* pitiless, ruthless

spifferare (**spiffero**) *tr* (coll) to blurt out || *intr* to blow in (*said of wind*)

spiffero *m* (coll) draft

spi·ga *f* (**ghe**) panicle (*of oats*); (bot) ear, spike; **a spiga** herringbone

spiga·to -ta *adj* herringbone

spighétta *f* braid; (bot) spikelet

spigionare (**spigióno**) *ref* to be or become vacant

spiglia·to -ta *adj* easy, free and easy

spi·go *m* (**-ghi**) lavender

spigolare (**spìgolo**) *tr* to glean

spigola·tóre -trice *mf* gleaner

spìgolo *m* corner; edge; (archit) arris

spilla *f* brooch, pin; **spilla da cravatta** tiepin; **spilla di sicurezza** safety pin

spillare *tr* to draw off, tap; to wheedle, worm (*money*) || *intr* to leak (*said of container*) || *intr* (ESSERE) to leak (*said of liquid*)

spillàti·co *m* (**-ci**) (law) pin money (*for one's wife*)

spillo *m* pin; gimlet; trifle; **a spillo** spikelike; **spillo da balia** or **di sicurezza** safety pin

spillóne *m* hatpin; bodkin

spilluzzicare §197 (**spillùzzico**) *tr* to pick at, nibble; to scrape together

spilorcería *f* stinginess

spilòr·cio -cia (**-ci -ce**) *adj* stingy || *mf* miser, tightwad

spilungó·ne -na *mf* lanky person

spina *f* thorn; quill, spine (*of porcupine*); bone (*of fish*); (fig) preoccupation, worry; **alla spina** (*beer*) on tap; **a spina di pesce** herringbone (*fabric*); **con una spina nel cuore** sick at heart; **essere sulle spine** to be on pins and needles; **spina della botte** tap; bunghole; **spina dorsale** spinal column; (fig) backbone; **spina elettrica** plug

spinà·cio *m* (**-ci**) spinach (*plant*); **spinaci** spinach (*as food*)

spinapésce *m*—**a spinapesce** herringbone

spina·to -ta *adj* barbed (*wire*); herringbone (*fabric*)

spìngere §126 *tr* to push, press; to prod, goad || *ref* to push; to reach

spi·no -na *adj* thorny || *m* thorn || *f* see **spina**

spinóne *m* griffon

spinó·so -sa [s] *adj* thorny

spinòtto *m* wrist pin

spinta *f* push; pressure; poke, prod; stress

spinterògeno *m* (aut) distributor unit, ignition system

spin·to -ta *adj* pushed; bent, inclined; (coll) risqué; (coll) far-out, offbeat || *f* see **spinta**

spintóne *m* (coll) push, shove

spionà·gio *m* (**-gi**) espionage, spying

spioncino *m* peephole

spió·ne -na *mf* spy, stool pigeon

spiovènte *adj* drooping; sloping; falling || *m* slope; drainage area (*of a mountain*)

spiòvere §216 *intr* to fall, to hang down (*said, e.g., of hair*); to flow down || *impers* (ESSERE)—**è spiovuto** it stopped raining

spira *f* turn (*of a coil*); coil (*of serpent*); a spire spiral

spirà·glio *m* (**-gli**) small opening; gleam (*of light or hope*)

spirale *adj* spiral || *f* spiral; hairspring; wreath (*of smoke*); **spirale di fumo** smoke ring

spirare *tr* to send forth; (lit) to inspire, infuse; (lit) to show (*kindness*) || *intr* to blow; to emanate; to die; to expire

spirita·to -ta *adj* possessed; wild, mad

spirìti·co -ca *adj* (**-ci -che**) spiritual; spiritualistic

spiritismo *m* spiritualism

spìrito *m* spirit; wit; mind; spirits, alcohol; sprite; **bello spirito** wit (*person*); **fare dello spirito** to be witty; to crack jokes; **l'ultimo spirito** (lit) one's last breath; **spirito di corpo** esprit de corps; **spirito di parte** partisanship; **spirito sportivo** sportsmanship

spiritosàggine [s] *f* witticism

spiritó·so -sa [s] *adj* witty; alcoholic

spirituale *adj* spiritual

spìzzi·co *m* (**-chi**)—**a spizzico** or **a spizzichi** little by little; a little at a time

splendènte *adj* resplendent, shining

splèndere §281 *intr* (ESSERE & AVERE) to shine

splèndi·do -da *adj* splendid; gorgeous; bright || *m*—**fare lo splendido** to be a big spender

splendóre *m* splendor; brightness; beauty

splène *m* (anat) spleen

spòcchia *f* haughtiness

spodestare (**spodèsto**) *tr* to dispossess; to dethrone; to oust

spoetizzare [ddzz] *tr* to disillusion

spòglia *f* slough (*of snake*); skin (*of onion*); husk (*of corn*); (lit) body; (lit) outer garment; **sotto mentite spoglie** under false pretense; **spoglie** spoils

spogliare §280 (**spòglio**) *tr* to undress, strip; to strip of armor; to defraud, deprive; to free; to check, examine; to husk (*corn*); to go through (*e.g., correspondence*) || *ref* to undress; to slough (*said, e.g., of a snake*); **spogliarsi di** to get rid of; to divest oneself of; to shake (*a habit*)

spogliarelli·sta *f* (**-ste**) stripteaser

spogliarèllo *m* striptease

spoglia·tóio *m* (**-tói**) dressing room; locker room

spò·glio -glia (**-gli -glie**) *adj* stripped, bare; free || *m* cast-off clothing; sorting; scrutiny; counting (*of votes*); **di spoglio** second-hand (*material*) || *f* see **spoglia**

spòla *f* bobbin; shuttle; **fare la spola** to shuttle

spolétta *f* bobbin, spool; (mil) fuse

spolmonare (spolmóno) *ref* (coll) to talk, sing, or shout oneself hoarse

spolpare (spólpo) *tr* to gnaw (*a bone*); to eat up (*fruit*); (fig) to fleece

spolverare (spólvero) *tr* to dust off, whisk; to powder, dust; to pounce

spolveratura *f* dusting; powdering; sprinkling, smattering (*of knowledge*); **dare una spolveratura a** to brush up on

spolverina *f* (coll) duster

spolverino *m* duster, smock; powder-sugar duster; pounce; (coll) whisk broom

spolverizzaménto [ddzz] *m* sprinkling (*with powder*)

spolverizzare [ddzz] *tr* to dust, powder, pounce

spólvero *m* dusting; powdering; pounce; smattering, sprinkling (*of knowledge*); display

spónda *f* bank (*of river*); side; cushion (*of billiard table*)

sponsale *adj* (lit) wedding || **sponsali** *mpl* (lit) wedding

spontàne·o -a *adj* spontaneous; artless

spopolare (spòpolo) *tr* to depopulate || *intr* to be a hit; to become depopulated or deserted

spoppare (spóppo) *tr* to wean

sporàdi·co -ca *adj* (**-ci -che**) sporadic

sporcacció·ne -na *adj* (coll) filthy || *mf* filthy person; (fig) dirty mouth

sporcare §197 (spórco) *tr* to dirty; to soil || *ref* to get dirty; to soil oneself; **sporcarsi la fedina** (coll) to get a black mark on one's record

sporcìzia *f* dirt, filth

spòr·co -ca (-chi -che) *adj* dirty, filthy; foul; **farla sporca** to pull a dirty trick || *m* dirt, filth

sporgènte *adj* leaning; protruding; beetle (*brow*)

sporgènza *f* prominence, projection

spòrgere §217 *tr* to stick out; to stretch out; to lodge (*a complaint*) || *intr* (ESSERE) to project, jut out || *ref* to lean out

spòrt *m* (spòrt) sport; game; **per sport** for fun, for pleasure

spòrta *f* shopping bag; bagful; basket; basketful; shopping; **a sporta** wide-brimmed (*hat*)

sportèllo *m* door; panel; window (*in bank, station, etc.*); wicket; branch (*of a bank*); (theat) box office

sportivi·tà *f* (**-tà**) sportsmanship

sporti·vo -va *adj* sporting; sportsman-like; athletic || *m* sportsman

spòr·to -ta *adj* projecting; jutting out || *m* projection; removable shutter (*on store door or window*) || *f* see **sporta**

spòsa *f* bride; wife; **andare in sposa a** to get married to; **sposa promessa** fiancée

sposali·zio -zia (-zi -zie) *adj* (lit) nuptial || *m* wedding

sposare (spòso) *tr* to marry; to unite; to embrace (*a cause*); to fit perfectly; to give in marriage || *ref* to get married, marry

spòso *m* bridegroom; **sposi** newlyweds

spossare (spòsso) *tr* to exhaust || *ref* to become worn out

spossatézza *f* exhaustion

spostaménto *m* shift; movement; displacement; change

spostare (spòsto) *tr* to move; to change, shift; to upset || *ref* to move; to shift; to get out of place; to be upset

sposta·to -ta *adj* ill-adjusted, out of place || *mf* misfit

spran·ga *f* (**-ghe**) bar, crossbar

sprangare §209 *tr* to bar, bolt

sprazzo *m* spray; flash; burst

sprecare §197 (sprèco) *tr* to waste; to miss (*an opportunity*) || *ref* to waste one's efforts

sprè·co m (-chi) waste; squandering

sprecó·ne -na *adj & mf* spendthrift

spregévole *adj* contemptible, despicable

spregiare §290 (sprègio) *tr* to despise

sprè·gio m (-gi) contempt, scorn

spregiudica·to -ta *adj* open-minded, unbiased || *m* open-minded person

sprèmere §123 *tr* to squeeze, press; **spremere le lacrime a** to move to tears || *ref*—**spremersi il cervello** to rack one's brain

spremifrut·ta m (-ta) squeezer

spremilimó·ni m (-ni) lemon squeezer

spremuta *f* squeezing; **spremuta d'arancia** orange juice

spretare (sprèto) *ref* to doff the cassock

sprezzante *adj* contemptuous, haughty

sprezzare (sprèzzo) *tr* (lit) to despise

sprèzzo *m* disdain, contempt

sprigionare (sprigióno) *tr* to exhale, emit; to free from prison || *ref* to free oneself; to escape, come forth, issue (*said, e.g., of steam*)

sprimacciare §128 *tr* to beat, fluff (*e.g., a pillow*)

sprizzare *tr* to spout; to sparkle with (*joy, health*) || *intr* (ESSERE) to spurt; to fly (*said of sparks*); to sparkle

sprizzo *m* sprinkle; spurt; spark

sprofondare (sprofóndo) *tr* to send to the bottom; to destroy, ruin; to sink || *intr* (ESSERE) to sink; to founder; to cave in; to be sunk (*e.g., in meditation*)

sprolò·quio m (-qui) long rigmarole

spronare (spróno) *tr* to spur, goad

spróne *m* spur; prodding; example; guimpe; buttress; abutment (*of bridge*); **a sprone battuto** at full speed; at once; **dar di sprone a** to spur on; **sprone di cavaliere** (bot) rocket larkspur

sproporziona·to -ta *adj* out of proportion, disproportionate

sproporzióne *f* disproportion

sproposita·to -ta *adj* out of proportion; excessive; gross (*error*)

spropòsito *m* blunder, gross error; excessive amount; **a sproposito** out of place; inopportunely

sprovvedu·to -ta *adj* deprived; brainless, witless

sprovvi·sto -sta *adj* deprived; devoid, lacking; **alla sprovvista** suddenly; unawares, off guard

spruzzabianche·rìa *m* (-**rìa**) sprinkler (*to sprinkle clothes*)

spruzzare *tr* to sprinkle, spray; to powder (*sugar*)

spruzzatóre *m* sprayer; (aut) nozzle (*of carburetor*)

spruzzo *m* spray; splash (*of mud*)

spudora·to -ta *adj* shameless; impudent

spugna *f* sponge; **dare un colpo di spugna** to wipe the slate clean; **gettare la spugna** to throw in the towel

spugnare *tr* to sponge; to swab

spugnatura *f* sponge bath

spugnó·so -sa [s] *adj* spongy

spulciare §128 *tr* to pick the fleas off; to scrutinize, examine minutely

spuma *f* foam, froth

spumante *adj* sparkling || *m* sparkling wine; champagne

spumare *intr* to froth

spumeggiante *adj* sparkling; vaporous; foamy

spumeggiare §290 (**spuméggio**) *intr* to foam

spumóne *m* spumoni

spumó·so -sa [s] *adj* foamy, frothy

spunta *f* check; check list; check mark

spuntare *tr* to blunt; to unpin; to overcome; to clip, trim; to check off; **spuntarla** to come out on top; to overcome || *intr* (ESSERE) to appear; to sprout; to rise; to well up (*said of tears*); to pop out; to break through || *ref* to become blunt; to die down

spuntino *m* bite, snack; **fare uno spuntino** to have a bite

spunto *m* sourness (*of wine*); (theat) cue; (sports) sprint; (fig) starting point, origin

spuntóne *m* spike; pike; crag

spurgare §209 *tr* to purge, clear; to clean up || *ref* to expectorate

spur·go *m* (-**ghi**) discharge; reject (*e.g., book*)

spù·rio -ria *adj* (-**ri -rie**) spurious

sputacchiare §287 *tr* to spit upon || *intr* to sputter

sputacchièra *f* spittoon, cuspidor

sputare *tr* to spit; to cough up; (fig) to spew (*venom*); **sputare sangue** to spit blood; (fig) to sweat blood || *intr* to spit

sputasentènze *mf* (-**ze**) wiseacre

sputo *m* spit, sputum; spitting

squadernare (**squadèrno**) *tr* to leaf through; **squadernare qlco a qlcu** to put s.th under the nose of s.o. || *ref* to come apart (*said of a book*)

squadra *f* square (*for measuring right angles*); squad, group; (mil) squadron; (sports) team; **a squadra** at right angles; **fuori squadra** out of kilter; **squadra di pompieri** fire company; **squadra mobile** flying squad

squadrare *tr* to square; (fig) to examine, study

squadriglia *f* (aer, nav) squadron

squadróne *m* squadron (*of cavalry*)

squagliare §280 *tr* to melt || *ref* to melt; **squagliarsela** to take French leave

squalìfi·ca *f* (-**che**) disqualification

squalificare §197 (**squalìfico**) *tr* to disqualify || *ref* to disqualify oneself; to prove to be unqualified

squàlli·do -da *adj* wretched, dreary, gloomy; faint (*smile*); (lit) emaciated

squallóre *m* wretchedness, dreariness, gloominess

squalo *m* shark

squama *f* scurf (*shed by the skin*); (bot, pathol, zool) scale

squamare *tr & ref* to scale

squamó·so -sa [s] *adj* scaly

squarciagóla *adv*—**a squarciagola** at the top of one's voice

squarciare §128 *tr* to rend, tear apart; to dispel (*a doubt*) || *ref* to become torn; to open

squàr·cio *m* (-**ci**) tear, rip; passage (*of book*)

squartare *tr* to quarter

squartatura *f* quartering

squassare *tr* to shake violently; to wreck

squattrina·to -ta *adj* penniless || *m* pauper

squilibra·to -ta *adj* unbalanced, deranged || *mf* mad or insane person

squili·brio *m* (-**bri**) lack of balance; **squilibrio mentale** insanity; unbalanced mental condition

squillante *adj* ringing, shrill; sharp

squillare *intr* to ring; to ring out; to blare

squillo *m* ring; peal; blare, blast (*of horn*); || *f* call girl

squinternare (**squintèrno**) *tr* to tear (*a book*) to pieces; (fig) to upset

squisi·to -ta *adj* exquisite

squittire §176 *intr* to squeak; to squeal

sradicare §197 (**sràdico**) *tr* to uproot; to eradicate; to pull (*a tooth*)

sragionare (**sragióno**) *intr* to talk nonsense

sregola·to -ta *adj* intemperate; dissolute

srotolare (**sròtolo**) *tr* to unroll

stàb·bio *m* (-**bi**) pen; manure, dung

stabbiòlo *m* pigpen

stàbile *adj* stable; real (*estate*); permanent; stock (*company*) || *m* building

stabiliménto *m* plant, factory; establishment; settlement, colony; conclusion (*of a deal*)

stabilire §176 *tr* to establish; to decide || *ref* to settle

stabili·tà *f* (-**tà**) stability, steadiness

stabilito *m* (law) agreement of sale (*drawn up by a broker*)

stabilizzare [ddzz] *tr & ref* to stabilize

stabilizza·tóre -trice [ddzz] *mf* stabilizing person || *m* (aer) stabilizer; (elec) voltage stabilizer

staccare §197 *tr* to detach; to unhitch; to outdistance; to draw (*a check*); to tear off; to take (*one's eyes*) away; to begin; to enunciate (*words*) || *intr* to stand out; (coll) to stop working || *ref* to come off; **staccarsi da** to come off (*e.g., the wall*); to leave (*one's home; the shore*); (aer) to take off from

stacciare §128 *tr* to sift, sieve

stàc·cio *m* (-ci) sieve
staccionata *f* fence; hurdle; stockade
stac·co *m* (-chi) tearing off; cut of
  cloth (*for a suit*); interval; **fare
  stacco** to stand out
stadèra *f* steelyard; **stadera a ponte**
  weighbridge
stàdia *f* leveling rod
stà·dio *m* (-di) stadium; stage
staffa *f* stirrup; heel (*of sock*); gaiter
  strap; clamp; (mach) bracket; **perdere le staffe** to lose one's nerve
staffétta *f* courier, messenger; pilot
  (*car*); **a staffetta** relay
staffière *m* groom, footman; servant
staffilare *tr* to whip, belt, lash
staffilata *f* lash
staffile *m* stirrup strap; whip
stàg·gio *m* (-gi) stay, upright
stagionale *adj* seasonal ‖ *mf* seasonal
  worker
stagionare (stagióno) *tr* to season, cure
stagiona·to -ta *adj* seasoned, ripe
stagióne *f* season; **da mezza stagione**
  spring-and-fall (*coat*); **di fine stagione** year-end (*sale*)
stagliare §280 *tr* to hack ‖ *ref* to stand
  out
staglia·to -ta *adj* sheer (*cliff*)
sta·gnàio *m* (-gnài) tinsmith; plumber
stagnante *adj* stagnant
stagnare *tr* to tin; to solder; to stanch
  ‖ *intr* to stagnate
stagnaro *m* var of stagnaio
stagnina *f* tin can
stagnino *m* (coll) var of stagnaio
sta·gno -gna *adj* watertight; airtight ‖
  m tin; pond, pool
stagnòla *f* tin foil; tin can
stàio *m* (stài) bushel (*container*); —
  staio (coll) top (*hat*) ‖ *m* (stàia *fpl*)
  bushel (*measure*); **a staia** in abundance
stalla *f* stable
stallìa *f* (com) lay day
stallière *m* stableman, stableboy
stallo *m* seat; stall; (chess) stalemate
stallóne *m* stallion
stamane, stamani or stamattina *adv*
  this morning
stambéc·co *m* (-chi) ibex
stambèr·ga *f* (-ghe) hovel
stambù·gio *m* (-gi) hole, hovel
stamburare *tr* to puff up, to boast
  about ‖ *intr* to drum
stame *m* (bot) stamen; thread, yarn
stamigna *f* cheesecloth
stampa *f* printing; print; (fig) print;
  (fig) mold; **stampe** printed matter
stampàg·gio *m* (-gi) (mach) stamping
stampare *tr* to stamp; to print; to impress; to publish ‖ *ref* (fig) to be
  ingraved
stampatèllo *m*—**in stampatello** in block
  letters; **scrivere in stampatello** to
  print (*with pen or pencil*)
stampa·to -ta *adj* printed; impressed ‖
  m printed form; **stampati** printed
  matter
stampa·tóre -trice *mf* printer
stampèlla *f* crutch
stamperìa *f* print shop

stampìglia *f* rubber stamp; billboard;
  overprint
stampigliare §280 *tr* to stamp; to overprint
stampinare *tr* to stencil
stampino *m* stencil
stampo *m* mold; stencil; stamp, kind;
  decoy
stanare *tr* to flush (*game*); (fig) to dig
  up
stancare §197 *tr* to tire, fatigue; to bore
  ‖ *ref* to tire, weary
stanchézza *f* tiredness, weariness
stan·co -ca *adj* (-chi -che) tired; tired
  out; (lit) left (*hand*)
standardizzare [ddzz] *tr* to standardize
stan·ga *f* (-ghe) bar; shaft (*of cart*);
  beam (*of plow*)
stangata *f* blow
stanghétta *f* small bar; bolt (*of lock*);
  temple (*of spectacles*); (mus) bar
stanòtte *adv* tonight; last night
stante *adj* being; standing; **a sé stante**
  by itself, independent ‖ *prep* because
  of; **stante che** since
stan·tìo -tìa *adj* (-tìi; -tìe) stale; musty
stantuffo *m* piston; plunger
stanza *f* room; stanza; **essere di stanza**
  (mil) to be stationed; **stanza da
  bagno** bath room; **stanza di compensazione** clearing house; **stanza di
  soggiorno** living room
stanziare §287 *tr* to allocate; to appropriate; to budget ‖ *ref* to settle
stanzino *m* small room; closet
stappare *tr* to uncork
stare §263 *intr* (ESSERE) to stay; to
  stand; to live; to be; to be located;
  to linger; to last; to stick (*e.g., to a
  rule*); (poker) to stand pat; **come
  sta?** how are you?; **lasciar stare** to
  leave alone; **lasciar stare che** to
  leave aside that; **non stare in sé dalla
  gioia** to be beside oneself with joy;
  sta bene! O.K.!; **starci** to fit, e.g.,
  ci stanno trecento persone three hundred people fit there; **starci di** to be
  in favor of, e.g., **io ci starei d'andare
  al cine** I would be in favor of going
  to the movies; **stare** + **ger** to be +
  ger, e.g., **stava leggendo** he was reading; **stare a** to be up to; to stand on
  (*ceremony*); to base oneself on;
  to take (*a joke*); to cost, e.g., **a
  quanto sta il prosciutto?** how much
  does the ham cost?; **stare a** + *inf* to
  keep + ger, e.g., **stai sempre a sognare** you always keep dreaming;
  to take + inf, e.g., **stette poco a
  decidere** he took little time to decide;
  stare a cuore (with *dat*) to deem important, e.g., **gli sta a cuore il lavoro**
  he deems his work important; **stare
  a pancia all'aria** to not do a stroke
  of work; **stare al proprio posto** to
  keep one's place; **stare a segno** to
  behave properly; **stare a vedere** to be
  possible, e.g., **sta a vedere che non
  viene?** could it be possible that he
  won't come?; **stare bene** to be well;
  to be well-off; (with *dat*) to fit, to
  become, e.g., **questo vestito gli sta**

bene this suit fits him well, this suit becomes him; to serve right, e.g., **gli sta bene!** it serves him right!; **stare comodo** to be at ease; to remain seated; **stare con** (fig) to be on the side of; **starsene** to stay apart, e.g., **se ne sta solo soletto** he stays apart or all alone; **stare fermo** to be quiet; to not move; **stare in forse** to doubt; to be doubtful; **stare sulle proprie** to stand aloof; **stare su** to stand erect; **stare su tardi** to stay up late; **stia comodo!** remain seated!

starna f gray partridge

starnazzare intr to flap its wings; to flutter; to cackle

starnutare intr to sneeze

starnuto m sneeze

stasare [s] tr to unplug, unblock

staséra [s] adv tonight, this evening

sta·si f (-si) (com) stagnation; (pathol) stasis

statale adj government; state || f government employee

stàti·co -ca (-ci -che) static || f statics

stati·no -na adj (coll) migratory || m itemized list; (educ) registration form

stati·sta m (-sti) statesman

statisti·co -ca (-ci -che) adj statistical || m statistician || f statistics; **fare una statistica (di)** to survey; **statistiche** statistics (data)

stati·vo -va adj nonmigratory; permanent || m stand (of microscope)

stato m state; condition; plight; frame (of mind); status; estate (social class); **di stato** public (e.g., school); **essere in stato di arresto** to be under arrest; **stati** extracts from vital statistics; **Stati Pontifici** Papal States; **Stati Uniti** United States; **stato civile** marital status; vital statistics; **stato confessionale** state under ecclesiastical rule; **stato cuscinetto** buffer state; **stato di preallarme** state of emergency; **stato di previsione** preliminary budget; **stato interessante** pregnancy; **stato maggiore** (mil) general staff

statoreattóre m ramjet engine

stàtua f statue

statuà·rio -ria (-ri -rie) adj statuary; statuesque || m sculptor

statunitènse adj & mf American (U.S.A.)

statura f stature; height

statuto m statute

stavòlta adv (coll) this time

stazionaménto m parking; **stazionamento vietato** no parking

stazionare (stazióno) intr to park

stazionà·rio -ria adj (-ri -rie) stationary

stazióne f station; bearing, posture; **stazione balneare** shore resort; **stazione climatica** health resort, spa; **stazione di rifornimento** service station; **stazione di tassametri** cab stand; **stazione estiva** summer resort; **stazione generatrice** power plant; **stazione orbitale** orbiting station; **stazione sanitaria** clinic

stazza f tonnage; (naut) displacement

stazzare tr (naut) to gauge; (naut) to displace

stazzonare (stazzóno) tr to crumple

steatite f French chalk

stéc·ca f (-che) small stick; slat (of shutter); rib (of umbrella); bone (of whale); carton (of cigarettes); rail (of fence); letter opener; chisel (of sculptor); (billiards) cue; (billiards) miscue; (surg) splint; **fare una stecca** (billiards) to miscue; (mus) to sing or play a sour note

steccadèn·ti m (-ti) (coll) toothpick

steccare §197 (stécco) tr to fence; to put in a splint || intr to play or sing a sour note; (billiards) to miscue

steccato m fence; (racing) inside track

stecchétto m small stick; **tenere a stecchetto** to keep on a strict diet; to keep short of money

stecchino m toothpick

stecchi·to -ta adj stiff; lean, lank; **dry** (twig); dumfounded

stéc·co m (-chi) stick, twig

stecconata f stockade; fence

stélla f star; rowel (of spur); speck of fat (in soup); (fig) sky; **a stella** star-shaped; stellar; **montare alle stelle** to be sky-high (said, e.g., of prices); **portare alle stelle** to praise to the skies; **stella alpina** edelweiss; **stella cadente** shooting star; **stella di mare** starfish; **stella filante** shooting star; confetti; **stella polare** polestar, lodestar

stellare adj stellar; (mach) radial || v (stéllo) tr to spangle with stars; to stud

stella·to -ta adj starry; star-spangled; star-shaped; studded

stellétta f (mil) star; (typ) asterisk; **guadagnarsi le stellette** (mil) to earn a promotion; **portare le stellette** (mil) to be in the service

stellina f starlet

stelloncino m (journ) short paragraph

stèlo m stem, stalk

stèm·ma m (-mi) coat of arms; genealogy (of a manuscript)

stemperare (stèmpero) tr to dilute; to blunt; to untemper; (lit) to waste || ref to melt; to become dull or blunt

stendardo m banner, standard

stèndere §270 tr to stretch; to hang up (laundry); to spread; to draw up (a document); (mil) to deploy; **stendere a terra** to knock down || ref to stretch out

stendibianche·rìa m (-rìa) clothes rack, clotheshorse

stenodattilògra·fo -fa mf shorthand typist

stenografare (stenògrafo) tr to take down in shorthand

stenografìa f shorthand, stenography

stenogràfi·co -ca adj (-ci -che) stenographic, shorthand

stenògra·fo -fa mf stenographer

stenòsi f (pathol) stricture

stenotipìa f stenotypy

stentare (stènto) tr to eke out (a living)

‖ *intr* to barely make ends meet; **stentare a** to hardly be able to; to find it hard to

stenta·to -ta *adj* hard; stunted; strained (*smile*)

stènto *m* privation; hardship; **a stento** hardly; with difficulty; **senza stento** without any trouble

stèr·co *m* (**-chi**) dung

stereofòni·co -ca *adj* (**-ci -che**) stereo, stereophonic

stereoscòpi·co -ca *adj* (**-ci -che**) stereoscopic

stereoscò·pio *m* (**-pi**) stereoscope

stereotipa·to -ta *adj* stereotyped

sterilizzare [ddzz] *tr* to sterilize

sterlina *f* pound sterling

sterminare (**stèrmino**) *tr* to exterminate

stermìna·to -ta *adj* immense, boundless

stermì·nio *m* (**-ni**) extermination; (**coll**) large amount, lots

stèrno *m* breastbone

sterpàglia *f* brushwood; undergrowth

stèrpo *m* dry twig; bramble

sterrare (**stèrro**) *tr* to excavate

sterratóre *m* digger

sterzare (**stèrzo**) *tr* to diminish by one third; to thin out (*woodland*); (**aut**) to steer ‖ *intr* to swerve

sterzata *f* swerve

stèrzo *m* handle bar; (**aut**) steering gear; (**aut**) steering wheel

stésa [s] *f* coat (*of paint*); string (*of clothes on line*)

stés·so -sa *adj* same, e.g., **lo stesso mese** the same month; very, e.g., **tuo fratello stesso** your very brother; **essere alle stesse** to be just the same; **io stesso** I myself; **lui stesso** he himself, etc.; **per sé stesso** by himself; **by itself** ‖ *pron* same; same thing; **fa lo stesso** it's all the same, it makes no difference

stesura [s] *f* drawing up (*of a contract*); **prima stesura** first draft

stetoscò·pio *m* (**-pi**) stethoscope

stìa *f* chicken coop

Stige *m* Styx

stì·gio -gia *adj* (**-gi -gie**) Stygian

stigmate *fpl* stigmata

stilare *tr* to draft properly

stile *m* style

stilè *adj invar* stylish

stilétto *m* dagger, stiletto

stilizzare [ddzz] *tr* to stylize

stilla *f* (**lit**) drop, droplet

stillare *tr* to exude; to distill ‖ *intr* (ESSERE) to ooze, drip, exude ‖ *ref*—**stillarsi il cervello** to rack one's brains

stillicì·dio *m* (**-di**) dripping; repetition

stilo *m* stylus; arm (*of steelyard*); dagger; gnomon (*of sundial*); (**poet**) style ‖ *f* (**coll**) fountain pen

stilogràfi·ca *f* (**-che**) fountain pen

stima *f* appraisal; esteem; (**naut**) dead reckoning; **a stima d'occhio** more or less

stimare *tr* to estimate; to deem; to esteem ‖ *ref* (**coll**) to think a lot of oneself

stima·tóre -trice *mf* appraiser; admirer

stìmmate *fpl* var of **stigmate**

stimolante *adj* & *m* stimulant

stimolare (**stìmolo**) *tr* to stimulate

stìmolo *m* influence; stimulus

stìn·co *m* (**-chi**) shinbone; shin; **stinco di santo** saintly person, saint; **rompere gli stinchi a** to annoy

stìngere §126 *tr, intr* (ESSERE) & *ref* to fade

stipa *f* kindling wood, brushwood

stipare *tr* & *ref* to crowd, jam

stipendiare §287 (**stipèndio**) *tr* to employ, hire; to pay a salary to

stipendia·to -ta *adj* salaried ‖ *mf* salaried person

stipèn·dio *m* (**-di**) pay, salary

stipétto *m* (**naut**) closet, cabinet

stìpite *m* jamb; stock, family; (**bot**) trunk (*of palm tree*)

stipo *m* cabinet

stipulare (**stìpulo**) *tr* to draw up (*a contract*); to stipulate

stiracchiare §287 *tr* to stretch; to eke out (*a living*); to twist (*a meaning*); to haggle over ‖ *intr* to haggle; to economize ‖ *ref* to stretch out

stirare *tr* to stretch; to iron, press ‖ *intr* to iron ‖ *ref* to stretch out

stira·tóre -trice *mf* ironer, presser

stiratura *f* ironing; stretching

stirerìa *f* ironing shop

stiro *m*—**ferro da stiro** see **ferro**

stirpe *f* family; birth, origin

stitichézza *f* constipation

stìti·co -ca *adj* (**-ci -che**) constipated; (**fig**) tight

stiva *f* (**naut**) hold; (**lit**) beam (*of plow*)

stivàg·gio *m* (**-gi**) stowage

stivale *m* boot; **dei miei stivali** goodfor-nothing; **lustrare gli stivali a qlcu** to lick s.o.'s boots

stivalétto *m* high shoe

stivalóne *m* boot; **stivaloni da equitazione** riding boots; **stivaloni da palude** hip boots

stivare *tr* to stow

stivatóre *m* stevedore

stizza *f* anger; irritation

stizzire §176 *tr* to anger, vex ‖ *ref* to get angry

stizzó·so -sa [s] *adj* peevish, irritable

stoccafisso *m* stockfish

stoccata *f* thrust (*with dagger or rapier*); dig, sarcastic remark; touch (*for money*)

stòc·co *m* (**-chi**) dagger; rapier; stalk (*of corn*)

Stoccólma *f* Stockholm

stòffa *f* cloth, material; (**fig**) stuff, makings

stoicismo *m* stoicism

stòi·co -ca (**-ci -che**) *adj* stoic, stoical ‖ *m* stoic; Stoic

stoino *m* doormat

stòla *f* stole

stòli·do -da *adj* foolish, silly

stoltézza *f* foolishness, silliness

stól·to -ta *adj* silly ‖ *mf* fool

stomacare §197 (**stòmaco**) *tr* to disgust; to nauseate

stomachévole *adj* disgusting, sickening

stòma·co m (-ci or -chi) stomach; maw (of animal); **dare di stomaco** to vomit

stonare (**stòno**) tr to sing or play out of tune; to upset || intr to sing or play out of tune; to be out of place; to not harmonize

stona·to -ta adj out-of-tune; upset; clashing (color)

stonatura f jarring sound; clash (of colors); lack of harmony

stóppa f tow; oakum; **di stoppa** flaxen; weak, trembling; **stoppa incatramata** oakum

stoppàc·cio m (-ci) wad

stóppie fpl stubble

stoppino m wick

stoppó·so -sa [s] adj stubby; stringy

stórcere §272 tr to twist; to twitch; to wrench (one's ankle); to roll (one's eyes) || ref to twist; to writhe; to bend

stordiménto m bewilderment; dizziness

stordire §176 tr to bewilder; to daze || intr to be bewildered || ref to dull one's senses

storditàggine f carelessness; mistake, blunder

stordi·to -ta adj careless; bewildered; amazed; dizzy || mf scatterbrain

stòria f history; story, tale; fact; **fare storie** to stand on ceremony; **un'altra storia** a horse of another color

stòri·co -ca (-ci -che) adj historical || m historian

storièlla f tale, short story; joke

storiografia f historiography

storióne m sturgeon

stormire §176 intr to rustle

stórmo m swarm, flock; (aer) group

stornare (**stórno**) tr to ward off; to dissuade; to divert (funds); to write off (as noncollectable)

stornèllo m Italian folksong; (orn) starling

stór·no -na adj dapple-gray || m (com) transfer; (orn) starling

storpiare §287 (**stòrpio**) tr to cripple; to clip (one's words)

stòr·pio -pia (-pi -pie) adj crippled || m cripple

stòr·to -ta adj twisted; crooked; crippled || f twist; dislocation; retort

stoviglie fpl dishes; **lavare le stoviglie** to wash the dishes

stra- pref adj extra-, e.g., **straordinario** extraordinary; over-, e.g., **stracarico** overloaded

stràbi·co -ca adj (-ci -che) crosseyed

strabiliante adj astonishing, amazing

strabiliare §287 tr to amaze || intr & ref to be amazed

strabismo m strabismus, squint

straboccare §197 (**strabócco**) intr to overflow

strabocchévole adj overflowing

strabuzzare [ddzz] tr (coll) to roll (one's eyes)

stracàri·co -ca adj (-chi -che) overloaded, overburdened

stracca f—**pigliare una stracca** to be dead tired

straccale m breeching (of harness); **straccali** (coll) suspenders

straccare §197 tr (coll) to tire

stracciaiò·lo -la m/f ragpicker

stracciare §128 tr to tear, rend; to comb (natural silk)

stràc·cio -cia (-ci -ce) adj torn, in rags; waste (paper) || m rag, tatter; tear, rend; combed silk

stracció·ne -na mf tatterdemalion

straccivéndo·lo -la mf ragpicker; rag dealer

strac·co -ca adj (-chi -che) tired; worn-out; **alla stracca** lazily || f see **stracca**

stracòt·to -ta adj overcooked, overdone || m stew

stracuòcere §144a tr to overcook, overdo

strada f roadway; street; **da strada** vulgar, common; **divorare la strada** to burn up the road; **essere in mezzo a una strada** to be in a bad way; **fare strada** to pave the way for; **farsi strada** to make one's way; **prender la strada** to set forth; **strada carrozzabile** carriage road; **strada dell'orto** easy way out; **strada ferrata** railroad; **strada maestra** main road; **tagliare la strada a** to stand in the way of; (aut) to cut in front of

stradale adj road; street; traffic (e.g., accident); highway (police) || m avenue || f highway patrol

stradà·rio m (-ri) street directory

strafalcióne m blunder, gross error

strafare §173 tr to overdo; to overcook

strafóro m drilled hole; **di straforo** stealthily

strafottènte adj unconcerned, nonchalant; arrogant, impudent

strafottènza f nonchalance, unconcern; arrogance, impudence

strage f butchery, massacre, carnage; (coll) multitude, lot

stragrande adj enormous, huge

stralciare §128 tr to prune, trim (grapevines); to eliminate, remove; (com) to liquidate

stràl·cio adj invar interim; emergency (e.g., law); liquidating || m (-ci) excerpt; clearance sale; **a stralcio at a bargain**

strale m (lit) arrow

strallo m (naut) stay

stralunare tr to roll (one's eyes)

straluna·to -ta adj upset; wild-eyed

stramazzare tr to fell || intr (ESSERE) to fall down

stramazzo m sluice; (coll) straw mattress

stramberìa f eccentricity

stram·bo -ba adj odd, queer, eccentric; crooked (legs); squint (eyes)

strame m litter; fodder

strampala·to -ta adj strange; preposterous, absurd

stranézza f strangeness; oddity

strangolare (**stràngolo**) tr to strangle; (naut) to furl

strangola·tóre -trice mf strangler

straniare §287 tr (lit) to draw away || ref to become estranged

straniè·ro -ra *adj* foreign, alien; (lit) strange || *mf* foreigner, alien

stra·no -na *adj* strange, odd; (lit) estranged

straordinà·rio -ria (-ri -rie) *adj* extraordinary; extra || *mf* temporary employee || *m* overtime

strapagare §209 *tr* to overpay; to pay too much for

strapazzare *tr* to rebuke, upbraid; to mishandle; to bungle || *ref* to overwork oneself

strapazza·to -ta *adj* crumpled; bungled; scrambled (*eggs*); overworked || *f* upbraiding, rebuke; fatigue

strapazzo *m* misuse; fatigue; excess; **da strapazzo** working (*clothes*); hackneyed, second-rate

strapèrdere §212 *tr & intr* to lose hopelessly || *intr* to be wiped out

strapiè·no -na *adj* chock-full

strapiombare (strapiómbo) *intr* to overhang, jut out

strapiómbo *m* overhang; **a strapiombo** sheer (*cliff*)

strapotènte *adj* overpowerful

strappare *tr* to pull; to tear, rend; to wring (*s.o.'s heart*); **strappare le lacrime a qlcu** to move s.o. to tears; **strappare qlco a qlcu** to pry s.th out of s.o.; to snatch s.th from s.o. || *ref* to tear (*e.g., one's hair*)

strappata *f* pull, tug, snatch

strappo *m* pull; tear, rip; infraction, breach; pulling away (*on a bicycle*); patch (*of sky*); **a strappi** in jerks; **strappo muscolare** pulled muscle; sprain

strapuntino *m* folding seat, jump seat; bucket seat; (naut) mattress

straríc·co -ca *adj* (**-chi -che**) (coll) immensely rich

straripare *intr* (ESSERE & AVERE) to overflow

strascicare §197 (**stràscico**) *tr* to drag; to shuffle; **strascicare le parole** to drawl

strascichì·o *m* (**-i**) shuffle (*of feet*)

stràsci·co *m* (**-chi**) train (*of skirt*); trail; sequel, aftermath; **a strascico** dragging

strascinare (stràscino) *tr* to drag || *ref* to drag oneself, drag

strascini·o *m* (**-i**) shuffle

stràscino *m* dragnet, trawl

stratagèm·ma *m* (**-mi**) stratagem

strategìa *f* strategy

stratègi·co -ca *adj* (**-ci -che**) strategic

stratè·go *m* (**-ghi**) strategist; general, commander

stratificare §197 (**stratìfico**) *tr* to stratify

strato *m* layer; coat, coating; stratum; (meteor) stratus

stratosfèra *f* stratosphere

strattóne *m* jerk, tug

stravagante *adj* extravagant; whimsical, capricious || *mf* eccentric

stravèc·chio -chia *adj* (**-chi -chie**) aged (*cheese, wine, etc.*); very old

stravincere §285 *tr* to overpower

straviziare §287 *intr* to be intemperate

stravì·zio *m* (**-zi**) intemperance, excess

stravòlgere §289 *tr* to roll (*the eyes*); to distort; to derange

straziante *adj* heartbreaking; excruciating (*pain*); horrible

straziare §287 *tr* to torture; to dismay; to mangle; to murder (*a language*)

strazia·to -ta *adj* torn, stricken

strà·zio *m* (**-zi**) suffering, pain; torture; shame; boredom; **fare strazio di** to squander

stré·ga *f* (**-ghe**) witch; sorceress

stregare §209 (**strégo**) *tr* to bewitch

stregóne *m* sorcerer; witch doctor

stregonerìa *f* witchcraft; sorcery

strègua *f* standard, criterion; **alla stregua di** on the basis of

strema·to -ta *adj* exhausted

strènna *f* Christmas gift, New Year's gift; special New Year's issue

strè·nuo -nua *adj* strenuous

strepitare (strèpito) *intr* to make a noise; to shout, make a racket

strèpito *m* noise, racket; **fare strepito** to make a hit

strepitó·so -sa [s] *adj* loud, noisy; resounding (*success*)

streptomicina *f* streptomycin

stressa·to -ta *adj* under stress

strétta *f* grasp, clench; tightening (*of brakes*); hold; press, crush; pang; mountain pass; **mettere alle strette** to drive into a corner; **stretta dei conti** rendering of accounts; **stretta di mano** handshake; **stretta finale** climax

strettézza *f* narrowness; **strettezze** straits, hardship

strét·to -ta *adj* narrow; tight; bare (*necessities*); pure (*e.g., dialect*); strict; clenched (*fist*); heavy (*heart*); minimum (*price*); (phonet) close || *m* straits, narrows || *f* see **stretta** || **stretto** *adv* tightly

strettóia *f* narrow stretch; hardship; bandage

strìa *f* stripe, streak

striare §119 *tr* to stripe, streak

stricnina *f* strychnine

stridènte *adj* jarring; clashing (*colors*); strident (*sound*)

strìdere §264 *tr* to grit (*one's teeth*) || *intr* to shriek; to squeak; to creak; to clash (*said of colors*); to croak (*said of raven*); to hoot (*said of owl*); to howl (*said of wind*) || *ref* (coll) to be resigned

strido *m* (**-di & -da** *fpl*) shriek; squeak

stridóre *m* shriek; creak, squeak; gnashing (*of teeth*)

stridu·lo -la *adj* shrill

strigare §209 *tr* to disentangle || *ref* to extricate oneself

strìglia *f* currycomb

strigliare §280 *tr* to curry; to upbraid || *ref* to groom oneself

strillare *tr* to shout; (coll) to scold; (coll) to hawk (*newspapers*) || *intr* to scream

strillo *m* shriek; shout, scream

strilló·ne -na *mf* loud-mouthed person || *m* newsdealer; newsboy, paperboy

striminzi·to -ta *adj* shrunken; tight; stunted; skinny

strimpellare (strimpèllo) *tr* to thrum; to thrum on

strinare *tr* to singe; to burn (*with a flatiron*)

strin·ga *f* (**-ghe**) lace; shoelace

stringa·to -ta *adj* terse, concise

stringere §265 *tr* to tighten; to grip; to shake, clasp (*a hand*); to drive into a corner; to squeeze; to embrace; to close (*an alliance, a deal*); to wring (*one's heart*); to clench (*the fist*); (*lit*) to gird (*a sword*); (*mus*) to accelerate; **stringere d'assedio** to besiege; **stringere i freni** to put the brakes on || *intr* to be tight; **il tempo stringe** time is running short; **stringi, stringi** at the very end, in conclusion || *ref* to squeeze close together; to shrink; to coagulate; to draw close; **stringersi a** to snuggle up to; **stringersi addosso a** to attack; **stringersi nelle spalle** to shrug one's shoulders

stringina·so [s] *m* (**-so**) pince-nez

stri·scia *f* (**-sce**) strip, band; trail; stripe; line; **a strisce** striped; **striscia d'atterramento** airstrip; **striscia di cuoio** strop

strisciante *adj* crawling; (*fig*) fawning

strisciare §128 *tr* to shuffle (*feet*); to graze; **strisciare una riverenza** to curtsy || *intr* to creep, crawl; to graze by || *ref* to fawn; **strisciarsi a** to rub one's back against

strisciata or **strisciatura** *f* sliding; trail

stri·scio *m* (**-sci**) rubbing; shuffling; **ballare di striscio** to shuffle; **da** or **di striscio** superficial (*wound*)

strisció *m* festoon; festooned sign; flatterer; **striscione d'arrivo** landing (*in gymnastics*); **striscione del traguardo** (sports) tape

striscióni *adv* crawling

stritolare (stritolo) *tr* to crush, smash

strizzalimó·ni *m*(**-ni**) lemon squeezer

strizzare *tr* to squeeze, press; to wink (*the eye*); **strizzare l'occhio** to wink

strizza·tóio *m* (**-tói**) wringer

strò·fa or **strò·fe** *f* (**-fe**) strophe

strofinàc·cio *m* (**-ci**) dust cloth

strofinare *tr* to rub; to polish || *ref* to rub oneself; to fawn

strofinata *f*—**dare una strofinata a** to give a lick and a promise to

strofiní·o *m* (**-i**) rubbing; wiping

stròla·ga *f* (**-ghe**) (orn) loon

strombatura *f* embrasure

strombazzare *tr* to glorify; **strombazzare i propri meriti** to toot one's own horn || *intr* to blast away on the trumpet

strombazza·tóre -trice *mf* show-off

strombettare (strombétto) *tr* to trumpet, toot

stroncare §197 (**strónco**) *tr* to break off; to break down; to eliminate; (fig) to criticize severely

stroncatura *f* devastating criticism

strònzio *m* strontium

strónzo *m* (vulg) turd

stropicciare §128 *tr* to rub (*hands*); to

drag, shuffle (*feet*); (coll) to crumple || *ref*—**stropicciarsene** (coll) to not give a hoot

stropicci·o *m* (**-i**) rubbing; shuffling

stròzza *f* (coll) gullet, throat

strozzare (stròzzo) *tr* to strangle; to stop up; to fleece, swindle || *ref* to choke; to narrow

strozza·to -ta *adj* choked; choking; strangulated (*hernia*)

strozzatura *f* narrowing

strozzinàg·gio *m* (**-gi**) usury

strozzino *m* usurer, loan shark

strùggere §266 *tr* to melt; to consume || *ref* to melt; to pine away; to be upset; **struggersi di** to be consumed by

struggiménto *m* melting; longing; torment

strumentale *adj* instrument (*flying*); capital (*goods*); instructional (*language, in multi-lingual regions*); (gram, mus) instrumental

strumentali·sta *mf* (**-sti -ste**) instrumentalist

strumentalizzare [ddzz] *tr* to use, take advantage of

strumentare (struménto) *tr* to orchestrate

struménto *m* instrument; tool, implement; **strumento a corda** stringed instrument; **strumento a fiato** wind instrument; **strumento di bordo** (aer) flight recorder

strusciare §128 *tr* to rub; to shuffle (*feet*); to crumple; to wear out || *ref*—**strusciarsi a** to fawn on

strutto *m* lard, shortening

struttura *f* structure

strutturare *tr* to organize, structure

struzzo *m* ostrich

stuccare §197 *tr* to putty; to stucco; to surfeit || *ref* to grow weary

stucchévole *adj* sickening

stuc·co -ca (**-chi -che**) *adj* bored; **stucco e ristucco** sick and tired || *m* putty; stucco; plaster of Paris; **rimanere di stucco** to be taken aback

studèn·te -téssa *mf* student

studenté·sco -sca (**-schi -sche**) *adj* student; student-like || *f* student body

studiare §287 *tr* to study; **studiarle tutte** to consider every angle || *intr* to study; to try || *ref* to try; to gaze at oneself

studia·to -ta *adj* affected, studied

stù·dio *m* (**-di**) study; school district; office (*of professional man*); studio; (hist) university; (lit) wish; (mus) étude; **a studio** on purpose; **essere allo studio** to be under consideration

studió·so -sa [s] *adj* studious || *m* scholar

stufa *f* stove, heater; hothouse

stufare *tr* to warm up, heat up; to stew; (coll) to bore

stufato *m* stew

stu·fo -fa *adj* (coll) bored, sick and tired || *f* see **stufa**

stuòia *f* mat; matting

stuòlo *m* throng, crowd; flock; (lit) army

stupefacènte *adj* amazing; habit-forming || *m* dope

stupefare §173 *tr* to amaze, astonish

stupefazióne *f* amazement, astonishment; stupefaction

stupèn·do -da *adj* stupendous

stupidàggine *f* stupidity; silliness; child's play, cinch

stùpi·do -da *adj* stupid; silly; (lit) amazed

stupire §176 *tr* to amaze || *ref* to be amazed

stupóre *m* amazement

stuprare *tr* to rape

stura *f* tapping; uncorking; **dar la stura a** to begin (*a speech*)

sturabottì·glie *m* (**-glie**) bottle opener

sturalavandi·ni *m* (**-ni**) plunger (*to open up clogged sink*)

sturare *tr* to uncork; to take the wax out of (*ears*); to open up (*clogged line*)

stuzzicadèn·ti *m* (**-ti**) toothpick

stuzzicare §197 (**stùzzico**) *tr* to pick (*e.g., one's teeth*); to bother; to excite, arouse; to tease; to sharpen (*appetite*)

su *adv* up; up; on top; upstairs; **da . . . in su** from . . . on, e.g., **dal mese scorso in su** from last month on; **di su** from upstairs; **in su** up; **metter su** to put on the fire; to instigate; **metter su bottega** to set up shop; **metter su casa** to set up housekeeping; **più su** higher; further up; **su!** come on!; let's go!; **su di** on; **su e giù** back and forth; up and down; **su per giù** more or less; **tirarsi su** to lift oneself up; to sit up; to get better, recover; **tirar su** to pick up; to grow, raise; **venir su** to grow; to come up || §4 *prep* on, upon; up; towards; over, above; onto; against; at, e.g., **sul far del giorno** at daybreak; on top of; out of, e.g., **due volte su tre** two times out of three; **mettere su superbia** to become proud; **stare sulle sue** to be reserved; **sul serio** in earnest; **su misura** made to order

suaccenna·to -ta *adj* above-mentioned

sub *m* (**sub**) (coll) skindiver

subàcque·o -a *adj* submarine

subaffittare *tr* to sublet

subaffitto *m* subletting, sublet; **prendere in subaffitto** to sublet

subaltèr·no -na *adj & m* subaltern; subordinate

subastare *tr* to auction off

sùbbia *f* stonecutter's chisel

subbù·glio *m* (**-gli**) turmoil, hubbub

subcosciènte *adj & m* subconscious

sùbdo·lo -la *adj* treacherous, deceitful

subentrare (**subéntro**) *intr* (ESSERE) (with *dat*) to succeed, follow

subire §176 *tr* to suffer; to undergo

subissare *tr* to ruin; to sink; to overwhelm || *intr* (ESSERE) to sink; to go to rack and ruin

subisso *m* ruin; (coll) lots, plenty

subitàne·o -a *adj* sudden

sùbi·to -ta *adj* (lit) sudden || *m*—**d'un subito** all of a sudden || **subito** *adv*

rapidly; immediately; right away; **subito al principio** at the very beginning; **subito dopo** right after; **subito prima** right before || *interj* right away!

sublima·to -ta *adj* sublimated || *m* **sublimato corrosivo** corrosive sublimate

sublime *adj & m* sublime

subodorare (**subodóro**) *tr* to suspect; to get wind of

subordinare (**subórdino**) *tr* to subordinate

subordina·to -ta *adj & m* subordinate || *f* subordinate clause

subornare (**subórno**) *tr* to bribe

substrato *m* substratum

suburba·no -na *adj* suburban

subùr·bio *m* (**-bi**) suburb

succedàne·o -a *adj & m* substitute

succèdere §132 (*pp* **succeduto** or **succèsso**) *intr* (ESSERE) (with *dat*) to succede, to follow || *ref* to follow one another, follow one after the other || (*pret* **succèssi**; *pp* **succèsso**) *intr* (ESSERE) to happen, to come to pass; (with *dat*) to happen to, to come over, e.g., **che gli è successo?** what happened to him?

successióne *f* succession; **in successione** in succession; in a row

successì·vo -va *adj* successive; next

successo *m* success; outcome

successóre *m* successor

successò·rio -ria *adj* (**-ri -rie**) inheritance (*tax*)

succhiare §287 *tr* to suck

succhièllo *m* gimlet

succhiétto *m* pacifier

sùc·chio *m* (**-chi**) suck, sucking; (bot) sap; (coll) gimlet

succiaca·pre *m* (**-pre**) goatsucker, whippoorwill

succin·to -ta *adj* scanty (*clothing*); succinct, concise

suc·co *m* (**-chi**) juice; (fig) gist

succó·so -sa [s] *adj* juicy; pithy

succursale *f* branch, branch office

sud *m* south

sudafrica·no -na *adj & mf* South African

sudamerica·no -na *adj & mf* South American

sudàmina *f* prickly heat

sudare *tr* to sweat; to ooze; **sudare il pane** to earn one's living by the sweat of one's brow; **sudare sette camicie** to toil very hard || *intr* to perspire, sweat; to reek

sudà·rio *m* (**-ri**) shroud

suda·to -ta *adj* wet with perspiration; hard-earned || *f* sweat, sweating

suddét·to -ta *adj* aforesaid, above

sùddi·to -ta *adj & mf* subject

suddivìdere §158 *tr* to subdivide

sud-èst *m* southeast

sudicerìa *f* filth, filthiness; smut

sùdi·cio -cia (**-ci -cie**) *adj* dirty, filthy || *m* dirt, filth

sudiciume *m* dirt, filth

sudi·sta *mf* (**-sti -ste**) Southerner

sudóre *m* sweat, perspiration

sud-òvest *m* southwest

sufficiènte *adj* sufficient, adequate; self-sufficient ‖ *m* sufficient

sufficiènza *f* sufficiency; self-sufficiency; (educ) minimum passing grade

suffisso *m* suffix

suffragare §209 *tr* to support; to pray for

suffragétta *f* suffragette

suffrà·gio *m* (-gi) suffrage

suffumicare §197 (**suffùmico**) *tr* to fumigate

suffumi·gio *m* (-gi) treatment by inhalation; fumigation

suggellare (**suggèllo**) *tr* to seal

suggèllo *m* seal

suggeriménto *m* suggestion

suggerire §176 *tr* to suggest; to prompt

suggeri·tóre -trice *mf* prompter ‖ *m* (baseball) coach

suggestionàbile *adj* suggestible

suggestionare (**suggestióno**) *tr* to influence by suggestion ‖ *ref*—**suggestionarsi a** + *inf* to talk oneself into + *ger*

suggestióne *f* suggestion; fascination

suggesti·vo -va *adj* suggestive; fascinating; (law) leading (*question*)

sùghero *m* cork

sugli §4

sugna *f* fat; lard

su·go *m* (-ghi) juice; gravy; gist, pith; **non c'è sugo** it's no fun; there's nothing to it; **senza sugo** pointless, dull

sugó·so -sa [s] *adj* juicy

sui §4

suici·da (-di -de) *adj* suicidal ‖ *mf* suicide (*person*)

suicidare *ref* to commit suicide

suici·dio *m* (-di) suicide (*act*)

sui·no -na *adj* swinish; see **carne** ‖ *m* swine

sul §4

sulfamìdi·co -ca (-ci -che) *adj* sulfa ‖ *m* sulfa drug

sulla §4

sulle §4

sulli §4

sullo §4

sulloda·to -ta *adj* above-mentioned

sultano *m* sultan

summentova·to -ta, summenziona·to -ta, sunnomina·to -ta *adj* above-mentioned

sunteggiare §290 (**suntéggio**) *tr* to summarize

sunto *m* résumé, summary

suo sua §6 *adj & pron poss* (**suòi sue**)

suòcera *f* mother-in-law

suòcero *m* father-in-law; **i suoceri** the in-laws

suòla *f* sole (*of shoe*); share (*of plow*); (naut) sliding ways; (rr) flange (*of rail*)

suòlo *m* ground; soil; floor ‖ *m* (**suola** *fpl*) (coll) layer; (coll) sole (*of shoe*)

suonare (**suòno**) *tr & intr var of* **sonare**

suòno *m* sound; (fig) ring; **a suon di bastonate** with a sound thrashing; **a suon di fischi** with loud boos; **suono armonico** (mus) overtone

suòno·stère·o *m* (-o) stereo tape player

suòra *f* nun, sister

super- *pref adj & mf* super-, e.g., **supersonico** supersonic; over-, e.g., **superallenamento** overtraining

superaffollaménto *m* overcrowding

superare (**sùpero**) *tr* to surpass; to cross; to overcome; to pass; to exceed; (cards) to trump

supera·to -ta *adj* out-of-date, passé

supèrbia *f* pride, haughtiness; **montare in superbia** to get a swelled head

superbió·so -sa [s] *adj* proud, haughty

supèr·bo -ba *adj* proud, haughty; superb; spirited ‖ **i superbi** the haughty ones

supercarburante *m* high-octane gas

supercolòsso *m* supercolossal film

superdònna *f*—**si dà arie di superdonna** she thinks she's hot stuff

supereterodina *f* superheterodyne

superficiale *adj* superficial; surface; cursory, perfunctory ‖ *m* superficial fellow

superfì·cie *f* (-ci & cie) surface; area; **superficie portante** airfoil

supèr·fluo -flua *adj* superfluous ‖ *m* surplus

super·io *m* (-io) superego

superióra *f* (eccl) mother superior

superióre *adj* superior; upper; higher; above; **superiore a** a higher than; more than; larger than ‖ *m* superior

superlati·vo -va *adj & m* superlative

superlavóro *m* overwork

supermercato *m* supermarket

supersòni·co -ca *adj* (-ci -che) supersonic

supèrstite *adj* surviving; remaining ‖ *mf* survivor

superstizióne *f* superstition

superstizió·so -sa [s] *adj* superstitious

superstrada *f* superhighway

superuòmo *m* superman

supervisióne *f* supervision

supervisóre *m* supervisor; (mov) director

supi·no -na *adj* supine; on one's back

suppellèttile *f* furnishings; equipment; fixtures; fund (*of knowledge*)

supplementare *adj* supplementary

suppleménto *m* supplement; (mil) reinforcement

supplènte *adj & mf* substitute

supplènza *f* substitute assignment

suppleti·vo -va *adj* additional; (gram) suppletive

sùppli·ca *f* (-che) supplication; plea; petition

supplicante *mf* supplicant

supplicare §197 (**sùpplico**) *tr* to beseech; to plead with; to appeal to

supplichévole *adj* beseeching, imploring

supplire §176 *tr* to replace ‖ *intr* (with *dat*) to supplement, make up for

suppliziare §287 *tr* to torture; to execute

suppli·zio *m* (-zi) torture, torment; **estremo supplizio** capital punishment

suppórre §218 *tr* to suppose

suppòrto *m* support, prop

suppositò·rio *m* (-ri) suppository

supposizióne _f_ supposition; presumption

suppó·sto -sta _adj_ alleged ‖ _m_ supposition ‖ _f_ suppository

suppurare _intr_ (ESSERE & AVERE) to suppurate

supremazìa _f_ supremacy

suprè·mo -ma _adj_ supreme

surclassare _tr_ to outclass

surgelare (surgèlo) _tr_ to quick-freeze

surreali·sta _mf_ (-sti -ste) surrealist

surrenale _adj_ adrenal (gland)

surrène _m_ (anat) adrenal gland

surriscaldare _tr_ to overheat

surrogare §209 **(surrògo)** _tr_ to replace

surroga·to -ta _adj_ replaceable ‖ _m_ makeshift, substitute, ersatz

suscettìbile _adj_ susceptible; touchy

suscitare (sùscito) _tr_ to rouse; to give rise to; to provoke

susina _f_ plum

susino _m_ plum tree

susseguènte _adj_ subsequent, following

susseguire (susséguo) _intr_ (ESSERE) (with _dat_) to follow ‖ _ref_ to follow one after the other

sussidiare §287 _tr_ to subsidize

sussidià·rio -ria (-ri -rie) _adj_ subsidiary; (nav) auxiliary ‖ _m_ supplementary text book; subsidiary

sussì·dio _m_ (-di) subsidy; assistance, relief; **sussidi audiovisivi** audio-visual aids; **sussidi didattici** teaching aids; **sussidio di disoccupazione** unemployment compensation

sussiè·go _m_ (-ghi) stiffness, haughtiness

sussistènza _f_ substance; subsistence; (mil) quartermaster corps

sussìstere §114 _intr_ (ESSERE & AVERE) to subsist; to be, exist

sussultare _intr_ to start, jump; to quake

sussulto _m_ start, jump; **sussulto di terremoto** earth tremor

sussurrare _tr_ to whisper; to murmur, mutter ‖ _intr_ to whisper; to rustle ‖ _ref_—**si sussurra** it is rumored

sussurra·tóre -trice _mf_ whisperer; grumbler

sussurrì·o _m_ (-i) whispering; murmur; rustle

sussurro _m_ whisper; murmur

susta _f_ temple (_of_ spectacles); (coll) spring

suvvìa _interj_ come!, come on!

svagare §209 _tr_ to entertain; to distract ‖ _ref_ to have a good time; to relax

svaga·to -ta _adj_ absent-minded; inattentive

sva·go _m_ (-ghi) entertainment, diversion; avocation, hobby

svaligiare §290 _tr_ to ransack; to rob; to pirate

svaligia·tóre -trice _mf_ thief, robber

svalutare (svàluto & svaluto) _tr_ to devaluate; to depreciate; to belittle ‖ _ref_ to depreciate

svalutazióne _f_ depreciation

svanìre §176 _intr_ (ESSERE) to evaporate; to vanish

svanì·to -ta _adj_ faded, evaporated; vanished; enfeebled

svantàg·gio _m_ (-gi) disadvantage

svantaggió·so -sa [s] _adj_ disadvantageous

svaporare (svapóro) _intr_ (ESSERE) to evaporate; to vanish

svaria·to -ta _adj_ varied; **svaria·ti -te** several

svarióne _m_ blunder, gross error

svasare _tr_ to transplant from a pot; to make (_e.g., a gown_) flare

svasa·to -ta _adj_ bell-mouthed, flaring

svecchiare §287 **(svècchio)** _tr_ to renew; to rejuvenate; to modernize

svedése [s] _adj_ Swedish; safety (_match_) ‖ _mf_ Swede ‖ _m_ Swedish

svéglia _f_ awakening; reveille; alarm clock; **dare la sveglia a** to wake up

svegliare §280 _tr_ & _ref_ to wake up

svegliarino _m_ alarm clock; (coll) rebuke

své·glio -glia _adj_ (-gli -glie) awake; alert ‖ _f_ see **sveglia**

svelare (svélo) _tr_ to reveal; to unveil ‖ _ref_ to reveal oneself; **svelarsi per** to reveal oneself to be

svèllere §267 _tr_ (lit) to eradicate

sveltézza _f_ quickness; slenderness

sveltire §176 _tr_ to make shrewd; to quicken, accelerate ‖ _ref_ to become smart

svèl·to -ta _adj_ quick; slender; brisk; quick-witted; **alla svelta** quickly; **svelto di lingua** loose-tongued; **svelto di mano** light-fingered ‖ **svelto** _interj_ quick!

svenare (svéno) _tr_ to bleed to death; (fig) to bleed ‖ _ref_ to bleed to death; (fig) to bleed oneself white

svéndere §281 _tr_ to sell below cost; to undersell

svéndita _f_ clearance sale

svenévole _adj_ maudlin, mawkish

svenevolézza _f_ maudlinness, mawkishness

sveniménto _m_ faint, swoon

svenire §282 _intr_ (ESSERE) to faint

sventagliare §280 _tr_ to fan; to flash, display

sventagliata _f_ blow with a fan; volley

sventare (svènto) _tr_ to foil, thwart; (naut) to spill (_a sail_)

sventa·to -ta _adj_ careless, thoughtless

svèntola _f_ fan (_to kindle fire_); (coll) box, slap; **a sventola** (_ears_) that stick out

sventolare (svèntolo) _tr_ to wave; to fan; to winnow ‖ _intr_ to flutter ‖ _ref_ to fan oneself

sventolì·o _m_ (-i) fluttering, flutter

sventraménto _m_ demolition; disembowelment; hernia

sventrare (svèntro) _tr_ to demolish; to disembowel; to draw (_a fowl_)

sventura _f_ misfortune, mishap; bad luck

sventura·to -ta _adj_ unfortunate, unlucky

sverginare (svérgino) _tr_ to deflower

svergognare (svergógno) _tr_ to put to shame; to unmask

svergogna·to -ta _adj_ shameless

svergolare (svérgolo) *tr & ref* to warp; (mach) to twist

svernare (svèrno) *intr* to winter

svérza [dz] *f* big splinter

sverzino [dz] *m* lash, whipcord

svestire (svèsto) *tr* to undress; to hull (rice); (fig) to strip ‖ *ref* to undress; **svestirsi di** to shed (e.g., leaves)

svettare (svétto) *tr* to pollard, top ‖ *intr* to stand out; to sway (said of a tree)

Svè·vo -va *adj & m* Swabian

Svèzia, la Sweden

svezzaménto *m* weaning

svezzare (svézzo) *tr* to wean; **svezzare da** to break (s.o.) of (e.g., a habit)

sviare §119 *tr* to turn aside; to lead astray ‖ *intr & ref* to go astray; to straggle; (rr) to run off the track

svignare *intr* (ESSERE) to slip away ‖ *ref*—**svignarsela** to sneak away

svilire §176 *tr* to devaluate

svillaneggiare §290 (svillanéggio) *tr* to insult, abuse

sviluppare *tr* to develop; to cause; (lit) to uncoil ‖ *intr* (ESSERE & AVERE) & *ref* to develop; to break out (said of fire)

sviluppo *m* development; puberty

svincolare (svìncolo) *tr* to free; to clear (at customs)

svìncolo *m*—**svincolo autostradale**

interchange; **svincolo doganale** customs clearance

svirilizzare [ddzz] *tr* (fig) to emasculate

svisare *tr* to alter, distort

sviscerare (svìscero) *tr* to eviscerate; to examine thoroughly ‖ *ref*—**sviscerarsi per** to be crazy about; to bow and scrape to

sviscera·to -ta *adj* ardent, passionate; obsequious

svista *f* slip, error, oversight

svitare *tr* to unscrew

svìzze·ro -ra *adj & mf* Swiss ‖ **la Svizzera** Switzerland

svocia·to -ta *adj* hoarse

svogliatézza *f* laziness; listlessness

svoglia·to -ta *adj* lazy; listless

svolazzare *intr* to flutter, flit

svolazzo *m* flutter; short flight; curlicue, flourish

svòlgere §289 *tr* to unwrap; to unfold; to unwind; to develop; to pursue (an activity); to dissuade ‖ *ref* to unwind; to free oneself; to develop; to take place; to unfold

svolgiménto *m* development; composition

svòlta *f* turn; curve; turning point

svoltare (svòlto) *tr* to unwrap ‖ *intr* to turn

svotare §257 or **svuotare** (svuòto) *tr* to empty

T

T, t [ti] *m & f* eighteenth letter of the Italian alphabet

tabac·càio -càia *mf* (-**cài -càie**) tobacconist

tabaccare §197 *intr* to take snuff

tabaccherìa *f* cigar store

tabacchièra *f* snuffbox

tabac·co *m* (-**chi**) tobacco; **tabacco da fiuto** snuff

tabarro *m* winter coat; cloak

tabèlla *f* tablet; list; schedule; (coll) clapper, noisemaker; **tabella di marcia** timetable

tabellare *adj* (typ) on wooden blocks; scheduled

tabellóne *m* board; bulletin board; (basketball) backboard

tabernàcolo *m* tabernacle

ta·bù *adj invar & m* (-**bù**) taboo

tàbula *f*—**far tabula rasa di** to make a clean sweep of

tabulare (tàbulo) *tr* to tabulate

tabulatóre *m* tabulator

tabulatrice *f* printer (of computer)

tac·ca *f* (-**che**) notch; size; kind; tally; blemish; (typ) nick; **di mezza tacca** middle-sized; mediocre; **tacca di mira** rear sight (of firearm)

tacca·gno -gna *adj* stingy, closefisted ‖ *mf* miser

taccheggia·tóre -trice *mf* shoplifter ‖ *f* prostitute, streetwalker

taccheggiatura *f* or **tacchég·gio** *m* (-**gi**) shoplifting

tacchétto *m* high heel; cleat (on soccer or football shoe)

tacchina *f* turkey hen

tacchino *m* turkey

tàc·cia *f* (-**ce**) notoriety

tacciare §128 *tr*—**tacciare di** to accuse of, charge with

tac·co *m* (-**chi**) heel; block; (typ) underlay; **battere i tacchi** to take to one's heels

taccóne *m* (coll) patch; (coll) hobnail; **battere il taccone** to take to one's heels

taccuino *m* pocketbook; notebook

tacére *m* silence; **mettere a tacere** to silence ‖ §268 *tr* to conceal, withhold; to imply, understand ‖ *intr* to keep quiet; to stop playing; to quiet down; to be silent; **far tacere** to silence; **taci!** (coll) shut up!

tachìmetro *m* tachometer; (aut) speedometer

tacitare (tàcito) *tr* to silence, satisfy (a creditor); to pay off

tàci·to -ta *adj* silent; tacit

tacitur·no -na *adj* taciturn

tafano *m* horsefly, gadfly

tafferù·glio *m* (-**gli**) scuffle

taffe·tà *m* (-**tà**) taffeta; **taffetà adesivo**

or **inglese** adhesive plaster, court plaster

tàglia f ransom, reward; size; build; tally; (mach) tackle

tagliabór·se m (-se) pickpocket

tagliabò·schi m (-schi) woodcutter, woodsman

tagliacar·te m (-te) letter opener, paper knife

tagli·àcque m (-àcque) cutwater (of bridge)

tagliaèrba adj invar grass-cutting

tagliafèr·ro m (-ro) cold chisel

taglialé·gna m (-gna) woodcutter

tagliama·re m (-re) cutwater (of ship)

tagliando m coupon

tagliapiè·tre m (-tre) stonecutter

tagliare §280 tr to cut; to cut down; to cut off; to pick (a pocket); to cross (finish line); to tailor (a suit); to blend (wine); to turn off (e.g., water); **tagliare a fette** to slice; **tagliare in due** to split; **tagliare i panni addosso a qlcu** to slander s.o.; **tagliare i ponti con** to sever relations with; **tagliare i viveri a** to cut off supplies from; **tagliare la corda** to run away; **tagliare la strada a** to stand in the way of; (aut) to cut in front of; **tagliare le gambe a** to make wobbly (said of wine) || intr to cut; to bite (said of cold); **tagliare per una scorciatoia** to take a shortcut || ref to cut oneself; to tear (said of material)

tagliasiga·ri m (-ri) cigar cutter

tagliata f cut; clearing; (mil) abatis; **tagliata ai capelli** haircut

tagliatèlle fpl noodles

taglia·to -ta adj cut; fashioned; **essere tagliato per** to be cut out for; **tagliato all'antica** old-fashioned; **tagliato con l'accetta** rough-hewn || f see **tagliata**

taglia·tóre -trice mf cutter

tagliènte adj cutting || m edge

taglière m carving board

taglierina f paper cutter

tà·glio m (-gli) cut; cutting; dressmaking; cutting edge; sharpness; blending (of wines); size; denomination (of paper money); crossing (of t); (bb) fore edge; **a due tagli** double-edged; **a tagli** by the slice; **dare un taglio a** to chop; **di taglio** edgewise; **rifare il taglio a** to sharpen; **taglio cesareo** Caesarean section; **taglio d'abito** suiting; **taglio dei capelli** haircut; **venire in taglio** to come in handy

tagliòla f trap

tagliuzzare tr to shred, cut into shreds

tailandése [s] adj & mf Thai

Tailàndia, la Thailand

tailleur m (tailleur) woman's tailored costume

talal·tro -tra pron indef another, some other

tàlamo m (lit) nuptial bed

talare adj ankle-length || f soutane, cassock

talché conj so that

---

talco m talcum; talcum powder

tale adj such; such a; that; **il tale** such and such a; **un tale** such a; a certain; **un tal quale** such a; a certain || pron so-and-so; **il tal dei tali** so-and-so; Mr. so-and-so; **il tale** that fellow; that guy; **quel tale** that fellow, that guy; **tale e quale** like; **tali e quali** exactly, word for word; **un tale** someone, a certain person

talèa f (hort) cutting

talènto m talent; inclination; **a proprio talento** gladly, willingly; **di mal talento** grudgingly; **andare a talento** a to suit, e.g., **non gli va a talento nulla** nothing suits him

talismano m talisman

tallire §176 intr (ESSERE & AVERE) to sprout

tallonare (**tallóno**) tr (sports) to be at the heels of

talloncino m coupon, stub

tallóne m heel; coupon, stub; tang (of knife); **tallone d'Achille** Achilles heel

talménte adv so, so much

talóra adv sometimes

talpa f mole

talu·no -na pron indef some; someone, somebody || **talu·ni -ne** adj & pron indef some

talvòlta adv sometimes

tamarindo m tamarind

tambureggiare §290 (**tamburéggio**) intr to drum; to beat down (said, e.g., of hail)

tamburèllo m tambour (for embroidering); (mus) tambourine

tamburino m drummer

tamburo m drum; barrel (of watch; of windlass); **a tamburo battente** on the spot

tamerice f tamarisk

Tamigi m Thames

tampóco adv—**né tampoco** (archaic) nor . . . either

tamponaménto m stopping, plugging; rear-end collision

tamponare (**tampóno**) tr to tampon, plug; to collide with; to hit from the rear; (surg) to tampon

tampóne m plug, tampon, pad; (mus) drumstick; (rr) buffer; (surg) tampon; **tampone di vapore** vapor lock

tana f burrow; den; hole; hovel; base (in children games)

tanàglie fpl var of **tenaglie**

tan·ca f (-che) can, jerry can; tank

tanfo m musty or stuffy smell

tangènte adj tangent || f tangent; (com) commission

tàngere §269 (lit) to touch

Tàngeri f Tangier

tànghero m boor, lout

tangíbile adj tangible

tàni·ca f (-che) var of **tanca**

tantino m—**un tantino** a little, e.g., **è un tantino arrabbiato** he is a little angry; a little bit, e.g., **un tantino di dolce** a little bit of cake

tan·to -ta adj & pron indef such, so much; as much; **a dir tanto** or **a far tanto** at the most; **ai tanti**

(*del mese*) on such and such a day (*of the month*); a tanto to such a point; to such a level; **e tanto** odd, e.g., **mille dollari e tanto** a thousand odd dollars; **è tanto** it has been a long time, e.g., **è tanto che lo conosco** it has been a long time since I made his acquaintance; **fra tanto** meanwhile; **senza tanto chiasso** without any noise; **tan·ti -te** many; so many; as many; a lot, e.g., **grazie tante!** thanks a lot! **tanti . . . che** so many . . . that; **tanti . . . quanti** as many . . . as; **tanto di guadagnato** so much the better || **tanto** *adv* so much; so; only, e.g., **tanto per passare il tempo** only to pass the time; anyhow; anyway; **nè tanto nè quanto** at all; **tant'è** it's the same; **tanto che** so much that, e.g., **mi ha annoiato tanto che l'ho mandato via** he bothered me so much that I dismissed him; **tanto . . . che** both . . . and, e.g., **tanto Maria che Roberto** both Mary and Robert; so much . . . that; **tanto fa** or **vale** it's all the same; **tanto meglio** so much the better; **tanto meno** so much the less; **tanto per cambiare** as usual; **tanto più . . . quanto più** the more . . . the more; **tanto . . . quanto** as . . . as || **s—ascoltare con tanto d'orecchie** to be all ears; **di tanto in tanto** from time to time

tapi·no -na *adj* (lit) wretched || *mf* (lit) wretch

tappa *f* stopping place; stop; stage, leg; (sports) lap; **bruciare le tappe** to press on, keep going; **fare tappa** to stop

tappabu·chi *mf* (**-chi**) makeshift, pinch hitter, substitute

tappare *tr* to cork, plug; to shut up tight || *ref* to shut oneself in; to plug (*e.g., one's ears*)

tapparèlla *f* (coll) inside rolling shutter

tappéto *m* rug, carpet; (sports) canvas, mat; **mettere al tappeto** (boxing) to knock out; **tappeto erboso** lawn, green; **tappeto verde** gambling table

tappezzare (**tappèzzo**) *tr* to paper (*a wall*); to upholster

tappezzerìa *f* wallpaper; upholstery; upholsterer's shop; tapestry; wallflower

tappezzière *m* paperhanger; upholsterer

tappo *m* (cork, stopper; cap; plug; **tappo a corona** bottle cap; **tappo a vite** screw cap

tara *f* tare

taràntola *f* tarantula

tarare *tr* to tare; to set, adjust

tara·to -ta *adj* net (*weight*); calibrated (*instrument*); sickly, weak

tarchia·to -ta *adj* stocky, sturdy

tardare *tr* to delay || *intr* to delay; to be late

tardi *adv* late; **al più tardi** at the latest; **a più tardi!** so long!; **fare tardi** to be late; **più tardi** later; later on; **sul tardi** in the late afternoon

tardi·vo -va *adj* late; retarded, slow; belated

tar·do -da *adj* slow; late; **di età tarda** of advanced years; **tardo d'ingegno** slow-witted

tardó·ne -na *adj* slow-moving || *mf* slowpoke || *f* old dame, middle-aged vamp

tar·ga *f* (**-ghe**) plate; nameplate; shield; (aut) license plate; (sports) trophy

targare §209 *tr* (aut) to register

targatura *f* (aut) registration

targhétta *f* nameplate

tariffa *f* tariff; rate; rates

tariffà·rio -ria (**-ri -rie**) *adj* tariff; rate || *m* price list; rate book

tarlare *tr* to eat (*said of woodworms or moths*) || *intr* (ESSERE) & *ref* to become worm-eaten; to become moth-eaten

tarlo *m* woodworm; moth; bookworm; (fig) gnawing

tarma *f* moth; clothes moth

tarmare *tr* to eat (*said of moths*) || *intr* (ESSERE) & *ref* to become moth-eaten

tarmici·da (**-di -de**) *adj* moth-repelling || *m* moth repellent

taròc·co *m* (**-chi**) tarot; tarok

tarpare *tr* to clip; **tarpare le ali a** to clip the wings of

tartagliare §280 *tr* & *intr* to stutter, stammer

tàrta·ro -ra *adj* Tartar || *m* tartar; Tartar || **Tartaro** *m* Tartarus

tartaru·ga *f* (**-ghe**) turtle, tortoise; tortoise shell

tartassare *tr* to ill-treat; to harass

tartina *f* slice of bread and butter; canapé

tartufo *m* truffle; (fig) tartuffe, hypocrite

ta·sca *f* (**-sche**) pocket; briefcase; **aver le tasche piene di** to be sick and tired of; **da tasca** pocket; **rompere le tasche a** (vulg) to bother, annoy; **tasca in petto** inside pocket

tascàbile *adj* pocket; vest-pocket

tascapane *m* knapsack, rucksack

tascata *f* pocketful

taschino *m* vest pocket, small pocket

tassa *f* tax; (coll) duty, fee; **tassa complementare** surtax; **tassa di circolazione** road-use tax; **tassa di registro** registration fee; **tassa scolastica** tuition

tassàbile *adj* taxable

tassàmetro *m* taximeter; **tassametro di parcheggio** parking meter

tassare *tr* to tax; to assess || *ref* to pledge money

tassati·vo -va *adj* positive; specific; peremptory

tassazióne *f* taxation; tax

tassèllo *m* dowel; inlay; plug; patch; reinforcement

tas·sì *m* (**-sì**) taxi, taxicab

tassi·sta *m* (**-sti**) taxi driver

tasso *m* stake (*anvil*); yew tree; (com) rate (*e.g., of interest*); (zool) badger; **tasso valutario fluttuante** (econ) fluctuation of currency rate

tastare *tr* to touch; to feel; to probe; **tastare il terreno** (fig) to see how the land lies

tastièra *f* keyboard; manual (*of organ*)

tasto *m* touch, feeling, feel; plug (*e.g., in watermelon*); key (*of piano or typewriter*); sample (*in drilling*); **tasto bianco** white key, natural; **toccare un tasto falso** to strike a sour note

tastóni *adv*—**a tastoni** gropingly

tàtti·co -ca (-ci -che) *adj* tactical; tactful ‖ *m* tactician ‖ *f* tactics; prudence; tactfulness

tatto *m* touch; tact

tatuàg·gio *m* **(-gi)** tattoo

tatuare (tàtuo) *tr* to tattoo

taumatur·go *m* **(-gi & -ghi)** wonder-worker

tauri·no -na *adj* taurine, bull-like; bull

tavèrna *f* tavern, inn

tavernière *f* tavernkeeper

tàvola *f* board, plank; slab; table; tablet; bookplate; list; **tavola a ribalta** drop-leaf table; **tavola armonica** (mus) sound board; **tavola calda** cafeteria, snack bar; **tavola da stirare** ironing board; **tavola di salvezza** (fig) last recourse, lifesaver; **tavola imbandita** open house; **tavola nera** blackboard; **tavola operatoria** operating table; **tavola pitagorica** multiplication table; **tavola reale** backgammon; **tavole di fondazione** charter (*of a charitable institution*)

tavolàc·cio *m* **(-ci)** wooden board (*on which soldiers on guard and prisoners used to sleep*)

tavolare (tàvolo) *tr* to board up

tavolata *f* tableful

tavolato *m* planking; plateau

tavolétta *f* small table; tablet; bar (*e.g., of chocolate*)

tavolière *m* chessboard table; card table; plateau, tableland

tavolino *m* small table; desk

tàvolo *m* table; desk; **tavolo di gioco** gambling table; **tavolo d'ufficio** office desk

tavolòzza *f* palette

tazza *f* cup; bowl

tazzina *f* demitasse

tazzóna *f* mug

te §5 *pron pers*

tè *m* **(tè)** tea; **tè danzante** tea dance, thé dansant

tèa *adj fem*—**rosa tea** tea rose

teatrale *adj* theatrical

teatro *m* theater; performance; drama; stage; (fig) scene; **che teatro!** what fun!; **teatro dell'opera** or **teatro lirico** opera house; **teatro di posa** (mov) studio; **teatro di prosa** legitimate theater

teatróne *m* large theater; (coll) excellent box office

Tèbe *f* Thebes

tè·ca *f* **(-che)** case; (eccl) reliquary

tecnicismo *m* technicality

tècni·co -ca (-ci -che) *adj* technical ‖ *m* technician; engineer ‖ *f* technique; technics

téco §5 *prep phrase* (lit) with you

tedé·sco -sca *adj* & *mf* **(-schi -sche)** German

tediare §287 **(tèdio)** *tr* to bore ‖ *ref* to get bored

tè·dio *m* **(-di)** dullness, tedium, boredom; **recare tedio a** to annoy, bother

tedió·so -sa [s] *adj* dull, tedious

tegame *m* pan; **al tegame** fried (*e.g., eggs*)

tegamino *m* small pan; **uova al tegamino** fried eggs

téglia *f* pan; baking pan

tégola *f* tile; (fig) blow

tégolo *m* tile

teièra *f* teapot, teakettle

tèk *m* teak

téla *f* linen; cloth; material; canvas, oil painting; (fig) plot, trap; (lit) weft; (theat) curtain; **far tela** (coll) to beat it; **tela batista** batiste; **tela cerata** oilcloth; **tela da imballaggio** burlap; **tela di ragno** cobweb; **tela di sacco** sackcloth; **tela greggia** gunny, burlap; **tela smeriglio** emery cloth

te·làio *m* **(-lài)** loom; frame; embroidery frame; sash; stretcher (*for oil painting*); (aut) chassis; **telaio di finestra** window sash

teleama·tóre -trice *mf* TV viewer

telear·ma *f* **(-mi)** guided missile

telecabina *f* cable car

telecàmera *f* TV camera

telecomanda·to -ta *adj* remote-control

telecomando *m* remote control

telecommentatóre *m* TV newscaster

telecròna·ca *f* **(-che)** TV broadcast; **telecronaca diretta** live broadcast

telecroni·sta *mf* **(-sti -ste)** TV news announcer, TV newscaster

telediffusióne *f* TV broadcasting

teledram·ma *m* **(-mi)** teleplay

telefèri·ca *f* **(-che)** cableway, telpherage

telefonare (telèfono) *tr* & *intr* to telephone ‖ *ref* to call one another

telefonata *f* telephone call

telefòni·co -ca *adj* **(-ci -che)** telephone

telefoni·sta *mf* **(-sti -ste)** telephone operator, central; telephone installer

telèfono *m* telephone; **telefono a gettone** pay telephone (*operated by tokens*); **telefono a moneta** pay telephone; **telefono interno** intercommunication system, intercom

telegèni·co -ca *adj* **(-ci -che)** telegenic, videogenic

telegiornale *m* TV newscast

telegrafare (telègrafo) *tr* & *intr* to telegraph

telegràfi·co -ca *adj* **(-ci -che)** telegraphic

telegrafi·sta *mf* **(-sti -ste)** telegrapher; telegraph installer

telègrafo *m* telegraph; **telegrafo di macchina** (naut) engine-room telegraph; **telegrafo ottico** heliograph; wigwag; **telegrafo senza fili** wireless

telegram·ma *m* **(-mi)** telegram

teleguida *f* remote control

teleguidare *tr* to control from a distance, to operate by remote control

Telèmaco *m* Telemachus

telèmetro *m* telemeter; range finder

teleobbiettivo *m* (phot) telephoto lens

telepatia *f* telepathy

teleproietto *m* guided missile

telericévere §141 *tr* to receive by TV; to teleview

teleschérmo *m* television screen

telescò·pio *m* (**-pi**) telescope
telescrivènte *f* teletypewriter; ticker
telescriventi·sta *mf* (**-sti -ste**) teletype operator
teleselezióne *f* (telp) direct distance dialing
telespetta·tóre -trice *mf* televiewer
teletrasméttere §198 *tr* to televise, telecast
teletrasmissióne *f* telecast
televisióne *f* television, TV
televisi·vo -va *adj* television, TV
televisóre *m* television set
tellina *f* sunset shell or clam
télo *m* piece of cloth; yardage, length of material; (mil) side (*of tent*)
tèlo *m* (lit) dart, arrow
telóne *m* canvas; (theat) curtain
tè·ma *m* (**-mi**) theme; (gram) stem
téma *f* (lit) fear; **per tema di** (lit) for fear of
temerarie·tà *f* (**-tà**) recklessness, rashness
temerà·rio -ria *adj* (**-ri -rie**) reckless, rash; ill-founded
temére (**témo** & **tèmo**) *tr* to fear; to respect ‖ *intr* to fear; **temere di** to be afraid to
temeri·tà *f* (**-tà**) temerity
temìbile *adj* frightening
tèmpera *f* tempera, distemper
temperala·pis *m* (**-pis**) or **temperamati·te** *m* (**-te**) pencil sharpener
temperaménto *m* middle course, compromise; temper, temperament
temperante *adj* temperate, moderate
temperanza *f* temperance
temperare (**tèmpero**) *tr* to mitigate; to temper; to sharpen (*a pencil*)
tempera·to -ta *adj* temperate; tempered (*metal*); watered (*wine*)
temperatura *f* temperature; **temperatura ambiente** room temperature
temperino *m* penknife, pocketknife
tempèsta *f* tempest, storm; **tempesta in un bicchier d'acqua** tempest in a teapot
tempestare (**tempèsto**) *tr* to pound; to pepper, pelt; to pester ‖ *intr* to storm
tempesta·to -ta *adj* studded, spangled
tempesti·vo -va *adj* timely
tempestó·so -sa [s] *adj* stormy, tempestuous
tèmpia *f* temple (*side of forehead*); **tempie** (lit) head
tempiale *m* temple (*in loom; of spectacles*)
tempière *m* Templar
tèm·pio *m* (**-pi** & **-pli**) temple (*edifice*)
tempi·sta *mf* (**-sti -ste**) person or athlete showing good timing; (mus) rhythmist
tèmpo *m* time; weather; age; period, stage; cycle (*of internal-combustion engine*); (gram) tense; (mus) tempo, (mus) movement; (sports) period; (theat, mov) part; **ad un tempo** at the same time; **al tempo che Berta filava** long ago; **a suo tempo** in due time; long ago; **a tempo debito** in due time; **a tempo e luogo** at the opportune time; **a tempo perso** in

one's spare time; **aver fatto il proprio tempo** to be outdated; **c'è sempre tempo** we are still in time; **col tempo** in time; **dare tempo al tempo** to allow time to heal things; **darsi del bel tempo** to have a good time; **da tempo** for a long time; **del tempo di** from the time of; **è scaduto il tempo utile** the time is up; **è tanto tempo** it's been a long time; **fa bel tempo** the weather is fine; **il Tempo** Father Time; **lasciare il tempo che trova** to have no effect; **molto tempo dopo** long afterward; **nel tempo che** while; **per tempo** early; **prima del tempo** formerly; **quanto tempo** how long; **sentire il tempo** to feel the weather in one's bones; **senza por tempo in mezzo** without any delay; **tempi che corrono** present times; **tempo fa** some time ago; **tempo legale** legal time limit; **tempo libero** leisure time; **tempo supplementare** (sports) overtime; **tempo un . . .** within (*e.g., one month*); **un tempo** long ago
temporale *adj* temporal ‖ *m* storm
temporàne·o -a *adj* temporary, provisional
temporeggiare §290 (**temporéggio**) *intr* to temporize
tèmpra *f* (metallurgy) tempering, temper; (mus) timbre; (fig) fiber, timber
temprare (**tèmpro**) *tr* to temper (*metal*); to harden, inure ‖ *ref* to become hardened or inured
tenace *adj* tenacious; tough
tenàcia *f* tenacity
tenaci·tà *f* (**-tà**) strength, resistance; tenacity
tenàglie *fpl* nippers, pincers, pliers; tongs; **a tenaglie** (mil) pincers (*e.g., action*)
tènda *f* curtain; awning; tent
tendènza *f* tendency; trend
tendenzió·so -sa [s] *adj* tendentious
tèn·der *m* (**-der**) (rr) tender
tèndere §270 *tr* to stretch; to tighten; to draw (*a bow*); to cast (*nets*); to lay (*snares*); to reach out (*one's hand*); to prick up (*one's ears*); to draw (*s.o.'s attention*); to set (*sail*) ‖ *intr* to aim; to lean; to tend; to tend to be
tendina *f* curtain, blind
tèndine *m* (anat) tendon
tendiscar·pe *m* (**-pe**) shoetree
tenditóre *m* turnbuckle; **tenditore della racchetta** (tennis) press
tendóne *m* big curtain; canvas; tent (*of circus*); (theat) curtain
tendòpo·li *f* (**-li**) tent city
tènebre *fpl* darkness
tenebró·so -sa [s] *adj* dark, gloomy
tenènte *m* lieutenant; (mil) first lieutenant; (nav) lieutenant junior grade; **tenente colonnello** (mil) lieutenant colonel; **tenente di vascello** (nav) lieutenant senior grade
tenére §271 *tr* to hold; to have; to keep; to stand (*e.g., rough sea*); to wear; to make (*a speech*); to follow

(*a course*); **tenere a battesimo** to stand for, sponsor; **tenere al corrente** to keep informed; **tenere a memoria** to remember; **tenere da conto** to hold in high esteem; to take good care of (*s.th*); **tenere d'occhio** to keep an eye on; **tenere la destra** to keep to the right; **tenere la strada** (aut) to hug the road; **tenere la testa a partito** to mend one's ways; **tenere le distanze** to keep aloof; **tenere mano a** to connive with; **tenere presente** to bear in mind; **tenere qlco a conto** to take good care of s.th ‖ *intr* to hold; to take root; **tenerci che** to be anxious for, e.g., **ci tengo che vinca le elezioni** I am anxious for him to win the elections; **tenere a destra** to keep to the right; **tenere alle apparenze** to stand on ceremony; to keep up appearances; **tenere da** to hail from; to take after; **tenere dietro a** to follow; to keep abreast of; **tenere duro** to hold fast; **tenere per** (sports) to be a fan of ‖ *ref* to hold; to hold on; to keep (*e.g., ready*); to regard oneself; **tenersi a** to adhere to (*e.g., a treaty*); to hold on to; to stick to; to follow; **tenersi a galla** to stay afloat; **tenersi al largo** (naut) to keep to the open sea; **tenersi al vento** (naut) to sail to leeward; (fig) to follow a safe course; **tenersi in piedi** to stand up; **tenersi per mano** to hold hands; **tenersi sulle proprie** to keep aloof

tenerézza *f* tenderness; fondness, endearment

tène·ro -ra *adj* tender ‖ *m* tender portion

tènia *f* tapeworm

teni·tóre -trice *mf* keeper

tènnis *m* tennis; **tennis da tavolo** table tennis, ping-pong

tenni·sta *mf* (**-sti -ste**) tennis player

tennìsti·co -ca *adj* (**-ci -che**) tennis

tenóne *m* tenon

tenóre *m* character, tone; tenor; alcoholic content; manner (*of living*); **tenore di vita** way of life; standard of living

tensióne *f* tension; **alta tensione** high tension; **tensione sanguigna** blood pressure

tentàcolo *m* tentacle

tentare (**tènto**) *tr* to try, attempt; to assay; to tempt; (lit) to touch

tentativo *m* attempt; **tentativo di furto** attempted robbery

tenta·tóre -trice *adj* tempting ‖ *m* tempter ‖ *f* temptress

tentazióne *f* temptation

tentennare (**tenténno**) *tr* to shake; to rock ‖ *intr* to shake; to wobble; to hesitate; to stagger

tentóne or **tentóni** *adv* blindly, gropingly; at random

tènue *adj* small (*intestine*); (lit) tenuous, thin

tenu·to -ta *adj* bound, obliged ‖ *f* capacity, volume; estate, farm; uniform; outfit; (sports) endurance, resistance; **a tenuta d'acqua** watertight; **a tenuta d'aria** airtight; **tenuta dei libri** bookkeeping; **tenuta di gala** (mil, nav) full-dress uniform; **tenuta di servizio** (mil) fatigues; **tenuta di strada** (aut) roadability

tenzóne *f* combat; poetic contest

teologìa *f* theology

teòlo·go *m* (**-gi**) theologian

teorè·ma *m* (**-mi**) theorem

teorèti·co -ca *adj* (**-ci -che**) theoretic(al)

teorìa *f* theory; (lit) series, row

teòri·co -ca (**-ci -che**) *adj* theoretical ‖ *m* theoretician

tèpi·do -da *adj* var of tiepido

tepóre *m* warmth

tèppa *f* underworld, rabble

teppi·sta *m* (**-sti**) hoodlum, hooligan

terapèuti·co -ca (**-ci -che**) *adj* therapeutic ‖ *f* therapeutics

terapìa *f* therapy; **terapia convulsivante** or **terapia d'urto** shock therapy

Terèsa *f* Theresa

tèrgere §162 *tr* (lit) to wipe

tergicristallo *m* windshield wiper

tergiversare (**tergivèrso**) *intr* to stall; to beat around the bush

tèr·go *m* (**-ghi**) back (*of a coin*); **a tergo** on the reverse side ‖ *m* (**-ga** *fpl*) (lit) back; **volgere le terga** (lit) to turn one's back

termale *adj* thermal (*e.g., waters*)

tèrme *fpl* spa, hot spring

tèrmi·co -ca *adj* (**-ci -che**) thermal; heat, heating

terminale *adj* & *m* terminal

terminare (**tèrmino**) *tr* to border; to end, terminate ‖ *intr* (ESSERE) to end, terminate

terminazióne *f* termination; completion; (gram) ending

tèrmine *m* border; marker; term; deadline; end; goal; boundary, bounds; (fig) point; **a termini di legge** according to law; **avere termine** to end; **in altri termini** in other words; **mezzo termine** half measure; **porre termine a** to put an end to; **portare a termine** to put through

terminologìa *f* terminology

termistóre *m* (elec) thermistor

tèrmite *f* termite

termoconvettóre *m* baseboard radiator

termocòppia *f* thermocouple

termodinàmi·co -ca (**-ci -che**) *adj* thermodynamic ‖ *f* thermodynamics

termòforo *m* heating pad

termòmetro *m* thermometer

termonucleare *adj* thermonuclear

tèr·mos *m* (**-mos**) thermos bottle

termosifóne *m* radiator; hot-water heating system; steam heating system

termòstato *m* thermostat

termovisièra *f* electric defroster

tèrno *m* tern (*in lotto*); **vincere un terno al lotto** to hit the jackpot

tèrra *f* earth; land; ground; world; city, town; dirt, soil; clay; **essere a terra** to be downcast; to be broke; to be flat (*said of a tire*); **rimanere a terra** to miss the boat; **sotto terra** underground; **terra bruciata** scorched earth; **terra di nessuno** no man's land; **terra di Siena** sienna; **terra ferma** terra firma; mainland; **terra terra** skimming the ground; (naut) close to the shore; (fig) mediocre, second-rate

terracòtta f (**terrecòtte**) terra cotta; earthenware

terrafèrma f mainland (as distinguished from adjacent islands); terra firma (dry land, not air or water)

terràglia f crockery; **terraglie** earthenware

terranò·va m (**-va**) Newfoundland (dog) || **Terranova** f Newfoundland

terrapieno m embankment

terrazza f terrace; **a terrazza** terraced

terrazza·no -na mf villager

terrazzo m balcony; terrace; ledge, shelf; terrazzo

terremota·to -ta adj hit by an earthquake || mf earthquake victim

terremòto m earthquake

terré·no -na adj terrestrial, earthly; ground-floor; first-floor || m ground floor; first floor; ground; soil; land, plot of ground; combat zone, terrain; **preparare il terreno** to work the soil; (fig) to pave the way; **scendere sul terreno** to fight a duel; **tastare il terreno** to feel one's way; **terreno di gioco** (sports) field

tèrre·o -a adj wan, sallow

terrèstre adj terrestrial; ground, land || m earthling

terrìbile adj terrible; awesome, awful

terric·cio m (**-ci**) soil; top soil

terriè·ro -ra adj land; landed

terrificare §197 (**terrifico**) tr to terrify

terrina f tureen

territò·rio m (**-ri**) territory

terróre m terror

terrorismo m terrorism

terrori·sta mf (**-sti -ste**) terrorist

terrorizzare [ddzz] tr to terrorize

terró·so -sa [s] adj dirty (e.g., spinach); dirty-earth (color); (chem) rare-earth (metal)

tèr·so -sa [s] adj clear

tèrza f third grade; (aut) third; (eccl) tierce; (rr) third class

terzaforzi·sta (**-sti -ste**) adj of the third force || m partisan of the third force

terzaròlo m (naut) reef

terzétto m trio

terzià·rio -ria adj (**-ri -rie**) tertiary

terzina f tercet

terzino m (soccer) back

tèr·zo -za adj & pron third || m third; third party || f see **terza**

terzùlti·mo -ma adj third from the end

tésa [s] f brim (of hat); snare, net

tesare [s] (**téso**) tr to pull taut

tè·schio m (**-schi**) skull

tè·si f (**-si**) thesis; dissertation

té·so -sa [s] adj taut, tight; strained; outstretched (hand); **con le orecchie tese** all ears || f see **tesa**

tesorería f treasury; liquid assets

tesorière m treasurer

tesò·ro m treasure; treasury; thesaurus; bank vault; **far tesoro di** to treasure, prize; **tesoro mio!** my darling!

Tèspi m Thespis

tèssera f card; domino (piece); **tessera** (of mosaic)

tessera·to -ta adj card-carrying; rationed || mf card-carrying member; holder of ration card

tèssere tr to weave; to spin

tèssile adj textile || m textile; **tessili** textile workers

tessilsac·co m (**-chi**) garment bag

tessi·tóre -trice mf weaver

tessitura f weaving; spinning mill; (mus) range; (fig) plot

tessuto m cloth, fabric; tissue

tèsta f head; mind; bulb (of garlic); spindle (of wheel); warhead (of torpedo); row (of bricks); **a testa** apiece; per capita; **a testa a testa** neck and neck; **fare di testa propria** to act on one's own; **fare la testa grossa a** to stun; to annoy; **levarsi di testa** to forget about; **mettersi in testa di** to get it into one's head to; **non avere testa di** + inf to not feel like + ger; **non sapere dove battere la testa** to not know which way to turn; **per una corta testa** by a neck; **rompersi la testa** to rack one's brains; **tenere testa a** to face up to; **testa coda** (aut) spin; **testa di ponte** (mil) bridgehead; **testa di sbarco** (mil) beachhead; **testa e croce** head or tails

testaménto m will, testament || **Antico** or **Vecchio Testamento** Old Testament; **Nuovo Testamento** New Testament

testardàggine f stubbornness

testar·do -da adj stubborn

testata f headboard (of bed); top; end (e.g., of beam); heading (of newspaper); butt with the head; nose (of rocket)

tèste m witness

testé adv (lit) a short time ago; (lit) presently, in a little while

testìcolo m testicle

testièra f headboard; crown (of harness); battering ram

testimòne m witness; **testimone di nozze** best man; **testimone di veduta** or **testimone oculare** eyewitness

testimonianza f testimony

testimoniare §287 (**testimònio**) tr to attest; to depose, testify; **testimoniare il falso** to bear false witness || intr to bear witness

testimò·nio m (**-ni**) (coll) witness

testina f small head; whimsical person; boiled head of veal; head (e.g., of tape recorder)

tèsto m text; pie dish; (coll) flower vase; **fare testo** to serve as a model

testó·ne -na m/f dolt; stubborn person

testuale adj textual; word-for-word

testùggine f turtle; tortoise

tètano m tetanus

tè·tro -tra adj (lit) gloomy, dark

tétta f (coll) teat

tettarèlla f nipple

tétto m roof; ceiling price; home; **senza tetto** homeless; **tetto a capanna** gable roof; **tetto a padiglione** hip roof; **tetto a una falda** lean-to roof; **tetto di paglia** thatched roof

tettóia f shed; pillared roof

tettóia-garage f (**tettóie-garage**) carport

tettùc·cio m (**-ci**) (aut) roof; (aut) top; **tettuccio a bulbo** dome; **tettuccio rigido** (aut) convertible top

ti §5 pron

tìbia f tibia, shinbone

tic m (**tic**) twitch; habit

ticchettì·o m (**-i**) click (of typewriter); patter (of rain); tick (of clock)

tìc·chio m (**-chi**) whim; tic; viciousness (of animal); blemish

tièpi·do -da adj tepid, lukewarm

tifo m typhus; **fare il tifo per** to root for; to be a fan of

tifoidèa f typhoid fever

tifóne m typhoon

tifó·so -sa [s] adj rooting || mf fan, rooter

ti·glio m (**-gli**) linden, lime; bast; fiber

tiglió·so -sa [s] adj tough, fibrous

tigna f ringworm; (coll) tightwad

tignòla f clothes moth

tigra·to -ta adj striped; tabby

tigre f tiger

timballo m pie, meat pie; timbale; (lit) drum

timbrare tr to stamp; to cancel (stamps)

timbro m stamp; character (of a writer); (mus) timbre; **timbro di gomma** rubber stamp; **timbro postale** postmark

timidézza f shyness, bashfulness; timidity

tìmi·do -da adj shy, bashful; timid || mf shy person

timo m (anat) thymus; (bot) thyme

timóne m rudder, helm; shaft, pole (of cart); **timone di direzione** (aer) rudder; **timone di profondità** (aer) elevator; (nav) diving plane (of submarine)

timonièra f (naut) pilot house

timonière m helmsman, steersman; coxswain

timonziè·ro -ra adj rudder; tail (feather) || f see **timoniera**

timora·to -ta adj conscientious; **timorato di Dio** God-fearing

timóre m fear; awe; **avere timore di** to fear

timoró·so -sa [s] adj timorous

tìmpano m (archit) tympanum; (anat) eardrum; (mus) kettledrum; **rompere i timpani a** to deafen

tin·ca f (**-che**) (ichth) tench

tinèllo m pantry; breakfast room

tìngere §126 tr to dye; to dirty, soil; to color || ref to dye (e.g., one's hair); to put on make-up; to become colored

tino m tub, vat

tinòzza f tub, washtub

tinta f paint; color; dye; shade; stain; **calcare le tinte** to exaggerate; **mezza tinta** halftone, shade; **vedere qlco a fosche tinte** to take a dim view of s.th; **vedere qlco a tinte rosee** to see s.th through rose-colored glasses

tintarèlla f (coll) suntan

tinteggiare §290 (**tintéggio**) tr to calci-

mine; to whitewash; to tint; to paint (e.g., a house)

tintinnare intr (ESSERE & AVERE) to jingle; to clink

tintinnì·o m (**-i**) jingling; clink

tin·to -ta adj dyed; tinged; soiled; (lit) dark || f see **tinta**

tintó·re -ra mf dyer; dry cleaner

tintorìa f dyeworks; dry cleaning establishment; dyeing

tintura f dyeing; dyestuff; tincture; smattering; **tintura di iodio** iodine

tìpi·co -ca adj (**-ci -che**) typical

tipificare §197 (**tipìfico**) tr to standardize

tipizzare [ddzz] tr to standardize

tipo adj invar typical, e.g., **famiglia tipo** typical family || m type; standard, model; fellow, guy; phylum (in taxonomy); character, card; **coi tipi di** printed in the shop of; **sul tipo di** similar to; **vero tipo** prototype, epitome

tipografìa f typography; print shop

tipogràfi·co -ca adj (**-ci -che**) typographical

tipògrafo m typographer; owner of print shop, printer

tipòmetro m (typ) line gauge

tiptologìa f table rapping (during séance); tapping in code (among jailbirds)

tiraba·ci m (**-ci**) (coll) spitcurl

tiràg·gio m (**-gi**) draft; **a tiraggio forzato** forced-draft

tiralìne·e m (**-e**) ruling pen

tirannìa f tyranny

tirànni·co -ca adj (**-ci -che**) tyrannical

tiran·no -na adj tyrannical || mf tyrant

tirante m brace; rod; strap; trace (of harness); **tirante degli stivali** bootstrap

tirapiè·di m (**-di**) hangman's assistant; underling

tirapu·gni m (**-gni**) brass knuckles

tirare tr to pull; to draw; to tug; to suck; to haul in (nets); to deserve (a slap); to pluck; to throw; to give (blows); to utter (oaths); to shoot (arrows, bullets); to stretch; to tighten (one's belt); to print; to make (an addition); (sports) to force (the pace); **tirare a lucido** to polish; **tirare a sé** to attract; **tirare a sorte** to draw lots for; **tirare fuori** to draw out; to pull out; to get out; **tirare giù** to lower; to jot down; (coll) to gulp down; **tirare gli orecchi a** to punish by yanking the ears of; **tirare il collo a** to wring the neck of; **tirare in ballo** to bring up (a subject); **tirare l'acqua al proprio mulino** to look out for number one; **tirare l'anima coi denti** to be at the end of one's rope; **tirare l'aria** to draw (said of a chimney); **tirare le cuoia** (slang) to kick the bucket; **tirare per i capelli** to drag by the hair; to push, coerce; **tirare per le lunghe** to stretch out; **tirare su** to lift; to raise (children); to pull up || intr to be too tight (said of clothes); to shoot; to blow (said of wind); to draw (said, e.g., of chimney); **tirare a** to tend toward, lean toward; **tirare a + inf** to try to + inf; **tirare a campare** (coll) to goldbrick; **tirare avanti** to go ahead; to manage to get along; **tirare di boxe** to box; **tirare diritto** to go straight ahead; **tirare di scherma** to fence; **tirare in lungo** to delay, linger; to dillydally; **tirare innanzi** to keep on going; to go ahead; **tirare sul prezzo** to haggle; **tirare via** to hurry along || *ref*— **tirarsi addosso** (coll) to bring upon oneself; **tirarsi dietro** to drag along; **tirarsi fuori da** to get out of (e.g., trouble); **tirarsi gente in casa** to keep open house; **tirarsi indietro** to move back; **tirarsi in là** to move aside; **tirarsi su** to get up; to recover; to roll up (one's sleeves); **tirarsi un colpo di rivoltella** to shoot oneself

tirastiva·li *m* (**-li**) bootjack

tirata *f* pull; stretch; tirade

tirati·ra *m* (**-ra**) (coll) yen; **fare a tiratira per** (coll) to scramble for

tira·to *-ta adj* taut; forced (smile); drawn (face); tight, closefisted; **tirato con short of** || *f* see **tirata**

tira·tóre -trice *mf* shot; **tiratore scelto** sharpshooter; **franco tiratore** sniper

tiratura *f* printing

tirchieria *f* stinginess

tir·chio -chia (**-chi -chie**) *adj* stingy, closefisted || *mf* miser

tirèlla *f* trace (of harness)

tirétto *m* (coll) drawer

tiritèra *f* rigmarole

tiro *m* pull; pair, brace (e.g., of oxen); throw; fire, shot; trick; **a tiro** within reach; **a un tiro di schioppo** within gunshot; **da tiro** draft; **fuori del tiro dell'orecchio** out of earshot; **tiro alla fune** tug of war; **tiro al piattello** trapshooting; **tiro a quattro** four-in-hand; **tiro a segno** rifle range; shooting gallery

tiroci·nio *m* (**-ni**) apprenticeship; internship; **tirocinio didattico** practice teaching

tiròide *f* thyroid

tirolése [s] *adj & mf* Tyrolean

tirrèni·co -ca *adj* (**-ci -che**) Tyrrhenian

Tirrèno *m* Tyrrhenian Sea

tisana *f* tea, infusion

tisi *f* consumption, tuberculosis

tìsi·co -ca *adj* (**-ci -che**) consumptive; stunted || *mf* consumptive

titàni·co -ca *adj* (**-ci -che**) titanic

titànio *m* titanium

titillare *tr* to tickle

titolare *adj* titular; regular, full-time || *m* owner, boss; incumbent || *v* (**titolo**) *tr* to name, call

titolo *m* title; heading; name; caption; entry (in dictionary); grade; fineness (of gold); (chem) titer; (educ) credit; **avere titolo a** to have a right to; **a titolo di** as, by way of; **titoli di testa** (mov) credits; **titolo al portatore** security payable to bearer; **titolo azionario** share; **titolo corrente** subtitle; **titolo di credito** instrument of

credit; certificate; deed; conveyance; **titolo di studio** degree, diploma; credits; **titolo di trasporto** travel document

titubare (**tìtubo**) *intr* to hesitate; to waver

tiziané·sco -sca *adj* (**-schi -sche**) titian; Titian

tì·zio *m* (**-zi**) fellow, guy

tizzo or **tizzóne** *m* brand, firebrand

to' *interj* here!; well!

tobò·ga *m* (**-ga**) toboggan

toccafèrro *m* tag (game)

toccamano *m* handshake (to close a deal); bribe, under-the-table tip

toccante *adj* touching, moving

toccare §197 (**tócco**) *tr* to touch; to reach; to concern; to push (a button); to play (an instrument); to feel; to hit (the target); to border on (e.g., the age of forty); **toccare con mano** to make sure of; **toccare il cielo col dito** to be in seventh heaven; **toccare nel vivo** to touch to the quick; **toccare terra** to land; **toccarne molte** to get a good thrashing; **toccato!** touché! || *intr* (ESSERE) to be touching; **toccare a** to be up to, e.g., **tocca a lui** it's up to him; to have to, e.g., **le tocca partire domani** she has to leave tomorrow; to deserve, e.g., **gli è toccato il premio** he deserved the prize || *ref* to meet, e.g., **gli estremi si toccano** extremes meet

toccasa·na [s] *m* (**-na**) cure-all, panacea

tocca·to -ta *adj* touché; touched in the head, nutty; **già toccato** abovementioned || *f* (mus) toccata

tóc·co -ca (**-chi -che**) *adj* touched, nutty; spoiled (fruit) || *m* touch; knock; one o'clock (P.M.); (coll) stroke

tòc·co *m* (**-chi**) chunk, piece; mortarboard; toque; **un bel tocco di ragazza** a buxom lass

tò·ga *f* (**-ghe**) gown, academic gown; (hist) toga

tògliere §127 *tr* to remove, take away; to take; to cut (telephone connection); to deduct; to take off; to preclude, prevent; **togliere a** to take away from; **togliere al cielo** (lit) to praise to the skies; **togliere di mezzo** to remove; to do away with; **togliere la parola a** to take the floor from; **togliere l'onore a** to dishonor; **togliere una spina dal cuore a** to relieve the heart and mind of || *intr*— **tolga Dio!** God forbid! || *ref* to take off (e.g., one's coat); to have (e.g., a tooth) pulled; to satisfy (a whim); **togliersi di mezzo** to get out of the way; **togliersi la vita** to take one's life; **togliersi qlcu dai piedi** to get rid of s.o.

tòlda *f* (naut) deck

tolemài·co -ca *adj* (**-ci -che**) Ptolemaic

tolétta *f* dressing table; dressing room; toilet, washroom; dress, gown; **fare toletta** or **farsi la toletta** to make one's toilet

tolleràbile *adj* tolerable

tollerante *adj* tolerant; liberal

tolleranza *f* tolerance; leeway

tollerare (tòllero) *tr* to tolerate; to bear, stand

tòl·to -ta *adj* taken; except, leaving out, e.g., **tolta sua figlia** leaving his daughter out ‖ *m*—**il mal tolto** ill-gotten goods

to·màio *m* (**-mài & -màia** *fpl*) or **to·màia** *f* (**-màie**) upper (*of shoe*)

tómba *f* tomb, grave

tombale *adj* grave (*e.g., stone*)

tombino *m* sewer inlet

tómbola *f* bingo; (coll) tumble

tombolare (tómbolo) *tr* (coll) to tumble down (*the steps*) ‖ *intr* (ESSERE) to fall headlong; (coll) to go to rack and ruin; (aer) to tumble

tómbolo *m* fall, tumble; bolster; lace pillow; (coll) fatso; **fare un tombolo** to go to rack and ruin; to lose one's position

Tommaso *m* Thomas

tòmo *m* volume; (coll) character

tòna·ca *f* (**-che**) (eccl) frock; (eccl) soutane; **gettare la tonaca alle ortiche** to doff the cassock

tonare §257 *intr* to peal; to thunder ‖ *impers* (ESSERE & AVERE)—**tuona** it is thundering

tondeggiante *adj* round; rounded; chubby; curvaceous

tondino *m* coaster; iron rod (*for reinforced concrete*); (archit) molding (*at top or bottom of column*); (archit) astragal

tón·do -da *adj* round; (typ) roman ‖ *m* round; circle; plate, dish; (typ) roman; **in tondo** around

tónfo *m* splash; thump

tòni·co -ca (**-ci -che**) *adj* tonic ‖ *m* tonic (*medicine*) ‖ *f* (mus) tonic

tonificare §197 (**tonìfico**) *tr* to invigorate

tonnara *f* tuna nets

tonnellàg·gio *m* (**-gi**) tonnage

tonnellata *f* ton; **tonnellata di stazza** displacement ton

tónno *m* tuna

tòno *m* tone; tune; hue; style; (mus) pitch; (mus) key; **darsi tono** to put on airs; **di tono** stylish; **fuori di tono** out of tune

tonsilla *f* tonsil

tonsura *f* tonsure

tón·to -ta *adj* (coll) dumb, stupid

topàia *f* rat's nest; hovel

topà·zio *m* (**-zi**) topaz

tòpi·co -ca (**-ci -che**) *adj* topical ‖ *f* topic; (coll) blunder

tòpo *m* mouse; rat; **topo campagnolo** field mouse; **topo d'acqua** water rat; **topo d'albergo** hotel thief; **topo d'auto** car thief; **topo di biblioteca** bookworm

topografia *f* topography

topolino *m* little mouse ‖ **Topolino** *m* Mickey Mouse

toporagno *m* shrew

tòppa *f* patch; keyhole

tòppo *m* stump; headstock (*of lathe*)

torace *m* thorax

tórba *f* peat

tórbi·do -da *adj* cloudy; murky ‖ *m* trouble; **pescare nel torbido** to fish in troubled waters; **torbidi** disorder

torbièra *f* peatbog

tòrcere §272 *tr* to twist; to wring; to bend, curve; to curl (*the lips*); to lead astray ‖ *intr* (ESSERE) to bend, curve ‖ *ref* to writhe; to bend over; **torcersi dalle risa** to split with laughter

torchiare §287 (**tòrchio**) *tr* to press

tòr·chio *m* (**-chi**) press; printing press

tòr·cia *f* (**-ce**) torch

torcicòllo *m* stiff neck; (orn) wryneck

torcinaso [s] *m* (vet) twitch

tórdo *m* thrush; simpleton

torèllo *m* young bull; (naut) garboard

torèro *m* bullfighter

tórlo *m* yolk

tórma *f* crowd, throng; herd

torménta *f* blizzard

tormentare (torménto) *tr* to torture; torment: to pester, nag ‖ *ref* to worry

torménto *m* torture, torment; pang; bore, pest, annoyance

tornacònto *m* interest, advantage

tornante *m* curve

tornare (tórno) *tr* (lit) to restore; (obs) to turn ‖ *intr* (ESSERE) to return; to go back; (coll) to jibe, agree, square; **tornare a** to be profitable to; **tornare a + inf** verb + again, e.g., **tornare a essere** to become again; **tornare a fare** to do again; **tornare a bomba** to return to the point; **tornare a galla** to come back to the surface; **tornare a gola** to repeat (*said of food*); **tornare a onore di qlcu** to do credit to s.o.; **tornare a pennello** to fit to a T; **tornare in sé** to come to; **tornare opportuno** or **utile a** to suit, e.g., **non gli tornò opportuno vendere la casa** it did not suit him to sell the house; **tornare utile** to come in handy; **tornare sulle proprie decisioni** to change one's mind

tornasóle *m* litmus

tornèllo *m* turnstile

tornèo *m* tournament, tourney

tór·nio *m* (**-ni**) lathe

tornire §176 *tr* to turn, turn up (*on a lathe*); to polish

tornitóre *m* lathe operator

tórno *m* turn; period (*of time*); **levarsi di torno** to get rid of; **torno torno** all around

tòro *m* bull; (archit, geom) torus; (lit) marital bed ‖ **Toro** *m* (astrol) Taurus

torpèdine *f* torpedo

torpedinièra *f* destroyer escort; torpedo-boat destroyer

torpè·do *f* (**-do**) (aut) touring car

torpedóne *m* bus, motor coach

tòrpi·do -da *adj* torpid, sluggish; numb

torpóre *m* torpor, sluggishness; numbness

tórre *f* tower; (chess) castle; (nav) turret; **torre campanaria** bell tower; **torre d'avorio** ivory tower; **torre di**

lancio (rok) gantry; **torre pendente** leaning tower

torrefare §173 *tr* to roast (*coffee*)

torreggiante *adj* towering

torreggiare §290 (**torréggio**) *intr* to tower

torrènte *m* torrent

torrenziale *adj* torrential

torrétta *f* turret; (nav) conning tower (*of submarine*); (archit) bartizan

tòrri·do -**da** *adj* torrid

torrióne *m* donjon; (nav) conning tower (*of battleship*)

torróne *m* nougat

torsióne *f* torsion

tórso *m* stalk; core (*of fruit*); torso, trunk; **a torso nudo** bare-chested

tórsolo *m* core; stalk; stem; **non vale un torsolo** it's not worth a fig

tórta *f* pie; cake, tart; **torta di mele** apple pie

tòrta *f* twist

tortièra *f* baking pan

tòr·to -**ta** *adj* twisted; crooked; gloomy (*face*) || *m* wrong; **a torto** unjustly; **avere torto** to be wrong; **avere torto marcio** to be dead wrong; **dar torto a** to lay the blame on; **fare torto a** to wrong, e.g., **fece torto al proprio fratello** he wronged his own brother; to bring discredit upon || *f* see **tòrta** || **torto** *adv* askance

tórtora *f* turtledove

tortuó·so -**sa** [s] *adj* winding; ambiguous; (fig) devious

tortura *f* torture

torturare *tr* to torture; to pester || *ref* to torment oneself; **torturarsi il cervello** to rack one's brain

tosare (**tóso**) *tr* to clip, crop; to shear; (fig) to fleece

tosa·tóre -**trice** *mf* clipper, shearer || *f* clippers; lawn mower

tosatura *f* sheepshearing; clip (*of wool*)

tosca·no -**na** *adj & mf* Tuscan || *m* stogy || **Toscana, la** Tuscany

tósse *f* cough; **tosse asinina** or **canina** whooping cough

tòssi·co -**ca** (-**ci** -**che**) toxic || *m* (archaic) poison

tossicòmane *mf* drug addict

tossicomanìa *f* drug addiction

tossina *f* toxin

tossire (**tósso**) & §176 *intr* to cough

tostapa·ne *m* (-**ne**) toaster

tostare (**tòsto**) *tr* to toast; to roast (*e.g., coffee*)

tò·sto -**sta** *adj* (lit) prompt; (lit) impudent; (lit) brazen (*face*) || **tosto** *adv* (lit) soon; **ben tosto** (lit) very soon; **tosto che** (lit) as soon as

tòt *adj pl invar* so many, that many || *pron invar* so much, that much

totale *adj & m* total

totalità·rio -**ria** *adj* (-**ri** -**rie**) total, complete; totalitarian

totalizzare [ddzz] *tr* to add up; to make (*so many points*)

totalizzatóre [ddzz] *m* pari-mutuel; betting window; (mach) totalizator

tòtano *m* squid; (orn) tattler

totocàlcio *m* soccer pool

tovàglia *f* tablecloth

tovagliòlo *m* napkin

tòz·zo -**za** *adj* stubby, stocky || *m* piece (*of fresh bread*); crust (*of bread*)

tra *prep* among; between

trabàccolo *m* small fishing boat

traballare *intr* to shake; to totter; to wobble; to stagger; to toddle

trabìccolo *m* frame for bedwarmer; jalopy; hulk

traboccante *adj* overflowing

traboccare §197 (**trabòcco**) *tr* to knock down || *intr* to overflow (*said of container*) || *intr* (ESSERE) to overflow (*said of liquid*) || *intr* (ESSERE & AVERE) to tip (*said of scales*); **far traboccare** to make (*the scales*) tip

trabocchétto *m* pitfall; trapdoor

trabóc·co *m* (-**chi**)—**trabocco di sangue** internal hemorrhage

tracagnòt·to -**ta** *adj* stubby, stocky || *mf* stocky person

tracannare *tr* to gulp down

tracchég·gio *m* (-**gi**) delay; (fencing) feint

tràc·cia *f* (-**ce**) track; trace, clue; trail; outline, plan; (lit) line, row; **buona traccia** right track; **fare la traccia a** to open the way for; **in** or **sotto traccia** concealed (*e.g., wiring*); **tracce** tinge; (chem) traces

tracciante *adj* tracer (*bullet*)

tracciare §128 *tr* to trace; to pave (*the way*); to outline; (lit) to track

tracciato *m* tracing, drawing; outline; map; layout

trachèa *f* trachea, windpipe

tracòlla *f* baldric; shoulder strap; **a tracolla** slung across the shoulders

tracòllo *m* collapse, debacle

tracotanza *f* arrogance

tradiménto *m* treason; treachery; **a tradimento** unawares, unexpectedly; treacherously

tradire §176 *tr* to betray; to fail (*a person; said of memory*) || *ref* to give oneself away

tradi·tóre -**trice** *adj* charming, seductive; treacherous; deceitful, faithless || *mf* traitor; betrayer || *f* traitress

tradizionale *adj* traditional

tradizióne *f* tradition

tradòtta *f* military train

tradurre §102 *tr* to translate

tradut·tóre -**trice** *mf* translator

traduzióne *f* translation

traènte *mf* (com) drawer

trafela·to -**ta** *adj* breathless, out of breath

traferro *m* (elec) air gap; (elec) spark gap

trafficante *m* dealer, trader; trafficker

trafficare §197 (**tràffico**) *tr* to sell; to traffic in || *intr* to trade, deal; to hustle

tràffi·co *m* (-**ci**) traffic

trafficó·ne -**na** *mf* hustler

trafiggere §104 *tr* to pierce, stab, transfix; to wound

trafila *f* routine; red tape; (mach) drawplate

trafilare *tr* to wiredraw

trafilétto *m* (journ) short feature, special item; (journ) notice

trafitta *f* stab wound; shooting pain

trafittura *f* stab; shooting pain

traforare (**trafòro** & **trafóro**) *tr* to bore; to pierce; to carve (*wood*); to pink (*leather*); to embroider with open work

trafóro *m* boring; tunnel; open work

trafugare §209 *tr* to purloin; to sneak off with

tragèdia *f* tragedy; **far tragedie** (coll) to make a fuss

traghettare (**traghétto**) *tr* to ferry

traghétto *m* ferry; **traghetto spaziale** space shuttle

tràgi·co -ca (**-ci -che**) *adj* tragic || *m* tragedian; **il tragico** (fig) the tragic

tragitto *m* journey; (obs) ferry

traguardo *m* sight; aim; goal; finish line; (phot) viewfinder; (sports) tape

traiettòria *f* trajectory; path

tràina *f* towline; **pescare alla traina** to troll

trainare (**tràino**) *tr* to drag, tug, pull

tràino *m* drag; load; trailer

tralasciare §128 *tr* to interrupt; to omit; **non tralasciare di** to not fail to

tràl·cio *m* (**-ci**) stem (*of vine*)

tralíc·cio *m* (**-ci**) ticking, bedtick; trellis; tower (*of high-tension line*)

tralice *m*—**in tralice** askance

tralignare *intr* (ESSERE & AVERE) to degenerate

tram *m* (**tram**) streetcar

trama *f* woof, weft; plot (*of play*); texture (*of cloth*)

tramà·glio *m* (**-gli**) trammel net

tramandare *tr* to hand down

tramare *tr* & *intr* to weave; to plot

trambusto *m* bustle

tramestí·o *m* (**-i**) bustle, confusion

tramèzza [ddzz] *f* partition

tramezzare (**tramèzzo**) [ddzz] *tr* to interpose; to partition

tramezzino [ddzz] *m* small partition; sandwich; sandwich man

tramèzzo [ddzz] *m* partition; side dish; (sew) insertion || *adv* in between; **tramezzo a** among

tràmite *m* intermediary; (lit) pass; **per tramite di** through || *prep* (coll) by; by means of

tramòg·gia *f* (**-ge**) hopper

tramontana *f* north wind; **perdere la tramontana** to lose one's bearings

tramontare (**tramónto**) *intr* (ESSERE) to set (*said, e.g., of sun*); to end

tramónto *m* setting; sunset; decline

tramortire §176 *tr* to stun || *intr* (ESSERE) to faint, swoon

trampolière *m* wading bird; (orn) stilt

tràmpoli *mpl* stilts

trampolino *m* diving board; springboard; ski jump; (fig) springboard

tramutare *tr* to transfer; to transform

tràn·cia *f* (**-ce**) slice; (mach) shears

tranèllo *m* trap, snare

trangugiare §290 *tr* to swallow; to gulp down

tranne *prep* except, save; **tranne che** unless

tranquillante *m* tranquilizer

tranquillare *tr* & *ref* (lit) to tranquilize; to calm down

tranquilli·tà *f* (**-tà**) tranquillity

tranquillizzare [ddzz] *tr* to tranquilize; to reassure || *ref* to become reassured

tranquíl·lo -la *adj* tranquil, calm; clear (*conscience*)

transatlànti·co -ca *adj* & *m* (**-ci -che**) transatlantic

transazióne *f* compromise

transènna *f* bar, barrier

transètto *m* (archit) transept

trànsfu·ga *m* (**-ghi**) (lit) deserter

transigere §165 *tr* to settle || *intr* to compromise

transistóre *m* transistor

transitàbile *adj* passable

transitare (**trànsito**) *intr* to move; to walk

transiti·vo -va *adj* transitive

trànsito *m* passage; traffic; (lit) passing; **di transito** transient

transitò·rio -ria *adj* (**-ri -rie**) temporary; transitory; transitional

transizióne *f* transition

transoceàni·co -ca *adj* (**-ci -che**) transoceanic

transòni·co -ca *adj* (**-ci -che**) transonic

transunto *m* abstract, summary (*of a document*)

trantràn *m* routine

tran·vài *m* (**-vài**) (coll) streetcar

tranvía *f* streetcar line

tranvià·rio -ria *adj* (**-ri -rie**) streetcar

tranvière *m* streetcar conductor; motorman

trapanare (**tràpano**) *tr* to drill; (surg) to trephine

tràpano *m* drill; (surg) trephine; **trapano a vite** automatic drill

trapassare *tr* to pierce; (fig) to grieve; (poet) to cross; (lit) to pass, spend || *intr* (ESSERE) to go through; to pass (*said of an inheritance*); (lit) to pass away; **trapassare da, per** or **al di là di** to come through (*said, e.g., of a nail, light*)

trapassato *m* (lit) deceased; **trapassato prossimo** past perfect

trapasso *m* crossing; transfer; transition; (lit) passing, death

trapelare (**trapélo**) *intr* (ESSERE) to ooze; to trickle out; to leak through; (fig) to leak out

trapè·zio *m* (**-zi**) trapeze; (geom) trapezoid

trapezòide *adj* trapezoidal || *m* trapezoid

trapiantare *tr* to transplant || *ref* to transfer

trapianto *m* transplantation; transplant; **trapianto cardiaco** heart transplant

tràppola *f* trap; (coll) gadget; (fig) lie; **trappola esplosiva** booby trap

trapunta *f* quilt

trapuntare *tr* to quilt; to embroider

trapun·to -ta *adj* quilted; embroidered; studded || *m* embroidery || *f* see **trapunta**

trarre §273 *tr* to pull; to drag; to draw; to bring; to deduct; to lead; to unsheathe (*a sword*); to heave (*a sigh*); to spin (*silk, wool*, etc.); **il dado è tratto** the die is cast; **trarre dalla prigione** to free from prison; **trarre d'impaccio** to get (*s.o.*) out of trouble; **trarre fuori** to extract; **trarre in inganno** to deceive; **trarre in rovina** to ruin; **trarre per mano** to lead by the hand || *intr* to kick (*said of a mule*); (lit) to run; (lit) to blow (*said of the wind*) || *ref* to take off (*e.g., one's hat*); **trarsi d'impaccio** to get out of trouble; **trarsi indietro** to pull back; **trarsi in disparte** to move aside

trasalire [s] §176 *intr* (ESSERE & AVERE) to start, jump

trasanda·to -ta *adj* untidy, slovenly

trasbordare (**trasbórdo**) *tr* to transfer, transship

trasbórdo *m* transfer, transshipment

trascéndere §245 *tr* to transcend || *intr* (ESSERE) to go to excesses

trascinare *tr* to drag; to stir; to enthrall; to lead astray; **trascinare la vita** to barely make ends meet || *ref* to drag oneself; to drag on

trascolorare (**trascolóro**) *tr* to discolor; to change the color of || *intr* (ESSERE) & *ref* to discolor; to change color

trascórrere §139 *tr* to pass (*time*); to skim through (*e.g., a book*); (lit) to go through || *intr* to go to excesses || *intr* (ESSERE) to elapse, pass

trascórso *m* slip (*e.g., of pen*); peccadillo

trascrìvere §250 *tr* to transcribe

trascrizióne *f* transcription; registration (*e.g., of a deed*)

trascuràbile *adj* negligible

trascurare *tr* to neglect; to fail; to disregard || *ref* to not take care of oneself

trascuratézza *f* negligence, neglect; carelessness; slovenliness

trascura·to -ta *adj* neglected; careless; slovenly

trasecolare (**trasècolo**) [s] *intr* (ESSERE & AVERE) to marvel, be astonished

trasferìbile *adj* transferable

trasferiménto *m* transfer; conveyance

trasferire §176 *tr* to transfer; to assign, convey || *ref* to move

trasfèrta *f* business trip; traveling expenses, per diem

trasfigurare *tr* to transfigure; to distort (*the truth*) || *ref* to be transfigured; to change countenance

trasfocatóre *m* (phot) zoom lens

trasfóndere §178 *tr* to transfuse; (fig) to instill

trasformàbile *adj* transformable; (aut) convertible

trasformare (**trasfórmo**) *tr* to transform; to alter || *ref* to transform oneself; to be converted

trasformati·vo -va *adj* (gram) transformational

trasformatóre *m* transformer

trasformazióne *f* transformation

trasformi·sta *mf* (**-sti -ste**) quick-change artist

trasfusióne *f* transfusion

trasgredire §176 *tr* & *intr* to transgress

trasgressióne *f* transgression

trasgressóre *m* transgressor

trasla·to -ta *adj* figurative; metaphorical; (lit) transferred || *m* figure of speech; metaphor

traslitterare (**traslìttero**) *tr* to transliterate

traslocare §197 (**traslòco**) *tr* to transfer; to move || *intr* & *ref* to move

traslò·co *m* (**-chi**) moving

traslùci·do -da *adj* translucent

trasméttere §198 *tr* to transmit; (rad) to broadcast

trasmetti·tóre -trice *mf* transmitter || *m* (naut) engine-room telegraph; (telg) sender

trasmigrare *intr* (ESSERE & AVERE) to transmigrate || *intr* (ESSERE) to pass, pass on

trasmissióne *f* transmission; conveyance; broadcast; telecast; **trasmissione del pensiero** thought transference

trasmittènte *adj* transmitting; broadcasting || *f* broadcasting station

trasmutare *tr* to transmute; to change

trasogna·to -ta [s] *adj* dreamy; daydreaming; dazed

trasparènte *adj* transparent || *m* transparency

trasparènza *f* transparence; **in trasparenza** against the light

trasparire §108 *intr* (ESSERE) to appear; to shine; to show through; to show, be revealed (*said of feelings*); **far trasparire** to reveal

traspirare *intr* to perspire || *intr* (ESSERE) to show, be revealed

traspirazióne *f* perspiration

traspórre §218 *tr* to transpose

trasportare (**traspòrto**) *tr* to transport; to carry away; to transfer; to translate; to postpone; (mus) to transpose; **lasciarsi trasportare** to be carried away || *ref* to move; (fig) to go back

trasporta·tóre -trice *mf* carrier || *m* (mach) conveyor belt; (phot) sprocket

traspòrto *m* transportation; transport; transfer; eagerness; moving; (mus) transposition; **trasporto funebre** funeral procession

trasposi·tóre -trice *mf* (mus) transposer

trassa·to -ta *adj* paying || *m* drawee

trastullare *tr* to amuse; to entice || *ref* to have a good time; to loiter

trastullo *m* play, game; fun; plaything

trasudare [s] *tr* to ooze; (fig) to exude || *intr* to ooze (*said of a wall*) || *intr* (ESSERE) to drip (*said of perspiration*)

trasversale *adj* transverse, cross || *f* crossroad

trasvèr·so -sa *adj* transverse || *m* transverse beam

trasvolare (**trasvólo**) *tr* to fly over, cross by air || *intr*—**trasvolare su** to skip over

trasvolata *f* non-stop flight

tratta *f* tug, pull; (rr) stretch; (com)

draft; (lit) crowd; **tratta dei neri** slave trade; **tratta delle bianche** white slavery

trattàbile adj negotiable; friendly, sociable

trattaménto m treatment; working conditions; food, spread; reception, welcome; **trattamento di favore** special treatment; **trattamento di quiescenza** retirement benefits

trattare tr to treat; to deal with; to transact; to wield; to play (an instrument); to work (e.g., iron); to deal in; **trattare qlcu da bugiardo** to call s.o. a liar; **trattare da cane** to treat like a dog || intr to bargain; **trattare di** to deal with; to take care of; to treat, handle || ref to take good care of oneself || impers (ESSERE) **si tratta di** it's question of

tratta·rio -ria mf (-ri -rie) drawee

trattativa f negotiation

trattato m treatise; treaty

trattazióne f treatment

tratteggiare §290 **(trattéggio)** tr to sketch; to outline; to hatch

trattég·gio m (-gi) hatching

trattenére §271 tr to keep; to entertain; to withhold; to hold back; to detain || ref to stop; to refrain; to remain

trattenimento m entertainment, party; delay

trattenuta f withholding; checkoff

trattino m dash; hyphen

trat·to -ta adj drawn, extracted || m stretch; span; passage; tract; gesture; throw (of dice); stroke (of pen); bearing; section; (chess) move; **a larghi tratti** in broad outline; **a tratti** from time to time; **a un tratto** all of a sudden; at the same time; **dare un tratto alla bilancia** to tip the scales; **tratti** features; **tratti del volto** features; **tratto di corda** strappado; **tratto di unione** hyphen; **tutto d'un tratto** all of a sudden; **un bel tratto** quite a while

trat·tóre -trice mf innkeeper; restaurateur || m tractor; **trattore a cingoli** caterpillar tractor || f tractor (vehicle)

trattorìa f inn, restaurant

tratturo m cow path

traumatizzare [ddzz] tr to traumatize

travagliare §280 tr to torment; to molest || intr & ref to toil, labor

travà·glio m (-gli) suffering; toil; trave (to inhibit horse being shod); **travaglio di parto** labor pains; **travaglio di stomaco** upset stomach

travasare tr to pour off; to decant; to transfer || ref to spill

travaso m pouring off; transfer; **travaso di bile** gall bladder attack; **travaso di sangue** hemorrhage

travatura f roof timbers; **travatura maestra** ridgepole

trave f beam; joist; **fare una trave d'un fuscello** to make a mountain out of a molehill

travedére §279 tr to glimpse || intr to be mistaken

travéggole fpl—**avere le traveggole** to see things; to see one thing for another

travèrsa f crossbar; crossroad; crosspiece; rung; bar (of goalpost); dam; rail (of fence); transom; slat (to hold bedspring); rubber pad; (rr) tie

traversare (travèrso) tr to cross

traversata f passage, crossing

traversìa f strong wind; **traversie** misfortunes

traversina f (rr) tie

travèr·so -sa adj cross; devious || m width; crossbar; (naut) beam; (naut) side; **a traverso** (naut) on the beam; **capire a traverso** to misunderstand; **di traverso** askance; crosswise; the wrong way || f see **traversa**

traversóne m large crossbar; westerly gale; side blow with saber

travestiménto m disguise; travesty

travestire (travèsto) tr to disguise; to travesty, parody || ref to disguise oneself

traviare §119 tr to lead astray || intr & ref to go astray

travicèllo m joist

travisare tr to distort

travolgènte adj impetuous; fascinating; sweeping

travòlgere §289 tr to overwhelm; to overturn; to sweep away

trazióne f traction

tre [e] adj & pron three; **le tre** three o'clock || m three; third (in dates)

trébbia f thresher; threshing

trebbiare §287 **(trébbio)** tr & intr to thresh

trebbiatrice f thresher, threshing machine

trebbiatura f threshing

tréc·cia f (-ce) plait; braid; **treccia a ciambella** bun, knot

trecentèsi·mo -ma adj, m & pron three hundredth

trecènto adj, m & pron three hundred || **il Trecento** the fourteenth century

tredicèsi·mo -ma adj, m & pron thirteenth || f Xmas bonus

trédici adj & pron thirteen; **le tredici** one P.M. || m thirteen; thirteenth (in dates)

trégua f truce; respite; **tregua atomica** nuclear test ban; **senza tregua** without letup

tremare (trèmo) intr to shake, tremble; to quiver; **far tremare** to shake

tremarèlla f—**avere la tremarella** (coll) to shake in one's boots

tremebón·do -da adj (lit) shaky

tremèn·do -da adj tremendous

trementina f turpentine

tremila adj, m & pron three thousand

trèmito m trembling; quivering

tremolare (trèmolo) intr to shake; to quiver; to flicker

trèmo·lo -la adj tremulous || m (bot) aspen; (mus) tremolo

trèno m train; quarter (of animal); set (of tires); threnody, lamentation; **treno accelerato** local; **treno di lusso** Pullman train; **treno direttissimo** express; **treno di vita** mode of life; mode of living; **treno merci** freight train; **treno stradale** tractor-trailer

trenodìa *f* threnody

trénta *adj & pron* thirty || *m* thirty; thirtieth (*in dates*)

trentèsi·mo -ma *adj, m & pron* thirtieth

trentìna *f* about thirty

Trènto *f* Trent

trepidare (trèpido) *intr* to fear; to worry

trepidazióne *f* fear, trepidation

treppiède *m* tripod; trivet

tré·sca *f* (-sche) intrigue; liaison

tréspolo *m* stool; pedestal; stand, perch; (coll) jalopy

triàngolo *m* triangle; **triangolo rettangolo** right triangle

tribolare (tribolo) *tr* to torment, afflict || *intr* to suffer

tribolazióne *f* tribulation, ordeal

tribórdo *m* (naut) starboard

tri·bù *f* (-bù) tribe

tribuna *f* rostrum, platform; (sports) grandstand; **tribuna stampa** press box

tribunale *m* court, tribunal; courthouse; **tribunale dei minorenni** juvenile court; **tribunale di prima istanza** court of first instance

tributare *tr* to bestow

tributà·rio -ria (-ri -rie) *adj* tributary; tax || *m* tributary

tributo *m* tribute; tax

triché·co *m* (-chi) walrus

triciclo *m* tricycle

tricolóre *adj & m* tricolor

tricòrno *m* cocked hat, tricorn

tricromìa *f* three-color printing; three-color print

tridènte *m* trident

trifase *adj* three-phase

trifocale *adj* trifocal

trifò·glio *m* (-gli) clover; three-leaf clover

trìfola *f* (coll) truffle

trìglia *f* red mullet

trigonometrìa *f* trigonometry

trilióne *m* trillion

trillare *intr* to trill; to vibrate

trillo *m* trill; ringing

trilogìa *f* trilogy

trimestrale *adj* quarterly

trimèstre *m* quarter; quarterly dues; quarterly payment; (educ) quarter, trimester

trimotóre *m* three-engine plane

trina *f* lace

trin·ca *f* (-che) (naut) gammoning; **di trinca** clearly, cleanly; **nuovo di trinca** brand-new

trincare §197 *tr* (coll) to gulp down, swill

trincèa *f* trench

trincerare (trincèro) *tr* to dig trenches in || *ref* to entrench oneself

trincétto *m* shoemaker's blade

trinchétto *m* (naut) foremast; (naut) foresail

trinciante *adj* cutting || *m* carving knife

trinciapòllo *m* meat shears

trinciare §128 *tr* to carve; to shred; to advance (*rash opinions*); to cut up

trinciato *m* smoking tobacco

trinciatrice *f* shredder; slicer

Trinità *f* Trinity

trionfale *adj* triumphal

trionfante *adj* triumphant

trionfare (triónfo) *intr* to triumph

triónfo *m* triumph; center piece; tidbit dish with three or four tiers; trump (*in game of tarot*)

triparti·to -ta *adj* tripartite

triplicare §197 **(trìplico)** *tr & ref* to triple

trìplice *adj* threefold

tri·plo -pla *adj & m* triple

trìpode *m* tripod

trippa *f* tripe; (coll) belly

tripudiare §287 *intr* to exult

tripù·dio *m* (-di) exultation

tris *m* (tris) (poker) three of a kind

trisàvola *f* great-great-grandmother

trisàvolo *m* great-great-grandfather; **trisavoli** great-great-grandparents

trisma *m* lockjaw

triste *adj* sad; gloomy, bleak

tristézza *f* sadness

tri·sto -sta *adj* wicked; wretched; poor (*figure*); (lit) sad

tritacar·ne *m* (-ne) meat grinder

tritaghiàc·cio *m* (-cio) ice crusher

tritare *tr* to chop; to grind; to mince, hash; to pound

tri·to -ta *adj* minced, hashed; worn, trite

tritòlo *m* T.N.T.

tritóne *m* (zool) newt; (fig) merman || **Tritone** *m* Triton

tritti·co *m* (-ci) triptych; export document in triplicate; trilogy

trittòn·go *m* (-ghi) triphthong

triturare *tr* to mince, hash

trivèlla *f* auger, drill; post-hole digger

trivellare (trivèllo) *tr* to drill, bore

triviale *adj* vulgar

triviali·tà *f* (-tà) vulgarity

trì·vio *m* (-vi) crossroads; trivium; **da trivio** vulgar

trofèo *m* trophy; (mil) insignia (*on headpiece*)

trògolo *m* trough

tròia *f* sow; slut || **Troia** *f* Troy

troia·no -na *adj & m* Trojan

trómba *f* trumpet; bugle, clarion; trunk (*of elephant*); leg (*of boot*); (anat) tube; (aut, rad) horn; **con le trombe nel sacco** crestfallen, dejected; **tromba d'aria** whirlwind; tornado; **tromba marina** waterspout; **tromba delle scale** stairwell

trombétta *f* trumpet

trombettière *m* (mil) trumpeter

trombetti·sta *m* (-sti) trumpet player

trombóne *m* trombone; blunderbuss

trombò·si *f* (-si) thrombosis

troncare §197 **(trónco)** *tr* to chop; to cut off; to clip (*words*); to break, sever; to block (*s.o.'s progress*); to apocopate

tronché·se [s] *m* wire cutter

trón·co -ca (-chi -che) *adj* truncate; oxytone; apocopated; exhausted, dead-tired; incomplete; **in tronco** in the middle; (*dismissal*) on the spot || *m* trunk; stub (*of receipt book*);

section (*of highway*); log; strain (*of a family*); (rr) branch; **tronco di cono** truncated cone; **tronco maggiore** (naut) lower mast

troncóne *m* stump

troneggiare §290 (**tronéggio**) *intr* to tower; to hold forth; **troneggiare su** to lord it over

trón·fio -fia *adj* (**-fi -fie**) haughty; bombastic

tròno *m* throne

tropicale *adj* tropical

tròpi·co *m* (**-ci**) tropic

troposfèra *f* troposphere

tròp·po -pa *adj & pron* too much; **trop·pi -pe** too many || *m* too much; **questo è troppo!** enough is enough! || **troppo** *adv* too; too much; **essere di troppo** to be in the way

tròta *f* trout

trottare (**tròtto**) *intr* to trot

trotterellare (**trotterèllo**) *intr* to trot along; to toddle

tròtto *m* trot; **piccolo trotto** jog trot

tròttola *f* top

trovare (**tròvo**) *tr* to find; to visit; **trovare a** or **da ridire** (**su**) to find fault (with); **trovi?** don't you think so? || *ref* to find oneself; to meet; to be; to be located; to happen, e.g., **mi trovai a passare di fronte a casa sua** I happened to pass in front of his house

trovaro·be *m* (**-be**) (theat) property man || *f* (theat) dresser

trovata *f* find; trick, gimmick

trovatèl·lo -la *mf* foundling, waif

trovatóre *m* troubadour

trovière *m* trouvère

truccare §197 *tr* to make up; to falsify; (aut) to soup up || *ref* to put on make-up

truccatura *f* make-up; trick, gimmick

truc·co *m* (**-chi**) make-up; trick, gimmick

truce *adj* fierce, cruel; menacing

trucidare (**trùcido**) *tr* to massacre

trùciolo *m* chip, shaving

truculènto *adj* truculent

truffa *f* cheat, fraud, swindle; **truffa all'americana** confidence game

truffare *tr* to cheat, swindle

truffa·tóre -trice *mf* cheat, swindler

truismo *m* truism

truògolo *m* var of **trogolo**

truppa *f* troop; soldiers; **di truppa** (mil) enlisted (*man or woman*); **in truppa** in a flock

tu §5 *pron pers;* **a tu per tu** face to face; **dare del tu a** to address in the familiar form

tuba *f* tuba; (hist) horn, trumpet; (joc) top hat, stovepipe; (anat) tube

tubare *intr* to coo

tubatura *f* piping, tubing; pipe, tube; pipeline

tubazióne *f* tubes, pipes

tubèrcolo *m* tubercle

tubercolosà·rio [s] *m* (**-ri**) tuberculosis sanitarium

tubercoló·si [s] (**-si**) tuberculosis

tubercoló·so -sa [s] *adj* tuberculous || *mf* T.B. patient

tùbero *m* tuber

tubétto *m* tube (*for pills or toothpaste*); spool

tubino *m* small tube; derby (hat)

tubo *m* tube; pipe; (anat) canal, duct; **a tubo** tubular; **tubo di scarico** exhaust pipe; **tubo di troppopieno** overflow; **tubo di ventilazione** air shaft

tubolare *adj* tubular || *m* tire (*for racing bicycle*)

tuffare *tr* to dip; to plunge || *ref* to plunge; to dive

tuffa·tóre -trice *mf* diver || *m* dive bomber

tuffétto *m* (orn) dabchick, grebe

tuffo *m* dive; plunge; throb; **a tuffo** (aer) diving; **scendere a tuffo** (aer) to dive; **tuffo ad angelo** (sports) swan dive; **tuffo d'acqua** downpour

tufo *m* tufa

tu·ga *f* (**-ghe**) (naut) deckhouse

tugù·rio *m* (**-ri**) hovel

tulipano *m* tulip

tumefare §173 *tr & ref* to swell

tumefazióne *f* swelling

tùmi·do -da *adj* tumid

tumóre *m* tumor

tùmulo *m* tomb; tumulus

tumulto *m* tumult, riot; commotion

tumultuó·so -sa [s] *adj* tumultuous

tungstèno *m* tungsten

tùni·ca *f* (**-che**) tunic

Tùnisi *f* Tunis

Tunisìa, la Tunisia

tunisi·no -na *adj & mf* Tunisian

tuo tua §6 *adj & pron poss* (**tuòi tue**)

tuòno *m* thunder

tuòrlo *m* yolk

turàcciolo *m* cork, stopper

turare *tr* to plug, stop; to cork

turba *f* crowd; mob; (pathol) upset

turbaménto *m* commotion, perturbation; disturbance, breach (*of law and order*)

turbante *m* turban

turbare *tr* to muddy; to disturb; to upset || *ref* to become cloudy; to become upset

turba·to -ta *adj* upset; disturbed; distracted

tùrbi·do -da *adj* turbid

turbina *f* turbine

turbinare (**tùrbino**) *tr* to separate in a centrifuge || *intr* to whirl

tùrbine *m* whirlwind; swarm; tumult

turbinó·so -sa [s] *adj* whirling; tumultuous

turboèli·ca *m* (**-ca**) turboprop

turbogètto *m* turbojet

turbolèn·to -ta *adj* turbulent

turbolènza *f* turbulence

turbomotrice *f* (rr) turbine engine

turboreattóre *m* turbojet

turcasso *m* quiver

turchése [s] *m* turquoise

Turchìa, la Turkey

turchinétto *m* bluing

turchi·no -na *adj* dark-blue || *m* dark blue

tur·co -ca (**-chi -che**) *adj* Turkish; **sedere alla turca** to sit cross-legged || *mf* Turk || *m* Turkish (*language*); **bestemmiare come un turco** to swear like a trooper; **fumare come un turco** to smoke like a steam engine

tùrgi·do ·da *adj* turgid

turibolo *m* thurible, censer

turismo *m* tourism

turi·sta *mf* (**-sti -ste**) tourist

turìsti·co ·ca *adj* (**-ci -che**) tourist; travel (*e.g., bureau*); traveler's (*check*)

turlupinare *tr* to hoodwink, swindle

turlupinatura *f* swindle, confidence game

turno *m* turn; shift; **a turno** in turn; **di turno** on duty; **fare a turno** to take turns

turpe *adj* base, abject; (lit) ugly

turpilò·quio *m* (**-qui**) foul language

turpitùdine *f* turpitude

tuta *f* overalls; **tuta antigravità** anti-G suit; **tuta da bambini** jumpers; **tuta spaziale** spacesuit

tutèla *f* guardianship; defense, protection

tutelare *adj* tutelary || *v* (**tutèlo**) *tr* to protect, defend

tùtolo *m* corncob

tu·tóre -trice *mf* guardian; protector

tuttavìa *adv* yet, nevertheless; (lit) always, continuously

tut·to -ta *adj* whole; all; full; **con tutto** in spite of, e.g., **con tutto quello che ho fatto per lui** in spite of all I have done for him; **del tutto** fully, completely; **è tutt'uno** it's all the same; **tutt'altro** completely different; on the contrary; **tutt'altro che** anything but; **tutti** every, e.g., **tutti gli scolari** every pupil; **tutti e due** both || *m* everything; whole; **con tutto che** although; **fare di tutto** to do everything possible; **in tutto** altogether || *pron* **tut·ti -te** all, everybody (*of a group*); **tutti** everybody || **tutto** *adv* quite; **tutt'a un tratto** all of a sudden; **tutto al contrario** quite the opposite

tuttofa·re *adj invar* of all trades; of all work || *m* (**-re**) factotum, jack-of-all-trades || *f* (**-re**) maid of all work

tuttóra *adv* yet, still

tziga·no -na *adj* & *mf* var of zigano

U

U, u [u] *m* & *f* nineteenth letter of the Italian alphabet

ubbia *f* prejudice, bias; complex; whim

ubbidiènte *adj* obedient

ubbidire §176 *tr* to obey || *intr* to obey; to respond (*said of a car*); (with *dat*) to obey, e.g., **gli ubbedì** he obeyed him

ubertó·so -sa [s] *adj* fruitful; fertile

ubicazióne *f* location

ubiquità *f* ubiquity; **non ho il dono dell'ubiquità** I can't be everywhere at the same time

ubì·quo -qua *adj* ubiquitous

ubriacare §197 *tr* to make drunk, intoxicate || *ref* to get drunk

ubriacatura or **ubriachèzza** *f* drunkenness, intoxication

ubria·co ·ca (**-chi -che**) *adj* drunk; **ubriaco fradicio** dead drunk || *mf* drunkard

ubriacó·ne -na *mf* drunkard

uccellare (**uccèllo**) *tr* to take in, cajole || *intr* to snare; to fowl; to hunt birds

uccèllo *m* bird; **uccello di bosco** fugitive; **uccello di galera** gallows bird; **uccello di passo** bird of passage

uccella·tóre -trice *mf* live-bird catcher

uccellièra *f* aviary; large birdcage

uccìdere §274 *tr* to kill || *ref* to kill oneself; to get killed; to kill one another

-ùccio -ùccia (**-uci -ucce**) *suf adj* not very, e.g., **calduccio** not very hot; rather, e.g., **magruccio** rather thin; poor little, e.g., **caruccio** poor little darling || *suf m* & *f* small e.g., **cappelluccio** small hat

uccisióne *f* killing; murder

ucci·so -sa *adj* killed || *mf* victim

ucci·sóre -ditrice *mf* killer

ucrai·no -na *adj* & *mf* Ukrainian || **l'Ucraina** *f* the Ukraine

udibile *adj* audible

udiènza *f* audience; hearing; **l'udienza è aperta!** the court is now in session!

udire §275 *tr* to hear; to listen to

udito *m* hearing

uditòfono *m* hearing aid

udi·tóre -trice *adj* hearing || *mf* (educ) auditor || *m* magistrate

uditò·rio ·ria (**-ri -rie**) *adj* auditory || *m* audience

ufficiale *adj* official || *m* official; officer; **primo ufficiale** (naut) first officer, mate; **ufficiale di giornata** (mil) officer of the day; **ufficiale di rotta** (aer, naut) navigator; **ufficiale giudiziario** clerk of the court; process server, bailiff; **ufficiale medico** (mil) medical officer

ufficiare §128 *tr* to officiate

uffi·cio *m* (**-ci**) duty; office; bureau; department (*of agency*); **d'ufficio** ex-officio; public, e.g., **avvocato d'ufficio** public defender; **ufficio di collocamento** placement bureau; **ufficio di compensazione** clearing house; **ufficio d'igiene** board of health

uffició·so -sa [s] *adj* unofficial; kindly; white (*lie*)

uffì·zio *m* (**-zi**) (eccl) office

ufo *m*—**a ufo** gratis, without paying

ugèllo *m* nozzle

ùg·gia *f* (**-ge**) darkness; gloom; dislike; **avere in uggia** to dislike

uggiolare (**ùggiolo**) *intr* to whine (*said of a dog*)

uggió·so -sa [s] *adj* gloomy; boring

ugnare *tr* to bevel; to miter

ugnatura *f* bevel; miter
ùgola *f* uvula; **bagnarsi l'ugola** (coll) to wet one's whistle
ugonòtto *m* Huguenot
uguaglianza *f* equality
uguagliare §280 *tr* to equal; to make equal; to equalize; to level; to compare || *ref* to compare oneself; to be equal; to be compared
uguale *adj* equal; same; even; level; **per me è uguale** it's the same to me || *m* equal; (math) equal sign
ùlcera *f* ulcer; sore
ulcerare (**ùlcero**) *tr & ref* to ulcerate
ùliva *f* var of **oliva**
ulterióre *adj* further, subsequent, ulterior
ùltima *f* latest news; last straw
ultimare (**ùltimo**) *tr* to complete, finish
ultimato *m* ultimatum
ultimissima *f* latest edition (*of newspaper*); **ultimissime** late news
ùlti·mo -ma *adj* last; final; latest; latter; farthest; ultimate; least; top (*floor*); **all'ultimo, dall'ultimo, nell'ultimo** or **sull'ultimo** lately; finally, at the end || *f see* **ultima**
ultimogèni·to -ta *adj* last-born || *mf* last-born child
ultra- *pref adj* and *m & f* ultra-, e.g., **ultraelevato** ultrahigh; super-, e.g., **ultrasonico** supersonic (*speed*)
ultracór·to -ta *adj* ultrashort
ultraròs·so -sa *adj & m* infrared
ultraterré·no -na *adj* ultramundane; unearthly
ultraviolét·to -ta *adj & m* ultraviolet
ululare (**ùlulo**) *intr* to howl
ululato *m* howl
umanésimo *m* humanism
umani·sta *mf* (**-sti -ste**) humanist
umani·tà *f* (**-tà**) humanity; **umanità** *fpl* humanities
umanità·rio -ria *adj & mf* (**-ri -rie**) humanitarian
uma·no -na *adj* human; humane || *m* human nature; **umani** human beings
um·bro -bra *adj & m* Umbrian
umettare (**umétto**) *tr* to moisten, dampen
umidìc·cio -cia *adj* (**-ci -ce**) dampish
umidi·tà *f* (**-tà**) humidity, dampness
ùmi·do -da *adj* humid, damp || *m* humidity, dampness; **in umido** stewed (*e.g., meat*)
ùmile *adj* humble || **gli umili** *mpl* the meek
umiliare §287 *tr* to humiliate, humble || *ref* to humble oneself
umiliazióne *f* humiliation
umiltà *f* humility
umóre *m* humor, mood, temper; whim; (bot) sap; **un bell'umore** (coll) quite a character
umorismo *m* humor
umori·sta *mf* (**-sti -ste**) humorist
umorìsti·co -ca *adj* (**-ci -che**) humorous; amusing, comic, funny
un (apocopated form of **uno**) §9 *indef art* a, an || §9 *numeral adj* one || §12 *reciprocal indef pron*—**l'un l'altro** each other, one another

unànime *adj* unanimous
unanimità *f* unanimity
unàni·mo -ma *adj* unanimous
uncinare *tr* to hook, grapple
uncinétto *m* small hook; crochet hook
uncino *m* hook; grapnel; clasp; pothook; (fig) pretext; **a uncino** hooked
undicèsi·mo -ma *adj, m & pron* eleventh
ùndici *adj & pron* eleven; **le undici** eleven o'clock || *m* eleven; eleventh (*in dates*); (soccer) squad
ùngere §183 *tr* to grease; to oil; to smear; to anoint; to flatter || *ref* to smear oneself
Ungheria, l' *f* Hungary
ungherése [*s*] *adj & mf* Hungarian
ùnghia *f* nail; fingernail; claw; hoof; fluke (*of anchor*); (fig) hairbreadth; **avere le unghie lunghe** to be light-fingered; **unghia del piede** toenail; **unghie** (fig) clutches
unghiata *f* nail scratch
unguènto *m* unguent, ointment
ùni·co -ca *adj* (**-ci -che**) only, sole; unique; single (*copy*); complete (*text*) || *f*—**l'unica** the only solution
unicòrno *m* unicorn
unificare §197 (**unìfico**) *tr* to unify; to standardize
unificazióne *f* unification; standardization
uniformare (**unifórmo**) *tr* to make uniform, standardize || *ref*—**uniformarsi a** to conform to; to comply with
unifórme *adj* uniform; standard || *f* uniform; **alta uniforme** (mil) full dress
unilaterale *adj* unilateral
unióne *f* union; agreement; **unione libera** free love
unire §176 *tr & ref* to unite
unìsono [*s*] *m* unison; **all'unisono** in unison
uni·tà *f* (**-tà**) unity; unit; **unità di misura** unit of measurement
unità·rio -ria (**-ri -rie**) *adj* unit (*e.g., price*); united || *m* Unitarian
uni·to -ta *adj* united; joined; compact; plain (*color*); consolidated
universale *adj* universal; last (*judgment*)
universi·tà *f* (**-tà**) university
università·rio -ria (**-ri -rie**) *adj* university; college || *mf* university or college student; university or college professor
univer·so -sa *adj* universal || *m* universe
unno *m* Hun
u·no -na §9 *indef art* a, an || §9 *numeral adj* one || *m* one || §10 *pron indef* one; **le una, la una,** or **l'una** one o'clock; **l'uno e l'altro** both; **l'uno o l'altro** either, either one; **per uno** in single file; **uno per uno** one by one; each other || §11 *correlative pron* one
un·to -ta *adj* greasy || *m* grease, fat; flattery; anointed one
untuosità [*s*] *f* greasiness; unction, unctuousness
untuó·so -sa [*s*] *adj* greasy; unctuous

unzióne f unction

uò·mo m (**-mini**) man; **come un sol uomo** to a man; **uomo d'affari** businessman; **uomo del giorno** man of the hour; **uomo della strada** man of the street; **uomo di chiesa** churchman; **uomo di fatica** laborer; **uomo di fiducia** trusted man; **uomo di mare** seaman; **uomo di paglia** straw man; **uomo di parola** man of his word; **uomo in mare!** man overboard!; **uomo meccanico** automaton; **uomo morto** (rr) deadman brake; **uomo nuovo** nouveau riche; **uomo rana** frogman

uòpo m—**all'uopo** if need be; **essere d'uopo** (lit) to be necessary

uòse [s] fpl leggings

uò·vo m (**-va** fpl) egg; **meglio un uovo oggi che una gallina domani** a bird in a hand is worth two in the bush; **rompere le uova nel paniere a qlcu** to spoil s.o.'s plans; **uovo affogato** poached egg; **uovo alla coque** soft-boiled egg; **uovo all'occhio di bue** fried egg; **uovo da tè** tea ball; **uovo strapazzato** scrambled egg

uragano m hurricane; storm (of applause); **uragano di neve** blizzard

Urali mpl Ural Mountains

uranife·ro -ra adj uranium-bearing

urànio m uranium

urbanésimo m urbanization, migration toward the cities

urbanisti·co -ca (**-ci -che**) adj city-planning || f city planning

urbani·tà f (**-tà**) urbanity, civility; city population

urbanizzare [ddzz] tr to urbanize

urba·no -na adj urban; urbane

urètra f urethra

urgènte adj urgent, pressing

urgènza f urgency; **d'urgenza** urgent; emergency (e.g., operation); **fare urgenza a** to urge

àrgere §276 tr to urge, press || intr to be urgent

urina f urine

urinà·rio -ria adj (**-ri -rie**) urinary

urlare tr to shout; to shout down || intr to howl; to shout, yell

urla·tóre -trice adj screaming || mf screamer; loud singer

ur·lo m howl || m (**-la** fpl) yell, scream

urna f urn; ballot box; (poet) grave; **urne** polls

-uro suf m (chem) -ide, e.g., **cloruro** chloride

urologìa f urology

urrà interj hurrah!

ursóne m Canada porcupine

urtare tr to hit; to bump; to annoy || intr—**urtare contro** to hit, strike against; **urtare in** to hit; to stumble into || ref to get annoyed; to clash; to bump into one another

urto m hit; bump; collision; onslaught; clash, disagreement; **urto di nervi** huff

Uruguai, l' m Uruguay

uruguaia·no -na adj & mf Uruguayan

usanza f usage, custom; habit, practice

usare tr to use, employ; to wear out;

(lit) to frequent; **usare** + inf to be accustomed to + ger || intr to be fashionable; **usare di** to use, employ || ref to become accustomed; **si usa** + inf it is customary to + inf

usa·to -ta adj used, second-hand; worn; worn-out; (lit) usual || m usage, custom; norm; second-hand goods

usbèr·go m (**-ghi**) hauberk; (fig) shield, protection

uscènte adj ending, terminating; retiring

uscière m receptionist; office boy, errand boy; (coll) court clerk; (coll) bailiff; (coll) tipstaff

ù·scio m (**-sci**) door; **infilar l'uscio** to take French leave; **metter tra l'uscio e il muro** (fig) to corner

uscire §277 intr (ESSERE) to go out, leave; to come out; to flow out; to escape; to turn out, ensue; **essere uscito** to be out; **uscire da** to leave; to run off (the track); **uscire dai gangheri** to get mad; **uscire dal comune** to be out of the ordinary; **uscire dal segno** to go too far; **uscire dal seminato** to go astray; **uscire di mente** to escape one's mind, e.g., **gli è uscito di mente** it escaped his mind; **uscire di sentimento** to pass out; **uscire di vita** to die; **uscire in** to lead into; **uscire per il rotto della cuffia** to barely make it

uscita f exit; outlay; quip, sally; gate (e.g., in an airport); (gram) ending; **all'uscita** on the way out; **buona uscita** severance pay; bonus; **libera uscita** day off (of servant); (mil) pass; **uscita di sicurezza** emergency exit

usignòlo m nightingale

u·so -sa adj (lit) accustomed || m practice; usage; use; wear; faculty; power (e.g., of hearing); (lit) intimate relations; **all'uso di** in the fashion of; **avere per uso di** to be wont to; **come d'uso** as usual; **farci l'uso** to get used to it!; **fuori d'uso** worn-out, out of commission; **uso esterno!** (pharm) not to be taken internally!

ustionare (**ustióno**) tr to burn, scorch

ustióne f burn

usuale adj usual; ordinary, common

usufruire §176 intr—**usufruire di** to have the use of; to enjoy

usura f usury; (mach) wear and tear; **ad usura** abundantly

usu·ràio -ràia (**-rài -ràie**) adj usurious || mf usurer, loanshark

usurpare tr to usurp

utensile adj tool, e.g., **macchina utensile** machine tool || m utensil; tool

utènte m user; customer, consumer

ùtero m uterus, womb

ùtile adj useful; usable; workable; legal, prescribed (e.g., time); **essere utile a** to help; **venire utile** to come in handy || m usefulness; profit, gain

utili·tà f (**-tà**) utility, usefulness; profit, gain

utilitària f economy car, compact

utilizzare [ddzz] tr to utilize

utopìa *f* utopia
utopi·sta *mf* (-sti -ste) utopian
utopisti·co -ca *adj* (-ci -che) utopian
uva *f* grapes; **un grano di uva passa** a raisin; **uva passa** raisins

uxorici·da *m* (-di) uxoricide || *f* (-de) murderer of one's husband
uxorici·dio *m* (-di) uxoricide; murder of one's husband
ùzzolo [ddzz] *m* whim, fancy, caprice

V

V, v [vu] *m & f* twentieth letter of the Italian alphabet
v. *abbr* (**vostro**) your
vacante *adj* vacant
vacanza *f* vacancy; vacation; **fare vacanza** to be on vacation; **vacanze** vacation
vacanzière *m* vacationer
vac·ca *f* (-che) cow
vac·càio *m* (-cài) cowboy; stable boy
vaccherìa *f* dairy farm
vacchétta *f* cowhide
vaccìna *f* cow manure; cow
vaccinare *tr* to vaccinate
vaccinazióne *f* vaccination
vacci·no -na *adj* cow; bovine || *m* vaccine || *f* see **vaccina**
vacillante *adj* vacillating
vacillare *intr* to totter; to vacillate; to shake; to flicker; to fail, e.g., **la memoria gli vacilla** his memory is failing; **far vacillare** to rock
vacui·tà *f* (-tà) vacuity
và·cuo -cua *adj* empty || *m* vacuum
vademè·cum *m* (-cum) almanac, ready-reference handbook
vagabondàg·gio *m* (-gi) vagrancy; wandering; rambling
vagabondare (**vagabóndo**) *intr* to wander, rove
vagabón·do -da *adj* wandering; vagabond || *mf* vagrant, bum, tramp; rover
vagare §209 *intr* to wander, ramble, rove
vagheggiare §290 (**vaghéggio**) *tr* to gaze fondly at; to cherish
vagire §176 *intr* to cry, whimper
vagìto *m* cry, whimper
và·glia *m* (-glia) money order || *f*—**di vaglia** worthy, capable
vagliare §280 *tr* to sift, bolt
và·glio *m* (-gli) sieve; **mettere al vaglio** to scrutinize
va·go -ga (-ghi -ghe) *adj* vague; vacant (*stare*); (*lit*) beautiful; (*lit*) roving; (*poet*) desirous || *m* vagueness; (*lit*) rover; (*anat*) vagus
vagonata *f* carload
vagóne *m* (rr) car; **vagone frigorifero** (rr) refrigerator car; **vagone letto** (rr) sleeping car, sleeper; **vagone ristorante** (rr) dining car; **vagone volante** (aer) flying boxcar
vàio vàia (vài vàie) *adj* dark-grey || *m* dark grey; (heral) vair; (zool) Siberian squirrel
vaiòlo *m* smallpox
valan·ga *f* (-ghe) avalanche
valènte *adj* capable, skillful; clever
valentìa *f* skill; cleverness

valentino *m* Valentine (*sweetheart*)
valènza *f* (chem) valence
valére §278 *tr* to win, get (*e.g., an honor for s.o.*); **che vale?** what's the use?; **valere la pena** to be worthwhile; **valere un Perù** to be worth a king's ransom || *intr* (ESSERE & AVERE) to be worth· to be of avail; to be valid; to mean; to be the equivalent; **far valere** to enforce; **farsi valere** to assert oneself; **tanto vale** it's all the same; **vale a dire** that is to say; **valere meglio** to be better || *ref*—**valersi di** to avail oneself of; to play on; to employ
valévole *adj* valid, good
valicare §197 (*s*) *tr* to cross, pass
vàli·co *m* (-chi) mountain pass; passage; opening (*in a hedge*)
validi·tà *f* (-tà) validity
vàli·do -da *adj* valid; able, able-bodied; strong
valigerìa *f* luggage; luggage store
valigétta *f* valise; **valigetta diplomatica** attaché case
vali·gia *f* (-ge) suitcase; traveling bag; **fare le valige** to pack one's bags; **valigia diplomatica** diplomatic pouch; attaché case; **valigia per abiti** suit carrier
vallata *f* valley
valle *f* valley; **a valle** downhill; downstream
vallétta *f* (telv) assistant
vallétto *m* valet; page; (telv) assistant
valló·ne -na *adj & mf* Walloon || *m* narrow valley
valóre *m* value; valor, bravery; force; (fig) jewel; (math) variable; **mettere in valore** to raise the value of; **valore di mercato** market value; **valore facciale** face value; **valore locativo** rental value; **valori valuables**; securities; **valori mobiliari** securities
valorizzare [ddzz] *tr* to enhance the value of
valoró·so -sa [s] *adj* brave, valiant
valuta *f* currency; (com) effective date; (com) value (*of promissory note*)
valutare *tr* to estimate, appraise; to value, prize; to count, reckon; to take into consideration
valutazióne *f* estimation, appraisal; evaluation
valva *f* (bot, zool) valve
vàlvola *f* (anat, mach) valve; (elec) fuse; (rad, telv) tube, valve; **valvola a galleggiante** ball cock; **valvola di sicurezza** safety valve; **valvola in testa** overhead valve
vàl·zer *m* (-zer) waltz

vamp f (vamp) vamp

vampa f flame; blaze; flash; flush

vampata f burst (of heat); blast (of hot air); flash, flush

vampiro m vampire

vanàdio m vanadium

vanaglòria f vainglory, boastfulness

vanaglorió·so -sa [s] adj vainglorious

vandalismo m vandalism

vànda·lo -la adj & m vandal || **Vandalo** m Vandal

vaneggiare §290 (vanéggio) intr to rave; to be delirious; (lit) to open, yawn

vanè·sio -sia adj (-si -sie) vain

van·ga f (-ghe) spade

vangare §209 tr to spade up; to dig with a spade

vangèlo m gospel || **Vangelo** m Gospel

vanghétto m spud

vaniglia f vanilla

vanilò·quio m (-qui) empty talk

vani·tà f (-tà) vanity

vanitó·so -sa [s] adj vain, conceited

va·no -na adj vain; (lit) empty, hollow; **in vano** in vain || m empty space; room

vantàg·gio m (-gi) advantage; profit; odds, handicap; discount; (coll) extra; (typ) galley; **a vantaggio di** on behalf of

vantaggió·so -sa [s] adj advantageous

vantare tr to boast of; to set up (a claim) || ref to boast; **vantarsi di** to brag about, vaunt

vanteria f brag, boast, vaunt

vanto m brag, boast; **aver vanto su** (lit) to overcome

vànvera f—**a vanvera** at random

vapóre m vapor; steam; locomotive; steamship; **a tutto vapore** at full speed

vaporétto m small river boat; vaporetto (in Venice)

vaporizzare [ddzz] tr to vaporize; to spray || intr (ESSERE) & ref to evaporate

vaporizzatóre [ddzz] m vaporizer; sprayer

vaporó·so -sa [s] adj vaporous

varaménto m assemblage (of prefab pieces)

varano m monitor lizard

varare tr to launch; to pass (a law); (coll) to back, promote (a candidate)

varcare §197 tr to cross || intr (poet) to pass (said of time)

var·co m (-chi) opening; mountain pass; breach; **attendere al varco** to lie in wait for; **cogliere al varco** to catch unawares; **fare varco in** to breach

varechina f (laundry) bleach

variàbile adj & f variable

variante f variant; detour; (aut) model

variare §287 tr & intr (ESSERE & AVERE) to vary

variazióne f variation

varicèlla f chicken pox

varicó·so -sa [s] adj varicose

variega·to -ta adj variegated

varie·tà m (-tà) (theat) vaudeville || f variety

và·rio -ria (-ri -rie) adj varied; various; variable; different; **va·ri -rie** several || m variety || **varie** fpl miscellanies || **va·ri -rie** pron indef several

variopin·to -ta adj multicolored

varo m (naut) launch

vas m (vas) subchaser

va·sàio m (-sài) potter

va·sca f (-sche) tub; basin; pool; **vasca da bagno** bathtub; **vasca dei pesci** aquarium; **vasca navale** (naut) basin

vascèllo m vessel, ship

vaselina or **vaselìna** f vaseline

vasellame m dishes; set of dishes; **vasellame da cucina** kitchen ware; **vasellame d'argento** silverware; **vasellame di porcellana** chinaware

vasèllo m (lit) vessel

vasi·stas m (-stas) transom

vaso m vase; vessel; jar, pot; nave (of church); hall (of building); (naut) shipway; (poet) cup; **vasi vinari** wine containers; **vaso da fiori** flowerpot; **vaso da notte** chamber pot; **vaso d'elezione** (eccl) chosen vessel (viz., Saint Paul)

vassallo m vassal; (obs) helper

vas·sóio m (-sói) tray; mortarboard

vasti·tà f (-tà) vastness

va·sto -sta adj spacious; vast; (fig) deep

vate m (lit) prophet, poet

vatica·no -na adj Vatican || **Vaticano** m Vatican

vaticinare (vatìcino & vaticìno) tr to prophesy

vatici·nio m (-ni) prophecy

ve §5 pron

V.E. abbr (Vostra Eccellenza) Your Excellency

vècchia f old woman

vecchiàia f old age

vecchièzza f old age

vèc·chio -chia (-chi -chie) adj old; elder; **vecchio come il cucco** as old as the hills || m old man; **vecchi** old people; **vecchio del mestiere** old hand || f see **vecchia**

véc·cia f (-ce) vetch

véce f stead, e.g., **in vece mia** in my stead; (lit) vicissitude; **fare le veci di** to act for or as

vedére m seeing; looks; view, opinion || §279 tr to see; to review; to look over; **chi s'è visto s'è visto!** good-by and good luck!; **dare a vedere** to make believe; **stare a vedere** to watch; observe; **non poter vedere** to not be able to stand; **non vedere l'ora di** to be hardly able to wait for; **vedere male qlcu** to be ill-disposed toward s.o. || intr—**stare a vedere** to wait and see; **vederci bene** to see (e.g., in the dark); **vederci chiaro** to look into it; **vedere di** to try to || ref to see oneself; to see each other; **vedersela brutta** to anticipate trouble

vedétta f lookout; (nav) vedette

védova f widow

vedovanza f widowhood

vedovile adj widow's; widower's || m dower

védo·vo -va *adj* widowed ‖ *m* widower ‖ *f* see **vedova**

veduta *f* view; (lit) eyesight; **di corte vedute** narrowminded; **di larghe vedute** broadminded

veemènte *adj* vehement; violent; impassioned

veemènza *f* vehemence; violence

vegetale *adj* vegetable ‖ *m* plant, vegetable

vegetare (végeto) *intr* to vegetate

vegetaria·no -na *adj & mf* vegetarian

vegetazióne *f* vegetation

vège·to -ta *adj* vigorous, spry

veggènte *adj* (obs) seeing ‖ *mf* fortuneteller ‖ *m* seer, prophet; **i veggenti** people having eyesight ‖ *f* seeress, prophetess

véglia *f* vigil, watch; wakefulness; evening party, soirée; party, crowd; **a veglia** unbelievable *(tale)*; **veglia danzante** dance; **veglia funebre** wake

vegliardo *m* old man

vegliare §280 (véglio) *tr* to keep watch over ‖ *intr* to stay awake; to keep watch; to stay up

veglióne *m* masked ball

veicolo *m* vehicle; carrier *(of disease)*

véla *f* sail; sailing; **alzare le vele** to set sail; **ammainare le vele** to take in sail; **a vela** under sail; **far vela** to set sail; **vela aurica** lugsail; **vela bermudiana** or **Marconi** jib; **vela maestra** mainsail

ve·làio *m* (-**lài**) sailmaker

velare *adj & f* (phonet) velar ‖ *v* **(vélo)** *tr* to veil; to cover; to muffle *(sound)*; to attenuate, reduce *(a shock)*; to dim, cloud; to conceal; (phot) to fog ‖ *ref* to cover oneself with a veil; to take the veil; to get dim, e.g., **gli si è velata la vista** his eyesight got dim

velà·rio *m* (-**ri**) (hist) velarium; (theat) curtain

vela·to -ta *adj* veiled; sheer *(hosiery)*

velatura *f* coating; (aer) airfoil; (naut) sails

veleggiare §290 (veléggio) *tr* (lit) to sail over *(the sea)* ‖ *intr* to sail; (aer) to glide

veleggiatóre *m* sailboat; (aer) glider

veléno *m* poison; (fig) venom

velenó·so -sa [s] *adj* poisonous; (fig) venomous

velétta *f* veil; (naut) topgallant

vèli·co -ca *adj* (-**ci -che**) sail, sailing

velièro *m* sailing ship

veli·no -na *adj* thin *(paper)* ‖ *f* carbon copy; onionskin; slant *(given to a news item)*

velìvo·lo -la *adj* (lit) gliding; (lit) sailing ‖ *m* (lit) airplane, aircraft

vellei·tà *f* (-**tà**) wild ambition, dream

vellicare §197 (vèllico) *tr* to tickle

vèllo *m* (lit) fleece; **vello d'oro** Golden Fleece

velló·so -sa [s] *adj* hairy

velluta·to -ta *adj* velvety

vellutino *m* thin velvet; velvet ribbon; **vellutino di cotone** velveteen

vellu·to -ta *adj* (lit) hairy ‖ *m* velvet; **velluto a coste** corduroy

vélo *m* veil; coating; film; skin *(e.g., of onion)*; (anat, bot) velum; (fig) body; **fare velo a** to becloud; to fog

velóce *adj* speedy, quick, fast; fleeting

velocipedastro *m* poor or reckless bicycle rider

veloci·sta *mf* (-**sti -ste**) (sports) sprinter

veloci·tà *f* (-**tà**) velocity; speed; (aut) speed; **a grande velocità** by express; **a piccola velocità** by freight; **velocità di crociera** cruising speed; **velocità di fuga** (rok) escape velocity

velòdromo *m* bicycle ring or track

véna *f* vein; grain *(in wood or stone)*; mood; streak *(of madness)*; **di vena** willingly; **essere in vena di** to be in the mood to

venale *adj* venal

venare (véno) *tr* to vein

vena·to -ta *adj* veined; streaked; suffused; **venato di sangue** bloodshot

venatura *f* veining; (fig) streak

vendémmia *f* vintage

vendemmiare §287 (vendémmio) *tr* to harvest *(grapes)* ‖ *intr* to gather grapes; (fig) to make a killing

vendemmia·tóre -trice *mf* vintager

véndere §281 *tr* to sell; **da vendere** plenty, more than enough; **vendere allo scoperto** (fin) to sell short; **vendere fumo** to peddle influence ‖ *intr* to sell; **vendere allo scoperto** (fin) to sell short ‖ *ref* to sell; **si vende for sale**

vendétta *f* vengeance; revenge; **gridare vendetta** to cry out for retribution

vendicare §197 (véndico) *tr* to avenge ‖ *ref* to get revenge

vendicati·vo -va *adj* vengeful, vindictive

vendica·tóre -trice *adj* avenging ‖ *mf* avenger

vendifu·mo *mf* (-**mo**) influence peddler

véndita *f* sale; shop; **in vendita** for sale; **vendita allo scoperto** (fin) short sale; **vendita per corrispondenza** catalogue sale

vendi·tóre -trice *mf* seller; clerk *(in store)* ‖ *m* salesman; **venditore ambulante** peddler; **venditore di fumo** influence peddler ‖ *f* saleslady

venefi·cio *m* (-**ci**) poisoning

venèfi·co -ca (-**ci -che**) *adj* poisonous; unhealthy ‖ *m* (lit) poisonmaker

veneràbile or **venerando** *adj* venerable

venerare (vènero) *tr* to venerate, revere; to worship

venerazióne *f* veneration; worship

vener·dì *m* (-**dì**) Friday ‖ **Venerdì Santo** Good Friday

Vènere *m* (astr) Venus ‖ *f* (mythol & fig) Venus

venè·reo -rea *adj* (-**rei -ree**) venereal

Venèzia *f* Venice; Venetia *(province)*

venezia·no -na *adj & mf* Venetian ‖ *f* Venetian blind

venezola·no -na *adj & mf* Venezuelan

vènia *f* (lit) forgiveness, pardon

venire §282 *intr* (ESSERE) to come; to turn out *(well or badly)*; to turn out to be; **che viene** next, e.g., **il mese che viene** next month; **come viene** as it is; **far venire** to send for; to give, cause; **un va e vieni** a backward-and-forward motion; **venire +** *ger* to keep + *ger*; **venire +** *pp* to be + *pp, e.g.,* **il portone viene aperto alle tre** the gate is opened at three; **venire a capo di** to solve; **venire ai ferri corti** to come into open conflict; **venire al dunque** or **al fatto** to come to the point; **venire alle corte** to get down to brass tacks; **venire alle mani** or **alle prese** to come to blows; **venire a parole** to have words; **venire a patti con** to come to terms with; **venire a proposito** to come in handy; **venire incontro a** to go to meet; **venire in possesso di** to come into possession of (*s.th*); to come into the hands of (*s.o.*); **venire meno** to faint; **venir meno a** to fail to keep (*one's word*); **venir su** to grow, come up; **venire via** to give way ‖ *ref*—**venirsene** to stroll along ‖ *impers* (with *dat*)—**viene da** feel the urge to, *e.g.,* **gli venne da starnutire** he felt the urge to sneeze; **gli è venuto da ridere** he felt the urge to laugh; **viene detto** blurt out, *e.g.,* **gli è venuto detto che non gli piaceva quel tipo** he blurted out that he did not like that fellow; **viene fatto di**+*inf* succeed in+*ger, e.g.,* **le venne fatto di convincerli** she succeeded in convincing them; **happen to** + *inf, e.g.,* **gli venne fatto di incontrarmi per istrada** he happened to meet me on the way

ventà·glio *m* (**-gli**) fan; (fig) spread; **a ventaglio** fanlike; **diramarsi a ventaglio** to fan out

ventaròla *f* weather vane

ventata *f* gust of wind; (fig) wave

ventènne *adj* twenty-year-old ‖ *mf* twenty-year-old person

ventèsi·mo -ma *adj, m & pron* twentieth

vénti *adj & pron* twenty; **le venti** eight P.M. ‖ *m* twenty; twentieth (*in dates*)

ventidue *adj & pron* twenty-two **le ventidue** ten P.M. ‖ *m* twenty-two; twenty-second (*in dates*)

ventilare (**ventìlo**) *tr* to air, ventilate; to winnow (*grain*); to discuss minutely; to air (*a subject*); to broach (*a subject*); to unfurl (*a flag*) ‖ *ref* to fan oneself

ventilatóre *m* fan, ventilator; vent; (min) ventilation shaft; (naut) funnel

ventilazióne *f* ventilation; winnowing

ventina *f* score; **una ventina (di)** twenty, about twenty

ventino *m* twenty-cent coin

ventiquattro *adj & pron* twenty-four; **le ventiquattro** twelve P.M. ‖ *m* twenty-four; twenty-fourth (*in dates*)

ventiquattrór·e *f* (**-re**) overnight bag; twenty-four-hour race; **ventiquattrore** *fpl* period of twenty-four hours

ventitré *adj & pron* twenty-three; **le ventitré** eleven P.M.; **portare il cappello alle ventitré** to wear one's hat cocked ‖ *m* twenty-three; twenty-third (*in dates*)

vènto *m* wind; air; guy wire; **presentarsi al vento** to sail into the wind; **farsi vento** to fan oneself; **a vento** windproof; wind-propelled; **col vento in prora** downwind; **col vento in poppa** upwind; favorably, famously

vèntola *f* fireside fan; lampshade; candle sconce; blade (*of fan*)

ventó·so -sa [*s*] *adj* windy ‖ *f* cupping glass; suction cup; (zool) sucker

vèntre *m* belly; **a ventre a terra** on one's belly; on one's face; at full speed (*said of a horse*)

ventrìcolo *m* ventricle

ventrièra *f* abdominal band or belt

ventrilòquia *f* ventriloquism

ventrìlo·quo -qua *mf* ventriloquist

ventuno *adj & pron* twenty-one; **le ventuno** nine P.M. ‖ *m* twenty-one; twenty-first (*in dates*); (cards) blackjack

ventu·ro -ra *adj* next ‖ *f* (lit) luck, fortune; (lit) good fortune; **alla ventura** at random, at a venture; **di ventura** of fortune, *e.g.,* **soldato di ventura** soldier of fortune

venustà *f* (lit) pulchritude

venu·to -ta *mf*—**nuovo venuto** newcomer; **primo venuto** firstcomer ‖ *f* coming, arrival

véra *f* curbstone (*of well*); (coll) wedding ring

verace *adj* true; truthful, veracious

veraci·tà *f* (**-tà**) veracity, truthfulness

veranda *f* veranda; porch

verbale *adj* verbal ‖ *m* minutes; ticket (*given by a policeman*); **mettere a verbale** to enter into the record

verbèna *f* verbena

vèrbo *m* verb; (lit) word ‖ **Verbo** *m* (theol) Word

verbosità [*s*] *f* verbiage, verbosity

verbó·so -sa [*s*] *adj* windy, longwinded, verbose

verda·stro -stra *adj* greenish

vérde *adj* green; young, youthful ‖ *m* green; **al verde** (coll) broke, penniless; **nel verde degli anni** in the prime of life

verdeggiante *adj* verdant

verderame *m* blue vitriol; verdigris

verdét·to -ta *adj* greenish ‖ *m* verdict

verdógno·lo -la *adj* greenish; sallow (*face*)

verdura *f* vegetables

verecóndia *f* modesty, bashfulness

verecón·do -da *adj* modest, bashful

vér·ga *f* (**-ghe**) switch; rod; ingot, bar; pole; penis; (eccl) staff, crosier; (naut) yard; **tremare a verga a verga** to shake like a leaf

vergare §209 (**vérgo**) *tr* to switch; to rule (*paper*); to stripe; to write

vergati·no -na *adj* thin (*paper*) ‖ *m* striped cloth

verga·to -ta *adj* striped; watermarked with stripes ‖ *m* (obs) serge

verginale *adj* maidenly, virginal

vérgine *adj & f* virgin ‖ **Vergine** *f* (eccl) Virgin; (astr) Virgo

verginità *f* virginity, maidenhood

vergógna *f* shame; **aver vergogna** to be

ashamed; **vergogne** privates ‖ *interj* for shame!

vergognare (**vergógno**) *ref* to be ashamed; to feel cheap; **vergognati!** shame on you!

vergognó·so -sa [s] *adj* ashamed; bashful; shameful

veridici·tà *f* (**-tà**) veracity

verìdi·co -ca *adj* (**-ci -che**) veracious

verìfi·ca *f* (**-che**) verification; control; **verifica fiscale** auditing (*of tax return*)

verificare §197 (**verìfico**) *tr* to verify; to control, check; to audit ‖ *ref* to come true; to happen

verifica·tóre -trice *mf* checker, inspector

verismo *m* verism (*as developed in Italy*)

veri·sta *adj & mf* (**-sti -ste**) verist

veri·tà *f* (**-tà**) truth; **in verità** truthfully, verily

veritiè·ro -ra *adj* truthful

vèrme *m* worm; (*mach*) thread; **verme solitario** tapeworm

vermì·glio -glia (**-gli -glie**) *adj* vermilion; ruby (*lips*) ‖ *m* vermilion

vèr·mut *m* (**-mut**) vermouth

vernàcolo *m* vernacular

vernice *f* varnish; paint; polish; patina; (*painting*) private viewing; (*fig*) veneer; **scarpe di vernice** patent-leather shoes; **vernice a olio** oil paint; **vernice a spruzzo** spray paint; **vernice da scarpe** shoe polish

verniciare §128 *tr* to varnish; to paint

vé·ro -ra *adj* true; real; right; pure; **non è vero?** isn't that so? La traduzione precedente è generalmente rimpiazzata da molte altre frasi. Se la prima espressione è negativa, la domanda equivalente a **non è vero?** sarà affermativa, per esempio, **Lei non lavora, non è vero?** You are not working, are you? Se la prima espressione è affermativa, la domanda sarà negativa, per esempio, **Lei lavora, non è vero?** You are working, are you not? or aren't you? Se la prima espressione contiene un ausiliare, la domanda conterrà l'ausiliare stesso senza infinito o senza participio passato, per esempio, **Arriveranno domani, non è vero?** They will arrive tomorrow, won't they? **Ha finito il compito, non è vero?** He has finished his homework, hasn't he? Se la prima espressione non contiene né un ausiliare, né una delle forme del verbo "to be" in funzione di copula, la domanda conterrà l'ausiliare "do" o "did" senza l'infinito del verbo, per esempio, **Lei è vissuto a Milano, non è vero?** You lived in Milano, did you not? **Lei non va mai al parco, non è vero?** You never go to the park, do you?; **non mi par vero** it seems unbelievable ‖ *m* truth; actuality; **a dire il vero** to tell the truth, as a matter of fact; **dal vero** from nature; **salvo il vero** if I am not mistaken ‖ *f* see **vera**

veróne *m* (*lit*) balcony

verosimiglianza *f* verisimilitude; probability, likelihood

verosìmile *adj* verisimilar; probable, likely

verricèllo *m* winch, windlass

vèrro *m* boar

verru·ca *f* (**-che**) wart

versaménto *m* spilling; payment; deposit

versante *m* depositor; slope, side

versare (**vèrso**) *tr* to pour; to spill; to shed; to pay; to deposit ‖ *intr* to overflow; **versare in gravi condizioni** to be in a bad way ‖ *ref* to spill; to pour (*said of people*); to empty (*said of a river*)

versàtile *adj* versatile; fickle

versa·to -ta *adj* versed; gifted; fully subscribed to (*e.g., stock of a corporation*)

verseggia·tóre -trice *mf* verse writer

versétto *m* verse (*of Bible*)

versificare §197 (**versìfico**) *tr & intr* to versify

versificazióne *f* versification

versióne *f* version; translation

vèrso *adj invar—***pollice verso** (hist) thumbs down ‖ *m* verse; local accent; voice, cry; reverse (*of coin*); verso (*of page*); line (*of poetry*); singsong; gesture; direction, way, manner; respect; **andare a verso** (with *dat*) to suit, e.g., **le sue maniere non gli vanno a verso** her manners do not suit him; **a verso** properly; **contro verso** against the grain; **fare un verso** to make faces; **per un verso** on one hand; **rifare il verso** (with *dat*) to mimick; **senza verso** without rhyme or reason; **verso sciolto** blank verse ‖ *prep* toward; near, around; about; for, toward; upon, in return for; as compared with; **verso di** toward

vèrtebra *f* vertebra

vertebrale *adj* vertebral; spinal

vertebra·to -ta *adj & m* vertebrate

vertènza *f* quarrel, dispute; **vertenza sindacale** labor dispute

vèrtere §283 *intr—***vertere su** to deal with, to turn on

verticale *adj & f* vertical

vèrtice *m* top, summit; vertex; summit conference

vertigine *f* vertigo, dizziness; **avere le vertigini** to feel dizzy

vertiginó·so -sa [s] *adj* dizzy; breathtaking

vérza [dz] *f* cabbage

verzière [dz] *m* (lit) fruit, vegetable, and flower garden; (coll) produce market

verzura [dz] *f* verdure

vesci·ca *f* (**-che**) bladder; blister; **vescica di vento** (fig) windbag; **vescica gonfiata** swellhead; **vescica natatoria** air bladder

vescichétta *f* blister; vescicle; **veschetta biliare** gall bladder

vescìcola *f* blister

vescovado *m* bishopric

véscovo *m* bishop

vè·spa *f* wasp, yellowjacket || *f* (-spe & -spa) motor scooter
ve·spàio *m* (-spài) wasp's nest; (fig) hornet's nest
vespasiano *m* public urinal
Vèspero *m* Vesper
vesperti·no -na *adj* (lit) evening
vèspro *m* (eccl) vespers; (lit) vespertide
vessare (vèsso) *tr* (lit) to oppress
vessatò·rio -ria *adj* (-ri -rie) vexatious
vessazióne *f* oppression
vessillo *m* flag
vestàglia *f* negligee, dressing gown; **vestaglia da bagno** bathrobe
vèste *f* dress; cover; (lit) body; **in veste di** in the quality of; as; in the guise of; **veste da camera** negligee, dressing gown; bathrobe; **veste talare** (eccl) long vestment; **vesti** clothes
vestià·rio *m* (-ri) wardrobe
vestìbolo *m* vestibule, lobby
vesti·gio *m* (-gi & -gia *fpl*) vestige, trace; (lit) footprint
vestire (vèsto) *tr* to dress; to don; to wear; to clothe; to cover, bedeck || *intr* to dress; to fit || *ref* to get dressed; to dress; to dress oneself; to buy one's own clothes
vesti·to -ta *adj* dressed; covered || *m* dress; suit; clothing; **vestiti** clothes; **vestito da donna** dress; **vestito da festa** Sunday best; **vestito da sera** evening clothes, formal suit; evening gown; **vestito da uomo** suit
Vesùvio, il Vesuvius
vetera·no -na *adj & mf* veteran
veterinà·rio -ria (-ri -rie) *adj* veterinary || *m* veterinarian || *f* veterinary medicine
vèto *m* veto; **porre il veto a** to veto
ve·tràio *m* (-tràì) glass manufacturer; glass dealer; glass blower
vetra·to -ta *adj* glass, glass-enclosed; sand (*paper*) || *m* glare ice, glaze || *f* glass door; glass window; glass enclosure; **vetrata a colori** or **vetrata istoriata** stained-glass window
vetreria *f* glassworks; **vetrerie** glassware
vetria·to -ta *adj* glassy; glass-covered
vetrificare §197 (vetrìfico) *tr* to vitrify || *ref* to become vitrified
vetrina *f* show window; showcase, glass cabinet; **mettersi in vetrina** to show off; **vetrine** (coll) eyeglasses
vetrini·sta *mf* (-sti -ste) window dresser
vetri·no -na *adj* glass-like; brittle, fragile || *m* slide (*of microscope*) || *f* see **vetrina**
vetriòlo *m* vitriol
vétro *m* glass; glassware; window pane; piece of glass; **vetro aderente** contact lens; **vetro infrangibile** (aut) safety glass; **vetro smerigliato** ground glass, frosted glass
vetrorèsina *f* fiberglass
vetró·so -sa [s] *adj* vitreous, glassy
vétta *f* peak; top, tip; limb (*of tree*); (naut) end (*of hawser*); **tremare come una vetta** to shake like a leaf
vet·tóre -trice *adj* leading, guiding; spreading, carrying || *m* carrier; (math, phys) vector

vettovagliare §280 *tr* to supply with food
vettovàglie *fpl* victuals, food; supplies
vettura *f* forwarding; coach; car; freight; **in vettura!** (rr) all aboard!; **prendere in vettura** to hire (*a conveyance*); **vettura belvedere** (rr) observation car; **vettura da turismo** (aut) pleasure car; **vettura di piazza** hack, hackney; **vettura letto** (rr) sleeping car; **vettura ristorante** (rr) diner
vetturétta *f* economy car, compact
vetturino *m* hackman, cab driver
vetu·sto -sta *adj* old, ancient
vezzeggiare §290 (vezzéggio) *tr* to coddle || *intr* (lit) to strut
vezzeggiati·vo -va *adj* endearing || *m* endearing expression; diminutive
vézzo *m* habit; caress; necklace; bad habit; **vezzi** fondling, petting; mawkish behavior; charms
vezzó·so -sa [s] *adj* graceful, charming; affected, mincing
vi §5
via *m* (vìa) starting signal; **dare il via a** to give the go-ahead to || *f* street; road, way; route; career; **dare la via a** to open the way to; **in via confidenziale** in confidence; **in via eccezionale** as an exception; **per via di** via, through; (coll) because of; **per via gerarchica** through administrative channels; **per via orale** orally; **per via rettale** rectally; **prendere la via** to be on one's way; **venire a via di fatto** to come to blows; **Via Crucis** Way of the Cross; **via d'acqua** waterway; **via di scampo** (fig) way out; **via d'uscita** way out; **Via Lattea** Milky Way; **vie di fatto** assault and battery; **vie legali** legal steps || *adv* away; (math) times, by; **e così via** and so on; **e via dicendo** and so on; **tirar via** to hurry along; **via via che** as || *prep* via, by way of
viadótto *m* viaduct
viaggiare §290 *intr* to travel; (com) to deal
viaggia·tóre -trice *adj* traveling; homing (*pigeon*) || *mf* traveler || *m* traveling salesman
viàg·gio *m* (-gi) travel; journey; trip; **buon viaggio!** bon voyage!; **viaggio d'andata e ritorno** round trip; **viaggio di prova** (naut) trial run, shakedown cruise
viale *m* boulevard
viandante *mf* (lit) wayfarer
vià·rio -ria *adj* (-ri -rie) road, highway
viàti·co *m* (-ci) viaticum
viavài *m* coming and going; hustle and bustle
vibrante *adj* vibrant; wiry; (phonet) vibrant || *f* (phonet) trill, vibrant
vibrare *tr* to jar; to deliver (*a blow*); to vibrate; (lit) to hurl || *intr* to vibrate
vibra·to -ta *adj* vibrant; resolute, vigorous || *m* vibrating sound
vibrazióne *f* vibration
vicariato *m* vicarage
vicà·rio *m* (-ri) vicar

vice- *pref adj* vice-, e.g., **vicereale** viceroyal || *pref m & f* vice-, e.g., **viceammiraglio** vice-admiral; assistant, e.g., **vicegovernatore** assistant governor; deputy, e.g., **vicesindaco** deputy mayor

vicediret·tóre -trice *mf* assistant manager

vicènda *f* vicissitude; rotation (*of crops*); **a vicenda** in turn

vicendévole *adj* mutual, reciprocal

vicepresidènte [s] *mf* vice president

vice·ré *m* (**-ré**) viceroy

vicevèrsa *adv* vice versa; (coll) instead, on the contrary

vichin·go -ga *adj & mf* (**-ghi -ghe**) Viking

vicinanza *f* nearness; **in vicinanza di** in the neighborhood of; **vicinanze** vicinity, neighborhood

vicinato *m* neighborhood

vici·no -na *adj* near; neighboring; next; close (*relative*) || *mf* neighbor || **vicino** *adv* nearby, near; **da vicino** closely; at close quarters; **vicino a** near; next to, close to

vicissitúdine *f* vicissitude

ví·co *m* (**-chi**) alley, lane; village; (lit) region

vìcolo *m* alley, court, place; **vicolo cieco** blind alley, dead end

videocassétta *f* video cassette

vidimare (**vìdimo**) *tr* to validate, visa; to sign

vidimazióne *f* validation, visa; signature

viennése [s] *adj & mf* Viennese

viepiù *adv* (lit) more and more

vietare (**vièto**) *tr* to forbid, prohibit

vieta·to -ta *adj* forbidden; **senso vietato** one way; **sosta vietata** no parking; no stopping; **vietato fumare** no smoking

Vietnam, il Vietnam

vietnami·ta *adj & mf* (**-ti -te**) Vietnamese

viè·to -ta *adj* (lit) old-fashioned; (coll) musty-smelling, rancid

vigènte *adj* current, in force

vigere §284 *intr* to be in force

vigèsi·mo -ma *adj* twentieth

vigilante *adj* watchful, vigilant || *m* watchman

vigilanza *f* vigilance; surveillance

vigilare (**vìgilo**) *tr* to watch; to watch over; to police || *intr* to watch; **vigilare che** to see to it that

vigila·tóre -trice *mf* inspector || *f* camp counselor; **vigilatrice sanitaria** child health inspector

vìgile *adj* (lit) watchful || *m* watch; **vigile del fuoco** fireman; **vigile urbano** policeman

vigìlia *f* fast; vigil; **la vigilia di** on the eve of, the night before

vigliaccherìa *f* cowardice

vigliac·co -ca (**-chi -che**) *adj* cowardly || *m* coward

vigna *f* vineyard

vignaiòlo *m* vine dresser

vignéto *m* vineyard

vignétta *f* vignette; **vignetta umoristica** cartoon

vignetti·sta *mf* (**-sti -ste**) cartoonist

vigógna *f* vicuña

vigóre *m* vigor; **in vigore** in force

vigoria *f* vigor

vigoró·so -sa [s] *adj* vigorous

vile *adj* cowardly; vile, low, cheap; base (*metal*)

vilificare §197 (**vilìfico**) *tr* to vilify

vilipèndere §148 *tr* to despise; to show scorn for

villa *f* villa; country house; one-family detached house; (lit) country

villàg·gio *m* (**-gi**) village; **villaggio del fanciullo** boys' town

villanata *f* boorishness

villanìa *f* boorishness, rudeness; insult

villa·no -na *adj* rude, churlish || *mf* boor, churl; (lit) peasant

villanzó·ne -na *mf* boor, uncouth person

villeggiante *mf* vacationist

villeggiare §290 (**villéggio**) *intr* to vacation

villeggiatura *f* vacation, summer vacation

villétta *f* or **villino** *m* bungalow

villó·so -sa [s] *adj* hairy

vil·tà *f* (**-tà**) baseness; cowardice

viluppo *m* tangle, twist

vìmine *m* withe, wicker, osier

vinàcce *fpl* pressed grapes

vi·nàio *m* (**-nài**) wine merchant

vincènte *adj* winning || *mf* winner

vincere §285 *tr* to overcome; to win; to convince; to check; to defeat; **vincere per un pelo** to nose out; **vincerla** to come out on top || *ref* to control oneself

vincetòssi·co *m* (**-ci**) swallowwort, tame poison

vinciper·di *m* (**-di**) giveaway

vìncita *f* gain; winnings

vinci·tóre -trice *adj* conquering, victorious || *mf* winner; conqueror; victor

vincolare *adj* binding; bound || *v* (**vìncolo**) *tr* to tie; to bind, obligate; to restrict the use of (*real-estate property*)

vìncolo *m* tie, bond; (law) entail; (law) restriction (*in a real-estate deed*)

vinìco·lo -la *adj* wine, wine-producing

vinile *m* vinyl

vino *m* wine; **vin caldo** mulled wine; **vino da pasto** table wine; **vino di marca** vintage wine; **vino di mele** cider

vin·to -ta *adj* vanquished, overcome, defeated; victorious (*battle*); **averla vinta su** to overcome; **darla vinta a qlcu** to let s.o. get away with murder; **darsi per vinto** to give in, yield || *m* vanquished person; **i vinti** the vanquished

viò·la *adj invar* violet || *m* (**-la**) violet (*color*) || *f* violet; (mus) viola; **viola del pensiero** pansy; **viola mammola** sweet violet

violacciòc·ca *f* (**-che**) (bot) wallflower

violà·ceo -cea *adj* violet

violare (**vìolo**) *tr* to violate; to run (*a blockade*)

violazióne *f* violation; **violazione di**

domicilio housebreaking, burglary; **violazione di proprietà** trespass

violentare (violènto) *tr* to violate, force; to do violence to; to rape

violèn·to -ta *adj* violent || *m* violent person

violènza *f* violence; **violenza carnale** rape

violét·to -ta *adj & m* violet || *f* (bot) violet

violini·sta *mf* (-sti -ste) violinist

violino *m* violin; **primo violino** concertmaster

violoncelli·sta *mf* (-sti -ste) violoncellist

violoncèllo *m* violoncello, cello

viòttolo *m* path

vipera *f* viper, adder

viràg·gio *m* (-gi) turn; (aer) banking; (naut) tacking; (phot) toning

virare *tr* to veer; to turn (*a winch*); (aer) to bank; (phot) to tone || *intr* to veer, steer; **virare di bordo** (naut) to put about; (naut) to tack

virata *f* turn, veer; (aer) banking; (naut) tacking

virginale *adj* var of **verginale**

virgì·nia *m* (-nia) Virginia tobacco || *f* (-nia) Virginia cigarette

virgola *f* comma; (*used in Italian to set off the decimal fraction from the integer*) decimal point; **doppia virgola** quotation mark

virgolétta *f* quotation mark

virgulto *m* (lit) shoot; (lit) shrub

virile *adj* virile

virilità *f* virility

viròla *f* (mach) male piece

virologìa *f* virology

vir·tù *f* (-tù) virtue; (lit) valor

virtuale *adj* virtual

virtualménte *adv* virtually, to all intents and purposes

virtuosismo [s] *m* virtuosity; showing off

virtuosità [s] *f* virtuosity

virtuó·so -sa [s] *adj* virtuous || *mf* virtuoso

virulèn·to -ta *adj* virulent

virulènza *f* virulence

vi·rus *m* (-rus) virus

vìsce·re *m* (-ri) internal organ; **visceri** entrails, viscera || **viscere** *fpl* entrails, viscera; (fig) heart, feeling; (fig) bowels (*of the earth*)

vi·schio *m* (-schi) mistletoe; birdlime; (fig) trap

vischió·so -sa [s] *adj* sticky, viscous; (com) steady

visci·do -da *adj* viscid; clammy; (fig) unctuous

vìsciola *f* sour cherry

vìsciolo *m* sour cherry tree

viscónte *m* viscount

viscontéssa *f* viscountess

viscó·so -sa [s] *adj* viscous, sticky || *f* viscose

visétto *m* small face; baby face

visìbile *adj* visible; obvious

visibì·lio *m* (-li) (coll) crowd; (coll) bunch; **andare in visibilio** to become ecstatic; **mandare in visibilio** to throw into ecstasy, enrapture

visibilità *f* visibility

visièra *f* visor; fencing mask; eyeshade; **visiera termica** (aut) electric defroster

visigò·to -ta *adj* Visigothic || *mf* Visigoth

visionà·rio -ria *adj & mf* (-ri -rie) visionary

visióne *f* vision; sight; (mov, telv) showing; **in visione gratuita** for free examination; **mandare qlco a qlcu in visione** to send s.th to s.o. for his (or her) opinion; **prendere visione di** to examine; to peruse

vi·sìr *m* (-sìr) vizier

visita *f* visit; visitation; **fare una visita** to pay a visit; **marcare visita** (mil) to report sick; **visita doganale** customs inspection

visitare (visìto) *tr* to visit; to inspect

visita·tóre -trice *mf* visitor || *f* social worker

visitazióne *f* visitation

visì·vo -va *adj* visual

viso *m* face; **far buon viso a cattivo gioco** to grin and bear it

visóne *m* mink

visóre *m* (phot) viewer; (phot) viewfinder

vi·spo -spa [s] *adj* brisk, lively

vissu·to -ta *adj* wordly-wise

vista *f* sight, eyesight; view; vista; glance; (poet) window; **a vista** exposed, visible; **a vista d'occhio** as far as the eye can see; **essere in vista** to be expected; to be imminent; to be in the limelight; **far vista di** to pretend to; **in vista di** in view of; **mettere in vista** to show off; **vista a volo d'uccello** bird's-eye view; **vista corta** poor eyesight

vistare *tr* to validate, visa

vi·sto -sta *adj*—**visto che** seeing that, inasmuch as || *m* visa; approval || *f* see **vista**

vistó·so -sa [s] *adj* showy, flashy; (fig) considerable

visuale *adj* visual || *f* view; line of sight

visualizzare [ddzz] *tr* to visualize

vita *f* life; livelihood; living; waist; **avere breve vita** to be short-lived; **fare la vita** to be a prostitute; **vita natural durante** for life; during one's lifetime

vitaiòlo *m* man about town; playboy, bon vivant

vitale *adj* vital

vitalità *f* vitality

vitalì·zio -zia (-zi -zie) *adj* life, lifetime || *m* life annuity

vitamina *f* vitamin

vite *f* (bot) grapevine; (mach) screw; **a vite** threaded; (aer) in a tailspin; **vite autofilettante** self-tapping screw; **vite del Canadà** woodbine, Virginia creeper; **vite per legno** wood screw; **vite per metallo** machine screw; **vite perpetua** (mach) endless screw, worm gear; **vite prigioniera** stud bolt

vitèllo *m* calf; veal

vitic·cio *m* (-ci) tendril

vìtre·o -a *adj* vitreous; glassy (*eyes*)

vìttima *f* victim

vitto *m* food; diet; **vitto e alloggio** room and board

vittòria *f* victory; **cantar vittoria** to crow; to crow too soon

vittorió·so -sa [s] *adj* victorious

vituperare (**vitùpero**) *tr* to vituperate

vituperévole *adj* contemptible, shameful

vituperèrio *m* (**-ri**) shame, infamy; insult; (lit) blame

viuzza *f* narrow street, lane

viva *interj* long live!

vivacchiare §287 *intr* (coll) to get along || *ref*—**si vivacchia** (coll) so, so

vivace *adj* lively, brisk; brilliant; vivacious

vivacità *f* liveliness, briskness; brilliancy, brightness; vivacity

vivaddìo *interj* yes, of course!; by Jove!

vivagno *m* selvage; edge

vi·vàio *m* (**-vài**) fishpond; fish tank; tree nursery; (fig) seedbed

vivanda *f* food

vivandiè·re -ra *mf* (mil) sutler

vivere *m* living; living; cost of living; **viveri** food, provisions; allowance || §286 *tr* to live; **vivere un brutto momento** to spend an uncomfortable moment || *intr* (ESSERE) to live; **vive** (typ) stet; **vivere alla giornata** to live from hand to mouth

vivézza *f* liveliness

vìvi·do -da *adj* vivid, lively

vivificare §197 (**vivìfico**) *tr* to vivify

vivisezionare (**vivisezióno**) *tr* to vivisect; to scrutinize

vivisezióne *f* vivisection

vi·vo -va *adj* alive; living; live, vivacious; lively; vivid; high (*flame*); bright (*light*); raw (*flesh*); sharp, acute (*pain*); hearty (*thanks*); outright (*expense*); gross (*weight*); brute (*strength*); modern (*language*); kinetic (*energy*); running (*water*) || *m* living being; heart (*of a question*); **al vivo** lively; lifelike; **i vivi e i morti** the quick and the dead; **toccare nel vivo** to sting to the quick || **viva** *interj* see viva

viziare §287 *tr* to spoil; to ruin; (law) to vitiate || *ref* to become spoiled

vizià·to -ta *adj* spoiled; ruined; stale (*air*)

vì·zio *m* (**-zi**) vice; defect; flaw; (law) vitiation

vizió·so -sa [s] *adj* vicious; defective || *mf* profligate

viz·zo -za *adj* withered

vocabolà·rio *m* (**-ri**) dictionary; vocabulary

vocàbolo *m* word

vocale *adj* vocal; (lit) sonorous || *f* vowel

vocalizzare [ddzz] *tr & ref* to vocalize

vocativo *m* vocative

vocazióne *f* vocation

vóce *f* voice; noise, roar; word; rumor; entry; tone; **ad alta voce** aloud; **a bassa voce** in a low voice; **a viva voce** by word of mouth; **a voce** orally; **dare una voce a** (coll) to call; **dare sulla voce a** to rebuke; to con-

tradict; **fare la voce grossa** to raise one's voice; **non avere voce in capitolo** to have no say; **schiarirsi la voce** to clear one's throat; **senza voce** hoarse; **sotto voce** in a low tone; **voce bianca** child's voice (*in singing*)

vociare *m* bawl || §128 (**vócio**) *intr* to bawl

vociferare (**vocìfero**) *intr* to vociferate, shout || *ref*—**si vocifera** it is rumored

vó·ga *f* (**-ghe**) fashion, vogue; energy, enthusiasm; rowing

vogare §209 (**vógo**) *tr & intr* to row

voga·tóre -trice *mf* rower || *m* oarsman; rowing machine

vòglia *f* wish; whim, fancy; willingness; birthmark; **aver voglia di** to feel like, have a notion to; **di buona voglia** willingly; **di mala voglia** unwillingly

voglió·so -sa [s] *adj* fanciful; (lit) desirous

vói §5 *pron pers* you; **voi altri** you, e.g., **voi altri americani** you Americans

voial·tri -tre *pron pl* you, e.g., **voialtri americani** you Americans

volano *m* shuttlecock; (mach) flywheel

volante *adj* flying; loose (*sheet*); free (*agent*) || *m* steering wheel; (mach) hand wheel; shuttlecock

volantino *m* leaflet; fringe; (mach) hand wheel

volare (**vólo**) *tr* (soccer) to overthrow || *intr* (ESSERE & AVERE) to fly

volata *f* flight; sprint; run; mouth (*of gun*); (tennis) volley; **di volata** in a hurry

volàtile *adj* volatile; flying (*animal*) || **volatili** *mpl* birds

volatilizzare [ddzz] *tr & intr* (ESSERE) to volatilize

volènte *adj*—**Dio volente** God willing; **volente o nolente** willy-nilly

volentièri *adv* gladly, willingly

volére *m* will, wish; **al volere di** at the bidding of || §288 *tr* to will; to want, desire; (lit) to believe, affirm; **l'hai voluto tu** it's your fault; **non vuol dire!** never mind!; **qui ti voglio** here's the rub, that's the trouble; **senza volere** without meaning to; **voglia Dio!** may God grant!; **voler bene** (with *dat*) to like; **volerci** to take, e.g., **ci vorranno due anni per finire questo palazzo** it will take two years to complete this building; **ce ne vogliono ancora tre** it takes three more of them; **voler dire** to mean; to try, e.g., **vuole piovere** it is trying to rain; **volere che** + *subj* to want + *inf*, e.g., **vuole che vengano** he wants them to come; **volere piuttosto** to prefer; **volere è potere** where there is a will there is a way; **voler male** (with *dat*) to dislike; **volerne a** to bear a grudge against; **vorrei** I should like, I'd like; **vuoi . . . vuoi** either . . . or

volgare *adj* vernacular, popular, common; vulgar || *m* vernacular

volgarì·tà *f* (**-tà**) vulgarity

volgarizzare [ddzz] *tr* to popularize
vòlgere §289 *tr* to turn; (lit) to translate || *intr* to turn; (lit) to go by; **volgere a** to turn toward; to draw near, to approach; **volgere in fuga** to take to flight || *ref* to turn; to devote oneself
vól·go *m* (**-ghi**) (lit) crowd, mob
volièra *f* aviary
voliti·vo *-va adj* volitional; strongminded, strong-willed
vólo *m* flight; fall; **al volo** on the spot; on the wing; **a volo d'uccello** as the crow flies; bird's-eye (*e.g.*, *view*); **di volo** at top speed, immediately; **in volo** aloft, in the air; **prendere il volo** to take flight; **volo a vela** or **volo planato** gliding; **volo strumentale** instrument flying; **volo veleggiato** gliding
volon·tà *f* (**-tà**) will; **di spontanea volontà** of one's own volition; **pieno di buona volontà** eager to please; **ultime volontà** last will and testament
volontariato *m* volunteer work; apprenticeship without pay; (mil) volunteer service
volontà·rio -ria *adj* (**-ri -rie**) voluntary || *m* volunteer
volonteró·so -sa [s] *adj* willing, welldisposed
volpacchiòtto *m* fox cub; (fig) sly fox
vólpe *f* fox; (agr) smut; **volpe argentata** silver fox
volpi·no -na *adj* fox; fox-colored; foxy || *m* Pomeranian
volpó·ne -na *mf* sly fox
vòlt *m* (**vòlt**) (elec) volt
vòl·ta *m* (**-ta**) (elec) volt || *f* turn; time; vault; roof (*of mouth*); **alla volta di** toward; **a volta di corriere** by return mail; **a volte** sometimes; **c'era una volta** once upon a time there was; **certe volte** sometimes; **dare di volta il cervello** to go crazy, e.g., **gli ha dato di volta il cervello** he went crazy; **dar la volta** to turn sour (*said of wine*); **due volte** twice; **molte volte** often; **per una volta tanto** only once; **poche volte** seldom; **tante volte** often; **tutto in una volta** at one swoop, at one stroke; in one gulp, in one swallow; **una volta** once; **una volta che** (coll) inasmuch as; **una volta per sempre** once and for all; **una volta tanto** for once; **volta a crociera** cross vault; **volta per volta** little by little; **volte** (math) times, e.g., **cinque volte cinque** five times five
voltafàc·cia *m* (**-cia**) volte-face; **fare voltafaccia** to wheel around (*said of a horse*)
voltagabbà·na *mf* (**-na**) turncoat
voltàg·gio *m* (**-gi**) voltage
voltài·co -ca *adj* (**-ci -che**) voltaic
voltare (**vòlto**) *tr, intr & ref* to turn
voltastòma·co *m* (**-chi**) (coll) nausea; **fare venire il voltastomaco a qlcu** (coll) to turn s.o.'s stomach
voltata *f* turn; curve

volteggiare §290 (**voltéggio**) *tr* to put (*a horse*) through its paces || *intr* to hover; to flit, flutter; (sports) to vault (*e.g., on horseback or trapeze*)
voltég·gio *m* (**-gi**) (sports) vaulting
vòltmetro *m* voltmeter
vólto *m* (lit) face
voltura *f* (com, law) transfer
volùbile *adj* fickle
volubilità *f* fickleness
volume *m* volume; bulk; mass
voluminó·so -sa [s] *adj* voluminous, bulky
volu·to -ta *adj* desired; intentional || *f* (archit) volute, scroll
volut·tà *f* (**-tà**) pleasure, enjoyment; voluptuousness
voluttuà·rio -ria *adj* (**-ri -rie**) luxury (*goods*)
voluttuó·so -sa [s] *adj* voluptuous, sensuous
vòmere *m* plowshare; trail spade (*of gun*)
vòmi·co -ca *adj* (**-ci -che**) emetic
vomitare (**vòmito**) *tr & intr* to vomit
vomitati·vo -va *adj & m* emetic
vòmito *m* vomit
vóngola *f* clam
vorace *adj* voracious
voraci·tà *f* (**-tà**) voracity
voràgine *f* chasm, gulf, abyss
vòrtice *m* vortex, whirlpool; whirlwind
vorticó·so -sa [s] *adj* whirling, swirling
vò·stro -stra §6 *adj & pron poss*
votare (**vóto**) *tr* to devote; to vote || *intr* to vote || *ref* to devote oneself
votazióne *f* vote, voting, poll; (educ) grades
voti·vo -va *adj* votive
vóto *m* vow; wish; votive offering; vote, ballot; grade, mark; **a pieni voti** with highest honors; **fare un voto** to make a vow; **pronunciare i voti** to take vows; **voto di fiducia** vote of confidence; **voto preferenziale** write-in vote; preferential ballot
vudù *m* voodoo
vuduì·sta *mf* (**-sti -ste**) voodoo (*person*)
vulcàni·co -ca *adj* (**-ci -che**) volcanic
vulcanizzare [ddzz] *tr* to vulcanize
vulcano *m* volcano
vulga·to -ta *adj* disseminated || **Vulgata** *f* Vulgate
vulneràbile *adj* vulnerable
vuotare (**vuòto**) *tr* to empty; **vuotare il sacco** to speak one's mind, unburden oneself || *ref* to empty
vuò·to -ta *adj* empty; devoid || *m* vacuum; emptiness; empty space; empty seat; empty feeling; empty (*e.g., container*); **a vuoto** in vain; wide of the mark; (*check*) without sufficient funds; **andare a vuoto** to fail; (mach) to idle; **cadere nel vuoto** to fall on deaf ears; **mandare a vuoto** to thwart; **sotto vuoto** in a vacuum; **vuoto d'aria** (aer) air pocket; **vuoto di cassa** deficit; **vuoto di potere** power vacuum

W

W, w ['doppjo 'vu] *m & f*
wà·fer *m* (**-fer**) wafer
water-clòset *m* (**-clòset**) flush toilet
watt *m* (**watt**) watt

watt·óra *m* (**-óra**) watt-hour
wèstern *m* (**wèstern**) (mov) western
whisky *m* (**whisky**) whiskey
wìgwam *m* (**wìgwam**) wigwam

X

X, x [iks] *m & f*
xèno *m* xenon
xenòfo·bo -ba *mf* xenophobe

xè·res *m* (**-res**) sherry
xerografìa *f* xerography
xeròfito *m* xerophyte

Y

Y, y ['ipsilon] *m & f*
yacht *m* (**yachts**) yacht
yak *m* (**yak**) yak

yànkee *m* (**yànkees**) Yankee
yìddish *adj invar & m* Yiddish

Z

Z, z ['dzeta] *m & f* twenty-first letter
  of the Italian alphabet
zabaióne [dz] *m* eggnog
zàcchera *f* splash of mud
zaffare *tr* to plug; to bung
zaffata *f* unpleasant whiff, stench; gust
zafferano [dz] *m* saffron
zaffiro [dz] *m* sapphire
zaffo *m* plug; bung; tampon
zàgara [dz] *f* orange blossom
zàino [dz] *m* knapsack; (mil) pack
zampa *f* paw; (culin) leg; **a quattro
  zampe** on all fours; **zampa di gallina**
  crow's-foot; illegible scrawl; **zampa
  di porco** crowbar
zampare *intr* to paw; to stamp
zampettare (**zampétto**) *intr* to toddle;
  to scamper
zampillare *intr* (ESSERE & AVERE) to
  spurt, gush, spring
zampillo *m* spurt, gush, spring
zampino *m* little paw; **metterci lo zampino** to put one's finger in the pie
zampiróne *m* slow-burning mosquito
  repellent; foul-smelling cigarette
zampógna *f* bagpipe
zampognare (**zampógno**) *intr* to pipe,
  play the bagpipe
zampóne *m* Modena salami (*stuffed
  forepaw of a hog*)
zanèlla *f* gully
zàngola *f* butter churn
zanna *f* tusk; fang; **mostrare le zanne**
  to show one's teeth
zanzara [dz] [dz] *f* mosquito
zanzarièra [dz] [dz] *f* mosquito net;
  window screen
zappa *f* hoe; **darsi la zappa sui piedi**

to cut one's nose off to spite one's
  face
zappare *tr* to hoe
zappatóre *m* hoer, digger; (mil) sapper
zar *m* (**zar**) czar
zàttera *f* raft; **zattera di salvataggio** life
  raft
zatterière *m* log driver
zavòrra [dz] *f* ballast; (fig) deadwood
zavorrare [dz] (**zavòrro**) *tr* to ballast
zàzzera *f* mop (*of hair*)
zèbra [dz] *f* zebra; **zebre** zebra crossing
zebra·to -ta [dz] *adj* zebra-striped
ze·bù [dz] *m* (**-bù**) zebu
zéc·ca *f* (**-che**) mint; (ent) tick; **nuovo
  di zecca** brand-new
zecchino *m* sequin, gold coin
zèfiro [dz] *m* zephyr
zelante [dz] *adj* zealous; studious || *mf*
  zealot; eager beaver
zèlo [dz] *m* zeal; **zelo pubblico** public
  spirit
zènit [dz] *m* zenith
zénzero [dz] [dz] *m* ginger
zép·po -pa *adj* crammed, jammed || *f*
  wedge; (fig) padding
zerbino [dz] *m* doormat; dandy
zerbinòtto [dz] *m* dandy, sporty fellow
zèro [dz] *m* zero
zìa *f* aunt
zibaldóne [dz] *m* notebook; collection
  of thoughts; (pej) hodgepodge
zibellino [dz] *m* sable
zibétto [dz] *m* civet cat; civet (*substance used in perfumery*)
zibibbo *m* raisin
ziga·no -na *adj & mf* gypsy
zìgomo [dz] *m* cheekbone

zigrinare [dz] *tr* to grain (*leather*); to mill, knurl (*metal*)

zigrina‧to ‧ta [dz] *adj* shagreened, grained (*leather*); knurled

zigzàg [dz] [dz] *m* (**zigzàg**) zigzag; **andare a zigzag** to zigzag

zigzagare §209 [dz] [dz] *intr* to zigzag

zimarra [dz] *f* cassock; (obs) overcoat

zimbèllo *m* decoy (*bird*); laughingstock

zincare §197 *tr* to zinc

zinco *m* zinc

zingaré‧sco ‧sca (-**schi** -**sche**) *adj* & *mf* gypsy

zinga‧ro ‧ra *mf* gypsy

zinnia [dz] *f* zinnia

zio *m* uncle; **zio d'America** rich uncle

zipolo *m* peg, bung

zircóne [dz] *m* zircon

zircònio [dz] *m* zirconium

zirlare *intr* to warble; to squeak (*said of mouse*)

zitèlla *f* old maid

zittire §176 *tr* & *intr* to hoot, hiss

zit‧to ‧ta *adj* silent; **far stare zitto** to hush up; **stare zitto** to keep quiet ‖ *m* whisper ‖ **zitto** *interj* quiet!; hush!; shut up!

zizzània [dz] [ddzz] *f* (bot) darnel; **seminar zizzania** to sow discord

zòccolo *m* clog, sabot; clump, clod; clodhopper; base (*of column*); pedestal; wide baseboard; (zool) hoof

zodiaco [dz] *m* zodiac

zolfanèllo *m* sulfur match

zolfara *f* var of **solfara**

zólfo *m* sulfur

zòlla *f* clod, clump; turf; lump, cube (*of sugar*)

zollétta *f* lump, cube (*of sugar*)

zòna [dz] *f* zone; area; girdle; band, stripe; ticker tape; (pathol) shingles; (telg) tape; **zona glaciale** frigid zone; **zona tropicale** tropics, tropical zone

zónzo [dz] [dz] *m*—**andare a zonzo** to stroll, loiter along

zoòfito [dz] *m* zoophite

zoologia [dz] *f* zoology

zoològi‧co ‧ca [dz] *adj* (-**ci** -**che**) zoological

zoòlo‧go ‧ga [dz] *mf* (-**gi** -**ghe**) zoologist

zootecnìa [dz] *f* animal husbandry

zootècni‧co ‧ca [dz] (-**ci** -**che**) *adj* livestock ‖ *m* livestock specialist

zoppicante *adj* limping; halting; shaky

zoppicare §197 (**zòppico**) *intr* to limp; to be shaky (*in one's studies*); to wobble

zoppicatura *f* limp; wobble

zòp‧po ‧pa *adj* crippled; lame; wobbly ‖ *mf* cripple; lame person

zòti‧co ‧ca [dz] (-**ci** -**che**) *adj* uncouth, boorish ‖ *m* churl, boor

zuc‧ca *f* (-**che**) pumpkin; (joc) pate; (coll) empty head

zuccata *f* bump with the head

zuccherare (**zùcchero**) *tr* to sweeten, sugar

zuccherièra *f* sugar bowl

zuccherifi‧cio *m* (-**ci**) sugar refinery

zuccheri‧no ‧na *adj* sugary ‖ *m* candy; sugar plum; sugar-coated pill

zùcchero *m* sugar; **zucchero filato** cotton candy; **zucchero in polvere** powdered sugar

zuccheró‧so ‧sa [s] *adj* sugary

zucchétto *m* scull cap; zucchetto

zucchi‧no ‧na *m* & *f* zucchini

zuccó‧ne ‧na *mf* dunce, dumbbell

zuffa *f* brawl, fight

zufolare (**zùfolo**) *tr* & *intr* to whistle

zùfolo *m* (mus) whistle, pipe

zu‧lù (-**lù**) [dz] *adj* & *mf* Zulu

zumare [dz] *tr* & *intr* (mov, telv) to zoom

zumata [dz] *f* (mov, telv) zoom

zuppa *f* soup; (fig) mess; **zuppa inglese** cake with brandy and whipped cream; **zuppa pavese** consommé with toast and eggs

zuppièra *f* tureen

zup‧po ‧pa *adj* drenched, soaked ‖ *f* see **zuppa**

Zurigo *f* Zurich

zuzzurulló‧ne ‧na [dz] [ddzz] *mf* overgrown child, just a big kid

PART TWO

Inglese-Italiano

La pronunzia dell'inglese

I simboli seguenti rappresentano approssimativamente tutti i suoni della lingua inglese.

VOCALI

SIMBOLO	SUONO	ESEMPIO
[æ]	Più chiuso della a in caso.	hat [hæt]
[ɑ]	Come la a in basso.	father ['fɑðər] proper ['prɑpər]
[ɛ]	Come la e in sella.	met [mɛt]
[e]	Più chiuso della e in ché. Specialmente in posizione finale, si pronunzia come se fosse seguita da [ɪ].	fate [fet] they [ðe]
[ə]	Come la seconda e nella parola francese gouvernement.	heaven ['hevən] pardon ['pɑrdən]
[i]	Come la i in nido.	she [ʃi] machine [mə'ʃin]
[ɪ]	Come la i in ritto.	fit [fɪt] beer [bɪr]
[o]	Più chiuso della o in sole. Specialmente in posizione finale, si pronunzia come se fosse seguito da [ʊ].	nose [noz] road [rod] row [ro]
[ɔ]	Meno chiuso della o in torre.	bought [bɔt] law [lɔ]
[ʌ]	Piuttosto simile alla eu nella parola francese peur	cup [kʌp] come [kʌm] mother ['mʌðər]
[ʊ]	Meno chiuso della u in insulto.	pull [pʊl] book [bʊk] wolf [wʊlf]
[u]	Come la u in acuto.	rude [rud] move [muv] tomb [tum]

DITTONGHI

SIMBOLO	SUONO	ESEMPIO
[aɪ]	Come ai in laico.	night [naɪt] eye [aɪ]
[aʊ]	Come au in causa.	found [faʊnd] cow [kaʊ]
[ɔɪ]	Come oi in poi.	voice [vɔis] oil [ɔɪl]

3

SIMBOLO	SUONO	ESEMPIO
[b]	Come la b in **bambino**. Suono bilabiale occlusivo sonoro.	bed [bɛd] robber [ˈrabər]
[d]	Come la d in **caldo**. Suono dentale occlusivo sonoro.	dead [dɛd] add [æd]
[dʒ]	Come la g in **gente**. Suono palatale affricato sonoro.	gem [dʒɛm] jail [dʒel]
[ð]	Come la d nella pronuncia castigliana di **nada**. Suono interdentale fricativo sonoro.	this [ðɪs] father [ˈfaðər]
[f]	Come la f in **fare**. Suono labiodentale fricativo sordo.	face [fes] phone [fon]
[g]	Come la g in **gatto**. Suono velare occlusivo sonoro.	go [go] get [gɛt]
[h]	Come la c aspirata nella pronuncia toscana di **casa**.	hot [hɒt] alcohol [ˈælkə ˌhɒl]
[j]	Come la i in **ieri** o la y in **yo-yo**. Semiconsonante di suono palatale sonoro.	yes [jes] unit [ˈjunɪt]
[k]	Come la c in **casa** ma accompagnato da un'aspirazione. Suono velare occlusivo sordo.	cat [kæt] chord [kɔrd] kill [kɪl]
[l]	Come la l in **latino**. Suono alveolare fricativo laterale sonoro.	late [let] allow [əˈlaʊ]
[m]	Come la m in **madre**. Suono bilabiale nasale sonoro.	more [mor] command [kəˈmænd]
[n]	Come la n in **notte**. Suono alveolare nasale sonoro.	nest [nɛst] manner [ˈmænər]
[ŋ]	Come la n in **manca**. Suono velare nasale sonoro.	king [kɪŋ] conquer [ˈkaŋkər]
[p]	Come la p in **patto** ma accompagnato da un'aspirazione. Suono bilabiale occlusivo sordo.	pen [pɛn] cap [kæp]
[r]	La r più comune in molte parti dell'Inghilterra e nella maggior parte degli Stati Uniti e del Canadà è un suono semivocalico articolato con la punta della lingua elevata verso la volta del palato. Questa consonante è debolissima in posizione intervocalica o alla fine di una sillaba, e può appena percepirsi. L'articolazione di questa consonante ha la tendenza di influenzare il suono delle vocali contigue. La r, preceduta dai suoni [ʌ] o [ə], dà il proprio colorito a questi suoni e sparisce completamente come suono consonantico.	run [rʌn] far [far] art [ɑrt] carry [ˈkæri] burn [bʌrn] learn [lʌrn] weather [ˈwɛðər]
[s]	Come la s in **sette**. Suono alveolare fricativo sordo.	send [sɛnd] cellar [ˈsɛlər]
[ʃ]	Come sc in **lasciare**. Suono palatale fricativo sordo.	shall [ʃæl] machine [məˈʃin]
[t]	Come la t in **tavolo** ma accompagnato da un'aspirazione. Suono dentale occlusivo sordo.	ten [tɛn] dropped [drɒpt]
[tʃ]	Come c in **cibo**. Suono palatale affricato sordo.	child [tʃaɪld] much [mʌtʃ] nature [ˈnetʃər]
[θ]	Come la z castigliana in **zapato**. Suono interdentale fricativo sordo.	think [θɪŋk] truth [truθ]
[v]	Come la v in **vento**. Suono labiodentale fricativo sonoro.	vest [vɛst] over [ˈovər] of [ɑv]

4

SIMBOLO	SUONO	ESEMPIO
[w]	Come la **u** in **quadro**. Suono labiovelare fricativo sonoro.	**work** [wʌrk] **tweed** [twid] **queen** [kwin]
[z]	Come la **s** in **asilo**. Suono alveolare fricativo sonoro.	**zeal** [zil] **busy** ['bɪzi] **his** [hɪz]
[ʒ]	Come la seconda **g** nella parola francese **garage**. Suono palatale fricativo sonoro.	**azure** ['eʒər] **measure** ['meʒər]

ACCENTO

L'accento tonico principale, indicato col segno grafico ˈ, e l'accento secondario, indicato col segno grafico ˌ, precedono la sillaba sulla quale cadono, per es., **fascinate** ['fæsɪˌnet].

La pronunzia delle parole composte

Nella parte inglese-italiano di questo Dizionario la pronunzia figurata di tutte le parole inglesi semplici è indicata in parentesi quadre dopo l'esponente immediatamente, secondo un nuovo adattamento dell'alfabeto fonetico internazionale.

Vi sono tre generi di parole composte in inglese: (1) le parole in cui gli elementi componenti si sono uniti per formare una parola solida, come per es., **steamboat** vapore; (2) la parole in cui gli elementi componenti sono uniti da un trattino, come per es., **high'-grade'** di qualità superiore; (3) le parole in cui gli elementi componenti rimangono graficamente indipendenti gli uni da gli altri, per es., **post card** cartolina postale. La pronunzia delle parole inglesi composte non è indicata in questo Dizionario qualora gli elementi componenti appaiono come esponenti indipendenti nella loro normale posizione alfabetica e mostrano quindi la loro pronunzia figurata. Solo gli accenti principali e secondari di tali parole sono indicati, come per es., **steam'boat'**, **high'-grade'**, **post' card'**. Se i due membri di una parola composta inglese solida non sono separati da un accento grafico, si usa un punto leggermente elevato sopra il rigo per indicarne la divisione, come per es., **la'dy·like'**.

Nei nomi in cui l'accento secondario cade sul membro **-man** o **-men**, le vocali di tali membri si pronunziano come nelle parole semplici **man** e **men**, come per es., **mailman** ['melˌmæn] e **mailmen** ['melˌmen]. Nei nomi in cui tali membri componenti non sono accentati, le loro vocali si pronunziano come se fossero un'e muta francese, come per es., **policeman** [pəˈlismən] e **policemen** [pəˈlismən]. In questo Dizionario la trascrizione fonetica di tali nomi non è stata indicata qualora il primo membro componente appaia come esponente con la sua pronunzia in alfabeto fonetico internazionale. Gli accenti sono ciò nondimeno indicati:

> **mail'man'** s (-men')
> **police'man'** s (-men')

La pronunzia dei participi passati

La pronunzia di una parola la cui desinenza è **-ed** (o **-d** dopo una e muta) non è indicata nel presente Dizionario, purché la pronunzia della parola stessa senza tale suffisso appaia con il suo esponente nella sua posizione alfabetica. In tale caso la pronunzia segue le regole indicate qui sotto. Si osservi che il raddoppiamento della vocale finale dopo una semplice vocale tonica non muta la pronunzia del suffisso **-ed**, per es.: **batted** ['bætɪd], **dropped** [drɑpt], **robbed** [rɑbd].

La desinenza **-ed** (o **-d** dopo una e muta) del preterito, del participio passato e di certi aggettivi ha tre pronunzie differenti, che dipendendo dal suono in cui il tema termina:

1) Se il tema termina in suono consonantico sonoro (che non sia [d]), cioè [b], [g], [l], [m], [n], [ŋ], [r], [v], [z], [ð], [ʒ] o [dʒ] o in un suono vocalico, l'**-ed** è pronunziato [d]:

SUONO IN CUI TERMINA IL TEMA	INFINITO	PRETERITO E PARTICIPIO PASSATO
[b]	**ebb** [ɛb] **rob** [rɑb] **robe** [rob]	**ebbed** [ɛbd] **robbed** [rɑbd] **robed** [robd]

SUONO IN CUI TERMINA IL TEMA	INFINITO	PRETERITO E PARTICIPIO PASSATO
[g]	egg [eg] sag [sæg]	egged [egd] sagged [sægd]
[l]	mail [mel] scale [skel]	mailed [meld] scaled [skeld]
[m]	storm [stɔrm] bomb [bɑm] name [nem]	stormed [stɔrmd] bombed [bɑmd] named [nemd]
[n]	tan [tæn] sign [saɪn] mine [maɪn]	tanned [tænd] signed [saɪnd] mined [maɪnd]
[ŋ]	hang [hæŋ]	hanged [hæŋd]
[r]	fear [fɪr] care [kɛr]	feared [fɪrd] cared [kerd]
[v]	rev [rev] save [sev]	revved [revd] saved [sevd]
[z]	buzz [bʌz] fuze [fjuz]	buzzed [bʌzd] fuzed [fjuzd]
[ð]	smooth [smuð] bathe [beð]	smoothed [smuðd] bathed [beðd]
[ʒ]	massage [mə'sɑʒ]	massaged [mə'sɑʒd]
[dʒ]	page [pedʒ]	paged [pedʒd]
suono vocalico	key [ki] sigh [saɪ] paw [pɔ]	keyed [kid] sighed [saɪd] pawed [pɔd]

2) Se il tema termina in un suono consonantico sordo (che non sia [t]), cioè [f], [k], [p], [s], [θ], [ʃ] o [tʃ], l'-ed si pronunzia [t]:

SUONO IN CUI TERMINA IL TEMA	INFINITO	PRETERITO E PARTICIPIO PASSATO
[f]	loaf [lof] knife [naɪf]	loafed [loft] knifed [naɪft]
[k]	back [bæk] bake [bek]	backed [bækt] baked [bekt]
[p]	cap [kæp] wipe [waɪp]	capped [kæpt] wiped [waɪpt]
[s]	hiss [hɪs] mix [mɪks]	hissed [hɪst] mixed [mɪkst]
[θ]	lath [læθ]	lathed [læθt]
[ʃ]	mash [mæʃ]	mashed [mæʃt]
[tʃ]	match [mætʃ]	matched [mætʃt]

3) Se il tema termina in un suono dentale, cioè [t] o [d], l'-ed si pronunzia [ɪd] o [əd]:

SUONO IN CUI TERMINA IL TEMA	INFINITO	PRETERITO E PARTICIPIO PASSATO
[t]	wait [wet] mate [met]	waited ['wetɪd] mated ['metɪd]
[d]	mend [mend] wade [wed]	mended ['mendɪd] waded ['wedɪd]

L'-ed di alcuni aggettivi aggiunto ad un tema che termina in suono consonantico (oltre a quelli che terminano in [d] o [t]), è ciò nonostante talvolta pronunziato [ɪd] e tale fenomeno è idicato con la piena pronunzia della parola in simboli dell'alfabeto fonetico internazionale, per es., blessed ['blɛsɪd], crabbed ['kræbɪd].

6

A, a [e] *s* prima lettera dell'alfabeto inglese

a [e] *art indef* un, uno, una, un'

aback [ə'bæk] *adv* all'indietro; **taken aback** colto alla sprovvista, sconcertato

aba·cus [ˈæbəkəs] *s* (**-cuses** or **-ci** [ˌsaɪ]) pallottoliere *m*; (archit) abaco

abaft [ə'bæft] or [ə'bɑft] *adv* a poppa ‖ *prep* dietro a

abandon [ə'bændən] *s* disinvoltura ‖ *tr* abbandonare

abase [ə'bes] *tr* umiliare, degradare

abash [ə'bæʃ] *tr* imbarazzare; sconcertare

abate [ə'bet] *tr* ridurre; omettere; (law) terminare ‖ *intr* diminuire, calmarsi

aba·tis [ˈæbətɪs] or [ə'bætɪs] *s* (**-tis** or **-tises**) (mil) tagliata

abattoir [ˈæbəˌtwɑr] *s* macello

abba·cy [ˈæbəsi] *s* (**-cies**) abbazia

abbess [ˈæbɪs] *s* badessa

abbey [ˈæbi] *s* badia, abbazia

abbot [ˈæbət] *s* abate *m*

abbreviate [ə'briviˌet] *tr* abbreviare, raccorciare

abbreviation [əˌbriviˈeʃən] *s* (*abbreviated form*) abbreviazione; (*shortening*) abbreviamento

A B C [ˌeˌbiˈsi] *s* (letterword) abbiccì *m*; **A B C's** abbecedario

abdicate [ˈæbdɪˌket] *tr* abdicare a ‖ *intr* abdicare

abdomen [ˈæbdəmən] or [æb'domən] *s* addome *m*

abduct [æb'dʌkt] *tr* rapire

abed [ə'bed] *adv* a letto

abet [ə'bet] *v* (*pret & pp* **abetted;** *ger* **abetting**) *tr* favoreggiare

abeyance [ə'be·əns] *s* sospensione; **in abeyance in** sospeso

ab·hor [æbˈhɔr] *v* (*pret & pp* **-horred;** *ger* **-horring**) *tr* aborrire

abhorrent [æbˈhɑrənt] or [æbˈhɔrənt] *adj* detestabile

abide [ə'baɪd] *v* (*pret & pp* **abode** or **abided**) *tr* aspettare; tollerare ‖ *intr* —**to abide by** attenersi a; rimanere fedele a

abili·ty [ə'bɪlɪti] *s* (**-ties**) abilità *f*, bravura

abject [ˈæbdʒɛkt] or [æb'dʒɛkt] *adj* abietto, turpe

abjure [æbˈdʒʊr] *tr* abiurare

ablative [ˈæblətɪv] *adj & s* ablativo

ablaut [ˈæblaʊt] *s* apofonia

ablaze [ə'blez] *adj* in fiamme; risplendente

able [ˈebəl] *adj* abile, esperto; **to be able to** + *inf* potere + *inf*

able-bodied [ˈebəlˈbɑdid] *adj* sano; forte

abloom [ə'blum] *adj & adv* in fiore

abnormal [æbˈnɔrməl] *adj* anormale

aboard [ə'bord] *adv* a bordo; **all aboard!** (rr) signori, in vettura!; **to go aboard** imbarcarsi; **to take aboard** imbarcare ‖ *prep* a bordo di; (*a bus, train, etc.*) in, su

abode [ə'bod] *s* abitazione, dimora

abolish [ə'balɪʃ] *tr* abolire

A-bomb [ˈeˌbam] *s* bomba atomica

abominable [ə'bamənəbəl] *adj* abominevole

abomination [əˌbamɪˈneʃən] *s* abominazione

aborigenes [ˌæbəˈrɪdʒɪˌniz] *spl* aborigeni *mpl*

abort [ə'bɔrt] *tr* terminare prematuramente; provocare un aborto in ‖ *intr* abortire

abortion [ə'bɔrʃən] *s* aborto

abound [ə'baʊnd] *intr* abbondare; **to abound in** or **with** abbondare di

about [ə'baʊt] *adv* circa, press'a poco; qua intorno; qua e' là; in direzione opposta; (coll) quasi; **to be about to** star sul punto di ‖ *prep* intorno a; circa a; addosso a; tutt'intorno a; riguardo a

about'-face' *interj* (mil) dietro front!

about'-face' or **about'-face'** *s* voltafaccia; (mil) dietro front *m* ‖ **about'-face'** *intr* fare dietro front

above [ə'bʌv] *adj* soprammenzionato; superiore ‖ *s*—**from above** dal cielo; dall'alto ‖ *adv* in alto; su; più sopra ‖ *prep* sopra, sopra a; più di; al di là di, oltre; **above all** soprattutto

above-mentioned [ə'bʌvˈmenʃənd] *adj* summenzionato, sunnominato

abrasive [ə'bresɪv] or [ə'brezɪv] *adj & s* abrasivo

abreast [ə'brest] *adj & adv* in fila, in linea; **to keep abreast of** tenersi alla pari con; essere al corrente di

abridge [ə'brɪdʒ] *tr* compendiare; ridurre

abroad [ə'brɔd] *adv* all'estero; all'aria aperta; **to be abroad** (*said of news*) circolare

abrupt [ə'brʌpt] *adj* brusco, improvviso; (*very steep*) scosceso

abscess [ˈæbses] *s* accesso

abscond [æb'skand] *intr* scappare; **to abscond with** svignarsela con

absence [ˈæbsəns] *s* assenza; **in the absence of** in mancanza di

absent [ˈæbsənt] *adj* assente ‖ [æbˌsent] *tr*—**to absent oneself** assentarsi

absentee [ˌæbsənˈti] *s* assente *mf*

absent-minded [ˈæbsəntˈmaɪndɪd] *adj* distratto, assente

absinth [ˈæbsɪnθ] *s* assenzio

absolute [ˈæbsəˌlut] *adj & s* assoluto

absolutely [ˈæbsəˌlutli] *adv* assolutamente, certamente ‖ [ˌæbsəˈlutli] *interj* certamente!

absolve [æb'salv] *tr* assolvere

absorb [æb'sɔrb] *tr* assorbire; **to be** or **become absorbed** essere assorto

absorbent [æb'sɔrbənt] *adj* assorbente; (*cotton*) idrofilo ‖ *s* sostanza assorbente

absorbing [æb'sɔrbɪŋ] *adj* interessantissimo

abstain [æb'sten] *intr* astenersi

abstemious [æb'stimi·əs] *adj* astemio

abstention [æb'stenʃən] *s* astensione; astenuto (*vote withheld*)

abstinent ['æbstinənt] *adj* astinente

abstract ['æbstrækt] *adj* astratto || *s* compendio, sommario || *tr* compendiare || (æb'strækt) *tr* astrarre; (*to steal*) sottrarre

abstruse [æb'strus] *adj* astruso

absurd [æb'sʌrd] or [æb'zʌrd] *adj* assurdo

absurdi·ty [æb'sʌrditi] or [æb'zʌrditi] *s* (**-ties**) assurdità *f*

abundant [ə'bʌndənt] *adj* abbondante

abuse [ə'bjus] *s* (*misuse*) abuso; maltrattamento; insulto || [ə'bjuz] *tr* (*to misuse, take unfair advantage of*) abusare di; maltrattare; insultare

abusive [ə'bjusiv] *adj* abusivo; insultante

abut [ə'bʌt] *v* (*pret & pp* **abutted;** *ger* **abutting**) *intr*—**to abut on** confinare con

abutment [ə'bʌtmənt] *s* rinfianco; (*at either end of bridge*) spalla; (*of buttresses of bridge*) sprone *m*

abysmal [ə'bizməl] *adj* abissale; (*e.g., ignorance*) sproposito

abyss [ə'bis] *s* abisso

academic [,ækə'demik] *adj* accademico

ac'ademic cos'tume *s* toga accademica

academician [ə,kædə'mi/ən] *s* accademico

ac'adem'ic year' *s* anno scolastico

acade·my [ə'kædəmi] *s* (**-mies**) accademia

accede [æk'sid] *intr* accedere; **to accede to** salire a; accedere a

accelerate [æk'sɛlə,ret] *tr & intr* accelerare

accelerator [æk'sɛlə,retər] *s* acceleratore *m*

accent ['æksent] *s* accento || ['æksent] or [æk'sent] *tr* accentare; (*to accentuate*) accentuare

ac'cent mark' *s* segnaccento, accento grafico

accentuate [æk'sent/u,et] *tr* accentuare

accept [æk'sept] *tr* accettare

acceptable [æk'septəbəl] *adj* accettabile

acceptance [æk'septəns] *s* accettazione

access ['æksɛs] *s* accesso

accessible [æk'sɛsibəl] *adj* accessibile; (*person*) abbordabile

accession [æk'sɛ/ən] *s* accessione, acquisto; (*e.g., to the throne*) adito

accesso·ry [æk'sɛsəri] *adj* accessorio || *s* (**-ries**) accessorio; (*to a crime*) complice *m*

accident ['æksidənt] *s* accidente *m*; **by accident** accidentalmente, per caso

accidental [,æksi'dentəl] *adj* accidentale || *s* (mus) accidente *m*

acclaim [ə'klem] *s* acclamazione, applauso || *tr & intr* acclamare, applaudire

acclimate ['ækli,met] *tr* acclimatare || *intr* acclimatarsi

accolade [,ækə'led] *s* accollata; (fig) elogio

accommodate [ə'kamə,det] *tr* (*to adjust, make fit*) accomodare; (*to pro-*

vide with a loan) venire incontro a; (*to supply with lodging*) alloggiare; (*to oblige*) favorire; (*to have room for*) aver posto per

accommodating [ə'kamə,detiŋ] *adj* servizievole, compiacente

accommodation [ə,kamə'de/ən] *s* (*favor*) favore *m*; (*loan*) prestito; (*adaptation*) adattamento; (*reconciliation*) conciliazione; (*compromise*) accomodamento; **accommodations** (*traveling space*) posto; (*in a hotel*) alloggio

accommoda'tion train' *s* treno accelerato

accompaniment [ə'kʌmpənimənt] *s* accompagnamento

accompanist [ə'kʌmpənist] *s* accompagnatore *m*

accompa·ny [ə'kʌmpəni] *v* (*pret & pp* **-nied**) *tr* accompagnare

accomplice [ə'kamplis] *s* complice *mf*

accomplish [ə'kampli/] *tr* compiere

accomplished [ə'kampli/t] *adj* (*completed*) compiuto, terminato; (*skilled*) finito, compiuto

accomplishment [ə'kampli/mənt] *s* (*completion*) esecuzione, realizzazione; (*something accomplished*) opera; (*acquired ability*) talento; (*military achievement*) prodezza; (*social skill*) compitezza

accord [ə'kord] *s* accordo; **in accord with** in conformità con; **of one's own accord** spontaneamente; **with one accord** di comune accordo || *tr* concedere || *intr* accordarsi

accordance [ə'kordəns] *s* accordo; **in accordance with** in conformità con

according [ə'kordiŋ] *adv*—**according as** a seconda che; **according to** secondo, a seconda di

accordingly [ə'kordiŋli] *adv* per conseguenza, perciò; in conformità

accordion [ə'kordiən] *s* fisarmonica

accost [ə'kost] or [ə'kast] *tr* accostare, abbordare

accouchement [ə'ku/mənt] *s* parto

account [ə'kaunt] *s* (*explanation*) versione; (*report*) resoconto; conto; (*statement*) estratto conto; **by all accounts** secondo la voce comune; **of account** d'importanza; **of no account** senza importanza; **on account** in acconto; **on account of** a causa di; **for l'amor di; on all accounts** in ogni modo; **on no account** in nessuna maniera; **to call to account** chiedere conto di; **to give a good account of oneself** comportarsi bene; **to take account of** prendere in considerazione; **to turn to account** trarre profitto da || *intr*—**to account for** render conto di; essere responsabile per

accountable [ə'kauntəbəl] *adj* responsabile; (*explainable*) spiegabile

accountant [ə'kauntənt] *s* contabile *mf*, ragioniere *m*

accounting [ə'kauntiŋ] *s* contabilità *f*, ragioneria

accouterments [ə'kutərmənts] *spl* (mil)

buffetterie *fpl;* (*trappings*) ornamenti *mpl*

accredit [ə'krɛdɪt] *tr* accreditare; **to accredit s.o. with s.th** ascrivere qlco a credito di qlcu

accrue [ə'kru] *intr* accumularsi; (*said of interest*) maturare

acculturation [ə,kʌlt/ə'reʃən] *s* acculturazione

accumulate [ə'kjumjə,let] *tr* accumulare || *intr* accumularsi

accuracy ['ækjərəsi] *s* esattezza, precisione; fedeltà *f*

accurate ['ækjərɪt] *adj* esatto, preciso; fedele

accursed [ə'kʌrsɪd] or [ə'kʌrst] *adj* maledetto

accusation [,ækjə'zeʃən] *s* accusa

accusative [ə'kjuzətɪv] *adj & s* accusativo

accuse [ə'kjuz] *tr* accusare

accustom [ə'kʌstəm] *tr* abituare

ace [es] *s* asso; **to be within an ace of** essere quasi sul punto di

ace' in the hole' *s* asso nella manica

acetate ['æsɪ,tet] *s* acetato

ace'tic ac'id [ə'sitɪk] *s* acido acetico

aceti·fy [ə'sɛtɪ,faɪ] *v* (*pret & pp* -fied) *tr* acetificare || *intr* acetificarsi

acetone ['æsɪ,ton] *s* acetone *m*

acetylene [ə'sɛtɪ,lin] *s* acetilene *m*

acet'ylene torch' *s* cannello ossiacetilenico

ache [ek] *s* dolore *m* || *intr* dolere, e.g., **my tooth aches** mi duole il dente

Acheron ['ækə,rɑn] *s* Acheronte *m*

achieve [ə't/iv] *tr* compiere, conseguire

achievement [ə't/ivmənt] *s* compimento; successo; (*exploit*) impresa, prodezza

Achil'les heel' [ə'kɪliz] *s* tallone *m* d'Achille

acid ['æsɪd] *adj & s* acido

acidi·fy [ə'sɪdɪ,faɪ] *v* (*pret & pp* -fied) *tr & intr* acidificare

acidity [ə'sɪdɪti] *s* acidità *f*

acid' test' *s* prova del fuoco

ack-ack ['æk'æk] *s* (slang) cannone antiaereo

acknowledge [æk'nɑlɪdʒ] *tr* riconoscere; (*receipt of a letter*) accusare; (*a claim*) ammettere; mostrare la gratitudine per; (law) certificare

acknowledgment [æk'nɑlɪdʒmənt] *s* riconoscimento; (*of receipt of a letter*) accusa, cenno

acme ['ækmi] *s* acme *f*

acolyte ['ækə,laɪt] *s* accolito

acorn ['ekɔrn] or ['ekərn] *s* ghianda

acoustic [ə'kustɪk] *adj* acustico || **acoustics** *s* acustica

acquaint [ə'kwent] *tr* mettere al corrente; **to be acquainted with** conoscere; essere al corrente di; **to become acquainted** (*with each other*) conoscersi

acquaintance [ə'kwentəns] *s* conoscenza; (*person*) conoscente *mf*, conoscenza

acquiesce [,ækwɪ'ɛs] *intr* acconsentire, accondiscendere

acquiescence [,ækwɪ'ɛsəns] *s* accondiscendenza

acquire [ə'kwaɪr] *tr* acquistare

acquisition [,ækwɪ'zɪʃən] *s* acquisto

acquit [ə'kwɪt] *v* (*pret & pp* acquitted; *ger* acquitting) *tr* (*to pay*) ripagare; (*to declare not guilty*) assolvere; **to acquit oneself** condursi

acquittal [ə'kwɪtəl] *s* assoluzione

acre ['ekər] *s* acro

acrid ['ækrɪd] *adj* acrido, pungente

acrobat ['ækrə,bæt] *s* acrobata *mf*

acrobatic [,ækrə'bætɪk] *adj* acrobatico || **acrobatics** *ssg* (e.g., *of a stunt pilot*) acrobazie *fpl;* **acrobatics** *spl* (*gymnastics*) acrobatica

acronym ['ækrənɪm] *s* acronimo, parola macedonia

acropolis [ə'krɑpəlɪs] *s* acropoli *f*

across [ə'krɔs] or [ə'krɑs] *adv* dall'altra parte; **to get an idea across to** farsi capire da || *prep* attraverso; (*on the other side of*) al di là di, dall'altra parte di; **to come across** (*a person*) imbattersi in; **to go across** attraversare

across'-the-board' *adj* generale

act [ækt] *s* atto; legge *f*; rappresentazione; **in the act** in flagrante || *tr* (*a drama*) rappresentare; (*a role*) recitare || *intr* (*on the stage*) recitare; (*to behave*) comportarsi; (*to perform special duties; to reach a decision*) agire; (*to have an effect*) reagire; **to act as** fungere da; **to act for** rimpiazzare; **to act on** eseguire; **to act up** (coll) fare il matto; non funzionare bene (*said, e.g., of a motor*); **to act up to** (coll) fare festa a

acting ['æktɪŋ] *adj* facente funzione, interino || *s* recita

action ['ækʃən] *s* azione; (*moving parts*) meccanismo; **to take action** iniziare azione; (law) intentare causa

activate ['æktɪ,vet] *tr* attivare

active ['æktɪv] *adj & s* attivo

activi·ty [æk'tɪvɪti] *s* (-ties) attività *f*

act' of God' *s* forza maggiore

actor ['æktər] *s* attore *m*

actress ['æktrɪs] *s* attrice *f*

actual ['ækt/u·əl] *adj* reale

actually ['ækt/u·əli] *adv* realmente, in realtà

actuar·y ['ækt/u,ɛri] *s* (-ies) attuario

actuate ['ækt/u,et] *tr* attuare, mettere in azione; (*to motivate*) stimolare

acuity [ə'kju·ɪti] *s* acuità *f*

acumen [ə'kjumən] *s* acume *m*

acupuncture ['ækju,pʌŋkt/ər] *s* agopuntura

acute [ə'kjut] *adj* acuto

ad [æd] *s* (coll) inserzione pubblicitaria

Adam ['ædəm] *s* Adamo; **not to know from Adam** non conoscere affatto

adamant ['ædəmənt] *adj* saldo, inflessibile

Ad'am's ap'ple *s* pomo d'Adamo

adapt [ə'dæpt] *tr* adattare

adaptation [,ædæp'teʃən] *s* adattamento; (e.g., *of a play*) rifacimento

add [æd] *tr* aggiungere; (*numbers*)

sommare ‖ *intr* aggiungere; far di conto; **to add up to** ammontare a; (coll) voler dire

adder ['ædər] *s* vipera

addict ['ædɪkt] *s* (*to drugs*) tossicomane *mf*; (*to a sport*) tifoso ‖ [ə'dɪkt] *tr* abituare; rendere propenso alla tossicomania; **to addict oneself to** darsi a, abbandonarsi a

addiction [ə'dɪkʃən] *s* dedizione; (*to drugs*) tossicomania; (*to sports*) tifo

add'ing machine' *s* calcolatrice *f*

addition [ə'dɪʃən] *s* addizione; (*building*) annessi *mpl*; **in addition** inoltre, per di più; **in addition to** oltre a

additive ['ædɪtɪv] *adj & s* additivo

address [ə'dres] or ['ædres] *s* (*speech*) discorso; (*place and destination of mail*) indirizzo; (*skill*) destrezza; (*formal request*) petizione; **to deliver an address** pronunciare un discorso ‖ [ə'dres] *tr* indirizzare; (*to speak to*) rivolgere la parola a

addressee [,ædre'si] *s* destinatario

address'ing machine' *s* macchina per indirizzi

adduce [ə'djus] or [ə'dus] *tr* addurre

adenoids ['ædə,nɔɪds] *spl* vegetazioni *fpl* adenoidi, adenoidi *fpl*

adept [ə'dept] *adj & s* esperto

adequate ['ædɪkwɪt] *adj* sufficiente; (*suitable*) conveniente

adhere [æd'hɪr] *intr* aderire

adherence [æd'hɪrəns] *s* aderenza

adherent [æd'hɪrənt] *adj & s* aderente *m*

adhesion [æd'hiʒən] *s* adesione; (pathol) aderenza

adhesive [æd'hisɪv] or [æd'hizɪv] *adj & s* adesivo

adhe'sive tape' *s* tela adesiva, cerotto

adieu [ə'dju] or [ə'du] *s* (**adieus** or **adieux**) addio ‖ *interj* addio!

adjacent [ə'dʒesənt] *adj* adiacente

adjective ['ædʒɪktɪv] *adj* aggettivale; accessorio, secondario ‖ *s* aggettivo

adjoin [ə'dʒɔɪn] *tr* confinare con ‖ *intr* essere confinanti

adjoining [ə'dʒɔɪnɪŋ] *adj* confinante; vicino, attiguo

adjourn [ə'dʒʌrn] *tr* aggiornare, rinviare ‖ *intr* rinviarsi

adjournment [ə'dʒʌrnmənt] *s* aggiornamento, rinvio

adjust [ə'dʒʌst] *tr* accomodare; regolare; (ins) liquidare ‖ *intr* accomodarsi

adjustable [ə'dʒʌstəbəl] *adj* regolabile

adjustment [ə'dʒʌstmənt] *s* aggiustamento; accomodamento; (ins) liquidazione del danno

adjutant ['ædʒətənt] *s* aiutante *mf*

ad-lib ['æd'lɪb] *v* (*pret & pp* **-libbed**; *ger* **-libbing**) *tr & intr* improvvisare

administer [æd'mɪnɪstər] *tr* amministrare; (*medicine*) somministrare; (*an oath*) dare ‖ *intr*—**to administer to** ministrare, prestare aiuto a

administrator [æd'mɪnɪs,tretər] *s* amministratore *m*

admirable ['ædmɪrəbəl] *adj* ammirabile, ammirevole

admiral ['ædmɪrəl] *s* ammiraglio

admiral·ty ['ædmɪrəlti] *s* (**-ties**) ammiragliato

admire [æd'maɪr] *tr* ammirare

admirer [æd'maɪrər] *s* ammiratore *m*

admissible [æd'mɪsɪbəl] *adj* ammissibile

admission [æd'mɪʃən] *s* ammissione; confessione; (*entrance fee*) prezzo d'ingresso; **to gain admission** arrivare a entrare

ad·mit [æd'mɪt] *v* (*pret & pp* **-mitted**; *ger* **-mitting**) *tr* ammettere; confessare ‖ *intr* dare l'ingresso; **to admit of** permettere, ammettere; consentire

admittance [æd'mɪtəns] *s* ammissione; permesso di entrare; **no admittance** divieto d'ingresso

admonish [æd'mɑnɪʃ] *tr* ammonire

ado [ə'du] *s* confusione, trambusto; **much ado about nothing** molto rumore per nulla; **to make a big ado** fare cerimonie

adobe [ə'dobi] *s* mattone crudo

adolescence [,ædə'lesəns] *s* adolescenza

adolescent [,ædə'lesənt] *adj & s* adolescente *mf*

adopt [ə'dɑpt] *tr* adottare

adoption [ə'dɑpʃən] *s* adozione

adorable [ə'dorəbəl] *adj* adorabile

adore [ə'dor] *tr* adorare

adorn [ə'dɔrn] *tr* adornare

adornment [ə'dɔrnmənt] *s* ornamento

adre'nal gland' [æd'rinəl] *s* glandola surrenale

Adriatic [,edri'ætɪk] or [,ædri'ætɪk] *adj* adriatico ‖ *adj & s* Adriatico

adrift [ə'drɪft] *adj & adv* alla deriva

adroit [ə'drɔɪt] *adj* destro

adult [ə'dʌlt] or ['ædʌlt] *adj & s* adulto

adulterate [ə'dʌltə,ret] *tr* adulterare

adulterer [ə'dʌltərər] *s* adultero

adulteress [ə'dʌltərɪs] *s* adultera

adulter·y [ə'dʌltəri] *s* (**-ies**) adulterio

advance [æd'væns] or [æd'vɑns] *adj* avanzato ‖ *s* avanzata; (*increase in price*) aumento; (*of money*) anticipo; **advances** approcci *mpl*; **in advance** in anticipo ‖ *tr* avanzare; aumentare; (*to make earlier*) anticipare; (*money*) anticipare; (*a clock*) mettere avanti ‖ *intr* avanzare; (said, e.g., of prices) aumentare

advanced [æd'vænst] or [æd'vɑnst] *adj* avanzato, progredito

advanced' stand'ing *s* trasferimento di voti scolastici

advancement [æd'vænsmənt] or [æd'vɑnsmənt] *s* progresso; promozione; (mil) avanzata

advance' public'ity *s* pubblicità *f* di lancio

advantage [æd'væntɪdʒ] or [æd'vɑntɪdʒ] *s* vantaggio; **to advantage in** maniera favorevole; **to take advantage of** approfittarsi di; abusare di ‖ *tr* avvantaggiare

advantageous [,ædvən'tedʒəs] *adj* vantaggioso

advent ['ædvent] *s* avvento

adventure [æd'ventʃər] s avventura || tr avventurare || intr avventurarsi

adventurer [æd'ventʃərər] s avventuriero

adventuresome [æd'ventʃərsəm] adj avventuroso

adventuress [æd'ventʃərɪs] s avventuriera

adventurous [æd'ventʃərəs] adj avventuroso

adverb ['ædvʌrb] s avverbio

adversar·y ['ædvər,seri] s (-ies) avversario

adverse [æd'vʌrs] or ['ædvʌrs] adj avverso, contrario

adversi·ty [æd'vʌrsɪti] s (-ties) avversità f

advertise ['ædvər,taɪz] or [,ædvər'taɪz] tr propagandare; reclamizzare || intr fare la pubblicità; inserire un annunzio; inserzionare

advertisement [,ædvər'taɪzmənt] or [æd'vʌrtɪsmənt] s annuncio pubblicitario, inserzione

advertiser ['ædvər,taɪzər] or [,ædvər'taɪzər] s inserzionista mf

advertising ['ædvər,taɪzɪŋ] s pubblicità f, pubblicismo

ad'vertising a'gent s pubblicista mf

ad'vertising campaign' s campagna pubblicitaria

ad'vertising man' s agente m di pubblicità, reclamista m

advice [æd'vaɪs] s consiglio; **a piece of advice** un consiglio

advisable [æd'vaɪzəbəl] adj consigliabile

advise [æd'vaɪz] tr consigliare; informare || intr—**to advise with** chiedere il consiglio di; avere una conferenza con

advisement [æd'vaɪzmənt] s considerazione; **to take under advisement** prendere in considerazione

adviser [æd'vaɪzər] s consigliere m

advisory [æd'vaɪzəri] adj consultivo

advocate ['ædvə,ket] s difensore m; (lawyer) avvocato || tr sostenere, propugnare

adze [ædz] s ascia

Aege'an Sea' [ɪ'dʒi·ən] s mare Egeo

aegis ['idʒɪs] s egida

Aeneid [i'ni·ɪd] s Eneide f

aerate ['eret] or ['e·ə,ret] tr aerare

aerial ['erɪ·əl] or [e'ɪrɪ·əl] adj aereo || ['erɪ·əl] s (rad & telv) antenna

aer'ial pho'tograph s aerofotogramma m

aerodrome ['erə,drom] s aerodromo

aerodynamic [,erodaɪ'næmɪk] adj aerodinamico || **aerodynamics** ssg aerodinamica

aeronaut ['erə,nɔt] s aeronauta m

aeronautic [,erə'nɔtɪk] adj aeronautico || **aeronautics** ssg aeronautica

aerosol ['erə,sɔl] s aerosol m

aerospace ['ero,spes] adj aerospaziale || s aerospazio

Aesop ['isəp] s Esopo

aesthete ['esθit] s esteta mf

aesthetic [es'θetɪk] adj estetico || **aesthetics** ssg estetica

afar [ə'fɑr] adv lontano; **from afar** da lontano

affable ['æfəbəl] adj affabile

affair [ə'fer] s affare m; (romance) relazione amorosa

affect [ə'fekt] tr influenzare; (to touch the heart of) commuovere; (to pretend to have) affettare

affectation [,æfek'teʃən] s affettazione

affected [ə'fektɪd] adj affettato

affection [ə'fekʃən] s affezione

affectionate [ə'fekʃənɪt] adj affettuoso, affezionato

affidavit [,æfɪ'devɪt] s affidavit m, dichiarazione sotto giuramento

affiliate [ə'fɪlɪ,et] adj & s affiliato || tr affiliare || intr affiliarsi

affini·ty [ə'fɪnɪti] s (-ties) affinità f

affirm [ə'fʌrm] tr affermare; confermare

affirmative [ə'fʌrmətɪv] adj affermativo || s affermativa

affix ['æfɪks] s affisso || [ə'fɪks] tr affiggere; (a signature) apporre; (e.g., blame) attribuire

afflict [ə'flɪkt] tr affliggere

affliction [ə'flɪkʃən] s afflizione

affluence ['æflu·əns] s opulenza, abbondanza

affluent ['æflu·ənt] adj opulento, abbondante; ricco || s affluente m

afford [ə'ford] tr permettersi il lusso di; (to furnish) provvedere; (to give) dare

affray [ə'fre] s rissa

affront [ə'frʌnt] s affronto || tr fare un affronto a

afghan ['æfgən] or ['æfgæn] s coperta di lana all'uncinetto || **Afghan** adj & s afgano

afield [ə'fild] adv sul campo; **far afield** lontano

afire [ə'faɪr] adj ardente; in fuoco, in fiamme

aflame [ə'flem] adj in fiamme

afloat [ə'flot] adj & adv a galla; a bordo; (drifting) alla deriva; (said of a rumor) in circolazione

afoot [ə'fut] adj & adv a piedi; in movimento, in moto

aforementioned [ə'for,menʃənd] or **aforesaid** [ə'for,sed] adj suddetto

afoul [ə'faul] adj & adv in collisione; **to run afoul of** finire nelle mani di, impigliarsi con

afraid [ə'fred] adj impaurito, spaventato; **to be afraid (of)** aver paura (di)

African ['æfrɪkən] adj & s africano

aft [æft] or [ɑft] adv a poppa; indietro

after ['æftər] or ['ɑftər] adj seguente; di poppa || adv dopo; (behind) dietro || prep dopo; dopo di; (in the manner of) secondo; **to run after** correre dietro a || conj dopo che

afterburner ['æftər,bʌrnər] or ['ɑftər-,bʌrnər] s (aer) postbruciatore m

af'ter-din'ner adj dopo la cena

aftereffect ['æftərɪ,fekt] or ['ɑftərɪ-,fekt] s conseguenza

af'ter-hours' adj dopo le ore di ufficio

af'ter-life' s aldilà m; vita susseguente

aftermath ['æftər‚mæθ] or ['ɑftər‚mæθ] s consequenze *fpl;* gravi conseguenze *fpl*

af'ter·noon' *adj* pomeridiano ‖ *s* pomeriggio

after-shaving ['æftər ‚ʃevɪŋ] or ['ɑftər‚ʃevɪŋ] *adj* dopobarba

af'ter-taste' *s* retrosapore *m*

af'ter·thought' *s* pensiero tardivo

afterward ['æftərwərd] or ['ɑftərwərd] *adv* dopo; **long afterward** molto tempo dopo

af'ter·while' *adv* fra un po'

again [ə'gen] *adv* di nuovo; ancora; un'altra volta; **again and again** ripetutamente; **as much again** due volte tanto, altrettanto; **to + inf + again** tornare a + *inf*, e.g., **to cook again** tornare a cuocere

against [ə'genst] *prep* contro; *(opposite)* in faccia a; **to be against** opporsi a; **to go against the grain** ripugnare

agape [ə'gep] *adj & adv* a bocca aperta

age [edʒ] *s* età *f; (old age)* vecchiaia; *(full term of life)* vita; *(historical or geological period)* evo; generazione; **of age** maggiorenne; **to come of age** diventare maggiorenne; **under age** minorenne ‖ *tr & intr* invecchiare

aged [edʒd] *adj* dell'età di ‖ ['edʒɪd] *adj* vecchio, invecchiato

ageless ['edʒlɪs] *adj* eternamente giovane, che non invecchia mai

agen·cy ['edʒənsɪ] *s* (-cies) azione; agenzia; mediazione; *(of government)* ente *m*

agenda [ə'dʒendə] *s* agenda, ordine *m* del giorno

agent ['edʒənt] *s* agente *m; (coll)* commesso viaggiatore, agente *m* di commercio; (rr) gestore *m*

Age' of Enlight'enment *s* illuminismo

agglomeration [ə‚glɑmə'reʃən] *s* agglomerazione

aggrandizement [ə'grændɪzmənt] *s* aumento, innalzamento

aggravate ['ægrə‚vet] *tr* aggravare; *(coll)* irritare, esasperare

aggregate ['ægrɪ‚get] *adj & s* aggregato, totale *m;* **in the aggregate** nel complesso ‖ *tr* aggregare; ammontare a

aggression [ə'greʃən] *s* aggressione

aggressive [ə'gresɪv] *adj* aggressivo, attivo

aggressor [ə'gresər] *s* aggressore *m*

aggrieve [ə'griv] *tr* affliggere

aghast [ə'gæst] or [ə'gɑst] *adj* atterrito

agile ['ædʒɪl] *adj* agile

agitate ['ædʒɪ‚tet] *tr* agitare ‖ *intr* agitarsi

agitator ['ædʒɪ‚tetər] *s* agitatore *m*

aglow [ə'glo] *adj* splendente

agnostic [æg'nɑstɪk] *adj & s* agnostico

ago [ə'go] *adv* fa, or, **a year ago** un anno fa; **long ago** molto tempo fa

agog [ə'gɑg] *adj & adv* ansioso; **to set agog** riempire di ansietà

agonize ['ægə‚naɪz] *intr* soffrire straziantemente; *(to struggle)* dibattersi

ago·ny ['ægənɪ] *s* (-nies) agonia

agrarian [ə'grerɪ·ən] *adj* agrario ‖ *s* membro del partito agrario

agree [ə'gri] *intr* aderire, andar d'accordo; *(to consent)* acconsentire; (gram) concordare; **to agree with** confarsi a, e.g., **eggs do not agree with him** le uova non gli si confanno

agreeable [ə'gri·əbəl] *adj* gentile; gradevole; *(willing to agree)* consenziente

agreement [ə'grimənt] *s* accordo; **in agreement** d'accordo

agriculture ['ægrɪ‚kʌltʃər] *s* agricoltura

agriculturist [‚ægrɪ'kʌltʃərɪst] *s (farmer)* agricoltore *m;* perito in agricoltura, agronomo

agronomy [ə'grɑnəmɪ] *s* agronomia

aground [ə'graund] *adv* alla riva; **to run aground** andare or dare in secca

ague ['egju] *s (chill)* brivido; febbre *f*

ahead [ə'hed] *adv* davanti, avanti; **to get ahead** (coll) andare avanti, aver successo; **to get ahead of** sorpassare; **to go ahead** avanzare; continuare

ahoy [ə'hɔɪ] *interj*—**ship ahoy!** ehi della barca!

aid [ed] *s* aiuto; assistente *m;* (mil) aiutante *m* di campo ‖ *tr* aiutare; **to aid and abet** essere complice di

aide [ed] *s* assistente *m*

aide-de-camp ['eddə'kæmp] *s* (**aides-de-camp**) aiutante *m* di campo

ail [el] *tr* affliggere; **what ails you?** che ha? ‖ *intr* soffrire, essere malato

aileron ['elə‚rɑn] *s* alerone *m*

ailing ['elɪŋ] *adj* ammalato

ailment ['elmənt] *s* malattia, indisposizione; *(chronic)* acciacco

aim [em] *s* mira; intento ‖ *tr (a gun)* puntare; *(words)* dirigere ‖ *intr* mirare; **to aim to** cercare di, aver l'intenzione di

air [er] *adj (e.g., pocket)* d'aria; *(e.g., show)* aeronautico ‖ *s* aria; **by air** per via aerea; **in the open air** all'aria aperta; **to be in the air** circolare; **to be on the air** (rad, telv) essere in onda; **to go on the air** (rad, telv) andare in onda; **to put on airs** darsi delle arie; **to take the air** andar fuori; **up in the air** incerto; (slang) arrabbiato ‖ *tr* aerare, ventilare

airborne ['er‚bɔrn] or ['er‚bɔrn] *adj* aerosostentato; aerotrasportato

air' brake' *s* freno ad aria compressa

air' cas'tle *s* castello in aria

air'-condi'tion *tr* climatizzare

air' condi'tioner *s* condizionatore *m*

air' condi'tioning *s* aria condizionata, climatizzazione

air-'cool' *tr* raffreddare con aria

air' corps' *s* aviazione, arma aeronautica

air'craft' *s* (-craft) aeromobile *m*

air'craft car'rier *s* portaerei *f*

airdrome ['er‚drom] *s* aerodromo

air'drop' *tr* paracadutare

air'field' *s* campo d'aviazione

air'foil' *s* superficie *f* portante, velatura

air' force' *s* forza aerea

air' gap' *s* (elec) intraferro

airing ['erɪŋ] s aerazione; passeggiata all'aria aperta; pubblica discussione

air' jack'et s (aer, naut) giubbotto salvagente

air' lane' s aerovia

air'lift' s ponte aereo, aerotrasporto || tr aerotrasportare

air'line' s linea aerea; tubo dell'aria

air' mail' s posta aerea

air'-mail' adj per via aerea || s lettera per posta aerea || adv per posta aerea || tr spedire per posta aerea

air'-mail let'ter s lettera per posta aerea

air'-mail stamp' s francobollo posta aerea

air'man s (-men) aviatore m, aviere m

air' mat'tress s materasso pneumatico

air'plane' s aeroplano, aereo

air'plane car'rier s portaerei f

air' pock'et s vuoto d'aria

air' pollu'tion s contaminazione atmosferica, inquinamento atmosferico

air' port' s aeroporto

air' pump' s pompa pneumatica

air' raid' s incursione aerea

air'-raid shel'ter s rifugio antiaereo

air'-raid warn'ing s allerta

air' ri'fle s fucile m ad aria compressa

air' serv'ice s aeroservizio

air' shaft' s tubo di ventilazione

air'ship' s aeronave f

airsickness ['er ,sɪknɪs] s male m d'aria

air' sleeve' s manica a vento

airspace ['er ,spes] s aerospazio

air'strip' s aviopista

air' ter'minal s aerostazione

air'tight' adj impermeabile all'aria, ermetico

air'waves' spl onde fpl, radioonde fpl

air'way' s aerovia; **airways** (rad) onda, onde fpl

air·y ['eri] adj (-ier; -iest) arioso; leggero; aereo

aisle [aɪl] s (between rows of seats) corsia; (of a church) navata laterale; (theat) canale m

ajar [ə'dʒɑr] adj socchiuso; in disaccordo

akimbo [ə'kɪmbo] adj & adv—**with arms akimbo** con le mani sui fianchi

akin [ə'kɪn] adj affine; congiunto

alabaster ['ælə ,bæstər] or ['ælə- ,bɑstər] s alabastro

à la carte [,ɑlə'kɑrt] adv alla carta

à la mode [,ɑlə'mod] or [,ælə'mod] adv alla moda; servito con gelato

alarm [ə'lɑrm] s allarme m || tr allarmare

alarm' clock' s sveglia

alas [ə'læs] or [ə'lɑs] interj ahimé!; povero me!

Albanian [æl'benɪ·ən] adj & s albanese mf

albatross ['ælbə ,trɔs] or ['ælbə ,trɑs] s albatro, diomedea

album ['ælbəm] s album m

albumen [æl'bjumən] s albume m

alchemy ['ælkəmi] s alchimia

alcohol ['ælkə ,hɔl] or ['ælkə ,hɑl] s alcole m

alcoholic [,ælkə'hɔlɪk] or [,ælkə'ha- lɪk] adj alcolico || s alcolizzato

alcove ['ælkov] s (recess) alcova; (in a garden) chiosco, padiglione m; cameretta attigua

alder ['ɔldər] s ontano, alno

al'der·man s (-men) assessore m municipale, consigliere m municipale

ale [el] s birra amara

alembic [ə'lembɪk] s alambicco

alert [ə'lʌrt] adj attento; vispo || s allerta; **to be on the alert** stare allerta || tr dare l'allerta a

Aleu'tian Is'lands [ə'luʃən] spl Isole Aleutine

Alexander [,ælɪg'zændər] or [,ælɪg- 'zɑndər] s Alessandro

Alexan'der the Great' s Alessandro Magno

Alexandrine [,ælɪg'zændrɪn] adj & s alessandrino

alfalfa [æl'fælfə] s (bot) erba medica

algae ['ældʒi] spl alghe fpl

algebra ['ældʒɪbrə] s algebra

algebraic [,ældʒɪ'bre·ɪk] adj algebrico

Algeria [æl'dʒɪrɪ·ə] s l'Algeria

Algerian [æl'dʒɪrɪ·ən] adj & s algerino

Algiers [æl'dʒɪrz] s Algeri f

alias ['elɪ·əs] s pseudonimo || adv alias

ali·bi ['ælɪ ,baɪ] s (-bis) alibi m

alien ['eljən] or ['elɪ·ən] adj straniero; (strange) strano || s straniero; (outsider) estraneo

alienate ['eljə ,net] or ['elɪ·ə ,net] tr alienare

alight [ə'laɪt] v (pret & pp **alighted** or **alit** [ə'lɪt]) intr scendere; **to alight on** or **upon** posarsi su

align [ə'laɪn] tr allineare || intr allinearsi

alike [ə'laɪk] adj uguali; **to look alike** assomigliarsi || adv nello stesso modo

alimen'tary canal' [,ælɪ'mentəri] s tubo digestivo

alimony ['ælɪ ,moni] s alimonia

alive [ə'laɪv] adj vivo, in vita; (lively) vivace; **alive to** conscio di; **alive with** brulicante di, pieno zeppo di; **look alive!** fa presto!

alka·li ['ælkə ,laɪ] s (-lis or -lies) alcali m

alkaline ['ælkə ,laɪn] or ['ælkəlɪn] adj alcalino

all [ɔl] adj indef tutto, tutto il, ogni || s tutto || pron tutto; tutti; **all of** tutti || adv completamente; **all but** quasi; **all in** (slang) stanco morto; **all in all** tutto considerato; **all the better** tanto meglio; **all the worse** tanto peggio; **far all that** per quello che, e.g., **for all that I know** per quello che io ne sappia; **in all** tutto contato; **it's all right!** va bene!; **not at all** niente affatto; prego

allay [ə'le] tr calmare, mitigare

all' clear' s fine f dell'allarme, cessato allarme

allegation [,ælɪ'geʃən] s asserzione, affermazione

allege [ə'ledʒ] tr asserire, affermare; addurre

allegiance [ə'lidʒəns] s fedeltà f, lealtà f

allegoric(al) [ˌælɪ'gɑrɪk(əl)] or [ˌælɪ-'gɔrɪk(əl)] *adj* allegorico
allego·ry ['ælɪˌgori] *s* (**-ries**) allegoria
aller·gy ['ælərdʒi] *s* (**-gies**) allergia
alleviate [ə'livi͜ˌet] *tr* alleviare
alley ['æli] *s* vicolo, calle *f*; (*for bowl-ing*) pista; (*tennis*) corridoio
All' Fools' Day' *s* primo d'aprile
all' fours' *spl*—**on all fours** a quattro gambe
alliance [ə'laɪ·əns] *s* alleanza
alligator ['ælɪˌgetər] *s* alligatore *m*
alliteration [əˌlɪtə're/ən] *s* allitterazione
all-knowing ['ɔl'no·ɪŋ] *adj* onnisciente
allocate ['æləˌket] *tr* assegnare; (*funds*) stanziare; (*to fix the place of*) allogare
allot [ə'lɑt] *v* (*pret & pp* **allotted**) *ger* **allotting**) *tr* distribuire, assegnare
all'-out' *adj* completo; (*ruthless*) acerrimo
allow [ə'lau] *tr* permettere; ammettere; concedere || *intr* **to allow for** prendere in considerazione
allowance [ə'lau·əns] *s* (*limited share*) assegno; concessione; (*reduction in price*) sconto; tolleranza; **to make allowance for** prendere in considerazione
alloy ['ælɔɪ] or [ə'lɔɪ] *s* lega; impurezza || [ə'lɔɪ] *tr* far lega di, legare; adulterare
all-powerful ['ɔl'pau·ərfəl] *adj* onnipotente
all' right' *adj* esatto; bene; in buona salute; (*slang*) dabbene
All' Saints'' Day' *s* Ognissanti *m*
All' Souls'' Day' *s* giorno dei morti
all'spice' *s* pimento, pepe *m* della Giamaica
all'-star' game' *s* partita sportiva in cui tutti i giocatori sono scelti fra i migliori
allude [ə'lud] *intr* alludere
allure [ə'lur] *s* fascino, incanto || *tr* affascinare, incantare
alluring [ə'lurɪŋ] *adj* affascinante, seducente
allusion [ə'lu/ən] *s* allusione
al·ly ['ælaɪ] *s* (**-lies**) alleato || [ə'laɪ] *v* (*pret & pp* **-lied**) *tr* alleare; associare; **to become allied** allearsi; imparentarsi || *intr* allearsi
almanac ['ɔlmə͜ˌnæk] *s* almanacco
almighty [ɔl'maɪti] *adj* onnipotente
almond ['ɑmənd] or ['æmənd] *s* (*nut*) mandorla; (*tree*) mandorlo
al'mond brittle' *s* croccante *m*
almost ['ɔlmost] or [ɔl'most] *adv* quasi
alms [ɑmz] *s* elemosina
aloe ['ælo] *s* aloe *m*
aloft [ə'lɔft] or [ə'lɑft] *adv* in alto, sopra; (*aer*) in volo; (*naut*) nell'alberatura
alone [ə'lon] *adj* solo; **let alone** senza menzionare; **to leave alone** non disturbare || *adv* solo, solamente
along [ə'lɔŋ] or [ə'lɑŋ] *adv* (*length-wise*) per il lungo; (*onward*) avanti; **all along** tutto il tempo; **along with**

con; **to get along** andar d'accordo; andarsene; avanzare; aver successo; **to take along** prendere con sè || *prep* lungo
along'side' *adv* a lato; **alongside of** a lato di || *prep* a lato di, vicino a
aloof [ə'luf] *adj* riservato, freddo; **to keep or stand aloof from** tenersi a distanza da || *adv* lontano; da solo
aloud [ə'laud] *adv* ad alta voce
alphabet ['ælfə͜ˌbet] *s* alfabeto
alpine ['ælpaɪn] *adj* alpino
Alps [ælps] *spl* Alpi *fpl*
already [ɔl'redi] *adv* già
Alsace [æl'ses] or [ˈælsæs] *s* l'Alsazia
Alsatian [æl'se/ən] *adj & s* alsaziano
also ['ɔlso] *adv* anche
altar ['ɔltər] *s* altare *m*
al'tar boy' *s* accolito, chierico
al'tar-piece' *s* pala d'altare
alter ['ɔltər] *tr* alterare; (*a male ani-mal*) castrare || *intr* diventare differente, cambiare
alteration [ˌɔltə're/ən] *s* alterazione, modifica
alternate ['ɔltərnɪt] or ['æltərnɪt] *s* sostituto, supplente *mf* || ['ɔltər͜ˌnet] or ['æltər͜ˌnet] *tr* alternare || *intr* alternarsi, avvicendarsi
al'ternating cur'rent *s* corrente alternata
alternator ['ɔltər͜ˌnetər] or ['æltər-ˌnetər] *s* alternatore *m*
although [ɔl'ðo] *conj* benchè, per quanto, malgrado
altimeter [æl'tɪmɪtər] or ['æltə͜ˌmitər] *s* altimetro
altitude ['æltɪ͜ˌtjud] or ['æltɪ͜ˌtud] *s* altitudine *f*
al·to ['ælto] *s* (**-tos**) contralto
altogether [ˌɔltə'geðər] *adv* completamente, affatto, tutt'insieme
altruist ['æltru·ɪst] *s* altruista *mf*
altruistic [ˌæltru'ɪstɪk] *adj* altruistico
alum ['æləm] *s* allume *m*
aluminum [ə'lumɪnəm] *s* alluminio
alum·na [ə'lʌmnə] *s* (**-nae** [ni]) diplomata, laureata
alum·nus [ə'lʌmnəs] *s* (**-ni** [nai]) diplomato, laureato
alveo·lus [æl'vi·ələs] *s* (**-li** [ˌlaɪ]) alveolo
always ['ɔlwɪz] or ['ɔlwez] *adv* sempre
amalgam [ə'mælgəm] *s* amalgama *m*
amalgamate [ə'mælgə͜ˌmet] *tr* amalgamare || *intr* amalgamarsi
amass [ə'mæs] *tr* ammassare
amateur ['æmə͜t/ər] *adj* da dilettante; *s* amatore *m*, dilettante *mf*
amaze [ə'mez] *tr* stupire, meravigliare
amazing [ə'mezɪŋ] *adj* straordinario
Amazon ['æmə͜ˌzɑn] or ['æməzən] *s* rio delle Amazzoni; (*myth*) Amazzone *f*
ambassador [æm'bæsədər] *s* ambasciatore *m*
ambassadress [æm'bæsədrɪs] *s* ambasciatrice *f*
amber ['æmbər] *s* ambra
ambigui·ty [ˌæmbɪ'gju·ɪti] *s* (**-ties**) ambiguità *f*
ambiguous [æm'bɪgju·əs] *adj* ambiguo

ambition [æm'bɪʃən] s ambizione

ambitious [æm'bɪʃəs] adj ambizioso

amble ['æmbəl] s ambio || intr ambiare

ambulance ['æmbjələns] s ambulanza

ambush ['æmbuʃ] s imboscata; **to lie in ambush** tendere un'imboscata || tr appostare || intr appostarsi

amelioration [ə‚miljə'reʃən] s miglioramento

amen ['e'men] or ['ɑ'men] s amen m || interj amen!

amenable [ə'minəbəl] or [ə'menəbəl] adj docile, aperto; (accountable) responsabile

amend [ə'mend] tr emendare || **amends** spl ammenda, contravvenzione; **to make amends for** fare ammenda per

amendment [ə'mendmənt] s emendamento

ameni·ty [ə'minɪti] or [ə'menɪti] s (-ties) amenità f

American [ə'merɪkən] adj & s americano

Americanize [ə'merɪkə‚naɪz] tr americanizzare

amethyst ['æmɪθɪst] s ametista

amiable ['emɪ·əbəl] adj amabile

amicable ['æmɪkəbəl] adj amichevole

amid [ə'mɪd] prep in mezzo a, fra, tra

amidship [ə'mɪd/ɪp] adv a mezzanave

amiss [ə'mɪs] adj erroneo, sbagliato || adv erroneamente; **to take amiss** offendersi, prendere in mala parte

ami·ty ['æmɪti] s (-ties) amicizia

ammeter ['æm‚mitər] s amperometro

ammonia [ə'monɪ·ə] s ammoniaca; acqua ammoniacale

ammunition [‚æmjə'nɪʃən] s munizione, munizioni fpl

amnes·ty ['æmnɪsti] s (-ties) amnistia || v (pret & pp -tied) tr amnistiare

amoeba [ə'mibə] s ameba

among [ə'mʌŋ] prep fra, tra, in mezzo a

amorous ['æmərəs] adj amoroso; erotico

amortize ['æmər‚taɪz] tr ammortare

amount [ə'maunt] s ammontare m || intr—**to amount to** ammontare a

ampere ['æmpɪr] s ampere m

am'pere-hour' s amperora m

amphibious [æm'fɪbɪ·əs] adj anfibio

amphitheater ['æmfɪ‚θi·ətər] s anfiteatro

ample ['æmpəl] adj ampio

amplifier ['æmplɪ‚faɪ·ər] s amplificatore m

ampli·fy ['æmplɪ‚faɪ] v (pret & pp -fied) tr amplificare

amplitude ['æmplɪ‚tjud] or ['æmplɪ‚tud] s ampiezza

am'plitude modula'tion s modulazione d'ampiezza

amputate ['æmpjə‚tet] tr amputare

amputee [‚æmpjə'ti] s chi ha subito l'amputazione di un arto

amuck [ə'mʌk] adv freneticamente; **to run amuck** dare in un accesso di pazzia; attaccare alla cieca

amulet ['æmjəlɪt] s amuleto

amuse [ə'mjuz] tr divertire

amusement [ə'mjuzmənt] s divertimento

amuse'ment park' s parco dei divertimenti, luna park m

amusing [ə'mjuzɪŋ] adj divertente

an [æn] or [ən] art indef var of a, used before words beginning with vowel or mute h

anachronism [ə'nækrə‚nɪzəm] s anacronismo

anaemia [ə'nimɪ·ə] s var of **anemia**

anaesthesia [‚ænɪs'θiʒə] s anestesia

anaesthetic [‚ænɪs'θetɪk] adj & s anestetico

anaesthetize [ə'nesθɪ‚taɪz] tr anestetizzare

analogous [ə'næləgəs] adj analogo

analo·gy [ə'nælədʒi] s (-gies) analogia

analy·sis [ə'nælɪsɪs] s (-ses [‚siz]) analisi f

analyst ['ænəlɪst] s analista mf

analytic(al) [‚ænə'lɪtɪk(əl)] adj analitico

analyze ['ænə‚laɪz] tr analizzare

anarchist ['ænərkɪst] s anarchico

anarchy ['ænərki] s anarchia

anathema [ə'næθɪmə] s anatema m

anatomic(al) [‚ænə'tɑmɪk(əl)] adj anatomico

anato·my [ə'nætəmi] s (-mies) anatomia

ancestor ['ænsestər] s antenato

ances·try ['ænsestri] s (-tries) lignaggio, prosapia

anchor ['æŋkər] s ancora; **to cast anchor** gettare l'ancora; **to ride at anchor** stare all'ancora; **to weigh anchor** salpare l'ancora, salpare || tr ancorare || intr ancorarsi, stare all'ancora

ancho·vy ['æntʃovi] s (-vies) acciuga

ancient ['enʃənt] adj antico || s vecchio, anziano; **the ancients** gli antichi

ancillary ['ænsɪ‚leri] adj dipendente; ausiliario, ausiliare

and [ænd] or [ənd] conj e, ed; **and so on, and so forth** e così via

Andean [æn'di·ən] or ['ændi·ən] adj andino || s abitante mf della regione andina

Andes ['ændiz] spl Ande fpl

andiron ['ænd‚aɪ·ərn] s alare m

anecdote ['ænɪk‚dot] s aneddoto

anemia [ə'nimɪ·ə] s anemia

anemic [ə'nimɪk] adj anemico

an'eroid barom'eter ['ænə‚rɔɪd] s barometro aneroide

anesthesia [‚ænɪs'θiʒə] s anestesia

anesthetic [‚ænɪs'θetɪk] adj & s anestetico

anesthetize [æ'nesθɪ‚taɪz] tr anestetizzare

aneurysm ['ænjə‚rɪzəm] s aneurisma m

anew [ə'nju] or [ə'nu] adv di nuovo, nuovamente

angel ['endʒəl] s angelo; (financial backer) (coll) finanziatore m

angelic(al) [æn'dʒelɪk(əl)] adj angelico

anger ['æŋgər] s ira, collera || tr adirare || intr adirarsi, incollerirsi

angle ['æŋgəl] s angolo; punto di vista

|| *intr* intrigare; **to angle for** darsi da fare per

an'gle i'ron *s* cantonale *m*, angolare *m*

angler ['æŋglər] *s* pescatore *m* alla lenza; (fig) intrigante *m*

Anglo-Saxon ['æŋglo'sæksən] *adj & s* anglosassone *mf*

an·gry ['æŋgri] *adj* (**-grier; -griest**) arrabbiato; (pathol) infiammato; **to become angry at** incollerirsi per; **to become angry with** adirarsi con

anguish ['æŋgwɪʃ] *s* angoscia, pena

angular ['æŋgjələr] *adj* angolare

anhydrous [æn'haɪdrəs] *adj* anidro

aniline ['ænɪlɪn] *or* ['ænɪ‚laɪn] *s* anilina

animal ['ænɪməl] *adj & s* animale *m*

an'imated cartoon' ['ænɪ‚metɪd] *s* cartone animato

animation [‚ænɪ'meʃən] *s* animazione

animosi·ty [‚ænɪ'mɑsɪti] *s* (**-ties**) animosità *f*

animus ['ænɪməs] *s* odio, malanimo

anion ['æn‚aɪ-ən] *s* anione *m*

anise ['ænɪs] *s* anice *f*

anisette [‚ænɪ'zɛt] *s* anisetta

ankle ['æŋkəl] *s* caviglia

an'kle·bone' *s* malleolo

an'kle support' *s* cavigliera

anklet ['æŋklɪt] *s* calzino corto; bracciale *m* da caviglia

annals ['ænəlz] *spl* annali *mpl*

annex ['ænɛks] *s* annesso, dipendenza || [ə'nɛks] *tr* annettere, appropriarsi di

annihilate [ə'naɪ‚let] *tr* annientare

anniversa·ry [‚ænɪ'vʌrsəri] *adj* anniversario || *s* (**-ries**) anniversario

annotate ['ænə‚tet] *tr* annotare

announce [ə'nauns] *tr* annunciare

announcement [ə'naunsmənt] *s* annuncio, partecipazione

announcer [ə'naunsər] *s* annunziatore *m*

annoy [ə'nɔɪ] *tr* annoiare, seccare

annoyance [ə'nɔɪ-əns] *s* fastidio, seccatura

annoying [ə'nɔɪ-ɪŋ] *adj* noioso

annual ['ænjʊ-əl] *adj* annuale || *s* annuario; pianta annuale

annui·ty [ə'nju·ɪti] *or* [ə'nu·ɪti] *s* (**-ties**) annualità *f*; (*for life*) vitalizio

an·nul [ə'nʌl] *v* (*pret & pp* **-nulled**; *ger* **-nulling**) *tr* annullare, cassare

annunciation [ə‚nʌnsɪ'eʃən] *s* annunzio || **Annunciation** *s* Annunciazione

anode ['ænod] *s* anodo

anoint [ə'nɔɪnt] *tr* ungere

anomalous [ə'nɑmələs] *adj* anomalo

anoma·ly [ə'nɑməli] *s* (**-lies**) anomalia

anonymi·ty [‚ænə'nɪmɪti] *s* (**-ties**) anonimia; **to preserve one's anonymity** serbare l'anonimo

anonymous [ə'nɑnɪməs] *adj* anonimo

another [ə'nʌðər] *adj & pron indef* un altro

answer ['ænsər] *or* ['ɑnsər] *s* risposta; (*to a problem*) soluzione || *tr* rispondere a; **this will answer your purpose** questo fa per Lei; **to answer back** (slang) dare una risposta a; **to answer the door** andare a rispondere

|| *intr* rispondere; corrispondere; essere responsabile; **to answer back** (slang) dare una rispostaccia

ant [ænt] *s* formica

antagonism [æn'tægə‚nɪzəm] *s* antagonismo

antagonize [æn'tægə‚naɪz] *tr* opporsi a; creare antagonismo in

antarctic [ænt'ɑrktɪk] *adj* antartico || **the Antarctic** la regione antartica

anteater ['ænt‚itər] *s* formichiere *m*

antecedent [‚æntɪ'sidənt] *adj & s* antecedente *m*; **antecedents** antenati *mpl*

antechamber ['æntɪ‚tʃembər] *s* anticamera

antedate ['æntɪ‚det] *tr* antidatare; (*to happen before*) antecedere

antelope [‚æntɪ‚lop] *s* antilope *f*

anten·na [æn'tɛnə] *s* (**-nae** [ni]) (*of insect*) antenna || *s* (**-nas**) (rad, telv) antenna

antepenult [‚æntɪ‚pinʌlt] *s* terzultima sillaba

anteroom ['æntɪ‚rum] *or* ['æntɪ‚rʊm] *s* anticamera, sala d'aspetto

anthem ['ænθəm] *s* inno

ant'hill' *s* formicaio

antholo·gy [æn'θɑlədʒi] *s* (**-gies**) antologia

anthracite ['ænθrə‚saɪt] *s* antracite *f*

anthrax ['ænθræks] *s* antrace *m*

anthropoid ['ænθrə‚pɔɪd] *adj* antropoide, antropomorfo

anthropology [‚ænθrə'pɑlədʒi] *s* antropologia

antiaircraft [‚æntɪ'er‚kræft] *or* [‚æntɪ'er‚krɑft] *adj* antiaereo

antibiotic [‚æntɪbaɪ'ɑtɪk] *adj & s* antibiotico

antibod·y ['æntɪ‚bɑdi] *s* (**-ies**) anticorpo

anticipate [æn'tɪsɪ‚pet] *tr* anticipare, prevedere; ripromettersi

anticipation [æn‚tɪsɪ'peʃən] *s* anticipazione, previsione

antics ['æntɪks] *spl* pagliacciate *fpl*, buffonate *fpl*

antidote ['æntɪ‚dot] *s* antidoto

antifreeze ['æntɪ‚friz] *s* anticongelante *m*

antiglare [‚æntɪ'gler] *adj* antiabbagliante

anti-G' suit' *s* tuta antigravità

antiknock [‚æntɪ'nɑk] *adj* antidetonante

antimissile [‚æntɪ'mɪsɪl] *adj* antimissile

antimony ['æntɪ‚moni] *s* antimonio

antinoise [‚æntɪ'nɔɪz] *adj* antirumore

antipa·thy [æn'tɪpəθi] *s* (**-thies**) antipatia

antipersonnel [‚æntɪ‚pʌrsə'nɛl] *adj* (*e.g., mine*) antiuomo

antiquarian [‚æntɪ'kwerɪ-ən] *adj & s* antiquario

antiquar·y ['æntɪ‚kweri] *s* (**-ies**) antiquario

antiquated ['æntɪ‚kwetɪd] *adj* antiquato

antique [æn'tik] *adj* antico, vecchio; antiquato || *s* oggetto d'epoca, antichità *f*

antique' deal'er s antiquario
antique' store' s negozio d'antiquariato
antiqui·ty [æn'tıkwıtı] s (-ties) antichità f
anti-Semitic [ˌæntısı'mıtık] adj antisemita
antiseptic [ˌæntı'septık] adj & s antisettico
antislavery [ˌæntı'sleværı] adj antischiavista
antitank [ˌæntı'tæŋk] adj anticarro
antitheft [ˌæntı'θeft] adj antifurto
antithe·sis [æn'tıθısıs] s (-ses [ˌsiz]) antitesi f
antitoxin [ˌæntı'taksın] s antitossina
antitrust [ˌæntı'trʌst] adj antitrust
antler ['æntlər] s corno di cervo
antonym ['æntonım] s antonimo
Antwerp ['æntwərp] s Anversa
anvil ['ænvıl] s incudine m
anxie·ty [æŋ'zaı·ətı] s (-ties) ansietà f; (psychol) angoscia
anxious ['æŋkjəs] adj ansioso; **anxious about** sollecito di; **anxious for** desideroso di
any ['enı] adj indef ogni, qualunque, qualsiasi; qualche, e.g., **do you know any boy who could help me?** conosce qualche ragazzo che possa aiutarmi?; di + art, e.g., **do you want any cheese?** vuole del formaggio?; **not . . . any** non . . . nessuno, e.g., **he does not read any newspaper** non legge nessun giornale || adv un po', e.g., **do you want any?** ne vuole un po'?; **not . . . any longer** non . . . più; **not . . . any more** non . . . più || pron ne, e.g., **do you want any?** ne vuole?
an'y·bod'y pron indef chiunque; (in interrogative sentences) qualcuno; **not . . . anybody** non . . . nessuno
an'y·how' adv in qualunque modo, comunque; in ogni caso; (haphazardly) alla rinfusa
an'y·one' pron indef chiunque; (in interrogative sentences) qualcuno; **not . . . anyone** non . . . nessuno
an'y·thing' s qualunque cosa || pron indef qualcosa; qualunque cosa; tutto quanto; checchessia; **anything at all** qualunque cosa; **not . . . anything** non . . . niente; **not . . . anything at all** non . . . niente affatto, non . . . nulla; **not . . . anything else** non . . . nient'altro
an'y·way' adv in qualunque modo, comunque; in ogni caso; (haphazardly) alla rinfusa
an'y·where' adv dovunque, in qualsiasi luogo; **not . . . anywhere** non . . . in nessun luogo
apace [ə'pes] adv presto, rapidamente
apart [ə'part] adv a parte, a pezzi; separatamente; **apart from** a parte da; oltre a; **to come apart** andare a pezzi, cadere a pezzi; **to set apart** mettere in disparte; **to take apart** smontare; **to tear apart** fare a pezzi; **to tell apart** distinguere
apartment [ə'partmənt] s appartamento; (single room) stanza

apart'ment house' s casa d'appartamenti
apathetic [ˌæpə'θetık] adj apatico
apathy ['æpəθı] s apatia
ape [ep] s scimmia antropomorfa; scimmia || tr imitare, scimmiottare
Apennines ['æpəˌnaınz] spl Appennini mpl
aperture ['æpərtʃər] s apertura
apex ['epeks] s (apexes or apices ['æpıˌsiz]) apice m
apheresis [ə'ferısıs] s aferesi f
aphorism ['æfəˌrızəm] s aforisma m
aphrodisiac [ˌæfrə'dızıˌæk] adj & s afrodisiaco
apiar·y ['epıˌerı] s (-ies) apiario
apiece [ə'pis] adv a testa, per persona; ciascuno
apish ['epıʃ] adj scimmiesco; da scimmia
aplomb [ə'plam] s disinvoltura, baldanza
apocalypse [ə'pakəˌlıps] s apocalisse f
apogee ['æpəˌdʒi] s apogeo
apologetic [əˌpalə'dʒetık] adj pieno di scuse
apologize [ə'paləˌdʒaız] intr chiedere scusa, scusarsi
apolo·gy [ə'palədʒı] s (-gies) scusa; (makeshift) surrogato
apoplectic [ˌæpə'plektık] adj & s apoplettico
apoplexy ['æpəˌpleksı] s apoplessia
apostle [ə'pasəl] s apostolo
apostrophe [ə'pastrəfı] s (mark) apostrofo; (rhet) apostrofe f
apothecar·y [ə'paθıˌkerı] s (-ies) farmacista mf
appall [ə'pɔl] tr sgomentare, sbigottire
appalling [ə'pɔlıŋ] adj sconcertante
appara·tus [ˌæpə'retəs] or [ˌæpə'rætəs] s (-tus or -tuses) apparato
apparel [ə'pærəl] s confezioni fpl, vestiario
apparent [ə'pærənt] or [ə'perənt] adj apparente; chiaramente visibile
apparition [ˌæpə'rıʃən] s apparizione f
appeal [ə'pil] s appello; (attraction) attrattiva, fascino || tr (a sentence) appellare contro || intr dare nell'occhio; **to appeal from** (law) appellarsi contro; **to appeal to** supplicare, pregare, piacere a, e.g., **his idea appeals to me** la sua idea mi piace
appear [ə'pır] intr apparire; (to seem) sembrare; (said of a book) uscire; (before the public) presentarsi; (law) comparire
appearance [ə'pırəns] s apparizione f; (of a book) pubblicazione f; (outward look) apparenza; (law) comparizione; **to keep up appearances** salvare le apparenze
appease [ə'piz] tr pacificare, placare; (a desire) soddisfare
appeasement [ə'pizmənt] s pacificazione, tranquillizzazione
appel'late court' [ə'pelıt] s corte f d'appello
appellation [ˌæpə'leʃən] s denominazione, nome m
append [ə'pend] tr allegare, aggiungere

appendage [ə'pɛndɪdʒ] *s* appendice *f*
appendicitis [ə,pɛndɪ'saɪtɪs] *s* appendicite *f*
appen·dix [ə'pɛndɪks] *s* (**-dixes** or **-dices** [dɪ,siz]) appendice *f*
appertain [,æpər'ten] *intr* spettare, riferirsi
appetite ['æpɪ,taɪt] *s* appetito
appetizer ['æpɪ,taɪzər] *s* (*drink*) aperitivo; (*food*) stimulante *m* dell'appetito
appetizing ['æpɪ,taɪzɪŋ] *adj* appetitoso
applaud *tr* applaudire, applaudire (with *dat*) || *intr* applaudire
applause [ə'plɔz] *s* applauso, applausi *mpl*
apple ['æpəl] *s* mela, pomo; (*tree*) melo, pomo
ap'plejack' *s* acquavite *f* di mele
ap'ple of dis'cord *s* pomo della discordia
ap'ple of one's eye' *s* pupilla degli occhi di qlcu, beniamino di qlcu
ap'ple pie' *s* torta di mele
ap'ple pol'isher *s* leccapiedi *mf*
ap'ple-sauce' *s* marmellata di mele; (*slang*) scemenza
appliance [ə'plaɪ·əns] *s* apparecchio, apparato; (*complicated instrument*) congegno; (*for domestic chores*) utensile *m*; (*act of applying*) applicazione
applicant ['æplɪkənt] *s* postulante *mf*, aspirante *m*, candidato
application [,æplɪ'keʃən] *s* applicazione; uso; richiesta, domanda
ap·ply [ə'plaɪ] *v* (*pret & pp* **-plied**) *tr* applicare; (*the brakes*) mettere; (*e.g., a nickname*) affibbiare || *intr* (*said of a rule*) essere applicabile; fare richiesta; **to apply for** sollecitare
appoint [ə'pɔɪnt] *tr* nominare; assegnare; (*to furnish*) ammobiliare
appointee [,æpɔɪn'ti] *s* persona nominata a una carica
appointive [ə'pɔɪntɪv] *adj* a nomina
appointment [ə'pɔɪntmənt] *s* nomina; (*position*) ufficio; (*agreement to meet*) appuntamento; **appointments** mobilia, arredamento; **by appointment** previo appuntamento
apportion [ə'porʃən] *tr* spartire, dividere proporzionatamente
appraisal [ə'prezəl] *s* stima, valutazione; (*of real estate*) estimo
appraise [ə'prez] *tr* stimare, valutare
appreciable [ə'priʃɪ·əbəl] *adj* apprezzabile, notevole
appreciate [ə'priʃɪ,et] *tr* apprezzare, valutare; (*to be grateful for*) gradire; (*to be aware of*) rendersi conto di; (*to raise in value*) valorizzare || *intr* aumentare di valore
appreciation [ə,priʃɪ'eʃən] *s* apprezzamento, valutazione; (*grateful recognition*) gradimento, riconoscenza; valorizzazione
appreciative [ə'priʃɪ,etɪv] *adj* grato, riconoscente
apprehend [,æprɪ'hɛnd] *tr* (*to fear*) temere; (*to understand*) comprendere; (*to arrest*) arrestare

apprehension [,æprɪ'hɛnʃən] *s* timore *m*, apprensione; comprensione; arresto
apprehensive [,æprɪ'hɛnsɪv] *adj* apprensivo
apprentice [ə'prɛntɪs] *s* apprendista *mf*, novizio || *tr* mettere in apprendistato; accettare in apprendistato
apprenticeship [ə'prɛntɪs,ʃɪp] *s* apprendistato, carovana
apprise or **apprize** [ə'praɪz] *tr* avvertire, avvisare; stimare, valutare
approach [ə'protʃ] *s* (*a coming near*) avvicinamento; (*of night*) avvicinarsi *m*, far *m*; approssimazione; (*access*) via d'accesso; (*to a problem*) impostazione; **approaches** approcci *mpl* || *tr* avvicinarsi a, avvicinare; fare approcci con || *intr* avvicinarsi, approssimarsi
approbation [,æprə'beʃən] *s* approvazione
appropriate [ə'proprɪ·ɪt] *adj* appropriato, acconcio || [ə'proprɪ,et] *tr* (*to take*) appropriarsi di; (*to set aside for some specific use*) stanziare
approval [ə'pruvəl] *s* approvazione, consenso; **on approval** in prova
approve [ə'pruv] *tr & intr* approvare
approximate [ə'praksɪmɪt] *adj* approssimato, approssimativo || [ə'praksɪ,met] *tr* approssimarsi a || *intr* approssimarsi
apricot ['eprɪ,kɑt] or ['æprɪ,kɑt] *s* color albicocca || *s* (*fruit*) albicocca; (*tree*) albicocco
April ['eprɪl] *s* aprile *m*
A'pril fool' *s* pesce *m* d'aprile
A'pril Fools' Day' *s* primo d'aprile
apron ['eprən] *s* grembiale *m*, grembiule *m*; **tied to the apron strings of** attaccato alle sottane di
apropos [,æprə'po] *adj* opportuno || *adv*—**apropos of** a proposito di
apse [æps] *s* abside *f*
apt [æpt] *adj* atto, appropriato; (*quick*) pronto; **to be apt to** essere propenso a, portato a
aptitude ['æptɪ,tjud] or ['æptɪ,tud] *s* attitudine *f*
ap'titude test' *s* esame *m* attitudinale
Apulia [ə'pjulɪ·ə] *s* la Puglia
aqualung ['ækwə,lʌŋ] *s* autorespiratore *m*
aquamarine [,ækwəmə'rin] *s* acquamarina
aquaplane ['ækwə,plen] *s* acquaplano || *intr* andare in acquaplano
aquari·um [ə'kwɛrɪ·əm] *s* (**-ums** or **-a** [ə]) acquario, vasca dei pesci
Aquarius [ə'kwɛrɪ·əs] *s* (astr) Acquario
aquatic [ə'kwætɪk] or [ə'kwɑtɪk] *adj* acquatico || *s* animale acquatico; pianta acquatica; **aquatics** sport acquatici
aqueduct ['ækwə,dʌkt] *s* acquedotto
aqueous ['ekwɪ·əs] or ['ækwɪ·əs] *adj* acquoso
aq'uiline nose' ['ækwɪ,laɪn] *s* naso aquilino
Arab ['ærəb] *adj & s* arabo
Arabic ['ærəbɪk] *adj & s* arabo

arbiter ['ɑrbɪtər] s arbitro
arbitrary ['ɑrbɪ‚treri] adj arbitrario
arbitrate ['ɑrbɪ‚tret] tr arbitrare || intr fare l'arbitro
arbitration [‚ɑrbɪ'treʃən] s arbitrato
arbitrator ['ɑrbɪ‚tretər] s arbitro
arbor ['ɑrbər] s pergola, pergolato; (mach) albero, asse m
arbore·tum [‚ɑrbə'ritəm] s (-tums or -ta [tə]) arboreto
arbutus [ɑr'bjutəs] s (Arbutus unedo) corbezzolo
arc [ɑrk] s arco; (elec) arco voltaico || intr (elec) formare un arco
arcade [ɑr'ked] s arcata, portico
arch [ɑrtʃ] adj malizioso || s arco; (anat) arco del piede || tr attraversare; arcuare || intr inarcarsi
archaeology [‚ɑrkɪ'ɑlədʒi] s archeologia
archaic [ɑr'ke·ɪk] adj arcaico
archaism ['ɑrke‚ɪzəm] or ['ɑrki‚ɪzəm] s arcaismo
archangel ['ɑrk‚endʒəl] s arcangelo
archbishop ['ɑrtʃ'bɪʃəp] s arcivescovo
archduke ['ɑrtʃ'djuk] or ['ɑrtʃ'duk] s arciduca m
archene·my ['ɑrtʃ'enɪmi] s (-mies) nemico giurato
archer ['ɑrtʃər] s arciere m
archery ['ɑrtʃəri] s tiro con l'arco
archetype ['ɑrkɪ‚taɪp] s archetipo, prototipo
archipela·go [‚ɑrkɪ'peləgo] s (-gos or -goes) arcipelago
architect ['ɑrkɪ‚tekt] s architetto
architectural [‚ɑrkɪ'tektʃərəl] adj architetturale, architettonico
architecture ['ɑrkɪ‚tektʃər] s architettura
archives ['ɑrkaɪvz] spl archivio
arch'way' s arcata
arc' lamp' s lampada ad arco
arctic ['ɑrktɪk] adj artico || the Arctic la regione artica
arc' weld'ing s saldatura ad arco
ardent ['ɑrdənt] adj ardente
ardor ['ɑrdər] s ardore m
arduous ['ɑrdʒʊ·əs] or ['ɑrdjʊ·əs] adj arduo
area ['erɪ·ə] s area
ar'ea code' s prefisso
Argentina [‚ɑrdʒən'tinə] s l'Argentina
Argentine ['ɑrdʒən‚tin] or ['ɑrdʒən‚taɪn] adj & s argentino || the Argentine l'Argentina
Argonaut ['ɑrgə‚nɔt] s argonauta m
argue ['ɑrgju] tr dibattere; (to indicate) indicare, provare; to argue out of dissuadere da; to argue s.o. into s.th persuadere qlcu di qlco || intr argomentare, discutere
argument ['ɑrgjəmənt] s discussione, argomentazione; (theme) argomento
argumentative [‚ɑrgjə'mentətɪv] adj litigioso
aria ['ɑrɪ·ə] or ['erɪ·ə] s aria
arid ['ærɪd] adj arido
aridity [ə'rɪdɪti] s aridità f
Aries ['eriz] or ['eri‚iz] s (astr) Ariete m

aright [ə'raɪt] adv correttamente; to set aright rettificare
arise [ə'raɪz] v (pret arose [ə'roz]; pp arisen [ə'rɪzən]) intr alzarsi; (to originate) provenire, trarre origine; (to occur) succedere, avvenire; (to be raised, as objections) avanzarsi
aristocra·cy [‚ærɪs'tɑkrəsi] s (-cies) aristocrazia
aristocrat [ə'rɪstə‚kræt] s aristocratico
aristocratic [ə‚rɪstə'krætɪk] adj aristocratico
Aristotelian [‚ærɪstə'tilɪ·ən] adj & s aristotelico
Aristotle ['ærɪ‚stɑtəl] s Aristotele m
arithmetic [ə'rɪθmətɪk] s aritmetica
arithmetical [‚ærɪθ'metɪkəl] adj aritmetico
arithmetician [‚ærɪθmə'trɪʃən] or [ə‚rɪθmə'trɪʃən] s aritmetico
ark [ɑrk] s arca
ark' of the cov'enant s arca dell'alleanza
arm [ɑrm] s braccio; (e.g., of a bear) zampa; (of a chair) bracciolo; (weapon) arma; arm in arm a braccetto; to be up in arms essere in armi; essere indignato; to lay down one's arms deporre le armi; to rise up in arms levarsi in armi; with open arms a braccia aperte || tr armare || intr armarsi
armament ['ɑrməmənt] s armamento
armature ['ɑrmə‚tʃər] s (of an animal) corazza; (of motor or dynamo) indotto; (of a buzzer or electric bell) ancora
arm'chair' s poltrona
Armenian [ɑr'minɪ·ən] adj & s armeno
armful ['ɑrm‚fʊl] s bracciata
arm'hole' s giro manica
armistice ['ɑrmɪstɪs] s armistizio
armlet ['ɑrmlɪt] s bracciale m
armor ['ɑrmər] s armatura, corazza || tr corazzare, blindare
ar'mored car' s carro armato
ar'mor plate' s lamiera di corazza
armor·y ['ɑrməri] s (-ies) armeria; arsenale m
arm'pit' s ascella
arm'rest' s bracciolo
ar·my ['ɑrmi] adj dell'esercito, militare || s (-mies) esercito; (two or more army corps) armata
ar'my corps' s corpo d'armata
aromatic [‚ærə'mætɪk] adj aromatico
around [ə'raʊnd] adv intorno; all'intorno; dappertutto; to turn around voltarsi || prep intorno a; (coll) vicino a; (approximately) (coll) circa
arouse [ə'raʊz] tr eccitare, incitare; svegliare
arpeg·gio [ɑr'pedʒo] s (-gios) arpeggio
arraign [ə'ren] tr citare, portare in giudizio; accusare
arrange [ə'rendʒ] tr disporre, sistemare; (a dispute) comporre, accomodare; (mus) ridurre, arrangiare
arrangement [ə'rendʒmənt] s disposizione, sistemazione; composizione, accomodamento; (mus) riduzione,

arrangiamento; arrangements preparazione, preparativi *mpl*

array [ə're] *s* ordine *m;* (*clothes*) abbigliamento; (mil) spiegamento, schiera ‖ *tr* disporre; abbigliare, adornare; (mil) spiegare, schierare

arrears [ə'rɪrz] *spl* arretrati *mpl;* **in arrears** in arretrato

arrest [ə'rest] *s* arresto; **under arrest** in arresto ‖ *tr* arrestare; (*the attention*) attrarre

arresting [ə'restɪŋ] *adj* interessante, che fa colpo

arrival [ə'raɪvəl] *s* arrivo; persona arrivata

arrive [ə'raɪv] *intr* arrivare

arrogance ['ærəgəns] *s* arroganza

arrogant ['ærəgənt] *adj* arrogante

arrogate ['ærə,get] *tr* (*to take without right*) arrogare per sé, arrogarsi; (*to claim for another*) attribuire ingiustamente

arrow ['æro] *s* freccia, saetta

ar'row·head' *s* punta di freccia; (bot) sagittaria

arsenal ['ɑrsənəl] *s* arsenale *m*

arsenic ['ɑrsɪnɪk] *s* arsenico

arson ['ɑrsən] *s* incendio doloso

art [ɑrt] *s* arte *f*

arter·y ['ɑrtəri] *s* (**-ies**) arteria

artful ['ɑrtfəl] *adj* artificioso; (*clever*) destro; (*crafty*) astuto

arthritic [ɑr'θrɪtɪk] *adj & s* artritico

arthritis [ɑr'θraɪtɪs] *s* artrite *f*

artichoke ['ɑrtɪ,tʃok] *s* carciofo

article ['ɑrtɪkəl] *s* articolo

articulate [ɑr'tɪkjəlɪt] *adj* articolato; facile di parola ‖ [ɑr'tɪkjə,let] *tr* articolare ‖ *intr* pronunziare in modo articolato

articulation [ɑr,tɪkjə'leʃən] *s* articolazione

artifact ['ɑrtɪ,fækt] *s* manufatto

artifice ['ɑrtɪfɪs] *s* artificio

artificial [,ɑrtɪ'fɪʃəl] *adj* artificiale

artillery [ɑr'tɪləri] *s* artiglieria

artil'lery·man *s* (**-men**) artigliere *m*, cannoniere *m*

artisan ['ɑrtɪzən] *s* artigiano

artist ['ɑrtɪst] *s* artista *mf*

artistic [ɑr'tɪstɪk] *adj* artistico

artistry ['ɑrtɪstri] *s* abilità artistica

artless ['ɑrtlɪs] *adj* ingenuo, naturale; ignorante; (*clumsy*) grossolano

arts' and crafts' *spl* arti *fpl* e mestieri *mpl*

art·y ['ɑrti] *adj* (**-ier; -iest**) (coll) interessato nell'arte con ostentazione

Aryan ['ɛrɪ·ən] or ['ɑrjən] *adj & s* ariano

as [æz] or [əz] *pron rel* che; **the same as** lo stesso che ‖ *adv* come; per esempio; **as . . . as** così . . . come; **as far as** fino a; **as far as I know** per quanto mi consta; **as for** in quanto a, per quanto concerne; **as is** (slang) com'è, nelle condizioni in cui si trova; **as long as** tanto che, mentre che; **as per** secondo; **as soon as** appena, non appena, non appena che; **as to** per quanto concerne; **as well** pure, anche; **as yet** ancora ‖ *prep* come; da; **as a rule** come regola ‖

conj come; mentre; dato che; per quanto; **as if** come se; **as it were** per così dire; **as though** come se

asbestos [æs'bestəs] *s* asbesto, amianto

ascend [ə'send] *tr* ascendere, scalare ‖ *intr* ascendere, salire

ascension [ə'senʃən] *s* ascensione, scalata ‖ **Ascension** *s* Ascensione

ascent [ə'sent] *s* scalata; salita; (*slope*) erta

ascertain [,æsər'ten] *tr* sincerarsi di, verificare

ascertainable [,æsər'tenəbəl] *adj* verificabile

ascetic [ə'setɪk] *adj* ascetico ‖ *s* asceta *m*

ascor'bic ac'id [ə'skɔrbɪk] *s* acido ascorbico

ascribe [ə'skraɪb] *tr* attribuire, imputare

aseptic [ə'septɪk] or [e'septɪk] *adj* asettico

ash [æʃ] *s* cenere *f;* (bot) frassino

ashamed [ə'ʃemd] *adj* vergognoso; **to be** or **feel ashamed** vergognarsi

ash'can' *s* pattumiera; (coll) bomba antisommergibile

ashen ['æʃən] *adj* cinereo

ashlar ['æʃlər] *s* bugna, bugnato

ashore [ə'ʃor] *adv* a terra; **to come ashore** andare a terra, sbarcare; **to run ashore** arenarsi

ash'tray' *s* portacenere *m*

Ash' Wednes'day *s* le Ceneri

Asia ['eʒə] or ['eʃə] *s* l'Asia *f*

A'sia Mi'nor *s* l'Asia *f* Minore

Asian ['eʒən] or ['eʃən] or **Asiatic** [,eʒɪ'ætɪk] or [,eʃɪ'ætɪk] *adj & s* asiatico

aside [ə'saɪd] *s* parola detta a parte; (theat) a parte *m* ‖ *adv* da parte; a parte; **aside from** (coll) eccetto; separato da; **to step aside** farsi da un lato

asinine ['æsɪnaɪn] *adj* (*like an ass*) asinino; (*stupid*) asinesco

ask [æsk] or [ɑsk] *tr* chiedere (with *dat*), domandare (with *dat*); invitare; (*a question*) fare; **to ask s.o. for s.th** chiedere or domandare qlco a qlcu; **to ask s.o. to** + *inf* chiedere a qlcu di + *inf* ‖ *intr* chiedere; **to ask about** chiedere informazioni di; **to ask for** chiedere, domandare; **to ask for it** (coll) andare in cerca di disgrazie; (coll) volerlo, e.g., **he asked for it** l'ha voluto

askance [ə'skæns] *adv* di traverso, di sbieco; (fig) con sospetto

asleep [ə'slip] *adj* addormentato; **to fall asleep** addormentarsi

asp [æsp] *s* aspide *m*

asparagus [ə'spærəgəs] *s* asparago; (as *food*) asparagi *mpl*

aspect ['æspekt] *s* aspetto; (*direction anything faces*) esposizione

aspen ['æspən] *s* pioppo tremolo, tremolo

aspersion [ə'spʌrʒən] or [ə'spʌrʃən] *s* diffamazione, calunnia; (eccl) aspersione

asphalt ['æsfɔlt] or ['æsfælt] *s* asfalto ‖ *tr* asfaltare

asphyxiate [æsˈfɪksɪ͵et] *tr* asfissiare
aspirant [əˈspaɪrənt] *or* [ˈæspɪrənt] *s* aspirante *mf*
aspire [əˈspaɪr] *intr* aspirare
aspirin [ˈæspɪrɪn] *s* aspirina
ass [æs] *s* asino
assail [əˈsel] *tr* assalire, assaltare
assassin [əˈsæsɪn] *s* assassino
assassinate [əˈsæsɪ͵net] *tr* assassinare
assassination [ə͵sæsɪˈneʃən] *s* assassinio
assault [əˈsɔlt] *s* assalto || *tr* assaltare
assault′ and bat′tery *s* vie *fpl* di fatto
assay [əˈse] *or* [ˈæse] *s* saggio, esame *m* || [əˈse] *tr* saggiare
assemblage [əˈsemblɪdʒ] *s* assemblea; (mach) montaggio
assemble [əˈsembəl] *tr* riunire; (mach) montare, mettere insieme || *intr* assembrarsi, riunirsi
assembler [əˈsemblər] *s* montatore *m*
assem′bly [əˈsemblɪ] *s* (**-blies**) assemblea, riunione; (mach) montaggio
assem′bly hall′ *s* sala di riunioni
assem′bly line′ *s* catena di montaggio
assem′bly-man *s* (**-men**) membro dell'assemblea legislativa
assent [əˈsent] *s* assenso || *intr* assentire
assert [əˈsʌrt] *tr* asserire; **to assert oneself** far valere i propri diritti
assertion [əˈsʌrʃən] *s* asserzione
assess [əˈses] *tr* stimare, valutare; (*for taxation or fine*) tassare
assessment [əˈsesmənt] *s* valutazione; tassazione
assessor [əˈsesər] *s* agente *m* delle tasse
asset [ˈæsət] *s* vantaggio; persona di valore; **assets** (com) attivo; (law) beni *mpl*
assiduous [əˈsɪdʒu·əs] *or* [əˈsɪdju·əs] *adj* assiduo
assign [əˈsaɪn] *s* cessionario || *tr* assegnare; (*e.g., a date*) fissare; (*a right*) trasferire
assignation [͵æsɪgˈneʃən] *s* assegnazione; trasferimento; (*date*) appuntamento amoroso
assignment [əˈsaɪnmənt] *s* assegnamento; (*of rights*) trasferimento; (*schoolwork*) compito
assimilate [əˈsɪmɪ͵let] *tr* assimilare || *intr* essere assimilato; assimilarsi
assist [əˈsɪst] *s* aiuto || *tr* aiutare, assistere
assistance [əˈsɪstəns] *s* assistenza, aiuto
assistant [əˈsɪstənt] *adj & s* assistente *m*
associate [əˈsoʃɪ·ɪt] *or* [əˈsoʃɪ͵et] *adj* associato || [əˈsoʃɪ·ɪt] *s* associato; membro limitato || [əˈsoʃɪ͵et] *tr* associare || *intr* associarsi
association [ə͵soʃɪˈeʃən] *s* associazione
assort [əˈsɔrt] *tr* assortire || *intr* associarsi
assortment [əˈsɔrtmənt] *s* assortimento
assuage [əˈswedʒ] *tr* alleviare
assume [əˈsum] *or* [əˈsjum] *tr* assumere; (*to appropriate*) usurpare; (*to pretend*) fingere; (*to suppose*) supporre
assumed [əˈsumd] *or* [əˈsjumd] *adj* supposto, immaginario

assumption [əˈsʌmpʃən] *s* (*arrogance*) aria, arroganza; (*thing taken for granted*) supposizione; (*of an undertaking*) assunzione
assurance [əˈʃurəns] *s* assicurazione, certezza; baldanza, fiducia in sè; (*too much boldness*) sicumera
assure [əˈʃur] *tr* assicurare
assuredly [əˈʃurɪdlɪ] *adv* sicuramente
astatine [ˈæstə͵tin] *s* astato
asterisk [ˈæstə͵rɪsk] *s* asterisco, stelloncino
astern [əˈstʌrn] *adv* a poppa, a poppavia
asthma [ˈæzmə] *or* [ˈæsmə] *s* asma
astonish [əˈstanɪʃ] *tr* meravigliare, stupefare
astonishing [əˈstanɪʃɪŋ] *adj* stupefacente, sorprendente
astound [əˈstaund] *tr* stupefare, sbalordire
astounding [əˈstaundɪŋ] *adj* stupefacente
astraddle [əˈstrædəl] *adv* a cavaliere, a cavalcioni
astray [əˈstre] *adv* sulla cattiva via; **to go astray** traviarsi; **to lead astray** traviare
astride [əˈstraɪd] *adj & adv* a cavaliere; (*said of a person*) a cavalcioni || *prep* a cavaliere di; a cavalcioni di
astrology [əˈstralədʒɪ] *s* astrologia
astronaut [ˈæstrə͵nɔt] *s* astronauta *mf*
astronautic [͵æstrəˈnɔtɪk] *adj* astronautico || **astronautics** *ssg* astronautica
astronomer [əˈstranəmər] *s* astronomo
astronomic(al) [͵æstrəˈnamɪk(əl)] *adj* astronomico
astronomy [əˈstranəmɪ] *s* astronomia
astute [əˈstjut] *or* [əˈstut] *adj* astuto
asunder [əˈsʌndər] *adv* a pezzi; **to tear asunder** separare, fare a pezzi
asylum [əˈsaɪləm] *s* asilo
asymmetry [əˈsɪmɪtrɪ] *s* asimmetria
at [æt] *or* [ət] *prep* a; in; a casa di, e.g., **at John's** a casa di Giovanni; da, e.g., **at Mary's** da Maria; di, e.g., **to be surprised at** essere sorpreso di; **to laugh at** ridersi di
atheist [ˈeθi·ɪst] *s* ateista *mf*
Athenian [əˈθinɪ·ən] *adj & s* ateniese *mf*
Athens [ˈæθɪnz] *s* Atene *f*
athirst [əˈθʌrst] *adj* assetato
athlete [ˈæθlit] *s* atleta *mf*
athletic [æθˈlɛtɪk] *adj* atletico || **athletics** *ssg & spl* atletica
Atlantic [ætˈlæntɪk] *adj* atlantico || *adj & s* Atlantico
atlas [ˈætləs] *s* atlante *m* || **Atlas** *s* Atlante *m*
atmosphere [ˈætməs͵fɪr] *s* atmosfera
atmospheric [͵ætməsˈfɛrɪk] *adj* atmosferico || **atmospherics** *spl* disturbi atmosferici
atom [ˈætəm] *s* atomo
at′om bomb′ *s* bomba atomica
atomic [əˈtamɪk] *adj* atomico
atom′ic age′ *s* era atomica
atom′ic sub′marine *s* sommergibile *m* nucleare
atomize [ˈætə͵maɪz] *tr* atomizzare

atomizer ['ætə‚maizər] s nebulizzatore *m*

at'om smash'er s acceleratore *m* di particelle

atone [ə'ton] *intr*—to atone for espiare

atonement [ə'tonmənt] s riparazione; espiazione

atop [ə'tɑp] *adv* in cima || *prep* in cima a

atrocious [ə'trofəs] *adj* atroce

atroci·ty [ə'trasiti] s (-ties) atrocità *f*

atro·phy ['ætrəfi] s atrofia || *v* (*pret & pp* ·phied) *tr* atrofizzare || *intr* atrofizzarsi

attach [ə'tætʃ] *tr* attaccare; (*to affix*) apporre; (*to attribute*) attribuire; (law) sequestrare; **to be attached to** essere legato a; fare parte di || *intr*—**to attach to** essere pertinente a

attaché [‚ætə'ʃe] or [ə'tæʃe] s attaché *m.*, addetto

attaché' case' s valigetta diplomatica

attachment [ə'tætʃmənt] s attacco, unione; affezione; (mach) accessorio; (law) sequestro

attack [ə'tæk] s attacco || *tr & intr* attaccare

attain [ə'ten] *tr* raggiungere || *intr*—**to attain to** raggiungere, conseguire

attainder [ə'tendər] s morte *f* civile

attainment [ə'tenmənt] s raggiungimento, realizzazione; (*accomplishment*) dote *f*

attempt [ə'tempt] s tentativo; (*attack*) attentato || *tr* tentare; (*s.o.'s life*) attentare a

attend [ə'tend] *tr* (*to be present at*) presenziare, presenziare a, assistere a; (*to accompany*) accompagnare; (*to take care of*; *to pay attention to*) assistere || *intr*—**to attend to** occuparsi di, attendere a

attendance [ə'tendəns] s (*attending*) presenza; (*company present*) concorso; **to dance attendance** essere al servizio completo

attendant [ə'tendənt] *adj* assistente; (*accompanying*) concomitante || *s* (*servant*) inserviente *mf*; presente *m*

attention [ə'tenʃən] s attenzione; (mil) attenti *m*; **attentions** attenzioni *fpl*; **to call s.o.'s attention to s.th** fare presente qlco a qlcu; **to stand at attention** stare sull'attenti || *interj* attenti!

attentive [ə'tentiv] *adj* attento, premuroso

attenuate [ə'tenju‚et] *tr* attenuare

attest [ə'test] *tr* attestare || *intr*—**to attest to** attestare, testimoniare

attic ['ætik] s attico, solaio || **Attic** *adj & s* attico

attire [ə'tair] s vestiti *mpl*, vestiario || *tr* vestire

attitude ['æti‚tjud] or ['æti‚tud] s atteggiamento, attitudine *f*; **to strike an attitude** atteggiarsi

attorney [ə'tʌrni] s avvocato; (*proxy*) procuratore *m*

attor'ney gen'eral s (**attor'neys gen'eral** *or* **attor'ney gen'erals**) procuratore *m* generale || **Attorney General** s (U.S.A.) ministro di grazia e giustizia

attract [ə'trækt] *tr* attrarre; (*attention*) chiamare

attraction [ə'trækʃən] s attrazione

attractive [ə'træktiv] *adj* attrattivo

attribute ['ætri‚bjut] s attributo || [ə'tribjut] *tr* attribuire

attrition [ə'triʃən] s attrito; diminuzione di numero

auburn ['ɔbərn] *adj & s* biondo fulvo, rosso tizianesco

auction ['ɔkʃən] s asta, incanto || *tr* vendere all'asta

auctioneer [‚ɔkʃə'nir] s banditore *m* || *tr & intr* vendere all'asta

audacious [ɔ'deʃəs] *adj* audace

audaci·ty [ɔ'dæsiti] s (-ties) audacia

audience ['ɔdi‚əns] s (*hearing*) udienza; uditorio, pubblico

au'dio fre'quency ['ɔdi‚o] s audiofrequenza

au'dio-vis'ual aids' *spl* sussidi audiovisivi

audit ['ɔdit] s verifica or esame *m* dei conti || *tr* esaminare i conti di; (*a class*) assistere a, come uditore || *intr* assistere a una classe come uditore

audition [ɔ'diʃən] s audizione || *tr* dare un'audizione a

auditor ['ɔditər] s revisore *m* dei conti; (educ) uditore *m*

auditorium [‚ɔdi'tori‚əm] s auditorio

auger ['ɔgər] s succhiello, trivella

aught [ɔt] s zero; **for aught I know** per quanto ne so || *adv* affatto

augment [ɔg'ment] *tr & intr* aumentare

augur ['ɔgər] s augure *m* || *tr & intr* vaticinare

augu·ry ['ɔgəri] s (-ries) augurio

august [ɔ'gʌst] *adj* augusto || **August** ['ɔgəst] s agosto

aunt [ænt] or [ɑnt] s zia

aurora [ə'rorə] s aurora

auspice ['ɔspis] s auspicio; **under the auspices of** sotto gli auspici di

austere [ɔ'stir] *adj* austero

Australia [ɔ'streljə] s l'Australia *f*

Australian [ɔ'streljən] *adj & s* australiano

Austria ['ɔstri‚ə] s l'Austria *f*

Austrian ['ɔstri‚ən] *adj & s* austriaco

authentic [ɔ'θentik] *adj* autentico

authenticate [ɔ'θenti‚ket] *tr* autenticare

author ['ɔθər] s autore *m*

authoress ['ɔθəris] s autrice *f*

authoritarian [ə‚θɔri'teri‚ən] or [ə‚θɔri'teri‚ən] *adj* autoritario || *s* persona autoritaria

authoritative [ə'θɔri‚tetiv] or [ə'θɔri‚tetiv] *adj* autorevole; autoritario

authori·ty [ə'θɔriti] or [ə'θɑriti] s (-ties) autorità *f*; **on good authority** da buona fonte, da fonte autorevole

authorize ['ɔθə‚raiz] *tr* autorizzare

authorship ['ɔθər‚ʃip] s paternità letteraria

au·to ['ɔto] s (-tos) (coll) auto *f*

autobiogra·phy [‚ɔtobai'agrəfi] or [‚ɔtobi'agrəfi] s (-phies) autobiografia

autobus ['ɔto ,bʌs] s autobus m
autocratic(al) [,ɔtə'krætɪk(əl)] adj autocratico
autograph ['ɔtə ,græf] or ['ɔtə ,graf] adj & s autografo || tr porre l'autografo su, firmare con firma autografa
automat ['ɔtə ,mæt] s ristorante m self-service a distribuzione automatica
automate ['ɔtə ,met] tr automatizzare
automatic [,ɔtə'mætɪk] adj automatico || s pistola automatica
automat'ic transmis'sion s trasmissione automatica
automation [,ɔtə'meʃən] s automazione
automa·ton [ɔ'tɑmə ,tɑn] s (-tons or -ta [tə]) automa m
automobile [,ɔtəmo'bil] or [,ɔtə'mobil] adj & s automobile f
automobile' show' s salone m dell'automobile
automotive [,ɔtə'motɪv] adj (self-propelled) automotore; automobilistico
autonomous [ɔ'tɑnəməs] adj autonomo
autonomy [ɔ'tɑnəmi] s autonomia
autop·sy ['ɔtɑpsi] s (-sies) autopsia
au'to trans'port rig' s autotreno per trasporto di automobili
autumn ['ɔtəm] s autunno
autumnal [ɔ'tʌmnəl] adj autunnale
auxilia·ry [ɔg'zɪljəri] adj & s (-ries) ausiliare m
avail [ə'vel] s utilità f; of no avail che non serve a nulla || tr servire (with dat); to avail oneself of servirsi di; approfittare di || intr servire
available [ə'veləbəl] adj disponibile; to make available to mettere alla disposizione di
avalanche ['ævə ,læntʃ] or ['ævə ,lɑntʃ] s valanga
avant-garde [əvɑ̃'gard] adj d'avanguardia
avant-gardism [ə'vɑ̃'gardɪzəm] s avanguardismo
avarice ['ævərɪs] s avarizia
avaricious [,ævə'rɪʃəs] adj avaro
avenge [ə'vendʒ] tr vendicare; to avenge oneself on vendicarsi di
avenue ['ævə ,nju] or ['ævənu] s viale m, corso
aver [ə'vʌr] v (pret & pp averred; ger averring) tr asserire, affermare
average ['ævərɪdʒ] adj medio || s media; (naut) avaria; (e.g., of goals) (sports) quoziente m; on the average di media || tr fare la media di; fare . . . di media, e.g., he averages one hundred dollars a week fa cento dollari di media alla settimana
averse [ə'vʌrs] adj avverso
aversion [ə'vʌrʒən] s avversione
avert [ə'vʌrt] tr (to ward off) evitare; (to turn away) distogliere
aviar·y ['ævɪ ,ɛri] s (-ies) aviario, voliera
aviation [,evɪ'eʃən] s aviazione
aviator ['evɪ ,etər] s aviatore m
avid ['ævɪd] adj avido
avidity [ə'vɪdɪti] s avidità f

avocation [,ævə'keʃən] s svago, passatempo
avoid [ə'vɔɪd] tr evitare
avoidable [ə'vɔɪdəbəl] adj evitabile
avow [ə'vau] tr confessare, ammettere
avowal [ə'vau·əl] s confessione, ammissione
await [ə'wet] tr aspettare, attendere
awake [ə'wek] adj sveglio || v (pret & pp awoke [ə'wok] or awaked) tr svegliare || intr svegliarsi
awaken [ə'wekən] tr svegliare || intr svegliarsi
awakening [ə'wekənɪŋ] s risveglio
award [ə'wɔrd] s (prize) premio; (decision by judge) sentenza || tr aggiudicare
aware [ə'wer] adj conscio, consapevole; to become aware of rendersi conto di
awareness [ə'wernɪs] s coscienza
awash [ə'wɑʃ] or [ə'wɔʃ] adj & adv a fior d'acqua
away [ə'we] adj distante, assente || adv lontano; via; continuamente; away back (coll) molto tempo fa; away from lontano da; to do away with disfarsi di, sopprimere; to get away scappare, sfuggire; to go away andarsene; to run away fuggire; to send away mandar via; to take away portar via
awe [ɔ] s estremo rispetto; sacro timore || tr infondere rispetto a; infondere un sacro timore a
aweigh [ə'we] adj (anchor) levato
awesome ['ɔsəm] adj grandioso, imponente
awestruck ['ɔ ,strʌk] adj pieno di sacro timore
awful ['ɔfəl] adj terribile; imponente || adv (coll) terribilmente
awfully ['ɔfəli] adv tremendamente, terribilmente; (coll) molto
awhile [ə'hwaɪl] adv un po', un po' di tempo
awkward ['ɔkwərd] adj (clumsy) goffo, maldestro; (unwieldly) scomodo; (embarrassing) imbarazzante
awl [ɔl] s punteruolo
awning ['ɔnɪŋ] s tenda; (in front of a store) tendone m
A.W.O.L. ['ewɔl] (acronym) or ['e·dʌbəl ,ju'o'el] (letterword) adj (mil) assente al contrappello
awry [ə'raɪ] adv—to go awry andare a capovoscio; to look awry guardare di sbieco
ax or **axe** [æks] s scure f; to have an axe to grind (coll) avere un interesse speciale
axiom ['æksɪ·əm] s assioma m
axiomatic [,æksɪ·ə'mætɪk] adj assiomatico
axis ['æksɪs] s (axes ['æksiz]) asse m
axle ['æksəl] s assale m, asse m
ax'le·tree' s assale m
ay [aɪ] s & adv sì m
Azores [ə'zorz] or ['ezorz] spl Azzorre fpl
azure ['æʒər] or ['eʒər] adj & s azzurro, blu m

B

B, b [bi] *s* seconda lettera dell'alfabeto inglese

baa [ba] *s* belato ‖ *intr* belare

babble ['bæbəl] *s* (*murmuring sound*) mormorio; (*senseless prattle*) balbettio ‖ *tr* (*e.g., a secret*) divulgare ‖ *intr* mormorare; balbettare; (*to talk idly*) parlare a vanvera

babe [beb] *s* bebè *m*, bambino; persona inesperta; (*slang*) ragazza

baboon [bæ'bun] *s* babbuino

ba·by ['bebi] *s* (**-bies**) bebè *m*, neonato; bambino; (*the youngest child*) piccolo ‖ *v* (*pret & pp* **-bied**) *tr* coccolare, ninnare

ba'by car'riage *s* carrozzella

ba'by grand' *s* piano a mezza coda

babyhood ['bebi,hud] *s* infanzia

babyish ['bebi·ɪʃ] *adj* infantile

Babylon ['bæbilən] *or* ['bæbɪ,lɑn] *s* Babilonia

ba'by sit'ter *s* bambinaia ad ore

ba'by teeth' *spl* denti *mpl* di latte

baccalaureate [,bækə'lɔrɪ·ɪt] *s* baccalaureato; servizio religioso prima del baccalaureato

bacchanal ['bækənəl] *adj* bacchico ‖ *s* baccanale *m*; (*person*) ubriacone *m*, bisboccione *m*

bachelor ['bætʃələr] *s* (*unmarried man*) scapolo, celibe *m*; (*holder of bachelor's degree*) diplomato; (*apprentice knight*) baccelliere *m*

bachelorhood ['bætʃələr,hud] *s* celibato

bacil·lus [bə'sɪləs] *s* (**-li** [laɪ]) bacillo

back [bæk] *adj* di dietro, posteriore; arretrato; contrario ‖ *s* dorso, schiena; parte *f* posteriore, didietro; (*of a sheet or coin*) tergo; (*of a knife*) costola; (*of a room*) fondo; (*of a book*) fine *f*; (*of a chair*) schienale *m*; **behind one's back** dietro le spalle di uno; **to turn one's back on** volgere la schiena a ‖ *adv* dietro; indietro; **a few weeks back** alcune settimane fa; **as far back as** sino da; **back of** dietro, dietro a; **to go back on one's word** mancare di parola; **to go back to** ritornare a; **to pay back** ripagare; **to send back** restituire ‖ *tr* appoggiare; far indietreggiare ‖ *intr* indietreggiare; rinculare; **to back down** rinunciarci; **to back off** *or* **out** ritirarsi; **to back up** (*said of a car*) fare marcia indietro

back'ache' *s* mal *m* di schiena

back'bite' *v* (*pret* **-bit**; *pp* **-bitten** *or* **-bit**) *tr* sparlare di ‖ *intr* sparlare

back'bit'er *s* maldicente *mf*

back'board' *s* (*basketball*) tabellone *m*

back'bone' *s* spina dorsale; (*of a book*) costola, dorso; (*fig*) fermezza

back'break'ing *adj* sfiancante

back'door' *adj* segreto, clandestino

back' door' *s* porta di dietro; (*fig*) mezzo clandestino

back'drop' *s* (theat) fondale *m*

backer ['bækər] *s* sostenitore *m*, difensore *m*; (com) finanziatore *m*

back'fire' *s* (*for firefighting*) controfuoco; (aut) ritorno di fiamma ‖ *intr* (aut) avere un ritorno di fiamma; (fig) raggiungere l'effetto opposto

back'ground' *s* fondo, sfondo; (precedenti *mpl;* origine *f*

back'ground mu'sic *s* musica di fondo

backhand ['bæk,hænd] *adj* obliquo ‖ *s* scrittura inclinata a sinistra; (tennis) rovescio

back'hand'ed *adj* obliquo; sarcastico; insincero

backing ['bækɪŋ] *s* appoggio; sostegno; (bb) dorso

back'ing light' *s* (aut) faro retromarcia; (theat) luce *f* per il fondale

back'lash' *s* reazione; contraccolpo; (mach) gioco

back'log' *s* ceppo; (fig) riserva

back' num'ber *s* numero arretrato; (coll) persona all'antica

back' pay' *s* paga arretrata, arretrati *mpl*

back' scratch'er *s* manina per grattare la schiena; (coll) leccapiedi *m*

back' seat' *s* (aut) faro sedile *m* posteriore; (fig) posizione secondaria

back'side' *s* dorso; didietro

back'slide' *v* (*pret & pp* **-slid** [,slɪd]) *intr* ricadere

back'spac'er *s* tasto ritorno

back'spin' *s* effetto

back'stage' *adj* dietro alle quinte ‖ *s* retroscena *m* ‖ *adv* a retroscena, dietro alle quinte

back'stairs' *adj* indiretto, segreto

back' stairs' *spl* scala di servizio

back'stitch' *s* impuntura ‖ *tr & intr* impunturare

back'stroke' *s* (swimming) bracciata sul dorso

back'swept wing' *s* ala a freccia

back' talk' *s* risposta impertinente

back'track' *intr* ritornare sulle proprie tracce; (fig) fare macchina indietro

back'up light' *s* (aut) faro retromarcia

backward ['bækwərd] *adj* ritroso; poco progredito, retrogrado ‖ *adv* a ritroso, all'indietro; verso il passato; alla rovescia; **backward and forward** (coll) completamente, perfettamente; **to go backward and forward** andare avanti e indietro

back'wash' *s* risacca

back'wa'ter *s* gora, ristagno; (fig) eremo

back'woods' *spl* zona boscosa lontana dai centri popolati

back'yard' *s* cortile *m* posteriore

bacon ['bekən] *s* pancetta

bacteria [bæk'tɪrɪ·ə] *spl* batteri *mpl*

bacterial [bæk'tɪrɪ·əl] *adj* batterico

bacteriologist [bæk,tɪrɪ'ɑlədʒɪst] *s* batteriologo

bacteriology [bæk,tɪrɪ'ɑlədʒi] *s* batteriologia

bad [bæd] *adj* (**worse** [wʌrs]; **worst** [wʌrst]) cattivo; (*coin*) falso; (*weather*) brutto; (*debt*) insolvibile; severo ‖ *s* male *m;* **from bad to**

worse da male in peggio || *adv* male;
to be too bad essere peccato; **to feel
bad** esser spiacente; sentirsi male; **to
look bad** aver brutta cera
bad' breath' *s* fiato cattivo
bad' egg' *s* (slang) cattivo soggetto
badge [bædʒ] *s* divisa; decorazione;
simbolo, placca
badger ['bædʒər] *s* tasso || *tr* molestare
badly ['bædlɪ] *adv* male; gravemente;
molto
bad'ly off' *adj* in cattive condizioni
badminton ['bædmɪntən] *s* badminton *m*
baffle ['bæfəl] *s* (mach) deflettore *m*;
(rad) schermo acustico || *tr* frustrare,
confondere
baffling ['bæflɪŋ] *adj* sconcertante
bag [bæg] *s* sacco; borsetta; (*of a
marsupial*) borsa; (hunt) presa; **bag
and baggage** con armi e bagagli; **to
be in the bag** (slang) averlo nel sacco;
to be left holding the bag (coll) es-
sere piantato in asso || *v* (*pret & pp*
bagged; *ger* bagging) *tr* insaccare;
(hunt) pigliare || *intr* (*to hang
loosely*) far pieghe
baggage ['bægɪdʒ] *s* bagaglio
bag'gage car' *s* bagagliaio
bag'gage check' *s* scontrino del bagaglio
bag'gage room' *s* deposito bagagli
bag-gy ['bægi] *adj* (-**gier; -giest**) come
un sacco
bag'pipe' *s* cornamusa, zampogna
bag'pip'er *s* zampognaro
bail [bel] *s* cauzione; libertà provvisoria sotto cauzione; (*bucket*) sassola
|| *tr* liberare sotto cauzione; **to bail
out** (*a boat*) sgottare || *intr*—**to bail
out** (aer) gettarsi col paracadute
bailiwick ['belɪwɪk] *s* (fig) sfera di
competenza
bait [bet] *s* esca; (fig) allettamento || *tr*
adescare; (fig) allettare
baize [bez] *s* panno verde
bake [bek] *tr* cuocere al forno || *intr*
cuocersi al forno; abbrustolirsi
bakelite ['bekə,laɪt] *s* bachelite *f*
baker ['bekər] *s* fornaio, panettiere *m*
bak'er's doz'en *s* tredici per ogni dozzina
baker-y ['bekəri] *s* (-**ies**) panetteria
bak'ing pan' ['bekɪŋ] *s* tortiera
bak'ing pow'der *s* lievito in polvere
bak'ing so'da *s* bicarbonato di soda
balance ['bæləns] *s* (*scales*) bilancia;
equilibrio; armonia; (*of watch*) bilanciere *m*; (*remainder; amount due*)
resto; (*of budget*) pareggio; **in the
balance** in bilico; **to lose one's balance** perdere l'equilibrio; **to strike a
balance** fare il bilancio || *tr* bilan-
ciare, pesare; (com) bilanciare, pa-
reggiare || *intr* bilanciarsi
bal'ance of pay'ments *s* bilancia dei
pagamenti
bal'ance of pow'er *s* equilibrio politico
bal'ance of trade' *s* bilancia commerciale
bal'ance sheet' *s* bilancio
balco-ny ['bælkəni] *s* (-**nies**) balcone
m; (theat) galleria

bald [bɔld] *adj* calvo; (*bare*) nudo;
(*unadorned*) semplice
bald' ea'gle *s* aquila col capo bianco
dell'America del Nord
baldness ['bɔldnɪs] *s* calvizie *f*
baldric ['bɔldrɪk] *s* tracolla
bale [bel] *s* balla; collo || *tr* imballare
baleful ['belfəl] *adj* minaccioso, funesto
balk [bɔk] *s* ostacolare || *intr* inte-
starsi, impuntarsi
Balkan ['bɔlkən] *adj* balcanico || **the
Balkans** i Balcani
balk-y ['bɔki] *adj* (-**ier; -iest**) caparbio,
ostinato
ball [bɔl] *s* palla; pallone *m*; sfera; (*of
the thumb*) polpastrello; (*of wool*)
gomitolo; (*projectile*) palla, pallottola; (*dance*) ballo; **on the ball**
(slang) capace, efficiente; (slang) in
gamba; **to play ball** giocare alla
palla; **to play ball** essere in
cooperazione con || *tr*—**to ball up**
(slang) confondere
ballad ['bæləd] *s* ballata
ball' and chain' *s* palla di piombo;
(fig) impedimento; (slang) moglie *f*
ball'-and-sock'et joint' ['bɔlən'sɑkɪt] *s*
giunto a sfere
ballast ['bæləst] *s* zavorra; (rr) pie-
trisco || *tr* zavorrare
ball' bear'ing *s* cuscinetto a sfere
ballet ['bæle] *s* balletto
ballistic [bə'lɪstɪk] *adj* balistico || **bal-
listics** *ssg* balistica
balloon [bə'lun] *s* pallone *m*; (*for children*) palloncino; (*in comic strip*)
fumetto
ballot ['bælət] *s* scheda elettorale; voto
|| *intr* votare, ballottare
bal'lot box' *s* bussola, urna
ball'play'er *s* giocatore *m* di palla, giocatore *m* di baseball
ball'-point pen' *s* penna a sfera
ball'room' *s* salone *m* da ballo
ballyhoo ['bælɪ,hu] *s* chiasso; monta-
tura || *tr* far chiasso a favore di
balm [bɑm] *s* balsamo
balm-y ['bɑmi] *adj* (-**ier; -iest**) bal-
samico; salubre; (slang) pazzo
balsam ['bɔlsəm] *s* balsamo; (*plant*)
balsamina
Baltic ['bɔltɪk] *adj* baltico
baluster ['bæləstər] *s* balaustro
balustrade [,bæləs'tred] *s* balaustrata
bamboo [bæm'bu] *s* bambù *m*
bamboozle [bæm'buzəl] *tr* ingannare,
raggirare
bamboozler [bæm'buzlər] *s* raggira-
tore *m*
ban [bæn] *s* bando; (*of marriage*) pubblicazione matrimoniale; (eccl) inter-
detto, scomunica || *v* (*pret & pp*
banned; *ger* banning) *tr* proibire
banal ['benəl] or [bə'næl] *adj* banale
banana [bə'nænə] *s* banana, (*tree*)
banano
band [bænd] *s* banda, striscia; (*of thin
cloth*) benda; (*of metal, rubber*) fascia, nastro; (*of hat*) nastro; (mus)
banda, fanfara; **to beat the band**
fortemente; abbondantemente || *tr*
unire || *intr*—**to band together** unire

bandage ['bændɪdʒ] s benda, bendaggio || tr fasciare

bandanna [bæn'dænə] s fazzolettone colorato

band'box' s cappelliera

bandit ['bændɪt] s bandito

band'mas'ter s capomusica m

bandoleer [,bændə'lɪr] s bandoliera

band' saw' s sega a nastro

band'stand' s chiosco della banda

band'wag'on s carrozzone m da circo; **to jump on the bandwagon** prendere le parti del vincitore

baneful ['benfəl] adj nocivo; funesto

bang [bæŋ] s rumore m, scoppio; (coll) energia; (pleasure) (slang) piacere m, eccitazione; **bangs** frangetta || adv tutto d'un colpo || tr sbattere || intr rimbombare || interj bum!

bang'-up' adj (slang) eccellente, di prim'ordine

banish ['bænɪʃ] tr sbandire, mettere al bando

banishment ['bænɪʃmənt] s bando, esilio

banister ['bænɪstər] s balaustra; **banisters** balaustrata

bank [bæŋk] s (of fish; of fog) banco; (of a river) sponda; (for coins) salvadanaio; (financial institution) banca, banco; (of earth, snow) mucchio, banco; (of clouds) cumulo; (aer) inclinazione laterale; (billiards) sponda || tr (a fire) coprire di cenere; (to pile up) ammonticchiare; (a curve) sopraelevare; (money) depositare || intr depositare denaro; (aer) inclinarsi lateralmente; **to bank on** (coll) contare su (di)

bank'book' s libretto bancario, libretto di deposito

banker ['bæŋkər] s banchiere m

banking ['bæŋkɪŋ] adj bancario || s attività bancaria; professione di banchiere

bank' note' s biglietto di banca

bank'roll' s rotolo di carta moneta; soldi mpl || tr (slang) finanziare

bankrupt ['bæŋkrʌpt] adj & s fallito; **to go bankrupt** andare in fallimento || tr dichiarare in fallimento; far fallire

bankrupt·cy ['bæŋkrʌptsi] s (-cies) fallimento

banner ['bænər] adj importante || s bandiera, stendardo; (journ) titolo in grassetto

banns [bænz] spl bandi mpl matrimoniali

banquet ['bæŋkwɪt] s banchetto || tr dar un banchetto a || intr banchettare

bantam ['bæntəm] adj piccolo || s pollo nano

ban'tam-weight' s peso gallo, bantam m

banter ['bæntər] s scherzo, facezia || intr scherzare, celiare

baptism ['bæptɪzəm] s battesimo

baptismal [bæp'tɪzməl] adj battesimale; (certificate) di battesimo

Baptist ['bæptɪst] adj & s battista mf

baptister·y ['bæptɪstəri] s (-ies) battistero

baptize [bæp'taɪz] or ['bæptaɪz] tr battezzare

bar [bɑr] s barra, sbarra; (of soap) saponetta; (of chocolate) tavoletta; (of sand) banco; (obstacle) barriera; bar m; (of public opinion) tribunale m; (legal profession) avvocatura; (of door or window) spranga; (of lead) (typ) lingotto; (mus) battuta; **behind bars** in guardina; **to be admitted to the bar** diventare avvocato; **to tend bar** fare il barista || prep eccetto, salvo; **bar none** senza eccezione || v (pret & pp **barred**; ger **barring**) tr sbarrare; sprangare; bloccare; escludere

bar' associa'tion s associazione dell'ordine degli avvocati

barb [bɑrb] s (of arrow) barbiglio

barbarian [bɑr'bɛri·ən] s barbaro

barbaric [bɑr'bærɪk] adj barbaro

barbarism ['bɑrbə,rɪzəm] s barbarismo

barbari·ty [bɑr'bærɪti] s (-ties) barbarie f

barbarous ['bɑrbərəs] adj barbaro, crudele

Bar'bary ape' ['bɑrbəri] s bertuccia

barbecue ['bɑrbɪ,kju] s arrosto allo spiedo || tr arrostire allo spiedo

barbed [bɑrbd] adj irto di punte; mordace, pungente

barbed' wire' s filo spinato

barber ['bɑrbər] s barbiere m; (who cuts and styles hair) parrucchiere m

bar'ber-shop' s barbieria, negozio di barbiere; negozio di parrucchiere

barbiturate [bɑr'bɪtʃə,ret] s barbiturato, barbiturico

bard [bɑrd] s bardo, poeta m

bare [bɛr] adj nudo; (head) a capo scoperto; (unconcealed) palese; (empty) vuoto; (wire) senza isolante; (unadorned) semplice; **to lay bare** mettere a nudo || tr denudare, scoprire

bare'back' adj & adv senza sella

barefaced ['bɛr,fest] adj impudente, sfacciato, spudorato

bare'foot' adj scalzo

barehanded ['bɛr,hændɪd] adj & adv a mani nude

bareheaded ['bɛr,hɛdɪd] adj a capo scoperto

barelegged ['bɛr,lɛgɪd] adj a gambe nude

barely ['bɛrli] adv appena, soltanto

bargain ['bɑrgɪn] s affare m, buon affare m; contrattazione; **at a bargain** a buon prezzo; **into the bargain** in soprappiù || intr—**to bargain away** vendere a buonissimo prezzo || intr contrattare, mercanteggiare; **to bargain for** aspettarsi

bar'gain sale' s vendita sottoprezzo

barge [bɑrdʒ] s barcone m, chiatta || intr—**to barge in** entrare senza chiedere permesso

baritone ['bærɪ,ton] adj di baritono || s baritono m

barium ['bɛri·əm] s bario

bark [bɑrk] s corteccia, scorza; (of dog) abbaiamento, latrato || tr (e.g., *insults*) lanciare ‖ *intr* abbaiare, latrare

bar'keep'er s barista *mf*

barker ['barkər] s banditore *m*, imbonitore *m*

barley ['barlɪ] s orzo

bar' mag'net s calamita a forma di barra allungata

bar'maid' s barista *f*

bar'man s (**-men**) barista *m*

barn [barn] s granaio; (*for hay*) fienile *m*; (*for livestock*) stalla

barnacle ['barnəkəl] s cirripede *m*

barn' owl' s civetta

barn'yard' s bassacorte *f*, aia

barn'yard fowl' s animale *m* da cortile ‖ *spl* animali *mpl* da cortile

barometer [bə'ramɪtər] s barometro

baron ['bærən] s barone *m*; (*industrialist*) cavaliere *m* d'industria

baroness ['bærənɪs] s baronessa

baroque [bə'rok] *adj* & s barocco

bar'rack-room' *adj* da caserma ‖ s camerata

barracks ['bærəks] *spl* caserma; camerata

barrage [bə'raʒ] s (*mil*) fuoco di sbarramento

barrel ['bærəl] s barile *m*, botte *f*; (*of gun*) canna; (*mach*) cilindro

bar'rel or'gan s organetto di Barberia

barren ['bærən] *adj* sterile; (*without vegetation*) brullo

barricade [,bærɪ'ked] s barricata ‖ *tr* barricare

barrier ['bærɪ-ər] s barriera

bar'rier reef' s barriera corallina

barring ['barɪŋ] *prep* eccetto, salvo

barrister ['bærɪstər] s (Brit) avvocato

bar'room' s bar *m*, cantina, mescita

bar'tend'er s barista, *mf*, barman *m*

barter ['bartər] s baratto ‖ *tr* & *intr* barattare, permutare

basalt [bə'sɔlt] s basalto

base [bes] *adj* basale; basso; servile; (*morally low*) turpe; (*metal*) vile, non prezioso ‖ s base *f*; (*in children's games*) tana; (*of a word*) radice *f* basale ‖ *tr* basare

base'ball' s baseball *m*, pallabase *f*

base'board' s basamento; (*of wall*) zoccolo

Basel ['bazəl] s Basilea

baseless ['beslɪs] *adj* infondato

basement ['besmənt] s scantinato, piano interrato

bashful ['bæʃfəl] *adj* timido

basic ['besɪk] *adj* fondamentale; (*chem*) basico

ba'sic commod'ities *spl* articoli *mpl* di prima necessità

basilica [bə'sɪlɪkə] s basilica

basin ['besɪn] s catino; vasca; (*of balance*) piatto; (*of river*) bacino; (*of harbor*) darsena

ba·sis ['besɪs] s (**-ses** [siz]) base *f*

bask [bæsk] *or* [bask] *intr* crogiolarsi

basket ['bæskɪt] *or* ['baskɪt] s cesta; (*sports*) cesto

bas'ket·ball' s pallacanestro *f*

Basque [bæsk] *adj* & s basco

bas-relief [,barɪ'lif] *or* [,bærɪ'lif] s bassorilievo

bass [bes] *adj* & s (mus) basso ‖ [bæs] s (ichth) pesce persico

bass' drum' s grancassa

bass' horn' s bassotuba *m*

bassinet ['bæsə,net] *or* [,bæsə'net] s culla a forma di cesto; carrozzina a forma di cesto

bas·so ['bæso] *or* ['baso] s (**-sos** *or* **-si** [si]) basso

bassoon [bə'sun] s fagotto

bass' vi'ol ['vaɪ-əl] s contrabbasso

bastard ['bæstərd] *adj* & s bastardo

baste [best] *tr* (*to sew*) imbastire; (*meat*) inumidire con acqua o grasso

bastion ['bæstʃən] *or* ['bæstɪ-ən] s bastione *m*

bat [bæt] s mazza; (*in cricket*) maglio; (coll) colpo; (zool) pipistrello ‖ *v* (*pret* & *pp* **batted**; *ger* **batting**) *tr* colpire con la mazza; **without batting an eye** (coll) senza batter ciglio

batch [bætʃ] s (*of bread*) infornata; gruppo, numero

bath [bæθ] *or* [baθ] s bagno; **to take a bath** fare il bagno

bathe [beð] *tr* bagnare, lavare ‖ *intr* bagnarsi, fare il bagno

bather ['beðər] s bagnante *mf*

bath'house' s (*individual*) cabina; spogliatoio

bath'ing beau'ty s bellezza in costume da bagno

bath'ing cap' s cuffia da bagno

bath'ing resort' s stazione balneare

bath'ing suit' s costume *m* da bagno

bath'ing trunks' *spl* mutandine *fpl* da bagno

bath'robe' s accappatoio

bath'room' s stanza da bagno

bath' salts' *spl* sali *mpl* da bagno

bath'tub' s bagno, vasca da bagno

baton [bæ'tan] *or* ['bætən] s bastone *m*; (mus) bacchetta

battalion [bə'tæljən] s battaglione *m*

batten ['bætən] *tr* assicella; piccola traversa; (naut) bietta ‖ *tr*—**to batten down the hatches** chiudere ermeticamente i boccaporti

batter ['bætər] s pasta, farina pastosa; (baseball) battitore *m* ‖ *tr* battere, tempestare di colpi; (*to wear out*) logorare

bat'tering ram' s ariete *m*

batter·y ['bætərɪ] s (**-ies**) (*primary cell*) pila; (*secondary cell*) accumulatore *m*; (*group of batteries*) batteria; (law) assalto; (mil & mus) batteria

battle ['bætəl] s battaglia; **to do battle** dar battaglia ‖ *tr* combattere contro ‖ *intr* combattere

bat'tle cry' s grido di guerra

battledore ['bætəl,dor] s racchetta; **battledore and shuttlecock** gioco del volano

bat'tle-field' s campo di battaglia

bat'tle-front' s fronte *m* di combattimento

battlement ['bætəlmənt] s merlatura

bat'tle roy'al s baruffa generale, zuffa generale

bat'tle-ship' s corazzata

battue [bæ'tu] *or* [bæ'tju] s (hunt) battuta

bat·ty [ˈbæti] *adj* (**-tier; -tiest**) (slang) pazzo, eccentrico

bauble [ˈbɔbəl] *s* bazzecola, gingillo

Bavaria [bəˈveri·ə] *s* la Baviera

Bavarian [bəˈveri·ən] *adj & s* bavarese *mf*

bawd [bɔd] *s* ruffiano; ruffiana

bawd·y [ˈbɔdi] *adj* (**-ier; -iest**) indecente, osceno

bawd'y·house' *s* casa di malaffare

bawl [bɔl] *s* grido; pianto || *tr*—to bawl out (slang) fare una ramanzina a || *intr* strillare; (coll) piangere

bay [be] *adj* baio || *s* baia; vano, alcova; (*recess in wall*) apertura nel muro; finestra sporgente; (*of dog*) latrato; cavallo baio; (bot) lauro; **at bay** in una posizione disperata || *intr* latrare

bayonet [ˈbe·ənɪt] *s* baionetta || *tr* dare baionettate a || *intr* dare baionettate

bay' win'dow *s* finestra sporgente; (slang) pancia

bazooka [bəˈzukə] *s* bazooka *m*

be [bi] *v* (*pres* **am** [æm], **is** [ɪz], **are** [ɑr]; *pret* **was** |wɑz| *or* |wʌz|, **were** |wʌr|; *pp* **been** |bɪn|) *intr* essere; fare, e.g., **to be a mason** fare il muratore; fare, e.g., **3 times 3 is 9** tre volte tre fa nove; **be as it may be** comunque sia; **here is** *or* **here are** ecco; **there are** ci sono; **there is** c'è; **to be** futuro, e.g., **my wife to be** la mia futura sposa; **to be ashamed** aver vergogna; **to be cold** aver freddo; **to be hot** aver caldo; **to be hungry** aver fame; **to be in** stare a casa; **to be in a hurry** aver fretta; **to be in with** (coll) essere amico intimo di; **to be off** andarsene; **to be out** essere fuori; **to be out of** (coll) non aver più; **to be right** aver ragione; **to be sleepy** aver sonno; **to be thirsty** avere sete; **to be up** essere alzato; **to be up to** essere all'altezza di; toccare, e.g., **it's up to you** tocca a Lei; **to be warm** avere caldo; **to be wrong** avere torto; sbagliarsi; **to be . . . years old** avere . . . anni || *aux* stare, e.g., **to be waiting** stare aspettando; essere, e.g., **the murder has been committed** l'omicidio è stato commesso; dovere, e.g., **he is to clean the stables tomorrow** domani deve pulire la stalla || *impers* essere, e.g., **it is necessary** è necessario; fare, e.g., **it is cold** fa freddo; **it is hot** fa caldo

beach [bitʃ] *s* spiaggia || *tr* (*a boat*) arenare || *intr* arenarsi

beach'comb' *intr* raccogliere relitti sulla spiaggia

beach'comb'er *s* girellone *m* di spiaggia

beach'head' *s* testa di sbarco

beach' robe' *s* accappatoio

beach' shoe' *s* sandalo da spiaggia

beach' umbrel'la *s* ombrellone *m* da spiaggia

beacon [ˈbikən] *s* faro || *tr* rischiarare; fare da guida a || *intr* brillare

bead [bid] *s* perlina; grano, chicco; (*drop*) goccia; **beads** (*in a necklace or rosary*) conterie *fpl*; **to count one's beads** recitare il rosario

beagle [ˈbigəl] *s* segugio, bracco

beak [bik] *s* becco; promontorio

beam [bim] *s* trave *f*; (*of balance*) braccio; (*of light*) raggio; (*ship's breadth*) larghezza; (*smile*) sorriso; (*radio signal*) fascio direttore; (*course indicated by radio beam*) aerovia; (naut) traverso || *tr* (*a radio signal*) dirigere; (*e.g., light*) irraggiare || *intr* raggiare

bean [bin] *s* fagiolo; (*of coffee*) chicco; (slang) testa

beaner·y [ˈbinəri] *s* (**-ies**) (slang) gargotta, taverna di secondo ordine

bean'pole' *s* puntello per i fagioli; (coll) palo del telegrafo

bear [bɛr] *s* orso; (astr) orsa; (com) ribassista *m*, giocatore *m* al ribasso || *v* (*pret* **bore** [bor]; *pp* **borne** [born]) *tr* (*to carry*) portare; (*to give birth to*) partorire; (*to sustain*) sostenere; (*to withstand*) sopportare; (*a grudge*) serbare; (*in mind*) tenere; (*interest*) produrre; (*to pay*) pagare; **to bear the date** aver la data; **to bear out** confermare; **to bear witness** testimoniare || *intr* (*to be productive*) fruttificare; (*to move*) dirigersi; (*to be oppressive*) fare pressione; **to bear down on** fare pressione su; avvicinarsi a; **to bear up** resistere; **to bear with** tollerare

bearable [ˈbɛrəbəl] *adj* tollerabile

beard [bɪrd] *s* barba; (*e.g., in wheat*) arista

bearded *adj* barbuto

beardless [ˈbɪrdlɪs] *adj* imberbe

bearer [ˈbɛrər] *s* portatore *m*

bearing [ˈbɛrɪŋ] *s* portamento; relazione; importanza; (mach) bronzina, cuscinetto; **bearings** orientamento; **to lose one's bearings** perdere la bussola; perdere l'orientamento

bearish [ˈbɛrɪʃ] *adj* (*like a bear*) orsino; (*e.g., prices*) in ribasso; (*market*) al ribasso; (*speculator*) ribassista

bear'skin' *s* pelle *f* dell'orso; (mil) colbacco

beast [bist] *s* bestia

beast·ly [ˈbistli] *adj* (**-lier; -liest**) bestiale || *adv* (coll) malissimo

beast' of bur'den *s* bestia da soma

beast' of prey' *s* animale *m* da rapina

beat [bit] *s* (*of heart*) battito; (*of policeman*) ronda; (*stroke*) colpo; (*habitual route*) cammino battuto; (mus) tempo; (phys) battimento || *v* (*pret* **beat**; *pp* **beat** *or* **beaten**) *tr* battere; percuotere; (*eggs*) frullare; (*to whip*) frustare; (coll) confondere; **beat it!** (slang) vattene!; **to beat a retreat** battere in ritirata; **to beat back** respingere; **to beat down** sopprimere; **to beat off** respingere; **to beat up** (*eggs*) frullare; (*people*) dargliene a || *intr* battere; pulsare; **to beat around the bush** (coll) menare il can per l'aia

beat'en path' [ˈbitən] *s* cammino battuto

beater [ˈbitər] *s* frullino

beati·fy [biˈæti‚faɪ] *v* (*pret & pp* **-fied**) *tr* beatificare

beating ['bitɪŋ] s battitura; (*whipping*) frustatura; (*throbbing*) pulsazione, battito; (*defeat*) sconfitta

beau [bo] s (**beaus** or **beaux** [boz]) (*dandy*) bellimbusto; (*girl's sweetheart*) spasimante m

beautician [bju'tɪ/ən] s estetista mf

beautiful ['bjutɪfəl] adj bello

beauti-fy ['bjutɪ,faɪ] v (pret & pp -fied) tr abbellire

beau-ty ['bjutɪ] s (-ties) bellezza

beau'ty con'test s concorso di bellezza

beau'ty par'lor s istituto di bellezza

beau'ty sleep' s primo sonno

beau'ty spot' s neo; posto pittoresco

beaver ['bivər] s castoro; pelle f di castoro; cappello a cilindro

because [bɪ'kɔz] conj perchè; **because of** a causa di

beck [bɛk] s gesto; **at the beck and call of** agli ordini di

beckon ['bɛkən] s gesto || tr fare gesto a || intr fare gesto

becloud [bɪ'klaʊd] tr annebbiare; oscurare

be-come [bɪ'kʌm] v (pret -came; pp -come) tr convenire a; stare bene a, e.g., **this hat becomes you** questo cappello Le sta bene || intr diventare; farsi; convertirsi, e.g., **water became wine** l'acqua si convertì in vino; succedere, e.g., **what became of my coat?** che è successo del mio pastrano?; essere, e.g., **what will become of me?** che sarà di me?; **to become accustomed** abituarsi; **to become angry** entrare in collera; **to become crazy** impazzire; **to become ill** ammalarsi

becoming [bɪ'kʌmɪŋ] adj conveniente; appropriato; acconcio; **this is very becoming to you** questo Le sta molto bene

bed [bɛd] s letto; (*layer*) strato; giacimento; **to go to bed** andare a letto; **to take to one's bed** mettersi a letto

bed' and board' s vitto e alloggio; pensione completa

bed'bug' s cimice f

bed'clothes' spl lenzuola fpl e coperte fpl, biancheria da letto

bed'cov'er s coperta da letto

bedding ['bedɪŋ] s lenzuola fpl e coperte fpl; (*litter*) lettiera; (*foundation*) fondamenta fpl

bedeck [bɪ'dɛk] tr ornare, adornare

bedev-il [bɪ'dɛvɪl] v (pret & pp -iled or -illed; ger -iling or -illing) tr tormentare diabolicamente; confondere

bed'fast' adj confinato a letto

bed'fel'low s compagno di letto; compagno di stanza; compagno

bedlam ['bedləm] s manicomio; pandemonio

bed' lin'en s biancheria da letto

bed'pan' s padella

bedridden ['bed,rɪdən] adj degente a letto

bed'room' s stanza da letto, camera da letto

bed'room slip'per s babbuccia, pantofola

bed'side' s capezzale m

bed'side man'ner s maniera di fare coi pazienti

bed'sore' s piaga da decubito

bed'spread' s coperta da letto

bed'spring' s rete f del letto; molla del letto

bed'stead' s fusto del letto

bed'tick' s traliccio

bed'time' s ora di coricarsi

bed'warm'er s scaldaletto

bee [bi] s ape f

beech [bit/] s faggio

beech'nut' s faggiola

beef [bif] s bue m, manzo; carne f di manzo; (*coll*) forza; (*slang*) lamentela || tr—**to beef up** (coll) rinforzare || intr (slang) lamentarsi

beef' cat'tle s manzi mpl da carne

beef'steak' s bistecca

beef' stew' s stufato di manzo

bee'hive' s alveare m

bee'keep'er s apicoltore m

bee'line' s—**to make a beeline for** (coll) andare direttamente verso

beer [bɪr] s birra

beer' saloon' s birreria

beeswax ['biz,wæks] s cera d'api

beet [bit] s barbabietola

beetle ['bital] adj sporgente, folto || s scarafaggio

bee'tle-browed' adj dalle sopracciglia folte

beet' su'gar s zucchero di barbabietola

be-fall [bɪ'fɔl] v (pret -fell ['fel]; pp -fallen ['fɔlən]) tr succedere a || intr succedere

befitting [bɪ'fɪtɪŋ] adj appropriato

before [bɪ'for] adv prima, prima d'ora || prep (in time) prima di; (in place) dinnanzi a, davanti a; **before Christ** avanti Cristo || conj prima che

before'hand' adv in anticipo; precedentemente

befriend [bɪ'frɛnd] tr diventare amico di, proteggere, favorire; aiutare

befuddle [bɪ'fʌdəl] tr confondere

beg [bɛg] v (pret & pp begged; ger begging) tr chiedere; implorare; (*alms*) mendicare; **I beg your pardon** Le chiedo scusa; **to beg s.o. for s.th** chiedere qlco a qlcu || intr chiedere la carità; **to beg for** sollecitare; **to beg off** scusarsi; **to go begging** rimanere invenduto

be-get [bɪ'gɛt] v (pret -got ['gɑt]; pp -gotten or -got; ger -getting) tr generare

beggar ['bɛgər] s accattone m, mendicante m

be-gin [bɪ'gɪn] v (pret -gan ['gæn]; pp -gun ['gʌn]; ger -ginning) tr & intr cominciare, iniziare; **beginning with** a partire da; **to begin with** per cominciare

beginner [bɪ'gɪnər] s principiante mf

beginning [bɪ'gɪnɪŋ] s inizio, origine f, principio, esordio

begrudge [bɪ'grʌdʒ] tr invidiare; concedere con riluttanza

beguile [bɪ'gaɪl] tr ingannare; sedurre; (*to delight*) divertire

behalf [bɪ'hæf] or [bɪ'hɑf] s—**on behalf of** nell'interesse di; a nome di

behave [bɪ'hev] *intr* comportarsi; comportarsi bene

behavior [bɪ'hevjər] *s* comportamento, condotta; funzionamento

behead [bɪ'hed] *tr* decapitare

behest [bɪ'hest] *s* ordine *m*, comando

behind [bɪ'haɪnd] *s* didietro; (slang) sedere *m* || *adv* dietro; (*in arrears*) in arretrato; **from behind** dal didietro || *prep* dietro a, dietro di; **behind time** in ritardo

be·hold [bɪ'hold] *v* (*pret & pp* **-held** ['held]) *tr* contemplare; ammirare || *interj* guarda!

behoove [bɪ'huv] *impers*—**it behooves him to** gli conviene di

being ['bi·ɪŋ] *adj* esistente; **for the time being** per ora || *s* essere *m*, ente *m*

belabor [bɪ'lebər] *tr* attaccare; (fig) ribattere, confutare; (fig) insistere su

belated [bɪ'letɪd] *adj* tardivo

belch [belt/] *s* rutto || *tr* eruttare, vomitare || *intr* ruttare

beleaguer [bɪ'ligər] *tr* assediare

bel·fry ['belfrɪ] *s* (**-fries**) (*tower*) campanile *m*; (*site of bell*) cella campanaria; (slang) testa

Belgian ['beldʒən] *adj & s* belga *mf*

Belgium ['beldʒəm] *s* il Belgio

be·lie [bɪ'laɪ] *v* (*pret & pp* **-lied** ['laɪd]; *ger* **-lying** ['laɪ·ɪŋ]) *tr* (*to misrepresent*) tradire; (*to prove false*) smentire

belief [bɪ'lif] *s* fede *f*, credenza

believable [bɪ'livəbəl] *adj* credibile

believe [bɪ'liv] *tr* credere || *intr* credere, aver fede; **to believe in** credere in

believer [bɪ'livər] *s* credente *mf*

belittle [bɪ'lɪtəl] *tr* menomare

bell [bel] *s* campana; (*for a door*) campanello; (*sound*) rintocco; (*on cattle*) campanaccio; (*of deer*) bramito || *intr* bramire

belladonna [,belə'dɑnə] *s* belladonna

bell'-bot'tom *adj* a campana

bell'boy' *s* cameriere *m*, ragazzo

belle [bel] *s* bella

belles-lettres [,bel'letrə] *spl* belle lettere

bell' glass' *s* campana di vetro

bell'hop' *s* cameriere *m*, ragazzo

bellicose ['belɪ,kos] *adj* bellicoso

belligerent [bə'lɪdʒərənt] *adj & s* belligerante *m*

bellow ['belo] *s* muggito; **bellows** mantice *m*; (*of camera*) soffietto || *tr* gridare || *intr* muggire

bell' ring'er ['rɪŋər] *s* campanaro

bellwether ['bel,weðər] *s* pecora guida

bel·ly ['belɪ] *s* (**-lies**) ventre *m*, pancia || *v* (*pret & pp* **-lied**) *intr* far pancia

bel'ly·ache' *s* (coll) mal *m* di pancia || *intr* (slang) lamentarsi

bel'ly·but'ton *s* (coll) ombelico

bel'ly dance' *s* (coll) danza del ventre

bel'ly flop' *s* panciata

bellyful ['belɪ,ful] *s*—**to have a bellyful** (slang) averne fino agli occhi

bel'ly·land' *intr* (aer) atterrare sul ventre

belong [bɪ'lɔŋ] or [bɪ'lɑŋ] *intr* appartenere; stare bene, e.g., **this chair belongs in this room** questa sedia sta bene in questa stanza

belongings [bɪ'lɔŋɪŋz] or [bɪ'lɑŋɪŋz] *spl* effetti *mpl* personali

beloved [bɪ'lʌvɪd] or [bɪ'lʌvd] *adj & s* diletto, amato

below [bɪ'lo] *adv* sotto; più sotto; sotto zero, e.g., **ten below** dieci gradi sotto zero || *prep* sotto, sotto di

belt [belt] *s* cintura, cinghia; (mach) nastro; (mil) cinturone *m*; (geog) fascia, zona; **to tighten one's belt** far cintura || *tr* cingere; (slang) staffilare

belt'ed tire' *s* copertone cinturato

belt' line' *s* linea di circonvallazione

beltway ['belt,we] *s* raccordo anulare

bemoan [bɪ'mon] *tr* lamentare; compiangere

bench [bent/] *s* banco, panca; tribunale *m*; (mach) banco di prova; **to be on the bench** (law) essere giudice

bend [bend] *s* curva; (*e.g., of pipe*) gomito, angolo || *v* (*pret & pp* **bent** [bent]) *tr* curvare; piegare; far piegare || *intr* deviare; piegare, piegarsi; **to bend over** inchinarsi

beneath [bɪ'niθ] *adv* sotto; più sotto || *prep* sotto, sotto di

benediction [,benɪ'dɪk/ən] *s* benedizione

benefactor ['benɪ,fæktər] or [,benɪ-'fæktər] *s* benefattore *m*

benefactress ['benɪ,fæktrɪs] or [,benɪ-'fæktrɪs] *s* benefattrice *f*

beneficence [bɪ'nefɪsəns] *s* beneficenza

beneficent [bɪ'nefɪsənt] *adj* caritatevole; benefico

beneficial [,benɪ'fɪ/əl] *adj* benefico

beneficiar·y [,benɪ'fɪ/ɪ,erɪ] *s* (**-ies**) beneficiario

benefit ['benɪfɪt] *s* beneficio; festa di beneficenza; **for the benefit of** a beneficio di || *tr & intr* beneficiare

benevolence [bɪ'nevələns] *s* benevolenza; carità *f*

benevolent [bɪ'nevələnt] *adj* benevolo; (*institution*) benefico

benign [bɪ'naɪn] *adj* benigno

bent [bent] *adj* curvo; **bent on** deciso a || *s* curva; tendenza, propensità *f*

Benzedrine ['benzɪ,drin] (trademark) *s* benzedrina

benzene ['benzin] *s* benzolo

benzine [ben'zin] *s* benzina

bequeath [bɪ'kwiθ] or [bɪ'kwið] *tr* legare, lasciare in eredità

bequest [bɪ'kwest] *s* legato, lascito

berate [bɪ'ret] *tr* redarguire

be·reave [bɪ'riv] *v* (*pret & pp* **-reaved** or **-reft** ['reft]) *tr* spogliare

bereavement [bɪ'rivmənt] *s* lutto, perdita

beret [bə're] or ['bere] *s* berretto

Berlin [bər'lɪn] *adj* berlinese || *s* Berlino

Berliner [bər'lɪnər] *s* berlinese *mf*

Bermuda [bər'mjudə] *s* le Bermude

ber·ry ['berɪ] *s* (**-ries**) (*dry seed*) chicco; (*fruit*) bacca

berserk [bʌr'sʌrk] *adj* infuriato || *adv* —**to go berserk** impazzire

berth [bʌrθ] *s (for a ship)* posto di ormeggio; *(bed)* cuccetta; *(coll)* posto

beryllium [bə'rɪlɪ-əm] *s* berillio

be·seech [bɪ'sitʃ] *v (pret & pp -**sought** ['sɔt] or -**seeched**) tr* supplicare

be·set [bɪ'sɛt] *v (pret & pp -***set**; ger -**setting**) tr* assediare, circondare; *(e.g., with problems)* assillare

beside [bɪ'saɪd] *adv* oltre, inoltre || *prep* vicino a; in confronto di; oltre a; **beside oneself** fuori di sé; **beside the point** fuori del seminato

besides [bɪ'saɪdz] *adv* inoltre; d'altronde || *prep* oltre a

besiege [bɪ'sidʒ] *tr* assediare; *(with questions)* bombardare

besmear [bɪ'smɪr] *tr* imbrattare, sgorbiare; sporcare

besmirch [bɪ'smʌrtʃ] *tr* insudiciare

bespatter [bɪ'spætər] *tr* inzaccherare

be·speak [bɪ'spik] *v (-***spoke** ['spok]; -**spoken**) tr* chiedere anticipatamente a; *(to show)* dimostrare

best [bɛst] *adj super* (il) migliore; ottimo || *s* meglio; **at best** nella miglior delle ipotesi; **to do one's best** fare del proprio meglio; **to get the best of** avere la meglio di; **to make the best of** adattarsi a || *adv super* meglio; **had best, e.g., I had best** dovrei || *tr* battere, riuscire superiore a

bestial ['bɛstjəl] or ['bɛstʃəl] *adj* bestiale

be·stir [bɪ'stʌr] *v (pret & pp -***stirred**; ger -**stirring**) tr* eccitare; **to bestir oneself** darsi da fare

best' man' *s* testimone *m* di nozze

bestow [bɪ'sto] *tr* accordare; conferire

best' sell'er *s* best-seller *m*

bet [bɛt] *s* scommessa || *v (pret & pp* **bet** or **betted**; ger **betting**) tr & intr* scommettere; **I bet** ci scommetto; **you bet** (coll) evidentemente

be·take [bɪ'tek] *v (pret -***took** ['tuk]; *pp* -**taken**) tr*—**to betake oneself** andare, dirigersi

be·think [bɪ'θɪŋk] *v (pret & pp -***thought** ['θɔt]) tr* **to bethink oneself** pensare; ricordarsi

Bethlehem ['bɛθlɪ-əm] or ['bɛθlɪ‚hɛm] *s* Betlemme *f*

betide [bɪ'taɪd] *tr* accadere a || *intr* accadere

betoken [bɪ'tokən] *tr* indicare, presagire

betray [bɪ'tre] *tr* tradire, ingannare; *(to reveal)* rivelare

betroth [bɪ'troð] or [bɪ'troθ] *tr* promettere in matrimonio a

betrothal [bɪ'troðəl] or [bɪ'troθəl] *s* fidanzamento

betrothed [bɪ'troðd] or [bɪ'troθt] *adj* fidanzato || *s* promesso sposo, fidanzato

better ['bɛtər] *adj comp* migliore; **to grow better** migliorare || *s*—**betters** superiori *mpl*; ottimati *mpl*; **to get the better of** avere la meglio di || *adv* meglio; **had better** dovere, e.g., **I had**

better dovrei; **to be better off** stare meglio; **to think better of** riconsiderare; **you ought to know better** dovrebbe vergognarsi || *tr* sorpassare; migliorare; **to better oneself** migliorare la propria situazione

bet'ter half' *s* metà *f*

betterment ['bɛtərmənt] *s* miglioramento

bettor ['bɛtər] *s* scommettitore *m*

between [bɪ'twin] *adv* in mezzo; **in between** in mezzo, fra i piedi || *prep* fra, tra

between'-decks' *s* interponte *m*

bev·el ['bɛvəl] *s (instrument)* falsa squadra; *(sloping part)* augnatura || *v (pret & pp* **-eled** or **-elled**; ger **-eling** or **-elling**) tr* augnare

beverage ['bɛvərɪdʒ] *s* bevanda

bev·y ['bɛvi] *s (-***ies**) (of women)* gruppo; *(of birds)* stormo

bewail [bɪ'wel] *tr* lamentare

beware [bɪ'wer] *tr* fare attenzione a, guardarsi da || *intr* fare attenzione, guardarsi

bewilder [bɪ'wɪldər] *tr* lasciar perplesso, confondere, disorientare

bewilderment [bɪ'wɪldərmənt] *s* perplessità *f*, disorientamento

bewitch [bɪ'wɪtʃ] *tr* stregare

beyond [bɪ'jɑnd] *s*—**the beyond** l'aldilà *m* || *adv* più lontano || *prep* al di là di; oltre a; più tardi di; **beyond a doubt** fuori dubbio; **beyond repair** irreparabile

bias ['baɪ·əs] *s* linea diagonale; pregiudizio; **on the bias** diagonalmente || *tr* prevenire

bib [bɪb] *s* bavaglino

Bible ['baɪbəl] *s* Bibbia

Biblical ['bɪblɪkəl] *adj* biblico

bibliogra·phy [‚bɪblɪ'ɑgrəfi] *s (-***phies**)* bibliografia

bibliophile ['bɪblɪ-ə‚faɪl] *s* bibliofilo

bicarbonate [baɪ'kɑrbə‚net] *s* bicarbonato

biceps ['baɪsɛps] *s* bicipite *m*

bicker ['bɪkər] *s* bisticcio, disputa || *intr* bisticciare, disputare

bicycle ['baɪsɪkəl] *s* bicicletta

bid [bɪd] *s* offerta; *(cards)* dichiarazione; *(coll)* invito || *v (pret* **bade** [bæd] or **bid**; *pp* **bidden** ['bɪdən] or **bid**; ger **bidding**) tr & intr* offrire; comandare; *(cards)* dichiarare

bidder ['bɪdər] *s* offerente *mf*; *(cards)* dichiarante *mf*; **the highest bidder** il miglior offerente

bidding ['bɪdɪŋ] *s* ordine *m*; offerte *fpl*; *(cards)* dichiarazione

bide [baɪd] *tr*—**to bide one's time** attendere l'ora propizia

biennial [baɪ'ɛnɪ·əl] *adj* biennale

bier [bɪr] *s* catafalco

bifocal [baɪ'fokəl] *adj* bifocale || **bifocals** *spl* occhiali *mpl* bifocali

big [bɪg] *adj (***bigger**; **biggest**)* grande; *(coll)* importante; *(coll)* stravagante; **big with child** incinta || *adv*—**to talk big** (coll) parlare con iattanza

bigamist ['bɪgəmɪst] *s* bigamo

bigamous ['bɪgəməs] *adj* bigamo

big-bellied ['bɪg ˌbelid] adj panciuto

Big' Dip'per s Gran Carro

big' game' s caccia grossa

big-hearted ['bɪg ˌhɑrtɪd] adj magnanimo, generoso

big' mouth' s (slang) sbraitone m

bigot ['bɪgət] s bigotto, bacchettone m

bigoted ['bɪgətɪd] adj (in religion) bigotto; intransigente

bigot·ry ['bɪgətri] s (-ries) bigottismo; intransigenza

big' shot' s (slang) pezzo grosso, (un) qualcuno

big' slam' s (bridge) grande slam m

big'-time op'erator s (slang) grosso trafficante

big' toe' s alluce m

big' wheel' s (slang) pezzo grosso

bike [baɪk] s (coll) bicicletta

bile [baɪl] s bile f

bilge [bɪldʒ] s sentina; (of barrel) ventre m

bilge'ways' spl parati mpl

bilingual [baɪ'lɪŋgwəl] adj bilingue

bilious ['bɪljəs] adj bilioso

bilk [bɪlk] tr defraudare

bill [bɪl] s (of bird) becco; (statement of charges) conto; (e.g., for electricity) bolletta; (menu) lista; (money) biglietto; (proposed law) disegno di legge; (handbill) annunzio; (law) atto; (theat) cartellone m; to fill the bill (coll) riempire i requisiti; to foot the bill (coll) pagare lo scotto || tr fare una lista di; mettere in conto a || intr (said of doves) beccuzzarsi; (said of lovers) baciucchiarsi

bill'board' s cartellone m; (rad, telv) titolo di testa

billet ['bɪlɪt] s (mil) alloggiamento; (mil) ordine m d'alloggiamento || tr (mil) alloggiare, accasermare

bill'fold' s portafoglio

bill'head' s intestazione di fattura

billiards ['bɪljərdz] s bigliardo

bil'ling clerk' s fatturista mf

billion ['bɪljən] s (U.S.A.) miliardo; (Brit) bilione m

bill' of exchange' s tratta

bill' of fare' s menu m, lista delle vivande

bill' of lad'ing ['ledɪŋ] s polizza di carico

bill' of rights' s dichiarazione dei diritti

bill' of sale' s atto di vendita

billow ['bɪlo] s ondata, cavallone m

bill'post'er s attacchino

bil·ly ['bɪli] s (-lies) manganello

bil'ly goat' s capro, caprone m

bimonthly [baɪ'mʌnθli] adj (occurring every two months) bimestrale; (occurring twice a month) bimensile

bin [bɪn] s cassone m; (for bread) madia; (e.g., for coal) deposito

binaural [baɪ'nɔrəl] adj biauricolare

bind [baɪnd] v (pret & pp bound [baʊnd]) tr legare; allacciare; (to bandage) fasciare; (to constipate) costipare; (a book) rilegare; (to oblige) obbligare; (mach) grippare

binder ['baɪndər] s rilegatore m; (cover) cartella

binder·y ['baɪndəri] s (-ies) rilegatoria

binding ['baɪndɪŋ] adj obbligatorio || s (of book) rilegatura; legatura; fasciatura

bind'ing post' s (elec) capocorda; (e.g., of battery) (elec) serrafilo

binge [bɪndʒ] s—to go on a binge (coll) far baldoria

bingo ['bɪngo] s tombola

binnacle ['bɪnəkəl] s abitacolo

binoculars [bɪ'nɑkjələrz] or [baɪ'nɑkjələrz] spl binocolo

biochemical [ˌbaɪ-ə'kemɪkəl] adj biochimico

biochemist [ˌbaɪ-ə'kemɪst] s biochimico

biochemistry [ˌbaɪ-ə'kemɪstri] s biochimica

biodegradable [ˌbaɪ-odɪ'gredəbəl] adj biodegradabile

biographer [baɪ'ɑgrəfər] s biografo

biographic(al) [ˌbaɪ-ə'græfɪk(əl)] adj biografico

biogra·phy [baɪ'ɑgrəfi] s (-phies) biografia

biologist [baɪ'ɑlədʒɪst] s biologo

biology [baɪ'ɑlədʒi] s biologia

biophysics [ˌbaɪ-ə'fɪzɪks] s biofisica

biop·sy ['baɪ ˌɑpsi] s (-sies) biopsia

bipartisan [baɪ'pɑrtɪzən] adj (system) bipartitico; (government) bipartito

biped ['baɪped] adj & s bipede m

birch [bʌrtʃ] s betulla || tr scudisciare

bird [bʌrd] s uccello; a bird in the hand is worth two in the bush un uovo oggi vale meglio di una gallina domani; birds of a feather gente f della stessa risma; to kill two birds with one stone pigliare due piccioni con una fava

bird' cage' s gabbia

birdie ['bʌrdi] s uccellino; (golf) giocata di un colpo sotto la media

bird'lime' s pania

bird' of pas'sage s uccello di passo

bird' of prey' s uccello da preda

bird'seed' s becchime m

bird's'-eye view' s vista a volo d'uccello

bird' shot' s pallini mpl da caccia

birth [bʌrθ] s nascita; to give birth to dare i natali a; mettere alla luce

birth' certif'icate s certificato di nascita

birth' control' s limitazione delle nascite

birth'day' s natalizio, compleanno; (of an event) anniversario

birth'mark' s voglia

birth'place' s patria; (e.g., city) luogo di nascita; to be the birthplace of dare i natali a

birth' rate' s natalità f

birth'right' s diritto acquisito sin dalla nascita

biscuit ['bɪskɪt] s panino soffice; (Brit) biscotto

bisect [baɪ'sekt] tr bisecare || intr (said of roads) incrociarsi

bisection [baɪ'sekʃən] s bisezione

bishop ['bɪʃəp] s vescovo; (chess) alfiere m

bishopric ['bɪʃəprɪk] s vescovado

bismuth ['bɪzməθ] *s* bismuto
bison ['baɪsən] or ['baɪzən] *s* bisonte *m*
bisulfate [baɪ'sʌlfet] *s* bisolfato
bisulfite [baɪ'sʌlfaɪt] *s* bisolfito
bit [bɪt] *s* (*of bridle*) morso; (*of key*) mappa; (*tool*) punta, trivella; (*small piece*) briciolo; **a bit un po'**; (coll) un momento; **a good bit** una buona quantità; **bit by bit** poco a poco; **to blow to bits** fare a pezzi; **to champ the bit** mordere il freno; **two bits** (slang) quarto di dollaro, cinque soldi
bitch [bɪtʃ] *s* cagna; (vulg) donnaccia || *intr* (slang) lamentarsi
bite [baɪt] *s* morso; (*mouthful*) boccone *m*; **to take a bite** fare uno spuntino; mangiare un boccone || *v* (*pret* **bit** [bɪt]; *pp* **bit** or **bitten** ['bɪtən]) *tr* mordere, addentare; pungere; (*the dust*) baciare || *intr* mordere; (*said of insects*) pungere; (*said of fish*) abboccare
biting ['baɪtɪŋ] *adj* mordace; pungente
bitter ['bɪtər] *adj* amaro; (*e.g., fight*) accanito; (*cold*) pungente || *s* amaro; **bitters** amaro
bit'ter end' *s*—**to the bitter end** fino alla fine; fino alla morte
bit'ter•en'der *s* (coll) intransigente *mf*
bitterness ['bɪtərnɪs] *s* amarezza
bit'ter•sweet' *adj* dolceamaro; (fig) agrodolce || *s* dulcamara
bitumen [bɪ'tjumən] or [bɪ'tumən] *s* bitume *m*
bivou•ac ['bɪvu‚æk] or ['bɪvwæk] *s* bivacco || *v* (*pret & pp* **-acked**; *ger* **-acking**) *intr* bivaccare
biweekly [baɪ'wikli] *adj* bisettimanale; quindicinale || *adv* ogni due settimane
biyearly [baɪ'jɪrli] *adj* semestrale || *adv* semestralmente
bizarre [bɪ'zɑr] *adj* bizzarro
blab [blæb] *s* chiacchierone *m* || *v* (*pret & pp* **blabbed**; *ger* **blabbing**) *tr* rivelare || *intr* chiacchierare
black [blæk] *adj* nero; (*without light*) buio || *s* nero; **to wear black** vestire a lutto, vestire di nero || *intr*—**to black out** perdere i sensi
black'-and-blue' *adj* livido e pesto
black'-and-white' *adj* in bianco e nero
black'ball' *s* palla nera, voto contrario || *tr* dare la palla nera a
black'ber'ry *s* (-ries) mora
black'bird' *s* merlo
black'board' *s* lavagna, tavola nera
black'cap' *s* capinera
black'damp' *s* putizza
Black' Death' *s* peste bubbonica
blacken ['blækən] *tr* annerire; (*shoes*) lucidare; (*reputation*) sporcare
black' eye' *s* occhio pesto; (fig) cattiva reputazione
blackguard ['blægɑrd] *s* canaglia
black'head' *s* comedone *m*
blackish ['blækɪʃ] *adj* nerastro
black'jack' *s* randello; (cards) ventuno || *tr* randellare
black' mag'ic *s* magia nera

black'mail' *s* ricatto || *tr* ricattare
blackmailer ['blæk‚melər] *s* ricattatore *m*
Black' Mari'a [mə'raɪ•ə] *s* (coll) furgone *m* cellulare
black' mar'ket *s* borsa nera
black' marketeer' [‚mɑrkɪ'tɪr] *s* borsanerista *mf*
blackness ['blæknɪs] *s* nerezza
black'out' *s* oscuramento; (theat) spegnitura; (pathol) svenimento passeggero
black' sheep' *s* (fig) pecora nera
black'smith' *s* fabbro
black' tie' *s* cravatta da smoking; smoking *m*
bladder ['blædər] *s* vescica
blade [bled] *s* (*of a leaf*) pagina; (*of grass*) stelo, filo; (*of oar*) pala; (*of turbine*) paletta; (*of fan*) ventola; (*of knife*) lama; (coll) caposcarico
blame [blem] *s* colpa; **to be to blame for** aver la colpa di; **to put the blame on s.o. for s.th** attribuire a qlcu la colpa di qlco; **you are to blame** è colpa Sua || *tr* biasimare, incolpare
blameless ['blemlɪs] *adj* innocente, senza colpa
blanch [blæntʃ] or [blɑntʃ] *tr* bianchire || *intr* impallidire
bland [blænd] *adj* blando; (*weather*) mite
blandish ['blændɪʃ] *tr* blandire
blank [blæŋk] *adj* (*not written on*) in bianco; (*e.g., stare*) vuoto; (*utter*) completo || *s* (*printed form*) modulo; (*cartridge*) cartuccia a salve; (*of the mind*) lacuna; **to draw a blank** (coll) non avere alcun successo || *tr*—**blank out** cancellare
blank' check' *s* assegno in bianco; (fig) carta bianca
blanket ['blæŋkɪt] *adj* generale, combinato || *s* coperta; (*of snow*) cappa || *tr* coprire con una coperta; oscurare
blank' verse' *s* verso sciolto
blare [bler] *s* squillo || *tr* proclamare; fare echeggiare || *intr* squillare; echeggiare
blaspheme [blæs'fim] *tr & intr* bestemmiare
blasphemous ['blæsfɪməs] *adj* bestemmiatore
blasphe•my ['blæsfɪmi] *s* (-mies) bestemmia
blast [blæst] or [blɑst] *s* (*of air*) raffica; (*of a horn*) squillo; (*blight*) rovina; scoppio, esplosione; **at full blast** a piena velocità || *tr* rovinare; fare scoppiare, far saltare || *intr* —**to blast off** (rok) lanciarsi
blast' fur'nace *s* altoforno
blast'off' *s* lancio di missile or di nave spaziale
blatant ['bletənt] *adj* (*noisy*) rumoroso; (*obtrusive*) palmare; (*flashy*) chiassoso
blaze [blez] *s* fiammata; splendore *m*; (*on a horse's head*) stella; **in a blaze** in fiamme || *tr* proclamare; **to blaze a**

trail marcare il cammino || *intr* divampare

bleach [blitʃ] *s* candeggio, candeggina || *tr* imbiancare, candeggiare

bleachers ['blitʃərz] *spl* posti *mpl* allo scoperto o di gradinata

bleak [blik] *adj* nudo, deserto; (*cold*) freddo; (*gloomy*) triste

blear·y ['blɪrɪ] *adj* (-ier; iest) (*sight*) cisposo; confuso; offuscato

bleat [blit] *s* belato || *intr* belare

bleed [blid] *v* (*pret & pp* **bled** [bled]) *tr* (*to draw blood from*) salassare; (*a tree*) estrare linfa da; (*coll*) sfruttare || *intr* sanguinare; (*said of a tree*) dar linfa; **to bleed to death** morire dissangu..to

blemish ['blemɪʃ] *s* difetto; macchia || *tr* danneggiare; macchiare

blend [blend] *s* mescolanza, miscuglio; (*of gasoline*) miscela || *v* (*pret & pp* **blended** or **blent** [blent]) *tr* mescolare, miscelare || *intr* mescolarsi, miscelarsi; armonizzare; fondersi

bless [bles] *tr* benedire; (*to endow*) dotare; (*to make happy*) allietare

blessed ['blesɪd] *adj* benedetto; beato; fortunato; dotato

bless'ed event' *s* lieto evento

blessing ['blesɪŋ] *s* benedizione

blight [blaɪt] *s* (*insect; disease*) piaga; rovina; (*fungus*) ruggine *f* || *tr* rovinare, guastare

blimp [blɪmp] *s* piccolo dirigibile

blind [blaɪnd] *adj* cieco; (*slang*) ubriaco || *s* persiana; tendina; (*decoy*) mascheratura; pretesto || *adv* alla cieca || *tr* accecare

blind' al'ley *s* vicolo cieco

blinder ['blaɪndər] *s* paraocchi *m*

blind' fly'ing *s* (aer) volo senza visibilità

blind'fold' *adj* bendato, cogli occhi bendati || *s* benda || *tr* bendare gli occhi a

blindly ['blaɪndlɪ] *adv* alla cieca

blind' man' *s* cieco

blind'man's buff' *s* mosca cieca

blindness ['blaɪndnɪs] *s* cecità *f*

blind' spot' *s* (anat) punto cieco; (rad) zona di silenzio; (fig) debole *m*

blink [blɪŋk] *s* batter *m* di ciglio; (*glimpse*) occhiata; (*glimmer*) barlume *m*; **on the blink** (slang) fuori servizio || *tr*—**to blink one's eyes** batter il ciglio || *intr* occhieggiare; (*to wink*) ammiccare; (*to flash on and off*) lampeggiare; **to blink at** ignorare; far finta di non vedere

blinker ['blɪŋkər] *s* (*at a crossing*) luce *f* intermittente; (*on a horse*) paraocchi *m*

blip [blɪp] *s* guizzo sullo schermo radar

bliss [blɪs] *s* beatitudine *f*, felicità *f*

blissful ['blɪsfəl] *adj* beato, felice

blister ['blɪstər] *s* vescica, bolla || *tr* coprire di vesciche; (fig) bollare || *intr* coprirsi di vesciche

blithe [blaɪð] *adj* gaio, giocondo

blitzkrieg ['blɪts,krig] *s* guerra lampo

blizzard ['blɪzərd] *s* tormenta, ventoneve *m*

bloat [blot] *tr* gonfiare || *intr* gonfiarsi

blob [blɑb] *s* (*lump*) zolla; (*of liquid*) macchia

block [blɑk] *s* (*e.g., of wood*) blocco; (*for chopping*) ceppo; (*pulley*) puleggia; ostacolo; (*of houses*) isolato; (typ) cliché *m* || *tr* bloccare; (*a hat*) mettere in forma; **to block up** tappare

blockade [blɑ'ked] *s* blocco; **to run a blockade** forzare il blocco || *tr* bloccare

block' and tack'le *s* bozzello

block'bust'er *s* (coll) superbomba

block'head' *s* imbecille *mf*

block' let'ter *s* carattere *m* stampatello

block' sig'nal *s* (rr) segnale di blocco

blond [blɑnd] *adj & s* biondo

blonde [blɑnd] *s* bionda

blood [blʌd] *s* sangue *m*; **in cold blood** a sangue freddo; **to draw blood** ferire, fare sanguinare

blood' bank' *s* emoteca

bloodcurdling ['blʌd ,kʌrdlɪŋ] *adj* orripilante

blood' do'nor *s* donatore *m* di sangue

blood'hound' *s* segugio

bloodless ['blʌdlɪs] *adj* esangue; (*e.g., revolution*) senza effusione di sangue

blood'mobile' [mo ,bil] *s* autoemoteca

blood' poi'soning *s* avvelenamento del sangue

blood' pres'sure *s* pressione sanguigna

blood' rela'tion *s* consanguineo

blood'shed' *s* spargimento di sangue, carneficina

blood'shot' *adj* iniettato di sangue

blood'stained' *adj* macchiato di sangue

blood'stream' *s* circolazione sanguigna

blood'suck'er *s* sanguisuga

blood' test' *s* esame *m* del sangue

blood'thirst'y *adj* assetato di sangue

blood' transfu'sion *s* trasfusione di sangue

blood' type' *s* gruppo sanguigno

blood' ves'sel *s* vaso sanguigno

blood·y ['blʌdɪ] *adj* (-ier; -iest) sanguinoso; (*bloodthirsty*) avido di sangue || *v* (*pret & pp* -ied) *tr* macchiare di sangue

bloom [blum] *s* fiore *m*; (*state of having open buds*) sboccio; (*youthful glow*) incarnato || *intr* fiorire; sbocciare

bloomers ['blumərz] *spl* pantaloni *mpl* femminili larghi fermati sotto il ginocchio

blossom ['blɑsəm] *s* fiore *m*; sboccio || *intr* sbocciare

blot [blɑt] *s* macchia || *v* (*pret & pp* **blotted**; *ger* **blotting**) *tr* macchiare; (*with blotting paper*) asciugare; **to blot out** cancellare; oscurare || *intr* macchiarsi; (*to be absorbent*) essere assorbente; (*said of a pen*) fare macchie

blotch [blɑtʃ] *s* chiazza, macchia || *tr* chiazzare

blotter ['blɑtər] *s* carta asciugante, carta assorbente; (*book*) registro

blouse [blaus] *s* blusa

blow [blo] *s* colpo; (*blast*) folata; (*of

horn) squillo; (*sudden reverse*) batosta; **at one blow** d'un sol colpo; **to come to blows** venire alle mani; **without striking a blow** senza colpo ferire ‖ *v* (*pret* **blew** [blu]; *pp* **blown**) *tr* soffiare, soffiare su; (*an instrument*) suonare; (*one's nose*) soffiarsi; **to blow in** sfondare; **to blow one's brains out** bruciarsi le cervella; **to blow open** aprire completamente; **to blow out** (*e.g., a candle*) spegnere; (*a fuse*) fondere; **to blow up** (*e.g., a mine*) far brillare; (*phot*) ingrandire ‖ *intr* soffiare; (*to pant*) ansimare; (*with an instrument*) suonare; (*to puff*) sbuffare; (slang) andarsene; **to blow hot and cold** cambiare d'opinione ogni cinque minuti; **to blow in** (coll) arrivare inaspettatamente; **to blow out** (said, *e.g., of a candle*) spegnersi; (*said of a fuse*) saltare, fondersi; (*said of a tire*) scoppiare; **to blow over** passare; **to blow up** saltar per aria; (*said of a storm*) scoppiare; (coll) perdere la pazienza, scoppiare d'ira

blow'out' *s* scoppio di un pneumatico
blow'pipe' *s* (*tube*) soffione *m*; (*peashooter*) cerbottana
blow'torch' *s* saldatrice *f* a benzina
blubber ['blʌbər] *s* grasso di balena ‖ *intr* piangere, lamentarsi
bludgeon ['blʌdʒən] *s* randello ‖ *tr* randellare
blue [blu] *adj* blu, azzurro; (*gloomy*) triste; (*e.g., laws*) puritanico ‖ *s* blu *m*, azzurro *m*; **out of the blue** inaspettatamente; **the blues** la malinconia; (mus) blues *m*; **to have the blues** essere giù di morale ‖ *tr* tingere di azzurro; (*a metal*) brunire
blue'ber'ry *s* (-ries) mirtillo
blue'bird' *s* uccello azzurro
blue' blood' *s* sangue *m* blu
blue' cheese' *s* gorgonzola americano
blue' chip' *s* (fin) azione di prim'ordine
blue' jay' *s* ghiandaia azzurra
blue' moon' *s*—**once in a blue moon** ad ogni morte di papa
blue'-pen'cil *v* (*pret* & *pp* -ciled or -cilled; *ger* -ciling or -cilling) *tr* correggere col lapis blu
blue'print' *s* riproduzione cianografica; (*plan*) piano ‖ *tr* riprodurre in cianografia; preparare dettagliatamente
blue'stock'ing *s* saccente *f*, sapientona
blue' streak' *s*—**like a blue streak** (coll) come un razzo
bluff [blʌf] *adj* scosceso; brusco, burbero ‖ *s* promontorio scosceso; bluff *m*; bluffatore *m* ‖ *intr* bluffare
bluing ['bluɪŋ] *s* turchinetto
bluish ['blu·ɪʃ] *adj* bluastro
blunder ['blʌndər] *s* errore *m* madornale ‖ *intr* pigliare un granchio
blunt [blʌnt] *adj* ottuso; (*plain-spoken*) franco ‖ *tr* rendere ottuso
bluntness ['blʌntnɪs] *s* ottusità *f*; franchezza
blur [blʌr] *s* macchia; offuscamento; confusione ‖ *v* (*pret* & *pp* **blurred**;

ger **blurring**) *tr* macchiare; (*the view*) offuscare
blurb [blʌrb] *s* annuncio pubblicitario
blurt [blʌrt] *tr*—**to blurt out** prorompere a dire, lasciarsi sfuggire
blush [blʌʃ] *s* rossore *m*; (*pinkish natural tinge*) incarnato ‖ *intr* arrossire; **to blush at** vergognarsi di
bluster ['blʌstər] *s* frastuono; (fig) boria ‖ *intr* (*said of the wind*) infuriare; fare il bravaccio
blustery ['blʌstəri] *adj* tempestuoso, violento; (*swaggering*) borioso
boar [bor] *s* verro; (*wild hog*) porco selvatico, cinghiale *m*
board [bord] *s* asse *m*; (*notice*) cartello; (*pasteboard*) cartone *m*; (*table*) tavola; (*meals*) vitto; (*group of administrators*) consiglio; (naut) bordo; **above board** franco; **in boards** rilegato; **on board** a bordo; (rr) in vettura; **to go by the board** andare in rovina; **to tread the boards** fare l'attore ‖ *tr* chiudere con assi; (*to provide with meals*) dare pensione a, tenere a dozzina; (*a ship*) salire a bordo di; (*a train*) salire su; (naut) abbordare ‖ *intr* essere a pensione
board' and lodg'ing *s* pensione completa
boarder ['bordər] *s* pensionante *mf*
board'ing house' *s* pensione di famiglia
board'ing school' *s* collegio di pensionanti
board' of direc'tors *s* consiglio d'amministrazione
board' of health' *s* ufficio d'igiene
board' of trade' *s* camera di commercio
board'walk' *s* passeggiata a mare
boast [bost] *s* millanteria, vanteria ‖ *intr* vantarsi
boastful ['bostfəl] *adj* millantatore
boat [bot] *s* nave *f*, battello; (*small ship*) barca, imbarcazione; (*dish*) salsiera; **in the same boat** nella stessa situazione
boat' hook' *s* alighiero
boat'house' *s* capannone *m* per i canotti
boating ['botɪŋ] *s* escursione in barca
boat'man *s* (-men) barcaiolo
boat' race' *s* regata
boatswain ['bosən] or ['bot,swen] *s* nostromo
bob [bab] *s* (*plumb*) piombino; (*short haircut*) taglio alla bebè; coda mozza (di cavallo); (*jerky motion*) strattone *m*; (*on pendulum of clock*) lente *f*; (*on fishing line*) sughero ‖ *v* (*pret* & *pp* **bobbed**; *ger* **bobbing**) *tr* tagliare alla bebè; far muovere a scatti ‖ *intr* muoversi a scatti; fare mossa; **to bob up** apparire
bobbin ['babɪn] *s* bobina
bob'by pin' ['babi] *s* forcina
bob'by-socks' *spl* (coll) calzini *mpl* da ragazza
bobbysoxer ['babi ,saksər] *s* (coll) ragazzina
bobolink ['babə ,lɪŋk] *s* doliconice *m*
bob'sled' *s* guidoslitta
bode [bod] *tr* & *intr* presagire
bodice ['badɪs] *s* giubbetto, copribusto

bodily [ˈbɑdɪli] *adj* fisico, corporeo ‖ *adv* fisicamente, corporeamente; di persona; in massa

bodkin [ˈbɑdkɪn] *s* punteruolo; (*for lady's hair*) spillone *m*

bod·y [ˈbɑdi] *s* (**-ies**) corpo; (*corpse*) cadavere *m*; (*of water*) massa; (*of people*) gruppo; (*of a liquid*) sostanza; (*of truck*) cassone *m*; (*of car*) carrozzeria; (*of tree*) tronco; (coll) persona; **in a body** in massa

bod′y-guard′ *s* (*of a high official*) guardia del corpo; (*e.g., of a movie star*) guardaspalle *m*

bod′y suit′ *s* calzamaglia

bog [bɑg] *s* pantano, palude *m* ‖ (*pret & pp* **bogged;** *ger* **bogging**) *intr*—**to bog down** impelagarsi

bogey·man [ˈbogiˌmæn] *s* (**-men** [mɛn]) babau *m*

bogus [ˈbogəs] *adj* (coll) falso, finto

Bohemian [boˈhimɪ·ən] *adj* boemo; da bohémien ‖ *s* boemo; (fig) bohémien *m*

boil [bɔɪl] *s* bollore *m*, ebollizione; (pathol) foruncolo; **to come to a boil** cominciare a bollire ‖ *tr* bollire; **to boil down** condensare ‖ *intr* bollire; **to boil away** evaporare completamente; **to boil down** condensarsi; **to boil over** andare per il fuoco

boiled′ ham′ *s* prosciutto cotto

boiler [ˈbɔɪlər] *s* caldaia; (*for cooking*) caldaio

boil′er·mak′er *s* calderaio

boiling [ˈbɔɪlɪŋ] *adj* bollente ‖ *s* bollore *m*, ebollizione

boisterous [ˈbɔɪstərəs] *adj* (*storm*) violento; (*loud*) rumoroso

bold [bold] *adj* (*daring*) coraggioso; (*impudent*) sfacciato; (*steep*) scosceso; (*clear, sharp*) netto

bold′face′ *s* (typ) neretto, grassetto

boldness [ˈboldnɪs] *s* coraggio, audacia; sfacciataggine *f*, impudenza

boll′ wee′vil [bol] *s* antonomo del cotone

bologna [bəˈlonə] or [bəˈlonjə] *s* mortadella

Bolshevik [ˈbʌlʃəvɪk] or [ˈbolʃəvɪk] *adj* & *mf* bolscevico

bolster [ˈbolstər] *s* cuscino; cuscinetto; (*support*) sostegno ‖ *tr* sorreggere; **to bolster up** sostenere

bolt [bolt] *s* (*arrow*) freccia; (*of lightning*) fulmine *m*; (*sliding bar*) chiavistello; (*threaded rod*) bullone *m*; (*of paper or cloth*) pezza, rotolo ‖ *adv*—**bolt upright** dritto come un fuso ‖ *tr* (*to swallow hurriedly*) ingollare; (*to fasten, e.g., a door*) sprangare; (*to fasten, e.g., two metal parts*) bullonare; (*e.g., a political party*) abbandonare ‖ *intr* (*said of people*) spiccare un salto; (*said of a horse*) prendere la mano; precipitarsi

bolt′ from the blue′ *s* fulmine *m* a ciel sereno

bomb [bɑm] *s* bomba; (*e.g., for spraying*) bombola ‖ *tr* bombardare

bombard [bɑmˈbɑrd] *tr* bombardare; (*with questions*) bersagliare

bombardment [bɑmˈbɑrdmənt] *s* bombardamento

bombast [ˈbɑmbæst] *s* ampollosità *f*

bombastic [bɑmˈbæstɪk] *adj* ampolloso

bomb′ cra′ter *s* cratere *m*

bomber [ˈbɑmər] *s* bombardiere *m*

bomb′proof′ *adj* a prova di bomba

bomb′shell′ *s* bomba; (fig) colpo di bomba, colpo di sorpresa

bomb′ shel′ter *s* rifugio antiaereo

bomb′sight′ *s* traguardo aereo

bona fide [ˈbonəˌfɑɪdə] *adj* sincero ‖ *adv* in buona fede

bonanza [bəˈnænzə] *s* (min) ricca vena; (coll) fortuna

bond [bɑnd] *s* legame *m*, vincolo; (*contractual obligation*) obbligazione; (*interest-bearing certificate*) buono, obbligazione; (*surety*) cauzione; **bonds** catene *fpl*; **in bond** sotto cauzione; (*said of goods*) in punto franco ‖ *tr* unire, connettere

bondage [ˈbɑndɪdʒ] *s* schiavitù *f*

bond′ed ware′house *s* deposito in punto franco

bond′hold′er *s* obbligazionista *mf*

bonds′man *s* (**-men**) garante *m*

bone [bon] *s* osso; (*of fish*) spina; (*of whale*) stecca; **bones** ossa *fpl*; **to have a bone to pick with** avere un conto da regolare con; **to make no bones about** (coll) ammettere; (coll) parlare esplicitamente ‖ *tr* disossare; cavare le spine a ‖ *intr*—**to bone up on** (coll) ripassare

bone′head′ *s* (coll) testa dura

boneless [ˈbonlɪs] *adj* senz'osso; (*fish*) senza spine

boner [ˈbonər] *s* (slang) errore *m* madornale

bonfire [ˈbɑnˌfaɪr] *s* falò *m*

bonnet [ˈbɑnɪt] *s* cappello da donna; (*of child*) berrettino

bonus [ˈbonəs] *s* gratifica; indennità *f*; (*to an outgoing employee*) buonuscita

bon·y [ˈboni] *adj* (**-ier; -iest**) (*having bones*) osseo; (*emaciated*) scarno; (*fish*) spinoso

boo [bu] *s* fischio, urlaccio ‖ *tr* & *intr* fischiare, disapprovare

boo·by [ˈbubi] *s* (**-bies**) stupido

boo′by hatch′ *s* (naut) portello; (slang) manicomio; (slang) prigione *f*

boo′by prize′ *s* premio dato al peggior giocatore

boo′by trap′ *s* (mil) trappola esplosiva; (fig) tranello

boogie-woogie [ˈbugiˈwugi] *s* bughi-bughi *m*

book [buk] *s* libro; (*e.g., of matches*) pacchetto; (mus) libretto; (fig) regole *fpl*; **the Book** la Bibbia; **to be in one's book** essere nelle grazie di; **to bring s.o. to book** fare una ramanzina a ‖ *tr* registrare; (*e.g., on a horse*) allibrare; (*e.g., a room*) prenotare; (*an actor*) scritturare

book′bind′er *s* rilegatore *m*

book′bind′er·y *s* (**-ies**) rilegatoria

book′bind′ing *s* rilegatura

book′case′ *s* scaffale *m*

book′ end′ *s* reggilibri *m*

bookie [ˈbuki] s (coll) allibratore m

booking [ˈbukɪŋ] s (of a trip) prenotazione; (of an actor) scrittura

book'ing clerk' s impiegato alla biglietteria

bookish [ˈbukɪʃ] adj studioso; libresco

book'keep'er s contabile mf

booklet [ˈbuklɪt] s libretto; (pamphlet) opuscolo

book'keep'ing s contabilità f

book'mak'er s (one who accepts bets) allibratore m

book'mark' s segnalibro

bookmobile [ˈbukmo͵bil] s bibliobus m

book'plate' s ex libris m

book' review' s rassegna, recensione

book'sell'er s libraio

book'shelf' s (-shelves) scaffale m

book'stand' s (rack) scansia; (stall) edicola

book'store' s libreria

book'worm' s (zool) tarlo dei libri; (fig) topo da biblioteca

boom [bum] s (of crane) braccio; (barrier) barriera galleggiante; (noise) bum m; (fin) boom m; (naut) boma; (mov, telv) giraffa || intr rimbombare; essere in condizioni floride

boomerang [ˈbumə͵ræŋ] s bumerang m

boom' town' s città f fungo

boon [bun] s fortuna, benedizione

boon' compan'ion s compagnone m

boor [bur] s bifolco, zotico

boorish [ˈburɪʃ] adj grossolano

boost [bust] s aumento; (coll) spinta || tr spingere in su; sostenere; (prices) alzare; parlare a favore di

booster [ˈbustər] s (backer) sostenitore m; propulsore m a razzo; (rok) propulsore m del primo stadio; (med) seconda iniezione

boot [but] s stivale m; (kick) calcio; (patch) (aut) pezza; **the boot is on the other foot** la situazione è rovesciata; **to be in the boots** of essere nella pelle di; **to boot** per di più; **to get the boot** (coll) essere messo sulla strada; **to lick the boots** of leccare i piedi a; **to wipe one's boots** on trattare come una pezza da piedi || tr dare un calcio a; **to boot out** (slang) buttar fuori

boot'black' s lustrascarpe m

booth [buθ] s (stall) banco da mercato; (for telephoning, voting) cabina

boot'jack' s tirastivali m

boot'leg' adj di contrabbando || s liquore m di contrabbando || v (pret & pp -legged; ger -legging) tr vendere di contrabbando || intr vendere alcol di contrabbando

bootlegger [ˈbut͵lɛgər] s contrabbandiere m di liquori

boot'lick'er [͵lɪkər] s (coll) leccapiedi mf

boot'strap' s tirante m degli stivali

boo-ty [ˈbuti] s (-ties) bottino

booze [buz] s (coll) bevanda alcolica || intr (coll) ubriacarsi

borax [ˈboræks] s borace m

border [ˈbordər] adj confinario, con-

finante || s bordo, margine m; (between two countries) confine m || tr bordare; confinare con || intr confinare

bor'der clash' s incidente m ai confini

bor'der-line' adj incerto || s frontiera

bore [bor] s (drill hole) buco, foro; (hollow part of gun) anima; (caliber) calibro; (dull person) seccatore m; (annoyance) seccatura; (mach) alesaggio || tr bucare, forare; seccare; (mach) alesare

boredom [ˈbordəm] s noia, tedio

boring [ˈborɪŋ] adj noioso || s trivellazione

born [bɔrn] adj nato, partorito; **to be born** nascere; **to be born again** rinascere; **to be born with a silver spoon in one's mouth** nascere con la camicia

borough [ˈbʌro] s borgata, comune m

borrow [ˈbaro] or [ˈbɔro] tr chiedere a or in prestito; prendere a or in prestito; ricevere a or in prestito; (to adopt) adottare; **to borrow trouble** preoccuparsi per nulla

borrower [ˈbaro-ər] or [ˈbɔro-ər] s chi riceve a prestito; (law) comodatario, prestatario

borrowing [ˈbaro-ɪŋ] or [ˈbɔro-ɪŋ] s prestito; prestito linguistico, forestierismo

bosom [ˈbuzəm] s petto, seno; (e.g., of the family) grembo, seno; (of shirt) pettorina

bos'om friend' s amico del cuore

Bosporus [ˈbaspərəs] s Bosforo

boss [bɔs] or [bas] s (coll) padrone m; (coll) direttore m; (coll) capintesta m; (coll) principale m; (archit) bugna, bozza || tr fare da padrone a || intr fare da padrone

boss-y [ˈbɔsi] or [ˈbasi] adj (-ier; -iest) autoritario

botanical [bəˈtænɪkəl] adj botanico

botanist [ˈbatənɪst] s botanico

botany [ˈbatəni] s botanica

botch [batʃ] s abborracciatura || tr abborracciare

both [boθ] adj entrambi i, tutti e due i || pron entrambi, tutti e due || conj del pari, al medesimo tempo; **both . . . and** tanto . . . quanto

bother [ˈbaðər] s (worry) noia, seccatura; (person) seccatore m || tr dar noia a, seccare || intr preoccuparsi; **to bother about** or **with** occuparsi di; **to bother to** + inf molestarsi di a + inf

bothersome [ˈbaðərsəm] adj incomodo

bottle [ˈbatəl] s bottiglia, fiasco || tr imbottigliare; **to bottle up** imbottigliare

bot'tle cap' s tappo a corona

bot'tle-neck' s collo di bottiglia; (traffic) congestione, imbottigliamento

bot'tle o'pener [ˈopənər] s apribottiglie

bottom [ˈbatəm] adj basso; (price, dollar) ultimo; infimo || s fondo; (of chair) sedile m; base f; (of bottle) culo; (of ship) scafo; **at bottom** in realtà; **to begin at the bottom** cominciare dalla gavetta; **to get at the bottom of** andare a fondo di; **to go to the bottom** andare a picco

bottomless ['batəmlɪs] *adj* senza fondo

boudoir [bu'dwar] *s* gabinetto di toletta (da signora)

bough [bau] *s* ramo

bouillon ['bujan] *s* brodo schietto

boulder ['boldər] *s* masso, roccia

boulevard ['bulə ,vard] *s* corso

bounce [bauns] *s* balzo; salto; elasticità *f*; (*of boat or plane*) piastrellamento; (fig) spirito; **to get the bounce** (slang) essere licenziato || *tr* far balzare; (slang) buttar fuori || *intr* rimbalzare; saltare; (aer, naut) piastrellare

bouncer ['baunsər] *s* (*in night club*) (slang) buttafuori *m*

bouncing ['baunsɪŋ] *adj* forte, vigoroso; grande, rumoroso

bound [baund] *adj* legato; collegato; obbligato; (bb) rilegato; (coll) risoluto; **bound for** destinato a, diretto per; **bound up in** or **with** in strette relazioni con; assorto in || *s* salto; rimbalzo; limite *m*; **bounds** zona limitrofa; **out of bounds** fuori limiti; al di là delle convenienze || *tr* delimitare

bounda•ry ['baundəri] *s* (**-ries**) confine *m*, limite *m*

bound'ary stone' *s* pietra di confine

boundless ['baundlɪs] *adj* illimitato, sconfinato

bountiful ['bauntɪfəl] *adj* generoso; abbondante

boun•ty ['baunti] *s* (**-ties**) dono generoso; generosità *f*, abbondanza; (*reward*) premio

bouquet [bu'ke] or [bo'ke] *s* mazzo, mazzolino; profumo, aroma *m*

bourgeois ['burʒwa'zi] *adj & s* borghese *mf*

bourgeoisie [,burʒwa'zi] *s* borghesia

bout [baut] *s* lotta, contesa; (*of illness*) attacco

bow [bau] *s* inchino, riverenza; (naut) prua; **to take a bow** ricevere gli applausi || *tr* chinare, piegare || *intr* inchinarsi; sottomettersi; **to bow and scrape** fare riverenze || [bo] *s* (*weapon*) arco; (*knot*) nodo; (mus) archetto; (*stroke of bow*) (mus) arcata || *tr & intr* (mus) suonare con l'archetto

bowdlerize ['baudlə ,raɪz] *tr* espurgare

bowel ['bau•əl] *s* budello; **bowels** viscere *fpl*

bow'el move'ment *s* evacuazione; **to have a bowel movement** andar di corpo

bower ['bau•ər] *s* pergolato

bowery ['bau•əri] *adj* frondoso

bowknot ['bo ,nat] *s* nodo scorsoio

bowl [bol] *s* (*dish*) ciotola; (*cup*) tazza; (*of pipe*) fornello; (*basin*) catino; (*amphitheater*) arena; (*ball*) boccia; (*delivery of ball*) bocciata; **bowls** bocce *fpl* || *tr* bocciare; **to bowl down** or **over** abbattere || *intr* giocare alle bocce

bowlegged ['bo ,lɛgd] or ['bo ,lɛgɪd] *adj* con le gambe storte

bowler ['bolər] *s* giocatore *m* di bocce

bowling ['bolɪŋ] *s* bocce *fpl*; bowling *m*, birilli *mpl*

bowl'ing al'ley *s* pista per il bowling; bowling *m*

bowl'ing green' *s* campo di bocce erboso

bowshot ['bo ,ʃat] *s* tiro d'arco

bowsprit ['bausprit] or ['bosprɪt] *s* (naut) bompresso

bow' tie' [bo] *s* cravatta a farfalla

bowwow ['bau ,wau] *interj* bau bau!

box [baks] *s* scatola; cassa; (*for jury*) banco; (*for sentry*) garitta; (*on coach*) cassetta; (*in stable*) posta; (*slap*) ceffone *m*; (*with fist*) pugno; (bot) bosso; (theat) palco, barcaccia; (baseball) posto del battitore; (typ) riquadratura || *tr* mettere in scatola; (*to slap*) schiaffeggiare; (*to hit with fist*) fare a pugilato con; **to box in** or **up** rinchiudere || *intr* fare a pugni; combattere

box'car' *s* vagone *m* merci coperto

boxer ['baksər] *s* pugile *m*

box'hold'er *s* palchettista *mf*

boxing ['baksɪŋ] *s* pugilato

box'ing gloves' *spl* guantoni *mpl* da pugilato

box' of'fice *s* sportello, biglietteria; (theat) incasso; (theat) successo

box'-of'fice hit' *s* grande successo

box' pleat' *s* (*of skirt*) cannone *m*

box' seat' *s* posto in palco

box'wood' *s* bosso

boy [bɔɪ] *s* ragazzo, giovane *m* || *interj* accidempoli!

boycott ['bɔɪkat] *s* boicottaggio || *tr* boicottare

boy'friend' *s* innamorato, amico

boyhood ['bɔɪhud] *s* fanciullezza

boyish ['bɔɪ•ɪʃ] *adj* giovanile

boy' scout' *s* giovane esploratore *m*

bra [bra] *s* (coll) reggiseno

brace [bres] *s* (*couple*) paio; (*device for maintaining tension*) tirante *m*; (*prop*) sostegno; (*tool*) trapano; (typ) graffa; **braces** (Brit) bretelle *fpl* || *tr* legare; serrare; puntellare; sostenere; invigorare; **to brace oneself** pigliare animo || *intr*—**to brace up** (coll) pigliare animo

brace' and bit' *s* menarola, trapano

bracelet ['breslɪt] *s* braccialetto

bracer ['bresər] *s* (coll) bicchierino

bracket ['brækɪt] *s* mensola; (*for lamp*) braccio; angolo; classifica; (typ) parentesi quadra || *tr* sostenere con mensola; mettere tra parentesi quadra; classificare

brackish ['brækɪʃ] *adj* salmastro

brad [bræd] *s* chiodino, punta

brag [bræg] *s* vanto || *v* (*pret & pp* **bragged**; *ger* **bragging**) *intr* vantare

braggart ['brægərt] *s* millantatore *m*

Brah•man ['bramən] *s* (**-mans**) bramino

braid [bred] *s* treccia; (*strip of cloth*) spighetta; (mil) cordellina || *tr* intrecciare; decorare con spighette

brain [bren] *s* cervello; **brains** cervello, intelligenza; **to rack one's brains** rompersi la testa ‖ *tr* far saltare le cervella di

brain'child' *s* (coll) parto dell'ingegno, idea geniale

brain' drain' *s* (coll) fuga di cervelli

brainless ['brenlɪs] *adj* senza testa

brain' pow'er *s* intelligenza

brain'storm' *s* (coll) ispirazione

brain' trust' *s* consiglio d'esperti

brain'wash'ing *s* lavaggio del cervello

brain' wave' *s* onda encefalica; (coll) idea geniale

brain'work' *s* lavoro intellettuale

brain-y ['breni] *adj* (-ier; -iest) intelligente

braise [brez] *tr* (culin) brasare

brake [brek] *s* freno; (*thicket*) macchia ‖ *tr & intr* frenare

brake' drum' *s* tamburo del freno

brake' lin'ing *s* ferodo

brake'man *s* (-men) frenatore *m*

brake' shoe' *s* ganascia

bramble ['bræmbəl] *s* rovo

bran [bræn] *s* crusca

branch [bræntʃ] *s* (*of tree*) branca, ramo; (*of river*) braccio; (*of a family*) ramo; (*of business*) filiale *f*; (rr) diramazione ‖ *intr* biforcarsi; **to branch off or out** ramificarsi, diramarsi

branch' line' *s* ferrovia di diramazione

branch' of'fice *s* succursale *f*

brand [brænd] *s* (*burning stick*) tizzone *m*; (*mark; stigma*) marchio; (*label; make*) marca ‖ *tr* (*to mark with a brand*) marchiare; (*to put a stigma on*) bollare; **to brand as** tacciare di

brandied ['brændid] *adj* conservato in acquavite

brand'ing i'ron *s* ferro da marchio

brandish ['brændɪʃ] *tr* brandire

brand'-new' *adj* nuovo fiammante

bran-dy ['brændi] *s* (-dies) cognac *m*, acquavite *f*

brash [bræʃ] *adj* (*too hasty*) avventato; (*insolent*) impudente ‖ *s* frammenti *mpl*; attacco (di malattia), indigestione

brass [bræs] *or* [brɑs] *s* ottone *m*; (coll) faccia tosta; (slang) alti ufficiali; **brasses** (mus) ottoni *mpl*

brass' band' *s* fanfara

brassiere [brə'zɪr] *s* reggiseno

brass' knuck'les *spl* tirapugni *m*

brass' tack' *s* chiodino *or* borchia d'ottone; **to get down to brass tacks** (coll) venire al sodo

brass-y ['bræsi] *or* ['brɑsi] *adj* (-ier; -iest) fatto d'ottone; sfacciato, impudente

brat [bræt] *s* marmocchio, monello

brava-do [brə'vado] *s* (-does *or* -dos) bravata

brave [brev] *adj* coraggioso ‖ *s* persona coraggiosa; guerriero indiano ‖ *tr* (*to defy*) sfidare; (*to meet with courage*) affrontare

bravery ['brevəri] *s* coraggio

bra-vo ['bravo] *s* (-vos) bravo; applauso ‖ *interj* bravo!

brawl [brɔl] *s* zuffa, rissa ‖ *intr* azzuffarsi, rissare

brawn [brɔn] *s* forza muscolare

brawn-y ['brɔni] *adj* (-ier; -iest) muscoloso

bray [bre] *s* raglio ‖ *intr* ragliare

braze [brez] *s* brasatura ‖ *tr* brasare

brazen ['brezən] *adj* d'ottone; (*shameless*) sfrontato; (*sound*) penetrante ‖ *tr*—**to brazen out or through** affrontare sfacciatamente

brazier ['breʒər] *s* caldano, braciere *m*; (*workman*) ottonaio

Brazil [brə'zɪl] *s* il Brasile

Brazilian [brə'zɪljən] *adj & s* brasiliano

Brazil' nut' *s* noce *f* del Brasile

breach [britʃ] *s* (*gap*) breccia; (*failure to observe a law*) infrazione ‖ *tr* fare breccia su, fare varco in

breach' of faith' *s* abuso di confidenza

breach' of prom'ise *s* rottura di promessa di matrimonio

breach' of the peace' *s* violazione dell'ordine pubblico

bread [brɛd] *s* pane *m*; **to break bread with** sedersi a tavola con ‖ *tr* impannare

bread' and but'ter *s* pane *m* e burro; (coll) pane quotidiano

bread' crumbs' *spl* pangrattato

breaded ['brɛdɪd] *adj* impannato

bread' knife' *s* coltello da pane

bread' line' *s* coda del pane

bread' stick' *s* grissino

breadth [brɛdθ] *s* (*width*) larghezza; (*scope*) ampiezza

bread'win'ner *s* sostegno della famiglia

break [brek] *s* interruzione, intervallo; omissione; (*breaking*) rottura; (*of bones*) frattura; (*of day*) fare *m*, spuntare *m*; (*sudden change*) mutamento; (*from jail*) evasione; (*luck*) (coll) fortuna; **to give s.o. a break** dare a qlcu l'opportunità ‖ *v* (*pret* **broke** [brok]; *pp* **broken**) *tr* (*to smash*) rompere, spezzare; (*to tame*) domare; (*to demote*) destituire; (*a record*) superare; (*to violate*) violare; (*to make bankrupt*) mandare al fallimento; (*to interrupt*) interrompere; (*to reduce the effects of*) attutire; (*to disclose*) rivelare; (*to bring to an end by force*) battere; (*a banknote*) cambiare; (*one's word*) mancare (*with dat*); (*a law*) rompere; **to break asunder** separare; **to break down** analizzare; **to break in** forzare; **to break open** forzare, scassinare; **to break up** dissolvere ‖ *intr* (*to divide*) rompersi; (*to burst*) scoppiare; (*said of voice of youngster*) cambiare; (*said of voice*) indebolirsi; (*said of a crowd*) disperdersi; (*said of weather*) rischiararsi; (*said of prices*) ribassare; (*to come into being*) scoppiare; (boxing) separarsi; **to break asunder** separarsi; **to break away** scappare; **to break down** abbattersi; (aut) essere *or* rimanere in panna; **to break even** fare patta; **to break in** irrompere; interrompere; **to break into** forzare; **to break into a run** incominciare a correre; **to break loose** liberarsi; (*said of a storm*) scatenarsi; **to break off** interrompere; **to break out** (*said of the skin*) avere un'eruzione; (*said, e.g., of war*) scoppiare; **to break through** aprirsi il varco; **to break up** disperdersi; **to break with** rompere le relazioni con

breakable ['brekəbəl] *adj* fragile

breakage ['brekɪdʒ] *s* rottura

break'down' *s* (*in negotiations*) rottura; (aut) panna; (chem) analisi *f*; (pathol) colasso

breaker ['brekər] *s* (*wave*) frangente *m*

breakfast ['brekfəst] *s* prima colazione || *intr* fare prima colazione

break'neck' *adj* pericoloso; **at breakneck speed** a rotta di collo, a rompicollo

break' of day' *s* alba

break'through' *s* (mil) penetrazione; (fig) scoperta sensazionale

break'up' *s* dispersione; dissoluzione; (*of a friendship*) rottura

break'wa'ter *s* diga, frangiflutti *m*

breast [brest] *s* petto; (*of female*) seno; (*source of emotions*) animo; **to make a clean breast of** fare una piena confessione di

breast'bone' *s* sterno

breast' drill' *s* trapano da petto

breast'feed' *v* (*pret & pp* **-fed** [fed]) *tr* allattare

breast'pin' *s* spilla

breast'stroke' *s* bracciata a rana

breath [breθ] *s* respiro, respirazione; (*odor*) alito; (*breeze*) soffio; (*whisper*) sussurro; (fig) vita; **out of breath** ansimante; **short of breath** corto di respiro; **to gasp for breath** respirare affannosamente; **under one's breath** sottovoce

breathe [brið] *tr* respirare; (*to whisper*) sussurrare; **to breathe one's last** esalare l'ultimo sospiro; **to not breathe a word** non dire una parola || *intr* respirare; **to breathe in** inspirare; **to breathe out** espirare

breath'ing spell' *s* attimo di respiro

breathless ['breθlɪs] *adj* senza fiato, ansimante; soffocante

breath'tak'ing *s* emozionante, commovente

breech [britʃ] *s* (*buttocks*) natiche *fpl*; (*rear part*) parte *f* posteriore; (*of gun*) culatta; **breeches** ['brɪtʃɪz] pantaloni *mpl* al ginocchio; pantaloni *mpl* da cavallo; **to wear the breeches** (coll) portare le brache

breed [brid] *s* razza; tipo; (*stock*) origine *f* || *v* (*pret & pp* **bred** [bred]) *tr* produrre; (*to raise*) allevare

breeder ['bridər] *s* allevatore *m*; riproduttore *m*

breeding ['bridɪŋ] *s* (*e.g., of livestock*) allevamento; educazione

breeze [briz] *s* brezza

breez·y ['brizi] *adj* (**-ier; -iest**) ventilato; (*brisk*) vivace, brioso

brethren ['breðrɪn] *spl* fratelli *mpl*

brevi·ty ['brevɪti] *s* (**-ties**) brevità *f*

brew [bru] *s* pozione; bevanda || *tr* (*beer*) fabbricare; (*to steep*) preparare; (*to plot*) complottare || *intr* (*said of beer*) fermentare; (*said of a storm*) prepararsi

brewer ['bru·ər] *s* birraio

brew'er's yeast' *s* lievito di birra

brewer·y ['bru·əri] *s* (**-ies**) birreria, fabbrica di birra

bribe [braɪb] *s* subornazione, bustarella || *tr* subornare, dare la bustarella a

briber·y ['braɪbəri] *s* (**-ies**) subornazione, corruzione

bric-a-brac ['brɪkə,bræk] *s* bric-a-brac *m*, cianfrusaglia, cianfrusaglie *fpl*

brick [brɪk] *s* mattone *m* || *tr* mattonare

brick'bat' *s* pezzo di mattone; (coll) insulto

brick'kiln' *s* fornace *f* per mattoni

bricklayer ['brɪk,le·ər] *s* muratore *m*

brick'yard' *s* deposito di mattoni

bridal ['braɪdəl] *adj* nuziale, da sposa

brid'al wreath' *s* serto nuziale

bride [braɪd] *s* sposa

bride'groom' *s* sposo

bridesmaid ['braɪdz,med] *s* damigella d'onore

bridge [brɪdʒ] *s* ponte *m*; (*of violin*) ponticello; (*on a ship*) ponte *m* di comando || *tr* gettare un ponte su; congiungere; **to bridge a gap** colmare una lacuna

bridge'head' *s* testa di ponte

bridle ['braɪdəl] *s* briglia || *tr* mettere la briglia a; (fig) frenare || *intr* drizzare il capo, insuperbirsi

bri'dle path' *s* strada cavalcabile

brief [brif] *adj* breve || *s* sommario; (law) esposto; (eccl) breve *m*; **briefs** slip *m* || *tr* dare istruzioni a, mettere al corrente

brief' case' *s* cartella, borsa d'avvocato

brier ['braɪ·ər] *s* radica; pipa di radica

brig [brɪg] *s* (naut) brigantino; (naut) prigione

brigade [brɪ'ged] *s* brigata

brigadier [,brɪgə'dɪr] *s* (coll) brigadier generale *m*, generale *m* di brigata

brigand ['brɪgənd] *s* brigante *m*

brigantine ['brɪgən,tin] *or* ['brɪgən,taɪn] *s* (naut) brigantino goletta

bright [braɪt] *adj* (*shining*) lucido; (*light*) brillante; (*lively*) vivo; intelligente; famoso; (*idea*) luminoso

brighten ['braɪtən] *tr* illuminare; ravvivare || *intr* illuminarsi; ravvivarsi; rischiararsi

bright' lights' *spl* luci *fpl* abbaglianti; (aut) fari *mpl* abbaglianti

brilliance ['brɪljəns] *or* **brilliancy** ['brɪljənsi] *s* splendore *m*, scintillio

brilliant ['brɪljənt] *adj* brillante

brim [brɪm] *s* (*e.g., of cup*) orlo; bordo; (*of hat*) ala, tesa || *v* (*pret & pp* **brimmed**; *ger* **brimming**) *intr* essere pieno sino all'orlo

brim'stone' *s* zolfo

brine [braɪn] *s* salamoia; acqua di mare

bring [brɪŋ] *v* (*pret & pp* **brought**

[brɔt]) *tr* far venire; provocare; (*to carry along*) portare con sè; **to bring about** causare; **to bring around** persuadere; **to bring back** restituire; **to bring down** far abbassare; (fig) umiliare; **to bring forth** dare alla luce; **to bring forward** (*an excuse*) addurre; (math) riportare; **to bring in** introdurre; far entrare; **to bring off** compiere; **to bring on** causare; **to bring oneself to** rassegnarsi a; **to bring out** (*to expose*) rivelare; (*to offer to the public*) presentare al pubblico; (*a book*) far uscire; **to bring to** far rinvenire; (*a ship*) fermare; **to bring together** riunire; **to bring up** (*children*) allevare, tirar su; (*to introduce*) allegare; (*to cough up*) rigettare

bringing-up ['brɪŋɪŋ'ʌp] *s* educazione

brink [brɪŋk] *s* orlo

briquet [brɪ'ket] *s* bricchetta

brisk [brɪsk] *adj* (*quick*) svelto; (*sharp*) acuto; (*invigorating*) frizzante; (*gunfire*) nutrito

bristle ['brɪsəl] *s* setola ‖ *intr* (*to be stiff*) irrigidirsi; (*said of hair*) rizzarsi; (*with anger*) adirarsi

bris-tly ['brɪsli] *adj* (*-tlier; -tliest*) irto di setole

British ['brɪtɪʃ] *adj* britannico ‖ **the British** i britannici, gl'inglesi

Britisher ['brɪtɪʃər] *s* britannico

Briton ['brɪtən] *s* britannico

Brittany ['brɪtəni] *s* la Bretagna

brittle ['brɪtəl] *adj* fragile, friabile; (*crisp*) croccante

broach [brɔtʃ] *s* (*pin*) spilla; (*spit*) spiedo; (*mach*) alesatore *m* ‖ *tr* perforare; (*a subject*) intavolare

broad [brɔd] *adj* largo; tollerante, liberale; (*daylight*) pieno; (*story*) grossolano; (*extensive*) lato; (*accent*) pronunciato

broad'cast' *s* disseminazione; (rad) radiodiffusione ‖ *v* (*pret & pp* -cast) *tr* disseminare, diffondere ‖ (*pret & pp* -cast or -casted) *tr* radiodiffondere

broad'casting sta'tion *s* stazione radiotrasmittente

broad'cloth' *s* (*wool*) panno di lana; (*cotton*) popeline *f*

broaden ['brɔdən] *tr* allargare, estendere ‖ *intr* allargarsi, estendersi

broad' jump' *s* salto in lunghezza

broadloom ['brɔd,lum] *adj* tessuto su telaio largo

broad-minded ['brɔd'maɪndɪd] *adj* di ampie vedute, liberale

broad-shouldered ['brɔd'ʃoldərd] *adj* largo di spalle

broad'side' *s* (nav) bordo; (nav) bordata; (*verbal criticism*) (coll) sfuriata; (*written criticism*) (coll) attacco violento

broad'sword' *s* spada da taglio

brocade [bro'ked] *s* broccato

broccoli ['brɑkəli] *s* broccolo; (*as food*) broccoli *mpl*

brochure [bro'ʃur] *s* opuscolo, libriccino

brogue [brog] *s* accento irlandese; scarpa forte e comoda

broil [brɔil] *s* cottura alla graticola; carne *f* cotta alla graticola; (*quarrel*) rissa, zuffa ‖ *tr* cucinare alla graticola; bruciare ‖ *intr* cucinare alla graticola; (*to quarrel*) rissare, azzuffarsi

broiler ['brɔilər] *s* graticola, gratella; (*chicken*) pollo da cucinare alla gratella or allo spiedo

broke [brok] *adj* (coll) al verde

broken ['brokən] *adj* rotto; fratturato; (*e.g., English*) parlato male; (*tamed*) domato

bro'ken-down' *adj* avvilito; rovinato

broken-hearted ['brokən'hartɪd] *adj* affranto

broker ['brokər] *s* sensale *m*; (*on the stock exchange*) agente *m* di cambio

brokerage ['brokərɪdʒ] *s* mediazione

bromide ['bromaɪd] *s* bromuro; (coll) banalità *f*

bromine ['bromin] *s* bromo

bronchitis [brɑŋ'kaɪtɪs] *s* bronchite *f*

bron-co ['brɑŋko] *s* (*-cos*) puledro brado

broncobuster ['brɑŋko,bʌstər] *s* domatore *m* di puledri bradi

bronze [brɑnz] *adj* bronzeo ‖ *s* bronzo ‖ *tr* bronzare ‖ *intr* abbronzarsi

brooch [brotʃ] *or* [brutʃ] *s* spilla

brood [brud] *s* covata, nidiata ‖ *tr* covare ‖ *intr* chiocciare; meditare; **to brood on** *or* **over** meditare con tristezza (su)

brook [bruk] *s* ruscello ‖ *tr*—**to brook no** non sopportare

broom [brum] *or* [brum] *s* scopa; (*shrub*) saggina

broom'corn' *s* sorgo

broom'stick' *s* manico di scopa

broth [brɔθ] *or* [brɑθ] *s* brodo

brothel ['brɑθəl] *or* ['brɑðəl] *s* postribolo, bordello

brother ['brʌðər] *s* fratello

brotherhood ['brʌðər,hud] *s* fratellanza; (*association*) confraternita

broth'er-in-law' *s* (**brothers-in-law**) cognato

brotherly ['brʌðərli] *adj* fraterno ‖ *adv* fraternamente

brow [brau] *s* ciglio; (*forehead*) fronte *f*; **to knit one's brow** aggrottare la fronte

brow'beat' *v* (*pret* -beat; *pp* -beaten) *tr* intimidire, intimorire

brown [braun] *adj* bruno; (*tanned*) abbronzato ‖ *s* color bruno ‖ *tr* colorare di bruno; abbronzare; (*metal*) brunire; (*culin*) dorare ‖ *intr* colorarsi di bruno; abbronzarsi; brunirsi; (culin) dorarsi

brownish ['braunɪʃ] *adj* brunastro

brown' stud'y *s*—**in a brown study** assorto in fantasticherie

brown' sug'ar *s* zucchero greggio

browse [brauz] *intr* (*said of cattle*) brucare; sfogliare; **to browse around** curiosare

bruise [bruz] *s* ammaccatura, contusione || *tr* ammaccare || *intr* ammaccarsi

brunet [bru'nɛt] *adj* bruno

brunette [bru'nɛt] *adj & s* bruna

brunt [brʌnt] *s* forza; scontro; peso

brush [brʌʃ] *s* pennello; spazzola; (*stroke*) pennellata; (*light touch*) tocco; (*brushwood*) macchia; (*brief encounter*) scaramuccia; (elec) spazzola || *tr* spazzolare; pennellare; **to brush aside** rigettare; **to brush up** ritoccare || *intr*—**to brush by** passar vicino; **to brush up on** ripassare

brush'-off' *s* (slang) scortesia; **to give the brush-off to** (slang) snobbare

brush'wood' *s* macchia, fratta

brusque [brʌsk] *adj* brusco

brusqueness ['brʌsknɪs] *s* bruschezza

Brussels ['brʌsəlz] *s* Bruxelles *f*

Brus'sels sprouts' *spl* cavolini *mpl*

brutal ['brutəl] *adj* brutale

brutali·ty [bru'tælɪti] *s* (-ties) brutalità *f*

brute [brut] *adj & s* bruto

brutish ['brutɪʃ] *adj* bruto

bubble ['bʌbəl] *s* bolla; (fig) chimera || *intr* bollire; (*to make a bubbling sound*) barbugliare; **to bubble over** traboccare

bub'ble bath' *s* bagno di schiuma

buccaneer [ˌbʌkə'nɪr] *s* bucaniere *m*

buck [bʌk] *s* (deer) cervo; (goat) caprone *m*; (sawhorse) cavalletto; (rabbit) coniglio maschio; (bucking) groppata; (dandy) damerino; (slang) dollaro; **to pass the buck** (coll) giocare a scaricabarile || *tr* resistere accanitamente || *intr* (said of a horse) fare salti da caprone; **to buck for** (slang) cercare di ottenere; **to buck up** (coll) rianimarsi, prender animo

bucket ['bʌkɪt] *s* secchio; bigoncia; (*e.g., of dredge*) benna; **to kick the bucket** (slang) tirare le cuoia

buck'et seat' *s* sedile *m*, strapuntino

buckle ['bʌkəl] *s* (clasp) fibbia, boccola; piega || *tr* affibbiare || *intr* piegarsi, curvarsi; **to buckle down** to (coll) mettersi di buzzo buono a

buck' pri'vate *s* (slang) soldato semplice

buckram ['bʌkrəm] *s* tela da fusto

buck'saw' *s* cavalletto

buck'shot' *s* pallini *mpl* da caccia

buck'tooth' *s* (-teeth) dente *m* in fuori, dente *m* sporgente

buck'wheat' *s* grano saraceno

bud [bʌd] *s* bocciolo, gemma; **to nip in the bud** troncare sul nascere || *v* (*pret & pp* budded; *ger* budding) *intr* sbocciare; nascere

Buddhism ['budɪzəm] *s* buddismo

bud·dy ['bʌdi] *s* (-dies) (coll) amico, compare *m*

budge [bʌdʒ] *tr* smuovere || *intr* muoversi

budget ['bʌdʒɪt] *s* bilancio || *tr* stanziare, preventivare; (*to schedule*) anticipare; (*time*) calcolare in anticipo

budgetary ['bʌdʒɪˌtɛri] *adj* preventivo, di bilancio

buff [bʌf] *adj* bruno giallastro; di pelle || *s* (leather) pelle gialla; dilet-

tante *m*; (mil) giacca di pelle gialla; (coll) pelle nuda || *tr* lucidare; (*to reduce the force of*) ammortizzare

buffa·lo ['bʌfəˌlo] *s* (-loes or -los) bufalo || *tr* (coll) intimidire

buffer ['bʌfər] *s* ammortizzatore *m*; cuscinetto; (worker) lucidatore *m*; (mach) lucidatrice *f*; (rr) respingente *m*

buff'er state' *s* stato cuscinetto

buffet [bu'fe] *s* (*piece of furniture*) credenza; (counter) buffet *m* || ['bʌfɪt] *s* pugno; schiaffo || *tr* dar pugni a; schiaffeggiare; lottare con; (*to push about*) sballottare

buffet' car' [bu'fe] *s* vagone *m* ristorante

buffoon [bə'fun] *s* buffone *m*

buffoner·y [bə'funəri] *s* (-ies) buffoneria

bug [bʌg] *s* insetto; (coll) germe *m*; (*in motor*) (slang) noia; (slang) pazzo; **to put a bug in the ear of** mettere una pulce nell'orecchio di || *v* (*pret & pp* bugged; *ger* bugging) *tr* (slang) installare un sistema d'ascolto nel telefono di; (*to annoy*) (slang) seccare || *intr*—**to bug out** (slang) andarsene

bug'bear' *s* spauracchio

bug·gy ['bʌgi] *adj* (-gier; -giest) pieno di cimici; (slang) pazzo || *s* (-gies) carrozzino

bug'house' *adj* (slang) pazzo || *s* (slang) manicomio

bugle ['bjugəl] *s* tromba, cornetta

bugler ['bjuglər] *s* trombettiere *m*

build [bɪld] *s* corporatura, taglia || *v* (*pret & pp* built [bɪlt]) *tr* costruire, edificare; fondare, basare; **to build up** sviluppare

builder ['bɪldər] *s* costruttore *m*; costruttore *m* edile

building ['bɪldɪŋ] *s* edificio, stabile *m*; costruzione; edilizia

build'ing and loan' associa'tion *s* società *f* di credito fondiario

build'ing lot' *s* (coll) terreno da costruzioni

build'ing trades' *spl* edilizia

build'-up' *s* concentrazione; sviluppo; processo di preparazione; propaganda favorevole

built'-in' *adj* (in a wall) murato; (in a cabinet) incassato, incorporato

built'-in clos'et *s* armadio a muro

built'-up' *adj* armato; popolato

bulb [bʌlb] *s* bulbo; (lamp) lampadina; (*of a lamp*) globo, cipolla

Bulgarian [bʌl'gɛrɪən] *adj & s* bulgaro

bulge [bʌldʒ] *s* protuberanza, sporgenza || *intr* sporgere, gonfiarsi

bulk [bʌlk] *s* volume *m*, massa; **in bulk** in blocco; sciolto || *intr* avere importanza; aumentare d'importanza

bulk'head' *s* diga; (naut) paratia

bulk·y ['bʌlki] *adj* (-ier; -iest) voluminoso

bull [bul] *s* toro; (*in the stockmarket*) rialzista *mf*; (slang) scemenza; (eccl) bulla || *tr*—**to bull the market** giocare al rialzo

bull'dog' *s* molosso

bulldoze ['bul‚doz] *tr* intimidire; (*land*) livellare

bulldozer ['bul‚dozər] *s* livellatrice *f*, apripista *m*

bullet ['bulɪt] *s* palla, pallottola

bulletin ['bulətɪn] *s* bollettino; (*of a school*) albo; (*journ*) comunicato

bul'letin board' *s* tabellone *m*

bul'let-proof' *adj* blindato

bull'fight' *s* corrida

bull'fight'er *s* torero

bull'finch' ['tʃ] *s* (*orn*) ciuffolotto

bull'frog' *s* rana americana

bull-headed ['bul‚hedɪd] *adj* testardo

bullion ['buljən] *s* lingotti *mpl* d'oro or d'argento; frangia d'oro; (*on an Italian general's hat*) greca

bullish ['bulɪʃ] *adj* ostinato; (*market*) al rialzo; (*speculator*) rialzista

bullock ['bulək] *s* manzo

bull'ring' *s* arena

bull's-eye ['bulz‚aɪ] *s* centro, tiro in pieno sul bersaglio; **to hit the bull's-eye** fare centro

bul·ly ['buli] *adj* (coll) eccellente ‖ *s* (-lies) bravaccio ‖ *v* (*pret & pp* -lied) *tr* intimidire

bulrush ['bul‚rʌʃ] *s* giunco; (Bibl) papiro

bulwark ['bulwərk] *s* baluardo; protezione ‖ *tr* proteggere

bum [bʌm] *adj* (slang) pessimo ‖ *s* (slang) vagabondo; **on the bum** (slang) rotto, fuori servizio ‖ *v* (*pret & pp* **bummed**; *ger* **bumming**) *tr* (slang) scroccare ‖ *intr* (slang) oziare; (slang) vivere d'elemosina; (slang) fare lo scroccatore

bumble ['bʌmbəl] *tr* abborracciare ‖ *intr* abborracciare; (*to stagger*) barcollare; (*to stumble*) balbettare; (*said of a bee*) ronzare

bum'blebee' *s* calabrone *m*

bump [bʌmp] *s* botta, botto; (*collision*) colpo, urto; (*swelling*) bernoccolo ‖ *tr* urtare; **to bump off** (slang) uccidere ‖ *intr* urtare, cozzare; **to bump into** incontrarsi con; cozzare contro

bumper ['bʌmpər] *adj* (coll) abbondante ‖ *s* bicchiere pieno fino all'orlo; (*aut*) paraurti *m*; (*rr*) respingente *m*

bumpkin ['bʌmpkɪn] *s* beota *m*

bumptious ['bʌmpʃəs] *adj* vanitoso, presuntuoso

bump·y ['bʌmpi] *adj* (-ier; -iest) (*road*) irregolare, ondulato; (*air*) agitato

bun [bʌn] *s* panino; (*of hair*) crocchia, treccia a ciambella

bunch [bʌntʃ] *s* (*of grapes*) grappolo; (*of keys*) mazzo; (*of grass*) ciuffo; (*of people*) gruppo; (*of twigs*) fastello; (*of animals*) branco ‖ *tr* (*things*) ammonticchiare; (*people*) raggruppare ‖ *intr* raggrupparsi

bundle ['bʌndəl] *s* fascio, fastello; (*package*) pacco; (*large package*) collo; (*bunch*) mucchio ‖ *tr* affastellare; impacchettare; ammucchiare; **to bundle off** or **out** cacciare precipitosamente; **to bundle up** infagottare ‖ *intr*—**to bundle up** infagottarsi

bung [bʌŋ] *s* spina, cannella

bungalow ['bʌŋgə‚lo] *s* casetta, villino, bungalow *m*

bung'hole' *s* spina, foro della botte

bungle ['bʌŋgəl] *s* abborracciatura ‖ *tr* abborracciare ‖ *intr* lavorare alla carlona

bungler ['bʌŋglər] *s* abborraccione *m*

bungling ['bʌŋglɪŋ] *adj* goffo; mal fatto ‖ *s* abborracciatura

bunion ['bʌnjən] *s* gonfiore *m* dell'alluce

bunk [bʌŋk] *s* letto a castello; (nav) cuccetta; (slang) sciocchezza ‖ *intr* dormire in cuccetta

bunk' bed' *s* letto a castello

bunker ['bʌŋkər] *s* (bin) carbonile *m*; (mil) casamatta; (golf) ostacolo

bun·ny ['bʌni] *s* (-nies) coniglietto

bunting ['bʌntɪŋ] *s* ornamento di bandiere; (nav) gala; (orn) zigolo

buoy [bɔɪ] or ['bu·i] *s* boa; (*life preserver*) salvagente *m* ‖ *tr*—**to buoy up** tenere a galla; (fig) rincuorare

buoyancy ['bɔɪ·ənsi] or ['bujənsi] *s* galleggiabilità *f*; (*cheerfulness*) allegria, esuberanza

buoyant ['bɔɪ·ənt] or ['bujənt] *adj* galleggiante; allegro, esuberante

bur [bʌr] *s* riccio, aculeo

burble ['bʌrbəl] *s* gorgoglio ‖ *intr* gorgogliare

burden ['bʌrdən] *s* carico, peso, fardello; (*of a speech*) tema *m*; (*chorus*) ritornello; (naut) portata ‖ *tr* caricare

bur'den of proof' *s* onere *m* della prova

burdensome ['bʌrdənsəm] *adj* oneroso

burdock ['bʌrdak] *s* lappa, lappola

bureau ['bjuro] *s* comò *m*; (*agency*) ufficio, servizio

bureaucra·cy [bju'rakrəsi] *s* (-cies) burocrazia

bureaucrat ['bjurə‚kræt] *s* burocrate *m*

burglar ['bʌrglər] *s* scassinatore *m*

bur'glar alarm' *s* campanello antifurto

burglarize ['bʌrglə‚raɪz] *tr* scassinare

bur'glar-proof' *adj* a prova di furto

burgla·ry ['bʌrgləri] *s* (-ries) furto con scasso, scassinatura

Burgundy ['bʌrgəndi] *s* la Borgogna; (*wine*) borgogna *m*

burial ['berɪ·əl] *s* sepoltura

bur'ial ground' *s* cimitero

burin ['bjurɪn] *s* burino, cesello

burlap ['bʌrlæp] *s* tela di iuta

burlesque [bʌr'lesk] *adj* burlesco ‖ *s* farsa, burlesque *m* ‖ *tr* parodiare

burlesque' show' *s* spettacolo di varietà, music-hall *m*

bur·ly ['bʌrli] *adj* (-lier; -liest) membruto, robusto

Burma ['bʌrmə] *s* la Birmania

burn [bʌrn] *s* bruciatura, scottatura ‖ *v* (*pret & pp* **burned** or **burnt** [bʌrnt]) *tr* bruciare; (*to set on fire*) dar fuoco a; (*bricks*) cuocere; **to burn down** radere al suolo; **to burn up** consumare; (*the road*) divorare; (coll) fare arrabbiare ‖ *intr* bruciare, bruciarsi; (*said of lights*) essere acceso, e.g., **the lights were burning** la luce era accesa; **to burn out** (*said of an electric bulb or a fuse*) bruciarsi;

to burn to (fig) agognare di; **to burn up** (coll) essere arrabiato; **to burn with** (e.g., envy) ardere di
burner ['bʌrnər] s (of gas fixture or lamp) becco; (of furnace) bruciatore m
burning ['bʌrnɪŋ] adj bruciante, scottante || s incendio; (ceramic) cottura finale
burn'ing ques'tion s questione di attualità palpitante
burnish ['bʌrnɪʃ] s lucidatura || tr brunire
burnt' al'mond [bʌrnt] s mandorla tostata
burp [bʌrp] s (coll) rutto || intr (coll) ruttare
burr [bʌr] s riccio, aculeo; (rough edge) bava; (dentist's drill) fresa
burrow ['bʌro] s tana, buca || intr imbucarsi, rintanarsi
bursar ['bʌrsər] s tesoriere universitario
burst [bʌrst] s esplosione; (e.g., of machine gun) raffica; (break) crepa; (of passion) accesso; (of speed) slancio || tr far scoppiare || intr scoppiare, esplodere; **to burst into** (e.g., a room) irrompere in; (e.g., angry words) esplodere in; **to burst out crying** scoppiare in lacrime; **to burst with laughter** scoppiare dalle risa
bur·y ['bɛri] v (pret & pp -ied) tr sotterrare; **to be buried in thought** essere immerso nel pensiero; **to bury the hatchet** fare la pace
bus [bʌs] s (buses or busses) bus m, autobus m || v (pret & pp bused or bussed) ger busing or bussing) tr trasportare con autobus
bus'boy' s secondo cameriere
bus·by ['bʌzbi] s (-bies) colbacco
bus' driv'er s conducente mf di autobus
bush [bʊʃ] s cespuglio, arbusto; **to beat around the bush** menare il can per l'aia
bushed [bʊʃt] adj (coll) stanco morto
bushel ['bʊʃəl] s staio
bushing ['bʊʃɪŋ] s (mach) bronzina
bush·y ['bʊʃi] adj (-ier; -iest) ricco di arbusti; (face) ispido
business ['bɪznɪs] adj commerciale || s occupazione; commercio; affare m, negozio; faccenda; impiego; **it is not your business** non è affare Suo; **to know one's business** sapere il fatto proprio; **to make it one's business to** proporsi di; **to mean business** (coll) farla sul serio; **to mind one's own business** impicciarsi degli affari propri
businesslike ['bɪznɪs‚laɪk] adj metodico; serio; efficace
busi'ness·man' s (-men') commerciante m, uomo d'affari
busi'ness suit' s abito da passeggio
busi'ness·wom'an s (wom'en) commerciante f
bus'man s (-men) guidatore m d'autobus
buss [bʌs] s bacione sonoro || tr (coll) baciare sonoramente
bus' stop' s fermata degli autobus

bust [bʌst] s busto; petto; (slang) fallimento; (slang) pugno || tr (slang) rompere; (slang) far fallire; (slang) colpire, dare pugni a; (mil) degradare
buster ['bʌstər] s (coll) ragazzo; (coll) rompitore m
bustle ['bʌsəl] s (on a dress) guardinfante m; attività f || intr affrettarsi
bus·y ['bɪzi] adj (-ier; -iest) occupato || v (pret & pp -ied) tr occupare, tenere occupato; **to busy oneself with** occuparsi di
bus'y·bod'y s (-ies) ficcanaso
bus'y sig'nal s (telp) segnale m d'occupato
but [bʌt] s ma m || adv solo, solamente; **but for** se non . . . per il prep eccetto, ad eccezione di, meno, se non; **all but** quasi || conj ma; che non, e.g., **I never go out in the rain but I catch a cold** non esco mai con la pioggia che non mi pigli un raffreddore
butcher ['bʊtʃər] s macellaio || tr macellare; massacrare
butch'er knife' s coltello da cucina, coltella
butch'er shop' s macelleria
butcher·y ['bʊtʃəri] s (-ies) macello; carneficina
butler ['bʌtlər] s cantiniere m, credenziere m
butt [bʌt] s (butting) cornata; (of rifle or gun) calcio; (of cigar) mozzicone m; (target) bersaglio; (end) estremità f; (of ridicule) zimbello; (cask) botte f || tr dare cornate a; cozzare contro || intr—**to butt into** (slang) intromettersi in
butter ['bʌtər] s burro || tr imburrare; **to butter up** (coll) adulare
but'ter·cup' s (bot) bottone m d'oro, ranuncolo
but'ter dish' s piattino per il burro
but'ter·fat' s grasso nel latte
but'ter·fly' s (-flies) farfalla
but'ter knife' s coltello per il burro
but'ter·milk' s latticello
but'ter sauce' s burro fuso
but'ter·scotch' s caramella al burro
buttocks ['bʌtəks] spl chiappe fpl, natiche fpl
button ['bʌtən] s bottone m || tr abbottonare
but'ton·hole' s occhiello, asola || tr attaccare un bottone a
but'ton·hook' s allacciabottoni m
buttress ['bʌtrɪs] s contrafforte m; piedritto || tr rinforzare
buxom ['bʌksəm] adj avvenente, procace
buy [baɪ] s compra || v (pret & pp bought [bɔt]) tr comprare; **to buy off** corrompere; **to buy out** comprare la parte di
buyer ['baɪ·ər] s compratore m
buzz [bʌz] s brusio, ronzio || tr volare a bassa quota sopra; (coll) fare una telefonata a || intr ronzare
buzzard ['bʌzərd] s (hawk) poiana; avvoltoio americano
buzzer ['bʌzər] s suoneria ronzante

buzz' saw' *s* sega circolare, segatrice *f* a disco
by [baɪ] *adv* oltre, e.g., **to speed by** correre velocemente oltre; **by and by** fra poco; **by and large** generalmente ‖ *prep* vicino a; di, durante, e.g., **by night** di notte, durante la notte; a, e.g., **they work by the hour** lavorano all'ora; (*not later than, through*) per; (*past*) in fronte a; (*through the agency of*) da; (*according to*) secondo; (*math*) per, volte; **by far** di molto; **by the way** a proposito
bygone ['baɪ‚gɒn] or ['baɪ‚gɑn] *adj & s* passato; **to let bygones be bygones** dimenticare il passato

bylaw ['baɪ‚lɔ] *s* legge *f* locale, regolamento di una società
by'-line' *s* (journ) firma
by'pass' *s* linea secondaria; (*detour*) deviazione ‖ *tr* fare una deviazione oltre a; (*a difficulty*) evitare
by'path' *s* sentiero secondario; sentiero privato
by'prod'uct *s* sottoprodotto
bystander ['baɪ‚stændər] *s* astante *m*, spettatore *m*
byway ['baɪ‚we] *s* via traversa
byword ['baɪ‚wʌrd] *s* proverbio; oggetto di obbrobrio
Byzantium [bɪ'zænʃɪ‚əm] or [bɪ'zæntɪ‚əm] *s* Bisanzio

C

C, c [si] *s* terza lettera dell'alfabeto inglese
cab [kæb] *s* vettura di piazza; tassì *m*; (*of truck or locomotive*) cabina
cabbage ['kæbɪdʒ] *s* cavolo, verza
cab' driv'er *s* autista *m* di piazza; (*of horse-drawn cab*) vetturino
cabin ['kæbɪn] *s* (*shed*) capanna; (*hut*) baracca; (aer, naut) cabina
cab'in boy' *s* mozzo
cabinet ['kæbɪnɪt] *s* (*piece of furniture*) vetrina; (*for a radio*) armadietto; (*small room; ministry of a government*) gabinetto
cab'inet-mak'er *s* ebanista *m*
cab'inet-mak'ing *s* ebanisteria
cable ['kebəl] *s* cavo; cablogramma; (elec) cablaggio ‖ *tr* cablare, mandare un cablogramma a
ca'ble address' *s* indirizzo telegrafico
ca'ble car' *s* funicolare *f*, teleferica
cablegram ['kebəl‚græm] *s* cablogramma *m*
caboose [kə'bus] *s* (rr) vagone *m* di coda
cab'stand' *s* stazione di tassametri
cache [kæʃ] *s* nascondiglio ‖ *tr* mettere in un nascondiglio
cachet [kæ'ʃe] *s* sigillo; (*distinguishing feature*) impronta
cackle ['kækəl] *s* (*of chickens*) coccodè *m*; (*of people*) chiacchierio ‖ *intr* fare coccodè; ciarlare
cac·tus ['kæktəs] *s* (**-tuses** or **-ti** [taɪ]) cactus *m*
cad [kæd] *s* mascalzone *m*
cadaver [kə'dævər] *s* cadavere *m*
cadaverous [kə'dævərəs] *adj* cadaverico
caddie ['kædi] *s* portamazze *m*
cadence ['kedəns] *s* cadenza
cadet [kə'det] *s* cadetto
cadmium ['kædmɪ‚əm] *s* cadmio
cadres ['kædrɪz] *spl* (mil) quadri *mpl*
Caesar'ean sec'tion [sɪ'zɛrɪ‚ən] *s* taglio cesareo
café [kæ'fe] *s* caffè *m*, bar *m*, ristorante *m*
ca·fé soci'ety *s* bel mondo

cafeteria [‚kæfə'tɪrɪ‚ə] *s* mensa, tavola calda, caffetteria
caffeine [kæ'fin] or ['kæfi‚ɪn] *s* caffeina
cage [kedʒ] *s* gabbia; (*of elevator*) cabina ‖ *tr* ingabbiare
ca·gey ['kedʒi] *adj* (**-gier; -giest**) (coll) astuto, cauto
cahoots [kə'huts] *s*—**to be in cahoots** (slang) far lega, essere in combutta; **to go cahoots** (slang) dividere in parti eguali
Cain [ken] *s* Caino; **to raise Cain** (slang) arrabbiarsi; (slang) fare una sfuriata
Cairo ['kaɪro] *s* il Cairo
caisson ['kesən] *s* cassone *m*; (archit) cassettone *m*
cajole [kə'dʒol] *tr* lusingare; persuadere con lusinghe
cajoler·y [kə'dʒoləri] *s* (**-ies**) lusinga
cake [kek] *s* dolce *m*; torta, pasta; (*with bread-like dough*) focaccia; (*of soap*) saponetta; (*of earth*) zolla; **to take the cake** (coll) essere il colmo ‖ *tr* incrostare ‖ *intr* indurirsi; incrostarsi
calabash ['kælə‚bæʃ] *s* zucca a fiasca
calaboose ['kælə‚bus] *s* (coll) gattabuia
calamitous [kə'læmɪtəs] *adj* calamitoso
calami·ty [kə'læmɪti] *s* (**-ties**) calamità *f*
calci·fy ['kælsɪ‚faɪ] *v* (*pret & pp* **-fied**) *tr* calcificare ‖ *intr* calcificarsi
calcium ['kælsɪ‚əm] *s* calcio
calculate ['kælkjə‚let] *tr* calcolare ‖ *intr* calcolare; **to calculate on** contare su
cal'culating machine' *s* (macchina) calcolatrice
calcu·lus ['kælkjələs] *s* (**-luses** or **-li** [‚laɪ]) (math, pathol) calcolo
calendar ['kæləndər] *s* calendario; (*agenda*) ordine *m* del giorno
calf [kæf] or [kɑf] *s* (**calves** [kævz] or [kɑvz]) vitello; (*of shoes or binding*) pelle *f* di vitello; (*of the leg*) polpaccio
calf'skin' *s* pelle *f* di vitello

caliber ['kælɪbər] s calibro
calibrate ['kælɪ‚bret] tr calibrare
cali·co ['kælɪ‚ko] s (-coes or -cos) cotone stampato, calico
California [‚kælɪ'fɔrnɪ·ə] s la California
calipers ['kælɪpərz] spl compasso a grossezze, calibro
caliph ['kelɪf] or ['kælɪf] s califfo
calisthenic [‚kælɪs'θenɪk] adj ginnastico || calisthenics spl ginnastica a corpo libero
calk [kɔk] tr var of caulk
call [kɔl] s chiamata; visita; (shout) grido, richiamo; (of bugle) squillo; (of telephone) colpo; (of ship) scalo; obbligo; vocazione; (com) richiesta; on call disponibile; within call a portata di voce || tr chiamare; convocare; (to awaken) svegliare; to call back richiamare; to call in (e.g., an expert) fare venire; (e.g., currency) domandare, esigere; to call off annullare; to call out chiamare; to call together convocare; to call up chiamare per telefono || intr chiamare; visitare; to call at passare per la casa di; (naut) fare scalo a; to call for venire a prendere; to call out gridare; to go calling andare a fare visite
cal′la lil′y ['kælə] s (Zantedeschia aethiopica) calla dei fioristi
call′boy′ s (in a hotel) fattorino; (theat) buttafuori m
caller ['kɔlər] s visitatore m
call′ girl′ s ragazza squillo
calling ['kɔlɪŋ] s appello; professione
call′ing card′ s biglietto da visita
call′ num′ber s numero telefonico; numero di biblioteca
callous ['kæləs] adj calloso; insensibile
callow ['kælo] adj inesperto, immaturo
call′ to arms′ s chiamata alle armi
call′ to the col′ors chiamata sotto la bandiera
callus ['kæləs] s callo
calm [kɑm] adj calmo, tranquillo || s calma || tr calmare, tranquillizzare || intr—to calm down calmarsi; (said of weather) abbonacciarsi
calmness ['kɑmnɪs] s calma, placidità f, tranquillità f
calomel ['kælə‚mel] s calomelano
calorie ['kælərɪ] s caloria
calum·ny ['kæləmnɪ] s (-nies) calunnia
Calvary ['kælvərɪ] s (Bib) Calvario
cam [kæm] s camma
camber ['kæmbər] s curvatura; convessità f || tr arcuare || intr curvarsi
cambric ['kembrɪk] s cambrì m
camel ['kæməl] s cammello
came·o ['kæmɪ‚o] s (-os) cammeo
camera ['kæmərə] s macchina fotografica; (mov) cinepresa
cam′era·man′ s (-men′) operatore m
camomile ['kæmə‚maɪl] s camomilla
camouflage ['kæmə‚flɑʒ] s mascheramento || tr mascherare, camuffare
camp [kæmp] s accampamento, campo || intr accamparsi
campaign [kæm'pen] s campagna || intr fare una campagna

campaigner [kæm'penər] s veterano; (pol) propagandista m
camp′ bed′ s letto da campo, branda
camper ['kæmpər] s campeggiatore m, campeggista mf
camp′fire′ s fuoco di accampamento
camp′ground′ s terreno per campeggio
camphor ['kæmfər] s canfora
camp′stool′ s seggiolino pieghevole
campus ['kæmpəs] s campo, terreno dell'università
cam′shaft′ s albero di distribuzione, albero a camme
can [kæn] s lattina, barattolo; (of gasoline or oil) bidone m || v (pret & pp canned; ger canning) tr inscatolare; (slang) licenziare || v (pret & cond could) aux I can speak English so parlare inglese; can he go now? se ne può andare ora?
Canada ['kænədə] s il Canadà
Canadian [kə'nedɪ·ən] adj & s canadese mf
canal [kə'næl] s canale m
canar·y [kə'nerɪ] s (-ies) canarino || Canaries spl Canarie fpl
can·cel ['kænsəl] v (pret & pp -celed or -celled; ger -celing or -celling) tr cancellare; annullare; revocare; (stamps) timbrare, annullare
cancellation [‚kænsə'leʃən] s cancellazione, annullamento; cassazione; (of a stamp) bollo
cancer ['kænsər] s cancro || Cancer s Cancro
cancerous ['kænsərəs] adj canceroso
candela·brum [‚kændə'lɑbrəm] s (-bra [brə] or -brums) candelabro
candid ['kændɪd] adj candido; sincero, franco
candida·cy ['kændɪdəsɪ] s (-cies) candidatura
candidate ['kændɪ‚det] s candidato; (for a degree) laureando
can′did cam′era s camera fotografica indiscreta
candied ['kændɪd] adj candito
candle ['kændəl] s candela || tr (eggs) sperare
can′dle·hold′er s var of candlestick
can′dle·light′ s luce f or lume m di candela
can′dle·pow′er s (phys) candela
can′dle·stick′ s (ornate) candeliere m; (plain) bugia
candor ['kændər] s candore m; ingenuità f
can·dy ['kændɪ] s (-dies) dolciumi mpl; a piece of candy un bombon || v (pret & pp -died) tr candire
can′dy box′ s bomboniera
can′dy dish′ s bomboniera; (three-tier-high) alzata
can′dy store′ s confetteria
cane [ken] s canna, giunco; (for walking) bastone m || tr bastonare; (chairs) impagliare
cane′ seat′ s sedia impagliata
cane′ sug′ar s zucchero di canna
canine ['kenaɪn] adj canino || s (tooth) canino; (dog) cane m
canister ['kænɪstər] s barattolo

canned' goods' *spl* conserve *fpl* alimentari; prodotti *mpl* in scatola

canned' mu'sic *s* (slang) musica su dischi

canner•y ['kænəri] *s* (-ies) fabbrica di conserve alimentari

cannibal ['kænɪbəl] *adj & s* cannibale *mf*, antropofago

canning ['kænɪŋ] *s* conservazione

cannon ['kænən] *s* cannone *m*

cannonade [ˌkænə'ned] *s* cannonata || *tr* cannoneggiare

can'non-ball' *s* palla da cannone

can'non fod'der *s* carne *f* da cannone

can•ny ['kæni] *adj* (-nier; -niest) astuto, fino; malizioso

canoe [kə'nu] *s* canoa, piroga

canon ['kænən] *s* canone *m*; (*priest*) canonico

canonical [kə'nɑnɪkəl] *adj* canonico || **canonicals** *spl* paramenti liturgici

canonize ['kænə̩naɪz] *tr* canonizzare

can'on law' *s* diritto canonico

canon•ry ['kænənri] *s* (-ries) canonicato

can' o'pener ['opənər] *s* apriscatole *m*

cano•py ['kænəpi] *s* (-pies) tenda; baldacchino; (*of sky*) (fig) volta

cant [kænt] *adj* ipocrita || *s* linguaggio ipocrita; gergo; (*slope*) inclinazione

cantaloupe ['kæntə̩lop] *s* melone *m*

cantankerous [kæn'tæŋkərəs] *adj* bisbetico, attaccabrighe

canteen [kæn'tin] *s* cantina, spaccio; (*metal bottle*) borraccia

canter ['kæntər] *s* piccolo galoppo || *intr* andare al piccolo galoppo

cantilever ['kæntɪ̩livər] *adj* a cantiliver || *s* trave *f* a sbalzo; (archit) trave *f* a mensola

cantle ['kæntəl] *s* arcione *m* posteriore

canton [kæn'tɑn] *s* cantone *m*; regione || *tr* accantonare

cantonment [kæn'tɑnmənt] *s* accantonamento

cantor ['kæntər] *s* cantore *m*

canvas ['kænvəs] *s* (*cloth*) olona; (*e.g. on open truck*) copertone *m*; (*painting*) tela; (naut) vela; **under canvas** (naut) a vele spiegate

canvass ['kænvəs] *s* discussione; dibattito; (pol) sollecitazione di voti || *tr* discutere; (*votes*) sollecitare; (*to investigate*) indagare; (com) fare la piazza a || *intr* discutere; sollecitare voti; indagare; (com) fare la piazza

canyon ['kænjən] *s* cañon *m*

cap [kæp] *s* berretto; cuffia; (*of academic costume*) berrettone *m*; (*of bottle*) tappo, capsula; (*e.g., of fountain pen*) cappuccio || *v* (*pret & pp* capped; *ger* capping) *tr* (*a person*) coprire il capo di; (*s.o.'s head*) coprire con il berretto; (*a bottle*) mettere il tappo a; terminare; **to cap the climax** essere il colmo

capabil•ty [ˌkepə'bɪlɪti] *s* (-ties) capacità *f*, abilità *f*

capable ['kepəbəl] *adj* capace, abile

capacious [kə'peʃəs] *adj* ampio, capace

capaci•ty [kə'pæsɪti] *s* (-ties) capacità

f; **filled to capacity** pieno zeppo; **in the capacity of** in veste di

cap' and bells' *spl* berretto a sonagli; scettro di buffone

cap' and gown' *s* costume accademico, toga e tocco

caparison [kə'pærɪsən] *s* bardatura || *tr* bardare

cape [kep] *s* cappa, mantello; (mil) mantella; (geog) capo

Cape' of Good' Hope' *s* Capo di Buona Speranza

caper ['kepər] *s* capriola; (bot) cappero; **to cut capers** far capriole; (fig) fare monellerie || *intr* fare capriole; saltellare

Cape' Town' *s* Città *f* del Capo

capital ['kæpɪtəl] *adj* capitale || *s* (*money*) capitale *m*; (*city*) capitale *f*; (*of column*) capitello

cap'ital expen'ditures *spl* spese *fpl* d'impianto

cap'ital goods' *spl* beni *mpl* strumentali

capitalism ['kæpɪtə̩lɪzəm] *s* capitalismo

capitalize ['kæpɪtə̩laɪz] *tr* capitalizzare; scrivere con la maiuscola || *intr*—**to capitalize on** approfittare di

cap'ital let'ter *s* lettera maiuscola

cap'ital pun'ishment *s* pena capitale

cap'ital stock' *s* capitale *m* sociale

capitol ['kæpɪtəl] *s* campidoglio

capitulate [kə'pɪtʃə̩let] *intr* capitolare

capon ['kepən] *s* cappone *m*

caprice [kə'pris] *s* capriccio, ghiribizzo

capricious [kə'prɪʃəs] *adj* capriccioso, estroso

Capricorn ['kæprɪ̩kɔrn] *s* Capricorno

capsize ['kæpsaɪz] *tr* capovolgere || *intr* capovolgersi

capstan ['kæpstən] *s* argano

cap'stone' *s* (archit) coronamento

capsule ['kæpsəl] *adj* in miniatura; riassuntivo || *s* capsula

captain ['kæptən] *s* capitano; (naut) comandante *m*; || *tr* capitanare

caption ['kæpʃən] *s* titolo; (mov) didascalia; (journ) leggenda

captivate ['kæptɪ̩vet] *tr* cattivare, affascinare

captive ['kæptɪv] *adj & s* prigioniero

captivi•ty ['kæp'tɪvɪti] *s* (-ties) cattività *f*, prigionia

captor ['kæptər] *s* persona che cattura

capture ['kæptʃər] *s* cattura, presa; (*person*) prigioniero; (*thing*) bottino || *tr* catturare; prendere

car [kɑr] *s* (*of train*) vagone *m*, vettura; (*automobile*) automobile *m* & *f*, macchina, vettura; (*of elevator*) cabina; (*of balloon*) navicella; (*for narrow-gauge track*) carrello

carafe [kə'ræf] *s* caraffa

caramel ['kærəməl] or ['kɑrməl] *s* (*burnt sugar*) caramello; (*candy*) caramella appiccicaticcia

carat ['kærət] *s* carato

caravan ['kærə̩væn] *s* carovana; (*covered vehicle*) furgone *m*

caravansa•ry [ˌkærə'vænsəri] *s* (-ries) caravanserraglio

caraway ['kærə̩we] *s* cumino

car'barn' *s* rimessa del tram

carbide ['kɑrbaɪd] s carburo

carbine ['kɑrbaɪn] s carabina

carbol'ic ac'id [kɑr'bɑlɪk] s acido fenico

carbon ['kɑrbən] s (in arc light, battery, auto cylinder) carbone m; carta carbone; (chem) carbonio

car'bon cop'y s copia a carbone, velina

car'bon diox'ide s anidride carbonica

car'bon monox'ide s ossido di carbonio, monossido di carbonio

car'bon pa'per s carta carbone

carbuncle ['kɑrbʌŋkəl] s (stone; boil) carbonchio; (boil) foruncolo

carburetor ['kɑrbə,retər] or ['kɑrbjə-,retər] s carburatore m

carcass ['kɑrkəs] s carcassa; (in state of decay) carogna

card [kɑrd] s (file) scheda; (post card) cartolina; (personal card) biglietto; (announcement) partecipazione; (playing card) carta da gioco; (coll) tipo divertente, bel tipo

card'board' s cartone m

card'-car'rying mem'ber s tesserato

card' case' s portatessere m

card' cat'alogue s schedario

card'hold'er s socio, tesserato

cardiac ['kɑrdɪ,æk] adj & s cardiaco

cardigan ['kɑrdɪgən] s panciotto a maglia

cardinal ['kɑrdɪnəl] adj cardinale, fondamentale || s cardinale m

card' in'dex s schedario

cardiogram ['kɑrdɪ·o,græm] s cardiogramma m

card' par'ty s riunione per giocare a carte

card'sharp' s baro

card' ta'ble s tavoliere m, tavolino da gioco

card' trick' s gioco di prestigio colle carte

care [ker] s cura, custodia; inquietudine f, preoccupazione; cautela; care of presso, e.g., R. Smith care of Jones R. Smith presso Jones; to take care of fare attenzione; to take care of prendersi cura di, badare a; to take care of oneself badare alla salute || intr curarsi, badare; I don't care non m'importa; to care about preoccuparsi di; to care for voler bene a; curarsi di; to care to volere

careen [kə'rin] s carenaggio || intr sbandare

career [kə'rɪr] adj di carriera || s carriera

care'free' adj spensierato

careful ['kerfəl] adj attento; diligente; premuroso; careful! faccia attenzione!

careless ['kerlɪs] adj trascurato; imprudente; indifferente

carelessness ['kerlɪsnɪs] s trascuratezza; imprudenza; indifferenza

caress [kə'res] s carezza || tr carezzare, accarezzare

caretaker ['ker,tekər] adj interinale, provvisorio || s custode m; guardiano; (of school) bidello

care'taker gov'ernment s governo interinale

care'worn' adj accasciato dalle preoccupazioni

car'fare' s passaggio, denaro per il tram; (small sum of money) spiccioli mpl

car·go ['kɑrgo] s (-goes or -gos) carico mercantile

car'go boat' s battello da carico

Caribbean [,kærɪ'bi·ən] or [kə-'rɪbɪ·ən] s Mare m dei Caraibi

caricature ['kærɪkət/ər] s caricatura || tr mettere in caricatura

carillon ['kærɪ,lɑn] or [kə'rɪljən] s carillon m || intr suonare il carillon

car'load' s vagone completo, vagonata

carnage ['kɑrnɪdʒ] s carnaio, carneficina

carnal ['kɑrnəl] adj carnale

carnation [kɑr'ne/ən] adj incarnato || s garofano; (color) incarnato

carnival ['kɑrnɪvəl] adj carnevalesco || s carnevale m; festa, spettacolo all'aperto

carob ['kærəb] s (fruit) carruba; (tree) carrubo

car·ol ['kærəl] s canzone f popolare; pastorella di Natale || v (pret & pp -oled or -olled; ger -oling or -olling) tr cantare

carom ['kærəm] s carambola || intr carambolare

carousal [kə'rauzəl] s baldoria, gozzoviglia

carouse [kə'rauz] intr fare baldoria, gozzovigliare

carousel [,kærə'zel] or [,kæru'zel] s giostra, carosello

carp ['kɑrp] s carpa || intr lagnarsi, criticare

carpenter ['kɑrpəntər] s falegname m

carpentry ['kɑrpəntrɪ] s falegnameria

carpet ['kɑrpɪt] s tappeto || tr coprire con un tappeto, tappetare

carpetbagger ['kɑrpɪt,bægər] s avventuriero; (hist) politicante m

car'pet sweep'er s spazzolone elettrico per tappeti

car'port' s tettoia-garage f

car'-ren'tal serv'ice s servizio di autonoleggi

carriage ['kærɪdʒ] s carrozza; (of gun) affusto; (of typewriter) carrello; (bearing) portamento; (mach) slitta

carrier ['kærɪ·ər] s portatore m; (person or organization in business of carrying goods) spedizioniere m; (of mail) postino; (e.g., on top of station wagon) portabagagli m; (of a disease) veicolo

car'rier pig'eon s piccione m viaggiatore

car'rier wave' s (rad) onda portante

carrion ['kærɪ·ən] s carogne fpl

carrot ['kærət] s carota

car·ry ['kærɪ] v (pret & pp -ried) tr portare; trasportare; (a burden) sopportare; (an election) guadagnare; (to keep in stock) avere in assortimento; to carry along portare con sé; to carry away trasportare; entusiasmare; to carry forward riportare; to carry out eseguire; to carry

through completare; **to carry weight** aver importanza || *intr* avere la portata (di), e.g., **this gun carries two miles** questo cannone ha la portata di due miglia; **to carry on** continuare; (coll) fare baccano

cart [kɑrt] *s* carro, carretto; (*for shopping*) carrello; **to put the cart before the horse** mettere il carro davanti ai buoi || *tr* trasportare col carro

carte blanche [ˈkɑrtˈblɑnʃ] *s* carta bianca

cartel [kɑrˈtɛl] *s* cartello

Carthage [ˈkɑrθɪdʒ] *s* Cartagine *f*

cart' horse' *s* cavallo da tiro

cartilage [ˈkɑrtɪlɪdʒ] *s* cartilagine *f*

carton [ˈkɑrtən] *s* cartone *m*; scatola di cartone; (*of cigarettes*) stecca

cartoon [kɑrˈtun] *s* disegno; caricatura; (*comic strip*) fumetto; (mov) disegno animato || *tr* fare caricature di

cartoonist [kɑrˈtunɪst] *s* disegnatore *m*; caricaturista *mf*

cartridge [ˈkɑrtrɪdʒ] *s* cartuccia; (*e.g., of camera*) caricatore *m*

car'tridge belt' *s* cartucciera; (mil) giberna

car'tridge clip' *s* serbatoio

cart'wheel' *s* ruota di carro; **to turn cartwheels** fare la ruota

carve [kɑrv] *tr* (*meats*) trinciare; scolpire, intagliare

carv'ing knife' *s* trinciante *m*

car' wash'er *s* lavamacchine *m*

cascade [kæsˈked] *s* cascata || *intr* cadere a mo' di cascata

case [kes] *s* (*box*) cassetta; (*of watch*) calotta; (*outer covering*) astuccio; (*instance*) caso; (gram) caso; (law) causa; (typ) cassa; **in case** in caso, nel caso; **in no case** in nessun modo || *tr* rinchiudere; (*to package*) impaccare; (slang) ispezionare

casement [ˈkesmənt] *s* telaio di finestra; finestra a gangheri

case' stud'y *s* casistica

cash [kæʃ] *s* contante *m*; **cash on delivery** spedizione contro assegno; **for cash** in contanti; a pronta cassa || *tr* (*a check*) cambiare, incassare || *intr* —**to cash in on** (coll) trarre profitto da

cash' box' *s* cassa

cashew [ˈkæʃu] *s* (*tree*) anacardio; (*nut*) mandorla indiana

cashier [kæˈʃɪr] *s* cassiere *m* || *tr* (*to dismiss*) silurare

cashier's' check' *s* assegno circolare

cash' reg'ister *s* registratore *m* cassa

casing [ˈkesɪŋ] *s* rivestimento; tubo di rivestimento; (*for salami*) budello; (*of tire*) copertone *m*

cask [kæsk] *or* [kɑsk] *s* barile *m*, botte *f*

casket [ˈkæskɪt] *or* [ˈkɑskɪt] *s* scrigno, cofanetto; (*coffin*) bara, cassa da morto

casserole [ˈkæsəˌrol] *s* tegame *m* di terracotta *or* vetro; (*food*) pasticcio, timballo

cassette [kəˈsɛt] *s* (mus) musicassetta; (mus & phot) caricatore *m*

cassock [ˈkæsək] *s* sottana, tonaca; **to doff the cassock** gettar la tonaca alle ortiche

cast [kæst] *or* [kɑst] *s* getto; lancio; forma; (mach) pezzo fuso; (surg) gesso; (theat) complesso artistico, cast *m* || *v* (*pret & pp* cast) *tr* gettare; fondere; (*a ballot*) dare; (*the roles*) distribuire; (*actors*) scegliere; **to cast aside** abbandonare; **to cast down** deprimere; **to cast lots** tirare a sorte; **to cast off** abbandonare; **to cast out** buttar fuori || *intr* tirare i dadi; **to cast off** (naut) mollare gli ormeggi

castanets [ˌkæstəˈnɛts] *spl* nacchere *fpl*

cast'a·way' *adj & s* naufrago; (fig) reprobo

caste [kæst] *or* [kɑst] *s* casta; **to lose caste** perdere prestigio

caster [ˈkæstər] *or* [ˈkɑstər] *s* ampollina, saliera, pepaiola; (*roller*) rotella per i mobili

castigate [ˈkæstɪˌget] *tr* castigare, punire; correggere

Castile [kæsˈtil] *s* (la) Castiglia

Castilian [kæsˈtɪljən] *adj & s* castigliano

casting [ˈkæstɪŋ] *or* [ˈkɑstɪŋ] *s* getto, getto fuso; (*in fishing*) pesca a getto

cast' i'ron *s* ghisa

cast'-i'ron *adj* fatto di ghisa; (*e.g., stomach*) fatto d'acciaio, di struzzo

castle [ˈkæsəl] *or* [ˈkɑsəl] *s* castello; (chess) torre *f* || *tr & intr* (chess) arroccare

cas'tle in Spain' *or* **cas'tle in the air'** *s* castello in aria

cast'off' *adj* abbandonato || *s* rigetto; persona abbandonata; (typ) stima

cas'tor oil' [ˈkæstər] *or* [ˈkɑstər] *s* olio di ricino

castrate [ˈkæstret] *tr* castrare

casual [ˈkæʒʊ·əl] *adj* casuale, fortuito; (*clothing*) semplice, sportivo

casually [ˈkæʒʊ·əli] *adv* con disinvoltura; (*by chance*) fortuitamente

casual·ty [ˈkæʒʊ·əlti] *s* (-ties) accidente *m*, disastro; vittima; **casualties** (*in war*) perdite *fpl*

casuist·ry [ˈkæʃ/ʊ·ɪstri] *s* (-ries) (*specious reasoning*) speciosità *f*; (philos) casistica

cat [kæt] *s* gatto; donna perfida; **to let the cat out of the bag** lasciarsi scappare il segreto

cataclysm [ˈkætəˌklɪzəm] *s* cataclisma *m*

catacomb [ˈkætəˌkom] *s* catacomba

catalogue [ˈkætəˌlɔg] *or* [ˈkætəˌlɑg] *s* catalogo || *tr* catalogare

cat'alogue sale' *s* vendita per corrispondenza

catalyst [ˈkætəlɪst] *s* catalizzatore *m*

catapult [ˈkætəˌpʌlt] *s* catapulta || *tr* catapultare

cataract [ˈkætəˌrækt] *s* cataratta

catarrh [kəˈtɑr] *s* catarro

catastrophe [kəˈtæstrəfi] *s* catastrofe *f*, disastro

cat'call' *s* urlo di disapprovazione

catch [kætʃ] *s* presa; cattura; *(of door)* paletto; *(in marriage)* partito; *(trick)* inganno; *(of fish)* pesca; *(mach)* nottolino ‖ *v (pret & pp* **caught** [kɔt]) *tr* prendere, acchiappare; *(a cold)* pigliare, buscarsi; **to catch hold of** afferrare; **to catch it** (coll) prendersele; **to catch oneself** contenersi; **to catch up** sorprendere sul fatto ‖ *intr* agganciarsi; *(said of a disease)* trasmettersi; **to catch on** capire l'antifona; **to catch up** mettersi al corrente; **to catch up with** raggiungere

catch'-as-catch'-can' *s* lotta libera americana

catch' ba'sin *s* ricettacolo di fogna

catcher ['kætʃər] *s* ricevitore *m*, catcher *m*

catching ['kætʃɪŋ] *adj (alluring)* seducente; *(infectious)* contagioso

catch'word' *s* slogan *m; (typ)* chiamata; *(typ)* esponente *m* in testa di pagina

catch·y ['kætʃi] *adj* (**-ier; -iest**) attraente, vivo; *(tricky)* insidioso

catechism ['kætɪ,kɪzəm] *s* catechismo

catego·ry ['kætɪ,gori] *s* (**-ries**) categoria

cater ['ketər] *intr* provvedere cibo; **to cater to** servire

cater-cornered ['kætər,kɔrnərd] *adj* diagonale ‖ *adv* diagonalmente

caterer ['ketərər] *s* provveditore *m*

caterpillar ['kætər,pɪlər] *s* bruco

cat'erpillar trac'tor *s* trattore *m* a cingoli

cat'fish' *s* pesce *m* gatto

cat'gut' *s* (mus) corda di minugia; *(surg)* catgut *m*, cattegù *m*

cathartic [kə'θɑrtɪk] *adj* & *s* catartico

cathedral [kə'θidrəl] *s* cattedrale *f*

catheter ['kæθɪtər] *s* catetere *m*

catheterize ['kæθɪtə,raɪz] *tr* cateterizzare

cathode ['kæθod] *s* catodo

catholic ['kæθəlɪk] *adj* cattolico; *(e.g., mind)* liberale ‖ **Catholic** *adj* & *s* cattolico

catkin ['kætkɪn] *s* (bot) amento, gattino

cat'nap' *s* corta siesta, sonnellino

cat-o'-nine-tails [,kætə'naɪn,telz] *s* gatto a nove code

cat's'-paw' *s* gonzo; *(breeze)* brezzolina

catsup ['kætsəp] *or* ['kætʃəp] *s* salsa piccante di pomodoro, ketchup *m*

cat'tail' *s* stiancia

cattle ['kætəl] *s* bestiame grosso

cat'tle·man *s* (**-men**) allevatore *m* di bestiame

cat·ty ['kæti] *adj* (**-tier; -tiest**) malizioso, maligno; felino, gattesco

cat'walk' *s* passerella, ballatoio

Caucasian [kɔ'keʒən] *or* [kɔ'keʃən] *adj* & *s* caucasico

caucus ['kɔkəs] *s* comitato elettorale; conciliabolo politico

cauldron ['kɔldrən] *s* calderone *m*

cauliflower ['kɔlɪ,flau·ər] *s* cavolfiore *m*

caulk [kɔk] *tr* calafatare, stoppare

cause [kɔz] *s* causa, cagione ‖ *tr* causare, cagionare; **to cause to** + *inf*, e.g., **she caused him to fall** l'ha fatto cadere

cause'way' *s* strada rialzata, scarpata

caustic ['kɔstɪk] *adj* caustico

cauterize ['kɔtə,raɪz] *tr* cauterizzare

caution ['kɔʃən] *s* cautela, prudenza; ammonizione ‖ *tr* ammonire

cautious ['kɔʃəs] *adj* prudente

cavalcade ['kævəl,ked] *or* [,kævəl-'ked] *s* cavalcata

cavalier [,kævə'lir] *or* ['kævə,lir] *adj* altero, sdegnoso; disinvolto ‖ *s* cavaliere *m*

caval·ry ['kævəlri] *s* (**-ries**) cavalleria

cav'alry·man *or* **cav'alry-man** *s* (**-men** *or* **-men**) cavalleggero, soldato di cavalleria

cave [kev] *s* caverna, grotta ‖ *intr*— **to cave in** sprofondarsi; *(to give in)* (coll) cedere; *(to become exhausted)* (coll) diventare spossato

cave'-in' *s* sprofondamento

cave' man' *s* troglodita *m*

cavern ['kævərn] *s* caverna

caviar ['kævɪ,ɑr] *or* [,kævɪ'ɑr] *s* caviale *m*

cav·il ['kævɪl] *v* (*pret & pp* **-iled** *or* **-illed**; *ger* **-iling** *or* **-illing**) *intr* cavillare

cavi·ty ['kævɪti] *s* (**-ties**) cavità *f; (in tooth)* carie *f*

cavort [kə'vɔrt] *intr* far capriole

caw [kɔ] *s* gracchiamento ‖ *intr* gracchiare

cease [sis] *tr* cessare, interrompere ‖ *intr* cessare, interrompersi; **to cease** + *ger* cessare di + *inf*

cease'-fire' *s* sospensione delle ostilità

ceaseless ['sislɪs] *adj* incessante

cedar ['sidər] *s* cedro; legno di cedro

cede [sid] *tr* cedere, trasferire

ceiling ['silɪŋ] *s* soffitto; (aer) altezza massima; **to hit the ceiling** (slang) uscire dai gangheri

ceil'ing price' *s* calmiere *m*, tetto

celebrate ['sɛlɪ,bret] *tr* celebrare ‖ *intr* celebrare; far festa

celebrated ['sɛlɪ,bretɪd] *adj* celebre, famoso

celebration [,sɛlɪ'breʃən] *s* celebrazione

celebri·ty [sɪ'lebrɪti] *s* (**-ties**) celebrità *f*

celery ['sɛləri] *s* sedano

celestial [sɪ'lestʃəl] *adj* celestiale, celeste

celibacy ['sɛləbəsi] *s* celibato

celibate ['sɛlə,bet] *or* ['sɛləbɪt] *adj* & *s* celibe *m; nubile f*

cell [sɛl] *s* (*e.g., of jail*) cella; *(of electric battery)* elemento; (biol, phys, pol) cellula

cellar ['sɛlər] *s* cantina; *(partly above ground)* seminterrato

cellist *or* **'cellist** [tʃelɪst] *s* violoncellista *mf*

cel·lo *or* **'cel·lo** ['tʃelo] *s* (**-los**) violoncello

cellophane ['sɛlə,fen] *s* cellofan *m*

celluloid ['sɛljə,lɔɪd] *s* celluloide *f*

Celtic ['sɛltɪk] *or* ['keltɪk] *adj* celtico ‖ *s* lingua celtica cement [sɪ'ment] s cemento || tr cementare

cemete·ry ['sɛmɪ ˌtɛri] s (-ries) cimitero

censer ['sɛnsər] s turibolo

censor ['sɛnsər] s censore m || tr censurare

censure ['sɛnʃər] s censura, critica || tr censurare, criticare

census ['sɛnsəs] s censo, censimento

cent [sent] s centesimo di dollaro, cent m; not to have a red cent to one's name non avere il becco di un quattrino

centaur ['sɛntɔr] s centauro

centennial [sɛn'tɛnɪ·əl] adj & s centenario

center ['sɛntər] s centro || tr centrare, concentrare || intr—to center on concentrarsi su

cen'ter·board' s chiglia mobile

cen'ter·piece' s centro tavola

cen'ter punch' s punzone m, punteruolo

centigrade ['sɛntɪ ˌgred] adj centigrado

centimeter ['sɛntɪ ˌmitər] s centimetro

centipede ['sɛntɪ ˌpid] s centopiedi m

cento ['sɛnto] s centone m

central ['sɛntrəl] adj centrale || s centrale f, centrale telefonica; (operator) telefonista m

Cen'tral Amer'ica s l'America Centrale

centralize ['sɛntrə ˌlaɪz] tr centralizzare || intr centralizzarsi

centu·ry ['sɛntʃəri] s (-ries) secolo

ceramic [sɪ'ræmɪk] adj ceramico || ceramics ssg ceramica; spl oggetti mpl di ceramica

cereal ['sɪrɪ·əl] adj cerealicolo || s (grain) cereale m; (uncooked breakfast food, e.g., cornflakes) fiocchi mpl; (breakfast food to be cooked) farina

cerebral ['sɛrɪbrəl] adj cerebrale

ceremonious [ˌsɛrɪ'monɪ·əs] adj cerimonioso

ceremo·ny ['sɛrɪ ˌmoni] s (-nies) cerimonia; to stand on ceremony fare cerimonie

certain ['sʌrtən] adj certo; for certain di or per certo; to be certain to + inf non mancare di + inf

certainly ['sʌrtənli] adv certamente; (gladly) con piacere

certain·ty ['sʌrtənti] s (-ties) certezza

certificate [sər'tɪfɪkɪt] s certificato; (com) titolo || [sər'tɪfɪ ˌket] tr certificare

cer'tified check' s assegno a copertura garantita

cer'tified cop'y s estratto; (as a formula on a document) per copia conforme

cer'tified pub'lic account'ant s esperto contabile

certi·fy ['sʌrtɪ ˌfaɪ] v (pret & pp -fied) tr certificare, garantire

cervix ['sʌrvɪks] s (cervices [sər'vaɪsɪz] cervice f

cessation [sɛ'seʃən] s cessazione

cesspool ['sɛs ˌpul] s pozzo nero

Ceylo·nese [ˌsilə'niz] adj & s (-nese) singalese mf

chafe [tʃef] s irritazione || tr (the hands) strofinare; irritare; (to wear away) logorare || intr irritarsi; logorarsi

chaff [tʃæf] or [tʃɑf] s lolla; pula; (joke) burla; (fig) loppa

chaf'ing dish' s fornello a spirito

cha·grin [ʃə'grɪn] s cruccio, dispiacere m || v (pret -grined or -grinned; ger -grining or -grinning) tr crucciare, affliggere

chain [tʃen] s catena; (e.g., for necklace) catenella || tr incatenare

chain' gang' s catena di forzati

chain' reac'tion s reazione a catena

chain' saw' s motosega

chain'-smoke' intr fumare come un turco

chain' store' s negozio a catena

chair [tʃɛr] s sedia, seggiola; (of important person) seggio; (at a university) cattedra; (chairman) presidente m, presidenza; to take the chair cominciare una riunione || tr (a meeting) presiedere

chair' lift' s seggiovia

chair'man s (-men) presidente m

chair'man·ship' s presidenza

chair'wom'an s (-wom'en) presidentessa

chalice ['tʃælɪs] s calice m

chalk [tʃɔk] s gesso || tr marcare or scrivere col gesso; to chalk up prendere appunti di; attribuire

chalk' talk' s conferenza illustrata

chalk·y ['tʃɔki] adj (-ier; -iest) gessoso

challenge ['tʃælɪndʒ] s sfida; (law) ricusazione; (mil) chi va là m || tr sfidare; (a juror) (law) ricusare; (mil) dare il chi va là a

chamber ['tʃembər] s camera, stanza; (of a palace) aula; (of a judge) gabinetto

chamberlain ['tʃembərlɪn] s ciambellano

cham'ber·maid' s cameriera

cham'ber of com'merce s camera di commercio

cham'ber pot' s orinale m

chameleon [kə'milɪ·ən] s camaleonte m

cham·ois ['ʃæmi] s (-ois) camoscio

champ [tʃæmp] s (slang) campione m || tr masticare rumorosamente; (the bit) mordere || intr masticare rumorosamente

champagne [ʃæm'pen] s champagne m, spumante m

champion ['tʃæmpɪ·ən] s campione m || tr difendere; farsi paladino di

championship ['tʃæmpɪ·ən ˌʃɪp] s campionato

chance [tʃæns] or [tʃɑns] adj casuale, fortuito || s occasione; caso; probabilità f; rischio; biglietto di lotteria; by chance per caso; not to stand a chance non avere la probabilità di riuscita; to take one's chances arrischiarsi; to wait for a chance attendere l'opportunità || intr succedere; to chance upon imbattersi in

chancel ['tʃænsəl] or ['tʃɑnsəl] s presbiterio, coro

chanceller·y ['tʃænsələri] or ['tʃɑnsələri] s (-ies) cancelleria

chancellor ['t∫ænsələr] or ['t∫ɑnsələr] s cancelliere m

chandelier [,∫ændə'lir] s lampadario

change [t∫endʒ] s cambiamento; (of clothes) muta; (of currency) cambio; (coins) spiccioli mpl; **for a change** tanto per cambiare; **to keep the change** tenere il resto ‖ tr cambiare, rimpiazzare; (clothes) cambiare, cambiarsi di ‖ intr cambiare, mutare

changeable ['t∫endʒəbəl] adj mutevole, variabile, incostante

change' of heart' s pentimento, conversione

change' of life' s menopausa

chan·nel ['t∫ænəl] s canale m; tubo, passaggio; stretto; (of river) alveo; (groove) solco; (rad, telv) canale m; **through channels** per via gerarchica ‖ v (pret & pp -neled or -nelled; ger -neling or -nelling) tr incanalare; (a river) incassare ‖ **the Channel** il Canale della Manica

chant [t∫ænt] or [t∫ant] s canto; salmodia; canzone f ‖ tr & intr cantare

chanticleer ['t∫æntɪ,klɪr] s il gallo

chaos ['ke·ɑs] s caos m

chaotic [ke'ɑtɪk] adj caotico

chap [t∫æp] s (fellow) individuo, tipo; (of skin) screpolatura; **chaps** pantaloni mpl di cuoio ‖ v (pret & pp chapped; ger chapping) tr screpolare ‖ intr screpolarsi

chapel ['t∫æpəl] s cappella

chaperon or **chaperone** ['∫æpə,ron] s accompagnatrice f (di signorina) ‖ tr accompagnare

chaplain ['t∫æplɪn] s cappellano

chaplet ['t∫æplɪt] s (wreath) corona, ghirlanda; rosario

chapter ['t∫æptər] s capitolo; (of a club) sezione

chap'ter and verse' s—**to give chapter and verse** citare le autorità

char [t∫ɑr] v (pret & pp charred; ger charring) tr carbonizzare; bruciare

character ['kærɪktər] s carattere m; lettera, scrittura; indole f; (theat) personaggio; (coll) tipo; **in character** caratteristico di lui (lei, loro, etc.)

char'acter ac'tor s caratterista m

char'acter ac'tress s caratterista f

char'acter assassina'tion s linciaggio morale

characteristic [,kærɪktə'rɪstɪk] adj caratteristico ‖ s caratteristica

characterize ['kærɪktə,raɪz] tr caratterizzare

char'coal' s carbone m di legna, carbone m dolce; (for sketching) carboncino; (sketch) disegno al carboncino

charge [t∫ɑrdʒ] s carica; incarico; responsabilità f; (indictment) accusa; costo; prezzo; debito; **in charge** in comando; **in charge of** a cura di; **to take charge of** prendersi cura di ‖ tr caricare; comandare; accusare; (a price) fare pagare; mettere in conto; **to charge s.o. with s.th** addebitare qlco a qlcu; accusare qlcu di qlco ‖ intr fare una carica

charge' account' s conto corrente

chargé d'affaires [∫ɑr'ʒe də'fer] s (chargés d'affaires) incaricato d'affari

charger ['t∫ɑrdʒər] s cavallo di battaglia; (of a battery) caricatore m

chariot ['t∫ærɪ·ət] s cocchio

charioteer [,t∫ærɪ·ə'tɪr] s auriga m

charis·ma [kə'rɪzmə] s (-mata [mətə]) fascino personale; (theol) carisma m

charitable ['t∫ærɪtəbəl] adj (person) caritatevole; (institution) caritativo

chari·ty ['t∫ærɪti] s (-ties) carità f; associazione di beneficenza

charlatan ['∫ɑrlətən] s ciarlatano

charlatanism ['∫ɑrlətən,ɪzəm] s ciarlataneria

Charlemagne ['∫ɑrlə,men] s Carlomagno

Charles [t∫ɑrlz] s Carlo

char'ley horse' ['t∫ɑrli] s (coll) crampo

charlotte ['∫ɑrlət] s charlotte f ‖ **Charlotte** s Carlotta

charm [t∫ɑrm] s fascino; amuleto; portafortuna m ‖ tr incantare, stregare

charming ['t∫ɑrmɪŋ] adj affascinante

charnel ['t∫ɑrnəl] adj orribile ‖ s ossario

chart [t∫ɑrt] s carta geografica; lista; diagramma m ‖ tr tracciare

charter ['t∫ɑrtər] s statuto; privilegio ‖ tr (a company) fondare; (a conveyance) noleggiare

char'ter mem'ber s socio fondatore

char'wom'an s (-wom'en) domestica per la pulizia

chase [t∫es] s inseguimento; caccia; (typ) telaio ‖ tr inseguire; cacciare; (to chisel) cesellare; **to chase away** scacciare ‖ intr—**to chase after** inseguire

chaser ['t∫esər] s cacciatore m; (coll) bibita da bersi dopo un liquore

chasm ['kæzəm] s abisso, baratro

chas·sis ['t∫æsi] s (-sis [siz]) telaio

chaste [t∫est] adj casto

chasten ['t∫esən] tr castigare

chastise [t∫æs'taɪz] tr castigare

chastity ['t∫æstɪti] s castità f

chat [t∫æt] s chiacchierata ‖ v (pret & pp chatted; ger chatting) intr chiacchierare

chatelaine ['∫ætə,len] s castellana

chattels ['t∫ætəlz] spl beni mpl mobili

chatter ['t∫ætər] s cicaleccio; balbettio; (of teeth) battito ‖ intr cicalare; balbettare; (said of teeth) battere

chat'ter·box' s chiacchierone m

chauffeur ['∫ofər] or [∫o'fʌr] s autista mf ‖ intr fare l'autista

cheap [t∫ip] adj a buon mercato, economico; (of poor quality) scadente; **to feel cheap** vergognarsi ‖ adv a buon mercato

cheapen ['t∫ipən] tr deprezzare; avvilire; rendere di cattivo gusto

cheapness ['t∫ipnəs] s buon mercato, prezzo basso

cheat [t∫it] s truffa; truffatore m ‖ tr imbrogliare, truffare ‖ intr truffare; (at cards) barare

check [t∫ek] s arresto, pausa; ostacolo;

esame *m*; verifica, controllo; (*of bank*) assegno; (*for baggage*) tagliando, scontrino; (*square pattern*) quadretto; (*fabric in squares*) tessuto a scacchi; (*in a restaurant*) conto; **in check** controllato, sotto controllo; (chess) sotto scacco ‖ *tr* fermare; confrontare; ispezionare; marcare; (*e.g., a coat*) depositare; disegnare a quadretti; (chess) dare scacco a; **to check off** controllare marcando; **to check on** controllare, verificare ‖ *intr* fermarsi; corrispondere perfettamente; **to check in** scendere (a un albergo); **to check out** andar via; pagare il conto; **to check up on** controllare

check′book′ *s* libretto d'assegni

checker [′tʃɛkər] *s* ispettore *m*; quadretto; (*in game of checkers*) pedina; **checkers** dama ‖ *tr* variegare; marcare a quadretti

check′er-board′ *s* scacchiera

check′ered *adj* (*e.g., career*) pieno di vicissitudini; (*marked with squares*) a scacchi; (*in color*) variegato

check′ing account′ *s* conto corrente

check′mate′ *s* scacco matto ‖ *tr* dare scacco matto a ‖ *interj* scacco matto!

check′off′ **dues**′ *spl* trattenute *fpl* sindacali

check′-out′ *s* (*from hotel room*) partenza; (*time*) ora della partenza; (*examination*) esame *m* di controllo; (*in a supermarket*) cassa

check′point′ *s* punto di ispezione

check′room′ *s* guardaroba *m*

check′up′ *s* (*of car*) ispezione; (*of patient*) esame *m* (fisico)

cheek [tʃik] *s* guancia, gota; (coll) faccia tosta

cheek′bone′ *s* zigomo

cheek·y [′tʃiki] *adj* (**-ier; -iest**) (coll) impudente, sfacciato

cheer [tʃɪr] *s* gioia, allegria; applauso; **of good cheer** di buon umore ‖ *tr* riempire di gioia, rallegrare; applaudire; ricevere con applausi ‖ *intr* rallegrarsi; **cheer up!** animo!, coraggio!

cheerful [′tʃɪrfəl] *adj* allegro, di buon umore; (*willing*) volonteroso

cheerless [′tʃɪrlɪs] *adj* tetro, triste

cheese [tʃiz] *s* formaggio ‖ *intr*—**cheese it!** (slang) scappa via!

cheese′ cake′ *s* torta di formaggio; (slang) pin-up girl *f*

cheese′cloth′ *s* etamine *f*, stamigna

chees·y [′tʃizi] *adj* (**-ier; -iest**) di formaggio; come il formaggio; (slang) meschino, di cattiva qualità

chef [ʃɛf] *s* chef *m*, capocuoco

chemical [′kɛmɪkəl] *adj* chimico ‖ *s* prodotto chimico

chemise [ʃə′miz] *s* sottoveste *f*

chemist [′kɛmɪst] *s* chimico

chemistry [′kɛmɪstri] *s* chimica

cherish [′tʃɛrɪʃ] *tr* accarezzare; (*a memory*) custodire; (*a hope*) nutrire

cher·ry [′tʃɛri] *s* (**-ries**) (*tree*) ciliegio; (*fruit*) ciliegia

cher·ub [′tʃɛrəb] *s* (**-ubim** [əbɪm] & **-ubs**) cherubino

chess [tʃɛs] *s* scacchi *mpl*

chess′board′ *s* scacchiera

chess′man′ *or* **chess′man** *s* (**-men**′ *or* **-men**) scacco

chest [tʃɛst] *s* petto; (*box*) cassapanca; (*furniture with drawers*) cassettone *m*; (*for money*) forziere *m*

chestnut [′tʃɛsnət] *s* (*tree, wood, color*) castagno; (*nut*) castagna

chest′ of drawers′ *s* cassettone *m*

cheval′ glass′ [ʃə′væl] *s* psiche *f*

chevalier [ˌʃɛvə′lɪr] *s* cavaliere *m*

chevron [′ʃɛvrən] *s* gallone *m*

chew [tʃu] *tr* masticare; **to chew the cud** ruminare; **to chew the rag** (slang) chiacchierare ‖ *intr* masticare

chew′ing gum′ *s* gomma da masticare

chic [ʃik] *adj* & *s* chic

chicaner·y [ʃɪ′kɛnəri] *s* (**-ies**) trucco, rigiro

chick [tʃɪk] *s* pulcino; (slang) ragazza

chicken [′tʃɪkən] *s* pollo, pollastro; (coll) giovane *mf*; **to be chicken** (slang) avere la fifa ‖ *intr*—**to chicken out** (coll) indietreggiare

chick′en coop′ *s* pollaio

chick′en feed′ *s* (slang) spiccioli *mpl*

chicken-hearted [′tʃɪkən‚hɑrtɪd] *adj* timido, fifone

chick′en pox′ *s* varicella

chick′en store′ *s* polleria

chick′en wire′ *s* rete metallica esagonale

chick′pea′ *s* cece *m*

chico·ry [′tʃɪkəri] *s* (**-ries**) cicoria

chide [tʃaɪd] *v* (*pret* **chided** *or* **chid** [tʃɪd]; *pp* **chided, chid,** *or* **chidden** [′tʃɪdən]) *tr* & *intr* rimproverare, correggere

chief [tʃif] *adj* principale, sommo, supremo ‖ *s* capo, comandante supremo; (slang) padrone *m*

chief′ exec′utive *s* capo del governo

chief′ jus′tice *s* presidente *m* di una corte; presidente *m* della corte suprema

chiefly [′tʃifli] *adv* principalmente

chief′ of staff′ *s* capo di stato maggiore

chief′ of state′ *s* capo dello stato

chieftain [′tʃiftən] *s* capo

chiffon [ʃɪ′fɑn] *s* velo trasparente, chiffon *m*; **chiffons** trine *fpl*

chiffonier [ˌʃɪfə′nɪr] *s* mobile *m* a cassettini, chiffonier *m*

chilblain [′tʃɪl‚blen] *s* gelone *m*

child [tʃaɪld] *s* (**children** [′tʃɪldrən]) bebè *mf*, bambino; figlio; discendente *mf*; **with child** incinta

child′birth′ *s* parto

childhood [′tʃaɪldhʊd] *s* infanzia

childish [′tʃaɪldɪʃ] *adj* infantile

childishness [′tʃaɪldɪʃnɪs] *s* puerilità *f*, infanzia

child′ la′bor *s* lavoro dei minorenni

childless [′tʃaɪldlɪs] *adj* senza figli

child′like′ *adj* infantile, innocente

child′s′ play′ *s* un gioco

child′ wel′fare *s* protezione dell'infanzia

Chile [′tʃɪli] *s* il Cile

Chilean [′tʃɪlɪ·ən] *adj* cileno

chil′i sauce′ [ˈtʃɪli] *s* salsa di pomodoro con peperoni

chill [tʃɪl] *adj* freddo; || *s* freddo; bri-
vido di freddo; freddezza; (*depres-
sion*) abbattimento || *tr* raffreddare;
(*a metal*) temprare; (fig) scoraggiare
|| *intr* raffreddarsi

chill·y [ˈtʃɪli] *adj* (*-ier; -iest*) fresco,
freddiccio; (*reception*) freddo

chime [tʃaɪm] *s* scampanio; **chimes**
campanello || *intr* scampanare; **to
chime in** cominciare a cantare al-
l'unisono; (coll) intromettersi

chime′ clock′ *s* orologio con carillon

chimney [ˈtʃɪmni] *s* camino; (*of factory*) ciminiera; **to smoke like a
chimney** fumare come un turco

chim′ney flue′ *s* tubo di stufa, canna
del camino

chim′ney pot′ *s* testa della canna fumaria, comignolo

chim′ney sweep′ *s* spazzacamino

chimpanzee [ˌtʃɪmpænˈzi] or [ˌtʃɪm-
pænˈzi] *s* scimpanzé *m*

chin [tʃɪn] *s* mento; **to keep one's chin
up** (coll) non perdersi di coraggio; **to
take it on the chin** (slang) subire
una sconfitta || *v* (*pret & pp* **chinned**;
ger **chinning**) *tr*—**to chin oneself** sol-
levarsi fino al mento (ai manubri) ||
intr (slang) chiacchierare

china [ˈtʃaɪnə] *s* porcellana || **China** *s*
la Cina

chi′na clos′et *s* armadio per le stoviglie

chi′na·ware′ *s* porcellana, stoviglie *fpl*

Chi·nese [tʃaɪˈniz] *adj* cinese || *s*
(*-nese*) cinese *mf*

Chi′nese lan′tern *s* lampioncino alla
veneziana

Chi′nese puz′zle *s* rebus *m*

chink [tʃɪŋk] *s* fessura

chin′ strap′ *s* sottogola

chintz [tʃɪnts] *s* chintz *m*

chip [tʃɪp] *s* scheggia; frammento; (*in
card games*) gettone *m*; (*of wood*)
truciolo; **chip off the old block** vero
figlio di suo padre (di sua madre);
chip on one's shoulder propensità *f*
a attaccar brighe || *v* (*pret & pp*
chipped; *ger* **chipping**) *tr* scheggiare;
to chip in contribuire || *intr* scheg-
giarsi

chipmunk [ˈtʃɪpˌmʌŋk] *s* tamia

chipper [ˈtʃɪpər] *adj* (coll) allegro, vivo

chiropodist [kaɪˈrɑpədɪst] or [kɪˈrɑpə-
dɪst] *s* callista *mf*, pedicure *mf*

chiropractice [ˈkaɪrəˌpræktɪs] *s* chiro-
pratica

chirp [tʃʌrp] *s* (*of birds*) cinguettio;
(*of crickets*) cri cri *m* || *intr* cinguet-
tare; fare cri cri

chis·el [ˈtʃɪzəl] *s* (*for wood and metal*)
scalpello; (*for metal*) cesello || *v*
(*pret & pp* **-eled** or **-elled**; *ger* **-eling**
or **-elling**) *tr* scalpellare; cesellare;
(slang) imbrogliare || *intr* (slang)
imbrogliare, fare l'imbroglione

chiseler [ˈtʃɪzələr] *s* scalpellino; cesel-
latore *m*; (slang) imbroglione *m*

chit-chat [ˈtʃɪt ˌtʃæt] *s* chiacchierata

chivalrous [ˈʃɪvəlrəs] *adj* cavalleresco

chivalry [ˈʃɪvəlri] *s* cavalleria

chive [tʃaɪv] *s* cipolla porraia

chloride [ˈklɔraɪd] *s* cloruro

chlorine [ˈklɔrin] *s* cloro

chloroform [ˈklɔrəˌfɔrm] *s* cloroformio
|| *tr* cloroformizzare

chlorophyll [ˈklɔrəfɪl] *s* clorofilla

chock [tʃɑk] *s* (*wedge*) bietta, cuneo

chock-full [ˈtʃɑkˈful] *adj* colmo, pieno
zeppo

chocolate [ˈtʃɔkəlɪt] or [ˈtʃɑkəlɪt] *s*
(*candy*) cioccolato; (*drink*) cioccolata

choc′olate bar′ *s* barretta di cioccolato

choice [tʃɔɪs] *adj* di prima scelta, su-
periore || *s* scelta; (*variety*) assorti-
mento

choir [kwaɪr] *s* coro

choir′boy′ *s* ragazzo cantore

choir′ loft′ *s* coro

choir′mas′ter *s* maestro di cappella

choke [tʃok] *s* strozzatura; (aut) far-
falla del carburatore || *tr* strozzare;
ostruire; (*an internal-combustion engine*) arricchire la miscela di; **to
choke back** trattenere; **to choke up**
tappare, ostruire || *intr* soffocarsi;
to choke up tapparsi; (coll) soffocarsi

choker [ˈtʃokər] *s* (*necklace*) (coll)
collana; (*scarf*) (coll) foulard *m*

cholera [ˈkɑlərə] *s* colera *m*

choleric [ˈkɑlərɪk] *adj* collerico

cholesterol [kəˈlestəˌrol] or [kəˈlestə-
ˌral] *s* colesterina

choose [tʃuz] *v* (*pret* **chose** [tʃoz]; *pp*
chosen [ˈtʃozən]) *tr* scegliere || *intr*
—**to choose to** decidere di

choos·y [ˈtʃuzi] *adj* (*-ier; -iest*) (coll)
di difficile contentatura

chop [tʃɑp] *s* colpo; (*of meat*) coto-
letta; **chops** labbra *fpl*, bocca || *v*
(*pret & pp* **chopped**; *ger* **chopping**)
tr tagliare; (*meat*) tritare; **to chop
off** troncare; **to chop up** sminuzzare

chopper [ˈtʃɑpər] *s* (*man*) tagliatore
m; interruttore automatico; coltello
da macellaio; (slang) elicottero;
choppers (slang) i denti

chop′ping block′ *s* tagliere *m*

chop·py [ˈtʃɑpi] *adj* (*-pier; -piest*)
(*wind*) variabile; (*sea*) agitato; (*style*)
instabile

choral [ˈkorəl] *adj* & *s* corale *m*

chorale [koˈral] *s* corale *m*

chord [kɔrd] *s* corda; (mus) accordo

chore [tʃor] *s* lavoro; lavoro spiacevole; **chores** faccende domestiche

choreography [ˌkɔriˈɑɡrəfi] *s* coreografia

chorine [koˈrin] *s* (slang) ballerina

chorus [ˈkorəs] *s* coro; (*group of
dancers*) corpo di ballo; (*of a song*)
ritornello

cho′rus girl′ *s* ballerina

cho′rus man′ *s* (**men′**) corista *m*

chow [tʃau] *s* (*dog*) chow chow *m*;
(slang) cibo, pappa

chowder [ˈtʃaudər] *s* zuppa di vongole;
zuppa di pesce

Christ [kraɪst] *s* Cristo

christen [ˈkrɪsən] *tr* battezzare

Christendom [ˈkrɪsəndəm] *s* cristianità
f

christening ['krɪsənɪŋ] s battesimo
Christian ['krɪstʃən] adj & s cristiano
Christianity [,krɪstʃɪ'ænɪti] s (*Christendom*) cristianità f; (*religion*) cristianesimo
Chris'tian name' s nome m di battesimo
Christmas ['krɪsməs] adj natalizio || s Natale m; **Merry Christmas!** Buon Natale!
Christ'mas card' s cartoncino natalizio
Christ'mas car'ol s pastorella di Natale
Christ'mas Eve' s vigilia di Natale
Christ'mas gift' s strenna natalizia
Christ'mas tree' s albero di Natale
chrome [krom] adj cromato || s cromo || tr cromare
chromium ['kromɪ·əm] s cromo
chromosome ['kromə,som] s cromosoma m
chronic ['krɑnɪk] adj cronico
chronicle ['krɑnɪkəl] s cronaca || tr fare la storia di
chronicler ['krɑnɪklər] s cronista mf
chronolo-gy [krə'nɑlədʒi] s (-gies) cronologia
chronometer [krə'nɑmɪtər] s cronometro
chrysanthemum [krɪ'sænθɪməm] s crisantemo
chub-by ['tʃʌbi] adj (-bier; -biest) paffuto
chuck [tʃʌk] s buffetto sotto il mento; (*cut of meat*) reale m; (*of lathe*) coppaia || tr accarezzare sotto il mento; (*to throw*) (coll) gettare
chuckle ['tʃʌkəl] s risatina || intr ridacchiare
chum [tʃʌm] s (coll) amico intimo; (coll) compagno di stanza || v (*pret & pp* **chummed;** *ger* **chumming**) intr (coll) essere amico intimo; essere compagno di stanza
chum-my ['tʃʌmi] adj (-mier; -miest) (coll) intimo, amicone
chump [tʃʌmp] s ciocco, ceppo; (coll) sciocco
chunk [tʃʌŋk] s grosso pezzo
church [tʃʌrtʃ] s chiesa
churchgoer ['tʃʌrtʃ,go·ər] s praticante mf
church'man s (-men) parrocchiano; (*clergyman*) sacerdote m
Church' of Eng'land s chiesa anglicana
church'yard' s camposanto
churl [tʃʌrl] s zotico, villano
churlish ['tʃʌrlɪʃ] adj villano
churn [tʃʌrn] s zangola || tr agitare violentemente, sbattere || intr (*said of water*) ribollire
chute [ʃut] s piano inclinato, canna; (*in a river*) cascata, rapida; paracadute m; (*into a swimming pool*) toboga m
Cicero ['sɪsə,ro] s Cicerone m
cider ['saɪdər] s sidro
cigar [sɪ'gɑr] s sigaro
cigar' case' s portasigari m
cigar' cut'ter s tagliasigari m
cigarette [,sɪgə'rɛt] s sigaretta
cigarette' butt' s cicca
cigarette' case' s portasigarette m
cigarette' hold'er s bocchino

cigarette' light'er s accendisigaro, accendino
cigarette' pa'per s cartina da sigarette
cigar' store' s tabaccheria, rivendita di sali e tabacchi
cinch [sɪntʃ] s (*on a horse*) sottopancia m; (*hold*) (coll) presa; (slang) giochetto || tr legare con una cinghia; (slang) agguantare
cinder ['sɪndər] s tizzone m; (slang) scoria; **cinders** cenere f
cin'der block' s concio di scoria
Cinderella [,sɪndə'rɛlə] s (la) Cenerentola
cinema ['sɪnəmə] s cine m, cinema m
cinnabar ['sɪnə,bɑr] s cinabro
cinnamon ['sɪnəmən] s cannella
cipher ['saɪfər] s zero; cifra; codice m; monogramma m || tr calcolare; (*to write in code*) cifrare
circle ['sʌrkəl] s cerchio; (*of theater*) prima galleria; (*of friends*) cerchia || tr cerchiare, compiere una rotazione intorno a
circuit ['sʌrkɪt] s circuito; (*district*) circoscrizione
cir'cuit break'er s salvamotore m, interruttore automatico
circuitous [sər'kju·ɪtəs] adj tortuoso
circuitry ['sʌrkɪtri] s (*plan*) schema m di montaggio; (*components*) elementi mpl di un circuito
circular ['sʌrkjələr] adj & s circolare f
circulate ['sʌrkjə,let] tr mettere in circolazione, diffondere || intr circolare
cir'culating li'brary s biblioteca circolante
circulation [,sʌrkjə'leʃən] s circolazione; (*of newspaper*) diffusione
circumcise ['sʌrkəm,saɪz] tr circoncidere
circumference [sər'kʌmfərəns] s circonferenza
circumflex ['sʌrkəm,flɛks] adj circonflesso || s accento circonflesso
circumscribe [,sʌrkəm'skraɪb] tr circoscrivere
circumspect ['sʌrkəm,spɛkt] adj circospetto
circumstance ['sʌrkəm,stæns] s circostanza; (*fact*) dettaglio; solennità f; **circumstances** condizioni fpl; dettagli mpl; condizioni economiche; **under no circumstances** = nessuna condizione; **under the circumstances** le cose essendo come sono
circumstantial [,sʌrkəm'stænʃəl] adj circostanziale, indiziario; (*incidental*) secondario; (*complete*) circostanziato
cir'cumstan'tial ev'idence s prova indiziaria
circumstantiate [,sʌrkəm'stænʃɪ,et] tr (*to support with particulars*) comprovare; (*to describe in detail*) circonstanziare
circumvent [,sʌrkəm'vɛnt] tr (*to surround*) accerchiare; (*to outwit*) circuire; (*a difficulty*) eludere, scansare
circus ['sʌrkəs] s circo equestre
cistern ['sɪstərn] s cisterna, serbatoio
citadel ['sɪtədəl] s cittadella
citation [saɪ'teʃən] s citazione

cite [saɪt] *tr* citare
cither [ˈsɪðər] *s* cetra
citizen [ˈsɪtɪzən] *s* cittadino; *(civilian)* civile *mf*
citizenship [ˈsɪtɪzən ˌʃɪp] *s* cittadinanza
citric [ˈsɪtrɪk] *adj* citrico
citron [ˈsɪtrən] *s* cedro; cedro candito
cit'rus fruit' [ˈsɪtrəs] *s* agrumi *mpl*
cit·y [ˈsɪti] *s* (-ies) città *f*
cit'y coun'cil *s* consiglio municipale
cit'y ed'itor *s* apocronista *m*
cit'y fa'thers *spl* maggiorenti *mpl;* consiglieri *mpl* municipali
cit'y hall' *s* municipio
cit'y plan'ning *s* urbanistica
cit'y room' *s* (journ) redazione
civic [ˈsɪvɪk] *adj* civico || civics *s* educazione civica
civil [ˈsɪvɪl] *adj* civile
civ'il engineer'ing *s* genio civile
civilian [sɪˈvɪljən] *adj & s* civile *mf,* borghese *mf*
civili·ty [sɪˈvɪlɪti] *s* (-ties) cortesia; civilities ossequi *mpl*
civilization [ˌsɪvɪlɪˈzeʃən] *s* civilizzazione, civiltà *f*
civilize [ˈsɪvɪˌlaɪz] *tr* civilizzare
civ'il law' *s* diritto civile
civ'il serv'ant *s* impiegato statale
civ'il war' *s* guerra civile || Civil War *s (of the U.S.A.)* guerra di secessione
claim [klem] *s* pretesa; richiesta; (min) concessione || *tr (one's rights)* rivendicare; *(one's property)* richiedere; dichiarare; to claim to be pretendere d'essere
claim' check' *s* tagliando
clairvoyance [klerˈvɔɪ·əns] *s* chiaroveggenza
clairvoyant [klerˈvɔɪ·ənt] *adj* chiaroveggente || *s* veggente *mf,* chiaroveggente *mf*
clam [klæm] *s* vongola || *intr*—to clam up (coll) essere muto come un pesce
clamber [ˈklæmər] *intr* arrampicarsi
clam·my [ˈklæmi] *adj* (-mier; -miest) coperto di sudore freddo; morbido
clamor [ˈklæmər] *s* clamore *m* || *intr* fare clamore
clamorous [ˈklæmərəs] *adj* clamoroso
clamp [klæmp] *s* graffa, morsetto; *(e.g., to hold a hose)* fascetta || *tr* assicurare con graffa, aggrappare; *(a tool)* montare || *intr*—to clamp down on (coll) fare pressione su, mettere i freni a
clan [klæn] *s* clan *m*
clandestine [klænˈdestɪn] *adj* clandestino
clang [klæŋ] *s* clangore *m* || *intr* risonare con clangore
clannish [ˈklænɪʃ] *adj* esclusivista, partigiano
clap [klæp] *s* applauso; *(of thunder)* scoppio || *v (pret & pp* clapped; *ger* clapping) *tr (the hands)* battere; *(e.g., in jail)* schiaffare; to clap shut || *intr* applaudire
clapper [ˈklæpər] *s* applauditore *m; (of bell)* batacchio
clap'trap' *s* imbonimento
claret [ˈklærɪt] *adj & s* chiaretto

clari·fy [ˈklærɪˌfaɪ] *v (pret & pp* -fied) *tr* chiarificare, chiarire
clarinet [ˌklærɪˈnɛt] *s* clarinetto
clarion [ˈklærɪ·ən] *adj* chiaro e metallico || *s* tromba, clarino
clash [klæʃ] *s* cozzo, urto; conflitto di opinioni || *intr* cozzare, urtarsi; essere in conflitto
clasp [klæsp] *or* [klɑsp] *s* gancio, fermaglio; *(hold)* presa; *(grip)* stretta || *tr* agganciare; *(to hold in the arms)* abbracciare; *(to grip)* stringere
class [klæs] *or* [klɑs] *s* classe *f* || *tr* classificare
class'book' *s* registro
classic [ˈklæsɪk] *adj & s* classico
classical [ˈklæsɪkəl] *adj* classico
classicism [ˈklæsɪˌsɪzm] *s* classicismo
classicist [ˈklæsɪsɪst] *s* classicista *mf*
classified [ˈklæsɪˌfaɪd] *adj* segreto
clas'sified ad' *s* annunzio economico
classi·fy [ˈklæsɪˌfaɪ] *v (pret & pp* -fied) *tr* classificare
class'mate' *s* compagno di scuola
class'room' *s* aula scolastica
class' strug'gle *s* lotta di classe
class·y [ˈklæsi] *adj* (-ier; -iest) (slang) di lusso, di prim'ordine
clatter [ˈklætər] *s (of dishes)* acciottolio; vocio, schiamazzo || *tr* acciottolare || *intr* fare schiamazzo
clause [klɔz] *s* clausola; (gram) proposizione
clavicle [ˈklævɪkəl] *s* clavicola
claw [klɔ] *s* artiglio; *(of lobster)* pinza; *(tool)* raffio; *(of hammer)* granchio; (coll) dita *fpl* || *tr* aggraffiare; artigliare
claw' ham'mer *s* levachiodi *m*
clay [kle] *s* argilla, creta
clay' pipe' *s* pipa di terracotta
clean [klin] *adj* pulito; *(precise)* netto; *(e.g., break)* completo || *adv* completamente || *tr* pulire; to clean out pulire, fare repulisti di; (slang) ripulire; to clean up pulire completamente; mettere in ordine || *intr* pulirsi, fare pulizia
clean' bill' of health' *s* patente sanitaria; (fig) esonero completo
clean'-cut' *adj* ben delineato, deciso
cleaner [ˈklinər] *s* pulitore *m,* smacchiatore *m; (machine)* pulitrice *f,* smacchiatrice *f;* to send to the cleaners (slang) spolpare
clean'ing fluid' *s* smacchiatore *m*
clean'ing wom'an *s* donna di servizio per fare la pulizia
clean·ly [ˈklɛnli] *adj* (-lier; -liest) pulito, netto
cleanse [klɛnz] *tr* pulire; detergere; purificare
cleanser [ˈklɛnzər] *s* detergente *m*
clean'-sha'ven *adj* sbarbato di fresco
clean'up' *s* pulizia; (slang) guadagno enorme
clear [klɪr] *adj* chiaro; evidente; completo; innocente; *(profit)* netto; clear of libero da || *s* posto libero; in the clear libero; esonerato; non in codice || *adv* chiaramente; completamente || *tr (e.g., trees)* rischiarare; *(e.g., peo-*

ple) sgombrare; (*the table*) sparecchiare; (*an obstacle*) superare; (*from guilt*) discolpare; (*a profit*) guadagnare; (*goods at customs*) svincolare; (*a ship through customs*) dichiarare il carico di; (*checks*) compensare; **to clear away** or **off** liberare; **to clear out** sgombrare, sbarazzare; **to clear up** spiegare; (*a doubt*) dissipare || *intr* rasserenarsi; (*said of a ship*) partire; **to clear away** or **off** sparire; **to clear out** (coll) andarsene; **to clear up** rasserenarsi

clearance [ˈklɪrəns] *s* liberazione; (*of a ship*) partenza; (*of goods through customs*) sdoganamento; (*of checks*) compensazione; (*of goods*) liquidazione; (*mach*) gioco

clear'ance sale' *s* liquidazione

clear'-cut' *adj* chiaro, distinto

clearing [ˈklɪrɪŋ] *s* (*open space*) radura; (*of checks*) compensazione

clear'ing house' *s* stanza di compensazione

cleat [klit] *s* bietta, cuneo; (*on the sole of shoe*) tacchetto; (naut) galloccia

cleavage [ˈklivɪdʒ] *s* divisione; fessura

cleave [kliv] *v* (*pret & pp* **cleft** [kleft] or **cleaved**) *tr* dividere, fendere || *intr* aderire, essere fedele

cleaver [ˈklivər] *s* scure *f*, accetta; (*of butcher*) spaccaossa *m*, fenditoio

clef [klef] *s* (mus) chiave *f*

cleft [kleft] *adj* diviso, fesso || *s* fessura, crepaccio

cleft' pal'ate *s* palato spaccato, gola lupina

clematis [ˈklemətɪs] *s* clematide *f*

clemen·cy [ˈklemənsi] *s* (*-cies*) clemenza

clement [ˈklemənt] *adj* clemente

clench [klentʃ] *s* stretta || *tr* stringere; afferrare

clergy [ˈklɜrdʒi] *s* clero

cler'gy·man *s* (*-men*) ecclesiastico

cleric [ˈklerɪk] *s* ecclesiastico, sacerdote *m*

clerical [ˈklerɪkəl] *adj* da impiegato; (*error*) burocratico; (*of clergy*) clericale || *s* ecclesiastico; **clericals** abiti ecclesiastici

cler'ical work' *s* lavoro d'ufficio

clerk [klɑrk] *s* impiegato, commesso; (*accountant*) contabile *mf*; (*e.g., in a record office*) ufficiale *m*; cancelliere *m*; (*copyist, typist*) scrivano

clever [ˈklevər] *adj* intelligente; bravo, abile; destro

cleverness [ˈklevərnɪs] *s* intelligenza; bravura, abilità *f*

clew [klu] *s* indizio, traccia; (*of yarn*) gomitolo; (naut) bugna

cliché [kliˈʃe] *s* cliché *m*, luogo comune

click [klɪk] *s* (*of camera or gun*) scatto; (*of typewriter*) battito, ticchettio || *tr* (*the tongue*) schioccare; (*the heels*) battere || *intr* ticchettare; (slang) andare d'accordo; (slang) avere fortuna

client [ˈklaɪənt] *s* cliente *mf*

clientele [ˌklaɪənˈtɛl] *s* clientela

cliff [klɪf] *s* rupe *f*, precipizio

climate [ˈklaɪmɪt] *s* clima *m*

climax [ˈklaɪmæks] *s* apice *m*; (*acute phase*) parossismo

climb [klaɪm] *s* salita; (*of a mountain*) scalata, ascensione || *tr* (*the stairs*) salire; (*a mountain*) scalare, ascendere || *intr* salire, arrampicarsi; **to climb down** discendere a carponi; (coll) ritirarsi

climber [ˈklaɪmər] *s* scalatore *m*; pianta rampicante; (*ambitious person*) (coll) arrampicatore *m*

clinch [klɪntʃ] *s* stretta, presa; (boxing) corpo a corpo *m* || *tr* (nails) ribattere, ribadire

clincher [ˈklɪntʃər] *s* chiodo per ribaditura; argomento decisivo

cling [klɪŋ] *v* (*pret & pp* **clung** [klʌŋ]) *intr* avviticchiare, attaccarsi; aderire, rimanere attaccato

cling'stone' peach' *s* pesca duracino

clinic [ˈklɪnɪk] *s* clinica

clinical [ˈklɪnɪkəl] *adj* clinico

clinician [klɪˈnɪʃən] *s* clinico

clink [klɪŋk] *s* tintinnio; (slang) gattabuia || *tr* (glasses) toccare || *intr* tintinnare

clinker [ˈklɪŋkər] *s* clinker *m*; mattone vetrificato; (slang) sbaglio

clip [klɪp] *s* (*of hair*) taglio; (*of wool*) tosatura; (speed) passo rapido; clip *f*, fermaglio; (*large clip*) fermacarte *m*; (*for cartridges*) caricatore *m*; (coll) colpo || *v* (*pret & pp* **clipped**; *ger* **clipping**) *tr* tagliare, tosare; (*words*) mangiare, storpiare; (paper) ritagliare; ritenere; (coll) battere || *intr* andare di buon passo

clipper [ˈklɪpər] *s* tagliatore *m*; (aer, naut) clipper *m*; **clippers** (*for hair*) tosatrice *f*; (*for nails*) pinze *fpl* per le unghie

clipping [ˈklɪpɪŋ] *s* taglio; (*from newspaper*) ritaglio

clique [klik] *s* cricca, chiesuola

cloak [klok] *s* mantello, manto; (fig) velo, maschera || *tr* ammantare, velare

cloak'-and-dag'ger *adj* d'avventura

cloak'-and-sword' *adj* di cappa e spada

cloak'room' *s* guardaroba *m*

clock [klɑk] *s* orologio; (*with pendulum*) pendolo, pendola; (*on stocking*) freccia || *tr* registrare, cronometrare

clock'mak'er *s* orologiaio

clock' tow'er *s* torre *f* dell'orologio

clock'wise' *adj & adv* nella direzione delle lancette dell'orologio

clock'work' *s* movimento d'orologeria; **like clockwork** come un orologio

clod [klɑd] *s* zolla; (fig) tonto

clod'hop'per *s* (shoe) scarpone *m*; (fig) villano, bifolco

clog [klɑg] *s* intoppo; (*to impede movement*) pastoia; scarpone *m*, zoccolo || *v* (*pret & pp* **clogged**; *ger* **clogging**) *tr* intoppare; (*to hold back*) impastoiare || *intr* otturarsi, ostruirsi

cloister [ˈklɔɪstər] *s* chiostro || *tr* rinchiudere in un chiostro

close [klos] *adj* vicino; (*translation*)

fedele; (*air in room*) male arieggiato; (*weather*) soffocante; (*stingy*) avaro; limitato, senza gioco; (*haircut*) corto; (*friend*) intimo; (*hit*) preciso; (*enclosed*) chiuso; (*narrow*) stretto || *adv* da vicino; **close** to vicino a || [kloz] *s* fine *f*, conclusione; **to bring to a close** concludere || *tr* chiudere; otturare; concludere; **to close down** chiudere completamente; **to close out** vendere in liquidazione; **to close up** bloccare || *intr* chiudersi; serrarsi; **to close down** chiudersi completamente; **to close in on** venire alle prese con; **to close up** bloccarsi; (*said of a wound*) rimarginarsi

close' call' [klos] *s* rischio scampato per miracolo

closed' chap'ter *s* affare chiuso

closed' cir'cuit *s* circuito chiuso

closed' sea'son *s* periodo di caccia o pesca vietata

closefisted ['klos'fɪstɪd] *adj* taccagno

close-fit'ing [klos] *adj* attillato

close-lipped ['klos'lɪpt] *adj* riservato

closely ['klosli] *adv* da vicino; strettamente; fedelmente; attentamente

close' quar'ters [klos] *spl* (*cramped space*) pigia pigia *m*; **at close quarters** a corpo a corpo

close' quote' [kloz] *s* fine *f* della citazione

close' shave' [klos] *s*—**to have a close shave** farsi fare la barba a contropelo; (coll) scamparla per un pelo

closet ['klazɪt] *s* armadio a muro; (*small private room*) gabinetto; (*for keeping clothing*) ripostiglio || *tr*—**to be closeted** with essere in conciliabolo con

close'-up' [klos] *s* (mov) primo piano

closing ['klozɪŋ] *s* fine *f*, conclusione

clos'ing price' *s* ultimo corso

clot [klɑt] *s* grumo, coagulo || *v* (*pret & pp* **clotted;** *ger* **clotting**) *intr* raggrumarsi, coagularsi

cloth [klɔθ] or [klɑθ] *s* panno, tessuto, stoffa; abito; (*for binding books*) tela; **the cloth** il clero

clothe [kloð] *v* (*pret & pp* **clothed** or **clad** [klæd]) *tr* vestire, rivestire, coprire

clothes [kloz] or [kloðz] *spl* vestiti *mpl*, abiti *mpl*; (*for a bed*) coltre *f*; **to change clothes** cambiarsi

clothes'bas'ket *s* cesto della biancheria

clothes'brush' *s* spazzola per vestiti

clothes' dry'er *s* asciugatrice *f*

clothes' hang'er *s* attaccapanni *m*

clothes'horse' *s* cavalletto per stendere il bucato; elegantone *m*

clothes'line' *s* corda per stendere il bucato

clothes' moth' *s* tarma, tignola

clothes'pin' *s* molletta

clothes' tree' *s* attaccapanni *m*

clothier ['kloðjər] *s* negoziante *m* di confezioni; mercante *m* di panno

clothing ['kloðɪŋ] *s* vestiti *mpl*, vestiario

cloud [klaud] *s* nuvola, nube *f*; (*great number*) nuvolo; macchia; sospetto

cloud' bank' *s* banco di nubi

cloud'burst' *s* acquazzone *m*, nubifragio

cloud'-capped' *adj* coperto di nubi

cloudless ['klaudlɪs] *adj* senza nubi

cloud·y ['klaudi] *adj* (**-ier; -iest**) nuvoloso, annuvolato; confuso; tenebroso

clout [klaut] *s* (coll) schiaffo || *tr* (coll) schiaffeggiare

clove [klov] *s* chiodo di garofano; (*of garlic*) spicchio

cloven-hoofed ['klovən'huft] *adj* dal piede biforcuto; demoniaco

clover ['klovər] *s* trifoglio; **in clover** come un papa

clo'ver-leaf' *s* (**-leaves** [,livz]) foglia di trifoglio; incrocio stradale a quadrifoglio

clown [klaun] *s* pagliaccio, buffone *m* || *intr* fare il pagliaccio

clownish ['klaunɪʃ] *adj* buffonesco, clownesco, claunesco

cloy [klɔɪ] *tr* saziare fino alla nausea

club [klʌb] *s* bastone *m*; circolo, società *f*; (*playing card*) fiore *m* || *v* (*pret & pp* **clubbed;** *ger* **clubbing**) *tr* bastonare || *intr*—**to club together** unirsi

club' car' *s* vagone *m* con servizio di buffet

club'house' *s* sede *f* di un circolo

club'man' *s* (**-men'**) frequentatore *m* di circoli

club'room' *s* sala delle riunioni

club' sand'wich *s* sandwich *m* a tre fette di pane con insalata

club'wom'an *s* (**-wom'en**) frequentatrice *f* di circoli

cluck [klʌk] *s* (il) chiocciare || *intr* chiocciare

clue [klu] *s* traccia, indizio

clump [klʌmp] *s* gruppo, massa; (*of earth*) zolla || *intr* camminare con passo pesante

clum·sy ['klʌmzi] *adj* (**-sier; -siest**) goffo, malaccorto, sgraziato

cluster | 'klʌstər] *s* gruppo; (*of grapes*) grappolo; (*of bees*) sciame *m*; (*of stars*) ammasso; (*of people*) folla || *tr* raggruppare || *intr* raggrupparsi

clutch [klʌtʃ] *s* presa; (*claw*) grinfia; (*of chickens*) covata; (mach) innesto; (aut) frizione; **clutches** grinfie *fpl*; **to throw out the clutch** innestare la marcia; **to throw the clutch out** disinnestare la marcia || *tr* afferrare, aggrappare || *intr*—**to clutch at** aggrapparsi a

clutter ['klʌtər] *tr*—**to clutter up** ingombrare alla rinfusa

coach [kotʃ] *s* carrozza, vettura; vagone *m*; (*automobile*) berlina; autobus *m*; (*trainer*) allenatore *m*; (*teacher*) ripetitore *m* || *tr* allenare; preparare

coach' house' *s* rimessa

coaching | 'kotʃɪŋ] *s* suggerimento; (*in school*) ripetizione; (sports) allenamento

coach'man *s* (**-men**) cocchiere *m*

coagulate [ko'ægjə‚let] *tr* coagulare || *intr* coagularsi

coal [kol] *s* carbone *m;* (*piece of burning wood*) tizzone *m;* **to call** or **haul over the coals** rimproverare || *tr* rifornire di carbone || *intr* rifornirsi di carbone; (naut) fare carbone

coal'bin' *s* carbonaia

coal' deal'er *s* (*wholesale*) negoziante *m* di carbone; (*retail*) carbonaio

coal' field' *s* bacino carbonifero

coal' gas' *s* gas *m* illuminante

coali'tion [‚ko·ə'lɪʃən] *s* coalizione

coal' mine' *s* miniera di carbone

coal' oil' *s* cherosene *m*

coal' scut'tle *s* secchio del carbone

coal' tar' *s* catrame *m*

coal' yard' *s* carbonaia, carboniera

coarse [kors] *adj* (*manners*) volgare, ordinario; (*unrefined*) greggio; (*lacking refinement in manners*) rozzo, grossolano

coast [kost] *s* costa; discesa a ruota libera; **the coast is clear** la via è libera || *tr* costeggiare || *intr* costeggiare; scendere a ruota libera

coastal ['kostəl] *adj* costiero

coaster ['kostər] *s* nave *f* di cabotaggio; (*amusement*) otto volante, montagna russa; (*small tray*) sottobicchiere *m*

coast'er brake' *s* freno a contropedale

coast' guard' *s* guardacoste *m*

coast'-guard cut'ter *s* guardacoste *m*

coast'ing trade' *s* cabotaggio

coast'land' *s* costa

coast'line' *s* linea costiera, litorale *m*

coast'wise' *adv* lungo la costa

coat [kot] *s* soprabito; cappotto; (*jacket*) giacca; (*hide of man and animals*) mantello; (*of paint*) mano *f;* (*layer*) strato || *tr* vestire, proteggere; ricoprire, coprire

coat'ed ['kotɪd] *adj* rivestito; (*tongue*) patinato

coat' hang'er *s* attaccapanni *m*

coating ['kotɪŋ] *s* rivestimento; (*of paint*) mano *f;* (*of cement*) strato; (*cloth*) tessuto per abiti

coat' of arms' *s* scudo, stemma *m*

coat'room' *s* guardaroba *m*

coat'tail' *s* falda

coax [koks] *tr* blandire; ottenere con lusinghe

cob [kab] *s* spiga di granturco; (*horse*) cavallo da tiro; (*swan*) cigno maschio

cobalt ['kobɔlt] *s* cobalto

cobble ['kabəl] *s* ciottolo || *tr* acciottolare; (*to mend*) raccomodare, riparare

cobbler ['kablər] *s* calzolaio, ciabattino; (*pie*) torta di frutta

cob'ble·stone' *s* ciottolo

cob'web' *s* tela di ragno, ragnatela

cocaine [ko'ken] *s* cocaina

cock [kak] *s* gallo; (*faucet*) rubinetto; (*of gun*) cane *m;* (*of the eye*) ammicco; (*of nose*) angolo (del naso) rivolto all'insù; (*of hay*) covone *m* || *tr* (*a gun*) armare; (*the head*) drizzare

cockade [ka'ked] *s* coccarda

cock-a-doodle-doo ['kakə‚dudəl'du] *s* chicchirichì *m*

cock'-and-bull' sto'ry *s* racconto incredibile

cocked' hat' *s* tricorno, cappello tricorno; **to knock into a cocked hat** (slang) distruggere completamente

cockeyed ['kak‚aɪd] *adj* strabico; (slang) sbilenco; (slang) sciocco, scemo

cockle ['kakəl] *s* (*mollusk*) cardio; (*weed*) loglio; (*boat*) barchetta; (*wrinkle*) grinza; **to warm the cockles of one's heart** far bene al cuore || *intr* raggrinzirsi

cock' of the walk' *s* gallo del pollaio

cock'pit' *s* (*of boat*) cabina; (aer) carlinga; (naut) cassero di poppa

cock'roach' *s* scarafaggio, blatta

cocks'comb' *s* cresta di gallo; berretto da buffone

cock'sure' *adj* ostinato; troppo sicuro di sé stesso

cock'tail' *s* cocktail *m*

cock'tail par'ty *s* cocktail *m*

cock·y ['kaki] *adj* (*-ier; -iest*) impudente, presuntuoso

cocoa ['koko] *s* (*bean*) cacao; (*drink*) cioccolata; (*tree*) cocco

coconut ['kokə‚nʌt] *s* noce *f* di cocco

co'conut palm' or **tree'** *s* cocco

cocoon [kə'kun] *s* bozzolo

cod [kad] *s* merluzzo

C.O.D. ['si'o'di] *s* (letterword) (**Collect on Delivery**) contro assegno

coddle ['kadəl] *tr* vezzeggiare

code [kod] *s* codice *m,* cifra; **in code** in codice, in cifra || *tr* mettere in codice or in cifra; cifrare

codex ['kodeks] *s* (*codices* ['kodɪ‚siz] or ['kadɪ‚siz]) codice *m*

cod'fish' *s* merluzzo

codger ['kadʒər] *s*—**old codger** (coll) vecchietto

codicil ['kadɪsɪl] *s* codicillo

codi·fy ['kadɪ‚faɪ] or ['kodɪ‚faɪ] *v* (*pret & pp -fied*) *tr* codificare

cod'-liver oil' *s* olio di fegato di merluzzo

coed ['co‚ɛd] *s* studentessa di scuola mista

coeducation [‚ko‚ɛdʒə'keʃən] *s* coeducazione

co'educa'tional school' [‚ko·ɛdʒə'keʃənəl] *s* scuola mista

coefficient [‚ko·ɪ'fɪʃənt] *s* coefficiente *m*

coerce [ko'ʌrs] *tr* forzare, costringere

coercion [ko'ʌrʃən] *s* coercizione

coexist [‚ko·ɪg'zɪst] *intr* coesistere

coffee ['kɔfi] or ['kafi] *s* caffè *m;* **ground coffee** caffè macinato; **roasted coffee** caffè torrefatto

cof'fee bean' *s* chicco di caffè

cof'fee-cake' *s* pasticcino (da mangiarsi con il caffè)

cof'fee grind'er *s* macinino da caffè, macinacaffè *m*

cof'fee grounds' *spl* fondi *mpl* di caffè

cof'fee house' *s* caffè *m*

cof'fee mak'er *s* macchinetta del caffè

cof'fee mill' s macinino del caffè, macinacaffè m

cof'fee-pot' s caffettiera

cof'fee shop' s caffè m

coffer ['kɔfər] or ['kɑfər] s forziere m; (ceiling) soffitto a cassettoni; (archit) cassettone m; **coffers** tesoro

coffin ['kɔfɪn] or ['kɑfɪn] s bara

cog [kɑg] s dente m d'ingranaggio; ruota dentata; **to slip a cog** fare un errore

cogent ['kodʒənt] adj convincente, persuasivo

cogitate ['kɑdʒɪ‚tet] tr & intr cogitare, ponzare

cognac ['konjæk] or ['kɑnjæk] s cognac m

cognate ['kɑgnet] adj consanguineo, parente, affine || s parola dello stesso ceppo linguistico; consanguineo, parente m

cognizance ['kɑgnɪzəns] or ['kɑnɪzəns] s conoscenza; **to take cognizance of** prendere conoscenza di

cognizant ['kɑgnɪzənt] or ['kɑnɪzənt] adj informato, al corrente

cog'wheel' s ruota dentata

cohabit [ko'hæbɪt] intr convivere; (archaic) coabitare

coheir [ko'er] s coerede mf

cohere [ko'hɪr] intr aderire; (fig) avere nesso

coherent [ko'hɪrənt] adj coerente

coiffeur [kwɑ'fʌr] s parrucchiere m per signora; (Brit) parrucchiere m

coiffure [kwɑ'fjur] s pettinatura || tr pettinare

coil [kɔɪl] s (of rope) rotolo; (of pipe) serpentino; (of wire) bobina, avvolgimento || tr arrotolare || intr arrotolarsi

coil' spring' s molla a spirale, molla elicoidale

coin [kɔɪn] s moneta; **to pay back in one's own coin** pagare della stessa moneta; **to toss a coin** giocare a testa o croce || tr (money) coniare, battere; (words) inventare, creare; **to coin money** battere moneta; (coll) fare soldoni

coincide [‚ko·ɪn'saɪd] intr coincidere

coincidence [ko'ɪnsɪdəns] s coincidenza

coke [kok] s coke m, carbone m coke

colander ['kɑləndər] or ['kɔləndər] s colabrodo, colapasta m

cold [kold] adj freddo; **it is cold** (said of weather) fa freddo; **to be cold** (said of a person) avere freddo || s freddo; (ailment) raffreddore m; **out in the cold** solo soletto; **to catch cold** pigliare freddo, pigliarsi un raffreddore

cold' blood' s—**in cold blood** a sangue freddo

cold'-blood'ed adj insensibile; (sensitive to cold) freddoloso; (animal) a sangue freddo

cold' chis'el s tagliaferro

cold' com'fort s magra consolazione

cold' cream' s crema emolliente

cold' cuts' spl salumi mpl, affettato

cold' feet' spl—**to get cold feet** (coll) perdersi d'animo

cold'-heart'ed adj—**to be coldhearted** avere il cuore duro

coldness ['koldnɪs] s freddezza

cold' shoul'der s—**to get the cold shoulder** (coll) essere trattato con freddezza; **to turn a cold shoulder on** (coll) trattare con freddezza

cold' snap' s freddo breve e improvviso

cold' stor'age s conservazione a freddo

cold' war' s guerra fredda

cold' wave' s ondata di freddo

coleslaw ['kol‚slɔ] s insalata di cavolo cappuccio

colic ['kɑlɪk] adj colico || s colica

coliseum [‚kɑlɪ'si·əm] s stadio, arena || **Coliseum** s Colosseo

collaborate [kə'læbə‚ret] intr collaborare

collaborationist [kə‚læbə'reʃənɪst] s collaborazionista mf

collaborator [kə'læbə‚retər] s collaboratore m

collapse [kə'læps] s (of business) fallimento; (e.g., of a roof) caduta; (of a person) collasso || tr piegare || intr (to shrink) restringersi, sgonfiarsi; (said of a business) fallire; (said of health) venir meno; (said, e.g., of a roof) cadere, crollare

collapsible [kə'læpsɪbəl] adj pieghevole, smontabile

collar ['kɑlər] s (of shirt) colletto; (for dog or horse) collare m; (ring) anello; (short piece of pipe) manicotto || tr afferrare per il collo, catturare

col'lar-band' s cinturino della camicia

col'lar-bone' s clavicola

collate [kə'let] or ['kɑlet] tr collazionare, confrontare

collateral [kə'lætərəl] adj collaterale; accessorio, addizionale || s collaterale m

colleague ['kɑlig] s collega mf

collect ['kɑlekt] s (eccl) colletta || [kə'lekt] adv contro assegno; (telp) pagamento all'abbonato chiamato || tr raccogliere, riunire; (e.g., stamps) collezionare; (mail) levare; (bills) incassare; (ideas) coordinare; (thoughts) riordinare; (e.g., classroom papers) raccogliere; (taxes) riscuotere; **to collect oneself** riprendersi, riprendere il controllo di sé stesso || intr (for the poor) fare la colletta; riunirsi, raccogliersi

collected [kə'lektɪd] adj raccolto; equilibrato, padrone di sè

collection [kə'lek/ən] s collezione; (for the poor) colletta; (of mail) levata; (heap) deposito; (of taxes) esazione; (of bills) riscossione

collec'tion a'gency s agenzia di riscossione

collective [kə'lektɪv] adj collettivo

collector [kə'lektər] s (of stamps) collezionista mf; (of taxes) esattore m; (of tickets) controllore m

college ['kɑlɪdʒ] s scuola superiore,

università *f;* (*e.g., of medicine*) facoltà *f;* (*electoral*) collegio

collide [kə'laɪd] *intr* collidere, scontrarsi

collie ['kɑlɪ] *s* collie *m*

collier ['kɑljər] *s* (*ship*) carboniera; (min) minatore *m* di carbone

collier·y ['kɑljərɪ] *s* (-ies) miniera di carbone

collision [kə'lɪʒən] *s* collisione

colloid ['kɑlɔɪd] *adj* colloidale ‖ *s* colloide *m*

colloquial [kə'lokwɪ·əl] *adj* familiare, colloquiale

colloquialism [kə'lokwɪ·ə‚lɪzəm] *s* espressione familiare

collo·quy ['kɑləkwɪ] *s* (-quies) colloquio

collusion [kə'luʒən] *s* collusione; **to be in collusion with** essere d'intelligenza con

cologne [kə'lon] *s* acqua di colonia, colonia ‖ **Cologne** *s* Colonia

colon ['kolən] *s* (anat) colon *m;* (gram) due punti *mpl*

colonel ['kʌrnəl] *s* colonnello

colonist ['kɑlənɪst] *s* colono, coloniale *m*

colonize ['kɑlə‚naɪz] *tr & intr* colonizzare

colonnade [‚kɑlə'ned] *s* colonnato

colo·ny ['kɑlənɪ] *s* (-nies) colonia

color ['kʌlər] *s* colore *m; off color* sbiadito, scolorito; (slang) sporco, volgare; **the colors** i colori, la bandiera; **to call to the colors** chiamare in servizio militare; **to change color** cambiar colore; arrossire; impallidire; **to give** or **lend color to** far parere probabile; **to lose color** impallidire; **to show one's colors** mostrarsi come si è; **under color of** sotto il pretesto di ‖ *tr* colorare; (fig) colorire ‖ *intr* arrossire

col'or-blind' *adj* daltonico

colored ['kʌlərd] *adj* colorato; (*person*) di colore; esagerato

colorful ['kʌlərfəl] *adj* colorito, espressivo

col'or guard' *s* guardia d'onore alla bandiera

coloring ['kʌlərɪŋ] *s* colorazione; colore *m;* pigmento; (fig) specie *f*

colorless ['kʌlərlɪs] *adj* incolore, incoloro

col'or photog'raphy *s* fotografia a colori

col'or ser'geant *s* sergente *m* portabandiera

col'or tel'evision *s* televisione a colori

colossal [kə'lɑsəl] *adj* colossale

colossus [kə'lɑsəs] *s* colosso

colt [kolt] *s* puledro

Columbus [kə'lʌmbəs] *s* Colombo

column ['kɑləm] *s* colonna

columnist ['kɑləmnɪst] *s* giornalista incaricato di una colonna speciale; articolista *mf*

coma ['komə] *s* coma *m*

comb [kom] *s* pettine *m;* (*for horse*) striglia; (*of hen* or *wave*) cresta; (*honeycomb*) favo ‖ *tr* pettinare;

(fig) esaminare minuziosamente ‖ *intr* (*said of waves*) frangersi

com·bat ['kɑmbæt] *s* combattimento ‖ ['kɑmbæt] or [kəm'bæt] *v* (*pret & pp* -bated or -batted; *ger* -bating or -batting) *tr & intr* combattere

combatant ['kɑmbətənt] *s* combattente *mf*

com'bat du'ty *s* servizio in zona di guerra

combination [‚kɑmbɪ'neʃən] *s* combinazione

combine ['kɑmbaɪn] *s* consorzio; (pol) coalizione; mieto-trebbiatrice ‖ [kəm'baɪn] *tr* combinare ‖ *intr* combinarsi

combin'ing form' *s* membro di parola composta

combo ['kɑmbo] *s* orchestrina

combustible [kəm'bʌstɪbəl] *adj & s* combustibile *m*

combustion [kəm'bʌstʃən] *s* combustione

come [kʌm] *v* (*pret* **came** [kem]; *pp* **come**) *intr* venire; arrivare; (*to become*) diventare; (*to amount*) ammontare; **come!** macchè!; **come along!** andiamo!; **come in!** avanti!; entri!; **come on!** andiamo!; avanti!, coraggio!; **to come about** accadere, succedere; **to come across** incontrarsi con; (slang) pagare; **to come around** cedere; mettersi d'accordo; (*said of health*) rimettersi; **to come at** raggiungere; (*to attack*) attaccare; **to come back** ritornare; **to come between** mettersi fra; **to come by** ottenere; **to come down** scendere; decadere; essere trasmesso; **to come down with** ammalarsi di; **to come forward** farsi avanti; **to come in** entrare, passare; **to come in for** ricevere; **to come into** ricevere; ereditare; **to come off** succedere; riuscire; **to come on** mostrarsi; migliorare; incontrarsi; **to come out** uscire; debuttare in società; andare a finire; **to come out with** uscire con; mostrare; **to come over** succedere a, e.g., **what came over him?** che gli è successo?; **to come through** riuscire; **to come to** riprendere i sensi; **to come under** essere di competenza di; appartenere a; **to come up** salire; **to come up to** salire fino a; avvicinarsi a; **to come up with** raggiungere; produrre, fornire; proporre

come'back' *s* (coll) ritorno; (slang) pronta risposta; **to stage a comeback** (coll) ritornare in auge

comedian [kə'midɪ·ən] *s* attore comico; (*author*) commediografo; (*amusing person*) commediante *mf*

comedienne [kə‚midɪ'ɛn] *s* attrice comica

come'down' *s* (coll) rovescio di fortuna

come·dy ['kɑmədɪ] *s* (-dies) commedia

come·ly ['kʌmlɪ] *adj* (-lier; -liest) bello, grazioso

comet ['kɑmɪt] *s* cometa

comfort ['kʌmfərt] *s* conforto, sollievo;

(ease) benessere *m* || *tr* confortare, alleviare

comfortable ['kʌmfərtəbəl] *adj* comodo, agiato; *(e.g., income)* (coll) bastante || *s* coltre *f*

comforter ['kʌmfərtər] *s* consolatore *m; (bedcover)* coltre *f;* sciarpa di lana || **the Comforter** lo Spirito Santo, lo Spirito Consolatore

comforting ['kʌmfərtɪŋ] *adj* confortante

com'fort sta'tion *s* latrina pubblica

comic ['kɑmɪk] *adj* comico || *s (actor)* comico; comicità *f;* **comics** fumetti *mpl*

comical ['kɑmɪkəl] *adj* comico

com'ic book' *s* libretto a fumetti

com'ic op'era *s* opera buffa

com'ic strip' *s* racconto umoristico a fumetti

coming ['kʌmɪŋ] *adj* venturo, prossimo; promettente || *s* venuta

com'ing out' *s* debutto in società; *(e.g., of stock)* emissione

comma ['kɑmə] *s* virgola

command [kə'mænd] *or* [kə'mɑnd] *s* comando; *(e.g., of a language)* padronanza || *tr* comandare, ordinare; *(to overlook)* dominare; *(to be able to have)* disporre di || *intr* avere il comando

commandant [ˌkɑmən'dænt] *or* [ˌkɑmən'dɑnt] *s* comandante *m*

commandeer [ˌkɑmən'dɪr] *tr* requisire

commander [kə'mændər] *or* [kə'mɑndər] *s (of knighthood)* commendatore *m;* (mil) comandante *m;* (nav) capitano di vascello

command'er in chief' *s* comandante *m* in capo

command'ing of'ficer *s* comandante *m*

commandment [kə'mændmənt] *or* [kə'mɑndmənt] *s* comandamento

command' mod'ule *s* (rok) modulo di comando

commando [kə'mændo] *s* guastatore *m*

commemorate [kə'mɛmə ˌret] *tr* commemorare, celebrare

commence [kə'mɛns] *tr* & *intr* cominciare

commencement [kə'mɛnsmənt] *s* inizio, esordio; *(in a school)* cerimonia per la distribuzione dei diplomi

commend [kə'mɛnd] *tr* lodare; *(to entrust)* raccomandare, affidare

commendable [kə'mɛndəbəl] *adj (person)* lodevole; *(act)* commendevole

commendation [ˌkɑmən'deʃən] *s* lode *f;* raccomandazione; (mil) citazione

comment ['kɑmɛnt] *s* commento || *tr* commentare || *intr* fare commenti; **to comment on** fare commenti su

commentar·y ['kɑmən ˌtɛri] *s* (-ies) commentario

commentator ['kɑmən ˌtetər] *s* commentatore *m*

commerce ['kɑmərs] *s* commercio

commercial [kə'mɜrʃəl] *adj* commerciale || *s* (rad, telv) programma *m* di pubblicità; (rad, telv) annunzio pubblicitario

commiserate [kə'mɪzə ˌret] *intr—to*

commiserate with commiserare, compiangere

commissar ['kɑmɪ ˌsɑr] *or* [ˌkɑmɪ'sɑr] *s* commissario del popolo

commissar·y ['kɑmɪ ˌsɛri] *s* (-ies) *(store)* economato; *(deputy)* commissario; *(in army)* intendente *m*

commission [kə'mɪʃən] *s* commissione; *(e.g., in army)* nomina, brevetto; autorità *f; (of a crime)* perpetrazione; (il) fare; **in commission** in servizio, in uso; **out of commission** fuori servizio || *tr* nominare, dare un brevetto a; autorizzare; *(a ship)* armare

commis'sioned of'ficer *s* (mil, nav) ufficiale *m*

commissioner [kə'mɪʃənər] *s* commissario; membro di una commissione

commis'sion mer'chant *s* sensale *m*

com·mit [kə'mɪt] *v (pret & pp -mitted; ger -mitting) tr* commettere, perpetrare; *(to deliver)* affidare, consegnare; *(to imprison)* mandare in prigione; *(an insane person)* internare, *(to refer)* rinviare; *(to involve)* compromettere; **to commit oneself** compromettersi; **to commit to memory** imparare a memoria; **to commit to writing** mettere in iscritto

commitment [kə'mɪtmənt] *s (act of committing)* commissione; *(to an asylum)* internamento; promessa; (law) mandato

committal [kə'mɪtəl] *s* consegna; promessa

committee [kə'mɪti] *s* comitato, commissione

commode [kə'mod] *s (chest of drawers)* cassettone *m; (washstand)* lavabo; seggetta, comoda

commodious [kə'modɪ·əs] *adj* spazioso; conveniente

commodi·ty [kə'mɑdɪti] *s* (-ties) merce *f;* articolo di prima necessità

commod'ity exchange' *s* borsa merci

common ['kɑmən] *adj* comune || *s* fondo comunale; pascolo comune; **commons** gente *f* non nobile; refettorio; **in common** in comune || **the Commons** la Camera dei Comuni

com'mon car'rier *s* impresa di trasporti pubblici

commoner ['kɑmənər] *s* plebeo, borghese *m;* membro della Camera dei Comuni

com'mon law' *s* consuetudine *f,* diritto consuetudinario

com'mon-law mar'riage *s* matrimonio basato sulla mera convivenza

commonly ['kɑmənli] *adv* generalmente

com'mon·place' *adj* banale, ordinario || *s* banalità *f,* cosa ordinaria

com'mon sense' *s* senso comune

com'mon-sense' *adj* giudizioso

com'mon stock' *s* azione ordinaria; azioni ordinarie

commonweal ['kɑmən ˌwil] *s* bene pubblico

com'mon·wealth' *s (citizens of a state)* cittadinanza; repubblica; *(one of the*

50 states of the U.S.A.) stato; comunità *f*, federazione

commotion [kə'moʃən] *s* agitazione

commune [kə'mjun] *s* comune *m* ‖ *intr* confabulare; (eccl) comunicarsi

communicate [kə'mjunɪ͵ket] *tr & intr* comunicare

communicating [kə'mjunɪ͵ketɪŋ] *adj* comunicante

communication [kə͵mjunɪ'keʃən] *s* comunicazione; **communications** sistema *m* di comunicazione; **mezzi** *mpl* di comunicazione

communicative [kə'mjunɪ͵ketɪv] *adj* comunicativo

Communion [kə'mjunjən] *s* Comunione; **to take Communion** comunicarsi

communiqué [kə͵mjunɪ'ke] or [kə'mjunɪ͵ke] *s* comunicato

communism ['kamjə͵nɪzəm] *s* comunismo

communist ['kamjənɪst] *s* comunista *mf*

communi-ty [kə'mjunɪti] *s* (**-ties**) (*people living together*) comunità *f*; (*sharing together*) comunanza; (*neighborhood*) circondario

commu′nity cen′ter *s* centro sociale

commu′nity chest′ *s* fondo di beneficenza

commuta′tion tick′et [͵kamjə'teʃən] *s* biglietto d'abbonamento

commutator ['kamjə͵tetər] *s* (switch) commutatore *m*; (*of dynamo or motor*) collettore *m*

commute [kə'mjut] *tr* commutare ‖ *intr* commutare; fare il pendolare

commuter [kə'mjutər] *s* pendolare *mf*

compact [kəm'pækt] *adj* compatto ‖ ['kampækt] *s* (*small case for face powder*) portacipria *m*; (*agreement*) accordo; (*small car*) utilitaria

companion [kəm'pænjən] *s* compagno; (*one of two items*) pendant *m*; (*lady*) dama di compagnia

compan′ion·ship′ *s* cameratismo

compan′ion·way′ *s* (naut) scaletta per andare sottocoperta

compa·ny ['kʌmpəni] *s* (**-nies**) compagnia; (coll) ospite *m* or ospiti *mpl*; (naut) equipaggio; **to bear company** accompagnare; **to be good company** essere simpatico; **to keep company** (*said of a couple*) andare insieme; **to keep company with** accompagnare; (coll) fare la corte a; **to part company** separarsi

comparable ['kampərəbəl] *adj* comparabile, paragonabile

comparative [kəm'pærətɪv] *adj* comparativo; (*e.g., anatomy*) comparato ‖ *s* (gram) comparativo

compare [kəm'per] *s*—**beyond compare** incomparabile ‖ *tr* confrontare; **compared to** a confronto di, in confronto a

comparison [kəm'pærɪsən] *s* confronto; (gram) comparazione; **in comparison with** in confronto a, a confronto di

compartment [kəm'partmənt] *s* compartimento; (naut) compartimento stagno; (rr) compartimento

compass ['kʌmpəs] *s* (*instrument for showing direction*) bussola; (*boundary*) limite *m*; (*range*) ambito; (*range of voice*) compasso; **compasses** (*drawing instrument*) compasso ‖ *tr* girare intorno a; comprendere; **to compass about** accerchiare

com′pass card′ *s* rosa dei venti

compassion [kəm'pæʃən] *s* compassione

compassionate [kəm'pæʃənɪt] *adj* compassionevole

com′pass saw′ *s* gattuccio

com·pel [kəm'pel] *v* (*pret & pp* **-pelled**; *ger* **-pelling**) *tr* forzare, obbligare

compelling [kəm'pelɪŋ] *adj* imperioso, coercitivo

compendious [kəm'pendɪ·əs] *adj* compendioso, conciso

compensate ['kampən͵set] *tr & intr* compensare

compensation [͵kampən'seʃən] *s* compensazione; (*pay*) pagamento; (*something given to offset a loss*) risarcimento, indennità *f*

compete [kəm'pit] *intr* competere

competence ['kampɪtəns] or **competency** ['kampɪtənsi] *s* (*fitness*) abilità *f*; (*money*) agiatezza; (*authority*) competenza

competent ['kampɪtənt] *adj* abile; competente

competition [͵kampɪ'tɪʃən] *s* competizione, gara; (*in business*) concorrenza

competitive [kəm'petɪtɪv] *adj* competitivo; (*based on competition*) di concorso

compet′itive pric′es *spl* prezzi *mpl* di concorrenza

competitor [kəm'petɪtər] *s* competitore *m*, concorrente *mf*; rivale *mf*

compilation [͵kampɪ'leʃən] *s* compilazione

compile [kəm'paɪl] *tr* compilare

complacence [kəm'plesəns] or **complacency** [kəm'plesənsi] *s* compiacenza; compiacenza di sé stesso

complacent [kəm'plesənt] *adj* compiaciuto o soddisfatto con sé stesso

complain [kəm'plen] *intr* lagnarsi

complainant [kəm'plenənt] *s* (law) querelante *mf*

complaint [kəm'plent] *s* lagnanza, reclamo; (*sickness*) malattia; (law) querela

complaisance [kəm'plezəns] or ['kamplɪ͵zæns] *s* compiacenza

complaisant [kəm'plezənt] or ['kamplɪ͵zænt] *adj* compiacente, cortese

complement ['kamplɪmənt] *s* complemento; (naut) equipaggio ‖ ['kamplɪ͵ment] *tr* completare

complete [kəm'plit] *adj* completo; (*done*) finito ‖ *tr* completare, finire

completion [kəm'pliʃən] *s* completamento, compimento

complex [kəm'pleks] or ['kampleks]

adj complesso, complicato ‖ [ˈkɑmpleks] *s* complesso

complexion [kəmˈplekʃən] *s (of skin)* carnagione; *(appearance)* aspetto; *(viewpoint)* punto di vista

compliance [kəmˈplaɪəns] *s* condiscendenza, arrendevolezza; **in compliance with** in conformità di

complicate [ˈkɑmplɪˌket] *tr* complicare

complicated [ˈkɑmplɪˌketɪd] *adj* complicato

complici·ty [kəmˈplɪsɪti] *s* (-ties) complicità *f*

compliment [ˈkɑmplɪmənt] *s* complimento, omaggio ‖ [ˈkɑmplɪˌment] *tr*—**to compliment s.o. on s.th** felicitarsi con qlcu per qlco; **to compliment s.o. with s.th** regalare qlco a qlcu

complimentary [ˌkɑmplɪˈmentəri] *adj* complimentoso, lusinghiero; *(free)* in omaggio, gratis; *(ticket)* di favore

com·ply [kəmˈplaɪ] *v (pret & pp -plied) intr* acconsentire, accondiscendere; **to comply with** accedere a

component [kəmˈponənt] *adj* componente, costituente ‖ *s (component part)* componente *m; (force)* componente *f*

compose [kəmˈpoz] *tr* comporre; **to be composed of** essere composto di; **to compose oneself** calmarsi

composed [kəmˈpozd] *adj* calmo, tranquillo

composer [kəmˈpozər] *s (peacemaker)* conciliatore *m;* (mus) compositore *m*

compos'ing stick' *s* (typ) compositoio

composite [kəmˈpɑzɪt] *adj & s* composto, composito

composition [ˌkɑmpəˈzɪʃən] *s* composizione; *(agreement)* compromesso

compositor [kəmˈpɑzɪtər] *s* compositore *m*

compost [ˈkɑmpost] *s* concime *m* naturale

composure [kəmˈpoʒər] *s* calma

compote [ˈkɑmpot] *s (stewed fruit)* composta; *(dish)* compostiera

compound [ˈkɑmpaʊnd] *adj* composto; *(fracture)* complesso; (archit, bot) composito ‖ *s* composto; parola composta; *(yard)* recinto ‖ [kɑmˈpaʊnd] *tr (to mix)* combinare; *(to settle)* comporre; *(interest)* capitalizzare

comprehend [ˌkɑmprɪˈhend] *tr* comprendere

comprehensible [ˌkɑmprɪˈhensɪbəl] *adj* comprensibile

comprehension [ˌkɑmprɪˈhenʃən] *s* comprensione

comprehensive [ˌkɑmprɪˈhensɪv] *adj* comprensivo

compress [ˈkɑmpres] *s* compressa ‖ [kəmˈpres] *tr* comprimere

compressed' air' *s* aria compressa

compression [kəmˈpreʃən] *s* compressione

comprise [kəmˈpraɪz] *tr* comprendere, includere; **to be comprised of** consistere di

compromise [ˈkɑmprəˌmaɪz] *s* compromesso ‖ *tr (a dispute)* transigere, comporre; *(to put in danger)* compromettere ‖ *intr* transigere, fare un compromesso

comptroller [kənˈtrolər] *s* economo, amministratore *m,* controllore *m*

compulsive [kəmˈpʌlsɪv] *adj* obbligatorio, coercitivo; (psychol) compulsivo

compulsory [kəmˈpʌlsəri] *adj* obbligatorio

compute [kəmˈpjut] *tr & intr* computare, calcolare

computer [kəmˈpjutər] *s* calcolatore *m;* elaboratore *m*

comrade [ˈkɑmræd] *or* [ˈkɑmrɪd] *s* camerata *m,* compagno

com'rade in arms' *s* compagno d'armi

con [kɑn] *s* contro ‖ *v (pret & pp conned; ger conning) tr* imparare a memoria; (slang) imbrogliare

concave [ˈkɑnkev] *or* [kɑnˈkev] *adj* concavo

conceal [kənˈsil] *tr* nascondere; *(to keep secret)* celare

concealment [kənˈsilmənt] *s* occultamento; *(place)* nascondiglio

concede [kənˈsid] *tr* concedere

conceit [kənˈsit] *s (high opinion of oneself)* presunzione; *(fanciful notion)* concetto sottile

conceited [kənˈsitɪd] *adj* vanitoso

conceivable [kənˈsivəbəl] *adj* concepibile

conceive [kənˈsiv] *tr & intr* concepire

concentrate [ˈkɑnsənˌtret] *s* concentrato ‖ *tr* concentrare ‖ *intr* concentrarsi; **to concentrate on** concentrarsi in

concentra'tion camp' [ˌkɑnsənˈtreʃən] *s* campo di concentrazione

concept [ˈkɑnsept] *s* concetto

conception [kənˈsepʃən] *s* concezione

concern [kənˈsʌrn] *s* interesse *m; (worry)* ansietà *f;* (firm) ditta, compagnia; **of concern** d'interesse ‖ *tr* concernere; **as concerns** circa; **to concern oneself** interessarsi; **to whom it may concern** a chiunque possa averne interesse

concerning [kənˈsʌrnɪŋ] *prep* riguardo a

concert [ˈkɑnsərt] *s* concerto ‖ [kənˈsʌrt] *tr & intr* concertare

con'cert·mas'ter *s* primo violino

concer·to [kənˈtʃerto] *s* (-tos *or* -ti [ti]) concerto

concession [kənˈseʃən] *s* concessione

conciliate [kənˈsɪliˌet] *tr* conciliare, conciliarsi con

concise [kənˈsaɪs] *adj* conciso

conclude [kənˈklud] *tr* concludere ‖ *intr* concludersi, terminare

conclusion [kənˈkluʒən] *s* conclusione; **in conclusion** per finire; **to try conclusions with** misurarsi con

conclusive [kənˈklusɪv] *adj* decisivo, convincente

concoct [kənˈkɑkt] *tr* preparare, confezionare; *(a story)* inventare

concoction [kɑnˈkɑkʃən] *s* preparazione, mescolanza; (unpleasant in taste) intruglio

concomitant [kən'kɑmɪtənt] adj concomitante || s fatto or sintomo concomitante

concord ['kɑŋkɔrd] s concordia, armonia; (treaty) accordo; (gram) concordanza

concourse ['kɑŋkors] s confluenza; (crowd) affluenza, concorso; (boulevard) viale m; (rr) salone m principale

concrete ['kɑŋkrit] or [kɑn'krit] adj concreto; fatto di cemento; solido || s cemento, calcestruzzo || tr (e.g., a sidewalk) cementare

con'crete mix'er s betoniera

con·cur [kɑn'kʌr] v (pret & pp -curred; ger -curring) intr (to work together) concorrere; (to agree) essere d'accordo, aderire

concurrence [kɑn'kʌrəns] s concorso; (agreement) accordo

concurrent [kɑn'kʌrənt] adj concomitante, simultaneo; cooperante; armonioso

concussion [kɑn'kʌʃən] s scossa, urto; (of brain) commozione cerebrale

condemn [kɑn'dem] tr condannare; (to take for public use) espropriare

condemnation [,kɑndem'neʃən] s condanna

condense [kɑn'dens] tr condensare || intr condensarsi

condescend [,kɑndɪ'send] intr condiscendere, degnarsi

condescending [,kɑndɪ'sendɪŋ] adj condiscendente

condescension [,kɑndɪ'senʃən] s condiscendenza, degnazione

condiment ['kɑndɪmənt] s condimento

condition [kɑn'dɪʃən] s condizione; clausola; **on condition that** a condizione che || tr condizionare; mettere in buone condizioni fisiche

conditional [kɑn'dɪʃənəl] adj & s condizionale m

condole [kɑn'dol] intr condolersi

condolence [kɑn'doləns] s condoglianza

condone [kɑn'don] tr condonare

conduce [kɑn'djus] or [kɑn'dus] intr contribuire, indurre

conducive [kɑn'djusɪv] or [kɑn'dusɪv] adj contribuente

conduct ['kɑndʌkt] s condotta; direzione || [kɑn'dʌkt] tr condurre; (an orchestra) dirigere; **to conduct oneself** condursi, comportarsi || intr dirigere

conductor [kɑn'dʌktər] s direttore m; (of a streetcar) fattorino, conduttore m; (phys) conduttore m; (rr) capotreno

conduit ['kɑndɪt] or ['kɑndu·ɪt] s condotto

cone [kon] s cono; (bot) pigna

Con'estoga wag'on ['kɑnɪ'stogə] s carriaggio coperto

confectioner [kɑn'fekʃənər] s confettiere m, pasticcere m

confec'tioners' sug'ar s zucchero in polvere finissimo

confectioner·y [kɑn'fekʃə,neri] s (-ies) confetteria, pasticceria; (candies) confetture fpl

confedera·cy [kɑn'fedərəsi] s (-cies) confederazione; lega

confederate [kɑn'fedərɪt] s alleato; (in crime) complice mf || [kɑn'fedə,ret] tr confederare || intr confederarsi

con·fer [kɑn'fʌr] v (pret & pp -ferred; ger -ferring) tr conferire || intr conferire, abboccarsi

conference ['kɑnfərəns] s conferenza

confess [kɑn'fes] tr confessare, ammettere || intr confessare, confessarsi

confession [kɑn'feʃən] s confessione

confessional [kɑn'feʃənəl] s confessionale m

confes'sion of faith' s professione di fede

confessor [kɑn'fesər] s confessore m

confetti [kɑn'feti] s coriandoli mpl

confide [kɑn'faɪd] tr confidare; (to entrust) affidare || intr confidarsi

confidence ['kɑnfɪdəns] s fiducia; sicurezza di sé; (boldness) baldanza; (secrecy) confidenza

confident ['kɑnfɪdənt] adj fiducioso; baldanzoso || s confidente mf

confidential [,kɑnfɪ'denʃəl] adj confidenziale

confine ['kɑnfaɪn] s confine m || [kɑn'faɪn] tr limitare; confinare; **to be confined** essere in altro stato; **to be confined to bed** dover stare a letto

confinement [kɑn'faɪnmənt] s confino; (childbirth) parto; (imprisonment) prigionia

confirm [kɑn'fʌrm] tr confermare; (eccl) cresimare

confirmed [kɑn'fʌrmd] adj (e.g., piece of news) confermato; (bachelor; drunkard) impenitente; inveterato; (e.g., invalid) cronico

confiscate ['kɑnfɪs,ket] tr confiscare

conflagration [,kɑnflə'greʃən] s conflagrazione

conflict ['kɑnflɪkt] s conflitto || [kɑn'flɪkt] intr lottare; essere in conflitto

conflicting [kɑn'flɪktɪŋ] adj contrastante; contraddittorio

confluence ['kɑnflu·əns] s confluenza

conform [kɑn'fɔrm] tr conformare || intr conformarsi

conformi·ty [kɑn'fɔrmɪti] s (-ties) conformità f; **in conformity with** in conformità di

confound [kɑn'faund] tr confondere || ['kɑn'faund] tr maledire; **confound it!** accidenti!

confounded [kɑn'faundɪd] or ['kɑn'faundɪd] adj maledetto; (hateful) odioso

confront [kɑn'frʌnt] tr affrontare, opporsi a; (to bring face to face) raffrontare; (to compare) confrontare

confrontation [,kɑnfrən'teʃən] s contestazione

confuse [kɑn'fjuz] tr confondere; **to get confused** confondersi

confusion [kɑn'fjuʒən] s confusione

congeal [kən'dʒil] tr congelare; coagulare ‖ intr congelarsi; (said, e.g., of blood) coagularsi

congenial [kən'dʒinjəl] adj (agreeable) simpatico; (having similar tastes) affine; (suited to one's needs or tastes) congeniale

congenital [kən'dʒɛntəl] adj congenito

con'ger eel' ['kaŋgər] s grongo

congest [kən'dʒɛst] tr congestionare ‖ intr essere congestionato

congestion [kən'dʒɛstʃən] s congestione

conglomerate [kən'glamərɪt] adj & s conglomerato ‖ [kən'glamə,ret] tr conglomerare ‖ intr conglomerarsi

congratulate [kən'grætʃə,let] tr congratularsi con

congratulation [kən,grætʃə'leʃən] s congratulazione, felicitazione

congregate ['kaŋgrɪ,get] intr congregarsi

congregation [,kaŋgrɪ'geʃən] s congregazione; fedeli mpl di una chiesa

congress ['kaŋgrɪs] s parlamento; congresso

con'gress·man s (-men) deputato al congresso degli S.U.

con'gress·wom'an s (-wom'en) deputatessa al congresso degli S.U.

conical ['kanɪkəl] adj conico

conjecture [kən'dʒɛktʃər] s congettura ‖ tr & intr congetturare

conjugate ['kandʒə,get] tr coniugare

conjugation [,kandʒə'geʃən] s coniugazione

conjunction [kən'dʒʌŋkʃən] s congiunzione

conjure [kən'dʒur] tr (to entreat) scongiurare ‖ ['kandʒər] or ['kʌndʒər] tr evocare, stregare; **to conjure up** evocare ‖ intr fare delle stregonerie

conk [kaŋk] intr—**to conk out** (slang) essere in panna; (slang) svenire

connect [kə'nɛkt] tr connettere, unire ‖ intr connettersi, essere associato; (said of public conveyances) operare in coincidenza

connect'ing rod' [kə'nɛktɪŋ] s (mach) biella

connection [kə'nɛkʃən] s connessione; unione, associazione; (of trains) coincidenza; (relative) parente mf; (e.g., of a water pipe) allacciamento; **in connection with** rispetto a

con'ning tow'er ['kanɪŋ] s (nav) torretta

conniption [kə'nɪpʃən] s (slang) attacco di rabbia

connive [kə'naɪv] intr essere connivente; **to connive at** chiudere un occhio su

connote [kə'not] tr indicare, suggerire

conquer ['kaŋkər] tr & intr conquistare

conqueror ['kaŋkərər] s conquistatore m

conquest ['kaŋkwɛst] s conquista

conscience ['kanʃəns] s coscienza; **in all conscience** a prezzo onesto; certamente

conscientious [,kanʃɪ'ɛnʃəs] adj coscienzioso

conscien'tious objec'tor [ab'dʒɛktər] s obiettore m di coscienza

conscious ['kanʃəs] adj (aware of one's existence) cosciente; (aware) conscio, consapevole; (lie) consapevole; **to become conscious** riprendere i sensi

consciousness ['kanʃəsnɪs] s coscienza, conoscenza; **to lose consciousness** perdere la conoscenza

conscript ['kanskrɪpt] s coscritto ‖ [kən'skrɪpt] tr coscrivere, arruolare

conscription [kən'skrɪpʃən] s coscrizione

consecrate ['kansɪ,kret] tr consacrare

consecutive [kən'sɛkjətɪv] adj consecutivo; di seguito

consensus [kən'sɛnsəs] s consenso

consent [kən'sɛnt] s consenso; **by common consent** per comune consenso ‖ intr consentire

consequence ['kansɪ,kwɛns] s conseguenza

consequential [,kansɪ'kwɛnʃəl] adj conseguente; importante, d'importanza; pomposo, pieno di sé

consequently ['kansɪ,kwɛntli] adv consequentemente, per conseguenza

conservation [,kansər've/ən] s conservazione; preservazione delle foreste

conservatism [kən'sʌrvə,tɪzəm] s conservatorismo

conservative [kən'sʌrvətɪv] adj conservatore; (cautious) cauto; (preserving) conservativo; (free from fads) tradizionale ‖ s conservatore m

conservato·ry [kən'sʌrvə,tori] s (-ries) (greenhouse) serra; (mus) conservatorio

conserve [kən'sʌrv] tr conservare

consider [kən'sɪdər] tr considerare

considerable [kən'sɪdərəbəl] adj (fairly large) considerevole; (worth thinking about) considerabile

considerate [kən'sɪdərɪt] adj riguardoso, premuroso

consideration [kən,sɪdə'reʃən] s considerazione; (reason) motivo; (money) pagamento; **in consideration of** a cagione di; in cambio di; **on no consideration** in nessuna maniera, mai; **under consideration** in considerazione, sotto esame; **without due consideration** senza riflessione, alla leggera

considering [kən'sɪdərɪŋ] adv tutto considerato ‖ prep per, visto ‖ conj considerando che, visto che

consign [kən'saɪn] tr consegnare; (to send) inviare; (to set apart) assegnare

consignee [,kansaɪ'ni] s consegnatario

consignment [kən'saɪnmənt] s consegna; **on consignment** in consegna

consist [kən'sɪst] intr—**to consist in** consistere in; **to consist of** consistere in, constare di

consisten·cy [kən'sɪstənsi] s (-cies) (firmness, amount of firmness) consistenza; (logical connection) coerenza

consistent [kən'sɪstənt] adj (holding firmly together) consistente; (agree-

ing with itself or oneself) conseguente, coerente; compatibile

consolation [ˌkɑnsəˈleʃən] *s* consolazione

console [ˈkɑnsol] *s* (*table*) console *f*; (*rad, telv*) mobile *m*; (*mus*) console *f* ‖ [kənˈsol] *tr* consolare

consonant [ˈkɑnsənənt] *adj* consonante, armonioso; (*gram*) consonantico ‖ *s* consonante *f*

consort [ˈkɑnsort] *s* consorte *mf* ‖ [kənˈsort] *intr* associarsi; (*to agree*) concordarsi

conspicuous [kənˈspɪkju‧əs] *adj* visibile, manifesto; notevole; (*too noticeable*) appariscente; **to make oneself conspicuous** farsi notare

conspira‧cy [kənˈspɪrəsi] *s* (-*cies*) cospirazione, congiura

conspire [kənˈspaɪr] *intr* cospirare, congiurare; (*to act together*) cooperare

constable [ˈkɑnstəbəl] *or* [ˈkʌnstəbəl] *s* poliziotto; (*keeper of a castle*) conestabile *m*

constancy [ˈkɑnstənsi] *s* costanza

constant [ˈkɑnstənt] *adj & s* costante *f*

constellation [ˌkɑnstəˈleʃən] *s* costellazione

constipate [ˈkɑnstɪˌpet] *tr* costipare

constipation [ˌkɑnstɪˈpeʃən] *s* costipazione

constituen‧cy [kənˈstɪtʃʊ‧ənsi] *s* (-*cies*) (*voters*) elettorato; (*district*) circoscrizione elettorale

constituent [kənˈstɪtʃʊ‧ənt] *adj* costituente ‖ *s* (*component*) parte *f* costituente; (*voter*) elettore *m*; (*of a chemical substance*) costituente *m*

constitute [ˈkɑnstɪˌtjut] *or* [ˈkɑnstɪˌtut] *tr* costituire

constitution [ˌkɑnstɪˈtjuʃən] *or* [ˌkɑnstɪˈtuʃən] *s* costituzione

constrain [kənˈstren] *tr* (*to force*) costringere; (*to restrain*) restringere, comprimere

constrict [kənˈstrɪkt] *tr* stringere, comprimere

construct [kənˈstrʌkt] *tr* costruire

construction [kənˈstrʌkʃən] *s* costruzione; (*meaning*) interpretazione

construe [kənˈstru] *tr* (*to interpret*) interpretare; (*to translate*) tradurre; (*gram*) analizzare

consul [ˈkɑnsəl] *s* console *m*

consular [ˈkɑnsələr] *or* [ˈkɑnsjələr] *adj* consolare

consulate [ˈkɑnsəlɪt] *or* [ˈkɑnsjəlɪt] *s* consolato

consult [kənˈsʌlt] *tr* consultare ‖ *intr* consultarsi

consultation [ˌkɑnsəlˈteʃən] *s* consultazione, conferenza

consume [kənˈsum] *or* [kənˈsjum] *tr* consumare; distruggere; **consumed with** (*passion*) arso di; (*curiosity*) assorbito da

consumer [kənˈsumər] *or* [kənˈsjumər] *s* consumatore *m*

consum'er goods' *spl* beni *mpl* di consumo

consumerism [kənˈsumər‧ˌɪzem] *s* consumismo

consummate [kənˈsʌmɪt] *adj* consumato ‖ [ˈkɑnsə‧ˌmet] *tr* consumare

consumption [kənˈsʌmpʃən] *s* (*decay*) consunzione; (*using up*) consumo; (*pathol*) consunzione

consumptive [kənˈsʌmptɪv] *adj* tubercolotico, tisico; (*wasteful*) logorante ‖ *s* tisico, etico

contact [ˈkɑntækt] *s* contatto; (*elec*) contatto; (*elec*) presa di corrente ‖ *tr* (*coll*) mettersi in contatto con ‖ *intr* (*coll*) mettersi in contatto

con'tact break'er *s* ruttore *m*

con'tact lens' *s* lente *f* a contatto

contagion [kənˈtedʒən] *s* contagio

contagious [kənˈtedʒəs] *adj* contagioso

contain [kənˈten] *tr* contenere; **to contain oneself** frenarsi

container [kənˈtenər] *s* recipiente *m*, contenitore *m*

contaminate [kənˈtæmɪˌnet] *tr* contaminare

contamination [kənˌtæmɪˈneʃən] *s* contaminazione

contemplate [ˈkɑntəmˌplet] *tr* contemplare; (*to think about*) meditare; (*to have in mind*) progettare, avere in mente ‖ *intr* meditare

contemplation [ˌkɑntəmˈpleʃən] *s* contemplazione; (*intention*) intenzione

contemporaneous [kənˌtempəˈreni‧əs] *adj* contemporaneo, coevo

contemporar‧y [kənˈtempəˌreri] *adj* contemporaneo, coevo ‖ *s* (-*ies*) contemporaneo

contempt [kənˈtempt] *s* (*despising*) disprezzo; (*condition of being despised*) dispregio; (*of the law*) disprezzo

contemptible [kənˈtemptɪbəl] *adj* disprezzabile, spregevole

contempt' of court' *s* (*law*) offesa alla magistratura, oltraggio al tribunale

contemptuous [kənˈtemptʃu‧əs] *adj* sprezzante, sdegnoso

contend [kənˈtend] *tr* dichiarare ‖ *intr* (*to argue*) disputare, contendere; (*to fight*) lottare

contender [kənˈtendər] *s* competitore *m*, concorrente *m*

content [kənˈtent] *adj* contento; (*willing*) pronto ‖ *s* contentezza ‖ [ˈkɑntent] *s* contenuto; **contents** contenuto ‖ [kənˈtent] *tr* contentare

contented [kənˈtentɪd] *adj* soddisfatto

contention [kənˈtenʃən] *s* disputa, litigio; contenzione

contentious [kənˈtenʃəs] *adj* litigioso

contentment [kənˈtentmənt] *s* contentezza

contest [ˈkɑntest] *s* contesa, controversia; (*game*) gara ‖ [kənˈtest] *tr* disputare, contestare ‖ *intr* combattere, fare resistenza

contestant [kənˈtestənt] *s* concorrente *m*; (*law*) contendente *m*

context [ˈkɑntekst] *s* contesto

contiguous [kənˈtɪgju‧əs] *adj* contiguo

continence [ˈkɑntɪnəns] *s* continenza

continent [ˈkɑntɪnənt] *adj & s* continente *m*; **on the Continent** nel continente europeo

continental [ˌkɑntɪ'nentəl] *adj & s* continentale *mf*

contingen·cy [kən'tɪndʒənsɪ] *s* (**-cies**) contingenza, congiuntura; (*chance*) eventualità *f*

contingent [kən'tɪndʒənt] *adj* eventuale; imprevisto; (*philos*) contingente; **to be contingent upon** dipendere da

continual [kən'tɪnju·əl] *adj* continuo

continuance [kən'tɪnjuəns] *s* continuazione; (*in office*) permanenza; (*law*) rinvio

continue [kən'tɪnju] *tr* continuare; (*to cause to remain*) mantenere; (*law*) rinviare ‖ *intr* continuare; rimanere

continu·i·ty [ˌkɑntɪ'nju·ɪtɪ] *or* [ˌkɑntɪ'nu·ɪtɪ] *s* (**-ties**) continuità *f*; (*mov & telv*) sceneggiatura; (*rad*) copione *m*

continuous [kən'tɪnju·əs] *adj* continuo

contin'uous show'ing *s* (*mov*) spettacolo permanente

contortion [kən'tɔrʃən] *s* contorsione; (*of facts*) distorsione

contour ['kɑntur] *s* contorno

con'tour line' *s* curva di livello, isoipsa

contraband ['kɑntrə͵bænd] *adj* di contrabbando ‖ *s* contrabbando

contrabass ['kɑntrə͵bes] *s* contrabbasso

contraceptive [ˌkɑntrə'septɪv] *adj & s* antifecondativo

contract ['kɑntrækt] *s* contratto ‖ ['kɑntrækt] *or* [kən'trækt] *tr* (*a business deal*) contrattare; (*marriage*) contrarre ‖ *intr* (*to shrink*) contrarsi; **to contract for** contrattare, appaltare

contraction [kən'trækʃən] *s* contrazione

contractor [kən'træktər] *s* (*person who makes a contract*) contraente *m*; (*person who contracts to supply material*) appaltatore *m*, imprenditore *m*; (*in building*) capomastro

contradict [ˌkɑntrə'dɪkt] *tr* contraddire

contradiction [ˌkɑntrə'dɪkʃən] *s* contraddizione

contradictory [ˌkɑntrə'dɪktərɪ] *adj* contraddittorio

contrail ['kɑn͵trel] *s* (*aer*) scia di condensazione

contral·to [kən'trælto] *s* (**-tos**) (*person*) contralto *mf*; (*voice*) contralto *m*

contraption [kən'træpʃən] *s* (coll) aggeggio

contra·ry ['kɑntrerɪ] *adj* contrario ‖ [kən'trerɪ] *adj* ostinato, caparbio ‖ ['kɑntrerɪ] *s* (**-ries**) contrario; **on the contrary** al contrario ‖ *adv* contrariamente

contrast ['kɑntræst] *s* contrasto ‖ [kən'træst] *tr* confrontare ‖ *intr* contrastare

contravene [ˌkɑntrə'vin] *tr* contraddire; (*a law*) contravvenire (with *dat*)

contribute [kən'trɪbjut] *tr* contribuire ‖ *intr* contribuire; (*to a newspaper*) collaborare

contribution [ˌkɑntrɪ'bjuʃən] *s* contribuzione; (*to a newspaper*) collaborazione

contributor [kən'trɪbjutər] *s* contributore *m*; (*to a newspaper*) collaboratore *m*

contrite [kən'traɪt] *adj* contrito

contrition [kən'trɪʃən] *s* contrizione

contrivance [kən'traɪvəns] *s* dispositivo, congegno; (*faculty*) invenzione; (*scheme*) artificio, piano

contrive [kən'traɪv] *tr* inventare; (*to scheme up*) macchinare; (*to bring about*) effettuare; **to contrive to** trovare il modo di

con·trol [kən'trol] *s* controllo; (*check*) freno; **controls** comandi *mpl*; **to get under control** riuscire a controllare ‖ *v* (*pret & pp* **-trolled**; *ger* **-trolling**) *tr* controllare

controller [kən'trolər] *s* controllore *m*; analista *mf* di gestione; economo; (*mach*) regolatore *m*; (*elec*) interruttore *m* di linea

control'ling in'terest *s* maggioranza delle azioni

control' stick' *s* leva di comando

controversial [ˌkɑntrə'vɑrʃəl] *adj* controverso, polemico, discusso

controver·sy ['kɑntrə͵vɑrsɪ] *s* (**-sies**) controversia

controvert ['kɑntrə͵vɑrt] *or* [ˌkɑntrə'vɑrt] *tr* contraddire

contumacious [ˌkɑntju'meʃəs] *or* [ˌkɑntu'meʃəs] *adj* ribelle, contumace

contuma·cy ['kɑntjuməsɪ] *or* ['kɑntuməsɪ] *s* (**-cies**) contumacia

contusion [kən'tjuʒən] *or* [kən'tuʒən] *s* contusione

conundrum [kə'nʌndrəm] *s* indovinello

convalesce [ˌkɑnvə'les] *intr* essere convalescente

convalescence [ˌkɑnvə'lesəns] *s* convalescenza

convalescent [ˌkɑnvə'lesənt] *adj & s* convalescente *mf*

con'vales'cent home' *s* convalescenziario

convene [kən'vin] *tr* convocare ‖ *intr* convenire

convenience [kən'vinjəns] *s* convenienza; (*comfort*) agio; (*anything that saves work*) conforto; **at your earliest convenience** quanto prima

convenient [kən'vinjənt] *adj* conveniente, adatto; comodo; **convenient to** (*near*) (coll) vicino a

convent ['kɑnvent] *s* convento di religiose

convention [kən'venʃən] *s* convenzione, assemblea; **conventions** (*customs*) convenzioni *fpl*

conventional [kən'venʃənəl] *adj* convenzionale

converge [kən'vɑrdʒ] *intr* convergere

conversant [kən'vɑrsənt] *adj* versato, esperto, dotto

conversation [ˌkɑnvər'seʃən] *s* conversazione

converse ['kɑnvʌrs] *adj & s* contrario ‖ [kən'vʌrs] *intr* conversare

conversion [kən'vʌrʒən] *s* conversione; (*unlawful appropriation*) malversazione

convert ['kɑnvʌrt] *s* convertito ‖ [kən'vʌrt] *tr* convertire; misappropriare ‖ *intr* convertirsi

convertible [kən'vʌrtɪbəl] *adj & s* convertibile *f*; (*aut*) trasformabile *f*, decappottabile *f*

convex ['kɑnveks] *or* [kɑn'veks] *adj* convesso

convey [kən've] *tr* (*to carry*) trasportare; (*liquids*) convogliare; (*sounds*) trasmettere; (*to express*) esprimere; (*e.g., property*) trasferire

conveyance [kən've·əns] *s* trasporto; veicolo; comunicazione; (*of property*) trasferimento; (*deed*) titolo di proprietà

convey'or belt' [kən've·ər] *s* trasportatore *m*

convict ['kɑnvɪkt] *s* condannato ‖ [kən'vɪkt] *tr* convincere, condannare

conviction [kən'vɪk/ən] *s* condanna; (*belief*) convinzione, convincimento

convince [kən'vɪns] *tr* convincere

convincing [kən'vɪnsɪŋ] *adj* convincente

convivial [kən'vɪvɪ·əl] *adj* (*festive*) conviviale; gioviale, bonaccione

convocation [ˌkɑnvə'ke/ən] *s* convocazione, assemblea

convoke [kən'vok] *tr* convocare

convoy ['kɑnvɔɪ] *s* (*of ships*) convoglio; (*of vehicles*) carovana ‖ *tr* convogliare

convulse [kən'vʌls] *tr* (*to shake*) scuotere; (*to throw into convulsions*) mettere in convulsioni; (*to cause to shake with laughter*) far torcere dalle risa

coo [ku] *intr* tubare, gemere

cook [kʊk] *s* cuoco ‖ *tr* cuocere; **to cook up** (*coll*) preparare, macchinare ‖ *intr* (*said of food*) cuocere; (*said of a person*) fare il cuoco

cook'book' *s* libro di cucina

cookie ['kʊkɪ] *s var of* **cooky**

cooking ['kʊkɪŋ] *s* culinaria

cook'out' *s* picnic *m*, spuntino all'aperto

cook'stove' *s* cucina economica

cook·y ['kʊkɪ] *s* (*-ies*) pasticcino, biscotto

cool [kul] *adj* fresco; calmo; (*not cordial*) freddo; (*bold*) sfacciato ‖ *s* fresco ‖ *tr* rinfrescare; **to cool one's heels** fare anticamera ‖ *intr* rinfrescarsi; **to cool off** rinfrescarsi; calmarsi

coolant ['kulənt] *s* miscela refrigerante

cooler ['kulər] *s* ghiacciaia; (*slang*) prigione

cool'-head'ed *adj* calmo, imperturbabile

coolish ['kulɪ/] *adj* freschetto

coon [kun] *s* procione *m*

coop [kup] *s* pollaio; cogliera; **to fly the coop** (*slang*) scapparsene ‖ *tr*—**to coop up** rinchiudere tra quattro mura

cooper ['kupər] *s* bottaio

cooperate [ko'ɑpə ˌret] *intr* cooperare

cooperation [ko ˌɑpə're/ən] *s* cooperazione

cooperative [ko'ɑpə ˌretɪv] *adj* cooperativo ‖ *s* cooperativa

coordinate [ko'ɔrdɪnɪt] *adj* coordinato; (*gram*) coordinativo ‖ *s* (*math*) coordinata ‖ [ko'ɔrdɪ ˌnet] *tr & intr* coordinare

coot [kut] *s* (*zool*) folaga; (*slang*) vecchio pazzo

cootie ['kutɪ] *s* (*slang*) pidocchio

cop [kɑp] *s* (*slang*) poliziotto ‖ *v* (*pret & pp* **copped**) *ger* **copping** *tr* (*slang*) rubare

copartner [ko'pɑrtnər] *s* consocio, socio

cope [kop] *intr*—**to cope with** tener testa a

cope'stone' *s* pietra da cimasa

copier ['kɑpɪ·ər] *s* (*person*) copista *mf*; imitatore *m*; (*machine*) duplicatore *m*

copilot ['ko ˌpaɪlət] *s* copilota *mf*

coping ['kopɪŋ] *s* coronamento, cimasa

cop'ing saw' *s* seghetto da traforo

copious ['kopɪ·əs] *adj* copioso

copper [kɑp'ər] *s* rame *m*; (*coin*) soldo; (*boiler*) calderone *m*; (*slang*) poliziotto

cop'per-head' *s* vipera (*Ancistrodon contortrix*)

cop'per-smith' *s* battirame *m*, calderaio

coppice ['kɑpɪs] *or* **copse** [kɑps] *s* boschetto

copulate ['kɑpjə ˌlet] *intr* copularsi, congiungersi carnalmente

cop·y ['kɑpɪ] *s* (*-ies*) copia; modello; manoscritto ‖ *v* (*pret & pp* **-ied**) *tr* copiare, imitare ‖ *intr* copiare; **to copy after** imitare

cop'y·book' *s* quaderno

copyist ['kɑpɪ·ɪst] *s* copista *mf*; imitatore *m*

cop'y·right' *s* copyright *m*, diritto di proprietà letteraria ‖ *tr* registrare; proteggere con copyright

cop'y·writ'er *s* copy-writer *m*, redattore *m* pubblicitario

coquetry ['kokətrɪ] *or* [ko'ketrɪ] *s* (*-ries*) civetteria

coquette [ko'ket] *s* civetta

coquettish [ko'ketɪ/] *adj* civettuolo

coral ['kɑrəl] *or* ['kɔrəl] *adj* corallino ‖ *s* corallo

cor'al reef' *s* banco di coralli

cord [kɔrd] *s* corda, fune *f*; (*corduroy*) tessuto cordonato; (*elec*) cordone *m* ‖ *tr* legare con corda

cordial ['kɔrdʒəl] *adj & s* cordiale *m*

corduroy ['kɔrdə ˌrɔɪ] *s* velluto a coste; **corduroys** pantaloni *mpl* alla cacciatora

core [kor] *s* (*of fruit*) torsolo; (*central part*) centro; (*of problem*) nocciolo; (*of earth*) barisfera, nucleo centrale; (*phys*) nucleo; **rotten to the core** guasto nelle ossa

corespondent [ˌkorɪs'pɑndənt] *s* coimputato in un processo di divorzio

cork [kɔrk] *s* (*bark*) sughero; (*stopper*) tappo, tappo di sughero ‖ *tr* tappare

cork' oak' *s* sughero

cork'screw' s cavatappi m

cormorant ['kɔrmərənt] s cormorano

corn [kɔrn] s granturco, mais m; (*kernel*) chicco; (*thickening of skin*) callo; (*whiskey*) whisky m di granturco; (Brit) grano; (Scot) avena; (slang) banalità f

corn' bread' s pane m di farina gialla

corn' cake' s omelette f di granturco

corn'cob' s tutolo

corn'cob pipe' s pipa fatta di un tutolo di pannocchia

corn'crib' s granaio per le pannocchie

corn' cure' s callifugo

cornea ['kɔrnɪə] s cornea

corner ['kɔrnər] s angolo; (*of street*) cantonata; situazione difficile; (*of the eye*) coda dell'occhio; (com) accaparramento, incetta, bagarinaggio; **to cut corners** tagliare le spese; **to turn the corner** passare il punto più pericoloso || *tr* mettere in una situazione difficile; (*the market*) incettare, accaparrare

cor'ner cup'board s cantoniera, armadio d'angolo

cor'ner stone' s pietra angolare; (*of new building*) prima pietra

cornet [kɔr'nɛt] s cornetta

corn' exchange' s borsa dei cereali

corn'field' s (in U.S.A.) campo di granturco; (*in England*) campo di grano; (*in Scotland*) campo di avena

corn'flakes' spl fiocchi mpl di granturco

corn' flour' s farina di granturco

corn'flow'er s fiordaliso

corn'husk' s brattea, cartoccio

cornice ['kɔrnɪs] s (*of house*) cornicione m; (*of room*) cornice f

corn' liq'uor s whisky m di granturco

corn' meal' s farina di granturco

corn' on the cob' s granturco servito in pannocchia

corn' plas'ter s cerotto per i calli

corn' silk' s barba del granturco

corn'stalk' s fusto di granturco

corn'starch' s amido di granturco

corn·y ['kɔrni] adj (**-ier; -iest**) (slang) banale, trito, triviale

coronation [,kɔrə'neʃən] or [,kɔrə-'neʃən] s incoronazione

coroner ['kɔrənər] or ['kɔrənər] s magistrato inquirente

cor'oner's in'quest s inchiesta giudiziaria dinanzi a giuria

coronet ['kɔrə,nɛt] or ['kɔrə,nɛt] s corona (non reale); diadema m

corporal ['kɔrpərəl] adj caporalesco || s caporale m

corporation [,kɔrpə'reʃən] s società anonima

corps [kɔr] s (**corps** [kɔrz]) corpo

corps' de bal'let s corpo di ballo

corpse [kɔrps] s cadavere m

corpulent ['kɔrpjələnt] adj corpulento

corpuscle ['kɔrpəsəl] s (anat) globulo; (phys) corpuscolo

cor·ral [kə'ræl] s recinto per bestiame || v (*pret & pp* **-ralled;** *ger* **-ralling**) tr mettere in un recinto; catturrare

correct [kə'rɛkt] adj corretto || tr correggere

correction [kə'rɛkʃən] s correzione

corrective [kə'rɛktɪv] adj & s correttivo

correctness [kə'rɛktnɪs] s correttezza

correlate ['kɑrə,let] or ['kɔrə,let] tr correlare || intr essere in correlazione

correlation [,kɑrə'leʃən] or [,kɔrə-'leʃən] s correlazione

correspond [,kɑrɪ'spand] or [,kɔrɪ-'spand] intr corrispondere

correspondence [,kɑrɪ'spandəns] or [,kɔrɪ'spandəns] s corrispondenza

correspond'ence school' s scuola per corrispondenza

correspondent [,kɑrɪ'spandənt] or [,kɔrɪ'spandənt] adj & s corrispondente mf

corridor ['kɑrɪdər] or ['kɔrɪdər] s corridoio

corroborate [kə'rabə,ret] tr corroborare

corrode [kə'rod] tr corrodere || intr corrodersi

corrosion [kə'roʒən] s corrosione

corrosive [kə'rosɪv] adj & s corrosivo

corrugated ['kɑrə,getɪd] or ['kɔrə-,getɪd] adj ondulato

corrupt [kə'rʌpt] adj corrotto || tr corrompere; (*a language*) imbarbarire || intr corrompersi

corruption [kə'rʌpʃən] s corruzione

corsage [kɔr'saʒ] s (*bodice*) corpetto; (*bouquet*) mazzolino di fiori da appuntarsi al vestito

corsair ['kɔr,ser] s corsaro

corset ['kɔrsɪt] s corsetto

Corsican ['kɔrsɪkən] adj & s corso

cortege [kɔr'teʒ] s corteggio

cor·tex ['kɔr,tɛks] s (**-tices** [tɪ,siz]) cortice f

cortisone ['kɔrtɪ,son] s cortisone m

corvette [kɔr'vɛt] s corvetta

cosmetic [kaz'metɪk] adj & s cosmetico

cosmic ['kazmɪk] adj cosmico

cosmonaut ['kazmə,nɔt] s cosmonauta mf

cosmopolitan [,kazmə'palɪtən] adj & s cosmopolita mf

cosmos ['kazməs] s cosmo

cost [kɔst] or [kast] s costo, prezzo; **at all costs** or **at any cost** ad ogni costo; **costs** (law) spese fpl processuali || v (*pret & pp* **cost**) intr costare

cost·ly ['kɔstli] or ['kastli] adj (**-lier; -liest**) costoso; (*sumptuous*) lussuoso

cost' of liv'ing s costo della vita

costume ['kastjum] or ['kastum] s costume m

cos'tume ball' s ballo in costume

cos'tume jew'elry s gioielli falsi

cot [kat] s (*narrow bed*) branda; (*cottage*) capanna, cabina

coterie ['kotəri] s gruppo; (*clique*) chiesuola

cottage ['katɪdʒ] s casetta, villino

cot'tage cheese' s ricotta americana

cot'ter pin' ['katər] s copiglia, coppiglia

cotton ['katən] s cotone m || intr—**to cotton up to** (coll) cominciare a provare della simpatia per; (coll) andare d'accordo con

cot'ton can'dy s zucchero filato

cot'ton gin' *s* sgranatrice *f*
cot'ton pick'er ['pɪkər] *s* chi raccoglie il cotone; macchina che raccoglie il cotone
cot'tonseed oil' *s* olio di semi di cotone
cot'ton waste' *s* cascame *m* di cotone
cot'ton-wood' *s* pioppo deltoide
couch [kautʃ] *s* canapè *m*, sofà *m*, divano ǁ *tr* esprimere
couch' grass' *s* gramigna
cougar ['kugər] *s* puma *m*
cough [kɔf] *or* [kɑf] *s* tosse *f* ǁ *tr*—**to cough up** sputare, sputare tossendo; (slang) dare, pagare ǁ *intr* tossire
cough' drop' *s* pastiglia per la tosse
cough' syr'up *s* sciroppo per la tosse
could [kud] *v aux*—**I could not come yesterday** non ho potuto venire ieri; **I could not see you tomorrow** non potrei vederLa domani; **it could not be so** non potrebbe essere così
council ['kaunsəl] *s* consiglio; (eccl) concilio
coun'cil·man *s* (-men) consigliere *m* or assessore *m* municipale
coun·sel ['kaunsəl] *s* consiglio; (law-yer) avvocato; **to keep one's counsel** essere riservato; **to take counsel with** consultarsi con ǁ *v* (*pret & pp* -seled *or* -selled) *ger* -seling *or* -selling *tr* consigliare ǁ *intr* consigliare; consigliarsi
counselor ['kaunsələr] *s* consigliere *m*; avvocato
count [kaunt] *s* conto; (*nobleman*) conte *m*; (law) capo d'accusa ǁ *tr* contare; **to count off by** (*twos, threes*) contare per (*due, tre*); **to count out** escludere; (boxing) contare ǁ *intr* contare; (*to be worth*) valere; **to count on** contare su
count'down' *s* conteggio alla rovescia
countenance ['kauntɪnəns] *s* espressione; (*face*) faccia; (*approval*) approvazione ǁ *tr* approvare, incoraggiare
counter ['kauntər] *adj* contrario ǁ *s* contatore *m*; (*token*) gettone *m*; (*table in store*) banco; (*opposite*) contrario ǁ *adv* contro, contrariamente ǁ *tr* contrariare, opporre ǁ *intr* (boxing) rispondere
coun'ter·act' *tr* contrariare, neutralizzare
coun'ter·attack' *s* contrattacco ǁ **coun'ter·attack'** *tr & intr* contrattaccare
coun'ter·bal'ance *s* contrappeso ǁ **coun'ter·bal'ance** *tr* controbilanciare
coun'ter·clock'wise *adj* antiorario ǁ *adv* in senso antiorario
coun'ter·es'pionage *s* controspionaggio
counterfeit ['kauntərfɪt] *adj* contraffatto ǁ *s* contraffazione; moneta falsa ǁ *tr & intr* contraffare
counterfeiter ['kauntər‚fɪtər] *s* contraffattore *m*
coun'ter·feit mon'ey *s* moneta falsa
countermand ['kauntər‚mænd] *or* ['kauntər‚mɑnd] *tr* (*troops*) dare un contrordine a; (*an order; a payment*) cancellare

coun'ter·march' *s* contromarcia ǁ *intr* fare contromarcia
coun'ter·offen'sive *s* controffensiva
coun'ter·pane' *s* sopraccoperta
coun'ter·part' *s* copia; (*person*) sosia
coun'ter·point' *s* (mus) contrappunto; (mus) controcanto
Coun'ter Reforma'tion *s* controriforma
coun'ter·rev'olu'tion *s* controrivoluzione
coun'ter·sign' *s* (*password*) parola d'ordine; (*signature*) controfirma ǁ *tr* controfirmare
coun'ter·sink' *v* (*pret & pp* -sunk) *tr* incassare, accecare
coun'ter·spy' *s* (-spies) membro del controspionaggio
coun'ter·stroke' *s* contraccolpo
coun'ter·weight' *s* contrappeso
countess ['kauntɪs] *s* contessa
countless ['kauntlɪs] *adj* innumerevole
countrified ['kʌntrɪ‚faɪd] *adj* rustico, rurale
coun·try ['kʌntri] *s* (-tries) (*land*) terreno; (*nation*) paese *m*; (*land of one's birth*) patria; (*rural region*) campagna
coun'try club' *s* circolo privato sportivo situato nei sobborghi
coun'try cous'in *s* campagnolo
coun'try estate' *s* tenuta
coun'try·folk' *s* campagnoli *mpl*
coun'try gen'tleman *s* proprietario terriero, signorotto di campagna
coun'try house' *s* casa di campagna
coun'try jake' *s* (coll) zoticone *m*
coun'try life' *s* vita rustica
coun'try·man *s* (-men) paesano, compaesano
coun'try·peo'ple *s* gente *f* di campagna
coun'try·side' *s* campagna
coun'try·wide' *adj* nazionale
coun'try·wom'an *s* (-wom'en) *s* paesana, compaesana
coun·ty ['kaunti] *s* (-ties) contea, distretto
coun'ty seat' *s* capoluogo di contea
coup [ku] *s* colpo; colpo di stato
coup de grâce [ku də 'grɑs] *s* colpo di grazia
coup d'état [ku de 'tɑ] *s* colpo di stato
coupe [kup] *or* **coupé** [ku'pe] *s* coupé *m*
couple ['kʌpəl] *s* (*of people or animals*) paio, coppia; (*of things*) paio; (*link*) unione ǁ *tr* accoppiare; (*to link*) unire, agganciare ǁ *intr* accoppiarsi
couplet ['kʌplɪt] *s* coppia di versi; (mus) couplet *m*
coupling ['kʌplɪŋ] *s* unione; (mach) giunto
coupon ['kupɑn] *or* ['kjupɑn] *s* coupon *m*, tagliando
courage ['kʌrɪdʒ] *s* coraggio; **to have the courage of one's convictions** avere il coraggio delle proprie opinioni
courageous [kə'redʒəs] *adj* coraggioso
courier ['kʌrɪ·ər] *or* ['kurɪ·ər] *s* corriere *m*
course [kors] *s* corso; (*part of meal*) portata; (*place for games*) campo;

(row) fila; **in due course** a tempo debito; **in the course of** durante, nel corso di; **of course** certamente, senza dubbio

court [kɔrt] s (*uncovered place surrounded by walls*) corte f, cortile m; (*royal residence; courtship*) corte f; (*short street*) vicolo; (*playing area*) campo; (law) corte f ǁ tr corteggiare; (*e.g., disaster*) andare in cerca di

courteous [ˈkʌrtɪ·əs] adj cortese

courtesan [ˈkʌrtɪzən] or [ˈkɔrtɪzən] s cortigiana, meretrice f

courte·sy [ˈkʌrtɪsɪ] s (-**sies**) cortesia, gentilezza; **through the courtesy of** con il gentile permesso di

court'house' s palazzo di giustizia

courtier [ˈkɔrtɪ·ər] s cortigiano

court' jest'er s buffone m di corte

court·ly [ˈkɔrtlɪ] adj (-**lier**; -**liest**) cortese, cortigiano; ossequioso

court'-mar'tial s (**courts-martial**) corte f marziale ǁ v (pret & pp -**tialed** or -**tialled**; ger -**tialing** or -**tialling**) tr sottomettere a corte marziale

court' plas'ter s taffettà m

court'room' s aula di giustizia

courtship [ˈkɔrtʃɪp] s corte f, corteggiamento

court'yard' s corte f, cortile m

cousin [ˈkʌzɪn] s cugino

cove [kov] s piccola baia, cala

covenant [ˈkʌvənənt] s convenzione, patto ǁ tr promettere solennemente

cover [ˈkʌvər] s (*lid*) coperchio; (*tablecloth; shelter*) coperto; (*of book*) copertina; **to take cover** nascondersi; **under cover** in segreto, segretamente; **under cover of** sotto la protezione di; **under separate cover** in busta a parte, in plico a parte ǁ tr coprire; puntare un'arma verso; (journ) riferire, riportare; **to cover up** coprire completamente ǁ intr (*said of paint*) spandersi

coverage [ˈkʌvərɪdʒ] s copertura; (journ) servizio giornalistico; (rad, telv) raggio di udibilità

coveralls [ˈkʌvər‚ɔlz] spl tuta

cov'er charge' s coperto

cov'ered wag'on s carro coperto da tendone

cov'er girl' s ragazza-copertina

covering [ˈkʌvərɪŋ] s copertura; involucro

covert [ˈkʌvərt] adj nascosto, segreto

cov'er-up' s dissimulazione; sotterfugio

covet [ˈkʌvɪt] tr desiderare, agognare

covetous [ˈkʌvɪtəs] adj cupido

covey [ˈkʌvɪ] s covata

cow [kau] s vacca; (*of seal, elephant, etc.*) femmina ǁ tr spaventare, intimidire

coward [ˈkau·ərd] s codardo, vile m

cowardice [ˈkau·ərdɪs] s codardia, viltà f

cowardly [ˈkau·ərdlɪ] adj codardo, vile ǁ adv vilmente

cow'bell' s campano, campanaccio

cow'boy' s cowboy m

cow'catch'er s (rr) cacciapietre m

cower [ˈkau·ər] intr rannicchiarsi

cow'herd' s guardiano d'armenti

cow'hide' s pelle f di vacca

cowl [kaul] s (*hood*) cappuccio; (*monk's cloak*) cappa; (*of car*) sostegno del cofano; (*of chimney*) cappello; (aer) cappottatura

cow'lick' s ritrosa

cow'pox' s (vet) vaiolo bovino

coxcomb [ˈkaks‚kom] s zerbinotto

coxwain [ˈkaksən] or [ˈkak‚swen] s timoniere m

coy [kɔɪ] adj timido, ritroso

co·zy [ˈkozɪ] adj (-**zier**; -**ziest**) comodo ǁ s (-**zies**) copriteiera m

C.P.A. [ˈsiˈpiˈe] s (letterword) (**certified public accountant**) esperto contabile

crab [kræb] s granchio; (aer) scarroccio; (*complaining person*) (coll) scontroso ǁ v (pret & pp **crabbed**; ger **crabbing**) intr (coll) lamentarsi

crab' apple' s mela selvatica; (*tree*) melo selvatico

crabbed [ˈkræbɪd] adj sgarbato; (*handwriting*) da gallina; (*style*) oscuro, ermetico

crab' louse' s piattola

crab·by [ˈkræbɪ] adj (-**bier**; -**biest**) scontroso, sgarbato

crack [kræk] adj (slang) di prim'ordine, eccellente ǁ s (*noise*) schiocco; (*break*) rottura, screpolatura, crepa; (*opening*) fessura; (slang) tentativo; (slang) barzelletta ǁ tr (*e.g., a whip*) schioccare; (*to break*) rompere, screpolare; (*oil*) ridurre con distillazione; (coll) risolvere; (*a safe*) (slang) forzare; (*a joke*) (slang) dire; **cracked up to be** (slang) avendo fama di ǁ intr (*to make a noise*) scricchiolare; (*to break*) rompersi, screpolarsi; (*said of voice*) diventare fesso; (slang) avere un esaurimento nervoso; **to crack down** (slang) essere severo; **to crack up** (slang) andare a pezzi

cracked [krækt] adj rotto, spezzato; (*voice*) fesso; (coll) pazzo

cracker [ˈkrækər] s cracker m, galletta

crack'er-bar'rel adj in piccolo, alla buona

crack'er·jack' adj (slang) di prim'ordine ǁ s (slang) persona di prim'ordine

cracking [ˈkrækɪŋ] s piroscissione

crackle [ˈkrækəl] s crepitio, crepito ǁ intr crepitare

crack'pot' adj & s (coll) mattoide mf

crack'-up' s accidente m; collisione; (*breakdown in health or in relations*) (coll) colasso; (aer) accidente m d'atterraggio

cradle [ˈkredəl] s culla; (*of handset*) forcella ǁ tr cullare

crad'le-song' s ninnananna

craft [kræft] or [krɑft] s (*skill*) abilità f; (*trade*) mestiere m; (*guile*) astuzia, furberia; (*ship*) nave f; aeronave

craftiness [ˈkræftɪnɪs] or [ˈkrɑftɪnɪs] s astuzia, furberia

crafts'man s (-**men**) operaio specializzato, artigiano

craft' un'ion *s* artigianato, sindacato artigiano

craft·y ['kræfti] or ['krɑfti] *adj* (-ier; -iest) astuto, furbo

crag [kræg] *s* roccia scoscesa, rupe *f*

cram [kræm] *v* (*pret & pp* **crammed**; *ger* **cramming**) *tr* (*to pack full*) riempire fino all'orlo; (*to stuff with food*) rimpinzare || *intr* rimpinzarsi; (coll) prepararsi un esame alla svelta

cramp [kræmp] *s* (*painful contraction*) crampo; (*bar with hooks*) grappa; (fig) ostacolo || *tr* ostacolare, restringere

cranberr·y ['kræn,beri] *s* (-ries) mirtillo

crane [kren] *s* (orn, mach) gru *f*; (*boom*) (telv, mov) giraffa || *tr* (*one's neck*) allungare || *intr* allungare il collo

crani·um ['kreni·əm] *s* (-a [ə]) cranio

crank [kræŋk] *s* manovella;. (aut) alzacristalli *m*; (coll) eccentrico || *tr* girare con la manovella; mettere in moto con la manovella

crank'case' *s* coppa dell'olio, carter *m*

crank'shaft' *s* albero a gomito

crank·y ['kræŋki] *adj* (-ier; -iest) irritabile; eccentrico

cran·ny ['kræni] *s* (-nies) (*crevice*) crepaccio; (*crack*) fessura

crape [krep] *s* crespo

crape'hang'er *s* (slang) pessimista uggioso, guastafeste *mf*

craps [kræps] *s* gioco dei dadi; **to shoot craps** giocare ai dadi

crash [kræʃ] *adj* (coll) d'emergenza || *s* (*noise*) scoppio, schianto; accidente *m*; (*collapse of business*) crac *m*, rovescio; (*bad landing*) atterraggio senza carrello || *tr* fracassare; **to crash the gate** (coll) entrare senza invito || *intr* fracassarsi; (com) fallire; **to cash into** investire, cozzare contro; **to cash through** sfondare

crash' dive' *s* immersione rapida di un sottomarino

crash' hel'met *s* casco

crass [kræs] *adj* crasso

crate [kret] *s* gabbia d'imballaggio || *tr* imballare in una gabbia

crater ['kretər] *s* cratere *m*

cravat [krə'væt] *s* cravatta

crave [krev] *tr* anelare; (*to beg*) implorare || *intr*—**to crave for** desiderare ardentemente

craven ['krevən] *adj & s* codardo

craving ['krevɪŋ] *s* anelito, desiderio

craw [krɔ] *s* gozzo

crawl [krɔl] *s* strisciamento, avanzata striscioni; (sports) crawl *m* || *intr* strisciare, avanzare striscioni; (*said of worms*) brulicare; (*said of insects*) formicolare; (*to feel creepy*) sentirsi il formicolio

crayfish ['krefɪʃ] *s* (*Palinurus vulgaris*) aragosta; (*Astacus; Cambarus*) gambero

crayon ['kre·ən] *s* pastello; disegno a pastello || *tr* disegnare a pastello

craze [krez] *s* mania, moda || *tr* fare impazzire

cra·zy ['krezi] *adj* (-zier; -ziest) pazzo, matto; **to be crazy about** (coll) esser matto per; **to drive crazy** fare impazzire

cra'zy bone' *s* osso rabbioso (del gomito)

creak [krik] *s* scricchiolio, cigolio || *intr* scricchiolare, cigolare

creak·y ['kriki] *adj* (-ier; -iest) stridente, cigolante

cream [krim] *s* crema, panna; (*finest part*) fior fiore *m* || *tr* rendere di consistenza cremosa; (*to remove cream from*) scremare; prendere il meglio di

creamer·y ['krimǝri] *s* (-ies) (*factory*) caseificio; (*store*) cremeria

cream' puff' *s* bignè *m*

cream·y ['krimi] *adj* (-ier; -iest) cremoso; butirroso

crease [kris] *s* piega, grinza || *tr* piegare, raggrinzire || *intr* piegarsi, raggrinzirsi, far pieghe

crease'-resis'tant *adj* antipiega

create [kri'et] *tr* creare

creation [kri'eʃǝn] *s* creazione; **the Creation** il creato

creative [kri'etɪv] *adj* creativo

creator [kri'etǝr] *s* creatore *m*

creature ['kritʃǝr] *s* creatura

credence ['kridǝns] *s* credenza

credentials [krɪ'denʃǝlz] *spl* lettere *fpl* credenziali; documento d'autorizzazione

credible ['kredɪbǝl] *adj* credibile

credit ['kredɪt] *s* credito; (*in a school*) unità *f* di promozione; (com) avere *m*; **credits** (mov, telv) titoli *mpl* di testa || *tr* accreditare; **to credit s.o. with** s.th attribuire qlco a qlcu

creditable ['kredɪtǝbǝl] *adj* lodevole

cred'it card' *s* carta di credito

creditor ['kredɪtǝr] *s* creditore *m*

cre·do ['krido] or ['kredo] *s* (-dos) credo

credulous ['kredʒǝlǝs] *adj* credulo

creed [krid] *s* credo

creek [krik] *s* fiumicello

creep [krip] *v* (*pret & pp* **crept** [krept]) *intr* strisciare, avanzare striscioni; (*to grow along a wall*) arrampicarsi; (*to feel creepy*) sentirsi il formicolio

creeper ['kripǝr] *s* strisciante *m*; (*plant*) rampicante *f*

creeping ['kripɪŋ] *adj* lento; (*plant*) rampicante

cremate ['krimet] *tr* cremare

cremato·ry ['krimǝ,tori] *adj* crematorio || *s* (-ries) forno crematorio

Creole ['kri·ol] *adj & s* creolo

crescent ['kresǝnt] *s* (*of Islam*) mezzaluna; (*of moon*) crescente *m*; (*roll*) cornetto

cress [kres] *s* crescione *m*

crest [krest] *s* cresta; (heral) stemma *m*, insegna

crestfallen ['krest,fɔlǝn] *adj* depresso

Cretan ['kritǝn] *adj & s* cretese *mf*

cretin ['kritǝn] *s* cretino

crevice ['krevɪs] *s* fessura, fenditura

crew [kru] *s* (*group working together*) personale *m*; (*group of workmen*;

mob) ciurma; (*of a ship or racing boat*) equipaggio; (sports) canottaggio

crew' cut' *s* capelli *mpl* a spazzola

crib [krɪb] *s* (*bed*) lettino; (*rack*) rastrelliera; (*building*) capanna, granaio; (coll) bigino ‖ *v* (*pret & pp* **cribbed**; *ger* **cribbing**) *tr* (coll) usare un bigino in ‖ *intr* (coll) usare un bigino; (coll) commettere un plagio

cricket ['krɪkɪt] *s* grillo; (sports) cricket *m*, palla a spatola

crier ['kraɪ·ər] *s* banditore *m*

crime [kraɪm] *s* delitto, crimine *m*

criminal ['krɪmɪnəl] *adj* criminale; (*code*) penale ‖ *s* delinquente *mf*

crimp [krɪmp] *s* piega, pieghettatura; **to put a crimp in** (slang) mettere i bastoni fra le ruote a ‖ *tr* pieghettare; (*the hair*) arricciare

crimson ['krɪmzən] *adj & s* cremisi *m* ‖ *intr* imporporarsi

cringe [krɪndʒ] *intr* rannicchiarsi; (*to fawn*) umiliarsi

crinkle ['krɪŋkəl] *tr* arricciare ‖ *intr* (*to rustle*) sfrusciare

cripple ['krɪpəl] *s* zoppo, sciancato ‖ *tr* storpiare; (*e.g., business*) paralizzare

cri·sis ['kraɪsɪs] *s* (-ses [siz]) crisi *f*

crisp [krɪsp] *adj* (*brittle*) croccante, friabile; (*air*) frizzante; (*sharp and clear*) acuto

criteri·on [kraɪ'tɪrɪ·ən] *s* (-a [ə] or -ons) criterio

critic ['krɪtɪk] *s* critico

critical ['krɪtɪkəl] *adj* critico

criticism ['krɪtɪ ˌsɪzəm] *s* critica

criticize ['krɪtɪ ˌsaɪz] *tr & intr* criticare

critique [krɪ'tik] *s* critica

croak [krok] *s* (*of frogs*) gracidio; (*of crows*) gracchiamento ‖ *intr* gracidare; gracchiare; (slang) crepare

Croat ['kro·æt] *s* croato

Croatian [kro'eʃən] *adj & s* croato

cro·chet [kro'ʃe] *s* lavoro all'uncinetto ‖ *v* (*pret & pp* -**cheted** ['ʃed]; *ger* -**cheting** ['ʃe·ɪŋ]) *tr & intr* lavorare all'uncinetto

crock [krak] *s* vaso di terracotta, giara, orcio

crockery ['krakəri] *s* vasellame *m* di terracotta, terracotta

crocodile ['krakə ˌdaɪl] *s* coccodrillo

croc'odile tears' *spl* lacrime *fpl* di coccodrillo

crocus ['krokəs] *s* croco

crone [kron] *s* vecchia incartapecorita

cro·ny ['kroni] *s* (-nies) amicone *m*, compare *m*

crook [krʊk] *s* (*hook*) uncino; (*staff*) pastorale *m*; (*bend*) curva; (*bend of pipe*) gomito; (coll) imbroglione *m* ‖ *tr* piegare ‖ *intr* piegarsi

crooked ['krʊkɪd] *adj* uncinato; curvo, piegato; (coll) disonesto

croon [krun] *intr* canterellare; cantare in modo sentimentale

crop [krap] *s* (*of bird*) gozzo; (*agricultural product, growing or harvested*) messe *f*; (*agricultural product harvested*) raccolto; (*riding whip*) fru-

stino; (*hair cut close*) capelli corti; gruppo ‖ *v* (*pret & pp* **cropped**; *ger* **cropping**) *tr* (*to cut the ends off of*) spuntare; (*to reap*) raccogliere; (*to cut short*) tosare ‖ *intr*—**to crop out** or **up** apparire inaspettatamente

crop'-dust'ing *s* fumigazione aerea

cropper ['krapər] *s* mietitore *m*; (*sharecropper*) mezzadro; **to come a cropper** (coll) fare una cascataccia; (coll) andare in rovina

croquet [kro'ke] *s* croquet *m*, pallamaglio *m & f*

croquette [kro'ket] *s* crocchetta

crosier ['kroʒər] *s* pastorale *m*

cross [krɔs] or [kras] *adj* trasversale, contrario, obliquo; (*irritable*) bisbetico, di cattivo umore; (*of mixed breed*) incrociato ‖ *s* croce *f*; (*crossing of breeds*) incrocio; **to take the cross** farsi crociato ‖ *tr* crociare, segnare con una croce; (*the street*) attraversare; (*e.g., the legs*) incrociare; (*to draw a line across*) barrare; (*to thwart*) ostacolare; **to cross oneself** farsi il segno della croce; **to cross one's mind** venire in mente a uno; **to cross out** cancellare ‖ *intr* incrociarsi

cross'bones' *spl* teschio e tibie incrociate (*simbolo della morte*)

cross'bow' *s* balestra

cross'breed' *v* (*pret & pp* -**bred** [ˌbred]) *tr* incrociare, ibridare

cross'-coun'try *adj* campestre; attraverso il paese

cross'-examina'tion *s* (law) confronto, interrogatorio in contraddittorio

cross-eyed ['krɔsˌaɪd] or ['krasˌaɪd] *adj* guercio, strabico

crossing ['krɔsɪŋ] or ['krasɪŋ] *s* incrocio; ostacolo; (*of the sea*) traversata; (*of a river*) guado; (rr) passaggio a livello

cross'patch' *s* (coll) bisbetico

cross'piece' *s* traversa

cross' ref'erence *s* richiamo, rimando

cross'road' *s* strada trasversale; **at the crossroads** al bivio; **crossroads** crocicchio

cross' sec'tion *s* sezione trasversale

cross' street' *s* traversa

cross' talk' *s* conversazione; (telp) diafonia

cross'word puz'zle *s* cruciverba *m*, parole incrociate

crotch [kratʃ] *s* inforcatura; (*of pants*) cavallo

crotchety ['kratʃɪti] *adj* bisbetico

crouch [krautʃ] *intr* accoccolarsi

croup [krup] *s* (pathol) crup *m*

crouton ['krutan] *s* crostino

crow [kro] *s* corvo, cornacchia; (*cry of rooster*) chicchirichì *m*; **as the crow flies** in linea retta, a volo d'uccello; **to eat crow** (coll) rimangiarsi le parole ‖ *intr* fare chicchirichì; **to crow over** vantarsi di, esultare per

crow'bar' *s* bastone *m* a leva

crowd [kraud] *s* folla; (*common people*) masse *fpl*; (coll) gruppo ‖ *tr* affollare; (to push) spingere || intr affollarsi; (to press forward) spingersi

crowded ['kraudɪd] adj affollato

crown [kraun] s corona; (of hat) cupola; (highest point) sommo || tr coronare; (checkers) damare; to **crown s.o.** (coll) battere qlcu sulla testa

crown' prince' s principe ereditario

crown' prin'cess s principessa ereditaria

crow's'-foot' s (-feet) zampa di gallina

crow's'-nest' s coffa, gabbia

crucial ['kruʃəl] adj cruciale, critico

crucible ['krusɪbəl] s crogiolo

crucifix ['krusɪfɪks] s crocefisso

crucifixion [ˌkrusɪ'fɪkʃən] s crocifissione

cruci·fy ['krusɪ ˌfaɪ] v (pret & pp -fied) tr crocifiggere

crude [krud] adj (raw) grezzo; (unripe) acerbo; (roughly made; uncultured) rozzo

crudi·ty ['krudɪti] s (-ties) rozzezza

cruel ['kruˑəl] adj crudele

cruel·ty ['kruˑəlti] s (-ties) crudeltà f

cruet ['kruˑɪt] s oliera

cruise [kruz] s crociera || tr navigare || intr andare in crociera; andare avanti e indietro

cruiser ['kruzər] s (nav) incrociatore m

cruising ['kruzɪŋ] adj di crociera

cruis'ing ra'dius s autonomia di crociera

cruller ['krʌlər] s frittella

crumb [krʌm] s briciola || tr sbriciolare; (e.g., a cutlet) impannare || intr sbriciolarsi

crumble ['krʌmbəl] tr sbriciolare, polverizzare || intr andare a pezzi, polverizzarsi, sbriciolarsi

crum·my ['krʌmi] adj (-mier; -miest) (slang) sporco; (miserable) (slang) schifoso; (e.g., joke) (slang) povero

crumple ['krʌmpəl] tr sgualcire, spiegazzare; to **crumple into a ball** appallottolare || intr spiegazzarsi

crunch [krʌntʃ] s crocchio; (coll) stretta, morsa || tr sgranocchiare || intr crocchiare

crusade [kru'sed] s crociata || intr crociarsi; (to take up a cause) farsi paladino

crusader [kru'sedər] s crociato; (of a cause) paladino

crush [krʌʃ] s pigiatura, schiacciatura; (crowd) calca; (coll) infatuazione || tr schiacciare; (to grind) frantumare; (to subdue) sottomettere; (to extract by squeezing) pigiare

crust [krʌst] s crosta; (slang) faccia tosta || tr incrostare || intr incrostare, incrostarsi

crustacean [krʌs'teʃən] s crostaceo

crust·y ['krʌsti] adj (-ier; -iest) crostoso; duro; rude

crutch [krʌtʃ] s gruccia, stampella; (fig) sostegno

crux [krʌks] s difficoltà f, busillis m; (crucial point) punto cruciale

cry [kraɪ] s (cries) (shout) grido; (fit of weeping) pianto; (entreaty) richiamo; (of animal) urlo; a **far cry** ben lontano, ben distinto; to **have a good cry** sfogarsi, piangere a calde lacrime || tr gridare; (to proclaim) bandire; to **cry down** disprezzare; to **cry one's heart out** piangere a calde lacrime; to **cry out** proclamare; to **cry up** elogiare || intr gridare, urlare; piangere; to **cry for** implorare

cry'ba'by s (-bies) piagnucolone m

crypt [krɪpt] s cripta

cryptic(al) ['krɪptɪk(əl)] adj segreto, occulto, misterioso

crystal ['krɪstəl] s cristallo

crys'tal ball' s globo di cristallo

crystalline ['krɪstəlɪn] or ['krɪstə ˌlaɪn] adj cristallino

crystallize ['krɪstə ˌlaɪz] tr cristallizzare || intr cristallizzarsi

cub [kʌb] s cucciolo; (of lion) leoncino; (of fox) volpicino, volpacchiotto

cubbyhole ['kʌbɪ ˌhol] s sgabuzzino, bugigattolo

cube [kjub] adj cubico || s cubo; (of sugar) zolla || tr elevare al cubo; (to shape) tagliare in quadretti

cubic ['kjubɪk] adj cubico

cub' report'er s giornalista novello

cuckold ['kʌkəld] adj & s cornuto, becco || tr cornificare

cuckoo ['kuku] adj (slang) pazzo || s cuculo

cuck'oo clock' s orologio a cucù

cucumber ['kjukʌmbər] s cetriolo

cud [kʌd] s mangime masticato; to **chew the cud** ruminare

cuddle ['kʌdəl] tr abbracciare affettuosamente || intr (to lie close) giacere vicino; (to curl up) rannicchiarsi, raggomitolarsi

cudg·el ['kʌdʒəl] s manganello, randello; to **take up the cudgels for** farsi paladino di || v (pret & pp -eled or -elled; ger -eling or -elling) tr bastonare, randellare; to **cudgel one's brains** rompersi la testa

cue [kju] s suggerimento, imbeccata; (billiards) stecca; to **miss a cue** (theat) mancare la battuta; (coll) non capire l'antifona || tr—to **cue s.o. (in) on** (coll) dare a qlcu informazioni su

cuff [kʌf] s (of shirt) polsino; (of trousers) risvolto; (slap) schiaffo || tr schiaffeggiare

cuff' links' spl bottoni doppi, gemelli mpl

cuirass [kwɪ'ræs] s corazza

cuisine [kwɪ'zin] s cucina

culinary ['kjulɪ ˌnɛri] adj culinario

cull [kʌl] s scarto || tr (to gather, pluck) cogliere; selezionare, scegliere

culminate ['kʌlmɪ ˌnet] intr culminare

culottes [ku'lɑts] spl gonna pantaloni

culpable ['kʌlpəbəl] adj colpevole

culprit ['kʌlprɪt] s colpevole m, imputato

cult [kʌlt] s culto

cultivate ['kʌltɪ ˌvet] tr coltivare

cultivated ['kʌltɪ,vetɪd] *adj* colto, coltivato

cultivation [,kʌltɪ'veʃən] *s* coltivazione, cultura

culture ['kʌltʃər] *s* cultura

cultured ['kʌltʃərd] *adj* colto

cul'tured pearl' *s* perla coltivata

culvert ['kʌlvərt] *s* chiavica

cumbersome ['kʌmbərsəm] *adj* ingombrante, incomodo; (*clumsy*) goffo

cumulative ['kjumjə,letɪv] *adj* cumulativo

cunning ['kʌnɪŋ] *adj* (*sly*) astuto; (*skillful*) abile; (*pretty*) bello; (*created with skill*) ben fatto, fine ‖ *s* astuzia; abilità *f*, destrezza

cup [kʌp] *s* tazza; (mach, sports) coppa; (eccl) calice *m*; **in one's cups** ubriaco ‖ *v* (*pret & pp* cupped) *ger* cupping) *tr* mettere ventose a; **to cup one's hands** foggiare le mani a mo' di conca

cupboard ['kʌbərd] *s* armadio a muro, dispensa; (*buffet*) credenza

Cupid ['kjupɪd] *s* Cupido

cupidity [kju'pɪdɪtɪ] *s* cupidigia

cup' of tea' *s* tazza di tè; (coll) forte *m*, e.g., **physics is not my cup of tea** la fisica non è il mio forte

cupola ['kjupələ] *s* cupola

cur [kʌr] *s* cane bastardo; (*despicable fellow*) canaglia, gaglioffo

curate ['kjurɪt] *s* curato

curative ['kjurətɪv] *adj* curativo

curator [kju'retər] *s* conservatore *m*

curb [kʌrb] *s* (*of bit*) barbazzale *m*; (*of pavement*) orlo del marciapiede; (*check*) freno ‖ *tr* frenare

curb'stone' *s* cordone *m*; (*of well*) sponda del pozzo

curd [kʌrd] *s* cagliata ‖ *tr* cagliare ‖ *intr* cagliarsi

curdle ['kʌrdəl] *tr* cagliare; (*the blood*) far gelare ‖ *intr* cagliarsi; (*said of custard*) impazzare

cure [kjur] *s* cura ‖ *tr* curare; (*e.g., meat*) conservare; (*wood*) stagionare

cure'-all' *s* panacea

curfew ['kʌrfju] *s* coprifuoco

curio ['kjurɪ,o] *s* (*-os*) curiosità *f*

curiosity [,kjurɪ'ɑsɪtɪ] *s* (*-ties*) curiosità *f*

curious ['kjurɪ·əs] *adj* curioso

curl [kʌrl] *s* (*of hair*) ricciolo; (*anything curled*) rotolo, spirale *f* ‖ *tr* arricciare; arrotolare; (*the lips*) torcere ‖ *intr* arricciarsi; arrotolarsi; **to curl up** raggomitolarsi

curlicue ['kʌrlɪ,kju] *s* ghirigoro

curl'ing i'ron *s* ferro da arricciare

curl'pa'per *s* bigodino

curly ['kʌrlɪ] *adj* (*-ier; -iest*) ricciuto

curmudgeon [kər'mʌdʒən] *s* bisbetico

currant ['kʌrənt] *s* (*seedless raisin*) uva passa di Corinto, uva sultanina; (*shrub and berry of genus Ribes*) ribes *m*

currency ['kʌrənsɪ] *s* (*-cies*) (*circulation*) circolazione; (*money*) denaro circolante; (*general use*) corso

current ['kʌrənt] *adj & s* corrente *f*

cur'rent account' *s* conto corrente

cur'rent events' *spl* attualità *fpl*, eventi *mpl* correnti

curriculum [kə'rɪkjələm] *s* (*-lums or -la* [lə]) programma *m*; piano educativo

curry ['kʌrɪ] *s* (*-ries*) (*spice*) curry *m* ‖ *v* (*pret & pp -ried*) *tr* (*a horse*) strigliare; (*leather*) conciare; **to curry favor** cercare di compiacere

cur'ry-comb' *s* striglia ‖ *tr* strigliare

curse [kʌrs] *s* maledizione; bestemmia ‖ *tr* maledire ‖ *intr* imprecare, bestemmiare

cursed ['kʌrsɪd] or [kʌrst] *adj* maledetto; (*hateful*) odiato

cursive ['kʌrsɪv] *adj & s* corsivo

cursory ['kʌrsərɪ] *adj* rapido, superficiale

curt [kʌrt] *adj* (*rude*) brusco, sgarbato; (*short*) breve, conciso

curtail [kər'tel] *tr* ridurre, restringere

curtain ['kʌrtən] *s* (*in front of stage*) sipario; (*for window*) tendina; (fig) cortina ‖ *tr* coprire con tenda; separare con tenda; coprire, nascondere

cur'tain call' *s* (theat) chiamata

cur'tain rais'er ['rezər] *s* (theat) avanspettacolo; (sports) incontro preliminare

cur'tain ring' *s* campanella

cur'tain rod' *s* bastone *m* su cui si fissano le tende

curtsy ['kʌrtsɪ] *s* (*-sies*) riverenza, inchino ‖ *v* (*pret & pp -sied*) *intr* fare la riverenza, inchinarsi

curve [kʌrv] *s* curva ‖ *tr* curvare ‖ *intr* curvarsi

curved [kʌrvd] *adj* curvo, curvato

cushion ['kuʃən] *s* cuscino; (*of billiard table*) mattonella ‖ *tr* proteggere, ammortizzare, attutire

cuspidor ['kʌspɪ,dɔr] *s* sputacchiera

cuss [kʌs] *s* (coll) bestemmia; (coll) tipo perverso ‖ *tr* maledire ‖ *intr* bestemmiare

custard ['kʌstərd] *s* crema

custodian [kəs'todɪ·ən] *s* (*caretaker*) custode *m*, guardiano *m*; (*person who is entrusted with s.th*) conservatore *m*; (*janitor of school*) bidello

custody ['kʌstədɪ] *s* (*-dies*) custodia; (*imprisonment*) arresto; **in custody** in prigione; **to take into custody** arrestare

custom ['kʌstəm] *s* costume *m*; (*customers*) clientela; **customs** dogana; diritti *mpl* doganali

customary ['kʌstə,merɪ] *adj* consueto, abituale

custom-built ['kʌstəm'bɪlt] *adj* fatto su misura; (*car*) fuori serie

customer ['kʌstəmər] *s* cliente *mf*

cus'tom-house' *adj* doganale ‖ *s* dogana

custom-made ['kʌstəm'med] *adj* fatto su misura

cus'toms inspec'tion *s* visita doganale

cus'toms of'ficer *s* doganiere *m*

cus'tom work' *s* lavoro fatto su misura

cut [kʌt] *adj* (*prices*) ridotto; **to be cut out for** essere tagliato per ‖ *s* taglio; (*reduction*) ribasso; (typ) cliché *m*;

(snub) (coll) affronto; (coll) assenza non autorizzata; (coll) parte *f*; **a cut above** (coll) un po' meglio di ‖ *tr* tagliare; *(cards)* alzare; *(prices)* ridurre; (coll) far finta di non riconoscere; (coll) marinare; **cut it out!** basta!; **to cut back** ridurre; **to cut off** tagliare; diseredare; (surg) amputare; **to cut short** interrompere; **to cut teeth** fare i denti; **to cut up** sminuzzare; criticare ‖ *intr* tagliare, tagliarsi; **to cut across** attraversare; **to cut in** interrompere; **to cut under** vendere sottoprezzo; **to cut up** (slang) fare il pagliaccio

cut-and-dried ['kʌtən'draɪd] *adj* monotono, stantio; bell'e fatto, fatto in anticipo

cutaneous [kju'teni·əs] *adj* cutaneo

cut'away' coat' ['kʌtə,we] *s* marsina da giorno

cut'back' *s* riduzione; eliminazione; (mov) ritorno dell'azione a un'epoca anteriore

cute [kjut] *adj* (coll) carino, grazioso; *(shrewd)* (coll) furbo

cut' glass' *s* cristallo intagliato

cuticle ['kjutɪkəl] *s* cuticola

cutlass ['kʌtləs] *s* sciabola

cutler ['kʌtlər] *s* coltellinaio

cutlery ['kʌtləri] *s* coltelleria

cutlet ['kʌtlɪt] *s* cotoletta; *(flat croquette)* polpetta

cut'off' *s* taglio; *(road)* scorciatoia; *(of cylinder)* otturatore *m*, chiusura dell'ammissione; *(of river)* braccio diretto

cut'out' *s* ritaglio; (aut) valvola di scappamento libero

cut'-rate' *adj* a prezzo ridotto

cutter ['kʌtər] *s* tagliatore *m*; (naut) cutter *m*

cut'throat' *adj* spietato; *(relentless)* senza posa ‖ *s* assassino

cutting ['kʌtɪŋ] *adj* tagliente ‖ *s* taglio; *(from a newspaper)* ritaglio;

(e.g., of prices) riduzione; (hort) talea

cut'ting board' *s* tagliere *m*; *(of dishwasher)* piano d'appoggio

cut'ting edge' *s* taglio

cuttlefish ['kʌtəl,fɪʃ] *s* seppia

cut'wat'er *s* *(of bridge)* tagliacque *m*; *(of boat)* tagliamare *m*

cyanamide [saɪ'ænə,maɪd] *s* cianamide *f*; cianamide *f* di calcio

cyanide ['saɪ·ə,naɪd] *s* cianuro

cycle ['saɪkəl] *s* ciclo; bicicletta; *(of internal combustion engine)* tempo; (phys) periodo ‖ *intr* andare in bicicletta

cyclic(al) ['saɪklɪk(əl)] or ['sɪklɪk(əl)] *adj* ciclico

cyclone ['saɪklon] *s* ciclone *m*

cyclops ['saɪklɑps] *s* ciclope *m*

cyclotron ['saɪklo ,trɑn] or ['sɪklo ,trɑn] *s* ciclotrone *m*

cylinder ['sɪlɪndər] *s* cilindro; *(container)* bombola

cyl'inder block' *s* monoblocco

cyl'inder bore' *s* alesaggio

cyl'inder head' *s* testa

cylindric(al) [sɪ'lɪndrɪk(əl)] *adj* cilindrico

cymbals ['sɪmbəls] *spl* piatti *mpl*

cynic ['sɪnɪk] *adj* & *s* cinico

cynical ['sɪnɪkəl] *adj* cinico

cynicism ['sɪnɪ,sɪzəm] *s* cinismo

cynosure ['saɪnə,ʃʊr] or ['sɪnə,ʃʊr] *s* centro dell'attenzione

cypress ['saɪprəs] *s* cipresso

Cyprus ['saɪprəs] *s* Cipro

Cyrus ['saɪrəs] *s* Ciro

cyst [sɪst] *s* ciste *f*, cisti *f*

czar [zɑr] *s* zar *m*

czarina [zɑ'rinə] *s* zarina

Czech [tʃɛk] *adj* & *s* ceco

Czecho-Slovak ['tʃɛko'slovæk] *adj* & *s* cecoslovacco

Czecho-Slovakia [,tʃɛkoslo'vækɪ·ə] *s* la Cecoslovacchia

D

D, d [di] *s* quarta lettera dell'alfabeto inglese

dab [dæb] *s* tocco; *(of mud)* schizzo; *(e.g., of butter)* spalmata ‖ *v* (pret & pp **dabbed**) *ger* **dabbing**) *tr* toccare leggermente; *(to apply a substance to)* spennellare

dabble ['dæbəl] *tr* spruzzare ‖ *intr* diguazzare; **to dabble in** occuparsi di; *(stocks)* speculare in

dad [dæd] *s* (coll) papà *m*

dad·dy ['dædi] *s* (-dies) (coll) papà *m*

daffodil ['dæfədɪl] *s* trombone *m*

daff·y ['dæfi] *adj* (-ier; -iest) (coll) pazzo

dagger ['dægər] *s* daga, pugnale *m*; (typ) croce *f*; **to look daggers at** fulminare con lo sguardo

dahlia ['dæljə] *s* dalia

dai·ly ['deli] *adj* quotidiano, diurno ‖ *s* (-lies) quotidiano ‖ *adv* giornalmente

dai'ly dou'ble *s* duplice *f*, accoppiata

dain·ty ['denti] *adj* (-ier; -tiest) delicato ‖ *s* (-ties) manicaretto

dair·y ['deri] *s* (-ies) *(store)* latteria; *(factory)* caseificio

dair'y farm' *s* vaccheria

dair'y·man *s* (-men) lattaio

dais ['de·ɪs] *s* predella

dai·sy ['dezi] *s* (-sies) margherita

dal·ly ['dæli] *v* (pret & pp -lied) *intr* *(to loiter)* bighellonare; *(to trifle)* scherzare

dam [dæm] *s* diga; *(for fishing)* pescaia; (zool) fattrice *f* ‖ *v* (pret & pp **dammed**; *ger* **damming**) *tr* arginare; ostruire; tappare

damage ['dæmɪdʒ] *s* danno, scapito; (fig) menomazione; (com) avaria; **damages** danni *mpl* ‖ *tr* danneggiare, ledere; sinistrare

damascene ['dæmə,sin] *or* [,dæmə-'sin] *adj* damasceno ‖ *s* damaschinatura ‖ *tr* damaschinare

dame [dem] *s* dama, signora; (slang) donna

damn [dæm] *s*—**I don't give a damn** (slang) me ne impipo; **that's not worth a damn** (slang) non vale un fico ‖ *tr* dannare, condannare ‖ *intr* maledire ‖ *interj* maledizione!

damnation [dæm'neʃən] *s* dannazione; (theol) condanna

damned [dæmd] *adj* dannato, maledetto ‖ **the damned** i dannati ‖ *adv* maledettamente

damp [dæmp] *adj* umido ‖ *s* umidità *f*; (firedamp) grisou *m* ‖ *tr* inumidire; umettare; (to muffle) smorzare; (waves) (elec) smorzare; **to damp s.o.'s enthusiasm** raffreddare gli spiriti di qlcu; scoraggiare qlcu

dampen ['dæmpən] *tr* inumidire; umettare; smorzare; (s.o.'s enthusiasm) raffreddare

damper ['dæmpər] *s* (of chimney) valvola di tiraggio; (fig) doccia fredda; (mus) smorzatore *m*; (mus) sordina

damsel ['dæmzəl] *s* damigella

dance [dæns] *or* [dɑns] *s* ballo, danza ‖ *tr* & *intr* ballare, danzare

dance' band' *s* orchestrina

dance' floor' *s* pista da ballo

dance' hall' *s* sala da ballo

dancer ['dænsər] *or* ['dɑnsər] *s* danzatore *m*; (expert or professional) ballerino

danc'ing part'ner *s* cavaliere *m*; dama

danc'ing par'ty *s* festa da ballo

dandelion ['dændɪ,laɪ·ən] *s* dente *m* di leone, soffione *m*

dandruff ['dændrəf] *s* forfora

dan·dy ['dændi] *adj* (-dier; -diest) (coll) eccellente, magnifico ‖ *s* (-dies) damerino, elegantone *m*

Dane [den] *s* danese *mf*

danger ['dendʒər] *s* pericolo

dangerous ['dendʒərəs] *adj* pericoloso

dangle ['dæŋgəl] *tr* dondolare ‖ *intr* penzolare, ciondolare

Danish ['denɪʃ] *adj* & *s* danese *m*

dank [dæŋk] *adj* umido

Danube ['dænjub] *s* Danubio

dapper ['dæpər] *adj* azzimato

dapple ['dæpəl] *adj* pezzato ‖ *tr* chiazzare

dap'ple-gray' *adj* storno

dare [der] *s* sfida ‖ *tr* sfidare ‖ *intr* osare; **I dare say** oserei dire; forse, e.g., **I dare say we will be done at seven** forse avremo finito alle sette; **to dare to** (to have the courage to) osare di, fidarsi a

dare'dev'il *s* scavezzacollo

daring ['derɪŋ] *adj* temerario, spericolato ‖ *s* audacia, temerarietà *f*

dark [dɑrk] *adj* scuro; (complexion) bruno; oscuro, segreto; (gloomy) tetro, fosco ‖ *s* oscurità *f*, scuro; tenebre *fpl;* **in the dark** al buio

Dark' Ag'es *spl* alto medio evo

dark-complexioned ['dɑrkkəm'plɛk-ʃənd] *adj* bruno

darken ['dɑrkən] *tr* scurire, oscurare ‖ *intr* scurirsi, oscurarsi

dark' horse' *s* vincitore imprevisto, outsider *m*

darkly ['dɑrkli] *adv* oscuramente; segretamente

dark' meat' *s* gamba o anca (di pollo o tacchino)

darkness ['dɑrknɪs] *s* oscurità *f*

dark'room' *s* camera oscura

darling ['dɑrlɪŋ] *adj* & *s* caro, amato

darn [dɑrn] *s* rammendo ‖ *tr* rammendare ‖ *interj* (coll) accidenti!

darned [dɑrnd] *adj* (coll) maledetto ‖ *adv* maledettamente; (coll) tremendamente

darnel ['dɑrnəl] *s* zizzania

darning ['dɑrnɪŋ] *s* rammendo

darn'ing nee'dle *s* ago da rammendo

dart [dɑrt] *s* freccia, dardo; (game) frecciolo ‖ *intr* dardeggiare; lanciarsi, precipitarsi

dash [dæʃ] *s* sciacquio; piccola quantità, sospetto; (spirit) brio; (typ, telg) trattino, lineetta ‖ *tr* lanciare; mescolare; (s.o.'s hopes) frustrare; deprimere; **to dash off** gettar giù; **to dash to pieces** fare a pezzi ‖ *intr* precipitarsi; **to dash against** gettarsi contro; **to dash by** passare a gran velocità; **to dash in** entrare come un razzo; **to dash off** *or* **out** andarsene in fretta; lanciarsi fuori

dash'board' *s* cruscotto; (in an open carriage) parafango

dashing ['dæʃɪŋ] *adj* impetuoso; vistoso ‖ *s* (of waves) sciacquio

dastard ['dæstərd] *adj* & *s* vile *mf*, codardo

da'ta proc'essing *s* elaborazione

date [det] *s* (time) data; (palm) palma da datteri; (fruit) dattero; (appointment) (coll) appuntamento; **out of date** fuori moda; **to date** sinora; **up to date** a giorno ‖ *tr* datare; (coll) avere un appuntamento con ‖ *intr*— **to date from** partire da

date' line' *s* linea del cambiamento di data

dative ['detɪv] *adj* & *s* dativo

datum ['detəm] *or* ['dætəm] *s* (data ['detə] *or* ['dætə]) dato

daub [dɔb] *s* imbratto ‖ *tr* imbrattare

daughter ['dɔtər] *s* figlia, figliola

daughter-in-law ['dɔtərɪn,lɔ] *s* (daughters-in-law) nuora

daunt [dɔnt] *tr* spaventare; intimidire

dauntless ['dɔntlɪs] *adj* intrepido

dauphin ['dɔfɪn] *s* delfino

davenport ['dævən,port] *s* sofà *m*, sofà *m* letto

davit ['dævɪt] *s* gru *f* per lancia

daw [dɔ] *s* cornacchia

dawdle ['dɔdəl] *intr* bighellonare

dawn [dɔn] *s* alba ‖ *intr* (said of the day) farsi, nascere, spuntare; **to dawn on** cominciare a apparire nella mente di

day [de] *adj* diurno; (student) esterno ‖ *s* giorno; (of travel, work, etc.)

giornata; **a few days ago** giorni fa; **any day now** da un giorno all'altro; **by day di** giorno; **the day after** il giorno dopo; **the day after tomorrow** dopodomani; **the day before yesterday** ieri l'altro; **to call it a day** (coll) finire di lavorare

day' bed' *s* sofà *m* letto

day'book' *s* brogliaccio

day'break' *s* far *m* del giorno

day'dream' *s* fantasticheria || *intr* fantasticare

day' la'borer *s* giornaliero

day'light' *s* luce *f* del giorno; alba; **in broad daylight** alla luce del sole; **to see daylight** comprendere; vedere la fine

day'light-sav'ing time' *s* ora legale, ora estiva

day' nurs'ery *s* asilo infantile

day' off' *s* giorno di vacanza; (*of servant*) libera uscita

day' of reck'oning *s* giorno di rendiconto; (*last judgment*) giorno del giudizio

day' shift' *s* turno diurno

day'time' *adj* diurno || *s* giornata

daze [dez] *s* stordimento; **in a daze** stordito || *tr* stordire

dazzle ['dæzəl] *s* abbagliamento || *tr* abbagliare

dazzling ['dæzlɪŋ] *adj* abbagliante

deacon ['dikən] *s* diacono

dead [dɛd] *adj* morto || *s*—**in the dead of** (*e.g., night*) nel pieno di; **the dead** i morti || *adv* (coll) completamente; (*abruptly*) (coll) di colpo

dead' beat' *adj* (coll) stanco morto

dead'beat' *s* (coll) scroccone *m*

dead' cen'ter *s* punto morto

dead'drunk' *adj* ubriaco fradicio

deaden ['dɛdən] *tr* attutire; (*e.g., s.o.'s senses*) ottundere

dead' end' *s* vicolo cieco

dead' let'ter *s* lettera morta; lettera non reclamata

dead'line' *s* termine *m*

dead'lock' *s* punto morto || *tr* portare al punto morto || *intr* giungere al punto morto

dead·ly ['dɛdli] *adj* (-**lier;** -**liest**) mortale; insopportabile

dead' pan' *s* (slang) faccia senza espressione

dead'pan' *adj* senza espressione

dead' reck'oning *s* (naut) stima

dead'wood' *s* legna secca; (fig) zavorra

deaf [dɛf] *adj* sordo; **to turn a deaf ear** fare orecchio da mercante

deaf'-and-dumb' *adj* sordomuto

deafen ['dɛfən] *tr* assordare, intronare

deafening ['dɛfənɪŋ] *adj* assordante

deaf'-mute' *s* sordomuto

deafness ['dɛfnɪs] *s* sordità *f*

deal [dil] *s* accordo; quantità *f*; (cards) mano, girata; (coll) affare *m*; (coll) trattamento; **a good deal (of)** or **a great deal (of)** moltissimo || *v* (*pret & pp* **dealt** [dɛlt]) *tr* (*a blow*) menare; (cards) fare, sfogliare; **to deal s.o. in** (coll) includere || *intr* mercanteggiare, commerciare; fare le

carte; **to deal with** trattare con; trattare di

dealer ['dilər] *s* commerciante *mf*, esercente *mf*; (cards) mazziere *m*

dean [din] *s* decano

dear [dir] *adj* (*beloved; expensive*) caro; **dear me!** povero me!; **Dear Sir** egregio Signore || *s* caro

dearie ['dɪri] *s* (coll) caro

dearth [dɑrθ] *s* scarsezza; insufficienza

death [dɛθ] *s* morte *f*; **to bleed to death** morire dissanguato; **to burn to death** morire bruciato; **to choke to death** morire di soffocazione; **to freeze to death** morire di gelo; **to put to death** dare la morte a; **to shoot to death** uccidere a fucilate; **to stab to death** scannare; **to starve to death** far morire di fame; morire di fame

death'bed' *s* letto di morte

death'blow' *s* colpo mortale

deathless ['dɛθlɪs] *adj* immortale, eterno

deathly ['dɛθli] *adj* mortale || *adv* mortalmente; assolutamente

death' pen'alty *s* pena di morte

death' rate' *s* mortalità *f*

death' rat'tle *s* rantolo della morte

death' ray' *s* raggio della morte

death' sen'tence *s* pena di morte

death' war'rant *s* pena di morte; fine *f* di ogni speranza

death'watch' *s* veglia mortuaria; (zool) orologio della morte

debacle [de'bakəl] *s* disastro; (*downfall*) tracollo; (*in a river*) sgelo repentino

de·bar [dɪ'bɑr] *v* (*pret & pp* -**barred;** *ger* -**barring**) *tr* escludere; proibire (with *dat*)

debark [dɪ'bɑrk] *tr & intr* sbarcare

debarkation [,dibɑr'keʃən] *s* sbarco

debase [dɪ'bes] *tr* degradare; adulterare

debatable [dɪ'betəbəl] *adj* discutibile

debate [dɪ'bet] *s* discussione || *tr & intr* discutere

debauch [dɪ'bɔtʃ] *s* dissolutezza, corruzione || *tr* corrompere

debauchee [,dɛbə'ʃi] or [,dɛbɔ't/i] *s* degenerato, vizioso

debauch·er·y [dɪ'bɔt/əri] *s* (-**ies**) dissolutezza, corruzione

debenture [dɪ'bɛntʃər] *s* (*bond*) obbligazione; (*voucher*) buono

debilitate [dɪ'bɪlɪ,tet] *tr* debilitare

debili·ty [dɪ'bɪlti] *s* (-**ies**) debolezza

debit ['dɛbɪt] *s* debito; (*debit side*) (com) dare *m* || *tr* addebitare

debonair [,dɛbə'nɛr] *adj* gioviale; cortese

debris [de'bri] *s* detrito, rottami *mpl*

debt [dɛt] *s* debito; **to run into debt** indebitarsi

debtor ['dɛtər] *s* debitore *m*

debut [de'bju] or ['debju] *s* debutto; **to make one's debut** debuttare || *intr* debuttare

debutante [,dɛbju'tɑnt] or ['dɛbjə,tænt] *s* debuttante *f*, esordiente *f*

decade ['dɛked] *s* decennio

decadence [dɪ'kedəns] *s* decadenza

decadent [dɪ'kedənt] *adj & s* decadente *mf*

decanter [dɪ'kæntər] *s* boccia

decapitate [dɪ'kæpɪ,tet] *tr* decapitare

decay [dɪ'ke] *s (decline)* decadimento; *(rotting)* marciume *m*, putredine *f*; *(of teeth)* carie *f* || *tr* imputridire || *intr* imputridire, marcire; *(said of teeth)* cariarsi

decease [dɪ'sis] *s* decesso || *intr* decedere

deceased [dɪ'sist] *adj & s* defunto

deceit [dɪ'sit] *s* inganno, frode *f*

deceitful [dɪ'sitfəl] *adj* ingannatore, menzognero, subdolo

deceive [dɪ'siv] *tr & intr* ingannare

decelerate [dɪ'selə,ret] *tr & intr* decelerare

December [dɪ'sembər] *s* dicembre *m*

decen·cy ['disənsi] *s* (**-cies**) decenza, pudore *m*; **decencies** convenienze *fpl*

decent ['disənt] *adj* decente; *(proper)* conveniente

decentralize [dɪ'sentrə,laɪz] *tr* decentrare

deception [dɪ'sepʃən] *s* inganno

deceptive [dɪ'septɪv] *adj* ingannevole

decide [dɪ'saɪd] *tr* decidere || *intr* decidere, decidersi

decimal ['desɪməl] *adj & s* decimale *m*

dec'imal point' *s* (*in Italian the comma is used to separate the decimal fraction from the integer*) virgola

decimate ['desɪ,met] *tr* decimare

decipher [dɪ'saɪfər] *tr* decifrare

decision [dɪ'sɪʒən] *s* decisione

decisive [dɪ'saɪsɪv] *adj* decisivo; *(resolute)* fermo

deck [dek] *s (of cards)* mazzo; *(naut)* coperta, tolda, ponte *m*; **on deck** (coll) pronto; (coll) prossimo || *tr—***to deck out** adornare; *(with flags)* imbandierare

deck' chair' *s* sedia a sdraio

deck' hand' *s* marinaio di coperta

deck'house' *s* (naut) tuga

deck'le edge' ['dekəl] *s* sbavatura

declaim [dɪ'klem] *tr & intr* declamare

declaration [,deklə'reʃən] *s* dichiarazione

declarative [dɪ'klærətɪv] *adj* declaratorio; (gram) enunciativo

declare [dɪ'kler] *tr* dichiarare || *intr* dichiararsi

declension [dɪ'klenʃən] *s* declinazione

declination [,deklɪ'neʃən] *s* declinazione

decline [dɪ'klaɪn] *s* decadenza; *(in prices)* ribasso; *(in health)* deperimento; *(of sun)* tramonto || *tr* declinare || *intr* declinare; decadere, scadere

declivi·ty [dɪ'klɪvɪti] *s* (**-ties**) declivio, pendice *f*

decode [dɪ'kod] *tr* decifrare

décolleté [,dekɔl'te] *adj* scollato

decompose [,dikəm'poz] *tr* decomporre || *intr* decomporsi

decomposition [,dikɑmpə'zɪʃən] *s* decomposizione

décor [de'kɔr] *s* decorazione; *(of a room)* stile *m*; (theat) scenario

decorate ['dekə,ret] *tr* decorare

decoration [,dekə'reʃən] *s* decorazione

decorator ['dekə,retər] *s* decoratore *m*

decorous ['dekərəs] or [dɪ'korəs] *adj* corretto, decoroso

decorum [dɪ'korəm] *s* decoro, correttezza

decoy [dɪ'kɔɪ] or ['dikɔɪ] *s* richiamo; *(for birds)* zimbello; *(person)* adescatore *m* || *tr (to lure)* adescare; *(to deceive)* abbindolare

decrease ['dikris] or [dɪ'kris] *s* diminuzione; *(of salary)* decurtazione || [dɪ'kris] *tr* decurtare || *intr* diminuire

decree [dɪ'kri] *s* decreto || *tr* decretare

de·cry [dɪ'kraɪ] *v* (*pret & pp* **-cried**) *tr* denigrare, screditare

dedicate ['dedɪ,ket] *tr* dedicare

dedication [,dedɪ'keʃən] *s* dedizione; *(inscription in a book)* dedica

deduce [dɪ'djus] or [dɪ'dus] *tr* dedurre

deduct [dɪ'dʌkt] *tr* dedurre, defalcare

deductible [dɪ'dʌktɪbəl] *adj* defalcabile || *s* (ins) franchigia

deduction [dɪ'dʌkʃən] *s* deduzione

deed [did] *s* fatto; *(exploit)* prodezza; (law) titolo || *tr* trasferire legalmente

deem [dim] *tr & intr* credere, giudicare

deep [dip] *adj* profondo; basso; *(woods)* folto; *(friendship)* intimo; **deep in debt** carico di debiti; **deep in thought** assorto in pensieri || *adv* profondamente; **deep into the night** a notte fatta; **to go deep into** approfondirsi in

deepen ['dipən] *tr* approfondire || *intr* approfondirsi

deep'-freeze' *tr* (*pret* **-froze** [froz]; *pp* **-frozen** [frozən]) *tr* surgelare

deep-laid ['dip,led] *adj* preparato astutamente

deep' mourn'ing *s* lutto stretto

deep-rooted ['dip,rutɪd] *adj* profondo

deep'-sea' fish'ing *s* pesca d'alto mare or d'altura

deep-seated ['dip,sitɪd] *adj* profondo, connaturato

Deep' South' *s* Profondo Sud

deer [dɪr] *s* cervo

deer'skin' *s* pelle *f* di daino

deface [dɪ'fes] *tr* sfigurare

defamation [,defə'meʃən] or [,difə'meʃən] *s* diffamazione

defame [dɪ'fem] *tr* diffamare

default [dɪ'fɔlt] *s* mancanza; *(failure to act)* inadempienza; **in default of** per mancanza di; **to lose by default** dichiarare forfeit || *tr* essere inadempiente a || *intr* essere inadempiente; (sports) dichiarare forfeit

defeat [dɪ'fit] *s* sconfitta, disfatta || *tr* sconfiggere, vincere

defeatism [dɪ'fitɪzəm] *s* disfattismo

defeatist [dɪ'fitɪst] *adj & s* disfattista *mf*

defecate ['defɪ,ket] *tr* defecare

defect [dɪ'fekt] or ['difekt] *s* vizio, difetto || [dɪ'fekt] *intr* defezionare

defection [dɪ'fekʃən] *s* defezione

defective [dɪ'fektɪv] *adj* difettivo, difettoso

defend [dɪ'fend] *tr* difendere, proteggere

defendant [dɪ'fendənt] *s* (law) imputato, querelato

defender [dɪ'fendər] *s* difensore *m*

defense [dɪ'fens] *s* difesa

defenseless [dɪ'fenslɪs] *adj* indifeso

defensive [dɪ'fensɪv] *adj* difensivo ‖ *s* difensiva

de·fer [dɪ'fʌr] *v* (*pret & pp* **-ferred**; *ger* **-ferring**) *tr* differire, rinviare ‖ *intr* rimettersi

deference ['defərəns] *s* deferenza

deferential [ˌdefə'renʃəl] *adj* deferente

deferment [dɪ'fʌrmənt] *s* differimento

defiance [dɪ'faɪəns] *s* opposizione, sfida; **in defiance of** a dispetto di

defiant [dɪ'faɪənt] *adj* provocante, ostile

deficien·cy [dɪ'fɪʃənsi] *s* (**-cies**) deficienza; (com) ammanco

deficient [dɪ'fɪʃənt] *adj* deficiente

deficit ['defɪsɪt] *adj* deficitario ‖ *s* deficit *m*, disavanzo

defile [dɪ'faɪl] or ['difaɪl] *s* gola, passo ‖ [dɪ'faɪl] *tr* profanare ‖ *intr* marciare in fila

define [dɪ'faɪn] *tr* definire

definite ['defɪnɪt] *adj* definito; (gram) determinativo, determinato

definition [ˌdefɪ'nɪʃən] *s* definizione

definitive [dɪ'fɪnɪtɪv] *adj* definitivo

deflate [dɪ'flet] *tr* sgonfiare; (*s.o.'s hopes*) deprimere; (*e.g., currency*) deflazionare

deflation [dɪ'fleʃən] *s* sgonfiamento; (*of prices*) deflazione

deflect [dɪ'flekt] *tr* far deflettere ‖ *intr* deflettere

deflower [dɪ'flau·ər] *tr* privare dei fiori; (*a woman*) deflorare

deforest [di'fɔrest] or [di'fɑrest] *tr* disboscare, smacchiare

deform [dɪ'fɔrm] *tr* deformare

deformed [dɪ'fɔrmd] *adj* deforme

deformi·ty [dɪ'fɔrmiti] *s* (**-ties**) deformità *f*

defraud [dɪ'frɔd] *tr* defraudare

defray [dɪ'fre] *tr* pagare

defrost [di'frɔst] or [di'frɑst] *tr* sgelare, sbrinare

defroster [di'frɔstər] or [di'frɑstər] *s* (aut) visiera termica

deft [deft] *adj* destro, lesto

defunct [dɪ'fʌŋkt] *adj* defunto

de·fy [dɪ'faɪ] *v* (*pret & pp* **-fied**) *tr* sfidare, provocare

degeneracy [dɪ'dʒenərəsi] *s* degenerazione

degenerate [dɪ'dʒenərɪt] *adj & s* degenerato ‖ [dɪ'dʒenəˌret] *intr* degenerare, tralignare

degrade [dɪ'gred] *tr* degradare

degrading [dɪ'gredɪŋ] *adj* degradante

degree [dɪ'gri] *s* grado; titolo accademico; **by degrees** a grado a grado; **to a degree** fino a un certo punto; troppo; **to take a degree** ricevere un titolo di studio

dehydrate [di'haɪdret] *tr* disidratare

deice [di'aɪs] *tr* sgelare

dei·fy ['di·ɪˌfaɪ] *v* (*pret & pp* **-fied**) *tr* deificare

deign [den] *intr* degnarsi

dei·ty ['di·ɪti] *s* (**-ties**) deità *f*; **the Deity** Dio

dejected [dɪ'dʒektɪd] *adj* demoralizzato

dejection [dɪ'dʒekʃən] *s* (*in spirits*) demoralizzazione; (*evacuation*) deiezione

delay [dɪ'le] *s* ritardo, proroga; dilazione; **without further delay** senza ulteriore indugio ‖ *tr* tardare; (*to put off*) differire ‖ *intr* tardare, ritardare

delayed'-ac'tion *adj* a azione differita

delectable [dɪ'lektəbəl] *adj* dilettevole

delegate ['delɪˌget] or ['delɪgɪt] *s* delegato, incaricato; (*to a convention*) congressista *mf* ‖ ['delɪˌget] *tr* delegare, incaricare

delegation [ˌdelɪ'geʃən] *s* delegazione

delete [dɪ'lit] *tr* cancellare, sopprimere

deletion [dɪ'liʃən] *s* cancellazione

deliberate [dɪ'lɪbərɪt] *adj* meditato; (*slow in deciding*) cauto; (*slow in moving*) lento ‖ [dɪ'lɪbəˌret] *tr & intr* deliberare

deliberately [dɪ'lɪbərɪtli] *adv* (*on purpose*) deliberatamente; (*without hurrying*) con ponderatezza

delica·cy ['delɪkəsi] *s* (**-cies**) delicatezza; (*choice food*) leccornia

delicatessen [ˌdelɪkə'tesən] *s* negozio di salumerie ‖ *spl* salumerie *fpl*, articoli alimentari scelti

delicious [dɪ'lɪʃəs] *adj* delizioso

delight [dɪ'laɪt] *s* gioia, delizia ‖ *tr* dilettare ‖ *intr* dilettarsi

delightful [dɪ'laɪtfəl] *adj* delizioso

delinquen·cy [dɪ'lɪŋkwənsi] *s* (**-cies**) colpa; (*offense*) delinquenza; (*in payment of a debt*) morosità *f*

delinquent [dɪ'lɪŋkwənt] *adj* colpevole; (*in payment*) moroso; non pagato ‖ *s* delinquente *m*; debitore moroso

delirious [dɪ'lɪri·əs] *adj* in delirio

deliri·um [dɪ'lɪri·əm] *s* (**-ums** or **-a** [ə]) delirio

deliver [dɪ'lɪvər] *tr* consegnare; (*a blow*) affibbiare; (*a speech*) fare; (*a letter*) recapitare; (*electricity or gas*) erogare; (*said of a pregnant woman*) partorire; (*said of a doctor*) assistere durante il parto

deliver·y [dɪ'lɪvəri] *s* (**-ies**) consegna; (*of mail*) distribuzione; (*of merchandise*) fornitura; (*of a speech*) dizione; (*childbirth*) parto; (sports) lancio

deliv'ery·man' *s* (**-men'**) fattorino

deliv'ery room' *s* sala parto

deliv'ery truck' *s* furgoncino

dell [del] *s* valletta

delouse [di'laus] or [di'lauz] *tr* spidocchiare

delude [dɪ'lud] *tr* illudere, ingannare

deluge ['deljudʒ] *s* diluvio, inondazione ‖ **the Deluge** il diluvio universale ‖ *tr* inondare

delusion [dɪ'luʒən] *s* illusione, inganno; (*psychopath*) allucinazione;

(psychopath) idea fissa; **delusions of grandeur** mania di grandezza

de luxe [dɪˈlʊks] or [dɪˈlʌks] *adj* di lusso || *adv* in gran lusso

delve [delv] *intr* frugare; **to delve into** approfondirsi in

demagnetize [diˈmægnɪˌtaɪz] *tr* smagnetizzare

demagogue [ˈdeməˌgag] *s* demagogo

demand [dɪˈmænd] or [dɪˈmand] *s* esigenza; (com) richiesta, domanda; **to be in demand** essere in richiesta || *tr* esigere

demanding [dɪˈmændɪŋ] or [dɪˈmandɪŋ] *adj* esigente, impegnativo

demarcate [dɪˈmarket] or [ˈdimarˌket] *tr* demarcare

démarche [deˈmarʃ] *s* progetto, piano

demean [dɪˈmin] *tr* degradare; **to demean oneself** comportarsi; degradarsi

demeanor [dɪˈminər] *s* condotta, contegno

demented [dɪˈmentɪd] *adj* demente

demigod [ˈdemɪˌgad] *s* semidio

demijohn [ˈdemɪˌdʒɑn] *s* damigiana

demilitarize [diˈmɪlɪtəˌraɪz] *tr* smilitarizzare

demimonde [ˈdemɪˌmand] *s* donne *fpl* della società equivoca

demise [dɪˈmaɪz] *s* decesso

demitasse [ˈdemɪˌtæs] or [ˈdemɪˌtas] *s* tazzina da caffè; (contents) caffè nero

demobilize [diˈmobɪˌlaɪz] *tr* smobilitare

democra·cy [dɪˈmɑkrəsi] *s* (-cies) democrazia

democrat [ˈdeməˌkræt] *s* democratico

democratic [ˌdeməˈkrætɪk] *adj* democratico

demolish [dɪˈmɑlɪʃ] *tr* demolire

demolition [ˌdeməˈlɪʃən] or [ˌdiməˈlɪʃən] *s* demolizione

demon [ˈdimən] *s* demonio

demoniacal [ˌdiməˈnaɪəkəl] *adj* demoniaco

demonstrate [ˈdemənˌstret] *tr & intr* dimostrare

demonstration [ˌdemənˈstreʃən] *s* dimostrazione

demonstrative [dɪˈmanstrətɪv] *adj* dimostrativo; (giving exhibition of emotion) espansivo

demonstrator [ˈdemənˌstretər] *s* (of a product) dimostratore *m*; (in a public gathering) dimostrante *m*; (product) prodotto usato da dimostratori

demoralize [dɪˈmarəˌlaɪz] or [dɪˈmɔrəˌlaɪz] *tr* demoralizzare

demote [dɪˈmot] *tr* retrocedere

demotion [dɪˈmoʃən] *s* retrocessione

de·mur [dɪˈmʌr] *v* (pret & pp -murred; ger -murring) *intr* sollevare obiezioni

demure [dɪˈmjʊr] *adj* modesto; sobrio

demurrage [dɪˈmʌrɪdʒ] *s* (com) controstallie *fpl*; (rr) sosta

den [den] *s* (of animals, thieves) tana; (little room) bugigattolo; (little room for studying or writing) studiolo; (of lions) (Bib) fossa

denaturalize [diˈnætʃərəˌlaɪz] *tr* snaturare; privare della nazionalità

dena'tured al'cohol [dɪˈnetʃərd] *s* alcole denaturato

denial [dɪˈnaɪəl] *s* diniego; (disavowal) smentita

denim [ˈdenɪm] *s* tessuto di cotone per tuta; **denims** tuta; (trousers) jeans *mpl*

denizen [ˈdenɪzən] *s* abitante *mf*

Denmark [ˈdenmark] *s* la Danimarca

denomination [dɪˌnamɪˈneʃən] *s* denominazione; categoria; (com) taglio; (eccl) confessione

denote [dɪˈnot] *tr* denotare, significare

denouement [denuˈma] *s* scioglimento

denounce [dɪˈnaʊns] *tr* denunziare

dense [dens] *adj* denso; stupido

densi·ty [ˈdensɪti] *s* (-ties) densità *f*

dent [dent] *s* ammaccatura; (in a gearwheel) tacca, dente *m*; **to make a dent** fare progresso; fare impressione || *tr* ammaccare; (fig) ferire

dental [ˈdentəl] *adj* dentale, dentario || *s* dentale *f*

den'tal floss' *s* filo cerato dentario

dentifrice [ˈdentɪfrɪs] *s* dentifricio

dentist [ˈdentɪst] *s* dentista *mf*

dentistry [ˈdentɪstri] *s* odontoiatria

denture [ˈdentʃər] *s* dentiera

denunciation [dɪˌnʌnsɪˈeʃən] or [dɪˌnʌnʃɪˈeʃən] *s* denunzia

de·ny [dɪˈnaɪ] *v* (pret & pp -nied) *tr* (to declare not to be true) negare; (to refuse) rifiutare; **to deny oneself to callers** sottrarsi alle visite || *intr* negare; rifiutare

deodorant [diˈodərənt] *adj & s* deodorante *m*

deo'dorant spray' *s* deodorante *m* spray

deodorize [diˈodəˌraɪz] *tr* deodorare

depart [dɪˈpart] *intr* partire, andarsene; (to diverge) dipartire

departed [dɪˈpartɪd] *adj* morto, defunto || **the departed** i defunti

department [dɪˈpartmənt] *s* dipartimento; (of government) ministero; (e.g., of a hospital) reparto; (of agency) sezione, ufficio

depart'ment store' *s* grandi magazzini *mpl*

departure [dɪˈpartʃər] *s* partenza; divergenza, deviazione

depend [dɪˈpend] *intr* dipendere; **to depend on** (to rely on) contare su; dipendere da

dependable [dɪˈpendəbəl] *adj* sicuro, fidato

dependence [dɪˈpendəns] *s* dipendenza; (trust) fiducia

dependen·cy [dɪˈpendənsi] *s* (-cies) dipendenza; (territory) possessione

dependent [dɪˈpendənt] *adj* dipendente; a carico; **to be dependent on** dipendere da || *s* persona a carico

depend'ent clause' *s* proposizione subordinata

depict [dɪˈpɪkt] *tr* descrivere, dipingere

deplete [dɪˈplit] *tr* esaurire

depletion [dɪˈpliʃən] *s* esaurimento

deplorable [dɪˈplorəbəl] *adj* deplorevole

deplore [dɪˈplor] *tr* deplorare

deploy [dɪˈplɔɪ] *tr* (mil) spiegare, stendere

deployment [dɪ'plɔɪmənt] *s* (mil) dispositivo, spiegamento

depolarize [di'polə‚raɪz] *tr* depolarizzare

depopulate [di'pɑpjə‚let] *tr* spopolare

deport [dɪ'port] *tr* deportare; **to deport oneself** comportarsi

deportation [‚dipor'teʃən] *s* deportazione

deportee [‚dipor'ti] *s* deportato

deportment [dɪ'portmənt] *s* condotta, comportamento

depose [dɪ'poz] *tr & intr* deporre

deposit [dɪ'pɑzɪt] *s* deposito; (*down payment*) caparra ‖ *tr* depositare ‖ *intr* depositarsi

depos'it account' *s* conto corrente

depositor [dɪ'pɑzɪtər] *s* versante *mf*; (*to the credit of an established account*) correntista *mf*

deposito‧ry [dɪ'pɑzɪ‚tori] *s* (**-ries**) deposito; (*person*) depositario

depos'it slip' *s* distinta di versamento

depot ['dipo] *or* ['depo] *s* magazzino; (mil) deposito; (rr) stazione

depraved [dɪ'prevd] *adj* depravato

depravi‧ty [dɪ'prævɪti] *s* (**-ties**) depravazione

deprecate ['deprɪ‚ket] *tr* deprecare

depreciate [dɪ'priʃɪ‚et] *tr* svalutare, deprezzare ‖ *intr* deprezzarsi

depreciation [dɪ‚priʃɪ'eʃən] *s* (*drop in value*) deprezzamento; (*disparagement*) disprezzo

depredation [‚deprɪ'deʃən] *s* depredazione

depress [dɪ'pres] *tr* deprimere; avvilire; (*prices*) far abbassare

depression [dɪ'preʃən] *s* depressione; (*gloom*) sconforto; (*slump*) crisi *f*

deprive [dɪ'praɪv] *tr* privare; **to deprive oneself** espropriarsi

depth [depθ] *s* profondità *f*; (*of a house or room*) lunghezza; (*of sea*) fondale *m*; (fig) vastità *f*; **in the depth of** nel cuor di; **to go beyond one's depth** non toccare più; (fig) andare oltre le proprie possibilità

depth' bomb' *s* (aer) bomba antisommergibile

depth' charge' *s* (nav) granata antisommergibile

depth' of hold' *s* (naut) puntale *m*

deputation [‚depjə'teʃən] *s* deputazione

deputize ['depjə‚taɪz] *tr* deputare

depu‧ty ['depjəti] *s* (**-ties**) deputato

derail [dɪ'rel] *tr* far deragliare ‖ *intr* deragliare, deviare

derailment [dɪ'relmənt] *s* deragliamento, deviamento

derange [dɪ'rendʒ] *tr* (*to disarrange*) dissestare; (*to make insane*) squilibrare, render pazzo

derangement [dɪ'rendʒmənt] *s* (*disorder*) disordine *m*; (*insanity*) squilibrio mentale, pazzia

der‧by ['dɑrbi] *s* (**-bies**) bombetta; (*race*) derby *m*

derelict ['derɪlɪkt] *adj* derelitto; negligente ‖ *s* derelitto; (naut) relitto

dereliction [‚derɪ'lɪkʃən] *s* (*in one's duty*) negligenza; (law) derelizione

deride [dɪ'raɪd] *tr* deridere, schernire, farsi beffe di

derision [dɪ'rɪʒən] *s* derisione, scherno

derisive [dɪ'raɪsɪv] *adj* derisorio

derivation [‚derɪ'veʃən] *s* derivazione

derivative [dɪ'rɪvətɪv] *adj & s* derivato

derive [dɪ'raɪv] *tr & intr* derivare

dermatology [‚dʌrmə'tɑlədʒɪ] *s* dermatologia

derogatory [dɪ'rɑgə‚tori] *adj* dispregiativo

derrick ['derɪk] *s* gru *f*; (naut) picco di carico

dervish ['dʌrvɪʃ] *s* dervis *m*

desalinization [di‚selɪnɪ'zeʃən] *s* desalazione

desalt [di'sɔlt] *tr* desalificare

descend [dɪ'send] *tr* discendere ‖ *intr* discendere; **to descend on** calare su, gettarsi su

descendant [dɪ'sendənt] *adj & s* discendente *mf*

descendent [dɪ'sendənt] *adj* discendente

descent [dɪ'sent] *s* (*slope*) china; (*decline*) declino; discesa; (*lineage*) stirpe *f*, discendenza; (*sudden raid*) calata

Descent' from the Cross' *s* Deposizione dalla Croce

describe [dɪ'skraɪb] *tr* descrivere

description [dɪ'skrɪpʃən] *s* descrizione

descriptive [dɪ'skrɪptɪv] *adj* descrittivo

de‧scry [dɪ'skraɪ] *v* (*pret & pp* **-scried**) *tr* avvistare

desecrate ['desɪ‚kret] *tr* profanare, dissacrare

desecration [‚desɪ'kreʃən] *s* profanazione, dissacrazione

desegregate [di'segrɪ‚get] *intr* sopprimere la segregazione razziale

desegregation [di‚segrɪ'geʃən] *s* desegregazione

desensitize [di'sensɪ‚taɪz] *tr* desensibilizzare

desert ['dezərt] *adj & s* deserto ‖ [dɪ'zɑrt] *s* merito; **he received his just deserts** ricevette quanto meritava ‖ *tr & intr* disertare

deserter [dɪ'zɑrtər] *s* disertore *m*

deserted [dɪ'zɛrtɪd] *adj* (*person*) abbandonato; (*place*) deserto

desertion [dɪ'zʌrʃən] *s* diserzione; abbandono del coniuge

deserve [dɪ'zɑrv] *tr & intr* meritare

deservedly [dɪ'zʌrvɪdli] *adv* meritatamente, meritevolmente

design [dɪ'zaɪn] *s* disegno; (*of a play*) congegno; **to have designs on** aver mire su ‖ *tr* disegnare; progettare ‖ *intr* disegnare; **designed for** destinato a

designate ['dezɪg‚net] *tr* designare

designer [dɪ'saɪnər] *s* disegnatore *m*

designing [dɪ'zaɪnɪŋ] *adj* intrigante, macchinatore ‖ *s* disegnazione

desirable [dɪ'zaɪrəbəl] *adj* desiderabile

desire [dɪ'zaɪr] *s* desiderio ‖ *tr* desiderare

desirous [dɪ'zaɪrəs] *adj* desideroso

desist [di'zɪst] *intr* desistere

desk [desk] *s* scrittoio; tavolo d'ufficio;

(*lectern*) leggio; (*of professor*) cattedra; (*of pupil*) banco; (com) cassa

desk'bound' *adj* sedentario; legato al tavolino

desk' pad' *s* blocco da tavolo; blocco per appunti

desolate ['desəlɪt] *adj* desolato, deserto; (*hopeless*) disperato; (*dismal*) lugubre || ['desə,let] *tr* desolare; devastare

desolation [,desə'leʃən] *s* desolazione; devastazione

despair [dɪ'sper] *s* disperazione; **to be in despair** disperarsi || *intr* disperare, disperarsi

despairing [dɪ'sperɪŋ] *adj* disperato

despera·do [,despə'redo] *or* [,despə'rɑdo] *s* (**-does** *or* **-dos**) fuorilegge disposto a tutto

desperate ['despərɪt] *adj* disposto a tutto; (*hopeless*) disperato; (*very bad*) atroce, terribile; (*bitter, excessive*) accanito; (*remedy*) estremo

desperation [,despə'reʃən] *s* disperazione

despicable ['despɪkəbəl] *adj* spregevole, incanaglito

despise [dɪ'spaɪz] *tr* sprezzare, disprezzare, vilipendere

despite [dɪ'spaɪt] *prep* malgrado

despoil [dɪ'spɔɪl] *tr* spogliare

desponden·cy [dɪ'spandənsi] *s* (**-cies**) scoraggiamento, abbattimento

despondent [dɪ'spandənt] *adj* scoraggiato, abbattuto

despot ['despat] *s* despota *m*

despotic [des'patɪk] *adj* dispotico

despotism ['despə,tɪzəm] *s* dispotismo

dessert [dɪ'zʌrt] *s* dessert *m*

dessert' spoon' *s* cucchiaio *or* cucchiaino da dessert

destination [,destɪ'neʃən] *s* destinazione

destine ['destɪn] *tr* destinare

desti·ny ['destɪni] *s* (**-nies**) destino

destitute ['destɪ,tjut] *or* ['destɪ,tut] *adj* (*poverty-stricken*) indigente; (*lacking*) privo

destitution [,destɪ'tjuʃən] *or* [,destɪ'tuʃən] *s* indigenza, miseria

destroy [dɪ'strɔɪ] *tr* distruggere

destroyer [dɪ'strɔɪ·ər] *s* (nav) cacciatorpediniere *m*

destruction [dɪ'strʌkʃən] *s* distruzione

destructive [dɪ'strʌktɪv] *adj* distruttivo

desultory ['desəl,tori] *adj* saltuario, sconnesso

detach [dɪ'tætʃ] *tr* staccare, distaccare; (mil) distaccare

detachable [dɪ'tætʃəbəl] *adj* staccabile; separabile

detached [dɪ'tætʃt] *adj* (*e.g., stub*) staccato; (*e.g., house*) distacco; (*aloof*) riservato, freddo; imparziale

detachment [dɪ'tætʃmənt] *s* distacco; imparzialità *f*; (mil) distaccamento

detail [dɪ'tel] *or* ['ditel] *s* dettaglio, ragguaglio; (mil) distaccamento || [dɪ'tel] *tr* dettagliare; (mil) distaccare

detain [dɪ'ten] *tr* detenere, trattenere

detect [dɪ'tekt] *tr* scoprire, discernere; (rad) rivelare

detection [dɪ'tekʃən] *s* scoperta; (rad) rivelazione

detective [dɪ'tektɪv] *s* detective *m*

detec'tive sto'ry *s* romanzo poliziesco, romanzo giallo

detector [dɪ'tektər] *s* (rad) detector *m*, rivelatore *m*

detention [dɪ'tenʃən] *s* detenzione

de·ter [dɪ'tʌr] *v* (*pret & pp* **-terred;** *ger* **-terring**) *tr* distogliere, impedire

detergent [dɪ'tɑrdʒənt] *adj & s* detergente *m*

deteriorate [dɪ'tɪrɪ·ə,ret] *tr* deteriorare || *intr* deteriorarsi, andar giù

determination [dɪ,tʌrmɪ'neʃən] *s* determinazione

determine [dɪ'tʌrmɪn] *tr* determinare

determined [dɪ'tʌrmɪnd] *adj* determinato, risoluto

deterrent [dɪ'tʌrənt] *s* deterrente *m*

detest [dɪ'test] *tr* detestare, odiare

dethrone [dɪ'θron] *tr* detronizzare

detonate ['detə,net] *or* ['ditə,net] *tr* far scoppiare || *intr* detonare

detonator ['detə,netər] *s* innesco

detour ['ditur] *or* [dɪ'tur] *s* deviazione || *tr* far deviare || *intr* deviare

detract [dɪ'trækt] *tr* detrarre || *intr—* **to detract from** diminuire

detractor [dɪ'træktər] *s* detrattore *m*

detriment ['detrɪmənt] *s* detrimento; **to the detriment of** a danno di

detrimental [,detrɪ'mentəl] *adj* pregiudizievole

deuce [djus] *or* [dus] *s* (cards) due *m*; **the deuce!** diavolo!

devaluate [di'vælju,et] *tr* svalutare

devaluation [di,vælju'eʃən] *s* devalutazione, svalutazione

devastate ['devəs,tet] *tr* devastare

devastating ['devəs,tetɪŋ] *adj* devastatore, devastante; (*e.g., reply*) schiacciante, annichilante

devastation [,devəs'teʃən] *s* devastazione

develop [dɪ'veləp] *tr* sviluppare; (phot) sviluppare, rivelare || *intr* svilupparsi; manifestarsi

developer [dɪ'veləpər] *s* (*e.g., of a new engine*) sfruttatore *m*; (*in real estate*) specialista *mf* in lottizzazione; (phot) sviluppatore *m*, rivelatore *m*

development [dɪ'veləpmənt] *s* sviluppo; valorizzazione; sfruttamento; (phot) rivelazione

deviate ['divi,et] *tr* sviare || *intr* deviare, sviarsi

deviation [,divi'eʃən] *s* deviazione

deviationism [,divi'eʃə,nɪzəm] *s* deviazionismo

deviationist [,divi'eʃənɪst] *s* deviazionista *mf*

device [dɪ'vaɪs] *s* dispositivo, congegno; (*trick*) stratagemma *m*; (*motto*) divisa, emblema *m*; **to leave s.o. to his own devices** lasciare che qlcu faccia come gli pare e piace

dev·il ['devəl] *s* diavolo; **between the devil and the deep blue sea** fra l'incudine e il martello; **to raise the devil** (slang) fare diavolo a quattro || *v* (*pret & pp* **-iled** *or* **-illed**) *ger*

-iling or **-illing**) *tr* condire con spezie o con pepe; (coll) infastidire
devilish ['devəlɪʃ] *adj* diabolico
devilment ['devəlmənt] *s* (*mischief*) diavoleria; (*evil*) cattiveria
devil·try ['devəltri] *s* (**-tries**) malvagità *f*, crudeltà *f*; (*mischief*) diavoleria
devious ['diːvɪ·əs] *adj* (*tricky*) traverso; (*roundabout*) tortuoso
devise [dɪ'vaɪz] *tr* ideare, inventare; (law) legare, disporre per testamento
devoid [dɪ'vɔɪd] *adj* sprovvisto
devolve [dɪ'vɑlv] *intr*—**to devolve on** ricadere su
devote [dɪ'vot] *tr* dedicare
devoted [dɪ'votɪd] *adj* devoto; dedito, dedicato
devotee [ˌdevə'ti] *s* devoto; (*fan*) fanatico, tifoso, entusiasta *mf*
devotion [dɪ'voʃən] *s* devozione; (*e.g., to work*) dedizione; **devotions** orazioni *mpl*, preghiere *fpl*
devour [dɪ'vaʊr] *tr* divorare
devout [dɪ'vaʊt] *adj* devoto; sincero
dew [dju] or [du] *s* rugiada
dew'drop' *s* goccia di rugiada
dew'lap' *s* giogaia
dew·y ['djuː·i] or ['duː·i] *adj* (**-ier; -iest**) rugiadoso
dexterity [deks'terɪti] *s* destrezza
diabetes [ˌdaɪ·ə'bitɪs] or [ˌdaɪ·ə'bitiz] *s* diabete *m*
diabetic [ˌdaɪ·ə'betɪk] or [ˌdaɪ·ə-'bitɪk] *adj* & *s* diabetico
diabolic(al) [ˌdaɪ·ə'bɑlɪk(əl)] *adj* diabolico
diadem ['daɪ·ə,dem] *s* diadema *m*
diaere·sis [daɪ'erɪsɪs] *s* (**-ses** [ˌsiz]) dieresi *f*
diagnose ['daɪ·əg'nos] or [ˌdaɪ·əg-'noz] *tr* diagnosticare
diagno·sis [ˌdaɪ·əg'nosɪs] *s* (**-ses** [siz]) diagnosi *f*
diagonal [daɪ'ægənəl] *adj* & *s* diagonale *f*
dia·gram ['daɪ·ə,græm] *s* diagramma *m*; (*drawing*) schema *m*; (*plan*) prospetto || *v* (*pret* & *pp* **-gramed** or **-grammed**; *ger* **-graming** or **-gramming**) *tr* diagrammare
dial ['daɪ·əl] *s* (*of watch*) quadrante *m*; (rad) tabella graduata, sintogramma *m*; (telp) disco combinatore || *tr* (rad) sintonizzare; (*a person*) (telp) chiamare; (*a number*) (telp) comporre; (*the phone*) (telp) comporre il numero di || *intr* (telp) comporre il numero
dialect ['daɪ·ə,lekt] *s* dialetto
dialing ['daɪ·əlɪŋ] *s* composizione del numero
dialogue ['daɪ·ə,lɔg] or ['daɪ·ə,lɑg] *s* dialogo
di'al tel'ephone *s* telefono automatico
di'al tone' *s* (telp) segnale *m* di via libera
diameter [daɪ'æmɪtər] *s* diametro
diametric(al) [ˌdaɪ·ə'metrɪk(əl)] *adj* diametrico, diametrale
diamond ['daɪmənd] *s* diamante *m*; (*figure of a rhombus*) losanga; (baseball) diamante *m*; **diamonds** (cards) quadri *mpl*

diaper ['daɪ·pər] *s* pannolino
diaphanous [daɪ'æfənəs] *adj* diafano
diaphragm ['daɪ·ə,fræm] *s* diaframma *m*; (telp) membrana
diarrhea [ˌdaɪ·ə'ri·ə] *s* diarrea
dia·ry ['daɪ·əri] *s* (**-ries**) diario
diastole [daɪ'æstəli] *s* diastole *f*
diathermy ['daɪ·ə,θʌrmi] *s* diatermia
dice [daɪs] *spl* dadi *mpl*; (*small cubes*) cubetti *mpl*; **no dice** (slang) niente da fare; (slang) risposta a picche
dice' cup' *s* bussolotto
dichloride [daɪ'klorɪd] *s* bicloruro
dichoto·my [daɪ'kɑtəmi] *s* (**-mies**) dicotomia
dickey ['dɪki] *s* camiciola; (*starched insert*) sparato; (bib) bavaglino
dictaphone ['dɪktə,fon] *s* dittafono
dictate ['dɪktet] *s* dettato || ['dɪktet] or [dɪk'tet] *tr* dettare
dictation [dɪk'teʃən] *s* dettato; (*act of ordering*) ordine *m*; **to take dictation** scrivere sotto dettatura
dictator ['dɪktetər] or [dɪk'tetər] *s* dittatore *m*
dictatorship ['dɪktetər,ʃɪp] or [dɪk-'tetər,ʃɪp] *s* dittatura
diction ['dɪkʃən] *s* dizione
dictionar·y ['dɪkʃən,eri] *s* (**-ies**) dizionario, vocabolario
dic·tum ['dɪktəm] *s* (**-ta** [tə]) detto, sentenza
didactic(al) [daɪ'dæktɪk(əl)] or [dɪ-'dæktɪk(əl)] *adj* didattico
die [daɪ] *s* (**dice** [daɪs]) dado; **the die is cast** il dado è tratto || *s* (**dies**) (*for stamping coins, medals,* etc.) stampo; (*for cutting threads*) filiera || *v* (*pret* & *pp* **died**; *ger* **dying**) *intr* morire; **to die hard** morire lentamente; morire lottando; **to die laughing** morire dalle risa; **to die off** morire uno per uno
die'-hard' *adj* & *s* intransigente *m*
die'sel oil' ['dizəl] *s* nafta, gasolio
die'stock' *s* girafiliera
diet ['daɪ·ət] *s* dieta, regime *m* || *intr* stare a dieta
dietetic [ˌdaɪ·ə'tetɪk] *adj* dietetico || **dietetics** *ssg* dietetica
dietitian [ˌdaɪ·ə'tɪʃən] *s* dietista *mf*
differ ['dɪfər] *intr* (*to be different*) differire, differenziarsi; **to differ with** dissentire da
difference ['dɪfərəns] *s* differenza; **to make no difference** fare lo stesso; **to split the difference** dividere la differenza; (fig) venire a un compromesso
different ['dɪfərənt] *adj* differente
differential [ˌdɪfə'renʃəl] *adj* & *s* differenziale *m*
differentiate [ˌdɪfə'renʃɪ,et] *tr* differenziare || *intr* differenziarsi
difficult ['dɪfɪ,kʌlt] *adj* difficile
difficul·ty ['dɪfɪ,kʌlti] *s* (**-ties**) difficoltà *f*
diffident ['dɪfɪdənt] *adj* timido, imbarazzato
diffuse [dɪ'fjus] *adj* diffuso || [dɪ'fjuz] *tr* diffondere || *intr* diffondersi
dig [dɪg] *s* (*poke*) botta, spintone *m*; (*jibe*) stoccata, fiancata || *v* (*pret* & *pp* **dug** [dʌg]; *ger* **digging**) *tr* sca-

vare, sterrare; **to dig up** dissodare; (*to uncover*) dissotterrare ‖ *intr* scavare; **to dig in** (mil) fortificarsi; **to dig into** (coll) sprofondarsi in

digest ['daɪdʒɛst] *s* compendio; (law) digesto ‖ [dɪ'dʒɛst] or [daɪ'dʒɛst] *tr* & *intr* digerire

digestible [dɪ'dʒɛstɪbəl] or [daɪ'dʒɛstɪbəl] *adj* digeribile, digestibile

digestion [dɪ'dʒɛstʃən] or [daɪ'dʒɛstʃən] *s* digestione

digestive [dɪ'dʒɛstɪv] or [daɪ'dʒɛstɪv] *adj* (*tube*) digerente ‖ *s* digestivo

digit ['dɪdʒɪt] *s* cifra, unità *f*; (*finger*) dito; (*toe*) dito del piede

dig'ital clock' *s* orologio a scatto

digitalis [ˌdɪdʒɪ'tælɪs] or [ˌdɪdʒɪ'telɪs] *s* (bot) digitale *f*; (pharm) digitalina

dignified ['dɪgnɪˌfaɪd] *adj* dignitoso, fiero, contegnoso

digni•fy ['dɪgnɪˌfaɪ] *v* (*pret* & *pp* -**fied**) *tr* (*to ennoble*) nobilitare; onorare, esaltare; dare la dignità a

dignitar•y ['dɪgnɪˌteri] *s* (-**ies**) dignitario; **dignitaries** dignità *fpl*

digni•ty ['dɪgnɪti] *s* (-**ties**) dignità *f*, decoro; **to stand on one's dignity** mantenere la propria dignità

digress [dɪ'grɛs] or [daɪ'grɛs] *intr* digredire, divagare

digression [dɪ'grɛʃən] or [daɪ'grɛʃən] *s* digressione, divagazione

dike [daɪk] *s* diga; (*in a river*) argine *m*; (*ditch*) fosso; scarpata

dilapidated [dɪ'læpɪˌdetɪd] *adj* dilapidato, decrepito

dilate [daɪ'let] *tr* dilatare ‖ *intr* dilatarsi

dilatory ['dɪləˌtori] *adj* lento, tardivo; (*e.g., strategy*) dilatorio

dilemma [dɪ'lɛmə] *s* dilemma *m*

dilettan•te [ˌdɪlə'tænti] *adj* dilettantesco ‖ *s* (-**tes** or -**ti** [ti]) dilettante *mf*

diligence ['dɪlɪdʒəns] *s* diligenza

diligent ['dɪlɪdʒənt] *adj* diligente

dill [dɪl] *s* (bot) aneto

dillydal•ly ['dɪlɪˌdæli] *v* (*pret* & *pp* -**lied**) *intr* farla lunga

dilute [dɪ'lut] or [daɪ'lut] *adj* diluito ‖ [dɪ'lut] *tr* diluire ‖ *intr* diluirsi

dilution [dɪ'luʃən] *s* diluizione

dim [dɪm] *adj* (**dimmer; dimmest**) (*light*) fioco; (*sight*) debole; (*memory*) vago; (*color*) smorzato; (*sound*) sordo; **to take a dim view of** avere una visione pessimistica di ‖ *v* (*pret* & *pp* **dimmed; ger dimming**) *tr* (*lights*) smorzare; **to dim the headlights** abbassare i fari

dime [daɪm] *s* moneta di dieci centesimi di dollaro

dimension [dɪ'mɛnʃən] *s* dimensione

diminish [dɪ'mɪnɪʃ] *tr* & *intr* diminuire, scemare

diminutive [dɪ'mɪnjətɪv] *adj* (*tiny*) minuscolo; (gram) diminutivo ‖ *s* diminutivo

dimly ['dɪmli] *adv* indistintamente

dimmer ['dɪmər] *s* smorzatore *m*; (aut) luce *f* di incrocio; **dimmers** fari *mpl* antiabbaglianti

dimple ['dɪmpəl] *s* fossetta

dimwit ['dɪmˌwɪt] *s* (slang) stupido, cretino

din [dɪn] *s* fragore *m*, frastuono ‖ *v* (*pret* & *pp* **dinned**; *ger* **dinning**) *tr* assordare; **to din s.th into s.o.'s ears** rintronare qlco nelle orecchie di qlcu

dine [daɪn] *tr* offrire un pranzo a; offire una cena a ‖ *intr* pasteggiare; cenare; **to dine out** mangiare fuori di casa

diner ['daɪnər] *s* commensale *m*; (rr) vettura ristorante; (U.S.A.) ristorante *m* a forma di vagone

ding-dong ['dɪŋˌdɔŋ] or ['dɪŋˌdɑŋ] *s* dindon *m*

din•gy ['dɪndʒɪ] *adj* (-**gier; -giest**) sporco, sbiadito

din'ing car' *s* vagone *m* ristorante

din'ing room' *s* sala da pranzo

dinner ['dɪnər] *s* cena; pranzo; (*formal meal*) banchetto

din'ner coat' or **jack'et** *s* smoking *m*

din'ner knife' *s* coltello da tavola

din'ner set' *s* servizio da tavola

din'ner ta'ble *s* desco

din'ner time' *s* ora di pranzo o di cena

dinosaur ['daɪnəˌsɔr] *s* dinosauro

dint [dɪnt] *s* tacca, ammaccatura; **by dint of** a forza di ‖ *tr* ammaccare

diocese ['daɪəˌsis] or ['daɪəsɪs] *s* diocesi *f*

diode ['daɪod] *s* diodo

dioxide [daɪ'aksaɪd] *s* biossido

dip [dɪp] *s* immersione; (*brief swim*) tuffo, nuotata; (*in a road*) depressione; inclinazione magnetica ‖ *v* (*pret* & *pp* **dipped**; *ger* **dipping**) *tr* immergere, tuffare; (*the flag*) abbassare; (*bread*) inzuppare ‖ *intr* immergersi, tuffarsi; inclinarsi; (*to drop down*) sparire subitamente; **to dip into** (*a book*) sfogliare; (*business*) mettersi in; (*a container of liquids*) intingere; **to dip into one's purse** spendere soldi

diphtheria [dɪf'θɪrɪ•ə] *s* difterite *f*

diphthong ['dɪfθɔŋ] or ['dɪfθɑŋ] *s* dittongo

diphthongize ['dɪfθɔŋˌgaɪz] or ['dɪfθɑŋˌgaɪz] *tr* & *intr* dittongare

diploma [dɪ'plomə] *s* diploma *m*

diploma•cy [dɪ'ploməsi] *s* (-**cies**) diplomazia

diplomat ['dɪpləˌmæt] *s* diplomatico

diplomatic [ˌdɪplə'mætɪk] *adj* diplomatico

dip'lomat'ic pouch' *s* valigia diplomatica

dipper ['dɪpər] *s* mestolo

dip'stick' *s* asta di livello

dire [daɪr] *adj* terribile, orrendo

direct [dɪ'rɛkt] or [daɪ'rɛkt] *adj* diretto; sincero ‖ *tr* dirigere; ordinare

direct' cur'rent *s* corrente continua

direct' dis'course *s* discorso diretto

direct' dis'tance di'aling *s* (telp) teleselezione *f*

direct' hit' *s* colpo centrato

direction [dɪ'rɛkʃən] or [daɪ'rɛkʃən] *s* direzione; **directions** istruzioni *fpl*; (*for use*) indicazioni *fpl* per l'uso

directional [dɪˈrekʃənəl] or [daɪˈrekʃənəl] *adj* direzionale

directive [dɪˈrektɪv] or [daɪˈrektɪv] *s* direttiva

direct' ob'ject *s* (gram) complemento diretto, complemento oggetto

director [dɪˈrektər] or [daɪˈrektər] *s* direttore *m*, gerente *m*; *(member of a governing body)* consigliere *m*

directorship [dɪˈrektərˌʃɪp] or [daɪˈrektərˌʃɪp] *s* direzione; amministrazione

directo·ry [dɪˈrektəri] or [daɪˈrektəri] *s* (-ries) *(board of directors)* direzione, direttorio; *(list of names and addresses)* rubrica, elenco; (telp) elenco dei telefoni, guida telefonica

dirge [dʌrdʒ] *s* canto funebre

dirigible [ˈdɪrɪdʒɪbəl] *adj & s* dirigibile *m*

dirt [dʌrt] *s* *(soil)* terra, suolo; *(dust)* polvere *m*; *(mud)* fango; *(accumulation of dirt)* sudiciume *m*, lerciume *m*; *(moral filth)* porcheria, sozzura; *(gossip)* pettegolezzi *mpl*; **to do s.o. dirt** (slang) calunniare qlcu

dirt'-cheap' *adj* a prezzo bassissimo

dirt' road' *s* strada di terra battuta

dirt·y [ˈdʌrti] *adj* (-ier, -iest) sporco, sudicio; fangoso; polveroso; *(e.g., spinach)* terroso; *(obscene)* sconcio, lurido; immondo || *v* (pret & pp -ied) *tr* sporcare, insudiciare, imbrattare

dir'ty lin'en *s* roba sporca; **to air one's dirty linen in public** mettere i panni al sole

dir'ty trick' *s* brutto tiro

disabili·ty [ˌdɪsəˈbɪlɪti] *s* (-ties) incapacità *f*, invalidità *f*

disabil'ity insur'ance *s* assicurazione invalidità

disable [dɪsˈebəl] *tr* mutilare, storpiare; *(a ship)* smantellare; (law) invalidare

disabuse [ˌdɪsəˈbjuz] *tr* disingannare

disadvantage [ˌdɪsədˈvæntɪdʒ] or [ˌdɪsədˈvɑntɪdʒ] *s* svantaggio

disadvantageous [dɪsˌædvənˈtedʒəs] *adj* svantaggioso

disagree [ˌdɪsəˈgri] *intr* discordare, disconvenire; *(to quarrel)* litigare, altercare; **to disagree with** non essere del parere di

disagreeable [ˌdɪsəˈgriˑəbəl] *adj* sgradevole

disagreement [ˌdɪsəˈgrimənt] *s* sconcordanza, dissidio, dissenso

disallow [ˌdɪsəˈlaʊ] *tr* non permettere, rifiutare

disappear [ˌdɪsəˈpɪr] *intr* sparire, scomparire

disappearance [ˌdɪsəˈpɪrəns] *s* scomparsa

disappoint [ˌdɪsəˈpɔɪnt] *tr* deludere, disilludere; **to be disappointed** rimanere deluso

disappointment [ˌdɪsəˈpɔɪntmənt] *s* delusione, disinganno, disappunto

disapproval [ˌdɪsəˈpruvəl] *s* disapprovazione, riprova

disapprove [ˌdɪsəˈpruv] *tr & intr* disapprovare

disarm [dɪsˈɑrm] *tr* disarmare || *intr* disarmare, disarmarsi

disarmament [dɪsˈɑrməmənt] *s* disarmo

disarming [dɪsˈɑrmɪŋ] *adj* ingraziante, simpatico

disarray [ˌdɪsəˈre] *s* disordine *m*, scompiglio; *(of apparel)* sciatteria || *tr* scomporre, scompigliare

disassemble [ˌdɪsəˈsembəl] *tr* smontare, sconnettere

disassociate [ˌdɪsəˈsoʃɪˌet] *tr* dissociare, disassociare

disaster [dɪˈzæstər] or [dɪˈzɑstər] *s* disastro, sinistro

disastrous [dɪˈzæstrəs] or [dɪˈzɑstrəs] *adj* disastroso

disavow [ˌdɪsəˈvaʊ] *tr* sconfessare

disavowal [ˌdɪsəˈvaʊˑəl] *s* sconfessione

disband [dɪsˈbænd] *tr* *(an assembly)* sciogliere; *(troops)* congedare; *(any group)* sbandare || *intr* sbandarsi

dis·bar [dɪsˈbɑr] *v* (pret & pp -barred; ger -barring) *tr* (law) radiare dall'albo degli avvocati

disbelief [ˌdɪsbɪˈlif] *s* incredulità *f*

disbelieve [ˌdɪsbɪˈliv] *tr* rifiutarsi di credere a || *intr* rifiutarsi di credere

disburse [dɪsˈbʌrs] *tr* sborsare

disbursement [dɪsˈbʌrsmənt] *s* sborso, disborso

discard [dɪsˈkɑrd] *s* scarto, scartina; **to put into the discard** scartare || *tr* scartare

discern [dɪˈzʌrn] or [dɪˈsʌrn] *tr* scernere, discernere, sceverare

discernible [dɪˈzʌrnɪbəl] or [dɪˈsʌrnɪbəl] *adj* discernibile

discerning [dɪˈzʌrnɪŋ] or [dɪˈsʌrnɪŋ] *adj* perspicace, oculato

discernment [dɪˈzʌrnmənt] or [dɪˈsʌrnmənt] *s* discernimento

discharge [dɪsˈtʃɑrdʒ] *s* *(of a load)* scarico; *(of a gun; of electricity)* scarica; *(of a prisoner)* liberazione; *(of a duty)* adempimento; *(of a debt)* pagamento; *(from a job)* licenziamento; (mil) foglio di congedo; (pathol) spurgo || *tr* scaricare; *(a duty)* adempiere; *(a prisoner)* liberare; *(a debt)* pagare; *(an employee)* licenziare; *(a patient)* lasciar uscire; *(a passenger from a ship)* sbarcare; *(a battery)* scaricare; (mil) congedare || *intr* scaricarsi; *(said, e.g., of a liquid)* sboccare; *(said of a gun, of a battery)* scaricarsi

disciple [dɪˈsaɪpəl] *s* discepolo

disciplinarian [ˌdɪsɪplɪˈnerɪˑən] *s* disciplinatore *m*; partigiano di una forte disciplina

disciplinary [ˈdɪsɪplɪˌneri] *adj* disciplinare

discipline [ˈdɪsɪplɪn] *s* disciplina; castigo || *tr* disciplinare; castigare

disclaim [dɪsˈklem] *tr* non riconoscere, negare

disclose [dɪsˈkloz] *tr* rivelare, scoprire

disclosure [dɪsˈkloʒər] *s* rivelazione, scoperta; divulgazione

discolor [dɪsˈkʌlər] *tr* scolorare, scolorire || *intr* scolorirsi

discoloration [dɪsˌkʌləˈreʃən] *s* discolorazione

discomfit [dɪs'kʌmfɪt] *tr* sconcertare, turbare; frustrare, battere, mettere in fuga

discomfiture [dɪs'kʌmfɪtʃər] *s* sconcerto, turbamento; frustrazione; disfatta

discomfort [dɪs'kʌmfərt] *s* disagio || *tr* incomodare

disconcert [,dɪskən'sʌrt] *tr* sconcertare

disconnect [,dɪskə'nɛkt] *tr* sconnettere; (elec) disinserire

disconsolate [dɪs'kɑnsəlɪt] *adj* sconsolato, desolato

discontent [,dɪskən'tɛnt] *adj & s* scontento || *tr* scontentare

discontented [,dɪskən'tɛntɪd] *adj* scontento

discontinue [,dɪskən'tɪnju] *tr* cessare, interrompere

discord ['dɪskɔrd] *s* discordia, dissidio

discordance [dɪs'kɔrdəns] *s* discordanza

discotheque [,dɪskə'tɛk] *s* discoteca

discount ['dɪskaunt] *s* sconto || ['dɪskaunt] or [dɪs'kaunt] *tr* scontare; (*news*) fare la tara a

dis'count rate' *s* tasso di sconto

discourage [dɪs'kʌrɪdʒ] *tr* scoraggiare, sconfortare; (*to dissuade*) sconsigliare

discouragement [dɪs'kʌrɪdʒmənt] *s* scoraggiamento; disapprovazione

discourse ['dɪskɔrs] or [dɪs'kɔrs] *s* discorso || [dɪs'kɔrs] *intr* discorrere

discourteous [dɪs'kʌrtɪ·əs] *adj* scortese

discourte·sy [dɪs'kʌrtəsi] *s* (*-sies*) scortesia

discover [dɪs'kʌvər] *tr* scoprire

discoverer [dɪs'kʌvərər] *s* scopritore *m*

discover·y [dɪs'kʌvəri] *s* (*-ies*) scoperta

discredit [dɪs'krɛdɪt] *s* discredito || *tr* screditare

discreditable [dɪs'krɛdɪtəbəl] *adj* indegno, disonorevole

discreet [dɪs'krit] *adj* discreto

discrepan·cy [dɪs'krɛpənsi] *s* (*-cies*) discrepanza, divario

discretion [dɪs'krɛʃən] *s* discrezione

discriminate [dɪs'krɪmɪ,net] *tr* di- scriminare || *intr*—to discriminate against fare delle discriminazioni contro

discrimination [dɪs,krɪmɪ'neʃən] *s* discriminazione

discriminatory [dɪs'krɪmɪnə,tori] *adj* discriminante

discuss [dɪs'kʌs] *tr & intr* discutere

discussion [dɪs'kʌʃən] *s* discussione

discus thrower ['dɪskəs 'θro·ər] *s* discobolo

disdain [dɪs'den] *s* disdegno || *tr* disdegnare, sdegnare

disdainful [dɪs'denfəl] *adj* sdegnoso

disease [dɪ'ziz] *s* malattia

diseased [dɪ'zizd] *adj* malato

disembark [,dɪsɛm'bark] *tr & intr* sbarcare

disembarkation [dɪs,ɛmbar'keʃən] *s* sbarco

disembowel [,dɪsɛm'bau·əl] *tr* sbudellare, sventrare

disenchant [,dɪsɛn'tʃænt] or [,dɪsɛn'tʃɑnt] *tr* disincantare

disenchantment [,dɪsɛn'tʃæntmənt] or [,dɪsɛn'tʃɑntmənt] *s* disinganno

disengage [,dɪsɛn'gɛdʒ] *tr* (*from a pledge*) svincolare; (*to disconnect*) sgranare, disinnestare; (mil) sganciare

disengagement [,dɪsɛn'gɛdʒmənt] *s* liberazione; disinnesto; svincolamento

disentangle [,dɪsɛn'tæŋgəl] *tr* disincagliare, districare

disentanglement [,dɪsɛn'tæŋgəlmənt] *s* districamento

disestablish [,dɪsɛs'tæblɪʃ] *tr* (*the Church*) separare dallo Stato

disfavor [dɪs'fevər] *s* disfavore *m*

disfigure [dɪs'fɪgjər] *tr* sfigurare, deturpare

disfigurement [dɪs'fɪgjərmənt] *s* deturpazione

disfranchise [dɪs'fræntʃaɪz] *tr* privare dei diritti civili

disgorge [dɪs'gɔrdʒ] *tr* vomitare; (*something illicitly obtained*) restituire; (*said of a river*) scaricare || *intr* vomitare; scaricarsi

disgrace [dɪs'gres] *s* vergogna; disgrazia || *tr* disonorare; privare del favore

disgraceful [dɪs'gresfəl] *adj* infamante, disonorante

disgruntle [dɪs'grʌntəl] *tr* scontentare, irritare

disgruntled [dɪs'grʌntəld] *adj* irritato, di cattivo umore

disguise [dɪs'gaɪz] *s* travestimento || *tr* travestire, dissimulare

disgust [dɪs'gʌst] *s* disgusto, schifo || *tr* disgustare, fare schifo a

disgusting [dɪs'gʌstɪŋ] *adj* disgustoso, schifoso

dish [dɪʃ] *s* piatto, **dishes** vasellame *m*; **to wash the dishes** fare i piatti || *tr* scodellare; (*to defeat*) (slang) sconfiggere; **to dish out** (slang) distribuire

dish'cloth' *s* canovaccio, strofinaccio

dishearten [dɪs'hartən] *tr* scoraggiare, disanimare, desolare

dishev·el [dɪ'ʃɛvəl] *v* (*pret & pp* -eled or -elled; *ger* -eling or -elling) *tr* scomporre, scarmigliare, scapigliare

dishonest [dɪs'ɑnɪst] *adj* disonesto

dishones·ty [dɪs'ɑnɪsti] *s* (*-ties*) disonestà *f*

dishonor [dɪs'ɑnər] *s* disonore *m* || *tr* disonorare; (com) rifiutare di pagare

dishonorable [dɪs'ɑnərəbəl] *adj* disonorevole, disonorante

dish'pan' *s* bacinella per lavare i piatti

dish'rack' *s* portapiatti *m*, sgocciolatoio

dish'rag' *s* canovaccio, strofinaccio

dish'towel' *s* canovaccio per le stoviglie

dish'wash'er *s* (*person*) sguattero, lavapiatti *m*; (*machine*) lavastoviglie *m & f*

dish'wa'ter *s* lavatura di piatti

disillusion [,dɪsɪ'luʒən] *s* disillusione || *tr* disilludere

disillusionment [,dɪsɪ'luʒənmənt] *s* disillusione

disinclination [dɪs,ɪnklɪ'neʃən] *s* riluttanza, avversione

disinclined [,dɪsɪn'klaɪnd] *adj* riluttante, avverso

disinfect [,dısın'fɛkt] *tr* disinfettare
disinfectant [,dısın'fɛktənt] *adj* & *s* disinfettante *m*
disingenuous [,dısın'dʒɛnjʊ-əs] *adj* poco schietto, insincero
disinherit [,dısın'hɛrıt] *tr* diseredare
disintegrate [dıs'ıntı,gret] *tr* disintegrare, disgregare || *intr* disintegrarsi, disgregarsi
disintegration [dıs,ıntı'greʃən] *s* disintegrazione, disgregamento
disin·ter [,dısın'tʌr] *v* (*pret* & *pp* **-terred;** *ger* **-terring**) *tr* dissotterrare
disinterested [dıs'ıntə,rɛstıd] or [dıs-'ıntrıstıd] *adj* disinteressato
disjunctive [dıs'dʒʌŋktıv] *adj* disgiuntivo
disk [dısk] *s* disco; (*of ski pole*) rotella
disk' jock'ey *s* presentatore *m* di un programma radiodiffuso di dischi
dislike [dıs'laık] *s* antipatia, avversione; **to take a dislike for** prendere in uggia || *tr* non piacere (with *dat*), e.g., **he dislikes wine** non gli piace il vino
dislocate ['dıslo,ket] *tr* spostare, mettere fuori posto; (*a bone*) slogare
dislodge [dıs'lɑdʒ] *tr* sloggiare
disloyal [dıs'lɔı-əl] *adj* sleale
disloyal·ty [dıs'lɔı-əltı] *s* (**-ties**) slealtà *f*
dismal ['dızməl] *adj* tetro, triste; cattivo, orribile
dismantle [dıs'mæntəl] *tr* smontare, smantellare; (*a fortress*) sguarnire
dismay [dıs'me] *s* costernazione || *tr* costernare
dismember [dıs'mɛmbər] *tr* smembrare
dismiss [dıs'mıs] *tr* congedare; (*to fire*) licenziare; (*a subject*) scartare; (*from the mind*) scacciare
dismissal [dıs'mısəl] *s* congedo; licenziamento
dismount [dıs'maunt] *tr* disarcionare || *intr* scendere, smontare
disobedience [,dısə'bidı-əns] *s* disubbidienza
disobedient [,dısə'bidı-ənt] *adj* disubbidiente
disobey [,dısə'be] *tr* disubbidire (with *dat*) || *intr* disubbidire
disorder [dıs'ɔrdər] *s* disordine *m* || *tr* disordinare, confondere
disorderly [dıs'ɔrdərlı] *adj* disordinato, confuso; (*unruly*) turbolento
disor'derly con'duct *s* contegno contrario all'ordine pubblico
disor'derly house' *s* bordello, lupanare *m*
disorganize [dıs'ɔrgə,naız] *tr* disorganizzare
disoriented [dıs'ɔrı,ɛntıd] *adj* disorientato
disown [dıs'on] *tr* disconoscere
disparage [dıs'pærıdʒ] *tr* svilire, deprezzare
disparagement [dıs'pærıdʒmənt] *s* discredito, deprezzamento
disparate ['dıspərıt] *adj* disparato
dispari·ty [dıs'pærıtı] *s* (**-ties**) disparità *f*, spareggio
dispassionate [dıs'pæʃənıt] *adj* spassionato

dispatch [dıs'pætʃ] *s* dispaccio || *tr* spedire; (*to dismiss*) congedare; uccidere; (*a meal*) (coll) liquidare
dis·pel [dıs'pɛl] *v* (*pret* & *pp* **-pelled;** *ger* **-pelling**) *tr* dissipare
dispensa·ry [dıs'pɛnsərı] *s* (**-ries**) dispensario
dispensation [,dıspɛn'seʃən] *s* (*dispensing*) distribuzione, dispensa; (*exemption*) dispensa
dispense [dıs'pɛns] *tr* (*medicines*) distribuire; (*justice*) amministrare; (*to distribute*) dispensare; (*to exempt*) esimere || *intr*—**to dispense with** fare a meno di; esimersi da
dispenser [dıs'pɛnsər] *s* dispensatore *m*; (*automatic*) distributore *m*
disperse [dıs'pʌrs] *tr* disperdere || *intr* dispersersi
dispersion [dı'spʌrʒən] or [dı'spɛrʃən] *s* dispersione
dispersive [dı'spʌrsıv] *adj* dispersivo
dispirit [dı'spırıt] *tr* scoraggiare
displace [dıs'ples] *tr* muovere; costringere a lasciare il proprio paese; (*to supplant*) rimpiazzare; (naut) dislocare
displaced' per'son *s* rifugiato politico
displacement [dıs'plɛsmənt] *s* spostamento; sostituzione; (*of a piston*) cilindrata; (naut) dislocamento
display [dıs'ple] *s* sfoggio, mostra || *tr* mostrare; (e.g., *in a store window*) mettere in mostra; (*to unfold*) spiegare; (*to show ostentatiously*) sfoggiare, ostentare; (*ignorance*) rivelare
display' cab'inet *s* bacheca
display' win'dow *s* mostra, vetrina
displease [dıs'pliz] *tr* dispiacere (with *dat*)
displeasing [dıs'plizıŋ] *adj* spiacevole
displeasure [dıs'plɛʒər] *s* dispiacere *m*; sfavore *m*
disposable [dıs'pozəbəl] *adj* (*available*) disponibile; (*made to be thrown away after use*) scartabile, da gettarsi via, usa e getta
disposal [dıs'pozəl] *s* disposizione; eliminazione; **to have at one's disposal** disporre di
dispose [dıs'poz] *tr* disporre; **to dispose of** disporre di; (*to get rid of*) sbarazzarsi di; vendere
disposed [dı'spozd] *adj*—**to be disposed to** essere disposto a
disposition [,dıspə'zıʃən] *s* disposizione; (*mental outlook*) indole *f*; tendenza; (mil) ordinamento
dispossess [,dıspə'zɛs] *tr* spodestare, bandire; (*to evict*) sfrattare
disproof [dıs'pruf] *s* confutazione
disproportionate [,dısprə'porʃənıt] *adj* sproporzionato
disprove [dıs'pruv] *tr* confutare
dispute [dıs'pjut] *s* disputa; **beyond dispute** incontestabile; **in dispute** in discussione || *tr* & *intr* disputare
disquali·fy [dıs'kwɑlı,faı] *v* (*pret* & *pp* **-fied**) *tr* squalificare
disquiet [dıs'kwaı-ət] *s* inquietudine *f* || *tr* inquietare, turbare
disquisition [,dıskwı'zıʃən] *s* disquisizione

disregard [ˌdɪsrɪ'gɑrd] s (of a rule) inosservanza; (of danger) disprezzo, noncuranza ‖ tr non fare attenzione a

disrepair [ˌdɪsrɪ'pɛr] s cattivo stato, rovina

disreputable [dɪs'rɛpjətəbəl] adj malfamato; disonorevole; (in bad condition) raso, logoro

disrepute [ˌdɪsrɪ'pjut] s cattiva fama; **to bring into disrepute** rovinare la reputazione di

disrespect [ˌdɪsrɪ'spɛkt] s mancanza di rispetto ‖ tr mancare di rispetto a

disrespectful [ˌdɪsrɪ'spɛktfəl] adj non rispettoso, irriverente

disrobe [dɪs'rob] tr svestire ‖ intr svestirsi, spogliarsi

disrupt [dɪs'rʌpt] tr disorganizzare; interrompere

disruption [dɪs'rʌpʃən] s rottura; disorganizzazione

dissatisfaction [ˌdɪssætɪs'fækʃən] s scontento, malcontento

dissatisfied [dɪs'sætɪsˌfaɪd] adj scontento, malcontento; insoddisfatto

dissatis·fy [dɪs'sætɪsˌfaɪ] v (pret & pp -fied) tr scontentare

dissect [dɪ'sɛkt] tr sezionare

dissemble [dɪ'sɛmbəl] tr & intr dissimulare

disseminate [dɪ'sɛmɪˌnet] tr disseminare, divulgare

dissension [dɪ'sɛnʃən] s dissensione

dissent [dɪ'sɛnt] s dissenso; (nonconformity) dissidio ‖ intr dissentire

dissenter [dɪ'sɛntər] s dissenziente m

dissertation [ˌdɪsər'teʃən] s dissertazione

disservice [dɪ'sʌrvɪs] s danno; cattivo servizio

dissidence ['dɪsɪdəns] s dissidenza

dissident ['dɪsɪdənt] adj & s dissidente m

dissimilar [dɪ'sɪmɪlər] adj dissimile

dissimilate [dɪ'sɪmɪˌlet] tr dissimilare ‖ intr dissimilarsi

dissimulate [dɪ'sɪmjəˌlet] tr & intr dissimulare

dissipate ['dɪsɪˌpet] tr dissipare ‖ intr dissiparsi; (to indulge oneself) darsi alla dissipatezza

dissipated ['dɪsɪˌpetɪd] adj dissipato

dissipation [ˌdɪsɪ'peʃən] s dissipazione

dissociate [dɪ'soʃɪˌet] tr dissociare ‖ intr dissociarsi

dissolute ['dɪsəˌlut] adj dissoluto

dissolution [ˌdɪsə'luʃən] s dissoluzione

dissolve [dɪ'zɑlv] tr sciogliere, disciogliere ‖ intr sciogliersi, disciogliersi

dissonance ['dɪsənəns] s dissonanza

dissuade [dɪ'swed] tr dissuadere

dissyllabic [ˌdɪsɪ'læbɪk] adj disillabo

dissyllable [dɪ'sɪləbəl] s disillabo

distaff ['dɪstæf] or ['dɪstaf] s rocca

dis'taff side' s ramo femminile di una famiglia

distance ['dɪstəns] s distanza; **a long distance** (fig) moltissimo; **in the distance** in lontananza; **to keep at a distance or to keep one's distance** mantenere le distanze ‖ tr distanziare

distant ['dɪstənt] adj distante; (relative) lontano; (aloof) freddo, riservato

distaste [dɪs'test] s ripugnanza

distasteful [dɪs'testfəl] adj ripugnante, sgradevole

distemper [dɪs'tɛmpər] s cimurro; (painting) tempera ‖ tr dipingere a tempera

distend [dɪs'tɛnd] tr stendere, distendere; gonfiare ‖ intr stendersi, distendersi; gonfiarsi

distension [dɪs'tɛnʃən] s distensione; gonfiamento

distill [dɪs'tɪl] tr distillare

distillation [ˌdɪstɪ'leʃən] s distillazione

distiller·y [dɪs'tɪlərɪ] s (-ies) distilleria

distinct [dɪs'tɪŋkt] adj distinto, chiaro; (not blurred) nitido

distinction [dɪs'tɪŋkʃən] s distinzione

distinctive [dɪs'tɪŋktɪv] adj distintivo

distinguish [dɪs'tɪŋgwɪʃ] tr distinguere

distinguished [dɪs'tɪŋgwɪʃt] adj distinto

distort [dɪs'tɔrt] tr distorcere; (the truth) svisare, snaturare

distortion [dɪs'tɔrʃən] s deformazione; (of the truth) alterazione, svisamento; (rad) distorsione

distract [dɪs'trækt] tr distrarre

distracted [dɪs'træktɪd] adj distratto; (irrational) turbato, sconvolto

distraction [dɪs'trækʃən] s distrazione

distraught [dɪs'trɔt] adj turbato, stordito

distress [dɪs'trɛs] s pena, dispiacere m; pericolo; (naut) difficoltà f ‖ tr sconfortare, affliggere

distressing [dɪs'trɛsɪŋ] adj penoso

distress' mer'chandise s merce f sotto costo

distress' sig'nal s segnale m di soccorso

distribute [dɪs'trɪbjut] tr distribuire

distribution [ˌdɪstrɪ'bjuʃən] s distribuzione, erogazione

distributor [dɪs'trɪbjətər] s distributore m; (aut) distributore m d'accensione

district ['dɪstrɪkt] s regione; (of a city) rione m, quartiere m; (administrative division) distretto ‖ tr dividere in distretti

dis'trict attor'ney s procuratore m generale

distrust [dɪs'trʌst] s diffidenza ‖ tr diffidare di

distrustful [dɪs'trʌstfəl] adj diffidente

disturb [dɪs'tʌrb] tr disturbare, turbare; disordinare

disturbance [dɪs'tʌrbəns] s disturbo, turbamento, perturbazione; disordine m

disuse [dɪs'jus] s disuso

ditch [dɪtʃ] s fossa, fossato ‖ tr scavare un fosso in; (rr) far deragliare; (slang) piantare in asso ‖ intr fare un ammaraggio forzato

dither ['dɪðər] s agitazione; **to be in a dither** (coll) essere agitato

dit·to ['dɪto] s (-tos) lo stesso; (ditto symbol) virgolette fpl ‖ adv ugualmente, idem ‖ tr copiare, duplicare

dit'to marks' spl virgolette fpl

dit·ty ['dɪtɪ] *s* (**-ties**) canzonetta

diva ['divə] *s* (mus) diva

divan ['daɪvæn] or [dɪ'væn] *s* divano

dive [daɪv] *s* tuffo; (*of a submarine*) immersione; (aer) picchiata; (coll) taverna; (com) discesa || *v* (*pret & pp* **dived** or **dove** [dov]) *intr* tuffarsi; (*said of submarine*) immergersi; (*to plunge*) lanciarsi; (aer) scendere in picchiata; **to dive for** (*e.g., pearls*) pescare

dive'-bomb' *tr* bombardare in picchiata || *intr* scendere a tuffo

dive' bomb'ing *s* bombardamento in picchiata

diver ['daɪvər] *s* tuffatore *m*; (*person who works under water*) palombaro; (orn) tuffetto

diverge [dɪ'vʌrdʒ] or [daɪ'vʌrdʒ] *intr* divergere

divers ['daɪvərz] *adj* diversi, vari

diverse [dɪ'vʌrs], [daɪ'vʌrs] or ['daɪvʌrs] *adj* (*different*) diverso; (*of various kinds*) multiforme

diversification [dɪ,vʌrsɪfɪ'keʃən] or [daɪ,vʌrsɪfɪ'keʃən] *s* diversificazione

diversi·fy [dɪ'vʌrsɪ,faɪ] or [daɪ'vʌrsɪ,faɪ] *v* (*pret & pp* **-fied**) *tr* diversificare || *intr* diversificarsi

diversion [dɪ'vʌrʒən] or [daɪ'vʌrʒən] *s* diversione; (*pastime*) svago

diversi·ty [dɪ'vʌrsɪtɪ] or [daɪ'vʌrsɪtɪ] *s* (**-ties**) diversità *f*

divert [dɪ'vʌrt] or [daɪ'vʌrt] *tr* deviare; (*to entertain*) divertire; (*money*) stornare, distrarre

diverting [dɪ'vʌrtɪŋ] or [daɪ'vʌrtɪŋ] *adj* divertente

divest [dɪ'vest] or [daɪ'vest] *tr* spogliare; spossessare; **to divest oneself of** spogliarsi di, espropriarsi di

divide [dɪ'vaɪd] *tr* spartiacque *m* || *tr* dividere || *intr* dividersi

dividend ['dɪvɪ,dend] *s* dividendo

dividers [dɪ'vaɪdərz] *spl* compasso a punte fisse

divination [,dɪvɪ'neʃən] *s* divinazione

divine [dɪ'vaɪn] *adj* divino || *s* sacerdote *m*, prete *m* || *tr* divinare

diviner [dɪ'vaɪnər] *s* divinatore *m*

diving ['daɪvɪŋ] *s* tuffo, immersione

div'ing bell' *s* campana da palombaro

div'ing board' *s* trampolino

div'ing suit' *s* scafandro

divin'ing rod' ['daɪvaɪnɪŋ] *s* bacchetta rabdomantica

divini·ty [dɪ'vɪnɪtɪ] *s* (**-ties**) divinità *f*; teologia; **the Divinity** Dio

divisible [dɪ'vɪsɪbəl] *adj* divisibile

division [dɪ'vɪʒən] *s* divisione

divisor [dɪ'vaɪzər] *s* divisore *m*

divorce [dɪ'vors] *s* divorzio; **to get a divorce** divorziare || *tr* (*a married couple*) divorziare; (*one's spouse*) divorziare da || *intr* divorziare

divorcé [dɪvor'se] *s* divorziato

divorcée [dɪvor'si] *s* divorziata

divulge [dɪ'vʌldʒ] *tr* divulgare

dizziness ['dɪzɪnɪs] *s* vertigine *f*, stordimento; confusione

diz·zy ['dɪzɪ] *adj* (**-zier; -ziest**) (*causing dizziness*) vertiginoso; (*suffering diz-*

ziness) preso da vertigine, stordito; (coll) stupido

do [du] *v* (*3rd pers* **does** [dʌz]; *pret* **did** [dɪd]; *pp* **done** [dʌn]; *ger* **doing** ['du·ɪŋ]) *tr* fare; (*a problem*) risolvere; (*a distance*) percorrere; (*to study*) studiare; (*to explore*) attraversare; (*to tire*) stancare; **to do one's best** fare del proprio meglio; **to do over** tornare a fare; ripetere; **to do right by** trattare bene; **to do s.o. out of s.th** (coll) portare via qlco a qlcu; **to do to death** mettere a morte; **to do up** (coll) impacchettare; stancare; (*one's hair*) farsi; vestire; (*a shirt*) lavare e stirare; **to have done** far fare || *intr* fare; agire; comportarsi; servire; bastare; stare; succedere; **how do you do?** come sta?; **that will do** basta; è sufficiente; **to have done with** non aver più nulla a che fare con; **to have nothing to do with** non aver nulla a che vedere con; **to have to do with** aver a che fare con, trattarsi di; **to do away with** togliere di mezzo; **to do for** servire da; **to do well** crescere bene; **to do without** fare a meno di || *v aux* used 1) in interrogative sentences: **Do you speak Italian?** Parla italiano?; 2) in negative sentences: **I do not speak Italian** Non parlo italiano; 3) to avoid repetition of a verb or full verbal expression: **Did you go to church this morning? Yes, I did.** È stato in chiesa questa mattina? Sì, ci sono stato; 4) to lend emphasis to a principal verb: **I do believe what you told me** Ci credo a quello che mi ha detto; 5) in inverted constructions after certain adverbs: **Seldom does he come to see me** Mi viene a vedere di raro; 6) in a supplicating tone with imperatives: **Do come in** entri per favore

docile ['dɑsɪl] *adj* docile

dock [dɑk] *s* (*wharf*) molo; (*waterway between two piers*) darsena; (*area including piers and waterways*) scalo portuario; (law) gabbia degli imputati || *tr* (*to deduct from the wages of*) fare una deduzione a; (*to deduct s.o.'s salary*) dedurre da; (*an animal*) scodare; (naut) attraccare || *intr* (aer) agganciarsi; (naut) attraccare

dockage ['dɑkɪdʒ] *s* attracco; (*charges*) diritti *mpl* di porto

docket ['dɑkɪt] *s* ordine *m* del giorno; (law) ruolo delle sentenze; **on the docket** (coll) pendente, in sospeso

dock' hand' *s* portuale *m*

docking ['dɑkɪŋ] *s* (aer) aggancio; (naut) attracco

dock'yard' *s* cantiere *m* navale

doctor ['dɑktər] *s* dottore *m*; (*physician*) medico || *tr* curare; aggiustare; falsificare; adulterare || *intr* esercitare la medicina; (coll) curarsi, prendere medicine

doctorate ['dɑktərɪt] *s* dottorato

doctrine ['dɑktrɪn] *s* dottrina

document ['dɑkjəmənt] *s* documento || ['dɑkjə,ment] *tr* documentare

documenta·ry [ˌdɑkjəˈmentəri] *adj* & *s* (**-ries**) documentario

documentation [ˌdɑkəmenˈteʃən] *s* documentazione

doddering [ˈdɑdərɪŋ] *adj* tremante, rimbambito

dodge [dɑdʒ] *s* scarto, schivata; (fig) stratagemma *m* ‖ *tr* schivare, evitare ‖ *intr* schivarsi; (fig) rispondere evasivamente; **to dodge around the corner** scantonare

do·do [ˈdodo] *s* (**-dos** or **-does**) (coll) rimbecillito

doe [do] *s* (*of deer*) cerva; (*of goat*) capretta; (*of rabbit*) coniglia

doeskin [ˈdoˌskɪn] *s* pelle *f* di daino, pelle *f* di dante; lana finissima

doff [dɑf] or [dɔf] *tr* (*one's hat*) togliersi; (*clothing*) deporre

dog [dɔg] or [dɑg] *s* cane *m*; **to go to the dogs** (coll) andare in malora; **to put on the dog** (coll) darsi delle arie ‖ *v* (*pret* & *pp* **dogged**; *ger* **dogging**) *tr* seguire; perseguitare

dog'catch'er *s* accalappiacani *m*

dog' days' *s* solleone *m*, canicola

doge [dodʒ] *s* doge *m*

dog'-ear' *s* orecchia, orecchio

dog'fight' *s* duello aereo

dogged [ˈdɔgɪd] or [ˈdɑgɪd] *adj* accanito

doggerel [ˈdɔgərəl] or [ˈdɑgərəl] *s* versi *mpl* da colascione

dog·gy [ˈdɔgi] or [ˈdɑgi] *adj* (**-gier**; **-giest**) vistoso; canino ‖ *s* (**-gies**) cagnolino

dog'house' *s* canile *m*; **to be in the doghouse** (slang) essere in disgrazia

dog' Lat'in *s* latino maccheronico

dogma [ˈdɔgmə] or [ˈdɑgmə] *s* dogma *m*

dogmatic [dɔgˈmætɪk] or [dɑgˈmætɪk] *adj* dogmatico

dog' rac'ing *s* corse *fpl* dei cani

dog' show' *s* mostra canina

dog's' life' *s* vita da cani

Dog' Star' *s* canicola

dog' tag' *s* (mil) piastrina, piastrino

dog'-tired' *adj* (coll) stanco morto

dog'tooth' *s* (**-teeth** [ˌtiθ]) canino

dog' track' *s* cinodromo

dog'watch' *s* (naut) quarto di solo due ore, gaettone *m*

dog'wood' *s* corniolo

doi·ly [ˈdɔɪli] *s* (**-lies**) centrino

doings [ˈdu�·ɪŋz] *spl* azioni *fpl*, fatti *mpl*

do'-it-your·self' *s* il fare tutto da sé

doldrums [ˈdɑldrəmz] *spl* calma equatoriale; inattività *f*; depressione

dole [dol] *s* elemosina; (*to the jobless*) sussidio di disoccupazione ‖ *tr*—**to dole out** distribuire parsimoniosamente

doleful [ˈdolfəl] *adj* lugubre, triste

doll [dɑl] *s* bambola ‖ *intr*—**to doll up** (slang) agghindarsi

dollar [ˈdɑlər] *s* dollaro

dol'lar·wise' *adv* in termini finanziari

dol·ly [ˈdɑli] *s* (**-lies**) pupattola; (*low, wheeled frame for moving heavy loads*) carrello; (mov, telv) carrello

‖ *v* (*pret* & *pp* **-lied**) *intr* (mov, telv) carrellare

dol'ly shot' *s* (mov, telv) carrellata

dolphin [ˈdɑlfɪn] *s* delfino

dolt [dolt] *s* gonzo, balordo

doltish [ˈdoltɪʃ] *adj* gonzo, balordo

domain [doˈmen] *s* dominio; (law) proprietà *f*; (fig) campo, orbita

dome [dom] *s* cupola

dome' light' *s* lampadario

domestic [dəˈmestɪk] *adj* & *s* domestico

domesticate [dəˈmestɪˌket] *tr* domesticare

domicile [ˈdɑmɪsɪl] or [ˈdɑmɪˌsaɪl] *s* domicilio ‖ *tr* domiciliare

dominance [ˈdɑmɪnəns] *s* dominio

dominant [ˈdɑmɪnənt] *adj* & *s* dominante *f*

dominate [ˈdɑmɪˌnet] *tr* & *intr* dominare

domination [ˌdɑmɪˈneʃən] *s* dominazione

domineer [ˌdɑmɪˈnɪr] *intr* spadroneggiare

domineering [ˌdɑmɪˈnɪrɪŋ] *adj* dispotico, tirannico

Dominican [dəˈmɪnɪkən] *adj* & *s* dominicano; (eccl) domenicano

dominion [dəˈmɪnjən] *s* dominio

domi·no [ˈdɑmɪˌno] *s* (**-noes** or **-nos**) (*costume and person*) domino; (*piece*) tessera di domino; **dominoes** (*game*) domino

don [dɑn] *s* signore *m*; don *m*; membro di un collegio universitario inglese ‖ *v* (*pret* & *pp* **donned**; *ger* **donning**) *tr* (*clothes*) mettersi, vestire

donate [ˈdonet] *tr* donare, dare

donation [doˈneʃən] *s* donazione

done [dʌn] *adj* fatto; finito; stanco; (culin) ben cotto, ben rosolato

done' for' *adj* (coll) stanco morto; (coll) rovinato; (coll) fuori combattimento; (coll) morto

donjon [ˈdʌndʒən] or [ˈdɑndʒən] *s* torrione *m*, maschio

Don Juan, [dɑn ˈwɑn] or [dɔn ˈhwɑn] *s* Don Giovanni

donkey [ˈdɑŋki] or [ˈdʌŋki] *s* asino, somaro

donnish [ˈdɑnɪʃ] *adj* pedante

donor [ˈdonər] *s* donatore *m*

doodle [ˈdudəl] *tr* & *intr* scarabocchiare, riempire di ghirigori

doom [dum] *s* destino; morte *f*, rovina; sentenza di morte; giudizio finale ‖ *tr* destinare; condannare; condannare a morte

doomsday [ˈdumzˌde] *s* giorno del giudizio

door [dor] *s* porta; (*of a carriage or automobile*) portiera, sportello; (*one part of a double door*) battente *m*; **behind closed doors** a porte chiuse; **to see to the door** accompagnare alla porta; **to show s.o. the door** mettere qlcu alla porta

door'bell' *s* campanello della porta

door' check' *s* chiusura automatica di porta, scontro

door'frame' *s* cornice *f*

door'head' s architrave m
door'jamb' s stipite m
door'keep'er s portinaio
door'knob' s maniglia della porta
door' knock'er s battente m
door' latch' s paletto
door'man' s (-men') portiere m, portinaio; (of large apartment house) guardaportone m
door'mat' s stoino, zerbino
door'nail' s borchione m; **dead as a doornail** morto e ben morto
door'post' s stipite m
door' scrap'er s raschietto
door'sill' s soglia
door'step' s gradino davanti la porta
door'stop' s paracolpi m
door'-to-door' adj (shipment) diretto; (selling) di porta in porta
door'way' s vano della porta; porta
dope [dop] s lubrificante m; (aer) vernice f; (slang) stupido, scemo; (slang) informazioni fpl; (slang) narcotico || tr (slang) narcotizzare; **to dope out** (slang) indovinare, decifrare, immaginare
dope' fiend' s (slang) tossicomane mf
dope'sheet' s giornaletto con le previsioni della corse ippiche
dormant ['dɔrmənt] adj dormente; latente
dor'mer win'dow ['dɔrmər] s abbaino
dormito·ry ['dɔrmɪ ,tori] s (-ries) dormitorio
dor·mouse ['dɔr ,maus] s (-mice [,maɪs]) ghiro
dosage ['dosɪdʒ] s dosatura
dose [dos] s dose f; (coll) boccone amaro || tr dosare; somministrare
dossier ['dɑsɪ ,e] s incartamento
dot [dɑt] s punto; **on the dot** (coll) in punto || v (pret & pp **dotted;** ger **dotting**) tr punteggiare; **to dot one's i's** mettere i punti sulle i
dotage ['dotɪdʒ] s rimbecillimento; **to be in one's dotage** essere rimbambito
dotard ['dotərd] s vecchio rimbambito
dote [dot] intr rimbambirsi; **to dote on** essere pazzo per
doting ['dotɪŋ] adj che ama alla follia; (from old age) rimbambito, rimbecillito
dots' and dash'es spl (telg) punti mpl e tratti mpl
dot'ted line' s linea punteggiata; **to sign on the dotted line** firmare inconsideratamente
double ['dʌbəl] adj doppio || s doppio; (bridge) contre m; **doubles** (tennis) doppio || tr raddoppiare; (bridge) contrare || intr raddoppiarsi; (bridge) contrare; (mov, theat) sostenere due ruoli; (mov) doppiare; **to double up** (said of two people) dividere la stessa camera, dividere lo stesso letto; piegarsi in due
double-barreled ['dʌbəl'bærəld] adj a due canne; (fig) a doppio fine
dou'ble bass' s contrabbasso
dou'ble bed' s letto matrimoniale
dou'ble boil'er s bagnomaria m

double-breasted ['dʌbəl'brestɪd] adj a doppio petto, doppiopetto
dou'ble chin' s pappagorgia
dou'ble-cross' tr (coll) tradire
dou'ble date' s (coll) appuntamento amoroso di due coppie
dou'ble-deal'ing adj doppio
dou'ble-deck'er s (bed) letto a castello; (sandwich) tramezzino doppio; autobus m a due piani; (naut) nave f due ponti; (aer) aereo due ponti
double-edged ['dʌbəl'edʒd] adj a due tagli, a doppio taglio
dou'ble en'try s (com) partita doppia
dou'ble fea'ture s (mov) programma m di due lungometraggio
double-header ['dʌbəl'hedər] s treno con due locomotive; due partite di baseball giocate successivamente
double-jointed ['dʌbəl'dʒɔɪntɪd] adj snodato
dou'ble-park' tr & intr parcheggiare in doppia fila
dou'ble-quick' adj & adv a passo di carica
dou'ble stand'ard s—**to have a double standard** usare due pesi e due misure
doublet ['dʌblɪt] s (close-fitting jacket) farsetto; (philol) doppione m
dou'ble-talk' s discorso incomprensibile; **to give s.o. double-talk** parlare evasivamente a qlcu || intr parlare evasivamente
dou'ble time' s paga doppia; (mil) passo di carica
doubleton ['dʌbəltən] s doppio
doubly ['dʌbli] adv doppiamente
doubt [daut] s dubbio; **beyond doubt** senza dubbio; **if in doubt** in caso di dubbio; **no doubt** senza dubbio || tr dubitare di || intr dubitare
doubter ['dautər] s incredulo
doubtful ['dautfəl] adj incerto; dubbioso
doubtless ['dautlɪs] adj indubitabile || adv senza dubbio; probabilmente
douche [duʃ] s irrigazione f; (instrument) irrigatore m || tr irrigare || intr fare irrigazioni
dough [do] s pasta di pane; (money) (slang) soldi mpl, quattrini mpl
dough'boy' s fantaccino americano
dough'nut' s ciambella; (with filling) sgonfiotto
dough-ty ['dauti] adj (-tier; -tiest) forte, coraggioso
dough-y ['do·i] adj (-ier; -iest) pastoso, molle
dour [daur] or [dur] adj triste, severo
douse [daus] tr immergere; bagnare; (the light) (coll) spegnere
dove [dʌv] s colomba, tortora
dovecote ['dʌv ,kot] s piccionaia
dove'tail' s coda di rondine || tr calettare a coda di rondine; (to make fit) adattare, far combaciare || intr (to fit) combaciare; corrispondere
dowager ['dau·ədʒər] s vedova titolata; vecchia signora austera; **queen dowager** regina madre
dow·dy ['daudi] adj (-dier; -diest) trasandato

dow·el ['dau·əl] *s* caviglia, tassello ‖ *v* (*pret & pp* **-eled** or **-elled**; *ger* **-eling** or **-elling**) *tr* tassellare

dower ['dau·ər] *s* (*widow's portion*) legittima, vedovile *m*; (*marriage portion; natural gift*) dote *f* ‖ *tr* dotare; assegnare un vedovile a

down [daun] *adj* che discende; basso; (*train*) che va al centro; depresso; finito; (*money, payment*) anticipato; (*storage battery*) esaurito ‖ *s* (*of fruit and human body*) lanugine *f*; (*of birds*) piumino; (*upset*) rovescio; discesa; (*sandhill*) duna ‖ *adv* giù; all'ingiù, in giù; dabbasso; a terra; al sud; (*in cash*) a contanti; **down and out** rovinato; senza una soldo; **down from** da; **down on one's knees** in ginocchio; **down to** fino a; **down under** agli antipodi; **down with . . . !** abasso . . . !; **to get down to work** mettersi seriamente al lavoro; **to go down** scendere; **to lie down** sdraiarsi; andare a letto; **to sit down** sedersi ‖ *prep* giù per; **down the river** a valle; **down the street** giù per la strada ‖ *tr* abbattere; (coll) buttar giù, tracannare

down'cast' *adj* mogio, sfiduciato

down'fall' *s* rovina, rovescio

down'grade' *adj & adv* in declivio, a valle ‖ *s* discesa; **to be on the downgrade** essere in declino ‖ *tr* attribuire minor importanza a; degradare

downhearted ['daun¸hɑrtɪd] *adj* scoraggiato, abbattuto

down'hill' *adj & adv* in declivio; **to go downhill** declinare

down' pay'ment *s* acconto

down'pour' *s* acquazzone *m*, rovescio

down'right' *adj* assoluto; completo; franco, diretto ‖ *adv* completamente

down'stairs' *adj* del piano di sotto ‖ *s* il piano di sotto; i piani di sotto ‖ *adv* dabbasso, di sotto, giù

down'stream' *adv* a valle

down'stroke' *s* corsa discendente

down'town' *adj* centrale ‖ *s* centro della città ‖ *adv* al centro della città

down' train' *s* treno discendente, treno che va al centro

down'trend' *s* tendenza al ribasso

downtrodden ['daun¸trɑdən] *adj* calpestato, oppresso

downward ['daunwərd] *adj & adv* all'ingiù

down·y ['dauni] *adj* (**-ier; -iest**) piumoso, lanuginoso; (*soft*) molle, morbido

dow·ry ['dauri] *s* (**-ries**) dote *f*

doze [doz] *s* pisolo ‖ *intr* dormicchiare; **to doze off** appisolarsi

dozen ['dʌzən] *s* dozzina

dozy ['dozi] *adj* sonnolento

drab [dræb] *adj* (**drabber; drabbest**) grigiastro; (*dull*) scialbo ‖ *s* colore grigiastro; (*fabric*) tela naturale; donna di malaffare

drach·ma ['drækmə] *s* (**-mas** or **-mae** [mi]) dramma

draft [dræft] or [drɑft] *s* corrente *f* d'aria; (*pulling*) tiro; (*in a chimney*)

tiraggio; (*sketch, outline*) schizzo; (*first form of a writing*) prima stesura; (*drink*) sorso, bicchiere *m*; (com) tratta, lettera di credito; (law) progetto, disegno; (naut) pesca; (mil) coscrizione *f*, leva; **on draft** alla spina ‖ *tr* disegnare; fare uno schizzo di; (*a document*) stendere; (mil) coscrivere; **to be drafted** essere di leva, andar coscritto

draft' age' *s* età *f* di leva

draft' beer' *s* birra alla spina

draft' board' *s* consiglio di leva

draft' dodg'er ['dadʒər] *s* renitente *m* alla leva, imboscato

draftee [¸dræf'ti] or [¸drɑf'ti] *s* coscritto

draft' horse' *s* cavallo da tiro

drafts'man *s* (**-men**) disegnatore *m*; (*man who draws up documents*) redattore *m*

draft' trea'ty *s* progetto di trattato

draft·y ['dræfti] or ['drɑfti] *adj* (**-ier; -iest**) pieno di correnti d'aria

drag [dræg] *s* (*sledge for conveying heavy bodies*) traino, treggia; (*on a cigarette*) boccata; (aer) resistenza aerodinamica; (naut) draga; (fig) noia; (*influence*) (slang) aderenze *fpl*; (*a bore*) (slang) rompiscatole *m* ‖ *v* (*pret & pp* **dragged**; *ger* **dragging**) *tr* strascinare, strascicare; (naut) rastrellare ‖ *intr* strascicare, strascicarsi; dilungarsi; **to drag on** andare per le lunghe

drag'net' *s* paranza; (fig) retata

dragon ['drægən] *s* drago, dragone *m*

drag'on-fly' *s* (**-flies**) libellula

dragoon [drə'gun] *s* (mil) dragone *m* ‖ *tr* forzare, costringere

drain [dren] *s* scolo; prosciugamento; (geog) spiovente *m*; (surg) drenaggio; (fig) salasso ‖ *tr* (*a liquid*) scolare; prosciugare; (*humid land; a wound*) drenare ‖ *intr* scolare; prosciugarsi; (geog) defluire

drainage ['drenɪdʒ] *s* drenaggio; (geog) displuvio, spartiacque *m*

drain'board' *s* scolatoio per le stoviglie

drain' cock' *s* rubinetto di scarico

drain'pipe' *s* tubo di scarico

drake [drek] *s* anatra maschio

dram [dræm] *s* dramma; bicchierino di liquore

drama ['drɑmə] or ['dræmə] *s* dramma *m*; (*art and genre*) drammatica

dramatic [drə'mætɪk] *adj* drammatico ‖ **dramatics** *ssg* drammatica; *spl* rappresentazione dilettantesca; comportamento drammatico

dramatist ['dræmətɪst] *s* drammaturgo

dramatize ['dræmə¸taɪz] *tr* drammatizzare

drape [drep] *s* tenda, cortina; (*of a curtain*) drappeggio; (*of a skirt*) taglio ‖ *tr* drappeggiare

draper·y ['drepəri] *s* (**-ies**) drapperia; negozio di tessuti; **draperies** tendaggi *mpl*

drastic ['dræstɪk] *adj* drastico

draught [dræft] or [drɑft] *s* & *tr* var of **draft**

draught' beer' *s* birra alla spina

draw [drɔ] *s* (*in a game*) patta; (*in a lottery*) sorteggio; (*act of drawing*) tiro; (*of chimney*) tiraggio; (*attraction*) attrazione; (*of a drawbridge*) ala || *v* (*pret* **drew** [dru]; *pp* **drawn** [drɔn]) *tr* (*a line*) tirare; (*to attract*) richiamare; (*butter*) fondere; (*a sword*) sguainare; (*a nail*) estrarre; (*people*) attrarre; (*a sigh*) emettere; (*a curtain*) far scorrere; (*a salary*) pigliare; (*a prize*) ricevere; (*a game*) impattare; (*in card games*) pescare; (*a drawbridge*) sollevare; (*said of a ship*) pescare; (*a comparison*) fare; (*a profit*) ricavare; (*a chicken*) sventrare; (*e.g., a picture*) disegnare, ritrarre; (*to sketch in words*) descrivere; (*a contract*) stipulare; (*interest*) ricevere; (com) spiccare, staccare; **to draw forth** far uscire; **to draw off** estrarre; (*a liquid*) spillare; **to draw** (*shoes*) on mettersi; **to draw** (*money*) **on** ritirare da; **to draw** (*a draft*) **on** domiciliare presso; **to draw oneself up** raddrizzarsi; **to draw out** (*to persuade to talk*) far parlare, tirar fuori le parole a; **to draw up** (*a document*) estendere; (mil) schierare || *intr* (*said of chimney*) tirare; impattare; sorteggiare un premio; aver attrazione; disegnare; **to draw aside** scostarsi; **to draw back** retrocedere, ritirarsi; **to draw near** avvicinarsi; volgere a; **to draw to a close** essere quasi finito; **to draw together** unirsi

draw'back' *s* inconveniente *m*

draw'bridge' *s* ponte levatoio

drawee [‚drɔ'i] *s* trattario, trassato

drawer [‚drɔ·ər] *s* disegnatore *m*; (com) traente *m* || [drɔr] *s* cassetto; **drawers** mutande *fpl*

drawing [‚drɔ·ɪŋ] *s* disegno; (*in a lottery*) sorteggio

draw'ing board' *s* tavolo da disegno

draw'ing card' *s* attrazione

draw'ing room' *s* salotto, salottino

draw'knife' *s* (-**knives** [‚naɪvz]) coltello a petto

drawl [drɔl] *s* accento strascicato || *tr* dire con accento strascicato || *intr* strascicare le parole

drawn' but'ter *s* burro fuso

drawn' work' *s* lavoro a giorno

dray [dre] *s* carro pesante; slitta, treggia; autocarro

drayage [‚dre·ɪdʒ] *s* carreggio

dray'man *s* (-**men**) carrettiere *m*

dread [drɛd] *adj* spaventoso, terribile || *s* spavento, terrore *m* || *tr* & *intr* temere

dreadful [‚drɛdfəl] *adj* spaventevole, terribile; (coll) orribile

dread'nought' *s* corazzata

dream [drim] *s* sogno; illusione, fantasticheria; **dream come true** sogno fatto realtà || *v* (*pret* & *pp* **dreamed** or **dreamt** [drɛmt]) *tr* sognare; **to dream up** (coll) immaginare, fantasticare || *intr* sognare

dreamer [‚drimər] *s* sognatore *m*

dream'land' *s* paese *m* dei sogni

dream·y [‚drimi] *adj* (-**ier**; -**iest**) sognante; (*visionary*) trasognato; vago

drear·y [‚drɪri] *adj* (-**ier**; -**iest**) squallido; triste; (*boring*) noioso

dredge [drɛdʒ] *s* draga || *tr* dragare; (culin) infarinare

dredger [‚drɛdʒər] *s* (*boat*) draga; (*container*) spolverino

dredging [‚drɛdʒɪŋ] *s* dragaggio

dregs [drɛgz] *spl* feccia

drench [drɛntʃ] *tr* infradiciare, inzuppare

dress [drɛs] *s* vestito; vestiti *mpl*; vestito da donna; abito; abito da cerimonia; (*of a bird*) piumaggio || *tr* vestire; adornare, decorare; (*hair*) pettinare; (*a wound*) medicare; (*leather*) conciare; (*food*) condire; (*a boat*) pavesare; **to dress down** (coll) rimproverare; **to get dressed** vestirsi || *intr* vestire; vestirsi; (mil) schierarsi; **to dress up** vestirsi da sera; farsi bello, mettersi in gala

dress' ball' *s* ballo di gala

dress' coat' *s* frac *m*

dresser [‚drɛsər] *s* toletta; (*sideboard*) credenza; **to be a good dresser** vestire con eleganza

dress' goods' *spl* stoffa per abiti

dressing [‚drɛsɪŋ] *s* ornamento; (*for food*) condimento, salsa; (*stuffing for fowl*) ripieno; (*fertilizer*) concime *m*; (*for a wound*) medicazione

dress'ing-down' *s* ramanzina

dress'ing gown' *s* vestaglia

dress'ing room' *s* spogliatoio, toletta; (theat) camerino

dress'ing sta'tion *s* posto di pronto soccorso

dress'ing ta'ble *s* toletta, specchiera

dress'mak'er *s* sarta, sarto per donna

dress'mak'ing *s* taglio, sartoria

dress' rehears'al *s* prova generale

dress' shirt' *s* camicia inamidata

dress' suit' *s* marsina

dress' u'niform *s* (mil) alta uniforme

dress·y [‚drɛsi] *adj* (-**ier**; **iest**) (coll) elegante, ricercato

dribble [‚drɪbəl] *s* goccia || *tr* (sports) palleggiare, dribblare || *intr* gocciolare; (*at the mouth*) sbavare; (sports) dribblare

driblet [‚drɪblɪt] *s* piccola quantità; **in driblets** col contagoccia

dried' beef' [draɪd] *s* carne seccata

dried' fruit' *s* frutta secca

drier [‚draɪ·ər] *s* (*for hair*) asciugacapelli *m*; (*for clothes*) asciugatrice *f*

drift [drɪft] *s* movimento; (*of sand, snow, etc.*) cumulo; (*snowdrift*) neve accumulata dal vento; tendenza, corrente *f*; intenzione; (aer, naut) deriva; (rad, telv) deviazione || *intr* andare alla deriva; (*said of snow*) accumularsi; (aer, naut) derivare, scadere

drift' ice' *s* ghiaccio alla deriva

drift'pin' *s* (mach) mandrino

drift'wood' *s* legname andato alla deriva

drill [drɪl] s esercizio; (*fabric*) tela cruda; (agr) seminatrice *f*; (mach) trapano, trivella; (mil) esercitazioni *fpl* militari ‖ *tr* trivellare; istruire; (mil) insegnare gli esercizi militari a ‖ *intr* addestrarsi; (mil) fare gli esercizi militari

drill'mas'ter s istruttore *m*

drill' press' s trapano a colonna

drink [drɪŋk] s bevanda; the drinks are on the house! paga il proprietario! ‖ *v* (*pret* **drank** [dræŋk]; *pp* **drunk** [drʌŋk]) *tr* bere; assorbire; **to drink down** tracannare; **to drink in** bere, assorbire; (*air*) aspirare ‖ *intr* bere; **to drink out of** bere da; **to drink to the health of** bere alla salute di

drinkable ['drɪŋkəbəl] *adj* bevibile, potabile

drinker ['drɪŋkər] s bevitore *m*

drinking ['drɪŋkɪŋ] s (il) bere

drink'ing foun'tain s fontanella pubblica

drink'ing song' s canzone bacchica

drink'ing straw' s cannuccia

drink'ing trough' s abbeveratoio

drink'ing wa'ter s acqua potabile

drip [drɪp] s sgocciolo, sgocciolatura ‖ *v* (*pret & pp* **dripped**) *ger* **dripping**) *intr* sgocciolare, stillare; (*said of perspiration*) trasudare

drip' cof'fee s caffè fatto con la macchinetta

drip'-dry' *adj* non-stiro

drip' pan' s (culin) ghiotta; (mach) coppa

dripping ['drɪpɪŋ] s gocciolio; **drippings** grasso che cola dall'arrosto

drive [draɪv] s scarrozzata; strada; passeggiata; impulso; forza, iniziativa; urgenza; spinta; campagna; (aut) trazione; (mach) trasmissione ‖ *v* (*pret* **drove** [drov]; *ger* **driven** ['drɪvən]) *tr* (a *nail*) ficcare, piantare; (*e.g., cattle*) condurre, menare; (*s.o. in a carriage or auto*) condurre, portare; spingere; stimulare; forzare; spingere a lavorare; (sports) colpire molto forte; **to drive away** scacciare; **to drive back** respingere; **to drive mad** far impazzire; **to drive out** scacciare ‖ *intr* fare una scarrozzata; **to drive at** parare a; voler dire; **to drive hard** lavorare sodo; **to drive in** entrare in automobile; (a *place*) entrare in automobile in; **to drive on the right** guidare a destra; **to drive out** uscire in macchina; **to drive up** arrivare in macchina

drive'-in' mov'ie the'ater s cineparco

drive'-in' res'taurant s ristorante *m* con servizio alla portiera

driv•el ['drɪvəl] s (*slobber*) bava; (*nonsense*) scemenza ‖ *v* (*pret* **-eled** or **-elled**; *ger* **-eling** or **-elling**) *intr* sbavare; dire scemenze

driver ['draɪvər] s guidatore *m*; (of a *carriage*) cocchiere *m*; (of a *locomotive*) macchinista *m*; (of *pack animals*) carrettiere *m*, mulattiere *m*

driv'er's li'cense s patente automobilistica

driv'er's seat' s posto di guida

drive' shaft' s albero motore

drive'way' s strada privata d'accesso; carrozzabile *f*

drive' wheel' s ruota motrice

driv'ing school' ['draɪvɪŋ] s autoscuola, scuola guida

drizzle ['drɪzəl] s pioviggine *f* ‖ *intr* pioviginare

droll [drol] *adj* buffo, spassoso

dromedar•y ['drɑmə,deri] s (**-ies**) dromedario

drone [dron] s fuco, pecchione *m*; (*hum*) ronzio; (of *bagpipe*) bordone *m*; areoplano teleguidato ‖ *tr* dire in tono monotono ‖ *intr* (*to live in idleness*) fare il fannullone; (*to buzz, hum*) ronzare

drool [drul] s (*slobber*) bava; (slang) scemenza ‖ *intr* sbavare; (slang) dire scemenze

droop [drup] s accasciamento ‖ *intr* (*to sag*) pendere; (*to lose spirit*) accasciarsi; (*said, e.g., of wheat*) avvizzire

drooping ['drupɪŋ] *adj* (*eyelid*) abbassato; (*shoulder*) spiovente; (fig) accasciato

drop [drɑp] s goccia; (*slope*) pendenza; (*earring*) pendente *m*; (in *temperature*) discesa; (*from an airplane*) lancio; (*trap door*) botola; (*gallows*) trabocchetto della forca; (*lozenge*) pastiglia; (*slit for letters*) buca; (*curtain*) tela; (in *prices*) calo; **a drop in the bucket** una goccia nell'oceano ‖ *v* (*pret & pp* **dropped**; *ger* **dropping**) *tr* lasciar cadere; (a *letter*) imbucare; (a *curtain*) abbassare; (a *remark*) lasciar scappare; (a *note*) scrivere; omettere; abbandonare; (*anchor*) gettare; (*from an airplane*) lanciare; (*from an automobile*) lasciare; (*from a list*) cancellare ‖ *intr* cadere; lasciarsi cadere; terminare; **to drop dead** cader morto; **to drop in** entrare un momento; **to drop off** sparire; addormentarsi; morire improvvisamente; **to drop out** scomparire; ritirarsi; dare le dimissioni

drop' cur'tain s telone *m*

drop' ham'mer s maglio

drop'-leaf' ta'ble s tavola a ribalta

drop'light' s lampada sospesa

drop'out' s studente *m* che abbandona permanentemente la scuola media

dropper ['drɑpər] s contagocce *m*

dropsical ['drɑpsɪkəl] *adj* idropico

dropsy ['drɑpsi] s idropisia

dross [drɔs] or [drɑs] s scoria; (fig) feccia

drought [draut] s siccità *f*; (*shortage*) mancanza

drove [drov] s branco; folla; **in droves** in massa

drover ['drovər] s mandriano

drown [draun] *tr & intr* affogare, annegare

drowse [drauz] *intr* sonnecchiare

drow•sy ['drauzi] *adj* (**-sier; -siest**) sonnolento, insonnolito

drub [drʌb] *v* (*pret & pp* **drubbed**; *ger* **drubbing**) *tr* bastonare; battere

drudge [drʌdʒ] *s* sgobbone *m* || *intr* sgobbare, sfacchinare

drudger·y [ˈdrʌdʒərɪ] *s* (-ies) lavoro ingrato, sfacchinata

drug [drʌg] *s* droga, medicina; narcotico; **drug on the market** merce *f* invendibile || *v* (*pret* & *pp* **drugged;** *ger* **drugging**) *tr* drogare, narcotizzare

drug' ad'dict *s* tossicomane *mf*

drug' addic'tion *s* tossicomania

druggist [ˈdrʌgɪst] *s* farmacista *mf*

drug' hab'it *s* tossicomania

drug'store' *s* farmacia

drug' traf'fic *s* traffico in stupefacenti

druid [ˈdruːɪd] *s* druida *m*

drum [drʌm] *s* (*cylinder; instrument*) tamburo; (*container*) fusto || *v* (*pret* & *pp* **drummed;** *ger* **drumming**) *tr* stamburare; **to drum up** (*customers*) farsi; (*enthusiasm*) creare || *intr* tambureggiare; (*with the fingers*) tamburellare

drum'beat' *s* rullo di tamburi

drum' corps' *s* banda di tamburi

drum'fire' *s* fuoco nutrito

drum'head' *s* membrana del tamburo

drum' ma'jor *s* tamburo maggiore

drummer [ˈdrʌmər] *s* (*salesman*) agente *m* viaggiatore; (*mus*) tamburo; (*mil*) tamburino

drum'stick' *s* bacchetta del tamburo; (*of cooked fowl*) coscia

drunk [drʌŋk] *adj* ubriaco; **to get drunk** ubriacarsi || *s* ubriaco; (*spree*) sbornia; **to go on a drunk** (coll) ubriacarsi

drunkard [ˈdrʌŋkərd] *s* ubriacone *m*

drunken [ˈdrʌŋkən] *adj* ubriaco

drunk'en driv'ing *s*—**to be arrested for drunken driving** esser arrestato per aver guidato in stato di ubriachezza

drunkenness [ˈdrʌŋkənnɪs] *s* ubriachezza, ebbrezza

dry [draɪ] *adj* (**drier; driest**) secco; (*boring*) arido; **to be dry** aver sete || *s* (**drys**) abolizionista *mf* || *v* (*pret* & *pp* **dried**) *tr* seccare; (*to wipe dry*) asciugare || *intr* seccarsi; **to dry up** prosciugarsi, essiccarsi; (slang) star zitto

dry' bat'tery *s* pila a secco; (*group of dry cells*) batteria a secco

dry' cell' *s* pila a secco

dry'-clean' *tr* lavare a secco, pulire a secco

dry' clean'er *s* tintore *m*

dry' clean'ing *s* lavaggio a secco, pulitura a secco

dry'-clean'ing estab'lishment *s* tintoria

dry' dock' *s* bacino di carenaggio

dryer [ˈdraɪər] *s* var of **drier**

dry'-eyed' *adj* a occhi asciutti

dry' farm'ing *s* coltivazione di terreno arido

dry' goods' *spl* tessuti *mpl*; aridi *mpl*

dry'-goods store' *s* drapperia, negozio di tessuti

dry' ice' *s* neve carbonica, ghiaccio secco

dry' law' *s* legge *f* proibizionista

dry' meas'ure *s* misura per solidi

dryness [ˈdraɪnɪs] *s* siccità *f*; (*e.g., of a speaker*) aridità *f*

dry' nurse' *s* balia asciutta

dry' run' *s* esercizio di prova; (mil) esercitazione senza munizioni

dry' sea'son *s* stagione arida

dry' wash' *s* roba lavata e asciugata ma non stirata

dual [ˈdjuːəl] or [ˈduːəl] *adj* & *s* duale *m*

duali·ty [djuˈælɪtɪ] or [duˈælɪtɪ] *s* (-ties) dualità *f*

dub [dʌb] *s* (slang) giocatore inesperto || *v* (*pret* & *pp* **dubbed;** *ger* **dubbing**) *tr* chiamare, affibbiare il nome di; (*a knight*) armare; (mov) doppiare

dubbing [ˈdʌbɪŋ] *s* doppiaggio

dubious [ˈdjuːbɪ·əs] or [ˈduːbɪ·əs] *adj* dubbioso; incerto

ducat [ˈdʌkət] *s* ducato

duchess [ˈdʌtʃɪs] *s* duchessa

duch·y [ˈdʌtʃɪ] *s* (-ies) ducato

duck [dʌk] *s* anatra; mossa rapida; (*in the water*) tuffo; (*dodge*) schivata; **ducks** pantaloni *mpl* di tela cruda || *tr* (*one's head*) abbassare rapidamente; (*in water*) tuffare; (*a blow*) schivare || *intr* tuffarsi; **to duck out** (coll) svignarsela

duckling [ˈdʌklɪŋ] *s* anatroccolo

ducks' and drakes' *s*—**to play ducks and drakes with** buttar via, sperperare

duck' soup' *s* (slang) cosa facilissima

duct [dʌkt] *s* tubo, condotto

ductile [ˈdʌktɪl] *adj* duttile

duct'less gland' [ˈdʌktlɪs] *s* ghiandola a secrezione interna

duct'work' *s* condotto, canalizzazione

dud [dʌd] *s* (slang) bomba inesplosa; (*person*) (slang) fallito; (*enterprise*) (slang) fallimento; **duds** (coll) vestito; roba

dude [djud] or [dud] *s* elegantone *m*

due [dju] or [du] *adj* dovuto; atteso, debito; pagabile; **due to** dovuto a; **to fall due** scadere; **when is the train due?** a che ora arriva il treno? || *s* spettanza; debito; **dues** (*of a member*) quota sociale; **to get one's due** ricevere quanto uno merita; **to give the devil his due** trattare ognuno con giustizia || *adv* in direzione, e.g., **due north** in direzione nord

duel [ˈdjuːəl] or [ˈduːəl] *s* duello; **to fight a duel** battersi a duello || *v* (*pret* & *pp* **dueled** or **duelled;** *ger* **dueling** or **duelling**) *intr* duellare

duelist or **duellist** [ˈdjuːəlɪst] or [ˈduːəlɪst] *s* duellante *mf*

dues-paying [ˈdjuz ˌpeɪɪŋ] or [ˈduz ˌpeɪɪŋ] *adj* regolare, effettivo

duet [djuˈɛt] or [duˈɛt] *s* duetto

duf'fel bag' [ˈdʌfəl] *s* sacca da viaggio

duke [djuk] or [duk] *s* duca *m*

dukedom [ˈdjukdəm] or [ˈdukdəm] *s* ducato

dull [dʌl] *adj* (*not sharp*) spuntato, senza filo; (*color*) spento, sbiadito; (*sound, pain*) sordo; (*stupid*) ebete, tonto; (*business*) inattivo; (*boring*) noioso, melenso; (*flat*) opaco, appannato || *tr* spuntare; sbiadire; inebetire; ottundere; (*enthusiasm*) raffreddare; (*pain*) alleviare || *intr* spuntarsi; sbiadirsi; inebetirsi; raffreddarsi

dullard ['dʌlərd] s stupido

duly ['djuli] or ['duli] adv debitamente

dumb [dʌm] adj (lacking the power to speak) muto; (coll) tonto, stupido

dumb′bell′ s manubrio; (slang) zuccone m, stupido

dumb′ crea′ture s animale m, bruto

dumb′ show′ s pantomima

dumb′wai′ter s montavivande m

dumfound [,dʌm'faund] tr interdire, lasciare esterrefatto

dum·my ['dʌmi] adj copiato; falso || s (-mies) (dress form) manichino; (in card games) morto; (figurehead) uomo di paglia, prestanome m; (skeleton copy of a book) menabò m; copia; (slang) stupido, tonto

dump [dʌmp] s immondezzaio; mucchio di spazzature; (mil) deposito munizioni; (min) montagnetta di scarico; **to be down in the dumps** (coll) avere le paturnie || tr scaricare; (to tip over) rovesciare; (com) scaricare sul mercato; (com) vendere sottocosto

dumping ['dʌmpɪŋ] s scarico; (com) dumping m

dumpling ['dʌmplɪŋ] s gnocco

dump′ truck′ s ribaltabile m

dump·y ['dʌmpi] adj (-ier; -iest) grassoccio, tarchiato

dun [dʌn] adj bruno grigiastro || s creditore importuno; (demand for payment) sollecitazione di pagamento || v (pret & pp dunned; ger dunning) tr sollecitare

dunce [dʌns] s ignorante mf, zuccone m

dunce′ cap′ s berretto d'asino

dune [djun] or [dun] s duna

dung [dʌŋ] s sterco, letame m || tr concimare con il letame

dungarees [,dʌŋɡə'riz] spl tuta di cotone blu

dungeon ['dʌndʒən] s carcere sotterraneo; (fortified tower) torrione m, maschio

dung′hill′ s letamaio

dunk [dʌŋk] tr inzuppare

du·o ['dju·o] or ['du·o] s (-os) duo

duode·num [,dju·ə'dinəm] or [,du·ə-'dinəm] s (-na [nə]) duodeno

dupe [djup] or [dup] s gonzo || tr gabbare, ingannare

du′plex house′ ['djuplɛks] or ['dupleks] s casa di due appartamenti

duplicate ['djuplɪkɪt] or ['duplɪkɪt] adj & s duplicato || ['djuplɪˌket] or ['duplɪˌket] tr duplicare

du′plicating machine′ s duplicatore m

duplici·ty [dju'plɪsɪti] or [du'plɪsɪti] s (-ties) duplicità f, doppiezza

durable ['djurəbəl] or ['durəbəl] adj durabile, duraturo

du′rable goods′ spl beni mpl durevoli

duration [dju're∫ən] or [du're∫ən] s durata

during ['djurɪŋ] or ['durɪŋ] prep durante

du′rum wheat′ ['durəm] or ['djurəm] s grano duro

dusk [dʌsk] s crepuscolo

dust [dʌst] s polvere f || tr (to free of dust) spolverare; (to sprinkle with dust) spolverizzare; **to dust off** (slang) rimettere in uso; (slang) spolverare le spalle a

dust′ bowl′ s regione polverosissima

dust′cloth′ s strofinaccio

dust′ cloud′ s polverone m

duster ['dʌstər] s (cloth) cencio; (light overgarment) spolverino

dust′ jack′et s sopraccoperta

dust′pan′ s pattumiera

dust′ rag′ s strofinaccio

dust·y ['dʌsti] adj (-ier; -iest) polveroso; grigiastro

Dutch [dʌt∫] adj olandese; (slang) tedesco || s (language) olandese m; (language) (slang) tedesco; **in Dutch** (slang) in disgrazia; (slang) nei pasticci; **the Dutch** gli olandesi; (slang) i tedeschi; **to go Dutch** (coll) pagare alla romana

Dutch′man s (-men) olandese m; (slang) tedesco

Dutch′ treat′ s invito alla romana

dutiable ['djutɪəbəl] or ['dutɪəbəl] adj soggetto a dogana

dutiful ['djutɪfəl] or ['dutɪfəl] adj obbediente, doveroso

du·ty ['djuti] or ['duti] s (-ties) dovere m; (task) funzione; dazio, dogana; **off duty** libero; in libera uscita; **on duty** in servizio; di guardia; **to do one's duty** fare il proprio dovere; **to take up one's duties** entrare in servizio

du′ty-free′ adj esente da dogana

dwarf [dwɔrf] adj & s nano || tr rimpiccolire || intr rimpiccolire; apparire più piccolo

dwarfish ['dwɔrfɪ∫] adj nano, da nano

dwell [dwel] v (pret & pp dwelled or dwelt [dwelt]) intr dimorare, abitare; **to dwell on** or **upon** intrattenersi su

dwelling ['dwelɪŋ] s abitazione, residenza

dwell′ing house′ s casa d'abitazione

dwindle ['dwɪndəl] intr diminuire; restringersi, consumarsi

dye [daɪ] s tinta, colore m || v (pret & pp dyed; ger dyeing) tr tingere

dyed-in-the-wool ['daɪdɪnðə,wul] adj tinto prima della tessitura; completo, intransigente

dyeing ['daɪ·ɪŋ] s tintura

dyer ['daɪ·ər] s tintore m

dye′stuff′ s tintura, materia colorante

dying ['daɪ·ɪŋ] adj morente

dynamic [daɪ'næmɪk] or [dɪ'næmɪk] adj dinamico

dynamite ['daɪnə,maɪt] s dinamite f || tr far saltare con la dinamite

dyna·mo ['daɪnə,mo] s (-mos) dinamo f

dynast ['daɪnæst] s dinasta m

dynas·ty ['daɪnæsti] s (-ties) dinastia

dysentery ['dɪsən,teri] s dissenteria

dyspepsia [dɪs'pɛpsɪ·ə] or [dɪs'pɛp/ə] s dispepsia

E

E, e [i] *s* quinta lettera dell'alfabeto inglese

each [it/] *adj indef* ogni ‖ *pron indef* ognuno, ciascuno; **each other** ci; vi; si; l'un l'altro ‖ *adv* l'uno; a testa

eager ['igər] *adj* (*enthusiastic*) ardente; **eager for** avido di; **eager to** + *inf* desideroso di + *inf*

ea'ger bea'ver *s* zelante *mf*

eagerness ['igərnis] *s* ardore *m;* brama

eagle ['igəl] *s* aquila

ea'gle owl' *s* gufo reale

eaglet ['iglit] *s* aquilotto

ear [ir] *s* orecchio; (*of corn*) pannocchia; (*of wheat*) spiga; **to be all ears** essere tutt'orecchi; **to prick up one's ears** tendere l'orecchio; **to turn a deaf ear** far l'orecchio da mercante

ear'ache' *s* mal *m* d'orecchi

ear'drop' *s* pendente *m*

ear'drum' *s* timpano

ear'flap' *s* paraorecchi *m*

earl [ʌrl] *s* conte *m*

earldom ['ʌrldəm] *s* contea

ear•ly ['ʌrli] (**-lier; -liest**) *adj* (*occurring before customary time*) di buon'ora; (*first in a series*) primo; (*far back in time*) remoto, antico; (*occurring in near future*) prossimo ‖ *adv* presto; per tempo, di buon'ora; **as early as** (*a certain time of day*) già a; (*a certain time or date*) fin da, già in; **as early as possible** quanto prima possibile; **early in** (*e.g., the month*) all'inizio di; **early in the morning** di mattina presto, di buon mattino; **early in the year** all'inizio dell'anno

ear'ly bird' *s* persona mattiniera

ear'ly mass' *s* prima messa

ear'ly ris'er *s* persona mattiniera

ear'mark' *s* contrassegno ‖ *tr* contrassegnare; assegnare a scopo speciale

ear'muff' *s* paraorecchi *m*

earn [ʌrn] *tr* guadagnare, guadagnarsi; (*to get one's due*) meritarsi; (*interest*) (com) produrre ‖ *intr* trarre profitto, rendere

earnest ['ʌrnist] *adj* serio; fervente; **in earnest** sul serio ‖ *s* caparra

ear'nest mon'ey *s* caparra

earnings ['ʌrniŋz] *s* guadagno; salario

ear'phone' *s* (*of sonar*) orecchiale *m;* (rad, telp) cuffia

ear'piece' *s* (*of eyeglasses*) susta; (telp) ricevitore *m*

ear'ring' *s* orecchino

ear'shot' *s* tiro dell'orecchio; **within earshot** a portata di voce

ear'split'ting *adj* assordante

earth [ʌrθ] *s* terra; **to come back to or down to earth** scendere dalle nuvole

earthen ['ʌrθən] *adj* di terra; di terracotta

ear'then•ware' *s* coccio, terraglie *fpl,* terracotta

earthling ['ʌrθliŋ] *s* terrestre *mf*

earthly ['ʌrθli] *adj* terreno, terrestre;

to be of no earthly use non servire assolutamente a niente

earthmover ['ʌrθ,muvər] *s* ruspa

earth'quake' *s* terremoto

earth'work' *s* terrapieno

earth'worm' *s* lombrico

earth•y ['ʌrθi] *adj* (**-ier; -iest**) terroso; (*coarse*) rozzo; pratico; sincero, diretto

ear' trum'pet *s* corno acustico

ear'wax' *s* cerume *m*

ease [iz] *s* facilità *f;* (*naturalness*) spigliatezza, disinvoltura; (*comfort*) benestare *m;* tranquillità *f;* **at ease!** (mil) riposo!; **with ease** con facilità ‖ *tr* facilitare; (*a burden*) alleggerire; (*to let up on*) rallentare; mitigare; **to ease out** licenziare con le buone maniere ‖ *intr* alleviarsi, mitigarsi, diminuire; rallentare

easel ['izəl] *s* cavalletto

easement ['izmənt] *s* attenuamento; (law) servitù *f*

easily ['izili] *adv* facilmente; senza dubbio; probabilmente

easiness ['izinis] *s* facilità *f;* disinvoltura; grazia, agilità *f;* indifferenza

east [ist] *adj* orientale, dell'est ‖ *s* est *m* ‖ *adv* verso l'est

Easter ['istər] *s* Pasqua

East'er egg' *s* uovo di Pasqua

East'er Mon'day *s* lunedì *m* di Pasqua

eastern ['istərn] *adj* orientale

East'er•tide' *s* tempo pasquale

eastward ['istwərd] *adv* verso l'est

eas•y ['izi] *adj* (**-ier; -iest**) facile; (*conducive to ease*) comodo, agiato; (*free from worry*) tranquillo; (*easygoing*) disinvolto, spigliato; (*not tight*) ampio; (*not hurried*) lento, moderato ‖ *adv* (coll) facilmente; (coll) tranquillamente; **to take it easy** (coll) riposarsi; (coll) non prendersela; (coll) andar piano

eas'y chair' *s* poltrona

eas'y•go'ing *adj* (*person*) comodone; (*horse*) sciolto nell'andatura

eas'y mark' *s* (coll) gonzo

eas'y mon'ey *s* denaro fatto senza fatica; soldi rubati

eas'y terms' *spl* facilitazioni *fpl* di pagamento

eat [it] *v* (*pret* **ate** [et]; *pp* **eaten** ['itən]) *tr* mangiare; **to eat away** smangiare; **to eat up** mangiarsi ‖ *intr* mangiare

eatable ['itəbəl] *adj* mangiabile ‖ **eatables** *spl* commestibili *mpl*

eaves [ivz] *spl* gronda

eaves'drop' *v* (*pret* & *pp* **-dropped;** *ger* **-dropping**) *intr* origliare

ebb [eb] *s* riflusso; decadenza ‖ *intr* (*said of the tide*) ritirarsi; decadere

ebb' and flow' *s* flusso e riflusso

ebb' tide' *s* riflusso, deflusso

ebon•y ['ebəni] *s* (**-ies**) ebano

ebullient [ɪˈbʌljənt] *adj* bollente

eccentric [ekˈsentrɪk] *adj* & *s* eccentrico

eccentrici·ty [ˌɛksən'trɪsɪti] *s* (**-ties**) eccentricità *f*, originalità *f*
ecclesiastic [ɪˌklizɪ'æstɪk] *adj* & *s* ecclesiastico
echelon ['ɛʃəˌlɑn] *s* scaglione *m*; (*mil*) scaglione *m* ‖ *tr* scaglionare
ech·o ['ɛko] *s* (**-oes**) eco *f* ‖ *tr* far eco a ‖ *intr* echeggiare, rieccheggiare
éclair [e'klɛr] *s* dolce ripieno di crema
eclectic [ɛk'lɛktɪk] *adj* & *s* eclettico
eclipse [ɪ'klɪps] *s* eclisse *f*, eclissi *f* ‖ *tr* eclissare
eclogue ['ɛklɔg] *or* ['ɛklɑg] *s* egloga
ecology [ɪ'kɑlədʒi] *s* ecologia
economic(al) [ˌikə'nɑmɪk(əl)] *or* [ˌɛkə'nɑmɪk(əl)] *adj* economico
economics [ˌikə'nɑmɪks] *or* [ˌɛkə'nɑmɪks] *s* economia (politica)
economist [ɪ'kɑnəmɪst] *s* economista *mf*
economize [ɪ'kɑnəˌmaɪz] *tr* & *intr* economizzare
econo·my [ɪ'kɑnəmi] *s* (**-mies**) economia
ecosystem ['ɛkoˌsɪstəm] *s* ecosistema *m*
ecsta·sy ['ɛkstəsi] *s* (**-sies**) estasi *f*
ecstatic [ɛk'stætɪk] *adj* estatico
ecumenic(al) [ˌɛkjə'mɛnɪk(əl)] *adj* ecumenico
eczema ['ɛksɪmə] *or* [ɛg'zimə] *s* eczema *m*
ed·dy ['ɛdi] *s* (**-dies**) turbine *m* ‖ *v* (*pret* & *pp* **-died**) *tr* & *intr* turbinare
edelweiss ['ɛdəlˌvaɪs] *s* stella alpina
edge [ɛdʒ] *s* (*of knife, sword, etc*) filo, tagliente *m*; (*border at which a surface terminates*) orlo, bordo; (*of a wound*) labbro, margine *m*; (*of a book*) taglio; (*of a tumbler*) giro; (*of clothing*) vivagno; (*of a table*) spigolo; (*slang*) vantaggio; **on edge** nervoso; **to have the edge on** (*coll*) avere il vantaggio su; **to set the teeth on edge** far allegare i denti ‖ *tr* affilare, aguzzare; orlare, bordare; **to edge out** riuscire ad eliminare ‖ *intr* avanzare lentamente
edgeways ['ɛdʒˌwez] *adv* di taglio; **to not let s.o. get a word in edgeways** non lasciar dire una parola a qlcu
edging ['ɛdʒɪŋ] *s* orlo, bordo
edg·y ['ɛdʒi] *adj* (**-ier; -iest**) acuto, angolare; nervoso, ansioso
edible ['ɛdɪbəl] *adj* mangereccio, mangiabile ‖ **edibles** *spl* commestibili *mpl*
edict ['idɪkt] *s* editto
edification [ˌɛdɪfɪ'keʃən] *s* edificazione
edifice ['ɛdɪfɪs] *s* edificio
edi·fy ['ɛdɪˌfaɪ] *v* (*pret* & *pp* **-fied**) *tr* edificare
edifying ['ɛdɪˌfaɪ·ɪŋ] *adj* edificante
edit ['ɛdɪt] *tr* redigere; (*e.g., a manuscript*) correggere; (*an edition*) curare; (*a newspaper*) dirigere; (*mov*) montare
edition [ɪ'dɪʃən] *s* edizione
editor ['ɛdɪtər] *s* (*of a newspaper or magazine*) direttore *m*, gerente *mf*; (*of an editorial*) redattore *m*, cronista *mf*; (*of a critical edition*) editore *m*; (*of a manuscript*) revisore *m*

editorial [ˌɛdɪ'torɪ·əl] *adj* editoriale ‖ *s* capocronaca *m*, articolo di fondo
ed'ito'rial staff' *s* redazione
ed'itor in chief' *s* gerente *mf* responsabile
educate ['ɛdʒʊˌket] *tr* educare, erudire
education [ˌɛdʒʊ'keʃən] *s* educazione; istruzione, insegnamento
educational [ˌɛdʒʊ'keʃənəl] *adj* educativo
educa'tional institu'tion *s* istituto di magistero
educator ['ɛdʒʊˌketər] *s* educatore *m*
eel [il] *s* anguilla; **to be as slippery as an eel** guizzare di mano come un'anguilla
ee·rie *or* **ee·ry** ['ɪri] *adj* (**-rier; -riest**) spettrale, pauroso
efface [ɪ'fes] *tr* cancellare; **to efface oneself** eclissarsi, mettersi in disparte
effect [ɪ'fɛkt] *s* effetto; (*main idea*) tenore *m*; **in effect** in vigore; in realtà; **to go into effect** *or* **to take effect** andare in vigore; **to put into effect** mandare ad effetto ‖ *tr* effettuare
effective [ɪ'fɛktɪv] *adj* efficace; (*actually in effect*) effettivo; (*striking*) che colpisce; **to become effective** entrare in vigore
effectual [ɪ'fɛktʃʊ·əl] *adj* efficace
effectuate [ɪ'fɛktʃʊˌet] *tr* effettuare
effeminacy [ɪ'fɛmɪnəsi] *s* effemminatezza
effeminate [ɪ'fɛmɪnɪt] *adj* effemminato
effervesce [ˌɛfər'vɛs] *intr* essere in effervescenza
effervescence [ˌɛfər'vɛsəns] *s* effervescenza
effervescent [ˌɛfər'vɛsənt] *adj* effervescente
effete [ɪ'fit] *adj* esausto, sterile
efficacious [ˌɛfɪ'keʃəs] *adj* efficace
effica·cy [ɛfɪkəsi] *s* (**-cies**) efficacia
efficien·cy [ɪ'fɪʃənsi] *s* (**-cies**) efficienza; (*mech*) rendimento, efficienza
effi'ciency engineer' *s* analista *mf* tempi e metodi
efficient [ɪ'fɪʃənt] *adj* efficiente; (*person*) abile; (*mech*) efficiente
effi·gy ['ɛfɪdʒi] *s* (**-gies**) effigie *f*
effort ['ɛfərt] *s* sforzo
effronter·y [ɪ'frʌntəri] *s* (**-ies**) sfrontatezza, sfacciataggine *f*
effusion [ɪ'fjuʒən] *s* effusione
effusive [ɪ'fjusɪv] *adj* espansivo
egg [ɛg] *s* uovo; (*slang*) bravo ragazzo ‖ *tr*—**to egg on** incitare
egg'beat'er *s* frullino, sbattiuova *m*
egg'cup' *s* portauovo
egg'head' *s* (*coll*) intellettuale *mf*
eggnog ['ɛgˌnɑg] *s* zabaione *m*
egg'plant' *s* melanzana, petonciano
egg'shell' *s* guscio d'uovo
egoism ['ɛgoˌɪzəm] *or* ['igoˌɪzəm] *s* egoismo
egoist ['ɛgo·ɪst] *or* ['igo·ɪst] *s* egoista *mf*
egotism ['ɛgoˌtɪzəm] *or* ['igoˌtɪzəm] *s* egotismo
egotist ['ɛgotɪst] *or* ['igotɪst] *s* egotista *mf*

egregious [ɪˈgridʒəs] *adj* gigantesco, tremendo, marchiano

egress [ˈigres] *s* uscita

Egypt [ˈidʒɪpt] *s* l'Egitto

Egyptian [ɪˈdʒɪpʃən] *adj & s* egiziano

ei′der down′ [ˈaɪdər] *s* piumino

ei′der duck′ *s* edredone *m*

eight [et] *adj, s & pron* otto || *s* otto; **eight o′clock** le otto

eighteen [ˈetˈtin] *adj, s & pron* diciotto

eighteenth [ˈetˈtinθ] *adj, s & pron* diciottesimo || *s (in dates)* diciotto

eighth [etθ] *adj & s* ottavo || *s (in dates)* otto

eight′ hun′dred *adj, s & pron* ottocento

eightieth [ˈetɪ·ɪθ] *adj, s & pron* ottantesimo

eight·y [ˈeti] *adj & pron* ottanta || *s (-ies)* ottanta *m;* **the eighties** gli anni ottanta

either [ˈiðər] *or* [ˈaɪðər] *adj* l'uno o l'altro; l'uno e l'altro; ciascuno; entrambi i, tutti e due || *pron* l'uno o l'altro; l'uno e l'altro; entrambi || *adv*—**not either** nemmeno || *conj*—**either . . . or** o . . . o

ejaculate [ɪˈdʒækjə‚let] *tr* esclamare; (physiol) emettere || *intr* esclamare; (physiol) avere un'eiaculazione

eject [ɪˈdʒɛkt] *tr* espellere, gettar fuori; *(to evict)* sfrattare

ejection [ɪˈdʒɛkʃən] *s* espulsione; *(of a tenant)* sfratto

ejec′tion seat′ *s* sedile *m* eiettabile

eke [ik] *tr*—**to eke out a living** sbarcare il lunario

elaborate [ɪˈlæbərɪt] *adj (done with great care)* elaborato; *(detailed)* minuzioso; *(ornate)* ornato || [ɪˈlæbə‚ret] *tr* elaborare || *intr*—**to elaborate on** *or* **upon** circonstanziare, particolareggiare

elapse [ɪˈlæps] *intr* passare, trascorrere

elastic [ɪˈlæstɪk] *adj & s* elastico

elasticity [ɪ‚læsˈtɪsɪti] *or* [‚ɪlæsˈtɪsɪti] *s* elasticità *f*

elated [ɪˈletɪd] *adj* esultante, gongolante

elation [ɪˈleʃən] *s* esultanza, gaudio

elbow [ˈelbo] *s* gomito; *(in a river)* ansa; *(of a chair)* braccio; **at one's elbow** sotto mano; **out at the elbows** coi gomiti logori; **to crook the elbow** alzare il gomito; **to rub elbows** stare gomito a gomito; **up to the elbows** fino al collo || *tr*—**to elbow one's way** aprirsi il passo a gomitate || *intr* dar gomitate

el′bow grease′ *s* (coll) olio di gomiti

el′bow patch′ *s* toppa al gomito

el′bow rest′ *s* bracciolo

el′bow·room′ *s* spazio sufficiente; libertà *f* d'azione

elder [ˈeldər] *adj* seniore, maggiore || *s* (bot) sambuco; (eccl) maggiore *m*

el′der·ber′ry *s (-ries)* sambuco; *(fruit)* bacca del sambuco

elderly [ˈeldərli] *adj* attempato, anziano

eld′er states′man *s* uomo di stato esperto

eldest [ˈeldɪst] *adj* (il) maggiore; (il) più vecchio

elect [ɪˈlɛkt] *adj & s* eletto; **the elect** gli eletti || *tr* eleggere

election [ɪˈlɛkʃən] *s* elezione

electioneer [ɪ‚lɛkʃəˈnɪr] *intr* fare una campagna elettorale

elective [ɪˈlɛktɪv] *adj* elettivo || *s* corso facoltativo

electorate [ɪˈlɛktərɪt] *s* elettorato

electric(al) [ɪˈlɛktrɪk(əl)] *adj* elettrico

elec′tric blend′er *s* frullatore *m*

elec′tric chair′ *s* sedia elettrica

elec′tric cord′ *s* piattina, filo elettrico

elec′tric eel′ *s* gimnoto

elec′tric eye′ *s* occhio elettrico

electrician [ɪ‚lɛkˈtrɪʃən] *or* [‚ɛlɛkˈtrɪʃən] *s* elettricista *m*

electricity [ɪ‚lɛkˈtrɪsɪti] *or* [‚ɛlɛkˈtrɪsɪti] *s* elettricità *f*

elec′tric me′ter *s* contatore *m* della luce

elec′tric per′cola′tor *s* caffettiera elettrica

elec′tric shav′er *s* rasoio elettrico

elec′tric shock′ *s* scossa elettrica, elettrosquasso

elec′tric tape′ *s* nastro isolante

elec′tric train′ *s* elettrotreno

electri·fy [ɪˈlɛktrɪ‚faɪ] *v (pret & pp -fied) tr (to provide with electric power)* elettrificare; *(to communicate electricity to; to thrill)* elettrizzare

electrocute [ɪˈlɛktrə‚kjut] *tr* fulminare con la corrente; far morire sulla sedia elettrica

electrode [ɪˈlɛktrod] *s* elettrodo

electrolysis [ɪ‚lɛkˈtrɑlɪsɪs] *or* [‚ɛlɛkˈtrɑlɪsɪs] *s* elettrolisi *f*

electrolyte [ɪˈlɛktrə‚laɪt] *s* elettrolito

electromagnet [ɪ‚lɛktrəˈmægnɪt] *s* elettrocalamita

electromagnetic [ɪ‚lɛktrəmægˈnɛtɪk] *adj* elettromagnetico

electromotive [ɪ‚lɛktrəˈmotɪv] *adj* elettromotore

electron [ɪˈlɛktrɑn] *s* elettrone *m*

electronic [ɪ‚lɛkˈtrɑnɪk] *or* [‚ɛlɛkˈtrɑnɪk] *adj* elettronico || **electronics** *s* elettronica

electroplating [ɪˈlɛktrə‚pletɪŋ] *s* galvanostegia

electrostatic [ɪ‚lɛktrəˈstætɪk] *adj* elettrostatico

electrotype [ɪˈlɛktrə‚taɪp] *s* stereotipia || *tr* stereotipare

eleemosynary [‚ɛlɪˈmɑsɪ‚nɛri] *adj* caritatevole, di beneficenza

elegance [ˈɛlɪgəns] *s* eleganza

elegant [ˈɛlɪgənt] *adj* elegante

elegiac [‚ɛlɪˈdʒaɪ‚æk] *adj* elegiaco

ele·gy [ˈɛlɪdʒi] *s (-gies)* elegia

element [ˈɛlɪmənt] *s* elemento; **to be out of one's element** essere fuori del proprio ambiente

elementary [‚ɛlɪˈmɛntəri] *adj* elementare

elephant [ˈɛlɪfənt] *s* elefante *m*

elevate [ˈɛlɪ‚vet] *tr* elevare, innalzare

elevated [ˈɛlɪ‚vetɪd] *adj* elevato || *s* ferrovia soprelevata, metropolitana soprelevata

elevation [‚ɛlɪˈveʃən] *s* elevazione; (surv) quota

elevator [ˈɛlɪ‚vetər] *s* ascensore *m;*

(for freight) montacarichi *m*; *(for hoisting grain)* elevatore *m* di grano; *(warehouse for storing grain)* deposito granaglie; *(aer)* timone *m* di profondità

eleven [ɪˈlɛvən] *adj & pron* undici ‖ *s* undici *m*; **eleven o'clock** le undici

eleventh [ɪˈlɛvənθ] *adj, s & pron* undicesimo ‖ *s* (*in dates*) undici *m*

elev'enth hour' *s* ultimo momento

elf [ɛlf] *s* (**elves** [ɛlvz]) elfo

elicit [ɪˈlɪsɪt] *tr* cavare, sottrarre

elide [ɪˈlaɪd] *tr* elidere

eligible [ˈɛlɪdʒɪbəl] *adj* eleggibile; accettabile

eliminate [ɪˈlɪmɪˌnet] *tr* eliminare

elision [ɪˈlɪʒən] *s* elisione

elite [eˈlit] *adj* eletto, scelto ‖ *s—***the elite** l'élite *f*

elk [ɛlk] *s* alce *m*

ellipse [ɪˈlɪps] *s* (geom) ellisse *f*

ellip·sis [ɪˈlɪpsɪs] *s* (**-ses** [siz]) (gram) ellissi *f*

elliptic(al) [ɪˈlɪptɪk(əl)] *adj* ellittico

elm [ɛlm] *s* olmo

elongate [ɪˈlɔŋget] *or* [ɪˈlɑŋget] *tr* allungare, prolungare

elope [ɪˈlop] *intr* fuggire con un amante

elopement [ɪˈlopmənt] *s* fuga con un amante

eloquence [ˈɛləkwəns] *s* eloquenza

eloquent [ˈɛləkwənt] *adj* eloquente

else [ɛls] *adj—***nobody else** nessun altro; **nothing else** nient'altro; **somebody else** qualcun altro; **something else** qualcosa d'altro; **what else** che altro; **who else** chi altro; **whose else** di che altra persona ‖ *adv—***how else** in che altra maniera; **or else** se no; altrimenti; **when else** in che altro momento; in che altro periodo; **where else** dove mai, da che parte

else'where' *adv* altrove

elucidate [ɪˈlusɪˌdet] *tr* dilucidare

elude [ɪˈlud] *tr* eludere

elusive [ɪˈlusɪv] *adj* elusivo; (*evasive*) fugace, sfuggente

emaciated [ɪˈmeʃɪˌetɪd] *adj* smunto, emaciato, macilento

emanate [ˈɛməˌnet] *tr & intr* emanare

emancipate [ɪˈmænsɪˌpet] *tr* emancipare

embalm [ɛmˈbɑm] *tr* imbalsamare

embankment [ɛmˈbæŋkmənt] *s* terrapieno

embar·go [ɛmˈbɑrgo] *s* (**-goes**) embargo ‖ *tr* mettere l'embargo a

embark [ɛmˈbɑrk] *intr* imbarcarsi

embarkation [ˌɛmbɑrˈkeʃən] *s* imbarco

embarrass [ɛmˈbærəs] *tr* imbarazzare, mettere a disagio; (*to impede*) imbarazzare, impacciare; mettere in difficoltà economiche

embarrassing [ɛmˈbærəsɪŋ] *adj* sconcertante; imbarazzante

embarrassment [ɛmˈbærəsmənt] *s* imbarazzo, disagio, confusione; impaccio; difficoltà finanziaria, dissesto

embas·sy [ˈɛmbəsi] *s* (**-sies**) ambasciata

em·bed [ɛmˈbɛd] *s* (*pret & pp* **-bedded**; *ger* **-bedding**) incastrare, incassare

embellish [ɛmˈbɛlɪʃ] *tr* imbellire

embellishment [ɛmˈbɛlɪʃmənt] *s* abbellimento; (fig) fioretto

ember [ˈɛmbər] *s* brace *f*; **embers** braci *fpl*

Em'ber days' *spl* tempora *fpl*

embezzle [ɛmˈbɛzəl] *tr* appropriare, malversare ‖ *intr* appropriarsi

embezzlement [ɛmˈbɛzəlmənt] *s* appropriazione indebita, malversazione; (*of public funds*) peculato

embezzler [ɛmˈbɛzlər] *s* malversatore *m*

embitter [ɛmˈbɪtər] *tr* amareggiare

emblazon [ɛmˈblezən] *tr* blasonare; celebrare

emblem [ˈɛmbləm] *s* emblema *m*

emblematic(al) [ˌɛmbləˈmætɪk(əl)] *adj* emblematico

embodiment [ɛmˈbɑdɪmənt] *s* incarnazione, personificazione

embod·y [ɛmˈbɑdi] *v* (*pret & pp* **-ied**) *tr* incarnare, personificare; incorporare

embolden [ɛmˈboldən] *tr* imbaldanzire

embolism [ˈɛmbəˌlɪzəm] *s* embolia

emboss [ɛmˈbɔs] *or* [ɛmˈbɑs] *tr* (*metal*) sbalzare; (*paper*) goffrare

embrace [ɛmˈbres] *s* abbraccio ‖ *tr* abbracciare ‖ *intr* abbracciarsi

embrasure [ɛmˈbreʒər] *s* (architt) strombatura; (mil) feritoia

embroider [ɛmˈbrɔɪdər] *tr* ricamare, trapuntare

embroider·y [ɛmˈbrɔɪdəri] *s* (**-ies**) ricamo, trapunto

embroil [ɛmˈbrɔɪl] *tr* ingarbugliare; (*to involve in contention*) coinvolgere

embroilment [ɛmˈbrɔɪlmənt] *s* imbroglio; (*in contention*) disaccordo

embry·o [ˈɛmbrɪˌo] *s* (**-os**) embrione *m*

embryology [ˌɛmbrɪˈɑlədʒi] *s* embriologia

embryonic [ˌɛmbrɪˈɑnɪk] *adj* embrionale

emcee [ˈɛmˈsi] *s* presentatore *m* ‖ *tr* presentare

emend [ɪˈmɛnd] *tr* emendare

emendation [ˌimɛnˈdeʃən] *s* emendamento

emerald [ˈɛmərəld] *s* smeraldo

emerge [ɪˈmɑrdʒ] *intr* emergere

emergence [ɪˈmɑrdʒəns] *s* emergenza

emergen·cy [ɪˈmɑrdʒənsi] *s* (**-cies**) emergenza

emer'gency brake' *s* freno a mano

emer'gency ex'it *s* uscita di sicurezza

emer'gency land'ing *s* atterragio di fortuna

emer'gency ward' *s* sala d'urgenza

emeritus [ɪˈmɛritəs] *adj* emerito

emersion [ɪˈmɑrʒən] *or* [ɪˈmɑrʃən] *s* emersione

emery [ˈɛməri] *s* smeriglio

em'ery cloth' *s* tela smeriglio

em'ery wheel' *s* mola a smeriglio

emetic [ɪˈmɛtik] *adj & s* emetico

emigrant [ˈɛmɪgrənt] *adj & s* emigrante *mf*

emigrate [ˈɛmɪˌgret] *intr* emigrare

émigré [emiˈgre] *or* [ˈɛmɪˌgre] *s* emigrato

eminence ['emɪnəns] s eminenza; (eccl) Eminenza

eminent ['emɪnənt] adj eminente

emissar·y ['emɪ ˌseri] s (-ies) emissario

emission [ɪ'mɪʃən] s emissione

emit [ɪ'mɪt] v (pret & pp emitted; ger emitting) tr emettere

emolument [ɪ'maljəmənt] s emolumento

emotion [ɪ'moʃən] s emozione

emotional [ɪ'moʃənəl] adj emotivo

emperor ['empərər] s imperatore m

empha·sis ['emfəsɪs] s (-ses [ˌsiz]) enfasi f, risalto

emphasize ['emfəˌsaɪz] tr dar rilievo a, sottolineare

emphatic [em'fætɪk] adj enfatico

emphysema [ˌemfɪ'simə] s enfisema m

empire ['empaɪr] s impero

empiric(al) [em'pɪrɪk(əl)] adj empirico

empiricist [em'pɪrɪsɪst] s empirista mf

emplacement [em'plesmənt] s piazzola, postazione

employ [em'plɔɪ] s impiego || tr impiegare, usare; valersi di

employee [em'plɔɪ·i] or [ˌemplɔɪ'i] s impiegato, dipendente mf

employer [em'plɔɪ·ər] s dirigente mf, datore m di lavoro

employment [em'plɔɪmənt] s impiego, occupazione

employ'ment a'gency s agenzia di collocamento

empower [em'pau·ər] tr autorizzare; permettere

empress ['emprɪs] s imperatrice f

emptiness ['emptɪnɪs] s vuoto

emp·ty ['empti] adj (-tier; -tiest) vuoto; (gun) scarico; (hungry) (coll) digiuno; (fig) esausto || v (pret & pp -tied) tr vuotare || intr vuotarsi

empty-handed ['empti'hændɪd] adj a mani vuote

empty-headed ['empti'hedɪd] adj dalla testa vuota, balordo

empyrean [ˌempɪ'ri·ən] adj & s empireo

emulate ['emjəˌlet] tr emulare

emulator ['emjəˌletər] s emulo

emulous ['emjələs] adj emulo

emulsi·fy [ɪ'mʌlsɪˌfaɪ] v (pret & pp -fied) tr emulsionare

emulsion [ɪ'mʌlʃən] s emulsione

enable [en'ebəl] tr abilitare, permettere (with dat)

enact [en'ækt] tr decretare; (a role) rappresentare

enactment [en'æktmənt] s legge f; (of a law) promulgazione; (of a play) rappresentazione

enam·el [ɪn'æməl] s smalto || v (pret & pp -eled or -elled; ger -eling or -elling) tr smaltare

enam'el·ware' s utensili mpl di cucina di ferro smaltato

enamor [en'æmər] tr innamorare; to become enamored of innamorarsi di

encamp [en'kæmp] tr accampare || intr accamparsi

encampment [en'kæmpmənt] s campeggio; (mil) accampamento

encase [en'kes] tr incassare

encephalitis [en ˌsefə'laɪtɪs] s encefalite f

enchain [en't'ʃen] tr incatenare

enchant [en't'ʃænt] or [en't'ʃɑnt] tr incantare

enchantment [en't'ʃæntmənt] or [en't'ʃɑntmənt] s incanto, malia

enchanting [en't'ʃæntɪŋ] or [en't'ʃɑntɪŋ] adj incantatore, incantevole

enchantress [en't'ʃæntrɪs] or [en't'ʃɑntrɪs] s incantatrice f, maliarda

enchase [en't'ʃes] tr incastonare

encircle [en'sʌrkəl] tr rigirare, girare intorno a; (mil) circondare

enclave ['enklev] s enclave f

enclitic [en'klɪtɪk] adj enclitico || s enclitica

enclose [en'kloz] tr rinchiudere; (in a letter) accludere, includere; to enclose herewith accludere alla presente

enclosure [en'klozər] s (land surrounded by fence) recinto, chiuso; (e.g., letter) allegato

encomi·um [en'komi·əm] s (-ums or -a [ə]) encomio, elogio

encompass [en'kʌmpəs] tr circondare; racchiudere, contenere

encore ['ɑŋkor] s bis m || tr (a performance) chiedere il bis di; (a performer) chiedere il bis a || interj bis!

encounter [en'kauntər] s (casual meeting) incontro; (combat) scontro || tr incontrare || intr scontrarsi

encourage [en'kʌrɪdʒ] tr incoraggiare; (to foster) favorire

encouragement [en'kʌrɪdʒmənt] s incoraggiamento; favoreggiamento

encroach [en'krot'ʃ] intr—to encroach on or upon invadere; usurpare; occupare il territorio di

encumber [en'kʌmbər] tr imbarazzare; ingombrare; (to load with debts, etc) gravare

encumbrance [en'kʌmbrəns] s imbarazzo; ingombro; gravame m

encyclical [en'sɪklɪkəl] or [en'saɪklɪkəl] s enciclica

encyclopedia [en ˌsaɪklə'pidɪ·ə] s enciclopedia

encyclopedic [en ˌsaɪklə'pidɪk] adj enciclopedico

end [end] s (extremity; concluding part) fine f; (e.g., of the week) fine f; (purpose) fine m; (part adjacent to an extremity) lembo; (small piece) pezza, avanzo; (of a beam) testata; (sports) estrema; at the end of in capo a; in fondo a; in the end alla fine, all'ultimo; no end (coll) moltissimo; no end of (coll) un mucchio di; to make both ends meet sbarcare il lunario; to no end senza effetto; to stand on end mettere in piedi, drizzare; mettersi diritto; (said of hair) drizzarsi; to the end that affinché || tr finire, terminare; to end up andare a finire || intr finire, terminare; to end up finire

endanger [en'dendʒər] tr mettere in pericolo

endear [en'dɪr] *tr* affezionare; **to endear oneself to** rendersi caro a

endeavor [en'devər] *s* tentativo, sforzo || *intr* tentare, sforzarsi

endemic [en'demɪk] *adj* endemico || *s* endemia

ending ['endɪŋ] *s* fine *f*, conclusione; (*gram*) terminazione, desinenza

endive ['endaɪv] *s* indivia

endless ['endlɪs] *adj* interminabile; sterminato; (*mach*) senza fine

end'most' *adj* estremo, ultimo

endorse [en'dɔrs] *tr* girare; (*fig*) approvare, confermare

endorsee [,endɔr'si] *s* giratario

endorsement [en'dɔrsmənt] *s* girata; approvazione, conferma

endorser [en'dɔrsər] *s* girante *mf*

endow |en'daʊ] *tr* dotare

endowment [en'daʊmənt] *adj* dotale || *s* (*of an institution*) dotazione; (*gift, talent*) dote *f*

end' pap'er *s* risguardo

endurance [en'djʊrəns] or [en'dʊrəns] *s* sopportazione, tolleranza; (*ability to hold out*) resistenza, forza; (*lasting time*) durata

endure [en'djʊr] or [en'dʊr] *tr* sopportare, tollerare; resistere (with *dat*) || *intr* durare, resistere

enduring [en'djʊrɪŋ] or [en'dʊrɪŋ] *adj* duraturo, durevole; paziente

enema ['enəmə] *s* clistere *m*

ene•my ['enəmi] *adj* nemico || *s* (-mies) nemico

en'emy al'ien *s* straniero nemico

energetic [,enər'dʒetɪk] *adj* energetico, vigoroso

ener•gy ['enərdʒi] *s* (-gies) energia

enervate ['enər,vet] *tr* snervare

enfeeble [en'fibəl] *tr* indebolire

enfold [en'fold] *tr* avvolgere; abbracciare

enforce [en'fɔrs] *tr* far osservare; ottenere per forza; (*e.g., obedience*) imporre; (*an argument*) far valere

enforcement [en'fɔrsmənt] *s* imposizione; (*of a law*) esecuzione

enfranchise [en'fræntʃaɪz] *tr* liberare; concedere il diritto di voto a

engage [en'gedʒ] *tr* occupare; riservare; (*s.o.'s attention*) attrarre; (*a gear*) ingranare; (*the enemy*) ingaggiare; (*to hire*) assumere; (*theat*) scritturare; **to be engaged, to be engaged to be married** essere fidanzato; **to engage s.o. in conversation** intavolare una conversazione con qlcu || *intr* essere occupato; essere impiegato; assumere un'obbligazione; (*mil*) impegnarsi; (*mach*) ingranare, incastrarsi

engaged [en'gedʒd] *adj* fidanzato; occupato, impegnato; (*column*) murato

engagement [en'gedʒmənt] *s* accordo; fidanzamento; impegno, contratto; (*appointment*) appuntamento; (*mil*) azione; (*mach*) innesto

engage'ment ring' *s* anello di fidanzamento

engaging [en'gedʒɪŋ] *adj* attrattivo

engender [en'dʒendər] *tr* ingenerare

engine ['endʒɪn] *s* macchina; (aut) motore *m*; (rr) locomotiva, motrice *f*

engineer [,endʒə'nɪr] *s* ingegnere *m*; (rr) macchinista *m*; (mil) zappatore *m*, geniere *m* || *tr* costruire; progettare

engineering [,endʒə'nɪrɪŋ] *s* ingegneria

en'gine house' *s* stazione dei pompieri

en'gine•man' *s* (-men) (rr) macchinista *m*

en'gine room' *s* sala macchine

en'gine-room' tel'egraph *s* (naut) telegrafo di macchina, trasmettitore *m*

England ['ɪŋglənd] *s* l'Inghilterra

Englander ['ɪŋgləndər] *s* nativo dell'Inghilterra

English ['ɪŋglɪʃ] *adj* inglese || *s* inglese *m*; (billiards) effetto; **the English** gli inglesi

Eng'lish Chan'nel *s* Canale *m* della Manica

Eng'lish dai'sy *s* margherita

Eng'lish horn' *s* (mus) corno inglese

Eng'lish•man *s* (-men) inglese *m*

Eng'lish-speak'ing *adj* di lingua inglese, anglofono

Eng'lish•wom'an *s* (-wom'en) inglese *f*

engraft [en'græft] or [en'grɑft] *tr* (hort) innestare; (fig) inculcare

engrave [en'grev] *tr* incidere

engraver [en'grevər] *s* incisore *m*

engraving [en'grevɪŋ] *s* incisione

engross [en'gros] *tr* preoccupare, assorbire; redigere ufficialmente, scrivere a grandi caratteri; monopolizzare

engrossing [en'grosɪŋ] *adj* assorbente

engulf [en'gʌlf] *tr* sommergere, inondare

enhance [en'hæns] or [en'hɑns] *tr* valorizzare; far risaltare

enigma [ɪ'nɪgmə] *s* enigma *m*

enigmatic(al) [,ɪnɪg'mætɪk(əl)] *adj* enigmatico

enjambment [en'dʒæmmənt] or [en'dʒæmbmənt] *s* inarcatura

enjoin [en'dʒɔɪn] *tr* ingiungere, intimare

enjoy [en'dʒɔɪ] *tr* godere; **to enjoy + ger** provar piacere in + *inf*; **to enjoy oneself** divertirsi

enjoyable [en'dʒɔɪ-əbəl] *adj* gradevole

enjoyment [en'dʒɔɪmənt] *s* (*pleasure*) piacere *m*; (*pleasurable use*) godimento

enkindle [en'kɪndəl] *tr* infiammare

enlarge [en'lɑrdʒ] *tr* aumentare; ingrossare; (phot) ingrandire || *intr* aumentare; **to enlarge on** or **upon** dilungarsi su

enlargement [en'lɑrdʒmənt] *s* aumento; ingrossamento; (phot) ingrandimento

enlighten [en'laɪtən] *tr* illustrare, illuminare

enlightenment [en'laɪtənmənt] *s* spiegazione, schiarimento || **Enlightenment** *s* illuminismo

enlist [en'lɪst] *tr* (*e.g., s.o.'s favor*) guadagnarsi; (*the help of a person*) ottenere; (mil) ingaggiare || *intr* (mil) ingaggiarsi, arruolarsi; **to enlist**

in (*a cause*) dare il proprio appoggio a

enlistment [ɛn'lɪstmənt] *s* arruolamento, ingaggio

enliven [ɛn'laɪvən] *tr* ravvivare

enmesh [ɛn'mɛʃ] *tr* irretire

enmi·ty ['ɛnmɪti] *s* (**-ties**) inimicizia

ennoble [ɛn'nobəl] *tr* nobilitare

ennui ['anwi] *s* noia, tedio

enormous [ɪ'nɔrməs] *adj* enorme

enormously [ɪ'nɔrməsli] *adv* enormemente

enough [ɪ'nʌf] *adj* abbastanza || *s* il sufficiente || *adv* abbastanza || *interj* basta!

enounce [ɪ'naʊns] *tr* enunciare; (*to declare*) affermare

enrage [ɛn'redʒ] *tr* infuriare, irritare

enrapture [ɛn'ræptʃər] *tr* mandare in visibilio, estasiare

enrich [ɛn'rɪtʃ] *tr* arricchire

enroll [ɛn'rol] *tr* arruolare, ingaggiare; (*a student*) iscrivere || *intr* arruolarsi, ingaggiarsi; (*said of a student*) iscriversi

enrollment [ɛn'rolmənt] *s* arruolamento, ingaggio; (*of a student*) iscrizione

en route [an 'rut] *adv* in cammino; **en route to** in via per

ensconce [ɛn'skans] *tr* nascondere; **to esconce oneself** rannicchiarsi, istallarsi comodamente

ensemble [an'sambəl] *s* insieme *m*; (*mus*) concertato

ensign ['ɛnsaɪn] *s* (*standard*) bandiera, insegna; (*badge*) distintivo || ['ɛnsən] *or* ['ɛnsaɪn] *s* guardamarina *m*

ensilage ['ɛnsɪlɪdʒ] *s* (*preservation of fodder*) insilamento; (*preserved fodder*) insilato

ensile [ɛn'saɪl] *or* [ɛn'saɪl] *tr* insilare

enslave [ɛn'slev] *tr* fare schiavo, asservire

enslavement [ɛn'slevmənt] *s* asservimento

ensnare [ɛn'sner] *tr* irretire

ensue [ɛn'su] *or* [ɛn'sju] *intr* risultare; seguire, conseguire

ensuing [ɛn'su·ɪŋ] *or* [ɛn'sju·ɪŋ] *adj* risultante, conseguente; seguente

ensure [ɛn'ʃur] *tr* assicurare, garantire

entail [ɛn'tel] *s* (law) obbligo || *tr* provocare, comportare; (law) obbligare

entangle [ɛn'tæŋgəl] *tr* intricare, imbrogliare, impigliare

entanglement [ɛn'tæŋgəlmənt] *s* groviglio, garbuglio

enter [ɛn'tər] *tr* (*a house*) entrare in; (*in the customhouse*) dichiarare; (*to make a record of*) registrare; (*a student*) iscrivere; iscriversi a; fare membro; (*to undertake*) intraprendere; **to enter s.o.'s head** passare per la testa a qlcu || *intr* entrare; (*theat*) entrare in scena; **to enter into** entrare in; (*a contract*) impegnarsi in; **to enter on** *or* **upon** intraprendere

enterprise ['ɛntər‚praɪz] *s* (*undertak-*

ing) impresa; (*spirit, push*) intraprendenza

enterprising ['ɛntər‚praɪzɪŋ] *adj* intraprendente

entertain [‚ɛntər'ten] *tr* divertire, intrattenere; (*guests*) ospitare; (*a hope*) accarezzare; (*a proposal*) considerare || *intr* ricevere

entertainer [‚ɛntər'tenər] *s* (*host*) ospite *mf*; (*in public*) attore *m*, cantante *mf*, fine dicitore *m*

entertaining [‚ɛntər'tenɪŋ] *adj* divertente

entertainment [‚ɛntər'tenmənt] *s* trattenimento, svago; spettacolo, attrazione; buon trattamento

enthrall [ɛn'θrɔl] *tr* affascinare, incantare; (*to subjugate*) asservire, soggiogare

enthrone [ɛn'θron] *tr* mettere sul trono, intronizzare; esaltare, innalzare

enthuse [ɛn'θuz] *or* [ɛn'θjuz] *tr* (coll) entusiasmare || *intr* (coll) entusiasmarsi

enthusiasm [ɛn'θuzɪ‚æzəm] *or* [ɛn'θjuzɪ‚æzəm] *s* entusiasmo

enthusiast [ɛn'θuzɪ‚æst] *or* [ɛn'θjuzɪ‚æst] *s* entusiasta *mf*, maniaco

enthusiastic [ɛn‚θuzɪ'æstɪk] *or* [ɛn‚θjuzɪ'æstɪk] *adj* entusiastico

entice [ɛn'taɪs] *tr* attrarre, provocare; tentare

enticement [ɛn'taɪsmənt] *s* attrazione, provocazione; tentazione

entire [ɛn'taɪr] *adj* intero

entirely [ɛn'taɪrli] *adv* interamente; (*solely*) solamente

entire·ty [ɛn'taɪrti] *s* (**-ties**) interezza; totalità *f*

entitle [ɛn'taɪtəl] *tr* dar diritto a; (*to give a name to*) intitolare

enti·ty ['ɛntɪti] *s* (**-ties**) (*something real; organization, institution*) ente *m*; (*existence*) entità *f*

entomb [ɛn'tum] *tr* seppellire

entombment [ɛn'tummənt] *s* sepoltura

entomology [‚ɛntə'malədʒɪ] *s* entomologia

entourage [‚antu'raʒ] *s* seguito

entrails ['ɛntrɛlz] *or* ['ɛntrəlz] *spl* visceri *mpl*

entrain [ɛn'tren] *tr* far salire sul treno || *intr* imbarcarsi sul treno

entrance ['ɛntrəns] *s* entrata, ingresso || [ɛn'træns] *or* [ɛn'trans] *tr* ipnotizzare, incantare

en'trance exam'ina'tion *s* esame *m* d'ammissione

entrancing [ɛn'trænsɪŋ] *or* [ɛn'transɪŋ] *adj* incantatore

entrant ['ɛntrənt] *s* nuovo membro; (sports) concorrente *mf*

en·trap [ɛn'træp] *v* (*pret & pp* **-trapped;** *ger* **-trapping**) *tr* intrappolare, irretire

entreat [ɛn'trit] *tr* implorare

entreat·y [ɛn'triti] *s* (**-ies**) implorazione, supplica

entree ['antre] *s* entrata, ingresso; (culin) prima portata

entrench [ɛn'trɛntʃ] *tr* trincerare || *intr*
—to entrench on *or* **upon** violare

entrust [en'trʌst] *tr* affidare, confidare

en·try ['entri] *s* (-**tries**) entrata; (*item*) partita, registrazione; (*in a dictionary*) lemma, esponente *m*; (*sports*) concorrente *mf*

entwine [en'twain] *tr* intrecciare || *intr* intrecciarsi

enumerate [ɪ'njumə,ret] *or* [ɪ'numə,ret] *tr* enumerare

enunciate [ɪ'nʌnsɪ,et] *or* [ɪ'nʌnʃɪ,et] *tr* enunciare, staccare

envelop [en'vɛləp] *tr* involgere

envelope ['envə,lop] *or* ['ɑnvə,lop] *s* (*for a letter*) busta; (*wrapper*) involucro

envenom [en'vɛnəm] *tr* avvelenare

enviable ['envi-əbəl] *adj* invidiabile

envious ['envi-əs] *adj* invidioso

environment [en'vairənmənt] *s* ambiente *m*; condizioni *fpl* ambientali

environs [en'vairənz] *spl* dintorni *mpl*, sobborghi *mpl*

envisage [en'vizidʒ] *tr* considerare, immaginare

envoi ['envɔi] *s* (pros) congedo

envoy ['envɔi] *s* inviato; (mil) parlamentare *m*; (pros) congedo

en·vy ['envi] *s* (-**vies**) invidia || *v* (*pret & pp* -**vied**) *tr* invidiare

enzyme ['enzaim] *or* ['enzim] *s* enzima *m*

epaulet *or* **epaulette** ['ɛpə,lɛt] *s* spallina

epenthe·sis [e'pɛnθɪsɪs] *s* (-**ses** [,siz]) epentesi *f*

ephemeral [ɪ'fɛmərəl] *adj* effimero

epic ['ɛpɪk] *adj* epico || *s* epica

epicure ['ɛpɪ,kjur] *s* epicureo

epicurean [,ɛpɪkju'ri·ən] *adj & s* epicureo

epidemic [,ɛpɪ'dɛmɪk] *adj* epidemico || *s* epidemia

epidermis [,ɛpɪ'dʌrmɪs] *s* epidermide *f*

epiglottis [,ɛpɪ'glɑtɪs] *s* epiglottide *f*

epigram ['ɛpɪ,græm] *s* epigramma *m*

epilepsy ['ɛpɪ,lɛpsi] *s* epilessia

epileptic [,ɛpɪ'lɛptɪk] *adj & s* epilettico

epilogue ['ɛpɪ,lɔg] *or* ['ɛpɪ,lɑg] *s* epilogo

Epiphany [ɪ'pɪfəni] *s* Epifania

Episcopalian [ɪ,pɪskə'peli·ən] *adj & s* episcopaliano

episode ['ɛpɪ,sod] *s* episodio

epistle [ɪ'pɪsəl] *s* epistola

epitaph ['ɛpɪ,tæf] *s* epitaffio

epithet ['ɛpɪ,θɛt] *s* epiteto

epitome [ɪ'pɪtəmi] *s* epitome *f*; (fig) prototipo, personificazione

epitomize [ɪ'pɪtə,maiz] *tr* epitomare; (fig) incarnare, personificare

epoch ['ɛpək] *or* ['ipɑk] *s* epoca

epochal ['ɛpəkəl] *adj* memorabile

ep'och-mak'ing *adj*—**to be epoch-making** fare epoca

Ep'som salt' ['ɛpsəm] *s* sale *m* inglese

equable ['ɛkwəbəl] *or* ['ikwəbəl] *adj* uniforme; tranquillo

equal ['ikwəl] *adj* uguale; **equal to** pari a, all'altezza di || *s* uguale *m* || *v* (*pret & pp* **equaled** *or* **equalled**; *ger* **equaling** *or* **equalling**) *tr* uguagliare

equali·ty [ɪ'kwɑliti] *s* (-**ties**) uguaglianza

equalize ['ikwə,laiz] *tr* uguagliare; (*to make uniform*) perequare, pareggiare

equally ['ikwəli] *adv* ugualmente

equanimity [,ikwə'nimiti] *s* equanimità *f*

equate [ɪ'kwet] *tr* mettere in forma di equazione; considerare uguale or uguali

equation [ɪ'kweʒən] *or* [ɪ'kweʃən] *s* equazione

equator [ɪ'kwetər] *s* equatore *m*

equatorial [,ikwə'tori·əl] *adj* equatoriale

equer·ry ['ɛkwəri] *or* [ɪ'kwɛri] *s* (-**ries**) scudiero

equestrian [ɪ'kwɛstri·ən] *adj* equestre || *s* cavallerizzo

equilateral [,ikwɪ'lætərəl] *adj* equilatero

equilibrium [,ikwɪ'lɪbrɪ·əm] *s* equilibrio

equinoctial [,ikwɪ'nɑkʃəl] *adj* equinoziale

equinox ['ikwɪ,nɑks] *s* equinozio

equip [ɪ'kwɪp] *v* (*pret & pp* **equipped**; *ger* **equipping**) *tr* equipaggiare; **to equip** (*e.g., a ship*) **with** munire di

equipment [ɪ'kwɪpmənt] *s* equipaggiamento; (*skill*) attitudine *f*, capacità *f*

equipoise ['ikwɪ,pɔiz] *or* ['ɛkwɪ,pɔiz] *s* equilibrio || *tr* equilibrare

equitable ['ɛkwɪtəbəl] *adj* equo

equi·ty ['ɛkwɪti] *s* (-**ties**) (*fairness*) equità *f*; valore *m* al netto; (*in a corporation*) interessenza azionaria

equivalent [ɪ'kwɪvələnt] *adj* equivalente || *s* equivalente *m*; (com) controvalore *m*

equivocal [ɪ'kwɪvəkəl] *adj* equivoco

equivocate [ɪ'kwɪvə,ket] *intr* giocare sulle parole, parlare in maniera equivoca

equivocation [ɪ,kwɪvə'keʃən] *s* equivocità *f*; equivoco

era ['ɪrə] *or* ['irə] *s* era, evo

eradicate [ɪ'rædɪ,ket] *tr* sradicare

erase [ɪ'res] *tr* cancellare

eraser [ɪ'resər] *s* gomma da cancellare; (*for blackboard*) spugna

erasure [ɪ'reʒər] *or* [ɪ'reʒər] *s* cancellatura; (*of a tape*) cancellazione

ere [er] *prep* (lit) prima di || *conj* (lit) prima che

erect [ɪ'rɛkt] *adj* dritto, eretto; (*hair*) irto || *tr* (*to set in upright position*) drizzare; (*a building*) erigere, costruire; (*a machine*) montare

erection [ɪ'rɛkʃən] *s* erezione

ermine ['ʌrmɪn] *s* ermellino; (fig) carica di giudice, toga, magistratura

erode [ɪ'rod] *tr* erodere || *intr* corrodersi, consumarsi

erosion [ɪ'roʒən] *s* erosione

erotic [ɪ'rɑtɪk] *adj* erotico

err [ʌr] *intr* errare; (*to be incorrect*) sbagliarsi

errand ['ɛrənd] *s* corsa, commissione; **to run an errand** fare una commissione

er'rand boy' *s* fattorino, galoppino

erratic [ɪ'rætɪk] *adj* erratico; strano, eccentrico

erra·tum [ɪ'retəm] or [ɪ'rɑtəm] *s* (-ta [tə]) errore *m* di stampa

erroneous [ɪ'roni-əs] *adj* erroneo

error ['erər] *s* errore *m*, sbaglio

erudite ['eru͵daɪt] or ['erju͵daɪt] *adj* erudito, dotto

erudition [͵eru'dɪʃən] or [͵erju'dɪʃən] *s* erudizione

erupt [ɪ'rʌpt] *intr* (said of a volcano) eruttare; (said of a skin rash) fiorire; (said of a tooth) spuntare; (fig) erompere

eruption [ɪ'rʌpʃən] *s* eruzione

escalate ['eskə͵let] *tr & intr* aumentare

escalation [͵eskə'leʃən] *s* aumento

escalator ['eskə͵letər] *s* scala mobile

escallop [es'kæləp] *s* (on edge of cloth) dentellatura, festone *m*; (mollusk) pettine *m* ‖ *tr* cuocere in conchiglia; cuocere al forno con salsa e pane grattugiato

escapade [͵eskə'ped] *s* scappatella

escape [es'kep] *s* (getaway) fuga; (from responsibility, duties, etc.) scampo ‖ *tr* sottrarsi a, eludere; **to escape s.o.** scappare da qlcu; scappar di mente a qlcu ‖ *intr* scappare; sprigionarsi; **to escape from** (a person) sfuggire a; (jail) evadere da

escapee [͵eskə'pi] *s* evaso

escape' lit'erature *s* letteratura di evasione

escapement [es'kepmənt] *s* scappamento

escape' veloc'ity *s* (rok) velocità *f* di fuga

escarpment [es'karpmənt] *s* scarpata

eschew [es't͡ʃu] *tr* evitare, rifuggire da

escort ['eskɔrt] *s* scorta; (of a woman or girl) compagno, cavaliere *m* ‖ [es'kɔrt] *tr* scortare

escutcheon [es'kʌt͡ʃən] *s* scudo; (plate in front of lock on door) bocchetta

Esk·imo ['eskɪ͵mo] *adj* eschimese ‖ *s* (-mos or -mo) eschimese *mf*

esopha·gus [i'safəgəs] *s* (-gi [͵d͡ʒaɪ]) esofago

espalier [es'pæljər] *s* spalliera

especial [es'peʃəl] *adj* speciale

espionage ['espɪ-ənɪd͡ʒ] or [͵espɪ-ə-'naʒ] *s* spionaggio

esplanade [͵esplə'ned] or [͵esplə'nad] *s* spianata, piazzale *m*

espousal [es'pauzəl] *s* sposalizio; (of a cause) adozione

espouse [es'pauz] *tr* sposare; (to advocate) abbracciare, adottare

esquire [es'kwaɪr] or ['eskwaɪr] *s* scudiero ‖ **Esquire** *s* titolo di cortesia usato generalmente con persone di riguardo

essay ['ese] *s* saggio

essayist ['ese-ɪst] *s* saggista *mf*

essence ['esəns] *s* essenza

essential [e'senʃəl] *adj & s* essenziale *m*

establish [es'tæblɪʃ] *tr* stabilire

establishment [es'tæblɪʃmənt] *s* stabilimento; fondazione; **the Establishment** l'autorità costituita

estate [es'tet] *s* stato; condizione sociale; (landed property) tenuta; (a

esteem [es'tim] *s* stima ‖ *tr* stimare

esthete ['esθit] *s* esteta *mf*

esthetic [es'θetɪk] *adj* estetico ‖ **esthetics** *ssg* estetica

estimable ['estɪməbəl] *adj* stimabile

estimate ['estɪ͵met] or ['estɪmɪt] *s* stima, valutazione; (statement of cost of work to be done) preventivo ‖ ['estɪ͵met] *tr* stimare, valutare; preventivare

estimation [͵estɪ'meʃən] *s* stima; **in my estimation** a mio parere

estimator ['estɪ͵metər] *s* preventivista *mf*

estrangement [es'trend͡ʒmənt] *s* alienazione, disaffezione

estuar·y ['est͡ʃu͵eri] *s* (-ies) estuario

etch [et͡ʃ] *tr & intr* incidere all'acquaforte

etcher ['et͡ʃər] *s* acquafortista *mf*

etching ['et͡ʃɪŋ] *s* acquaforte *f*

eternal [ɪ'tʌrnəl] *adj* eterno

eterni·ty [ɪ'tʌrnɪti] *s* (-ties) eternità *f*

ether ['iθər] *s* etere *m*

ethereal [ɪ'θɪrɪ-əl] *adj* etereo

ethical ['eθɪkəl] *adj* etico

ethics ['eθɪks] *ssg* etica

Ethiopian [͵iθɪ'opɪ-ən] *adj & s* etiope *mf*

ethnic(al) ['eθnɪk(əl)] *adj* etnico

ethnography [eθ'nɑgrəfi] *s* etnografia

ethnology [eθ'nɑləd͡ʒi] *s* etnologia

ethyl ['eθɪl] *s* etile *m*

ethylene ['eθɪ͵lin] *s* etilene *m*

etiquette ['etɪ͵ket] *s* etichetta

étude [e't͡jud] *s* (mus) studio

etymology [͵etɪ'mɑləd͡ʒi] *s* etimologia

ety·mon ['etɪ͵mɑn] *s* (-mons or -ma [mə]) etimo

eucalyp·tus [͵jukə'lɪptəs] *s* (-tuses or -ti [taɪ]) eucalipto

Eucharist ['jukərɪst] *s* Eucaristia

eugenics [ju'd͡ʒenɪks] *ssg* eugenetica

eulogistic [͵julə'd͡ʒɪstɪk] *adj* elogiativo

eulogize ['julə͵d͡ʒaɪz] *tr* elogiare

eulo·gy ['juləd͡ʒi] *s* (-gies) elogio; elogio funebre

eunuch ['junək] *s* eunuco

euphemism ['jufɪ͵mɪzəm] *s* eufemismo

euphemistic [͵jufɪ'mɪstɪk] *adj* eufemistico

euphonic [ju'fanɪk] *adj* eufonico

eupho·ny ['jufəni] *s* (-nies) eufonia

euphoria [ju'forɪ-ə] *s* euforia

euphuism ['jufju͵ɪzəm] *s* eufuismo

Europe ['jurəp] *s* l'Europa

European [͵jurə'pi-ən] *adj & s* europeo

euthanasia [͵juθə'neʒə] *s* eutanasia

evacuate [ɪ'vækju͵et] *tr & intr* evacuare

evacuation [ɪ͵vækju'eʃən] *s* evacuazione

evacuee [ɪ'vækju͵i] or [ɪ͵vækju'i] *s* sfollato

evade [ɪ'ved] *tr* eludere ‖ *intr* evadere

evaluate [ɪ'vælju͵et] *tr* valutare

evaluation [ɪ͵vælju'eʃən] *s* valutazione

Evangel [ɪ'vænd͡ʒəl] *s* Vangelo

evangelic(al) [͵ivæn'd͡ʒelɪk(əl)] or [͵evən'd͡ʒelɪk(əl)] *adj* evangelico

Evangelist [ɪ'vændʒəlɪst] s evangelista m

evaporate [ɪ'væpə,ret] tr & intr evaporare

evasion [ɪ'veʒən] s evasione; (subterfuge) scappatoia

evasive [ɪ'vesɪv] adj evasivo

eve [iv] s vigilia; **on the eve of** la vigilia di

even ['ivən] adj (smooth) piano, regolare; (number) pari; uguale, uniforme; (temperament) calmo, placido; **even with** a livello di; **to be even** mettersi in pari; **to get even** prendersi la rivincita || adv anche; fino, perfino; pure; esattamente; magari; **even as** proprio mentre; **even if** anche se, quando pure; **even so** anche se così; **even though** quantunque; **even when** anche quando; **not even** neppure, nemmeno; **to break even** impattare || tr spianare; **to even up** bilanciare

evening ['ivnɪŋ] adj serale || s sera, serata; **all evening** tutta la sera; **every evening** tutte le sere; **in the evening** la sera

eve'ning clothes' spl vestito da sera

eve'ning gown' s vestito da sera da signora

eve'ning star' s espero

e'ven·song' s (eccl) vespro

event [ɪ'vent] s avvenimento; (outcome) evenienza; (public function) manifestazione; (sports) prova; **at all events** or **in any event** in ogni caso; **in the event that** in caso che, se

eventful [ɪ'ventfəl] adj ricco di avvenimenti; movimentato

eventual [ɪ'ventʃʊ·əl] adj finale

eventu·al·i·ty [ɪ,ventʃʊ'ælɪti] s (-ties) eventualità f, evenienza

eventually [ɪ'ventʃʊ·əli] adv finalmente, alla fine

eventuate [ɪ'ventʃʊ,et] intr risultare; accadere

ever ['evər] adv (at all times) sempre; (at any time) mai; **as ever** come sempre; **as much as ever** tanto come prima; **ever since** (since that time) sin da; da allora in poi; **ever so** molto; **ever so much** moltissimo; **hardly ever** or **scarcely ever** quasi mai; **not . . . ever** non . . . mai

ev'er·glade' s terreno paludoso coperto di erbe

ev'er·green' adj & s sempreverde m & f; **evergreens** decorazione di sempreverdi

ev'er·last'ing adj eterno; incessante; (lasting indefinitely) duraturo; (wearisome) noioso || s eternità f; (bot) semprevivo

ev'er·more' adv eternamente; **for evermore** per sempre

every ['evri] adj tutti i; (each) ogni, ciascuno; (being each in a series) ogni, e.g., **every three days** ogni tre giorni; **every bit** (coll) in tutto e per tutto, e.g., **every bit a man** un uomo in tutto e per tutto; **every now and then** di quando in quando; **every once in a while** una volta ogni tanto;

every other day ogni secondo giorno; **every which way** (coll) da tutte le parti; (coll) in disordine

ev'ery·bod'y pron indef ognuno, tutti

ev'ery·day' adj di ogni giorno; quotidiano; ordinario

ev'ery·man' s l'uomo qualunque || pron chiunque

ev'ery·one' or **ev'ery one'** pron indef ciascuno, tutti

ev'ery·thing' pron indef tutto, ogni cosa, tutto quanto

ev'ery·where' adv dappertutto, dovunque

evict [ɪ'vɪkt] tr sfrattare, sloggiare

eviction [ɪ'vɪkʃən] s sfratto, sloggio

evidence ['evɪdəns] s evidenza; (law) prova

evident ['evɪdənt] adj evidente

evil ['ivəl] adj cattivo, malvagio || s male m; disgrazia

evildoer ['ivəl,du·ər] s malfattore m, malvagio

e'vil·do'ing s malafatta, malvagità f

e'vil eye' s iettatura, malocchio

evil-minded ['ivəl'maɪndɪd] adj malintenzionato

e'vil one', **the** il nemico

evince [ɪ'vɪns] tr mostrare, manifestare

evoke [ɪ'vok] tr evocare

evolution [,evə'luʃən] s evoluzione

evolve [ɪ'vɑlv] tr sviluppare || intr evolversi

ewe [ju] s pecora

ewer ['ju·ər] s brocca

ex [eks] prep senza includere

exacerbation [ɪg,zæsər'beʃən] s esulcerazione, esacerbazione

exacerbate [ɪg'zæsər,bet] tr esacerbare, esulcerare

exact [eg'zækt] adj esatto || tr esigere

exacting [eg'zæktɪŋ] adj esigente

exaction [eg'zækʃən] s esazione

exactly [eg'zæktli] adv esattamente; (sharp, on the dot) in punto

exactness [eg'zæktnɪs] s esattezza

exaggerate [eg'zædʒə,ret] tr esagerare

exalt [eg'zɔlt] tr elevare, esaltare

exam [eg'zæm] s (coll) esame m

examination [eg,zæmɪ'neʃən] s esame m; **to take an examination** sostenere un esame

examine [eg'zæmɪn] tr esaminare

examiner [eg'zæmɪnər] s esaminatore m

example [eg'zæmpəl] or [eg'zɑmpəl] s esempio; (precedent) precedente m; (of mathematics) problema m; **for example** per esempio

exasperate [eg'zæspə,ret] tr esasperare

excavate ['ekskə,vet] tr scavare

exceed [ek'sid] tr eccedere

exceedingly [ek'sidɪŋli] adv estremamente, sommamente

ex·cel [ek'sel] v (pret & pp -celled; ger -celling) tr sorpassare || intr eccellere

excellence ['eksələns] s eccellenza

excellen·cy ['eksələnsi] s (-cies) eccellenza; **Your Excellency** Sua Eccellenza

excelsior [ek'selsɪ·ər] s trucioli mpl per imballaggio

except [ek'sept] prep eccetto; **except**

for tranne, ad eccezione di; **except that** eccetto che || *tr* eccettuare

exception [ek'sepʃən] *s* eccezione; **to take exception** obiettare; scandalizzarsi; **with the exception of** a esclusione di, eccetto

exceptional [ek'sepʃənəl] *adj* eccezionale

excerpt ['eksʌrpt] *or* [ek'sʌrpt] *s* brano, selezione || [ek'sʌrpt] *tr* scegliere, selezionare

excess ['ekses] *or* [ek'ses] *adj* eccedente || [ek'ses] *s* (*amount or degree by which one thing exceeds another*) eccedente *m*, eccedenza; (*excessive amount; immoderate indulgence; unlawful conduct*) eccesso; **in excess of** più di

ex'cess bag'gage *s* bagaglio eccedente

ex'cess fare' *s* (rr) supplemento

excessive [ek'sesɪv] *adj* eccessivo

ex'cess-prof'its tax' *s* tassa sui sopraprofitti

exchange [eks'tʃendʒ] *s* scambio; (*place for buying and selling*) borsa; (*transactions in the currencies of two different countries*) cambio; (telp) centrale *f*, centralino; **in exchange for** in cambio di || *tr* scambiare, scambiarsi; **to exchange blows** venire alle mani; **to exchange greetings** salutarsi

exchequer [eks'tʃekər] *or* ['ekstʃekər] *s* erario, tesoro

ex'cise tax' [ek'saɪz] *or* ['eksaɪz] *s* imposta sul consumo

excitable [ek'saɪtəbəl] *adj* eccitabile

excite [ek'saɪt] *tr* eccitare

excitement [ek'saɪtmənt] *s* eccitazione

exciting [ek'saɪtɪŋ] *adj* emozionante; (*stimulating*) eccitante

exclaim [eks'klem] *tr & intr* esclamare

exclamation [ˌeksklə'meʃən] *s* esclamazione

exclama'tion mark' *or* **point'** *s* punto esclamativo

exclude [eks'klud] *tr* escludere

excluding [eks'kludɪŋ] *prep* a esclusione di, senza contare

exclusion [eks'kluʒən] *s* esclusione; **to the exclusion of** tranne, salvo

exclusive [eks'klusɪv] *adj* esclusivo; **exclusive of** escluso, senza contare || *s* (journ) esclusiva

excommunicate [ˌekskə'mjunɪˌket] *tr* scomunicare

excommunication [ˌekskəˌmjunɪ'keʃən] *s* scomunica

excoriate [eks'korɪˌet] *tr* criticare aspramente, vituperare

excrement ['ekskrəmənt] *s* escremento

excruciating [eks'kruʃɪˌetɪŋ] *adj* (*e.g., pleasure*) estremo; (*e.g., pain*) atroce, lancinante, straziante

exculpate ['ekskʌlˌpet] *or* [eks'kʌlpet] *tr* scolpare, scagionare

excursion [eks'kʌrʒən] *or* [eks'kʌrʃən] *s* escursione, gita

excursionist [eks'kʌrʒənɪst] *or* [eks'kʌrʃənɪst] *s* escursionista *mf*

excusable [eks'kjuzəbəl] *adj* scusabile

excuse [eks'kjus] *s* scusa || [eks'kjuz] *tr* scusare; esentare; (*a debt*) rimettere

execute ['eksɪˌkjut] *tr* (*to carry out; to produce*) eseguire; (*to put to death*) giustiziare; (law) rendere esecutorio

execution [ˌeksɪ'kjuʃən] *s* esecuzione; (*e.g., of a criminal*) esecuzione capitale

executioner [ˌeksɪ'kjuʃənər] *s* giustiziere *m*, boia *m*, carnefice *m*

executive [eg'zekjətɪv] *adj* esecutivo || *s* esecutivo; (*of a school, business, etc.*) dirigente *mf*

Exec'utive Man'sion *s* palazzo del governatore; residenza del capo del governo statunitense

executor [eg'zekjətər] *s* (law) esecutore testamentario

executrix [eg'zekjətrɪks] *s* (law) esecutrice testamentaria

exemplary [eg'zempləri] *or* ['egzəmˌpleri] *adj* esemplare

exempli-fy [eg'zemplɪˌfaɪ] *v* (*pret & pp* **-fied**) *tr* esemplificare

exempt [eg'zempt] *adj* esente || *tr* esimere, esentare

exemption [eg'zempʃən] *s* esenzione

exercise ['eksərˌsaɪz] *s* esercizio; cerimonia; **to take exercise** fare del moto || *tr* esercitare; (*care*) usare; (*to worry*) preoccupare || *intr* esercitarsi

exert [eg'zʌrt] *tr* (*e.g., power*) esercitare; **to exert oneself** sforzarsi

exertion [eg'zʌrʃən] *s* sforzo, tentativo; (*active use*) uso, esercizio

exhalation [ˌeks-hə'leʃən] *s* (*of gas, vapors*) esalazione; (*of air from lungs*) espirazione

exhale [eks'hel] *or* [eg'zel] *tr* (*gases, vapors, etc.*) esalare; (*air from lungs*) espirare || *intr* esalare; espirare

exhaust [eg'zost] *s* scarico, scappamento; tubo di scarico or scappamento || *tr* (*to wear out*) spossare, finire; (*to use up*) esaurire, dar fondo a; vuotare

exhaust' fan' *s* aspiratore *m*

exhaustion [eg'zostʃən] *s* esaurimento; estenuazione; (sports) cotta

exhaustive [eg'zostɪv] *adj* esauriente

exhaust' man'ifold *s* collettore *m* di scarico

exhaust' pipe' *s* tubo di scarico

exhaust' valve' *s* valvola di scappamento

exhibit [eg'zɪbɪt] *s* esposizione; (law) documento in giudizio || *tr* esibire

exhibition [ˌeksɪ'bɪʃən] *s* esibizione

exhibitor [eg'zɪbɪtər] *s* espositore *m*

exhilarating [eg'zɪləˌretɪŋ] *adj* esilarante

exhort [eg'zort] *tr* esortare

exhume [eks'hjum] *or* [eg'zjum] *tr* esumare, dissotterrare

exigen-cy ['eksɪdʒənsi] *s* (**-cies**) esigenza

exigent ['eksɪdʒənt] *adj* esigente

exile ['egzaɪl] *or* ['eksaɪl] *s* esilio; (*person*) esule *mf* || *tr* esiliare

exist [eg'zɪst] *intr* esistere

existence [eg'zɪstəns] *s* esistenza

existing [eg'zɪstɪŋ] *adj* esistente

exit ['egzɪt] *or* ['eksɪt] *s* uscita || *intr* uscire

exodus ['ɛksədəs] s esodo

exonerate [eg'zɑnə‚ret] tr (from an obligation) esonerare; (from blame) scagionare

exorbitant [eg'zɔrbɪtənt] adj esorbitante

exorcise ['ɛksɔr‚saɪz] tr esorcizzare

exotic [eg'zɑtɪk] adj esotico

expand [ɛks'pænd] tr (a metal) dilatare; (gas) espandere; (to enlarge) allargare, ampliare; (to unfold) spiegare; (math) svolgere, sviluppare || intr dilatarsi; espandersi; allargarsi, ampliarsi; spiegarsi, estendersi

expanse [ɛks'pæns] s vastità f

expansion [ɛks'pænʃən] s espansione

expansive [ɛks'pænsɪv] adj espansivo

expatiate [ɛks'peʃɪ‚et] intr dilungarsi

expatriate [ɛks'petrɪ‚ɪt] adj esiliato || s esule mf || [ɛks'petri‚et] tr esiliare; **to expatriate oneself** espatriare

expect [ɛks'pɛkt] tr aspettare, attendere; (coll) credere, supporre; **expect it** aspettarselo, aspettarsela

expectan•cy [ɛks'pɛktənsɪ]. s (-cies) aspettativa, aspettazione

expect'ant moth'er [ɛks'pɛktənt] s futura madre

expectation [‚ɛkspɛk'teʃən] s aspettativa

expectorate [ɛks'pɛktə‚ret] tr & intr espettorare

expedien•cy [ɛks'pidɪ‚ənsɪ]. s (-cies) industria, ingegno; opportunismo, vantaggio personale

expedient [ɛks'pidɪ‚ənt] adj conveniente; vantaggioso; (acting with self-interest) opportunista || s espediente m

expedite ['ɛkspɪ‚daɪt] tr sbrigare, accelerare; (a document) dar corso a

expedition [‚ɛkspɪ'dɪʃən] s spedizione; (speed) celerità f

expeditionary [‚ɛkspɪ'dɪʃən‚ɛri] adj (e.g., corps) di spedizione

expeditious [‚ɛkspɪ'dɪʃəs] adj spicciativo, spiccio

ex•pel [ɛks'pɛl] v (pret & pp **-pelled;** ger **-pelling**) tr espellere, scacciare

expend [ɛks'pɛnd] tr spendere, consumare

expendable [ɛks'pɛndəbəl] adj spendibile; da buttarsi via; (mil) da sacrificare

expenditure [ɛks'pɛndɪt‚ʃər] s spesa

expense [ɛks'pɛns] s spesa; **at the expense of** al costo di; **expenses** spese fpl; **to meet expenses** far fronte alle spese

expense' account' s conto delle spese risarcibili

expensive [ɛks'pɛnsɪv] adj caro, costoso

experience [ɛks'pɪrɪ‚əns] s esperienza || tr sperimentare, provare

experienced [ɛks'pɪrɪ‚ənst] adj esperto, sperimentato

experiment [ɛks'pɛrɪmənt] s esperimento || [ɛks'pɛrɪ‚mɛnt] intr sperimentare

expert ['ɛkspərt] adj & s esperto

expertise [‚ɛkspər'tiz] s maestria

expiate ['ɛkspɪ‚et] tr espiare

expiation [‚ɛkspɪ'eʃən] s espiazione

expire [ɛks'paɪr] tr espirare || intr (to breathe out) espirare; (said of a contract) scadere; (to die) morire

explain [ɛks'plen] tr spiegare; **to explain away** giustificare; dar ragione di || intr spiegare, spiegarsi

explainable [ɛks'plenəbəl] adj spiegabile

explanation [‚ɛksplə'neʃən] s spiegazione, delucidazione

explanatory [ɛks'plænə‚tori] adj esplicativo

explicit [ɛks'plɪsɪt] adj esplicito

explode [ɛks'plod] tr far scoppiare; (a theory) smontare || intr scoppiare

exploit [ɛks'plɔɪt] or ['ɛksplɔɪt] s impresa, prodezza || [ɛks'plɔɪt] tr utilizzare, sfruttare

exploitation [‚ɛksplɔɪ'teʃən] s utilizzazione, sfruttamento

exploration [‚ɛksplə'reʃən] s esplorazione

explore [ɛks'plor] tr esplorare

explorer [ɛks'plorər] s esploratore m

explosion [ɛks'ploʒən] s esplosione, scoppio; (of a theory) confutazione

explosive [ɛks'plosɪv] adj & s esplosivo

exponent [ɛks'ponənt] s esponente m

export ['ɛksport] adj di esportazione || s esportazione, articolo di esportazione || [ɛks'port] or ['ɛksport] tr & intr esportare

exportation [‚ɛkspor'teʃən] s esportazione

exporter ['ɛksportər] or [ɛks'portər] s esportatore m

expose [ɛks'poz] tr esporre; (to unmask) smascherare

exposé [‚ɛkspo'ze] s rivelazione scandalosa, smascheramento

exposition [‚ɛkspə'zɪʃən] s esposizione; interpretazione, commento

expostulate [ɛks'pʌstʃə‚let] intr protestare; **to expostulate with** lagnarsi con

exposure [ɛks'poʒər] s (disclosure) rivelazione; (situation with regard to sunlight) esposizione; (phot) esposizione

expo'sure me'ter s (phot) fotometro, esposimetro

expound [ɛks'paund] tr esporre

express [ɛks'prɛs] adj espresso || s (rr) celere m, rapido, direttissimo; **by express** per espresso, a grande velocità || adv per espresso, a grande velocità || tr esprimere; mandare per espresso; (to squeeze out) spremere; **to express oneself** esprimersi

ex'press com'pany s servizio corriere

expression [ɛks'prɛʃən] s espressione

expressive [ɛks'prɛsɪv] adj espressivo

expressly [ɛks'prɛsli] adv espressamente

express'man s (-men) fattorino di servizio corriere

express'way' s autostrada

expropriate [ɛks'propri‚et] tr espropriare

expulsion [ɛks'pʌlʃən] s espulsione

expunge [eks'pʌndʒ] *tr* espungere

expurgate ['ekspər‚get] *tr* espurgare

exquisite ['ekskwızıt] *or* [eks'kwızıt] *adj* squisito; intenso

ex'serv'ice-man' *s* (-men') ex combattente *m*

extant ['ekstənt] *or* [eks'tænt] *adj* ancora esistente

extemporaneous [eks‚tempə'renı-əs] *adj* estemporaneo; (*made for the occasion*) improvvisato

extempore [eks'tempəri] *adj* improvvisato || *adv* senza preparazione

extemporize [eks'tempə‚raız] *tr & intr* improvvisare

extend [eks'tend] *tr* allungare; estendere; (*e.g., aid*) offrire; (*payment of a debt*) dilazionare || *intr* estendersi

extended [eks'tendıd] *adj* esteso; prolungato

extension [eks'tenʃən] *s* estensione; prolungamento; (com) proroga; (telp) derivazione

exten'sion lad'der *s* scala porta, scala a prolunga

exten'sion ta'ble *s* tavola allungabile

exten'sion tel'ephone' *s* telefono interno

extensive [eks'tensıv] *adj* (*wide*) vasto; (*lengthy*) lungo; (*characterized by extention*) estensivo

extent [eks'tent] *s* estensione; to a certain extent fino a un certo punto; to a great extent in larga misura; to the full extent all'estremo limite

extenuate [eks'tenju‚et] *tr* (*to make seem less serious*) attenuare; (*to underrate*) sottovalutare

exterior [eks'tırı-ər] *adj & s* esteriore *m*

exterminate [eks'tʌrmı‚net] *tr* sterminare

external [eks'tʌrnəl] *adj* esterno || externals *spl* esteriorità *f*, di fuori *m*

extinct [eks'tıŋkt] *adj* estinto

extinction [eks'tıŋkʃən] *s* estinzione

extinguish [eks'tıŋgwıʃ] *tr* estinguere

extinguisher [eks'tıŋgwı-ər] *s* estintore *m*

extirpate ['ekstər‚pet] *or* [eks'tʌrpet] *tr* estirpare

ex•tol [eks'tol] *or* [eks'tɑl] *v* (*pret & pp* -tolled; *ger* -tolling) *tr* inneggiare

extort [eks'tort] *tr* estorcere

extortion [eks'torʃən] *s* estorsione

extra ['ekstrə] *adj* extra; (*spare*) di scorta || *s* (*of a newspaper*) edizione straordinaria; (*something additional*) soprappiù *m*; (theat) figurante *mf* || *adv* straordinariamente

ex'tra charge' *s* supplemento

extract ['ekstrækt] *s* estratto || [eks-'trækt] *tr* (*to pull out*) estrarre; (*to take from a book*) scegliere, selezionare

extraction [eks'trækʃən] *s* estrazione

extracurricular [‚ekstrəkə'rıkjələr] *adj* fuori del programma normale

extradition [‚ekstrə'dıʃən] *s* estradizione

ex'tra-dry' *adj* molto secco, brut

ex'tra fare' *s* supplemento al biglietto

ex'tra·mar'ital *adj* extraconiugale

extramural [‚ekstrə'mjurəl] *adj* fuori della scuola, interscolastico; fuori delle mura

extraneous [eks'trenı-əs] *adj* estraneo

extraordinary [eks‚ekstrə'ordı‚nerı] *or* [eks'trordı‚nerı] *adj* straordinario

extrapolate [eks'træpə‚let] *tr & intr* estrapolare

extrasensory [‚ekstrə'sensəri] *adj* extrasensoriale

extravagance [eks'trævəgəns] *s* prodigalità *f*; (*wildness, folly*) stravaganza

extravagant [eks'trævəgənt] *adj* prodigo; (*wild, foolish*) stravagante

extreme [eks'trim] *adj & s* estremo; in the extreme in massimo grado; to go to extremes andare agli estremi

extremely [eks'trimli] *adv* estremamente, in sommo grado

extreme' unc'tion *s* Estrema Unzione

extremist [eks'trimıst] *adj & s* estremista *mf*

extremi•ty [eks'tremıti] *s* (-ties) estremità *f*; (*great want*) estrema necessità; extremities estremi *mpl*; (*hands and feet*) estremità *fpl*

extricate ['ekstrı‚ket] *tr* districare

extrinsic [eks'trınsık] *adj* estrinseco

extrovert ['ekstrə‚vʌrt] *s* estroverso

extrude [eks'trud] *tr* estrudere || *intr* protrudere

exuberant [eg'zubərənt] *or* [eg'zjubərənt] *adj* esuberante

exude [eg'zud] *or* [ek'sud] *tr & intr* trasudare, stillare

exult [eg'zʌlt] *intr* esultare, tripudiare

exultant [eg'zʌltənt] *adj* esultante

eye [aı] *s* occhio; (*of hook and eye*) occhiello; to catch one's eye attirare l'attenzione di qlcu; to feast one's eyes on deliziarsi la vista con; to lay eyes on riuscire a vedere; to make eyes at fare gli occhi dolci a; to roll one's eyes stralunare gli occhi; to see eye to eye andare perfettamente d'accordo; to shut one's eyes to chiudere un occhio a; far finta di non vedere; without batting an eye senza batter ciglio || *v* (*pret & pp* eyed; *ger* eying or eyeing) *tr* occhieggiare; to eye up and down guardare da capo a piedi

eye'ball' *s* globo oculare

eye'bolt' *s* bullone *m* ad anello

eye'brow' *s* sopracciglio; to raise one's eyebrows inarcare le sopracciglia

eye'cup' *s* occhiera

eye'drop'per *s* contagocce *m*

eyeful ['aı‚ful] *s* vista, colpo d'occhio; (coll) bellezza

eye'glass' *s* (*of optical instrument*) lente *f*, oculare *m*; (*eyecup*) occhiera; eyeglasses occhiali *mpl*

eye'lash' *s* ciglio

eyelet ['aılıt] *s* occhiello, maglietta, asola; (*hole to look through*) feritoia

eye'lid' *s* palpebra

eye' o'pener ['opənər] *s* affare *m* che apre gli occhi; (coll) bicchierino bevuto di mattina presto

eye'piece' s oculare m
eye'shade' s visiera
eye' shad'ow s rimmel m
eye'sight' s—**within eyeshot** a portata di vista
eye'sight' s vista; (*range*) capacità visiva
eye' sock'et s occhiaia, orbita
eye'sore' s pugno in un occhio

eye'strain' s vista affaticata
eye'-test chart' s tabella optometrica
eye'tooth' s (-**teeth**) dente canino; **to cut one's eyeteeth** (coll) fare esperienza; **to give one's eyeteeth for** (coll) dare un occhio della testa per
eye'wash' s (*flattery*) burro, lusinga; (pharm) collirio; (slang) balla
eye' wit'ness s testimone m oculare

F

F, f [ef] s sesta lettera dell'alfabeto inglese
fable ['febəl] s favola
fabric ['fæbrɪk] s stoffa, tessuto; fabbrica, struttura
fabricate ['fæbrɪ,ket] tr fabbricare
fabrication [,fæbrɪ'keʃən] s fabbricazione; falsificazione, invenzione
fabulous ['fæbjələs] adj favoloso
façade [fə'sɑd] s facciata
face [fes] s volto, viso, faccia; (*surface*) superficie f; (*of coin*) diritto; (*of precious stone*) faccetta; (*of water*) mostra; (*grimace*) smorfia; (*of building*) facciata, (typ) occhio; **in the face of** di fronte a; **to have a long face** fare il muso lungo; **to keep a straight face** contenere le risa; **to show one's face** farsi vedere || tr far fronte a, fronteggiare; (*a wall*) ricoprire; (*a suit*) foderare; **facing of** fronte a || intr—**to face about** voltarsi, fare dietro front; **to face on** dare a; **to face up to** guardare in faccia
face' card' s figura
face' lift'ing s plastica facciale
facet ['fæsɪt] s faccetta; (fig) faccia
facetious [fə'siʃəs] adj faceto
face' val'ue s valore m facciale
facial ['feʃəl] adj facciale || s massaggio facciale
fa'cial tis'sue s velina detergente
facilitate [fə'sɪlɪ,tet] tr facilitare
facili·ty [fə'sɪlɪti] s (-**ties**) facilità f; **facilities** (*installations*) attrezzature fpl; (*for transportation*) mezzi mpl; (*services*) servizi mpl
facing ['fesɪŋ] s rivestimento
facsimile [fæk'sɪmɪli] s facsimile m
fact [fækt] s fatto; **in fact** in realtà; **the fact is that** il fatto si è che
faction ['fækʃən] s fazione; discordia
factional ['fækʃənəl] adj fazioso; (*partisan*) partigiano
factionalism ['fækʃənə,lɪzəm] s partigianeria; parzialità f
factor ['fæktər] s fattore m || tr scomporre in fattori
facto·ry ['fæktəri] s (-**ries**) fabbrica
factual ['fæktʃu·əl] adj effettivo, reale
facul·ty ['fækəlti] s (-**ties**) facoltà f
fad [fæd] s moda passeggera
fade [fed] tr stingere || intr (*said of colors*) stingersi, sbiadire; (*said of*

sounds, sight, radio signals, memory, etc.) svanire, affievolirsi; (*said of beauty*) sfiorire
fade'-out' s affievolimento, affievolirsi m; (mov) chiusura in dissolvenza; (rad, telv) evanescenza
fading ['fedɪŋ] s affievolimento; (mov) dissolvenza; (rad, telv) evanescenza
fag [fæg] s schiavo del lavoro; (coll) sigaretta || tr—**to fag out** stancare
fagot ['fægət] s fascina, fastello
fail [fel] s—**without fail** senza meno || tr mancare (with dat); (*a student*) riprovare, (*an examination*) farsi bocciare in || intr fallire, venire a meno; (*said of a student*) farsi riprovare; (*said of a motor*) rompersi, fermarsi; (com) cadere in fallimento; **to fail to** mancare di
failure ['feljər] s insuccesso; insufficienza; (*student*) bocciato; (com) fallimento
faint [fent] adj debole; **to feel faint** sentirsi mancare || s svenimento || intr svenire
faint-hearted ['fent'hɑrtɪd] adj codardo, timido
fair [fer] adj giusto, onesto; (*moderately large*) discreto; (*even*) liscio; (*civil*) gentile; (*hair*) biondo; (*complexion*) chiaro; (*sky, weather*) sereno || s (*exhibition*) fiera; (*carnival*) sagra || adv direttamente; **to play fair** agire onestamente
fair'ground' s terreno dell'esposizione, campo della fiera
fairly ['ferli] adv giustamente, imparzialmente; discretamente, abbastanza; completamente
fair-minded ['fer'maɪndɪd] adj equanime, equo, giusto
fairness ['fernɪs] s giustizia, imparzialità f; bellezza; (*of complexion*) bianchezza
fair' play' s comportamento leale
fair' sex' s bel sesso
fair'-weath'er adj—**a fair-weather friend** un amico del tempo felice
fair·y ['feri] adj fatato || s (-**ies**) fata; (slang) finocchio
fair'y god'mother s buona fata
fair'y·land' s terra delle fate
fair'y tale' s fiaba, racconto delle fate
faith [feθ] s fede f; **to break faith with** venir meno alla parola data a; **to keep faith with** tener fede alla parola

data a; **to pin one's faith on** porre tutte le proprie speranze su; **upon my faith!** in fede mia!

faithful ['feθfəl] *adj* fedele || **the faithful** i fedeli

faithless ['feθlɪs] *adj* infedele, sleale

fake [fek] *adj* falso, finto || *s* contraffazione; (*person*) imbroglione *m* || *tr & intr* contraffare, falsificare

faker ['fekər] *s* (coll) imbroglione *m*

falcon ['fɔkən] or ['fɔlkən] *s* falcone *m*

falconer ['fɔkənər] or ['fɔlkənər] *s* falconiere *m*

falconry ['fɔkənrɪ] or ['fɔlkənrɪ] *s* falconeria

fall [fɔl] *adj* autunnale || *s* caduta; (*of water*) cataratta, cascata; (*of prices*) ribasso; (*autumn*) autunno; **falls** cataratta, cascate *fpl* || *v* (*pret* **fell** [fel]; *pp* **fallen** ['fɔlən]) *intr* cadere; discendere; **to fall apart** farsi a pezzi; **to fall back** (mil) ripiegare; **to fall behind** rimanere indietro; **to fall down** cadere; stramazzare; **to fall due** scadere; **to fall flat** stramazzare; essere un insuccesso; **to fall for** (slang) lasciarsi abbindolare da; (slang) innamorarsi di; **to fall in** (*said of a building*) crollare; (mil) allinearsi; **to fall in with** imbattersi in; mettersi d'accordo con; **to fall off** ritirarsi; diminuire; **to fall out** accadere; essere in disaccordo; (mil) rompere i ranghi; **to fall out of** cadere da; **to fall out with** inimicarsi con; **to fall over** cadere; (coll) adulare; **to fall through** fallire; **to fall to** cominciare; (coll) cominciare a mangiare; (*said, e.g., of an inheritance*) ricadere su; **to fall under** rientrare in

fallacious [fə'leʃəs] *adj* fallace

falla·cy ['fæləsɪ] *s* (*-cies*) fallacia

fall' guy's (slang) testa di turco

fallible ['fælɪbəl] *adj* fallibile

fall'ing star's stella cadente

fall'out's pulviscolo radioattivo

fall'out shel'ter's rifugio antiatomico

fallow ['fælo] *adj* incolto; **to lie fallow** rimanere incolto || *s* maggese *m* || *tr* maggesare

false [fɔls] *adj* falso; (*hair, teeth, etc.*) posticcio, finto || *adv* falsamente; **to play false** tradire

false' bot'tom's doppio fondo

false' col'ors *spl* apparenze mentite

false' face's maschera; (*ugly false face*) mascherone *m*

false'-heart'ed ['fɔls'hɑrtɪd] *adj* perfido

falsehood ['fɔls-hʊd] *s* falsità *f*, falso

false' pretens'es *spl* falso, impostura; **under false pretenses** allegando ragioni false

falset·to [fɔl'seto] *s* (*-tos*) (*voice*) falsetto; (*person*) cantante *m* in falsetto

falsi·fy ['fɔlsɪ,faɪ] *v* (*pret & pp* **-fied**) *tr* falsificare; (*to disprove*) smentire || *intr* mentire

falsi·ty ['fɔlsɪtɪ] *s* (*-ties*) falsità *f*

falter ['fɔltər] *s* vacillamento; (*in speech*) balbettio || *intr* vacillare; balbettare

fame [fem] *s* fama

famed [femd] *adj* famoso

familiar [fə'mɪljər] *adj* familiare; intimo; **to be familiar with** (*people*) aver pratica con; (*things*) aver pratica di

familiari·ty [fə,mɪlɪ'ærɪtɪ] *s* (*-ties*) familiarità *f*, dimestichezza

familiarize [fə'mɪljə,raɪz] *tr* far conoscere

fami·ly ['fæmɪlɪ] *adj* familiare; **in the family way** (coll) in altro stato || *s* (*-lies*) famiglia

fam'ily man's (*men'*) padre *m* di famiglia

fam'ily name's cognome *m*

fam'ily tree's albero genealogico

famine ['fæmɪn] *s* carestia

famished ['fæmɪʃt] *adj* famelico; **to be famished** avere una fame da lupo

famous ['feməs] *adj* famoso; (coll) eccellente

fan [fæn] *s* ventaglio; (elec) ventilatore *m*; (coll) tifoso, patito || *v* (*pret & pp* **fanned;** *ger* **fanning**) *tr* sventagliare; (*to winnow*) vagliare; (*fire, passions*) attizzare || *intr* sventagliarsi; **to fan out** (*said of a road*) diramarsi a ventaglio

fanatic [fə'nætɪk] *adj & s* fanatico

fanatical [fə'nætɪkəl] *adj* fanatico

fanaticism [fə'nætɪ,sɪzəm] *s* fanatismo

fan' belt's (aut) cinghia del ventilatore

fancied ['fænsɪd] *adj* immaginario

fancier ['fænsɪ·ər] *s* maniaco, tifoso; (*of animals*) conoscitore *m*, allevatore *m*

fanciful ['fænsɪfəl] *adj* fantasioso, estroso; immaginario

fan·cy ['fænsɪ] *adj* (*-cier; -ciest*) immaginario; immaginativo; ornamentale; di lusso; fantasioso, estroso || *s* fantasia; (*whim*) grillo, estro; **to take a fancy to** prendere una passione per || *v* (*pret & pp* **-cied**) *tr* immaginare

fan'cy ball's ballo in costume

fan'cy dress's costume *m*

fan'cy foods' *spl* cibi *mpl* di lusso

fan'cy-free' *adj* libero dai lacci dell'amore

fan'cy skat'ing *s* pattinaggio artistico

fan'cy·work's (sew) ricamo ornamentale

fanfare ['fænfer] *s* fanfara

fang [fæŋ] *s* zanna; (*of reptile*) dente velenoso

fan'light's lunetta

fantastic(al) [fæn'tæstɪk(əl)] *adj* fantastico

fanta·sy ['fæntəzi] or ['fæntəsi] *s* (*-sies*) fantasia

far [fɑr] *adj* distante; **on the far side of** dall'altra parte di || *adv* lontano; **as far as** fino a; **as far as I am concerned** per quanto mi riguardi; **as far as I know** per quanto io sappia; **by far** di gran lunga; **far and near** in lungo e in largo; **far away** molto lontano; **far be it from me** Dio me ne scampi e liberi; **far better** molto meglio; molto migliore; **far different** molto differente; **far from** lontano da; **far from it** tutto al contrario; **far into** fino al fondo di; **far into the night** fino a tarda ora; **far more** molto più; **far off** lontanissimo; **how far** quanto lontano; **how far is it?** a che distanza è da qui?; **in so far as** in quanto; **thus far** sinora; **to go far towards** contribuire molto a

faraway ['farǝ‚we] *adj* distante, lontano; distratto

farce [fɑrs] *s* farsa

farcical ['fɑrsɪkǝl] *adj* farsesco

fare [fer] *s* prezzo della corsa; passeggero; (*food*) vitto || *intr* andare, e.g., **how did you fare?** come Le è andata?

Far' East' *s* Estremo Oriente

fare'well' *s* congedo, commiato; **to bid farewell to** or **to take farewell of** prender commiato da || *interj* addio!

far-fetched ['fɑr'fetʃt] *adj* peregrino, campato in aria

far-flung ['fɑr'flʌŋ] *adj* ampio; d'ampia distribuzione

farm [fɑrm] *adj* agricolo || *s* fattoria, tenuta || *tr* (*land*) coltivare || *intr* fare l'agricoltore or l'allevatore

farmer ['fɑrmǝr] *s* agricoltore *m*, contadino

farm' hand' *s* bracciante *m*

farm'house' *s* casa colonica, masseria

farming ['fɑrmɪŋ] *s* agricoltura, coltivazione

farm'yard' *s* aia

far'-off' *adj* lontano

far-reaching ['fɑr'ritʃɪŋ] *adj* di grande portata

far-sighted ['fɑr'saɪtɪd] *adj* lungimirante; perspicace; presbite

farther ['fɑrðǝr] *adj* più lontano; addizionale || *adv* più lontano, più in là; inoltre; **farther on** più oltre

farthest ['fɑrðɪst] *adj* (il) più lontano; ultimo || *adv* al massimo

farthing ['fɑrðɪŋ] *s* (Brit) quarto di centesimo

Far' West' *s* (U.S.A.) lontano Occidente

fascinate ['fæsɪ‚net] *tr* affascinare

fascinating ['fæsɪ‚netɪŋ] *adj* incantatore, affascinante

fascism ['fæʃɪzǝm] *s* fascismo

fascist ['fæʃɪst] *adj & s* fascista *mf*

fashion ['fæʃǝn] *s* voga, moda; foggia, maniera; alta società; **after a fashion** in certo modo; **in fashion** di moda; **out of fashion** fuori moda; **to go out of fashion** passare di moda || *tr* fare, foggiare

fashionable ['fæʃǝnǝbǝl] *adj* elegante, alla moda

fash'ion design'ing *s* alta moda

fash'ion plate' *s* figurino

fash'ion show' *s* sfilata di moda

fast [fæst] or [fɑst] *adj* veloce; (*clock*) che corre, in anticipo; (*color*) solido; (*friend*) fedele || *s* digiuno; **to break fast** rompere il digiuno || *adv* rapidamente, fortemente; (*asleep*) profondamente; **to hold fast** tenersi saldo; **to live fast**

condurre una vita dissoluta || *intr* digiunare, fare vigilia

fast' day' *s* giorno di magro

fasten ['fæsǝn] or ['fɑsǝn] *tr* fissare; attaccare; (*a door*) sbarrare; (*a nickname; blows*) affibbiare; (*a dress*) allacciarsi || *intr* attaccarsi

fastener ['fæsǝnǝr] or ['fɑsǝnǝr] *s* legaccio, laccio; (*snap, clasp*) fermaglio; (*for papers*) fermacarte *m*

fastidious [fæs'tɪdɪ‐ǝs] *adj* schizzinoso; meticoloso

fasting ['fæstɪŋ] or ['fɑstɪŋ] *s* digiuno

fat [fæt] *adj* (**fatter; fattest**) grasso; (*productive*) forte, ricco, pingue; **to get fat** ingrassare || *s* grasso, unto; (*of pork*) sugna

fatal ['fetǝl] *adj* fatale

fatalism ['fetǝ‚lɪzǝm] *s* fatalismo

fatalist ['fetǝlɪst] *s* fatalista *mf*

fatali·ty [fǝ'tælɪti] *s* (**-ties**) (*in an accident*) morte *f*; accidente *m* mortale; fatalità *f*

fate [fet] *s* fato; **the Fates** le Parche || *tr* predestinare

fated ['fetɪd] *adj* destinato

fateful ['fetfǝl] *adj* fatidico, fatale

fat'head' *s* (coll) zuccone *m*

father ['fɑðǝr] *s* padre *m*; (*male ancestor*) antenato || *tr* procreare; creare; assumere la paternità di

fatherhood ['fɑðǝr‚hud] *s* paternità *f*

fa'ther-in-law' *s* (**fathers-in-law**) suocero

fa'ther·land' *s* patria

fatherless ['fɑðǝrlɪs] *adj* orfano di padre; senza padre

fatherly ['fɑðǝrli] *adj* paterno

Fa'ther's Day' *s* festa del papà

Fa'ther Time' *s* il Tempo

fathom ['fæðǝm] *s* braccio || *tr* sondare

fathomless ['fæðǝmlɪs] *adj* senza fondo; imponderabile

fatigue [fǝ'tig] *s* fatica, strapazzo; (mil) comanda || *tr* stancare, affaticare

fatigue' clothes' *spl* (mil) tenuta di servizio, tenuta di fatica

fatten ['fætǝn] *tr & intr* ingrassare

fat·ty ['fæti] *adj* (**-tier; -tiest**) grasso; (pathol) adiposo || *s* (**-ties**) (coll) tombolo

fatuous ['fætʃʊ‐ǝs] *adj* fatuo

faucet ['fɔsɪt] *s* rubinetto

fault [fɔlt] *s* (*misdeed, blame*) colpa; (*defect*) difetto, magagna; (geol) faglia; (sports) fallo; **it's your fault** è colpa Sua; **to a fault** all'eccesso; **to find fault with** trovare a ridire sul conto di

fault'find'er *s* ipercritico, criticone *m*

fault'find'ing *adj* criticone || *s* ipercritica

faultless ['fɔltlɪs] *adj* perfetto, inappuntabile

fault·y ['fɔlti] *adj* (**-ier; -iest**) manchevole, difettoso

faun [fɔn] *s* fauno

fauna ['fɔnǝ] *s* fauna

favor ['fevǝr] *s* favore *m*; (*letter*) pregiata; **do me the favor to** mi faccia il piacere di; **by your favor** col Suo permesso; **favors** regali *mpl* di festa; **to be in favor with** essere nelle grazie di; **to be out of favor** cadere in disgrazia || *tr* favorire; (coll) assomigliare (with *dat*)

favorable ['fevərəbəl] *adj* favorevole

favorite ['fevərɪt] *adj & s* favorito

favoritism ['fevərɪ‚tɪzəm] *s* favoritismo

fawn [fɔn] *s* cerbiatto || *intr*—**to fawn on** adulare, strusciarsi a

faze [fez] *tr* (coll) perturbare

fear [fɪr] *s* paura; **for fear of** per paura di; **for fear that** per paura che; **no fear** non c'è pericolo; **to be in fear of** aver timore di || *tr & intr* temere

fearful ['fɪrfəl] *adj* pauroso, timorato; (coll) spaventoso

fearless ['fɪrlɪs] *adj* impavido

feasible ['fizɪbəl] *adj* fattibile, possibile

feast [fist] *s* festa; (*sumptuous meal*) festino, banchetto || *tr* intrattenere || *intr* banchettare; **to feast on** rallegrarsi alla vista di

feat [fit] *s* fatto, prodezza

feather ['feðər] *s* penna; (*soft and fluffy structure covering bird*) piuma; (*type*) qualità *f*, conio; (*tuft*) pennacchio; **in fine feather** di buon umore; in buona salute || *tr* impennare; coprire di piume; (naut) spalare; (aer) bandierare; **to feather one's nest** arricchirsi

feath'er bed' *s* letto di piume

feath'er-bed'ding *s* impiego di mano d'opera non necessaria richiesto da un sindacato operaio

feath'er-brain' *s* cervello di gallina

feath'er-edge' *s* (*of board*) augnatura; (*of sharpened tool*) filo morto

feath'er-weight' *s* peso piuma

feathery ['feðərɪ] *adj* piumato; leggero

feature ['fitʃər] *s* fattezza; caratteristica; (journ) articolo principale; (mov) attrazione; **features** fattezze *fpl* || *tr* caratterizzare; mettere in evidenza; (coll) immaginare

fea'ture film' *s* lungometraggio

fea'ture sto'ry *s* articolo di spalla

February ['fɛbru‚ɛrɪ] *s* febbraio

feces ['fisɪz] *spl* feci *fpl*

feckless ['fɛklɪs] *adj* debole; inetto

federal ['fɛdərəl] *adj* federale || *s* federalista *mf*

federate ['fɛdə‚ret] *adj* federato || *tr* federare || *intr* federarsi

federation [‚fɛdə'reʃən] *s* federazione

federative ['fɛdə‚retɪv] or ['fɛdərətɪv] *adj* federativo

fedora [fɪ'dorə] *s* cappello floscio di feltro

fed' up' [fɛd] *adj* stanco e stufo; **to be fed up with** averne fin sopra gli occhi di

fee [fi] *s* onorario; (*charge allowed by law*) diritto; (*tip*) mancia; (*for tuition*) tassa; (*for admission*) ingresso || *tr* pagare

feeble ['fibəl] *adj* debole, fievole

feeble-minded ['fibəl'maɪndɪd] *adj* rimbecillito; debole, vacillante

feed [fid] *s* mangime *m;* (coll) mangiata; (mach) dispositivo d'alimentazione || *v* (*pret & pp* fed [fɛd]) *tr* nutrire; (*a machine*) alimentare; (*cattle*) pascere; (theat) imbeccare || *intr* mangiare; **to feed upon** nutrirsi di

feed'back' *s* (*of a computer*) ritorno d'informazioni; (electron) reazione

feed' bag' *s* musetta

feed' pump' *s* pompa di alimentazione

feed' trough' *s* (*for cattle*) vasca; (*for hogs*) trogolo

feed' wire' *s* cavo di alimentazione

feel [fil] *s* sensazione; (*touch*) tocco; (*vague mental impression*) senso || *v* (*pret & pp* felt [fɛlt]) *tr* sentire; (e.g., with the hands) palpare, toccare; (*s.o.'s pulse*) tastare || *intr* (sick, tired, etc.) sentirsi; **to feel bad** sentirsi male; (*to be unhappy*) essere spiacente; **to feel cheap** vergognarsi; **to feel comfortable** sentirsi a proprio agio; **to feel for** cercare di toccare; avere compassione per; **to feel like** aver voglia di; **to feel safe** sentirsi al sicuro; **to feel sorry** essere spiacente; pentirsi; **to feel sorry for** aver compassione di; pentirsi di

feeler ['filər] *s* (*hint*) sondaggio; **feelers** (*of insect*) antenne *fpl;* (*of mollusk*) tentacoli *mpl;* **to put out feelers** (fig) tastare il terreno

feeling ['filɪŋ] *s* (*with senses*) senso; (*impression, emotion*) sentimento, sensazione; opinione

feign [fen] *tr* fingere; inventare; imitare || *intr* far finta; **to feign to be** fingersi

feint [fent] *s* finta || *intr* fare una finta

feldspar ['fɛld‚spar] *s* feldspato

felicitate [fə'lɪsɪ‚tet] *tr* felicitarsi con

felicitous [fə'lɪsɪtəs] *adj* felice, indovinato; eloquente

fell [fɛl] *adj* crudele, mortale || *tr* (*trees*) abbattere

felloe ['fɛlo] *s* cerchione *m;* (*part of the rim*) gavello

fellow ['fɛlo] *s* compagno; collega *m;* (*of a society*) membro, socio; (*holder of fellowship*) borsista *mf;* (coll) tipo, tizio; (coll) innamorato; **good fellow** buon diavolo; galantuomo

fel'low cit'izen *s* concittadino

fel'low coun'try-man *s* (**-men**) concitadino

fel'low crea'ture *s* prossimo

fel'low-man' *s* (**-men'**) prossimo

fel'low mem'ber *s* consocio

fellowship ['fɛlo‚ʃɪp] *s* compagnia; (*for study*) borsa di studio

fel'low trav'eler *s* simpatizzante *mf;* criptocomunista *mf;* compagno di viaggio

felon ['fɛlən] *s* criminale *mf;* (pathol) patereccio, giradito

felo-ny ['fɛlənɪ] *s* (**-nies**) delitto doloso

felt [fɛlt] *s* feltro

felt' board' *s* lavagna di panno

felt'-tip pen' *s* pennarello

female ['fimel] *adj* (*sex*) femminile;

(animal, plant, piece of a device)
femmina || *s* femmina

feminine ['fɛmɪnɪn] *adj & s* femminile *m*

feminism ['fɛmɪ ˌnɪzəm] *s* femminismo

fence [fɛns] *s* steccato, staccionata; *(for stolen goods)* ricettatore *m*; *(carp)* squadra di guida; *(sports)* scherma; **on the fence** *(coll)* indeciso || *tr* recingere || *intr* tirare di scherma

fencing ['fɛnsɪŋ] *s* scherma; *(fig)* schermaglia

fenc'ing mask' *s* visiera

fend [fɛnd] *tr*—**to fend off** parare || *intr*—**to fend for oneself** *(coll)* badare a sé stesso

fender ['fɛndər] *s (of trolley car)* salvagente *m*; *(of fireplace)* parafuoco; *(aut)* parafango; *(naut)* parabordo

fennel ['fɛnəl] *s* finocchio

ferment ['fɜrmɛnt] *s* fermento || [fər'mɛnt] *tr & intr* fermentare

fern [fɜrn] *s* felce *f*

ferocious [fə'roʃəs] *adj* feroce

ferocity [fə'rɑsɪti] *s* ferocia

ferret ['fɛrɪt] *s* furetto || *tr*—**to ferret out** scovare || *intr* indagare

Fer'ris wheel' ['fɛrɪs] *s* ruota *(del parco dei divertimenti)*

fer·ry ['fɛri] *s (-ries)* traghetto; nave *f* traghetto || *v (pret & pp -ried) tr* traghettare || *intr* attraversare

fer'ry·boat' *s* nave *f* traghetto, ferryboat *m*

fertile ['fɜrtɪl] *adj* fertile

fertilize ['fɜrtɪ ˌlaɪz] *tr* fertilizzare; *(to impregnate)* fecondare

fertilizer ['fɜrtɪ ˌlaɪzər] *s* fertilizzante *m*; *(e.g., of flowers)* fecondatore *m*

fervent ['fɜrvənt] *adj* fervente, fervido

fervid ['fɜrvɪd] *adj* fervido

fervor ['fɜrvər] *s* fervore *m*

fester ['fɛstər] *s* ulcera, piaga || *tr* corrompere || *intr* suppurare; *(fig)* corrompersi

festival ['fɛstɪvəl] *adj* festivo || *s* festa; *(of music)* festival *m*

festive ['fɛstɪv] *adj* festivo

festivi·ty [fɛs'tɪvɪti] *s (-ties)* festività *f*

festoon [fɛs'tun] *s* festone *m* || *tr* ornare di festoni

fetch [fɛtʃ] *tr* andare a prendere; *(a price)* fruttare, vendersi per

fetching ['fɛtʃɪŋ] *adj (coll)* cattivante, attraente

fete [fɛt] *s* festa || *tr* festeggiare

fetid ['fɛtɪd] *or* ['fitɪd] *adj* fetido

fetish ['fitɪʃ] *or* ['fɛtɪʃ] *s* feticcio

fetlock ['fɛtlɑk] *s* nocca; *(tuft of hair)* barbetta

fetter ['fɛtər] *s* ceppo, catena || *tr* mettere ai ceppi, incatenare

fettle ['fɛtəl] *s* stato, condizione; **in fine fettle** in buone condizioni

fetus ['fitəs] *s* feto

feud [fjud] *s* antagonismo; odio ereditario || *intr* essere in lotta

feudal ['fjudəl] *adj* feudale

feudalism ['fjudə ˌlɪzəm] *s* feudalismo

fever ['fivər] *s* febbre *f*

feverish ['fivərɪʃ] *adj* febbrile

few [fju] *adj & pron* pochi; **a few** alcuni; **quite a few** molti

fiancé [ˌfi·ɑn'se] *s* fidanzato

fiancée [ˌfi·ɑn'se] *s* fidanzata

fias·co [fɪ'æsko] *s (-cos or -coes)* fiasco

fib [fɪb] *s* menzogna, frottola || *v (pret & pp fibbed; ger fibbing)* intr raccontar frottole

fiber ['faɪbər] *s* fibra; *(fig)* tempra

fi'ber·glass' *s* vetroresina

fibrous ['faɪbrəs] *adj* fibroso

fickle ['fɪkəl] *adj* volubile, incostante, mobile

fiction ['fɪkʃən] *s (invention)* finzione; *(branch of literature)* novellistica

fictional ['fɪkʃənəl] *adj* immaginario

fictionalize ['fɪkʃənə ˌlaɪz] *tr* romanzare

fictitious [fɪk'tɪʃəs] *adj* fittizio

fiddle ['fɪdəl] *s* violino; **fit as a fiddle** in perfetta salute || *tr (coll)* suonare sul violino; **to fiddle away** *(coll)* sprecare || *intr (coll)* suonare il violino; **to fiddle with** *(coll)* giocherellare con

fiddler ['fɪdlər] *s (coll)* violinista *mf*

fiddling ['fɪdlɪŋ] *adj* triviale, futile, insignificante

fideli·ty [faɪ'dɛlɪti] *or* [fɪ'dɛlɪti] *s (-ties)* fedeltà *f*

fidget ['fɪdʒɪt] *intr* agitarsi; **to fidget with** giocherellare con

fidgety ['fɪdʒɪti] *adj* irrequieto

fiduciar·y [fɪ'dju ʃɪ ˌɛri] *or* [fɪ'duʃɪ ˌɛri] *adj* fiduciario || *s (-ies)* fiduciario

fie [faɪ] *interj* vergogna!

fief [fif] *s* feudo

field [fild] *adj (mil)* da campagna || *s* campo; *(sports)* terreno; *(min)* giacimento; *(of motor or dynamo)* (elec) induttore *m*; *(phys)* campo

fielder ['fildər] *s (outfielder)* giocatore *m* del campo esterno

field' glass'es *spl* binocolo

field' hock'ey *s* hockey *m* su prato

field' mag'net *s* induttore *m*, calamita induttrice

field' mar'shal *s (mil)* maresciallo di campo

field' mouse' *s* topo di campagna

field'piece' *s* pezzo da campagna

fiend [find] *s* diavolo; *(coll)* addetto, tifoso

fiendish ['findɪʃ] *adj* diabolico

fierce [fɪrs] *adj* fiero, feroce; *(wind)* furioso; *(coll)* maledetto

fierceness ['fɪrsnɪs] *s* ferocia

fier·y ['faɪri] *or* ['faɪ·əri] *adj (-ier; -iest)* ardente, focoso

fife [faɪf] *s* piffero

fifteen ['fɪf'tin] *adj, s & pron* quindici *m*

fifteenth ['fɪf'tinθ] *adj, s & pron* quindicesimo || *s (in dates)* quindici *m*

fifth [fɪfθ] *adj, s & pron* quinto || *s (in dates)* cinque *m*

fifth' col'umn *s* quinta colonna

fiftieth ['fɪftɪ·ɪθ] *adj, s & pron* cinquantesimo

fif·ty ['fɪfti] *adj & pron* cinquanta || *s (-ties)* cinquanta *m*; **the fifties** gli anni cinquanta

fif'ty-fif'ty *adv*—**to go fifty-fifty** fare a metà

fig [fɪg] *s* fico

fight [faɪt] *s* lotta; baruffa; combattimento; spirito combattivo; (sports) incontro; **to pick a fight with** attaccar briga con ‖ *v* (*pret & pp* **fought** [fɔt]) *tr* lottare con; combattere contro; opporsi a ‖ *intr* lottare; combattere; **to fight shy of** cercar di evitare

fighter ['faɪtər] *s* lottatore *m*; (*warrior*) combattente *m*; (aer) caccia *m*

fig' leaf' *s* foglia di fico

figment ['fɪgmənt] *s* finzione

figurative ['fɪgjərətɪv] *adj* (fa) figurativo; (rhet) figurato

figure ['fɪgjər] *s* figura; numero; prezzo; **to be good at figures** far bene di conto; **to cut a figure** fare una buona figura; **to keep one's figure** conservare la linea ‖ *tr* figurare; immaginare; raffigurare; supporre, calcolare; **to figure out** calcolare; decifrare ‖ *intr* apparire; **to figure on** (coll) contare su

fig'ure-head' *s* uomo di paglia, prestanome *m*; (naut) polena

fig'ure of speech' *s* figura retorica

fig'ure skat'ing *s* pattinaggio artistico

figurine [ˌfɪgjəˈrin] *s* figurina

filament ['fɪləmənt] *s* filamento

filbert ['fɪlbərt] *s* (*tree*) nocciolo, avellano; (*nut*) nocciola, avellana

filch [fɪltʃ] *tr* rubacchiare

file [faɪl] *s* (*row*) fila; (*tool*) lima; (*folder*) filza; (*room*) archivio; (*of cards*) schedario ‖ *tr* mettere in fila; limare; archiviare, schedare; (journ) trasmettere ‖ *intr* sfilare; **to file for** fare domanda di

file' clerk' *s* schedarista *mf*

filet [fɪ'le] or ['fɪle] *s* filetto ‖ *tr* tagliare in filetti

filial ['fɪlɪəl] or ['fɪljəl] *adj* filiale

filiation [ˌfɪlɪ'eʃən] *s* filiazione

filibuster ['fɪlɪ ˌbʌstər] *s* (*tactics*) ostruzionismo; (*speech*) discorso ostruzionista; (*person making such a speech*) ostruzionista *mf*; (*buccaneer*) filibustiere *m* ‖ *tr* fare ostruzionismo contro ‖ *intr* fare dell'ostruzionismo

filigree ['fɪlɪ ˌgri] *adj* filigranato ‖ *s* filigrana ‖ *tr* lavorare in filigrana

filing ['faɪlɪŋ] *s* (*of documents*) schedatura; limatura; **filings** limatura

fil'ing cab'inet *s* schedario

fil'ing card' *s* cartellino, scheda

fill [fɪl] *s* sazietà *f*; (*place filled with earth*) terrapieno; **to have or get one's fill** mangiare a sazietà ‖ *tr* riempire; (*an order*) eseguire; (*a hole*) otturare; (*a tooth*) piombare; (*a tire*) gonfiare; (*a place*) occupare; (*with sand*) interrare; **to fill out** (*a form*) riempire; **to fill up** (aut) fare il pieno di ‖ *intr* riempirsi; **to fill in** prendere il posto; **to fill up** riempirsi

filler ['fɪlər] *s* ripieno; (*person*) riempitore *m*; (*painting*) mestica; (journ) articolo riempitivo

fillet ['fɪlɪt] *s* nastro, fascia; (*for hair*) nastro; (archit) listello ‖ *tr* filettare

‖ ['fɪle] or ['fɪlɪt] *s* (*of meat or fish*) filetto ‖ *tr* tagliare a filetti

filling ['fɪlɪŋ] *s* (*of a tooth*) impiombatura; (*of turkey*) ripieno

fill'ing sta'tion *s* stazione di rifornimento

fillip ['fɪlɪp] *s* stimolo; colpetto col dito ‖ *tr* dare un colpetto col dito a; (fig) stimulare

fil·ly ['fɪli] *s* (-**lies**) puledra

film [fɪlm] *s* pellicola; (mov, phot) pellicola, film *m* ‖ *tr* filmare

film' li'brary *s* cineteca, filmoteca

film'strip' *s* filmina

film·y ['fɪlmi] *adj* (-**ier**; -**iest**) sottile, delicato; (*look*) annebbiato

filter ['fɪltər] *s* filtro ‖ *tr & intr* filtrare

filtering ['fɪltərɪŋ] *s* filtrazione

fil'ter pa'per *s* carta da filtro

fil'ter tip' *s* filtro, bocchino filtro

filth [fɪlθ] *s* sporco, sporcizia

filth·y ['fɪlθi] *adj* (-**ier**; -**iest**) sporco, sudicio

filth'y lu'cre ['lukər] *s* il vile metallo

filtrate ['fɪltret] *s* liquido filtrato ‖ *tr & intr* filtrare

fin [fɪn] *s* pinna; (slang) biglietto da cinque dollari

final ['faɪnəl] *adj* finale; (*last in a series*) ultimo; definitivo, insindacabile ‖ *s* esame *m* finale; **finals** (sports) finale *f*

finale [fɪ'nɑli] *s* (mus) finale *m*

finalist ['faɪnəlɪst] *s* finalista *mf*

finally ['faɪnəli] *adv* finalmente

finance [fɪ'næns] or ['faɪnæns] *s* finanza; **finances** finanze *fpl* ‖ *tr* finanziare

financial [fɪ'nænʃəl] or [faɪ'nænʃəl] *adj* finanziario

financier [ˌfɪnən'sɪr] or [ˌfaɪnən'sɪr] *s* finanziere *m*

financing [fɪ'nænsɪŋ] or ['faɪnænsɪŋ] *s* finanziamento

finch [fɪntʃ] *s* fringuello

find [faɪnd] *s* trovata ‖ *v* (*pret & pp* **found** [faʊnd]) *tr* trovare; rinvenire; (*s.o. innocent or guilty*) dichiarare; **to find out** venire a sapere ‖ *intr* (law) sentenziare; **to find out about** informarsi su

finder ['faɪndər] *s* (phot) mirino; (astr) cannochiale cercatore

finding ['faɪndɪŋ] *s* scoperta; (law) sentenza

fine [faɪn] *adj* buono; bello; fino, fine ‖ *s* multa ‖ *adv* (coll) benissimo; **to feel fine** (coll) sentirsi benissimo ‖ *tr* multare

fine' arts' *spl* belle arti

fineness ['faɪnnɪs] *s* finezza; (*of metal*) titolo

fine' print' *s* testo in caratteri minuti

finer·y ['faɪnəri] *s* (-**ies**) ornamenti *mpl*, fronzoli *mpl*; abito vistoso

fine-spun ['faɪn ˌspʌn] *adj* sottile

finesse [fɪ'nes] *s* finezza; (bridge) impasse *f* ‖ *tr* fare l'impasse a ‖ *intr* fare l'impasse

fine'-tooth comb' *s* pettine fitto; **to go over with a fine-tooth comb** esaminare minuziosamente

finger ['fɪŋgər] s dito; **to have a finger in the pie** avere le mani in pasta; **to put one's finger on the spot** mettere il dito nella piaga; **to slip between the fingers** sfuggire di tra le dita; **to snap one's fingers at** infischiarsi di; **to twist around one's little finger** fare ciò che si vuole di || tr toccare con le dita; (to pilfer) rubacchiare; (slang) mostrare a dito

fin'ger board' s (mus) tastiera

fin'ger bowl' s sciacquadita m

fingering ['fɪŋgərɪŋ] s palpeggiamento; (mus) diteggiatura

fin'ger mark' s ditata

fin'ger-nail' s unghia

fin'ger-print' s impronta digitale || tr prendere le impronte digitali di

fin'ger-tip' s polpastrello; **to have at one's fingertips** avere sulla punta delle dita, sapere a menadito

finical ['fɪnɪkəl] or **finicky** ['fɪnɪki] adj pignolo, schizzinoso

finish ['fɪnɪʃ] s fine f; finitura; (sports) finale m || tr finire; **to finish off** distruggere || intr finire; **to finish + ger** finire di + inf; **to finish by + ger** finire per + inf

fin'ishing school' s scuola di perfezionamento per signorine

fin'ishing touch' s ultimo tocco

finite ['faɪnaɪt] adj finito

Finland ['fɪnlənd] s la Finlandia

Finlander ['fɪnləndər] s finlandese mf

Finn [fɪn] s (member of a Finnish-speaking group of people) finnico; (native or inhabitant of Finland) finlandese mf

Finnic ['fɪnɪk] adj & s finnico

Finnish ['fɪnɪʃ] adj finlandese || s (language) finlandese m

fir [fʌr] s abete m

fire [faɪr] s fuoco; (destructive burning) incendio; **to be on fire** ardere; **to be under enemy fire** essere sotto tiro nemico; **to catch fire** infiammarsi; **to hang fire** essere in sospeso; **to open fire** aprire il fuoco; **to set on fire, to set fire to** dar fuoco a; **under fire** sotto fuoco nemico; accusato || tr accendere; (an oven) scaldare; (bricks) cuocere; (a weapon) sparare; (the imagination) riscaldare; (an employee) (coll) licenziare || intr accendersi; **to fire on** far fuoco su; **to fire up** attivare una caldaia

fire' alarm' s avvisatore m d'incendio

fire'arm' s arma da fuoco

fire'ball' s palla da cannone esplosiva; (lightning) lampo a forma di globo infocato; meteorite m a forma di globo infocato

fire'boat' s lancia dei pompieri

fire'box' s (of a boiler) fornello; (to give alarm) stazione d'allarme

fire'brand' s tizzone m; (fig) fiaccola della discordia

fire'brick' s mattone refrattario

fire' brigade' s corpo di pompieri vòlontari

fire'bug' s (coll) incendiario

fire' com'pany s corpo dei pompieri;

compagnia d'assicurazioni contro gli incendi

fire'crack'er s mortaretto

fire'damp' s grisou m

fire' depart'ment s corpo dei pompieri

fire'dog' s alare m

fire' drill' s esercitazione in caso d'incendio

fire' en'gine s autopompa

fire' escape' s scala di sicurezza

fire' extin'guisher s estintore m

fire'fly' s (-flies) lucciola

fire'guard' s parafuoco

fire' hose' s manichetta

fire'house' s caserma dei pompieri

fire' hy'drant s bocca d'incendi

fire' insur'ance s assicurazione contro gli incendi

fire' i'rons spl arnesi mpl del camino

fire'man s (-men) (man who extinguishes fires) pompiere m, vigile m del fuoco; (stoker) fochista m

fire'place' s camino

fire'plug' s bocca da incendio, idrante m

fire'proof' adj incombustibile || tr rendere incombustibile

fire' sale' s vendita di merce avariata dal fuoco

fire' screen' s parafuoco

fire' ship' s brulotto

fire'side' s focolare m

fire'trap' s edificio senza mezzi adeguati per combattere incendi

fire' wall' s paratia antincendio

fire'wa'ter s (coll) acquavite f

fire'wood' s legna

fire'works' spl fuochi mpl artificiali

firing ['faɪrɪŋ] s (of furnace) alimentazione; (of bricks) cottura; (of a gun) sparo; (of soldiers) tiro; (of an internal-combustion engine) accensione; (of an employee) (coll) licenziamento

fir'ing line' s linea del fuoco

fir'ing or'der s (aut) ordine m d'accensione

fir'ing pin' s percussore m

fir'ing squad' s (for saluting at a burial) plotone m d'onore; (for executing) plotone m d'esecuzione

firm [fʌrm] adj forte, fermo || s ditta, compagnia

firmament ['fʌrməmənt] s firmamento

firm' name' s ragione f sociale

firmness ['fʌrmnɪs] s fermezza

first [fʌrst] adj primo || s primo; (aut) prima; (mus) voce f principale; **at first** sulle prime; **from the first da** bel principio || adv prima; **first of all** per prima cosa

first' aid' s pronto soccorso

first'-aid' kit' s cassetta farmaceutica d'urgenza

first'-aid' sta'tion s posto di pronto soccorso

first'-born' adj & s primogenito

first'-class' adj di prim'ordine, soprafino || adv in prima classe

first' cous'in s cugino primo

first'-day cov'er s busta primo giorno

first' draft' s brutta copia

first' fin'ger s dito indice
first' floor' s pianoterra m
first' fruits' spl primizie fpl
first' lieuten'ant s tenente m
firstly ['fʌrstli] adv in primo luogo
first' mate' s (naut) primo ufficiale, comandante m in seconda, secondo
first' name' s nome m di battesimo
first' night' s (theat) prima
first' of'ficer s (naut) primo ufficiale, comandante m in seconda, secondo
first'-rate' adj di prima forza; eccellente || adv (coll) benissimo
first'-run' adj di prima visione
fiscal ['fɪskəl] adj (pertaining to public treasury) fiscale; finanziario || s avvocato fiscale
fis'cal year' s esercizio finanziario
fish [fɪʃ] s pesce m; to be like a fish out of water essere come un pesce fuor d'acqua; to be neither fish nor fowl non essere né carne né pesce; to drink like a fish bere come una spugna || tr pescare || intr pescare; to fish for compliments cercare di farsi fare dei complimenti; to go fishing andare alla pesca; to take fishing portare con sé alla pesca
fish'bone' s lisca, spina di pesce
fish'bowl' s vaschetta per i pesci rossi
fisher ['fɪʃər] s pescatore m; (zool) martora canadese
fish'er·man s (-men) pescatore m; (boat) peschereccio
fisher·y ['fɪʃəri] s (-ies) (activity) pesca; (business) pescheria; (grounds) riserva di pesca, luogo dove si pesca
fish' glue' s colla di pesce
fish'hook' s amo
fishing ['fɪʃɪŋ] adj da pesca || s pesca
fish'ing reel' s mulinello
fish'ing rod' s canna di pesca
fish'ing tack'le s attrezzatura da pesca
fish'line' s lenza
fish' mar'ket s pescheria
fish'pool' s peschiera
fish' spear' s fiocina
fish' sto'ry s (coll) fandonia; to tell fish stories spararle grosse
fish'tail' s (aut) imbardata (aer) spedalata || intr (aut) imbardare; (aer) compiere una spedalata
fish'wife' s (-wives') pescivendola; (foul-mouthed woman) ciana
fish'worm' s lombrico
fish·y ['fɪʃi] adj (-ier; -iest) che sa di pesce; (coll) dubbioso, inverosimile
fission ['fɪʃən] s (biol) scissione; (phys) fissione
fissionable ['fɪʃənəbəl] adj fissionabile
fissure ['fɪʃər] s fenditura; (in rock) crepaccio
fist [fɪst] s pugno; (typ) indice m; to shake one's fist at mostrare i pugni a
fist'fight' s scontro a pugni
fist'ful' s pugno, manciata
fisticuff ['fɪstɪˌkʌf] s pugno; fisticuffs scontro a pugni
fit [fɪt] adj (fitter; fittest) indicato; idoneo, adatto; in buona salute; fit to be tied (coll) infuriato, arrabbia-

tissimo; fit to eat mangiabile; to feel fit sentirsi in buona salute; to see fit giudicare conveniente || s equipaggiamento; (of a suit) taglio; (of one piece with another) incastro; (of coughing) accesso; (of anger) attacco; by fits and starts a pezzi e a bocconi || v (pret & pp fitted; ger fitting) tr adattare; quadrare a; andar bene a; equipaggiare; preparare; servire a; esser d'accordo con; to fit out or up attrezzare, equipaggiare || intr stare; incastrare; (said of clothes) cascare; entrare; to fit in entrarci
fitful ['fɪtfəl] adj capriccioso; incostante, irregolare
fitness ['fɪtnɪs] s convenienza; idoneità f; buona salute
fitter ['fɪtər] s aggiustatore m; (of machinery) montatore m; (of clothing) sarto che mette in prova
fitting ['fɪtɪŋ] adj appropriato, adatto, conveniente || s adattamento; (of a garment) prova; tubo adattabile; (carp) incastro; fittings accessori mpl; utensili mpl; (iron trimmings) ferramenta fpl
five [faɪv] adj & pron cinque || s cinque m; five o' clock le cinque
five' hun'dred adj, s & pron cinquecento
five'-year plan' s piano quinquennale
fix [fɪks] s—in a tight fix (coll) nei pasticci; to be in a fix (coll) star fresco, essere nei guai || tr riparare; fissare; (a meal) preparare; (a bayonet) inastare; (attention) attrarre, fermare; (hair) mettere a posto; (coll) arrangiare || intr fissarsi, stabilirsi; to fix on scegliere
fixed [fɪkst] adj fisso; (time) improrogabile; (coll) arrangiato
fixing ['fɪksɪŋ] adj fissativo || s (fastening) attacco; (phot) fissaggio; with all the fixings (coll) con tutti i contorni
fix'ing bath' s bagno di fissaggio
fixture ['fɪkstʃər] s infisso; accessorio; (of a lamp) guarnizione; fixtures (e.g., of a store) suppellettili fpl
fizz [fɪz] s effervescenza; gazosa; (Brit) spumante m || intr frizzare
fizzle ['fɪzəl] s (coll) fiasco || intr crepitare; (coll) fare fiasco
flabbergast ['flæbərˌɡæst] tr (coll) sbalordire, lasciare stupefatto
flab·by ['flæbi] adj (-bier; -biest) floscio, flaccido, cascante
flag [flæɡ] s bandiera || v (pret & pp flagged; ger flagging) tr imbandierare; segnalare; (rr) far fermare || intr ammosciarsi, afflosciarsi
flageolet [ˌflædʒəˈlɛt] s flautino
flag'man s (-men) (rr) manovratore m
flag' of truce' s bandiera parlamentaria
flag'pole' s pennone m
flagrant ['fleɡrənt] adj flagrante; scandaloso
flag'ship' s nave ammiraglia
flag'staff' s pennone m
flag' sta'tion s (rr) stazione facoltativa
flag'stone' s lastra di pietra

flag' stop' s (rr) fermata facoltativa

flail [flel] s correggiato || tr battere col correggiato; battere

flair [fler] s fiuto, istinto

flak [flæk] s fuoco antiaereo

flake [flek] s falda; (of snow) fiocco, falda; (of cereal) fiocco; || tr sfaldare; (fish) scagliare || intr sfaldarsi

flak·y ['fleki] adj (-ier; -iest) a falde, faldoso

flamboyant [flæm'bɔɪ·ənt] adj sgargiante; (archit) fiammeggiante

flame [flem] s fiamma || tr & intr fiammeggiare

flamethrower ['flem,θro·ər] s lanciafiamme m

flaming ['flemɪŋ] adj fiammeggiante; appassionato; (culin) alla fiamma

flamin·go [flə'mɪŋgo] s (-gos or -goes) fenicottero, fiammingo

flammable ['flæməbəl] adj infiammabile

Flanders ['flændərz] s le Fiandre

flange [flændʒ] s (e.g., on a pipe) flangia; (on I beam) bordo; (of a wheel) cerchione m

flank [flæŋk] s fianco || tr fiancheggiare

flannel ['flænəl] s flanella

flap [flæp] s (in clothing) falda; (of hat) tesa; (of book) risvolto; (of pocket) patta; (of shoe) linguetta; (blow) colpo; (of a table) pannello; (of the counter in a store) ribalta; (of wings) alata || v (pret & pp flapped; ger flapping) tr battere, sbattere; (to move violently) sbatacchiare || intr penzolare

flare [fler] s vampa; scintillio; (of a dress) svasatura; (mil) fuoco di segnalazione; **flares** (trousers) calzoni mpl a zampe d'elefante || tr svasare || intr scintillare; (said of a garment) scampanare; **to flare up** divampare; (said of an illness) aggravarsi, infiammarsi

flare'-up' s vampa, fiammata; (of an illness) recrudescenza; scoppio d'ira, accesso di collera

flash [flæʃ] s (of light) sprazzo; (of lightning) lampo, baleno; (of hope) raggio; (of joy) accesso; (journ, phot) flash m; (fig) lampo; **flash in the pan** fuoco di paglia || tr (powder) accendere; (a sword) brandire; (journ) diffondere; (e.g., money) (coll) ostentare || intr lampeggiare, balenare, folgorare; **to flash by** passare come un lampo

flash'back' s flashback m

flash' bulb' s lampada lampo

flash' cube' s cuboflash m

flash' flood' s inondazione torrenziale

flashing ['flæʃɪŋ] s metallo per coprire la conversa; commessura metallica fra tetto e comignolo

flash'light' s lampadina tascabile; (of a lighthouse) luce f intermittente; (phot) fotolampo, lampeggiatore m

flash'light bulb' s lampada per fotolampo

flash·y ['flæʃi] adj (-ier; -iest) sgargiante, chiassoso, vistoso

flask [flæsk] or [flɑsk] s fiasco, fiasca; (for laboratory use) beuta

flat [flæt] adj (flatter; flattest) piano; (nose) camuso; (boat) a fondo piatto; (surface) liscio; (beer) svanito; (tire) sgonfio; (denial) deciso; (mus) bemolle; (coll) al verde || s (flat surface) piatto; (flat area) piano; (apartment) appartamento; (mus) bemolle m; (coll) gomma a terra || adv—**to fall flat** fallire

flat'boat' s chiatta

flat'car' s (rr) pianale m

flat-footed ['flæt,fʊtɪd] adj dai piedi piatti; (coll) inflessibile

flat'head' s (of a bolt) testa piatta; (coll) testa di legno

flat'i'ron s ferro da stiro

flat' race' s corsa piana

flatten ['flætən] tr schiacciare; distendere || intr appiattirsi; indebolirsi; **to flatten out** appiattirsi; (aer) porsi in linea orizzontale di volo

flatter ['flætər] tr adulare, lusingare; (to make seem more attractive) favorire || intr adulare

flatterer ['flætərər] s adulatore m, lusingatore m

flattering ['flætərɪŋ] adj lusinghiero

flatter·y ['flætəri] s (-ies) lusinga

flat' tire' s gomma a terra

flat'top' s portaerei f

flatulence ['flætʃələns] s flatulenza

flat'ware' s argenteria, vasellame m

flaunt [flɔnt] or [flɑnt] tr sfoggiare, ostentare

flautist ['flɔtɪst] s flautista mf

flavor ['flevər] s sapore m, gusto; condimento || tr insaporire; condire; aromatizzare, profumare

flavoring ['flevərɪŋ] s condimento, sapore m

flaw [flɔ] s difetto, menda, fallo; (crack) incrinatura

flawless ['flɔlɪs] adj senza difetti

flax [flæks] s lino

flaxen ['flæksən] adj di lino; biondo

flax'seed' s linosa

flay [fle] tr scorticare, scoiare

flea [fli] s pulce f

flea'bite' s morso di pulce; (fig) inezia, seccatura secondaria

fleck [flɛk] s macchia; efelide f || tr chiazzare, macchiare

fledgling ['flɛdʒlɪŋ] s uccellino appena nato; (fig) pivello

flee [fli] v (pret & pp fled [flɛd]) tr & intr fuggire, sfuggire

fleece [flis] s vello; (e.g., of clouds) bioccolo || tr tosare; (fig) pelare

fleec·y ['flisi] adj (-ier; -iest) lanoso; (sky) a pecorelle

fleet [flit] adj rapido || s flotta

fleeting ['flitɪŋ] adj fugace, passeggero

Fleming ['flɛmɪŋ] s fiammingo

Flemish ['flɛmɪʃ] adj & s fiammingo

flesh [flɛʃ] s carne f; (of fruit) polpa; **in the flesh** in carne ed ossa; **to lose flesh** dimagrire; **to put on flesh** ingrassare

flesh' and blood' s (relatives) carne f della carne, i miei, i suoi, etc.; il corpo umano

flesh-colored [ˈflɛʃ ˌkʌlərd] *adj* color carne

fleshiness [ˈflɛʃɪnɪs] *s* carnosità *f*

fleshless [ˈflɛʃlɪs] *adj* scarno

flesh'pot' *s* piatto di carne; locale *m* di dissoluzione; **fleshpots** vita dissoluta

flesh' wound' *s* ferita superficiale

flesh-y [ˈflɛʃi] *adj* (**-ier; -iest**) carnoso; polposo

flex [flɛks] *tr* piegare || *intr* piegarsi

flexible [ˈflɛksɪbəl] *adj* flessibile; (*joint*) a snodo

flick [flɪk] *s* schiocco; (*slang*) pellicola cinematografica || *tr* schioccare

flicker [ˈflɪkər] *s* fiamma tremolante; (*of eyelids*) battito; (*of hope*) bagliore *m* || *intr* tremolare; vacillare

flier [ˈflaɪ·ər] *s* aviatore *m*; (*venture*) (*coll*) impresa rischiosa; (*coll*) foglio volante

flight [flaɪt] *s* fuga; (*of an airplane*) volo; (*of birds*) stormo; (*of stairs*) rampa; (*of fancy*) slancio; **to put to flight** mettere in fuga; **to take flight** prendere la fuga

flight' deck' *s* ponte *m* di volo

flight-y [ˈflaɪti] *adj* (**-ier; -iest**) frivolo; volubile

flim-flam [ˈflɪm ˌflæm] *s* (*coll*) imbroglio, truffa || *v* (*pret & pp* **-flammed;** *ger* **-flamming**) *tr* (*coll*) imbrogliare, truffare

flim-sy [ˈflɪmzi] *adj* (**-sier; -siest**) leggero; (*material*) di scarsa consistenza; (*excuse*) inconsistente

flinch [flɪntʃ] *intr* indietreggiare; **without flinching** senza scomporsi

fling [flɪŋ] *s* tiro; ballo scozzese; **to go on a fling** darsi alla pazza gioia; **to have a fling at** tentare di fare; **to have one's fling** correre la cavallina || *v* (*pret & pp* **flung** [flʌŋ]) *tr* sbattere, scagliare; (*e.g., in jail*) schiaffare; **to fling open** spalancare; **to fling shut** chiudere improvvisamente

flint [flɪnt] *s* selce *f*, pietra focaia

flint'lock' *s* fucile *m* a pietra focaia

flint-y [ˈflɪnti] *adj* (**-ier; -iest**) pietroso; (*unmerciful*) spietato; duro come un macigno

flip [flɪp] *adj* (**flipper; flippest**) impertinente || *s* buffetto; salto mortale || *v* (*pret & pp* **flipped;** *ger* **flipping**) *tr* sbattere in aria; muovere d'un tratto **to flip a coin** giocare a testa e croce; **to flip shut** (*e.g., a fan*) chiudere improvvisamente

flippancy [ˈflɪpənsi] *s* leggerezza

flippant [ˈflɪpənt] *adj* scanzonato, leggero

flirt [flʌrt] *s* (*woman*) civetta; (*man*) vagheggino || *intr* (*said of a woman*) civettare; (*said of a man*) fare il damerino; **to flirt with** flirtare con; (*an idea*) accarezzare; (*death*) giocare con

flit [flɪt] *v* (*pret & pp* **flitted;** *ger* **flitting**) *intr* svolazzare, volteggiare; passare rapidamente, volare

flitch [flɪtʃ] *s* fetta di pancetta

float [flot] *s* (*raft*) galleggiante *m*; (*of mason*) cazzuola; carro allegorico || *tr* far galleggiare; (*a business*) lanciare; (*stocks, bonds*) emettere || *intr* galleggiare, tenersi a galla

floating [ˈflotɪŋ] *adj* galleggiante

flock [flak] *s* (*of birds*) stormo; (*of sheep*) gregge *m*; (*of people*) stuolo; (*of wool*) fiocco; (*fig*) mucchio || *intr* affollarsi, riunirsi, radunarsi

floe [flo] *s* tavola di ghiaccio

flog [flag] *v* (*pret & pp* **flogged;** *ger* **flogging**) *tr* battere, fustigare

flood [flʌd] *s* (*caused by rain*) diluvio; (*sudden rise of river*) piena, fiumana; (*of tide*) flusso || *tr* inondare; (*aut*) ingolfare || *intr* straripare; (*aut*) ingolfarsi || **the Flood** il diluvio universale

flood'gate' *s* (*of a canal*) chiusa; (*of a dam*) saracinesca

flood'light' *s* riflettore *m*

flood' tide' *s* flusso

floor [flor] *s* (*inside bottom surface of room*) pavimento; (*story of building*) piano; (*of the sea, a swimming pool, etc.*) fondo; (*of the exchange*) recinto delle grida; (*of an assembly hall*) emiciclo; (*naut*) madiere *m*; **to ask for the floor** chiedere la parola; **to have the floor** avere la parola; **to take the floor** prendere la parola || *tr* pavimentare; abbattere, gettare al suolo; (*coll*) confondere; (*coll*) vincere

flooring [ˈflorɪŋ] *s* palco, impiantito

floor' mop' *s* redazza

floor' plan' *s* pianta

floor' show' *s* spettacolo di caffè concerto

floor'walk'er *s* direttore *m* di sezione

floor' wax' *s* cera da pavimenti

flop [flap] *s* (*coll*) fiasco || *v* (*pret & pp* **flopped;** *ger* **flopping**) *tr* lasciar cadere; sbattere || *intr* lasciarsi cadere; (*coll*) fare fiasco; **to flop over** (*to change sides*) cambiare casacca

flora [ˈflorə] *s* flora

floral [ˈflorəl] *adj* floreale

Florence [ˈflorəns] *or* [ˈflɑrəns] *s* Firenze *f*

Florentine [ˈflɑrən ˌtin] *or* [ˈflɔrən-ˌtin] *adj & s* fiorentino

florescence [floˈrɛsəns] *s* infiorescenza

florid [ˈflɑrɪd] *or* [ˈflɔrɪd] *adj* florido

florist [ˈflɔrɪst] *s* fiorista *mf*, fioraio

floss [flɔs] *or* [flɑs] *s* lanugine *f*; (*of corn*) barba

floss-y [ˈflɔsi] *or* [ˈflɑsi] *adj* (**-ier; -iest**) serico; (*downy*) lanuginoso; (*coll*) vistoso

flotsam [ˈflɑtsəm] *s* relitti gettati a mare

flot'sam and jet'sam *s* relitti *mpl* di naufragio; (*trifles*) cianfrusaglie *fpl*; gentaglia, vagabondi *mpl*

flounce [flaʊns] *s* balza, falda, falpalà *m* || *tr* ornare di falpalà || *intr—*to **flounce out** andarsene irosamente

flounder [ˈflaʊndər] *s* (*ichth*) passera || *intr* dibattersi

flour [flaʊr] *adj* farinoso || *s* farina || *tr* infarinare

flourish [ˈflʌrɪʃ] *s* (*with the sword*) mulinello; (*with the pen*) ghirigoro; (*as part of signature*) svolazzo; (*mus*) fioritura || *tr* (*one's sword*) roteare || *intr* rifiorire, prosperare

flourishing ['flʌrɪ/ɪŋ] *adj* prosperoso

flour' mill' *s* mulino per grano

floury ['flauri] *adj* farinoso; infarinato

flout [flaut] *tr* burlarsi di || *intr* burlare, motteggiare

flow [flo] *s* flusso; (*of a river*) regime *m* || *intr* fluire; (*said of tide*) montare; (*said of hair in the air*) ondeggiare; **to flow into** gettarsi in, sfociare in; **to flow over** traboccare; **to flow with** abbondare di

flower ['flau-ər] *s* fiore *m* || *tr* infiorare || *intr* fiorire

flow'er bed' *s* aiola fiorita

flow'er gar'den *s* giardino

flow'er girl' *s* fioraia; (*at a wedding*) damigella d'onore

flow'er-pot' *s* vaso da fiori

flow'er shop' *s* negozio di fiori

flow'er show' *s* esposizione di fiori

flow'er-stand' *s* portafiori *m*

flowery ['flau-əri] *adj* fiorito

flowing ['flo-ɪŋ] *adj* (*water*) corrente; (*language*) scorrevole; (*e.g., hair*) fluente; (*e.g., lines of a dress*) filante

flu [flu] *s* influenza

fluctuate ['flʌktʃu,et] *intr* fluttuare, ondeggiare; (*said of prices*) oscillare

flue [flu] *s* gola, fumaiolo

fluency ['flu-ənsi] *s* facilità *f* di parola

fluent ['flu-ənt] *adj* (*speaker*) facondo; (*style*) fluido

fluently ['flu-əntli] *adv* correntemente

fluff [flʌf] *s* lanugine *f*; vaporosità *f*; (*of an actor*) papera || *tr* sprimacciare || *intr* sprimacciarsi; (*coll*) impaperarsi

fluff·y ['flʌfi] *adj* (**-ier; -iest**) lanuginoso; vaporoso

fluid ['flu-ɪd] *adj* & *s* fluido

flu'id drive' *s* trasmissione idraulica

fluidity [flu'ɪdɪti] *s* fluidità *f*

fluke [fluk] *s* (*of anchor*) marra, dente *m*; (*in billiards*) colpo fortunato; (*ichth*) passera

flume [flum] *s* gora; condotta forzata

flunk [flʌŋk] *s* (*coll*) bocciatura || *tr* (*coll*) bocciare; (*a course*) (*coll*) farsi bocciare in || *intr* (*coll*) fare fiasco; **to flunk out** (*coll*) farsi bocciare

flunk·y ['flʌŋki] *s* (**-ies**) valletto; parassita *m*

fluor ['flu-ɔr] *s* fluorite *f*

fluorescence [,flu-ə'rɛsəns] *s* fluorescenza

fluorescent [,flu-ə'rɛsənt] *adj* fluorescente

fluoridation [,flu-ərɪ'defən] *s* fluorizzazione

fluoride ['flu-ə,raɪd] *s* fluoruro

fluorine ['flu-ə,rin] *s* fluoro

fluoroscope ['flu-ərə,skop] *s* schermo fluorescente

fluorspar ['flu-ər,spar] *s* spatofluore *m*

flur·ry ['flʌri] *s* (**-ries**) agitazione; (*of wind*) raffica; (*of rain*) acquazzone *m*; (*of snow*) turbine *m* || *v* (*pret & pp* **-ried**) *tr* agitare

flush [flʌʃ] *adj* livellato; contiguo; prospero, ben provvisto; abbondante; vigoroso; (*full to overflowing*) rigurgitante; arrossito; **flush with** allo stesso livello che || *s* (*of water*) flusso improvviso; (*in the cheeks*) caldana, scalmana; (*of spring*) germogliare *m*; (*of joy*) ebbrezza; (*of youth*) rigoglio; (*in poker*) colore *m* || *adv* rasente, raso || *tr* (*to cause to blush*) far arrossire; lavare con un getto d'acqua; (*e.g., a rabbit*) snidare || *intr* essere accaldato; (*to blush*) arrossire; (*to gush*) zampillare

flush' tank' *s* sciacquone *m*

flush' toi'let *s* gabinetto a sciacquone

fluster ['flʌstər] *s* nervosismo, eccitazione || *tr* innervosire, eccitare

flute [flut] *s* (*of a column*) scanalatura; (*mus*) flauto || *tr* scanalare

flutist ['flutɪst] *s* flautista *mf*

flutter ['flʌtər] *s* svolazzo; agitazione; sensazione || *intr* frullare; svolazzare; agitarsi; (*said of the heart*) palpitare; (*said of the heartbeat*) essere irregolare

flux [flʌks] *s* (*flow*) flusso; (*for fusing metals*) fondente *m*

fly [flaɪ] *s* (**flies**) mosca; (*of trousers*) finta; (*for fishing*) mosca artificiale || *v* (*pret* **flew** [flu]; *pp* **flown** [flon]) *tr* (*an airplane*) pilotare, far volare; trasportare a volo; (*e.g., an ocean*) trasvolare; (*a flag*) battere || *intr* volare; fuggire, scappare; (*said of a flag*) ondeggiare; **to fly away** involarsi; **to fly into a rage** andare in eccessi; **to fly off** volare via; scappare; **to fly over** trasvolare; **to fly shut** chiudersi improvvisamente

fly'blow' *s* uovo di mosca

fly'-by-night' *adj* poco raccomandabile; di breve durata

fly'catch'er *s* (*orn*) pigliamosche *m*

flyer ['flaɪ-ər] *s* var of **flier**

fly'-fish' *intr* pescare con le mosche artificiali

flying ['flaɪ-ɪŋ] *adj* volante; rapido; in fuga; (*start*) lanciato || *s* volo

fly'ing boat' *s* idrovolante *m* a scafo centrale

fly'ing but'tress *s* contrafforte *m*

fly'ing col'ors *spl* successo; **with flying colors** a bandiere spiegate

fly'ing field' *s* campo d'aviazione

fly'ing sau'cer *s* disco volante

fly'ing sick'ness *s* male *m* d'aria

fly'ing squad' *s* squadra mobile

fly'ing time' *s* ore *fpl* di volo

fly'leaf' *s* (**-leaves**) (*bb*) guardia

fly' net' *s* (*for a bed*) moschettiera; (*for a horse*) scacciamosche *m*

fly'pa'per *s* carta moschicida

fly'speck' *s* macchia di mosca; macchiolina

fly' swat'ter ['swatər] *s* scacciamosche *m*

fly'trap' *s* pigliamosche *m*

fly'wheel' *s* volano

foal [fol] *s* puledro || *intr* (*said of a mare*) figliare

foam [fom] *s* schiuma || *intr* schiumare

foam' rub'ber *s* gommapiuma

foam·y ['fomi] *adj* (-ier; -iest) spumoso, schiumeggiante

fob [fab] *s* taschino per l'orologio; (*chain*) catenina per l'orologio || *v* (*pret & pp* **fobbed;** *ger* **fobbing**) *tr*—**to fob off s.th on s.o.** rifilare qlco a qlcu

f.o.b. or **F.O.B.** [,ɛf,o'bi] *adv* (letter-word) (**free on board**) franco

focal ['fokəl] *adj* focale

fo·cus ['fokəs] *s* (-cuses or -ci [saɪ]) fuoco; (*of a disease*) focolaio || *v* (*pret & pp* -cused or -cussed; *ger* -cusing or -cussing) *tr* mettere a fuoco; (*attention*) concentrare || *intr* convergere

fodder ['fadər] *s* foraggio

foe [fo] *s* nemico

fog [fag] or [fɔg] *s* nebbia; (phot) velo || *v* (*pret & pp* **fogged;** *ger* **fogging**) *tr* annebbiare; (phot) velare || *intr* annebbiarsi; (phot) velarsi

fog' bank' *s* banco di nebbia

fog'bound' *adj* avvolto nella nebbia

fog·gy ['fagi] or ['fɔgi] *adj* (-gier; -giest) annebbiato; nebbioso; (*idea*) vago; (phot) velato; **it is foggy** fa nebbia

fog'horn' *s* sirena da nebbia

foible ['fɔɪbəl] *s* debolezza, debole *m*

foil [fɔɪl] *s* (*thin sheet of metal*) foglia; (*of mirror*) argentatura; contrasto, risalto; (*sword*) fioretto || *tr* sventare; (*a mirror*) argentare

foist [fɔɪst] *tr*—**to foist s.th on s.o.** rifilare qlco a qlcu

fold [fold] *s* piega; drappeggio; (*for sheep*) ovile *m*; (*of sheep; of the faithful*) gregge *m*; (geol) corrugamento || *tr* piegare; (*the arms*) incrociare; **to fold up** ripiegare || *intr* piegarsi; **to fold up** (coll) fare fallimento

folder ['foldər] *s* (*pamphlet*) pieghevole *m*; (*cover*) portacarte *m*

folding ['foldɪŋ] *adj* pieghevole

fold'ing cam'era *s* macchina fotografica a soffietto

fold'ing chair' *s* sedia pieghevole

fold'ing cot' *s* branda

fold'ing door' *s* porta a libro

fold'ing seat' *s* strapuntino

foliage ['folɪ·ɪdʒ] *s* fogliame *m*

foli·o ['folɪ,o] *adj* in-folio || *s* (-os) foglio; (*book*) in-folio || *tr* numerare

folk [fok] *adj* popolare || *s* (**folk** or **folks**) gente *f*; **your folks** i Suoi

folk'lore' *s* folclore *m*

folk' mu'sic *s* musica folcloristica

folk' song' *s* canzone *f* tradizionale

folk·sy ['foksi] *adj* (-sier; -siest) socievole; alla buona, alla mano

folk'ways' *spl* costumi *mpl* tradizionali

follicle ['falɪkəl] *s* follicolo

follow ['falo] *tr* seguire; (*to keep up with*) interessarsi di; **to follow suit** seguire l'esempio; (*cards*) rispondere al colore || *intr* seguire; derivare; **as follows** come segue; **it follows** ne risulta

follower ['falo·ər] *s* seguace *m*; discepolo; partigiano

following ['falo·ɪŋ] *adj* susseguente || *s* seguito; aderenti *mpl*

fol'low-up' *adj* susseguente; ricordativo; da continuarsi || *s* prosecuzione; lettera ricordativa

fol·ly ['fali] *s* (-lies) follia; **follies** rivista di varietà

foment [fo'ment] *tr* fomentare

fond [fand] *adj* appassionato; (*of food*) ghiotto; **to become fond of** appassionarsi di

fondle ['fandəl] *tr* accarezzare, vezzeggiare

fondness ['fandnɪs] *s* tenerezza; passione

font [fant] *s* acquasantiera, pila; fonte *f* battesimale; (typ) fondita

food [fud] *adj* alimentare || *s* cibo, vitto; (*for animals*) mangiare *m*; **food for thought** materia di che pensare

food' store' *s* negozio di commestibili

food'stuffs' *spl* commestibili *mpl*

fool [ful] *s* scemo, sciocco; (*jester*) buffone *m*; (*person imposed on*) vittima, zimbello; **to make a fool of** beffarsi di; **to play the fool** fare lo stupido || *tr* infinocchiare, ingannare; **to fool away** sprecare || *intr* giocare, fare per gioco; **to fool around** perdere il proprio tempo; **to fool with** giocherellare con

fooler·y ['fuləri] *s* (-ies) pazzia, buffonata

fool'har'dy *adj* (-dier; -diest) temerario

fooling ['fulɪŋ] *s* scherzo; **no fooling** senza scherzi, parlando sul serio

foolish ['fulɪʃ] *adj* sciocco; matto

fool'proof' *adj* a tutta prova; infallibile

fools'cap' *s* berretto a sonagli; carta formato protocollo

fool's' er'rand *s* impresa inutile

fool's' par'adise *s* felicità immaginaria

foot [fut] *s* (**feet** [fit]) piede *m*; (*of an animal*) zampa; (*of horse*) zoccolo; **to drag one's feet** procedere a passo di lumaca; **to put one's best foot forward** fare del proprio meglio; **to put one's foot down** farsi valere, imporsi; **to put one's foot in it** (coll) fare una topica; **to stand on one's own two feet** agire indipendentemente; **to tread under foot** calcare || *tr* (*the bill*) pagare; **to foot it** andare a piedi; ballare

footage ['futɪdʒ] *s* distanza or lunghezza in piedi; (*of film measured in meters*) metraggio

foot'-and-mouth' disease' *s* (vet) afta epizootica

foot'ball' *s* (*ball*) pallone *m*; (*game*) pallovale *f*; (*soccer*) calcio, football *m*

foot'board' *s* (*support for foot*) predellino; (*of bed*) spalliera

foot' brake' *s* freno a pedale

foot'bridge' *s* passerella, ponte riservato ai pedoni

foot'fall' *s* passo

foot'hill' *s* collina ai piedi di una montagna

foot'hold' s stabilità f; **to gain a foot-hold** prender piede

footing ['futɪŋ] s piede m, e.g., **he lost his footing** perse piede; **on a friendly footing** in relazioni amichevoli; **on an equal footing** su un piede di parità; **on a war footing** su un piede di guerra

foot'lights' spl luci fpl della ribalta; (fig) ribalta, scena

foot'loose' adj completamente libero

foot'man s (-men) staffiere m

foot'mark s orma

foot'note' s rimando, rinvio

foot'path s sentiero

foot'print' s orma, pesta

foot' race' s corsa podistica

foot'rest' s pedana

foot' rule' s regolo di un piede

foot' soldier' s fante m, fantaccino

foot'sore' adj coi piedi stanchi

foot'step' s passo; **to follow in the footsteps of** seguire le orme di

foot'stone' s pietra tombale a piè di un sepolcro; (archit) pietra di sostegno

foot'stool' s sgabello

foot' warm'er s scaldino

foot'wear' s calzature fpl

foot'work' s allenamento delle gambe; (fig) manovra delicata

foot'worn' adj (road) battuto; (person) spedato

foozle ['fuzəl] s schiappinata || tr & intr mancare completamente

fop [fɑp] s bellimbusto, gagà m

for [fɔr] prep per; malgrado, e.g., **for all his wealth** malgrado tutta la sua ricchezza; come, e.g., **he uses his house for an office** adopera la casa come ufficio; di, e.g., **time for bed** ora di andare a letto; da, e.g., **he has been here for three days** è qui da tre giorni; per amor di; **to go for a walk** andare a fare una passeggiata || conj perché, poiché

forage ['fɑrɪdʒ] or ['fɔrɪdʒ] adj foraggero || s foraggio || tr foraggiare || intr andare in cerca di foraggio

foray ['fɑre] or ['fɔre] s razzia, scorreria || intr razziare

for·bear [fɔr'bɛr] v (pret -bore ['bor]; pp -borne ['born]) tr astenersi da || intr essere longanime

forbearance [fɔr'bɛrəns] s longanimità f, tolleranza; astensione

for·bid [fɔr'bɪd] v (pret -bade ['bæd] or -bad ['bæd]; pp -bidden ['bɪdən]; ger -bidding) tr proibire, vietare || intr—**God forbid!** Dio ci scampi!

forbidding [fɔr'bɪdɪŋ] adj severo, sinistro

force [fɔrs] s forza; (staff of workers) forza, personale m; (phys) forza; **by force of** a forza di; **by main force** con tutte le sue forze; **in force** vigente; in gran numero; **to join forces** allearsi || tr forzare; obbligare; **to force back** respingere; **to force open** forzare; **to force s.th on s.o.** obbligare qlcu a accettare qlco

forced [fɔrst] adj forzato; studiato

forced' air' s aria sotto pressione

forced' draft' s tiraggio forzato

forced' land'ing s atterraggio forzato

forced' march' s marcia forzata

forceful ['fɔrsfəl] adj vigoroso, energico

for·ceps ['fɔrsəps] s (-ceps or -cipes [sɪ,piz]) (dent, surg) pinze fpl; (obstet) forcipe m

force' pump' s pompa premente

forcible ['fɔrsɪbəl] adj impetuoso, energico; efficace

ford [fɔrd] s guado || tr guadare

fore [fɔr] adj davanti; (naut) prodiero || s davanti m; (naut) prua; **to the fore** alla ribalta; d'attualità || adv prima; (naut) a proravia || interj attenzione!

fore' and aft' adv a poppa e a prua

fore'arm' s avambraccio || **fore·arm'** tr premunire; prevenire

fore'bears' spl antenati mpl

forebode [fɔr'bod] tr (to portend) preannunziare; (to have a presentiment of) presentire

foreboding [fɔr'bodɪŋ] s preannunzio; presentimento

fore'cast' s pronostico || v (pret & pp -cast or -casted) tr pronosticare

forecastle ['foksəl], ['fɔr,kæsəl] or ['fɔr,kɑsəl] s castello, pozzetto

fore·close' tr escludere, precludere; (a mortgage) (law) precludere il riscatto di

fore·doom' tr condannare all'insuccesso

fore' edge' s (bb) taglio

fore'fa'ther s antenato

fore'fin'ger s dito indice

fore'front' s—**in the forefront** all'avanguardia

fore·go' v (pret -went'; pp -gone') tr & intr precedere

fore·go'ing adj precedente, anteriore

fore'gone' conclu'sion s conclusione inevitabile; decisione già scontata

fore'ground' s primo piano

forehanded ['fɔr,hændɪd] adj previdente; (thrifty) risparmiatore

forehead ['fɑrɪd] or ['fɔrɪd] s fronte f

foreign ['fɑrɪn] or ['fɔrɪn] adj straniero; (product; affairs) estero; **foreign to** estraneo a

for'eign affairs' spl affari esteri

for'eign-born' adj nato all'estero

foreigner ['fɑrɪnər] or ['fɔrɪnər] s straniero, forestiero

for'eign exchange' s divise fpl; (money) valuta

for'eign min'ister s ministro degli affari esteri

for'eign of'fice s ministero degli affari esteri

for'eign serv'ice s servizio diplomatico e consolare; (Brit) servizio militare in paesi d'oltremare

fore'leg' s zampa anteriore

fore'lock' s ciuffo sulla fronte; **to take time by the forelock** acchiappare l'occasione

fore'man s (-men) sorvegliante m, capomastro; presidente m dei giurati

fore'mast ['fɔrməst], ['fɔr,mæst] or ['fɔr,mɑst] s trinchetto

foremost ['fɔr,most] adj primo, principale, più importante

fore'noon' *adj* mattinale || *s* mattina

fore'part' *s* parte *f* anteriore; prima parte

fore'paw' *s* zampa anteriore

fore'quar'ter *s* quarto anteriore

fore'run'ner *s* precursore *m*, predecessore *m*, foriero

fore-sail [ˈforsəl] or [ˈforˌsel] *s* trinchetto

fore-see' *v* (*pret* **-saw'**; *pp* **-seen'**) *tr* prevedere

foreseeable [forˈsiːəbəl] *adj* prevedibile

fore-shad'ow *tr* presagire

fore-short'en *tr* scorciare

fore'sight *s* (*prudence*) previdenza; (*foreknowledge*) previsione

fore'sight'ed *adj* previdente

fore'skin' *s* prepuzio

forest [ˈfɑrɪst] or [ˈfɔrɪst] *adj* forestale || *s* foresta, bosco

fore-stall' *tr* prevenire; anticipare; (*to buy up*) accaparrare

for'est rang'er [ˈrendʒər] *s* guardaboschi *m*, guardia forestale

forestry [ˈfɑrɪstri] or [ˈfɔrɪstri] *s* selvicoltura

fore'taste' *s* pregustazione || *tr* pregustare

fore-tell' *v* (*pret & pp* **-told'**) *tr* predire, presagire, preannunziare

fore'thought' *s* premeditazione; previdenza

forever [forˈevər] *adv* per sempre; continuamente

fore-warn' *tr* prevenire, preavvertire

fore'word' *s* avvertenza, prefazione

forfeit [ˈforfɪt] *adj* perduto || *s* perdita, confisca; multa; (*article deposited*) pegno; **forfeits** (*game*) pegni *mpl* || *tr* decadere da

forfeiture [ˈforfɪtʃər] *s* perdita di un pegno

forgather [forˈgæðər] *intr* riunirsi; incontrarsi

forge [fordʒ] *s* fucina, forgia || *tr* forgiare; (*a lie*) inventare; (*e.g., handwriting*) falsificare || *intr* forgiare; commettere un falso; **to forge ahead** farsi strada

forger·y [ˈfordʒəri] *s* (**-ies**) falsificazione, falso, contraffazione

for-get [forˈget] *v* (*pret* **-got** [ˈgɑt]; *pp* **-got** or **-gotten** [ˈgɑtən]) *tr* dimenticare; **forget it!** non si preoccupi!; **to forget oneself** venir meno alla propria dignità; **to forget** to passare di mente a (qlcu) di, e.g., **he forgot to turn off the lights** gli è passato di mente di spegnere la luce

forgetful [forˈgetfəl] *adj* (*apt to forget*) smemorato; (*neglectful*) dimentico, immemore

forgetfulness [forˈgetfəlnɪs] *s* (*inability to recall*) smemorataggine *f*; (*neglectfulness*) dimenticanza

for-get'-me-not' *s* nontiscordardimé *m*

forgivable [forˈgɪvəbəl] *adj* perdonabile

for-give [forˈgɪv] *v* (*pret* **-gave'**; *pp* **-giv'en**) *tr* perdonare

forgiveness [forˈgɪvnɪs] *s* perdono

forgiving [forˈgɪvɪŋ] *adj* clemente

for-go [forˈgo] *v* (*pret* **-went**; *pp* **-gone**) *tr* rinunciare (*with dat*)

fork [fork] *s* (*pitchfork*) forca, forcone *m*; (*of a bicycle*) forcella; (*for eating*) forchetta; (*of a tree or road*) biforcazione, diramazione || *tr* muovere col forcone; inforcare; **to fork out** (*slang*) cacciar fuori || *intr* biforcarsi, diramarsi

forked [forkt] *adj* biforcuto

fork'-lift truck' *s* carrello elevatore a forca

forlorn [forˈlorn] *adj* abbandonato; disperato; miserabile

forlorn' hope' *s* impresa disperata

form [form] *s* forma; (*paper to be filled out*) formulario; (*construction to give shape to cement*) cassaforma || *tr* formare || *intr* formarsi

formal [ˈforməl] *adj* formale; di gala, da sera, da etichetta

for'mal attire' *s* vestito da cerimonia

for'mal call' *s* visita di prammatica

formali·ty [forˈmælɪti] *s* (**-ties**) formalità *f*; (*excessive adherence to rules*) formalismo

for'mal par'ty *s* ricevimento di gala

for'mal speech' *s* discorso ufficiale

format [ˈformæt] *s* formato

formation [forˈmeʃən] *s* formazione

former [ˈformər] *adj* (*preceding*) anteriore; (*long past*) passato, antico; (*having once been*) già, ex; (*of two*) primo; **the former** quello

formerly [ˈformərli] *adv* già, prima, in tempi passati

form'fit'ting *adj* aderente al corpo

formidable [ˈformɪdəbəl] *adj* formidabile

formless [ˈformlɪs] *adj* informe

form' let'ter *s* lettera a formulario, stampato

formu·la [ˈformjələ] *s* (**-las** or **-lae** [ˌli]) formula

formulate [ˈformjəˌlet] *tr* formulare

for-sake [forˈsek] *v* (*pret* **-sook** [ˈsuk]; *pp* **-saken** [ˈsekən]) *tr* abbandonare

fort [fort] *s* forte *m*, fortezza

forte [fort] *s* forte *m*

forth [forθ] *adv* avanti; **and so forth** e così via; **from this day forth** da oggi in poi; **to go forth** uscire

forth'com'ing *adj* prossimo; immediatamente disponibile

forth'right' *adj* diretto || *adv* direttamente; senza ambagi; immediatamente

forth'with' *adv* immediatamente

fortieth [ˈfortɪɪθ] *adj*, *s & pron* quarantesimo

fortification [ˌfortɪfɪˈkeʃən] *s* fortificazione

forti·fy [ˈfortɪˌfaɪ] *v* (*pret & pp* **-fied**) *tr* fortificare; aumentare il livello alcolico di

fortitude [ˈfortɪˌtjud] or [ˈfortɪˌtud] *s* fortezza, fermezza

fortnight [ˈfortnaɪt] or [ˈfortnɪt] *s* quindicina, due settimane

fortress [ˈfortrɪs] *s* fortezza, forte *m*

fortuitous [forˈtjuˌɪtəs] or [forˈtuˌɪtəs] *adj* fortuito, occasionale

fortunate [ˈfortʃənɪt] *adj* fortunato

fortune [ˈfortʃən] *s* fortuna; **to make a fortune** farsi un patrimonio; **to tell**

s.o. his fortune leggere il futuro a qlcu

for'tune hunt'er *s* cacciatore *m* di dote

for'tune-tel'ler *s* indovino, cartomante *mf*

for·ty ['fɔrtɪ] *adj & pron* quaranta || *s* (-ties) quaranta *m;* **the forties** gli anni quaranta

fo·rum ['forəm] *s* (-rums or -ra [rə]) foro

forward ['forwərd] *adj* avanzato; precoce; impertinente || *s* (soccer) avanti *m* || *adv* avanti; **to bring forward** mettere in luce; riportare; **to come forward** avanzare; **to look forward to** anticipare il piacere di || *tr* inoltrare, trasmettere; promuovere

fossil ['fɑsɪl] *adj & s* fossile *m*

foster ['fɔstər] & ['fɑstər] *adj* adottivo; di latte || *tr* allevare; promuovere

fos'ter home' *s* famiglia adottiva

foul [faul] *adj* sporco; (air) viziato; (wind) contrario; (weather; breath) cattivo; (baseball) fuori linea di gioco || *s* (of boats) urto, collisione; (baseball) palla colpita fuori linea di gioco; (boxing) colpo basso; (sports) fallo || *adv* slealmente; (baseball) fuori linea di gioco; **to fall foul of** entrare in collisione con; urtarsi con; **to run foul of** avere una controversia con || *tr* sporcare; otturare; (baseball) colpire fuori linea di gioco || *intr* (said of two boats) entrare in collisione; (said, e.g., of a rope) imbrogliarsi

foul-mouthed ['faul'mauðd] or ['faul'mauθt] *adj* sboccato, osceno

foul' play' *s* reato; (sports) gioco sleale

found [faund] *tr* fondare; (to melt, to cast) fondere

foundation [faun'deʃən] *s* fondazione; (endowment) dotazione; (charitable) patronato; (masonry support) platea, fondamenta *fpl;* (make-up) fondo tinta; (fig) fondatezza

founder ['faundər] *s* fondatore *m;* (of family) capostipite *m;* (of metals) fonditore *m* || *intr* (said of a ship) affondare; (said of a horse) azzopparsi; (to fail) fare fiasco

foundling ['faundlɪŋ] *s* trovatello

found'ling hos'pital *s* brefotrofio

found·ry ['faundrɪ] *s* (-ries) fonderia

found'ry-man *s* (-men) fonditore *m*

fount [faunt] *s* fonte *f*

fountain ['fauntən] *s* fonte *f*, fontana; (of knowledge) pozzo

foun'tain·head' *s* sorgente *f*

foun'tain pen' *s* penna stilografica

foun'tain syringe' *s* clistere *m* a pera

four [for] *adj & pron* quattro || *s* quattro; **four o'clock** le quattro; **on all fours** gattoni, carponi

four'-cy'cle *adj* a quattro tempi

four'-cyl'inder *adj* a quattro cilindri

four'-flush' *intr* (coll) millantare

fourflusher ['for,flʌʃər] *s* (coll) millantatore *m*

four-footed ['for'futɪd] *adj* quadrupede

four' hun'dred *adj, s & pron* quattro-

cento || **the Four Hundred** l'alta società

four'-in-hand' *s* cravatta a cappio; tiro a quattro

four'-lane' *adj* a quattro corsie

four'-leaf clo'ver *s* quadrifoglio

four-legged ['for'lɛgɪd] or ['for'lɛgd] *adj* a quattro zampe; (schooner) (coll) a quattro alberi

four'-letter word' *s* parolaccia di quattro lettere

four'-mo'tor plane' *s* quadrimotore *m*

four'-o'clock' *s* (bot) bella di notte

four' of a kind' *s* (cards) poker *m*

four'post'er *s* letto a baldacchino

four'score' *adj* ottanta

foursome ['forsəm] *s* gruppo di quattro giocatori

fourteen ['for'tin] *adj, s & pron* quattordici *m*

fourteenth ['for'tinθ] *adj, s & pron* quattordicesimo || *s* (in dates) quattordici *m*

fourth [forθ] *adj, s & pron* quarto || *s* (in dates) quattro

fourth' estate' *s* quarto potere

four'-way' *adj* a quattro orifizi; **fra quattro persone;** quadruplice

fowl [faul] *s* pollo || *intr* uccellare

fowl'ing piece' *s* fucile *m* da caccia

fox [fɑks] *s* volpe *f* || *tr* (coll) ingannare

fox'glove' *s* digitale *f*

fox'hole' *s* buca ricovero

fox'hound' *s* segugio

fox' hunt' *s* caccia alla volpe

fox' ter'rier *s* fox-terrier *m*

fox'-trot' *s* (of a horse) piccolo trotto; (dance) fox-trot *m*

fox·y ['fɑksɪ] *adj* (-ier; -iest) volpino, astuto

foyer ['fɔɪ·ər] *s* (of a private house) ingresso, vestibolo; (theat) ridotto

fracas ['frekəs] *s* lite *f*, tumulto

fraction ['frækʃən] *s* frazione; frammento

fractional ['frækʃənəl] *adj* frazionario; insignificante

fractious ['frækʃəs] *adj* litigioso, permaloso; indisciplinato

fracture ['fræktʃər] *s* frattura || *tr* fratturare; (e.g., an arm) fratturarsi, rompersi || *intr* fratturarsi

fragile ['frædʒɪl] *adj* fragile

fragment ['frægmənt] *s* frammento; (e.g., of a movie) spezzone *m* || *tr* frammentare, spezzare

fragmenta'tion bomb' [,frægmən'teʃən] *s* bomba dirompente

fragrant ['fregrənt] *adj* fragrante

frail [frel] *adj* (not robust) gracile; (easily broken) fragile; (morally weak) debole || *s* canestro di giunco

frail·ty ['freltɪ] *s* (-ties) fragilità *f;* (of a person) debolezza

frame [frem] *s* (of picture) cornice *f;* (of glasses) montatura; (structure) ossatura; (of a building) ingabbiatura, impalcatura; (for embroidering) telaio; (of a window) intelaiatura; (of mind) stato; (of government) sistema *m;* (mov) inquadratura; (phot) fotogramma *m;* (aer) ordinata;

(naut) costa ‖ *tr* (*to put in a frame*) incorniciare; montare; costruire; inventare; esprimere; (slang) architettare un' accusa contro

frame′ house′ *s* casa con l'ossatura di legno

frame′-up′ *s* (slang) complotto per incriminare un innocente

frame′work′ *s* intelaiatura, impalcatura; palificazione

franc [fræŋk] *s* franco

France [fræns] *or* [frɑns] *s* la Francia

Frances [′frænsɪs] *or* [′frɑnsɪs] *s* Francesca

franchise [′fræntʃaɪz] *s* diritto di voto; concessione; (*privilege*) franchigia

Francis [′frænsɪs] *or* [′frɑnsɪs] *s* Francesco

Franciscan [fræn′sɪskən] *adj* & *s* francescano

frank [fræŋk] *adj* sincero, schietto ‖ *s* affrancatura postale; lettera affrancata; (*franking privilege*) franchigia postale ‖ *tr* affrancare ‖ **Frank** *s* (*member of Frankish tribe*) franco; (*masculine name*) Franco

frankfurter [′fræŋkfərtər] *s* salsiccia di Francoforte, Frankfurter *m*

frankincense [′fræŋkɪn‚sens] *s* olibano

Frankish [′fræŋkɪʃ] *adj* & *s* franco

frankness [′fræŋknɪs] *s* franchezza

frantic [′fræntɪk] *adj* frenetico

frappé [fræ′pe] *adj* & *s* frappé *m*

frat [fræt] *s* (slang) associazione di studenti

fraternal [frə′tʌrnəl] *adj* fraterno

fraterni-ty [frə′tʌrnɪti] *s* (*-ties*) (*brotherliness*) fraternità *f*; sodalizio; (eccl) confraternita; (U.S.A.) associazione di studenti

fraternize [′frætər‚naɪz] *intr* fraternizzare

fraud [frɔd] *s* truffa, frode *f*; (*person*) (coll) truffatore *m*

fraudulent [′frɔdjələnt] *adj* fraudolento; (*conversion*) indebito

fraught [frɔt] *adj*—**fraught with** carico di, gravido di

fray [fre] *s* zuffa, rissa, lotta ‖ *intr* sfilacciarsi, logorarsi

freak [frik] *s* (*sudden fancy*) capriccio, ticchio; (*person, animal*) fenomeno

freakish [′frikɪʃ] *adj* capriccioso; strano, grottesco

freckle [′frekəl] *s* lentiggine *f*, efelide *f*

freckle-faced [′frekəl‚fest] *adj* lentigginoso

freckly [′frekli] *adj* lentigginoso

Frederick [′fredərɪk] *s* Federico

free [fri] *adj* (**freer** [′fri-ər]; **freest** [′fri-ɪst]) libero; gratis; franco; sciolto; esente; generoso; **to be free with** essere prodigo di; **to set free** liberare ‖ *adv* liberamente; in libertà; gratis ‖ *v* (*pret* & *pp* **freed** [frid]; *ger* **freeing** [′fri-ɪŋ]) *tr* liberare; (*from customs*) svincolare; esimere

freebooter [′fri‚butər] *s* pirata *m*

free′born′ *adj* nato in libertà; proprio di un popolo libero

freedom [′fridəm] *s* libertà *f*

free′dom of speech′ *s* libertà *f* di parola

free′dom of the press′ *s* libertà *f* di stampa

free′dom of the seas′ *s* libertà *f* di navigazione

free′dom of wor′ship *s* libertà religiosa

free′ en′terprise *s* economia libera

free′-for-all′ *s* rissa, tafferuglio

free′ hand′ *s* libertà assoluta

free′-hand′ *adj* a mano libera

freehanded [′fri′hændɪd] *adj* liberale, generoso

free′ lance′ *s* giornalista *mf* pubblicista; scrittore *m* che lavora senza contratto; soldato di ventura

free′load′er *s* (coll) mangiatore *m* a sbafo

free′ port′ *s* porto franco

free′ serv′ice *s* manutenzione gratuita

free′-spo′ken *adj* franco, aperto

free′stone′ *adj* spiccagnolo ‖ *s* pesca spicca

free′think′er *s* libero pensatore

free′ thought′ *s* libero pensiero

free′ trade′ *s* libero scambio

free′trad′er *s* liberoscambista *mf*

free′way′ *s* autostrada

free′ will′ *s* libero arbitrio

freeze [friz] *s* gelo, gelata; (*e.g., of prices*) blocco ‖ *v* (*pret* **froze** [froz]; *pp* **frozen**) *tr* gelare; (*credits, rentals, etc.*) bloccare ‖ *intr* gelarsi; (*said of brakes*) inchiodarsi; morire assiderato; (*to become immobilized*) irrigidirsi

freeze′-dry′ *v* (*pret* & *pp* **-dried**) *tr* liofilizzare

freezer [′frizər] *s* congelatore *m*; (*for making ice cream*) sorbettiera

freight [fret] *s* carico; (*charge*) porto; (naut) nolo; **by freight** come carico mercantile; (rr) a piccola velocità ‖ *tr* spedire come carico

freight′ car′ *s* vagone *m* or carro merci

freighter [′fretər] *s* speditore *m*; nave *f* da carico

freight′ plat′form *s* (rr) banchina adibita al traffico merci

freight′ sta′tion *s* (rr) stazione merci

freight′ train′ *s* treno merci, merci *m*

freight′ yard′ *s* (rr) scalo merci

French [frentʃ] *adj* & *s* francese *m*; **the French** i francesi

French′ bread′ *s* pane *m* a bastone

French′ chalk′ *s* pietra da sarto

French′ door′ *s* porta a vetri

French′ dress′ing *s* salsa verde con aceto

French′ fried′ pota′toes *spl* patate fritte affettate

French′ horn′ *s* (mus) corno

French′ leave′ *s*—**to take French leave** andarsene all'inglese, filare all'inglese

French′man *s* (*-men*) francese *m*

French′ tel′ephone *s* microtelefono

French′ toast′ *s* pane dorato al salto

French′ win′dow *s* portafinestra

French′wom′an *s* (*-wom′en*) francese *f*

frenzied ['frɛnzɪd] *adj* frenetico

fren·zy ['frɛnzɪ] *s* (-zies) frenesia

frequen·cy ['frikwənsɪ] *s* (-cies) frequenza

fre′quency modula′tion *s* modulazione di frequenza

frequent ['frikwənt] *adj* frequente || [frɪ'kwɛnt] or ['frikwənt] *tr* frequentare, praticare

frequently ['frikwəntlɪ] *adv* frequentemente

fres·co ['frɛsko] *s* (-coes or -cos) affresco || *tr* affrescare

fresh [frɛʃ] *adj* fresco; (*water*) dolce; (*new*) nuovo; (*wind*) moderato; (*inexperienced*) novizio; (*cheeky*) (slang) sfacciato || *adv* recentemente, di recente; **fresh in** (coll) appena arrivato; **fresh out** (coll) appena esaurito

freshen ['frɛʃən] *tr* rinfrescare || *intr* rinfrescarsi

freshet ['frɛʃɪt] *s* piena, crescita

fresh′man *s* (-men) (*newcomer*) novizio; (educ) matricola

freshness ['frɛʃnɪs] *s* freschezza; (*of air*) frescura; (*cheek*) (slang) sfacciataggine *f*

fresh′-wa′ter *adj* d'acqua dolce; poco conosciuto; piccolo

fret [frɛt] *s* (*interlaced design*) fregio, greca; irritazione; (mus) tasto || *v* (*pret & pp* **fretted;** *ger* **fretting**) *tr* fregiare || *intr* fremere, trepidare, agitarsi

fretful ['frɛtfəl] *adj* irritabile, permaloso

fret′work′ *s* greca

Freudianism ['frɔɪdɪ·ə‚nɪzəm] *s* freudismo

friar ['fraɪ·ər] *s* frate *m*

friar·y ['fraɪ·ərɪ] *s* (-ies) convento di frati

fricassee [‚frɪkə'si] *s* fricassea

friction ['frɪkʃən] *s* frizione; disaccordo, dissenso

fric′tion tape′ *s* nastro isolante

Friday ['fraɪdɪ] *s* venerdì *m*

fried [fraɪd] *adj* fritto

fried′ egg′ *s* uovo al tegame, uovo occhio di manzo

friend [frɛnd] *s* amico; **to be friends with** essere amico di; **to make friends** allacciare amicizie; **to make friends with** fare l'amicizia di

friend·ly ['frɛndlɪ] *adj* (-lier; -liest) amico, amichevole

friendship ['frɛndʃɪp] *s* amicizia

frieze [friz] *s* (archit) fregio

frigate ['frɪgɪt] *s* fregata

fright [fraɪt] *s* spavento; **to take fright at** spaventarsi di

frighten ['fraɪtən] *tr* intimorire, spaventare; **to frighten away** mettere in fuga, sgomentare || *intr* spaventarsi

frightful ['fraɪtfəl] *adj* spaventevole, orribile; (coll) enorme

frightfulness ['fraɪtfəlnɪs] *s* spavento; terrorismo

frigid ['frɪdʒɪd] *adj* freddo; (*zone*) glaciale

frigidity [frɪ'dʒɪdɪtɪ] *s* (fig) frigidezza; (pathol) frigidità *f*

frill [frɪl] *s* pieghettatura; (*of birds and other animals*) collarino; (*in dress, speech, etc.*) affettazione

fringe [frɪndʒ] *s* frangia; (*in dressmaking*) volantino; (*on curtains*) balza; **on the fringe of** all'orlo di || *tr* orlare

fringe′ ben′efits *spl* assegni *mpl*, benefici *mpl* marginali

fripper·y ['frɪpərɪ] *s* (-ies) (*finery*) fronzoli *mpl*; ostentazione; (*trifles*) cianfrusaglie *fpl*

frisk [frɪsk] *tr* perquisire; (slang) derubare || *intr* fare capriole

frisk·y ['frɪskɪ] *adj* (-ier; -iest) gaio, vivace

fritter ['frɪtər] *s* frittella; frammento || *tr*—**to fritter away** sprecare

frivolous ['frɪvələs] *adj* frivolo

friz [frɪz] *s* (frizzes) ricciolo || *v* (*pret & pp* **frizzed;** *ger* **frizzing**) *tr* arricciare

frizzle ['frɪzəl] *s* ricciolo || *tr* arricciare || *intr* arricciarsi

friz·zly ['frɪzlɪ] *adj* (-zlier; -zliest) crespo, riccio

fro [fro] *adv*—**to and fro** avanti e indietro; **to go to and fro** andare e venire

frock [frɑk] *s* gabbano; (*smock*) grembiule *m*; blusa; (*of priest*) tonaca

frock′ coat′ *s* finanziera

frog [frɑg] or [frɔg] *s* rana; (*button and loop on a garment*) alamaro; (*in throat*) raschio

frog′man′ *s* (-men′) sommozzatore *m*, uomo rana

frol·ic ['frɑlɪk] *s* scherzo, monelleria || *v* (*pret & pp* **-icked;** *ger* **-icking**) *intr* scherzare, folleggiare

frolicsome ['frɑlɪksəm] *adj* scherzoso

from [frʌm], [frɑm] or [frəm] *prep* da; e.g., **I am from New York** sono di New York; da parte di; a, e.g., **to take s.th away from s.o.** portar via qlco a qlcu

front [frʌnt] *adj* frontale, anteriore; di fronte || *s* fronte *m & f*; (*of a building*) prospetto; (*of a book*) principio; (*of a shirt*) sparato; (e.g., *of wealth*) apparenza; (theat) boccascena *m*; (mil) fronte *m*; **in front of** dinanzi a; **to put on a front** (coll) fare ostentazione; **to put up a bold front** (coll) farsi coraggio || *tr* (*to face*) fronteggiare; (*to confront*) affrontare; (*to supply with a front*) coprire; servire da facciata a || *intr*—**to front on** dare su

frontage ['frʌntɪdʒ] *s* facciata, veduta; terreno di fronte alla casa

front′ door′ *s* porta d'entrata

front′ drive′ *s* (aut) trazione anteriore

frontier [frʌn'tɪr] *adj* limitrofo || *s* frontiera

fron′tiers′man *s* (-men) pioniere *m*

frontispiece ['frʌntɪs‚pis] *s* (*of book*) pagina illustrata di fronte al frontispizio; (*of building*) facciata

front′ mat′ter *s* (*of book*) parte *f* preliminare

front′-page′ *tr* stampare in prima pagina

front′ porch′ *s* porticato

front' room' s stanza con vista sulla strada
front' row' s prima fila
front' seat' s posto in una delle file davanti; (aut) sedile m anteriore
front' steps' spl scalinata d'ingresso
front' view' s vista sulla strada
frost [frɔst] or [frɑst] s gelo, brina, gelata; (fig) freddezza; (slang) fiasco ‖ tr agghiacciare; (with sugar) glassare; (glass) smerigliare
frost'bite' s congelamento
frost'ed glass' s vetro smerigliato
frosting ['frɔstɪŋ] or ['frɑstɪŋ] s glassatura; (of glass) smerigliatura
frost·y ['frɔsti] or ['frɑsti] adj (-ier; -iest) brinato; (hair) canuto; (fig) gelido
froth [frɔθ] or [frɑθ] s schiuma; (fig) frivolezza ‖ intr schiumare; (at the mouth) avere la schiuma
froth·y ['frɔθi] or ['frɑθi] adj (-ier; -iest) spumoso; frivolo
froward ['frowərd] adj indocile
frown [fraun] s aggrottare m delle ciglia; (of disapproval) cipiglio ‖ intr aggrottare le ciglia; **to frown at** or **on** disapprovare
frows·y or **frowz·y** ['frauzi] adj (-ier; -iest) sporco; puzzolente
fro'zen foods' ['frozən] spl cibi congelati; cibi surgelati
frugal ['frugəl] adj parsimonioso; (in food and drink) frugale
fruit [frut] adj (tree) fruttifero; (dish) da frutta ‖ s (such as apple) frutto; (collectively) frutta, e.g., **I like fruit** mi piace la frutta; (fig) frutto
fruit' cake' s torta con noci e canditi
fruit' cup' s macedonia di frutta
fruit' dish' s fruttiera, portafrutta m
fruit' fly' s moscerino del vino
fruitful ['frutfəl] adj fruttuoso
fruition [fru'ɪʃən] s realizzazione; **to come to fruition** giungere a buon fine
fruit' jar' s vaso da frutta
fruit' juice' s sugo or spremuta di frutta
fruitless ['frutlɪs] adj infruttuoso
fruit' sal'ad s macedonia di frutta
fruit' stand' s bancarella da fruttivendolo
fruit' store' s negozio di frutta
frumpish ['frʌmpɪʃ] adj trasandato
frustrate ['frʌstret] tr frustrare
fry [fraɪ] s (fries) fritto ‖ v (pret & pp fried) tr & intr friggere
fry'ing pan' s padella; **out of the frying pan into the fire** dalla padella nella brace
fudge [fʌdʒ] s dolce m di cioccolato
fuel ['fju·əl] s combustibile m; (fig) cibo ‖ v (pret & pp fueled or fuelled; ger fueling or fuelling) tr rifornire di carburante ‖ intr rifornirsi di carburante
fuel' cell' s cellula elettrogena
fu'el oil' s nafta, olio pesante
fu'el tank' s serbatoio del carburante
fugitive ['fjudʒɪtɪv] adj & s fuggiasco, fuggitivo
fugue [fjug] s (mus) fuga
ful·crum ['fʌlkrəm] s (-crums or -cra [krə]) fulcro

fulfill [ful'fɪl] tr (to carry out) eseguire; (an obligation) mantenere; (to bring to an end) completare
fulfillment [ful'fɪlmənt] s adempimento; realizzazione
full [ful] adj pieno; (speed) tutto; (garment) ampio; (voice) spiegato; (of food) sazio; (member) effettivo; **full of aches and pains** pieno d'acciacchi; **full of fun** divertentissimo; **full of play** pieno di vita ‖ s pieno; colmo; **in full** per esteso, in pieno; **to the full** completamente ‖ adv completamente; **full many** (a) moltissimi; **full well** perfettamente ‖ tr follare
full-blooded [ˌful'blʌdɪd] adj vigoroso; purosangue
full-blown ['ful'blon] adj completamente sbocciato; maturo
full-bodied ['ful'badɪd] adj forte, ricco
full' dress' s vestito da sera; (mil) tenuta di gala, alta uniforme
full-faced ['ful'fest] adj paffuto; (view) intero; (typ) grassetto
full-fledged ['ful'fledʒd] adj completamente sviluppato; vero, autentico
full-grown ['ful'gron] adj completamente sviluppato, adulto
full' house' s (theat) piena; (poker) full m
full'-length' mir'ror s specchiera
full'-length mov'ie s lungometraggio
full' moon' s luna piena
full' name' s nome m e cognome m
full'-page' adj di tutta una pagina
full' pow'ers spl pieni poteri
full' sail' adv a vele spiegate
full'-scale' adj in grandezza naturale; completo
full-sized ['ful'saɪzd] adj in grandezza naturale
full' speed' adv a tutta velocità
full' stop' s fermata; (gram) punto
full' swing' s piena attività
full' tilt' adv a tutta forza
full'-time' adj a orario completo
fully ['fuli] or ['fulli] adv completamente, del tutto
fulsome ['fulsəm] or ['fʌlsəm] adj basso, volgare; nauseante
fumble ['fʌmbəl] tr (a ball) lasciar cadere ‖ intr titubare; andare a tentoni; (in one's pocket) cercare alla cieca
fume [fjum] s fumo, vapore m, esalazione ‖ tr affumicare ‖ intr fumare, esalare fumo; (to show anger) irritarsi
fumigate ['fjumɪˌget] tr fumigare
fumigation [ˌfjumɪ'geʃən] s fumigazione
fun [fʌn] s divertimento, spasso; **to be fun** essere divertente; **to have fun** divertirsi; **to make fun of** prendersi gioco di
function ['fʌŋkʃən] s funzione ‖ intr funzionare, marciare, camminare
functional ['fʌŋkʃənəl] adj funzionale
functionalism ['fʌŋkʃənəlˌɪzəm] s funzionalismo
functionar·y ['fʌŋkʃəˌnɛri] s (-ies) funzionario

fund [fʌnd] s fondo; (of knowledge) suppellettile f || tr (debts) consolidare

fundamental [ˌfʌndəˈmentəl] adj fondamentale || s fondamento

fundamentalist [ˌfʌndəˈmentəlɪst] adj & s scritturale m

funeral [ˈfjunərəl] adj funebre, funerario || s funerale m, trasporto funebre; **it's not my funeral** (slang) non sono affari miei

fu'neral direc'tor s imprenditore m di pompe funebri

fu'neral home' or **par'lor** s impresa di pompe funebri

fu'neral serv'ice s ufficio dei defunti

funereal [fjuˈnɪrɪ·əl] adj funebre

fungous [ˈfʌŋgəs] adj fungoso

fungus [ˈfʌŋgəs] s **(funguses** or **fungi** [ˈfʌndʒaɪ]) fungo

funicular [fjuˈnɪkjələr] adj & s funicolare f

funk [fʌŋk] s (coll) paura; (coll) codardo; **in a funk** (coll) con una paura matta

fun·nel [ˈfʌnəl] s imbuto; (smokestack) fumaiolo; (for ventilation) manica a vento || v (pret & pp -neled or -nelled; ger -neling or -nelling) tr incanalare

funnies [ˈfʌniz] spl pagine fpl fumetti

fun·ny [ˈfʌni] adj **(-nier; -niest)** comico, buffo; (coll) strano; **to strike as funny** parere strano or buffo a

fun'ny bone' s osso rabbioso (del gomito); **to strike s.o.'s funny bone** far ridere qlcu

fur [fʌr] s pelo; (garment) pelliccia; (on the tongue) patina

furbelow [ˈfʌrbə ˌlo] s falpalà m

furbish [ˈfʌrbɪʃ] tr lustrare; mettere a nuovo; **to furbish up** rinfrescare

furious [ˈfjurɪ·əs] adj furioso

furl [fʌrl] tr (a flag) incazzottare; (naut) raccogliere, strangolare

fur-lined [ˈfʌr ˌlaɪnd] adj foderato di pelliccia

furlong [ˈfʌrlɔŋ] or [ˈfʌrlɑŋ] s un ottavo di miglio terrestre

furlough [ˈfʌrlo] s licenza || tr licenziare

furnace [ˈfʌrnɪs] s fornace f; (to heat a house) caldaia del calorifero

furnish [ˈfʌrnɪʃ] tr fornire; ammobiliare

furnishings [ˈfʌrnɪʃɪŋz] spl mobilia; (things to wear) accessori mpl da uomo

furniture [ˈfʌrnɪtʃər] s mobili mpl, mobilia; (naut) attrezzatura; **a piece of furniture** un mobile

fur·ni·ture deal'er s mobiliere m

furor [ˈfjurɔr] s furore m

furrier [ˈfʌrɪ·ər] s pellicciaio

furrier·y [ˈfʌrɪ·əri] s (-ies) pellicceria

furrow [ˈfʌro] s solco || tr solcare

further [ˈfʌrðər] adj più lontano; ulteriore || adv oltre; più; inoltre || tr favorire, incoraggiare

furtherance [ˈfʌrðərəns] s avanzamento, incoraggiamento

furthermore [ˈfʌrðər ˌmor] adv inoltre

furthest [ˈfʌrðɪst] adj (il) più lontano || adv al massimo

furtive [ˈfʌrtɪv] adj furtivo

fu·ry [ˈfjuri] s (-ries) furia

furze [fʌrz] s ginestra spinosa

fuse [fjuz] s (for igniting an explosive) miccia; (for detonating an explosive) spoletta; (elec) fusibile m; **to burn out a fuse** bruciare un fusibile || tr fondere || intr fondersi; (elec) saltare

fuse' box' s valvoliera

fuselage [ˈfjuzələdʒ] or [ˌfjuzəˈlɑʒ] s fusoliera

fusible [ˈfjuzɪbəl] adj fusibile

fusillade [ˌfjuzɪˈled] s fucileria; (fig) gragnola || tr attaccare con fuoco di fucileria

fusion [ˈfjuʒən] s fusione

fuss [fʌs] s agitazione inutile; (coll) alterco per nulla; **to make a fuss** accogliere festosamente; fare molte storie; **to make a fuss over** aver un alterco su || tr disturbare || intr agitarsi per un nonnulla

fuss·y [ˈfʌsi] adj (-ier; -iest) (person) pignolo, meticoloso; (object) carico di fronzoli; (writing) complicato

fustian [ˈfʌstʃən] s fustagno; (fig) verbosità f, magniloquenza

fust·y [ˈfʌsti] adj (-ier; -iest) ammuffito, che sa di muffa; antico, sorpassato

futile [ˈfjutɪl] adj (unproductive) sterile; (unimportant) futile

futili·ty [fjuˈtɪlɪti] s (-ties) sterilità f; futilità f

future [ˈfjutʃər] adj futuro || s futuro; **futures** contratto con consegna a termine; **in the near future** nel prossimo avvenire

fuze [fjuz] s (for igniting an explosive) miccia; (for detonating an explosive) spoletta; (elec) fusibile m || tr innestare la spoletta a

fuzz [fʌz] s lanugine f, peluria; (in corners) polvere f; (slang) poliziotto; (slang) polizia

fuzz·y [ˈfʌzi] adj (-ier; -iest) lanuginoso; coperto di polvere; (indistinct) confuso

G

G, g [dʒi] s settima lettera dell'alfabeto inglese

gab [gæb] s (coll) parlantina || v (pret & pp **gabbed;** ger **gabbing**) intr (coll) chiacchierare

gabardine [ˈgæbər ˌdin] s gabardine f

gabble [ˈgæbəl] s barbugliamento || intr barbugliare

gable [ˈgebəl] s (archit) timpano

ga'ble roof' s tetto a due falde, tetto a capanna

gad [gæd] v (pret & pp **gadded;** ger **gadding**) intr bighellonare

gad'about' adj ozioso || s vagabondo, bighellone m; fannullone m

gad'fly' s (-flies) tafano, moscone m

gadget ['gædʒɪt] s congegno, dispositivo, macchinetta

Gaelic ['gelɪk] adj & s gaelico

gaff [gæf] s arpione m; (naut) picco; **to stand the gaff** (slang) aver pazienza

gag [gæg] s bavaglio; (joke) barzelletta; (theat) battuta improvvisata || v (pret & pp **gagged**; ger **gagging**) tr imbavagliare; soffocare || intr sentirsi venire la nausea

gage [gedʒ] s (pledge) pegno; (challenge) sfida

gaie·ty ['ge·ɪti] s (-ties) gaiezza

gaily ['geli] adv allegramente

gain [gen] s profitto; (increase) aumento || tr guadagnare; (to reach) raggiungere; (altitude) prendere || intr (said of a patient) migliorare; (said of a watch) correre; **to gain on** guadagnare terreno su; sorpassare

gainful ['genfəl] adj rimunerativo

gain·say v (pret & pp **-said** [,sed] or [,sed]) tr disdire, misconoscere; negare

gait [get] s portamento, andatura

gaiter ['getər] s ghetta

gala ['gælə] or ['gelə] adj di gala || s gala m & f, festa

galax·y ['gæləksɪ] s (-ies) galassia

gale [gel] s (of wind) bufera; (of laughter) scoppio; **to weather the gale** resistere alla tempesta

gall [gɔl] s fiele m; bile f; cistifellea; scorticatura; (gallnut) galla; (audacity) (coll) faccia tosta || tr irritare || intr irritarsi; (naut) logorarsi

gallant ['gælənt] or [gə'lænt] adj galante || ['gælənt] adj (brave) valoroso; (grand) magnifico; (showy) festivo || s prode m; (man attentive to women) galante m

gallant·ry ['gæləntrɪ] s (-ries) galanteria; valore m

gall' blad'der s vescichetta biliare

gall'-blad'der attack' s travaso di bile

galleon ['gælɪ·ən] s galeone m

galler·y ['gælərɪ] s (-ies) galleria; tribuna; (cheapest seats in theater) loggione m

galley ['gælɪ] s (vessel) galera; (kitchen) (aer) cucina; (kitchen) (naut) cambusa; (galley proof) (typ) bozza in colonna; (tray) (typ) vantaggio

gal'ley proof' s bozza in colonna

gal'ley slave' s galeotto

Gallic ['gælɪk] adj gallo, gallico

galling ['gɔlɪŋ] adj irritante

gallivant ['gælɪ,vænt] intr andare a spasso; fare il galante

gall'nut' s galla

gallon ['gælən] s gallone m

galloon [gə'lun] s gallone m, nastro

gallop ['gæləp] s galoppo; **at a gallop** al galoppo || tr far galoppare || intr galoppare

gal·lows ['gæloz] s (-lows or -lowses) forca; (min) castelletto

gal'lows bird' s (coll) remo di galera, pendaglio da forca

gall'stone' s calcolo biliare

galore [gə'lor] adv in abbondanza

galosh [gə'lɑʃ] s stivaletto di gomma

galvanize ['gælvə,naɪz] tr galvanizzare

gal'vanized i'ron s ferro zincato

gambit ['gæmbɪt] s gambetto

gamble ['gæmbəl] s azzardo; (game) gioco d'azzardo || tr giocare; **to gamble away** giocarsi || intr giocare d'azzardo; (com) speculare

gambler ['gæmblər] s giocatore m; speculatore m

gambling ['gæmblɪŋ] s gioco (d'azzardo)

gam'bling den' s bisca

gam'bling house' s casa da gioco

gam·bol ['gæmbəl] s salto, capriola || v (pret & pp **-boled** or **-bolled**; ger **-boling** or **-bolling**) intr saltare, far capriole

gambrel ['gæmbrəl] s garretto

gam'brel roof' s tetto a mansarda

game [gem] adj da caccia, coraggioso; (leg) (coll) zoppo; (coll) pronto || s (amusement) gioco; (contest) partita; (any sport) sport m; (wild animals hunted) selvaggina; (any pursuit) attività f; (object of pursuit) bersaglio; (bridge) manche f; **the game is up** il gioco è fallito; **to make game of** farsi gioco di; **to play the game** giocare onestamente

game' bag' s carniere m

game'cock' s gallo da combattimento

game'keep'er s guardacaccia m

game' of chance' s gioco d'azzardo

game' preserve' s bandita di caccia

game' war'den s guardacaccia m

gamut ['gæmət] s (mus, fig) gamma

gam·y ['gemɪ] adj (-ier; -iest) coraggioso; (culin) che sa di selvatico

gander ['gændər] s papero, oca

gang [gæŋ] adj multiplo || s (of workers) ganga; (of thugs) cricca || intr—**to gang up** riunirsi; **to gang up against** or **on** (coll) gettarsi insieme contro

gangling ['gæŋglɪŋ] adj dinoccolato

gangli·on ['gæŋglɪ·ən] s (-ons or -a [ə]) ganglio

gang'plank' s palanca, plancia

gangrene ['gæŋgrin] s cancrena || tr far andare in cancrena || intr andare in cancrena

gangster ['gæŋstər] s gangster m

gang'way' s (passageway) corridoio; (gangplank) passerella, scalandrone m; (in ship's side) barcarizzo || interj lasciar passare!

gan·try ['gæntrɪ] s (-tries) (of crane) cavalletto; (rr) ponte m delle segnalazioni; (rok) piattaforma verticale, torre f di lancio

gap [gæp] s (pass) passo; (in a wall) breccia; (interval) lacuna; (between two points of view) abisso; (mach) gioco

gape [gep] or [gæp] s apertura; (yawn) sbadiglio; sguardo di meraviglia || intr stare a bocca aperta; **to gape at** guardare a bocca aperta

garage [gə'rɑʒ] s rimessa

garb [gɑrb] s veste f || tr vestire

garbage ['gɑrbɪdʒ] s pattume m, immondizia, immondizie fpl

gar'bage can' s portaimmondizie m

gar'bage collec'tor s spazzaturaio, spazzino, netturbino

garble ['garbəl] tr falsare, mutilare

garden ['gardən] s (of vegetables) orto; (of flowers) giardino

gardener ['gardnər] s (of vegetables) ortolano; (of flowers) giardiniere m

gardenia [gar'dini-ə] s gardenia

gardening ['gardnɪŋ] s orticoltura; giardinaggio

gar'den par'ty s trattenimento in giardino

gargle ['gargəl] s gargarismo || intr gargarizzare

gargoyle ['gargɔɪl] s doccione m, gargolla

garish ['gerɪʃ] or ['gærɪʃ] adj appariscente; abbagliante

garland ['garlənd] s ghirlanda || tr inghirlandare

garlic ['garlɪk] s aglio

garment ['garmənt] s capo di vestiario

gar'ment bag' s tessilsacco

garner ['garnər] tr mettere in granaio; (to get) acquistarsi; (to hoard) incettare

garnet ['garnɪt] adj & s granata

garnish ['garnɪʃ] s guarnizione; || tr guarnire; (law) sequestrare

garret ['gærɪt] s sottotetto, soffitta

garrison ['gærɪsən] s guarnigione, presidio || tr presidiare

garrote [gə'rat] or [gə'rot] s strangolamento; garrotta || tr strangolare; giustiziare con la garrotta

garrulous ['gærələs] or ['gærjələs] adj garrulo, loquace

garter ['gartər] s giarrettiera

gas [gæs] s gas m; (coll) benzina; (slang) successo; (slang) chiacchiere fpl || v (pret & pp **gassed**; ger **gassing**) tr fornire di gas; (mil) gassare; (slang) divertire || intr emettere gas; (slang) chiacchierare; **to gas up** fare il pieno

gas'bag' s involucro per il gas; (coll) chiacchierone m

gas' burn'er s becco a gas; (on a stove) fornello a gas

Gascony ['gæskəni] s la Guascogna

gaseous ['gæsɪ-əs] adj gassoso

gas' fit'ter s gassista m

gash [gæʃ] s sfregio || tr sfregiare

gas' heat' s calefazione a gas

gas'hold'er s gassometro

gasi•fy ['gæsɪ ,faɪ] v (pret & pp **-fied**) tr gassificare || intr gassificarsi

gas' jet' s fornello a gas; fiamma

gasket ['gæskɪt] s guarnizione

gas'light' s luce f del gas

gas' main' s tubatura principale del gas

gas' mask' s maschera antigas

gas' me'ter s contatore m del gas

gasoline ['gæsə ,lin] or [,gæsə'lin] s benzina

gas'oline' deal'er s benzinaio

gas'oline' pump' s colonnetta, distributore m di benzina

gasp [gæsp] or [gɑsp] s respirazione affannosa; (of death) rantolo || tr dire affannosamente || intr boccheggiare

gas' range' s cucina a gas, fornello a gas

gas'-sta'tion attend'ant s benzinaio

gas' stove' s cucina a gas

gas' tank' s gassometro; (aut) serbatoio di benzina

gastric ['gæstrɪk] adj gastrico

gastronomy [gæs'trɑnəmi] s gastronomia

gas' works' s officina del gas

gate [get] s porta; (in fence or wall) cancello; (of sluice) saracinesca; (in an airport or station) uscita, (rr) barriera; (sports, theat) incasso totale; **to crash the gate** (coll) fare il portoghese

gate'keep'er s portiere m; (rr) guardabarriere m

gate'way' s passaggio, entrata

gather ['gæðər] tr raccogliere, cogliere; (news) raccapezzare; (dust) coprirsi di; (e.g., a shawl) avvolgere; (speed) aumentare (di); concludere, dedurre; (signatures) (bb) riunire; (sew) increspare || intr riunirsi; raccogliersi; accumularsi

gathering ['gæðərɪŋ] s riunione; (bb) raccolta e piegatura; (pathol) ascesso; (sew) pieghettatura

gaud•y ['gɔdi] adj (-ier; -iest) chiassoso, vistoso

gauge [gedʒ] s misura; calibro; (for liquids) indicatore m di livello; (of carpenter) graffietto; indice m; diametro; (aut) spia; (rr) scartamento || tr misurare; calibrare; (naut) stazzare

Gaul [gɔl] s gallo

gaunt [gɔnt] or [gɑnt] adj magro, emaciato; (e.g., landscape) desolato

gauntlet ['gɔntlɪt] or ['gɑntlɪt] s guanto; guanto di ferro; guantone m, manopola; **to run the gauntlet** (fig) esporsi alla critica; **to take up the gauntlet** raccogliere il guanto; **to throw down the gauntlet** gettare il guanto

gauze [gɔz] s garza

gavel ['gævəl] s martello, martelletto

gavotte [gə'vat] s gavotta

gawk [gɔk] s sciocco || intr guardare a bocca aperta

gawk•y ['gɔki] adj (-ier; -iest) sgraziato, goffo

gay [ge] adj gaio; brillante; dissipato; (slang) omosessuale

gaye•ty ['ge-ɪti] s (-ties) gaiezza

gaze [gez] s sguardo fisso || intr fissare lo sguardo

gazelle [gə'zel] s gazzella

gazette [gə'zet] s gazzetta

gazetteer [,gæzə'tɪr] s dizionario geografico

gear [gɪr] s utensili mpl, attrezzi mpl; (mechanism) meccanismo, dispositivo; (aut) marcia; (mach) ingranaggio **out of gear** disingranato; (fig) disturbato; **to throw into gear** ingranare; **to throw out of gear** disingranare; (fig) disturbare || tr adattare || intr adattarsi

gear' box' s scatola del cambio

gear'shift' s cambio di velocità

gear'shift lev'er s leva del cambio

gear'wheel' s ruota dentata

gee [dʒi] interj oh!; che bellezza!; **gee up!** (command to a draft animal) arri!

Gei'ger count'er [ˈgaɪgər] s contatore m Geiger

gel [dʒɛl] s gel m || v (pret & pp **gelled**; ger **gelling**) intr gelatinizzarsi

gelatine [ˈdʒɛlətɪn] s gelatina

geld [gɛld] v (pret & pp **gelded** or **gelt** [gɛlt]) tr castrare

gem [dʒɛm] s gemma, gioia

Gemini [ˈdʒɛmɪˌnaɪ] spl i Gemelli

gender [ˈdʒɛndər] s (gram) genere m; (coll) sesso

gene [dʒin] s (biol) gene m

genealo-gy [ˌdʒɛnɪˈælədʒi] or [ˌdʒini-ˈælədʒi] s (-gies) genealogia

general [ˈdʒɛnərəl] adj & s generale m

gen'eral deliv'ery s fermo in posta, fermo posta m

generalissi-mo [ˌdʒɛnərəˈlɪsɪmo] s (-mos) generalissimo

generali-ty [ˌdʒɛnəˈrælɪti] s (-ties) generalità f

generalize [ˈdʒɛnərəˌlaɪz] tr & intr generalizzare

generally [ˈdʒɛnərəli] adv in genere, generalmente

gen'eral part'ner s accomandatario

gen'eral practi'tioner s medico generico

generalship [ˈdʒɛnərəlˌʃɪp] s generalato; strategia, abilità f militare; abilità amministrativa

gen'eral staff' s stato maggiore

generate [ˈdʒɛnəˌret] tr (offspring; electricity) generare; (math) originare

gen'erat'ing sta'tion s centrale elettrica

generation [ˌdʒɛnəˈreʃən] s generazione

generative [ˈdʒɛnəˌretɪv] adj generativo

gen'erative gram'mar s grammatica generativa

generator [ˈdʒɛnəˌretər] s generatore m; (elec) generatrice f

generic [dʒɪˈnɛrɪk] adj generico

generous [ˈdʒɛnərəs] adj generoso; abbondante, copioso

gene-sis [ˈdʒɛnɪsɪs] s (-ses [ˌsiz]) genesi f || **Genesis** s (Bib) Genesi m

genetic [dʒɪˈnɛtɪk] adj genetico || **genetics** ssg genetica

Geneva [dʒɪˈnivə] s Ginevra

Genevan [dʒɪˈnivən] adj & s ginevrino

genial [ˈdʒinɪəl] adj affabile, geniale

genie [ˈdʒini] s genio

genital [ˈdʒɛnɪtəl] adj genitale || **genitals** spl genitali mpl

genitive [ˈdʒɛnɪtɪv] adj & s genitivo

genius [ˈdʒinjəs] or [ˈdʒini-əs] s (geniuses) genio || s (genii) [ˈdʒini-ˌaɪ] (spirit; deity) genio

Genoa [ˈdʒɛno-ə] s Genova

genocide [ˈdʒɛnəˌsaɪd] s (act) genocidio; (person) genocida mf

Geno-ese [ˌdʒɛnoˈiz] adj genovese || s (-ese) genovese mf

genre [ˈʒɑnrə] adj (e.g., painting) di genere || s genere m

genteel [dʒɛnˈtil] adj (well-bred) beneducato; (affectedly polite) manieroso, manierato

gentian [ˈdʒɛnʃən] s genziana

gentile [ˈdʒɛntɪl] or [ˈdʒɛntaɪl] adj gentilizio || [ˈdʒɛntaɪl] adj & s non circonciso; non ebreo; cristiano; (pagan) gentile

gentili-ty [dʒɛnˈtɪlɪti] s (-ties) distinzione, raffinatezza

gentle [ˈdʒɛntəl] adj (e.g., manner) gentile; (e.g., wind) dolce, soave; (wellborn) bennato; (tap) leggero

gen'tle-folk s gente f per bene

gen'tle-man s (-men) signore m; (attendant to a person of high rank) gentiluomo; (well-mannered man) gentleman m

gen'tleman in wait'ing s gentiluomo di camera

gentlemanly [ˈdʒɛntəlmənli] adj signorile

gen'tleman of the road' s brigante m; vagabondo

gen'tlemen's agree'ment s accordo fondato sulla buona fede

gen'tle sex' s gentil sesso

gentry [ˈdʒɛntri] s gente f per bene

genuine [ˈdʒɛnjuˌɪn] adj genuino

genus [ˈdʒinəs] s (genera [ˈdʒɛnərə] or **genuses**) genere m

geographer [dʒɪˈɑgrəfər] s geografo

geographic(al) [ˌdʒɪ-əˈgræfɪk(əl)] adj geografico

geogra-phy [dʒɪˈɑgrəfi] s (-phies) geografia

geologic(al) [ˌdʒɪ-əˈlɑdʒɪk(əl)] adj geologico

geologist [dʒɪˈɑlədʒɪst] s geologo

geolo-gy [dʒɪˈɑlədʒi] s (-gies) geologia

geometric(al) [ˌdʒɪ-əˈmɛtrɪk(əl)] adj geometrico

geometrician [dʒɪˌɑmɪˈtrɪʃən] s geometra mf

geome-try [dʒɪˈɑmɪtri] s (-tries) geometria

George [dʒɔrdʒ] s Giorgio

geranium [dʒɪˈrenɪ-əm] s geranio

geriatrics [ˌdʒɛrɪˈætrɪks] ssg geriatria

germ [dʒʌrm] s germe m

German [ˈdʒʌrmən] adj & s tedesco

germane [dʒərˈmen] adj pertinente

Germanize [ˈdʒʌrməˌnaɪz] tr germanizzare

Ger'man mea'sles s rosolia, rubeola

Ger'man sil'ver s alpacca

Germany [ˈdʒʌrməni] s la Germania

germ' car'rier s portatore m di germi

germ' cell' s cellula germinale

germicidal [ˌdʒʌrmɪˈsaɪdəl] adj germicida

germicide [ˈdʒʌrmɪˌsaɪd] s germicida m

germinate [ˈdʒʌrmɪˌnet] intr germinare

germ' war'fare s guerra batteriologica

gerontology [ˌdʒɛrɑnˈtɑlədʒi] s gerontologia

gerund [ˈdʒɛrənd] s gerundio

gestation [dʒɛsˈteʃən] s gestazione

gesticulate [dʒɛsˈtɪkjəˌlet] intr gesticolare

gesticulation [dʒes‚tɪkjəˈleʃən] s gesti-colazione

gesture [ˈdʒestʃər] s gesto || intr ge-stire, gesticolare

get [gɛt] v (pret got [gɑt]; pp got or gotten [ˈgɑtən]; ger getting) tr otte-nere; ricevere; prendere; andare a comprare; procacciare; riportare; procurarsi; riscuotere; guadagnare; **to get across** far capire; **to get back** riacquistare; **to get down** staccare; (to swallow) trangugiare; **to get off** togliere, cavare; **to get s.o. to** + inf indurre che qlcu + subj; **to get done** far fare; **to have got** (coll) avere; **to have got to** + inf (coll) dovere + inf || intr (to become) diventare, farsi; (to arrive) arrivare, venire; **to get out** (said of a convalescent) alzarsi; **to get along** andarsene; andare avanti; tirare avanti, giostrare; aver suc-cesso; **to get along in years** essere avanti con gli anni; **to get along with** andare d'accordo con; **to get angry** arrabbiarsi; **to get around** uscire; di-vulgarsi; rigirare; **to get away** scap-pare, darsela a gambe; **to get away with** s.th scappare con qlco; (coll) farla franca; **to get back** ritornare; ricuperare; **to get back at** (coll) ven-dicarsi di; **to get behind** rimanere indietro; (to support) appoggiare, patrocinare; **to get better** migliorare; **to get by** passare oltre; (to succeed) arrivare a farcela; passare inosser-vato; **to get even with** rifarsi con, prendersi la rivincita con; **to get going** mettersi in moto; **to get in** entrare; rientrare; arrivare; **to get in deeper and deeper** cacciarsi nei pa-sticci; **to get in with** diventare amico di; **to get married** sposarsi; **to get off** andarsene; smontare da; **to get old** invecchiare; **to get on** andare avanti; andare d'accordo; **to get out** uscire; propagarsi; **to get out of** (a car) uscire da; (trouble) trarsi di; **to get out of the way** togliersi di mezzo; **to get run over** essere investito; **to get through** finire; arrivare; farsi capire; **to get to be** finire per essere; **to get under way** mettersi in cammino; **to get up** alzarsi; **to not get over it** (coll) non arrivare a rassegnarsi

get'-a-way' s fuga; (sports) partenza

get'-to-geth'er s riunione, crocchio

get'up' s (coll) stile m, presentazione; (coll) costume m, abbigliamento

gewgaw [ˈgjugo] s cianfrusaglia

geyser [ˈgaɪzər] s geyser m

ghast-ly [ˈgæstli] or [ˈgɑstli] adj (-lier; -liest) orribile, orrendo; spettrale

gherkin [ˈgʌrkɪn] s cetriolino

ghet-to [ˈgeto] s (-tos or -toes) ghetto

ghost [gost] s spettro, fantasma m; **not a ghost of** nemmeno l'ombra di; **to give up the ghost** rendere l'anima

ghost-ly [ˈgostli] adj (-lier; -liest) spet-trale, fantomatico

ghost' sto'ry s storia di fantasmi

ghost' town' s città morta

ghost' writ'er s collaboratore anonimo

ghoul [gul] s spirito necrofago; ladro di tombe

ghoulish [ˈgulɪʃ] adj demoniaco, maca-bro

GI [ˈdʒiˈaɪ] (letterword) (General Issue) s (GI's) soldato degli Stati Uniti

giant [ˈdʒaɪ‑ənt] adj & s gigante m

giantess [ˈdʒaɪ‑əntɪs] s gigantessa

gibberish [ˈdʒɪbərɪʃ] or [ˈgɪbərɪʃ] s linguaggio inintelligibile

gibbet [ˈdʒɪbɪt] s forca || tr impiccare sulla forca; (to hold up to scorn) mettere alla berlina

gibe [dʒaɪb] s scherno, frecciata || intr schernire; **to gibe at** beffarsi di

giblets [ˈdʒɪblɪts] spl rigaglie fpl

giddiness [ˈgɪdɪnɪs] s vertigine f; fri-volezza

gid-dy [ˈgɪdi] adj (-dier; -diest) verti-ginoso; preso dalle vertigini; frivolo

gift [gɪft] s regalo; (natural ability) dono, dote f; (for Christmas) strenna

gifted [ˈgɪftɪd] adj dotato

gift' horse'—**never look a gift horse in the mouth** a caval donato non si guarda in bocca

gift' of gab' s (coll) facondia; **to have the gift of gab** (coll) avere la lingua sciolta

gift' pack'age s pacco-dono

gift' shop' s negozio di regali

gift'-wrap' v (pret & pp -wrapped; ger -wrapping) tr incartare in carta spe-ciale per regali

gigantic [dʒaɪˈgæntɪk] adj gigantesco

giggle [ˈgɪgəl] s risolino || intr ridere scioccamente, ridacchiare

gigo-lo [ˈdʒɪgəˌlo] s (-los) gigolo

gild [gɪld] v (pret & pp gilded or gilt [gɪlt]) tr dorare, indorare

gilding [ˈgɪldɪŋ] s doratura

gill [gɪl] s (of fish) branchia || [dʒɪl] s quarto di pinta

gilt [gɪlt] adj & s dorato

gilt-edged [ˈgɪltˌedʒd] adj a bordo dorato; di primissima qualità

gimcrack [ˈdʒɪmˌkræk] adj di nessun valore || s cianfrusaglia

gimlet [ˈgɪmlɪt] s succhiello

gimmick [ˈgɪmɪk] s (slang) trucco

gin [dʒɪn] s (liquor) gin m; (trap) trappola; (mach) arganello; (tex) sgranatrice f di cotone || v (pret & pp ginned; ger ginning) tr ginnare, sgranare

ginger [ˈdʒɪndʒər] s zenzero; (coll) energia, vivacità f

gin'ger ale' s gazosa allo zenzero

gin'ger-bread' s pan di zenzero; orna-mento di cattivo gusto

gingerly [ˈdʒɪndʒərli] adj cauto || adv con cautela

gin'ger-snap' s biscotto allo zenzero

gingham [ˈgɪŋəm] s rigatino

giraffe [dʒɪˈræf] or [dʒɪˈrɑf] s giraffa

girandole [ˈdʒɪrənˌdol] s girandola

gird [gʌrd] v (pret & pp girt [gʌrt] or girded) tr cingere; (to equip) dotare; (to prepare) preparare; (to surround) circondare

girder [ˈgʌrdər] s longherina

girdle [ˈgʌrdəl] s reggicalze m, zona, fascetta ‖ tr fasciare; circondare

girl [gʌrl] s fanciulla; ragazza

girl′ friend′ s amica, innamorata

girlhood [ˈgʌrlhud] s adolescenza, giovinezza

girlish [ˈgʌrlɪʃ] adj fanciullesco; da ragazza

girl′ scout′ s giovane esploratrice f

girth [gʌrθ] s circonferenza; fascia; (to hold a saddle) sottopancia m

gist [dʒɪst] s sugo, nocciolo, essenza

give [gɪv] s elasticità f ‖ v (pret gave [gev]; pp given [ˈgɪvən]) tr dare; (trouble) causare; (a play) rappresentare; (a speech; fruit; a sigh) fare; **to give away** distribuire gratuitamente; (to reveal) lasciarsi sfuggire; (a bride) accompagnare all'altare; (coll) tradire; **to give back** restituire; **to give forth** (odors) emettere; **to give oneself up** darsi; **to give up** cedere; (a position) abbandonare ‖ intr dare; cedere; (said, e.g., of a rope) rompersi; **to give in** cedere; darsi per vinto; **to give out** esaurirsi; venir meno; **to give up** darsi per vinto

give′-and-take′ s compromesso; conversazione briosa

give′a·way′ s premio gratuito; rivelazione involontaria; (game) vinciperdi m; (rad, tely) programma m a premi

given [ˈgɪvən] adj dato; **given that** dato che, concesso che

giv′en name′ s nome m di battesimo

giver [ˈgɪvər] s donatore m; dispensatore m

gizzard [ˈgɪzərd] s magone m

glacial [ˈgleʃəl] adj glaciale

glacier [ˈgleʃər] s ghiacciaio

glad [glæd] adj (gladder; gladdest) felice, lieto, contento; **to be glad (to)** essere felice (di)

gladden [ˈglædən] tr rallegrare

glade [gled] s radura

glad′ hand′ s (coll) accoglienza calorosa

gladiator [ˈglædɪˌetər] s gladiatore m

gladiola [ˌglædɪˈolə] or [gləˈdaɪ·ələ] s gladiolo

gladly [ˈglædlɪ] adv volentieri, di buon grado

gladness [ˈglædnɪs] s contentezza

glad′ rags′ s (coll) panni mpl da festa; (coll) vestito da sera

glamorous [ˈglæmərəs] adj affascinante, attraente

glamour [ˈglæmər] s fascino, malia

glam′our girl′ s ragazza sci-sci

glance [glæns] or [glɑns] s occhiata, guardata; **at first glance** a prima vista ‖ intr lanciare uno sguardo; **to glance at** dare un'occhiata a; **to glance off** sorvolare su; deviare da; **to glance over** dare una scorsa a

gland [glænd] s ghiandola

glanders [ˈglændərz] spl morva

glare [gler] s splendore m, luce f abbagliante; sguardo minaccioso ‖ intr risplendere; lanciare occhiatacce; **to glare at** fare la faccia feroce a

glare′ ice′ s vetrato

glaring [ˈglerɪŋ] adj risplendente, abbagliante; (look) torvo; evidente

glass [glæs] or [glɑs] s vetro; (tumbler) bicchiere m; (mirror) specchio; (glassware) cristalleria; **glasses** occhiali mpl

glass′ blow′er [ˈblo·ər] s vetraio

glass′ case′ s vetrinetta

glass′ cut′ter s tagliatore m di cristallo; (tool) diamante m tagliavetro

glass′ door′ s porta a vetri

glassful [ˈglæsful] or [ˈglɑsful] s bicchiere m

glass′house′ s vetreria; (fig) casa di vetro

glass′ware′ s vetreria, cristalleria

glass′ wool′ s vetro filato

glass′work′er s vetraio

glass′works′ s vetreria, cristalleria

glass·y [ˈglæsɪ] or [ˈglɑsɪ] adj (-ier; -iest) vetriato, vetroso

glaze [glez] s vernice vitrea; smalto; (of ice) superficie invetriata; (culin) glassa ‖ tr smaltare; invetriare; (culin) glassare

glazier [ˈgleʒər] s vetraio

gleam [glim] s barlume m, raggio ‖ intr baluginare

glean [glin] tr spigolare, racimolare; (to gather facts) raccogliere

glee [gli] s gioia, esultanza

glee′ club′ s società f corale

glib [glɪb] adj (glibber; glibbest) loquace; (tongue) facile, sciolto

glide [glaɪd] s scivolata; (aer) volo a vela, volo planato; (mus) legamento ‖ intr scivolare; (aer) librarsi, planare; **to glide away** scorrere

glider [ˈglaɪdər] s (aer) libratore m, veleggiatore m

glimmer [ˈglɪmər] s barlume m ‖ intr brillare, luccicare; tralucere

glimmering [ˈglɪmərɪŋ] adj tenue, tremulo ‖ s luce fioca; barlume m

glimpse [glɪmps] s occhiata; **to catch a glimpse of** intravedere ‖ tr travedere

glint [glɪnt] s scintillio ‖ intr scintillare

glisten [ˈglɪsən] s scintillio, luccichio ‖ intr scintillare, luccicare

glitter [ˈglɪtər] s luccichio ‖ intr rilucere, sfolgorare

gloaming [ˈglomɪŋ] s crepuscolo (vespertino)

gloat [glot] intr guardare con maligna soddisfazione; **to gloat over** godere di

global [ˈglobəl] adj globale; universale; globulare

globe [glob] s globo; (with map of earth) mappamondo

globe-trotter [ˈglobˌtratər] s giramondo

globule [ˈglabjul] s globulo

glockenspiel [ˈglakənˌʃpil] s vibrafono

gloom [glum] s oscurità f; malinconia, uggia

gloom·y [ˈglumɪ] adj (-ier; -iest) lugubre, triste, tetro

glori·fy [ˈglorɪˌfaɪ] v (pret & pp -fied) tr glorificare; (to enhance) esaltare

glorious ['glɔrɪ·əs] *adj* glorioso; magnifico, splendido

glo·ry ['glɔri] *s* (**-ries**) gloria; **to go to glory** morire ‖ *v* (*pret & pp* **-ried**) *intr* gloriarsi

gloss [glɔs] or [glɑs] *s* lucentezza, patina; (*commentary*) glossa ‖ *tr* satinare, patinare; (*to annotate*) glossare; **to gloss over** nascondere, discolpare

glossa·ry ['glɑsəri] *s* (**-ries**) glossario

gloss·y ['glɔsi] or ['glɑsi] *adj* (**-ier**; **-iest**) lucido; (*paper*) satinato

glottal ['glɑtəl] *adj* articolato alla glottide

glottis ['glɑtɪs] *s* glottide *f*

glove [glʌv] *s* guanto

glove' compart'ment *s* cassetto portaoggetti

glow [glo] *s* fuoco, incandescenza; splendore *m*, scintillio; calore *m*; colorito acceso ‖ *intr* essere incandescente; (*said of cheeks*) avvampare; (*said of cat's eyes*) fosforeggiare

glower ['glau·ər] *s* sguardo torvo ‖ *intr* guardare col viso torvo

glowing ['glo·ɪŋ] *adj* incandescente; acceso; entusiasta, entusiastico

glow'worm' ['glo·] *s* lucciola; lampiride *m*

glucose ['glukos] *s* glucosio

glue [glu] *s* colla, mastice *m* ‖ *tr* incollare, ingommare

glue'pot' *s* pentolino per la colla

gluey ['glu·i] *adj* (**gluier; gluiest**) attaccaticcio; (*smeared with glue*) incollato

glum [glʌm] *adj* (**glummer; glummest**) tetro, accigliato

glut [glʌt] *s* abbondanza; eccesso; **there is a glut on the market** il mercato è saturo ‖ *v* (*pret & pp* **glutted**; *ger* **glutting**) *tr* saziare; (*the market*) saturare; (*a channel*) otturare

glutton ['glʌtən] *adj & s* ghiottone *m*

gluttonous ['glʌtənəs] *adj* ghiotto

glutton·y ['glʌtəni] *s* (**-ies**) ghiottoneria, golosità *f*

glycerine ['glɪsərɪn] *s* glicerina

G'-man' *s* (**-men'**) agente *m* federale

gnarl [nɑrl] *s* nodo ‖ *tr* torcere ‖ *intr* ringhiare

gnarled [nɑrld] *adj* nodoso; (*wrinkled*) grinzoso

gnash [næʃ] *tr* digrignare ‖ *intr* digrignare i denti

gnat [næt] *s* moscerino, pappataci *m*

gnaw [nɔ] *tr* rosicchiare, rodere ‖ *intr* —**to gnaw at** (fig) rimordere

gnome [nom] *s* gnomo

go [go] *s* (**goes**) andata; energia; (*for traffic*) via libera; **it's a go** è un affare fatto; **it's all the go** (coll) è all'ultimo grido; **it's no go** (coll) è impossibile; **on the go** in continuo andare e venire; **to make a go of** (coll) aver successo con ‖ *v* (*pret* **went** [wɛnt]; *pp* **gone** [gɔn] or [gɑn]) *tr* (coll) sopportare; (coll) scommettere; (coll) pagare; **to go it alone** fare da sé ‖ *intr* andare; (*to operate*) camminare, funzionare; (*e.g., mad*) diventare; (*said of numbers*) entrare; **gone!** vendutol; **so it goes** così va il mondo; **to be going to** + *inf* andare a + *inf*, e.g., **I am going to New York to see him** vado a New York a vederlo; (*to express futurity*) use *fut ind*, e.g., **I am going to stay home today** starò a casa oggi; **to be gone** essere andato; esser morto; **to go against** opporsi a; **to go ahead** andar avanti; tirare avanti; **to go around** andare in giro; **to go away** andarsene; **to go back** tornare; **to go by** passare per; regolarsi su; (*said of time*) passare; **to go down** discendere; (*said of a boat*) affondare; **to go fishing** andare a pescare; **to go for** vendersi per; andare a pigliare, attaccare; favorire; **to go get** andare a pigliare; **to go house hunting** andare in cerca di una casa; **to go hunting** andare a caccia; **to go in** entrare in; (*to fit in*) starci in; **to go in for** dedicarsi a; **to go into** investigare; darsi a, dedicarsi a; (*gear*) (aut) ingranare; **to go in with** associarsi con; **to go off** andarsene; aver luogo; (*said of a bomb*) esplodere; (*said of a rifle*) sparare; (*said of a trap*) scattare; **to go on** continuare, protrarsi; **to go on** + *ger* continuare a + *inf*; **to go out** uscire; passare di moda; (*said, e.g., of fire*) spegnersi; (*to strike*) mettersi in sciopero; **to go over** aver successo; leggere; esaminare; **to go over to** passare ai ranghi di; **to go skiing** andare a sciare; **to go swimming** andare a nuotare, andare al bagno; **to go through** esperimentare; (*to examine carefully*) rovistare; (*said, e.g., of a plan or a project*) aver successo; (*a fortune*) dissipare; **to go through a red light** passare la strada col semaforo rosso; **to go with** andare con, accompagnare; (*a girl*) essere l'amico di; **to go without** fare a meno di

goad [god] *s* pungolo ‖ *tr* pungolare; (fig) spronare

go'-ahead' *adj* intraprendente ‖ *s* via *m*

goal [gol] *s* meta; (football) gol *m*

goalie ['goli] *s* portiere *m*

goal'keep'er *s* portiere *m*

goal' line' *s* linea di porta

goal' post' *s* montante *m*

goat [got] *s* capra; (*male*) becco; (coll) capro espiatorio; **to get the goat of** (coll) irritare

goatee [go'ti] *s* barbetta, pizzo

goat'herd' *s* capraio

goat'skin' *s* pelle *f* di capra

goat'suck'er *s* caprimulgo

gob [gɑb] *s* massa informe; **gobs** (coll) mucchio, quantità *f* enorme

gobble ['gɑbəl] *s* gloglottio ‖ *tr* ingozzare; **to gobble up** (coll) trangugiare; (coll) impadronirsi di ‖ *intr* trangugiare; (*said of a turkey*) gloglottare

gobbledegook ['gɑbəldɪ‚guk] *s* linguaggio oscuro

go'-between' *s* intermediario; (*pander*) mezzano; (poet) pronubo

goblet ['gɑblɪt] *s* coppa

goblin ['gɑblɪn] *s* folletto

go'-by' *s*—**to give s.o. the go-by** (coll) schivare qlcu

go'-cart' *s* carrettino; (*walker*) girello

god [gɑd] s dio; **God forbid** Dio ci scampi; **God grant** voglia Dio; **God willing** se Dio vuole

god'child' s (-chil'dren) figlioccio

god'daugh'ter s figlioccia

goddess ['gɑdɪs] s dea, diva

god'fa'ther s padrino

God'-fear'ing adj timorato di Dio

God'for·sak'en adj miserabile; (place) sperduto, fuori di mano

god'head' s deità f || **Godhead** s Ente Supremo, Dio

godless ['gɑdlɪs] adj ateo; malvagio || **the godless** i senza Dio

god·ly ['gɑdli] adj (-lier; -liest) devoto, pio

god'moth'er s madrina

God's' a'cre s camposanto

god'send' s manna, provvidenza

god'son' s figlioccio

God'speed' s successo, buona fortuna

go-getter ['go ˌgɛtər] s (coll) persona intraprendente

goggle ['gɑgəl] intr stralunare gli occhi

goggle-eyed ['gɑgəl ˌaɪd] adj dagli occhi sporgenti

goggles ['gɑgəlz] spl occhiali mpl da protezione

going ['go·ɪŋ] adj in moto, in funzione; **going on** quasi, e.g., **it is going on seven o'clock** sono quasi le sette || s andata; progresso

go'ings on' s (coll) comportamento, contegno; (coll) avvenimenti mpl

goiter ['gɔɪtər] s gozzo

gold [gold] adj aureo, d'oro || s oro

gold'beat'er s battiloro

gold'brick' s imitazione, frode f; (slang) fannullone m

gold' dig'ger ['dɪgər] s cercatore m d'oro; (coll) donna unicamente interessata nel denaro

golden ['goldən] adj aureo, d'oro; (gilt) dorato; (fig) splendido

gold'en age' s età f dell'oro

gold'en calf' s vitello d'oro

Gold'en Fleece' s vello d'oro

gold'en mean' s aurea mediocrità

gold'en·rod' s (bot) verga d'oro

gold'en rule' s regola della carità cristiana

gold'en wed'ding s nozze fpl d'oro

gold-filled ['gold ˌfɪld] adj otturato in oro

gold'finch' s cardellino

gold'fish' s pesce rosso

goldilocks ['gɔldɪ ˌlɑks] s bionda; (bot) ranuncolo

gold' leaf' s oro in foglia

gold' mine' s miniera d'oro

gold' plate' s vasellame m d'oro

gold'-plate' tr dorare

gold' rush' s febbre f dell'oro

gold'smith' s orefice m

gold' stand'ard s regime aureo

golf [gɑlf] s golf m || intr giocare a golf

golf' cart' s mini-auto f per campi da golf

golf' club' s mazza; associazione di giocatori di golf

golfer ['gɑlfər] s giocatore m di golf

golf' links' spl campo di golf

Golgotha ['gɑlgəθə] s il Golgota

gondola ['gɑndələ] s gondola

gondolier [ˌgɑndə'lɪr] s gondoliere m

gone [gɔn] or [gɑn] adj partito; rovinato; andato; morto; **gone on** (coll) innamorato di

gong [gɔŋ] or [gɑŋ] s gong m

goo [gu] s (coll) sostanza appiccicaticcia

good [gud] adj (better; best) buono; **good and . . .** (coll) molto, e.g., **good and cheap** molto a buon mercato; **good for** buono per; responsabile per; (equivalent) valido per; **to be good at** esser bravo a; **to be no good** (coll) non servire a nulla; (coll) essere un perdigiorno; **to make good** avere successo; (one's promise) mantenere; (a debt) pagare; (damages) indennizzare || s bene m; utile m, profitto; **for good** per sempre; **for good and all** una volta per sempre; **goods** merce f, mercanzia; **the good** il bene; i buoni; **to catch with the goods** (coll) cogliere in flagrante; **to deliver the goods** (slang) mantenere le promesse; **to do good** fare del bene; **to the good** come profitto; come attivo; **what is the good of . . . ?** a che serve . . . ?

good' afternoon' s buon pomeriggio

good'-by [ˌgud'baɪ] s addio || interj addio!; arrivederci!

good' day' s buon giorno

good' deed' s buona azione

good' egg' s (slang) bonaccione m, gran brava persona

good' eve'ning s buona sera; buona notte

good' fel'low s buon ragazzo

good'-fel'low·ship' s cameratismo

good'-for-noth'ing adj inutile, senza valore || s pelandrone m, inetto

Good' Fri'day s Venerdì Santo

good' grac'es spl buone grazie

good-hearted ['gud'hɑrtɪd] adj di buon cuore

good'-hum'ored adj di buon umore

good'-look'ing adj bello

good' looks' s bellezza

good·ly ['gudli] adj (-lier; -liest) bello; di buona qualità; ampio, considerevole

good' morn'ing s buon giorno

good-natured ['gud'netʃərd] adj bonaccione, affabile

goodness ['gudnɪs] s bontà f; **for goodness sake!** per amor di Dio!; **goodness knows!** chi sa mai! || interj Dio mio!

good' night' s buona notte

good'-sized' adj piuttosto grande

good' speed' s buona fortuna

good'-tem'pered adj di carattere mite, gioviale

good' time' s periodo gradevole; **to have a good time** divertirsi; **to make good time** andare di buon passo

good' turn' s favore m, servizio

good' will' s buona volontà; (com) reputazione; (com) clientela

good·y ['gudi] adj (coll) troppo buono || s (-ies) (coll) santerello; **goodies**

(coll) ghiottonerie *fpl* || *interj* (coll) bene!, benissimo!

gooey ['gu·i] *adj* (**gooier; gooiest**) (slang) attaccaticcio

goof [guf] *s* (slang) sciocco || *tr* (slang) rovinare; **to goof up** (*an opportunity*) (slang) mancare || *intr* (slang) pigliare un granchio; **to goof off** (slang) battere la fiacca; **to goof up** (slang) farla grossa

goof·y ['gufi] *adj* (**-ier; -iest**) (slang) sciocco

goon [gun] *s* (slang) scemo; (coll) crumiro, gaglioffo, terrorista *m*

goose [gus] *s* (**geese** [gis]) oca; **the goose hangs high** tutto va per il meglio; **to cook one's goose** rompere le uova nel paniere di qlcu; **to kill the goose that lays the golden eggs** uccidere la gallina delle uova d'oro || *s* (**gooses**) ferro di stiro per sarto

goose'ber'ry *s* (**-ries**) uva spina; (*berry*) bacca d'uva spina

goose' egg' *s* (slang) zero; (*lump on the head*) (coll) bernoccolo

goose' flesh' *s* pelle *f* d'oca

goose'neck' *s* collo d'oca

goose' pim'ples *spl* pelle *f* d'oca

goose' step' *s* passo dell'oca

gopher ['gofər] *s* scoiattolo di terra, citillo

gore [gor] *s* sangue coagulato; (*in a garment*) gherone *m* || *tr* (*with a horn*) incornare; inserire gheroni in

gorge [gɔrdʒ] *s* gola, burrone *m*; (*meal*) mangiata || *tr* rimpinzare || *intr* rimpinzarsi

gorgeous ['gɔrdʒəs] *adj* splendido, magnifico

gorilla [gə'rɪlə] *s* gorilla *m*

gorse [gɔrs] *s* gineprone *m*

gor·y ['gori] *adj* (**-ier; -iest**) sanguinolento

gosh [gaʃ] *interj* perbacco!

goshawk ['gas‚hɔk] *s* sparviere *m*, astore *m*

gospel ['gaspəl] *s* vangelo || **Gospel** *s* Vangelo

gos'pel truth' *s* santissima verità

gossamer ['gasəmər] *s* ragnatela; (*variety of gauze*) garza finissima; tessuto impermeabile finissimo

gossip ['gasɪp] *s* maldicenza; (*person*) pettegolo; **piece of gossip** maldicenza || *intr* spettegolare

gossipy ['gasɪpi] *adj* pettegolo

Goth [gaθ] *s* Goto

Gothic ['gaθɪk] *adj & s* gotico

gouge [gaudʒ] *s* (*cut made with a gouge*) scanalatura; (*tool*) sgorbia; (coll) truffa || *tr* sgorbiare; (coll) truffare

goulash ['gulaʃ] *s* gulasch *m*

gourd [gord] *or* [gurd] *s* zucca

gourmand ['gurmənd] *s* ghiottone *m*

gourmet ['gurme] *s* buongustaio

gout [gaut] *s* gotta, podagra

gout·y ['gauti] *adj* (**-ier; -iest**) gottoso

govern ['gʌvərn] *tr* governare; (gram) reggere

governess ['gʌvərnɪs] *s* governante *f*, istitutrice *f*

government ['gʌvərnmənt] *s* governo; (gram) reggenza

governmental [‚gʌvərn'mentəl] *adj* governativo

governor ['gʌvərnər] *s* governatore *m*; (mach) regolatore *m*

governorship ['gʌvərnər‚ʃɪp] *s* governatorato

gown [gaun] *s* (*of a woman*) vestito; (*academic*) toga; (*of a physician or patient*) gabbanella; (*of a priest*) veste *f* talare

grab [græb] *s* presa; **up for grabs** (coll) pronto a esser pigliato || *v* (*pret & pp* **grabbed**; *ger* **grabbing**) *tr* pigliare, afferrare

grace [gres] *s* (*charm; favor*) grazia; (*pardon*) mercé *f*; (*prayer*) benedicite *m*; (com) dilazione; **to say grace** recitare il benedicite; **with good grace** di buona voglia || *tr* adornare

graceful ['gresfəl] *adj* grazioso, vezzoso, leggiadro

grace' note' *s* (mus) appoggiatura

gracious ['greʃəs] *adj* grazioso; misericordioso || *interj* Dio buono!

gradation [gre'deʃən] *s* gradazione; (*step in a series*) passo

grade [gred] *s* grado; (*slope*) pendenza; (*mark in school*) voto; **to make the grade** raggiungere la meta || *tr* selezionare; (*a student*) dare un voto a; (*land*) spianare

grade' cros'sing *s* (rr) passaggio a livello

grade' school' *s* scuola elementare

gradient ['gredɪ·ənt] *adj* in pendenza || *s* pendenza; (phys) gradiente *m*

gradual ['grædʒu·əl] *adj* graduale

graduate ['grædʒu·ɪt] *adj* graduato; superiore; (*student*) laureato; (*candidate for degree*) laureando || ['grædʒu‚et] *tr* graduare; laureare, diplomare || *intr* laurearsi, diplomarsi

grad'uate school' *s* facoltà *f* di studi avanzati

graduation [‚grædʒu'eʃən] *s* graduazione; laurea; cerimonia della consegna delle lauree

graft [græft] *or* [graft] *s* (hort) innesto; (surg) trapianto; (coll) prevaricazione || *tr* (hort) innestare; (surg) trapiantare || *intr* (coll) prevaricare

gra'ham bread' ['gre·əm] *s* pane *m* integrale

grain [gren] *s* chicco; (*of sand*) granello; (*cereal seeds*) granaglie *fpl*; (*in wood*) venatura; (*in stone*) grana; **against the grain** di cattivo verso || *tr* granulare; (*leather*) zigrinare; (*metal*) granire

grain' el'evator *s* elevatore *m* di grano; (*building*) deposito di cereali

graining ['grenɪŋ] *s* venatura

gram [græm] *s* grammo

grammar ['græmər] *s* grammatica

grammarian [grə'merɪ·ən] *s* grammatico

gram'mar school' *s* scuola elementare

grammatical [grə'mætɪkəl] *adj* grammatico

gramophone ['græmə ‚fon] *s* (trade-mark) grammofono

grana·ry ['grænəri] *s* (-ries) granaio

grand [grænd] *adj* grandioso; grande, famoso

grand'aunt' *s* prozia

grand'child' *s* (-chil'dren) nipote *mf*

grand'daugh'ter *s* nipote *f*

grand' duch'ess *s* granduchessa

grand' duke' *s* granduca *m*

grandee [græn'di] *s* grande *m*

grandeur ['grændʒər] *or* ['grændʒur] *s* grande *m*, grandiosità *f*

grand'fa'ther *s* nonno; (*forefather*) antenato

grand'father's clock' *s* grande orologio a pendolo

grandiose ['grændɪ ‚os] *adj* grandioso

grand' ju'ry *s* giuria investigativa

grand' lar'ceny *s* furto importante

grand' lodge' *s* grande oriente *m*

grandma ['grænd ‚ma], ['græm ‚ma] *or* ['græmə] *s* (coll) nonna

grand'moth'er *s* nonna

grand'neph'ew *s* pronipote *m*

grand'niece' *s* pronipote *f*

grand' op'era *s* opera, opera lirica

grandpa ['grænd ‚pa], ['græn ‚pa] *or* ['græmpə] *s* (coll) nonno

grand'par'ent *s* nonno, nonna

grand' pian'o *s* pianoforte *m* a coda

grand'son' *s* nipote *m*

grand'stand' *s* tribuna

grand' to'tal *s* somma totale; importo globale

grand'un'cle *s* prozio

grand' vizier' *s* gran visir *m*

grange [grendʒ] *s* (*farm*) fattoria; (*organization of farmers*) sindacato di agricoltori

granite ['grænɪt] *s* granito

grant [grænt] *or* [grant] *s* concessione; (*sum of money*) sovvenzione; trapasso di proprietà || *tr* concedere; (*a wish*) esaudire; (*a permit*) rilasciare; (*law*) trasferire; **to take for granted** ammettere come vero; trattare con indifferenza

grantee [græn'ti] *or* [gran'ti] *s* concessionario; beneficiario

grant'-in-aid' *s* (grants'-in-aid') sussidio governativo a un ente pubblico; borsa di studio

grantor [græn'tər] *or* [gran'tər] *s* concedente *m*, concessore *m*

granular ['grænjələr] *adj* granulare

granulate ['grænjə ‚let] *tr* granulare || *intr* diventare granulato

gran'ulated sug'ar *s* zucchero cristallizzato

granule ['grænjul] *s* granulo

grape [grep] *s* chicco d'uva; (*vine*) vite *f*; **grapes** uva

grape' ar'bor *s* pergolato

grape'fruit' *s* pompelmo

grape' juice' *s* succo d'uva

grape'shot' *s* mitraglia

grape'vine' *s* vite *f*; **by the grapevine** di bocca in bocca; (mil) attraverso la radio fante

graph [græf] *or* [graf] *s* (*diagram*) grafico; (gram) segno grafico

graphic(al) ['græfɪk(əl)] *adj* grafico

graphite ['græfaɪt] *s* grafite *f*

graph' pa'per *s* carta millimetrata

grapnel ['græpnəl] *s* uncino; (*anchor*) grappino

grapple ['græpəl] *s* uncino; lotta corpo a corpo || *tr* uncinare || *intr* combattere; **to grapple with** lottare con

grap'pling i'ron *s* raffio, grappino

grasp [græsp] *or* [grasp] *s* impugnatura; (*power*) possesso; **to have a good grasp of** sapere a fondo; **within the grasp of** nei limiti della comprensione di || *tr* (*with hand*) impugnare; (*to get control of*) impadronirsi di; (fig) capire || *intr*—**to grasp at** cercare di afferrare

grasping ['græspɪŋ] *or* ['graspɪŋ] *adj* tenace; avido, cupido

grass [græs] *or* [gras] *s* erba; (*pasture land*) pastura; (*lawn*) tappeto erboso; **to go to grass** (*said of cattle*) andare al pascolo; andare in vacanza; ritirarsi; andare in rovina; morire; **to not let the grass grow under one's feet** non dormire in piuma

grass' court' *s* campo da tennis d'erba

grass'hop'per *s* cavalletta

grass'-roots' *adj* popolare

grass' seed' *s* semente *f* d'erba

grass' wid'ow *s* donna separata dal marito

grass·y ['græsi] *or* ['grasi] *adj* (-ier; -iest) erboso

grate [gret] *s* (*for cooking*) griglia; (*at a window*) grata || *tr* mettere una grata a; (*one's teeth*) digrignare; (*e.g., cheese*) grattugiare || *intr* stridere, cigolare; **to grate on one's nerves** dare sui nervi di qlcu

grateful ['gretfəl] *adj* riconoscente; (*pleasing*) piacevole, gradito

grater ['gretər] *s* grattugia

grati·fy ['grætɪ ‚faɪ] *v* (pret & pp -fied) *tr* gratificare, soddisfare

gratifying ['grætɪ ‚faɪ-ɪŋ] *adj* soddisfacente, piacevole

grating ['gretɪŋ] *adj* irritante; (*sound*) stridente || *s* inferriata

gratis ['gretɪs] *or* ['grætɪs] *adj* gratuito || *adv* gratis

gratitude ['grætɪ ‚tjud] *or* ['grætɪ ‚tud] *s* gratitudine *f*, riconoscenza

gratuitous [grə'tju·ɪtəs] *or* [grə'tu·ɪtəs] *adj* gratuito

gratui·ty [grə'tju·ɪti] *or* [grə'tu·ɪti] *s* (-ties) mancia, regalia

grave [grev] *adj* grave || *s* tomba, sepolcro, fossa

gravedigger ['grev ‚dɪgər] *s* becchino

gravel ['grævəl] *s* ghiaia; (pathol) renella

grav'en im'age ['grevən] *s* idolo

grave'stone' *s* pietra tombale

grave'yard' *s* cimitero, camposanto

gravitate ['grævɪ ‚tet] *intr* gravitare

gravitation [‚grævɪ'teʃən] *s* gravitazione

gravi·ty ['grævɪti] *s* (-ties) gravità *f*

gravure [grə'vjur] *or* ['grevjur] *s* fotoincisione

gra·vy ['grevi] *s* (-vies) (*juice from*

cooking *meat*) sugo; (*sauce made with it*) salsa, intingolo; (slang) guadagni *mpl* facili

gra'vy boat' *s* salsiera

gra'vy train' *s* (slang) greppia, mangiatoia

gray [gre] *adj* grigio; (*gray-haired*) canuto || *s* grigio; cavallo grigio || *intr* incanutire

gray'beard' *s* vecchio

gray-haired ['gre ,herd] *adj* canuto

gray'hound' *s* levriere *m*

grayish ['gre·ɪʃ] *adj* grigiastro

gray' mat'ter *s* materia grigia

graze [grez] *tr* (*to touch lightly*) sfiorare; (*to scratch lightly*) scalfire; (*grass*) brucare; (*cattle*) pascere, pascolare || *intr* pascere, brucare

grease [gris] *s* grasso, unto || [gris] or [griz] *tr* ingrassare, ungere

grease' cup' [gris] *s* coppa dell'olio

grease' gun' [gris] *s* ingrassatore *m*

grease' lift' [gris] *s* piattaforma di lubrificazione

grease' paint' [gris] *s* cerone *m*

grease' pit' [gris] *s* fossa di riparazione

greas·y ['grisi] or ['grizi] *adj* (-ier; -iest) grasso, unto, untuoso

great [gret] *adj* grande; (coll) eccellente || **the great** i grandi

great'-aunt' *s* prozia

Great' Bear' *s* Orsa Maggiore

Great' Brit'ain ['brɪtən] *s* la Gran Bretagna

Great' Dane' *s* danese *m*, alano

Great'er New York' *s* Nuova York e i suoi sobborghi

great'-grand'child' *s* (-chil'dren) pronipote *mf*

great'-grand'daught'er *s* pronipote *f*

great'-grand'fa'ther *s* bisnonno

great'-grand'moth'er *s* bisnonna

great'-grand'par'ent *s* bisnonno, bisnonna

great'-grand'son' *s* pronipote *m*

greatly ['gretli] *adv* molto

great'-neph'ew *s* pronipote *m*

greatness ['gretnɪs] *s* grandezza

great'-niece' *s* pronipote *f*

great'-un'cle *s* prozio

Grecian ['griʃən] *adj* & *s* greco

Greece [gris] *s* la Grecia

greed [grid] *s* avarizia, avidità *f*

greediness ['gridɪnɪs] *s* bramosia

greed·y ['gridi] *adj* (-ier; -iest) avaro; ingordo, bramoso

Greek [grik] *adj* & *s* greco

green [grin] *adj* verde; (fig) verde, inesperto || *s* verde *m*; (*lawn*) tappeto erboso; **greens** verdura, insalata

green'back' *s* (U.S.A.) biglietto di banca

green' earth' *s* verdaccio

greener·y ['grinəri] *s* (-ies) (*foliage*) vegetazione; (*hothouse*) serra

green'-eyed' *adj* dagli occhi verdi; (coll) geloso

green'gage' *s* regina claudia

green'horn' *s* (slang) pivello, sempliciotto

green'house' *s* serra

greenish ['grinɪʃ] *adj* verdastro

Greenland ['grinlənd] *s* la Groenlandia

green' light' *s* semaforo verde; (coll) via *m*

greenness ['grinnɪs] *s* verdore *m*, verdezza; inesperienza

green' pep'per *s* peperone *m* verde

greensward ['grin,sword] *s* tappeto erboso

green' thumb' *s* abilità *f* speciale per il giardinaggio

green' veg'etables *spl* verdura

green'wood' *s* bosco verde

greet [grit] *tr* salutare; ricevere; (*e.g., one's ears*) offrirsi a

greeting ['gritɪŋ] *s* saluto; accoglienza || **greetings** *interj* saluti!

greet'ing card' *s* cartolina d'auguri

gregarious [grɪ'geri·əs] *adj* (*living in the midst of others*) gregario; (*sociable*) sociale

Gregorian [grɪ'gori·ən] *adj* gregoriano

grenade [grɪ'ned] *s* granata

grenadier [,grenə'dɪr] *s* granatiere *m*

grenadine [,grenə'din] *s* granatina

grey [gre] *adj*, *s* & *intr* var of gray

grid [grɪd] *s* (*network*) rete *f*; (*on map*) reticolato; (electron) griglia

griddle ['grɪdəl] *s* tegame *m*

grid'dle·cake' *s* frittella cotta in teglia, crêpe *m*

grid'i'ron *s* griglia; campo di football; (theat) graticola

grief [grif] *s* affanno, dolore *m*; disgrazia; **to come to grief** andare in rovina

grievance ['grivəns] *s* lagnanza; motivo di lagnanza

grieve [griv] *tr* affliggere || *intr* affliggersi, dolersi; **to grieve over** soffrire per

grievous ['grivəs] *adj* doloroso, penoso; (*error*) grave; (*deplorable*) deplorevole

griffin ['grɪfɪn] *s* grifo, grifone *m*

grill [grɪl] *s* griglia || *tr* mettere alla griglia; (coll) interrogare insistentemente

grille [grɪl] *s* inferriata; (aut) mascherina, calandra

grill'room' *s* grill-room *m*, rosticceria

grim [grɪm] *adj* (grimmer; grimmest) (*stern*) accigliato; (*fierce*) feroce; (*sinister*) sinistro; (*unyielding*) implacabile

grimace ['grɪməs] or [grɪ'mes] *s* smorfia, sberleffo || *intr* fare le boccacce

grime [graɪm] *s* sporco; (*soot*) fuliggine *f*

grim·y ['graɪmi] *adj* (-ier; -iest) sporco; fuligginoso

grin [grɪn] *s* sorriso; (*malicious in intent*) ghigno || *v* (pret & pp grinned; ger grinning) *intr* sorridere; ghignare

grind [graɪnd] *s* macinata; (*laborious work*) (coll) macina; (slang) sgobbone *m* || *v* (pret & pp ground [graʊnd]) *tr* macinare; (*to sharpen*) molare; (*lenses*) smerigliare; (*meat*) tritare; opprimere; (*a crank*) girare; (mach) rettificare || *intr* macinare; frantumarsi; cigolare; (coll) sgobbare

grinder ['graɪndər] *s* (*to sharpen tools*) mola; (*to grind coffee*) macinino;

(*back tooth*) molare *m*; (*person*) molatore *m*

grind'stone' *s* mola; **to keep one's nose to the grindstone** lavorare senza posa

grin·go ['grɪŋgo] *s* (**-gos**) (*disparaging*) gringo

grip [grɪp] *s* (*grasp*) presa; (*with hand*) stretta; (*handle*) impugnatura; **to come to grips** venire alle prese || *v* (*pret & pp* **gripped;** *ger* **gripping**) *tr* stringere; impugnare; attirare l'attenzione di

gripe [graɪp] *s* (coll) lamentela; (naut) rizza; **gripes** colica || *intr* (coll) lamentarsi, brontolare

grippe [grɪp] *s* influenza

gripping ['grɪpɪŋ] *adj* interessantissimo, affascinante

gris·ly ['grɪzli] *adj* (**-lier; -liest**) orribile, spaventoso

grist [grɪst] *s* (*grain to be ground*) macinata; (*ground grain*) farina; (coll) mucchio; **to be grist to the mill of** (coll) fare comodo a

gristle ['grɪsəl] *s* cartilagine *f*

gris·tly ['grɪsli] *adj* (**-tlier; -tliest**) cartilaginoso

grist'mill' *s* mulino

grit [grɪt] *s* sabbia, arenaria; (fig) forza d'animo || *v* (*pret & pp* **gritted;** *ger* **gritting**) *tr* (*one's teeth*) far stridere, digrignare

grit·ty ['grɪti] *adj* (**-tier; -tiest**) sabbioso, granuloso; (fig) forte, coraggioso

griz·zly ['grɪzli] *adj* (**-zlier; -zliest**) brizzolato, canuto || *s* (**-zlies**) orso grigio

groan [gron] *s* gemito || *intr* gemere; (*to be overburdened*) essere sovraccarico

grocer ['grosər] *s* droghiere *m*; pizzicagnolo; proprietario di negozio di generi alimentari

grocer·y ['grosəri] *s* (**-ies**) (*store selling spices, soap, etc.*) drogheria; (*store selling cheese, cold cuts, etc.*) negozio di pizzicagnolo; negozio di generi alimentari; **groceries** generi *mpl* alimentari, commestibili *mpl*

grog [grag] *s* grog *m*

grog·gy ['grɑgi] *adj* (**-gier; -giest**) (coll) groggy, intontito

groin [grɔɪn] *s* (anat) inguine *m*; (archit) costolone *m*

groom [grum] *s* mozzo di stalla; (*bridegroom*) sposo || *tr* rassettare; (*horses*) rigovernare; (pol) preparare per le elezioni

grooms'man *s* (**-men**) compare *m* di nozze

groove [gruv] *s* scanalatura; (*of a pulley*) gola; (*of a phonograph record*) solco; (fig) routine *f* || *tr* scanalare, incavare

grope [grop] *intr* brancicare; (*for words*) cercare; **to grope for** cercare a tastoni

gropingly ['gropɪŋli] *adv* a tastoni

gross [gros] *adj* (*thick*) spesso; (*coarse*) volgare; (*fat*) grosso; (*error*) mar-

chiano; (*without deductions*) lordo || *s* grossa || *tr* fare un incasso lordo di

grossly ['grosli] *adv* approssimativamente; totalmente

gross' na'tional prod'uct *s* reddito nazionale

grotesque [gro'tɛsk] *adj & s* grottesco

grot·to ['grato] *s* (**-toes** or **-tos**) grotta

grouch [graʊtʃ] *s* (coll) malumore *m*; (coll) persona stizzosa || *intr* (coll) brontolare

grouch·y ['graʊtʃi] *adj* (**-ier; -iest**) (coll) stizzoso, brontolone

ground [graʊnd] *s* (*earth, soil, land*) terra; (*piece of land*) terreno; (*basis*) causa, fondatezza; (elec) terra, massa; (fig) occasione, motivo; **grounds** giardini *mpl*, terreno; (*of coffee*) fondi *mpl*; **on the ground of** per motivo di; **to break ground** dare la prima palata; (fig) mettere la prima pietra; **to fail to the ground** cadere al suolo; (fig) fallire; **to gain ground** guadagnar terreno; **to give ground** ceder terreno; **to lose ground** perder terreno; **to stand one's ground** non indietreggiare || *tr* fondare; (elec) mettere a massa; **to be grounded** (*said of an airplane*) essere forzato di rimanere a terra; **to be well grounded** essere bene al corrente || *intr* incagliarsi

ground' connec'tion *s* messa a terra

ground' crew' *s* (aer) personale *m* di servizio

ground' floor' *s* pianterreno

ground' glass' *s* vetro smerigliato

ground' hog' *s* marmotta americana

ground' lead' [lid] *s* (elec) collegamento a massa

groundless ['graʊndlɪs] *adj* infondato

ground' meat' *s* carne tritata

ground' plan' *s* progetto, pianta

ground' swell' *s* mareggiata

ground' wire' *s* filo di terra, filo di massa

ground'work' *s* fondamento, base *f*

group [grup] *adj* collettivo || *s* gruppo; (aer) stormo || *tr* raggruppare || *intr* raggrupparsi

grouse [graʊs] *s* gallo cedrone; (slang) brontolio || *intr* (slang) brontolare

grout [graʊt] *s* stucco || *tr* stuccare

grove [grov] *s* boschetto

grov·el ['grʌvəl] or ['gravəl] *v* (*pret & pp* **-eled** or **-elled;** *ger* **-eling** or **-elling**) *intr* umiliarsi

grow [gro] *v* (*pret* **grew** [gru]; *pp* **grown** [gron]) *tr* (*plants*) coltivare; (*animals*) allevare; (*a beard*) farsi crescere || *intr* crescere; svilupparsi; nascere; venir su; (*to become*) diventare; farsi; **to grow angry** arrabbiarsi; **to grow old** invecchiare; **to grow out of** (*fashion*) passare di; originare da; **to grow up** svilupparsi

growing ['gro·ɪŋ] *adj* crescente; (*pains*) di crescenza; (*child*) in crescita

growl [graʊl] *s* ringhio; brontolio || *intr* (*said of animals*) ringhiare; brontolare

grown'-up' *adj* adulto, grande || *s* (grown-ups) adulto

growth [groθ] *s* crescita, sviluppo; aumento; (pathol) escrescenza

growth' stock' *s* azione *f* che promette di aumentare di valore

grub [grʌb] *s* (drudge) sgobbone *m*; larva di coleottero; (coll) mangiare *m* || *v* (pret & pp grubbed; ger grubbing) *tr* scavare, zappare, dissodare || *intr* cercare assiduamente; scavare; sgobbare

grub·by ['grʌbi] *adj* (-bier; -biest) sporco; bacato; infestato di larve

grudge [grʌdʒ] *s* rancore *m*; **to have a grudge against** nutrire rancore contro || *tr* (to spend unwillingly) lesinare; invidiare

grudgingly ['grʌdʒɪŋli] *adv* di cattiva voglia

gru·el ['gru·əl] *s* farinata d'avena || *v* (pret & pp -eled or -elled; ger -eling or -elling) *tr* estenuare

gruesome ['grusəm] *adj* raccapricciante

gruff [grʌf] *adj* brusco, burbero; (voice) rauco, roco

grumble ['grʌmbəl] *s* brontolio || *intr* brontolare, borbottare

grump·y ['grʌmpi] *adj* (-ier; -iest) di cattivo umore, scontroso

grunt [grʌnt] *s* grugnito || *intr* grugnire

G-string ['dʒi,strɪŋ] *s* (loincloth) perizoma *m*; (worn by a female entertainer) triangolino di stoffa; (mus) corda di sol

guarantee [,gærən'ti] *s* garanzia; (guarantor) garante *mf* || *tr* garantire

guarantor ['gærən,tɔr] *s* garante *mf*

guaran·ty ['gærənti] *s* (-ties) garanzia || *v* (pret & pp -tied) *tr* garantire

guard [gɑrd] *s* guardia; (safeguard) protezione; (in a prison) guardia carceraria; (of a sword) guardamano; (football) mediano; **off guard** alla sprovvista; **on guard** in guardia; di fazione; **to mount a guard** montare la guardia; **under guard** ben custodito || *tr* guardare || *intr* fare la sentinella; **to guard against** guardarsi di

guarded ['gɑrdɪd] *adj* (remark) prudente

guard'house' *s* locale *m* di detenzione; (mil) corpo di guardia

guardian ['gɑrdɪ·ən] *adj* tutelare || *s* guardiano; (law) tutore *m*

guard'ian an'gel *s* angelo custode

guardianship ['gɑrdɪ·ən,ʃɪp] *s* protezione; (law) tutela

guard'rail' *s* guardavia *m*; (naut) parapetto

guard'room' *s* (mil) corpo di guardia

guards'man *s* (-men) guardia

guerrilla [gə'rɪlə] *s* guerrigliero

guerril'la war'fare *s* guerriglia

guess [gɛs] *s* congettura, supposizione || *tr* & *intr* congetturare, supporre; (to estimate correctly) indovinare; (coll) credere; **I guess so** credo di sì

guess'work' *s* congettura

guest [gɛst] *s* invitato, ospite *m*; (of a hotel) cliente *mf*; (of a boarding house) pensionante *mf*

guest' book' *s* albo d'onore; (in a hotel) registro

guffaw [gə'fɔ] *s* sghignazzata || *intr* sghignazzare

Guiana [gɪ'ɑnə] or [gɪ'ænə] *s* la Guayana

guidance ['gɑɪdəns] *s* guida, governo; **for your guidance** per Sua norma

guide [gɑɪd] *s* guida || *tr* guidare

guide'board' *s* indicatore *m* stradale

guide'book' *s* guida

guid'ed mis'sile ['gɑɪdɪd] *s* telearma, teleproietto, missile teleguidato

guide' dog' *s* cane *m* conduttore di un cieco

guide'line' *s* falsariga; corda fissa; linea di condotta, direttiva

guide'post' *s* indicatore *m* stradale

guide' word' *s* esponente *m* in testa di pagina

guidon ['gɑɪdən] *s* guidone *m*

guild [gɪld] *s* associazione mutua; (hist) gilda

guild'hall' *s* palazzo delle corporazioni

guile [gɑɪl] *s* astuzia, frode *f*

guileful ['gɑɪlfəl] *adj* astuto, insidioso

guileless ['gɑɪllɪs] *adj* sincero, innocente

guillotine ['gɪlə,tin] *s* ghigliottina || [,gɪlə'tin] *tr* ghigliottinare

guilt [gɪlt] *s* colpa, reità *f*

guiltless ['gɪltlɪs] *adj* innocente

guilt·y ['gɪlti] *adj* (-ier; -iest) colpevole, reo

guimpe [gɪmp] or [gæmp] *s* sprone *m*

guinea ['gɪni] *s* ghinea; gallina faraona || **Guinea** *s* la Guinea

guin'ea fowl' *s* gallina faraona

guin'ea pig' *s* porcellino d'India, cavia; (fig) cavia

guise [gɑɪz] *s* aspetto; veste *f*; **under the guise of** in guisa di

guitar [gɪ'tɑr] *s* chitarra

guitarist [gɪ'tɑrɪst] *s* chitarrista *mf*

gulch [gʌltʃ] *s* burrone *m*

gulf [gʌlf] *s* golfo; abisso

Gulf' Stream' *s* corrente *f* del Golfo

gull [gʌl] *s* gabbiano; (coll) credulone *m* || *tr* darla da bere a

gullet ['gʌlɪt] *s* gargarozzo; esofago

gullible ['gʌlɪbəl] *adj* credulone

gul·ly ['gʌli] *s* (-lies) borro, zanella

gulp [gʌlp] *s* sorsata || *tr*—**to gulp down** (food) ingoiare; (drink) tracannare; (fig) ingoiare, tranguiare

gum [gʌm] *s* gomma; (mucus on eyelids) cispa; **gums** (anat) gengive *fpl* || *v* (pret & pp gummed; ger gumming) *tr* ingommare; **to gum up** (slang) guastare || *intr* secernere gomma

gum' ar'abic *s* gomma arabica

gum'boil' *s* flemmone *m* gengivale

gum' boot' *s* stivale *m* da palude

gum'drop' *s* caramella alla gelatina di frutta, pasticca di gomma, drop *m*

gum·my ['gʌmi] *adj* (-mier; -miest) gommoso, vischioso; (eyelid) cisposo

gumption ['gʌmpʃən] *s* (coll) iniziativa; (coll) coraggio, fegato

gum'shoe' *s* caloscia; (slang) poliziotto || *v* (pret & pp -shoed; ger -shoeing)

intr (slang) camminare silenziosamente
gun [gʌn] *s* (*rifle*) fucile *m*; (*revolver*)
revolver *m*; (*pistol*) rivoltella; (*e.g.,
for spraying*) rivoltella; **to stick to
one's guns** tener duro ‖ *v* (*pret & pp*
gunned; *ger* **gunning**) *tr* far fuoco su,
freddare; (*a motor*) (slang) accelerare rapidamente ‖ *intr* andare a
caccia; sparare; **to gun for** andare a
caccia di
gun'boat' *s* cannoniera, esploratore *m*
gun' car'riage *s* affusto
gun'cot'ton *s* fulmicotone *m*
gun'fire' *s* fuoco, tiro
gun'man *s* (**-men**) bandito, sicario
gun' met'al *s* bronzo da cannoni; acciaio brunito
gunnel ['gʌnəl] *s* (naut) frisata
gunner ['gʌnər] *s* artigliere *m*, servente
m
gunnery ['gʌnəri] *s* artiglieria, tiro
gunnysack ['gʌni ,sæk] *s* sacco di tela
greggia
gunpoint ['gʌn ,pɔint] *s* mirino; **at gunpoint** a mano armata, e.g., **he was
held up at gunpoint** subì una rapina
a mano armata
gun'pow'der *s* polvere nera or pirica
gun'run'ner *s* contrabbandiere *m* di
armi da fuoco
gun'shot' *s* schioppettata; revolverata;
within gunshot a tiro di schioppo
gun'shot' wound' *s* schioppettata
gun'smith' *s* armaiolo
gun'stock' *s* cassa del fucile
gunwale ['gʌnəl] *s* frisata
gup·py ['gʌpi] *s* (**-pies**) lebiste *m*
gurgle ['gʌrgəl] *s* gorgoglio, borboglio
‖ *intr* gorgogliare, borbogliare; (*said
of a human being*) barbugliare
gush [gʌʃ] *s* getto, fiotto ‖ *intr* zampillare, sgorgare; (coll) dare in effu-
sioni
gusher ['gʌʃər] *s* pozzo di petrolio;
(coll) persona espansiva
gushing ['gʌʃɪŋ] *adj* zampillante, sgor-
gante; (coll) espansivo ‖ *s* zampillo;
(coll) espansione, effusione

gush·y ['gʌʃi] *adj* (**-ier; -iest**) (coll)
espansivo, effusivo
gusset ['gʌsɪt] *s* gherone *m*
gust [gʌst] *s* (*of wind*) raffica; (*of
smoke*) ondata, zaffata; (*of noise*)
esplosione; (*of anger*) sfuriata
gusto ['gʌsto] *s* gusto; entusiasmo
gust·y ['gʌsti] *adj* (**-ier; -iest**) a raffiche, burrascoso
gut [gʌt] *s* budello; **guts** budello;
(slang) fegato, coraggio ‖ *v* (*pret &
pp* **gutted**; *ger* **gutting**) *tr* sparare,
spanciare; distruggere l'interno di
gutta-percha ['gʌtə'pʌrt[ə] *s* gutta-
perca
gutter ['gʌtər] *s* (*on side of road*)
cunetta; (*in street*) rigagnolo; (*of
roof*) doccia, grondaia; (fig) bassifondi *mpl*
gut'ter-snipe' *s* monello
guttural ['gʌtərəl] *adj & s* gutturale *f*
guy [gai] *s* cavo di sicurezza; (coll)
tipo, tizio ‖ *tr* burlarsi di
guzzle ['gʌzəl] *tr & intr* trincare, bere
a garganella
guzzler ['gʌzlər] *s* ubriacone *m*
gym [dʒɪm] *s* (coll) palestra
gymnasi·um [dʒɪm'nezi·əm] *s* (**-ums** or
-a [ə]) palestra
gymnast ['dʒɪmnæst] *s* ginnasta *mf*
gymnastic [dʒɪm'næstɪk] *adj* ginnastico
‖ **gymnastics** *spl* ginnastica
gynecologist [,gaɪnə'kɑlədʒɪst], [,dʒaɪ-
nə'kɑlədʒɪst] or [,dʒɪnə'kɑlədʒɪst] *s*
ginecologo
gyp [dʒɪp] *s* (coll) imbroglio; (*person*)
(coll) imbroglione *m* ‖ *v* (*pret & pp*
gypped; *ger* **gypping**) *tr* imbrogliare
gypsum ['dʒɪpsəm] *s* gesso
gyp·sy ['dʒɪpsi] *adj* zingaresco, zingaro
‖ *s* (**-sies**) zingaro ‖ **Gypsy** *s* (*language*) zingaresco
gypsyish ['dʒɪpsi·ɪʃ] *adj* zingaresco
gyrate ['dʒaɪret] *intr* turbinare
gyrocompass ['dʒaɪro ,kʌmpəs] *s* giro-
bussola
gyroscope ['dʒaɪrə ,skop] *s* giroscopio

H

H, h [etʃ] *s* ottava lettera dell'alfabeto
inglese
haberdasher ['hæbər ,dæʃər] *s* cami-
ciaio; (*dealer in notions*) merciaio
haberdasher·y ['hæbər ,dæʃəri] *s* (**-ies**)
camiceria; merceria
habit ['hæbɪt] *s* abitudine *f*; (*addiction*) vizio; (*garb*) saio; **to be in the
habit of** aver l'usanza di
habitat ['hæbɪ ,tæt] *s* habitat *m*
habitation [,hæbɪ'teʃən] *s* abitazione
habit-forming ['hæbɪt ,formɪŋ] *adj*
(*e.g., drugs*) stupefacente; (*e.g., T.V.*)
assuefacente, che fa venire il vizio
habitual [hə'bɪtʃʊ·əl] *adj* abituale
habitué [hə ,bɪtʃʊ'e] *s* habitué *m*

hack [hæk] *s* (*cut*) taglio; (*notch*)
tacca; (*cough*) tosse secca; cavallo
da nolo; vettura di piazza; (*nag*)
ronzino; (*poor writer*) scribacchino ‖
tr tagliare; stagliare
hack'man *s* (**-men**) vetturino
hackney ['hækni] *s* cavallo da sella;
vettura di piazza
hackneyed ['hæknid] *adj* banale, trito
hack'saw' *s* seghetto per metalli
haddock ['hædək] *s* eglefino
haft [hæft] or [hɑft] *s* impugnatura
hag [hæg] *s* (*ugly old woman*) megera;
(*witch*) strega
haggard ['hægərd] *adj* sparuto, macilento; (*wild-looking*) stralunato

haggle ['hægəl] *intr* mercanteggiare
hagiographer [,hægi'ɑgrəfər] or [,hedʒi'ɑgrəfər] *s* agiografo
hagiography [,hægi'ɑgrəfi] or [,hedʒi-'ɑgrəfi] *s* agiografia
Hague, The [heg] *s* L'Aia *f*
hail [hel] *s* (*precipitation*) grandine *f*; (*greeting*) saluto; **within hail** a portata di voce || *tr* salutare; accogliere; chiamare; (*e.g.*, *blows*) far cadere || *intr* grandinare; **to hail from** venire da || *interj* salute!; salve!
hail'-fel'low *adj* gioviale
Hail' Mar'y *s* Ave Maria, avemaria
hail'stone' *s* chicco di grandine
hail'storm' *s* grandinata
hair [her] *s* capelli *mpl*; (*of animals*) pelame *m* or pelo; **a hair** (*a single filament*) un capello or un pelo; **to a hair** a perfezione; **to get in one's hair** (slang) dare sui nervi a qlcu; **to let one's hair down** (slang) parlare francamente; (slang) comportarsi alla buona; **to make one's hair stand on end** far rizzare i capelli a qlcu; **to not turn a hair** non scomporsi; **to split hairs** cercare il pelo nell'uovo
hair'breadth' *s* spessore *m* di un capello; **to escape by a hairbreadth** scamparla per un pelo
hair'brush' *s* spazzola per i capelli
hair'cloth' *s* cilicio
hair'cut' *s* taglio dei capelli; **to get a haircut** farsi tagliare i capelli
hair'do' *s* (-dos) acconciatura
hair'dress'er *s* parrucchiere *m* per signora; pettinatrice *f*
hair' dri'er *s* asciugacapelli *m*
hair' dye' *s* tintura per i capelli
hairless ['herlɪs] *adj* pelato, calvo
hair' net' *s* rete *f* per i capelli
hair'pin' *s* forcella, forcina, molletta
hair-raising ['her,rezɪŋ] *adj* orripilante
hair' re·mov'er *s* depilatorio
hair' restor'er [rɪ'stɔrər] *s* rigeneratore *m* per i capelli
hair' rib'bon *s* nastro per i capelli
hairsplitting ['her,splɪtɪŋ] *adj* meticoloso, pignolo
hair'spring' *s* spirale *f*
hair' styl'ing *s* pettinatura per signora
hair·y ['herɪ] *adj* (**-i·er; -i·est**) peloso, villoso, irsuto
hake [hek] *s* merluzzo, nasello
halberd ['hælbərd] *s* alabarda
halberdier [,hælbər'dɪr] *s* alabardiere *m*
halcyon ['hælsɪ·ən] *adj* calmo, pacifico
hale [hel] *adj* sano, robusto || *tr* trascinare a viva forza
half [hæf] or [hɑf] *adj* mezzo; **a half** or **half a** mezzo; **half the** la metà di || *s* (**halves** [hævz] or [hɑvz]) metà *f*; (arith) mezzo; **in half** a metà; **to go halves** fare a metà || *adv* mezzo, e.g., **half asleep** mezzo addormentato; a metà, e.g., **half finished** a metà finito; **half past** e mezzo or e mezza, e.g., **half past three** le tre e mezzo or le tre e mezza; **half . . . half** metà . . . metà
half'-and-half' *adj* mezzo e mezzo || *s* mezza crema e mezzo latte; mezza

birra chiara e mezza scura || *adv* a metà, in parti uguali
half'back' *s* (football) mediano; (soccer) laterale *m*
half-baked ['hæf,bekt] or ['hɑf,bekt] *adj* mezzo cotto; (*ideas*) infondato, inesperto
half' bind'ing *s* rilegatura in mezza pelle
half'-blood' *s* meticcio; fratellastro; sorellastra
half'-breed' *s* meticcio
half' broth'er *s* fratellastro
half-cocked ['hæf,kɑkt] or ['hɑf,kɑkt] *adj* immaturo, precipitato || *adv* (coll) precipitatamente
half' fare' *s* mezza corsa
half'-full' *adj* mezzo pieno
half-hearted ['hæf,hɑrtɪd] or ['hɑf,hɑrtɪd] *adj* indifferente, freddo
half'-hol'iday *s* mezza festa
half' hose' *s* calzini *mpl* corti
half'-hour' *s* mezz'ora; **on the half-hour** ogni trenta minuti allo scoccare dell'ora e della mezz'ora
half'-length' *adj* a mezzo busto || *s* ritratto a mezzo busto
half'life' *s* (phys) vita media
half'-mast' *s*—**at half-mast** a mezz'asta
half'moon' *s* mezzaluna
half' mourn'ing *s* mezzo lutto
half' note' *s* (mus) minima
half' pay' *s* mezza paga
halfpen·ny ['hepənɪ] or ['hepnɪ] *s* (-nies) mezzo penny
half' pint' *s* mezza pinta; (slang) mezza cartuccia, mezza calzetta
half'-seas o'ver *adj*—**to be half-seas over** (slang) essere sbronzato
half' shell' *s*—**on the half shell** in conchiglia
half' sis'ter *s* sorellastra
half' sole' *s* mezza suola
half'-sole' *tr* mettere la mezza suola a
half'-staff' *s*—**at half-staff** a mezz'asta
half'-timbered ['hæf,tɪmbərd] or ['hɑf,tɪmbərd] *adj* in legno e muratura
half' ti'tle *s* occhiello, occhietto
half'tone' *s* mezzatinta
half'-track' *s* semicingolato
half'truth' *s* mezza verità, mezza bugia
half'way' *adj* a metà strada; parziale, mezzo || *adv* a metà strada; **halfway through** nel mezzo di; **to meet halfway** fare concessioni mutue
half-witted ['hæf,wɪtɪd] or ['hɑf,wɪtɪd] *adj* mezzo scemo
halibut ['hælɪbət] *s* ippoglosso
halide ['hælaɪd] or ['helaɪd] *s* alogenuro
halitosis [,hælɪ'tosɪs] *s* alito cattivo, fiato puzzolente
hall [hɔl] *s* (*passageway*) corridoio; (*entranceway*) vestibolo; (*large meeting room*) salone *m*; (*assembly room of a university*) aula magna; (*building of a university*) edificio
halleluiah or **hallelujah** [,hælɪ'lujə] *s* alleluia *m* || *interj* alleluia!
hall'mark' *s* punzone *m* di garanzia; (fig) contrassegno, caratteristica
hal·lo [hə'lo] *s* (-los) grido || *interj* ehi!
hallow ['hælo] *tr* santificare

hallowed ['hæləd] *adj* consacrato
Halloween or **Hallowe'en** [ˌhælo'in] *s* vigilia di Ognissanti
hallucination [həˌlusɪ'neʃən] *s* allucinazione
hall'way' *s* corridoio; entrata
ha·lo ['helo] *s* (*-los* or *-loes*) alone *m*
halogen ['hælədʒən] *s* alogeno
halt [hɔlt] *adj* zoppicante || *s* fermata; **to call a halt** dare ordine di fermarsi; **to come to a halt** fermarsi || *tr* fermare || *intr* fermarsi, esitare || *interj* altolà!
halter ['hɔltər] *s* (*for leading horse*) cavezza; (*noose*) capestro; (*hanging*) impiccagione; corpino bagno di sole
halting ['hɔltɪŋ] *adj* zoppicante; esitante
halve [hæv] or [hɑv] *tr* dimezzare
halyard ['hæljərd] *s* (naut) drizza
ham [hæm] *s* (*part of leg behind knee*) polpaccio; (*thigh and buttock*) coscia; (*cured meat from hog's hind leg*) prosciutto; (slang) istrione *m;* (slang) radioamatore *m;* **hams** natiche *fpl*
ham' and eggs' *spl* uova *fpl* col prosciutto
hamburger ['hæmˌbʌrgər] *s* hamburger *m*
hamlet ['hæmlɪt] *s* frazione, paese *m* || **Hamlet** *s* Amleto
hammer ['hæmər] *s* martello; (*of gun*) cane *m;* (*of piano*) martelletto; **under the hammer** all'asta pubblica || *tr* martellare; **to hammer out** battere; portare a fine faticosamente || *intr* martellare; **to hammer away** lavorare accanitamente
hammock ['hæmək] *s* amaca
hamper ['hæmpər] *s* cesta || *tr* imbarazzare, intralciare
hamster ['hæmstər] *s* criceto
ham·string ['hæmˌstrɪŋ] *v* (*pret & pp* **-strung**) *tr* azzoppare; tagliare i garretti a; (fig) impastoiare
hand [hænd] *adj* manuale; fatto a mano || *s* mano *f;* (*workman*) garzone *m,* operaio; (*way of writing*) scrittura; (*signature*) firma; (*clapping of hands*) applauso; (*of clock or watch*) lancetta; (*all the cards in one's hand*) gioco; (*a round of play*) smazzata, mano *f;* (*player*) giocatore *m;* (*skill*) destrezza; (*side*) lato; **all hands** (naut) tutto l'equipaggio; (coll) tutti *mpl;* **at first hand** direttamente; **at hand** a portata di mano; **hand in glove** in perfetta unione; **hand in hand** tenendosi per mano; **hands up!** le mani in alto!; **hand to hand** corpo a corpo; **in hand** tra le mani; **in his own hand** di proprio pugno; **on hand** disponibile; **on hands and knees** (*crawling*) a gattoni; (*beseeching*) in ginocchio; **on the one hand** da un canto; **on the other hand** per contro; **to change hands** cambiare di mano; **to clap hands** battere le mani; **to eat out of one's hand** essere sottomesso a qlcu; **to get out of hand** diventare incontrollabile; **to have a hand in** prender parte a; **to have one's hands**
full essere occupatissimo; **to hold hands** tenersi per mano; **to hold up one's hands** (*as a sign of surrender*) alzare le mani; **to join hands** darsi la mano; **to keep one's hands off** non mettere il naso in; **to lend a hand** dare una mano; **to live from hand to mouth** vivere alla giornata; **to not lift a hand** non alzare un dito; **to play into the hands of** fare il gioco di; **to shake hands** darsi la mano; **to show one's hand** scoprire il proprio gioco; **to take in hand** prendere in mano; (*a matter*) prendere in esame; **to throw up one's hands** darsi per vinto; **to try one's hand** mettere la propria abilità alla prova; **to turn one's hand to** dedicarsi a; **to wash one's hands of** lavarsi le mani di; **under my hand** di mia firma autografa; **under the hand and seal of** firmato di pugno da || *tr* dare, porgere; **to hand down** tramandare; **to hand in** consegnare; **to hand on** trasmettere; **to hand out** distribuire
hand'bag' *s* borsetta
hand' bag'gage *s* valigie *fpl* a mano
hand'ball' *s* palla a mano
hand'bill' *s* manifestino, foglio volante
hand'book' *s* manuale *m;* guida; (*of a particular field*) prontuario
hand'breadth' *s* palmo
hand'car' *s* (rr) carrello a mano
hand'cart' *s* carretto a mano
hand'cuffs' *spl* manette *fpl* || *tr* mettere le manette a
handful ['hændˌful] *s* manata, manciata
hand' glass' *s* lente *f* di ingrandimento; specchietto
hand' grenade' *s* bomba a mano
handi·cap ['hændɪˌkæp] *s* svantaggio; (sports) handicap *m* || *v* (*pret & pp* **-capped;** *ger* **-capping**) *tr* andicappare
handicraft ['hændɪˌkræft] or ['hændɪˌkrɑft] *s* destrezza manuale; artigianato
handiwork ['hændɪˌwʌrk] *s* lavoro fatto a mano; opera, lavoro
handkerchief ['hæŋkərtʃɪf] or ['hæŋkərˌtʃif] *s* fazzoletto
handle ['hændəl] *s* manico; (*of a sword*) impugnatura; (*of a door*) maniglia; (*of a drawer*) pomolo; (*of a hand organ*) manovella; espediente *m;* **to fly off the handle** (slang) uscire dai gangheri || *tr* maneggiare; manovrare, dirigere; commerciare in || *intr* comportarsi
handle'bar' *s* manubrio
handler ['hændlər] *s* (sports) allenatore *m*
hand'made' *adj* fatto a mano
hand'maid' or **hand'maid'en** *s* domestica, serva; (fig) ancella
hand'-me-down' *adj* smesso || *s* vestito smesso or di seconda mano
hand' or'gan *s* organetto, organino, organetto di Barberia
hand'out' *s* elemosina di cibo; articolo distribuito gratis; comunicato stampa
hand-picked ['hændˌpɪkt] *adj* colto a mano; scelto specialmente

hand'rail' s guardamano, passamano
hand'saw' s sega a mano
hand'set' s microtelefono
hand'shake' s stretta di mano
handsome ['hænsəm] adj bello; considerevole; generoso
hand'spring' s capriola, salto mortale fatto toccando il terreno con le mani
hand'-to-hand' adj corpo a corpo
hand'-to-mouth' adj precario, da un giorno all'altro
hand'work' s lavoro fatto a mano
hand'writ'ing s scrittura
hand'wrought' adj lavorato a mano
hand·y ['hændɪ] adj (-ier; -iest) (easy to handle) maneggevole; (within easy reach) vicino; (skillful) destro, abile; **to come in handy** tornare utile
hand'y·man' s (-men') factotum m
hang [hæŋ] s maniera di cadere; **to get the hang of** (coll) imparare a adoperare; **to not give a hang** (coll) non importare un fico a || v (pret & pp **hung** [hʌŋ]) tr sospendere; (laundry) stendere; (to attach) attaccare; (a door or window) mettere sui cardini; (one's head) abbassare; **hang it!** (coll) al diavolo!; **to hang up** appendere; sospendere il progresso di || intr pendere, penzolare; esitare; essere sospeso; essere attaccato; **to hang around** ciondolare, oziare, gironzolare; **to hang on** essere sospeso a; dipendere da; persistere; (s.o.'s words) pendere; **to hang out** sporgersi; (slang) raccogliersi; (slang) vivere; **to hang over** esser sospeso; (to threaten) minacciare; **to hang together** mantenersi uniti; **to hang up** (telp) riattaccare || v (pret **hanged** or **hung**) tr (to execute) impiccare || intr impiccarsi
hangar ['hæŋər] or ['hæŋgɑr] s rimessa; (aer) aviorimessa, hangar m
hanger ['hæŋər] s gancio, uncino; (for clothes) attaccapanni m
hang'er-on' s (hangers-on) seguace mf; seccatore m; (sponger) parassita m
hanging ['hæŋɪŋ] adj pendente, pensile || s impiccagione; **hangings** parati mpl
hang'man s (-men) boia m
hang'nail' s pipita delle unghie
hang'out' s (coll) ritrovo abituale
hang'o'ver s mal m di testa dopo una sbornia
hank [hæŋk] s matassa
hanker ['hæŋkər] intr agognare
Hannibal ['hænɪbəl] s Annibale m
haphazard [,hæp'hæzərd] adj fortuito, a caso || adv a caso; alla carlona
hapless ['hæplɪs] adj sfortunato
happen ['hæpən] intr succedere; **to happen along** sopravvenire; **to happen on** incontrarsi per caso con; **to happen to** + inf per caso + ind, e.g., I **happened to see her at the theater** l'ho incontrata per caso a teatro
happening ['hæpənɪŋ] s avvenimento, fatto
happily ['hæpɪli] adv felicemente; fortunatamente

happiness ['hæpɪnɪs] s felicità f; gioia, piacere m
hap·py ['hæpi] adj (-pier; -piest) lieto, felice, contento; **to be happy to** avere il piacere di
hap'py-go-luck'y adj spensierato
hap'py me'dium s giusto mezzo
Hap'py New Year' interj buon anno!, felice anno nuovo!
harangue [hə'ræŋ] s arringa, concione || tr & intr arringare
harass ['hærəs] or [hə'ræs] tr bersagliare; tartassare, tormentare
harbinger ['hɑrbɪndʒər] s foriero; annunzio || tr annunziare
harbor ['hɑrbər] adj di porto, portuario || s porto || tr albergare; (love or hatred) nutrire; (e.g., a criminal) dare ricetto a
har'bor mas'ter s capitano di porto
hard [hɑrd] adj duro; (difficult) difficile; (work) improbo; (solder) forte; (hearing or breathing) grosso; (drinker) impenitente; (liquor) fortemente alcolico; **to be hard on** essere severo con; (to wear out fast) logorare rapidamente || adv duro; forte; molto; **hard upon** subito dopo
hard'-and-fast' adj inflessibile
hard-bitten ['hɑrd'bɪtən] adj duro, incallito
hard-boiled ['hɑrd'bɔɪld] adj (egg) sodo; (coll) duro
hard' can'dy s caramelle fpl; **piece of hard candy** caramella
hard' cash' s denaro contante
hard' ci'der s sidro fermentato
hard' coal' s antracite f
hard'-earned' adj guadagnato a stento
harden ['hɑrdən] tr indurire || intr indurirsi
hardening ['hɑrdənɪŋ] s indurimento; (metallurgy) tempra
hard' facts' spl realtà f
hard-fought ['hɑrd'fɔt] adj accanito
hard-headed ['hɑrd'hedɪd] adj astuto; ostinato, caparbio
hard-hearted ['hɑrd'hɑrtɪd] adj dal cuore duro
hardihood ['hɑrdɪ,hʊd] s forza, coraggio; insolenza
hardiness ['hɑrdɪnɪs] s ardire m; vigore m, robustezza fisica
hard' la'bor s lavori forzati
hard' luck' s mala sorte
hard'-luck' sto'ry s storia delle proprie disgrazie
hardly ['hɑrdli] adv appena, quasi no; (with great difficulty) a malapena, a fatica; **hardly ever** quasi mai
hardness ['hɑrdnɪs] s durezza
hard'-of-hear'ing adj duro d'orecchio
hard-pressed ['hɑrd'prest] adj oppresso; **to be hard-pressed for** essere a corto di
hard' rub'ber s ebanite f
hard' sauce' s miscela di burro e zucchero
hard'-shell crab' s granchio con la corazza
hardship ['hɑrd/ɪp] s pena, privazione; **hardships** privazioni fpl, strettezze fpl

hard'tack' *s* galletta

hard' times' *spl* strettezze *fpl*

hard' to please' *adj* di difficile contentatura

hard' up' *adj* (coll) in urgente bisogno; **to be hard up for** (coll) essere a corto di

hard'ware' *s* ferramenta *fpl;* macchinario

hard'ware store' *s* negozio di ferramenta

hard-won ['hɑrd,wʌn] *adj* (*victory, battle*) conquistato con molti sforzi; (*money*) acquistato con molti sforzi

hard'wood' *s* legno forte

hard'wood floor' *s* pavimento di legno, parquet *m*

har·dy ['hɑrdi] *adj* (**-dier; -diest**) forte, resistente; (*rash*) temerario; (hort) resistente al freddo

hare [hɛr] *s* lepre *f*

harebrained ['hɛr,brend] *adj* scervellato, sventato

hare'lip' *s* labbro leporino

harem ['hɛrəm] *s* arem *m*

hark [hɑrk] *intr* ascoltare; **to hark back** (*said of hounds*) ritornare sulla pista; riandare col pensiero ‖ *interj* ascolta!

harken ['hɑrkən] *intr* ascoltare

harlequin ['hɑrləkwɪn] *s* arlecchino

harlot ['hɑrlət] *s* meretrice *f*, baldracca

harm [hɑrm] *s* danno ‖ *tr* rovinare; nuocere (with *dat*), fare del male (with *dat*)

harmful ['hɑrmfəl] *adj* nocivo

harmless ['hɑrmlɪs] *adj* innocuo

harmonic [hɑr'mɑnɪk] *adj* armonico ‖ *s* (phys) armonica ‖ **harmonics** *ssg* armonica; *spl* suoni armonici

harmonica [hɑr'mɑnɪkə] *s* armonica a bocca

harmonious [hɑr'monɪ·əs] *adj* armonioso

harmonize ['hɑrmə,naɪz] *tr* intonare; (mus) armonizzare ‖ *intr* intonarsi; (mus) cantare all'unisono

harmo·ny ['hɑrməni] *s* (**-nies**) armonia

harness ['hɑrnɪs] *s* bardatura, finimenti *mpl*; (fig) routine *f*; **to die in the harness** morire sulla breccia ‖ *tr* bardare, imbrigliare; (*a waterfall*) captare

har'ness mak'er *s* sellaio

har'ness race' *s* corsa al trotto, corsa di cavalli col sulky

harp [hɑrp] *s* arpa ‖ *intr*—**to harp on** ripetere ostinatamente

harpist ['hɑrpɪst] *s* arpista *mf*

harpoon [hɑr'pun] *s* rampone *m* ‖ *tr* & *intr* arpionare

harpsichord ['hɑrpsɪ,kɔrd] *s* arpicordo, clavicembalo

har·py ['hɑrpi] *s* (**-pies**) arpia

harrow ['hæro] *s* erpice *m* ‖ *tr* (agr) erpicare; (fig) tormentare

harrowing ['hæro·ɪŋ] *adj* straziante

har·ry ['hæri] *v* (*pret* & *pp* **-ried**) *tr* saccheggiare; tormentare

harsh [hɑrʃ] *adj* (*to touch*) ruvido; (*to taste or hearing*) aspro; inclemente

harshness ['hɑrʃnɪs] *s* ruvidezza; asprezza; inclemenza

harum-scarum ['hɛrəm'skɛrəm] *adj* & *s* scervellato

harvest ['hɑrvɪst] *s* raccolta, mietitura ‖ *tr* raccogliere, mietere

harvester ['hɑrvɪstər] *s* (*person*) mietitore *m*; (*machine*) mietitrice *f*

har'vest home' *s* fine *f* della mietitura; festa dei mietitori; canzone *f* dei mietitori

har'vest moon' *s* luna di settembre

has-been ['hæz,bɪn] *s* (*person*) fallito; (*thing*) anticaglia

hash [hæʃ] *s* polpettone *m* ‖ *tr* tritare

hash' house' *s* osteria di terz'ordine

hashish ['hæʃiʃ] *s* ascisc *m*

hasp [hæsp] or [hɑsp] *s* boncinello

hassle ['hæsəl] *s* (coll) rissa, disputa

hassock ['hæsək] *s* cuscino poggiapiedi

haste [hest] *s* premura; **in haste** di premura; **to make haste** fare presto

hasten ['hesən] *tr* affrettare ‖ *intr* affrettarsi

hast·y ['hesti] *adj* (**-ier; -iest**) frettoloso; precipitato

hat [hæt] *s* cappello; **to keep under one's hat** (coll) mantenere il segreto su; **to throw one's hat in the ring** (coll) dichiarare la propria candidatura

hat'band' *s* nastro del cappello

hat' block' *s* forma da cappelli

hat'box' *s* cappelliera

hatch [hætʃ] *s* (*brood*) nidiata; (*shading line*) tratteggio; (*trap door*) porta a ribalta; (*lower half of door*) mezza porta; (naut) boccaporto ‖ *tr* (*eggs*) covare; (*a drawing*) tratteggiare; complottare, tramare ‖ *intr* schiudersi

hat'check girl' *s* guardarobiera

hatchet ['hætʃɪt] *s* accetta; **to bury the hatchet** fare la pace

hatch'way' *s* (*trap door*) porta a ribalta; (naut) boccaporto

hate [het] *s* odio ‖ *tr* & *intr* odiare

hateful ['hetfəl] *adj* odioso

hat'pin' *s* spillone *m*

hat'rack' *s* attaccapanni *m*

hatred ['hetrɪd] *s* odio, livore *m*

hatter ['hætər] *s* cappellaio

haughtiness ['hɔtɪnɪs] *s* superbia

haugh·ty ['hɔti] *adj* (**-tier; -tiest**) superbo, sprezzante

haul [hɔl] *s* (*tug*) tiro; (*amount caught*) retata; (*distance transported*) percorso, pezzo ‖ *tr* trasportare; tirare; (naut) alare

haunch [hɔntʃ] or [hɑntʃ] *s* fianco; anca; (*hind quarter of an animal*) coscia; (*same used for food*) cosciotto

haunt [hɔnt] or [hɑnt] *s* ritrovo, nido ‖ *tr* frequentare assiduamente; perseguitare

haunt'ed house' *s* casa frequentata dai fantasmi

haute couture [ot ku'tyr] *s* alta moda

have [hæv] *s*—**the haves and the have-nots** gli abbienti e i nullatenenti ‖ *v* (*pret & pp* had [hæd]) *tr* avere; (*a dream*) fare; (*to get, take*) prendere, ottenere, ricevere; **to have got** (coll) avere; **to have got to** + *inf* (coll) dovere + *inf*; **to have it in for** (coll) serbar rancore per; **to have it out with** avere a che dire con; **to have on** portare; **to have (s.th) to do with** avere (qlco) a che fare con, e.g., **I don't want to have anything to do with him** non voglio aver nulla a che fare con lui; **to have** + *inf* fare + *inf*, e.g., **I had him pay the bill** gli ho fatto pagare il conto; **to have** + *pp* fare + *inf*, e.g., **I had my watch repaired** ho fatto aggiustare l'orologio ‖ *intr*—**to have at** attaccare, mettersi di buzzo buono con; **to have to** + *inf* dovere + *inf*; **to have to do with** avere a che fare con; trattare di, e.g., **this book has to do with superstition** questo libro tratta di superstizione ‖ *v aux* avere, e.g., **he has studied his lesson** ha studiato la sua lezione

havelock ['hævlɑk] *s* coprinuca *m*

haven ['hevən] *s* porto; asilo

haversack ['hævər,sæk] *s* bisaccia; (mil) zaino

havoc ['hævək] *s* rovina; **to play havoc with** rovinare; scompigliare

haw [hɔ] *s* (*of hawthorn*) bacca; (*in speech*) esitazione ‖ *intr* voltare a sinistra ‖ *interj* voltare a sinistra!

hawk [hɔk] *s* falco; (*mortarboard*) sparviere *m;* (coll) persona rapace ‖ *tr* imbonire; (*newspapers*) strillare; **to hawk up** sputare raschiandosi la gola ‖ *intr* fare il merciaiolo ambulante; schiarirsi la gola

hawker ['hɔkər] *s* merciaiolo ambulante

hawse [hɔz] *s* (naut) cubia; (*hole*) (naut) occhio di cubia; (naut) altezza di cubia

hawse'hole' *s* occhio di cubia

hawser ['hɔzər] *s* cavo, gomena

haw'thorn' *s* biancospino

hay [he] *s* fieno; **to hit the hay** (slang) andare a letto; **to make hay while the sun shines** battere il ferro fin ch'è caldo

hay' fe'ver *s* febbre *f* da fieno, raffreddore *m* da fieno

hay'field' *s* prato seminato a fieno

hay'fork' *s* forcone *m;* (mach) rastrello

hay'loft' *s* fienile *m*

haymow ['he,mɑu] *s* fienile *m*

hay'rack' *s* rastrelliera

hay'ride' *s* gita notturna in carro da fieno

hay'seed' *s* semente *f* d'erba; (coll) semplicione *m*, campagnolo

hay'stack' *s* meta, pagliaio

hay'wire' *adj* (coll) disordinato, in confusione; (coll) impazzito ‖ *s* filo per legare il fieno

hazard ['hæzərd] *s* pericolo; (*chance*) rischio; (golf) ostacolo ‖ *tr* rischiare; (*an opinion*) arrischiare

hazardous ['hæzərdəs] *adj* pericoloso

haze [hez] *s* foschia; (fig) confusione ‖ *tr* far la matricola a

hazel ['hezəl] *adj* nocciola ‖ *s* (*tree*) nocciolo; (*fruit*) nocciola

ha'zel·nut' *s* nocciola

hazing ['hezɪŋ] *s* vessazione, angheria; (*at university*) matricola

ha·zy ['hezi] *adj* (*-zier; -ziest*) nebbioso; confuso

H-bomb ['et∫,bɑm] *s* bomba H

he [hi] *s* (**hes**) maschio ‖ *pron pers* (**they**) lui, egli, esso

head [hed] *s* testa, capo; (*of bed*) testiera; (*caption*) testata; (*of a nail*) cappello; (*on a glass of beer*) schiuma; (*of a boil*) punta purulenta; (*e.g., of cattle*) capo; **at the head of** a capo di; **from head to foot** da capo a piedi; **head over heels** a gambe levate; completamente; **heads or tails** testa o croce; **over one's head** al di sopra della capacità intellettuale di qlcu; (*going to a higher authority*) al di sopra di qlcu; **to be out of one's head** (coll) esser matto; **to bring to a head** far giungere alla crisi; **to come into one's head** passar per la mente a qlcu; **to go to one's head** dare al cervello a qlcu; **to keep one's head** non perdere la testa; **to keep one's head above water** arrivare a sbarcare il lunario; **to not make head or tail of** non riuscire a raccapezzarsi su ‖ *tr* dirigere, comandare; essere alla testa di ‖ *intr*—**to head towards** dirigersi verso

head'ache' *s* mal di capo, emicrania

head'band' *s* fascia sul capo; (bb) capitello; (typ) filetto

head'board' *s* testiera del letto

head' cheese' *s* salame *m* di testa

head'dress' *s* acconciatura

header ['hedər] *s*—**to take a header** (coll) gettarsi a capofitto

head'first' *adv* a capofitto

head'gear' *s* copricapo; (*for protection*) casco

head'hunt'er *s* cacciatore *m* di teste

heading ['hedɪŋ] *s* intestazione; (*of a chapter of a book*) titolo; (journ) testata, capopagina *m*

headland ['hedlənd] *s* promontorio

headless ['hedlɪs] *adj* senza testa

head'light' *s* (naut, rr) fanale *m;* (aut) faro

head'line' *s* (*of a page of a book*) titolo; (journ) testata ‖ *tr* intestare; fare pubblicità a

head'lin'er *s* (slang) attrazione principale

head'long' *adj* precipitoso ‖ *adv* a precipizio; a capofitto

head'man *s* (**-men**) capo; giustiziere *m*

head'mas'ter *s* direttore *m* di un collegio per ragazzi

head'most' *adj* primo, più avanzato

head' of'fice *s* sede *f* centrale

head' of hair' *s* capigliatura

head'-on' *adj* frontale ‖ *adv* di fronte, frontalmente

head'phones' *spl* cuffia

head'piece' *s* (*any covering for the head*) copricapo; (*helmet*) elmo; (*brains, judgment*) testa; (*of bed*) spalliera; (*headset*) cuffia; (typ) testata

head'quar'ters *s* sede *f* centrale, direzione; (mil) quartier *m* generale

head'rest' *s* poggiatesta *m*, testiera

head'set' *s* cuffia

head'ship' *s* direzione

head'stone' *s* pietra angolare; (*on a grave*) pietra tombale

head'stream' *s* affluente *m* principale

head'strong' *adj* testardo, ostinato

head'wait'er *s* capocameriere *m*

head'wa'ters *spl* fonti *fpl* or sorgenti *fpl* d'un fiume

head'way' *s* progresso; to make headway progredire

head'wear' *s* copricapo

head'wind' *s* vento di prua

head'work' *s* lavoro intellettuale

head·y ['hɛdi] *adj* (-ier; -iest) eccitante; impetuoso; violento; (*clever*) astuto; intossicante

heal [hil] *tr* sanare, guarire; purificare || *intr* risanarsi, guarire; (*said of a wound*) rimarginare

healer ['hilər] *s* guaritore *m*

health [hɛlθ] *s* salute *f*; to radiate health sprizzare salute da tutti i pori; to your health! alla Sua salute!

health' depart'ment *s* sanità *f*

healthful ['hɛlθfəl] *adj* salutare

health' insur'ance *s* assicurazione malattia

health·y ['hɛlθi] *adj* (-ier; -iest) sano; salubre

heap [hip] *s* mucchio; (coll) insalata, mare *m* || *tr* ammucchiare; to heap s.th upon s.o. colmare qlcu di qlco; to heap with colmare di

hear [hɪr] *v* (*pret & pp* heard [hʌrd]) *tr* udire; to hear it said sentirlo dire || *intr* udire; hear!, hear! bravo!; to hear about sentir parlare di; to hear from aver notizie di; to hear of sentir parlare di; to hear that sentir dire che

hearer ['hɪrər] *s* ascoltatore *m*

hearing ['hɪrɪŋ] *s* (*sense*) udito, orecchio; (*act*) udienza; in the hearing of in presenza di; within hearing a portata d'orecchio

hear'ing aid' *s* uditofono

hear'say' *s* diceria; by hearsay per sentito dire

hearse [hʌrs] *s* carro, carrozzone *m*, or furgone *m* funebre

heart [hɑrt] *s* cuore *m*; (*e.g., of lettuce*) grumolo; after one's heart di gusto di qlcu; by heart a memoria; heart and soul di tutto cuore; to break the heart of spezzare il cuore di; to die of a broken heart morire di crepacuore; to eat one's heart out piangere silenziosamente; to get to the heart of sviscerare il nocciolo di; to have one's heart in one's work lavorare di buzzo buono; to have one's heart in the right place avere buone intenzioni; to lose heart scoraggiarsi; to open one's heart to aprire il cuore a; to take heart prender coraggio; to take to heart prendersi a cuore; to

wear one's heart on one's sleeve parlare a cuore aperto; with one's heart in one's mouth col cuore in bocca

heart'ache' *s* angustia, angoscia

heart' attack' *s* attacco cardiaco

heart'beat' *s* battito del cuore

heart'break' *s* angoscia straziante

heart'break'er *s* rubacuori *m*

heartbroken ['hɑrt,brokən] *adj* col cuore spezzato

heart'burn' *s* bruciore *m* di stomaco

heart' disease' *s* mal *m* di cuore

hearten ['hɑrtən] *tr* rincuorare

heart' fail'ure *s* (*death*) arresto cardiaco; collasso cardiaco

heartfelt ['hɑrt,fɛlt] *adj* sentito

hearth [hɑrθ] *s* focolare *m*

hearth'stone' *s* pietra del focolare

heartily ['hɑrtɪli] *adv* di cuore, cordialmente; saporitamente

heartless ['hɑrtlɪs] *adj* senza cuore, insensibile

heart' mur'mur *s* soffio al cuore

heart-rending ['hɑrt,rɛndɪŋ] *adj* da far male al cuore

heart'sick' *adj* afflitto, sconsolato

heart'strings' *spl* precordi *mpl*

heart'-to-heart' *adj* cuore a cuore

heart' trans'plant *s* trapianto cardiaco

heart'wood' *s* cuore *m* del legno

heart·y ['hɑrti] *adj* (-ier; -iest) cordiale, di cuore; abbondante; (*eater*) grande

heat [hit] *adj* termico || *s* calore *m*; (*of room, house, etc.*) riscaldamento; (zool) fregola; (sports) batteria; (fig) fervore *m*; in heat (zool) in amore || *tr* scaldare, riscaldare; (fig) eccitare || *intr* riscaldarsi; (fig) accalorarsi

heated ['hitɪd] *adj* accalorato

heater ['hitər] *s* riscaldatore *m*; (*for central heating*) calorifero; (*to heat hands or bed*) scaldino; (*to heat water in tub*) scaldabagno

heath [hiθ] *s* (*shrub*) brugo, erica; (*tract of land*) brughiera

hea·then ['hiðən] *adj* pagano; irreligioso || *s* (-then or -thens) pagano

heathendom ['hiðəndəm] *s* (*worship*) paganesimo; (*land*) pagania

heather ['hɛðər] *s* erica, brugo

heating ['hitɪŋ] *adj* di riscaldamento || *s* riscaldamento

heat'ing pad' *s* termoforo

heat' light'ning *s* lampo di caldo

heat' shield' *s* (rok) scudo termico

heat'stroke' *s* colpo di calore

heat' wave' *s* ondata di caldo

heave [hiv] *s* sollevamento, sforzo; heaves (vet) bolsaggine *f* || *v* (*pret & pp* heaved or hove [hov]) *tr* sollevare, alzare; rigettare; (*a sigh*) emettere || *intr* alzarsi e abbassarsi; (*said of one's chest*) palpitare; avere conati di vomito

heaven ['hɛvən] *s* cielo; for heaven's sake! or good heavens! per amor del cielo!; heavens (*firmament*) cielo || Heaven *s* cielo

heavenly ['hɛvənli] *adj* celeste

heav'enly bod'y *s* corpo celeste

heav·y ['hɛvi] *adj* (-ier; -iest) (*of great*

weight) pesante; (*liquid*) denso; (*cloth, sea*) grosso; (*traffic*) forte; (*serious*) grave; (*crop*) abbondante; (*rain*) dirotto; (*features*) grossolano; (*heart*) stretto; (*ponderous*) macchinoso; (*industry*) grande; (*stock market*) abbattuto || *adv* (coll) pesantemente; **to hang heavy** (*said of time*) passar lentamente

heav'y-du'ty *adj* extraforte

heavy-hearted ['hɛvɪ'hɑrtɪd] *adj* afflitto, triste

heav'y-set' *adj* forte, corpulento

heav'y-weight' *s* peso massimo

Hebrew ['hibru] *adj & s* ebreo; (*language*) ebraico

hecatomb ['hɛkə‚tom] or ['hɛkə‚tum] *s* ecatombe *f*

heckle ['hɛkəl] *tr* interrompere con domande imbarazzanti

hectic ['hɛktɪk] *adj* febbrile

hedge [hɛdʒ] *s* barriera; (*of bushes*) siepe *f*; (*in stock market*) operazione controbilanciante || *tr* circondare con siepe; **to hedge in** circondare || *intr* evitare di compromettersi; (com) coprirsi

hedge'hog' *s* (zool) riccio; (*porcupine*) (zool) porcospino

hedge'hop' *v* (*pret & pp* -hopped; *ger* hopping) *intr* volare a volo radente

hedgehopping ['hɛdʒ‚hɑpɪŋ] *s* volo radente

hedge'row' [ro] *s* siepe *f*

heed [hid] *s* attenzione; **to take heed** fare attenzione || *tr* badare a || *intr* fare attenzione, badare

heedless [hidlɪs] *adj* sbadato

heehaw ['hi‚hɔ] *s* (*of donkey*) raglio d'asino; risata || *intr* ragliare; ridere fragorosamente

heel [hil] *s* (*of shoe, of foot*) calcagno, tallone *m*; (*of stocking or shoe*) tallone *m*; (*raised part of shoe below heel*) tacco; (coll) farabutto; **down at the heel** mal ridotto; **to cool one's heels** aspettare a lungo; **to kick up one's heels** darsi alla pazza gioia; **to show a clean pair of heels** or **to take to one's heels** battere i tacchi

heeler ['hilər] *s* politicante *mf*

heft·y ['hɛfti] *adj* (-ier; -iest) (*heavy*) pesante; (*strong*) forte

hegemon·y [hɪ'dʒɛməni] or ['hɛdʒɪ‚moni] *s* (-ies) egemonia

hegira [hɪ'dʒaɪrə] or ['hɛdʒɪrə] *s* fuga

heifer ['hɛfər] *s* manza, giovenca

height [haɪt] *s* altezza; (*e.g., of folly*) colmo

heighten ['haɪtən] *tr* innalzare; (*to increase the amount of*) accrescere, aumentare || *intr* aumentare

heinous ['henəs] *adj* nefando, odioso

heir [ɛr] *s* erede *m*

heir' appar'ent *s* (**heirs' appar'ent**) erede necessario

heirdom ['ɛrdəm] *s* eredità *f*

heiress ['ɛrɪs] *s* ereditiera, erede *f*

heirloom ['ɛr‚lum] *s* cimelio di famiglia

Helen ['hɛlən] *s* Elena

helicopter ['hɛlɪ‚kɑptər] *s* elicottero

heliport ['hɛlɪ‚port] *s* eliporto

helium ['hili·əm] *s* elio

helix ['hilɪks] *s* (**helixes or helices** ['hɛlɪ‚siz]) spirale *f*; (geom) elica

hell [hɛl] *s* inferno

hell-bent ['hɛl'bɛnt] *adj* (coll) risoluto; **to be hell-bent on** (coll) avere un chiodo in testa di

hell'cat' *s* arpia, megera

hellebore ['hɛlɪ‚bor] *s* elleboro

Hellene ['hɛlin] *s* greco

Hellenic [hɛ'lɛnɪk] or [hɛ'linɪk] *adj* ellenico

hell'fire' *s* fuoco dell'inferno

hellish ['hɛlɪʃ] *adj* infernale

hel·lo [hɛ'lo] *s* saluto || *interj* ciao!; (*on telephone*) pronto!

helm [hɛlm] *s* barra del timone; ruota del timone; timone *m* || *tr* dirigere

helmet ['hɛlmɪt] *s* (mil) elmetto; (sports) casco; (hist) elmo

helms'man *s* (-men) timoniere *m*

help [hɛlp] *s* aiuto; (*relief*) rimedio, e.g., **there's no help for it** non c'è rimedio; servitù *f*; impiegati *mpl*; operai *mpl*; **to come to the help of** venire in aiuto di || *tr* aiutare; soccorrere, mitigare; (*to wait on*) servire; **it can't be helped** non c'è rimedio; **so help me God!** Dio mi sia testimonio!; **to help down** aiutare a scendere; **to help s.o. with his coat** aiutare qlcu a mettersi il cappotto; **to help oneself** servirsi da solo; **to help up** aiutare a salire; aiutare ad alzarsi; **to not be able to help** + *ger* non poter fare a meno di + *inf*, e.g., **he can't help laughing** non può fare a meno di ridere || *intr* aiutare || *interj* aiuto!

helper ['hɛlpər] *s* aiutante *m*; (*in a shop*) garzone *m*, lavorante *m*

helpful ['hɛlpfəl] *adj* utile, servizievole

helping ['hɛlpɪŋ] *s* (*of food*) razione

helpless ['hɛlpɪs] *adj* (*weak*) debole; (*powerless*) impotente; senza risorse; (*confused*) perplesso; (*situation*) irrimediabile

help'mate' *s* compagno; (*wife*) compagna

heiter-skelter ['hɛltər'skɛltər] *adj & adv* in fretta e furia; alla rinfusa

hem [hɛm] *s* (*any edge*) orlo; (*of skirt*) basta, pedana; (*of suit*) falda || *v* (*pret & pp* hemmed; *ger* hemming) *tr* orlare, bordare; **to hem in** insaccare || *intr* esitare; **to hem and haw** esitare; essere evasivo

hemisphere ['hɛmɪ‚sfɪr] *s* emisfero

hemistich ['hɛmɪ‚stɪk] *s* emistichio

hem'line' *s* orlo della gonna

hem'lock' *s* (herb and poison) cicuta; (*Tsuga canadensis*) abete *m* del Canada

hemoglobin [‚hɛmə'globɪn] or [‚himə-'globɪn] *s* emoglobina

hemophilia [‚hɛmə'fɪlɪ·ə] or [‚himə-'fɪlɪ·ə] *s* emofilia

hemorrhage ['hɛmərɪdʒ] *s* emorragia

hemorrhoids ['hɛmə‚rɔɪdz] *spl* emorroidi *fpl*

hemostat ['hɛmə‚stæt] or ['himə‚stæt] *s* pinza emostatica

hemp [hɛmp] *s* canapa

hemstitch ['hem,stɪtʃ] *s* orlo a giorno || *tr & intr* orlare a giorno

hen [hen] *s* gallina

hence [hens] *adv* di qui; da ora; quindi; di qui a, e.g., **three weeks hence** di qui a tre settimane

hence'forth' *adv* d'ora innanzi

hench·man ['hentʃmən] *s* (**-men** [mən]) accolito; politicante *m*

hen'house' *s* pollaio

henna ['henə] *s* henna || *tr* tingere con la henna

hen'peck' *tr* (*a husband*) trovare a ridire con

hen'pecked' hus'band *s* marito dominato dalla moglie

her [hʌr] *adj poss* suo, il suo || *pron pers* la, lei; **to her le**, a lei

herald ['herəld] *s* araldo; annunziatore *m* || *tr* annunziare

heraldic [he'rældɪk] *adj* araldico

herald·ry ['herəldri] *s* (**-ries**) (*office*) consulta araldica; (*science*) araldica; (*coat of arms*) blasone *m*

herb [ʌrb] or [hʌrb] *s* erba; erba medicinale

herbaceous [hʌr'befəs] *adj* erbaceo

herbage ['ʌrbɪdʒ] or ['hʌrbɪdʒ] *s* erba; (*law*) erbatico

herbalist ['hʌrbəlɪst] or ['ʌrbəlɪst] *s* erborista *mf*

herbari·um [hʌr'berɪ·əm] *s* (**-ums** or **-a** [ə]) erbario

herb' doc'tor *s* erborista *mf*

herculean [hʌr'kjulɪ·ən] or [,hʌrkju-'li·ən] *adj* erculeo

herd [hʌrd] *s* (*of sheep*) gregge *m*; (*of cattle*) mandria; (*of men*) torma *f* || *tr & intr* imbrancare

herds'man *s* (**-men**) (*of cattle*) mandriano, vaccaio; (*of sheep*) pastore *m*

here [hɪr] *adj* presente || *s*—**the here and the hereafter** la vita presente e l'aldilà || *adv* qui, qua; **here and there** qua e là; **here is** or **here are** ecco; **that's neither here not there** ciò non ha nulla a che vedere || *interj* presente!

hereabouts ['hɪrə,bauts] *adv* qua vicino

here·af'ter *s* aldilà *m* || *adv* d'ora innanzi; nel futuro

here·by' *adv* con la presente

hereditary [hɪ'redɪ,teri] *adj* ereditario

heredi·ty [hɪ'redtɪ] *s* (**-ties**) eredità *f*

here·in' *adv* qui; in questo posto

here·of' *adv* di questo

here·on' *adv* in questo; su questo

here·sy ['herəsi] *s* (**-sies**) eresia

heretic ['heretɪk] *adj & s* eretico

heretical [hɪ'retɪkəl] *adj* eretico

heretofore [,hɪrtu'for] *adv* sinora

here·u·pon' *adv* su questo; in questo; immediatamente dopo

here·with' *adv* accluso; con la presente

heritage ['herɪtɪdʒ] *s* eredità *f*

hermetic(al) [hʌr'metɪk(əl)] *adj* ermetico

hermit ['hʌrmɪt] *s* eremita *m*

hermitage ['hʌrmɪtɪdʒ] *s* eremitaggio

herni·a ['hʌrnɪ·ə] *s* (**-as** or **-ae** [,i]) ernia

he·ro ['hɪro] *s* (**-roes**) eroe *m*

heroic [hɪ'ro·ɪk] *adj* eroico || **heroics** *spl* linguaggio altisonante

heroin ['hero·ɪn] *s* (pharm) eroina

heroine ['hero·ɪn] *s* eroina

heroism ['hero,ɪzəm] *s* eroismo

heron ['herən] *s* airone *m*

herring ['herɪŋ] *s* aringa

her'ring·bone' *s* (*in fabrics*) spina di pesce; (*in hardwood floors*) spiga

hers [hʌrz] *pron poss* il suo; **of hers** suo

herself [hʌr'self] *pron pers* lei stessa; sé stessa; si, e.g., **she enjoyed herself** si divertì; **with herself** con sé

hertz [hʌrts] *s* hertz *m*

hesitan·cy ['hezɪtənsi] *s* (**-cies**) titubanza, esitanza

hesitant ['hezɪtənt] *adj* esitante

hesitate ['hezɪ,tet] *intr* esitare, titubare; (*to stutter*) balbettare

hesitation [,hezɪ'tefən] *s* esitazione

heterodox ['hetərə,dɑks] *adj* eterodosso

heterodyne ['hetərə,daɪn] *s* eterodina

heterogeneous [,hetərə'dʒɪnɪ·əs] *adj* eterogeneo

hew [hju] *v* (*pret* **hewed**; *pp* **hewed** or **hewn**) *tr* tagliare; (*a passage*) aprirsi; (*a statue*) abbozzare; **to hew down** abbattere || *intr*—**to hew close to the line** (coll) filare diritto

hex [heks] *s* strega; incantesimo || *tr* stregare, incantare

hexameter [heks'æmɪtər] *s* esametro

hey [he] *interj* ehi!

hey'day' *s* apogeo

hia·tus [haɪ'etəs] *s* (**-tuses** or **-tus**) (*gap*) lacuna; (gram) iato

hibernate ['haɪbər,net] *intr* ibernare; (*said of people*) svernare

hibiscus [hɪ'bɪskəs] or [haɪ'bɪskəs] *s* ibisco

hic·cup ['hɪkəp] *s* singhiozzo || *v* (*pret & pp* **-cuped** or **-cupped**; *ger* **-cuping** or **-cupping**) *intr* singhiozzare

hick [hɪk] *adj & s* (coll) rustico

hicko·ry ['hɪkəri] *s* (**-ries**) hickory *m*

hidden ['hɪdən] *adj* nascosto

hide [haɪd] *s* cuoio, pelle *f*; **hides** cuoio; **neither hide nor hair** nemmeno una traccia; **to tan s.o.'s hide** (coll) dargliele sode a qlcu || *v* (*pret* **hid** [hɪd]; *pp* **hid** or **hidden** ['hɪdən]) *tr* nascondere || *intr* nascondersi; **to hide out** (coll) rintanarsi

hide'-and-seek' *s* rimpiattino; **to play hide-and-seek** giocare a rimpiattino or a nascondino

hide'bound' *adj* retrogrado, conservatore

hideous ['hɪdɪ·əs] *adj* orribile, brutto

hide'out' *s* nascondiglio

hiding ['haɪdɪŋ] *s* nascondere *m*; (*place*) nascondiglio; **in hiding** nascosto

hid'ing place' *s* nascondiglio

hie [haɪ] *v* (*pret & pp* **hied**; *ger* **hieing** or **hying**) *tr*—**hie thee home** affrettati a tornare a casa || *intr* affrettarsi

hierar·chy ['haɪ·ə,rɑrki] *s* (**-chies**) gerarchia

hieroglyphic [,haɪ·ərə'glɪfɪk] *adj & s* geroglifico

hi-fi ['haɪ'faɪ] adj di alta fedeltà ‖ s alta fedeltà

higgledy-piggledy ['hɪgəldɪ'pɪgəldɪ] adj confuso ‖ adv alla rinfusa

high [haɪ] adj alto; (color) forte; (merry) allegro; (luxurious) lussuoso; (coll) ubriaco; (culin) frollo; **high and dry** abbandonato; **high and mighty** (coll) arrogante ‖ adv molto; riccamente; **to aim high** mirare in alto; **to come high** essere caro ‖ s (aut) quarta, diretta; **on high** in cielo

high' al'tar s altare m maggiore

high'ball' s whiskey con ghiaccio e gazosa ‖ intr (slang) andare di carriera

high' blood' pres'sure s ipertensione

high'born' adj di nobile lignaggio

high'boy' s cassettone alto

high'brow' s intellettuale mf; (coll) intellettualoide mf

high'chair' s seggiolino per bambini

high' command' s comando supremo

high' cost' of liv'ing s carovita m, caroviveri m

high'er educa'tion s insegnamento universitario, istruzione superiore

higher-up [,haɪ·ər'ʌp] s (coll) superiore m

high' explo'sive s esplosivo ad alta potenza

highfalutin [,haɪfə'lutən] adj (coll) pomposo, pretenzioso

high' fidel'ity s high fidelity, alta fedeltà

high'-fre'quency [adj] ad alta frequenza

high' gear' s (aut) presa diretta

high'-grade' adj di qualità superiore

high-handed ['haɪ'hændɪd] adj arbitrario

high' hat' s cappello a cilindro

high'-hat' adj (coll) snob m ‖ v (pret & pp -hatted; ger -hatting) tr (coll) snobbare

high'-heeled' shoe' ['haɪ ,hild] s scarpa coi tacchi alti

high' horse' s comportamento arrogante; **to get up on one's high horse** darsi delle grandi arie

high' jinks' ['dʒɪŋks] s (slang) pagliacciata, gazzarra

high' jump' s salto in altezza

highland ['haɪlənd] adj montagnoso ‖ **highlands** spl regione montagnosa

high' life' s high-life f, alta società

high'light' s punto culminante ‖ tr mettere in risalto

highly ['haɪlɪ] adv altamente, molto; (paid) profumatamente; **to speak highly of** parlar molto bene di

High' Mass' s messa cantata

high-minded ['haɪ'maɪndɪd] adj magnanimo

highness ['haɪnɪs] s altezza ‖ **Highness** s Altezza

high' noon' s mezzogiorno in punto; (fig) sommo

high-pitched ['haɪ'pɪt/t] adj acuto; intenso, emozionante

high-powered ['haɪ'pau·ərd] adj ad alta potenza; (binoculars) ad alto ingrandimento

high'pres'sure adj ad alta pressione ‖ tr sollecitare con insistenza

high-priced ['haɪ'praɪst] adj caro, di alto prezzo

high' priest' s sommo sacerdote

high' rise' s edificio di molti piani

high'road' s strada principale

high'school' s scuola media; (in Italy) liceo

high' sea' s alto mare; **high seas** alto mare

high' soci'ety s l'alta società

high'-sound'ing adj altisonante

high'-speed' adj ad alta velocità

high-spirited ['haɪ'spɪrɪtɪd] adj fiero, vivace, focoso

high-strung ['haɪ'strʌŋ] adj teso, nervoso

high'-test' fuel' s supercarburante m

high' tide' s alta marea; punto culminante

high' time' s ora, e.g., **it is high time for you to go** è proprio ora che Lei se ne vada; (coll) baldoria

high' trea'son s (against the sovereign) lesa maestà; (against the state) alto tradimento

high' wa'ter s alta marea; (in a river) straripamento

high'way' adj autostradale ‖ s autostrada

high'way'man s (-men) grassatore m

hijack ['haɪ,dʒæk] tr rubare; (e.g., an airplane) dirottare ‖ intr effettuare un dirottamento

hijacker ['haɪ,dʒækər] s ladro a mano armata; (e.g., of an airplane) dirottatore m

hijacking ['haɪ,dʒækɪŋ] s furto a mano armata; dirottamento

hike [haɪk] s (for pleasure) gita, camminata; (increase) aumento; (mil) marcia ‖ tr tirar su; aumentare ‖ intr fare una gita; (mil) fare una marcia

hiker ['haɪkər] s camminatore m

hilarious [hɪ'lɛrɪ·əs] or [haɪ'lɛrɪ·əs] adj ilare; (e.g., joke) allegro, divertente

hill [hɪl] s collina ‖ tr rincalzare

hillbil·ly ['hɪl,bɪlɪ] s (-lies) (coll) montanaro rustico

hillock ['hɪlək] s poggio, collinetta

hill'side' s pendio

hill'top' s cima

hill·y ['hɪlɪ] adj (-ier; -iest) collinoso; ripido

hilt [hɪlt] s impugnatura, elsa; **up to the hilt** completamente

him [hɪm] pron pers lo; lui; **to him** gli, a lui

himself [hɪm'sɛlf] pron pers lui stesso; sé stesso; si, e.g., **he enjoyed himself** si è divertito; **with himself** con sé

hind [haɪnd] adj posteriore, di dietro ‖ s cerva

hinder ['hɪndər] tr ostacolare, impedire

hindmost ['haɪnd,most] adj ultimo

hind'quar'ter s quarto posteriore

hindrance ['hɪndrəns] s ostacolo, impedimento

hind'sight' s senno di poi
Hindu ['hɪndu] adj & s indù mf
hinge [hɪndʒ] s cardine m; (bb) cerniera; (philately) listello gommato; punto principale ‖ tr munire di cardini ‖ intr—**to hinge on** dipendere da
hin•ny ['hɪnɪ] s (-nies) bardotto
hint [hɪnt] s insinuazione; **to take the hint** capire l'antifona ‖ tr & intr insinuare; **to hint at** alludere a
hinterland ['hɪntər,lænd] s retroterra m, entroterra m
hip [hɪp] adj—**to be hip to** (slang) essere al corrente di ‖ s anca, fianco; (of a roof) spigolo
hip'bone' s ileo, osso iliaco
hipped [hɪpt] adj (livestock) zoppicante; (roof) a padiglione; **hipped on** (coll) ossessionato per
hippie ['hɪpɪ] s capellone m
hip•po ['hɪpo] s (-pos) (coll) ippopotamo
hippodrome ['hɪpə,drom] s ippodromo
hippopota•mus [,hɪpə'patəməs] s (-muses or -mi [,maɪ]) ippopotamo
hip' roof' s tetto a padiglione
hire [haɪr] s paga, salario; nolo; **for hire** a nolo ‖ tr (help) impiegare; (a conveyance) noleggiare ‖ intr—**to hire out** mettersi a servizio
hired' girl' s lavorante f di campagna
hired' hand' s lavorante mf
hired' man' s (men') lavorante m di campagna
hireling ['haɪrlɪŋ] adj venale ‖ s persona prezzolata
his [hɪz] adj poss suo, il suo ‖ pron poss il suo
Hispanic [hɪs'pænɪk] adj ispano
Hispanist ['hɪspənɪst] s ispanista mf
hiss [hɪs] s (of fire, wind, serpent, etc.) sibilo; (of disapproval) fischio, zittio ‖ tr zittire ‖ intr zittire; sibilare; (said of a kettle) fischiare
histology [hɪs'taledʒɪ] s istologia
historian [hɪs'torɪ•ən] s storico
historic(al) [hɪs'tarɪk(əl)] or [hɪs-'tɔrɪk(əl)] adj storico
histo•ry ['hɪstərɪ] s (-ries) storia
histrionic [,hɪstrɪ'ɑnɪk] adj teatrale; (artificial, affected) istrionico, teatrale ‖ **histrionics** s istrionismo, teatralità f
hit [hɪt] s colpo; successo; (sarcastic remark) frecciata; **to be a hit** far furore; **to make a hit with** fare ottima impressione con ‖ v (pret & pp hit; ger hitting) tr colpire; (to bump) cozzare; (the target) toccare, imbroccare, infilare; (with a car) metter sotto; (a certain speed) andare a ‖ intr battere; **to hit on** (s.th new) imbroccare; **to hit out** attaccare
hit'-and-run' adj (driver) colpevole di mancato soccorso
hit'-and-run' driv'er s pirata m della strada
hitch [hɪtʃ] s (jerk) strattone m; (knot) nodo; difficoltà f, ostacolo; ‖ tr (to tie) attaccare; (oxen) aggiogare; (slang) sposare
hitch'hike' intr fare l'autostop

hitch'hik'er s autostoppista mf
hitch'ing post' s palo per attaccare un cavallo
hither ['hɪðər] adv qua, qui; **hither and thither** qua e là
hith'er•to' adv sinora
hit'-or-miss' adj fatto alla carlona
hit' rec'ord s disco di grande successo
hive [haɪv] s (box for bees) alveare m; (swarm) sciame m; **hives** orticaria ‖ tr (bees) raccogliere
hoard [hord] s cumulo; (of money) gruzzolo ‖ tr & intr custodire gelosamente; tesaurizzare
hoarding ['hordɪŋ] s ammassamento, tesaurizzazione
hoarfrost ['hor,frɔst] s brina
hoarse [hors] adj rauco, svociato
hoarseness ['horsnɪs] s raucedine f
hoar•y ['horɪ] adj (-ier; -iest) canuto, incanutito
hoax [hoks] s mistificazione ‖ tr mistificare
hob [hab] s mensola del focolare; **to play hob with** (coll) mettere a soqquadro
hobble ['habəl] s zoppicamento; (to tie legs of animal) pastoia ‖ tr far zoppicare; imbarazzare; mettere le pastoie a ‖ intr zoppicare
hob•by ['habɪ] s (-bies) svago, passatempo; **to ride a hobby** dedicarsi troppo alla propria occupazione favorita
hob'by-horse' s cavallo a dondolo
hob'gob'lin s folletto
hob'nail' s brocca, bulletta
hob-nob ['hab,nab] v (pret & pp -nobbed; ger -nobbing) intr essere amiconi; **to hobnob with** essere intimo di
ho•bo ['hobo] s (-bos or -boes) girovago, vagabondo
Hob'son's choice' ['habsənz] s scelta fra quanto viene offerto o niente
hock [hak] s garretto; (coll) pegno; **in hock** (coll) impegnato, al monte di pietà ‖ tr tagliare i garretti a; (coll) impegnare
hockey ['hakɪ] s hockey m
hock'ey play'er s hockeista m, discatore m
hock'shop' s (coll) negozio di prestiti su pegno
hocus-pocus ['hokəs'pokəs] s (meaningless formula) abracadabra m; gherminella
hod [had] s vassoio; secchio per il carbone
hod' car'rier s manovale m
hodgepodge ['hadʒ,padʒ] s farragine f
hoe [ho] s marra, zappa ‖ tr & intr zappare
hog [hag] or [hɔg] s suino, porco, maiale m ‖ v (pret & pp hogged; ger hogging) tr (slang) mangiarsi il meglio di
hoggish ['hagɪʃ] or ['hɔgɪʃ] adj maialesco; egoista
hogs'head' s barilozzo di sessantatré galloni
hog'wash' s broda da maiali

hoist [hɔɪst] *s* montacarichi *m;* (*lift*) spinta ‖ *tr* alzare, rizzare; (*a flag*) inastare; (*naut*) issare

hoity-toity [ˈhɔɪtiˈtɔɪti] *adj* arrogante, altezzoso

hokum [ˈhokəm] *s* (coll) fandonie *fpl;* (coll) sentimentalismo volgare

hold [hold] *s* presa, piglio; (*handle*) impugnatura; autorità *f*, ascendente *m;* (*wrestling*) presa; (aer) cabina bagagli; (mus) corona; (naut) cala, stiva; **to take hold of** afferare; impossessarsi di ‖ *v* (*pret & pp* **held** [held]) *tr* tenere; (*to hold up*) sostenere; (*e.g., with a pin*) assicurare; (*a rank*) rivestire; contenere; (*a meeting*) avere; (*a note*) (mus) filare; **to hold back** trattenere; **to hold in** trattenere; **to hold one's own** non perdere terreno; **to hold over** differire; **to hold up** reggere, sostenere; (*to rob*) (coll) derubare, rapinare ‖ *intr* stare; (*to cling*) reggere; restare valido; **hold on!** un momento!; **to hold back** frenarsi; **to hold forth** fare un discorso; **to hold off** astenersi; mantenersi a distanza; **to hold on** continuare; **to hold on to** attaccarsi a; **to hold out** tener duro, resistere; **to hold out for** mantenersi fermo per

holder [ˈholdər] *s* possessore *m*, detentore *m;* (*e.g., for a cigar*) bocchino; (*e.g., for a pot*) manico, impugnatura

holding [ˈholdɪŋ] *s* possesso; **holdings** valori *mpl*, patrimonio

hold'ing com'pany *s* società finanziaria

hold'up' *s* (*delay*) interruzione; (coll) rapina a mano armata; (fig) furto

hold'up man' *s* grassatore *m*

hole [hol] *s* buco; (*in cheese*) occhio; (*in a road*) buca; (*den*) tana; (*burrow*) fossa; **in a hole** in grane, in difficoltà; **to burn a hole in one's pocket** (*said of money*) scorrere attraverso le mani bucate di qlcu; **to pick holes in** trovare a ridire su ‖ *intr*—**to hole up** (coll) imbucarsi

holiday [ˈhɑlɪˌde] *s* giorno festivo, festa; vacanza

holiness [ˈholnɪs] *s* santità *f;* **his Holiness** sua Santità

Holland [ˈhɑlənd] *s* l'Olanda *f*

Hollander [ˈhɑləndər] *s* olandese *mf*

hollow [ˈhɑlo] *adj* vuoto; (*sound*) sordo; (*eyes, cheeks*) infossato; vano, futile ‖ *s* buca, cavità *f;* (*small valley*) valletta ‖ *adv*—**to beat all hollow** (coll) battere completamente ‖ *tr* scavare

hol·ly [ˈhɑli] *s* (-**lies**) agrifoglio

holly'hock' *s* altea, malvone *m*

holm' oak' [hom] *s* leccio

holocaust [ˈhɑləˌkɔst] *s* olocausto

holster [ˈholstər] *s* fondina

ho·ly [ˈholi] *adj* (-**lier; -liest**) santo; (*writing*) sacro; (*water*) benedetto

Ho'ly Ghost' *s* Spirito Santo

ho'ly or'ders *spl* ordini sacri; **to take holy orders** entrare in un ordine religioso

Ho'ly Rood' [rud] *s* Santa Croce

Ho'ly Scrip'ture *s* Sacra Scrittura

Ho'ly See' *s* Santa Sede

Ho'ly Sep'ulcher *s* Santo Sepolcro

Ho'ly Thurs'day *s* l'Ascensione; il giovedì santo

ho'ly wa'ter *s* acqua benedetta, acquasanta

Ho'ly Writ' *s* Sacra Scrittura

homage [ˈhɑmɪdʒ] or [ˈɑmɪdʒ] *s* omaggio

homburg [ˈhɑmbʌrg] *s* lobbia *m & f*

home [hom] *adj* casalingo, domestico; nazionale ‖ *s* casa, dimora; (*fatherland*) patria; (*for the sick, aged, etc.*) ricovero; (sports) meta, traguardo; **at home** a casa; (*at ease*) a proprio agio; (sports) nel proprio campo; **away from home** fuori di casa; **make yourself at home** stia comodo; **to be at home** (*to receive callers*) ricevere ‖ *adv* a casa; **to see home** accompagnare a casa; **to strike home** toccare nel vivo

home'bod'y *s* (-**ies**) persona casalinga

homebred [ˈhomˌbred] *adj* domestico; rozzo; semplice

home'brew' *s* bevanda fatta in casa

home-coming [ˈhomˌkʌmɪŋ] *s* ritorno a casa

home' coun'try *s* paese *m* natale

home' deliv'ery *s* trasporto a domicilio

home' front' *s* fronte domestico

home'land' *s* paese natio

homeless [ˈhomlɪs] *adj* senza tetto

home' life' *s* vita familiare

home-loving [ˈhomˌlʌvɪŋ] *adj* casalingo

home·ly [ˈhomli] *adj* (-**lier; -liest**) (*not goodlooking*) brutto; (*not elegant*) semplice, scialbo

homemade [ˈhomˈmed] *adj* fatto in casa

homemaker [ˈhomˌmekər] *s* casalinga

home' of'fice *s* sede *f* centrale ‖ **Home Office** *s* (Brit) ministero degli interni

homeopath [ˈhomiˌ ə ˌpæθ] or [ˈhɑmiə ˌpæθ] *s* omeopatico

home' plate' *s* casa base

home' port' *s* porto d'iscrizione (nel registro marittimo)

home' rule' *s* autogoverno

home' run' *s* colpo che permette al battitore di percorrere tutte le basi del diamante fino alla casa base

home-sick [ˈhomsɪk] *adj* nostalgico; **to be homesick for** sentire la nostalgia per

home'sick'ness *s* nostalgia

homespun [ˈhomˌspʌn] *adj* filato a casa; semplice

home'stead' *s* casa e terreno

home'stretch' *s* (sports) dirittura d'arrivo; (fig) fase *f* finale

home'town' *s* città *f* natale

homeward [ˈhomwərd] *adj* di ritorno ‖ *adv* verso casa; verso la patria

home'work' *s* lavoro a domicilio; (*of a student*) dovere *m*, esercizio

homey [ˈhomi] *adj* (**homier; homiest**) intimo, comodo

homicidal [ˌhɑmɪˈsaɪdəl] *adj* omicida

homicide [ˈhɑmɪˌsaɪd] *s* (*act*) omicidio; (*person*) omicida *mf*

homi·ly [ˈhɑmɪli] *s* (-**lies**) omelia

homing ['homɪŋ] *adj* (*pigeon*) viaggiatore; (*weapon*) cercatore del bersaglio

hominy ['hɑmɪnɪ] *s* granturco macinato

homogenei·ty [ˌhoməʤɪˈni·ɪtɪ] or [ˌhɑmeʤɪˈni·ɪtɪ] *s* (-ties) omogeneità *f*

homogeneous [ˌhoməˈʤɪnɪ·əs] or [ˌhɑməˈʤɪnɪ·əs] *adj* omogeneo

homogenize [həˈmɑʤəˌnaɪz] *tr* omogeneizzare

homonym ['hɑmənɪm] *s* omonimo

homonymous [həˈmɑnɪməs] *adj* omonimo

homosexual [ˌhoməˈsɛkʃʊ·əl] *adj* & *s* omosessuale *mf*

hone [hon] *s* cote *f* || *tr* affilare

honest ['ɑnɪst] *adj* onesto; guadagnato onestamente; integro, schietto

honesty ['ɑnɪstɪ] *s* onestà *f*; (bot) lunaria

hon·ey ['hʌnɪ] *adj* melato, dolce | *s* miele *m*; nettare *m*; (coll) caro | *v* (*pret* & *pp* -eyed or -ied) *tr* dire parole melate a

hon'ey·bee' *s* ape domestica

hon'ey·comb' *s* favo || *tr* crivellare

honeyed ['hʌnɪd] *adj* melato

hon'eydew mel'on *s* melone *m* dolce dalla scorza liscia

hon'ey lo'cust *s* acacia a tre spine

hon'ey·moon' *s* luna di miele || *intr* andare in viaggio di nozze

honeysuckle ['hʌnɪˌsʌkəl] *s* caprifoglio

honk [hɑŋk] or [hɔŋk] *s* (of wild goose) schiamazzo; (of automobile horn) suono del clacson || *tr* (aut) suonare || *intr* schiamazzare; (aut) suonare

honkytonk ['hɑŋkɪˌtɑŋk] or ['hɔŋkɪˌtɔŋk] *s* (coll) locale notturno rumoroso

honor ['ɑnər] *s* onore *m* || *tr* onorare; (com) accettare e pagare

honorable ['ɑnərəbəl] *adj* (upright) onorato; (bringing honor; worthy of honor) onorevole

honorari·um [ˌɑnəˈrɛrɪ·əm] *s* (-ums or -a [ə]) onorario

honorary ['ɑnəˌrɛrɪ] *adj* onorario

honorific [ˌɑnəˈrɪfɪk] *adj* onorifico || *s* titolo onorifico; formula di gentilezza

hon'or sys'tem *s* sistema scolastico basato sulla parola d'onore

hood [hud] *s* cappuccio; cappuccio di toga universitaria; (of carriage) soffietto; (aut) cofano; (slang) gangster *m* || *tr* incappucciare

hoodlum ['hudləm] *s* (slang) facinoroso, gangster *m*, teppista *m*

hoodoo ['hudu] *s* (body of primitive rites) vuduismo; (bad luck) iettatura; (person who brings bad luck) iettatore *m* || *tr* iettare

hood'wink' *tr* turlupinare, imbrogliare

hooey ['hu·ɪ] *s* (coll) sciocchezze *fpl*

hoof [huf] or [huf] *s* zoccolo, unghia; on the hoof (cattle) vivo || *tr*—to hoof it (slang) camminare; ballare

hoof'beat' *s* rumore *m* degli zoccoli

hook [huk] *s* gancio; (for fishing) amo;

(to join two things) agganciamento; (for pulling) raffio, rampino; (curve) curva; (of hook and eye) uncinello; (boxing) hook *m*, gancio; by hook or by crook di riffa o di raffa; to swallow the hook abboccare all'amo || *tr* agganciare; (to bend) curvare; (fish) pigliare; (to wound with the horns) incornare; to hook up agganciare; (e.g., a loudspeaking system) montare || *intr* agganciarsi; curvarsi

hookah ['hukə] *s* narghilè *m*

hook' and eye' *s* uncinello e occhiello

hook' and lad'der *s* autoscala

hooked' rug' *s* tappeto fatto all'uncinetto

hook'nose' *s* naso gobbo

hook'up' *s* (electron) diagramma *m*, schema *m* di montaggio; (rad, telv) rete *f*

hook'worm' *s* anchilostoma *m*

hooky ['hukɪ] *s*—to play hooky marinare la scuola

hooligan ['hulɪgən] *s* teppista *m*

hooliganism ['hulɪgənˌɪzəm] *s* teppismo

hoop [hup] or [hup] *s* cerchio || *tr* cerchiare

hoop' skirt' *s* crinolina

hoot [hut] *s* grido della civetta; grido di derisione || *tr* zittire || *intr* stridere; to hoot at fischiare

hoot' owl' *s* allocco

hop [hɑp] *s* salto, saltello; (aer) breve volo; (bot) luppolo; (coll) corsa; hops (dried flowers of hop vine) luppolo || *v* (*pret* & *pp* hopped; *ger* hopping) *tr* saltare su; (aer) trasvolare || *intr* saltellare; saltellare su un piede; to hop over saltare su; fare una corsa a

hope [hop] *s* speranza || *tr* & *intr* sperare; to hope for sperare

hope' chest' *s* corredo da sposa

hopeful ['hopfəl] *adj* (feeling hope) fiducioso; (giving hope) promettente

hopeless ['hoplɪs] *adj* disperato

hopper ['hɑpər] *s* tramoggia

hop'scotch' *s* gioco del mondo

horde [hord] *s* orda

horehound ['hor,haund] *s* marrubio; pastiglie *fpl* per la tosse al marrubio

horizon [həˈraɪzən] *s* orizzonte *m*

horizontal [ˌhɑrɪˈzɑntəl] or [ˌhɔrɪˈzɑntəl] *adj* & *s* orizzontale *f*

hormone ['hɔrmon] *s* ormone *m*

horn [hɔrn] *s* corno; (aut) clacson *m*, avvisatore acustico; (mus) corno; (trumpet) (slang) tromba; to blow one's horn cantare le proprie lodi; to lock horns lottare, disputare; to pull in one's horns battere in ritirata || *intr*—to horn in (slang) intromettersi (in)

horned' owl' [hɔrnəd] *s* allocco

hornet ['hɔrnɪt] *s* calabrone *m*

hor'net's nest' *s* vespaio; to stir up a hornet's nest suscitare un vespaio

horn' of plen'ty *s* corno dell'abbondanza

horn'pipe' *s* clarinetto contadinesco inglese fatto di corno di bue

horn'-rimmed glass'es ['hɔrn'rɪmd] *spl* occhiali cerchiati di corno or con la montatura di corno

horn-y ['hɔrni] *adj* (**-ier; -iest**) corneo; (*callous*) calloso; (*having hornlike projections*) cornuto; (*slang*) preso da desiderio lussurioso

horoscope ['hɑrə‚skop] *or* ['hɔrə‚skop] *s* oroscopo

horrible ['hɑrɪbəl] *or* ['hɔrɪbəl] *adj* orrendo, orribile

horrid ['hɑrɪd] *or* ['hɔrɪd] *adj* orrido, orribile

horri-fy ['hɑrɪ‚faɪ] *or* ['hɔrɪ‚faɪ] *v* (*pret & pp* **-fied**) *tr* inorridire

horror ['hɑrər] *or* ['hɔrər] *s* orrore *m;* **to have a horror of** provare orrore per

hors d'oeuvre [ɔr 'dʌrv] *s* (**hors d'oeuvres** [ɔr 'dʌrvz]) *s* antipasto

horse [hɔrs] *s* cavallo; (*of carpenter*) cavalletto; **hold your horses!** (coll) aspetti un momento!; **to back the wrong horse** (coll) puntare sul perdente; **to be a horse of another color** (coll) essere un altro paio di maniche || *intr—***to horse around** (slang) giocherellare; (slang) fare tiri burloni

horse'back' *s—***on horseback** a cavallo || *adv—***to ride horseback** montare a cavallo

horse' block' *s* montatoio

horse'break'er *s* domatore *m* di cavalli

horse'car' *s* tram a cavalli

horse' chest'nut *s* (*tree*) ippocastano; (*nut*) castagna d'India

horse' deal'er *s* mercante *m* di cavalli

horse' doc'tor *s* veterinario

horse'fly' *s* (**-flies**) tafano

horse'hair' *s* crine *m* di cavallo; (*fabric*) cilicio

horse'hide' *s* cuoio di cavallo

horse'laugh' *s* risataccia

horse'man *s* (**-men**) cavallerizzo

horsemanship ['hɔrsmən‚ʃɪp] *s* equitazione, maneggio

horse' meat' *s* carne equina

horse' op'era *s* western *m*

horse' pis'tol *s* pistola da sella

horse'play' *s* gioco violento, tiro burlone

horse'pow'er *s* cavallo vapore inglese

horse' race' *s* corsa ippica

horse'rad'ish *s* cren *m*, barbaforte *m*

horse' sense' *s* (coll) senso comune

horse'shoe' *s* ferro di cavallo

horse'shoe mag'net *s* calamita a ferro di cavallo

horse'shoe nail' *s* chiodo da cavallo

horse' show' *s* concorso ippico

horse' thief' *s* ladro di cavalli

horse'-trade' *intr* trafficare

horse'whip' *s* staffile *m* || *v* (*pret & pp* **-whipped**; *ger* **-whipping**) *tr* staffilare

horse'wom'an *s* (**-wom'en**) amazzone *f*

hors-y ['hɔrsi] *adj* (**-ier; -iest**) equestre; (*interested in horses*) appassionato ai cavalli; (coll) goffo

horticulture ['hɔrtɪ‚kʌltʃər] *s* orticoltura

horticulturist [‚hɔrtɪ'kʌltʃərɪst] *s* orticoltore *m*

hose [hoz] *s* (*stocking*) calza; (*sock*) calzino corto; (*flexible tube*) manica || **hose** *spl* calze *fpl*

hosier ['hoʒər] *s* calzettaio

hosiery ['hoʒəri] *s* calze *fpl*; calzificio

hospice ['hɑspɪs] *s* ospizio

hospitable ['hɑspɪtəbəl] *or* [hɑs'pɪtəbəl] *adj* ospitale

hospital ['hɑspɪtəl] *s* ospedale *m*

hospitali-ty [‚hɑspɪ'tælɪti] *s* (**-ties**) ospitalità *f*

hospitalize ['hɑspɪtə‚laɪz] *tr* ospedalizzare

host [host] *s* ospite *m;* (*at an inn*) oste *m;* (*army*) milizia; (*crowd*) folla || **Host** *s* (eccl) ostia

hostage ['hɑstɪdʒ] *s* ostaggio

hostel ['hɑstəl] *s* ostello della gioventù

hostel·ry ['hɑstəlri] *s* (**-ries**) albergo

hostess ['hostɪs] *s* ospite *f*, padrona di casa; (*e.g., on a bus*) accompagnatrice *f*, guida *f*; (aer) assistente *f* di volo

hostile ['hɑstɪl] *adj* ostile

hostili-ty [hɑs'tɪlɪti] *s* (**-ties**) ostilità *f*

hostler ['hɑslər] *or* ['ɑslər] *s* stalliere *m*

hot [hɑt] *adj* (**hotter; hottest**) caldo; (*reception*) caloroso; (*e.g., pepper*) piccante; (*fresh*) fresco; (*pursuit*) impetuoso; (*in rut*) in calore; (coll) radioattivo; **to be hot** (*said of a person*) aver caldo; (*said of the weather*) fare caldo; **to make it hot for** (coll) dare del filo da torcere a

hot' air' *s* aria calda; (slang) fumo

hot'-air fur'nace *s* impianto di riscaldamento ad aria calda

hot' baths' *spl* terme *fpl*

hot'bed' *s* (*e.g., of revolt*) focolaio; (hort) semenzaio, letto caldo

hot'-blood'ed *adj* ardente; impetuoso

hot' cake' *s* frittella; **to sell like hot cakes** vendersi come se fosse regalato

hot' dog' *s* Frankfurter *m*, Würstel *m*

hotel [ho'tɛl] *adj* alberghiero || *s* albergo

ho-tel'keep'er *s* albergatore *m*

hot'head' *s* testa calda

hotheaded ['hɑt‚hɛdɪd] *adj* esaltato, scalmanato

hot'house' *s* serra

hot' plate' *s* fornello elettrico, scaldavivande *m*

hot' springs' *spl* terme *fpl*

hot-tempered ['hɑt'tɛmpərd] *adj* impulsivo, irascibile

hot' wa'ter *s—***to be in hot water** (coll) essere nei guai

hot'-wa'ter boil'er *s* caldaia del termosifone

hot'-wa'ter bot'tle *s* borsa dell'acqua calda

hot'-wa'ter heat'er *s* scaldabagno

hot'-wa'ter heat'ing *s* riscaldamento a circolazione di acqua calda

hound [haund] *s* bracco; **to follow the hounds** *or* **to ride to hounds** andare a caccia alla volpe || *tr* perseguitare

hour [aur] *s* ora; **by the hour** a ore; **in an evil hour** in un brutto momento; **on the hour** ogni ora al suonar dell'ora; **to keep late hours** andare a letto tardi

hour'glass' s clessidra

hour' hand' s lancetta delle ore

hourly ['aurlɪ] adj orario || adv ogni ora; spesso

house [haus] s **(houses** ['hauzɪz]) casa; (*legislative body*) camera; (*size of audience*) concorso di pubblico; teatro; **to keep house** fare le faccende domestiche; **to put one's house in order** migliorare il proprio comportamento; accomodare le proprie faccende || [hauz] tr allogare

house' arrest' s arresto a domicilio

house'boat' s casa galleggiante

house'break'er s scassinatore m

housebreaking ['haus,brekɪŋ] s violazione di domicilio, scasso

housebroken ['haus,brokən] adj (e.g., *cat*) che è stato addestrato a tenersi pulito

house'clean'ing s pulizia della casa; (fig) pulizia, repulisti m

house'coat' s vestaglia da casa

house' cur'rent s corrente f di rete

house'fly' s **(-flies)** mosca domestica

houseful ['haus,ful] s casa piena

house' fur'nishings spl arredi domestici

house'hold' adj domestico || s famiglia

house'hold'er s capo della famiglia

house'-hunt' intr—**to go house-hunting** andare in cerca di casa

house'keep'er s governante f

house'keep'ing s faccende domestiche; **to set up housekeeping** metter su casa

house'keeping apart'ment s appartamentino

house'maid' s domestica

house' me'ter s contatore domestico

house'moth'er s maestra in pensionato per studenti

house' of cards' s castello di carte

house' of ill' repute' s casa di malaffare

house' paint'er s imbianchino

house' physi'cian s medico residente

house'top' s tetto; **to shout from the housetops** proclamare ai quattro venti

housewarming ['haus,wormɪŋ] s festa per l'inaugurazione di una casa

house'wife' s **(-wives)** donna di casa

house'work' s faccende domestiche

housing ['hauzɪŋ] s (*of a horse*) gualdrappa; (*dwelling*) abitazioni fpl; (carp) alloggiamento; (mach) gabbia, custodia; (aut) coppa; (*of transmission*) (aut) scatola

hous'ing short'age s crisi f degli alloggi

hovel ['hʌvəl] or ['hɑvəl] s catapecchia, stamberga; (*shed*) baracca

hover ['hʌvər] or ['hɑvər] intr librarsi; (*on the lips*) trapelare; (fig) ondeggiare, esitare

how [hau] adv come; (*at what price*) a quanto; **how early** quando, a che ora; **how else** in che altro modo; **how far** fino a dove; quanto, e.g., **how far is it to the station?** quanto c'è da qui alla stazione?; **how long** quanto tempo; **how many** quanti; **how much**

quanto; **how often** quante volte; **how old are you?** quanti anni ha?; **how soon** quando, a che ora; **how** + adj quanto + adj, e.g., **how beautiful she is!** quanto è bella!

how-ev'er adv comunque; in qualunque modo; per quanto . . . , e.g., **however wrong he may be** per quanto torto possa avere || conj come, e.g., **do it however you want** lo faccia come vuole

howitzer ['hau-ɪtsər] s obice m

howl [haul] s ululato, urlo; scoppio di risa || tr gridare; **to howl down** sopraffare a grida; || intr ululare, urlare

howler ['haulər] s urlatore m; (coll) strafalcione m, topica

hoyden ['hɔɪdən] s ragazzaccia

hub [hʌb] s mozzo; (fig) centro

hubbub ['hʌbəb] s putiferio, fracasso

hub'cap' s (aut) calotta della ruota

huckleber·ry ['hʌkəl,berɪ] s **(-ries)** mirtillo

huckster ['hʌkstər] s venditore m ambulante; trafficante m

huddle ['hʌdəl] s conferenza segreta || intr affollarsi, accalcarsi

hue [hju] s tono, tinta; **hue and cry** grido d'indignazione

huff [hʌf] s stizza; **in a huff** di cattivo umore || tr (checkers) buffare

hug [hʌg] s abbraccio || v (pret & pp **hugged;** ger **hugging**) tr abbracciare; (e.g., *a wall*) costeggiare || intr abbracciarsi

huge [hjudʒ] adj smisurato, immane

huh [hʌ] interj eh!

hulk [hʌlk] s scafo, carcassa; (*unwieldy object*) trabiccolo

hulking ['hʌlkɪŋ] adj grosso e goffo

hull [hʌl] s (*of ship or hydroplane*) scafo; (*of dirigible*) intelaiatura; (*of airplane*) fusoliera; (e.g., *of a nut*) guscio || tr sgusciare; (rice) brillare

hullabaloo ['hʌləbə,lu] or [,hʌləbə'lu] s fracasso, baccano

hum [hʌm] s canterellio; (*of bee, machine, etc.*) ronzio || v (pret & pp **hummed;** ger **humming**) tr canterellare || intr canterellare; (*to buzz*) ronzare; (coll) vibrare, essere attivo

human ['hjumən] adj umano

hu'man be'ing s essere umano

humane [hju'men] adj umano; compassionevole

humanist ['hjumənɪst] adj umanistico || s umanista mf

humanitarian [hju,mænɪ'terɪ·ən] adj & s umanitario

humani·ty [hju'mænɪtɪ] s **(-ties)** umanità f; **humanities** (*of Greece and Rome*) studi umanistici; (*literature, art, philosophy*) scienze umanistiche

hu'man·kind' s genere umano

humble ['hʌmbəl] or ['ʌmbəl] adj umile || tr umiliare

hum'ble pie' s—**to eat humble pie** accettare un'umiliazione

hum'bug' s frottola; (*person*) impostore m || v (pret & pp **-bugged;** ger

-bugging) *tr* imbrogliare ‖ *intr* fare l'imbroglione

hum'drum' *adj* noioso, monotono

humer·us ['hjumərəs] *s* (**-i** [,aɪ]) omero

humid ['hjumɪd] *adj* umido

humidifier [hju'mɪdɪ,faɪ-ər] *s* evaporatore *m*

humidi·fy [hju'mɪdɪ,faɪ] *v* (*pret & pp* **-fied**) *tr* inumidire

humidity [hju'mɪdɪti] *s* umidità *f*

humiliate [hju'mɪlɪ,et] *tr* umiliare

humiliating [hju'mɪlɪ,etɪŋ] *adj* umiliante

humility [hju'mɪlɪti] *s* umiltà *f*

hummingbird ['hʌmɪŋ,bʌrd] *s* colibrì *m*

humor ['hjumər] or ['jumər] *s* umore *m*; umorismo; **out of humor** di cattivo umore ‖ *tr* adattarsi alle fisime di, assecondare

humorist ['hjumərɪst] or ['jumərɪst] *s* umorista *mf*

humorous ['hjumərəs] or ['jumərəs] *adj* umoristico

hump [hʌmp] *s* gobba; (*in the ground*) monticello

hump'back' *s* gobba; (*person*) gobbo

humus ['hjuməs] *s* humus *m*

hunch [hʌntʃ] *s* gobba; (*premonition*) (coll) sospetto ‖ *tr* piegare ‖ *intr* accovacciarsi

hunch'back' *s* gobba; (*person*) gobbo

hundred ['hʌndrəd] *adj, s & pron* cento; **a hundred** or **one hundred** cento; **by the hundreds** a centinaia

hundredth ['hʌndrədθ] *adj, s & pron* centesimo

hun'dred·weight' *s* cento libbre

Hungarian [hʌŋ'gerɪ·ən] *adj & s* ungherese *mf*

Hungary ['hʌŋgəri] *s* l'Ungheria *f*

hunger ['hʌŋgər] *s* fame *f* ‖ *intr* aver fame; **to hunger for** aver un desiderio ardente di, agognare

hun'ger strike' *s* sciopero della fame

hun·gry ['hʌŋgri] *adj* (**-grier; -griest**) affamato; **to be hungry** aver fame; **to go hungry** andare a digiuno

hunk [hʌŋk] *s* (coll) bel pezzo

hunt [hʌnt] *s* caccia; **on the hunt for** a caccia di ‖ *tr* cacciare; (*to look for*) cercare ‖ *intr* andare a caccia; cercare; **to go hunting** andare a caccia; **to hunt for** cercare

hunter ['hʌntər] *s* cacciatore *m*; (*dog*) cane *m* da caccia

hunting ['hʌntɪŋ] *adj* da caccia ‖ *s* caccia

hunt'ing box' *s* capanno

hunt'ing dog' *s* cane *m* da caccia

hunt'ing ground' *s* terreno di caccia

hunt'ing horn' *s* corno da caccia

hunt'ing jack'et *s* cacciatora

hunt'ing lodge' *s* (*hut*) capanno; villino da caccia

hunt'ing sea'son *s* stagione della caccia

huntress ['hʌntrɪs] *s* cacciatrice *f*

hunts'man *s* (**-men**) cacciatore *m*

hurdle ['hʌrdəl] *s* (*hedge*) siepe *f*; (*wooden frame*) barriera; (sports, fig) ostacolo; **hurdles** corsa ad ostacoli ‖ *tr* saltare, superare

hur'dle race' *s* corsa agli ostacoli

hurl [hʌrl] *s* lancio ‖ *tr* lanciare; **to hurl back** respingere

hurrah [hu'rɑ] or **hurray** [hu're] *s* viva *m* ‖ *tr* applaudire ‖ *intr* gridare urrà ‖ *interj* evviva!, urrà!; **hurrah for . . . !** viva . . . !

hurricane ['hʌri,ken] *s* uragano

hurried ['hʌrid] *adj* frettoloso

hur·ry ['hʌri] *s* (**-ries**) fretta; **to be in a hurry** avere fretta ‖ *v* (*pret & pp* **-ried**) *tr* affrettare, sollecitare ‖ *intr* affrettarsi; **to hurry after** correr dietro a; **to hurry away** andarsene di furia; **to hurry back** ritornare presto; **to hurry up** spicciarsi

hurt [hʌrt] *adj* (*injured*) ferito; (*offended*) risentito ‖ *s* (*harm*) danno; (*injury*) ferita; (*pain*) dolore *m* ‖ *v* (*pret & pp* **hurt**) *tr* (*to harm*) fare male a; (*to injure*) ferire; (*to offend*) offendere; (*to pain*) dolere (with *dat*) ‖ *intr* fare male, dolere; aver male, e.g., **my head hurts** ho male alla testa

hurtle ['hʌrtəl] *intr* sferrarsi, scagliarsi, precipitarsi

husband ['hʌzbənd] *s* marito ‖ *tr* amministrare con economia

hus'band·man *s* (**-men**) agricoltore *m*

husbandry ['hʌzbəndri] *s* agricoltura; (*management of domestic affairs*) governo, economia domestica

hush [hʌʃ] *s* silenzio ‖ *tr* far tacere; **to hush up** (*a scandal*) soffocare ‖ *intr* tacere ‖ *interj* zitto!

hushaby ['hʌʃə,baɪ] *interj* fa' la nanna!

hush'-hush' *adj* segretissimo

hush' mon'ey *s* prezzo del silenzio

husk [hʌsk] *s* guscio; (*of corn*) spoglia ‖ *tr* sgusciare; (*rice*) brillare; (*corn*) scartocciare, spogliare

husk·y ['hʌski] *adj* (**-ier; -iest**) forte; (*voice*) rauco

hus·sy ['hʌzi] or ['hʌsi] *s* (**-sies**) poca di buono; ragazza impudente

hustle ['hʌsəl] *s* vigore *m*; (slang) traffico ‖ *tr* forzare, spingere ‖ *intr* affrettarsi, scalmanarsi; (slang) trafficare; (*said of a prostitute*) (slang) accostare un cliente

hustler ['hʌslər] *s* (*go-getter*) persona intraprendente; (slang) trafficone *m*, imbroglione *m*; (slang) passeggiatrice *f*

hut [hʌt] *s* casolare *m*, casupola

hyacinth ['haɪ-əsɪnθ] *s* giacinto

hybrid ['haɪbrɪd] *adj & s* ibrido

hybridize ['haɪbrɪ,daɪz] *tr & intr* ibridare

hy·dra ['haɪdrə] *s* (**-dras** or **-drae** [dri]) idra

hydrant ['haɪdrənt] *s* idrante *m*; (*water faucet*) rubinetto

hydrate ['haɪdret] *s* idrato ‖ *tr* idratare ‖ *intr* idratarsi

hydraulic [haɪ'drɔlɪk] *adj* idraulico ‖ **hydraulics** *s* idraulica

hydrau'lic ram' *s* pompa idraulica

hydriodic [,haɪdrɪ'ɑdɪk] *adj* iodidrico

hydrobromic [,haɪdrə'bromɪk] *adj* bromidrico

hydrocarbon [ˌhaɪdrəˈkɑrbən] s idrocarburo

hydrochloric [ˌhaɪdrəˈklorɪk] adj cloridrico

hydroelectric [ˌhaɪdro·ɪˈlektrɪk] adj idroelettrico

hydrofluoric [ˌhaɪdrəfluˈɑrɪk] or [ˌhaɪdrəfluˈɔrɪk] adj fluoridrico

hydrofoil [ˈhaɪdrəˌfɔɪl] s superficie idrodinamica; (winglike member) aletta idrodinamica; (vessel) aliscafo, idroplano

hydrogen [ˈhaɪdrədʒən] s idrogeno

hy'drogen bomb' s bomba all'idrogeno

hy'drogen perox'ide s perossido d'idrogeno, acqua ossigenata

hy'drogen sul'fide s solfuro d'idrogeno

hydrometer [haɪˈdrɑmɪtər] s areometro

hydrophobia [ˌhaɪdrəˈfobɪ·ə] s idrofobia

hydroplane [ˈhaɪdrəˌplen] s (aer) idrovolante m; (naut) idroscivolante m, idroplano

hydroxide [haɪˈdrɑksaɪd] s idrossido

hyena [haɪˈinə] s iena

hygiene [ˈhaɪdʒin] or [ˈhaɪdʒɪˌin] s igiene f

hygienic [ˌhaɪdʒɪˈenɪk] or [haɪˈdʒɪnɪk] adj igienico

hymn [hɪm] s inno

hymnal [ˈhɪmnəl] s innario

hyperacidity [ˌhaɪpərəˈsɪdɪti] s iperacidità f

hyperbola [haɪˈpʌrbələ] s (geom) iperbole f

hyperbole [haɪˈpʌrbəli] s (rhet) iperbole f

hyperbolic [ˌhaɪpərˈbɑlɪk] adj iperbolico

hypersensitive [ˌhaɪpərˈsensɪtɪv] adj ipersensibile

hypertension [ˌhaɪpərˈtɛnʃən] s ipertensione

hyphen [ˈhaɪfən] s trattino

hyphenate [ˈhaɪfəˌnet] tr unire con trattino; scrivere con trattino

hypno·sis [hɪpˈnosɪs] s (-ses [siz]) ipnosi f

hypnotic [hɪpˈnɑtɪk] adj & s ipnotico

hypnotism [ˈhɪpnəˌtɪzəm] s ipnotismo

hypnotize [ˈhɪpnəˌtaɪz] tr ipnotizzare

hypochondriac [ˌhaɪpəˈkɑndrɪˌæk] or [ˌhɪpəˈkɑndrɪˌæk] s ipocondriaco

hypocri·sy [hɪˈpɑkrəsi] s (-sies) ipocrisia

hypocrite [ˈhɪpəkrɪt] s ipocrita

hypocritical [ˌhɪpəˈkrɪtɪkəl] adj ipocrita

hypodermic [ˌhaɪpəˈdʌrmɪk] adj ipodermico

hyposulfite [ˌhaɪpəˈsʌlfaɪt] s iposolfito

hypotenuse [haɪˈpɑtɪˌnus] or [haɪˈpɑtɪˌnjus] s ipotenusa

hypothesis [haɪˈpɑθɪsɪs] s (-ses [ˌsiz]) ipotesi f

hypothesize [haɪˈpɑθɪˌsaɪz] tr ipotizzare

hypothetic(al) [ˌhaɪpəˈθetɪk(əl)] adj ipotetico

hyssop [ˈhɪsəp] s issopo

hysteria [hɪsˈtɪrɪ·ə] s isterismo

hysteric [hɪsˈterɪk] adj isterico || **hysterics** s isterismo

hysterical [hɪsˈterɪkəl] adj isterico

I

I, i [aɪ] s nona lettera dell'alfabeto inglese

I [aɪ] pron pers (we [wi]) io; **it is I** sono io

iambic [aɪˈæmbɪk] adj giambico

iam·bus [aɪˈæmbəs] s (-bi [baɪ]) giambo

I'-beam' s putrella

Iberian [aɪˈbɪrɪ·ən] adj iberico || s abitante mf dell'Iberia; lingua iberica

ibex [ˈaɪbeks] s (**ibexes** or **ibices** [ˈɪbɪˌsiz]) stambecco

ice [aɪs] s ghiaccio; **to break the ice** rompere il ghiaccio; **to cut no ice** (coll) non avere importanza; **to skate on thin ice** cacciarsi in una situazione delicata || tr gelare; (to cover with icing) glassare || intr gelarsi

ice' age' s epoca glaciale

ice' bag' s borsa di ghiaccio

iceberg [ˈaɪsˌbʌrg] s borgognone m, montagna di ghiaccio

ice'boat' s slitta a vela; (icebreaker) rompighiaccio

icebound [ˈaɪsˌbaʊnd] adj chiuso dal ghiaccio

ice'box' s ghiacciaia

ice'break'er s rompighiaccio

ice' buck'et s secchiello da ghiaccio

ice'cap' s calotta glaciale

ice'-cold' adj gelido, ghiacciato

ice' cream' s gelato, sorbetto

ice'-cream cone' s cono gelato

ice'-cream freez'er s gelatiera

ice'-cream par'lor s gelateria

ice' cube' s cubetto di ghiaccio

ice' hock'ey s hockey m su ghiaccio

Iceland [ˈaɪslənd] s l'Islanda f

Icelander [ˈaɪsˌlændər] or [ˈaɪsləndər] s islandese mf

Icelandic [aɪsˈlændɪk] adj islandese || s (language) islandese m

ice'man' s (-men') venditore m di ghiaccio

ice' pack' s banco di ghiaccio; (ice bag) borsa di ghiaccio

ice' pick' s rompighiaccio

ice' shelf' s tavolato di ghiaccio

ice' skate' s pattino da ghiaccio

ice' wa'ter s acqua gelata

ichthyology [ˌɪkθɪˈɑlədʒi] s ittiologia

icicle [ˈaɪsɪkəl] s ghiacciolo

icing [ˈaɪsɪŋ] s glassa; (meteor) gelo

iconoclast [aɪˈkɑnəˌklæst] s iconoclasta mf

iconoscope [aɪ'kɑnə‚skop] *s* (trademark) iconoscopio
icy ['aɪsi] *adj* (**icier; iciest**) ghiacciato; (*e.g., wind, hands*) gelido; (fig) glaciale
idea [aɪ'di‚ə] *s* idea
ideal [aɪ'di‚əl] *adj & s* ideale *m*
idealist [aɪ'di‚əlɪst] *adj & s* idealista *mf*
idealistic [aɪ‚dɪ‚əl'ɪstɪk] *adj* idealistico
idealize [aɪ'di‚ə‚laɪz] *tr* idealizzare
identic(al) [aɪ'dentɪk(əl)] *adj* identico
identification [aɪ‚dentɪfɪ'keʃən] *s* identificazione, riconoscimento
identifica'tion card' *s* carta d'identità
identifica'tion tag' *s* piastrina
identi·fy [aɪ'dentɪ‚faɪ] *v* (*pret & pp* **-fied**) *tr* identificare
identi·ty [aɪ'dentɪti] *s* (**-ties**) identità *f*
ideolo·gy [‚aɪdɪ'ɑlədʒi] *or* [‚ɪdɪ'ɑlədʒɪ] *s* (**-gies**) ideologia
ides [aɪdz] *spl* idi *mpl & fpl*
idio·cy ['ɪdɪ‚əsi] *s* (**-cies**) idiozia
idiom ['ɪdɪ‚əm] *s* (*expression that is contrary to the usual patterns of the language*) locuzione idiomatica, idiotismo; (*style of language*) lingua, idioma *m*; (*style of an author*) stile *m*; (*character of a language*) indole *f*
idiomatic [‚ɪdɪ‚ə'mætɪk] *adj* idiomatico
idiosyncra·sy [‚ɪdɪ‚ə'sɪnkrəsi] *s* (**-sies**) eccentricità *f*, originalità *f*; (med) idiosincrasia
idiot ['ɪdɪ‚ət] *s* idiota *mf*
idiotic [‚ɪdɪ'ɑtɪk] *adj* idiota
idle ['aɪdəl] *adj* (*unemployed*) disoccupato; (*machine*) fermo; (*capital*) giacente; (*time*) perso; (*talk*) vano; (*lazy*) fannullone, ozioso; **to run idle** girare a vuoto || *tr*—**to idle away** (*time*) sprecare || *intr* poltrire, fare il fannullone; (aut) girare al minimo
idleness ['aɪdəlnɪs] *s* ozio
idler ['aɪdlər] *s* fannullone *m*
idling ['aɪdlɪŋ] *s* (*of motor*) minimo
idol ['aɪdəl] *s* idolo
idola·try [aɪ'dɑlətri] *s* (**-tries**) idolatria
idolize ['aɪdə‚laɪz] *tr* idolatrare
idyll ['aɪdəl] *s* idillio
idyllic [aɪ'dɪlɪk] *adj* idilliaco
if [ɪf] *conj* se; as if come se; even if anche se; if so se è così; if true se è vero
ignis fatuus ['ɪgnɪs'fætʃʊ‚əs] *s* (**ignes fatui** ['ɪgniz'fætʃʊ‚aɪ]) fuoco fatuo
ignite [ɪg'naɪt] *tr* infiammare || *intr* infiammarsi
ignition [ɪg'nɪʃən] *s* ignizione; (aut) accensione
igni'tion switch' *s* (aut) chiavetta dell'accensione
igni'tion sys'tem *s* (aut) apparecchiatura d'accensione
ignoble [ɪg'nobəl] *adj* ignobile
ignominious [‚ɪgnə'mɪnɪ‚əs] *adj* ignominioso
ignoramus [‚ɪgnə'reməs] *s* ignorante *mf*
ignorance ['ɪgnərəns] *s* ignoranza
ignorant ['ɪgnərənt] *adj* ignorante; **to be ignorant of** ignorare

ignore [ɪg'nor] *tr* (*a person; a person's kindness*) ignorare
ill [ɪl] *adj* (**worse** [wʌrs]; **worst** [wʌrst]) malato; **to take ill** cadere malato || *adv* male; **to take ill** prendere in mala parte
ill-advised ['ɪləd'vaɪzd] *adj* inconsulto, sconsiderato
ill'-at-ease' *adj* imbarazzato, spaesato
ill-bred ['ɪl'bred] *adj* maleducato
ill-considered ['ɪlkən'sɪdərd] *adj* sconsiderato
ill-disposed ['ɪldɪs'pozd] *adj* maldisposto, malintenzionato
illegal [ɪ'ligəl] *adj* illegale
illegible [ɪ'ledʒɪbəl] *adj* illeggibile
illegitimate [‚ɪlɪ'dʒɪtɪmɪt] *adj* illegittimo
ill' fame' *s* pessima fama
ill-fated ['ɪl'fetɪd] *adj* infausto
ill-gotten ['ɪl'gɑtən] *adj* male acquistato
ill-humored ['ɪl'hjumərd] *adj* di cattivo umore
illicit [ɪ'lɪsɪt] *adj* illecito
illitera·cy [ɪ'lɪtərəsi] *s* (**-cies**) analfabetismo; (*mistake*) solecismo; ignoranza
illiterate [ɪ'lɪtərɪt] *adj* (*uneducated*) illetterato; (*unable to read or write*) analfabeta || *s* analfabeta *mf*
ill-mannered ['ɪl'mænərd] *adj* screanzato, ineducato
illness ['ɪlnɪs] *s* malattia
illogical [ɪ'lɑdʒɪkəl] *adj* illogico
ill-spent ['ɪl'spent] *adj* sprecato
ill-starred ['ɪl'stɑrd] *adj* nato sotto una cattiva stella; sfortunato, funesto
ill-tempered ['ɪl'tempərd] *adj* di cattivo umore
ill-timed ['ɪl'taɪmd] *adj* inopportuno
ill'-treat' *tr* maltrattare, tartassare
illuminate [ɪ'lumɪ‚net] *tr* illuminare; (*a manuscript*) miniare
illumination [ɪ‚lumɪ'neʃən] *s* illuminazione; (*in manuscript*) miniatura
illusion [ɪ'luʒən] *s* illusione
illusive [ɪ'lusɪv] *adj* illusorio
illusory [ɪ'lusəri] *adj* illusorio
illustrate ['ɪləs‚tret] *or* [ɪ'lʌstret] *tr* illustrare
illustration [‚ɪləs'treʃən] *s* illustrazione
illustrator ['ɪləs‚tretər] *s* illustratore *m*
illustrious [ɪ'lʌstrɪ‚əs] *adj* illustre
ill' will' *s* astio, ruggine *f*, malevolenza
image ['ɪmɪdʒ] *s* immagine *f*; **the very image of** il ritratto parlante di
image·ry ['ɪmɪdʒri] *or* ['ɪmɪdʒəri] *s* (**-ries**) (*mental images*) fantasia; (*images collectively*) immagini *fpl*; (rhet) linguaggio figurato
imaginary [ɪ'mædʒɪ‚neri] *adj* immaginario
imagination [ɪ‚mædʒɪ'neʃən] *s* immaginazione
imagine [ɪ'mædʒɪn] *tr & intr* immaginare; (*to conjecture*) immaginarsi; **imagine!** si figuri!
imbalance [ɪm'bæləns] *s* scompenso
imbecile ['ɪmbɪsɪl] *adj & s* imbecille *mf*

imbecili·ty [ˌɪmbɪˈsɪlɪti] s (-ties) imbecillità f, imbecillaggine f

imbibe [ɪmˈbaɪb] tr (to drink) bere; assorbire || intr bere

imbue [ɪmˈbju] tr imbevere

imitate [ˈɪmɪˌtet] tr imitare

imitation [ˌɪmɪˈteʃən] adj (e.g., jewelry) falso || s imitazione

imitator [ˈɪmɪˌtetər] s imitatore m

immaculate [ɪˈmækjəlɪt] adj immacolato

immaterial [ˌɪməˈtɪrɪəl] adj immateriale; poco importante; **it's immaterial to me** a me fa lo stesso

immature [ˌɪməˈtjur] or [ˌɪməˈtur] adj immaturo

immeasurable [ɪˈmeʒərəbəl] adj incommensurabile, smisurato

immediacy [ɪˈmidɪˌəsi] s immediatezza

immediate [ɪˈmidɪ·ɪt] adj immediato

immediately [ɪˈmidɪ·ɪtli] adv immediatamente

immemorial [ˌɪmɪˈmorɪ·əl] adj immemorabile

immense [ɪˈmens] adj immenso

immerge [ɪˈmʌrdʒ] intr sommergersi

immerse [ɪˈmʌrs] tr immergere

immersion [ɪˈmʌrʃən] or [ɪˈmʌrʒən] s immersione

immigrant [ˈɪmɪgrənt] adj & s immigrante m

immigrate [ˈɪmɪˌgret] intr immigrare

immigration [ˌɪmɪˈgreʃən] s immigrazione

imminent [ˈɪmɪnənt] adj imminente

immobile [ɪˈmobɪl] or [ɪˈmobɪl] adj immobile

immobilize [ɪˈmobɪˌlaɪz] tr immobilizzare

immoderate [ɪˈmɑdərɪt] adj smodato, sregolato

immodest [ɪˈmɑdɪst] adj immodesto

immoral [ɪˈmɑrəl] adj immorale

immortal [ɪˈmɔrtəl] adj & s immortale mf

immortalize [ɪˈmɔrtəˌlaɪz] tr eternare, immortalare

immune [ɪˈmjun] adj immune

immunize [ˈɪmjəˌnaɪz] or [ɪˈmjunaɪz] tr immunizzare

imp [ɪmp] s diavoletto; (child) frugolo

impact [ˈɪmpækt] s impatto

impair [ɪmˈper] tr danneggiare; (to weaken) indebolire

impan·el [ɪmˈpænəl] v (pret & pp -eled or -elled; ger -eling or -elling) tr iscrivere nella lista dei giurati; (a jury) selezionare

impart [ɪmˈpɑrt] tr (a secret) far conoscere; (knowledge) impartire; (motion) imprimere

impartial [ɪmˈpɑrʃəl] adj imparziale

impassable [ɪmˈpæsəbəl] or [ɪmˈpɑsəbəl] adj impraticabile, intransitabile

impasse [ɪmˈpæs] or [ˈɪmpæs] s vicolo cieco, impasse f

impassible [ɪmˈpæsɪbəl] adj impassibile

impassioned [ɪmˈpæʃənd] adj caloroso, veemente

impassive [ɪmˈpæsɪv] adj impassibile

impatience [ɪmˈpeʃəns] s impazienza

impatient [ɪmˈpeʃənt] adj impaziente

impeach [ɪmˈpitʃ] tr accusare; (a public official) sottoporre a un'inchiesta; (a statement) mettere in dubbio

impeachment [ɪmˈpitʃmənt] s accusa; inchiesta

impeccable [ɪmˈpekəbəl] adj impeccabile

impecunious [ˌɪmpɪˈkjunɪ·əs] adj indigente

impedance [ɪmˈpidəns] s impedenza

impede [ɪmˈpid] tr impedire, intralciare

impediment [ɪmˈpedɪmənt] s impedimento; ostacolo

im·pel [ɪmˈpel] v (pret & pp -pelled or -pelled; ger -peling or -pelling) tr spingere, forzare

impending [ɪmˈpendɪŋ] adj imminente, incombente

impenetrable [ɪmˈpenɪtrəbəl] adj impenetrabile

impenitent [ɪmˈpenɪtənt] adj impenitente || s persona impenitente

imperative [ɪmˈperɪtɪv] adj (commanding) imperativo; (urgent) imperioso || s imperativo

imperceptible [ˌɪmpərˈseptɪbəl] adj impercettibile

imperfect [ɪmˈpʌrfɪkt] adj & s imperfetto

imperfection [ˌɪmpərˈfekʃən] s imperfezione

imperial [ɪmˈpɪrɪ·əl] adj imperiale || s (goatee) barbetta, mosca; (top of coach) imperiale m

imperialist [ɪmˈpɪrɪ·əlɪst] adj & s imperialista mf

imper·il [ɪmˈperɪl] v (pret & pp -iled or -illed; ger -iling or -illing) tr mettere in pericolo

imperious [ɪmˈpɪrɪ·əs] adj imperioso

imperishable [ɪmˈperɪʃəbəl] adj imperituro, duraturo

impersonate [ɪmˈpʌrsəˌnet] tr (to pretend to be) spacciarsi per; (on the stage) impersonare

impertinence [ɪmˈpʌrtɪnəns] s impertinenza

impertinent [ɪmˈpʌrtɪnənt] adj impertinente

impetuous [ɪmˈpetʃʊ·əs] adj impetuoso

impetus [ˈɪmpɪtəs] s impeto, foga

impie·ty [ɪmˈpaɪ·əti] s (-ties) empietà f

impinge [ɪmˈpɪndʒ] intr—**to impinge on** or **upon** violare; (said, e.g., of the sun) ferire; (the imagination) colpire

impious [ˈɪmpɪ·əs] adj empio

impish [ˈɪmpɪʃ] adj indiavolato

implant [ɪmˈplænt] tr innestare; instillare, istillare

implement [ˈɪmplɪmənt] s utensile m, strumento || [ˈɪmplɪˌment] tr completare, mettere in opera; (to provide with implements) attrezzare

implicate [ˈɪmplɪˌket] tr implicare

implicit [ɪmˈplɪsɪt] adj implicito; (unquestioning) assoluto, cieco

implied [ɪmˈplaɪd] adj implicito

implore [ɪmˈplor] tr (a person; pardon)

implorare; (to entreat) raccomandarsi a

im·ply [ɪm'plaɪ] v (pret & pp -plied) tr voler dire, significare; implicare, sottintendere

impolite [ˌɪmpə'laɪt] adj scortese

import ['ɪmport] s importazione; articolo d'importazione; importanza || [ɪm'port] or ['ɪmport] tr importare; significare || intr importare

importance [ɪm'pɔrtəns] s importanza

important [ɪm'pɔrtənt] adj importante

importation [ˌɪmpor'teʃən] s importazione

importer [ɪm'portər] s importatore m

importunate [ɪm'pɔrtʃənɪt] adj importuno

importune [ˌɪmpor'tjun] or [ɪm'pɔrtʃun] tr importunare

impose [ɪm'poz] tr imporre || intr—to impose on or upon abusare di; abusare della gentilezza di

imposing [ɪm'pozɪŋ] adj imponente

imposition [ˌɪmpə'zɪʃən] s imposizione; abuso; abuso della gentilezza; inganno

impossible [ɪm'pɑsɪbəl] adj impossibile

impostor [ɪm'pɑstər] s impostore m

imposture [ɪm'pɑstʃər] s impostura

impotence ['ɪmpətəns] s impotenza

impotent ['ɪmpətənt] adj impotente

impound [ɪm'paʊnd] tr rinchiudere, recintare; (water) raccogliere; (law) sequestrare, confiscare

impoverish [ɪm'pɑvərɪʃ] tr impoverire

impracticable [ɪm'præktɪkəbəl] adj impraticabile; (intractable) intrattabile

impractical [ɪm'præktɪkəl] adj poco pratico

impregnable [ɪm'pregnəbəl] adj inespugnabile, imprendibile

impregnate [ɪm'pregnet] tr impregnare

impresari·o [ˌɪmprɪ'sɑri‚o] s (-os) impresario

impress [ɪm'pres] tr (to affect in mind or feelings) impressionare; (to produce by pressure; to fix on s.o.'s mind) imprimere; (mil) arruolare

impression [ɪm'preʃən] s impressione

impressionable [ɪm'preʃənəbəl] adj impressionabile

impressive [ɪm'presɪv] adj impressionante, imponente

imprint ['ɪmprɪnt] s impronta; (typ) indicazione dell'editore || [ɪm'prɪnt] tr imprimere

imprison [ɪm'prɪzən] tr imprigionare

imprisonment [ɪm'prɪzənmənt] s prigione, prigionia

improbable [ɪm'prɑbəbəl] adj improbabile

imprompt·u [ɪm'prɑmptju] or [ɪm'prɑmptu] adj improvvisato || s improvvisazione; (mus) impromptu m || adv all'improvviso

improper [ɪm'prɑpər] adj (erroneous) improprio; (inappropriate; unseemly) scorretto; (math) improprio

improve [ɪm'pruv] tr migliorare; (an opportunity) approfittare di || intr migliorare; to improve on or upon perfezionare

improvement [ɪm'pruvmənt] s miglioramento, perfezionamento; (in real estate) miglioria; (e.g., of time) buon uso

improvident [ɪm'prɑvɪdənt] adj improvvido, improvidente

improvise ['ɪmprə‚vaɪz] tr & intr improvvisare

imprudence [ɪm'prudəns] s imprudenza

imprudent [ɪm'prudənt] adj imprudente

impudence ['ɪmpjədəns] s impudenza, sfrontatezza, sfacciataggine f

impudent ['ɪmpjədənt] adj sfrontato, sfacciato, spudorato

impugn [ɪm'pjun] tr impugnare

impulse ['ɪmpʌls] s impulso

impulsive [ɪm'pʌlsɪv] adj impulsivo

impunity [ɪm'pjunɪti] s impunità f

impure [ɪm'pjur] adj impuro

impuri·ty [ɪm'pjurɪti] s (-ties) impurità f

impute [ɪm'pjut] tr imputare

in [ɪn] adj interno; (coll) moderno, alla moda || s relazione; the ins and outs tutti i dettagli || adv dentro; a casa; in ufficio; in here qui dentro; in there lì dentro; to be in essere a casa; to be in for essere destinato a; to be in with essere in intimità con || prep in; (within) dentro a; (over, through) per; di, e.g., the best in the class il migliore della classe; dressed in vestito di; in so far as per quanto; in that per quanto, dato che

inability [ˌɪnə'bɪlɪti] s inabilità f

inaccessible [ˌɪnæk'sesɪbəl] adj inaccessibile

inaccura·cy [ɪn'ækjərəsi] s (-cies) inesattezza, imprecisione

inaccurate [ɪn'ækjərɪt] adj inesatto

inaction [ɪn'ækʃən] s inazione

inactive [ɪn'æktɪv] adj inattivo

inadequate [ɪn'ædɪkwɪt] adj inadeguato, inadatto

inadvertent [ˌɪnəd'vʌrtənt] adj disattento; inavvertito

inadvisable [ˌɪnəd'vaɪzəbəl] adj poco consigliabile

insane [ɪn'en] adj insensato, assurdo

inanimate [ɪn'ænɪmɪt] adj inanimato

inappreciable [ˌɪnə'priʃɪ‚əbəl] adj inapprezzabile

inappropriate [ˌɪnə'propri‚ɪt] adj non appropriato, improprio

inarticulate [ˌɪnɑr'tɪkjəlɪt] adj (sounds, words) inarticolato; (person) incapace di esprimersi

inasmuch as [ˌɪnəs'mʌt‚ʃ ‚æz] conj dato che, visto che, in quanto che

inattentive [ˌɪnə'tentɪv] adj disattento

inaugural [ɪn'ɔgjərəl] adj inaugurale || s discorso inaugurale

inaugurate [ɪn'ɔgjə‚ret] tr inaugurare

inauguration [ɪn‚ɔgjə'reʃən] s inaugurazione; (investiture of a head of government) assunzione dei poteri

inborn ['ɪn‚bɔrn] adj innato, ingenito

inbreeding ['ɪn‚bridɪŋ] s incrocio fra animali o piante affini

incandescent [ˌɪnkən'desənt] adj incandescente

incapable [ɪn'kepəbəl] *adj* incapace

incapacitate [ˌɪnkə'pæsɪˌtet] *tr* inabilitare; (law) interdire

incapaci·ty [ˌɪnkə'pæsɪti] *s* (**-ties**) incapacità *f*

incarcerate [ɪn'kɑrsəˌret] *tr* incarcerare

incarnate [ɪn'kɑrnɪt] *or* [ɪn'kɑrnet] *adj* incarnato || [ɪn'kɑrnet] *tr* incarnare

incarnation [ˌɪnkɑr'neʃən] *s* incarnazione

incendiarism [ɪn'sendɪ-əˌrɪzəm] *s* incendio doloso; (*agitation*) sobillazione

incendiar·y [ɪn'sendɪˌeri] *adj* incendiario || *s* (**-ies**) incendiario; (fig) sobillatore *m*

incense ['ɪnsens] *s* incenso || *tr* (*to burn incense for*) incensare || [ɪn'sens] *tr* irritare, esasperare

in'cense burn'er *s* (*person*) incensatore *m*; (*vessel*) incensiere *m*

incentive [ɪn'sentɪv] *adj & s* incentivo

inception [ɪn'sepʃən] *s* principio

incertitude [ɪn'sɑrtɪˌtjud] *or* [ɪn'sɑrtɪˌtud] *s* incertezza

incest ['ɪnsest] *s* incesto

incestuous [ɪn'sest/ʊ-əs] *adj* incestuoso

inch [ɪntʃ] *s* pollice *m*; **to be within an inch of** essere a due dita da || *intr*—**to inch ahead** spingersi avanti poco a poco

incidence ['ɪnsɪdəns] *s* incidenza

incident ['ɪnsɪdənt] *adj* incidente, incidentale || *s* incidente *m*

incidental [ˌɪnsɪ'dentəl] *adj* incidentale || *s* elemento incidentale; **incidentals** piccole spese

incidentally [ˌɪnsɪ'dentəli] *adv* incidentalmente, per inciso; a proposito

incinerator [ɪn'sɪnəˌretər] *s* inceneritore *m*

incision [ɪn'sɪʒən] *s* incisione

incisive [ɪn'saɪsɪv] *adj* incisivo

incite [ɪn'saɪt] *tr* incitare, stimulare

inclemen·cy [ɪn'klemənsi] *s* (**-cies**) inclemenza

inclination [ˌɪnklɪ'neʃən] *s* inclinazione

incline ['ɪnklaɪn] *or* [ɪn'klaɪn] *s* declivio || [ɪn'klaɪn] *tr* inclinare || *intr* inclinarsi

inclose [ɪn'kloz] *tr* includere, accludere; **to inclose herewith** accludere alla presente

inclosure [ɪn'kloʒər] *s* (*land surrounded by fence*) recinto; (*e.g., letter*) allegato

include [ɪn'klud] *tr* includere; **including** incluso, e.g., **three books including the grammar** tre libri inclusa la grammatica

inclusive [ɪn'klusɪv] *adj* incluso, e.g., **until next Friday inclusive** fino a venerdì prossimo incluso; **inclusive of** inclusivo di, e.g., **price inclusive of freight** prezzo inclusivo delle spese di trasporto

incogni·to [ɪn'kɑgnɪˌto] *adj* incognito || *s* (**-tos**) incognito || *adv* in incognito

incoherent [ˌɪnko'hɪrənt] *adj* incoerente

incombustible [ˌɪnkəm'bʌstɪbəl] *adj* incombustibile

income ['ɪnkʌm] *s* reddito, provento

in'come tax' *s* imposta sul reddito

incoming ['ɪnˌkʌmɪŋ] *adj* entrante; futuro; (*tide*) ascendente || *s* entrata

incomparable [ɪn'kɑmpərəbəl] *adj* incomparabile, impareggiabile

incompatible [ˌɪnkəm'pætɪbəl] *adj* incompatibile

incomplete [ˌɪnkəm'plit] *adj* incompleto, tronco, scompleto

incomprehensible [ˌɪnkɑmprɪ'hensɪbəl] *adj* incomprensibile

inconceivable [ˌɪnkən'sivəbəl] *adj* inconcepibile

inconclusive [ˌɪnkən'klusɪv] *adj* inconcludente

incongruous [ɪn'kɑŋgru-əs] *adj* incongruo

inconsequential [ɪnˌkɑnsɪ'kwenʃəl] *adj* (*lacking proper sequence of thought or speech*) inconseguente; (*trivial*) di poca importanza

inconsiderate [ˌɪnkən'sɪdərɪt] *adj* inconsiderato, sconsiderato

inconsisten·cy [ˌɪnkən'sɪstənsi] *s* (**-cies**) inconsistenza

inconsistent [ˌɪnkən'sɪstənt] *adj* inconsistente, inconseguente

inconsolable [ˌɪnkən'soləbəl] *adj* inconsolabile, sconsolato

inconspicuous [ˌɪnkən'spɪkju-əs] *adj* poco appariscente, poco apparente

inconstant [ɪn'kɑnstənt] *adj* incostante

incontinence [ɪn'kɑntɪnəns] *s* incontinenza

incontrovertible [ɪnˌkɑntrə'vʌrtɪbəl] *adj* incontrovertibile

inconvenience [ˌɪnkən'vini-əns] *s* scomodo, incomodo || *tr* scomodare

inconvenient [ˌɪnkən'vini-ənt] *adj* incomodo, inconveniente

incorporate [ɪn'kɔrpəˌret] *tr* incorporare; costituire in società anonima || *intr* incorporarsi; costituirsi in società anonima

incorrect [ˌɪnkə'rekt] *adj* scorretto

increase ['ɪnkris] *s* aumento; crescita; **to be on the increase** essere in aumento || [ɪn'kris] *tr* aumentare; (*by propagation*) moltiplicare || *intr* aumentare; moltiplicarsi

increasingly [ɪn'krisɪŋli] *adv* sempre più

incredible [ɪn'kredɪbəl] *adj* incredibile

incredulous [ɪn'kredʒələs] *adj* incredulo

increment ['ɪnkrɪmənt] *s* aumento, incremento

incriminate [ɪn'krɪmɪˌnet] *tr* incriminare

incrust [ɪn'krʌst] *tr* incrostare

incubate ['ɪnkjəˌbet] *tr* incubare || *intr* essere in incubazione; (*said, e.g., of a hen*) covare; (fig) covare

incubator ['ɪnkjəˌbetər] *s* incubatrice *f*

inculcate [ɪn'kʌlket] *or* ['ɪnkʌlˌket] *tr* inculcare

incumben·cy [ɪnˈkʌmbənsi] s (-cies) incombenza

incumbent [ɪnˈkʌmbənt] adj—**to be incumbent on** incombere a, spettare a || s titolare mf

incunabula [ˌɪnkjʊˈnæbjələ] spl (beginnings) origini fpl; (early printed books) incunaboli mpl

in·cur [ɪnˈkʌr] v (pret & pp -curred; ger -curring) tr incorrere in; (a debt) assumere, contrarre

incurable [ɪnˈkjʊrəbəl] adj & s incurabile mf

incursion [ɪnˈkʌrʒən] or [ɪnˈkʌrʃən] s incursione, scorreria

indebted [ɪnˈdetɪd] adj indebitato; obbligato

indecen·cy [ɪnˈdisənsi] s (-cies) indecenza, sconcezza

indecent [ɪnˈdisənt] adj indecente, sconveniente

indecisive [ˌɪndɪˈsaɪsɪv] adj indeciso; (e.g., event) non decisivo

indeed [ɪnˈdid] adv difatti, infatti || interj davvero!

indefatigable [ˌɪndɪˈfætɪgəbəl] adj indefesso, infaticabile

indefensible [ˌɪndɪˈfensɪbəl] adj indifendibile, insostenibile

indefinable [ˌɪndɪˈfaɪnəbəl] adj indefinibile

indefinite [ɪnˈdefɪnɪt] adj indefinito

indelible [ɪnˈdelɪbəl] adj indelebile

indemnification [ɪnˌdemnɪfɪˈkeʃən] s indennità f, indennizzo

indemni·fy [ɪnˈdemnɪˌfaɪ] v (pret & pp -fied) tr indennizzare

indemni·ty [ɪnˈdemnɪti] s (-ties) indennità f, indennizzo

indent [ɪnˈdent] tr frastagliare, dentellare; (typ) far rientrare

indentation [ˌɪndenˈteʃən] s frastaglio, dentellatura; (typ) accapo

indenture [ɪnˈdentʃər] s scrittura pubblica; contratto di apprendista || tr obbligare per contratto

independence [ˌɪndɪˈpendəns] s indipendenza

independent [ˌɪndɪˈpendənt] adj & s indipendente mf

indescribable [ˌɪndɪˈskraɪbəbəl] adj indescrivibile

indestructible [ˌɪndɪˈstrʌktɪbəl] adj indistruttibile

indeterminate [ˌɪndɪˈtʌrmɪnɪt] adj indeterminato

index [ˈɪndeks] s (indexes or indices [ˈɪndɪˌsiz]) indice m; (typ) indice m indicatore || tr mettere un indice a; mettere all'indice || Index s Indice m

in'dex card' s scheda di catalogo

in'dex fin'ger s dito indice

India [ˈɪndɪə] s l'India f

In'dia ink' s inchiostro di china

Indian [ˈɪndɪən] adj & s indiano

In'dian club' s clava di ginnastica

In'dian corn' s granoturco

In'dian file' s fila indiana || adv in fila indiana

In'dian O'cean s Oceano Indiano

In'dian sum'mer s estate f di San Martino

In'dian wres'tling s braccio di ferro

In'dia pa'per s carta bibbia, carta d'India

In'dia rub'ber s cacciù m

indicate [ˈɪndɪˌket] tr indicare

indication [ˌɪndɪˈkeʃən] s indicazione

indicative [ɪnˈdɪkətɪv] adj & s indicativo

indicator [ˈɪndɪˌketər] s indicatore m, indice m

indict [ɪnˈdaɪt] tr accusare

indictment [ɪnˈdaɪtmənt] s accusa, atto d'accusa

indifferent [ɪnˈdɪfərənt] adj indifferente; (not particularly good) passabile

indigenous [ɪnˈdɪdʒɪnəs] adj indigeno

indigent [ˈɪndɪdʒənt] adj indigente || **the indigent** gli indigenti

indigestion [ˌɪndɪˈdʒestʃən] s indigestione

indignant [ɪnˈdɪgnənt] adj indignato

indignation [ˌɪndɪgˈneʃən] s indignazione

indigni·ty [ɪnˈdɪgnɪti] s (-ties) indignità f

indi·go [ˈɪndɪˌgo] adj indaco || s (-gos or -goes) indaco

indirect [ˌɪndɪˈrekt] or [ˌɪndaɪˈrekt] adj indiretto

in'direct dis'course s discorso indiretto

indiscernible [ˌɪndɪˈzʌrnɪbəl] or [ˌɪndɪˈsʌrnɪbəl] adj indiscernibile

indiscreet [ˌɪndɪsˈkrit] adj indiscreto

indispensable [ˌɪndɪsˈpensəbəl] adj indispensabile, imprescindibile

indispose [ˌɪndɪsˈpoz] tr indisporre

indisposed [ˌɪndɪsˈpozd] adj (disinclined) mal disposto; (slightly ill) indisposto

indissoluble [ˌɪndɪˈsɑljəbəl] adj indissolubile

indistinct [ˌɪndɪsˈtɪŋkt] adj indistinto

indite [ɪnˈdaɪt] tr redigere

individual [ˌɪndɪˈvɪdʒuəl] adj individuale || s individuo

individuali·ty [ˌɪndɪˌvɪdʒuˈælɪti] s (-ties) individualità f; (person of distinctive character) individuo

Indochina [ˈɪndoˈtʃaɪnə] s l'Indocina f

Indo-Chi·nese [ˈɪndoˈtʃaɪˈniz] adj indocinese || s (-nese) indocinese mf

Indo-European [ˈɪndoˌjʊrəˈpiən] adj & s indoeuropeo

indolent [ˈɪndələnt] adj indolente

Indonesia [ˌɪndoˈniʒə] or [ˌɪndoˈniʒə] s l'Indonesia f

Indonesian [ˌɪndoˈniʒən] or [ˌɪndoˈniʒən] adj & s indonesiano

indoor [ˈɪnˌdor] adj situato in casa; da farsi in casa

indoors [ˈɪnˈdorz] adv dentro, a casa, al coperto

indorse [ɪnˈdors] tr (com) girare; (fig) appoggiare, approvare

indorsee [ˌɪndorˈsi] s giratario

indorsement [ɪnˈdorsmənt] s (com) girata; (fig) appoggio, approvazione

indorser [ɪnˈdorsər] s girante mf

induce [ɪnˈdjus] or [ɪnˈdus] tr indurre

inducement [ɪnˈdjusmənt] or [ɪnˈdusmənt] s stimolo, incentivo

induct [ɪn'dʌkt] *tr* installare; iniziare; (mil) arruolare

induction [ɪn'dʌkʃən] *s* iniziazione; (elec & log) induzione; (mil) arruolamento

indulge [ɪn'dʌldʒ] *tr* indulgere (with *dat*) || *intr* cedere, lasciarsi andare; **to indulge in** abbandonarsi a; permettersi il lusso di

indulgence [ɪn'dʌldʒəns] *s* compiacenza; intemperanza, abbandono; (*leniency*) indulgenza

indulgent [ɪn'dʌldʒənt] *adj* indulgente

industrial [ɪn'dʌstrɪəl] *adj* industriale

industrialist [ɪn'dʌstrɪəlɪst] *s* industriale *m*

industrialize [ɪn'dʌstrɪə,laɪz] *tr* industrializzare

industrious [ɪn'dʌstrɪəs] *adj* industrioso, laborioso

indus•try [ˈɪndʌstrɪ] *s* (**-tries**) industria

inebriation [ɪn,ibrɪ'eʃən] *s* ubriachezza

inedible [ɪn'edɪbəl] *adj* immangiabile

ineffable [ɪn'efəbəl] *adj* ineffabile

ineffective [,ɪnɪ'fektɪv] *adj* inefficace; (*person*) incapace

ineffectual [,ɪnɪ'fektʃʊ•əl] *adj* inefficace

inefficient [,ɪnɪ'fɪʃənt] *adj* inefficiente

ineligible [ɪn'elɪdʒɪbəl] *adj* ineleggibile

inequali•ty [,ɪnɪ'kwɑlɪti] *s* (**-ties**) disuguaglianza

inequi•ty [ɪn'ekwɪti] *s* (**-ties**) ingiustizia

ineradicable [,ɪnɪ'rædɪkəbəl] *adj* inestirpabile

inertia [ɪn'ʌrʃe] *s* inerzia

inescapable [,ɪnes'kepəbəl] *adj* ineluttabile, inderogabile

inevitable [ɪn'evɪtəbəl] *adj* inevitabile

inexact [,ɪneg'zækt] *adj* inesatto

inexcusable [,ɪneks'kjuzəbəl] *adj* inescusabile

inexhaustible [,ɪneg'zɔstɪbəl] *adj* inesauribile

inexorable [ɪn'eksərəbəl] *adj* inesorabile

inexpedient [,ɪnek'spidɪ•ənt] *adj* inopportuno

inexpensive [,ɪnek'spensɪv] *adj* poco costoso, a buon mercato

inexperience [,ɪnek'spɪrɪ•əns] *s* inesperienza

inexplicable [ɪn'eksplɪkəbəl] *adj* inesplicabile

inexpressible [,ɪnek'spresɪbəl] *adj* indicibile, inesprimibile

infallible [ɪn'fælɪbəl] *adj* infallibile

infamous [ˈɪnfəməs] *adj* infame

infa•my [ˈɪnfəmi] *s* (**-mies**) infamia

infan•cy [ˈɪnfənsi] *s* (**-cies**) infanzia

infant [ˈɪnfənt] *adj* infantile; (*in the earliest stage*) (fig) nascente || *s* neonato, bebè *m*

infantile [ˈɪnfən,taɪl] or [ˈɪnfəntɪl] *adj* infantile

infan•try [ˈɪnfəntri] *s* (**-tries**) fanteria

in'fantry•man *s* (**-men**) fante *m*

infatuated [ɪn'fætʃʊ,etɪd] *adj* infatuato

infect [ɪn'fekt] *tr* infettare

infection [ɪn'fekʃən] *s* infezione

infectious [ɪn'fekʃəs] *adj* infettivo

in•fer [ɪn'fʌr] *v* (*pret & pp* **-ferred;** *ger* **-ferring**) *tr* inferire; (coll) dedurre, supporre

inferior [ɪn'fɪrɪ•ər] *adj & s* inferiore *m*

inferiority [ɪn,fɪrɪ'ɑrɪti] *s* inferiorità *f*

inferior'ity com'plex *s* complesso di inferiorità

infernal [ɪn'fʌrnəl] *adj* infernale

infest [ɪn'fest] *tr* infestare

infidel [ˈɪnfɪdəl] *adj & s* infedele *mf*

infideli•ty [,ɪnfɪ'delɪti] *s* (**-ties**) infedeltà *f*

in'field *s* campo interno, diamante *m*

infiltrate [ɪn'fɪltret] or [ˈɪnfɪl,tret] *tr* infiltrarsi in || *intr* infiltrarsi

infinite [ˈɪnfɪnɪt] *adj & s* infinito

infinitive [ɪn'fɪnɪtɪv] *adj* infinitivo || *s* infinito

infini•ty [ɪn'fɪnɪti] *s* (**-ties**) infinità *f*; (math) infinito

infirm [ɪn'fʌrm] *adj* infermo; (*not firm*) debole

infirma•ry [ɪn'fʌrməri] *s* (**-ries**) infermeria

infirmi•ty [ɪn'fʌrmɪti] *s* (**-ties**) infermità *f*

inflame [ɪn'flem] *tr* infiammare || *intr* infiammarsi

inflammable [ɪn'flæməbəl] *adj* infiammabile

inflammation [,ɪnflə'meʃən] *s* infiammazione

inflate [ɪn'flet] *tr* gonfiare; (*currency, prices*) inflazionare || *intr* gonfiarsi

inflation [ɪn'fleʃən] *s* inflazione; (*of a tire*) gonfiatura

inflect [ɪn'flekt] *tr* curvare; (*voice*) modulare; (gram) flettere

inflection [ɪn'flekʃən] *s* inflessione; (gram) flessione

inflexible [ɪn'fleksɪbəl] *adj* inflessibile

inflict [ɪn'flɪkt] *tr* infliggere, inferire

influence [ˈɪnflu•əns] *s* influenza || *tr* influire su, influenzare

influential [,ɪnflu'enʃəl] *adj* influente

influenza [,ɪnflu'enzə] *s* influenza

inform [ɪn'fɔrm] *tr* informare || *intr* dare informazioni; **to inform on** denunziare, fare la spia contro

informal [ɪn'fɔrməl] *adj* non ufficiale, ufficioso; (*unceremonious*) alla buona, familiare

informant [ɪn'fɔrmənt] *s* informatore *m*; (*informer*) delatore *m*; (ling) fonte *f* orale, informatore *m*

information [,ɪnfər'meʃən] *s* informazioni *fpl*; conoscenze *fpl*

informational [,ɪnfər'meʃənəl] *adj* informativo

informed' sour'ces *spl* fonti *fpl* attendibili

informer [ɪn'fɔrmər] *s* (*informant*) informatore *m*; (*spy*) delatore *m*

infraction [ɪn'frækʃən] *s* infrazione

infrared [,ɪnfrə'red] *adj & s* infrarosso

infrequent [ɪn'frikwənt] *adj* infrequente

infringe [ɪn'frɪndʒ] *tr* violare || *intr* **to infringe on** or **upon** violare, contravvenire a

infringement [ɪn'frɪndʒmənt] *s* infrazione

infuriate [ɪnˈfjʊrɪ ˌet] *tr* infuriare
infuse [ɪnˈfjuz] *tr* infondere
infusion [ɪnˈfjuʒən] *s* infusione
ingenious [ɪnˈdʒinjəs] *adj* ingegnoso
ingenui·ty [ˌɪndʒɪˈnu·ɪti] *or* [ˌɪndʒɪˈnju·ɪti] *s* ingegnosità *f*
ingenuous [ɪnˈdʒɛnju·əs] *adj* ingenuo
ingenuousness [ɪnˈdʒɛnju·əsnɪs] *s* ingenuità *f*
ingest [ɪnˈdʒɛst] *tr* ingerire
ingoing [ˈɪnˌgoɪŋ] *adj* entrante
ingot [ˈɪngət] *s* lingotto, massello
ingraft [ɪnˈgræft] *or* [ɪnˈgrɑft] *tr* (hort & surg) innestare; (fig) inculcare
ingrate [ˈɪngret] *s* ingrato
ingratiate [ɪnˈgreʃɪ ˌet] *tr*—**to ingratiate oneself with** ingraziarsi
ingratiating [ɪnˈgreʃɪ ˌetɪŋ] *adj* attraente, affascinante, insinuante
ingratitude [ɪnˈgrætɪ ˌtjud] *or* [ɪnˈgrætɪ ˌtud] *s* ingratitudine *f*
ingredient [ɪnˈgridɪ·ənt] *s* ingrediente *m*
in'grown nail' [ˈɪngron] *s* unghia incarnita
ingulf [ɪnˈgʌlf] *tr* sommergere, inondare
inhabit [ɪnˈhæbɪt] *tr* abitare, popolare
inhabitant [ɪnˈhæbɪtənt] *s* abitante *mf*
inhale [ɪnˈhel] *tr & intr* inspirare
inherent [ɪnˈhɪrənt] *adj* inerente
inherit [ɪnˈhɛrɪt] *tr & intr* ereditare
inheritance [ɪnˈhɛrɪtəns] *s* eredità *f*
inheritor [ɪnˈhɛrɪtər] *s* erede *mf*
inhibit [ɪnˈhɪbɪt] *tr* inibire
inhospitable [ɪnˈhɑspɪtəbəl] *or* [ˌɪnhɑsˈpɪtəbəl] *adj* inospitale
inhuman [ɪnˈhjumən] *adj* inumano
inhumane [ˌɪnhjuˈmen] *adj* inumano
inimical [ɪˈnɪmɪkəl] *adj* nemico
iniqui·ty [ɪˈnɪkwɪti] *s* (**-ties**) iniquità *f*
ini·tial [ɪˈnɪʃəl] *adj & s* iniziale *f* ‖ *v* (*pret* **-tialed** *or* **-tialled**; *ger* **-tialing** *or* **-tialling**) *tr* siglare
initiate [ɪˈnɪʃɪ ˌet] *tr* iniziare
initiation [ɪ ˌnɪʃɪˈeʃən] *s* iniziazione
initiative [ɪˈnɪʃɪ·ətɪv] *or* [ɪˈnɪʃətɪv] *s* iniziativa
inject [ɪnˈdʒɛkt] *tr* iniettare; introdurre
injection [ɪnˈdʒɛkʃən] *s* iniezione
injudicious [ˌɪndʒuˈdɪʃəs] *adj* avventato, sconsiderato
injunction [ɪnˈdʒʌŋkʃən] *s* ingiunzione
injure [ˈɪndʒər] *tr* (*to harm*) danneggiare; (*to wound*) ferire; (*to offend*) offendere, ingiuriare
injurious [ɪnˈdʒʊrɪ·əs] *adj* dannoso, offensivo, ingiurioso
inju·ry [ˈɪndʒəri] *s* (**-ries**) (*harm*) danno; (*wound*) ferita, lesione; offesa, ingiuria
injustice [ɪnˈdʒʌstɪs] *s* ingiustizia
ink [ɪŋk] *s* inchiostro ‖ *tr* inchiostrare
inkling [ˈɪŋklɪŋ] *s* sentore *m*, indizio
ink'stand' *s* (*container*) calamaio; (*stand*) calamaiera
ink'well' *s* calamaio
ink·y [ˈɪŋki] *adj* (**-ier**; **-iest**) nero come l'inchiostro; nero d'inchiostro
inlaid [ˈɪn ˌled] *or* [ˌɪnˈled] *adj* intarsiato, incrostato

inland [ˈɪnlənd] *adj & s* interno ‖ *adv* verso l'interno
in'-law' *s* affine *mf*
in·lay [ˈɪn ˌle] *s* intarsio, tassello ‖ [ɪnˈle] *or* [ˈɪn ˌle] *v* (*pret & pp* **-laid**) *tr* intarsiare
in'let *s* (*of the shore*) insenatura; (*entrance*) ammissione
in'mate' *s* (*patient, e.g., in an insane asylum*) internato; (*in a jail*) prigioniero
inn [ɪn] *s* taverna, osteria
innate [ɪˈnet] *or* [ˈɪnet] *adj* innato
inner [ˈɪnər] *adj* interno, interiore; intimo, profondo
in'ner·spring' mat'tress *s* materasso a molle
in'ner tube' *s* camera d'aria
inning [ˈɪnɪŋ] *s* (baseball) turno
inn'keep'er *s* locandiere *m*, oste *m*
innocence [ˈɪnəsəns] *s* innocenza
innocent [ˈɪnəsənt] *adj & s* innocente *mf*
innovate [ˈɪnə ˌvet] *tr* innovare
innovation [ˌɪnəˈveʃən] *s* innovazione
innuen·do [ˌɪnjuˈɛndo] *s* (**-does**) sottinteso, insinuazione
innumerable [ɪˈnjumərəbəl] *or* [ɪˈnumərəbəl] *adj* innumerevole
inoculate [ɪnˈɑkjə ˌlet] *tr* inoculare; (*e.g., with hatred*) inoculare; permeare
inoculation [ɪn ˌɑkjəˈleʃən] *s* inoculazione
inoffensive [ˌɪnəˈfɛnsɪv] *adj* inoffensivo
inopportune [ɪn ˌɑpərˈtjun] *or* [ɪn ˌɑpərˈtun] *adj* inopportuno
inordinate [ɪnˈɔrdɪnɪt] *adj* smoderato
inorganic [ˌɪnɔrˈgænɪk] *adj* inorganico
in'pa'tient *s* degente *mf*
in'put' *s* entrata; (elec, mach) energia immessa
inquest [ˈɪnkwɛst] *s* inchiesta
inquire [ɪnˈkwaɪr] *tr* domandare, chiedere ‖ *intr*—**to inquire about, after,** *or* **for** chiedere di; **to inquire into** investigare
inquir·y [ɪnˈkwaɪri] *or* [ˈɪnkwɪri] *s* (**-ies**) indagine *f*, inchiesta
inquisition [ˌɪnkwɪˈzɪʃən] *s* inquisizione
inquisitive [ɪnˈkwɪzɪtɪv] *adj* indagatore, curioso
in'road' *s* incursione, invasione
insane [ɪnˈsen] *adj* pazzo, matto
insane' asy'lum *s* manicomio
insani·ty [ɪnˈsænɪti] *s* (**-ties**) pazzia, follia, demenza
insatiable [ɪnˈseʃəbəl] *adj* insaziabile
inscribe [ɪnˈskraɪb] *tr* iscrivere; (*a book*) dedicare; (geom) inscrivere
inscription [ɪnˈskrɪpʃən] *s* scritta, iscrizione; (*of a book*) dedica
inscrutable [ɪnˈskrutəbəl] *adj* imperscrutabile
insect [ˈɪnsɛkt] *s* insetto
insecticide [ɪnˈsɛktɪ ˌsaɪd] *adj & s* setticida *m*
insecure [ˌɪnsɪˈkjur] *adj* malsicuro
inseparable [ɪnˈsɛpərəbəl] *adj* inseparabile

insert ['ınsʌrt] *s* inserzione; (*circular*) inserto || [ın'sʌrt] *tr* inserire

insertion [ın'sʌr/ən] *s* inserzione; (*in lunar orbit*) immissione; (*of lace*) tramezzo

in·set ['ın‚set] *s* intercalazione || [ın-'set] or ['ın‚set] *v* (*pret & pp* **-set;** *ger* **-setting**) *tr* intercalare

in'shore' *adj & adv* vicino alla spiaggia

in'side' *adj* interno; privato, confidenziale || *s* interno; **insides** (coll) interiora *fpl;* **to be on the inside** avere informazioni confidenziali || *adv* dentro; all'interno; **inside of** dentro, dentro a, dentro di; **to turn inside out** rovesciare, voltare il diritto al rovescio || *prep* dentro, dentro a

in'side flap' *s* (bb) risvolto

insider [‚ın'saıdər] *s* persona informata

in'side track' *s* (racing) steccato; **to have the inside track** (coll) trovarsi in una situazione vantaggiosa

insidious [ın'sıdı·əs] *adj* insidioso

in'sight' *s* intuito, penetrazione

insigni·a [ın'sıgnı·ə] *s* (-a or -as) distintivo; (*distinguishing sign*) segno

insignificant [‚ınsıg'nıfıkənt] *adj* insignificante

insincere [‚ınsın'sır] *adj* insincero

insinuate [ın'sınju‚et] *tr* insinuare

insist [ın'sıst] *intr* insistere

insofar as [‚ınso'far‚æz] *conj* per quanto

insolence ['ınsələns] *s* insolenza

insolent ['ınsələnt] *adj* insolente

insoluble [ın'saljəbəl] *adj* insolubile

insolven·cy [ın'salvənsi] *s* (-cies) insolvenza

insomnia [ın'samnı·ə] *s* insonnia

insomuch [‚ınso'mʌt/] *adv* fino al punto; **insomuch as** giacché, visto che; **insomuch that** fino al punto che

inspect [ın'spekt] *tr* ispezionare

inspection [ın'spek/ən] *s* ispezione

inspector [ın'spektər] *s* ispettore *m*

inspiration [‚ınspı're/ən] *s* ispirazione

inspire [ın'spaır] *tr & intr* ispirare

install [ın'stɔl] *tr* istallare

installment [ın'stɔlmənt] *s* rata; (*of a book*) dispensa; **in installments** a rate

install'ment plan' *s* pagamento rateale; **on the installment plan** con facilitazioni di pagamento

instance ['ınstəns] *s* esempio; (law) istanza; **for instance** per esempio

instant ['ınstənt] *adj* istantaneo || *s* istante *m;* mese *m* corrente

instantaneous [‚ınstən'tenı·əs] *adj* istantaneo

instantly ['ınstəntli] *adv* immediatamente, istantaneamente

instead [ın'sted] *adv* invece; **instead of** invece di

in'step' *s* collo del piede

instigate ['ınstı‚get] *tr* istigare

instigation [‚ınstı'ge/ən] *s* istigazione

in·still' *tr* instillare, istillare

instinct ['ınstıŋkt] *s* istinto

instinctive [ın'stıŋktıv] *adj* istintivo

institute ['ınstı‚tjut] or ['ınstı‚tut] *s* istituto || *tr* istituire

institution [‚ınstı'tju/ən] or [‚ınstı-'tu/ən] *s* istituzione

institutionalize [‚ınstı'tju/ənə‚laız] or [‚ınstı'tu/ənə‚laız] *tr* istituzionalizzare

instruct [ın'strʌkt] *tr* istruire

instruction [ın'strʌk/ən] *s* istruzione

instructive [ın'strʌktıv] *adj* istruttivo

instructor [ın'strʌktər] *s* istruttore *m*

instrument ['ınstrəmənt] *s* strumento; (law) istrumento || ['ınstrə‚ment] *tr* strumentare

instrumental [‚ınstrə'mentəl] *adj* strumentale; **to be instrumental in** contribuire a

instrumentalist [‚ınstrə'mentəlıst] *s* strumentista *mf*

instrumentali·ty [‚ınstrəmən'tælıti] *s* (-ties) mediazione, aiuto

in'strument fly'ing *s* volo strumentale

in'strument pan'el *s* (aut) cruscotto

insubordinate [‚ınsə'bɔrdınıt] *adj* insubordinato

insufferable [ın'sʌfərəbəl] *adj* insoffribile

insufficient [‚ınsə'fı/ənt] *adj* insufficiente

insular [‚ınsələr] or ['ınsjulər] *adj* insulare; (*e.g., attitude*) gretto

insulate ['ınsə‚let] *tr* isolare

in'sulating tape' ['ınsəletıŋ] *s* nastro isolante

insulation [‚ınsə'le/ən] *s* isolamento

insulator ['ınsə‚letər] *s* isolatore *m*

insulin ['ınsəlın] *s* insulina

insult ['ınsʌlt] *s* insulto || [ın'sʌlt] *tr* insultare, insolentire

insulting [ın'sʌltıŋ] *adj* insultante

insurance [ın'/urəns] *s* assicurazione

insure [ın'/ur] *tr* assicurare

insurer [ın'/urər] *s* assicuratore *m*

insurgent [ın'sʌrdʒənt] *adj & s* insorgente *mf*

insurmountable [‚ınsər'mauntəbəl] *adj* insormontabile

insurrection [‚ınsə'rek/ən] *s* insurrezione

insusceptible [‚ınsə'septıbəl] *adj* non suscettibile

intact [ın'tækt] *adj* intatto, integro

in'take' *s* (*place of taking in*) entrata; (*act of taking in*) ammissione; (mach) presa, immissione, aspirazione

in'take man'ifold' *s* collettore *m* d'ammissione

intangible [ın'tændʒıbəl] *adj* intangibile; (fig) vago, inafferrabile

integer ['ıntıdʒər] *s* numero intero

integral ['ıntıgrəl] *adj* integrale; (*part of a whole*) integrante || *s* (math) integrale *m*

integration [‚ıntı'gre/ən] *s* integrazione

integrity [ın'tegrıti] *s* integrità *f*

intellect ['ıntə‚lekt] *s* intelletto

intellectual [‚ıntə'lekt/u·əl] *adj & s* intellettuale *mf*

intelligence [ın'telıdʒəns] *s* intelligenza; informazione, conoscenza intel'ligence bu'reau *s* ufficio spionaggi

intel'ligence quo'tient *s* quoziente *m* d'intelligenza

intelligent [ɪn'telɪdʒənt] *adj* intelligente

intelligentsia [ɪn,telɪ'dʒentsɪ·ə] or [ɪn,telɪ'gentsɪ·ə] *s* intellighenzia, intellettualità *f*

intelligible [ɪn'telɪdʒɪbəl] *adj* intelligibile, comprensibile

intemperance [ɪn'tempərəns] *s* intemperanza, sregolatezza

intemperate [ɪn'tempərɪt] *adj* intemperante; (*climate*) rigoroso

intend [ɪn'tend] *tr* intendere, prefiggersi; (*to mean for a particular purpose*) destinare; (*to signify*) voler dire

intendance [ɪn'tendəns] *s* intendenza

intendant [ɪn'tendənt] *s* intendente *m*

intended [ɪn'tendɪd] *adj & s* (coll) promesso, promessa

intense [ɪn'tens] *adj* intenso

intensi·fy [ɪn'tensɪ·faɪ] *v* (*pret & pp* -fied) *tr* intensificare, rinforzare; (phot) rinforzare ǁ *intr* intensificarsi, rinforzarsi

intensi·ty [ɪn'tensɪti] *s* (-ties) intensità *f*

intensive [ɪn'tensɪv] *adj* intensivo

intent [ɪn'tent] *adj* intento, attento; intent on deciso a ǁ *s* (*purpose*) intento, scopo; (*meaning*) significato; to all intents and purposes virtualmente, in realtà

intention [ɪn'tenʃən] *s* intenzione

intentional [ɪn'tenʃənəl] *adj* intenzionale, deliberato

intentionally [ɪn'tenʃənəli] *adv* apposta, deliberatamente

in·ter [ɪn'tʌr] *v* (*pret & pp* -terred; -terring) *tr* interrare, inumare

interact [,ɪntər'ækt] *intr* esercitare un'azione reciproca

interaction [,ɪntər'ækʃən] *s* azione reciproca

inter·breed [,ɪntər'brid] *s* (*pret & pp* -bred ['bred]) *tr* incrociare ǁ *intr* incrociarsi

intercalate [ɪn'tʌrkə,let] *tr* intercalare

intercede [,ɪntər'sid] *intr* intercedere

intercept [,ɪntər'sept] *tr* intercettare

interceptor [,ɪntər'septər] *s* (*person*) intercettatore *m*; (aer) intercettore *m*

interchange ['ɪntər,tʃendʒ] *s* interscambio; (*on a highway*) svincolo autostradale ǁ [,ɪntər'tʃendʒ] *tr* scambiare ǁ *intr* scambiarsi

intercollegiate [,ɪntərkə'lidʒɪ·ɪt] *adj* interscolastico, fra università

intercom ['ɪntər,kam] *s* citofono

intercourse ['ɪntər,kors] *s* comunicazione; (*of products, ideas, etc.*) scambio; (*copulation*) copula, coito; to have intercourse accoppiarsi sessualmente

intercross [,ɪntər'kras] or [,ɪntər'kras] *tr* incrociare ǁ *intr* incrociarsi

interdict ['ɪntər,dɪkt] *s* interdetto ǁ [,ɪntər'dɪkt] *tr* interdire; to interdict s.o. from + *ger* interdire a qlcu di + *inf*

interest ['ɪntərɪst] or ['ɪntrɪst] *s* in-

teresse *m;* the interests i potenti ǁ ['ɪntərɪst], ['ɪntrɪst] or ['ɪntə,rest] *tr* interessare

interested ['ɪntrɪstɪd] or ['ɪntə,restɪd] *adj* interessato

interesting ['ɪntrɪstɪŋ] or ['ɪntə,restɪŋ] *adj* interessante

interfere [,ɪntər'fɪr] *intr* interferire; (sports) ostacolare l'azione; to interfere with interferire in

interference [,ɪntər'fɪrəns] *s* interferenza

interim ['ɪntərɪm] *adj* interino ǁ *s* interim *m;* in the interim frattanto

interior [ɪn'tɪrɪ·ər] *adj & s* interno

interject [,ɪntər'dʒekt] *tr* interporre ǁ *intr* interporsi

interjection [,ɪntər'dʒekʃən] *s* interposizione; esclamazione; (gram) interiezione

interlard [,ɪntər'lard] *tr* infiorare, lardellare

interline [,ɪntər'laɪn] *tr* scrivere nell'interlinea di; (*a garment*) foderare con ovattina

interlining ['ɪntər,laɪnɪŋ] *s.* soppanno

interlink [,ɪntər'lɪŋk] *tr* concatenare

interlock [,ɪntər'lak] *tr* connettere ǁ *intr* connettersi

interlope [,ɪntər'lop] *intr* intromettersi; trafficare senza permesso

interloper [,ɪntər'lopər] *s* intruso

interlude ['ɪntər,lud] *s* interludio; (theat) intermezzo

intermarriage [,ɪntər,mærɪdʒ] *s* matrimonio tra consanguinei; matrimonio fra membri di razze diverse

intermediar·y [,ɪntər'midɪ,eri] *adj* intermediario ǁ (-ies) *s* intermediario

intermediate [,ɪntər'midɪ·ɪt] *adj* intermedio

interment [ɪn'tʌrmənt] *s* inumazione

intermingle [,ɪntər'mɪŋgəl] *tr* mescolare ǁ *intr* mescolarsi

intermission [,ɪntər'mɪʃən] *s* interruzione; (theat) intervallo

intermittent [,ɪntər'mɪtənt] *adj* intermittente

intermix [,ɪntər'mɪks] *tr* mescolare ǁ *intr* mescolarsi

intern ['ɪntʌrn] *s* interno ǁ [ɪn'tʌrn] *tr* internare

internal [ɪn'tʌrnəl] *adj* interno

inter'nal-combus'tion en'gine *s* motore *m* a combustione interna, motore *m* a scoppio

inter'nal rev'enue *s* fisco

international [,ɪntər'næʃənəl] *adj* internazionale

in'terna'tional date' line' *s* linea del cambiamento di data

internationalize [,ɪntər'næʃənə,laɪz] *tr* internazionalizzare

internecine [,ɪntər'nisɪn] *adj* micidiale, sanguinario

internee [,ɪntər'ni] *s* internato

internist [ɪn'tʌrnɪst] *s* internista *mf*

internment [ɪn'tʌrnmənt] *s* internamento

internship ['ɪntʌrn,ʃɪp] *s* tirocinio in un ospedale, internato

interpellate [ˌɪntər'pelet] or [ɪn'tʌrpɪˌlet] tr interpellare

interplanetary [ˌɪntər'plænəˌteri] adj interplanetario

interplay ['ɪntərˌple] s azione reciproca

interpolate [ɪn'tʌrpəˌlet] tr interpolare

interpose [ˌɪntər'poz] tr frapporre

interpret [ɪn'tʌrprɪt] tr interpretare

interpreter [ɪn'tʌrprətər] s interprete mf

interrogate [ɪn'terəˌget] tr & intr interrogare

interrogation [ɪnˌterə'geʃən] s interrogazione

interroga'tion mark' or **point'** s punto interrogativo

interrupt [ˌɪntə'rʌpt] tr interrompere

interruption [ˌɪntə'rʌpʃən] s interruzione

interscholastic [ˌɪntərskə'læstɪk] adj interscolastico

intersect [ˌɪntər'sekt] tr intersecare || intr intersecarsi

intersection [ˌɪntər'sekʃən] s (of streets, roads, etc.) crocevia m; (geom) intersezione

intersperse [ˌɪntər'spʌrs] tr cospargere, inframezzare

interstellar [ˌɪntər'stelər] adj interstellare

interstice [ɪn'tʌrstɪs] s interstizio

intertwine [ˌɪntər'twaɪn] tr intrecciare || intr intrecciarsi

interval ['ɪntərvəl] s intervallo; **at intervals** a intervalli; di tanto in tanto

intervene [ˌɪntər'vin] intr intervenire; (to happen) succedere

intervening [ˌɪntər'vinɪŋ] adj—**in the intervening time** nel frattempo

intervention [ˌɪntər'venʃən] s intervenzione

interview ['ɪntərˌvju] s intervista || tr intervistare

inter·weave [ˌɪntər'wiv] v (pret -wove ['wov] or -weaved; pp -wove, -woven or -weaved) tr intessere

intestate [ɪn'testet] or [ɪn'testɪt] adj intestato

intestine [ɪn'testɪn] s intestino

inthrall [ɪn'θrɔl] tr affascinare, incantare; (to subjugate) asservire, soggiogare

inthrone [ɪn'θron] tr mettere sul trono, intronizzare; esaltare, innalzare

intima·cy ['ɪntɪməsi] s (-cies) intimità f

intimate ['ɪntɪmɪt] adj & s intimo || ['ɪntɪˌmet] tr insinuare

intimation [ˌɪntɪ'meʃən] s insinuazione

intimidate [ɪn'tɪmɪˌdet] tr intimidire

into ['ɪntu] or ['ɪntu] prep in; verso; contro

intolerant [ɪn'talərənt] adj & s intollerante mf, insofferente mf

intomb [ɪn'tum] tr inumare, seppellire

intombment [ɪn'tummənt] s sepoltura

intonation [ˌɪnto'neʃən] s intonazione

intone [ɪn'ton] tr intonare || intr salmodiare

intoxicant [ɪn'taksɪkənt] s bevanda alcoolica

intoxicate [ɪn'taksɪˌket] tr ubriacare; esilarare; (to poison) avvelenare, intossicare

intoxication [ɪnˌtaksɪ'keʃən] s ubriachezza; ebbrezza, allegria; (poisoning) avvelenamento, intossicazione

intractable [ɪn'træktəbəl] adj intrattabile

intransigent [ɪn'trænsɪdʒənt] adj & s intransigente mf

intransitive [ɪn'trænsɪtɪv] adj intransitivo

intravenous [ˌɪntrə'vinəs] adj intravenoso, endovenoso

intrench [ɪn'trentʃ] tr & intr var of entrench

intrepid [ɪn'trepɪd] adj intrepido

intrepidity [ˌɪntrɪ'pɪdɪti] s intrepidezza

intricate ['ɪntrɪkɪt] adj intricato

intrigue [ɪn'trig] or ['ɪntrig] s intrigo; tresca, intrigo amoroso; (theat) intreccio || [ɪn'trig] tr incuriosire || intr intrigare; trescare

intrinsic(al) [ɪn'trɪnsɪk(əl)] adj intrinseco

introduce [ˌɪntrə'djus] or [ˌɪntrə'dus] tr introdurre; (a product) lanciare; (a person) presentare

introduction [ˌɪntrə'dʌkʃən] s introduzione; presentazione

introductory [ˌɪntrə'dʌktəri] adj introduttivo

introit ['ɪntro·ɪt] s (eccl) introito

introspective [ˌɪntrə'spektɪv] adj introspettivo

introvert ['ɪntrəˌvʌrt] adj & s introverso

intrude [ɪn'trud] intr intrudersi, intrufolarsi

intruder [ɪn'trudər] s intruso; importuno

intrusion [ɪn'truʒən] s intrusione

intrusive [ɪn'trusɪv] adj invadente

intrust [ɪn'trʌst] tr affidare, confidare

intuition [ˌɪntu·'ɪʃən] or [ˌɪntju·'ɪʃən] s intuizione, intuito

inundate ['ɪnənˌdet] tr inondare

inundation [ˌɪnən'deʃən] s inondazione

inure [ɪn'jur] tr indurire, assuefare || intr entrare in vigore; **to inure to** ridondare in favore di

invade [ɪn'ved] tr invadere

invader [ɪn'vedər] s invasore m

invalid [ɪn'vælɪd] adj (non valid) invalido || ['ɪnvəlɪd] adj (person) invalido; (thing) povero; (diet) per malati || ['ɪnvəlɪd] s invalido

invalidate [ɪn'vælɪˌdet] tr invalidare

invalidity [ˌɪnvə'lɪdɪti] s invalidità f

invaluable [ɪn'vælju·əbəl] adj inestimabile, inapprezzabile

invariable [ɪn'veri·əbəl] adj invariabile

invasion [ɪn'veʒən] s invasione

invective [ɪn'vektɪv] s invettiva

inveigh [ɪn've] intr—**to inveigh against** inveire contro

inveigle [ɪn'vegəl] or [ɪn'vigəl] tr sedurre, abbindolare

invent [ɪn'vent] tr inventare

invention [ɪn'venʃən] s invenzione

inventiveness [ɪnˈvɛntɪvnɪs] *s* inventiva
inventor [ɪnˈvɛntər] *s* inventore *m*
invento·ry [ˈɪnvənˌtori] *s* (**-ries**) inventario || *v* (*pret & pp* **-ried**) *tr* inventariare
inverse [ɪnˈvʌrs] *adj & s* inverso
inversion [ɪnˈvʌrʒən] *or* [ɪnˈvʌrʃən] *s* inversione
invert [ˈɪnvʌrt] *s* invertito || [ɪnˈvʌrt] *tr* invertire
invertebrate [ɪnˈvʌrtɪˌbret] *or* [ɪnˈvʌrtɪbrɪt] *adj & s* invertebrato
invest [ɪnˈvɛst] *tr* investire || *intr* fare un investimento; fare investimenti
investigate [ɪnˈvɛstɪˌget] *tr* investigare
investigation [ɪnˌvɛstɪˈgeʃən] *s* investigazione
investigator [ɪnˈvɛstɪˌgetər] *s* investigatore *m*
investment [ɪnˈvɛstmənt] *s* (*of money*) investimento; (*e.g., with an office*) investitura; (*siege*) assedio
investor [ɪnˈvɛstər] *s* investitore *m*
inveterate [ɪnˈvɛtərɪt] *adj* inveterato
invidious [ɪnˈvɪdɪ·əs] *adj* irritante, odioso
invigorate [ɪnˈvɪgəˌret] *tr* invigorire
invigorating [ɪnˈvɪgəˌretɪŋ] *adj* ritemprante, ricostituente, rinforzante
invincible [ɪnˈvɪnsɪbəl] *adj* invincibile
invisible [ɪnˈvɪzɪbəl] *adj* invisibile
invis'ible ink' *s* inchiostro simpatico
invitation [ˌɪnvɪˈteʃən] *s* invito
invite [ɪnˈvaɪt] *tr* invitare
inviting [ɪnˈvaɪtɪŋ] *adj* invitante, attrattivo; (*food*) appetitoso; accogliente
invoice [ˈɪnvɔɪs] *s* fattura; **as per invoice** secondo fattura || *tr* fatturare
invoke [ɪnˈvok] *tr* invocare; (*a spirit*) evocare
involuntary [ɪnˈvɑlənˌteri] *adj* involontario
involve [ɪnˈvɑlv] *tr* involvere, includere; occupare; (*to bring unpleasantness upon*) implicare, coinvolgere; complicare
invulnerable [ɪnˈvʌlnərəbəl] *adj* invulnerabile
inward [ˈɪnwərd] *adj* interno || *adv* al di dentro, verso l'interno
iodide [ˈaɪ·əˌdaɪd] *s* ioduro
iodine [ˈaɪ·əˌdin] *s* iodio || [ˈaɪ·əˌdaɪn] *s* tintura di iodio
ion [ˈaɪ·ən] *or* [ˈaɪ·ɑn] *s* ione *m*
ionize [ˈaɪ·əˌnaɪz] *tr* ionizzare
IOU [ˈaɪ·oˈju] *s* (letterword) (**I owe you**) cambiale *f*, pagherò *m*
I.Q. [ˈaɪˈkju] *s* (letterword) (**intelligence quotient**) quoziente *m* d'intelligenza
Iranian [aɪˈreni·ən] *adj & s* iraniano
Ira·qi [ɪˈrɑki] *adj* iracheno *s* (**-qis**) iracheno
irate [ˈaɪret] *or* [aɪˈret] *adj* irato
ire [aɪr] *s* ira, collera
Ireland [ˈaɪrlənd] *s* l'Irlanda *f*
iris [ˈaɪrɪs] *s* iride *f*
I'rish·man *s* (**-men**) irlandese *m*
I'rish stew' *s* stufato all'irlandese
I'rish·wom'an *s* (**-wom'en**) irlandese *f*
irk [ʌrk] *tr* infastidire, annoiare

irksome [ˈʌrksəm] *adj* fastidioso
iron [ˈaɪ·ərn] *adj* ferreo || *s* ferro; (*to press clothes*) ferro da stiro; **irons** ferri *mpl;* **strike while the iron is hot** batti il ferro fin ch'è caldo || *tr* (*clothes*) stirare; **to iron out** (*a difficulty*) (coll) appianare
i'ron-bound' *adj* ferrato; (*unyielding*) ferreo, inflessibile; (*rock-bound*) roccioso, scabroso
ironclad [ˈaɪ·ərnˌklæd] *adj* corazzato, blindato; inflessibile, ferreo
i'ron constitu'tion *s* salute *f* di ferro
i'ron cur'tain *s* cortina di ferro
i'ron horse' *s* locomotiva a vapore
ironic(al) [aɪˈrɑnɪk(əl)] *adj* ironico
ironing [ˈaɪ·ərnɪŋ] *s* stiratura; roba stirata; roba da stirare
i'roning board' *s* tavolo o asse *m* da stiro
i'ron lung' *s* polmone *m* d'acciaio
i'ron·ware' *s* ferrame *m*
i'ron will' *s* volontà *f* di ferro
i'ron·work' *s* lavoro in ferro; **ironworks** *ssg* ferriera
i'ron·work'er *s* ferraio; metalmeccanico, siderurgico
iro·ny [ˈaɪrəni] *s* (**-nies**) ironia
irradiate [ɪˈrediˌet] *tr* irradiare || *intr* irradiare, irradiarsi
irrational [ɪˈræʃənəl] *adj* irrazionale
irrecoverable [ˌɪrɪˈkʌvərəbəl] *adj* irrecuperabile
irredeemable [ˌɪrɪˈdiməbəl] *adj* irredimibile
irrefutable [ˌɪrɪˈfjutəbəl] *adj* irrefutabile
irregular [ɪˈrɛgjələr] *adj* irregolare || *s* (mil) irregolare *m*
irrelevance [ɪˈrɛləvəns] *s* irrilevanza
irrelevant [ɪˈrɛləvənt] *adj* irrilevante
irreligious [ˌɪrɪˈlɪdʒəs] *adj* irreligioso
irremediable [ˌɪrɪˈmidɪ·əbəl] *adj* irrimediabile
irremovable [ˌɪrɪˈmuvəbəl] *adj* irremovibile, inamovibile
irreplaceable [ˌɪrɪˈplesəbəl] *adj* insostituibile
irrepressible [ˌɪrɪˈprɛsɪbəl] *adj* irreprimibile, incontenibile
irreproachable [ˌɪrɪˈprotʃəbəl] *adj* irreprensibile
irresistible [ˌɪrɪˈzɪstɪbəl] *adj* irresistibile
irrespective [ˌɪrɪˈspɛktɪv] *adj*—**irrespective of** senza riguardo a
irresponsible [ˌɪrɪˈspɑnsɪbəl] *adj* irresponsabile
irretrievable [ˌɪrɪˈtrivəbəl] *adj* irrecuperabile
irreverent [ɪˈrɛvərənt] *adj* irriverente
irrevocable [ɪˈrɛvəkəbəl] *adj* irrevocabile
irrigate [ˈɪrɪˌget] *tr* irrigare
irrigation [ˌɪrɪˈgeʃən] *s* irrigazione
irritant [ˈɪrɪtənt] *adj & s* irritante *m*
irritate [ˈɪrɪˌtet] *tr* irritare
irritation [ˌɪrɪˈteʃən] *s* irritazione
irruption [ɪˈrʌpʃən] *s* irruzione
isinglass [ˈaɪzɪŋˌglæs] *or* [ˈaɪzɪŋˌglɑs] *s* (*gelatine*) colla di pesce; mica
Islam [ˈɪsləm] *or* [ɪsˈlɑm] *s* l'Islam *m*

island ['aɪlənd] *adj* isolano ‖ *s* isola; (*for safety of pedestrians*) salvagente *m*

islander ['aɪləndər] *s* isolano

isle [aɪl] *s* isoletta

isolate ['aɪsə,let] *or* ['ɪsə,let] *tr* isolare

isolation [,aɪsə'leʃən] *or* [,ɪsə'leʃən] *s* isolamento

isolationist [,aɪsə'leʃənɪst] *or* [,ɪsə'leʃənɪst] *s* isolazionista *mf*

isosceles [aɪ'sɑsə,liz] *adj* isoscele

isotope ['aɪsə,top] *s* isotopo

Israel ['ɪzrɪ-əl] *s* l'Israele *m*

Israe·li [ɪz'reli] *adj* israeliano ‖ *s* (*-lis* [liz]) israeliano

Israelite ['ɪzrɪ-ə,laɪt] *adj & s* israelita *mf*

issuance ['ɪʃu-əns] *s* (*of stamps, stocks, bonds, etc.*) emissione; (*e.g., of clothes*) distribuzione; (*of a law*) emanazione

issue ['ɪʃu] *s* (*outlet*) uscita; distribuzione; (*result*) conseguenza; (*offspring*) prole *f*; (*of a magazine*) puntata, fascicolo; (*of a bond*) emissione; (*yield*) prodotto; (*of a law*) promulgazione; (*pathol*) flusso; **at issue** in discussione; **to face the issue** affrontare la situazione; **to force the issue** forzare la soluzione; **to take issue with** non essere d'accordo con, dissentire da ‖ *tr* (*e.g., a book*) pubblicare; (*bonds, orders*) emettere; (*a communiqué*) diramare; (*e.g., food*) distribuire ‖ *intr* uscire; **to issue from** provenire da

isthmus ['ɪsməs] *s* istmo

it [ɪt] *pron pers* esso, essa; lo, la; **it is**

I sono io; **it is raining** piove; **it is four o'clock** sono le quattro

Italian [ɪ'tæljən] *adj & s* italiano

Ital'ian-speak'ing *adj* italofono

italic [ɪ'tælɪk] *adj* (*typ*) corsivo ‖ **italics** *s* (*typ*) corsivo ‖ **Italic** *adj* italico

italicize [ɪ'tælɪ,saɪz] *tr* stampare in carattere corsivo; sottolineare

Italy ['ɪtəli] *s* l'Italia *f*

itch [ɪtʃ] *s* prurito; (*pathol*) rogna; (*eagerness*) (fig) pizzicore *m* ‖ *tr* prudere, e.g., **his foot itches him** gli prude il piede ‖ *intr* (*said of a part of body*) prudere; (*said of a person*) avere il prurito; **to itch to** avere il pizzicore di

itch·y ['ɪtʃi] *adj* (*-ier; -iest*) che prude; (pathol) rognoso

item ['aɪtəm] *s* articolo; notizia; (*on the agenda*) questione; (slang) notizia scottante

itemize ['aɪtə,maɪz] *tr* dettagliare, specificare

itinerant [aɪ'tɪnərənt] *or* [ɪ'tɪnərənt] *adj* itinerante, ambulante ‖ *s* viaggiatore *m*, viandante *m*

itinerar·y [aɪ'tɪnə,reri] *or* [ɪ'tɪnə,reri] *adj* itinerario ‖ *s* (*-ies*) itinerario

its [ɪts] *adj & pron poss* il suo

itself [ɪt'sɛlf] *pron pers* sé stesso; si, e.g., **it opened itself** si è aperto

ivied ['aɪvɪd] *adj* coperto di edera

ivo·ry ['aɪvəri] *adj* d'avorio ‖ *s* (*-ries*) avorio; **ivories** (slang) tasti *mpl* del piano; (slang) palle *fpl* da bigliardo; (*dice*) (slang) dadi *mpl*; (slang) denti *mpl*

i'vory tow'er *s* torre *f* d'avorio

ivy ['aɪvi] *s* (**ivies**) edera

J

J, j [dʒe] *s* decima lettera dell'alfabeto inglese

jab [dʒæb] *s* puntata; (*prick*) puntura; (*with elbow*) gomitata ‖ *v* (*pret & pp* **jabbed**; *ger* **jabbing**) *tr* pugnalare; pungere; dare una gomitata a ‖ *intr* dare colpi

jabber ['dʒæbər] *s* borbottamento, ciarla ‖ *tr & intr* borbottare, ciarlare

jack [dʒæk] *s* (*for lifting heavy objects*) cricco, martinetto; (*jackass*) asino; (*device for turning a spit*) girarrosto; (*to remove a boot*) cavastivali *m*; (cards) fante *m*; (bowling) pallino; (rad & telv) jack *m*; (elec) presa; (slang) soldi *mpl*; **every man jack** ognuno, tutti *mpl* ‖ **Jack** *s* marinaio; (coll) buonuomo ‖ *tr*—**to jack up** alzare col cricco; (*prices*) (coll) alzare

jackal ['dʒækəl] *s* sciacallo

jack'ass' *s* asino

jack'daw' *s* cornacchia

jacket ['dʒækɪt] *s* giacca; (*of boiled*

potatoes) buccia; (*of book*) sopraccoperta; (*metal casing*) camicia

jack'ham'mer *s* martello perforatore

jack'-in-the-box' *s* scatola a sorpresa

jack'knife' *s* (**-knives**) coltello a serramanico; (sports) salto a pesce

jack'-of-all-trades' *s* factotum *m*

jack-o'-lantern ['dʒækə,læntərn] *s* lanterna a forma di testa umana fatta con una zucca; fuoco fatuo

jack'pot' *s* monte *m* premi; **to hit the jackpot** (slang) vincere un terno al lotto

jack' rab'bit *s* lepre nordamericana di taglia grande

jack'screw' *s* cricco a verme

jack'-tar' *s* (coll) marinaio

jade [dʒed] *adj* di giada, come la giada ‖ *s* (*ornamental stone*) giada; (*worn-out horse*) ronzino; (*disreputable woman*) donnaccia ‖ *tr* logorare

jad'ed ['dʒedɪd] *adj* logoro, stanco; (*appetite*) stucco

jag [dʒæg] *s* slabbratura; **to have a jag on** (slang) avere la sbornia

jagged ['dʒægɪd] *adj* dentato, slabbrato

jaguar ['dʒægwɑr] *s* giaguaro

jail [dʒel] *s* prigione *f*; **to break jail** evadere dal carcere ‖ *tr* carcerare

jail'bird' *s* galeotto, remo di galera

jail'break' *s* evasione *f* dal carcere

jailer ['dʒelɑr] *s* carceriere *m*

jalop·y [dʒə'lɑpi] *s* (**-ies**) carcassa, trespolo, trabiccolo

jam [dʒæm] *s* stretta, compressione; (*in traffic*) imbottigliamento; (*preserve*) marmellata, confettura; (*difficult situation*) (coll) pasticcio ‖ *v* (*pret & pp* **jammed;** *ger* **jamming**) *tr* stipare; (*e.g., one's finger*) schiacciare, schiacciarsi; (rad) disturbare; **to jam on the brakes** bloccare i freni ‖ *intr* schiacciarsi; (*said of firearms*) incepparsi; (mach) grippare

jamb [dʒæm] *s* stipite *m*

jamboree [ˌdʒæmbə'ri] *s* riunione nazionale di giovani esploratori; (coll) riunione

James [dʒemz] *s* Giacomo

jamming ['dʒæmɪŋ] *s* radiodisturbo

jam-packed ['dʒæm'pækt] *adj* gremito, pieno fino all'orlo

jangle ['dʒæŋgəl] *s* suono stridente; (*quarrel*) baruffa ‖ *tr* fare suoni stridenti con ‖ *intr* stridere; litigare

janitor ['dʒænɪtɑr] *s* portiere *m*

janitress ['dʒænɪtrɪs] *s* portinaia

January ['dʒænjuˌɛri] *s* gennaio

ja·pan [dʒə'pæn] *s* lacca giapponese; oggetto di lacca ‖ *v* (*pret & pp* **-panned;** *ger* **-panning**) *tr* laccare ‖

Japan *s* il Giappone

Japa·nese [ˌdʒæpə'niz] *adj* giapponese ‖ *s* (**-nese**) giapponese *mf*

Jap'anese bee'tle *s* scarabeo giapponese

Jap'anese lan'tern *s* lampioncino alla veneziana

Jap'anese persim'mon *s* cachi *m*

jar [dʒɑr] *s* barattolo; (*earthenware container*) orcio, giara; discordanza; (*jolt*) scossa; (fig) brutta sorpresa; **on the jar** (*said of a door*) socchiuso ‖ *v* (*pret & pp* **jarred;** *ger* **jarring**) *tr* scuotere; far stridere ‖ *intr* vibrare; stridere; essere in conflitto; **to jar on** irritare

jardiniere [ˌdʒɑrdɪ'nɪr] *s* (*pot*) vaso da fiori; giardiniera

jargon ['dʒɑrgən] *s* gergo

jasmine ['dʒæsmɪn] *or* ['dʒæzmɪn] *s* gelsomino

jasper ['dʒæspər] *s* diaspro

jaundice ['dʒɔndɪs] *or* ['dʒɑndɪs] *s* itterizia; (fig) invidia

jaundiced ['dʒɔndɪst] *or* ['dʒɑndɪst] *adj* itterico; (fig) invidioso

jaunt [dʒɔnt] *or* [dʒɑnt] *s* passeggiata, gita

jaun·ty ['dʒɔnti] *or* ['dʒɑnti] *adj* (**-tier; -tiest**) disinvolto; elegante

Java·nese [ˌdʒævə'niz] *adj* giavanese ‖ *s* (**-nese**) giavanese *m*

javelin ['dʒævlɪn] *or* ['dʒævəlɪn] *s* giavellotto

jaw [dʒɔ] *s* mascella, mandibola; (mach) ganascia; **jaws** fauci *fpl*; gola, stretta ‖ *tr* (slang) rimproverare ‖

intr (slang) chiacchierare; (slang) fare la predica

jaw'bone' *s* mascella, mandibola

jaw'break'er *s* (coll) parola difficile da pronunciare; (coll) caramella durissima; (mach) frantoio a mascelle

jay [dʒe] *s* (orn) ghiandaia; (coll) sempliciotto

jay'walk' *intr* attraversare la strada contro la luce rossa del semaforo

jay'walk·er *s* (coll) pedone distratto che attraversa la strada contro la luce rossa del semaforo

jazz [dʒæz] *s* jazz *m*; (slang) spirito ‖ *tr*—**to jazz up** (slang) dar vita a

jazz' band' *s* orchestra jazz

jealous ['dʒɛləs] *adj* geloso; (*envious*) invidioso; vigilante

jealous·y ['dʒɛləsi] *s* (**-ies**) gelosia; invidia; vigilanza

jean [dʒin] *s* tela cruda; **jeans** pantaloni *mpl* di tela cruda

jeep [dʒip] *s* gip *f*, jeep *f*

jeer [dʒɪr] *s* beffa ‖ *tr* beffare ‖ *intr* beffarsi; **to jeer at** motteggiare

Jeho'vah's Wit'nesses [dʒɪ'hovəs] *spl* Testimoni di Geova

jell [dʒɛl] *s* gelatina ‖ *intr* (*to congeal*) gelatinizzarsi; (*to become substantial*) cristallizzarsi

jel·ly ['dʒɛli] *s* (**-lies**) gelatina ‖ *v* (*pret & pp* **-lied**) *tr* gelatinizzare ‖ *intr* gelatinizzarsi

jel'ly-fish' *s* medusa; (*weak person*) (coll) fiaccone *m*

jeopardize ['dʒɛpərˌdaɪz] *tr* compromettere, mettere a repentaglio

jeopardy ['dʒɛpərdi] *s* pericolo, repentaglio

jeremiad [ˌdʒɛrɪ'maɪˌæd] *s* geremiade

Jericho ['dʒɛrɪˌko] *s* Gerico *f*

jerk [dʒʌrk] *s* strattone *m*, scatto; **tic** *m*; (*stupid person*) scempio, sciocco; **by jerks** a scatti ‖ *tr* tirare a strattoni; (*meat*) essiccare ‖ *intr* sobbalzare

jerked' beef' *s* fetta di carne di bue essicata

jerkin ['dʒʌrkɪn] *s* giubbetto

jerk'wa'ter *adj* di scarsa importanza

jerk·y ['dʒʌrki] *adj* (**-ier; -iest**) sussultante; (*style*) disuguale

Jerome [dʒə'rom] *s* Gerolamo

jersey ['dʒʌrzi] *s* jersey *m*, maglione *m*

Jerusalem [dʒɪ'rusələm] *s* Gerusalemme *f*

jest [dʒɛst] *s* scherzo, burla; **in jest** per celia ‖ *intr* scherzare

jester ['dʒɛstər] *s* motteggiatore *m*, burlone *m*; (hist) buffone *m*

Jesuit ['dʒɛʒuˌɪt] *or* ['dʒɛzjuˌɪt] *adj & s* gesuita *m*

Jesuitic(al) [ˌdʒɛʒu'ɪtɪk(əl)] *or* [ˌdʒɛzju'ɪtɪk(əl)] *adj* gesuitico

Jesus ['dʒizəs] *s* Gesù *m*

Je'sus Christ' *s* Gesù *m* Cristo

jet [dʒet] *adj* di giaietto ‖ *s* (*of a fountain*) zampillo; (*stream shooting forth from nozzle*) getto; (*mineral; lustrous black*) giaietto; (aer) aereo a getto ‖ *v* (*pret & pp* **jetted;** *ger* **jetting**) *tr* spruzzare ‖ *intr* zampillare; volare in aereo a getto

jet' age' *s* era dell'aviogetto

jet'-black' *adj* nero come il carbone

jet' bomb'er *s* bombardiere *m* a reazione

jet' coal' *s* carbone a lunga fiamma

jet' en'gine *s* motore *m* a reazione

jet' fight'er *s* caccia *m* a reazione

jet'lin'er *s* aviogetto da trasporto passeggeri

jet' plane' *s* aviogetto

jet' propul'sion *s* gettopropulsione

jetsam ['dʒɛtsəm] *s* relitto

jet' stream' *s* corrente *f* a getto; scappamento di motore a razzo

jettison ['dʒɛtɪsən] *s* (naut) alleggerimento ‖ *tr* (naut) alleggerirsi di; (fig) disfarsi di

jet-ty ['dʒɛti] *s* (-ties) gettata; (*wharf*) molo, imbarcadero

Jew [dʒu] *s* giudeo

jewel ['dʒu·əl] *s* pietra preziosa; (*valuable personal ornament*) gioia, gioiello; (*of a watch*) rubino; (*costume jewelry*) gioia finta; (fig) valore *m*, gioiello

jew'el case' *s* scrigno, portagioie *m*

jeweler or **jeweller** ['dʒu·ələr] *s* gioielliere *m*, orefice *m*

jewelry ['dʒu·əlrɪ] *s* gioielli *mpl*

jew'elry shop' *s* gioielleria

Jewess ['dʒu·ɪs] *s* giudea

Jewish ['dʒu·ɪʃ] *adj* giudeo

jews'-harp or **jew's-harp** ['dʒuz,harp] *s* scacciapensieri *m*

jib [dʒɪb] *s* (*of a crane*) (mach) braccio (di gru); (naut) fiocco, vela Marconi

jib' boom' *s* asta di fiocco

jibe [dʒaɪb] *s* burla, beffa ‖ *intr* beffarsi; accordarsi; **to jibe at** beffarsi di

jif-fy ['dʒɪfi] *s*—**in a jiffy** (coll) in men che non si dica

jig [dʒɪg] *s* (*dance*) giga; **the jig is up** (slang) tutto è perduto

jigger ['dʒɪgər] *s* bicchierino di liquore d'un'oncia e mezza; (*flea*) pulce *f* tropicale; (*gadget*) (coll) aggeggio; (naut) bozzello; (min) crivello

jiggle ['dʒɪgəl] *s* scossa ‖ *tr* scuotere, agitare ‖ *intr* scuotersi

jig' saw' *s* sega da traforo

jig'saw puz'zle *s* gioco di pazienza, rompicapo

jilt [dʒɪlt] *tr* piantare

jim-my ['dʒɪmi] *s* (-mies) piccolo piede di porco ‖ *v* (*pret* & *pp* -mied) *tr* scassinare; **to jimmy open** scassinare

jingle ['dʒɪŋgəl] *s* sonaglio, bubbolo; (*sound*) rumore *m* di sonagliera; cantilena, rima infantile ‖ *tr* far suonare ‖ *intr* tintinnare

jin-go ['dʒɪŋgo] *adj* sciovinista ‖ *s* (-goes) sciovinista *mf*; **by jingo!** perbacco!

jingoism ['dʒɪŋgo,ɪzəm] *s* sciovinismo

jinx [dʒɪŋks] *s* iettatura; (*person*) iettatore *m* ‖ *tr* portare la iettatura a

jitters ['dʒɪtərz] *spl* (coll) nervosismo; **to have the jitters** (coll) essere nervoso

jittery ['dʒɪtəri] *adj* nervoso

job [dʒab] *s* (*piece of work*) lavoro;

(*task*) mansione; (*employment*) posto, impiego; (slang) furto; **by the job** a cottimo; **on the job** (slang) attento, sollecito; **to be out of a job** essere disoccupato; **to lie down on the job** (slang) dormire sul lavoro

job' anal'ysis *s* valutazione delle mansioni

jobber ['dʒabər] *s* grossista *mf*; (*pieceworker*) lavoratore *m* a cottimo; (*funzionario disonesto*) funzionario disonesto

job'hold'er *s* impiegato; (*in the government*) burocrate *m*

jobless ['dʒablɪs] *adj* disoccupato

job' lot' *s* (com) saldo

job' print'er *s* piccolo tipografo non specializzato

job' print'ing *s* piccolo lavoro tipografico

jockey ['dʒaki] *s* fantino ‖ *tr* (*a horse*) montare; manovrare; (*to trick*) abbindolare

jockstrap ['dʒak,stræp] *s* sospensorio

jocose [dʒo'kos] *adj* giocoso

jocular ['dʒakjələr] *adj* scherzoso

jog [dʒag] *s* spinta; piccolo trotto ‖ *v* (*pret* & *pp* **jogged**; *ger* **jogging**) *tr* spingere leggermente; (*the memory*) rinfrescare ‖ *intr* barcarellarsi; **to jog along** continuare col solito tran tran

jog' trot' *s* piccolo trotto; (fig) tran tran *m*

John [dʒan] *s* Giovanni *m*

John' Bull' *s* il tipico inglese; gli inglesi, il popolo inglese

John' Han'cock ['hænkak] *s* (coll) la firma

johnnycake ['dʒani,kek] *s* pane *m* di granturco

John'ny-come'-late'ly *s* (coll) ultimo arrivato

John'ny-jump'-up' *s* violetta, viola del pensiero

John'ny-on-the-spot' *s* (coll) persona sempre pronta

John' the Bap'tist *s* San Giovanni Battista

join [dʒɔɪn] *tr* giungere, congiungere; associarsi a; unire; (*e.g., a party*) farsi membro di; (*the army*) arruolarsi in; (*battle*) ingaggiare; (*to empty into*) sfociare in ‖ *intr* congiungersi, unirsi; (*said, e.g., of two rivers*) confluire

joiner ['dʒɔɪnər] *s* falegname *m*; membro di molte società

joint [dʒɔɪnt] *adj* congiunto ‖ *s* (*in a pipe*) giuntura; (*of bones*) giuntura, articolazione; (*hinge of book*) brachetta; (*in woodwork*) incastro, commettitura; (*of meat*) taglio; (mach) snodo; (*gambling den*) (slang) bisca; (elec) innesto; (slang) bettola; **out of joint** slogato; (fig) fuori luogo; **to throw** (*e.g., one's arm*) **out of joint** slogarsi

joint' account' *s* conto in comune

joint' commit'tee *s* commissione mista

jointly ['dʒɔɪntli] *adv* unitamente

joint' own'er *s* condomino

joint'-stock' com'pany *s* società *f* per azioni a responsabilità illimitata

joist [dʒɔɪst] *s* trave *f*

joke [dʒok] *s* burla, barzelletta; (*trifling matter*) cosa da nulla; (*person laughed at*) zimbello; **to tell a joke** raccontare una barzelletta; **to play a joke on** fare uno scherzo a || *tr*—**to joke one's way into** ottenere dicendo barzellette || *intr* burlare, dire storielle; **joking aside** senza scherzi

joker ['dʒokər] *s* burlone *m*, fumista *m*; (*wise guy*) saputello; (*hidden provision*) clausola ingannatrice; (*cards*) matta

jol·ly ['dʒɑlɪ] *adj* (**-lier; -liest**) allegro, gaio || *adv* (coll) molto || *v* (*pret & pp* **-lied**) *tr* (coll) prendersi gioco di

jolt [dʒolt] *s* scossa || *tr* scuotere || *intr* sobbalzare

Jonah ['dʒonə] *s* Giona; (fig) uccello di mal augurio

jongleur ['dʒɑŋglər] *s* giullare *m*

jonquil ['dʒɑŋkwɪl] *s* giunchiglia

Jordan ['dʒɔrdən] *s* (*country*) la Giordania; (*river*) Giordano

Jordanian [dʒɔr'denɪ·ən] *adj & s* giordano

josh [dʒɑʃ] *tr & intr* (coll) canzonare

jostle ['dʒɑsəl] *s* spintone *m* || *tr* spingere || *intr* scontrarsi; farsi strada a gomitate

jot [dʒɑt] *s*—**I don't care a jot for** non mi importa un fico di || *v* (*pret & pp* **jotted**; *ger* **jotting**) *tr*—**to jot down** notare, gettar giù

jounce [dʒauns] *s* scossa || *tr* scuotere || *intr* sobbalzare

journal ['dʒʌrnəl] *s* (*newspaper*) giornale *m*; (*magazine*) rivista; (*daily record*) diario; (com) giornale *m*; (mach) perno; (naut) giornale *m* di bordo

journalese [ˌdʒʌrnə'liz] *s* linguaggio giornalistico

journalism ['dʒʌrnə·ˌlɪzəm] *s* giornalismo

journalist ['dʒʌrnəlɪst] *s* giornalista *mf*

journey ['dʒʌrni] *s* viaggio || *intr* viaggiare

jour'ney·man *s* (**-men**) operaio specializzato

joust [dʒʌst] *or* [dʒust] *or* [dʒaust] *s* giostra || *intr* giostrare

jovial ['dʒovɪ·əl] *adj* gioviale

jowl [dʒaul] *s* (*cheek*) guancia; (*jawbone*) mascella; (*of cattle*) giogaia; (*of fowl*) bargiglio; (*of fat person*) pappagorgia

joy [dʒɔɪ] *s* gioia, allegria; **to leap with joy** ballare dalla gioia

joyful ['dʒɔɪfəl] *adj* gioioso, festoso; **joyful over** lieto di

joyless ['dʒɔɪlɪs] *adj* senza gioia

joyous ['dʒɔɪ·əs] *adj* gioioso

joy' ride' *s* (coll) gita in auto; (coll) gita all'impazzata in auto

jubilant ['dʒubɪlənt] *adj* esultante

jubilation [ˌdʒubɪ'leʃən] *s* giubilo

jubilee ['dʒubɪˌli] *s* (*jubilation*) giubilo; (eccl) giubileo

Judaism ['dʒude·ˌɪzəm] *s* giudaismo

judge [dʒʌdʒ] *s* giudice *m* || *tr & intr* giudicare; **judging by** a giudicare da

judge' ad'vocate *s* avvocato militare; avvocato della marina da guerra

Judgeship ['dʒʌdʒʃɪp] *s* carica di giudice

judgment ['dʒʌdʒmənt] *s* giudizio; (*legal decision*) sentenza

judg'ment day' *s* giorno del giudizio

judg'ment seat' *s* banco dei giudici; tribunale *m*

judicature ['dʒudɪkətʃər] *s* carica di giudice

judicial [dʒu'dɪʃəl] *adj* giudiziario; (*becoming a judge*) giudizioso

judiciar·y [dʒu'dɪʃɪˌeri] *adj* giudiziario || *s* (**-ies**) (*judges collectively*) magistratura; (*judicial branch*) potere giudiziario

judicious [dʒu'dɪʃəs] *adj* giudizioso

jug [dʒʌg] *s* brocca, boccale *m*; (*narrow-necked vessel*) orcio; (*jail*) (slang) prigione

juggle ['dʒʌgəl] *s* gioco di prestigio || *tr* fare il giocoliere con; (*documents, facts*) alterare frodolentamente; **to juggle away** ghermire, trafugare || *intr* fare il giocoliere; fare l'imbroglione

juggler ['dʒʌglər] *s* giocoliere *m*, prestigiatore *m*; impostore *m*

juggling ['dʒʌglɪŋ] *s* giochi *mpl* di prestigio

Jugoslav ['jugo'slɑv] *adj & s* iugoslavo, jugoslavo

Jugoslavia [ˌjugo'slɑvɪ·ə] *s* la Iugoslavia, la Jugoslavia

jugular ['dʒʌgjələr] *or* ['dʒugjələr] *adj & s* giugulare *f*

juice [dʒus] *s* sugo; (*natural fluid of an animal body*) succo; (slang) elettricità *f*; (slang) benzina; **to stew in one's own juice** (coll) annegarsi nel proprio sugo

juic·y ['dʒusi] *adj* (**-ier; -iest**) sugoso, succoso; (*spicy*) piccante

jukebox ['dʒuk ˌbɑks] *s* grammofono a gettone, juke-box *m*

julep ['dʒulɪp] *s* bibita di menta col ghiaccio; (pharm) giulebbe *m*

julienne [ˌdʒulɪ'en] *s* giuliana

July [dʒu'laɪ] *s* luglio

jumble ['dʒʌmbəl] *s* intrico, garbuglio || *tr* ingarbugliare

jum·bo ['dʒʌmbo] *adj* (coll) enorme || *s* (**-bos**) (*person*) (coll) elefante *m*; (*thing*) (coll) oggetto enorme

jump [dʒʌmp] *s* salto; (*in a parachute*) lancio; (*of prices*) sbalzo; (*start*) soprassalto; **on the jump** in moto; **to get or to have the jump on** (coll) avere il vantaggio su || *tr* saltare; (*a horse*) far saltare; (*prices*) alzare; uscire da, e.g., **the train jumped the track** il treno uscì dalle rotaie; (*to attack*) (coll) balzare su; (checkers) suffiare || *intr* saltare; (*from surprise*) trasalire; (*said of prices*) salire; (*in a parachute*) lanciarsi; **to jump at** (*e.g., an offer*) afferrare; **to jump on** saltare su; (coll) sgridare, arrabbiarsi con; **to jump over** oltrepassare; (*a page*) saltare; **to jump to a conclusion** arrivare precipitosamente a una conclusione

jumper ['dʒʌmpər] *s* saltatore *m*; camiciotto; **jumpers** tuta da bambini

jump'ing jack' [ˈdʒʌmpɪŋ] s marionetta

jump'ing-off' place' s fine f del mondo; (fig) trampolino, punto di partenza

jump' seat' s strapuntino

jump' spark' s scintilla elettrica; (of induction coil) (elec) scintilla d'intraferro

jump' wire' s filo elettrico di contatto

jump·y [ˈdʒʌmpi] adj (-ier; -iest) nervoso, eccitato

junction [ˈdʒʌŋkʃən] s congiunzione; (of two rivers) confluenza; (carp) commettitura; (rr) raccordo ferroviario

juncture [ˈdʒʌŋktʃər] s giuntura; (occasion) congiuntura; (moment) momento

June [dʒun] s giugno

jungle [ˈdʒʌŋgəl] s giungla

junglegym [ˈdʒʌŋgəl ˌdʒɪm] s (trademark) castello

junior [ˈdʒunjər] adj minore, di minore età; giovane; (in American university) del penultimo anno; figlio, e.g., **John H. Smith, Junior** Giovanni H. Smith, figlio ‖ s minore m; socio secondario; studente m del penultimo anno

jun'ior col'lege s scuola universitaria unicamente di primo biennio

jun'ior high' school' s scuola media; ginnasio

juniper [ˈdʒunipər] s ginepro

ju'niper ber'ry s coccola di ginepro

junk [dʒʌŋk] s roba vecchia, ferro vecchio; (Chinese ship) giunca; (naut) carne salata ‖ tr (slang) gettar via

junk' deal'er s robivecchi m

junket [ˈdʒʌŋkɪt] s budino di giuncata; (outing) viaggio di piacere; viaggio pagato a spese del tesoro ‖ intr far un viaggio di piacere; far un viaggio a spese del tesoro

junk'man' s (-men') ferravecchio; rigattiere m

junk' room' s ripostiglio

junk' shop' s negozio di robivecchi

junk'yard' s cantiere m di ferravecchio

juridical [dʒuˈrɪdɪkəl] adj giuridico

jurisdiction [ˌdʒurɪsˈdɪkʃən] s giurisdizione

jurisprudence [ˌdʒurɪsˈprudəns] s giurisprudenza

jurist [ˈdʒurɪst] s giurista mf

juror [ˈdʒurər] s giurato

ju·ry [ˈdʒuri] s (-ries) giuria

ju'ry box' s banco della giuria

ju'ry·man s (-men) giurato

just [dʒʌst] adj giusto ‖ adv giustamente, giusto; appena; proprio; **just as** come, proprio come; **just beyond** un po' più in là (di); **just now** poco fa, or ora; **just out** appena uscito, appena pubblicato

justice [ˈdʒʌstɪs] s giustizia; (judge) giudice m; **to bring to justice** arrestare e condannare; **to do justice to** render giustizia a; apprezzare bastantemente

jus'tice of the peace' s giudice m conciliatore

justifiable [ˈdʒʌstɪ ˌfaɪ·əbəl] adj giustificabile

justi·fy [ˈdʒʌstɪ ˌfaɪ] v (pret & pp (-fied) tr giustificare; (typ) giustificare

justly [ˈdʒʌstli] adj giustamente

jut [dʒʌt] v (pret & pp jutted; ger jutting) intr—**to jut out** strapiombare, sporgere

jute [dʒut] s iuta ‖ **Jute** s Juto

juvenile [ˈdʒuvənɪl] or [ˈdʒuvə ˌnaɪl] adj giovanile; minorile ‖ s giovane mf; libro per la gioventù; (theat) amoroso

ju'venile court' s tribunale m per i minorenni

ju'venile delin'quency s delinquenza minorile

juvenilia [ˌdʒuvəˈnɪli·ə] spl opere fpl giovanili; libri mpl per ragazzi

juxtapose [ˌdʒʌkstəˈpoz] tr giustapporre

K

K, k [ke] s undicesima lettera dell'alfabeto inglese

kale [kel] s verza; (slang) cocuzza, soldi mpl

kaleidoscope [kəˈlaɪdə ˌskop] s caleidoscopio

kangaroo [ˌkæŋgəˈru] s canguro

katydid [ˈketɪdɪd] s grossa cavalletta verde nordamericana

kedge [kedʒ] s (naut) ancorotto

keel [kil] s chiglia ‖ intr—**to keel over** (naut) abbattersi in carena, capovolgersi; (fig) svenire

keelson [ˈkelsən] or [ˈkilsən] s (naut) controchiglia

keen [kin] adj (sharpened) affilato; (wind; wit) tagliente, mordente; (eyes) penetrante; (ears; mind) acuto,

fine; (eager) entusiasta; intenso, vivo; (slang) meraviglioso; **to be keen on** essere appassionato per

keep [kip] s mantenimento; (of medieval castle) torrione m, maschio; **for keeps** (coll) seriamente; (coll) per sempre; **to earn one's keep** guadagnarsi la vita ‖ v (pret & pp **kept** [kept]) tr mantenere; (watch) fare; (one's word) mantenere; (to withhold) trattenere; (accounts) tenere; (servants, guests) avere; (a garden) coltivare; (a business) esercitare; (a holiday) festeggiare; (to support) sostentare; (a secret; one's seat) serbare; (to decide to purchase) prendere **to keep away** tener lontano; **to keep back** trattenere; (a secret) man

tenere; **to keep down** reprimere; (*expenses*) ridurre al minimo; **to keep s.o. from** + *ger* impedire a qlcu di + *inf*; **to keep in** tener chiuso; **to keep off** tenere a distanza; (*e.g., moisture*) non lasciar penetrare; **to keep s.o. informed about s.th** tenere qlcu al corrente di qlco; **to keep s.o. waiting** fare aspettare qlcu; **to keep up** mantenere, sostenere || *intr* **to keep** + *ger* continuare a + *inf*; **to keep away** tenersi lontano; **to keep from** + *ger* evitare di + *inf*; **to keep informed (about)** tenersi al corrente (di); **to keep in with** (coll) stare nelle buone grazie di; **to keep off** stare lontano (da); (*the grass*) non calpestare; **to keep on** + *ger* seguitare a + *inf*; **to keep out** star fuori, non entrare; **to keep out of** non entrare in; (*danger*) stare lontano da; non immischiarsi in; **to keep quiet** stare tranquillo; **to keep to** (*left or right*) tenere; **to keep to oneself** stare in disparte; **to keep up** continuare; **to keep up with** stare alla pari con; (*e.g., the news*) tenersi al corrente di
keeper ['kipər] *s* (*of a shop*) tenitore *m*; guardiano; (*of a game preserve*) guardacaccia *m*; (*of a magnet*) àncora
keeping ['kipɪŋ] *s* custodia; (*of a holiday*) celebrazione; **in keeping with** in armonia con; **in safe keeping** in luogo sicuro; **out of keeping with** in cattivo accordo con
keep'sake' *s* ricordo
keg [keg] *s* barilotto, botticella
ken [ken] *s* portata; **beyond the ken of** al di là dell'ambito di
kennel ['kenəl] *s* canile *m*
kep•i ['kepi] or ['kepi] *s* (**-is**) chepì *m*
kept' wo'man [kept] *s* (**wom'en**) mantenuta
kerchief ['kʌrtʃɪf] *s* fisciù *m*
kernel ['kʌrnəl] *s* (*of a nut*) gheriglio; (*of wheat*) chicco; (fig) nucleo
kerosene ['kerə,sin] or [,kerə'sin] *s* cherosene *m*, petrolio da illuminazione
kerplunk [kər'plʌŋk] *interj* patapum!
ketchup ['ketʃəp] *s* salsa piccante di pomodoro, ketchup *m*
kettle ['ketəl] *s* marmitta, paiolo; (*teakettle*) bricco, teiera
ket'tle•drum' *s* timpano
key [ki] *adj* chiave; chiave || *s* chiave *f*; (*of piano, typewriter, etc.*) tasto; (*cotter pin*) chiavetta, coppiglia; (*reef*) isolotto; (*tone of voice*) tono; (fig, mus) chiave *f*; (bot) samara; (telg) tasto trasmettitore, manipolatore *m*; **off key** stonato || *tr* aggiustare; inchiavardare; **to key up** eccitare, portare al parossismo
key'board' *s* tastiera
key'hole' *s* toppa, buco della serratura; (*of a clock*) buco della chiave
key'note' *s* (mus) tono; (fig) principio informatore
key'note address' *s* discorso d'apertura
key'punch op'era'tor *s* perforatore *m*
key' ring' *s* portachiavi *m*

key'stone' *s* chiave *f* di volta
key' word' *s* parola chiave
kha•ki ['kaki] or ['kæki] *adj* cachi || *s* (**-kis**) cachi *m*
khedive [kə'div] *s* kedivè *m*
kibitz ['kɪbɪts] *intr* (coll) dare consigli non richiesti
kibitzer ['kɪbɪtsər] *s* (*at a card game*) (coll) consigliere *m* importuno; (coll) ficcanaso *mf*
kibosh ['kaɪbɑʃ] or [kɪ'bɑʃ] *s* (coll) sciocchezza; **to put the kibosh on** (coll) impossibilitare
kick [kɪk] *s* calcio, pedata; (*of a gun*) rinculo; (*complaint*) (slang) protesta; (*of liquor*) (slang) forza; **to get a kick out of** (slang) pigliar piacere da || *tr* prendere a calci; (*a ball*) calciare; (*one's feet*) battere; **to kick out** (coll) sbatter fuori a pedate; **to kick up a row** scatenare un putiferio || *intr* calciare; (*said of an animal*) scalciare, trarre; (*said of a firearm*) rinculare; (coll) lamentarsi; **to kick against the pricks** dar calci al vento; **to kick off** (football) dare il calcio d'inizio
kick'back' *s* (coll) contraccolpo; (coll) intrallazzo, bustarella
kick'off' *s* calcio d'inizio
kid [kɪd] *s* capretto; (coll) piccolo; **kids** guanti *mpl* or scarpe *fpl* di capretto || *v* (*pret & pp* **kidded**; *ger* **kidding**) *tr* (coll) prendere in giro; **to kid oneself** (coll) farsi illusioni || *intr* (coll) dirlo per scherzo
kidder ['kɪdər] *s* (coll) burlone *m*
kid' gloves' *spl* guanti *mpl* di capretto; **to handle with kid gloves** trattare con la massima cautela
kid'nap' *v* (*pret & pp* **-naped** or **-napped**; *ger* **-naping** or **-napping**) *tr* rapire, sequestrare
kidnaper or **kidnapper** ['kɪd,næpər] *s* rapitore *m* a scopo d'estorsione
kidnaping or **kidnapping** ['kɪd,næpɪŋ] *s* rapimento a scopo di estorsione
kidney ['kɪdni] *s* rene *m*; (culin) rognone *m*; (*temperament*) carattere *m*; (*kind*) tipo
kid'ney bean' *s* fagiolo
kid'ney stone' *s* calcolo renale
kill [kɪl] *s* uccisione; (*game killed*) cacciagione; (coll) fiumicello; **for the kill** per il colpo finale || *tr* uccidere; eliminare; (*a bill*) bocciare; (fig) opprimere
killer ['kɪlər] *s* uccisore *m*
kill'er whale' *s* orca
killing ['kɪlɪŋ] *adj* mortale; (*exhausting*) opprimente; (coll) molto divertente || *s* uccisione; (*game killed*) cacciagione; (coll) fortuna; **to make a killing** (coll) fare una fortuna da un giorno all'altro
kill'-joy' *s* guastafeste *mf*
kiln [kɪl] or [kɪln] *s* forno, fornace *f*
kil•o ['kilo] or ['kilo] *s* (**-os**) chilogrammo; chilometro
kilocycle ['kɪlə,saɪkəl] *s* chilociclo
kilogram ['kɪlə,græm] *s* chilogrammo
kilo•hertz ['kɪlə,hʌrts] *s* (**-hertz**) chilohertz

kilometer ['kɪlə ˌmitər] or [kɪ'lɑmɪtər] s chilometro

kilowatt ['kɪlə ˌwɑt] s kilowatt m, chilowatt m

kilowatt-hour ['kɪlə ˌwɑt'aʊr] s (**kilo-watt-hours**) chilowattora m

kilt [kɪlt] s gonnellino

kilter ['kɪltər] s—**to be out of kilter** (coll) essere fuori squadra

kimo·no [kɪ'monə] or [kɪ'mono] s (**-nos**) chimono

kin [kɪn] s (*family relationship*) parentela; (*relatives*) parenti *mpl*; **of kin** parente, affine; **the next of kin** il parente più prossimo, i parenti più prossimi

kind [kaɪnd] *adj* gentile; **kind to** buono con || s genere m, specie f; **a kind of** una specie di; **all kinds of** (coll) ogni sorta di; **in kind** in natura; **kind of** (coll) quasi, piuttosto; **of a kind** dello stesso stampo; (*mediocre*) di poco valore

kindergarten ['kɪndər ˌgartən] s scuola materna, giardino d'infanzia

kindergartner ['kɪndər ˌgartnər] s allievo della scuola d'infanzia; (*teacher*) maestra giardiniera

kind-hearted ['kaɪnd'hartɪd] *adj* gentile, di buon cuore

kindle ['kɪndəl] *tr* accendere || *intr* accendersi

kindling ['kɪndlɪŋ] s accensione; legna minuta

kin'dling wood' s legna minuta per accendere il fuoco

kind·ly ['kaɪndli] *adj* (**-lier; -liest**) gentile; (*climate*) benigno; favorevole || *adv* gentilmente; cordialmente; per gentilezza; **to not take kindly to** non accettare di buon grado

kindness ['kaɪndnɪs] s gentilezza; **have the kindness to** abbia la bontà di

kindred ['kɪndrɪd] *adj* imparentato; affine || s parentela; affinità f

kinescope ['kɪnɪ ˌskop] s (trademark) cinescopio

kinetic [kɪ'netɪk] or [kaɪ'netɪk] *adj* cinetico || **kinetics** s cinetica

kinet'ic en'ergy s forza viva, energia cinetica

king [kɪŋ] s re m; (*checkers*) dama; (cards, chess) re m

king'bolt' s perno

kingdom ['kɪŋdəm] s regno

king'fish'er s martin pescatore m

king·ly ['kɪŋli] *adj* (**-lier; -liest**) reale; (*stately*) maestoso || *adv* regalmente

king'pin' s birillo centrale; (aut) perno dello sterzo; (fig) figura principale

king' post' s (archit) ometto, monaco

king's' e'vil s scrofola

kingship ['kɪŋʃɪp] s regalità f

king'-size' *adj* extra-grande

king's' ran'som s ricchezza di Creso

kink [kɪŋk] s (*in a rope*) arricciatura; (*in hair*) crespatura; (*soreness in neck*) torcicollo; (*flaw*) ostacolo; (*mental twist*) ghiribizzo || *tr* attorcigliare || *intr* attorcigliarsi

kink·y ['kɪŋki] *adj* (**-ier; -iest**) attorcigliato; (*hair*) crespo

kinsfolk ['kɪnz ˌfok] s parentado

kinship ['kɪnʃɪp] s parentela; affinità f

kins'man s (**-men**) parente m

kins'wom'an s (**-wom'en**) parente f

kipper ['kɪpər] s aringa affumicata || *tr* (*herring or salmon*) affumicare

kiss [kɪs] s bacio; (*billiards*) rimpallo leggerissimo; (*confection*) meringa || *tr* baciare; **to kiss away** (*tears*) asciugare con baci || *intr* baciare, baciarsi; (billiards) rimpallare leggermente

kit [kɪt] s (*case*) cassetta dei ferri; (*tools*) ferri *mpl* del mestiere; (*set of supplies*) corredo; (*of small tools*) astuccio; (*of a traveler*) borsa da viaggio; (*pail*) secchio; **the whole kit and caboodle** (coll) tutti quanti

kitchen ['kɪtʃən] s cucina

kitchenette [ˌkɪtʃə'net] s cucinetta

kitch'en gar'den s orto

kitch'en-maid' s sguattera

kitch'en police' s (mil) corvè f di cucina

kitch'en range' s cucina economica

kitch'en sink' s acquaio

kitch'en-ware' s utensili *mpl* di cucina

kite [kaɪt] s cervo volante, aquilone m; (orn) nibbio

kith' and kin' [kɪθ] *spl* amici *mpl* e parenti *mpl*

kitten ['kɪtən] s gattino

kittenish ['kɪtənɪʃ] *adj* giocattolone, civettuolo

kit·ty ['kɪti] s (**-ties**) gattino; (cards) piatto || *interj* micio!

kleptomaniac [ˌkleptə'menɪ ˌæk] s cleptomane mf

knack [næk] s abilità f, destrezza

knapsack ['næp ˌsæk] s zaino

knave [nev] s furfante m; (cards) fante m

knaver·y ['nevəri] s (**-ies**) furfanteria

knead [nid] *tr* maneggiare, intridere; (*a muscle*) massaggiare

knee [ni] s ginocchio; (*of trousers*) ginocchiera; (mach) gomito; **to bring s.o. to his knees** ridurre qlcu all'obbedienza; **to go down on one's knees** (**to**) gettarsi in ginocchio (davanti a)

knee' breech'es [ˌbrɪtʃɪz] *spl* calzoni *mpl* al ginocchio

knee'cap' s rotula, patella; (*protective covering*) ginocchiera

knee'-deep' *adj* fino al ginocchio

knee'-high' *adj* fino al ginocchio

knee' jerk' s riflesso patellare

kneel [nil] *v* (*pret & pp* **knelt** [nelt] or **kneeled**) *intr* inginocchiarsi

knee'pad' s ginocchiera

knee'pan' s rotula, patella

knell [nɛl] s rintocco funebre, campana a morto; **to toll the knell of** annunciare la morte di || *intr* suonare a morto

knickers ['nɪkərz] *spl* knickerbockers *mpl*, calzoni *mpl* alla zuava

knickknack ['nɪk ˌnæk] s soprammobile m; gingillo, ninnolo

knife [naɪf] s (**knives** [naɪvz]) coltello; (*of a paper cutter*) mannaia; (*of a milling machine*) fresa; **to go under the knife** essere sulla tavola operatoria || *tr* accoltellare; mettere il coltello nella schiena di

knife' sharp'ener s affilatoio

knife' switch' *s* (elec) coltella
knight [naɪt] *s* cavaliere *m*; (chess) cavallo || *tr* armare cavaliere
knight-errant [ˈnaɪtˈerənt] *s* (**knights-errant**) cavaliere *m* errante
knighthood [ˈnaɪt·hʊd] *s* cavalleria
knightly [ˈnaɪtli] *adj* cavalleresco
knit [nɪt] *v* (*pret & pp* **knitted** or **knit**; *ger* **knitting**) *tr* lavorare a maglia; (*to join*) unire; (*e.g., the brow*) corrugare || *intr* lavorare a maglia; fare la calza; unirsi; (*said of a bone*) saldarsi
knitting [ˈnɪtɪŋ] *s* maglia, lavoro a maglia
knit'ting machine' *s* macchina per maglieria
knit'ting mill' *s* maglieria
knit'ting nee'dle *s* ferro da calza
knit'wear' *s* maglieria
knit'wear store' *s* maglieria
knob [nɑb] *s* (*lump*) bozza, protuberanza; (*of a door*) maniglia; (*on furniture*) pomolo; (*hill*) collinetta rotondeggiante; (rad, telv) manopola, pulsante *m*
knock [nɑk] *s* colpo; (*on a door*) tocco; (slang) attacco, critica || *tr* battere; (*repeatedly*) sbatacchiare; (slang) attaccare, criticare; **to knock down** (*with a punch*) stendere a terra; (*a wall*) diroccare; (*to the highest bidder*) aggiudicare; (*e.g., a machine*) smontare; **to knock off** (*work*) (slang) sospendere; (slang) terminare; (slang) uccidere; **to knock out** mettere fuori combattimento || *intr* battere; (aut) battere in testa; (slang) criticare; **to knock about** (slang) gironzolare; **to knock against** urtare contro; **to knock at** (*e.g., a door*) battere a, bussare a; **to knock off** (slang) cessare di lavorare
knock'down' *adj* (*blow*) knock down, che atterra; (*dismountable*) smontabile || *s* (*blow*) colpo che atterra; (*discount*) sconto
knocker [ˈnɑkər] *s* (*on a door*) battaglio, bussatoio; (coll) criticone *m*
knock-kneed [ˈnɑkˌnid] *adj* con le gambe a X [iks]
knock'out' *s* pugno che mette fuori combattimento; fuori combattimento; (coll) pezzo di giovane
knock'out drops' *spl* (slang) narcotico
knoll [nol] *s* poggio, rialzo
knot [nɑt] *s* nodo; (*worn as an ornament*) fiocco; (*in wood*) nocchio; gruppo; protuberanza; (*tie*) nodo;

(naut) nodo; **to tie the knot** (coll) sposarsi || *v* (*pret & pp* **knotted**; *ger* **knotting**) *tr* annodare; (*the brow*) corrugare || *intr* annodarsi
knot'hole' *s* buco lasciato da un nodo (nel legno)
knot-ty [ˈnɑti] *adj* (**-tier; -tiest**) nodoso; (fig) spinoso
know [no] *s*—**to be in the know** (coll) essere al corrente || *v* (*pret* **knew** [nju] or [nu]; *pp* **known**) *tr & intr* (*by reasoning or learning*) sapere; (*by the senses or by perception; through acquaintance or recognition*) conoscere; **as far as I know** per quanto io ne sappia; **to know about** essere al corrente di; **to know best** essere il miglior giudice; **to know how** to + *inf* sapere + *inf*; **to know it all** (coll) sapere tutto; **to know what's what** (coll) saperla lunga; **you ought to know better** dovresti vergognarti
knowable [ˈno·əbəl] *adj* conoscibile
know'-how' *s* sapere *m*, abilità *f*
knowingly [ˈno·ɪŋli] *adv* con conoscenza di causa; (*on purpose*) apposta
know'-it-all' *adj & s* (coll) saputello
knowledge [ˈnɑlɪdʒ] *s* (*faculty*) scibile *m*, sapere *m*, sapienza; (*awareness, acquaintance, familiarity*) conoscenza; **to have a thorough knowledge of** conoscere a fondo; **to my knowledge** per quanto io ne sappia; **with full knowledge** con conoscenza di causa; **without my knowledge** a mia insaputa
knowledgeable [ˈnɑlɪdʒəbəl] *adj* intelligente, bene informato
knuckle [ˈnʌkəl] *s* nocca; foro del cardine, cardine *m*; **knuckles** pugno di ferro || *intr*—**to knuckle down** (coll) lavorare di impegno; **to knuckle under** (coll) darsi per vinto
knurl [nʌrl] *s* granitura || *tr* godranare, zigrinare
Koran [koˈrɑn] or [koˈræn] *s* Corano
Korea [koˈri·ə] *s* la Corea
Korean [koˈri·ən] *adj & s* coreano
kosher [ˈkoʃər] *adj* kasher, casher, puro secondo la legge giudaica; (coll) autentico
kowtow [ˈkaʊˈtaʊ] or [ˈkoˈtaʊ] *intr* inchinarsi servilmente
Kremlin [ˈkremlɪn] *s* Cremlino
Kremlinology [ˌkremlɪˈnɑlədʒi] *s* Cremlinologia
kudos [ˈkjudas] or [ˈkudas] *s* (coll) gloria, fama, approvazione

I

L, l [el] *s* dodicesima lettera dell'alfabeto inglese
la-bel [ˈlebəl] *s* marca, etichetta; (*descriptive word*) qualifica || *v* (*pret & pp* **-beled** or **-belled**; *ger* **-beling** or **-belling**) *tr* etichettare; qualificare
labial [ˈlebɪ·əl] *adj & s* labiale *f*

labor [ˈlebər] *adj* operaio || *s* lavoro; (*toil*) fatica; (*childbirth*) parto; (*body of wage earners*) manodopera; (*class as contrasted with management*) prestatori *mpl* d'opera, lavoro; **labors** fatiche *fpl*; **to be in labor** avere le doglie || *intr* lavorare; (*to exert one-*

self) travagliare; (*said of a ship*) rollare e beccheggiare; **to labor for** lottare per; **to labor under** soffrire di

laborato·ry [ˈlæbərəˌtori] *s* (**-ries**) laboratorio

la′bor dispute′ *s* vertenza sindacale

labored [ˈlebərd] *adj* elaborato, artificiale; penoso, difficile

laborer [ˈlebərər] *s* lavoratore *m*; (*unskilled worker*) bracciante *m*, manovale *m*, uomo di fatica

laborious [ləˈborɪ·əs] *adj* laborioso

la′bor un′ion *s* sindacato

Labourite [ˈlebəˌraɪt] *s* laburista *mf*

labyrinth [ˈlæbɪrɪnθ] *s* labirinto

lace [les] *s* (*cord or string*) stringa; (*netlike ornament*) trina, merletto; (*braid*) gallone *m* || *tr* stringare; merlettare; (coll) fustigare

lace′work′ *s* trina, merletto, pizzo

lachrymose [ˈlækrɪˌmos] *adj* lacrimoso

lacing [ˈlesɪŋ] *s* stringa, cordone *m*; gallone *m*; (coll) battuta, frustata

lack [læk] *s* mancanza, scarsezza, difetto || *tr* mancare di, scarseggiare di || *intr* mancare, scarseggiare, difettare

lackadaisical [ˌlækəˈdezɪkəl] *adj* letargico, indifferente

lackey [ˈlæki] *s* lacchè *m*

lacking [ˈlækɪŋ] *prep* privo di

lack′lus′ter *adj* smorto, spento

laconic [ləˈkɑnɪk] *adj* laconico

lacquer [ˈlækər] *s* lacca || *tr* laccare

lac′quer spray′ *s* lacca spray

lac′quer ware′ *s* oggetti *mpl* laccati

lacu·na [leˈkjunə] *s* (**-nas** or **-nae** [ni]) lacuna

lac·y [ˈlesi] *adj* (**-ier**; **-iest**) simile al merletto

lad [læd] *s* ragazzo, fanciullo

ladder [ˈlædər] *s* scala; (*stepladder hinged on top*) scaleo; (*stepping stone*) (fig) scalino

lad′der truck′ *s* autocarro di pompieri munito di scale

la′dies′ man′ *s* beato fra le donne

la′dies′ room′ *s* gabinetto per signore

ladle [ˈledəl] *s* ramaiolo, mestolo; (*of tinsmith*) cucchiaio || *tr* scodellare

la·dy [ˈledi] *s* (**-dies**) signora, dama

la′dy·bug′ *s* coccinella

la′dy·fin′ger *s* savoiardo, lingua di gatto

la′dy-in-wait′ing *s* (**ladies-in-waiting**) dama di corte

la′dy-kil′ler *s* rubacuori *m*

la′dy·like′ *adj* signorile; **to be ladylike** comportarsi come una signora

la′dy-love′ *s* amata

la′dy of the house′ *s* padrona di casa

ladyship [ˈlediˌʃɪp] *s* signoria

la′dy′s maid′ *s* cameriera personale della signora

lag [læg] *s* ritardo || *v* (*pret* & *pp* **lagged**; *ger* **lagging**) *intr* ritardare; **to lag behind** rimanere indietro

la′ger beer′ [ˈlɑgər] *s* birra invecchiata

laggard [ˈlægərd] *s* tardo, pigro

lagoon [ləˈgun] *s* laguna

laid′ pa′per [led] *s* carta vergata

laid′ up′ *adj* messo da parte; (naut) disarmato; (coll) costretto a letto

lair [lɛr] *s* tana, covo

laity [ˈle·ɪti] *s* laicato

lake [lek] *adj* lacustre || *s* lago

lamb [læm] *s* agnello

lambaste [læmˈbest] *tr* (*to thrash*) sferzare; (*to reprimand*) riprovare

lamb′ chop′ *s* cotoletta d'agnello

lambkin [ˈlæmkɪn] *s* agnellino; (fig) innocente *mf*

lamb′skin′ *s* (*leather*) pelle *f* d'agnello; (*skin with its wool*) agnello

lame [lem] *adj* zoppo; difettoso; (*disabled*) invalido; (*excuse*) dèbole || *tr* azzoppare

lament [ləˈment] *s* lamento; lamento funebre || *tr* lamentare || *intr* lamentarsi

lamentable [ˈlæməntəbəl] or [ləˈmentəbəl] *adj* lamentevole

lamentation [ˌlæmənˈteʃən] *s* lamentazione

laminate [ˈlæmɪˌnet] *tr* laminare

lamp [læmp] *s* lampada

lamp′black′ *s* nerofumo

lamp′ chim′ney *s* tubo di vetro di lampada a petrolio

lamp′light′ *s* luce *f* di lampada

lamp′light′er *s* lampionaio

lampoon [læmˈpun] *s* satira || *tr* satireggiare

lamp′post′ *s* colonna del lampione

lamp′shade′ *s* paralume *m*, ventola

lamp′wick′ *s* lucignolo

lance [læns] or [lɑns] *s* lancia; (surg) lancetta || *tr* (*with an oxygen lance*) tagliare col cannello ossidrico; (surg) sbrigliare, incidere col bisturi

lance′ rest′ *s* resta

lancet [ˈlænsɪt] or [ˈlɑnsɪt] *s* (surg) lancetta

land [lænd] *adj* terrestre; (*wind*) di terra || *s* terra; **on land, on sea, and in the air** per mare, per terra e nel cielo; **to make land** toccare terra; **to see how the land lies** tastare terreno || *tr* sbarcare; (aer) fare atterrare; (coll) pigliare || *intr* sbarcare; (*to come to rest*) andare a finire; (naut) toccar terra; (aer) atterrare; **to land on one's feet** cadere in piedi; **to land on one's head** andare a gambe all'aria; **to land on the moon** allunare; **to land on the water** ammarare

land′ breeze′ *s* vento di terra

landed [ˈlændɪd] *adj* (*owning land*) terriero; (*real estate*) immobile

land′fall′ *s* (*sighting land*) avvistamento; terra avvistata; (*landslide*) frana

land′ grant′ *s* terreno ricevuto in dono dallo stato

land′hold′er *s* proprietario terriero

landing [ˈlændɪŋ] *s* (*of passengers*) sbarco; (*place where passengers and goods are landed*) imbarcadero; (*of stairway*) pianerottolo; (aer, naut) atterraggio

land′ing bea′con *s* radiofaro d'atterraggio

land′ing card′ *s* cartoncino di sbarco

land′ing craft′ *s* imbarcazione da sbarco

land′ing field′ *s* campo d'atterraggio

land'ing flap' s (aer) iposostentatore m

land'ing gear' s (aer) carrello d'atterraggio

land'ing strip' s (aer) pista d'atterraggio

land'la'dy s (-dies) (of an apartment) padrona di casa; (of a lodging house) affittacamere f; (of an inn) ostessa

landlocked ['lænd ,lɑkt] adj circondato da terra

land'lord' s (of an apartment) padrone m di casa; (of a lodging house) affittacamere m; (of an inn) oste m

land·lubber ['lænd ,lʌbər] s marinaio d'acqua dolce

land'mark' s (boundary stone) pietra di confine; (distinguishing landscape feature) punto di riferimento; (fig) pietra miliare

land' of'fice s ufficio del catasto

land'-office busi'ness s (coll) sacco d'affari

land'own'er s proprietario terriero

landscape ['lænd ,skep] s paesaggio || tr abbellire

land'scape gar'dener s giardiniere m ornamentale

land'scape paint'er s paesista mf

landscapist ['lænd ,skepɪst] s paesista mf

land'slide' s frana; (fig) vittoria strepitosa

landward ['lændwərd] adv verso terra, verso la costa

land' wind' s vento di terra

lane [len] s (narrow street) vicolo, viuzza; (of a highway) corsia; (naut) rotta; (aer) corridoio

langsyne [,læŋ'saɪn] s (Scotch) tempo passato || adv (Scotch) molto tempo fa

language ['læŋgwɪdʒ] s lingua; (style of language) linguaggio; (of a special group of people) gergo

lan'guage lab'oratory s laboratorio linguistico

languid ['læŋgwɪd] adj languido

languish ['læŋgwɪʃ] intr languire; affettare languore

languor ['læŋgər] s languore m

languorous ['læŋgərəs] adj languido; (causing languor) snervante

lank [læŋk] adj scarnito, sparuto

lank·y ['læŋki] adj (-ier; -iest) scarnito, sparuto

lantern ['læntərn] s lanterna

lan'tern slide' s diapositiva

lanyard ['lænjərd] s (naut) drizza; (mil) aghetto, cordellina

lap [læp] s (of human body or clothing) grembo; (with the tongue) leccata; (of the waves) sciacquio; (sports) giro, tappa; **in the lap of** in mezzo a, e.g., **in the lap of luxury** in mezzo alle delicatezze || v (pret & pp **lapped;** ger **lapping**) tr lappare; (said, e.g., of waves) lambire; (to fold) piegare; (to overlap) sovrapporre; **to lap up** lappare; (coll) accettare con entusiasmo || intr sovrapporsi; **to lap against** (said of the waves) lambire; **to lap over** traboccare

lap'board' s tavolino da lavoro da tenersi sulle ginocchia

lap' dissolve' s (mov) dissolvenza incrociata

lap' dog' s cagnolino da salotto

lapel [lə'pɛl] s risvolto

Lap'land' s la Lapponia

Laplander ['læp ,lændər] s lappone mf

Lapp [læp] s lappone mf; (language) lappone m

lap' robe' s coperta da viaggio

lapse [læps] s (interval) spazio di tempo; (fall, decline) caduta; (of memory) perdita; errore m; (ins) risoluzione; (law) decadenza || intr cadere, ricadere; cadere in disuso; (said of time) passare; (ins) risolversi; (law) decadere

lap'wing' s pavoncella

larce·ny ['lɑrsəni] s (-nies) furto

larch [lɑrtʃ] s larice m

lard [lɑrd] s strutto || tr lardellare

larder ['lɑrdər] s dispensa

large [lɑrdʒ] adj grande, grosso || s— **at large** in libertà

large' intes'tine s intestino crasso

largely ['lɑrdʒli] adv in gran parte

large'-scale' adj su larga scala

lariat ['lærɪ·ət] s lazo, laccio

lark [lɑrk] s allodola; (coll) burla; **to go on a lark** (coll) far festa

lark'spur' s (rocket larkspur) sprone m di cavaliere; (field larkspur) consolida reale

lar·va ['lɑrvə] s (-vae [vi]) larva

laryngitis [,lærɪn'dʒaɪtɪs] s laringite f

laryngoscope [lə'rɪŋgə ,skop] s laringoscopio

larynx ['lærɪŋks] s (**larynxes** or **larynges** [lə'rɪndʒiz]) laringe f

lascivious [lə'sɪvɪ·əs] adj lascivo

lasciviousness [lə'sɪvɪ·əsnɪs] s lascivia

laser ['lezər] s (acronym) (**light amplification by stimulated emission of radiation**) laser m

lash [læʃ] s (cord on end of whip) sverzino; (blow with whip; scolding) staffilata; (of animal's tail) colpo; (eyelash) ciglio; (fig) assalto || tr (to whip) frustare; (to bind) legare; (to shake) agitare; (to attack with words) staffilare || intr lanciarsi; **to lash out at** attaccare violentemente

lashing ['læʃɪŋ] s legatura; (severe scolding) staffilata; (fastening with a rope) (naut) rizza

lass [læs] s ragazza, giovane f; innamorata

las·so ['læso] or [læ'su] s (-sos or -soes) lasso, lazo || tr pigliare col lasso

last [læst] or [lɑst] adj ultimo, passato; (most recent) scorso; **before last** ieralltro, e.g., **the night before last** ieralltro notte; **every last one** tutti senza eccezione; **last but one** penultimo || s ultima persona; ultima cosa; fine f; (for holding shoes) forma; **at last** alla fine; **at long last!** finalmente; **stick to your last!** fa' il mestiere tuo!; **the last of the month** alla fine del mese; **to breathe one's last** dare l'ultimo sospiro; **to see the last of s.o.** vedere qlcu per l'ultima volta; **to the last** fino alla fine || *adv* ultimo, per ultimo, alla fine || *intr* durare, continuare

lasting ['læstɪŋ] *or* ['lɑstɪŋ] *adj* duraturo, durevole

lastly ['læstli] *or* ['lɑstli] *adv* finalmente, in conclusione

last'-min'ute news' *s* notizie *fpl* dell'ultima ora

last' name' *s* cognome *m*

last' night' *adv* ieri sera; la notte scorsa

last' quar'ter *s* ultimo quarto

last' sleep' *s* ultimo sonno

last' straw' *s* ultima, colmo

Last' Sup'per *s* Ultima Cena

last will' and tes'tament *s* ultime volontà *fpl*

last' word' *s* ultima parola; *(latest style)* ultima novità, ultimo grido

latch [læt∫] *s* saliscendi *m*; *(wooden)* nottola || *tr* chiudere col saliscendi

latch'key' *s* chiave *f* per saliscendi

latch'string' *s*—**the latchstring is out** faccia come fosse a casa Sua

late [let] *adj (happening after the usual time)* tardo; *(person)* in ritardo; *(hour of the night)* avanzato; *(news)* dell'ultima ora, recente; *(incumbent of an office)* predecessore, ex, passato; *(coming toward the end of a period)* tardivo; *(deceased)* defunto, fu; **in the late 30's, 40's, etc.** verso la fine del decennio che va dal 1930, 1940, etc. al 1940, 1950, etc.; **of late** recentemente; **to be late in** + *ger* essere in ritardo a + *inf*; **to grow late** farsi tardi; **to keep late hours** fare le ore piccole || *adv* tardi; in ritardo; **late in** *(the week, the month, etc.)* alla fine di; **late in life** a un'età avanzata

latecomer ['let,kʌmər] *s* ritardatario

lateen' sail' [læ'tin] *s* vela latina

lately ['letli] *adv* recentemente

latent ['letənt] *adj* latente

later ['letər] *adj comp* più tardi; *(event)* susseguente; **later than** posteriore a || *adv comp* più tardi; **later on** più tardi; **see you later** (coll) arrivederci, a ben presto

lateral ['lætərəl] *adj* laterale

lath [læθ] *or* [lɑθ] *s* listello, striscia di legno || *tr* mettere listelli su

lathe [leð] *s* tornio

lather ['læðər] *s* schiuma di sapone; schiuma || *tr* insaponare; (coll) bastonare || *intr* schiumare

lathery ['læðəri] *adj* schiumoso

lathing ['læθɪŋ] *or* ['lɑθɪŋ] *s* costruzione con listelli

Latin ['lætɪn] *or* ['lætən] *adj & s* latino

Lat'in Amer'ica *s* l'America latina

Lat'in-Amer'ican *adj* dell'America latina

Lat'in Amer'ican *s* abitante *mf* dell'America latina

latitude ['lætɪ,tjud] *or* ['lætɪ,tud] *s* latitudine *f*

latrine [lə'trin] *s* latrina militare

latter ['lætər] *adj (more recent)* posteriore; *(of two)* secondo; **the latter** questo; **the latter part of** la fine di

lattice ['lætɪs] *s* graticcio || *tr* munire di graticcio, graticciare

lat'tice gird'er *s* trave *f* a traliccio

lat'tice·work' *s* graticcio, traliccio

Latvia ['lætvɪ·ə] *s* la Lettonia

laud [lɔd] *tr* lodare

laudable ['lɔdəbəl] *adj* lodevole

laudanum ['lɔdənəm] *or* ['lɔdnəm] *s* laudano

laudatory ['lɔdə,tori] *adj* lodativo

laugh [læf] *or* [lɑf] *s* riso || *tr*—**to laugh away** dissipare ridendo; **to laugh off** prendere sotto gamba, non dare importanza a || *intr* ridere, ridersi; **to laugh at** ridersi di; **to laugh up one's sleeve** ridere sotto i baffi

laughable ['læfəbəl] *or* ['lɑfəbəl] *adj* risibile

laughing ['læfɪŋ] *or* ['lɑfɪŋ] *adj* che ride; **to be no laughing matter** non esserci niente da ridere || *s* riso

laugh'ing gas' *s* gas *m* esilarante

laugh'ing·stock' *s* ludibrio, zimbello

laughter ['læftər] *or* ['lɑftər] *s* riso

launch [lɔnt∫] *or* [lɑnt∫] *s (of a ship)* varo; *(of a rocket)* lancio; (naut) lancia, scialuppa || *tr (to throw; to send forth)* lanciare; (naut) varare || *intr* lanciarsi

launching ['lɔnt∫ɪŋ] *or* ['lɑnt∫ɪŋ] *s* lancio; *(of a ship)* varo

launch'ing pad' *s* piattaforma di lancio

launder ['lɔndər] *or* ['lɑndər] *tr* lavare e stirare || *intr* riuscire dopo il lavaggio

launderer ['lɔndərər] *or* ['lɑndərər] *s* lavandaio stiratore *m*

laundress ['lɔndrɪs] *or* ['lɑndrɪs] *s* lavandaia stiratrice *f*

laundromat ['lɔndrə,mæt] *or* ['lɑndrə-,mæt] *s* (trademark) lavanderia a gettone

laun·dry ['lɔndri] *or* ['lɑndri] *s* (**-dries**) lavanderia; *(clothing)* bucato

laun'dry·man' *s* (**-men'**) lavandaio

laun'dry·wom'an *s* (**-wom'en**) lavandaia

laureate ['lɔrɪ·ɪt] *adj* laureato || *s* laureato; poeta laureato

lau·rel ['lɔrəl] *or* ['lɑrəl] *s* lauro, alloro; **laurels** (fig) alloro; **to rest or sleep on one's laurels** dormire sugli allori || *v (pret & pp* **-reled** *or* **-relled;** *ger* **-reling** *or* **-relling)** *tr* laureare

lava ['lɑvə] *or* ['lævə] *s* lava

lava·to·ry ['lævə,tori] *s* (**-ries**) *(room)* gabinetto da bagno; *(bowl)* lavabo; *(toilet)* gabinetto di decenza, cesso

lavender ['lævəndər] *s* lavanda

lavish ['lævɪ∫] *adj* prodigo || *tr* prodigare, profondere

law [lɔ] *s (of man, of nature, of science)* legge *f*; *(study, profession of law)* diritto; **to enter the law** farsi avvocato; **to go to law** ricorrere alla legge; **to lay down the law** dettar legge; **to maintain law and order** mantenere la pace interna; **to practice law** fare l'avvocato

law-abiding ['lɔ·ə,baɪdɪŋ] *adj* osservante della legge

law'break'er *s* violatore *m* della legge

law' court' s tribunale m di giustizia

lawful ['lɔfəl] adj legale, legittimo

lawless ['lɔlɪs] adj illegale; (unbridled) sfrenato

law'mak'er s legislatore m

lawn [lɔn] s tappeto erboso; (fabric) batista

lawn' mow'er s tosatrice f

law' of'fice s ufficio d'avvocato

law' of na'tions s diritto delle genti

law' of the jun'gle s legge f della giungla

law' stu'dent s studente m di legge

law'suit' s causa, lite f, processo

lawyer ['lɔjər] s avvocato, legale m

lax [læks] adj (in morals) lasso, rilassato; (rope) lento; (negligent) trascurato; vago, indeterminato

laxative ['læksətɪv] adj purgativo || s purga, purgante m

lay [le] adj (not belonging to the clergy) laico; (not having special training) non dotto, profano || s configurazione, disposizione || v (pret & pp **laid** [led]) tr mettere, collocare; (snares) tendere; (one's eyes; a stone) porre; (blame) dare, gettare; (a bet) fare; (for consideration) presentare; (the table) imbandire; (said of a hen) deporre; (plans) impostare; (to locate) disporre; **to be laid in** (said of a scene) aver luogo in; **to lay aside** mettere da parte; **to lay down** dichiarare; (one's life) dare; (one's arms) deporre; **to lay low** abbattere, uccidere; **to lay off** (workers) licenziare; (to measure) marcare; (slang) lasciare in pace; **to lay open** rivelare; (to a danger) esporre; **to lay out** estendere; preparare, disporre; (a corpse) comporre; (money) (coll) sborsare; **to lay over** posporre; **to lay up** mettere da parte; obbligare a letto; (naut) disarmare || intr (said of a hen) fare le uova; **to lay about** dar botte da orbi; **to lay for** (slang) attendere al varco; **to lay off** (coll) cessare di lavorare; **to lay over** trattenersi, fermarsi; **to lay to** (naut) navigare alla cappa

lay' broth'er s frate m secolare; converso

lay' day' s (com) stallia

layer ['le·ər] s (of paint) mano f; (of bricks) testa; (e.g., of rocks) strato, falda; (anat) pannicolo; (hort) propaggine f || tr (hort) propagginare

lay'er cake' s dolce m a strati

layette [le'ɛt] s corredino

lay'fig'ure s manichino

laying ['le·ɪŋ] s posa; (of eggs) deporre m; (of a wire) tendere m

lay'man s (-men) (member of the laity) laico, secolare m; (not a member of a special profession) laico, profano

lay'off' s (dismissal of workers) licenziamento; (period of unemployment) disoccupazione

lay' of the land' s andamento generale

lay'out' s piano; (sketch) tracciato; (of tools) armamentario; (coll) residenza; (typ) menabò m; (coll) banchetto, festino

lay'o'ver s fermata in un viaggio

lay' sis'ter s suora al secolo; conversa

laziness ['lezɪnɪs] s pigrizia

la-zy ['lezi] adj (-zier; -ziest) pigro

la'zy-bones' s (coll) poltrone m

lea [li] s (fallow land) maggese m; (meadow) prato

lead [lɛd] adj plumbeo || s piombo; (of lead pencil) mina; (for sounding depth) (naut) scandaglio; (typ) interlinea || [lɛd] v (pret & pp **leaded**; ger **leading**) tr impiombare; (typ) interlineare || [lid] s (foremost place) primato; (guidance) guida, direzione; (leash) guinzaglio; (journ) testata; (cards) mano f, prima mano; (elec) conduttore m; (mach) passo; (min) filone m; (rad, telv) filo d'entrata; (theat) ruolo principale; (theat) primo attore; (theat) prima attrice; **to take the lead** prendere il comando || [lid] v (pret & pp **led** [lɛd]) tr condurre, portare; (to command) comandare, essere alla testa di; (an orchestra) dirigere; (a good or bad life) fare; (s.o. into vice) trascinare; (cards) cominciare a giocare; (elec, mach) anticipare; **to lead astray** forviare || intr essere in testa, guidare; prendere l'offensiva; (said of a road) condurre; (cards) cominciare a giocare; **to lead to** risultare in; **to lead up to** andare a condurre a

leaden ['lɛdən] adj (of lead; like lead) plumbeo; (sluggish) tardo; (with sleep) carico; triste

leader ['lidər] s capo, comandante m; (ringleader) capobanda m; (of an orchestra) direttore m; (among animals) guidaiolo; (in a dance) ballerino guidaiolo; (sports) capintesta m; (journ) articolo di fondo

lead'er dog' s cane m guida di ciechi

leadership ['lidər‚ʃɪp] s comando, direzione; doti fpl di comando

leading ['lidɪŋ] adj principale; primo; dirigente, preeminente

lead'ing ar'ticle s articolo di fondo

lead'ing edge' s (aer) bordo d'attacco

lead'ing la'dy s prima attrice

lead'ing man' s (men') primo attore

lead'ing ques'tion s domanda suggestiva, domanda orientatrice

lead'ing strings' spl dande fpl

lead'-in wire' ['lid‚ɪn] s filo d'antenna

lead' pen'cil ['lɛd] s lapis m, matita

leaf [lif] s (leaves [livz]) (of plant) foglia; (of vine) pampino; (of paper) foglio; (of double door) battente m; (of table) asse m a ribalta; **to turn over a new leaf** ricominciare una nuova vita || intr fogliare; **to leaf through** sfogliare

leafless ['liflɪs] adj senza foglie

leaflet ['liflɪt] s manifestino, volantino; (of plant) foglietta

leaf' spring' s molla a balestra

leaf'stalk' s picciolo

leaf-y ['lifi] adj (-ier; -iest) foglioso, frondoso

league [lig] s lega || tr associare || intr associarsi

League′ of Na′tions s Società f delle Nazioni

leak [lik] s (*in a roof*) stillicidio; (*in a ship*) falla; (*of water, gas, steam*) fuga; (*of electricity*) dispersione; buco, fessura; (*of news*) filtrazione; **to spring a leak** avere una perdita; (*naut*) cominciare a far acqua ‖ *tr* (*gas, liquids*) perdere, lasciar scappare; (*news*) lasciar trapelare ‖ *intr* (*said of water, gas etc.,*) perdere, scappare; (*said of a barrel*) spillare; (*naut*) fare acqua; **to leak away** (*said of money*) andarsene; **to leak out** (*said of news*) trapelare

leakage ['likɪdʒ] s perdita, fuoruscita, fuga; (*elec*) dispersione; (*com*) colaggio

leak·y ['liki] adj (-ier; -iest) che perde; (*naut*) che fa acqua; (*coll*) indiscreto

lean [lin] adj magro, secco; (*gasoline mixture*) povero ‖ v (*pret & pp* **leaned** or **leant** [lɛnt]) *tr* inclinare; appoggiare ‖ *intr* pendere, inclinarsi; (*fig*) inclinare, tendere; **to lean against** appoggiarsi a, addossarsi a; **to lean back** sdraiarsi; **to lean on** appoggiarsi su; **to lean out (of)** sporgersi (da); **to lean over backwards** fare di tutto; **to lean toward** (fig) tendere a, avere un′inclinazione per

leaning ['linɪŋ] adj inclinato, pendente ‖ s inclinazione

lean′ing tow′er s torre f pendente

lean′-to′ s (-tos) tetto a una falda

leap [lip] s salto, balzo; **by leaps and bounds** a passi da gigante; **leap in the dark** salto nel vuoto ‖ v (*pret & pp* **leaped** or **leapt** [lɛpt]) *tr* saltare ‖ *intr* saltare; (*said of one′s heart*) balzare

leap′frog′ s cavallina; **to play leapfrog** giocare alla cavallina

leap′ year′ s anno bisestile

learn [lʌrn] v (*pret & pp* **learned** or **learnt** [lʌrnt]) *tr* imparare; imparare a memoria; (*news*) apprendere ‖ *intr* istruirsi, apprendere

learned ['lʌrnɪd] adj dotto; (*word*) colto

learn′ed jour′nal s rivista scientifica

learn′ed soci′ety s associazione di eruditi

learn′ed word′ s parola dotta

learn′ed world′ s mondo di dotti

learner ['lʌrnər] s apprendista mf; studente m; (*beginner*) principiante mf

learning ['lʌrnɪŋ] s istruzione; (*scholarship*) erudizione

lease [lis] s locazione, contratto d′affitto; **a new lease on life** nuove prospettive di felicità; vita nuova (dopo una malattia) ‖ *tr* locare; prendere in affitto ‖ *intr* affittare

lease′hold′ adj affittato ‖ s beni mpl sotto locazione

leash [liʃ] s guinzaglio; **to strain at the leash** mordere il freno ‖ *tr* frenare, controllare

least [list] adj minore, menomo, minimo ‖ s (il) meno; **at least** or **at the least** per lo meno, quanto meno;

not in the least nient′affatto ‖ adv meno

leather ['lɛðər] s cuoio

leath′er·back′ tur′tle s tartaruga di mare

leath′er goods′ store′ s pelletteria

leathery ['lɛðəri] adj coriaceo

leave [liv] s (*permission*) permesso; (*permission to be absent*) licenza; (*farewell*) commiato; **on leave** in licenza; **to take French leave** andarsene all′inglese; **to take leave (of)** prender congedo (da) ‖ v (*pret & pp* **left** [lɛft]) *tr* (*to go away from*) lasciare, uscire da; (*to let stay*) lasciare; (*to bequeath*) lasciare in testamento; **leave it to me!** lasciami fare!; **to be left** restare, e.g., **the door was left open** la porta restò aperta; **there is no bread left** non c′è più pane; **to leave alone** lasciare in pace; **to leave no stone unturned** cercare ogni possibilità; **to leave off** abbandonare, lasciare; **to leave out** omettere; **to leave things as they are** lasciar stare le cose ‖ *intr* andarsene; (*said of a conveyance*) partire

leaven ['lɛvən] s lievito ‖ *tr* lievitare; (fig) impregnare, permeare

leavening ['lɛvənɪŋ] s lievito

leave′ of ab′sence s licenza; (*without pay*) aspettativa

leave′-tak′ing s commiato

leavings ['livɪŋz] spl rifiuti mpl

Leba·nese [,lɛbə'niz] adj libanese ‖ s (-nese) libanese mf

Lebanon ['lɛbənən] s il Libano

lecher ['lɛtʃər] s libertino

lecherous ['lɛtʃərəs] adj libidinoso

lechery ['lɛtʃəri] s lussuria

lectern ['lɛktərn] s leggio

lecture ['lɛktʃər] s conferenza; (*tedious reprimand*) pistolotto ‖ *tr* dare una conferenza a; sermoneggiare ‖ *intr* fare una conferenza; sermoneggiare

lecturer ['lɛktʃərər] s conferenziere m

ledge [lɛdʒ] s cornice f, cornicione m

ledger ['lɛdʒər] s (com) libro mastro

ledg′er line′ s (mus) rigo supplementare

lee [li] s (*shelter*) rifugio; (naut) parte f sottovento; **lees** feccia

leech [litʃ] s mignatta, sanguisuga; **to stick like a leech** attaccarsi come una sanguisuga

leek [lik] s porro

leer [lɪr] s occhiata lussuriosa or maligna ‖ *intr*—**to leer at** guardare di sbieco, sbirciare

leer·y ['lɪri] adj (-ier; -iest) sospettoso

leeward ['liwərd] or ['lu·ərd] adj di sottovento ‖ s sottovento, poggia ‖ adv sottovento

lee′way′ s (aer, naut) deriva, scarroccio; (in time) (coll) tolleranza; (coll) libertà f d′azione

left [lɛft] adj sinistro; (pol) di sinistra ‖ s sinistra; (boxing) sinistro ‖ adv alla sinistra

left′ field′ s fuoricampo di sinistra

left′-hand′ drive′ s guida a sinistra

left-handed ['lɛft'hændɪd] adj (*individual*) mancino; (*awkward*) goffo;

(*compliment*) ambiguo; (*mach*) sinistrorso

leftish [ˈleftɪʃ] *adj* sinistrista

leftist [ˈleftɪst] *adj* di sinistra ‖ *s* membro della sinistra

left'o'ver *adj & s* rimanente *m;* **left-overs** resti *mpl*

left'-wing' *adj* di sinistra

left-winger [ˈleftˈwɪŋər] *s* (coll) membro dell'estrema sinistra; (coll) membro della sinistra

leg [leg] *s* (*of man, animal, table, chair; of trousers*) gamba; (*of fowl; of lamb*) coscia; (*of boot*) gambale *m;* (*of a journey*) tappa; **to be on one's last legs** essere agli estremi, essere ridotto alla disperazione; **to not have a leg to stand on** (coll) non avere la minima giustificazione; **to pull the leg of** (coll) prendere in giro, burlarsi di; **to shake a leg** (coll) affrettarsi; (*to dance*) (coll) ballare; **to stretch one's legs** sgranchirsi le gambe

lega·cy [ˈlegəsi] *s* (-**cies**) legato

legal [ˈligəl] *adj* legale

legali·ty [lɪˈgælɪti] *s* (-**ties**) legalità *f*

legalize [ˈligəˌlaɪz] *tr* legalizzare

le'gal ten'der *s* denaro a corso legale

legate [ˈlegɪt] *s* legato

legatee [ˌlegəˈti] *s* legatario

legation [lɪˈgeʃən] *s* legazione

legend [ˈledʒənd] *s* leggenda

legendary [ˈledʒənˌderi] *adj* leggendario

legerdemain [ˌledʒərdɪˈmen] *s* gioco di prestigio; (*trickery*) imbroglio

legging [ˈlegɪŋ] *s* gambale *m*

leg·gy [ˈlegi] *adj* (-**gier; -giest**) dalle gambe lunghe

leg'horn' *s* cappello di paglia di Firenze; gallina bianca livornese ‖ **Leghorn** *s* Livorno

legible [ˈledʒɪbəl] *adj* leggibile

legion [ˈlidʒən] *s* legione *f*

legislate [ˈledʒɪs‚let] *tr* ordinare per mezzo di legge ‖ *intr* legiferare

legislation [ˌledʒɪsˈleʃən] *s* legislazione

legislative [ˈledʒɪs‚letɪv] *adj* legislativo

legislator [ˈledʒɪs‚letər] *s* legislatore *m*

legislature [ˈledʒɪs‚letʃər] *s* legislatura; corpo legislativo

legitimacy [lɪˈdʒɪtɪməsi] *s* legittimità *f*

legitimate [lɪˈdʒɪtɪmɪt] *adj* legittimo ‖ [lɪˈdʒɪtɪ‚met] *tr* legittimare

legit'imate dra'ma *s* teatro serio

legitimize [lɪˈdʒɪtɪ‚maɪz] *tr* legittimare

leg' of lamb' *s* cosciotto d'agnello

legume [ˈlegjum] *or* [lɪˈgjum] *s* (*pod*) legume *m;* (*table vegetables*) legumi *mpl;* (bot) leguminose *fpl*

leg'work' *s* lavoro che involve molto cammino

leisure [ˈlidʒər] *or* [ˈlɛʒər] *s* ozio; **at leisure** senza fretta; disoccupato; **at one's leisure** quando si abbia un po' di tempo libero

lei'sure class' *s* gente agiata

lei'sure hours' *spl* ore *fpl* d'ozio

leisurely [ˈlidʒərli] *or* [ˈlɛʒərli] *adj* lento ‖ *adv* lentamente, a tempo perso

lei'sure time' *s* tempo libero

lemon [ˈlemən] *s* limone *m;* (*car*) (coll) catorcio

lemonade [ˌleməˈned] *s* limonata

lem'on squeez'er *s* spremilimoni *m*

lend [lend] *s* (*pret & pp* **lent** [lent]) *tr* prestare; (*a hand*) dare

lender [ˈlendər] *s* prestatore *m*

lend'ing li'brary *s* biblioteca circolante

length [lɛŋθ] *s* lunghezza; (*of time*) durata; **at length** finalmente; **to go to any lengths** fare quanto è possibile; essere disposto a tutto; **to keep at arm's length** (*someone else*) tenere a distanza (qlcu); (*said of oneself*) tenere a distanza

lengthen [ˈlɛŋθən] *tr* allungare ‖ *intr* allungarsi

length'wise' *adj* longitudinale ‖ *adv* per il lungo

length·y [ˈlɛŋθi] *adj* (-**ier; -iest**) lungo, prolungato

lenien·cy [ˈlini‚ənsi] *s* (-**cies**) indulgenza

lenient [ˈliniˌənt] *adj* indulgente, clemente

lens [lenz] *s* lente *f;* (*of the eye*) cristallino

Lent [lent] *s* quaresima

Lenten [ˈlentən] *adj* quaresimale

lentil [ˈlentəl] *s* lenticchia

Leo [ˈli·o] *s* (astr) il Leone

leopard [ˈlepərd] *s* leopardo

leotard [ˈli·əˌtard] *s* calzamaglia

leper [ˈlepər] *s* lebbroso

leprosy [ˈleprəsi] *s* lebbra

leprous [ˈleprəs] *adj* lebbroso; (*of an animal or plant*) squamoso

Lesbian [ˈlezbɪ‚ən] *adj* lesbico ‖ *s* lesbico; (*female homosexual*) lesbica

lesbianism [ˈlezbɪ‚ə‚nɪzəm] *s* lesbismo

lese majesty [ˈlizˈmædʒɪsti] *s* delitto di lesa maestà

lesion [ˈliʒən] *s* lesione *f*

less [les] *adj* minore ‖ *adv* meno; **less and less** sempre meno; **less than** meno che; (*followed by numeral or personal pron*) meno di; (*followed by verb*) meno di quanto ‖ *s* meno

lessee [lesˈi] *s* locatario; (*of business establishment*) concessionario

lessen [ˈlesən] *tr* diminuire, ridurre ‖ *intr* diminuire, ridursi

lesser [ˈlesər] *adj comp* minore

lesson [ˈlesən] *s* lezione *f*

lessor [ˈlesər] *s* locatore *m*

lest [lest] *conj* per paura che

let [let] *v* (*pret & pp* **let**; *ger* **letting**) *tr* permettere; (*to rent*) affittare; **let** + *inf* che + *subj*, e.g., **let him go** che vada; **let alone** tanto meno; senza menzionare; **let good enough alone** essere contento dell'onesto; **let us** + *inf* = 1st *pl impv*, e.g., **let us sing** cantiamo; **to let** da affittare; **to let alone** lasciare in pace; **to let be** lasciar stare; **to let by** lasciar passare; **to let down** far scendere; deludere; tradire; abbandonare; **to let fly** (*insults*) lanciare; **to let go** lasciar libero; vendere; **to let in** fare entrare; **to let it go at that** non parlarne più; **to let know** far sapere; **to**

let loose sciogliere; **to let out** lasciar uscire; (*a secret*) divulgare; (*a scream*) lasciarsi scappare; (*to enlarge*) allargare; affittare; **to let through** lasciar passare; **to let up** lasciar salire; lasciar alzare || *intr* affittare; **to let down** diminuire gli sforzi; **to let go of** disfarsi di; **to let on** (coll) fare finta; **to not let on** (coll) non lasciar trapelare; **to let out** (*said, e.g., of school*) terminare; **to let up** (coll) cessare; (coll) diminuire

let'down' *s* diminuzione; smacco, umiliazione; delusione

lethal ['liθəl] *adj* letale

lethargic [lɪ'θɑrdʒɪk] *adj* letargico

lethar∙gy ['lɛθərdʒi] *s* (**-gies**) letargo

Lett [lɛt] *s* lettone *mf*; (*language*) lettone *m*

letter ['lɛtər] *s* lettera; **letters** (*literature*) lettere *fpl*, letteratura; **to the letter** alla lettera || *tr* marcare con lettere

let'ter box' *s* cassetta delle lettere

let'ter car'rier *s* postino

let'ter drop' *s* buca delle lettere

let'ter-head' *s* capolettera *m*; (*paper with printed heading*) carta da lettera intestata

lettering ['lɛtərɪŋ] *s* iscrizione; lettere *fpl*

let'ter of cred'it *s* lettera di credito

let'ter o'pener ['opənər] *s* tagliacarte *m*

let'ter pa'per *s* carta da lettere

let'ter-per'fect *adj* alla lettera; che sa alla perfezione

let'ter-press' *s* stampato in tipografia || *adv* a stampa tipografica

let'ter scales' *spl* pesalettere *m*

let'ter-word' *s* sigla

Lettish ['lɛtɪʃ] *adj* & *s* lettone *m*

lettuce ['lɛtɪs] *s* lattuga

let'up' *s* (coll) pausa, sosta; (coll) tregua; **without letup** (coll) senza posa

leucorrhea [ˌlukə'riə] *s* leucorrea

leukemia [lu'kimɪə] *s* leucemia

Levant [lɪ'vænt] *s* levante *m*

levee ['lɛvi] *s* (*embankment*) argine *m*; (*reception*) ricevimento

lev∙el ['lɛvəl] *adj* piano; livellato; equilibrato; **level with** a livello di; **one's level best** (coll) il proprio meglio || *s* (*instrument*) livella; (*degree of elevation*) livello; (*flat surface*) spianata, pianura; **on the level** (slang) onesto; onestamente; **to find one's level** trovare il proprio ambiente || *v* (*pret* & *pp* **-eled** or **-elled**; *ger* **-eling** or **-elling**) *tr* livellare; (*to flatten out*) spianare; (*e.g., prices*) pareggiare, ragguagliare; (*a gun*) puntare; (coll) gettare a terra; (fig) dirigere || *intr*— **to level off** (aer) volare orizzontalmente

level-headed ['lɛvəl'hɛdɪd] *adj* equilibrato

lev'eling rod' *s* stadia

lever ['livər] or ['lɛvər] *s* leva || *tr* far leva su || *intr* far leva

leverage ['lɛvərɪdʒ] or ['livərɪdʒ] *s* azione di una leva; (fig) potere *m*

leviathan [lɪ'vaɪ·əθən] *s* leviatano

levitation [ˌlɛvɪ'teʃən] *s* levitazione

levi∙ty ['lɛvɪti] *s* (**-ties**) leggerezza

lev∙y ['lɛvi] *s* (**-ies**) (*of taxes*) esazione; (*of money*) tributo; (*of troops*) leva || *v* (*pret* & *pp* **-ied**) *tr* (*a tax*) imporre; (*soldiers*) reclutare; (*war*) fare

lewd [lud] *adj* (*lustful*) lascivo; osceno

lexical ['lɛksɪkəl] *adj* lessicale

lexicographer [ˌlɛksɪ'kɑgrəfər] *s* lessicografo

lexicographic(al) [ˌlɛksɪko'græfɪk(əl)] *adj* lessicografico

lexicography [ˌlɛksɪ'kɑgrəfi] *s* lessicografia

lexicology [ˌlɛksɪ'kɑlədʒi] *s* lessicologia

lexicon ['lɛksɪkən] *s* lessico

liabili∙ty [ˌlaɪ·ə'bɪlɪti] *s* (**-ties**) svantaggio; responsabilità *f*; (*e.g., to disease*) tendenza; (com) passivo; **liabilities** debiti *mpl*; (com) passivo

liabil'ity insur'ance *s* assicurazione sulla responsabilità civile

liable ['laɪəbəl] *adj* (*e.g., to disease*; *e.g., to make mistakes*) soggetto; responsabile; probabile; (*e.g., to a fine*) passibile

liaison ['li·əˌzɑn] or [li'ezən] *s* legame *m*; relazione illecita; (mil, nav) collegamento; (phonet) legamento

li'aison of'ficer *s* ufficiale *m* di collegamento

liar ['laɪ·ər] *s* bugiardo, mentitore *m*

libation [laɪ'beʃən] *s* (joc) libazione, bevuta

li∙bel ['laɪbəl] *s* diffamazione; (*defamatory writing*) libello || *v* (*pret* & *pp* **-beled** or **-belled**; *ger* **-beling** or **-belling**) *tr* diffamare

libelous ['laɪbələs] *adj* diffamatorio

liberal ['lɪbərəl] *adj* liberale; (*translation*) libero || *s* liberale *mf*

liberali∙ty [ˌlɪbə'rælɪti] *s* (**-ties**) liberalità *f*; (*breadth of mind*) ampiezza di vedute

liberal-minded ['lɪbərəl'maɪndɪd] *adj* liberale, tollerante

liberate ['lɪbəˌret] *tr* liberare

liberation [ˌlɪbə'reʃən] *s* liberazione

liberator ['lɪbəˌretər] *s* liberatore *m*

libertine ['lɪbərˌtin] *adj* & *s* libertino

liber∙ty ['lɪbərti] *s* (**-ties**) libertà *f*; **to take the liberty to** permettersi di

liberty-loving ['lɪbərti'lʌvɪŋ] *adj* amante della libertà

libidinous [lɪ'bɪdɪnəs] *adj* libidinoso

libido [lɪ'bido] or [lɪ'baɪdo] *s* libidine *f*; (psychoanal) libido *f*

Libra ['lɪbrə] or ['laɪbrə] *s* (astr) Bilancia

librarian [laɪ'brɛrɪ·ən] *s* bibliotecario

librar∙y ['laɪˌbrɛri] or ['laɪbrəri] *s* (**-ies**) biblioteca; (*room in a house*; *collection of books*) libreria

li'brary num'ber *s* segnatura

li'brary sci'ence *s* biblioteconomia

libret∙to [lɪ'breto] *s* (**-tos**) (mus) libretto

Libya ['lɪbɪ·ə] *s* la Libia

license ['laɪsəns] *s* licenza; (aut) patente *f* || *tr* dare la licenza a

li'cense num'ber s numero di targa di circolazione

li'cense plate' or **tag'** s targa di circolazione

licentious [laɪˈsɛn/əs] adj licenzioso

lichen [ˈlaɪkən] s lichene m

lick [lɪk] s leccata, leccatura; (coll) esplosione di energia; (coll) velocità f; (coll) battitura; (coll) ripulita; **to give a lick and a promise to** (coll) fare rapidamente e con poca attenzione ‖ tr leccare; (said of waves, flames, etc.) lambire; (to defeat) (coll) battere, vincere; (e.g., with a stick) (coll) bastonare

licorice [ˈlɪkərɪs] s liquirizia

lid [lɪd] s coperchio; (eyelid) palpebra; (curb) (coll) restrizione, freno; (hat) (slang) cappello

lie [laɪ] s menzogna; **to catch in a lie** pigliare in castagna; **to give the lie to** smentire ‖ v (pret & pp **lied**; ger **lying**) tr—**to lie oneself out of** or **to lie one's way out of** trarsi fuori da (un impaccio) con una menzogna ‖ intr mentire ‖ v (pret **lay** [le]; pp **lain** [len]; ger **lying**) intr essere sdraiato; trovarsi; (in the grave) giacere; **to lie down** sdraiarsi

lie' detec'tor s macchina della verità

lien [lin] or [ˈli·ən] s diritto di pegno, diritto di garanzia

lieu [lu] s—**in lieu of** in luogo di

lieutenant [luˈtɛnənt] s luogotenente m; (mil) tenente m; (nav) tenente m di vascello

lieuten'ant colo'nel s (mil) tenente m colonnello

lieuten'ant command'er s (nav) capitano di corvetta

lieuten'ant gen'eral s (mil) generale m di corpo d'armata

lieuten'ant gov'ernor s (USA) vicegovernatore m

lieuten'ant jun'ior grade' s (nav) sottotenente m di vascello

life [laɪf] adj (animate) vitale; (lifelong) perpetuo; (annuity) vitalizio; (working from nature) dal vero ‖ s (lives [laɪvz]) vita; (of an insurance policy) forza; **for life** a vita; **for the life of me** per quanto io provi; **the life and soul of** (e.g., the party) l'anima di; **to come to life** tornare a sé; riprender vita; **to depart this life** passar a miglior vita; **to run for one's life** scappare a tutta corsa

life' annu'ity s rendita vitalizia

life' belt' s cintura di salvataggio

life'boat' s imbarcazione di salvataggio, lancia di salvataggio

life' buoy' s salvagente m

life' float' s zattera di salvataggio

life'guard' s bagnino

life' impris'onment s ergastolo

life' insur'ance s assicurazione sulla vita

life' jack'et s cintura or giubbotto di salvataggio

lifeless [ˈlaɪflɪs] adj inanimato; (in a faint) esanime; senza vita

life'like' adj (e.g., portrait) parlante; naturale

life' line' s sagola di salvataggio; (fig) linea di comunicazione vitale

life'long' adj perpetuo, a vita

life' of Ri'ley s vita del michelaccio

life' of the par'ty s anima della festa

lifer [ˈlaɪfər] s (slang) ergastolano

life' raft' s zattera di salvataggio

life'sav'er s salvatore m della vita; (something that saves from a predicament) ancora di salvezza

life' sen'tence s condanna all'ergastolo

life'-size' adj in grandezza naturale

life'time' adj vitalizio ‖ s corso della vita

life' vest' s (air, naut) giubbotto salvagente or di salvataggio

life'work' s lavoro di tutta una vita

lift [lɪft] s sollevamento; (act of helping) aiuto; (ride) passaggio; (apparatus) elevatore m; (aer) portanza ‖ tr sollevare, alzare; (one's hat) levarsi; rimuovere; (coll) plagiare; (coll) rubare; (fire) (mil) sospendere ‖ intr sollevare, sollevarsi; (said, e.g., of fog) dissiparsi

lift'-off' s (aer) decollo verticale

lift' truck' s carrello elevatore

ligament [ˈlɪgəmənt] s legamento

ligature [ˈlɪgət/ər] s legatura

light [laɪt] adj (in weight) leggero; (hair) biondo; (complexion) chiaro; (oil) fluido; (naut) con poco carico; (room) chiaro, illuminato; (beer) chiaro; **light in the head** (dizzy) allegro; (silly) scimunito; **to make light of** prendere sotto gamba ‖ s luce f; (to light a cigarette) fuoco; (to control traffic) segnale m; (shining example) luminare m; (lighthouse) faro; (window) luce f; **according to one's lights** secondo l'intelligenza che il buon Dio gli (le) ha dato; **against the light** controluce; **in this light** sotto questo punto di vista; **lights** esempio; (of sheep) polmone m; **to come to light** venire alla luce; **to shed** or **throw light on** mettere in luce; **to strike a light** accendere un fiammifero ‖ v (pret & pp **lighted** or **lit** [lɪt]) tr (to furnish with illumination) illuminare; (to ignite) accendere; **to light up** illuminare ‖ intr illuminarsi; accendersi; (said, e.g., of a bird) posarsi; (from a car) scendere; **to light into** (coll) gettarsi contro; **to light out** (slang) darsela a gambe; **to light upon** imbattersi in ‖ adv senza bagagli; senza carico

light' bulb' s lampadina

light-complexioned [ˈlaɪtkəmˈplɛk/ənd] adj dal colorito chiaro

lighten [ˈlaɪtən] tr alleggerire, sgravare; illuminare; (to cheer up) rallegrare ‖ intr alleggerirsi; (to become less dark) illuminarsi; (to give off flashes of lightning) lampeggiare

lighter [ˈlaɪtər] s accenditore m; (naut) burchio

light-fingered [ˈlaɪtˈfɪŋgərd] adj svelto di mano, con le mani lunghe

light-footed ['laɪt'futɪd] *adj* agile

light-headed ['laɪt'hedɪd] *adj* (*dizzy*) allegro; (*simple*) scemo

light-hearted ['laɪt'hɑrtɪd] *adj* allegro

light'house' *s* faro

lighting ['laɪtɪŋ] *s* illuminazione

lightly ['laɪtlɪ] *adv* alla leggera

light' me'ter *s* esposimetro

lightness ['laɪtnɪs] *s* (*in weight*) leggerezza; (*in illumination*) chiarezza

light·ning ['laɪtnɪŋ] *s* lampo, fulmine *m* ‖ *v* (*ger* -ning) *intr* lampeggiare

light'ning arrest'er [ə'restər] *s* scaricatore *m*

light'ning bug' *s* lucciola

light'ning rod' *s* parafulmine *m*

light' op'era *s* operetta

light'ship' *s* battello-faro

light-struck ['laɪt ˌstrʌk] *adj* che ha preso luce

light'weight' *adj* leggero; da mezza stagione, e.g., **lightweight coat** cappotto da mezza stagione

light'-year' *s* anno luce

likable ['laɪkəbəl] *adj* simpatico

like [laɪk] *adj* uguale, simile; uguale a, simile a, e.g., **this hat is like mine** questo cappello è simile al mio; (*elec*) di segno uguale; **like father like son** tale il padre quale il figlio; **to feel like** + *ger* aver voglia di + *inf*; **to look like** assomigliare a; sembrare, e.g., **it looks like rain** sembra che pioverà ‖ *s* (*liking*) preferenza; (*fellow man*) simile *m*; **and the like e cose dello stesso genere; to give like for like** rendere pane per focaccia ‖ *adv* come; **like enough** (coll) probabilmente ‖ *prep* come ‖ *conj* (coll) come; come se; (coll) che, e.g., **it seems like he is afraid** sembra che abbia paura ‖ *tr* voler bene (with *dat*), e.g., **I like her very much** le voglio molto bene; trovar piacere in, e.g., **I like music** trovo piacere nella musica; piacere (with *dat*), e.g., **John likes apples** le mele piacciono a Giovanni; **to like best** *or* **better** preferire; **to like it** in trovarsi a proprio agio in; **to like to** + *inf* piacere (with *dat*) + *inf*, e.g., **she likes to dance** le piace ballare; gradire che + *subj*, e.g., **I should like him to pay a visit to my parents** gradirei che facesse una visita ai miei genitori ‖ *intr* volere, desiderare, e.g., **as you like** come desidera; **if you like** se vuole

likelihood ['laɪklɪˌhud] *s* probabilità *f*

like·ly ['laɪklɪ] *adj* (-lier; -liest) probabile; verosimile; a proposito; promettente; **to be likely to** + *inf* essere probabile che + *fut*, e.g., **Mary is likely to get married in the spring** è probabile che Maria si sposerà in primavera ‖ *adv* probabilmente

like-minded ['laɪk'maɪndɪd] *adj* dello stesso parere, della stessa opinione

liken ['laɪkən] *tr* paragonare

likeness ['laɪknɪs] *s* (*picture*) ritratto; (*similarity*) rassomiglianza; apparenza

like'wise' *adv* ugualmente; inoltre; **to do likewise** fare lo stesso

liking ['laɪkɪŋ] *s* simpatia; **to be to the liking of** essere di gusto di; **to have a liking for** (*things*) prendere gusto per; (*people*) affezionarsi a

lilac ['laɪlək] *adj* & *s* lilla *m*

Lilliputian [ˌlɪlɪ'pjuʃən] *adj* & *s* lillipuziano

lilt [lɪlt] *s* canzone *f* a cadenza; movimento a cadenza; (*in verse*) cadenza

lil·y ['lɪlɪ] *s* (-ies) giglio; **to gild the lily** cercare di migliorare quanto è già perfetto

lil'y of the val'ley *s* mughetto

li'ma bean' ['laɪmə] *s* fagiolo bianco

limb [lɪm] *s* (*of body*) membro, arto; (*of tree*) ramo; (*of cross*) braccio; **to be out on a limb** (coll) essere nei guai

limber ['lɪmbər] *adj* agile ‖ *intr*—**to limber up** sciogliersi i muscoli, sgranchirsi le gambe

lim·bo ['lɪmbo] *s* (-bos) esilio; dimenticatoio; (theol) limbo

lime [laɪm] *s* (*calcium oxide*) calce *f*; (*Citrus aurantifolia*) limetta agra; (*linden tree*) tiglio ‖ *tr* gessare

lime'kiln' *s* fornace *f* da calce

lime'light' *s*—**to be in the limelight** essere in vista

limerick ['lɪmərɪk] *s* canzoncina umoristica di cinque versi

lime'stone' *s* calcare *m*

limit ['lɪmɪt] *s* limite *m*; (coll) colmo; **to go to the limit** andare agli estremi ‖ *tr* limitare

limitation [ˌlɪmɪ'teʃən] *s* limitazione

lim'ited-ac'cess high'way ['lɪmɪtɪd] *s* autostrada, strada con corsia d'accesso

lim'ited com'pany *s* società *f* a responsabilità limitata

lim'ited mon'archy *s* monarchia costituzionale

limitless ['lɪmɪtlɪs] *adj* illimitato

limousine ['lɪməˌzin] *or* [ˌlɪmə'zin] *s* berlina

limp [lɪmp] *adj* floscio; debole ‖ *s* zoppicatura ‖ *intr* zoppicare

limpid ['lɪmpɪd] *adj* limpido

linage ['laɪnɪdʒ] *s* (typ) numero di linee

linchpin ['lɪntʃˌpɪn] *s* acciarino

linden ['lɪndən] *s* tiglio

line [laɪn] *s* linea; (e.g., *of people*) fila; (*of trees*) filare *m*; (*for fishing*) lenza; (*written or printed*) rigo, riga; (*wrinkle*) ruga; (*of goods*) ramo; (naut) gherlino; **all along the line** su tutta la linea; **in line** allineato; sotto controllo; **in line with** secondo; **out of line** fuori d'allineamento; (slang) in disaccordo; **to bring into line** far filare; **to draw the line at** fermarsi a; stabilire il limite a; **to fall in line** conformarsi; allinearsi; **to have a line on** (coll) aver informazioni su; **to read between the lines** leggere fra le righe; **to stand in line** fare la coda; **to toe the line** filare diritto; **to wait in line** fare la fila ‖ *tr* rigare; (e.g., *the street*) schierare lungo; (*a suit*) foderare; (*a brake*) rivestire; **to line up** allineare; trovare, scovare ‖ *intr*

—**to line up** mettersi in fila; fare la coda

lineage ['lɪnɪ·ɪdʒ] s lignaggio

lineaments ['lɪnɪ·əmənts] spl lineamenti mpl

linear ['lɪnɪ·ər] adj lineare

line'man s (-men) (elec) guardafili m; (sports) guardalinee m; (surv) assistente geometra m

linen ['lɪnən] adj di tela di lino || s (fabric) tela di lino, lino; (yarn) filo di lino; biancheria

lin'en clos'et s guardaroba m per la biancheria

line' of fire' s (mil) linea di tiro

line' of least' resist'ance s principio del minimo sforzo; **to follow the line of least resistance** prendere la via più facile

line' of sight' s visuale f; (mil) linea di mira

liner ['laɪnər] s transatlantico

line'-up' s disposizione f; (of prisoners) allineamento; (sports) formazione

linger ['lɪŋgər] intr indugiare, soffermarsi; (to be tardy) tardare; rimanere in vita; **to linger over** contemplare

lingerie [ˌlænʒə'ri] s biancheria intima

lingering ['lɪŋgərɪŋ] adj prolungato

lingual ['lɪŋgwəl] adj linguale || s suono linguale

linguist ['lɪŋgwɪst] s poliglotto; (specialist in linguistics) glottologo

linguistic [lɪŋ'gwɪstɪk] adj linguistico || **linguistics** s linguistica, glottologia

lining ['laɪnɪŋ] s (of a coat) fodera; (of auto brake) guarnizione; (of a furnace) rivestimento interno; (of wall) rivestimento

link [lɪŋk] s anello, maglia; unione; (of sausage) nocco; **links** campo di golf || tr connettere || intr connettersi

linnet ['lɪnɪt] s fanello

linotype ['laɪnə,taɪp] s linotype f || tr comporre in linotipia

lin'otype op'erator s linotipista mf

linseed ['lɪn,sid] s linosa

lin'seed oil' s olio di lino

lint [lɪnt] s peluria, sfilacciatura; (for dressing wounds) filaccia

lintel ['lɪntəl] s architrave m

lion ['laɪən] s leone m; celebrità f; **to beard the lion in his den** affrontare l'avversario a casa sua; **to put one's head in the lion's mouth** cacciarsi nei pericoli

lioness ['laɪ·ənɪs] s leonessa

lion-hearted ['laɪ·ən ,hɑrtɪd] adj cuor di leone, coraggioso

lionize ['laɪ·ə ,naɪz] tr festeggiare come una celebrità

li'on's den' s fossa dei leoni

li'on's share' s parte f del leone

lip [lɪp] s labbro; (of a jar) beccuccio; (slang) linguaggio insolente; **to smack one's lips** leccarsi le labbra

lip'read' v (pret & pp -read [,rɛd]) tr leggere le labbra di || intr leggere le labbra

lip' read'ing s labiolettura

lip' serv'ice s omaggio non sentito

lip'stick' s rossetto per le labbra, matita per le labbra

lique·fy ['lɪkwɪ ,faɪ] v (pret & pp -fied) tr & intr liquefare

liqueur [lɪ'kʌr] s liquore m

liquid ['lɪkwɪd] adj liquido || s liquido; (phonet) liquida

liquidate ['lɪkwɪ ,det] tr & intr liquidare

liquidity [lɪ'kwɪdɪti] s liquidità f

liq'uid meas'ure s misura di capacità per liquidi

liquor ['lɪkər] s distillato alcolico, bevanda alcolica; (broth) brodo

Lisbon ['lɪzbən] s Lisbona

lisp [lɪsp] s pronuncia blesa || intr parlare bleso

lissome ['lɪsəm] adj flessibile, agile

list [lɪst] s lista, elenco; (border) orlo; (selvage) cimossa, vivagno; (naut) sbandamento; **lists** lizza; **to enter the lists** entrare in lizza || tr elencare, listare || intr (naut) sbandare, andare alla banda

listen ['lɪsən] intr ascoltare; obbedire; **to listen in** ascoltare una conversazione; (rad) captare una comunicazione; **to listen to** ascoltare; obbedire a, prestare attenzione a; **to listen to reason** intendere ragione

listener ['lɪsənər] s ascoltatore m; radioascoltatore m

lis'tening post' s (mil) posto di ascolto

listless ['lɪstlɪs] adj svogliato

list' price' s prezzo di catalogo

lita·ny ['lɪtəni] s (-nies) litania

liter ['litər] s litro

literacy ['lɪtərəsi] s abilità f di leggere e scrivere; istruzione

literal ['lɪtərəl] adj letterale

literary ['lɪtə ,rɛri] adj letterario; (individual) letterato

literate ['lɪtərɪt] adj che sa leggere e scrivere; (educated) istruito; (well-read) letterato || s persona che sa leggere e scrivere; letterato

literature ['lɪtərət/ər] s letteratura; (printed matter) opuscoli pubblicitari

lithe [laɪθ] adj flessibile, agile

lithium ['lɪθɪ·əm] s litio

lithograph ['lɪθə ,græf] or ['lɪθə ,grɑf] s litografia || tr litografare

lithographer [lɪ'θɑgrəfər] s litografo

lithography [lɪ'θɑgrəfi] s litografia

Lithuania [,lɪθu'enɪ·ə] s la Lituania

Lithuanian [,lɪθu'enɪ·ən] adj & s lituano

litigant ['lɪtɪgənt] adj & s litigante mf

litigate ['lɪtɪ ,get] tr & intr litigare

litigation [,lɪtɪ'geʃən] s litigio; (lawsuit) lite f, causa

litmus ['lɪtməs] s tornasole m

lit'mus pa'per s cartina al tornasole

litter ['lɪtər] s disordine m; (scattered rubbish) pattume m; (young brought forth at one birth) figliata; (of puppies) cucciolata; (bedding for animals) strame m; (stretcher; bed carried by men or animals) lettiga, portantina || tr mettere in disordine; spargere rifiuti per; coprire di strame || intr partorire

lit'ter•bug' s sparpagliatore m di rifiuti

littering ['lɪtərɪŋ] s—**no littering** vietato gettare rifiuti

little ['lɪtəl] adj (in size) piccolo; (in amount) poco, e.g., **little salt** poco sale; **a little un po'** di, e.g., **a little salt un po'** di sale; **the little ones** i piccini || s poco; **a little un po'**; **to make little of** farsi gioco di; non pigliar sul serio; **to think little of** non tener di conto || adv poco; **little by little** poco a poco, mano a mano

Lit'tle Bear' s Orsa minore

Lit'tle Dip'per s Piccolo Carro

lit'tle fin'ger s mignolo; **to twist around one's little finger** maneggiare come un fantoccio

lit'tle•neck' s piccola vongola (Venus mercenaria)

lit'tle owl' s civetta

lit'tle peo'ple adj fate fpl; folletti mpl

Lit'tle Red Rid'inghood' ['raɪdɪŋ ,hʊd] s Cappuccetto Rosso

lit'tle slam' s (bridge) piccolo slam

liturgic(al) [lɪ'tʌrdʒɪk(əl)] adj liturgico

litur•gy ['lɪtərdʒi] s (-gies) liturgia

livable ['lɪvəbəl] adj abitabile; socievole; tollerabile

live [laɪv] adj vivo; (flame) ardente; di attualità; (elec) sotto tensione; (telv) in diretta || [lɪv] tr vivere; **to live down** (one's past) far dimenticare; **to live it up** (coll) darsi alla bella vita, scialare; **to live out** (e.g., a war) sopravvivere (with dat) || intr vivere; **to live from hand to mouth** vivere alla giornata; **to live high** darsi alla bella vita; **to live on** continuare a vivere; (e.g., vegetables) vivere di; vivere alle spalle di; **to live up to** (one's promises) compiere; (one's earnings) spendere

live' coal' [laɪv] s brace f

livelihood ['laɪvlɪ ,hʊd] s vita; **to earn one's livelihood** guadagnarsi la vita

livelong ['lɪv ,lɔŋ] or ['lɪv ,lɑŋ] adj—**all the livelong day** tutto il santo giorno

live•ly ['laɪvli] adj (-lier; -liest) vivo, vivace; (color) vivido; (resilient) elastico; (tune) brioso

liven ['laɪvən] tr animare || intr animarsi, rianimarsi

liver ['lɪvər] s abitante mf; (anat) fegato

liver•y ['lɪvəri] s (-ies) livrea

liv'ery•man s (-men) stalliere m

liv'ery sta'ble s stallaggio

livestock ['laɪv ,stɑk] adj zootecnico || s bestiame m

live' wire' [laɪv] s (elec) filo carico di corrente; (slang) persona energica

livid ['lɪvɪd] adj livido; (with anger) incollerito

living ['lɪvɪŋ] adj vivo; (conditions) abitativo || s vivere m; **to earn a living** guadagnarsi la vita

liv'ing quar'ters spl abitazione, alloggio

liv'ing room' s stanza di soggiorno

liv'ing wage' s salario sufficiente per vivere

lizard ['lɪzərd] s lucertola

load [lod] s peso, carico; **loads of** (coll) un mucchio di; **to get a load of** (slang) stare a vedere; (slang) stare a sentire; **to have a load on** (slang) essere ubriaco || tr caricare || intr caricarsi

loaded ['lodɪd] adj caricato; (slang) ubriaco fradicio; (slang) ricchissimo

load'ed dice' spl dadi truccati

load'stone' s magnetite f; (fig) calamita

loaf [lof] s (loaves [lovz]) pane m; (molded mass) forma; (of sugar) pane m; (long and thin loaf) filone m || intr batter fiacca, oziare

loafer ['lofər] s fannullone m

loam [lom] s ricca argilla sabbiosa; terra da fonderia

loan [lon] s prestito; **to hit for a loan** (coll) dare una stoccata a || tr prestare

loan' shark' s (coll) strozzino

loan' word' s (ling) prestito

loath [loθ] adj poco disposto; **nothing loath** molto volentieri

loathe [loð] tr detestare, aborrire

loathsome ['loðsəm] adj abominevole, disgustoso

lob [lab] s (tennis) pallonetto || v (pret & pp lobbed; ger lobbing) tr (tennis) dare un pallonetto a

lob•by ['labi] s (-bies) anticamera, vestibolo; sollecitazione di voti || v (pret & pp -bied) intr sollecitare voti, influenzare il voto dietro le quinte

lobbyist ['labi ,ɪst] s politicante m che cerca di influenzare il voto dietro le quinte

lobe [lob] s lobo

lobster ['labstər] s (Palinurus vulgaris) aragosta; (Hommarus vulgaris) astice m

lob'ster pot' s nassa per aragoste

local ['lokəl] adj locale || s treno accelerato; notizia di interesse locale; (of a union) sezione

locale [lo'kæl] s località f

locali•ty [lo'kælɪti] s (-ties) località f

localize ['lokə ,laɪz] tr localizzare

lo'cal op'tion s referendum m locale sulla vendita di alcolici

locate [lo'ket] or ['loket] tr (to discover the location of) localizzare; (to place, settle) situare, stabilire; (to ascribe a location to) individuare || intr stabilirsi

location [lo'keʃən] s localizzazione; posizione; sito; **on location** (mov) in esterno

lock [lak] s serratura; (of a canal) chiusa; (of hair) ciocca; (of a firearm) percussore m; (mach) freno; **lock, stock, and barrel** (coll) completamente; **under lock and key** sotto chiave || tr chiudere a chiave; serrare; (a boat) far passare per una chiusa; unire; abbracciare; **to lock in** chiudere sotto chiave; **to lock out** chiudere fuori; (workers) sbarrare dal lavoro; **to lock up** chiudere a chiave; incarcerare

locker ['lakər] s armadietto a chiave; (in the form of a chest) bauletto

lock'er room' s spogliatoio
locket ['lakɪt] s medaglione m
lock'jaw' s tetano, trisma m
lock' nut' s controdado
lock'out' s serrata
lock'smith' s magnano, fabbro
lock' step' s—**to march in lock step** marciare a passo serrato
lock' stitch' s punto a filo doppio
lock' ten'der s guardiano di chiusa
lock'up' s prigione; (typ) messa in forma
lock' wash'er s rondella di sicurezza
locomotive [,lokə'motɪv] s locomotiva
lo·cus ['lokəs] s (**-ci** [saɪ]) luogo
locust ['lokəst] s (ent) locusta; (*cicada*) (ent) cicala; (bot) robinia
lode [lod] s filone m, vena
lode'star' s stella polare; guida
lodge [ladʒ] s casetta; padiglione m da caccia; albergo; (*e.g., of Masons*) loggia || tr alloggiare, ospitare; depositare; contenere; (*a complaint*) sporgere || intr alloggiare; essere contenuto, trovarsi; andar a finire
lodger ['ladʒər] s inquilino
lodging ['ladʒɪŋ] s alloggio
loft [lɔft] or [laft] s (*attic*) solaio; (*hayloft*) fienile m; (*in theater or church*) galleria
loft·y ['lɔfti] or ['lafti] adj (**-ier; -iest**) alto, elevato; (*haughty*) orgoglioso
log [lɔg] or [lag] s ceppo, ciocco; (naut) solcometro; (aer, naut) giornale m di bordo; **to sleep like a log** dormire della grossa || v (*pret & pp* **logged;** *ger* **logging**) tr registrare; (*a speed*) fare; (*a distance*) percorrere
logarithm ['lɔgə,rɪðəm] or ['lagə,rɪðəm] s logaritmo
log'book' s (aer, naut) libro di bordo
log' cab'in s capanna di tronchi
log' chip' s (naut) barchetta
log' driv'er s zatteriere m
log' driv'ing ['draɪvɪŋ] s fluitazione
logger ['lɔgər] or ['lagər] s taglialegna m; trattore m per trasporto tronchi
log'ger·head' s testone m; **at loggerheads** in lite
loggia ['lodʒə] s loggia
logic ['ladʒɪk] s logica
logical ['ladʒɪkəl] adj logico
logician [lo'dʒɪʃən] s logico
logistic(al) [lo'dʒɪstɪk(əl)] adj logistico
logistics [lo'dʒɪstɪks] s logistica
log'jam' s ingorgo fluviale dovuto a ammasso di tronchi; (fig) ristagno
log' line' s (naut) sagola
log'roll' intr barattare favori politici
log'wood' s campeggio
loin [lɔɪn] s lombo; **to gird up one's loins** prepararsi per l'azione
loin'cloth' s perizoma m, copripudende m
loiter ['lɔɪtər] tr—**to loiter away** (*time*) sprecare in ozio || intr bighellonare, trastullarsi
loiterer ['lɔɪtərər] s perdigiorno
loll [lal] intr sdraiarsi pigramente, adagiarsi pigramente; pendere
lollipop ['lalɪ,pap] s caramella sullo stecchetto, lecca-lecca m

Lombard ['lambard] or ['lambərd] adj & s lombardo; (hist) longobardo
Lom'bardy pop'lar s pioppo italico
London ['lʌndən] adj londinese || s Londra
Londoner ['lʌndənər] s londinese mf
lone [lon] adj solo; solitario
loneliness ['lonlinɪs] s solitudine f
lone·ly ['lonli] adj (**-lier; -liest**) solingo, solo, solitario
lonesome ['lonsəm] adj solitario
lone' wolf' s (coll) orso, solitario
long [lɔŋ] or [laŋ] (**longer** ['lɔŋgər] or ['laŋgər]; **longest** ['lɔŋgɪst] or ['laŋgɪst]) adj lungo; **three meters long** lungo tre metri || adv molto, molto tempo; **as long as** mentre; (*provided*) fin tanto che; (*inasmuch as*) dato che; **before long** fra poco; **how long?** quanto?; **long ago** molto tempo fa; **long before** molto prima; **long since** molto tempo fa; **no longer** non più; **so long!** (coll) ciao!, arrivederci!; **so long as** fino a che, finché || intr anelare; **to long for** sviscerarsi per, sospirare per
long'boat' s (naut) lancia
long'-dis'tance adj (telp) interurbano, intercomunale; (sports) di fondo; (aer) a distanza
long'-drawn'-out' adj prolungato
longeron ['landʒərən] s longherone m
longevity [lan'dʒɛvɪti] s longevità f
long' face' s (coll) faccia triste, muso lungo
long'hair' adj & s (coll) intellettuale mf; (coll) musicomane mf
long'hand' adj (scritto) a mano || s scrittura a mano; **in longhand** scritto a mano
longing ['lɔŋɪŋ] or ['laŋɪŋ] adj bramoso, anelante || s brama, anelito
longitude ['landʒɪ,tjud] or ['landʒɪ,tud] s longitudine f
long-lived ['lɔŋ'laɪvd], ['lɔŋ'lɪvd], ['laŋ'laɪvd] or ['laŋ'lɪvd] adj (*person*) longevo, di lunga vita; (*e.g., rumor*) di lunga durata
long'-play'ing rec'ord s disco di grande durata
long'-range' adj a lunga portata
long'shore'man s (**-men**) portuale m, scaricatore m
long'stand'ing adj vecchio, che esiste da lungo tempo
long'-suf'fering adj paziente, longanime
long' suit' s (cards) serie lunga; (fig) forte m
long'-term' adj a lunga scadenza
long'-wind'ed adj verboso; (*speech*) chilometrico
look [luk] s (*appearance*) aspetto; (*glance*) sguardo; (*search*) ricerca; **looks** aspetto, apparenza; **to take a look at** dare un'occhiata a || tr guardare; (*one's age*) mostrare; **to look daggers at** fulminare con lo sguardo; **to look up** (*e.g., in a dictionary*) cercare; andare a visitare; venire a visitare || intr guardare; cercare; parere; **look out!** attenzione!; **to look after** badare a; occuparsi di; **to look at** guardare; **to look back** riguardare;

(fig) guardare al passato; **to look down on s.o.** guardare qlcu dall'alto in basso; **to look for** cercare; aspettarsi; **to look forward to** anticipare il piacere di; **to look ill** avere una brutta cera; **to look in** passare per la casa di; **to look into** esaminare a fondo; **to look like** sembrare, parere; **to look out** fare attenzione; **to look out for** aver cura di; **to look out of** guardare da; **to look out on** dare su; **to look through** guardare per; (*a book*) sfogliare; **to look toward** dare su; **to look up to** ammirare, guardare con ammirazione; **to look well** avere una buona cera; fare figura

looker-on [ˌlʊkərˈɑn] or [ˌlʊkərˈɔn] s (**lookers-on**) astante m

look'ing glass' [ˈlʊkɪŋ] s specchio

look'out' s guardia; (*person; watch kept; place from which a watch is kept*) vedetta; (*concern*) (coll) affare m; **to be on the lookout** stare in guardia; **to be on the lookout for** essere in cerca di

loom [lum] s telaio ‖ *intr* apparire indistintamente; pararsi dinanzi; apparire

loon [lun] s scemo; fannullone m; (orn) (*Gavia*) strolaga

loon·y [ˈluni] adj (**-ier; -iest**) (slang) pazzo ‖ s (**-ies**) (slang) pazzo

loop [lup] s cappio; (*e.g., of a road*) tortuosità f; (*for fastening a button*) occhiello; (aer) cerchio o giro della morte; (phys) ventre m; ‖ *tr* fare cappi in; annodare; **to loop the loop** (aer) fare il giro della morte ‖ *intr* avanzare tortuosamente, girare

loop'hole' s (*narrow opening*) feritoia; (*means of evasion*) scappatoia

loose [lus] adj libero, sciolto; (*available*) disponibile; (*not firm*) rilasciato; (*tooth*) che balla; (*unchaste*) facile; (*garment*) ampio; (*soil*) smosso; (*translation*) libero; (*rein*) lento; **to become loose** sciogliersi; **to break loose** mettersi in libertà; **to have loose bowels** avere la diarrea; **to turn loose** liberare ‖ s—**to be on the loose** (coll) essere in libertà; (coll) correre la cavallina ‖ *tr* sciogliere; slegare; lanciare

loose' change' s spiccioli mpl

loose' end' s capo sciolto; **at loose ends** indeciso; disoccupato, senza nulla da fare

loose'-leaf' adj a fogli mobili

loosen [ˈlusən] *tr* snodare; rilasciare; smuovere; allentare; (*the bowels*) liberare dalla stitichezza ‖ *intr* snodarsi; rilasciarsi; smuoversi; allentarsi

looseness [ˈlusnɪs] s scioltezza; (*in morals*) rilassamento

loose-tongued [ˈlusˈtʌŋd] adj sciolto di lingua; linguacciuto, maldicente

loot [lut] s bottino ‖ *tr* saccheggiare

lop [lɑp] v (*pret & pp* **lopped**; *ger* **lopping**) *tr* lasciar cadere, lasciar penzolare; **to lop off** mozzare; (*a tree*) potare; (*a vine*) stralciare ‖ *intr* penzolare

lopsided [ˈlɑpˈsaɪdɪd] adj che pende da una parte; asimmetrico, sproporzionato

loquacious [loˈkweʃəs] adj loquace

lord [lɔrd] s signore m; (Brit) lord m ‖ *tr*—**to lord it over** signoreggiare su

lord·ly [ˈlɔrdli] adj (**-lier; -liest**) signorile, magnifico; altero, disdegnoso, arrogante

Lord's' Day', the la domenica, il giorno del Signore

lordship [ˈlɔrdʃɪp] s signoria

Lord's' Prayer' s paternostro

Lord's' Sup'per s Eucarestia; Ultima Cena

lore [lor] s tradizioni fpl popolari; cognizioni fpl

lorgnette [lɔrnˈjet] s occhialetto, lorgnette f; binocolo da teatro col manico

lor·ry [ˈlɑri] s (**-ries**) (rr) vagoncino; (Brit) camion m

lose [luz] v (*pret & pp* **lost** [lɔst] or [lɑst]) *tr* perdere; (*said of a physician*) non riuscire a salvare; **to lose heart** perdersi d'animo; **to lose oneself** perdersi, smarrirsi ‖ *intr* perdere; (*said of a watch*) ritardare; **to lose out** rimetterci

loser [ˈluzər] s perdente mf

losing [ˈluzɪŋ] adj perdente ‖ **losings** spl perdite fpl

loss [lɔs] or [lɑs] s perdita; **to be at a loss** essere perplesso; **to be at a loss to** + *inf* non saper come + *inf*; **to sell at a loss** vendere in perdita

loss' of face' s perdita di faccia

lost [lɔst] or [lɑst] adj perduto; **lost in thought** assorto in sè stesso; **lost to** perso per; insensibile a

lost'-and-found' depart'ment s ufficio degli oggetti smarriti

lost' sheep' s percorella smarrita

lot [lɑt] s (*for building*) lotto; (*fate*) sorte f; (*parcel, portion*) partita; (*of people*) gruppo; (coll) grande quantità f; (coll) tipo, soggetto; **a lot (of)** or **lots of** (coll) molto, molti; **to cast** or **to throw in one's lot with** condividere la sorte di; **to draw** or **to cast lots** tirare a sorte

lotion [ˈloʃən] s lozione

lotter·y [ˈlɑtəri] s (**-ies**) lotteria, riffa

lotto [ˈlɑto] s tombola, lotto

lotus [ˈlotəs] s loto

loud [laʊd] adj forte; (*noisy*) rumoroso; (*voice*) alto; (*garish*) sgargiante, chiassoso, appariscente; (*foul-smelling*) puzzolente ‖ adv a voce alta; rumorosamente

loud-mouthed [ˈlaʊdˌmaʊθt] or [ˈlaʊdˌmaʊðd] adj chiassone

loud'speak'er s altoparlante m

lounge [laʊndʒ] s divano, sofà m; sala soggiorno; ridotto ‖ *intr* oziare, star senza far niente; bighellonare; **to lounge around** bighellonare

lounge' liz'ard s (slang) damerino, bellimbusto, gagà m

louse [laʊs] s (**lice** [laɪs]) pidocchio ‖ *tr*—**to louse up** (slang) rovinare

lous·y [ˈlaʊzi] adj (**-ier; -iest**) pidocchioso; (*mean; bungling*) (coll) schifoso; *(filthy)* (coll) sporco; **lousy with** *(e.g., money)* (slang) pieno di

lout [laut] *s* gaglioffo, tanghero

louver ['luvər] *s* sportello girevole di persiana; (aut) feritoia per ventilazione

lovable ['lʌvəbəl] *adj* amabile

love [lʌv] *s* amore *m;* (tennis) zero; **not for love nor money** a nessun prezzo; **to be in love (with)** essere innamorato (di); **to make love to** fare l'amore con ‖ *tr* amare; voler bene a; piacere (with *dat*), e.g., **she loves short skirts** le piacciono le sottane corte

love' affair' *s* passione, amori *mpl*

love'bird' *s* (orn) inseparabile *m;* **love-birds** (slang) amanti appassionati

love' child' *s* figlio naturale

love' feast' *s* agape *f*

loveless ['lʌvlɪs] *adj* senza amore

lovelorn ['lʌv,lɔrn] *adj* abbandonato dalla persona amata

love·ly ['lʌvli] *adj* (-lier; -liest) bello; (coll) delizioso

love' match' *s* matrimonio d'amore

love' po'tion *s* filtro d'amore

lover ['lʌvər] *s* amante *m;* *(e.g., of music)* amico, appassionato

love' seat' *s* amorino

love'sick' *adj* malato d'amore

love'sick'ness *s* mal *m* d'amore

love' song' *s* canzone *f* d'amore

loving ['lʌvɪŋ] *adj* affezionato, amoroso; **your loving son** il vostro affezionato figlio

lov'ing-kind'ness *s* tenera sollecitudine

low [lo] *adj* basso; *(deep)* profondo; *(diet)* magro; *(visibility)* cattivo; *(dress)* scollato; *(dejected)* abbattuto; *(fire)* lento; *(flame; speed)* piccolo; **to lay low** ammazzare; abbattere; **to lie low** rimanere nascosto; attendere ‖ *s* punto basso; prezzo minimo; *(of cow)* muggito; (aut) prima velocità; (meteor) depressione ‖ *adv* basso, a basso, in basso ‖ *intr (said of a cow)* muggire

low'born' *adj* di umili origini

low'boy' *s* cassettone basso con le gambe corte

low'brow' *adj* & *s* (coll) ignorante *mf*

low'-cost' hous'ing *s* case *fpl* popolari

Low' Coun'tries, the i Paesi Bassi

low'-down' *adj* (coll) basso, vile ‖ **low'-down'** *s* (coll) semplice verità *f,* notizie *fpl* confidenziali

lower ['lo·ər] *adj* inferiore, disotto ‖ *tr* abbassare; *(prices)* ribassare ‖ *intr* diminuire; discendere ‖ ['lau·ər] *intr* aggrottare le ciglia; *(said of the weather)* imbronciarsi

low'er berth' ['lo·ər] *s* cuccetta inferiore

low'er case' ['lo·ər] *s* (typ) cassa inferiore

lower-case ['lo·ər,kes] *adj* (typ) minuscolo

low'er mid'dle class' ['lo·ər] *s* piccola borghesia

lowermost ['lo·ər,most] *adj* (il) più basso, (l') infimo

low'-fre'quency *adj* a bassa frequenza

low' gear' *s* prima velocità, prima

lowland ['loland] *s* pianura ‖ **Low-lands** *spl* Scozia meridionale, bassa Scozia

low·ly ['loli] *adj* (-lier; -liest) umile

Low' Mass' *s* messa bassa

low-minded ['lo'maɪndɪd] *adj* vile, basso

low-necked ['lo'nɛkt] *adj* scollato

low-pitched ['lo'pɪtʃt] *adj (sound)* basso, grave; *(roof)* poco inclinato

low'-pres'sure *adj* a bassa pressione

low-priced ['lo'praɪst] *adj* a buon mercato, a basso prezzo

low' shoe' *s* scarpa bassa

low'-speed' *adj* di piccola velocità

low-spirited ['lo'spɪrɪtɪd] *adj* depresso

low' tide' *s* bassa marea; (fig) punto più basso

low' visibil'ity *s* scarsa visibilità

low' wa'ter *s* (low tide) bassa marea; *(of a river)* magra

loyal ['lɔɪ·əl] *adj* leale

loyalist ['lɔɪ·əlɪst] *s* lealista *mf*

loyal·ty ['lɔɪ·əlti] *s* (-ties) lealtà *f*

lozenge ['lazɪndʒ] *s* losanga; *(candy cough drop)* pasticca, pastiglia

LP ['ɛl'pi] *s* (letterword) (trademark) disco di grande durata

lubricant ['lubrɪkənt] *adj* & *s* lubrificante *m*

lubricate ['lubrɪ,ket] *tr* lubrificare; *(e.g., one's hands)* ungersi

lubrication [,lubrɪ'keʃən] *s* lubrificazione

lubricous ['lubrɪkəs] *adj* lubrico; incerto, incostante

lucerne [lu'sʌrn] *s* erba medica

lucid ['lusɪd] *adj* lucido

Lucifer ['lusɪfər] *s* Lucifero

luck [lʌk] *s (good or bad)* sorte *f;* *(good)* sorte *f,* fortuna; **down on one's luck** in cattive condizioni; **in luck** fortunato; **out of luck** sfortunato; **to bring luck** portare (buona) fortuna; **to try one's luck** tentare la sorte; **worse luck** disgraziatamente

luckily ['lʌkɪli] *adv* fortunatamente

luckless ['lʌklɪs] *adj* sfortunato

luck·y ['lʌki] *adj* (-ier; -iest) fortunato; *(supposed to bring luck)* portafortuna; *(foretelling good luck)* di buon augurio; **to be lucky** aver fortuna

luck'y hit' *s* (coll) colpo di fortuna

lucrative ['lukrətɪv] *adj* lucrativo

ludicrous ['ludɪkrəs] *adj* ridicolo

lug [lʌg] *s* manico; *(pull)* tiro; **to put the lug on s.o.** (slang) batter cassa a qlcu ‖ *v* *(pret & pp* lugged; *ger* lugging) *tr* tirarsi dietro; (coll) introdurre a sproposito

luggage ['lʌgɪdʒ] *s* *(used in traveling)* bagaglio; *(found in a store)* valigeria

lug'gage store' *s* valigeria

lugubrious [lu'gubrɪ·əs] *or* [lu'gjubrɪ·əs] *adj* lugubre

lukewarm ['luk,wɔrm] *adj* tiepido

lull [lʌl] *s* momento di calma, calma ‖ *tr* calmare, pacificare; addormentare

lulla·by ['lʌlə,baɪ] *s* (-bies) ninnananna

lumbago [lʌm'bego] *s* lombaggine *f*

lumber ['lʌmbər] s legname m, legno da costruzione; cianfrusaglie fpl ‖ intr muoversi pesantemente
lum'ber-jack' s boscaiolo
lum'ber jack'et s giaccone m
lum'ber-man s (-men) (dealer) commerciante m in legname; (man who cuts down lumber) boscaiolo
lum'ber room' s ripostiglio
lum'ber-yard' s deposito legnami
luminar-y ['lumɪˌnɛri] s (-ies) luminare m
luminous ['lumɪnəs] adj luminoso
lummox ['lʌməks] s (coll) sciumunito
lump [lʌmp] s grumo; mucchio; cumulo; (swelling) bernoccolo; (of sugar) zolletta; (in one's throat) groppo; (coll) stupidone m; in the lump in blocco; nell'insieme ‖ tr mescolare; (to make into lumps) raggrumare; to lump it (coll) mandarla giù
lumpish ['lʌmpɪʃ] adj grumoso; goffo; balordo
lump' sum' s ammontare unico, somma globale
lump-y ['lʌmpi] adj (-ier; -iest) grumoso; (person) pesante, ottuso; (sea) agitato
luna-cy ['lunəsi] s (-cies) pazzia
lunar ['lunər] adj lunare
lu'nar land'ing s allunaggio
lu'nar mod'ule s modulo lunare
lu'nar rov'er s auto f lunare
lunatic ['lunətɪk] adj & s demente mf
lu'natic asy'lum s manicomio
lu'natic fringe' s estremisti mpl fanatici
lunch [lʌntʃ] s (regular midday meal) seconda colazione; (light meal) spuntino, merenda ‖ intr fare colazione; fare uno spuntino
lunch' bas'ket s portavivande m
luncheon ['lʌntʃən] s seconda colazione; pranzo ufficiale
luncheonette [ˌlʌntʃə'nɛt] s tavola calda
lunch'eon meat' s insaccati mpl
lunch'room' s tavola calda
lung [lʌŋ] s polmone m
lunge [lʌndʒ] s slancio; (fencing) affondo ‖ intr slanciarsi
lurch [lʌrtʃ] s barcollamento; (at close of a game) cappotto; (naut) sbandata; to leave in the lurch piantare

in asso ‖ intr barcollare; (naut) sbandare
lure [lur] s esca; (fig) insidie fpl ‖ tr adescare; to lure away distogliere, sviare
lurid ['lurɪd] adj (fiery) ardente, acceso; sensazionale; (gruesome) orripilante
lurk [lʌrk] intr stare in agguato, nascondersi; (fig) essere latente
luscious ['lʌʃəs] adj delizioso; lussuoso, lussureggiante; voluttuoso
lush [lʌʃ] adj lussureggiante, lussuoso
lust [lʌst] s desiderio sfrenato; libidine f, lussuria ‖ intr—to lust after or for aver sete di
luster ['lʌstər] s (gloss) lustro, lucentezza; (glory) lustro, onore m
lus'ter-ware' s ceramiche smaltate
lustful ['lʌstfəl] adj lussurioso
lustrous ['lʌstrəs] adj lucido
lust-y ['lʌsti] adj (-ier; -iest) vigoroso, gagliardo
lute [lut] s (mus) liuto; (chem) luto
Lutheran ['luθərən] adj & s luterano
luxuriance [lʌg'ʒurɪ-əns] s rigoglio
luxuriant [lʌg'ʒurɪ-ənt] adj lussureggiante; (imagery) ridondante
luxuriate [lʌg'ʒurɪˌet] or [lʌk'ʃurɪˌet] intr lussureggiare; trovare piacere
luxurious [lʌg'ʒurɪ-əs] or [lʌk'ʃurɪ-əs] adj lussuoso, fastoso
luxu-ry ['lʌkʃəri] or ['lʌgʒəri] s (-ries) lusso, sfarzo
lye [laɪ] s ranno, lisciva
lying ['laɪ-ɪŋ] adj menzognero ‖ s il mentire
ly'ing-in' hos'pital s clinica ostetrica, maternità f
lymph [lɪmf] s linfa
lymphatic [lɪm'fætɪk] adj linfatico
lynch [lɪntʃ] tr linciare
lynching ['lɪntʃɪŋ] s linciaggio
lynx [lɪŋks] s lince f
lynx-eyed ['lɪŋksˌaɪd] adj dagli occhi di lince
lyonnaise [ˌlaɪ-ə'nez] adj (culin) alla maniera di Lione
lyre [laɪr] s lira
lyric ['lɪrɪk] adj lirico ‖ s lirica; (words of a song) parole fpl
lyrical ['lɪrɪkəl] adj lirico
lyricism ['lɪrɪˌsɪzəm] s lirismo
lyricist ['lɪrɪsɪst] s (writer of words for songs) paroliere m; (poet) lirico

M

M, m [ɛm] s tredicesima lettera dell'alfabeto inglese
ma'am [mæm] or [mɑm] s (coll) signora
macadam [mə'kædəm] s macadàm m
macadamize [mə'kædəˌmaɪz] tr macadamizzare
macaroni [ˌmækə'roni] s maccheroni mpl
macaroon [ˌmækə'run] s amaretto
macaw [mə'kɔ] s ara

mace [mes] s mazza; (spice) macis m & f
mace' bear'er s mazziere m
machination [ˌmækɪ'neʃən] s macchinazione, macchina
machine [mə'ʃin] s macchina ‖ tr fare a macchina
machine' gun' s mitragliatrice f
machine'-gun' v (pret & pp -gunned; ger -gunning) tr mitragliare
machine'-made' adj fatto a macchina

machiner·y [mə'ʃinəri] s (**-ies**) macchinario, meccanismo

machine' screw' s vite f per metallo

machine' shop' s officina meccanica

machine' tool' s macchina utensile

machinist [mə'ʃinɪst] s meccanico; (nav) secondo macchinista

mackerel ['mækərəl] s maccarello

mack'erel sky' s cielo a pecorelle

mackintosh ['mækɪn,taʃ] s impermeabile m

mad [mæd] adj (**madder; maddest**) (angry; rabid) arrabbiato; (insane; foolish) pazzo, folle; furioso; **to be mad about** (coll) andar pazzo per; **to drive mad** far impazzire; **to go mad** impazzire; (said of a dog) diventare idrofobo

madam ['mædəm] s signora

mad'cap' s mattoide m, rompicollo

madden ['mædən] tr (to make angry) inferocire; (to make insane) fare impazzire

made-to-order ['medtə'ɔrdər] adj fatto apposta; (clothing) fatto su misura

made'-up' adj inventato; (using cosmetics) truccato

mad'house' s manicomio

mad'man' s (**-men'**) pazzo

madness ['mædnɪs] s rabbia; pazzia

Madonna lily [mə'dɑnə] s giglio

maelstrom ['melstrəm] s vortice m

magazine ['mægə,zin] or [,mægə'zin] s (periodical) rivista, giornale m; (warehouse) magazzino; (for cartridges) caricatore m; (for powder) polveriera; (naut) santabarbara; (phot) magazzino

maggot ['mægət] s larva di dittero

Magi ['medʒaɪ] spl Re Magi

magic ['mædʒɪk] adj magico ‖ s magia; illusionismo; **as if by magic** come per incanto

magician [mə'dʒɪʃən] s (entertainer) illusionista mf; (sorcerer) mago

magistrate ['mædʒɪs,tret] s magistrato

magnanimous [mæg'nænɪməs] adj magnanimo

magnesium [mæg'niʃi/ɪ·əm] or [mæg-'niʒi·əm] s magnesio

magnet ['mægnɪt] s calamita, magnete m

magnetic [mæg'netɪk] adj magnetico

magnetism ['mægnɪ,tɪzəm] s magnetismo

magnetize ['mægnɪ,taɪz] tr calamitare, magnetizzare

magne·to [mæg'nito] s (**-tos**) magnete m

magnificent [mæg'nɪfɪsənt] adj magnifico

magni·fy ['mægnɪ,faɪ] v (pret & pp **-fied**) tr ingrandire; (to exaggerate) magnificare

mag'nifying glass' s lente f d'ingrandimento

magnitude ['mægnɪ,tjud] or ['mægnɪ,tud] s grandezza

magpie ['mæg,paɪ] s gazza

mahlstick ['mɑl,stɪk] or ['mɔl,stɪk] s appoggiamano

mahoga·ny [mə'hɑgəni] s (**-nies**) mogano

Mahomet [mə'hɑmɪt] s Maometto

maid [med] s (girl) ragazza; (servant) cameriera, domestica

maiden ['medən] s pulzella

maid'en·hair' s (bot) capelvenere m

maid'en·head' s imene m

maidenhood ['medən,hud] s verginità f

maid'en la'dy s zitella

maid'en name' s nome m da signorina

maid'en voy'age s viaggio inaugurale

maid'-in-wait'ing s (**maids-in-waiting**) (of a princess) damigella d'onore; (of a queen) dama d'onore

maid' of hon'or s (attendant at a wedding; attendant of a princess) damigella d'onore; (attendant of a queen) dama d'onore

maid'serv'ant s domestica, ancella

mail [mel] s posta; (of armor) maglia; **by return mail** a volta di corriere ‖ tr impostare

mail'bag' s sacco postale

mail'boat' s battello postale

mail'box' s cassetta or buca delle lettere

mail' car' s vagone m postale

mail' car'rier s postino, portalettere m

mail'ing list' s indirizzario

mail'ing per'mit s abbonamento postale

mail'man' s (**-men'**) portalettere m

mail' or'der s ordinazione per corrispondenza

mail'-order house' s ditta che fa affari unicamente per corrispondenza

mail'plane' s areoplano postale

mail' train' s treno postale

maim [mem] tr mutilare

main [men] adj principale, maggiore ‖ s condotta principale; **in the main** principalmente, per lo più

main' clause' s proposizione principale

main' course' s piatto forte

main' deck' s ponte m principale

mainland ['men,lænd] or ['menlənd] s terra ferma, continente m

main' line' s (rr) linea principale

mainly ['menli] adv principalmente

mainmast ['menmæst], ['men,mæst] or ['men,mast] s albero maestro

mainsail ['mensəl] or ['men,sel] s vela maestra

main'spring' s molla motrice; (fig) molla

main'stay' s (naut) strallo di maestra; (fig) cardine m

main' street' s strada principale

maintain [men'ten] tr mantenere

maintenance ['mentɪnəns] s mantenimento; (upkeep) manutenzione

maître d'hôtel [,metər do'tel] s (butler) maggiordomo; (headwaiter) capocameriere m

maize [mez] s mais m

majestic [mə'dʒɛstɪk] adj maestoso

majes·ty ['mædʒɪsti] s (**-ties**) maestà f

major ['medʒər] adj maggiore ‖ s (educ) specializzazione; (mil) maggiore m ‖ intr (educ) specializzarsi

major·do·mo [,medʒər'domo] s (**-mos**) maggiordomo

ma'jor gen'eral s generale m di divisione

majori·ty [mə'dʒɑrɪti] or [mə'dʒɔrɪti] *adj* maggioritario ‖ *s* (**-ties**) (*being of full age*) maggiore età *f;* (*larger number or part*) maggioranza; (mil) grado di maggiore

make [mek] *s* (*brand*) marca; (*form*) stile *m;* produzione; **on the make** (slang) tirando l'acqua al proprio mulino ‖ *v* (*pret & pp* **made** [med]) *tr* fare; (*a train*) pigliare; (*a circuit*) chiudere; essere, e.g., **she will make a good typist** sarà una buona dattilografa; **to make** + *inf* fare + *inf,* e.g., **she made him study** lo fece studiare; **to make into** trasformare in; **to make known for** sapere; **to make of** pensare di; **to make oneself known** darsi a conoscere; **to make out** decifrare; (*a prescription*) scrivere, preparare; (*a check*) riempire; **to make over** convertire; (com) trasferire; **to make up** preparare, comporre; (*a story*) inventare; (*lost time*) riguadagnare; (typ) impaginare; (theat) truccare ‖ *intr* essere fatto; **to make away with** rubare; disfarsi di; **to make believe that** + *ind* far finta di + *inf,* e.g., **he made believe (that) he was sleeping** fece finta di dormire; **to make for** avvicinarsi a; attaccare; (*better relations*) contribuire a cementare; **to make much of** (coll) fare le feste a; **to make off** andarsene; **to make off with** svignarsela con; **to make out** (coll) farcela; **to make toward** incamminarsi verso; **to make up** truccarsi; fare la pace; **to make up for** compensare per, supplire a; **to make up to** (coll) ingraziarsi; (coll) fare la corte a

make'-be·lieve' *adj* immaginario ‖ *s* finzione, sembianza

maker ['mekər] *s* fabbricante *mf,* costruttore *m* ‖ **Maker** *s* Fattore *m*

make'shift' *adj* improvvisato, di fortuna ‖ *s* espediente *m,* ripiego; (*person*) tappabuchi *mf*

make'-up' *s* composizione, costituzione; truccatura, cosmetico; (typ) impaginazione; (journ) caratteristica

make'-up man' *s* truccatore *m*

make'-up test' *s* esame *m* di riparazione

make'weight' *s* giunta, contentino; (fig) supplemento, di più *m*

making ['mekɪŋ] *s* fabbricazione; costituzione; causa del successo; **makings** materiale *m;* (*potential*) stoffa

maladjusted [ˌmælə'dʒʌstɪd] *adj* spostato

mala·dy ['mælədi] *s* (**-dies**) malattia

malaise [mæ'lez] *s* malessere *m*

malapropos [ˌmælæprə'po] *adj* inopportuno ‖ *adv* a sproposito

malaria [mə'lɛrɪ·ə] *s* malaria

Malay ['mele] or [mə'le] *adj & s* malese *mf*

malcontent ['mælkən‚tent] *adj & s* malcontento

male [mel] *adj & s* maschio

malediction [ˌmælɪ'dɪk/ən] *s* maledizione

malefactor ['mælɪ‚fæktər] *s* malfattore *m*

male' nurse' *s* infermiere *m*

malevolent [mə'lɛvələnt] *adj* malevolo

malfeasance [mæl'fizəns] *s* reato di pubblico funzionario

malice ['mælɪs] *s* malizia; (law) dolo; **to bear malice** serbar rancore; **with malice prepense** (law) con premeditazione

malicious [mə'lɪ/əs] *adj* malizioso, maligno

malign [mə'laɪn] *adj* maligno ‖ *tr* calunniare

malignan·cy [mə'lɪgnənsi] *s* (**-cies**) malignità *f;* (pathol) malignità *f*

malignant [mə'lɪgnənt] *adj* maligno

maligni·ty [mə'lɪgnɪti] *s* (**-ties**) malignità *f*

malinger [mə'lɪŋgər] *intr* fingersi ammalato, darsi malato (per sottrarsi al proprio dovere)

mall [mɔl] or [mæl] *s* viale *m;* (*strip of land in a boulevard*) aiola

mallet ['mælɪt] *s* maglio; (*of a stone cutter*) mazzuolo

mallow ['mælo] *s* malva

malnutrition [ˌmælnju'trɪ/ən] or [ˌmælnu'trɪ/ən] *s* malnutrizione

malodorous [mæl'odərəs] *adj* puzzolente

malpractice [mæl'præktɪs] *s* incuria, negligenza; (*of physician or lawyer*) negligenza colposa

malt [mɔlt] *s* malto

maltreat [mæl'trit] *tr* maltrattare

mamma ['mɑmə] or [mə'mɑ] *s* (coll) mamma

mammal ['mæməl] *s* mammifero

mammalian [mæ'melɪ·ən] *adj & s* mammifero

mammoth ['mæməθ] *adj* mastodontico ‖ *s* mammut *m*

man [mæn] *s* (**men** [mɛn]) uomo; (*in chess*) pedina; (*in checkers*) pezzo; **a man** uno, e.g., **a man can get lost in this town** uno può perdersi in questa città; **as one man** come un sol uomo; **man alive!** accidenti!; **man and wife** marito e moglie; **to be one's own man** essere completamente indipendente ‖ *v* (*pret & pp* **manned;** *ger* **manning**) *tr* (*a boat*) equipaggiare; (*a fortress*) guarnire; (*a cannon*) manneggiare

man' about town' *s* vitaiolo

manacle ['mænəkəl] *s*—**manacles** manette *fpl* ‖ *tr* ammanettare

manage ['mænɪdʒ] *tr* (*a business*) gestire; (*e.g., a tool*) maneggiare ‖ *intr* sbrogliarsela; **to manage to** fare in modo di; ingegnarsi a; **to manage to get along** barcamenarsi

manageable ['mænɪdʒəbəl] *adj* maneggevole

management ['mænɪdʒmənt] *s* direzione, gestione; (*executives collectively*) classe *f* dirigente; direzione; (*college course*) economia aziendale

manager ['mænədʒər] *s* direttore *m,* gerente *mf;* (theat) impresario; (sports) procuratore *m,* manager *m*

managerial [ˌmænə'dʒɪrɪ·əl] *adj* direttoriale, imprenditoriale

man'aging ed'itor s gerente m responsabile, redattore m in capo

mandate ['mændet] s mandato ‖ tr dare in mandato a

mandatory ['mændə‚tori] adj obbligatorio

mandolin ['mændəlɪn] s mandolino

mandrake ['mændrek] s mandragola

mandrel ['mændrəl] s (mach) mandrino

mane [men] s criniera

maneuver [mə'nuvər] s manovra ‖ tr manovrare; intr manovrare; (aer, nav) evoluire; (fig) intrigare

manful ['mænfəl] adj maschile, risoluto

manganese ['mæŋgə‚nis] or ['mæŋgə‚niz] s manganese m

mange [mendʒ] s rogna

manger ['mendʒər] s presepio

mangle ['mæŋgəl] tr straziare, lacerare

man-gy ['mendʒi] adj (-gier; -giest) rognoso; (squalid) misero

man'han'dle tr malmenare, maltrattare

man'hole' s passo d'uomo, pozzetto

manhood ['mænhud] s virilità f; uomini mpl, umanità f

man'hunt' s caccia all'uomo

mania ['menɪə] s mania

maniac ['menɪ‚æk] adj & s maniaco

manicure ['mænɪ‚kjur] s (treatment) manicure f; (manicurist) manicure mf ‖ tr (a person) curare le mani di; (the hands) curare

manicurist ['mænɪ‚kjurɪst] s manicurista mf, manicure mf

manifest ['mænɪ‚fest] adj manifesto ‖ s (naut) manifesto di carico ‖ tr manifestare

manifes·to [‚mænɪ'festo] s (-toes) manifesto

manifold ['mænɪ‚fold] adj molteplice ‖ s copia; carta velina; (aut, mach) collettore m

manikin ['mænɪkɪn] s manichino; (dwarf) nano

man' in the moon' s faccia di uomo che appare nella luna piena

man' in the street' s uomo qualunque, uomo della strada

manipulate [mə'nɪpjə‚let] tr manipolare

man'kind' s genere umano ‖ **man'kind'** s il sesso maschile

manliness ['mænlɪnɪs] s virilità f

man·ly ['mænli] adj (-lier; -liest) maschio, virile

manned' space'ship s astronave pilotata

mannequin ['mænɪkɪn] s (figure) manichino; (person) indossatrice f

manner ['mænər] s maniera; **by all manner of means** in tutti i modi; **in a manner of speaking** in una certa maniera; **in the manner of** alla moda di; **manners** maniere, fpl, educazione; **to the manner born** avvezzo sin dalla nascita

mannish ['mænɪʃ] adj maschile; (woman) mascolino

man' of God' s santo; profeta m; (priest) uomo al servizio di Dio

man' of let'ters s letterato

man' of means' s uomo danaroso

man' of parts' s uomo di talento

man' of straw' s uomo di paglia

man' of the world' s uomo di mondo

man-of-war [‚mænəv'wor] s (men-of-war [‚menəv'wor] nave f da guerra

manor ['mænər] s maniero; feudo

man'or house' s maniero, palazzo

man' o'verboard interj uomo in mare!

man'pow'er s manodopera; (mil) effettivo

mansard ['mænsard] s mansarda

man'serv'ant s (men'serv'ants) servo, servitore m

mansion ['mænʃən] s palazzo, palazzina; (manor house) maniero

man'slaugh'ter s omicidio colposo

mantel ['mæntəl] s parte f anteriore dei pilastri del camino; (shelf above it) mensola

man'tel·piece' s mensola del camino

man'tis shrimp' ['mæntɪs] s canocchia

mantle ['mæntəl] s mantello, cappa ‖ tr ammantare; (to conceal) nascondere ‖ intr (to blush) arrossire

manual ['mænju·əl] adj manuale ‖ s (book) manuale m; (mil) esercizio; (mus) tastiera d'organo

man'ual train'ing s istruzione nelle arti e mestieri

manufacture [‚mænjə'fæktʃər] s fabbricazione; (thing manufactured) manufatto ‖ tr fabbricare

manufacturer [‚mænjə'fæktʃərər] s fabbricante mf, industriale m

manure [mə'njur] or [mə'nur] s letame m ‖ tr concimare

manuscript ['mænjə‚skript] adj & s manoscritto

many ['meni] adj & pron molti; **a good many** or **a great many** un buon numero; **as many . . . as tanti . . .** quanti; **as many as** fino a, e.g., **they sell as many as five thousand dozen** vendono fino a cinquemila dozzine; **how many** quanti; **many a** molti, e.g., **many a day** molti giorni; **many another** molti altri; **many more** molti di più; **so many** tanti; **too many** troppi; **twice as many** altrettanti, il doppio

many-sided ['meni‚sardɪd] adj multilaterale; versatile

map [mæp] s mappa; (of a city) piano ‖ v (pret & pp mapped; ger mapping) tr tracciare la mappa di; mostrare sulla mappa; **to map out** fare il piano di

maple ['mepəl] s acero

maquette [mæ'ket] s plastico

mar [mar] v (pret & pp marred; ger marring) tr deturpare, sfigurare

maraud [mə'rod] tr & intr predare

marauder [mə'rodər] s predone m

marble ['marbəl] adj marmoreo ‖ s marmo; (little ball of glass) bilia; **marbles** bilie fpl; **to lose one's marbles** (slang) mancare una rotella a qlcu ‖ tr marmorizzare

march [martʃ] s marcia; (hist) marca; **to steal a march on** guadagnare il vantaggio su || *tr* far marciare || *intr* marciare || **March** *s* marzo

marchioness ['marʃənis] *s* marchesa

mare [mer] *s* (*female horse*) cavalla; (*female donkey*) asina

margarine ['mardʒərin] *s* margarina

margin ['mardʒin] *s* margine *m*; (*econ*) scoperto

mar'gin stop' *s* marginatore *m*

marigold ['mæri ‚gold] *s* fiorrancio

marihuana or **marijuana** [‚mari-'hwanə] *s* marijuana

marina [mə'rinə] *s* porto turistico di imbarcazioni, porticciolo turistico

marinate ['mæri ‚net] *tr* marinare

marine [mə'rin] *adj* marino, marittimo || *s* marina; soldato di fanteria da sbarco; **marines** fanteria da sbarco; **tell that to the marines!** (coll) va a raccontarlo ai frati!

mariner ['mærinər] *s* marinaio

marionette [‚mæri∙ə'net] *s* marionetta

mar'ital sta'tus ['mæritəl] *s* stato civile

maritime ['mæri ‚taim] *adj* marittimo

marjoram ['mardʒərəm] *s* origano; (*sweet marjoram*) maggiorana

mark [mark] *s* segno; (*brand*) marca; (*of punctuation*) punto; (*in an examination*) voto; (*sign made by illiterate person*) croce *f*; (*landmark*) segnale *m*; (*target*) bersaglio; (*spot*) macchia; (*starting point in a race*) linea di partenza; (*of confidence*) voto; (*coin*) marco; impronta; **to be beside the mark** essere fuori del seminato; **to hit the mark** colpire il bersaglio; **to leave one's mark** lasciare la propria impronta; **to make one's mark** raggiungere il successo; **to miss the mark** fallire il colpo; **to toe the mark** mettersi in fila; filare diritto || *tr* marcare, segnare, contrassegnare; (*a student*) dar il voto a; (*a test*) esaminare; improntare; notare, avvertire; **to mark down** mettere in iscritto; ribassare il prezzo di

mark'down' *s* riduzione di prezzo

market ['markit] *s* mercato; **to bear the market** giocare al ribasso; **to bull the market** giocare al rialzo; **to play the market** giocare in borsa; **to put on the market** lanciare sul mercato || *tr* mettere sul mercato

marketable ['markitəbəl] *adj* commerciabile, vendibile

marketing ['markitiŋ] *s* compravendita; marketing *m*

mar'ket-place' *s* piazza del mercato

mar'ket price' *s* prezzo corrente

mark'ing gauge' ['markiŋ] *s* graffietto

marks'man *s* (-men) tiratore *m*; **a good marksman** un tiratore scelto

marksmanship ['marksmən ‚ʃip] *s* qualità *f* di tiratore scelto

mark'up' *s* margine *m* di rivendita

marl [marl] *s* marna || *tr* marnare

marmalade ['marmə ‚led] *s* marmellata d'arance

marmot ['marmət] *s* marmotta

maroon [mə'run] *adj* & *s* marrone *m* || *tr* abbandonare (*in un luogo deserto*)

marquee [mar'ki] *s* pensilina

marquess ['markwis] *s* marchese *m*

marque•try ['markətri] *s* (-tries) intarsio

marquis ['markwis] *s* marchese *m*

marquise [mar'kiz] *s* marchesa; (Brit) pensilina

marriage ['mæridʒ] *s* matrimonio

marriageable ['mæridʒəbəl] *adj* adatto al matrimonio; (*woman*) nubile

mar'riage por'tion *s* dote *f*

mar'riage rate' *s* nuzialità *f*

mar'ried life' *s* vita coniugale

marrow ['mæro] *s* midollo

mar•ry ['mæri] *v* (*pret* & *pp* **-ried**) *tr* sposare; **to get married to** sposarsi con || *intr* sposarsi; **to marry into** (e.g., *a noble family*) imparentarsi con; **to marry the second time** risposarsi

Mars [marz] *s* Marte *m*

Marseilles [mar'selz] *s* Marsiglia

marsh [marʃ] *s* palude *f*, lama

mar•shal ['marʃəl] *s* direttore *m* di una sfilata; maestro di cerimonie; (mil) maresciallo; (U.S.A.) ufficiale *m* di giustizia || *v* (*pret* & *pp* **-shaled** or **-shalled**; *ger* **-shaling** or **-shalling**) *tr* introdurre cerimoniosamente; mettere in buon ordine

marsh' mal'low *s* (bot) altea

marsh'mal'low *s* dolce *m* di gelatina e zucchero

marsh•y ['marʃi] *adj* (-ier; -iest) paludoso, palustre

marten ['martən] *s* (*Martes martes*) martora; (*Martes zibellina*) zibellino

martial ['marʃəl] *adj* marziale

mar'tial law' *s* legge *f* marziale

Martian ['marʃən] *adj* & *s* marziano

martin ['martin] *s* rondicchio

martinet [‚marti'net] or ['marti ‚net] *s* pignolo

martyr ['martər] *s* martire *mf*

martyrdom ['martərdəm] *s* martirio

mar•vel ['marvəl] *s* meraviglia || *v* (*pret* & *pp* **-veled** or **-velled**; *ger* **-veling** or **-velling**) *intr* meravigliarsi; **to marvel at** stupirsi di, meravigliarsi di

marvelous ['marvələs] *adj* meraviglioso

Marxist ['marksist] *adj* & *s* marxista *mf*

mascara [mæs'kærə] *s* bistro, rimmel *m*

mascot ['mæskət] *s* mascotte *f*

masculine ['mæskjəlin] *adj* & *s* maschile *m*

mash [mæʃ] *s* (*crushed mass*) poltiglia; (*to form wort*) decotto d'orzo germinato; (e.g., *for poultry*) intriso || *tr* schiacciare; impastare

mashed' pota'toes *spl* purè *m* di patate

masher ['mæʃər] *s* utensile *m* per schiacciare; (slang) pappagallo

mask [mæsk] or [mask] *s* maschera; (phot) mascherina || *tr* mascherare; (phot) mettere una mascherina a || *intr* mascherarsi

masked' ball' *s* ballo in maschera

mason ['mesən] *s* muratore *m* || **Mason** *s* massone *m*

mason•ry ['mesənri] *s* (-ries) arte *f* del

muratore; muratura || **Masonry** s massoneria

masquerade [ˌmæskə'red] or [ˌmɑskə-'red] s mascherata; (disguise) maschera; (pretense) finzione || intr mascherarsi; **to masquerade as** mascherarsi da; farsi passare per

mass [mæs] s massa; (celebration of the Eucharist) messa; **in the mass** nell'insieme; **the masses** le masse || tr ammassare || intr ammassarsi, accumularsi

massacre ['mæsəkər] s massacro, strage f || tr massacrare, trucidare

massage [mə'sɑʒ] s massaggio || tr massaggiare

masseur [mæ'sœr] s massaggiatore m

masseuse [mæ'sœz] s massaggiatrice f

massive ['mæsɪv] adj massiccio; (e.g., dose) massivo; solido

mass' me'dia ['midɪ-ə] s mezzi mpl di comunicazione di massa

mass' meet'ing s assemblea popolare; adunanza in massa

mass' produc'tion s produzione in serie

mast [mæst] or [mɑst] s (post) palo; (agr) ghiande fpl, faggiole fpl; (naut) albero; **before the mast** come marinaio semplice

master ['mæstər] or ['mɑstər] s (employer) padrone m; (male head of household) capo di casa; (man who possesses some special skill) maestro; (title of respect for a boy) signorino; (naut) capitano || tr dominare; (a language) possedere

mas'ter bed'room s camera da letto padronale

mas'ter blade' s foglia maestra (di una balestra)

mas'ter build'er s capomastro

masterful ['mæstərfəl] or ['mɑstərfəl] adj autoritario; provetto, magistrale

mas'ter key' s chiave maestra

masterly ['mæstərli] or ['mɑstərli] adj magistrale || adv magistralmente

mas'ter mechan'ic s mastro meccanico

mas'ter-mind' s mente direttiva || tr organizzare, dirigere

mas'ter of cer'emonies s maestro di cerimonia; (in a night club, radio, etc.) presentatore m

mas'ter-piece' s capolavoro

mas'ter ser'geant s (mil) sergente m maggiore

mas'ter stroke' s colpo da maestro

mas'ter-work' s capolavoro

master·y ['mæstəri] or ['mɑstəri] s (-ies) (command of a subject) dominio; (skill) maestria

mast'head' s (journ) titolo; (naut) testa d'albero

masticate ['mæstɪˌket] tr masticare

mastiff ['mæstɪf] or ['mɑstɪf] s mastino

masturbate ['mæstərˌbet] tr masturbare || intr masturbarsi

mat [mæt] s (for floor) tappeto, stuoia; (under a dish) tondo, sottocoppa, centrino; (before a door) stoino, zerbino; (around a picture) bordo di cartone; (sports) materas-

sino; (typ) flan m; flano || v (pret & pp **matted;** ger **matting**) tr coprire di stuoie; arruffare || intr arruffarsi

match [mætʃ] s (counterpart) uguale m; (suitably associated pair) paio; (light) fiammifero; (wick) miccia; (prospective mate) partito; (sports) partita, gara; **to be a match for** essere pari a, fare fronte a; **to meet one's match** trovare un degno rivale || tr uguagliare, pareggiare; (colors) combinare; (in pairs) appaiare; giocarsi, e.g., **to match s.o. for the drinks** giocarsi le bevande con qlcu || intr corrispondersi, fare il paio

match'box' s scatola di fiammiferi; (of wax matches) scatola di cerini

matchless ['mætʃlɪs] adj incomparabile, senza pari

match'mak'er s paraninfo

mate [met] s compagno; (husband or wife) consorte mf; (to a female) maschio; (to a male) femmina; (chess) scacco matto; (naut) primo ufficiale || tr appaiare; (chess) dar scacco matto a; **to be well mated** esser ben appaiato || intr accoppiarsi

material [mə'tɪrɪ-əl] adj materiale; importante || s materiale m, materia; (cloth, fabric) tela, stoffa; **materials** occorrente m

materialist [mə'tɪrɪ-əlɪst] s materialista mf

materialize [mə'tɪrɪ-əˌlaɪz] intr materializzarsi

matériel [mə'tɪrɪ'ɛl] s materiale m; materiale bellico

maternal [mə'tʌrnəl] adj materno

maternity [mə'tʌrnɪti] s maternità f

mater'nity ward' s maternità f

mathematical [ˌmæθɪ'mætɪkəl] adj matematico

mathematician [ˌmæθɪmə'tɪʃən] s matematico

mathematics [ˌmæθɪ'mætɪks] s matematica

matinée [ˌmætɪ'ne] s mattinata, diurna

mat'ing sea'son s calore m

matins ['mætɪnz] spl mattutino

matriarch ['metrɪˌɑrk] s matrona dignitosa; donna che possiede l'autorità matriarcale

matricidal [ˌmetrɪ'saɪdəl] or [ˌmætrɪ-'saɪdəl] adj matricida

matricide ['metrɪˌsaɪd] or ['mætrɪ-ˌsaɪd] s (act) matricidio; (person) matricida mf

matriculate [mə'trɪkjəˌlet] tr immatricolare || intr immatricolarsi

matriculation [məˌtrɪkjə'leʃən] s immatricolazione, iscrizione

matrimonial [ˌmætrɪ'monɪ-əl] adj matrimoniale

matrimo·ny ['mætrɪˌmoni] s (-nies) matrimonio

ma·trix ['metrɪks] or ['mætrɪks] s (-trices [trɪˌsiz] or -trixes) matrice f

matron ['metrən] s matrona; direttrice f; guardiana

matronly ['metrənli] adj matronale

matter ['mætər] s (physical substance) materia; (pus) materia; (affair, busi-

ness) faccenda; *(material of a book)* contenuto; *(reason)* motivo; *(copy for printer)* manoscritto; *(printed material)* stampati *mpl;* **a matter of** un caso di; **for that matter** per quanto riguarda ciò; **in the matter** al soggetto; **no matter** non importa; **no matter how** non importa come; **no matter when** non importa quando; **no matter where** non importa dove; **what is the matter?** cosa succede?; **what is the matter with you?** cosa ha? || *intr* importare

mat′ter of course′ *s*—**as a matter of course** come se nulla fosse, come se fosse una cosa naturale

mat′ter of fact′ *s*—**as a matter of fact** in realtà, a onor del vero

matter-of-fact [′mætərəv ‚fækt] *adj* prosaico, pratico

mattock [′mætək] *s* piccone *m*

mattress [′mætrɪs] *s* materasso

mature [məˈtʃʊr] or [məˈtʊr] *adj* maturo; *(due)* scaduto || *tr* maturare || *intr* maturare; (com) scadere

maturity [məˈtʊrɪti] or [məˈtʊrɪti] *s* maturità *f;* (com) scadenza

maudlin [′mɔdlɪn] *adj* sentimentale, lagrimoso; piagnucoloso e ubriaco

maul [mɔl] *tr* maltrattare, bistrattare

maulstick [′mɔl‚stɪk] *s* appoggiamano

maundy [′mɔndi] *s* lavanda

Maun′dy Thurs′day *s* giovedì santo

mausole·um [‚mɔsəˈli·əm] *s* (**-ums** or **-a** [ə]) mausoleo

maw [mɔ] *s (e.g., of a hog)* stomaco; *(of carnivorous mammal)* fauci *fpl; (of fowl)* gozzo; (fig) bocca, fauci *fpl*

mawkish [′mɔkɪʃ] *adj (sickening)* nauseante; *(sentimental)* svenevole

maxim [′mæksɪm] *s* massima

maximum [′mæksɪməm] *adj & s* massimo

may [me] *v aux*—**it may be** può essere; **may I come in?** si può?; **may you be happy!** possa tu essere felice! || **May** *s* maggio

maybe [′mebi] *adv* forse

May′ Day′ *s* primo maggio; festa della primavera; (hist) calendimaggio *(in Florence)*

mayhem [′mehem] or [′me·əm] *s* mutilazione dolosa

mayonnaise [‚me·əˈnez] *s* maionese *f*

mayor [′me·ər] or [mer] *s* sindaco

mayoress [′me·ərɪs] or [′merɪs] *s* donna sindaco

May′pole *s* maio, maggio, palo per le danze di calendimaggio

May′pole dance′ *s* ballo figurato con nastri per la festa di primavera

May′ queen′ *s* reginetta di maggio

maze [mez] *s* dedalo, labirinto

me [mi] *pron* me; mi; **to me** mi; **a me**

meadow [′medo] *s* prato

mead′ow·land *s* prateria

meager [′migər] *adj* magro

meal [mil] *s (food)* pasto; *(unbolted grain)* farina

meal′time *s* ora del pasto

mean [min] *adj (intermediate)* medio;

(low in rank) basso, umile; *(shabby)* misero; *(of poor quality)* inferiore; *(stingy)* taccagno; *(nasty)* villano; *(vicious, as a horse)* intrattabile; (coll) indisposto; (coll) vergognoso; (slang) splendido; **no mean** eccellente || *s* media, termine medio; **by all means** certamente, senza dubbio; **by means of** per mezzo di; **by no means** in nessuna maniera; **means** beni *mpl; (agency)* mezzo, maniera; **to live on one's means** vivere di rendita || *v (pret & pp* **meant** [ment]) *tr* significare, voler dire; **to mean to** pensare || *intr*—**to mean well** aver buone intenzioni

meander [mɪˈændər] *s* meandro || *intr* serpeggiare, vagare

meaning [′minɪŋ] *s* senso, significato

meaningful [′minɪŋfəl] *adj* significativo

meaningless [′minɪŋlɪs] *adj* senza senso, senza significato

meanness [′minnɪs] *s* viltà *f,* bassezza; *(stinginess)* meschinità *f; (lowliness)* umiltà *f,* povertà *f*

mean′time′ *s*—**in the meantime** nel frattempo || *adv* frattanto, intanto

mean′while′ *s & adv* var of **meantime**

measles [′mizəlz] *s* morbillo; *(German measles)* rosolia

measly [′mizli] *adj* (**-slier; -sliest**) col morbillo; (coll) miserabile

measurable [′meʒərəbəl] *adj* misurabile

measure [′meʒər] *s* misura; *(legislative bill)* progetto di legge; (mus) battuta; **in a measure** in un certo senso; **to take the measure of** prendere le misure di; giudicare accuratamente || *tr* misurare; *(a distance)* percorrere; **to measure out** somministrare || *intr* misurare; **to measure up to** essere all'altezza di

measurement [′meʒərmənt] *s* misura; **to take s.o.'s measurements** prendere le misure di qlcu

meas′uring cup′ *s* vetro graduato

meat [mit] *s* carne *f; (food in general)* cibo; *(of nut)* gheriglio; (fig) sostanza, midollo

meat′ball′ *s* polpetta

meat′ grind′er *s* tritacarne *m*

meat′ loaf′ *s* polpettone *m*

meat′ mar′ket *s* macelleria

meat·y [′miti] *adj* (**-ier; -iest**) carnoso, polputo; (fig) sostanzioso

Mecca [′mekə] *s* la Mecca; **the Mecca** (fig) la Mecca

mechanic [mɪˈkænɪk] *s* meccanico; (aut) motorista *m*

mechanical [mɪˈkænɪkəl] *adj* meccanico; *(machinelike)* (fig) macchinale

mechan′ical engineer′ing *s* ingegneria meccanica

mechan′ical pen′cil *s* matita automatica

mechanics [mɪˈkænɪks] *s* meccanica

mechanism [′mekə‚nɪzəm] *s* meccanismo, congegno

mechanize [′mekə‚naɪz] *tr* meccanizzare

medal [′medəl] *s* medaglia

medallion [mɪˈdæljən] *s* medaglione *m*

meddle ['mɛdəl] *intr* intromettersi

meddler ['mɛdlər] *s* ficcanaso

meddlesome ['mɛdəlsəm] *adj* invadente, indiscreto

median ['midɪ·ən] *adj* medio, mediano || *s* punto medio, numero medio

me'dian strip' *s* spartitraffico

mediate ['midɪ‚et] *tr (a dispute)* comporre; *(parties)* pacificare || *intr (to be in the middle)* mediare; fare da paciere

mediation [‚midɪ'eʃən] *s* mediazione

mediator ['midɪ‚etər] *s* mediatore *m*

medical ['mɛdɪkəl] *adj* medico; *(student)* di medicina

medicinal [mə'dɪsɪnəl] *adj* medicinale

medicine ['mɛdɪsɪn] *s* medicina

med'icine cab'inet *s* armadietto farmaceutico

med'icine kit' *s* cassetta farmaceutica

med'icine man' *s* (**men'**) stregone indiano

medieval [‚midɪ'ivəl] *or* [‚mɛdɪ'ivəl] *adj* medievale

medievalist [‚midɪ'ivəlɪst] *or* [‚mɛdɪ'ivəlɪst] *s* medievalista *mf*

mediocre ['midɪ‚okər] *or* [‚midɪ'okər] *adj* mediocre

mediocri·ty [‚midɪ'akrɪti] *s* (**-ties**) mediocrità *f*

meditate ['mɛdɪ‚tet] *tr & intr* meditare

meditation [‚mɛdɪ'teʃən] *s* meditazione

Mediterranean [‚mɛdɪtə'renɪ·ən] *adj & s* Mediterraneo

medi·um ['midɪ·əm] *adj* medio; *(heat)* moderato; *(meat)* cotto moderatamente || *s* (**-ums** *or* **-a** [ə]) *(middle state; mean)* media; mezzo; *(in spiritualism)* medium *m*; **media** *(of communication)* media *mpl*; **through the medium of** per mezzo di

medlar ['mɛdlər] *s (tree)* nespolo; *(fruit)* nespola

medley ['mɛdli] *s* farragine *f*, mescolanza; *(mus)* pot-pourri *m*

medul·la [mɪ'dʌlə] *s* (**-lae** [li]) midollo

meek [mik] *adj* mansueto, umile

meekness ['miknɪs] *s* mansuetudine *f*

meerschaum ['mɪrʃəm] *or* ['mɪrʃəm] *s* schiuma; pipa di schiuma

meet [mit] *adj* conveniente || *s* incontro || *v* (*pret & pp* **met** [mɛt]) *tr* incontrare, incontrarsi con; *(to become acquainted with)* fare la conoscenza di; riunirsi con; *(to cope with)* sopperire a; *(said of a public carrier)* fare coincidenza con; andar incontro a; *(one's obligations)* far fronte a; *(bad luck)* avere; **to meet the eyes of** presentarsi agli occhi di || *intr* incontrarsi; riunirsi; conoscersi; **till we meet again** arrivederci; **to meet with** incontrare, incontrarsi con; *(an accident)* avere; *(said of a public carrier)* fare coincidenza con

meeting ['mitɪŋ] *s* riunione, ritrovo; seduta, convegno; *(political)* comizio; *(e.g., of two rivers)* confluenza; duello

meet'ing of the minds' *s* accordo, consonanza di voleri

meet'ing place' *s* luogo di riunione

megacycle ['mɛgə‚saɪkəl] *s* megaciclo

megaphone ['mɛgə‚fon] *s* megafono, portavoce *m*

megohm ['mɛg‚om] *s* megaohm *m*

melancholia [‚mɛlən'kolɪ·ə] *s* melanconia, malinconia

melanchol·y ['mɛlən‚kali] *adj* malinconico || *s* (**-ies**) malinconia

melee ['mele] *or* ['mele] *s (fight)* mischia; confusione

mellow ['mɛlo] *adj (fruit)* maturo; *(wine)* pastoso; *(voice)* soave, melodioso || *tr* raddolcire || *intr* raddolcirsi

melodic [mɪ'ladɪk] *adj* melodico

melodious [mɪ'lodɪ·əs] *adj* melodioso

melodramatic [‚mɛlədrə'mætɪk] *adj* melodrammatico

melo·dy ['mɛlədi] *s* (**-dies**) melodia

melon ['mɛlən] *s* melone *m*, popone *m*

melt [mɛlt] *tr* sciogliere; *(metals)* fondere; *(fig)* intenerire || *intr* sciogliersi; fondersi; *(fig)* intenerirsi; **to melt away** svanire; **to melt into** convertirsi in, diventare; *(tears)* struggersi in

melt'ing pot' *s* crogiolo

member ['mɛmbər] *s* membro

membership ['mɛmbər‚ʃɪp] *s* associazione; numero di membri

membrane ['mɛmbren] *s* membrana

memen·to [mɪ'mɛnto] *s* (**-tos** *or* **-toes**) oggetto ricordo

mem·o ['mɛmo] *s* (**-os**) (coll) memorandum *m*

memoir ['mɛmwar] *s* memoria, memoriale *m*; biografia; **memoirs** memorie *fpl*

memoran·dum [‚mɛmə'rændəm] *s* (**-dums** *or* **-da** [ə]) memorandum *m*

memorial [mɪ'morɪ·əl] *adj* commemorativo || *s* sacrario; *(petition)* memoriale *m*

Memo'rial Day' *s* giorno dei caduti

memorialize [mɪ'morɪ·ə‚laɪz] *tr* commemorare

memorize ['mɛmə‚raɪz] *tr* imparare a memoria

memo·ry ['mɛməri] *s* (**-ries**) memoria; **to commit to memory** imparare a memoria

menace ['mɛnɪs] *s* minaccia || *tr & intr* minacciare

ménage [me'naʒ] *s* casa; *(housekeeping)* economia domestica

menagerie [mə'næʒəri] *or* [mə'nædʒəri] *s* serraglio

mend [mɛnd] *s* riparo; **to be on the mend** migliorare || *tr (to repair)* raccomodare, riparare; *(to patch)* rammendare; *(fig)* correggere || *intr* correggersi

mendacious [mɛn'deʃəs] *adj* mendace

mendicant ['mɛndɪkənt] *adj & s* mendicante *mf*

menfolk ['mɛn‚fok] *spl* uomini *mpl*

menial ['minɪ·əl] *adj* basso, servile || *s* servitore *m*, servo

menses ['mɛnsiz] *spl* mestruazione, mestrui *mpl*

men's' fur'nishings *spl* articoli *mpl* d'abbigliamento maschile

men's' room' *s* gabinetto per signori

menstruate ['mɛnstru ,et] *intr* avere le mestruazioni

men'tal arith'metic ['mɛntəl] *s* calcolo mentale

men'tal hos'pital *s* manicomio

men'tal ill'ness *s* malattia mentale

men'tal reserva'tion *s* riserva mentale

men'tal test' *s* test *m* mentale

mention ['mɛnʃən] *s* menzione ‖ *tr* menzionare; **don't mention it** non c'è di che

menu ['mɛnju] or ['menju] *s* menu *m*, lista

meow [mɪ'au] *s* miagolio ‖ *intr* miagolare

Mephistophelian [,mɛfɪstə'filɪ-ən] *adj* mefistofelico

mercantile ['mʌrkən ,til] or ['mʌrkən- ,taɪl] *adj* mercantile

mercenar·y ['mʌrsə ,nɛri] *adj* mercenario ‖ *s* (-ies) mercenario

merchandise ['mʌrtʃən ,daɪz] *s* mercanzia, merce *f*

merchant ['mʌrtʃənt] *adj* mercantile ‖ *s* mercante *m*, commerciante *mf*

mer'chant-man *s* (-men) mercantile *m*

mer'chant marine' *s* marina mercantile

merciful ['mʌrsɪfəl] *adj* misericordioso

merciless ['mʌrsɪlɪs] *adj* spietato

mercu·ry ['mʌrkjəri] *s* (-ries) mercurio ‖ **Mercury** *s* Mercurio

mer·cy ['mʌrsi] *s* (-cies) misericordia; **at the mercy of** alla mercé di

mere [mɪr] *adj* mero, puro

meretricious [,mɛrɪ'trɪʃəs] *adj* vistoso, chiassoso, sgargiante; artificiale, falso, finto

merge [mʌrdʒ] *tr* fondere ‖ *intr* fondersi; (*said of two roads*) convergere; **to merge into** convertirsi lentamente in

merger ['mʌrdʒər] *s* fusione

meridian [mə'rɪdɪ-ən] *adj* meridiano; culminante ‖ *s* meridiano; apogeo

meringue [mə'ræŋ] *s* meringa

merit ['mɛrɪt] *s* merito ‖ *tr* meritare

meritorious [,mɛrɪ'tori-əs] *adj* meritorio

merlon ['mʌrlən] *s* merlo

mermaid ['mʌr ,med] *s* sirena

mer'man' *s* (-men') tritone *m*

merriment ['mɛrɪmənt] *s* allegria

mer·ry ['mɛri] *adj* (-rier; -riest) allegro, giocondo; **to make merry** divertirsi

Mer'ry Christ'mas *interj* Buon Natale!

mer'ry-go-round' *s* giostra, carosello; (*of parties*) serie ininterrotta

mer'ry-mak'er *s* festaiolo

mesh [mɛʃ] *s* (*network*) rete *f*; (*each open space of net*) maglia; (mach) ingranaggio; **meshes** rete *f* ‖ *tr* irretire; (mach) ingranare ‖ *intr* irretirsi; (mach) ingranarsi

mess [mɛs] *s* (*dirty condition*) disordine *m*; (*meal for a group of people*) mensa, rancio; porzione; **to get into a mess** mettersi nei pasticci; **to make a mess of** rovinare ‖ *tr* sporcare; disordinare; rovinare ‖ *intr* mangiare in comune; **to mess around** (coll) perdersi in cose inutili

message ['mɛsɪdʒ] *s* messaggio

messenger ['mɛsəndʒər] *s* messaggero; (*person who goes on an errand*) fattorino; (mil) portaordini *m*

mess' hall' *s* mensa

Messiah [mə'saɪ-ə] *s* Messia *m*

mess' kit' *s* gavetta, gamella

mess'mate' *s* compagno di rancio

mess' of pot'tage ['pɑtɪdʒ] *s* (Bib & fig) piatto di lenticchie

Messrs. ['mɛsərz] *pl* of **Mr.**

mess·y ['mɛsi] *adj* (-ier; -iest) disordinato; sporco

metal ['mɛtəl] *adj* metallico ‖ *s* metallo

metallic [mɪ'tælɪk] *adj* metallico

metallurgy ['mɛtə ,lʌrdʒi] *s* metallurgia

met'al pol'ish *s* lucido per metalli

met'al·work' *s* lavoro di metallo

metamorpho·sis [,mɛtə'mɔrfəsɪs] *s* -ses [,siz]) metamorfosi *f*

metaphony [mə'tæfəni] *s* metafonia, metafonesi *f*

metaphor ['mɛtəfər] or ['mɛtə ,fɔr] *s* metafora

metaphorical [,mɛtə'farɪkəl] or [,mɛtə'fɔrɪkəl] *adj* metaforico

metathe·sis [mɪ'tæθɪsɪs] *s* (-ses [,siz]) metatesi *f*

mete [mit] *tr*—**to mete out** distribuire

meteor ['mitɪ-ər] *s* meteora

meteoric [,mitɪ'arɪk] or [,mitɪ'ɔrɪk] *adj* meteorico; (fig) rapidissimo, folgorante

meteorite ['mitɪ-ə ,raɪt] *s* meteorite *m* & *f*

meteorology [,mitɪ-ə'ralədʒi] *s* meteorologia

meter ['mitər] *s* (*unit of length; verse*) metro; (*instrument for measuring gas, water, etc.*) contatore *m*; (mus) tempo ‖ *tr* misurare col contatore

me'ter read'er *s* lettore *m*, letturista *m*

methane ['mɛθen] *s* metano

method ['mɛθəd] *s* metodo

methodic(al) [mɪ'θɑdɪk(əl)] *adj* metodico

Methodist ['mɛθədɪst] *adj* & *s* metodista *mf*

Methuselah [mɪ'θuzələ] *s* Matusalemme *m*

meticulous [mɪ'tɪkjələs] *adj* meticoloso

metric(al) ['mɛtrɪk(əl)] *adj* metrico

metronome ['mɛtrə ,nom] *s* metronomo

metropolis [mɪ'trapəlɪs] *s* metropoli *f*

metropolitan [,mɛtrə'palɪtən] *adj* & *s* metropolitano

mettle ['mɛtəl] *s* disposizione, temperamento; brio, animo; **to be on one's mettle** impegnarsi a fondo

mettlesome ['mɛtəlsəm] *adj* brioso

mew [mju] *s* miagolio; (orn) gabbiano; **mews** scuderie *fpl*

Mexican ['mɛksɪkən] *adj* & *s* messicano

Mexico ['mɛksɪ ,ko] *s* il Messico

mezzanine ['mɛzə ,nin] *s* mezzanino

mica ['maɪkə] *s* mica

microbe ['maɪkrob] *s* microbio

microbiology [,maɪkrəbaɪ'alədʒi] *s* microbiologia

microcard ['maɪkrə ,kard] *s* microscheda

microfarad [ˌmaɪkrə'færæd] s microfarad m

microfilm ['maɪkrəˌfɪlm] s microfilm m || tr microfilmare

microgroove ['maɪkrəˌgruv] adj microsolco · || s microsolco; disco microsolco

microphone ['maɪkrəˌfon] s microfono

microscope ['maɪkrəˌskop] s microscopio

microscopic [ˌmaɪkrə'skɑpɪk] adj microscopico

microwave ['maɪkrəˌwev] s microonda

mid [mɪd] adj mezzo, la metà di, e.g., **mid October** la metà di ottobre

mid'day' adj di mezzogiorno || s mezzogiorno

middle ['mɪdəl] adj medio, mezzo || s mezzo, metà f; (of human body) cintura; **about the middle of** verso la metà di; **in the middle of** nel mezzo di

mid'dle age' s mezza età || **Middle Ages** spl Medio Evo

mid'dle class' s ceto medio, borghesia

Mid'dle East' s Medio Oriente

Mid'dle Eng'lish s inglese m medievale parlato fra il 1150 e il 1500

mid'dle fin'ger s dito medio

mid'dle-man' s (-men') intermediario

middling ['mɪdlɪŋ] adj mediocre, passabile || s (coarsely ground wheat) farina grossa integrale; **middlings** articoli mpl di qualità mediocre || adv moderatamente

mid·dy ['mɪdi] s (-dies) aspirante m di marina

mid'dy blouse' s marinara

midget ['mɪdʒɪt] s nano

midland ['mɪdlənd] adj centrale, interno || s regione centrale

mid'night' adj di mezzanotte; **to burn the midnight oil** studiare a lume di candela || s mezzanotte f

midriff ['mɪdrɪf] s diaframma m; (middle part of body) cintura, vita

mid'ship'man s (-men) aspirante m di marina

midst [mɪdst] s mezzo, centro; **in the midst of** in mezzo a

mid'stream' s—**in midstream** in mezzo al fiume

mid'sum'mer s cuore m dell'estate

mid'way' adj situato a metà strada || s metà strada; viale m principale di un' esposizione || adv a metà strada

mid'week' s mezzo della settimana

mid'wife' s (-wives') levatrice f

mid'win'ter s cuore m dell'inverno

mid'year' adj nel nezzo dell'anno || s mezzo dell'anno; **midyears** (coll) esami mpl nel mezzo dell'anno scolastico

mien [min] s aspetto, portamento

miff [mɪf] s (coll) battibecco || tr (coll) offendere

might [maɪt] s forza, potenza; **with might and main** a tutta forza || v aux used to form the potential, e.g., **he might change his mind** è possibile che cambi opinione

might·y ['maɪti] adj (-ier; -iest) po-

tente; (huge) grandissimo || adv (coll) moltissimo, grandemente

migraine ['maɪgren] s emicrania

migrate ['maɪgret] intr migrare

migratory ['maɪgrəˌtori] adj migratore

milch [mɪltʃ] adj lattifero

mild [maɪld] adj dolce, mite, gentile; (disease) leggero

mildew ['mɪlˌdju] or ['mɪlˌdu] s (mold) muffa; (plant disease) peronospora

mile [maɪl] s miglio terrestre; miglio marino

mileage ['maɪlɪdʒ] s distanza in miglia

mile'age tick'et s biglietto calcolato in miglia simile al biglietto chilometraggio

mile'post' s colonnina miliare

mile'stone' s pietra miliare

milieu [mɪl'ju] s ambiente m

militancy ['mɪlɪtənsi] s bellicismo; spirito militante

militant ['mɪlɪtənt] adj & s militante mf

militarism ['mɪlɪtəˌrɪzəm] s militarismo

militarist ['mɪlɪtərɪst] adj & s militarista mf

militarize ['mɪlɪtəˌraɪz] tr militarizzare

military ['mɪlɪˌteri] adj militare || s— **the military** le forze armate

mil'itary acad'emy s scuola allievi ufficiali, accademia militare

mil'itary police' s polizia militare

militate ['mɪlɪˌtet] intr militare

militia [mɪ'lɪʃə] s milizia

mili'tia-man s (-men) miliziano

milk [mɪlk] adj lattifero; di latte; **al latte** || s latte m || tr mungere; (fig) spillare || intr dare latte

milk' can' s bidone m per il latte

milk' choc'olate s cioccolato al latte

milk' diet' s regime latteo

milking ['mɪlkɪŋ] s mungitura

milk'maid' s lattaia

milk'man' s (-men') lattaio

milk' of hu'man kind'ness s grande compassione

milk' pail' s secchio da latte

milk' shake' s frappé m or frullato di latte

milk'sop' s effeminato

milk'weed' s vincetossico

milk·y ['mɪlki] adj (-ier; -iest) latteo; (whitish) lattiginoso

Milk'y Way' s Via Lattea

mill [mɪl] s (for grinding grain) mulino; (for making fabrics) filanda; (for cutting wood) segheria; (for refining sugar) zuccherificio; (for producing steel) acciaieria; (to grind coffee) macinino; (part of a dollar) millesimo; **to put through the mill** mettere a dura prova || tr (grains) macinare; (coins) zigrinare; (steel) laminare; (ore) frantumare; (with a milling machine) fresare; (chocolate) frullare || intr—**to mill about** or **around** girare intorno

millennial [mɪ'lɛniəl] adj millenario

milleni·um [mɪˈlenɪ·əm] s (-ums or -a [ə]) millennio

miller [ˈmɪlər] s mugnaio; (ent) tignola notturna

millet [ˈmɪlɪt] s panico, miglio

milliampere [ˌmɪlɪˈæmpɪr] s milliampere m

milliard [ˈmɪljərd] or [ˈmɪljɑrd] s (Brit) miliardo, bilione m

milligram [ˈmɪlɪˌgræm] s milligrammo

millimeter [ˈmɪlɪˌmitər] s millimetro

milliner [ˈmɪlɪnər] s modista

milliner·y [ˈmɪlɪˌnerɪ] or [ˈmɪlɪnərɪ] s (-ies) cappelli mpl per signora; modisteria; articoli mpl di modisteria

mil′linery shop′ s modisteria

milling [ˈmɪlɪŋ] s (of grain) macinatura; (of coins) granitura; (mach) fresatura

mill′ing machine′ s fresatrice f

million [ˈmɪljən] adj milione di, milioni di || s milione m

millionaire [ˌmɪljənˈer] s milionario

millionth [ˈmɪljənθ] adj, s & pron milionesimo

millivolt [ˈmɪlɪˌvolt] s millivolt m

mill′pond′ s gora

mill′race′ s corrente f che aziona il mulino; canale m di presa

mill′stone′ s mola, macina, palmento; (fig) peso, gravame m

mill′ wheel′ s ruota del mulino

mill′work′ s lavoro di falegnameria; lavoro di falegnameria fatto a macchina

mime [maɪm] s mimo || tr mimare

mimeograph [ˈmɪmɪ·əˌgræf] or [ˈmɪmɪ·əˌgrɑf] s (trademark) ciclostile m || tr ciclostilare

mim·ic [ˈmɪmɪk] s mimo, imitatore m || v (pret & pp -icked; ger -icking) tr imitare, scimmiottare

mimic·ry [ˈmɪmɪkrɪ] s (-ries) mimica; (biol) mimetismo

minaret [ˌmɪnəˈret] or [ˈmɪnəˌret] s minareto

mince [mɪns] tr tagliuzzare, triturare; (words) pronunziare con affettazione; **to not mince one's words** non aver peli sulla lingua

mince′meat′ s carne tritata; **to make mincemeat of** annientare completamente

mince′ pie′ s torta di frutta secca e carne tritata

mind [maɪnd] s mente f; opinione; **to bear in mind** tener presente; **to be not in one's right mind** essere fuori di senno; **to be of one mind** essere d'accordo; **to be out of one's mind** essere impazzito; **to change one's mind** cambiare d'opinione; **to go out of one's mind** impazzire; **to have a mind to** aver voglia di; **to have in mind** to pensare a; **to have on one's mind** avere in mente; **to lose one's mind** uscire di mente; **to make up one's mind** decidersi; **to my mind** a mio modo di vedere; **to say whatever comes to one's mind** dire quanto salta in testa, e.g., John always says whatever comes to his mind Gio-

vanni dice sempre quanto gli salta in testa; **to set one's mind on** risolversi a; **to slip one's mind** scappare di mente (with dat), e.g., **it slipped his mind** gli è scappato di mente; **to speak one's mind** dire la propria opinione; **with one mind** unanimemente || tr (to take care of) occuparsi di; obbedire (with dat); **do you mind the smoke?** Le disturba il fumo?; **mind your own business** si occupi degli affari Suoi || intr osservare, fare attenzione; rincrescere, e.g., **do you mind if I go?** Le rincresce se vado?; **never mind** non si preoccupi

mindful [ˈmaɪndfəl] adj memore

mind′ read′er s lettore m del pensiero

mind′ read′ing s lettura del pensiero

mine [maɪn] s (e.g., of coal) miniera; (mil & nav) mina || pron poss il mio; mio || tr minare; (earth) scavare; (ore) estrarre || intr lavorare una miniera; (mil & nav) minare

mine′ detec′tor s rivelatore m di mine

mine′field′ s campo minato

mine′lay′er s posamine m

miner [ˈmaɪnər] s minatore m

mineral [ˈmɪnərəl] adj & s minerale m

mineralogy [ˌmɪnəˈrælədʒɪ] s mineralogia

min′eral wool′ s cotone m or lana minerale

mine′ sweep′er s dragamine m

mingle [ˈmɪŋgəl] tr mescolare; unire || intr mescolarsi, associarsi

miniature [ˈmɪnɪ·ətʃər] or [ˈmɪnɪtʃər] s miniatura; **to paint in miniature** miniare, dipingere in miniatura

min′iature golf′ s minigolf m

miniaturization [ˌmɪnɪ·ətʃərɪˈzeʃən] or [ˌmɪnɪtʃərɪˈzeʃən] s miniaturizzazione

minimal [ˈmɪnɪməl] adj minimo

minimize [ˈmɪnɪˌmaɪz] tr minimizzare

minimum [ˈmɪnɪməm] adj & s minimo

min′imum wage′ s salario minimo

mining [ˈmaɪnɪŋ] adj minerario || s estrazione di minerali; (nav) posa di mine

minion [ˈmɪnjən] s servo; favorito, beniamino

min′ion of the law′ s poliziotto

miniskirt [ˈmɪnəˌskɑrt] s minigonna

minister [ˈmɪnɪstər] s ministro; pastore m protestante || tr & intr ministrare

ministerial [ˌmɪnɪsˈtɪrɪ·əl] adj ministeriale

minis·try [ˈmɪnɪstrɪ] s (-tries) ministero; sacerdozio

mink [mɪŋk] s visone m

minnow [ˈmɪno] s pesciolino; (ichth) ciprino

minor [ˈmaɪnər] adj minore || s minore m, minorenne mf; (educ) corso secondario

minori·ty [mɪˈnɑrɪtɪ] or [mɪˈnɔrɪtɪ] adj minoritario || s (-ties) (smaller number or part; group differing in race, etc., from majority) minoranza; (under legal age) minorità f

minstrel [ˈmɪnstrəl] s (hist) menestrello; (U.S.A.) comico vestito da nero

minstrel·sy ['mɪnstrəlsɪ] s (-sies) giulleria; poesia giullaresca

mint [mɪnt] s zecca; (plant) menta; (losenge) mentina; (fig) miniera d'oro ‖ tr coniare

minuet [,mɪnjʊ'et] s minuetto

minus ['maɪnəs] adj meno ‖ s meno, perdita ‖ prep meno, senza

minute [maɪ'njut] or [maɪ'nut] adj minuto ‖ ['mɪnɪt] adj fatto in un minuto ‖ s minuto; momento; **minutes** processo verbale; **to write up the minutes** tenere i verbali; **up to the minute** al corrente; dell'ultima ora

min'ute hand' ['mɪnɪt] s sfera or lancetta dei minuti

minutiae [mɪ'njuʃɪ‚i] or [mɪ'nuʃɪ‚i] spl minuzie fpl

minx [mɪŋks] s sfacciata, civetta

miracle ['mɪrəkəl] s miracolo

mir'acle play' s sacra rappresentazione

miraculous [mɪ'rækjələs] adj miracoloso

mirage [mɪ'rɑʒ] s miraggio

mire [maɪr] s limo, mota

mirror ['mɪrər] s specchio ‖ tr specchiare, riflettere

mirth [mʌrθ] s allegria, gioia

mir·y ['maɪrɪ] adj (-ier; -iest) fangoso, limaccioso

misadventure [,mɪsəd'ventʃər] s disavventura, contrattempo

misanthrope ['mɪsən‚θrop] s misantropo

misanthropy [mɪs'ænθrəpɪ] s misantropia

misapprehension [,mɪsæprɪ'henʃən] s malinteso

misappropriation [,mɪsə‚proprɪ'eʃən] s malversazione

misbehave [,mɪsbɪ'hev] intr comportarsi male

misbehavior [,mɪsbɪ'hevɪ‚ər] s cattiva condotta

miscalculation [,mɪskælkjə'leʃən] s calcolo errato

miscarriage [mɪs'kærɪdʒ] s (of justice) errore m; (of a letter) disguido; (pathol) aborto

miscar·ry [mɪs'kærɪ] v (pret & pp -ried) intr (said of a project) fallire; (said of a letter) smarrirsi; (pathol) abortire

miscellaneous [,mɪsə'lenɪ‚əs] adj miscellaneo

miscella·ny ['mɪsə‚lenɪ] s (-nies) miscellanea

mischief ['mɪstʃɪf] s (harm) danno; (disposition to annoy) malizia; (prankishness) birichinata

mis'chief-mak'er s mettimale mf

mischievous ['mɪstʃɪvəs] adj dannoso; malizioso; birichino

misconception [,mɪskən'sepʃən] s concetto erroneo, fraintendimento

misconduct [mɪs'kɑndʌkt] s cattiva condotta; (of a public official) malgoverno m ‖ [,mɪskən'dʌkt] tr male amministrare; **to misconduct oneself** comportarsi male

misconstrue [,mɪskən'stru] or [mɪs-'kɑnstru] tr fraintendere

miscount [mɪs'kaunt] s conteggio erroneo ‖ tr & intr contare male

miscue [mɪs'kju] s sbaglio; (in billiards) stecca ‖ intr steccare; (theat) sbagliarsi di battuta

mis·deal ['mɪs‚dil] s distribuzione sbagliata ‖ [mɪs'dil] v (pret & pp -dealt [dɛlt]) tr & intr distribuire erroneamente

misdeed [mɪs'did] or ['mɪs‚did] s misfatto, malfatto

misdemeanor [,mɪsdɪ'minər] s cattiva condotta; (law) delitto colposo

misdirect [,mɪsdɪ'rekt] or [,mɪsdaɪ-'rekt] tr dare un indirizzo sbagliato a; (a letter) mettere un indirizzo sbagliato su

misdoing [mɪs'du‚ɪŋ] s misfatto

miser ['maɪzər] s avaro, spilorcio

miserable ['mɪzərəbəl] adj miserabile, miserevole; (coll) malissimo; (coll) schifoso

miserly ['maɪzərlɪ] adj spilorcio

miser·y ['mɪzərɪ] s (-ies) miseria

misfeasance [mɪs'fizəns] s infrazione della legge; abuso di autorità commesso da pubblico funzionario

misfire [mɪs'faɪr] s difetto di esplosione; (aut) difetto d'accensione ‖ intr (said of a gun) fare cilecca; (aut) dare accensione irregolare; (fig) fallire

mis·fit ['mɪs‚fɪt] s vestito che non va bene; (person) spostato, pesce m fuor d'acqua ‖ [mɪs'fɪt] v (pret & pp -fitted; ger -fitting) intr andar male

misfortune [mɪs'fɔrtʃən] s disgrazia

misgiving [mɪs'gɪvɪŋ] s dubbio, timore m, cattivo presentimento

misgovern [mɪs'gʌvərn] tr amministrare male

misguided [mɪs'gaɪdɪd] adj fuorviato; (e.g., kindness) sconsigliato

mishap ['mɪshæp] or [mɪs'hæp] s accidente m, infortunio

misinform [,mɪsɪn'fɔrm] tr dare informazioni errate a

misinterpret [,mɪsɪn'tɜrprɪt] tr interpretare male, trasfigurare

misjudge [mɪs'dʒʌdʒ] tr & intr giudicare male

mis·lay [mɪs'le] v (pret & pp -laid [,led]) tr (e.g., tile) applicare in maniera sbagliata; (e.g., papers) smarrire, mettere al posto sbagliato

mis·lead [mɪs'lid] v (pret & pp -led [,led]) tr sviare, traviare

misleading [mɪs'lidɪŋ] adj ingannatore

mismanagement [mɪs'mænɪdʒmənt] s malgoverno

misnomer [mɪs'nomər] s termine improprio

misplace [mɪs'ples] tr mettere fuori di posto; (trust) riporre erroneamente

misprint ['mɪs‚prɪnt] s errore m di stampa, refuso ‖ [mɪs'prɪnt] tr stampare erroneamente

mispronounce [,mɪsprə'nauns] tr pronunciare in modo erroneo

mispronunciation [,mɪsprə‚nʌnsɪ-

misquote [mɪs'kwot] *tr* citare incorrettamente

misrepresent [,mɪsreprɪ'zent] *tr* travisare, snaturare; (pol) rappresentare slealmente

miss [mɪs] *s* sbaglio, omissione; tiro fuori bersaglio; signorina || *tr* (*a train, an opportunity*) perdere; (*the target*) fallire; (*an appointment*) mancare; (*the point*) non vedere, non capire; per poco, e.g., **the car missed hitting him** l'automobile non l'ha investito per poco || *intr* sbagliare, fallire; mancare il bersaglio || **Miss** *s* signorina, la signorina

missal ['mɪsəl] *s* messale *m*

misshapen [mɪs'ʃepən] *adj* deforme, malfatto

missile ['mɪsɪl] *adj* missilistico || *s* missile *m*

mis'sile launch'er *s* lanciamissili *m*

missing ['mɪsɪŋ] *adj* mancante; assente; (*in action*) disperso

mis'sing link' *s* anello di congiunzione

miss'ing per'son *s* disperso

mission ['mɪʃən] *s* missione *f*

missionar·y ['mɪʃən,ɛri] *adj* missionario || *s* (**-ies**) (eccl) missionario; (dipl) incaricato in missione

missive ['mɪsɪv] *s* missiva

mis·spell [mɪs'spel] *v* (*pret & pp* **-spelled** or **-spelt** ['spelt]) *tr & intr* scrivere male

misspelling [mɪs'spelɪŋ] *s* errore *m* di ortografia

misspent [mɪs'spent] *adj* sprecato

misstatement [mɪs'stetmənt] *s* dichiarazione inesatta

misstep [mɪs'step] *s* passo falso

miss·y ['mɪsi] *s* (**-ies**) (coll) signorina

mist [mɪst] *s* caligine *f*, foschia; (*of tears*) velo; (*of smoke, vapors, etc.*) nuvola

mis·take [mɪs'tek] *s* errore *m*, sbaglio; **and no mistake** (coll) di sicuro; **by mistake** per sbaglio; **to make a mistake** sbagliarsi || *v* (*pret* **-took** ['tʊk]; *pp* **-taken**) *tr* fraintendere; **to be mistaken for** essere preso per; **to mistake for** pigliare per

mistaken [mɪs'tekən] *adj* errato, sbagliato; **to be mistaken** essere in errore, sbagliarsi

mister ['mɪstər] *s* (mil, nav) signore *m*; (coll) marito || *interj* (coll) signore!; (coll) Lei!; (coll) buonuomo! || **Mister** *s* Signore *m*

mistletoe ['mɪsəl,to] *s* vischio

mistreat [mɪs'trit] *tr* maltrattare

mistreatment [mɪs'tritmənt] *s* maltrattamento

mistress ['mɪstrɪs] *s* (*of a household*) signora, padrona; (*paramour*) amante *f*, ganza; (Brit) maestra di scuola

mistrial [mɪs'traɪəl] *s* processo viziato da errore giudiziario

mistrust [mɪs'trʌst] *s* diffidenza || *tr* diffidare di || *intr* diffidarsi

mistrustful [mɪs'trʌstfəl] *adj* diffidente

mist·y ['mɪsti] *adj* (**-ier**; **-iest**) fosco, brumoso; (fig) vago, confuso

misunder·stand [,mɪsʌndər'stænd] *v* (*pret & pp* **-stood** ['stʊd]) *tr* fraintendere, equivocare

misunderstanding [,mɪsʌndər'stændɪŋ] *s* malinteso

misuse [mɪs'jus] *s* abuso; (*of funds*) malversazione || [mɪs'juz] *tr* abusare di; (*funds*) malversare

misword [mɪs'wʌrd] *tr* comporre male

mite [maɪt] *s* obolo; (ent) acaro

miter ['maɪtər] *s* (carp) ugnatura; (carp) giunto a quartabuono; (eccl) mitra || *tr* tagliare a quartabuono, ugnare; giungere a quartabuono

mi'ter box' *s* cassetta per ugnature

mi'ter joint' *s* giunto a quartabuono

mitigate ['mɪtɪ,get] *tr* mitigare

mitten ['mɪtən] *s* manopola, muffola

mix [mɪks] *tr* mescolare; (*colors*) mesticare; (*dough*) impastare; (*salad*) condire; **to mix up** confondere || *intr* confondersi, mescolarsi

mixed [mɪkst] *adj* misto; (*candy*) assortito; (coll) confuso

mixed' com'pany *s* riunione *f* di ambo i sessi

mixed' drink' *s* miscela di liquori diversi

mixed' feel'ing *s* sentimento ambivalente

mixed' met'aphor *s* metafora incongruente

mixer ['mɪksər] *s* (mach) mescolatrice *f*; **to be a good mixer** essere socievole

mixture ['mɪkstʃər] *s* mistura, mescolanza; (aut) miscela, carburazione

mix'-up' *s* confusione; (coll) baruffa

mizzen ['mɪzən] *s* mezzana

moan [mon] *s* gemito || *intr* gemere

moat [mot] *s* fosso, fossato

mob [mab] *s* turba || *v* (*pret & pp* **mobbed**; *ger* **mobbing**) *tr* assaltare; affollarsi intorno a; (*a place*) affollare

mobile ['mobɪl] or ['mobil] *adj* mobile

mo'bile home' *s* caravan *m*, roulotte *f*

mobility [mo'bɪlɪti] *s* mobilità *f*

mobilization [,mobɪlɪ'zeʃən] *s* mobilitazione

mobilize ['mobɪ,laɪz] *tr & intr* mobilitare

mob' rule' *s* legge *f* della teppa

mobster ['mabstər] *s* gangster *m*

moccasin ['makəsɪn] *s* mocassino

Mo'cha cof'fee ['mokə] *s* caffè *m* moca

mock [mak] *adj* finto, imitato || *s* dileggio, burla || *tr* deridere, canzonare; ingannare || *intr* motteggiare; **to mock** at farsi gioco di

mocker·y ['makəri] *s* (**-ies**) dileggio, scherno; (*subject of derision*) zimbello; (*poor imitation*) contraffazione

mock'-hero'ic *adj* eroicomico

mockingbird ['makɪŋ,bʌrd] *s* mimo

mock' or'ange *s* gelsomino selvatico

mock' tur'tle soup' *s* finto brodo di tartaruga

mock'-up' *s* modello dimostrativo

mode [mod] *s* modo, maniera; (*fashion*) moda; (gram) modo

mod·el ['madəl] *adj* modello, e.g., **model student** studente modello || *s* modello; (*woman serving as subject for artists*) modello *f*; (*woman wearing clothes at fashion show*) indossatrice *f* || *v* (*pret & pp* **-eled** or **-elled**; *ger* **-eling** or **-elling**) *tr* modellare || *intr* modellarsi; fare il manichino

mod'el air'plane *s* aeromodello

mo'del-air'plane build'er *s* aeromodellista *mf*

mod'eling clay' *s* plastilina

moderate ['madərɪt] *adj* moderato || ['madə,ret] *tr* moderare; (*a meeting*) presiedere a || *intr* moderarsi

moderator ['madə,retər] *s* moderatore *m*; (*mediator*) arbitro; (*phys*) moderatore *m*

modern ['madərn] *adj* moderno

modernize ['madər,naɪz] *tr* modernizzare, rimodernare

modest ['madɪst] *adj* modesto

modes·ty ['madɪsti] *s* (**-ties**) modestia

modicum ['madɪkəm] *s* piccola quantità

modi·fy ['madɪ,faɪ] *v* (*pret & pp* **-fied**) *tr* modificare; (*gram*) determinare

modish ['modɪʃ] *adj* alla moda

modulate ['madʒə,let] *tr & intr* modulare

modulation [,madʒə'leʃən] *s* modulazione

mohair ['mo,her] *s* mohair *m*

Mohammedan [mo'hæmɪdən] *adj & s* maomettano

Mohammedanism [mo'hæmɪdə,nɪzəm] *s* maomettismo

moist [mɔɪst] *adj* umido; lacrimoso

moisten ['mɔɪsən] *tr* inumidire || *intr* inumidirsi

moisture ['mɔɪstʃər] *s* umidità *f*

molar ['molər] *s* molare *m*

molasses [mə'læsɪz] *s* melassa

mold [mold] *s* stampo, forma; (*fungus*) muffa; humus *m*; (fig) indole *f* || *tr* plasmare, conformare; (*to make moldy*) fare ammuffire || *intr* ammuffire

molder ['moldər] *s* modellatore *m* || *intr* sgretolarsi; polverizzarsi

molding ['moldɪŋ] *s* modellato; (archit, carp) modanatura

mold·y ['moldi] *adj* (**-ier; -iest**) ammuffito

mole [mol] *s* (*pier*) molo; (*harbor*) darsena; (*spot on skin*) neo; (*small mammal*) talpa

molecule ['malɪ,kjul] *s* molecola

mole'hill' *s* mucchio di terra sopra la tana di talpe

mole'skin' *s* pelle *f* di talpa; (*fabric*) fustagno di prima qualità

molest [mə'lest] *tr* molestare; fare proposte disoneste a

moll [mal] *s* (slang) ragazza della malavita; (slang) puttana

molli·fy ['malɪ,faɪ] *v* (*pret & pp* **-fied**) *tr* pacificare, placare

mollusk ['maləsk] *s* mollusco

mollycoddle ['malɪ,kadəl] *s* effeminato || *tr* viziare, coccolare

Mo'lotov cock'tail ['malə,tɔf] *s* bottiglia Molotov

molt [molt] *s* muda || *intr* andare in muda

molten ['moltən] *adj* fuso

molybdenum [mə'lɪbdɪnəm] or [,malɪb'dinəm] *s* molibdeno

moment ['momənt] *s* momento; **at any moment** da un momento all'altro

momentary ['momən,teri] *adj* momentaneo

momentous [mo'mentəs] *adj* grave, importante

momen·tum [mo'mentəm] *s* (**-tums** or **-ta** [tə]) slancio; (mech) momento

monarch ['manərk] *s* monarca *m*

monarchic(al) [mə'narkɪk(əl)] *adj* monarchico

monarchist ['manərkɪst] *adj & s* monarchico

monar·chy ['manərki] *s* (**-chies**) monarchia

monaster·y ['manəs,teri] *s* (**-ies**) monastero

monastic [mə'næstɪk] *adj* monastico, monacale

monasticism [mə'næstɪ,sɪzəm] *s* monachesimo

Monday ['mʌndi] *s* lunedì *m*

monetary ['manɪ,teri] *adj* monetario; pecuniario

money ['mʌni] *s* denaro; **to be in the money** esser carico di soldi; **to make money** far quattrini

mon'ey-bag' *s* borsa per denaro; **moneybags** (coll) riccone sfondato

moneychanger ['mʌnɪ,tʃendʒər] *s* cambiavalute *m*

moneyed ['mʌnid] *adj* danaroso

moneylender ['mʌni,lendər] *s* prestatore *m* di denaro

mon'ey-mak'er *s* capitalista *mf*; affare vantaggioso

mon'ey or'der *s* vaglia *m*

Mongolian [maŋ'golɪən] *adj & s* mongolo

mon·goose ['maŋgus] *s* (**-gooses**) mangusta

mongrel ['mʌŋgrəl] or ['maŋgrəl] *adj* ibrido || *s* ibrido; cane bastardo

monitor ['manɪtər] *s* (educ) capoclasse *mf*; (rad, telv) monitore *m* || *tr* osservare; (*a signal*) controllare; (*a broadcast*) ascoltare

monk [mʌŋk] *s* monaco

monkey ['mʌŋki] *s* scimmia; **to make a monkey of** farsi gioco di || *intr*—**to monkey around** (coll) oziare; **to monkey around with** (coll) giocherellare con

mon'key-shines' *spl* (slang) monellerie *fpl*, pagliacciate *fpl*

mon'key wrench' *s* chiave *f* inglese

monkhood ['mʌŋkhud] *s* monacato

monkshood ['mʌŋks,hud] *s* (bot) aconito

monocle ['manəkəl] *s* monocolo

monogamy [mə'nagəmi] *s* monogamia

monogram ['manə,græm] *s* monogramma *m*

monograph ['manə,græf] or ['manə,graf] *s* monografia

monolithic [,manə'lɪθɪk] *adj* monolitico

monologue ['manə‚lɔg] or ['manə‚lag] s monologo

monomania [‚manə'menɪ‚ə] s monomania

monomial [mə'nomɪ‚əl] s monomio

monopolize [mə'napə‚laɪz] tr monopolizzare, accaparrare

monopo‧ly [mə'napəlɪ] s (-lies) monopolio, privativa

monorail ['manə‚rel] s monorotaia

monosyllable ['manə‚sɪləbəl] s monosillabo

monotheist ['manə‚θi‧ɪst] adj & s monoteista mf

monotonous [mə'natənəs] adj monotono

monotype ['manə‚taɪp] s (method) monotipia; (typ) monotipo

monoxide [mə'naksaɪd] s monossido m

monseigneur [‚mansen'jœr] s monsignore m

monsignor [man'sinjər] s (-monsignors or **monsignori** [‚mɑnsi'njori]) (eccl) monsignore m

monsoon [man'sun] s monsone m

monster ['manstər] adj mostruoso || s mostro

monstrance ['manstrəns] s ostensorio

monstrosi‧ty [man'strasɪti] s (-ties) mostruosità f

monstrous ['manstrəs] adj mostruoso

month [mʌnθ] s mese m

month‧ly ['mʌnθli] adj mensile || s (-lies) rivista mensile; **monthlies** (coll) mestruazione || adv mensilmente

monument ['manjəmənt] s monumento

moo [mu] s muggito || intr muggire

mood [mud] s umore m, vena; (gram) modo; **moods** luna, malumore m

mood‧y ['mudi] adj (-ier; -iest) triste, malinconico; lunatico, capriccioso

moon [mun] s luna; **once in a blue moon** ad ogni morte di papa || tr—**to moon away** (time) (coll) sprecare || intr—**to moon about** (coll) gingillarsi, baloccarsi; (to daydream about) (coll) sognarsi di

moon'beam' s raggio di luna

moon'light' s chiaro m di luna

moon'light'ing s secondo lavoro notturno

moon'shine' s chiaro di luna; (coll) chiacchiere fpl, balle fpl; (coll) whisky m distillato illegalmente

moon'shot' s lancio alla luna

moon'stone' s lunaria

moor [mur] s brughiera, landa || tr ormeggiare || intr ormeggiarsi || **Moor** s moro

Moorish ['murɪʃ] adj moresco

moor'land' s brughiera, landa

moose [mus] s (moose) alce americano

moot [mut] adj controverso, discutibile

mop [map] s scopa di filacce; (naut) redazza; (of hair) zazzera || v (pret & pp mopped; ger mopping) tr (a floor) pulire, asciugare; (one's brow) asciugarsi; **to mop up** rastrellare

mope [mop] intr andare rattristato

mopish ['mopɪʃ] adj triste, avvilito

moral ['marəl] or ['mɔrəl] adj morale || s (of a fable) morale f; **morals** (ethics) morale f; (modes of conduct) costumi mpl

morale [mə'ræl] or [mə'rɑl] s morale m

morali‧ty [mə'rælɪti] s (-ties) moralità f

mor'als charge' s accusa di oltraggio al pudore

morass [mə'ræs] s palude f

moratori‧um [‚marə'tori‧əm] or [‚mɔrə'tori‧əm] s (-ums or -a [ə]) moratoria

morbid ['mɔrbɪd] adj (gruesome) orribile; (feelings; curiosity; pertaining to disease; pathologic) morboso

mordacious [mɔr'deʃəs] adj mordace

mordant ['mɔrdənt] adj & s mordente m

more [mor] adj & s più m || adv più; **more and more** sempre più; **more than** più di; (followed by verb) più di quanto; **the more . . . the less** tanto più . . . quanto meno

more‧o'er adv per di più, inoltre

Moresque [mo'resk] adj moresco

morgue [mɔrg] s deposito, obitorio; (journ) archivio di un giornale, frigorifero

moribund ['mɔrɪ‚bʌnd] or ['mɑrɪ‚bʌnd] adj moribondo

morning ['mɔrnɪŋ] adj mattiniero || s mattina, mattino; **good morning** buon giorno; **in the morning** di mattina

morn'ing coat' s giacca nera a code

morn'ing-glo'ry s (-ries) convolvolo; (Ipomea) campanella; (Convolvulus tricolor) bella di giorno

morn'ing sick'ness s vomito di gravidanza

morn'ing star' s Lucifero, stella del mattino

Moroccan [mə'rakən] adj & s marocchino

morocco [mə'rako] s (leather) marocchino || **Morocco** s il Marocco

moron ['morɑn] s deficiente mf

morose [mə'ros] adj tetro, imbronciato

morphine ['mɔrfin] s morfina

morphology [mɔr'falədʒi] s morfologia

morrow ['maro] or ['mɔro] s—**on the morrow** l'indomani, il giorno seguente; domani

morsel ['mɔrsəl] s boccone m, bocconcino; pezzetto

mortal ['mɔrtəl] adj & s mortale m

mortality [mɔr'tælɪti] s mortalità f; (death or destruction on a large scale) moria

mortar ['mɔrtər] s (mixture of lime or cement) malta, calcina; (bowl) mortaio; (mil) mortaio, lanciabombe m

mor'tar‧board' s sparviere m; (cap) tocco accademico

mortgage ['mɔrgɪdʒ] s ipoteca || tr ipotecare

mortgagee [‚mɔrgɪ'dʒi] s creditore m ipotecario

mortgagor ['mɔrgɪdʒər] s debitore m ipotecario

mortician [mɔr'tɪʃən] s impresario di pompe funebri

morti-fy ['mɔrtɪ,faɪ] v (pret & pp -fied) tr mortificare; **to be mortified** vergognarsi

mortise ['mɔrtɪs] s intaccatura, incastro || tr incassare, incastrare

mor'tise lock' s serratura incastrata

mortuar-y ['mɔrtʃu,eri] adj mortuario || s (-ies) camera mortuaria

mosaic [mo'ze-ɪk] s mosaico

Moscow ['mɑskau] or ['mɑsko] s Mosca

Moses ['moziz] or ['mozis] s Mosè m

Mos-lem ['mɑzləm] or ['mɑsləm] adj musulmano || s (-lems or -lem) musulmano

mosque [mɑsk] s moschea

mosqui-to [məs'kito] s (-toes or -tos) zanzara

mosqui'to net' s zanzariera

moss [mɔs] or [mɑs] s musco

moss'back' s (coll) ultraconservatore m, fossile m

moss-y ['mɔsi] or ['mɑsi] adj (-ier; -iest) muscoso

most [most] adj il più di, la maggior parte di || s la maggioranza, i più; **most of** la maggior parte di; **to make the most of** trarre il massimo da || adv più, maggiormente, al massimo

mostly ['mostli] adv per lo più, maggiormente, al massimo

motel [mo'tel] s motel m, autostello

moth [mɔθ] or [mɑθ] s falena; (clothes moth) tarma

moth'ball' s pallina antitarmica

moth-eaten ['mɔθ,itən] or ['mɑθ,itən] adj tarmato; antiquato

mother ['mʌðər] adj (love, tongue) materno; (country) natio; (church, company) madre || s madre f; (elderly woman) (coll) zia || tr fare da madre a; creare; procreare; assumere la maternità di

moth'er coun'try s madrepatria

Moth'er Goose' s supposta autrice di una raccolta di favole infantili

motherhood ['mʌðər,hud] s maternità f

moth'er-in-law' s (moth'ers-in-law') suocera

moth'er-land' s madrepatria

motherless ['mʌðərlɪs] adj orfano di madre, senza madre

mother-of-pearl ['mʌðərəv'pʌrl] adj madreperlaceo || s madreperla

motherly ['mʌðərli] adj materno

Moth'er's Day' s giorno della madre, festa della mamma

moth'er supe'rior s madre superiora

moth'er tongue' s madrelingua; (language from which another language is derived) lingua madre

moth'er wit' s intelligenza nativa

moth' hole' s tarlatura

moth-y ['mɔθi] or ['mɑθi] adj (-ier; -iest) tarmato

motif [mo'tif] s motivo

motion ['moʃən] s movimento; (e.g., of a dancer) movenza, mossa; (in parliamentary procedure) mozione; **in motion** in moto || intr fare cenno

motionless ['moʃənlɪs] adj immobile

mo'tion pic'ture s pellicola cinematografica; **motion pictures** cinematografia

mo'tion-picture' adj cinematografico

motivate ['motɪ,vet] tr animare, incitare

motive ['motɪv] adj motivo; (producing motion) motore || s motivo; (incentive) movente m

mo'tive pow'er s forza motrice; impianto motore; (rr) insieme m di locomotive

motley ['mɑtli] adj eterogeneo; variato, variopinto

motor ['motər] adj motore; (operated by motor) motorizzato; (pertaining to motor vehicles) motoristico || s motore m; (aut) macchina || intr viaggiare in macchina

mo'tor-boat' s motobarca, motoscafo

mo'tor-bus' s torpedone m; autobus m

motorcade ['motər,ked] s carovana di automobili

mo'tor-car' s automobile f

mo'tor-cy'le s motocicletta

motorist ['motərɪst] s automobilista mf

motorize ['motə,raɪz] tr motorizzare

mo'torman s (-men) guidatore m di tram; guidatore m di locomotore

mo'tor sail'er s motoveliero

mo'tor scoot'er s motoretta

mot'or ship' s motonave f

mo'tor truck' s autocarro, camion m

mo'tor ve'hicle s motoveicolo

mottle ['mɑtl] tr chiazzare, screziare

mot-to ['mɑto] s (-toes or -tos) motto, divisa

mould [mold] s, tr, & intr var of **mold**

mound [maund] s monticello, collinetta

mount [maunt] s monte m, montagna; (horse for riding) cavalcatura, monta; (setting for a jewel) montatura; supporto; (for a picture) incorniciatura || tr montare; (a wall) scalare; (theat) allestire || intr montare; (to climb) salire

mountain ['mauntən] s montagna; **to make a mountain out of a molehill** fare di un bruscolo una trave, fare d'una mosca un elefante

moun'tain climb'ing s alpinismo

mountaineer [,mauntə'nɪr] s montanaro

mountainous ['mauntənəs] adj montagnoso

moun'tain rail'road s ferrovia a dentiera

moun'tain range' s catena di montagne

moun'tain sick'ness s mal m di montagna

mountebank ['maunti,bæŋk] s ciarlatano

mounting ['mauntɪŋ] s (act) il montare, montaggio; (setting) montatura; (mach) supporto

mourn [morn] tr (the loss of s.o.) piangere; (a misfortune) lamentare || intr piangere; vestire a lutto

mourner ['mornər] s persona in lutto; (penitent sinner) penitente mf;

(*woman hired to attend a funeral or funerals*) prefica

mourn'er's bench' s banco dei penitenti

mournful ['mɔrnfəl] *adj* luttuoso, funesto; (*gloomy*) lugubre

mourning ['mɔrnɪŋ] s lutto; **to be in mourning** portare il lutto

mourn'ing band' s bracciale *m* a lutto

mouse [maʊs] s (**mice** [maɪs]) topo, sorcio

mouse'hole' s topaia; piccolo buco

mouser ['maʊzər] s cacciatore *m* di topi

mouse'trap' s trappola per topi

moustache [məs'tæʃ] or [məs'taʃ] s baffi *mpl*, mustacchi *mpl*

mouth [maʊθ] s (**mouths** [maʊðz]) bocca; **by mouth** per via orale; **to be born with a silver spoon in one's mouth** essere nato con la camicia; **to make one's mouth water** fare venire a qlcu l'acquolina in bocca

mouthful ['maʊθ,fʊl] s boccata

mouth' or'gan s armonica a bocca

mouth'piece' s (*of wind instrument*) bocchetta; (*of bridle*) imboccatura; (*of megaphone*) boccaglio; (*of cigarette*) bocchino; (*of telephone*) imboccatura; (*spokesman*) portavoce *m*

mouth'wash' s sciacquo, risciacquo

movable ['muvəbəl] *adj* mobile, movibile; (*law*) mobiliare

move [muv] s movimento; (*change of residence*) trasloco; (*step*) passo; (*e.g., in chess*) mossa; **on the move** in moto, in movimento; **to get a move on** (coll) affrettarsi || *tr* muovere; (*the bowels*) provocare l'evacuazione di; (*to prompt*) spingere; (*to stir the feelings of*) emozionare, commuovere; (*law*) proporre; (com) svendere; **to move up** (*a date*) anticipare || *intr* muoversi; passare; (*to another house*) traslocare; (*to another city*) trasferirsi; (*said of goods*) avere una vendita; (*said of the bowels*) evacuare; procedere; (*law*) presentare una mozione; (coll) andarsene; **to move away** andarsene; trasferirsi; **to move back** tirarsi indietro; **to move in** avanzare; (*society*) frequentare; **to move off** allontanarsi

movement ['muvmənt] s movimento; (*of a watch*) meccanismo; (*of the bowels*) evacuazione; (mus) movimento, tempo

movie ['muvi] s (coll) film *m*, pellicola

movie-goer ['movi,go·ər] s frequentatore *m* del cinema

mov'ie house' s (coll) cinematografo

mov'ie-land' s (coll) cinelandia

moving ['muvɪŋ] *adj* commovente, emozionante || s trasporto; (*from one house to another*) trasloco

mov'ing pic'ture s film *m*, pellicola

mov'ing stair'case' s scala mobile

mow [mo] v (*pret* mowed; *pp* mowed or mown) *tr & intr* falciare

mower ['mo·ər] s falciatore *m*; (mach) falciatrice *f*

Mr. ['mɪstər] s (**Messrs.** ['mesərz]) Signore *m*

Mrs. ['mɪsɪz] s Signora

much [mʌtʃ] *adj & pron* molto; **as much . . . as** tanto . . . quanto; **too much** troppo || *adv* molto; **however much** per quanto; **how much** quanto; **too much** troppo; **very much** moltissimo

mucilage ['mjusɪlɪdʒ] s colla; (*gummy secretion in plants*) mucillagine *f*

muck [mʌk] s letame *m*; (*dirt*) sudiciume *m*; (min) materiale *m* di scoria

muck'rake' *intr* (coll) sollevare scandali

mucous ['mjukəs] *adj* mucoso

mucus ['mjukəs] s muco

mud [mʌd] s fango, melma, limo; **to sling mud at** calunniare

muddle ['mʌdəl] s confusione, guazzabuglio || *tr* confondere, intorbidire || *intr*—**to muddle through** arrangiarsi; cavarsela alla meno peggio in

mud'dle-head' s (coll) semplicione *m*

mud-dy ['mʌdi] *adj* (-**dier** -**diest**) fangoso, melmoso; (*obscure*) torbido || v (*pret & pp* -**died**) *tr* turbare, intorbidare; (*to soil with mud*) infangare

mud'guard' s parafango

mud'hole' s pozzanghera, fangaia

mud' slide' s smottamento

mudslinger ['mʌd,slɪŋɡər] s calunniatore *m*

muff [mʌf] s manicotto || *tr* (coll) mancare; (*to handle badly*) (coll) abborracciare; (sports) mancare di pigliare

muffin ['mʌfɪn] s panino soffice

muffle ['mʌfəl] *tr* infagottare, imbacuccare; (*a sound*) velare, smorzare

muffler ['mʌflər] s sciarpa; (aut) silenziatore *m*, marmitta

mufti ['mʌfti] s—**in mufti** in borghese

mug [mʌɡ] s tazzona; (slang) muso, grugno || v (*pret & pp* **mugged**) *ger* **mugging**) *tr* (slang) fotografare; (slang) attaccare proditoriamente || *intr* fare le smorfie

mug-gy ['mʌɡi] *adj* (-**gier**; -**giest**) afoso, opprimente

mulat-to [mju'læto] or [mə'læto] s (-**toes**) mulatto

mulber-ry ['mʌl,beri] s (-**ries**) (*tree*) gelso; (*fruit*) mora di gelso

mulct [mʌlkt] *tr* defraudare

mule [mjul] s mulo; (*slipper*) pianella

muleteer [,mjulə'tɪr] s mulattiere *m*

mulish ['mjulɪʃ] *adj* testardo

mull [mʌl] *tr* (*wine*) scaldare aggiungendo spezie || *intr*—**to mull over** pensarci sopra, rinvangare

mulled' wine' s vino caldo

mullion ['mʌljən] s colonnina che divide una bifora

multigraph ['mʌltɪ,ɡræf] or ['mʌltɪ,ɡraf] s (trademark) poligrafo || *tr* poligrafare

multilateral [,mʌltɪ'lætərəl] *adj* multilaterale

multimotor [,mʌltɪ'motər] s plurimotore *m*

multiple ['mʌltɪpəl] *adj & s* multiplo

multiplici-ty [,mʌltɪ'plɪsɪti] s (-**ties**) molteplicità *f*

multi-ply ['mʌltɪ,plaɪ] v (*pret & pp* -**plied**) *tr* moltiplicare || *intr* moltiplicarsi

multistage ['mʌltɪ ,stedʒ] *adj* (rok) pluristadio

multitude ['mʌltɪ ,tjud] or ['mʌltɪ ,tud] *s* moltitudine *f*

mum [mʌm] *adj* zitto; **mum's the word!** acqua in bocca!; **to keep mum** stare zitto || *interj* zitto!

mumble ['mʌmbəl] *tr* biascicare || *intr* farfugliare

mummer·y ['mʌməri] *s* (-ies) buffonata, mascherata

mum·my ['mʌmi] *s* (-mies) mummia

mumps [mʌmps] *s* orecchioni *mpl*

munch [mʌntʃ] *tr* sgranocchiare

mundane ['mʌndén] *adj* mondano

municipal [mju'nɪsɪpəl] *adj* municipale

municipali·ty [mju ,nɪsɪ'pælɪti] *s* (-ties) municipio

munificent [mju'nɪfɪsənt] *adj* munifico

munition [mju'nɪʃən] *s* munizione || *tr* fornire di munizioni

muni'tion dump' *s* deposito munizioni

mural ['mjurəl] *adj* murale || *s* pittura murale

murder ['mʌrdər] *s* omicidio || *tr* assassinare

murderer ['mʌrdərər] *s* omicida *m*

murderess ['mʌrdərɪs] *s* omicida *f*

murderous ['mʌrdərəs] *adj* omicida, crudele, sanguinario

murk·y ['mʌrki] *adj* (-ier; -iest) fosco, tenebroso; brumoso, nebbioso

murmur ['mʌrmər] *s* mormorio || *tr & intr* mormorare

Mur'phy bed' ['mʌrfi] *s* letto a scomparsa

muscle ['mʌsəl] *s* muscolo

muscular ['mʌskjələr] *adj* muscolare; (*having well-developed muscles*) muscoloso

muse [mjuz] *s* musa; **the Muses** le Muse || *intr* meditare, rimuginare

museum [mju'zi·əm] *s* museo

mush [mʌʃ] *s* pappa, polentina; (fig) leziosaggine *f*, sdolcinatura

mush'room *s* fungo || *intr* venir su come i funghi; **to mushroom into** diventare rapidamente

mush'room cloud' *s* fungo atomico

mush·y ['mʌʃi] *adj* (-ier; -iest) polposo, spappolato; (fig) sdolcinato, sentimentale

music ['mjuzɪk] *s* musica; **to face the music** (coll) affrontare le conseguenze; **to set to music** mettere in musica

musical ['mjuzɪkəl] *adj* musicale

mu'sical com'edy *s* operetta, commedia musicale

musicale [,mjuzɪ'kæl] *s* serata musicale

mu'sic box' *s* scatola armonica

mu'sic cab'inet *s* scaffaletto per la musica

mu'sic hall' *s* salone *m* da concerti; (Brit) teatro di varietà, music-hall *m*

musician [mju'zɪʃən] *s* musicista *mf*

musicianship [mju'zɪʃən ,ʃɪp] *s* abilità *f* musicale, virtuosismo

musicologist [,mjuzɪ'kɑlədʒɪst] *s* musicologo

musicology [,mjuzɪ'kɑlədʒi] *s* musicologia

mu'sic stand' *s* portamusica *m*

musk [mʌsk] *s* muschio

musk' deer' *s* mosco

musket ['mʌskɪt] *s* moschetto

musketeer [,mʌskɪ'tɪr] *s* moschettiere *m*

musk'mel'on *s* melone *m*

musk' ox' *s* bue muschiato

musk'rat' *s* ondatra, topo muschiato

muslin ['mʌzlɪn] *s* mussolina

muss [mʌs] *tr* (*the hair*) scompigliare, arruffare; (*clothing*) (coll) sciupare

mussel ['mʌsəl] *s* mussolo

Mussulman ['mʌsəlmən] *adj & s* mussulmano

muss·y ['mʌsi] *adj* (-ier; -iest) (coll) arruffato, scompigliato

must [mʌst] *s* (*new wine*) mosto; (*mold*) muffa; (coll) cosa assolutamente indispensabile || *v aux*—**I must go now** devo andarmene ora; **it must be Ann** deve essere Anna; **she must be ill** dev'essere malata; **they must have known it** devono averlo saputo

mustache [məs'tæʃ], [məs'tɑʃ] or ['mʌstæʃ] *s* baffi *mpl*, mustacchi *mpl*

mustard ['mʌstərd] *s* mostarda

mus'tard plas'ter *s* senapismo

muster ['mʌstər] *s* adunata, rivista; **to pass muster** passar ispezione || *tr* chiamare a raccolta; riunire; **to muster in** arruolare; **to muster out** congedare; **to muster up courage** prendere coraggio a quattro mani

mus'ter roll' *s* ruolo; (naut) appello

mus·ty ['mʌsti] *adj* (-tier; -tiest) (*moldy*) ammuffito; (*stale*) stantio; (fig) ammuffito, stantio

mutation [mju'teʃən] *s* mutazione

mute [mjut] *adj & s* muto || *tr* mettere la sordina a

mutilate ['mjutɪ ,let] *tr* mutilare

mutineer [,mjutɪ'nɪr] *s* ammutinato

mutinous ['mjutɪnəs] *adj* ammutinato

muti·ny ['mjutɪni] *s* (-nies) ammutinamento || *v* (*pret & pp* -nied) *intr* ammutinarsi

mutt [mʌt] *s* (slang) cane bastardo; (slang) scemo

mutter ['mʌtər] *tr & intr* borbottare

mutton ['mʌtən] *s* montone *m*

mut'ton chop' *s* cotoletta di montone

mutual ['mutʃu·əl] *adj* mutuo, vicendevole

mu'tual aid' *s* mutualità *f*

mu'tual fund' *s* fondo comune di investimento

muzzle ['mʌzəl] *s* (*of animal*) muso; (*device to keep animal from biting*) museruola; (*of firearm*) bocca || *tr* mettere la museruola a; (fig) imbavagliare

my [maɪ] *adj poss* mio, il mio || *interj* (coll) corbezzoli!

myriad ['mɪrɪ·əd] *s* miriade *f*

myrrh [mʌr] *s* mirra

myrtle ['mʌrtəl] *s* mirto, mortella

myself [maɪ'sɛlf] *pron pers* io stesso; me, me stesso; mi, e.g., **I hurt myself** mi sono fatto male

mysterious [mɪsˈtɪrɪ·əs] *adj* misterioso

myster·y [ˈmɪstəri] *s* (**-ies**) mistero

mystic [ˈmɪstɪk] *adj & s* mistico

mystical [ˈmɪstɪkəl] *adj* mistico

mysticism [ˈmɪstɪ ˌsɪzəm] *s* misticismo

mystification [ˌmɪstɪfɪˈkeʃən] *s* mistificazione

mysti·fy [ˈmɪstɪ ˌfaɪ] *v* (*pret & pp*

-fied) *tr* avvolgere. nel mistero; (*to hoax*) mistificare

myth [mɪθ] *s* mito

mythical [ˈmɪθɪkəl] *adj* mitico

mythological [ˌmɪθəˈlɑdʒɪkəl] *adj* mitologico

mytholo·gy [mɪˈθɑlədʒi] *s* (**-gies**) mitologia

N

N, n [en] *s* quattordicesima lettera dell'alfabeto inglese

nab [næb] *v* (*pret & pp* **nabbed;** *ger* **nabbing**) *tr* (slang) afferrare, agguantare

nag [næg] *s* ronzino ‖ *v* (*pret & pp* **nagged;** *ger* **nagging**) *tr & intr* tormentare, infastidire

naiad [ˈne·æd] or [ˈnaɪ·æd] *s* naiade *f*

nail [nel] *s* (*of finger or toe*) unghia; (*of metal*) chiodo; **to hit the nail on the head** cogliere nel giusto ‖ *tr* inchiodare

nail'brush' spazzolino per le unghie

nail' file' *s* lima per le unghie

nail' pol'ish *s* smalto per le unghie

nail' set' *s* punzone *m*

naïve [nɑˈiv] *adj* candido, ingenuo

naked [ˈnekɪd] *adj* nudo, ignudo; **to strip naked** denudare; denudarsi; **with the naked eye** a occhio nudo

name [nem] *s* nome *m*; (*first name*) nome *m*; (*last name*) cognome *m*; fama, reputazione; titolo; lignaggio; **in the name of** nel nome di; **to call s.o. names** coprire qlco di ingiurie; **to go by the name of** essere conosciuto sotto il nome di; **to make a name for oneself** farsi un nome; **what is your name?** come si chiama Lei? ‖ *tr* nominare; menzionare; battezzare; (*a price*) fissare

name' day' *s* onomastico

nameless [ˈnemlɪs] *adj* senza nome, anonimo

namely [ˈnemli] *adv* cioè, vale a dire

name'plate' *s* targa, targhetta

namesake [ˈnem ˌsek] *s* omonimo; persona chiamata in onore di qualcun altro

nan'ny goat' [ˈnæni] *s* capra

nap [næp] *s* lanugine *f*; (*pile*) pelo; pisolino, sonnellino; **to take a nap** schiacciare un sonnellino ‖ *v* (*pret & pp* **napped;** *ger* **napping**) *intr* sonnecchiare; **to catch napping** cogliere alla sprovvista

napalm [ˈnepɑm] *s* napalm *m*

nape [nep] *s* nuca

naphtha [ˈnæfθə] *s* nafta

napkin [ˈnæpkɪn] *s* tovagliolo

nap'kin ring' *s* portatovagliolo

Naples [ˈneplz] *s* Napoli *f*

Napoleonic [nə ˌpoliˈɑnɪk] *adj* napoleonico

narcissus [nɑrˈsɪsəs] *s* narciso

narcotic [nɑrˈkɑtɪk] *adj & s* narcotico

narrate [næˈret] *tr* narrare

narration [næˈreʃən] *s* narrazione

narrative [ˈnærətɪv] *adj* narrativo ‖ *s* narrazione; (*genre*) narrativa

narrator [næˈretər] *s* narratore *m*

narrow [ˈnæro] *adj* stretto; limitato; (*illiberal*) meschino, ristretto ‖ **narrows** *spl* stretti *mpl* ‖ *tr* limitare, restringere ‖ *intr* limitarsi, restringersi

nar'row escape' *s*—**to have a narrow escape** scamparla bella

nar'row-gauge' *adj* a scartamento ridotto

narrow-minded [ˈnæroˈmaɪndɪd] *adj* gretto, ristretto d'idee

nasal [ˈnezəl] *adj & s* nasale *f*

nasturtium [nəˈstʌrʃəm] *s* nasturzio

nas·ty [ˈnæsti] or [ˈnɑsti] *adj* (**-tier; -tiest**) brutto, cattivo; sgradevole, orribile; sudicio; (*foul*) perfido

natatorium [ˌnetəˈtorɪəm] *s* piscina

nation [ˈneʃən] *s* nazione

national [ˈnæʃənəl] *adj & s* nazionale *mf*

na'tional an'them *s* inno nazionale

na'tional debt' *s* debito pubblico

na'tional hol'iday *s* festa nazionale

nationalism [ˈnæʃənə ˌlɪzəm] *s* nazionalismo

nationali·ty [ˌnæʃənˈælɪti] *s* (**-ties**) nazionalità *f*

nationalize [ˈnæʃənə ˌlaɪz] *tr* nazionalizzare

na'tion-wide' *adj* su scala nazionale

native [ˈnetɪv] *adj* nativo, indigeno, oriundo; (*language*) materno ‖ *s* indigeno, nativo

na'tive land' *s* patria, paese natio

nativi·ty [nəˈtɪvɪti] *s* (**-ties**) nascita, natività *f* ‖ **Nativity** *s* Natività *f*

Nato [ˈneto] *s* (acronym) (**North Atlantic Treaty Organization**) la **N.A.T.O.**

nat·ty [ˈnæti] *adj* (**-tier; -tiest**) accurato, elegante

natural [ˈnætʃərəl] *adj* naturale ‖ *s* imbecille *mf*; (mus) bequadro; (mus) tono naturale; (mus) tasto bianco; **a natural** (coll) proprio quello che ci vuole

naturalism [ˈnætʃərə ˌlɪzəm] *s* naturalismo

naturalist [ˈnætʃərəlɪst] *s* naturalista *mf*

naturalization [ˌnætʃərəlɪˈzeʃən] *s* naturalizzazione

nat'uraliza'tion pa'pers *spl* documenti *mpl* di naturalizzazione

naturalize ['nætʃərə‚laɪz] tr naturalizzare

naturally ['nætʃərəli] adv naturalmente

nature ['netʃər] s natura; **from nature** dal vero

naught [nɔt] s niente m; zero; **to come to naught** ridursi al nulla; **to set at naught** disprezzare

naughty ['nɔti] adj (**-tier; -tiest**) cattivo, disubbidiente; (joke) di cattivo genere

nausea ['nɔʃɪ‚ə] or ['nɔsɪ‚ə] s nausea

nauseate ['nɔʃɪ‚et] or ['nɔsɪ‚et] tr nauseare || intr essere nauseato

nauseating ['nɔʃɪ‚etɪŋ] or ['nɔsɪ‚etɪŋ] adj nauseabondo, stomachevole

nauseous ['nɔʃɪ‚əs] or ['nɔsɪ‚əs] adj nauseabondo

nautical ['nɔtɪkəl] adj nautico, marittimo, marino

naval ['nevəl] adj navale

na'val acad'emy s accademia navale

na'val of'ficer s ufficiale m di marina

na'val sta'tion s base f navale

nave [nev] s navata centrale; (of a wheel) mozzo

navel ['nevəl] s ombelico

na'vel or'ange s arancia (con depressione alla sommità)

navigability [‚nævɪgə'bɪlɪti] s navigabilità f; (of a ship) manovrabilità f

navigable ['nævɪgəbəl] adj (river) navigabile; (ship) manovrabile

navigate ['nævɪ‚get] tr & intr navigare

navigation [‚nævɪ'geʃən] s navigazione

navigator ['nævɪ‚getər] s navigatore m; (in charge of navigating ship or plane) ufficiale m di rotta

navy ['nevi] adj blu marino || s (**-vies**) marina (da guerra)

na'vy bean' s fagiolo secco

na'vy blue' s blu marino

na'vy yard' s arsenale m

nay [ne] s no; voto negativo || adv no; anzi

Nazarene [‚næzə'rin] adj & s nazareno; **the Nazarene** il Nazzareno

Nazi ['natsi] or ['nætsi] adj & s nazista mf

N-bomb ['ɛn‚bam] s bomba al neutrone

Neapolitan [‚ni‚ə'palɪtən] adj & s napoletano

neap' tide' [nip] s marea di quadratura

near [nɪr] adj vicino, prossimo; intimo; esatto || adv vicino, da vicino || prep vicino a, accanto a; **to come near** avvicinarsi a || tr avvicinarsi a || intr avvicinarsi

nearby ['nɪr‚baɪ] adj vicino || adv vicino, qui vicino

Near' East' s Medio Oriente

nearly ['nɪrli] adv quasi; (a little more or less) press'a poco; per poco non, e.g., **he nearly died** per poco non morì

near-sighted ['nɪr'saɪtɪd] adj miope

near'-sight'ed-ness s miopia

neat [nit] adj netto, pulito; elegante, accurato; puro

neat's'-foot oil' s olio di piede di bue

Nebuchadnezzar [‚nɛbjəkəd'nɛzər] s Nabucodonosor m

nebula ['nɛbjələ] s (**-lae** [‚li] or **-las**) nebulosa

nebular ['nɛbjələr] adj nebulare

nebulous ['nɛbjələs] adj nebuloso

necessary ['nɛsɪ‚sɛri] adj necessario

necessitate [nɪ'sɛsɪ‚tet] tr necessitare, esigere

necessitous [nɪ'sɛsɪtəs] adj bisognoso

necessity [nɪ'sɛsɪti] s (**-ties**) necessità f

neck [nɛk] s collo; (of a horse) incollatura; (of violin) manico; (of mountain) gola, passo; **neck and neck** testa a testa; **to stick one's neck out** (coll) esporsi al pericolo; **to win by a neck** vincere per una corta testa || intr (slang) abbracciarsi, sbaciucchiarsi

neck'band' s colletto

neckerchief ['nɛkər‚tʃɪf] s fazzoletto da collo

necklace ['nɛklɪs] s collana

neck'line' s giro collo, scollatura

necktie ['nɛk‚taɪ] s cravatta

neck'tie pin' s spilla da cravatta

necrology [nɛ'krɑlədʒi] s (**-gies**) necrologia

necromancy ['nɛkrə‚mænsi] s necromanzia

nectar ['nɛktər] s nettare m

née or **nee** [ne] adj nata

need [nid] s necessità f, bisogno; povertà f; **if need be** se ci fosse bisogno; **in need** in strettezze || tr aver bisogno di || intr necessitare, essere in necessità || v aux—**to need (to)** + inf dovere + inf

needful ['nidfəl] adj necessario

needle ['nidəl] s ago; (of phonograph) puntina; **to look for a needle in a haystack** cercare l'ago nel pagliaio || tr cucire; (fig) aguzzare, eccitare

nee'dle bath' s bagno a doccia filiforme

nee'dle-case' s agoraio

nee'dle-point' s merletto; ricamo su canovaccio

needless ['nidlɪs] adj inutile

nee'dle-work' s lavoro di cucito; (embroidery) ricamo; (needlepoint) merletto

needs [nidz] adv necessariamente; **it must needs be** dev'essere proprio così

needy ['nidi] adj (**-ier; -iest**) bisognoso, indigente || **the needy** i bisognosi

ne'er-do-well ['nɛrdu‚wɛl] adj & s buono a nulla

negate ['nɛget] or [nɪ'get] tr invalidare; negare

negation [nɪ'geʃən] s negazione

negative ['nɛgətɪv] adj negativo || s negativa; (elec) polo negativo; (gram) negazione || tr respingere, votare contro; neutralizzare

neglect [nɪ'glɛkt] s negligenza, trascuratezza || tr trascurare; **to neglect to** trascurare di; dimenticarsi di

neglectful [nɪ'glɛktfəl] adj negligente, trascurato

négligée or **negligee** [‚nɛglɪ'ʒe] s veste f da camera or vestaglia per signora

negligence ['nɛglɪdʒəns] s negligenza, trascuratezza

negligent ['neglɪdʒənt] *adj* negligente, trascurato

negligible ['neglɪdʒɪbəl] *adj* trascurabile, insignificante

negotiable [nɪ'goʃɪ·əbəl] *adj* negoziabile; (*security*) al portatore; (*road*) transitabile

negotiate [nɪ'goʃɪ‚et] *tr* negoziare; (*to overcome*) superare || *intr* negoziare

negotiation [nɪ‚goʃɪ'eʃən] *s* negoziazione, negoziato

Ne·gro ['nigro] *adj* negro || *s* (**-groes**) negro, nero

neigh [ne] *s* nitrito || *intr* nitrire

neighbor ['nebər] *adj* vicino, adiacente || *s* vicino; (*fellow man*) prossimo || *tr* essere vicino a || *intr* essere vicino

neighborhood ['nebər‚hud] *s* vicinanza, vicinato; **in the neighborhood of** nei pressi di; (coll) a un dipresso, all'incirca

neighboring ['nebərɪŋ] *adj* vicino, attiguo; (*country*) limitrofo

neighborly ['nebərli] *adj* da buon vicino, socievole

neither ['niðər] or ['naɪðər] *adj indef* nessuno dei due, e.g., **neither boy** nessuno dei due ragazzi || *pron indef* nessuno dei due, nè l'uno nè l'altro || *conj* neppure, nemmeno, e.g., **neither do I** nemmeno io; **neither . . . nor** nè . . . nè

neme·sis ['nemɪsɪs] *s* (**-ses** [‚sɪz]) nemesi *f* || **Nemesis** *s* Nemesi *f*

neologism [ni'ɑlə‚dʒɪzəm] *s* neologismo

neomycin [‚ni·ə'maɪsɪn] *s* neomicina

ne'on lamp' ['ni·ɑn] *s* lampada al neon

neophyte ['ni·ə‚faɪt] *s* neofita *mf*

nepenthe [nɪ'penθɪ] *s* nepente *f*

nephew ['nefju] or ['nevju] *s* nipote *m*

Nepos ['nipɑs] or ['nepɑs] *s* Nipote *m*

Neptune ['nept/un] or ['neptjun] *s* Nettuno

neptunium [nep't/uni·əm] or [nep'tjuni·əm] *s* (chem) nettunio

Nero ['niro] *s* Nerone *m*

nerve [nʌrv] *adj* nervoso || *s* nervo; (*courage*) coraggio; (*boldness*) (coll) faccia tosta; **to get on one's nerves** dare ai nervi di qlcu; **to lose one's nerve** perdere le staffe

nerve-racking ['nʌrv‚rækɪŋ] *adj* irritante, esasperante

nervous ['nʌrvəs] *adj* nervoso

nerv'ous break'down *s* esaurimento nervoso

nervousness ['nʌrvəsnɪs] *s* nervosismo

nerv·y ['nʌrvi] *adj* (**-ier; -iest**) (*strong*) forte, vigoroso; audace; (coll) insolente, sfacciato

nest [nest] *s* nido; (*of hen*) cova; (*retreat*) rifugio; (*hangout*) tana; (*brood*) nidiata; **to feather one's nest** farsi il gruzzolo || *tr* (e.g., *tables*) mettere l'uno nell'altro || *intr* nidificare

nest' egg' *s* endice *m*; (fig) gruzzolo

nestle ['nesəl] *tr* annidare || *intr* annidarsi, nidificare; (*to cuddle up*) rannicchiarsi

net [net] *adj* netto || *s* rete *f*; (*snare*) laccio, trappola; guadagno netto ||

tr prendere con la rete; (*a sum of money*) fare un guadagno netto di

nether ['neðər] *adj* inferiore, infero

Netherlander ['neðər‚lændər] or ['neðərləndər] *s* olandese *mf*

Netherlands, The ['neðərləndz] *spl* i Paesi Bassi

netting ['netɪŋ] *s* rete *f*

nettle ['netəl] *s* ortica || *tr* irritare, provocare

net'work' *s* rete *f*

neuralgia [nju'rældʒə] or [nu'rældʒə] *s* nevralgia

neurology [nju'rɑlədʒi] or [nu'rɑlədʒi] *s* neurologia

neuro·sis [nju'rosɪs] or [nu'rosɪs] (**-ses** [sɪz]) *s* neurosi *f*

neurotic [nju'rɑtɪk] or [nu'rɑtɪk] *adj & s* neurotico

neuter ['njutər] or ['nutər] *adj* neutro || *s* genere neutro

neutral ['njutrəl] or ['nutrəl] *adj* neutro; (*not aligned*) neutrale || *s* neutrale *m*; (mach) folle *m*

neutralist ['njutrəlɪst] or ['nutrəlɪst] *adj & s* neutralista *mf*

neutrality [nju'trælɪti] or [nu'trælɪti] *s* neutralità *f*

neutralize ['njutrə‚laɪz] or ['nutrə‚laɪz] *tr* neutralizzare

neutron ['njutrɑn] or ['nutrɑn] *s* neutrone *m*

neu'tron bomb' *s* bomba al neutrone

never ['nevər] *adv* mai, giammai; non . . . mai; **never mind** non importa

nev'er-more' *adv* mai più

nevertheless [‚nevərðə'les] *adv* ciò nonostante, ciò nondimeno, tuttavia

new [nju] or [nu] *adj* nuovo; **what's new?** che c'è di nuovo?

new' arri'val *s* nuovo venuto; (*baby*) neonato

new'born' *adj* neonato; (e.g., *faith*) rinato

New'cas'tle *s*—**to carry coals to Newcastle** portare l'acqua al mare, portare vasi a Samo

newcomer ['nju‚kʌmər] or ['nu‚kʌmər] *s* nuovo venuto

New' Eng'land *s* la Nuova Inghilterra

newfangled ['nju'fæŋgəld] or ['nu‚fæŋgəld] *adj* all'ultima moda; di nuovo conio, di nuova invenzione

Newfoundland ['njufənd‚lænd] or ['nufənd‚lænd] *s* la Terranova || [nju'faundlənd] or [nu'faundlənd] *s* (*dog*) terranova *m*

newly ['njuli] or ['nuli] *adv* di recente, di fresco

new'ly·wed' *s* sposino or sposina; **the newlyweds** gli sposi

new' moon' *s* luna nuova, novilunio

news [njuz] or [nuz] *s* notizie *fpl*; **a news item** una notizia; **a piece of news** una notizia

news' a'gency *s* agenzia d'informazioni

news'beat' *s* colpo giornalistico

news'boy' *s* strillone *m*

news'cast' *s* notiziario

news'cast'er *s* annunziatore *m*, radiocommentatore *m*, telecommentatore *m*

news' con'ference *s* conferenza stampa

news' cov'erage s reportaggio

news'deal'er s venditore m di giornali

news'man' s (-men') (reporter) giornalista m; giornalaio

newsmonger ['njuz͵mʌŋgər] or ['nuz͵mʌŋgər] s persona pettegola, gazzettino

news'pa'per adj giornalistico || s giornale m

news'pa'per·man' s (-men') giornalista m

news'print' s carta da giornale

news'reel' s cinegiornale m

news'stand' s chiosco, edicola

news'week'ly s (-lies) settimanale m d'informazione

news'wor'thy adj degno d'essere pubblicato, di viva attualità

news·y ['njuzi] or ['nuzi] adj (-ier; -iest) (coll) informativo

New' Tes'tament s Nuovo Testamento

New' Year's' card' s cartolina d'auguri di capodanno

New' Year's' Day' s il capo d'anno, il capodanno

New' Year's' Eve' s la vigilia di capodanno, la sera di San Silvestro

New' York' [jɔrk] adj nuovayorchese || s New York f, Nuova York

New' York'er ['jɔrkər] s nuovayorchese mf

New' Zea'land ['ziland] adj neozelandese || s la Nuova Zelanda

New' Zea'lander ['zilandər] s neozelandese mf

next [nɛkst] adj prossimo, seguente; (month) prossimo, entrante || adv la prossima volta; dopo, in seguito; **next to** vicino a; **next to nothing** quasi nulla; **to come next** essere il prossimo

next'-door' adj della casa vicina || **next'-door'** adv nella casa vicina

next' of kin' s (next' of kin') parente più prossimo

niacin ['naɪ·əsɪn] s niacina

Niag'ara Falls' ['naɪ'ægərə] spl le Cascate del Niagara

nib [nɪb] s becco; punta; **his nibs** (slang & pej) sua eccellenza

nibble ['nɪbəl] s piccolo morso || tr & intr mordicchiare, sbocconcellare; (said of a fish) abboccare

nice [naɪs] adj (pleasant) simpatico, gentile; (requiring skill) buono, bello; (fine) sottile; (refined) raffinato, per bene; (fussy) esigente, difficile; rispettabile; (weather) bello; (attractive) bello; **nice . . . and** (coll) bello, e.g., **it is nice and warm** fa un bel caldo

nice-looking ['naɪs'lukɪŋ] adj bello, attraente

nicely ['naɪsli] adv precisamente, esattamente; (coll) benissimo

nice·ty ['naɪsəti] s (-ties) esattezza, precisione; **to a nicety** con la massima precisione

niche [nɪtʃ] s nicchia

Nicholas ['nɪkələs] s Nicola m

nick [nɪk] s intaccatura; (of a dish) slabbratura; **in the nick of time** al

momento giusto || tr intaccare; (to cut) tagliare; (a dish) slabbrare

nickel ['nɪkəl] s nichel m; moneta americana di cinque cents || tr nichelare

nick'el plate' s nichelatura

nick'el-plate' tr nichelare

nicknack ['nɪk͵næk] s soprammobile m; gingillo, ninnolo

nick'name' s nomignolo, soprannome m || tr soprannominare

nicotine ['nɪkə͵tin] s nicotina

niece [nis] s nipote f

nif·ty ['nɪfti] adj (-tier; -tiest) (coll) elegante; (coll) eccellente

niggard ['nɪgərd] adj & s spilorcio

night [naɪt] adj notturno || s notte f; **at** or **by night** di notte; **the night before last** l'altra notte; **to make a night of it** (coll) fare le ore piccole

night'cap' s berretto da notte; bicchierino di liquore che si beve prima di coricarsi

night' club' s night-club m

night' driv'ing s il guidare di notte

night'fall' s crepuscolo; **at nightfall** sul cader della notte, all'imbrunire

night'gown' s camicia da notte

nightingale ['naɪtn͵gel] s usignolo

night' latch' s serratura a molla

night' let'ter s telegramma notturno

night'long' adj di tutta la notte || adv tutta la notte

nightly ['naɪtli] adj di notte; di ogni notte || adv di notte; ogni notte

night'mare' s incubo

nightmarish ['naɪt͵merɪʃ] adj raccapricciante

night' owl' s (coll) nottambulo

night' school' s scuola serale

night'shirt' s camicia da notte

night'time' s notte f

night'walk'er s nottambulo; vagabondo notturno; (prostitute) passeggiatrice f

night' watch' s guardia notturna

night' watch'man s (-men) guardiano notturno

nihilist ['naɪ·ɪlɪst] s nichilista mf

nil [nɪl] s nulla m, niente m

Nile [naɪl] s Nilo

nimble ['nɪmbəl] adj agile, svelto

Nimrod ['nɪmrɑd] s Nembrod m

nincompoop ['nɪnkəm͵pup] s babbeo, tonto, semplicione m

nine [naɪn] adj & pron nove || s nove m; **nine o' clock** le nove

nine' hun'dred adj, s & pron novecento

nineteen ['naɪn'tin] adj, s & pron diciannove m

nineteenth ['naɪn'tinθ] adj & s diciannovesimo; (century) decimonono || s (in dates) diciannove m || pron diciannovesimo

ninetieth ['naɪntɪ·ɪθ] adj, s & pron novantesimo

nine·ty ['naɪnti] adj & pron novanta || s (-ties) novanta m; **the gay nineties** il decennio scapestrato dal 1890 al 1900

ninth [naɪnθ] adj, s & pron nono || s (in dates) nove m

nip [nɪp] s morso, pizzicotto; freddo pungente; (of liquor) bicchierino, sorso; **nip and tuck** testa a testa ‖ *v* (*pret* & *pp* **nipped;** *ger* **nipping**) *tr* pizzicare, mordere; (*to squeeze*) spremere; (*to freeze*) gelare; (*liquor*) sorseggiare; **to nip in the bud** arrestare di bel principio ‖ *intr* bere a sorsi

nipple ['nɪpəl] *s* capezzolo; (*of rubber*) tettarella; (*mach*) corto tubo filettato a entrambe le estremità, manicotto, cappuccio

Nippon [nɪ'pɑn] *or* ['nɪpɑn] *s* il Giappone

Nippon·ese [ˌnɪpə'niz] *adj* nipponico ‖ *s* (**-ese**) Giapponese *mf*

nip·py ['nɪpi] *adj* (**-pier; -piest**) mordente, pizzicante; gelato

nirvana [nɪr'vɑnə] *s* il nirvana

nit [nɪt] *s* lendine *m*; pidocchio

niter ['naɪtər] *s* nitro

nit'-pick' *intr* (coll) cercare il pelo nell'uovo

nitrate ['naɪtret] *s* nitrato; (agr) nitrato di soda; (agr) nitrato di potassio

ni'tric ac'id ['naɪtrɪk] *s* acido nitrico

nitride ['naɪtraɪd] *s* azoturo, nitruro

nitrogen ['naɪtrədʒən] *s* azoto

nitroglycerin [ˌnaɪtrə'glɪsərɪn] *s* nitroglicerina

ni'trous ox'ide ['naɪtrəs] *s* ossidulo di azoto

nitwit ['nɪtˌwɪt] *s* (slang) baggiano

no [no] *adj* nessuno; **no admittance** vietato l'ingresso; **no doubt** senza dubbio; **no matter** non importa; **no parking** divieto di sosta; **no smoking** vietato fumare; **no thoroughfare** divieto di transito; **no use** inutilmente; **with no** senza ‖ *s* no; voto negativo ‖ *adv* non; **no longer** non . . . più; **no sooner** non appena

Noah ['no·ə] *s* Noè *m*

nob·by ['nɑbi] *adj* (**-bier; -biest**) (slang) elegante; (slang) eccellente

nobili·ty [no'bɪlɪti] *s* (**-ties**) nobiltà *f*

noble ['nobəl] *adj* & *s* nobile *m*

no'ble·man *s* (**-men**) nobile *m*, nobiluomo

no'ble·wom'an *s* (**-wom'en**) nobile *f*, nobildonna

nobod·y ['no ˌbɑdi] *or* ['nobədi] *s* (**-ies**) nessuno, illustre sconosciuto ‖ *pron indef* nessuno; **nobody but** nessun altro che; **nobody else** nessun altro

nocturnal [nɑk'tʌrnəl] *adj* notturno

nod [nɑd] *s* cenno d'assenso, cenno del capo; (*of person going to sleep*) crollo del capo ‖ *v* (*pret* & *pp* **nodded;** *ger* **nodding**) *tr* (*one's head*) inclinare; **to nod assent** fare cenno di sì ‖ *intr* inclinare il capo; (*to drowse*) assopirsi

node [nod] *s* nodo; protuberanza; (phys) nodo

**no'-good' ** *adj* & *s* (coll) buono a nulla *m*

nohow ['no ˌhaʊ] *adv* (coll) in nessuna maniera

noise [nɔɪz] *s* rumore *m* ‖ *tr* divulgare

noiseless ['nɔɪzlɪs] *adj* silenzioso

nois·y ['nɔɪzi] *adj* (**-ier; -iest**) rumoroso, chiassoso

nomad ['nomæd] *adj* & *s* nomade *m*

no' man's' land' *s* terra di nessuno

nominal ['nɑmɪnəl] *adj* nominale; simbolico

nominate ['nɑmɪˌnet] *tr* presentare la candidatura di; (*to appoint*) nominare, designare

nomination [ˌnɑmɪ'neʃən] *s* candidatura; nomina

nominative ['nɑmɪnətɪv] *adj* & *s* nominativo

nominee [ˌnɑmɪ'ni] *s* candidato designato

nonbelligerent [ˌnɑnbə'lɪdʒərənt] *adj* & *s* non belligerante *m*

nonbreakable [nɑn'brekəbəl] *adj* infrangibile

nonce [nɑns] *s*—**for the nonce** per l'occasione

nonchalance ['nɑnʃələns] *or* [ˌnɑnʃə'lɑns] *s* disinvoltura, indifferenza

nonchalant ['nɑnʃələnt] *or* [ˌnɑnʃə'lɑnt] *adj* disinvolto, indifferente

noncom ['nɑnˌkɑm] *s* (coll) sottufficiale *m*

noncombatant [nɑn'kɑmbətənt] *adj* non combattente ‖ *s* persona non combattente

non'commis'sioned of'ficer [ˌnɑnkə'mɪʃənd] *s* sottufficiale *m*

noncommittal [ˌnɑnkə'mɪtəl] *adj* ambiguo, evasivo

non compos mentis ['nɑn 'kɑmpəs 'mentɪs] *adj* pazzo; (law) incapace

nonconformist [ˌnɑnkən'fɔrmɪst] *s* anticonformista *mf*, nonconformista *mf*

nondelivery [ˌnɑndɪ'lɪvəri] *s* mancata consegna

nondescript ['nɑndɪˌskrɪpt] *adj* indefinibile, inclassificabile

none [nʌn] *pron indef* nessuno; **none of** nessuno di; **none other** nessun altro ‖ *adv* non; affatto, niente affatto; **none the less** ciò nonostante, nondimeno

nonenti·ty [nɑn'entɪti] *s* (**-ties**) inesistenza; (*person*) nullità *f*

nonfiction [nɑn'fɪkʃən] *s* letteratura non romanzesca

nonfulfillment [ˌnɑnfʊl'fɪlmənt] *s* mancanza di esecuzione

nonintervention [ˌnɑnɪntər'venʃən] *s* non intervento

nonmetal ['nɑnˌmetəl] *s* metalloide *m*

nonpayment [nɑn'pemənt] *s* mancato pagamento

non·plus [nɑn'plʌs] *or* [nɑn'plʌs] *s* perplessità *f* ‖ *v* (*pret* & *pp* **-plussed** *or* **plused;** *ger* **-plussing** *or* **-plusing**) *tr* lasciare perplesso

nonprofit [nɑn'prɑfɪt] *adj* senza scopo lucrativo

nonrefillable [ˌnɑnrɪ'fɪləbəl] *adj* (*prescription*) non ripetibile; (*e.g., bottle*) non ricaricabile

nonresident [nɑn'rezɪdənt] *s* persona di passaggio, non residente *mf*

nonresidential [nɑnˌrezɪ'denʃəl] *adj* commerciale, non residenziale

nonscientific [nɑnˌsaɪən'tɪfɪk] *adj* non scientifico

nonsectarian [ˌnɑnsek'tɛrɪ-ən] *adj* che non segue nessuna confessione religiosa

nonsense ['nɑnsens] *s* sciocchezza, assurdità *f*, nonsenso

nonsensical [nɑn'sensɪkəl] *adj* sciocco, assurdo, illogico

nonskid ['nɑn'skɪd] *adj* antiderapante

nonstop ['nɑn'stɑp] *adj & adv* senza scalo

nonsupport [ˌnɑnsə'port] *s* mancato pagamento degli alimenti

noodle ['nudəl] *s* (slang) scemo; (slang) testa; **noodles** tagliatelle *fpl*

noo'dle soup' *s* tagliatelle *fpl* in brodo

nook [nʊk] *s* angolo, ˌantuccio

noon [nun] *s* mezzogiorno; **at high noon** a mezzogiorno in punto

no one or **no-one** ['no ˌwʌn] *pron indef* nessuno; **no one else** nessun altro

noontime ['nun ˌtaɪm] *s* mezzogiorno

noose [nus] *s* laccio, nodo scorsoio

nor [nɔr] *conj* nè

Nordic ['nɔrdɪk] *adj* nordico

norm [nɔrm] *s* norma, media, tipo

normal ['nɔrməl] *adj* normale ‖ *s* condizione normale; norma; (geom) normale *f*

Norman ['nɔrmən] *adj & s* normanno

Normandy ['nɔrməndɪ] *s* la Normandia

Norse [nɔrs] *adj* norvegese; scandinavo ‖ *s* (*ancient Scandinavian language*) scandinavo; (*language of Norway*) norvegese *m;* **the Norse** gli scandinavi; i norvegesi

Norse'man *s* (**-men**) normanno

north [nɔrθ] *adj* del nord, settentrionale ‖ *s* nord *m* ‖ *adv* al nord, verso il nord

North' Amer'ica *s* l'America del Nord

North' Amer'ican *adj & s* nordamericano

north'east' *adj* di nord-est ‖ *s* nord-est *m* ‖ *adv* al nord-est

north'east'er *s* vento di nord-est

northern ['nɔrðərn] *adj* settentrionale; (*Hemisphere*) boreale

North' Kore'a *s* la Corea del Nord

North' Pole' *s* polo nord

northward ['nɔrθwərd] *adv* verso il nord

north'west' *adj* di nord-ovest ‖ *s* nord-ovest *m* ‖ *adv* al nord-ovest

north'wind' *s* vento del nord, aquilone *m*

Norway ['nɔrwe] *s* la Norvegia

Norwegian [nɔr'widʒən] *adj & s* norvegese *mf* ‖ *s* (*language*) norvegese *m*

nose [noz] *s* naso; (*of missile*) testata; **to blow one's nose** soffiarsi il naso; **to count noses** contare il numero dei presenti; **to follow one's nose** andare a lume di naso; **to lead by the nose** menare per il naso; **to look down one's nose at** (coll) guardare dall'alto in basso; **to pay through the nose** pagare un occhio della testa; **to pick one's nose** mettersi le dita nel naso; **to speak through the nose** parlare nel naso; **to thumb one's nose at** fare marameo a; **to turn up one's nose at** guardare dall'alto in basso, guardare

con disprezzo ‖ *tr* fiutare; **to nose out** vincere per un pelo ‖ *intr* fiutare; **to nose about** curiosare

nose' bag' *s* musetta

nose'band' *s* museruola di cavallo

nose'bleed' *s* sangue *m* dal naso

nose' cone' *s* ogiva

nose' dive' *s* (*of prices*) subita discesa; (aer) discesa in picchiata

nose'-dive' *intr* discendere in picchiata

nosegay ['noz ˌge] *s* mazzolino di fiori

nose' glass'es *spl* occhiali *mpl* a stringinaso

nose' ring' *s* nasiera

nose'wheel' *s* (aer) ruota del carrello anteriore

no'-show' *s* (coll) passeggero che si è prenotato e non parte

nostalgia [nɑ'stældʒə] *s* nostalgia

nostalgic [nɑ'stældʒɪk] *adj* nostalgico

nostril ['nɑstrɪl] *s* narice *f*

nos·y ['nozi] *adj* (**-ier; -iest**) (coll) curioso

not [nɑt] *adv* no; non; **not at all** niente affatto; **not yet** non ancora; **to think not** credere di no; **why not?** come no?

notable ['notəbəl] *adj* notevole, notabile ‖ *s* notabile *m*

notarize ['notə ˌraɪz] *tr* munire di fede notarile

nota·ry ['notəri] *s* (**-ries**) notaio

notch [nɑtʃ] *s* tacca; (*in mountain*) passo; (coll) tantino; **notches** (coll) di gran lunga, e.g., **notches above** di gran lunga migliore ‖ *tr* intaccare

note [not] *s* nota, annotazione; (*currency*) banconota; (*communication*) memorandum *m;* (*of bird*) canto; (*tone of voice*) tono; (*reputation*) riguardo; (*short letter*) biglietto, letterina; (mus) nota; (com) cambiale *f* ‖ *tr* notare, annotare; osservare

note'book' *s* (*for school*) quaderno; taccuino, notes *m*

noted ['notɪd] *adj* ben noto, eminente

note' pa'per *s* carta da lettera

note'wor'thy *adj* notevole

nothing ['nʌθɪŋ] *s* niente *m*, nulla; **for nothing** gratis; inutilmente; **next to nothing** quasi niente ‖ *pron indef* niente, nulla, non . . . niente, non . . . nulla; **nothing else** nient'altro; **to make nothing of it** non farne caso ‖ *adv* per nulla; **nothing less** non meno

notice ['notɪs] *s* attenzione; notizia, notifica; annunzio, preavviso; (*in newspaper*) trafiletto; (law) disdetta; **on short notice** senza preavviso; (com) a breve scadenza; **to escape the notice of** passare inavvertito a; **to serve notice to** far sapere a, far constatare a ‖ *tr* osservare, notare, prendere nota di

noticeable ['notɪsəbəl] *adj* notevole; (*e.g., difference*) percettibile

noti·fy ['notɪ ˌfaɪ] *v* (*pret & pp* **-fied**) *tr* informare, far sapere

notion ['noʃən] *s* nozione; (*whim*) capriccio; **notions** mercerie *fpl;* **to have a notion to** aver voglia di

notorie·ty [ˌnotə'raɪ-ɪti] *s* (**-ties**) (*state*

of being well known) notorietà *f*; cattiva fama

notorious [no'torɪ·əs] *adj* (*generally known*) notorio; (*unfavorably known*) famigerato

no'-trump' *adj & s* senza atout *m*

notwithstanding [ˌnɑtwɪð'stændɪŋ] *or* [ˌnɑtwɪθ'stændɪŋ] *adv* ciò nonostante ‖ *prep* malgrado ‖ *conj* sebbene

nougat ['nugət] *s* torrone *m*

noun [naʊn] *s* nome *m*, sostantivo

nourish ['nʌrɪʃ] *tr* nutrire

nourishing ['nʌrɪʃɪŋ] *adj* nutriente

nourishment ['nʌrɪʃmənt] *s* nutrimento

novel ['nɑvəl] *adj* nuovo, novello, insolito, originale ‖ *s* romanzo

novelist ['nɑvəlɪst] *s* romanziere *m*

novel·ty ['nɑvəlti] *s* (-ties) novità *f*; **novelties** chincaglierie *fpl*

November [no'vɛmbər] *s* novembre *m*

novice ['nɑvɪs] *s* novizio

novitiate [no'vɪʃɪ·ɪt] *s* noviziato

novocaine ['novəˌken] *s* novocaina

now [naʊ] *s* presente *m* ‖ *adv* adesso; **from now on** d'ora in poi; **just now** un momento fa; **now and then** di tempo in tempo; **now that** visto che ‖ *conj* visto che, dato che

nowadays ['nɑʊ·əˌdez] *adv* al giorno d'oggi, oggidì

no'way' *adv* in nessun modo; nient'affatto

no'where' *adv* da nessuna parte; **nowhere else** da nessun'altra parte, in nessun altro luogo

noxious ['nɑkʃəs] *adj* nocivo

nozzle ['nɑzəl] *s* (*of hose or pipe*) boccaglio; (*of tea pot, gas burner*) becco; (*of gun*) bocca; (*of sprinkling can*) bocchetta; (*aut, mach*) becco; (*slang*) naso

nth [enθ] *adj* ennesimo; **to the nth degree** all'ennesima potenza

nuance [nju'ɑns] *or* ['nju·ɑns] *s* sfumatura

nub [nʌb] *s* protuberanza; (*of coal*) pezzo; (*coll*) nocciolo, cuore *m*

nuclear ['njuklɪ·ər] *or* ['nuklɪ·ər] *adj* nucleare

nu'clear fis'sion *s* fissione nucleare

nu'clear fu'sion *s* fusione nucleare

nu'clear test' ban' *s* accordo per la tregua atomica

nucle·us ['njuklɪ·əs] *or* ['nuklɪ·əs] *s* (-i [ˌaɪ] *or* -uses) nucleo

nude [njud] *or* [nud] *adj* nudo ‖ *s*—**in the nude** nudo

nudge [nʌdʒ] *s* gomitatina ‖ *tr* dare di gomito a

nudist ['njudɪst] *or* ['nudɪst] *adj & s* nudista *mf*

nudi·ty ['njudɪti] *or* ['nudɪti] *s* (-ties) nudità *f*

nugget ['nʌgɪt] *s* pepita

nuisance ['njusəns] *or* ['nusəns] *s* noia, seccatura; (*person*) seccatore *m*, pittima *mf*

null [nʌl] *adj* nullo; **null and void** invalido

nulli·fy ['nʌlɪˌfaɪ] *v* (*pret & pp* -fied) *tr* annullare, invalidare

nulli·ty ['nʌlɪti] *s* (-ties) nullità *f*

numb [nʌm] *adj* intorpidito; (*from cold*) intirizzito; **to become numb** intorpidirsi ‖ *tr* intorpidire

number ['nʌmbər] *s* numero; (*for sale*) articolo di vendita; (*publication*) fascicolo; (*of a serial*) dispensa, puntata; **a number of** parecchi; **beyond** *or* **without number** senza numero, infiniti ‖ *tr* numerare, contare; **his days are numbered** i suoi giorni sono contati ‖ *intr*—**to number among** essere tra

numberless ['nʌmbərlɪs] *adj* innumerevole

numeral ['njumərəl] *or* ['numərəl] *adj* numerale ‖ *s* numero

numerical [nju'mɛrɪkəl] *or* [nu'mɛrɪkəl] *adj* numerico

numerous ['njumərəs] *or* ['numərəs] *adj* numeroso

numskull ['nʌmˌskʌl] *s* (*coll*) stupido

nun [nʌn] *s* monaca, religiosa

nuptial ['nʌpʃəl] *adj* nuziale ‖ **nuptials** *spl* nozze *fpl*

nurse [nʌrs] *s* infermiera; (*to suckle a child*) nutrice *f*; (*to take care of a child*) bambinaia ‖ *tr* (*to minister to*) curare; allattare; allevare; (*e.g., hatred*) covare ‖ *intr* fare l'infermiera

nurser·y ['nʌrsəri] *s* (-ies) stanza dei bambini; (*shelter for children*) asilo infantile; (*hort*) vivaio

nurs'ery·man *s* (-men) orticoltore *m*

nurs'ery rhyme' *s* canzoncina per i più piccini

nurs'ery school' *s* scuola materna

nursing ['nʌrsɪŋ] *adj* infermieristico ‖ *s* allattamento; professione d'infermiera

nurs'ing bot'tle *s* biberon *m*, poppatoio

nurs'ing home' *s* convalescenziario; ospizio dei vecchi, gerontocomio

nurture ['nʌrtʃər] *s* allevamento; nutrimento ‖ *tr* allevare; alimentare; (*e.g., hope*) accarezzare

nut [nʌt] *s* noce *f*; (*eccentric*) (*slang*) esaltato, pazzoide *m*; (*mus*) capotasto; (*mach*) madrevite *f*, dado; **a hard nut to crack** un osso duro da rodere; **to be nuts for** (*coll*) essere pazzo per

nut'crack'er *s* schiaccianoci *m*

nutmeg ['nʌtˌmɛg] *s* noce moscata

nutrition [nju'trɪʃən] *or* [nu'trɪʃən] *s* (*process*) nutrizione; (*food*) nutrimento

nutritious [nju'trɪʃəs] *or* [nu'trɪʃəs] *adj* nutriente

nut'shell' *s* guscio di noce; **in a nutshell** in breve, in poche parole

nut·ty ['nʌti] *adj* (-tier; -tiest) che sa di noci; (*slang*) pazzo; **nutty about** (*slang*) pazzo per

nuzzle ['nʌzəl] *tr* toccare col muso, ammusare ‖ *intr* (*said of swine*) grufolare; (*said of other animals*) stare muso a muso, ammusare; (*to snuggle*) rannicchiarsi

nylon ['naɪlɑn] *s* nailon *m*

nymph [nɪmf] *s* ninfa

O

O, o [o] *s* quindicesima lettera del-l'alfabeto inglese

O *interj* o!, oh!

oaf [of] *s* balordo, scemo, imbecille *mf*

oak [ok] *s* quercia

oaken ['okən] *adj* di quercia, quercino

oakum ['okəm] *s* stoppa incatramata

oar [or] *s* remo; **to lie** or **rest on one's oars** dormire sugli allori; non lavorare più || *tr* spingere coi remi || *intr* remare

oar'lock' *s* scalmo

oars'man *s* (-men) rematore *m*

oa·sis [o'esɪs] *s* (-ses [siz]) oasi *f*

oat [ot] *s* avena; **oats** (*seeds*) avena; **to feel one's oats** (coll) essere pieno di vita; (coll) sentirsi importante; **to sow one's wild oats** correre la cavallina

oath [oθ] *s* giuramento; **on oath** sotto giuramento; **to take an oath** giurare, prestar giuramento

oat'meal' *s* (*breakfast food*) fiocchi *mpl* d'avena; farina d'avena

obdurate ['abdjərɪt] *adj* indurito, inesorabile; impenitente, incallito

obedience [o'bidɪ·əns] *s* obbedienza, ubbidienza

obedient [o'bidɪ·ənt] *adj* ubbidiente

obeisance [o'besəns] or [o'bisəns] *s* saluto rispettoso; omaggio

obelisk ['abəlɪsk] *s* obelisco

obese [o'bis] *adj* obeso

obesity [o'bisrti] *s* obesità *f*

obey ['obe] *tr* ubbidire (with *dat*), ubbidire || *intr* ubbidire

obfuscate [ab'fʌsket] or ['abfəs,ket] *tr* offuscare

obituar·y [o'bɪtʃʊ,ɛri] *adj* necrologico || *s* (-ies) necrologia

object ['abdʒɪkt] *s* oggetto || [ab-'dʒɛkt] *tr* obiettare || *intr* fare obiezioni, obiettare

objection [ab'dʒɛkʃən] *s* obiezione

objectionable [ab'dʒɛkʃənəbəl] *adj* reprensibile; (*e.g., odor*) sgradevole; offensivo

objective [ab'dʒɛktɪv] *adj* & *s* obiettivo

obligate ['ablɪ,get] *tr* obbligare

obligation [,ablɪ'geʃən] *s* obbligo, obbligazione

oblige [ə'blaɪdʒ] *tr* obbligare; favorire; **much obliged** obbligatissimo

obliging [ə'blaɪdʒɪŋ] *adj* compiacente, accomodante, servizievole

oblique [ə'blik] *adj* obliquo; indiretto

obliterate [ə'blɪtə,ret] *tr* obliterare; spegnere, distruggere

oblivion [ə'blɪvɪ·ən] *s* oblio

oblivious [ə'blɪvɪ·əs] *adj* (*forgetful*) dimentico; (*unaware*) ignaro

oblong ['ɑblɑŋ] or ['ɑblɔŋ] *adj* oblungo

obnoxious [ɑb'nɑkʃəs] *adj* detestabile

oboe ['obo] *s* oboe *m*

oboist ['obo·ɪst] *s* oboista *mf*

obscene [ɑb'sin] *adj* osceno

obsceni·ty [ɑb'sɛnɪti] or [ɑb'sɪnɪti] *s* (-ties) oscenità *f*, sconcezza

obscure [əb'skjʊr] *adj* oscuro || *tr* oscurare

obscuri·ty [əb'skjʊrɪti] *s* (-ties) oscurità *f*

obsequies ['ɑbsɪkwiz] *spl* esequie *fpl*

obsequious [əb'sikwɪ·əs] *adj* ossequioso, servile

observance [əb'zʌrvəns] *s* osservanza; **observances** pratiche *fpl*; cerimonie *fpl*

observation [,ɑbzər'veʃən] *s* osservazione; osservanza

observa'tion car' *s* (rr) vettura belvedere

observato·ry [əb'zʌrvə,tori] *s* (-ries) osservatorio

observe [əb'zʌrv] *tr* osservare

observer [əb'zʌrvər] *s* osservatore *m*

obsess [əb'sɛs] *tr* ossessionare

obsession [əb'sɛʃən] *s* ossessione

obsolescent [,ɑbsə'lɛsənt] *adj* che sta cadendo in disuso

obsolete ['ɑbsə,lit] *adj* disusato

obstacle ['ɑbstəkəl] *s* ostacolo

obstetrical [ɑb'stɛtrɪkəl] *adj* ostetrico

obstetrics [ɑb'stɛtrɪks] *s* ostetricia

obstina·cy [ɑb'stɪnəsi] *s* (-cies) ostinazione

obstinate ['ɑbstɪnɪt] *adj* ostinato

obstreperous [ɑb'strɛpərəs] *adj* turbolento; rumoroso

obstruct [əb'strʌkt] *tr* ostruire

obstruction [əb'strʌkʃən] *s* ostruzione

obtain [əb'ten] *tr* ottenere || *intr* prevalere, essere in voga

obtrusive [əb'trusɪv] *adj* intruso, importuno; sporgente

obtuse [əb'tjus] or [əb'tus] *adj* ottuso

obviate ['ɑbvɪ,et] *tr* ovviare (with *dat*)

obvious ['ɑbvɪ·əs] *adj* ovvio, palmare

occasion [ə'keʒən] *s* occasione; **on occasion** di quando in quando || *tr* occasionare

occasional [ə'keʒənəl] *adj* saltuario; (*e.g., verses*) d'occasione

occasionally [ə'keʒənəli] *adv* occasionalmente, di tanto in quanto

occident ['ɑksɪdənt] *s* occidente *m*

occidental [,ɑksɪ'dɛntəl] *adj* & *s* occidentale *mf*

occlud'ed front' [ə'kludɪd] *s* fronte occluso

occlusion [ə'kluʒən] *s* occlusione

occlusive [ə'klusɪv] *adj* occlusivo || *s* occlusiva

occult [ə'kʌlt] or ['ɑkʌlt] *adj* occulto

occupancy ['ɑkjəpənsi] *s* occupazione, presa di possesso; (*tenancy*) locazione

occupant ['ɑkjəpənt] *s* occupante *m*; (*tenant*) inquilino

occupation [,ɑkjə'peʃən] *s* occupazione

occupational [,ɑkjə'peʃənəl] *adj* occupazionale; (*e.g., disease*) professionale, del lavoro

occu·py ['ɑkjə,paɪ] *v* (*pret* & *pp* **-pied**) *tr* occupare; (*to dwell in*) abitare

oc·cur [ə'kʌr] *v* (*pret* & *pp* **-curred;**

ger -curring) *intr* accadere, succedere; incontrarsi; *(to come to mind)* venir in mente, e.g., **it occurs to me** mi viene in mente

occurrence [ə'kʌrəns] *s* evento, avvenimento; apparizione

ocean ['oʃən] *s* oceano

o'cean lin'er *s* transatlantico

o'clock [ə'klɑk] *adv* secondo l'orologio; **it is one o'clock** è la una; **it is two o'clock** sono le due

octane ['ɑkten] *adj* ottanico || *s* ottano

octave ['ɑktɪv] *or* ['ɑktev] *s* ottava

Octavian [ɑk'tevɪ-ən] *s* Ottaviano

October [ɑk'tobər] *s* ottobre *m*

octo-pus ['ɑktəpəs] *s* (**-puses** *or* **-pi** [ˌpaɪ]) *(small)* polpo; *(large)* piovra; *(fig)* piovra

ocular ['ɑkjələr] *adj & s* oculare *m*

oculist ['ɑkjəlɪst] *s* oculista *mf*

odd [ɑd] *adj* *(number)* dispari; strambo, bizzarro; *(not matching)* scompagnato, spaiato; strano; e rotti, e.g., **three hundred odd** tre cento e rotti || **odds** *ssg or spl* probabilità *f*; *(advantage)* vantaggio, superiorità *f*; **at odds** in disaccordo; **it makes no odds** fa lo stesso; **the odds are** la quota è; **to set at odds** seminare zizzania fra

oddi·ty ['ɑdɪti] *s* (**-ties**) stranezza

odd' jobs' *spl* lavori saltuari

odd' lot' *s* (fin) compravendita di meno di cento unità

odds' and ends' *spl* un po' di tutto

odious ['odɪ-əs] *adj* odioso

odor ['odər] *s* odore *m*; **to be in bad odor** aver cattiva fama

odorless ['odərlɪs] *adj* inodoro

odorous ['odərəs] *adj* odoroso

Odysseus [o'dɪsjus] *or* [o'dɪsɪ-əs] *s* Odisseo

Odyssey ['ɑdɪsi] *s* Odissea

Oedipus ['ɛdɪpəs] *or* ['idɪpəs] *s* Edipo

of [ʌv] *or* [əv] *prep* di, e.g., **the lead of the pencil** la mina della matita; a, e.g., **to think of** pensare a; meno, e.g., **a quarter of ten** le dieci meno un quarto

off [ɔf] *or* [ɑf] *adj* *(wrong)* sbagliato; *(slightly abnormal)* matto, pazzo; inferiore; *(electricity)* tagliato; *(agreement)* sospeso; libero, in libertà; distante; destro; *(season)* morto || *adv* via; fuori, lontano, distante; **to be off** mettersi in marcia || *prep* da; fuori da; al disotto di; lontano da; distolto da, e.g., **his eyes were off the target** i suoi occhi erano distolti dal bersaglio; (naut) al largo di

offal ['ɑfəl] *or* ['ɔfəl] *s* *(of butchered animal)* frattaglie *fpl*; rifiuti *mpl*

off' and on' *adv* di tempo in tempo

off'beat' *adj* insolito, originale

off' chance' *s* possibilità remota

off'-col'or *adj* scolorito; indisposto; *(joke)* di dubbio gusto

offend [ə'fɛnd] *tr & intr* offendere

offender [ə'fɛndər] *s* offensore *m*

offense [ə'fɛns] *s* offesa; **to take offense (at)** offendersi (di)

offensive [ə'fɛnsɪv] *adj* offensivo || *s* offensiva

offer ['ɔfər] *or* ['ɑfər] *s* offerta || *tr* offrire; *(thanks)* porgere; *(resistance)* opporre || *intr* offrirsi

offering ['ɔfərɪŋ] *or* ['ɑfərɪŋ] *s* offerta

off'hand' *adj* fatto all'improvviso; sbrigativo, alla buona || *adv* all'improvviso; bruscamente

office ['ɔfɪs] *or* ['ɑfɪs] *s* ufficio; funzione, incombenza; *(of a doctor)* gabinetto; *(of a lawyer)* studio; (eccl) uffizio; **through the good offices of** per tramite di

of'fice boy' *s* fattorino

of'fice-hold'er *s* pubblico funzionario

of'fice hours' *spl* orario d'ufficio

officer ['ɔfɪsər] *or* ['ɑfɪsər] *s* *(in a corporation)* funzionario; *(policeman)* agente *m*; (mil, nav, naut) ufficiale *m*; **officer of the day** (mil) ufficiale *m* di giornata

of'fice seek'er ['sikər] *s* aspirante *m* a un ufficio pubblico

of'fice supplies' *spl* articoli *mpl* di cancelleria

official [ə'fɪʃəl] *adj* ufficiale || *s* funzionario, ufficiale *m*

officiate [ə'fɪʃɪˌet] *intr* ufficiare

officious [ə'fɪʃəs] *adj* invadente, inframettente; **to be officious** essere un impiccione

offing ['ɔfɪŋ] *or* ['ɑfɪŋ] *s*—**in the offing** al largo; (fig) in preparazione, probabile

off'-lim'its *adj* proibito; **off-limits to** ingresso proibito a

off'-peak' heat'er *s* (elec) scaldabagno azionato unicamente in periodi di consumo minimo

off'-peak' load' *s* (elec) carico di consumo minimo

off'print' *s* estratto

off'set' *s* compensazione; (typ) offset *m* || **off'set'** *v* *(pret & pp* **-set;** *ger* **-setting)** *tr* compensare; stampare in offset

off'shoot' *s* *(of plant)* germoglio; *(of family or race)* discendente *mf*; *(branch)* ramo; (fig) conseguenza

off'shore' *adj* *(wind)* di terra; *(fishing)* vicino alla costa; *(island)* costiero || *adv* al largo

off'side' *adv* (sports) fuori gioco

off'spring' *s* discendente *m*; prole *f*; figlio; figli *mpl*

off'stage' *adv* tra le quinte

off'-the-rec'ord *adj* confidenziale || *adv* confidenzialmente

often ['ɔfən] *or* ['ɑfən] *adv* sovente, spesso; **how often?** quante volte?; **once too often** una volta di troppo

ogive ['odʒaɪv] *or* [o'dʒaɪv] *s* ogiva

ogle ['ogəl] *tr* adocchiare, occhieggiare

ogre ['ogər] *s* orco

ohm [om] *s* ohm *m*

oil [ɔɪl] *adj* *(pertaining to edible oil)* oleario; *(e.g., well)* di petrolio; *(e.g., lamp)* a olio; *(tanker)* petroliero; *(field)* petrolifero || *s* olio; petrolio; **to burn the midnight oil** studiare a lume di candela; **to pour oil on troubled waters** pacificare; **to strike oil** trovare petrolio || *tr* oliare; lubrificare; ungere ‖ *intr* (*said of a motorship*) fare petrolio

oil' burn'er *s* bruciatore *m* a gasolio

oil'can' *s* oliatore *m*

oil'cloth' *s* incerata, tela cerata

oil' field' *s* giacimento petrolifero

oil' lamp' *s* lampada a petrolio

oil'man *s* (**-men**) (*retailer*) mercante *m* di petrolio; (*operator*) petroliere *m*

oil' paint'ing *s* quadro a olio

oil' slick' *s* macchia d'olio

oil' tank'er *s* petroliera

oil' well' *s* pozzo di petrolio

oil•y ['ɔɪlɪ] *adj* (**-ier; -iest**) oleoso; untuoso

ointment ['ɔɪntmənt] *s* unguento

O.K. [o'ke] *adj* (*coll*) corretto ‖ *s* (*coll*) approvazione ‖ *adv* (*coll*) benissimo, d'accordo ‖ *v* (*pret & pp* **O.K.'d**; *ger* **O.K.'ing**) *tr* (*coll*) dare l'approvazione a ‖ *interj* benissimo!

okra ['okrə] *s* (bot) ibisco esculento; (bot) baccello dell'ibisco esculento

old [old] *adj* vecchio; antico, vetusto; **how old is . . . ?** quanti anni ha . . .?; **of old** anticamente; **to be . . . years old** avere . . . anni

old' age' *s* vecchiaia

old' boy' *s* vecchietto arzillo; (Brit) vecchio mio

old'-clothes'man' *s* (**-men**) rigattiere *m*

old' coun'try *s* madre patria

old-fashioned ['old'fæʃənd] *adj* all'antica; fuori moda

old' fo'gey or **old' fo'gy** ['fogi] *s* (**-gies**) uomo di idee antiquate, reazionario

Old' Glo'ry *s* la bandiera degli Stati Uniti

Old' Guard' *s* (U.S.A.) parte *f* più conservatrice di un partito

old' hand' *s* vecchio del mestiere

old' maid' *s* zitella

old' mas'ter *s* grande maestro; quadro di un gran maestro

old' moon' *s* luna calante

old' salt' *s* lupo di mare

old' school' *s* gente *f* all'antica

old' school' tie' *s* (Brit) cravatta coi colori della propria scuola; (fig) tradizionalismo

Old' Tes'tament *s* Antico Testamento

old'-time' *adj* all'antica; del tempo antico

old-timer ['old'taɪmər] *s* (coll) veterano; (coll) vecchio

old' wives' tale' *s* superstizione da donnicciole; racconto di vecchie comari

Old' World' *s* mondo antico

oleander [,olɪ'ændər] *s* oleandro

oligar•chy ['olɪ,garkɪ] *s* (**-chies**) oligarchia

olive ['olɪv] *adj* oleario; (*color*) olivastro ‖ *s* (*tree*) ulivo; (*fruit*) oliva

ol'ive branch' *s* ramoscello d'olivo

ol'ive grove' *s* oliveto

ol'ive oil' *s* olio d'oliva

Oliver ['olɪvər] *s* Oliviero

ol'ive tree' *s* olivo

Olympiad [o'lɪmpɪ,æd] *s* olimpiade *f*

Olympian [o'lɪmpɪ-ən] *adj* olimpico ‖ *s* deità olimpica; giocatore olimpico

Olympic [o'lɪmpɪk] *adj* olimpico, olimpionico

omelet or **omelette** ['aməlɪt] or ['amlɪt] *s* frittata, omelette *f*

omen ['omən] *s* augurio

ominous ['amɪnəs] *adj* infausto, ominoso

omission [o'mɪʃən] *s* omissione

omit [o'mɪt] *v* (*pret & pp* **omitted;** *ger* **omitting**) *tr* omettere

omnibus ['amnɪ,bʌs] or ['amnɪbəs] *adj* di interesse generale ‖ *s* bus *m*; volume collettivo

omnipotent [am'nɪpətənt] *adj* onnipotente

omniscient [am'nɪʃənt] *adj* onnisciente

omnivorous [am'nɪvərəs] *adj* onnivoro

on [an] or [ɔn] *prep* addosso, su, with his hat on col cappello addosso: in uso, in funzione; (*light*) acceso; (*deal*) fatto, concluso; (*e.g., game*) già cominciato; **what is on at the theater?** che cosa si dà al teatro? ‖ *adv* su; avanti; dietro, e.g., **to drag on** tirarsi dietro; **and so on** e così via; **come on!** va via!; **farther on** più in là; **later on** più tardi; **to be on to s.o.** (coll) scoprire il gioco di qlcu; **to have on** avere addosso; **to . . . on** continuare a, e.g., **the band played on** la banda continuò a suonare; **to put on** mettersi ‖ *prep* su, sopra; a, e.g., **on foot** a piedi; **on his arrival** al suo arrivo; sotto, e.g., **on my responsibility** sotto la mia responsabilità; contro, e.g., **an attack on the government** un attacco contro il governo; da, e.g., **on good authority** da buona fonte; **on all sides** da tutte le parti; verso, e.g., **to march on the capital** marciare verso la capitale; dopo, e.g., **victory on victory** vittoria dopo vittoria

on' and on' *adv* senza cessa

once [wʌns] *s* una volta; volta, e.g., **this once** questa volta ‖ *adv* una volta; mai, e.g., **if this once becomes known** se questo si risaprisse mai; **all at once** repentinamente; **at once** subito; allo stesso tempo; **for once** almeno una volta; **once and again** ripetutamente; **once in a blue moon** ad ogni morte di papa; **once in a while** di tanto in tanto; **once upon a time there was** c'era una volta ‖ *conj* se appena; una volta che

once'-o'ver *s* (coll) occhiata rapida; **to give s.th the once-over** (coll) esaminare qlco rapidamente; (coll) pulire qlco superficialmente

one [wʌn] *adj* uno; un certo, e.g., **one Smith** un certo Smith; unico e.g., **one price** prezzo unico ‖ *s* uno ‖ *pron* uno, e.g., **how can one live here?** come è possibile che uno viva qui?; si, e.g., **how does one go to the museum?** come si va al museo?; **I for one** per lo meno io; **it's all one and the same to me** per me fa lo stesso; **my little one** piccolo mio; **one and all** tutti; **one another** si, e.g., **they wrote one another** si scrissero;

l'un(o) l'altro, e.g., **they looked at one another** si guardarono l'un l'altro; **one o'clock** la una; **one's** il suo, il proprio; **the blue hat and the red one** il cappello blu e quello rosso; **the one and only** l'unico; **the one that** chi, quello che; **this one** questo; **that one** quello; **to make one** unire

one'-eyed' *adj* monocolo

one'-horse' *adj* a un solo cavallo; (coll) da nulla, poco importante

one'-man' show' *s* personale *f*

onerous ['ɑnərəs] *adj* oneroso

one-self *pron* sé stesso; se; si; **to be oneself** essere normale; comportarsi normalmente

one-sided ['wʌn'saɪdɪd] *adj* unilaterale; ingiusto; parziale

one'-track' *adj* a un solo binario; (coll) unilaterale, limitato

one'-way' *adj* a senso unico; (ticket) semplice, d'andata

onion ['ʌnjən] *s* cipolla; **to know one's onions** (coll) conoscere i propri polli

on'ion·skin' *s* carta pelle aglio, carta velina

on'look'er *s* presente *m*, spettatore *m*

only ['onlɪ] *adj* solo, unico ‖ *adv* solo, soltanto, non . . . più di; **not only . . . but also** non solo . . . ma anche ‖ *conj* ma; se non che

on'set' *s* attacco; (beginning) inizio; **at the onset** dapprincipio

onslaught ['ɑn,slɔt] or ['ɔn,slɔt] *s* attacco

on'to *prep* su, sopra a; **to be onto** (coll) rendersi conto del gioco di

onward ['ɑnwərd] or **onwards** ['ɑnwərdz] *adv* avanti, più avanti

onyx ['ɑnɪks] *s* onice *m*

ooze [uz] *s* trasudazione; liquido per concia ‖ *tr* sudare ‖ *intr* trasudare; (said, e.g., of blood) stillare; (said, e.g., of air) filtrare; (fig) trapelare

opal ['opəl] *s* opale *m*

opaque [o'pek] *adj* opaco; (writer's style) oscuro; stupido

open ['opən] *adj* aperto, scoperto; (job) vacante; (time) libero; (hunting season) legale; indeciso; manifesto; (hand) liberale; (needlework) a giorno; **to break** or **to crack open** forzare; **to throw open** aprire completamente ‖ *s* apertura; (in the woods) radura; **in the open** all'aperto; all'aria aperta; in alto mare; apertamente ‖ *tr* aprire; (an account) impostare; **to open up** spalancare; (one's eyes) sbarrare ‖ *intr* aprire, aprirsi; (theat) esordire; **to open into** sboccare in; **to open on** dare su; **to open up** sbottonarsi

o'pen-air' *adj* all'aria aperta

open-eyed ['opən,aɪd] *adj* con gli occhi aperti; meravigliato; fatto con piena conoscenza

open-handed ['opən'hændɪd] *adj* generoso, liberale

open-hearted ['opən'hɑrtɪd] *adj* franco, sincero; gentile

o'pen house' *s* tavola imbandita; **to keep open house** aver sempre ospiti

opening ['opənɪŋ] *s* apertura; (of dress) giro collo; (e.g., of sewer) imbocco; (in the woods) radura; (vacancy) posto vacante; (beginning) inizio; (chance to say something) occasione

o'pening night' *s* debutto, prima

o'pening num'ber *s* primo numero

o'pening price' *s* prezzo d'apertura

open-minded ['opən'maɪndɪd] *adj* di larghe vedute; imparziale

o'pen se'cret *s* segreto di Pulcinella

o'pen shop' *s* officina che impiega chi non è membro del sindacato

o'pen·work' *s* traforo

opera ['ɑpərə] *s* opera

op'era glass'es *spl* binocolo da teatro

op'era hat' *s* gibus *m*

op'era house' *s* teatro dell'opera

operate ['ɑpə,ret] *tr* (a machine) far funzionare; (a shop) gestire; operare ‖ *intr* funzionare; operare; **to operate on** (surg) operare

operatic [,ɑpə'rætɪk] *adj* operistico

op'erating expens'es *spl* spese *fpl* di ordinaria amministrazione

op'erating room' *s* sala operatoria

op'erating ta'ble *s* tavola operatoria

operation [,ɑpə're∫ən] *s* operazione; funzionamento, marcia

opera'tions research' *s* ricerca operativa

operator ['ɑpə,retər] *s* operatore *m*; (of a conveyance) conduttore *m*, conducente *mf*; (com) gestore *m*; (telp) telefonista *mf*; (surg) chirurgo operatore; (slang) faccendiere *m*

opiate ['opɪ·ɪt] or ['opɪ,et] *adj & s* oppiato

opinion [ə'pɪnjən] *s* opinione; **in my opinion** a mio modo di vedere; **to have a high opinion of** avere una grande stima di

opinionated [ə'pɪnjə,netɪd] *adj* ostinato, testardo, dogmatico

opium ['opɪ·əm] *s* oppio

o'pium den' *s* fumeria d'oppio

opossum [ə'pɑsəm] *s* opossum *m*

opponent [ə'ponənt] *s* avversario

opportune [,ɑpər'tjun] or [,ɑpər'tun] *adj* opportuno

opportunist [,ɑpər'tjunɪst] or [,ɑpər'tunɪst] *s* opportunista *mf*

opportuni·ty [,ɑpər'tjunɪtɪ] or [,ɑpər'tunɪtɪ] *s* (-ties) opportunità *f*, occasione

oppose [ə'poz] *tr* opporsi a

opposite ['ɑpəsɪt] *adj* opposto; di rimpetto, e.g., **the house opposite** la casa di rimpetto ‖ *s* contrario ‖ *prep* di faccia a, di rimpetto a

op'posite num'ber *s* persona di grado corrispondente

opposition [,ɑpə'zɪ∫ən] *s* opposizione

oppress [ə'pres] *tr* opprimere

oppressive [ə'presɪv] *adj* oppressivo; opprimente, soffocante

oppressor [ə'presər] *s* oppressore *m*

opprobrious [ə'probrɪ·əs] *adj* obbrobrioso

opprobrium [ə'probrɪ·əm] s obbrobrio
optic ['aptɪk] adj ottico || **optics** ssg ottica
optical ['aptɪkəl] adj ottico
optician [ap'tɪʃən] s ottico, occhialaio
optimism ['aptɪ‚mɪzəm] s ottimismo
optimist ['aptɪmɪst] s ottimista mf
optimistic [‚aptɪ'mɪstɪk] adj ottimistico
option ['apʃən] s opzione
optional ['apʃənəl] adj facoltativo
optometrist [ap'tamɪtrɪst] s optometrista mf
opulent ['apjələnt] adj opulento
or [or] conj o; (or else) oppure
oracle ['arəkəl] or ['ɔrəkəl] s oracolo
oracular [o'rækjələr] adj profetico; ambiguo; misterioso; sentenzioso
oral ['orəl] adj orale
orange ['arɪndʒ] or ['ɔrɪndʒ] adj di arance; arancio || s arancia
orangeade [‚arɪndʒ'ed] or [‚ɔrɪndʒ·'ed] s aranciata
or'ange blos'som s zagara
or'ange grove' s aranceto
or'ange juice' s sugo d'arancia
or'ange squeez'er s spremiagrumi m
or'ange tree' s arancio
orang-outang [o'ræŋʊ‚tæŋ] s orango
oration [o're ʃən] s orazione, discorso
orator ['arətər] or ['ɔrətər] s oratore m
oratorical [‚arə'tarɪkəl] or [‚ɔrə'tɔrɪ·kəl] adj oratorio
oratori·o [‚arə'torɪ‚o] or [‚ɔrə'tɔrɪ‚o] s (-os) (mus) oratorio
orato·ry ['arə‚tori] or ['ɔrə‚tori] s (-ries) oratoria; (eccl) oratorio
orb [ɔrb] s orbe m
orbit ['ɔrbɪt] s orbita; **to go into orbit** entrare in orbita || tr mettere in orbita; orbitare intorno a || intr orbitare
or'biting sta'tion s stazione orbitale
orchard ['ɔrtʃərd] s frutteto
orchestra ['ɔrkɪstrə] s orchestra; (parquet) platea
orchestral [ɔr'kestrəl] adj orchestrale
or'chestra pit' s golfo mistico
or'chestra seat' s poltrona di platea
orchestrate ['ɔrkɪs‚tret] tr orchestrare
orchid ['ɔrkɪd] s orchidea
ordain [ɔr'den] tr predestinare; decretare; (eccl) ordinare
ordeal [ɔr'dil] or [ɔr'di·əl] s sfacchinata; (hist) ordalia
order ['ɔrdər] s ordine m; compito, e.g., **a big order** un compito difficile; (com) commessa, ordinazione; (mil) consegna; **in order that** affinché; **in order to** + inf per + inf; **made to order** fatto su misura; **to get out of order** guastarsi; **to give an order** dare un ordine; (com) fare una commessa || tr (e.g., a drink) ordinare; (a person) ordinare (with dat); (e.g., a suit of clothes) fare fare; **to order around** mandare attorno; **to order s.o. away** mandar via qlcu
or'der blank' s cedola d'ordinazione
order·ly ['ɔrdərli] adj ordinato; disciplinato || s (-lies) (in a hospital) in-

serviente mf; (mil) ordinanza, attendente m
ordinal ['ɔrdɪnəl] adj & s ordinale m
ordinance ['ɔrdɪnəns] s ordinanza
ordinary ['ɔrdɪ‚neri] adj ordinario
ordnance ['ɔrdnəns] s artiglieria; bocche fpl da fuoco; munizionamento
ore [or] s minerale m (metallifero)
organ ['ɔrgən] s organo
organ·dy ['ɔrgəndi] s (-dies) organdì m
or'gan grind'er s suonatore m d'organetto
organic [ɔr'gænɪk] adj organico
organism ['ɔrgə‚nɪzəm] s organismo
organist ['ɔrgənɪst] s organista mf
organization [‚ɔrgənɪ'zeʃən] s organizzazione
organize ['ɔrgə‚naɪz] tr organizzare
organizer ['ɔrgə‚naɪzər] s organizzatore m
or'gan loft' s palco, galleria per l'organo
orgasm ['ɔrgæzəm] s orgasmo
or·gy ['ɔrdʒi] s (-gies) orgia
orient ['orɪ·ənt] s oriente m || **Orient** s Oriente m || **orient** ['orɪ‚ent] tr orientare, orizzontare
oriental [‚orɪ'entəl] adj orientale || **Oriental** s orientale mf
orifice ['arɪfɪs] or ['ɔrɪfɪs] s orifizio
origin ['arɪdʒɪn] or ['ɔrɪdʒɪn] s origine f, provenienza
original [ə'rɪdʒɪnəl] adj & s originale mf
originate [ə'rɪdʒɪ‚net] tr originare || intr originare, originarsi
oriole ['orɪ‚ol] s oriolo, rigogolo
Ork'ney Is'lands ['ɔrkni] spl Orcadi fpl
ormolu ['ɔrmə'lu] s (alloy) similoro; (gold powder) polvere f d'oro; (gilded metal) bronzo dorato
ornament ['ɔrnəmənt] s ornamento || ['ɔrnə‚ment] tr ornamentare
ornamental [‚ɔrnə'mentəl] adj ornamentale
ornate [ɔr'net] or ['ɔrnet] adj ornato; (style) elaborato
ornithologist [‚ɔrnɪ'θalədʒɪst] s ornitologo
orphan ['ɔrfən] adj & s orfano || tr rendere orfano
orphanage ['ɔrfənɪdʒ] s (institution) orfanotrofio; (condition) orfanezza
Orpheus ['ɔrfjus] or ['ɔrfɪ·əs] s Orfeo
orthodox ['ɔrθə‚daks] adj ortodosso
orthogra·phy [ɔr'θagrəfi] s (-phies) ortografia
oscillate ['asɪ‚let] intr oscillare
osier ['oʒər] s vimine m; (bot) vinco
osmosis [az'mosɪs] or [as'mosɪs] s osmosi f
osprey ['aspri] s falco pescatore
ossi·fy ['asɪ‚faɪ] v (pret & pp -fied) tr ossificare || intr ossificarsi
ostensible [as'tensɪbəl] adj apparente, preteso
ostentatious [‚asten'teʃəs] adj ostentato
osteopathy [‚asti'apəθi] s osteopatia
ostracism ['astrə‚sɪzəm] s ostracismo

ostracize ['ɑstrə‚saɪz] *tr* dare l'ostra-cismo a, ostracizzare
ostrich ['ɑstrɪtʃ] *s* struzzo
Othello [o'θɛlo] *or* [ə'θɛlo] *s* Otello
other ['ʌðər] *adj & pron indef* altro || *adv*—**other than** diversamente che
otherwise ['ʌðər‚waɪz] *adv* altrimenti; differentemente
otter ['ɑtər] *s* lontra
ottoman ['ɑtəmən] *s* (*fabric*) otto-mano; (*sofa*) ottomana; cuscino per i piedi || **Ottoman** *adj & s* ottomano
ouch [autʃ] *interj* ahi!
ought [ɔt] *s* qualcosa; zero; **for ought I know** per quanto io sappia || *v aux* is rendered in Italian by the condi-tional of *dovere,* e.g., **you ought to be ashamed** dovresti vergognarti
ounce [auns] *s* oncia
our [aur] *adj poss* nostro, il nostro
ours [aurz] *pron poss* il nostro
ourselves [aur'sɛlvz] *pron pers* noi stessi; ci, ce, **we enjoyed ourselves** ci siamo divertiti
oust [aust] *tr* espellere; (*a tenant*) sfrattare
out [aut] *adj* erroneo; esterno; fuori pratica; svenuto; ubriaco; finito; (*book*) pubblicato; (*lights*) spento; fuori moda; introvabile; palmare; di permesso, e.g., **my night out** la mia serata di permesso; (*e.g., at the knees*) frusto; (sports) fuori gioco || *s* d'uscita; **to be on the outs** or **at outs with** (coll) essere in disac-cordo con || *adv* fuori, all'infuori; all'aria libera; **out for** in cerca di; **out of** fuori, fuori di; di; da; (*e.g., money*) a corto di, senza; su, e.g., **two students out of three** due stu-denti su tre || *prep* fuori di; per, lungo || *interj* fuori!
out' and away' *adv* di gran lunga
out'-and-out' *adj* perfetto, completo || *adv* perfettamente, completamente
out'bid' *v* (*pret* -**bid**; *pp* -**bid** *or* -**bidden**) *ger* -**bidding**) *tr* fare un'of-ferta migliore di; (bridge) fare una dichiarazione più alta di
out'board mo'tor *s* fuoribordo, motore *m* fuoribordo
out'break' *s* insurrezione; (*of hives*) eruzione; (*of anger, of war*) scoppio
out'build'ing *s* dipendenza
out'burst' *s* (*of tears, of laughter*) scop-pio; (*of energy*) impeto, slancio
out'cast' *s* vagabondo reietto
out'come' *s* risultato
out'cry' *s* (-**cries**) grido, chiasso
out'dat'ed *adj* fuori moda
out'dis'tance *tr* distanziare
out'do' *v* (*pret* -**did**; *pp* -**done**) *tr* sor-passare; **to outdo oneself** sorpassare sé stesso
out'door' *adj* all'aria aperta
out'doors' *s* aria libera, aperta cam-pagna || *adv* all'aria aperta, fuori di casa
out'er space' ['autər] *s* spazio cosmico
out'field' *s* (baseball) campo esterno
out'field'er *s* (baseball) esterno
out'fit' *s* equipaggiamento; (*female cos-*

tume) insieme *m;* (*of bride*) corredo; (*group*) (coll) corpo; (com) compa-gnia || *v* (*pret & pp* -**fitted**; *ger* -**fitting**) *tr* equipaggiare
out'flow' *s* efflusso
out'go'ing *adj* in partenza; (*tide*) de-crescente; (*character*) espansivo || *s* efflusso
out'grow' *v* (*pret* -**grew**; *pp* -**grown**) *tr* essere troppo grande per; sorpassare in statura; perdere l'interesse per || *intr* protrudere
out'growth' *s* risultato, conseguenza; crescita
outing ['autɪŋ] *s* gita, scampagnata
outlandish [aut'lændɪʃ] *adj* strano, bizzarro; dall'aspetto straniero; (*re-mote, far away*) in capo al mondo
out'last' *tr* sopravvivere (with *dat*)
out'law' *s* fuorilegge *mf* || *tr* proscri-vere; dichiarare illegale
out'lay' *s* disborso || **out·lay'** *v* (*pret & pp* -**laid**) *tr* sborsare
out'let' *s* uscita; (*e.g., of river*) sbocco; (com) mercato; (elec) presa di cor-rente; (fig) sfogo
out'line' *s* contorno; traccia, tracciato; sagoma, profilo; prospetto || *tr* de-lineare; tracciare, tratteggiare; sago-mare, profilare; prospettare
out'live' *tr* sopravvivere (with *dat*)
out'look' *s* prospettiva; (*watch*) guar-dia; (*mental view*) modo di vedere, opinione
out'ly'ing *adj* lontano, fuori di mano; periferico
outmoded [‚aut'modɪd] *adj* fuori moda, antiquato
out'num'ber *tr* superare in numero
out'-of-date' *adj* fuori moda
out'-of-door' *adj* all'aria aperta
out'-of-doors' *adj* all'aria aperta || *s* aria aperta || *adv* all'aria aperta; fuori di casa
out'-of-print' *adj* esaurito
out'-of-the-way' *adj* appartato, fuori mano; inusitato, strano
out' of tune' *adj* stonato || *adv* fuori di tono
out' of work' *adj* disoccupato
out'pa'tient *s* paziente *mf* esterno
out'post' *s* (mil) posto avanzato
out'put' *s* produzione; (elec) uscita; (mach) rendimento, potenza utile
out'rage *s* oltraggio, indecenza || *tr* oltraggiare; (*a woman*) violare
outrageous [aut'redʒəs] *adj* oltrag-gioso; (*excessive*) eccessivo; atroce, feroce
out'rank' *tr* superare in grado
out'rid'er *s* battistrada *m*
out'right' *adj* completo, intero || *adv* completamente; apertamente; sul colpo, sull'istante
out'set' *s* inizio, principio
out'side' *adj* esterno; (*unlikely*) impro-babile; (*price*) massimo || *s* esterno, di fuori *m;* aspetto esteriore; vita fuori del carcere || *adv* fuori, di fuori; **outside of** fuori di || *prep* fuori di; (coll) all'infuori di

outsider [,aut'saɪdər] *s* estraneo, intruso; (sports) outsider *m*

out'skirts' *spl* sobborghi *mpl*, periferia

out'spo'ken *adj* franco, esplicito

out'stand'ing *adj* saliente, eminente; *(debt)* arretrato, non pagato

outward ['autwərd] *adj* esterno, superficiale || *adv* al di fuori

out'weigh' *tr* pesare più di; eccedere in importanza

out'wit' *v* (*pret & pp* -witted; *ger* -witting) *tr* farla in barba di; *(a pursuer)* far perdere la traccia or la pista a

oval ['ovəl] *adj & s* ovale *m*

ova·ry ['ovəri] *s* (-ries) ovaia

ovation [o've/ən] *s* ovazione

oven ['ʌvən] *s* forno

over ['ovər] *adj* superiore; esterno; finito, concluso || *adv* su, sopra; dall'altra parte; dall'altra sponda; al rovescio; di nuovo; *(at the bottom of a page)* continua; qui, e.g., **hand over the money** dammi qui il denaro; **over again** di nuovo; **over against** contro; **over and over** ripetutamente; **over here** qui; **over there** là || *prep* su, sopra; dall'altra parte di; attraverso, per; *(a certain number)* più di; a causa di; **over and above** in eccesso di

o'ver·all' *adj* completo, totale || **overalls** *spl* tuta

o'ver·bear'ing *adj* arrogante, prepotente

o'ver·board' *adv* in acqua; **man overboard!** uomo in mare!; **to go overboard** andare agli estremi

o'ver·cast' *adj* annuvolato || *s* cielo annuvolato || *v* (*pret & pp* -cast) *tr* coprire, annuvolare

o'ver·charge' *s* prezzo eccessivo; sovraccarico; (elec) carica eccessiva || **o'ver·charge'** *tr* far pagare eccessivamente; sovraccaricare

o'ver·coat' *s* soprabito, pastrano

o'ver·come' *v* (*pret* -came; *pp* -come) *tr* vincere, sopraffare; *(e.g., passions)* frenare; opprimere

o'vercon'fidence *s* sicumera

o'ver·crowd' *tr* gremire

o'ver·do' *v* (*pret* -did; *pp* -done) *tr* esagerare; strafare; esaurire; *(meat)* stracuocere || *intr* esaurirsi

o'ver·dose' *s* dose eccessiva

o'ver·draft' *s* assegno allo scoperto

o'ver·draw' *v* (*pret* -drew; *pp* -drawn) *tr* *(a check)* emettere allo scoperto; *(a character)* esagerare la descrizione di

o'ver·due' *adj* in ritardo; (com) in sofferenza, scaduto

o'ver·eat' *v* (*pret* -ate; *pp* -eaten) *tr & intr* mangiare troppo

o'ver·exer'tion *s* sforzo eccessivo

o'ver·expose' *tr* sovresporre

o'ver·expo'sure *s* sovresposizione

o'ver·flow' *s* *(of a river)* piena, straripamento; *(excess)* sovrabbondanza; *(e.g., of a fountain)* trabocco; *(outlet)* tubo di troppopieno || **o'ver·flow'** *intr* *(said of a river)* straripare; *(said of a container)* traboccare

o'ver·fly' *v* (*pret* -flew; *pp* -flown) *tr* sorvolare; *(a target)* oltrepassare

o'ver·grown' *adj* cresciuto troppo; coperto, denso

o'ver·hang' *s* strapiombo || **o'ver·hang'** *v* (*pret & pp* -hung) *tr* sovrastare (with *dat*); sovrastare; *(to threaten)* minacciare; pervadere, permeare || *intr* sovrastare, strapiombare

o'ver·haul' *s* riparazione; esame *m*, revisione || *tr* riparare; esaminare, ripassare, rivedere; raggiungere, mettersi alla pari con

o'ver·head' *adj* in alto, sopra la testa; aereo; elevato, pensile; generale || **o'ver·head'** *adv* in alto, di sopra || **o'ver·head'** *s* spese *fpl* generali

o'ver·head projec'tor *s* lavagna luminosa

o'ver·head valve' *s* valvola in testa

o'ver·hear' *v* (*pret & pp* -heard) *tr* sentire per caso, udire per caso

o'ver·heat' *tr* surriscaldare || *intr* surriscaldarsi; eccitarsi

overjoyed [,ovər'dʒɔɪd] *adj* felicissimo; **to be overjoyed** non stare in sé dalla contentezza

overland ['ovər ,lænd] or ['ovərlənd] *adj & adv* per via di terra

o'ver·lap' *v* (*pret & pp* -lapped; *ger* -lapping) *tr* sovrapporre, estendersi sopra || *intr* sovrapporsi, estendersi; coincidere parzialmente

o'ver·load' *s* sovraccarico || **o'ver·load'** *tr* sovraccaricare, stracaricare

o'ver·look' *tr* sovrastare su, dominare; ispezionare, sorvegliare; passare sopra, trascurare; dare su, e.g., **the window overlooks the street** la finestra dà sulla strada

o'ver·lord' *s* dominatore *m* || *tr* dominare despoticamente

overly ['ovərli] *adv* eccessivamente

o'ver·night' *adj* per la notte, per solo una notte || **o'ver·night'** *adv* durante la notte; la notte prima

o'vernight bag' *s* astuccio di toletta per la notte

o'ver·pass' *s* cavalcavia, viadotto

o'ver·pop'ulate' *tr* sovrappopolare

o'ver·pow'er *tr* sopraffare

o'ver·pow'ering *adj* schiacciante

o'ver·produc'tion *s* sovrapproduzione

o'ver·rate' *tr* sopravvalutare

o'ver·run' *v* (*pret* -ran; *pp* -run; *ger* -running) *tr* invadere, infestare; inondare; *(one's time)* oltrepassare, eccedere

o'ver·sea' or **o'ver·seas'** *adj* di oltremare || **o'ver·sea'** or **o'ver·seas'** *adv* oltremare, al di là dei mari

o'ver·see' *v* (*pret* -saw; *pp* -seen) *tr* sorvegliare

o'ver·seer' *s* sorvegliante *mf*

o'ver·shad'ow *tr* oscurare, eclissare

o'ver·shoe' *s* soprascarpa

o'ver·shoot' *v* (*pret & pp* -shot) *tr* *(the target)* oltrepassare; *(said of water)* scorrere sopra; **to overshoot oneself** andare troppo in là || *intr* (aer) atterrare lungo e richiamare

o'ver·sight' *s* sbadataggine *f*, svista; sorveglianza, supervisione o'ver•sleep' v (pret & pp -slept) tr (a certain hour) dormire oltre || intr dormire troppo a lungo

o'ver•step' v (pret & pp -stepped; ger -stepping) tr eccedere, oltrepassare

o'ver•stock' tr riempire eccessivamente

o'ver•sup•ply' s (-plies) fornitura superiore alla richiesta || o'ver•sup•ply' v (pret & pp -plied) tr fornire in quantità superiore alla richiesta

overt ['ovʌrt] or [o'vʌrt] adj palmare, chiaro, manifesto

o'ver•take' v (pret -took; pp -taken) tr raggiungere, sorpassare; sorprendere

o'ver-the-count'er adj (securities) venduto direttamente al compratore

o'ver•throw' s rovesciamento; disfatta || o'ver•throw' v (pret -threw; pp -thrown) tr rovesciare, sconfiggere

o'ver•time' adj supplementare, fuori orario || s straordinario; (sports) tempo supplementare || adv fuori orario

o'ver•tone' s (mus) suono armonico; (fig) sottinteso

o'ver•trump' s taglio con atout più alto || o'ver•trump' tr & intr tagliare con atout più alto

overture ['ovərt∫ər] s apertura; (mus) preludio, sinfonia

o'ver•turn' s rovesciamento || o'ver•turn' tr rovesciare, travolgere || intr rovesciarsi, ribaltarsi

overweening [,ovər'winiŋ] adj presuntuoso, vanitoso; esagerato, eccessivo

o'ver•weight' adj troppo grasso; oltrepassante i limiti di peso || o'ver•weight' s sovraccarico; preponderanza; eccesso di peso

overwhelm [,ovər'hwelm] tr schiacciare, debellare; coprire; (e.g., with kindness) colmare, ricolmare

o'ver•work' s lavoro straordinario; superlavoro || o'ver•work' tr far lavorare eccessivamente || intr lavorare eccessivamente

Ovid ['avɪd] s Ovidio

ow [au] interj ahi!

owe [o] tr dovere || intr essere in debito

owing ['o·ɪŋ] adj dovuto; owing to a causa di

owl [aul] s gufo, barbagianni m

own [on] adj proprio, e.g., my own brother il mio proprio fratello || s il proprio; on one's own (coll) per proprio conto; (without anybody's advice) di testa propria; to come into one's own entrare in possesso del proprio; essere riconosciuto per quanto si vale; to hold one's own non perdere terreno; essere pari || tr possedere; riconoscere || intr—to own up to confessare

owner ['onər] s padrone m, proprietario, titolare m

ownership ['onər,∫ɪp] s proprietà f

own'er's li'cence s permesso di circolazione

ox [aks] s (oxen ['aksən]) bue m

ox'cart' s carro tirato da buoi

oxide ['aksaɪd] s ossido

oxidize ['aksɪ,daɪz] tr ossidare || intr ossidarsi

oxygen ['aksɪdʒən] s ossigeno

ox'ygen mask' s maschera respiratoria

ox'ygen tent' s tenda ad ossigeno

oxytone ['aksɪ,ton] adj tronco, ossitono || s ossitono

oyster ['ɔɪstər] adj di ostriche || s ostrica

oys'ter bed' s ostricaio, banco di ostriche

oys'ter cock'tail s ostriche fpl servite in valva

oys'ter fork' s forchettina da ostriche

oys'ter-house' s ristorante m per la vendita delle ostriche

oys'ter-knife' s coltello per aprire le ostriche

oys'ter-man s (-men) ostricaio

oys'ter shell' s conchiglia d'ostrica

oys'ter stew' s brodetto d'ostriche

ozone ['ozon] s ozono

P

P, p [pi] s sedicesima lettera dell'alfabeto inglese

pace [pes] s passo, andatura; (of a horse) ambio; to keep pace with andare di pari passo con; to put s.o. through his paces mettere qlcu a dura prova; to set the pace for fare l'andatura per; dare l'esempio a || tr misurare a passi, percorrere; to pace the floor andare avanti e indietro per la stanza || intr camminare lentamente; andare al passo; (said of a horse) ambiare

pace'mak'er s battistrada m; (in races) chi stabilisce il passo; (med) pacemaker m

pacific [pə'sɪfɪk] adj pacifico || Pacific adj & s Pacifico

pacifier ['pæsɪ,faɪ-ər] s paciere m; (teething ring) succhietto, tettarella

pacifism ['pæsɪ,fɪzəm] s pacifismo

pacifist ['pæsɪfɪst] adj & s pacifista mf

paci•fy ['pæsɪ,faɪ] v (pret & pp -fied) tr pacificare

pack [pæk] s fardello, pacco; (of merchandise) balla; (of lies) mucchio; (of cards) mazzo; (of thieves) banda; (of dogs) muta; (of animals) branco; (of birds) stormo; (of cigarettes) pacchetto; (of ice) banchiglia; (of people) turba || tr affardellare, impaccare; (to wrap) imballare; ammucchiare; (in cans) mettere in conserva; (people) stipare; (a trunk) fare; to pack in stipare; to pack off mandare via || intr ammucchiarsi, pigiarsi, accalcarsi; **to pack up** fare il baule

package ['pækɪdʒ] *s* pacco, collo; (*small*) pacchetto || *tr* impacchettare

pack' an'imal *s* bestia da soma

packer ['pækər] *s* imballatore *m*; (*of canned goods*) proprietario (di fabbrica di conserve alimentari)

packet ['pækɪt] *s* pacchetto; (*boat*) vapore *m* postale

packing ['pækɪŋ] *s* imballaggio; (*on shoulders of suit*) spallina; (*mach*) stoppa; (*ring*) (mach) guarnizione

pack'ing box' or **case'** *s* cassa d'imballaggio

pack'ing house' *s* fabbrica di conserve alimentari; fabbrica di carne in conserva

pack'ing slip' *s* foglio d'imballaggio

pack'sad'dle *s* basto

pack'thread' *s* spago d'imballaggio

pack'train' *s* fila di animali da soma

pact [pækt] *s* patto

pad [pæd] *s* cuscinetto, tampone *m*; imbottitura; (*of writing paper*) blocco da annotazioni; (*of an animal*) superficie *f* plantare, zampa; (*of a water lily*) foglia; (*rok*) piattaforma || *v* (*pret & pp* **padded**; *ger* **padding**) *tr* imbottire, ovattare; (*e.g., a speech*) infarcire || *intr* camminare pesantemente

pad'ding *s* imbottitura

paddle ['pædəl] *s* pagaia; (*of waterwheel*) pala || *tr* remare; (*to spank*) bastonare || *intr* remare; (*to splash*) diguazzare

pad'dle wheel' *s* ruota a pale

paddock ['pædək] *s* prato d'allenamento, paddock *m*

pad'lock' *s* lucchetto || *tr* chiudere col lucchetto

pagan ['pegən] *adj & s* pagano

paganism ['pegə,nɪzəm] *s* paganesimo

page [pedʒ] *s* (*of a book*) pagina; (*at court*) paggio; (*in hotels*) fattorino, valletto || *tr* impaginare; (*in hotels*) chiamare, far chiamare

pageant ['pædʒənt] *s* parata, corteo, spettacolo

pageant·ry ['pædʒəntri] *s* (**-ries**) pompa, fasto

paginate ['pædʒɪ,net] *tr* impaginare

pail [pel] *s* secchio

pain [pen] *s* dolore *m*; **on pain of** sotto pena di; **to take pains** to prendersi cura di; **to take pains not to** guardarsi da || *tr & intr* dolere

painful ['penfəl] *adj* doloroso, penoso

pain'kill'er *s* (coll) analgesico

painless ['penlɪs] *adj* indolore

painstaking ['penz,tekɪŋ] *adj* meticoloso

paint [pent] *s* (*for pictures*) colore *m*; (*for a house*) vernice *f*; (*make-up*) trucco || *tr* dipingere; (*a house*) verniciare, tinteggiare || *intr* (*with make-up*) dipingersi; essere pittore

paint'box' *s* scatola da colori

paint'brush' *s* pennello

painter ['pentər] *s* (*of pictures*) pittore *m*; (*of a house*) verniciatore *m*; (naut) barbetta

painting ['pentɪŋ] *s* pittura, dipinto

paint' remov'er [rɪ'muvər] *s* solvente *m* per levar la vernice

paint' thin'ner *s* diluente *m*

pair [per] *s* paio; (*of people*) coppia || *tr* appaiare, accoppiare || *intr* appaiarsi, accoppiarsi

pair' of scis'sors *s* forbici *fpl*

pair' of trou'sers *s* calzoni *mpl*

pajamas [pə'dʒɑməz] or [pə'dʒæməz] *spl* pigiama *m*

Pakistan [,pɑkɪ'stɑn] *s* il Pakistan

Pakistani [,pɑkɪ'stɑni] *adj & s* pachistano

pal [pæl] *s* (coll) compagno || *v* (*pret & pp* **palled**; *ger* **palling**) *intr* (coll) essere compagni

palace ['pælɪs] *s* palazzo

palatable ['pælətəbəl] *adj* gustoso, appetitoso; accettabile

palatal ['pælətəl] *adj & s* palatale *f*

palate ['pælɪt] *s* palato

pale [pel] *adj* pallido || *s* palo; (*enclosure*) recinto; (fig) ambito || *intr* impallidire

pale'face' *s* faccia pallida

palette ['pælɪt] *s* tavolozza

palfrey ['pɔlfri] *s* palafreno

palisade [,pælɪ'sed] *s* palizzata; (*line of cliffs*) dirupo

pall [pɔl] *s* panno mortuario; (*of smoke*) cappa || *tr* saziare, infastidire || *intr* saziarsi, perdere l'appetito

pall'bear'er *s* chi accompagna il feretro; chi porta il feretro

palliate ['pælɪ,et] *tr* attenuare, alleviare

pallid ['pælɪd] *adj* pallido

pallor ['pælər] *s* pallore *m*

palm [pɑm] *s* (*tree and leaf*) palma; (*of hand; measure*) palmo; **to carry off the palm** riportare la palma; **to grease the palm of** ungere le ruote a || *tr* far sparire nella mano; nascondere; **to palm off s.th on s.o.** rifilare qlco a qlcu

palmet·to [pæl'meto] *s* (**-tos** or **-toes**) palmeto

palmist ['pamɪst] *s* chiromante *mf*

palmistry ['pamɪstri] *s* chiromanzia

palm' leaf' *s* palma, foglia di palma

palm' oil' *s* olio di palma

Palm' Sun'day *s* Domenica delle Palme

palpable ['pælpəbəl] *adj* palpabile

palpitate ['pælpɪ,tet] *intr* palpitare

pal·sy ['pɔlzi] *s* (**-sies**) paralisi *f* || *v* (*pret & pp* **-sied**) *tr* paralizzare

pal·try ['pɔltri] *adj* (**-trier; -triest**) vile, meschino, irrisorio

pamper ['pæmpər] *tr* viziare; (*the appetite*) saziare

pamphlet ['pæmflɪt] *s* opuscolo, libello

pan [pæn] *s* padella, casseruola; (*of a balance*) coppa, piatto; (phot) bacinella || *v* (*pret & pp* **panned**; *ger* **panning**) *tr* friggere; (*gold*) vagliare in padella; (*salt*) estrarre in salina; (coll) criticare || *intr* essere estratto; **to pan out** (coll) riuscire || **Pan** *s* Pan *m*

panacea [,pænə'si·ə] *s* panacea

Pan'ama Canal' ['pænə,mɑ] *s* Canale *m* di Panama

Pan'ama hat' s panama m
Panamanian [ˌpænə'mɛnɪ·ən] or [ˌpænə'mɑnɪ·ən] adj & s panamegno
pan'cake' s frittella ‖ intr (aer) atterrare a piatto
pan'cake land'ing s atterraggio a piatto
pancreas ['pænkrɪ·əs] s pancreas m
pander ['pændər] s mezzano ‖ intr ruffianeggiare; **to pander to** favorire, assecondare i desideri di
pane [pen] s pannello, vetro di finestra
pan·el ['pænəl] s pannello; gruppo che discute in faccia al pubblico, telequiz m; discussione pubblica; (of door or window) specchio; (law) lista di giurati ‖ v (pret & pp -eled or -elled; ger -eling or -elling) tr coprire di pannelli
pan'el discus'sion s colloquio di esperti in faccia al pubblico
panelist ['pænəlɪst] s partecipante mf a una discussione in faccia al pubblico
pan'el lights' spl luci fpl del cruscotto
pan'el truck' s camioncino
pang [pæŋ] s (sharp pain) spasimo; (of remorse) tormento
pan'han'dle s manico della padella ‖ intr accattare, mendicare
pan·ic ['pænɪk] adj & s panico ‖ v (pret & pp -icked; ger -icking) tr riempire di panico ‖ intr essere colto dal panico
pan'ic-strick'en adj morto di paura, in preda al panico
pano·ply ['pænəplɪ] s (-plies) panoplia; abbigliamento in pompa magna
panorama [ˌpænə'ræmə] or [ˌpænə'rɑmə] s panorama m
pan·sy ['pænzɪ] s (-sies) viola del pensiero
pant [pænt] s anelito, affanno; **pants** pantaloni mpl, calzoni mpl; **to wear the pants** portare i calzoni ‖ intr ansare; (said of heart) palpitare
panthe'ism ['pænθɪ ˌɪzəm] s panteismo
pantheon ['pænθɪ ˌɑn] or ['pænθɪ·ən] s panteon m, pantheon m
panther ['pænθər] s pantera
panties ['pæntɪz] spl mutandine fpl
pantomime ['pæntə ˌmaɪm] s pantomima
pan·try ['pæntrɪ] s (-tries) dispensa
pap [pæp] s pappa
papa·cy ['pepəsɪ] s (-cies) papato
Pa'pal States' ['pepəl] spl Stati mpl pontifici
paper ['pepər] adj di carta, cartaceo ‖ s carta; (newspaper) giornale m; (of a student) tema m, saggio; (of a scholar) dissertazione; **on paper** per iscritto ‖ tr (a wall) tappezzare
pa'per·back' s libro in brossura
pa'per·boy' s giornalaio, strillone m
pa'per clip' s fermaglio per le carte, clip m
pa'per cone' s cartoccino
pa'per cut'ter s rifilatrice f
pa'per doll' s pupazzetto di carta
pa'per·hang'er s tappezziere m
pa'per knife' s tagliacarte m
pa'per mill' s cartiera
pa'per mon'ey s carta moneta

pa'per prof'its spl guadagni mpl non realizzati su valori non venduti
pa'per tape' s (of teletype) nastro di carta; (of computer) nastro perforato
pa'per·weight' s fermacarte m
pa'per work' s lavoro a tavolino
papier-mâché [ˌpepərmə'ʃe] s cartapesta
paprika [pæ'prɪkə] or ['pæprɪkə] s paprica
papy·rus [pə'paɪrəs] s (-ri [raɪ]) papiro
par [pɑr] adj alla pari, nominale; normale ‖ s parità f, valore m nominale; **at par** alla pari
parable ['pærəbəl] s parabola
parabola [pə'ræbələ] s parabola
parachute ['pærə ˌʃut] s paracadute m ‖ intr lanciarsi col paracadute
par'a·chute jump' s lancio col paracadute
parachutist ['pærə ˌʃutɪst] s paracadutista mf
parade [pə'red] s parata, sfilata; ostentazione, sfoggio ‖ tr ostentare, sfoggiare; disporre in parata ‖ intr fare mostra di sé; (mil) sfilare
paradise ['pærə ˌdaɪs] s paradiso
paradox ['pærə ˌdɑks] s paradosso
paradoxical [ˌpærə'dɑksɪkəl] adj paradossale
paraffin ['pærəfɪn] s paraffina
paragon ['pærə ˌgɑn] s paragone m
paragraph ['pærə ˌgræf] or ['pærə ˌgrɑf] s paragrafo, capoverso; (in a newspaper) trafiletto; (of law) comma m
parakeet ['pærə ˌkit] s parrocchetto
paral·lel ['pærə ˌlɛl] adj parallelo ‖ s (geog, fig) parallelo; (geom) parallela; **parallels** (typ) sbarrette fpl verticali ‖ v (pret & pp -leled or -lelled; ger -leling or -lelling) tr collocare parallelamente; correre parallelo a; confrontare
par'allel bars' spl parallele fpl
paraly·sis [pə'rælɪsɪs] s (-ses [ˌsiz]) paralisi f
paralytic [ˌpærə'lɪtɪk] adj & s paralitico
paralyze ['pærə ˌlaɪz] tr paralizzare
paramount ['pærə ˌmaunt] adj capitale, supremo
paramour ['pærə ˌmur] s amante mf
paranoiac [ˌpærə'nɔɪ·æk] adj & s paranoico
parapet ['pærə ˌpɛt] s parapetto
paraphernalia [ˌpærəfər'nɛlɪ·ə] spl roba, cose fpl; attrezzi mpl, aggeggi mpl
parasite ['pærə ˌsaɪt] s parassita m
parasitic(al) [ˌpærə'sɪtɪk(əl)] adj parassitico, parassitario
parasol ['pærə ˌsɔl] or ['pærə ˌsɑl] s parasole m, ombrellino da sole
par'a·troop'er s paracadutista m
par'a·troops' spl truppe fpl paracadutiste
parboil ['pɑr ˌbɔɪl] tr bollire parzialmente; (fig) far bollire
parcel ['pɑrsəl] s pacchetto; (of land) appezzamento ‖ v (pret & pp -celed or -celled; ger -celing or -celling) tr

impacchettare; **to parcel out** dividere, distribuire

par'cel post' s servizio pacchi postali

parch [part∫] tr bruciare; (land) inaridire; (e.g., beans) essiccare; **to be parched** bruciare dalla sete ‖ intr arrostirsi; inaridire

parchment ['part∫mənt] s pergamena

pardon ['pardən] s perdono, grazia; **I beg your pardon** scusi ‖ tr perdonare; (an offense) graziare

pardonable ['pardənəbəl] adj perdonabile, veniale

par'don board' s ufficio per la decisione delle grazie

pare [per] tr (fruit, potatoes) sbucciare, pelare; (nails) tagliare; (expenses) ridurre

parent ['perənt] adj madre, principale ‖ s genitore m or genitrice f; (fig) origine f; **parents** genitori mpl

parentage ['perəntɪdʒ] s discendenza, lignaggio

parenthesis [pə'renθɪsɪs] s (-ses [,siz]) parentesi f; **in parenthesis** tra parentesi

parenthetically [,pærən'θetɪkəli] adv tra parentesi

parenthood ['perənt,hʊd] s paternità f or maternità f

pariah [pə'rai·ə] or ['parɪ·ə] s paria m

pari-mutuel ['pærɪ'mjut/ʊ·əl] s totalizzatore m

par'ing knife' ['perɪŋ] s coltello per sbucciare

Paris ['pærɪs] s Parigi f

parish ['pærɪ∫] s parrocchia

parishioner [pə'rɪ∫ənər] s parrocchiano

Parisian [pə'rɪʒən] adj & s parigino

parity ['pærɪti] s parità f

park [park] s parco ‖ tr parcare, parcheggiare ‖ intr parcare, parcheggiare, stazionare

parking ['parkɪŋ] s posteggio, parcheggio; **no parking** divieto di parcheggio

park'ing lights' spl luci fpl di posizione

park'ing lot' s posteggio, parcheggio

park'ing me'ter s parchimetro

park'ing tick'et s contravvenzione per parcheggio abusivo

park'way' s boulevard m

parlay ['parli] or ['par'le] tr rigiocare

parley ['parli] s trattativa, conferenza ‖ intr parlamentare

parliament ['parlɪmənt] s parlamento

parlor ['parlər] s salotto; (of beautician or undertaker) salone m; (of convent) parlatorio

par'lor car' s vettura salone

par'lor game' s gioco di società

par'lor pol'itics s politica da caffè

Parmesan [,parmɪ'zæn] adj & s parmigiano

Parnassus [par'næsəs] s (poetry; poets) parnaso; il Parnaso

parochial [pə'rokɪ·əl] adj parrocchiale; ristretto, limitato; (school) confessionale

parody ['pærədi] s (-dies) parodia f ‖ v (pret & pp -died) tr parodiare

parole [pə'rol] s parola d'onore; libertà f condizionale, condizionale f ‖ tr mettere in libertà condizionale

paroxytone [pær'aksɪ,ton] adj parossitono ‖ s parola parossitona

par-quet [par'ke] s pavimento di legno tassellato, tassellato; (theat) platea ‖ v (pret & pp -queted ['ked]; ger -queting ['ke·ɪŋ]) tr pavimentare in legno tassellato

par'quet cir'cle s poltroncine fpl

parricide ['pærɪ,saɪd] s (act) patricidio, parricidio; (person) patricida mf, parricida mf

parrot ['pærət] s pappagallo ‖ tr scimmiottare, fare il pappagallo a

par-ry ['pæri] s (-ries) parata f ‖ v (pret & pp -ried) tr parare; (fig) evitare

parse [pars] tr (gram) analizzare grammaticalmente

parsimonious [,parsɪ'monɪ·əs] adj parsimonioso

parsley ['parsli] s prezzemolo

parsnip ['parsnɪp] s pastinaca

parson ['parsən] s parroco; pastore m protestante

part [part] s parte f; (of a machine) pezzo, organo; (of hair) riga; **for my part** per parte mia; **on the part of** da parte di; **part and parcel** parte f integrante; **parts** abilità f, dote f; regione f, paesi mpl; **to do one's part** fare il proprio dovere ‖ adv parzialmente, in part ‖ tr dividere, separare; **to part company** separarsi; **to part one's hair** farsi la riga ‖ intr separarsi; **to part from** separarsi da, dividersi da; **to part with** rinunciare a

par-take [par'tek] v (pret -took ['tuk]; pp -taken) tr condividere ‖ intr—**to partake in** partecipare a; **to partake of** condividere

parterre [par'ter] s aiola; (theat) platea

Parthenon ['parθɪ,nan] s Partenone m

partial ['par∫əl] adj parziale

participate [par'tɪsɪ,pet] intr partecipare; **to participate in** partecipare a

participation [par,tɪsɪ'pe/ən] s partecipazione

participle ['partɪ,sɪpəl] s participio

particle ['partɪkəl] s particella

particular [pər'tɪkjələr] adj (belonging to a single person) particolare; (exacting) esigente, fastidioso ‖ s particolare m; **in particular** specialmente, particolarmente

part'ing adj (words) di commiato; (last) ultimo ‖ s commiato; separazione

partisan ['partɪzən] adj & s partigiano

partition [par'tɪ∫ən] s partizione, divisione; (or house) tramezzo ‖ tr dividere; tramezzare

partner ['partnər] s (in sports) compagno; (in dancing) cavaliere m, dama; (husband or wife) consorte mf; (com) socio

partnership ['partnər,∫ɪp] s associazione; (com) società f

part' of speech' s parte f del discorso

partridge ['partrɪdʒ] s pernice f

part' time' adj a orario ridotto, a ore

par-ty ['parti] adj comune; di gala ‖ s (-ties) festa, ricevimento, trattenimento; (of people) gruppo; (indi-

vidual) persona; (*pol*) partito; (*law*) contraente *mf;* (*mil*) distaccamento; **to be a party to** prendere parte a; essere complice di

par'ty girl' *s* ragazza che fa la vita

par-ty-go'er *s* frequentatore *m* di trattenimenti

part'y line' *s* (*boundary*) linea di confine; (*of Communist party*) politica del partito; (*telp*) linea in coutenza

pass [pæs] or [pɑs] *s* passaggio; (*state*) stato, situazione; (*free ticket*) ingresso gratuito; (*leave of absence given to a soldier*) congedo, permesso; (*of a hypnotist*) gesto; (*between mountains*) passo; (*slang*) tentativo d'abbraccio; **a pretty pass** (*coll*) un bell'affare || *tr* (*a course in school*) passare; (*to promote*) promuovere; (*a law*) approvare; (*a sentence*) pronunciare; (*an opinion*) esprimere, avanzare; (*to excrete*) evacuare; far muovere; **to pass by** non fare attenzione a; **to pass off** (*e.g., bogus money*) azzeccare; **to pass on** trasmettere; **to pass out** distribuire; **to pass over** omettere || *intr* (*to go*) passare; (*said of a law*) essere approvato; (*said of a student*) essere promosso; (*to be accepted*) farsi passare; (*said, e.g., of two trains*) incrociarsi; **to come to pass** accadere, succedere; **to pass as** passare per; **to pass away** morire; **to pass out** (*slang*) svenire; **to pass over** or **through** attraversare, passare per

passable ['pæsəbəl] or ['pɑsəbəl] *adj* praticabile; (*by boat*) navigabile; (*adequate*) passabile; (*law*) promulgabile

passage ['pæsɪdʒ] *s* passaggio; (*of a law*) approvazione; (*ticket*) biglietto di passaggio; (*of the bowels*) evacuazione

pass'book' *s* libretto di banca; libretto della cassa di risparmio

passenger ['pæsəndʒər] *s* passeggero

passer-by ['pæsər'baɪ] or ['pɑsər'baɪ] *s* (**passers-by**) passante *mf*

passing ['pæsɪŋ] or ['pɑsɪŋ] *adj* (*fleeting*) fuggente; (*casual*) incidentale; (*grade*) che concede la promozione || *s* passaggio; (*death*) morte *f;* promozione

passion ['pæʃən] *s* passione

passionate ['pæʃənɪt] *adj* appassionato; (*hot-tempered*) collerico; veemente, ardente

passive ['pæsɪv] *adj & s* passivo

pass'key' *s* chiave maestra; (*for use of hotel help*) comunella

Pass'o'ver *s* Pasqua ebraica

pass'port' *s* passaporto

pass'word' *s* parola d'ordine

past [pæst] or [pɑst] *adj* passato, scorso; ex, **past president** ex presidente || *s* passato || *adv* oltre; al di fuori; al di là || *prep* oltre; al di là di; dopo (di); **past belief** incredibile; **past cure** incurabile; **past hope** senza speranza; **past recovery** incurabile; **past three o'clock** le tre passate

paste [pest] *s* (*dough*) pasta; (*adhesive*) colla; diamante *m* artificiale || *tr* incollare; (*slang*) dare pugni a

paste'board' *s* cartone *m*

pastel [pæs'tel] *adj & s* pastello

pasteurize ['pæstə,raɪz] *tr* pastorizzare

pastime ['pæs,taɪm] or ['pɑs,taɪm] *s* diversione, passatempo

pastor ['pæstər] or ['pɑstər] *s* pastore *m*, sacerdote *m*

pastoral ['pæstərəl] or ['pɑstərəl] *adj* pastorale || *s* (*poem, letter*) pastorale *f;* (*crosier*) pastorale *m*

pas·try ['pestri] *s* (**-tries**) pasticceria

pas'try cook' *s* pasticciere *m*

pas'try shop' *s* pasticceria

pasture ['pæstʃər] or ['pɑstʃər] *s* pastura, pascolo || *tr* condurre al pascolo || *intr* brucare

past·y ['pesti] *adj* (**-ier; -iest**) pastoso; flaccido

pat [pæt] *s* colpetto; (*of butter*) panetto || *v* (*pret & pp* **patted;** *ger* **patting**) *tr* accarezzare leggermente; battere leggermente; **to pat on the back** elogiare, incoraggiare battendo sulla spalla

patch [pætʃ] *s* (*on a suit or shoes*) toppa; (*in a tire*) pezza; (*on wound*) benda; (*of ground*) appezzamento; (*small area*) lembo || *tr* rammendare; **to patch up** (*an argument*) comporre; (*to produce crudely*) raffazzonare

patent ['petənt] *adj* patente, palmare || ['pætənt] *adj* brevettato || *s* (*of invention*) brevetto; (*sole right*) privativa || *tr* brevettare

pat'ent leath'er [pætənt] *s* copale *m & f*, pelle *f* di vernice

pat'ent med'icine [pætənt] *s* specialità *f* medicinale

pat'ent right' [pætənt] *s* proprietà brevettata

paternal [pə'tʌrnəl] *adj* paterno

paternity [pə'tʌrnɪti] *s* paternità *f*

path [pæθ] or [pɑθ] *s* via battuta, sentiero; (*fig*) via

pathetic [pə'θetɪk] *adj* patetico

path'find'er *s* esploratore *m*

pathology [pə'θɑlədʒi] *s* patologia

pathos ['peθɑs] *s* patos *m*, pathos *m*

path'way' *s* sentiero, cammino

patience ['peʃəns] *s* pazienza

patient ['peʃənt] *adj & s* paziente *mf*

patriarch ['petri,ɑrk] *s* patriarca *m*

patrician [pə'trɪʃən] *adj & s* patrizio

patricide ['pætri,saɪd] *s* (*act*) parricidio; (*person*) parricida *mf*

Patrick ['pætrɪk] *s* Patrizio

patrimo·ny ['pætri,moni] *s* (**-nies**) patrimonio

patriot ['petri·ət] or ['pætri·ət] *s* patriota *m*

patriotic [,petri'ɑtɪk] or [,pætri'ɑtɪk] *adj* patriottico

patriotism ['petri·ə,tɪzəm] or ['pætri·ə,tɪzəm] *s* patriottismo

pa·trol [pə'trol] *s* (*group*) pattuglia; (*individual*) soldato or agente *m* di pattuglia || *v* (*pret & pp* **-trolled;** *ger* **-trolling**) *tr & intr* pattugliare

patrol'man *s* (**-men**) agente *m*, poliziotto

patrol' wag'on s carrozzone m cellulare, cellulare m

patron ['petrən] or ['pætrən] s patrono, sostenitore m; (customer) cliente mf

patronize ['petrə‚naɪz] or ['pætrə‚naɪz] tr (to support) sostenere; trattare con condiscendenza; essere cliente abituale di

pa'tron saint' s patrono

patter ['pætər] s (e.g., of rain) battito; (of feet) scalpiccio; (speech) chiaccherio ‖ intr battere, picchiettare; chiaccherare

pattern ['pætərn] s modello; disegno; (of flight) procedura ‖ tr modellare

pat•ty ['pæti] s (-ties) pasticcino; (meat cake) polpetta

paucity ['pɔsɪti] s pochezza, scarsità f, insufficienza

Paul [pɔl] s Paolo

paunch [pɔntʃ] s pancia

paunch•y ['pɔntʃi] adj (-ier; -iest) pancuto

pauper ['pɔpər] s povero, indigente mf

pause [pɔz] s pausa; (of a tape recorder) arresto momentaneo; **to give pause (to)** dar di che pensare (a) ‖ intr far pausa, fermarsi; (to hesitate) esitare, vacillare

pave [pev] tr pavimentare, lastricare; **to pave the way (for)** aprire il cammino (a)

pavement ['pevmənt] s pavimentazione, lastricato; (sidewalk) marciapiede m

pavilion [pə'vɪljən] s padiglione m; (of circus) tendone m

paw [pɔ] s zampa ‖ tr (to touch with paws) dar zampate a; (to handle clumsily) maneggiare goffamente; (coll) palpeggiare ‖ intr zampare

pawn [pɔn] s (security) pegno; (tool of another person) pedina; (chess) pedina, pedone m; (fig) ostaggio ‖ tr dare in pegno, impegnare

pawn'bro'ker s prestatore m su pegno

pawn'shop' s agenzia di prestiti su pegno, monte m di pietà

pawn' tick'et s ricevuta di pegno, polizza del monte di pietà

pay [pe] s pagamento; (wages) paga, salario; (mil) soldo ‖ v (pret & pp **paid** [ped]) tr pagare; (wages) conguagliare; (one's respects) presentare; (a visit) fare; (a bill) saldare; (attention) fare, presentare; **to pay back** ripagare; (fig) pagare pan per focaccia a; **to pay for** pagare; **to pay off** liquidare; (in order to discharge) pagare e licenziare; **to pay up** saldare ‖ intr pagare; valere la pena; **pay as you enter** pagare all'ingresso; **pay as you go** pagare le tasse per trattenuta; **pay as you leave** pagare all'uscita

payable ['pe·əbəl] adj pagabile

pay' boost' s aumento di salario

pay'check' s assegno in pagamento del salario; salario, paga

pay'day' s giorno di paga

payee [pe'i] s beneficiario

pay' en'velope s bustapaga

payer ['pe·ər] s pagatore m

pay'load' s peso utile

pay'mas'ter s ufficiale m pagatore

payment ['pemənt] s pagamento

pay'off' s pagamento, regolamento; (coll) conclusione

pay' phone' s telefono a moneta

pay'roll' s lista degli impiegati; libro paga

pay' sta'tion s telefono pubblico

pea [pi] s pisello

peace [pis] s pace f; **to hold one's peace** tacere, stare zitto

peaceable ['pisəbəl] adj pacifico

peaceful ['pisfəl] adj pacifico

peace'mak'er s paciere m

peace' of mind' s serenità f d'animo

peace' pipe' s calumet m della pace

peach [pitʃ] s pesca; (coll) persona or cosa stupenda

peach' tree' s pesco

peach•y ['pitʃi] adj (-ier; -iest) (coll) stupendo

pea'cock' s pavone m

peak [pik] s picco; (of traffic) punta; (of one's career) sommo

peak' hour' s ora di punta

peak' load' s carico delle ore di punta, carico massimo

peal [pil] s (of bells) squillo; (of gun) rombo; (of laughter) scoppio; (of thunder) scroscio ‖ intr scampanare, squillare

pea'nut' s nocciolina americana; (plant) arachide f

pea'nut but'ter s pasta d'arachidi

pear [per] s (fruit) pera; (tree) pero

pearl [parl] s perla; (mother-of-pearl) madreperla; colore perlaceo

pearl' oys'ter s ostrica perlifera

pear' tree' s pero

peasant ['pezənt] adj & s contadino

pea'shoot'er s cerbottana

pea' soup' s minestra di piselli; (coll) nebbione m

peat [pit] s torba

pebble ['pebəl] s ciottolo

peck [pɛk] s beccata; misura di due galloni; **a peck of trouble** un mare di guai ‖ tr beccare ‖ intr beccare; **to peck at** beccucciare

peculation [‚pekjə'leʃən] s malversazione, peculato

peculiar [pɪ'kjuljər] adj peculiare; (odd) strano

pedagogue ['pedə‚gɑg] s pedagogo

pedagogy ['pedə‚godʒi] or ['pedə‚gadʒi] s pedagogia

ped•al ['pedəl] s pedale m ‖ v (pret & pp **-aled** or **-alled;** ger **-aling** or **-alling**) tr spingere coi pedali ‖ intr pedalare

pedant ['pedənt] s pedante mf

pedantic [pɪ'dæntɪk] adj pedantesco

pedant•ry ['pedəntri] s (-ries) pedanteria

peddle ['pedəl] tr vendere di porta in porta ‖ intr fare il venditore ambulante

peddler ['pedlər] s venditore m or merciaiolo ambulante

pedestal ['pedɪstəl] s piedistallo
pedestrian [pɪ'destrɪ·ən] adj pedestre || s pedone m
pediatrics [,pidɪ'ætrɪks] or [,pedɪ-'ætrɪks] s pediatria
pedigree ['pedɪ,gri] s albero genealogico; discendenza, lignaggio
pediment ['pedɪmənt] s frontone m
peek [pik] s sbirciata || intr sbirciare
peel [pil] s scorza, buccia; (of baker) pala || tr sbucciare; **to keep one's eyes peeled** (slang) tenere gli occhi aperti || intr pelarsi
peep [pip] s sbirciata; (sound) pigolio || intr guardare attraverso una fessura; (said of birds) pigolare; (to begin to appear) fare capolino
peep'hole' s spioncino
Peep'ing Tom' s guardone m
peep' show' s cosmorama m
peer [pɪr] s pari m, uguale m; (Brit) pari m || intr guardare da vicino
peerless ['pɪrlɪs] adj senza pari
peeve [piv] s (coll) seccatura, irritazione || tr (coll) seccare, irritare
peevish ['pivɪʃ] adj irritabile
peg [peg] s (to plug holes) zipolo; (pin) cavicchio; (mus) bischero; (coll) grado; **to take down a peg** (coll) fare abbassare la testa a || v (pret & pp **pegged**; ger **pegging**) tr fissare con cavicchi; (prices) stabilizzare || intr—**to peg away** lavorare di lena
peg' leg' s gamba di legno
Peking ['pi'kɪŋ] s Pechino f
Peking·ese [,pikɪ'niz] adj pechinese || s (-ese) pechinese mf
pelf [pelf] s (pej) denaro rubacchiato, maltolto
pelican ['pelɪkən] s pellicano
pellet ['pelɪt] s pallottola; (for shotgun) pallino; (pill) pillola
pell-mell ['pel'mel] adj confuso, disordinato || adv alla rinfusa
Peloponnesian [,peləpə'niʃən] adj & s peloponnesiaco
pelt [pelt] s pelle grezza; (blow) colpo || tr scagliare contro; (to beat) battere violentemente || intr battere, scrosciare
pen [pen] s (enclosure) recinto; (for writing) penna; (pen point) pennino || v (pret & pp **penned**; ger **penning**) tr scrivere a penna; (to compose) redigere || v (pret & pp **penned** or **pent**; ger **penning**) tr recintare
penalize ['pinə,laɪz] tr punire; (sports) penalizzare
penal·ty ['penəlti] s (-ties) punizione; (fine) multa; (for late payment) penale f; **under penalty of** sotto pena di
pen'alty goal' s calcio di rigore
penance ['penəns] s penitenza
penchant ['penʃənt] s propensione
pen·cil ['pensəl] s matita; (of rays) fascio || v (pret & pp **-ciled** or **-cilled**; ger **-ciling** or **-cilling**) tr scrivere a matita; (med) pennellare
pen'cil sharp'ener s temperalapis m
pendent ['pendənt] adj pendente, sospeso || s pendente m, ciondolo

pending ['pendɪŋ] adj imminente; **in sospeso** || prep durante; fino a
pendulum ['pendʒələm] s pendolo
pen'dulum bob' s lente f
penetrate ['penɪ,tret] tr & intr penetrare
penguin ['peŋgwɪn] s pinguino
pen'hold'er s portapenne m
penicillin [,penɪ'sɪlɪn] s penicillina
peninsula [pe'nɪnsələ] s penisola
peninsular [pə'nɪnsələr] adj & s peninsulare
penitence ['penɪtəns] s penitenza
penitent ['penɪtənt] adj & s penitente mf
pen'knife' s (-knives) temperino
penmanship ['penmən,ʃɪp] s calligrafia
pen' name' s nome m di penna, pseudonimo
pennant ['penənt] s pennone m
penniless ['penɪlɪs] adj povero in canna, senza un soldo
pennon ['penən] s pennone m
pen·ny ['peni] s (-nies) (U.S.A.) centesimo || s (pence [pens]) (Brit) penny m
pen'ny pinch'er ['pɪntʃər] s spilorcio
pen' pal' s amico corrispondente
pen'point' s pennino; (of ball-point pen) punta
pension ['penʃən] s pensione || tr pensionare, mettere in pensione
pensioner ['penʃənər] s pensionato
pensive ['pensɪv] adj pensieroso
Pentecost ['pentɪ,kɔst] or ['pentɪ,kast] s la Pentecoste
penthouse ['pent,haus] s appartamento di lusso sul tetto; tettoia
pent-up ['pent,ʌp] adj represso
penult ['pinʌlt] s penultima
penum·bra [pɪ'nʌmbrə] s (-brae [bri] or -bras) penombra
penurious [pɪ'nurɪ·əs] adj taccagno, meschino; indigente
penury ['penjəri] s taccagneria; estrema povertà, miseria
pen'wip'er s nettapenne m
people ['pipəl] spl popolo, gente f; (relatives) famiglia; gente f del popolo; si, e.g., **people say** si dice || ssg (peoples) nazione, popolazione || tr popolare
pep [pep] s (coll) animo, brio || v (pret & pp **pepped**; ger **pepping**) tr—**to pep up** (coll) dar animo a
pepper ['pepər] s pepe m || tr pepare; (to pelt) tempestare
pep'per·box' s pepaiola
pep'per·mint' s menta piperita
per [pʌr] prep per; (for each) il, e.g., **three dollars per meter** tre dollari il metro; **as per** secondo
perambulator [pər'æmbjə,letər] s carrozzella, carrozzino
per capita [pər 'kæpɪtə] per persona, a testa
perceive [pər'siv] tr percepire
percent [pər'sent] s percento, per cento
percentage [pər'sentɪdʒ] s percento, percentuale f; (coll) vantaggio
perception [pər'sɛpʃən] s percezione

perch [pʌrtʃ] s (*roost*) posatoio; (*horizontal rod*) ballatoio; (ichth) pesce persico || *intr* appollaiarsi

percolator ['pʌrkə,letər] s caffettiera filtro a circolazione

percus'sion cap' [pər'kʌʃən] s capsula di percussione

per diem [pər 'daɪ-əm] s assegno giornaliero

perdition [pər'dɪʃən] s perdizione

perennial [pə'rɛnɪ-əl] adj perenne || s pianta perenne

perfect ['pʌrfɪkt] adj & s perfetto || [pər'fɛkt] tr perfezionare

perfidious [pər'fɪdɪ-əs] adj perfido

perfi·dy ['pʌrfɪdɪ] s (-dies) perfidia

perforate ['pʌrfə,ret] tr perforare

perforation [,pʌrfə'reʃən] s perforazione; (*of postage stamp*) dentellatura

perforce [pər'fors] adv per forza, necessariamente

perform [pər'form] tr (*a task*) eseguire; (*a promise*) adempiere; (*to enact*) rappresentare || *intr* recitare; (*said, e.g., of a machine*) funzionare

performance [pər'forməns] s esecuzione; (*of a machine*) funzionamento; (*deed*) atto di prodezza; (theat) rappresentazione

performer [pər'formər] s esecutore m; attore m; acrobata mf

perform'ing arts' spl arti fpl dello spettacolo

perfume ['pʌrfjum] s profumo || [pər'fjum] tr profumare

perfumer·y [pər'fjuməri] s (-ies) profumeria

perfunctory [pər'fʌŋktəri] adj superficiale, pro forma; indifferente

perhaps [pər'hæps] adv forse

per·il ['pɛrəl] s pericolo || v (pret & pp -iled or -illed; ger -iling or -illing) tr mettere in pericolo

perilous ['pɛrɪləs] adj pericoloso

period ['pɪrɪ-əd] s periodo; mestruazione; (*in school*) ora; (sports) tempo; (gram) punto

pe'riod cos'tume s costume m dell'epoca

periodic [,pɪrɪ'ɑdɪk] adj periodico

periodical [,pɪrɪ'ɑdɪkəl] adj & s periodico

peripher·y [pə'rɪfəri] s (-ies) periferia

periscope ['pɛrɪ,skop] s periscopio

perish ['pɛrɪʃ] intr perire

perishable ['pɛrɪʃəbəl] adj deteriorabile

periwig ['pɛrɪ,wɪg] s parrucca

perjure ['pʌrdʒər] tr—to perjure oneself spergiurare, giurare il falso

perju·ry ['pʌrdʒəri] s (-ries) spergiuro

perk [pʌrk] tr (*the head, the ears*) alzare; **to perk oneself up** agghindarsi || *intr*—**to perk up** ringalluzzirsi

permanence ['pʌrmənəns] s permanenza

permanen·cy ['pʌrmənənsi] s (-cies) permanenza

permanent ['pʌrmənənt] adj permanente || s permanente f, ondulazione permanente

per'manent fix'ture s cosa or persona permanente

per'manent ten'ure s inamovibilità f

per'manent way' s (rr) sede f stradale ed armamento

permeate ['pʌrmɪ,et] tr permeare || *intr* permearsi

permissible [pər'mɪsɪbəl] adj permissibile

permission [pər'mɪʃən] s permesso

per·mit ['pʌrmɪt] s permesso; patente f, licenza || [pər'mɪt] v (pret & pp -mitted; ger -mitting) tr permettere

permute [pər'mjut] tr permutare

pernicious [pər'nɪʃəs] adj pernicioso

pernickety [pər'nɪkɪti] adj (coll) incontentabile, meticoloso

perorate ['pɛrə,ret] intr perorare

peroxide [pər'ɑksaɪd] s perossido; perossido d'idrogeno

perox'ide blonde' s bionda ossigenata

perpendicular [,pʌrpən'dɪkjələr] adj & s perpendicolare f

perpetrate ['pʌrpɪ,tret] tr (*a crime*) perpetrare; (*a blunder*) commettere

perpetual [pər'pɛtʃu-əl] adj perpetuo

perpetuate [pər'pɛtʃu,et] tr perpetuare

perplex [pər'plɛks] tr lasciare perplesso

perplexed [pər'plɛkst] adj perplesso

perplexi·ty [pər'plɛksɪti] s (-ties) perplessità f

per se [pər 'si] di per se

persecute ['pʌrsɪ,kjut] tr perseguitare

persevere [,pʌrsɪ'vɪr] intr perseverare

Persian ['pʌrʒən] adj & s persiano

Per'sian Gulf' s Golfo Persico

persimmon [pər'sɪmən] s diospiro virginiano; cachi m

persist [pər'sɪst] or [pər'zɪst] intr persistere

persistent [pər'sɪstənt] or [pər'zɪstənt] adj persistente

person ['pʌrsən] s persona; **no person** nessuno

personage ['pʌrsənɪdʒ] s personaggio; persona

personal ['pʌrsənəl] adj personale; (*goods*) mobile || s inserzione personale; trafiletto di società

personali·ty [,pʌrsə'nælɪti] s (-ties) personalità f; offesa personale

personal'ity cult' s culto della personalità

per'sonal prop'erty s beni mpl mobili

personi·fy [pər'sɑnɪ,faɪ] v (pret & pp -fied) tr personificare

personnel [,pʌrsə'nɛl] s personale m

per'son-to-per'son call' s (telp) chiamata con preavviso

perspective [pər'spɛktɪv] s prospettiva

perspicacious [,pʌrspɪ'keʃəs] adj perspicace

perspire [pər'spaɪr] intr sudare

persuade [pər'swed] tr persuadere

persuasion [pər'sweʒən] s persuasione; fede religiosa

pert [pʌrt] adj impertinente, sfacciato; vivace

pertain [pər'ten] intr appartenere; (*to have reference*) riferirsi

pertinacious [,pʌrtɪ'neʃəs] adj pertinace

pertinent ['pʌrtɪnənt] *adj* pertinente
perturb [pər'tʌrb] *tr* perturbare
Peru [pə'ru] *s* il Perù
perusal [pə'ruzəl] *s* attenta lettura
peruse [pə'ruz] *tr* leggere attentamente
pervade [pər'ved] *tr* pervadere
perverse [pər'vʌrs] *adj* perverso; (*obstinate*) ostinato
perversion [pər'vʌrʒən] *s* perversione
perversi·ty [pər'vʌrsɪti] *s* (**-ties**) perversità *f*; contrarietà *f*
pervert ['pʌrvərt] *s* pervertito, degenerato || [pər'vʌrt] *tr* pervertire, degenerare
pes·ky ['peski] *adj* (**-kier; -kiest**) (coll) noioso, molesto
pessimism ['pesɪ‚mɪzəm] *s* pessimismo
pessimist ['pesɪmɪst] *s* pessimista *mf*
pessimistic [‚pesɪ'mɪstɪk] *adj* pessimistico
pest [pest] *s* peste *f*, pestilenza; insetto; animale nocivo; (*person*) peste *f*, seccatore *m*
pester ['pestər] *tr* seccare, annoiare
pest'house' *s* lazzaretto
pesticide ['pestɪ‚saɪd] *s* insetticida *m*
pestiferous [pest'ɪfərəs] *adj* pestifero
pestilence ['pestɪləns] *s* pestilenza
pestle ['pesəl] *s* pestello
pet [pet] *s* animale favorito; beniamino || *v* (*pret & pp* **petted**; *ger* **petting**) *tr* accarezzare || *intr* (coll) pomiciare
petal ['petəl] *s* petalo
petard [pɪ'tard] *s* petardo
pet'cock' *s* chiavetta
Peter ['pitər] *s* Pietro; **to rob Peter to pay Paul** fare un buco per tapparne un altro || *intr*—**to peter out** (coll) affievolirsi
petition [pɪ'tɪʃən] *s* petizione || *tr* rivolgere un'istanza a
pet' name' *s* nomignolo vezzeggiativo
Petrarch ['pitrark] *s* Petrarca *m*
petri·fy ['petrɪ‚faɪ] *v* (*pret & pp* **-fied**) *tr* pietrificare || *intr* pietrificarsi
petrol ['petrəl] *s* (Brit) benzina
petroleum [pɪ'troli‚əm] *s* petrolio
pet' shop' *s* negozio di animali domestici
petticoat ['petɪ‚kot] *s* sottoveste *f*; (coll) sottana, gonnella
pet·ty ['peti] *adj* (**-tier; -tiest**) insignificante, minore; meschino
pet'ty cash' *s* cassa delle piccole spese
pet'ty lar'ceny *s* furterello
pet'ty of'ficer *s* (nav) sottufficiale *m* di marina
petulant ['petjələnt] *adj* stizzoso, irritabile
pew [pju] *s* banco di chiesa
pewter ['pjutər] *s* peltro; oggetti *mpl* di peltro
phalanx ['felæŋks] *or* ['fælæŋks] *s* falange *f*
phantasm ['fæntæzəm] *s* fantasma *m*
phantom ['fæntəm] *s* fantasma *m*
Pharaoh ['fero] *s* Faraone *m*
pharisee ['færɪ‚si] *s* fariseo || **Pharisee** *s* fariseo
pharmaceutical [‚farmə'sutɪkəl] *adj* farmaceutico

pharmacist ['farməsɪst] *s* farmacista *mf*
pharma·cy ['farməsi] *s* (**-cies**) farmacia
pharynx ['færɪŋks] *s* faringe *f*
phase [fez] *s* fase *f* || *tr* mettere in fase; sincronizzare; **to phase in** mettere in operazione gradualmente; **to phase out** eliminare gradualmente
pheasant ['fezənt] *s* fagiano
phenobarbital [‚fino'barbɪ‚tæl] *s* acido fenil-etilbarbiturico, barbiturato
phenomenal [fɪ'namɪnəl] *adj* fenomenale
phenome·non [fɪ'namɪ‚nan] *s* (**-na** [nə]) fenomeno
phial ['faɪ‚əl] *s* fiala
philanderer [fɪ'lændərər] *s* donnaiolo
philanthropist [fɪ'lænθrəpɪst] *s* filantropo
philanthro·py [fɪ'lænθrəpi] *s* (**-pies**) filantropia
philatelist [fɪ'lætəlɪst] *s* filatelico
philately [fɪ'lætəli] *s* filatelia
Philip ['fɪlɪp] *s* Filippo
Philippine ['fɪlɪ‚pin] *adj* filippino || **Philippines** *spl* isole *fpl* Filippine
Philistine [fɪ'lɪstɪn], ['fɪlɪ‚stin] *or* ['fɪlɪ‚staɪn] *adj & s* filisteo
philologist [fɪ'lalədʒɪst] *s* filologo
philology [fɪ'lalədʒi] *s* filologia
philosopher [fɪ'lasəfər] *s* filosofo
philosophic(al) [‚fɪlə'safɪk(əl)] *adj* filosofico
philoso·phy [fɪ'lasəfi] *s* (**-phies**) filosofia
philter ['fɪltər] *s* filtro
phlebitis [flɪ'baɪtɪs] *s* flebite *f*
phlegm [flem] *s* (*secretion*) muco, catarro; (*self-possession*) flemma; apatia
phlegmatic(al) [fleg'mætɪk(əl)] *adj* flemmatico
Phoebus ['fibəs] *s* Febo
Phoenician [fɪ'nɪʃən] *or* [fɪ'nɪʃən] *adj & s* fenicio
phoenix ['finɪks] *s* fenice *f*
phone [fon] *s* (coll) telefono || *tr & intr* (coll) telefonare
phone' call' *s* chiamata telefonica
phonetic [fo'netɪk] *adj* fonetico || **phonetics** *s* fonetica
phonograph ['fonə‚græf] *or* ['fonə‚graf] *s* fonografo
phonology [fə'nalədʒi] *s* fonologia
pho·ny ['foni] *adj* (**-nier; -niest**) (coll) falso || *s* (**-nies**) (coll) frode *f*; (*person*) (coll) impostore *m*
phosphate ['fasfet] *s* fosfato
phosphorescent [‚fasfə'resənt] *adj* fosforescente
phospho·rus ['fasfərəs] *s* (**-ri** [‚raɪ]) fosforo
pho·to ['foto] *s* (**-tos**) (coll) foto *f*
photo·cop·y ['fotə‚kapi] *s* (**-ies**) fotocopia || *tr* fotocopiare
pho'toelec'tric cell' [‚foto·ɪ'lektrɪk] *s* cellula fotoelettrica
photoengraving [‚foto·en'greviŋ] *s* fotoincisione
pho'to fin'ish *s* photofinish *m*, arrivo con fotografia

photogenic [ˌfotoˈdʒɛnɪk] *adj* fotogenico

photograph [ˈfotəˌgræf] *or* [ˈfotəˌgrɑf] *s* fotografia || *tr* fotografare || *intr*—to photograph well riuscire in fotografia

photographer [fəˈtɑgrəfər] *s* fotografo

photography [fəˈtɑgrəfi] *s* fotografia

photojournalism [ˌfotəˈdʒʌrnəˌlɪzəm] *s* giornalismo fotografico

pho'to-play' *s* dramma adattato per il cinematografo

photostat [ˈfotəˌstæt] *s* (trademark) copia fotostatica || *tr* riprodurre fotostaticamente

phototube [ˈfotəˌtjub] *or* [ˈfotəˌtub] *s* fototubo

phrase [frez] *s* (gram) locuzione; (mus) frase *f* || *tr* esprimere, formulare || *intr* (mus) fraseggiare

phrenology [frɪˈnɑlədʒi] *s* frenologia

Phyllis [ˈfɪlɪs] *s* Fillide *f*

phy·lum [ˈfaɪləm] *s* (-la [lə]) phylum *m*, tipo

phys·ic [ˈfɪzɪk] *s* purgante *m* || *v* (*pret* & *pp* -icked; *ger* -icking) *tr* dare il purgante a, purgare

physical [ˈfɪzɪkəl] *adj* fisico

physician [fɪˈzɪʃən] *s* medico

physicist [ˈfɪzɪsɪst] *s* fisico

physics [ˈfɪzɪks] *s* fisica

physiognomy [ˌfɪziˈɑgnəmi] *or* [ˌfɪziˈɑnəmi] *s* fisionomia

physiological [ˌfɪziəˈlɑdʒɪkəl] *adj* fisiologico

physiology [ˌfɪziˈɑlədʒi] *s* fisiologia

physique [fɪˈzik] *s* fisico

pi [paɪ] *s* (math) pi greco; (typ) tipi scartati || *v* (*pret* & *pp* pied; *ger* piing) *tr* (typ) scompaginare, scomporre

pian·o [pɪˈæno] *s* (-os) piano

picaresque [ˌpikəˈrɛsk] *adj* picaresco

picayune [ˌpikəˈjun] *adj* meschino, minore, di poca importanza

picco·lo [ˈpikəˌlo] *s* (-los) ottavino

pick [pɪk] *s* (tool) piccone *m*; (choice) scelta; (the best) fiore *m*; (mus) plettro || *tr* scavare; (to scratch at) grattare; (to gather) cogliere; (to pluck) spennare; (to pull apart) separare; (one's teeth) stuzzicarsi; (a bone) rosicchiare; (to choose) scegliere; (a lock) scassinare; (a pocket) tagliare, rubare; (mus) pizzicare; **to pick a fight** attaccare briga; **to pick faults** trovare a ridire; **to pick out** scegliere, distinguere; discriminare; **to pick s.o. to pieces** (coll) tagliare i panni addosso a qlcu; **to pick up** sollevare; (to find) trovare; (to learn) arrivare a sapere; (a radio signal) captare; (speed) acquistare || *intr* usare il piccone; **to pick at** (food) spilluzzicare; (coll) criticare; **to pick on** (coll) scegliere; (coll) criticare; **to pick up** (coll) migliorarsi

pick'ax' *s* piccone *m*

picket [ˈpikɪt] *s* picchetto || *tr* rinchiudere con palizzata; (to hitch) legare; (to post) (mil) mettere di picchetto; (e.g., a factory) picchettare

pick'et fence' *s* steccato

pick'et line' *s* corteo di scioperanti; corteo di dimostranti

pickle [ˈpikəl] *s* salamoia, sottaceto; (cucumber) cetriolo sottaceto; **to get into a pickle** (coll) cacciarsi in un imbroglio || *tr* mettere sottaceto; (metallurgy) decapare

pick-me-up [ˈpikmiˌʌp] *s* (coll) spuntino; (coll) bevanda stimulante

pick'pock'et *s* borseggiatore *m*, borsaiolo

pick'up' *s* sollevamento; (in speed) accelerazione; (of phonograph) pick-up *m*, fonorivelatore *m*; (aut) camioncino; (coll) persona conosciuta per caso; (coll) miglioramento

pick'-up-sticks' *spl* sciangai *m*

pic·nic [ˈpiknɪk] *s* picnic *m* || *v* (*pret* & *pp* -nicked; *ger* -nicking) *intr* fare merenda all'aperto

pictorial [pɪkˈtɔriəl] *adj* pittorico; illustrato; (of magazine) a rotocalco || *s* rivista illustrata

picture [ˈpiktʃər] *s* illustrazione, disegno; (painting) quadro, dipinto; (of a person) ritratto; fotografia; film *m*, pellicola || *tr* fare il ritratto di, disegnare; dipingere; fotografare; descrivere; immaginare, immaginarsi

pic'ture frame' *s* cornice *f*

pic'ture gal'lery *s* pinacoteca, galleria di quadri, quadreria

pic'ture post' card' *s* cartolina illustrata

pic'ture show' *s* cinematografo; mostra di quadri

picturesque [ˌpiktʃəˈrɛsk] *adj* pittoresco

pic'ture tube' *s* tubo televisivo

pic'ture win'dow *s* finestra panoramica

piddling [ˈpidlɪŋ] *adj* insignificante

pie [paɪ] *s* (with fruit) torta; (with meat) timballo; (orn) pica || *v* (*pret* & *pp* pied; *ger* pieing) *tr* (typ) scompaginare, scomporre

piece [pis] *s* pezzo; (e.g., of cloth) pezza; **a piece of advice** un consiglio; **a piece of baggage** un collo; **a piece of furniture** un mobile *m*; **a piece of news** una notizia; **by the piece** a cottimo; **to break to pieces** frantumare; frantumarsi; **to cut to pieces** fare a pezzi; **to fall to pieces** cadere a pezzi; **to fly to pieces** rompersi in mille pezzi; **to give s.o. a piece of one's mind** dirne a qlcu di tutti i colori; **to go to pieces** perdere il controllo di sé stesso; **to take to pieces** confutare punto per punto || *tr* rappezzare, mettere insieme || *intr* (coll) mangiucchiare

piece'meal' *adv* poco a poco

piece'work' *s* lavoro a cottimo

piece'work'er *s* cottimista *mf*

pier [pɪr] *s* (of a bridge) pila; (over water) molo; (archit) pilastro, pilone *m*

pierce [pɪrs] *tr* forare, bucare; penetrare; (to stab) trapassare || *intr* penetrare

piercing [ˈpɪrsɪŋ] *adj* acuto; (eyes) penetrante; (pain) lancinante

pier' glass' s specchiera

pie·ty ['paɪ·əti] s (-ties) pietà f

piffle ['pɪfəl] s (coll) fesserie fpl

pig [pɪg] s maiale m, porco; (metallurgy) lingotto, massello; **to buy a pig in the poke** comprare il gatto nel sacco

pigeon ['pɪdʒən] s piccione m

pi'geon·hole' s nicchia nella piccionaia; (for filing) casella || tr (to lay aside for later time) archiviare; (to shelve, e.g., an application) insabbiare

pi'geon house' s colombaia, piccionaia

piggish ['pɪgɪʃ] adj porcino, maialesco

pig'gy·back' ['pɪgɪ,bæk] adv sulle spalle, sulla schiena; (rr) su carrello stradale per trasporto carri

pig'head'ed adj ostinato, cocciuto

pig' i'ron s ghisa, ferro grezzo

pigment ['pɪgmənt] s pigmento || tr pigmentare || intr pigmentarsi

pig'pen' s porcile m

pig'skin' s pelle f di maiale; (coll) pallone m da football, sfera di cuoio

pig'sty' s (-sties) porcile m

pig'tail' s codino; (of girl) treccia; treccia di tabacco

pike [paɪk] s (weapon) picca; (road) autostrada; (ichth) luccio

piker ['paɪkər] s (coll) uomo piccino

pile [paɪl] s (heap) pila; (for burning a corpse) pira; (large building) mole f; (beam) palo; (of carpet) pelo; (of money) (slang) gruzzolo; (coll) mucchio; **piles** emorroidi fpl || tr ammucchiare, accumulare; **to pile up** ammonticchiare || intr accumularsi; **to pile into** pigiarsi in; **to pile up** accumularsi

pile' driv'er s battipalo, berta

pilfer ['pɪlfər] tr & intr rubacchiare

pilgrim ['pɪlgrɪm] s pellegrino

pilgrimage ['pɪlgrɪmɪdʒ] s pellegrinaggio

pill [pɪl] s pillola; amara pillola; (coll) rompiscatole mf; **to sugar-coat the pill** addolcire la pillola

pillage ['pɪlɪdʒ] s saccheggio, rapina || tr & intr saccheggiare, rapinare

pillar ['pɪlər] s pilastro, colonna; **from pillar to post** da Erode a Pilato

pill'box' s scatoletta per le pillole; (mil) casamatta

pillo·ry ['pɪləri] s (-ries) gogna, berlina || v (pret & pp -ried) tr mettere alla berlina

pillow ['pɪlo] s cuscino, guanciale m

pil'low·case' s federa

pilot ['paɪlət] adj pilota || s pilota m; (of locomotive) respingente m || tr pilotare

pi'lot light' s fiammella automatica

pimp [pɪmp] s ruffiano, lenone m

pimple ['pɪmpəl] s bitorzolo

pim·ply ['pɪmpli] adj (-plier; -pliest) bitorzoluto

pin [pɪn] s (of metal) spillo; (peg) caviglia; (adornment) spilla; (linchpin) acciarino; (of key) mappa; (clothespin) molletta; (bowling pin) birillo; **to be on pins and needles** stare sulle spine || tr appuntare; (to hold) immobilizzare; **to pin s.o. down** forzare qlcu a rivelare i propri piani **to pin s.th on s.o.** (coll) dare la colpa a qlcu per qlco

pinafore ['pɪnə,for] s grembiulino

pinaster [paɪ'næstər] s pino marittimo

pin'ball machine' s biliardino

pince-nez ['pæns,ne] s occhiali mpl a stringinaso

pincers ['pɪnsərz] ssg or spl tenaglie fpl; (zool) pinze fpl

pinch [pɪntʃ] s (squeeze) pizzicotto; (of tobacco) presa; (of salt) pizzico; (hardship) strettoia; **in a pinch in caso di necessità** || tr stringere, pizzicare; (to press) comprimere; ridurre alle strettezze; (slang) rubare; (slang) arrestare || intr stringere; (to be stingy) fare l'avaro

pin'cush'ion s puntaspilli m

pine [paɪn] s pino || intr—**to pine away** struggersi; **to pine for** spasimare per

pine'ap'ple s ananas m

pine' cone' s pigna

pine' nee'dle s ago del pino

ping [pɪŋ] s rumore secco; rumore metallico || intr fare un rumore secco or metallico

pin'head' s capocchia di spillo; (slang) testa quadra

pin'hole' s forellino

pink [pɪŋk] adj rosa || s color m rosa; condizione perfetta; (bot) garofano || tr orlare a zig-zag; (to stab) perforare

pin' mon'ey s denaro per le piccole spese

pinnacle ['pɪnəkəl] s pinnacolo

pin'point' adj di precisione || s punta di spillo || tr mettere in rilievo

pin'prick' s puntura di spillo

pint [paɪnt] s pinta

pintle ['pɪntəl] s maschietto

pin'up' s pin-up-girl f

pin'wheel' s girandola

pioneer [,paɪə'nɪr] s pioniere m || tr aprire la via a || intr fare il pioniere

pioneering [,paɪə'nɪrɪŋ] adj pionieristico

pious ['paɪ·əs] adj pio, devoto

pip [pɪp] s (seed) seme m; (vet) pipita

pipe [paɪp] s tubo, canna; (of stove) cannone m; (for smoking) pipa; (mus) legno; (mus) cornamusa || tr suonare; cantare ad alta voce; fischiare; condurre in una tubatura; munire di tubatura || intr suonare la zampogna; **to pipe down** (slang) stare zitto

pipe' clean'er s scovolino

pipe' dream' s castello in aria

pipe' line' s oleodotto; (fig) fonte f (d'informazioni)

pipe' or'gan s organo a canne

piper ['paɪpər] s zampognaro; **to pay the piper** pagare lo scotto

pipe' wrench' s chiave f per tubi

piping ['paɪpɪŋ] adj (voice) acuto; (sound) di cornamusa || s tubatura; suono di cornamuse; suono acuto; (on cakes) fregio; (on garments) cordoncino ornamentale || *adv*—**piping hot** scottante, bollente

pippin ['pɪpɪn] *s* mela renetta; *(seed)* seme *m*; *(fig)* gran brava persona

piquant ['pikənt] *adj* piccante

pique [pik] *s* picca, ripicco || *tr* offendere, eccitare

pira·cy ['paɪrəsi] *s* (-**cies**) pirateria

pirate ['paɪrɪt] *s* pirata *mf* || *tr* derubare; *(a book)* svaligiare, pubblicare illegalmente || *intr* pirateggiare

pirouette [ˌpɪru'et] *s* piroetta || *intr* piroettare

Pisces ['paɪsiz] *or* ['pɪsiz] *s* (astr) Pesci *mpl*

pistol ['pɪstəl] *s* pistola

piston ['pɪstən] *s* pistone *m*

pis'ton displace'ment *s* cilindrata

pis'ton ring' *s* segmento elastico

pis'ton rod' *s* *(of a steam engine)* biella d'accoppiamento; *(of a motor)* asta del pistone, biella

pis'ton stroke' *s* corsa dello stantuffo

pit [pɪt] *s* *(in the ground)* buca; *(trap)* trappola; *(of fruit)* nocciolo; *(of stomach)* bocca; *(scar)* buttero; *(in exchange)* recinto delle grida; *(for fights)* arena; *(theat)* platea; *(min)* miniera; *(aut)* fossa di riparazione || *v* *(pret & pp* **pitted**; *ger* **pitting**) *tr* infossare; butterare; opporre; *(to remove pits from)* snocciolare

pitch [pɪtʃ] *s* *(black sticky substance)* pece *f*; *(throw)* lancio; *(of a roof)* pendenza, inclinazione; *(of a boat)* beccheggio; *(of a screw)* passo; *(of sound)* altezza || *tr* lanciare; *(a tent)* rizzare || *intr* beccheggiare; **to pitch in** (coll) mettersi al lavoro; (coll) cominciare a mangiare

pitch' ac'cent *s* accento di altezza

pitch' at'titude *s* assetto longitudinale

pitch'-dark' *adj* nero come la pece

pitched' bat'tle *s* battaglia campale

pitcher ['pɪtʃər] *s* brocca; (baseball) lanciatore *m*

pitch'fork' *s* forca, tridente *m*; **to rain pitchforks** (coll) piovere a dirotto

pitch' pipe' *s* (mus) corista *m*

pit'fall' *s* trappola, trabocchetto

pith [pɪθ] *s* midollo; *(strength)* (fig) forza; *(fig)* succo, essenza

pith·y ['pɪθi] *adj* (-**ier**; -**iest**) midolloso; succoso, essenziale

pitiful ['pɪtɪfəl] *adj* pietoso

pitiless ['pɪtɪlɪs] *adj* spietato

pit·y ['pɪti] *s* (-**ies**) pietà *f*; **it is a pity that** è un peccato che; **what a pity!** che peccato! || *v* *(pret & pp* -**ied**) *tr* aver pietà di

Pius ['paɪ·əs] *s* Pio

pivot ['pɪvət] *s* asse *m*, perno; *(fig)* asse *m* || *tr* imperniare || *intr* imperniarsi; **to pivot on** fare perno su; dipendere da

placard ['plækɑrd] *s* manifesto, affisso || *tr* affiggere

place [ples] *s* luogo; locale *m*; *(court)* piazzetta; *(short street)* vicolo; residenza; sito, luogo, località *f*; *(point)* punto; *(space occupied)* posto; *(office)* posto, impiego; **in no place**

da nessuna parte; **in place** a posto; **in place of** al posto di, invece di; **in the first place** in primo luogo; **in the next place** in secondo luogo; **to know one's place** saper stare al proprio posto; **to take place** aver luogo || *tr* piazzare, mettere; *(to find employment for)* collocare; *(to identify)* ravvisare || *intr* (sports) piazzarsi

place·bo [plə'sibo] *s* (-**bos** *or* -**boes**) rimedio fittizio

place' card' *s* segnaposto

placement ['plesmənt] *s* *(e.g., of furniture)* collocazione; *(employment)* collocamento

place' name' *s* toponimo

place' of busi'ness *s* ufficio, negozio

placid ['plæsɪd] *adj* placido

plagiarism ['pledʒəˌrɪzəm] *s* plagio

plagiarize ['pledʒəˌraɪz] *tr* plagiare

plague [pleg] *s* peste bubbonica; *(widespread affliction)* piaga, flagello || *tr* infestare, appestare; tormentare

plaid [plæd] *s* tessuto scozzese

plain [plen] *adj* piano; aperto; evidente, esplicito; semplice; *(undyed)* naturale; comune, ordinario; **in plain English** senz'ambagi; **in plain view** di fronte a tutti || *s* pianura

plain'-clothes' man' *s* (-**men**) agente *m* in borghese

plains'man *s* (-**men**) abitante *m* della pianura

plaintiff ['plentɪf] *s* querelante *mf*

plaintive ['plentɪv] *adj* lamentevole

plan [plæn] *s* piano, progetto || *v* *(pret & pp* **planned**; *ger* **planning**) *tr & intr* progettare

plane [plen] *adj* piano || *m* piano; *(tool)* pialla; (aer) aeroplano; (aer) ala d'aeroplano; (bot) platano || *tr* piallare || *intr* andare in areoplano

plane' sick'ness *s* male *m* d'aria

planet ['plænɪt] *s* pianeta *m*

plane' tree' *s* platano

plan'ing mill' *s* officina di piallatura

plank [plæŋk] *s* tavola, asse *m*; *(of political party)* piattaforma || *tr* coprire d'assi; cucinare sulla graticola e servire sul tagliere; **to plank down** *(e.g., money)* (coll) snocciolare

plant [plænt] *or* [plɑnt] *s* *(factory)* impianto, stabilimento; *(e.g., of a college)* complesso di edifici; (bot) pianta; (mach) apparato motore; (slang) trappola || *tr* *(e.g., a tree)* piantare; *(seeds)* seminare; *(to stock)* fornire

plantation [plæn'teʃən] *s* piantagione

planter ['plæntər] *s* piantatore *m*; (mach) piantatrice *f*

plaster ['plæstər] *or* ['plɑstər] *s* *(gypsum)* gesso; *(mixture to cover walls)* intonaco, malta; *(poultice)* impiastro || *tr* ingessare; intonacare; impiastrare; *(with posters)* affiggere, ricoprire

plas'ter·board' *s* cartone *m* di gesso

plas'ter cast' *s* (sculp) gesso; (surg) ingessatura

plas'ter of Par'is *s* gesso, stucco

plastic ['plæstɪk] *adj & s* plastico

plate 237 **plug**

plate [plet] *s* (*dish*) piatto; (*sheet of metal*) placca, piastra; (*thin sheet of metal*) placca; (*of auto license*) targa; (*of condenser*) armatura; (*tableware*) vasellame *m* d'argento, vasellame *m* d'oro; dentiera; (*baseball*) casa base; (phot) lastra; (typ) cliché *m* ‖ *tr* (with gold or silver) placcare; (with armor) blindare, corazzare

plateau [plæ'to] *s* altipiano

plate' glass' *s* lastrone *m*

platen ['plætən] *s* rullo

platform ['plæt‚fɔrm] *s* piattaforma; (*for speaker*) tribuna, palco; (*for passengers*) (rr) marciapiede *m*; (*at end of car*) (rr) piattaforma

plat'form car' *s* (rr) pianale *m*

platinum ['plætɪnəm] *s* platino

plat'inum blonde' *s* bionda platinata

platitude ['plætɪ‚tjud] or ['plætɪ‚tud] *s* trivialità *f*, banalità *f*

Plato ['pleto] *s* Platone *m*

platoon [plə'tun] *s* plotone *m*

platter ['plætər] *s* piatto di portata; (slang) disco di grammofono

plausible ['plɔzɪbəl] *adj* plausibile; (*person*) credibile, attendibile

play [ple] *s* gioco; libertà *f* d'azione; recreazione; turno, volta; (theat) dramma *m*; (mach) gioco ‖ *tr* giocare; giocare contro; causare, produrre; (*a drama*) rappresentare; (*a character*) fare la parte di; (*to wield*) esercitare; (mus) suonare; **to play back** (*e.g., a tape*) riprodurre; **to play down** diminuire l'importanza di; **to play one off against another** mettere uno contro l'altro; **to play up** dare importanza a ‖ *intr* giocare; (*to act*) giocare, comportarsi; (theat) recitare; (mus) suonare; (mach) aver gioco; **to play on** continuare a giocare; continuare a suonare; valersi di; **to play safe** non prendere rischi; **to play sick** fare il malato; **to play up to** fare la corte a

play'back' *s* riproduzione; apparechiatura di riproduzione

play'bill' *s* (theat) programma *m*

play'boy' *s* playboy *m*, gaudente *m*

player ['ple‑ər] *s* giocatore *m*; (theat) attore *m*; (mus) suonatore *m*

play'er pian'o *s* pianola

playful ['plefəl] *adj* giocoso

playgoer ['ple‚go‑ər] *s* frequentatore *m* del teatro

play'ground' *s* parco di ricreazione; (*resort*) posto di villeggiatura

play'house' *s* teatro; casa di bambole

play'ing card' ['ple‑ɪŋ] *s* carta da gioco

play'ing field' *s* campo da gioco

play'mate' *s* compagno di gioco

play'-off' *s* (sports) spareggio

play'pen' *s* recinto, box *m*

play'thing' *s* giocattolo

play'time' *s* ricreazione

playwright ['ple‚raɪt] *s* drammaturgo, commediografo

play'writ'ing *s* drammaturgia

plaza ['plæzə] or ['plɑzə] *s* piazzale *m*

plea [pli] *s* scusa; richiesta, domanda; (law) dichiarazione

plead [plid] *v* (*pret & pp* **pleaded** or **pled** [pled]) *tr* (*ignorance*) dichiarare; (*a case*) perorare ‖ *intr* supplicare; argomentare; **to plead guilty** dichiararsi colpevole

pleasant ['plɛzənt] *adj* piacevole; (*person*) simpatico

pleasant·ry ['plɛzəntri] *s* (-ries) facezia, motto

please [pliz] *tr* piacere (with *dat*) ‖ *intr* piacere; **as you please** come vuole; **if you please** per favore; **please** per cortesia; **to be pleased to** avere il piacere di; **to be pleased with** essere soddisfatto con; **to do as one pleases** fare come par e piace

pleasing ['plizɪŋ] *adj* piacevole

pleasure ['plɛʒər] *s* piacere *m*; desiderio; **what is your pleasure?** cosa desidera?

pleas'ure car' *s* vettura da turismo

pleat [plit] *s* piega ‖ *tr* piegare, pieghettare

plebeian [plɪ'bi‑ən] *adj & s* plebeo

plebiscite ['plɛbɪ‚saɪt] *s* plebiscito

pledge [plɛdʒ] *s* pegno; promessa; voto; (*person*) ostaggio; (*toast*) brindisi *m*; **as a pledge** in pegno; **to take the pledge** giurare d'astenersi dal bere ‖ *tr* dare in pegno; (*to bind*) far promettere a

plentiful ['plɛntɪfəl] *adj* abbondante

plenty ['plɛnti] *s* abbondanza ‖ *adv* (coll) abbastanza

pleurisy ['plʊrɪsi] *s* pleurite *f*

pliable ['plaɪ‑əbəl] *adj* flessibile, pieghevole; docile

pliers ['plaɪ‑ərz] *ssg* or *spl* pinze *fpl*

plight [plaɪt] *s* condizione or situazione precaria ‖ *tr*—**to plight one's troth** fidanzarsi

plod [plɑd] *v* (*pret & pp* **plodded;** *ger* **plodding**) *tr* percorrere pesantemente ‖ *intr* camminare pesantemente; (*to drudge*) sgobbare

plot [plɑt] *s* (*of ground*) appezzamento; (*of a play*) trama, intreccio; (*evil scheme*) cospirazione, trama ‖ *v* (*pret & pp* **plotted;** *ger* **plotting**) *tr* fare il piano di; macchinare; preparare la trama di; (aer, naut) fare il punto di ‖ *intr* tramare, cospirare

plover ['plʌvər] or ['plovər] *s* piviere *m*

plow [plau] *s* aratro; (*for snow*) spazzaneve *m* ‖ *tr* arare; (*e.g., water*) solcare; (*snow*) spazzare; **to plow back** reinvestire ‖ *intr* arare; aprirsi la via; camminare pesantemente

plow'man *s* (-men) aratore *m*; contadino

plow'share' *s* vomere *m*

pluck [plʌk] *s* strattone *m*; coraggio; (*giblets*) frattaglie *fpl* ‖ *tr* (*to snatch*) tirare; (*e.g., fruit*) svellere; (*a fowl*) spennare; (mus) pizzicare ‖ *intr* tirare; **to pluck up** farsi coraggio

pluck·y ['plʌki] *adj* (-ier; -iest) coraggioso

plug [plʌg] *s* tappo, zaffo; tavoletta di

tabacco; bocca da incendi; (elec) spina; (horse) (slang) ronzino; (slang) raccomandazione || v (pret & pp **plugged**; ger **plugging**) tr tappare, otturare; colpire; inserire; (slang) fare la pubblicità di; **to plug in** (elec) innestare, connettere || intr (coll) sgobbare

plum [plʌm] s (fruit) susina; (tree) susino; (slang) cosa bellissima; (slang) colpo di fortuna

plumage ['plumɪdʒ] s piumaggio

plumb [plʌm] adj appiombo || s piombino || adv appiombo; (coll) completamente || tr determinare la verticale col piombino; assodare

plumb' bob' s piombino

plumber ['plʌmər] s installatore m, idraulico

plumbing ['plʌmɪŋ] s impianto idraulico; mestiere m d'idraulico; sondaggio

plumb'ing fix'tures spl rubinetteria, impianti mpl sanitari

plumb' line' s filo a piombo

plum' cake' s panfrutto

plume [plum] s piuma; (tuft of feathers) pennacchio || tr coprire di piume; **to plume oneself on** piccarsi di; **to plume one's feathers** pulirsi le penne

plummet ['plʌmɪt] s piombino || intr cadere a piombo

plump [plʌmp] adj grassoccio, paffuto; franco || s caduta || adv francamente || intr cadere a piombo

plum' pud'ding s budino con uva passa

plum' tree' s susino

plunder ['plʌndər] s (act) saccheggio; (loot) bottino || tr & intr saccheggiare

plunge [plʌndʒ] s (fall) caduta; (dive) nuotata, tuffo || tr gettare; tuffare; (e.g., a knife) configgere || intr (to rush) precipitarsi; (to gamble) (coll) darsi al gioco; (fig) ripiombare

plunger ['plʌndʒər] s tuffatore m; (for clearing clogged drains) stura-lavandini m; (mach) stantuffo; (coll) giocatore temerario

plunk [plʌŋk] adv (coll) proprio; (coll) con un colpo secco || tr (coll) gettare; lasciar cadere; (mus) pizzicare || intr (coll) lasciarsi cadere

plural ['plurəl] adj & s plurale m

plus [plʌs] adj superiore; (elec) positivo; (coll) con lode || s più m; soprappiù m || prep più

plush [plʌʃ] adj di lusso || s peluche f, felpa

Plutarch ['plutɑrk] s Plutarco

Pluto ['pluto] s Plutone m

plutonium [plu'tonɪəm] s plutonio

ply [plaɪ] s (plies) spessore m; (layer) strato; (of rope) legnolo || v (pret & pp **plied**) tr (a trade) esercitare; (a tool) maneggiare; (to assail) premere, incalzare || intr lavorare assiduamente; **to ply between** fare la spola tra

ply'wood' s legno compensato

pneumatic [nju'mætɪk] or [nu'mætɪk] adj pneumatico

pneumat'ic drill' s martello perforatore or pneumatico

pneumonia [nju'monɪ·ə] or [nu'monɪ·ə] s polmonite f

poach [potʃ] tr (eggs) affogare || intr cacciare or pescare di frodo

poacher ['potʃər] s bracconiere m; pescatore m di frodo

pock [pɑk] s buttero

pocket ['pɑkɪt] adj tascabile || s tasca; (billiards) buca; (aer) vuoto; (min) deposito || tr intascare; (e.g., one's pride) ingoiare

pock'et-book' s portafoglio; (woman's purse) borsetta

pock'et book' s libro tascabile

pock'et-hand'kerchief s fazzoletto

pock'et-knife' s (-knives) temperino

pock'et mon'ey s spiccioli mpl

pock'mark' s buttero

pod [pɑd] s baccello; (aer) contenitore m

poem ['po·ɪm] s poesia; (of some length) poema m

poet ['po·ɪt] s poeta m

poetess ['po·ɪtɪs] s poetessa

poetic [po'ɛtɪk] adj poetico || **poetics** ssg poetica

poetry ['po·ɪtri] s poesia

pogrom ['pogrəm] s pogrom m

poignancy ['pɔɪnjənsi] or ['pɔɪnənsi] s strazio; intensità f

poignant ['pɔɪnjənt] or ['pɔɪnənt] adj straziante; intenso

point [pɔɪnt] s (sharp end) punta; (something essential) essenziale m; (hint) suggerimento; (dot, decimal point, spot, degree, instant, position of compass) punto; (coll) costrutto; **beside the point** fuori del seminato; **in point of** per quanto concerne; **to come to the point** venire al sodo; **to get the point** capire l'antifona; **to make a point of** dar importanza a; insistere di; **to stretch a point** fare un'eccezione, fare uno strappo alla regola; **to the point** a proposito || tr (e.g., a weapon) puntare; (to sharpen) aguzzare; (to dot) punteggiare; (to give force to) dare enfasi a; (with mortar) rinzaffare || intr puntare; **to point at** puntare il dito a; **to point to** mostrare a dito

point'blank' adj & adv a bruciapelo

pointed ['pɔɪntɪd] adj appuntito; personale, diretto, acuto

pointer ['pɔɪntər] s (rod) bacchetta; indice m, indicatore m; cane m da punta, pointer m; (coll) direttiva

poise [pɔɪz] s equilibrio, stabilità f; dignità f || tr equilibrare || intr equilibrarsi, stare in equilibrio

poison ['pɔɪzən] s veleno || tr avvelenare

poi'son i'vy s edera del Canada, tossicodendro

poisonous ['pɔɪzənəs] adj velenoso

poke [pok] s spinta, urto; (with elbow) gomitata; (slang) polentone m || tr (to prod) spingere, urtare; (the head) sporgere; (the fire) attizzare; **to poke fun at** burlarsi di; **to poke one's nose into** ficcare il naso in || intr (to jab) urtare; (to thrust oneself) ficcarsi; (to pry) ficcare il naso; **to poke around** gironzolare; **to poke out** spuntare, protrudere

poker ['pokər] s (game) poker m; (bar) attizzatoio

pok'er face' s faccia impassibile

pok·y ['poki] adj (-ier; -iest) (coll) lento; (coll) meschino, modesto || (-ies) s (slang) gattabuia

Poland ['polənd] s la Polonia

po'lar bear' ['polər] s orso bianco

polarize ['polə‚raɪz] tr polarizzare

pole [pol] s palo; (long rod) pertica; (of wagon) timone m; (for jumping) asta; (astr, biol, elec, geog, math) polo || tr (a boat) spingere con un palo || intr spingere una barca con un palo || **Pole** s polacco

pole'cat' s puzzola

pole' lamp' s lampada a stelo

pole'star' s stella polare

pole' vault' s salto coll'asta

police [pə'lis] s polizia || tr vigilare, proteggere; (mil) pulire

police'man s (-men) agente m di polizia, vigile urbano

police' state' s governo poliziesco

police' sta'tion s commissariato di polizia

poli·cy ['palɪsi] s (-cies) politica; (ins) polizza

polio ['polɪ‚o] s (coll) polio f

polish ['palɪʃ] s lustro, lucentezza; (for shoes or furniture) cera; (fig) raffinatezza, eleganza || tr pulire; (e.g., a stone) levigare; **to polish off** (slang) finire; **to polish up** (slang) migliorare || intr pulirsi; diventar lucido || **Polish** ['polɪʃ] adj & s polacco

polisher ['palɪʃər] s lucidatore m; (mach) lucidatrice f

polite [pə'laɪt] adj raffinato, cortese

politeness [pə'laɪtnɪs] s cortesia

politic ['palɪtɪk] adj prudente; (expedient) diplomatico

political [pə'lɪtɪkəl] adj politico

politician [‚palɪ'tɪʃən] s politico; (pej) politicante m, politicastro

politics ['palɪtɪks] ssg or spl politica

poll [pol] s votazione; (registering of votes) scrutinio; lista elettorale; (analysis of public opinion) referendum m, sondaggio; (head) testa; **to go to the polls** andare alle urne; **to take a poll** fare un'inchiesta || tr ricevere i voti di; contare i voti di; (a tree) potare; fare un'inchiesta di

pollen ['palən] s polline m

pollinate ['palɪ‚net] tr fecondare col polline

poll'ing booth' ['polɪŋ] s cabina elettorale

polliwog ['palɪ‚wag] s girino

poll' tax' s capitazione

pollute [pə'lut] tr insudiciare; (to defile) desecrare, profanare; (e.g., the environment) inquinare, contaminare

pollution [pə'luʃən] s inquinamento, contaminazione

poll' watch'er s rappresentante m di lista

polo ['polo] s polo

po'lo play'er s giocatore m di polo, polista m

po'lo shirt' s maglietta, polo

polygamist [pə'lɪgəmɪst] s poligamo

polygamous [pə'lɪgəməs] adj poligamo

polyglot ['palɪ‚glat] adj & s poliglotto

polygon ['palɪ‚gan] s poligono

polynomial [‚palɪ'nomɪ‚əl] adj polinomiale || s polinomio

polyp ['palɪp] s (pathol, zool) polipo

polytheist ['palɪ‚θiɪst] s politeista mf

polytheistic [‚palɪθi'ɪstɪk] adj politeistico

pomade [pə'med] or [pə'mad] s pomata

pomegranate ['pam‚grænɪt] s (shrub) melograno; (fruit) melagrana

pom·mel ['pʌməl] or ['paməl] s (of sword) pomello; (of saddle) arcione m || v (pret & pp -meled or -melled; ger -meling or -melling) tr prendere a pugni

pomp [pamp] s pompa

pompadour ['pampə‚dor] or ['pampə‚dur] s acconciatura a ciuffo

pompous ['pampəs] adj pomposo

pon·cho ['pant∫o] s (-chos) poncho

pond [pand] s stagno

ponder ['pandər] tr & intr ponderare; **to ponder over** pensare sopra

ponderous ['pandərəs] adj ponderoso

poniard ['panjərd] s pugnale m

pontiff ['pantɪf] s pontefice m

pontifical [pan'tɪfɪkəl] adj pontificale

pontoon [pan'tun] s (boat) chiatta, pontone m; (aer) galleggiante m

po·ny ['poni] s (-nies) pony m; (glass and drink) bicchierino; (for cheating) (slang) bigino

poodle ['pudəl] s barbone m, cane m barbone

pool [pul] s (pond) stagno; (puddle) pozza; (for swimming) piscina; (game) biliardo; (com) cartello, consorzio; (com) fondo comune || tr mettere in un fondo comune || intr formare un cartello or un consorzio

pool'room' s sala da biliardo

pool' ta'ble s tavolo da biliardo

poop [pup] s poppa; (deck) casseretto

poor [pur] adj povero; (inferior) scadente || **the poor** spl i poveri

poor' box' s cassetta per l'elemosina

poor'house' s asilo dei poveri

poorly ['purli] adv male

pop [pap] s scoppio; (soda) gazzosa || v (pret & pp popped; ger popping) tr far scoppiare; **to pop the question** (coll) fare la domanda di matrimonio || intr esplodere con fragore; **to pop in** fare una capatina, entrare all'improvviso

pop'corn' s pop-corn m

pope [pop] s papa m

popeyed ['pap‚aɪd] adj con gli occhi sporgenti; con gli occhi fuori dalle orbite

pop'gun' s fucile m ad aria compressa

poplar ['paplər] s pioppo

pop·py ['papi] s (-pies) papavero

pop'py·cock' s (coll) scemenza

popsicle ['pɑpsɪkəl] s (trademark) gelato da passeggio

populace ['pɑpjələs] s gente f, popolino

popular ['pɑpjələr] adj popolare

popularize ['pɑpjələ‚raɪz] tr divulgare, volgarizzare

populate ['pɑpjə‚let] tr popolare

population [‚pɑpjə'leʃən] s popolazione

populous ['pɑpjələs] adj popoloso

porcelain ['pɔrsəlɪn] or ['pɔrslɪn] s porcellana

porch [pɔrtʃ] s portico

porcupine ['pɔrkjə‚paɪn] s (Hystrix cristata) istrice m & f, porcospino; (Erethizon dorsatum) ursone m, porcospino americano

pore [pɔr] s poro || intr—to pore over studiare minutamente

pork [pɔrk] s carne f di maiale

pork' butch'er shop' s salumeria

pork'chop' s cotoletta di maiale

porous ['pɔrəs] adj poroso

po'rous plas'ter s cataplasma m

porphy•ry ['pɔrfɪri] s (-ries) porfido

porpoise ['pɔrpəs] s focena; (dolphin) delfino

porridge ['pɑrɪdʒ] or ['pɔrɪdʒ] s pappa, farinata

port [pɔrt] adj portuario || s (harbor; wine) porto; (naut) babordo, sinistra; (opening in side of ship) portello; (round opening) (naut) oblò m

portable ['pɔrtəbəl] adj portabile

portal ['pɔrtəl] s portale m

portend [pɔr'tɛnd] tr presagire

portent ['pɔrtɛnt] s presagio

portentous [pɔr'tɛntəs] adj sinistro, funesto, premonitore; (amazing) portentoso

porter ['pɔrtər] s (doorman) portiere m; (man who carries luggage) facchino; (of a sleeper) conduttore m; (in a store) inserviente mf; (beverage) birra scura e amara

portfoli•o [pɔrt'folɪ‚o] s (-os) cartella; (office; holdings) portafoglio

port'hole' s (opening in side of ship) portello; (round opening) (naut) oblò m

porti•co ['pɔrtɪ‚ko] s (-cos or -coes) portico

portion ['pɔrʃən] s porzione; (dowry) dote f || tr—to portion out dividere, ripartire

port•ly ['pɔrtli] adj (-lier; -liest) obeso, corpulento

port' of call' s scalo

portrait ['pɔrtret] or ['pɔrtrɪt] s ritratto

portray [pɔr'tre] tr ritrarre

portrayal [pɔr'tre‚əl] s delineazione; ritratto

Portugal ['pɔrtʃəgəl] s il Portogallo

Portu•guese ['pɔrtʃə‚giz] adj portoghese || s (-guese) portoghese mf

pose [poz] s posa || tr (a question) avanzare; (a model) mettere in posa || intr posare; **to pose as** posare a, atteggiarsi a

posh [pɑʃ] adj (coll) di lusso

position [pə'zɪʃən] s posizione; rango; impiego, posto; **to be in a position to** essere in grado di

positive ['pɑzɪtɪv] adj positivo || s positivo; (phot) positiva

possess [pə'zɛs] tr possedere

possession [pə'zɛʃən] s possedimento; (of mental faculties) possesso; **possessions** (wealth) beni mpl

possessive [pə'zɛsɪv] adj possessivo; (e.g., mother) opprimente, soffocante

possible ['pɑsɪbəl] adj possibile

possum ['pɑsəm] s opossum m; **to play possum** (coll) fare il morto

post [post] s (mail) posta; (pole) palo; (in horse racing) linea di partenza; posizione, rango; (job) posto; (mil) presidio || tr mettere in una lista; impostare; tenere al corrente; **post no bills** divieto d'affissione

postage ['postɪdʒ] s affrancatura

post'age me'ter s affrancatrice f

post'age stamp' s francobollo

postal ['postəl] adj postale

post'al card' s cartolina postale

pos'tal per'mit s abbonamento postale

post'al sav'ings bank' s cassa di risparmio postale

post'al scale' s pesalettere m

post' card' s cartolina illustrata; cartolina postale

post'date' tr postdatare

poster ['postər] s cartellone m, manifesto pubblicitario

posterity [pɑs'tɛrɪti] s posterità f

postern ['postərn] adj posteriore || s posteriela

post' exchange' s spaccio militare

post'haste' adv al più presto possibile

posthumous ['pɑst‚uməs] adj postumo

post'man s (-men) portalettere m

post'mark' s bollo, timbro postale || tr bollare, timbrare

post'mas'ter s ricevitore m postale

post'master gen'eral s (postmasters general) ministro delle poste

post-mortem ['post'mɔrtəm] adj postumo || s autopsia

post' of'fice s ufficio postale

post'-office box' s casella postale

postpaid ['post‚ped] adj franco di porto

postpone [post'pon] tr differire, posporre

postscript ['post‚skrɪpt] s poscritto

postulant ['pɑstʃələnt] s postulatore m, postulante mf

posture ['pɑstʃər] s portamento; posa || intr posare

post'war' adj del dopoguerra

po•sy ['pozi] s (-sies) fiore m; (nosegay) mazzolino di fiori

pot [pɑt] s pentola, pignatta; pitale m, orinale m; (in gambling) (coll) piatto; **to go to pot** andare a gambe all'aria

potash ['pɑt‚æʃ] s potassa

potassium [pə'tæsɪ‚əm] s potassio

pota•to [pə'teto] s (-toes) patata

pota'to om'elet s omelette f con patate

potbellied ['pɑt‚belɪd] adj panciuto

poten•cy ['potənsi] s (-cies) potenza

potent ['potənt] adj potente

potentate ['potən,tet] s potentato
potential [pə'tenʃəl] adj & s potenziale m
pot'hold'er s patta, presa
pot'hook' s uncino
potion ['poʃən] s pozione
pot'luck' s—**to take potluck** mangiare quello che passa il convento
pot' shot' s colpo sparato a casaccio
potter ['patər] s vasaio
pot'ter's clay' s argilla per stoviglie
pot'ter's field' s cimitero dei poveri
potter·y ['patəri] s (-ies) vasellame m; fabbrica di vasellame; ceramica
pouch |pautʃ] s sacchetto, borsa; (of kangaroo) borsa
poultice ['poltis] s cataplasma m
poultry ['poltri] s pollame m
poul'try·man s (-men) pollivendolo
pounce [pauns] intr—**to pounce on** balzare su
pound ['paund] s libbra; lira sterlina; (for stray animals) recinto || tr battere, picchiare; tempestare di colpi; (to crush) polverizzare || intr battere
pound' cake' s dolce m fatto con una libbra di burro, una di zucchero ed una di farina
pound' ster'ling s lira sterlina
pour [por] tr versare; (e.g., tea) servire; (wine) mescere; (stones upon an enemy) far piovere || intr fluire; (to rain) diluviare; **to pour in** affluire; **to pour out** uscire in massa
pout [paut] s broncio || intr tenere il broncio
poverty ['pavərti] s povertà f
POW ['pi'o'dʌbl ,ju] s (letterword) (prisoner of war) prigioniero di guerra
powder ['paudər] s polvere f; (for the face) cipria; (med) polverina || tr incipriare; (to sprinkle with powder) spolverizzare
pow'dered sug'ar s zucchero in polvere
pow'der puff' s piumino
pow'der room' s toletta
powdery ['paudəri] adj polveroso; fragile; (snow) farinoso
power ['pau·ər] s (ability, authority) potere m; forza, energia; (nation) potenza; (math, phys) potenza; **in power** al potere; **the powers that be** i potenti || tr azionare
pow'er·boat' s barca a motore
pow'er brake' s (aut) servofreno
pow'er com'pany s compagnia di elettricità
pow'er drive' s picchiata
powerful ['pau·ərfəl] adj poderoso
pow'er·house' s centrale elettrica
powerless ['pau·ərlis] adj impotente
pow'er line' s elettrodotto
pow'er mow'er s motofalciatrice f
pow'er of attor'ney s procura legale
pow'er plant' s stazione f generatrice; (aut) gruppo motore
pow'er steer'ing s servosterzo
pow'er tool' s apparecchiatura a motore
pow'er vac'uum s vuoto di potere
practical ['præktikəl] adj pratico

prac'tical joke' s scherzo da prete
practically ['præktikəli] adv (in a practical manner; virtually, really) praticamente; più o meno, quasi
practice ['præktis] s pratica; (of a profession) esercizio; (e.g., of a doctor) clientela; (process of doing something) prassi f; (habitual performance) abitudine f || tr praticare, esercitare || intr esercitarsi, praticare; (to be active in a profession) esercitare; **to practice as** esercitare la professione di
practitioner [præk'tiʃənər] s professionista mf
Prague [prag] or [preg] s Praga
prairie ['preri] s prateria
prai'rie dog' s cinomio
prai'rie wolf' s coyote m
praise [prez] s lode f, elogio || tr lodare, elogiare; **to praise to the skies** levare alle stelle
praise'wor'thy adj lodevole
pram [præm] s (coll) carrozzella
prance [præns] or [prɑns] s caracollo || intr caracollare; (to caper) ballonzolare
prank [præŋk] s burla, tiro
prate [pret] intr cianciare
prattle ['prætəl] s ciancia, chiacchierio || intr cianciare, parlare a vanvera
pray [pre] tr & intr pregare
prayer [prer] s preghiera
prayer' book' s libro di preghiere
preach [pritʃ] tr & intr predicare
preacher ['pritʃər] s predicatore m
preamble ['pri,æmbəl] s preambolo
precarious [pri'keri·əs] adj precario
precaution [pri'koʃən] s precauzione
precede [pri'sid] tr & intr precedere
precedent ['presidənt] s precedente m
precept ['prisept] s precetto
precinct ['prisiŋkt] s distretto; circoscrizione elettorale; **precincts** dintorni mpl
precious ['preʃəs] adj prezioso || adv— **precious little** (coll) molto poco
precipice ['presipis] s precipizio
precipitate [pri'sipi,tet] adj precipitoso || s precipitato || tr & intr precipitare
precipitous [pri'sipitəs] adj precipitoso, a precipizio
precise [pri'sais] adj preciso
precision [pri'siʒən] s precisione
preclude [pri'klud] tr precludere; escludere
precocious [pri'koʃəs] adj precoce
predatory ['predə,tori] adj da preda, predatore
predicament [pri'dikəmənt] s situazione critica or imbarazzante
predict [pri'dikt] tr predire
prediction [pri'dikʃən] s predizione
predispose [,pridis'poz] tr predisporre
predominant [pri'dɑminənt] adj predominante
preeminent [pri'eminənt] adj preminente
preempt [pri'empt] tr occupare or acquistare in precedenza
preen [prin] tr (feathers, fur) lisciarsi;

to preen oneself agghindarsi, attillarsi

prefabricate [pri'fæbri,ket] *tr* prefabbricare

preface ['prɛfɪs] *s* prefazione ‖ *tr* prefazionare; essere la prefazione di

pre-fer [prɪ'fʌr] *v* (*pret & pp* **-ferred;** *ger* **-ferring**) *tr* preferire; (*to advance*) promuovere; (*law*) presentare, avanzare

preferable ['prɛfərəbəl] *adj* preferibile

preference ['prɛfərəns] *s* preferenza

preferred' stock' *s* azioni *fpl* privilegiate

prefix ['prifɪks] *s* prefisso ‖ *tr* prefiggere

pregnan·cy ['prɛgnənsi] *s* (**-cies**) gravidanza

pregnant ['prɛgnənt] *adj* incinta, gravida; (fig) gravido

prehistoric [,prihɪs'tɑrɪk] or [,prihɪs-'tɔrɪk] *adj* preistorico

prejudice ['prɛdʒədɪs] *s* pregiudizio; preconcetto; **without prejudice** senza detrimento ‖ *tr* (*to harm*) pregiudicare; predisporre; **to prejudice against** prevenire contro

prejudicial ['prɛdʒə'dɪ/əl] *adj* pregiudizievole

prelate ['prɛlɪt] *s* prelato

preliminar·y [prɪ'lɪmɪ,nɛri] *adj* preliminare ‖ *s* (**-ies**) preliminare *m*

prelude ['prɛljud] or ['prɪlud] *s* preludio ‖ *tr* preludere a ‖ *intr* preludere

premeditate [pri'mɛdɪ,tet] *tr* premeditare

premier [prɪ'mɪr] or ['primɪ·ər] *s* primo ministro, presidente *m* del consiglio

premiere [prə'mjɛr or [prɪ'mɪr] *s* prima; prima attrice

premise ['prɛmɪs] *s* premessa; **on the premises** nella proprietà, sul luogo; **premises** proprietà *f*

premium ['primɪ·əm] *s* premio; **at a premium** in gran richiesta; **a prezzo altissimo**

premonition [,primə'nɪ/ən] *s* presentimento; indizio

preoccupation [pri,ɑkjə'pe/ən] *s* preoccupazione

preoccu·py [pri'ɑkjə,paɪ] *v* (*pret & pp* **-pied**) *tr* preoccupare; (*to occupy beforehand*) occupare prima

prepaid [pri'ped] *adj* pagato in anticipo; franco di porto

preparation [,prɛpə're/ən] *s* preparazione; (*for a trip*) preparativo; (pharm) preparato

preparatory [prɪ'pærə,tori] *adj* preparatorio

prepare [prɪ'pɛr] *tr* preparare ‖ *intr* prepararsi

preparedness [prɪ'pɛrɪdnəs] or [prɪ-'pɛrdnɪs] *s* preparazione; preparazione militare

pre·pay [pri'pe] *v* (*pret & pp* **-paid**) *tr* pagare anticipatamente

preponderant [prɪ'pɑndərənt] *adj* preponderante

preposition [,prɛpə'zɪ/ən] *s* preposizione

prepossessing [,pripə'zɛsɪŋ] *adj* simpatico, attraente, piacevole

preposterous [prɪ'pɑstərəs] *adj* assurdo, ridicolo

prep' school' [prɛp] *s* (coll) scuola preparatoria

prerecorded [,priri'kɔrdɪd] *adj* (rad & telv) a registrazione differita

prerequisite [pri'rɛkwɪzɪt] *s* requisito

prerogative [prɪ'rɑgətɪv] *s* prerogativa

presage ['prɛsɪdʒ] *s* presagio ‖ [prɪ-'sɛdʒ] *tr* presagire

Presbyterian [,prɛzbɪ'tɪrɪ·ən] *adj & s* presbiteriano; Presbiteriano

prescribe [prɪ'skraɪb] *tr & intr* prescrivere

prescription [prɪ'skrɪp/ən] *s* prescrizione; (pharm) ricetta

presence ['prɛzəns] *s* presenza; **in the presence of** alla presenza di

present ['prɛzənt] *adj* presente ‖ *s* presente *m*, regalo ‖ [prɪ'zɛnt] *tr* presentare; **present arms!** presentat'arm!; **to present s.o. with s.th** regalare qlco a qlcu

presentable [prɪ'zɛntəbəl] *adj* presentabile

presentation [,prɛzən'te/ən] or [,prizən'te/ən] *s* presentazione; (theat) rappresentazione

presenta'tion cop'y *s* copia d'omaggio

presentiment [prɪ'zɛntɪmənt] *s* presentimento

presently ['prɛzəntli] *adv* fra poco; attualmente

preserve [prɪ'zʌrv] *s* (*for hunting*) riserva; **preserves** conserva, marmellata ‖ *tr* preservare; conservare

preserved' fruit' *s* frutta in conserva

preside [prɪ'zaɪd] *intr* presiedere; **to preside over** presiedere, presiedere a

presiden·cy ['prɛzɪdənsi] *s* (**-cies**) presidenza

president ['prɛzɪdənt] *s* presidente *m*; (*of a university*) rettore *m*

press [prɛs] *s* pressione; (*crowd*) folla; (*closet*) armadio; (mach) pressa; (typ) stampa; **to go to press** andare in macchina ‖ *tr* (*to push*) spingere, premere; (*to squeeze*) spremere; (*to embrace*) abbracciare; forzare; costringere; urgere, sollecitare; (*to iron*) stirare ‖ *intr* premere; avanzare

press' a'gent *s* agente pubblicitario

press' con'ference *s* conferenza stampa

pressing ['prɛsɪŋ] *adj* pressante, urgente ‖ *s* (*of records*) incisione

press' release' *s* comunicato stampa

pressure ['prɛ/ər] *s* pressione; tensione, urgenza ‖ *tr* pressare, incalzare con insistenza

pres'sure cook'er ['kʊkər] *s* pentola a pressione

pressurize ['prɛ/ə,raɪz] *tr* pressurizzare

prestige [prɛs'tiʒ] or ['prɛstɪdʒ] *s* prestigio

prestigious [prɛ'stɪdʒɪ·əs] or [prɛ-'stɪdʒəs] *adj* onorato, stimato

presumably [prɪ'zuməbli] or [prɪ'zjuməbli] *adv* presumibilmente

presume [prɪ'zum] or [prɪ'zjum] *tr* presumere; **to presume to** prendersi la libertà di || *intr* assumere; **to presume on** or **upon** abusare di

presumption [prɪˈzʌmp/ən] *s* presunzione; supposizione

presumptuous [prɪˈzʌmpt/u-əs] *adj* presuntuoso

presuppose [ˌprisəˈpoz] *tr* presupporre

pretend [prɪˈtend] *tr* fingere, fare finta di || *intr* fingere; **to pretend to** (*e.g., the throne*) pretendere a

pretender |prɪˈtendər| *s* pretendente *mf;* impostore *m*

pretense [prɪˈtens] or [ˈpritɛns] *s* pretesa; finzione; **under false pretenses** allegando ragioni false; **under pretense of** sotto l'apparenza di

pretentious [prɪˈtɛn/əs] *adj* pretenzioso

preterit |ˈprɛtərɪt| *adj* passato, preterito || *s* passato remoto, preterito

pretext |ˈpritɛkst| *s* pretesto

pretonic [priˈtɑnɪk] *adj* pretonico

pret·ty |ˈprɪti| *adj* (**-tier; -tiest**) grazioso, arino; (*e.g., sum of money*) (coll) bello || *adv* abbastanza; molto; **sitting pretty** (slang) ben messo

prevail [prɪˈvel] *intr* prevalere; **to prevail on** or **upon** persuadere

prevailing [prɪˈvelɪŋ] *adj* prevalente

prevalent |ˈprɛvələnt| *adj* comune

prevaricate [prɪˈværɪˌket] *intr* mentire

prevent [prɪˈvent] *tr* impedire; **to prevent from** + *ger* impedire (with *dat*) di + *inf* or che + *subj*

prevention [prɪˈvɛn/ən] *s* prevenzione

preventive [prɪˈventɪv] *adj* preventivo || *s* rimedio preventivo

preview [ˈpriˌvju] *s* indizio; (*private showing*) (mov) anteprima; (*showing of brief scenes for advertising*) (mov) scene *fpl* di prossima programmazione

previous [ˈprivi·əs] *adj* previo, precedente || *adv* precedentemente; **previous to** prima di

prewar [ˈpriˌwɔr] *adj* anteguerra

prey [pre] *s* preda; **to be prey to** essere preda di || *intr* predare; **to prey on** or **upon** predare, sfruttare; preoccupare

price [praɪs] *s* prezzo; **at any price** a qualunque costo || *tr* chiedere il prezzo di; fissare il prezzo di

price′ control′ *s* calmiere *m*

price′ cut′ting *s* riduzione di prezzo

price′ fix′ing *s* regolamento dei prezzi

price′ freez′ing *s* congelamento dei prezzi

priceless [ˈpraɪslɪs] *adj* inestimabile; (coll) molto divertente

price′ list′ *s* listino prezzi

price′ tag′ *s* cartellino del prezzo

price′ war′ *s* guerra dei prezzi

prick [prɪk] *s* punta; puntura; **to kick against the pricks** tirare calci al vento || *tr* bucare, forare; pungere; (*to goad*) spronare; (*the ears*) ergere; (*said, e.g., of the conscience*) rimordere (with *dat*)

prick·ly [ˈprɪkli] *adj* (**-lier; -liest**) spinoso, pungente

prick′ly heat′ *s* sudamina

prick′ly pear′ *s* ficodindia *m*

pride [praɪd] *s* orgoglio; arroganza; **the**

pride of il fiore di || *tr*—**to pride oneself on** or **upon** inorgoglırsi di

priest [prist] *s* prete *m,* sacerdote *m*

priesthood [ˈpristˌhud] *s* sacerdozio

priest·ly [ˈpristli] *adj* (**-lier; -liest**) sacerdotale

prig [prɪg] *s* pedante *mf,* moralista *mf*

prim [prɪm] *adj* (**primmer; primmest**) formale, corretto, compito

prima·ry [ˈpraɪˌmeri] or [ˈpraɪmərɪ] *adj* primario || *s* (**-ries**) elezione preferenziale; (elec) bobina primaria; (elec) primario

prime [praɪm] *adj* primo; originale; di prima qualità || *s* (*earliest part*) inizio; (*best period*) fiore *m;* (*choicest part*) fior fiore *m;* (math) numero primo; (*mark*) (math) primo || *tr* preparare; (*a pump*) adescare; (*a firearm*) innescare; (*a canvas*) mesticare; (*a wall*) dare la prima mano a; (*to supply with information*) istruire

prime′ min′ister *s* primo ministro

primer [ˈpraɪmər] *s* sillabario, abbecedario || [ˈpraɪmər] *s* innesco, detonatore *m*

primeval [praɪˈmivəl] *adj* primordiale

primitive [ˈprɪmɪtɪv] *adj* primitivo

primp [prɪmp] *tr* agghindare || *intr* agghindarsi

prim′rose′ *s* primula

prim′rose path′ *s* sentiero dei piaceri

prince [prɪns] *s* principe *m;* **to live like a prince** vivere da principe

prince′ roy′al *s* principe ereditario

princess |ˈprɪnsɪs| *s* principessa

principal |ˈprɪnsɪpəl| *adj* principale || *s* (*chief*) padrone *m,* principale *m;* (*of school*) direttore *m,* preside *m;* (*actor*) primo attore; (com) capitale *m;* (law) mandante *mf*

principle |ˈprɪnsɪpəl| *s* principio; **on principle** per principio

print [prɪnt] *s* stampa; (*cloth*) tessuto stampato; (*printed matter*) stampato; (*newsprint*) giornale *m;* (*mark made by one's thumb*) impronta; (phot) positiva; **in print** stampato; disponibile; **out of print** esaurito || *tr* stampare, tirare; (*to write in print*) scrivere in stampatello; (*in the memory*) imprimere

print′ed cir′cuit *s* circuito stampato

print′ed mat′ter *s* stampati *mpl*

printer [ˈprɪntər] *s* stampatore *m;* (*of computer*) tabulatrice *f*

print′er's dev′il *s* apprendista *m* tipografo

print′er's ink′ *s* inchiostro da stampa

printing [ˈprɪntɪŋ] *s* stampa; stampato; tiratura, edizione; (*writing in printed letters*) stampatello

prior [ˈpraɪ·ər] *adj* anteriore, precedente || *s* priore *m* || *adv* prima; **prior to** prima di

prior·ty [praɪˈɑrɪti] or [praɪˈɔrɪti] *s* (**-ties**) priorità *f*

prism [ˈprɪzəm] *s* prisma *m*

prison [ˈprɪzən] *s* prigione, carcere *m*

prisoner [ˈprɪzənər] or [ˈprɪznər] *s* prigioniero

pris′on van′ *s* furgone *m* cellulare

pris·sy ['prɪsɪ] *adj* (-sier; -siest) sman-
ceroso, smorfioso
priva·cy ['praɪvəsɪ] *s* (-cies) ritiro; segreto; **to have no privacy** non esser
mai lasciato in pace
private ['praɪvɪt] *adj* privato, personale
|| *s* soldato semplice; **in private** pri-
vatamente; **privates** pudende *fpl*
pri'vate eye' *s* poliziotto privato
pri'vate first' class' *s* soldato scelto
pri'vate hos'pital *s* clinica
priv'ate view'ing *s* (mov) anteprima;
(painting) vernice *f*
privet ['prɪvɪt] *s* ligustro
privilege ['prɪvɪlɪdʒ] *s* privilegio
priv·y ['prɪvɪ] *adj* privato; **privy to**
segretamente a conoscenza di || *s*
(-ies) latrina
prize [praɪz] *s* premio; (nav) preda ||
tr valutare, stimare
prize' fight' *s* incontro di pugilato
prize' fight'er *s* pugile *m*, pugilista *m*
prize' ring' *s* ring *m*, quadrato
pro [pro] *s* (**pros**) pro; voto favorevole; argomento favorevole; (coll)
professionista *m;* **the pros and the
cons** il pro e il contro
probabili·ty [,prɑbə'bɪlɪtɪ] *s* (-ties)
probabilità *f*
probable ['prɑbəbəl] *adj* probabile
probate ['probet] *s* omologazione di
un testamento; copia autentica di un
testamento || *tr* (*a will*) omologare
probation [pro'beʃən] *s* prova; periodo
di prova; (law) condizionale *f*, libertà
vigilata; (educ) provvedimento disciplinare
probe [prob] *s* inchiesta; (surg) sonda
|| *tr* indagare; sondare
problem ['prɑbləm] *s* problema *m*
procedure [pro'sidʒər] *s* procedura
proceed ['prosid] *s*—**proceeds** provento
|| [pro'sid] *intr* procedere
proceeding [pro'sidɪŋ] *s* procedimento;
proceedings atti *mpl*; (law) procedi-
menti *mpl*
process ['proses] *s* processo; **in the
process of time** in processo di tempo
|| *tr* trattare
procession [pro'seʃən] *s* processione
proc'ess serv'er *s* ufficiale giudiziario
proclaim [pro'klem] *tr* proclamare
proclitic [pro'klɪtɪk] *adj* proclitico ||
s parola proclitica
procrastinate [pro'kræstɪ,net] *tr & intr*
procrastinare
procure [pro'kjur] *tr* ottenere || *intr*
ruffianeggiare
prod [prɑd] *s* pungolo, stimolo || *v*
(*pret & pp* **prodded;** *ger* **prodding**)
tr stimolare, pungolare, incitare
prodigal ['prɑdɪgəl] *adj & s* prodigo
prodigious [pro'dɪdʒəs] *adj* prodigioso
prodi·gy ['prɑdɪdʒɪ] *s* (-gies) prodigio
produce ['prodjus] *or* ['prodʌs] *s* pro-
duzione; prodotti *mpl* agricoli || [pro-
'djus] *or* [pro'dus] *tr* produrre;
(theat) presentare
producer [pro'djusər] *or* [pro'dusər] *s*
produttore *m;* (*of a play*) impresario;
(mov) produttore *m*
product ['prɑdəkt] *s* prodotto

production [pro'dʌkʃən] *s* produzione
profane [pro'fen] *adj* profano; bla-
sfemo || *tr* profanare
profani·ty [pro'fænɪtɪ] *s* (-ties) bestemmia
profess [pro'fes] *tr & intr* professare
profession [pro'feʃən] *s* professione
professor [pro'fesər] *s* professore *m*
proffer ['prɑfər] *s* offerta || *tr* offrire
proficient [pro'fɪʃənt] *adj* abile, competente
profile ['profaɪl] *s* profilo || *tr* profilare
profit ['prɑfɪt] *s* profitto; vantaggio; **at
a profit** con guadagno || *tr* avvantag-
giare; giovare (with *dat*) || *intr* av-
vantaggiarsi; **to profit by** approfittare
di
profitable ['prɑfɪtəbəl] *adj* vantaggioso
prof'it and loss' *s* profitti *mpl* e perdite
fpl
profiteer [,prɑfɪ'tɪr] *s* profittatore *m* ||
intr fare il profittatore
prof'it shar'ing *s* cointeressenza, partecipazione agli utili
prof'it tak'ing *s* realizzo
profligate ['prɑflɪgɪt] *adj & s* dissoluto; prodigo
pro for'ma in'voice ['fɔrmə] *s* fattura
fittizia
profound [pro'faund] *adj* profondo
profuse [pro'fjus] *adj* profuso, abbondante; **profuse in** prodigo di
proge·ny ['prɑdʒənɪ] *s* (-nies) prole *f*
progno·sis [prɑg'nosɪs] *s* (-ses [siz])
prognosi *f*
prognostic [prɑg'nɑstɪk] *s* pronostico
prognosticate [prɑg'nɑstɪ,ket] *tr* pronosticare
pro·gram ['progræm] *s* programma
m || *v* (*pret & pp* **-gramed** *or*
-grammed; *ger* **-graming** *or*
-gramming) *tr* programmare
programmer ['progræmər] *s* pannellista
mf, programmatore *m*
progress ['prɑgres] *s* progresso; **in
progress** in corso; **to make progress**
fare dei progressi || [prə'gres] *intr*
progredire; migliorare
progressive [prə'gresɪv] *adj* (*proceeding step by step*) progressivo; pro-
gressista || *s* progressista *mf*
prohibit [pro'hɪbɪt] *tr* proibire
prohibition [,pro·ə'bɪʃən] *s* proibi-
zione; (hist) proibizionismo
project ['prɑdʒekt] *s* progetto || [prə-
'dʒekt] *tr* (*to propose, plan*) progettare; (*light, a shadow, etc.*) proiettare
|| *intr* sporgere, protrudere
projectile [prə'dʒektɪl] *s* proiettile *m*
projection [prə'dʒekʃən] *s* proiezione,
sporgenza
projector [prə'dʒektər] *s* (*apparatus*)
proiettore *m;* (*person*) progettista *mf*
proletarian [,prolɪ'terɪ·ən] *adj & s*
proletario
proliferate [prə'lɪfə,ret] *intr* proliferare
prolific [prə'lɪfɪk] *adj* prolifico
prolix ['proliks] *or* [pro'lɪks] *adj* pro-
lisso
prologue ['prolɔg] *or* ['prolɑg] *s* pro-
logo

prolong [pro'lɔŋ] or pro'laŋ] *tr* prolungare

promenade [ˌprɑmɪ'ned] or [ˌprɑmɪ'nɑd] *s* passeggiata; ballo di gala ‖ *tr & intr* passeggiare

promenade' deck' *s* ponte *m* passeggiata

prominent ['prɑmɪnənt] *adj* prominente

promise ['prɑmɪs] *s* promessa ‖ *tr & intr* promettere

prom'ising young' man' *s* giovane *m* di belle speranze

prom'issory note' ['prɑmɪ ˌsori] *s* cambiale *f*, pagherò *m*

promonto·ry ['prɑmən ˌtori] *s* (**-ries**) promontorio

promote [prə'mot] *tr* promuovere

promotion [prə'moʃən] *s* promozione

prompt [prɑmpt] *adj* pronto ‖ *tr* incitare, istigare; (theat) suggerire

prompter ['prɑmptər] *s* suggeritore *m*, rammentatore *m*

prompt'er's box' *s* buca del suggeritore

promptness ['prɑmptnɪs] *s* prontezza

promulgate ['prɑməl ˌget] or [pro'mʌlget] *tr* promulgare

prone [pron] *adj* prono

prong [prɔŋ] or [praŋ] *s* punta; (*of fork*) dente *m*; (*of pitchfork*) rebbio

pronoun ['pronaun] *s* pronome *m*

pronounce [prə'nauns] *tr* pronunziare

pronounced [prə'naunst] *adj* pronunziato, marcato

pronouncement [prə'naunsmənt] *s* dichiarazione ufficiale

pronunciamen·to [prə ˌnʌnsɪ·ə'mento] *s* (**-tos**) pronunciamento

pronunciation [prə ˌnʌnsɪ'eʃən] or [prə ˌnʌn/ɪ'eʃən] *s* pronunzia

proof [pruf] *adj*—**proof against** a prova di ‖ *s* prova; (*of alcoholic beverages*) gradazione; (typ) bozza

proof'read'er *s* correttore *m* di bozze

prop [prɑp] *s* sostegno, puntello; (*pole*) palo; **props** attrezzi *mpl* teatrali ‖ *v* (*pret & pp* **propped**; *ger* **propping**) *tr* sostenere, puntellare

propaganda [ˌprɑpə'gændə] *s* propaganda

propagate ['prɑpə ˌget] *tr* propagare ‖ *intr* propagarsi

pro·pel [prə'pel] *v* (*pret & pp* **-pelled**; *ger* **-pelling**) *tr* propulsare, spingere, azionare; (*a rocket*) propellere

propeller [prə'pelər] *s* elica

propensi·ty [prə'pensɪti] *s* (**-ties**) propensione

proper ['prɑpər] *adj* appropriato, corretto; decente, convenevole; (gram) proprio; **proper to** proprio di

proper·ty ['prɑpərti] *s* (**-ties**) proprietà *f*; **properties** attrezzi *mpl* teatrali

prop'erty man' *s* trovarobe *m*, attrezzista *m*

prop'erty own'er *s* proprietario fondiario

prophe·cy ['prɑfɪsi] *s* (**-cies**) profezia

prophe·sy ['prɑfɪ ˌsai] *v* (*pret & pp* **-sied**) *tr* profetizzare

prophet ['prɑfɪt] *s* profeta *m*

prophetess ['prɑfɪtɪs] *s* profetessa

prophylactic [ˌprofɪ'læktɪk] *adj* profilattico ‖ *s* rimedio profilattico; preservativo

propitiate [prə'pɪʃɪ ˌet] *tr* propiziare

propitious [prə'pɪʃəs] *adj* propizio

prop'jet' *s* turboelica *m*

proportion [prə'porʃən] *s* proporzione; **in proportion as** a misura che; **in proportion to** in proporzione a; **out of proportion** sproporzionato ‖ *tr* proporzionare, commensurare

proportionate [prə'porʃənɪt] *adj* proporzionato

proposal [prə'pozəl] *s* proposta; proposta di matrimonio

propose [prə'poz] *tr* proporre ‖ *intr* fare una proposta di matrimonio; **to propose to** chiedere la mano di; proporsi di + *inf*

proposition [ˌprɑpə'zɪʃən] *s* proposizione, proposta; (coll) progetto ‖ *tr* fare delle proposte indecenti a

propound [prə'paund] *tr* proporre

proprietary [prə'praɪ·ə ˌteri] *adj* padronale; esclusivo, patentato

proprietor [prə'praɪ·ətər] *s* proprietario

proprietress [prə'praɪ·ɪtrɪs] *s* proprietaria

proprie·ty [prə'praɪ·əti] *s* (**-ties**) correttezza, decoro; **proprieties** convenzioni *fpl* sociali

propulsion [prə'pʌlʃən] *s* propulsione

prorate [pro'ret] *tr* rateizzare

prosaic [pro'ze·ɪk] *adj* prosaico

proscribe [pro'skraɪb] *tr* proscrivere

prose [proz] *adj* prosaico ‖ *s* prosa

prosecute ['prɑsɪ ˌkjut] *tr* eseguire; (law) processare

prosecutor ['prɑsɪ ˌkjutər] *s* esecutore *m*; (law) querelante *m*; (law) avvocato d'accusa

proselyte ['prɑsɪ ˌlaɪt] *s* proselito

prose' writ'er *s* prosatore *m*

prosody ['prɑsədi] *s* prosodia, metrica

prospect ['prɑspekt] *s* vista; prospettiva; candidato; probabile cliente *m*; **prospects** speranze *fpl* ‖ *intr* fare il cercatore; **to prospect for** fare il cercatore di

prospectus [prə'spektəs] *s* prospetto

prosper ['prɑspər] *tr & intr* prosperare

prosperi·ty [prɑs'perɪti] *s* (**-ties**) prosperità *f*, benessere *m*

prosperous ['prɑspərəs] *adj* prospero

prostitute ['prɑstɪ ˌtjut] or ['prɑstɪ ˌtut] *s* prostituta ‖ *tr* prostituire

prostrate ['prɑstret] *adj* prostrato ‖ *tr* prostrare

prostration [prɑs'treʃən] *s* prostrazione

protagonist [pro'tægənɪst] *s* protagonista *mf*

protect [prə'tekt] *tr* proteggere

protection [prə'tekʃən] *s* protezione

protégé ['protə ˌʒe] *s* protetto, favorito

protégée ['protə ˌʒe] *s* protetta, favorita

protein ['proti·ɪn] or ['protɪn] *s* proteina

pro tempore [pro'tempə ˌri] *adj* provvisorio, interinale

protest ['protest] *s* protesta; (com)

protesto ‖ [pro'test] *tr & intr* protestare

Protestant ['pratıstənt] *adj & s* protestante *mf*

protester [prə'testər] *s* protestatario

prothonotar·y [pro'θanə,teri] *s* (-ies) (law) cancelliere *m* capo

protocol ['protə,kal] *s* protocollo

protoplasm ['protə,plæzəm] *s* protoplasma *m*

prototype ['protə,taıp] *s* prototipo

proto·zoon [,protə'zo·an] *s* (-zoa ['zo·ə]) protozoo

protract [pro'trækt] *tr* prolungare

protractor [pro'træktər] *s* rapportatore *m*

protrude [pro'trud] *intr* sporgere

proud [praud] *adj* fiero; arrogante; maestoso, magnifico

proud' flesh' *s* tessuto di granulazione

prove [pruv] *v* (*pret* proved; *pp* proved or proven) *tr* provare; (*ore*) analizzare; (law) omologare; (math) fare la prova di ‖ *intr* risultare

proverb ['pravərb] *s* proverbio

provide [prə'vaıd] *tr* provvedere ‖ *intr*—to provide for provvedere a; (*to be ready for*) prepararsi a

provided [prə'vaıdıd] *conj* a condizione che, purché; **provided that** a condizione che, purché

providence ['pravıdəns] *s* provvidenza

providential [,pravı'denʃəl] *adj* provvidenziale

providing [prə'vaıdıŋ] *conj* var of **provided**

province ['pravıns] *s* provincia; (fig) pertinenza, competenza

provision [prə'vıʒən] *s* provvedimento; clausola; **provisions** viveri *mpl*

provi·so [prə'vaızo] *s* (-sos or -soes) stipulazione, clausola

provoke [prə'vok] *tr* provocare; contrariare, irritare

prow [prau] *s* prora, prua

prowess ['prau·ıs] *s* prodezza; maestria

prowl [praul] *intr* andare in cerca di preda; vagabondare

prowler ['praulər] *s* vagabondo; ladro

proximity [prak'sımıti] *s* prossimità *f*

prox·y ['praksi] *s* (-ies) procura; (*person*) procuratore *m*

prude [prud] *s* pudibondo

prudence ['prudəns] *s* prudenza

prudent ['prudənt] *adj* prudente

pruder·y ['prudəri] *s* (-ies) attitudine pudibonda

prudish ['prudıʃ] *adj* pudibondo

prune [prun] *s* prugna secca ‖ *tr* potare

pry [praı] *v* (*pret & pp* pried) *tr*—to pry (open) forzare con una leva; **to pry s.th out of s.o.** strappare qlco a qlcu ‖ *intr* intromettersi, cacciarsi

psalm [sam] *s* salmo

pseudo ['sudo] or ['sjudo] *adj* falso, finto, sedicente

pseudonym ['sudənım] or ['sjudənım] *s* pseudonimo

psychiatrist [saı'kaı·ətrıst] *s* psichiatra *mf*

psychiatry [saı'kaı·ətri] *s* psichiatria

psychic ['saıkık] *adj* psichico ‖ *s* medium *mf*

psychoanalysis [,saıko·ə'nælısıs] *s* psicanalisi *f*

psychoanalyze [,saıko'ænə,laız] *tr* psicanalizzare

psychologic(al) [,saıko'ladʒık(əl)] *adj* psicologico

psychologist [saı'kalədʒıst] *s* psicologo

psycholo·gy [saı'kalədʒi] *s* (-gies) psicologia

psychopath ['saıkə,pæθ] *s* psicopatico

psycho·sis [saı'kosıs] *s* (-ses [siz]) psicosi *f*

psychotic [saı'katık] *adj* psicotico

pub [pʌb] *s* (Brit) taverna, bar *m*

puberty ['pjubərti] *s* pubertà *f*

public ['pʌblık] *adj & s* pubblico

pub'lic-address' sys'tem *s* sistema *m* d'amplificazione per discorsi in pubblico

publication [,pʌblı'keʃən] *s* pubblicazione

pub'lic convey'ance *s* veicolo di servizi pubblici

publicity [pʌb'lısıti] *s* pubblicità *f*

publicize ['pʌblı,saız] *tr* pubblicare, divulgare

pub'lic li'brary *s* biblioteca comunale

pub'lic-opin'ion poll' *s* sondaggio d'opinioni

pub'lic pros'ecutor *s* pubblico ministero

pub'lic school' *s* (U.S.A.) scuola dell'obbligo; (Brit) scuola privata, collegio

pub'lic serv'ant *s* funzionario pubblico

pub'lic speak'ing *s* oratoria

pub'lic spir'it *s* civismo

pub'lic toi'let *s* gabinetto pubblico

pub'lic util'ity *s* impresa di servizio pubblico; **public utilities** azioni emesse da imprese di servizi pubblici

publish ['pʌblıʃ] *tr* pubblicare

publisher ['pʌblıʃər] *s* editore *m*; (journ) direttore *m* responsabile

pub'lishing house' *s* casa editrice

pucker ['pʌkər] *s* grinza ‖ *tr* raggrinzire ‖ *intr* raggrinzirsi

pudding ['pudıŋ] *s* budino, torta

puddle ['pʌdəl] *s* pozza, pozzanghera ‖ *intr* diguazzare

pudg·y ['pʌdʒi] *adj* (-ier; -iest) grassoccio

puerile ['pju·ərıl] *adj* puerile

Puerto Rican ['pwerto'rikən] *adj & s* portoricano

puff [pʌf] *s* soffio, sbuffo; (*e.g., of cigar*) boccata; (*pad*) piumino; (*exaggerated praise*) pistolotto; (culin) bignè *m* ‖ *tr* sbuffare; gonfiare; adulare ‖ *intr* soffiare, sbuffare; (*to breathe heavily*) ansimare, ansare; gonfiarsi; tirare boccate

puff' paste' *s* pasta sfoglia

pugilist ['pjudʒılıst] *s* pugile *m*

pug-nosed ['pʌg'nozd] *adj* camuso

puke [pjuk] *tr & intr* (slang) vomitare

pull [pul] *s* tiro; (*act of drawing in*) tirata; (*handle*) tirante *m*; (slang) influenza, appoggi *mpl* ‖ *tr* tirare; (*a tooth*) cavare; (*a muscle*) strappare;

(a punch) (coll) limitare la forza di; **to pull apart** fare a pezzi; **to pull down** abbattere; degradare; **to pull on** (e.g., one's pants) infilarsi; **to pull oneself together** ricomporsi; **to pull s.o.'s leg** beffarsi di qlcu || intr tirare; **to pull apart** andare a pezzi; **to pull at** tirare; **to pull away** andarsene; **to pull for** (coll) fare il tifo per; **to pull in** (said of a train) arrivare, entrare in stazione; **to pull out** (said of a train) partire; **to pull through** guarire, riuscire a cavarsela; **to pull up** to avanzare fino a

pullet ['pulɪt] s pollastra

pulley ['pulɪ] s puleggia, carrucola

pulp [pʌlp] s polpa; (for making paper) pasta

pulpit ['pulpɪt] s pulpito

pulsate ['pʌlset] intr pulsare

pulsation [pʌl'seʃən] s pulsazione

pulse [pʌls] s polso; **to feel or take the pulse of** tastare il polso a

pulverize ['pʌlvə‚raɪz] tr polverizzare

pum'ice stone' s ['pʌmɪs] s pomice f, pietra pomice

pum·mel ['pʌməl] v (pret & pp -meled or -melled; ger -meling or -melling) tr prendere a pugni

pump [pʌmp] s pompa; (slipper) scarpina || tr pompare; (coll) cavare un segreto a; **to pump up** pompare

pumpkin ['pʌmpkɪn] or ['pʌŋkɪn] s zucca

pump-priming ['pʌmp‚praɪmɪŋ] s stimolo governativo per sostentare l'economia

pun [pʌn] s gioco di parole || v (pret & pp punned; ger punning) intr fare giochi di parole

punch [pʌntʃ] s pugno; (tool) punteruolo, punzone m; (drink) ponce m; (coll) forza || tr dare un pugno a; (metal) punzonare; (a ticket) perforare || **Punch** s Pulcinella m; **pleased as Punch** soddisfattissimo

punch' bowl' s vaso per il ponce

punch' card' s scheda perforata

punch' clock' s orologio di controllo

punch'-drunk' adj stordito

punched' tape' s nastro perforato

punch'ing bag' s sacco

punch' line' s perfinire m, motto finale

punctilious [pʌŋk'tɪlɪ‚əs] adj cerimonioso, pignolo

punctual ['pʌŋktʃʊ‚əl] adj puntuale

punctuate ['pʌŋktʃʊ‚et] tr punteggiare

punctuation [‚pʌŋktʃʊ'eʃən] s punteggiatura

punctua'tion mark' s segno d'interpunzione

puncture ['pʌŋktʃər] s puntura; (hole) bucatura; **to have a puncture** avere una gomma a terra || tr bucare, perforare || intr essere bucato

punct'ure-proof' adj antiperforante

pundit ['pʌndɪt] s esperto, autorità f

pungent ['pʌndʒənt] adj pungente

punish ['pʌnɪʃ] tr punire

punishment ['pʌnɪʃmənt] s punizione, castigo

punk [pʌŋk] adj (slang) di pessima

---

qualità || s esca; (decayed wood) legno marcio; (slang) malandrino

punster ['pʌnstər] s freddurista mf

punt [pʌnt] s (football) calcio dato al pallone prima che tocchi il terreno

pu·ny ['pjuni] adj (-nier; -niest) insignificante, meschino; (weak) debole

pup [pʌp] s cucciolo

pupil ['pjupəl] s allievo, scolaro; (anat) pupilla

puppet ['pʌpɪt] s marionetta, burattino; (fig) fantoccio

puppeteer [‚pʌpɪ'tɪr] s burattinaio

pup'pet gov'ernment s governo fantoccio or pupazzo

pup'pet show' s spettacolo di marionette

pup·py ['pʌpi] s (-pies) cucciolo

pup'py love' s amore m giovanile

purchase ['pʌrtʃəs] s compra, acquisto; (grip) presa, leva || tr comprare, acquistare

pur'chasing pow'er s potere m d'acquisto

pure [pjur] adj puro

purgative ['pʌrgətɪv] adj purgativo || s purga

purge [pʌrdʒ] s purga || tr purgare

puri·fy ['pjurɪ‚faɪ] v (pret & pp -fied) tr purificare || intr purificarsi

puritan ['pjurɪtən] adj & s puritano || **Puritan** adj & s puritano

purity ['pjurɪti] s purezza

purloin [pər'lɔɪn] tr & intr rubare

purple ['pʌrpəl] adj purpureo || s porpora

purport ['pʌrport] s senso, significato || [pər'port] tr significare; **to purport to** + inf pretendere di + inf

purpose ['pʌrpəs] s scopo, fine m; **on purpose** apposta; **to good purpose** con buoni risultati; **to no purpose** inutilmente; **to serve one's purpose** fare al caso proprio

purposely ['pʌrpəsli] adv a bella posta, apposta

purr [pʌr] s ronfare m || intr fare le fusa

purse [pʌrs] s borsa; (woman's handbag) borsetta; (for men) borsetto || tr (one's lips) arricciare

purser ['pʌrsər] s commissario di bordo

purse' snatch'er [‚snætʃər] s borsaiolo

purse' strings' spl cordini mpl della borsa; **to hold the purse strings** controllare le spese

purslane ['pʌrslen] or ['pʌrslɪn] s (bot) porcellana

pursue [pər'su] or [pər'sju] tr perseguire; (to harass) perseguitare; (a career) proseguire

pursuit [pər'sut] or [pər'sjut] s inseguimento, caccia; occupazione, esercizio

pursuit' plane' s caccia m

purvey [pər've] tr provvedere, fornire

pus [pʌs] s pus m

push [puʃ] s spinta; (advance) avanzata; (coll) impulso, energia || tr premere, spingere; (a product) promuovere la vendita di; dare impulso a; (narcotics) (slang) spacciare; **to**

push around (coll) dare spintoni a; (fig) fare pressione su; **to push back** ricacciare ∥ intr spingere; **to push ahead** avanzarsi a spintoni, avanzarsi; **to push on** avanzare

push' but'ton s pulsante m, bottone m

push'-button con'trol s controllo a pulsanti

push'cart' s carretto a mano

pusher ['puʃər] adj spingente; (aer) propulsivo ∥ s spingitore m; (aer) aeroplano a elica propulsiva; (slang) spacciatore m di stupefacenti

pushing ['puʃɪŋ] adj aggressivo, intraprendente

puss [pus] s micio

puss' in the cor'ner s gioco dei quattro cantoni

puss·y ['pusi] s (-ies) micio

puss'y wil'low s salice americano a gattini

pustule ['pʌstʃul] s pustola

put [put] v (pret & pp put; ger putting) tr mettere; (to estimate) stimare; (a question) rivolgere; (to throw) lanciare; imporre; **to put across** (slang) far accettare; **to put aside, away** or **by** mettere da parte; **to put down** annotare; (to suppress) reprimere; **to put off** differire; evadere; **to put on** (clothes) mettersi; (a brake) azionare; (to assume) fingere; (airs) darsi; **to put out** spegnere; imbarazzare; incomodare; deludere; annoiare, irritare; (of a game) espellere; **to put it over on s.o.** fargliela a qlcu; **to put off** rinviare; **to put over** mandare ad effetto; **to put to flight** mettere in fuga; **to put to shame** svergognare; **to put through** portare a termine; **to put up** offrire; mettere in conserva; alloggiare; costruire; (money) contribuire; (coll) incitare ∥ intr dirigersi; **to put to sea** mettersi in mare; **to put up** prendere alloggio; **to put up with** tollerare

put'-out' adj sconcertato, seccato

putrid ∣ 'pjutrɪd] adj putrido

Putsch [putʃ] s tentativo di sollevazione, sollevazione

putter ['pʌtər] intr occuparsi di inezie; **to putter about** andare avanti e indietro

put·ty ['pʌti] s (-ties) stucco, mastice m ∥ v (pret & pp -tied) tr stuccare

put'ty knife' s spatola

put'-up' adj (coll) complottato

puzzle ['pʌzəl] s enigma m; (toy) indovinello ∥ tr rendere perplesso, confondere; **to puzzle out** decifrare ∥ intr essere perplesso

puzzler ['pʌzlər] s enigma m

puzzling ['pʌzlɪŋ] adj enigmatico

pyg·my ['pɪgmi] s (-mies) pigmeo

pylon s pilone m

pyramid ['pɪrəmɪd] s piramide f ∥ tr (e.g., costs) aumentare gradualmente; (one's money) aumentare giocando in margine

pyre [paɪr] s pira

Pyrenees ['pɪrɪ ,niz] spl Pirenei mpl

pyrites [paɪ'raɪtiz] or ['paɪraɪts] s pirite f

pyrotechnics [,paɪrə'tekniks] spl pirotecnica

python ['paɪθən] or ['paɪθən] s pitone m

pythoness ['paɪθənɪs] s pitonessa

pyx [pɪks] s (eccl) pisside f

Q

Q, q [kju] s diciassettesima lettera dell'alfabeto inglese

quack [kwæk] adj falso ∥ s medicastro; ciarlatano; qua qua m ∥ intr (said of a duck) fare qua qua

quacker·y ['kwækəri] s (-ies) ciarlataneria

quadrangle ['kwad ,ræŋɡəl] s quadrangolo

quadrant ['kwadrənt] s quadrante m

quadruped ['kwadru ,ped] adj & s quadrupede m

quadruple ['kwadrupəl] or [kwa'drupəl] adj quadruplo; (alliance) quadruplice ∥ s quadruplo ∥ tr quadruplicare ∥ intr quadruplicarsi

quaff [kwaf] or [kwæf] s lungo sorso ∥ tr & intr bere a lunghi sorsi

quail [kwel] s quaglia ∥ intr sgomentarsi

quaint [kwent] adj strano, strambo, originale; all'antica ma bello

quake [kwek] s terremoto ∥ intr tremare, sussultare

Quaker ['kwekər] adj & s quacchero, quacquero

Quak'er meet'ing s riunione di quaccheri; (coll) riunione in cui si parla poco

quali·fy ['kwalɪ ,faɪ] v (pret & pp -fied) tr qualificare; (for a profession) abilitare ∥ intr qualificarsi; abilitarsi

quali·ty ['kwalɪti] s (-ties) qualità f; (of a sound) timbro

qualm [kwam] s scrupolo di coscienza; preoccupazione; nausea

quanda·ry ['kwandəri] s (-ries) incertezza, perplessità f

quanti·ty ['kwantɪti] s (-ties) quantità f

quan·tum ['kwantəm] adj quantistico ∥ s (-ta [tə]) quanto

quarantine ['kwarən ,tin] or ['kwɔrən ,tin] s quarantena ∥ tr mettere in quarantena

quar·rel ['kwarəl] or ['kwɔrəl] s litigio, diverbio; **to have no quarrel with** non essere in disaccordo con; **to pick a quarrel with** venire a diverbio con ∥ v (pret & pp -reled or -relled; ger -reling or -relling) intr litigare

quarrelsome ['kwɑrəlsəm] or ['kwɔrəl-səm] *adj* litigioso, rissoso

quar·ry ['kwɑri] or ['kwɔri] *s* (-ries) cava; (*game*) selvaggina, cacciagione || *v* (*pret & pp* -ried) *tr* cavare

quart [kwɔrt] *s* quarto di gallone

quarter ['kwɔrtər] *adj* quarto || *s* quarto; moneta di un quarto di dollaro; (*three months*) trimestre *m*; (*of town*) quartiere *m*; **a quarter after one** l'una e un quarto; **a quarter of an hour** un quarto d'ora; **a quarter to one** l'una meno un quarto; **at close quarters** corpo a corpo; **quarters** quartiere *m* || *tr* squartare; (*soldiers*) accasermare

quar'ter-deck' *s* cassero

quar'ter-hour' *s* quarto d'ora; **on the quarter-hour** ogni quindici minuti allo scoccare del quarto d'ora

quarter·ly ['kwɔrtərli] *adj* trimestrale || *s* (-lies) pubblicazione trimestrale || *adv* trimestralmente

quar'ter·mas'ter *s* (mil) intendente *m* militare; (nav) secondo capo

quartet [kwɔr'tɛt] *s* quartetto

quartz [kwɔrts] *s* quarzo

quasar ['kwesɑr] *s* (astr) radiostella

quash [kwɑʃ] *tr* sopprimere; annullare

quaver ['kwevər] *s* tremito; (mus) tremolo; (mus) croma || *intr* tremare

quay [ki] *s* molo

queen [kwin] *s* regina; (*in cards*) donna; (chess) regina

queen' bee' *s* ape regina; (fig) basilessa

queen' dow'ager *s* regina vedova

queen·ly ['kwinli] *adj* (-lier; -liest) da regina; regio

queen' moth'er *s* regina madre

queen' post' *s* monaco

queen's' Eng'lish *s* inglese corretto

queer [kwɪr] *adj* strano, curioso; poco bene, indisposto; falso; (slang) omosessuale || *s* (slang) finocchio || *tr* rovinare, mettere in pericolo

quell [kwɛl] *tr* soffocare, domare; (*pain*) calmare

quench [kwɛntʃ] *tr* (*fire, thirst*) spegnere, estinguere; (*rebellion*) soffocare; (elec) ammortizzare

que·ry ['kwɪri] *s* (-ries) domanda; punto interrogativo; dubbio || *v* (*pret & pp* -ried) *tr* interrogare; (typ) apporre punto interrogativo a

quest [kwɛst] *s* ricerca; **in quest of** in cerca di

question ['kwɛstʃən] *s* domanda; problema *m*, quesito; (*matter*) questione; **beyond question** senza dubbio; **out of the question** impossibile; **this is beside the question** questo non c'entra; **to ask a question** fare una domanda; **to be a question of** trattarsi di; **to call in** or **into question** mettere in dubbio; **without question** senza dubbio || *tr* interrogare; mettere in dubbio; (pol) interpellare

questionable ['kwɛstʃənəbəl] *adj* discutibile

ques'tion mark' *s* punto interrogativo

questionnaire [,kwɛstʃən'ɛr] *s* questionario

queue [kju] *s* (*of hair*) codino; (*of people*) coda || *intr* fare la coda

quibble ['kwɪbəl] *intr* sottilizzare

quick [kwɪk] *adj* pronto, sollecito; sbrigativo; veloce, rapido; vivo || *s*— **the quick and the dead** i vivi e i morti; **to cut to the quick** toccare nel vivo

quicken ['kwɪkən] *tr* sveltire; animare; ravvivare

quick'lime' *s* calce viva

quick' lunch' *s* tavola calda

quickly ['kwɪkli] *adv* svelto, alla svelta; presto

quick'sand' *s* sabbia mobile

quick'-set'ting *adj* a presa rapida

quick'sil'ver *s* argento vivo

quick'work' *s* (naut) opera viva

quiet ['kwaɪət] *adj* quieto; silenzioso; (com) calmo; **to keep quiet** stare zitto || *s* quiete *f*, tranquillità *f*; pace *f*, calma || *tr* quietare; calmare || *intr*— **to quiet down** quietarsi, calmarsi

quill [kwɪl] *s* penna d'oca; (*basal part of feather*) calamo; (*e.g., of porcupine*) aculeo

quilt [kwɪlt] *s* trapunta, imbottita || *tr* trapuntare

quince [kwɪns] *s* cotogna; (*tree*) cotogno

quinine ['kwaɪnaɪn] *s* (*alkaloid*) chinina; (*salt of the alkaloid*) chinino

quinsy ['kwɪnzi] *s* angina

quintessence [kwɪn'tɛsəns] *s* quintessenza

quintet [kwɪn'tɛt] *s* quintetto

quintuplet [kwɪn'tjuplɛt] or [kwɪn-'tuplɛt] *s* gemello nato da un parto quintuplice

quip [kwɪp] *s* frizzo, uscita || *v* (*pret & pp* quipped; *ger* quipping) *tr & intr* uscire a dire, dire come battuta

quire [kwaɪr] *s* ventiquattro fogli; (bb) quinterno

quirk [kwʌrk] *s* stranezza, manierismo; (*quibble*) cavillo; (*sudden turn*) mutamento improvviso

quit [kwɪt] *adj* libero; **to be quits** esser pari; **to call it quits** finirla, farla finita || *v* (*pret & pp* quit or quitted; *ger* quitting) *tr* abbandonare || *intr* andarsene; abbandonare l'impiego; smettere (di + *inf*)

quite [kwaɪt] *adv* completamente; molto, del tutto

quitter ['kwɪtər] *s* persona che abbandona facilmente

quiver ['kwɪvər] *s* fremito; (*to hold arrows*) faretra, turcasso || *intr* fremere, tremare

quixotic [kwɪks'ɑtɪk] *adj* donchisciottesco

quiz [kwɪz] *s* (quizzes) esame *m*; interrogatorio || *v* (*pret & pp* quizzed; *ger* quizzing) *tr* esaminare; interrogare

quiz' game' *s* quiz *m*

quiz' pro'gram *s* programma *m* di quiz

quiz' sec'tion *s* (educ) classe *f* a base di esercizi (e non di conferenze)

quizzical ['kwɪzɪkəl] *adj* strano, curioso; (*derisive*) canzonatore

quoin [kɔɪn] or [kwɔɪn] *s* cantone *m*,

pietra angolare; (*piece of wood*) zeppa; (typ) serraforme *m* || *tr* fissare con serraforme

quoit [kwɔɪt] or [kɔɪt] *s* anello di corda o di metallo da lanciarsi come gioco; **quoits** *ssg* gioco consistente nel lancio di anelli su di un piolo

quondam [ˈkwɑndæm] *adj* quondam

quorum [ˈkwɔrəm] *s* quorum *m*

quota [ˈkwotə] *s* (*share*) quota; (*of*

imports) contingentamento; (*of persons*) contingente *m*

quotation [kwoˈteʃən] *s* (*from a book*) citazione; (*of prices*) quotazione

quota'tion mark' *s* doppia virgola, virgoletta

quote [kwot] *s* citazione, richiamo || *tr & intr* citare, richiamare; (com) quotare; **quote cito**

quotient [ˈkwoʃənt] *s* quoziente *m*

R

R, r [ɑr] *s* diciottesima lettera dell'alfabeto inglese

rabbet [ˈræbɪt] *s* scanalatura, incastro || *tr* scanalare, incastrare

rab·bi [ˈræbaɪ] *s* (**-bis**) rabbino

rabbit [ˈræbɪt] *s* coniglio

rab'bit ears' *spl* (telv) doppia antenna a stilo

rabble [ˈræbəl] *s* gentaglia, marmaglia

rab'ble-rous'er [ˈrauzər] *s* arruffapopoli *m*

rabies [ˈrebiz] or [ˈrebɪˌiz] *s* rabbia

raccoon [ræˈkun] *s* procione *m*

race [res] *s* (*branch of human stock*) razza; (*contest in speed*) corsa; (*contest of any kind*) gara; (*channel*) canale *m* di adduzione || *tr* far correre; gareggiare (in velocità) çon; (*a motor*) imballare || *intr* correre; fare le corse; (*said of a motor*) imballarsi; (naut) fare le regate

race' horse' *s* cavallo da corsa

race' ri'ot *s* contestazione di razza

race' track' *s* pista

racial [ˈreʃəl] *adj* razziale

rac'ing car' *s* automobile *f* da corsa

rack [ræk] *s* (*to hang clothes*) attaccapanni *m*; (*framework to hold fodder, baggage, guns, etc.*) rastrelliera; (mach) cremagliera; **to go to rack and ruin** andare a rotoli || *tr* tormentare, torturare; **to rack off** (*wine*) travasare; **to rack one's brains** rompersi il capo, lambiccarsi il cervello

racket [ˈrækɪt] *s* racchetta; (*noise*) chiasso, gazzarra; (coll) racket *m*; **to raise a racket** fare gazzarra

racketeer [ˌrækɪˈtɪr] *s* chi è nel racket; (*engaged in extortion*) ricattatore *m* || *intr* essere nel racket; fare il ricattatore

rack' rail'way *s* ferrovia a cremagliera

rac·y [ˈresi] *adj* (**-ier; -iest**) pungente, vigoroso; piccante

radar [ˈredɑr] *s* radar *m*

radiant [ˈredɪənt] *adj* raggiante, radioso

radiate [ˈredɪˌet] *tr* irradiare || *intr* irradiarsi

radiation [ˌredɪˈeʃən] *s* radiazione

radia'tion sick'ness *s* malattia causata da radiazione atomica

radiator [ˈredɪˌetər] *s* radiatore *m*

ra'diator cap' *s* tappo del radiatore

radical [ˈrædɪkəl] *adj* radicale || *s*

radicale *mf*; (chem, math) radicale *m*

radi·o [ˈredɪˌo] *s* (**-os**) radio *f*; radiogramma *m* || *tr* radiotrasmettere

radioactive [ˌredɪˌoˈæktɪv] *adj* radioattivo

ra'dio am'ateur *s* radioamatore *m*

ra'dio announc'er *s* radioannunciatore *m*

ra'dio bea'con *s* radiofaro

ra'dio·broad'cast *s* radiodiffusione || *tr* radiodiffondere

ra'dio com'pass *s* radiobussola

ra'dio·fre'quency *s* radiofrequenza

ra'dio lis'tener *s* radioascoltatore *m*

radiology [ˌredɪˈɑlədʒi] *s* radiologia

ra'dio net'work *s* rete *f*

ra'dio news'caster *s* radiocronista *mf*

ra'dio·pho'to *s* (**-tos**) (coll) radiofoto *f*

ra'dio set' *s* radioricevente *f*

ra'dio sta'tion *s* stazione radio

radish [ˈrædɪʃ] *s* ravanello

radium [ˈredɪəm] *s* radio

radi·us [ˈredɪˌəs] *s* (**-i** [ˌaɪ] or **-uses**) (anat) radio; (fig, geom) raggio; **within a radius of** entro un raggio di

raffle [ˈræfəl] *s* riffa || *tr* sorteggiare

raft [ræft] or [rɑft] *s* zattera; (coll) mucchio

rafter [ˈræftər] or [ˈrɑftər] *s* puntone *m*

rag [ræg] *s* straccio; **to chew the rag** (slang) chiacchierare

ragamuffin [ˈrægəˌmʌfɪn] *s* straccione *m*

rag' doll' *s* bambola di pezza

rage [redʒ] *s* rabbia; **to be all the rage** furoreggiare; **to fly into a rage** montare in bestia || *intr* infuriare

ragged [ˈrægɪd] *adj* cencioso; (*torn*) stracciato; (*edge*) rozzo, scabroso

ragpicker [ˈrægˌpɪkər] *s* cenciaiolo, straccivendolo

rag'weed' *s* (bot) ambrosia

raid [red] *s* irruzione, razzia || *tr* scorrere || *intr* scorrazzare

rail [rel] *s* (*of fence*) stecca, traversa; (*fence*) stecconata; (*railing*) ringhiera; (rr) rotaia; **by rail** per ferrovia; **rails** titoli *mpl* ferroviari || *intr* inveire; **to rail at** inveire contro

rail'car' *s* automotrice *f*

rail' fence' *s* stecconata fatta di traverse piallate alla buona

rail'head' *s* fine *f* della linea ferroviaria

railing ['reliŋ] *s* ringhiera

rail'road' *adj* ferroviaria ‖ *s* ferrovia ‖ *tr* trasportare in ferrovia; (*a bill*) far passare precipitosamente; (coll) imprigionare falsamente

rail'road cros'sing *s* passaggio a livello

rail'road·er *s* ferroviere *m*

rail'way' *s* ferrovia, strada ferrata

raiment ['remənt] *s* (lit) abbigliamento

rain [ren] *s* pioggia; **rain or shine** con qualunque tempo ‖ *tr* fare piovere; (lit) piovere; **to rain cats and dogs** piovere a catinelle; **to rain out** far sospendere per via della pioggia ‖ *intr* piovere

rainbow ['ren‚bo] *s* arcobaleno

rain'coat' *s* impermeabile *m*

rain'fall' *s* acquazzone *m*; piovosità *f*

rain·y ['reni] *adj* (-ier; -iest) piovoso, piovano

rain'y day' *s* giorno piovoso; (fig) tempi *mpl* difficili

raise [rez] *s* aumento ‖ *tr* levare, rialzare; (*children, animals*) allevare; (*to build*) tirare su; (*a question*) sollevare; (*the dead*) risollevare; (*to increase*) aumentare; (*money*) raccogliere; (*a siege*) togliere; (*at cards*) rilanciare; (*anchor*) salpare; (math) elevare

raisin ['rezən] *s* grano d'uva passa, grano d'uva secca; **raisins** uva passa, uva secca

rake [rek] *s* rastrello; (*person*) porcaccione *m*, libertino ‖ *tr* rastrellare; **to rake in money** far soldoni

rake'-off' *s* (coll) compenso illecito, bustarella; (coll) sconto

rakish ['rekɪʃ] *adj* libertino; brioso, vivace; **to wear one's hat at a rakish angle** portare il cappello sulle ventitré

ral·ly ['ræli] *s* (-lies) riunione, comizio; adunata; ricupero ‖ *v* (*pret & pp* -lied) *tr* riunire, chiamare a raccolta; rianimare ‖ *intr* riunirsi; rianimarsi; (*said of stock prices*) rialzarsi, rimettersi in forze; **to rally to the side of** correre all'aiuto di

ram [ræm] *s* (*male sheep*) montone *m*; (mil) ariete *m*; (nav) sperone *m*; (mach) maglio del battipalo ‖ *v* (*pret & pp* **rammed;** *ger* **ramming**) *tr* battere, sbattere contro; cacciare, conficcare; forzare; (nav) speronare ‖ *intr*—**to ram into** sbattere contro

ramble ['ræmbəl] *s* girata ‖ *intr* (*to wander around*) gironzolare; vagare; (*said of a vine*) crescere disordinatamente; (*said, e.g., of a river*) serpeggiare; (fig) scorrazzare, divagare

rami·fy ['ræmɪ‚faɪ] *v* (*pret & pp* -fied) *tr* ramificare ‖ *intr* ramificarsi

ram'jet en'gine *s* statoreattore *m*

ramp [ræmp] *s* rampa

rampage ['ræmpedʒ] *s* stato d'eccitazione; **to go on a rampage** infierire, comportarsi furiosamente

rampart ['ræmpɑrt] *s* baluardo, muraglione *m*

ram'rod' *s* (*for ramming*) (mil) bacchetta; (*for cleaning*) (mil) scovolo

ram'shack'le *adj* cadente, in rovina

ranch [ræntʃ] *s* fattoria agricola

rancid ['rænsɪd] *adj* rancido

rancor ['ræŋkər] *s* rancore *m*

random ['rændəm] *adj* fortuito; **at random** alla rinfusa, a casaccio

range [rendʒ] *s* (row) fila; (rank) classe *f*; (*distance*) portata; campo di tiro a segno; raggio d'azione; (*scope*) gamma; (*for grazing*) pascolo; (*stove*) fornello, cucina economica; **within range of** alla portata di ‖ *tr* allineare; ordinare; passare attraverso; mandare al pascolo ‖ *intr* variare, fluttuare; estendersi; trovarsi; (mil) portare; **to range over** percorrere; (fig) trattare

range' find'er *s* telemetro

rank [ræŋk] *adj* esuberante; grossolano; denso, spesso; puzzolente; eccessivo; completo, assoluto ‖ *s* rango, grado; (row) fila, schiera; **ranks** truppe *fpl*, ranghi *mpl* ‖ *tr* arrangiare, allineare; classificare; avere rango superiore a ‖ *intr* avere il massimo rango; **to rank high** avere un'alta posizione; **to rank low** avere una posizione bassa; **to rank with** essere allo stesso livello di

rank' and file' *s* truppa; massa

rankle ['ræŋkəl] *tr* irritare ‖ *intr* inasprirsi

ransack ['rænsak] *tr* (*to search thoroughly*) frugare, rovistare; (*to pillage*) svaligiare, saccheggiare

ransom ['rænsəm] *s* taglia, riscatto ‖ *tr* riscattare

rant [rænt] *intr* farneticare, parlare a vanvera

rap [ræp] *s* colpo, colpetto; **I don't care a rap** non m'importa un fico; **to take the rap** (slang) prendersi la colpa ‖ *v* (*pret & pp* **rapped;** *ger* **rapping**) *tr* dare colpi a; battere; **to rap out** (*e.g., a command*) lanciare ‖ *intr* dare colpi, bussare

rapacious [rə'peʃəs] *adj* rapace

rape [rep] *s* rapimento; (*of a woman*) stupro; (bot) ravizzone *m* ‖ *tr* rapire; forzare, violentare

rapid ['ræpɪd] *adj* rapido ‖ **rapids** *spl* rapide *fpl*

rap'id-fire' *adj* a tiro rapido

rapidity [rə'pɪdəti] *s* rapidità *f*

rapier ['repɪ‚ər] *s* spada, stocco

rapt [ræpt] *adj* assorto; estatico

rapture ['ræptʃər] *s* rapimento, estasi *f*

rare [rer] *adj* raro; (*thinly distributed*) rado; (gas) rarefatto; (*meat*) al sangue; (gem) prezioso

rare'-earth' met'al *s* metallo delle terre rare

rare·fy ['rerɪ‚faɪ] *v* (*pret & pp* -fied) *tr* rarefare ‖ *intr* rarefarsi

rarely ['rerli] *adv* di rado, raramente

rascal ['ræskəl] *s* briccone *m*, birbante *m*

rash [ræʃ] *adj* temerario, precipitato ‖ *s* eruzione; (fig) mucchio

rasp [ræsp] *or* [rɑsp] *s* raspa; rumore

m di raspa || *tr* raspare; irritare; dire con voce roca || *intr* fare rumore raspante

raspber·ry ['ræz‚beri] or ['rɑz‚beri] *s* (-ries) lampone *m*; (slang) pernacchia

rat [ræt] *s* ratto; (*to give fullness to hair*) posticcio; (slang) traditore *m*; **to smell a rat** (coll) subodorare un inganno

ratchet ['rætʃɪt] *s* nottolino

rate [ret] *s* (*of interest*) saggio, tasso; prezzo; costo; velocità *f;* (*degree of action*) ragione; tariffa; **at any rate** ad ogni modo; **at the rate of** in ragione di || *tr* valutare, classificare || *intr* essere considerato; essere classificato

rate' of exchange' *s* corso del cambio

rather ['ræðər] or ['rɑðər] *adv* piuttosto; a preferenza; per meglio dire; bensì; discretamente; **rather than** piuttosto di || *interj* e come!

rati·fy ['rætɪ‚faɪ] *v* (*pret & pp* -**fied**) *tr* ratificare, sancire

rating ['retɪŋ] *s* classifica; (nav) grado; (com) valutazione

ra·tio ['reʃo] or ['reʃɪ‚o] *s* (-**tios**) ragione, rapporto; proporzione

ration ['reʃən] or ['ræʃən] *s* razione || *tr* razionare

rational ['ræʃənəl] *adj* razionale

ra'tion book' *s* tessera di razionamento

rat' poi'son *s* veleno per i topi

rat' race' *s* (coll) corsa dei barbieri

rattle ['rætəl] *s* (*sharp sounds*) fracasso; (*child's toy*) sonaglio; (*noisemaking device*) raganella; (*in throat*) rantolo || *tr* scuotere; (*to confuse*) sconcertare; **to rattle off** dire rapidamente, snocciolare || *intr* risuonare, scuotersi; cianciare

rat'tle·snake' *s* serpente *m* a sonagli

rat'trap' *s* trappola per topi; (*hovel*) topaia; (*jam*) (fig) frangente *m*

raucous ['rɔkəs] *adj* rauco

ravage ['rævɪdʒ] *s* distruzione; **ravages** (*of time*) oltraggio || *tr* distruggere, disfare

rave [rev] *intr* farneticare, delirare; infuriare; andare in estasi; **to rave about** levare alle stelle

raven ['revən] *s* corvo

ravenous ['rævənəs] *adj* famelico

ravine [rə'vin] *s* canalone *m*, burrone *m*

ravish ['rævɪʃ] *tr* incantare, entusiasmare; rapire; (*a woman*) stuprare

raw [rɔ] *adj* crudo; (*e.g., silk*) grezzo; (*flesh*) vivo; inesperto

raw' deal' *s* trattamento brutale e ingiusto

raw'hide' *s* pelle greggia

raw' mate'rial *s* materia prima

ray [re] *s* raggio; (*fish*) razza

rayon ['re‚ɑn] *s* raion *m*

raze [rez] *tr* radere al suolo

razor ['rezər] *s* rasoio

ra'zor blade' *s* lametta

ra'zor strop' *s* coramella

razz [ræz] *s* (slang) pernacchia || *tr* (slang) prendere in giro

reach [ritʃ] *s* portata; estensione; **out of reach (of)** fuori della portata (di); oltre alle possibilità (di); **fuori tiro** (di); **within reach of** alla portata di || *tr* raggiungere; toccare; (*customers*) guadagnare || *intr* estendere la mano; **to reach for** cercare di raggiungere

react [rɪ'ækt] *intr* reagire

reaction [rɪ'ækʃən] *s* reazione

reactionar·y [rɪ'ækʃə‚neri] *adj* reazionario || *s* (-**ies**) reazionario

reactor [rɪ'æktər] *s* reattore *m*

read [rid] *v* (*pret & pp* **read** [rɛd]) *tr* leggere; (*s.o.'s thoughts*) leggere in; **to read over** ripassare || *intr* leggere; saper leggere; essere concepito, e.g., **your cable reads thus** il vostro telegramma è concepito così; leggersi, e.g., **this books reads easily** questo libro si legge facilmente; **to read on** continuare a leggere

reader ['ridər] *s* lettore *m;* libro di lettura, sillabo

readily ['rɛdɪli] *adv* velocemente; facilmente; di buona voglia

reading ['ridɪŋ] *s* lettura; dizione

read'ing desk' *s* leggio

read'ing glass' *s* lente *f* d'ingrandimento; **reading glasses** occhiali *mpl* per la lettura

read'ing lamp' *s* lampada da scrittoio

read'ing room' *s* sala di lettura

read·y ['rɛdi] *adj* (-**ier** -**iest**) pronto; disponibile; **to make ready** preparare; prepararsi || *v* (*pret & pp* -**ied**) *tr* preparare || *intr* prepararsi

read'y cash' *s* denaro contante

read'y-made cloth'ing *s* confezioni *fpl*

read'y-made suit' *s* vestito già fatto

reaffirm [‚ri·ə'fʌrm] *tr* riaffermare

reagent [rɪ'edʒənt] *s* reagente *m*

real ['ri·əl] *adj* effettivo, reale

re'al estate' *s* beni *mpl* immobili, proprietà *f* immobiliare

re'al-estate' *adj* immobiliare, fondiario

realism ['ri·ə‚lɪzəm] *s* realismo

realist ['ri·əlɪst] *s* realista *mf*

realistic [‚ri·ə'lɪstɪk] *adj* realistico

reali·ty [rɪ'ælɪti] *s* (-**ies**) realtà *f*

realize ['ri·ə‚laɪz] *tr* rendersi conto di; concretare; realizzare || *intr* convertire proprietà in contanti

realm [rɛlm] *s* regno

realtor ['ri·əl‚tər] or ['ri·əltər] *s* (trademark) agente *m* d'immobili membro dell'associazione nazionale

realty ['ri·əlti] *s* proprietà *f* immobiliare

ream [rim] *s* risma; **reams** pagine *fpl* e pagine || *tr* alesare

reamer ['rimər] *s* (mach) alesatore *m;* (dentistry) fresa

reap [rip] *tr & intr* (*to cut*) mietere; (*to gather*) raccogliere

reaper ['ripər] *s* (*person*) mietitore *m;* (mach) mietitrice *f*

reappear [‚ri·ə'pɪr] *intr* ricomparire, riapparire

reappearance [‚ri·ə'pɪrəns] *s* riapparizione, ricomparsa

reapportionment [‚ri·ə'porʃənmənt] *s* ridistribuzione

rear [rɪr] *adj* posteriore, di dietro || *s*

retro, di dietro; posteriore *m*; (mil) retroguardia || *tr* alzare, elevare; allevare, educare || *intr* (*said of a horse*) impennarsi

rear' ad'miral *s* contrammiraglio

rear' drive' *s* trazione posteriore

rear' end' *s* retro, di dietro; (coll) posteriore *m*; (aut) retrotreno

rearmament [ri'ɑrməmənt] *s* riarmo

rear'-view mir'ror *s* specchietto retrovisivo

rear' win'dow *s* (aut) lunetta posteriore

reason ['rizən] *s* ragione; **by reason of** per causa di; **to bring s.o. to reason** indurre qlcu alla ragione; **to stand to reason** esser logico || *tr* & *intr* ragionare

reasonable ['rizənəbəl] *adj* ragionevole

reassessment [ˌri·ə'sɛsmənt] *s* rivalutazione

reassure [ˌri·ə'ʃʊr] *tr* rassicurare, riassicurare

reawaken [ˌri·ə'wekən] *tr* risvegliare || *intr* risvegliarsi

rebate ['ribet] *or* [ri'bet] *s* ribasso || *tr* ribassare

rebel ['rɛbəl] *adj* & *s* ribelle *mf* || **re·bel** [ri'bɛl] *v* (*pret* & *pp* **-belled;** *ger* **-belling**) *intr* ribellarsi

rebellion [ri'bɛljən] *s* ribellione

rebellious [ri'bɛljəs] *adj* ribelle

re·bind [ri'baɪnd] *v* (*pret* & *pp-* **bound** ['baʊnd]) *tr* rifasciare; (bb) rilegare

rebirth ['ribʌrθ] *or* [ri'bʌrθ] *s* rinascita

rebore [ri'bor] *tr* rialesare, rettificare

rebound ['ri,baʊnd] *or* [ri'baʊnd] *s* rimbalzo || [ri'baʊnd] *intr* rimbalzare

rebroad'casting sta'tion *s* stazione ripetitrice

rebuff [ri'bʌf] *s* rifiuto || *tr* respingere, rifiutare

rebuild [ri'bɪld] *v* (*pret* & *pp* **-built** ['bɪlt]) *tr* ricostruire, riedificare

rebuke [ri'bjuk] *s* rabbuffo || *tr* rabbuffare

re·but [ri'bʌt] *v* (*pret* & *pp* **-butted;** *ger* **-butting**) *tr* confutare

rebuttal [ri'bʌtəl] *s* confutazione

recall [ri'kɔl] *or* ['rikɔl] *s* richiamo; revoca || [ri'kɔl] *tr* richiamare; ricordare, ricordarsi di; richiamare alla memoria

recant [ri'kænt] *tr* ritrattare || *intr* ritrattarsi

re·cap ['ri,kæp] *or* [ri'kæp] *v* (*pret* & *pp* **-capped;** *ger* **-capping**) *tr* ricapitolare, riepilogare; (*a tire*) rifare il battistrada a

recapitulation [ˌrikə,pɪtʃə'leʃən] *s* ricapitolazione, riepilogo

re·cast ['ri,kæst] *or* ['ri,kɑst] *s* rifusione || [ri'kæst] *or* [ri'kɑst] *v* (*pret* & *pp* **-cast**) *tr* rifondere

recede [ri'sid] *intr* ritirarsi, allontanarsi; recedere, retrocedere; (*said, e.g., of chin*) sfuggire

receipt [ri'sit] *s* ricevimento; (*acknowledgment of payment*) ricevuta; (*recipe*) ricetta; **receipts** incasso, introito *tr* quietanzare

receive [ri'siv] *tr* ricevere; (*stolen* goods*) ricettare; (*to have inflicted upon one*) subire || *intr* ricevere

receiver [ri'sivər] *s* ricevitore *m*; ricettatore *m*; (law) curatore *m* fallimentare; (telp) auricolare *m*

receiv'ing set' *s* apparecchio radioricevente

receiv'ing tell'er *s* cassiere *m* incaricato delle riscossioni

recent ['risənt] *adj* recente

recently ['risəntli] *adv* recentemente, di recente

receptacle [ri'sɛptəkəl] *s* recipiente *m*; (elec) presa

reception [ri'sɛpʃən] *s* accoglienza; (*function*) ricevimento

recep'tion desk' *s* ufficio informazioni, bureau *m*

receptionist [ri'sɛpʃənɪst] *s* accoglitrice *f*; (*male*) usciere *m*

receptive [ri'sɛptɪv] *adj* ricettivo

recess [ri'sɛs] *or* ['risɛs] *s* intermezzo, interludio; ora di ricreazione; (*in a line*) rientranza; (*in a wall*) nicchia, alcova; (fig) recesso || [ri'sɛs] *tr* aggiornare, dare vacanza a; incassare, mettere in una nicchia || *intr* aggiornarsi, prendersi vacanza

recession [ri'sɛʃən] *s* ritirata; processione finale; (com) recessione

recipe ['rɛsɪ,pi] *s* ricetta

reciprocal [ri'sɪprəkəl] *adj* reciproco

reciprocity [ˌrɛsɪ'prɑsɪti] *s* reciprocità *f*

recital [ri'saɪtəl] *s* narrazione; (*of music or poetry*) recital *m*

recite [ri'saɪt] *tr* raccontare; (*music or poetry*) recitare

reckless ['rɛklɪs] *adj* temerario, spericolato

reckon ['rɛkən] *tr* calcolare; considerare; (coll) supporre || *intr* contare; **to reckon with** prevedere, tener conto di

reclaim [ri'klem] *tr* (*land*) sanare, prosciugare; (*substances*) rigenerare; (fig) rigenerare

recline [ri'klaɪn] *tr* reclinare || *intr* reclinarsi, adagiarsi

recluse [ri'klus] *or* ['rɛklus] *adj* & *s* recluso

recognition [ˌrɛkəg'nɪʃən] *s* riconoscimento

recognize ['rɛkəg,naɪz] *tr* riconoscere

recoil [ri'kɔɪl] *s* indietreggiamento; (*of a firearm*) rinculo || *intr* indietreggiare; rinculare

recollect [ˌrɛkə'lɛkt] *tr* & *intr* ricordare

recollection [ˌrɛkə'lɛkʃən] *s* ricordo

recommend [ˌrɛkə'mɛnd] *tr* raccomandare

recompense ['rɛkəm,pɛns] *s* ricompensa || *tr* ricompensare

reconcile ['rɛkən,saɪl] *tr* riconciliare; **to reconcile oneself** rassegnarsi

reconnaissance [ri'kɑnɪsəns] *s* ricognizione

reconnoiter [ˌrɛkə'nɔɪtər] *or* [ˌrikə'nɔɪtər] *tr* & *intr* perlustrare

reconsider [ˌrikən'sɪdər] *tr* riconsiderare

reconstruct [ˌrikən'strʌkt] *tr* ricostruire

reconversion [ˌrikən'vʌrʒən] *s* riconversione

record ['rɛkərd] *s* registrazione; annotazione; (*official report*) verbale *m*, protocollo; (*criminal*) fedina sporca; (*of a phonograph*) disco; (*educ*) documenti *mpl* scolastici; (*sports*) record *m*, primato; **off the record** confidenziale; confidenzialmente; **records** annali *mpl*, documenti *mpl*; **to break a record** battere un record ‖ [rɪ'kɔrd] *tr* registrare; mettere a verbale; (*e.g., a song*) incidere

rec′ord break′er *s* (sports) primatista *mf*

rec′ord chang′er ['tʃendʒər] *s* cambiadischi *m*

recorder [rɪ'kɔrdər] *s* (*apparatus*) registratore *m*; (law) cancelliere *m*; (mus) flauto a imboccatura a tubo

rec′ord hold′er *s* (sports) primatista *mf*

recording [rɪ'kɔrdɪŋ] *s* registrazione; (*of a record*) incisione; (*record*) disco

record′ing sec′retary *s* cancelliere *m*

rec′ord play′er *s* giradischi *m*

recount ['ri,kaunt] *s* nuovo conteggio ‖ [ri'kaunt] *tr* (*to count again*) ricontare ‖ [rɪ'kaunt] *tr* (*to narrate*) raccontare

recourse [rɪ'kɔrs] or ['rikɔrs] *s* ricorso; (com) rivalsa; **to have recourse to** ricorrere a

recover [rɪ'kʌvər] *tr* ricuperare, riacquistare; (*a substance*) rigenerare; **to recover consciousness** riaversi, riprendere conoscenza ‖ *intr* rimettersi; guadagnare una causa

recover·y [rɪ'kʌvəri] *s* (-ies) ricupero; guarigione; **past recovery** incurabile

recreant ['rɛkrɪ·ənt] *adj* & *s* codardo; traditore *m*

recreation [ˌrɛkrɪ'eʃən] *s* ricreazione

recruit [rɪ'krut] *s* recluta ‖ *tr* & *intr* reclutare

rectangle ['rɛk,tæŋɡəl] *s* rettangolo

rectifier ['rɛktə,faɪ·ər] *s* rettificatore *m*; (elec) raddrizzatore *m*

recti·fy ['rɛktɪ,faɪ] *v* (*pret* & *pp* **-fied**) *tr* rettificare; (elec) raddrizzare

rectitude ['rɛktɪ,tud] or ['rɛktɪ,tjud] *s* rettitudine *f*

rec·tum ['rɛktəm] *s* (-tums or -ta [tə]) retto

recumbent [rɪ'kʌmbənt] *adj* sdraiato

recuperate [rɪ'kjupə,ret] *tr* ricuperare ‖ *intr* ristabilirsi, rimettersi

re·cur [rɪ'kʌr] *v* (*pret* & *pp* **-curred**; *ger* **-curring**) *intr* ricorrere; ritornare; tornare a mente

recurrent [rɪ'kʌrənt] *adj* ricorrente

recycle [ri'saɪkəl] *tr* riconvertire; (*e.g., in chemical industry*) riciclare

red [rɛd] *adj* (**redder; reddest**) rosso ‖ *s* rosso; **in the red** in debito, in rosso ‖ **Red** *adj* & *s* (*Communist*) rosso

red′bait′ *tr* dare del comunista a

red′bird′ *s* cardinale *m*

red-blooded ['rɛd,blʌdɪd] *adj* sanguigno; vigoroso

red′breast′ *s* pettirosso

red′bud′ *s* siliquastro

red′cap′ *s* (Brit) poliziotto militare; (U.S.A.) facchino

red′ cell′ *s* globulo rosso

red′ cent′ *s*—**to not have a red cent** (coll) non avere il becco di un quattrino

Red′ Cross′ *s* Croce Rossa

redden ['rɛdən] *tr* arrossare ‖ *intr* arrossire

redeem [rɪ'dim] *tr* redimere; (*a promise*) disimpegnare

redeemer [rɪ'dimər] *s* redentore *m*

redemption [rɪ'dɛmpʃən] *s* redenzione; disimpegno

red-handed ['rɛd'hændɪd] *adj*—**to be caught red-handed** esser colto sul fatto or con le mani nel sacco

red′head′ *s* persona dai capelli rossi

red′ her′ring *s* argomento usato per sviare l'attenzione; aringa affumicata

red′-hot′ *adj* rovente, incandescente; fresco fresco, appena uscito

rediscover [ˌridɪs'kʌvər] *tr* riscoprire

red′-let′ter *adj* memorabile

red′-light′ dis′trict *s* quartiere *m* delle case di tolleranza

red′ man′ *s* pellerossa *m*

re·do ['ri'du] *v* (*pret* **-did** ['dɪd]; *pp* **-done** ['dʌn]) *tr* rifare

redolent ['rɛdələnt] *adj* fragrante, profumato; **redolent of** che sa di

redoubt [rɪ'daut] *s* (mil) ridotta

redound [rɪ'daund] *intr* ridondare

red′ pep′per *s* pepe *m* di Caienna

redress [rɪ'drɛs] or ['ridrɛs] *s* riparazione, risarcimento ‖ [rɪ'drɛs] *tr* riparare, risarcire

red′skin′ *s* pellerossa *mf*

red′ tape′ *s* trafila, burocrazia

reduce [rɪ'djus] or [rɪ'dus] *tr* ridurre; diluire; (mil) retrocedere; (*a hernia*) (surg) sbrigliare ‖ *intr* ridursi; (*to lose weight*) dimagrire

reducing [rɪ'djusɪŋ] or [rɪ'dusɪŋ] *adj* dimagrante; (chem) riducente

reduction [rɪ'dʌkʃən] *s* riduzione

redundant [rɪ'dʌndənt] *adj* ridondante

red′wood′ *s* sequoia

reed [rid] *s* (*stalk*) calamo; (*plant*) canna; (mus) linguetta; (mus) strumento a linguetta

reedit [ri'ɛdɪt] *tr* rifondere

reef [rif] *s* scoglio, barriera; (naut) terzarolo; (min) vena, filone *m* ‖ *tr* (*sail*) imbrogliare

reefer ['rifər] *s* giacchetta a doppio petto; (slang) sigaretta di marijuana

reek [rik] *intr* puzzare; sudare, evaporare, fumare

reel [ril] *s* (*spool*) bobina; (*sway*) vacillamento; (*for fishing*) mulinello; **off the reel** senza esitazione ‖ *tr* bobinare; **to reel off** rifilare ‖ *intr* barcollare

reelection [ˌri·ɪ'lɛkʃən] *s* rielezione

reenlist [ˌri·ɛn'lɪst] *tr* arruolare di nuovo ‖ *intr* arruolarsi di nuovo

reen·try [rɪ'ɛntri] *s* (-tries) rientro

reexamination [ˌri·ɛɡ,zæmɪ'neʃən] *s* riesame *m*

re·fer [rɪ'fʌr] v (pret & pp **-ferred;** ger **-ferring**) tr riferire || intr riferirsi

referee [ˌrefə'ri] s arbitro || tr & intr arbitrare

reference ['refərəns] s riferimento; (testimonial) referenza; (e.g., in a book) rinvio, rimando

ref'erence book' s libro di consultazione

referen·dum [ˌrefə'rendəm] s (**-dums** or **-da** [də]) referendum m

refill ['rifɪl] s ricambio || [rɪ'fɪl] tr riempire di nuovo

refine [rɪ'faɪn] tr raffinare

refinement [rɪ'faɪnmənt] s raffinatezza; (of oil) raffinatura

refiner·y [rɪ'faɪnəri] s (**-ies**) raffineria

reflect [rɪ'flekt] tr riflettere || intr riflettere, riflettersi

reflection [rɪ'flekʃən] s riflessione

reflex ['rifleks] adj riflesso || s riflesso; (camera) reflex m

reflexive [rɪ'fleksɪv] adj riflessivo

reforestation [ˌrifɔrɪs'teʃən] or [ˌrifɔrɪs'teʃən] s rimboschimento

reform [rɪ'fɔrm] s riforma || tr riformare || intr correggersi

reformation [ˌrefər'meʃən] s riforma || **Reformation** s—**the Reformation** la Riforma

reformato·ry [rɪ'fɔrmə.tori] adj riformativo || s (**-ries**) riformatorio

reformer [rɪ'fɔrmər] s riformatore m

reform' school' s riformatorio

refraction [rɪ'frækʃən] s rifrazione

refrain [rɪ'fren] s ritornello, intercalare m || intr astenersi

refresh [rɪ'freʃ] tr rinfrescare; ristorare || intr ristorarsi

refreshing [rɪ'freʃɪŋ] adj rinfrescante; ristoratore; ricreativo

refreshment [rɪ'freʃmənt] s rinfresco

refrigerate [rɪ'frɪdʒə.ret] tr refrigerare

refrigerator [rɪ'frɪdʒə.retər] s refrigerante m, frigorifero

refrig'erator car' s vagone frigorifero

re·fuel [rɪ'fjul] v (pret & pp **-fueled** or **-fuelled;** ger **-fueling** or **-fuelling**) tr rifornire di carburante || intr rifornirsi di carburante

refuge ['refjudʒ] s rifugio; scampo; **to take refuge (in)** rifugiarsi (in)

refugee [ˌrefju'dʒi] s rifugiato

refund ['rifʌnd] s rifusione || [rɪ'fʌnd] tr (to repay) rifondere || [rɪ'fʌnd] tr (bonds) consolidare; (to fund anew) rifondere

refurnish [rɪ'fʌrnɪʃ] tr riammobiliare

refusal [rɪ'fjuzəl] s rifiuto

refuse ['refjus] s rifiuto, spazzatura || [rɪ'fjuz] tr rifiutare; **to refuse to** rifiutarsi di

refute [rɪ'fjut] tr smentire, confutare

regain [rɪ'gen] tr riguadagnare; **to regain consciousness** tornare in sé

regal ['rigəl] adj reale, regale

regale [rɪ'gel] tr intrattenere, rallegrare

regalia [rɪ'geljə] spl (of royalty) prerogative fpl reali; alta uniforme

regard [rɪ'gɑrd] s riguardo; (look)

sguardo; (esteem) rispetto; **in regard to** rispetto a; **regards** rispetti mpl; **warm regards** cordiali saluti mpl; **without regard to** senza considerare || tr considerare; osservare; concernere; **as regards** per quanto concerne

regarding [rɪ'gɑrdɪŋ] prep per quanto concerne

regardless [rɪ'gɑrdlɪs] adj incurante || adv ciò nonostante; costi quello che costi; **regardless of** malgrado

regatta [rɪ'gætə] s regata

regen·cy ['ridʒənsi] s (**-cies**) reggenza

regenerate [rɪ'dʒenə.ret] tr rigenerare || intr rigenerarsi

regent ['ridʒənt] s reggente mf

regicide ['redʒɪ.saɪd] s (act) regicidio; (person) regicida mf

regiment ['redʒɪmənt] s reggimento || ['redʒɪ.ment] tr irregimentare

regimental [ˌredʒɪ'mentəl] adj reggimentale || **regimentals** spl uniforme f reggimentale

region ['ridʒən] s regione

register ['redʒɪstər] s registro; (for controlling the flow of air) regolatore m dell'aria || tr registrare; (e.g., a student) iscrivere; (e.g., anger) dimostrare; (a letter) raccomandare || intr registrarsi; iscriversi; fare impressione

reg'istered let'ter s raccomandata

reg'istered nurse' s infermiera diplomata

registrar ['redʒɪs.trɑr] s registratore m, archivista mf; (of deeds) ricevitore m

registration [ˌredʒɪs'treʃən] s registrazione; (e.g., of a student) iscrizione; (of mail) raccomandazione

registra'tion fee' s diritto di segreteria

re·gret [rɪ'gret] s pentimento, rammarico; **regrets** scuse fpl || v (pret & pp **-gretted;** ger **-gretting**) tr rimpiangere; **to regret** to essere spiacente di

regrettable [rɪ'gretəbəl] adj deplorevole

regular ['regjələr] adj regolare; (life) regolato; (coll) vero || s cliente m abituale; (mil) effettivo

regularity [ˌregju'lærɪti] s regolarità f

regularize ['regjələ.raɪz] tr regolarizzare

regulate ['regjə.let] tr regolare

regulation [ˌregjə'leʃən] s regolazione; (rule) regolamento

rehabilitate [ˌrihə'bɪlɪ.tet] tr riabilitare

rehearsal [rɪ'hʌrsəl] s prova

rehearse [rɪ'hʌrs] tr provare || intr fare le prove

rehiring [ri'haɪrɪŋ] s riassunzione

reign [ren] s regno || intr regnare

reimburse [ˌri·ɪm'bʌrs] tr rimborsare

rein [ren] s redine f; **to give full rein to** dare briglia sciolta a || tr guidare con le redini; frenare

reincarnation [ˌri·ɪnkɑr'neʃən] s reincarnazione

reindeer ['ren.dɪr] s renna

reinforce [ˌri·ɪn'fors] tr rinforzare; (a wall) armare

re'inforced con'crete s cemento armato

reinforcement [ˌri·ɪn'forsmənt] *s* rinforzo

reinstate [ˌri·ɪn'stet] *tr* reintegrare

reiterate [rɪ'ɪtəˌret] *tr* reiterare

reject ['rɪdʒɛkt] *s* rigetto, rifiuto; **rejects** scarti *mpl* ‖ [rɪ'dʒɛkt] *tr* rigettare; (*to refuse*) rifiutare

rejection [rɪ'dʒɛkʃən] *s* rigetto; rifiuto

rejoice [rɪ'dʒɔɪs] *intr* rallegrarsi

rejoin [rɪ'dʒɔɪn] *tr* raggiungere; (*to reunite*) riunire; (*to reply*) rispondere

rejoinder [rɪ'dʒɔɪndər] *s* risposta; (*law*) controreplica

rejuvenation [rɪ ˌdʒuvɪ'neʃən] *s* ringiovanimento

rekindle [rɪ'kɪndəl] *tr* riaccendere

relapse [rɪ'læps] *s* ricaduta ‖ *intr* ricadere

relate [rɪ'let] *tr* mettere in relazione; (*to tell*) narrare

relation [rɪ'leʃən] *s* relazione; (*account*) resoconto; (*relative*) parente *mf*; (*kinship*) parentela; **in relation to** or **with** in relazione a

relationship [rɪ'leʃənˌʃɪp] *s* rapporto, relazione; (*kinship*) parentela

relative ['rɛlətɪv] *adj* relativo ‖ *s* congiunto, parente *mf*

relativity [ˌrɛlə'tɪvɪti] *s* relatività *f*

relax [rɪ'læks] *tr* rilasciare, rilassare ‖ *intr* rilasciarsi, rilassarsi

relaxation [ˌrilæks'eʃən] *s* distensione; (*entertainment*) ricreazione

relaxa'tion of ten'sion *s* distensione

relaxing [rɪ'læksɪŋ] *adj* rilassante; divertente

relay ['rile] *or* [rɪ'le] *s* (elec) relè *m*; (rad) ripetitore *m*; (mil, sports) staffetta; (sports) corsa a staffetta ‖ *v* (*pret & pp -layed*) *tr* trasmettere, ritrasmettere ‖ [rɪ'le] *v* (*pret & pp -laid*) *tr* rimettere, porre di nuovo

re'lay race' *s* corsa a staffetta

release [rɪ'lis] *s* (*e.g., from jail*) liberazione; (*from obligation*) disimpegno; (*for publication*) autorizzazione; (*mov*) distribuzione; (*journ*) comunicato; (aer) lancio; (mach) scappamento ‖ *tr* liberare; disimpegnare; autorizzare la pubblicazione di; (mov) distribuire; (*a bomb*) (aer) lanciare; **to release s.o. from a debt** rimettere un debito a qlcu

relent [rɪ'lɛnt] *intr* placarsi

relentless [rɪ'lɛntlɪs] *adj* implacabile

relevant ['rɛlɪvənt] *adj* pertinente

reliable [rɪ'laɪ·əbəl] *adj* (*person*) fidato; (*source*) attendibile

reliance [rɪ'laɪ·əns] *s* fiducia, fede *f*

relic ['rɛlɪk] *s* reliquia

relief [rɪ'lif] *s* sollievo; sussidio; (*prominence; projection*) rilievo; (mil) cambio; **in relief** in rilievo; **on relief** sotto sussidio

relieve [rɪ'liv] *tr* (*e.g., pain*) alleviare; (*e.g., a load*) sgravare; (mil) rilevare

religion [rɪ'lɪdʒən] *s* religione

religious [rɪ'lɪdʒəs] *adj* religioso

relinquish [rɪ'lɪŋkwɪʃ] *tr* abbandonare

relish ['rɛlɪʃ] *s* piacere *m*, gusto; sapore *m*, aroma *m*; (culin) condimento ‖ *tr* gustare, apprezzare; dare gusto a

reluctance [rɪ'lʌktəns] *s* riluttanza

reluctant [rɪ'lʌktənt] *adj* riluttante

re·ly [rɪ'laɪ] *v* (*pret & pp -lied*) *intr* fare assegnamento; **to rely on** fidarsi di, fondarsi su

remain [rɪ'men] *s*—**remains** resti *mpl*; resti *mpl* mortali ‖ *intr* restare, rimanere

remainder [rɪ'mendər] *s* resto, restante *m*; (*unsold books*) fondi *mpl* di libreria ‖ *tr* vendere come rimanenza

re·make [rɪ'mek] *v* (*pret & pp -made* ['med]) *tr* rifare

remark [rɪ'mɑrk] *s* osservazione, rimarco ‖ *tr & intr* osservare; **to remark on** fare osservazioni su

remarkable [rɪ'mɑrkəbəl] *adj* notevole

remar·ry [rɪ'mæri] *v* (*pret & pp -ried*) *intr* riprendere moglie, risposarsi

reme·dy ['rɛmɪdi] *s* (*-dies*) rimedio ‖ *v* (*pret & pp -died*) *tr* rimediare (*with dat*)

remember [rɪ'mɛmbər] *tr* ricordare di; (*to send greetings to*) ricordare ‖ *intr* ricordare, ricordarsi

remembrance [rɪ'mɛmbrəns] *s* rimembranza, ricordo

remind [rɪ'maɪnd] *tr* rammentare

reminder [rɪ'maɪndər] *s* promemoria

reminisce [ˌrɛmɪ'nɪs] *intr* ricordare il passato

reminiscence [ˌrɛmɪ'nɪsəns] *s* reminiscenza

remiss [rɪ'mɪs] *adj* negligente

re·mit [rɪ'mɪt] *v* (*pret & pp -mitted*; *ger -mitting*) *tr* rimettere; (*to a lower court*) (law) rinviare

remittance [rɪ'mɪtəns] *s* rimessa

remnant ['rɛmnənt] *s* (*remaining quantity*) rimanente *m*; (*of cloth*) scampolo; vestigio; **remnants** (*of merchandise*) rimanenze *fpl*, fondi *mpl* di magazzino

remod·el [rɪ'mɑdəl] *v* (*pret & pp -eled* or *-elled*; *ger -eling* or *-elling*) *tr* rimodellare; ricostruire

remonstrance [rɪ'mɑnstrəns] *s* rimostranza

remonstrate [rɪ'mɑnstret] *intr* protestare, rimostrare; **to remonstrate with** rimostrare a

remorse [rɪ'mɔrs] *s* rimorso

remorseful [rɪ'mɔrsfəl] *adj* tormentato dal rimorso, pentito

remote [rɪ'mot] *adj* remoto

remote' control' *s* telecomando

removable [rɪ'muvəbəl] *adj* amovibile

removal [rɪ'muvəl] *s* rimozione; trasferimento; (*dismissal*) destituzione

remove [rɪ'muv] *tr* rimuovere; (*one's jacket*) togliersi, cavarsi; (*from office*) destituire; eliminare ‖ *intr* trasferirsi; andarsene

remuneration [rɪ ˌmjunə'reʃən] *s* rimunerazione

renaissance [ˌrɛnə'sɑns] *or* [rɪ'nesəns] *s* rinascimento, rinascita ‖ **Renaissance** *s* Rinascimento

rend [rɛnd] *v* (*pret & pp rent* [rɛnt]) *tr* (*to tear*) stracciare; (*to split*) fendere, squarciare

render ['rɛndər] *tr* (*justice*) rendere;

(a service) fare; (aid) prestare; (a bill) presentare; (to translate) tradurre; (a piece of music) interpretare; (e.g., fat) struggere

rendez•vous ['rɑndə‚vu] s (-vous [‚vuz]) appuntamento; (in space) incontro ‖ v (pret & pp -voused [‚vud]; ger -vousing [‚vu·ɪŋ]) intr incontrarsi

rendition [ren'dɪʃən] s restituzione, resa; traduzione; interpretazione

renege [rɪ'nɪg] s rifiuto ‖ intr rifiutare; (coll) venire meno

renew [rɪ'nju] or [rɪ'nu] tr rinnovare ‖ intr rinnovarsi

renewal [rɪ'nju·əl] or [rɪ'nu·əl] s rinnovo, rinnovamento

renounce [rɪ'nauns] tr rinunziare (with dat); ripudiare

renovate ['renə‚vet] tr rinnovare; (a building) restaurare; (a room) rimettere a nuovo

renown [rɪ'naun] s rinomanza

renowned [rɪ'naund] adj rinomato

rent [rent] adj scisso ‖ s fitto, pigione; (tear) squarcio ‖ tr locare, dare a pigione ‖ intr prendere a pigione

rental ['rentəl] s affitto

renter ['rentər] s affittuario, locatario

renunciation [rɪ‚nʌnsɪ'eʃən] or [rɪ‚nʌnʃɪ'eʃən] s rinunzia

reopen [ri'opən] tr riaprire ‖ intr riaprirsi

reopening [ri'opənɪŋ] s riapertura

reorganize [ri'ɔrgə‚naɪz] tr riorganizzare ‖ intr riorganizzarsi

repair [rɪ'per] s riparazione; **in good repair** in buono stato ‖ tr riparare ‖ intr riparare, dirigersi

repair'man' s (-men') aggiustatore m

repaper [ri'pepər] tr ritappezzare

reparation [‚repə're ʃən] s riparazione

repartee [‚repər'ti] s replica arguta, rimando

repast [rɪ'pæst] or [rɪ'pɑst] s pasto

repatriate [ri'petrɪ‚et] tr rimpatriare

re•pay [ri'pe] v (pret & pp -paid ['ped]) tr ripagare

repayment [rɪ'pemənt] s rimborso; risarcimento, compensazione

repeal [rɪ'pil] s revoca, abrogazione ‖ tr revocare, abrogare

repeat [rɪ'pit] s ripetizione ‖ tr ripetere ‖ intr ripetere; (said of food) tornare a gola

re•pel [rɪ'pel] v (pret & pp -pelled; ger -pelling) tr respingere, ricacciare; ripugnare (with dat)

repent [rɪ'pent] tr pentirsi di ‖ intr pentirsi, ravvedersi

repentance [rɪ'pentəns] s pentimento

repentant [rɪ'pentənt] adj pentito

repercussion [‚ripər'kʌʃən] s ripercussione

reperto•ry ['repər‚tori] s (-ries) (com) magazzino; (theat) repertorio

repetition [‚repɪ'tɪʃən] s ripetizione

repine [rɪ'paɪn] intr lamentarsi

replace [rɪ'ples] tr (to put back) rimettere; (to take the place of) rimpiazzare

replaceable [rɪ'plesəbəl] adj sostituibile

replacement [rɪ'plesmənt] s rimpiazzo, sostituzione; **as a replacement for al** posto di

replenish [rɪ'plenɪʃ] tr rifornire

replete [rɪ'plit] adj pieno zeppo

replica ['replɪkə] s replica

re•ply [rɪ'plaɪ] s (-plies) risposta ‖ v (pret & pp -plied) tr & intr rispondere

report [rɪ'port] s rapporto, informazione; voce f, rumore m; (of a physician) responso; (of a firearm) detonazione ‖ tr riportare, rapportare; denunziare ‖ intr fare un rapporto; fare il cronista; presentarsi; **to report sick** (mil) marcare visita

report' card' s pagella

reportedly [rɪ'portɪdli] adv secondo la voce comune

reporter [rɪ'portər] s cronista mf, reporter m

reporting [rɪ'portɪŋ] s reportage m

repose [rɪ'poz] s riposo ‖ tr posare, riporre ‖ intr riposare

reprehend [‚reprɪ'hend] tr riprovare, rimproverare

represent [‚reprɪ'zent] tr rappresentare

representation [‚reprɪsen'teʃən] s rappresentazione; protesta; **representations** dichiarazioni fpl

representative [‚reprɪ'zentətɪv] adj rappresentativo ‖ s rappresentante mf; (pol) deputato

repress [rɪ'pres] tr reprimere

repression [rɪ'preʃən] s repressione

reprieve [rɪ'priv] s tregua temporanea; sospensione della pena capitale ‖ tr accordare una tregua a; sospendere l'esecuzione di

reprimand ['reprɪ‚mænd] or ['reprɪ‚mɑnd] s sgridata, ramanzina ‖ tr sgridare, rimproverare

reprint ['rɪ‚prɪnt] s ristampa; (offprint) estratto ‖ [ri'prɪnt] tr ristampare

reprisal [rɪ'praɪzəl] s rappresaglia

reproach [rɪ'protʃ] s rimprovero; vituperio ‖ tr rimproverare; **to reproach s.o. for s.th** rimproverare qlcu di qlco, rimproverare qlco a qlcu

reproduce [‚riprə'djus] or [‚riprə'dus] tr riprodurre ‖ intr riprodursi

reproduction [‚riprə'dʌkʃən] s riproduzione

reproof [rɪ'pruf] s rimprovero

reprove [rɪ'pruv] tr rimproverare; disapprovare

reptile ['reptɪl] s rettile m

republic [rɪ'pʌblɪk] s repubblica

republican [rɪ'pʌblɪkən] adj & s repubblicano

repudiate [rɪ'pjudɪ‚et] tr ripudiare; rinnegare

repugnant [rɪ'pʌgnənt] adj ripugnante

repulse [rɪ'pʌls] s rifiuto; sconfitta ‖ tr rifiutare; (e.g., an enemy) sconfiggere

repulsive [rɪ'pʌlsɪv] adj ripulsivo

reputation [‚repjə'teʃən] s reputazione

repute [rɪ'pjut] *s* reputazione, fama ‖ *tr* reputare

reputedly [rɪ'pjutɪdli] *adv* secondo l'opinione corrente

request [rɪ'kwɛst] *s* domanda, richiesta; **at the request of** su domanda di ‖ *tr* richiedere

Requiem ['rikwɪ,ɛm] or ['rɛkwɪ,ɛm] *adj* di Requiem ‖ *s* Requiem *m* & *f*; **Messa di Requiem**

require [rɪ'kwaɪr] *tr* richiedere

requirement [rɪ'kwaɪrmənt] *s* requisito; richiesta, fabbisogno

requisite ['rɛkwɪzɪt] *adj* requisito, richiesto ‖ *s* requisito

requisition [,rɛkwɪ'zɪʃən] *s* requisizione

requital [rɪ'kwaɪtəl] *s* contraccambio

requite [rɪ'kwaɪt] *tr* (*e.g., an injury*) contraccambiare; (*a person*) contraccambiare (with *dat*)

re-read [ri'rid] *v* (*pret* & *pp* **-read** ['rɛd]) *tr* rileggere

resale ['ri,sel] or [ri'sel] *s* rivendita

rescind [rɪ'sɪnd] *tr* annullare, cancellare; (law) rescindere

rescue ['rɛskju] *s* salvataggio, liberazione; **to go to the rescue of** andare al soccorso di ‖ *tr* salvare, liberare, soccorrere

research [rɪ'sʌrtʃ] or ['risʌrtʃ] *s* ricerca, indagine *f* ‖ *intr* investigare

re-sell [ri'sel] *v* (*pret* & *pp* **-sold** ['sold]) *tr* rivendere

resemblance [rɪ'zɛmbləns] *s* somiglianza

resemble [rɪ'zɛmbəl] *tr* somigliare (with *dat*), rassomigliare (with *dat*); **to resemble one another** rassomigliarsi

resent [rɪ'zɛnt] *tr* (*a remark*) risentirsi per; (*a person*) risentirsi con

resentful [rɪ'zɛntfəl] *adj* risentito

resentment [rɪ'zɛntmənt] *s* risentimento

reservation [,rɛzər'veʃən] *s* riserva; (*e.g., for a room*) prenotazione

reserve [rɪ'zʌrv] *s* riserva; (*self-restraint*) riserbo, contegno ‖ *tr* riservare; prenotare

reservist [rɪ'zʌrvɪst] *s* riservista *m*

reservoir ['rɛzər,vwar] *s* serbatoio, cisterna; (*large storage place for supplying community with water*) bacino di riserva; (fig) pozzo

re-set [ri'sɛt] *v* (*pret* & *pp* **-set**; *ger* **-setting**) *tr* rimettere a posto; (*a watch*) regolare; (*a gem*) incastonare di nuovo; (*a machine*) rimontare

re-ship [ri'ʃɪp] *v* (*pret* & *pp* **-shipped**; *ger* **-shipping**) *tr* rispedire; (*on a ship*) reimbarcare ‖ *intr* reimbarcarsi

reshipment [ri'ʃɪpmənt] *s* rispedizione; (*on a ship*) reimbarco

reside [rɪ'zaɪd] *intr* risiedere

residence ['rɛzɪdəns] *s* residenza

resident ['rɛzɪdənt] *adj* & *s* residente *mf*

residential [,rɛzɪ'dɛnʃəl] *adj* residenziale

residue ['rɛzɪ,dju] or ['rɛsɪ,du] *s* residuo

resign [rɪ'zaɪn] *tr* rassegnare, abbandonare; **to be resigned to** rassegnarsi a ‖ *intr* dimettersi, rassegnare le dimissioni

resignation [,rɛzɪg'neʃən] *s* (*from a job*) dimissione; (*submission*) rassegnazione

resin ['rɛzɪn] *s* resina

resist [rɪ'zɪst] *tr* resistere (with *dat*) ‖ *intr* resistere

resistance [rɪ'zɪstəns] *s* resistenza

resole [ri'sol] *tr* risolare

resolute ['rɛzə,lut] *adj* risoluto

resolution [,rɛzə'luʃən] *s* risoluzione; **good resolutions** buoni propositi

resolve [rɪ'zɔlv] *s* risoluzione ‖ *tr* risolvere ‖ *intr* risolversi

resonance ['rɛzənəns] *s* risonanza

resort [rɪ'zɔrt] *s* (*appeal*) ricorso; (*for vacation*) centro di villeggiatura ‖ *intr* ricorrere

resound [rɪ'zaʊnd] *intr* risonare

resounding [rɪ'zaʊndɪŋ] *adj* risonante; (*success*) strepitoso

resource [rɪ'sɔrs] or ['risɔrs] *s* risorsa

resourceful [rɪ'sɔrsfəl] *adj* ingegnoso

respect [rɪ'spɛkt] *s* rispetto; **respects** rispetti *mpl*, ossequi *mpl*; **with respect to** rispetto a ‖ *tr* rispettare

respectable [rɪ'spɛktəbəl] *adj* rispettabile; onesto, per bene

respectful [rɪ'spɛktfəl] *adj* rispettoso

respecting [rɪ'spɛktɪŋ] *prep* rispetto a

respective [rɪ'spɛktɪv] *adj* rispettivo

respiratory ['rɛspɪrə,tori] or [rɪ'spaɪrə,tori] *adj* respiratorio

respire [rɪ'spaɪr] *tr* & *intr* respirare

respite ['rɛspɪt] *s* tregua, requie *f*; (*reprieve*) proroga, dilazione

resplendent [rɪ'splɛndənt] *adj* risplendente

respond [rɪ'spand] *intr* rispondere

response [rɪ'spans] *s* risposta

responsibil·ty [rɪ,spansɪ'bɪlɪti] *s* (-ties) responsabilità *f*

responsible [rɪ'spansɪbəl] *adj* responsabile; (*job*) di fiducia; **responsible for** responsabile di

responsive [rɪ'spansɪv] *adj* rispondente; (*e.g., to affection*) sensibile; (*e.g., motor*) che risponde

rest [rɛst] *s* riposo; (*what remains*) resto; (mus) pausa; **at rest** in riposo; tranquillo, in pace; (*dead*) morto; **the rest** il resto, gli altri; **to come to rest** andare a finire; **to lay to rest** sotterrare ‖ *tr* riposare; (*to direct one's eyes*) dirigere; (*faith*) porre ‖ *intr* riposarsi, riposare; appoggiarsi; **to rest assured (that)** esser sicuro (che); **to rest on** aver fiducia in; basarsi su; (*one's laurels*) dormire su

restaurant ['rɛstərənt] or ['rɛstə,rant] *s* ristorante *m*

restful ['rɛstfəl] *adj* riposante, tranquillo

rest' home' *s* casa di riposo

rest'ing place' *s* luogo di riposo; (*of a staircase*) pianerottolo; (*of the dead*) ultima dimora

restitution [,rɛstɪ'tjuʃən] or [,rɛstɪ'tuʃən] *s* restituzione

restive ['rɛstɪv] *adj* irrequieto; (*e.g.,* *horse*) recalcitrante

restless ['rɛstlɪs] *adj* irrequieto; (*night*) insonne, in bianco

restock [rɪ'stɑk] *tr* rifornire; (*e.g., with fish*) ripopolare

restoration [ˌrɛstə'reʃən] *s* restaurazione

restore [rɪ'stor] *tr* restaurare, ripristinare

restrain [rɪ'stren] *tr* ritenere, frenare; limitare

restraint [rɪ'strent] *s* restrizione, controllo, ritegno; detenzione

restrict [rɪ'strɪkt] *tr* restingere, limitare

restriction [rɪ'strɪkʃən] *s* restrizione

rest' room' *s* toletta; gabinetto di decenza

restructuring [rɪ'strʌktʃərɪŋ] *s* ristrutturazione

result [rɪ'zʌlt] *s* risultato || *intr* risultare; **to result in** risolversi in, concludersi con

resume [rɪ'zum] *or* [rɪ'zjum] *tr* riprendere || *intr* ricominciare

résumé [ˌrɛzu'me] *or* [ˌrɛzju'me] *s* sunto, riassunto

resumption [rɪ'zʌmpʃən] *s* ripresa

resurface [rɪ'sʌrfɪs] *tr* mettere copertura nuova a || *intr* riemergere

resurrect [ˌrɛzə'rɛkt] *tr & intr* risuscitare

resurrection [ˌrɛzə'rɛkʃən] *s* risurrezione

resuscitate [rɪ'sʌsɪˌtet] *tr* rendere alla vita

retail ['ritel] *adj & adv* al dettaglio, al minuto || *s* dettaglio || *tr* dettagliare, vendere al minuto || *intr* vendere or vendersi al minuto

retailer ['ritelər] *s* dettagliante *mf*

retain [rɪ'ten] *tr* ritenere; (*a lawyer*) assicurarsi i servizi di

retaliate [rɪ'tælɪˌet] *intr* fare rappresaglie; **to retaliate for** ricambiare

retaliation [rɪˌtælɪ'eʃən] *s* rappresaglia

retard [rɪ'tɑrd] *s* ritardo || *tr* ritardare

retch [rɛtʃ] *intr* avere sforzi di vomito

reticence ['rɛtɪsəns] *s* riservatezza

reticent ['rɛtɪsənt] *adj* riservato, taciturno

retina ['rɛtɪnə] *s* retina

retinue ['rɛtɪˌnju] *or* ['rɛtɪˌnu] *s* seguito, corteggio

retire [rɪ'taɪr] *tr* ritirare; (*an employee*) giubilare, mettere a riposo || *intr* ritirarsi; andare a riposo; (*to go to bed*) andare a letto

retired [rɪ'taɪrd] *adj* (*employee*) in pensione; (*officer*) a riposo

retirement [rɪ'taɪrmənt] *s* ritiro; (*of an employee*) pensionamento, quiescenza

retort [rɪ'tɔrt] *s* risposta per le rime; controreplica; (*chem*) storta || *tr* rispondere per le rime a || *intr* rispondere per le rime

retouch [rɪ'tʌtʃ] *tr* ritoccare

retrace [rɪ'tres] *tr* ripercorrere; **to retrace one's steps** ritornare sui propri passi

retract [rɪ'trækt] *tr* ritrattare, disdire || *intr* disdirsi

re·tread ['riˌtred] *s* pneumatico col copertone ricostruito || [rɪ'tred] *v* (*pret & pp* **-treaded**) *tr* ricostruire il copertone di || *v* (*pret* **-trod** ['trɑd]; *pp* **-trod** *or* **-trodden**) *tr* ripercorrere || *intr* rimettere il piede

retreat [rɪ'trit] *s* (*seclusion*) ritiro; (mil) ritirata; (eccl) esercizio spirituale; **to beat a retreat** battere in ritirata || *intr* ritirarsi

retrench [rɪ'trɛntʃ] *tr* ridurre, tagliare; (mil) trincerare || *intr* ridurre le spese; (mil) trincerarsi

retribution [ˌrɛtrɪ'bjuʃən] *s* ricompensa; (theol) giudizio finale

retributive [rɪ'trɪbjətɪv] *adj* retributivo

retrieve [rɪ'triv] *tr* riguadagnare, riconquistare; (*to repair*) risarcire; (hunt) riportare || *intr* riportare la presa

retriever [rɪ'trivər] *s* cane *m* da presa

retroactive [ˌrɛtro'æktɪv] *adj* retroattivo

retrofiring [ˌrɛtro'faɪrɪŋ] *s* accensione dei retrorazzi

retrogress ['rɛtrəˌgrɛs] *intr* regredire; retrocedere

retrorocket [ˌrɛtro'rɑkɪt] *s* retrorazzo

retrospect ['rɛtrəˌspɛkt] *s* esame retrospettivo; **in retrospect** retrospettivamente

retrospective [ˌrɛtrə'spɛktɪv] *adj* retrospettivo

re·try [rɪ'traɪ] *v* (*pret & pp* **-tried**) *tr* (*a person*) riprocessare; (*a case*) ritentare

return [rɪ'tʌrn] *adj* di ritorno; ripetuto || *s* restituzione; ritorno; profitto; (*of income tax*) dichiarazione; risposta; rapporto ufficiale; (*of an election*) responso; (sports) rimando, rimessa; **in return (for)** in cambio (di); **many happy returns of the day!** cento di questi giorni!; **returns** (*of an election*) responso, risultato || *tr* tornare, ritornare restituire; (*a favor*) contraccambiare; (*a profit*) dare; (*thanks; a decision*) rendere; (sports) ribattere || *intr* tornare; rispondere

return' ad'dress *s* indirizzo del mittente

return' bout' *s* (boxing) rivincita

return' mail' *s*—**by return mail** a volta di corriere, a giro di posta

return' tick'et *s* biglietto di ritorno; (Brit) biglietto di andata e ritorno

reunification [riˌjunɪfɪ'keʃən] *s* riunione, unificazione

reunion [ri'junjən] *s* riunione

reunite [ˌriju'naɪt] *tr* riunire || *intr* riunirsi

rev [rɛv] *s* (coll) giro || *v* (*pret & pp* **revved**; *ger* **revving**) *tr*—**to rev up** (coll) imballare || *intr* (coll) accelerare, imballarsi

revamp [ri'væmp] *tr* rinnovare, rappezzare

reveal [rɪ'vil] *tr* rivelare, svelare

reveille ['rɛvəli] *s* sveglia, levata

rev·el ['rɛvəl] *s* baldoria || *v* (*pret &*

pp **-eled** or **-elled; ger -eling** or
-elling) *intr* gozzovigliare; bearsi
revelation [‚revə'leʃən] *s* rivelazione
|| **Revelation** *s* (Bib) Apocalisse *f*
revel·ry ['revəlri] *s* (**-ries**) baldoria
revenge [ri'vendʒ] *s* vendetta || *tr* ven-
dicare
revengeful [ri'vendʒfəl] *adj* vendicativo
revenue ['revə‚nju] or ['revə‚nu] *s*
entrata, profitto; (*government income*) entrate *fpl* erariali
rev'enue cut'ter *s* motobarca della
guardia di finanza
rev'enue stamp' *s* marca da bollo
reverberate [ri'vʌrbə‚ret] *intr* river-
berarsi; (*said, e.g., of sound*) riper-
cuotersi, risonare; (*said of an echo*)
rimbalzare
revere [ri'vir] *tr* venerare, riverire
reverence ['revərəns] *s* riverenza || *tr*
ossequiare
reverend ['revərənd] *adj* & *s* reverendo
reverent ['revərənt] *adj* reverente
reverie ['revəri] *s* sogno, fantasticheria
reversal [ri'vʌrsəl] *s* inversione, cambio; (law) annullamento
reverse [ri'vʌrs] *adj* rovescio, con-
trario; (mach) di retromarcia || *s*
contrario; (*rear*) dietro; (*misfortune*)
side of a coin not bearing principal
design) rovescio; (mach) retromarcia
|| *tr* invertire; rovesciare; mettere in
marcia indietro; **to reverse oneself**
cambiare d'opinione; **to reverse the
charges** far pagare al destinatario;
(telp) far pagare al numero chiamato
|| *intr* invertirsi
revert [ri'vʌrt] *intr* ritornare
review [ri'vju] *s* (*critical article*) recensione; (*magazine*) rivista; (educ)
ripasso, ripetizione; (mil) rivista ||
tr recensire; rivedere; (*a lesson*) ripassare; (mil) passare in rassegna
revile [ri'vail] *tr* insultare, offendere
revise [ri'vaiz] *s* revisione; (typ) se-
conda bozza || *tr* rivedere; correg-
gere
revision [ri'viʒən] *s* revisione
revisionism [ri'viʒə‚nizəm] *s* revisionismo
revival [ri'vaivəl] *s* ripresa delle forze;
(*restoration*) ripristino; (*of learning*) rinascimento; risveglio religioso;
(theat, mov) ripresa
revive [ri'vaiv] *tr* ravvivare; (*a custom*) ripristinare; (theat) dare la
ripresa di || *intr* ravvivarsi; risorgere
revoke [ri'vok] *tr* revocare
revolt [ri'volt] *s* rivolta || *tr* rivoltare
|| *intr* rivoltarsi
revolting [ri'voltiŋ] *adj* rivoltante
revolution [‚revə'luʃən] *s* rivoluzione
revolutionar·y [‚revə'luʃə‚neri] *adj* ri-
voluzionario || *s* (**-ies**) rivoluzionario
revolve [ri'vʌlv] *tr* far rotare; (*in one's
mind*) rivolgere || *intr* girare, rotare
revolver [ri'vʌlvər] *s* rivoltella
revolv'ing book'case *s* scaffale *m* girevole
revolv'ing cred'it *s* credito rotativo
revolv'ing door' *s* porta girevole

revolv'ing fund' *s* fondo rotativo
revue [ri'vju] *s* rivista
revulsion [ri'vʌlʃən] *s* ripugnanza, avversione; (med) revulsione
reward [ri'word] *s* premio, ricompensa; (*money offered for capture*)
taglia; (*for return of articles lost*)
mancia competente || *tr* premiare,
ricompensare
rewarding [ri'wordiŋ] *adj* rimunerativo; gradevole
re-wind [ri'waind] *s* (*of a tape*) ribo-
binazione || *v* (*pret* & *pp* **-wound**
[waund]) *tr* ribobinare
re-write [ri'rait] *v* (*pret* **-wrote** ['rot];
pp **-written** ['ritən]) *tr* riscrivere;
(*news*) rimaneggiare, correggere
rhapso·dy ['ræpsədi] *s* (**-dies**) rapsodia
rheostat ['ri·ə‚stæt] *s* reostato
rhesus ['risəs] *s* reso
rhetoric ['retərik] *s* retorica
rhetorical [ri'tarikəl] or [ri'tɔrikəl]
adj retorico
rheumatic [ru'mætik] *adj* & *s* reuma-
tico
rheumatism ['rumə‚tizəm] *s* reumatismo
Rhine [rain] *s* Reno
Rhineland ['rain‚lænd] *s* la Renania
rhine'stone' *s* gemma artificiale
rhinoceros [rai'nasərəs] *s* rinoceronte
m
Rhodes [rodz] *s* Rodi *f*
Rhone [ron] *s* Rodano
rhubarb ['rubarb] *s* rabarbaro; (slang)
baruffa
rhyme [raim] *s* rima; **without rhyme or
reason** senza capo né coda || *tr* &
intr rimare
rhythm ['riðəm] *s* ritmo
rhythmic(al) ['riðmik(əl)] *adj* ritmico
rial·to [ri'ælto] *s* (**-tos**) mercato || **the
Rialto** il ponte di Rialto; il centro
teatrale di New York
rib [rib] *s* costola; (*cut of meat*) costata; (*of umbrella*) stecca; (*of leaf*)
nervatura; (aer, archit) centina;
(naut) costa || *v* (*pret* & *pp* **ribbed;**
ger **ribbing**) *tr* (slang) prendersi
gioco di
ribald ['ribəld] *adj* volgare, indecente
ribbon ['ribən] *s* nastro; (*decoration*)
nastrino; **ribbons** (*shreds*) brandelli
mpl
rice [rais] *s* riso
rich [ritʃ] *adj* ricco; (*food*) nutrito,
grasso; (*wine*) generoso; (*voice*)
caldo; (*color*) vivo; (*odor*) forte;
(coll) divertente; (coll) assurdo; **to
strike it rich** trovare la miniera d'oro
|| **riches** *spl* ricchezze *fpl*; **the rich** i
ricchi
rickets ['rikits] *s* rachitismo
rickety ['rikiti] *adj* (*object*) sganghe-
rato; (*person*) vacillante; (*suffering
from rickets*) rachitico
rid [rid] *v* (*pret* & *pp* **rid;** *ger* **ridding**)
tr liberare, sbarazzare; **to get rid of**
liberarsi di, sbarazzarsi di
riddance ['ridəns] *s* liberazione; **good
riddance!** che sollievo!
riddle ['ridəl] *s* enigma *m*, indovi-

nello; (*sieve*) crivello ‖ *tr* crivellare; (*to sift*) vagliare; (*s.o.'s reputation*) rovinare; **to riddle with** crivellare di

ride [raɪd] *s* scarrozzata; cavalcata; gita ‖ *v* (*pret* **rode** [rod]; *pp* **ridden** [ˈrɪdən]) *tr* cavalcare, montare, montare su; (*e.g., a bus*) andare in; (*the waves*) galleggiare su; attraversare; tiranneggiare; farsi gioco di; **to ride down** travolgere; sorpassare; **to ride out** uscire felicemente da ‖ *intr* cavalcare; fare una passeggiata, fare una gita; (*to float*) galleggiare; **to let ride** lasciar correre; **to ride on** dipendere da

rider [ˈraɪdər] *s* cavallerizzo; ciclista *mf*; viaggiatore *m*, passeggero

ridge [rɪdʒ] *s* (*of mountains*) crinale *m*, dorsale *f*; (*of roof*) displuvio; (*agr*) porca

ridge'pole' *s* trave maestra, colmo

ridicule [ˈrɪdɪˌkjul] *s* ridicolo; **to expose to ridicule** porre in ridicolo ‖ *tr* ridicolizzare

ridiculous [rɪˈdɪkjələs] *adj* ridicolo

rid'ing boot' *s* stivalone *m* d'equitazione

rid'ing school' *s* maneggio

rife [raɪf] *adj* comune, prevalente; **rife with** pieno di

riffraff [ˈrɪfˌræf] *s* gentaglia

rifle [ˈraɪfəl] *s* fucile *m*; cannone rigato ‖ *tr* (*a place*) svaligiare; (*a person*) derubare; (*a gun*) rigare

rifle' range' *s* tiro a segno

rift [rɪft] *s* crepa, fessura; disaccordo

rig [rɪg] *s* attrezzatura, equipaggio; impianto di sondaggio (per il petrolio); (*outfit*) tenuta ‖ *v* (*pret & pp* **rigged**; *ger* **rigging**) *tr* attrezzare, equipaggiare; guarnire; abbigliare in maniera strana

rigging [ˈrɪgɪŋ] *s* (naut) padiglione *m*; (*tackle*) (naut) rizza; (coll) vestiti *mpl*

right [raɪt] *adj* giusto; corretto; (*mind*) sano; destro, diritto; (geom) retto; (geom) perpendicolare; **right or wrong** a torto o a ragione; **to be all right** star bene di salute; **to be right** aver ragione ‖ *s* diritto; quanto è giusto, (il) giusto; (*in a company*) interessenza; (*right hand*) destra; (*turn*) giro a destra; (boxing) diritto; (tex) dritto; (pol) destra; **by right** in giustizia; **on the right** alla destra; **to be in the right** aver ragione ‖ *adv* direttamente; completamente; immediatamente; proprio, precisamente, correttamente, giustamente; bene; alla destra; (coll) molto; **all right** benissimo ‖ *tr* drizzare; correggere; rimettere a posto ‖ *intr* drizzarsi

righteous [ˈraɪtʃəs] *adj* retto; virtuoso

right' field' *s* (baseball) campo destro

rightful [ˈraɪtfəl] *adj* giusto; legittimo

right'-hand drive' *s* guida a destra

right-handed [ˈraɪtˈhændɪd] *adj* che usa la destra; destrorso

right'-hand man' *s* braccio destro

rightist [ˈraɪtɪst] *adj* conservatore ‖ *s* conservatore *m*, membro della destra

rightly [ˈraɪtli] *adv* correttamente; giustamente; **rightly or wrongly** a torto o a ragione

right' mind' *s*—**in one's right mind** nel pieno possesso delle proprie facoltà, con la testa a posto

right' of way' *s* precedenza; (law) servitù *f* di passaggio; (rr) sede *f*

rights' of man' *s* diritti *mpl* dell'uomo

right'-wing *adj* della destra

right-winger [ˈraɪtˈwɪŋər] *s* membro della destra, conservatore *m*

rigid [ˈrɪdʒɪd] *adj* rigido

rigmarole [ˈrɪgməˌrol] *s* sproloquio

rigorous [ˈrɪgərəs] *adj* rigoroso

rile [raɪl] *tr* irritare, esasperare

rill [rɪl] *s* rigagnolo

rim [rɪm] *s* orlo, bordo; (*of a wheel*) cerchione *m*

rime [raɪm] *s* brina; (*in verse*) rima ‖ *tr* brinare; rimare ‖ *intr* rimare

rind [raɪnd] *s* (*of animals*) cotenna; (*of fruit or cheese*) scorza

ring [rɪŋ] *s* (*for finger*) anello; (*anything round*) cerchio; (*circular course*) pista; (*of people*) crocchio; (*of evildoers*) combriccola; (*of anchor*) anello; (*sound of bell*) squillo; (*loud sound of bell*) scampanellata; (*of small bell; of glassware*) tintinnio; (*act of ringing*) sonata; (telp) chiamata; (fig) suono; (boxing) quadrato; (mach) ghiera; (fig, taur) arena; **to run rings around** essere molto migliore di ‖ *v* (*pret & pp* **ringed**) *tr* accerchiare; mettere un anello a ‖ *intr* formare cerchi ‖ *v* (*pret* **rang** [ræŋ]; *pp* **rung** [rʌŋ]) *tr* sonare; squillare; tintinnare; chiamare al telefono; **to ring up** chiamare al telefono; (*a sale*) battere sul registratore di cassa ‖ *intr* sonare; squillare; tintinnare; chiamare; (*said of one's ears*) fischiare; **to ring for** chiamare col campanello; **to ring off** terminare una conversazione telefonica; **to ring up** chiamare al telefono

ring-around-a-rosy [ˈrɪŋəˌraʊndəˈrozi] *s* girotondo

ringing [ˈrɪŋɪŋ] *adj* alto, sonoro ‖ *s* accerchiamento; squillo; tintinnio; (*in the ears*) fischio

ring'lead'er *s* capobanda *m*

ringlet [ˈrɪŋlɪt] *s* anellino

ring'mas'ter *s* direttore *m* di circo equestre

ring'side' *s* posto vicino al quadrato

ring'worm' *s* tigna

rink [rɪŋk] *s* pattinatoio

rinse [rɪns] *s* risciacquatura ‖ *tr* risciacquare

riot [ˈraɪət] *s* sommossa, tumulto; profusione; **to be a riot** (coll) essere divertentissimo; **to run riot** sfrenarsi; (*said of plants*) crescere disordinatamente ‖ *intr* tumultuare; darsi alle gozzoviglie

rioter [ˈraɪətər] *s* rivoltoso

rip [rɪp] *s* sdrucitura; (*open seam*) scucitura ‖ *v* (*pret & pp* **ripped**; *ger* **ripping**) *tr* sdrucire; (*to open the* *seam of)* scucire || *intr* sdrucirsi; scucirsi; **to rip out with insults** (coll) prorompere in improperi

ripe [raɪp] *adj* maturo; *(lips)* turgido; *(cheese)* stagionato; pronto

ripen [ˈraɪpən] *tr & intr* maturare

ripple [ˈrɪpəl] *s* increspatura; *(sound)* mormorio || *tr* increspare || *intr* incresparsi; mormorare

rise [raɪz] *s (of prices, temperature)* aumento; *(of a road)* salita; *(of ground)* elevazione; *(of a heavenly body)* levata; *(in rank)* ascesa; *(of a step)* alzata; *(of a stream)* sorgente *f;* *(of water)* crescita; **to get a rise out of** (coll) farsi rispondere per le rime da; **to give rise to** dar origine a || *v (pret* **rose** [roz]; *pp* **risen** [ˈrɪzən]) *intr (said of the sun)* sorgere; rialzarsi; *(said of plants)* crescere; *(said of the wind)* alzarsi; *(said of a building)* ergersi; *(to return from the dead)* risorgere; *(to increase)* aumentare; **to rise above** alzarsi al di sopra di; essere al di sopra di; **to rise to** sorgere all'altezza di

riser [ˈraɪzər] *s (of step)* alzata; *(upright)* montante *m;* **early riser** persona mattiniera; **late riser** dormiglione *m*

risk [rɪsk] *s* rischio; **to run or take a risk** correre un rischio || *tr* rischiare

risk·y [ˈrɪski] *adj (-ier, -iest)* rischioso

risqué [rɪsˈke] *adj* audace, spinto

rite [raɪt] *s* rito; **last rites** riti *mpl* funebri

ritual [ˈrɪtʃʊ·əl] *adj & s* rituale *m*

ri·val [ˈraɪvəl] *s* rivale *mf* || *v (pret & pp* **-valed** or **-valled;** *ger* **-valing** or **-valling)** *tr* rivaleggiare con

rival·ry [ˈraɪvəlri] *s (-ries)* rivalità *f*

river [ˈrɪvər] *s* fiume *m;* **down the river** a valle; **up the river** a monte

riv·er ba·sin *s* bacino fluviale

riv·er·bed *s* letto di fiume

riv·er front *s* riva di fiume

riv·er·head *s* sorgente *f* di fiume

riv·er·side *adj* rivierasco || *s* riva del fiume

rivet [ˈrɪvɪt] *s* ribattino; *(of scissors)* perno || *tr* ribadire; *(s.o.'s attention)* concentrare

roach [rotʃ] *s* scarafaggio

road [rod] *adj* stradale || *s* strada; via; (naut) rada; **to be in the road of** ostacolare il cammino a; **to burn up the road** divorare la strada; **to get out of the road** togliersi di mezzo

roadability [ˌrodəˈbɪlɪti] *s* tenuta di strada

road·bed *s (of highway)* piattaforma; (rr) massicciata, infrastruttura

road·block *s* (mil) barricata; (fig) impedimento

road·house *s* taverna su autostrada

road· la·borer *s* cantoniere *m*

road· map *s* carta stradale

road· roll·er *s* compressore *m* stradale, rullo compressore

road· serv·ice *s* servizio di assistenza stradale

road·side *s* bordo della strada

road·side inn *s* taverna posta su autostrada

road· sign *s* indicatore *m* stradale

road·stead *s* rada

road·way *s* carreggiata; strada

roam [rom] *s* vagabondaggio || *tr* girovagare per || *intr* girovagare

roar [ror] *s* ruggito, muggito; boato, fragore *m* || *intr* muggire; **to roar with laughter** fare una risata

roast [rost] *s* arrosto; torrefazione || *tr* arrostire; *(coffee)* tostare, torrefare; (coll) farsi beffe di || *intr* arrostirsi

roast· beef *s* rosbif *m*

roast·ed pea·nut *s* nocciolina americana abbrustolita

roast· pork *s* arrosto di maiale

rob [rab] *v (pret & pp* **robbed;** *ger* **robbing)** *tr & intr* derubare

robber [ˈrabər] *s* ladro, malandrino

robber·y [ˈrabəri] *s (-ies)* furto

robe [rob] *s (of a woman)* vestito; *(of a professor)* toga; *(of a priest)* abito talare; *(dressing gown)* vestaglia; *(for lap)* coperta da viaggio; **robes** vestiti *mpl* || *tr* vestire || *intr* vestirsi

robin [ˈrabɪn] *s* pettirosso

robot [ˈrobat] *s* robot *m*

robust [roˈbʌst] *adj* robusto

rock [rak] *s* roccia; *(any stone)* pietra; *(sticking out of water)* scoglio; *(one that is thrown)* sasso; *(hill)* rocca; (slang) pietra preziosa; **on the rocks** (coll) in rovina; (coll) al verde; *(said, e.g., of whiskey)* sul ghiaccio || *tr* far vacillare; dondolare || *intr* vacillare; dondolare

rock·bot·tom *adj* (l') ultimo; (il) minimo

rock· can·dy *s* zucchero candito

rock· crys·tal *s* cristallo di rocca

rocker [ˈrakər] *s (curved piece at bottom of rocking chair)* dondolo; sedia a dondolo; (mach) bilanciere *m;* **off one's rocker** (slang) matto

rocket [ˈrakɪt] *s* razzo || *intr* partire come un razzo

rock·et launch·er [ˈlɔntʃər] or [ˈlɑntʃər] *s* lanciarazzo

rock· gar·den *s* giardino piantato fra le rocce

rock·ing chair *s* sedia a dondolo

rock·ing horse *s* cavallo a dondolo

rock· salt *s* salgemma *m*

rock· wool *s* cotone *m* or lana minerale

rock·y [ˈraki] *adj (-ier, -iest)* roccioso; traballante; (coll) debole

rod [rad] *s* verga, bacchetta; scettro; punizione; *(bar)* asta; *(for fishing)* canna da pesca; (anat, biol) bastoncino; (mach) biella; (surv) biffa; (Bib) razza, tribù *f;* (slang) pistola; **spare the rod and spoil the child** la madre pietosa fa la piaga cancrenosa

rodent [ˈrodənt] *adj & s* roditore *m*

rod·man *s (-men)* *s* aiutante *m* geometra

roe [ro] *s* capriolo; *(of fish)* uova *fpl*

rogue [rog] *s* furfante *m;* *(scamp)* picaro

rogues'' gal'lery s collezione di fotografie di malviventi

rôle or **role** [rol] s ruolo, parte f; **to play a role** fare la parte

roll [rol] s (of film, paper, etc.) rotolo, bobina; (of fat) strato; (roller) rotella; (of bread) panino; ondulazione; (noise) rullio, rullo; (of a boat) rollio; (of thunder) rombo; (list) ruolo; (of money) (slang) fascio; **to call the roll** fare la chiama || tr far rotolare; (one's r's) arrotare; (one's eyes) stralunare; (e.g., dough) spianare; (steel) laminare; (to wrap) arrotolare; (a drum) rullare; **to roll back** (prices) ridurre; **to roll out** spianare; srotolare; **to roll up** (one's sleeves) arrotolarsi; accumulare; aumentare || intr rotolare; rullare; arrotolarsi; raggomitolarsi; **to roll on** passare; **to roll out** srotolarsi; (to get out of bed) (slang) alzarsi

roll' call' s chiama, appello

roller ['rolər] s rotella; (for hair) bigodino; rotolo; (wave) ondata lunga

roll'er bear'ing s cuscinetto a rotolamento

roll'er coast'er s montagne russe

roll'er skate' s pattino a rotelle

roll'er-skate' intr pattinare coi pattini a rotelle

roll'er tow'el s bandinella

roll'ing mill' ['rolɪŋ] s laminatoio

roll'ing pin' s matterello

roll'ing stock' s (rr) materiale m rotabile

roll'-top desk' s scrivania a piano scorrevole

roly-poly ['roli'poli] adj grassoccio

roman ['romən] adj (typ) romano, tondo || s (typ) carattere romano, tondo || **Roman** adj & s romano

Ro'man can'dle s candela romana

Ro'man Cath'olic Church' s Chiesa Cattolica Apostolica Romana

romance [ro'mæns] or ['romæns] s romanzo; sentimentalità f; idillio, intrigo amoroso; (mus) romanza || [ro'mæns] intr scrivere romanzi; raccontare romanzi; fare il romantico || **Romance** ['romæns] or [ro'mæns] adj romanzo, neolatino

Ro'man Em'pire s Impero Romano

romanesque [,romən'esk] adj romantico || **Romanesque** adj & s romanico

Ro'man nose' s naso aquilino

romantic [ro'mæntɪk] adj romantico

romanticism [ro'mæntɪ,sɪzəm] s romanticismo

romanticist [ro'mæntɪsɪst] s romantico

romp [romp] intr ruzzare

rompers ['rompərz] spl pagliaccetto

roof [ruf] or [ruf] s (of house) tetto; (of heaven) volta; (of car) tetto, padiglione m; **to hit the roof** (slang) andare fuori dai gangheri; **to raise the roof** (slang) fare molto chiasso; (slang) protestare violentemente || tr ricoprire con tetto

roofer ['rufər] or ['rufər] s conciatetti m

roof' gar'den s giardino pensile

rook [ruk] s (bird) cornacchia; (in chess) torre f || tr truffare

rookie ['ruki] s novizio; (mil) recluta

room [rum] or [rum] s stanza, camera; vano, locale m; posto, spazio; opportunità f; **to make room far** luogo || intr alloggiare

room' and board' s vitto e alloggio

room' clerk' s impiegato d'albergo assegnato alle prenotazioni

roomer ['rumər] or ['rumər] s inquilino

room'ing house' s casa con camere d'affittare

room'mate' s compagno di stanza

room-y ['rumi] or ['rumi] adj (-ier; -iest) ampio, spazioso

roost [rust] s (perch) ballatoio; (house for chickens) pollaio; (place for resting) posto di riposo; **to rule the roost** essere il gallo del pollaio || intr appollaiarsi; andare a dormire

rooster ['rustər] s gallo

root [rut] or [rut] s radice f; **to get to the root of** andare al fondo di; **to take root** metter radici || tr inchiodare, piantare || intr radicare; (said of swine) grufolare; **to root for** fare il tifo per

rooter ['rutər] or ['rutər] s tifoso

rope [rop] s fune f, corda; (of a hangman) capestro; laccio, lasso; **to know the ropes** (coll) conoscere la faccenda a fondo, saperla lunga || tr legare con fune; prendere al laccio; **to rope in** (slang) imbrogliare

rope'danc'er or **rope'walk'er** s funambolo

rosa-ry ['rozəri] s (-ries) rosario

rose [roz] adj & s rosa

rose'bud' s bottoncino di rosa

rose'bush' s rosaio

rose'-col'ored adj color di rosa

rose'-colored glass'es spl occhiali mpl rosa

rose' gar'den s roseto

rosemar-y ['roz,meri] s (-ies) rosmarino

rose' of Shar'on ['ʃɛrən] s altea

rosette [ro'zet] s rosetta; (archit) rosone m

rose' win'dow s rosone m

rose'wood' s palissandro

rosin ['rozɪn] s colofonia

roster ['rostər] s ruolino; orario scolastico

rostrum ['rostrəm] s tribuna

ros-y ['rozi] adj (-ier; -iest) rosa, roseo

rot [rot] s marcio; (coll) stupidaggine f || v (pret & pp rotted; ger rotting) tr & intr imputridire

ro'tary en'gine ['rotəri] s motore rotativo

ro'tary press' s rotativa

rotate ['rotet] or [ro'tet] tr & intr rotare

rotation [ro'teʃən] s rotazione; **in rotation** in successione, a turno

rote [rot] s ripetizione macchinale; **by rote** a memoria

rot'gut' s (slang) acquavite f di infima qualità

rotisserie [ro'tɪsəri] *s* girarrosto a motore

rotten ['rɑtən] *adj* marcio, fradicio; corrotto

rotund [ro'tʌnd] *adj* (*plump*) rotondetto; (*voice*) profondo; (*speech*) enfatico

rouge [ruʒ] *s* belletto, rossetto || *tr* dare il belletto a || *intr* darsi il belletto

rough [rʌf] *adj* scabroso; (*sea*) agitato; (*crude*) rozzo, rude; (*road*) accidentato; approssimativo || *tr*—**to rough it** vivere primitivamente; **to rough up** malmenare

rough'cast' *s* intonaco; modello disgrossato || *v* (*pret & pp* **-cast**) *tr* (*a wall*) intonacare; disgrossare, dirozzare

rough' cop'y *s* brutta copia

rough-hew ['rʌf'hju] *tr* digrossare, dirozzare

roughly ['rʌfli] *adv* aspramente; rozzamente; approssimativamente

round [raund] *adj* rotondo || *s* tondo; (*of applause; of guns*) salva; (*of a single gun*) colpo, tiro; (*of a chair*) piolo; (*of a doctor*) giro; (*of a policeman*) ronda; serie *f*; (*of golf*) partita; (*e.g., of bridge*) mano *f*; cerchio; (*boxing*) ripresa || *adv* intorno; dal principio alla fine || *prep* intorno a; attraverso || *tr* (*to make round*) arrotondare; circondare; (*a corner*) scantonare; **to round off** arrotondare; completare, perfezionare; **to round up** raccogliere; (*cattle*) condurre

roundabout ['raundə,baut] *adj* indiretto || *s* giacca attillata; via traversa; giro di parole; (Brit) giostra; (Brit) anello stradale

round'house' *s* rimessa per locomotive

round-shouldered ['raund'ʃoldərd] *adj* dalle spalle spioventi

round'-trip tick'et *s* biglietto d'andata e ritorno

round'up' *s* (*of cattle*) riunione; (*of criminals*) retata; (*of facts*) riassunto

rouse [rauz] *tr* svegliare; suscitare; (*game*) scovare || *intr* svegliarsi

rout [raut] *s* sconfitta, rotta || *tr* sconfiggere, mettere in rotta || *intr* grufolare

route [rut] or [raut] *s* via, rotta; itinerario || *tr* istradare

routine [ru'tin] *adj* ordinario || *s* trafila, routine *f*

rove [rov] *intr* vagabondare, vagare

rover ['rovər] *s* vagabondo

row [rau] *s* piazzata, scenata; (*clamor*) (coll) baccano; **to raise a row** (coll) fare baccano || [ro] *s* fila; (*of figures*) finca; (*e.g., of trees*) filare *m*; **in a row** in continuazione, di seguito || *tr* vogare || *intr* remare, vogare

rowboat ['ro,bot] *s* barca a remi

row·dy ['raudi] *adj* (**-dier; -diest**) turbolento || *s* (**-dies**) attaccabrighe *mf*

rower ['ro·ər] *s* rematore *m*

rowing ['ro·ɪŋ] *s* (*action*) voga; (*sport*) canottaggio

royal ['rɔɪ·əl] *adj* reale, regio

royalist ['rɔɪ·əlɪst] *adj* sostenitore del re || *s* realista *mf*

royal·ty ['rɔɪ·əlti] *s* (**-ties**) regalità *f*; membro della famiglia reale; nobiltà *f*; diritto d'autore; diritto d'inventore; percentuale *f* sugli utili

rub [rʌb] *s* frizione; difficile *m*; **here's the rub** qui sta il busillis || *v* (*pret & pp* **rubbed**; *ger* **rubbing**) *tr* fregare; **to rub elbows with** stare giunto a gomiti con; **to rub out** cancellare con la gomma; (slang) togliere di mezzo || *intr* sfregare; **to rub off** venir via sfregando; cancellarsi

rubber ['rʌbər] *s* gomma, caucciù *m*; gomma da cancellare; (*overshoe*) caloscia; (*in cards*) rubber *m*; (sports) bella

rub'ber band' *s* elastico

rub'ber·neck' *s* (coll) ficcanaso; (coll) turista curioso || *intr* (coll) allungare il collo

rub'ber plant' *s* albero del caucciù

rub'ber stamp' *s* timbro di gomma; (coll) persona che approva inconsultamente

rub'ber-stamp' *tr* timbrare; (coll) approvare inconsultamente

rubbish ['rʌbɪʃ] *s* spazzatura; immondizia; (fig) detrito; (coll) sciocchezza

rubble ['rʌbəl] *s* (*broken stone*) pietrisco; (*masonry*) mistura di malta e pietrame; (*broken bits*) calcinacci *mpl*

rub'down' *s* fregagione

rube [rub] *s* (slang) contadino gonzo

ru·by ['rubi] *adj* vermiglio || *s* (**-bies**) *s* rubino

rudder ['rʌdər] *s* timone *m*; (aer) timone *m* di direzione

rud·dy ['rʌdi] *adj* (**-dier; -diest**) rubicondo

rude [rud] *adj* rude, sgarbato

rudiment ['rudɪmənt] *s* rudimento

rue [ru] *tr* lamentare, rimpiangere

rueful ['rufəl] *adj* lamentevole; triste

ruffian ['rʌfɪ·ən] *s* ribaldo

ruffle ['rʌfəl] *s* increspatura; (*of drum*) rullo; (sew) gala, crespa || *tr* increspare; arruffare; irritare; (*a drum*) far rullare; (sew) guarnire di gala or crespa

rug [rʌg] *s* tappeto

rugged ['rʌgɪd] *adj* aspro, irregolare; rugoso; rozzo; forte; tempestuoso

ruin ['ru·ɪn] *s* rovina || *tr* rovinare, mandare in rovina

rule [rul] *s* regola; dominazione; (*reign*) regno; (law) ordinanza; (typ) filetto; **as a rule** in generale || *tr* governare; dominare; (*with lines*) rigare; (law) deliberare; **to rule out** escludere || *intr* governare; regnare; **to rule over** governare

rule' of thumb' *s* regola basata sull'esperienza; **by rule of thumb** secondo la propria esperienza

ruler ['rulər] *s* governante *m*, dominatore *m*; (*for ruling lines*) riga, regolo

ruling ['rulɪŋ] *adj* dirigente || *s* (*ruled lines*) rigatura; (law) decisione

rum [rʌm] *s* rum *m*; (*any alcoholic drink*) acquavite *f*

Rumanian [ru'menɪ·ən] *adj & s* rumeno

rumble ['rʌmbəl] *s* rimbombo; (*of the intestines*) gorgoglio; (*slang*) rissa fra ganghe rivali ‖ *intr* rimbombare; gorgogliare

ruminate ['rumɪ ‚net] *tr & intr* ruminare

rummage ['rʌmɪdʒ] *tr & intr* rovistare, frugare

rum'mage sale' *s* vendita di cianfrusaglie

rumor ['rumər] *s* voce *f*, diceria ‖ *tr* vociferare; **it is rumored** che corre voce che

rump [rʌmp] *s* anca; posteriore *m;* (*of beef*) quarto posteriore

rumple ['rʌmpəl] *s* piega ‖ *tr* spiegazzare, sgualcire ‖ *intr* sgualcirsi

rumpus ['rʌmpəs] *s* tumulto; rissa; **to raise a rumpus** fare baccano

run [rʌn] *s* corsa; percorso; produzione; (*e.g., in a stocking*) smagliatura; direzione; (*spell*) serie *f;* (*in cards*) scala; (*of goods*) richiesta; (*on a bank*) afflusso; **in the long run** a lungo andare; **on the run** (coll) di corsa; in fuga; **the common run of men** la media della gente; **to give s.o. a run for his money** dare a qlcu del filo da torcere; essere denaro ben speso per qlcu, e.g., **that sweater gave me a run for my money** quello sweater è stato denaro ben speso per me; **to have a long run** tenere il cartellone per lungo tempo; **to have the run of** avere la libertà di andare e venire per ‖ *v* (*pret* **ran** [ræn]; *pp* **run**; *ger* **running**) *tr* muovere; (*a horse*) far correre; (*the street*) vivere liberamente in; (*game*) inseguire; trasportare; (*a machine*) far camminare; (*a store*) esercire; (*a candidate*) portare; (*a risk*) correre; (*a blockade*) violare; mettere, ficcare; (*a line*) tirare; **to run down** cacciare; esaminare; trovare; (*a pedestrian*) investire; denigrare, criticare; **to run in** (*a machine*) rodare; (*slang*) schiaffare in prigione; **to run off** creare di getto; cacciare; (*typ*) tirare; **to run up** ammassare ‖ *intr* correre; scappare; (*in a race*) arrivare; (*said of a candidate*) portarsi; passare; (*said of knitted material*) smagliarsi; (*said of a liquid*) scorrere; (*said of a color*) sbavare; (*said of fish*) migrare; funzionare; (*to become*) diventare; (*to be worded*) essere del tenore; (com) decorrere; (theat, mov) durare in cartellone; **to run across** imbattersi in; **to run aground** incagliarsi; **to run away** fuggire; (*said of a horse*) prendere la mano; **to run down** (*said of a liquid*) scorrere; (*said of a battery, a watch*) scaricarsi; (*in health*) sciuparsi; **to run for** presentarsi candidato per; **to run in the family** essere una caratteristica familiare; **to run into** imbattersi in; ammontare a; (*to follow*) succedersi a; **to run off the track** (rr) uscire dalle rotaie; **to run out** aver termine; scadere; esaurirsi;

to run out of rimanere senza; **to run over** oltrepassare; (*e.g., with a car*) investire; **to run through** trapassare; (*a fortune*) dilapidare; esaminare rapidamente

run'a·way' *adj* fuggiasco; (*horse*) che ha preso la mano ‖ *s* fuggiasco; cavallo che ha preso la mano; fuga

run'-down' *adj* esausto; negletto, cadente; (*watch, battery*) scarico

rung [rʌŋ] *s* (*of chair or ladder*) piolo

runner ['rʌnər] *s* corridore *m;* messaggero; fattorino, messo; (*of sleigh*) pattino; (*of ice skate*) lama; (*rug*) guida; (*on a table*) striscia di pizzo; (*in stocking*) smagliatura

run'ner-up' *s* (**runners-up**) finalista *mf* secondo

running ['rʌnɪŋ] *adj* in corsa; da corsa; (*water*) corrente; (*vine*) rampicante; (*knot*) scorsoio; (*sore*) purulento; (*writing*) corsivo; consecutivo; (*start*) (sports) lanciato ‖ *s* corsa; (*of a business*) esercizio; direzione; funzionamento; **to be in the running** avere possibilità di vittoria

run'ning board' *s* (aut) pedana

run'ning head' *s* titolo corrente

run·ny ['rʌni] *adj* (-**nier**; -**niest**) (liquid) scorrevole; (*color*) sbavante; **to have a runny nose** avere la goccia al naso

run'off' *s* ballottaggio

run-of-the-mill ['rʌnəvðə'mɪl] *adj* ordinario, corrente

run'proof' *adj* indemagliabile

runt [rʌnt] *s* nanerottolo; animale deperito

run'way' *s* pista; (*of a stream*) letto; (*for animals*) chiusa; (aut) corsia

rupture ['rʌptʃər] *s* rottura; (pathol) ernia ‖ *tr* rompere; causare un'ernia a ‖ *intr* rompersi; soffrire di ernia

ru'ral free' deliv'ery ['rʊrəl] *s* distribuzione postale campestre

ruse [ruz] *s* astuzia, stratagemma *m*

rush [rʌʃ] *adj* urgente ‖ *s* fretta; slancio, corsa; (*of blood*) ondata; (*rushing of persons to a new mine*) febbre *f;* (bot) giunco; **in a rush** in fretta e furia ‖ *tr* affrettare; portare di fretta; spingere; (coll) fare la corte a; **to rush through** fare di fretta; (*e.g., a bill through Congress*) far approvare di fretta ‖ *intr* lanciarsi; affrettarsi; passare velocemente; **to rush through** (*a book*) leggere velocemente; (*one's work*) fare in fretta; (*a town*) attraversare velocemente

rush'-bot'tomed chair' *s* sedia di giunchi

rush' can'dle *s* lumicino con lo stoppino fatto di midollo di giunco

rush' hour' *s* ora di punta

russet ['rʌsɪt] *adj* color cannella

Russia ['rʌʃə] *s* la Russia

Russian ['rʌʃən] *adj & s* russo

rust [rʌst] *s* ruggine *f;* (fig) torpore *m* ‖ *tr* arrugginire ‖ *intr* arrugginirsi

rustic ['rʌstɪk] *adj & s* rustico

rustle ['rʌsəl] *s* fruscio; (*of leaves*) stormire *m* ‖ *tr* far frusciare; far stormire; (*cattle*) (coll) rubare ‖ *intr* frusciare; stormire; (coll) lavorare di buzzo buono

rust·y ['rʌstɪ] *adj* (-ier; -iest) rugginoso; color ruggine; fuori pratica

rut [rʌt] *s* (*track*) solco, carrareccia; (*of animals*) fregola; (il) solito tran

ruthless ['ruθlɪs] *adj* spietato

rye [raɪ] *s* segala; whiskey *m* di segala

S

S, s [es] *s* diciannovesima lettera dell'alfabeto inglese

Sabbath ['sæbəθ] *s* (*of Jews*) sabato; (*of Christians*) domenica; **to keep the Sabbath** osservare il riposo domenicale

sabbat'ical year' [sə'bætɪkəl] *s* anno di congedo; (Bib) anno sabbatico

saber ['sebər] *s* sciabola

sa'ber rat'tling *s* minacce *fpl* di guerra

sable ['sebəl] *adj* nero ‖ *s* zibellino; **sables** vestiti di lutto

sabotage ['sæbə‚taʒ] *s* sabotaggio ‖ *tr* & *intr* sabotare

saccharin ['sækərɪn] *s* saccarina

sachet ['sæʃe] *or* [sæ'ʃe] *s* sacchetto profumato (per la biancheria)

sack [sæk] *s* sacco; (*of an employee*) (slang) licenziamento; (slang) letto ‖ *tr* insaccare; (*to lay waste*) saccheggiare, mettere a sacco; (slang) licenziare

sack'cloth' *s* tela di sacco; (*for penitence*) sacco, cilicio; **in sackcloth and ashes** pentito e contrito

sacrament ['sækrəmənt] *s* sacramento

sacramental [‚sækrə'mentəl] *adj* sacramentale

sacred ['sekrəd] *adj* sacro

sacrifice ['sækrɪ‚faɪs] *s* sacrificio; **at a sacrifice** in perdita ‖ *tr* sacrificare; (com) svendere

sacrilege ['sækrɪlɪdʒ] *s* sacrilegio

sacrilegious [‚sækrɪ'lɪdʒəs] *or* [‚sækrɪ'lidʒəs] *adj* sacrilego

sacristan ['sækrɪstən] *s* sagrestano

sacris·ty ['sækrɪstɪ] *s* (-ties) sagrestia

sad [sæd] *adj* (sadder; saddest) triste; (*bad*) cattivo; (*color*) tetro

sadden ['sædən] *tr* rattristare ‖ *intr* rattristarsi

saddle ['sædəl] *s* sella ‖ *tr* insellare; **to saddle with** gravare di

sad'dle·bag' *s* fonda

saddlebow ['sædəl‚bo] *s* arcione *m* anteriore

sad'dle·cloth' *s* gualdrappa

saddler ['sædlər] *s* sellaio

sad'dle·tree' *s* arcione *m*

sadist ['sædɪst] *or* ['sedɪst] *s* sadico

sadistic [sæ'dɪstɪk] *or* [se'dɪstɪk] *adj* sadico

sadness ['sædnɪs] *s* tristezza

sad' sack' *s* (coll) marmittone *m*

safe [sef] *adj* sicuro; cauto; (*distance*) rispettoso; **safe and sound** sano e salvo ‖ *s* cassaforte *f*

safe'-con'duct *s* salvacondotto

safe'-depos'it box' *s* cassetta di sicurezza

safe'guard' *s* salvaguardia ‖ *tr* salvaguardare

safe·ty ['seftɪ] *adj* di sicurezza ‖ *s* (-ties) sicurezza; (*of a gun*) sicura; **to reach safety** mettersi in salvo

safe'ty belt' *s* (*of a worker*) imbraca; (aer, aut) cintura di sicurezza; (naut) cintura di salvataggio

safe'ty glass' *s* vetro infrangibile

safe'ty is'land *s* salvagente *m*

safe'ty match' *s* fiammifero svedese

safe'ty pin' *s* spillo di sicurezza

safe'ty ra'zor *s* rasoio di sicurezza

safe'ty valve' *s* valvola di sicurezza

saffron ['sæfrən] *s* zafferano

sag [sæg] *s* cedimento; depressione; (*of a rope*) allentamento ‖ *v* (*pret* & *pp* sagged; *ger* sagging) *intr* curvarsi; cedere, afflosciarsi; allentarsi; (*said of prices*) calare

sagacious [sə'geʃəs] *adj* sagace

sage [sedʒ] *adj* saggio, savio ‖ *s* saggio, savio; (bot) salvia

sage'brush' *s* artemisia

Sagittarius [‚sædʒɪ'terɪ‑əs] *s* Sagittario

sail [sel] *s* vela; (*of windmill*) ala; gita a vela; **to set sail** far vela; **under full sail** a piena velatura ‖ *tr* veleggiare, navigare; (*a boat*) far navigare ‖ *intr* veleggiare, navigare; far vela; volare; (*said of a vessel*) partire; **to sail into** (coll) attaccare

sail'boat' *s* nave *f* a vela, veliero

sail'cloth' *s* tela di olona

sailing ['selɪŋ] *adj* in partenza ‖ *s* partenza; navigazione; navigazione a vela

sail'ing ship' *s* veliero

sail'mak'er *s* velaio

sailor ['selər] *s* marinaio

saint [sent] *adj* & *s* santo ‖ *tr* santificare, canonizzare

saint'hood *s* santità *f*

saintliness ['sentlɪnɪs] *s* santità *f*

Saint' Vi'tus's dance' ['vaɪtəsəz] *s* (pathol) ballo di San Vito

sake [sek] *s* causa, interesse *m*; **for the sake of** per il bene di, per l'amor di

salaam [sə'lɑm] *s* salamelecco ‖ *tr* fare salamelecchi a

salable ['seləbəl] *adj* vendibile

salacious [sə'leʃəs] *adj* salace

salad ['sæləd] *s* insalata

sal'ad bowl' *s* insalatiera

sal'ad oil' *s* olio da tavola

sala·ry ['sælərɪ] *s* (-ries) stipendio

sale [sel] *s* vendita; (*at reduced prices*) svendita, saldo; **for sale** in vendita; si vende, si vendono

sales'clerk' *s* commesso, impiegato

sales'la'dy *s* (**-dies**) commessa, impiegata

sales'man *s* (**-men**) venditore *m;* commesso; (*traveling*) piazzista *m*

sales'man·ship' *s* arte *f* di vendere

sales' promo'tion *s* promozione delle vendite, promotion *f*

sales'room' *s* sala di esposizione; sala di vendita

sales' talk' *s* discorso da venditore; (*e.g., of a barker*) imbonimento

sales' tax' *s* imposta sulle vendite

saliva [sə'laɪvə] *s* saliva

sallow ['sælo] *adj* giallastro, olivastro

sal·ly ['sæli] *s* (**-lies**) escursione, gita; (*outburst*) esplosione; (*witty remark*) uscita; (mil) sortita ‖ *v pret & pp* **-lied**) *intr* fare una sortita; **to sally forth** balzar fuori

salmon ['sæmən] *s* salmone *m*

salon [sæ'lɒn] *s* salone *m*

saloon [sə'lun] *s* taverna; (*on a passenger vessel*) salone *m*

saloon' keep'er *s* taverniere *m*

salt [sɒlt] *s* sale *m;* **to be worth one's salt** valere il pane che si mangia ‖ *tr* salare; (*cattle*) dare sale a; **to salt away** (coll) metter via, conservare

salt' bed' *s* salina

salt'cel'lar *s* saliera

saltine [sɒl'tin] *s* galletta salata

saltish ['sɒltɪʃ] *adj* salmastro

salt'pe'ter (*potassium nitrate*) salnitro; (*sodium nitrate*) nitro del Cile

salt' shak'er *s* saliera

salt·y ['sɒlti] *adj* (**-ier; -iest**) salato

salubrious [sə'lubrɪ·əs] *adj* salubre

salutation [ˌsæljə'teʃən] *s* saluto

salute [sə'lut] *s* saluto ‖ *tr* salutare

salvage ['sælvɪdʒ] *s* ricupero ‖ *tr* ricuperare

salvation [sæl've/ən] *s* salvezza

Salva'tion Ar'my *s* Esercito della Salvezza

salve [sæv] *or* [sɑv] *s* unguento ‖ *tr* lenire, alleviare

sal·vo ['sælvo] *s* (**-vos** *or* **-voes**) salva

Samaritan [sə'mærɪtən] *adj & s* samaritano

same [sem] *adj & pron indef* medesimo, stesso; **it's all the same to me** a me fa lo stesso; **just the same** lo stesso, ugualmente; **same . . . as** lo stesso . . . che

sameness ['semnɪs] *s* uniformità *f;* monotonia

sample ['sæmpəl] *s* campione *m*, saggio ‖ *tr* (*to take a sample of*) campionare; (*to taste*) assaggiare; provare

sam'ple cop'y *s* esemplare *m* di campione

sancti·fy ['sæŋktɪˌfaɪ] *v* (*pret & pp* **-fied**) *tr* santificare

sanctimonious [ˌsæŋktɪ'monɪ·əs] *adj* che affetta devozione ipocrita

sanction ['sæŋkʃən] *s* sanzione ‖ *tr* sanzionare

sanctuar·y ['sæŋktʃʊˌɛri] *s* (**-ies**) santuario; **to take sanctuary** prendere asilo, rifugiarsi

sand [sænd] *s* sabbia ‖ *tr* insabbiare;

(*to polish*) smerigliare; cospergere di sabbia

sandal ['sændəl] *s* sandalo

san'dal·wood' *s* sandalo

sand'bag' *s* sacchetto a terra

sand'bank' *s* banco di sabbia

sand' bar' *s* cordone *m* litorale, banco di sabbia

sand'blast' *s* sabbiatura ‖ *tr* pulire con sabbiatura, sabbiare

sand'box' *s* cassone *m* pieno di sabbia; (rr) sabbiera

sand'glass' *s* orologio a polvere *or* a sabbia

sand'pa'per *s* carta vetrata ‖ *tr* pulire con carta vetrata

sand'stone' *s* arenaria

sandwich ['sændwɪtʃ] *s* panino imbottito, tramezzino ‖ *tr* inserire

sand'wich man' *s* tramezzino, uomo sandwich

sand·y ['sændi] *adj* (**-ier; -iest**) sabbioso; (*hair*) biondo rossiccio

sane [sen] *adj* sensato

sanguinary ['sæŋgwɪnˌɛri] *adj* sanguinario

sanguine ['sæŋgwɪn] *adj* fiducioso; (*complexion*) sanguigno

sanitary ['sænɪˌtɛri] *adj* sanitario

san'itary nap'kin *s* pannolino igienico

sanitation [ˌsænɪ'teʃən] *s* sanità *f*

sanity ['sænɪti] *s* sanità *f* di mente

Santa Claus ['sæntəˌklɒz] *s* Babbo Natale

sap [sæp] *s* linfa, succhio; (mil) trincea; (coll) scemo ‖ *v* (*pret & pp* **sapped**) *ger* **sapping**) *tr* scavare; insidiare, minare; (*to weaken*) indebolire

sapling ['sæplɪŋ] *s* alberello; (*youth*) giovanetto

sapphire ['sæfaɪr] *s* zaffiro

Saracen ['særəsən] *adj & s* saraceno

sarcasm ['sɑrkæzəm] *s* sarcasmo

sarcastic [sɑr'kæstɪk] *adj* sarcastico

sardine [sɑr'din] *s* sardina; **packed in like sardines** pigiati come le acciughe

Sardinia [sɑr'dɪnɪ·ə] *s* la Sardegna

Sardinian [sɑr'dɪnɪ·ən] *adj & s* sardo

sarsaparilla [ˌsɑrsəpə'rɪlə] *s* salsapariglia

sash [sæʃ] *s* sciarpa; (*around one's waist*) fusciacca; (*of window*) telaio

sash' win'dow *s* finestra a ghigliottina

sas·sy ['sæsi] *adj* (**-sier; -siest**) (coll) impertinente; (*pert*) (coll) vivace

satchel ['sætʃəl] *s* sacca; (*of schoolboy*) cartella

sateen [sæ'tin] *s* satin *m*

satellite ['sætəˌlaɪt] *s* satellite *m*

satiate ['seʃɪˌet] *tr* saziare

satin ['sætən] *s* raso

satire ['sætaɪr] *s* satira

satiric(al) [sə'tɪrɪk(əl)] *adj* satirico

satirist ['sætɪrɪst] *s* satirico

satirize ['sætɪˌraɪz] *tr* satireggiare

satisfaction [ˌsætɪs'fækʃən] *s* soddisfazione

satisfactory [ˌsætɪs'fæktəri] *adj* soddisfacente

satis·fy ['sætɪsˌfaɪ] *v* (*pret & pp* **-fied**) *tr & intr* soddisfare

saturate ['sætʃəˌret] *tr* saturare

Saturday ['sætərdi] s sabato

Saturn ['sætərn] s (astr) Saturno

sauce [sɔs] s salsa; (of fruit) conserva; (of chocolate) crema; (coll) insolenza, impertinenza || tr condire; rendere piccante || [sɔs] or [sæs] tr (coll) rispondere con impertinenza a

sauce'pan' s casseruola

saucer ['sɔsər] s piattino

sau•cy ['sɔsi] adj (-cier; -ciest) impertinente; (pert) vivace

sauerkraut ['saur,kraut] s sarcrauti mpl, crauti mpl

saunter ['sɔntər] s giro, bighellonata || intr girandolare, bighellonare

sausage ['sɔsɪdʒ] s salsiccia

savage ['sævɪdʒ] adj & s selvaggio

savant ['sævənt] s erudito

save [sev] prep tranne, salvo || tr salvare; (money) risparmiare; (to set apart) serbare; **to save face** salvare le apparenze || intr fare economia

saving ['sevɪŋ] adj economico; che redime || **savings** spl risparmi mpl, economie fpl || **saving** prep eccetto, salvo

sav'ings account' s conto di risparmio

sav'ings and loan' associa'tion s cassa di risparmio che concede mutui

sav'ings bank' s cassa di risparmio

savior ['sevjər] s salvatore m

Saviour ['sevjər] s Salvatore m

savor ['sevər] s sapore m || tr assaporare; (to flavor) saporire || intr odorare; **to savor of** sapere di; odorare di

savor•y ['sevəri] adj (-ier; -iest) saporoso; piccante; delizioso || s (-ies) (bot) santoreggia

saw [sɔ] s (tool) sega; detto, proverbio || tr segare

saw'buck' s cavalletto

saw'dust' s segatura

saw'horse' s cavalletto

saw'mill' s segheria

Saxon ['sæksən] adj & s sassone m

saxophone ['sæksə,fon] s sassofono

say [se] s dire m; **to have no say** non aver voce in capitolo; **to have one's say** esprimere la propria opinione; **to have the say** avere l'ultima parola || v (pret & pp **said** [sed]) tr dire; **I should say so!** certamente!; **it is said** si dice; **no sooner said than done** detto fatto; **that is to say** vale a dire; **to go without saying** essere ovvio

saying ['se·ɪŋ] s detto, proverbio

scab [skæb] s crosta; (strikebreaker) crumiro

scabbard ['skæbərd] s guaina, fodero

scab•by ['skæbi] adj (-bier; -biest) crostoso; (animal) rognoso; (slang) vile

scabrous ['skæbrəs] adj scabroso

scads [skædz] spl (slang) un mucchio

scaffold ['skæfəld] s impalcatura; (to execute a criminal) patibolo

scaffolding ['skæfəldɪŋ] s incastellatura, ponteggio

scald [skɔld] tr scottare; (e.g., milk) cuocere al disotto del punto d'ebollizione

scale [skel] s (e.g., of map) scala; piatto della bilancia; (of fish) squama; **on a large scale** in grande scala; **scales** bilancia; **to tip the scales** far inclinare la bilancia || tr squamare; (to incrust) incrostare; (to weigh) pesare; scalare; graduare; ridurre a scala || intr squamarsi; scrostarsi

scallion ['skæljən] s scalogno

scallop ['skɑləp] or ['skæləp] s (for cooking) conchiglia; (mollusk) pettine m; (slice of meat) scaloppina; (on edge of cloth) dentello, smerlo || tr (fish) cuocere in conchiglia; dentellare, smerlare

scalp [skælp] s cuoio capelluto || tr scotennare; (tickets) fare il bagarinaggio di

scalpel ['skælpəl] s scalpello

scalper ['skælpər] s bagarino

scal•y ['skeli] adj (-ier; -iest) squamoso; scrostato

scamp [skæmp] s cattivo soggetto, briccone m

scamper ['skæmpər] intr sgambettare; **to scamper away** darsela a gambe

scan [skæn] v (pret & pp **scanned**; ger **scanning**) tr scrutare; dare un'occhiata a; (verse) scandire; (telv) analizzare, scandire, esplorare

scandal ['skændəl] s scandalo

scandalize ['skændə,laɪz] tr scandalizzare

scandalous ['skændələs] adj scandaloso

Scandinavian [,skændɪ'nevɪ·ən] adj & s scandinavo

scanning ['skænɪŋ] s (telv) esplorazione

scan'ning line' s (telv) riga di analisi

scant [skænt] adj scarso; corto || tr diminuire; lesinare

scant•y ['skænti] adj (-ier; -iest) appena sufficiente; povero, magro; (clothing) succinto

scapegoat ['skep,got] s capro espiatorio

scar [skɑr] s cicatrice f; (fig) sfregio || v (pret & pp **scarred**; ger **scarring**) tr segnare, marcare; sfregiare || intr cicatrizzarsi

scarce [skɛrs] adj scarso, raro; **to make oneself scarce** (coll) non farsi vedere

scarcely ['skɛrsli] adv appena; a mala pena; non . . . affatto; **scarcely ever** raramente; non . . . affatto

scarci•ty ['skɛrsɪti] s (-ties) scarsità f, scarsezza; carestia

scare [skɛr] s spavento || tr spaventare, impaurire; **to scare away** fare scappare per lo spavento; **to scare up** (money) (coll) metter insieme

scare'crow' s spaventapasseri m

scarf [skɑrf] s (scarfs or scarves [skɑrvz]) sciarpa; cravattone m; (cover for table) centro, striscia

scarf'pin' s spilla da cravatta

scarlet ['skɑrlɪt] adj scarlatto

scar'let fe'ver s scarlattina

scar•y ['skeri] adj (-ier; -iest) (timid) (coll) fifone; (causing fright) (coll) spaventevole

scathing ['skeðɪŋ] *adj* severo, bruciante

scatter ['skætər] *tr* disperdere, sparpagliare || *intr* disperdersi, sparpagliarsi

scatterbrained ['skætər‚brend] *adj* scervellato, stordito

scenari·o [sɪ'nɛrɪ‚o] *or* [sɪ'nɑrɪ‚o] *s* (-os) scenario

scenarist [sɪ'nɛrɪst] *or* [sɪ'nɑrɪst] *s* scenarista *mf*, sceneggiatore *m*

scene [sin] *s* (*view*) paesaggio; (*place*) scena; (theat) scena, quadro; **behind the scenes** dietro le quinte; **to make a scene** fare una scenata

scener·y ['sinəri] *s* (-ies) paesaggio; (theat) scenario

scenic ['sinɪk] *or* ['sɛnɪk] *adj* pittoresco; (*pertaining to the stage*) scenico

scent [sɛnt] *s* odore *m*; profumo; (*sense of smell*) fiuto, odorato; (*trail*) traccia, pista || *tr* profumare; (*to detect*) fiutare, annusare

scepter ['sɛptər] *s* scettro

sceptic ['skɛptɪk] *adj* & *s* scettico

sceptical ['skɛptɪkəl] *adj* scettico

scepticism ['skɛptɪ‚sɪzəm] *s* scetticismo

schedule ['skɛdjʊl] *s* lista; programma *m*; (*of trains, planes, etc.*) orario || *tr* programmare; mettere in orario

scheme [skim] *s* schema *m*; piano, progetto; (*plot*) trama || *tr* progettare; tramare

schemer ['skimər] *s* progettista *mf*; (*underhanded*) manipolatore *m*, concertatore *m*

scheming ['skimɪŋ] *adj* intrigante, scaltro

schism ['sɪzəm] *s* scisma *m*

schist [ʃɪst] *s* scisto

scholar ['skɑlər] *s* (*pupil*) alunno; detentore *m* di una borsa di studio; (*learned person*) dotto, studioso

scholarly ['skɑlərli] *adj* erudito, studioso

scholarship ['skɑlər‚ʃɪp] *s* erudizione; (*money*) borsa di studio

scholasticism [skə'læstɪ‚sɪzəm] *s* scolastica

school [skul] *s* scuola; (*of a university*) facoltà *f*; (*of fish*) banco || *tr* istruire, insegnare

school' age' *s* età scolastica

school'bag' *s* cartella

school' board' *s* comitato scolastico

school'boy' *s* alunno, scolaro

school' bus' *s* scuolabus *m*

school' day' *s* giorno di scuola; durata della giornata scolastica

school'girl' *s* alunna, scolara

school'house' *s* scuola, edificio scolastico

schooling ['skulɪŋ] *s* istruzione

school'mas'ter *s* maestro di scuola; direttore scolastico

school'mate' *s* compagno di scuola, condiscepolo

school'room' *s* aula scolastica

school'teach'er *s* maestro

school' year' *s* anno scolastico

schooner ['skunər] *s* goletta

sciatica [saɪ'ætɪkə] *s* (pathol) sciatica

science ['saɪ‚əns] *s* scienza

sci'ence fic'tion *s* fantascienza

sci'ence-fic'tion *adj* fantascientifico

scientific [‚saɪ‚ən'tɪfɪk] *adj* scientifico

scientist ['saɪ‚əntɪst] *s* scienziato

scimitar ['sɪmɪtər] *s* scimitarra

scintillate ['sɪntɪ‚let] *intr* scintillare

scion ['saɪ‚ən] *s* rampollo, discendente *m*

scissors ['sɪzərz] *ssg or spl* forbici *fpl*

scoff [skɔf] *or* [skɑf] *s* dileggio, beffa || *intr* burlarsi; **to scoff at** burlarsi di, dileggiare

scold [skold] *s* megera || *tr* & *intr* sgridare, rimproverare

scoop [skup] *s* (*ladlelike utensil*) paletta; (*kitchen utensil*) cucchiaio, cucchiaione *m*; cucchiaiata; palettata; (*of dredge*) benna; (*hollow*) buco; (naut) gottazza; (journ) primizia, esclusiva; (coll) colpo || *tr* vuotare a cucchiaiate; (journ) battere; (naut) gottare; **to scoop out** (*e.g., sand*) scavare; (*soup*) scodellare

scoot [skut] *s* (coll) corsa || *intr* (coll) correre precipitosamente

scooter ['skutər] *s* monopattino

scope [skop] *s* ampiezza; lunghezza; **to give full scope to** dare piena libertà d'azione

scorch [skɔrtʃ] *s* scottatura || *tr* bruciacchiare; bruciare, inaridire; (fig) ferire || *intr* bruciarsi

scorching ['skɔrtʃɪŋ] *adj* bruciante

score [skor] *s* (*in a game*) punteggio; (*in an examination*) nota; linea, segno, marca; (*twenty*) ventina; (mus) partitura; **scores** un mucchio; **to keep score** segnare il punteggio; **to settle a score** (fig) saldare un conto || *tr* raggiungere il punteggio di, fare; marcare; guadagnare; (*to censure*) sgridare, rimproverare; (mus) orchestrare

score'board' *s* quadro del punteggio

score'keep'er *s* segnapunti *m*

scorn [skɔrn] *s* disdegno, disprezzo || *tr* & *intr* disdegnare, disprezzare

scornful ['skɔrnfəl] *adj* disdegnoso

Scorpio ['skɔrpi‚o] *s* Scorpione *m*

scorpion ['skɔrpɪ‚ən] *s* scorpione *m*

Scot [skɑt] *s* scozzese *mf*

Scotch [skɑtʃ] *adj* scozzese || *s* scozzese *m*; whisky *m* scozzese; **the Scotch** gli scozzesi

Scotch'man *s* (-men) scozzese *m*

Scotch' pine' *s* pino silvestre

Scotch' tape' *s* (trademark) nastro autoadesivo Scotch

scot'-free' *adj* impune; **to get off scot-free** farla franca

Scotland ['skɑtlənd] *s* la Scozia

Scottish ['skɑtɪʃ] *adj* scozzese || *s* scozzese *mf*; **the Scottish** gli scozzesi

scoundrel ['skaundrəl] *s* birbante *m*, farabutto, manigoldo

scour [skaur] *tr* sgrassare fregando, pulire fregando; (*the countryside*) battere

scourge [skʌrdʒ] *s* sferza; (fig) flagello || *tr* sferzare

scout [skaut] *s* esplorazione; giovane esploratore *m;* giovane esploratrice *f;* (mil) ricognitore *m;* (nav) esploratore *m;* (slang) tipo || *tr* esplorare, riconoscere; cercar di trovare; disdegnare

scouting ['skautɪŋ] *s* scoutismo

scowl [skaul] *s* cipiglio || *intr* aggrottare le ciglia; guardare torvamente

scram [skræm] *v* (*pret & pp* **scrammed;** *ger* **scramming**) *intr* (coll) tagliare la corda; **scram!** (coll) vattene!, (coll) escimi di tra i piedi!

scramble ['skræmbəl] *s* ruffa, gara || *tr* (*to grab up*) arraffare; confondere, mescolare; (*eggs*) strapazzare || *intr* arrampicarsi; (*to struggle*) azzuffarsi

scram'bled eggs' *spl* uova strapazzate

scrap [skræp] *s* pezzetto, frammento; ritaglio, rottame *m;* (coll) baruffa; **scraps** avanzi *mpl;* || *v* (*pret & pp* **scrapped;** *ger* **scrapping**) *tr* scartare || *intr* (coll) fare baruffa

scrap'book' *s* album *m* di ritagli (di giornale o fotografie)

scrape [skrep] *s* impiccio, imbroglio; baruffa || *tr* raschiare, graffiare; **to scrape together** racimolare || *intr* raschiare; **to scrape along** vivacchiare; **to scrape through** passare per il rotto della cuffia

scraper ['skrepər] *s* raschietto

scrap' i'ron *s* rottami *mpl* di ferro

scrap' pa'per *s* carta straccia; carta da appunti

scratch [skrætʃ] *s* graffio, scalfittura; scarabocchio; (billiards) punto perduto; (sports) linea di partenza; **from scratch** da bel principio; dal niente; **up to scratch** soddisfacente || *tr* graffiare, grattare; (*e.g., a horse*) cancellare || *intr* graffiare; (*said of a chicken*) raspare; (*said of a pen*) grattare

scratch' pad' *s* quaderno per appunti

scratch' pa'per *s* carta da appunti

scrawl [skrɔl] *s* scarabocchio || *tr & intr* scarabocchiare

scraw·ny ['skrɔni] *adj* (**-nier; -niest**) ossuto, scarno

scream [skrim] *s* grido, strillo; cosa divertentissima; persona divertentissima || *intr* gridare, strillare

screech [skritʃ] *s* stridio || *intr* stridere

screech' owl' *s* gufo; (barn owl) barbagianni *m*

screen [skrin] *s* (*movable partition*) paravento; (*in front of fire*) parafuoco; rete metallica; (*sieve*) vaglio; (mov; phys) schermo; (telv) teleschermo || *tr* schermare; riparare, proteggere; (*to sieve*) vagliare; (*a film*) proiettare; (*to adapt*) (mov) sceneggiare

screen' grid' *s* (rad, telv) griglia schermo

screen' test' *s* provino

screw [skru] *s* vite *f;* giro di vite; (*of a boat*) elica; **to have a screw loose** (slang) avere una rotella fuori di posto; **to put the screws on** far pressione su || *tr* avvitare; (*to twist*)

torcere; **to screw up** (slang) rovinare; **to screw up one's courage** prendere il coraggio a quattro mani || *intr* avvitarsi

screw'ball' *s* (slang) pazzoide *m,* svitato

screw'driv'er *s* cacciavite *m*

screw' eye' *s* occhiello a vite

screw' jack' *s* martinetto a vite

screw' propel'ler *s* elica

screw·y ['skru·i] *adj* (**-ier; -iest**) (slang) pazzo; (slang) fuori di posto, strano

scribble ['skrɪbəl] *s* scarabocchio || *tr & intr* scarabocchiare

scribe [skraɪb] *s* (*Jewish scholar*) scriba *m;* copista *mf* || *tr* tracciare, incidere

scrimmage ['skrɪmɪdʒ] *s* ruffa; (*football*) azione

scrimp [skrɪmp] *tr & intr* lesinare

script [skrɪpt] *s* scrittura, scrittura a mano; manoscritto; testo; (*e.g., of a play*) copione *m;* (typ) carattere *m* inglese

scriptural ['skrɪptʃərəl] *adj* scritturale, biblico

scripture ['skrɪptʃər] *s* scrittura || **Scripture** Scrittura

script'writ'er *s* soggettista *mf*

scrofula ['skrɑfjələ] *s* scrofola

scroll [skrol] *s* rotolo di carta, rotolo di pergamena; (*of violin*) riccio; (archit) voluta, cartoccio

scroll'work' *s* ornamentazione a voluta

scro·tum ['skrotəm] *s* (**-ta** [tə] or **-tums**) scroto

scrub [skrʌb] *s* boscaglia; alberelli *mpl;* animale bastardo; persona di poco conto; (*act of scrubbing*) fregata; (sports) giocatore *m* di riserva || *v* (*pret & pp* **scrubbed;** *ger* **scrubbing**) *tr* pulire, fregare

scrub' oak' *s* rovere basso

scrub'wom'an *s* (**-wom'en**) lavatrice *f,* donna a giornata

scruff [skrʌf] *s* nuca, collottola

scruple ['skrupəl] *s* scrupolo

scrupulous ['skrupjələs] *adj* scrupoloso

scrutinize ['skrutɪ ˌnaɪz] *tr* scrutare, disaminare

scruti·ny ['skrutɪni] *s* (**-nies**) attento esame, disamina

scuff [skʌf] *s* graffio, logorio || *tr* logorare, graffiare

scuffle ['skʌfəl] *s* zuffa, rissa || *intr* azzuffarsi, collottolare

scull [skʌl] *s* (*oar*) remo a bratto; (*boat*) canotto || *tr* spingere a bratto || *intr* vogare a bratto

sculler·y ['skʌləri] *s* (**-ies**) retrocucina

scul'lery maid' *s* sguattera

scullion ['skʌljən] *s* sguattero

sculptor ['skʌlptər] *s* scultore *m*

sculptress ['skʌlptrɪs] *s* scultrice *f*

sculpture ['skʌlptʃər] *s* scultura || *tr & intr* scolpire

scum [skʌm] *s* schiuma; (slag) scoria; (*rabble*) feccia, gentaglia || *v* (*pret & pp* **scummed;** *ger* **scumming**) *tr & intr* schiumare

scum·my [ˈskʌmi] *adj* (-mier; -miest) spumoso; (coll) vile, schifoso

scurf [skʌrf] *s* (*shed by the skin*) squama; incrostazione

scurrilous [ˈskʌrɪləs] *adj* scurrile

scur·ry [ˈskʌri] *v* (*pret & pp* -ried) *intr* affrettarsi; **to scurry around** dimenarsi

scur·vy [ˈskʌrvi] *adj* (-vier; -viest) spregevole, meschino || *s* scorbuto

scuttle [ˈskʌtəl] *s* (*for coal*) secchio; (*trap door*) botola; corsa, fuga; (naut) boccaporto || *tr* aprire una falla in, affondare || *intr* affrettarsi, darsi alla corsa

scut'tle·butt' *s* (naut) barilozzo dell'acqua; (coll) rumore *m*, diceria

scuttling [ˈskʌtlɪŋ] *s* autoaffondamento

Scylla [ˈsɪlə] *s* Scilla; **between Scylla and Charybdis** fra Scilla e Cariddi

scythe [saɪð] *s* falce *f*

sea [si] *s* mare *m*; (*wave*) maroso; **at sea** in alto mare; **by the sea** a mare, sulla costa; **to follow the sea** farsi marinaio; **to put to sea** prendere il largo

sea'board' *adj* costiero || *s* litorale *m*

sea' breeze' *s* brezza marina

sea'coast' *s* costa, litorale *m*

sea' dog' *s* (seal) foca; (sailor) lupo di mare

seafarer [ˈsiˌfɛrər] *s* marinaio; viaggiatore marittimo

sea'food' *s* pesce *m*; (shellfish) frutti *mpl* di mare

seagoing [ˈsiˌgoˑɪŋ] *adj* di alto mare

sea' gull' *s* gabbiano

seal [sil] *s* sigillo; (*sea animal*) foca; (fig) suggello || *tr* sigillare, apporre i sigilli a; (fig) suggellare

sea' legs' *spl*—**to have good sea legs** avere piede marino

sea' lev'el *s* livello del mare

seal'ing wax' *s* ceralacca

seal'skin' *s* pelle *f* di foca

seam [sim] *s* (*abutting of edges*) giuntura; (stitches) costura, cucitura; (scar) cicatrice *f*; (wrinkle) ruga; (in metal) commettitura; (min) filone *m*, vena

sea'man *s* (-men) marinaio

sea' mile' *s* miglio marino

seamless [ˈsimlɪs] *adj* senza giuntura; (stockings) senza cucitura

seamstress [ˈsimstrɪs] *s* cucitrice *f*

seam·y [ˈsimi] *adj* (-ier; -iest) pieno di cuciture; basso, sordido; (unpleasant) spiacevole

séance [ˈseˑɑns] *s* seduta spiritica

sea'plane' *s* idrovolante *m*

sea'port' *s* porto di mare

sea' pow'er *s* potenza navale

sear [sɪr] *adj* secco || *s* scottatura || *tr* scottare, bruciare; (*to brand*) marcare a fuoco; inaridire; (fig) indurire

search [sʌrtʃ] *s* ricerca, investigazione; (*frisking a person*) perquisizione; **in search of** in cerca di || *tr* cercare, investigare; perquisire, frugare || *intr* investigare; **to search for** cercare; **to search into** investigare

searching [ˈsʌrtʃɪŋ] *adj* (e.g., *inspec-*

tion) profondo; (e.g., *glance*) indagatore, penetrante

search'light' *s* proiettore *m*, riflettore *m*; (mil) fotoelettrica

search' war'rant *s* mandato di perquisizione

sea'scape' *s* vista del mare; (painting) marina

sea' shell' *s* conchiglia

sea'shore' *s* costa, marina, mare *m*

sea'sick' *adj*—**to be seasick** aver mal di mare

sea'sick'ness *s* mal *m* di mare

sea'side' *s* costa, riviera, marina

season [ˈsizən] *s* stagione; **in season** di stagione; **in season and out of season** sempre, continuamente; **out of season** fuori stagione || *tr* (food) condire; (*to mature*) stagionare; (e.g., *wood*) stagionare

seasonal [ˈsizənəl] *adj* stagionale

seasoning [ˈsizənɪŋ] *s* condimento; (of wood) stagionamento

sea'son's greet'ings *spl* migliori auguri *mpl* per le feste natalizie

sea'son tick'et *s* biglietto d'abbonamento

seat [sit] *s* sedia; (*part of chair*) sedile *m*; (*of human body*) sedere *m*; (*of pants*) fondo; sito, posto; (e.g., *of government*) sede *f*; (in parliament) seggio; (e.g., *of learning*) centro; (rr, theat) posto || *tr* far sedere; aver posti per; (*a chair*) mettere il sedile a; (pants) mettere il fondo a; (*an official*) insediare; (mach) installare; **to be seated** essere seduto; **to seat oneself** sedersi

seat' belt' *s* cintura di sicurezza

seat' cov'er *s* guaina, foderina

seat'ing room' *s* posti *mpl* a sedere

sea' wall' *s* diga

sea'way' *s* via marittima; alto mare; mare grosso; rotta percorsa; via di fiume accessibile a navi da trasporto

sea'weed' *s* alga marina; pianta marina

sea'wor'thy *adj* atto a tenere il mare

secede [sɪˈsid] *intr* separarsi, distaccarsi

secession [sɪˈsɛʃən] *s* secessione

seclude [sɪˈklud] *tr* appartare; isolare

seclusion [sɪˈkluʒən] *s* reclusione; solitudine *f*, intimità *f*

second [ˈsɛkənd] *adj & pron* secondo; **to be second to none** non cederla a nessuno || *s* secondo; (*in a duel*) padrino; (in dates) due *m*; (aut, mus) seconda; **seconds** (com) articoli *mpl* di seconda qualità; **to have seconds on** servirsi una seconda volta di || *tr* assecondare; (*a motion*) appoggiare || *adv* in secondo luogo

secondar·y [ˈsɛkənˌdɛri] *adj* secondario || *s* (-ies) (elec) secondario

sec'ond-best' *adj* (il) migliore dopo il primo; **to come off second-best** arrivare secondo

sec'ond-class' *adj* di seconda qualità; (aer, naut, rr) di seconda classe

sec'ond hand' *s* lancetta dei secondi

sec'ond·hand' *adj* di seconda mano, d'occasione

sec'ond lieuten'ant *s* sottotenente *m*
sec'ond-rate' *adj* di seconda categoria; (*inferior*) da strapazzo
sec'ond sight' *s* chiaroveggenza
sec'ond wind' [wɪnd] *s*—to get one's second wind riprendere fiato
secre·cy ['sikrəsi] *s* (-cies) segretezza; in secrecy in segreto
secret ['sikrɪt] *adj* & *s* segreto; in secret in segreto
secretar·y ['sɛkrɪ ˌtɛri] *s* (-ies) segretario; (*desk*) scrittoio
se'cret bal'lot *s* scrutinio segreto
secrete [sɪ'krit] *tr* nascondere; (physiol) secernere
secretive ['sikrɪtɪv] or [sɪ'kritɪv] *adj* riservato, poco comunicativo
sect [sɛkt] *s* setta
sectarian [sɛk'tɛri·ən] *adj* & *s* settario
section ['sɛkt/ən] *s* sezione; (*of city*) rione *m*; (*of fruit*) spicchio; (*of highway*) tronco; (rr) tratta ‖ *tr* sezionare
sectional ['sɛkʃənəl] *adj* (e.g., bookcase) componibile; sezionale; locale, regionale
secular ['sɛkjələr] *adj* & *s* secolare *m*
secularism ['sɛkjələ ˌrɪzəm] *s* laicismo
secure [sɪ'kjʊr] *adj* salvo, sicuro ‖ *tr* ottenere; assicurare; fissare; (law) garantire
securi·ty [sɪ'kjʊrɪti] *s* (-ties) sicurezza; protezione; garanzia; (*person*) garante *m*; securities valori *mpl*, titoli *mpl*
sedan [sɪ'dæn] *s* (aut) berlina
sedan' chair' *s* bussola, portantina
sedate [sɪ'det] *adj* calmo, posato
sedation [sɪ'deʃən] *s* ritorno alla calma; stato di calma mentale
sedative ['sɛdətɪv] *adj* & *s* sedativo
sedentary ['sɛdən ˌtɛri] *adj* sedentario
sedge [sɛdʒ] *s* carice *m*
sediment ['sɛdɪmənt] *s* sedimento
sedition [sɪ'dɪʃən] *s* sedizione
seditious [sɪ'dɪʃəs] *adj* sedizioso
seduce [sɪ'djus] or [sɪ'dus] *tr* sedurre
seducer [sɪ'djusər] or [sɪ'dusər] *s* seduttore *m*, corruttore *m*
seduction [sɪ'dʌkʃən] *s* seduzione
seductive [sɪ'dʌktɪv] *adj* seduttore
sedulous ['sɛdjələs] *adj* diligente
see [si] *s* (eccl) sede *f* ‖ *v* (*pret* saw [sɔ]; *pp* seen [sin]) *tr* vedere; to see off andare ad accompagnare; to see through portare a termine ‖ *intr* vedere; see here! faccia attenzione!; to see after prender cura di; to see through conoscere il gioco di
seed [sid] *s* seme *m*, semenza; to go to seed andare in semenza; deteriorarsi ‖ *tr* seminare; (*fruit*) togliere i semi da ‖ *intr* seminare; produrre semi
seed'bed' *s* semenzaio; (fig) vivaio
seeder ['sidər] *s* (*person*) seminatore *m*; (*machine*) seminatrice *f*
seedling ['sidlɪŋ] *s* piantina da trapianto
seed·y ['sidi] *adj* (-ier; -iest) pieno di semi; (*unkempt*) malmesso, malvestito
seeing ['si·ɪŋ] *conj* visto che, dato che

See'ing Eye' dog' *s* cane *m* guida per ciechi
seek [sik] *v* (*pret* & *pp* sought [sɔt]) *tr* cercare, ricercare; to be sought after essere ricercato; to seek to cercare di
seem [sim] *intr* parere, sembrare
seemingly ['simɪŋli] *adv* apparentemente
seem·ly ['simli] *adj* (-lier; -liest) decoroso; appropriato
seep [sip] *intr* colare, filtrare
seer [sɪr] *s* profeta *m*, veggente *m*
see'saw' *s* altalena; (*motion*) viavai *m* ‖ *intr* altalenare
seethe [siθ] *intr* bollire
segment ['sɛgmənt] *s* segmento
segregate ['sɛgrɪ ˌget] *tr* segregare
segregation [ˌsɛgrɪ'geʃən] *s* segregazione
segregationist [ˌsɛgrɪ'geʃənɪst] *s* segregazionista *mf*
Seine [sen] *s* Senna
seismograph ['saɪzmə ˌgræf] or ['saɪzmə ˌgraf] *s* sismografo
seismology [saɪz'mɑlədʒi] *s* sismologia
seize [siz] *tr* afferrare; impossessarsi di; (*with one's clenched fist*) impugnare; comprendere; (law) sequestrare, confiscare
seizure ['siʒər] *s* conquista, cattura; (*of an illness*) attacco; (law) sequestro, pignoramento
seldom ['sɛldəm] *adj* di raro, raramente
select [sɪ'lɛkt] *adj* scelto, selezionato ‖ *tr* prescegliere, selezionare
selectee [sɪ ˌlɛk'ti] *s* (mil) recluta
selection [sɪ'lɛkʃən] *s* selezione, scelta
selective [sɪ'lɛktɪv] *adj* selettivo
self [sɛlf] *adj* stesso ‖ *s* (selves [sɛlvz]) sé stesso; io, personalità *f*; all by one's self senza aiuto altrui ‖ *pron* sé stesso
self'-abuse' *s* abuso delle proprie forze; masturbazione
self'-addressed' *adj* col nome e l'indirizzo del mittente
self'-cen'tered *adj* egocentrico
self'-con'scious *adj* imbarazzato, vergognoso, timido
self'-control' *s* padronanza di sé stesso, autocontrollo
self'-defense' *s* autodifesa; in self-defense in legittima difesa
self'-deni'al *s* abnegazione
self'-deter'mina'tion *s* autodeterminazione
self'-dis'cipline *s* autodisciplina
self'-ed'ucat'ed *adj* autodidatta
self'-employed' *adj* che lavora in proprio
self'-ev'i·dent *adj* evidente, lampante
self'-ex·plan'a·tor·y *adj* ovvio, che si spiega da sé
self'-gov'ernment *s* autogoverno; controllo sopra sé stesso
self'-im·por'tant *adj* presuntuoso
self'-in·dul'gence *s* intemperanza
self'-in'terest *s* egoismo, interesse *m*
selfish ['sɛlfɪʃ] *adj* egoista
selfishness ['sɛlfɪʃnɪs] *s* egoismo

selfless ['sɛlflɪs] *adj* disinteressato; altruista
self'-liq'ui-dat'ing *adj* autoammortizzabile
self'-love' *s* amor proprio
self'-made' *adj* che si è fatto da sé
self'-por'trait *s* autoritratto
self'-pos-sessed' *adj* calmo, padrone di sé
self'-pres'er-va'tion *s* conservazione
self'-pro-pelled' *adj* semovente
self'-re-li'ant *adj* pieno di fiducia in sé stesso
self'-re-spect' *s* rispetto di sé stesso
self'-right'eous *adj* che si considera più morale degli altri, ipocrita
self'-sac'ri-fice' *s* sacrificio di sé, spirito di sacrificio
self'-same' *adj* stesso e medesimo
self'-sat'is-fied' *adj* contento di sé
self'-seek'ing *adj* egoista || *s* egoismo
self'-serv'ice *s* autoservizio
self'-start'er *s* motorino d'avviamento
self'-styled' *adj* sedicente
self'-support' *s* indipendenza economica
self'-tap'ping screw' *s* vite *f* autofilettante
self'-taught' *adj* autodidatta
self'-threading ['sɛlf'θrɛdɪŋ] *adj* autofilettante
self'-willed' *adj* ostinato, caparbio
self'-wind'ing *adj* a carica automatica
sell [sɛl] *v* (*pret & pp* **sold** [sold]) *tr* vendere; (*an idea*) fare accettare; **to sell off** svendere, liquidare; **to sell out** smerciare; vendere a stralcio; (coll) tradire || *intr* vendere, vendersi; fare il venditore; **to sell off** (*said of the stock market*) essere in ribasso; **to sell out** vendere a stralcio; vendersi
seller ['sɛlər] *s* venditore *m*
Selt'zer wa'ter ['sɛltsər] *s* selz *m*
selvage ['sɛlvɪdʒ] *s* cimosa, vivagno
semantic [sɪ'mæntɪk] *adj* semantico || **semantics** *s* semantica
semaphore ['sɛmə,for] *s* semaforo
semblance ['sɛmbləns] *s* apparenza, specie *f*; apparizione
semen ['simən] *s* sperma *m*
semester [sɪ'mɛstər] *adj* semestrale || *s* semestre *m*
semicircle ['sɛmɪ,sʌrkəl] *s* semicircolo
semicolon ['sɛmɪ,kolən] *s* punto e virgola
semiconductor [,sɛmɪkən'dʌktər] *s* semiconduttore *m*
semiconscious [,sɛmɪ'kɑnʃəs] *adj* mezzo cosciente
semifinal [,sɛmɪ'faɪnəl] *s* semifinale *f*
semilearned [,sɛmɪ'lʌrnɪd] *adj* semidotto
semimonth-ly [,sɛmɪ'mʌnθli] or [,sɛmaɪ'mʌnθli] *adj* quindicinale || *s* (-lies) rivista quindicinale
seminar ['sɛmɪ,nɑr] or [,sɛmɪ'nɑr] *s* seminario
seminar-y ['sɛmɪ,nɛri] *s* (-ies) seminario
Semite ['sɛmaɪt] or ['simaɪt] *s* semita *mf*

Semitic [sɪ'mɪtɪk] *adj* semitico || *s* lingua semitica; (*family of languages*) semitico
semitrailer ['sɛmɪ,trelər] *s* semirimorchio
semiweek-ly [,sɛmi'wikli] or [,sɛmaɪ'wikli] *adj* bisettimanale || *s* (-lies) periodico bisettimanale
semiyearly [,sɛmi'jɪrli] or [,sɛmaɪ'jɪrli] *adj* semestrale || *adv* due volte all'anno
senate ['sɛnɪt] *s* senato
senator ['sɛnətər] *s* senatore *m*
send [sɛnd] *v* (*pret & pp* **sent** [sɛnt]) *tr* inviare, mandare; spedire; (*e.g., a punch*) lanciare; **to send back** rimandare; **to send forth** emettere; **to send packing** licen iare su due piedi || *intr* (rad) trasmettere; **to send for** mandare a chiamare, far venire
sender ['sɛndər] *s* speditore *m*, mittente *m*; (telg) trasmettitore *m*
send'-off' *s* (coll) addio affettuoso; (coll) lancio
senility [sɪ'nɪlɪti] *s* (pathol) senilismo
senior ['sinjər] *adj* maggiore, più anziano; seniore, di grado più elevato; dell'ultimo anno, laureando; senior, il vecchio || *s* maggiore *m*; seniore *m*, persona di grado più elevato; studente *m* dell'ultimo anno, laureando
sen'ior cit'izen *s* vecchio, pensionato
seniority [sin'jɑrɪti] or [sin'jɔrɪti] *s* anzianità *f*
sensation [sɛn'seʃən] *s* sensazione
sensational [sɛn'seʃənəl] *adj* sensazionale
sense [sɛns] *s* senso; **in a sense** in un certo senso; **to come to one's senses** riprendere il giudizio; **to make sense out of** arrivare a capire; **to take leave of one's senses** perdere il ben dell'intelletto || *tr* intuire; comprendere
senseless ['sɛnslɪs] *adj* (*unconscious*) privo di sensi; (*meaningless*) insensato, privo di senso
sense' or'gan *s* organo di senso
sensibili-ty [,sɛnsɪ'bɪlɪti] *s* (-ties) sensibilità *f*; **sensibilities** suscettibilità *f*
sensible ['sɛnsɪbəl] *adj* sensato; (*keenly aware*) sensibile; cosciente
sensitive ['sɛnsɪtɪv] *adj* sensitivo, sensibile; delicato
sensitize ['sɛnsɪ,taɪz] *tr* sensibilizzare
sensory ['sɛnsəri] *adj* sensorio
sensual ['sɛnʃʊ-əl] *adj* sensuale
sensuous ['sɛnʃʊ-əs] *adj* sensuale
sentence ['sɛntəns] *s* (gram) frase; (law) sentenza, condanna || *tr* sentenziare, condannare
sentiment ['sɛntɪmənt] *s* sentimento
sentimental [,sɛntɪ'mɛntəl] *adj* sentimentale
sentimentalism [,sɛntɪ'mɛntəl,izəm] *s* sentimentalismo
sentinel ['sɛntɪnəl] *s* sentinella; **to stand sentinel** montare di sentinella
sen-try ['sɛntri] *s* (-tries) sentinella
sen'try box' *s* garitta, casotto
separate ['sɛpərɪt] *adj* separato ||

['sepə‚ret] *tr* separare || *intr* separarsi

separation [‚sepə're∫ən] *s* separazione

Sephardic [sı'fɑrdık] *adj* sefardita

September [sep'tembər] *s* settembre *m*

septic ['septık] *adj* settico

sep'tic tank' *s* fossa settica

sepulcher ['sepəlkər] *s* sepolcro

sequel ['sikwəl] *s* seguito

sequence ['sikwəns] *s* serie *f*, sequenza, successione; conseguenza; (cards, eccl, mov) sequenza; (gram) correlazione

sequester [sı'kwestər] *tr* isolare, appartare; (law) sequestrare

sequin ['sikwın] *s* lustrino

ser·aph ['serəf] *s* (**-aphs** or **-aphim** [əfım]) serafino

Serbian ['sʌrbı·ən] *adj & s* serbo

Serbo-Croatian [‚sʌrbokro'e∫ən] *adj & s* serbocroato

sere [sır] *adj* secco, appassito

serenade [‚serə'ned] *s* serenata || *tr* fare la serenata a || *intr* fare la serenata

serene [sı'rin] *adj* sereno

serenity [sı'renıti] *s* serenità *f*

serf [sʌrf] *s* servo della gleba

serfdom ['sʌrfdəm] *s* servitù *f* della gleba

serge [sʌrdʒ] *s* saia

sergeant ['sɑrdʒənt] *s* sergente *m*

ser'geant at arms' *s* (**ser'geants at arms'**) ufficiale *m* delegato a mantenere l'ordine

ser'geant ma·jor *s* (**sergeants major** or **sergeant majors**) (in U.S. Army) sergente *m* maggiore; (in Italian Army) maresciallo

serial ['sırı·əl] *adj* a puntate, a dispense || *s* periodico; romanzo a puntate; programma *m* a serie

se'rial num'ber *s* matricola; (of a book) segnatura; (aut) matricola di telaio

se·ries ['sıriz] *s* (**-ries**) serie *f*; (works dealing with the same topic) collana; **in series** (elec) in serie

serious ['sırı·əs] *adj* serio

seriousness ['sırı·əsnıs] *s* serietà *f*; **in all seriousness** molto sul serio

sermon ['sʌrmən] *s* sermone *m*

sermonize ['sʌrmə‚naız] *tr & intr* sermonare

serpent ['sʌrpənt] *s* serpente *m*

se·rum ['sırəm] *s* (**-rums** or **-ra** [rə]) siero

servant ['sʌrvənt] *s* servo, domestico; (civil servant) funzionario; (fig) servitore *m*

serv'ant girl' *s* serva, domestica

serv'ant prob'lem *s* crisi *f* ancillare

serve [sʌrv] *s* (in tennis) servizio || *tr* servire; (a sentence) espiare; (to suffice) bastare (with dat); (a writ) notificare; **to serve s.o. right** stare bene (with dat), e.g., **it serves him right** gli sta bene || *intr* servire; **to serve as** fare da

service ['sʌrvıs] *s* servizio; (of a writ) notifica; (branch of the armed forces) arma; **at your service** per servirLa || *tr* rifornire, riparare

serviceable ['sʌrvısəbəl] *adj* utile; durevole; pratico; riparabile

serv'ice club' *s* casa del soldato

serv'ice-man' *s* (**-men'**) militare *m*; riparatore *m*, aggiustatore *m*

serv'ice mod'ule *s* modulo di servizio

serv'ice rec'ord *s* stato di servizio

serv'ice sta'tion *s* stazione di servizio or di rifornimento

serv'ice-sta'tion attend'ant *s* benzinaio

serv'ice stripe' *s* gallone *m*

servile ['sʌrvıl] *adj* servile

servitude ['sʌrvı‚tjud] or ['sʌrvı‚tud] *s* servitù *f*; lavori forzati

sesame ['sesəmi] *s* sesamo; **open sesame** apriti sesamo

session ['se∫ən] *s* sessione *f*, seduta

set [set] *adj* determinato, preordinato; abituale; fisso, rigido; (ready) pronto; meditato, studiato || *s* (e.g., of books) collezione, serie *f*; (e.g., of chess) gioco; set *m*, insieme *m*, completo; (of tires) treno; (of horses) pariglia; (of tennis) partita; (of dishes) servizio; (of kitchen utensils) batteria; posizione, atteggiamento; (of a garment) linea; (e.g., of cement) presa; (of people) gruppo; (of thieves) genia; (of sails) muta; (of lines) (geom) fascio; (rad, telv) apparato; (theat, mov) set *m* || *v* (pret & pp **set**; ger **setting**) *tr* porre, deporre; mettere; (fire) dare; (a table) imbandire; (a watch) regolare; (s.o. a certain number of tricks) far cadere di; (a price) fissare; (a gem) incastonare; (a fracture) mettere a posto; (a saw) allicciare; (a trap) tendere; (hair) acconciare; stabilire; insediare; (to plant) piantare; (a sail) tendere; (e.g., milk) rapprendere; calibrare, tarare; (cement) solidificare; (typ) comporre; **to set back** ritardare; (a clock) mettere indietro; **to set forth** descrivere; **to set one's heart on** desiderare ardentemente; **to set store by** tenere in gran conto; **to set up** metter su; impiantare; (drinks) (slang) pagare || *intr* (said, e.g., of the sun) tramontare; (said of a liquid) solidificarsi; (said of cement) fare presa; (said of milk) rapprendersi; (said of a hen) covare; (said of a garment) cascare; (said of hair) prendere la piega; **to set about** mettersi a; **to set out** porsi in cammino; **to set out to** mettersi a; **to set to work** mettersi a lavorare; **to set upon** attaccare

set'back' *s* rovescio, contrarietà *f*

set'screw' *s* vite *f* di pressione

setting ['setıŋ] *s* (environment) ambiente *m*; (of a gem) montatura; (of cement) presa; (e.g., of the sun) tramonto; (theat) scenario; (mus) arrangiamento

set'ting-up' ex'ercises *spl* ginnastica da camera

settle ['setəl] *tr* determinare, risolvere; sistemare, regolare; (a bill) liquidare; installarsi in, colonizzare; calmare; (a liquid) far depositare; (law) conciliare || *intr* mettersi d'accordo; saldare un conto; stanziarsi, domiciliarsi; fermarsi, posare; (*said of a liquid*) depositare, calmarsi; solidificarsi; **to settle down to work** mettersi a lavorare di buzzo buono; **to settle on** scegliere, fissare

settlement ['setəlmənt] *s* stabilimento; sistemazione, regolamento; colonia, comunità *f*; (*of a building*) infossamento; agenzia di beneficenza

settler ['setlər] *s* fondatore *m*; colono; conciliatore *m*

set'up' *s* portamento; (*e.g., of tools*) disposizione; quanto è necessario per mescolare una bibita alcolica; (coll) incontro truccato

seven ['sevən] *adj & pron* sette || *s* sette *m*; **seven o'clock** le sette

sev'en hun'dred *adj & pron* settecento

seventeen ['sevən'tin] *adj, s & pron* diciassette

seventeenth ['sevən'tinθ] *adj, s & pron* diciassettesimo || *s* (*in dates*) diciassette *m*

seventh ['sevənθ] *adj, s & pron* settimo || *s* (*in dates*) sette *m*

seventieth ['sevənti·ıθ] *adj, s & pron* settantesimo

seven·ty ['sevənti] *adj & pron* settanta || *s* (*-ties*) settanta *m*; **the seventies** gli anni settanta

sever ['sevər] *tr* tagliare, mozzare; (*relations*) troncare || *intr* separarsi

several ['sevərəl] *adj* parecchi, vari; rispettivi || *spl* parecchi *mpl*

sev'erance pay' ['sevərəns] *s* buonuscita, indennità *f* di licenziamento

severe [sı'vır] *adj* severo; (*weather*) rigido; (*pain*) acuto; (*illness*) grave

sew [so] *v* (*pret* sewed; *pp* sewed or sewn) *tr & intr* cucire

sewage ['su·ıdʒ] or ['sju·ıdʒ] *s* acque *fpl* di scolo or di rifiuto

sewer ['su·ər] or ['sju·ər] *s* fogna, chiavica

sewerage ['su·ərıdʒ] or ['sju·ərıdʒ] *s* fognatura; drenaggio, rimozione delle acque di rifiuto

sew'ing machine' ['so·ıŋ] *s* macchina da cucire

sex [seks] *s* sesso

sex' appeal' *s* attrattiva fisica, sex appeal *m*

sextant ['sekstənt] *s* sestante *m*

sextet [seks'tet] *s* sestetto

sexton ['sekstən] *s* sagrestano

sexual ['seks[u·ə]l] *adj* sessuale

sex·y ['seksi] *adj* (*-ier; -iest*) (coll) erotico; (coll) procace

shab·by ['ʃæbi] *adj* (*-bier; -biest*) (*clothes*) frusto; (*house*) malandato; (*person*) malvestito; (*deal*) cattivo

shack [ʃæk] *s* baracca

shackle ['ʃækəl] *s* ceppo; (*to tie an animal*) pastoia; (fig) ostacolo; **shackles** ceppi *mpl*, manette *fpl* || *tr* mettere in ceppi; (fig) inceppare

shad [ʃæd] *s* alosa

shade [ʃed] *s* ombra; (*of lamp*) paralume *m*; (*of window*) tendina; (*for the eyes*) visiera; (*hue*) tinta, sfumatura; **a shade of** un po' di; **shades** tenebre *fpl*; ombre *fpl* || *tr* ombreggiare; sfumare, digradare; (*a price*) ribassare leggermente

shadow ['ʃædo] *s* ombra || *tr* ombreggiare; (*to follow*) pedinare; **to shadow forth** adombrare, preannunciare

shadowy ['ʃædo·i] *adj* ombroso, ombreggiato; illusorio, chimerico

shad·y ['ʃedi] *adj* (*-ier; -iest*) ombroso; spettrale; (coll) losco; **to keep shady** (slang) starsene lontano

shaft [ʃæft] or [ʃɑft] *s* (*of arrow*) asta; (*of feather*) rachide *f*; (*of light*) raggio; (*handle*) manico; (*of wagon*) stanga, timone *m*; (*of motor*) albero; (*of column*) fusto; (*of elevator*) pozzo; (*in a mountain*) camino; (min) fornello; (fig) frecciata

shag·gy ['ʃægi] *adj* (*-gier; -giest*) peloso, irsuto; (*unkempt*) trasandato; (*cloth*) ruvido

shag'gy dog' sto'ry *s* storiella senza capo né coda

shake [ʃek] *s* scossa; stretta di mano; momento, istante *m*; **the shakes** la tremarella || *v* (*pret* shook [ʃuk]; *pp* shaken) *tr* scuotere; scrollare; (*s.o.'s hands*) serrare; (*e.g., with a mixer*) sbattere; agitare, perturbare; eludere, disfarsi di || *intr* tremare; (*to totter*) traballare, tentennare; scuotere; darsi la mano

shake'down' *s* estorsione, concussione; (*bed*) lettuccio di fortuna

shake'down' cruise' *s* (naut) viaggio di prova

shaker ['ʃekər] *s* (*e.g., for sugar*) spolverino; (*for cocktails*) sbattighiaccio, shaker *m*

shake'-up' *s* cambiamento completo, riorganizzazione, rimaneggiamento

shak·y ['ʃeki] *adj* (*-ier; -iest*) tremebondo; traballante, zoppicante

shall [ʃæl] *v* (*cond* should [ʃud]) *v aux* si usa per formare (1) il futuro dell'indicativo, per es., **I shall do it** lo farò; (2) il futuro perfetto dell'indicativo, per es., **I shall have done it** l'avrò fatto; (3) espressioni di obbligo o necessità, per es., **what shall I do?** che devo fare?, che vuole che faccia?

shallow ['ʃælo] *adj* basso, poco profondo; leggero, superficiale

sham [ʃæm] *adj* falso, finto || *s* frode *f*, contraffazione || *v* (*pret & pp* shammed; *ger* shamming) *tr & intr* fingere

sham' bat'tle *s* finta battaglia

shambles ['ʃæmbəlz] *s* macello; confusione, disordine

shame [ʃem] *s* vergogna; **shame on you!** vergogna!; **what a shame!** che peccato! || *tr* svergognare, disonorare

shame'faced' *adj* timido, vergognoso

shameful ['ʃemfəl] *adj* vergognoso

shameless ['ʃemlıs] *adj* sfrontato, impudente, svergognato

shampoo [ʃæm'pu] *s* shampoo *m* ‖ *tr* fare lo shampoo a

shamrock ['ʃæmrɑk] *s* trifoglio irlandese

shanghai ['ʃæŋhaɪ] *or* [ʃæŋ'haɪ] *tr* imbarcare a viva forza ‖ **Shanghai** *s* Sciangai *f*

shank [ʃæŋk] *s* fusto; (*of tool*) codolo; (*stem*) gambo; (*of bird*) zampa; (*of anchor*) fuso; (coll) principio; (coll) fine *f*; **to ride shank's mare** andare col cavallo di San Francesco

shan·ty ['ʃæntɪ] *s* (*-ties*) bicocca

shan'ty·town' *s* bidonville *f*

shape [ʃep] *s* forma; **in bad shape** in cattive condizioni; **out of shape** sformato ‖ *tr* formare, foggiare; plasmare, conformare ‖ *intr* formarsi; **to take shape** prender forma

shapeless ['ʃeplɪs] *adj* informe

shape·ly ['ʃeplɪ] *adj* (*-lier; -liest*) ben fatto, formoso

share [ʃer] *s* parte *f*; interesse *m*; (*of stock*) azione *f*; (*of plow*) suola; **to go shares** dividere in parti eguali ‖ *tr* (*to enjoy jointly*) condividere; (*to apportion*) ripartire ‖ *intr* partecipare, prender parte

sharecropper ['ʃer,krɑpər] *s* mezzadro

share'hold'er *s* azionista *mf*

shark [ʃɑrk] *s* pescecane *m*; (*schemer*) piovra; (slang) esperto

sharp [ʃɑrp] *adj* affilato, acuto; angoloso; (*e.g., curve*) forte; distinto, ben delineato; (*taste*) pungente, salato; (*pain*) vivo; (*words*) mordace; (slang) elegante ‖ *s* (mus) diesis *m* ‖ *adv* acutamente; in punto, e.g., **at seven o'clock sharp** alle sette in punto

sharpen ['ʃɑrpən] *tr* affilare; (*a pencil*) fare la punta a ‖ *intr* affilarsi

sharpener ['ʃɑrpənər] *s* (*person*) affilatore *m*; (*machine*) affilatrice *f*

sharper ['ʃɑrpər] *s* gabbamondo

sharp'shoot'er *s* tiratore scelto

shatter ['ʃætər] *tr* frantumare; sfracellare; (*health*) rovinare; (*nerves*) sconvolgere; distruggere ‖ *intr* frantumarsi, andare in pezzi

shat'ter·proof' *adj* infrangibile

shave [ʃev] *s* rasatura; **to have a close shave** scapparla or scamparla bella ‖ *tr* (*the face*) radere, sbarbare; (*wood*) piallare; (*to scrape*) sfiorare; (*prices*) ridurre; (*a lawn*) tosare ‖ *intr* rasarsi

shaving ['ʃevɪŋ] *adj* da barba, per barba, e.g., **shaving cream** crema da or per barba ‖ *s* rasatura; **shavings** trucioli *mpl*

shav'ing brush' *s* pennello da barba

shav'ing soap' *s* sapone *m* per la barba

shawl [ʃɔl] *s* scialle *m*

she [ʃi] *s* (**shes**) femmina ‖ *pron pers* (**they**) essa, lei

sheaf [ʃif] *s* (**sheaves** [ʃivz]) covone *m*; (*of paper*) fascio

shear [ʃɪr] *s* lama di cesoia; tagliatura; **shears** cesoie *fpl* ‖ *v* (*pret* **sheared**; *pp* **sheared** *or* **shorn** [ʃorn]) *tr* (*sheep*) tosare; (*cloth*) tagliare; **to shear s.o. of** privare qlcu di

sheath [ʃiθ] *s* (**sheaths** [ʃiðz]) guaina, coperta; (*of a sword*) fodero

sheathe [ʃið] *tr* rinfoderare, inguainare

shed [ʃed] *s* portico, tettoia; (geog) spartiacque *m*, versante *m* ‖ *v* (*pret* & *pp* **shed**; *ger* **shedding**) *tr* (*e.g., blood*) spargere, versare; (*light*) dare, fare; (*feathers*) spogliarsi di, lasciar cadere

sheen [ʃin] *s* lucentezza

sheep [ʃip] *s* (**sheep**) pecora; **sheep's eyes** occhio di triglia; **to separate the sheep from the goats** separare i buoni dai cattivi

sheep'dog' *s* cane *m* da pastore

sheepish ['ʃipɪʃ] *adj* timido, goffo; pecoresco, pedissequo

sheep'skin' *s* pelle *f* di pecora; (*parchment*) cartapecora; (bb) bazzana; (coll) diploma *m*

sheer [ʃɪr] *adj* trasparente, fino, velato; puro; (*cliff*) stagliato ‖ *adv* completamente ‖ *intr* deviare

sheet [ʃit] *s* (*for bed*) lenzuolo; (*of paper*) foglio; (*of metal*) lamina; (*of water*) specchio; (naut) scotta

sheet' light'ning *s* lampeggio all'orizzonte

sheet' met'al *s* lamiera

sheet' mu'sic *s* spartito non rilegato

sheik [ʃik] *s* sceicco; (*great lover*) (slang) rubacuori *m*

shelf [ʃelf] *s* (**shelves** [ʃelvz]) scaffale *m*, scansia; (*ledge*) terrazzo, ripiano; banco di sabbia; **on the shelf** in disparte, dimenticato

shell [ʃel] *s* (*of egg or crustacean*) guscio; (*of mollusk*) conchiglia; (*of vegetable*) baccello; proietto, proiettile *m*; (*cartridge*) cartuccia; (*of a cartridge*) bossolo; (*framework*) armatura; (*of boiler*) involucro; imbarcazione da regata, schifo, iole *f* ‖ *tr* (*vegetables*) sgranare; bombardare, cannoneggiare; **to shell out** (slang) tirar fuori

shel·lac [ʃə'læk] *s* gomma lacca ‖ *v* (*pret* & *pp* **-lacked**; *ger* **-lacking**) *tr* verniciare con gomma lacca; (slang) dare una batosta a

shell'fish' *ssg* (*-fish*) frutto di mare; crostaceo; *spl* frutti *mpl* di mare; crostacei *mpl*

shell' hole' *s* cratere *m*

shell' shock' *s* psicosi traumatica bellica

shelter ['ʃeltər] *s* rifugio, ricovero; **to take shelter** rifugiarsi ‖ *tr* raccogliere, ospitare, dare rifugio a

shelve [ʃelv] *tr* mettere sullo scaffale; (*a bill*) insabbiare; mettere a riposo

shepherd ['ʃepərd] *s* pastore *m* ‖ *tr* guardare, curarsi di

shep'herd dog' *s* cane *m* da pastore

shepherdess ['ʃepərdɪs] *s* pastora

sherbet ['ʃɑrbɪt] *s* sorbetto

sheriff ['ʃerɪf] *s* sceriffo

sher·ry ['ʃerɪ] *s* (*-ries*) xeres *m*

shield [ʃild] *s* scudo; (*for armpit*) sottoascella *m*; (*badge*) scudetto; (elec) schermo ‖ *tr* proteggere; (elec) schermare

shift [ʃɪft] *s* cambio, cambiamento;

(*period of work*) turno; (*group of workmen*) operai *mpl* di turno, squadra di lavoro; espediente *m*, sotterfugio || *tr* cambiare; spostare; (*blame*) riversare; || *intr* cambiare; spostarsi; fare da sé; vivere di espedienti; (rr) manovrare; (aut) cambiare marcia

shift' key' *s* tasto maiuscole

shiftless [′ʃɪftlɪs] *adj* pigro, ozioso

shift·y [′ʃɪfti] *adj* (**-ier; -iest**) astuto; evasivo; pieno d'espedienti; (*glance*) sfuggente

shilling [′ʃɪlɪŋ] *s* scellino

shimmer [′ʃɪmər] *s* luccichio || *intr* luccicare, mandare bagliori

shim·my [′ʃɪmi] *s* (**-mies**) (*dance*) shimmy *m*; (aut) farfallamento delle ruote, shimmy *m* || *intr* ballare lo shimmy; vibrare

shin [ʃɪn] *s* stinco; (*of cattle*) cannone *m* || *v* (*pret* & *pp* **shinned; ger shinning**) *tr* arrampicarsi su || *intr* arrampicarsi

shin'bone' *s* stinco, tibia

shine [ʃaɪn] *s* splendore *m*; luce *f*; bel tempo; lucidatura, lucido; **to take a shine to** (coll) prender simpatia per || *v* (*pret* & *pp* **shined**) *tr* pulire, lucidare || *v* (*pret* & *pp* **shone** [ʃon]) *tr* (*e.g., a flashlight*) dirigere i raggi di || *intr* brillare, luccicare, risplendere; (*to excel*) essere brillante, eccellere

shiner [′ʃaɪnər] *s* (slang) occhio pesto

shingle [′ʃɪŋgəl] *s* assicella di copertura; (*to cover a wall*) mattoncino di rivestimento; (Brit) greto ciottoloso; (coll) capelli *mpl* alla bebé; **shingles** (pathol) erpete *m*, zona; **to hang out one's shingle** (coll) aprire un ufficio professionale || *tr* coprire di assicelle or mattoncini; (*hair*) tagliare alla bebé

shining [′ʃaɪnɪŋ] *adj* brillante, lucente

shin·y [′ʃaɪni] *adj* (**-ier; -iest**) lucente, lucido; (*paper*) patinato

ship [ʃɪp] *s* nave *f*, bastimento; aeronave *f*; aeroplano; (*crew*) equipaggio || *v* (*pret* & *pp* **shipped; ger shipping**) *tr* imbarcare; mandare, spedire; (*oars*) disarmare; (*water*) imbarcare || *intr* imbarcarsi

ship'board' *s*—**on shipboard** a bordo

ship'build'er *s* costruttore *m* navale

ship'build'ing *s* architettura navale

ship'mate' *s* compagno di bordo

shipment [′ʃɪpmənt] *s* invio, spedizione

ship'own'er *s* armatore *m*

shipper [′ʃɪpər] *s* speditore *m*, spedizioniere *m*, mittente *m*

shipping [′ʃɪpɪŋ] *s* imbarco; spedizione; (naut) trasporto marittimo

ship'ping clerk' *s* speditore *m*

ship'ping room' *s* ufficio impaccatura

ship'shape' *adj* & *adv* in perfette condizioni

ship'side' *s* molo

ship's' pa'pers *spl* documenti *mpl* di bordo

ship'wreck' *s* naufragio; (*remains*) relitto || *tr* far naufragare || *intr* naufragare

ship'yard' *s* cantiere *m* navale

shirk [ʃʌrk] *tr* (*work*) evitare; (*responsibility*) sottrarsi a || *intr* imboscarsi

shirt [ʃʌrt] *s* camicia; **to keep one's shirt on** (slang) non perdere la calma; **to lose one's shirt** (slang) perdere la camicia

shirt' front' *s* sparato

shirt' sleeve' *s* manica di camicia

shirt'tail' *s* falda della camicia

shirt'waist' *s* blusa da donna

shiver [′ʃɪvər] *s* brivido || *intr* rabbrividire, battere i denti

shoal [ʃol] *s* secca, banco di sabbia

shock [ʃak] *s* urto, collisione; scossa; scossa elettrica; (pathol) shock *m* || *tr* scuotere; (*to strike against*) urtare; scandalizzare, indignare; dare la scossa elettrica a; (fig) scioccare

shock' absorb'er [æb′sɔrbər] *s* ammortizzatore *m* di colpi

shocking [′ʃakɪŋ] *adj* disgustoso, scandalizzante

shock' ther'apy *s* terapia d'urto

shock' troops' *spl* truppe *fpl* d'assalto

shod·dy [′ʃadi] *adj* (**-dier; -diest**) scadente, falso

shoe [ʃu] *s* scarpa; (*horseshoe*) ferro da cavallo; (*of a tire*) copertone *m*; (*of brake*) ganascia, ceppo || *v* (*pret* & *pp* **shod** [ʃad]) *tr* calzare; (*a horse*) ferrare

shoe'black' *s* lustrascarpe *m*

shoe'horn' *s* corno da scarpe, calzatoio

shoe'lace' *s* laccio delle scarpe

shoe'mak'er *s* calzolaio

shoe' pol'ish *s* crema or cera da scarpe

shoe'shine' *s* lucidatura, lustramento di scarpe

shoe' store' *s* calzoleria

shoe'string' *s* laccio delle scarpe; **on a shoestring** con quattro soldi

shoe'tree' *s* tendiscarpe *m*

shoo [ʃu] *tr* fare sciò a || *intr* fare sciò

shoot [ʃut] *s* (*e.g., with a firearm*) tiro; gara di tiro; (*chute*) scivolo; (rok) lancio; (bot) getto, virgulto || *v* (*pret* & *pp* **shot** [ʃat]) *tr* (*any missile*) tirare; (*a bullet*) sparare; (*to execute with a bullet*) fucilare; (*to fling*) lanciare; (*the sun*) prendere l'altezza di; (*dice*) gettare; (mov, telv) girare, riprendere; **to shoot down** (*a plane*) abbattere; **to shoot up** (coll) terrorizzare sparando a casaccio || *intr* tirare, sparare; passare rapidamente; nascere; (*said of pain*) dare fitte; (mov) cinematografare; **to shoot at** tirare a; (coll) cercare di ottenere

shoot'ing gal'lery *s* tiro a segno

shoot'ing match' *s* gara di tiro a segno; (slang) tutto, ogni cosa

shoot'ing star' *s* stella cadente

shop [ʃap] *s* (*store*) negozio, rivendita; (*workshop*) officina; **to talk shop** parlare del proprio lavoro || *v* (*pret* & *pp* **shopped; ger shopping**) *intr* fare la spesa; **to go shopping** andare a fare la spesa; **to shop around** cercare un'occasione di negozio in negozio

shop'girl' *s* venditrice *f*

shop'keep'er s negoziante mf

shoplifter ['ʃɑp,lɪftər] s taccheggiatore m

shopper ['ʃɑpər] s compratore m

shopping ['ʃɑpɪŋ] s compra; (purchases) compre fpl, shopping m

shop'ping bag' s sporta, shopping m

shop'ping cen'ter s centro d'acquisto, ipermercato

shop'ping dis'trict s zona commerciale

shop'win'dow s vetrina

shop'worn' adj sciupato, usato

shore [ʃor] s costa, riva; spiaggia, lido; (fig) regione; (support) sostegno, puntello || tr puntellare

shore' din'ner s pranzo di pesce

shore' leave' s (naut) franchigia

shore'line' s frangia costiera

shore' patrol' s polizia della marina

short [ʃort] adj (in stature) piccolo, basso; (in space, time) breve; (scanty) scarso; succinto; (in quantity) poco, piccolo; (rude) brusco; **in a short time** in breve; **in short** per farla breve; **on short notice** senza preavviso; **short of breath** corto di fiato; **to be short of** scarseggiare di || s (elec) cortocircuito; (mov) cortometraggio; **shorts** (underwear) mutande fpl; (sports attire) calzoncini mpl, shorts mpl || adv brevemente; bruscamente; (com) allo scoperto, e.g., **to sell short** vendere allo scoperto; **to run short of** essere a corto di; **to stop short** fermarsi di colpo || tr (elec) causare un cortocircuito in || intr (elec) andare in cortocircuito

shortage ['ʃortɪdʒ] s mancanza; (of food) carestia; (from pilfering) ammanco

short'cake' s torta di pasta frolla; torta ricoperta di frutta fresca

short'-change' tr non dare il cambio giusto a; (coll) imbrogliare

short'-cir'cuit s (elec) cortocircuito

short'-cir'cuit tr mandare in cortocircuito; (coll) rovinare || intr andare in cortocircuito

short'com'ing s difetto, manchevolezza

short'cut' s scorciatoia

shorten ['ʃortən] tr raccorciare, abbreviare || intr raccorciarsi, abbreviarsi

shortening ['ʃortənɪŋ] s raccorciamento; (culin) grasso, strutto

short'hand' adj stenografico || s stenografia; **to take shorthand** stenografare

short'hand' typ'ist s stenodattilografo

short-lived ['ʃort'laɪvd] or ['ʃort'lɪvd] adj effimero, di breve vita

shortly ['ʃortli] adv in breve, brevemente; fra poco; bruscamente; **shortly after** poco dopo

short'-range' adj di corta portata

short' sale' s vendita allo scoperto

short-sighted ['ʃort'saɪtɪd] adj miope; (fig) miope

short'stop' s (baseball) interbase m

short' sto'ry s novella

short-tempered ['ʃort'tempərd] adj irascibile

short'-term' adj a breve scadenza

short'wave' adj alle onde corte || s onda corta

short' weight' s—**to give short weight** rubare sul peso

shot [ʃɑt] s tiro, sparo; (cartridge) cartuccia; (for cannon) palla; (pellets of lead) pallini mpl; (person) tiratore m; (hypodermic injection) iniezione; (of liquor) bicchierino; (phot) istantanea; (sports) peso; (mov) inquadratura; **not by a long shot** nemmeno a pensarci; **to start like a shot** partire come una palla da cannone; **to take a shot at** tirare un colpo a; (to attempt to) provarsi a

shot'gun' s schioppo, fucile m da caccia

shot' put' s lancio del peso

should [ʃʊd] v aux si usa nelle seguenti situazioni: 1) per formare il condizionale presente, per es., **if I should wait for him, I should miss the train** se lo aspettassi, perderei il treno; 2) per formare il perfetto del condizionale, per es., **if I had waited for him, I should have missed the train** se lo avessi aspettato, avrei perso il treno; 3) per indicare la necessità di un'azione, per es., **he should go at once** dovrebbe andare immediatamente; **he should have gone immediately** sarebbe dovuto andare immediatamente

shoulder ['ʃoldər] s spalla; (of highway) banchina; **across the shoulder** a bandoliera; **to put one's shoulders to the wheel** mettersi a lavorare di buzzo buono; **to turn a cold shoulder to** volgere le spalle a || tr portare sulle spalle; (a responsibility) addossarsi; spingere con le spalle

shoul'der blade' s scapola

shoul'der strap' s spallina; (mil) tracolla

shout [ʃaʊt] s urlo, grido || tr urlare, gridare; **to shout down** far tacere a forza di strilli || intr gridare

shove [ʃʌv] s spintone m || tr spingere || intr spingere, dare spintoni; **to shove off** allontanarsi dalla riva; (slang) andarsene

shovel ['ʃʌvəl] s pala || v (pret & pp -eled or -elled; ger -eling or -elling) tr spalare || intr lavorare di pala

show [ʃo] s mostra; apparenza; traccia; ostentazione; (mov, telv, theat) spettacolo; **to make a show of** dar spettacolo di; **to steal the show from** ricevere tutti gli applausi invece di || tr mostrare, esporre, (a movie) presentare; dimostrare, insegnare; provare; (to register) segnare; (one's feelings) manifestare; (to the door) accompagnare; **to show in** fare entrare; **to show off** mettere in mostra || intr mostrarsi; presentarsi, apparire; (said of a horse) (sports) arrivare terzo, piazzarsi; **to show off** mettersi in mostra; **to show up** (coll) mostrarsi; (coll) farsi vedere

show' bill' s cartellone m

show'boat' s battello per spettacoli teatrali

show' busi'ness *s* industria dello spettacolo

show'case' *s* bacheca, vetrina

show'down' *s* carte scoperte; chiarificazione

shower ['ʃau·ər] *s* (*of rain*) acquazzone *m*; (*shower bath*) doccia; (*e.g., for a bride*) ricevimento cui i partecipanti devono portare un regalo; (fig) pioggia || *tr* innaffiare; **to shower with** colmare di || *intr* diluviare; fare la doccia

show'er bath' *s* doccia

show' girl' *s* ballerina, girl *f*

show'man *s* (**-men**) impresario teatrale; persona che ha molta scena

show'-off' *s* reclamista *m*, strombazzatore *m*

show'piece' *s* capolavoro, oggetto d'arte

show'place' *s* luogo celebre; **to be a showplace** (*said, e.g., of a house*) essere arredato perfettamente

show'room' *s* sala di mostra

show' win'dow *s* vetrina

show·y ['ʃo·i] *adj* (**-ier; -iest**) vistoso, sgargiante

shrapnel ['ʃræpnəl] *s* shrapnel *m*

shred [ʃred] *s* brano, brandello; ritaglio; (fig) granello; **to cut to shreds** fare a brandelli || *v* (*pret & pp* **shredded** *or* **shred**; *ger* **shredding**) *tr* fare a brandelli; (*paper*) tagliuzzare

shrew [ʃru] *s* (*woman*) bisbetica; (*animal*) toporagno

shrewd [ʃrud] *adj* astuto, scaltro

shriek [ʃrik] *s* strido; strillo; risata stridula || *intr* stridere; strillare

shrill [ʃrɪl] *adj* stridulo, squillante

shrimp [ʃrɪmp] *s* gamberetto; (*person*) omiciattolo, nanerottolo

shrine [ʃraɪn] *s* santuario, sacrario

shrink [ʃrɪŋk] *v* (*pret* **shrank** [ʃræŋk] *or* **shrunk** [ʃrʌŋk]; *pp* **shrunk** *or* **shrunken**) *tr* contrarre, restringere || *intr* contrarsi, restringersi; ritirarsi

shrinkage ['ʃrɪŋkɪdʒ] *s* restringimento; (*in weight*) calo

shriv·el ['ʃrɪvəl] *v* (*pret & pp* **-eled** *or* **-elled**; *ger* **-eling** *or* **-elling**) *tr* raggrinzire; (*from heat*) raccartocciare; (*to wither*) avvizzire || *intr* raggrinzirsi; accartocciarsi; avvizzire; **to shrivel up** incartapecorire

shroud [ʃraud] *s* sudario, lenzuolo funebre; (fig) cappa || *tr* avvolgere

Shrove' Tues'day [ʃrov] *s* martedì grasso

shrub [ʃrʌb] *s* arbusto

shrubber·y ['ʃrʌbəri] *s* (**-ies**) arbusti *mpl*, cespugli *mpl*

shrug [ʃrʌg] *s* scrollata di spalle || *v* (*pret & pp* **shrugged**; *ger* **shrugging**) *tr* scrollare; **to shrug one's shoulders** scrollare le spalle || *intr* fare spallucce

shudder ['ʃʌdər] *s* brivido, fremito || *intr* rabbrividire, fremere

shuffle ['ʃʌfəl] *s* (*of cards*) mescolata; turno di fare il mazzo; (*of feet*) strascichio; evasione || *tr* mescolare; strisciare, strascicare || *intr* fare il

mazzo; scalpicciare; ballare di striscio; **to shuffle off** strascicarsi, scalpicciare; **to shuffle out of** evadere da

shun [ʃʌn] *v* (*pret & pp* **shunned**; *ger* **shunning**) *tr* evitare, schivare

shunt [ʃʌnt] *tr* sviare; (elec) shuntare; (rr) deviare

shut [ʃʌt] *adj* chiuso || *v* (*pret & pp* **shut**; *ger* **shutting**) *tr* chiudere, serrare; **to shut in** rinchiudere; **to shut off** (*e.g., gas*) tagliare; **to shut up** tappare; imprigionare; (coll) fare star zitto || *intr* chiudersi; **to shut up** (coll) stare zitto, tacere

shut'down' *s* chiusura

shutter ['ʃʌtər] *s* (*outside a window*) persiana, gelosia; (*outside a store window*) serranda, saracinesca; (phot) otturatore *m*

shuttle ['ʃʌtəl] *s* spola, navetta || *intr* fare la spola

shut'tle-cock' *s* volano, volante *m*

shut'tle train' *s* treno che fa la spola fra due stazioni

shy [ʃaɪ] *adj* (**shyer** *or* **shier**; **shyest** *or* **shiest**) timido; (*fearful*) schivo, ritroso; corto, a corto, e.g., **he is shy of funds** è a corto di denaro || *v* (*pret & pp* **shied**) *intr* ritirarsi; schivarsi; (*said of a horse*) adombrarsi; **to shy away** tenersi discosto

shyster ['ʃaɪstər] *s* (coll) azzeccagarbugli *m*

Sia·mese [ˌsaɪ·ə'miz] *adj* siamese || *s* (**-mese**) siamese *mf*

Si'amese twins' *spl* fratelli *mpl* siamesi

Siberian [saɪ'bɪrɪ·ən] *adj & s* siberiano

sibilant ['sɪbɪlənt] *adj & s* sibilante *f*

sibyl ['sɪbɪl] *s* sibilla

sic [sɪk] *adv* sic || [sɪk] *v* (*pret & pp* **sicked**; *ger* **sicking**) *tr* aizzare; **sick 'em!** va!; **to sick on** aizzare contro

Sicilian [sɪ'sɪljən] *adj & s* siciliano

Sicily ['sɪsɪli] *s* la Sicilia

sick [sɪk] *adj* ammalato; nauseato; (*bored*) stucco; **sick at heart** con una spina nel cuore; **to be sick and tired** averne sin sopra i capelli; **to be sick at one's stomach** avere la nausea; **to take sick** cader malato || *tr* (*a dog*) aizzare

sick'bed' *s* letto d'ammalato

sicken ['sɪkən] *tr* ammalare; disgustare || *intr* ammalarsi

sickening ['sɪkənɪŋ] *adj* stomachevole

sick' head'ache *s* emicrania accompagnata da nausea

sickle ['sɪkəl] *s* falce messoria, falcetto

sick' leave' *s* congedo per motivi di salute

sick·ly ['sɪkli] *adj* (**-lier; -liest**) cagionevole, malaticcio

sickness ['sɪknɪs] *s* malattia; nausea

side [saɪd] *adj* laterale || *s* parte *f*, lato; (*e.g., of a coin*) faccia; (*slope*) versante *m*; (*of human body, of a ship*) fianco; **to take sides** parteggiare || *intr* parteggiare; **to side with** schierarsi dalla parte di

side'board' *s* credenza

side'burns' *spl* basette *fpl*, favoriti *mpl*

side'car' s motocarrozzetta; carrozzino laterale (di motocarrozzetta)

side' dish' s portata extra

side' door' s porta laterale

side' effect' s effetto secondario

side'-glance' s occhiata di sbieco

side' is'sue s questione secondaria

side'line' s linea laterale; impiego secondario; attività secondaria

sidereal [saɪˈdɪrɪ·əl] adj siderale

side'sad'dle adv all'amazzone

side' show' s spettacolo secondario di baraccone; affare secondario

side'slip' intr (aer) scivolare d'ala

side'split'ting adj che fa sbellicare dalle risa

side' step' s passo laterale; scartata

side'-step' v (pret & pp -stepped; ger -stepping) tr evitare || intr farsi da parte; fare una scartata

side'track' s binario morto di smistamento || tr sviare; (rr) smistare

side' view' s vista di profilo

side'walk' s marciapiede m

side'walk cafè' s caffè m con tavolini all'aperto

sideward [ˈsaɪdwərd] adj obliquo, a sghembo || adv verso un lato; di sghembo

side'ways' adj sghembo || adv di sghembo; di fianco

side' whisk'ers spl favoriti mpl

siding [ˈsaɪdɪŋ] s (rr) diramazione, binario morto, raccordo ferroviario

sidle [ˈsaɪdəl] intr andare al lato; muoversi furtivamente

siege [sidʒ] s assedio; (of illness) ricorrenza d'attacchi; **to lay siege to** cingere d'assedio, assediare

siesta [si'ɛstə] s siesta; **to take a siesta** fare la siesta

sieve [sɪv] s vaglio, setaccio || tr vagliare, setacciare

sift [sɪft] tr (flour) abburattare; setacciare; (to scatter with a sieve) spolverare; (fig) vagliare

sigh [saɪ] s sospiro || tr mormorare sospirando || intr sospirare; **to sigh for** sospirare

sight [saɪt] s vista, visione; spettacolo, veduta; (opt) mira, traguardo; (mil) mirino, tacca di mira; (coll) mucchio; **a sight of** (coll) molto; **at first sight** a prima vista; **at sight** ad apertura di libro; (com) a vista; **out of sight** fuori di vista; lontano dagli occhi; (prices) astronomico; **sights** luoghi mpl interessanti; **sight unseen** senza averlo visto prima, a occhi chiusi; **to be a sight** (coll) essere un orrore; **to catch sight of** arrivare a intravedere; **to know by sight** conoscere di vista; **to not be able to stand the sight of s.o.** not poter vedere qlcu nemmeno dipinto || tr avvistare; (a weapon) mirare || intr mirare, prendere di mira; osservare attentamente

sight' draft' s (com) tratta a vista

sight'-read' v (pret & pp -read [ˌrɛd]) tr & intr leggere a libro aperto

sight'see'ing adj turistico || s turismo, visite fpl turistiche

sightseer [ˈsaɪtˌsi·ər] s turista mf

sign [saɪn] s segno; segnale m; (e.g., on a store) insegna, cartello; **signs** tracce fpl || tr firmare; ingaggiare; indicare, segnalare || intr firmare; fare segno; **to sign off** (rad, telv) terminare la trasmissione; **to sign up** iscriversi

sig·nal [ˈsɪgnəl] adj insigne, segnalato || s segnale m || v (pret & pp -naled or -nalled; ger -naling or -nalling) tr segnalare || intr fare segnalazioni

sig'nal corps' s (mil) armi fpl di trasmissione

sig'nal tow'er s (rr) posto di blocco

signato·ry [ˈsɪgnəˌtori] s (-ries) firmatario

signature [ˈsɪgnətʃər] s firma; segno musicale; (typ) segnatura

sign'board' s cartellone m

signer [ˈsaɪnər] s firmatario

sig'net ring' s [ˈsɪgnɪt] s anello col sigillo

significance [sɪgˈnɪfɪkəns] s importanza; (meaning) significato

significant [sɪgˈnɪfɪkənt] adj importante

signi·fy [ˈsɪgnɪˌfaɪ] v (pret & pp -fied) tr significare

sign'post' s palo indicatore

silence [ˈsaɪləns] s silenzio || tr far tacere; (mil) ridurre al silenzio

silent [ˈsaɪlənt] adj silenzioso, tacito

sil'ent mov'ie s cinema muto

silhouette [ˌsɪlu'ɛt] s silhouette f, silueta

silicon [ˈsɪlɪkən] s silicio

silicone [ˈsɪlɪˌkon] s silicone m

silk [sɪlk] adj di seta || s seta; **to hit the silk** (slang) gettarsi col paracadute

silken [ˈsɪlkən] adj serico, di seta

silk' hat' s cappello a cilindro

silk'screen proc'ess s serigrafia

silk'-stock'ing adj & s aristocratico

silk'worm' s baco da seta, filugello

silk·y [ˈsɪlki] adj (-ier; -iest) di seta; come la seta

sill [sɪl] s basamento; (of a door) soglia; (of a window) davanzale m

sil·ly [ˈsɪli] adj (-lier; -liest) sciocco, scemo

si·lo [ˈsaɪlo] s (-los) silo || tr insilare

silt [sɪlt] s sedimento

silver [ˈsɪlvər] adj d'argento; (voice) argentino; (plated with silver) argentato || s argento || tr inargentare

sil'ver-fish' s (ent) lepisma

sil'ver foil' s foglia d'argento

sil'ver fox' s volpe argentata

sil'ver lin'ing s spiraglio di speranza

sil'ver plate' s vasellame m d'argento; argentatura

sil'ver screen' s (mov) schermo

sil'ver-smith' s argentiere m

sil'ver spoon' s ricchezza ereditata; **to be born with a silver spoon in one's mouth** esser nato con la camicia

sil'ver-ware' s argenteria

sil'ver-chest' s portaposate m

similar [ˈsɪmɪlər] adj simile

similari·ty [ˌsɪmɪˈlærɪti] s (-ties) similarità f, somiglianza

simile [ˈsɪmɪli] s similitudine f

simmer ['sɪmər] *tr* cuocere a fuoco lento || *intr* cuocere a fuoco lento; (fig) ribollire; **to simmer down** (slang) calmarsi

simper ['sɪmpər] *s* sorriso scemo || *intr* fare un sorriso scemo

simple ['sɪmpəl] *adj* semplice

simple-minded ['sɪmpəl'maɪndɪd] *adj* semplicione, scemo

simpleton ['sɪmpəltən] *s* semplicione *m*

simulate ['sɪmjə‚let] *tr* simulare

simultaneous [‚saɪməl'teni‧əs] or [‚sɪməl'teni‧əs] *adj* simultaneo

sin [sɪn] *s* peccato || *v* (*pret & pp* **sinned;** *ger* **sinning**) *intr* peccare

since [sɪns] *adv* da allora, da allora in poi; da tempo fa || *prep* da || *conj* dacché; poiché, dato che

sincere [sɪn'sɪr] *adj* sincero

sincerity [sɪn'sɛrɪti] *s* sincerità *f*

sine [saɪn] *s* (math) seno

sinecure ['saɪnɪ‚kjur] or ['sɪnɪ‚kjur] *s* sinecura

sinew ['sɪnju] *s* tendine *m*; (fig) nerbo

sinful ['sɪnfəl] *adj* (*person*) peccatore; (*act, intention, etc.*) peccaminoso

sing [sɪŋ] *v* (*pret* **sang** [sæŋ] or **sung** [sʌŋ]; *pp* **sung**) *tr* cantare; **to sing to sleep** ninnare || *intr* cantare; (*said, e.g., of the ears*) fischiare

singe [sɪndʒ] *v* (*ger* **singeing**) *tr* strinare, bruciacchiare

singer ['sɪŋər] *s* cantante *mf*; (*in night club*) canzonettista *mf*

single ['sɪŋgəl] *adj* unico, solo; (*room*) a un letto; (*bed*) a una piazza; (*man*) celibe; (*woman*) nubile; (*combat*) corpo a corpo; semplice, sincero || **singles** *ssg* singolare *m* || *tr* scegliere; **to single out** individuare

single-breasted ['sɪŋgəl'brestɪd] *adj* a un petto, monopetto

sin'gle entry' *s* partita semplice

sin'gle file' *s* fila indiana

single-handed ['sɪŋgəl'hændɪd] *adj* da solo, senza aiuto altrui

sin'gle-phase' *adj* (elec) monofase

sin'gle room' *s* camera a un letto

sin'gle-track' *adj* (rr) a binario semplice; (fig) di corte vedute

sing'song' *adj* monotono || *s* cantilena

singular ['sɪŋgjələr] *adj & s* singolare *m*

sinister ['sɪnɪstər] *adj* sinistro

sink [sɪŋk] *s* acquaio; (*sewer*) scolo, fogna; (fig) sentina || *v* (*pret* **sank** [sæŋk] or **sunk** [sʌŋk]; *pp* **sunk**) *tr* sprofondare; infiggere; (*a well*) scavare; (*in tone*) abbassare; (*a boat*) mandare a picco; rovinare; investire; perdere || *intr* sprofondarsi; abbassarsi; (*said, of the sun, prices, etc.*) calare; andare a picco; lasciarsi cadere; (*in vice*) impantanarsi; (*said of one's cheeks*) infossarsi; (*in thought*) perdersi; **to sink down** sedersi; **to sink in** penetrare

sink'ing fund' *s* fondo d'ammortamento

sinner ['sɪnər] *s* peccatore *m*

Sinology [sɪ'nɑlədʒi] *s* sinologia

sinuous ['sɪnju‧əs] *adj* sinuoso

sinus ['saɪnəs] *s* seno

sip [sɪp] *s* sorso || *v* (*pret & pp* **sipped;** *ger* **sipping**) *tr* sorbire, sorseggiare

siphon ['saɪfən] *s* sifone *m* || *tr* travasare con un sifone

si'phon bot'tle *s* sifone *m*

sir [sʌr] *s* signore *m*; (Brit) sir *m*; **Dear Sir** Illustrissimo signore; (com) Egregio signore

sire [saɪr] *s* (*king*) sire *m*; padre *m*, stallone *m* || *tr* generare

siren ['saɪrən] *s* sirena

sirloin ['sʌrlɔɪn] *s* lombata, lombo

sirup ['sɪrəp] or ['sʌrəp] *tr* sciroppo

sis‧sy ['sɪsi] *s* (-sies) effeminato

sister ['sɪstər] *adj* (*ship*) gemello; (*language*) sorella; (*corporation*) consorella || *s* sorella; (*nun*) suora, monaca

sis'ter-in-law' *s* (*sis'ters-in-law'*) cognata

Sis'tine Chap'el ['sɪstɪn] *s* Cappella Sistina

sit [sɪt] *v* (*pret & pp* **sat** [sæt]; *ger* **sitting**) *intr* sedere; posare; (*said of a hen*) covare; (*said of a jacket*) stare; essere in sessione; **to sit down** sedersi; **to sit in on** partecipare a; assistere a; **to sit still** stare tranquillo; **to sit up** alzarsi; (coll) essere sorpreso

sit'-down strike' *s* sciopero bianco

site [saɪt] *s* sito, luogo, posizione

sitting ['sɪtɪŋ] *s* seduta; (*of a court*) sessione; (*of a hen*) covata; (*serving of a meal*) turno

sit'ting duck' *s* (slang) facile bersaglio

sit'ting room' *s* soggiorno

situate ['sɪt/ʊ‚et] *tr* situare

situation [‚sɪt/ʊ'eʃən] *s* situazione, posizione; posto

sitz' bath' [sɪts] *s* semicupio

six [sɪks] *adj & pron* sei || *s* sei *m*; **at sixes and sevens** in disordine; **six o'clock** le sei

six' hun'dred *adj, s & pron* seicento

sixteen ['sɪks'tin] *adj, s & pron* sedici *m*

sixteenth ['sɪks'tinθ] *adj, s & pron* sedicesimo || *s* (*in dates*) sedici *m*

sixth [sɪksθ] *adj, s & pron* sesto || *s* (*in dates*) sei *m*

sixtieth ['sɪkstɪ‧ɪθ] *adj, s & pron* sessantesimo

six‧ty ['sɪksti] *adj & pron* sessanta || *s* (-ies) sessanta *m*; **the sixties** gli anni sessanta

sizable ['saɪzəbəl] *adj* considerevole

size [saɪz] *s* grandezza; quantità *f*; (*of person or garment*) taglia; (*of shoes*) numero; (*of hat*) giro; (*of a pipe*) diametro; (*for gilding*) colla; (fig) situazione || *tr* misurare, classificare secondo grandezza; incollare; **to size up** (coll) stimare, giudicare

sizzle ['sɪzəl] *s* sfrigolio || *intr* sfriggere

skate [sket] *s* pattino; (slang) tipo || *intr* pattinare; **to skate on thin ice** andare in cerca di disgrazie

skat'ing rink' *s* pattinatoio

skein [sken] *s* gomitolo, matassa

skeleton ['skelɪtən] *adj* scheletrico || *s* scheletro

skel'eton key' *s* chiave maestra

skeptic ['skeptɪk] *adj & s* scettico

skeptical ['skeptɪkəl] *adj* scettico

sketch [sketʃ] *s* schizzo, disegno; abbozzo, bozzetto; (theat) scenetta ‖ *tr* schizzare, disegnare; abbozzare

sketch'book' *s* album *m* di schizzi; quaderno per abbozzi

skew [skju] *adj* obliquo ‖ *s* movimento obliquo; (chisel) scalpello a taglio obliquo ‖ *tr* tagliare di sghembo ‖ *intr* (to swerve) deviare; (to look obliquely) guardare di sghembo

skew' chis'el *s* scalpello a taglio obliquo

skewer ['skju-ər] *s* spiedino ‖ *tr* mettere allo spiedo

ski [ski] *s* (skis or ski) sci *m* ‖ *intr* sciare

ski' boot' *s* scarpa da sci

skid [skɪd] *s* (device to check a wheel) scarpa; (skidding forward) slittamento; (skidding sideway) sbandamento; (aer, mach) pattino ‖ *v* (pret & pp skidded; ger skidding) *tr* frenare ‖ *intr* (forward) slittare; (sideways) sbandare

skid' row' [ro] *s* quartiere malfamato

skier ['ski-ər] *s* sciatore *m*

skiff [skɪf] *s* skiff *m*, singolo

skiing ['ski-ɪŋ] *s* sci *m*

ski' jump' *s* salto con gli sci; trampolino di salto

ski' lift' *s* sciovia

skill [skɪl] *s* destrezza, perizia

skilled [skɪld] *adj* abile, esperto

skilled' la'bor *s* manodopera qualificata

skillet ['skɪlɪt] *s* padella

skillful ['skɪlfəl] *adj* destro, abile

skim [skɪm] *v* (pret & pp skimmed; ger skimming) *tr* (milk) scremare; (e.g., broth) sgrassare; (to graze) sfiorare; (the ground) radere; (a page) trascorrere ‖ *intr* sfiorare; **to skim over** scorrere

ski' mask' *s* passamontagna *m*

skimmer ['skɪmər] *s* schiumaiola; (hat) canottiera

skim' milk' *s* latte scremato or magro

skimp [skɪmp] *tr* lesinare ‖ *intr* economizzare, risparmiare

skimp·y ['skɪmpi] *adj* (-ier; -iest) corto, scarso; taccagno

skin [skɪn] *s* pelle *f*; (rind) scorza; (of onion) spoglia; **by the skin of one's teeth** (coll) per il rotto della cuffia; **soaked to the skin** bagnato fino alle ossa; **to have a thin skin** offendersi facilmente ‖ *v* (pret & pp skinned; ger skinning) *tr* pelare, spellare; (e.g., one's knee) spellarsi; (slang) tosare; **to skin alive** (slang) scotennare; (slang) battere in pieno

skin'-deep' *adj* a fior di pelle

skin'-div'er *s* nuotatore subacqueo, sub *m*; (mil) sommozzatore *m*

skin'flint' *s* avaro

skin' game' *s* truffa

skin·ny ['skɪni] *adj* (-nier; -niest) magro, scarno

skin' test' *s* cutireazione

skip [skɪp] *s* salto ‖ *v* (pret & pp skipped; ger skipping) *tr* (a fence; a meal) saltare; (a subject) sorvolare; (school) (coll) marinare ‖ *intr* saltare, salterellare; (said of typewriter) saltare uno spazio; (coll) svignarsela

ski' pole' *s* racchetta da sci

skipper ['skɪpər] *s* capitano, comandante *m*

skirmish ['skʌrmɪʃ] *s* scaramuccia ‖ *intr* battersi in una scaramuccia

skirt [skʌrt] *s* sottana, gonna; (edge) orlo; (woman) (slang) gonnella ‖ *tr* orlare; costeggiare; (a subject) evitare

ski' run' *s* pista da sci

skit [skɪt] *s* (theat) quadretto comico

skittish ['skɪtɪʃ] *adj* bizzarro, balzano; timido; (horse) ombroso

skulduggery [skʌl'dʌgəri] *s* trucco disonesto

skull [skʌl] *s* cranio, teschio

skull' and cross'bones *s* due tibie incrociate ed un teschio

skull'cap' *s* papalina

skunk [skʌŋk] *s* puzzola, moffetta; (coll) puzzone *m*

sky [skaɪ] *s* (skies) cielo; firmamento; **to praise to the skies** portare al cielo

sky'div'er *s* paracadutista *mf*

sky'jack'er *s* pirata *m* dell'aria

sky'lark' *s* allodola ‖ *intr* (coll) darsi alla pazza gioia

sky'light' *s* lucernario

sky'line' *s* linea dell'orizzonte; (of city) profilo

sky'rock'et *s* razzo ‖ *intr* salire come un razzo

sky'scrap'er *s* grattacielo

sky'writ'ing *s* scrittura pubblicitaria aerea

slab [slæb] *s* (of stone) lastra, lastrone *m*; (of wood) tavola; (slice) fetta

slack [slæk] *adj* lento, allentato; negligente, indolente; (fig) fiacco, morto ‖ *s* lentezza; negligenza; stagione morta, inattività *f*; **slacks** pantaloni *mpl* da donna; pantaloni sciolti ‖ *tr* allentare; trascurare; (lime) spegnere ‖ *intr* rilasciarsi; essere negligente; **to slack up** rallentare

slacker ['slækər] *s* fannullone *m*; (mil) imboscato

slag [slæg] *s* scoria

slake [slek] *tr* spegnere

slalom ['slɑləm] *s* slalom *m*

slam [slæm] *s* colpo; (of door) sbatacchiamento; (in cards) cappotto; (coll) strapazzata ‖ *v* (pret & pp slammed; ger slamming) *tr* sbattere, sbatacchiare; (coll) strapazzare ‖ *intr* sbattere, sbatacchiare

slam'bang' *adv* (coll) con gran rumore, precipitosamente

slander ['slændər] *s* calunnia, maldicenza ‖ *tr* calunniare, diffamare

slanderous ['slændərəs] *adj* calunnioso, diffamatorio

slang [slæŋ] *s* gergo

slant [slænt] *s* inclinazione; punto di vista ‖ *tr* inclinare; (news) snaturare ‖ *intr* inclinarsi; deviare

slap [slæp] *s* manata; *(in the face)* schiaffo, ceffone *m*; *(noise)* rumore *m*; insulto ‖ *v (pret & pp* **slapped;** *ger* **slapping)** *tr* dare una manata a; schiaffeggiare

slap'dash' *adj* raffazzonato, fatto a casaccio ‖ *adv* a casaccio

slap'hap'py *adj (punch-drunk)* stordito; *(giddy)* allegro, brillo

slap'stick' *adj* buffonesco ‖ *s* bastone *m* d'Arlecchino; buffonata

slash [slæʃ] *s* sfregio; *(of prices)* riduzione ‖ *tr* sfregiare; *(cloth)* tagliare; *(prices)* ridurre

slat [slæt] *s* travicello, regolo; *(for bed)* traversa; *(of shutter)* stecca

slate [slet] *s* ardesia, lavagna; lista elettorale; **clean slate** buon certificato ‖ *tr* coprire con tegole d'ardesia; proporre la nomina di; *(to schedule)* mettere in cantiere

slate' roof' *s* tetto d'ardesia

slattern ['slætərn] *s (slovenly woman)* sciamannona; *(harlot)* puttana

slaughter ['slɔtər] *s* eccidio, carneficina ‖ *tr* sgozzare, scannare

slaugh'ter-house' *s* macello, scannatoio

Slav [slav] *or* [slæv] *adj & s* slavo

slave [slev] *adj & s* schiavo ‖ *intr* lavorare come uno schiavo

slave' driv'er *s* negriere *m*

slavery ['slevəri] *s* schiavitù *f*

slave' trade' *s* tratta degli schiavi

Slavic ['slɑvɪk] *or* ['slævɪk] *adj & s* slavo

slay [sle] *v (pret* **slew** [slu]; *pp* **slain** [slen])** *tr* scannare, uccidere

slayer ['sle·ər] *s* uccisore *m*

sled [slɛd] *s* slittino, slitta ‖ *v (pret & pp* **sledded;** *ger* **sledding)** *intr* slittare

sledge' ham'mer *s* [slɛdʒ] *s* mazza

sleek [slik] *adj* liscio, lustro; elegante ‖ *tr* lisciare, ammorbidire

sleep [slip] *s* sonno; **to go to sleep** addormentarsi; **to put to sleep** addormentare; uccidere con un anestetico ‖ *v (pret & pp* **slept** [slɛpt])** *tr* dormire; aver posto a dormire per; **to sleep it over** dormirci sopra; **to sleep off a hangover** smaltire una sbornia dormendo ‖ *intr* dormire; **to sleep in** dormire fino a tardi; passare la notte a casa; **to sleep out** passare la notte fuori di casa

sleeper ['slipər] *s (person)* dormiente *mf*; *(beam, timber)* trave *f*

sleep'ing bag' *s* sacco a pelo

sleep'ing car' *s* vettura letto

sleep'ing pill' *s* sonnifero

sleepless ['sliplɪs] *adj* insonne; *(night)* bianco

sleep'walk'er *s* sonnambulo

sleep·y ['slipi] *adj* (-ier; -iest) insonnolito, sonnolento; **to be sleepy** aver sonno

sleep'y-head' *s* dormiglione *m*

sleet [slit] *s* nevischio ‖ *impers* **it is sleeting** cade il nevischio

sleeve [sliv] *s* manica; *(of phonograph record)* busta; *(mach)* manicotto; **to laugh in or up one's sleeve** ridere sotto i baffi

sleigh [sle] *s* slitta ‖ *intr* andare in slitta

sleigh' bells' *spl* bubboli *mpl* da slitta, sonagliera da slitta

sleigh' ride' *s* passeggiata in slitta

sleight' of hand' [slaɪt] *s* gioco di prestigio

slender ['slɛndər] *adj* smilzo, snello; esiguo, esile

sleuth [sluθ] *s* segugio

slew [slu] *s* (coll) mucchio

slice [slaɪs] *s* fetta; *(of an orange)* spicchio ‖ *tr* tagliare a fette; (fig) fendere

slick [slɪk] *adj* liscio, lustro; scivoloso; astuto; (slang) ottimo ‖ *s* posto scivoloso; (coll) rivista stampata su carta patinata ‖ *tr* lisciare, lustrare; **to slick up** (coll) acconciare

slicker ['slɪkər] *s* impermeabile *m* di tela cerata; (coll) furbo di tre cotte

slide [slaɪd] *s* scivolata, scivolone *m*; *(chute)* scivolo; *(landslide)* frana; *(for projection)* diapositiva; *(of a microscope)* vetrino; *(mach)* guida; *(of a slide rule)* (mach) cursore *m* ‖ *v (pret & pp* **slid** [slɪd])** *tr* far scivolare ‖ *intr* sdrucciolare, scivolare; *(said of a car)* pattinare, slittare; **to let slide** lasciar correre

slide' fas'tener *s* chiusura lampo

slide' projec'tor *s* diascopio

slide' rule' *s* regolo calcolatore

slide' valve' *s* (mach) cassetto di distribuzione

slid'ing door' *s* porta scorrevole

slid'ing scale' *s* scala mobile

slight [slaɪt] *adj* leggero, lieve; delicato ‖ *s* noncuranza, disattenzione; affronto ‖ *tr* fare con negligenza; *(to snub)* trattare con noncuranza, snobbare

slim [slɪm] *adj* (**slimmer; slimmest**) sottile; magro

slime [slaɪm] *s* melma; *(e.g., of a snail)* bava

slim·y ['slaɪmi] *adj* (-ier; -iest) melmoso; bavoso; sudicio

sling [slɪŋ] *s (to shoot stones)* fionda; *(naut)* braca; **in a sling** *(arm)* al collo ‖ *v (pret & pp* **slung** [slʌŋ])** *tr* gettare; lanciare; *(freight)* imbracare; sospendere; mettere a bandoliera

sling'shot' *s* fionda

slink [slɪŋk] *v (pret & pp* **slunk** [slʌŋk])** *intr* andare furtivamente; **to slink away** eclissarsi

slip [slɪp] *s* scivolone *m*; svista, errore *m*; *(in prices)* discesa; *(underdress)* sottoveste *f*; *(pillowcase)* federa; *(of paper)* pezzo; *(space between two wharves)* darsena, imbarcatoio; *(form)* modulo; personcina; *(inclined plane)* (naut) scalo d'alaggio; (bot) innesto; **to give the slip to** eludere ‖ *v (pret & pp* **slipped;** *ger* **slipping)** *tr* infilare; liberare; liberarsi da; omettere; **to slip off** togliersi; **to slip on** mettersi; **to slip one's mind** dimenticarsi di, e.g., **it slipped my mind** me ne sono dimenticato ‖ *intr* scivolare, scorrere; sdrucciolare; sbagliare; peggiorare; **to let slip** lasciarsi sfuggire; **to slip away** svignarsela; **to slip by** (said of time) passare, fuggire; **to slip out of s.o.'s hands** sgusciare dalle mani di qlcu; **to slip up** sbagliarsi

slip′cov′er s fodera

slip′knot′ s nodo scorsoio

slip′ of the tongue′ s errore m nel parlare

slipper ['slɪpər] s pantofola

slippery ['slɪpəri] adj sdrucciolevole, scivoloso; evasivo; incerto

slip′shod′ adj trasandato, mal fatto

slip′-up′ s (coll) sbaglio

slit [slɪt] s taglio, fenditura || v (pret & pp **slit**; ger **slitting**) tr tagliare, fendere; **to slit the throat of** sgozzare

slob [slɑb] s (slang) rozzo, villanzone m

slobber ['slɑbər] s bava; sdolcinatura || intr sbavare; parlare sdolcinatamente

sloe [slo] s (shrub) prugnolo; (fruit) prugnola

slogan ['slogən] s slogan m

sloop [slup] s cutter m

slop [slɑp] s pastone m; (slang) sbobba || v (pret & pp **slopped**; ger **slopping**) tr versare, imbrodare || intr rovesciarsi, scorrere; (slang) perdersi in smancerie

slope [slop] s costa, pendice f; (of mountain or roof) spiovente m || tr inclinare || intr digradare, scendere

slop·py ['slɑpi] adj (-pier; -piest) fangoso; bagnato; (slovenly) sciatto; (done badly) abborracciato

slot [slɑt] s scanalatura; (for letters) buca; (e.g., on a broadcasting schedule) posizione

sloth [sloθ] or [slɔθ] s pigrizia; (zool) bradipo, poltrone m

sloth′ful adj poltrone m

slot′ machine′ s macchina a gettone

slouch [slautʃ] s postura goffa; persona goffa; (coll) poltrone m || intr muoversi goffamente; **to slouch in a chair** sdraiarsi

slouch′ hat′ s cappello floscio

slough [slau] s pantano; (fig) abisso || [slʌf] s (of snake) spoglia; (pathol) crosta || tr—**to slough off** spogliarsi di || intr sbucciarsi, cadere

Slovak ['slovæk] or [slo′væk] adj & s slovacco

sloven·ly ['slʌvənli] adj (-lier; -liest) sciatto, trasandato

slow [slo] adj lento; (sluggish) tardo; (clock) indietro, in ritardo; (in understanding) tardivo || adv piano || tr rallentare || intr rallentarsi; (said of a watch) ritardare

slow′down′ s sciopero pignolo

slow′ mo′tion s—**in slow motion** al rallentatore

slow′-motion projec′tor s rallentatore m

slow′poke′ s (coll) poltrone m

slug [slʌg] s (heavy piece of metal) lingotto; (metal disk) gettone m; (fig) poltrone m; (zool) lumaca; (coll) colpo, mazzata || v (pret & pp

slugged; ger **slugging**) tr picchiare sodo

sluggard ['slʌgərd] s poltrone m

sluggish ['slʌgɪʃ] adj pigro, indolente; lento, fiacco

sluice [slus] s canale m; stramazzo

sluice′ gate′ s paratoia

slum [slʌm] s bassifondi mpl || v (pret & pp **slummed**; ger **slumming**) intr visitare i bassifondi

slumber ['slʌmbər] s dormiveglia m, sonnellino || intr dormire, dormicchiare

slump [slʌmp] s depressione, crisi f; (in prices) ribasso, calo || intr impantanarsi; peggiorare; (said of prices) ribassare, calare

slur [slʌr] s insulto, macchia; critica; (mus) legatura || v (pret & pp **slurred**; ger **slurring**) tr pronunziare indistintamente; (a subject) sorvolare; insultare, calunniare; (mus) legare

slush [slʌʃ] s poltiglia di neve; fanghiglia; (fig) sdolcinatezza

slut [slʌt] s cagna; (slovenly woman) sciamannona; troia, puttana

sly [slaɪ] adj (slyer or slier; slyest or sliest) furbo; insidioso; (hiding one's true feelings) sornione; **on the sly** furtivamente

smack [smæk] s schiaffo; (of whip or lips) schiocco; (taste) traccia, sapore m; (coll) bacio collo schiocco || adv di colpo, direttamente || tr dare uno schiaffo a; colpire; (the whip or one's lips) schioccare; schioccare un bacio a || intr—**to smack of** sapere di

small [smɔl] adj piccolo; povero; basso, umile; (change) spicciolo; (typ) minuscolo

small′ arms′ spl armi fpl portatili

small′ busi′ness s piccolo commercio

small′ cap′ital s (typ) maiuscoletto

small′ change′ s spiccioli mpl

small′ fry′ s minutaglia; bambini mpl; gente f di poca importanza

small′ hours′ spl ore fpl piccole

small′ intes′tine s intestino tenue

small-minded ['smɔl′maɪndɪd] adj di corte vedute, gretto

small′ of the back′ s fine f della schiena, reni fpl

smallpox ['smɔl‚pɑks] s vaiolo

small′ talk′ s conversazione futile

small′-time′ adj di poca importanza

small′-town′ adj di provincia

smart [smɑrt] adj intelligente; scaltro, furbo; (pain) acuto; (in appearance) elegante; (pert) impertinente; (coll) grande, abbondante || s dolore acuto, sofferenza || intr bruciare; dolere; soffrire

smart′ al′eck ['ælɪk] s saputello

smart′ set′ s bel mondo

smash [smæʃ] s sconquasso; colpo; collisione; rovina, fallimento; (tennis) smash m, schiacciata || tr sconquassare; sfracellare; rompere; (tennis) schiacciare || intr sconquassarsi; sfracellarsi; andare in rovina; **to smash into** scontrarsi con

smash′ hit′ s successone m

smash'-up' *s* sconquasso

smattering ['smætərɪŋ] *s* infarinatura, spolvero

smear [smɪr] *s* macchia, imbrattatura; calunnia; (bact) striscio || *tr* imbrattare; spalmare; calunniare

smear' campaign' *s* campagna di vilipendio

smell [smel] *s* odore *m;* (*sense*) olfatto, odorato; profumo || *v* (*pret &* *pp* smelled *or* smelt) *tr* fiutare, odorare || *intr* odorare; (*to stink*) puzzare; profumare; to smell of odorare di; puzzare di

smell'ing salts' *spl* sali aromatici

smell·y ['smeli] *adj* (-ier; -iest) puzzolente

smelt [smelt] *s* (ichth) eperlano || *tr &* *intr* fondere

smile [smaɪl] *s* sorriso || *intr* sorridere

smiling ['smaɪlɪŋ] *adj* sorridente

smirk [smʌrk] *s* ghigno || *intr* ghignare

smite [smaɪt] *v* (*pret* smote [smot]; *pp* smitten ['smɪtən] *or* smit [smɪt]) *tr* colpire; percuotere; affliggere, castigare

smith [smɪθ] *s* fabbro

smith·y ['smɪθi] *s* (-ies) fucina

smit'ten [smɪt] *adj* afflitto; innamorato

smock [smɑk] *s* camice *m;* (*of mechanic*) camiciotto

smock' frock' *s* blusa da lavoro

smog [smɑg] *s* foschia, smog *m*

smoke [smok] *s* fumo; to go up in smoke andare in cenere || *tr* affumicare; (*tobacco*) fumare; to smoke out cacciare col fumo; scoprire || *intr* fumare; (*said, e.g., of the earth*) fumigare

smoke'-filled room' *s* stanza da riunioni piena di fumo

smoke'less pow'der ['smoklɪs] *s* polvere *f* senza fumo

smoker ['smokər] *s* fumatore *m;* salone *m* fumatori; (rr) vagone *m* fumatori

smoke' rings' *spl* anelli *mpl* di fumo

smoke' screen' *s* cortina di fumo

smoke'stack' *s* fumaiolo

smoking ['smokɪŋ] *s* (il) fumare; no smoking vietato fumare

smok'ing car' *s* vagone *m* fumatori

smok'ing jack'et *s* giacca da casa

smok'ing room' *s* stanza per fumatori

smok·y ['smoki] *adj* (-ier; -iest) fumoso

smolder ['smoldər] *s* fumo derivante da fuoco che cova || *intr* (*said of fire or passion*) covare; (*said of s.o.'s eyes*) ardere

smooch [smutʃ] *intr* (coll) baciarsi, baciucchiarsi

smooth [smuð] *adj* liscio, levigato; (*face*) glabro; di consistenza uniforme; (*flat*) piano; senza interruzioni; tranquillo; elegante; (*sound*) armonioso; (*taste*) gradevole; (*wine*) abboccato; (*sea*) calmo; (*style*) fluido || *tr* lisciare, levigare; appianare, facilitare; calmare; to smooth away appianare

smooth-faced ['smuð ,fest] *adj* (*beardless*) glabro; liscio

smooth-spoken ['smuð,spokən] *adj* mellifluo

smooth·y ['smuði] *s* (-ies) galante *m*

smother ['smʌðər] *tr* affogare, soffocare

smudge [smʌdʒ] *s* macchia, imbrattatura || *tr* macchiare, imbrattare; (*a garden*) affumicare

smudge' pot' *s* apparecchiatura per affumicare

smug [smʌg] *adj* (smugger; smuggest) pieno di sé stesso; liscio, lisciato

smuggle ['smʌgəl] *tr* contrabbandare || *intr* praticare il contrabbando

smuggler ['smʌglər] *s* contrabbandiere *m*

smuggling ['smʌglɪŋ] *s* contrabbando

smut [smʌt] *s* sudiciume *m;* oscenità *f;* (agr) volpe *f,* golpe *f*

smut·ty ['smʌti] *adj* (-tier; -tiest) sudicio; osceno; (agr) malato di volpe

snack [snæk] *s* spuntino, merenda; porzione

snack' bar' *s* tavola calda

snag [snæg] *s* tronco sommerso; protuberanza, sporgenza; (*tooth*) dente rotto; (fig) intoppo, ostacolo; to hit a snag incontrare un ostacolo || *v* (*pret & pp* snagged; *ger* snagging) *tr* fare uno straccio a; (fig) ostacolare

snail [snel] *s* chiocciola, lumaca; at a snail's pace come una lumaca

snake [snek] *s* serpente *m;* (*nonvenomous*) biscia

snake' in the grass' *s* pericolo nascosto; (*person*) serpe *f* in seno

snap [snæp] *s* (*sharp sound*) schiocco; (*bite*) morso; (*fastener*) bottone automatico; (*of cold weather*) breve periodo; (*manner of speaking*) tono tagliente; (phot) istantanea; (coll) vigore *m;* (coll) cosa da nulla || *v* (*pret & pp* snapped; *ger* snapping) *tr* schioccare; chiudere di colpo; spezzare di colpo; (*a picture*) scattare; to snap one's fingers at infischiarsi di; to snap up afferrare; (*a person*) tagliare la parola a || *intr* schioccare; (*to crack*) rompersi di colpo; to snap at cercare di mordere; (*a bargain*) cercare di afferrare; to snap out of it (coll) riprendersi; to snap shut chiudersi di colpo

snap'drag'on *s* (bot) bocca di leone

snap' fas'tener *s* bottone automatico

snap' judg'ment *s* decisione presa senza riflessione

snap·py ['snæpi] *adj* (-pier; -piest) mordente, mordace; (coll) vivo, vivace; (coll) elegante; to make it snappy (slang) sbrigarsi

snap'shot' *s* istantanea

snare [sner] *s* laccio, lacciolo; (*of a drum*) corda

snare' drum' *s* cassa rullante

snarl [snɑrl] *s* (*of a dog*) ringhio; groviglio; (*of traffic*) ingorgo; (fig) confusione || *tr* urlare con un ringhio; (*to tangle*) aggrovigliare; complicare || *intr* ringhiare; aggrovigliarsi; complicarsi

snatch [snætʃ] *s* strappo, strappone *m;* presa; pezzetto; momentino || *tr &*

intr strappare; **to snatch at** cercare di afferrare; **to snatch from** strappare a

sneak [snik] *s* furfante *m* || *tr* mettere di nascosto; pigliare di nascosto || *intr*—**to sneak in** entrare di nascosto; **to sneak out** svignarsela

sneaker ['snikər] *s* furfante *m*; scarpetta da ginnastica

sneak' thief' *s* ladro, topo

sneak·y ['sniki] *adj* (-ier; -iest) furtivo

sneer [snɪr] *s* ghigno || *intr* sogghignare; **to sneer at** beffarsi si

sneeze [sniz] *s* starnuto || *intr* starnutare; **not to be sneezed at** (coll) non essere disprezzabile

snicker ['snɪkər] *s* risatina || *intr* fare una risatina

snide [snaɪd] *adj* malizioso

sniff [snɪf] *s* fiuto, fiutata; (*scent*) odore *m* || *tr* fiutare || *intr* aspirare rumorosamente; (*with emotion*) moccicare; **to sniff at** annusare; mostrare disprezzo per

sniffle ['snɪfəl] *s* moccio; **to have the sniffles** moccicare || *intr* moccicare

snip [snɪp] *s* taglio; pezzetto; (*person*) (coll) mezza cartuccia || *v* (*pret & pp* **snipped;** *ger* **snipping**) *tr* tagliuzzare

snipe [snaɪp] *s* tiro di nascosto; (orn) beccaccino || *intr* sparare in appostamento; attaccare da lontano

sniper ['snaɪpər] *s* franco tiratore, cecchino

snippet ['snɪpɪt] *s* ritaglio, frammento; (fig) mezza cartuccia

snip·py ['snɪpi] *adj* (-pier; -piest) frammentario; (coll) corto, brusco; (coll) arrogante

snitch [snɪtʃ] *tr & intr* (coll) graffignare, sgraffignare

sniv·el ['snɪvəl] *s* moccio; singhiozzo, piagnisteo; falsa commozione || *v* (*pret & pp* **-eled** or **-elled;** *ger* **-eling** or **-elling**) *intr* singhiozzare, piagnucolare; (*to have a runny nose*) moccicare, avere il moccio

snob [snɑb] *s* snob *mf*

snobbery ['snɑbəri] *s* snobismo

snobbish ['snɑbɪʃ] *adj* snobistico

snoop [snup] *s* (coll) ficcanaso || *intr* (coll) ficcare il naso

snoop·y ['snupi] *adj* (-ier; -iest) (coll) curioso, invadente

snoot [snut] *s* (slang) naso

snoot·y ['snuti] *adj* (-ier; -iest) (coll) snobistico

snooze [snuz] *s* (coll) sonnellino || *intr* (coll) fare un sonnellino

snore [snor] *s* russamento || *intr* russare

snort [snɔrt] *s* sbuffo || *intr* sbuffare

snot [snɑt] *s* (slang) moccio

snot·ty ['snɑti] *adj* (-tier; -tiest) (coll) snobistico; (coll) arrogante; (slang) moccioso

snout [snaʊt] *s* muso; (*of pig*) grugno; (*of person*) muso, grugno

snow [sno] *s* neve *f* || *intr* nevicare

snow'ball' *s* palla di neve || *tr* gettare palle di neve a || *intr* aumentare come una palla di neve

snow'blind' *adj* accecato dalla neve

snow'bound' *adj* prigioniero della neve

snow-capped ['sno͵kæpt] *adj* coperto di neve

snow'drift' *s* banco di neve

snow'fall' *s* nevicata

snow' fence' *s* barriera contro la neve

snow'flake' *s* fiocco di neve

snow' flur'ry *s* neve portata da raffiche

snow' line' *s* limite *m* delle nevi perenni

snow'man' *s* (-men') uomo di neve

snow'plow' *s* spazzaneve *m*

snow'shoe' *s* racchetta da neve

snow'slide' *s* valanga

snow'storm' *s* bufera di neve

snow' tire' *s* gomma da neve, pneumatico da neve

snow'-white' *adj* bianco come la neve

snow·y ['sno·i] *adj* (-ier; -iest) nevoso

snub [snʌb] *s* affronto || *v* (*pret & pp* **snubbed;** *ger* **snubbing**) *tr* snobbare

snub·by ['snʌbi] *adj* (-bier; -biest) camuso, rincagnato

snuff [snʌf] *s* fiutata; tabacco da fiuto; (*of a candlewick*) moccolo; **up to snuff** (coll) soddisfacente; (coll) bene || *tr* fiutare; tabaccare; (*a candle*) smoccolare; **to snuff out** spegnere; (fig) soffocare

snuff'box' *s* tabacchiera

snuffers ['snʌfərz] *spl* smoccolatoio

snug [snʌg] *adj* (**snugger; snuggest**) comodo; (*dress*) attillato; compatto; (*well-off*) agiato; (*sum*) discreto; (*sheltered*) ben protetto; (*well-hidden*) nascosto

snuggle ['snʌgəl] *intr* rannicchiarsi; **to snuggle up to** stringersi a

so [so] *adv* così; così o tanto + *adj* or *adv*; per quanto; **and so** certamente; pure; **and so on** e così via; **or so** più o meno; **to think so** credere di sì; **so as to** + *inf* per + *inf*; **so far** sinora, finora; **so long!** arrivederci!; **so many** tanti; **so much** tanto; **so so** così così; **so that** in maniera che, di modo che; **so to speak** per così dire || *conj* cosicché || *interj* bene!; basta!; così!

soak [sok] *s* bagnata; (*toper*) (slang) ubriacone *m* || *tr* bagnare, inzuppare; imbevere; (coll) ubriacare; (slang) far pagare un prezzo esorbitante a; **to soak up** assorbire; **soaked to the skin** bagnato fino alle ossa || *intr* stare a molle, macerare; inzupparsi

so'-and-so' *s* (-sos) tal *m* dei tali; tal cosa

soap [sop] *s* sapone *m* || *tr* insaponare

soap'box' *s* cassa di sapone; tribuna improvvisata

soap'box or'ator *s* oratore *m* che parla da una tribuna improvvisata

soap' bub'ble *s* bolla di sapone

soap' dish' *s* portasapone *m*

soap' flakes' *spl* sapone *m* a scaglie

soap' op'era *s* (coll) trasmissione radiofonica o televisiva lacrimogena

soap' pow'der *s* sapone *m* in polvere

soap'stone' *s* pietra da sarto

soap'suds' *spl* saponata

soap·y ['sopi] *adj* (-ier; -iest) saponoso

soar [sor] *intr* spaziare, slanciarsi; (aer) librarsi

sob [sɑb] *s* singhiozzo || *v* (*pret & pp* **sobbed;** *ger* **sobbing**) *tr* dire a singhiozzi || *intr* singhiozzare

sober ['sobər] *adj* sobrio; non ubriaco || *intr* smaltire la sbornia; **to sober down** calmarsi; **to sober up** smaltire la sbornia

sobriety [so'braɪ·əti] *s* sobrietà *f*

sobriquet ['sobrɪ‚ke] *s* nomignolo

sob′ sis′ter *s* giornalista lacrimogeno

sob′ sto′ry *s* storia lacrimogena

so′-called′ *adj* cosiddetto

soccer ['sɑkər] *s* calcio, football *m*

sociable ['soʃəbəl] *adj* sociale, socievole

social ['soʃəl] *adj* sociale || *s* riunione sociale

so′cial climb′er ['klaɪmər] *s* arrampicatore *m* sociale

so′cial con′tract *s* patto sociale

socialism ['soʃə‚lɪzəm] *s* socialismo

socialist ['soʃəlɪst] *s* socialista *mf*

socialite ['soʃə‚laɪt] *s* persona che appartiene all'alta società

So′cial Reg′ister *s* (trademark) annuario dell'alta società

so′cial secu′rity *s* sicurezza sociale

so′cial work′er *s* visitatrice *f*, assistente *mf* sociale

socie·ty [sə'saɪ·əti] *s* (**-ties**) società *f*; (*companionship or company*) compagnia

soci′ety ed′itor *s* cronista mondano

sociology [‚sosɪ'ɑlədʒi] or [‚soʃɪ'ɑlədʒi] *s* sociologia

sock [sɑk] *s* calzino; (slang) colpo forte; (slang) attore *m* di prim'ordine; (slang) spettacolo eccezionale || *tr* (slang) dare un forte colpo a

socket ['sɑkɪt] *s* (*of eye*) occhiaia; (*of tooth*) alveolo; (*of candlestick*) bocciolo; (*wall socket*) (elec) presa di corrente; (elec) portalampada *m*

sock′et wrench′ *s* chiave *f* a tubo

sod [sɑd] *s* zolla; terreno erboso || *v* (*pret & pp* **sodded;** *ger* **sodding**) *tr* piotare

soda ['sodə] *s* soda

so′da crack′er *s* galletta fatta al bicarbonato

so′da wa′ter *s* soda, gazosa

sodium ['sodɪ·əm] *adj* sodico || *s* sodio

sofa ['sofə] *s* sofà *m*, divano

so′fa bed′ *s* sofà *m* letto

soft [sɔft] or [sɑft] *adj* molle; (*smooth*) morbido; (*iron*) dolce; (*hat*) floscio; (*person*) rammollito; (coll) facile

soft′-boiled′ egg′ ['sɔft'bɔɪld] or ['sɑft'bɔɪld] *s* uovo alla coque

soft′ coal′ *s* carbone bituminoso

soft′ drink′ *s* bibita

soften ['sɔfən] or ['sɑfən] *tr* mollificare, rammollire; (fig) intenerire || *intr* intenerirsi

softener ['sɔfənər] or ['sɑfənər] *s* ammorbidente *m*

soft′ land′ing *s* allunaggio morbido

soft′-ped′al *v* (*pret & pp* **-aled** or **-alled;** *ger* **-aling** or **-alling**) *tr* mettere in sordina; (coll) moderare

soft′-shell crab′ *s* mollecca

soft′ soap′ *s* sapone *m* molle; (coll) adulazione

soft′-soap′ *tr* (coll) insaponare

sog·gy ['sɑgi] *adj* (**-gier; -giest**) rammollito, inzuppato

soil [sɔɪl] *s* suolo, terreno; territorio; (*spot*) macchia; (*filth*) porcheria, lordura || *tr* sporcare, macchiare || *intr* sporcarsi, macchiarsi

soil′ pipe′ *s* tubo di scarico

soiree or **soirée** [swɑ're] *s* serata

sojourn ['sodʒʌrn] *s* soggiorno || ['sodʒʌrn] or [so'dʒʌrn] *intr* soggiornare

solace ['sɑlɪs] *s* conforto || *tr* confortare, consolare

solar ['solər] *adj* solare

so′lar bat′tery *s* batteria solare

solder ['sɑdər] *s* saldatura; lega per saldatura || *tr* saldare

sol′dering i′ron *s* saldatoio

soldier ['soldʒər] *s* (*man of rank and file*) soldato; (*man in military service*) militare *m* || *intr* fare il soldato

sol′dier of for′tune *s* soldato di ventura

soldier·y ['soldʒəri] *s* (**-ies**) soldatesca

sold-out ['sold‚aut] *adj* esaurito; (*e.g., theater*) completo

sole [sol] *adj* solo, unico; esclusivo || *s* (*of foot*) pianta; (*of stocking*) soletta; (*of shoe*) suola; (*fish*) sfoglia || *tr* solare

solely ['solli] *adv* solamente

solemn ['sɑləm] *adj* solenne

solicit [sə'lɪsɪt] *tr* sollecitare; adescare, accostare

solicitor [sə'lɪsɪtər] *s* sollecitatore *m*; agente *m*; (law) procuratore *m*

solicitous [sə'lɪsɪtəs] *adj* sollecito

solicitude [sə'lɪsɪ‚tjud] or [sə'lɪsɪ‚tud] *s* sollecitudine *f*

solid ['sɑlɪd] *adj* solido; (*not hollow*) sodo; (*e.g., clouds*) denso; (*wall*) pieno, massiccio; (*word*) con grafia unita; intero; unanime, solidale; (*good*) buono; (*e.g., gold*) puro, massiccio

solidity [sə'lɪdɪti] *s* solidità *f*

sol′id-state′ *adj* transistorizzato, senza valvole

solilo·quy [sə'lɪləkwi] *s* (**-quies**) soliloquio

solitaire ['sɑlɪ‚ter] *s* solitario

solitar·y ['sɑlɪ‚teri] *adj* solitario; unico || *s* (**-ies**) persona solitaria

sol′itary confine′ment *s* segregazione cellulare

solitude ['sɑlɪ‚tjud] or ['sɑlɪ‚tud] *s* solitudine *f*

so·lo ['solo] *adj* solo, solitario; (mus) solista || *s* (**-los**) (mus) solo

soloist ['solo·ɪst] *s* solista *mf*

so′ long′ *interj* (coll) ciao!; (coll) addio!; (coll) arrivederci!

solstice ['sɑlstɪs] *s* solstizio

soluble ['sɑljəbəl] *adj* solubile

solution [sə'luʃən] *s* soluzione

solvable ['sɑlvəbəl] *adj* risolvibile

solve [sɑlv] *tr* risolvere, sciogliere

solvency ['sɑlvənsɪ] s solvenza
solvent ['sɑlvənt] adj & s solvente m
somber ['sɑmbər] adj tetro
some [sʌm] adj indef qualche; di + art, e.g., **some apples** delle mele; (coll) forte, grande || pron indef alcuni, taluni; ne, e.g., **I have some** ne ho
some'bod'y pron indef taluno, qualcuno; **somebody else** qualcun altro || s (-ies) (coll) qualcuno
some'day' adv qualche giorno
some'how' adv in qualche modo; **somehow or other** in un modo o nell'altro
some'one' pron indef qualcuno, taluno; **someone else** qualcun altro
somersault ['sʌmər ,sɔlt] s salto mortale || intr fare un salto mortale
something ['sʌmθɪŋ] pron indef qualcosa; **something else** qualcos'altro || adv un po'; (coll) molto, moltissimo
some'time' adj antico, di un tempo || adv un giorno o l'altro, uno di questi giorni
some'times' adv talora, talvolta
some'way' adv in qualche modo
some'what' s qualcosa || adv piuttosto, un po'
some'where' adv in qualche luogo, da qualche parte; a qualche momento; **somewhere else** altrove
somnambulist [sam'næmbjəlɪst] s sonnambulo
somnolent ['sɑmnələnt] adj sonnolento
son [sʌn] s figlio
sonar ['sonɑr] s ecogoniometro, sonar m
song [sɔŋ] or [sɑŋ] s canto, canzone f; **for a song** per un soldo
song'bird' s uccello canoro
Song' of Songs' s Cantico dei Cantici
songster ['sɑŋstər] s cantante m, canzonettista f
songstress ['sɑŋstrɪs] s cantante f, canzonettista f
song'writ'er s canzoniere m
son'ic boom' ['sɑnɪk] s boato sonico
son'-in-law' s (sons'-in-law') genero
sonnet ['sɑnɪt] s sonetto
son·ny ['sʌnɪ] s (-nies) figliolo
sonori·ty [sə'nɑrɪtɪ] or [sə'nɔrɪtɪ] s (-ties) sonorità f
soon [sun] adv in breve, ben presto; subito, presto; **as soon as** non appena, quanto prima; **as soon as possible** quanto prima; **I had sooner** preferirei; **how soon?** quando?; **soon after** poco dopo; **sooner or later** prima o poi, tosto o tardi
soot [sut] or [sut] s fuliggine f
soothe [suð] tr calmare, lenire
soothsayer ['suð ,se·ər] s indovino
soot·y ['sutɪ] or ['sutɪ] adj (-ier; -iest) fuliggginoso
sop [sɑp] s (soaked food) zuppa; (bribe) dono, offa || v (pret & pp **sopped**; ger **sopping**) tr intingere, inzuppare; **to sop up** assorbire
sophisticated [sə'fɪstɪ ,ketɪd] adj sofisticato, smaliziato
sophistication [sə ,fɪstɪ'keʃən] s eccessiva ricercatezza; gusti mpl raffinati

sophomore ['sɑfə ,mor] s studente m del secondo anno, fagiolo
sophomoric [,sɑfə'mɔrɪk] adj saputello, presuntuoso; ingenuo, imberbe
sopping ['sɑpɪŋ] adv—**sopping wet** inzuppato
sopran·o [sə'præno] or [sə'prɑno] adj per soprano, da soprano || s (-os) soprano mf
sorcerer ['sɔrsərər] s mago, stregone m
sorceress ['sɔrsərɪs] s maga, strega
sorcer·y ['sɔrsərɪ] s (-ies) stregoneria
sordid ['sɔrdɪd] adj sordido
sore [sor] adj irritato; indolenzito; estremo, grave; **to be sore at** (coll) aversela con || s piaga, ulcera; dolore m, afflizione; **to open an old sore** riaprire una ferita
sorely ['sorlɪ] adv penosamente; gravemente, urgentemente
soreness ['sornɪs] s dolore m, afflizione
sore' spot' s (fig) piaga
sore' throat' s mal m di gola
sorori·ty [sə'rɑrɪtɪ] or [sə'rɔrɪtɪ] s (-ties) associazione femminile universitaria
sorrel ['sɑrəl] or ['sɔrəl] adj sauro
sorrow ['sɑro] or ['sɔro] s dolore m, cordoglio || intr affliggersi, provar cordoglio; **to sorrow for** rimpiangere
sorrowful ['sɑrəfəl] or ['sɔrəfəl] adj doloroso
sor·ry ['sɑrɪ] or ['sɔrɪ] adj (-rier; -riest) spiacente, desolato, dolente; povero, cattivo; **to be sorry** dolersi; dispiacere a, e.g., **he is sorry** gli dispiace || interj mi dispiace!, scusi!
sort [sɔrt] s tipo, specie f; maniera; **a sort of** di una specie di; **out of sorts** depresso; ammalato; di mal umore; **sort of** (coll) piuttosto; (coll) un certo, e.g., **sort of a headache** un certo mal di testa || tr assortire; (mail) smistare
so'-so' adj passabile || adv così così
sot [sɑt] s ubriacone m
soubrette [su'bret] s (theat) soubrette f
soul [sol] s anima; **upon my soul!** sulla mia parola!
sound [saund] adj sano; solido, forte; valido, buono; (sleep) profondo; valido, legale; onesto || s suono; rumore m; (of an animal) verso; (passage of water) stretto; (surg) sonda; (ichth) vescica natatoria; **within sound of** alla portata di || adv profondamente || tr (an instrument) sonare; pronunciare; (e.g., s.o.'s chest) auscultare; (praises) cantare; (to measure) sondare || intr sonare; parere, sembrare; fare uno scandaglio; **to sound like** avere il suono di; dare l'impressione di, parere
sound' bar'rier s muro del suono
sound' film' s pellicola sonora
soundly ['saundlɪ] adv solidamente; profondamente; completamente
sound'proof' adj a prova di suono || tr insonorizzare

sound' track' s (mov) sonoro, colonna sonora

sound' truck' s autoveicolo con impianto sonoro

sound' wave' s onda sonora

soup [sup] s zuppa, minestra

soup' dish' s piatto fondo

soup' kitch'en s asilo dei poveri che serve zuppa gratuitamente

soup'spoon' s cucchiaio (da minestra)

sour [saur] adj acido; (fruit) acerbo || tr inacidire || intr inacidirsi

source [sors] s fonte f, sorgente f

source' lan'guage s lingua di partenza

source' mate'rial s fonti fpl originali

sour' cher'ry s (fruit) amarena; (tree) amareno

sour' grapes' interj l'uva è verde!

south [sauθ] adj meridionale, del sud || s sud m, meridione m || adv verso il sud

South' Amer'ica s l'America f del Sud

South' Amer'ican adj & s sudamericano

southeast [ˌsauθˈist] adj di sud-est || s sud-est || adv al sud-est

southern [ˈsʌðərn] adj meridionale

South'ern Cross' s Croce f del Sud

southerner [ˈsʌðərnər] s meridionale mf

South' Kore'a s la Corea del Sud

south'paw' adj & s (coll) mancino

South' Pole' s Polo sud

South' Vietnam-ese' [vɪˌetnəˈmiz] adj vietnamita del sud || s (-ese) vietnamita mf del sud

southward [ˈsauθwərd] adv verso il sud

south'west' adj di sud-ovest || s sud-ovest m || adv al sud-ovest

souvenir [ˌsuvəˈnɪr] or [ˈsuvəˌnɪr] s ricordo, memoria

sovereign [ˈsavrɪn] or [ˈsʌvrɪn] adj sovrano || s (king) sovrano; (queen; coin) sovrana

sovereign-ty [ˈsavrɪnti] or [ˈsʌvrɪnti] s (-ties) sovranità f

soviet [ˈsovɪˌet] or [ˌsovɪˈet] adj sovietico || s soviet m

So'viet Rus'sia s la Russia Sovietica

sow [sau] s porca, troia || [so] v (pret sowed; pp sown or sowed) tr seminare

soybean [ˈsɔɪˌbin] s soia; seme m di soia

spa [spɑ] s terme fpl

space [spes] adj spaziale || s spazio; periodo; **after a space** dopo un po' || tr spaziare; **to space out** diradare

space' bar' s barra spaziatrice, spaziatrice f

space' cen'ter s cosmodromo

space'craft' s astronave f

space' flight' s volo spaziale

space'man' s (-men') navigatore m spaziale

spacer [ˈspesər] s spaziatrice f, barra spaziatrice

space'ship' s astronave f

space'suit' s scafandro astronautico, tuta spaziale

spacious [ˈspeʃəs] adj spazioso

spade [sped] s vanga; (cards) picca; **to call a spade a spade** dire pane al pane, vino al vino || tr vangare

spade'work' s lavoro preliminare

spaghetti [spəˈgeti] s spaghetti mpl

Spain [spen] s la Spagna

span [spæn] s (of the hand) spanna; (of time) tratto; (of a bridge) campata, luce f; (of horses) paio; (aer) apertura || v (pret & pp spanned; ger spanning) tr misurare a spanne; attraversare, oltrepassare; (said of time) abbracciare

spangle [ˈspæŋgəl] s lustrino || tr tempestare di lustrini; (with bright objects) stellare || intr brillare

Spaniard [ˈspænjərd] s spagnolo

Spanish [ˈspænɪʃ] adj & s spagnolo; **the Spanish** gli spagnoli

Span'ish-Amer'ican adj & s ispano-americano

Span'ish broom' s ginestra

Span'ish fly' mosca cantaride

Span'ish om'elet s frittata di pomodori, cipolle e peperoni

Span'ish-speak'ing adj di lingua spagnola

spank [spæŋk] tr sculacciare

spanking [ˈspæŋkɪŋ] adj rapido; forte; (coll) eccellente, straordinario || s sculacciata

spar [spɑr] s (mineral) spato; (naut) asta, pennone m; (aer) longherone m || v (pret & pp sparred; ger sparring) intr fare la box

spare [sper] adj di riserva; libero, in eccesso; (e.g., diet) frugale; (lean) magro || tr salvare, risparmiare; perdonare; (to do without) fare a meno di, privarsi di; **to have . . . to spare** aver . . . d'avanzo; **to spare oneself** risparmiarsi

spare' parts' s pezzi mpl di ricambio

spare' room' s camera per gli ospiti

spare' tire' s ruota di scorta, pneumatico di scorta

spare' wheel' s ruota di scorta

sparing [ˈsperɪŋ] adj economico; (scanty) scarso

spark [spɑrk] s scintilla; traccia || tr (coll) rianimare; (coll) corteggiare || intr scintillare

spark' coil' s bobina d'accensione

spark' gap' s (elec) traferro, intraferro

sparkle [ˈspɑrkəl] s scintilla; (luster) scintillio; allegria, vivacità f || intr scintillare; (said, e.g., of eyes) brillare, luccicare; (said of wine) frizzare, spumeggiare

sparkling [ˈspɑrklɪŋ] adj scintillante; (wine) frizzante, spumeggiante; (water) gassoso

spark' plug' s candela

sparrow [ˈspæro] s passero

sparse [spɑrs] adj rado

Spartan [ˈspɑrtən] adj & s spartano

spasm [ˈspæzəm] s spasmo; sprazzo d'energia

spasmodic [spæzˈmɑdɪk] adj spasmodico; intermittente, a sprazzi

spastic [ˈspæstɪk] adj & s spastico

spat [spæt] s litigio, battibecco; **spats**

ghette *fpl* || *v* (*pret & pp* **spatted; ger spatting**) *intr* avere un battibecco

spatial ['speʃəl] *adj* spaziale

spatter ['spætər] *tr* schizzare, spruzzare || *intr* gocciolare

spatula ['spætʃələ] *s* spatola

spawn [spɔn] *s* prole *f*, progenie *f*; risultato || *tr* produrre, generare || *intr* (ichth) deporre le uova

spay [spe] *tr* asportare le ovaie a

speak [spik] *v* (*pret* **spoke** [spok]; *pp* **spoken**) *tr* (*a language*) parlare; (*the truth*) dire || *intr* parlare; **so to speak** per così dire; **speaking!** al telefono!; **to speak of** importante, che valga parlarne; **to speak out** dire la propria opinione

speak'-eas'y *s* (**-ies**) bar clandestino

speaker ['spikər] *s* conferenziere *m*, oratore *m*; (*of a language*) parlante *mf*; (pol) presidente *m*; (rad) altoparlante *m*

speaking ['spikɪŋ] *adj* parlante; **to be on speaking terms** parlarsi || *s* parlare *m*, discorso

speak'ing tube' *s* tubo acustico

spear [spɪr] *s* lancia; (*for fishing*) arpione *m*; (*of grass*) stelo || *tr* trafiggere con la lancia

spear' gun' *s* fucile subacqueo

spear'head' *s* punta di lancia || *tr* condurre, dirigere

spear'mint' *s* menta romana spicata

special ['speʃəl] *adj* speciale || *s* prezzo speciale; treno speciale

spe'cial deliv'ery *s* espresso

spe'cial draw'ing rights' *spl* (econ) diritti *mpl* speciali di prelievo

specialist ['speʃəlɪst] *s* specialista *mf*

specialize ['speʃə‚laɪz] *tr* specializzare || *intr* specializzarsi

spe'cial part'ner *s* accomandante *mf*

special‧ty ['speʃəlti] *s* (**-ties**) specialità *f*

spe‧cies ['spisiz] *s* (**-cies**) specie *f*

specific [spɪ'sɪfɪk] *adj & s* specifico

specification [‚spesɪfɪ'keʃən] *s* specifica; (com) capitolato

specif'ic grav'ity *s* peso specifico

speci‧fy ['spesɪ‚faɪ] *v* (*pret & pp* **-fied**) *tr* specificare

specimen ['spesɪmən] *s* esemplare *m*; (coll) tipo

specious ['spiʃəs] *adj* specioso

speck [spek] *s* macchiolina; (*of dust*) granello; (*of hope*) filo || *tr* macchiettare

speckle ['spekəl] *s* macchiolina || *tr* macchiettare, picchiettare

spectacle ['spektəkəl] *s* spettacolo; **spectacles** occhiali *mpl*

spectator ['spektetər] *or* [spek'tetər] *s* spettatore *m*

specter ['spektər] *s* spettro

spec‧trum ['spektrəm] *s* (**-tra** [trə] *or* **-trums**) spettro; (fig) gamma

speculate ['spekjə‚let] *intr* speculare

speech [spitʃ] *s* parola, parlata; (*before an audience*) discorso; (*of an actor*) elocuzione; **in speech** oralmente

speech' clin'ic *s* clinica per la correzione dei difetti del linguaggio

speechless ['spitʃlɪs] *adj* senza parole, muto

speed [spid] *s* velocità *f*; (aut) marcia || *tr* accelerare, affrettare || *intr* accelerare, affrettarsi; guidare oltre la velocità massima

speed'boat' *s* motoscafo da corsa

speeding ['spidɪŋ] *s* eccesso di velocità

speed' king' *s* asso del volante

speed' lim'it *s* limite *m* di velocità

speedometer [spi'dɑmɪtər] *s* tachimetro; (*to record the distance covered*) contachilometri *m*

speed'-up' *s* accelerazione

speed'way' *s* (*highway*) autostrada; (*for races*) pista

speed‧y ['spidi] *adj* (**-ier; -iest**) veloce, rapido

spell [spel] *s* malia, incantesimo; fascino; turno; attacco; periodo di tempo; **to cast a spell on** incantare || *v* (*pret & pp* **spelled** *or* **spelt** [spelt]) *tr* compitare; scrivere in tutte lettere; voler dire; **to spell out** (coll) spiegare dettagliatamente || *intr* scrivere, sillabare || *v* (*pret & pp* **spelled**) *tr* rimpiazzare

spell'bind' *v* (*pret & pp* **-bound**) *tr* affascinare

spell'bind'er *s* oratore *m* abbagliante

spelling ['spelɪŋ] *adj* ortografico || *s* (*act*) compitazione; (*way a word is spelled*) grafia; (*subject of study*) ortografia

spell'ing bee' *s* gara di ortografia

spelunker [spɪ'lʌŋkər] *s* esploratore *m* di caverne

spend [spend] *v* (*pret & pp* **spent** [spent]) *tr* spendere; (*time*) passare

spender ['spendər] *s* spenditore *m*

spend'ing mon'ey *s* denaro per le piccole spese personali

spend'thrift' *s* sprecone *m*, spendaccione *m*

sperm [spʌrm] *s* sperma *m*

sperm' whale' *s* capodoglio

spew [spju] *tr & intr* vomitare

sphere [sfɪr] *s* sfera

spherical ['sferɪkəl] *adj* sferico

sphinx [sfɪŋks] *s* (**sphinxes** *or* **sphinges** ['sfɪndʒiz]) sfinge *f*

spice [spaɪs] *s* droga; spezie *fpl*; (fig) gusto, sapore *m* || *tr* drogare; dare gusto a, rendere piccante

spick-and-span ['spɪkənd'spæn] *adj* ordinato e pulito

spic‧y ['spaɪsi] *adj* (**-ier; -iest**) drogato; piccante

spider ['spaɪdər] *s* ragno

spi'der-web' *s* ragnatela

spiff‧y ['spɪfi] *adj* (**-ier; -iest**) (slang) elegante, bello

spigot ['spɪgət] *s* (*peg*) zipolo; (*faucet*) rubinetto

spike [spaɪk] *s* chiodo, chiodone *m*; (*sharp-pointed piece*) spuntone *m*; (rr) arpione *m*; (bot) spiga || *tr* inchiodare; mettere chiodi a; (*a rumor*) porre fine a; (coll) alcolizzare

spill [spɪl] *s* rovesciamento; liquido rovesciato; (coll) caduta || *v* (*pret & pp* **spilled** *or* **spilt** [spɪlt]) *tr* rovesciare, spandere; versare; (naut) sventare; (coll) far cadere; (slang) snocciolare || intr rovesciarsi; versarsi

spill'way' s sfioratore m, stramazzo

spin [spɪn] s giro; (twirl) mulinello; corsa; **to go into a spin** (aer) cadere a vite || v (pret & pp **spun** [spʌn]; ger **spinning**) tr far girare; (e.g., thread) filare; **to spin out** prolungare; **to spin a yarn** raccontare una storia || intr girare; (said of a top) prillare; filare

spinach ['spɪnɪt∫] or ['spɪnɪdʒ] s spinacio; (leaves used as food) spinaci mpl

spi'nal col'umn ['spaɪnəl] s spina dorsale, colonna vertebrale

spi'nal cord' s midollo spinale

spindle ['spɪndəl] s (rounded rod) fuso; (shaft, axle) asse m; balaustro

spine [spaɪn] s spina; spina dorsale; (bb) costola; (fig) forza, carattere m

spineless ['spaɪnlɪs] adj senza spine; senza carattere

spinet ['spɪnɪt] s spinetta

spinner ['spɪnər] s filatore m; (machine) filatrice f

spinning ['spɪnɪŋ] adj filante || s filatura; rotazione

spin'ning mill' s filanda

spin'ning wheel' s filatoio

spinster ['spɪnstər] s zitella

spi·ral ['spaɪrəl] adj & s spirale f || v (pret & pp **-raled** or **-ralled**; ger **-raling** or **-ralling**) intr muoversi lungo una spirale

spi'ral stair'case s scala a chiocciola

spire [spaɪr] s (of a steeple) guglia, freccia; (of grass) foglia; (spiral) spirale f

spirit ['spɪrɪt] s spirito; valore m, vigore m; bevanda spiritosa; **out of spirits** giù di morale || tr—**to spirit away** portar via misteriosamente

spirited ['spɪrɪtɪd] adj brioso; (horse) superbo, vivace

spir'it lamp' s lampada a spirito

spiritless ['spɪrɪtlɪs] adj senza anima, senza vita

spir'it lev'el s livella a bolla d'aria

spiritual ['spɪrɪt∫u·əl] adj spirituale; (séance) spiritico

spiritualism ['spɪrɪt∫uə‚lɪzəm] s spiritismo; (philos) spiritualismo

spiritualist ['spɪrɪt∫u·əlɪst] s spiritista mf; (philos) spiritualista mf

spirituous ['spɪrɪt∫u·əs] adj alcolico

spit [spɪt] s sputo; (for roasting) spiedo, schidione m; punta; **the spit and image of** (coll) il ritratto parlante di || v (pret & pp **spat** [spæt] or **spit**; ger **spitting**) tr & intr sputare

spite [spaɪt] s dispetto, ripicco; **in spite of** a dispetto di, a onta di; **out of spite** per picca || tr far dispetto a; offendere; contrariare

spiteful ['spaɪtfəl] adj dispettoso

spit'fire' s persona collerica; (woman) bisbetica

spit'ting im'age s (coll) ritratto parlante

spittoon [spɪ'tun] s sputacchiera

splash [splæ∫] s schizzo, spruzzo; (of mud) zacchera; (sound) tonfo; **to make a splash** fare molto sci-sci || tr & intr sguazzare

splash'down' s (rok) ammaraggio, urto con l'acqua

spleen [splin] s cattivo umore, bile f; (anat) milza, splene m

splendid ['splɛndɪd] adj splendido; ottimo, magnifico

splendor ['splɛndər] s splendore m

splice [splaɪs] s giuntura || tr giuntare

splint [splɪnt] s stecca || tr steccare

splinter ['splɪntər] s scheggia || tr scheggiare || intr scheggiarsi

splin'ter group' s gruppo dissidente

split [splɪt] adj spaccato; diviso || s spaccatura; fessura; rottura, divisione; **splits** (sports) spaccato || v (pret & pp **split**; ger **splitting**) tr spaccare; dividere; **to split one's sides with laughter** scoppiare dalle risa || intr scindersi, dividersi; **to split up** separarsi

splitting ['splɪtɪŋ] adj che fende; che si fende; violento, fortissimo || s—**splittings** frammenti mpl

splotch [splɑt∫] s macchia, chiazza || tr macchiare, chiazzare

splurge [splʌrdʒ] s ostentazione || intr fare ostentazione; fare una spesa matta

splutter ['splʌtər] s crepitio; (utterance) barbugliamento || tr barbugliare || intr crepitare; barbugliare

spoil [spɔɪl] s spoglia, bottino; **spoils** (mil) spoglie fpl; (pol) profitto, vantaggio || v (pret & pp **spoiled** or **spoilt** [spɔɪlt]) tr rovinare, sciupare; (a child) viziare; (food) deteriorare || intr guastarsi, andare a male

spoilage ['spɔɪlɪdʒ] s deterioramento

spoiled [spɔɪld] adj (child) viziato; (food) andato a male, passato

spoils' sys'tem s sistema politico secondo il quale le cariche vanno al partito vincitore

spoke [spok] s (of a wheel) raggio; (of a ladder) piolo

spokes'man s (-men) portavoce m

sponge [spʌndʒ] s spugna; **to throw in the sponge** (slang) gettare la spugna || tr pulire con spugna; assorbire; (coll) scroccare || intr assorbire; **to sponge off** (coll) vivere alle spalle di

sponge' bath' s spugnatura

sponge' cake' s pan m di Spagna

sponger ['spʌndʒər] s scroccatore m

sponge' rub'ber s gommapiuma

spon·gy ['spʌndʒɪ] adj (-gier; -giest) spugnoso

sponsor ['spɑnsər] s patrocinatore m; (of a charitable institution) patrono; (godfather) padrino; (godmother) madrina || tr patrocinare; (rad, telv) offrire

sponsorship ['spɑnsər‚∫ɪp] s patrocinio

spontaneous [spɑn'tenɪ·əs] adj spontaneo

spoof [spuf] *s* mistificazione; parodia || *tr* mistificare; parodiare || *intr* mistificare; fare una parodia

spook [spuk] *s* (coll) spettro

spook·y [ˈspuki] *adj* (**-ier; -iest**) (coll) spettrale; (*horse*) (coll) nervoso

spool [spul] *s* spola, rocchetto

spoon [spun] *s* cucchiaio; (*lure*) cucchiaino; **born with a silver spoon in one's mouth** nato con la camicia || *tr* servire col cucchiaio || *intr* (coll) limonare

spoonerism [ˈspunəˌrɪzəm] *s* papera

spoon'-feed' *v* (*pret & pp* **-fed**) *tr* nutrire col cucchiaino; (fig) coccolare

spoonful [ˈspunˌful] *s* cucchiaiata

spoon·y [ˈspuni] *adj* (**-ier; -iest**) (coll) svenevole

sporadic(al) [spəˈrædɪk(əl)] *adj* sporadico

spore [spor] *s* spora

sport [sport] *adj* sportivo || *s* sport *m;* gioco; (*laughingstock*) zimbello; (*gambler*) (coll) giocatore *m;* (*person who behaves in a sportsmanlike manner*) (coll) spirito sportivo; (*flashy fellow*) (coll) tipo fino; (biol) mutazione; **to make sport of** farsi gioco di || *tr* (coll) sfoggiare; **to sport away** dissipare || *intr* divertirsi; giocare; farsi beffe

sport' clothes' *spl* vestiti *mpl* sport

sport'ing chance' *s* pari opportunità *f* di vincere

sport'ing goods' *spl* articoli *mpl* sportivi

sport'ing house' *s* (coll) bordello

sports'cast'er *s* annunziatore sportivo

sports' fan' *s* appassionato agli spettacoli sportivi, tifoso

sports'man *s* (**-men**) sportivo

sports'man·ship' *s* sportività *f,* spirito sportivo

sports' news' *s* notiziario sportivo

sports'wear' *s* articoli *mpl* d'abbigliamento sportivo

sports'writ'er *s* cronista sportivo

sport·y [ˈsporti] *adj* (**-ier; -iest**) (coll) elegante; (coll) sportivo; (coll) appariscente

spot [spɑt] *s* macchia; luogo, punto, posto; (*e.g., of tea*) goccia; **spots** locali *mpl;* **on the spot** sul posto; (*right now*) seduta stante; (slang) in difficoltà; **to hit the spot** (slang) soddisfare completamente || *v* (*pret & pp* **spotted;** *ger* **spotting**) *tr* macchiare; spargere; (coll) riconoscere || *intr* macchiare; macchiarsi

spot' cash' *s* pronta cassa

spot'-check' *tr* fare un breve sondaggio di; controllare rapidamente

spot' check' *s* breve sondaggio; rapido controllo

spotless [ˈspɑtlɪs] *adj* immacolato, senza macchia

spot'light' *s* riflettore *m;* (aut) proiettore *m;* **to be in the spotlight** (fig) essere il centro d'attenzione

spot' remov'er [rɪˈmuvər] *s* smacchiatore *m*

spot' weld'ing *s* saldatura per punti

spouse [spauz] *or* [spaus] *s* consorte *mf*

spout [spaut] *s* (*to carry water from roof*) doccia; (*of jar, pitcher, etc.*) becco, beccuccio; (*jet*) zampillo, getto || *tr & intr* sprizzare, zampillare; (coll) declamare

sprain [spren] *s* distorsione || *tr* distorcere, distorcersi

sprawl [sprɔl] *intr* sdraiarsi

spray [spre] *s* spruzzo; (*of the sea*) schiuma; (*device*) spruzzatore *m;* (*twig*) ramoscello || *tr & intr* spruzzare

sprayer [ˈspreər] *s* spruzzatore *m,* schizzetto, vaporizzatore *m;* (hort) irroratrice *f*

spray' gun' *s* pistola a spruzzo; (hort) irroratrice *f*

spray' paint' *s* vernice *f* a spruzzo

spread [sprɛd] *s* espansione; diffusione; differenza; tappeto, coperta; elasticità *f;* (*of the wings of bird or airplane*) apertura; cibo da spalmare; (coll) festino; (journ) articolo di fondo or pubblicitario su varie colonne || *v* (*pret & pp* **spread**) *tr* tendere, estendere; (*one's legs*) divaricare; (*wings*) spiegare; spargere, cospargere; (*the table*) preparare; (*butter*) spalmare; diffondere || *intr* estendersi; spiegarsi; spargersi; spalmarsi; diffondersi

spree [spri] *s* baldoria, bisboccia; **to go on a spree** darsi alla pazza gioia

sprig [sprɪg] *s* ramoscello

spright·ly [ˈspraɪtli] *adj* (**-lier; -liest**) brioso, vivace

spring [sprɪŋ] *adj* primaverile; sorgivo; a molla || *s* (*season*) primavera; (*issue of water from earth*) fonte *f,* polla; (*elastic device*) molla; elasticità *f;* (*leap*) salto; (*crack*) fenditura; (aut) balestra || *v* (*pret* **sprang** [spræŋ] *or* **sprung** [sprʌŋ]; *pp* **sprung**) *tr* (*e.g., a lock*) far scattare; (*a leak*) aprire; (*a mine*) far brillare || *intr* saltare; (*said of a metal spring*) scattare; scaturire, zampillare; nascere, derivare; esplodere; **to spring forth** or **up** sorgere

spring'board' *s* pedana, trampolino

spring' chick'en *s* pollo giovanissimo; (slang) ragazzina

spring' fe'ver *s* indolenza primaverile

spring' mat'tress *s* materasso a molle

spring' tide' *s* marea di sizigia

spring'time' *s* primavera

sprinkle [ˈsprɪŋkəl] *s* spruzzo, spruzzatina; (*small amount*) pizzico || *tr* spruzzare; (*e.g., sugar*) spolverizzare || *intr* sprizzare; piovigginare

sprinkler [ˈsprɪŋklər] *s* annaffiatoio; (*person*) annaffiattore *m*

sprinkling [ˈsprɪŋklɪŋ] *s* sprizzo, spruzzo; (*with holy water*) aspersione; (*with powder*) spolverizzamento; (*e.g., of knowledge*) spolvero, spolveratura; (*of people*) piccolo numero

sprin'kling can' *s* annaffiatoio

sprint [sprɪnt] *s* (sports) scatto, volata || *intr* (sports) scattare

sprite [spraɪt] *s* spirito folletto

sprocket ['sprɑkɪt] *s* moltiplica; (phot) trasportatore *m*

sprout [spraut] *s* germoglio || *intr* germogliare; crescere rapidamente

spruce [sprus] *adj* elegante, attillato || *s* abete rosso || *tr* attillare, azzimare || *intr* attillarsi, azzimarsi

spry [spraɪ] *adj* (**spryer** or **sprier;** **spryest** or **spriest**) vegeto

spud [spʌd] *s* vanghetto, tagliaradici *m;* (coll) patata

spun' glass' *s* lana di vetro

spunk [spʌŋk] *s* (coll) coraggio, fegato

spur [spʌr] *s* sperone *m;* (rr) raccordo ferroviario; (fig) pungolo; **on the spur of the moment** lì per lì || *v* (*pret & pp* **spurred;** *ger* **spurring**) *tr* spronare; **to spur on** spronare, incitare

spurious ['spjurɪ·əs] *adj* spurio

spurn [spʌrn] *s* disprezzo, sdegno; rifiuto || *tr* disprezzare, sdegnare; rifiutare

spurt [spʌrt] *s* spruzzo, zampillo; (*sudden burst*) scatto repentino || *intr* sprizzare, zampillare; scattare

sputter ['spʌtər] *s* barbugliamento; (*sizzling*) crepitio || *tr* barbugliare || *intr* barbugliare; crepitare

spu·tum ['spjutəm] *s* (**-ta** [tə]) sputo

spy [spaɪ] *s* (**spies**) spia || *v* (*pret & pp* **spied**) *tr* spiare; osservare || *intr* fare la spia; **to spy on** spiare

spy'glass' *s* cannocchiale *m*

spying ['spaɪ·ɪŋ] *s* spionaggio

squabble ['skwɑbəl] *s* battibecco || *intr* litigare

squad [skwɑd] *s* squadra

squadron ['skwɑdrən] *s* (*of cavalry*) squadrone *m;* (aer, nav) squadriglia; (mil) squadra

squalid ['skwɑlɪd] *adj* sordido; squallido, misero

squall [skwɔl] *s* groppo, turbine *m;* urlo || *intr* gridare, urlare

squalor ['skwɑlər] *s* sordidezza; squallore *m,* miseria

squander ['skwɑndər] *tr* scialacquare, dilapidare, sperperare

square [skwer] *adj* quadrato, e.g., **two square miles** due miglia quadrate; di ... di lato, e.g., **two miles square** di due miglia di lato; ad angolo retto; solido; saldato; (coll) onesto; (coll) diretto; (coll) sostanzioso; (slang) all'antica; **to get square with** (coll) fargliela pagare a || *s* quadrato; (*small square, e.g., of checkerboard*) quadretto; (*city block*) isolato; (*open area in city*) piazza, piazzale *m;* (*of carpenter*) squadra; **on the square** ad angolo retto; (coll) onesto || *adv* ad angolo retto; (coll) onestamente || *tr* squadrare; dividere in quadretti; elevare al quadrato; quadrare; (*a debt*) saldare; **to square with** adattare a || *intr* quadrare; **to square off** prepararsi, mettersi in posizione difensiva

square' dance' *s* danza figurata americana

square' meal' *s* (coll) pasto abbondante

square' root' *s* radice quadrata

square' shoot'er ['ʃutər] *s* (coll) persona onesta

squash [skwɑʃ] *s* spappolamento; (bot) zucca; (sports) squash *m* || *tr* spappolare; spiaccicare; (*e.g., a rumor*) sopprimere; (*a person*) (coll) ridurre al silenzio || *intr* spiaccicarsi

squash·y ['skwɑʃi] *adj* (**-ier; -iest**) tenero; (*ground*) fangoso, pantanoso; (*fruit*) maturo

squat [skwɑt] *adj* tozzo || *v* (*pret & pp* **squatted;** *ger* **squatting**) *intr* accocolarsi; stabilirsi illegalmente su territorio altrui; stabilirsi su terreno pubblico per ottenerne titolo

squatter ['skwɑtər] *s* intruso

squaw [skwɔ] *s* squaw *f;* (coll) donna

squawk [skwɔk] *s* schiamazzo; (slang) lamento stridulo || *intr* schiamazzare; (slang) lamentarsi strillando

squaw' man' *s* bianco sposato con una pellerossa

squeak [skwik] *s* strido; cigolio || *intr* stridere; cigolare; (*said of a mouse*) squittire; **to squeak through** farcela per il rotto della cuffia

squeal [skwil] *s* strido || *intr* stridere; (slang) cantare, fare il delatore

squealer ['skwilər] *s* (slang) delatore *m*

squeamish ['skwimɪʃ] *adj* pudibondo; scrupoloso; (*easily nauseated*) schiltoso, schizzinoso

squeeze [skwiz] *s* spremuta; stretta, abbraccio; **to put the squeeze on** (coll) far pressione su || *tr* premere; spremere, pigiare; stringere || *intr* stringere; **to squeeze through** aprirsi il passo attraverso; (fig) farcela a pena

squeezer ['skwizər] *s* spremifrutta *m*

squelch [skwɛltʃ] *s* osservazione schiacciante || *tr* schiacciare

squid [skwɪd] *s* calamaro, totano

squint [skwɪnt] *s* tendenza losca; (coll) occhiata; (pathol) strabismo || *tr* (*one's eyes*) socchiudere || *intr* socchiudere gli occhi; guardare furtivamente

squint-eyed ['skwɪnt‚aɪd] *adj* guercio, losco; malevolo

squire [skwaɪr] *s* (*of a lady*) cavalier *m* servente; (Brit) proprietario terriero; (U.S.A.) giudice *m* conciliatore || *tr* (*a woman*) accompagnare

squirm [skwʌrm] *s* contorsione || *intr* contorcersi; mostrare imbarazzo; **to squirm out of** cavarsela da

squirrel ['skwʌrəl] *s* scoiattolo

squirt [skwʌrt] *s* schizzo; (*instrument*) schizzetto; (coll) saputello || *tr & intr* schizzare

stab [stæb] *s* pugnalata; (*of pain*) fitta; **to make a stab at** (coll) provare || *v* (*pret & pp* **stabbed;** *ger* **stabbing**) *tr* pugnalare, trafiggere || *intr* pugnalare

stabilize ['stebəl‚aɪz] *tr* stabilizzare

stab' in the back' *s* pugnalata nella schiena or alle spalle

stable [ˈstebəl] *adj* stabile ‖ *s* stalla; (*of race horses*) scuderia

sta'ble-boy' *s* stalliere *m*

stack [stæk] *s* pila; (*of hay or straw*) pagliaio; (*of firewood*) catasta; (*of books*) scaffale *m*; camino; (coll) mucchio, sacco ‖ *tr* ammonticchiare, accatastare

stadi-um [ˈstedɪ·əm] *s* (**-ums** or **-a** [ə]) stadio

staff [stæf] or [stɑf] *s* bastone *m;* asta, albero; personale *m*, corpo; (mil) stato maggiore; (mus) rigo, pentagramma *m* ‖ *tr* dotare di personale

staff' of'ficer *s* ufficiale *m* di stato maggiore

stag [stæg] *adj* per signori soli ‖ *s* (deer) cervo; maschio; (coll) signore *m* ‖ *adv* senza compagna

stage [stedʒ] *s* fase *f*, stadio; tappa, giornata; (coach) diligenza; teatro; piattaforma; (*of microscope*) piatto portaoggetti; (theat) scena, palcoscenico; **by easy stages** poco a poco; **to go on the stage** diventare attore ‖ *tr* mettere in scena; organizzare

stage'coach' *s* diligenza

stage'craft' *s* scenotecnica

stage' door' *s* (theat) ingresso degli artisti

stage' fright' *s* tremarella

stage'hand' *s* macchinista *m*

stage' left' *s* (theat) la sinistra della scena guardando il pubblico

stage' man'ager *s* direttore *m* di scena

stage' right' *s* (theat) la destra della scena guardando il pubblico

stage'-struck' *adj* innamorato del teatro

stage' whis'per *s* a parte *m*

stagger [ˈstægər] *tr* far traballare; impressionare; (*troops; hours*) scaglionare ‖ *intr* traballare

stag'gering *adj* traballante; impressionante, stupefacente

staging [ˈstedʒɪŋ] *s* impalcatura; (theat) messa in scena

stagnant [ˈstægnənt] *adj* stagnante

staid [sted] *adj* serio, grave

stain [sten] *s* macchia; tinta; colorante *m* ‖ *tr* macchiare; tingere; colorare ‖ *intr* macchiarsi

stained' glass' *s* vetro colorato

stained'-glass window' *s* vetrata a colori

stainless [ˈstenlɪs] *adj* immacolato; (steel) inossidabile

stair [ster] *s* scala

stair'case' *s* scala

stair'way' *s* scala

stair'well' *s* tromba delle scale

stake [stek] *s* picchetto; (e.g., of cart) staggio; (to support a plant) puntello; (in gambling) puglia, giocata; **at stake** in gioco; **to die at the stake** morire sul rogo; **to pull up stakes** (coll) andarsene, traslocare ‖ *tr* picchettare; puntellare; attaccare a un palo; arrischiare; (coll) aiutare; **to stake out** picchettare; (slang) tenere sotto sorveglianza; **to stake out a claim** avanzare una pretesa

stale [stel] *adj* stantio; (air) viziato; (fig) ritrito

stale'mate' *s* (chess) stallo; **to reach a stalemate** essere in una posizione di stallo ‖ *tr* mettere in una posizione di stallo

stalk [stɔk] *s* stelo; (of corn) stocco; (of salad) piede *m* ‖ *tr* braccare ‖ *intr* avanzare furtivamente; camminare con andatura maestosa

stall [stɔl] *s* (in a stable) posta; (booth in a market) bancarella; (seat) stallo; (space in a parking lot) spazio per il parcheggio ‖ *tr* (an animal) stallare; (a car) parcheggiare; (a motor) far fermare; **to stall off** eludere, tenere a bada ‖ *intr* impantanarsi; stare nella posta; (said of a motor) fermarsi; (to temporize) menare il can per l'aia

stallion [ˈstæljən] *s* stallone *m*

stalwart [ˈstɔlwərt] *adj* forte, gagliardo ‖ *s* sostenitore *m*

stamen [ˈstemən] *s* stame *m*

stamina [ˈstæmɪnə] *s* forza, vigore *m*

stammer [ˈstæmər] *s* balbuzie *f* ‖ *tr* & *intr* balbettare

stammerer [ˈstæmərər] *s* balbuziente *mf*

stamp [stæmp] *s* (postage stamp) francobollo; (device to show that a fee has been paid) timbro, bollo; impressione; carattere *m*; sigillo; (tool for stamping coins) conio; (tool for crushing ore) maglio ‖ *tr* timbrare, stampigliare, bollare; sigillare; coniare; (one's foot) battere, pestare; imprimere; caratterizzare; (mach) stampare; **to stamp out** spegnere, sopprimere ‖ *intr* battere il piede; (said of a horse) zampare

stampede [stæmˈpid] *s* fuga precipitosa ‖ *tr* precipitarsi verso; far fuggire precipitosamente ‖ *intr* precipitarsi

stamp'ing ground' *s* (coll) luogo di ritrovo abituale

stamp' pad' *s* tampone *m*

stamp'-vend'ing machine' *s* distributore automatico di francobolli

stance [stæns] *s* posizione

stanch [stɑntʃ] *adj* leale; forte; a tenuta d'acqua ‖ *s* chiusa ‖ *tr* arrestare il flusso da; (blood) stagnare

stand [stænd] *s* posizione; resistenza, difesa; tribuna, palco; sostegno, supporto; (booth in market) posteggio; posto di sosta ‖ *v* (pret & pp stood [stʊd]) *tr* mettere in piedi; reggere, sostenere; sopportare, tollerare; (one's ground) mantenere; (a chance) avere; (watch) fare; (coll) pagare; **to stand off** tenere a distanza ‖ *intr* stare; essere alto; fermarsi; stare in piedi; trovarsi; aver forza; essere; (e.g., apart) tenersi; **to stand back of** spalleggiare; **to stand by** appoggiare; **to stand for** rappresentare, voler dire; appoggiare, favorire; tenere a battesimo; (coll) tollerare; **to stand in line** fare la fila or la coda; **to stand in with** (coll) essere nelle buone grazie di; **to stand out** stagliarsi, distaccarsi, risaltare; **to stand up** tenersi in piedi; resistere, durare; **to stand up to** affrontare

standard [ˈstændərd] *adj* (usual) normale; uniforme, standard; *(language)* corretto, preferito || *s* standard *m; (model)* modello, campione *m; (flag)* stendardo

stand·ard·bear′er *s* portabandiera *m*

standardize ['stændər‚daɪz] *tr* standardizzare

stand′ard of liv′ing *s* tenore *m* di vita

stand′ard time′ *s* ora ufficiale, ora legale

standee [stæn'di] *s* passeggero in piedi; spettatore *m* in piedi

stand′-in′ *s* (mov) controfigura; **to have a stand-in with** (coll) essere nelle buone grazie di

standing ['stændɪŋ] *adj (jump)* da fermo, in piedi; fermo; *(water)* stagnante; vigente, permanente; *(idle)* fuori uso || *s* posizione, rango, situazione; classifica; **in good standing** riconosciuto da tutti; **of long standing** vecchio, da lungo tempo

stand′ing ar′my *s* esercito permanente

stand′ing room′ *s* posto in piedi

standpatter ['stænd‚pætər] *s* (coll) seguace *mf* dell'immobilismo

stand′point′ *s* punto di vista

stand′still′ *s* fermata; riposo; **to come to a standstill** fermarsi

stanza ['stænzə] *s* stanza

staple ['stepəl] *adj* principale || *s* articolo di prima necessità; elemento indispensabile; *(e.g., to hold wire)* cavallotino, cambretta; *(to fasten papers)* grappetta; fibra tessile || *tr* aggraffare

stapler ['steplər] *s* cucitrice *f* a grappe

star [stɑr] *s (any heavenly body, except the moon, appearing in the sky)* astro; *(heavenly body radiating self-produced energy)* stella; *(actor)* divo; *(actress)* diva, stella *(athlete)* asso; (fig, mov) stella; (typ) stelletta; **to thank one's lucky stars** ringraziare la propria stella || *v (pret & pp starred; ger starring) tr* costellare, stellare; presentare come stella; (typ) marcare con stelletta || *intr* primeggiare

starboard ['stɑrbərd] *or* ['stɑr‚bɔrd] *adj* di dritta, di tribordo || *s* dritta, tribordo || *adv* a dritta, a tribordo

starch [stɑrtʃ] *s* amido, fecola; *(in laundering)* salda; (coll) forza || *tr* inamidare

starch·y ['stɑrtʃi] *adj (-ier; -iest)* amidaceo; *(e.g., collar)* inamidato; *(manner)* sostenuto, contegnoso

star′ dust′ *s* polveri *fpl* meteoriche; (fig) polvere *f* di stelle

stare [stɛr] *s* sguardo fisso || *intr* rimirare; **to stare at** fissare gli occhi addosso a

star′fish′ *s* stella di mare

star′gaze′ *intr* guardare le stelle; sognare ad occhi aperti

stark [stɑrk] *adj* completo; desolato; severo, serio; duro, rigido || *adv* completamente

stark′-na′ked *adj* nudo e crudo

starlet ['stɑrlɪt] *s* stellina, divetta

star′light′ *s* lume *f* delle stelle

starling ['stɑrlɪŋ] *s* storno, stornello

Stars′ and Stripes′ *s* bandiera stellata

Star′-Spangled Ban′ner *s* bandiera stellata

star′ sys′tem *s* (mov) divismo

start [stɑrt] *s* inizio, principio; partenza; linea di partenza; *(sudden jerk)* sussulto, soprassalto; *(advantage)* vantaggio; *(spurt)* scatto || *tr* iniziare, principiare; mettere in moto; dare il via a; *(a conversation)* intavolare; *(game)* stanare || *intr* iniziare, principiare; mettersi in moto; incamminarsi; *(to be startled)* trasalire, sussultare; **to start** + *ger* mettersi a + *inf;* **to start** + *ger* + **again** rimettersi a + *inf;* **to start after** andare in cerca di

starter ['stɑrtər] *s (of a venture)* iniziatore *m;* partente *m;* (aut) motorino d'avviamento; (sports) mossiere *m*

starting ['stɑrtɪŋ] *adj* di partenza || *s* messa in marcia

start′ing crank′ *s* manovella d'avviamento

start′ing point′ *s* punto di partenza

startle ['stɑrtəl] *tr* far trasalire || *intr* trasalire, sussultare

startling ['stɑrtlɪŋ] *adj* allarmante, sorprendente

starvation [stɑr'veʃən] *s* fame *f,* inedia, inanizione

starva′tion wag′es *spl* paga da fame

starve [stɑrv] *tr* affamare; far morire di fame; **to starve out** prendere per fame || *intr* essere affamato; morire di fame

starving ['stɑrvɪŋ] *adj* famelico

state [stet] *adj* statale; ufficiale; di gala, di lusso || *s* condizione; stato; gala, pompa; **to lie in state** essere esposto in camera ardente; **to live in state** vivere sfarzosamente || *tr* dichiarare, affermare; *(a problem)* impostare

stateless ['stetlɪs] *adj* apolide

state·ly ['stetli] *adj (-lier; -liest)* maestoso, imponente

statement ['stetmənt] *s* dichiarazione, affermazione; comunicazione; (com) estratto conto

state′ of mind′ *s* stato d'animo

state′room′ *s* cabina; (rr) compartimento privato

states′man *s* (-men) statista *m,* uomo di stato

static ['stætɪk] *adj* statico; (rad) atmosferico || *s* disturbi *mpl* atmosferici

station ['steʃən] *s* stazione; rango, condizione || *tr* stazionare

sta′tion a′gent *s* capostazione *m*

stationary ['steʃən‚eri] *adj* stazionario

sta′tion break′ *s* (rad, telv) intervallo

stationer ['steʃənər] *s* cartolaio

stationery ['steʃən‚eri] *s (writing paper)* carta da lettere; *(writing materials)* cancelleria

sta′tionery store′ *s* cartoleria

sta′tion house′ *s* posto di polizia

sta′tion·mas′ter *s* capostazione *m*

sta′tion wag′on *s* giardinetta

statistical [stə'tɪstɪkəl] *adj* statistico

statistician [‚stætɪs'tɪʃən] *s* statistico

statistics [stə'tɪstɪks] *ssg* (*science*) statistica; *spl* (*data*) statistiche *fpl*
statue ['stæt/ʊ] *s* statua
statuesque [ˌstæt/ʊ'esk] *adj* statuario
stature ['stæt/ər] *s* statura
status ['stetəs] *s* stato, condizione; condizione sociale
sta'tus sym'bol *s* simbolo della posizione sociale
statute ['stæt/ʊt] *s* legge *f*; regolamento
stat'ute of limita'tions *s* legge *f* che governa la prescrizione
statutory ['stæt/ʊ ˌtori] *adj* legale
staunch [stɔnt/] or [stɑnt/] *adj, s & tr* var of **stanch**
stave [stev] *s* (*of barrel*) doga; (*of ladder*) piolo; (mus) rigo, pentagramma *m* ‖ *v* (*pret & pp* staved or stove [stov]) *tr* bucare; (*to smash*) sfondare; **to stave off** tenere a bada
stay [ste] *s* permanenza, soggiorno; (*brace*) staggio; (*of corset*) stecca di balena; sostegno; (law) sospensione; (naut) strallo ‖ *tr* fermare; sospendere; poner freno a ‖ *intr* stare; mantenersi; restare, rimanere; (*at a hotel*) sostare; **to stay up** stare alzato
stay'-at-home' *adj* casalingo ‖ *s* persona casalinga
stead [stɛd] *s* posto; **in his stead** in suo luogo; **to stand in good stead** esser utile
stead'fast' *adj* fermo, risoluto
stead·y ['stedi] *adj* (-ier; -iest) stabile, fermo; regolare, costante; abituale; calmo, sicuro ‖ *v* (*pret & pp* -ied) *tr* rinforzare; calmare ‖ *intr* rinforzarsi; calmarsi
steak [stek] *s* bistecca
steal [stil] *s* (coll) furto ‖ *v* (*pret* stole [stol]; *pp* stolen) *tr* rubare; involare; (*the attention*) cattivare ‖ *intr* rubare; **to steal away** svignarsela; **to steal out** uscire di soppiatto; **to steal upon** approssimarsi silenziosamente a
stealth [stelθ] *s* clandestinità *f*; **by stealth** di straforo, di soppiatto
steam [stim] *adj* a vapore ‖ *s* vapore *m*; fumo; **to get up steam** aumentare la pressione; **to let off steam** scaricare la pressione; (slang) sfogarsi ‖ *tr* (*a steamship*) guidare; esalare; esporre al vapore; (*e.g., glasses*) appannare ‖ *intr* dar vapore, fumigare; bollire; (*to become clouded*) appannarsi; andare a vapore; **to steam ahead** avanzare a tutto vapore
steam'boat' *s* vapore *m*
steam' en'gine *s* macchina a vapore
steamer ['stimər] *s* vapore *m*
steam'er rug' *s* coperta da viaggio
steam'er trunk' *s* bauletto da cabina
steam' heat' *s* riscaldamento a vapore
steam' roll'er *s* rullo compressore; (fig) rullo compressore
steam'ship' *s* piroscafo, vapore *m*
steam' shov'el *s* escavatore *m* a vapore
steam' ta'ble *s* tavola riscaldata a vapore per mantenere calde le vivande
steed [stid] *s* destriere *m*

steel [stil] *adj* d'acciaio; (*industry*) siderurgico ‖ *s* acciaio; (*bar*) stecca d'acciaio; (*for sharpening knives*) affilacoltelli *m*; (fig) spada, brando ‖ *tr* acciaiare; **to steel oneself** corazzarsi, indurirsi; armarsi di coraggio
steel' wool' *s* paglia di ferro
steel'works' *spl* acciaieria
steelyard ['stil ˌjɑrd] or ['stiljərd] *s* stadera
steep [stip] *adj* erto, scosceso, ripido; (*price*) alto ‖ *tr* immergere, saturare, imbevere
steeple ['stipəl] *s* campanile *m*; (*spire*) cuspide *f*, guglia
stee'ple-chase' *s* corsa ad ostacoli
stee'ple-jack' *s* aggiustatore *m* di campanili
steer [stɪr] *s* bue *m*, manzo ‖ *tr* governare, guidare; (aer) pilotare ‖ *intr* governare; **to steer clear of** evitare
steerage ['stɪrɪdʒ] *s* (naut) alloggio passeggeri di terza classe
steer'ing wheel' *s* (aut) volante *m*, sterzo; (naut) ruota del timone
stellar ['stelər] *adj* stellare; (*role*) da stella
stem [stem] *s* (*of pipe, of key*) cannello; (*of goblet*) gambo; (*of column*) fusto; (*of spoon*) manico; (*of watch*) corona; (*of a word*) tema *m*; (*of note*) (mus) gamba; (bot) peduncolo, stelo; (bot) gambo; **from stem to stern** da poppa a prua ‖ *v* (*pret & pp* stemmed) *ger* stemming) *tr* togliere il gambo a; (*to check*) arrestare; (*to dam up*) arginare; (*to plug*) otturare; (*the tide*) risalire, andare contro ‖ *intr* originare, derivare
stem'-win'der *s* orologio a corona
stench [stent/] *s* tanfo, fetore *m*
sten·cil ['stensəl] *s* stampo, stampino; parole *fpl* a stampo ‖ *v* (*pret & pp* -ciled or -cilled) *ger* -ciling or -cilling) *tr* stampinare
stenographer [stə'nɑɡrəfər] *s* stenografo
stenography [stə'nɑɡrəfi] *s* stenografia
step [step] *s* passo; (*footprint*) orma, impronta; (*of ladder*) piolo; (*of staircase*) gradino; (*of carriage*) montatoio; **step by step** passo passo; **to watch one's step** fare molta attenzione ‖ *v* (*pret & pp* stepped) *ger* stepping) *tr* scaglionare; **to step off** misurare a passi ‖ *intr* camminare, andare a passi; mettere il piede; **to step aside** scostarsi; **to step back** indietreggiare; **to step on it** (slang) fare presto; **to step on the gas** (coll) accelerare; **to step on the starter** avviare il motore
step'broth'er *s* fratellastro, fratello consanguineo
step'child' *s* (-children [ˌt/ɪldrən]) figliastro
step'daugh'ter *s* figliastra
step'fa'ther *s* patrigno
step'lad'der *s* scala a gradini or a libretto
step'moth'er *s* matrigna
steppe [step] *s* steppa

step'ping stone' s passatoio, pietra per guadare; (fig) gradino

step'sis'ter s sorellastra

step'son' s figliastro

stere·o ['stɛrɪ ‚o] or ['stɪrɪ ‚o] adj stereofonico; stereoscopico || s (-os) musica stereofonica; sistema stereofonico; fotografia stereoscopica

stereotyped ['stɛrɪ·ə‚taɪpt] or ['stɪrɪ·ə‚taɪpt] adj stereotipato

sterile ['stɛrɪl] adj sterile

sterilize ['stɛrɪ ‚laɪz] tr sterilizzare

sterling ['stʌrlɪŋ] adj di lira sterlina; d'argento; puro; eccellente || s argento .925; vasellame m d'argento puro

stern [stʌrn] adj severo || s poppa

stet [stɛt] v (pret & pp **stetted;** ger **stetting**) tr marcare con la parola "vive"

stethoscope ['stɛθə ‚skop] s stetoscopio

stevedore ['stivə ‚dor] s stivatore m

stew [stju] or [stu] s stufato, guazzetto || tr stufare || intr cuocere a fuoco lento; (coll) preoccuparsi

steward ['stju·ərd] or ['stu·ərd] s amministratore m, agente m; maggiordomo; (aer, naut) cambusiere m, cameriere m

stewardess ['stju·ərdɪs] or ['stu·ərdɪs] s (naut) cameriera; (aer) hostess f, assistente f di volo

stewed' fruit' s composta di frutta

stewed' toma'toes spl pomodori mpl in umido

stick [stɪk] s stecco; legno; bacchetta; bastone m; (e.g., of candy) cannello; (naut) albero; (typ) compositoio; **in the sticks** (coll) in casa del diavolo || v (pret & pp **stuck** [stʌk]) tr pungere; ficcare, infiggere; attaccare; confondere; **to be stuck** essere insabbiato; essere attaccato; (fig) essere confuso; **to stick out** (the head) sporgere; (the tongue) cacciare; **to stick up** (slang) assaltare a mano armata, rapinare || intr rimanere attaccato; persistere; (said of glue) appiccicarsi; (to one opinion) tenersi; star; **to stick out** sporgere; **to stick together** rimanere uniti; **to stick up** risaltare; (said, e.g., of quills) rizzarsi; **to stick up for** (coll) stare dalla parte di

sticker ['stɪkər] s etichetta gommata; spina; persona zelante; (coll) busillis m

stick'ing plas'ter s cerotto

stick'pin' s spilla da cravatta

stick'up' s (slang) grassazione

stick·y ['stɪki] adj (-ier; -iest) attaccaticcio; vischioso; (weather) afoso, soffocante; (fig) difficile

stiff [stɪf] adj rigido, duro; forte; (price) alto; denso || s (slang) cadavere m; **poor stiff** (slang) povero diavolo

stiff' col'lar s colletto duro

stiffen ['stɪfən] tr irrigidire || intr irrigidirsi

stiff' neck' s torcicollo; ostinazione

stiff'-necked' adj testardo

stiff' shirt' s camicia inamidata

stifle ['staɪfəl] tr soffocare

stigma ['stɪgmə] s (-mas or -mata [mətə]) stigma m

stigmatize ['stɪgmə ‚taɪz] tr stigmatizzare

still [stɪl] adj fermo, tranquillo; silenzioso; (wine) non spumante || s calma; distillatore m; distilleria; (phot) fotografia singola || adv ancora; tuttora || conj tuttavia || tr calmare || intr calmarsi

still'birth' s parto di infante nato morto

still'born' adj nato morto

still' life' s (lifes') natura morta

stilt [stɪlt] s trampolo; (in water) palafitta; (orn) trampoliere m

stilted ['stɪltɪd] adj elevato; pomposo

stimulant ['stɪmjələnt] adj & s stimulante m, eccitante m

stimulate ['stɪmjə ‚let] tr stimulare

stimu·lus ['stɪmjələs] s (-li [‚laɪ]) stimolo

sting [stɪŋ] s puntura; (of insect) pungiglione; (fig) scottatura || v (pret & pp **stung** [stʌŋ]) tr & intr pungere

stin·gy ['stɪndʒi] adj (-gier; -giest) tirchio, taccagno

stink [stɪŋk] s puzza || v (pret stank [stæŋk] or **stunk** [stʌŋk]; pp stunk) tr far puzzare || intr puzzare; **to stink of money** (slang) aver soldi a palate

stinker ['stɪŋkər] s (slang) puzzone m

stint [stɪnt] s limite m; lavoro assegnato, compito || intr lesinarsi

stipend ['staɪpɛnd] s stipendio; assegno di studio, presalario

stipulate ['stɪpjə ‚let] tr stipulare

stir [stʌr] s agitazione, movimento; (poke) spinta; **to create a stir** creare una sensazione || v (pret & pp **stirred;** ger **stirring**) tr mescolare; muovere; (fire) ravvivare; (pity) fare; **to stir up** eccitare, svegliare; (to rebellion) sommuovere || intr muoversi, agitarsi

stirring ['stʌrɪŋ] adj commovente

stirrup ['stʌrəp] or ['stɪrəp] s staffa

stitch [stɪtʃ] s punto; maglia; (pain) fitta; (bit) poco, po' m; **to be in stitches** (coll) sbellicarsi dalle risa || tr cucire; aggraffare || intr cucire

stock [stɑk] adj regolare, comune; banale, ordinario; di bestiame; borsistico; azionario; (aut) di serie; (theat) stabile || s provvista, scorta; capitale m sociale; azione f; azioni fpl, titoli mpl; (of tree) tronco; (of family; of anchor; of anvil) ceppo; razza, famiglia; materia prima; (of rifle) cassa; (broth) brodo; (handle) manico; (livestock) bestiame m; (theat) compagnia stabile; **in stock** in magazzino, disponibile; **out of stock** esaurito; **stocks** gogna, berlina; **to take stock** fare l'inventario; **to take stock in** (coll) aver fede in || tr fornire; fornire di bestiame; fornire di pesci || intr—**to stock up** fare rifornimenti

stockade [stɑ'ked] s staccionata

stock'breed'er s allevatore m di bestiame

stock'bro'ker s agente m di cambio

stock' car' s automobile f di serie; (rr) carro bestiame

stock' com'pany s (theat) compagnia stabile; (com) società anonima

stock' div'idend s dividendo pagato in azioni

stock' exchange' s borsa valori

stock'fish' s stoccafisso

stock'hold'er s azionista mf

stock'holder of rec'ord s azionista mf registrato nei libri della compagnia

Stockholm ['stɑkhom] s Stoccolma

stocking ['stɑkɪŋ] s calza

stock' in trade' s stock m; ferri mpl del mestiere

stock' mar'ket s borsa valori

stock'pile' s riserva, scorta || tr mettere in riserva || intr mettere in riserva materie prime

stock' rais'ing s allevamento bestiame

stock'room' s magazzino, deposito

stock·y ['stɑki] adj (-ier; -iest) tozzo, tarchiato

stock'yard' s chiuso per il bestiame

stoic ['sto·ɪk] adj & s stoico

stoicism ['sto·ɪ,sɪzəm] s stoicismo

stoke [stok] tr (fire) attizzare; (a furnace) caricare

stoker ['stokər] s fochista m

stolid ['stɑlɪd] adj impassibile

stomach ['stʌmək] s stomaco || tr (fig) digerire

stone [ston] s sasso, pietra; (of fruit) osso; (pathol) calcolo || tr lapidare; affilare con la pietra; (fruit) snocciolare

stone'-broke' adj (coll) senza un soldo, senza il becco di un quattrino

stone'-deaf' adj sordo come una campana

stone'ma'son s tagliapietra m

stone' quar'ry s cava di pietra

stone's throw' s tiro di sasso; **within a stone's throw** a un tiro di schioppo

ston·y ['stoni] adj (-ier; -iest) di sasso, sassoso, pietroso

stooge [studʒ] s (theat) spalla; (slang) complice mf

stool [stul] s sgabello, seggiolino; gabinetto; (mass evacuated) feci fpl

stool' pi'geon s piccione m di richiamo; (slang) spia

stoop [stup] s curvatura, inclinazione; scalini mpl d'ingresso || intr inclinarsi, piegarsi; degnarsi, umiliarsi

stoop-shouldered ['stup'ʃoldərd] adj con le spalle cadenti

stop [stɑp] s fermata, sosta; arresto; otturazione, blocco; cessazione; ostacolo; (of a check) fermo; (restraint) freno; (of organ) registro; **to come to a stop** fermarsi; cessare; **to put a stop to** metter fine a || v (pret & pp **stopped**; ger **stopping**) tr fermare, cessare; arrestare, sospendere; tappare, otturare; (a check) mettere il fermo a; **to stop up** tappare, otturare || intr fermarsi; arrestarsi; (said of a ship) fare scalo; (at an hotel) scendere; **to stop + ger** smettere di or cessare di + inf

stop'cock' s rubinetto di arresto

stop'gap' adj provvisorio || s soluzione provvisoria; (person) tappabuchi m

stop'light' s (traffic light) semaforo; (aut) luce f di stop

stop'o'ver s fermata intermedia

stoppage ['stɑpɪdʒ] s fermata, arresto; (of work, wages, etc.) sospensione

stopper ['stɑpər] s tappo, turacciolo

stop' sign' s segnale m di fermata

stop'watch' s cronometro a scatto

storage ['storɪdʒ] s magazzinaggio; (place for storing) magazzino; (of a computer) memoria

stor'age bat'tery s (elec) accumulatore m

store [stor] s negozio; magazzino; (supply) scorta; **in store** in serbo; **to set store by** dare molta importanza a || tr immagazzinare; **to store away** accumulare

store'house' s magazzino, deposito; (of knowledge) miniera

store'keep'er s negoziante m

store'room' s magazzino; (naut) dispensa

stork [stork] s cicogna

storm [stɔrm] s tempesta, temporale m; (on the Beaufort scale) burrasca; (mil) assalto; (fig) scoppio || tr assaltare || intr tempestare; imperversare; (mil) andare all'attacco

storm' cloud' s nuvolone m

storm' door' s controporta

storm' sash' s controfinestra

storm' troops' spl truppe fpl d'assalto

storm' win'dow s controfinestra

storm·y ['stɔrmi] adj (-ier; -iest) tempestoso, burrascoso; (fig) inquieto, violento

sto·ry ['stori] s (-ries) storia, racconto, romanzo; (plot) trama; (level) piano; (coll) storia, menzogna || v (pret & pp **-ried**) tr istoriare

sto'ry-tell'er s narratore m, novelliere m; (coll) mentitore m

stoup [stup] s (eccl) acquasantiera

stout [staut] adj grasso, obeso; forte, robusto; leale; coraggioso || s birra nera forte

stout-hearted ['staut,hɑrtɪd] adj coraggioso

stove [stov] s (for warmth) stufa; (for cooking) fornello, cucina economica

stove'pipe' s tubo della stufa, cannone m; (hat) (coll) tuba

stow [sto] tr mettere in riserva; riempire; (naut) stivare || intr—**to stow away** imbarcarsi clandestinamente

stowage ['sto·ɪdʒ] s stivaggio; (place) stiva

stow'a·way' s passeggero clandestino

straddle ['strædəl] s divaricamento || tr (a horse) cavalcare; (the legs) divaricare; favorire entrambe le parti in || intr cavalcare; stare a gambe divaricate; (coll) tenere il piede tra due staffe

strafe [strɑf] or [stref] s attacco violento || tr attaccare con fuoco aereo; bombardare violentemente; (slang) punire

straggle ['strægəl] *intr* sbandarsi, sviarsi; sparpagliarsi, essere sparpagliato

straggler ['stræglər] *s* ritardatario

straight [stret] *adj* diritto, ritto; *(e.g., shoulders)* quadro; candido, franco; *(honest, upright)* retto; inalterato; *(hair; whiskey)* liscio; **to set s.o. straight** mettere qlcu sulla retta via; mostrare la verità a qlcu ‖ *s* rettilinea; *(cards)* scala ‖ *adv* dritto; sinceramente; rettamente; **straight ahead** sempre diritto; **straight away** immediatamente; **to go straight** vivere onestamente

straighten ['stretən] *tr* ordinare; raddrizzare ‖ *intr* raddrizzarsi

straight' face' *s* faccia seria

straight' flush' *s* (cards) scala reale

straight'for'ward *adj* diretto; onesto

straight' man' *s* (theat) spalla

straight' ra'zor *s* rasoio a mano libera

straight'way' *adv* immediatamente

strain [stren] *s* sforzo; fatica eccessiva; tensione, pressione; strappo muscolare; tono, stile *m*; *(family)* famiglia; tendenza, vena; *(coll)* lavoro severo; *(mus)* aria, melodia ‖ *tr* passare, colare; *(e.g., a rope)* tirare al massimo; *(one's ear)* tendere; *(a muscle)* strappare; *(the ankle)* slogare; *(e.g., words)* storcere, forzare ‖ *intr* colare, filtrare; tendersi, tirare; sforzarsi; fare resistenza; **to strain at** tirare; resistere a

strained [strend] *adj* (smile) stentato; *(relations)* teso

strainer ['strenər] *s* scolatoio

strait [stret] *s* stretto; **straits** stretto; (fig) strettezze *fpl*; **to be in dire straits** essere nei frangenti

strait' jack'et *s* camicia di forza

strait'-laced' *adj* puritano, pudibondo

strand [strænd] *s* sponda, lido; *(of metal cable)* trefolo; *(of rope)* legnolo; *(of pearls)* filo ‖ *tr* sfilare; *(e.g., a rope)* ritorcere, intrecciare; *(e.g., a boat)* lasciare incagliato; **to be stranded** trovarsi incagliato

stranded ['strændɪd] *adj* (ship) incagliato, arenato; *(e.g., rope)* ritorto, intrecciato

strange [strendʒ] *adj* strano; straniero; non abituato; inusitato

stranger ['strendʒər] *s* forestiero; nuovo venuto, intruso

strangle ['stræŋgəl] *tr* strangolare; soffocare ‖ *intr* strangolarsi; soffocarsi

strap [stræp] *s* (of leather) correggia; *(for holding things together)* tirante *m*; *(shoulder strap)* bretella; *(for passengers to hold on to)* manopola; *(to hold a sandal)* guiggia; *(to hold a baby)* falda; *(strop)* coramella ‖ *v* *(pret & pp* **strapped;** *ger* **strapping)** *tr* legare con correggia or tirante; *(a razor)* affilare

strap'hang'er *s* (coll) passeggero senza posto a sedere

strapping ['stræpɪŋ] *adj* robusto; (coll) grande, enorme

stratagem ['strætedʒəm] *s* stratagemma *m*

strategic(al) [strə'tidʒɪk(əl)] *adj* strategico

strategist ['strætɪdʒɪst] *s* stratego

strate·gy ['strætɪdʒi] *s* (-gies) strategia

strati·fy ['strætɪ͵faɪ] *v* (*pret & pp* **-fied)** *tr* stratificare ‖ *intr* stratificarsi

stratosphere ['strætə͵sfɪr] or ['stretə͵sfɪr] *s* stratosfera

stra·tum ['stretəm] or ['strætəm] *s* (-ta [tə] or **-tums)** strato

straw [strɔ] *adj* di paglia; di nessun valore; falso, fittizio ‖ *s* paglia; *(for drinking)* cannuccia; **I don't care a straw** non mi importa un fico; **to be the last straw** essere il colmo

straw'ber·ry *s* (-ries) fragola

straw'hat' *s* cappello di paglia; *(with hard crown)* paglietta

straw' man' *s* (figurehead) uomo di paglia; *(scarecrow)* spaventapasseri *m*

straw' mat'tress *s* pagliericcio

straw' vote' *s* votazione esplorativa

stray [stre] *adj* sbandato, randagio; casuale, fortuito ‖ *s* animale randagio ‖ *intr* sviarsi; (fig) sbandarsi

streak [strik] *s* stria; *(of light)* raggio; *(of madness)* ramo, vena; *(of luck)* (coll) periodo; **like a streak** (coll) come un lampo ‖ *tr* striare, venare ‖ *intr* striarsi, venarsi; andare come un lampo

stream [strim] *s* corrente *f*; *(of light)* raggio; *(of people)* fiumana, torrente *m*; *(of cars)* fila ‖ *intr* colare; filtrare, penetrare; *(said of a flag)* fluttuare

streamer ['strimər] *s* pennone *m*; nastro; raggio di luce

streamlined ['strim͵laɪnd] *adj* aerodinamico; (aer) carenato

stream'lin'er *s* treno dal profilo aerodinamico

street [strit] *adj* stradale ‖ *s* via, strada

street'car' *s* tram *m*

street' clean'er *s* spazzino; (mach) spazzatrice *f*

street' clothes' *spl* vestiti *mpl* da passeggio; vestito da passeggio

street' floor' *s* pianterreno

street'light' *s* lampione *m*

street' map' *s* pianta della città; stradario

street' sign' *s* segnale *m* stradale

street' sprin'kler *s* carro annaffiatoio

street' walk'er *s* passeggiatrice *f*

strength [strɛŋθ] *s* forza; resistenza; *(of spirituous liquors)* gradazione; (com) tendenza al rialzo; (mil) numero; **on the strength of** basandosi su

strengthen ['strɛŋθən] *tr* rinforzare; (fig) convalidare, rinsaldare ‖ *intr* rinforzarsi, ingagliardirsi

strenuous ['strɛnjʊ·əs] *adj* vigoroso; strenuo

stress [strɛs] *s* enfasi *f*, importanza; spinta; tensione, preoccupazione; accento; (mech) sollecitazione; **to lay**

stress on mettere in rilievo ‖ *tr (a word)* accentare, accentuare; *(to emphasize)* accentuare; *(mech)* sollecitare

stress' ac'cent *s* accento di intensità

stretch [stretʃ] *s* tiro, tirata; *(in time or space)* periodo; *(of road)* tratto, percorrenza; *(of imagination)* sforzo; *(rr)* tratta; *(slang)* periodo di detenzione; **at a stretch** di un tiro ‖ *tr* tirare; tendere, distendere; *(the imagination)* forzare; *(facts)* esagerare; *(money)* stiracchiare; *(one's legs)* sgranchirsi; *(the truth)* esagerare; **to stretch oneself** sdraiarsi ‖ *intr* estendersi; stiracchiarsi; distendersi; **to stretch out** sdraiarsi

stretcher ['stretʃər] *s (for a painting)* telaio; *(tool)* tenditore *m*, tenditoio; *(to carry wounded)* barella, lettiga

stretch'er-bear'er *s* portantino

strew [stru] *v (pret* **strewed;** *pp* **strewed** or **strewn)** *tr* spargere, cospargere; disseminare

stricken ['strɪkən] *adj* afflitto; ferito; danneggiato

strict [strɪkt] *adj* stretto, severo

stricture ['strɪktʃər] *s* aspra critica; *(pathol)* stenosi *f*

stride [straɪd] *s* passo; andatura; **rapid strides** grandi passi *mpl;* **to hit one's stride** avanzare a andatura regolare; **to take s.th in one's stride** fare qlco senza sforzi ‖ *v (pret* **strode** [strod]; *pp* **stridden** ['strɪdən]) *tr* attraversare a grandi passi; attraversare di un salto ‖ *intr* camminare a grandi passi; *(majestically)* incedere

strident ['straɪdənt] *adj* stridente

strife [straɪf] *s* discordia; concorrenza

strike [straɪk] *s (blow)* colpo; *(stopping of work)* sciopero; *(discovery of oil, ore, etc.)* scoperta; *(of fish)* abboccatura; colpo di fortuna ‖ *v (pret & pp* **struck** [strʌk]) *tr* colpire, percuotere; infiggere; *(a match)* strofinare; *(fire)* accendere; fare impressione su; incontrare improvvisamente; *(e.g., ore)* scoprire; *(roots)* mettere; *(a coin)* coniare; andare in sciopero contro; arrivare a; *(a posture)* prendere; *(the hour)* scoccare; cancellare, eliminare; *(sails)* calare; *(attention)* richiamare; **to strike it rich** scoprire una miniera; avere un colpo di fortuna ‖ *intr* dare un colpo; cadere; *(said of a bell)* suonare; accendersi; scioperare; *(mil)* attaccare; **to strike out** mettersi in marcia; *(to fail)* (fig) fallire, venir meno

strike'break'er *s* crumiro

striker ['straɪkər] *s* battitore *m; (clapper in clock)* martelletto; *(worker)* scioperante *m*

striking ['straɪkɪŋ] *adj* impressionante, sorprendente; notevole; scioperante

strik'ing pow'er *s* potere *m* d'assalto

string [strɪŋ] *s* spago, cordicella; *(e.g., of apron)* laccio; *(of pearls)* filo; *(of onions; of lies)* filza; *(row)* fila, infilata; *(mus)* corda; **no strings attached** *(coll)* senza condizioni;

strings strumenti *mpl* a corda; *(coll)* condizioni *fpl;* **to pull strings** usare influenza ‖ *v (pret & pp* **strung** [strʌŋ]) *tr* legare; allacciare; infilare; infilzare; *(a racket)* munire di corde; *(to stretch)* tendere; *(a musical instrument)* mettere le corde a; *(slang)* ingannare; **to string along** *(slang)* menare per il naso; **to string up** impiccare ‖ *intr*—**to string along with** *(slang)* andare d'accordo con

string' bean' *s* fagiolino

stringed' in'strument *s* strumento a corda

stringent ['strɪndʒənt] *adj* stringente; urgente; severo

string' quartet' *s* quartetto d'archi

strip [strɪp] *s* striscia; *(of metal)* lamina; *(of land)* lingua ‖ *v (pret & pp* **stripped;** *ger* **stripping)** *tr* spogliare; denudare; *(a fruit)* pelare; *(a ship)* sguarnire; *(tobacco)* togliere le nervature da; scortecciare; *(thread)* spanare; **to strip of** spogliare di ‖ *intr* spogliarsi; denudarsi; fare lo spogliarello

stripe [straɪp] *s* stria, striscia, riga, lista; tipo, qualità *f; (mil)* gallone *m* ‖ *tr* striare, filettare, rigare

strip' min'ing *s* sfruttamento minerario a cielo aperto

strip'tease' *s* spogliarello

stripteaser ['strɪp,tizər] *s* spogliarellista

strive [straɪv] *v (pret* **strove** [strov]; *pp* **striven** ['strɪvən]) *intr* sforzarsi; lottare; **to strive to** sforzarsi di

stroke [strok] *s* colpo; *(of bell or clock)* rintocco; *(of pen)* tratto, frego; *(of brush)* pennellata; *(of arms in swimming)* bracciata; colpo apoplettico; *(caress)* carezza; *(with oar)* vogata; *(of oar or paddle)* palata; *(of a master)* tocco; *(of a piston)* corsa; *(keystroke)* battuta; *(of genius)* lampo; *(of the hour)* scocco; **to not do a stroke of work** non muovere un dito ‖ *tr* accarezzare

stroll [strol] *s* passeggiata; **to take a stroll** fare una passeggiata ‖ *intr* fare una passeggiata, andare a zonzo; errare

stroller ['strolər] *s* girovago; carrozzella; *(itinerant performer)* (theat) guitto

strong [strɔŋ] or [strɑŋ] *adj* forte, vigoroso; valido; acceso, zelante; *(butter)* rancido; *(cheese)* piccante; *(com)* sostenuto

strong'box' *s* cassaforte *f*

strong' drink' *s* bevanda alcolica

strong'hold' *s* piazzaforte *f*

strong' man' *s (in a circus)* maciste *m; (leader)* anima; dittatore *m*

strong-minded ['strɔŋ,maɪndɪd] or ['strɑŋ,maɪndɪd] *adj* volitivo

strong'point' *s* luogo fortificato

strontium ['strɑn/ɪ-əm] *s* stronzio

strop [strɑp] *s* coramella, affilarasoio ‖ *v (pret & pp* **stropped;** *ger* **stropping)** *tr* affilare

strophe ['strofi] *s* strofa, strofe *f*

struc'tural steel' ['strʌktʃərəl] *s* profilato di acciaio

structure ['strʌktʃər] *s* struttura; edificio || *tr* strutturare

struggle ['strʌgəl] *s* lotta; sforzo || *intr* lottare; sforzare, dibattersi

strum [strʌm] *v* (*pret & pp* **strummed;** *ger* **strumming**) *tr & intr* strimpellare

strumpet ['strʌmpɪt] *s* sgualdrina, puttana

strut [strʌt] *s* controvento, puntello, saettone *m;* incedere impettito; (aer) montante || *v* (*pret & pp* **strutted;** *ger* **strutting**) *intr* pavoneggiarsi, fare la ruota

strychnine ['strɪknaɪn] *or* ['strɪknɪn] *s* stricnina

stub [stʌb] *s* (*of tree*) coppo; (*e.g., of cigar*) mozzicone *m;* (*of a check*) matrice *f,* madre *f* || *v* (*pret & pp* **stubbed;** *ger* **stubbing**) *tr* sradicare; **to stub one's toe** inciampare

stubble ['stʌbəl] *s* (*of beard*) pelo ispido; **stubbles** stoppie *fpl*

stubborn ['stʌbərn] *adj* (*headstrong*) testardo; (*resolute*) accanito; (*e.g., resistance*) ostinato; (*e.g., illness*) ribelle; (*soil*) ingrato

stuc·co ['stʌko] *s* (**-coes** *or* **-cos**) stucco || *tr* stuccare

stuck [stʌk] *adj* infisso; attaccato; (*glued*) incollato; (*unable to continue*) in panna; **stuck on** (slang) invaghito di

stuck'-up' *adj* (coll) presuntuoso, arrogante

stud [stʌd] *s* (*in upholstery*) borchia; bottone *m* da sparato; (*of walls*) montante *m;* (*stallion*) stallone *m;* (*for mares*) monta; (archit) bugna, bugnato *f* || *v* (*pret & pp* **studded;** *ger* **studding**) *tr* cospergere; (*with stars*) costellare; (*with jewels*) incastonare, ingioiellare

stud' bolt' *s* prigioniero

stud'book' *s* registro della genealogia

student ['stjudənt] *or* ['studənt] *adj* studentesco || *s* studente *m;* scolaro; (*investigator*) studioso

stu'dent bod'y *s* scolaresca

stud'horse' *s* stallone *m*

studied ['stʌdid] *adj* premeditato; (*affected*) studiato

studi·o ['studɪˌo] *or* ['stjudɪˌo] *s* (**-os**) studio

studious ['stjudɪ·əs] *or* ['studɪ·əs] *adj* studioso; assiduo, zelante

stud·y ['stʌdi] *s* (**-ies**) studio || *v* (*pret & pp* **-ied**) *tr & intr* studiare

stuff [stʌf] *s* roba, cosa; stoffa; materiale *m;* (*nonsense*) scemenze *fpl;* medicina; (coll) mestiere *m* || *tr* riempire, inzeppare; (*one's stomach*) rimpinzare; (*e.g., poultry*) farcire; (*e.g., salami*) insaccare; (*a dead animal*) impagliare; **to stuff up** intasare || *intr* rimpinzarsi

stuffed' shirt' *s* persona altezzosa

stuffing ['stʌfɪŋ] *s* ripieno

stuff·y ['stʌfi] *adj* (**-ier; -iest**) soffocante, opprimente; (*nose*) chiuso; pedante

stumble ['stʌmbəl] *intr* incespicare, inciampare; sbagliare, impaperarsi; **to stumble on** *or* **upon** intopparsi in

stum'bling block' *s* inciampo, scoglio

stump [stʌmp] *s* (*of tree*) toppo, ceppo; (*e.g., of arm*) moncherino, moncone *m;* (*of cigar, candle*) mozzicone *m;* dente rotto; tribuna popolare; (*for drawing*) sfumino; **up a stump** (coll) completamente perplesso || *tr* mozzare; lasciare perplesso; (coll) fare discorsi politici in

stump' speech' *s* discorso politico

stun [stʌn] *v* (*pret & pp* **stunned;** *ger* **stunning**) *tr* tramortire; (fig) sbalordire

stunning ['stʌnɪŋ] *adj* (*blow*) che stordisce; sbalorditivo, magnifico

stunt [stʌnt] *s* atrofia; creatura striminzita; bravata, prodezza; (*for publicity*) montatura || *tr* striminzire; arrestare la crescita di || *intr* fare delle acrobazie

stunt'ed *adj* striminzito

stunt' fly'ing *s* acrobazia aerea

stunt' man' *s* (mov) controfigura

stupe·fy ['stjupɪˌfaɪ] *or* ['stupɪˌfaɪ] *v* (*pret & pp* **-fied**) *tr* istupidire, intontire

stupendous [stju'pɛndəs] *or* [stu'pɛndəs] *adj* stupendo

stupid ['stjupɪd] *or* ['stupɪd] *adj* stupido, ebete, scemo

stupor ['stjupər] *or* ['stupər] *s* torpore *m,* stupore *m*

stur·dy ['stʌrdi] *adj* (**-dier; -diest**) forte; (*robust*) tarchiato; risoluto

sturgeon ['stʌrdʒən] *s* storione *m*

stutter ['stʌtər] *s* tartagliamento || *tr & intr* tartagliare

sty [staɪ] *s* (**sties**) porcile *m;* (pathol) orzaiolo

style [staɪl] *s* stile *m;* tono; (*mode of living*) treno || *tr* chiamare col nome di

stylish ['staɪlɪʃ] *adj* alla moda, di tono

sty·mie ['staɪmi] *v* (*pret & pp* **-mied;** *ger* **-mieing**) *tr* ostacolare, contrastare

styp'tic pen'cil ['stɪptɪk] *s* matita emostatica

Styx [stɪks] *s* Stige *m*

suave [swɑv] *or* [swev] *adj* soave

subaltern [səb'ɔltərn] *adj & s* subalterno

subcommittee ['sʌbkəˌmɪti] *s* sottocommissione

subconscious [səb'kɑnʃəs] *adj & s* subcosciente *m*

subconsciousness [səb'kɑnʃəsnɪs] *s* subcosciente *m,* subcoscienza

sub'deb' *s* (coll) signorina più giovane di una debuttante

subdivide ['sʌbdɪˌvaɪd] *or* [ˌsʌbdɪ'vaɪd] *tr* suddividere || *intr* suddividersi

subdue [səb'dju] *or* [səb'du] *tr* soggiogare, sottomettere; (*color, voice*) attenuare

subdued [səb'djud] *or* [səb'dud] *adj* (*voice*) sommesso; (*light*) tenue

subheading ['sʌb‚hedɪŋ] s sottotitolo; (journ) sommario

subject ['sʌbdʒɪkt] adj soggetto; **subject to** (e.g., a cold) soggetto a; (e.g., a fine) passibile di ‖ s soggetto, materia, proposito; (of a ruler) suddito; (gram, med, philos) soggetto ‖ [səb-'dʒɛkt] tr sottomettere

sub'ject cat'alogue s catalogo per materie

sub'ject in'dex s indice m per materie

subjection [səb'dʒɛkʃən] s soggezione

subjective [səb'dʒɛktɪv] adj soggettivo

sub'ject mat'ter s soggetto

subjugate ['sʌbdʒə‚get] tr soggiogare

subjunctive [səb'dʒʌŋktɪv] adj & s congiuntivo

sublease ['sʌb‚lis] s subaffitto ‖ [‚sʌb-'lis] tr subaffittare

sub-let [sʌb'let] or [sʌb‚let] v (pret & pp -let; ger -letting) tr subaffittare

sub-machine' gun' [‚sʌbmə'ʃin] s mitra m

submarine ['sʌbmə‚rin] adj & s sottomarino

sub'marine chas'er ['tʃesər] s caccia-sommergibili m

submerge [səb'mʌrdʒ] tr sommergere ‖ intr sommergersi

submersion [səb'mʌrʒən] or [səb-'mʌrʃən] s sommersione

submission [səb'mɪʃən] s sottomissione

submissive [səb'mɪsɪv] adj sottomesso

sub-mit [səb'mɪt] v (pret & pp -mitted; ger -mitting) tr sottomettere; presentare, deferire; osservare rispettosamente ‖ intr sottomettersi

subordinate [səb'ɔrdɪnɪt] adj & s subordinato ‖ [səb'ɔrdɪ‚net] tr subordinare

suborna'tion of per'jury [‚sʌbər'neʃən] s subornazione

subplot ['sʌb‚plɑt] s intreccio secondario

subpoena or **subpena** [sʌb'pinə] or [sə'pinə] s mandato di comparizione ‖ tr citare

sub rosa [sʌb'rozə] adv in segreto

subscribe [səb'skraɪb] tr sottoscrivere ‖ intr sottoscrivere; **to subscribe to** sottoscrivere a; (a magazine) abbonarsi a; (an opinion) approvare

subscriber [səb'skraɪbər] s sottoscrittore m; abbonato

subscription [sʌb'skrɪpʃən] s sottoscrizione; (e.g., to a newspaper) abbonamento; (e.g., to club) quota

subsequent ['sʌbsɪkwənt] adj susseguente, posteriore

subservient [səb'sʌrvɪ‚ənt] adj subordinato; ossequioso, servile

subside [səb'saɪd] intr calmarsi; (said of water) decrescere

subsidiar·y [səb'sɪdɪ‚erɪ] adj sussidiario ‖ s (-ies) sussidiario

subsidize ['sʌbsɪ‚daɪz] tr sussidiare, sovvenzionare; (by bribery) subornare

subsi·dy ['sʌbsɪdɪ] s (-dies) sussidio, sovvenzione

subsist [səb'sɪst] intr sussistere

subsistence [səb'sɪstəns] s sussistenza

subsoil ['sʌb‚sɔɪl] s sottosuolo

substance ['sʌbstəns] s sostanza

substandard [sʌb'stændərd] adj inferiore al livello normale

substantial [səb'stænʃəl] adj considerevole; ricco, influente; (food) sostanzioso; (e.g., reason) sostanziale

substantiate [səb'stænʃɪ‚et] tr provare, verificare; dare prova di, sostanziare

substantive ['sʌbstəntɪv] adj & s sostantivo

substation ['sʌb‚steʃən] s ufficio postale secondario; (elec) sottostazione

substitute ['sʌbstɪ‚tjut] or [‚sʌbstɪ‚tut] adj provvisorio, interino ‖ s (thing) sostituto, surrogato; (person) sostituto, supplente mf; **beware of substitutes** guardarsi dalle contraffazioni ‖ tr—**to substitute for** sostituire (qlco or qlcu) a ‖ intr—**to substitute for** sostituire, rimpiazzare, e.g., **he substituted for the teacher** sostituì il maestro

substitution [‚sʌbstɪ'tjuʃən] or [‚sʌbstɪ'tuʃən] s sostituzione; (by fraud) contraffazione

substra·tum [sʌb'strætəm] s (-ta [tə]) sostrato, substrato

subterfuge ['sʌbtər‚fjudʒ] s sotterfugio

subterranean [‚sʌbtə'reni‚ən] adj & s sotterraneo

subtitle ['sʌb‚taɪtəl] s sottotitolo; (journ) titolo corrente; (mov) didascalia ‖ tr dare una didascalia a

subtle ['sʌtəl] adj sottile

subtle·ty ['sʌtəltɪ] s (-ties) sottigliezza

subtract [səb'trækt] tr sottrarre

subtraction [sʌb'trækʃən] s sottrazione

suburb ['sʌbʌrb] s suburbio, sobborgo; **the suburbs** la periferia

suburban [sə'bʌrbən] adj suburbano

suburbanite [sə'bʌrbə‚naɪt] s abitante mf dei suburbi

subvention [səb'venʃən] s sovvenzione ‖ tr sovvenzionare

subversive [səb'vʌrsɪv] adj & s sovversivo

subvert [səb'vʌrt] tr sovvertire

subway ['sʌb‚we] s sotterranea, metropolitana, metrovia; sottopassaggio

sub'way sta'tion s stazione della metropolitana

succeed [sək'sid] tr succedere (with dat), subentrare (with dat) ‖ intr riuscire; **to succeed to** (the throne) succedere a

success [sək'ses] s successo, riuscita

successful [sək'sesfəl] adj felice, fortunato; che ha avuto successo

succession [sək'seʃən] s successione; **in succession** in seguito, uno dopo l'altro

successive [sək'sesɪv] adj successivo

succor ['sʌkər] s soccorso ‖ tr soccorrere

succotash ['sʌkə‚tæʃ] s verdura di fagioli e granturco

succumb [sə'kʌm] intr soccombere

such [sʌtʃ] adj & pron indef tale, simile; **such a** un simile, un tale; **such**

a + *adj* tanto + *adj*, e.g., **such a beautiful story** una storia tanto bella; **such as** tale quale, come
suck [sʌk] *s* succhio || *tr* succhiare; (*air*) aspirare; **to suck in** (in slang) ingannare
sucker ['sʌkər] *s* lattante *mf;* (bot) succhione *m;* (mach) pistone *m;* (coll) fesso, pollo, minchione *m*
suckle ['sʌkəl] *tr* allattare; nutrire || *intr* poppare
suck'ling pig' ['sʌklɪŋ] *s* maiale *m* di latte
suction ['sʌkʃən] *s* aspirazione
suc'tion cup' *s* ventosa
suc'tion pump' *s* pompa aspirante
sudden ['sʌdən] *adj* subito, improvviso; **all of a sudden** all'improvviso
suddenly ['sʌdənli] *adv* all'improvviso
suds [sʌdz] *spl* saponata; schiuma; (coll) birra
sue [su] or [sju] *tr* querelare || *intr* querelarsi; **to sue for damages** chiedere i danni; **to sue for peace** chiedere la pace
suede [swed] *s* pelle scamosciata
suet ['su·ɪt] or ['sju·ɪt] *s* grasso, sego
suffer ['sʌfər] *tr* soffrire; (*e.g., heavy losses*) subire || *intr* soffrire, patire
sufferance ['sʌfərəns] *s* tolleranza
suffering ['sʌfərɪŋ] *adj* sofferente || *s* sofferenza, strazio, patimento
suffice [sə'faɪs] *intr* bastare
sufficient [sə'fɪʃənt] *adj* sufficiente
suffix ['sʌfɪks] *s* suffisso
suffocate ['sʌfə‚ket] *tr & intr* soffocare
suffrage ['sʌfrɪdʒ] *s* suffragio
suffragette [‚sʌfrə'dʒɛt] *s* suffragetta
suffuse [sə'fjuz] *tr* soffondere
sugar ['ʃugər] *adj* (water) zucchero; (*industry*) zuccherino || *s* zucchero || *tr* zuccherare
sug'ar beet' *s* barbabietola da zucchero
sug'ar bowl' *s* zuccheriera
sug'ar cane' *s* canna da zucchero
sug'ar-coat' *tr* inzuccherare; (*e.g., the pill*) addolcire
sug'ar ma'ple *s* acero
sug'ar-plum' *s* zuccherino
sug'ar spoon' *s* cucchiaino per lo zucchero
sug'ar tongs' *spl* mollette *fpl* per lo zucchero
sugary ['ʃugəri] *adj* zuccherino, zuccheroso
suggest [səg'dʒɛst] *tr* suggerire
suggestion [səg'dʒɛstʃən] *s* suggerimento; (psychol) suggestione; ombra, traccia
suggestive [səg'dʒɛstɪv] *adj* suggestivo; (*risqué*) scabroso
suicidal [‚su·ɪ'saɪdəl] or [‚sju·ɪ'saɪdəl] *adj* suicida
suicide ['su·ɪ‚saɪd] or ['sju·ɪ‚saɪd] *s* (*person*) suicida *mf;* (*act*) suicidio; **to commit suicide** suicidarsi
suit [sut] or [sjut] *s* vestito da uomo; (*of a lady*) tailleur *m;* (*of cards*) seme *m*, colore *m;* (*for bathing*) costume *m;* corte *f*, corteggiamento; domanda, supplica; (law) causa; **to follow suit** seguire l'esempio; (cards)

rispondere a colore || *tr* adattarsi (with *dat*); convenire (with *dat*); **suit yourself** faccia come vuole || *intr* convenire, andare a proposito
suitable ['sutəbəl] or ['sjutəbəl] *adj* indicato, conveniente
suit'case' *s* valigia
suite [swit] *s* gruppo, serie *f;* serie *f* di stanze; (*of furniture*) mobilia; (*retinue*) seguito; (mus) suite *f*
suiting ['sutɪŋ] or ['sjutɪŋ] *s* taglio d'abito
suit' of clothes' *s* completo maschile
suitor ['sutər] or ['sjutər] *s* pretendente *m;* (law) querelante *mf*
sul'fa drugs' ['sʌlfə] *spl* sulfamidici *mpl*
sulfate ['sʌlfet] *s* solfato
sulfide ['sʌlfaɪd] *s* solfuro
sulfite ['sʌlfaɪt] *s* solfito
sulfur ['sʌlfər] *adj* solfireo || *s* zolfo; color *m* zolfo
sulfuric [sʌl'fjurɪk] *adj* solforico
sul'fur mine' *s* solfara
sulfurous ['sʌlfərəs] *adj* solforoso
sulk [sʌlk] *s* broncio || *intr* imbronciarsi
sulk·y ['sʌlki] *adj* (**-ier; -iest**) imbronciato ||*s* (**-ies**) (*in horse racing*) sediolo, sulky *m*
sullen ['sʌlən] *adj* bieco, triste, tetro
sul·ly ['sʌli] *v* (*pret & pp* **-lied**) *tr* insudiciare, insozzare
sulphur ['sʌlfər] *adj & s* var of **sulfur**
sultan ['sʌltən] *s* sultano
sul·try ['sʌltri] *adj* (**-trier; -triest**) soffocante; infocato, appassionato
sum [sʌm] *s* somma; sommario; problema *m* di aritmetica || *v* (*pret & pp* **summed;** *ger* **summing**) *tr* sommare; **to sum up** riepilogare
sumac or **sumach** ['Jumæk] or ['sumæk] *s* (bot) sommacco
summarize ['sʌmə‚raɪz] *tr* riassumere
summa·ry ['sʌməri] *adj* sommario || *s* (**-ries**) sommario, sunto
summer ['sʌmər] *adj* estivo || *s* estate *f* || *intr* passare l'estate
sum'mer resort' *s* stazione estiva
summersault ['sʌmər‚sɔlt] *s & intr* var of **somersault**
sum'mer school' *s* scuola estiva
summery ['sʌməri] *adj* estivo
summit ['sʌmɪt] *s* sommità *f*
sum'mit con'ference *s* riunione al vertice
summon ['sʌmən] *tr* convocare, invitare; evocare; (law) compulsare
summons ['sʌmənz] *s* ordine *m*, comando; (law) citazione || *tr* (law) citare
sumptuous ['sʌmptʃu·əs] *adj* sontuoso
sun [sʌn] *s* sole *m;* **place in the sun** posto al sole || *v* (*pret & pp* **sunned;** *ger* **sunning**) *tr* esporre al sole || *intr* prendere il sole
sun' bath' *s* bagno di sole
sun'beam' *s* raggio di sole
sun'burn' *s* abbronzatura || *v* (*pret & pp* **-burned** or **-burnt**) *tr* abbronzare || *intr* abbronzarsi

sundae ['sʌndi] *s* gelato con sciroppo, frutta o noci

Sunday ['sʌndi] *adj* domenicale ‖ *s* domenica

Sun'day best' *s* (coll) vestito da festa

Sun'day's child' *s* bambino nato con la camicia

Sun'day school' *s* scuola domenicale della dottrina

sunder ['sʌndər] *tr* separare

sun'di'al *s* meridiana

sun'down' *s* tramonto

sundries ['sʌndriz] *spl* generi *mpl* diversi

sundry ['sʌndri] *adj* vari, diversi

sun'fish' *s* pesce *m* mola, pesce *m* luna

sun'flow'er *s* girasole *m*

sun'glass'es *spl* occhiali *mpl* da sole

sunken ['sʌŋkən] *adj* affondato, sommerso; (*hollow*) incavato

sun' lamp' *s* sole *m* artificiale

sun'light' *s* luce *f* del sole

sun'lit' *adj* illuminato dal sole

sun-ny ['sʌni] *adj* (**-nier; -niest**) solatio, soleggiato; allegro, ridente; **it is sunny** fa sole

sun'ny side' *s* parte soleggiata; lato buono; **on the sunny side of** (*e.g., thirty*) al disotto dei . . . anni

sun' porch' *s* veranda a solatio

sun'rise' *s* sorgere *m* del sole; **from sunrise to sunset** dall'alba al tramonto

sun'set' *s* tramonto

sun'shade' *s* tenda; parasole *m*

sun'shine' *s* sole *m*, luce *f* del sole; **in the sunshine** al sole

sun'spot' *s* macchia solare

sun'stroke' *s* insolazione

sun' tan' *s* tintarella

sun'tan lo'tion *s* pomata antisole, abbronzante *m*

sun'up' *s* sorgere *m*, levare *m* del sole

sun' vi'sor *s* (aut) aletta parasole, parasole *m*

sup [sʌp] *v* (*pret & pp* **supped; ger supping**) *intr* cenare

super ['supər] *adj* (coll) superficiale; (coll) di prim'ordine, super ‖ *s* (coll) sovrintendente *m*; (coll) articolo di prim'ordine, super

superabundant [,supərə'bʌndənt] *adj* sovrabbondante

superannuated [,super'ænju,etid] *adj* giubilato, pensionato; messo a riposo per limiti di età; antiquato

superb [su'pʌrb] *or* [sə'pʌrb] *adj* superbo

supercar-go ['supər,kargo] *s* (**-goes**) (naut) sopraccarico

supercharge [,supər't/ardʒ] *tr* sovralimentare

supercilious [,supər'sili-əs] *adj* altero, arrogante

superficial [,supər'fi/əl] *adj* superficiale

superfluous [su'pʌrflu-əs] *adj* superfluo

su'per·high'way *s* autostrada

superhuman [,supər'hjumən] *adj* sovrumano

superimpose [,supərim'poz] *tr* sovrapporre

superintendent [,supərin'tendənt] *s* soprintendente *m; (of schools)* provveditore *m*

superior [sə'pɪrɪ-ər] *or* [su'pɪrɪ-ər] *adj* superiore; di superiorità; (typ) esponente ‖ *s* superiore *m*

superiority [sə,pɪrɪ'ɑrɪti] *or* [su,pɪrɪ-'ɑrɪti] *s* superiorità *f*

superlative [sə'pʌrlətɪv] *or* [su'pʌrlə-tɪv] *adj & s* superlativo

su'per·man' *s* (**-men**) superuomo

supermarket [,supər'markɪt] *s* supermercato

supernatural [,supər'næt/ərəl] *adj* soprannaturale

superpose [,supər'poz] *tr* sovrapporre

supersede [,supər'sid] *tr* rimpiazzare, sostituire

supersensitive [,supər'sensɪtɪv] *adj* ipersensibile

supersonic [,supər'sɑnɪk] *adj* supersonico

superstition [,supər'stɪ/ən] *s* superstizione

superstitious [,supər'stɪ/əs] *adj* superstizioso

supervene [,supər'vin] *intr* sopravvenire

supervise ['supər,vaɪz] *tr* sorvegliare, dirigere

supervision [,supər'vɪ/ən] *s* supervisione, sorveglianza, direzione

supervisor ['supər,vaɪzər] *s* supervisore *m*, sorvegliante *mf*; ispettore *m*

supper ['sʌpər] *s* cena

sup'per·time' *s* ora di cena

supplant [sə'plænt] *tr* rimpiazzare

supple ['sʌpəl] *adj* flessibile; docile

supplement ['sʌplɪmənt] *s* supplemento ‖ ['sʌpli,ment] *tr* completare, supplire (**with** *dat*)

suppliant ['sʌpli-ənt] *adj & s* supplicante *mf*

supplicant ['sʌplɪkənt] *s* supplicante *mf*

supplication [,sʌpli'ke/ən] *s* supplica

supplier [sʌ'plaɪ-ər] *s* fornitore *m*

sup·ply [sə'plaɪ] *s* (**-plies**) rifornimento, fornitura; provvista, scorta; (com) offerta; **supplies** rifornimento *mpl*, vettovaglie *fpl* ‖ *v* (*pret & pp* **-plied**) *tr* fornire, provvedere; (*food*) vettovagliare

supply' and demand' *s* domanda ed offerta

support [sə'port] *s* sostegno, appoggio; puntello, rincalzo; mantenimento ‖ *tr* sostenere, appoggiare; puntellare; (*a cause*) caldeggiare; mantenere

supporter [sə'portər] *s* fautore *m*, sostenitore *m; (jockstrap)* sospensorio; giarrettiera; fascia elastica

suppose [sə'poz] *tr* supporre; ammettere; **suppose we take a walk?** che ne dice se facessimo una passeggiata?; **to be supposed to** aver fama di essere; **to suppose so** credere di sì

supposed [sə'pozd] *adj* presunto

supposition [,sʌpə'zɪ/ən] *s* supposizione

supposito·ry [sə'pazɪ,tori] *s* (**-ries**) suppositorio, supposta

suppress [sə'pres] *tr* sopprimere

suppression [sə'preʃən] s soppressione
suppurate ['sʌpjə‚ret] intr suppurare
supreme [sə'prim] or [su'prim] adj supremo, sommo
Supreme' Court' s (in Italy) Corte f di Cassazione; (in U.S.A.) tribunale m di ultima istanza
surcharge ['sʌr‚tʃɑrdʒ] s soprapprezzo; soprattassa; sovraccarico; (philately) sovrastampa || [‚sʌr'tʃɑrdʒ] or ['sʌr‚tʃɑrdʒ] tr sovraccaricare
sure [ʃur] adj sicuro; **to be sure!** certamente!, senza dubbio! || interj (coll) certamente!; **sure enough!** (coll) difatti
sure-footed ['ʃjur'futɪd] adj dal piede sicuro
sure' thing' s (coll) successo garantito || adv (coll) certamente || interj (coll) di sicuro!
sure·ty ['ʃurti] or ['ʃurɪti] s (-ties) malleveria
surf [sʌrf] s frangente m
surface ['sʌrfɪs] adj superficiale || s superficie f || tr rifinire; spianare; ricoprire || intr emergere
sur'face mail' s posta ordinaria
surf'board' s tavola per il surfing
surfeit ['sʌrfɪt] s eccesso; sazietà f || tr saziare, rimpinzare || intr saziarsi, rimpinzarsi
surf'ing s surfing m
surge [sʌrdʒ] s ondata; fiotto; (elec) sovratensione || intr ondeggiare, fluttuare; (said, e.g., of a crowd) affluire
surgeon ['sʌrdʒən] s (medico) chirurgo
surger·y ['sʌrdʒəri] s (-ies) chirurgia; sala operatoria
surgical ['sʌrdʒɪkəl] adj chirurgico
sur·ly ['sʌrli] adj (-lier; -liest) arcigno, imbronciato
surmise [sər'maɪz] or ['sʌrmaɪz] s congettura, supposizione || [sər'maɪz] tr & intr congetturare, supporre
surmount [sər'maunt] tr sormontare; coronare
surname ['sʌr‚nem] s cognome m; (added name) soprannome m || tr dare il cognome a; soprannominare
surpass [sər'pæs] or [sər'pas] tr sorpassare, superare
surplice ['sʌrplɪs] s cotta
surplus ['sʌrplʌs] adj eccedente || s sopravanzo, eccedenza
surprise [sər'praɪz] adj insperato, improvviso || s sorpresa || tr sorprendere
surprise' par'ty s improvvisata
surprising [sər'praɪzɪŋ] adj sorprendente
surrender [sə'rendər] s resa || tr arrendere || intr arrendersi
surren'der val'ue s (ins) valore m di riscatto
surreptitious [‚sʌrəp'tɪʃəs] adj clandestino, nascosto, furtivo
surround [sə'raund] tr circondare, contornare; (mil) aggirare
surrounding [sə'raundɪŋ] adj circostante, circonvicino || **surroundings** spl dintorni mpl; ambiente m

surtax ['sʌr‚tæks] s sovrimposta, soprattassa; imposta complementare
surveillance [sər'veləns] or [sər'veljəns] s sorveglianza, vigilanza
survey ['sʌrve] s quadro generale, schizzo; indagine f; (of opinion) sondaggio; rapporto; rilievo topografico; perizia || [sʌr've] or ['sʌrve] tr fare un'indagine di; sondare; rilevare; misurare || intr fare un rilievo
sur'vey course' s corso di rassegna generale
surveyor [sər've·ər] s livellatore m, geometra m
survival [sər'vaɪvəl] s sopravvivenza
survive [sər'vaɪv] tr sopravvivere (with dat) || intr sopravvivere
surviving [sər'vaɪvɪŋ] adj superstite
survivor [sər'vaɪvər] s sopravvissuto, superstite mf
survivorship [sər'vaɪvər‚ʃɪp] s (law) sopravvivenza
susceptible [sə'septɪbəl] adj suscettibile, ricettivo; impressionabile; **susceptible to** (e.g., colds) soggetto a
suspect ['sʌspekt] or [səs'pekt] adj sospetto || ['sʌspekt] s sospetto || [səs'pekt] tr sospettare
suspend [səs'pend] tr sospendere || intr essere sospeso; fermarsi; fermare i pagamenti
suspenders [səs'pendərz] spl bretelle fpl
suspense [səs'pens] s sospensione; sospeso; **in suspense** in sospeso
suspen'sion bridge' [səs'penʃən] s ponte sospeso
suspicion [səs'pɪʃən] s sospetto
suspicious [səs'pɪʃəs] adj (subject to suspicion) sospetto; (inclined to suspect) sospettoso
sustain [səs'ten] tr sostenere, sorreggere; (with food) sostentare; (a conversation) mantenere; (a loss) soffrire; (law) confermare
sustenance ['sʌstɪnəns] s sostentamento
sutler ['sʌtlər] s (mil) vivandiere m
swab [swab] s (mil) scovolo; (naut) redazza; (surg) batuffolo di cotone || v (pret & pp swabbed; ger swabbing) tr pulire con la redazza; spugnare; assorbire col cotone
swaddle ['swadəl] tr fasciare
swad'dling clothes' spl fasce fpl del neonato
swagger ['swægər] s spavalderia || intr fare lo spavaldo
swain [swen] s innamorato; (lad) contadinotto
swallow ['swalo] s (of liquid) sorso; (of food) boccone m; (orn) rondine f || tr & intr tranguglare, inghiottire
swal'low-tailed' coat' ['swalo‚teld] s frac m, marsina, abito a coda di rondine
swal'low-wort' s vincetossico
swamp [swamp] s pantano, palude f || tr inondare, sommergere
swamp·y ['swampi] adj (-ier; -iest) paludoso, pantanoso
swan [swan] s cigno
swan' dive' s volo dell'angelo

swank [swæŋk] *adj* (coll) elegante, vistoso ‖ *s* (coll) eleganza vistosa

swan's-down ['swɑnz,daʊn] *s* piuma di cigno, piumino; mollettone *m*

swan' song' *s* canto del cigno

swap [swɑp] *s* scambio, baratto ‖ *v* (*pret* & *pp* swapped; *ger* swapping) *tr* & *intr* scambiare, barattare

swarm [swɔrm] *s* sciame *m* ‖ *intr* sciamare; (fig) formicolare

swarth·y ['swɔrði] or ['swɔrθi] *adj* (-ier; -iest) olivastro, abbronzato

swashbuckler ['swɑʃ,bʌklər] *s* spadaccino, rodomonte *m*

swat [swɑt] *s* colpo ‖ *v* (*pret* & *pp* swatted; *ger* swatting) *tr* colpire; (*a fly*) schiacciare

sway [swe] *s* dondolio, ondeggiamento; dominio ‖ *tr* dondolare, fare oscillare; influenzare; dominare ‖ *intr* dondolarsi, ondulare; oscillare

swear [swer] *v* (*pret* swore [swor]; *pp* sworn [sworn]) *tr* giurare; (*to secrecy*) fare giurare; to swear in fare prestar giuramento a; to swear off giurare di rinunziare a; to swear out a warrant ottenere un atto di accusa sotto giuramento ‖ *intr* giurare; (*to blaspheme*) bestemmiare; to swear at maledire; to swear by giurare su, avere certezza di; to swear to dichiarare sotto giuramento; giurare di + *inf*

swear'word' *s* bestemmia, parolaccia

sweat [swet] *s* sudata; sudore *m* ‖ *v* (*pret* & *pp* sweat or sweated) *tr* sudare; far sudare; to sweat it out (slang) farcela fino alla fine; to sweat off (*weight*) perdere sudando ‖ *intr* sudare

sweater ['swetər] *s* maglione *m*, golf *m*, sweater *m*

sweat' shirt' *s* maglione *m* da ginnastica

sweat·y ['sweti] *adj* (-ier; -iest) sudato; che fa sudare

Swede [swid] *s* svedese *mf*

Sweden ['swidən] *s* la Svezia

Swedish ['swidɪʃ] *adj* & *s* svedese *m*

sweep [swip] *s* scopata; movimento circolare; estensione; curva; (*of wind*) soffio; (*of well*) mazzacavallo; to make a clean sweep of far piazza pulita di ‖ *v* (*pret* & *pp* swept [swept]) *tr* spazzare, scopare; percorrere con lo sguardo; (*eyes*) dirigere; travolgere ‖ *intr* scopare; passare; estendersi; dragare

sweeper ['swipər] *s* spazzino; (*machine*) spazzatrice *f*; (nav) dragamine *m*

sweeping ['swipɪŋ] *adj* esteso; travolgente, decisivo ‖ sweepings *spl* spazzatura

sweep'-sec'ond *s* lancetta dei secondi a perno centrale

sweep'stakes' *ssg* or *spl* lotteria abbinata alle corse dei cavalli

sweet [swit] *adj* dolce; (*butter*) senza sale; (*cider*) analcolico; to be sweet on (coll) essere innamorato di ‖

sweets *spl* dolci *mpl;* (coll) patate *fpl* dolci ‖ *adv* dolcemente; to smell sweet saper di buono

sweet'bread' *s* animella

sweet'bri'er *s* eglantina

sweeten ['switən] *tr* inzuccherare; raddolcire; purificare ‖ *intr* raddolcirsi; purificarsi

sweet'heart' *s* innamorato; innamorata; caro, amore *m*

sweet' mar'joram *s* maggiorana

sweet'meats' *spl* dolci *mpl*, confetti *mpl*

sweet' pea' *s* pisello odoroso

sweet' pota'to *s* batata, patata americana; (mus) ocarina

sweet-scented ['swit,sentɪd] *adj* odoroso, profumato

sweet' tooth' *s* debole *m* per i dolci

sweet-toothed ['swit,tuθt] *adj* goloso

sweet' wil'liam *s* garofano barbuto

swell [swel] *adj* (slang) elegante; (slang) eccellente, di prim'ordine ‖ *s* gonfiore *m*; onda, ondata; aumento; (mus) crescendo; (slang) elegantone *m* ‖ *v* (*pret* swelled; *pp* swelled or swollen ['swolən]) *tr* gonfiare, ingrossare; aumentare ‖ *intr* gonfiare, ingrossarsi; aumentare; (*said of the sea*) alzarsi; (*with pride*) montarsi

swelled' head' *s* borioso; to have a swelled head montarsi, essere pieno di sé

swelter ['sweltər] *intr* soffocare dal caldo

swept'back wing' *s* ala a freccia

swerve [swʌrv] *s* scarto, sbandamento ‖ *tr* sviare ‖ *intr* scartare, sbandare

swift [swɪft] *adj* rapido ‖ *s* rondone *m* ‖ *adv* rapidamente

swig [swɪg] *s* (coll) sorso ‖ *v* (*pret* & *pp* swigged; *ger* swigging) *tr* & *intr* (coll) bere a grandi sorsi

swill [swɪl] *s* imbratto; risciacquatura ‖ *tr* tracannare, trincare ‖ *intr* bere a lunghi sorsi

swim [swɪm] *s* nuoto; the swim (*in social activities*) la corrente ‖ *v* (*pret* swam [swæm]; *pp* swum [swʌm]; *ger* swimming) *tr* traversare a nuoto ‖ *intr* nuotare; essere inondato; (*said of one's head*) girare, e.g., her head is swimming le gira la testa

swimmer ['swɪmər] *s* nuotatore *m*

swimming ['swɪmɪŋ] *s* nuoto

swim'ming pool' *s* piscina

swim'ming trunks' *spl* mutandine *fpl* da bagno

swim'suit' *s* costume *m* da bagno

swindle ['swɪndəl] *s* truffa, imbroglio ‖ *tr* truffare, imbrogliare

swine [swaɪn] *s* suino, maiale *m*, porco; swine *spl* suini *mpl*

swing [swɪŋ] *s* oscillazione; dondolio; curva; (*suspended seat*) altalena; alternarsi *m*; piena attività; (boxing) sventola; (mus) swing *m*; free swing libertà *f* d'azione; in full swing (coll) in piena attività ‖ *v* (*pret* & *pp* swung [swʌŋ]) *tr* (e.g., one's arms) dondolare, oscillare; *(a weapon)* brandire; *(e.g., a club)* rotare; far girare; appendere; *(a deal)* (coll) riuscire ad ottenere || *intr* dondolare, dondolarsi, oscillare; girare; essere sospeso; cambiare; *(boxing)* dare una sventola; **to swing open** aprirsi di colpo

swing'ing door' ['swɪŋɪŋ] *s* porta oscillante

swinish ['swaɪnɪʃ] *adj* porcino

swipe [swaɪp] *s* (coll) colpo forte || *tr* (coll) dare un forte colpo a; (slang) portare via, rubare

swirl [swʌrl] *s* turbine *m*, vortice *m* || *tr* far girare || *intr* turbinare

swirling ['swʌrlɪŋ] *adj* vorticoso

swish [swɪʃ] *s (of whip)* schiocco; *(of silk)* fruscio || *tr (a whip)* schioccare; || *intr* schioccare; frusciare

Swiss [swɪs] *adj* svizzero || *s* svizzero; **the Swiss** gli svizzeri

Swiss' chard' ['tʃɑrd] *s* bietola

Swiss' cheese' *s* groviera

Swiss' Guards' *spl* guardie *fpl* svizzere

switch [swɪtʃ] *s* verga; vergata; *(false hair)* posticcio; cambio, trapasso; (elec) interruttore *m*; (rr) scambio || *tr* battere, frustare; (elec) commutare; (rr) deviare; (fig) girare; **to switch off** *(light, radio, etc.)* spegnere; **to switch on** *(light, radio, etc.)* accendere || *intr* fustigare; cambiare; (rr) deviare

switch'back' *s* strada a zigzag; (rr) tracciato a zigzag

switch'blade knife' *s* coltello a serramanico

switch'board' *s* quadro

switch'board op'erator *s* centralinista *mf*

switch'ing en'gine *s* locomotiva da manovra

switch'man *s* (-men) deviatore *m*

switch'yard' *s* stazione smistamento

Switzerland ['swɪtsərlənd] *s* la Svizzera

swiv·el ['swɪvəl] *s* perno, gancio girevole || *v (pret & pp -eled or -elled; ger -eling or -elling) intr* girare

swiv'el chair' *s* sedia girevole

swoon [swun] *s* deliquio, svenimento || *intr* svenire

swoop [swup] *s* calata a piombo || *intr* calare a piombo, piombare

sword [sord] *s* spada; **at swords' points** pronti a incrociare le spade; **to put to the sword** passare a fil di spada

sword' belt' *s* cinturone *m*

sword' cane' *s* bastone animato

sword'fish' *s* pesce *m* spada

swords'man *s* (-men) spadaccino

sword' swal'lower ['swɑlo·ər] *s* giocoliere *m* che ingoia spade

sword' thrust' *s* stoccata

sworn [sworn] *adj* giurato

sycophant ['sɪkəfənt] *s* adulatore *m*; parassita *mf*

syllable ['sɪləbəl] *s* sillaba

sylla·bus ['sɪləbəs] *s* (-bi [,baɪ]) sillabo, sommario scolastico

syllogism ['sɪlə,dʒɪzəm] *s* sillogismo

sylph [sɪlf] *s* silfo; silfide *f*; (fig) silfide

sylvan ['sɪlvən] *adj* silvano

symbol ['sɪmbəl] *s* simbolo

symbolic(al) [sɪm'bɑlɪk(əl)] *adj* simbolico

symbolism ['sɪmbə,lɪzəm] *s* simbolismo

symbolize ['sɪmbə,laɪz] *tr* simboleggiare

symmetric(al) [sɪ'metrɪk(əl)] *adj* simmetrico

symme·try ['sɪmɪtri] *s* (-tries) simmetria

sympathetic [,sɪmpə'θetɪk] *adj* simpatetico; ben disposto

sympathize ['sɪmpə,θaɪz] *intr*—**to sympathize with** aver compassione di; mostrar comprensione per; *(to be in accord with)* simpatizzare con

sympa·thy ['sɪmpəθi] *s* (-thies) compassione, commiserazione; **to be in sympathy with** essere d'accordo con; **to extend one's sympathy to** fare le condoglianze a

sym'pathy strike' *s* sciopero di solidarietà

symphonic [sɪm'fɑnɪk] *adj* sinfonico

sympho·ny ['sɪmfəni] *s* (-nies) sinfonia

symposi·um [sɪm'pozɪ·əm] *s* (-a [ə]) simposio, colloquio

symptom ['sɪmptəm] *s* sintomo

synagogue ['sɪnə,gɔg] or ['sɪnə,gɑg] *s* sinagoga

synchronize ['sɪŋkrə,naɪz] *tr & intr* sincronizzare

synchronous ['sɪŋkrənəs] *adj* sincrono

syncopation [,sɪŋkə'peʃən] *s* sincope *f*

syncope ['sɪŋkə,pi] *s* (phonet) sincope *f*

syndicate ['sɪndɪkɪt] *s* sindacato || ['sɪndɪ,ket] *tr* organizzare in un sindacato

synonym ['sɪnənɪm] *s* sinonimo

synonymous [sɪ'nɑnɪməs] *adj* sinonimo

synop·sis [sɪ'nɑpsɪs] *s* (-ses [siz]) sinossi *f*; (mov) sinopsi *f*

synoptic(al) [sɪ'nɑptɪk(əl)] *adj* sinottico

syntax ['sɪntæks] *s* sintassi *f*

synthe·sis ['sɪnθɪsɪs] *s* (-ses [,siz]) sintesi *f*

synthesize ['sɪnθɪ,saɪz] *tr* sintetizzare

synthetic(al) [sɪn'θetɪk(əl)] *adj* sintetico

syphilis ['sɪfɪlɪs] *s* sifilide *f*

Syria ['sɪrɪ·ə] *s* la Siria

Syrian ['sɪrɪ·ən] *adj & s* siriano

syringe [sɪ'rɪndʒ] or ['sɪrɪndʒ] *s (fountain syringe)* schizzetto; *(for hypodermic injections)* siringa || *tr* schizzettare; iniettare

syrup ['sɪrəp] or ['sʌrəp] *s* sciroppo

system ['sɪstəm] *s* sistema *m*

systematic(al) [,sɪstə'mætɪk(əl)] *adj* sistematico

systematize ['sɪstəmə,taɪz] *tr* ridurre a sistema

systole ['sɪstəli] *s* sistole *f*

T

T, t [ti] s ventesima lettera dell'alfabeto inglese; **to fit to a T** calzare come un guanto

tab [tæb] s (*strap*) linguetta; (*of a pocket*) patta; targa; (*label*) etichetta; **to keep tabs on** (coll) sorvegliare; **to pick up the tab** (coll) pagare il conto

tab·by ['tæbi] s (**-bies**) gatto tigrato; gatta; (*spinster*) zitella; vecchia pettegola

tabernacle ['tæbər,nækəl] s tabernacolo

table ['tebəl] s tavola; (*food*) mensa; (*people at a table*) tavolata; (*synopsis*) quadro, prospetto; (*list or catalogue*) indice m; **to turn the tables** rovesciare la posizione; **under the table** ubriaco fradicio ‖ tr aggiornare, rinviare

tab·leau ['tæblo] s (**-leaus** or **-leaux** [loz]) quadro vivente

ta'ble·cloth' s tovaglia

table d'hôte ['tɑbəl'dot] s pasto a prezzo fisso

tableful ['tebəl,ful] s (*persons*) tavolata; (*food*) tavola apparecchiata

ta'ble·land' s tavoliere m

ta'ble lin'en s biancheria da tavola

ta'ble man'ners spl maniere fpl a tavola

ta'ble of con'tents s indice m delle materie

ta'ble·spoon' s cucchiaio

tablespoonful ['tebəl,spun,ful] s cucchiaiata

tablet ['tæblɪt] s (*writing pad*) blocco; (*slab*) lapide f; (*flat rigid sheet*) tabella, tavoletta; (pharm) disco, pastiglia

ta'ble talk' s conversazione familiare a tavola

ta'ble ten'nis s ping-pong m, tennis m da tavolo

ta'ble·ware' s servizio da tavola

ta'ble wine' s vino da pasto

tabloid ['tæbloɪd] s giornale m a carattere sensazionale

taboo [tə'bu] adj & s tabù m ‖ tr proibire assolutamente

tabulate ['tæbjə,let] tr tabulare

tabulator ['tæbjə,letər] s tabulatore m, incolonnatore m

tachometer [tə'kɑmɪtər] s tachimetro

tacit ['tæsɪt] adj tacito

taciturn ['tæsɪ,tʌrn] adj taciturno

tack [tæk] s bulletta; cambio di direzione; (naut) virata; (sew) imbastitura ‖ tr imbullettare; attaccare; (naut) bordeggiare; (sew) imbastire ‖ intr virare; mutare di direzione

tackle ['tækəl] s attrezzatura; (mach) taglia, paranco; (gear) (naut) padiglione m ‖ tr attaccare, affrontare; (sports) placcare, bloccare

tack·y ['tæki] adj (**-ier; -iest**) appiccicaticcio; (coll) trasandato

tact [tækt] s tatto

tactful ['tæktfəl] adj pieno di tatto

tactical ['tæktɪkəl] adj tattico

tactician [tæk'tɪʃən] s tattico

tactics ['tæktɪks] ssg (mil) tattica ‖ spl tattica

tactless ['tæktlɪs] adj che non ha tatto, indiscreto

tadpole ['tæd,pol] s girino

taffeta ['tæfɪtə] s taffettà m

taffy ['tæfi] s caramella, zucchero d'orzo; (coll) lisciata

tag [tæg] s etichetta; (*on a shoelace*) punta dell'aghetto; conclusione; (*last words of speech*) pistolotto finale; epiteto; frase fatta; (*of hair*) ciocca; (*in writing*) ghirigoro; (*game*) toccaferro ‖ v (pret & pp **tagged;** ger **tagging**) tr etichettare; (*to fine*) multare; aggiungere; soprannominare; accusare; stabilire il prezzo di; (coll) pedinare ‖ intr seguire da presso

tag' end' s (e.g., *of day*) fine f; estremità logorata; avanzo

tail [tel] s coda; fine f; (*of coin*) croce f; **tails** falde fpl, frac m; **to turn tails** darsela a gambe ‖ tr attaccare; finire; (coll) pedinare

tail' assem'bly s (aer) impennaggio

tail' end' s coda, fine f

tail'light' s fanale m di coda

tailor ['telər] s sarto ‖ tr (*a suit*) tagliare, confezionare; (*one's conduct*) adattare ‖ intr fare il sarto

tailoring ['telərɪŋ] s sartoria

tai'lor-made' adj fatto su misura

tai'lor shop' s sartoria

tail'piece' s coda, estremità f; (mus) cordiera; (typ) fusello finale

tail'race' s canale m di scarico

tail'spin' s avvitamento

tail'wind' s (aer) vento di coda; (naut) vento in poppa

taint [tent] s macchia; infezione ‖ tr macchiare, infettare, corrompere

take [tek] s presa; (*of fish*) retata; (mov) presa; ripresa; (slang) incasso ‖ v (pret **took** [tuk]; pp **taken**) tr prendere, pigliare; ricevere, accettare; portare; (*to get by force*) portar via; (*a nap*) schiacciare; (*a bath*) fare; (*a joke*) stare a; (*an examination*) sostenere; (*one's own life*) togliersi; (*to deduct*) cavare; (*a purchase*) comprare; (*to convey*) portare; (*time*) impiegare; (*a step, a walk*) fare; (*a subject*) studiare; (*a responsibility, role, etc.*) assumere; (*an oath*) prestare; (*root*) mettere; (*exception*) sollevare; credere; (*e.g., a photograph*) fare, scattare; (slang) fregare; **it takes** ci vuole, ci vogliono; **to take amiss** prendere a male; **to take apart** scomporre; smontare; **to take back** riprendere; **to take down** abbassare; smontare; prender nota di; **to take for** prendere per; **to take from** portar via a; **to take in** (*to admit*) ammettere, ricevere; (*to encompass*) includere; (*a dress*) restringere; (*to cheat*) ingannare; (*water*) fare; (*a point of inter-*

est) visitare; **to take it** accettare, ammettere; (slang) resistere; **to take off** (*e.g., one's coat*) togliersi; portar via; scontare, defalcare; (slang) imitare; **to take on** ingaggiare; assumere; intraprendere; accettare la sfida di; **to take out** cavare, togliere; (*e.g., a girl*) portar fuori; (*e.g., a patent*) ottenere; **to take over** rilevare; (slang) imbrogliare; **to take place** aver luogo; **to take s.o.'s eye** attrarre l'attenzione di qlcu; **to take the place of** sottentrare a; **to take up** cominciare a studiare; sollevare, tirar su; (*a duty*) assumere; (*time, space*) occupare || *intr* prendere; scattare; darsi; diventare; **to take after** rassomigliare a; **to take off** (coll) partire, andarsene; (aer) decollare, involare; **to take up with** (coll) fare amicizia con; (coll) vivere con; **to take well** riuscire bene in fotografia

take'off' *s* parodia; (aer) decollaggio; (mach) presa di forza

tal'cum pow'der ['tælkəm] *s* talco

tale [tel] *s* storia, racconto; favola, fiaba; (*lie*) bugia, frottola; (*piece of gossip*) maldicenza

tale'bear'er *s* pettegolo

talent ['tælənt] *s* talento; persona di talento; gente *f* di talento

talented ['tæləntɪd] *adj* dotato di talento, dotato d'ingegno

tal'ent scout' *s* scopritore *m* di talenti

talk [tɔk] *s* chiacchierata; discorso, conferenza; (*language*) parlata; (*gossip*) pettegolezzo; **to cause talk** originare pettegolezzi || *tr* parlare; convincere parlando; **to talk up** elogiare || *intr* parlare; discutere; **to talk on** discutere; continuare a parlare; **to talk up** parlare apertamente

talkative ['tɔkətɪv] *adj* loquace

talker ['tɔkər] *s* parlatore *m*

talkie ['tɔki] *s* (coll) parlato

talk'ing machine' *s* grammofono

talk'ing pic'ture *s* film parlato

tall [tɔl] *adj* alto; (coll) stravagante, esagerato

tallow ['tælo] *s* sego

tal·ly ['tæli] *s* (-lies) tacca, taglia || *v* (*pret & pp* -lied) *tr* contare, registrare || *intr* riscontrare

tal'ly sheet' *s* foglio di spunta

talon ['tælən] *s* artiglio

tambourine [,tæmbə'rin] *s* tamburello

tame [tem] *adj* addomesticato; docile, mansueto; mite || *tr* addomesticare; domare; (*water power*) captare

tamp [tæmp] *tr* pigiare, comprimere; (*e.g., ground*) costipare

tamper ['tæmpər] *s* (*person*) pigiatore *m*; (*tool*) mazzeranga || *intr* intrigare; **to tamper with** (*a lock*) forzare; (*a document*) manomettere; (*a witness*) corrompere

tampon ['tæmpɑn] *s* (surg) tampone *m* || *tr* (surg) tamponare

tan [tæn] *adj* marrone; (*by sun*) abbronzato || *v* (*pret & pp* **tanned**) *ger* **tanning**) *tr* (*leather*) conciare; abbronzare; (coll) picchiare, sculacciare

tandem ['tændəm] *adj & adv* in tandem || *s* tandem *m*

tang [tæŋ] *s* sapore *m* piccante; odore *m* forte; traccia; (*of knife*) tallone *m*; (*sound*) tintinnio

tangent ['tændʒənt] *adj* tangente || *s* tangente *f*; **to fly off at a tangent** cambiare improvvisamente d'idea

tangerine [,tændʒə'rin] *s* mandarino

tangible ['tændʒɪbəl] *adj* tangibile

Tangier [tæn'dʒɪr] *s* Tangeri *f*

tangle ['tæŋgəl] *s* intrico; (coll) litigio || *tr* intricare || *intr* intricarsi; (coll) litigare

tank [tæŋk] *s* conserva, serbatoio; (mil) carro armato

tankard ['tæŋkərd] *s* boccale *m*

tank' car' *s* (rr) carro botte

tanker ['tæŋkər] *s* petroliera; (aer) aerocisterna

tank' farm'ing *s* idroponica

tank' truck' *s* autocisterna

tanner ['tænər] *s* conciapelli *m*

tanner·y ['tænəri] *s* (-ies) conceria

tantalize ['tæntə,laɪz] *tr* stuzzicare con vane promesse

tantamount ['tæntə,maunt] *adj* equivalente

tantrum ['tæntrəm] *s* bizze *fpl*

tap [tæp] *s* colpetto, buffetto; (*in a keg*) spina, cannella; (*faucet*) rubinetto; (elec) presa; (mach) maschio; **on tap** alla spina; (coll) disponibile; **taps** (mil) silenzio || *v* (*pret & pp* **tapped**) *ger* **tapping**) *tr* battere; picchiare, picchiettare; (*from a barrel*) spillare; mettere il cannello a; (*resources*) usare; (*a telephone*) intercettare; (*water, electricity*) derivare; (mach) maschiare || *intr* picchiare

tap' dance' *s* tip tap *m*

tap'-dance' *intr* ballare il tip tap

tape [tep] *s* nastro; (sports) striscione *m* del traguardo || *tr* legare con nastro; misurare col metro a nastro; registrare su nastro magnetico

tape' meas'ure *s* metro a nastro; nastro per misurare

tape' play'er *s* riproduttore *m* a nastro magnetico

taper ['tepər] *s* cerino || *tr* affusolare || *intr* affusolarsi; **to taper off** rastremarsi; diminuire in intensità; diminuire a poco a poco

tape'-re·cord' *tr* registrare su nastro magnetico

tape' record'er *s* magnetofono, registratore *m* a nastro

tapes·try ['tæpɪstri] *s* (-tries) tappezzeria || *v* (*pret & pp* -tried) *tr* tappezzare

tape'worm' *s* verme solitario, tenia

tappet ['tæpɪt] *s* (aut) punteria

tap'room' *s* taverna, osteria

tap'root' *s* radice *f* a fittone

tap' wa'ter *s* acqua corrente

tap' wrench' *s* giramaschio

tar [tɑr] *s* catrame *m* || *v* (*pret & pp* **tarred**; *ger* **tarring**) *tr* incatramare

tar·dy ['tɑrdɪ] adj (-dier; -diest) in ritardo; lento

tare [ter] s tara || tr tarare

target ['tɑrgɪt] s segno, bersaglio

tar'get date' s data progettata

tar'get lan'guage s lingua obbiettivo, lingua di arrivo

tar'get prac'tice s esercizio di tiro a segno

tariff ['tærɪf] s (duties) tariffa doganale; (charge or fare) tariffa

tarnish ['tɑrnɪʃ] s ossidazione; (fig) macchia || tr appannare || intr appannarsi, perdere il lustro

tar' pa'per s carta atramata

tarpaulin ['tɑrpɔlɪn] s telone m impermeabile incatramato

tarragon ['tærəgən] s dragoncello

tar·ry ['tɑri] adj incatramato || ['tæri] v (pret & pp -ried) intr rimanere; ritardare

tart [tɑrt] adj acido, pungente || s torta; (slang) puttana

tartar ['tɑrtər] s tartaro; cremore m di tartaro; (shrew) megera; **to catch a tartar** imbattersi in un muso duro

Tartarus ['tɑrtərəs] s Tartaro

task [tæsk] or [tɑsk] s compito, incarico; **to take to task** rimproverare

task' force' s gruppo formato per una missione speciale

task'mas'ter s sorvegliante m; sorvegliante severo

tassel ['tæsəl] s nappa; (bot) ciuffo

taste [test] s gusto, sapore m; buon gusto; (sampling, e.g., of wine) assaggio; esperienza; **to one's taste** a genio di qlcu || tr gustare, assaggiare || intr sentire, sapere; **to taste of** degustare; sapere di

tasteless ['testlɪs] adj insipido; di cattivo gusto

tast·y ['testi] adj (-ier; -iest) saporito; (coll) di buon gusto

tatter ['tætər] s brandello, sbrendolo || tr sbrindellare

tattered ['tætərd] adj sbrindellato

tattle ['tætəl] s chiacchiera; (gossip) pettegolezzo || intr chiacchierare; spettegolare

tat'tle·tale' adj rivelatore || s gazzetta, chiacchierone m

tattoo [tæ'tu] s tatuaggio; (mil) ritirata || tr tatuare

taunt [tɔnt] or [tɑnt] s rimprovero sarcastico, insulto || tr rimproverare sarcasticamente, insultare

Taurus ['tɔrəs] s (astr) Toro

taut [tɔt] adj teso, tirato

tavern ['tævərn] s osteria

taw·dry ['tɔdri] adj (-drier; -driest) vistoso, sgargiante, pacchiano

taw·ny ['tɔni] adj (-nier; -niest) falbo, fulvo

tax [tæks] s tassa, imposta || tr tassare; (s.o.'s patience) mettere a dura prova

taxable ['tæksəbəl] adj tassabile

tax'able in'come s imponibile m

taxation [tæk'seʃən] s imposizione, tassazione, contribuzione

tax' collec'tor s esattore m delle imposte

tax' deduc'tion s detrazione

tax'-ex·empt' adj esente da tasse

tax' evad'er [ɪ'vedər] s evasore m

tax·i ['tæksi] s (-is) tassì m || v (pret & pp -ied; ger -iing or -ying) tr far rullare || intr andare in tassì; (aer) rullare

tax'i·cab' s tassì m

tax'i driv'er s tassista m

tax'i·plane' s aeroplano da noleggio, aerotassì m

taxi stand' s posteggio di tassì

tax'pay'er s contribuente mf

tax' rate' s imponibilità f

tea [ti] s tè m; (medicinal infusion) tisana; (beef broth) brodo di carne

tea' bag' s sacchetto di tè

tea' ball' s uovo da tè

tea'cart' s servitore m

teach [titʃ] v (pret & pp **taught** [tɔt]) tr & intr insegnare

teacher ['titʃər] s maestro, insegnante mf

teach'ers col'lege s scuola magistrale

teach'er's pet' s beniamino del maestro

teaching ['titʃɪŋ] adj insegnante || s insegnamento, dottrina

teach'ing aids' spl sussidi mpl didattici

teach'ing staff' s corpo insegnante

tea'cup' s tazza da tè

tea' dance' s tè m danzante

teak [tik] s tek m

tea'ket'tle s bricco del tè

team [tim] s (e.g., of horses) pariglia; (sports) squadra, equipaggio || tr apparigliare; tirare o trasportare con pariglia || intr—**to team up** unirsi, associarsi

team'mate' s compagno di squadra

teamster ['timstər] s (of horses) carrettiere m; (of truck) camionista m, autotrenista m

team'work' s affiatamento, collaborazione

tea'pot' s teiera

tear [tɪr] s lacrima; **to hold back one's tears** ingoiare le lacrime; **to laugh away one's tears** cambiare dal pianto al riso || [ter] s strappo || [ter] v (pret **tore** [tor]; pp **torn** [torn]) tr strappare, stracciare; (one's heart) squarciare; (to wound) sbranare; (one's hair) strapparsi; **to tear apart** rompere in due; separare; **to tear down** demolire; (a piece of equipment) smontare; **to tear off** staccare; **to tear to pieces** dilaniare; fare a pezzi; **to tear up** (a piece of paper) stracciare; (a street) scavare || intr strapparsi, stracciarsi; **to tear along** precipitarsi; correre all'impazzata

tear' bomb' [tɪr] s bomba lacrimogena

tearful ['tɪrfəl] adj lacrimoso

tear' gas' [tɪr] s gas lacrimogeno

tear-jerker ['tɪr ˌdʒʌrkər] s (coll) storia lacrimogena

tear-off ['ter ˌɔf] adj da staccarsi, perforato

tea'room' s sala da tè

tear' sheet' [ter] s copia di annuncio pubblicitario

tease [tiz] tr stuzzicare, molestare;

(*hair*) accotonare; (*e.g., wool*) cardare

tea'spoon' *s* cucchiaino

teaspoonful ['ti ,spun ,fʊl] *s* cucchiaino

teat [tit] *s* capezzolo

tea'time' *s* l'ora del tè

tea' wag'on *s* servitore *m*

technical ['tɛknɪkəl] *adj* tecnico

technicali·ty [,tɛknɪ'kælɪti] *s* (**-ties**) tecnicismo; dettaglio tecnico

technician [tɛk'nɪʃən] *s* tecnico

technics ['tɛknɪks] *ssg or spl* tecnica

technique [tɛk'nik] *s* tecnica

ted'dy bear' ['tɛdi] *s* orsacchiotto

tedious ['tidɪ·əs] *or* ['tidʒəs] *adj* tedioso, noioso

tee [ti] *adj* fatto a T ‖ *s* giunto a tre vie; (*golf*) piazzola di partenza ‖ *tr*— **to tee off** (*slang*) cominciare ‖ *intr*— **to be teed off** (*slang*) essere arrabbiato; **to tee off** (*golf*) colpire la palla dalla piazzola di partenza; **to tee off on** (*slang*) rimproverare severamente

teem [tim] *intr* brulicare; piovere a dirotto; **to teem with** abbondare di

teeming ['timɪŋ] *adj* brulicante; (*rain*) torrenziale

teen-ager ['tin ,edʒər] *s* giovane *mf* dai 13 ai 19 anni

teens [tinz] *spl* numeri inglesi che finiscono in -teen (dal 13 al 19); **to be in one's teens** avere dai 13 ai 19 anni

tee·ny ['tini] *adj* (**-nier; -niest**) (coll) piccolo, piccolissimo

teeter ['titər] *s* altalena, dondolio ‖ *intr* dondolarsi, oscillare

teethe [tið] *intr* mettere i denti

teething ['tiðɪŋ] *s* dentizione

teeth'ing ring' *s* dentaruolo

teetotaler [ti'totələr] *s* astemio

tele·cast ['tɛlɪ ,kæst] *or* ['tɛlɪ ,kɑst] *s* teletrasmissione ‖ *v* (*pret & pp* **-cast** *or* **-casted**) *tr & intr* teletrasmettere

telegram ['tɛlɪ ,græm] *s* telegramma *m*

telegraph ['tɛlɪ ,græf] *or* ['tɛlɪ ,grɑf] *s* telegrafo ‖ *tr & intr* telegrafare

tel'egraph pole' *s* palo del telegrafo

Telemachus [tɪ'lɛməkəs] *s* Telemaco

telemeter [tɪ'lɛmɪtər] *s* telemetro ‖ *tr* misurare col telemetro

telepathy [tɪ'lɛpəθi] *s* telepatia

telephone ['tɛlɪ ,fon] *s* telefono ‖ *tr & intr* telefonare

tel'ephone book' *s* elenco *or* guida dei telefoni

tel'ephone booth' *s* cabina telefonica

tel'ephone call' *s* chiamata telefonica, colpo di telefono

tel'ephone direc'tory *s* elenco *or* guida dei telefoni

tel'ephone exchange' *s* centrale telefonica

tel'ephone op'erator *s* centralinista *mf*, telefonista *mf*

tel'ephone receiv'er *s* ricevitore *m*

tel'ephoto lens' ['tɛlɪ ,foto] *s* teleobbiettivo

teleplay ['tɛlɪ ,ple] *s* teledramma *m*

teleprinter ['tɛlɪ ,prɪntər] *s* telescrivente *f*

telescope ['tɛlɪ ,skop] *s* telescopio ‖ *tr* snodare; condensare ‖ *intr* essere snodabile; (*in a collision*) incastrarsi

tel'etype screen' *s* telescrivente *f* ‖ *tr & intr* trasmettere per telescrivente

teletype ['tɛlɪ ,taɪp] *s* telescrivente *f* ‖ *tr & intr* trasmettere per telescrivente

teleview ['tɛlɪ ,vju] *tr* telericevere

televiewer ['tɛlɪ ,vju·ər] *s* telespettatore *m*

televise ['tɛlɪ ,vaɪz] *tr* teletrasmettere

television ['tɛlɪ ,vɪʒən] *adj* televisivo ‖ *s* televisione

tel'evision screen' *s* teleschermo

tel'evision set' *s* televisore *m*

tell [tɛl] *v* (*pret & pp* **told** [told]) *tr* dire; (*to narrate*) raccontare; (*to count*) contare; distinguere; **I told you so!** te l'avevo detto!; **to tell off** (coll) dire il fatto suo ‖ *intr* dire; prevedere; avere effetto; **to tell on** (*s.o.'s health*) pesare a, e.g., **age was telling on his health** l'età pesava alla sua salute; (coll) denunciare

teller ['tɛlər] *s* narratore *m*; (*of bank*) cassiere *m*; (*of votes*) scrutatore *m*

temper ['tɛmpər] *s* indole *f*, temperamento; umore *m*; calma; (metallurgy) tempra; **to keep one's temper** mantenersi calmo; **to lose one's temper** perdere la pazienza ‖ *tr* temprare ‖ *intr* temprarsi

temperament ['tɛmpərəmənt] *s* indole *f*, temperamento, carattere *m*

temperamental [,tɛmpərə'mɛntəl] *adj* emotivo, capriccioso

temperance ['tɛmpərəns] *s* (*self-restraint in action*) temperanza; (*abstinence from alcoholic beverages*) sobrietà *f*

temperate ['tɛmpərɪt] *adj* temperato

temperature ['tɛmpərət/ər] *s* temperatura

tempest ['tɛmpɪst] *s* tempesta; **tempest in a teapot** tempesta in un bicchier d'acqua

tempestuous [tɛm'pɛst/u·əs] *adj* tempestoso

temple ['tɛmpəl] *s* (*place of worship*) tempio; (*of spectacles*) susta, stanghetta; (anat) tempia

tem·po ['tɛmpo] *s* (**-pos** *or* **-pi** [pi]) (mus) tempo; (fig) ritmo

temporal ['tɛmpərəl] *adj* temporale

temporary ['tɛmpə ,rɛri] *adj* temporaneo, provvisorio, transitorio, interino

temporize ['tɛmpə ,raɪz] *intr* temporeggiare

tempt [tɛmpt] *tr* tentare

temptation [tɛmp'te/ən] *s* tentazione

tempter ['tɛmptər] *s* tentatore *m*

tempting ['tɛmptɪŋ] *adj* tentatore

ten [tɛn] *adj & pron* dieci ‖ *s* dieci *m*; **ten o'clock** le dieci

tenable ['tɛnəbəl] *adj* difendibile

tenacious [tɪ'ne/əs] *adj* tenace

tenant ['tɛnənt] *s* inquilino, pigionante *mf*; (*of land*) fittavolo

tend [tɛnd] *tr* riguardare, governare; accudire (with *dat*), e.g., **he tends the fire** accudisce al fuoco ‖ *intr* tendere; **to tend to** propendere verso; **one's own business**) attendere a; **to tend to + inf** tendere a + *inf*

tenden·cy ['tɛndənsi] *s* (**-cies**) tendenza, propensione

tender ['tɛndər] *adj* tenero; sensibile, dolorante || *s* offerta; (naut) nave *f* rifornimento; (naut) lancia; (rr) carboniera || *tr* offrire

tender-hearted ['tɛndər ,hɑrtɪd] *adj* dal cuore tenero

ten'der·loin' *s* filetto || **Tenderloin** *s* rione *m* della mala vita

tenderness ['tɛndərnɪs] *s* tenerezza

tendon ['tɛndən] *s* tendine *m*

tendril ['tɛndrɪl] *s* viticcio

tenement ['tɛnɪmənt] *s* appartamento; casa; casamento

ten'ement house' *s* casamento

tenet ['tɛnɪt] *s* dogma *m*, dottrina

tennis ['tɛnɪs] *s* tennis *m*

ten'nis court' *s* campo da tennis

ten'nis play'er *s* tennista *mf*

tenor ['tɛnər] *s* tenore *m*

tense [tɛns] *adj* teso || *s* (gram) tempo

tension ['tɛnʃən] *s* tensione *f*

tent [tɛnt] *s* tenda; (*of circus*) tendone *m*

tentacle ['tɛntəkəl] *s* tentacolo

tentative ['tɛntətɪv] *adj* a titolo di prova; (*smile*) esile

tenth [tɛnθ] *adj, s & pron* decimo || *s* (*in dates*) dieci *m*

tenuous ['tɛnju·əs] *adj* tenue

tenure ['tɛnjər] *s* (*in office*) rafferma; (*permanency of employment*) inamovibilità *f*; (law) possesso

tepid ['tɛpɪd] *adj* tiepido

tercet ['tʌrsɪt] *s* terzina

term [tʌrm] *s* vocabolo, voce *f*; periodo, durata; termine *m*; (com) scadenza; **terms** condizioni *fpl*; **to be on good terms** essere in buone relazioni; **to come to terms** venire a patti || *tr* chiamare, definire

termagant ['tʌrməgənt] *s* megera

terminal ['tʌrmɪnəl] *adj* terminale || *s* (*end or extremity*) terminale *m*; (elec) morsetto; (rr) capolinea *m*

terminate ['tʌrmɪ ,nɛt] *tr & intr* terminare

terminus ['tʌrmɪnəs] *s* termine *m*, fine *m*; (rr) capolinea *m*

termite ['tʌrmaɪt] *s* termite *f*

terrace ['tɛrəs] *s* terrazza, terrazzo; (agr) gradino, scaglione *m*

terra firma ['tɛrə 'fʌrmə] *s* terra ferma

terrain [tɛ'ren] *s* terreno

terrestrial [tə'rɛstrɪ·əl] *adj* terrestre

terrific [tə'rɪfɪk] *adj* terrificante; (coll) tremendo

terri·fy ['tɛrɪ ,faɪ] *v* (*pret & pp* -fied) *tr* terrificare, inorridire

territo·ry ['tɛrɪ ,tori] *s* (-ries) territorio

terror ['tɛrər] *s* terrore *m*

terrorize ['tɛrə ,raɪz] *tr* terrorizzare; dominare col terrore

ter'ry cloth' ['tɛri] *s* tessuto a spugna

terse [tʌrs] *adj* conciso, terso

tertiary ['tʌrʃɪ ,ɛri] *or* ['tʌrʃəri] *adj* terziario

test [tɛst] *s* prova, saggio; esame *m* || *tr* provare, saggiare; esaminare; (*e.g., a machine*) collaudare

testament ['tɛstəmənt] *s* testamento || **Testament** *s* Testamento Nuovo

test' ban' *s* interdizione degli esperimenti nucleari

test' flight' *s* volo di prova

testicle ['tɛstɪkəl] *s* testicolo

testi·fy ['tɛstɪ ,faɪ] *v* (*pret & pp* -fied) *tr & intr* testimoniare

testimonial [,tɛstɪ'moni·əl] *s* (*certificate*) benservito, referenza; (*expression of esteem*) segno di gratitudine

testimo·ny ['tɛstɪ ,moni] *s* (-nies) testimonianza

test' pat'tern *s* (telv) monoscopio

test' pi'lot *s* pilota *m* collaudatore

test' tube' *s* provetta

tetanus ['tɛtənəs] *s* tetano

tether ['tɛðər] *s* cavezza, pastoia; **at the end of one's tether** al limite delle proprie risorse || *tr* legare; incavezzare, impastoiare

tetter ['tɛtər] *s* eczema *m*, impetigine *f*

text [tɛkst] *s* testo; tema *m*

text'book' *s* libro di testo

textile ['tɛkstɪl] *or* ['tɛkstaɪl] *adj & s* tessile *m*

textual ['tɛkst ʃu·əl] *adj* testuale

texture ['tɛkstʃər] *s* (*of cloth*) trama; caratteristica, proprietà *f*

Thai ['tɑ·i] *or* ['taɪ] *adj & s* tailandese *mf*

Thailand ['taɪlənd] *s* la Tailandia

Thames [tɛmz] *s* Tamigi *m*

than [ðæn] *conj* di, e.g., **he is faster than you** è più veloce di te; (*before a verb*) di quanto, e.g., **he is smarter than I thought** è più intelligente di quanto pensavo; che, e.g., **he had barely begun to eat than it was time to leave** non aveva appena cominciato a mangiare che era ora di andarsene

thank [θæŋk] *s*—**thanks** ringraziamenti *mpl*; **thanks to** grazie a, in grazia di || *tr* ringraziare || **thanks** *interj* grazie!

thankful ['θæŋkfəl] *adj* grato

thankless ['θæŋklɪs] *adj* ingrato

Thanksgiv'ing Day' [,θæŋks'gɪvɪŋ] *s* giorno del Ringraziamento

that [ðæt] *adj dem* (those) quel; codesto; **that one** quello, quello là || *pron dem* (those) quello; codesto || *pron rel* che, quello che, il quale; **that is** cioè; **that's that** (coll) ecco fatto, ecco tutto || *adv* (coll) tanto, così; **that far** così lontano; **that many** tanti; **that much** tanto || *conj* che

thatch [θætʃ] *s* paglia, copertura di paglia; (*hair*) capigliatura || *tr* coprire di paglia

thaw [θɔ] *s* sgelo || *tr* sgelare || *intr* sgelarsi

the [ðə], [ðɪ], *or* [ði] *art def* il; al, e.g., **one dollar the dozen** un dollaro alla dozzina || *adv*—**so much the worse for him** tanto peggio per lui; **the more . . . the more** quanto più . . . tanto più

theater ['θi·ətər] *s* teatro

the'ater·go'er *s* frequentatore *m* abituale del teatro

the'ater news' *s* cronaca teatrale

theatrical [θɪ'ætrɪkəl] *adj* teatrale

Thebes [θibz] *s* Tebe *f*

thee [ði] *pron pers* (Bib; poet) ti; te

theft [θɛft] *s* furto, ruberia

their [ðeɪr] *adj poss* il loro, loro
theirs [ðeɪrz] *pron poss* il loro
them [ðem] *pron pers* li; loro; **to them** loro
theme [θim] *s* tema *m*, soggetto; saggio; (mus) tema *m*
theme' song' *s* (mus) tema *m* centrale; (rad) sigla musicale
them·selves' *pron pers* essi stessi, loro stessi; si, e.g., **they enjoyed themselves** si divertirono
then [ðen] *adj* allora, di allora || *s* quel tempo; **by then** a quell'epoca; **from then on** da quel giorno in poi || *adv* allora; indi, poi; **then and there** a quel momento
thence [ðens] *adv* indi, quindi; da lì; da allora in poi
thence'forth' *adv* da allora in poi
theolo·gy [θi'ɑlədʒi] *s* (**-gies**) telogia
theorem [θi·ərəm] *s* teorema *m*
theoretical [ˌθi·ə'rɛtɪkəl] *adj* teoretico
theo·ry ['θi·əri] *s* (**-ries**) teoria
therapeutic [ˌθerə'pjutɪk] *adj* terapeutico || **therapeutics** *ssg* terapeutica
thera·py ['θerəpi] *s* (**-pies**) terapia
there [ðer] *adv* lì, là; **there are** ci sono; **there is** c'è; ecco, e.g., **there it is** eccolo
there'abouts' *adv* circa, approssimativamente, giù di lì
there'af'ter *adv* in seguito, dipoi
there'by' *adv* quindi, perciò, così
therefore ['ðerfɔr] *adv* per questo, quindi, dunque
there'in' *adv* lì; in quel rispetto
there'of' *adv* di ciò, da ciò
Theresa [tə'risə] or [tə'resə] *s* Teresa
there'upon' *adv* su questo; a quel momento; come conseguenza
thermal ['θʌrməl] *adj* (*water*) termale; (*capacity*) termico
thermistor [θər'mɪstər] *s* (elec) termistore *m*
thermocouple ['θʌrmo ˌkʌpəl] *s* termocoppia
thermodynamic [ˌθʌrmodaɪ'næmɪk] *adj* termodinamico || **thermodynamics** *ssg* termodinamica
thermometer [θər'mɑmɪtər] *s* termometro
thermonuclear [ˌθʌrmo'njuklɪ·ər] or [ˌθʌrmo'nukli·ər] *adj* termonucleare
ther'mos bot'tle ['θʌrməs] *s* termos *m*
thermostat ['θʌrmə ˌstæt] *s* termostato
thesau·rus [θɪ'sɔrəs] *s* (**-ri** [raɪ] or **-ruses**) tesoro, lessico, compendio
these [ðiz] *pl* of **this**
the·sis ['θisɪs] *s* (**-ses** [siz]) tesi *f*
Thespis ['θespɪs] *s* Tespi *m*
they [ðe] *pron pers* essi, loro
thick [θɪk] *adj* spesso, grosso; folto, denso; pieno, coperto; viscoso; stupido; (coll) intimo || *s* spessore *m*; **in the thick of** nel folto di; **through thick and thin** nei tempi buoni e cattivi
thicken ['θɪkən] *tr* ispessire; ingrossare; infoltire || *intr* ispessirsi; ingrossarsi; (*said of a plot*) complicarsi
thicket ['θɪkɪt] *s* boscaglia, macchia
thick-headed ['θɪk ˌhɛdɪd] *adj* indietro, stupido

thick'set' *adj* tarchiato; (*hedge*) fitto, denso
thief [θif] *s* (**thieves** [θivz]) ladro
thieve [θiv] *intr* rubare
thiev·y ['θivəri] *s* (**-ies**) furto
thigh [θaɪ] *s* coscia
thigh'bone' *s* femore *m*
thimble ['θɪmbəl] *s* ditale *m*
thin [θɪn] *adj* (**thinner**; **thinnest**) (*paper, ice*) sottile; (*lean*) magro, smilzo; (*e.g., hair*) rado; (*air*) fine; (*excuse*) tenue; (*voice*) esile; (*wine*) leggero, annacquato || *v* (*pret & pp* **thinned**; *ger* **thinning**) *tr* assottigliare; (*paint*) diluire || *intr* assottigliarsi; **to thin out** (*said of a crowd; one's hair*) diradarsi
thine [ðaɪn] *adj & pron poss* (Bib & poet) tuo, il tuo
thing [θɪŋ] *s* cosa; **not to get a thing out of** non riuscire a capire; non cavare un briciolo d'informazione da; **of all things!** che cosa!; che sorpresa!; **the thing** l'ultima moda; **things** roba; **to see things** avere allucinazioni
think [θɪŋk] *v* (*pret & pp* **thought** [θɔt]) *tr* pensare; credere; **to think it over** ripensarci; **to think nothing of it** non darci la minima importanza; **to think of** (*to have as an opinion of*) pensare di, e.g., **what do you think of that doctor?** cosa ne pensa di quel medico?; **to think out** decifrare; **to think up** immaginare || *intr* pensare; **to think not** credere di no; **to think of** (*to turn one's thoughts to*) pensare a, e.g., **he is thinking of the future** pensa al futuro; (*to imagine*) immaginare; **to think so** credere di sì; **to think well of** avere una buona opinione di
thinkable ['θɪŋkəbəl] *adj* pensabile
thinker ['θɪŋkər] *s* pensatore *m*
third [θʌrd] *adj, s & pron* terzo || *s* terzo; (*in dates*) tre *m*; (aut) terza
third' degree' *s* interrogatorio di terzo grado
third' rail' *s* (rr) rotaia elettrificata di contatto
third'-rate' *adj* di terz'ordine
Third' World' *s* Terzo Mondo
thirst [θʌrst] *s* sete *f* || *intr* aver sete; **to thirst for** aver sete di
thirst·y ['θʌrsti] *adj* (**-ier**; **-iest**) assetato, sitibondo; **to be thirsty** avere sete
thirteen ['θʌr'tin] *adj, s & pron* tredici *m*
thirteenth ['θʌr'tinθ] *adj, s & pron* tredicesimo || *s* (*in dates*) tredici *m*
thirtieth ['θʌrtɪ·ɪθ] *adj, s & pron* trentesimo || *s* (*in dates*) trenta *m*
thir·ty ['θʌrti] *adj & pron* trenta || *s* (**-ties**) trenta *m*; **the thirties** gli anni trenta
this [ðɪs] *adj dem* (**these**) questo; **this one** questo, questo qui || *pron dem* (**these**) questo, questo qui || *adv* (coll) tanto, così
thistle ['θɪsəl] *s* cardo
thither ['θɪðər] or ['ðɪðər] *adv* là, da quella parte

Thomas ['tɑməs] *s* Tommaso

thong [θɔŋ] or [θaŋ] *s* coreggia

thorax ['θoræks] *s* (-raxes or -races [rə ,siz]) torace *m*

thorn [θɔrn] *s* spina

thorn·y ['θɔrni] *adj* (-ier; -iest) spinoso

thorough ['θʌro] *adj* completo, esauriente

thor'ough·bred' *adj* di razza; (*horse*) purosangue || *s* individuo di razza; (*horse*) purosangue *mf*

thor'ough·fare' *s* passaggio; **no thoroughfare** divieto di passaggio

thor'ough·go'ing *adj* completo, esauriente

thoroughly ['θʌroli] *adv* a fondo

those [ðoz] *pl* of **that**

thou [ðau] *pron pers* (Bib; poet) tu || *tr* dare del tu a

though [ðo] *adv* tuttavia || *conj* malgrado, sebbene; **as though** come se

thought [θɔt] *s* pensiero; **perish the thought!** (coll) nemmeno a pensarci!

thoughtful ['θɔtfəl] *adj* pensieroso, riflessivo; (*considerate*) sollecito

thoughtless ['θɔtlɪs] *adj* irriflessivo; sconsiderato; (*reckless*) incurante

thought' transfer'ence *s* trasmissione del pensiero

thousand ['θauzənd] *adj, s & pron* mille *m*; **a thousand** or **one thousand** mille *m*

thousandth ['θauzəndθ] *adj, s & pron* millesimo

thralldom ['θrɔldəm] *s* schiavitù *f*

thrash [θræʃ] *tr* battere; (agr) trebbiare; **to thrash out** discutere a fondo || *intr* agitarsi, dibattersi

thread [θred] *s* filo; (mach) filetto, verme *m*; **to lose the thread of** perdere il filo di || *tr* infilare; (fig) pervadere; (mach) filettare, impanare; **to thread one's way through** aprirsi il passaggio attraverso

thread'bare' *adj* frusto, logoro

threat [θret] *s* minaccia

threaten ['θretən] *tr & intr* minacciare

threatening ['θretənɪŋ] *adj* minaccioso; (*e.g., letter*) minatorio

three [θri] *adj & pron* tre || *s* tre *m*; **three o'clock** le tre

three'-cor'nered *adj* triangolare; (*hat*) a tre punte

three' hun'dred *adj, s & pron* trecento

threepenny ['θrepəni] or ['θrɪpəni] *adj* del valore di tre penny; di nessun valore

three'-phase' *adj* trifase

three'-ply' *adj* a tre spessori

three' R's' [ɑrz] *spl* lettura, scrittura e aritmetica

three'score' *adj* sessanta

three' thou'sand *adj, s & pron* tre mila *mpl*

threno·dy ['θrenədi] *s* (-dies) trenodia

thresh [θreʃ] *tr* (agr) trebbiare; **to thresh out** discutere a fondo || *intr* trebbiare; battere

thresh'ing machine' *s* trebbiatrice *f*

threshold ['θreʃold] *s* soglia

thrice [θraɪs] *adv* tre volte; molto

thrift [θrɪft] *s* economia

thrift·y ['θrɪfti] *adj* (-ier; -iest) eco-

nomo, economico; vigoroso; prospero

thrill [θrɪl] *s* fremito d'emozione; esperienza emozionante || *tr* emozionare || *intr* emozionarsi; vibrare

thriller ['θrɪlər] *s* (coll) thrilling *m*

thrilling ['θrɪlɪŋ] *adj* emozionante, thrilling

thrive [θraɪv] *v* (pret **thrived** or **throve** [θrov]; *pp* **thrived** or **thriven** ['θrɪvən]) *intr* prosperare, fiorire

throat [θrot] *s* gola; **to clear one's throat** schiarirsi la voce

throb [θrɑb] *s* battito, palpito, tuffo || *v* (pret & pp **throbbed**; *ger* **throbbing**) *intr* palpitare, pulsare

throe [θro] *s* agonia, travaglio, spasimo; **in the throes of** nel travaglio di; (*e.g., battle*) nel momento più penoso di

throne [θron] *s* trono

throng [θrɔŋ] or [θraŋ] *s* folla, stuolo || *intr* affollarsi

throttle ['θrɑtəl] *s* (of locomotive) leva di comando; (of motorcycle) manetta; (of car) acceleratore *m*; (mach) valvola di controllo || *tr* soffocare; (mach) regolare

through [θru] *adj* diretto, senza fermate; **to be through** aver finito; **to be through with** farla finita con || *adv* attraverso; da una parte all'altra; completamente; *prep* attraverso, per; durante; fino alla fine di; per mezzo di

through·out' *adv* completamente, da un capo all'altro; dappertutto || *prep* durante tutto, e.g., **throughout the afternoon** durante tutto il pomeriggio; per tutto, e.g., **throughout the house** per tutta la casa

throw [θro] *s* getto, tiro, lancio; gettata; coperta leggera || *v* (pret **threw** [θru]; *pp* **thrown**) *tr* gettare, tirare, lanciare; (a shadow) proiettare; (the current) connettere; (said of a horse) disarcionare; (wrestling) gettare a terra; (a game) (coll) perdere intenzionalmente; (coll) stupire; **to throw away** gettar via; perdere; **to throw back** rigettare; ritardare; **to throw in** (the clutch) innestare; (coll) aggiungere; **to throw oneself into** darsi a; **to throw out** sbatter fuori; (the clutch) disinnestare; **to throw over** abbandonare || *intr* gettare, tirare, lanciare; **to throw up** vomitare

thrum [θrʌm] *v* (pret & pp **thrummed**; *ger* **thrumming**) *intr* tambureggiare; (mus) far scorrere la mano sulle corde di uno strumento

thrush [θrʌʃ] *s* tordo

thrust [θrʌst] *s* (push) spinta; botta; (with dagger) pugnalata; (with sword) stoccata || *v* (pret & pp **thrust**) *tr* spingere; conficcare, configgere; **to thrust oneself** (e.g., into a conversation) ficcarsi

thru'way' *s* autostrada

thud [θʌd] *s* tonfo || *v* (pret & pp **thudded**; *ger* **thudding**) *intr* fare un rumore sordo

thug [θʌg] *s* fascinoroso

thumb [θʌm] *s* pollice *m*; **all thumbs** maldestro, goffo; **thumbs down** pollice verso; **to twiddle one's thumbs** girare i pollici, essere ozioso; **under the thumb of** sotto l'influenza di || *tr* sporcare con le dita; (*a book*) sfogliare; **to thumb a ride** chiedere l'autostop; **to thumb one's nose** (at) fare marameo (a)

thumb' in'dex *s* margine *m* a scaletta

thumb'nail' *adj* breve, conciso || *s* unghia del pollice

thumb'screw' *s* vite *f* ad aletta

thumb'tack' *s* puntina

thump [θʌmp] *s* tonfo || *tr* battere, percuotere || *intr* battere; cadere con un tonfo; camminare a passi pesanti; (*said of the heart*) palpitare violentemente

thumping [ˈθʌmpɪŋ] *adj* (coll) straordinario, eccezionale; (coll) grande

thunder [ˈθʌndər] *s* tuono; (*of applause*) scroscio; (*of a cannon*) rombo || *tr* lanciare || *intr* tonare, rombare; (fig) scrosciare

thun'der·bolt' *s* folgore *f*, fulmine *m*

thun'der·clap' *s* scroscio di tuono

thunderous [ˈθʌndərəs] *adj* fragoroso

thun'der·show'er *s* acquazzone *m* accompagnato da tuoni

thun'der·storm' *s* temporale *m*

thun'der·struck' *adj* attonito

Thursday [ˈθʌrsdi] *s* giovedì *m*

thus [ðʌs] *adv* così; **thus far** sino qui

thwack [θwæk] *s* colpo || *tr* colpire

thwart [θwɔrt] *adj* obliquo || *adv* di traverso || *tr* contrariare, sventare

thy [ðaɪ] *adj poss* (Bib; poet) tuo, il tuo

thyme [taɪm] *s* timo

thy'roid gland' [ˈθaɪrɔɪd] *s* tiroide *f*

thyself [ðaɪˈsɛlf] *pron* (Bib; poet) te stesso; te, ti

tiara [taɪˈɑrə] or [taɪˈɛrə] *s* (*female adornment*) diadema *m*; (eccl) tiara

tick [tɪk] *s* (*of pillow*) fodera; (*of mattress*) guscio; (*of clock*) ticchettio; (*dot*) punto; (ent) zecca; **on tick** (coll) a credito || *intr* fare ticchettio; **to make s.o. tick** mandare avanti qlcu

ticker [ˈtɪkər] *s* telescrivente *f*; (slang) orologio; (slang) cuore *m*

tick'er tape' *s* nastro della telescrivente

ticket [ˈtɪkɪt] *s* biglietto; (*e.g., of pawnbroker*) polizza; (*slip of paper or identifying tag*) bolletta, bollettino; (*summons*) verbale *m*; (*e.g., to indicate price*) etichetta; lista dei candidati; **that's the ticket** (coll) questo è quello che fa

tick'et a'gent *s* bigliettaio

tick'et of'fice *s* biglietteria

tick'et scalp'er [ˈskælpər] *s* bagarino

tick'et win'dow *s* sportello

ticking [ˈtɪkɪŋ] *s* traliccio

tickle [ˈtɪkəl] *s* solletico || *tr* solleticare; divertire || *intr* avere il solletico

ticklish [ˈtɪklɪʃ] *adj* sensibile al solletico; delicato; permaloso; **to be ticklish** soffrire il solletico

tick-tock [ˈtɪk ˌtɑk] *s* tic tac *m*

tid'al wave' [ˈtaɪdəl] *s* onda di marea; (fig) ondata

tidbit [ˈtɪd ˌbɪt] *s* bocconcino

tiddlywinks [ˈtɪdli ˌwɪŋks] *s* gioco della pulce

tide [taɪd] *s* marea; **to go against the tide** andare contro la corrente; **to stem the tide** fermare la corrente || *tr* portare sulla cresta delle onde; **to tide over** aiutare; (*a difficulty*) sormontare

tide'wa'ter *s* marea; costa marina

tidings [ˈtaɪdɪŋz] *spl* notizie *fpl*

ti·dy [ˈtaɪdi] *adj* (**-dier; -diest**) pulito, ordinato || *s* (**-dies**) cofanetto, astuccio; appoggiacapo || *v* (*pret & pp* **-died**) *tr* rassettare, mettere in ordine || *intr* rassettarsi

tie [taɪ] *s* laccio, nodo, vincolo; (*in games*) patta; (*necktie*) cravatta; (architecture) traversa; (rr) traversina; (mus) legatura || *v* (*pret & pp* **tied**; *ger* **tying**) *tr* allacciare, annodare; legare; confinare; (*a game*) impattare; (*a person*) impattarla con; **to be tied up** essere occupato; **to tie down** confinare, limitare; **to tie up** legare; impedire; (*e.g., traffic*) intasare || *intr* allacciare; (*in games*) impattare

tie' beam' *s* catena

tie'pin' *s* spilla da cravatta

tier [tɪr] *s* gradinata; ordine *m*, livello

tiff [tɪf] *s* screzio, litigio

tiger [ˈtaɪgər] *s* tigre *f*

ti'ger lil'y *s* giglio cinese

tight [taɪt] *adj* teso; stretto; compatto; impermeabile, ermetico; pieno; (*game*) (coll) serrato; (coll) tirato; (slang) ubriaco || **tights** *spl* calzamaglia || *adv* strettamente; **to hold tight** tenere stretto

tighten [ˈtaɪtən] *tr* (*e.g., one's belt*) tirare; (*e.g., a screw*) stringere || *intr* tirarsi; stringersi

tight-fisted [ˈtaɪtˈfɪstɪd] *adj* taccagno

tight'-fit'ting *adj* attillato

tight'rope' *s* corda tesa

tight' squeeze' s—to be in a tight squeeze (coll) essere alle strette

tight'wad' *s* (coll) spilorcio

tigress [ˈtaɪgrɪs] *s* tigre femmina

tile [taɪl] *s* mattonella; (*for floor*) piastrella; (*for roof*) tegola, coppo || *tr* coprire di mattonelle; coprire di piastrelle; coprire di coppi

tile' roof' *s* tetto di tegole

till [tɪl] *s* cassetto dei soldi || *prep* fino a || *conj* fino a che . . . non, fino a che, sinché . . . non, sinché || *tr* lavorare, coltivare

tilt [tɪlt] *s* inclinazione; giostra, torneo; **full tilt** di gran carriera; a tutta forza || *tr* inclinare; (*a lance*) mettere in resta; attaccare || *intr* inclinarsi; giostrare; **to tilt at** combattere con

timber [ˈtɪmbər] *s* legno, legname *m* da costruzione; alberi *mpl*; (fig) tempra

tim'ber·land' *s* bosco destinato a produrre legname

tim'ber line' *s* linea della vegetazione

timbre ['tɪmbər] s (phonet & phys) timbro

time [taɪm] s tempo; ora, e.g., **what time is it?** che ora è?; volta, e.g., **three times** tre volte; giorni mpl, e.g., **in our time** ai giorni nostri; momento; ultima ora; ore pl lavorative; periodo, e.g., **Xmas time** periodo natalizio; **for a long time** da lungo; **for the time being** per ora, per il momento; **in time** presto; col tempo; **on time** a tempo; a rate; (said, e.g., **of a bus**) in orario; **times** volte, e.g., **seven times seven** sette volte sette; **to bide one's time** aspettare l'ora propizia; **to do time** (coll) essere in prigione; **to have a good time** divertirsi; **to have no time for** non poter sopportare; **to lose time** (said of a watch) ritardare; **to make time** avanzare rapidamente; guadagnare terreno; **to pass the time of day** fare una chiacchierata; salutarsi; **to take one's time** fare le cose senza fretta; **to tell time** leggere l'orologio || tr fissare il momento di; calcolare il tempo di; (sports) cronometrare

time' bomb' s bomba a orologeria
time'card' s cartellino di presenza
time' clock' s orologio di controllo (delle presenze)
time' expo'sure s (phot) posa
time' fuse' s spoletta a tempo
time'keep'er s marcatempo; orologio; (sports) cronometrista mf
timeless ['taɪmlɪs] adj senza fine, eterno
time·ly ['taɪmli] adj (-lier; -liest) opportuno, tempestivo
time'piece' s orologio; cronometro
time' sig'nal s segnale orario
time'ta'ble s orario; tabella di marcia
time'work' s lavoro a ore
time'worn' adj logorato dal tempo
time' zone' s fuso orario
timid ['tɪmɪd] adj timido, pavido
tim'ing gears' ['taɪmɪŋ] spl ingranaggi mpl di distribuzione
timorous ['tɪmərəs] adj timoroso
tin [tɪn] s (element) stagno; (tin plate; can) latta || v (pret & pp **tinned**; ger **tinning**) tr stagnare
tin' can' s latta
tincture ['tɪŋktʃər] s tintura
tin' cup' s tazzina metallica
tinder ['tɪndər] s esca
tin'der·box' s cassetta con l'esca e l'acciarino; persona eccitabile; (fig) polveriera
tin' foil' s stagnola
ting-a-ling ['tɪŋə,lɪŋ] s dindìn m
tinge [tɪndʒ] s sfumatura; pizzico; punta || v (ger **tingeing** or **tinging**) tr sfumare; dare una traccia di sapore a
tingle ['tɪŋgəl] s formicolio, pizzicore m || intr informicolirsi; pizzicare; (said of the ears) ronzare; (with enthusiasm) fremere
tin' hat' s (slang) elmetto
tinker ['tɪŋkər] s calderaio, ramaio || intr armeggiare
tinkle ['tɪŋkəl] s tintinnio || tr far tintinnare || intr tintinnare

tin' plate' s latta
tin' roof' s tetto di lamiera di latta
tinsel ['tɪnsəl] s orpello, lustrino
tin'smith' s lattoniere m, stagnino
tin' sol'dier s soldatino di piombo
tint [tɪnt] s tinta, sfumatura || tr tinteggiare
tin'ware' s articoli mpl di latta
ti·ny ['taɪni] adj (-nier; -niest) piccino
tip [tɪp] s punta; (of mountain) vetta; (of umbrella) gorbia; (of shoe) mascherina; (of cigarette) bocchino; (of shoestring) aghetto; colpetto; (fee) mancia; informazione confidenziale; inclinazione || v (pret & pp **tipped**; ger **tipping**) tr mettere la punta a; inclinare, rovesciare; (one's hat) levarsi; dare la mancia a; toccare, battere; (the scales) far traboccare; **to tip in** (bb) inserire fuori testo; **to tip off** (coll) dare informazioni confidenziali a || intr inclinarsi; dare la mancia
tip'cart' s carro ribaltabile
tip'-off' s (coll) avvertimento confidenziale
tipped'-in' adj (bb) fuori testo
tipple ['tɪpəl] intr sbevucchiare
tip'staff' s usciere m
tip·sy ['tɪpsi] adj (-sier; -siest) brillo
tip'toe' s punta di piedi || v (pret & pp **-toed**; ger **-toeing**) intr camminare in punta di piedi
tirade ['taɪred] s tirata
tire [taɪr] s gomma, pneumatico; (of metal) cerchione m || tr stancare || intr stancarsi; infastidirsi
tire' chain' s catena antineve
tired [taɪrd] adj stanco, stracco
tire' gauge' s manometro della pressione delle gomme
tireless ['taɪrlɪs] adj infaticabile
tire' pres'sure s pressione (delle gomme)
tire' pump' s pompa (per i pneumatici)
tiresome ['taɪrsəm] adj faticoso; (boring) noioso
tissue ['tɪʃu] s tessuto; tessuto finissimo, velina
tis'sue pa'per s carta velina
titanium [taɪ'teni·əm] or [tɪ'teni·əm] s titanio
tithe [taɪð] s decima || tr imporre la decima su; pagare la decima su
Titian ['tɪʃən] adj tizianesco || s Tiziano
title ['taɪtəl] s titolo; (sports) campionato || tr intitolare
ti'tle deed' s titolo di proprietà
ti'tle·hold'er s campione m, primatista mf
ti'tle page' s frontespizio
ti'tle role' s (theat) ruolo principale
tit'mouse' s (-mice) (orn) cincia
titter ['tɪtər] s risatina || intr ridacchiare
titular ['tɪtʃələr] adj titolare
TNT ['ti,en'ti] s (letterword) tritolo
to [tu], [tʊ] or [tə] adv—**to and fro** da una parte all'altra, avanti e indietro; **to come** to tornare in sè || prep a, e.g., **he is going to Rome** va a Roma; **he gave a kiss to his mother**

diede un bacio a sua madre; **she is learning to sew** impara a cucire; per, e.g., **he has been a true friend to me** è stato un vero amico per me; da, e.g., **there is still a lot of work to do** c'è ancora molto lavoro da fare; con, e.g., **she was very kind to me** è stata molto gentile con me; in, e.g., **we went to church** siamo andati in chiesa; fino a, e.g., **to see s.o. to the station** accompagnare qlcu fino alla stazione; in confronto di, e.g., **the accounts are nothing to what really happened** le storie non sono nulla, in confronto di quanto è realmente successo; meno, e.g., **ten minutes to seven** le sette meno dieci

toad [tod] s rospo

toad'stool' s agarico, fungo velenoso

to-and-fro [tu-ənd'fro] adj avanti e indietro

toast [tost] s (drink to s.o.'s health) brindisi m; a piece of toast una fetta di pane tostato || tr tostare; brindare alla salute di || intr tostarsi; brindare

toaster ['tostər] s (of bread) tostapane m; persona che fa un brindisi

toast'mas'ter s persona che annuncia i brindisi, maestro di cerimonie

tobac·co [tə'bæko] s (-cos) tabacco

tobacconist [tə'bækənɪst] s tabaccaio

tobac'co pouch' s borsa da tabacco

toboggan [tə'bɑgən] s toboga m

tocsin ['tɑksɪn] s campana a martello; scampanata d'allarme

today [tu'de] s & adv oggi m

toddle ['tɑdəl] s passo vacillante || intr traballare, trotterellare

tod·dy ['tɑdi] s (-dies) ponce m

to-do [tə'du] s (-dos) (coll) daffare m, rumore m

toe [to] s dito del piede; (of shoe) punta || v (pret & pp **toed**; ger **toeing**) tr—**to toe the line** filare diritto

toe'nail' s unghia del piede

together [tu'gɛðər] adv insieme; **to bring together** riunire; riconciliare; **to call together** chiamare a raccolta; **to stick together** (coll) rimanere uniti, stare insieme

togs [tɑgz] spl vestiti mpl

toil [tɔɪl] s travaglio, sfacchinata; **toils** reti fpl, lacci mpl || intr travagliare, sfacchinare

toilet ['tɔɪlɪt] s toletta; gabinetto, ritirata; **to make one's toilet** farsi la toletta

toi'let pa'per s carta igienica

toi'let pow'der s polvere f di talco

toi'let soap' s sapone m da toletta

toi'let wa'ter s acqua da toletta

token ['tokən] s segno, marca; ricordo; (used as money) gettone m; **by the same token** per di più; **in token of** in segno di, come prova di

tolerance ['tɑlərəns] s tolleranza

tolerate ['tɑlə‚ret] tr tollerare

toll [tol] s (of bell) rintocco; (e.g., for passage over bridge) pedaggio; (tax) dazio; (compensation for grinding grains) molenda; (number of victims) perdite fpl; (telp) tariffa inter-

urbana || tr (a bell) sonare a morto; (the faithful) chiamare a raccolta || intr sonare a morto

toll' bridge' s ponte m a pedaggio

toll' call' s (telp) chiamata interurbana

toll'gate' s barriera di pedaggio; (in a turnpike) casello

toma·to [tə'meto] or [tə'mɑto] s (-toes) pomodoro

toma'to juice' s sugo di pomodoro

tomb [tum] s tomba

tomboy ['tɑm‚bɔɪ] s maschietta

tomb'stone' s pietra tombale, lapide f

tomcat ['tɑm‚kæt] s gatto maschio

tome [tom] s tomo

tomorrow [tu'mɑro] or [tu'mɔro] s domani m; **the day after tomorrow** dopodomani m || adv domani

tom-tom ['tɑm‚tɑm] s tam-tam m

ton [tʌn] s tonnellata; **tons** (coll) montagne fpl

tone [ton] s tono; (fig) tenore m || tr intonare; **to tone down** (colors) smorzare; (sounds) sfumare || intr intonarsi; **to tone down** moderarsi; **to tone up** rinforzarsi

tone' po'em s poema sinfonico

tongs [tɑŋz] or [tɑŋz] spl tenaglie fpl; (e.g., for sugar) molle fpl

tongue [tʌŋ] s (language) lingua; (of bell) battaglio; (of shoe) linguetta; (of wagon) timone m; (anat) lingua; (carp) maschio; **tongue in cheek** poco sinceramente; **to hold one's tongue** mordersi la lingua; **to speak with forked tongue** essere di due lingue

tongue' depres'sor s abbassalingua m

tongue'-lash'ing s sgridata

tongue' twist'er s scioglilingua m

tonic ['tɑnɪk] adj & s tonico

tonight [tu'naɪt] s questa sera, questa notte || adv stasera; stanotte

tonnage ['tʌnɪdʒ] s tonnellaggio, stazza

tonsil ['tɑnsəl] s tonsilla

ton·y ['toni] adj (-ier; -iest) (slang) elegante, di lusso

too [tu] adv (also) anche, pure; (more than enough) troppo; **too bad!** peccato!; **too many** troppi; **too much** troppo

tool [tul] s utensile m, attrezzo; (person) strumento; (of lathe) punta || tr lavorare; (bb) decorare

tool' bag' s borsa degli attrezzi

tool'box' s cassetta attrezzi

tool'mak'er s attrezzista m

tool'shed' s barchessa

toot [tut] s (of horn) suono; (of locomotive) fischio; (of car's horn) colpo; (coll) gazzarra || tr strombettare; **to toot one's own horn** bazzare i propri meriti || intr strombettare

tooth [tuθ] s (teeth [tiθ]) dente m

tooth'ache' s mal m di denti

tooth'brush' s spazzolino da denti

toothless ['tuθlɪs] adj sdentato

tooth'paste' s pasta dentifricia

tooth'pick' s stuzzicadenti m

tooth' pow'der s polvere dentifricia

top [tɑp] s cima, sommo, vertice m; (upper part of anything) disopra m;

(*of mountain, tree*) vetta; (*of box*) coperchio; (*beginning*) principio; (*of bottle*) imboccatura; (*of a bridge*) testata; (*of wagon*) mantice *m*; (*of car*) tetto; (*of wall*) coronamento; (*toy*) trottola; (naut) gabbia; **at the top of one's voice** a perdifiato; **from top to bottom** daccapo a piedi, dal principio alla fine; **on top of** in cima di; subito dopo; **the tops** (coll) il migliore, il fiore; **to blow one's top** (slang) dare in escandescenze; **to sleep like a top** dormire come un ghiro ‖ *v* (*pret & pp* **topped**; *ger* **topping**) *tr* (*a tree*) svettare; coronare; superare

topaz ['topæz] *s* topazio

top' bil'ling *s*—**to get top billing** essere artista di cartello; (journ) ricevere il posto più importante

top' boot' *s* stivale *m* a tromba

top'coat' *s* soprabito di mezza stagione

toper ['topər] *s* ubriacone *m*

topgal'lant sail' [ˌtap'gælənt] *s* (naut) pappafico, veletta

top' hat' *s* cappello a staio or a cilindro

top'-heav'y *adj* troppo pesante in cima, sovraccarico in cima

topic ['tapɪk] *s* topica, tema *m*

top'knot' *s* crocchia

topless ['taplɪs] *adj* (*mountain*) di cui non si vede la vetta, eccelso; (*bathing suit*) topless

top'mast' *s* (naut) alberetto

top'most' *adj* il più alto

topogra·phy [tə'pɑgrəfi] *s* (**-phies**) topografia

topple ['tapəl] *tr* abbattere, rovesciare ‖ *intr* rovesciarsi, cadere

top' prior'ity *s* priorità massima

topsail ['tapsəl] or ['tap ˌsel] *s* (naut) gabbia

top'-se'cret *adj* segretissimo

top'soil' *s* strato superiore del terreno

topsy-turvy ['tapsi'tʌrvi] *adj* rovesciato; confuso ‖ *s* soqquadro ‖ *adv* a soqquadro

torch [tɔrtʃ] *s* fiaccola, torcia; **to carry the torch for** (slang) amare disperatamente

torch'bear'er *s* portatore *m* di fiaccola; (fig) capo, guida *m*

torch'light' *s* luce *f* di fiaccola

torch' song' *s* canzone *f* triste d'amore non corrisposto

torment ['tɔrment] *s* tormento ‖ [tɔr'ment] *tr* tormentare

torna·do [tɔr'nedo] *s* (**-dos** or **-does**) tornado, tromba d'aria

torpe·do [tɔr'pido] *s* (**-does**) siluro ‖ *tr* silurare

torpe'do boat' *s* motosilurante *f*

torpe'do-boat destroy'er *s* torpediniera

torrent ['tarənt] or ['tɔrənt] *s* torrente *m*

torrid ['tarɪd] or ['tɔrɪd] *adj* torrido

torsion ['tɔrʃən] *s* torsione

tor'sion bar' *s* barra di torsione

tor·so ['tɔrso] *s* (**-sos**) torso

tortoise ['tɔrtəs] *s* tartaruga

tor'toise shell' *s* tartaruga

torture ['tɔrtʃər] *s* tortura ‖ *tr* torturare

toss [tɔs] or [tas] *s* lancio, getto ‖ *tr* lanciare, gettare; (*to fling about*) sballottare; (*one's head*) alzare sdegnosamente; agitare; rivoltare; (*an opinion*) avventare; **to toss off** fare rapidamente; (*e.g., a drink*) buttar giù; **to toss up** (*a coin*) gettar in aria, gettare a testa e croce; (coll) rigettare ‖ *intr* agitarsi, dimenarsi; **to toss and turn** (*in bed*) girarsi; **to toss up** giocare a testa e croce

toss'up' *s* testa e croce; (coll) eguale probabilità *f*

tot [tat] *s* bambino, piccolo

to·tal ['totəl] *adj* totale; (*e.g., loss*) completo ‖ *s* totale *m* ‖ *v* (*pret & pp* **-taled** or **-talled**; *ger* **-taling** or **-talling**) *tr* ammontare a; (*to make a total of*) sommare

totalitarian [toˌtælɪ'teri·ən] *adj* totalitario ‖ *s* aderente *mf* al totalitarismo

totter ['tatər] *s* vacillamento ‖ *intr* vacillare

touch [tʌtʃ] *s* (*act*) tocco; (*sense*) tatto; (*of an illness*) leggero attacco; (*slight amount*) punta; (*for money*) (slang) stoccata; **to get in touch with** mettersi in contatto con; **to lose one's touch** perdere il tocco personale ‖ *tr* toccare; raggiungere; riguardare; (*for a loan*) dare una stoccata a; **to touch on** menzionare; **to touch up** ritoccare ‖ *intr* toccare; **to touch down** (aer) atterrare

touching ['tʌtʃɪŋ] *adj* toccante, commovente ‖ *prep* riguardo a

touch'stone' *s* pietra di paragone

touch' type'writing *s* dattilografia a tatto

touch·y ['tʌtʃi] *adj* (**-ier; -iest**) suscettibile, permaloso; delicato, precario, rischioso

tough [tʌf] *adj* duro; forte; (*luck*) cattivo; violento ‖ *s* malvivente *m*

toughen ['tʌfən] *tr* indurire ‖ *intr* indurirsi

tough' luck' *s* disdetta, sfortuna

tour [tur] *s* gita, viaggio; (sports) giro; (mil) turno; (theat) tournée *f* ‖ *tr* girare; (theat) portare in tournée ‖ *intr* girare; (theat) andare in tournée

tour'ing car' ['turɪŋ] *s* automobile *f* da turismo

tourist ['turɪst] *adj* turistico ‖ *s* turista *mf*

tournament ['turnəmənt] or ['tʌrnəmənt] *s* torneo

tourney ['turni] or ['tʌrni] *s* torneo ‖ *intr* giostrare

tourniquet ['turnɪˌket] or ['tʌrnɪˌke] *s* laccio emostatico

tousle ['tauzəl] *tr* spettinare

tow [to] *s* rimorchio; (*e.g., of hemp*) stoppa; **to take in tow** prendere a rimorchio ‖ *tr* rimorchiare

toward(s) [tord(z)] or [tə'word(z)] *prep* (*in the direction of*) verso; (*in respect to*) per; (*near*) vicino a; (*a certain hour*) su, verso

tow'boat' *s* rimorchiatore *m*

tow' car' *s* rimorchiatore *m*

tow·el ['tau·əl] *s* asciugamano; (*of paper*) salvietta; **to throw in the**

towel (slang) gettare la spugna || *v* (*pret & pp* **-eled** *or* **-elled;** *ger* **-eling** *or* **-elling)** *tr* asciugare

tow'el rack' *s* portaasciugamani *m*

tower ['tau·ər] *s* torre *f* || *intr* torreggiare

towering ['tau·ərɪŋ] *adj* torreggiante; gigantesco; eccessivo

towline ['to‚laɪn] *s* cavo di rimorchio

town [taun] *s* città *f;* (*townspeople*) cittadinanza; **in town** in città

town' clerk' *s* segretario municipale

town' coun'cil *s* consiglio comunale

town' cri'er *s* banditore *m* municipale

town' hall' *s* municipio

township ['taun∫ɪp] *s* suddivisione di contea

towns'man *s* (**-men**) cittadino; concittadino

towns'peo'ple *spl* cittadini *mpl;* gente *f* di città

town' talk' *s* dicerie *fpl,* pettegolezzi *mpl*

tow'path' *s* strada d'alaggio

tow'rope' *s* corda da rimorchio

tow' truck' *s* autogru *f*

toxic ['taksɪk] *adj & s* tossico

toy [tɔɪ] *adj* giocattolo; di giocattoli || *s* giocattolo; (*trifle*) nonnulla *m;* (*trinket*) gingillo || *intr* giocare; **to toy with** (*to play with*) giocare con; (*to trifle, e.g., with food*) baloccarsi con; (*an idea*) accarezzare; (*to flirt with*) flirtare con

toy' bank' *s* salvadanaio

toy' sol'dier *s* soldatino di piombo

trace [tres] *s* traccia, vestigio; (*racing*) tracciato; (*of harness*) tirella; (fig) ombra || *tr* tracciare; (*e.g., s.o.'s ancestry*) rintracciare; (*a pattern*) lucidare

trac'er bul'let ['tresər] *s* pallottola tracciante

trache·a ['treki·ə] *s* (**-ae** [‚i]) trachea

tracing ['tresɪŋ] *s* tracciato

track [træk] *s* (*of foot*) traccia, pesta; (*rut*) solco, rotaia; (*of boat*) scia; corso; (*course followed by boat*) rotta; (*of tape recorder*) pista; (*of tractor*) cingolo; (*of ideas*) successione; (*width of a vehicle measured from wheel to wheel*) (aut) carreggiata; (rr) binario; (*track and field*) (sports) atletica leggera; (*for horses*) (sports) galoppatoio; (*for running*) (sports) pista, corsia; **to keep track of** non perder di vista; **to lose track of** perder di vista; **to make tracks** (coll) affrettarsi; **to stop in one's tracks** (coll) fermarsi di colpo || *tr* rintracciare, seguire le tracce di; lasciare tracce su; **to track down** rintracciare

track'ing sta'tion ['trækɪŋ] *s* (rok) stazione di avvistamento

track'less trol'ley ['træklɪs] *s* filobus *m*

track' meet' *s* incontro di atletica leggera

track'walk'er *s* (rr) guardialinee *m*

tract [trækt] *s* stratto, opuscolo, trattatello; (anat) tubo, canale *m*

traction ['træk∫ən] *s* trazione

trac'tion com'pany *s* società *f* di trasporti urbani

tractor ['træktər] *s* trattore *m;* (*of a tractor-trailer*) motrice *f*

trac'tor-trail'er *s* treno stradale

trade [tred] *s* commercio; affare *m;* occupazione, mestiere *m;* (*people*) commercianti *mpl,* professionisti *mpl;* mercato; (*customers*) clientela; (*in slaves*) tratta || *tr* mercanteggiare; cambiare; **to trade in** dare come pagamento parziale || *intr* trafficare, commerciare; comprare; **to trade in** lavorare in; **to trade on** approfittarsi di

trade'mark' *s* marca *or* marchio di fabbrica

trade' name' *s* ragione sociale

trader ['tredər] *s* trafficante *m*

trade' school' *s* scuola d'avviamento professionale, scuola d'arti e mestieri

trades'man *s* (**-men**) commerciante *m;* artigiano

trade' un'ion *s* sindacato di lavoratori

trade' un'ionist *s* sindacalista *mf*

trade' winds' *spl* alisei *mpl*

trad'ing post' *s* centro di scambi commerciali; (*in stock exchange*) posto delle compravendite

trad'ing stamp' *s* buono premio

tradition [trə'dɪ∫ən] *s* tradizione

traditional [trə'dɪ∫ənəl] *adj* tradizionale

traduce [trə'djus] *or* [trə'dus] *tr* calunniare

traf-fic ['træfɪk] *s* traffico, circolazione; commercio; comunicazione || *v* (*pret & pp* **-ficked;** *ger* **-ficking**) *intr* trafficare

traf'fic cir'cle *s* raccordo a circolazione rotatoria

traf'fic court' *s* tribunale *m* della polizia stradale

traf'fic is'land *s* isola spartitraffico

traf'fic jam' *s* intralcio del traffico, ingorgo stradale

traf'fic light' *s* semaforo

traf'fic man'ager *s* dirigente *m* del traffico; (rr) gestore *m* di stazione

traf'fic sign' *s* segnale *m* di circolazione stradale, cartello indicatore

traf'fic tick'et *s* contravvenzione per violazione del traffico

tragedian [trə'dʒɪdɪ·ən] *s* tragico

trage·dy ['trædʒɪdɪ] *s* (**-dies**) tragedia

tragic ['trædʒɪk] *adj* tragico

trail [trel] *s* sentiero; (*track*) traccia, pista; (*of robe*) strascico, coda; (*of smoke*) pennacchio; (*left by an airplane*) striscia; (*of people*) codazzo || *tr* strascicare; essere sulla fatta di; (*e.g., dust on the road*) sollevare; (*mud*) lasciar cadere || *intr* strascicare; (*said, e.g., of a snake*) strisciare; (*said of a plant*) arrampicarsi; **to trail off** mutare; (*to weaken*) affievolirsi

trailer ['trelər] *s* traino; (*to haul freight*) semirimorchio; (*for living*) carovana, roulotte *f;* (bot) rampicante *m*

train [tren] *s* (*of vehicles*) convoglio; (*of robe*) strascico; (*of thought*) or-

dine *m; (of people)* coda; (rr) treno
|| *tr* addestrare, impratichire; *(a
weapon)* puntare, rivolgere; *(a
horse)* scozzonare; *(e.g., a dog)* ammaestrare; *(a plant)* far crescere;
(sports) allenare || *intr* addestrarsi;
ammaestrarsi; (sports) allenarsi
trained' nurse' *s* infermiera diplomata
trainer ['trenər] *s* allenatore *m*
training ['trenɪŋ] *s* esercizio, esercitazione; (sports) allenamento
train'ing camp' *s* campo addestramento
train'ing school' *s* scuola di addestramento professionale; riformatorio
train'ing ship' *s* nave *f* scuola
trait [tret] *s* tratto, caratteristica
traitor ['tretər] *s* traditore *m*
traitress ['tretrɪs] *s* traditrice *f*
trajecto·ry [trə'dʒɛktəri] *s* (**-ries**)
traiettoria
tramp [træmp] *s* lunga camminata;
vagabondo; *(hussy)* sgualdrina || *tr*
attraversare; calpestare || *intr* cam-
minare a passi fermi; fare il vagabondo
trample ['træmpəl] *tr* calpestare; (fig)
conculcare || *intr—***to trample on** or
upon calpestare
trampoline ['træmpə,lin] *s* trampolino
di olona per salti mortali
tramp' steam'er *s* carretta
trance [træns] or [trɑns] *s* trance *f;
(dazed condition)* estasi *f*
tranquil ['træŋkwɪl] *adj* tranquillo
tranquilize ['træŋkwɪ,laɪz] *tr* tranquil-
lizzare || *intr* tranquillizzarsi
tranquilizer ['træŋkwɪ,laɪzər] *s* tranquillante *m*
tranquillity [træn'kwɪlɪti] *s* tranquillità
f
transact [træn'zækt] or [træns'ækt] *tr*
sbrigare, trattare
transaction [træn'zækʃən] or [træns-
'ækʃən] *s* disbrigo, operazione
transatlantic [,trænsət'læntɪk] *adj & s*
transatlantico
transcend [træn'sɛnd] *tr* trascendere,
sorpassare || *intr* eccellere
transcribe [træn'skraɪb] *tr* trascrivere
transcript ['trænskrɪpt] *s* copia; traduzione; (educ) copia ufficiale del certificato di studi
transcription [træn'skrɪpʃən] *s* trascrizione
transept ['trænsɛpt] *s* transetto
trans·fer ['trænsfər] *s* trasferimento;
passaggio; *(pattern)* rapporto; *(of
funds)* giro; *(of real estate)* compra-
vendita; (law) voltura || [træns'fʌr]
or ['trænsfər] *v (pret & pp* **-ferred;**
ger **-ferring)** *tr* trasferire, trasportare; *(funds)* stornare; *(a design)*
rapportare; *(real estate)* compraven-
dere || *intr* trasferirsi; cambiare di
treno
trans'fer tax' *s* tassa di successione;
tassa sulla compravendita
transfix [træns'fɪks] *tr* trafiggere; paralizzare, inchiodare
transform [træns'fɔrm] *tr* trasformare;
(elec) trasformare || *intr* trasformarsi
transforma'tional gram'mar [,trænsfər-

'meʃənəl] *s* grammatica trasforma-
tiva
transformer [træns'fɔrmər] *s* trasfor-
matore *m*
transfusion [træns'fjuʒən] *s* trasfusione
transgress [træns'grɛs] *tr* trasgredire;
(a limit or boundry) oltrepassare ||
intr peccare
transgression [træns'grɛʃən] *s* trasgressione; peccato
transient ['trænʃənt] *adj* passeggero,
temporaneo; di passaggio || *s* ospite
mf di passaggio
transistor [træn'zɪstər] *s* transistore *m*
transit ['trænsɪt] or ['trænzɪt] *s* transito
transition [træn'zɪʃən] *s* transizione
transitional [træn'zɪʃənəl] *adj* di transizione
transitive ['trænsɪtɪv] *adj* transitivo ||
s verbo transitivo
transitory ['trænsɪ,tori] *adj* transitorio
translate [træns'let] or ['trænslet] *tr*
tradurre; convertire; *(to transfer)* tra-
sportare || *intr* tradursi
translation [træns'leʃən] *s* traduzione;
trasformazione; (telg) ritrasmissione
translator [træns'letər] *s* traduttore *m*
transliterate [træns'lɪtə,ret] *tr* traslitterare
translucent [træns'lusənt] *adj* traslu-
cido; (fig) chiaro
transmission [træns'mɪʃən] *s* trasmissione; (aut) trasmissione
trans·mit [træns'mɪt] *v (pret & pp*
-mitted; *ger* **-mitting)** *tr & intr* trasmettere
transmitter [træns'mɪtər] *s* trasmettitore *m*
transmit'ting set' *s* emittente *f*
transmit'ting sta'tion *s* stazione tra-
smettitrice
transmute [træns'mjut] *tr & intr* trasmutare
transom ['trænsəm] *s (crosspiece)* traversa; *(window over door)* vasistas
m; (naut) specchio di poppa
transparen·cy ['træns'pɛrənsi] *s* (**-cies**)
trasparenza; *(design on a translucent
substance)* trasparente *m;* (phot) diapositiva
transparent [træns'pɛrənt] *adj* trasparente
transpire [træns'paɪr] *intr (to happen)*
avvenire; *(to perspire)* traspirare; *(to
become known)* trapelare
transplant [træns'plænt] or [træns-
'plɑnt] *tr* trapiantare || *intr* trapian-
tarsi
transport ['trænspɔrt] *s* trasporto;
mezzo di trasporto || [træns'pɔrt] *tr*
trasportare
transportation [,trænspɔr'teʃən] *s* trasporto; trasporti *mpl*, locomozione;
biglietto di trasporto
trans'port work'er *s* ferrotranviere *m*
transpose [træns'poz] *tr* trasporre;
(mus) trasportare
trans·ship [træns'ʃɪp] *v (pret & pp*
-shipped; *ger* **-shipping)** *tr* trasbordare
trap [træp] *s* trappola, tranello;

(*double-curved pipe*) sifone *m;* (slang) bocca; (sports) congegno lanciapiattelli || *v* (*pret* & *pp* **trapped;** ger **trapping**) *tr* intrappolare, accalappiare

trap' door' *s* trabocchetto, botola; (theat) ribalta

trapeze [trəˈpiz] *s* (sports) trapezio

trapezoid [ˈtræpɪˌzɔɪd] *s* (geom) trapezio, trapezoide *m*

trapper [ˈtræpər] *s* cacciatore *m* di animali da pelliccia con trappole

trappings [ˈtræpɪŋz] *spl* ornamenti *mpl;* (*for a horse*) gualdrappa

trap'shoot'ing *s* tiro al piattello

trash [træʃ] *s* immondizia, spazzatura; (*nonsense*) sciocchezze *fpl;* (*junk*) ciarpame *m;* (*worthless people*) gentaglia

trash' can' *s* portaimmondizie *m*

travail [ˈtrævel] *or* [trəˈvel] *s* travaglio; travaglio di parto

trav·el [ˈtrævəl] *s* viaggio; traffico; (mach) corsa || *v* (*pret* & *pp* **-eled** *or* **-elled;** ger **-eling** *or* **-elling**) *tr* viaggiare per, percorrere || *intr* viaggiare; muoversi; (coll) andare

trav'el a'gency *s* ufficio turistico

traveler [ˈtrævələr] *s* viaggiatore *m*

trav'eler's check' *s* assegno viaggiatori

trav'eling bag' *s* sacca da viaggio

trav'eling expens'es *spl* spese *fpl* di viaggio; (*per diem*) trasferta

trav'eling sales'man *s* (**-men**) commesso viaggiatore

traverse [ˈtrævərs] *or* [trəˈvʌrs] *tr* attraversare

traves·ty [ˈtrævɪsti] *s* (**-ties**) parodia || *v* (*pret* & *pp* **-tied**) *tr* parodiare

trawl [trɔl] *s* (*fishing net*) rete *f* a strascico; (*fishing line*) lenza al traino || *tr* & *intr* pescare con la rete a strascico; pescare con la lenza al traino

trawling [ˈtrɔlɪŋ] *s* pesca con la rete a strascico; pesca con la lenza al traino

tray [tre] *s* guantiera, vassoio; (chem, phot) bacinella

treacherous [ˈtrɛtʃərəs] *adj* traditore, subdolo; incerto, pericoloso

treacher·y [ˈtrɛtʃəri] *s* (**-ies**) tradimento

tread [trɛd] *s* (*step*) passo; (*of shoe*) suola; (*of tire*) battistrada *m;* (*of stairs*) pedata || *v* (*pret* **trod** [trɑd]; *pp* **trodden** [ˈtrɑdən] *or* **trod**) *tr* calpestare; (*the boards*) calcare; accoppiarsi con || *intr* camminare; **to tread on** calpestare

treadle [ˈtrɛdəl] *s* pedale *m*

tread'mill' *s* ruota azionata col camminare; (fig) lavoro ingrato

treason [ˈtrizən] *s* tradimento

treasonable [ˈtrizənəbəl] *adj* traditore

treasure [ˈtrɛʒər] *s* tesoro || *tr* far tesoro di

treasurer [ˈtrɛʒərər] *s* tesoriere *m*

treas'ure hunt' *s* caccia al tesoro

treasur·y [ˈtrɛʒəri] *s* (**-ies**) tesoreria; tesoro, erario

treat [trit] *s* trattenimento; (*something affording pleasure*) piacere *m,* diletto || *tr* trattare; (*to cure*) curare, medi-

care; offrire un trattenimento a || *intr* trattare; pagare per il trattenimento

treatise [ˈtritɪs] *s* trattato

treatment [ˈtritmənt] *s* trattamento; (*of a theme*) trattazione

trea·ty [ˈtriti] *s* (**-ties**) trattato

treble [ˈtrɛbəl] *adj* (*threefold*) triplo; (mus) soprano || *s* (*person*) soprano *mf;* (*voice*) soprano || *tr* triplicare || *intr* triplicarsi

tree [tri] *s* albero

tree' farm' *s* bosco ceduo

tree' frog' *s* raganella

treeless [ˈtrilɪs] *adj* spoglio, senza alberi

tree'top' *s* cima dell'albero

trellis [ˈtrɛlɪs] *s* traliccio, graticcio

tremble [ˈtrɛmbəl] *s* tremito || *intr* tremare

tremendous [trɪˈmɛndəs] *adj* tremendo

tremor [ˈtrɛmər] *or* [ˈtrimər] *s* tremito; (*of earth*) scossa

trench [trɛntʃ] *s* fosso, canale *m;* (mil) trincea

trenchant [ˈtrɛntʃənt] *adj* mordace, caustico; vigoroso; incisivo

trench' coat' *s* trench *m*

trench' mor'tar *s* lanciabombe *m*

trend [trɛnd] *s* tendenza, orientamento || *intr* tendere, dirigersi

Trent [trɛnt] *s* Trento *f*

trespass [ˈtrɛspəs] *s* (law) intrusione, violazione di proprietà || *intr* entrare senza diritto, intrudersi; peccare; **no trespassing** divieto di passaggio; **to trespass against** peccare contro; **to trespass on** entrare abusivamente in; (*e.g., s.o.'s time*) abusare di; violare

tress [trɛs] *s* treccia

trestle [ˈtrɛsəl] *s* cavalletto; viadotto a cavalletti; ponte *m* a cavalletti

trial [ˈtraɪəl] *s* tentativo, prova; (law) giudizio, processo; **on trial** in prova; (law) sotto processo; **to bring to trial** sottoporre a processo

tri'al and er'ror *s* metodo per tentativo; **by trial and error** a tastoni

tri'al balloon' *s* pallone *m* sonda

tri'al by ju'ry *s* processo con giuria

tri'al ju'ry *s* giuria civile o processuale

tri'al or'der *s* (com) ordine *m* di prova

tri'al run' *s* viaggio di prova

triangle [ˈtraɪˌæŋɡəl] *s* triangolo; (*in drafting*) quartabuono

tribe [traɪb] *s* tribù *f*

tribunal [trɪˈbjunəl] *or* [traɪˈbjunəl] *s* tribunale *m*

tribune [ˈtrɪbjun] *s* tribuna

tributar·y [ˈtrɪbjəˌtɛri] *adj* tributario || *s* (**-ies**) tributario

tribute [ˈtrɪbjut] *s* tributo; **to pay tribute to** (*e.g., beauty*) rendere omaggio a

trice [traɪs] *s* momento, istante *m;* **in a trice** in un batter d'occhio

trick [trɪk] *s* gherminella, inganno; trucco, tiro, scherzo; (*knack*) abilità *f;* (*feat*) atto; (*set of cards won*) presa; turno; (coll) piccola; **to be up to one's old tricks** farne una delle sue; **to play a dirty trick on** fare un brutto tiro a|| *tr* giocare, ingannare

tricker·y ['trɪkəri] *s* (-ies) gherminella, inganno

trickle ['trɪkəl] *s* gocciolio, filo || *intr* gocciolare; (*said of people*) andare or venire alla spicciolata; (*said of news*) trapelare

trickster ['trɪkstər] *s* imbroglione *m*

trick·y ['trɪki] *adj* (-ier; -iest) ingannatore; (*machine*) complicato; (*ticklish to deal with*) delicato

tried [traɪd] *adj* fedele, provato

trifle ['traɪfəl] *s* bazzecola, bagattella; (*small amount of money*) piccolezza, miseria; **a trifle** un po' || *tr*—**to trifle away** sprecare || *intr* gingillarsi; **to trifle with** giocherellare con; scherzare con; divertirsi con

trifling ['traɪflɪŋ] *adj* futile; insignificante, trascurabile

trifocal [traɪ'fokəl] *adj* trifocale || **trifocals** *spl* occhiali *mpl* trifocali

trigger ['trɪɡər] *s* (*of a firearm*) grilletto; (*of any device*) leva di sgancio || *tr* (*a gun*) far sparare; (fig) scatenare

trigonometry [,trɪɡə'nɑmɪtri] *s* trigonometria

trill [trɪl] *s* trillo, gorgheggio; vibrazione; (*speech sound*) (phonet) vibrante *f* || *tr* gorgheggiare; pronunziare con vibrazione || *intr* trillare, gorgheggiare

trillion ['trɪljən] *s* trilione *m*

trilo·gy ['trɪlədʒi] *s* (-gies) trilogia

trim [trɪm] *adj* (**trimmer; trimmest**) lindo, azzimato || *s* condizione; buona condizione; (*dress*) vestito; (*of hair*) taglio, sfumatura; decorazione, ornamento; (*of sails*) orientamento; (aut) attrezzatura della carrozzeria || *v* (*pret & pp* **trimmed**; *ger* **trimming**) *tr* tagliare; (*an edge*) rifilare; adattare; arrangiare; (*Christmas tree*) decorare; (*hair*) sfumare; (*a tree*) potare; ordinare, assettare; (*a sail*) orientare; (aer) equilibrare; (mach) sbavare; (coll) improverare; (coll) bastonare; (*to defeat*) (coll) battere, vincere

trimming ['trɪmɪŋ] *s* ornamento, guarnizione; (coll) battitura, batosta; **trimmings** guarnizioni *mpl*; (mach) sbavatura; (mach) rifilatura

trini·ty ['trɪnɪti] *s* (-ties) (*group of three*) triade *f* || **Trinity** *s* Trinità *f*

trinket ['trɪŋkɪt] *s* (*small ornament*) ninnolo, gingillo; **trinkets** (*trivial objects*) paccottiglia

tri·o ['tri·o] *s* (-os) terzetto

trip [trɪp] *s* viaggio; corsa; (*stumble*) inciampata; (*act of causing s.o. to stumble*) sgambetto; (*error*) passo falso; passo agile || *v* (*pret & pp* **tripped**; *ger* **tripping**) *tr* far inciampare, far cadere; fare lo sgambetto a; cogliere in fallo; (mach) far scattare || *intr* inciampare; fare un passo falso; avanzare saltellando, saltellare; **to trip over** inciampare in

tripartite [traɪ'pɑrtaɪt] *adj* tripartito

tripe [traɪp] *s* trippa; (slang) sciocchezze *fpl*

trip'ham'mer *s* maglio meccanico

triphthong ['trɪfθɔŋ] or ['trɪfθɑŋ] *s* trittongo

triple ['trɪpəl] *adj & s* triplo || *tr* triplicare || *intr* triplicarsi

triplet ['trɪplɪt] *s* (*offspring*) nato da un parto trigemino; (mus, poet) terzina

triplicate ['trɪplɪkɪt] *adj* triplicato || *s* triplice copia || ['trɪplɪ,ket] *tr* triplicare

tripod ['traɪpɑd] *s* (*e.g., for a camera*) treppiede *m*; (*stool with three legs*) tripode *m*

triptych ['trɪptɪk] *s* trittico

trite [traɪt] *adj* trito, ritrito

triumph ['traɪ·əmf] *s* trionfo || *intr* trionfare

trium'phal arch' [traɪ'ʌmfəl] *s* arco trionfale

trivia ['trɪvɪ·ə] *spl* banalità *f*, futilità *f*

trivial ['trɪvɪ·əl] *adj* insignificante, futile, banale

Trojan ['trodʒən] *adj & s* troiano

Tro'jan Horse' *s* cavallo di Troia

Tro'jan War' *s* guerra troiana

troll [trol] *tr & intr* pescare con la lenza al traino, pescare con il cucchiaino

trolley ['trɑli] *s* asta di presa, trolley *m*; carrozza tranviaria, tram *m*

trol'ley bus' *s* filobus *m*

trol'ley car' *s* vettura tranviaria, tram *m*

trol'ley pole' *s* trolley *m*

trollop ['trɑləp] *s* (*slovenly woman*) sciattona; (*hussy*) sgualdrina

trombone ['trɑmbon] *s* trombone *m*

troop [trup] *s* truppa, gruppo; (*of animals*) branco; (*of cavalry*) squadrone *m*; **troops** soldati *mpl* || *intr* raggrupparsi; marciare insieme

trooper ['trupər] *s* soldato di cavalleria; poliziotto a cavallo; **to swear like a trooper** bestemmiare come un turco

tro·phy ['trofi] *s* (-phies) trofeo; (*any memento*) ricordo

tropic ['trɑpɪk] *adj* tropicale || *s* tropico; **tropics** zona tropicale

tropical ['trɑpɪkəl] *adj* tropicale

troposphere ['trɑpə,sfɪr] *s* troposfera

trot [trɑt] *s* trotto || *v* (*pret & pp* **trotted**; *ger* **trotting**) *tr* far trottare; **to trot out** (coll) squadernare, esibire || *intr* trottare

troth [troθ] or [troθ] *s* promessa di matrimonio; **by my troth** affé di Dio; **in troth** in verità; **to plight one's troth** impegnarsi; dare la parola

troubadour ['trubə,dor] or ['trubə,dur] *s* trovatore *m*

trouble ['trʌbəl] *s* disturbo, fastidio; inconveniente *m*, grattacapo; disordine *m*, conflitto; (*of a mechanical nature*) panna, guasto; **not to be worth the trouble** non valere la pena; **that's the trouble** questo è il male; **the trouble is that** il guaio è che; **to be in trouble** essere nei guai; **to be**

looking for trouble andare a cercarsi le grane; **to get into trouble** mettersi nei pasticci; **to have trouble in** + ger durar fatica a + inf; **to take the trouble** incomodarsi || tr molestare, disturbare; (e.g., water) intorbidare; dar del filo da torcere a; **to be troubled with** soffrire di; **to trouble oneself** scomodarsi

trouble' light' s lampada di soccorso

trou·ble·mak'er s mettimale mf

troubleshooter ['trʌbəl͵ʃutər] s localizzatore m di guasti; (in disputes) paciere m, conciliatore m

troubleshooting ['trʌbəl͵ʃutɪŋ] s localizzazione dei guasti; (of disputes) composizione

troublesome ['trʌbəlsəm] adj molesto; difficile

trouble' spot' s luogo di disordini, polveriera

trough [trɔf] or [trɔf] s (to knead bread) madia; (for feeding pigs) trogolo; (for feeding animals) mangiatoia; (for watering animals) abbeveratoio; (gutter) doccia; (between two waves) cavo

troupe [trup] s troupe f

trouper ['trupər] s membro della troupe; vecchio attore; tipo di cui ci si può fidare

trousers ['trauzərz] spl pantaloni mpl

trousseau [tru'so] or ['truso] s (-seaux or -seaus) corredo da sposa

trout [traut] s trota

trouvère [tru'vɛr] s troviero

trowel ['trau·əl] s cazzuola, mestola

Troy [trɔɪ] s Troia

truant ['tru·ənt] s fannullone m; **to play truant** marinare la scuola

truce [trus] s tregua

truck [trʌk] s autocarro, camion m; (tractor-trailer) autotreno; (van) furgone m; (to be moved by hand) carretto; verdura per il mercato; (mach, rr) carrello; (coll) robaccia; (coll) relazioni fpl || tr trasportare per autocarro, autotrasportare

truck'driv'er s camionista m

truck' farm' s fattoria agricola per la produzione degli ortaggi

truculent ['trʌkjələnt] or ['trukjələnt] adj truculento

trudge [trʌdʒ] intr camminare; **to trudge along** camminare laboriosamente, scarpinare

true [tru] adj vero; esatto, conforme; legittimo; infallibile; a livello; **to come true** verificarsi; **true to life** conforme alla realtà

true' cop'y s copia conforme

true-hearted ['tru͵hɑrtɪd] adj fedele

true'love knot' s nodo d'amore

truffle ['trʌfəl] or ['trufəl] s tartufo

truism ['tru·ɪzəm] s truismo

truly ['truli] adv veramente; correttamente; **yours truly** distinti saluti

trump [trʌmp] s (cards) atout m; (Italian cards) briscola; **no trump** senza atout || tr superare; (cards) pigliare con un atout or con una briscola; **to**

trump up inventare, fabbricare || intr giocare un atout or una briscola

trumpet ['trʌmpɪt] s tromba; (toy) trombetta; **to blow one's own trumpet** cantare le proprie lodi || tr strombazzare || intr sonar la tromba; strombazzare; (said of an elephant) barrire

truncheon ['trʌntʃən] s bastone m del comando; (Brit) manganello

trunk [trʌŋk] s (of living body, tree, family, railroad) tronco; (for clothes) baule m; (of elephant) tromba; (aut) bagagliaio; (archit) fusto; (telp) linea principale; **trunks** pantaloncini mpl

trunk' hose' s (hist) brache fpl

truss [trʌs] s (to support a roof) capriata, incavallatura; (based on cantilever system) intralicciatura; (for reducing a hernia) cinto, brachiere m; (bot) infiorescenza || tr legare, assicurare

trust [trʌst] s fede f; speranza; fiducia, custodia; (com) trust m, consorzio; (law) fedecommesso; **in trust** in deposito; come fedecommesso; **on trust** a credito || tr fidarsi di; credere (with dat); (to entrust) dare in deposito a; dare a credito a || intr credere; fidarsi, prestar fede; **to trust in** (e.g., a friend) fidarsi di; (God) aver fede in

trust' com'pany s compagnia fedecommissaria; banca di deposito

trustee [trʌs'ti] s amministratore m; fiduciario; (of a university) curatore m; (of an estate) fedecommissario

trusteeship [trʌs'ti͵ɪp] s amministrazione; (law) fedecommisso; (pol) amministrazione fiduciaria

trustful ['trʌstfəl] adj fiducioso

trust'wor'thy adj fidato, di fiducia

trust·y ['trʌsti] adj (-ier; -iest) fidato || s (-ies) carcerato degno di fiducia

truth [truθ] s verità f; **in truth** in verità

truthful ['truθfəl] adj verace, veritiero

try [traɪ] s (tries) tentativo, prova || v (pret & pp tried) tr provare; (s.o.'s patience) mettere a dura prova; (a person) (law) processare; (a case) (law) giudicare; **to try on** (clothes) provare; **to try out** provare, esperimentare || intr cercare, tentare; **to try out for** cercare di ottenere il posto di; (sports) cercare di farsi accettare in; **to try to** cercare di

trying ['traɪ·ɪŋ] adj duro, penoso, difficile

tryst [trɪst] or [traɪst] s appuntamento

T'-shirt' s maglietta

tub [tʌb] s tino, bigoncia; vasca da bagno; (clumsy boat) (slang) carretta; (fat person) (slang) bombolo

tube [tjub] or [tub] s tubo; (e.g., for toothpaste) tubetto; (of tire) camera d'aria; (anat) tuba, tromba; (coll) ferrovia sotterranea

tuber ['tjubər] or ['tubər] s tubero

tubercle ['tjubərkəl] or ['tubərkəl] s tubercolo

tuberculosis [tju͵bɑrkjəˈlosɪs] or [tu-͵bɑrkjəˈlosɪs] *s* tubercolosi *f*

tuck [tʌk] *s* basta ‖ *tr* ripiegare; **to tuck away** nascondere; (slang) fare una scorpacciata di; **to tuck in** rincalzare; **to tuck up** rimboccare

tucker [ˈtʌkər] *s* collarino di merletto ‖ *tr*—**to tucker out** (coll) stancare

Tuesday [ˈtjuzdɪ] or [ˈtuzdɪ] *s* martedì *m*

tuft [tʌft] *s* (*of feathers*) pennacchio; (*of hair*) cernecchio; (*of flowers*) cespo; (*fluffy threads*) fiocco, nappa ‖ *tr* impunture; adornare di fiocchi ‖ *intr* crescere a cernecchi

tug [tʌg] *s* strattone *m*, strappata; (*struggle*) lotta; (*boat*) rimorchiatore *m* ‖ *v* (*pret & pp* **tugged**) *ger* **tugging**) *tr* tirare; (*a boat*) rimorchiare ‖ *intr* tirare con forza; lottare

tug'boat' *s* rimorchiatore *m*

tug' of war' *s* tiro alla fune

tuition [tjuˈɪʃən] or [tuˈɪʃən] *s* (*instruction*) insegnamento; tassa scolastica

tulip [ˈtjulɪp] or [ˈtulɪp] *s* tulipano

tumble [ˈtʌmbəl] *s* rotolone *m*, ruzzolone *m*; (*somersault*) salto mortale; caduta; disordine *m*, confusione; (*confused heap*) mucchio ‖ *intr* rotolare, ruzzolare; cadere, capitombolare; gettarsi; rigirarsi; **to tumble down** cadere in rovina; **to tumble to** (coll) rendersi conto di

tum'ble-down' *adj* dilapidato

tumbler [ˈtʌmblər] *s* (*acrobat*) saltimbanco; (*glass*) bicchiere *m*; (*in a lock*) levetta; (*toy*) misirizzi *m*

tumor [ˈtjumər] or [ˈtumər] *s* tumore *m*

tumult [ˈtjumʌlt] or [ˈtumʌlt] *s* tumulto

tun [tʌn] *s* botte *f*, barile *m*

tuna [ˈtunə] *s* tonno

tune [tjun] or [tun] *s* (*air*) aria; (*manner of speaking*) tono; **in tune** intonato; **out of tune** stonato; **to change one's tune** cambiare di tono ‖ *tr* intonare; **to tune in** (rad) sintonizzare; **to tune out** (rad) interrompere la sintonizzazione di; **to tune up** (*a motor*) mettere a punto; (mus) intonare

tuner [ˈtunər] or [ˈtjunər] *s* (rad) sintonizzatore *m*; (mus) accordatore *m*

tungsten [ˈtʌŋstən] *s* tungsteno

tunic [ˈtjunɪk] or [ˈtunɪk] *s* tunica

tun'ing coil' [ˈtjunɪŋ] or [ˈtunɪŋ] *s* bobina di sintonia

tun'ing fork' *s* diapason *m*, corista *m*

Tunis [ˈtjunɪs] or [ˈtunɪs] *s* Tunisi *f*

Tunisia [tjuˈnɪʒə] or [tuˈnɪʒə] *s* la Tunisia

Tunisian [tjuˈnɪʒən] or [tuˈnɪʒən] *adj & s* tunisino

tun·nel [ˈtʌnəl] *s* tunnel *m*, traforo, galleria; (min) galleria ‖ *v* (*pret & pp* **-neled** or **-nelled**) *ger* **-neling** or **-nelling**) *tr* costruire un passaggio attraverso o sotto a

turban [ˈtʌrbən] *s* turbante *m*

turbid [ˈtʌrbɪd] *adj* turbido

turbine [ˈtʌrbɪn] or [ˈtʌrbaɪn] *s* turbina

turbojet [ˈtʌrboˌdʒɛt] *s* turboreattore *m*

turboprop [ˈtʌrboˌprɑp] *s* turboelica *m*

turbulent [ˈtʌrbjələnt] *adj* turbolento

tureen [tuˈrin] or [tjuˈrin] *s* terrina

turf [tʌrf] *s* zolla erbosa; (peat) torba; **the turf** il campo delle corse; **le corse**, il turf

turf'man *s* (**-men**) amatore *m* delle corse ippiche

Turk [tʌrk] *s* turco

turkey [ˈtʌrki] *s* tacchino ‖ **Turkey** *s* la Turchia

turk'ey vul'ture *s* (Cathartes aura) avvoltoio americano

Turkish [ˈtʌrkɪʃ] *adj & s* turco

Turk'ish tow'el *s* asciugamano spugna

turmoil [ˈtʌrmɔɪl] *s* subbuglio

turn [tʌrn] *s* giro; (*time for action*) turno, volta; (*change of direction*) voltata; (*bend*) svolta, curva; (*of events*) piega; servizio; inclinazione, attitudine *f*; (*of key*) mandata; (*of coil*) spira; (coll) colpo, sussulto; (aer, naut) virata; **at every turn** a ogni piè sospinto; **in turn** a tua (Sua, vostra, etc.) volta; **to be one's turn** toccare a qlcu, e.g., **it's your turn** tocca a Lei; **to take turns** fare a turno ‖ *tr* girare, voltare; (soil) rovesciare; cambiare; (*to make sour*) coagulare; (*to translate*) tradurre; (e.g., *ten years*) raggiungere; (e.g., *one's eyes*) volgere; (*on a lathe*) tornire; (e.g., *a coat*) rivoltare; (*to twist*) torcere; (*the wheel*) (aut) sterzare; **to turn against** mettere su contro; **to turn around** rigirare; (*s.o.'s words*) ritorcere; **to turn aside** sviare; **to turn away** cacciare via; **to turn back** ricacciare; restituire; (*the clock*) ritardare; **to turn down** ripiegare; (*the light*) abbassare; (*an offer*) rifiutare; **to turn in** ripiegare; denunziare; rassegnare; **to turn off** (e.g., *light*) spegnere, smorzare; (gas, water, etc.) tagliare; (e.g., *a faucet*) chiudere; **to turn on** (e.g., *light, radio, etc.*) accendere; (e.g., *a faucet*) aprire; **to turn out** mettere alla porta; (animals) fare uscire dalla stalla; rivoltare; (light) spegnere; produrre, fabbricare; **to turn up** ripiegare in su, rimboccare; (*on a lathe*) tornire; tirar su; (*a card*) scoprire; trovare; (e.g., *the radio*) alzare ‖ *intr* girare; svoltare, e.g., **turn left at the corner** svolti a sinistra all'angolo; girarsi; cambiare; fermentare; cambiare di colore; diventare; (naut) virare; **to turn against** voltarsi contro; inimicarsi con; **to turn around** fare una giravolta; **to turn aside** or **away** sviarsi; **to turn back** ritornare; retrocedere; **to turn down** piegarsi in giù; rovesciarsi; **to turn in** piegarsi, ripiegarsi; tornare a casa; (coll) andare a dormire; **to turn into** sfogare in; trasformarsi in; **to turn on** voltarsi contro; girarsi su; dipendere da; occuparsi di; **to turn**

out riuscire; **to turn out to be** manifestarsi; riuscire ad essere; **to turn over** rotolarsi; rovesciarsi; **to turn up** voltarsi all'insù; alzarsi; apparire, farsi vedere

turn'buck'le s tenditore m

turn'coat' s voltagabbana mf; **to become a turncoat** voltar gabbano

turn'down' adj (collar) rovesciato ‖ s rifiuto

turn'ing point' s punto decisivo

turnip ['tʌrnɪp] s rapa

turn'key' s secondino, carceriere m

turn' of life' s menopausa

turn' of mind' s disposizione naturale

turn'out' s (gathering of people) concorso; (crowd) folla; produzione; (outfit) vestito; stile m, moda; (in a road) slargo, piazzola; (horse and carriage) equipaggio; (rr) binario laterale

turn'over' s (upset) rovesciamento, ribaltamento; (of customers) movimento di clienti; (of business) giro d'affari; rotazione di lavoratori; (com) ciclo operativo

turn'pike' s autostrada a pedaggio

turn' sig'nal s (aut) indicatore m di direzione, lampeggiatore m

turnstile ['tʌrn‚staɪl] s tornello

turn'ta'ble s (of phonograph) piatto rotante; (rr) piattaforma girevole

turpentine ['tʌrpən‚taɪn] s trementina

turpitude ['tʌrpɪ‚tjud] or ['tʌrpɪ‚tud] s turpitudine f

turquoise ['tʌrkɔɪz] or ['tʌrkwɔɪz] s turchese m

turret ['tʌrɪt] s torretta

turtle ['tʌrtəl] s tartaruga; **to turn turtle** rovesciarsi, capovolgersi

tur'tle-dove' s tortora

Tuscan ['tʌskən] adj & s toscano

Tuscany ['tʌskəni] s la Toscana

tusk [tʌsk] s zanna

tussle ['tʌsəl] s lotta, zuffa ‖ intr lottare, azzuffarsi

tutor ['tjutər] or ['tutər] s istitutore privato, ripetitore m; (guardian) tutore m ‖ tr dare ripetizione a ‖ intr dare ripetizioni; studiare con un ripetitore

tuxe·do [tʌk'sido] s (-dos) smoking m

twaddle ['twadəl] s sciocchezze fpl ‖ intr dire sciocchezze

twang [twæŋ] s (of musical instrument) suono vibrato; (of voice) timbro nasale ‖ tr pizzicare; dire con un timbro nasale ‖ intr parlare con voce nasale

twang·y ['twæŋi] adj (-ier; -iest) (tone) metallico; (voice) nasale

tweed [twid] s tweed m; **tweeds** abito di tweed

tweet [twit] s pigolio ‖ intr pigolare

tweeter ['twitər] s altoparlante m per alte audiofrequenze, tweeter m

tweezers ['twizərz] spl pinzette fpl

twelfth [twelfθ] adj, s & pron dodicesimo ‖ s (in dates) dodici m

Twelfth'-night' s vigilia dell'Epifania; sera dell'Epifania

twelve [twelv] adj & pron dodici ‖ s dodici m; **twelve o'clock** le dodici

twentieth ['twentɪ‚ɪθ] adj, s & pron ventesimo ‖ s (in dates) venti m

twen·ty ['twenti] adj & pron venti ‖ s (-ties) venti m; **the twenties** gli anni venti

twice [twaɪs] adv due volte

twice'-told' adj detto più di una volta; detto e ridetto

twiddle ['twɪdəl] tr—**to twiddle one's thumbs** rigirare i pollici, oziare

twig [twɪg] s ramoscello; **twigs** sterpi mpl

twilight ['twaɪ‚laɪt] adj crepuscolare ‖ s crepuscolo

twill [twɪl] s diagonale m ‖ tr tessere in diagonale

twin [twɪn] adj & s gemello

twine [twaɪn] s spago ‖ tr intrecciare ‖ intr intrecciarsi

twinge [twɪndʒ] s punta, dolore acuto

twinkle ['twɪŋkəl] s scintillio; batter m d'occhio ‖ intr scintillare

twin'-screw' adj a due eliche

twirl [twʌrl] s giro, mulinello ‖ tr girare; (slang) lanciare ‖ intr girare rapidamente, frullare

twist [twɪst] s curva; giro; viluppo, intreccio; tendenza, inclinazione; (yarn) ritorno; (e.g., of lemon) fettina; (dance) twist m ‖ tr intrecciare; torcere; (e.g., the face) contorcere; (the meaning) stravolgere, stiracchiare; girare ‖ intr intrecciarsi; torcersi, divincolarsi; girare; serpeggiare; **to twist and turn** (in bed) girarsi e rigirarsi

twister ['twɪstər] s (coll) tromba d'aria

twit [twɪt] v (pret & pp **twitted;** ger **twitting**) tr ridicolizzare

twitch [twɪtʃ] s tic m; (jerk) strattone m; (to restrain a horse) torcinaso ‖ intr contrarsi; tremare; **to twitch at** tirare

twitter ['twɪtər] s garrito, cinguettio; (chatter) chiacchierio; ansia, agitazione ‖ intr garrire, cinguettare; chiacchierare; tremare d'ansia

two [tu] adj & pron due ‖ s due m; **to put two and two together** arrivare alle logiche conclusioni; **two o'clock** le due

two'-cy'cle adj a due tempi

two'-cyl'inder adj a due cilindri

two-edged ['tu‚edʒd] adj a doppio filo

two'fold' adj duplice, doppio

two' hun'dred adj, s & pron duecento

twosome ['tusəm] s coppia

two'-time' tr (slang) fare le corna a

two'-way ra'dio s ricetrasmettitore m

tycoon [taɪ'kun] s magnate m

type [taɪp] s tipo; (typ) carattere m; (pieces collectively) (typ) caratteri mpl ‖ tr scrivere a macchina; simbolizzare ‖ intr scrivere a macchina

type'face' s stile m di carattere

type'script' s dattiloscritto

typesetter ['taɪp‚setər] s (person) compositore m; (machine) compositrice f

type′write′ v (pret **-wrote;** pp **-written**) tr & intr dattilografare, scrivere a macchina
type′writ′er s (machine) macchina da scrivere; (typist) dattilografo
type′writ′ing s dattilografia, scrittura a macchina; lavoro battuto a macchina
ty′phoid fe′ver [ˈtaɪfɔɪd] s febbre f tifoide
typhoon [taɪˈfun] s tifone m
typical [ˈtɪpɪkəl] adj tipico
typi·fy [ˈtɪpɪˌfaɪ] v (pret & pp **-fied**) tr simbolizzare

typist [ˈtaɪpɪst] s dattilografo
typographic(al) [ˌtaɪpəˈgræfɪk(əl)] adj tipografico
typograph′ical er′ror s errore m di stampa
typography [taɪˈpɑgrəfi] s tipografia
tyrannic(al) [tɪˈrænɪk(əl)] or [taɪˈrænɪk(əl)] adj tirannico
tyrannous [ˈtɪrənəs] adj tiranno
tyrant [ˈtaɪrənt] s tiranno
ty·ro [ˈtaɪro] s (**-ros**) principiante m
Tyrrhe′nian Sea′ [tɪˈrinɪ·ən] s Mare Tirreno

U

U, u [ju] s ventunesima lettera dell'alfabeto inglese
ubiquitous [juˈbɪkwɪtəs] adj ubiquo
udder [ˈʌdər] s mammella
ugliness [ˈʌglɪnɪs] s bruttezza
ug·ly [ˈʌgli] adj (**-lier; -liest**) brutto
Ukraine, the [ˈjukren] or [juˈkren] s l'Ucraina f
Ukrainian [juˈkrenɪ·ən] adj & s ucraino
ulcer [ˈʌlsər] s piaga, ulcera; (corrupting element) (fig) piaga
ulcerate [ˈʌlsəˌret] tr ulcerare ‖ intr ulcerarsi
ulterior [ʌlˈtɪrɪ·ər] adj ulteriore; (motive) nascosto, secondo
ultimate [ˈʌltɪmɪt] adj ultimo
ultima·tum [ˌʌltɪˈmetəm] s (**-tums** or **-ta** [tə]) ultimato
ultimo [ˈʌltɪˌmo] adv del mese scorso
ul′tra-high fre′quency [ˈʌltrəˈhaɪ] s frequenza ultraelevata
ultrashort [ˌʌltrəˈʃɔrt] adj ultracorto
ultraviolet [ˌʌltrəˈvaɪ·əlɪt] adj & s ultravioletto
umbil′ical cord′ [ʌmˈbɪlɪkəl] s cordone m ombelicale
umbrage [ˈʌmbrɪdʒ] s—**to take umbrage at** adombrarsi per
umbrella [ʌmˈbrɛlə] s ombrello, paracqua m; (mil) ombrello
umbrel′la stand′ s portaombrelli m
Umbrian [ˈʌmbrɪ·ən] adj & s umbro
umlaut [ˈumlaut] s metafonesi f; (mark) dieresi f ‖ tr cambiare il timbro di; scrivere con dieresi
umpire [ˈʌmpaɪr] s arbitro ‖ tr arbitrare ‖ intr fare l'arbitro
UN [ˈjuˈɛn] s (letterword) (**United Nations**) ONU f
unable [ʌnˈebəl] adj incapace; **to be unable to** essere impossibilitato a, non potere
unabridged [ˌʌnəˈbrɪdʒd] adj integrale, non abbreviato
unaccented [ʌnˈæksɛntɪd] or [ˌʌnækˈsɛntɪd] adj non accentato, atono
unacceptable [ˌʌnəkˈsɛptəbəl] adj inaccettabile
unaccountable [ˌʌnəˈkauntəbəl] adj irresponsabile; inesplicabile
unaccounted-for [ˌʌnəˈkauntɪd ˌfɔr]

adj (e.g., failure) inesplicato; (e.g., soldier) irreperibile, mancante
unaccustomed [ˌʌnəˈkʌstəmd] adj (unusual) insolito; non abituato
unafraid [ˌʌnəˈfred] adj impavido
unaligned [ˌʌnəˈlaɪnd] adj non impegnato
unanimity [ˌjunəˈnɪmɪti] s unanimità f
unanimous [juˈnænɪməs] adj unanime
unanswerable [ʌnˈænsərəbəl] adj per cui non vi è risposta; (argument) irrefutabile, incontestabile
unappreciative [ˌʌnəˈpriʃɪˌetɪv] adj sconoscente, ingrato
unapproachable [ˌʌnəˈprotʃəbəl] adj inabbordabile; incomparabile
unarmed [ʌnˈɑrmd] adj disarmato, inerme
unascertainable [ʌnˌæsərˈtenəbəl] adj non verificabile
unassailable [ˌʌnəˈseləbəl] adj inattaccabile
unassembled [ˌʌnəˈsɛmbəld] adj smontato
unassuming [ˌʌnəˈsumɪŋ] or [ˌʌnəˈsjumɪŋ] adj modesto, semplice
unattached [ˌʌnəˈtæt/t] adj indipendente; (loose) sciolto; non sposato; non fidanzato
unattainable [ˌʌnəˈtenəbəl] adj inarrivabile, irraggiungibile
unattractive [ˌʌnəˈtræktɪv] adj poco attraente
unavailable [ˌʌnəˈveləbəl] adj non disponibile
unavailing [ˌʌnəˈvelɪŋ] adj futile
unavoidable [ˌʌnəˈvɔɪdəbəl] adj inevitabile, ineluttabile
unaware [ˌʌnəˈwer] adj inconsapevole, ignaro ‖ adv inaspettatamente; (unknowingly) inavvertitamente
unawares [ˌʌnəˈwerz] adv inaspettatamente; (unknowingly) inavvertitamente
unbalanced [ʌnˈbælənst] adj sbilanciato, squilibrato
unbandage [ʌnˈbændɪdʒ] tr sbendare
un·bar [ʌnˈbɑr] v (pret & pp **-barred;** ger **-barring**) tr disserrare il chiavistello di
unbearable [ʌnˈberəbəl] adj insopportabile, insostenibile

unbeatable [ʌn'bitəbəl] *adj* imbattibile
unbecoming [ˌʌnbɪ'kʌmɪŋ] *adj* sconveniente, indegno; (*e.g.*, *hat*) disadatto, che non sta bene
unbelievable [ˌʌnbɪ'livəbəl] *adj* incredibile
unbeliever [ˌʌnbɪ'livər] *s* miscredente *mf*
unbending [ʌn'bɛndɪŋ] *adj* inflessibile
unbiased [ʌn'baɪ·əst] *adj* imparziale, spassionato
un·bind [ʌn'baɪnd] *v* (*pret & pp* **-bound** ['baʊnd]) *tr* slegare
unbleached [ʌn'blit/t] *adj* non candeggiato, al colore naturale
unbolt [ʌn'bolt] *tr* (*a door*) togliere il chiavistello a; sbullonare
unborn [ʌn'bɔrn] *adj* nascituro
unbosom [ʌn'buzəm] *tr* (*a secret*) rivelare; **to unbosom oneself** aprire il proprio animo, sfogarsi
unbound [ʌn'baʊnd] *adj* sciolto, libero; (*book*) non rilegato
unbreakable [ʌn'brekəbəl] *adj* infrangibile
unbridle [ʌn'braɪdəl] *tr* sbrigliare
unbuckle [ʌn'bʌkəl] *tr* sfibbiare
unburden [ʌn'bʌrdən] *tr* scaricare; **to unburden oneself (of)** vuotare il sacco (di)
unburied [ʌn'bɛrid] *adj* insepolto
unbutton [ʌn'bʌtən] *tr* sbottonare
uncalled-for [ʌn'kɔld ˌfɔr] *adj* superfluo, gratuito; fuori di posto, sconveniente
uncanny [ʌn'kæni] *adj* misterioso, straordinario
uncared-for [ʌn'kɛrd ˌfɔr] *adj* negletto, trascurato
unceasing [ʌn'sisɪŋ] *adj* incessante
unceremonious [ˌʌnsɛrɪ'moni·əs] *adj* senza cerimonie
uncertain [ʌn'sʌrtən] *adj* incerto
uncertain·ty [ʌn'sʌrtənti] *s* (**-ties**) incertezza
unchain [ʌn't/en] *tr* scatenare, sferrare
unchangeable [ʌn't/endʒəbəl] *adj* immutabile
uncharted [ʌn't/ɑrtɪd] *adj* inesplorato
unchecked [ʌn't/ɛkt] *adj* incontrollato
uncivilized [ʌn'sɪvɪˌlaɪzd] *adj* incivile
unclad [ʌn'klæd] *adj* svestito
unclaimed [ʌn'klemd] *adj* non reclamato; (*letter*) giacente
unclasp [ʌn'klæsp] *or* [ʌn'klɑsp] *tr* sfibbiare
unclassified [ʌn'klæsɪˌfaɪd] *adj* non classificato; non secreto
uncle ['ʌŋkəl] *s* zio
unclean [ʌn'klin] *adj* immondo
un·clog [ʌn'klɑg] *v* (*pret & pp* **-clogged;** *ger* **-clogging**) *tr* disintasare
unclouded [ʌn'klaʊdɪd] *adj* sereno, senza nubi
uncollectible [ˌʌnkə'lɛktɪbəl] *adj* inesigibile
uncomfortable [ʌn'kʌmfərtəbəl] *adj* scomodo, disagevole
uncommitted [ˌʌnkə'mɪtɪd] *adj* non impegnato
uncommon [ʌn'kɑmən] *adj* raro, straordinario

uncompromising [ʌn'kɑmprəˌmaɪzɪŋ] *adj* intransigente
unconcerned [ˌʌnkən'sʌrnd] *adj* indifferente, noncurante
unconditional [ˌʌnkən'dɪ/ənəl] *adj* incondizionato
uncongenial [ˌʌnkən'dʒini·əl] *adj* antipatico, sgradito
unconquerable [ʌn'kɑŋkərəbəl] *adj* inconquistabile, inespugnabile
unconscionable [ʌn'kɑn/ənəbəl] *adj* senza scrupoli; eccessivo
unconscious [ʌn'kɑn/əs] *adj* (*without awareness*) inconscio, inconsapevole; (*temporarily devoid of consciousness*) incosciente; (*unintentional*) involontario
unconsciousness [ʌn'kɑn/əsnɪs] *s* incoscienza
unconstitutional [ˌʌnkɑnstɪ'tju/ənəl] *or* [ˌʌnkɑnstɪ'tu/ənəl] *adj* incostituzionale
uncontrollable [ˌʌnkən'troləbəl] *adj* incontrollabile, ingovernabile
unconventional [ˌʌnkən'vɛn/ənəl] *adj* non convenzionale, anticonformista
uncork [ʌn'kɔrk] *tr* stappare
uncouple [ʌn'kʌpəl] *tr* sganciare, disconnettere
uncouth [ʌn'kuθ] *adj* zotico, incivile, pacchiano
uncover [ʌn'kʌvər] *tr* scoprire
unction ['ʌŋk/ən] *s* unzione; (fig) untuosità *f*
unctuous ['ʌŋkt/u·əs] *adj* untuoso
uncultivated [ʌn'kʌltɪˌvetɪd] *adj* incolto
uncultured [ʌn'kʌlt/ərd] *adj* incolto, rozzo
uncut [ʌn'kʌt] *adj* non tagliato; (*book*) intonso
undamaged [ʌn'dæmɪdʒd] *adj* indenne, illeso
undaunted [ʌn'dɔntɪd] *adj* imperterrito, impavido
undeceive [ˌʌndɪ'siv] *tr* disingannare
undecided [ˌʌndɪ'saɪdɪd] *adj* indeciso
undefeated [ˌʌndɪ'fitɪd] *adj* invitto
undefended [ˌʌndɪ'fɛndɪd] *adj* indifeso
undefensible [ˌʌndɪ'fɛnsɪbəl] *adj* insostenibile
undefiled [ˌʌndɪ'faɪld] *adj* puro, immacolato
undeniable [ˌʌndɪ'naɪ·əbəl] *adj* innegabile, indubitato
under ['ʌndər] *adj* di sotto; (*lower*) inferiore; (*clothing*) intimo, personale || *adv* sotto; più sotto; **to go under** affondare; cedere; (coll) fallire || *prep* sotto; sotto a; (*e.g.*, *20 years old*) meno di; **under full sail** a vele spiegate; **under lock and key** sotto chiave; **under oath** sotto giuramento; **under penalty of death** sotto pena di morte; **under sail** a vela; **under separate cover** in plico separato; **under steam** sotto pressione; **under the hand and seal of** firmato di pugno di; **under the weather** (coll) un po' indisposto; **under way** già iniziato
un'der·age' *adj* minorenne
un'der·arm' pad' *s* sottoascella *m*

un'der·bid' *v* (*pret & pp* **-bid;** *ger* **-bidding**) *tr* fare un'offerta inferiore a quella di

un'der·brush' *s* sottobosco

un'der·car'riage *s* (aut) telaio; (aer) carrello d'atterraggio

un'der·clothes' *spl* biancheria intima

un'der·consump'tion *s* sottoconsumo

un'der·cov'er *adj* segreto

un'der·cur'rent *s* (*of water*) corrente subacquea; (*of air*) corrente *f* inferiore; (fig) controcorrente *f*

underdeveloped [ˌʌndərdɪˈveləpt] *adj* sottosviluppato

un'der·dog' *s* chi è destinato ad avere la peggio; vittima; **the underdogs** i diseredati

un'der·done' *adj* non cotto abbastanza

un'der·es'timate *tr* sottovalutare

un'der·gar'ment *s* indumento intimo

un'der·go' *v* (*pret* **-went;** *pp* **-gone**) *tr* (*a test*) passare, sottostare (with *dat*); (*surgery*) subire, sottoporsi a; soffrire

un'der·grad'uate *adj* (*student*) non ancora laureato; (*course*) per studenti non ancora laureati ‖ *s* studente universitario che non ha ancora ricevuto il primo diploma

un'der·ground' *adj* sotterraneo; segreto ‖ *s* regione sotterranea; macchia, resistenza ‖ *adv* sottoterra; alla macchia, segretamente

un'der·growth' *s* sterpaglia

underhanded [ˈʌndərˈhændəd] *adj* subdolo, di sottomano

un'der·line' *or* **un'der·line'** *tr* sottolineare

underling [ˈʌndərlɪŋ] *s* tirapiedi *m*

un'der·mine' *tr* scalzare, minare

underneath [ˌʌndərˈniθ] *adj* inferiore ‖ *s* disotto ‖ *adv* sotto, di sotto ‖ *prep* sotto a, sotto

undernourished [ˌʌndərˈnʌrɪʃt] *adj* denutrito, malnutrito

un'der·pass' *s* sottopassaggio

un'der·pay' *s* (*pret & pp* **-paid**) *tr & intr* pagare insufficientemente

un'der·pin' *v* (*pret & pp* **-pinned;** *ger* **-pinning**) *tr* rincalzare

underprivileged [ˌʌndərˈprɪvɪlɪdʒd] *adj* derelitto, diseredato

un'der·rate' *tr* sottovalutare

un'der·score' *tr* sottolineare

un'der·sea' *adj* sottomarino ‖ *adv* sotto il mare

un'der·seas' *adv* sotto il mare

un'der·sec'retar'y *s* (**-ies**) sottosegretario

un'der·sell' *v* (*pret & pp* **-sold**) *tr* vendere a prezzo minore di; (*to sell for less than actual value*) svendere

un'der·shirt' *s* camiciola, canottiera

undersigned [ˈʌndərˌsaɪnd] *adj* sottoscritto

un'der·skirt' *s* sottogonna

un'der·stand' *v* (*pret & pp* **-stood**) *tr* capire, comprendere; sottintendere; (*to accept as true*) constare, e.g., **he understands that you are wrong** gli consta che Lei ha torto ‖ *intr* capire, comprendere

understandable [ˌʌndərˈstændəbəl] *adj* comprensibile

understanding [ˌʌndərˈstændɪŋ] *adj* comprensivo, tollerante ‖ *s* (*mind*) intelletto; (*knowledge*) conoscenza; comprensione, intendimento; (*agreement*) intesa, accordo

understatement [ˌʌndərˈstetmənt] *s* sottovalutazione

un'der·stud'y *s* (**-ies**) (theat) doppio, sostituto ‖ *v* (**-ied**) *tr* (*an actor*) fare il doppio di

un'der·take' *v* (*pret* **-took;** *ger* **-taken**) *tr* intraprendere; (*to promise*) promettere

undertaker [ˈʌndərˈtekər] *or* [ˈʌndərˌtekər] *s* impresario ‖ [ˈʌndərˌtekər] *s* impresario di pompe funebri

undertaking [ˌʌndərˈtekɪŋ] *s* (*task*) impresa; (*promise*) promessa ‖ [ˈʌndərˌtekɪŋ] *s* impresa di pompe funebri

un'der·tone' *s* bassa voce; (*background sound*) ronzio di fondo; tono; colore smorzato

un'der·tow' *s* (*on the beach*) risacca; (*countercurrent below surface*) controcorrente *f*

un'der·wa'ter *adj* subacqueo ‖ *adv* sottacqua

un'der·wear' *s* biancheria intima

un'der·world' *s* (*criminal world*) malavita, teppa; (*abode of spirits*) ade *m*, averno; mondo sotterraneo; mondo sottomarino; antipodi *mpl*

un'der·write' *v* (*pret* **-wrote;** *pp* **-written**) *tr* sottoscrivere; (*to insure*) assicurare

un'der·writ'er *s* sottoscrittore *m*; (ins) assicuratore *m*

undeserved [ˌʌndɪˈzʌrvd] *adj* immeritato

undesirable [ˌʌndɪˈzaɪrəbəl] *adj & s* indesiderabile *mf*

undetachable [ˌʌndɪˈtætʃəbəl] *adj* non movibile

undeveloped [ˌʌndɪˈveləpt] *adj* (*land*) non sfruttato; (*country*) sottosviluppato

undigested [ˌʌndɪˈdʒestɪd] *adj* non digerito

undignified [ʌnˈdɪgnɪˌfaɪd] *adj* poco decoroso

undiscernible [ˌʌndɪˈzʌrnɪbəl] *or* [ˌʌndɪˈsʌrnɪbəl] *adj* impercettibile

undisputed [ˌʌndɪˈspjutəd] *adj* indiscusso, incontrastato

un·do' [ʌnˈdu] *v* (*pret* **-did;** *pp* **-done**) *tr* sfare, disfare; rovinare; (*a package*) aprire; (*a knot*) sciogliere

undoing [ʌnˈduˌɪŋ] *s* rovina

undone [ʌnˈdʌn] *adj* non finito; **to come undone** disfarsi; **to leave nothing undone** non tralasciare di fare nulla

undoubtedly [ʌnˈdautidli] *adv* indubbiamente, senza dubbio

undress [ˈʌnˌdres] *or* [ʌnˈdres] *s* vestaglia; vestito da ogni giorno ‖ [ʌnˈdres] *tr* spogliare, svestire; (*a* *wound*) sbendare ‖ *intr* spogliarsi, svestirsi

undrinkable [ʌn'drɪŋkəbəl] *adj* imbevibile, non potabile

undue [ʌn'dju] or [ʌn'du] *adj* indebito; immeritato; eccessivo

undulate ['ʌndjəˌlet] *intr* ondulare

unduly [ʌn'djuli] or [ʌn'duli] *adv* indebitamente, eccessivamente

unearned [ʌn'ɑrnd] *adj* non guadagnato col lavoro; immeritato; non ancora guadagnato

un'earned in'crement *s* plusvalenza

unearth [ʌn'ɑrθ] *tr* dissotterrare

unearthly [ʌn'ɑrθli] *adj* ultraterreno; spettrale; impossibile, straordinario

uneasy [ʌn'izi] *adj* (*worried*) preoccupato; (*constrained*) scomodo; (*not conducive to ease*) inquietante, a disagio

uneatable [ʌn'itəbəl] *adj* immangiabile

uneconomic(al) [ˌʌnikə'nɑmɪk(əl)] or [ˌʌnɛkə'nɑmɪk(əl)] *adj* antieconomico

uneducated [ʌn'ɛdjəˌketɪd] *adj* ineducato

unemployed [ˌʌnɛm'plɔɪd] *adj* disoccupato, incollocato; improduttivo ‖ **the unemployed** i disoccupati

unemployment [ˌʌnɛm'plɔɪmənt] *s* disimpiego, disoccupazione

unemploy'ment compensa'tion *s* sussidio di disoccupazione

unending [ʌn'ɛndɪŋ] *adj* interminabile

unequal [ʌn'ikwəl] *adj* disuguale, impari; **to be unequal to** (*a task*) non essere all'altezza di

unequaled or **unequalled** [ʌn'ikwəld] *adj* ineguagliato

unerring [ʌn'ɑrɪŋ] or [ʌn'ɛrɪŋ] *adj* infallibile; corretto, preciso

unessential [ˌʌnɛ'sɛn∫əl] *adj* non essenziale

uneven [ʌn'ivən] *adj* disuguale, ineguale; (*number*) dispari

uneventful [ˌʌnɪ'vɛntfəl] *adj* senza avvenimenti importanti; (*life*) tranquillo

unexceptionable [ˌʌnɛk'sɛp∫ənəbəl] *adj* ineccepibile, irreprensibile

unexpected [ˌʌnɛk'spɛktɪd] *adj* insospettato, imprevisto

unexplained [ˌʌnɛk'splend] *adj* inesplicato

unexplored [ˌʌnɛk'splord] *adj* inesplorato

unexposed [ˌʌnɛk'spozd] *adj* (phot) non esposto alla luce

unfading [ʌn'fedɪŋ] *adj* immarcescibile; imperituro

unfailing [ʌn'felɪŋ] *adj* immancabile, infallibile; (*inexhaustible*) inesauribile; (*dependable*) sicuro

unfair [ʌn'fɛr] *adj* ingiusto; disonesto, sleale

unfaithful [ʌn'feθfəl] *adj* infedele

unfamiliar [ˌʌnfə'mɪljər] *adj* poco pratico; poco abituale, strano; non conosciuto

unfasten [ʌn'fæsən] or [ʌn'fɑsən] *tr* sfibbiare, sciogliere

unfathomable [ʌn'fæðəməbəl] *adj* insondabile

unfavorable [ʌn'fevərəbəl] *adj* sfavorevole

unfeeling [ʌn'filɪŋ] *adj* insensibile

unfetter [ʌn'fɛtər] *tr* sciogliere dalle catene

unfinished [ʌn'fɪnɪ/t] *adj* incompiuto; grezzo, non rifinito; (*business*) inevaso

unfit [ʌn'fɪt] *adj* disadatto; inabile

unfledged [ʌn'flɛdʒd] *adj* implume

unfold [ʌn'fold] *tr* schiudere; (*e.g., a newspaper*) spiegare ‖ *intr* schiudersi; svolgersi

unforeseeable [ˌʌnfor'si·əbəl] *adj* imprevedibile

unforeseen [ˌʌnfor'sin] *adj* imprevisto

unforgettable [ˌʌnfər'gɛtəbəl] *adj* indimenticabile

unforgivable [ˌʌnfər'gɪvəbəl] *adj* imperdonabile

unfortunate [ʌn'fɔrtjənɪt] *adj* & *s* disgraziato, sfortunato

unfounded [ʌn'faundɪd] *adj* infondato

un-freeze [ʌn'friz] *v* (*pret* -froze; *pp* -frozen) *tr* disgelare; (*credit*) sbloccare

unfriend·ly [ʌn'frɛndli] *adj* (-lier; -liest) mal disposto, ostile; sfavorevole

unfruitful [ʌn'frutfəl] *adj* infruttuoso

unfulfilled [ˌʌnfəl'fɪld] *adj* incompiuto

unfurl [ʌn'fɑrl] *tr* spiegare, dispiegare

unfurnished [ʌn'fɑrnɪ/t] *adj* smobiliato

ungainly [ʌn'genli] *adj* sgraziato, maldestro

ungentlemanly [ʌn'dʒɛntəlmənli] *adj* indegno di un gentleman

ungird [ʌn'gɑrd] *tr* discingere

ungodly [ʌn'gɑdli] *adj* irreligioso, empio; (*dreadful*) (coll) atroce

ungracious [ʌn'gre∫əs] *adj* rude, scortese; (*task*) sgradevole

ungrammatical [ˌʌngrə'mætɪkəl] *adj* sgrammaticato

ungrateful [ʌn'gretfəl] *adj* ingrato

ungrudgingly [ʌn'grʌdʒɪŋli] *adv* di buon grado, volentieri

unguarded [ʌn'gɑrdɪd] *adj* incustodito, indifeso; incauto, imprudente

unguent ['ʌŋgwənt] *s* unguento

unhappiness [ʌn'hæpɪnɪs] *s* infelicità *f*

unhap·py [ʌn'hæpi] *adj* (-pier; -piest) infelice, sfortunato

unharmed [ʌn'hɑrmd] *adj* illeso

unharness [ʌn'hɑrnɪs] *tr* togliere i finimenti a

unhealth·y [ʌn'hɛlθi] *adj* (-ier; -iest) malsano

unheard-of [ʌn'hɑrd ˌʌv] *adj* (*unknown*) sconosciuto; inaudito

unhinge [ʌn'hɪndʒ] *tr* sgangherare; (fig) sconvolgere

unhitch [ʌn'hɪt/] *tr* sganciare; (*a horse*) staccare

unho·ly [ʌn'holi] *adj* (-lier; -liest) empio; terribile, atroce

unhook [ʌn'huk] *tr* sganciare

unhoped-for [ʌn'hopt ˌfor] *adj* insperato

unhorse [ʌn'hors] *tr* disarcionare

unhurt [ʌn'hʌrt] *adj* incolume, illeso

unicorn ['junɪ ˌkɔrn] *s* unicorno

unification [ˌjunɪfɪ'keʃən] *s* unificazione

uniform ['junɪ ˌfɔrm] *adj* & *s* uniforme *f* ‖ *tr* uniformare

uni·fy ['junɪ ˌfaɪ] *v* (*pret* & *pp* **-fied**) *tr* unificare

unilateral [ˌjunɪ'lætərəl] *adj* unilaterale

unimpeachable [ˌʌnɪm'pitʃəbəl] *adj* irrefutabile; irreprensibile

unimportant [ˌʌnɪm'pɔrtənt] *adj* poco importante

uninhabited [ˌʌnɪn'hæbɪtɪd] *adj* inabitato, disabitato

uninspired [ˌʌnɪn'spaɪrd] *adj* senza ispirazione, prosaico

unintelligent [ˌʌnɪn'telɪdʒənt] *adj* non intelligente; stupido

unintelligible [ˌʌnɪn'telɪdʒɪbəl] *adj* inintelligibile

uninterested [ʌn'ɪntrɪstɪd] *or* [ʌn-'ɪntə ˌrestɪd] *adj* non interessato

uninteresting [ʌn'ɪntrɪstɪŋ] *or* [ʌn-'ɪntə ˌrestɪŋ] *adj* poco interessante

uninterrupted [ˌʌnɪntə'rʌptɪd] *adj* ininterrotto

union ['junjən] *s* unione; unione matrimoniale; (*of workers*) sindacato

unionize ['junjə ˌnaɪz] *tr* organizzare in un sindacato ‖ *intr* organizzarsi in un sindacato

un'ion shop' *s* fabbrica che assume solo sindacalisti

un'ion suit' *s* combinazione

unique [ju'nik] *adj* unico

unison ['junɪsən] *or* ['junɪzən] *s* unisono; **in unison** all'unisono

unit ['junɪt] *adj* unitario ‖ *s* unità *f*; (*mach, elec*) gruppo

unite [ju'naɪt] *tr* unire ‖ *intr* unirsi

united [ju'naɪtɪd] *adj* unito

Unit'ed King'dom *s* Regno Unito

Unit'ed Na'tions *spl* Organizzazione delle Nazioni Unite

Unit'ed States' *adj* statunitense ‖ **the United States** *ssg* gli Stati Uniti

uni·ty ['junɪtɪ] *s* (**-ties**) unità *f*

universal [ˌjunɪ'vʌrsəl] *adj* universale

u'niver'sal joint' *s* giunto cardanico

universe ['junɪ ˌvʌrs] *s* universo

universi·ty [ˌjunɪ'vʌrsɪtɪ] *adj* universitario ‖ *s* (**-ties**) università *f*

unjust [ʌn'dʒʌst] *adj* ingiusto

unjustified [ʌn'dʒʌstɪ ˌfaɪd] *adj* ingiustificato

unkempt [ʌn'kempt] *adj* spettinato; trascurato

unkind [ʌn'kaɪnd] *adj* scortese; duro, crudele

unknowable [ʌn'no·əbəl] *adj* inconoscibile

unknowingly [ʌn'no·ɪŋlɪ] *adv* inconsapevolmente

unknown [ʌn'non] *adj* sconosciuto ‖ *s* incognito; (*math*) incognita

Un'known Sol'dier *s* Milite Ignoto

unlace [ʌn'les] *tr* slacciare

unlatch [ʌn'lætʃ] *tr* tirare il saliscendi a

unlawful [ʌn'lɔfəl] *adj* illegale

unleash [ʌn'liʃ] *tr* sguinzagliare; (fig) scatenare

unleavened [ʌn'levənd] *adj* azzimo

unless [ʌn'les] *conj* se non che, salvo che

unlettered [ʌn'letərd] *adj* ignorante; (*illiterate*) analfabeta

unlike [ʌn'laɪk] *adj* dissimile, differente; dissimile da, e.g., **a copy unlike the original** una copia dissimile dall'originale; (elec) di segno contrario ‖ *prep* diversamente da, a differenza di; **it was unlike him to arrive late** non era cosa normale per lui arrivare in ritardo

unlikely [ʌn'laɪklɪ] *adj* improbabile

unlimber [ʌn'lɪmbər] *tr* mettere in batteria ‖ *intr* prepararsi a fare fuoco; (fig) prepararsi

unlimited [ʌn'lɪmɪtɪd] *adj* illimitato

unlined [ʌn'laɪnd] *adj* (*e.g., coat*) non foderato; (*paper*) non rigato

unload [ʌn'lod] *tr* scaricare; (*passengers*) sbarcare; (*to get rid of*) liberarsi di ‖ *intr* scaricare; sbarcare

unloading [ʌn'lodɪŋ] *s* discarica; sbarco

unlock [ʌn'lɑk] *tr* aprire

unloose [ʌn'lus] *tr* rilasciare; sciogliere

unloved [ʌn'lʌvd] *adj* poco amato

unlovely [ʌn'lʌvlɪ] *adj* poco attraente

unluck·y [ʌn'lʌkɪ] *adj* (**-ier; -iest**) sfortunato, disgraziato

un·make [ʌn'mek] *v* (*pret* & *pp* **-made** ['med]) *tr* disfare; deporre

unmanageable [ʌn'mænɪdʒəbəl] *adj* incontrollabile

unmanly [ʌn'mænlɪ] *adj* non virile, effemminato; codardo

unmannerly [ʌn'mænərlɪ] *adj* scortese

unmarketable [ʌn'mɑrkɪtəbəl] *adj* invendibile

unmarriageable [ʌn'mærɪdʒəbəl] *adj* che non si può sposare; non adatto al matrimonio

unmarried [ʌn'mærɪd] *adj* scapolo; (*female*) nubile

unmask [ʌn'mæsk] *or* [ʌn'mɑsk] *tr* smascherare ‖ *intr* smascherarsi

unmatchable [ʌn'mætʃəbəl] *adj* impareggiabile

unmatched [ʌn'mætʃd] *adj* impareggiabile; (*unpaired*) sparigliato

unmentionable [ʌn'menʃənəbəl] *adj* innominabile

unmerciful [ʌn'mʌrsɪfəl] *adj* spietato

unmesh [ʌn'meʃ] *tr* disingranare ‖ *intr* disingranarsi

unmindful [ʌn'maɪndfəl] *adj* immemore; incurante

unmistakable [ˌʌnmɪs'tekəbəl] *adj* inconfondibile

unmitigated [ʌn'mɪtɪ ˌgetɪd] *adj* completo; assoluto, perfetto

unmixed [ʌn'mɪkst] *adj* puro

unmoor [ʌn'mur] *tr* disormeggiare

unmoved [ʌn'muvd] *adj* immoto; fisso, immobile; (fig) impassibile

unmuzzle [ʌn'mʌzəl] *tr* togliere la museruola a

unnamed [ʌn'nemd] *adj* innominato

unnatural [ʌn'nætʃərəl] *adj* contro natura, snaturato; innaturale, affettato

unnecessary [ʌn'nɛsə ˌsɛri] *adj* inutile

unnerve [ʌn'nʌrv] *tr* snervare

unnoticeable [ʌn'notɪsəbəl] *adj* impercettibile

unnoticed [ʌn'notɪst] *adj* inosservato

unobserved [ˌʌnəb'zʌrvd] *adj* inosservato

unobtainable [ˌʌnəb'tenəbəl] *adj* non ottenibile, irraggiungibile

unobtrusive [ˌʌnəb'trusɪv] *adj* discreto, riservato

unoccupied [ʌn'ɑkjə ˌpaɪd] *adj* libero, disponibile; (*not busy*) disoccupato

unofficial [ˌʌnə'fɪʃəl] *adj* non ufficiale, ufficioso

unopened [ʌn'opənd] *adj* non aperto, chiuso; (*letter*) non dissuggellato; (*book*) intonso

unorthodox [ʌn'ɔrθə ˌdɑks] *adj* non ortodosso

unpack [ʌn'pæk] *tr* spaccare, sballare

unpalatable [ʌn'pælətəbəl] *adj* di gusto spiacevole

unparalleled [ʌn'pærə ˌlɛld] *adj* incomparabile, senza pari

unpardonable [ʌn'pardənəbəl] *adj* imperdonabile

unpatriotic [ˌʌnpetrɪ'ɑtɪk] or [ˌʌnpætrɪ'ɑtɪk] *adj* antipatriottico

unperceived [ˌʌnpər'sivd] *adj* inosservato

unperturbable [ˌʌnpər'tʌrbəbəl] *adj* imperterrito, imperturbato

unpleasant [ʌn'plɛsənt] *adj* spiacevole; (*person*) antipatico

unpopular [ʌn'pɑpjələr] *adj* impopolare

unpopularity [ʌn ˌpɑpjə'læriti] *s* impopolarità *f*

unprecedented [ʌn'prɛsɪ ˌdɛntɪd] *adj* senza precedenti, inaudito

unprejudiced [ʌn'prɛdʒədɪst] *adj* senza pregiudizio, imparziale

unpremeditated [ˌʌnprɪ'mɛdɪ ˌtɛtɪd] *adj* impremeditato

unprepared [ˌʌnprɪ'pɛrd] *adj* impreparato

unprepossessing [ˌʌnprɪpə'zɛsɪŋ] *adj* poco attraente, antipatico

unpresentable [ˌʌnprɪ'zɛntəbəl] *adj* impresentabile

unpretentious [ˌʌnprɪ'tɛnʃəs] *adj* modesto, senza pretese

unprincipled [ʌn'prɪnsɪpəld] *adj* senza principi

unproductive [ˌʌnprə'dʌktɪv] *adj* improduttivo

unprofitable [ʌn'prɑfɪtəbəl] *adj* infruttuoso

unpronounceable [ˌʌnprə'naʊnsəbəl] *adj* impronunziabile

unpropitious [ˌʌnprə'pɪʃəs] *adj* inauspicato

unpublished [ʌn'pʌblɪʃt] *adj* inedito

unpunished [ʌn'pʌnɪʃt] *adj* impunito

unqualified [ʌn'kwɑlɪ ˌfaɪd] *adj* inabile, inidoneo; assoluto, completo

unquenchable [ʌn'kwɛntʃəbəl] *adj* inappagabile, inestinguibile

unquestionable [ʌn'kwɛstʃənəbəl] *adj* indiscutibile

unrav·el [ʌn'rævəl] *v* (*pret & pp* -eled or -elled; *ger* -eling or -elling) *tr* dipanare || *intr* districarsi; chiarirsi

unreachable [ʌn'ritʃəbəl] *adj* irraggiungibile

unreal [ʌn'riəl] *adj* irreale

unreali·ty [ˌʌnri'ælti] *s* (-ties) irrealità *f*

unreasonable [ʌn'rizənəbəl] *adj* irragionevole

unrecognizable [ʌn'rɛkəg ˌnaɪzəbəl] *adj* irriconoscibile

unreel [ʌn'ril] *tr* svolgere, srotolare || *intr* srotolarsi

unrefined [ˌʌnrɪ'faɪnd] *adj* non raffinato, greggio; volgare, ordinario

unrelenting [ˌʌnrɪ'lɛntɪŋ] *adj* inesorabile, inflessibile; indefesso

unreliable [ˌʌnrɪ'laɪ·əbəl] *adj* malfido; (*news*) inattendibile

unremitting [ˌʌnrɪ'mɪtɪŋ] *adj* incessante, costante

unrented [ʌn'rɛntɪd] *adj* da affittare

unrepeatable [ˌʌnrɪpitəbəl] *adj* irripetibile

unrepentant [ˌʌnrɪ'pɛntənt] *adj* impenitente

unrequit'ed love' [ˌʌnrɪ'kwaɪtɪd] *s* amore non corrisposto

unresponsive [ˌʌnrɪ'spɑnsɪv] *adj* apatico, insensibile

unrest [ʌn'rɛst] *s* agitazione

un·rig [ʌn'rɪg] *v* (*pret & pp* -rigged; *ger* -rigging) *tr* (naut) disarmare

unrighteous [ʌn'raɪtʃəs] *adj* ingiusto

unripe [ʌn'raɪp] *adj* immaturo

unrivaled or **unrivalled** [ʌn'raɪvəld] *adj* senza pari

unroll [ʌn'rol] *tr* srotolare

unromantic [ˌʌnro'mæntɪk] *adj* poco romantico

unruffled [ʌn'rʌfəld] *adj* calmo, imperturbabile

unruly [ʌn'ruli] *adj* turbolento; indisciplinato, insubordinato

unsaddle [ʌn'sædəl] *tr* (*a horse*) dissellare; (*a rider*) scavalcare

unsafe [ʌn'sef] *adj* malsicuro, pericolante

unsaid [ʌn'sɛd] *adj* non detto, taciuto; **to leave unsaid** passare sotto silenzio

unsalable [ʌn'seləbəl] *adj* invendibile

unsanitary [ʌn'sænɪ ˌtɛri] *adj* antigienico

unsatisfactory [ʌn ˌsætɪs'fæktəri] *adj* poco soddisfacente

unsatisfied [ʌn'sætɪs ˌfaɪd] *adj* insoddisfatto, inappagato

unsavory [ʌn'sevəri] *adj* insipido; (fig) disgustoso, nauseabondo

un·say [ʌn'se] *v* (*pret & pp* -said [sɛd']) *tr* disdire

unscathed [ʌn'skeðd] *adj* incolume

unscheduled [ʌn'skɛdʒuld] *adj* non in elenco; (*event*) fuori programma; (*e.g., flight*) fuori orario; (*phase of production*) non programmato

unscientific [ˌʌnsaɪ·ən'tɪfɪk] *adj* poco scientifico

unscrew [ʌn'skru] *tr* svitare || *intr* svitarsi

unscrupulous [ʌn'skrupjələs] *adj* senza scrupoli

unseal [ʌn'sil] *tr* dissigillare

unseasonable [ʌn'siːzənəbəl] *adj* fuori stagione; inopportuno

unseasoned [ʌn'siːzənd] *adj* scondito; (*crop*) immaturo; (*crew*) inesperto

unseat [ʌn'siːt] *tr* (*a rider*) scavalcare, disarcionare; (*e.g., a congressman*) far perdere il seggio a, defenestrare

unseemly [ʌn'siːmli] *adj* disdicevole, sconveniente

unseen [ʌn'siːn] *adj* non visto, inosservato; nascosto, occulto; invisibile

unselfish [ʌn'sɛlfɪʃ] *adj* disinteressato

unsettled [ʌn'sɛtəld] *adj* disabitato; disorganizzato; disordinato, erratico; indeciso; (*bill*) da pagare

unshackle [ʌn'ʃækəl] *tr* liberare

unshaken [ʌn'ʃeɪkən] *adj* inconcusso

unshapely [ʌn'ʃepli] *adj* senza forma, deforme

unshaven [ʌn'ʃevən] *adj* non rasato

unshatterable [ʌn'ʃætərəbəl] *adj* infrangibile

unsheathe [ʌn'ʃiːð] *tr* sguainare

unshod [ʌn'ʃɑd] *adj* scalzo; (*horse*) sferrato

unshrinkable [ʌn'ʃrɪŋkəbəl] *adj* irrestringibile

unsightly [ʌn'saɪtli] *adj* ripugnante, brutto

unsinkable [ʌn'sɪŋkəbəl] *adj* insommergibile

unskilled [ʌn'skɪld] *adj* inesperto

un'skilled la'bor *s* lavoro manuale; mano d'opera non specializzata

unskillful [ʌn'skɪlfəl] *adj* maldestro

unsnarl [ʌn'snɑrl] *tr* sbrogliare

unsociable [ʌn'soʃəbəl] *adj* insocievole

unsold [ʌn'sold] *adj* invenduto

unsolder [ʌn'sɑdər] *tr* dissaldare

unsophisticated [ˌʌnsə'fɪstɪˌketɪd] *adj* semplice, puro

unsound [ʌn'saund] *adj* malsano, malato; (*decayed*) guasto, imputridito; falso, fallace; (*sleep*) leggero

unsown [ʌn'son] *adj* incolto, non seminato

unspeakable [ʌn'spikəbəl] *adj* indicibile; (*atrocious*) innominabile, inqualificabile

unsportsmanlike [ʌn'sportsmən,laɪk] *adj* antisportivo

unstable [ʌn'stebəl] *adj* instabile

unsteady [ʌn'stɛdi] *adj* malfermo; incostante; irregolare

unstinted [ʌn'stɪntɪd] *adj* generoso, senza limiti

unstitch [ʌn'stɪtʃ] *tr* scucire

un·stop [ʌn'stɑp] *v* (*pret* & *pp* **-stopped;** *ger* **-stopping**) *tr* stasare

unstressed [ʌn'strest] *adj* non accentuato; (*e.g., syllable*) non accentato

unstrung [ʌn'strʌŋ] *adj* (*beads*) sfilato; (*instrument*) allentato; (*person*) snervato

unsuccessful [ˌʌnsək'sɛsfəl] *adj* (*person*) sfortunato; (*deal*) mancato; **to be unsuccessful** fallire

unsuitable [ʌn'sutəbəl] or [ʌn'sjutəbəl] *adj* inappropriato

unsurpassable [ʌnsər'pæsəbəl] or [ˌʌnsər'pɑsəbəl] *adj* insuperabile

unsuspected [ˌʌnsəs'pɛktɪd] *adj* insospettato

unswerving [ʌn'swʌrvɪŋ] *adj* diritto, fermo, costante

unsympathetic [ˌʌnsɪmpə'θɛtɪk] *adj* indifferente, che non mostra comprensione

unsystematic(al) [ˌʌnsɪstə'mætɪk(əl)] *adj* senza sistema

untactful [ʌn'tæktfəl] *adj* senza tatto

untamed [ʌn'temd] *adj* indomito

untangle [ʌn'tæŋgəl] *tr* sgrovigliare

unteachable [ʌn'titʃəbəl] *adj* indocile; refrattario agli studi

untenable [ʌn'tɛnəbəl] *adj* insostenibile

unthankful [ʌn'θæŋkfəl] *adj* ingrato

unthinkable [ʌn'θɪŋkəbəl] *adj* impensabile

unthinking [ʌn'θɪŋkɪŋ] *adj* irriflessivo

untidy [ʌn'taɪdi] *adj* disordinato

un-tie [ʌn'taɪ] *v* (*pret* & *pp* **-tied;** *ger* **-tying**) *tr* sciogliere; (*a knot*) slacciare, snodare ‖ *intr* sciogliersi

until [ʌn'tɪl] *prep* fino, fino a ‖ *conj* fino a che, finché

untillable [ʌn'tɪləbəl] *adj* incoltivabile

untimely [ʌn'taɪmli] *adj* intempestivo; (*death*) prematuro

untiring [ʌn'taɪrɪŋ] *adj* instancabile

untold [ʌn'told] *adj* non detto, non raccontato; incalcolabile; (*inexpressable*) indicibile

untouchable [ʌn'tʌtʃəbəl] *adj & s* intoccabile *mf*

untouched [ʌn'tʌtʃt] *adj* intatto; insensibile; non menzionato

untoward [ʌn'tord] *adj* sfavorevole; sconveniente, disdicevole

untrammeled or **untrammelled** [ʌn'træməld] *adj* non inceppato

untried [ʌn'traɪd] *adj* non provato

untroubled [ʌn'trʌbled] *adj* tranquillo

untrue [ʌn'tru] *adj* falso

untrustworthy [ʌn'trʌst,wʌrði] *adj* infido, malfido

untruth [ʌn'truθ] *s* falsità *f*, menzogna

untruthful [ʌn'truθfəl] *adj* falso, menzognero

untwist [ʌn'twɪst] *tr* districare ‖ *intr* districarsi

unusable [ʌn'juzəbəl] *adj* inservibile

unused [ʌn'juzd] *adj* inutilizzato; **unused to** [ʌn'justu] disavvezzo a

unusual [ʌn'juʒu·əl] *adj* insolito

unutterable [ʌn'ʌtərəbəl] *adj* impronunciabile; indicibile

unvanquished [ʌn'væŋkwɪʃt] *adj* invitto

unvarnished [ʌn'vɑrnɪʃt] *adj* non verniciato; puro, semplice

unveil [ʌn'vel] *tr* svelare; (*a statue*) scoprire, inaugurare ‖ *intr* scoprirsi

unveiling [ˌʌn'velɪŋ] *s* scoprimento

unvoiced [ʌn'vɔɪst] *adj* non espresso; (*phonet*) sordo

unwanted [ʌn'wɑntɪd] *adj* non desiderato

unwarranted [ʌn'wɑrəntɪd] *adj* ingiustificato

unwary [ʌn'weri] *adj* incauto

unwavering [ʌn'wevərɪŋ] *adj* fermo, incrollabile

unwelcome [ʌn'wɛlkəm] *adj* malaccetto, sgradito

unwell [ʌn'wɛl] *adj* poco bene; **to be**

unwell (*said of a woman*) (coll) avere le mestruazioni

unwholesome [ʌn'holsəm] *adj* malsano

unwieldy [ʌn'wildi] *adj* ingombrante

unwilling [ʌn'wɪlɪŋ] *adj* riluttante

unwillingly [ʌn'wɪlɪŋli] *adv* a malincuore, a controvoglia

un-wind [ʌn'waɪnd] *v* (*pret & pp* -wound* ['waund]) *tr* svolgere || *intr* svolgersi; (*said of a watch*) scaricarsi; (*said of a person*) rilasciarsi

unwise [ʌn'waɪz] *adj* malaccorto

unwished-for [ʌn'wɪʃt,fɔr] *adj* indesiderato, non augurato

unwitting [ʌn'wɪtɪŋ] *adj* involontario

unwonted [ʌn'wʌntid] *adj* insolito

unworldly [ʌn'wʌrdli] *adj* (*not of this world*) non terrestre; (*not interested in things of this world*) non mondano; (*naive*) semplice

unworthy [ʌn'wʌrði] *adj* indegno

un-wrap [ʌn'ræp] *v* (*pret & pp* -wrapped; *ger* -wrapping) *tr* scartare, svolgere, scartocciare

unwrinkled [ʌn'rɪŋkəld] *adj* senza una grinza

unwritten [ʌn'rɪtən] *adj* orale; non scritto; (*blank*) in bianco

unyielding [ʌn'jildɪŋ] *adj* inflessibile

unyoke [ʌn'jok] *tr* liberare dal giogo

up [ʌp] *adj* che va verso la città; diretto al nord; al corrente; finito, terminato; alto; su; (*sports*) pari; **to be up and about** essere in piedi || *s* salita; vantaggio; aumento; **ups and downs** alti e bassi *mpl* || *adv* su; in alto; alla pari; **to be up** essere alzato; (*in sports or games*) essere avanti; **to be up in arms** essere in armi; essere indignato; **to be up to a person** toccare a una persona; **to get up** alzarsi; **to go up** salire; **to keep up** mantenere; continuare; **to keep up with** mantenersi alla pari con; up above lassù; up against (coll) contro; up against it (coll) in una strettoia; up to fino a; (*capable of*) (coll) all'altezza di; (*scheming*) (coll) tramando; what's up? che succede? || *prep* su; sopra; fino a; to go up a river risalire un fiume

up-and-coming ['ʌpən'kʌmɪŋ] *adj* promettente

up-and-doing ['ʌpən'du·ɪŋ] *adj* (coll) intraprendente; (coll) attivo

up-and-up ['ʌpən'ʌp] *s*—**on the up-and-up** (coll) aperto; (coll) apertamente; (coll) in ascesa

up-braid' *tr* rimproverare, strapazzare

upbringing ['ʌp,brɪŋɪŋ] *s* educazione

up'coun'try *adj* all'interno || *s* interno || *adv* verso l'interno

up-date' *tr* aggiornare

upheaval [ʌp'hivəl] *s* sommovimento; (geol) sconvolgimento tellurico

up'hill' *adj* erto, scosceso; arduo, faticoso || *adv* in salita, all'insù

up-hold' *v* (*pret & pp* -held) *tr* alzare; sostenere; difendere

upholster [ʌp'holstər] *tr* tappezzare

upholsterer [ʌp'holstərər] *s* tappezziere *m*

upholster·y [ʌp'holstəri] *s* (-ies) tappezzeria; (*e.g., of cushions*) imbottitura; (aut) selleria

up'keep' *s* manutenzione; spese *fpl* di manutenzione

upland ['ʌplənd] *or* ['ʌplænd] *adj* alto, elevato || *s* terreno elevato

up'lift' *s* elevazione; miglioramento sociale; edificazione || **up'lift'** *tr* elevare

upon [ʌ'pɒn] *prep* su, sopra, in; **upon** + *ger* non appena + *pp*, e.g., **upon arising** non appena alzato; **upon my word!** sulla mia parola!

upper ['ʌpər] *adj* superiore, disopra; (*town*) soprano; (*river*) alto || *s* disopra *m*; (*of shoe*) tomaia; (rr) (coll) cuccetta; **on one's uppers** ridotto al verde

up'per berth' *s* cuccetta superiore

up'per case' *s* (typ) cassa delle maiuscole, cassa superiore

up'per-case' *adj* (typ) maiuscolo

up'per classes *spl* classi *fpl* elevate

up'per hand' *s* vantaggio; **to have the upper hand** prendere il disopra

up'per·most' *adj* (il) più alto; principale || *adv* principalmente, in primo luogo

uppish ['ʌpɪʃ] *adj* (coll) arrogante, snob

up·raise' *tr* alzare, tirare su

up'right' *adj* ritto, verticale; dabbene, onesto || *s* staggio, montante *m* || *adv* verticalmente

uprising [ʌp'raɪzɪŋ] *or* ['ʌp,raɪzɪŋ] *s* sollevazione, insurrezione

up'roar' *s* gazzarra, cagnara, fracasso

uproarious [ʌp'rori·əs] *adj* tumultuoso; (*noisy*) rumoroso; (*funny*) comico

up-root' *tr* sradicare

up·set' *adj* rovesciato; scompigliato; (*emotionally*) scombussolato; (*stomach*) imbarazzato || **up'set'** *s* (*overturn*) rovesciamento; (*defeat*) rovescio; (*disorder*) scompiglio; (*illness*) imbarazzo, disturbo || **up·set'** *v* (*pret & pp* -set; *ger* -setting) *tr* rovesciare; scompigliare; indisporre || *intr* rovesciarsi, ribaltarsi

upset' price' *s* prezzo minimo di vendita di un oggetto all'asta

upsetting [ʌp'setɪŋ] *adj* sconcertante

up'shot' *s* conclusione; essenziale *m*

up'side *s* disopra *m*

up'side down' *adv* alla rovescia; **a gambe all'aria**; a soqquadro

up'stage' *adj* al fondo della scena; altiero, arrogante || *adv* al fondo della scena || *tr* trattare altezzosamente; (theat) rubare la scena a

up'stairs' *adj* del piano di sopra || *s* piano di sopra || *adv* su, al piano di sopra

upstanding [ʌp'stændɪŋ] *adj* diritto; forte; onorevole

up'start' *s* arrivato, nuovo ricco

up'stream' *adv* a monte, controcorrente

up'stroke' *s* (*in handwriting*) tratto ascendente; (mach) corsa ascendente

up'swing' *s* (*in prices*) ascesa; miglioramento; **to be on the upswing** migliorare

up'-to-date' *adj* recentissimo; moderno; dell'ultima ora

up'town' *adj* della parte più alta della città || *adv* nella parte più alta della città

up'trend' *s* tendenza al rialzo

up'turn' *s* rivolta; (com) rialzo

upturned [ʌp'tʌrnd] *adj* rivolto all'insù; (*upside down*) capovolto

upward ['ʌpwərd] *adj* ascendente || *adv* all'insù; **upward of** più di

U'ral Moun'tains ['jurəl] *spl* Urali *mpl*

uranium [ju'reni·əm] *s* uranio

urban ['ʌrbən] *adj* urbano

urbane [ʌr'ben] *adj* urbano

urbanite ['ʌrbə,naɪt] *s* abitante *mf* di una città

urbanity [ʌr'bænɪti] *s* urbanità *f*

urbanize ['ʌrbə,naɪz] *tr* urbanizzare

ur'ban renew'al *s* ricostruzione urbanistica

urchin ['ʌrtʃɪn] *s* monello, birichino

ure·thra [ju'riθrə] *s* (**-thras** or **-thrae** [θri]) uretra

urge [ʌrdʒ] *s* stimolo || *tr* urgere, sollecitare, spronare; (*to endeavor to persuade*) esortare; (*an enterprise*) accelerare || *intr*—**to urge against** opporsi a

urgen·cy ['ʌrdʒənsi] *s* (**-cies**) urgenza

urgent ['ʌrdʒənt] *adj* urgente; (*desire*) prepotente

urinal ['jurɪnəl] *s* (*receptacle*) orinale *m*; (*for a bedridden person*) pappagallo; (*place*) orinatoio, vespasiano

urinary ['jurɪ,neri] *adj* urinario

urinate ['jurɪ,net] *tr* & *intr* orinare

urine ['jurɪn] *s* urina

urn [ʌrn] *s* urna; (*for making coffee*) caffettiera; (*for making tea*) samovar *m*

urology [ju'rɑlədʒi] *s* urologia

Uruguay ['jurə,gwe] or ['jurə,gwaɪ] *s* l'Uruguai *m*

Uruguayan [,jurə'gwe·ən] or [,jurə'gwaɪ·ən] *adj* & *s* uruguaiano

us [ʌs] *pron pers* ci; noi; **to us** ci, a noi, per noi

U.S.A. ['ju'es'e] *s* (letterword) (**United States of America**) S.U.A. *mpl*

usable ['juzəbəl] *adj* servibile, adoperabile

usage ['jusɪdʒ] or ['juzɪdʒ] *s* uso, usanza; (*of a language*) uso

use [jus] *s* uso, impiego, usanza; **in use** in uso, in servizio; **it's no use** non giova; **out of use** disusato; **to be of no use** non servire a nulla; **to have**

no use for non aver bisogno di; non poter soffrire; **to make use of** servirsi di; **what's the use?** a che pro? || [juz] *tr* usare, impiegare, servirsi di; **to use badly** maltrattare; **to use up** consumare, esaurire || *intr*—**used to** translated in Italian in three ways: (1) by the imperfect indicative, e.g., **he used to go to church at seven o'clock** andava in chiesa alle sette; (2) by the imperfect indicative of **solere**, e.g., **he used to smoke all day** soleva fumare tutto il giorno; (3) by the imperfect indicative of **avere l'abitudine di**, e.g., **he used to go to the shore** aveva l'abitudine di andare alla spiaggia

used [juzd] *adj* uso, usato; **to get used to** ['juzdtu] or ['justu] fare la mano a, abituarsi a

useful ['jusfəl] *adj* utile

usefulness ['jusfəlnɪs] *s* utilità *f*

useless ['juslɪs] *adj* inutile, inservibile

user ['juzər] *s* utente *mf*

usher ['ʌʃər] *s* (*doorkeeper*) portiere *m*; (hist) cerimoniere *m*; (theat) maschera; (mov) lucciola || *tr* introdurre; **to usher in** annunciare, introdurre

U.S.S.R. ['ju'es'es'ɑr] *s* (letterword) (**Union of Soviet Socialist Republics**) U.R.S.S. *f*

usual ['juʒu·əl] *adj* usuale, abituale; **as usual** come il solito

usually ['juʒu·əli] *adv* usualmente

usurp [ju'zʌrp] *tr* usurpare

usu·ry [juʒəri] *s* (**-ries**) usura

utensil [ju'tensɪl] *s* utensile *m*

uter·us ['jutərəs] *s* (**-i** [,aɪ]) utero

utilitarian [,jutɪlɪ'teri·ən] *adj* utilitario

utili·ty [ju'trlɪti] *s* (**-ties**) utilità *f*; compagnia di servizi pubblici

utilize ['jutɪ,laɪz] *tr* utilizzare

utmost ['ʌt,most] *adj* sommo; estremo; massimo || *s*—**the utmost** il massimo; **to do one's utmost** fare tutto il possibile; **to the utmost** al massimo limite

utopia [ju'topɪ·ə] *s* utopia

utopian [ju'topɪ·ən] *adj* utopistico || *s* utopista *mf*

utter ['ʌtər] *adj* completo, totale || *tr* proferire, pronunziare; (*a sigh*) dare, fare

utterly ['ʌtərli] *adv* completamente

uxoricide [ʌk'sɔrɪ,saɪd] *s* (*husband*) uxoricida *m*; (*act*) uxoricidio

uxorious [ʌk'sɔrɪ·əs] *adj* eccessivamente innamorato della propria moglie; dominato dalla moglie

V

V, v [vi] *s* ventiduesima lettera dell'alfabeto inglese

vacan·cy ['vekənsi] *s* (**-cies**) (*emptiness*) vuoto; (*unfilled position*) vacanza; (*unfilled job*) posto vacante; (*in a building*) appartamento libero;

(*in a hotel*) camera libera; **no vacancy** completo

vacant ['vekənt] *adj* (*empty*) vuoto; (*position*) vacante; (*expression of the face*) vago

vacate ['veket] *tr* sgombrare; (*a posi-*

tion) ritirarsi da; (law) annullare; **to vacate one's mind of worries** liberarsi dalle preoccupazioni || *intr* sloggiare; (coll) andarsene

vacation [ve'keʃən] *s* vacanza, villeggiatura; **vacanze** *fpl* || *intr* estivare, villeggiare

vacationer [ve'keʃənər] *s* villeggiante *mf*, vacanziere *m*

vacationist [ve'keʃənɪst] *s* villeggiante *mf*, vacanziere *m*

vaca'tion with pay' *s* vacanze *fpl* pagate

vaccinate ['væksɪˌnet] *tr* vaccinare

vaccination [ˌvæksɪ'neʃən] *s* vaccinazione

vaccine [væk'sin] *s* vaccino

vacillate ['væsɪˌlet] *intr* vacillare

vacillating ['væsɪˌletɪŋ] *adj* vacillante

vacui·ty [væ'kju·ɪti] *s* (**-ties**) vacuità *f*

vacu·um ['vækju·əm] *s* (**-ums** *or* **-a** [ə]) vuoto; **in a vacuum** sotto vuoto || *tr* pulire con l'aspirapolvere

vac'uum clean'er *s* aspirapolvere *m*

vac'uum-pack'ed *adj* confezionato sotto vuoto

vac'uum tube' *s* tubo elettronico

vagabond ['vægəˌbɑnd] *adj* & *s* vagabondo

vagar·y [və'geri] *s* (**-ies**) capriccio

vagran·cy ['vegrənsi] *s* (**-cies**) vagabondaggio

vagrant ['vegrənt] *adj* & *s* vagabondo

vague [veg] *adj* vago

va'gus nerve' ['vegəs] *s* (anat) vago

vain [ven] *adj* vano; (*conceited*) vanitoso; **in vain** in vano

vainglorious [ven'glorɪ·əs] *adj* vanaglorioso

valance ['væləns] *s* balza, mantovana

vale [vel] *s* valle *f*

valedictorian [ˌvælɪdɪk'torɪ·ən] *s* studente *m* che pronuncia il discorso di commiato

valence ['veləns] *s* (chem) valenza

valentine ['vælənˌtaɪn] *s* (*sweetheart*) valentino; (*card*) cartolina di San Valentino

valet ['vælɪt] *or* ['væle] *s* valletto

valiant ['væljənt] *adj* valoroso

valid ['vælɪd] *adj* valido

validate ['vælɪˌdet] *tr* convalidare, vidimare; (sports) omologare

validation [ˌvælɪ'deʃən] *s* convalida, vidimazione; (sports) omologazione

validi·ty [və'lɪdɪti] *s* (**-ties**) validità *f*

valise [və'lis] *s* valigetta

valley ['væli] *s* valle *f*, vallata; (*of roof*) linea di compluvio

valor ['vælər] *s* valore *m*, coraggio

valorous ['vælərəs] *adj* valoroso

valuable ['vælju·əbəl] *or* ['væljəbəl] *adj* (*having monetary worth*) prezioso; pregevole, pregiato || **valuables** *spl* valori *mpl*

value ['vælju] *s* valore *m*; importanza; (com) valuta, valore *m*; **an excellent value** un acquisto eccellente || *tr* stimare, valutare

value'-added tax' *s* imposta sul valore aggiunto

valueless ['væljulɪs] *adj* senza valore

valve [vælv] *s* (anat, mach, rad, telv)

valvola; (bot, zool) valva; (mus) pistone *m*

valve' gears' *spl* meccanismo di distribuzione

valve'-in-head' en'gine *s* motore *m* a valvole in testa

valve' lift'er ['lɪftər] *s* alzavalvole *m*

valve' seat' *s* sede *f* della valvola

valve' spring' *s* molla di valvola

valve' stem' *s* stelo di comando della valvola

vamp [væmp] *s* parte *f* anteriore della tomaia; (*patchwork*) rabberciatura; (*female*) vamp *f* || *tr* (*a shoe*) rimontare; rabberciare; (*to concoct*) inventare, raffazzonare; (*an accompaniment*) improvvisare; (*said of a female*) sedurre

vampire ['væmpaɪr] *s* vampiro; (*female*) vamp *f*

van [væn] *s* camionetta, autofurgone *m*; (mil & fig) avanguardia

vanadium [və'nedɪ·əm] *s* vanadio

vandal ['vændəl] *adj* & *s* vandalo || **Vandal** *adj* & *s* Vandalo

vandalism ['vændəˌlɪzəm] *s* vandalismo

vane [ven] *s* (*weathervane*) banderuola; (*of windmill, of turbine*) pala; (*of feather*) barba

vanguard ['vænˌgɑrd] *s* avanguardia; **in the vanguard** all'avanguardia

vanilla [və'nɪlə] *s* vaniglia

vanish ['vænɪʃ] *intr* svanire

van'ishing cream' ['vænɪ/ɪŋ] *s* crema evanescente

vani·ty ['vænɪti] *s* (**-ties**) vanità *f*; (*table*) toletta; (*case*) astuccio di toletta

vanquish ['væŋkwɪʃ] *tr* superare, vincere

van'tage ground' ['væntɪdʒ] *s* posizione favorevole

vapid ['væpɪd] *adj* insipido

vapor ['vepər] *s* vapore *m*; (*visible vapor*) vapori *mpl*

vaporize ['vepəˌraɪz] *tr* vaporizzare || *intr* vaporizzarsi

va'por lock' *s* tampone *m* di vapore

vaporous ['vepərəs] *adj* vaporoso

va'por trail' *s* scia di condensazione

variable ['verɪ·əbəl] *adj* & *s* variabile *f*

variance ['verɪ·əns] *s* divario, differenza; **at variance with** (*a thing*) differente da; differentemente da; (*a person*) in disaccordo con

variant ['verɪ·ənt] *adj* & *s* variante *f*

variation [ˌverɪ'eʃən] *s* variazione

varicose ['verɪˌkos] *adj* varicoso

varied ['verid] *adj* vario, svariato

variegated ['verɪˌgetɪd] *or* ['verɪˌgetɪd] *adj* variegato, screziato

varie·ty [və'raɪ·ɪti] *s* (**-ties**) varietà *f*

vari'ety show' *s* spettacolo di varietà

varnish ['vɑrnɪʃ] *s* vernice *f* || *tr* verniciare; (fig) dare la vernice a

variola [və'raɪ·ələ] *s* (pathol) vaiolo

various ['verɪ·əs] *adj* vari; (*varicolored*) vario, variegato

varsi·ty ['vɑrsɪti] *adj* (sports) universitario || *s* (**-ties**) (sports) squadra numero uno

var·y ['vɛrɪ] v (pret & pp **-ied**) tr & intr variare

vase [ves] or [vez] s vaso

vaseline ['væsə‚lin] s (trademark) vaselina

vassal ['væsəl] adj & s vassallo

vast [væst] or [vɑst] adj vasto

vastly ['væstli] or ['vɑstli] adv enormemente

vastness ['væstnɪs] or ['vɑstnɪs] s vastità f

vat [væt] s tino, bigoncia

Vatican ['vætɪkən] adj vaticano ‖ s Vaticano

Vat'ican Cit'y s Città f del Vaticano

vaudeville ['vodvɪl] or ['vodəvɪl] s spettacolo di varietà; (theatrical piece) vaudeville m, commedia musicale

vault [vɔlt] s volta; (underground chamber) cantina; (of a bank) camera di sicurezza; (burial chamber) cripta; (of heaven) cappa; (leap) salto ‖ tr formare a mo' di volta; saltare ‖ intr saltare

vaunt [vɔnt] or [vɑnt] s vanto, vanteria ‖ tr vantare di ‖ intr vantarsi

veal [vil] s vitello

veal' chop' s scaloppa, cotoletta di vitello

veal' cut'let s scaloppina

vedette [vɪ'dɛt] s (nav) vedetta; (mil) sentinella avanzata

veer [vɪr] s virata ‖ tr far cambiare di direzione a ‖ intr virare; (said of the wind) cambiare di direzione

vegetable ['vɛdʒɪtəbəl] adj vegetale ‖ s (plant) vegetale m; (edible plant) ortaggio; **vegetables** verdura, erbe fpl, erbaggi mpl, ortaggi mpl

veg'etable gar'den s orto

veg'etable soup' s minestra di verdura

vegetarian [‚vɛdʒɪ'tɛrɪ·ən] adj & s vegetariano

vegetate ['vɛdʒɪ‚tɛt] intr vegetare

vehemence ['vi·ɪməns] s veemenza

vehement ['vi·ɪmənt] adj veemente

vehicle ['vi·ɪkəl] s veicolo

vehic'ular traf'fic [vɪ'hɪkjələr] s circolazione stradale

veil [vel] s velo; **to take the veil** prendere il velo ‖ tr velare

vein [ven] s vena; (streak) venatura; (of ore) filone m ‖ tr venare

velar ['vilər] adj & s velare f

vellum ['vɛləm] s pergamena

veloci·ty [vɪ'lɑsɪti] s (-ties) velocità f

velvet ['vɛlvɪt] adj di velluto ‖ s velluto; (slang) guadagno al gioco; (coll) situazione all'acqua di rose

velveteen [‚vɛlvɪ'tin] s vellutino di cotone

velvety ['vɛlvɪti] adj vellutato

vend [vɛnd] tr vendere; (to peddle) fare il venditore ambulante di

vend'ing machine' s distributore automatico

vendor ['vɛndər] s venditore m

veneer [və'nɪr] s impiallacciatura, piallaccio; (fig) vernice f ‖ tr impiallacciare

venerable ['vɛnərəbəl] adj venerabile

venerate ['vɛnə‚ret] tr venerare

venereal [vɪ'nɪrɪ·əl] adj venereo

Venetia [vɪ'niʃɪ·ə] or [vɪ'niʃə] s (province) Venezia

Venetian [vɪ'niʃən] adj & s veneziano

Vene'tian blind' s veneziana, persiana avvolgibile

Venezuelan [‚vɛnɪ'zwilən] adj & s venezolano

vengeance ['vɛndʒəns] s vendetta; **with a vengeance** violentemente; eccessivamente

vengeful ['vɛndʒfəl] adj vendicativo

Venice ['vɛnɪs] s Venezia

venire·man [vɪ'naɪrɪmən] s (-men) membro di un collegio di giurati

venison ['vɛnɪsən] or ['vɛnɪzən] s carne f di cervo

venom ['vɛnəm] s veleno

venomous ['vɛnəməs] adj velenoso

vent [vɛnt] s sfiatatoio; (of jacket) spacco; **to give vent to** dare sfogo a ‖ tr sfogare, sfuriare; mettere uno sfiatatoio a; **to vent one's spleen** sfogare la bile

vent' hole' s apertura di sfogo

ventilate ['vɛntɪ‚let] tr ventilare

ventilator ['vɛntɪ‚letər] s ventilatore m

ventricle ['vɛntrɪkəl] s ventricolo

ventriloquist [vɛn'trɪləkwɪst] s ventriloquo

venture ['vɛntʃər] s azzardo, avventura rischiosa; **at a venture** alla ventura ‖ tr avventurare ‖ intr avventurarsi, arrischiarsi

venturesome ['vɛntʃərsəm] adj (risky) rischioso; (daring) avventuroso

venturous ['vɛntʃərəs] adj avventuroso

vent' win'dow s (aut) deflettore m

venue ['vɛnju] s (law) posto dove ha avuto luogo il reato; (law) luogo dove si riunisce la corte; **change of venue** cambio di giurisdizione

Venus ['vinəs] s (very beautiful woman) venere f; (astr) Venere m; (myth) Venere f

veracious [vɪ're ʃəs] adj verace

veraci·ty [vɪ'ræsɪti] s (-ties) veridicità f

veranda or **verandah** [və'rændə] s veranda

verb [vʌrb] adj verbale ‖ s verbo

verbalize ['vʌrbə‚laɪz] tr esprimere con parole; (gram) convertire in forma verbale ‖ intr essere verboso

verbatim [vər'betɪm] adj letterale ‖ adv parola per parola, testualmente

verbena [vər'binə] s (bot) verbena

verbiage ['vʌrbɪ·ɪdʒ] s verbosità f; (style of wording) espressione

verbose [vər'bos] adj verboso

verdant ['vʌrdənt] adj verde, verdeggiante

verdict ['vʌrdɪkt] s verdetto

verdigris ['vʌrdɪ‚grɪs] s verderame m

verdure ['vʌrdʒər] s verde m

verge [vʌrdʒ] s orlo, limite m; bordo; (of a column) fusto; **on the verge of** al punto di; all'orlo di ‖ intr —**to verge on** costeggiare, rasentare

verification [‚vɛrɪfɪ'keʃən] s verifica

veri·fy ['vɛrɪ ˌfaɪ] v (pret & pp -fied) tr verificare, confermare

verily ['vɛrɪli] adv in verità

veritable ['vɛrɪtəbəl] adj vero

vermilion [vər'mɪljən] adj & s vermiglio

vermin ['vʌrmɪn] ssg (person) persona abominevole ‖ spl (animals or persons) insetti mpl

vermouth [vər'muθ] or ['vʌrmuθ] s vermut m

vernacular [vər'nækjələr] adj volgare ‖ s volgare m, vernacolo; (language peculiar to a class or profession) gergo

versatile ['vʌrsətɪl] adj (person) versatile; (tool or device) a vari usi

verse [vʌrs] s verso; (Bib) versetto

versed [vʌrst] adj versato

versification [ˌvʌrsɪfɪ'keʃən] s versificazione

versi·fy ['vʌrsɪ ˌfaɪ] v (pret & pp -fied) tr & intr versificare

version ['vʌrʒən] s versione

ver·so ['vʌrso] s (-sos) (of coin) rovescio; (of page) verso

versus ['vʌrsəs] prep contro; in confronto a

verte·bra ['vʌrtɪbrə] s (-brae [ˌbri] or -bras) vertebra

vertebrate ['vʌrtə ˌbret] adj & s vertebrato

ver·tex ['vʌrtɛks] s (-texes or -tices [tɪ ˌsiz]) vertice m

vertical ['vʌrtɪkəl] adj & s verticale f

ver'tical hold' s (telv) regolatore m del sincronismo verticale

ver'tical sta'bilizer s (aer) deriva

verti·go ['vʌrtɪ ˌgo] s (-goes or -gos) vertigine f

verve [vʌrv] s verve f, brio

very ['vɛri] adj (utter) grande, completo; (precise) vero e proprio; (mere) stesso, e.g., his very brother suo fratello stesso ‖ adv molto, e.g., to be very rich essere molto ricco

vesicle ['vɛsɪkəl] s vescichetta

vesper ['vɛspər] s vespro; vespers vespri mpl ‖ Vesper s Vespero

ves'per bell' s campana a vespro

vessel ['vɛsəl] s (ship) nave f, vascello; (container) vaso; (anat) vaso; (fig) vasello

vest [vɛst] s (of man's suit) panciotto, gilè m; (of woman's garment) corpino ‖ tr vestire; to vest (authority) in concedere a; to vest with investire di ‖ intr vestirisi; to vest in passare a

vest'ed in'terest s interesse acquisito

vestibule ['vɛstɪ ˌbjul] s vestibolo

vestige ['vɛstɪdʒ] s vestigio

vestment ['vɛstmənt] s (eccl) paramento

vest'-pock'et adj da tasca, tascabile

ves·try ['vɛstri] s (-tries) sagrestia; (chapel) cappella; giunta esecutiva della chiesa episcopaliana

ves'try·man s (-men) membro della giunta esecutiva della chiesa episcopaliana

Vesuvius [vɪ'suvɪ·əs] or [vɪ'sjuvɪ·əs] s il Vesuvio

vetch [vɛtʃ] s veccia; (grass pea) cicerchia

veteran ['vɛtərən] adj & s veterano

veterinarian [ˌvɛtərɪ'nɛrɪ·ən] s veterinario

veterinar·y ['vɛtərɪ ˌnɛri] adj veterinario ‖ s (-ies) veterinario

ve·to ['vito] s (-toes) veto ‖ tr porre il veto a

vex [vɛks] tr irritare, tormentare

vexation [vɛk'seʃən] s fastidio, contrarietà f

vexatious [vɛk'seʃəs] adj irritante, fastidioso; (law) vessatorio

vexing ['vɛksɪŋ] adj noioso, fastidioso, irritante

via ['vaɪ·ə] prep via, per via di

viaduct ['vaɪ·ə ˌdʌkt] s viadotto

vial ['vaɪ·əl] s fiala, boccetta

viand ['vaɪ·ənd] s vivanda, manicaretto

viati·cum [vaɪ'ætɪkəm] s (-cums or -ca [kə]) (eccl) viatico

vibrate ['vaɪbret] tr & intr vibrare

vibration [vaɪ'breʃən] s vibrazione

vicar ['vɪkər] s vicario

vicarage ['vɪkərɪdʒ] s residenza del vicario; (office; duties) vicariato

vicarious [vaɪ'kɛrɪ·əs] or [vɪ'kɛrɪ·əs] adj sostituto; (punishment) ricevuto in vece di altra persona; (power) delegato; (enjoyment) di riflesso

vice [vaɪs] s vizio

vice'-ad'miral s viceammiraglio, ammiraglio di squadra

vice'-pres'ident s vicepresidente m

viceroy ['vaɪsrɔɪ] s viceré m

vice versa ['vaɪsi 'vʌrsə] or ['vaɪsə 'vʌrsə] adv viceversa

vicini·ty [vɪ'sɪnɪti] s (-ties) vicinanze fpl, paraggi mpl

vicious ['vɪʃəs] adj vizioso; maligno, malvagio; (dog) cattivo, che morde; (horse) selvaggio; (headache) tremendo; (reasoning; circle) vizioso

victim ['vɪktɪm] s vittima

victimize ['vɪktɪ ˌmaɪz] tr fare una vittima di; ingannare; (hist) sacrificare

victor ['vɪktər] s vincitore m

victorious [vɪk'torɪ·əs] adj vittorioso

victo·ry ['vɪktəri] s (-ries) vittoria

victuals ['vɪtəlz] spl vettovaglie fpl

vid'eo cassette' ['vɪdɪ ˌo] s videocassetta

vid'eo sig'nal s segnale m video

vid'eo tape' s nastro televisivo

vie [vaɪ] v (pret & pp vied; ger vying) intr gareggiare; to vie for disputarsi

Vien·nese [ˌviɪ·ə'niz] adj viennese ‖ s (-nese) viennese mf

Vietnam [ˌviɛt'nam] s il Vietnam

Vietnam·ese [vɪ ˌɛtnə'miz] adj vietnamita ‖ s (-ese) vietnamita mf; (language) vietnamita m

view [vju] s vista; (picture) veduta; prospetto; esame m; punto di vista; to be on view (said of a corpse) essere esposto; to keep in view non perdere di vista; to take a dim view of avere un'opinione scettica di; with a view to con lo scopo di ‖ tr guardare, osservare; considerare

viewer ['vju·ər] s spettatore m; (telv) telespettatore m; (phot) visore m; (phot) proiettore m di diapositive

view'find'er s (phot) traguardo, visore m

view'point' s punto di vista

vigil ['vɪdʒɪl] s vigilia; **to keep vigil** vegliare

vigilance ['vɪdʒɪləns] s vigilanza

vigilant ['vɪdʒɪlənt] adj vigilante

vignette [vɪn'jet] s vignetta

vigor ['vɪgər] s vigore m, gagliardia

vigorous ['vɪgərəs] adj vigoroso

Viking ['vaɪkɪŋ] s vichingo

vile [vaɪl] adj vile, malvagio; (wretchedly bad) orribile; disgustoso, ripugnante; (filthy) sporco; (poor) povero, basso

vili·fy ['vɪlɪ,faɪ] v (pret & pp -fied) tr vilificare

villa ['vɪlə] s villa

village ['vɪlɪdʒ] s villaggio, paese m

villager ['vɪlɪdʒər] s paesano

villain ['vɪlən] s scellerato; (of a play) cattivo, anima nera

villainous ['vɪlənəs] adj vile, infame

villain·y ['vɪləni] s (-ies) scelleratezza, malvagità f

vim [vɪm] s vigore m, brio

vinaigrette [,vɪnə'gret] s boccetta dell'aceto aromatico

vinaigrette' sauce' s salsa verde

vindicate ['vɪndɪ,ket] tr scolpare; difendere, sostenere; (e.g., a claim) rivendicare

vindictive [vɪn'dɪktɪv] adj vendicativo

vine [vaɪn] s (climber) rampicante f; (grape plant) vite f

vine'dress'er s vignaiolo

vinegar ['vɪnɪgər] s aceto

vinegarish ['vɪnɪgərɪʃ] adj acetoso; (fig) acre, mordace

vinegary ['vɪnɪgəri] adj acetoso; (fig) irritabile, irascibile

vineyard ['vɪnjərd] s vigna, vigneto

vintage ['vɪntɪdʒ] s vendemmia; vino di annata eccezionale; (fig) edizione f

vintager ['vɪntɪdʒər] s vendemmiatore m

vin'tage wine' s vino di marca

vin'tage year' s buona annata

vintner ['vɪntnər] s produttore m di vino; vinaio

vinyl ['vaɪnɪl] or ['vɪnɪl] s vinile m

violate ['vaɪə,let] tr violare

violation [,vaɪə'leʃən] s violazione

violence ['vaɪələns] s violenza

violent ['vaɪələnt] adj violento

violet ['vaɪəlɪt] adj violetto || s (color) violetto, viola; (bot) violetta; (Viola odorata) viola mammola

violin [,vaɪə'lɪn] s violino

violinist [,vaɪə'lɪnɪst] s violinista mf

violoncellist [,vaɪələn'tʃelɪst] or [,vɪələn'tʃelɪst] s violoncellista mf

violoncel·lo [,vaɪələn'tʃelo] or [,vɪələn'tʃelo] s (-los) violoncello

VIP ['vi'aɪ'pi] s (letterword) (Very Important Person) persona di maggiore riguardo

viper ['vaɪpər] s vipera; (any snake) serpe f; (spiteful person) vipera

vira·go [vɪ'rego] s (-goes or -gos) megera, donna dal caratteraccio impossibile

virgin ['vʌrdʒɪn] adj & s vergine f || **Virgin** s Vergine f

vir'gin birth' s parto verginale della Madonna; (zool) partenogenesi f

Virgin'ia creep'er [vər'dʒɪnɪ·ə] s vite f del Canada

virginity [vər'dʒɪnɪti] s virginità f

Virgo ['vʌrgo] s (astr) Vergine f

virility [vɪ'rɪlɪti] s virilità f

virology [vaɪ'rɑlədʒi] s virologia

virtual ['vʌrtʃu·əl] adj virtuale

virtue ['vʌrtʃu] s virtù f

virtuosi·ty [,vʌrtʃu'ɑsɪti] s (-ties) virtuosità f, virtuosismo

virtuo·so [,vʌrtʃu'oso] s (-sos or -si [si]) virtuoso

virtuous ['vʌrtʃu·əs] adj virtuoso

virulence ['vɪrjələns] s virulenza

virulent ['vɪrjələnt] adj virulento

virus ['vaɪrəs] s virus m

visa ['vizə] s visto || tr vistare

visage ['vɪzɪdʒ] s faccia; apparenza

vis-à-vis [,vizə'vi] adj l'uno di fronte all'altro || adv vis-à-vis || prep di fronte a

viscera ['vɪsərə] spl visceri mpl, viscere fpl

viscount ['vaɪkaunt] s visconte m

viscountess ['vaɪkauntɪs] s viscontessa

viscous ['vɪskəs] adj viscoso

vise [vaɪs] s morsa

visé ['vize] or [vi'ze] s & tr var of visa

visible ['vɪzɪbəl] adj visibile

Visigoth ['vɪzɪ,gɑθ] s visigoto

vision ['vɪʒən] s visione; (sense) vista

visionar·y ['vɪʒə,neri] adj visionario || s (-ies) visionario

visit ['vɪzɪt] s visitare; affliggere, colpire; (a punishment) far ricadere || intr visitare; (to chat) fare un chiacchierata

visitation [,vɪzɪ'teʃən] s visitazione; punizione divina, visita del Signore

vis'iting card' s biglietto da visita

vis'iting hours' spl orario delle visite

vis'iting nurse' s infermiera che visita i pazienti a domicilio

visitor ['vɪzɪtər] s visitatore m

visor ['vaɪzər] s visiera; (fig) maschera

vista ['vɪstə] s vista, prospettiva

visual ['vɪʒu·əl] adj visivo, visuale

vis'ual acu'ity s acutezza visiva

visualize ['vɪʒu·ə,laɪz] tr formare l'immagine mentale di; (to make visible) visualizzare

vital ['vaɪtəl] adj vitale; (deadly) mortale || **vitals** spl organi vitali

vitality [vaɪ'tælɪti] s vitalità f

vitalize ['vaɪtə,laɪz] tr animare, infondere vita a

vi'tal statis'tics spl statistiche fpl anagrafiche

vitamin ['vaɪtəmɪn] s vitamina

vitiate ['vɪʃɪ,et] tr viziare

vitreous ['vɪtrɪ·əs] adj vitreo, vetroso

vitriolic [,vɪtrɪ'ɑlɪk] adj di vetriolo; (fig) caustico

vituperate [vaɪ'tupə,ret] or [vaɪ'tjupə,ret] tr vituperare

viva ['viva] s evviva || *interj* viva!
vivacious [vɪ've∫əs] or [vaɪ've∫əs] *adj* vivace
vivaci·ty [vɪ'væsiti] or [vaɪ'væsiti] s (-ties) vivacità f, gaiezza
viva voce ['vaɪvə 'vosi] *adv* a viva voce
vivid ['vɪvɪd] *adj* vivido
vivi·fy ['vɪvɪ ,faɪ] v (*pret* & *pp* -fied) *tr* vivificare
vivisection [,vɪvɪ'sek∫ən] s vivisezione
vixen ['vɪksən] s volpe femmina; (*ill-tempered woman*) megera
vizier [vɪ'zɪr] or ['vɪzjər] s visir m
vocabular·y [vo'kæbjə ,leri] s (-ies) vocabolario
vocal ['vokəl] *adj* vocale; (*inclined to express oneself freely*) che si fa sentire, loquace; (*e.g., outburst*) verbale
vocalist ['vokəlɪst] s cantante mf; (*of jazz*) vocalist mf
vocalize ['vokə ,laɪz] *tr* vocalizzare || *intr* vocalizzarsi
vocation [vo'ke∫ən] s vocazione; professione, impiego
voca'tional educa'tion s istruzione professionale
vocative ['vakətɪv] s vocativo
vociferate [vo'sɪfə ,ret] *intr* vociferare
vociferous [vo'sɪfərəs] *adj* rumoroso, vociferante
vogue [vog] s voga, moda; in vogue in voga, di moda
voice [vɔɪs] s voce f; (*of animals*) verso; in a loud voice a voce alta; in a low voice a voce bassa; to give voice to esprimere; with one voice con una sola voce || *tr* esprimere; (phonet) sonorizzare || *intr* sonorizzarsi
voiced [vɔɪst] *adj* (phonet) sonoro
voiceless ['vɔɪslɪs] *adj* senza voce; muto; (phonet) sordo, duro
void [vɔɪd] *adj* (*useless*) inutile; (*empty*) vuoto; (law) invalido, nullo; void of sprovvisto di || s vuoto; (*gap*) buco || *tr* vuotare; (*the bowels*) evacuare; annullare || *intr* andare di corpo
volatile ['valətɪl] *adj* volatile; instabile; (*disposition*) volubile, incostante
volatilize ['valətɪ ,laɪz] *tr* volatilizzare || *intr* volatilizzarsi
volcanic [val'kænɪk] *adj* vulcanico
volca·no [val'keno] s (-noes or -nos) vulcano
volition [və'lɪ∫ən] s volontà f; of one's own volition di propria volontà
volley ['vali] s (*e.g., of bullets*) scarica, sventagliata; (tennis) volata || *tr* colpire a volo || *intr* colpire la palla a volo
vol'ley·ball' s pallavolo f
volplane ['val ,plen] s planata || *intr* planare
volt [volt] s volt m
voltage ['voltidʒ] s voltaggio
volt'age divid'er [dɪ'vaɪdər] s divisore m del voltaggio
voltaic [val'te·ɪk] *adj* voltaico
volte-face ['vɔlt'fas] s voltafaccia m

volt'me'ter s voltmetro
voluble ['valjəbəl] *adj* locuace
volume ['valjəm] s volume m; to speak volumes avere molta importanza; essere molto espressivo
voluminous [və'luminəs] *adj* voluminoso
voluntar·y ['valən ,teri] *adj* volontario || s (-ies) assolo di organo
volunteer [,valən'tɪr] *adj* & s volontario || *tr* dare or dire volontariamente || *intr* offrirsi; arruolarsi come volontario; to volunteer to + *inf* offrirsi di + *inf*
voluptuar·y [və'lʌptʃu ,eri] *adj* voluttuoso || s (-ies) sibarita m, epicureo
voluptuous [və'lʌptʃu·əs] *adj* voluttuoso
volute [və'lut] s voluta
vomit ['vamɪt] s vomito || *tr* & *intr* vomitare, rigettare
voodoo ['vudu] *adj* di vudù || s (*practice*) vudù m; (*person*) vuduista mf
voracious [və're∫əs] *adj* vorace
voracity [və'ræsiti] s voracità f
vor·tex ['vortəks] s (-texes or -tices [tɪ ,siz]) vortice m
vota·ry ['votəri] s (-ries) persona legata da un voto; amante mf, appassionato
vote [vot] s voto; to put to the vote mettere ai voti; to tally the votes procedere allo scrutinio dei voti || *tr* votare; dichiarare; to vote down respingere; to vote in eleggere; to vote out scacciare || *intr* votare
vote' get'ter ['getər] s accaparratore m di voti; slogan m che conquista voti
voter ['votər] s elettore m
vot'ing machine' ['votɪŋ] s macchina per registrare lo scrutinio dei voti
votive ['votɪv] *adj* votivo
vo'tive of'fering s voto, ex voto, offerta votiva
vouch [vautʃ] *tr* garantire || *intr*—to vouch for (*s.th*) garantire; (*s.o.*) rendersi garante per, garantire per
voucher ['vautʃər] s garante mf; (*certificate*) ricevuta, pezza d'appoggio
vouch·safe' *tr* concedere, accordare || *intr*—to vouchsafe to + *inf* degnarsi di + *inf*
voussoir [vu'swar] s cuneo
vow [vau] s voto; to take vows pronunciare i voti || *tr* promettere; (*vengeance*) giurare || *intr* fare un voto
vowel ['vau·əl] s vocale f
voyage ['vɔɪ·ɪdʒ] s viaggio; (*by sea*) traversata || *tr* attraversare || *intr* viaggiare
voyager ['vɔɪ·ɪdʒər] s viaggiatore m, passeggero
vulcanize ['vʌlkə ,naɪz] *tr* vulcanizzare
vulgar ['vʌlgər] *adj* volgare; comune, popolare
vulgari·ty [vʌl'gæriti] s (-ties) volgarità f
Vul'gar Lat'in s latino volgare
Vulgate ['vʌlget] s Vulgata
vulnerable ['vʌlnərəbəl] *adj* vulnerabile
vulture ['vʌltʃər] s avvoltoio

W

W, w ['dʌbəl ˌju] *s* ventitreesima lettera dell'alfabeto inglese

wad [wɑd] *s* (*of cotton*) batuffolo, bioccolo; (*of money*) mazzetta, rotolo; (*of tobacco*) pallottola; (*in a gun*) stoppaccio ‖ *v* (*pret & pp* **wadded;** *ger* **wadding**) *tr* arrotolare; (*shot*) comprimere; (fig) imbottire

waddle ['wɑdəl] *s* andatura a mo' di anitra ‖ *intr* sculettare

wade [wed] *tr* guadare ‖ *intr* guadare; avanzare faticosamente; sguazzare; **to wade into** (coll) attaccare violentemente; **to wade through** procedere a stento per; leggere con difficoltà

wad'ing bird' ['wedɪŋ] *s* trampoliere *m*

wafer ['wefər] *s* disco adesivo di carta per chiudere lettere; (*cake*) wafer *m*, cialda; (eccl, med) ostia

waffle ['wɑfəl] *s* cialda

waf'fle i'ron *s* schiacce *fpl*

waft [wæft] or [wɑft] *tr* portare leggermente or a volo ‖ *intr* librarsi, spandersi

wag [wæg] *s* (*of head*) cenno; (*of tail*) scodinzolio; (*person*) burlone *m* ‖ *v* (*pret & pp* **wagged;** *ger* **wagging**) *tr* (*the head*) scuotere; (*the tail*) dimenare ‖ *intr* scodinzolare

wage [wedʒ] *s* salario, paga; **wages** salario, paga; ricompensa; prezzo, e.g., **the wages of sin is death** la morte è il prezzo del peccato ‖ *tr* (*war*) fare

wage' earn'er ['ʌrnər] *s* salariato

wager ['wedʒər] *s* scommessa; **to lay a wager** fare una scommessa ‖ *tr & intr* scommettere

wage'work'er *s* lavoratore salariato

waggish ['wægɪʃ] *adj* scherzoso, comico, burlone

Wagnerian [vɑg'nɪrɪ-ən] *adj & s* wagneriano

wagon ['wægən] *s* carro, carretto; (*e.g., Conestoga wagon*) carriaggio; furgone *m;* carrozzone *m;* **to be on the wagon** (slang) astenersi dal bere; **to hitch one's wagon to a star** avere altissime ambizioni

wag'tail' *s* (orn) ballerina, cutrettola

waif [wef] *s* (*foundling*) trovatello; abbandonato; animale smarrito

wail [wel] *s* gemito, lamento ‖ *intr* gemere, lamentarsi

wain·scot ['wenskət] or ['wenskɑt] *s* pannello per rivestimenti ‖ *v* (*pret & pp* **-scoted** or **-scotted;** *ger* **-scoting** or **-scotting**) *tr* rivestire di pannelli di legno

waist [west] *s* vita, cintura; blusa, camicetta, corpetto

waist'band' *s* cintola

waist'cloth' *s* perizoma *m*

waistcoat ['west ˌkot] or ['westkət] *s* corpetto, gilè *m*

waist'line' *s* vita, cintura; **to keep or watch one's waistline** conservare la linea

wait [wet] *s* attesa; **to lie in wait** attendere al varco ‖ *tr* (*one's turn*) attendere ‖ *intr* attendere, aspettare; **to wait for** attendere, aspettare; **to wait on** servire; **to wait up for** (coll) aspettare alzato

wait'-and-see' pol'icy *s* attendismo

waiter ['wetər] *s* cameriere *m;* (*tray*) vassoio

wait'ing list' *s* lista di aspettativa

wait'ing room' *s* sala d'aspetto

waitress ['wetrɪs] *s* cameriera

waive [wev] *tr* (*one's rights*) rinunciare (with *dat*); differire; mettere da parte

waiver ['wevər] *s* rinuncia

wake [wek] *s* (*any watch*) veglia; (*watch by a dead body*) veglia funebre; (*of a boat*) solco, scia; **in the wake of** come risultato di; nelle orme di ‖ *v* (*pret* **waked** or **woke** [wok]; *pp* **waked**) *tr* svegliare ‖ *intr* svegliarsi; **to wake to** darsi conto di; **to wake up** svegliarsi

wakeful ['wekfəl] *adj* sveglio; insonne

waken ['wekən] *tr* svegliare ‖ *intr* svegliarsi

wale [wel] *s* segno lasciato da una frustata, vescica; (*in fabric*) riga, costa

Wales [welz] *s* la Galles

walk [wɔk] *s* (*act*) camminata; (*distance*) cammino; (*for pleasure*) passeggiata; (*gait*) andatura; (*line of work*) attività *f*, mestiere *m;* (*sidewalk*) marciapiede *m;* (*in a garden*) sentiero; (*yard for domestic animals to exercise in*) recinto; (sports) marcia; **to go for a walk** andare a fare una passeggiata ‖ *tr* (*a street*) percorrere; (*a horse*) passeggiare; (*a patient*) far camminare; (*a heavy piece of furniture*) abbambinare; **to walk off** (*a headache*) far passare camminando ‖ *intr* camminare; passeggiare; (*said of a horse*) andare al passo; (sports) marciare; **to walk away from** andarsene a piedi da; **to walk off with** rubare; vincere con facilità; **to walk out** uscire in segno di protesta; (coll) mettersi in sciopero; **to walk out on** (coll) piantare in asso

walkaway ['wɔkə ˌwe] *s* facile vittoria

walker ['wɔkər] *s* camminatore *m;* (*to teach a baby to walk*) girello

walkie-talkie ['wɔki'tɔki] *s* trasmettitore-ricevitore *m* portatile

walk'ing pa'pers *spl*—**to give s.o. his walking papers** (coll) dare gli otto giorni a qlcu

walk'-in refrig'erator *s* cella frigorifera

walk'ing stick' *s* bastone *m* da passeggio

walk'-on' *s* (*actor*) figurante *m*, comparsa; (*role*) particina

walk'out' *s* sciopero

walk'o'ver *s* facile vittoria, passeggiata

wall [wɔl] *s* muro; (*between rooms; of a vein*) parete *f;* (*rampart*) muraglia; **to drive to the wall** ridurre alla disperazione; **to go to the wall** perdere; fare fallimento || *tr* murare; **to wall up** circondare con muro

wall'board' *s* pannello da costruzione

wallet ['wɑlɪt] *s* portafoglio

wall'flow'er *s* violacciocca gialla; **to be a wallflower** fare tappezzeria

Walloon [wɑ'lun] *adj & s* vallone *mf*

wallop ['wɑləp] *s* (coll) colpo violento; (coll) effetto || *tr* (coll) dare un colpo violento a; (coll) battere completamente

wallow ['wɑlo] *s* diguazzamento; (*place*) brago, pantano || *intr* diguazzare; (*in wealth*) nuotare

wall'pa'per *s* tappezzeria || *tr* tappezzare

walnut ['wɔlnət] *s* (*tree; wood*) noce *m*; (*fruit*) noce *f*

walrus ['wɔlrəs] or ['wælrəs] *s* tricheco

Walter ['wɔltər] *s* Gualtiero

waltz [wɔlts] *s* valzer *m* || *tr* ballare il valzer con; (coll) condurre con disinvoltura || *intr* ballare il valzer

wan [wɑn] *adj* (**wanner; wannest**) (*face*) smunto, sparuto, smorto; (*light*) debole

wand [wɑnd] *s* bacchetta

wander ['wɑndər] *tr* vagare per || *intr* vagare, vagabondare; errare

wanderer ['wɑndərər] *s* vagabondo; pellegrino

Wan'dering Jew' *s* ebreo errante

wan'der·lust' *s* passione del vagabondaggio

wane [wen] *s* decadenza, declino; calare *m* della luna; **on the wane** in declino; (*moon*) calante || *intr* decadere, declinare; (*said of the moon*) calare

wangle ['wæŋgəl] *tr* (coll) ottenere con l'astuzia, rimediare; (coll) falsificare; **to wangle one's way out of** (coll) tirarsi fuori da . . . con l'astuzia || *intr* (coll) arrangiarsi

want [wɑnt] or [wɔnt] *s* bisogno, necessità *f*; domanda; miseria; **for want of** a causa della mancanza di; **to be in want** essere in miseria; **to be in want of** aver bisogno di || *tr* volere, desiderare; mancare; aver bisogno di || *intr* desiderare; **to be wanting** mancare, e.g., **three cards are wanting** mancano tre carte; **to want for** aver bisogno di

want' ad' *s* annunzio economico

wanton ['wɑntən] *adj* di proposito, deliberato; arbitrario; licenzioso, sfrenato; (*archaic*) lussureggiante

war [wɔr] *s* guerra; **to go to war** entrare in guerra; (*said of a soldier*) andare in guerra; **to wage war** fare la guerra || *v* (*pret & pp* **warred;** *ger* **warring**) *intr* guerreggiare; **to war on** fare la guerra a

warble ['wɔrbəl] *s* gorgheggio || *intr* gorgheggiare

warbler ['wɔrblər] *s* canterino; uccello canoro; (orn) beccafico

war' cloud' *s* minaccia di guerra

ward [wɔrd] *s* (*of city*) distretto; (*division of hospital*) corsia; (*separate building in hospital*) padiglione *m*;

(*guardianship*) tutela; (*minor*) pupillo; (*of lock*) scontro || *tr*—**to ward off** stornare, schermirsi da

warden ['wɔrdən] *s* guardiano; (*of jail*) direttore *m*; (*in wartime*) capofabbricato

ward' heel'er *s* politicantuccio

ward'robe *s* guardaroba *m*

ward'robe trunk' *s* baule *m* armadio

ward'room' *s* (nav) quadrato

ware [wer] *s* vasellame *m*; **wares** merce *f*

war' ef'fort *s* sforzo bellico

ware'house' *s* deposito, magazzino

ware'house'man *s* (**-men**) magazziniere *m*

war'fare' *s* guerra

war'head' *s* (mil) testa

war'horse' *s* cavallo di battaglia; (coll) veterano

warily ['werɪli] *adv* con cautela

wariness ['werɪnɪs] *s* cautela

war'like' *adj* guerresco, guerriero

war' loan' *s* prestito di guerra

war' lord' *s* generalissimo

warm [wɔrm] *adj* caldo; (*lukewarm*) tiepido; (*clothes*) che tiene caldo; (*with anger*) acceso; **to be warm** (*said of a person*) avere caldo; (*said of the weather*) fare caldo || *tr* scaldare, riscaldare; (*s.o.'s heart*) slargare; **to warm up** riscaldare || *intr* scaldarsi, riscaldarsi; **to warm up** (*said, e.g., of a room*) riscaldarsi; (*with emotion*) eccitarsi, accalorarsi; **to warm up to** prender simpatia per

warm-blooded ['wɔrm'blʌdɪd] *adj* (*animal*) a sangue caldo; impetuoso, ardente

war' memo'rial *s* monumento ai caduti

warmer ['wɔrmər] *s* scaldino

warm-hearted ['wɔrm'hɑrtɪd] *adj* caloroso, cordiale

warm'ing pan' *s* scaldaletto

warmonger ['wɔr,mʌŋgər] *s* guerrafondaio

war' moth'er *s* madrina di guerra

warmth [wɔrmθ] *s* calore *m*, tepore *m*; foga, entusiasmo

warm'up' *s* preparazione; (*of radio, engine, etc.*) riscaldamento

warn [wɔrn] *tr* avvertire, mettere in guardia; (*to admonish*) ammonire; informare; **to warn off** intimare di allontanarsi (da)

warn'ing *adj* di avvertimento || *s* avvertimento, ammonimento; (law) diffida

war' nose' *s* acciarino, testa

war' of nerves' *s* guerra dei nervi

War' of the Roses' *s* Guerra delle due Rose

warp [wɔrp] *s* (*of a fabric*) ordito; (*of a board*) svergolamento, curvatura; aberrazione mentale; (naut) gherlino || *tr* curvare, svergolare; (*a fabric*) ordire; falsare, alterare; (naut) tirare col gherlino || *intr* curvarsi; falsarsi, alterarsi; (naut) alare

war'path' *s*—**to be on the warpath** essere sul sentiero della guerra, prepararsi alla guerra; (*to be angry*) essere arrabiato, essere di cattivo umore

war'plane' s aeroplano da guerra

war' prof'iteer s pescecane m

warrant ['wɑrənt] or ['wɔrənt] s garanzia; certificato; ricevuta; (com) nota di pegno; (law) ordine m, mandato ‖ tr garantire; autorizzare

warrantable ['wɑrəntəbəl] or ['wɔrəntəbəl] adj giustificabile, legittimo

war'rant of'ficer s sottufficiale m

warran·ty ['wɑrənti] or ['wɔrənti] s (-ties) garanzia; autorizzazione

warren ['wɑrən] or ['wɔrən] s conigliera; (fig) formicaio

warrior ['wɑrjər] or ['wɑrjər] s guerriero

Warsaw ['wɔrsɔ] s Varsavia

war'ship' s nave f da guerra

wart [wɔrt] s verruca

war'time' s tempo di guerra

war'-torn' adj devastato dalla guerra

war' to the death' s guerra a morte

war·y ['weri] adj (-ier; -iest) guardingo

wash [wɑʃ] or [wɔʃ] s lavata; (clothes washed or to be washed) bucato; (rushing movement of water) sciacquio; (dirty water) lavatura; (painting) mano f di colore; (aer, naut) scia ‖ tr lavare; (dishes) rigovernare; (said of sea or river) bagnare; **to be washed up** essere finito; **to wash away** (soil of river bank) dilavare; portar via ‖ intr lavarsi; fare il bucato; essere lavabile; (said of waves) battere

washable ['wɑʃəbəl] or ['wɔʃəbəl] adj lavabile

wash'-and-wear' adj non-stiro

wash'ba'sin s conca, catinella

wash'bas'ket s cesto del bucato

wash'board' s asse m da lavanda; (baseboard) battiscopa m

wash'bowl' s conca, catinella

wash'cloth' s pezzuola per lavarsi

wash'day' s giorno del bucato

washed-out ['wɑʃt‚aʊt] or ['wɔʃt‚aʊt] adj slavato; (coll) stanco; (coll) abbattuto, accasciato

washed-up ['wɑʃt‚ʌp] or ['wɔʃt‚ʌp] adj (coll) finito

washer ['wɑʃər] or ['wɔʃər] s (person) lavatore m; (machine) lavatrice f; (under head of bolt) rondella, rosetta; (ring to prevent leakage) guarnizione

wash'er·man s (-men) lavatore m

wash'er·wom'an s (-wom'en) lavatrice f, lavandaia

wash' goods' spl tessuti mpl lavabili

washing ['wɑʃɪŋ] or ['wɔʃɪŋ] s lavata, lavaggio, lavanda; (of clothes) bucato; **washings** lavaggio

wash'ing machine' s lavabiancheria, lavatrice f

wash'ing so'da s soda da lavare

wash'out' s erosione; (aer) svergolamento negativo; (coll) rovina completa

wash'rag' s pezzuola per lavarsi; straccio di cucina

wash'room' s gabinetto, toletta

wash'stand' s lavabo, lavamano

wash'tub' s mastello, lavatoio

wash' wa'ter s lavatura

wasp [wɑsp] s vespa

waste [west] s spreco; (refuse) scarico, rifiuto; (desolate country) landa; (excess material) scarto; (for wiping machinery) cascame m di cotone; **to go to waste** essere sciupato; **to lay waste** devastare ‖ tr perdere, sciupare, sprecare ‖ intr—**to waste away** intristire, consumarsi

waste'bas'ket s cestino della carta straccia

wasteful ['westfəl] adj dispendioso; distruttivo

waste'pa'per s cartastraccia

waste' pipe' s tubo di scarico

waste' prod'uct s scarto; (body excretion) escremento

wastrel ['westrəl] s sciupone m; spendaccione m, prodigo

watch [wɑtʃ] s orologio; (lookout) guardia; (mil) guardia; (naut) turno; **to be on the watch for** essere all'erta per; **to keep watch over** vegliare su ‖ tr (to look at) osservare; (to oversee) vigilare; guardare; fare attenzione a ‖ intr guardare; (to keep awake) vegliare; **to watch for** fare attenzione a; **to watch out fare** attenzione; **to watch out for** fare attenzione a; essere all'erta per; **to watch over** sorvegliare; **watch out!** attenzione!

watch'band' s cinturino dell'orologio

watch'case' s cassa dell'orologio

watch' charm' s ciondolo dell'orologio

watch' crys'tal s cristallo dell'orologio

watch'dog' s cane m da guardia; (fig) guardiano

watch'dog' commit'tee s comitato di sorveglianza

watchful ['wɑtʃfəl] adj vigile

watchfulness ['wɑtʃfəlnɪs] s vigilanza

watch'mak'er s orologiaio

watch'man s (-men) guardiano, sorvegliante m; (at night) guardia notturna, metronotte m

watch' night' s notte f di San Silvestro; ufficio religioso della vigilia di Capodanno

watch' pock'et s taschino dell'orologio

watch'tow'er s torre f d'osservazione

watch'word' s parola d'ordine, consegna; slogan m

water ['wɔtər] or ['wɑtər] s acqua; **of the first water** di prim'ordine; (e.g., a thief) della più bell'acqua; **to back water** retrocedere; **to be in deep water** essere in cattive acque; **to fish in troubled waters** pescare nel torbido; **to hold water** aver fondamento; **to keep above water** (fig) tenersi a galla; **to make water** (to urinate) urinare; (naut) fare acqua; **to throw cold water on** scoraggiare ‖ tr bagnare; dare acqua a; (cattle) abbeverare; (wine) annacquare ‖ intr abbeverarsi; (said of the mouth) aver l'acquolina; (said, e.g., of a ship) fare acqua; (said of the eyes) lacrimare

wa'ter bug' s bacherozzolo
wa'ter car'rier s acquaiolo
wa'ter·col'or s acquerello
wa'ter-cooled' adj a raffreddamento ad acqua
wa'ter·course' s corso d'acqua
wa'ter·cress' s crescione m
wa'ter cure' s cura delle acque
wa'ter·fall' s cascata
wa'ter·front' s riva, banchina
wa'ter gap' s gola, passo
wa'ter ham'mer s colpo d'ariete
wa'ter heat'er s scaldabagno, scaldaacqua m
wa'ter ice' s granita
wa'tering can' s annaffiatoio
wa'tering place' s stabilimento balneare; stazione termale; (drinking place) abbeveratoio
wa'tering pot' s annaffiatoio
wa'tering trough' s abbeveratoio
wa'ter jack'et s camicia d'acqua
wa'ter lil'y s nenufaro
wa'ter line' s linea di galleggiamento or d'acqua; linea di livello
wa'ter main' s tubo di flusso principale
wa'ter·mark' s linea di livello massimo; (in paper) filigrana
wa'ter·mel'on s cocomero, anguria
wa'ter me'ter s contatore m dell'acqua
wa'ter mill' s mulino ad acqua
wa'ter pipe' s tubo dell'acqua
wa'ter po'lo s pallanuoto f
wa'ter pow'er s forza idrica
wa'ter·proof' adj & s impermeabile m
wa'ter·repel'lent adj idrorepellente
wa'ter·shed' s spartiacque m, displuvio
wa'ter ski' s idrosci m
wa'ter sof'tener s decalcificatore m
wa'ter·spout' s (to carry water from roof) pluviale m; (meteor) tromba marina
wa'ter sys'tem s (of a river) sistema m fluviale; (of city) conduttura dell'acqua, impianto idrico
wa'ter·tight' adj stagno, ermetico; (fig) perfetto, inconfutabile
wa'ter tow'er s torre f serbatoio
wa'ter wag'on s (mil) carro dell'acqua; **to be on the water wagon** (slang) astenersi dal bere
wa'ter·way' s via d'acqua, idrovia
wa'ter wheel' s ruota or turbina idraulica; (of steamboat) ruota a pale
wa'ter wings' spl galleggiante m per nuotare
wa'ter·works' s impianto idrico; (pumping station) impianto di pompaggio
watery ['wɒtəri] or ['wɑtəri] adj acquoso; lacrimoso; povero, insipido; umido, acquitrinoso
watt [wɑt] s watt m
watt'-hour' s ('-hours) wattora m
wattle ['wɑtəl] s (of bird) bargiglio
watt'me'ter s wattmetro
wave [wev] s onda; (of cold; of feeling) ondata; (of the hand) cenno; (of hair) onda, ondulazione || tr (a flag) sventolare; (the hair) ondulare; (the hand) fare cenno con; **to wave aside** fare cenno di allontanarsi da; (e.g., a

proposal) rifiutare || intr ondeggiare; fare cenni con la mano
wave'length' s lunghezza d'onda
wave' mo'tion s movimento ondulatorio
waver ['wevər] intr ondeggiare, oscillare; (to hesitate) titubare, tentennare; (to totter) pencolare
wav·y ['wevi] adj (-ier; -iest) (sea) ondoso; (hair) ondulato
wax [wæks] s cera; (fig) fantoccio || tr incerare; (a recording) (coll) registrare || intr aumentare; diventare; (said of the moon) crescere; **to wax indignant** indignarsi
wax' pa'per s carta cerata, carta oleata
wax'works' s museo di statue di cera
way [we] s maniera, modo; via; condizione; **across the way** di fronte; **a good way** un buon tratto; **all the way** fino alla fine della strada; completamente; **all the way to** fino a; **any way** ad ogni modo; **by the way** a proposito; **in a way** in un certo modo; fino a un certo punto; **in every way** per ogni verso; **in this way** in questa maniera; **one way** senso unico; **on the way to** andando a; **on the way out** uscendo; diminuendo, sparendo; **out of the way** eliminato; fuori mano; strano; irregolare; **that way** in quella direzione; per di lì; in quella maniera; **this way** in questa direzione; per di qui; in questa maniera; **to be in the way** essere d'impaccio; **to feel one's way** avanzare a tentoni; **to force one's way** aprirsi il passo a viva forza; **to get out of the way** togliersi di mezzo; **to give way** ritirarsi, cedere; (said of a rope) rompersi; **to give way to** cedere a, darsi a; **to go out of one's way** darsi da fare, disturbarsi; **to have one's way** vincerla; **to keep out of the way** stare fuori dai piedi; **to know one's way around** conoscere bene la via; (fig) sapere il fatto proprio; **to know one's way to** sapere andare a; **to lead the way** guidare, fare da guida; prendere l'iniziativa; **to lose one's way** perdersi; **to make one's way** avanzare; fare carriera; **to make way for** far largo a; **to mend one's ways** mettere la testa a partito; **to not know which way to turn** non sapere a che santo votarsi; **to put out of the way** togliere di mezzo; **to see one's way to** vedere la possibilità di; **to take one's way** andarsene; **to wind one's way through** andare a zig zag per; **to wing one's way** andare a volo; **under way** in moto; in cammino, avviato; **way in** entrata; **way out** uscita; **ways** modi mpl, maniere fpl; (naut) scalo; **which way?** da che parte?; in che modo?, per dove?
way'bill' s lettera di vettura
wayfarer ['we ˌfɛrər] s viandante m
way'lay' v (pret & pp -laid) tr tendere un agguato a; fermare improvvisamente
way' of life' s tenore m di vita

way'side' s bordo della strada; **to fall by the wayside** cadere per istrada; (fig) fare fiasco

way' sta'tion s stazione con fermata facoltativa

way' train' s treno omnibus

wayward ['wewərd] adj indocile, caparbio; irregolare; capriccioso

we [wi] pron pers noi; noialtri, e.g., **we Italians** noialtri italiani

weak [wik] adj debole

weaken ['wikən] tr indebolire, infiacchire || intr indebolirsi, infiacchirsi

weakling ['wiklɪŋ] s debolino, rammollito

weak-minded ['wik'maɪndəd] adj irresoluto; scemo

weakness ['wiknɪs] s debolezza, fiacchezza; (liking) debole m

wealth [wɛlθ] s ricchezza

wealth·y ['wɛlθi] adj (-ier; -iest) ricco

wean [win] tr svezzare, slattare; **to wean away from** disavvezzare da

weanling ['winlɪŋ] adj appena svezzato || s bambino or animale appena svezzato

weapon ['wɛpən] s arma

weaponry ['wɛpənri] s armi fpl, armamento

wear [wer] s uso, servizio; (clothing) vestiti mpl, indumenti mpl; (wasting away from use) consumo, logorio; (lasting quality) durata, durabilità f; **for everyday wear** per ogni giorno || v (pret **wore** [wor]; pp **worn** [worn]) tr portare, avere indosso; (to cause to deteriorate) logorare, consumare; (to tire) stancare; **to wear out** logorare, strusciare; (a horse) sfiancare; (one's patience) esaurire; (s.o.'s hospitality) abusare di || intr logorarsi, consumarsi; **to wear off** diminuire, sparire; **to wear out** logorarsi; stancarsi; esaurirsi; **to wear well** essere di ottima durata

wear' and tear' [ter] s logorio

weariness ['wɪrɪnɪs] s fatica, stanchezza

wear'ing appar'el ['wɛrɪŋ] s abbigliamento, articoli mpl d'abbigliamento

wearisome ['wɪrɪsəm] adj affaticante; (tedious) noioso

wea·ry ['wɪri] adj (-rier; -riest) stanco || v (pret & pp -ried) tr stancare || intr stancarsi

weasel ['wizəl] s donnola

wea'sel words' spl parole fpl ambigue

weather ['wɛðər] s tempo; maltempo; **to be under the weather** (coll) non sentirsi bene; (to be slightly drunk) (coll) essere alticcio || tr (lumber) stagionare; (adversities) superare, resistere (with dat)

weather-beaten ['wɛðər,bitən] adj segnato dalle intemperie

weath'er bu'reau s servizio meteorologico

weath'er·cock' s banderuola

weath'er fore'cast s previsioni fpl del tempo, bollettino metereologico

weath'er·man' s (-men') metereologo

weath'er report' s bollettino metereologico

weath'er strip'ping ['strɪpɪŋ] s guarnizione a nastro per inzeppare

weath'er vane' s banderuola, ventarola

weave [wiv] s tessitura || v (pret **wove** [wov] or **weaved**; pp **wove** or **woven** ['wovən]) tr tessere; (fig) inserire; **to weave one's way** aprirsi un varco serpeggiando || intr tessere; serpeggiare

weaver ['wivər] s tessitore m

web [wɛb] s tessuto; (of spider) tela; (of rail) anima, gambo; (zool) membrana; (fig) rete f, maglia

web-footed ['wɛb,futɪd] adj palmipede

wed [wɛd] v (pret & pp **wed** or **wedded**; ger **wedding**) tr sposare; (said of the groom) impalmare; (said of the bride) andare in sposa || intr sposarsi

wedding ['wɛdɪŋ] adj nuziale || s sposalizio, nozze fpl, matrimonio

wed'ding cake' s torta nuziale

wed'ding day' s giorno di nozze

wed'ding invita'tion s invito a nozze

wed'ding march' s marcia nuziale

wed'ding ring' s fede f, vera

wedge [wɛdʒ] s cuneo; (of pie) spicchio; (to split wood) bietta; (to hold a wheel) scarpa || tr incuneare

wed'lock s matrimonio

Wednesday ['wɛnzdi] s mercoledì m

wee [wi] adj piccolo piccolo

weed [wid] s malerba, erbaccia; (coll) sigaretta; (slang) marijuana; **weeds** vestito da lutto, gramaglie fpl || tr sarchiare, mondare

weeder ['widər] s (agr) estirpatore m

weed'ing hoe' s sarchio, zappa

weed'-kill'er s diserbante m

week [wik] s settimana; **week in, week out** una settimana dopo l'altra

week'day' s giorno feriale

week'end' s fine-settimana m, fine f di settimana, week-end m || intr passare il fine-settimana

week·ly ['wikli] adj settimanale || s (-lies) settimanale m || adv settimanalmente

weep [wip] v (pret & pp **wept** [wɛpt]) tr piangere; **to weep oneself to sleep** addormentarsi piangendo; **to weep one's eyes out** piangere a calde lacrime || intr piangere; **to weep for joy** piangere di gioia

weeper ['wipər] s piagnone m; (hired mourner) prefica

weep'ing wil'low s salice m piangente

weep·y ['wipi] adj (-ier; -iest) piangente, lacrimoso

weevil ['wivəl] s curculione m

weft [wɛft] s (yarns running across warp) trama; (fabric) tela, tessuto

weigh [we] tr pesare; (anchor) levare; (to make heavy) appesantire; (fig) soppesare, ponderare; **to weigh down** piegare || intr pesare; gravitare; **to weigh in** (sports) pesarsi; **to weigh upon** gravare a

weigh'bridge' s stadera

weight [wet] s peso; (fig) peso; **to carry weight** aver del peso; **to lose weight** diminuire di peso; **to put on weight** crescere di peso; **to throw**

one's **weight around** far sentire la propria importanza || *tr* appesantire; (*statistically*) ponderare, dare un certo peso a

weightless ['wetlɪs] *adj* senza peso, imponderabile

weightlessness ['wetlɪsnɪs] *s* imponderabilità *f*

weight·y ['weti] *adj* (**-ier; -iest**) pesante; importante

weir [wɪr] *s* sbarramento; (*for catching fish*) pescaia

weird [wɪrd] *adj* soprannaturale, misterioso; strano, bizzarro

welcome ['welkəm] *adj* benvenuto; gradito; **you are welcome** (*i.e., gladly received*) sia il benvenuto; (*in answer to thanks*) prego; **you are welcome to it** è a Sua disposizione; **you are welcome to your opinion** pensi come la vuole || *s* benvenuto || *tr* dare il benvenuto a; accettare; gradire || *interj* benvenuto!

weld [weld] *s* saldatura autogena; (bot) guaderella || *tr* saldare || *intr* saldarsi

welder ['weldər] *s* saldatore *m*; (*machine*) saldatrice *f*

welding ['weldɪŋ] *s* saldatura autogena

wel·fare *s* benessere *m*; (*effort to improve living conditions*) beneficenza, assistenza; **to be on welfare** ricevere assistenza pubblica

welfare state' *s* stato sociale o assistenziale

well [wel] *adj* bene; in buona salute || *s* pozzo; (*for ink*) pozzetto, serbatoio; (*spring*) sorgente *f*; (*shaft for stairs*) tromba || *adv* bene; **as well** pure; **as well . . . as** tanto . . . come; **as well as** tanto come, non meno che || *tr* —**to well up** sgorgare || *interj* beh!; bene!; allora!, dunque!

well-appointed ['welə'pɔɪntɪd] *adj* ben ammobiliato

well-attended ['welə'tendɪd] *adj* molto frequentato

well-behaved ['welbɪ'hevd] *adj* beneducato; **to be well-behaved** comportarsi bene

well'-be'ing *s* benessere *m*

well'born' *adj* bennato

well-bred ['wel'bred] *adj* educato, costumato

well-disposed ['weldɪs'pozd] *adj* bendisposto

well-done ['wel'dʌn] *adj* benfatto; (*meat*) ben cotto

well-fixed ['wel'fɪkst] *adj* (coll) agiato, abbiente

well-formed ['wel'fɔrmd] *adj* benfatto

well-founded ['wel'faundɪd] *adj* fondato

well-groomed ['wel'grumd] *adj* (*person*) curato; (*horse*) ben governato

well-heeled ['wel'hild] *adj* (coll) agiato, benestante

well-informed ['welɪn'fɔrmd] *adj* bene informato

well-intentioned ['welɪn'tɛnʃənd] *adj* benintenzionato

well'-kept' *adj* ben conservato; (*person*) benportante; (*secret*) ben mantenuto

well-known ['wel'non] *adj* notorio, ben noto

well-meaning ['wel'minɪŋ] *adj* benevolo, benintenzionato

well-nigh ['wel'naɪ] *adv* quasi

well'-off' *adj* agiato, benestante

well-preserved ['welprɪ'zʌrvd] *adj* ben conservato; (*person*) benportante

well-read ['wel'red] *adj* colto, che ha letto molto

well-spoken ['wel'spokən] *adj* (*person*) raffinato nel parlare; (*word*) a proposito

well'spring' *s* sorgente *f*

well' sweep' *s* mazzacavallo del pozzo

well-tempered ['wel'tempərd] *adj* ben temperato

well-thought-of ['wel'θɔt,ɑv] *adj* tenuto in alta considerazione

well-timed ['wel'taɪmd] *adj* opportuno

well-to-do ['weltə'du] *adj* benestante

well-wisher ['wel'wɪʃər] *s* amico, sostenitore *m*

well-worn ['wel'worn] *adj* (*clothing*) liso, consunto, trito; (*argument*) logoro, banale; portato con eleganza

welsh [welʃ] *intr*—**to welsh on** (*a promise*) (slang) mancare a; (*a person*) (slang) fregare || **Welsh** *adj* & *s* gallese *mf*; **the Welsh** i gallesi

Welsh'man *s* (**-men**) gallese *m*

Welsh' rab'bit or **rare'bit** ['rerbɪt] *s* fonduta fatta con la birra servita su pane abbrustolito

welt [welt] *s* (*finish along a seam*) costa; (*of shoe*) guardolo; (*wale from a blow*) riga, sferzata

welter ['weltər] *s* guazzabuglio; confusione; (*a tumbling about*) rotolio || *intr* rotolarsi, guazzare

wel'ter·weight' *s* (boxing) peso welter, peso medio-leggero

wench [wentʃ] *s* ragazza, giovane *f*

wend [wend] *tr*—**to wend one's way** dirigere i propri passi

werewolf ['wɪr,wulf] *s* lupo mannaro

west [west] *adj* occidentale || *s* ovest *m*, occidente *m* || *adv* verso l'ovest

western ['westərn] *adj* occidentale || *s* western *m*

West' In'dies ['ɪndɪz] *spl* Indie *fpl* Occidentali

westward ['westwərd] *adv* verso l'ovest

wet [wet] *adj* (**wetter; wettest**) bagnato; (*paint*) fresco; (*damp*) umido; (*rainy*) piovoso; che permette la vendita delle bevande alcoliche || *s* umidità *f*; antiproibizionista *mf* || *v* (*pret* & *pp* **wet** or **wetted**; *ger* **wetting**) *tr* bagnare || *intr* bagnarsi

wet' blan'ket *s* guastafeste *mf*

wether ['weðər] *s* castrone *m*

wet' nurse' *s* nutrice *f*, balia

whack [hwæk] *s* (slang) colpo, percossa; (slang) prova, tentativo || *tr* (slang) percuotere

whale [hwel] *s* balena; **a whale of** (slang) gigantesco, e.g., **a whale of a lie** una bugia gigantesca; enorme, e.g., **a whale of a difference** una differenza enorme || *tr* (coll) battere || *intr* pescare balene

whale'bone' *s* osso di balena, fanone *m*

wharf [hwɔrf] *s* (**wharves** [hwɔrvz] or **wharfs**) molo

what [hwɑt] *adj interr* che; quale || *adj rel* quello . . . che; il . . . che, e.g., **wear what tie you prefer** mettiti la cravatta che preferisci || *pron interr* che; quale; **what else?** che altro?; **what if . . .?** e se . . .?; **what of it?** e che me ne importa? || *pron rel* quello che; **what's what** (coll) tutta la situazione || *interj* **what a . . .!** che . . .!, e.g., **what a beautiful day!** che splendida giornata!

what·ev'er *adj* qualsiasi; qualunque || *pron* quanto; che; quello che

what'not' *s* scaffaletto

wheal [hwil] *s* vescichetta

wheat [hwit] *s* grano, frumento

wheedle ['hwidəl] *tr* adulare; persuadere con lusinghe; (*money*) spillare

wheel [hwil] *s* ruota; (*of cheese*) forma; (coll) bicicletta; **at the wheel** al volante; in controllo || *tr* roteare; portare in carrozzella || *intr* girare

wheelbarrow ['hwil,bæro] *s* carriola

wheel'base' *s* passo

wheel'chair' *s* carrozzella

wheel' col'umn *s* (aut) piantone *m* di guida

wheeler-dealer ['hwilər'dilər] *s* (slang) grande affarista *m*

wheel' horse' *s* cavallo di timone; lavoratore *m* di fiducia

wheelwright ['hwil,raɪt] *s* carradore *m*

wheeze [hwiz] *s* affanno; (pathol) rantolo || *intr* respirare affannosamente; (pathol) rantolare

whelp [hwelp] *s* cucciolo || *tr & intr* figliare, partorire

when [hwen] *adv & conj* quando

whence [hwens] *adv* donde, di dove || *conj* donde; per che ragione

when·ev'er *conj* ogniqualvolta, qualora

where [hwer] *adv & conj* dove

whereabouts ['hwerə,bauts] *s* luogo dove uno si trova || *adv & conj* dove

whereas [hwer'æz] *conj* mentre; visto che, considerato che

where·by' *adv* per cui, col quale

wherever [hwer'evər] *adv* dove mai || *conj* dovunque

wherefore ['hwerfor] *s* perché *m* || *adv* perché || *conj* per cui, percome

where·from' *adv* donde

where·in' *adv* dove; in che modo || *conj* dove; nel quale

where·of' *adv* di che || *conj* di che; del quale

where·upon' *adv* sul che; laonde, dopodiché

wherewithal ['hwerwɪð,ɔl] *s* mezzi *mpl*

whet [hwet] *v* (*pret & pp* **whetted;** *ger* **whetting**) *tr* affilare; (*the appetite*) aguzzare

whether ['weðər] *conj* se; **whether or no** ad ogni modo, in ogni caso; **whether or not** che . . . o che non

whet'stone' *s* pietra da affilare

whey [hwe] *s* scotta

which [hwɪtʃ] *adj interr* quale || *adj rel* il (la, etc.) quale || *pron interr* che; quale; **which is which** qual'è l'uno e qual'è l'altro || *pron rel* che; il quale; quello che

which·ev'er *adj & pron rel* qualunque

whiff [hwɪf] *s* (*of air*) soffio; fiutata; (*trace of odor*) zaffata; **to get a whiff of** sentire l'odore di || *intr* soffiare; (*said of a smoker*) dare boccate

while [hwaɪl] *s* tempo; **a long while** un bel pezzo; **a while ago** un tratto fa; **to be worth one's while** valere la pena || *conj* mentre || *tr*—**to while away** passare piacevolmente

whim [hwɪm] *s* capriccio, estro

whimper ['hwɪmpər] *s* piagnucolio || *tr & intr* piagnucolare

whimsical ['hwɪmzɪkəl] *adj* capriccioso, estroso, stravagante

whine [hwaɪn] *s* (*of dog*) guaito; (*of person*) piagnucolio || *intr* (*said of a dog*) guaire, uggiolare; (*said of a person*) piagnucolare

whin·ny ['hwɪni] *s* (**-nies**) nitrito || *v* (*pret & pp* **-nied**) *intr* nitrire

whip [hwɪp] *s* frusta; uova *fpl* sbattute con frutta || *v* (*pret & pp* **whipped** or **whipt;** *ger* **whipping**) *tr* frustare, battere; (*eggs*) frullare; (coll) vincere, sconfiggere; **to whip off** (coll) buttar giù; **to whip out** tirar fuori rapidamente; **to whip up** (coll) preparare in quattro e quattr'otto; (coll) eccitare, incitare

whip'cord' *s* cordino della frusta; (*fabric*) saia a diagonale

whip' hand' *s* mano che tiene la frusta; vantaggio, posizione vantaggiosa

whip'lash' *s* scudisciata

whipped' cream' *s* panna montata

whipper-snapper ['hwɪpər,snæpər] *s* pivello

whippet ['hwɪpɪt] *s* piccolo levriere

whip'ping boy' ['hwɪpɪŋ] *s* testa di turco

whip'ping post' *s* palo per la fustigazione

whippoorwill [,hwɪpər'wɪl] *s* caprimulgo, succiacapre *m*

whir [hwʌr] *s* ronzio || *v* (*pret & pp* **whirred;** *ger* **whirring**) *intr* ronzare; volare ronzando

whirl [hwʌrl] *s* giro improvviso; corsa; mulinello; (fig) successione || *tr & intr* mulinare; **my head whirls** mi gira la testa

whirligig ['hwʌrlɪ,gɪg] *s* turbine *m;* (*carrousel*) giostra; (*toy*) girandola; (ent) ragno d'acqua

whirl'pool' *s* risucchio, mulinello

whirl'wind' *s* turbine *m*, tromba d'aria

whirlybird ['hwʌrli,bʌrd] *s* (coll) elicottero

whish [hwɪʃ] *s* fruscio || *intr* frusciare

whisk [hwɪsk] *s* scopatina || *tr* scopare, spolverare; (*eggs*) sbattere; **to whisk out of sight** far sparire || *intr* guizzare

whisk' broom' *s* scopetta per i vestiti, spolverino

whiskers ['hwɪskərz] *spl* barba; (*on side of man's face*) basette *fpl;* (*of cat*) baffi *mpl*

whiskey ['hwɪski] *s* whisky *m*

whisper ['hwɪspər] s sussurro, bisbiglio, mormorio; **in a whisper** in un sussurro ‖ *tr & intr* sussurrare, bisbigliare, mormorare

whisperer ['hwɪspərər] s sussurrone m

whispering ['hwɪspərɪŋ] *adj* di maldicenze ‖ s sussurro; maldicenza

whistle ['hwɪsəl] s fischio; **to wet one's whistle** (coll) bagnarsi l'ugola ‖ *tr* fischiare ‖ *intr* fischiare, zufolare; **to whistle for** chiamare con un fischio; (*money*) aspettare in vano

whis'tle stop' s stazioncina, paesetto

whit [hwɪt] s—**not a whit** niente affatto

white [hwaɪt] *adj* bianco ‖ s bianco; **whites** (pathol) leucorrea

white'cap' s frangente m, cavallone m, onda crespa

white' coal' s carbone bianco

white'-col'lar *adj* impiegatizio

white' feath'er s—**to show the white feather** mostrarsi vile

white' goods' *spl* biancheria da casa; articoli *mpl* di cotone; apparecchi *mpl* elettrodomestici

white-haired ['hwaɪt‚herd] *adj* dai capelli bianchi; (coll) favorito

white' heat' s calor bianco

white' lead' [lɛd] s biacca

white' lie' s bugia innocente

white' meat' s bianco, carne f del petto

whiten ['hwaɪtən] *tr* imbiancare, sbiancare ‖ *intr* imbiancarsi, sbiancarsi; impallidire

whiteness ['hwaɪtnɪs] s bianchezza

white' plague' s tubercolosi f

white' slav'ery s tratta delle bianche

white' tie' s cravatta da frac; marsina, abito da cerimonia

white'wash' s imbiancatura; (fig) copertura ‖ *tr* imbiancare, intonacare; (fig) coprire

white' wa'ter lil'y s ninfea

whither ['hwɪðər] *adv* dove, a che luogo ‖ *conj* dove

whiting ['hwaɪtɪŋ] s (ichth) nasello; (ichth) merlango

whitish ['hwaɪtɪʃ] *adj* biancastro

whitlow ['hwɪtlo] s patereccio

Whitsuntide ['hwɪtsən‚taɪd] s settimana di Pentecoste

whittle ['hwɪtəl] *tr* digrossare; **to whittle away or down** ridurre gradualmente

whiz or **whizz** [hwɪz] s sibilo; (coll) asso ‖ v (pret & pp whizzed) ger whizzing) *intr*—**to whiz by** passare sibilando; passare come una freccia

who [hu] *pron interr* chi; **who else?** chi altri?; **who goes there?** (mil) chi va là?; **who's who** chi è l'uno e chi è l'altro; chi è la gente importante ‖ *pron rel* chi; il quale

whoa [hwo] or [wo] *interj* fermo!

who∙ev'er *pron rel* chiunque

whole [hol] *adj* tutto, intero; sano, intatto; **made out of the whole cloth** completamente immaginario ‖ s tutto; **as a whole** nell'insieme; **on the whole** in generale

wholehearted ['hol‚hɑrtɪd] *adj* molto sincero, generoso

whole' note' s (mus) semibreve f

whole'sale' *adj & adv* all'ingrosso ‖ s ingrosso ‖ *tr* vendere all'ingrosso ‖ *intr* vendersi all'ingrosso

wholesaler ['hol‚selər] s grossista mf

wholesome ['holsəm] *adj* (beneficial) salutare; (in good health) sano

wholly ['holi] *adv* interamente

whom [hum] *pron interr* chi ‖ *pron rel* che; il quale

whom∙ev'er *pron rel* chiunque

whoop [hup] or [hwup] s urlo; (pathol) urlo della pertosse; **to not be worth a whoop** (coll) non valere un fico secco ‖ *tr*—**to whoop it up** (slang) fare il diavolo a quattro ‖ *intr* urlare

whoop'ing cough' ['hupɪŋ] or ['hʊpɪŋ] s pertosse f

whopper ['hwɑpər] s (coll) enormità f; (coll) fandonia, bugia enorme

whopping ['hwɑpɪŋ] *adj* (coll) enorme

whore [hor] s puttana ‖ *intr*—**to whore around** puttaneggiare; andare a puttane

whortleber∙ry ['hwʌrtəl‚beri] s (-ries) mirtillo

whose [huz] *pron interr* di chi ‖ *pron rel* di chi; del quale; di cui

why [hwaɪ] s (whys) perché m; **the whys and the wherefores** il perché e il percome ‖ *adv* perché ‖ *interj* diamine!; **why, certainly!** certamente!; **why, yes!** evidentemente!

wick [wɪk] s stoppino, lucignolo

wicked ['wɪkɪd] *adj* malvagio; (mischievous) cattivo; (dreadful) terribile, bestiale

wicker ['wɪkər] *adj* di vimini ‖ s vimine m

wicket ['wɪkɪt] s (small door) portello; (ticket window) sportello; (of a canal) chiusa; (cricket) porta; (croquet) archetto

wide [waɪd] *adj* largo, esteso; (eyes) aperto; (sense of a word) lato ‖ *adv* largamente; completamente; lontano; **wide of the mark** lontano dal bersaglio

wide'-an'gle *adj* grandangolare

wide'-awake' *adj* sveglio

widen ['waɪdən] *tr* slargare, estendere ‖ *intr* slargarsi, estendersi

wide'-o'pen *adj* spalancato; (to a gambler) accessibile

wide'-spread' *adj* (e.g., arms) aperto; diffuso

widow ['wɪdo] s vedova; (cards) morto ‖ *tr* lasciar vedova

widower ['wɪdo∙ər] s vedovo

widowhood ['wɪdo‚hud] s vedovanza

wid'ow's mite' s obolo della vedova

wid'ow's weeds' *spl* gramaglie *fpl* vedovili

width [wɪdθ] s larghezza

wield [wild] *tr* (e.g., a sword) brandire; (e.g., a hammer) maneggiare; (power) esercitare

wife [waɪf] s (wives [waɪvz]) moglie f

wig [wɪg] s parrucca

wiggle ['wɪgəl] s dimenio; (of fish)

guizzo ‖ *tr* dimenare ‖ *intr* dimenarsi; guizzare

wig'wag' *s* segnalazione con bandierine ‖ *v* (*pret & pp* **-wagged**; *ger* **-wagging**) *tr & intr* segnalare con bandierine

wigwam ['wɪgwɑm] *s* tenda a cupola dei pellirosse, wigwam *m*

wild [waɪld] *adj* (*animal*) feroce; (*e.g.*, *berry*) selvatico; (*barbarous*) selvaggio; (*violent*) furioso; (*mad*) pazzo; (*unruly*) discolo, indisciplinato; (*extravagant*) pazzesco; (*shot or throw*) lanciato all'impazzata; **wild about** pazzo per ‖ *s* regione deserta; **the wild** la foresta; **wilds** regioni selvagge ‖ *adv* pazzamente; **to go wild** andare in delirio; **to run wild** crescere all'impazzata; correre senza freno

wild' boar' *s* cinghiale *m*

wild' card' *s* matta

wild'cat' *s* gatto selvatico; lince *f*; impresa arrischiata ‖ *v* (*pret & pp* **-catted**; *ger* **-catting**) *tr & intr* esplorare per conto proprio

wild'cat strike' *s* sciopero non autorizzato dal sindacato

wilderness ['wɪldərnɪs] *s* deserto

wild-eyed ['waɪld ˌaɪd] *adj* stralunato; (*scheme*) pazzesco

wild'fire' *s* fuoco greco; fuoco fatuo; **to spread like wildfire** crescere come la gramigna; (*said of news*) spargersi come il baleno

wild' flow'er *s* fiore *m* di campo

wild' goose' *s* oca selvatica

wild'-goose' chase' *s* ricerca della luna nel pozzo

wild'life' *s* animali *spl* selvatici

wild' oat' *s* avena selvatica; **to sow one's wild oats** correre la cavallina

wild' ol'ive *s* olivastro, oleastro

wile [waɪl] *s* stratagemma *m*, inganno; (*cunning*) astuzia ‖ *tr* allettare; **to wile away** passare piacevolmente

will [wɪl] *s* volontà *f*, volere *m*; (*law*) testamento; **at will** a volontà ‖ *tr* volere; (*law*) legare ‖ *intr* volere; **do as you will** faccia come vuole ‖ *v* (*pret & cond* **would**) *aux* **she will leave tomorrow** partirà domani; **a cactus plant will live two months without water** una pianta grassa può vivere due mesi senz'acqua

willful ['wɪlfəl] *adj* volontario; ostinato

willfulness ['wɪlfəlnɪs] *s* volontarietà *f*; ostinatezza

William ['wɪljəm] *s* Guglielmo

willing ['wɪlɪŋ] *adj* volenteroso; **to be willing** essere disposto

willingly ['wɪlɪŋli] *adv* di buon grado, volentieri

willingness ['wɪlɪŋnɪs] *s* buona voglia, propensione

will-o'-the-wisp ['wɪləðə'wɪsp] *s* fuoco fatuo; (*fig*) illusione, chimera

willow ['wɪlo] *s* salice *m*

willowy ['wɪlo ˌi] *adj* pieghevole; (*slender*) snello; pieno di giunchi

will' pow'er *s* forza di volontà

willy-nilly ['wɪli'nɪli] *adv* volente o nolente

wilt [wɪlt] *tr* far appassire ‖ *intr* appassire, avvizzire

wil-y ['waɪli] *adj* (**-ier**; **-iest**) astuto, scaltro

wimple ['wɪmpəl] *s* soggolo

win [wɪn] *s* vittoria, vincita ‖ *v* (*pret & pp* **won** [wʌn]; *ger* **winning**) *tr & intr* guadagnare; **to win out** vincere, aver successo

wince [wɪns] *s* sussulto ‖ *intr* sussultare

winch [wɪntʃ] *s* verricello; (*handle*) manovella; (naut) molinello

wind [wɪnd] *s* vento; (*gas in intestines*) vento; (*breath*) fiato, tenuta; **to break wind** scoreggiare; **to get wind of** subodorare; **to sail close to the wind** (naut) andare all'orza; **to take the wind out of the sails of** sconcertare; **winds** (mus) fiati *mpl* ‖ *tr* far perdere il fiato a ‖ [waɪnd] *v* (*pret & pp* **wound** [waʊnd]) *tr* (*to wrap up*) arrotolare; (*thread, wool*) dipanare, aggomitolare; (*a clock*) caricare; (*a handle*) far girare; **to wind one's way through** serpeggiare per; **to wind up** arrotolare; eccitare; finire, portare a termine ‖ *intr* serpeggiare, snodarsi

windbag ['wɪnd ˌbæg] *s* (*of a bagpipe*) otre *m*; (fig) parolaio, otre *m* di vento

windbreak ['wɪnd ˌbrek] *s* frangivento

wind' cone' *s* manica a vento

winded ['wɪndɪd] *adj* senza fiato

windfall ['wɪnd ˌfɔl] *s* frutta abbattuta dal vento; provvidenza, manna del cielo

wind'ing sheet' ['waɪndɪŋ] *s* lenzuolo funebre

wind'ing stairs' ['waɪndɪŋ] *spl* scala a chiocciola

wind' in'strument [wɪnd] *s* (mus) strumento a fiato

windlass ['wɪndləs] *s* verricello

windmill ['wɪnd ˌmɪl] *s* mulino a vento; (*air turbine*) aeromotore *m*; **to tilt at windmills** combattere i mulini a vento

window ['wɪndo] *s* finestra; (*of ticket office*) sportello; (*of car or coach*) finestrino

win'dow dress'er *s* vetrinista *mf*

win'dow dress'ing *s* vetrinistica; (fig) facciata, apparenza

win'dow en'velope *s* busta a finestrella

win'dow frame' *s* intelaiatura della finestra

win'dow-pane' *s* vetro, invetriata

win'dow sash' *s* intelaiatura della finestra

win'dow screen' *s* zanzariera

win'dow shade' *s* tendina avvolgibile

win'dow-shop' *v* (*pret & pp* **-shopped**; *ger* **-shopping**) *intr* guardare nelle vetrine senza comprare

win'dow sill' *s* davanzale *m* della finestra

windpipe ['wɪnd ˌpaɪp] *s* trachea

windproof ['wɪnd ˌpruf] *adj* resistente al vento

windshield ['wɪnd ˌʃild] *s* parabrezza *m*

wind'shield wash'er *s* lavacristallo

wind'shield wip'er s tergicristallo

windsock ['wɪnd‚sɑk] s (aer) manica a vento

windstorm ['wɪnd‚stɔrm] s bufera di vento

wind' tun'nel [wɪnd] s (aer) galleria aerodinamica

wind-up ['waɪnd‚ʌp] s conclusione

windward ['wɪndwərd] s orza, sopravvento; **to turn to windward** mettersi al sopravvento

Wind'ward Is'lands spl Isole fpl Sopravvento

wind·y ['wɪndi] adj (-ier; -iest) ventoso; verboso, ampolloso; **it is windy** fa vento

wine [waɪn] s vino || tr offrire vino a || intr bere del vino

wine' cel'lar s cantina

wine'glass' s bicchiere da vino

winegrower ['waɪn‚groˌər] s vinificatore m, viticoltore m

wine' press' s torchio per l'uva

winer·y ['waɪnəri] s (-ies) stabilimento vinicolo

wine'shop' s fiaschetteria

wine'skin' s otre m

wine' stew'ard s sommelier m

winetaster ['waɪn‚testər] s degustatore m di vini

wing [wɪŋ] s ala; (unit of air force) aerobrigata; (theat) quinta; **to take wing** levarsi a volo; **under one's wing** sotto la protezione di qlcu || tr ferire nell'ala; **to wing one's way** volare, portarsi a volo

wing' chair' s poltrona a orecchioni

wing' col'lar s colletto per marsina

wing' nut' s (mach) galletto

wing'span' s (of airplane) apertura alare

wing'spread' s (of bird) apertura alare

wink [wɪŋk] s ammicco; **in a wink** in un batter d'occhio; **to not sleep a wink** non chiudere occhio; **to take forty winks** (coll) schiacciare un pisolino || tr (the eye) strizzare || intr ammiccare, strizzare l'occhio; (to blink) battere le ciglia; **to wink at** ammiccare a; far finta di non vedere

winner ['wɪnər] s vincitore m

winning ['wɪnɪŋ] adj vincente, vincitore; attraente, simpatico || **winnings** spl vincita

winnow ['wɪno] tr ventilare, brezzare; (fig) vagliare || intr svolazzare

winsome ['wɪnsəm] adj attraente

winter ['wɪntər] adj invernale || s inverno || intr svernare

win'ter-green' s tè m del Canadà; olio di gaulteria

win·try ['wɪntri] adj (-trier; -triest) invernale; freddo

wipe [waɪp] tr forbire, detergere; (to dry) asciugare; **to wipe away** (tears) asciugare; **to wipe off** pulire, forbire; **to wipe out** distruggere completamente; (coll) eliminare

wiper ['waɪpər] s strofinaccio; (mach) camma; (elec) contatto scorrevole

wire [waɪr] s filo metallico; telegramma m; (coll) telegrafo; **to pull wires** manovrare di dietro le quinte || tr legare con filo metallico; attrezzare l'elettricità in; (coll) mandare per telegrafo; (coll) telegrafare || intr (coll) telegrafare

wire' cut'ter s pinza tagliafili

wire' entan'glement s reticolato di filo spinato

wire' gauge' s calibro da fili

wire-haired ['waɪr‚herd] adj a pelo ruvido

wireless ['waɪrlɪs] adj senza fili || s telegrafo senza fili; telegrafia senza fili

wire' nail' s chiodo da falegname

wirepulling ['waɪr‚pʊlɪŋ] s manovra dietro alle quinte

wire' record'er s magnetofono a filo

wire' screen' s rete metallica

wire'tap' v (pret & pp -tapped; ger -tapping) tr (a conversation) intercettare

wiring ['waɪrɪŋ] s sistema m di fili elettrici

wir·y ['waɪri] adj (-ier; -iest) fatto di filo; (hair) ispido; (tone) metallico, vibrante; (sinewy) segaligno

wisdom ['wɪzdəm] s senno, sapienza, saggezza

wis'dom tooth' s dente m del giudizio

wise [waɪz] adj saggio, sapiente; (decision) giudizioso; **to be wise to** (slang) accorgersi del gioco di; **to get wise** (slang) mangiare la foglia; (slang) diventare impertinente || s modo, maniera; **in no wise** in nessun modo || tr—**to wise up** (slang) avvertire || intr—**to wise up** (slang) accorgersi

wiseacre ['waɪz‚ekər] s sapientone m

wise'crack' s (coll) spiritosaggine f || intr (coll) dire spiritosaggini

wise' guy' s (slang) sputasentenze m

wish [wɪʃ] s desiderio; augurio; **to make a wish** formulare un desiderio || tr desiderare; augurare; **to wish s.o. a good day** dare il buon giorno a qlcu || intr desiderare; **to wish for** desiderare

wish'bone' s forcella

wishful ['wɪʃfəl] adj desideroso

wish'ful think'ing s pio desiderio

wistful ['wɪstfəl] adj melanconico, pensoso, meditabondo

wit [wɪt] s spirito; (person) bellospirito; (understanding) senso; **to be at one's wits' end** non sapere a che santo votarsi; **to have one's wits about one** avere presenza di spirito; **to live by one's wits** vivere di espedienti

witch [wɪtʃ] s strega

witch'craft' s stregoneria

witch' doc'tor s stregone m

witch'es' Sab'bath s sabba m

witch' ha'zel s (shrub) amamelide f; (liquid) estratto di amamelide

witch' hunt' s caccia alle streghe

with [wɪð] or [wɪθ] prep con; a, e.g., **with open arms** a braccia aperte; di, e.g., **covered with silk** coperto di seta; **to be satisfied with the performance** essere contento della rappresentazione; da, e.g., **with the In-**

dians dagli indiani; **to part with** separarsi da

with·draw' v (pret -drew; pp -drawn) tr ritirare || intr ritirarsi

withdrawal [wɪð'drɔ·əl] or [wɪθ'drɔ·əl] s ritiro, ritirata; (of funds) prelevamento

wither ['wɪðər] tr intisichire; (with a glance) incenerire || intr avvizzire, intisichire

with·hold' v (pret & pp -held) tr trattenere; (information) sottacere; (payment) defalcare; (permission) negare

withhold'ing tax' s imposta trattenuta

with·in' adv dentro, didentro || prep entro, entro di, dentro a, dentro di; fra; in; (a time period) nel giro di

with·out' adv fuori || prep senza; fuori, fuori di; **to do without** fare a meno di; **without** + ger senza + inf, e.g., **without saying a word** senza dire una parola; **senza che** + subj, e.g., **she fell without anyone helping her** cadde senza che nessuno l'aiutasse

with·stand' v (pret & pp -stood) tr resistere (with dat), reggere (with dat)

witness ['wɪtnɪs] s testimone mf; **in witness whereof** in fé di che; **to bear witness** far fede || tr (to be present at) presenziare; (to attest) testimoniare, firmare come testimone

wit'ness stand' s banco dei testimoni

witticism ['wɪtɪ‚sɪzəm] s motto, battuta spiritosa, spiritosaggine f

wittingly ['wɪtɪŋli] adv consapevolmente

wit·ty ['wɪti] adj (-tier; -tiest) spiritoso, divertente

wizard ['wɪzərd] s mago

wizardry ['wɪzərdri] s magia

wizened ['wɪzənd] adj raggrinzito

woad [wod] s (bot) guado

wobble ['wɑbəl] s oscillazione, dondolio || intr oscillare, dondolare; (said of a chair) zoppicare; (fig) titubare

wob·bly ['wɑbli] adj (-blier; -bliest) oscillante, zoppo, malfermo

woe [wo] s disgrazia, afflizione, sventura; || interj—**woe is me!** ahimè!

woebegone ['wobɪ‚gɑn] or ['wobɪ‚gɑn] adj triste, abbattuto

woeful ['wofəl] adj sfortunato, disgraziato; (of poor quality) orribile

wolf [wulf] s (wolves [wulvz]) lupo; (coll) dongiovanni m; **to cry wolf** gridare al lupo; **to keep the wolf from the door** tener lontana la miseria || tr & intr mangiare come un lupo

wolf'hound' s cane m da pastore alsaziano

wolfram ['wulfrəm] s wolframio

wolf's-bane or **wolfsbane** ['wulfs‚ben] s (bot) aconito

wolverine [‚wulvə'rin] s (zool) ghiottone m

woman ['wumən] s (women ['wɪmɪn]) donna

womanhood ['wumən‚hud] s (quality) femminilità f; (women collectively) donne fpl, sesso femminile

womanish ['wumənɪʃ] adj femminile; (effeminate) effeminato

wom'an·kind' s sesso femminile

womanly ['wumənli] adj (-lier; -liest) femminile, muliebre

wom'an suf'frage s suffragio alle donne

woman-suffragist ['wumən's‚frədʒɪst] s suffragista mf

womb [wum] s utero; (fig) seno

womenfolk ['wɪmɪn‚fok] spl le donne

wonder ['wʌndər] s (something strange and surprising) meraviglia; (feeling) ammirazione; (miracle) prodigio, miracolo; **for a wonder** cosa strana; **no wonder that** non fa meraviglia che; **to work wonders** fare miracoli || tr—**to wonder that** meravigliarsi che; **to wonder how, if, when, where, who, why** domandarsi or chiedersi come, se, quando, dove, chi, perché || intr meravigliarsi; chiedersi; **to wonder at** ammirare

won'der drug' s medicina miracolosa

wonderful ['wʌndərfəl] adj meraviglioso

won'der·land' s paese m delle meraviglie

wonderment ['wʌndərmənt] s sorpresa, meraviglia, stupore m

won'der·work'er s taumaturgo

wont [wʌnt] or [wont] adj abituato, solito || s abitudine f, costume m

wonted ['wʌntɪd] or ['wontɪd] adj solito, abituale

woo [wu] tr (a woman) corteggiare; (to seek to win) allettare; (good or bad consequences) andare in cerca di

wood [wud] s legno; (firewood) legna; (keg) barile m; **out of the woods** fuori pericolo; al sicuro; **woods** bosco, selva

woodbine ['wud‚baɪn] s (honeysuckle) abbracciabosco; (Virginia creeper) vite f del Canadà

wood' carv'ing s intaglio in legno, statua in legno

wood'chuck' s marmotta americana

wood'cock' s beccaccia

wood'cut' s silografia

wood'cut'ter s boscaiolo

wooded ['wudɪd] adj legnoso, boschivo

wooden ['wudən] adj di legno; duro, rigido; inespressivo

wood' engrav'ing s silografia

wooden-headed ['wudən‚hedɪd] adj (coll) dalla testa dura

wood'en leg' s gamba di legno

wood'en shoe' s zoccolo

wood' grouse' s gallo cedrone

woodland ['wudlənd] adj boschivo || s foresta, bosco

wood'man s (-men) boscaiolo

woodpecker ['wud‚pekər] s picchio

wood'pile' s legnaia

wood' screw' s vite f per legno

wood'shed' s legnaia

woods'man s (-men) abitatore m dei boschi; boscaiolo

wood'wind' s strumento a fiato di legno

wood'work' s lavoro in legno; parti fpl di legno

wood'work'er s ebanista m, falegname m

wood'worm' s tarlo

wood·y ['wʊdi] *adj* (**-ier; -iest**) boscoso, alberato; (*like wood*) legnoso

wooer ['wu·ər] *s* corteggiatore *m*

woof [wuf] *s* (*yarns running across warp*) trama; (*fabric*) tessuto

woofer ['wufər] *s* altoparlante *m* per basse audiofrequenze, woofer *m*

wool [wʊl] *s* lana

woolen ['wʊlən] *adj* di lana || *s* tessuto di lana; **woolens** laneria

woolgrower ['wʊl‚gro·ər] *s* allevatore *m* di pecore

wool·ly ['wʊli] *adj* (**-ier; -liest**) di lana; lanoso; (coll) confuso

word [wʌrd] *s* parola; **by word of mouth** oralmente; **to be as good as one's word** essere di parola; **to have a word with** dire quattro parole a; **to have word from** aver notizie da; **to keep one's word** essere di parola; **to leave word** lasciar detto; **to send word** that mandare a dire che; **words** (*quarrel*) baruffa || *tr* esprimere, formulare || **Word** *s* (theol) Verbo

word' count' *s* conto lessicale

word' forma'tion *s* formazione delle parole

wording ['wʌrdɪŋ] *s* fraseologia, dicitura

word' or'der *s* disposizione delle parole in una frase

word'stock' *s* lessico

word·y ['wʌrdi] *adj* (**-ier; -iest**) verboso, parolaio

work [wʌrk] *s* lavoro; (*of art, fortification, etc.*) opera; **at work** al lavoro, in ufficio; (*in operation*) in servizio; **out of work** senza lavoro, disoccupato; **to give s.o. the works** (slang) trattare male; (slang) ammazzare; **to shoot the works** (slang) scialare; **works** opificio; meccanismo; (*of clock*) castello || *tr* far funzionare; lavorare, maneggiare; (*e.g., a miracle*) operare; (*e.g., iron*) trattare; **work up** preparare; stimulare, eccitare || *intr* lavorare; (*said of a machine*) funzionare; (*said of a remedy*) avere effetto; **to work loose** sciogliersi; **to work out** andare a finire; (*said of a problem*) sciogliersi; (*said of a total*) ammontare; (sports) allenarsi

workable ['wʌrkəbəl] *adj* (*feasible*) praticabile; (*e.g., iron*) lavorabile

work'bench' *s* banco

work'book' *s* manuale *m* d'istruzioni; (*for students*) quaderno d'esercizi

work'box' *s* cassetta dei ferri del mestiere; (*for needlework*) cestino da lavoro

work'day' *adj* lavorativo; ordinario, di tutti i giorni || *s* (*working day*) giorno feriale, giornata lavorativa

worked-up ['wʌrkt'ʌp] *adj* sovreccitato

worker ['wʌrkər] *s* lavorante *m*, lavoratore *m*, operaio

work' force' *s* mano *f* d'opera

work'horse' *s* cavallo da tiro; (*tireless worker*) lavoratore indefesso

work'house' *s* carcere *m* con lavoro obbligatorio; (Brit) istituto dei poveri

work'ing class' *s* classe operaia

work'ing condi'tions *spl* trattamento, condizioni *fpl* di lavoro

work'ing girl' *s* ragazza lavoratrice

work'ing hours' *spl* orario di lavoro

working'man *s* (**-men**) lavoratore *m*

work'ing or'der *s* buone condizioni, efficienza

work'ing-wom'an *s* (**-wom'en**) operaia, lavoratrice *f*

work'man *s* (**-men**) lavoratore *m*; (*skilled worker*) operaio specializzato

workmanship ['wʌrkmən‚ʃɪp] *s* fattura; (*work executed*) opera

work' of art' *s* opera d'arte

work'out' *s* (sports) esercizio, allenamento

work'room' *s* (*for manual work*) officina; (*study*) gabinetto, laboratorio

work'shop' *s* officina

work' stop'page *s* sospensione del lavoro

world [wʌrld] *adj* mondiale || *s* mondo; **a world of** un monte di; **for all the world** per tutto l'oro del mondo; **in the world** al mondo; **since the world began** da che mondo è mondo; **the other world** l'altro mondo; **to bring into the world** mettere al mondo; **to see the world** conoscere il mondo; **to think the world of** tenere in altissima considerazione

world' affairs' *spl* relazioni *fpl* internazionali

world·ly ['wʌrldli] *adj* (**-lier; -liest**) mondano, secolare

world'ly-wise' *adj* vissuto

world's' fair' *s* esposizione *f* mondiale

world' war' *s* guerra mondiale

world'-wide' *adj* mondiale

worm [wʌrm] *s* verme *m* || *tr* liberare dai vermi; **to worm a secret out of s.o.** carpire un segreto a qlcu; **to worm one's way into** insinuarsi in

worm-eaten ['wʌrm‚itən] *adj* tarlato, bacato

worm' gear' *s* meccanismo a vite perpetua, ingranaggio elicoidale

worm'wood' *s* assenzio; (fig) amarezza

worm·y ['wʌrmi] *adj* (**-ier; -iest**) verminoso; (*worm-eaten*) bacato; (*groveling*) vile, strisciante

worn [worn] *adj* usato; (*look*) stanco, esausto

worn'-out' *adj* logoro, scalcinato; (*by illness*) consunto; (fig) trito

worrisome ['wʌrisəm] *adj* preoccupante; (*inclined to worry*) preoccupato

wor·ry ['wʌri] *s* (**-ries**) preoccupazione, inquietudine *f*; (*trouble*) fastidio || *v* (*pret & pp* **-ried**) *tr* preoccupare, inquietare; **to be worried** essere impensierito || *intr* preoccuparsi, inquietarsi; **don't worry!** non si preoccupi!

worse [wʌrs] *adj & s* peggiore *m*, peggio || *adv* peggio; **worse and worse** di male in peggio

worsen ['wʌrsən] *tr & intr* peggiorare

wor·ship ['wʌrʃɪp] *s* venerazione, adorazione; servizio religioso; **your Worship** La Signoria Vostra || *v* (*pret &*

pp **-shiped** or **-shipped; ** *ger* **-shiping** or **-shipping**) *tr* venerare, adorare

worshiper or **worshipper** ['wʌr/ɪpər] *s* adoratore *m;* (*in church*) devoto, fedele *m*

worst [wʌrst] *adj* (il) peggiore; pessimo || *s* peggio, peggiore *m;* **at worst** alla peggio; **if worst comes to worst** alla peggio; **to get the worst** averne la peggio || *adv* peggio

worsted ['wustɪd] *adj* di lana pettinata || *s* tessuto di lana pettinata

wort [wʌrt] *s* mosto di malto; pianta, erba

worth [wʌrθ] *adj* che vale, da, e.g., **worth ten dollars** da dieci dollari; **to be worth** valere; essere di pregio; **to be worth** + *ger* valere la pena (di) + *inf*, e.g., **it is worth reading** vale la pena (di) leggerlo || *s* pregio, valore *m;* **a dollar's worth** un dollaro di

worthless ['wʌrθlɪs] *adj* senza valore; inutile; inservibile; (*person*) indegno

worth'while' *adj* meritevole, meritevole d'attenzione

wor·thy ['wʌrðɪ] *adj* (**-thier; -thiest**) degno, meritevole || *s* (**-thies**) maggiorente *mf*

would [wud] *v aux* **they said they would come** dissero che sarebbero venuti; **he would buy it if he had the money** lo comprerebbe se avesse i soldi; **would you be so kind to** avrebbe la cortesia di; **he would spend every winter in Florida** passava tutti gli inverni in Florida; **would that . . . !** oh se . . . !, volesse il cielo che . . . !, magari . . . !

would'-be' *adj* preteso, sedicente; (*intended to be*) inteso

wound [wund] *s* ferita || *tr* ferire

wounded ['wundɪd] *adj* ferito || **the wounded** i feriti

wow [wau] *s* distorsione acustica di suono riprodotto; (slang) successone *m* || *tr* (slang) entusiasmare || *interj* (coll) accidenti!

wrack [ræk] *s* naufragio; vestigio; (*seaweed*) alghe marine gettate sulla spiaggia; **to go to wrack and ruin** andare completamente in rovina

wraith [reθ] *s* spettro, fantasma *m*

wrangle ['ræŋgəl] *s* baruffa, alterco || *intr* altercare, rissare

wrap [ræp] *s* sciarpa; mantello || *v* (*pret & pp* **wrapped;** *ger* **wrapping**) *tr* involgere; impaccare; **to be wrapped up in** essere assorto in; **to wrap up** avvolgere; (*in paper*) incartare; (*in clothing*) imbaccucare; (coll) concludere || *intr*—**to wrap up** imbaccucarsi, avvolgersi

wrapper ['ræpər] *s* veste *f* da camera, peignoir *m;* (*of newspaper*) fascia, fascetta; (*of cigars*) involto

wrap'ping pa'per ['ræpɪŋ] *s* carta d'impacco or d'imballaggio

wrath [ræθ] or [raθ] *s* ira; vendetta

wrathful ['ræθfəl] or ['raθfəl] *adj* collerico, iracondo

wreak [rik] *tr* (*vengeance*) infliggere; (*anger*) scaricare

wreath [riθ] *s* (**wreaths** [riðz]) ghirlanda; (*of laurel*) laurea; (*of smoke*) spirale *f*

wreathe [rið] *tr* inghirlandare; avviluppare; (*a garland*) intessere || *intr* (*said of smoke*) innalzarsi in spire

wreck [rek] *s* rottame *m*, relitto; naufragio; rovina; catastrofe *f*, disastro; (fig) rottame *m*, relitto || *tr* far naufragare; distruggere, rovinare; (*a train*) fare scontrare, fare deragliare; (*a building*) demolire

wreckage ['rekɪdʒ] *s* rottami *mpl*, relitti *mpl;* rovine *fpl*

wrecker ['rekər] *s* (*tow truck*) autogrù *f;* (*housewrecker*) demolitore *m*

wreck'ing ball' *s* martello demolitore

wreck'ing car' *s* autogrù *f*

wrecking' crane' *s* (rr) carro gru

wren [ren] *s* scricciolo

wrench [rentʃ] *s* chiave *f;* (*pull*) tiro; (*of a joint*) distorsione || *tr* torcere, distorcere; (*one's limb*) torcersi, distorcersi

wrest [rest] *tr* strappare, togliere a viva forza; (*to twist*) torcere

wrestle ['resəl] *s* lotta, combattimento || *intr* fare la lotta, lottare

wrestler ['restlər] *s* lottatore *m*

wrestling ['reslɪŋ] *s* lotta

wretch [retʃ] *s* disgraziato, tapino

wretched ['retʃɪd] *adj* (*pitiable*) misero, disgraziato, tapino; (*poor, worthless*) miserabile

wriggle ['rɪgəl] *s* (e.g., *of a snake*) guizzo; dondolio || *tr* dondolare, dimenare || *intr* guizzare; dimenarsi; **to wriggle out of** sgattaiolare da, divincolarsi da

wrig·gly ['rɪglɪ] *adj* (**-glier; -gliest**) che si contorce; (fig) evasivo

wring [rɪŋ] *v* (*pret & pp* **wrung** [rʌŋ]) *tr* torcere; (*wet clothing*) strizzare; (*one's heart*) stringersi; (e.g., *one's hands*) torcersi; **to wring the truth out of** strappare la verità a

wringer ['rɪŋər] *s* strizzatoio

wrinkle ['rɪŋkəl] *s* (*on skin*) ruga; (*on fabric*) crespa, grinza; (coll) trovata, espediente *m* || *tr* corrugare, raggrinzire; (*fabric*) increspare

wrin'kle-proof' *adj* antipiega, ingualcibile

wrin·kly ['rɪŋklɪ] *adj* (**-klier; -kliest**) rugoso, grinzoso

wrist [rist] *s* polso

wrist'band' *s* polso

wrist' pin' *s* spinotto

wrist' watch' *s* orologio da polso

writ [rit] *s* scritto; (law) ordine *m*

write [rait] *v* (*pret* **wrote** [rot]; *pp* **written** ['rɪtən]) *tr* scrivere; **to write down** mettere in iscritto; (*to disparage*) menomare; **to write off** (*a debt*) cancellare; (com) stornare; **to write up** redigere, scrivere in pieno; (*to ballyhoo*) scrivere le lodi di || *intr* scrivere; **to write back** rispondere per lettera

write'-in-vote' *s* voto per candidato il cui nome non è nella lista

writer ['raitər] *s* scrittore *m*

write'-up' s descrizione scritta, conto; stamburata, elogio; (com) valutazione eccessiva

writhe [raɪð] intr contorcersi, spasimare, dibattersi

writing [ˈraɪtɪŋ] s lo scrivere; (something written) scritto; (characters written) scrittura; professione di scrittore; at this writing scrivendo questa mia; in one's own writing di proprio pugno; to put in writing mettere in iscritto

writ'ing desk' s scrittoio

writ'ing mate'rials spl l'occorrente m per scrivere, oggetti mpl di cancelleria

writ'ing pa'per s carta da lettere

writ'ten ac'cent [ˈrɪtən] s accento grafico

wrong [rɔŋ] or [rɑŋ] adj sbagliato, erroneo; (awry) guasto; (step) falso; cattivo, ingiusto; there is nothing wrong with him non ha niente; to be wrong (mistaken) aver torto; (guilty) aver la colpa ‖ s torto; to be in the wrong essere in errore; to do wrong fare del male; commettere un'ingiustizia ‖ adv male; (backward) alla rovescia; to go wrong andare alla rovescia; andare per la cattiva strada ‖ tr far torto a, offendere, maltrattare

wrongdoer [ˈrɔŋˌduˌər] or [ˈrɑŋˌduˌər] s peccatore m, trasgressore m

wrongdoing [ˈrɔŋˌduˌɪŋ] or [ˈrɑŋˌduˌɪŋ] s peccato, offesa, trasgressione

wrong' num'ber s (telp) numero sbagliato; you have the wrong number Lei si è sbagliato di numero

wrong' side' s rovescio; (of street) altra parte; to get out of bed on the wrong side alzarsi di malumore; wrong side out alla rovescia

wrought' i'ron [rɔt] s ferro battuto

wrought'-up' adj sovreccitato

wry [raɪ] adj (wrier; wriest) sbieco, storto; pervertito, alterato; ironico

wry'neck' s (orn & pathol) torcicollo

X

X, x [eks] s ventiquattresima lettera dell'alfabeto inglese

Xanthippe [zænˈtɪpi] s Santippe f

Xavier [ˈzævɪˌər] or [ˈzevɪˌər] s Saverio

xebec [ˈzibek] s (naut) sciabecco

xenon [ˈzinɑn] or [ˈzenɑn] s xeno

xenophobe [ˈzenəˌfob] s xenofobo

Xenophon [ˈzenəfən] s Senofonte m

xerography [zɪˈrɑgrəfi] s xerografia

xerophyte [zɪrəˌfaɪt] s xerofito

Xerxes [ˈzʌrksɪs] s Serse m

Xmas [ˈkrɪsməs] s Natale m

x-ray [ˈeksˌre] adj radiografico ‖ s raggio X; (photograph) radiogramma m, radiografia ‖ tr radiografare

xylograph [ˈzaɪləˌgræf] or [ˈzaɪləˌgraf] s silografia

xylophone [ˈzaɪləˌfon] s silofono

Y

Y, y [waɪ] s venticinquesima lettera dell'alfabeto inglese

yacht [jɑt] s yacht m, panfilo

yacht' club' s club m nautico, associazione velica

yak [jæk] s yak m ‖ v (pret & pp yakked; ger yakking) intr (slang) ciarlare, chiacchierare

yam [jæm] s igname m; (sweet potato) patata dolce, batata

yank [jæŋk] s tiro, strattone m ‖ tr dare uno strattone a, tirare ‖ intr dare uno strattone, tirare

Yankee [ˈjæŋki] adj & s yankee mf

yap [jæp] s guaito; (slang) chiacchierio, ciancia ‖ v (pret & pp yapped; ger yapping) intr latrare, guaire; (slang) chiacchierare, ciarlare

yard [jɑrd] s cortile m; recinto; yard m, iarda; (naut) pennone m; (rr) scalo smistamento

yard'arm' s estremità f del pennone

yard' goods' spl tessuti mpl in pezza

yard'mas'ter s (rr) capo dello scalo smistamento

yard'stick' s stecca di una iarda di lunghezza; (fig) metro

yarn [jɑrn] s filo, filato; (coll) storia

yarrow [ˈjæro] s millefoglie m

yaw [jɔ] s (naut) straorzata; (aer) imbardata ‖ intr (naut) straorzare, guizzare; (aer) imbardare

yawl [jɔl] s barca a remi; (naut) iolla

yawn [jɔn] s sbadiglio ‖ intr sbadigliare; (said, e.g., of a hole) vaneggiare, aprirsi

yea [je] s & adv sì m

yean [jin] intr (said of sheep or goat) partorire

year [jɪr] s anno; to be . . . years old avere . . . anni; year in, year out un anno dopo l'altro

year'book' s annuario

yearling [ˈjɪrlɪŋ] adj di un anno di età ‖ s animale m di un anno di età

yearly ['jɪrlɪ] *adj* annuale || *adv* annualmente

yearn [jʌrn] *intr* smaniare, sospirare; **to yearn for** anelare per

yearning ['jʌrnɪŋ] *s* anelo, sospiro ardente

yeast [jist] *s* lievito

yeast' cake' *s* compressa di lievito

yell [jel] *s* urlo || *tr* gridare || *intr* urlare

yellow ['jelo] *adj* giallo; (*newspaper*) sensazionale; (*cowardly*) (coll) vile || *s* giallo; giallo d'uovo || *intr* ingiallire

yellowish ['jelo·ɪʃ] *adj* giallastro

yel'low-jack'et *s* vespa, calabrone *m*

yel'low streak' *s* (coll) vena di codardia

yelp [jelp] *s* guaito || *intr* guaire

yeo'man *s* (-men) (naut) sottufficiale *m*; (Brit) piccolo proprietario terriero

yeo'man of the guard' *s* guardia del servizio reale

yeo'man's serv'ice *s* lavoro onesto

yes [jes] *s* sì *m*; **to say yes** dire di sì || *adv* sì || *v* (*pret & pp* **yessed**; *ger* **yessing**) *tr* dire di sì a || *intr* dire di sì

yes' man' *s* (coll) persona che approva sempre; (coll) leccapiedi *m*

yesterday ['jestərdɪ] *or* ['jestər,de] *s & adv* ieri *m*

yet [jet] *adv* ancora; tuttavia; **as yet** sinora; **nor yet** nemmeno; **not yet** non ancora || *conj* ma, però, pure

yew' tree' [ju] *s* tasso

Yiddish ['jɪdɪʃ] *adj & s* yiddish *m*

yield [jild] *s* rendimento, resa; (*crop*) raccolto; (com) reddito, gettito || *tr* rendere, fruttare || *intr* rendere, fruttare, produrre; (*to surrender*) cedere, arrendersi; sottomettersi; cedere il posto

yodeling *or* **yodelling** ['jodəlɪŋ] *s* tirolesa

yoke [jok] *s* (*contrivance*) giogo; (*pair*, e.g., *of oxen*) paio; (*of shirt*) sprone *m*; (naut) barra del timone; **to throw off the yoke** scuotere il giogo || *tr* aggiogare

yokel ['jokəl] *s* zoticone *m*

yolk [jok] *s* tuorlo

yonder ['jandər] *adj* situato lassù; situato laggiù || *adv* lassù; laggiù

yore [jor] *s*—**of yore** del tempo antico, del tempo in cui Berta filava

you [ju] *pron pers* Lei; tu; Le, La; te, ti; voi; vi; Loro || *pron indef* si, e.g., **you eat at' noon** si mangia a mezzogiorno

young [jʌŋ] *adj* (**younger** ['jʌŋgər]; **youngest** ['jʌŋgɪst]) giovane || **the young** i giovani

young' hope'ful *s* giovane *m* di belle speranze

young' la'dy *s* giovane *f*; (*married*) giovane signora

young' man' *s* giovane *m*, giovanotto

young' peo'ple *s* i giovani

youngster ['jʌŋstər] *s* giovanetto; (*child*) bambino

your [jur] *adj* Suo, il Suo; tuo, il tuo; vostro, il vostro

yours [jurz] *pron poss* Suo, il Suo; tuo, il tuo; vostro, il vostro; **of yours** Suo; **very truly yours** distinti saluti

your·self [jur'self] *pron pers* (**-selves** ['selvz]) Lei stesso; sé stesso; si, e.g., **are your enjoying yourself?** si diverte?

youth [juθ] *s* (**youths** [juðs] *or* [juðz]) gioventù *f*, giovinezza; (*person*) giovane *mf*; i giovani

youthful ['juθfəl] *adj* giovane, giovanile

yowl [jaul] *s* urlo || *intr* urlare

Yugoslav ['jugo'slav] *adj & s* iugoslavo

Yugoslavia ['jugo'slavɪ·ə] *s* la Iugoslavia

Yule [jul] *s* il Natale; le feste natalizie

Yule' log' *s* ceppo

Yuletide ['jul,taɪd] *s* le feste natalizie

Z

Z, z [zi] *s* ventiseiesima lettera dell'alfabeto inglese

za·ny ['zenɪ] *adj* (**-nier; -niest**) comico, buffonesco || *s* (**-nies**) buffone *m*, pagliaccio

zeal [zil] *s* zelo, entusiasmo

zealot ['zelət] *s* zelante *mf*, fanatico

zealotry ['zelətri] *s* fanatismo

zealous ['zeləs] *adj* zelante, volenteroso

zebra ['zibrə] *s* zebra

ze'bra cross'ing *s* zebre *fpl*

zebu ['zibju] *s* zebù *m*

zenith ['zinɪθ] *s* zenit *m*

zephyr ['zefər] *s* zefiro

ze·ro ['ziro] *s* (**-roes**) zero || *tr*—**zero in** (mil) aggiustare il mirino di || *intr*—**to zero in on** (mil) concentrare il fuoco su

ze'ro grav'ity *s* gravità *f* zero

ze'ro hour' *s* ora zero

zest [zest] *s* entusiasmo; (*flavor*) aroma *m*, sapore *m*

Zeus [zus] *s* Zeus *m*

zig-zag ['zɪg,zæg] *adj & adv* a zigzag || *s* zigzag *m*; serpentina || *v* (*pret & pp* **-zagged**; *ger* **-zagging**) *intr* zigzagare; serpeggiare

zinc [zɪŋk] *s* zinco

zinnia ['zɪnɪ·ə] *s* zinnia

Zionism ['zaɪ·ə,nɪzəm] *s* sionismo

zip [zɪp] *s* (coll) sibilo; (coll) energia, vigore *m* || *v* (*pret & pp* **zipped**; *ger* **zipping**) *tr* chiudere con cerniera lampo; aprire con cerniera lampo; (coll) portare rapidamente; **to zip up** (*to add zest to*) dare gusto a || *intr* aprirsi con cerniera lampo; sibilare; (coll) filare, correre; **to zip by** (coll) passare come un lampo

zip′ code′ s codice m di avviamento postale
zipper [ˈzɪpər] s cerniera or serratura lampo
zircon [ˈzʌrkɑn] s zircone m
zirconium [zərˈkonɪ·əm] s zirconio
zither [ˈzɪθər] s cetra tirolese
zodiac [ˈzodɪ ˌæk] s zodiaco
zone [zon] s zona; distretto postale ‖ tr dividere in zone
zoo [zu] s giardino zoologico
zoologic(al) [ˌzo·əˈlɑdʒɪk(əl)] adj zoologico

zoologist [zoˈɑlədʒɪst] s zoologo
zoology [zoˈɑlədʒi] s zoologia
zoom [zum] s ronzio; (aer) cabrata, impennata; (mov, telv) zumata ‖ tr (aer) far cabrare, fare impennare; (mov, telv) zumare ‖ intr ronzare; (aer) cabrare, impennarsi; (mov, telv) zumare
zoom′ lens′ s (phot) transfocatore m
zoophite [ˈzo·ə ˌfaɪt] s zoofito
Zu·lu [ˈzulu] adj zulù ‖ s (-lus) zulù mf
Zurich [ˈzurɪk] s Zurigo f

Special Offer
Buy a Bantam Book
for only 50¢.

Now you can have Bantam's catalog filled with hundreds of titles plus take advantage of our unique and exciting bonus book offer. A special offer which gives you the opportunity to purchase a Bantam book for only 50¢. Here's how!

By ordering any five books at the regular price per order, you can also choose any other single book listed (up to a $5.95 value) for just 50¢. Some restrictions do apply, but for further details why not send for Bantam's catalog of titles today!

Just send us your name and address and we will send you a catalog!
